PORTABLE MOVIE GUIDE

VARIETY®

PORTABLE MOVIE GUIDE

Updated Edition

Abridged from the *Variety® Movie Guide*
(Perigee Books edition, 2000)

The Editors of *Variety*

BERKLEY BOULEVARD BOOKS, NEW YORK

VARIETY PORTABLE MOVIE GUIDE, UPDATED EDITION

Abridged from the *Variety® Movie Guide* (Perigee Books edition, 2000).

A Berkley Boulevard Book / published by arrangement with
Variety, a division of The Cahners Publishing Company

PRINTING HISTORY
Berkley Boulevard edition / July 2000

All rights reserved.
Copyright © 2000 by Variety.
Book design by Tiffany Kukec.
Cover design by Matt Tepper.
Front cover photos: (clockwise) Katharine Hepburn; Jim Carrey in *Liar, Liar* (Yoram Kahana); Mike Myers in *Austin Powers* (New Line); Roberto Benigni (Ron Davis); *Star Wars Episode 1* (Lucasfilm); Humphrey Bogart; Kim Basinger in *L.A. Confidential*. Back cover photos: (left to right) James Cameron (Ron Davis); *The Full Monty*; Tom Hanks in *Saving Private Ryan*; Bette Davis. Spine photo: Gwyneth Paltrow in *Shakespeare in Love* (Miramax). All photos courtesy of Shooting Star®.
This book may not be reproduced in whole or in part, by mimeograph or any other means, without permission.
For information address: The Berkley Publishing Group, a division of Penguin Putnam Inc., 375 Hudson Street, New York, New York 10014.

The Penguin Putnam Inc. World Wide Web site address is
http://www.penguinputnam.com

ISBN: 0-425-17550-2

BERKLEY BOULEVARD
Berkley Boulevard Books are published by The Berkley Publishing Group, a division of Penguin Putnam Inc., 375 Hudson Street, New York, New York 10014.
BERKLEY BOULEVARD and its logo
are trademarks belonging to Penguin Putnam Inc.

PRINTED IN THE UNITED STATES OF AMERICA

10 9 8 7 6 5 4 3 2 1

Introduction

WELCOME TO THE eighth edition of *Variety Movie Guide,* the only one of its kind to combine a you-were-there-at-the-time feel with an unrivaled "trade" orientation to the reviews.

The current volume contains some 8,700 reviews selected from the 57,000-plus published by *Variety* over the past 93 years, from January 1907 to December 1999. The earliest review included is of D. W. Griffith's *Judith of Bethulia* (1914); the most recent, *The Hurricane.* The paper is the longest unbroken source of film criticism in existence.

The present edition includes just over 100 extra reviews selected from the period since the last edition closed, i.e., December 1999. Foreign-language movies—only some 420, for lack of space—are entered under their original titles, cross-referenced by English title(s). The emphasis is on accepted classics, both old and new. Especially in the early days, many of these were reviewed in a hard-nosed trade style very different to criticism from the sixties onward. When a film was reviewed twice (a common practice in *Variety*'s early history), preference has been given to the first, reflecting opinion at its original unspooling.

Reviewers' now-meaningless box-office predictions ("Fort Knox, move over"—*A Star Is Born*) have been cut out, as well as plot revelations. Minor changes to tenses have been made so that reviews "read" from a modern viewpoint, and any obscure contemporary references or pointless prejudices (especially during the two world wars and the McCarthy period) have been toned down or deleted. Until the mid-thirties, when *Variety* reviews began to take on their unique shape and structure, editing has been considerably heavier. Early reviews were more like scattergun essays: "film criticism" as we now know it did not arrive until the thirties.

Although *Variety* has occasionally included accents on foreign names, this book adheres to tradition by omitting them.

The following are the main criteria used:

- FILM TITLE. The original title in country of origin ("majority" country in the case of co-productions) or, for foreign productions shot in English, the English title (e.g., Bergman's *The Touch,* Leone's *The Good, the Bad and the Ugly*). When a film has subsequently had a title change, and is now better known under that title, the latter is used (e.g., *Murder My Sweet,* originally released out-of-town in 1944 as *Farewell, My Lovely*). The form of the title is that used on the print itself, not the officially registered one nor that on secondary material like posters or press handouts. So-called "possessory credits" are omitted (e.g., *Billy Rose's Jumbo* is listed as *Jumbo*), but are cross-indexed. A film's subsidiary title ("handle"), a growing trend since the eighties and the habit of sequels, is put on a separate line. a.k.a. ("also known as") is a general dumping ground for other release titles, video titles, and TV titles, but not production titles. The book is self-indexing, with entries in strict letter-by-letter A-Z order; those starting with numerals are positioned as if the figures were spelt out. To be included, a film has to have received a theatrical showing somewhere at some time in its life. Direct-to-video and TV movies are not included.

- YEAR. The year of first public release in its country of origin (or, with co-productions, "majority" country). Sneaks and out-of-town tryouts don't count; end-of-year Oscar-qualifying runs do. If a film never got a proper theatrical release, we've used the year of its first showing on the festival circuit, which nowadays is virtually an alternative exhibition chain. Establishing some films' opening dates is still problematical.

- RUNNING TIME. The hardest nut to crack, as secondary materials (press handouts, festival catalogues, producers' claims) are often wildly inaccurate, and during the era of roadshow epics the intermission was often permed into the running time. *Variety* reviewers now time all films themselves, but no running time should be taken as gospel. Movies are trimmed, speeded up by projectionists, cut for TV and generally mangled; more recently there has been a trend toward issuing longer versions for TV and homevideo (the so-called director's cut).

- COUNTRY OF ORIGIN. The second hardest nut. The rule here has been where the money actually came from, rather than where a film was shot, what passport the director had, what language the cast spoke in, or a movie's "cultural identity." With co-productions, the first country listed is the "majority" one (which decides its official title—see above). In the case of many British and American movies, especially since the fifties, whether some are UK/US, US/UK or even UK or US is virtually impossible to define.

- VIDEO. A nightmare keeping track of. Films that have been released on video (at one time or another) carry the symbol Ⓥ.

- LASERDISC AND DVD. The symbol ⊙ denotes the film has been released on laserdisc and/or DVD. In text annotations, the term ''homevideo'' includes video, laser, and DVD.

- WIDESCREEN. Films originally shown in an aspect ratio of 2:1 or greater—such as CinemaScope, Panavision widescreen, Todd-AO, etc.—are marked ▭. (Standard American so-called widescreen is only 1.85:1, and does not qualify; and almost all films in VistaVision—a variable ratio—were projected in less than 2:1.)

- SILENT. Films originally shown without a synchronized dialogue track are indicated with the symbol ⊗.

- DIRECTOR. The film's officially credited director or codirectors. Some productions are in fact the work of several hands (especially during Hollywood's studio era); only well-known uncredited contributions are listed in square parentheses. Second-unit or dance-number directors are occasionally included up top or in the text, if their contribution merits it.

- CAST LISTS. For space reasons, these have been limited to a maximum of six—ideally, in their original order of billing, with the sixth slot sometimes used for an interesting name hidden way down in the cast. For consistency, actors who later changed names are listed by their latest moniker.

- PRODUCTION COMPANY. More and more difficult, thanks to the growing complexity of production credits (''A so-and-so presentation, in association with so-and-so, of a so-and-so production, with the participation of so-and-so,'' etc.). The general rule, as in deciding the country of origin, has been to list those companies that actually stumped up the cash, but in a world of pre-buys and lengthy development periods, that too is often difficult to decide. For space reasons, an abbreviated version of companies' names is used. Companies that simply distributed the finished product are not included (unless, in the case of major studios, they basically funded it via the producer's private shingle), nor those credited as "in association with."

- ACADEMY AWARDS/NOMINATIONS. Includes winners and nominations in all feature categories. The date is of the Oscar award, not of the actual ceremony (generally held the following spring).

—DEREK ELLEY
London 1998

Glossary

THE FOLLOWING IS a guide to ninety-three years of *Variety* "slan-guage" as occurs in the selected reviews; it is not exhaustive and is intended especially for non-American and more general readers.

Variety's snazzy coinages and neologisms are a goulash of pub-lishing and showbiz/movie jargon, foreign words, Yiddish, street slang, contractions, and acronyms that since the mid-thirties (when the reviews took on a recognizable style) have acquired a reputation and life of their own (e.g., "whodunit," "helmer," "chopsocky").

Many of the words have long vanished from use in the paper (along with the slang that inspired them); new ones are still being invented. The only rule is that they sound "right" and carry on the tradition of sharp, compressed, flavorful prose. As a further aid for general readers, we have also included some words that are just movie jargon or archaic slang rather than pure *Variety* slanguage.

a.d. assistant director
a.k. ass-kisser
a.k.a. also known as
alky alcoholic
ancillary non-theatrical business, i.e., homevideo, TV
ankle leave, quit
anent regarding
anklebiter child
auds audiences
avoirdupois weight

back-to-back (two or more films shot) at the same time or without a break between
beaucoup much
b.b. big business
beer stube bar

belter boxer
b.f. boyfriend
Big Apple New York
Blighty UK
burley burlesque, music hall
b.o. box office (income)
bow debut, praise
b.r. bankroll, sum of money

cannon gun
carny carnival
Chi Chicago
chick girl
chili Mexican
chirp(er) sing(er)
chopsocky martial arts (film)
chore job, routine assignment
chump crazy (in love)
cleff(er) compose(r)

click hit, success
coin money, finance
contempo contemporary
coprod coproduction

d.a. district attorney
dick detective
doughboy infantry soldier
d.p. director of photography
dualer double-billed feature film

femme female, woman
fest festival
filmer filmmaker
flap flapper
flivver car
f/x special effects

G $1,000
gat gun
g.f. girlfriend
g.m. general manager
gob sailor
gorefest orgy of violence
Gotham New York
gyp swindler, cheat

habiliments clothing
helm(er) direct(or)
histrionics performance(s)
histrionically performance-wise
hoke hokum
hoke-up over-act
hoofology dancing
hotcha excellent
hoyden(ish) tomboy(ish)
h.s. high school

indie independent (production or company), i.e., not by an established major studio

ink sign
i.r. inquiring reporter, investigative reporter
Italoater spaghetti western

j.d. juvenile delinquent
jitterbug (1940s) jazz dance(r), nervous person

kayo knockout
keptive "kept" woman

legit(imate) theatrical, theater, stage
legiter stage play
legituner stage musical
lense(r) photograph(er)
limn portray
lingo language, dialogue
longhair highbrow, intellectual
lower case minor (quality)
LST landing ship tank (a WWII landing craft)

manse mansion
medico doctor
meg(aphoner) direct(or)
megger director
meller melodrama(tic)
milquetoast meek man
m.o. modus operandi
moniker name
moppet child

nabes suburbs
negative cost production cost
newshen female reporter
nitery night club

oater Western
ofay white man
oke okay
one-shot one-off
o.o. once-over
opp opposite
org organization, large company
Oz Australia(n)
ozoner drive-in theater

p.a. press agent
pactee contract player
Par Paramount
p.d. production designer
pen penitentiary, prison
Pennsy Pennsylvania
perf performance
photog photographer
p.i. private investigator
pic picture, movie
pix pictures, movies
plat platinum blonde
p.m. professional model
pol politician
p.o.v. point of view
p.r. public relations
prexy (company) president
prez president
profesh profession
programmer B-movie fodder
pug boxer

quondam one time

ridic ridiculous
rod-man gunman
RR railroad

s.a. sex appeal
sagebrush saga Western
sauce alcohol

Scandi Scandinavia(n)
schtick comic routine(s)
scripter scriptwriter
sec secretary
seg segment
segue link, follow on
sheet screen, newspaper
shingle production company (often attached to a major studio)
shutterbug photographer
single single woman
slugfest fight
smokeater fireman
sock(eroo) excellent, powerful
solon lawmaker
speak speakeasy
spec spectacle
stepping dancing
stew drinking bout
stock repertory theater
sudser soap opera
super super-production
switcheroo (plot) twist

tab tabloid
tapster tap-dancer
tech credits technical credits, i.e., photography, editing, art direction, etc.
ten-twent-thirt/10-20-30 amateurish (acting)
terp(ing) danc(ing)
terpsichore dancing
thesp(ing) actor, act(ing)
thespically performance-wise
thespics acting
tint(ed) color(ed)
tintuner showbiz musical
topkick boss
topper boss

topline(r) star
trick work special effects
troubadour singer
trouping acting
tube TV
tuner musical
20th 20th Century-Fox

U Universal
unreel play
unspool play
upper case major (quality)

vaude vaudeville
vet veteran

vignetting describing
vis-à-vis (romantic/sexual/
  billing) partner
v.o. voiceover

warbling singing
WB Warner Bros.
w.k. well-known

yahoo redneck
yak joke
yclept played by
yegg thief
yock joke

zaftig luscious, juicy

ABBA
THE MOVIE
1977, 94 mins, Sweden/Australia ⓥ
D: Lasse Hallstrom **A:** Anni-Frid Lyngstad, Agnetha Faltskog, Benny Andersson, Bjorn Ulvaeus, Bruce Barry, Robert Hughes (Polar Music/Grundy)

Handsomely produced, smooth, fast, and wittily edited musical entertainment that is a bit of a documentary both of Swedish group ABBA's Australian tour and of its four personable performers' background and work methods. There's also a slight but funny story about an Aussie disk jockey's chasing of the group and being most of the way thwarted in his attempts to do a taped interview with the Swedes.

ABBOTT AND COSTELLO IN HOLLYWOOD
1945, 83 mins, US ⓥ
D: S. Sylvan Simon **A:** Bud Abbott, Lou Costello, Frances Rafferty, Robert Stanton, Jean Porter, Warner Anderson (M-G-M)

Duo portrays the role of barber and shineboy in a tonsorial establishment who get the yen to be actor's agents when they see the easy life one of the latter has. When the agent turns down a youngster with a nice voice, they take him on, and before the film unwinds they have him set in a picture, but not before they almost wreck the studio and upset the personnel therein.

ABBOTT AND COSTELLO MEET DR. JEKYLL AND MR. HYDE
1953, 76 mins, US ⓥ
D: Charles Lamont **A:** Bud Abbott, Lou Costello, Boris Karloff, Craig Stevens, Helen Westcott, Reginald Denny (Universal)

A rousing good time for Abbott and Costello fans is contained in this spoof on fiction's classic bogeyman. The fat and thin comics combat Boris Karloff as the fictional dual personality in the very broad doings, and Karloff's takeoff on the character adds to the chuckles dished out by A&C.

ABBOTT AND COSTELLO MEET FRANKENSTEIN
1948, 82 mins, US ⓥ ⊙
D: Charles T. Barton **A:** Bud Abbott, Lou Costello, Lon Chaney, Bela Lugosi, Glenn Strange, Lenore Aubert (Universal)

The comedy team battles it out with the studio's roster of bogeymen in a rambunctious fracas that is funny and, at the same time, spine-tingling. Stalking through the piece to add menace are such characters as the Frankenstein Monster, the Wolf Man, and Dracula.

ABBOTT AND COSTELLO . . . MEET THE INVISIBLE MAN
1951, 82 mins, US
D: Charles Lamont **A:** Bud Abbott, Lou Costello, Nancy Guild, Arthur Franz, Adele Jergens, Sheldon Leonard (Universal)

Team's stock double takes and bewhiskered gags are still fulsome, but the hackneyed quips achieve a new gloss in this entry. The yarn is tied around the efforts of fighter Arthur Franz to clear himself of a murder rap. He hires private eyes Abbott and Costello to help him in his mission. When Franz injects himself with a serum possessing powers of invisibility, a flock of amusing sequences are touched off. Best of these is a scene in which Costello KO's the champ (with the invisible man's help).

ABDICATION, THE
1974, 103 mins, UK
D: Anthony Harvey **A:** Liv Ullmann, Peter Finch, Cyril Cusack, Graham Crowden, Michael Dunn, Paul Rogers (Warner)

The Abdication is a period film in more ways than one. The Ruth Wolff script from her play, based on the 17th-century abdication of Queen Christina of Sweden, has been directed by Anthony Harvey, like a trite 1930s sobsister melodrama, with dainty debauchery and titillating tease straight from 1920s women's pulp magazines. Peter Finch plays a Vatican-based cardinal assigned to investigate the background and the motivations of Liv Ullmann, who has quit her throne after converting to Roman Catholicism late in 1655.

ABIE'S IRISH ROSE
1928, 129 mins, US ⊗
D: Victor Fleming **A:** Jean Hersholt, Charles Rogers, Nancy Carroll, J. Farrell MacDonald, Bernard Gorcey (Paramount)

Anne Nichols' play has been translated literally from the stage, and the picture adds nothing, while it does detract a good deal. The picture takes over two hours to lead up to what in substance is a

1

rather feeble gag, when the antagonistic fathers, Jewish and Irish, at length come around on Christmas Eve to see the offspring of their cast-off children. The outstanding performance is that of Jean Hersholt as Solomon Levy. Nancy Carroll and Charles Rogers make a charming pair of young people.

ABIE'S IRISH ROSE
1928, 80 mins, US
D: Victor Fleming **A:** Jean Hersholt, Charles Rogers, Nancy Carroll, J. Farrell MacDonald, Bernard Gorcey (Paramount)

Use of added sound makes *Abie* a different matter. Most of the serious religious material is eliminated and the story treatment greatly lightened. Accompanying score is skillfully done, an accompaniment that holds to the action in its varying moods and introduces a certain humor with its switch from Irish to Jewish themes, military ideas in the war scenes, and the like. Also the footage has been cut 49 minutes and the story moves much faster.

ABIE'S IRISH ROSE
1946, 96 mins, US
D: A. Edward Sutherland **A:** Joanne Dru, Richard Norris, Michael Chekhov, J. M. Kerrigan (United Artists/Crosby)

Fundamentally the story is a topical misfit. It opens with ultramodern young Abie Levy meeting USO-camp shows entertainer Rosemary Murphy in a V-E Day London mix-up, resulting in their marriage by an army chaplain (incidentally Protestant, so as to get in all the three faiths, which didn't exist in the original play by Anne Nichols). Papa Levy is patently a prosperous Bronx department-store owner; his place of business, his household, and his friends bespeak prosperity. But thereafter this premise falls apart; for he has the prejudices of a pushcart peddler, and barrister Isaac Cohen (George E. Stone) and Mrs. Levy (Vera Gordon, who, somehow, manages a slightly more restrained characterization) are depicted as narrow-minded nitwits.

ABILENE TOWN
1946, 91 mins, US ⓥ
D: Edwin L. Marin **A:** Randolph Scott, Ann Dvorak, Edgar Buchanan, Rhonda Fleming, Lloyd Bridges (United Artists)

Fundamentally a story about the violent conflict of interests between the cattlemen and newly arrived homesteaders. *Abilene Town* focuses interest on the evolution of this Kansas village from the familiar reckless cowboy town into a more peaceful community. Abilene is located where the Chisholm Trail ends. It's where cattle were placed on trains for the packinghouse cities. Randolph Scott chips in with one of his best western characterizations as the marshal, a law officer who really whips the community into line. Ann Dvorak clicks as the dancehall entertainer, equally adept at warbling and stepping.

ABOMINABLE DOCTOR PHIBES, THE
1971, 94 mins, UK ⓥ ⊙
D: Robert Fuest **A:** Vincent Price, Joseph Cotten, Virginia North, Terry-Thomas, Hugh Griffith, Peter Jeffrey (American International)

The Abominable Doctor Phibes stars Vincent Price as a living corpse, out for revenge on the nine medics in attendance when his wife died in surgery. Anachronistic period-horror-musical-camp-fantasy is a fair description, loaded with comedic gore of the type that packs theaters and drives child psychologists up the walls. Joseph Cotten also stars as an intended victim who foils the plot. Price's makeup, by Trevor Crole-Rees, is outstanding in depicting without revulsion the look of a living corpse covered with scars.

A BOUT DE SOUFFLE (BREATHLESS)
1960, 89 mins, France ⓥ ⊙
D: Jean-Luc Godard **A:** Jean Seberg, Jean-Paul Belmondo, Henri-Jacques Huet, Jean-Pierre Melville, Liliane David, Daniel Boulanger (SNC)

This film, a first pic by a film critic, shows the immediate influence of Yank actioners and sociopsycho thrillers but has its own personal style. All of this adds up to a production resembling such pix as *Gun Crazy, They Live by Night,* and *Rebel Without a Cause.* But it has local touches in its candor, lurid lingo, frank love scenes, and general tale of a young childish hoodlum (Jean-Paul Belmondo) whose love for a boyish-looking, semi-intellectual American girl (Jean Seberg) is his undoing. Seberg lacks emotive projection but it helps in her role of a dreamy little Yank abroad playing at life. Her boyish prettiness is real help. Belmondo is excellent as the cocky hoodlum.

ABOUT LAST NIGHT . . .
1986, 113 mins, US ⓥ ⊙
D: Edward Zwick **A:** Rob Lowe, Demi

Moore, James Belushi, Elizabeth Perkins, George DiCenzo, Michael Alldredge (TriStar-Delphi IV & V)

About Last Night ... has little to do with perversity, let alone *Sexual Perversity in Chicago*, the David Mamet play on which it ostensibly is based. Film lacks much of Mamet's grittiness, but is likable in its own right. Focus of the story is on Danny (Rob Lowe) and Debbie (Demi Moore), who meet, move in together, separate, and get back together with an ease and casualness that makes it both appealing and disturbing. As the sour note, James Belushi is probably the high point of the film. His performance borrows much from his late brother (John) in its outrageousness and unpredictability.

ABOVE SUSPICION
1943, 90 mins, US Ⓥ
D: Richard Thorpe **A:** Joan Crawford, Fred MacMurray, Conrad Veidt, Basil Rathbone, Reginald Owen, Richard Ainley (M-G-M)

After establishing Fred MacMurray and Joan Crawford as newlywed Americans in England, planning a honeymoon in south of Germany just prior to outbreak of the war, yarn has British secret service drafting them for mission to secure vital confidential plans for a secret weapon, a magnetic mine. Both MacMurray and Crawford competently handle their roles, despite drawbacks of script material. Conrad Veidt clicks solidly in major supporting spot, along with brief appearances of Basil Rathbone as a Gestapo leader.

ABOVE THE LAW
1988, 99 mins, US ⊙
D: Andrew Davis **A:** Steven Seagal, Pam Grier, Henry Silva, Ron Dean, Daniel Faraldo, Sharon Stone (Warner)

Above the Law is an ultraviolent actioner with Steven Seagal playing an aikido-chopping cop on a one-man crusade to clean up Chi streets. When he's taken off the trail of a suspected drug dealer, he smells a rat or two at the top of his chain of command. With a couple dozen stunt persons and an earthy, warm, and supportive partner (Pam Grier), Seagal kicks, kills, and crushes with his skillful hands one handful after another of street hoods who try to thwart his mission. Quiet moments like the ones with Seagal and his emotional wife (Sharon Stone) comprise about 1 percent of the film.

ABRAHAM LINCOLN
1930, 93 mins, US Ⓥ ⊙
D: D. W. Griffith **A:** Walter Huston, Una Merkel, Kay Hammond, Jason Robards, Ian Keith, Hobart Bosworth (United Artists)

Abraham Lincoln is a startlingly superlative accomplishment. Next to the direction by D. W. Griffith, with only a tiny margin separating, is Walter Huston's Abraham Lincoln: young, aging, and aged; playful, fighting, grief-stricken; commanding, pleading. The assassination of Lincoln is classically melodramatic.

ABSENCE OF MALICE
1981, 116 mins, US Ⓥ ⊙ ▭
D: Sydney Pollack **A:** Paul Newman, Sally Field, Bob Balaban, Melinda Dillon, Luther Adler, Barry Primus (Columbia)

Absence of Malice is the flip side of *All the President's Men,* a splendidly disturbing look at the power of sloppy reporting to inflict harm on the innocent. This is, quite simply, a whale of a good story with something important to say. For that, much of the credit undoubtedly should go to writer Kurt Luedtke, a veteran newsman himself. Sally Field is a workaday reporter on a Miami paper, trying to stay on top of a breaking story about the mysterious disappearance of a local longshore labor leader. Paul Newman is the son of a mobster whose late father kept him straight and out of the rackets, running a legitimate business. But he still has unsavory family ties, and Bob Balaban, the head of a federal task force investigating the case, believes a little pressure on Newman might force his help in solving the disappearance.

1981: Nominations: Best Actor (Paul Newman), Supp. Actress (Melinda Dillon), Original Screenplay

ABSENT-MINDED PROFESSOR, THE
1961, 90 mins, US Ⓥ ⊙
D: Robert Stevenson **A:** Fred MacMurray, Nancy Olson, Keenan Wynn, Tommy Kirk, Leon Ames, Ed Wynn (Walt Disney)

On the surface, Walt Disney's *The Absent-Minded Professor* is a comedy-fantasy of infectious absurdity. But deeply rooted within the screenplay is a subtle protest against the detached, impersonal machinery of modern progress. The Professor (Fred MacMurray) is an easygoing, likable smalltown chemist who comes up with a practical discovery, a gooey substance endowed with the elusive quality of antigravity. He dubs it flubber (flying rubber) and proceeds to put it to use in incongruous ways. MacMurray is ideally cast as the car-hopping prof, and plays the role with warmth and gusto.

1961: Nominations: Best B&W Cinematography, B&W Art Direction, Special Effects

ABSOLUTE BEGINNERS
1986, 107 mins, UK Ⓥ ⊙ ▭
D: Julien Temple **A:** Eddie O'Connell, Patsy Kensit, David Bowie, James Fox, Ray Davies, Steven Berkoff (Virgin/Goldcrest/Palace)

Absolute Beginners is a terrifically inventive original musical for the screen. Daring attempt to portray the birth of teenagedom in London, 1958, almost exclusively through song is based upon Colin MacInnes cult novel about teen life and pop fashion in the percolating moments just before the youth cultural explosion in the early 1960s. Tenuous story line is a typical one of teen love achieved, lost, and regained, and is used as a mere string to which a constant parade of musical numbers and flights of fancy are attached.

ABSOLUTE POWER
1997, 120 mins, US Ⓥ ⊙ ▭
D: Clint Eastwood **A:** Clint Eastwood, Gene Hackman, Ed Harris, Laura Linney, Judy Davis, Scott Glenn (Malpaso/Castle Rock/Columbia)

Absolute Power is a high-toned potboiler, a reasonably engrossing and entertaining suspenser for most of its running time, but one that is undercut by too many coincidences and some whoppingly farfetched developments in the home stretch. A veteran master thief, Luther (Clint Eastwood) witnesses a murder of a woman that the US president (Gene Hackman) participates in. While senior homicide detective Seth Frank (Ed Harris) analyzes the perplexing evidence, Luther decides to turn the tables on the all-powerful establishment. No-frills direction seems almost charmingly old-fashioned at times. There's an excellent, very simply shot tête-à-tête between Luther and Seth in a cafe, in which the thief adroitly deflects the detective's suspicions of him.

ABSOLUTION
1981, 95 mins, UK Ⓥ ⊙
D: Anthony Page **A:** Richard Burton, Dominic Guard, Billy Connolly, Dai Bradley, Andrew Keir, Willoughby Gray (Kastner-O'Donovan)

Absolution is a dull, gloomy, nasty, contrived marketplace misfit, apparently designed to ride on Richard Burton's shirttails. Or in this case his cassock, since the actor portrays a stern, super-devout priest-teacher in a Catholic boarding school for boys. Gist of Anthony Shaffer's melodramatic plot has to do with a catch-22 test of Burton's faith as two embittered students, taking advantage of the secrecy of the confessional box, conspire to drive him round the bend and to an unwitting killing.

ABYSS, THE
1989, 140 mins, US Ⓥ ⊙ ▭
D: James Cameron **A:** Ed Harris, Mary Elizabeth Mastrantonio, Michael Biehn, Leo Burmester, Todd Graff, Kimberly Scott (20th Century-Fox)

A first-rate underwater suspenser with an otherworldly twist, The Abyss suffers from a payoff unworthy of its buildup. Same sensibilities that enable writer-director James Cameron to deliver riveting, supercharged action segments get soggy when the aliens turn out to be friendly. The Abyss has plenty of elements in its favor, not least the performances by Harris as the compassionate crewleader and Mastrantonio as his steel-willed counterpart. Not even the $50 million-plus pic's elaborate technical achievements can overshadow these two. [In 1993 a 171-min. version, The Abyss: Special Edition, was released. Restored footage was spread throughout the pic but primarily during the final two reels, including the original ending.]

1989: Best Visual Effects
Nominations: Best Cinematography, Art Direction, Sound

ACCATTONE
1961, 116 mins, Italy Ⓥ ⊙
D: Pier Paolo Pasolini **A:** Franco Citti, Silvana Corsini, Franca Pasut, Paola Guidi, Adele Cambria, Mario Cipriani (Arco/Cino Del Duca)

Tale is essentially about Accattone, a sort of Roman rebel without a cause who lives from hand to mouth in the daily pursuit of the wherewithal to live, preferably accomplished without manual labor, and sometimes with the unsavory financial support of local prostitutes. Pasolini's actors, practically every one of them taken from life (many are reenacting their slum selves), are all excellent. Franco Citti is especially standout as the sleepy-eyed Accattone, a definite find. A Bach musical adaptation effectively counterpoints action, especially in a fight scene.

ACCIDENT
1967, 105 mins, UK Ⓥ ⊙
D: Joseph Losey **A:** Dirk Bogarde, Stanley Baker, Jacqueline Sassard, Michael York, Vivien Merchant, (London)

The team that turned *The Servant* into a success took another novel as their plot material—Nicholas Mosley's *Accident*—and jacked it into a haunting study in relationships. It starts with a car crash splitting that night air of the quiet countryside outside Oxford. A male student has been killed, and his female companion, a campus gal, is taken into the neighboring mansion, occupied by the university teacher (Dirk Bogarde) who has been instructing them both in philosophy. The accident sparks the prolonged flashback that explores the tight-knit relationship of this enclosed community.

ACCIDENTAL HERO
See: Hero

ACCIDENTAL TOURIST, THE
1988, 121 mins, US Ⓥ ⊙ ▭
D: Lawrence Kasdan **A:** William Hurt, Kathleen Turner, Geena Davis, Amy Wright, Bill Pullman, Ed Begley Jr. (Warner)

The Accidental Tourist is a slow, sonorous, and largely satisfying adaptation of Anne Tyler's bestseller of one man's intensely self-contained passage from a state of grief to one of newfound love. William Hurt is an uptight, travel-book writer from the slightly eccentric, financially comfortable Leary family of unmarried middle-aged siblings in this essentially simple narrative story awash in warmth and wisdom about the emotional human animal.
1988: Best Supp. Actress (Geena Davis)
Nominations: Best Picture, Score, Adapted Screenplay

ACCUSED, THE
1949, 101 mins, US Ⓥ
D: William Dieterle **A:** Loretta Young, Robert Cummings, Wendell Corey, Sam Jaffe, Douglas Dick, Sara Allgood (Paramount)

The Accused exploits fear and emotional violence into a high-grade melodrama. An unbalanced but attractive student is on the make for his professor. By guile he induces her to ride with him to the beach. He attempts to attack her and she, in a moment of surrender to violence, bashes his head in with a tire iron. The crime is concealed to make it look like he had died in a dive over the sea cliff. Loretta Young's portrayal of the distraught professor plays strongly for sympathy. It's an intelligent delineation, gifting the role with life.

ACCUSED, THE
1988, 110 mins, US Ⓥ ⊙
D: Jonathan Kaplan **A:** Kelly McGillis, Jodie Foster, Bernie Coulson, Leo Rossi, Ann Hearn, Carmen Argenziano (Paramount)

The Accused is a dry case study of a rape incident whose only impact comes from the sobering crime itself, not the dramatic treatment. Screenplay is designed to pose questions about the thin line between sexual provocation and assault, seduction and force, and observation of and participation in a crime. Pic begins with a bloodied, disheveled Jodie Foster stumbling out of a roadhouse. A young patron calls the police to report an incident, and in short order three men plead guilty to the reduced charge of reckless endangerment rather than rape. Lawyer (Kelly McGillis) abruptly decides to pursue the matter much further by prosecuting some of the onlookers in the bar for criminal solicitation.
1988: Best Actress (Jodie Foster)

ACE IN THE HOLE
1951, 111 mins, US Ⓥ
D: Billy Wilder **A:** Kirk Douglas, Jan Sterling, Bob Arthur, Porter Hall, Frank Cady, Richard Benedict (Paramount)

The grim story of an unscrupulous reporter who wins brief fame at the expense of a cave-in victim is rather graphically unfolded in *Ace in the Hole*. Douglas enacts the heel reporter ably, giving it color to balance its unsympathetic character. Jan Sterling also is good in a role that has no softening touches, and Benedict's victim portrayal is first-rate. Billy Wilder's direction captures the feel of morbid expectancy that always comes out in the curious that flock to scenes of tragedy.
1951: Nomination: Best Story & Screenplay

ACES HIGH
1976, 114 mins, UK/FRANCE Ⓥ
D: Jack Gold **A:** Malcolm McDowell, Christopher Plummer, Simon Ward, Peter

Firth, John Gielgud, Trevor Howard (EMI/Fisz)

Pic is based on R. C. Sheriff's 1929 London and Broadway stage play, *Journey's End*, a classic on the theme of the futility and boredom of trench warfare in which some men cracked up while others found ways, like the bottle, of averting crack-up. *Aces High* packs little of the involving emotional credibility and impact of the play. Malcolm McDowell is both brave and scared and dependent on whiskey to sustain him as a credible leader of machine-gun fodder.

ACES
IRON EAGLE III
1992, 98 mins, US ⓥ ⊙
D: John Glen A: Louis Gossett Jr., Rachel McLish, Paul Freeman, Horst Buchholz, Christopher Cazenove, Sonny Chiba (Seven Arts/Carolco)

Aces is an action-packed, campy entry in Lou Gossett's *Iron Eagle* series. Best in its cartoonish moments, this follow-up helmed by James Bond director John Glen notably introduces the beautiful bodybuilder Rachel McLish. McLish is terrific in action scenes and merely needs intensive coaching on her acting.

ACE VENTURA, PET DETECTIVE
1994, 93 mins, US ⓥ ⊙
D: Tom Shadyac A: Jim Carrey, Courteney Cox, Sean Young, Dan Marino, Noble Winningham, Udo Kier (Morgan Creek/Warner)

Ace spoofs the detective genre by posting Carrey as a goofball private gumshoe whose specialty is finding missing pets. Pic scores points for its peppy, unpretentious quest to wrest laughs out of less-than-sparkling material. Best gags involve Ventura's menagerie-packed apartment and animallike qualities, including high-revved senses of taste, smell, and sexual appetite.

ACE VENTURA: WHEN NATURE CALLS
1995, 92 mins, US ⓥ ⊙
D: Steve Oedekerk A: Jim Carrey, Ian McNeice, Simon Callow, Maynard Eziashi, Bob Gunton, Sophie Okonedo (Morgan Creek/Warner)

As fresh, brash, and outrageous as the original. Plot is the least of concerns in the sequel. It's your basic boy gets bat, boy loses bat, boy gets bat back yarn, an opportunity to take this unlikely screen hero into satire, spoof, utter juvenilia, total tastelessness, and, believe it or not, social

commentary. It's a death-defying hodge-podge anchored by the complete confidence of star Jim Carrey.

ACROSS 110TH STREET
1972, 102 mins, US ⓥ
D: Barry Shear A: Anthony Quinn, Yaphet Kotto, Anthony Franciosa, Paul Benjamin, Ed Bernard, Richard Ward (Film Guarantors/United Artists)

Across 110th Street is not for the squeamish. Those portions of it which aren't bloody violent are filled in by the squalid location sites in New York's Harlem or equally unappealing ghetto areas, leaving no relief from depression and oppression.

ACROSS THE BRIDGE
1957, 103 mins, UK
D: Ken Annakin A: Rod Steiger, David Knight, Marla Landi, Noel Willman, Bernard Lee, Eric Pohlmann (IFP)

Across the Bridge is a gripping character study of an arrogant man who, through his own crookedness, folly, and greed, topples from power to degrading death as a gutter outcast. Complicated goings-on are background to a remarkable study of mental and physical decay by Steiger. As the Mexican police chief, Noel Willman gives a wily, subtle performance which, because of its very restraint, contrasts admirably with the Steiger technique.

ACROSS THE PACIFIC
1942, 86 mins, US ⓥ
D: John Huston A: Humphrey Bogart, Sydney Greenstreet, Mary Astor, Victor Sen Yung, Keye Luke, Richard Loo (Warner)

The yarn never gets into the Pacific Ocean, despite the title. After Humphrey Bogart is court-martialed out of the army coast artillery, he shifts to Canada in attempt to enlist in the Dominion artillery. Turned down, he gets passage on a Jap freighter bound for Panama and the Orient. Although picture does not quite hit the edge-of-seat tension engendered by *Maltese Falcon*, it's a breezy and fast-paced melodrama. Huston directs deftly from thrill-packed script by [Richard] Macauley.

ACROSS THE WIDE MISSOURI
1951, 78 mins, US ⓥ
D: William A. Wellman A: Clark Gable, Ricardo Montalban, John Hodiak, Adolphe Menjou, Maria Elena Marques, J. Carrol Naish (M-G-M)

The color lensing of the rugged outdoor locations backgrounding the story of beaver trappers and Indians in the early west brings the sites to the screen with breathtaking beauty. Critically, though, the presentation is choppy and episodic, and the device of having the Indian dialogue lengthily translated, is dull and boring. Plot finds Gable, a rough-and-ready trapper, taking Marques as a bride because he believes it will help him get into some untouched beaver country. Gable, the wife, and other trappers make the long trek and, upon arrival, are temporarily repulsed by young Indians led by Ricardo Montalban.

ACT OF VIOLENCE
1949, 82 mins, US
D: Fred Zinnemann **A:** Van Heflin, Robert Ryan, Janet Leigh, Phyllis Thaxter, Mary Astor, Berry Kroeger (M-G-M)

Story concerns two vets. Van Heflin has come out of the war with honors, while his comrades, all but one, were killed in a Nazi prison camp. Robert Ryan, crippled and vengeful, pursues Heflin to make him answer for betraying his buddies. Heflin and Ryan deliver punchy performances. A standout is the brassy, blowsy femme created by Mary Astor, a woman of the streets who gives Heflin shelter during his wild flight from fate.

ACTORS AND SIN
1952, 85 mins, US
D: Ben Hecht **A:** Edward G. Robinson, Marsha Hunt, Dan O'Herlihy, Eddie Albert, Tracey Roberts, Jenny Hecht (Hecht/United Artists)

Written, produced, and directed by Ben Hecht, *Actors and Sin* is an overall title for two stories separately tagged. *Actor's Blood* largely wastes the talents of Edward G. Robinson and Marsha Hunt. *Woman of Sin* is a genuinely amusing burlesque of prewar Hollywood.

ACTOR'S REVENGE, AN
See: Yukinojo Henge

ACTRESS, THE
1953, 89 mins, US
D: George Cukor **A:** Spencer Tracy, Jean Simmons, Teresa Wright, Anthony Perkins, Ian Wolfe, Kay Williams (M-G-M)

A warm, humorous motion picture has been made from Ruth Gordon's chronicle of her New England girlhood. Jean Simmons plays the title role, and portrays perfectly the teenage agonies and joys of a girl who must become an actress at all cost, yet stands in awe of a papa who,

though seeming to have no sympathy for such youthful ambitions, is the one who comes through to make them possible at the finale. Spencer Tracy is fine as the father, a man who desires better things for his family than he can provide on the miserly stipend he makes as a clerk. As a balance wheel in the family, Teresa Wright's mother is top-notch.
1950: Nomination: B&W Costume Design

ADAM HAD FOUR SONS
1941, 108 mins, US
D: Gregory Ratoff **A:** Ingrid Bergman, Warner Baxter, Susan Hayward, Fay Wray (Columbia)

This details the history of a typical American family kept intact by the father through the panic of 1907 and the First World War. The unanimous loyalties of the group, through prosperity and reversals, are broadly etched to result in moderately satisfactory entertainment. Ingrid Bergman turns in a persuasive and sympathetic performance. Warner Baxter does well as the head of the household, steeped in the good old American belief that family bonds are unbreakable.

ADAM'S RIB
1950, 103 mins, US
D: George Cukor **A:** Spencer Tracy, Katharine Hepburn, Judy Holliday, Tom Ewell, David Wayne, Jean Hagen (M-G-M)

Adam's Rib is a bright comedy success, belting over a succession of sophisticated laughs. Setup has Spencer Tracy as an assistant d.a., married to femme attorney Katharine Hepburn. He believes no woman has the right to take shots at another femme. Hepburn believes a woman has the same right to invoke the unwritten law as a man. They do courtroom battle over their theories when Tracy is assigned to prosecute Judy Holliday. This is the sixth Metro teaming of Tracy and Hepburn. A better realization of type than Holliday's portrayal of a dumb Brooklyn femme doesn't seem possible.
1950: Nomination: Best Story & Screenplay

ADDAMS FAMILY, THE
1991, 99 mins, US
D: Barry Sonnenfeld **A:** Anjelica Huston, Raul Julia, Christopher Lloyd, Dan Hedaya, Elizabeth Wilson, Christina Ricci (Paramount)

Despite inspired casting and nifty visual trappings, the eagerly awaited *Ad-*

dams Family figures as a major disappointment. First-time director Barry Sonnenfeld never really gets past the skeletal plot, which plays like a collection of sitcom one-liners augmented by feature-film special effects.

1991: Nomination: Best Costume Design

ADDAMS FAMILY VALUES
1993, 93 mins, US Ⓥ ⊙

D: Barry Sonnenfeld **A:** Anjelica Huston, Raul Julia, Christopher Lloyd, Joan Cusack, Christina Ricci, Carol Kane (Paramount)

The big-screen sequel shares many of the pluses and minuses of the 1991 excursion. It remains perilously slim in the story department but glides over the thin ice with technical razzle-dazzle and an exceptionally winning cast. Huston and Julia are one of the truly magical screen couples; it is a sublime pairing of effortless grace. Cusack is a lively addition, playing her black widow character as a princess with an attitude.

1993: Nomination: Best Art Direction

ADDICTION, THE
1995, 82 mins, US Ⓥ

D: Abel Ferrara **A:** Lili Taylor, Christopher Walken, Annabella Sciorra, Edie Falco, Paul Calderon, Fredro Star (Fast)

Vampires go for their Ph.D.s in *The Addiction,* a horror show that's heady in both senses of the word. Abel Ferrara's maverick entry in the never-dead genre is dramatically surprising, stylishly made in black-and-white ,and well acted, especially by Lili Taylor in the leading role. Even when the narrative road turns bumpy, what holds the picture together is Taylor. Stalking around in shades most of the time, Taylor makes palpable her character's intense suffering at the outset as well as, later on, her superhuman strength and resolve.

ADJUSTER, THE
1991, 102 mins, Canada Ⓥ ⊙ ⊡

D: Atom Egoyan **A:** Elias Koteas, Arsinee Khanjian, Maury Chaykin, Gabrielle Rose, Jennifer Dale, David Hemblen (Alliance/Ego)

In its escalating quest for eccentricity, Atom Egoyan's analysis of voyeurism is profoundly shallow. Noah (Elias Koteas), an insurance adjuster, is a wedded philanderer who exploits the vulnerability of female clients who've lost their homes to fires. His mate Hera (played by Egoyan's mate, Arsinee Khanjian) is a film censor

who secretly videotapes porn flicks for he sister Sete (Rose Sarkisyan), a matron with betwixt desires. These frigid spouses ren their model home to a couple (Maury Chaykin, Gabrielle Rose) who stiffly stag their sexual fantasies in absurd and even tually violent acts. Their characters have potential that the script never develops.

ADMIRABLE CRICHTON, THE (US: PARADISE LAGOON)
1957, 93 mins, UK

D: Lewis Gilbert **A:** Kenneth More, Dian Cilento, Cecil Parker, Sally Ann Howes Martita Hunt, Jack Watling (Moder Screen Play)

A peer takes his three daughters off or a yachting cruise with a few friends an domestic staff. They are shipwrecked an marooned on an uncharted island. Crich ton (More), the impeccable butler, i obliged to take complete control, becaus of the inefficiency of the other castaways Although More lacks the requisite statur of an English butler, his personality make a more human and sympathetic figure o the servant who has a firmer sense of snob values than his master. Cecil Parker, alter nately genial and pompous as the father is perhaps more in keeping with the pe riod.

ADVENTURE
1945, 130 mins, US

D: Victor Fleming **A:** Clark Gable, Gree Garson, Joan Blondell, Thomas Mitchell Tom Tully, Richard Haydn (M-G-M)

Film shows a new Gable. He has many of the old mannerisms, but director Victor Fleming makes him overly boisterous and stubborn, a seafaring man who would toss aside his new bride of a few days like she was just another girl in port. Garson dominates every scene, even when being browbeaten by the obstinate mate. She effects the transition from the prim, standoffish office gal into a life-loving femme who refuses to let her man get away.

ADVENTURE FOR TWO
See: The Demi-Paradise

ADVENTURE OF SHERLOCK HOLMES'S SMARTER BROTHER, THE
1975, 91 mins, UK Ⓥ

D: Gene Wilder **A:** Gene Wilder, Madeline Kahn, Marty Feldman, Dom DeLuise, Leo McKern, Roy Kinnear (20th Century-Fox)

Gene Wilder joins Mel Brooks in that elusive pantheon of madcap humor, by virtue of Wilder's script, title characterization, and directorial debut, all of which are outstanding. Wilder's script sends the famous Holmes (played by Douglas Wilmer) and Dr. Watson (Thorley Walters) ostensibly out of England, in order to fool Professor Moriarty (Leo McKern).

ADVENTURERS, THE
1970, 171 mins, US Ⓥ ⌷
D: Lewis Gilbert **A:** Bekim Fehmiu, Charles Aznavour, Alan Badel, Candice Bergen, Thommy Berggren, Ernest Borgnine (Paramount)

The Adventurers is a classic monument to bad taste. Film is marked by profligate and squandered production opulence; inferior, imitative, and curiously old-hat direction; banal, ludicrous dialogue; substandard, lifeless, and embarrassing acting; cornball music; indulgent, gratuitous, and boring violence; and luridly nonerotic sex. Harold Robbins's guesswho novel about the jet set and South American politics was as commercial as it was trashy; film version may be fairly said to make the novel look better.

ADVENTURES AT RUGBY
See: Tom Brown's Schooldays

ADVENTURES IN BABYSITTING
1987, 99 mins, US Ⓥ ⊚
D: Chris Columbus **A:** Elisabeth Shue, Maia Brewton, Keith Coogan, Anthony Rapp, Vincent D'Onofrio, Penelope Ann Miller (Touchstone)

Ferris Bueller meets *Risky Business* in this teen dream set in (where else?) the suburbs of Chicago. Chris Columbus weighs in adequately in his directorial debut, thanks to a fresh, solid lead performance from Elisabeth Shue. Yet the film can never rise above the leaden script.

ADVENTURES OF BARON MUNCHAUSEN, THE
1989, 125 mins, UK/W. Germany Ⓥ ⊚
D: Terry Gilliam **A:** John Neville, Eric Idle, Jonathan Pryce, Oliver Reed, Sting, Robin Williams (Prominent/Laura)

A fitting final installment in Terry Gilliam's trilogy begun with *Time Bandits* and continued with *Brazil, The Adventures of Baron Munchausen* shares many of those films' strengths and weaknesses, but doesn't possess the visionary qualities of the latter. The film offers a continual feast for the eyes, and not enough for the funny bone or the heart. Set in Europe in the 18th century, tale begins with a city under intense siege by the Turks. Gilliam takes the viewer into the exquisite palace of the sultan, whose ferocity is aroused when he loses a bet to a visiting baron (John Neville). With the help of his variously and superhumanly gifted gang of four, the Baron makes off with the sultan's entire treasure, but his city is left to suffer the consequences.

1989: Nominations: Best Art Direction, Costume Design, Makeup, Visual Effects

ADVENTURES OF BARRY MCKENZIE, THE
1972, 117 mins, Australia
D: Bruce Beresford **A:** Barry Crocker, Barry Humphries, Paul Bertram, Dennis Price, Avice Landon, Peter Cook (Longford)

Satirist Barry Humphries has put his talents to a film, as coauthor and costar. The result is what one would expect if the Marx Brothers were put into an Aussiebrand *Carry On* pic. Barry Crocker plays title role of the gauche young Aussie visiting Britain for the first time. His turns of phrases are witty and original, often with a bawdy tinge, and although much is in the Australian vernacular (frequently invented by Humphries), few are likely to miss the drift of the remarks.

ADVENTURES OF BUCKAROO BANZAI ACROSS THE 8TH DIMENSION, THE
1984, 103 mins, US Ⓥ ⊚ ⌷
D: W. D. Richter **A:** Peter Weller, John Lithgow, Ellen Barkin, Jeff Goldblum, Christopher Lloyd, Rosalind Cash (Sherwood)

The Adventures of Buckaroo Banzai plays more like an experimental film than a Hollywood production aimed at a mass audience. It violates every rule of storytelling and narrative structure in creating a self-contained world of its own. First-time director W. D. Richter and writer Earl Mac Rauch have created a comic-book world chock-full of references, images, pseudoscientific ideas, and plain mumbo jumbo. As the great one (Buckaroo), Peter Weller presents a moving target that is tough to hit. Also very funny is Jeff Goldblum, coming as if from another dimension as every mother's Jewish son.

ADVENTURES OF DON JUAN
1949, 110 mins, US Ⓥ ⊚
D: Vincent Sherman **A:** Errol Flynn, Viveca Lindfors, Robert Douglas, Raymond Burr, Alan Hale, Ann Rutherford (Warner)

The loves and escapades of the fabulous Don Juan are particularly adapted to the screen abilities of Errol Flynn and he gives them a flair that pays off strongly. Viveca Lindfors costars as the queen and she brings a compelling beauty to the role. Top action is reached in the deadly duel between Flynn and Robert Douglas, the crooked prime minister, climaxing with a long leap down a huge flight of castle stairs.

1949: Best Color Costume Design
Nomination: Best Color Art Direction

ADVENTURES OF FORD FAIRLANE, THE

1990, 104 mins, US Ⓥ ⊙ ▭
D: Renny Harlin **A:** Andrew Dice Clay, Wayne Newton, Priscilla Presley, Morris Day, Lauren Holly, Robert Englund (20th Century-Fox/Silver)

Surprisingly funny and expectedly rude, this first starring vehicle by vilified stand-up comic Andrew Dice Clay has a decidedly lowbrow humor that is a sort of modern equivalent of that of the Three Stooges. Clay plays Ford Fairlane, a private eye specializing in cases involving rock acts (hence his overused nickname, the rock-and-roll detective). The film's most significant find, undoubtedly, is Lauren Holly, who brings a lot of flash and charisma to a difficult role as Fairlane's longing girl Friday. Also, Robert Englund (a.k.a. Freddy Krueger) plays a sadistic killer, sans makeup.

ADVENTURES OF HUCK FINN, THE

1993, 108 mins, US Ⓥ ⊙
D: Stephen Sommers **A:** Elijah Wood, Courtney B. Vance, Robbie Coltrane, Jason Robards, Ron Perlman, Dana Ivey (Walt Disney)

Disney's remake of Mark Twain's classic *The Adventures of Huckleberry Finn* is a timely, literate, and handsome film. However, the acting of the two leads fails to provide the electrifying and stirring mood that the tale deserves. Elijah Wood stars as the roguish Huck Finn, living with the Widow Douglas (Dana Ivey). The film improves considerably once Huck encounters Jim (Courtney B. Vance), the runaway slave. The two drifters strike up a unique friendship as they start their fateful journey down the Mississippi. Fortunately, the two central roles are surrounded by a marvelous ensemble of supporting actors: the brilliant Jason Robards and Robbie Coltrane as the King and the Duke, respectively, Ron Perlman as the nasty Pap Finn,

Ivey as the Widow Douglas, and Lau Bundy as the precocious Susan Wilks.

ADVENTURES OF HUCKLEBERRY FINN, THE

1960, 90 mins, US Ⓥ ▭
D: Michael Curtiz **A:** Tony Randall, Edd Hodges, Archie Moore, Patty McCo mack, Neville Brand, Mickey Shaugh nessy (M-G-M)

Mark Twain's Huckleberry Finn is a boy. Eddie Hodges's Huck isn't. Therei lurks the basic reason this production the Twain classic is not all it could, ar should, be. An equal share of the rap mu be shouldered by director Michael Curti not only for the youthful star's shortcom ings in the role, but for a general slack, disturbing shortage of vitality noticeable several key junctures. An extremely co orful and experienced cast has been a sembled. These include Tony Randa whose work as the roguish King is a d lightful balance of whimsy and threat. Ar Archie Moore, the light-heavyweig champion of the world, who brings tl story its only moments of real warmth ar tenderness.

ADVENTURES OF MARCO POLO, THE

1938, 100 mins, US
D: Archie Mayo **A:** Gary Cooper, Sigr Gurie, Basil Rathbone, George Barbie Binnie Barnes, Ernest Truex (Goldwy United Artists)

A glamorous figure in history, whic places him in the 13th century as the fir European to visit the Orient, Marco Po has been portrayed as traveler, adventure merchant, diplomat. He probably was of these and a first-class liar besides. Ro ert E. Sherwood, who penned the scree script, conceives him also as an arde lover and politician. Gary Cooper fits tl character to the apex of his six-feet-tw The plot is strictly melodrama, starti with Ahmed (Basil Rathbone) as a conni ing prime minister to the Chinese rule Kublai Kahn (George Barbier). Marc Polo is admitted to the court and the glimpses the beautiful princess, who much taken with his height and easy ma ner of lovemaking behind the Chine fountain.

ADVENTURES OF MARK TWAIN, THE

1944, 130 mins, US
D: Irving Rapper **A:** Fredric Marc Alexis Smith, Donald Crisp, Alan Hale,

Aubrey Smith, John Carradine (Warner)

So rich and full was the life of Mark Twain, born Sam Clemens, that it requires two hours-plus to tell the full tale. It is a film that has its measure of symbolism: linking the humorist's lifetime of 75 years to appearances of Halley's Comet. In between Clemens adventures as a river boatman, journeyman reporter, and western goldruster, only to find sudden fame with his saga of the jumping frogs. Soon follow renown and fortune as Tom Sawyer, Huck Finn, and the rest of his funny books capture the hearts and the minds of all America.
1944: Nominations: Best B&W Art Direction, Scoring of a Dramatic Picture, Special Effects

ADVENTURES OF PRISCILLA, QUEEN OF THE DESERT, THE
1994, 102 mins, AUSTRALIA Ⓥ ⊙
D: Stephan Elliott **A:** Terence Stamp, Hugo Weaving, Guy Pearce, Bill Hunter, Sarah Chadwick, Mark Holmes (PFE/Latent Image/Specific)

A cheerfully vulgar and bitchy, but essentially warmhearted road movie with a difference, which boasts an amazing star turn by Terence Stamp as a transsexual, Stephan Elliott's second feature is a lot of fun. The plot of *Priscilla* isn't as important as the outlandish, wicked dialogue, the wild costumes and makeup, and the general high spirits of the entire enterprise. Dressed in femme clothes throughout, Stamp gives one of his best perfs as the bereaved woman whose latent masculinity occasionally shows through her graciously elegant exterior.
1994: Best Costume Design

ADVENTURES OF QUENTIN DURWARD, THE
See: Quentin Durward

ADVENTURES OF ROBIN HOOD, THE
1938, 104 mins, US Ⓥ ⊙
D: Michael Curtiz, William Keighley **A:** Errol Flynn, Olivia de Havilland, Basil Rathbone, Claude Rains, Patric Knowles, Eugene Pallette (Warner)

Cinematic pageantry at its best, a highly imaginative telling of folklore in all the hues of Technicolor. Played with intensity by an excellent company of actors, an illusion of fairy-story quality is retained throughout. Teamed with Olivia de Havilland as Marian, Flynn is an ardent suitor and a gallant courtier.

1938: Best Interior Decoration (Carl Jules Weyl), Original Score, Editing
Nomination: Best Picture

ADVENTURES OF SADIE, THE
See: Our Girl Friday

ADVENTURES OF SHERLOCK HOLMES, THE
1939, 71 mins, US Ⓥ ⊙
D: Alfred Werker **A:** Basil Rathbone, Nigel Bruce, Ida Lupino, Alan Marshal, E. E. Clive, George Zucco (20th Century-Fox)

Choice of Basil Rathbone as Sherlock was a wise one. Nigel Bruce as Dr. Watson is equally expert. With the two key characters thus capably handled, the film has the additional asset of being well conceived and grippingly presented. George Zucco offers a splendid characterization as the archcriminal and Ida Lupino is highly competent as the sole romantic figure in the mystery fable.

ADVENTURES OF THE ROCKETEER, THE
See: The Rocketeer

ADVENTURES OF TOM SAWYER, THE
1938, 93 mins, US Ⓥ
D: Norman Taurog **A:** Tommy Kelly, Jackie Moran, Ann Gillis, May Robson, Walter Brennan, Victor Jory (Selznick/United Artists)

Adventures of Tom Sawyer is in Technicolor and contains visual beauty and appeal in addition to a faithful and nearly literal adaptation of the Mark Twain story. Casting of the picture was reportedly a laborious job, in the course of which hundreds of boys were tested before Tommy Kelly, from the Bronx, NY, was selected for the role of Tom. His early scenes show self-consciousness but in the final sequences when he is being pursued by Injun Joe, Kelly performs like a veteran. Walter Brennan is a standout among the adult players.
1938: Nomination: Art Direction

ADVISE AND CONSENT
1962, 140 mins, US Ⓥ ▭
D: Otto Preminger **A:** Henry Fonda, Charles Laughton, Don Murray, Walter Pidgeon, Gene Tierney, Peter Lawford (Columbia)

Preminger has endowed his production with wholly capable performers. Henry Fonda as the secretary-of-state nominee, Charles Laughton as a southern-smooth rebellious Solon, Don Murray as the focal point of the homo-suicidal scandal, and Walter Pidgeon as a majority leader fighting in best stentorian tradition in Fonda's behalf all register firmly. The characterizations come through with fine clarity. Disturbing is lack of sufficiently clear motivation for the nub of the action. The settings are powerfully real. A Senate hearing room, the Senate itself, a party home in immediate Washington, and varying apartments plus a place in DC suburbia all have the look of genuineness.

AFFAIRS OF SUSAN, THE
1945, 110 mins, US
D: William A. Seiter **A:** Joan Fontaine, George Brent, Dennis O Keefe, Don DeFore, Walter Abel, Rita Johnson (Paramount)

In this tale about the four loves of Susan Darell (Joan Fontaine), producer Hal B. Wallis has invested the picture with considerable production values, but making the story and action the thing. Fontaine's sparkle in this first comedienne role is impressive. She swings easily from plain Jane to the seasoned-actress type, then to the glamorous, and finally to the intellectual. Top male contribution is Brent, as the producer. He's a fine combination of the hard-boiled showman and admiring husband.
1945: Nomination: Best Original Story

AFFAIR TO REMEMBER, AN
1957, 115 mins, US ⓥ ⊙ ▭
D: Leo McCarey **A:** Cary Grant, Deborah Kerr, Richard Denning, Neva Patterson, Cathleen Nesbitt, Robert Q. Lewis (20th Century-Fox)

Adding comedy lines, music, color, and CinemaScope, Jerry Wald and Leo McCarey turn this remake of the 1939 *Love Affair* into a winning film that is alternately funny and tenderly sentimental. *An Affair to Remember,* using plenty of attractive settings (on and off the USS *Constitution*), is still primarily a film about two people; and since those two happen to be Cary Grant and Deborah Kerr, the bittersweet romance sparkles and crackles with high spirits.
1957: Nominations: Best Cinematography, Costume Design, Score of a Dramatic Picture, Song ("An Affair to Remember")

AFRAID OF THE DARK
1992, 91 mins, UK/France ⓥ ⊙
D: Mark Peploe **A:** James Fox, Fanny Ardant, Paul McGann, Clare Holman, Robert

Stephens, Susan Wooldridge (Telescope/ Ariane/Cine Cinq)

Bernardo Bertolucci scripter Mark Peploe makes an ambitious bow behind the lens with *Afraid of the Dark,* a tricky mix of slasher movie and psychodrama that's strong on tease but weak on final delivery. Double-headed plot centers on an 11-year-old (Ben Keyworth), whose dad (James Fox) is a cop and mother (Fanny Ardant) is blind. For pure technique (and Hitchcock/Michael Powell homework), Peploe can't be faulted.

AFRICAN FURY
See: Cry, the Beloved Country

AFRICAN QUEEN, THE
1951, 104 mins, UK ⓥ ⊙
D: John Huston **A:** Humphrey Bogart, Katharine Hepburn, Robert Morley, Peter Bull, Theodore Bikel, Walter Gotell (Horizon/Romulus)

This story of adventure and romance, experienced by a couple in Africa just as World War I got under way, is an engrossing motion picture. Just offbeat enough in story, locale, and star teaming of Humphrey Bogart and Katharine Hepburn to stimulate the imagination. It is a picture with an unassuming warmth and naturalness. The independent production unit took stars and cameras to Africa to film C. S. Forester's novel, *African Queen,* against its actual background. Performance-wise, Bogart has never been seen to better advantage. Nor has he ever had a more knowing, talented film partner than Hepburn.
1951: Best Actor (Humphrey Bogart).
Nominations: Best Director, Actress (Katharine Hepburn), Screenplay

AFRICA TEXAS STYLE
1967, 110 mins, US ⓥ
D: Andrew Marton **A:** Hugh O'Brian, John Mills, Nigel Green, Tom Nardini, Adrienne Corri (Paramount/Ivan Tors)

Shot entirely in Kenya, director Andrew Marton, scripter Andy White, and cameraman Paul Beeson have thoroughly caught the feeling of Africa. Story twirls about the subject of game ranching, the domestication and breeding of wild animal life as a potentially huge source of meat and as a means of preserving many of Africa's rapidly vanishing species of wild beasts.

AFTER DARK, MY SWEET
1990, 114 mins, US ⓥ ⊙ ▭
D: James Foley **A:** Jason Patric, Rachel

Ward, Bruce Dern, George Dickerson, James Cotton, Corey Carrier (Avenue)

Director-cowriter James Foley has given this near-perfect adaptation of a Jim Thompson novel a contempo setting and emotional realism that make it as potent as a snakebite. Foley's take on *After Dark, My Sweet* feels right from the first frame, as ex-boxer and nuthouse escapee Kid Collins (Jason Patric) shambles into a desert town with a cardboard bundle under his arm, accompanied by his own desultory narration of Thompson's pungent first-person prose. In a bar he meets Fay Anderson (Rachel Ward), who tortures and tests him with her wit before taking him home. Ward is at her direct and provocative best, and Patric is enigmatic and affecting as the bruised drifter. Dern has his best role in years as the grasping conman Uncle Bud, and actually evokes some sympathy for the weasely character.

AFTERGLOW
1997, 113 mins, US ⓥ ⊙
D: Alan Rudolph A: Julie Christie, Nick Nolte, Lara Flynn Boyle, Jonny Lee Miller (Sand Castle 5/Elysian Dreams)

Followers of Alan Rudolph's career will rejoice at *Afterglow,* an incurably romantic comedy-drama. Jeffrey Byron (Jonny Lee Miller) is a self-centered twentysomething careerist with a sexually frustrated wife, Marianne (Lara Flynn Boyle). Amorous Lucky Mann (Nick Nolte), a repair contractor, experiences his own marital problems with longtime spouse Phyllis (Julie Christie), a former B-movie actress. Lucky arrives at the Byrons' apartment to do some minor repairs, and Marianne becomes instantly infatuated with him. This modern fairy tale needed four spectacular performers; unfortunately, it has only two. Christie dominates every scene she is in, rendering the witty, often wickedly funny lines with a suave irony. She is ably supported by Nolte, in a flashy, equally demanding role. Boyle is too harsh and one-dimensional, and Miller is pale and a bit stiff.

1997: Nomination: Best Actress (Julie Christie).

AFTER HOURS
1985, 97 mins, US ⓥ ⊙
D: Martin Scorsese A: Griffin Dunne, Rosanna Arquette, Verna Bloom, Thomas Chong, Linda Fiorentino, Teri Garr (Geffen/Double Play)

The cinema of paranoia and persecution reaches an apogee in *After Hours,* a nightmarish black comedy from Martin Scorsese. This anxiety-ridden picture would have been pretty funny if it didn't play like a confirmation of everyone's worst fears about contemporary urban life. A description of one rough night in the life of a mild-mannered New York computer programmer, film is structured like a Pilgrim's Progress through the anarchic, ever-treachous streets of SoHo. Every corner represents a turn for the worse, and by the end of the night, he's got to wonder, like Kafka's K, if he might not actually be guilty of something.

AFTER THE FOX
1966, 102 mins, UK/Italy ⓥ ▭
D: Vittorio De Sica A: Peter Sellers, Britt Ekland, Lidia Brazzi, Paola Stoppa, Victor Mature, Martin Balsam (Delegate/Nancy)

Peter Sellers is in nimble, lively form in this whacky comedy which, though sometimes strained, has a good comic idea and gives the star plenty of scope for his usual range of impersonations. Neil Simon's screenplay is uneven but naturally has a good quota of wit, and Vittorio De Sica's direction plays throughout for laughs.

AFTER THE THIN MAN
1936, 107 mins, US ⓥ
D: W. S. Van Dyke A: William Powell, Myrna Loy, James Stewart, Elissa Landi, Joseph Calleia, Jessie Ralph (M-G-M)

First thing everyone will want to know about this one is whether it is as good as *The Thin Man,* and the answer is that it is and it isn't. It has the same stars, William Powell and Myrna Loy; the same style of breezy direction by W. S. Van Dyke; almost as many sparkling lines of dialogue and amusing situations; but it hasn't, and probably couldn't have, the same freshness and originality of its predecessor. The two leading players seem to have a swell time throughout. They do a bedroom scene that is packed with laughs, but that is topped by a subsequent sequence when, having slept through an entire day, they have their breakfast in the evening and appear unable, or unwilling, to adjust themselves to the passing of time.

1936: Nomination: Best Screenplay

AGAINST ALL ODDS
1984, 128 mins, US ⓥ ⊙
D: Taylor Hackford A: Rachel Ward, Jeff Bridges, James Woods, Alex Karras, Jane Greer, Richard Widmark (Columbia)

If not for a somewhat murky and mis-

anthropic ending, *Against All Odds* would
stand as a well-engineered second try at
1947's *Out of the Past*. Jeff Bridges is a
fading pro footballer with shady connections to James Woods, a small-time L.A.
bookie-hood who has been keeping house
with Rachel Ward until she stabs him and
gets away. The action ranges all the way
to remote Mexican areas whose scenic
moods are captured nicely by cinematographer Donald Thorin.
1984: Nomination: Best Song ("Against
All Odds (Take a Look at Me Now)")

AGATHA
1979, 98 mins, UK ⊗ ▭
D: Michael Apted **A:** Dustin Hoffman,
Vanessa Redgrave, Timothy Dalton, He-
len Morse, Celia Gregory, Paul Brooke
(Warner/First Artists)

Billed as an imaginary solution to an
authentic mystery, Kathleen Tynan's original story fills in the gaps of Agatha Christie's well-publicized disappearance in
1926. Christie, portrayed by Vanessa Redgrave in superlative fashion, is confronted
with the breakdown of her marriage to war
hero Timothy Dalton. She flees to a remote health spa, where she sets in motion
a unique form of revenge. *Agatha* packs a
surprise twist that the real Agatha Christie
might have envied.
1979: Nomination: Best Costume Design

L' AGE D'OR
(AGE OF GOLD)
1930, 65 mins, France ⊗
D: Luis Bunuel **A:** Gaston Modot, Lya
Lys, Max Ernst, Pierre Prevert, Jose Arti-
gas, Jacques Brunius (Vicomte de Noail-
les)

Luis Bunuel's second effort created
such a furor when first shown in Paris [on
Oct. 28, 1930] that, after a stormy run, it
was finally banned by the French government. Bunuel's film was offensive to both
society and church. Bunuel's anger at society, particularly its attitude on morality,
seems not only dated today, but laugh provoking. (Review is of a 1964 screening at
Lincoln Center, NY, first showing of pic
in the US.) The behavior of his libidinous
hero and heroine, played by Gaston Modot
and Lya Lys in a style straight out of *A
Fool There Was,* wouldn't cause raised
eyebrows today at a Flatbush cocktail
party. As antique as his comments on morality now seem, those Bunuel makes
against religion are still marked by violence, blasphemy, and vilification.

AGENT 8 3/4
See: Hot Enough for June

AGE OF CONSENT
1932, 80 mins, US
D: Gregory La Cava **A:** Dorothy Wilson,
Richard Cromwell, Eric Linden, Arline
Judge, John Halliday (Radio)

Picture marks the first release of Dorothy Wilson, the stenographer in the Radio coast studio offices who was
skyrocketed from her typewriter into semi-
stardom. The newcomer reveals a remarkable aptitude for natural acting. Story is a
sexy tale, dealing in often sprightly manner with the adolescent amours of a coed
campus and its environs. Cast is made up
of young people, with just the leavening
in the professor character, deftly handled
as usual by John Halliday. Central male
characters are played by Richard Cromwell, an excellent choice as the young
hero, and Eric Linden, once more a philandering student highflier.

AGE OF CONSENT
1969, 103 mins, Australia ⊗
D: Michael Powell **A:** James Mason, He-
len Mirren, Jack MacGowran, Neva Carr-
Glyn, Antonia Katsaros, Frank Thring
(Nautilus)

Bradley Morahan (James Mason) is a
famous Australian painter. He proceeds to
the Great Barrier Reef to settle in a
broken-down shack on a dream island.
The only other inhabitants are a gin-
sodden old hag, her granddaughter Cora
(Helen Mirren), and Isabel Marley (Antonia Katsaros), a man-hungry spinster.
The film has plenty of corn, is sometimes
too slow, repetitious, and badly edited, almost as if scenes had been deleted. Yet the
picture has immense charm.

AGE OF GOLD
See: L'Age d'Or

AGE OF INNOCENCE, THE
1993, 136 mins, US ⊗ ⊙ ▭
D: Martin Scorsese **A:** Daniel Day-Lewis,
Michelle Pfeiffer, Winona Ryder, Miriam
Margolyes, Richard E. Grant, Alec Mc-
Cowen (Columbia)

An extraordinarily sumptuous piece of
filmmaking, *The Age of Innocence* is a
faithful adaptation of Edith Wharton's
classic 1921 Pulitzer Prize–winning novel,
which is both a blessing and a bit of a
curse. The material remains cloaked by the
very propriety, stiff manners, and emotional starchiness the picture delineates in
such copious detail in its portrait of an im-

14

possible romance set in the upper reaches of New York society in the 1870s. In his attempt to define an era through a thwarted romance set among the trappings of the very rich, director Martin Scorsese conjures up the cinematic worlds of Max Ophuls, notably *Madame de . . . ,* and Luchino Visconti, particularly *Senso* and *The Leopard*. For a director previously associated mostly with the violence of the lower classes of New York, it's a notable attempt to stretch, and admirable in many ways. Day-Lewis cuts an impressive figure, and the two principal female roles are superbly filled.
1993: Best Costume Design
Nominations: Best Supp. Actress (Winona Ryder), Adapted Screenplay, Art Direction, Original Score

AGNES OF GOD
1985, 98 mins, US Ⓥ ⊙ ▭
D: Norman Jewison **A:** Jane Fonda, Anne Bancroft, Meg Tilly, Anne Pitoniak, Winston Rekert, Gratien Gelinas (Columbia-Delphi IV)

John Pielmeier penned the screenplay from his own 1982 play about a young nun who is found to have given birth and then strangled the baby at an isolated convent. A psychiatrist, played by Jane Fonda, is appointed to determine whether or not the young woman (Meg Tilly) is fit to stand trial. In her aggressive quest for the facts in the case, Fonda goes head to head with Mother Superior Anne Bancroft. Fonda's relentless interrogating, mannered chain-smoking, and enforced two dimensionality cause her to become tiresome very early on. Bancroft gives a generally highly engaging performance. Tilly brings a convincing innocence and sincerity to the role that would be hard to match.
1985: Nominations: Best Actress (Anne Bancroft), Supp. Actress (Meg Tilly), Original Score

AGONY AND THE ECSTASY, THE
1965, 136 mins, US Ⓥ ▭
D: Carol Reed **A:** Charlton Heston, Rex Harrison, Diane Cilento, Harry Andrews, Alberto Lupo, Adolfo Celi (International Classics/20th Century-Fox)

Against a backdrop of political-religious upheaval during the Italian Renaissance, *The Agony and the Ecstasy* focuses on the personal conflict between sculptor-painter Michelangelo and his patron, Pope Julius II. Scripter Philip Dunne has zeroed in on a four-year span during which the painter labored on the ceiling frescoes for the Sistine Chapel. Rex Harrison is outstanding as the Pope. Charlton Heston's Michelangelo is, in its own way, also outstanding. Combination of austere garb, thinned face, short hair and beard, plus underplaying in early scenes, effectively submerge the Heston image fostered by his earlier epix.
1965: Nominations: Best Color Cinematography, Color Costume Design, Color Art Direction, Original Music Score, Sound

AGUIRRE, DER ZORN GOTTES (AGUIRRE, WRATH OF GOD)
1973, 95 mins, W. Germany Ⓥ ⊙
D: Werner Herzog **A:** Klaus Kinski, Cecilia Rivera, Ruy Guerra, Helena Rojo, Del Negro, Peter Berling (Herzog)

Independent West German filmmaker Werner Herzog has trekked down a river in Peru to resurrect the ancient conquistadores of Spain in a sort of parable on human need for power and warping of the best intentions when they are implemented by the sword or by fanatics. The acting is properly larger than life, especially Klaus Kinski as the title character, a lean, driven, but imposing man.

AGUIRRE, WRATH OF GOD
See: Aguirre, Der Zorn Gottes

AI NO CORRIDA
See: L'Empire des Sens

AIR AMERICA
1990, 112 mins, US Ⓥ ⊙ ▭
D: Roger Spottiswoode **A:** Mel Gibson, Robert Downey Jr., Nancy Travis, Ken Jenkins, David Marshall Grant, Lane Smith (Carolco)

Spectacular action sequences and engaging perfs by Mel Gibson and Robert Downey Jr. make this big-budgeter entertaining and provocative. It's probably news to most even at this late date that the CIA, through its proprietary Air America, was using drug money to finance the war in Southeast Asia and condoning the refining and exportation of heroin both to GIs in that part of the world and to the American public. Air America became known as "a dope airline," as Christopher Robbins's 1979 sourcebook puts it, and the filmmakers don't shrink from showing Gibson knowingly flying opium and cynically justifying it as essential to the US war effort.

AIR FORCE
1943, 124 mins, US Ⓥ

D: Howard Hawks **A:** John Ridgely, Gig Young, Arthur Kennedy, Harry Carey, Charles Drake, John Garfield (Warner)

Air Force is the saga of a Flying Fortress (the *Mary Ann,* a Boeing B-17). It is gripping, informative, entertaining, thrilling. It is a patriotic heartthrob in celluloid without preaching; it is inspirational without being phony in its emotions. Perhaps the best-known cast component is John Garfield and it's all the more effective that the principals are not as well known. Harry Carey gives a corking performance as the veteran crew chief, a career sergeant from way back.

1943: Best Editing
Nominations: Best Original Screenplay, B&W Cinematography, Special Effects

AIR FORCE ONE
1997, 124 mins, US Ⓥ ⊙ ▭

D: Wolfgang Petersen **A:** Harrison Ford, Gary Oldman, Glenn Close, Wendy Crewson, Paul Guilfoyle, William H. Macy (Radiant/Beacon/Columbia)

Seeing the president of the United States as a kick-butt action hero sums up the appeal of this preposterously pulpy but quite entertaining suspense meller. A prologue shows a Yank-Russian commando raid snaring fascistic leader Gen. Radek (Jurgen Prochnow). No sooner has Air Force One taken off for the trip home than it is taken over by a bunch of Radek faithful led by the fanatical Ivan (Gary Oldman). President James Marshall (Harrison Ford) seems to escape in an emergency pod. Marshall, however—Vietnam vet and Medal of Honor winner that he is—has not jumped ship, but has become a guerrilla fighter on board his own aircraft. Key scenes are shot and edited to pulse-quickening effect, which casts into shadow the numerous objections one can easily raise to the film: that it is a wildly jingoistic American imperialist exercise, a more covert *Rambo*-like fantasy projection for Vietnam-era men, or that the admittedly clever scenario could have sorely used some wit and humor.

1997: Nominations: Best Editing, Sound

AIRHEADS
1994, 91 mins, US Ⓥ ⊙

D: Michael Lehmann **A:** Brendan Fraser, Steve Buscemi, Adam Sandler, Joe Mantegna, Chris Farley, Amy Locane (20th Century-Fox/Island World)

There's plenty of sound and fury in *Airheads,* and while it would be extreme to say it adds up to nothing, the antic musical lark certainly doesn't have a lot on its mind. An absurdist variation on *Dog Day Afternoon,* the picture is a rather good-natured view of Generation X and the pursuit of rock-and-roll stardom.

AIR MAIL
1932, 85 mins, US

D: John Ford **A:** Pat O'Brien, Ralph Bellamy, Russell Hopton, Slim Summerville, Gloria Stuart, Lilian Bond (Universal)

Picture is a fund of interesting atmosphere about the air-mail service. Duke Talbot (Pat O'Brien) is a great flier and the bravest of the brave, in the air or on the ground. But he's a vainglorious showoff for one thing and a double-crossing lover. His disreputable affair with the wife of one of his service mates earns him the enmity of Mike Miller (Ralph Bellamy) in charge of the Desert Station post in the heart of the Rocky Mountains. The stunt stuff is breathtaking. O'Brien and Bellamy give strong, simple handling to the main roles.

AIRPLANE!
1980, 88 mins, US Ⓥ ⊙

D: Jim Abrahams, David Zucker, Jerry Zucker **A:** Robert Hays, Julie Hagerty, Lloyd Bridges, Peter Graves, Leslie Nielsen, Robert Stack (Paramount)

Airplane! is what they used to call a laff riot. Made by team that turned out *Kentucky Fried Movie,* this spoof of disaster features beats any other film for sheer number of comic gags. Writer-director leave no cliché unturned as they lay waste to the *Airport*-style disaster cycle, among other targets. From the clever *Jaws* takeoff opening to the final, irreverent title card laughs come thick and fast.

AIRPLANE II THE SEQUEL
1982, 85 mins, US ⊙

D: Ken Finkleman **A:** Robert Hays, Julie Hagerty, Lloyd Bridges, Peter Graves, William Shatner, Chad Everett (Paramount)

It can't be said that *Airplane II* is no better or worse than its predecessor. It is far worse, but might seem funnier had there been no original. In the first *Airplane,* Jim Abrahams, David Zucker, and Jerry Zucker had a fresh satirical crack at that hoary old genre, the airborne disaster film. But they wisely chose not to tackle a sequel, leaving incoming writer-director

Ken Finkleman a tough task for his feature debut.

AIRPORT
1970, 137 mins, US Ⓥ ⊙ ▭
D: George Seaton **A:** Burt Lancaster, Dean Martin, Jean Seberg, Jacqueline Bisset, George Kennedy, Helen Hayes (Universal)

Based on the novel by Arthur Hailey, overproduced by Ross Hunter with a cast of stars as long as a jet runway, and adapted and directed by George Seaton in a glossy, slick style, *Airport* is a handsome, often dramatically involving $10 million epitaph to a bygone brand of filmmaking. However, the ultimate dramatic situation of a passenger-loaded jetliner with a psychopathic bomber aboard that has to be brought into a blizzard-swept airport with runway blocked by a snow-stalled plane actually does not create suspense because the audience knows how it's going to end.
1970: Best Supp. Actress (Helen Hayes) **Nominations:** Best Picture, Supp. Actress (Maureen Stapleton), Screenplay, Cinematography, Costume Design, Art Direction, Editing, Original Score, Sound

AIRPORT 80 THE CONCORDE
See: The Concorde Airport 79

AIRPORT 1975
1974, 106 mins, US Ⓥ ▭
D: Jack Smight **A:** Charlton Heston, Karen Black, George Kennedy, Efrem Zimbalist Jr., Susan Clark, Gloria Swanson (Universal)

Airport 1975 gathers its specimens into a 747 jetliner which collides midair with a private plane, precipitating a complicated rescue effort. Charlton Heston's formula characterization is, quite literally, Messiah-ex-machina. Jack Smight's direction has the refreshing pace of a filmmaker who knows his plot can crash unless he hurries.

AIRPORT 77
1977, 113 mins, US Ⓥ ⊙ ▭
D: Jerry Jameson **A:** Jack Lemmon, Lee Grant, Brenda Vaccaro, Joseph Cotten, Olivia de Havilland, James Stewart (Universal)

The story peg here has James Stewart, a billionaire who has converted his home to museum status, loading his private plane with priceless paintings and a broader quality of people for a junket to the estate. However, Lemmon's copilot Robert Foxworth has joined with Monte Markham and Michael Pataki to hijack the plane for the artwork.
1977: Nominations: Best Costume Design, Art Direction

AIRPORT THE CONCORDE
See: The Concorde Airport 79

AIRPORT III
See: Airport 77

AKAHIGE
(RED BEARD)
1965, 188 mins, Japan Ⓥ ⊙ ▭
D: Akira Kurosawa **A:** Toshiro Mifune, Yuzo Kayama, Tsutomu Yamazaki, Kyoko Kagawa, Miyuki Kuwano, Kinuyo Tanaka (Kurosawa/Toho)

It's hokum lifted to the highest denominator, the banal made into near art by great skill and craftsmanship by the Japanese master. The main plot is the old chestnut about the enterprising young doctor and the misunderstood old curmudgeon, in this case Red Beard (Toshiro Mifune). Slowly, as Kurosawa interweaves several plots, understanding for his methods grows as human relations triumph over sheer medical know-how.

AKENFIELD
1975, 95 mins, UK Ⓥ ▭
D: Peter Hall **A:** Garrow Shand, Peggy Cole, Barbara Tilney, Lyn Brooks, Ida Page, Ted Dedman (Angle Films)

Adapted from Ronald Blythe's social study of a Suffolk village, this is the story of three generations of farm laboring, intercutting flashbacks with present day to demonstrate that the more things change, the more they remain the same. It is funny and touching and seldom less than engrossing.

AKIRA
1988, 124 mins, Japan Ⓥ ⊙
D: Katsuhiro Otomo (sup.) (Akira Committee)

A lavish animation extravaganza produced at a cost of $8 million, this futuristic exploration is a follow-up by author-director Katsuhiro Otomo to his tremendously popular comic books. A remarkable technical achievement in every respect, from the imaginative and detailed design of tomorrow to the booming Dolby effects on the soundtrack, pic's only drawback is the slight stiffness in the drawing of human movement.

ALADDIN
1992, 90 mins, US Ⓥ ⊙
D: John Musker, Ron Clements (Walt Disney)

Floridly beautiful, shamelessly derivative, and infused with an irreverent, sophisticated comic flair thanks to Robin Williams's vocal calisthenics, *Aladdin* represents the ultimate synthesis of filmmaking and marketing, extracting winning elements from Disney's last two animated hits (*The Little Mermaid* and *Beauty and the Beast*) as well as more venerable sources, particularly the 1940 *Thief of Bagdad*. Lyricist Tim Rice filled in seamlessly on three of the six songs after Howard Ashman's death, and while Alan Menken's score may not be as instantly hummable as *Beauty*'s, it's still impressive, with two showstoppingly elaborate numbers.
1992: Best Original Score, Song ("A Whole New World")
Nominations: Best Song ("Friends Like Me"), Sound, Sound Effects Editing

ALAMO, THE
1960, 192 mins, US Ⓥ ▱
D: John Wayne [John Ford] **A:** John Wayne, Richard Widmark, Laurence Harvey, Frankie Avalon, Richard Boone, Linda Cristal (Batjac)

Producer-director-star John Wayne has loaded the telling of the tale with happy homilies on American virtues and patriotic platitudes under life-and-death fire which smack of yesteryear theatricalism rather than the realism of modern battle drama. In spite of the painstaking attempts to explore the characters of the picture's three principal heroes (Bowie, Crockett, Travis), there is an absence of emotional feeling, of a sense of participation. With the rousing battle sequence at the climax (for which a goodly share of credit must go to second unit director Cliff Lyons) the picture really commands rapt attention.
1960: Best Sound (Samuel Goldwyn Studio Sound Dept, Todd-AO Sound Dept)
Nominations: Best Picture, Supp. Actor (Chill Wills), Color Cinematography, Editing, Score of a Dramatic Picture, Song ("The Green Leaves of Summer")

ALAMO BAY
1985, 98 mins, US Ⓥ ⊙
D: Louis Malle **A:** Amy Madigan, Ed Harris, Ho Nguyen, Donald Moffat, Truyen V. Tran, Rudy Young (Tri-Star/Delphi III)

Alamo Bay is a failed piece of social consciousness. The peripatetic Louis Malle hasn't managed to shed any meaningful light on his current subject, that of the conflict between refugee Vietnamese and local fisherfolk around Galveston Bay, Texas, circa 1979–81. Malle dared to place an exceedingly unsympathetic character at the center of his drama. Here it is Ed Harris, a bruising, philandering, unreflective lout who resents the intrusion of Vietnamese into his community.

ALAN SMITHEE FILM—BURN, HOLLYWOOD, BURN, AN
1997, 86 mins, US Ⓥ ⊙
D: Arthur Hiller **A:** Ryan O'Neal, Coolio, Chuck D, Eric Idle, Harvey Weinstein, Richard Jeni (Cinergi/Hollywood)

The Alan Smithee pseudonym used by the Directors Guild of America when a filmmaker wants to decline credit has popped up on more than 30 films in as many years. New effort is extremely consistent with the Smithee oeuvre to date. The negative of a $212 million action extravaganza called *Trio*, starring Sylvester Stallone, Whoopi Goldberg, and Jackie Chan, produced by blowhard producer James Edmunds (Ryan O'Neal), has been destroyed by its director, Smithee (Eric Idle), after the film was taken away from him by Edmunds. With Smithee now interned in the Keith Moon Psychiatric Institute in his native England, [what is promised] is an "autopsy" of the film. Docu-like approach, in which things are described more than shown, becomes tiresome and prevents the picture from developing a rhythm of its own. Film teems with minor in-jokes, few of which will mean anything to poeple outside Hollywood.

ALBERT, R.N.
1953, 88 mins, UK
D: Lewis Gilbert **A:** Anthony Steel, Jack Warner, Robert Beatty, William Sylvester, Guy Middleton, Anton Diffring (Eros)

The setting is a German camp for Allied naval officers, the action taking place late in 1944. The camp is regarded by its German masters as escape-proof and admittedly various attempts to breakout have been frustrated by alert prison guards. That is, until one of the internees hits on the idea of making a dummy to cover up for an absentee. The result is Albert, R.N., with a papier-mâché head and a wire-framed body. A solid all-around cast admirably fits into the plot.

AL CAPONE
1959, 105 mins, US Ⓥ
D: Richard Wilson A: Rod Steiger, Fay Spain, James Gregory, Martin Balsam, Nehemiah Persoff, Murvyn Vye (Allied Artists)

A tough, ruthless, and generally unsentimental account of the most notorious gangster of the Prohibition-repeal era, *Al Capone* is also a very well-made picture. There isn't much motivation given for Capone, at least not in the usual sense. But the screenplay does supply reasons and they are more logical than the usual once-over-lightly on the warped-youth bit. Capone, played by Rod Steiger, is shown as an amoral personality with a native genius for leadership and organization. Steiger's performance is mostly free of obvious technique, getting inside the character both physically and emotionally.

ALEKSANDR NYEVSKI
(ALEXANDER NEVSKY)
1938, 87 mins, USSR Ⓥ ⊙
D: Sergei Eisenstein, Dmitri Vasiliev A: Nikolai Cherkasov, Nikolai Okhlopkov, Andrei Abrikosov, Valentina Ivashova, Dmitri Orlov, Varvara Massalitinova (Mosfilm)

Huge reservoirs of manpower and materials have been thrown into this epic production, which is lavish in scope, theme, performance, and wealth of production detail, but despite its magnificence and scale the picture lacks the qualities which first marked director Sergei Eisenstein's technique. Analogy is drawn to present-day politics, and meaning and purpose of the entire production are shaped toward threats against any Russian invader. Saga relates of times in the early 1200s when Russia was overrun by Tartars in the east and Teutonic Knights from Germany on the west. Of the numerous honored artists in the film, Nikolai Cherkasov, as Prince Alexander, fulfills the requirements of the part in every respect. He is kingly, commanding, human, and gives a performance not easily forgotten.

ALEXANDER NEVSKY
See: Aleksandr Nyevski

ALEXANDER'S RAGTIME BAND
1938, 105 mins, US
D: Henry King A: Tyrone Power, Alice Faye, Don Ameche, Ethel Merman, Jack Haley, Jean Hersholt (20th Century-Fox)

Irving Berlin's *Alexander's Ragtime Band* is a grand filmusical that stirs and thrills, a medley of more than 30 pieces, selected from some 600 which Berlin has composed. Although the story opens back in 1911, the narrative moves swiftly through the years. None of the characters ages a single gray hair in 25 years. Richard Sherman conceived the story idea with a central figure, a San Francisco bandmaster who adopts the name of Alexander. It is strictly fiction, with only slight similarity to the Berlin bio. Berlin supervised the musical angles and, in addition, tossed off three new numbers, "Now It Can Be Told," "My Walking Stick," and "Marching Along with Time."
1938: Best Score (Alfred Newman)
Nominations: Best Picture, Original Story (Irving Berlin), Art Direction, Editing, Song ("Now It Can Be Told")

ALEXANDER THE GREAT
1956, 143 mins, US Ⓥ ▭
D: Robert Rossen A: Richard Burton, Fredric March, Claire Bloom, Danielle Darrieux, Harry Andrews, Stanley Baker (Rossen/United Artists)

It took Alexander the Great some 10 years to conquer the known world back in the fourth century B.C. It seems to take Robert Rossen almost as long to recreate on film this slice of history. Despite the length, however, he has fashioned a spectacle of tremendous size. Rossen is not always able to hold interest in his story and action, resulting in some long, dull stretches. Nor do the players have much chance to be more than puppets against the giant sweep of the spectacle.

ALEX IN WONDERLAND
1970, 110 mins, US
D: Paul Mazursky A: Donald Sutherland, Ellen Burstyn, Meg Mazursky, Glenna Sergent, Viola Spolin, Federico Fellini (M-G-M)

This fictional account of the personal and professional travails of a hotshot film director, played by Donald Sutherland, is partly admirable, partly realized, but also partly dull and somewhat déjà vu to boot. Sutherland attempts to retain his integrity amid the trappings of fame and too expensive Beverly Hills living accommodations.

ALFIE
1966, 114 mins, UK Ⓥ ▭
D: Lewis Gilbert A: Michael Caine, Shelley Winters, Millicent Martin, Julia Foster, Jane Asher, Shirley Anne Field (Sheldrake)

Alfie pulls few punches. With dialogue and situations that are humorous, tangy, raw, and, ultimately, often moving, the film may well shock. But behind its alleycat philosophy, there's some shrewd sense, some pointed barbs, and a sharp moral. Story concerns a glib, cynical young Cockney whose passion in life is chasing dames of all shapes, sizes, and dispositions, providing they are accommodating. Caine brings persuasiveness and a sardonic, thoroughly shabby, and humorous charm to the role. The two best performances among the women come from Julia Foster, becomingly wistful throughout, and Vivien Merchant as the married woman who suffers an abortion.
1966: Nominations: Best Picture, Actor (Michael Caine), Supp. Actress (Vivien Merchant), Screenplay, Song ("Alfie")

ALFRED THE GREAT
1969, 122 mins, UK ⊗ ▭
D: Clive Donner **A:** David Hemmings, Michael York, Prunella Ransome, Colin Blakely, Julian Glover, Ian McKellen (M-G-M)
    Idea was to show that Alfred, Prince of Wessex, who became the first and only British king to be called "the Great," was not just a guy who burned the cakes. Result is a film which hasn't the power or the passion to be a lavish historical film saga. David Hemmings plays the title role with intelligence, and does his best to suggest the inner complexities of the man, but he is under age for the role and rarely matches the stature of the man he is portraying.

ALGIERS
1938, 93 mins, US ⊗
D: John Cromwell **A:** Charles Boyer, Hedy Lamarr, Sigrid Gurie, Joseph Calleia, Gene Lockhart, Alan Haleei (Wanger/United Artists)
    Charles Boyer creates an interesting portrait of a continental gangster, jewel thief, and tough guy in *Algiers*. Other meritorious aspects include John Cromwell's direction and the first appearance in an American-made film of Hedy Lamarr. Film is a remake of *Pépé le Moko* (1937), a French picture directed by Julien Duvivier in which Jean Gabin starred. Boyer is a Parisian youth who is hunted by police and finally located in the native section of Algiers. So long as he stays within the prescribed area and lives and moves among the natives, without attempting escape to

the European section, he is allowed his liberty. In performances by a fine cast, Lamarr comes next to Boyer in a photo finish.
1938: Nominations: Best Actor (Charles Boyer), Supp. Actor (Gene Lockhart), Cinematography, Art Direction

ALI
See: Angst Essen Seele Auf

ALIBI
1929, 90 mins, US
D: Roland West **A:** Chester Morris, Harry Stubbs, Mae Busch, Eleanor Griffith, Irma Harrison, Regis Toomey (United Artists/Roland West)
    Jolt-packed crook melodrama in dialogue. From the human-interest standpoint picture belongs to Chester Morris, virile stage juvenile. In this picture he is a cruel, cold-blooded gangster. There are loose ends and desultory passages in *Alibi*, but in general it has tempo and is punched with some gripping sequences. Police atmosphere and detail have realism and the ring of authenticity.
1928/29: Nominations: Best Picture, Actor (Chester Morris)

ALICE
1990, 106 mins, US ⊗
D: Woody Allen **A:** Mia Farrow, Joe Mantegna, Alec Baldwin, Blythe Danner, Judy Davis, William Hurt (Orion)
    If *Stardust Memories* was Woody Allen's *8 1/2* and *Radio Days* his *Amarcord,* then *Alice* is his *Juliet of the Spirits*. It's a subtler, gentler retelling of Federico Fellini's tale of a pampered but unappreciated housewife who learns to shed her illusions by giving in to her fantasies. Performances are strong all around, with a succession of top actors making the most of their brief turns. But the center of the pic is Farrow, who's funny and touching.
1990: Nomination: Best Original Screenplay

ALICE ADAMS
1935, 95 mins, US ⊗ ☉
D: George Stevens **A:** Katharine Hepburn, Fred MacMurray, Fred Stone, Evelyn Venable, Frank Albertson, Ann Shoemaker (RKO)
    Translating Booth Tarkington's sometimes poignant and pathetic 1921 novel of the pretending, wistful Alice, whose economic background almost proves too much of a hurdle to surmount, must have been a yeoman task. That George Stevens

direction captures the wistfulness of Katharine Hepburn's superb histrionism, and yet has not sacrificed audience values at the altar of too much drabness and prosaic realism, is an achievement of no small order.

1935: Nominations: Best Picture, Actress (Katharine Hepburn)

ALICE DOESN'T LIVE HERE ANYMORE
1974, 112 mins, US ⓥ ⊙

D: Martin Scorsese **A:** Ellen Burstyn, Kris Kristofferson, Billy Green Bush, Diane Ladd, Lelia Goldoni, Harvey Keitel (Warner)

Alice Doesn't Live Here Anymore takes a group of well-cast film players and largely wastes them on a smaller-than-life film—one of those little-people dramas that make one despise little people. Script establishes Ellen Burstyn as the lovingly slovenly wife of Billy Green Bush, who gets killed near their New Mexico tract home. Burstyn decides to return to her long-ago Monterey origins. Eventually, just over an hour into the proceedings, enter Kris Kristofferson. The last half of the film is, indeed, a picture; but as a whole it's a distended bore.

1974: Best Actress (Ellen Burstyn)
Nominations: Best Supp. Actress (Diane Ladd), Original Screenplay

ALICE IN WONDERLAND
1951, 74 mins, US ⓥ ⊙

D: Clyde Geronimi, Hamilton Luske, Wilfred Jackson (Walt Disney)

The Mad Hatter, the March Hare, the Caterpillar, the Cheshire Cat, Tweedledee and Tweedledum, the White Rabbit, the Walrus and the Carpenter, the Queen of Hearts and other remembered characters are enchantingly projected as Alice strolls through her dream world to the accompaniment of ballads and musical nonsense. Young Kathryn Beaumont enchants as the voice of Alice, Ed Wynn (Mad Hatter), Jerry Colonna (March Hare), Richard Haydn (Caterpillar, a particular standout in his smoke-ring alphabet scene with Alice), Sterling Holloway (Cheshire Cat), Bill Thompson (White Rabbit), Pat O'Malley (Tweedle Twins) and Verna Felton (Queen of Hearts) are among those whose tonal tricks help sell the pen-and-ink people.

1951: Nomination: Scoring of a Musical Picture

ALICE'S ADVENTURES IN WONDERLAND
1972, 96 mins, UK ⓥ ▭

D: William Sterling **A:** Fiona Fullerton, Michael Crawford, Ralph Richardson, Flora Robson, Peter Sellers, Robert Helpmann (Fox-Rank)

A major disappointment. Superior stylistic settings and often terrific process effects are largely wasted by the limp, lifeless pacing of adapter-director William Sterling. Even the John Barry–Don Black score of 16 tunes is confined to key largo. Fiona Fullerton is a pleasantly bland Alice as are all other players. The film just lies there, and dies there, for 96 minutes.

ALICE'S RESTAURANT
1969, 111 mins, US ⓥ ▭

D: Arthur Penn **A:** Arlo Guthrie, Pat Quinn, James Broderick, Michael McClanathan, Geoff Outlaw, Tina Chen (United Artists/Florin)

Alice's Restaurant is the phantasmagorial account of the misadventures of a young folk singer in his brushes with the law and his draft board. Based on folk singer Arlo Guthrie's 18-minute, 20-second hit recording, ''Alice's Restaurant Massacree'' in which he limned some of his real-life experiences, the whole is a rather weird collection of episodes loosely strung together. Some of the acting is very good, but Arlo's performance is of the uncertain type and he appears to be living in a world of his own.

1969: Nomination: Best Director

ALIEN
1979, 124 mins, US ⓥ ⊙ ▭

D: Ridley Scott **A:** Tom Skerritt, Sigourney Weaver, Veronica Cartwright, Harry Dean Stanton, John Hurt, Ian Holm (20th Century-Fox/Brandywine)

Plainly put, *Alien* is an old-fashioned scary movie set in a highly realistic sci-fi future, made all the more believable by expert technical craftmanship. The price paid for the excitement, and it's a small one, is very little involvement with the characters themselves. But it really doesn't matter when the screaming starts. In contrast to the glamorous, adventurous outerspace life often depicted in sci-fi, *Alien* initially presents a mundane commercial spacecraft with crew members like Yaphet Kotto bitching and moaning about wages and working conditions. The tedium is shared by captain Tom Skerritt, his aide Sigourney Weaver, and the rest of the crew, played by a generally good cast in cardboard roles.

1979: Best Visual Effects
Nomination: Best Art Direction

ALIEN NATION
1988, 94 mins, US Ⓥ ⊙ ▭
D: Graham Baker **A:** James Caan, Mandy Patinkin, Terence Stamp, Kevyn Major Howard, Leslie Bevis, Peter Jason (20th Century-Fox)

Solid performances by leads James Caan and his humanoid buddy-cop partner Mandy Patinkin move this production beyond special effects, clever alien makeup, and car chases. There's a lot of violence and noise in this futuristic adaptation of a drug-pusher story, but also a compelling human-humanoid drama. Pic doesn't quite sustain a heart-pounding, eerie tone throughout.

ALIEN RESURRECTION
1997, 108 mins, US Ⓥ ⊙ ▭
D: Jean-Pierre Jeunet **A:** Sigourney Weaver, Winona Ryder, Ron Perlman, Dominique Pinon, Michael Wincott, Dan Hedaya (20th Century-Fox/Brandywine)

Tiptoeing into weird Freudian areas and moments of grotesquerie new even to this series, *Alien Resurrection*, the fourth entry in the franchise, is a cold though sometimes wildly imaginative and jokey scarefest held back by a lack of emotional engagement at its center. On board the United Systems Military's colossal *Auriga* spaceship, led by obsessive Gen. Perez (Dan Hedaya), is Ellen Ripley (Sigourney Weaver), from whose chest surgeons delicately remove a baby alien queen. It's 200 years later from *Alien 3·* and the USM plans to raise tame aliens for some nefarious purpose. Ripley was cloned from preserved blood samples in order to birth the queen with which she was impregnated in the last picture. Then arrives the *Betty*, a grungy commercial freighter crewed by six hardnosed mercenaries. As soon as the crew has delivered their load—alien eggs with human hosts attached—things start to go wrong, and the storyline settles into a straightforward escape drama. Movie is frequently gripping and always highly watchable, but its interest in Ripley's half-human personality and her maternal bond with the queen leads to some of the most intriguing—and cheesiest—stuff in the picture, as if the pic is afraid to enter the darkened rooms whose doors it keeps opening.

ALIENS
1986, 137 mins, US Ⓥ ⊙ ▭
D: James Cameron **A:** Sigourney Weaver, Carrie Henn, Michael Biehn, Lance Henriksen, Paul Reiser, Jenette Goldstein (20th Century-Fox/Brandywine)

Aliens proves a very worthy follow-up to Ridley Scott's 1979 sci-fi shocker, *Alien*. James Cameron's vault into the big time makes up for lack of surprise with sheer volume of thrills and chills; emphasis is decidedly on the plural aspect of the title. Although film accomplishes everything it aims to do, overall impression is of a film made by an expert craftsman, while Scott clearly had something of an artist in him. Weaver does a smashing job.

1986: Best Visual Effects, Sound Effects Editing
Nominations: Best Actress (Sigourney Weaver), Art Direction, Editing, Original Music Score, Sound

ALIEN 3
1992, 115 mins, US Ⓥ ⊙ ▭
D: David Fincher **A:** Sigourney Weaver, Charles S. Dutton, Charles Dance, Paul McGann, Brian Glover, Ralph Brown (20th Century-Fox/Brandywine)

The shape-shifting *Alien* trilogy reverts back to the form of the first film in this third close encounter, a muddled effort offering little more than visual splendor to recommend it. Music-video director David Fincher doesn't reveal much finesse with actors in his big-screen debut, and the screenplay proves fraught with lapses in reason, motivation, and logic. Weaver's character is so encumbered with baggage that she can't really showcase the qualities (particularly evident in the second film) that made the audience empathize with her.

1992: Nomination: Best Visual Effects

ALIVE
1993, 127 mins, US Ⓥ ⊙
D: Frank Marshall **A:** Ethan Hawke, Vincent Spano, Josh Hamilton, Bruce Ramsay, John Haymes Newton, David Kriegel (Touchstone/Paramount)

The true story (already told by 1976 Par release *Survive!*) of a 1970s plane crash in which the survivors, a rugby team, held on for more than two months in the subfreezing Andes largely by eating the corpses of the victims. Marshall and writer John Patrick Shanley deal with the topic seriously, exploring the survivors' desperation as well as their reluctance, down to an ethical debate prior to the initial meal, to engage in cannibalism.

ALL ABOUT EVE
1950, 138 mins, US Ⓥ ⊙
D: Joseph L. Mankiewicz A: Bette Davis, Anne Baxter, George Sanders, Celeste Holm, Gary Merrill, Thelma Ritter (20th Century-Fox)

Baxter plays a starry-eyed would-be actress who, by extraordinary design, finally meets Bette Davis, her histrionic idol (through the kind offices of Celeste Holm). She is taken into the household, machinates an understudy chore, and in return is ruthless in her pitch for both the beau and the husband of the two women who most befriended her. The basic story is garnished with exceedingly well-cast performances wherein Davis does not spare herself, makeup-wise, in the aging-star assignment.
1950: Best Picture, Director, Supp. Actor (George Sanders), Screenplay, Sound Recording, B&W Costume Design
Nominations: Best Actress (Anne Baxter, Bette Davis), Supp. Actress (Celeste Holm, Thelma Ritter), B&W Cinematography, Art Direction, Editing, Original Music Score

ALL ABOUT MY MOTHER
See: Todo Sobre Mi Madre

ALLAN QUATERMAIN AND THE LOST CITY OF GOLD
1987, 99 mins, US Ⓥ ⊙ ▱
D: Gary Nelson, Newt Arnold A: Richard Chamberlain, Sharon Stone, James Earl Jones, Henry Silva, Robert Donner, Aileen Marson (Cannon)

Quatermain (Richard Chamberlain) receives a gold piece from a dying man that inspires him to trek to East Africa in search of his brother Robeson (Martin Rabbett). Joining him are his archaeologist girlfriend (Sharon Stone) and African warrior (James Earl Jones), a comic-relief mystic (Robert Donner camping it up), and five expendable bearers. Film relies frequently on a very phony gimmick of a spear-proof tunic and story completely runs out of gas once the heroes arrive at their destination.

ALL FALL DOWN
1962, 111 mins, US
D: John Frankenheimer A: Eva Marie Saint, Warren Beatty, Karl Malden, Angela Lansbury, Brandon de Wilde (M-G-M)

Within John Houseman's production of *All Fall Down* there are some truly memorable passages, moments and scenes of great pith, poignancy, truth, and sensitivity. How disheartening it is, then, that the sum total is an artfully produced, cinematically rich, historically noteworthy, dramatically uneven near miss. A 16-year-old boy (Brandon de Wilde) who idolizes his emotionally unstable older brother (Warren Beatty) is the pivotal figure in William Inge's screenplay based on James Leo Herlihy's novel.

ALL I DESIRE
1953, 79 mins, US
D: Douglas Sirk A: Barbara Stanwyck, Richard Carlson, Lyle Bettger, Marcia Henderson, Maureen O'Sullivan, Lori Nelson (Universal)

Plot concerns the return of a mother to the family she ran away from 10 years previously for a fling at the stage. Homecoming is to see her daughter in the high-school graduation play, but, secretly, the mother hopes for a reconciliation. The Ross Hunter production and Douglas Sirk's direction pull all stops to make the picture a 79-minute excursion into sentimentality. With help of Barbara Stanwyck's performance, the soap-operish tear-jerking is palatable.

ALLIGATOR
1980, 94 mins, US Ⓥ
D: Lewis Teague A: Robert Forster, Robin Riker, Michael Gazzo, Dean Jagger, Henry Silva, Jack Carter (Group 1)

Alligator is bloody and boisterous, featuring the only man-eating monster in memory named Ramone. Dumb as it is, director Lewis Teague brings some pluses to the pic. Robert Forster, as a detective, and Riker are amiable leads, never taking the film too seriously. Tech credits are cheap but serviceable.

ALL MY SONS
1948, 98 mins, US
D: Irving Reis A: Edward G. Robinson, Burt Lancaster, Mady Christians, Howard Duff, Louisa Horton, Arlene Francis (Universal)

All My Sons is a serious, thoughtful study, loaded with dramatic dynamite. Chester Erskine's approach to the Arthur Miller play benefits from the broader movement permitted by the screen. Edward G. Robinson gives an effective performance as the small-town manufacturer who sends defective parts to the army air forces. Burt Lancaster, as his war-embittered son, shades the assignment with just the right amount of intensity.

ALL NEAT IN BLACK STOCKINGS
1969, 106 mins, UK
D: Christopher Morahan A: Victor Henry, Susan George, Jack Shepherd, Clare Kelly, Anna Cropper (Warner)

Victor Henry plays an exuberant young window cleaner with a lack of responsibility and a roving eye for the girls. Falling for a suburban chick that he picks up in a local tavern, he realizes that this is the real thing. But he's thwarted by her overpossessive widowed mother. There's not much to be done with such an anecdote, but brighten it up with smart dialogue and standout performances. This one gets neither. Aforementioned Henry brings some humor and guts to the antihero's role.

ALL NIGHT LONG
1981, 88 mins, US ⓥ
D: Jean-Claude Tramont A: Gene Hackman, Barbra Streisand, Diane Ladd, Dennis Quaid, Annie Girardot, William Daniels (Universal)

A weary premise and a hackneyed theme are given some wry, offbeat twists in *All Night Long*. Plot is the same old middle-age-blues song, with Hackman chucking his dreary job, wife, and lifestyle in favor of a younger woman and new reputation as a goofy carefree iconoclast. Familiar targets, such as uptight career businessmen, frivolous middle-class society ladies, and sterile suburbia are knocked with easy precision. Hackman brings even more to his role than might have been apparent in the script. Playing a clearly subordinate role, Streisand is more subdued than usual and effective as such.

ALL OF ME
1984, 93 mins, US ⓥ ⊙
D: Carl Reiner A: Steve Martin, Lily Tomlin, Victoria Tennant, Madolyn Smith, Richard Libertini, Dana Elcar (Kings Road)

All of Me plays more like an old-fashioned screwball comedy than a contempo film, its premise of a woman dying and her soul inhabiting half of another person's body in the same vein as *Here Comes Mr. Jordan*. When he is not arranging divorce settlements for rich husbands, Roger Cobb (Steve Martin) is a jazz guitarist. Martin's troubles really start on his 38th birthday when he inherits the soul of departing heiress and first-rank crank Edwina Cutwater (Lily Tomlin). For all its clowning, *All of Me* makes some good points about taking chances and doing what you want in life. Tomlin undergoes a transformation from a crabby sheltered poor little rich girl to a compassionate woman. It's a measure of her performance that even as a sourpuss she's irresistible.

ALL QUIET ON THE WESTERN FRONT
1930, 152 mins, US ⓥ ⊙
D: Lewis Milestone A: Lew Ayres, Louis Wolheim, John Wray, Raymond Griffith, Slim Summerville, Russell Gleason (Universal)

A harrowing, gruesome, morbid tale of war, compelling in its realism, bigness, and repulsiveness. The story carries a group of German schoolboys, enthused by their professor's plea for fealty to country, from their training days through warfare to their deaths. In sum one might say it's due to Lewis Milestone's direction and let it go at that. But there are standout performances, even in bits.
1929/30: Best Picture, Director
Nominations: Best Writing, Cinematography (Arthur Edeson)

ALL THAT HEAVEN ALLOWS
1955, 89 mins, US
D: Douglas Sirk A: Jane Wyman, Rock Hudson, Agnes Moorehead, Conrad Nagel, Virginia Grey, Gloria Talbott (Universal)

Although this story of a long-suffering woman who, at 40 or so, finds romance with a man between 10 and 15 years her junior, is hardly designed to ignite prairie fires, scripter Peg Fenwick nevertheless has managed to turn the story into a slightly offbeat yarn with some interesting overtones that accent the social prejudices of a small town. Jane Wyman is appealing and properly long-suffering. Hudson is handsome and somewhat wooden.

ALL THAT JAZZ
1979, 123 mins, US ⓥ ⊙
D: Bob Fosse A: Roy Scheider, Jessica Lange, Ann Reinking, Cliff Gorman, John Lithgow, Erzebet Foldi (20th Century-Fox/Columbia)

All That Jazz is a self-important, ego-maniacal, wonderfully choreographed, often compelling film that portrays the energetic life, and preoccupation with death, of a director-choreographer who ultimately suffers a heart attack. Roy Scheider gives a superb performance, creating a character filled with nervous energy.
1979: Best Art Direction, Adapted Score, Editing, Costume Design

Nominations: Best Picture, Director, Actor (Roy Scheider), Original Screenplay, Cinematography

ALL THAT MONEY CAN BUY
See: The Devil and Daniel Webster

ALL THE BROTHERS WERE VALIANT
1953, 94 mins, US ⓥ
D: Richard Thorpe **A:** Robert Taylor, Stewart Granger, Ann Blyth, Betta St. John, Keenan Wynn, James Whitmore (M-G-M)

Special effects are used to advantage to spotlight the high romance of adventuring on the bounding main. Film's big moments include the excitement stirred up by the dangers of 19th-century whaling and the climactic mass battle with mutineers aboard a sailing vessel. Stars Robert Taylor, Stewart Granger, and Ann Blyth are competent but the people they portray haven't enough depth or reality to come robustly alive.
1953: Nomination: Best Color Cinematography

ALL THE FINE YOUNG CANNIBALS
1960, 112 mins, US ▭
D: Michael Anderson **A:** Robert Wagner, Natalie Wood, Susan Kohner, George Hamilton, Pearl Bailey (M-G-M)

Under scrutiny is the accelerated world of troubled youth where a one-night stand invariably results in pregnancy, fame, or attempted suicide. More specifically, the scenario explores the affairs of two young couples (Natalie Wood–George Hamilton and Robert Wagner–Susan Kohner) who eventually learn to live with the fact that they share a mutual tax deduction in the form of a bouncing babe who bounced out of the premarital union of one half of each partnership (Wagner and Wood). Best emoting is done by Pearl Bailey, but even she can barely cope with a preposterous role of a celebrated blues singer who dies of a broken heart when jilted by that man who played horn for her.

ALL THE KING'S MEN
1949, 109 mins, US ⓥ ⊙
D: Robert Rossen **A:** Broderick Crawford, John Derek, Joanne Dru, John Ireland, Mercedes McCambridge, Shepperd Strudwick (Columbia)

The rise and fall of a backwoods political messiah is given graphic celluloid treatment in *All the King's Men*. As a great man using the opinionless, follow-the-leader instinct of the more common voter, Broderick Crawford does a standout performance. The story is told through the eyes of John Ireland, newspaperman. He becomes a devotee pursuing the Crawford career from small time into big time. Joanne Dru appears to advantage as a friend of Ireland's, but the most compelling of the femme players is Mercedes McCambridge, the mistress to the great man.
1949: Best Picture, Actor (Broderick Crawford), Supp. Actress (Mercedes McCambridge)
Nominations: Best Director, Supp. Actor (John Ireland), Screenplay, Editing

... ALL THE MARBLES
(UK: THE CALIFORNIA DOLLS)
1981, 113 mins, US ⓥ
D: Robert Aldrich **A:** Peter Falk, Vicki Frederick, Laurene Landon, Burt Young, Tracy Reed, Richard Jaeckel (M-G-M/Aldrich)

By any measure *Marbles* is a major disappointment, given the deft casting of Peter Falk as a seedy, selfish, and demanding manager of a couple of tag-team women wrestlers (Vicki Frederick and Laurene Landon). For some odd reason, however, director Robert Aldrich and writer Mel Frohman have chosen to portray women's wrestling as a serious sport, aiming for another *Rocky*-like climb from obscurity to triumph. It never works for a minute.

ALL THE PRESIDENT'S MEN
1976, 138 mins, US ⓥ ⊙
D: Alan J. Pakula **A:** Dustin Hoffman, Robert Redford, Jack Warden, Martin Balsam, Hal Holbrook, Jason Robards (Warner/Wildwood)

Some ingenious direction by Alan J. Pakula and scripting by William Goldman remove much of the inherent dramatic lethargy in any story of reporters running down a story. Thus, *All the President's Men*, from the Bob Woodward and Carl Bernstein book about their experiences uncovering the Watergate coverup for *The Washington Post*, emerges close to being an American *Z*. Robert Redford and especially Dustin Hoffman excel in their starring roles. Jason Robards, as *Post* exec editor Ben Bradlee, provides an excellent characterization, backed up strongly by Jack Warden and Martin Balsam as senior editors.
1976: Best Supp. Actor (Jason Robards), Adapted Screenplay, Art Direction, Sound

Nominations: Best Picture, Director, Supp. Actress (Jane Alexander), Editing

ALL THE RIGHT MOVES
1983, 91 mins, US Ⓥ ⊙
D: Michael Chapman A: Tom Cruise, Craig T. Nelson, Lea Thompson, Charles Cioffi, Paul Carafotes, Christopher Penn (20th Century-Fox)

A smash directorial debut by well-known cinematographer Michael Chapman, *All the Right Moves* crackles with authenticity. The story is centered on characters fighting to get out of a dying Pennsylvania mill town to make a better life for themselves. A welcome surprise is the touching relationship between high-school senior Cruise and his father. For once, here's a pop in a redneck town who treats his son like a human being, and Charles Cioffi, however brief his screen time, conveys a durable dignity.

ALL THE WAY
See: The Joker Is Wild

ALL THIS AND HEAVEN TOO
1940, 140 mins, US Ⓥ
D: Anatole Litvak A: Bette Davis, Charles Boyer, Jeffrey Lynn, Barbara O Neil, Virginia Weidler, Helen Westley (Warner)

Heaven is film theatre at its best. In the two starring roles are Bette Davis, as the young French governess, Henriette Deluzy-Desportes, and Charles Boyer, giving one of his best performances as the Duc de Praslin. The tragedy of their love affair, which resulted in the murder of the Duchesse de Praslin (Barbara O'Neil), the suicide of the duc, and the subsequent glimpse of some happiness for Henriette, is strong fare, involving delicate psychological shadings and understandings. Davis is off the screen during the briefest interludes. In her scenes with Boyer, she retains an outward composure which only intensifies her real feelings, never completely expressed. It is acting so restrained that a single overdrawn passage or expression would shatter the illusion.
1940: Nominations: Best Picture, Supp. Actress (Barbara O Neil), B&W Cinematography

ALL THROUGH THE NIGHT
1942, 107 mins, US Ⓥ
D: Vincent Sherman A: Humphrey Bogart, Conrad Veidt, Karen Verne, Jane Darwell, Frank McHugh, Peter Lorre (Warner)

Gripping espionage melodrama highlights three bad boys, with Humphrey Bogart this time working on the side of the law, order, and liberty in trying to clean up a nest of Nazi-spies and fifth columnists. Two other toughies are sinister, soft-spoken Peter Lorre and immaculate, iron-fist-in-velvet-glove Nazi agent Conrad Veldt, both first-rate.

ALMOST AN ANGEL
1990, 95 mins, US Ⓥ ⊙ ▭
D: John Cornell A: Paul Hogan, Elias Koteas, Linda Kozlowski, Charlton Heston, Doreen Lang, Joe Dallesandro (Paramount/Ironbark)

Almost an Angel is simply a no-effort vanity project with only Paul Hogan's easygoing charm to fill the space between the sprocket holes. Instead of stretching his acting muscles, Hogan assigns himself the comfortable role of an electronics expert/cracksman just released from prison who turns into an inveterate do-gooder. Kozlowski, styled plain with dark hair, is wasted as the mildest of romantic interests.

ALMOST PERFECT AFFAIR, AN
1979, 93 mins, US Ⓥ
D: Michael Ritchie A: Keith Carradine, Monica Vitti, Raf Vallone, Christian De Sica, Dick Anthony Williams (Paramount)

The emotions director Michael Ritchie is parlaying in this slim fable, which revolve around tender egos and unlimited ambition, are universal. But the details are so specific, and so grounded in film-industry reality, that the larger implications may be lost. Focus is the intriguing relationship between Vitti and Carradine, which starts out as a one-nighter and turns into a brief, but ill-fated romance.

ALONG CAME JONES
1945, 90 mins, US
D: Stuart Heisler A: Gary Cooper, Loretta Young, William Demarest, Dan Duryea, Frank Sully, Russell Simpson (International)

For his first independent production, Gary Cooper turned out a better-than-average western. Cooper plays a mild-mannered cowpoke who drifts into a small town with his sidekick (William Demarest), thus precipitating a situation in which he's mistaken for a notorious road agent. Cooper, actually, can't even handle a gun, but the inevitable result finds him the unwitting and indirect cause of the holdupman's slaying. And, of course, he gets the latter's girl (Young). Cooper plays his usually languid self impressively.

ALONG THE GREAT DIVIDE

1951, 88 mins, US Ⓥ

D: Raoul Walsh **A:** Kirk Douglas, Virginia Mayo, John Agar, Walter Brennan, Ray Teal, Hugh Sanders (Warner)

In his first western, Kirk Douglas is a US marshal, interested only in enforcing the letter of the law. Plot is concerned with Douglas bringing in a prisoner charged with rustling and murder, and the efforts of a cattle baron to take justice into his own hands. Douglas tries hard with his characterization and would have brought it off successfully had the scripting stuck to straight western action and not gone off in mental maneuverings.

ALPHABET MURDERS, THE

1966, 85 mins, UK

D: Frank Tashlin **A:** Tony Randall, Anita Ekberg, Robert Morley, Maurice Denham, Guy Rolfe, Sheila Allen (M-G-M British)

This British translation of one of Agatha Christie's better-known whodunits, *The A.B.C. Murders,* gets the broad comedy treatment. Much of the suspense of Christie's writing is lost in converting to comedy, and as a result is no more than a parody of the original, insufficiently clever to be outstanding. Tony Randall, as Hercule Poirot, delivers a very definite characterization in making his way through the plot haze of a series of murders.

ALPHAVILLE
UNE ETRANGE AVENTURE DE
LEMMY CAUTION

1965, 98 mins, France/Italy Ⓥ

D: Jean-Luc Godard **A:** Eddie Constantine, Anna Karina, Akim Tamiroff, Laszlo Szabo, Howard Vernon, Jean-Louis Comolli (Chaumiane/Filmstudio)

The most prolific of French filmmakers and ex–New Wavers, Jean-Luc Godard, has come up with an adventurous-philosophical pic with this one. He takes a popular actor and uses his screen personage in a new way. That Yank who became a star over here [in France] playing in parody G-man pi, Eddie Constantine is shown in some future city where human feelings have been all but done away with and where the powerful leader is a super computer. Anna Karina has the right doll-like appearance as the robot who slowly feels long-forgotten human feelings coming back. Godard again shows his uncompromising, intellectual, unorthodox methods for a pic that is both piquant and sketchy.

ALTERED STATES

1980, 102 mins, US Ⓥ ⊙

D: Ken Russell **A:** William Hurt, Blair Brown, Bob Balaban, Charles Haid, Drew Barrymore (Warner)

Altered States is an exciting combo science fiction–horror film. Direction by Ken Russell has energy to spare, with appropriate matchup of his baroque visual style to special-effects-intensive material. Tall tale concerns a young psychophysiologist, Edward Jessup (William Hurt), working in New York and later at Harvard on dangerous experiments involving human consciousness. Using himself as the subject, Jessup makes use of a sensory-deprivation tank to hallucinate back to the event of his birth and beyond, regressing into primitive stages of human evolution. Hurt's feature film debut is arresting, especially during the grueling climactic sequence.

1980: Nominations: Best Original Score, Sound

ALVAREZ KELLY

1966, 110 mins, US Ⓥ ▭

D: Edward Dmytryk **A:** William Holden, Richard Widmark, Janice Rule, Patrick O'Neal, Victoria Shaw, Roger C. Carmel (Columbia)

Based on a true US Civil War incident, *Alvarez Kelly* concerns a successful cattle grab engineered by Southern forces and executed under the noses of Northern troops. Outdoor action sequences, including an exciting stampede, enliven a tame script, routinely directed and performed erratically.

ALVIN PURPLE

1973, 97 mins, Australia Ⓥ

D: Tim Burstall **A:** Graeme Blundell, George Whaley, Penne Hackforth-Jones, Elli Maclure, Jacki Weaver, Jenny Hagen (Hexagon)

Alvin Purple is a young man whom women find irresistible. This comedy, made in Melbourne with local actors, is beautifully scripted by Aussie playwright Alan Hopgood with double entendres and situations abounding. Pace is slick and the pic never sags. In the title role Graeme Blundell gives a thoroughly convincing performance.

ALWAYS

1985, 105 mins, US Ⓥ ⊙ ▭

D: Henry Jaglom **A:** Patrice Townsend, Henry Jaglom, Joanna Frank, Alan Rachins, Melissa Leo, Bob Rafelson (Jagtown/International Rainbow)

Henry Jaglom's confessional comedy about his divorce from actress Patrice Townsend. The two star, more or less, as themselves, and are joined by two other couples who are, respectively, near the beginning and toward the middle of the marriage process for an alternately awkward, painful, loving, and farcical July Fourth weekend. Mainly, picture is wall-to-wall talk about what went wrong between Jaglom and Townsend, about emotional happiness and lack of same, about sexual matters, and many related topics.

ALWAYS
1989, 121 mins, US Ⓥ ⊙
D: Steven Spielberg **A:** Richard Dreyfuss, Holly Hunter, Brad Johnson, John Goodman, Audrey Hepburn, Keith David (Universal/United Artists/Amblin)

Always is a relatively small-scale, engagingly casual, somewhat silly, but always entertaining fantasy. Richard Dreyfuss charmingly inherits the lead role of a pilot returned from the dead in this remake of the 1943 Spencer Tracy pic *A Guy Named Joe* set among firefighters in national parks. Holly Hunter's dispatcher and semiskilled aspiring pilot, lacking the womanly grace Irene Dunne brought to the part, comes off as gawky and ditzy in the early parts of *Always*. Bereavement seems to visibly mature the actress, whose emotional struggle between the memory of Dreyfuss and new love Brad Johnson becomes spirited and gripping.

AMADEUS
1984, 158 mins, US Ⓥ ⊙ ⊡
D: Milos Forman **A:** F. Murray Abraham, Tom Hulce, Elizabeth Berridge, Simon Callow, Roy Dotrice, Christine Ebersole (Zaentz)

On a production level and as an evocation of a time and place, *Amadeus* is loaded with pleasures, the greatest of which derive from the on-location filming in Prague, the most 18th century of all European cities. The stature and power the work possessed onstage have been noticeably diminished, and Milos Forman's handling is perhaps too naturalistic for what was conceived as a highly stylized piece. *Amadeus* is Shaffer's fictionalized account of the relationship between Viennese court composer Antonio Salieri and Wolfgang Amadeus Mozart, during the 10 final years of the latter's life. It is a caustic study of the collision between mediocrity and genius. Fueling the fire of Salieri's fury is Mozart's offensive personality. In opposition to the idealized, romanticized 19th-century view of the composer, the character is an outlandish vulgarian.
1984: Best Picture, Director, Actor (F. Murray Abraham), Adapted Screenplay, Art Direction, Sound, Costume Design, Makeup
Nominations: Best Actor (Tom Hulce), Cinematography, Editing

LES AMANTS
1958, 90 mins, France Ⓥ ⊙ ⊡
D: Louis Malle **A:** Jeanne Moreau, Alain Cluny, Jean-Marc Bory, Judith Magre, Jose-Luis Villalonga, Gaston Modot (NEF)

A comedy of manners is mixed with an attempt at outright eroticism in this film. Neither is completely successful; only exploitation chances are its 20-minute love scene between a young wife and a young man in the house and grounds of the husband who happens to be at home during the tryst. The lovers snuggle, moan, and even take a bath together, but the lack of dimension in the characters dissipates the impact. Direction dwells on too many unessential points and lacks the true feel for this woman's plight to make her emotional release effective drama. Jeanne Moreau displays some insight into her character, which is more than most of the men can do.

AMARCORD
1973, 125 mins, Italy/France Ⓥ
D: Federico Fellini **A:** Pupella Maggio, Magali Noel, Armando Brancia, Ciccio Ingrassia, Nandino Orfei, Luigi Rossi (FC/PECF)

Amarcord is probably the first time an established film director went before cameras with one concept in mind and then created an almost entirely different picture. Instead of lensing a nostalgic look at the past to recapture the happy simplicity of existence before mechanization, the maestro did just the opposite. With a loose reference to his boyhood years in the very Italian province of Romagna (Fellini was born in Rimini), he has looked back as much in anger as in sorrow and has recreated provincial life in the early 1930s with unsparing emphasis on the inadequacies of man and existence.
1974: Best Foreign Language Film

AMATEUR

1994, 105 mins, US/UK/France Ⓥ ⊙

D: Hal Hartley **A:** Isabelle Huppert, Martin Donovan, Elina Lowensohn, Damian Young, Chuck Montgomery, David Simonds (True Fiction/Zenith/UGC)

A former nun who writes erotic stories, an amnesiac with a criminal past, and the most notorious porno actress in the world bounce off each other with tasty results in Hal Hartley's *Amateur*. Just as quirky and idiosyncratic as the Gotham-based writer/director's earlier efforts, this one pushes the spiky humor a bit more to the fore. Viewers not in tune with the filmmaker's approach may find the comic elements forced and contrived, since they are often based on absurd conceits. But Hartley's technique is now so refined and precise that he easily achieves his desired effects.

AMAZING DR. CLITTERHOUSE, THE

1938, 87 mins, US

D: Anatole Litvak **A:** Edward G. Robinson, Claire Trevor, Humphrey Bogart, Allen Jenkins, Donald Crisp, Gale Page (Warner)

The producers have retained the basic idea from the play of a veteran physician whose study of the physiological effects of crime on its habitués takes him on a series of ventures with a skilled gang of crooks. But in many respects it is an outright gangster film with the medico's study of criminals as the excuse for carefully diagramming the gang's operations. Edward G. Robinson, in the role of the criminal medico, is at his best. Humphrey Bogart's interpretation of the gangster chief is top-flight.

AMAZING GRACE AND CHUCK

1987, 115 mins, US Ⓥ ⊙

D: Mike Newell **A:** Jamie Lee Curtis, Alex English, Gregory Peck, William L. Petersen, Joshua Zuehlke (Tri-Star/Rastar/Turnstar)

Amazing Grace and Chuck is destined to go down in history as the camp classic of the antinuke genre. Little League baseball pitcher Chuck Murdock announces, "I can't play because of nuclear weapons." Boston Celtics star Amazing Grace Smith (played by Denver Nuggets' great Alex English) promptly gives up his $1-million-per-year salary to join Chuck in protest of nukes. In no time hundreds of athletes on both sides of the Iron Curtain are refusing to play until the ultimate weapon is eliminated.

AMAZING PANDA ADVENTURE, THE

1995, 84 mins, US Ⓥ ⊙ ▭

D: Christopher Cain **A:** Stephen Lang, Ryan Slater, Yi Ding, Huang Fei (Warner)

The script is a mix of the trite and the true. Ryan (Ryan Slater) is off on spring break to see his dad (Stephen Lang), an American working on a preserve in China to rescue the panda population. To save the preserve, its staffers must come up with a panda cub to show that they're accomplishing something, but the only known cub has been captured by poachers.

AMAZON

1992, 91 mins, Finland/US Ⓥ ▭

D: Mika Kaurismaki **A:** Kari Vaananen, Robert Davi, Rae Dawn Chong, Minna, Aili Sovio, Rui Polanah (Villealfa/Noema)

Shot in CinemaScope with an international B-movie cast playing foreigners at the ends of their ropes in the Brazilian jungle, *Amazon* plays like a second feature that might have been made in the 1960s by Sam Fuller or Gordon Douglas starring Burt Reynolds or Stuart Whitman. Visually, film is always stimulating but storytelling is wildly uneven, and director Mika Kaurismaki has an uncertain command of pic's tone.

AMAZON WOMEN ON THE MOON

1987, 85 mins, US Ⓥ ⊙

D: Joe Dante, Carl Gottlieb, Peter Horton, John Landis **A:** Rosanna Arquette, Ralph Bellamy, Carrie Fisher, Griffin Dunne, Steve Guttenberg, Russ Meyer (Universal)

Amazon Women on the Moon is irreverent, vulgar, and silly and has some hilarious moments and some real groaners, too. John Landis and company have found some 1980s things to satirize—like yuppies, the vidcassette biz, dating, condoms—done up in a way that's not particularly shocking anymore.

AMBUSHERS, THE

1968, 101 mins, US Ⓥ ⊙

D: Henry Levin **A:** Dean Martin, Senta Berger, Janice Rule, James Gregory, Albert Salmi, Kurt Kasznar (Columbia/Meadway-Claude)

This third Matt Helm pic starts out with a silly double entendre, then shifts for last half to tedious plot resolution. While production values remain strong, acting, writing, and direction are pedestrian.

AMERICA AMERICA
1963, 177 mins, US
D: Elia Kazan A: Stathis Giallelis, Frank
Wolf, Harry Davis, Linda Marsh, Paul
Mann, Lou Antonio (Warner)

Elia Kazan gives a penetrating, thorough,
and profoundly affecting account of the
hardships endured and surmounted at the
turn of the century by a young Greek lad in
attempting to fulfill his cherished dream of
getting to America from the old country. In
the all-important focal role of the young man
with the dream, Stathis Giallelis, an unknown, makes a striking screen debut. Virtually everyone is memorable.
1963: Best B&W Art Direction
Nominations: Best Picture, Director,
Original Story & Screenplay

AMERICAN BEAUTY
1999, 122 mins, US Ⓥ ⊙ ▭
D: Sam Mendes A: Kevin Spacey, An-
nette Bening, Thora Birch, Wes Bentley,
Mena Suvari, Peter Gallagher (Jinks-
Cohen/DreamWorks)

An acerbic, darkly comic critique of
social conventions, *American Beauty* represents a stunning card of introduction for
screenwriter Alan Ball and director Sam
Mendes. Landscape is the familiar one of
small-town America, of houses with white
picket fences racked by hostility, tension,
noncommunication, and perversity. This is
intended not as a revelation but as a given,
starting point for a tale in which nearly
every important character metamorphoses
in an utterly unpredictable way. Lester
Burnham (Kevin Spacey), a self-described
loser, has lost interest in his job, his beautiful, high-strung wife Carolyn (Annette
Bening), and sullen school-age daughter
Jane (Thora Birch). Lester becomes smitten by Jane's best friend, Angela (Mena
Suvari), and begins pumping iron and
smoking dope with a strange young man,
Ricky Fitts (Wes Bentley), who has
moved in next door. The ensemble of actors could not be better.
1999: Best Picture, Director, Best Actor
(Kevin Spacey), Original Screenplay, Cinematography
Nominations: Best Actress (Annette Bening), Film Editing, Original Score

AMERICAN FLYERS
1985, 114 mins, US Ⓥ ▭
D: John Badham A: Kevin Costner, David
Grant, Rae Dawn Chong, Alexandra Paul,
Janice Rule, Luca Bercovici (Warner)

Story of two brothers who untangle
their mixed emotions as they compete in
a grueling bicycle race, *American Flyers*

is most entertaining when it rolls along
unencumbered by big statements. Unfortunately, overblown production just pumps
hot air in too many directions and comes
up limp. Basic conflict between under-
achiever David (David Grant) and older
brother Marcus (Kevin Costner), a fierce
competitor and no-nonsense sports doctor,
is crammed into a hotbed of family problems including a career-woman mother
(Janice Rule) who emotionally abandoned
her dying husband.

AMERICAN FRIENDS
1991, 95 mins, UK Ⓥ ⊙
D: Tristram Powell A: Michael Palin,
Connie Booth, Trini Alvarado, Alfred Molina, David Calder (Millenium/Mayday)

Easy on the eyes and on the emotions,
American Friends is a slim vignette about
two American women who fall for a reserved Oxford don. Pic opens in the 1860s
at a stuffy Oxford college where bachelor
classics don Francis Ashby (Michael Palin)
is setting off for a walking vacation in
Switzerland. Atop the Alps, he meets two
Americans, Caroline (Connie Booth) and
her doe-eyed ward, Elinor (Trini Alvarado). Lack of dramatic tension can be
blamed, in part, on the ex–Monty Python
trouper's performance. Although yarn is
based on an actual event discovered in his
great-grandfather Edward's travel diaries,
Palin is too lightweight for such a key role.

AMERICAN GIGOLO
1980, 117 mins, US Ⓥ
D: Paul Schrader A: Richard Gere, Lauren
Hutton, Hector Elizondo, Nina Van Pallandt, Bill Duke, Brian Davies (Paramount)

A hot subject, cool style, and overly
contrived plotting don't all mesh in *American Gigolo*. Paul Schrader's third outing
as a director is betrayed by a curious, uncharacteristic evasiveness at its core. As
with several of Schrader's other scripts,
this one charts the course of a loner, a solo
driver navigating in a sea of sharks ready
to eat him alive. Rarely offscreen, Gere is
notably convincing in look and manner.
Very low-key, Hutton is not quite up to
the difficult part of a woman-with-
everything who throws it all over for her
questionable lover.

AMERICAN GRAFFITI
1973, 109 mins, US Ⓥ ⊙ ▭
D: George Lucas A: Richard Dreyfuss,
Ron Howard, Paul Le Mat, Charles Martin
Smith, Cindy Williams, Candy Clark
(Universal)

Set in 1962 but reflecting the culmination of the 1950s, the film is a most vivid recall of teenage attitudes and mores. Against this chrome-and-neon backdrop is told the story of one long summer night in the lives of four school chums: Richard Dreyfuss, on his last night before leaving for an eastern college; Ron Howard, less willing to depart the presence of Cindy Williams; Charles Martin Smith, a bespectacled fumbler whose misadventures with pubescent swinger Candy Clark are as touching as they are hilarious; and Paul Le Mat, 22 years old on a birth certificate but still strutting as he did four years earlier.

1973: Nominations: Best Picture, Director, Supp. Actress (Candy Clark), Original Screenplay, Editing

AMERICAN GUERRILLA IN THE PHILIPPINES, AN
(I SHALL RETURN)
1950, 104 mins, US
D: Fritz Lang **A:** Tyrone Power, Micheline Presle, Tom Ewell, Bob Patten, Jack Elam, Robert Barrat (20th Century-Fox)

A story of the Second World War in the Pacific, from the spring of 1942 up to General MacArthur's return to the islands, it is neatly staged. The Philippine locales supply a lush tropical dressing to brighten the heroics of a small band of Americans and natives who fight the US cause against the invading Japs. Fritz Lang's direction develops a strong sense of expectancy and suspense in the storytelling.

AMERICAN HEART
1992, 113 mins, US ⓥ ⊙
D: Martin Bell **A:** Jeff Bridges, Edward Furlong, Lucinda Jenney, Don Harvey, Tracey Kapinsky, Maggie Welsh (Avenue/ Asis-Heller)

First fictional feature from Martin Bell is rooted in an elemental story about an irresponsible, ex-con father and his teenage son, who is so ignored he must fend for himself on the streets. Around the edges are a host of observations about the sorry state of urban America, and grafted on is a bit of crime melodrama that provides some conventional chase and shoot-'em-up action. The pic could have used a dash of reality-heightening poetry to lift it out of the ordinary.

AMERICAN IN PARIS, AN
1951, 113 mins, US ⓥ ⊙
D: Vincente Minnelli **A:** Gene Kelly, Leslie Caron, Oscar Levant, Georges Guetary, Nina Foch, Eugene Borden (M-G-M)

An American in Paris is one of the most imaginative musical confections turned out by Hollywood. Kelly's diversified dancing is great as ever and his thesping is standout. But he reveals new talents in this one with his choreography. There's a lengthy ballet to the film's title song for the finale, which is a masterpiece of design, lighting, costumes, and color photography. It's a unique blending of classical and modern dance with vaude-style tapping. Caron is a beauteous, lissome number with an attractively pert personality and plenty of SA. She scores neatly with her thesping, particularly in the appealing love scenes with Kelly, and displays standout dancing ability.

1951: Best Picture, Story & Screenplay, Color Cinematography, Color Art Direction, Score for a Musical Picture, Color Costume Design
Nominations: Director, Editing

AMERICANIZATION OF EMILY, THE
1964, 115 mins, US ⓥ
D: Arthur Hiller **A:** James Garner, Julie Andrews, Melvyn Douglas, James Coburn, Joyce Grenfell, Edward Binns (M-G-M)

Emily, with Julie Andrews in title role as an English motor-pool driver in World War II, takes place immediately before the Normandy invasion. Most of the action unspools in London, where Garner, a lieutenant commander who makes avowed cowardice his career, is subordinate to Melvyn Douglas, an erratic admiral. Pic is primarily interesting for the romance between Andrews and Garner, the former struggling against being Americanized through her contact with the outgoing and freewheeling Garner.

1964: Nominations: Best B&W Cinematography, B&W Art Direction

AMERICAN ME
1992, 125 mins, US ⓥ
D: Edward James Olmos **A:** Edward James Olmos, William Forsythe, Pepe Serna, Danny De La Paz, Evelina Fernandez, Cary-Hiroyuki Tagawa (Universal/ YOY)

The criminal life is portrayed with all the glamour of a mug shot in *American Me,* a powerful indictment of the cycle of violence bred by the prisons and street culture. Long section detailing life at Folsom State Prison (where the company shot for three weeks) is as fascinating as it is disturbing. Film sketches racial divisions within the pen, the rise of the so-called

Mexican Mafia, how drugs are smuggled inside, the scams that can make life there safer, and how men inside control things outside. Olmos makes for a mesmerizing, implacable Santana, one of the least romanticized film gangsters since Paul Muni's Scarface.

AMERICAN NINJA
1985, 95 mins, US Ⓥ ⊙
D: Sam Firstenberg A: Michael Dudikoff, Steve James, Judie Aronson, Guich Koock, John Fujioka, Don Stewart (Cannon)

Michael Dudikoff is the titular hero, a sullen GI named Joe who arrives at US army base Fort Sonora with a chip on his shoulder. He quickly alienates everyone except the pretty daughter of the commanding officer, Patricia Hickock (Judie Aronson). Director Sam Firstenberg stages the numerous action scenes well, but engenders little interest in the nonstory.

AMERICAN NINJA 2
THE CONFRONTATION
1987, 89 mins, US Ⓥ ⊙
D: Sam Firstenberg A: Michael Dudikoff, Steve James, Larry Poindexter, Gary Conway, Jeff Weston, Michelle Botes (Golan-Globus)

Globe-trotting army hardbodies Michael Dudikoff and Steve James arrive on a small Caribbean island to investigate the disappearance of four US Marines. It turns out that a local drug kingpin is kidnapping soldiers and others to turn them into genetically reengineered ninja assassins who will do his bidding worldwide. All this merely provides an excuse for an ample number of martial-arts showdowns between the heroes and the black-robed baddies.

AMERICAN NINJA 3
BLOOD HUNT
1989, 90 mins, US Ⓥ ⊙
D: Cedric Sundstrom A: David Bradley, Steve James, Marjoe Gortner, Michele Chan, Yehuda Efroni, Calvin Yung (Breton)

With karate expert David Bradley replacing Michael Dudikoff in the leading role, series continues with a rehash of the enjoyable second entry, as top international martial-arts combatants gather on a tropical isle for a tournament. As before, the island plays host to an evil entrepreneur (Marjoe Gortner). Even for this level of by-the-numbers action filmmaking, Cedric Sundstrom's script is incredibly lame, and his staging of chopsocky violence is little better.

AMERICAN PIE
1999, 95 mins, US Ⓥ ⊙
D: Paul Weitz A: Jason Biggs, Shannon Elizabeth, Alyson Hannigan, Chris Klein, Natasha Lyonne, Thomas Ian Nicholas (Universal)

A film with a one-track mind, American Pie has but a single ambition—to be the king of gross-out comedy. The premise: four seniors, sick of their virginity, resolve to divest themselves of their innocence by prom night. They include Jim (Jason Biggs), something of an oaf; Kevin (Thomas Ian Nicholas), who's already reached third base with his blond g.f. Vicky (Tara Reid); skinny Finch (Eddie Kaye Thomas), who has no apparent prospects, and Oz (Chris Klein), whose advantageous looks and jock status are mitigated by an underlying propriety and shyness. Film succeeds in its elementary mission due to its relentless bluntness and fundamental realism about teenage human behavior. Largely no-name cast is game and gamy.

AMERICAN PRESIDENT, THE
1995, 113 mins, US Ⓥ ⊙ ▭
D: Rob Reiner A: Michael Douglas, Annette Bening, Martin Sheen, Michael J. Fox, David Paymer, Richard Dreyfuss (Wildwood/Castle Rock/Universal)

A romantic comedy about the dating problems of the world's most powerful man, The American President is genial middlebrow fare that coasts a long way on the charm of its two stars. Michael Douglas plays the embodiment of every liberal's dream, an attractive, dashing, sensitive, humane, and smart president of the United States. A widower with a young daughter, he has his attention diverted to his personal life when he meets crack lobbyist Sydney Ellen Wade (Annette Bening). Some of Bening's best comic moments are in her embarrassed but flattered reactions to his admiring advances.
1995: Nomination: Original Musical or Comedy Score

AMERICAN ROMANCE, AN
1944, 151 mins, US
D: King Vidor A: Brian Donlevy, Ann Richards, Walter Abel, John Qualen, Horace McNally (M-G-M)

One of Metro's greatest efforts (claimed to be two years in the making and cost over $3 million), this film is Brian Donlevy's baby from opening to closing, as the Czech immigrant who runs the gamut from poverty to become a wealthy industrialist. The one fault with *Romance* is that it is much too long in the telling.

AMERICAN SUCCESS
See: The American Success Company

AMERICAN SUCCESS COMPANY, THE
(AKA: AMERICAN SUCCESS COMPANY; SUCCESS)
1979, 94 mins, US/W. Germany
D: William Richert **A:** Jeff Bridges, Belinda Bauer, Ned Beatty, Bianca Jagger, Steven Keats, John Glover (Columbia/Geria)

Although almost everything that happens on screen is done with considerable style and a morbid sense of humor, lack of overall point ultimately sinks the picture. Jeff Bridges here plays the mild-mannered son-in-law of tycoon Ned Beatty. Called a loser by his boss and under the thumb of gorgeous wife Belinda Bauer, youth decides to turn the tables on them by assuming the guise of a gangsterish tough guy.

AMERICAN TAIL, AN
1986, 80 mins, US Ⓥ ⊙
D: Don Bluth (Amblin)

The film endeavors to tell the story of Russian immigrants, who happen in this case to be mice of the Mousekewitz clan, and their flight in the late 1800s to the United States. Cartoons with ambitions even this noble are as rare as Steven Spielberg films that lose money, but every character and every situation presented herein have been seen a thousand times before.
1986: Nomination: Best Song ("Somewhere Out There')

AMERICAN TAIL: FIEVEL GOES WEST, AN
1991, 74 mins, US Ⓥ ⊙
D: Phil Nibbelink, Simon Wells (Amblin)

Complete with legendary James Stewart voicing broken-down lawdog Wylie Burp, *An American Tail: Fievel Goes West* is an amiable sequel to the 1986 animated smash featuring the Russian immigrant mouse. The expansive shift to the Old West is welcome, as is the slowing of the pace to accommodate the relaxed, drawling, and almost comatose personality of Fievel's hero/mentor Wylie Burp. Phillip Glasser's sweet rendition of the mouse's voice is a major asset, as are the voice

parts of Dom DeLuise, as Fievel's scene-stealing companion; John Cleese, as the unctuously villainous Cat R. Waul; and Amy Irving, as the brassy saloon entertainer Miss Kitty.

AMERICAN TRAGEDY, AN
1931, 96 mins, US
D: Josef von Sternberg **A:** Phillips Holmes, Sylvia Sidney, Francis Dee, Irving Pichel, Frederick Burton, Claire McDowell (Paramount)

An American Tragedy's relations to the book [by Theodore Dreiser] upon which it is based are decidedly strained. As von Sternberg has seen fit to present it, this celluloid structure is slow, heavy, and not always interesting drama. There is not a performance in the cast of any real interest. The film spends a third or more of its 96 minutes on the trial. It's a big and theatrically good atmospheric scene, but the entire burden is on Phillips Holmes, as the floundering victim, a role he is incapable of upholding for the camera. On the sympathetic end is Sylvia Sidney as the trusting Roberta, an accomplishment she mainly brings off by means of a wistful smile.

AMERICAN WEREWOLF IN LONDON, AN
1981, 97 mins, US Ⓥ ⊙
D: John Landis **A:** David Naughton, Jenny Agutter, Griffin Dunne, John Woodvine, Brian Glover, Frank Oz (Universal/Lycanthrope)

A clever mixture of comedy and horror which succeeds in being both funny and scary, *An American Werewolf in London* possesses an overriding eagerness to please that prevents it from becoming off-putting. Bumming around Europe, two American students (David Naughton and Griffin Dunne) are attacked by a fierce beast, and after the good-natured humor of this prelude, audience is instantly sobered up when Dunne is killed and Naughton is heavily gashed and gored. Naughton is visited by the undead Dunne, who urges his friend to commit suicide or turn into a werewolf with the next full moon. Naughton ignores the advice and, sure enough, undergoes a complete transformation on camera, a highlight in which talents of special makeup effects designer Rick Baker are shown in full flower.
1981: Best Makeup

AMISTAD
1997, 152 mins, US Ⓥ ⊙ ▷
D: Steven Spielberg A: Morgan Freeman, Anthony Hopkins, Matthew Mc-Conaughey, Nigel Hawthorne, Djimon Hounsou, Pete Postlethwaite (Dream-Works)

Amistad is an artistically solid, if not always dramatically exciting, chronicle of the 1839 rebellion on board the Spanish slave ship of the title. Aiming to instruct as well as entertain, pic lacks the subtlety of tone and simplicity of form that made *Schindler's List* so special. Though there are a number of trials, Spielberg shrewdly avoids the routine format of courtroom drama, instead seamlessly integrating the numerous characters and their particular stands on the case. Morgan Freeman is totally wasted as former slave Joadson, a fictional character that's a composite of several historical figures. Matthew Mc-Conaughey renders a passable performance as a shady lawyer. Anthony Hopkins, as John Quincy Adams, former president and son of founding father John Adams, shines throughout.
1997: Nominations: Best Supp. Actor (Anthony Hopkins), Cinematography, Original Dramatic Score, Costume Design

AMITYVILLE 3-D
(AKA: AMITYVILLE: THE DEMON)
1983, 105 mins, US Ⓥ ⊙
D: Richard Fleischer A: Tony Roberts, Tess Harper, Robert Joy, Candy Clark, John Beal, Meg Ryan (De Laurentiis)

Amityville 3-D proudly announces that it is not a sequel to *The Amityville Horror* or *Amityville II*. Even so, there is hardly anything original about the picture. A new cast of characters and the addition of 3-D does little to pump new life, supernatural or otherwise, into this tired genre. This time around a doubting Thomas journalist (Tony Roberts) and his partner (Candy Clark) expose an occult hoax only to have their intervention literally backfire on them. The story moves along at a snail's pace, enlivened from time to time by some nice special effects and 3-D images. The film would have worked better played for laughs.

AMITYVILLE HORROR, THE
1979, 117 mins, US Ⓥ ⊙
D: Stuart Rosenberg A: James Brolin, Margot Kidder, Rod Steiger, Don Stroud, Natasha Ryan (American International)

Taken from the Jay Anson tome, San-dor Stern's script deals faithfully with the supposedly true (but since challenged) story of the Lutz family, who move into a home in Amityville, NY, at a knocked-down price because of its bloody history. The Lutzes fled 28 days later in terror. Stepfather James Brolin, mother Margot Kidde, and moppets Natasha Ryan, Meeno Peluce, and K. C. Martel sympathetically play the happy innocent family.
1979: Nomination: Best Original Score

AMITYVILLE: THE DEMON
See: Amityville 3-D

AMITYVILLE II
THE POSSESSION
1982, 104 mins, US Ⓥ ⊙
D: Damiano Damiani
A: Burt Young, Rutanya Alda, James Olson, Jack Magner, Diane Franklin, Andrew Prine (Orion/De Laurentiis)

It is never quite explained in the context of the film whether this is a prequel, sequel, or entirely new version of the Amityville story. No matter. We still have the same house of horrors about to be occupied by a family who, as usual, never think to leave the house once it starts taking on a personality of its own. There are actually two films meandering in this mess, one a second-rate horror flick about a family in peril, and another that is a slight variation on the demon-possessed *Exorcist* theme.

AMOROUS ADVENTURES OF MOLL FLANDERS, THE
1965, 123 mins, UK
D: Terence Young A: Kim Novak, Richard Johnson, Angela Lansbury, George Sanders, Leo McKern, Vittorio De Sica (Paramount)

A sprawling, brawling, gaudy, bawdy, tongue-in-cheek comedy that seeks to caricaturize an 18th-century London wench's desire to be a gentlewoman and her varying exploits thereof. Starring Kim Novak in title role, it has sex and color, slapstick and lusty, busty characterization, action that is sometimes very funny and, again, equally unfunny. Richard Johnson gives colorful and romantic vigor to the highwayman character.

AMOROUS PRAWN, THE
1962, 89 mins, UK
D: Anthony Kimmins A: Ian Carmichael, Joan Greenwood, Cecil Parker, Dennis Price, Robert Beatty, Liz Fraser (British Lion/Covent Garden)

Nondemanding light entertainment, cheerfully put over by a reliable cast of popular British thesps. General Fitzadam (Cecil Parker) is a bit short of cash. His wife hits on the idea of converting his military headquarters in Scotland into a guest house. Two major complications develop. One is the sudden, unexpected return of the general. The second occurs when an unexpected guest turns up who is revealed as the minister of state for war. Parker produces one of his typical, bumbly performances, but Joan Greenwood, as his wife, is not so peppily in character as she normally is in this sort of drawing-room farce. Ian Carmichael does a shrewd job as the wily corporal who becomes maître d'hôtel in the scheme.

UN AMOUR DE SWANN
(SWANN IN LOVE)
1984, 110 mins, France/W. Germany Ⓥ

D: Volker Schlondorff A: Jeremy Irons, Ornella Muti, Alain Delon, Fanny Ardant, Marie-Christine Barrault, Anne Bennent

The makers of this adaptation seemed to have their sights held at a reasonable level—only *Swann in Love,* the second part of the first volume of Marcel Proust's monumental book. Schlondorff fails because he has no substantial style of his own. His fastidious application makes for a film of attractive surfaces and little depth or feeling. In other words, it's fairly dull. The performances might have salvaged the film, but Jeremy Irons is not up to the difficult central role. One tires of his foppish single-mindedness and tends to side with poor Odette, lusciously but vaguely incarnated by Ornella Muti. (Both are dubbed into French.) Alain Delon is both marvelously comic and touching as Charlus, the middle-aged homosexual aristocrat.

L'AMOUR, L'APRES-MIDI
(CHLOE IN THE AFTERNOON)
1972, 95 mins, France Ⓥ ⊙

D: Eric Rohmer A: Bernard Verley, Zouzou, Francoise Verley, Daniel Ceccaldi, Malvina Penne, Barbette Ferrier (Films du Losange/Barbet Schroeder)

Eric Rohmer adds another plus to his record with this latest moral tale. It's a witty story of a self-satisfied, middle-class white-collar man (Bernard Verley) who almost gives in to Chloe, a free-living, impulsive woman (Zouzou), who barges in on him and whom he has not seen in years. Verley is right as the slightly puffy but still good-looking architect who has

found a good relationship with his wife, Hélène (Francoise Verley). It is his free afternoons that lead to his problems with the woman and his near seduction.

ANACONDA
1997, 89 mins, US Ⓥ ⊙ ▭

D: Luis Llosa A: Jennifer Lopez, Ice Cube, Jon Voight, Eric Stoltz, Jonathan Hyde, Owen Wilson (Cinema Line/Columbia)

Despite some game efforts by a fine cast dominated by a brazenly over-the-top Jon Voight, *Anaconda* is a silly and plodding *Jaws* rip-off about a 40-foot man-eating snake on the prowl in the Brazilian rain forest. A documentary crew sets out on a river journey to find a legendary tribe. Early on, they bring aboard an unexpected guest: Paul Sarone (Voight), an aggressively charismatic fellow who offers to guide his rescuers but has a very different agenda in mind. Sporting a scarred face, an arrogant leer and a tricky accent meant to identify him as a Paraguayan, Voight is a lot more fun, and much more convincing, than the animatronic anaconda, which comes off looking like a cartoonish bit player from *Who Framed Roger Rabbit?* Eric Stoltz spends most of the pic off camera while his character is asleep below deck, recovering from injuries. It's hard to shake the suspicion that, while his costars continued to labor, Stoltz was free to go off and do two or three indie movies.

ANALYZE THIS
1999, 103 mins, US Ⓥ ⊙

D: Harold Ramis A: Robert De Niro, Billy Crystal, Lisa Kudrow, Joe Viterelli, Chazz Palminteri, Bill Macy

A shrink pushes a mobster to get in touch with the good fella inside him in this sometimes funny situation comedy in which the mechanics of the situation eventually overwhelm the comedy. Paul Vitti (De Niro), a New York mob kingpin, is suffering from anxiety attacks and coerces his shrink, therapist Ben Sobel (Crystal), into being on 24-hour call to attend to his crises. The timing is inconvenient for Sobel, as he's headed for Miami to marry broadcaster Laura MacNamara (Lisa Kudrow). Vitti precipitates a Florida gangland hit that aborts Sobel's wedding and ups the ante between Vitti and his New York rival Primo Sindone (Chazz Palminteri). De Niro's precise comic timing and colorful line readings constitute pic's greatest pleasure. Once the action returns to Gotham, the plot machinery starts becoming far too visible.

ANASTASIA
1956, 105 mins, US Ⓥ ⊙ ⊡
D: Anatole Litvak A: Ingrid Bergman, Yul Brynner, Helen Hayes, Akim Tamiroff, Martita Hunt, Felix Aylmer (20th Century-Fox)

The stage hit *Anastasia* has been made into a wonderfully moving and entertaining motion picture from start to finish, and the major credit inevitably must go to Ingrid Bergman, who turns in a great performance. Yul Brynner as General Bounine, the tough Russian exile, etches a strong and convincing portrait that stands up perfectly to Bergman's Anastasia, and Helen Hayes has great dignity as the Empress. Brynner and a group of conspirators are working in Paris to produce an Anastasia who might help them collect the $10 million deposited in England by the czar's family. Bergman bears an amazing resemblance to the czar's youngest daughter, who was supposed to have been killed by the Reds in 1918. Bergman first resists, then begins to recover her regal bearing and her memories.
1956: Best Actress (Ingrid Bergman)
Nomination: Best Scoring of a Dramatic Picture

ANASTASIA
1997, 94 mins, US Ⓥ ⊙ ⊡
D: Don Bluth, Gary Goldman (Fox Family)

This ambitious, serious—but not particularly stimulating—animated musical feature attempts to graft warm and cuddly family-film motifs onto turbulent aspects of modern history. Pre-credits prologue establishes Anastasia (voiced by Kirsten Dunst, sung by Lacey Chabert) as the beloved daughter of Czar Nicholas in 1916, but attributes Russia's social unrest entirely to the sinister sorcerer Rasputin (Christopher Lloyd, sung by Jim Cummings). Anastasia is next seen as a beautiful young woman (Meg Ryan, sung by Liz Callaway) emerging from a People's Orphanage a decade later. Needing a supreme villain, the filmmakers resurrect Rasputin, who has his evil powers restored by his chatty pet bat. He unleashes his demons upon the train carrying Anastasia to Paris, making for an action-packed railway setpiece. Nonetheless, the film's impact is moderate at best.

1997: Nominations: Best Original Musical Score, Original Song ("Journey to the Past")

ANATOLIAN SMILE, THE
See: America America

ANATOMY OF A MURDER
1959, 160 mins, US Ⓥ ⊙
D: Otto Preminger A: James Stewart, Lee Remick, Ben Gazzara, Arthur O'Connell, Eve Arden, Kathryn Grant (Columbia/Carlyle)

Wendell Mayes screenplay is a large reason for the film's general excellence. In swift, brief strokes it introduces a large number of diverse characters and sets them in motion. An army lieutenant (Ben Gazzara) has killed a tavern operator whom he suspects of attempting to rape his wife (Lee Remick). James Stewart, former district attorney and now a privately practicing attorney in a small Michigan city, is engaged for the defense. Preminger purposely creates situations that flicker with uncertainty, that may be evaluated in different ways. Motives are mixed and dubious, and, therefore, sustain interest.
1959: Nominations: Best Picture, Actor (James Stewart), Supp. Actor (Arthur O'Connell, George C. Scott), Screenplay, B&W Cinematography, Editing

ANCHORS AWEIGH
1945, 138 mins, US Ⓥ ⊙
D: George Sidney A: Frank Sinatra, Kathryn Grayson, Gene Kelly, Jose Iturbi, Dean Stockwell, Pamela Britton (M-G-M)

Anchors Aweigh is solid musical fare. The production numbers are zingy; the songs are extremely listenable; the color treatment outstanding. Two of the potent entertainment factors are the tunes and Gene Kelly's hoofing. Jule Styne and Sammy Cahn cleffed five new numbers, three of which are given the Frank Sinatra treatment for boff results. In the dance department Kelly sells top terping. There is a clever Tom and Jerry sequence combining Kelly's live action with a cartoon fairy story. Kelly also combines three Spanish tunes into another sock number executed with little Sharon McManus. His third is a class tango. Kathryn Grayson figures importantly in the score with her vocaling.
1945: Best Score for a Musical Picture
Nominations: Best Picture, Actor (Gene Kelly), Color Cinematography, Song ("I Fall in Love Too Easily")   •

AND BABY MAKES THREE
1949, 83 mins, US
D: Henry Levin **A:** Robert Young, Barbara Hale, Robert Hutton, Janis Carter, Billie Burke (Columbia/Santana)

Fun starts confusingly but mood warms up as footage unfolds and plotline becomes clear. Robert Young has been divorced by Barbara Hale. It's a hurry-up Reno untying and Hale is ready to do a quick rebound marriage when she faints on the way to the altar. Pregnancy is the diagnosis. This upsets wedding plans with Robert Hutton and complications also develop when Young announces he'll fight for partial custody. Young is his usual able self. Hale delights as the would-be mother.

ANDERSON TAPES, THE
1971, 98 mins, US ⓥ ⊙
D: Sidney Lumet **A:** Sean Connery, Dyan Cannon, Martin Balsam, Alan King, Ralph Meeker, Christopher Walken (Columbia)

Sean Connery plays an ex-con who schemes to burglarize an entire apartment house on Manhattan's plush upper East Side. With backing from a new breed of organized mobster, led by Alan King, Connery recruits a band of diverse helpmates ranging from a homosexual antique dealer (Martin Balsam) to a fellow ex-con just released after 40 years in prison (Stan Gottlieb). Scripter Frank Pierson with director Sidney Lumet has injected broadly comic aspects and the laughs work without reducing suspense.

AND GOD CREATED WOMAN
1988, 94 mins, US ⓥ ⊙
D: Roger Vadim **A:** Rebecca DeMornay, Vincent Spano, Frank Langella, Donovan Leitch, Judith Chapman (Crow/Vestron)

A remake in name only of his first feature, made 32 years earlier, Roger Vadim's new film is considerably more legitimate dramatically than one might expect. Vadim tells a modestly involving tale about how a woman with two strikes against her gives herself a shot at life through a combination of sex, imagination, energy, and plenty of scheming. DeMornay throws herself deeply into the part as a lifelong loser determined to win at all costs.

...AND GOD CREATED WOMAN
See: Et Dieu ... Crea la Femme

...AND JUSTICE FOR ALL
1979, 120 mins, US ⓥ ⊙
D: Norman Jewison **A:** Al Pacino, Jack Warden, John Forsythe, Lee Strasberg, Christine Lahti, Jeffrey Tambor (Columbia)

...*And Justice for All* is a film that attempts to alternate between comedy and drama, handling neither one incompetently, but also not excelling at either task. Centering on the impossible circumstances a sensitive lawyer encounters when dealing with the complexities and corruption of the American judicial system, pic is another good vehicle for Al Pacino.
1979: Nominations: Best Actor (Al Pacino), Original Screenplay

ANDREI RUBLEV
See: Andrei Rublyov

ANDREI RUBLYOV
1971, 180 mins, USSR ⓥ ▭
D: Andrei Tarkovsky **A:** Anatoli Solonitsyn, Ivan Lapikov, Nikolai Grinko, Nikolai Sergeyev, Irma Raush, Nikolai Burlyayev (Mosfilm)

Film is a brilliantly fashioned fresco of 15th-century Russia built around the life of a noted icon painter, Andrei Rublev. It catches the medieval brutality and man's awakening cognizance of a need for change. In black-and-white, the film suddenly bursts into color to show Rublev's actual icons. It avoids an academic aspect and displays a director of exceptional talent in Andrei Tarkovsky, whose next film after this is *My Name Is Ivan*.

ANDROCLES AND THE LION
1952, 98 mins, US ⓥ
D: Chester Erskine **A:** Jean Simmons, Alan Young, Victor Mature, Robert Newton, Maurice Evans, Elsa Lanchester (RKO)

Bernard Shaw's satirical comedy on Romans and Christians provides the basis for a fair film offering. Picture is a curious mixture of basic comedy and Shavian wit. The first filming of a Shaw play in Hollywood, the presentation has the confined feeling of having been made indoors. The familiar story deals with Androcles' love of animals, a feeling that saves the Greek tailor when he frees a lion from a thorn and later meets that lion in the Roman arena.

ANDROID
1982, 80 mins, US ⓥ ⊙
D: Aaron Lipstadt **A:** Klaus Kinski, Brie Howard, Norbert Weisser, Crofton Hardester, Kendra Kirchner, Don Opper (New World)

Obsessed researcher Klaus Kinski inhabits a remote space station in the year 2036 with his android assistant, Max 404, played by cowriter Don Opper. Doctor is on the verge of perfecting his masterpiece, a perfect robot who happens to be a beautiful blonde, and who will render Max obsolete. Onto the craft from a prison ship come three escaped convicts with no precise plans but with dangerous personalities. Although there are the obligatory fight scenes and nudity, film works mainly due to the unusual interaction between the all-too-human Max robot and those around him.

ANDROMEDA STRAIN, THE
1971, 130 mins, US Ⓥ ⊙ ▭
D: Robert Wise **A:** Arthur Hill, David Wayne, James Olson, Kate Reid, Paula Kelly, George Mitchell (Universal)

The Andromeda Strain is a high-budget science-fact melodrama, marked by superb production, an excellent score, an intriguing story premise, and an exciting conclusion. But Nelson Gidding's adaptation of the Michael Crichton novel is too literal and talky. In four acts representing days, a team of civilian medics attempt to find and isolate an unknown phenomenon which has killed most of a desert town near the place where a space satellite has fallen to earth. Arthur Hill, David Wayne, James Olson, and Kate Reid are the specialists racing against time. The glacial internal plot evolution is not at all relieved by the performances. Hill is dull; Wayne is dull; Olson caroms from another dull character to a petulant kid; and Reid's unexplained-until-later epilepsy condition does not generate much interest.
1971: Nominations: Best Art Direction, Editing

AND SOON THE DARKNESS
1970, 100 mins, UK Ⓥ
D: Robert Fuest **A:** Pamela Franklin, Michele Dotrice, Sandor Eles, John Nettleton, Clare Kelly, Hanna-Maria Pravda (Associated British)

Story concerns two young British girls pedaling through a dull, flat, deserted part of France. One's a pert miss (Michele Dotrice), her chum is a more down-to-earth girl (Pamela Franklin). After a tiff the two separate. Franklin, lonely and remorseful, returns to find Dotrice. But she is missing. The film mainly concerns the trouble Franklin gets into while trying to solve the problem of what happened to her friend.

French atmosphere is conveyed excellently but overall there's a leering, sinister feeling about this piece which is repellent.

AND THEN THERE WERE NONE
1945, 97 mins, US Ⓥ
D: Rene Clair **A:** Barry Fitzgerald, Walter Huston, Louis Hayward, Roland Young, June Duprez, C. Aubrey Smith (20th Century-Fox)

Plot concerns itself with 10 assorted characters, each with a bad spot in his past, who are marooned on a lonely island off the English coast. Like the nursery rhyme, the number is decimated by sudden death until only two leave the island alive. Victims are mysteriously gathered in the spot by a mad judge who fancies himself as a dispenser of justice. Picture rarely rises to moments of suspense and despite the killings it gives the appearance of nothing ever happening as directed by Rene Clair.

AND WOMAN . . . WAS CREATED
See: Et Dieu . . . Crea la Femme

ANDY WARHOL'S FRANKENSTEIN
See: Flesh for Frankenstein

ANGEL
1937, 98 mins, US
D: Ernst Lubitsch **A:** Marlene Dietrich, Herbert Marshall, Melvyn Douglas, Edward Everett Horton, Herbert Mundin, Ernest Cossart (Paramount)

Angel is a drama more than it is comedy. The story seriously portrays a girl of the old world who loves her husband and home, yet must graze around in strange pastures. Authors seek to accentuate that a woman can love two men at the same time. Dietrich is glamour in double dress. This time she is wearing eyelashes you could hang your hat on and every now and then the star flicks 'em as though a dust storm was getting in her way. Marshall is excellent as the duped husband. The usual, smooth performance is obtained from Douglas as the persistent lover.

ANGEL
1982, 90 mins, Ireland Ⓥ ⊙
D: Neil Jordan **A:** Stephen Rea, Alan Devlin, Veronica Quilligan, Peter Caffrey, Honor Heffernan, Ray McAnally (MPCI)

Angel carries knockout power. A story of retribution set against the troubles in Northern Ireland, which are kept way in the background, it's an impressive pic debut for director-scripter Neil Jordan. A saxophonist with a traveling band unwittingly observes the murder of the band's manager (involved in extortion payoffs) and that of a deaf-and-dumb girl witness. The musician, vigorously played by Stephen Rea, is obsessed to hunt down the murderers and does so, becoming a murderer himself several times over.

ANGEL AND THE BADMAN
1947, 100 mins, US Ⓥ ⊙
D: James Edward Grant **A:** John Wayne, Gail Russell, Harry Carey, Bruce Cabot, Irene Rich, Lee Dixon (Republic)

John Wayne's first production effort is loaded with sharp performances, honest writing, and direction. Story essentials deal with a hot gunman of the early west who is succored by a family of Quakers when he falls wounded on its doorstep. There is a gradual absorption of the family's formula for living by the bad man, and in the end he turns to the soil and the religion in a perfectly believable manner. Wayne does his best job since *Stagecoach* as the gunman. Gail Russell has never been seen to better advantage as the frank and honest Quaker girl who falls in love and actually pursues the gunman.

ANGELA'S ASHES
1999, 145 mins, US Ⓥ ⊙
D: Alan Parker **A:** Emily Watson, Robert Carlyle, Joe Breen, Ciaran Owens, Michael Legge, Ronnie Masterson (Dirty Hands/Universal/Paramount)

Alan Parker's film version of *Angela's Ashes* artfully evokes the physical realities of Irish poverty, but mostly misses the humor, lyricism, and emotional charge of Frank McCourt's memoir. Film opens with the McCourts' miserable lives in Brooklyn during the Depression, establishing the unemployable, alcoholic Dad (Robert Carlyle), his incapable wife Angela (Emily Watson), and the resourceful five-year-old Frank (Joe Breen) and his younger brother Malachy. When baby Margaret dies, the family returns to Ireland and proceeds to Limerick, Angela's hometown and poverty capital of Ireland. At 10, Frank (Ciaran Owens) is felled by typhoid but has his literary ability recognized. At 16, Frank (Michael Legge) realizes he must return to New York. The leavening that young Frank's humorous outlook provided in the book is seldom evident, making the tale considerably grimmer on-screen than it was on the page.
1999: Nomination: Best Original Score

ANGEL AT MY TABLE, AN
1990, 156 mins, New Zealand/Australia Ⓥ ⊙
D: Jane Campion **A:** Kerry Fox, Alexia Keogh, Karen Fergusson, Melina Bernecker, Glynis Angell, William Brandt (Hibiscus)

Jane Campion comes up with a touching and memorable biography of New Zealand author Janet Frame, originally made as a three-part TV miniseries (each part 52 minutes). In the 1950s, Frame spent eight years in a mental home undergoing shock treatment for wrongly diagnosed schizophrenia. A potentially painful and harrowing film is imbued with gentle humor and great compassion, which makes every character come vividly alive. Campion constructs the film in a series of short, sometimes elliptical scenes.

EL ANGEL EXTERMINADOR (THE EXTERMINATING ANGEL)
1962, 95 mins, Mexico Ⓥ
D: Luis Bunuel **A:** Silvia Pinal, Enrique Rambal, Jacqueline Andere, Jose Baviera, Augusto Benedico, Luis Beristain (Uninci/Films 59)

A group of rich people go to a friend's home for late supper after the opera. The servants leave and the group notices suddenly that they lack the will or the ability to get out of the house. Drugs, cabalistic signs, and attempts to marshal the people into action all seem to fail as they slowly sink into near violence. Pic may be a razor-sharp look at purgatory. The symbols may have or not have any true, clear meaning, but do have shock value. The pic is of a piece and brilliantly utilized by director Luis Bunuel.

ANGEL FACE
1953, 91 mins, US
D: Otto Preminger **A:** Robert Mitchum, Jean Simmons, Mona Freeman, Herbert Marshall, Leon Ames, Barbara O'Neil (RKO)

Jean Simmons portrays the title role of a young lady behind whose beautiful face is a diseased mind that plots to murder her wealthy stepmother (Barbara O'Neil). Drawn into this scheme, although innocently, is Robert Mitchum. Mitchum and Simmons make a good team, both delivering the demands of the script and Preminger's direction ably.

ANGEL HEART
1987, 113 mins, US Ⓥ ⊙
D: Alan Parker **A:** Mickey Rourke, Robert

De Niro, Lisa Bonet, Charlotte Rampling (Carolco/Winkast-Union)

Even if it may be a specious work at its core, *Angel Heart* still proves a mightily absorbing mystery, a highly exotic telling of a small-time detective's descent into hell, with Faustian theme, heavy bloodletting, and pervasive grimness. Based on William Hjortsberg's novel *Falling Angel*, Alan Parker's screenplay, set in 1955, has seedy Gotham gumshoe Mickey Rourke engaged by mysterious businessman Robert De Niro to locate a certain Johnny Favorite, a big-band singer from the prewar days who, De Niro says, failed to live up to the terms of a contract. Rourke follows his leads to New Orleans, and particularly the jazz and voodoo elements within its black community.

ANGEL OF VENGEANCE
See: Ms. 45

ANGEL ON MY SHOULDER
1946, 100 mins, US ⓥ
D: Archie Mayo **A:** Paul Muni, Anne Baxter, Claude Rains, George Cleveland, Onslow Stevens (United Artists)

Paul Muni is the murdered gangster, turning in a performance that measures up to past credits and giving film plenty of zip. Awakening in hell after being bumped, Muni wants out so he can get revenge on his killer. Claude Rains, as Satan, sees chance to even things with a crime-busting earthly judge who's the double for Muni. The two take off for earth and the fun starts. Rains shines as the Devil, shading the character with a likable puckishness good for both sympathy and chuckles. Anne Baxter is excellent as the troubled fiancée.

ANGELS AND INSECTS
1995, 117 mins, US/UK ⓥ
D: Philip Haas **A:** Mark Rylance, Kristin Scott Thomas, Patsy Kensit, Jeremy Kemp, Douglas Henshall, Annette Badland (Samuel Goldwyn/Playhouse)

A curious, vastly uneven analysis of the early cracking in the armor of Victorian society, *Angels and Insects* gets off the ground only when the warped and weird final moves of A. S. Byatt's story come into play. Awkwardly filmed and erratically acted, this English-lensed second feature by US director Philip Haas begins poorly but develops a degree of narrative and thematic interest in the final reels. Set in 1862, entire narrative is played out at the lovely country estate of Reverend Har-

ald Alabaster (Jeremy Kemp), an aging thinking man whose enduring faith has been called into question by the recently published theories of Charles Darwin.

ANGELS AND THE PIRATES
See: Angels in the Outfield

ANGELS IN THE OUTFIELD
1951, 99 mins, US
D: Clarence Brown **A:** Paul Douglas, Janet Leigh, Keenan Wynn, Donna Corcoran, Lewis Stone, Spring Byington (M-G-M)

Clarence Brown has carved a tremendously satisfying film from a script that, from every evidence, could have gone completely haywire if handled clumsily, dealing as it does with fantasy. Religious angle also presented a delicate situation, but Brown has handled it all masterfully. Pivotal character is Paul Douglas, who plays one of the most tyrannical, blasphemous managers in the history of baseball. His team is in seventh place and is headed into the subbasement when somebody unknown to Douglas intercedes with the Angel Gabriel.

ANGELS IN THE OUTFIELD
1994, 102 mins, US ⓥ
D: William Dear **A:** Danny Glover, Tony Danza, Brenda Fricker, Christopher Lloyd, Ben Johnson, Jay O. Sanders (Walt Disney)

Angels in the Outfield shows scant devotion to the 1951 film on which it's based. Updated for nonnuclear families of the nineties, the story centers on a foster child, Roger (Joseph Gordon-Levitt), whose shiftless father says he may be able to reclaim him when the boy's favorite baseball team, the last-place California Angels, wins the pennant. Roger offers up a prayer to make it so, and the stars twinkle in response, sending down a wild-eyed, honest-to-you-know-who angel, Al (Christopher Lloyd), whom only Roger can see. William Dear doesn't shy away from overblown sentimentality after a rather slow and grim first act, as glowing winged figures pop up all over the field.

ANGELS ONE FIVE
1952, 97 mins, UK
D: George More O'Ferrall **A:** Jack Hawkins, Michael Denison, Dulcie Gray, Andrew Osborn, Cyril Raymond, John Gregson (Templar/Associated British)

Action of *Angels One Five* takes place during the period described by Winston Churchill as Britain's finest hour, when a handful of fighter pilots (the few against the many) stemmed the air invasion by Nazi war planes. Breaking away from the more conventional treatment, the script watches the progress of the battle, not from the perspective of the actual combats, but from the messages received by and emanating from the operational control room.

ANGELS OVER BROADWAY
1940, 78 mins, US Ⓥ ⊙
D: Ben Hecht, Lee Garmes **A:** Douglas Fairbanks Jr., Rita Hayworth, Thomas Mitchell, John Qualen, George Watts (Columbia)

Angels over Broadway is a synthetic tale of Broadway nightlife and the characters that roam around Times Square. Writer-director-producer Ben Hecht gets little movement in the unwinding, and depends too much on stage technique in trying to put over his points. An embezzler (John Qualen) is saved from committing suicide by a zany playwright (Mitchell) who proceeds to try to help the former out of his jam and give him a new lease on life. Douglas Fairbanks Jr. is a slick youth who shills for a big poker game, and sets his sights for Qualen, who he assumes is a rural hick. There's much byplay between the trio and a girl who moves in (Rita Hayworth).
1940: Nomination: Best Original Screenplay

ANGEL STREET
See: Gaslight (1940 B&W)

ANGELS WITH DIRTY FACES
1938, 97 mins, US Ⓥ ⊙
D: Michael Curtiz **A:** James Cagney, Pat O'Brien, Humphrey Bogart, Ann Sheridan, George Bancroft, Billy Halop (Warner)

Cagney is the tenderloin toughie who's the idol of the gutter-bred youngsters because of his criminal exploits and cocky belligerence. O'Brien is the priest who was a boyhood chum of Cagney's and who seeks to save the neighborhood kids from trying to emulate their gangster hero. Cagney and O'Brien form an irresistible team. Their personalities and acting styles offer both a blend and an eloquent contrast. Cagney has a swagger and an awgo-to-hell pugnacity. O'Brien gives an eminently credible performance of the mild-mannered, two-fisted, compassionate priest. The *Dead End* kids are as rambunctious as usual.

1938: Nominations: Best Director, Actor (James Cagney), Original Story

ANGIE
1994, 107 mins, US Ⓥ ⊙ ▭
D: Martha Coolidge **A:** Geena Davis, Stephen Rea, James Gandolfini, Aida Turturro, Philip Bosco, Jenny O'Hara (Hollywood)

Angie is a skin-deep feel-good movie about such less-than-breezy issues as a broken engagement, childbirth, single motherhood, infant infirmities, and discovering brutal truths about your parents. On the bright side is a star performance from Geena Davis in which the dazzling actress remains center screen virtually at all times, as well as an appealing turn by Stephen Rea as a wry Irish suitor who sticks around as long as it suits him. On the downside, pic goes mushy soft when confronted with its assorted heavy issues.

ANGI VERA
1979, 96 mins, Hungary
D: Pal Gabor **A:** Veronika Pap, Erzsi Pasztor, Tamas Dunai, Eva Szabo, Laszlo Halasz, Laszlo Horvath (Objektiv)

A cool treatment of early Communist-party training of selected people to fit into various areas of the new socialist regime at its beginnings in 1948, it is mainly about an innocent 18-year-old girl and her corruption by the hard-line, puritanical, Stalinist outlooks of the day. The good playing, the perceptive direction (despite its lack of more dramatic sweep), and its theme make this film an engrossing look at the period.

ANGRY HILLS, THE
1959, 105 mins, UK ▭
D: Robert Aldrich **A:** Robert Mitchum, Elisabeth Mueller, Stanley Baker, Gia Scala, Theodore Bikel, Donald Wolfit (M-G-M)

The Angry Hills, set in Greece, is a rather confused yarn. Robert Mitchum plays an American war correspondent who is hunted by Gestapo chief Stanley Baker and fifth columnist Theodore Bikel when he arrives in Athens as Greece is about to fall to the Nazis. Both Baker and Mitchum give very sound performances.

ANGRY SILENCE, THE
1960, 95 mins, UK
D: Guy Green **A:** Richard Attenborough, Pier Angeli, Michael Craig, Bernard Lee, Alfred Burke, Penelope Horner (Beaver)

The Angry Silence details the impact of industrial unrest on individuals, told with

passion, integrity, and guts, but without false theatrical gimmicks. Plot concerns a worker in a factory where there has been no trouble until a political troublemaker moves in. Insidiously he stirs up unrest, makes one of the workers his catspaw, creates a wildcat strike, and then quietly moves on to spread his poison in other factories. The main victim of the strike is played by Richard Attenborough, who, because he refuses to be pushed around, is sent to Coventry (shunned by his workmates) and is beaten up, and his family intimidated. Attenborough has done nothing better on the screen for a long time. That goes, too, for Pier Angeli as his wife.
1960: Nomination: Best Original Screenplay

ANGST ESSEN SEELE AUF (FEAR EATS THE SOUL; ALI)
1974, 94 mins, W. Germany
D: Rainer Werner Fassbinder **A:** Brigitte Mira, El Hedi Ben Salem, Barbara Valentin, Irm Hermann, Peter Gauhe, Rainer Werner Fassbinder (Tango)

Racism is the theme but done in a low-profile way that creates an internal unease rather than easy outrage at outright racists. A sixtyish widow one day wanders into a bar catering to Arab workers. She meets a thirtyish, handsome, bearded Arab worker who asks her to dance. They sympathize and somehow their mutual loneliness makes them friends. Her grown children are outraged; people she works with as a cleaning woman also shun her, as do tradespeople. Film is played with reserve. Technically flawless, deceptively simple, and avoiding excesses, it is about problems that are timely and timeless in implications.

ANIMAL CRACKERS
1930, 97 mins, US ⓥ ⊙
D: Victor Heerman **A:** Groucho Marx, Harpo Marx, Chico Marx, Zeppo Marx, Lillian Roth, Margaret Dumont (Paramount)
First give Paramount extreme credit for reproducing *Animal Crackers* intact from the stage, without too much of the songs and musical numbers. Among the Marx boys there is no preference. Groucho shines; Harpo remains a pantomimic clown who ranks with the highest; Chico adds an unusual comedy sense to his dialogue as well as business and piano playing; and Zeppo, if in on a split, is lucky.

ANIMAL FARM
1954, 72 mins, UK ⓥ ⊙
D: John Halas, Joy Batchelor (animation) John F. Reed (Halas & Batchelor)

Human greed, selfishness, and conniving are lampooned in *Animal Farm* with the pigs behaving in a piglike manner and the head pig, named Napoleon, corrupting and perverting an honest revolt against evil social conditions into a new tyranny as bad as, and remarkably similar to, the old regime. In short, this cartoon feature is a sermon against all that is bestial in politics and rotten in the human will to live in luxury at the expense of slaves. Made in Britain, the cartoon is vividly realized pictorially.

ANNA AND THE KING
1999, 147 mins, US ⓥ ▭
D: Andy Tennant **A:** Jodie Foster, Chow Yun-fat, Bai Ling, Tom Felton, Syed Alwi, Randall Duk Kim (Fox 2000)

Jodie Foster makes a valiant effort at bringing a contemporary edge to the role of 19th-century schoolteacher Anna Leonowens in *Anna and the King,* the third major screen version of the popular tale. But this is a schmaltzy, ultraelaborate, overly long production, consciously conceived as old-fashioned family entertainment. The most notable element is the large cast of Asian actors, beginning with the effective Hong Kong star Chow Yun-fat as King Mongkut. Production is designed to soothe and gratify everyone in the manner of fifties and sixties big-budget epics. Foster moves gracefully in period costumes and commands the screen charismatically. She enjoys strong chemistry with Chow, who impresses with his handsome presence and dignified stillness.
1999: Nominations: Best Art Direction, Costume Design

ANNA AND THE KING OF SIAM
1946, 128 mins, US ⓥ
D: John Cromwell **A:** Irene Dunne, Rex Harrison, Linda Darnell, Lee J. Cobb, Gale Sondergaard (20th Century-Fox)

A rather faithful screen adaptation of Margaret Landon's biography, intelligently handled to spellbind despite its long footage. *Anna* tells a straightforward narrative, bringing in the natural humor, suspense, and other dramatic values of the story of an English widow who finds herself confronted with the many problems of educating the children and some of the wives of the King of Siam. The monarch, himself, needs some education, and Anna

sees that he gets it. Irene Dunne does a superb enactment of Anna. Rex Harrison shines particularly in his American film debut. It's a sustained characterization of the King of Siam that makes the role real. **1946:** Best B&W Cinematography, B&W Interior Decoration (Lyle R. Wheeler, William Darling)
Nominations: Best Supp. Actress (Gale Sondergaard), Screenplay, Scoring of a Dramatic Picture

ANNA CHRISTIE
1923, 87 mins, US ⊗
D: John Griffith Wray **A:** Blanche Sweet, William Russell, George F. Marion, Eugenie Besserer (Ince/Associated First National)

Anna Christie is a picture that is as different from the regular run of screen productions as the Eugene O'Neill play it is based on is to the majority of hits and near hits that come to the spoken stage. There is one mistake John Griffith Wray makes in the direction. In the usual picture fashion he tries to force his leading woman to overshadow the character role. Blanche Sweet isn't the Anna Christie Pauline Lord was on the stage, but George Marion as Chris so far overshadows the leading woman that the director is undoubtedly forced to take the extremes he does to keep her in the eye of the audience. But that is not good direction.

ANNA CHRISTIE
1930, 86 mins, US ⊗
D: Clarence Brown **A:** Greta Garbo, George F. Marion, Marie Dressler, Charles Bickford (M-G-M)

Hollywood closely follows the Eugene O'Neill play. Infinite care in developing each sequence, just the proper emphasis on characterizations, and a part that exactly fits Greta Garbo put *Anna Christie* safely in the realm of the superlative. "Garbo talks" is, beyond quarrel, an event. La Garbo's accent is nicely edged with a Norse "yah," but once the ear gets the pitch it's okay. George Marion, as in the original Ince production, plays the old sentiment-hungry seagoing father. Charles Bickford as the Irish sailor of massive muscles and primitive ideals is magnificent. Perhaps the greatest surprise is Marie Dressler, who steps out of her usual straight slapstick to stamp herself an actress.
1929/30: Nominations: Best Director, Actress (Greta Garbo), Cinematography

ANNA KARENINA
1935, 95 mins, US ⊗
D: Clarence Brown **A:** Greta Garbo, Fredric March, Freddie Bartholomew, Basil Rathbone, Maureen O'Sullivan, May Robson (M-G-M)

Greta Garbo starred in this story once before in 1927. Silent film was titled *Love* and John Gilbert had the role now handled by Fredric March. March handles his assignment firmly and with understanding and the film in toto is a more honest and sincere rendition of the Tolstoy classic than the silent. Garbo, too, seems to have grown since 1927. There is no flaw to be found in her rendition of the love-racked Russian girl, Anna.

ANNA KARENINA
1948, 139 mins, UK ⊗
D: Julien Duvivier **A:** Vivien Leigh, Ralph Richardson, Kieron Moore, Hugh Dempster (London)

Fine as this fourth production of Tolstoy's novel is (Fox 1915, Metro 1927 and 1935), it misses greatness and has tedious stretches. It would appear that far too much attention was paid to the sets and the artistic structure at the expense of the players. Leigh dominates the picture, as she rightly should with her beauty, charm, and skill. It isn't her fault that eyes remain dry and hearts unwrung when she moves to inevitable tragedy, as the neglected wife and discarded lover. Richardson's portrayal of the priggish, unlikable husband is masterly yet uneven.

ANNA LUCASTA
1949, 86 mins, US
D: Irving Rapper **A:** Paulette Goddard, William Bishop, Oscar Homolka, John Ireland, Broderick Crawford (Columbia/Security)

Anna Lucasta, reverting the tale from the legit Negro cast to an all-white ensemble, is no bowl of Wheaties for the kiddies. It's about a greedy family that has thrown out the youngest daughter believing she has sinned. She is brought back when the family sees the chance of conning some money by wedding her off to a southern farmer. Paulette Goddard performs competently, although her physical accoutrements do not measure up to the lush requirements of the part.

ANNE AND MURIEL
See: Deux Anglaises et le Continent

43

L'ANNEE DERNIERE A MARIENBAD
(LAST YEAR AT MARIENBAD)
1961, 93 mins, France/Italy ⓥ ▱
D: Alain Resnais **A:** Delphine Seyrig, Giorgio Albertazzi, Sacha Pitoeff

This is a difficult, daring film that takes plenty of patience from any audience, including the most aesthetic. A man sees a woman in a fashionable German hotel that looks like an old château. He keeps asking her if she remembers last year, and they are seen in different periods, mixing the present with the past and the varying versions of the past. Director Alain Resnais's aim seems to be to lay bare the impossibility of true remembrance.

ANNE OF GREEN GABLES
1934, 80 mins, US
D: George Nicholls Jr. **A:** Anne Shirley, Tom Brown, O. P. Heggie, Helen Westley, Sara Haden, Murray Kinnell (RKO)

Anne of Green Gables is wholesome, sympathetic, romantic, and dramatic, packing many a heart tug and tear-jerk. It did much to establish Anne Shirley, who took her professional nom de screen from her character in the L. M. Montgomery classic. Homespun setting is almost idyllic in a natural, bucolic Prince Edward Island (Canada) locale.

ANNE OF THE INDIES
1951, 81 mins, US
D: Jacques Tourneur **A:** Jean Peters, Louis Jourdan, Debra Paget, Herbert Marshall, Thomas Gomez, James Robertson Justice (20th Century-Fox)

As the femme pirate who sailed the Caribbean seas as the dreaded Captain Providence, Jean Peters outdoes the best Ruth Roland tradition and looks good while doing it. There's nothing ludicrous about her performance in the type of action usually handed to males. The film plays along at an imaginative pace under Jacques Tourneur's direction. Sea battles are expertly staged to make the most of such actionful moments. Jourdan supplies a good hero and Thomas Gomez a colorful Blackbeard.

ANNE OF THE THOUSAND DAYS
1970, 145 mins, UK ⓥ ▱
D: Charles Jarrott **A:** Richard Burton, Genevieve Bujold, Irene Papas, Anthony Quayle, John Colicos, Michael Hordern (Universal)

With Richard Burton as Henry VIII and Genevieve Bujold in the title role of Anne Boleyn, *Anne of the Thousand Days* is a stunning-acted, sumptuous, grand-scale widescreen drama of the royal bedchamber and political intrigues that created the Church of England. Although Burton's portrayal is sensitive, vivid, and arresting, it is still basically an unsympathetic role. There is a basically stagy pace to the drama that makes it more static and less cinematic than it might have been.
1969: Best Costume Design
Nominations: Best Picture, Actor (Richard Burton), Actress (Genevieve Bujold), Supp. Actor (Anthony Quayle), Screenplay, Cinematography, Art Direction, Original Score, Sound

ANNIE
1982, 128 mins, US ⓥ ⊙ ▱
D: John Huston **A:** Albert Finney, Carol Burnett, Aileen Quinn, Ann Reinking, Bernadette Peters, Tim Curry (Columbia)

Many people said John Huston was an odd choice to direct *Annie* and he proves them right. In an effort to be more realistic *Annie* winds up exposing just how weak a story it had to start with, not helped here by the music. In the title role, little Aileen Quinn acquits herself quite well. Carol Burnett gets most of what chuckles there are as the drunken Miss Hannigan, who runs the orphanage. Albert Finney is best of the bunch as Daddy Warbucks.
1982: Nominations: Best Art Direction, Original Song & Score

ANNIE GET YOUR GUN
1950, 107 mins, US
D: George Sidney **A:** Betty Hutton, Howard Keel, Louis Calhern, J. Carrol Naish, Edward Arnold, Keenan Wynn (M-G-M)

Annie Get Your Gun is socko musical entertainment on film, just as it was on the Broadway stage. Ten of the *Annie* Irving Berlin hits are used and two are reprised. *Annie* is Wild West, shooting, Indians, daredevil riding, and action, never slowing a minute.
1950: Best Score for a Musical Picture
Nominations: Best Color Cinematography, Color Art Direction, Editing

ANNIE HALL
1977, 93 mins, US ⓥ ⊙
D: Woody Allen **A:** Woody Allen, Diane Keaton, Tony Roberts, Carol Kane, Paul Simon, Colleen Dewhurst (United Artists)

Woody Allen's four romantic comedies with Diane Keaton strike a chord of believability that makes them nearly the 1970s equivalent of the Tracy-Hepburn

films. *Annie Hall* is by far the best, a touching and hilarious three-dimensional love story. The gags fly by in almost non-stop profusion, but there is an undercurrent of sadness and pain reflecting a maturation of style. The script is loosely structured, virtually a two-character running conversation between Allen and Keaton as they meet, fall in love, quarrel, and break up.
1977: Best Picture, Director, Actress (Diane Keaton), Original Screenplay
Nomination: Best Actor (Woody Allen)

ANNIE OAKLEY
1935, 79 mins, US Ⓥ
D: George Stevens **A:** Barbara Stanwyck, Preston Foster, Melvyn Douglas, Moroni Olsen, Pert Kelton, Andy Clyde (RKO)
Comedy drama has the colorful background of Buffalo Bill's wild-west show. The film recounts the events which led to Annie's joining Buffalo Bill, and tells a tale of romantic interest involving Annie and two of the troupe's figures, played by Preston Foster and Melvyn Douglas. After early scenes, where she plays a backwoods girl effectively, Barbara Stanwyck does little enough for the picture, probably because the material gives her few opportunities.

ANNIVERSARY, THE
1968, 95 mins, UK Ⓥ
D: Roy Ward Baker **A:** Bette Davis, Sheila Hancock, Jack Hedley, James Cossins, Elaine Taylor, Christian Roberts (Hammer)
Derived from Bill McIllwraith's legit original, this was turned into a vehicle for the extravagant tantrums of Bette Davis, in her most ghoulish mood. This, together with its modish black-comedy lines and bold situation, is its chief asset. Davis sinks her teeth into the role of the ultrapossessive ma and hurls it out with splendid panache and flamboyance, but some might find her outsize portrayal too stark to carry conviction. She bosses it over a family of three sons, all of whom are in an advanced stage of spinelessness.

ANOTHER COUNTRY
1984, 90 mins, UK Ⓥ ☉
D: Marek Kanievska **A:** Rupert Everett, Colin Firth, Michael Jenn, Robert Addie, Rupert Wainwright, Anna Massey (Goldcrest)
Story is supposedly based on the early friendship of Guy Burgess and Donald MacLean, who, in the 1950s, spied for the USSR while working for the British government. Contention is that the homosexuality of Burgess, called Bennett here, made him as much an outsider in the claustrophobic atmosphere of the British upper crust as did MacLean's Marxism. Film is marvelously acted down the line, with Rupert Everett a standout as the tormented Bennett.

ANOTHER 48 HRS.
1990, 95 mins, US Ⓥ ☉
D: Walter Hill **A:** Eddie Murphy, Nick Nolte, Brion James, Kevin Tighe, Ed O'Ross, David Anthony Marshall (Paramount/Eddie Murphy)
Pic's really misnamed, since it's not *Another 48 Hrs.* but the same *48 Hrs.,* the 1982 mismatched buddy action pic. Director Walter Hill, reprising those chores, knows the terrain and tills it with all the familiar elements: bawdy humor, cannonloud gunplay, hissable bad guys, and plenty of action. Eddie Murphy and Nick Nolte manage to recapture some of their initial chemistry, but for the most part, the film is curiously flat in part due to a jumped plot that's so quickly tied up at the end it seems everyone was in a hurry to get their checks and get out of town.

ANOTHER MAN ANOTHER CHANCE
See: Un Autre Homme une Autre Chance

ANOTHER PART OF THE FOREST
1948, 106 mins, US
D: Michael Gordon **A:** Fredric March, Dan Duryea, Edmond O'Brien, Ann Blyth, Florence Eldridge, Dona Drake (Universal)
Another Part of the Forest backtracks 20 years from *The Little Foxes,* Lillian Hellman's play, showing the same family of Hubbards and how they got to be the way they are in *Foxes.* Picture opens 15 years after close of the Civil War, in a small southern town where the Hubbards aren't accepted socially, due to Hubbard père (Fredric March) having run salt at $8 a pound during the war to Confederates who badly needed the commodity. March delivers to tremendous effect as the father. Florence Eldridge makes her portrayal count, particularly as the mother who in the end admits she dislikes every one of her children. Edmond O'Brien, as the elder son, is seen in the best role of his career.

ANOTHER STAKEOUT
1993, 109 mins, US Ⓥ ⊙ ▱
D: John Badham **A:** Richard Dreyfuss, Emilio Estevez, Rosie O'Donnell, Dennis Farina, Marcia Strassman, Madeleine Stowe (Touchstone)

A purely escapist entertainment, John Badham's *Another Stakeout,* a sequel to his 1987 hit, is sillier and less plausible than the first movie, but it's also funnier. Scripter Jim Kouf's new comedy-adventure picks up Chris Lecce (Richard Dreyfuss) and Bill Reimers (Emilio Estevez), the two Seattle police detectives, six years later. The eternally feuding cops are appointed to locate Lu Delano (Cathy Moriarty), a missing key witness in the trial of a Las Vegas mobster. This time around, their team also includes Gina Garrett (Rosie O'Donnell), an assertive, tough-talking assistant DA, who insists on bringing along her dog.

ANOTHER TIME ANOTHER PLACE
1983, 101 mins, UK Ⓥ ⊙
D: Michael Radford **A:** Phyllis Logan, Giovanni Mauriello, Gian Luca Favilla, Claudio Rosini, Paul Young, Gregor Fisher (Umbrella)

It's not often that a British film is realized with as much creative integrity as *Another Time Another Place.* The plot springs from the cultural difference between the inhabitants of a bleak Scottish agricultural village and a trio of Italians confined to the community during the World War II. One Italian in particular, the passionate Neopolitan Luigi (Giovanni Mauriello) by seeming to offer an alternative to an emotionally cold marriage and a laborious penny-pinching life. Central to the film's effectiveness is the performance of Logan as the girl entranced.

ANOTHER WOMAN
1988, 84 mins, US Ⓥ ⊙
D: Woody Allen **A:** Gena Rowlands, Mia Farrow, Ian Holm, Blythe Danner, Gene Hackman, Martha Plimpton (Rollins/Joffe)

Woody Allen once again explores the human condition via the inner turmoil of gifted New Yorkers. Story deals with a very successful, often idolized character who discovers around the time of her 50th birthday that she has made many mistakes, but people have been more or less too deferential to confront her. Gena Rowlands plays Marion Post, head of a graduate philosophy department, married to a doctor.

She takes an apartment downtown in which to write a book, and begins overhearing analysis sessions from the psychiatrist's office next door.

ANOTHER YOU
1991, 94 mins, US Ⓥ ⊙
Dir Maurice Phillips **A:** Richard Pryor, Gene Wilder, Mercedes Ruehl, Stephen Lang, Vanessa Williams, Phil Rubenstein (Tri-Star)

Gene Wilder's frantic routines can't compensate for Richard Pryor's sadly depleted energy in *Another You,* and producer Ziggy Steinberg's feeble script is given slapdash direction by the man who replaced Peter Bogdanovich on what is billed a "film by Maurice Phillips" (the best joke in the film). The setup isn't without promise, as the "mentally challenged" Wilder is released from a sanitarium into the dubious care of Hollywood street hustler Pryor, who's been ordered to do community service as a condition of his parole. Some amiable, if predictable, gags about Wilder's readjustment to the sleazy outside world give way all too quickly to tiresome plot mechanics.

NOUS LA LIBERTE, A
1931, 93 mins, France Ⓥ
D: Rene Clair **A:** Henri Marchand, Raymond Cordy, Rolla France, Paul Olivier, Jacques Shelley, Germaine Aussey (Tobis)

Rene Clair has applied a technical formula similar to that of his preceding productions, *Sous les Toits de Paris* and *Le Million,* to subject matter which constitutes social satire. That is, his film has a minimum of dialogue and a good deal of accompanying music. This film is really in two parts. One half is social, and really the backbone of the picture. The other part, which practically constitutes an independent story, is a love affair. Like most Clair films, it contains much footage devoted to chases.

ANTHONY ADVERSE
1936, 139 mins, US Ⓥ
D: Mervyn LeRoy **A:** Fredric March, Olivia de Havilland, Edmund Gwenn, Claude Rains, Anita Louise, Louise Hayward (Warner)

In transmuting the Hervey Allen bestseller to the screen, the producers were faced with the unusual problem of too much material. They have maneuvered a straightforward and comparatively logical story. Fredric March as Adverse is an ace choice, playing the role to the hilt. Olivia

de Havilland has, perhaps, the next important role as Adverse's wife, Angela. She handles it acceptably, especially in the emotional scenes. Claude Rains does a splendid job as Don Luis.
1936: Best Supp. Actress (Gale Sondergaard), Cinematography, Score, Editing **Nominations:** Best Picture, Art Direction, Assistant Director (William Cannon)

ANTONIA'S LINE
1995, 93 mins, Belgium/UK/Netherlands ⓥ
D: Marleen Gorris **A:** Willeke Van Ammelrooy, Els Dottermans, Jan Decleir, Marina De Graaf, Mil Seghers, Jan Steen
Marleen Gorris's idealized perspective on an independent-minded woman who comes to live in a small Dutch farming community, *Antonia's Line* is a feel-good fairy tale that will appeal to many women. Gorris narrates the lives of five generations of women who work, have kids, and bond with each other and some of the more decent males in the vicinity, as season follows season in a natural rhythm of birth and death. In the title role, Van Ammelrooy provides a strong center to the rambling story, both feminine and authoritative.
1995: Best Foreign Language Film

ANTONY AND CLEOPATRA
1972, 158 mins, UK/Spain/Switzerland ⓥ ▭
D: Charlton Heston **A:** Charlton Heston, Hildegard Neil, Eric Porter, John Castle, Fernando Rey, Freddie Jones (Folio/Izaro/Filmtransac)
Charlton Heston has come up with a very creditable retelling of the Bard's Antony and Cleopatra passion. The finished film is a neat balance of close-up portraiture and panoramic action; the big battle sequences on land and sea are impressive achievements and the Spanish location landscape provides a stunning backdrop. Hildegard Neil proves one of Cleo's more convincing screen incarnations. Heston himself as Antony very often succeeds in capturing the nobility of the character.

ANTZ
1998, 83 mins, US ⓥ ⊙
D: Eric Darnell, Tim Johnson (DreamWorks/PDI)
Antz is a dazzling delight, a sort of *Metropolis* meets *Microcosmos* with a commoner-princess lovers-on-the-run romance at its core. Appropriately enough for a feature toplining Woody Allen, the picture starts on an analyst's couch, as meek worker ant Z (Allen) complains about his upbringing as "the middle child in a family of 5 million." The physical grandeur of the ants' underground totalitarian world is dazzlingly displayed, as countless workers are driven to extremes by Gen. Mandible (Gene Hackman), a martinet with dreams of even greater glory. The queen's daughter, Princess Bala (Sharon Stone), unhappily engaged to Mandible, goes slumming and asks an unsuspecting Z to dance. Vocal performances are outstanding across the board, while the backgrounds are magnificently designed with detail and bold, clear colors that continually provide feasts for the eyes.

ANYBODY'S WOMAN
1930, 80 mins, US
D: Dorothy Arzner **A:** Ruth Chatterton, Clive Brook, Paul Lukas, Huntly Gordon (Paramount)
It's mainly the unsympathetic role handed Clive Brook that takes the big punch out of the story. It starts out far more promisingly than it develops. Brook has just become divorced. He is tossed into the society of a chorus girl. She falls for his philosophy that probably a bad girl like her would make the best wife in the long run. The social-ostracism angle is also overdone, as is Ruth Chatterton's interpretation of the tough-chorus-girl role.

ANY GIVEN SUNDAY
1999, 162 mins, US ⓥ ⊙ ▭
D: Oliver Stone **A:** Al Pacino, Cameron Diaz, Dennis Quaid, James Woods, Jamie Foxx, LL Cool J (Ixtlan/The Donners/Warner)
A hyperkinetic, testosterone-and-adrenaline-drenched look at professional football, *Any Given Sunday* is Oliver Stone's most purely enjoyable film in years. The story begins by plunging the viewer headlong into a bitterly fought game, played out in agonizing fashion for Miami's "Sharks." Then more crises erupt off the field than during games. The Sharks' savvy veteran coach, Tony D'Amato (Al Pacino), has sacrificed his wife and kids to his job. Christina Pagniacci (Cameron Diaz) has inherited the team with her alcoholic mother (Ann-Margret) and has a ruthless bottom-line mentality. Main figures' private lives are sketched in quick, clear strokes. Stone and cowriter John Logan are able to make sharp observations about the generational,

racial, and attitudinal divides in American life. Music from myriad sources contributes to the sensory overload.

ANY NUMBER CAN PLAY
1949, 102 mins, US
D: Mervyn LeRoy A: Clark Gable, Alexis Smith, Wendell Corey, Audrey Totter, Mary Astor, Lewis Stone (M-G-M)

Pic's thesis maintains that gambling is legitimate if you're a winner. Yarn develops the point via a domestic break between Clark Gable, as the legalized-gambling-house operator, and his collegiate son who is ashamed of his pappy's profession. Gable effectively projects the hard-playing gambler with no sympathy for his son's idealistic gripings.

ANYTHING CAN HAPPEN
1952, 107 mins, US
D: George Seaton A: Jose Ferrer, Kim Hunter, Kurt Kasznar, Eugenie Leontovich, Oscar Karlweis, Nick Dennis (Paramount)

Anything Can Happen is a heartwarming comedy, engagingly acted, slickly produced and directed. Film concerns a lovable group of Near Eastern immigrants and their devotion to the new homeland in America. It shows Jose Ferrer's arrival in the new, strange country, his struggles with the English language, his shy courting of an American (Kim Hunter), and his eventual ownership of a California orange grove on which he is privileged to pay US taxes.

ANYTHING GOES
1936, 90 mins, US
D: Lewis Milestone A: Bing Crosby, Ethel Merman, Charles Ruggles, Ida Lupino, Grace Bradley, Arthur Treacher (Paramount)

Cole Porter's lyrics, which were the essence and chief asset of the original [1934] stage *Anything Goes,* have been replaced by plot motion in this adaptation. Only "I Get a Kick Out of You" and "You're the Top" are used. The title song is in also, but just for thematic and strictly instrumental use. There are four new numbers. Ethel Merman equals her job in the stage version, which means aces. But Charlie Ruggles as the gag gangster is miscast. With the story opening in a cabaret and finishing in a production scene, with most of the bulk in between taking place on a big ocean liner, the production is lavish. Crosby is fine singing "Sailor Beware"

alone. And he's also there when it comes to getting his quota of laughs.

ANYTHING GOES
1956, 106 mins, US
D: Robert Lewis A: Bing Crosby, Donald O'Connor, Zizi Jeanmaire, Mitzi Gaynor, Phil Harris, Kurt Kasznar (Paramount)

While there are Cole Porter songs and the legit handle is still carried, there's scant resemblance to Paramount's 1936 film version, in which Crosby also starred with Ethel Merman. Script provides Crosby with plenty of those sotto voce, throwaway cracks he and his fans dote on. Plot, simply, has Crosby and O'Connor agreeing to do a B'way musical together after European vacations. Abroad, each signs a femme star and the remainder concerns fitting the gals in with previous plans. Jeanmaire has two ballets that are clicks. Gaynor belts the title tune staged by Ernie Platt to score solidly in her solo showcasing.

ANY WEDNESDAY
1966, 109 mins, US Ⓥ
D: Robert Ellis Miller A: Jane Fonda, Jason Robards, Dean Jones, Rosemary Murphy, Ann Prentiss, Jack Fletcher (Warner)

An outstanding sophisticated comedy about marital infidelity. Zesty adaptation wisely distributes the comedy emphasis among all four principals—Jason Robards, the once-a-week philanderer; Jane Fonda, his two-year Wednesday date; Dean Jones, whose arrival rocks Robards's dreamboat; and Rosemary Murphy, recreating in superior fashion her original Broadway role as Robards's wife.

ANYWHERE BUT HERE
1999, 114 mins, US Ⓥ ◉ ▭
D: Wayne Wang A: Susan Sarandon, Natalie Portman, Eileen Ryan, Ray Baker, John Diehl, Shawn Hatosy (Fox 2000)

Centering on the turbulent but loving relationship between a single mother and her rebellious teenage daughter, *Anywhere but Here* is a sumptuously crafted but old-fashioned comedy-drama. Natalie Portman lends excellent support to Susan Sarandon's turn as her eccentric but ultimately self-sacrificing mother. Adele (Sarandon) and 14-year-old Ann (Portman) are heading for the promised land of Beverly Hills. They're leaving Bay City, WI, a provincial town Adele finds suffocating. Ann is furious over losing the cozy family and social life she enjoyed. Adele is pushing her daughter into acting, hoping that life in Los Angeles will fulfill her dreams. The revelation here is Portman, whose casting was reportedly Sarandon's condition for making the movie. Portman is a natural performer who brings rough edges to any role she plays. Wayne Wang directs with clarity.

ANY WHICH WAY YOU CAN
1980, 116 mins, US ⓥ ⊙
D: Buddy Van Horn A: Clint Eastwood, Sondra Locke, Ruth Gordon, William Smith, Harry Guardino, Geoffrey Lewis (Warner)

Any Which Way You Can is a benign continuation of *Every Which Way But Loose*. Clint Eastwood, Sondra Locke, Geoffrey Lewis, Ruth Gordon, and numerous supporting players all repeat their characterizations. Eastwood's Philo Beddoe swears off his lucrative sideline career, better to settle down with Ma Gordon, a significantly tamed Locke, and orangutan chum Clyde. However, the mob makes him an offer he can't refuse to battle he-man William Smith, and the two, despite having become good pals, end up in an epic brawl.

ANZIO
1968, 117 mins, Italy ⓥ ▭
D: Edward Dmytryk Act Robert Mitchum, Peter Falk, Robert Ryan, Arthur Kennedy, Earl Holliman, Mark Damon (Columbia)

Anzio, based on the World War II campaign in Italy, suffers from flat writing, stock performances, uninspired direction, and dull pacing. Produced by Dino De Laurentiis, film would seem to be a large-scale war epic, but it really is a pale tale of a small group of men trapped behind German lines. Robert Mitchum stars in a cast that is far better in potential than in reality.

APA
(FATHER)
1966, 96 mins, Hungary ⓥ ⊙
D: Istvan Szabo A: Miklos Gabor, Klari Tolnay, Andras Balint, Dani Erdelyi, Kati Solyom, Zsuzsa Rathonyi (Mafilm III)

The growth of a youth into manhood is explored here via the use of real and imaginary flashbacks to life with father, a doctor who died just after the end of the last World War, leaving his young son with a number of confused memories. As he grows, the child becomes slowly obsessed by the father's continuing influence on his life, and he unconsciously begins inventing wartime exploits with the partisans and other exaggerated achievements to further the hero image, which, he finds, rubs off on him with his fellow pupils. This is real, solid, moving yet unsentimental stuff and its integration of the 1956 Hungarian uprising is apt and honest, as are such other topics as early befuddlement with Marxism or the problems of a Jewish minority in Budapest.

APACHE
1954, 86 mins, US ⓥ
D: Robert Aldrich A: Burt Lancaster, Jean Peters, John McIntire, Charles Bronson, John Dehner, Paul Guilfoyle (United Artists)

Production is based on history, retelling story of a die-hard Apache who waged one-man war against the United States and thereafter became a tribal legend. While its roots are historic, the James R. Webb screenplay from Paul I. Wellman novel, *Bronco Apache,* gives it good old outdoor action punch true to western film tradition. Main plot switch is viewing Indian from sympathetic angle. Lancaster and Jean Peters play their Indian roles understandingly without usual screen stereotyping.

APARAJITO
(THE UNVANQUISHED)
1957, 108 mins, India ⓥ
D: Satyajit Ray A: Kanu Bannerjee, Karuna Bannerjee, Pinaki Sen Gupta, Sumiran Ghosjal (Epic)

As the second in Satyajit Ray's trilogy of Indian life, *Aparajito* is a worthy successor to the first film, *Pather Panchali.* It doesn't have quite the tension or quite the variety of mood but it has a special brooding quality and a more explicit conflict between East and West. The story simply continues to follow the fortunes and misfortunes of one Brahman family, which has moved to the holy city of Banares, where the father, movingly played by Kanu Bannerjee, contracts a fatal illness. The mother, played by sad-eyed Karuna Bannerjee, is forced to take work as a rich family's cook until a priestly uncle takes her and her little son, played by Pinaki Sen Gupta, back to a small village. The little boy, however, wins a scholarship to a Calcutta university. The city tears the young man, played by Sumiran Ghosjal, from his mother and she becomes ill.

APARTMENT, THE

1960, 124 mins, US Ⓥ ⊙ ▭
D: Billy Wilder **A:** Jack Lemmon, Shirley MacLaine, Fred MacMurray, Ray Walston, Edie Adams, Jack Kruschen (Mirisch/United Artists)

Billy Wilder furnishes *The Apartment* with a one-hook plot that comes out high in comedy, wide in warmth, and long in running time. Lemmon is a lonely insurance clerk with a convenient, if somewhat antiquated, apartment which has become the rendezvous point for five of his bosses and their amours. In return, he's promoted to a 27th-floor wood-paneled office complete with key to the executive washroom. When he falls in love with Shirley MacLaine, an elevator girl who's playing Juliet to top executive Fred MacMurray's Romeo, he turns in his washroom key. The screenplay fills every scene with touches that spring only from talented, imaginative filmmakers. *Apartment* is all Lemmon, with a strong twist of MacLaine. The actor uses comedy as it should be used, to evoke a rainbow of emotions. MacLaine, in pixie hairdo, is a prize who's worth the fight being waged for her affections.
1960: Best Picture, Director, Original Story & Screenplay, B&W Art Direction, Editing
Nominations: Best Actor (Jack Lemmon), Actress (Shirley MacLaine), Supp. Actor (Jack Kruschen), B&W Cinematography, Sound

APARTMENT FOR PEGGY

1948, 96 mins, US
D: George Seaton **A:** Jeanne Crain, William Holden, Edmund Gwenn, Gene Lockhart, Griff Barnett, Randy Stuart (20th Century-Fox)

Jeanne Crain is perfect casting for the young wife of William Holden, veteran studying under the GI bill. She gives the role a thoroughly believable reading that comes off big and Holden's work matches. Edmund Gwenn completes the star trio, socking over his professor-of-philosophy role with such deft understanding it's a joy to watch.

APARTMENT ZERO

1989, 124 mins, UK Ⓥ ⊙
D: Martin Donovan **A:** Colin Firth, Hart Bochner, Dora Bryan, Liz Smith, Fabrizio Bentivoglio, Cipe Lincovsky (Summit)

Apartment Zero emerges as a genuinely creepy, disturbing, and gripping psychological piece. Story's fundamental opposition is between Colin Firth, the nervously repressed, emotionally constipated British cinephile, and Hart Bochner, a charming, loose, American rascal whom Firth takes into his lovely flat as a boarder when finances demand it. Both actors are excellent.

APOCALYPSE NOW

1979, 153 mins, US ⊙ ▭
D: Francis Coppola **A:** Marlon Brando, Robert Duvall, Martin Sheen, Frederic Forrest, Dennis Hopper, Sam Bottoms (Omni Zoetrope/United Artists)

Alternately a brilliant and bizarre film, Francis Coppola's *Apocalypse Now* offers the definitive validation to the old saw war is hell. Coppola's vision of hell on earth hews closely to Joseph Conrad's novella *Heart of Darkness*, and therein lies the $40-million film's principal commercial defect. An exhilarating action-adventure exercise for two thirds of its 139 minutes, *Apocalypse* abruptly shifts to surrealistic symbolism for its denouement. Result will be many spectators left in the lurch. It's the first film to directly excoriate US involvement in the Vietnam War. Coppola's wisest decision was to narrow the focus on the members of the patrol-boat crew entrusted with taking intelligence assassin Martin Sheen on a hazardous mission upriver into Cambodia. There Sheen hopes to track down and terminate with extreme prejudice Marlon Brando, a megalomaniac officer. Robert Duvall appears midway as an air-force helicopter commander who's a surfing nut, and has his boys riding the waves in the midst of flak attacks. These and some otherworldly, nighttime river excursions contain a wacky, manic energy that serves *Apocalypse* well.
1979: Best Cinematography, Sound
Nominations: Best Picture, Director, Supp. Actor (Robert Duvall), Screenplay, Art Direction, Editing

APOLLO 13

1995, 140 mins, US Ⓥ ⊙ ▭
D: Ron Howard **A:** Tom Hanks, Kevin Bacon, Bill Paxton, Gary Sinise, Ed Harris, Kathleen Quinlan (Universal/Imagine)

With its rah-rah, gung-ho, can-do attitude and cast full of good-looking young white men in buzz cuts, this engrossing account of NASA's most perilous moon shot embodies what many consider to be old-fashioned American virtues in a virtually pristine state. Scarcely embellishing the story of how three astronauts barely avoided becoming the first Americans to die in outer space, director Ron Howard and his team walk a narrative line that's almost as narrow as the course of the mission itself. Casting Hanks as Lovell gives the film a human center, someone with whom the audience can feel at home. Bacon brings a colorful cockiness to the one *Top Gun*–style flier in the bunch, while Paxton is obliged to suffer quietly with a high fever. Harris's coiled tension provides a strong focus of attention in the control room, and Kathleen Quinlan gives depth of feeling to the necessarily compartmentalized role of Lovell's omen-fearing wife.

1995: Best Sound, Best Film Editing
Nominations: Best Picture, Best Supporting Actor (Ed Harris), Screenplay Adaptation, Original Dramatic Score, Best Art Direction, Best Sound, Visual Effects

APOSTLE, THE
1997, 133 mins, US Ⓥ ⊙
D: Robert Duvall **A:** Robert Duvall, Farrah Fawcett, Miranda Richardson, Todd Allen, John Beasley, June Carter Cash (Butchers Run)

Robert Duvall's third—and best—directorial effort is a sharply observed exploration of a middle-aged preacher who embarks on a redemptive odyssey after committing a crime. A devout Texan Pentecostal preacher, Sonny Dewey (Duvall) lives a seemingly happy life with his beautiful wife, Jessie (Farrah Fawcett). But Jessie is cheating on him with a younger minister, Horace (Todd Allen). Sonny strikes Horace with a bat at a softball game and gets on a bus to Louisiana. He baptizes himself as "the Apostle" to God and, in the predominantly black town of Bayou Boutte, LA, conquers his inner demons by organizing a grass-roots church until his estranged wife discovers his whereabouts. Duvall renders a superlative and modulated performance, one that allows the audience to feel an immediate connection with his character, even when his motives are dubious.

1997: Nomination: Best Actor (Robert Duvall)

L'APPAT
(FRESH BAIT)
1995, 117 mins, France
D: Bertrand Tavernier **A:** Marie Gillain, Olivier Sitruk, Bruno Putzulu, Richard Berry, Philippe Duclos, Clothilde Courau

Fresh Bait captures the twisted symbiosis whereby three reasonably nice and normal French kids become a clumsy death squad. Bertrand Tavernier's conscientious look at moral bankruptcy, as demonstrated by murders as chillingly excessive as they are pointless, does a sober, fairly suspenseful job of deglamorizing violence. Coscripters Tavernier and ex-wife Colo Tavernier O'Hagan have updated a true story that stunned the nation in 1984. Tightly knit ensemble cast is good, particularly Putzulu as the dim-bulb sponger who takes things literally. Extensive use of nocturnal, roving handheld camera renders the proceedings upclose, fluid, and intimate.

APPLAUSE
1929, 80 mins, US Ⓥ
D: Rouben Mamoulian **A:** Helen Morgan, Joan Peers, Fuller Mellish Jr., Jack Cameron, Henry Wadsworth, Dorothy Cumming (Paramount)

This is the real old burlesque, in its background, people, and atmosphere. Helen Morgan is Kitty Darling, a fading star of burlesque, aging on the stage as her daughter, born in a dressing room, grows up. Joan Peers comes to the front toward the finish as the daughter, April. Earlier and in the convent scenes she doesn't convince. The picture was made at Paramount's Long Island studio.

APPLEGATES, THE
See: Meet the Applegates

APPOINTMENT, THE
1969, 100 mins, US Ⓥ
D: Sidney Lumet **A:** Omar Sharif, Anouk Aimee, Lotte Lenya, Fausto Tozzi, Ennio Balbo (M-G-M/Marpol)

Omar Sharif plays a Roman lawyer who falls for a colleague's fiancée, a mannequin played by Anouk Aimee, and eventually marries her, undeterred by his pal's fear that she's secretly a high-priced call girl. Soon, however, suspicion begins to gnaw and he begins to tail his spouse. Flat writing and an overrigid performance by Sharif in a crucial role, which at times skirts the laughable, seriously flaw what might otherwise have been an intriguing love tale cum suspenser.

APPOINTMENT FOR LOVE
1941, 88 mins, US
D: William A. Seiter **A:** Charles Boyer, Margaret Sullavan, Rita Johnson, Eugene Pallette, Ruth Terry, Cecil Kellaway (Universal)

Producer Bruce Manning, who also collaborated on the script with Felix Jackson, points up the romantic adventure while injecting numerous refreshing episodes to the oft-told tale of newlywed problems. Charles Boyer falls in love with Margaret Sullavan, seriously immersed in the practice of medicine and with very novel and unusual ideas about marriage and continuance of separate careers. Sullavan takes a separate apartment in the same building with Boyer, explaining this unusual procedure as a result of a difference in time schedules in their work. William Seiter paces the film with an expert hand, deftly timing the smacko laugh lines and situations for brightest effect.

1941: Nomination: Best Sound

APPOINTMENT WITH DANGER

1951, 90 mins, US

D: Lewis Allen **A:** Alan Ladd, Phyllis Calvert, Paul Stewart, Jan Sterling, Jack Webb, Henry Morgan (Paramount)

Exploits of the Postal Inspection Service furnish Alan Ladd with a good cops-and-robbers actioner. Film deals with government detectives tracking down the killers of a fellow postal inspector and preventing a million-dollar mail robbery. Ladd is right at home as the tight-lipped, tough inspector assigned to the case. There is a neat contrasting byplay in the nun character done by Phyllis Calvert as costar, which adds an offbeat note to the meller plot.

APPOINTMENT WITH DEATH

1988, 108 mins, US Ⓥ

D: Michael Winner **A:** Peter Ustinov, Lauren Bacall, Carrie Fisher, John Gielgud, Piper Laurie, Hayley Mills (Cannon)

Peter Ustinov hams his way through *Appointment with Death* one more time as ace Belgian detective "Hercuool Pwarow," but neither he nor glitz can lift the pic from an impression of little more than a routine whodunit. Even the normally amusing Ustinov looks a bit jaded. There simply are not enough murders to sustain the interest of even the most avid Agatha Christie fan.

APPRENTICESHIP OF DUDDY KRAVITZ, THE

1974, 120 mins, Canada Ⓥ ⌷

D: Ted Kotcheff **A:** Richard Dreyfuss, Micheline Lanctot, Jack Warden, Randy Quaid, Joseph Wiseman, Denholm Elliott (International Cinemedia/Center/CFDC)

Director Ted Kotcheff has taken Mordecai Richler's novel by the scruff of the neck and worked a zesty but somewhat muted nostalgic look at a nervy Jewish kid on the make in the 1940s. Kravitz, played by a continually grinning, scratching, nervous-making, yet vulnerable Richard Dreyfuss, comes across effectively and with force.

1974: Nomination: Best Adapted Screenplay

APRIL FOOLS, THE

1969, 95 mins, US Ⓥ ⌷

D: Stuart Rosenberg **A:** Jack Lemmon, Catherine Deneuve, Peter Lawford, Jack Weston, Myrna Loy, Charles Boyer (Cinema Center/Jalem)

Jack Lemmon is both funny and touching as the mild-mannered stockbroker, tied to a nothing of a wife. Given a big promotion by his boss (Peter Lawford), he meets the latter's wife (Catherine Deneuve) at a stultifying cocktail party. She's bored and he doesn't know her real identity but they depart for a night of self-discovery. Deneuve, in her first American film, is worth just looking at.

APT PUPIL

1998, 111 mins, US Ⓥ ⊙ ⌷

D: Bryan Singer **A:** Ian McKellen, Brad Renfro, Bruce Davison, Elias Koteas, Joe Morton, Jan Triska (Bad Hat Harry/Phoenix/TriStar)

A creepy, well-acted story of contagious evil, *Apt Pupil* has more than enough chilling dramatic scenes to rivet the attention but suffers from some hokey contrivances and underlying insufficiencies of motivation. In 1984, 16-year-old Todd Bowden (Brad Renfro) becomes fascinated by the Holocaust and recognizes a grizzled local resident as one Kurt Dussander (Ian McKellen), a former officer at the Paten concentration camp, where 90,000 died. Under threat of turning him in, Todd commands the Nazi to tell him the brutal truth. "I want to hear about it. Everything. Everything they're afraid to show us in school." The main shortcoming is a failure to take Todd's fascination with Dussander far enough, to analyze the attraction evil has for him and, by extension, the potential anyone may have for inhuman acts under certain circumstances. As it is, Todd's motivation seems to stem from little more than a sadistic desire to humiliate the old man for his crimes.

APUR SANSAR
(THE WORLD OF APU)
1959, 105 mins, India ⓥ
D: Satyajit Ray A: Soumitra Chatterjee, Sharmila Tagore, Shapan Mukerjee, Alkoe Chakravarty (Ray)

Film is the final one of a trilogy on Indian life in the 1930s, following the life of a young boy and his family. This entry compares with its predecessors in knowing insight, poetics, and ability, but surpasses them in craftsmanship. Here the boy, Apu (Soumitra Chatterjee), is seen after he has finished schooling at 23. In a visit to his cousin's wedding he is talked into marrying the girl himself when the bridegroom has a fit during the ceremony. Script then deals with the love that grows between the newlyweds, the wife's death in childbirth, the husband's anguish and wanderings and refusal to see his son, and finally his determination to win the boy over after some years.

ARAB, THE
1924, 75 mins, US ⊗
D: Rex Ingram A: Ramon Novarro, Alice Terry, Maxudian, Jerrold Robertshaw, Jean De Limur (Metro-Goldwyn)

This is the finest sheik film of them all. As a sheik Ramon Novarro is the acme. Surrounded as he is by genuine men of the desert, for the scenes were shot in Algiers and the mobs are all natives in their natural environments, he seems as bona fide as the Arabs themselves. Alice Terry is the wistful, frightened, assailed little Christian whose winsomeness and piety make the presentation plausible, romantic, and attractive.

ARABELLA
1969, 88 mins, Italy ▭
D: Mauro Bolognini A: Virna Lisi, James Fox, Margaret Rutherford, Terry-Thomas, Paola Borboni, Giancarlo Giannini (Universal/Malenotti)

Arabella, Italian-produced with an English and Italian cast, is a series of episodes none too adroitly woven together which focus on the larcenous activities of Virna Lisi as she tries to help her Italian princess-grandma (Margaret Rutherford) pay taxes dating back to 1895. There are bright flashes of comedy, and as many long sequences of contrived and amateurish action, which add up to a mildly amusing film.

ARABESQUE
1966, 107 mins, US/UK ⓥ ▭
D: Stanley Donen A: Gregory Peck, Sophia Loren, Alan Badel, Kieron Moore, Carl Duering, John Merivale (Universal/Donen)

Arabesque packs the names of Gregory Peck and Sophia Loren and a foreign-intrigue theme, but doesn't always progress on a true entertainment course. Fault lies in a shadowy plotline and confusing characters. Peck tries valiantly with a role unsuited to him and Loren displays her usual lush and plush presence. If her part is an enigma to Peck, it is to the spectator, too. Menace is provided by Alan Badel and Kieron Moore.

ARABIAN NIGHT
1995, 72 mins, US/UK ⓥ ⊙ ▭
D: Richard Williams (Allied Filmmakers)

As with any fable, there are forces of light and darkness at odds in the animated romantic adventure Arabian Night. The good can be seen in some outstanding, complex, and eye-popping animation—perhaps the last great work to be done in this area prior to the advent of computer assists. The bad news is that, although its production history dates back as early as 1968, the film gives the overriding sense that there were still both visual and story refinements needed to bring the work fully to fruition. The story is relatively straightforward. In ancient Baghdad, the realm is about to be beset by the mighty hordes of the warrior One-Eye (voiced by Kevin Dorsey). Court magician Zigzag (Vincent Price) is in league with the tyrant for the hand of the appropriately named King Nod's daughter, Princess Yum Yum (Jennifer Beals). Legend has it that the city will be protected as long as the three gold balls on the tallest minaret shine upon the town. Zigzag winds up with them. It then falls upon Yum Yum and the humble young cobbler Tack (Matthew Broderick) to retrieve the orbs and save the empire from doom.

ARACHNOPHOBIA
1990, 109 mins, US ⓥ ⊙
D: Frank Marshall A: Jeff Daniels, Harley Jane Kozak, John Goodman, Julian Sands, Stuart Pankin, Brian McNamara (Tangled Web/Amblin)

Arachnophobia expertly blends horror and tongue-in-cheek comedy in the tale of a small California coastal town overrun by Venezuelan killer spiders. Frank Marshall's sophisticated feature directing debut never indulges in ultimate gross-out effects and carefully chooses both its victims and its means of depicting their dispatch. *Arachnophobia* cleverly follows the route of a prehistoric male spider hitching a ride to California and escaping to the farm of newly arrived town doctor Jeff Daniels. The droll John Goodman has a relatively small part as the town's magnificently slobby and incompetent exterminator. Daniels is the one with the arachnophobia, which, like James Stewart's trauma in Hitchcock's *Vertigo*, must be agonizingly overcome in the spectacular climax.

ARCH OF TRIUMPH
1948, 120 mins, US ⑫
D: Lewis Milestone **A:** Charles Boyer, Ingrid Bergman, Charles Laughton, Louis Calhern, Michael Romanoff, Ruth Warrick (Enterprise)

A frank romantic item, laid in a setting of Paris intrigue just before open war with the Western Allies broke out. The surcharged atmosphere of pre-Polish aggression and its repercussions in the City of Light that suddenly grows into blackout is a dramatic background for the Boyer-Bergman romance. Charles Laughton is rather wasted as a Nazi menace, obviously the victim of the cutting room shears, as was Ruth Warrick, the American dilettante.

ARIA
1987, 98 mins, US/UK ⑫ ⊙
D: Nicolas Roeg, Charles Sturridge, Jean-Luc Godard, Julien Temple, Bruce Beresford, Robert Altman, Franc Roddam, Ken Russell, Derek Jarman, Bill Bryden **A:** Theresa Russell, Nicola Swain, Buck Henry, Julie Hagerty, Tilda Swinton, John Hurt (RVP/Virgin)

Aria, a string of selections from 10 operas illustrated by 10 directors, is a film that could not have happened without the advent of music videos. Producer Don Boyd instructed the directors to create something new out of the emotion and content expressed in the music. The arias were the starting point. Individual segments are stunning but they come in such speedy succession that overall it is not a fully satisfying film experience. Selections also represent a variety of filmmaking styles from Bruce Beresford's rather pedestrian working of a love theme from Korngold's *Die tote Stadt* to Ken Russell's

characteristically excessive treatment of an idea distilled from Puccini's *Turandot*.

ARISTOCATS, THE
1970, 78 mins, US
D: Wolfgang Reitherman (Walt Disney)

A good animated feature, an original period comedy with drama about a feline family rescued from the plans of an evil butler who would prefer his mistress not to leave her fortune to the cats. Helped immeasurably by the voices of Phil Harris, Eva Gabor, Sterling Holloway, Scatman Crothers, and others, plus some outstanding animation, songs, sentiment, some excellent dialogue, and even a touch of psychedelia. Harris, who gave *Jungle Book* a lot of its punch, is even more prominent here as the voice of an alley cat who rescues Gabor and her three kittens. Gabor's voice and related animation are excellent, ditto that for two hound dogs, Pat Buttram and George Lindsey.

ARIZONA DREAM
1992, 142 mins, France ⑫ ⊙
D: Emir Kusturica **A:** Johnny Depp, Jerry Lewis, Faye Dunaway, Lili Taylor, Vincent Gallo, Paulina Porizkova (Constellation/UGC/Hachette Premiere)

Despite gorgeous, sometimes surreal visuals and the valiant efforts of an interesting cast, Emir Kusturica's *Arizona Dream* is heavy going. Award-winning Sarajevo-born helmer's first English-lingo pic tackles dreams and flight only to alternately soar and crash. Johnny Depp anchors the overlong pic as an unambitious 23-year-old fish-and-game warden. Depp's uncle (Jerry Lewis) is about to take a bride three decades his junior (Paulina Porizkova) and wants Depp to be his best man and stay on to work at his Cadillac dealership. Depp finds himself torn between seductive, half-mad widow Faye Dunaway and Dunaway's equally unstable stepdaughter, heiress Lili Taylor.

ARMAGEDDON
1998, 150 mins, US ⑫ ⊙ ▭
D: Michael Bay **A:** Bruce Willis, Billy Bob Thornton, Liv Tyler, Ben Affleck, Will Patton, Steve Buscemi (Bruckheimer/Touchstone)

Bruce Willis saves the world but can't save *Armageddon*. Despite its frequently incoherent staging, this $150 million sci-fi actioner nonetheless has the Willis juice and Jerry Bruckheimer–Michael Bay bad-boy ingredients. Pic plays like *Con Air Goes to*

Outer Space, with Doomsday approached like a giant videogame and a jingoistic, thank-you-America-for-saving-the-world message. Deciding to implant a nuke or two in a giant asteroid threatening the earth, NASA recruits the world's top oil driller, Harry S. Stamper (Willis). Stamper agrees on the condition that he can select his own team, mostly miscreants with bad attitudes. Bay's cutting style resembles a machine gun stuck in the firing position for 2 1/2 hours. Film's performance style consists of yelling above the ambient noise, which is usually considerable. All tech credits are predictably gigantic.

ARMED AND DANGEROUS
1986, 88 mins, US Ⓥ ◉
D: Mark L. Lester **A:** John Candy, Eugene Levy, Robert Loggia, Kenneth McMillan, Meg Ryan, Brion James (Columbia)

Armed and Dangerous is a broad farce. Candy plays one of L.A.'s finest until he's wrongfully kicked off the force for corruption. He winds up at Guard Dog Security, where he teams with shyster lawyer Levy on a new career. Company, it turns out, is under the thumb of the mob headed by union honcho Robert Loggia. It's all pretty basic stuff delivered with a minimum of imagination.

ARMORED CAR ROBBERY
1950, 67 mins, US Ⓥ
D: Richard Fleischer **A:** Charles McGraw, Adele Jergens, William Talman, Douglas Fowley, Steve Brodie, Don McGuire (RKO)

Charles McGraw heads the cast as Cordell, a tough cop out to run down a gang that robbed an armored car and killed his policeman buddy. Police work on closing in on the gang is interesting and believable, and there's considerable suspense in the various close escapes the crooks have.

ARMS AND THE GIRL
See: Red Salute

ARMY OF DARKNESS
EVIL DEAD 3
1993, 95 mins, US Ⓥ ◉
D: Sam Raimi **A:** Bruce Campbell, Embeth Davidtz, Marcus Gilbert, Ian Abercrombie, Richard Grove, Michael Earl Reid (De Laurentiis/Renaissance)

Blending almost nonstop violence with humorous parody, Sam Raimi's latest excursion into horror kitsch seems more like an irreverent *A Connecticut Yankee in King Arthur's Court.* The Yank, however, is equipped with a chain saw for an arm and a '73 Oldsmobile instead of a steed. Bruce Campbell and his car are plunked down in the midst of an Arthurian war, where Campbell ingratiates himself with Arthur. The only way for him to get back to California is by retrieving a sacred book. On his quest he runs across various obstacles, including the evil dead (who turn the maiden he's sweet on into a witch). Wizardry and special effects abound.

ARNELO AFFAIR, THE
1947, 86 mins, US
D: Arch Oboler **A:** John Hodiak, George Murphy, Frances Gifford, Dean Stockwell, Eve Arden, Warner Anderson (M-G-M)

Strictly speaking this is not a whodunit, nor can it be cataloged as a psychological suspense picture. Anne (Frances Gifford) finds herself attracted to Tony Arnelo (John Hodiak), nitery owner with a disreputable background who is a client of her lawyer husband Ted (George Murphy). Subordinated by Ted to his work, her almost hypnotic fascination for Arnelo drives her to see him daily. When another of Arnelo's amours turns up murdered, she is involved and he uses this as a means to bring her to him. There's never a question as to who committed the murder, but the crime is secondary to its effect on the characters involved.

AROUND THE WORLD IN EIGHTY DAYS
1956, 175 mins, US Ⓥ ◉ ▭
D: Michael Anderson **A:** David Niven, Cantinflas, Robert Newton, Shirley MacLaine, Charles Boyer, Ronald Colman (Todd)

Phileas Fogg and company proceed from London to Paris, thence via balloon to Spain and the bullfights; from there to Marseilles and India, where Fogg and Passepartout rescue beautiful Shirley MacLaine from death on a funeral pyre; to Hong Kong, Japan, San Francisco, across the country by train to New York (notwithstanding an Indian attack), and thence back to England. Todd-AO system here, for the first time, is properly used and fills the screen with wondrous effects. Images are extraordinarily sharp and depth of focus is striking in many scenes. David Niven, as Fogg, is the perfect stereotype of the unruffled English gentleman. Matching him is Mexican star Cantinflas (Mario Moreno) as Passepartout. There's rarely been a picture that can boast of so many star names in bit parts. Saul Bass's final titles are a tribute to the kind of taste and imagination, the ingenuity, and the splendor that mark this entire Todd production.

1956: Best Picture, Adapted Screenplay, Color Cinematography, Scoring of a Dramatic Picture, Editing

Nominations: Best Director, Color Costume Design, Color Art Direction

ARRANGEMENT, THE
1969, 125 mins, US ⓥ ▱

D: Elia Kazan **A:** Kirk Douglas, Faye Dunaway, Deborah Kerr, Richard Boone, Hume Cronyn, Dianne Hull (Warner/Athena)

One man is responsible for a confused, overly contrived, and overlong film peopled with a set of characters about whom the spectator couldn't care less. In a four-way plunge, Elia Kazan produced and directed from his own screenplay based upon his own 1967 novel. The talents of cast are taxed but they almost rise above their assignments. Douglas plays a successful Los Angeles advertising man, apparently a wizard account exec, wed to Kerr, a long-suffering wife who tries to understand her husband's obsession for Dunaway, with whom he's been carrying on a tumultous affair.

ARROWHEAD
1953, 105 mins, US ⓥ ⊙

D: Charles Marquis Warren **A:** Charlton Heston, Jack Palance, Katy Jurado, Brian Keith, Mary Sinclair, Milburn Stone (Paramount)

The southwest frontier is the setting for this good outdoor actioner. Plot is laid in Texas during 1878 in and around Fort Clark, historical old cavalry post, and Nat Holt films his production on the actual sites described in W. R. Burnett's novel *Adobe Walls*. Principals involved are Charlton Heston, army scout and bitter enemy of the Apaches, particularly Jack Palance, a chief's son who has aroused the braves and is leading them on the warpath. Katy Jurado, as a Mexican-Apache attracted to Heston but spying on him, gives the story s.a. touches, while Mary Sinclair furnishes a more ladylike part as an army widow also interested in the scout.

ARROWSMITH
1931, 108 mins, US ⓥ

D: John Ford **A:** Ronald Colman, Helen Hayes, Richard Bennett, A. E. Anson, Clarence Brooks, Myrna Loy (Goldwyn)

That portion of the citizenry which has read the Sinclair Lewis novel will probably be in sympathy with the filmization. Those who haven't will not be prone to deem this macabre tale entertainment. The responsible factors include complete elimination of the novel's exposé of the medical profession; unusual length; a tendency on the part of the director, John Ford, too often to disregard or overlook tempo; and an unhappy ending. But above all these things is the inability of Colman to convince as the intense scientist. Helen Hayes, as the nurse who becomes the promising physician's wife is wholly delightful.

1931/32: Nominations: Best Picture, Adaptation, Cinematography, Art Direction

ARSENE LUPIN
1932, 64 mins, US

D: Jack Conway **A:** John Barrymore, Lionel Barrymore, Karen Morley, John Miljan, Tully Marshall, Henry Armetta (M-G-M)

First screen appearance of John and Lionel Barrymore together and their fine acting lifts the production to a high artistic level. But the action often is allowed to lapse for dangerously long intervals while the two Barrymores elaborate their interpretation of the super thief (John) and the dogged detective (Lionel). Femme lead is played by Karen Morley with a beautiful balance of reticence and occasional emphasis.

ARSENE LUPIN RETURNS
1938, 81 mins, US

D: George Fitzmaurice **A:** Melvyn Douglas, Virginia Bruce, Warren William, John Halliday, Nat Pendleton, Monty Woolley (M-G-M)

Supposedly killed by the police long ago, the gendarme mystifier, Lupin, is found to have merely retired and gone legit. He is played by Melvyn Douglas, whose two associates, Nat Pendleton and E. E. Clive, a couple of mugs, help him in his pseudocrime reentry. Whole thing is deftly handled.

ARSENIC AND OLD LACE
1944, 118 mins, US ⓥ ⊙

D: Frank Capra **A:** Cary Grant, Priscilla Lane, Raymond Massey, Jack Carson, Peter Lorre, Edward Everett Horton (Warner)

The majority of the action is confined

to the home of the two amiably nutty aunts who believe it's kind to poison people they come in contact with and their non-violently insane brother who thinks he's Teddy Roosevelt. Cary Grant and Priscilla Lane open the picture getting married but are delayed in their honeymoon when Grant finds his two screwy aunts have been bumping off people in their house, burying them in the cellar, and even holding thoughtful funeral ceremonies for them. The laughs that surround his efforts to get John Alexander, the Teddy Roosevelt of the picture, committed to an institution, troubles that come up when a maniacal long-lost brother shows up after a world tour of various murders with a phony doctor, and other plot elements make for diversion of a very agreeable character.

ARTHUR
1981, 117 mins, US ⓥ ⊙
D: Steve Gordon **A:** Dudley Moore, Liza Minnelli, John Gielgud, Geraldine Fitzgerald, Jill Eikenberry, Stephen Elliott (Orion)

Arthur is a sparkling entertainment which attempts, with a large measure of success, to resurrect the amusingly artificial conventions of 1930s screwball romantic comedies. Dudley Moore is back in top-*10* form as a layabout drunken playboy who finds himself falling in love with working-class girl Liza Minnelli just as he's being forced into an arranged marriage with a society WASP. As Moore's eternally supportive but irrepressibly sarcastic valet, John Gielgud gives a priceless performance.

1981: Best Supp. Actor (John Gielgud), Song ("Best That You Can Do")
Nominations: Best Actor (Dudley Moore), Original Screenplay

ARTHUR 2
ON THE ROCKS
1988, 113 mins, US ⓥ ⊙
D: Bud Yorkin **A:** Dudley Moore, Liza Minnelli, John Gielgud, Geraldine Fitzgerald, Paul Benedict, Cynthia Sikes (Warner)

Arthur 2 is not as classy a farce as the original, but still manages to be an amusing romp. Five years into their marriage and living the enviable Park Avenue lifestyle, wife Linda (Liza Minnelli) finds she's unable to conceive and goes about adopting a baby. Minnelli loses some of

her working-class sassiness, though credit is due her for carrying plot's best scenes.

ARTICLE 99
1992, 100 mins, US ⓥ ⊙
D: Howard Deutch **A:** Ray Liotta, Kiefer Sutherland, Forest Whitaker, Lea Thompson, Kathy Baker, Eli Wallach (Orion/Gruskoff-Levy)

With didactic intent behind a rabble-rousing story, filmmakers admirably draw attention to the scandalous condition of health care at the nation's Veterans Administration hospitals while aiming for the seriocomic tone of *MASH, Catch-22,* and *The Hospital.* Screenplay presents a villainous bureaucracy ruled by hospital director John Mahoney. Opposing him are the irreverent but dedicated can-do doctors led by surgeon Ray Liotta. Lenser Richard Bowen has given the film a rough, vérité look.

ARTISTS AND MODELS
1937, 95 mins, US
D: Raoul Walsh **A:** Jack Benny, Ida Lupino, Richard Arlen, Gail Patrick, Ben Blue, Judy Canova (Paramount)

Artists and Models is so replete with a cavalcade of radio, nitery, vaudeville, and revuesque ingredients that it's much to the credit of all concerned that this madcap musical shapes up as well as it does. This is Benny's first solo starrer and it's also a departure for him in that he's assigned the major romantic interest. Benny is cast as an advertising-agency head. Arlen is his biggest (and practically only) account. Because Lupino is a professional model, she's first snubbed by Arlen for a ritzy ad campaign. Lupino hies to Miami posing as a socialite, in order to impress that being a pro model isn't a liability.

1937: Nomination: Best Song ("Whispers in the Dark")

ARTISTS AND MODELS
1955, 108 mins, US ⓥ ⊙
D: Frank Tashlin **A:** Dean Martin, Jerry Lewis, Shirley MacLaine, Dorothy Malone, Eddie Mayehoff, Anita Ekberg (Paramount)

Comedic diversion in the Martin and Lewis manner has been put together in this overdone, slaphappy mélange of gags and gals. Costarring with the comedy team are Shirley MacLaine and Dorothy Malone. The former tackles her role of model with a bridling cuteness but has a figure to take the viewer's mind off her facial expression. Ditto Dorothy Malone, her artist roommate. Dean Martin is an artist and Jerry Lewis is a would-be writer of kiddie stories, both starving in NY.

ART OF LOVE, THE
1965, 99 mins, US
D: Norman Jewison **A:** James Garner, Dick Van Dyke, Elke Sommer, Angie Dickinson, Ethel Merman, Carl Reiner (Universal/Cherokee)

Ross Hunter's pic starts out as pure film satire aimed only at light, bright comedy entertainment. It grows into a garbled mixture of coquettish comedy that has sidesplitting moments, some unusually fine character performances, but so much of everything it never once settles down to a consistent point of view. Story is of would-be American artist Dick Van Dyke who gives up to return to the rich fiancée in America who is paying his bills—and those of his roommate, would-be author James Garner. Garner is so devastated at the loss of his meal ticket, he tries everything to keep Van Dyke in Paris.

AS GOOD AS IT GETS
1997, 138 mins, US Ⓥ ⊙
D: James L. Brooks **A:** Jack Nicholson, Helen Hunt, Greg Kinnear, Cuba Gooding Jr., Skeet Ulrich, Shirley Knight (Gracie/TriStar)

James L. Brooks's sitcom roots are all too apparent in this sporadically funny romantic comedy with all the dramatic plausibility and tonal consistency of a TV variety show. Middle-aged curmudgeon Melvin Udall (Jack Nicholson) defines himself as the neighbor from hell by tossing a little dog down a garbage chute and gleefully assailing Fido's gay owner, Simon (Greg Kinnear), and the latter's black friend, Frank (Cuba Gooding Jr.). From the beginning, it is clear that the story has only one potential trajectory, the gradual humanization of Melvin. The door to his self-awakening is opened by, of all things, Simon's dog, which he comes to love and opens something in the scrooge's heart. Nicholson's performance is wonderfully enjoyable when Melvin remains an irascible s.o.b. but becomes unfathomable in its would-be tender moments.
1997: Best Actor (Jack Nicholson), Best Actress (Helen Hunt)
Nominations: Best Picture, Supp. Actor (Greg Kinnear), Original Screenplay, Editing, Original Comedy Score

ASHANTI
1979, 117 mins, Switzerland Ⓥ ⊠
D: Richard Fleischer **A:** Michael Caine, Peter Ustinov, Beverly Johnson, Omar Sharif, Rex Harrison, William Holden (Vuille)

A polished but lackluster adventure entertainment. Michael Caine and Beverly Johnson are World Health Organization medics on a visit to an African tribe when the lady becomes a prize catch of Arabian slave trader Peter Ustinov. Caine's retrieval odyssey thereafter is variously aided by Rex Harrison as an ambiguous go-between, William Holden as a mercenary helicopter pilot, and Indian actor Kabir Bedi as a Bedouin with his own score to settle with Ustinov. All acquit themselves with professional grace but unremarkable impact.

ASHES AND DIAMONDS
See: Popiol I Diament

ASH WEDNESDAY
1973, 99 mins, US Ⓥ
D: Larry Peerce **A:** Elizabeth Taylor, Henry Fonda, Helmut Berger, Keith Baxter, Maurice Teynac, Maggie Blye (Sagittarius/Paramount)

Ash Wednesday is a jolting tearjerker about middle-age marital trauma, compounded by the superficial and spiritual uplift of cosmetic surgery. Elizabeth Taylor stars as the fiftyish wife of Henry Fonda, and Helmut Berger is featured as her brief Italian-resort affair after the beautification process has restored her surface charm.

ASK A POLICEMAN
1939, 83 mins, UK
D: Marcel Varnel **A:** Will Hay, Graham Moffatt, Moore Marriott, Glennis Lorimer, Peter Gawthorne, Charles Oliver (Gainsborough)

Bits of *Dr. Syn* (1937), with George Arliss, and *The Ghost Train* (1931) blend happily with amusing dialogue and situations usually associated with Will Hay and his two stooges, the fat boy and old man. A village police station becomes the center of interest when it's discovered there's been no crime there for over 10 years. The sergeant (Hay) in command of two subordinates (Graham Moffatt, Moore Marriott), hearing they're likely to be transferred or fired because of lack of business, plans to frame one or two cases. Planting a keg of brandy on the beach, to stage a smuggler's racket, they discover another, real contraband keg. From then on it's a wild chase between the three nitwits and a band headed by the local squire (Charles Oliver) which is carrying on a lucrative clandestine trade.

AS LONG AS THEY'RE HAPPY
1955, 95 mins, UK
D: J. Lee Thompson **A:** Jack Buchanan, Janette Scott, Jean Carson, Brenda Banzie, Diana Dors, Susan Stephen (Rank)

Jack Buchanan repeats his original stage role as the stockbroker head of the family whose wife and three daughters are overwhelmed by the arrival of a Hollywood crooner at their suburban London home. Around these characters, the plot develops into a hearty and good-humored romp, without much attention to story line. Nine songs by Sam Coslow get full treatment and they strike an effective note. There is a delightful guest bit by Diana Dors.

ASPHALT JUNGLE, THE
1950, 112 mins, US ⓥ ⊙
D: John Huston **A:** Sterling Hayden, Louis Calhern, James Whitmore, Jean Hagen, Sam Jaffe, Marilyn Monroe (M-G-M)

The Asphalt Jungle is a study in crime, hard-hitting in its exposé of the underworld. Ironic realism is striven for and achieved in the writing, production, and direction. An audience will quite easily pull for the crooks in their execution of the million-dollar jewelry theft around which the plot is built. The actual heist is a suspenseful piece of filming, as is the following police chase and gradual disintegration of the gang. Sterling Hayden and Louis Calhern star as contrasting criminals, the former a mean, bitter hood who dreams of restoring an old Kentucky horse farm, and Calhern a crooked attorney who needs money to continue satisfying his desire for curvy blondes and high living.
1950: Nominations: Best Director, Supp. Actor (Sam Jaffe), Screenplay, B&W Cinematography

ASSASSIN, THE
See: Point of No Return

ASSASSINATION BUREAU LIMITED, THE
1969, 106 mins, UK/US ⓥ
D: Basil Dearden **A:** Oliver Reed, Diana Rigg, Telly Savalas, Curt Jurgens, Philippe Noiret, Warren Mitchell (Paramount)

As a comedy thriller, film stands high, if the spectator isn't too meticulous about expository details, particulary the whys and wherefores of a determined young femme reporter (Diana Rigg) who decides that a strange outbreak of highly professional, apparently motiveless killings must be the work of a single organization. Entire cast play their respective roles broadly and each gives a good account of himself.

ASSASSINATION OF TROTSKY, THE
1972, 105 mins, FRANCE/ITALY ⓥ
D: Joseph Losey **A:** Richard Burton, Alain Delon, Romy Schneider, Valentina Cortese, Luigi Vannucchi, Giorgio Albertazzi (Cinettel/CIAC/De Laurentiis)

The last days (1940) in the life of the Russian revolutionary figure Leon Trotsky are traced in this fairly cryptic film. But there is too much forced symbolism, diffuse characterization, and a sort of schematic feel sans enough interplay of people, historical perspective, or new insights into this political or psychological murder. Richard Burton sometimes catches a cantankerous and surface aspect of the aging revolutionary.

ASSASSINS
1995, 132 mins, US ⓥ ⊙
D: Richard Donner **A:** Sylvester Stallone, Antonio Banderas, Julianne Moore, Anatoly Davydov (Silver/Warner)

A not-much-fun high-tech actioner, *Assassins* has a body temperature that matches those of its coldly ruthless leading characters. As steely and well tooled as the fancy firearms that Sylvester Stallone and Antonio Banderas fire so frequently, this contrived hide-and-seek suspenser about a veteran hit man and the young hotshot who would bump him off is a simplistic reworking of *The Gunfighter* in modern dress. Stallone is playing his usual strong, morose, silent type who has an ounce of compassion and tenderness buried somewhere under the beefcake. Banderas bounces and gesticulates all over the screen, injecting some welcome humor into the proceedings.

ASSAULT OF THE KILLER BIMBOS
1988, 81 mins, US ⓥ ⊙
D: Anita Rosenberg **A:** Christina Whitaker, Elizabeth Kaitan, Tammara Souza, Nick Cassavetes, Griffin O'Neal, Jamie Bozian (Titan)

Assault of the Killer Bimbos is the kind

of engagingly dumb, slyly hip pic that is tailor-made for cult enjoyment. Chief bimbos are played by Christina Whitaker and Elizabeth Kaitan as go-go dancers in a dead-end nightclub who are mistakenly taken for murderers after their boss gets bumped off by hoods. On the lam to Mexico, they pick up a willing hostage truck-stop waitress Tammara Souza and three cartoonish surf bums played by Jamie Bozian and movie-biz brats Nick Cassavetes and Griffin O'Neal.

ASSAULT ON A QUEEN
1966, 106 mins, US Ⓥ ▭
D: Jack Donohue **A:** Frank Sinatra, Virna Lisi, Anthony Franciosa, Richard Conte, Alf Kjellin, Errol John (Seven Arts/Sinatra)

The admittedly wild-eyed adventures of an odd assortment of moral derelicts who salvage a submarine with the intent of robbing the *Queen Mary* (hence the title). Only Kjellin is able to create a well-rounded character and is outstanding as the apparently bland German, holding in control his diabolic intent. Sinatra and Lisi are very good in roles that make few demands on their acting ability.

ASSAULT ON PRECINCT 13
1976, 91 mins, US Ⓥ ▭
D: John Carpenter **A:** Austin Stoker, Darwin Joston, Laurie Zimmer, Martin West, Tony Burton, Kim Richards (CKK)

Novelty of a gang swearing a blood oath to destroy a precinct station and all inside is sufficiently compelling for the gory-minded to assure acceptance. Precinct station is within hours of closing to move to new quarters, which explains why only a single cop and a policewoman remains to hold down the fort, abetted by two prisoners who are temporarily incarcerated on their way to death row in Salinas. John Carpenter's direction of his screenplay, after a pokey opening half, is responsible for realistic movement.

ASSIGNMENT, THE
1977, 97 mins, SWEDEN Ⓥ
D: Mats Arehn **A:** Thomas Hellberg, Christopher Plummer, Carolyn Seymour, Fernando Rey, Per Oscarsson, Walter Gotell (Nordisk/Svensk/SFI)

Story about a young Swedish diplomat sent to a violence-torn Latin American state as mediator. From the moment of his arrival, it is clear that everybody distrusts him and most want him killed. Film, fortunately, preaches no moral, but in its mix of solid little chills and thrills, it features both tender compassion, rage against injustice, and a lot of subdued humor.

ASSIGNMENT PARIS
1952, 84 mins, US
D: Robert Parrish **A:** Dana Andrews, Marta Toren, George Sanders, Audrey Totter, Sandro Giglio, Willis Bouchey (Columbia)

A topical thriller of newspaper work under the handicaps of the Iron Curtain. Dana Andrews, Marta Toren, George Sanders, and Audrey Totter are newspaper people attached to the Paris office of a stateside paper, involved in the tale of intrigue. Spy-chase angles are mixed with romantic involvements, plus some speaking out against Communist rule in such countries as Hungary.

ASTRONAUT'S WIFE, THE
1999, 109 mins, US Ⓥ ⊙
D: Rand Ravich **A:** Johnny Depp, Charlize Theron, Joe Morton, Clea DuVall, Donna Murphy, Nick Cassavetes (Mad Chance/New Line)

The Astronaut's Wife is an aggressively stylish but dramatically flaccid drama that plays like an upscale reprise of a fifties sci-fi potboiler. Johnny Depp stars as NASA shuttle pilot Spencer Armacost, a vet space jock with a beautiful school-teacher wife, Jillian (Charlize Theron). Out in space, Armacost and fellow astronaut Alex Streck (Nick Cassavetes) run into trouble during a routine repair of a malfunctioning satellite. Both men survive but are unconscious when they are brought back to Earth. Jillian's peace of mind is undermined by what she views as strange behavior on the part of her husband. She's also unsettled by his increased lustiness, and discovers she is pregnant with twins. Theron hits the right balance of strong-willed resilience and moist-eyed vulnerability. Depp is aptly ambiguous in what amounts to a supporting role.

ASYLUM
1972, 88 mins, UK Ⓥ ⊙
D: Roy Ward Baker **A:** Peter Cushing, Britt Ekland, Herbert Lom, Patrick Magee, Robert Powell, Barbara Parkins (Amicus)

Herewith a trim little chiller, with a moderate quota of blood and mayhem, polished performances, and smooth direction. It also boasts some imaginative props, like the lopped-off limbs, etc., of Sylvia Syms metaphysically killing her murderer and errant husband, Richard

Todd, and his sweetie Barbara Parkins. The plot is essentially about a young shrink's (Robert Powell) voyage of discovery in an insane asylum. Very few of the key thesps remain robust and vertical by the windup, for which scripter Robert Bloch comes up with an effective trick ending.

AS YOU DESIRE ME
1932, 70 mins, US Ⓥ
D: George Fitzmaurice **A:** Greta Garbo, Melvyn Douglas, Erich von Stroheim, Owen Moore, Hedda Hopper, Rafaela Ottiano (M-G-M)

A romantic problem play interestingly played by the fascinating Greta Garbo, treated in a manner of high drama. Story has to do with an Italian countess driven into a mental fog which has blotted out her past. She is recognized 10 years later in her wanderings as a music-hall singer by the painter who had done her portrait as a bride, and by him brought back to her grief-stricken husband. Garbo's performance is always absorbing, vivid in its acting, and compelling in appeal. Owen Moore grabs the acting honors among the men, while Erich von Stroheim fails signally to make himself the man you love to hate by revealing an accent of blended Yorkville and Ninth Avenue.

ATAME!
(TIE ME UP! TIE ME DOWN!)
1990, 101 mins, Spain Ⓥ ⊙
D: Pedro Almodovar **A:** Victoria Abril, Antonio Banderas, Loles Leon, Julieta Serrano, Francisco Rabal, Rossy de Palma (El Deseo)

This film harks back to Pedro Almodovar's earlier features where sexuality was a central theme. Yarn concerns Ricki (Antonio Banderas), a 23-year-old man who is released from a mental institution. He sees a picture of Marina (Victoria Abril) in a film-buff magazine. She is a hooker and porno actress he once paid to spend a night with, and Ricki decides to marry her. Ricki forces his way into her apartment and declares his intentions. After a scuffle, he decides to tie her to the bed, certain that she will learn to love him. The relationship between the protagonists gradually shifts from that of captor and captured to lovers. Almodovar's inventive direction, superb lensing by Jose Luis Alcaine, a fine score by Ennio Morricone, and top technical credits make pic a pleasure to watch. Abril and Banderas are compelling to watch as the central couple.

AT CLOSE RANGE
1986, 111 mins, US Ⓥ ▭
D: James Foley **A:** Sean Penn, Christopher Walken, Mary Stuart Masterson, Christopher Penn, Millie Perkins, Candy Clark (Hemdale)

A downbeat tale of brutal family relations. Violent without being gratuitous, story introduces young Brad (Sean Penn) as just another rather tough kid with an eye for a new girl (the charming Mary Stuart Masterson) and fiercely protective of his brother (Christopher Penn). Along comes Brad's father (Christopher Walken) who has a reputation as a criminal. Intrigued by his seemingly exciting parent, Brad Jr. is encouraged to form his own gang to carry out more modest heists.

AT FIRST SIGHT
1999, 128 mins, US Ⓥ ⊙
D: Irwin Winkler **A:** Val Kilmer, Mira Sorvino, Kelly McGillis, Steven Weber, Bruce Davison, Nathan Lane (M-G-M)

Schmaltzy Val Kilmer–Mira Sorvino starrer about a blind man who recovers, then loses, his sight. An accomplished, high-strung Gotham-based architect, Amy (Sorvino) heads to a small upstate spa. There she meets Virgil (Kilmer), a blind masseur who releases her stress and her passion. She begins pushing an experimental surgery developed by Dr. Charles Aaron (Bruce Davison) aimed at restoring sight to those who have been blind since childhood. Irwin Winkler is a director of little subtlety; this material could have used a lighter touch. Screenplay leaves little to the imagination. Kilmer acquits himself admirably; Sorvino, however, frequently seems to be struggling not to appear awkward.

ATLANTIC CITY
1980, 104 mins, Canada/France/US Ⓥ ⊙
D: Louis Malle **A:** Burt Lancaster, Susan Sarandon, Michel Piccoli, Kate Reid, Robert Joy, Hollis McLaren (Cine-Neighbor/Selta)

Film is blessed with a spare, intriguing script by Yank John Guare, which always skirts impending clichés and predictability by finding unusual facets in his characters and their actions. The film is well limned by Burt Lancaster as a small-time, megalomaniacal, aging mafia hood, Susan Sarandon as an ambitious young woman, Kate Reid as a fading moll, and Robert Joy and Hollis McLaren as Sarandon's husband and young sister. Atlantic City is also a character as director Louis Malle

adroitly uses decrepit old and new facades.
1981: Nominations: Best Picture, Director, Actor (Burt Lancaster), Actress (Susan Sarandon), Original Screenplay

ATLANTIS, THE LOST CONTINENT
1961, 91 mins, US Ⓥ
D: George Pal **A:** Anthony Hall, Joyce Taylor, Frank de Kova, John Dall (M-G-M)

A tired, shopworn melodrama out of Gerald Hargreaves play. There is an astonishing similarity to the stevereevesian spectacles. An ordeal by fire and water ritual conducted in a great, crowded stadium seems almost a replica of gladiatorial combat in the Colosseum. When Atlantis is burning to a cinder at the climax, one can almost hear Nero fiddling. Even Russ Garcia's score has that pompous, martial Roman air about it. And at least several of the mob spectacle scenes have been lifted from Roman screen spectacles of the past (the 1951 version of *Quo Vadis* looks like the source). The acting is routine.

AT LONG LAST LOVE
1975, 118 mins, US
D: Peter Bogdanovich **A:** Burt Reynolds, Cybill Shepherd, Madeline Kahn, Duilio Del Prete, Eileen Brennan, John Hillerman (20th Century-Fox/Copa De Oro)

Peter Bogdanovich's experiment with a mostly singing 1930s upper-class romance, is a disappointing and embarrassing waste of talent. Utilizing 16 Cole Porter songs, many of them not heard for years and all of them replete with additional lyrics hardly ever used, writer-producer-director Bogdanovich tries to float a bubble of gaiety. The principals sang their numbers while being filmed, with orchestrations dubbed in later, in an attempt to eliminate the lifelessness of postsync when it is done poorly.

ATOMIC CITY, THE
1952, 84 mins, US
D: Jerry Hopper **A:** Gene Barry, Lydia Clarke, Michael Moore, Nancy Gates, Lee Aaker, Houseley Stevenson Jr. (Paramount)

Taut suspense and an interesting setting are features that make *The Atomic City* an effective spy thriller. Story is concerned with the kidnapping by foreign agents of the son of Gene Barry, a nuclear physicist at Los Alamos. Price for the boy's return is the formula for manufacturing atom bombs. Hopper's direction gets a tight grip on the plot and injects a continually building suspense as the FBI and the father grasp for clues that might lead them to the boy and the kidnappers.

AT PLAY IN THE FIELDS OF THE LORD
1991, 187 mins, US Ⓥ Ⓞ
D: Hector Babenco **A:** Tom Berenger, Aidan Quinn, Kathy Bates, John Lithgow, Daryl Hannah, Tom Waits (Zaentz)

At Play in the Fields of the Lord is how half-breed Cheyenne mercenary Lewis Moon describes his location to missionaries before he parachutes into the Amazon jungle to seek his essence among a tribe called the Niaruna. Tale that follows, a challenging, cerebral, and beautifully controlled take on Peter Matthiessen's revered 1965 novel, amounts to a cry of warning against interference with a delicate ecological and cultural balance. Central to this telling are two men: a callous, brooding jungle rat (Tom Berenger) and his nemesis (Aidan Quinn), a dedicated evangelical worker.

ATTACK
1956, 107 mins, US Ⓥ
D: Robert Aldrich **A:** Jack Palance, Eddie Albert, Lee Marvin, Robert Strauss, Richard Jaeckel, Buddy Ebsen (Associates & Aldrich)

Attack presents a cowardly officer who's murdered by his men. Entire film is treated with a hard realism that pays off in gutsy entertainment. It's a grim, extremely tough account of an infantry company during the Battle of the Bulge in World War II, brightly projected by the fine characterizations contributed by the cast. Scoring exceptionally strong is Lee Marvin, the opportunistic colonel who keeps the coward in command because he will be useful after the war in politics.

ATTACK OF THE 50-FOOT WOMAN
1958, 65 mins, US Ⓥ Ⓞ
D: Nathan Hertz **A:** Allison Hayes, William Hudson, Yvette Vickers, Roy Gordon, George Douglas, Ken Terrell (Allied Artists)

A minor offering for the sci-fi trade where demands aren't too great. The production is the story of a femme who overnight grows into a murderous giantess, out to get husband who's cheating with another woman. Growth was caused by ray burns suffered when she's seized by huge monster. Allison Hayes takes title role as a mentally disturbed woman who has been in a sanitarium.

ATTACK OF THE KILLER TOMATOES
1979, 87 mins, US ⊗
D: John De Bello **A:** David Miller, George Wilson, Sharon Taylor, Jack Riley (Four Square)

Attack of the Killer Tomatoes, a low-budget indie production made by a group of young San Diego filmmakers, isn't even worthy of sarcasm. Plot, if it can be called that, concerns sudden growth spurt of tomatoes and their rampage. Only saving grace is the satire pic's opening titles. Thereafter it's all downhill, rapidly.

AT THE CIRCUS
1939, 86 mins, US ⊗
D: Edward Buzzell **A:** Groucho Marx, Chico Marx, Harpo Marx, Margaret Dumont, Florence Rice, Kenny Baker (M-G-M)

The Marx Bros. revert to the rousing physical comedy and staccato gag dialogue of their earlier pictures in *At the Circus.* Story is slight but unimportant. Kenny Baker, owner of a circus, is harassed by pursuing James Burke, who wants to foreclose the mortgage he holds on the outfit. When Baker's bankroll is stolen, Chico and Harpo call in Groucho to straighten out the difficulties. Groucho winds up by selling the circus for one performance to Margaret Dumont, Baker's rich aunt and Newport social leader.

AT THE EARTH'S CORE
1976, 89 mins, UK ⊗
D: Kevin Connor **A:** Doug McClure, Peter Cushing, Caroline Munro, Cy Grant, Godfrey James, Sean Lynch (Amicus)

At the Earth's Core, from the Edgar Rice Burroughs novel, is a fast-paced, slightly tongue-in-cheek tale about stalwart hero Doug McClure's battles with underground monsters. There's old-fashioned rooting interest in the outlandish exploits of McClure and his doddering old professor sidekick, Peter Cushing, who goes through the entire ordeal carrying his umbrella. Pic takes place in the Victorian era, charmingly evoked at the beginning.

AUDREY ROSE
1977, 112 mins, US ⊗ ⊡
D: Robert Wise **A:** Marsha Mason, Anthony Hopkins, John Beck, Susan Swift, Norman Lloyd, John Hillerman (United Artists)

Frank De Felitta's novel and screen-play of reincarnation comes to the screen fully realized in all creative aspects. Film takes upper-middle-class couple Marsha Mason and John Beck into a nightmare of torment when daughter Susan Swift begins acting strangely. Anthony Hopkins menaces as the outsider who has a mysterious influence on the child.

AUGUST
1996, 93 mins, UK ⊗
D: Anthony Hopkins **A:** Anthony Hopkins, Kate Burton, Leslie Phillips, Gawn Grainger, Rhian Morgan, Hugh Lloyd (Majestic/Newcomm/Granada)

In *August,* Anthony Hopkins has decided to transpose the action of Chekhov's *Uncle Vanya* to his native Wales, circa 1890, for his film-directing debut. The good news is that the Chekhovian class system works just fine for that corner of the British Isles. But that's as good as it gets. The essential story remains intact. It's well performed by a fine ensemble cast, although the director indulges himself a tad as an actor.

AUNTIE MAME
1958, 143 mins, US ⊗ ⊙ ⊡
D: Morton Da Costa **A:** Rosalind Russell, Forrest Tucker, Coral Browne, Fred Clark, Roger Smith, Joanna Barnes (Warner)

Auntie Mame is a faithfully funny re-cording of the hit play. Rosalind Russell recreates the title role for the film. She is a high class or at least rich bohemian. She mixes Greek Orthodox bishops with Gertrude Stein–type females, for her own amusement, directing this chorus of mixed voices with a cigarette holder loaded with gems as phony as most of her guests. Life is a banquet is her philosophy. Russell scores because her native intelligence augments her sharp comedy sense.

1958: Nominations: Best Picture, Actress (Rosalind Russell), Supp. Actress (Peggy Cass), Color Cinematography, Art Direction, Editing

AUNT JULIA AND THE SCRIPTWRITER
See: Tune in Tomorrow

AU REVOIR, LES ENFANTS
1987, 104 mins, France/W. Germany ⊗ ⊙
D: Louis Malle **A:** Gaspard Manesse, Raphael Fejto, Francine Racette, Stanislas Carre de Malberg, Philippe Morier-Genoud, François Berleand

This moving, quasi-autobiographical drama set in a provincial Catholic boarding school in the last months of World War II assumes the dimensions of tragedy when the Gestapo disrupts the cloistered routine to arrest the school fathers and three Jewish children they are hiding there under false names. Basis of the film is a true incident that haunted director Louis Malle ever since his schoolboy days in a similar religious establishment near Fontainebleau. Malle said this was the film he wanted to make ever since the beginning of his career, and he did not betray his subject matter.

AUSTIN POWERS INTERNATIONAL MAN OF MYSTERY
1997, 89 mins, US Ⓥ ⊙ ▱
D: Jay Roach **A:** Mike Myers, Elizabeth Hurley, Michael York, Mimi Rogers, Robert Wagner, Seth Green (Moving Pictures/Eric's Boy/New Line)

An all-stops spoof, this is one of the goofiest movies to come down the pike in a long time. A loving paean to Bond, Flint, Helm, and their ilk, this film knows its turf and only missteps when it ventures into more contemporary territory. The mythic Powers (Mike Myers) is a bespectacled, mop-topped, fruggin' Carnaby Street–tailored agent. Back in 1967, he went toe to toe with Dr. Evil (also Myers), a bald, scarred criminal uberboss, who jumped into a cryogenic chamber. The British secret service also put their operative into deep freeze. Thirty years later, Evil returns and so does the 000-agent. Back in action, Powers is teamed with Vanessa Kensington (Elizabeth Hurley), the daughter of his former partner (Mimi Rogers). The tale barrels along with the hijack of missiles and the demand for $100 billion not to use them. Myers gets a real workout playing both the title role and his arch enemy. The strong supporting cast connects perfectly with the material, with Hurley displaying a true penchant for comedy.

AUSTIN POWERS THE SPY WHO SHAGGED ME
1999, 95 mins, US Ⓥ ⊙ ▱
D: Jay Roach **A:** Mike Myers, Heather Graham, Michael York, Robert Wagner, Rob Lowe, Seth Green (Eric's Boy/Moving Pictures/Team Todd/New Line)

Expanded in every aspect save inspiration, the follow-up to the 1997 sleeper tickles the funny bone ably enough, yet feels like a quickie in the writing. The world is again imperiled by arch-nemesis Dr. Evil (Myers). Worse, he's used time travel to steal the "mojo" (read sexual potency) from our superhero. Soon Austin (Myers) is tripping back to the Paisley Age, where curvaceous agent Felicity Shagwell (Heather Graham) is his new ally. Among the better new wrinkles are Evil's whiny teenage son Scott's (Seth Green) reunion with nefarious Dad on *The Jerry Springer Show* and a steamy chess game with bodacious enemy spy Ivana Humpalot (Kristen Johnston). But major added characters—Dr. E's diminutive clone Mini-Me (Verne J. Troyer) and repulsive Scottish hit man Fat Bastard (Myers)—are just middling conceits. Graham is a sexy, game partner without much comic flair of her own.

1999: Nomination: Best Makeup

AUTHOR! AUTHOR!
1982, 110 mins, US Ⓥ
D: Arthur Hiller **A:** Al Pacino, Dyan Cannon, Tuesday Weld, Alan King, Bob Dishy, Bob Elliott (20th Century-Fox)

Author! Author! is rather a mess, but a quite amiable one. This *Kramer vs. Kramer* multiplied by five kids by no means approaches its full comic or emotional potential, but Israel Horovitz's marvelous screenplay and Al Pacino's warm performance provide constant pleasure. Pacino plays a New York playwright who's attempting to get his first play in two years off the ground. Heart of the film, however, lies in Pacino's domestic life. His wife (Tuesday Weld) leaves him for another man, stranding kids of their own as well as from her previous three marriages.

UN AUTRE HOMME UNE AUTRE CHANCE (ANOTHER MAN ANOTHER CHANCE)
1977, 132 mins, FRANCE Ⓥ
D: Claude Lelouch **A:** James Caan, Genevieve Bujold, Francis Huster, Susan Tyrrell, Jennifer Warren (Films 13/Ariane/Artistes Associes)

A sort of valentine to American western films with James Caan and Genevieve Bujold for the he-she interest. It's a Frenchman's perspective on the US. It begins with a passage in steerage to America by Bujold in the 1870s. James Caan is an American veterinarian, happy in his work. Caan and Bujold finally fall in love. There are some simple observations of life in the west but not imitative of the general oater.

They are at ease and inventive in their roles of headstrong, piquant woman settler and relaxed charmer.

AUTUMN AFTERNOON, AN
See: Samma No Aji

AUTUMN SONATA
See: Hostsonat

AVALANCHE
1978, 91 mins, US ⊗

D: Corey Allen A: Rock Hudson, Mia Farrow, Robert Forster, Jeanette Nolan, Rick Moses, Steve Franken (New World)

Rock Hudson and Mia Farrow head the cast of characters gathered at a ski lodge beneath an uneasy cornice of snow. Eventually, the whole mountaintop comes down on the crowd of skaters, skiers, and sledders. Using a lot of archive footage of an actual massive avalanche, director Corey Allen and crew have done a very good job of creating realistic scenes.

AVALON
1990, 126 mins, US ⊗ ⊙

D: Barry Levinson A: Leo Fuchs, Eve Gordon, Lou Jacobi, Armin Mueller-Stahl, Elizabeth Perkins, Joan Plowright (Tri-Star/Baltimore)

Dealing with an extended Jewish family headed by brothers who left Europe in the early 20th century, *Avalon* seeks to recapture both a period (the post–World War II era, as television became king) and the essence of family life, with all its feuding, pettiness, and tumult. Still, beyond the beautiful photography, spotless classic cars, and slavishly detailed sets, the film lacks focus or a real reason for being. The patriarch of the central nuclear family is Sam Krichinsky (Armin Mueller-Stahl).
1990: Nominations: Best Original Screenplay, Cinematography, Original Score, Costume Design

AVANTI!
1972, 143 mins, US ⊗

D: Billy Wilder A: Jack Lemmon, Juliet Mills, Clive Revill, Edward Andrews, Gianfranco Barra, Franco Angrisano (Phalanx/Jalem)

In casting Jack Lemmon as an American corporation executive come to Italy to claim the body of his father, killed when he drove his car off a high cliff, Billy Wilder has the perfect foil for the building situations, marking the fifth time pair teamed up in a picture. Basic situation takes form as Lemmon discovers another person also met her death in the tragic accident, his father's longtime English mistress. He meets a chubby English dumpling (Mills) who he learns is the daughter of the lady in question. Lemmon displays his usual aptitude in a frantic role. Mills is a happy choice, endowing part with warmth and understanding.

AVENGERS, THE
1998, 89 mins, US ⊗ ⊙

D: Jeremiah Chechik A: Ralph Fiennes, Uma Thurman, Sean Connery, Patrick Macnee, Jim Broadbent, Fiona Shaw (Warner)

The Avengers is a pretty thin cuppa Earl Grey. Pic makes a game effort at reviving the popular '60s British spy serial. What's missing is chemistry: the right blend of seriousness and whimsy and charmingly compelling interplay between leads Ralph Fiennes and Uma Thurman, who turn in lackluster perfs. Steed's (Fiennes) controllers bring him together with the chic, agile Emma Peel (Thurman) to combat the predation of an out-of-control project called Prospero, which threatens to wreak havoc on Britain's weather. Chief culprit is Sir August de Wynter (Sean Connery), a maniacal aristo who plans to reduce Britain to an arctic wasteland unless the nation forks over 10 percent of its GNP. Production designer Stuart Craig provides an imaginative look that deftly balances the '60s and the '90s. Don MacPherson's script tries for the same, but its version of the Steed-Peel pas de deux is like champagne that's lost its fizz.

AVIATOR, THE
1985, 96 mins, US ⊗

D: George Miller A: Christopher Reeve, Rosanna Arquette, Jack Warden, Sam Wanamaker, Scott Wilson, Tyne Daly (United Artists)

The Aviator does not fly. Script is flat, costars Christopher Reeve and Rosanna Arquette fail to overcome unattractive characters, and the production's inherent flavor 1920s Stearman biplanes is too quickly sacrificed for a drama of survival in a desolate wilderness.

L'AVVENTURA
1960, 143 mins, Italy/France ⊗ ⊙

D: Michelangelo Antonioni A: Gabriele Ferzetti, Monica Vitti, Lea Massari, Dominique Blanchar, Renzo Ricci, Dorothy De Poliolo (Cino del Duca/PCE/Lyre)

On the heels of Federico Fellini's *La Dolce Vita*, which also castigated the emptiness and decadence of Italian high life, this one is more personal and less symbolic. But it is long, grave, and sometimes overemphatic. A group of idle rich go off on a cruise. Sandro (Gabriele Ferzetti) is involved with an erratic, mystical girl, Anna (Lea Massari), who showers him with love. But she disappears when they land on a barren island. Her lover tries to follow her trail, accompanied by the missing girl's friend Claudia (Monica Vitti), a poor girl. A love affair develops. Vitti stands out as the poorer girl whose hope is that this affair is more than an adventure.

AWAKENING, THE
1980, 102 mins, UK ⑰ ⊚
D: Mike Newell **A:** Charlton Heston, Susannah York, Jill Townsend, Stephanie Zimbalist, Patrick Drury (Orion)

It seems that there was once a certain Egyptian Queen Kara, dead at 18, buried, amid the usual riches, in an isolated tomb bearing a DO NOT DISTURB sign. Story possesses a strange fascination for archaeologist Charlton Heston, who finally penetrates the chamber centuries later. It's hokum through and through. Veteran lenser Jack Cardiff contributes a highly professional sheen but first-time feature director Mike Newell exhibits a jumpy, disjointed style.

AWAKENINGS
1990, 121 mins, US ⑰ ⊚
D: Penny Marshall **A:** Robin Williams, Robert De Niro, Julie Kavner, Ruth Nelson, John Heard, Penelope Ann Miller (Columbia)

Robin Williams joins Robert De Niro in enacting the story of neurologist Oliver Sacks, who in 1966 encountered a group of statuelike paralytics in a Bronx hospital and insisted something could be done for them. Williams wins permission to test a new drug and is able to awaken Leonard Lowe (De Niro). But the miracle cure proves temporary. Enacting the shy, fidgety doctor, Williams extends the extraordinary dramatic gifts he displayed in *Dead*

Poets Society. De Niro has this visceral, demanding role by the tail.
1990: Nominations: Best Picture, Actor (Robert De Niro), Adapted Screenplay

AWFULLY BIG ADVENTURE, AN
1995, 110 mins, UK ⑰ ⊚
D: Mike Newell **A:** Alan Rickman, Hugh Grant, Georgina Cates, Alun Armstrong, Peter Firth, Prunella Scales (Portman)

A dour, antisentimental, coming-of-age story set amid a small-time theatrical company in postwar Liverpool, this rather disagreeable look at the irresponsible and corrupting behavior of adults toward youthful protégés is both somewhat confusing and unpalatable, despite the strong talent involved. Exceedingly understated storytelling style keeps the film's ultimate concerns out of sight for longer than most viewers will be willing to wait.

AWFUL TRUTH, THE
1937, 90 mins, US ⑰ ⊚
D: Leo McCarey **A:** Irene Dunne, Cary Grant, Ralph Bellamy, Robert Allen, Cecil Cunningham, Alexander D'Arcy (Columbia)

When hubby Cary Grant isn't satisfied with simple, innocent explanation of where and how wife Irene Dunne spent the night away from home while he—faithful fellow—was feigning a trip to Florida and playing poker with pals around the corner, the couple obtain a divorce. The divorcée starts tagging around with an ardent oil-rich Oklahoman (Ralph Bellamy), who spikes up the film with a lot of spontaneous comedy as a simple, rustic soul accustomed to staying always within the shadow of his mother's trailing skirts. Meanwhile, Grant has started looping around with an heiress. The timing Leo McCarey plotted for the fast comedy lines is flawless.
1937: Best Director
Nominations: Best Picture, Actress (Irene Dunne), Supp. Actor (Ralph Bellamy), Screenplay

BABE, THE
1992, 113 mins, US Ⓥ ⊙

D: Arthur Hiller **A:** John Goodman, Kelly McGillis, Trini Alvarado, Bruce Boxleitner, Peter Donat, James Cromwell (Universal/Waterhorse)

Despite Haxell Wexler's alluring lensing, this thinly dramatized, overly episodic Babe Ruth biopic resembles a tele-that has lost its way onto the big reen. Lovable-TV-star-erstwhile-movie-character-actor John Goodman plays one of America's most endearing folk heroes. Goodman has an exuberant, bumptious charm ideally suited to the overgrown child he's playing. Pic is so infatuated with the Babe, warts and all, that it fails to bring to life the feelings of his first wife (Trini Alvarado). His satisfying second marriage to a practical-minded showgirl (saucy Kelly McGillis) brings out a new strain of maturity in Ruth, but it's hardly big-league-pic material.

BABE
1995, 94 mins, Australia/US Ⓥ ⊙

D: Chris Noonan **A:** James Cromwell, Magda Szubanski (Kennedy Miller/Universal)

Babe is a dazzling family entertainment with enormous charm and breathtaking technical innovation. The Australia-set tale of a piglet who becomes a championship sheep dog is unexpectedly enthralling, relayed from the animals' perspective. It's done in a wholly unselfconscious manner with a combination of animatronic wizardry and human voice-overs. Initially, it's a bit of a shocker to watch a family drama unfold in which the cast comprises real-life, fuzzy creatures and where humans get the pet roles. Nonetheless, you can't stop watching.

1995: Best Visual Effects
Nominations: Best Picture, Best Supp. Actor (James Cromwell), Director, Screenplay Adaptation, Film Editing, Best Art Direction

BABE
PIG IN THE CITY
1998, 97 mins, Australia/US Ⓥ ⊙

D: George Miller **A:** Magda Szubanski, James Cromwell, Mary Stein, Mickey Rooney, Julie Godfrey (Kennedy Miller/Universal)

There is plenty of fun in this $80 million cinematic menagerie, consummate screen magic and a series of well-intentioned messages that sidestep the cloying and saccharine. After Babe earns his stripes as a champion sheep "dog," life back on the farm resumes. But a freak accident results in farmer Hoggett (James Cromwell) falling down a well and being unable to work. The solution to the financial plight is to accept an invitation, with a generous fee attached, for Babe to demonstrate his herding prowess at a fair far away in the big city. Pic straddles the animal and human worlds, invests the non-humans with emotional qualities and flips the image by turning the more traditional cast members into well-observed Hogarthian creatures with bestial qualities. The seamless mix of real and animatronic animals is a testament to the vision of the creative team.

BABES IN ARMS
1939, 93 mins, US Ⓥ ⊙

D: Busby Berkeley **A:** Mickey Rooney, Judy Garland, Charles Winninger, Guy Kibbee, June Preisser (M-G-M)

Film version of the Rodgers and Hart musical has been considerably embellished. Basic idea is there, and two songs are retained. Otherwise, it's a greatly enhanced piece of entertainment, with Mickey Rooney having a field day parading his versatile talents. He sings, dances, gives out with a series of imitations including Clark Gable, Lionel Barrymore, and President Roosevelt. With Judy Garland he sings "Good Morning," a new tune by Nacio Herb Brown and producer Arthur Freed.

1939: Nominations: Best Actor (Mickey Rooney), Score

BABES IN TOYLAND
1934, 79 mins, US Ⓥ ⊙

D: Charles Rogers, Gus Meins **A:** Stan Laurel, Oliver Hardy, Charlotte Henry, Felix Knight, Henry Brandon, Marie Wilson (Roach/M-G-M)

Babes in Toyland is far away from the Victor Herbert original operetta. The arithmetic song and "March of the Toys" are the only outstanding survivors of Herbert's score, and these are merely background. Of the original book there is no trace at all. This is not a musical brought to the screen. It is a fairy story in technique and treatment, but a gorgeous fairy tale which gives everything to Laurel and Hardy and to which, in return, they give their happiest best.

BABES IN TOYLAND
1961, 106 mins, US Ⓥ
D: Jack Donohue A: Ray Bolger, Tommy Sands, Annette Funicello, Ed Wynn, Tommy Kirk, Kevin Corcoran (Walt Disney)

Walt Disney's first live-action musical, a lavish translation to the screen of Victor Herbert's operetta, is an expensive gift, brightly wrapped and intricately packaged. The Disney concept of *Toyland* falls somewhere in that never-never land where the techniques of the stage, the live-action screen, and the animated cartoon overlap. Ray Bolger delivers a sly, rollicking, congenially menacing portrayal. Sands and Funicello are rather wooden as the young lovers, but each has an opportunity to display vocal prowess and capable choreographic footwork. Ed Wynn and Tommy Kirk score as toymaker and assistant.

BABES ON BROADWAY
1942, 121 mins, US Ⓥ ◉
D: Busby Berkeley A: Mickey Rooney, Judy Garland, Richard Quine, Fay Bainter (M-G-M)

Teamed with Judy Garland in a filmusical that is very similar to their previous efforts, Rooney is as fresh as the proverbial daisy at the end of two hours of strenuous theatrical calisthenics. He dances, sings, acts, and does imitations—dozens of them. There isn't time to catch one's breath from the opening moment to the closing fade-out of Rooney and Garland giving their all in one of those Metro production numbers, where the stage, the scenery, the actors, and some of the audience are doing a gigantic revolution around the camera. In between, there is related a story about young performers battling for their chance on Broadway.
1942: Nomination: Best Song (''How About You?'')

BABETTE'S FEAST
See: Babettes Gaestebud

BABETTES GAESTEBUD
(BABETTE'S FEAST)
1987, 102 mins, Denmark Ⓥ ◉
D: Gabriel Axel A: Stephane Audran, Jean-Philippe Lafont, Gudmar Wivesson, Jarl Kulle, Bibi Andersson, Ebbe Rode (Panorama)

A rousing yarn of delicate philosophical overtones about a French female chef

de cuisine of five-star repute, exiled after the Paris uprisings of 1871, who survives as a maid and cook to a couple of devout elderly spinster daughters on the remote and rugged Scandinavian North Sea coast. Story has its title character (France's Stephane Audran) given a fling at preparing and serving up one final great dinner by blowing on it her entire winnings from a lottery ticket. Sweden's Jarl Kulle matches Audran in wit and depth, although the two are never seen together.
1988: Best Foreign Film

BABY BOOM
1987, 103 mins, US Ⓥ ◉
D: Charles Shyer A: Diane Keaton, Harold Ramis, Sam Wanamaker, James Spader, Pat Hingle, Sam Shepard (United Artists)

A transparent and one-dimensional parable about a power-devouring female careerist and the unwanted bundle of joy that turns her obsessive fast-track life in Gotham upside down. Constructed almost entirely upon facile and familiar media clichés about parenting and the super-yuppie set, *Baby Boom* has the superficiality of a project inspired by a lame *New York* magazine cover story and sketched out on a cocktail napkin at Spago's.

BABY DOLL
1956, 114 mins, US Ⓥ
D: Elia Kazan A: Karl Malden, Carroll Baker, Eli Wallach, Mildred Dunnock, Lonny Chapman (Newtown)

Except for moments of humor that are strictly inherent in the character of the principals, *Baby Doll* plays off against a sleazy, dirty, depressing southern background. Over it hangs a feeling of decay, expertly nurtured by director Elia Kazan. *Baby Doll* is based on a 1941 Tennessee Williams vignette. Story briefly has Carroll Baker, an immature teenager, married to middle-aged Karl Malden, who runs a cotton gin. Eli Wallach—owner of the gin—proceeds to seduce Baker. Malden, who has promised not to touch his young wife until one year after their marriage, finds Baker and Wallach together in the house and goes berserk with jealousy. Baker's performance captures all the animal charm, the naïveté, the vanity, contempt, and rising passion of Baby Doll. Wallach plays it to the hilt. Malden is cast to perfection.
1956: Nominations: Best Actress (Carroll Baker), Supp. Actress (Mildred Dunnock),

Adapted Screenplay, B&W Cinematography

BABY FACE NELSON
1957, 85 mins, US Ⓥ
D: Don Siegel **A:** Mickey Rooney, Carolyn Jones, Cedric Hardwicke, Leo Gordon, Anthony Caruso, Jack Elam (Fryman-ZS/United Artists)

Nelson was a member of the notorious Dillinger gang that scourged the midwest circa 1933. The script makes him a ruthless, trigger-happy, cold-blooded killer. The versatile Mickey Rooney is not particularly convincing as the pint-sized Nelson. More impressive is Carolyn Jones's portrayal of Rooney's loyal moll.

BABYFEVER
1994, 110 mins, US Ⓥ ⊙
D: Henry Jaglom **A:** Victoria Foyt, Matt Salinger, Dinah Lenney, Eric Roberts, Frances Fisher, Zack Norman (Jagtoria)

Henry Jaglom fashions a stylistic blend of fictional story, based on his own experience, and documentary, using interviews with many women, that emerges as overly long, fractured, and only intermittently entertaining. Victoria Foyt (Jaglom's wife) stars as an attractive middle-aged career woman who can't make up her mind whether she wants to have a baby with James (Matt Salinger), her sensitive b.f. Just when she is about to make a commitment, old flame Anthony (Eric Roberts) reappears with a proposition that confuses her even more.

BABY, IT'S YOU
1983, 105 mins, US Ⓥ ⊙
D: John Sayles **A:** Rosanna Arquette, Vincent Spano, Joanna Merlin, Jack Davidson, Nick Ferrari, Dolores Messina (Double Play)

Despite some strong thematic material and a vibrant central performance, *Baby, It's You* remains an essentially unfulfilled romantic drama. John Sayles's third directorial outing can't recoup from the ultimately unbelievable pairing of leading characters. Film has an elegantly dressed Italian street kid with the mysterious name of Sheik pursue, win, lose, and, at length, haunt the emotional life of a bright, ambitious, and terribly attractive high-school drama student, Jill. In spite of being a character who could have used more fleshing out in the writing, it's Rosanna Arquette who makes *Baby, It's You* persistently watchable. Vincent Spano

does a good turn, but unavoidably suffers from miscasting opposite Arquette.

BABYLON
1980, 95 mins, UK Ⓥ
D: Franco Rosso **A:** Brinsley Forde, Karl Howman, Trevor Laird

Like the reggae music that pulses through it, *Babylon* is rich, rough, and real. And like the streetlife of the young black Londoners it portrays, it's threatening, touching, violent, and funny. This one seems to explode in the gut with a powerful mix of pain and pleasure.

BABY MAKER, THE
1970, 109 mins, US Ⓥ
D: James Bridges **A:** Barbara Hershey, Collin Wilcox-Horne, Sam Groom, Scott Glenn, Jeannie Berlin, Lili Valenty (National General/Wise)

Collin Wilcox-Horne and Sam Groom are a barren couple who hire Barbara Hershey to bear his child. This in turn shatters the girl's relationship with Scott Glenn, both of whom are from the love generation. Development of an emotional relationship between Hershey and Groom is more than implicit, while Wilcox-Horne is excellent in a multifaceted performance: sometimes warm and loving, occasionally on the verge of jealousy, but always sincere in her character's motivations and reactions.

1970: Nomination: Best Original Song Score

BABY OF MACON, THE
1993, 122 mins, Netherlands/France Ⓥ
D: Peter Greenaway **A:** Julia Ormond, Ralph Fiennes, Philip Stone, Jonathan Lacey, Don Henderson, Jeff Nuttall (Allarts/UGC)

Peter Greenaway's *The Baby of Macon* is all fluff and no filling. Visually sumptuous and laden with religious refs and Brechtian devices, this elaborate but overlong film-of-a-play about the birth of a 17th-century miracle child and his short-lived period of grace plays like a tired rerun of the director's previous extravaganzas. Entire film takes place on a single giant set that includes audience and performers, gathered for an elaborate theatrical masque to celebrate fertility.

BABY'S DAY OUT
1994, 98 mins, US Ⓥ ⊙
D: Patrick Read Johnson **A:** Joe Mantegna, Lara Flynn Boyle, Joe Pantoliano, Brian Haley, Cynthia Nixon, Fred Dalton Thompson (20th Century-Fox)

Offering from writer-producer John

Hughes is a tired retread of past comic formulas played a pitch higher, a rhythm faster. A trio of kidnappers (Joe Mantegna, Joe Pantoliano, Brian Haley) pose as baby photographers to gain access to the home of an old-money Chicago couple (Lara Flynn Boyle and Matthew Glave). At an opportune moment they snatch the infant son and hide out until their ransom demands are met. The foolproof plan goes awry when 9-month-old Bennington August Cottwell IV, a.k.a. Baby Bink, crawls out of an apartment window and into the hustle bustle of downtown.

BABY
SECRET OF THE LOST LEGEND
1985, 95 mins, US Ⓥ ⊙ ▱
D: B.W.L. Norton A: William Katt, Sean Young, Patrick McGoohan, Julian Fellowes, Kyalo Mativo, Hugh Quarshie (Touchstone)
A huggable prehistoric hatchling is discovered by a young American couple in an African rain forest. Story has an engaging performance from William Katt, who plays the sportswriter husband of paleontologist Sean Young. Latter, whose maternal and scientific instincts propel events, is rather bland. Evil foil is Patrick McGoohan as a rival, ruthless paleontologist who enlists the aid of a rapacious revolutionary army to capture Baby's towering brontosaurus mama.

BABY-SITTERS CLUB, THE
1995, 94 mins, US Ⓥ
D: Melanie Mayron A: Schuyler Fisk, Bre Blair, Rachael Leigh Cook, Larisa Oleynik, Tricia Joe, Stacey Linn Ramsower (Scholastic/Beacon)
A warm, cuddly, and earnest tale of modern youth. It centers on the seven young girls who comprise the title group and their efforts to open up a summer daycare camp for their charges. The most serious plot thread involves group leader Kristy (Schuyler Fisk) and her sub-rosa relationship with her estranged father (Peter Horton). The picture's problem is that it is small in every way. Tyro director Melanie Mayron does yeoman work, eliciting perky performances from a predominantly untried cast.

BABY THE RAIN MUST FALL
1965, 93 mins, US Ⓥ ⊙
D: Robert Mulligan A: Lee Remick, Steve McQueen, Don Murray, Paul Fix, Josephine Hutchinson, Ruth White (Park Place/Solar)

Chief assets are outstanding performances by its stars and an emotional punch that lingers. Steve McQueen is exactly right as irresponsible rockabilly singer, Lee Remick portrays his wife sensitively, and newcomer Kimberly Block is charming and unaffected as their six-year-old daughter. Remick is vividly alive in spontaneous-appearing scenes with daughter. But director Robert Mulligan apparently was so determined to avoid soap-opera clichés that he did not permit actress to register negative emotion beyond look of distraught unhappiness even though sad events should have allowed room for tears.

BACHELOR, THE
1999, 101 mins, US Ⓥ ⊙
D: Gary Sinyor A: Chris O'Donnell, Renee Zellweger, Hal Holbrook, James Cromwell, Artie Lange, Edward Asner (Segan/New Line)
You don't have to know and love Buster Keaton's 1925 farce *Seven Chances* to dislike the modern remake *The Bachelor*. A mirthless and inept romantic comedy about a young man who must marry within a day if he's to inherit $100 million, new pic is woefully misconceived on virtually every level. Jimmy Shannon (Chris O'Donnell) is a good-looking but uninteresting confirmed bachelor who, after three years with g.f. Anne (Renee Zellweger), reaches the relationship's crossroads. The will of his grandfather (Peter Ustinov) reveals he inherits only if he marries by 6:05 P.M. on his 30th birthday, the very next day. Jimmy rushes off to propose to Anne. She's not convinced so Jimmy tracks down former girlfriends. O'Donnell's Jimmy is bland as can be, and Zellweger comes off far less well than in her other major films.

BACHELOR AND THE BOBBY-
SOXER, THE
1947, 94 mins, US Ⓥ ⊙
D: Irving Reis A: Cary Grant, Myrna Loy, Shirley Temple, Rudy Vallee, Ray Collins, Harry Davenport (RKO)
Tossed together are a lady judge, a playboy artist, and an impressionable teenager. Grant, the artist, has already had a brush with the judge, Myrna Loy, so when the judge's kid sister, Shirley Temple, is found in the artist's apartment late at night, he's in plenty of trouble. Court psychiatrist proposes that he be assigned to escort her around until she gets over her crush. Chuckles get heartier and heartier

as adult Grant plays at being a juvenile at basketball games, school picnics, etc. It's done with slapstick touch that pays off.
1947: Best Original Screenplay

BACHELOR FATHER
1931, 84 mins, US
D: Robert Z. Leonard **A:** Marion Davies, Ralph Forbes, C. Aubrey Smith, Ray Milland, Guinn Williams, David Torrence (M-G-M)

Marion Davies plays debonair comedy with just a touch of rowdiness, relieved at the other extreme with the merest suggestion of under-the-surface sentiment. C. Aubrey Smith delivers a screen portrait that is a gem, while Ralph Forbes brings a suave gentility to the juvenile lead in admirable contrast to the flamboyant playing of the star.

BACHELOR FLAT
1961, 92 mins, US ▭
D: Frank Tashlin **A:** Tuesday Weld, Richard Beymer, Terry-Thomas, Celeste Holm, Francesca Bellini, Howard McNear (20th Century-Fox)

Frivolous, farcical concoction. Terry-Thomas is the archaeology professor situated in California, where he is on the verge of wedlock with a roving fashion designer (Celeste Holm) who is abroad on business as the nuptial date approaches. T-T's path to the altar is complicated by: (1) the unscheduled advent of Tuesday Weld, who is Holm's daughter, unbeknownst to the prof; (2) regular invasions of his bachelor quarters by campus cuties; (3) the irresponsible advice of cynical student-neighbor Richard Beymer, who has a crush on Tuesday; (4) the singleness-of-purpose of Beymer's dachshund, a typical bona-Fido determined to bury the professor's prize possession—a rare dinosaur bone. Except for Terry-Thomas, whose comic intuition and creativity is responsible for most of the merriment, it is the supporting cast, rather than the principals, that comes through on the comedy end. The dachshund, incidentally, is an accomplished low comedienne.

BACHELOR GIRL APARTMENT
See: Any Wednesday

BACHELOR IN PARADISE
1961, 109 mins, US ▭
D: Jack Arnold **A:** Bob Hope, Lana Turner, Janis Paige, Jim Hutton, Paula Prentiss, Agnes Moorehead (M-G-M)

The screenplay is a no-depth (but easy to take) yarn which has Bob Hope as a writer. He goes to a newly developed California community to learn something about what makes American women tick. The women in town, all young marrieds and pretty, take to him, either for his counsel on marital affairs or a flirtation walk now and then. Actually, though, Hope is innocent of any romantic hanky-panky and eventually announces his love for Lana Turner, the only single girl in the vicinity.

BACHELOR MOTHER
1939, 80 mins, US ⓥ ⊙
D: Garson Kanin **A:** Ginger Rogers, David Niven, Charles Coburn, Frank Albertson, E. E. Clive (RKO)

Story is a rather ordinary Cinderella yarn, gaining substance and strength through adroit direction, excellently tempoed lines and situations, and top-notch cast performances. Ginger Rogers blossoms forth as a most competent comedienne. David Niven delivers strongly as the romantic interest. Picking up a baby on the steps of a foundling home, Rogers finds her excuses inadequate and she's tabbed as the unwed mother of the child. Niven becomes curiously interested in the foundling, and gradually develops romantic inclinations toward Rogers.
1939: Nomination: Best Original Story (Felix Jackson)

BACHELOR OF HEARTS
1958, 94 mins, UK
D: Wolf Rilla **A:** Hardy Kruger, Sylvia Syms, Ronald Lewis, Miles Malleson, Eric Barker, Barbara Steele (Independent Artists)

A facetious, rather embarrassing glimpse of life at Cambridge University. The thin yarn has Hardy Kruger as a German student on an exchange scholarship system. The wisecracks mostly depend on the young German's inability to understand the English idiom or the traditional behavior at the university. Kruger has a pleasant personality to make his slight love affair with Sylvia Syms acceptable.

BACHELOR PARTY, THE
1957, 92 mins, US ⓥ
D: Delbert Mann **A:** Don Murray, E. G. Marshall, Jack Warden, Philip Abbott, Carolyn Jones, Patricia Smith (United Artists/Norma)

The title tips that the comedy will come from the international institution of giving the groom-to-be his last fling as a single man. The script gets it all in the drinking dinner, the stag movies, the pub crawling, the visit to a strip show, and finally, the calling on a professional lady. Each sequence is vividly etched. Cast is headed by Don Murray. He's good as a reluctant member of the bachelor party, the round of tawdry revelry is seen through his eyes. One scene even involving Murray temporarily with a sexpot Greenwich Village character, played with great vitality by Carolyn Jones.

1957: Nomination: Best Supp. Actress (Carolyn Jones)

BACHELOR PARTY
1984, 106 mins, US ⓥ ⊙
D: Neal Israel **A:** Tom Hanks, Tawny Kitaen, Adrian Zmed, George Grizzard, Barbara Stuart, Robert Prescott (Aspect Ratio/ Twin Continental)

Bachelor Party is too contrived to capture the craziness it strains for and ultimately becomes offensive rather than funny. Filled with cartoon caricatures instead of people, picture is built around a prenuptial celebration that seems to bring the worst out in people. Rick (Tom Hanks) is marrying Debbie (Tawny Kitaen) and Rick's friends decide to throw a bash for their departing pal. While the film offers predictable shenanigans, such as a donkey snorting cocaine and an attempted suicide with an electric razor, main reason to see the pic is for Hanks's performance. He's all over the place, practically spilling off the screen with an overabundance of energy.

BACKBEAT
1994, 100 mins, UK ⓥ ⊙
D: Iain Softley **A:** Sheryl Lee, Stephen Dorff, Ian Hart, Gary Bakewell, Chris O'Neill, Scot Williams (Scala/PFE/Forthcoming)

The early, prefame days of the Beatles are a great subject for a film, but the potential has been only partly realized in *Backbeat*. This energetic, dramatically potent look at the band's Hamburg days, with special emphasis on the little-known original fifth Beatle, Stuart Sutcliffe, lacks a crucial, heightened artistic quality and point of view that would have given it real distinction. The screenplay focuses on John Lennon's relationship with his best friend, Sutcliffe, a young man of James Dean looks but little musical ability who left the group. For the most part, pic has been well cast. Returning as Lennon after his successful outing in *The Hours and Times*, Ian Hart is again terrifically effec-

tive, catching John's rebellious attitude. American actor Stephen Dorff also scores strongly as Sutcliffe.

BACKDRAFT
1991, 135 mins, US ⓥ ⊙ ▭
D: Ron Howard **A:** Kurt Russell, William Baldwin, Robert De Niro, Donald Sutherland, Jennifer Jason Leigh, Scott Glenn (Universal/Imagine)

Director Ron Howard torches off more thrilling scenes in *Backdraft* than any Saturday matinee serial ever dared. Visually, pic often is exhilarating, but it's shapeless and dragged down by corny, melodramatic characters and situations. Ex-fireman Gregory Widen's script about Chicago smokeaters begins with a scene of the two central characters as boys in 1971. This provides shorthand for later formulaic conflicts between fire-fighting brothers Kurt Russell and William Baldwin. Widen uncertainly blends tiresome family quarrels with a suspense plot involving fire-department investigator Robert De Niro's search for a mysterious arsonist. The spectacular fire scenes are done with terrifying believability (usually with the actors in the same shot as the fire effects) and a kind of sci-fi grandeur.

1991: Nominations: Best Sound, Sound Effects Editing, Visual Effects

BACK IN THE USSR
1992, 89 mins, US
D: Deran Sarafian **A:** Frank Whaley, Natalya Negoda, Roman Polanski, Andrew Divoff, Dey Young, Brian Blessed (Largo)

Back in the USSR is an amateurish adventure about the Russian underworld shot entirely in Moscow. This attempt to capitalize on perestroika stumbles over a weak script, wooden acting, and inferior tech credits. Story involves vacationing young American Frank Whaley, whose amorous pursuits lead him into a cops-and-robbers escapade. Russian actress Natalya Negoda is the love interest, and Roman Polanski plays the chief villain. In an obvious attempt at humor, nightclub owner Polanski is shown in one scene relishing nubile maidens onstage.

BACKLASH
1956, 83 mins, US
D: John Sturges **A:** Richard Widmark, Donna Reed, William Campbell, John McIntire, Barton MacLane, Edward C. Platt (Universal)

Regulation western drama. Story period is early Arizona soon after the Civil

War, and most of the location lensing was done in that state for picturesque visual values. Identification of five white men killed in an Apache raid and of one who escaped, plus the whereabouts of $60,000 in gold the party was supposed to have had, puts the plot in gear. Jim Slater (Widmark) wants to make sure his no-good father (John McIntire) is one of the dead and not, as he secretly fears, the one who escaped with the coin. Karyl Orton (Reed) is on the search for the money, believing her husband, one of the dead, had an interest in it.

BACK ROADS
1981, 94 mins, US Ⓥ ▱
D: Martin Ritt A: Sally Field, Tommy Lee Jones, Michael Gazzo, M. Emmet Walsh (Warner)

Plot focuses on southern hooker Sally Field who meets down-on-his-luck boxer Tommy Lee Jones in the course of a working night. Pair decide to leave Alabama for the promising California shores. Thrust of the film is their adventures hitchhiking along the road. Although both stars rise above script contrivances, they are somehow never an affecting romantic pair. All of their shared troubles would seem to make a great love story but they never share enough really intimate moments to carry it off.

BACK STREET
1932, 86 mins, US
D: John M. Stahl A: Irene Dunne, John Boles, June Clyde, George Meeker, ZaSu Pitts, Shirley Grey (Universal)

This saga of Ray Schmidt who lives in a shadowy "back street," and has an illicit relationship with Walter Saxel, leaps off the screen and smacks the viewer above the gray matter and under the heart. Her ready acquiesce to every demand of her lover (John Boles) despite his own imminent marriage, "for family reasons," is as natural in its artlessness as having a cup of coffee, and yet it is packed with human interest. Dunne is the personification of "a real woman." Boles, too, is very effective, deftly highlighting the somewhat selfish man who makes heavy demands of his mistress and yet as genuinely in love as the No. 2 woman in his life.

BACK STREET
1941, 89 mins, US
D: Robert Stevenson A: Charles Boyer, Margaret Sullavan, Richard Carlson, Frank McHugh, Tim Holt, Esther Dale (Universal)

Second picturization of Fannie Hurst's novel retains all of the tear-jerking qualities of the author's original work. Generating strong sympathy for the plight of a woman unable to enjoy the security of marriage, picture carries hefty dramatic punch. Margaret Sullavan delivers a strong and sympathetic characterization as the most willing victim of love and devotion. Charles Boyer provides a deft and restrained portrayal of the man willing to share his time and affections between wife and mistress.

BACK TO BATAAN
1945, 95 mins, US Ⓥ ⊙
D: Edward Dmytryk A: John Wayne, Anthony Quinn, Beulah Bondi, Fely Franquelli, Richard Loo, Philip Ahn (RKO)

Plot spans time from fall of Bataan and Corregidor to the American landings on Leyte, and depicts adventures of John Wayne as a colonel leading Filipino patriots in undercover sabotage against the islands' temporary conquerors. Love interest is given over to Anthony Quinn, portraying the descendant of the Filipino hero, Bonifacio, and Fely Franquelli. Quinn does a particularly outstanding job, as does Franquelli. Wayne makes a stalwart leader for the guerrillas, commendably underplaying the role for best results.

BACK TO THE FUTURE
1985, 116 mins, US Ⓥ ⊙
D: Robert Zemeckis A: Michael J. Fox, Christopher Lloyd, Crispin Glover, Lea Thompson, Claudia Wells, Thomas F. Wilson (Amblin)

The central winning elements in the scenario are twofold; hurtling the audience back to 1955, which allows for lots of comparative, pop-culture humor, and delivering a 1985 teenager (Michael J. Fox) at the doorstep of his future parents when they were 17-year-old kids. That encounter is a delicious premise, especially when the young hero's mother-to-be develops the hots for her future son and his future father is a bumbling wimp. Film is also sharply anchored by zestful byplay between Fox's Arthurian knight figure and Christopher Lloyd's Merlin-like, crazed scientist. Performances by the earnest Fox, the lunatic Lloyd, the deceptively passionate Lea Thompson, and, particularly, the bumbling-to-confident Glover, who runs away with the picture, merrily keep the ship sailing.

1985: Best Sound Effects Editing
Nominations: Best Original Screenplay,
Sound, Song ("Power of Love")

BACK TO THE FUTURE PART II
1989, 107 mins, US ⊗ ⊙
D: Robert Zemeckis **A:** Michael J. Fox,
Christopher Lloyd, Lea Thompson, Thomas F. Wilson, Harry Waters Jr., Elisabeth Shue (Amblin/Universal)

The energy and heart which Robert Zemeckis and strong-writing partner Bob Gale poured into the ingenious story of part one is diverted into narrative mechanics and camera wizardry in *Future II*. The story starts exactly where the original left off, with Michael J. Fox's Marty McFly and Christopher Lloyd's visionary inventor Dr. Emmett Brown taking off in their flying DeLorean time machine for 2015 on an urgent mission to save Fox's children from a terrible fate. Zemeckis's fascination with having characters interact at different ages of their lives hurts the film visually, and strains credibility past the breaking point, by forcing him to rely on some very cheesy makeup designs.
1989: Nomination: Best Visual Effects

BACK TO THE FUTURE PART III
1990, 118 mins, US ⊗ ⊙
D: Robert Zemeckis **A:** Michael J. Fox,
Christopher Lloyd, Mary Steenburgen, Thomas F. Wilson, Lea Thompson, Elisabeth Shue (Amblin)

Back to the Future Part III recovers the style, wit, and grandiose fantasy elements of the original. Michael J. Fox's Marty McFly in his time-traveling DeLorean finds himself in the midst of a band of charging Indians in John Ford country, Monument Valley 1885. His mission is to bring back Doc (Christopher Lloyd). Doc's offbeat romance with Mary Steenburgen's Clara Clayton, a spinster schoolmarm who shares his passion for Jules Verne, is funny, touching, and exhilarating. The fun of this meta-western is partly the recognition of elements familiar from genre classics. Fox reexperiences all this, literally flying through the screen (at an incongruous Monument Valley drive-in) into every western fan's dream of being a character in a real western.

BAD
1977, 105 mins, US ⊗
D: Jed Johnson **A:** Carroll Baker, Perry King, Susan Tyrrell, Stefania Cassini, Cyrinda Foxe, Mary Boylan (New World)

Watching Andy Warhol's *Bad* is a compellingly revolting experience. This is among the blackest of black comedies, featuring Carroll Baker as a Queens housewife who supplements her home electrolysis business by arranging for young girls to do repulsive errands for clients, killing dogs, retarded babies, etc. Don't see it after eating.

BAD AND THE BEAUTIFUL, THE
1952, 116 mins, US ⊗ ⊙
D: Vincente Minnelli **A:** Kirk Douglas, Lana Turner, Walter Pidgeon, Dick Powell, Barry Sullivan, Gloria Grahame (M-G-M)

Contemporary Hollywood is the setting for *The Bad and the Beautiful*. Kirk Douglas scores as the ruthless individual out to prove he is the best when it comes to making pictures. Swung along with him is Lana Turner, the drunken, inferiority-complexed daughter of a former screen great; Dick Powell, the self-satisfied southern professor-writer who is pulled into the Hollywood mill; and Barry Sullivan, who, as an embryo director, gets Douglas his first chance and is double-crossed for the helping hand.
1952: Best Supp. Actress (Gloria Grahame), Screenplay, B&W Cinematography, B&W Art Direction, B&W Costume Design
Nomination: Best Actor (Kirk Douglas)

BAD BEHAVIOUR
1993, 100 mins, UK ⊗
D: Les Blair **A:** Stephen Rea, Sinead Cusack, Philip Jackson, Clare Higgins, Phil Daniels, Saira Todd (Channel 4/Parallax)

Stephen Rea heads a strong cast, crisply directed, in *Bad Behaviour*, a delightful comedy of manners set among a group of north Londoners. Working, in the style of Mike Leigh, from an improvised script, helmer Les Blair juggles his small cast with great dexterity, playing down the line with no feel of treading water. The pic is character, not knockabout, comedy, but this is a group of mild eccentrics you want to follow to the end.

BAD BLOOD
1982, 105 mins, UK/New Zealand ⊗
D: Mike Newell **A:** Jack Thompson, Carol Burns, Dennis Lill, Donna Akersten, Martyn Sanderson, Marshall Napier (Southern)

Story revolves around Stan (Jack Thompson) and Dorothy Graham (Carol Burns), gun-happy dairy farmers who by 1941 have become ostracized by their neighbors in the isolated, close-knit New Zealand town of Kowhiterangi. A gunpoint confrontation with two neighbors forces constable Ted Best (Dennis Lill) to confiscate Thompson's rifle, backed by a trio of fellow officers. When the gendarmes invade Thompson's farmhouse, his last refuge from a world of his own making, the inevitable violence ensues. Direction by Mike Newell stands out for conveying more meaning with pictures than words, though the film stumbles somewhat through the narrative until the carnage begins.

BAD BOY BUBBY
1993, 112 mins, Australia/Italy Ⓥ ◉
D: Rolf De Heer A: Nicholas Hope, Claire Benito, Ralph Cotterill, Carmel Johnson, Natalie Carr, Norman Kaye (Bubby/Fandango)
A very original dramatic comedy with something to offend just about everybody. Bubby's crazy mother (Claire Benito), a religious freak, has kept her son (Nicholas Hope) in isolation from the outside world for the first 35 years of his life. Living in a grubby, windowless room, they bathe each other and even have sex together, an act Bubby has been raised to regard as normal. This strange existence is interrupted by the arrival of Bubby's long-lost father (Ralph Cotterill), a ragged priest heavily into booze and sex. He quickly displaces Bubby in mom's bed, and the younger man's jealousy and frustration erupts in violence. Hope gives a brave and sometimes astonishing performance as the naive wild child.

BAD BOYS
1983, 123 mins, US Ⓥ ◉
D: Rick Rosenthal A: Sean Penn, Reni Santoni, Esai Morales, Eric Gurry, Jim Moody, Ally Sheedy (EMI)
Bad Boys is a troubling and often riveting drama about juvenile delinquency. Director Rick Rosenthal does a top-notch job of bringing to life the seedy, hopeless environment of a jail for juvenile offenders and has gotten some terribly convincing performances from his young cast, notably topliner Sean Penn. Penn is nothing short of terrific in the key role, which, given a minimal amount of dialogue, calls for him to rely primarily on his emotional and physical abilities.

BAD BOYS
1995, 118 mins, US Ⓥ ◉
D: Michael Bay A: Martin Lawrence, Will Smith, Tea Leoni, Tcheky Karyo, Theresa Randle, Joe Pantoliano (Columbia)
Marcus Burnett (Martin Lawrence) and Mike Lowrey (Will Smith) are longtime friends who have been undercover partners on the Miami police force for six years. In a zingy sequence, some dazzlingly efficient crooks penetrate the bowels of the police department to make off with $100 million in heroin the heroes recently confiscated in their career bust. With 72 hours to solve the case before the feds step in, Marcus and Mike plausibly suspect a corrupt ex-cop of being in on the job, but he's knocked off by the real mastermind, cold-blooded Frenchman Fouchet (Tcheky Karyo), as is Max (Karen Alexander), a gorgeous high-class hooker and ex-girlfriend of Mike's. Marcus is forced to impersonate his best friend in order to advance the case. This central ruse serves as the basis of much of the humor. Throughout, pic is punctuated by the requisite number of intimidations, beatings, shootings, explosions, and chases, all staged with knowing panache by 30-year-old first-time helmer Michael Bay.

BAD COMPANY
1972, 91 mins, US Ⓥ
D: Robert Benton A: Jeff Bridges, Barry Brown, Jim Davis, David Huddleston, John Savage, Jerry Houser (Jaffilms/Paramount)
Bad Company is an excellent film that combines wry humor and gritty action with in-depth characterizations of two youths on the lam in the Civil War west. It's an intriguing story of the maturing-under-fire of Barry Brown, a midwest draft dodger but otherwise of good character, who gradually develops the educated, pragmatic survival instinct necessary in the Old West. In this he is influenced primarily by Jeff Bridges, a more primitive con-artist character who knows the ropes of street fighting and finagling.

BAD COMPANY
1995, 108 mins, US Ⓥ ◉ ▭
D: Damian Harris A: Ellen Barkin, Laurence Fishburne, Frank Langella, Michael Beach, Gia Carides, David Odgen Stiers (Touchstone)
Bad Company seemingly has no more noble ambition than to give audiences the interracial sex only hinted at in *The Pelican Brief*'s chaste pairing of Julia Roberts and Denzel Washington. But with its uninvolving story, listless delivery, and un-

sympathetic characters played by leads Laurence Fishburne and Ellen Barkin, would-be suspenser fails even on the erotic level. Story opens with ex-CIA troubleshooter Nelson Crowe (Fishburne) getting a new job at a company headed by Margaret Wells (Barkin) and Vic Grimes (Frank Langella). Couple's shady firm specializes in using former government sleuths to do the dirty work of corporations and other private predators. Barkin and Fishburne do capable work in roles that require only one-note shrewishness from her, stolid taciturnity from him.

BAD DAY AT BLACK ROCK
1954, 81 mins, US Ⓥ ⊙ ▭
D: John Sturges **A:** Spencer Tracy, Robert Ryan, Anne Francis, Dean Jagger, Walter Brennan, Ernest Borgnine (M-G-M)

Considerable excitement is whipped up in this suspense drama. Besides telling a yarn of tense suspense, the picture is concerned with a social message on civic complacency. To the tiny town of Black Rock, one hot summer day in 1945, comes Spencer Tracy, war veteran with a crippled left arm. He wants to find a Japanese farmer and give to him the medal won by his son in an action that left the latter dead and Tracy crippled. Tracy is greeted with an odd hostility and his own life is endangered when he puts together the reason for the cold, menacing treatment.
1955: Nominations: Best Director, Actor (Spencer Tracy), Screenplay

BAD GIRL
1931, 90 mins, US
D: Frank Borzage **A:** Sally Eilers, James Dunn, Minna Gombell, William Pawley, Frank Darien (Fox)

Story tells of two kids (Sally Eilers and James Dunn) who meet on a Coney Island boat and delve into marriage after a night in his boardinghouse room; Dorothy (Eilers) is consequently kicked out of a parentless home by her brother. Then Eddie (Dunn) gives up his dream of a radio shop of his own to furnish a new flat for his wife with the added complication of the baby which she has kept a secret from her inarticulate husband.
1931/32: Best Director, Adaptation
Nomination: Best Picture

BAD GIRLS
1994, 99 mins, US Ⓥ ⊙
D: Jonathan Kaplan **A:** Madeleine Stowe, Mary Stuart Masterson, Andie MacDow-

ell, Drew Barrymore, James Russo, James LeGros (20th Century-Fox)

Even though the sight of four comely cowgirls strapping on six-guns and thundering across the plains has its undeniable kick, the bad news is that *Bad Girls* drinks from an empty trough of wit and style. The five script and story writers were unfortunately unable to come up with much interesting for the feisty femmes to do, providing director Jonathan Kaplan, who replaced original helmer Tamra Davis, with an insurmountable problem. Film looks like what it is—four Hollywood actresses duded up in western gear, riding horses, and toting pistols.

BAD GIRLS
See: Les Biches

BAD GUYS
1986, 86 mins, US Ⓥ
D: Joel Silberg **A:** Adam Baldwin, Mike Jolly, Michelle Nicastro, Ruth Buzzi, James Booth, Dutch Mann (Tomorrow)

Bad Guys is a poorly scripted, would-be comedy attempting to cash in on the popularity of wrestling. Merest pretext of a story has young cops Adam Baldwin and Mike Jolly suspended from the L.A. police. After tasteless footage detailing their odd jobs (including a leering stint as male strippers), they turn their wrestling avocation into a full-time job under the tutelage of pretty reporter-turned-manager Michelle Nicastro. Topliner Baldwin is unrecognizable here with blond-dyed hair. He doesn't have the body weight to be convincing as a wrestler. Costar Jolly is bland while Nicastro looks out of place.

BAD INFLUENCE
1990, 99 mins, US Ⓥ ⊙
D: Curtis Hanson **A:** Rob Lowe, James Spader, Lisa Zane, Christian Clemenson, Kathleen Wilhoite, Tony Maggio (Epic/Sarlui-Diamant/PRO)

Bad Influence proves a reasonably taut, suspenseful thriller that provides its share of twists before straying into silliness. Rob Lowe doesn't really project enough menace or charisma to pull off his role as Alex, a baby-faced psycho who slowly leads Michael (James Spader) through a liberating fantasy that ultimately turns into a yuppie nightmare. Spader delivers a terrific performance, and some of the scenes have tremendous impact, especially when via video he discovers the depth of Alex's depravity, as fantasy turns into fatal attraction.

BADLANDERS, THE
1958, 85 mins, US Ⓥ ▱
D: Delmer Daves **A:** Alan Ladd, Ernest Borgnine, Katy Jurado, Claire Kelly, Nehemiah Persoff, Kent Smith (M-G-M)

A truly original frontier drama, a suspense melodrama on one level and a huge horselaugh on another, with each element playing off on the other. The heroes are two ex-cons with little but revenge and larceny in their hearts. It is the plan of one of them (Alan Ladd) to rob a gold mine, and he enlists the other (Ernest Borgnine) in support.

BADLANDS
1973, 95 mins, US Ⓥ ⊙
D: Terrence Malick **A:** Martin Sheen, Sissy Spacek, Warren Oates, Alan Vint, Ramon Bieri, Gary Littlejohn (Pressman-Williams)

Badlands is a uniquely American fairy tale, a romantic account set in the late 1950s of a 15-year-old girl's journey into violence and out of love with a 25-year-old South Dakota garbageman turned thrill killer. Pic is told through the girl's eyes as she narrates in dumb *Teen Romance* style the saga of her hero, a James Dean carbon, who kills her father and whisks her away on a flight into myth that ends in the badlands of Montana. Written, produced, and directed by Terrence Malick, pic is his first feature and it's an impressive debut.

BAD LIEUTENANT
1992, 96 mins, US Ⓥ ⊙
D: Abel Ferrara **A:** Harvey Keitel, Frankie Thorn, Zoe Lund, Anthony Ruggiero, Victoria Bastel, Robin Burrows (Pressman)

Abel Ferrara's uncompromising *Bad Lieutenant* is the harrowing journey of a corrupt NY cop into the depths, with an extraordinary and uninhibited perf by Harvey Keitel in the title role. Foulmouthed cop Keitel is almost constantly sniffing, smoking, or injecting drugs he's stolen from police busts while also indulging in alchohol and time-outs for sex. Turning point for him is being assigned to the case of a gang-raped nun. He's a lapsed Catholic who makes light of the event, but when nun Frankie Thorn (in an unadorned, affecting performance) forgives her assailants, Keitel faces a religious crisis of conscience.

BAD NEWS BEARS, THE
1976, 102 mins, US Ⓥ ⊙
D: Michael Ritchie **A:** Walter Matthau, Tatum O'Neal, Vic Morrow, Joyce Van Patten, Ben Piazza, Jackie Earle Haley (Paramount)

The Bad News Bears is an extremely funny adult-child comedy film. Walter Matthau stars to perfection as a bumbling baseball coach in the sharp production about the foibles and follies of Little League athletics. Tatum O'Neal also stars as Matthau's ace pitcher. Michael Ritchie's film has the correct balance of warmth and empathy to make the gentle social commentary very effective.

BAD NEWS BEARS GO TO JAPAN, THE
1978, 91 mins, US Ⓥ ⊙
D: John Berry **A:** Tony Curtis, Jackie Earle Haley, Tomisaburo Wakayama, Hatsune Ishihara, George Wyner, Lonny Chapman (Paramount)

The dangers inherent in sequel making are clearly apparent in *The Bad News Bears Go to Japan,* third in the series of junior baseball antics that began with the smash *Bad News Bears* in 1976. The boys are taken in by yet another hustler, this time Tony Curtis as a Hollywood agent out for big bucks via promoting a game between the Bears and the Japanese all-star Little Leaguers. Formula is strictly standard, with Curtis inviting the enmity of the kids, with exception of moppet Scoody Thornton, only to be reformed before the final game. Japanese locations at least add a different look.

BAD SEED, THE
1956, 127 mins, US Ⓥ ⊙
D: Mervyn LeRoy **A:** Nancy Kelly, Patty McCormack, Henry Jones, Eileen Heckart, Evelyn Varden, William Hopper (Warner)

This melodrama about a child with an inbred talent for homicide is pretty unpleasant stuff on its own. The screenplay varies little from the [Maxwell] Anderson legit piece. Some of the casting is from the stage success, too, with young Patty McCormack as the innocent-looking murderess and Nancy Kelly as her distraught mother. Both are outstanding.
1956: Nominations: Best Actress (Nancy Kelly), Supp. Actress (Eileen Heckart, Patty McCormack), B&W Cinematography

BAD TIMING
1980, 123 mins, UK Ⓥ ⊙ ▱
D: Nicolas Roeg **A:** Art Garfunkel, Theresa Russell, Harvey Keitel, Denholm Elliott, Daniel Massey, Dana Gillespie (Recorded Picture/Rank)

Technically flashy and teeming with degenerate chic, this downbeat tale of two destructively selfish lovers is unrelieved by its tacked-on thriller ending, and deals purely in despair. Every scene is shot with at least one eye and one ear to the editing table: results are generally masterful but at times obtrusively pretentious. Director Nicolas Roeg's visual sense remains a peculiar talent.

BAILIFF, THE
See: Sansho Dayu

BAISERS VOLES
(STOLEN KISSES)
1968, 90 mins, France ⓥ
D: Francois Truffaut **A:** Jean-Pierre Leaud, Delphine Seyrig, Claude Jade, Michel Lonsdale, Daniel Ceccaldi, Claire Duhamel (Films du Carrosse/Artistes Associes)

That timid, yet engaging, adolescent of *The 400 Blows,* played again by Jean-Pierre Leaud, is now in his twenties and cashiered out of the military. He comes home to a series of jobs that carry him through adventures that encompass his final winning of a childhood girlfriend (Claude Jade) as his wife, plus his first amorous adventure with the wife (Delphine Seyrig) of one of the men (Michel Lonsdale) he works for. The slice-of-life pic also has neat slices of observation, tasteful presentation, and easeful acting that avoid banality.

LA BALANCE
1982, 102 mins, France ⓥ
D: Bob Swaim **A:** Nathalie Baye, Philippe Leotard, Richard Berry, Christophe Malavoy, Maurice Ronet, Tcheky Karyo (Ariane/Films A2)

La Balance is a taut, engrossing crime drama. Ironically, the film, with its purportedly factual overlay of details about contemporary Paris police and underworld mentalities, and its telling, unglossy use of the city, was written and directed by an American, Bob Swaim. His tale centers on the methods of plainclothes detective squads that operate in different sectors of the capital and rely heavily on a network of local informers to nip crime in the bud. The acting is especially fine, with the big surprise being Nathalie Baye, at last breaking out of a syndrome of wholesome roles; as the streetwise young whore, she is real and affecting.

BALCONY, THE
1963, 84 mins, US ⓥ ⊙
D: Joseph Strick **A:** Shelley Winters, Peter Falk, Lee Grant, Peter Brocco, Jeff Corey, Ruby Dee (Walter Reade-Sterling/Allen Hodgdon)

This is never an easy film to watch, but also it is never boring or pretentious, and often it is acidly funny. Most of the action, located in an unnamed city in the throes of a bloody revolution, takes place in a highly special kind of brothel, equipped like a movie studio with sets, costumes, rear projection devices, etc., which permit the patrons to enact their darkest fantasies (they can also pay with credit cards). Presiding over the macabre revels is Shelley Winters. The peace of the brothel is shattered with the arrival of the police chief, Peter Falk, the madame's occasional lover who is fighting a last-ditch stand outside to destroy the revolution.

1963: Nomination: B&W Cinematography

BALLADA O SOLDATYE
(BALLAD OF A SOLDIER)
1960, 85 mins, USSR ⓥ ⊙
D: Grigori Chukhrai **A:** Vladimir Ivashov, Zhanna Prokhorenko, Antonina Maksimova, Nikolai Kryuchkov, Yevgeni Urbanski (Mosfilm)

This is a war film done in a poetic style with a purportedly pacifistic outlook. A 19-year-old Russian soldier, during the last war, gets a four-day pass and sets out for his home to see his mother and fix the roof. But he gets into a series of adventures and manages to arrive home only for a few minutes to talk to his mother. On this slim thread, the director has woven a series of tender sketches emphasizing the lurking terror, uselessness, and hopelessness of war.

BALLAD OF A SOLDIER
See: Ballada O Soldatye

BALLAD OF CABLE HOGUE, THE
1970, 121 mins, US ⓥ ⊙
D: Sam Peckinpah **A:** Jason Robards, Stella Stevens, David Warner, Strother Martin, Slim Pickens, L. Q. Jones (Warner)

The Ballad of Cable Hogue is a Damon Runyonesque oater comedy from Sam Peckinpah. Jason Robards is the title character, a charming desert rat; Stella Stevens is the cowtown harlot with the heart of gold; and David Warner is a preacher of sorts.

BALLAD OF LITTLE JO, THE
1993, 120 mins, US Ⓥ ⊙
D: Maggie Greenwald **A:** Suzy Amis, Bo Hopkins, Ian McKellen, David Chung, Carrie Snodgress, Rene Auberjonois (Fine Line/PFE/JoJo)

Suzy Amis's superlative performance dominates every frame of *The Ballad of Little Jo,* an earnest drama about a woman who disguises herself as a man to survive hardship in the Old West. But this well-intentioned, revisionist frontier saga is too solemn and dramatically unexciting. Greenwald brings a contemporary feminist vision to the saga. But despite her efforts to demystify the Old West, she ends up mythologizing her heroine as a symbol of pioneering endurance.

BALLAD OF NARAYAMA, THE
See: Narayama Bushi-ko [1958]

BALLAD OF NARAYAMA, THE
See: Narayama Bushi-ko [1983]

BALLAD OF THE SAD CAFE, THE
1991, 100 mins, US/UK Ⓥ
D: Simon Callow **A:** Vanessa Redgrave, Keith Carradine, Cork Hubbert, Rod Steiger, Austin Pendleton, Beth Dixon (Merchant-Ivory/Film Four)

Simon Callow makes an assured feature directing debut adapting Carson McCullers's novella *The Ballad of the Sad Cafe,* a demanding, abstract fable.

Amelia (Vanessa Redgrave) is a violent, mannishly styled woman who threw out her husband (Keith Carradine) on their wedding night and has become a legendary figure in her little southern town in the 1930s. With cropped hair and unglamorous makeup, Redgrave throws herself into the role with uncensored force.

Carradine brings a naturalism to his embittered role as the ex-con and spurned spouse. Catalyst in the piece is the fantasy character of Cousin Lymon (Cork Hubbert), a hunchbacked dwarf who pops up out of nowhere claiming to be Redgrave's cousin.

BALL OF FIRE
1941, 110 mins, US Ⓥ ⊙
D: Howard Hawks **A:** Gary Cooper, Barbara Stanwyck, Oscar Homolka, Dana Andrews, Dan Duryea, Henry Travers (RKO/Samuel Goldwyn)

Gag on which the whole thing is based is Gary Cooper's professorial efforts to write a learned piece on slang for an encyclopedia. He needs, for research purposes, someone who's hep to the last syllable of the lingo and brings into a sanctum, where he and seven colleagues are working on the encyclopedia, a burlesque stripper (Barbara Stanwyck). She upsets and excites the eight old men in the expected manner. Much of the dialogue is rapid-fire slang, plenty labored, but frequently good for laughs.

1941: Nominations: Best Actress (Barbara Stanwyck), Original Story, Scoring of a Dramatic Picture, Sound

BALTIMORE BULLET, THE
1980, 103 mins, US Ⓥ
D: Robert Ellis Miller **A:** James Coburn, Omar Sharif, Bruce Boxleitner, Ronee Blakely, Jack O'Halloran, Calvin Lockhart (Avco Embassy)

James Coburn and Bruce Boxleitner limn a kind of father-son pool-hustling team who make their living traveling through the country taking advantage of local would-be billiard sharks. Ronee Blakely is picked up by the pair along the way for moral support and fulfills the limited duties asked of her. Situations are just too inane to take seriously and not funny enough to be laughed at.

BALTO
1995, 77 mins, US Ⓥ
D: Simon Wells **A:** Miriam Margolyes, Lola Bates-Campbell (Amblin/Universal)

Balto is an average, at best, animated yarn. Live-action wraparounds help frame the story of Balto (voiced by Kevin Bacon), a stray half dog, half wolf who helps guide a sled carrying medication to a town full of sick kids in Alaska. The villain, Steele (Jim Cummings), deeply resents Balto, vying with him for the affection of Jenna (Bridget Fonda). Balto has an assortment of friends that includes a Russian goose named Boris (Bob Hoskins) and two landlocked polar bears, Muk and Luk (Phil Collins). Director Simon Wells and a quartet of writers fall flat with much of the humor, only occasionally delivering laughs. James Horner's blaring score does work overtime to create a sense of excitement.

BAMBI
1942, 70 mins, US Ⓥ ⊙
D: David Hand (Walt Disney)

Bambi is gemlike in its reflection of the color and movement of sylvan plant and animal life. The transcription of nature in its moments of turbulence and peace heightens the brilliance of the canvas. The story is full of tenderness and the characters tickle the heart. Thumper, the rabbit, steals the picture. It's a regret that there wasn't much more of him in the picture. In this story of Bambi and his friends of the forest, the span of the central character is from birth to the period when he reaches full buckhood. The dramatic highlights of Bambi's career include the death of his mother by gunshot (a scene of deep pathos) and his fight to the death with another buck over the doe Faline.

1942: Nominations: Best Scoring of a Dramatic Picture, Song (''Love Is a Song''), Sound

BANANAS
1971, 82 mins, US ⓥ ⊙
D: Woody Allen **A:** Woody Allen, Louise Lasser, Carlos Montalban, Natividad Abascal, Jacobo Morales, Miguel Suarez (United Artists)

Bananas is chock-full of sight gags, one-liners, and swiftly executed unnecessary excursions into vulgarity whose humor for the most part can't make up for content. Woody Allen, as bumbling New Yorker working for an automation film, is rejected by his activist sweetheart Louise Lasser who is involved in revolutions, particularly in fictional San Marcos, where dictator Carlos Montalban has seized control. Allen, disconsolate, bids farewell to parents Charlotte Rae and Stanley Ackerman while they are performing a medical operation. Landing in San Marcos, he is feted by Montalban, who is setting him up as a pigeon to be erased supposedly by revolutionary Jacobo Morales's men.

BANDIDO
1956, 91 mins, US ▭
D: Richard Fleischer **A:** Robert Mitchum, Ursula Thiess, Gilbert Roland, Zachary Scott, Rodolfo Acosta, Henry Brandon (Bandido/United Artists)

Gunrunning in Mexico back in 1916 sets up a round of adventurous action. Robert Mitchum is a likable, not-always-understandable sort of hero-heavy who likes war because it gives him a chance to make some money gunrunning, besides finding amusement. The male end of the cast draws notable help from the presence of Gilbert Roland, leader of the rebels for whom the gunrunner is trying to obtain arms by hijacking a shipment being brought in by Zachary Scott for the Regulares.

BANDITI A ORGOSOLO (THE BANDITS OF ORGOSOLO)
1961, 98 mins, Italy
D: Vittorio De Seta **A:** Michele Cossu, Peppeddu Cuccu, Vittorina Pisano (Titanus)

Fine initial effort by young Italian filmmaker Vittorio De Seta, *Orgosolo* tells of vain efforts of a Sardinian shepherd to escape from his fate. He is unjustly involved in a theft-and-murder episode, with the police hunting him and his flock of sheep over hill and valley. Animals die and the shepherd, already partly resigned, accompanies his brother to the village where they lived. Then he takes to the hills again, where circumstances now force him to steal others' sheep and become what to the outside world is merely a bandit. Pace is keyed to setting and people, slow and not overly talkative.

BANDIT OF SHERWOOD FOREST, THE
1946, 85 mins, US
D: George Sherman, Henry Levin **A:** Cornel Wilde, Anita Louise, Jill Esmond, Edgar Buchanan, George Macready, Henry Daniell (Columbia)

Technicolor spectacle of high adventure in Sherwood Forest. It's a costume western, in effect, offering the fictional escapades of the son of Robin Hood, a hard-riding, hard-loving hombre who uses his trusty bow and arrow to right injustice and tyranny back in the days of feudal England. There is considerable ineptness in writing, production, and direction but it still stands up as okay escapist film fare for the not-too-critical. Wilde is properly swashbuckling as the hero.

BANDIT QUEEN
1994, 121 mins, India/UK ⓥ
D: Shekhar Kapur **A:** Seema Biswas, Nirmal Pandey, Manoj Bajpai, Rajesh Vivek, Govind Namdeo, Saurabh Shukla (Kaleidoscope/Channel 4)

True story of a femme bandit who eluded the Indian authorities for five years makes initially leisurely but finally gripping viewing. Phoolan Devi finally surrendered to the police in January 1983, accused of murder and kidnapping. Pic is based on the dictated prison diaries of the woman herself, who, after a change of government, was finally released in February 1994 to local superstar status. Comprehension isn't helped by sometimes choppy editing in the early going, but once the story moves into high gear, helmer

Shekhar Kapur brings out his big guns to often stunning effect. Biswas is terrific in the title role, moving from tough to tender with natural ease.

BANDITS OF ORGOSOLO, THE
See: Banditi a Orgosolo

BAND OF ANGELS
1957, 125 mins, US
D: Raoul Walsh A: Clark Gable, Yvonne De Carlo, Sidney Poitier, Efrem Zimbalist Jr., Patric Knowles, Carolle Drake (Warner)

Subject of miscegenation is explored and developed in this colorful production of the Old South which deals with a young woman of quality discovering that her mother was a slave. Beautiful and realistic backgrounds are achieved through locationing in Louisiana. Clark Gable's characterization is reminiscent of his Rhett Butler in *Gone with the Wind,* although there is obviously no paralleling of plot. As former slave runner turned New Orleans gentleman, with bitter memories of his earlier days, he contributes a warm, decisive portrayal that carries tremendous authority. Yvonne De Carlo is beautiful as the mulatto. Sidney Poitier impresses as Gable's educated protégé.

BANDOLERO!
1968, 107 mins, US ⓥ ▭
D: Andrew V. McLaglen A: James Stewart, Dean Martin, Raquel Welch, George Kennedy, Andrew Prine, Will Geer (20th Century-Fox)

Bandolero! is a dull western meller. Dean Martin heads an outlaw group which includes Will Geer, Tom Heaton, Sean McClory, and Clint Ritchie. Pretitle bank heist, in which Raquel Welch's husband is killed, lands the group in George Kennedy's jail, awaiting hanging by itinerant executioner Guy Raymond. Stewart, Martin's older brother, takes Raymond's place in order to effect gang's escape. Welch is got up to look like a Mexican Sophia Loren. Her makeup is distressingly false looking, her accent more so.

BAND WAGON, THE
1953, 112 mins, US ⓥ ⊙
D: Vincente Minnelli A: Fred Astaire, Cyd Charisse, Oscar Levant, Nanette Fabray, Jack Buchanan, James Mitchell (M-G-M)

Plot is the one about a dancing film star whose pictures aren't selling. A couple of writing pals conceive a stage musical for him and the rest of the story is concerned with making the show a success after a flop tryout and weeks of rewriting and new starts. Twelve songs from various Broadway musicals are either chirped or terped. Showing up as an imaginative highlight is "Girl Hunt," the modern-jazz-ballet finale done to a turn by Fred Astaire and Cyd Charisse. A takeoff in dance on the Mickey Spillane type of private eye, the number is a new cleffing for the picture by Howard Dietz and Arthur Schwartz, credited with all of the songs.
1953: Nominations: Best Story & Screenplay, Color Costume Design, Scoring of a Musical Picture

BANK BREAKER, THE
See: Kaleidoscope

BANK DETECTIVE, THE
See: The Bank Dick

BANK DICK, THE
1940, 69 mins, US ⓥ ⊙
D: Edward Cline A: W. C. Fields, Cora Witherspoon, Una Merkel, Jessie Ralph, Franklin Pangborn, Grady Sutton (Universal)

Story is credited to Mahatma Kane Jeeves, Fields's own humorous nom de plume. It's a deliberate rack on which to hang the varied Fieldsian comedic routines. The unexpected hero of a bank robbery, he is rewarded with the job of detective to guard against future holdups. He involves his prospective son-in-law as a temporary embezzler to buy wildcat mining stock, and then holds off the bank examiner via the Mickey Finn route. Repeat bank robbery again results in Fields accepting hero honors, the reward, and sudden riches from a film directing contract. Several times Fields reaches into satirical pantomime reminiscent of Charlie Chaplin's best efforts during his Mutual and Essanay days. Directorial guidance by Cline (graduate of the Keystone Kop school) smacks over every gag line and situation to the fullest extent.

BANK HOLIDAY
1938, 86 mins, UK
D: Carol Reed A: John Lodge, Margaret Lockwood, Hugh Williams, Rene Ray, Linden Travers, Merle Tottenham (Gainsborough)

A young nurse, Catherine (Margaret Lockwood), has planned to spend an illicit weekend with a man. Her patient dies in childbirth and her pity for the forlorn husband changes her whole life. In the hectic rush of London's termini, she joins her waiting lover. The tragedy she has left behind mars her pleasure; she flees her lover and saves the widower from suicide. Interspersed are many rich characters: a Cockney family with squabbling kids, two young soldiers on leave, entrants for a beauty prize, one trying to get over a jilt, another aping society and making all the judges. None is overdrawn and all are depicted with human interest.

BARABBAS
1962, 144 mins, Italy ⊛ ⊙
D: Richard Fleischer **A:** Anthony Quinn, Silvana Mangano, Arthur Kennedy, Jack Palance, Vittorio Gassman, Ernest Borgnine (De Laurentiis)

The film tells the story of Barabbas, thief and murderer, who was replaced, in jail and on the Cross, by Jesus Christ. Barabbas's conscience plagues him. In a struggling, almost bovine manner he tries to find the truth about the new wave of faith that is sweeping the country. Where the film hits the bell is in Fleischer's bold, dramatic handling of certain scenes, allied to some slick lensing by Aldo Tonti. The scenes in the Rome gladiatorial pit, sharply etched by Jack Palance as the top boy, have an urgent excitement, with Palance's sadism matched only by Quinn's bewildered concentration. Quinn is first-class in a role which could have become monotonous.

BARBARELLA
1968, 98 mins, France/Italy ⊛ ⊙ ⊡
D: Roger Vadim **A:** Jane Fonda, John Phillip Law, Anita Pallenberg, Milo O'Shea, David Hemmings, Marcel Marceau (Marianne/De Laurentiis)

Based on what has been called an adult comic strip, the production is flawed with a cast that is not particularly adept at comedy, a flat script, and direction that can't get this beached whale afloat. Jane Fonda stars in the title role, and comes across as an ice-cold, antiseptic, wide-eyed girl who just can't say no. Fonda's abilities are stretched to the breaking point along with her clothes. John Phillip Law is inept as a simp angel, while Anita Pallenberg, as the lesbian queen, fares better because of a well-defined character.

BARBARIAN AND THE GEISHA, THE
1958, 105 mins, US ⊛ ⊡
D: John Huston **A:** John Wayne, Eiko Ando, Sam Jaffe, So Yamamura, Morita, Hiroshi Yamato (20th Century-Fox)

The Barbarian and the Geisha is an Oriental pageant of primitive beauty based on the true story of the exploits of the first US consul to establish headquarters in Japan. Japan was a forbidden kingdom to outsiders in 1856 when US consul-general Townsend Harris (John Wayne) arrived under orders to open the door on the hermetically sealed country, armed only with his own personality and accompanied only by his European translator (Sam Jaffe). Wayne gains the confidence of the local noble (Soh Yamamura) who, to make Wayne's isolation easier, delivers a geisha (Eiko Ando) to the non-Nipponese barbarian.

BARBAROSA
1982, 90 mins, US ⊛ ⊡
D: Fred Schepisi **A:** Willie Nelson, Gary Busey, Isela Vega, Gilbert Roland, Danny De La Paz, Alma Martinez (Universal/Associated)

Australian director Fred Schepisi does a careful job of bringing the western legend to light with endearing performances from actors Willie Nelson and Gary Busey. Nelson limns the renowned title character, who in essence is nothing more than a sensitive outlaw forever eluding the assassination attempts of his wife's overprotective family.

BARBARY COAST
1935, 97 mins, US ⊛ ⊙
D: Howard Hawks **A:** Miriam Hopkins, Edward G. Robinson, Joel McCrea, Walter Brennan, Frank Craven, Brian Donlevy (Goldwyn/United Artists)

Sam Goldwyn picked *Barbary Coast* as a title and called in Ben Hecht and Charles MacArthur to write a story to fit. Result is a picture that has all it takes to get along in thoroughbred company. Miriam Hopkins arrives in Frisco to meet the man she is going to marry. Learning he has been killed over a gambling loss, she throws herself toward Edward G. Robinson, the town's underworld leader. Story makes Hopkins a partially unsympathetic character until she falls in love with a young prospector. It is mostly Hopkins's picture but Robinson and Joel McCrea are also strong.
1935: Nomination: Best Cinematography

BARB WIRE
1996, 99 mins, US ⊛ ⊙
D: David Hogan **A:** Pamela Anderson Lee, Temuera Morrison, Victoria Rowell, Jack Noseworthy, Xander Berkely, Udo

Kier (Propaganda/Dark Horse/PolyGram)

If not a great action film, this cartoon-like starring vehicle for Pamela Anderson Lee offers enough choreographed fight sequences, heavy artillery, and fleeting glimpses of the star's august body parts to satisfy the raging hormones of its target young male audience. Pic is set in the year 2017, in the midst of America's second civil war, in Steel Harbor, home of a sneaky yet stylish joint called the Hammerhead Bar & Grille, owned by the aloof and amoral Barb Wire (Lee). *Barb Wire* is a ride that is definitely fun while it lasts.

BARCELONA
1994, 100 mins, US Ⓥ ⊙
D: Whit Stillman **A:** Taylor Nichols, Chris Eigeman, Tushka Bergen, Mira Sorvino, Pep Munne, Nuria Badia (Westly/Castle Rock)

A verbal tale of two well-spoken American men posted in the beautiful seaport city during what is described as the last decade of the cold war, this sophisticated picture possesses a strong authorial voice and an appealing intelligence in its handling of affairs of the heart and its Americans-abroad theme. Perhaps the film's most singular achievement is the portrayal of the manifold ways from subtle to overt in which anti-American sentiments were vented overseas during a certain period in the seventies and eighties.

BAREFOOT CONTESSA, THE
1954, 128 mins, US Ⓥ
D: Joseph L. Mankiewicz **A:** Humphrey Bogart, Ava Gardner, Edmond O'Brien, Marius Goring, Valentina Cortese, Rossano Brazzi (United Artists/Figaro)

Sharpness of the characters, the high-voltage dialogue, the cynicism and wit and wisdom of the story, the spectacular combination of the immorally rich and the immorally sycophantic—these add up to a click feature from writer-director Joseph L. Mankiewicz. Ava Gardner is the contessa of the title, discovered in a second-rate flamenco nitery in Madrid. The trio of discoverers: Humphrey Bogart as a writer-director and determined member of Alcoholics Anonymous; Edmond O'Brien, as a glib, nervous, perspiring combination of press agent and (apparent) procurer; and Warren Stevens, the rich producer.
1954: Best Supp. Actor (Edmond O'Brien)
Nomination: Best Story & Screenplay

BAREFOOT IN THE PARK
1967, 104 mins, US Ⓥ ⊙
D: Gene Saks **A:** Robert Redford, Jane Fonda, Charles Boyer, Mildred Natwick, Herb Edelman, Mabel Albertson (Paramount)

Adapted by Neil Simon from his stage smash, retaining Robert Redford and Mildred Natwick from the original cast, and adding Jane Fonda and Charles Boyer to round out the principals, this is a thoroughly entertaining comedy delight about young marriage. Redford is outstanding, particularly adept in light comedy. Fonda is excellent, ditto Natwick, her mother. A genuine surprise casting is Boyer, as the bohemian who lives in the attic above the newlyweds top-floor flat.
1967: Nomination: Best Supp. Actress (Mildred Natwick)

BARFLY
1987, 99 mins, US Ⓥ ⊙
D: Barbet Schroeder **A:** Mickey Rourke, Faye Dunaway, Alice Krige, Jack Nance, J. C. Quinn, Frank Stallone (Coppola/Cannon)

Barfly is a low-life fairy tale, an ethereal seriocomedy about gutter existence from the pen of one who's been there, Charles Bukowski, spiked with unexpected doses of humor, much of it due to Mickey Rourke's quirky, unpredictable, most engaging performance as the boozy hero. He meets a terribly attractive fellow alcoholic, Wanda (Faye Dunaway), who immediately takes him in and keeps him well plied with drink and sex, to the extent they are both interested in and capable of the latter.

BARKLEYS OF BROADWAY, THE
1949, 102 mins, US Ⓥ ⊙
D: Charles Walters **A:** Fred Astaire, Ginger Rogers, Oscar Levant, Billie Burke, Gale Robbins, George Zucco (M-G-M)

With Fred Astaire and Ginger Rogers *The Barkleys of Broadway* is an ace dance fest. The screen's most complementary dance team glides through five dance numbers with the grace and apparent spontaneity that is their trademark when appearing together. Sixth dance number is done solo by Astaire. It is the combination of special effects and Astaire hoofing in a dance that spellbinds into standout terping. Plot is a more or less standard story of a Broadway star team of man and wife who have a misunderstanding, separate, and then get back together for the finale.

1949: Nomination: Best Color Cinematography

BARQUERO
1970, 108 mins, US
D: Gordon Douglas **A:** Lee Van Cleef, Forrest Tucker, Warren Oates, Kerwin Mathews, Mariette Hartley, Marie Gomez (United Artists)

Barquero is a taut, bloody-as-a-slaughterhouse western morality play with Lee Van Cleef as the fierce pioneering individualist pitted against Warren Oates, the personification of evil dressed all in black. Oates is the twitchy, sadistic leader of a band of mercenaries from the Mexican Revolution. Van Cleef is the barquero who has hand-built and operates a primitive ferry across a river.

BARRETTS OF WIMPOLE STREET, THE
1934, 110 mins, US ♥ ☉
D: Sidney Franklin **A:** Norma Shearer, Fredric March, Charles Laughton, Maureen O'Sullivan, Katherine Alexander, Una O'Connor (M-G-M)

The romance between Elizabeth Barrett (Norma Shearer) and Robert Browning (Fredric March) is a beautiful exposition in its ethereal and physically rehabilitating effect on the ailing Barrett. The unnatural love of Papa Barrett is graphically depicted by Charles Laughton, as the psychopathic, hateful character whose twisted affections for his children, especially daughter Elizabeth, almost prove her physical and spiritual undoing. The confining locale of London's Wimpole Street in 1845 limits the action to the interior of the Barretts' home, but the general persuasiveness of all the histrionics achieves much in offsetting the lack of physical action.
1934: Nominations: Best Picture, Actress (Norma Shearer)

BARRETTS OF WIMPOLE STREET, THE
1957, 104 mins, US/UK ▭
D: Sidney Franklin **A:** Jennifer Jones, John Gielgud, Bill Travers, Virginia McKenna, Jean Anderson, Vernon Gray (M-G-M)

Sidney Franklin, who directed the original screen version starring Norma Shearer and Fredric March, helms this production. Jennifer Jones, while a surprisingly healthy-looking Elizabeth, plays the invalid literary figure with great skill. Bill Travers's Browning, the vigorous, colorful poet who managed to court and win the delicate Elizabeth under the nose of her despotic father, is personable and competent enough. John Gielgud, the father with an almost incestuous attachment for his daughter, repeats the role originally done by Charles Laughton with all the stern menace it requires.

BARRY LYNDON
1975, 184 mins, UK ♥ ☉
D: Stanley Kubrick **A:** Ryan O'Neal, Marisa Berenson, Patrick Magee, Hardy Kruger, Gay Hamilton, Leonard Rossiter (Hawk/Warner)

Stanley Kubrick's series of film morality plays continues with *Barry Lyndon,* a most elegant and handsome adaptation of William Makepiece Thackeray's 19th-century novel. Ryan O'Neal's excellent performance captures the shallow opportunism of the title character. Kubrick's outstanding landscapes in rich, cool tones overpower the antlike people crawling about; his interiors, hot and uncomfortable despite their plushness, seem unnatural in contrast. This cinematic mural bears repeated and sustained watching without ever really commanding and demanding acute attention.
1975: Best Cinematography, Art Direction, Costume Design, Adapted Scoring
Nominations: Best Picture, Director, Adapted Screenplay

BARTLEBY
1971, 78 mins, UK ♥ ☉
D: Anthony Friedmann **A:** Paul Scofield, John McEnery, Thorley Walters, Colin Jeavons, Raymond Mason, Charles Kinross (Pantheon)

Bartleby is virtually a duel between Scofield and John McEnery, who plays a young audit clerk, a fallout from society. He gets a job with Scofield, who patiently employs him but is astounded at the young man's attitude. Very politely he insists that he "prefers not to do" this or that. Baffled, Scofield does everything possible to get through to the young man but is thwarted and eventually, irritated, fires him. But Bartleby prefers not to go. This modestly budgeted picture, from Herman Melville's story, is intriguing because of the two main performances.

BARTON FINK
1991, 116 mins, US ♥ ☉
D: Joel Coen **A:** John Turturro, John Goodman, Judy Davis, Michael Lerner, John Mahoney (20th Century-Fox/Circle)

Hermetic tale of a genius playwright's brief stint as a studio contract writer is a painstakingly miniaturist work that can be read any number of ways. Title character, played with a creepily growing sense of dread by John Turturro, is a gravely serious New York dramatist. In Hollywood he is assigned a Wallace Beery wrestling programmer. Scene after scene is filled with a ferocious strength and humor. Michael Lerner's performance as a Mayer-like studio overlord is sensational. Goodman is marvelous as the folksy neighbor, rolling his tongue around pages of wonderful dialogue. Judy Davis nicely etches a woman who has a way with difficult writers, and John Mahoney turns up as a near dead ringer for William Faulkner in his Hollywood period.

1991: Nominations: Best Supp. Actor (Michael Lerner), Art Direction, Costume Design

BASIC INSTINCT
1992, 127 mins, US Ⓥ ⊙ ▭
D: Paul Verhoeven **A:** Michael Douglas, Sharon Stone, George Dzundza, Jeanne Tripplehorn, Denis Arndt, Leilani Sarelle (Carolco/Canal Plus)

Basic Instinct is grade-A pulp fiction. This erotically charged thriller about the search for an ice-pick murderer in San Francisco rivets attention through its sleek style, attractive cast doing and thinking kinky things, and story, which is as weirdly implausible as it is intensely visceral. Tale gets off to a slambang start when, at the peak of mutual sexual excitement, an unidentifiable blonde ties up her lover's hands and does him in. Back on the streets of San Francisco, detective Michael Douglas and partner George Dzundza head up the coast to quiz the dead man's g.f., the fabulously wealthy and sexy Sharon Stone, who has published a novel in which an identical murder is depicted. The very tough and ice-cold Stone quickly begins tantalizing Douglas, who has recently gone cold turkey off cigarettes, booze, drugs, and sex.

1992: Nominations: Best Editing, Original Score

BASIL THE GREAT MOUSE DETECTIVE
See: The Great Mouse Detective

BASKETBALL DIARIES, THE
1995, 102 mins, US Ⓥ
D: Scott Kalvert **A:** Leonardo DiCaprio, Bruno Kirby, Lorraine Bracco, Ernie Hudson, Patrick McGaw, Juliette Lewis (Island)

The Basketball Diaries is a weak-tea rendition of Jim Carroll's much-admired cult tome about his teenage drug addiction. Leonardo DiCaprio's Jim Carroll is part of a mischievous quartet of boys, three of whom form the nucleus of the hottest Catholic hoopsters in Gotham. Jim's descent into mad-dog heroin addiction is presented as a road cleared by recreational cocaine indulgence and an idiotic use of downers right before a basketball game, which gets him and his buddy Mickey (Mark Wahlberg) kicked off the team and briefly expelled from school, and also leads to Jim's being booted out by his hardworking mother (Lorraine Bracco). From there the story becomes a tour through hell that's been visited before by any number of films and often in more compelling fashion.

BASKET CASE
1982, 90 mins, US Ⓥ ⊙
D: Frank Henenlotter **A:** Kevin Van Hentenryck, Terri Susan Smith, Beverly Bonner, Robert Vogel, Diana Browne, Lloyd Pace (Ievens-Henenlotter)

Basket Case is an ultracheap monster film created with a tongue-in-cheek approach. Picture concerns a young man Duane (Kevin Van Hentenryck) who comes to the Big Apple carrying a large wicker basket. A lengthy mid-film flashback reveals he is seeking out revenge, carried out by his Siamese-twin monstrous brother Belial (residing in the basket), killing off the three doctors who separated them surgically at age 10. Acting styles vary (creating intentional camp humor), but the leads are fine. Tech credits are a drawback, particularly the variable sound recording, grainy blowup from 16mm, and shrill musical score.

BASKET CASE 2
1990, 89 mins, US Ⓥ ⊙
D: Frank Henenlotter **A:** Kevin Van Hentenryck, Annie Ross, Kathryn Meisle, Heather Rattray, Matt Mitler, Ted Sorel (Shapiro Glickenhaus)

Basket Case 2 is a hilarious genre spoof. Here Frank Henenlotter's paying homage to Tod Browning's 1932 classic Freaks. Annie Ross as Granny Ruth is a crusader for the rights of unique individuals (i.e. freaks) and welcomes the Siamese-twin brothers Kevin and Belial into her home in Staten Island. Weird menagerie of youngsters, mostly crazy variations on the Elephant Man by makeup whiz Gabe Bartalos, are treated very sympathetically at first, but as in Browning's film their potential for scaring the audience also is exploited. Casting coup is Annie Ross, the legendary jazz singer, who is a lot of fun as the demented granny who goads her freakish charges to fight back.

BASKET CASE 3
THE PROGENY
1992, 90 mins, US Ⓥ

D: Frank Henenlotter **A:** Annie Ross, Kevin Van Hentenryck, Dan Biggers, Gil Roper, Tina Louise Hilbert, James O'Doherty (Shapiro Glickenhaus)

Henenlotter's mix of wild overacting, cartoon color scheme, and heavy-handed message regarding tolerance is tough to take for the uninitiated. His fans will enjoy seeing the growing menagerie of creatures, including the cute/grotesque progeny. Van Hentenryck acts way over the top, while Ross literally dominates the film with her intensity and gets to lead the monsters in a singalong of the golden oldie "Personality." Heroine Hilbert makes a good impression in a Jekyll and Hyde role. Creature effects are quite inventive.

BASTARD OUT OF CAROLINA
1996, 97 mins, US Ⓥ

D: Anjelica Huston **A:** Jennifer Jason Leigh, Ron Eldard, Jena Malone, Glenne Headly, Lyle Lovett, Dermot Mulroney (TNT)

An absorbing, sometimes wrenching tale of growing up poor and abused in the 1950s south, *Bastard out of Carolina* is a quality item, with nonexploitative handling of potent material, strong work by debuting helmer Anjelica Huston, and striking perfs from young newcomer Jena Malone, Jennifer Jason Leigh, and others. Story looks behind Tobacco Road clichés to evoke the complex weave of love, hardship, and family bonds that conditioned the life of poor whites in the days before New South prosperity kicked in. Anne Meredith's script preserves the key ingredients of the tale while skillfully imposing dramatic structure and economy.

BAT, THE
1926, 91 mins, US Ⓥ

D: Roland West **A:** Tullio Carminati, Jewel Carmen, Louise Fazenda, Emily Fitzroy, Arthur Houseman, Jack Pickford (West/United Artists)

The mystery concerns the death of a bank president, the theft of $200,000, the disappearance of the young cashier, and the mysterious criminal whose sign is the shadow of bat projected from the front of an electric flashlight. This criminal is behind a thousand suspicious actions but meantime, every member of the cast is suspected of having been the culprit. An Italian actor named Tullio Carminati gives a performance as the detective that is one of the best things done by a newcomer to the screen. Louise Fazenda draws her share of laughs with the hokey maid's part, while Eddie Gribbon is good for a giggle or so as the hick detective.

BATAAN
1943, 113 mins, US Ⓥ

D: Tay Garnett **A:** Robert Taylor, George Murphy, Thomas Mitchell, Robert Nolan, Robert Walker, Desi Arnaz (M-G-M)

Bataan is a melodramatic reenactment of the last-ditch stand of an American patrol detailed to guard a road in the Philippines following the evacuation of Manila. Picture pulls no punches in displaying the realistically grim warfare.

Robert Taylor gives a strong performance as the commanding sergeant, but picture focuses attention on screen debut of Robert Walker, who smacks over an arresting portrayal as the sensitive and sympathetic young sailor who attaches himself to the outfit to get a crack at the Japs.

LA BATAILLE DU RAIL
(BATTLE OF THE RAILS)
1946, 90 mins, France

D: Rene Clement **A:** Jean Daurand, Tony Laurent, Clarieux, Jacques Desagneaux, Leray, Lozach (Cooperative Generale)

A lengthy documentary recording the bitter fight which French railway workers waged against the Germans, *Rails* primarily offers audiences a bird's-eye view of how French transportation employees utilized sabotage to obstruct the Nazis from securing maximum advantages from the Gallic railway system. However, in an effort to overly emphasize the workers' resistance, the glorification of the trainmen frequently steps beyond the bounds of logic.

BATHING BEAUTY
1944, 102 mins, US Ⓥ ⊙

D: George Sidney **A:** Red Skelton, Esther Williams, Basil Rathbone, Bill Goodwin, Ethel Smith, Jean Porter (M-G-M)

Bathing Beauty is produced in the lush, lavish, manner that is as familiar as the Metro trademark. Esther Williams is pulled to stardom by her swimsuit straps. The former swimming champ displays her aquatic and acting abilities in the role of a collegienne who travels the rocky road of love with songwriter Red Skelton. Skelton is his usual effervescent self. His two specialty numbers are especially funny: one, where he attends a ballet dancing class with the girls of the school, dressed in a short, fluffy, pink dress with dancing slippers; the other, his impression of a gal getting up in the morning, prettying herself and dressing. Water-ballet costumes by Irene Sharaff, and the water ballet, produced under the supervision of John Murray Anderson, are memorable.

BATMAN
1966, 105 mins, US ⑰ ⊙
D: Leslie Martinson **A:** Adam West, Burt Ward, Lee Merriwether, Cesar Romero, Burgess Meredith, Frank Gorshin (20th Century-Fox)

Batman is packed with action, clever sight gags, interesting complications, and goes all out with batmania: batplane, batboat, batcycle, etc. Humor is stretched to the limit, color is comic-strip sharp, and script retrieves every trick from the highly popular teleseries oatbag, adding a few more sophisticated touches. It's Batman and Robin against his four arch-enemies, Catwoman, the Joker, the Penguin, and the Riddler. Quartet have united and are out to take over the world.

BATMAN
1989, 126 mins, US ⑰ ⊙
D: Tim Burton **A:** Michael Keaton, Jack Nicholson, Kim Basinger, Robert Wuhl, Pat Hingle, Billy Dee Williams (Guber-Peters/Warner)

Director Tim Burton effectively echoes the visual style of the original Bob Kane comics while conjuring up a nightmarish world of his own. Going back to the source elements of the cartoon figure, the production will appeal to purists. In a striking departure from his usual amiable comic style, Michael Keaton captures the haunted intensity of the character, and seems particularly lonely and obsessive without Robin around to share his exploits. The gorgeous Kim Basinger takes the sidekick's place, in a determined bow to heterosexuality which nonetheless leaves Batman something less than enthusiastic. It comes as no surprise that Jack Nicholson steals every scene in a sizable role as the hideously disfigured Joker. What keeps the film arresting is the visual

stylization. It was a shrewd choice for Burton to emulate the jarring angles and creepy lighting of film noir.
1989: Best Art Direction

BATMAN & ROBIN
1997, 130 mins, US ⊙
D: Joel Schumacher **A:** Arnold Schwarzenegger, George Clooney, Chris O'Donnell, Uma Thurman, Alicia Silverstone, Michael Gough (Warner)

Batman loses altitude and velocity in this fourth installment of Warner Bros.' hugely successful series. The villains, Arnold Schwarzenegger and especially Uma Thurman, remain the highlights here, as the rest of the gargantuan production lacks the dash and excitement that would have given the franchise a boost. Narrative drive and humor are also in short supply. The black-caped duo battle Mr. Freeze (Schwarzenegger), a warrior bedecked in climate-controlled armor for whom revenge is the word, as it is for a nerdy horticulturalist (Thurman) who emerges from a near-fatal incident in the curvy form of an outrageously sexy vamp, Poison Ivy. Midsection is woefully low on conflict and incident. The climax is a protracted sequence as thunderously numbing as that of any other $100 million film in recent memory.

BATMAN FOREVER
1995, 121 mins, US ⑰ ⊙
D: Joel Schumacher **A:** Val Kilmer, Tommy Lee Jones, Jim Carrey, Nicole Kidman, Chris O'Donnell, Michael Gough (Warner)

An enormous fun-house ride, the second *Batman* sequel succeeds on some basic levels while coming up short on others. On the plus side, the tone has lightened up after criticism of the last outing, Val Kilmer seamlessly slides into the Dark Knight's cape, and the film boasts considerable action and visual splendor. In the negative column, that action isn't as involving as it should be, and there are so many characters the movie can't adequately service them all. Two-Face (Tommy Lee Jones)—a onetime district attorney gone bad after being scarred by acid—terrorizes Gotham. After grappling with Two-Face and his minions, Batman encounters a criminal psychologist, Dr. Chase Meridian (Nicole Kidman), with her own designs on Gotham's hero. That ongoing romance overlaps with the introduction of Dick Grayson (Chris O'Donnell), a teenage circus acrobat who is taken in

by Batman alter ego Bruce Wayne. A final thread involves Jim Carrey's transformation from an addled inventor into the villainous Riddler. Carrey continues the tradition of villainous scene-stealing in the Batman movies, and overshadows Jones, who aside from a wild cackle has little to do.
1995: Nominations: Cinematography, Best Sound, Best Sound Effects Editing

BATMAN RETURNS
1992, 126 mins, US Ⓥ ⊙
D: Tim Burton **A:** Michael Keaton, Danny DeVito, Michelle Pfeiffer, Christopher Walken, Michael Gough, Cristi Conaway (Warner)

Many nonfans of *Batman* will find this sequel superior in several respects. Batman's new foes, Penguin and Catwoman, are both fascinating creations, wonderfully played. Much of the film is massively inventive and spiked with fresh, perverse humor. On the performance side, the deck is stacked entirely in favor of the villains. Briskly waddling, cawing his rude remarks, and conveying decades' worth of resentment and bitterness, DeVito makes Penguin very much his own. Endearingly klutzy initially as Selina, Pfeiffer looks amazing in her skintight, S&M-like leather skin. Wild-maned Walken has the right comic understatement and sangfroid as Shreck, an in-joke on the German actor Max Schreck (1922's *Nosferatu*).
1992: Nominations: Best Makeup, Visual Effects

LA BATTAGLIA DI ALGERI
(THE BATTLE OF ALGIERS)
1966, 122 mins, Italy/Algeria Ⓥ ⊙ ▱
D: Gillo Pontecorvo **A:** Jean Martin, Yacef Saadi, Brahim Haggiag, Tommaso Neri, Fawzia El-Kader, Michele Kerbash (Igor/Casbah)

Graphic, straightforward, realistic reenactment of the events that led to the birth of a free Algerian nation. Backdrop of documentarylike treatment of Algerian strife between 1954 and final liberation in 1962 is shown via restaging skillfully blended with newsreel clips. Gray reel quality gives pic an authentic flavor throughout, and adds to dramatic impact of many of its sequences. Up front, but not as spotlit as in usual pix of this kind, are some key characters drawn from life but guided here to heighten dramatic effect. There are no stars and there is no glamour.

*BATTERIES NOT INCLUDED
1987, 106 mins, US Ⓥ ⊙
D: Matthew Robbins **A:** Hume Cronyn, Jessica Tandy, Frank McRae, Elizabeth Pena, Michael Carmine, Dennis Boutsikaris (Universal/Amblin)

*Batteries Not Included could have used more imaginative juices to distinguish it from other, more enchanting Spielbergian pics where lovable mechanical things solve earthly human dilemmas. Still, it's suitable entertainment for kids. Scene here is in one of the crumbling neighborhoods of Manhattan where some tenants of an old and much beloved brownstone are being harassed to move out. The most stubborn of the holdouts is an irascible café owner (Hume Cronyn) and his senile wife (Jessica Tandy). Tandy is visited in the middle of the night by a couple of miniature flying saucers which become little angels, repairing all that the local hoods have broken on any number of their rampages.

BATTLE BENEATH THE EARTH
1968, 91 mins, US Ⓥ
D: Montgomery Tully **A:** Kerwin Mathews, Viviane Ventura, Robert Ayres, Peter Arne, Martin Benson, Al Mulock (M-G-M)

Atomic destruction is given a new twist. Premise deals with the Chinese burrowing beneath the US from Hawaii in a vast complex of tunnels that extend under all major installations and population centers. Once this system is completed and atomic warheads planted, the US will be virtually wiped out and a new civilization built by the Chinese. Kerwin Mathews as an American commander detailed to counter the danger does a good job and Martin Benson is properly menacing as the Chinese general planning the giant scheme.

BATTLE BEYOND THE STARS
1980, 104 mins, US Ⓥ ⊙
D: Jimmy T. Murakami **A:** Richard Thomas, Robert Vaughn, George Peppard, John Saxon, Darlanne Fluegel, Sybil Danning (New World)

In unfolding its saga of how the peace-loving bunch on a small planet rebuffs a vicious band of bad guys, *Battle* incorporates touches of an old-fashioned western, horror pics, and even a touch of softcore. Principal characterizations are skin-deep. Dialogue takes the form of relaxed banter with a minimum of homilies. George Peppard has fun as a Scotch-tippling cowboy from Earth who turns up as one of the mercenaries hired by the planet's earnest young soldier (Richard Thomas). John Saxon is hilarious as the chief bad guy.

BATTLE CRY
1955, 147 mins, US ⓥ ⊙ ▭
D: Raoul Walsh **A:** Van Heflin, Aldo Ray, Mona Freeman, Nancy Olson, Tab Hunter, Dorothy Malone (Warner)

Amatory, rather than military, action is the mainstay of this saga of the United States Marines. While overboard in length, this comes from the detailing of several sets of romantics, each interesting in itself, plus the necessary battle action to indicate the basis is rather grim warfare. Of the romantic pairings, the most impression is made by Aldo Ray and Nancy Olson, not only because it occupies the main portion of the film's second half, but also because of the grasp the two stars have on their characters.
1955: Nomination: Best Scoring of a Dramatic Picture

BATTLE FOR ANZIO
See: Anzio

BATTLE FOR RUSSIA, THE
1943, 80 mins, US
D: Frank Capra (US War Department)

In *The Battle for Russia,* Lieutenant Colonel Frank Capra, of the Special Service Division, Army Service Forces, turns out by far the most notable in the series of *Why We Fight* army orientation pictures. *Russia* is a brilliant compilation of carefully edited footage culled, in the latter instance, from official Soviet sources and from newsreel and Signal Corps film. Keyed to General Douglas MacArthur's statement that "The scale and grandeur of the [Russian] effort mark it as the greatest military achievement in all history," this documentary is primarily the story of the titanic struggle that preceded the successful defense of Stalingrad.

BATTLE FOR THE PLANET OF THE APES
1973, 88 mins, US ⓥ ▭
D: J. Lee Thompson **A:** Roddy McDowall, Claude Akins, Natalie Trundy, Severn Darden, Lew Ayres, John Huston (20th Century-Fox)

The fifth and last film of the series depicts the confrontation between the apes and the nuclear-mutated humans inhabiting a large city destroyed in previous episode. Roddy McDowall encores as the apes' leader, having his own tribal strife

with Claude Akins, a militant troublemaker. Lew Ayres has a good bit, and John Huston appears in another pompous cameo as an aged philosopher of future generations who sets the flashback motif for the story.

BATTLEGROUND
1949, 118 mins, US ⓥ
D: William A. Wellman **A:** Van Johnson, John Hodiak, Ricardo Montalban, George Murphy, James Whitmore, Leon Ames (M-G-M)

Film deals with a segment of the Battle of the Bulge. Through sharp focus on a group of characters it exposes all the gripping disappointments and foxhole dreams and aspirations of the battle-wearied foot soldier. The cast performs in inspired manner. Murphy is the 35-year-old Pop, who is being discharged but finds himself a civilian in no-man's-land. Johnson plays the carefree GI, and with great credibility. Other standouts include John Hodiak as the newspaperman who enlisted and Montalban as the Mexican-American.
1949: Best Screenplay & Story, B&W Cinematography
Nominations: Best Picture, Director, Supp. Actor (James Whitmore), Editing

BATTLE HELL
See: Yangtse Incident

BATTLE HYMN
1956, 108 mins, US ▭
D: Douglas Sirk **A:** Rock Hudson, Anna Kashfi, Dan Duryea, Don DeFore, Martha Hyer, Jock Mahoney (Universal)

The inspirational story of a young clergyman is neatly integrated with fighter-pilot action in *Battle Hymn.* Rock Hudson, as Colonel Dean Hess, the minister whose story is told, heads the excellent cast. Perhaps best known of Hess's deeds were his efforts in behalf of the Korean children left orphans and homeless in the wake of the fighting in that country.

BATTLE OF ALGIERS, THE
See: La Battaglia di Algeri

BATTLE OF BRITAIN
1969, 133 mins, UK ⓥ ⊙
D: Guy Hamilton **A:** Laurence Olivier, Trevor Howard, Michael Caine, Ralph Richardson, Susannah York, Michael Redgrave (United Artists)

Battle sequences in the air are splendidly conceived and sweepingly dramatic, though sometimes repetitious. The $12-million-plus film strikes a happy medium between action and human interest. Standouts among the stars are Laurence Olivier as Sir Hugh Dowding, Fighter Command's supremo, and Trevor Howard as the tight-lipped, dedicated Air Vice-Marshall Keith Park.

BATTLE OF MIDWAY
See: Midway

BATTLE OF THE BULGE
1965, 167 mins, US ⓥ ⊙ ☐
D: Ken Annakin **A:** Henry Fonda, Robert Shaw, Robert Ryan, Dana Andrews, Telly Savalas, George Montgomery (Warner/United States)

Based on the pivotal action which precipitated the end of the Second World War in Europe, but otherwise fictionalized, *Battle of the Bulge* is a rousing, commercial battlefield action-drama of the emotions and activities of US and German forces. Script pits hard-charging German tank commander Robert Shaw against a US military hierarchy topped by Robert Ryan, intelligence chief Dana Andrews, and latter's assistant (Henry Fonda). Shaw is outstanding in a multifaceted role.

BATTLE OF THE RAILS
See: La Bataille du Rail

BATTLE OF THE RIVER PLATE
1956, 119 mins, UK ⓥ ☐
D: Michael Powell, Emeric Pressburger **A:** John Gregson, Anthony Quayle, Peter Finch, Ian Hunter, Jack Gwillim, Bernard Lee (Arcturus/Rank)

Defeat of the *Graf Spee* was the first major naval victory for Britain in the last big war. Apart from the strategy involved, it was also an exercise in subterfuge and diplomacy. All these points are neatly and simply brought out in the Michael Powell–Emeric Pressburger filmization. The battle sequences, in which the lightweight British cruisers close in on the *Graf Spee* and force the enemy to take shelter in Montevideo Harbor, are powerful, exciting, and technically impressive. Peter Finch gets the plum role as the German captain, who emerges as a warm, sincere, and kindly person.

BATTLE OF THE SEXES, THE
1914, 60 mins, US ⊗
D: D. W. Griffith **A:** Donald Crisp, Robert Harron, Lillian Gish, Mary Alden, Owen Moore, Fay Tincher (Reliance)

The story is a familiar but intimate tale vividly illustrated on the screen. Griffith keeps it alive every moment. A family of four—father, mother, son, and daughter—are living in an apartment house. To the same floor comes an adventuress, who is planted there to make a play for the husband (Donald Crisp). The woman (Fay Tincher) goes to work by leaving her door ajar and her skirt slightly lifted as the husband starts out. From this beginning the story pictures a mistress, a broken home, a heartbroken mother (Mary Alden), and two sad children (Robert Harron and Lillian Gish). As a middle-aged woman, called upon to pantomimically represent all the emotions, including an impulse toward insanity upon the discovery of her husband's unfaithfulness, Alden is superb.

BATTLE OF THE VILLA FIORITA, THE
1965, 111 mins, US ☐
D: Delmer Daves **A:** Maureen O'Hara, Rossano Brazzi, Richard Todd, Phyllis Calvert, Olivia Hussey, Maxine Audley (Warner)

The Battle of the Villa Fiorita is a beautifully photographed and well-mounted production which falls short artistically by switching gears. Daves's script (from Rumer Godden's novel) propels Maureen O'Hara into affair with Italian composer Rossano Brazzi. The lovers hie to Italian villa and set up housekeeping. At this point concept shifts to attempts by her kids (Martin Stephens and Elizabeth Dear) to break it up, joined later by Brazzi's moppet, Olivia Hussey. Idea is played for laffs, from juves' trek from England through hunger strikes, faked illness, and other gambits.

BATTLESHIP POTEMKIN
See: Bronenosets Potyomkin

BATTLING BUTLER
1926, 75 mins, US ⊗
D: Buster Keaton **A:** Buster Keaton, Sally O'Neil, Snitz Edwards, Francis McDonald (Keaton/M-G-M)

Keaton opens up as a pampered son of wealth. A disgusted father sends him out to rough it, and he goes plus a foreign car, valet, and an elaborate camping outfit. Here he meets the girl (Sally O'Neil), whose backwoods dad and brother think little of Alfred (Keaton) until the valet (Snitz Edwards) bridges the breach by explaining his young boss is Battling Butler, the lightweight boxer, about to fight the champ in his division. Circumstances force the meek scion into marriage and he has to migrate to the genuine Butler's training quarters to make it look on the level.

BAT 21
1988, 105 mins, US Ⓥ ⊙
D: Peter Markle **A:** Gene Hackman, Danny Glover, Jerry Reed, David Marshall Grant, Clayton Rohner, Erich Anderson (Tri-Star/Vision/Eagle)

The true story of an officer forced to parachute into enemy-infested jungle during the Vietnam War and survive on his own until a rescue can be attempted, this is a straightforward, surprisingly somber picture that sticks to the facts. This $10 million venture recounts the exceptional efforts of a reconnaissance flier (Danny Glover) to keep tabs on the downed missile intelligence expert (Gene Hackman) who has never before seen actual combat or come face-to-face with the enemy. Glover turns in a solid job but, as with Hackman, he remains one-dimensional.

BAT WHISPERS, THE
1931, 82 mins, US Ⓥ ⊙
D: Roland West **A:** Chester Morris, Una Merkel, Chance Ward, Richard Tucker, Wilson Benge, DeWitt Jennings (Art Cinema/United Artists)

Of the clutching-hand school, *The Bat Whispers,* in its talking version, is a good picture in the class division, for shivers and smiles. Chester Morris has little to do. At the finale the audience is halted by a cry from the screen not to leave, and, as a sort of epilogue, Morris reappears to request the audience not to divulge the identity of the Bat in the picture.

**BAWANG BIE JI
(FAREWELL TO MY CONCUBINE; FAREWELL MY CONCUBINE)**
1993, 170 mins, Hong Kong Ⓥ ⊙
D: Chen Kaige **A:** Leslie Cheung, Zhang Fengyi, Gong Li, Lu Qi, Ying Da, Ge You (Tomson)

A seductively lensed but emotionally uninvolving drama about two male Peking Opera stars and the ex-prostitute who comes between them. Long-arced story line spans 50 years of modern Chinese history. From the earliest scenes, at the Peking Opera training school, Chen's helming is consciously operatic in style. There's a stagy, unreal quality that mirrors the tight, enclosed universe in which the homosexual Douzi's (Cheung) friendship and rift with fellow student and eventual male-roles star Shitou (Zhang Fengyi) over his marriage to Juxian (Gong Li) is played out. But there's little attempt to dig deep into the political and historical background, and the script skirts around any

real examination of Douzi's sexual identity. As the male half of the duo, mainland actor Zhang anchors the movie in a powerful, shaded performance. Cheung, well cast as the tragic gay, does his best in an underwritten part. Gong, strong in several scenes, is also shackled by a script that's too stop/go.
1993: Nominations: Best Foreign Language Film, Cinematography

BAXTER!
1973, 105 mins, UK
D: Lionel Jeffries **A:** Patricia Neal, Jean-Pierre Cassel, Britt Ekland, Lynn Carlin, Scott Jacoby, Sally Thomsett (Anglo-EMI/Group W/Hanna-Barbera)

Baxter! is a good tearjerker about a young boy with a psychosomatic speech defect plus a bad family problem. Well directed by Lionel Jeffries, the British-lensed drama stars Patricia Neal as a speech therapist, Britt Ekland and Jean-Pierre Cassel as lovers who help Scott Jacoby in the title character role, and Lynn Carlin, as the boy's mother. Neal's dancing voice and eyes are as magnificent as ever. Carlin is particularly excellent as the mother.

BAY BOY
1984, 104 mins, Canada Ⓥ ⊙
D: Daniel Petrie **A:** Liv Ullmann, Kiefer Sutherland, Alan Scarfe, Mathieu Carriere, Peter Donat, Isabelle Mejias (ICC)

Canadian-born director Daniel Petrie had long cherished making a film about his early days in Nova Scotia. Setting is a coastal mining community circa 1937. Principals are a family of nonminers barely eking out an existence during the Depression. Kiefer Sutherland has the pivotal part of a teenager whose family envision his future with the clergy. The family travails—father's precarious fortunes, brother's debilitating disease, mother's profound religious guilt, etc.— are cut with humorous vignettes and insights.

BEACHES
1988, 123 mins, US Ⓥ ⊙
D: Garry Marshall **A:** Bette Midler, Barbara Hershey, John Heard, Spalding Gray, Lainie Kazan, James Read (Touchstone/Silver Screen Partners IV/South-All Girl)

Story of this engaging tearjerker is one of a profound friendship between two wildly mismatched women, a lower-class Jew (Bette Midler) from the Bronx whose every breath is showbiz, and a San Francisco blueblood (Barbara Hershey) destined for a pampered but troubled life. Men, marriages, and career vicissitudes come and go, but their bond ultimately cuts through it all. Midler's strutting, egotistical, self-aware character gets off any number of zingers, but Hershey plays her more emotionally untouchable part with an almost severe gravity.

1988: Nomination: Best Art Direction

BEACH PARTY
1963, 104 mins, US ⓥ ▱
D: William Asher A: Robert Cummings, Dorothy Malone, Frankie Avalon, Annette Funicello, Harvey Lembeck, Jody McCrea (American International)

Beach Party is a bouncy bit of lightweight fluff, attractively cast, beautifully set (Malibu Beach), and scored throughout with a big twist beat. It has a kind of direct, simpleminded cheeriness. Plot is pegged on a study of teenage sex habits undertaken by anthropologist Cummings on the beach at Malibu. What complications there are center around the romantic problems of a group of young surfers, principally Frankie Avalon and Annette Funicello. Story is padded out with some lovely surf-riding sequences and a whole string of Les Baxter songs.

BEACH RED
1967, 105 mins, US
D: Cornel Wilde A: Cornel Wilde, Rip Torn, Burr DeBenning, Patrick Wolfe, Jean Wallace, Jaime Sanchez (United Artists)

In contrast to many professedly antiwar films, *Beach Red* is indisputably sincere in its war-is-hell message. Except for brief reveries of civilian life, the film focuses entirely on a single dreary campaign by an American unit out to take a Japanese-held island in the Pacific. The trouble with the screenplay, adapted from Peter Bowman's 1945 novel, is that little is substituted for wisely avoided clichés. The central characters are spokesmen for differing points of view, not real, full-bodied people.

1967: Nomination: Best Editing

BEAN
1997, 90 mins, UK ⓥ ⊙
D: Mel Smith A: Rowan Atkinson, Peter MacNicol, Pamela Reed, Harris Yulin, Burt Reynolds, John Mills (Working Title/PolyGram)

The half-hour, almost silent British comedy series *Bean* segues to the big screen, aiming squarely at the U.S. market, with mostly satisfactory results. Rowan Atkinson's Mr. Bean is a Mr. Average who lives alone and dresses conservatively in jacket and tie. Though possessed of a child's innocence, he has an evil streak and often provokes the catastrophes that follow inevitably in his wake. Bean works as a security guard in Britain's National Gallery. His employers have to find a way to get rid of him, and their chance comes with a request from a small Los Angeles art gallery which seeks an art scholar to officiate at an unveiling, and the National sends Mr. Bean. Atkinson boasts a full-on comic personality that on the screen is a bit daunting at times.

BEAST, THE
1988, 109 mins, US ⓥ
D: Kevin Reynolds A: George Dzundza, Jason Patric, Steven Bauer, Stephen Baldwin, Don Harvey, Kabir Bedi (A&M)

A harrowing, tightly focused war film that becomes a moving, near-biblical allegory, *The Beast* represents a stellar achievement for all involved. Pic explores a single fictional incident set in 1981, the second year of the Russian occupation of Afghanistan. A Russian tank gets trapped after its brutal decimation of a nearby Afghan village, and the surviving villagers, who've discovered a weapon capable of destroying a tank, decide to track it down for revenge.

BEAST FROM 20,000 FATHOMS, THE
1953, 80 mins, US ⓥ ⊙
D: Eugene Lourie A: Paul Christian, Paula Raymond, Cecil Kellaway, Kenneth Tobey, Donald Woods, Lee Van Cleef (Warner)

Producers have created a prehistoric monster that makes Kong seem like a chimpanzee. It's a gigantic amphibious beast that towers above some of New York's highest buildings. The sight of the beast stalking through Gotham's downtown streets is awesome. Special credit should go to Ray Harryhausen for the socko technical effects. Screenplay has a documentary flavor, which Jack Russell's camera captures expertly.

BEASTMASTER, THE
1982, 118 mins, US ⓥ ⊙
D: Don Coscarelli A: Marc Singer, Tanya Roberts, Rip Torn, John Amos, Josh Milrad, Rod Loomis (M-G-M/United Artists)

When *The Beastmaster* begins, it is very hard to tell what it is all about. An hour later it is very hard to care what it is all about. Another hour later it is very hard to remember what it was all about. From the early confusion, in which it seems that a cow gives birth to a baby boy, Marc Singer emerges as Dar. Singer's destiny is to go after the villains led by Rip Torn to avenge the destruction of the village.

BEASTMASTER 2
THROUGH THE PORTAL OF TIME
1991, 107 mins, US Ⓥ ⊙
D: Sylvio Tabet **A:** Marc Singer, Kari Wuhrer, Wings Hauser, Sarah Douglas, Charles Young (Republic/Films 21)

Despite this low-budget sequel's silly dialogue and cheesy special effects, *Beastmaster 2* is a mildly engaging tongue-in-cheek fantasy about mythical characters traveling through a time warp to battle it out in the mean streets of contempo L.A. Blond, lithely muscular Marc Singer returns in his loincloth title role as a sort of violent St. Francis figure accompanied by a tiger, an eagle, and two ferrets who help him out of scrapes with the evil rulers of his desert abode. Singer maintains a winning simplicity despite all the sword-and-sorcery hokum.

BEAST WITH FIVE FINGERS, THE
1946, 90 mins, US Ⓥ
D: Robert Florey **A:** Robert Alda, Andrea King, Peter Lorre, Victor Francen (Warner)

The Beast with Five Fingers is a weird, Grand Guignol-ish conconction. Victor Francen, as a semi-invalid concert pianist, lives in a gloomy villa in northern Italy. His companions are his secretary, Peter Lorre; his nurse, Andrea King; a composer friend, Robert Alda; and his attorney, David Hoffman. A good deal of the plot is projected through Lorre's eyes, without any explanation of the switches from straight narration to scenes registered by Lorre's deranged mind. He chases a ghoulish hand around the library several times, catching it finally and hammering it down in a bloodcurdling scene.

BEAST WITHIN, THE
1982, 90 mins, US Ⓥ
D: Philippe Mora **A:** Ronny Cox, Bibi Besch, Paul Clemens, Don Gordon, R. G. Armstrong, Kitty Moffat (M-G-M/United Artists)

Honeymooning, Ronny Cox and Bibi Besch get their car stuck in the woods and she gets raped by something with hairy legs. Fastforward 17 years to find them

parents of that most dreaded of monsters—a teenager. The teenager (Paul Clemens) is bad sick and starts to chomp people. There does come a time when Clemens has to get on with being a bigtime monster. Thanks to Thomas R. Burman's makeup effects, this sequence actually creates chills as the boy's head bubbles and bursts and his skin pops and stretches.

BEAT THE DEVIL
1953, 100 mins, UK/Italy Ⓥ ⊙ ⊠
D: John Huston **A:** Humphrey Bogart, Jennifer Jones, Gina Lollobrigida, Robert Morley, Peter Lorre, Edward Underdown (Romulus/Santana)

In an easy sort of way, the story describes the adventures of a bunch of uranium exploiteers who want to get hold of some valuable land in Africa. While they're waiting for a passage from Italy, their go-between (Humphrey Bogart) becomes involved with a young couple, played by Jennifer Jones and Edward Underdown. There are carefully timed laughs in the script as well as intended comedy situations that misfire. Bogart's virile performance is handsomely matched by Jones's pert and vivacious study. Gina Lollobrigida gives a provocative portrayal as Bogart's wife.

BEAU BRUMMELL
1924, 120 mins, US Ⓥ ⊗
D: Harry Beaumont **A:** John Barrymore, Mary Astor, Willard Louis, Irene Rich, Alec B. Francis, Carmel Myers (Warner)

This has John Barrymore at the head of a cast that holds some strong picture names. Irene Rich as the Duchess of York would have undoubtedly made a much better Lady Margery than Mary Astor, who does not display any great histrionic ability. Willard Louis as George, Prince of Wales, walks away with practically every scene in which he appears. Carmel Myers as a vamp is a modern vamp rather than one of the period in which the action is laid. As for Barrymore, there are flashes in his characterization of the London dandy that are inspired, and there are other moments when he does not seem to get over at all.

BEAU GESTE
1926, 129 mins, US ⊗
D: Herbert Brenon **A:** Ronald Colman, Neil Hamilton, Ralph Forbes, Alice Joyce, Mary Brian, Noah Beery (Paramount)

Beau Geste is a man's picture. The story revolves around three brothers and their love for each other. And a great looking trio—Ronald Colman, Neil Hamilton, and Ralph Forbes. Beyond that the love interest is strictly secondary, practically nil. The picture is all story. In fact, only one cast member seems to rise above the scenario. This is Noah Beery as the bestial sergeant major. There can be no question that Beery is the outstanding figure of the picture.

BEAU GESTE
1939, 114 mins, US ♥ ⊙
D: William A. Wellman **A:** Gary Cooper, Ray Milland, Robert Preston, Brian Donlevy, Susan Hayward, J. Carrol Naish (Paramount)

Beau Geste has been produced with vigorous realism and spectacular sweep. Director William Wellman has focused attention on the melodramatic and vividly gruesome aspects of the story. Gary Cooper is okay in the title spot. Ray Milland and Robert Preston work hard and competently. Trio are overshadowed by the vivid Brian Donlevy as the savagely brutal sergeant of the legion.
1939: Nominations: Best Supp. Actor (Brian Donlevy), Art Direction

BEAU GESTE
1966, 105 mins, US ♥ ▭
D: Douglas Heyes **A:** Guy Stockwell, Doug McClure, Leslie Nielsen, Telly Savalas, David Mauro, Robert Wolders (Universal)

Third time out for one of the most memorable silent films still packs hardy entertainment. The production is an expertly made translation of Percival Christopher Wren's novel of the French Foreign Legion in a lonely Sahara outpost, distinguished by good acting, fine photographic values, and fast direction. Guy Stockwell delineates the title role.

LE BEAU SERGE
(HANDSOME SERGE)
1958, 97 mins, France ♥
D: Claude Chabrol **A:** Gerard Blain, Jean-Claude Brialy, Michele Meritz, Bernadette Lafont, Edmond Beauchamp, Claude Cerval (Ajym)

An important new French director, Claude Chabrol, is unveiled in this pic. A young man goes back to his hometown. Here he finds an old friend has become a hopeless alcoholic. He at first blames it on his wife but then finds that the boy's disorientation comes from a stillborn, idiotic first child and the general provincialism

and lack of moral or spiritual strength in the small, inbred town.

BEAUTIFUL BLONDE FROM BASHFUL BEND, THE
1949, 76 mins, US ♥
D: Preston Sturges **A:** Betty Grable, Cesar Romero, Rudy Vallee, Olga San Juan, Sterling Holloway, Hugh Herbert (20th Century-Fox)

Blonde is basically a rather silly western farce, loosely concocted. Producer-director-writer Preston Sturges plays his script with frantic slapstick, stressing raw, bawdy comedy rather than genuine humor. Betty Grable is the dancehall gal who knows how to handle a gun and gets into trouble because of it. The boyfriend is Cesar Romero. Grable is out to kill him for two-timing but, in a dark room, shoots a judge in the posterior by mistake.

BEAUTIFUL GIRLS
1996, 110 mins, US ♥
D: Ted Demme **A:** Matt Dillon, Noah Emmerich, Annabeth Gish, Lauren Holly, Timothy Hutton, Rosie O'Donnell, Uma Thurman, Natalie Portman (Woods)

This startlingly uneventful compendium of thickheaded boy-talk and female tolerance squanders a fine cast on incredibly ordinary characters and situations. The talk is almost single-mindedly about sex and relationships, redundantly and routinely so. The mesmerizing, quicksilver work of young actress Portman is the single best reason to see the film. Hutton is easygoing and likable, while Thurman has no trouble making her dazzler dazzling.

BEAUTIFUL THING
1996, 89 mins, UK ♥
D: Hettie Macdonald **A:** Linda Henry, Glen Berry, Scott Neal, Ben Daniels, Tameka Empson, Anna Karen (World/Channel 4)

Ken Loach meets Mike Leigh in *Beautiful Thing,* an often rough-and-ready but infectiously funny working-class comedy, with a feel-good gay theme, set in a southeast London housing project. Fresh performances from a largely unknown cast make this low-budget version of Jonathan Harvey's 1994 off–West End legit hit. At heart, it's a working-class dramedy with a couple of gay characters, propelled by a sense of humor that comes as much from its noncorrect approach to the subject as from its one-liners.

BEAUTY AND THE BEAST
1991, 85 mins, US Ⓥ

D: Gary Trousdale, Kirk Wise

A lovely film that ranks with the best of Disney's animated classics, *Beauty and the Beast* is a tale freshly retold. *Beauty* engages the emotions with an unabashed sincerity that manages to avoid the pitfalls of triteness and corn. Belle, magnificently voiced by Paige O'Hara, is a brainy young woman kidnapped by the Beast. She finds her initial aversion overcome by a growing appreciation of his inner beauty and sensitivity. While the usually soft-spoken Robby Benson might seem an odd choice for the voice of the Beast, his booming bass voice in the early sections and the increasingly boyish timbre of his voice in the later parts perfectly capture the character's complexity. Songs are witty, charming, richly orchestrated, and smoothly integrated into the plot. The first-rate animation staff bring a strikingly three-dimensional look to the film.
1991: Best Song ("Beauty and the Beast"), Original Score
Nominations: Best Picture, Song ("Belle," "Be Our Guest"), Sound

BEAUTY AND THE BEAST
See: La Belle et la Bete

BEAUTY JUNGLE, THE
1964, 114 mins, UK ⌑

D: Val Guest A: Ian Hendry, Janette Scott, Ronald Fraser, Edmund Purdom, Jean Claudio, Kay Walsh (Rank)

There's some lively, if not oversubtle, comedy in this yarn of a pretty stenographer (Janette Scott) entering a seaside pier contest. She wins and becomes regular contestant at such junkets who progresses steadily around the familiar circuit and gets into the big-time league of big money, overblown publicity, commercialism, and spurious glitter. Ian Hendry, as the poor man's Svengali, is brisk and credible, while Ronald Fraser, as his lenser buddy, also turns in a ripe performance.

BEAVIS AND BUTT-HEAD DO AMERICA
1996, 80 mins, US Ⓥ ⊙

D: Mike Judge, Yvette Kaplan (anim.) (MTV/Paramount)

The good news is that *Beavis and Butt-head Do America* doesn't suck. The bad news is that it doesn't rule, either. To stretch things out for feature length, director Mike Judge sends Beavis and Butt-head on a cross-country odyssey. Among the notables who lend their vocal talents to the enterprise: Robert Stack, as a stern ATF agent, and Cloris Leachman, as a sweet little old lady. The animation is slightly more sophisticated than on the TV show, though it remains, by movie standards, minimalist at best. That, of course, is part of the joke.

BECAUSE OF HIM
1946, 100 mins, US

D: Richard Wallace A: Deanna Durbin, Franchot Tone, Charles Laughton (Universal)

Film is a merry mélange of music, comedy, and drama. Durbin, despite her role as a stagestruck waitress through most of the plot, is gowned to perfection and looks ditto. Music plays a minor part in the film, with the star's vocal efforts limited to three songs, but seldom has she been in finer voice. Plot revolves around Durbin's attempt to inveigle her way into a top Broadway production. Laughton grabs the acting honors in a sterling portrayal of the actor whose every gesture would look well between two slices of rye.

BECKET
1964, 148 mins, UK Ⓥ ⊙ ⌑

D: Peter Glenville A: Richard Burton, Peter O'Toole, John Gielgud, Donald Wolfit, Gino Cervi, Paolo Stoppa (Paramount/Keep)

A very fine, perhaps great, motion picture. The screenplay owes much to Jean Anouilh's stage script. The modern psychology of Anouilh lends fascination to these 12th-century shenanigans by investing them with special motivational insights. The basic story is, of course, the murder on December 29, 1170, in the cathedral of Canterbury of its archbishop, Becket, by barons from the entourage of Henry II. In the title role, Richard Burton gives a generally convincing and resourceful performance. As Henry II, Peter O'Toole emerges with the fatter role, and the more colorful. The king is an unhappy monarch whose only satisfying companionship has been provided by the Saxon Becket. Hating-loving, miserably lonely when deserted by his friend, O'Toole makes of the king a tormented, many-sided, baffled, believable human being.
1964: Best Adapted Screenplay
Nominations: Best Picture, Director, Actor (Richard Burton, Peter O'Toole), Supp. Actor (John Gielgud), Color Cinematography, Color Costume Design, Color Art

Direction, Editing, Original Music Score, Sound

BECKY SHARP
1935, 84 mins, US Ⓥ
D: Rouben Mamoulian **A:** Miriam Hopkins, Cedric Hardwicke, Nigel Bruce, Frances Dee, Alan Mowbray, G. P. Huntley Jr. (Pioneer/RKO)

The first full-length talker in highly improved Technicolor, it's a tribute to the new process and to Robert Edmond Jones's beautiful splashes of multitone visual values. The pastel shades of the interior properties, the faithful reproduction even of the femmes' makeup, the gay carnival splashes of color such as that in the Brussels waltz-quadrille scene (climaxed by Napoleon's Waterloo return) impress optically, but the story falls flat dramatically and the dialogue is likewise fraught with too much discordant stridency of tone. Miriam Hopkins at times fairly shrieks her way through the footage. As the calculating Becky, her role of a temptress is neither lurid nor winsome.
1935: Nomination: Best Actress (Miriam Hopkins)

BED AND BOARD
See: Domicile Conjugal

BEDAZZLED
1967, 104 mins, UK Ⓥ ⊙ ▭
D: Stanley Donen **A:** Peter Cook, Dudley Moore, Eleanor Bron, Raquel Welch, Robert Russell, Barry Humphries (20th Century-Fox)

Bedazzled is a fantasy of a London short-order cook madly in love with a waitress, who is offered seven wishes by the devil in return for his soul. Stanley Donen production is pretty much the work of two of its three stars, Peter Cook and Dudley Moore. Pair scripted from Cook's original story, and Moore also composed music score. Eleanor Bron is third star, plus Raquel Welch, whose brief appearance is equaled only by her scant attire.

BEDFORD INCIDENT, THE
1965, 102 mins, US Ⓥ
D: James B. Harris **A:** Richard Widmark, Sidney Poitier, James MacArthur, Martin Balsam, Wally Cox, Eric Portman (Bedford/Columbia)

The Bedford Incident is an excellent sea drama based on a day-to-day reality of the Cold War, the monitoring of Russian submarine activity by US Navy destroyers. The production, made at England's Shepperton Studios, has salty scripting and solid performances, including one of the finest in Widmark's career. Widmark's skipper is that rare breed whom the crew not only follows, but worships. The character of this sea dog is drawn out by Sidney Poitier, as a wise-guy magazine writer, and Martin Balsam, a reserve medic back on active duty. Poitier does an excellent job in both the light and serious aspects of his role, and manages to leave a personal stamp on his scenes.

BEDKNOBS AND BROOMSTICKS
1971, 117 mins, US Ⓥ ⊙
D: Robert Stevenson **A:** Angela Lansbury, David Tomlinson, Roddy McDowall, Sam Jaffe, John Ericson, Bruce Forsyth (Walt Disney)

The magic of Walt Disney lingers magnificently on in *Bedknobs and Broomsticks*.

The setting is a quaint old-world English seaside village during the earlier days of World War II. Three Cockney kids (Roy Snart, Ian Weighill, and Cindy O'Callaghan) are evacuated there and are as appalled by the dullness of it all as they are by the eccentricities and rules of Angela Lansbury, with whom they are billeted. Then they discover she is studying witchcraft with the idea of using it against the Germans should they invade. Life takes on a rosier hue. They learn to perform all sorts of magic, fly to London on a bedstead, and spend a joyous time in the never-never land.
1971: Best Special Visual Effects
Nominations: Best Costume Design, Art Direction, Original Song Score, Song ("The Age of Not Believing")

BED OF ROSES
1996, 87 mins, US Ⓥ ⊙
D: Michael Goldenberg **A:** Christian Slater, Mary Stuart Masterson, Pamela Segall, Josh Brolin, Ally Walker, Debra Monk (New Line)

Sweet but uninspired, *Bed of Roses* is a genial, old-fashioned romance with very little to recommend it other than earnest, likable performances by leads Christian Slater and Mary Stuart Masterson. Sprinkled with fairy-tale trappings—from the premise to Michael Convertino's score—pic proves a relatively straightforward tale about a young, career-driven woman whose life ends up being transformed by one simple act of kindness.

BEDROOM WINDOW, THE
1986, 112 mins, US ⊗ ⊙ ▭
D: Curtis Hanson **A:** Steve Guttenberg, Elizabeth McGovern, Isabelle Huppert, Paul Shenar, Wallace Shawn, Carl Lumbly (De Laurentiis)

Cast against type, Steve Guttenberg plays a malleable young executive carrying on an affair with his boss's wife, the sexy Sylvia (Isabelle Huppert). During a tryst at Guttenberg's apartment one night after a party, Huppert, looking out his bedroom window, sees a girl (Elizabeth McGovern) being assaulted outside. Guttenberg ultimately becomes a suspect in the rash of rape-and-murder cases, forcing him in the Hitchcock tradition to begin his own investigation in trying to prove who the real killer is. Curtis Hanson's screenplay involves several ingenious plot twists. Unfortunately, a lot of coincidences and just plain stupid actions by Guttenberg are relied upon to keep the pot boiling.

BEDSIDE MANNER
1945, 79 mins, US ⊗
D: Andrew L. Stone **A:** John Carroll, Ruth Hussey, Charles Ruggles, Ann Rutherford, Claudia Drake (United Artists)

Bedside Manner is a well-contrived, streamlined comedy of the overworked medico profession in wartimes. At least that is the clothes rack on which is strung a ludicrous romance between a femme doctor and a war worker. Plot pits Charles Ruggles against his niece (Ruth Hussey), another medico, in the former's frantic effort to have her assist him with his overworked practice. This central motive is speeded along by the romance between Hussey and John Carroll, the airplane test pilot, to an almost wacky degree. Hussey steals the picture. Ruggles, as usual, lends infectious humor to the role of overworked physician.

BED SITTING ROOM, THE
1970, 90 mins, UK ⊗
D: Richard Lester **A:** Rita Tushingham, Ralph Richardson, Peter Cook, Dudley Moore, Spike Milligan, Michael Hordern (United Artists)

A play by Spike Milligan and John Antrobus serves as an ideal springboard for an offbeat antiwar film by Richard Lester which, miraculously, manages to convey its grim message with humor. Sketchlike pic catches glimpses and comments of the 20-odd survivors of a London shredded by an A-bomb as they dig out of their holes to try and cope with the gray new world before they, too, become animals.

BEDTIME STORY
1941, 83 mins, US
D: Alexander Hall **A:** Fredric March, Loretta Young, Robert Benchley, Allyn Joslyn, Eve Arden, Helen Westley (Columbia)

Picture is a combo of slick scripting, fast-paced direction, and excellent performances. Maximum entertainment is provided in the breezy exposition of the marital problems of producer-playwright March and his star-wife Young. The wife desires to retire to their farm in Connecticut, while the energetic March hatches a new play in which he wants Young to star. Both Young and the audience are kept intrigued by the inventive devices concocted by the playwright in trying to swing his wife into the new play.

BEDTIME STORY
1964, 99 mins, US ⊗
D: Ralph Levy **A:** Marlon Brando, David Niven, Shirley Jones, Dody Goodman, Aram Stephan, Marie Windsor (Universal)

Bedtime Story will divert the less discriminating. Some of the lines snap and crackle, and several of the situations (done with slapstick overtones) in which Brando and Niven find themselves involved as con men in competition on the French Riviera are broadly funny. The screenplay has Niven as a big-time operator and Brando a relatively petty practitioner of the confidence art who comes to challenge the king of the mountain in his own backyard. The mercenary contest centers around American soap queen Shirley Jones, who turns out to be merely the penniless winner of a soap-queen contest. Brando wins the girl, but he loses the histrionic contest to Niven, whose effortless flair for sophisticated comedy is not matched by his co-star.

BEETHOVEN
1992, 88 mins, US ⊗ ⊙
D: Brian Levant **A:** Charles Grodin, Bonnie Hunt, Dean Jones, Oliver Platt, Stanley Tucci, Nicholle Tom (Universal)

Six-year-olds and animal-rights activists should warm up to the titular big slobbering dog, his perfect family, and the crises that brings them together. The real star is a 185-pound St. Bernard. Stolen as a puppy, he stumbles into the Newton family's life. They are a demographically perfect group, with an uptight dad

(Charles Grodin) who reluctantly agrees to adopt the beast. Beethoven grows and, as only movie dogs can, manages to help the kids' lives in various creative ways, even as he mangles the house and antagonizes Dad.

BEETHOVEN'S 2ND
1993, 88 mins, US Ⓥ ⊙
D: Rod Daniel **A:** Charles Grodin, Bonnie Hunt, Nicholle Tom, Christopher Castle, Sarah Rose Karr, Debi Mazar (Universal)

Beethoven's 2nd does better than just double up its mediocre forebear, creating what amounts to a live-action cartoon with a strong *101 Dalmatians* riff that should play particularly well among moppets. Pic begins with a lonely Beethoven meeting his dream dog and having puppies, only to have the pooch taken away by her evil owner, Regina (Debi Mazar). The Newton kids start raising the puppies, concealing them from Dad, before Regina becomes determined to cash in on a second front by selling the purebred litter. The dog actors (more than 100 play the puppies at various stages, per the production notes) outemote their two-footed counterparts.

1993: Nomination: Best Song ("The Day I Fall in Love")

BEETLEJUICE
1988, 92 mins, US Ⓥ ⊙
D: Tim Burton **A:** Alec Baldwin, Geena Davis, Michael Keaton, Jeffrey Jones, Winona Ryder, Sylvia Sidney (Geffen)

Beetlejuice springs to life when the raucous and repulsive Betelgeuse (Michael Keaton) rises from his moribund state to wreak havoc on fellow spooks and mortal enemies. Geena Davis and Alec Baldwin live in a big barn of a house that they are lovingly restoring. But they drown—and are consigned to an afterlife that keeps them stuck at home, forever invisible to anyone not similarly situated. Their beloved house is sold to a rich New York financier (Jeffrey Jones) and his wife, the affected artiste (Catherine O'Hara). Help comes via a cryptically written book for the newly deceased but better yet, from this freak of a character named Betelgeuse.

1988: Best Makeup

BEFORE AND AFTER
1996, 107 mins, US Ⓥ ⊙
D: Barbet Schroeder **A:** Meryl Streep, Liam Neeson, Edward Furlong, Julia Weldon, Alfred Molina, Daniel Von Bargen (Hollywood)

Before and After is so afraid of violating basic pieties that it ends up saying nothing. The tough question of how solid, intelligent, well-meaning parents respond when their child commits a horrible crime is softened by a crucial qualifier: the child isn't guilty. Carolyn (Meryl Streep) is an established pediatrician, Ben (Liam Neeson) a successful artist. Their well-ordered life is upended when a local policeman brings the news that their son, Jacob (Edward Furlong), was the last person seen with a teen girl who's been murdered, and he's now missing. The script at every turn falls back on mushy affirmations of family rather than taking the risk of exploring conflicts that reveal the bitterest divisions between one family member and another, and between family and community.

BEFORE SUNRISE
1995, 101 mins, US Ⓥ ⊙
D: Richard Linklater **A:** Ethan Hawke, Julie Delpy (Castle Rock/Detour)

A lovely, rather risky concept isn't entirely fulfilled in the telling of *Before Sunrise*. As their train is speeding toward Vienna, a young American fellow, Jesse (Ethan Hawke), begins chatting with a lovely French student, Céline (Julie Delpy). Jesse convinces Céline to detrain with him in Vienna so they can get to know each other better. What's commendable about Linklater's approach here is the real-time, in-depth aspect of portraying a burgeoning relationship. But while attractive and enthusiastic, Jesse is ultimately a regular guy who lacks the quirks and distinctiveness that would make him a resonant personality. By contrast, Delpy's Céline is a beautiful creation, a young lady seemingly mature beyond her years.

BEFORE THE RAIN
1994, 115 mins, UK/France/Macedonia ▭
D: Milcho Manchevski **A:** Katrin Cartlidge, Rade Serbedzija, Gregoire Colin, Labina Mitevska, Silvija Stojanovska (Aim/Noe/Varder)

Before the Rain attempts to answer the tragic riddle of why the Balkan states are perpetually at war. *Rain* depicts senseless ethnic hatred as endemic in the region. Film is divided into three parts. In *Words,* the young Greek Orthodox monk Kiril (Gregoire Colin), living in an ancient monastery, shelters and hides an Albanian girl, Zamira (Labina Mitevska). The modernity of the second episode, *Faces,* comes as a shock. Anne (Katrin Cartlidge), who works in a London photo agency, is torn between her Macedonian lover, Aleksandar (Rade Serbedzija), a Pulitzer Prize–winning war photographer, and her sweet, boring husband, Nick (Jay Villiers). *Pictures* takes the story back to Macedonia and brings the threads together.

1994: Nomination: Best Foreign Language Film

BEFORE WINTER COMES
1969, 107 mins, UK
D: J. Lee Thompson A: David Niven, Topol, Anna Karina, John Hurt, Anthony Quayle, Ori Levy (Columbia/Windward)

An unevenly scripted, confusingly directed drama about the treatment of displaced persons in Austria immediately following V-E Day. David Niven turns in his usual competent professional job as a major assigned to run a camp for displaced persons during the spring of 1945. Topol is the multilingual magician whom Niven chooses to assist him in deciding who should be turned over to American and who to Russian authorities. Topol exudes a romantic masculinity not without sexual charm at the same time that he shows a formidable comedic timing and grace.

BEGGAR'S OPERA, THE
1953, 94 mins, UK ⊗
D: Peter Brook A: Laurence Olivier, Stanley Holloway, George Devine, Hugh Griffith, Athene Syler, Dorothy Tutin (British Lion)

A bold experiment that does not come off, *The Beggar's Opera* is an example of the uneasy partnership between screen and opera. At constant intervals, events are brought to a standstill by the John Gay lyrics, and attractive though they are in their own right, they do not merge too happily in the film. Apart from Olivier and Stanley Holloway, the singing voices of the cast are dubbed by leading British vocalists and the contrast is clear and distinct. Olivier's light baritone, pleasant enough in its own way, is no match for the other voices. This apart, his performance is as robust and as lively as could be expected. Holloway is a polished singer as well as being a first-class thesper and his is one of the best individual contributions to the pic. Arthur Bliss's score is outstanding.

BEGINNING OR THE END, THE
1947, 110 mins, US
D: Norman Taurog A: Brian Donlevy, Robert Walker, Tom Drake, Audrey Totter, Hume Cronyn, Beverly Tyler (M-G-M)

The Beginning or the End tells its portentous tale in broad strokes of masterful scripting and production. It brings an appreciation of how science and big business were mobilized by America to achieve the atomic bomb; the rallying around Dr. J. Robert Oppenheimer (whom Hume Cronyn expertly impersonates); the questioning by young Tom Drake whether he was doing the right thing. Brian Donlevy is capital as General Groves, eclipsed only by Godfrey Tearle's extraordinary personation of President Roosevelt.

BEGIN THE BEGUINE
See: Volver a Empezar

BEGUILED, THE
1971, 105 mins, US ⊗ ⊙
D: Don Siegel A: Clint Eastwood, Geraldine Page, Elizabeth Hartman, Jo Ann Harris, Darleen Carr, Mae Mercer (Malpaso/Universal)

Eastwood eschews his usual action character to portray a wounded Union soldier recuperating within the confines of a small school for southern girls run by Geraldine Page. His presence cues a series of diverse sexual frustrations, and his wily handling of the ladies sparks jealousies of melodramatic proportions. Pic is essentially black comedy, but treatment is consistently heavy-handed. Eastwood is not called upon to do much emoting; that is left in spades to the ladies. Page, per usual, runs away with the honors.

BEHIND THE GREEN DOOR
1972, 72 mins, US ⊗
D: Jim Mitchell, Art Mitchell A: Marilyn Chambers, George S. McDonald, Johnny Keyes, Ben Davidson (Mitchell Brothers)

Football fans attracted to the hardcore debut of Oakland Raider pro Ben Davidson should flag him for box-office clipping. His fully clothed cameo appearance is hardly worth the time. But sports fans won't go away entirely disappointed, since ex-middleweight-boxing champ Johnny Keyes goes all the way. Marilyn Chambers makes her hardcore debut in *Behind the Green Door*. Unfortunately, she never has enough to say to judge whether she qualifies as an actress.

BEHIND THE RISING SUN
1943, 86 mins, US ⊗
D: Edward Dmytryk A: Margo, Tom Neal, J. Carrol Naish, Robert Ryan, Gloria Holden (RKO)

A good drama of inside info on Jap in-doctrination and thinking. Story is an in-timate affair of a Jap family of the upper class, and the impress of the conquests in Asia and war against the United States on both father and son. Father is influential newspaper publisher (J. Carrol Naish), while son is Cornell-educated Tom Neal.

BEHOLD A PALE HORSE
1964, 119 mins, US ⓥ
D: Fred Zinnemann A: Gregory Peck, Anthony Quinn, Omar Sharif, Raymond Pellegrin, Paola Stoppa, Mildred Dunnock (Columbia)

Pale Horse is rooted in the Spanish Civil War and essentially concerns a Spanish guerrilla (Gregory Peck) who continues to live the war alone. He is thrown again into the fray in a personal attack against a vain and arrogant police captain (Anthony Quinn) who has vowed his death. Peck surges with force and energy in a characterization that ranks among the better in his long career. There is also an excellent performance from Quinn. Omar Sharif shows a warm, sensitive side in this film, playing the role of a young priest torn between obligations of personal morality and the official laws of government.

BEING HUMAN
1994, 125 mins, US/UK ⓥ ⊚
D: Bill Forsyth A: Robin Williams, John Turturro, Anna Galiena, Vincent D'Onofrio, Hector Elizondo, Lorraine Bracco (Warner/Enigma)

Being Human never comes alive. Forsyth has built this curiosity out of five historical vignettes centered upon a character named Hector (Williams). He's a caveman in the Bronze Age, a slave during the Roman Empire, a traveler fleeing war in the Middle Ages, a Portuguese adventurer during the Age of Exploration, and a hapless divorced man in contempo New York—but in any era he's a meek, ineffectual wimp who can't make a decision or stand up for himself. Never in the film has Williams's inspired, manic personality been so suppressed, never has he seemed to bland.

BEING JOHN MALKOVICH
1999, 112 mins, UK/US ⓥ ⊚
D: Spike Jonze A: John Cusack, Cameron Diaz, Catherine Keener, Orson Bean, Mary Kay Place, John Malkovich (Propaganda/Single Cell/Gramercy)

Music-video and commercials creator Spike Jonze makes a bracingly original feature-film debut with *Being John Malkovich*, a metaphysical comic love story. What makes it so fresh is the decision to treat the most surreal inventions in real terms, placing writer Charlie Kaufman's peculiar universe in everyday New York City. Street puppeteer Craig Schwartz (John Cusack), married to frumpy pet-store staffer Lotte (Cameron Diaz) and driven to find a job, becomes a filing clerk on a Manhattan building's low-ceilinged 7 1/2th floor, where he is smitten by Maxine (Catherine Keener) and finds a tunnel behind a cabinet in his office. Exploring this, Craig is sucked into the head of John Malkovich, viewing the world through the actor's eyes for 15 minutes before being spat out into a ditch off the New Jersey Turnpike. The endlessly resourceful script never lets up, and Jonze draws rich, enjoyable performances from the entire cast. **1999: Nominations:** Best Director, Supp. Actress (Catherine Keener), Original Screenplay

BEING THERE
1979, 130 mins, US ⓥ ⊚
D: Hal Ashby A: Peter Sellers, Shirley MacLaine, Melvyn Douglas, Jack Warden, Richard Basehart (United Artists/Lorimar)

Being There is a faithful but nonetheless imaginative adaptation of Jerzy Kosinski's quirky comic novel which takes Sellers from his position as a childlike, unblinking naif who can't read or write to that of a valued adviser to an industrial giant and ultimately to the brink of a presidential nomination. Sellers's performance stands as the centerpiece of the film, and it's a beauty. Shirley MacLaine is subtle and winning. Melvyn Douglas almost steals the film with his spectacular performance as the dying financial titan. **1979:** Best Supp. Actor (Melvyn Douglas) **Nomination:** Best Actor (Peter Sellers)

BELL, BOOK AND CANDLE
1958, 106 mins, US ⓥ ⊚
D: Richard Quine A: James Stewart, Kim Novak, Jack Lemmon, Ernie Kovacs, Hermione Gingold, Elsa Lanchester (Phoenix/Columbia)

The offbeat story is concerned with witches and warlocks operating against today's world of skepticism and realism. James Stewart is the straight man thrust by chance into a group of people, headed by Novak, for whom incantations, spells, and sorcery are as commonplace as processed foods. Novak literally weaves a spell on Stewart to make him fall in love with her.

The hazard of the story is that there is really only one joke. This was sustained in the play by Van Druten's witty dialogue. It is undercut in the picture by backgrounds that are too often as weird as the situations.

1958: Nominations: Best Costume Design, Art Direction

BELLBOY, THE
1960, 72 mins, US ⓥ ⊙
D: Jerry Lewis A: Jerry Lewis, Alex Gerry, Bob Clayton, Bill Richmond, Sonny Sands, Milton Berle (Paramount)

From an artistic standpoint, *The Bellboy* is minor-league screen comedy, the victim of its energetic star's limited craftsmanship. The picture is a series of silly sequences, with no story, no plot. It follows Jerry Lewis, as a bellboy at Miami's fashionable Fontainebleau Hotel, through a number of zany misadventures in which he speaks not a word of dialogue. Several of the sequences are amusing, but too many are dependent upon climactic sight gags anticipated well in advance of the punch.

BELLE DE JOUR
1967, 102 mins, France/Italy ⓥ ⊙
D: Luis Bunuel A: Catherine Deneuve, Jean Sorel, Michel Piccoli, Genevieve Page, Francisco Rabal, Pierre Clementi (Paris/Five)

Luis Bunuel comes up with a crackling look at a supposedly well-married, comely girl who begins to give way to masochistic leanings, working by day in a sporting house, if a good wife by night. Catherine Deneuve has the fine, luminous features to help make her heroine always coherent, rigorous, and forthright enough to clarify the dual life. Jean Sorel is properly attractive and weak as her husband. Michel Piccoli is an outspoken friend who sees through the heroine as effectively as the many perverted clients in her bagnio life.

LA BELLE ET LA BETE (BEAUTY AND THE BEAST)
1946, 110 mins, France ⓥ ⊙
D: Jean Cocteau A: Josette Day, Jean Marais, Mila Parely, Nane Germon, Michel Auclair, Marcel Andre (Paulve)

Unduly slow pace and repetitious use of trick sets hurts chances of this film. Story, a fairy tale in medieval costumes, shows Josette Day in a Cinderella part falling in love with a monster who turns into a Prince Charming upon death. Picture is geared more for the arty crowd than the masses.

BELLE OF NEW YORK, THE
1952, 82 mins, US ⓥ
D: Charles Walters A: Fred Astaire, Vera-Ellen, Marjorie Main, Keenan Wynn, Alice Pearce, Clinton Sundberg (M-G-M)

A film musical usually can get by with the lightest plot if the dance numbers and tunes are sock, but *Belle* has an even lighter plot than usual, and the numbers are just ordinary. Script has Astaire as an early–New York playboy who falls for a Bowery mission worker (Vera-Ellen) and changes his ways, even getting employment to prove he is worthy of her pure, honest affection.

BELLE OF THE NINETIES
1934, 75 mins, US
D: Leo McCarey A: Mae West, Roger Pryor, John Mack Brown, Katherine DeMille, John Miljan (Paramount)

Mae West's opera is as ten-twent-thirt as its mauve-decade time and locale. The melodramatics are put on a bit thick, including the archvillain, who is an arch-renegade, a would-be murderer, a welcher, an arsonist, and everything else in the book of ye-good-old-time mellers. Just like she makes stooges of almost anybody assigned to bandy-talk with her, West dittoes with her principal support, including Roger Pryor, the fave vis-à-vis, John Mack Brown as the good-time Charlie, and John Miljan, a villyun of darkest mien.

BELLE OF THE YUKON
1944, 83 mins, US
D: William A. Seiter A: Randolph Scott, Gypsy Rose Lee, Dinah Shore, Charles Winninger, William Marshall (RKO)

Belle of the Yukon is a typical backstage filmusical, utilizing a Yukon dance hall for setting. Yarn spins with tongue-in-cheek attitude and in general light vein. Randolph Scott is a reformed confidence man who fled north and opened a successful dancehall-gambling establishment at Malamute. Gypsy Rose Lee, deserted by Scott in his flight, arrives as head of a new entertainment unit and is intrigued by his reformation to again fall in love with him.

BELLES OF ST. TRINIAN'S, THE
1954, 91 mins, UK ⓥ
D: Frank Launder A: Alastair Sim, Joyce Grenfell, George Cole, Hermione Baddeley, Betty Ann Davies, Renee Houston (British Lion/London)

Inspired by Ronald Searle's British cartoons about the little horrors of a girls' school, *The Belles of St. Trinian's* never lives up to the promise of the opening reel. Frank Launder and Sidney Gilliat have concocted an involved yarn about a plot to steal the favorite horse in a big race which is foiled by the girls in the fourth form after a battle royal with the sixth form. As both the headmistress and her bookmaker brother, Alastair Sim rarely reaches comedy heights. Joyce Grenfell, however, as a police spy posing as a games teacher, is good for plenty of laughs. Best individual contribution is by George Cole, playing a wide-shouldered wiseguy.

BELL FOR ADANO, A
1945, 103 mins, US
D: Henry King **A:** Gene Tierney, John Hodiak, William Bendix, Richard Conte (20th Century-Fox)

John Hersey's story of an American major's administration of a town in Sicily, and his attempts to return it to its peaceful prewar status, has not been tampered with or elaborated upon. The film has some very beautiful, inspired moments, and finishes off with several scenes of emotional brilliance. John Hodiak presents the right hard-boiled type of civil-affairs officer, determined to bring spiritual rebirth (through the return of its city-hall bell) to the community. Gene Tierney, too, as the blond fisherman's daughter, has a certain quiet grace without always bringing sufficient poignancy to the role. William Bendix, as the major's orderly, plays the part in subdued fashion for the most convincing portrayal of the three leads.

BELLISSIMA
1952, 130 mins, Italy Ⓥ
D: Luchino Visconti **A:** Anna Magnani, Walter Chiari, Tina Apicella, Gastone Renzelli, Arturo Bragaglia, Alessandro Blasetti (Bellissima)

Story was suggested to writer Cesare Zavattini (*Miracle in Milan*) during the casting of recent Italian films. In telling about the attempts by a Rome worker's wife to get her little girl a film role, it launches some sharp barbs at the Roman film milieu. Magnani runs the thespian gamut in this one, in her colorful portrayal of the mother's role, with splendid support from comedian Walter Chiari. Latter here plays a straight part as a likable studio profiteer. The scene in which he tries and fails to seduce her on an excursion is one of pic's highlights.

BELL JAR, THE
1979, 107 mins, US Ⓥ
D: Larry Peerce **A:** Marilyn Hassett, Julie Harris, Anne Jackson, Barbara Barrie, Donna Mitchell, Robert Klein (Avco Embassy)

The Bell Jar, based on the late poet Sylvia Plath's autobiographical novel, evokes neither understanding nor sympathy for the plight of its heroine, Esther Greenwood, the epitome of a straight-A, golden-girl overachiever, who is mentally coming apart at the seams. As played by Marilyn Hassett, Esther emerges as a selfish, morbid little prig. Larry Peerce's direction provides a sense of headachy dullness 15 minutes into the film.

BELLS ARE RINGING
1960, 126 mins, US Ⓥ ⊙ ▭
D: Vincente Minnelli **A:** Judy Holliday, Dean Martin, Fred Clark, Eddie Foy, Jean Stapleton, Frank Gorshin (M-G-M)

Better Broadway musicals than *Bells Are Ringing* have come to Hollywood, but few have been translated to the screen so effectively. It's a pleasant yarn from which several rather inspired musical numbers spring. Holliday's outstanding turn occurs when she demonstrates her verve and versatility on the amusing "I'm Goin' Back (Where I Can Be Me, at the Bonjour Tristesse Brassiere Factory)." Holliday steals show with a performance of remarkable variety and gusto as a girl who takes her switchboard and humanity seriously, Martin is excellent as her writer friend, displaying more animation than customary.
1960: Nomination: Best Scoring of a Dramatic Picture

BELLS GO DOWN, THE
1943, 86 mins, UK
D: Basil Dearden **A:** Tommy Trinder, James Mason, Mervyn Johns, Philippa Hiatt, Finlay Currie, Beatrice Varley (Ealing)

This film depicts the activities of life in the London Auxiliary Fire Service. Viewed as a mere low comedy, *The Bells Go Down* ambles along amiably. There is a running commentary patterned on the lines of those made familiar by Quentin Reynolds, and the fire scenes alternate with the wisecracking of Tommy Trinder, which are often without provocation. Thrillingly effective conflagration scenes deserve a large share of the honors.

BELLS OF ST. MARY'S, THE
1945, 126 mins, US Ⓥ ⊙
D: Leo McCarey A: Bing Crosby, Ingrid Bergman, Henry Travers, Ruth Donnelly, Rhys Williams, Una O'Connor (RKO/Rainbow)

The Bells of St. Mary's is warmly sentimental, has a simple story leavened with many laughs, and bears comparison with *Going My Way*. Bing Crosby's Father O'Malley is the same priest character seen in *Way*, and *Bells* tells of his new assignment as parish priest at the parochial school, St. Mary's. Ingrid Bergman again demonstrates her versatility as the sister in charge. Her clashes with Crosby—all good-mannered—over proper methods of educating children, her venture into athletics, and coaching of a youngster to return a good left hook instead of the other cheek, are moments that will have an audience alternately laughing and sniffling.
1945: Best Sound Recording
Nominations: Best Picture, Director, Actor (Bing Crosby), Actress (Ingrid Bergman), Editing, Scoring of a Dramatic Picture, Song ("Aren't You Glad You're You?")

BELLY OF AN ARCHITECT, THE
1987, 118 mins, UK Ⓥ ⊙
D: Peter Greenaway A: Brian Dennehy, Chloe Webb, Lambert Wilson, Sergio Fantoni (Callender/Film Four/British Screen)

The Belly of an Architect is a visual treat, almost an homage to the style of Rome's architecture, lensed with skill and packed with esoteric nuances, but doubts about the story and the skill of the acting linger. The belly in question is the stomach of a US architect, played by a suitably paunchy Brian Dennehy, who becomes convinced he is being slowly poisoned by his wife (Chloe Webb) who is having an affair with a rival Italian architect (Lambert Wilson). Dennehy makes an admirable effort as the troubled architect, but the rest of the cast—mostly European—turn in generally poor efforts.

BELOVED ENEMY
1936, 90 mins, US Ⓥ
D: H. C. Potter A: Merle Oberon, Brian Aherne, Karen Morley, Jerome Cowan, David Niven, Henry Stephenson (Goldwyn/United Artists)

Beloved Enemy is a Hollywood version of how peace was restored betwen the British and Irish in 1921. The collaborators of *Beloved Enemy* have conceived a romantic tragedy between the leader of the Irish insurrectionists and the titled daughter of a British conciliator, and the result is more fantastic than anything G. A. Henty ever invented. Merle Oberon and Brian Aherne are surprisingly well suited to each other, and the romantic episodes are charmingly played. Oberon is lovely to look upon and speaks her lines with fine enunciation. Aherne plays the young Irish rebel with humorous ease.

BELOVED INFIDEL
1959, 123 mins, US ▭
D: Henry King A: Gregory Peck, Deborah Kerr, Eddie Albert, Philip Ober, Herbert Rudley, John Sutton (20th Century-Fox)

The protracted and stormy Sheilah Graham–F. Scott Fitzgerald romance in the 1930s is brought to the screen. This is primarily a film about a sharp, aggressive film columnist who falls in love with a man who is her intellectual superior. The characters go mostly unexplained and this makes for a superficiality which deprives them of sympathy. Problem is primarily with Peck, who brings to Fitzgerald the kind of clean-cut looks and youthful appearance that conflict with the image of a has-been novelist. Kerr can't overcome the artificiality of the part or the situation, and after a while the affair just peters out and becomes dull.

BEN
1972, 83 mins, US Ⓥ
D: Phil Karlson A: Lee H. Montgomery, Joseph Campanella, Arthur O'Connell, Rosemary Murphy, Meredith Baxter, Kaz Garas (Cinerama/Crosby)

Willard has a tension-packed sequel in *Ben*, which takes up minutes after Willard, the man who trained rats, was killed off by his rodents in original entry. Ben, the rat heavy of the other, plays title role here. Chief protagonist is a young boy played by Lee H. Montgomery, who befriends Ben. Latter's army of rats obey his orders, and they create a reign of terror as they indulge in a wave of killing.
1972: Nomination: Best Song ("Ben")

BEND OF THE RIVER
1952, 91 mins, US Ⓥ
D: Anthony Mann A: James Stewart, Arthur Kennedy, Julie Adams, Rock Hudson, Lori Nelson, Jay C. Flippen (Universal)

Basic plotline deals with a band of settlers who make a long, wagon-train trek into Oregon to claim the country from the wilderness. James Stewart is the wagon-train guide. He rescues Arthur Kennedy, a former Missouri raider, from a hanging and the latter joins the party. Stewart's handling of his role has punch. Kennedy socks his likable heavy role. Julie Adams fulfills romantic demands of her top femme role, and Rock Hudson pleasantly projects the part of a young gambler who joins the settlers.

BENEATH THE PLANET OF THE APES
1970, 95 mins, US ⓥ ⊙ ☒
D: Ted Post **A:** James Franciscus, Kim Hunter, Maurice Evans, Linda Harrison, Charlton Heston, Victor Buono (20th Century-Fox/Apjac)

This sequel to the 1968 smash *Planet of the Apes* is hokey and slapdash. James Franciscus is yet another space explorer who crash-lands, centuries out of time. Dialogue, acting, and direction are substandard. Heston appears in some new footage, and Franciscus looks just like a twin brother by this time, in face and in voice.

BENEATH THE 12-MILE REEF
1953, 102 mins, US ⓥ ☒
D: Robert D. Webb **A:** Robert Wagner, Terry Moore, Gilbert Roland, J. Carrol Naish, Richard Boone, Peter Graves (20th Century-Fox)

Set among the sponge-diving Greek colony at Tarpon Springs, FL, the squeeze lensing [of CinemaScope] gives punch in the display of underwater wonders, the seascapes, and the brilliant, beautiful sunrises and sunsets of the Florida Gulf coast. Robert Wagner and Terry Moore are likable, so the shallowness of their performances is no serious handicap to the entertainment. Scoring resoundingly is Gilbert Roland, colorful Greek diver and father of Wagner. Angela Clarke also clicks as the wife and mother.
1953: Nomination: Best Color Cinematography

BENEATH THE VALLEY OF THE ULTRA VIXENS
1979, 93 mins, US ⓥ ⊙
D: Russ Meyer **A:** Francesca Kitten Natividad, Anne Marie, Ken Kerr, June Mack, Lola Langusta (RM International)

For the fanciers of pneumatic pulchritude, Russ Meyer is back with *Beneath the Valley of the Ultra Vixens*. Briefly, the strand of plot concerns Lavonia (Francesca Kitten Natividad), whose only fault is enthusiasm and her unsatisfactory sex re-

lationship with her man, Lamar (Ken Kerr). In the course of curing Lamar so that he will straighten up and satisfy, Lavonia has a hot time with everybody in town. This is the umpteenth in Meyer's vixen series. But are they satire, as Meyer would have one believe, or fantasy, or both? If anything, they are funny, and though a bit too long, Meyer, who does everything (directs, edits, photographs, and produces), keeps the action fast and furious.

BENEFIT OF THE DOUBT
1993, 90 mins, US ⓥ ⊙
D: Jonathan Heap **A:** Donald Sutherland, Amy Irving, Rider Strong, Christopher McDonald, Graham Greene, Theodore Bikel (Monument)

Suspense is not the strongest suit of this lackluster psychological thriller. Initially interesting setup has Frank Braswell (Donald Sutherland) paroled after 22 years in prison. Accused of killing his wife, Frank's conviction was helped by the testimony of his daughter Karen (Amy Irving), who still believes he is guilty. Karen dreads the return of her father. The chief problem is that a half hour into the movie, the pivotal dirty family secrets are disclosed and the story has nowhere to go. When the first murder makes its scheduled stop, one can sniff red herring a mile away. Cast against type, Irving gives a startling performance. The usually reliable Sutherland is surprisingly timid and inexpressive.

BEN-HUR
1959, 212 mins, US ⓥ ⊙ ☒
D: William Wyler, [Andrew Marton, Richard Thorpe] **A:** Charlton Heston, Jack Hawkins, Stephen Boyd, Haya Harareet, Hugh Griffith, Sam Jaffe (M-G-M)

The big difference between *Ben-Hur* and other spectacles, biblical or otherwise, is its sincere concern for human beings. This has been accomplished without sacrificing the impact of the spectacle elements. The famous chariot race between Ben-Hur, the Prince of Judea, and Messala, the Roman tribune, directed by Andrew Marton and Yakima Canutt, represents some 40 minutes of the most hair-raising excitement ever witnessed. Charlton Heston is excellent as the brawny yet kindly Ben-Hur, who survives the life of a galley slave to seek revenge on his enemy Messala. Stephen Boyd, as Messala, is not the standard villain, but succeeds in giving understanding to this position in his dedication to the Roman Empire. The film took 10 months to complete at Rome's Cinecitta Studios. The 300 sets are one of the highlights of the film, particularly the massive arena for the chariot sequence. The musical score by Miklos Rozsa also contributes to the overall excellence of the giant project.

1959: Best Picture, Director, Actor (Charlton Heston), Supp. Actor (Hugh Griffith), Color Cinematography, Color Art Direction, Sound, Scoring of a Dramatic Picture, Editing, Special Effects, Color Costume Design
Nomination: Best Adapted Screenplay

BEN-HUR
A TALE OF THE CHRIST
1925, 128 mins, US ⓥ ⊙ ⊗
D: Fred Niblo **A:** Ramon Novarro, Francis X. Bushman, May McAvoy, Betty Bronson, Carmel Myers (M-G-M)

Ben-Hur is a picture that rises above spectacle, even though it is spectacle. On the screen it isn't the chariot race or the great battle scenes between the fleet of Rome and the pirate galleys of Golthar. It is the tremendous heartthrobs that one experiences leading to those scenes that make them great. The Mary of Betty Bronson is without doubt the most tremendous individual score that any actress has ever made, with but a single scene with a couple of close-ups. And in the color scenes she appears simply superb. Then, as for Ramon Novarro: anyone who sees him in this picture will have to admit that he is without doubt a man's man and 100 percent of that. Francis X. Bushman does a comeback in the role of the heavy (Messala) that makes him stand alone.

BENJI
1974, 85 mins, US ⓥ
D: Joe Camp **A:** Patsy Garrett, Allen Fiuzat, Cynthia Smith, Peter Breck, Edgar Buchanan (Mulberry Square)

Benji is a dog's picture from first to last. From the moment he pokes his head through a broken door in a deserted house where he has his pad until he's adopted by the family whose two children he saves from kidnappers, interest rests squarely on the head of this pooch, of uncertain parentage. Much of the footage is shot from about 18 inches above the ground, upward from Benji's point of view, and innovation is fascinating.
1974: Nomination: Best Song ("I Feel Love")

BENNY & JOON
1993, 98 mins, US ⓥ ⊙
D: Jeremiah Chechik **A:** Johnny Depp, Mary Stuart Masterson, Aidan Quinn, Julianne Moore, Oliver Platt, C.C.H. Pounder (M-G-M)

Johnny Depp and Mary Stuart Masterson render such startling performances in the romantic fable *Benny & Joon* they almost overcome being in a not particularly well-written or directed effort. Masterson stars as Juniper ("Joon"), the mentally ill sister of Benny (Aidan Quinn), an auto mechanic who takes care of her. The quick-witted Joon spends her days at home, painting with passion. This frail equilibrium is shattered when Sam (Depp), a modern-day clown in the mold of Chaplin and Keaton, shows up and changes the rules of the game. The pic's strength lies more in the nuances of the relationships than in the smooth flow of an episodic narrative.

BENNY GOODMAN STORY, THE
1955, 116 mins, US ⓥ
D: Valentine Davies **A:** Steve Allen, Donna Reed, Berta Gersten, Herbert Anderson, Robert F. Simon (Universal)

The Benny Goodman Story is of the same stripe as Universal's previously socko bandleader saga, *The Glenn Miller Story*. If the romantics of the script and Steve Allen and Donna Reed's interpretations lack a bit, they are sufficiently glossed over because the major canvas is the saga of the Chicago youth with the licorice stick and his dedication to the cause of a new exciting tempo, later interpreted as "swing." The close-ups on the very poor Jewish family and Goodman's humble environments are not glossed over. In the same idiom there is no fanfare about the interracial mixing, socially or professionally.

BEQUEST TO THE NATION
1973, 115 mins, UK ▭
D: James Cellan Jones **A:** Glenda Jackson, Peter Finch, Michael Jayston, Anthony Quayle, Margaret Leighton, Dominic Guard (Universal)

This is a deliberate, though stylish and genteel, deglamorizing of the affair between Lord Nelson and Lady Hamilton which scandalized England. Production is based on Terence Rattigan's adaptation of his own play, and never completely escapes its legit origins. The story-as-is permits Jackson to display a variety of her dramatic abilities. Finch is slightly less effective as Nelson, though he manages to project the complex facets of character.

BERKELEY SQUARE
1933, 87 mins, US
D: Frank Lloyd **A:** Leslie Howard, Heather Angel, Valerie Taylor, Irene Browne, Alan Mowbray, Juliette Compton (Fox)

Berkeley Square is an imaginative, beautiful, and well-handled production. Leslie Howard in the same role he played on the stage is as near perfection as can be hoped for in screen characterization. Story of *Berkeley Square* is still another variation on Mark Twain's *A Connecticut Yankee in King Arthur's Court*. Where Twain used the idea of flashing a character into another century for fun, Peter Standish (Howard) moves back into a spot used by one of his forefathers and falls in love with a gal of that period. It's a new kind of love story. Heather Angel, as the girl, turns in a splendid performance.
1932/33: Nomination: Best Actor (Leslie Howard)

BERLIN EXPRESS
1948, 86 mins, US ⓥ ⊙
D: Jacques Tourneur **A:** Merle Oberon, Robert Ryan, Charles Korvin, Paul Lukas, Robert Coote, Reinhold Schunzel (RKO)

Most striking feature of this production is its extraordinary background of war-ravaged Germany. With a documentary eye, this film etches a powerfully grim picture of life amid the shambles. Chief defect of the screenplay is its failure to break away from the formula of anti-Nazi films. The Nazis, now underground, are still the heavies but it's difficult to get excited about such a group of ragged hoodlums. Their motivation in the pic, moreover, is never explained satisfactorily as they set about kidnapping a prominent German democrat, played by Paul Lukas. Ryan establishes himself as a first-rate actor in this film.

BEST FOOT FORWARD
1943, 93 mins, US ⓥ
D: Edward Buzzell **A:** Lucille Ball, Tommy Dix, Nancy Walker, June Allyson, Gloria de Haven, Chill Wills (M-G-M)

This filmusical version of George Abbott's stage production retains all of the youthful enthusiasm and spontaneity of the original, with addition of Harry James and his orchestra for generous supply of his trumpeteering and jump music. Metro

displays a number of new faces and teenage talent including five—Tommy Dix, Nancy Walker, June Allyson, Kenny Bowers, and Jack Jordan—from the original stage cast. Scholastic zest and pep, and the musical interludes, successfully carry the extremely fragile story premise.

BEST FRIENDS
1982, 116 mins, US ⓥ ⊙
D: Norman Jewison **A:** Burt Reynolds, Goldie Hawn, Jessica Tandy, Barnard Hughes, Audra Lindley, Keenan Wynn (Warner)

Best Friends is a very engaging film. Addressing the problems two writers in a professional and personal relationship encounter when they decide to get married, almost all of the picture's funny moments are underscored by the more serious issues they face from themselves, their families, and society as a "married couple." Both stars are tremendously aided by an intelligent screenplay from Valerie Curtin and Barry Levinson, who are said to have based at least part of this work on their own relationship. They leave Hawn and Reynolds more than enough room to inject their own nuances.
1982: Nomination: Best Original Song ("How Do You Keep the Music Playing?")

BEST LITTLE WHOREHOUSE IN TEXAS, THE
1982, 114 mins, US ⓥ ⊙ ▭
D: Colin Higgins **A:** Burt Reynolds, Dolly Parton, Dom DeLuise, Charles Durning, Jim Nabors, Robert Mandan (Universal-RKO)

The Best Little Whorehouse in Texas is just about everything it's meant to be—a couple of diverting hours in the dark. Rollicking, good-natured, a bit spicy, and with just enough heart to avoid seeming totally synthetic, the $26-million adaptation of the 1978 Broadway hit ideally teams powerhouse stars Burt Reynolds and Dolly Parton.
1982: Nomination: Best Supp. Actor (Charles Durning)

BEST MAN, THE
1964, 102 mins, US ⓥ
D: Franklin J. Schaffner **A:** Henry Fonda, Cliff Robertson, Edie Adams, Margaret Leighton, Shelley Berman, Lee Tracy (United Artists)

Gore Vidal's provocative drama of political infighting on the national level has been skillfully converted to film. Vidal's straightforward, sharply drawn scenario describes the bitter struggle for a party's presidential nomination between an ambitious self-righteous character assassin (many will see him as a Nixon-McCarthy composite) and a scrupulous intellectual (of Stevensonian essence). Between these two antagonists, portrayed with conviction and sensitivity by Cliff Robertson and Henry Fonda respectively, stands the imposing figure of the mortally ill but still politically virile ex-president, a character likely to be associated with Harry S. Truman. Lee Tracy repeats his Broadway characterization in the role and just about steals the show with his expressive, colorful portrayal.

1964: Nomination: Best Supp. Actor (Lee Tracy)

BEST OF CINERAMA, THE
1963, 141 mins, US ⌂
Prod Merian C. Cooper, Thomas Conroy (Cinerama)

Derived from *This Is Cinerama, Cinerama Holiday, 7 Wonders of the World, Search for Paradise,* and *Cinerama South Seas Adventure,* this is out-and-out travelogue. Opening picks up the well-remembered roller-coaster sequence. Close attention is paid to fast movement, other rapido being caught in such sequences as bobsledding at St. Moritz, acrobatic water skiing in Florida, surfboarding at Waikiki. Other highlights include such sequences as La Scala Opera House in Milan, with the triumphal scene from *Aida;* gondola ride through Venice and St. Mark's Square; men jumping from a 100-foot tower in the New Hebrides with vines bound around their ankles.

BEST OF ENEMIES, THE
1961, 104 mins, UK/Italy ⌂
D: Guy Hamilton **A:** David Niven, Alberto Sordi, Michael Wilding, Amedeo Nazzari, Harry Andrews, David Opatoshu (Columbia)

A wartime comedy, with a gently serious undertone for those who seek it. Locale is the Ethiopian desert in 1941. David Niven, a British major, and his pilot RAF officer Michael Wilding, are captured by an Italian patrol, led by an Italian officer (Alberto Sordi). He releases them on condition that they let his patrol move freely to a nearby fort. Back in base, Niven is ordered to attack the fort and does so reluctantly. From then on it's a hilarious, cat-and-mouse game, with captor and captive alternating as the fortunes of war

sway. The serious undertone? That war is crazy. Niven, debonair, nonchalant, and skilfully underplaying, is matched excellently by Sordi, playing his first English-speaking role.

BEST OF EVERYTHING, THE
1959, 122 mins, US Ⓥ ⌂
D: Jean Negulesco **A:** Hope Lange, Stephen Boyd, Suzy Parker, Martha Hyer, Diane Baker, Joan Crawford (20th Century-Fox)

Amanda (Joan Crawford), a successful career woman, is having an affair with a married man (unseen). One of her co-workers, Barbara (Martha Hyer), is also involved with another married man (Donald Harron). Gregg (Suzy Parker) is having an affair with stage producer David (Louis Jourdan), who jilts her to take up (extramaritally, of course) with Judy (Myrna Hansen). To continue, April (Diane Baker) becomes pregnant (out of wedlock) by Dexter (Robert Evans), who proposes they solve this problem by visiting an abortionist. Caroline (Hope Lange) is jilted by Eddie (Brett Halsey) for a rich girl. Sex, it will be seen, occupies a large part of this film. Jean Negulesco's direction is firm-handed at keeping the overwrought story from getting overheated.

BEST SELLER
1987, 110 mins, US Ⓥ ⊙
D: John Flynn **A:** James Woods, Brian Dennehy, Victoria Tennant, Allison Balson, Paul Shenar, George Coe (Hemdale)

Best Seller combines the sinister appeal of James Woods at his cold-blooded best with the gruffly lovable persona of Brian Dennehy as a literary cop; on the level of detective thriller, it's a real page-turner. Dennehy is Dennis Meechum, a cop who writes a book based on a famous unsolved case. Seventeen years after the incident, he is a lonely burnout case. Into the picture comes mystery man Cleve (Woods), full of unctuous charm and foreboding stares. He presents himself as a former hit man who worked for a pillar of L.A. society. The body of the film has Cleve bringing Meechum around the country, providing different details in his story, while Meechum takes it all down in a book.

BEST SHOT
See: Hoosiers

BEST THINGS IN LIFE ARE FREE, THE
1956, 104 mins, US ▭
D: Michael Curtiz A: Gordon MacRae, Dan Dailey, Sheree North, Ernest Borgnine, Tommy Noonan, Murvyn Vye (20th Century-Fox)

In *The Best Things in Life Are Free*, producer Henry Ephron and director Michael Curtiz went on the reasonably sound theory that in telling the story of Tin Pan Alley's fabulous team of Buddy DeSylva, Lew Brown, and Ray Henderson, all that was necessary was to fill the widescreen with a huge potpourri of their works. It catches little of the Jazz Age feeling, except in its costumes and the frantic shimmy and Black Bottom numbers, and the songwriting trio barely come to life as real people. It's a sparkling string of hits that's presented with all the nostalgic attention they deserve. Performances are top caliber, from Gordon MacRae's and Dan Dailey's pleasant crooning, to Ernest Borgnine's clowning and Sheree North's agile terp routines.
1956: Nomination: Best Scoring of a Musical Picture

BEST YEARS OF OUR LIVES, THE
1946, 163 mins, US Ⓥ ◉
D: William Wyler A: Fredric March, Myrna Loy, Dana Andrews, Teresa Wright, Harold Russell, Cathy O'Donnell (RKO/Goldwyn)

The postwar saga of the soda jerk who became an army officer; the banker who was mustered out as the sergeant; and a seaman who came back to glory minus both hands. Inspired casting has newcomer Harold Russell, a real-life amputee, pacing the seasoned trouper, and Fredric March, for personal histrionic triumphs. But all the other performances are equally good. Myrna Loy is the small-town bank veepee's beauteous wife. Teresa Wright plays their daughter, who goes for the already-married Dana Andrews with full knowledge of his wife (Virginia Mayo, who does a capital job as the cheating looker). Cathy O'Donnell does her sincerely-in-love chore with the same simplicity as Harold Russell, the $200-a-month war-pensioned hero, who, since he has lost his hands in combat, spurns O'Donnell because he never wants to be a burden. The pace of the picture is a bit leisurely. Almost a full hour is required to set the mood and the motivation, but never does it pall. Not a line or scene is spurious.
1946: Best Picture, Director, Actor (Fredric March), Supp. Actor (Harold Russell), Screenplay, Scoring of a Dramatic Picture, Editing, Special Award (Harold Russell)
Nomination: Best Sound

LA BETE HUMAINE
1939, 96 mins, France Ⓥ
D: Jean Renoir A: Jean Gabin, Simone Simon, Fernand Ledoux, Carette, Jean Renoir, Blanchette Brunoy (Paris)

La Bete Humaine is French production at its best. Jean Renoir, in filming Emile Zola's penetrating study of a man obsessed by an irrepressible desire to kill, has captured that repression in all of its nuances. Jean Gabin, as the humble locomotive engineer, knows and is haunted by his desire to strangle when the urge strikes his numbed brain. Ledoux is the station chief and Simone Simon is his unfaithful wife. Ledoux murders his wife's lover before her eyes. Gabin and Ledoux's wife become lovers, she aware that Gabin knows who committed the murder. She tells Gabin he must kill her husband or he will kill them both.

BETHUNE
THE MAKING OF A HERO
1990, 115 mins, Canada/China/France Ⓥ
D: Phillip Borsos A: Donald Sutherland, Helen Mirren, Helen Shaver, Harrison Liu, Anouk Aimee, Ronald Pickup (Filmline/August 1st/Parmentier/Belstar)

This c. $18-million political saga is a thorough documenting of the life of Canadian doctor Norman Bethune, a hero in China for his medical input during the long march in Mao Tse-tung's revolution. The film belongs to Donald Sutherland, who delivers a stunning performance as the complex and controversial surgeon. Harrison Liu delivers a fine performance as Bethune's protégé, Dr. Fong, but Helen Shaver (as a missionary in China) and Helen Mirren (as Bethune's wife) pale beside Sutherland.

BETRAYAL
1983, 95 mins, UK Ⓥ
D: David Jones A: Jeremy Irons, Ben Kingsley, Patricia Hodge (Horizon)

Betrayal is an absorbing, quietly amusing chamber drama for those attuned to Harold Pinter's way with words. In laying out his study of a rather conventional ménage-à-trois among two male best friends and the wife of one of them, Pinter's gambit was to present it in reverse chronological order. Tale thus starts in the present and gradually steps backward over the course of nine years. Kingsley comes across best, as the film only springs fully to life when he's onscreen.

1983: Nomination: Best Adapted Screenplay

BETRAYED
1988, 127 mins, US Ⓥ ⊙
D: Constantin Costa-Gavras **A:** Debra Winger, Tom Berenger, John Heard, Betsy Blair, John Mahoney, Ted Levine (United Artists)

Betrayed is a political thriller that is more political than thrilling but never less than absorbing due to the combustible subject matter, that of the white-supremacist movement. Debra Winger has come up from Texas as a combine girl. Local farmer Tom Berenger quickly takes a shine to the new gal in town, while she responds to the warmth of his family life. Winger soon hops back to Chicago to brief her superiors at the FBI on her progress in infiltrating the group suspected of perpetrating murder. Berenger proves forceful and properly unpredictable in his vulnerable macho role, and entire cast is nicely low-keyed.

BETRAYED
See: When Strangers Marry

BETSY, THE
1978, 125 mins, US Ⓥ
D: Daniel Petrie **A:** Laurence Olivier, Robert Duvall, Katharine Ross, Tommy Lee Jones, Jane Alexander, Lesley-Anne Down (Allied Artists/Robbins)

There's something too classy about this version of the Harold Robbins novel. It's too tame. And too solemn. The script has four main interests: cars, sex, money, and power. It's an American movie. Laurence Olivier is retired auto tycoon Loren Hardeman Sr., now interested in manufacturing a revolutionary car, one too efficient, too practical, and too benevolent for American industry. Through a series of flashbacks, Olivier ages from 40 to 90. Complete with midwest accent, he's on target, maybe too much so. Ditto for Robert Duvall as his grandson and current president of the auto company, Jane Alexander as Duvall's wife, and Katharine Ross as Olivier's daughter-in-law and lover. Tommy Lee Jones as a daredevil race driver plays his role with a mixture of edginess and off handedness—a com-

bination of Burt Reynolds and Harvey Keitel. His style—it's got a sense of humor and a campy quality to it—seems more to the point. It's almost trashy. (Now, that's Harold Robbins.)

BETSY'S WEDDING
1990, 98 mins, US Ⓥ ⊙
D: Alan Alda **A:** Alan Alda, Madeline Kahn, Molly Ringwald, Ally Sheedy, Anthony LaPaglia, Joe Pesci (Touchstone/Silver Screen Partners IV)

From a bolt of ordinary cloth Alan Alda fashions a thoroughly engaging matrimonial romp in *Betsy's Wedding*. Most of the action comes from the clash of personalities and wills as unconventional daughter Betsy (Molly Ringwald) announces her plans to wed boyfriend Jake (Dylan Walsh), and everyone jumps into the act. Overreaching dad (Alda) wants a big, wonderful Italian-Jewish wedding, and plans accelerate into a one-upmanship contest when Jake's wealthy WASP parents try to take the reins.

BETTER TOMORROW, A
See: Yinghung Bunsik

BETTER TOMORROW II, A
See: Yinghung Bunsik II

BETTY BLUE
See: 37°2 le Matin

BETWEEN HEAVEN AND HELL
1956, 94 mins, US ▭
D: Richard Fleischer **A:** Robert Wagner, Terry Moore, Broderick Crawford, Buddy Ebsen, Robert Keith, Brad Dexter (20th Century-Fox)

A good, hard-hitting action film, replete with the usual heroics but also full with the ugly realization that the men who fought World War II were far from perfect. The film captures the sights and sounds of the Pacific fighting and generates a good deal of tension and excitement. Not all of it is believable, and Wagner's final rushing down the Jap-infested mountain is almost ludicrous as he sideswipes one Jap party after the other. Wagner gives a good, low-key performance as the boy who gets busted to private after he hits an officer who has killed the men in his patrol. Broderick Crawford is loud and overbearing as the psycho colonel.

BETWEEN THE LINES
1977, 101 mins, US Ⓥ
D: Joan Micklin Silver **A:** John Heard, Lindsay Crouse, Jeff Goldblum, Jill Ei-

kenberry, Bruno Kirby, Gwen Welles (Midwest/Silver)

A fresh and uncluttered look at what goes on behind the scenes at a grubby, underfinanced but undaunted little newspaper. Where it is strong is partially due to the excellently written script, partially due to the overall first-rate acting by the entire cast. It's a series of interrelationships, professionally and romantically, between staff photographer Lindsay Crouse and top investigative reporter John Heard; reporter-cum-bookwriter Stephen Collins and staffer Gwen Welles; plus the story of an underpaid and overworked rock-music critic Jeff Goldblum, copyboy and would-be reporter Bruno Kirby, and the other oddballs who work for the newspaper, due to be taken over any day by a communications conglomerate.

BETWEEN TWO WORLDS
1944, 112 mins, US
D: Edward A. Blatt A: John Garfield, Paul Henreid, Sydney Greenstreet, Eleanor Parker, Edmund Gwenn, George Tobias (Warner)

An artistic transcription of *Outward Bound*, the Broadway stage hit of 1925, this film was earlier brought to the screen in 1930. A 1944 opening has been provided here, the locale being an unidentified port in England from which a small assorted group of persons is preparing to sail for America. Unable to leave because his papers aren't in order is Paul Henreid. He and his wife, played with much feeling by Eleanor Parker, take to the gas pipe, both wanting to die together. Meantime, in an air raid the bus carrying others to the evacuation ship is destroyed. From here the action shifts to a mystery ship which, it finally becomes evident, is bound for the Great Beyond, with Henreid, Parker, and the group that had been killed in the bomb raid. On reaching High Olympus and judgment day, Sydney Greenstreet enters the scene as the examiner, taking his new arrivals one by one. His performance is outstanding, and the sequence represents a productional, directional, and acting triumph.

BEVERLY HILLBILLIES, THE
1993, 93 mins, US Ⓥ ⊙
D: Penelope Spheeris A: Diedrich Bader, Dabney Coleman, Erika Eleniak, Cloris Leachman, Rob Schneider, Lea Thompson (20th Century-Fox)

Just as corny and stupid as the long-running TV series, pic version has been cleverly cast and shrewdly skewed to appeal jointly to original fans of the show and younger viewers only vaguely familiar with it. Taking officious control of the newly rich family's affairs when they arrive in BevHills are toadying banker Mr. Drysdale and prim secretary Miss Hathaway, roles neatly filled by TV-friendly Dabney Coleman and Lily Tomlin. Latter is given the assignment of finding a suitable wife for the widowed Jed (Jim Varney), who is now one of the most eligible men in America. It's all pretty thin, scattershot stuff, but the ingratiating naïveté of the characters and the aw-shucks friendliness of the cast are disarming.

BEVERLY HILLS COP
1984, 105 mins, US Ⓥ ⊙
D: Martin Brest A: Eddie Murphy, Judge Reinhold, Lisa Eilbacher, John Ashton, Ronny Cox, Steven Berkoff (Paramount)

Beverly Hills Cop is more cop show than comedy riot. Expectations that Eddie Murphy's street brand of rebelliousness would devastate staid and glittery Beverly Hills are not entirely met in a film that grows increasingly dramatic as Murphy's recalcitrant cop from Detroit runs down the killers of his best friend. Strong assists come from a deceptively likable performance from Judge Reinhold as a naive Beverly Hills detective, from by-the-book chief Ronny Cox, and from the serpentine villainy of Steven Berkoff, who plays an art dealer involved in nefarious endeavors.
1984: Nomination: Best Original Screenplay

BEVERLY HILLS COP II
1987, 102 mins, US Ⓥ ⊙ ▭
D: Tony Scott A: Eddie Murphy, Judge Reinhold, Jurgen Prochnow, Ronny Cox, John Ashton, Brigitte Nielsen (Paramount/Murphy)

Beverly Hills Cop II is a noisy, numbing, unimaginative, heartless remake of the original film. Getting Eddie Murphy back to Beverly Hills from his native Detroit turf is the critical wounding of police captain Ronny Cox by a group of rich baddies committing the Alphabet Crimes, a series of violent robberies at heavily guarded locations. Murphy keeps things entertainingly afloat with his sassiness and raunchy one-liners, take-charge brazenness, and innate irreverence. Murphy's a hoot in numerous scenes, but less so than on other occasions because of the frosty context for his shenanigans.

BEVERLY HILLS COP III
1994, 109 mins, US Ⓥ ⊙
D: John Landis **A:** Eddie Murphy, Judge Reinhold, Hector Elizondo, Timothy Carhart, John Saxon, Bronson Pinchot (Paramount)

The third installment of the *Beverly Hills Cop* series boasts a return to form by Eddie Murphy and a breezy and witty first half, though the film runs out of steam before the end. Murphy is reunited with an old Beverly Hills crony, Billy Rosewood (Judge Reinhold), and a new cop buddy played by Hector Elizondo. The focus of the action is a theme park called WonderWorld. Screenwriter Steven E. de Souza has a lark lampooning the squeaky-clean Americana atmosphere of these entertainments as well as those overwrought Universal crash-bam-boom thrill rides.

BEWITCHED
1945, 65 mins, US
D: Arch Oboler **A:** Phyllis Thaxter, Edmund Gwenn, Henry H. Daniels Jr., Horace McNally, Minor Watson (M-G-M)

Produced on a low budget, with a sterling cast of actor's actors, this picture just oozes with class. Climax follows climax, strong performance follows strong performance in this thrilling psychopathic study of a girl obsessed by an inner voice that drives her to murder. Phyllis Thaxter carries the major burden in this one, and Oboler's direction guides her to new dramatic heights. She's in fast company here, with Edmund Gwenn, costarred in the role of a psychiatrist, registering tellingly. Yarn is told in flashbacks, an eerie musical score by Bronislau Kaper adding to the suspense.

BEYOND A REASONABLE DOUBT
1956, 80 mins, US Ⓥ
D: Fritz Lang **A:** Dana Andrews, Joan Fontaine, Sidney Blackmer, Barbara Nichols, Philip Bourneuf, Shepperd Strudwick (RKO)

A trick ending wraps up the melodrama in *Beyond a Reasonable Doubt* but comes a little too late to revive interest in a tale that relies too often on pat contrivance. Dana Andrews is a writer engaged to Joan Fontaine, daughter of newspaper publisher Sidney Blackmer. The latter talks Andrews into going along with his scheme for showing up the fallacy of circumstantial evidence. In brief, Blackmer plans to plant evidence that will get Andrews arrested, tried, and convicted for the murder of a burlesque stripper. Scheme works as planned, except at the crucial moment Blackmer gets himself killed.

BEYOND BEDLAM
1994, 88 mins, UK Ⓥ
D: Vadim Jean **A:** Craig Fairbrass, Elizabeth Hurley, Keith Allen, Anita Dobson, Craig Kelly, Jesse Birdsall (Metrodome)

Beyond Bedlam is an ambitious Brit horror schlocker that seems to have mislaid its script halfway. Careening, often stylish meltdown of everything from Thomas Harris shavings to Elm Street and Clive Barker offshoots starts with a bang but trails off into a whimper as the pic abandons all logic in the second half. Shot largely in an abandoned sanitarium in north London, the $3-million production has an umbral, high-gloss visual style in its early going.

BEYOND RANGOON
1995, 99 mins, US Ⓥ ⊙ ▱
D: John Boorman **A:** Patricia Arquette, Frances McDormand, Spalding Gray, Aung Ko, Victor Slezak, Adelle Lutz (Castle Rock/Columbia)

Another of John Boorman's ambitious explorations of a remote foreign culture, physically handsome effort was originally planned with Meg Ryan as its star. In the end, Patricia Arquette took on the role of Laura Bowman, an American doctor. With her sister Andy (Frances McDormand), Laura is in Burma in 1988 when the peaceful protests against the military government begin reaching a crescendo. In the first of numerous melodramatic contrivances, Laura manages to lose her passport and be left behind when her sister and the rest of her touring party beat a hasty retreat from the country. Seeking a safe haven away from the capital, she escapes with ostensible guide Aung Ko, a former professor and political dissident. The momentary excitement of the large-scale action sequences notwithstanding, the film never goes more than halfway in satisfying on all its levels of concentration as psychological exploration of Laura's inner journey, as exposé of a little-dramatized political situation, and as pure adventure tale.

BEYOND REASONABLE DOUBT
1980, 127 mins, New Zealand Ⓥ ▱
D: John Laing **A:** David Hemmings, John Hargreaves, Martyn Sanderson, Grant

Tilly, Diana Rowan, Ian Watkin (Endeavour)

For 10 years the New Zealand public lived with the murder mystery surrounding the deaths of Jeanette and Harvey Crewe. After an unprecedented two trials, Arthur Thomas was found guilty. He was pardoned late in 1979. If the aim was to persuade us that a tough cop, hell-bent on a conviction, manipulated murder evidence even to the extent of planting a cartridge case at the scene of the crime to implicate Thomas, then it strikes a bull's-eye. Roles have been sharply cast to have look-alikes doubling for the real-life protagonists. David Hemmings brings a chillingly vindictive venom to the role of the cop. John Hargreaves is suitably bewildered as Thomas, the rather simple young farmer who can't believe it's happening to him.

BEYOND THE CLOUDS
See: *Par Dela Les Nuages*

BEYOND THE FOREST
1949, 95 mins, US ⊛
D: King Vidor **A:** Bette Davis, Joseph Cotten, David Brian, Ruth Roman, Regis Toomey (Warner)

Beyond the Forest gives Bette Davis a chance to portray the neurotic femme she does so well. The character of Rosa Moline, a woman who yearns for broader vistas than those supplied by the Wisconsin mill town to which she is tied, furnishes plenty of bite for the Davis technique and she belts it across. Joseph Cotten is the small-town-minded doctor married to Rosa. His chore as the doctor is quiet and effective and David Brian is colorful as the man on whom Rosa has set her sights.
1949: Nomination: Best Scoring of a Dramatic Picture

BEYOND THE LIMIT
See: *The Honorary Consul*

BEYOND THE POSEIDON ADVENTURE
1979, 122 mins, US ⊛ ⊡
D: Irwin Allen **A:** Michael Caine, Sally Field, Telly Savalas, Peter Boyle, Jack Warden, Karl Malden (Warner)

Beyond the Poseidon Adventure comes off as a virtual remake of the 1972 original, without that film's mounting suspense and excitement. Recap of original premise, a luxury liner turned upside down by gigantic tidal wave, is accomplished in a few seconds. New plot turn pits salvage tug operators Michael Caine, Karl Malden, and Sally Field against evildoer Telly Savalas for looting rights to the big boat.

BEYOND THE VALLEY OF THE DOLLS
1970, 109 mins, US ⊛ ⊡
D: Russ Meyer **A:** Dolly Read, Cynthia Myers, Marcia McBroom, John La Zar, Michael Blodgett, David Gurian (20th Century-Fox)

This trashy, gaudy, soundstage vulgarity about low life among the high life is as funny as a burning orphanage. Dolly Read, Cynthia Myers, and Marcia McBroom head a busty cast as three pop singers who come to swinging Hollywood with manager David Gurian. Michael Blodgett plays a film-hero louse, Edy Williams a sex goddess, Erica Gavin the obligatory lesbian, and Duncan McLeod an unscrupulous lawyer. The sole good running gag involves Williams and Gurian; she's ready for sex anyplace except in bed.

B.F.'S DAUGHTER
1948, 107 mins, US
D: Robert Z. Leonard **A:** Barbara Stanwyck, Van Heflin, Charles Coburn, Keenan Wynn, Richard Hart, Margaret Lindsay (M-G-M)

It's a boy-meets-girl story, backgrounded against the period from the early thirties into the war years. Barbara Stanwyck has been stunningly gowned and beautifully photographed. Heflin gives an expressive interpretation as the poor, liberal college professor and lecturer who falls in love with and marries the daughter of an industrial giant.

BHOWANI JUNCTION
1956, 110 mins, US ⊛ ⊡
D: George Cukor **A:** Ava Gardner, Stewart Granger, Bill Travers, Abraham Sofaer, Francis Matthews, Peter Illing (M-G-M)

Metro went to Pakistan to shoot a film about India. The journey paid rich dividends, for the sense of realism in the film is one of the best things about it. *Bhowani Junction,* starring Ava Gardner as an Anglo-Indian, and Stewart Granger as a British colonel who falls in love with her, is a horse of many colors. Picture goes off in quite a few directions, ranging from romance and action to a halfhearted attempt to explain the Indians and a more serious effort to dramatize the social twilight into which the British withdrawal from India tossed a small group of people who were of mixed Indian and British blood.

BIBLE
IN THE BEGINNING..., THE
1966, 174 mins, Italy/US Ⓥ ⊙ ▭
D: John Huston **A:** Michael Parks, Ulla Bergryd, Richard Harris, John Huston, Stephen Boyd, George C. Scott (De Laurentiis/20th Century-Fox)

The world's oldest story—the origins of mankind, as told in the Book of Genesis—is put upon the screen by director John Huston and producer Dino De Laurentiis with consummate skill, taste, and reverence. Huston's rich voice functions in narration, and he also plays Noah with heartwarming humility, compassion, and humor. Richard Harris plays the jealous and remorseful Cain with a sure feeling, while Franco Nero's Abel conveys in very brief footage the image of a sensitive, obedient young man whose murder provoked a supreme outrage. The 45-minute sequence devoted to Noah and the Flood is, in itself, a triumph in filmmaking. It plays dramatically and fluidly, and belies monumental logistics of production.
1966: Nomination: Best Original Song Score

BICENTENNIAL MAN
1999, 131 mins, US Ⓥ ⊙
D: Chris Columbus **A:** Robin Williams, Sam Neill, Embeth Davidtz, Oliver Platt, Wendy Crewson, Hallie Kate Eisenberg (1492 Pictures/Touchstone/Columbia)

An ambitious tale handled in a dawdling, sentimental way, *Bicentennial Man* filters the prescient vision of sci-fi writer Isaac Asimov through the touchy-feely sensibility of Robin Williams. Story of a robot's 200-year journey to become a human being benefits from compelling thematic notions and visual effects, but bogs down in slack storytelling and an insipidly conventional approach. Williams is Andrew, a genial domestic robot acquired by an upscale Bay Area family. The head of the family, Sir (Sam Neill), suspects there might be more to Andrew than metal, fiberglass, and wire, and the robot becomes the confidant of Sir's daughter Little Miss (Embeth Davidtz). When Sir dies, Andrew sets out to locate others of his ilk. Back in San Francisco, he finds bouncy femme robot Galatea and her benign owner, Rupert Burns (Oliver Platt). Williams expresses personality as well as anyone could under the circumstances.
1999: Nomination: Best Makeup

LES BICHES
1968, 100 mins, France/Italy Ⓥ
D: Claude Chabrol **A:** Stephane Audran, Jacqueline Sassard, Jean-Louis Trintignant, Nane Germon, Henri Attal, Dominique Zardi (Boetie/Alexandra)

Here, director Claude Chabrol deals with lesbianism and bisexuality but still within a psychological and even suspense envelope. A rich and bored woman (Stephane Audran) picks up a Left Bank hippie girl (Jacqueline Sassard). She seduces her in an adroit, daring scene. Then she takes her to her villa in St. Tropez. There are two deadbeats living there who are her clowns. Into this setup comes a young architect (Jean-Louis Trintignant), who first seduces the hippie girl and then is seduced in turn by the rich woman. The gripping second part develops the strange relationships.

BICYCLE THIEF, THE
See: Ladri di Biciclette

BICYCLE THIEVES
See: Ladri di Biciclette

IL BIDONE
1955, 100 mins, Italy/France Ⓥ ⊙
D: Federico Fellini **A:** Broderick Crawford, Richard Basehart, Franco Fabrizi, Giulietta Masina, Sue Ellen Blake, Giacomo Gabrielli (Titanus/SGC)

Controversial pic tells of three small-time swindlers and some of their exploits in fleecing gullible Romans of their hard-earned coin. Pic centers on the sad loneliness which characterizes the lives of these men, and especially that of Augusto (Broderick Crawford). Film is full of symbolism and contains some powerful moments, as well as bitingly satirical sequences such as a cocktail-party brawl in a rich swindler's apartment. General audiences are bound to note a general tediousness, only here and there relieved by a humorous or human touch.

BIG
1988, 102 mins, US Ⓥ ⊙
D: Penny Marshall **A:** Tom Hanks, Elizabeth Perkins, John Heard, Jared Rushton, Robert Loggia, David Moscow (20th Century-Fox/Gracie)

A 13-year-old junior-high kid, Josh (David Moscow), is transformed into a 35-year-old's body (Tom Hanks) by a carnival wishing machine in this pic, which unspools with enjoyable genuineness and ingenuity. Immediate dilemma, since go-

ing back to school is not an option and his mom thinks he's an intruder and doesn't buy into the explanation that he's changed into a man, is to escape to anonymous New York City and hide out in a seedy hotel. Pretty soon, the viewer forgets that what's happening on screen has no basis in reality. The characters are having too much fun enjoying life away from responsibility.
1988: Nominations: Best Actor (Tom Hanks), Original Screenplay

BIG BAD MAMA
1974, 83 mins, US Ⓥ
D: Steve Carver **A:** Angie Dickinson, William Shatner, Tom Skerritt, Susan Sennett, Robbie Lee, Noble Willingham (New World)
The plotline is flimsy at best, opening circa 1932 with Angie Dickinson posturing as a hard-bitten mother, rumrunner, bank robber, jewel thief, kidnapper, and queen bee in the sack. *Big Bad Mama* is mostly rehashed *Bonnie and Clyde*, with a bit more blood and Angie Dickinson taking off her clothes for sex scenes with the crooks in her life.

BIG BLUE, THE
See: Le Grand Bleu

BIG BOSS, THE
See: Tang Shan Daxiong

BIG BRASS RING, THE
1999, 104 mins, US Ⓥ Ⓒ
D: George Hickenlooper **A:** William Hurt, Nigel Hawthorne, Miranda Richardson, Irene Jacob, Ewan Stewart, Gregg Henry (Pfilmco/Millennium)
A serious-minded, emotionally distant study of political intrigue and personal betrayal, *The Big Brass Ring* offers interesting ideas but lacks dramatic plausibility and character motivation. A good cast, fresh St. Louis settings, lively dialogue, and resonant themes remaining from Orson Welles's original script keep the film watchable. The gubernatorial race between Blake Pellarin (William Hurt) and his competitor is in its final week when a potential trip wire turns up in the form of Kim Mennaker (Nigel Hawthorne), a former senator and Pellarin's unofficial stepfather. Mennaker has been living in exile in Havana after his gay exploits finished his political career. An aggressive journalist, Cela Brandini (Irene Jacob), tries to pry additional info out of Pellarin. Hurt is plausible as an attractive if opaque political figure, and Hawthorne has a good time as a grand dirty old man.

BIG BRAWL, THE
1980, 95 mins, US/Hong Kong Ⓥ ▭
D: Robert Clouse **A:** Jackie Chan, Jose Ferrer, Kristine DeBell, Mako, Rosalind Chao, Mary Ellen O'Neill (Warner/Golden Harvest)
Hong Kong martial-arts star Jackie Chan makes an amiable American film debut in *The Big Brawl*, an amusing chopsocky actioner whose appeal is not limited to the usual audience for this genre. Key ingredient here is humor. Story is set in Chicago, 1938, and filmed with engagingly artificial style that resembles vintage gangster pix.

BIG BROADCAST, THE
1932, 80 mins, US
D: Frank Tuttle **A:** Stuart Erwin, Bing Crosby, George Burns, Gracie Allen, Leila Hyams (Paramount)
It's an all-star show with a flock of the biggest air favorites. Bing Crosby, Burns and Allen, Kate Smith, Boswell Sisters, Arthur Tracy (the Street Singer), Donald Novis, and the Vincent Lopez and Cab Calloway orchestras are as varied a galaxy of radio favorites as they are ether-renowned. Crosby and Burns and Allen alone went to the coast to participate in the actual production, having lines and parts, with the rest shot in the east and cut in for their specialties. The chief fault with *Broadcast* is that it's not a feature film but a succession of talking shorts. The story is rather childish.

BIG BROADCAST OF 1936, THE
1935, 97 mins, US
D: Norman Taurog **A:** Jack Oakie, George Burns, Gracie Allen, Lyda Roberti, Bing Crosby, Ethel Merman (Paramount)
Names are in and out as fast and as often as a firefly's taillight. There just isn't time for a plot, and probably best that none was attempted. Jack Oakie, Burns and Allen, Lyda Roberti, Wendy Barrie, Henry Wadsworth, C. Henry Gordon, and a few others carry on whatever yarn there is and they play it lightly, as required. You have to look quickly to see such names as Bing Crosby, Ethel Merman, Ray Noble's band, Amos 'n Andy, Boland and Ruggles, and Bill Robinson. These and other specialty turns are worked into the continuity via a crazy television gag.
1935: Nomination: Best Dance Direction

("Elephant Number—It's the Animal in Me")

BIG BROADCAST OF 1937, THE
1936, 100 mins, US
D: Mitchell Leisen **A:** Jack Benny, George Burns, Gracie Allen, Martha Raye, Shirley Ross, Ray Milland (Paramount)

The third in the *Big Broadcast* series from Paramount, this one far outdistances the two that precede it. There are enough comedians of one form or another in *Broadcast* to make it a hit solely on the strength of the laughs: Jack Benny, Martha Raye, Bob Burns, and Burns and Allen are the prominents poking at audience ribs. Burns's best scenes are those in which he bursts in on radio programs which are on the air, while looking for conductor Leopold Stokowski. Benny plays the manager of the radio studios.

BIG BROADCAST OF 1938, THE
1938, 88 mins, US
D: Mitchell Leisen **A:** W. C. Fields, Martha Raye, Dorothy Lamour, Shirley Ross, Lynne Overman, Bob Hope (Paramount)

With the rejuvenated W. C. Fields at his inimitable best in a streamlined production which combines spectacle, melody, and dance, *Big Broadcast of 1938* is pictorially original and alluring. The outstanding moment is a contribution by Kirsten Flagstad, of the Metropolitan Opera company, singing an aria from *Die Walküre*. Surrounding Fields and the diva is a company of players who turn in a full quota of laughs and musical numbers. Martha Raye, Dorothy Lamour, Shirley Ross, Lynne Overman, Bob Hope, Ben Blue, Leif Erikson, Rufe Davis, and Grace Bradley are clicks.
1938: Best Song ("Thanks for the Memory")

BIG BUS, THE
1976, 88 mins, US Ⓥ ▭
D: James Frawley **A:** Joseph Bologna, Stockard Channing, John Beck, Rene Auberjonois, Ned Beatty, Jose Ferrer (Paramount)

Heading the cast of this overkill spoof is Joseph Bologna, good as a down-and-out bus driver whose chance to make a comeback is the nuclear-powered behemoth designed by Stockard Channing and father Harold Gould. Suffice it to say that no cliché is left unattached.

BIG BUSINESS
1988, 97 mins, US Ⓥ ◉
D: Jim Abrahams **A:** Bette Midler, Lily Tomlin, Fred Ward, Edward Herrmann, Michele Placido, Barry Primus (Touchstone/Silver Screen Partners III)

Big Business is a shrill, unattractive comedy which stars Bette Midler and Lily Tomlin, who play two sets of twins mixed up at birth. They have distinctly different comic styles, with the former's loud brashness generally dominating the latter's sly skittishness. Of the four performances by the two leads, the one easiest to enjoy is Midler's as venal corporate boss. Dressed to the nines and sporting a mincing but utterly determined walk, Midler tosses off her waspish one-liners with malevolent glee, stomping on everyone in her path. There are moments of delight as well in her other characterization as a country bumpkin who has always yearned for the material pleasures of Babylon. Tomlin has her moments, too, but her two sweetly flaky, nay-saying characters for a while seem so similar.

BIG CARNIVAL
See: Ace in the Hole

BIG CHILL, THE
1983, 103 mins, US Ⓥ ◉
D: Lawrence Kasdan **A:** Tom Berenger, Glenn Close, Jeff Goldblum, William Hurt, Kevin Kline, JoBeth Williams (Carson/Columbia)

The Big Chill is an amusing, splendidly acted but rather shallow look at what's happened to the generation formed by the 1960s. Framework has seven old college friends gathering for the funeral of another old pal, who has committed suicide in the home of happily married Glenn Close and Kevin Kline. Others in attendance are: sharp-looking Tom Berenger, who has gained fame on TV; Jeff Goldblum, horny wiseacre who writes for *People* magazine; William Hurt, the Jake Barnes of the piece by virtue of having been strategically injured in Vietnam; Mary Kay Place, a successful career woman; and JoBeth Williams, whose older husband returns home to the two kids. Also provocatively on hand is Meg Tilly, much younger girlfriend of the deceased.
1983: Nominations: Best Picture, Supp.

Actress (Glenn Close), Original Screenplay

BIG CLOCK, THE
1948, 95 mins, US
D: John Farrow A: Ray Milland, Charles Laughton, Maureen O'Sullivan, George Macready, Elsa Lanchester, Dan Tobin (Paramount)

There are weaknesses lurking in this pic, namely a too patly tailored yarn and some spotty acting, but the pace is so redhot that there's no time or inclination, during the unfolding, to question coincidental or misplaced mugging. Laughton, in this instance, is the topkick in a gigantic publishing house. Toiling under him is Ray Milland, editor of a crime mag. Goaded by insane jealousy, Laughton kills his mistress and scurries for cover. Laughton is aware that he's been sighted by his unknown rival. As he sees it, there's only one way out, and that's to locate the sole witness. Milland, of course, is hired for that job, and his desperate efforts are directed toward covering his own tracks while pinning the goods on the real murderer. Laughton, unfortunately, overplays his hand so that his tycoon-sans-heart takes on the quality of parodying the real article.

BIG COMBO, THE
1955, 86 mins, US
D: Joseph H. Lewis A: Cornel Wilde, Richard Conte, Brian Donlevy, Jean Wallace, Robert Middleton, Lee Van Cleef (Security/Theodora)

This is another saga of the honest cop who lets nothing sway him from the self-appointed task of smashing a crime syndicate and its leader. It is done with grim melodramatics that are hard-hitting despite a rambling, not-too-credible plot. One torture scene in particular will shock the sensibilities and cause near nausea. Performances are in keeping with the bare-knuckle direction by Joseph Lewis and, on that score, are good. Low-key photography by John Alton and a noisy, jazzy score by David Raksin are in keeping with the film's tough mood.

BIG COUNTRY, THE
1958, 166 mins, US
D: William Wyler A: Gregory Peck, Jean Simmons, Carroll Baker, Charlton Heston, Burl Ives, Charles Bickford (United Artists/Anthony Worldwide)

The Big Country lives up to its title. The camera has captured a vast section of the southwest with such fidelity that the long stretches of dry country, in juxtaposition to tiny western settlements, and the giant canyon country in the arid area, have been recorded with almost three-dimensional effect. Although the story is dwarfed by these outpourings, The Big Country is nonetheless armed with a serviceable, adult-western yarn. Basically it concerns the feud between Major Henry Terrill (Charles Bickford) and Rufus Hannassey (Burl Ives), rugged individualists who covet the same watering area for their cattle. The water spot is open to both camps since it is the property of Julie Maragon (Jean Simmons). Into the atmosphere of hate and vengeance comes Gregory Peck, a genteel eastern dude. Jerome Moross's musical score is on the plus side.
1958: Best Supp. Actor (Burl Ives)
Nomination: Best Score of a Dramatic Picture

BIG EASY, THE
1986, 108 mins, US
D: Jim McBride A: Dennis Quaid, Ellen Barkin, Ned Beatty, John Goodman, Ebb Roe Smith, Lisa Jane Persky (Kings Road)

Until conventional plot contrivances begin to spoil the fun, The Big Easy is a snappy, sassy battle of the sexes in the guise of a melodrama about police corruption. Buildup is quite engaging. In the classic screwball-comedy tradition of opposites irresistibly attracting, brash New Orleans homicide detective Dennis Quaid puts the make on Ellen Barkin, a northern import assigned by the d.a.'s office to investigate possible illegal activities in the department. Not necessarily the likeliest of couples, Quaid and Barkin bring great energy and an offbeat wired quality to their roles.

BIG FISHERMAN, THE
1959, 180 mins, US
D: Frank Borzage A: Howard Keel, Susan Kohner, John Saxon, Martha Hyer, Herbert Lom, Ray Stricklyn (Buena Vista)

The Big Fisherman is a pious but plodding account of the conversion to Christianity of Simon-Peter, the apostle called "the fisher of men." There is plenty of opportunity for both spectacle and sex, and it is all the more curious, considering its big budget and leisurely production schedule, that both are almost absent. Although the title seems to make Simon-Peter the central character, the film is only incidentally about him. His part in the story is his influence on two young lovers,

John Saxon as an Arab prince and Susan Kohner as the daughter of Herod by an Arab princess. Kohner and Saxon make a handsome young couple. But their problems seem trivial against the turbulent era. Howard Keel is handsomely picturesque as Simon-Peter, and shows he can hold his own as a straight actor.

BIG FIX, THE
1978, 108 mins, US ℗
D: Jeremy Paul Kagan **A:** Richard Dreyfuss, Susan Anspach, Bonnie Bedelia, John Lithgow, Ofelia Medina, F. Murray Abraham (Universal)

In *The Big Fix,* Richard Dreyfuss delivers what is for him a particularly relaxed and confident performance as Moses Wine, the 1970s answer to Philip Marlowe, Lew Archer, and Sam Spade. Simply as a detective thriller, *The Bix Fix* has strong appeal. As a centerpiece it has a tough, cynical, intelligent detective, an independent man with a rat hole for an apartment, a personal life in need of some investigating, and a full supply of wisecracks. Briefly, the film finds Dreyfuss employed by Susan Anspach, a campaign worker for a gubernatorial candidate. Someone is trying to sabotage the election. Dreyfuss is a natural for the case because he knew people in the radical movement.

BIG GAMBLE, THE
1961, 98 mins, US ▭
D: Richard Fleischer **A:** Stephen Boyd, Juliette Greco, David Wayne, Gregory Ratoff, Fernand Ledoux, Sybil Thorndike (Zanuck/20th Century-Fox)

A short but invaluable course on how not to drive a 10-ton truck through French Equitorial Africa is offered in *The Big Gamble*. Outside of a heap of dramatic jeopardy and some interesting scenic views of the Dark Continent, there isn't a great deal in this picture to entice the average customer. Irwin Shaw's original screenplay launches itself in Dublin, where newlyweds Marie (Juliette Greco) and Vic (Stephen Boyd) are seeking funds from the latter's family to finance a trucking venture in Africa. They get the money, but they also inherit milquetoast bankclerk cousin Samuel (David Wayne) who decides to accompany them in order to protect the family investment. Balance of the film depicts the trio's oversea and overland misadventures in reaching their destination.

BIGGER SPLASH, A
1975, 105 mins, UK
D: Jack Hazan **A:** David Hockney, Peter Schlesinger, Celia Birtwell, Mo McDermott, Henry Geldzahler, Kasmin (Buzzy)

A Bigger Splash is a revealing last ripple of the so-called life style of Swinging London invented mainly by journalists. Jack Hazan uses painter David Hockney, his art dealer in the US, and his fashion-creator friend and the latter's wife. It has Hockney breaking with a boyfriend and not being able to work as his friends worry and his American dealer exhorts him. Real people play themselves around a partly fictionalized tale. Hockney was noted for his color and specialization in California subjects. The gay life around him is indicated with style and taste.

BIGGER THAN LIFE
1956, 95 mins, US ▭
D: Nicholas Ray **A:** James Mason, Barbara Rush, Walter Matthau, Robert F. Simon, Christopher Olsen, Roland Winters (20th Century-Fox)

Bigger Than Life exposes the good and bad in cortisone. A great deal of care is taken to give both sides of the case, while telling a gripping, dramatic story of people that become very real. The performances are standout, with Barbara Rush earning particular praise as Mason's wife. Mason is exceptionally fine as the modestly circumstanced grade-school teacher who undergoes a series of experiments with cortisone in the hope he can be cured of a usually fatal disease. He begins to overdose himself and some startling personality changes occur. Christopher Olsen scores with his tremendously effective study of Mason's young son.

BIGGEST BUNDLE OF THEM ALL, THE
1968, 105 mins, US ▭
D: Ken Annakin **A:** Vittorio De Sica, Raquel Welch, Robert Wagner, Godfrey Cambridge, Francesco Mule, Edward G. Robinson (M-G-M)

Title refers to the theft of $5 million in platinum ingots by a gang composed of a deported Italian mobster and four amateurs. What appeals most is the general ineptitude of the would-be criminals as they seek to rob the train bearing the ingots. Vittorio De Sica pumps plenty of heart and humor into his role of the erstwhile Chicago mobster who attends the funeral in Naples of a Chi comrade-in-arms and finds himself kidnapped by four strangers, headed by American Robert Wagner. Wagner handles himself satisfactorily, and Raquel Welch is his voluptuous girlfriend, still playing bikini queen.

BIG GIRLS DON'T CRY . . . THEY GET EVEN
1992, 102 mins, US ⓥ
D: Joan Micklin Silver **A:** Hillary Wolf, David Strathairn, Margaret Whitton, Griffin Dunne, Patricia Kalember, Adrienne Shelly (New Line)

This tale of a teenage girl overlooked by her parents never escapes its sitcom premise and finally gives in to an ending so hackneyed it practically defines the term. The film struggles under its heavy-handed screenplay, featuring a stilted narration by teen protagonist Hillary Wolf that's a mix of bad one-liners and romance-novel angst. Wolf resides with her uncaring mother (Margaret Whitton), rich stepfather (David Strathairn), and three step-siblings, while her biological father (Griffin Dunne) is estranged from his kind second wife (Patricia Kalember) and shacked up with his pregnant, much younger New Age g.f. (Adrienne Shelly). Muddle gets worse when Wolf flees to the woods with her stepbrother (Dan Futterman) to escape a family trip to Hawaii, with the rest of her extended family in hot pursuit.

BIGGLES
1986, 108 mins, UK ⓥ ⊙
D: John Hough **A:** Neil Dickson, Alex Hyde-White, Fiona Hutchinson, Peter Cushing, Marcus Gilbert, William Hootkins (Compact Yellowbill)

This stylish romp combining World War I heroics and the currently in-vogue plot device of time travel has food-service entrepreneur Jim Ferguson (Alex Hyde-White) inexplicably hurled across the decades. Trouble is, he doesn't know when this phenomenon will recur, which makes for some amusing (and not-so) juxtapositions of past and present. Best bit is his drop into a French convent under siege, attired only in a bath towel. Ferguson keeps meeting up with Biggles (Neil Dickson), a dashing, WWI British aviator who's out to stop the Hun from implementing a hi-tech secret weapon, which, as they find out later, is akin to a big microwave oven for men and machinery. Ferguson is aided and advised in the present by Colonel Raymond (Peter Cushing), who somehow knows what's going on.

Neil Dickson as Biggles steals the film. Technically, pic is top-notch, especially aerial sequences using vintage biplanes.

BIG HANGOVER, THE
1950, 82 mins, US ⓥ
D: Norman Krasna **A:** Van Johnson, Elizabeth Taylor, Percy Waram, Fay Holden, Leon Ames, Edgar Buchanan (M-G-M)

Norman Krasna, as writer-director-producer, does a good job. Story is that of a young idealist, graduating from law school and about to enter a rich, socialite law firm. He has a peculiar allergy to liquor. Meantime, the daughter of the law firm's senior partner has taken the law grad in hand to cure him of his drink allergy, with the inevitable romantic complications. Elizabeth Taylor is warm and appealing as the amateur psychiatrist. Van Johnson, too, is rather subdued and serious here, to just as warming effect.

BIG HEART, THE
See: Miracle on 34th Street

BIG HEAT, THE
1953, 89 mins, US ⓥ ⊙
D: Fritz Lang **A:** Glenn Ford, Gloria Grahame, Jocelyn Brando, Alexander Scourby, Lee Marvin, Jeanette Nolan (Columbia)

It's the story of a cop, a homicide sergeant, who busts up the crime syndicate strangling his city and its administration. Because he prefers to do his job and collect his pay honestly, he finds the going tough. So tough that his wife is murdered by an auto bomb intended for him, his child is threatened with kidnapping, and he loses his police job because of pressure from higher-ups. Ford's portrayal of the homicide sergeant is honest and packs much wallop. Lang's direction builds taut suspense, throwing unexpected, and believable, thrills at the audience. Gloria Grahame's character, that of a gangster's sweetie, is choice and she makes it a colorful, important part of the picture.

BIG HIT, THE
1998, 91 mins, US ⓥ ⊙
D: Che-Kirk Wong **A:** Mark Wahlberg, Lou Diamond Phillips, Christina Applegate, Avery Brooks, Bokeem Woodbine, China Chow (Amen-Ra/Zide-Perry/Lion Rock/TriStar)

Combine the high-energy pyrotechnic choreography of a Hong Kong actioner with the plight of a banal sitcom schnook and you have *The Big Hit*. A fleet piece of sock-'em entertainment, this film's kinetic force plows through myriad plot holes and inconsistencies with game abandon. The conceit is that the contract killer is a bighearted lug who wants to be liked and have a normal family life once he arrives home from "the office." Strapped to keep up payments on his suburban tract, Mel (Mark Wahlberg) reluctantly agrees to do a moonlighting job for pal Cisco (Lou Diamond Phillips). It's a snatch-and-grab of Japanese-American Jiro Nishi's (Sab Shimono) teenage daughter, Keiko (China Chow), with a cool $1 million ransom attached. But Keiko just happens to be the goddaughter of Cisco's boss, Paris (Avery Brooks), so Cisco figures out a way to cover his tracks and implicate Mel as the ringleader. Wahlberg's hangdog look and pained expression is perfectly employed for wry comic effect. Phillips glories in Cisco's flamboyance.

BIG HOUSE, THE
1930, 84 mins, US
D: George Hill **A:** Chester Morris, Wallace Beery, Lewis Stone, Robert Montgomery, Leila Hyams, Karl Dane (Cosmopolitan)

Wallace Beery, Chester Morris, and Robert Montgomery are a great trio in the big house, where each is serving a stretch for homicide, forgery, and manslaughter, respectively. Prison life on the half shell is plainly exposed. The big wallop is the prison revolt. The hand grenades, barrages, stench bombs, tractor attacks, and other means to conquer rebellious prisoners, with variations in the dungeon, etc., are all graphically dovetailed into the tense story.
1929/30: Best Writing (Frances Marion), Sound
Nominations: Best Picture, Actor (Wallace Beery)

BIG JAKE
1971, 109 mins, US Ⓥ
D: George Sherman **A:** John Wayne, Richard Boone, Maureen O'Hara, Patrick Wayne, Christopher Mitchum, Bruce Cabot (Batjac)

Big Jake is an extremely slick and commercial John Wayne starrer, this time as a long-gone husband out to rescue a grandson from kidnapper Richard Boone. Harry Julian Fink and R. M. Fink's original story and script is well structured and fleshed out with solid dialogue. It opens with a 10-person slaughter 13 minutes into the film. Maureen O'Hara, as a strong-willed woman whose husband (Wayne) has long

since departed, sends for him to track down Boone's gang, which has kidnapped grandson John Ethan Wayne (the star's own eight-year-old son). Wayne and Boone snarl extremely well at each other.

BIG JIM MCLAIN
1952, 90 mins, US Ⓥ ⊙
D: Edward Ludwig **A:** John Wayne, Nancy Olson, James Arness, Alan Napier, Veda Ann Borg, Hans Conried (Wayne-Fellows/Warner)

Honolulu forms the setting for a story of the work to exposé Communist activities. The picture was rushed into the market and bears evidence of that haste. Continuity is choppy, the script sketchy and lacking in clarity. John Wayne and James Arness are crack investigators for the House Committee on Un-American Activities. When it is learned the Communists are threatening in the islands, the pair is dispatched there to get evidence against the Red cells.

BIG KNIFE, THE
1955, 111 mins, US
D: Robert Aldrich **A:** Jack Palance, Ida Lupino, Wendell Corey, Shelley Winters, Jean Hagen, Rod Steiger (Associates & Aldrich)

Film is an inside Hollywood story. It's sometimes so brittle and brutal as to prove disturbing. Rod Steiger vividly interprets the Janus aspects of the studio head who knows when to con and cajole Jack Palance into a 14-year deal. He has no compunction about staging an accidental death of one of those casting-couch contractees (Shelley Winters), foiled by his laconic and resourceful publicity director.

BIG LEBOWSKI, THE
1998, 127 mins, US Ⓥ ⊙
D: Joel Coen **A:** Jeff Bridges, John Goodman, Julianne Moore, Steve Buscemi, Peter Stormare, David Huddleston (Working Title/PolyGram)

Spiked with wonderfully funny sequences and some brilliantly original notions, *The Big Lebowski* adds up to considerably less than the sum of its often scintillating parts. The Dude (Jeff Bridges), whose real name is Lebowski, is beaten up by two goons looking for a multimillionaire known as the Big Lebowski, whose wife owes their boss money. The Dude, goaded on by his Vietnam vet bowling buddy Walter (John Goodman), tracks down the other Lebowski (David Huddleston) and meets his sexpot young wife Bunny (Tara Reid). The Dude is soon paged by Lebowski to deliver a $1 million ransom for the return of his wife, who has been kidnapped. Bridges throws himself into the leading role with glee, and as the blustery Walter, Goodman is vastly entertaining. There is an astonishing cameo by John Turturro as a flamboyant Latin sex offender who suddenly turns up at the bowling alley.

BIG MAN, THE
(US: CROSSING THE LINE)
1990, 115 mins, UK Ⓥ ⊙
D: David Leland A: Liam Neeson, Joanne Whalley-Kilmer, Ian Bannen, Billy Connolly, Maurice Roeves, Hugh Grant (Miramax)

Though unquestionably well intentioned, *The Big Man* has a depressing theme and ultraviolent conclusion. The early scenes, set in a depressed Scottish village where an abandoned coal mine and mass unemployment reflect the aftermath of Britain's crippling miners' strike, look promising. Liam Neeson comes on strong as the unemployed Danny, who was imprisoned during the strike for hitting a policeman. His best friend, Frankie (an engaging straight turn from Scottish comedian Billy Connolly), acts as a runner for Mason (Ian Bannen), a corrupt businessman who needs Danny to fight for him. Motives for the fight, a bare-knuckle affair with no rules, are obscure. The fight, when it comes, is one of the most grueling ever caught on film.

BIG MEAT EATER
1982, 77 mins, Canada Ⓥ
D: Chris Windsor A: George Dawson, Andrew Gillies, Big Miller, Stephen Dimopoulos, Georgina Hegedos (BDC Entertainment)

A delightfully unpretentious musical comedy which defies classification, although billed as a bizarre new-wave comedy. The small-town parable about progress owes something to both Canadian humorist Stephen Leacock and to Harold Lloyd. The principal figure is a cheery family butcher who has invented a new universal language and is a great booster for his hometown of Burquitlam.

BIG NIGHT, THE
1951, 70 mins, US
D: Joseph Losey A: John Barrymore Jr., Preston Foster, Joan Lorring, Howard St. John, Dorothy Comingore, Philip Bourneuf (Waxman/United Artists)

John Barrymore Jr. is the star of this story, ineptly scripted. Direction pars the writing and the playing is in keeping. Plotline that can be sorted out of the muddled script gets under way on Barrymore's 17th birthday. His father (Preston Foster) is brutally caned, without resisting, by Howard St. John, a disliked sports columnist. Barrymore, disturbed by the incident, later that night takes a pistol from his father's bar and goes looking for St. John. Much footage is involved with the people he encounters and side adventures during a night of wandering.

BIG NOISE, THE
1928, 77 mins, US ⊗
D: Allan Dwan A: Chester Conklin, Alice White, Bodil Rosing, Sam Hardy, Jack Egan, Ned Sparks (First National)

There isn't a newspaperman anywhere who won't enjoy this picture. Whether it's a slap or burlesque on a tabloid daily's methods, or a sort of satirical dreamland idea of bringing a boob into the limelight, to let him sink back into the darkness of the tenement, it's fine either way. There is much subtlety to it all of the while. Chester Conklin's playing is no small part of this.

BIG PARADE, THE
1925, 150 mins, US Ⓥ ⊙
D: King Vidor A: John Gilbert, Renee Adoree, Hobart Bosworth, Claire McDowell, Claire Adams, Karl Dane (M-G-M)

King Vidor had a tough subject to deal with. He knew that he would have to show the horrors of war, and therefore worked his story out in such a manner that it has plenty of comedy relief and a love sequence. John Gilbert's performance is a superb thing, while Renee Adoree, as the little French peasant, figuratively lives the role. The same may as well be said for Karl Dane and Tom O'Brien, for it is the excellent work of all these players and the manner in which Vidor has handled them that lift this production far above the ordinary.

BIG PICTURE, THE
1989, 99 mins, US Ⓥ
D: Christopher Guest A: Kevin Bacon, Emily Longstreth, J. T. Walsh, Jennifer Jason Leigh, Martin Short, Michael McKean (Aspen/Columbia)

A surprisingly genial, good-natured satire on contemporary Hollywood mores, *The Big Picture* displays a keen eye for the silliness of film-biz customs, lingo, and attitudes. Kevin Bacon and Emily Longstreth are appealing enough in the leads, but it is in the supporting roles that things come alive, thanks to Jennifer Jason Leigh, almost unrecognizable as an avant-garde hip-hoppy dancer, J. T. Walsh as the super-cool but shallow studio boss, and Teri Hatcher as the starlet with a perfect body. Cameos by the likes of John Cleese, Elliott Gould, Eddie Albert, June Lockhart, Roddy McDowall, and Stephen Collins help root the picture in its setting.

BIG RED ONE, THE
1980, 111 mins, US Ⓥ ⊙
D: Samuel Fuller **A:** Lee Marvin, Mark Hamill, Robert Carradine, Bobby DiCicco, Stephane Audran, Kelly Ward (Lorimar)

The Big Red One was 2 years in the making and 35 years in Samuel Fuller's head. It's a terrific war yarn, a picture of palpable raw power which manages both intense intimacy and great scope at the same time. The story of the 1st Infantry Division's exploits in North Africa and Europe between 1942 and 1945, fast-paced pic attempts to tell entire story of the European land war through the eyes of five foot soldiers. Approach eschews usual sociological analysis used in many war pix. These men are there for one reason only, to survive the war.

BIG SKY, THE
1952, 140 mins, US Ⓥ
D: Howard Hawks **A:** Kirk Douglas, Dewey Martin, Elizabeth Threatt, Arthur Hunnicutt, Hank Worden, Jim Davis (Winchester/RKO)

Pic is a gigantic outdoor epic, but its impact is dissipated by the marathon running time. Kirk Douglas is cast as a Kentucky mountaineer. Story involves his joining a keelboat expedition up the Missouri River in the 1830s. The long trip is filled with the usual obstacles, warring Indians, treacherous white men, nature's forces, etc.

1952: Nominations: Best Supp. Actor (Arthur Hunnicutt), B&W Cinematography

BIG SLEEP, THE
1946, 113 mins, US Ⓥ ⊙
D: Howard Hawks **A:** Humphrey Bogart, Lauren Bacall, John Ridgely, Martha Vickers, Dorothy Malone, Peggy Knudsen (Warner)

Brittle Chandler characters have been transferred to the screen with punch by Howard Hawks's production and direction, providing full load of rough, tense action most of the way. Humphrey Bogart as Philip Marlowe and Lauren Bacall as Vivian, Marlowe's chief romantic interest, make a smooth team to get over the amatory play and action in the script. Hawks has given story a staccato pace in the development, using long stretches of dialogueless action and then whipping in fast talk between characters. This helps to punch home high spots of suspense, particularly in latter half of picture. There are six deaths to please whodunit fans, plenty of lusty action, both romantic and physical, as Bogart matches wits with dealers in sex literature, blackmail, gambling, and murder.

BIG SLEEP, THE
1978, 99 mins, UK Ⓥ ⊙
D: Michael Winner **A:** Robert Mitchum, Sarah Miles, Richard Boone, Candy Clark, Joan Collins, Edward Fox (United Artists)

This remake transplants Raymond Chandler's *The Big Sleep* from 1940s California to 1970s London. Mitchum is hired by wealthy cripple James Stewart to probe possible blackmail. This leads him into the tangled lives of the client's daughters—seminympho Candy Clark and the more mature Sarah Miles. Latter has a relationship with gambler Oliver Reed, whose wife, Diana Quick, has disappeared. The production is handsome, but in the updating and relocation a lot has been lost. In particular, gone is the 1940s L.A. feel. Only Clark seems to project the requisite spoiled-rotten youthful spark. Nearly every other principal seems beyond the point of really caring.

BIG SQUEEZE, THE
1996, 82 mins, US Ⓥ
D: Marcus De Leon **A:** Peter Dobson, Lara Flynn Boyle, Luca Bercovici, Danny Nucci, Teresa Dispina, Sam Vlahos (Zeta)

A film noir formula is updated to modern, multicultural L.A. Witty, light-fingered script centers on a Chicano bar where Tanya (Lara Flynn Boyle) pops Coronas behind the bar while husband Henry (Luca Bercovici) sits on his duff. Tanya really gets miffed when she accidentally discovers that he's also sitting on $130,000 he never bothered to mention. Enter Benny (Peter Dobson), an indigent yet slick opportunist who hits on the slinky barmaid. Tanya herself bunks in, platonically, with Jesse (Danny Nucci). She puts out feelers to Benny to see if they can hook hubby in a handy sting. True to noir-scam form, Benny soon has Jesse drawn into his nefarious plan (unbeknownst to Tanya), and it's not long before all are at one another's throats. What makes this work is that De Leon immediately establishes a breezy, nonviolent tone and sticks to it without sacrificing atmosphere or tension.

BIG STEAL, THE
1949, 78 mins, US ⊘ ⊙
D: Don Siegel **A:** Robert Mitchum, Jane Greer, William Bendix, Patric Knowles, Ramon Novarro (RKO)

Steal was lensed on location in and around Mexico City. It gains added sight interest from this, as well as strengthened melodramatics. Footage is one long chase through Mexico. Robert Mitchum is chasing Patric Knowles and, in turn, is being chased by William Bendix. All are interested in a $300,000 army payroll, stolen from Mitchum by Knowles.

BIG STEAL, THE
1990, 100 mins, Australia
D: Nadia Tass **A:** Ben Mendelsohn, Claudia Karvan, Steve Bisley, Marshall Napier, Tim Robertson (Cascade)

Ben Mendelsohn is Danny, a shy 18-year-old who wants two things: to own a Jaguar and to date Joanna (Claudia Karvan). Danny's father gives him a 1963 Nissan Cedric the family has owned for years. Danny decides to trade this in for a 1973 Jag in time for his first date. Teens here are incredibly unsophisticated compared with 18-year-olds in Hollywood teen comedies, and that's part of the film's charm. Mendelsohn and Karvan are quite sweet in their roles.

BIG STORE, THE
1941, 94 mins, US ⊘
D: Charles Riesner **A:** Groucho Marx, Chico Marx, Harpo Marx, Tony Martin, Virginia Grey, Margaret Dumont (M-G-M)

A large department store serves as background for this display of familiar Marxian comedy. Groucho gets a job as bodyguard-detective for Tony Martin, co-owner of the store, when manager Douglass Dumbrille tries to get Martin out of the way. The frères Marx then proceed to romp through the store in their usual slaphappy manner, taking advantage of the numerous props available for comedy purposes. Harp solo by Harpo, staged between mirrors to obtain unusual effects both musically and comedically, is most original.

BIG STREET, THE
1942, 88 mins, US ⊘
D: Irving Reis **A:** Henry Fonda, Lucille Ball, Agnes Moorehead, Barton MacLane, Eugene Pallette, Sam Levene (RKO)

Taken from a story by Damon Runyon, this is a Cinderella-like fable of a Broadway café-singing gold digger who becomes more human long after a fall cripples her for life. Scripter Leonard Spigelgass makes the transition from the grasping, selfish little beauty to a bitter disillusioned girl entirely lifelike, albeit a prolonged affair. Lucille Ball comes through with high laurels. Henry Fonda, as the mooning but intensely loyal Little Pinks, is at his best.

BIG TIME OPERATORS
See: The Smallest Show on Earth

BIG TOP PEE-WEE
1988, 86 mins, US ⊘ ⊙
D: Randal Kleiser **A:** Pee-Wee Herman [Paul Reubens], Kris Kristofferson, Valeria Golino, Penelope Ann Miller, Susan Tyrrell, Terrence Mann (Paramount)

Big Top Pee-Wee again demonstrates that Pee-Wee Herman is one very strange screen personality; he previously scored with his 1985 feature debut, *Pee-Wee's Big Adventure*. Surrounded by animals as strange as himself, Herman pursues a career in agricultural extravagance with the help of his goggled talking pig Vincent (amusingly voiced by Wayne White). A storm brings a broken-down circus to Herman's farm, adding a menagerie of freakish animals and people to his already curious collection. Kris Kristofferson oversees the visitors and keeps them rallied with hearty circus sayings, along with explanations of how he came to marry his miniature wife (Susan Tyrrell), whom he carries around in his pocket. Very little of this is interesting or amusing on paper, which must have been a real challenge to director Randal Kleiser.

BIG TRAIL, THE
1930, 125 mins, US ⊘ ▭
D: Raoul Walsh **A:** John Wayne, Marguerite Churchill, El Brendel, Tully Marshall, Tyrone Power Sr., David Rollins (Fox)

A big-screen effort and an elegantly directed job by Raoul Walsh. But the recurrence of the same things, interrupted now and then by a "big scene," such as the river or cliff crossing, or El Brendel's dragged-in comedy with his mother-in-law, or the simple romance and the silly melodrama, commences to weary. This leaves the historical portion, the Oregon Trail, as the single interesting part. Young John Wayne, wholly inexperienced, shows it, but also suggests he can be built up.

BIG TROUBLE IN LITTLE CHINA
1986, 99 mins, US Ⓥ ⊙ ⊟
D: John Carpenter A: Kurt Russell, Kim Cattrall, Dennis Dun, James Hong, Victor Wong, Kate Burton (20th Century-Fox)

Story is promising, involving an ancient Chinese magician Lo Pan (James Hong) who controls an evil empire beneath San Francisco's Chinatown. Director John Carpenter seems to be trying to make an action-adventure along the lines of *Indiana Jones and the Temple of Doom*. The effect goes horribly awry. Leading the cast is Kurt Russell, who looks embarrassed, and should be, playing his CB philosophizing truck-driver character as a cross between a swaggering John Wayne, adventurous Harrison Ford, and wacky Bill Murray.

BIG WEDNESDAY
1978, 126 mins, US Ⓥ ⊙ ⊟
D: John Milius A: Jan-Michael Vincent, William Katt, Gary Busey, Patti D'Arbanville, Lee Purcell, Robert Englund (A-Team/Warner)

This film about three Malibu surfers in the 1960s has been branded major statement and it's got Big Ideas about adolescence, friendship, and the 1960s. The film revolves around three friends, Jan-Michael Vincent, William Katt, and Gary Busey. Each is a noted surfer, with Vincent something of a legend. The movie is divided into four movements, with each section moving ahead a few years. It climaxes at the final segment, Big Wednesday, when the surf has swelled to unknown proportions and the three reunite as men to again conquer the ocean.

BILL & TED'S BOGUS JOURNEY
1991, 98 mins, US Ⓥ ⊙
D: Peter Hewitt A: Keanu Reeves, Alex Winter, William Sadler, Joss Ackland, Pam Grier, George Carlin (Interscope/Nelson)

In aptly named *Bill & Ted's Bogus Journey,* the characters of the dopey, sweet-spirited dudes from San Dimas, CA, go undeveloped in a sequel that contrives another elaborate but nonexcellent adventure. This time, evil robot versions of Bill and Ted (Alex Winter and Keanu Reeves) have been sent from the future to kill the duo before their band, Wyld Stallyns, can win a local talent contest and inspire a Bill and Ted following that changes the world.

BILL & TED'S EXCELLENT ADVENTURE
1989, 90 mins, US Ⓥ ⊟
D: Stephen Herek A: Keanu Reeves, Alex Winter, George Carlin, Terry Camilleri, Dan Shor (Nelson/Interscope)

Keanu Reeves (Ted) and Alex Winter (Bill) play San Dimas "dudes" so close they seem wired together. Preoccupied with plans for "a most triumphant video" to launch their two-man rock band, the Wyld Stallyns, they're suddenly, as Bill put it, "in danger of flunking most heinously" out of history. A cosmic benefactor offers them a chance to travel back through history and gather up the speakers they need for an awesome presentation. They end up jamming Napoleon, Billy the Kid, Sigmund Freud, Socrates, Joan of Arc, Genghis Khan, Abraham Lincoln, and Mozart into their time-traveling phone booth. Reeves, with his beguilingly blank face and loose-limbed, happy-go-lucky physical vocabulary, and Winter, with his golden curls, gleefully good vibes, and "bodacious" vocabulary, propel this adventure as long as they can.

BILLIE
1965, 86 mins, US Ⓥ ⊟
D: Don Weis A: Patty Duke, Jim Backus, Jane Greer, Warren Berlinger, Billy De Wolfe, Charles Lane (Chrislaw/United Artists)

Patty Duke stars as the tomboy who complicates her family life before shedding athletic gear for maiden attire. Ronald Alexander adapted his *Time Out for Ginger* legiter of the early 1950s, cutting some characters to focus on Duke, the younger daughter of understanding Jane Greer and bumbling Jim Backus, who shines in field meets via a mental gimmick. Coach Charles Lane uses her to goad his less proficient males, including Warren Berlinger, to whom the gal eventually reveals her secret and gives her heart. Duke has an infectious personality which comes across.

BILLION DOLLAR BRAIN
1967, 111 mins, UK Ⓥ ⊟
D: Ken Russell A: Michael Caine, Karl Malden, Francoise Dorleac, Oscar Homolka, Ed Begley (United Artists)

Plot takes too long to get moving, and when it does it is quite incredible and hard to follow. Harry Palmer (Michael Caine) is instructed to take a package containing mysterious eggs to Finland, and meets up with a former American CIA man, Ed Newbigin (Karl Malden), whose life he has saved in the past. It doesn't matter so much that the story line offends belief—so do the Bond gambols—but it is deployed by director Ken Russell with such abrupt speed that it doesn't make immediate sense in its own frivolous terms. Francoise Dorleac introduces a touch of glamor as an agent who might be working for anybody.

BILL OF DIVORCEMENT, A
1932, 75 mins, US Ⓥ
D: George Cukor A: John Barrymore, Billie Burke, Katharine Hepburn, David Manners, Bramwell Fletcher (Radio)

Standout here is the smash impression made by Katharine Hepburn in her first picture assignment. She has a vital something that sets her apart from the picture galaxy. John Barrymore distinguishes himself anew in a part far from his accustomed range. For Billie Burke, the role of the distracted wife holds out small promise of flourish and histrionic parade, but she looks miraculously fresh and young, giving much charm to the character of the secondary femme character. David Manners as the heroine's young sweetheart is another happy choice.

BILL OF DIVORCEMENT, A
1940, 70 mins, US
D: John Farrow A: Maureen O'Hara, Adolphe Menjou, Fay Bainter, Herbert Marshall, May Whitty, C. Aubrey Smith (RKO)

Clemence Dane's play, originally turned out by RKO, skyrocketed Katharine Hepburn into prominence and marquee lights. Maureen O'Hara, a capable Irish actress imported by Erich Pommer and Charles Laughton, essays the Hepburn role in this remake with utmost confidence and ability. Story is of a woman's sacrifice of love, marriage, and an anticipated family in order to care for her demented father. O'Hara takes fullest advantage of a meaty role which is attention arresting and rich in acting opportunity. Menjou provides an excellent characterization of the father (previously handled by John Barrymore). Fay Bainter delivers her usual warmful and sincere performance as the wife.

BILLY BATHGATE
1991, 106 mins, US Ⓥ ⊙
D: Robert Benton A: Dustin Hoffman, Nicole Kidman, Loren Dean, Bruce Willis, Steven Hill, Stanley Tucci (Touchstone)

This refined, intelligent drama about thugs appeals considerably to the head but has little impact in the gut. Tom Stoppard's tight, neatly arcing screenplay kicks off powerfully with Schultz (Dustin Hoffman), arguably the king of the New York underworld in 1935, taking his once-trusted top enforcer (Bruce Willis) for a nocturnal tugboat ride, tying him up, and planting his feet in cement. Observing this showdown from close range is Billy (Loren Dean), a nervy kid. The personal drama mainly concerns Billy earning a place in the gang and vowing to take care of the beautiful Drew Preston (Nicole Kidman), the dead enforcer's former girlfriend. Despite Dean's alert, open performance, Billy remains an opaque witness to events that are unfolding over his head. Hoffman's performance also is problematic. There is a stiffness that sets his impersonation apart from his best contempo characterizations. Kidman comes on strongly, showing both girlish frivolousness and steely resolve.

BILLY BUDD
1962, 123 mins, US/UK Ⓥ ▭
D: Peter Ustinov A: Robert Ryan, Peter Ustinov, Melvyn Douglas, Terence Stamp, Ronald Lewis, David McCallum (Allied Artists)

Billy Budd is the allegorical tale of the clash of an incredibly good-hearted young foretopman and an inhumanly sadistic master-at-arms aboard a British fighting vessel in 1797, and the issue of moral justice vs. the wartime military code that arises when the former is condemned to hang for killing the latter, though recognized even by those who sit in judgment upon him as being spiritually innocent. The clash between Budd and his tormentor, Claggart—archetypes of good and evil—has been carried off well by Terence Stamp and Robert Ryan under Ustinov's guidance. Where Ustinov has slipped is in the development and delineation of the character he himself plays—the overly conscientious Captain Vere.
1962: Nomination: Best Supp. Actor (Terence Stamp)

BILLY JACK
1971, 115 mins, US Ⓥ ⊙
D: T. C. Frank [Tom Laughlin] A: Tom

Laughlin, Delores Taylor, Clark Howat, Bert Freed, Julie Webb, Ken Tobey (National Student)

Leading character is a half-breed named Billy Jack, guardian of the red man's rights and nemesis of any white who may intrude on these rights. He finds plenty of opportunity to assert himself, what with defending wild horses on the Arizona reservation, wild kids, a school on the reservation, and the actions of residents of a neighboring town violently opposed both to the school and Billy himself. Screenplay attempts to encompass too many story facets. Result is that the action frequently drags and interest palls as some of the young people in the school, many of them white, spout their philosophy and question the behavior of the whites. Tom Laughlin, as the invincible defender, is first-rate.

BILLY JACK GOES TO WASHINGTON

1977, 155 mins, US ▭

D: T. C. Frank [Tom Laughlin] **A:** Tom Laughlin, Delores Taylor, E. G. Marshall, Teresa Laughlin, Sam Wanamaker, Lucie Arnaz (Taylor-Laughlin)

Billy Jack Goes to Washington, a remake of the 1939 Frank Capra classic *Mr. Smith Goes to Washington,* compensates for its lack of subtlety with an angry attack on governmental corruption. In the old James Stewart role of the innocent-turned-senator, Tom Laughlin is fighting against the scheme of political boss Sam Wanamaker and corrupt fellow senator E. G. Marshall to exploit a planned nuclear plant for their financial gain. By comparison with the brilliance of the Capra version, the pic is much flatter and largely devoid of performing or visual nuances.

BILLY LIAR

1963, 98 mins, UK ⓥ ▭

D: John Schlesinger **A:** Tom Courtenay, Julie Christie, Wilfred Pickles, Mona Washbourne, Finlay Currie, Rodney Bewes (Vic/Anglo-Amalgamated)

Billy Liar is an imaginative, fascinating film. It is perhaps unfair to label the film as entirely realistic, since it moves into a world of Walter Mitty–like fantasy, and that is its only weakness. These scenes lack impact. Billy Liar (Tom Courtenay) is a daydreaming young man who is an incorrigible liar, dreaming dreams and, whenever possible, retreating into an invented world where he is the dictator of an imagined slice of Ruritania. Of the three girls with whom he is involved, Julie Christie is the only one who really understands him. Christie turns in a glowing performance. Helen Fraser and Gwendolyn Watts provide sharply contrasting performances as the other young women in Billy Liar's complicated, muddled existence.

BILLY MADISON

1995, 89 mins, US ⓥ

D: Tamra Davis **A:** Adam Sandler, Darren McGavin, Bridgette Wilson, Bradley Whitford, Josh Mostel, Norm McDonald (Universal)

Adam Sandler's title character is the son of a hotel magnate (Darren McGavin) who slobs around a huge estate with his friends, drinking beer, lounging in the pool, and staging inane pranks. When his dad decides to retire, Billy—who slid through school on bribes—must pass all 12 grades, two weeks at a time, to prevent his father from leaving the company to an insidious aide. Sandler (who also scripted, with Tim Herlily) delivers the expected adult-among-children scenes and, unfortunately, plenty of material on the level of bodily-excretion gags and gay jokes directed at the high-school principal (Josh Mostel). They tend to obscure some of the more clever bits. Sandler and director Tamra Davis bring a certain manic energy and no-holds-barred attitude to the proceedings but still feel like they're stretching sketch material to feature length.

BILLY ROSE'S JUMBO

See: Jumbo

BILLY THE KID

1930, 95 mins, US ▭

D: King Vidor **A:** John Mack Brown, Wallace Beery, Kay Johnson, Karl Dane, Wyndham Standing, Russell Simpson (M-G-M)

Billy the Kid is replete with gunfights and anticlimaxes. At least on two occasions it looks as if the feature is finished but it keeps right on going. There's little or no love interest, albeit the script intimates that the Kid would like to fall for best friend's wife. That her fiancé is shot on their wedding day is the reason the Kid swears vengeance upon one half of the state of New Mexico and they have to call in the cavalry to halt his ensuing feud with the Donovan mob.

BILLY TWO HATS

1974, 99 mins, US ⓥ

D: Ted Kotcheff **A:** Gregory Peck, Desi

Arnaz Jr., Jack Warden, Sian Barbara Allen, David Huddleston, John Pearce (Algonquin)

This is a fresh, different oater (the first filmed in Israel) that opens with violence and contains some throughout but never lingers lovingly on mayhem and gore. A Scot and a young half Indian (Billy Two Hats, because his white father was an important man) commit a robbery. They get away, but the far-off Scot is shot in the leg with a buffalo gun. The lad makes a rough stretcher and hauls him behind his horse. Gregory Peck, almost unrecognizable behind a broad Highland brogue and a bushy beard, is splendid.

BILOXI BLUES
1988, 106 mins, US ⓥ ⊙ ▭
D: Mike Nichols A: Matthew Broderick, Christopher Walken, Matt Mulhern, Michael Dolan, Penelope Ann Miller, Markus Flanagan (Rastar/Universal)

Biloxi Blues is an agreeable but hardly inspired film version of Neil Simon's second installment of his autobiographical trilogy. World War II barracks comedy provokes just mild laughs and smiles rather than the guffaws Simon's work often elicits in the theater. Playing a character perched precisely on the point between adolescence and manhood, Broderick is enjoyable all the way. Penelope Ann Miller is adorable as the girl who inspires love at first sight, while the most intriguing performance comes from Christopher Walken.

BINGO LONG TRAVELING ALL-STARS AND MOTOR KINGS, THE
1976, 110 mins, US ⓥ
D: John Badham A: Billy Dee Williams, James Earl Jones, Richard Pryor, Rico Dawson, Sam Birmingham Brison, Jophery Brown (Motown/Pan-Arts)

Billy Dee Williams and James Earl Jones are superb as leaders of a barnstorming black baseball team circa 1939. Based on a William Brashler novel, the script is an adroit mix of broad comedy and credible dramatic conflict. Among the standout featured players is Richard Pryor, shifting amusingly from Cuban to Indian heritages as a way to break the black barrier.

BIRD
1988, 161 mins, US ⓥ ⊙
D: Clint Eastwood A: Forest Whitaker, Diane Venora, Michael Zelniker, Samuel E. Wright, Keith David (Malpaso/Warner)

In taking on a biopic of late jazz great

Charlie Parker, Clint Eastwood has had to chart bold new territory for himself as a director, and he has pulled it off in most impressive fashion. That Parker (Forest Whitaker), who died in 1955 at 34, was the greatest sax man of them all is virtually undisputed, but he also lived a messy complicated life, mixing drug addiction and a multitude of women with an ongoing attempt at a home life with his wife Chan (Diane Venora) and their two children. Naturally, the prolific artist's music provides the continuing thread for the film, and jazzman Lennie Niehaus does a sensational job in blending Bird's actual sax solos with fresh backups by contemporary musicians. Whitaker makes an imposing likable, very hip genius. Venora is so riveting that her occasional long absences from the story are sorely missed.
1988: Best Sound

BIRDCAGE, THE
1996, 119 mins, US ⓥ ⊙
D: Mike Nichols A: Robin Williams, Gene Hackman, Nathan Lane, Dianne Wiest, Hank Azaria, Christine Baranski (United Artists)

It may not have seemed that the world needed a remake of *La Cage aux Folles*, but Mike Nichols and Elaine May, in their first official screen collaboration, have scored with a riotous comedy whose irreverent topicality is one of its most refreshing components. Armand (Robin Williams) runs the hugely successful boîte, where the family-oriented drag revue is headed by Starina, otherwise known as Albert (Nathan Lane). The two have enjoyed a strong personal and professional relationship for 20 years and have successfully raised Armand's son, Val (Dan Futterman). Complications click in when Val's future father-in-law, Republican Senator Keeley (Gene Hackman), cofounder of the Coalition for Moral Order, and his prim-and-proper wife (Dianne Wiest) and daughter, Barbara (Calista Flockhart), drop in on the menagerie in Miami, and the impending visit throws the household into a tizzy. The filmmakers have strayed from the structure and characters of the original nary at all, but have adapted it all to a contempo American context with dizzying skill.

BIRDMAN OF ALCATRAZ
1962, 147 mins, US ⓥ ⊙
D: John Frankenheimer A: Burt Lancaster, Karl Malden, Thelma Ritter, Neville

Brand, Telly Savalas, Edmond O'Brien (United Artists/Harold Hecht)

Birdman of Alcatraz is not really a prison picture in the traditional and accepted sense of the term. Penetrating and affecting screenplay delicately and artfully sketches the 53-year imprisonment of the 72-year-old "Birdman," Stroud, illustrating the highlights and lowlights of that terrible, yet miraculously ennobling span. Lancaster gives a superbly natural, unaffected performance. His running clash with the narrow-minded and vengeful warden Shoemaker is a highlight of the film, culminating in a powerful scene depicting their opposing views on penology. Karl Malden is excellent as the warden.
1962: Nominations: Best Actor (Burt Lancaster), Supp. Actor (Telly Savalas), Supp. Actress (Thelma Ritter), B&W Cinematography

BIRD OF PARADISE
1932, 80 mins, US Ⓥ
D: King Vidor **A:** Dolores Del Rio, Joel McCrea, John Halliday, Lon Chaney Jr., Skeets Gallagher, Bert Roach (Radio)

The old perennial stands the test of the innumerable South Seas pictures that have been done since its stage production way back yonder. Outside of its romantic side, the subject's greatest asset is the truly fine performance of Dolores Del Rio as the savage princess Luana, admirably supplemented by the playing of the stalwart Joel McCrea. Spectacular side of the production has received handsome treatment by director King Vidor. Possibilities for stunning tropical Hawaiian scenery have been realized to the fullest.

BIRD OF PARADISE
1951, 100 mins, US
D: Delmer Daves **A:** Louis Jourdan, Debra Paget, Jeff Chandler, Everett Sloane, Jack Elam, Maurice Schwartz (20th Century-Fox)

Bird of Paradise makes another trip to the screen. Essentials of the drama are still there, plus a beautiful Technicolor camera job, haunting island music, and the use of actual locales. Louis Jourdan and Debra Paget play the roles of the white man and native girl. There's another strong casting in Jeff Chandler, seen in the new character of a native who returns to his island after a try at stateside living. Paget hits a high level in her performance as the Princess Kalua. She as well as the other players give their characters considerable sincerity.

BIRD ON A WIRE
1990, 110 mins, US Ⓥ ⊙ ▭
D: John Badham **A:** Mel Gibson, Goldie Hawn, David Carradine, Bill Duke, Joan Severance, Stephen Tobolowsky (Badham-Cohen/Interscope)

Only the chemistry of Goldie Hawn and Mel Gibson makes the film watchable. Gibson plays a schnook who's been hiding out for 15 years under an FBI witness relocation program. The man he fingered (David Carradine) is just out of prison. Contrived and thoroughly unconvincing plot cog has Gibson discovered incognito by old flame Hawn at the Detroit gas station where he works just as Carradine and partner Duke catch up with him. Resulting shoot-out throws Hawn and Gibson together on the lam for the rest of the pic. Main kudos go to British designer Philip Harrison, who's allowed to run hog-wild in a large-scale climax set at a zoo exhibit depicting a Brazilian rain forest.

BIRDS, THE
1963, 120 mins, US Ⓥ ⊙
D: Alfred Hitchcock **A:** Rod Taylor, Tippi Hedren, Jessica Tandy, Suzanne Pleshette, Veronica Cartwright, Charles McGraw (Universal)

Beneath all of this elaborate feather bedlam lies a Hitch cock-and-bull story that's essentially a fowl ball. The premise is fascinating. The idea of billions of birdbrains refusing to eat crow any longer and adopting the hunt-and-peck system, with Homo sapiens as their ornithological target, is fraught with potential. Cinematically, Hitchcock & Co. have done a masterful job of meeting this formidable challenge. But dramatically, *The Birds* is little more than a shocker-for-shock's-sake. An unnecessary elaborate romantic plot has been cooked up and then left suspended. It involves a young bachelor attorney (Rod Taylor), his sister (Veronica Cartwright), their mother (Jessica Tandy), and a plucky, mysterious playgirl (Tippi Hedren). Aside from the birds, the film belongs to Hedren, who makes an auspicious screen bow.
1963: Nomination: Best Special Effects

BIRDY
1984, 120 mins, US Ⓥ ⊙
D: Alan Parker **A:** Matthew Modine, Nicolas Cage, John Harkins, Sandy Baron, Karen Young, Bruno Kirby (A&M/Tri-Star)

Birdy is a heavy adult drama about best friends and the aftereffects of war, but it takes too long to live up to its ambitious premise. Matthew Modine stars as the title character, who, psychologically ill and institutionalized, spends much of his time naked, curled up in birdlike positions and speaking to no one. These posturings stem from a childhood affinity to birds which he shared to a significant degree with Nicolas Cage, who himself is banged up from the fighting, but is brought in to try to communicate with his boyhood pal.

BIRTHDAY PARTY, THE
1968, 123 mins, UK ⊗
D: William Friedkin **A:** Robert Shaw, Patrick McGee, Dandy Nichols, Sydney Tafler (Continental/Palomar)

Harold Pinter's comedy of menace has been transfered to the screen as an intellectual exercise in verbal gymnastics. Robert Shaw is the frightened lost soul, put upon as humanity's nonconformist. It appears that prior to vegetating the past year at Dandy Nichols's boardinghouse, he may have been a piano player and a deserting member of a criminal organization. Sydney Tafler and cohort Patrick McGee are the organization men sent to get Shaw. On these bones, Pinter fleshes out his philosophy of the complex fictions people employ.

BIRTH OF A NATION, THE
(AKA: THE CLANSMAN)
1915, 187 mins, US ⊗ ⊙ ⊗
D: D. W. Griffith **A:** Henry B. Walthall, Miriam Cooper, Mae Marsh, Lillian Gish, Ralph Lewis, George Siegmann (Griffith/Epoch/Dixon)

The Birth of a Nation is the main title David Wark Griffith gave to his version of Thomas Dixon's story of the south, The Clansman. The story involves: the Camerons of the south and the Stonemans of the north and Silas Lynch, the mulatto lieutenant governor; the opening and finish of the Civil War; the scenes attendant upon the assassination of Abraham Lincoln; the period of carpetbagging days and union reconstruction following Lee's surrender; and the terrorizing of the southern whites by the newly freed blacks and the rise of the Ku Klux Klan. All these, including some wonderfully well-staged battle scenes taken at night, are realistically, graph___lly, and most superbly depicted by th___ra. Henry Walthall makes a ___ightforward character of the ___l and handles his big scenes ___v. Mae Marsh as the pet sis-___markable work as the little

girl who loves the south and loves her brother. Ralph Lewis as the leader of the House who helps Silas Lynch rise to power. George Siegmann gets all there can be gotten out of the despicable character of Lynch. Walter Long makes Gus, the renegade Negro, a hated, much-despised type, his acting and makeup being complete. The Birth of a Nation is said to have cost $300,000.

BIRTH OF A NATION, THE
1930, 108 mins, US
D: D. W. Griffith (Griffith)

The original score, assembled by J. C. Breil, has been recorded for [this sound reissue]. But though tuneful, the music seems shallow in its tenderness and short of the sweeping spectacle that's the essence of this crossroads production. There is the blare of the Klan's trumpet as the horses and men gallop, and this ride remains a big thrill. There are also battle effects.

BIRTH OF THE BLUES
1941, 80 mins, US
D: Victor Schertzinger **A:** Bing Crosby, Mary Martin, Brian Donlevy, Carolyn Lee, Eddie Rochester Anderson, J. Carrol Naish (Paramount)

Birth of the Blues has everything from melody to comedy. A saga of Basin Street, New Orleans, cradle of the Dixieland jazz idiom, it projects its story with bounce and gusto; forthright in its allegiance to a then-unorthodox jazz style; plus arresting romance, a plug-ugly cabaret menace, and a wealth of cavalcade jazzapation. Bing Crosby is the licorice-stick disciple who adheres to his premise that the colored man's levee music, at the foot of Basin Street, is bound to sweep the country.
1941: Nomination: Best Scoring of a Musical Picture

BIRUMA NO TATEGOTO
(THE BURMESE HARP; HARP OF BURMA)
1956, 116 mins, Japan ⊗
D: Kon Ichikawa **A:** Rentaro Mikuni, Shoji Yasui, Tatsuya Mihashi, Taniye Kitabayashi, Yunosuke Ito (Nikkatsu)

Offbeater concerns the last days of the war in Burma and is about a Japanese private who decides to stay on to bury all the Japanese dead strewn over the land. Film concerns how his captive mates learn of his resolve and try to talk him into going back with them. Film has a good narrative style, but has oversimplified storytelling.

Direction is restrained but lacks the power to make this an unusual plea.

BISHOP'S WIFE, THE
1947, 106 mins, US 🔇 ⊙
D: Henry Koster **A:** Cary Grant, Loretta Young, David Niven, Monty Woolley, Gladys Cooper, Elsa Lanchester (RKO)

While a fantasy, there are no fantastic heavenly manifestations. There's a humanness about the characters, even the angel, that beguiles full attention. Cary Grant is the angel of the piece. Role, with the exception of a minor miracle or two, is potently pointed to indicate character could have been a flesh-and-blood person, a factor that embellishes sense of reality as the angel sets about answering the troubled prayers of Episcopalian bishop (David Niven). Loretta Young gives a moving performance as the wife whose life is touched by an angel without her knowledge of his heavenly origin.
1947: Best Sound Recording
Nominations: Best Picture, Director, Editing, Scoring of a Dramatic Picture

BITCH, THE
1979, 90 mins, UK 🔇
D: Gerry O'Hara **A:** Joan Collins, Michael Coby, Kenneth Haigh, Ian Hendry, Carolyn Seymour, Sue Lloyd (Brent Walker)
The Bitch offers more mock orgasm than plot as it oscillates between the disco floor and the sack or the pool, shower, or wherever a couple can couple. Not to mince about, the production, scripted and feverishly directed by Gerry O'Hara, is corny and coarse, but at least mercifully brief at 90 minutes. Joan Collins does her spoiled-nympho-rich-girl turn with assurance.

BITE THE BULLET
1975, 131 mins, US 🔇 ⊙ ▭
D: Richard Brooks **A:** Gene Hackman, Candice Bergen, James Coburn, Ben Johnson, Ian Bannen, Jan-Michael Vincent (Columbia)
Bite the Bullet is an excellent, literate action drama probing the diverse motivations of participants in an endurance horse race. The contestants include Gene Hackman and James Coburn as ex–San Juan Hill Rough Riders; Candice Bergen as a former resident of Jean Willes frontier pleasure shanty, seeking money to help her imprisoned lover; vagabond Ben Johnson desperately wanting to be somebody for a brief moment in life.

1975: Nominations: Best Original Song Score, Sound

BITTER HARVEST
1963, 96 mins, UK 🔇
D: Peter Graham Scott **A:** Janet Munro, John Stride, Anne Cunningham, Alan Badel, William Lucas, Barbara Ferris (Independent Artists)

The story of the country innocent (Janet Munro) who gets caught up in the dizzy pitfalls of London nightlife is a conventional yarn. Munro is given opportunities to portray innocence, gaiety, cupidity, depression, vanity, fear, cunning, tenderness, harshness, wonder, and anger. All the emotions are fleeting but the star helps to mold them into a well-drawn picture of an innocent who learns quickly. John Stride is solid, charming, and resourceful as the infatuated bartender. Alan Badel makes a brief but telling contribution as a steely, unscrupulous theater boss.

BITTER MOON
1992, 139 mins, France/UK 🔇 ⊙
D: Roman Polanski **A:** Peter Coyote, Emmanuelle Seigner, Hugh Grant, Kristin Scott Thomas, Victor Bannerjee, Sophie Patel (RP/Burrill)

Roman Polanski approaches rock bottom with *Bitter Moon*, a phony slice of *huis clos* drama between two couples aboard a Euro liner. Initial focus is on a couple of hoity-toity Brits (Hugh Grant, Kristin Scott Thomas). Things start to go awry when they help a distraught young femme, Mimi (Emmanuelle Seigner). Grant is accosted by her American hubby (Peter Coyote), a wheelchair-bound misanthrope. Pic settles into a series of long flashbacks detailing Coyote-Seigner's tempestuous love life. Pic holds a certain awful fascination as Polanski careens every which way with the material. Coyote gives a scenery-chewing performance. Seigner is eye-popping in the sex scenes.

BITTER SWEET
1933, 76 mins, UK 🔇
D: Herbert Wilcox **A:** Anna Neagle, Fernand Gravet, Esme Percy, Clifford Heatherly, Ivy St. Helier, Miles Mander (British & Dominions/United Artists)

Direction hampers Anna Neagle, a stunning blonde of compelling grace, but here permitted no emotional range. Fernand Gravet is young, dark and a vital type. Support role here doesn't bring out his engaging personality in full. Clifford Heatherly does the Vienna cafe proprietor,

Herr Schlick, contributing a splendidly flexible performance with a capital knack of legitimate comedy. Ivy St. Helier plays the soubrette role to the hilt. Continuity takes many liberties with the operetta script, usually without improving it. The leads handle several numbers agreeably.

BITTER SWEET
1940, 92 mins, US ⓥ
D: W. S. Van Dyke A: Jeanette MacDonald, Nelson Eddy, George Sanders, Ian Hunter, Felix Bressart (M-G-M)
Bitter Sweet is a super-elaborate production providing a background for the fetching Noel Coward songs, in his highly successful operetta. The story's an obvious and static romance from the time music teacher Eddy elopes with his pupil (MacDonald); takes her to Vienna while he writes an operetta; and his tragic death just as his work is to be presented. The love scenes between the couple are staid and cold. Both MacDonald and Eddy interpret Coward's numbers in excellent style.

BITTER TEA OF GENERAL YEN, THE
1933, 87 mins, US ⓥ
D: Frank Capra A: Barbara Stanwyck, Nils Asther, Gavin Gordon, Toshia Mori, Walter Connolly, Richard Loo (Columbia)
A queer story of a romance in China between a Chinese and a white woman. The Chinese warlord is a curious and rather questionable human composition of a poet, philosopher, and bandit. He speaks rather fluent English and essays somewhat dainty American mannerisms, especially in manipulating a handkerchief. Nils Asther plays the role. Barbara Stanwyck is the white girl. Pleasant enough and for the first half, where she repulses the Chinaman, gathers some audience sympathy. Subsequently, where the photography attempts to simulate that the girl, in her dreams, loves the Chinese, the role fails her. Besides which, as a New England missionary type, Stanwyck does not fit. Walter Connolly takes the acting honors as the adventurous American financial adviser of General Yen.

BITTER VICTORY
1958, 97 mins, France/US ▢
D: Nicholas Ray A: Richard Burton, Curt Jurgens, Ruth Roman, Raymond Pellegrin, Anthony Bushell, Christopher Lee (Transcontinental/Laffont)
A literary, hard-hitting screenplay sets up a deadly struggle between two British army officers during the Second World War African campaign. Conflict between Captain Leith and Major Brand derives from fact that Leith knows of Brand's basic cowardice in action, and also from jealousy over Brand's wife, with whom Leith has had an affair. Brand tries twice indirectly to bring about Leith's death. Script is basically flawed by the unclearly delineated key character of the major and Curt Jurgens's competent, straightforward performance is less successful because of it.

BLACK AND WHITE IN COLOR
See: La Victoire en Chantant

BLACK ARROW, THE
1948, 76 mins, US ⓥ
D: Gordon Douglas A: Louis Hayward, Janet Blair, George Macready, Edgar Buchanan (Columbia)
Using Robert Louis Stevenson's *The Black Arrow* for the takeoff, Columbia has made an action-filled cloak-and-dagger romance. The picture is virtually a western of lethal combat, hard riding, intrigue, and deep-dyed villainy all in when-knighthood-was-in-flower terms. Maybe it isn't exactly art, but it is good entertainment.

BLACKBEARD'S GHOST
1968, 106 mins, US ⓥ ⊙
D: Robert Stevenson A: Peter Ustinov, Dean Jones, Suzanne Pleshette, Elsa Lanchester, Joby Baker, Elliott Reid (Walt Disney)
Lively and entertaining Walt Disney production features Peter Ustinov in a tour de farce title role as the restless spirit of the famed pirate. Robert Stevenson's direction is highlighted by several very amusing chase and special-effects sequences. Ustinov plays his part to the hilt: mugging and cutting up, as the wandering spirit who must do a good deed to achieve repose. Joby Baker is the lead heavy, and Pleshette's presence lends a romantic, also sympathetic touch to the proceedings.

BLACKBEARD, THE PIRATE
1952, 98 mins, US ⓥ ⊙
D: Raoul Walsh A: Robert Newton, Linda Darnell, William Bendix, Keith Andes, Torin Thatcher, Richard Egan (RKO)
A rollicking swashbuckler stacked with high adventure, extensive swordplay, and all the things big pirate pictures are made of. It's the 17th century on the Spanish Main again. Torin Thatcher, a reformed pirate, has been commissioned by the King of England to rid the seas of Robert

("Blackbeard") Newton. Keith Andes, a young sailor of fortune out to collect some reward money, allows himself to be shanghaied. Also going aboard is Thatcher's adopted daughter (Linda Darnell).

BLACK BEAUTY
1933, 63 mins, US
D: Phil Rosen **A:** Esther Ralston, Alexander Kirkland, Hale Hamilton, Gavin Gordon, Don Alvarado, George Walsh (Monogram)

This is a picturization of that classic juvenile story first published in 1877. A tear element figures as the horse, hero of the tale, gets rough breaks, one after another. Not laid on with unnatural thickness but, rather, strikes a note of sympathy, which stands as an asset. Two particularly sympathetic characters, as done by Esther Ralston and Alexander Kirkland, are the wealthy widow and the boyish owner of Black Beauty.

BLACK BEAUTY
1946, 74 mins, US ⊗
D: Max Nosseck **A:** Mona Freeman, Richard Denning, Evelyn Ankers, Charles Evans, J. M. Kerrigan, Moyna Macgill (Alson/20th Century-Fox)

A standard among horse yarns, dealing with a young girl's love for a colt that she rears, the story, backgrounded by the English countryside in the late 19th century, mostly concerns the heartaches that result when the animal is forced into the hands of others and subsequently encounters the downtrail as a job horse. Mona Freeman is properly impetuous and eager, while Denning is bedeviled by the script, as are all the others. Direction is frequently poor. Acting by some lesser characters is unusually bad.

BLACK BEAUTY
1971, 106 mins, UK/W. Germany/Spain ⊗
D: James Hill **A:** Mark Lester, Uschi Glas, Walter Slezak, Peter Lee Lawrence, John Nettleton, Patrick Mower (CCC Filmkunst/Chilton Films/Emiliano Piedra Tigon British/German Cinerama)

Continental producers have taken their first crack at this bestseller. In their attempt to please all audiences, in too many different lands, the filmmakers have ridden off in all directions at once. The heavies hamming up their parts, probably intended to suit Spanish tastes. An oversweet saccharine streak of German heart and soul oozes through the picture. Still another element, quite foreign to the original story, is unsuccessfully aimed at Yank preferences: to some extent, this charming horse saga emerges as a rough-riding western. Director James Hill does little to save this one from disintegrating into self-contradiction. Film's assets are the noble title horse with its great equestrian stunts and the appealing landscape, exquisitely color-lensed by Fernando Arribas.

BLACK BEAUTY
1994, 85 mins, US ⊗
D: Caroline Thompson **A:** Sean Bean, David Thewlis, Jim Carter, Peter Davison, Alun Armstrong, John McEnery (Warner)

Affecting, rather grave rendition of the children's perennial. Debuting director Caroline Thompson has brought considerable feeling and care to this story of a fine horse's often difficult life in Victorian England. Work's notable feature is its first-person narration from the point of view of Black Beauty, which soon proves charming and lends the film what worldview it has. By closely following the book, Thompson has had to face its extremely episodic nature, a problem that has not entirely been surmounted either in the scripting or the editing.

BLACK BELT JONES
1974, 85 mins, US ⊗
D: Robert Clouse **A:** Jim Kelly, Gloria Hendry, Scatman Crothers, Alan Weeks, Eric Laneuville, Andre Phillipe (Warner)

The story strand pits a group of graceful black martial-arts students against some cliché white gangsters, neither side taking things seriously. Kelly, between the thousands of body blows given and taken, has time for Gloria Hendry, equally adept at physical jousting and providing a good romantic interest.

BLACK BIRD, THE
1926, 76 mins, US ⊗
D: Tod Browning **A:** Lon Chaney, Renee Adoree, Owen Moore, Doris Lloyd (M-G-M)

Lon Chaney plays a dual role, that of a crook and of his brother, a Limehouse missionary. Although the reverend fellow is crippled up plenty, the curse is taken off by one shot showing the crook throwing his arm and leg out of joint and then assuming the role of the man whom the world thought to be his brother. The crook falls in love with a music-hall performer, while a flashier crook from the West End also goes for the same girl. It's a good melodrama, excellently produced.

BLACK BIRD, THE
1975, 98 mins, US ⊗

D: David Giler A: George Segal, Stephane Audran, Lionel Stander, Lee Patrick, Elisha Cook Jr., Felix Silla (Columbia/Rastar)

This satirical contemporary update of Dashiell Hammett's novel *The Maltese Falcon* emerges as fair whimsy. George Segal, as Sam Spade's son, has inherited the detective agency. The search for the elusive Maltese Falcon is reinstated, bringing in all sorts of mysterious characters. There are lots of smiles, many chuckles, and a few strong laughs.

BLACKBOARD JUNGLE
1955, 100 mins, US ⊗ ⊙

D: Richard Brooks A: Glenn Ford, Anne Francis, Louis Calhern, Vic Morrow, Sidney Poitier, Margaret Hayes (M-G-M)

An angry picture that flares out in moral and physical rage. The main issue is the juvenile bum who terrorizes schoolrooms and teachers. The strong-among-the-evil element, here represented by Vic Morrow, is already beyond any reform. The good, represented by Sidney Poitier, has had no stimulus to awaken his leadership abilities because he is a Negro. Glenn Ford, Morrow, and Poitier are so real in their performances that the picture alternatingly has the viewer pleading, indignant, and frightened before the conclusion.

1955: Nominations: Best Screenplay, B&W Cinematography, B&W Art Direction, Editing

BLACK CAT, THE
(UK: HOUSE OF DOOM)
1934, 65 mins, US ⊙

D: Edgar G. Ulmer A: Boris Karloff, Bela Lugosi, David Manners, Julie Bishop, Andy Devine, John Carradine (Universal)

Story is confused and confusing, and while, with the aid of heavily shadowed lighting and mausoleumlike architecture, a certain eeriness has been achieved, it's all a poor imitation of things seen before. Boris Karloff occupies a spooky manor. Bela Lugosi is a batty doctor. Clash of the two eyebrow-squinting nuts involves an American bridal couple temporarily caught in the manor. It is the playful notion of nasty Karloff to make the bride Exhibit A in a devil cult of which he is the head, and it is the revenge of Lugosi to torture his enemy by skinning him alive.

BLACK CAULDRON, THE
1985, 80 mins, US ⊗ ⊠

D: Ted Berman, Richard Rich (Walt Disney)

The $25-million animated *Cauldron* is not very original. The characters, though cute and cuddly and sweet and mean and ugly and simply awful, don't really have much to do that would remain of interest to any but the youngest minds. Story line is fairly stock sword-and-sorcery, with a band of likable youngsters, animals, and creatures forced to tackle an evil mob of monsters.

BLACK CHRISTMAS
1974, 93 mins, Canada ⊗

D: Bob Clark A: Olivia Hussey, Keir Dullea, Margot Kidder, Andrea Martin, John Saxon, Marian Waldman (August)

Black Christmas, a bloody, senseless kill-for-kicks feature, exploits unnecessary violence in a university sorority house. Its slow-paced, murky tale involves an obscene telephone caller who apparently delights in killing the girls off one by one, even the hapless housemother.

BLACK FURY
1935, 94 mins, US ⊗

D: Michael Curtiz A: Paul Muni, Karen Morley, William Gargan, Barton MacLane, John Qualen, J. Carrol Naish (Warner)

Pennsy coal-mining background is basically a masculine setting for intra-industry politics. The fomenting anti-unionists who generate ill will for benefit of ultimate strike-breaking maneuvers is the means for bringing in the strong-arm coal-mine police, the scabs, etc. They become the abstract composite villain. There are times when the footage is slow and Paul Muni's Polish brogue too thick but in the main the general result is arresting. J. Carrol Naish is excellent as the strike fomenter.

BLACK HOLE, THE
1979, 97 mins, US ⊗ ⊙ ⊠

D: Gary Nelson A: Maximilian Schell, Anthony Perkins, Robert Forster, Joseph Bottoms, Yvette Mimieux, Ernest Borgnine (Walt Disney)

The black hole itself gets short shrift. Most of the pic is devoted to setting up the story of mad scientist Maximilian Schell. An exploration ship stumbles on both Schell and the nearby black hole. What ensues is sometimes talky but never dull. The most attractive and sympathetic

characters are not human at all. George F. McGinnis has constructed a bevy of robots that establish a mechanical world all their own.
1979: Nominations: Best Cinematography, Visual Effects

BLACK JACK
1979, 106 mins, UK
D: Ken Loach **A:** Jean Franval, Stephen Hirst, Louise Cooper, Andrew Bennett (Kestrel)

Basically an adventure yarn set in northern England in 1750, this suffers from a meandering plotline, but that hardly matters, as it is continuously engrossing, and enlivened with a wry wit. After miraculously surviving a hanging, Black Jack, a gigantic Frenchman with few words of English, endearingly played by Jean Franval, takes along a young boy (Stephen Hirst) to speak for him. The main plot concerns a girl (Louise Cooper) whose irrational behavior has caused her wealthy parents to commit her to a privately run madhouse.

BLACK LEGION, THE
1937, 80 mins, US Ⓥ
D: Archie Mayo **A:** Humphrey Bogart, Dick Foran, Erin O'Brien-Moore, Ann Sheridan, Robert Barrat, Helen Flint (Warner)

A melodrama which gives the emotions a rough going-over. The action includes floggings, the burning of a chicken farm, destruction of a drugstore, a neophyte's taking of the oath of allegiance amid a woodland gathering of the Clan, and the behind-the-scenes machinations of the Michigan hooded order's promoters. Humphrey Bogart is a young workman in a large machine-making plant who, out of disappointment at losing the foremanship to another with a non-American name, joins the hooded order and eventually degenerates into becoming its murderous tool.

BLACKMAIL
1929, 88 mins, UK Ⓥ ⊙
D: Alfred Hitchcock **A:** Anny Ondra, Sara Allgood, Charles Paton, Donald Calthrop, John Longden, Cyril Ritchard (British International)

Blackmail has no speed or pace and very little suspense. Everything's openface. It's a story that has been told in different disguises—the story of a girl who kills a man trying to assault her. The girl, Anny Ondra, leaves her steady, a regular

Scotland Yard dick, to join the other half of the flirtation. The other half asks the girl upstairs to see his studio, he being an artist. She foolishly assents, and then follows the jam. In performance the standout is Donald Calthrop as the rat crook. He looks it. Ondra is excellent as the girl.

BLACKMAIL
1939, 80 mins, US
D: H. C. Potter **A:** Edward G. Robinson, Ruth Hussey, Gene Lockhart, Bobs Watson, Guinn Williams, John Wray (M-G-M)

Blackmail starts and finishes with spectacular oil-well fires. In between there's some lusty and actionful melodrama. Robinson rehabilitates himself after escape from a chain gang. Prospering as head of an oil-well firefighting business, he's a staid and happy family man. Gene Lockhart strolls into town, and after confessing to Robinson he committed the crime for which Robinson was sentenced, doublecrosses Robinson, who goes back to serve his sentence. Tortured in the chain gang, and discovering his wife and son are destitute while Lockhart enjoys wealth from the oil well, Robinson escapes.

BLACK MARBLE, THE
1980, 112 mins, US Ⓥ ⊡
D: Harold Becker **A:** Robert Foxworth, Paula Prentiss, Harry Dean Stanton, Barbara Babcock, James Woods, Christopher Lloyd (Avco Embassy)

Joseph Wambaugh at last comes close to presenting police as human, even humorous beings, capable of balancing remorse, regret, and romance without becoming total psychotics. Robert Foxworth is teamed on a burglary detail with Paula Prentiss. Barbara Babcock's show dog is kidnapped and she proves superb in the role of a lonely, sex-starved woman with her whole life wrapped up in her schnauzer. Much of the credit for making the picture work goes to Harry Dean Stanton as the dognapper, driven to his dirty deed by debt.

BLACK NARCISSUS
1947, 100 mins, UK Ⓥ ⊙
D: Michael Powell, Emeric Pressburger **A:** Deborah Kerr, Sabu, David Farrar, Kathleen Byron, Flora Robson, Jean Simmons (Archers)

Cynics may dub this lavish production *Brief Encounter in the Himalayas* and not without reason. The picture resolves itself into the story of two sex-starved women

and a man. And since the women are nuns, there can be no happy ending except perhaps in the spiritual sense. Five sisters of an Anglo-Catholic order open a school and hospital in a remote Himalayan village. They occupy an ancient palace, once known as the House of Women, built on a ledge 6,000 feet in the air. The nuns find their task overwhelming and Deborah Kerr, as the sister in charge, has to call for help on the cynical British agent, David Farrar, in spite of her instinctive antagonism. Production has gained much through being in color, Jack Cardiff's photography being outstanding. Most effective acting comes from Kathleen Byron as the neurotic half-crazed Sister Ruth.
1947: Best Color Cinematography, Color Art Direction

BLACK ORCHID, THE
1959, 94 mins, US Ⓥ
D: Martin Ritt **A:** Sophia Loren, Anthony Quinn, Mark Richman, Ina Balin, Virginia Vincent, Frank Puglia (Paramount)

Martin Ritt's honest direction tells an intricately drawn story with a smooth, authoritative hand. As the widower who falls in love with the pretty widow, Anthony Quinn is excellent, uniting charm with strength. Sophia Loren plays with notable feeling, convincingly portraying the mother, the widow, and the bride. The musical score by Alessandro Cicognini aptly points up contrasts in the story.

BLACK ORPHEUS
See: Orfeu Negro

BLACKOUT
See: Contraband

BLACK PIRATE, THE
1926, 88 mins, US Ⓥ ⊗
D: Albert Parker **A:** Douglas Fairbanks, Billie Dove, Donald Crisp, Anders Randolf, Tempe Piggott, Sam De Grasse (Elton/United Artists)

Douglas Fairbanks's initial feature shot completely in color. Fairbanks is up and down the screen with his acrobatics, the punch being his taking of a merchant vessel single-handed as a pirate. His best athletic bit is the manner in which he rips the sails by mounting to the cross arms, piercing the wide sail with his sword, grabbing the hilt and descending to the deck, his momentum retarded by the sword ripping the canvas as he comes down.

BLACK RAIN
1989, 126 mins, US Ⓥ ⊙ ▭
D: Ridley Scott **A:** Michael Douglas,

Andy Garcia, Ken Takakura, Kate Capshaw, Yusaku Matsuda, John Spencer (Paramount)

Since this is a Ridley Scott film, *Black Rain* is about 90 percent atmosphere and 10 percent story. But what atmosphere! This gripping crime thriller about hardboiled NY cop Michael Douglas tracking a yakuza hood in Osaka, Japan, boasts magnificent lensing and powerfully baroque production design. Douglas is utterly believable as a reckless and scummy homicide detective who takes kickbacks from drug dealers and resorts to the most brutal methods to capture escaped counterfeiter Yusaka Matsuda.
1989: Best Sound
Nomination: Best Sound Effects Editing

BLACK RAINBOW
1990, 113 mins, UK Ⓥ
D: Mike Hodges **A:** Rosanna Arquette, Jason Robards, Tom Hulce, Mark Joy, Ron Rosenthal, John Bennes (Goldcrest)

This enjoyable supernatural thriller is set in the fundamentalist society of crumbling industrial towns where folks have a deep-rooted faith in the spiritualist movement. Pic opens with journalist Tom Hulce tracking down traveling clairvoyant Rosanna Arquette. During one act Arquette receives a message from a murdered man to pass on to his wife in the audience. Unfortunately he is not dead and his wife gets rather upset. Later that night the man is killed in his home. Hulce sets about uncovering the scoop. Arquette is excellent as the strange but seductive Martha. She has an ethereal quality combined with innate sexuality.

BLACK ROBE
1991, 100 mins, Canada/Australia Ⓥ ⊙
D: Bruce Beresford **A:** Lothaire Bluteau, Aden Young, Sandrine Holt, August Schellenberg, Tantoo Cardinal, Frank Wilson (Alliance/Samson)

First official coproduction between Canada and Australia is a gripping and tragic story. Saga begins in 1634 at Fort Champlain, where newly arrived French Jesuit priest Lothaire Bluteau (whom the Indians call Black Robe because of his austere garb), is assigned to a difficult and dangerous journey 1,500 miles north to the mission outpost of Ihonatiria. Director Bruce Beresford and writer Brian Moore have made this intriguing yarn a small epic of endurance. The production has an austere beauty and thoughtful approach. Bluteau gives a moving performance in the central role.

BLACK ROSE, THE
1950, 120 mins, UK Ⓥ
D: Henry Hathaway **A:** Tyrone Power, Orson Welles, Cecile Aubry, Jack Hawkins, Michael Rennie, Herbert Lom (20th Century-Fox)

Black Rose is the story of Saxon revolt against Norman domination, 200 years after the conquest. The central figure in the Saxon fight is Walter of Gurnie (Tyrone Power), the illegitimate son of a Saxon peer. In a picture of warring, there is only the suggestion of battle. Perhaps one good scene, with some honest-to-goodness cinematic bloodletting, might have done something to increase the tempo of the picture. Power is credible in the lead role, while Welles underplays effectively the part of Bayan.
1950: Nomination: Best Color Costume Design

BLACK STALLION, THE
1979, 118 mins, US Ⓥ ⊙
D: Carroll Ballard **A:** Kelly Reno, Mickey Rooney, Teri Garr (United Artists)

A perfect gem. Based on Walter Farley's 1941 novel, Carroll Ballard's feature debut is rich in adventure, suspense, and mythical elements. Ballard's camera eye and powers of sequence conceptualization are manifestly extraordinary. Set in 1949, opening sees the American boy Alec (Kelly Reno) on a ship. Also on board is "the Black," a stallion owned by a menacing Arab. After both end up overboard, Alec and the horse find sanctuary on a deserted Mediterranean island and establish rapport. After rescue, Alec's mother (Teri Garr) naturally doesn't understand her son's now nearly symbiotic relationship with Black. Horse escapes, later to be found at farm of retired racehorse trainer Mickey Rooney.
1979: Nominations: Best Supp. Actor (Mickey Rooney), Editing

BLACK STALLION RETURNS, THE
1983, 93 mins, US Ⓥ ⊙
D: Robert Dalva **A:** Kelly Reno, Vincent Spano, Allen Garfield, Woody Strode, Ferdy Mayne, Teri Garr (Zoetrope)

The Black Stallion Returns is little more than a contrived, cornball story that most audiences will find to be an interminable bore. Much of the charm and innocence of the original are absent here as now young teen-hero Kelly Reno follows the unlikeliest of searches through the Sahara Desert for his devoted horse.

BLACK SUNDAY
1977, 143 mins, US Ⓥ ⊙ ▭
D: John Frankenheimer **A:** Robert Shaw, Bruce Dern, Marthe Keller, Fritz Weaver, Steven Keats, Bekim Fehmiu (Paramount)

Black Sunday is an intelligent and meticulous depiction of an act of outlandish terrorism—the planned slaughter of the Super Bowl stadium audience. The motivations of stars Robert Shaw, as an Israeli guerrilla, Black September activist Marthe Keller, and mentally unbalanced pilot Bruce Dern are handled with unusual dramatic depth, which displays the gray areas of real life.

BLACK SWAN, THE
1942, 83 mins, US
D: Henry King **A:** Tyrone Power, Maureen O'Hara, Laird Cregar, Thomas Mitchell, George Sanders, Anthony Quinn (20th Century-Fox)

This is a lusty story of English buccaneers who plunder women and the Spanish Main with equal facility. Some of the pirates reform, while the others meet their just desserts at sword's end or the gallows. Thus chief pirate Laird Cregar winds up as the honest governor of Jamaica; his chief aide (Tyrone Power) likewise turns pure, even winning the love of Maureen O'Hara; Thomas Mitchell also winds up a reformed pirate, while such brutes as George Sanders and Anthony Quinn, as a one-eyed scourge of the sea, become dead pirates.
1942: Best Color Cinematography

BLACK TENT, THE
1956, 93 mins, UK
D: Brian Desmond Hurst **A:** Anthony Steel, Donald Sinden, Anna Maria Sandri, Andre Morell, Ralph Truman, Donald Pleasence (Rank)

An entertaining adventure yarn during World War II colorfully limned in story's actual Libyan desert setting. David Holland (Anthony Steel), wounded in tank action, is taken in by the Bedouins. He falls in love with sheik's daughter, whom he weds after learning the British whom he hoped to rejoin have been beaten back. He decides to make his home with the tribe. Later the Britisher persuades the sheik to help him carry on guerrilla warfare behind the German lines.

BLACK WATCH, THE
1929, 91 mins, US
D: John Ford **A:** Victor McLaglen, Myrna Loy, David Rollins, Roy D'Arcy, Walter Long, Mitchell Lewis (Fox)

Tale is that of the Scottish Captain King (Victor McLaglen), who is ordered to India to prevent a native uprising. He gets into a drunken brawl, during which he supposedly kills a fellow serviceman, the ruse being an escape among the pack of fanatics planning to overthrow British rule. The natives worship a woman (Myrna Loy) as their goddess, who, in turn, succumbs to the brawn of King. Director John Ford's best work is the opening of a Scottish officers' dinner on the eve of war, with bagpipes wailing. Joseph August's camerawork is superb.

BLACK WIDOW
1987, 103 mins, US ⓥ ⊙
D: Bob Rafelson **A:** Debra Winger, Theresa Russell, Sami Frey, Dennis Hopper, Nicol Williamson, Diane Ladd (Mark/Americent/American Entertainment)

Theresa Russell makes an exceptionally handsome living by marrying wealthy men, murdering them, then collecting the settlements from the wills. Conscientious, disheveled Justice Department agent Debra Winger thinks she smells a rat and begs permission to pursue the case. The most intriguing aspect is the barely submerged sexual jealousy the overworked government employee feels for the sexy, utterly confident manipulator of sex and lives. Winger and Russell are both talented and watchable young actresses, so the picture has a lot going for it thanks to their casting alone.

BLACK WIDOW
1954, 95 mins, US ⊡
D: Nunnally Johnson **A:** Ginger Rogers, Van Heflin, Gene Tierney, George Raft, Peggy Ann Garner, Reginald Gardiner (20th Century-Fox)

Once the business of murder is gotten down to, *Black Widow* takes a firm and unrelenting grip on audience attention. Nanny, a young girl (Peggy Ann Garner), comes to Gotham with a yen to break into the big time and winds up the murder victim. Brought into the web are: Lottie (Ginger Rogers), a top-rung legit actress who finds evil delight in meddling into others' lives; Peter (Van Heflin), producer of Lot-

tie's current play, whose assistance to Nanny backfires into odious involvement in her murder; Gene Tierney, as Heflin's wife; and Bruce (George Raft), the detective on the prowl for a murderer.

BLACK WINDMILL, THE
1974, 106 mins, UK ⓥ ⊡
D: Don Siegel **A:** Michael Caine, Donald Pleasence, Delphine Seyrig, Clive Revill, John Vernon, Joss Ackland (Universal)

Don Siegel's filmmaking takes a dip in *The Black Windmill*, a British espionage drama with Michael Caine as an agent whose son has been kidnapped by one of his own spy colleagues. All principal players are well cast, but the production fizzles in its final half hour because the story premise gets clobbered by clumsy and ineffective resolution and execution.

BLACULA
1972, 92 mins, US ⓥ ⊙
D: William Crain **A:** William Marshall, Vonetta McGee, Denise Nicholas, Thalmus Rasulala, Gordon Pinsent, Charles McCauley (American International)

Count Dracula has a black counterpart. A pair of interior decorators have purchased all the furnishings of Castle Dracula and shipped them to America, including the locked coffin in which Blacula is resting. William Marshall portrays title role with a flourish.

BLADE
1998, 121 mins, US ⓥ ⊙ ⊡
D: Stephen Norrington **A:** Wesley Snipes, Stephen Dorff, Kris Kristofferson, N'Bushe Wright, Donal Logue, Udo Kier (Amen Ra/New Line)

The edge is off *Blade*, which toplines Wesley Snipes as a Marvel Comics-derived vampire slayer. Though slick and diverting in some aspects, increasingly silly pic has trouble meshing disparate elements—horror, superhero fantasy, straight-up action—into a workable whole. A young man lured into a vampire dance club is saved by the sudden appearance of Blade—Snipes in a sort of black leather RoboCop ensemble. Protag leaves behind a charred undead man. When this figure is delivered to the morgue, he provides an unpleasant surprise for hematologist Karen (N'Bushe Wright) and her ex-boyfriend co-worker (Tim Guinee). Wounded Karen is taken by Blade to the warehouse lair he shares with grizzled mortal Whistler (Kris Kristofferson), his loyal partner in creature killing. The ghoul

136

eatery-cum-discos are the brainchild of young Turk vampire Frost (Stephen Dorff), who wants to rock the boat and instigate a full-fledged "vampire apocalypse."

BLADE RUNNER
1982, 114 mins, US Ⓥ ⊙ ▭
D: Ridley Scott **A:** Harrison Ford, Rutger Hauer, Sean Young, Edward James Olmos, M. Emmet Walsh, Daryl Hannah (Warner/Ladd)

Ridley Scott's reported $30-million picture is a stylistically dazzling film noir set in November 2019 in a brilliantly imagined Los Angeles marked by both technological wonders and horrendous squalor. Replicants, robots designed to supply off-world slave labor, are outlawed on earth. But a few of them have infiltrated L.A., and retired enforcer Harrison Ford is recruited to eliminate them before they can do any damage. Dramatically, film is virtually taken over at the midway point by top replicant Rutger Hauer. The massive, albino-looking Hauer takes off after Ford, and the villain here is so intriguing and charismatic that one almost comes to prefer him to the more stolid hero.
1982: Nominations: Best Art Direction, Visual Effects

BLAIR WITCH PROJECT, THE
1999, 87 mins, US Ⓥ ⊙
D: Daniel Myrick, Eduardo Sanchez **A:** Heather Donahue, Michael Williams, Joshua Leonard, Bob Griffith, Jim King, Sandra Sanchez (Haxan)

An intensely imaginative piece of filmmaking that also delivers the goods as a dread-drenched horror movie, ultralowbudgeter *The Blair Witch Project* puts a clever modern twist on the fear of things that go bump in the night. An opening title informs that in October 1994, three young filmmakers hiked into the Black Hills Forest in Maryland to shoot a docu about the gruesome legend of the Blair witch and were never heard from again. But their footage was found, and constitutes the present feature. Visuals are handheld, jittery color video images taken by the bossy director and project organizer, Heather, or black-and-white 16mm shots lensed by the troupe's tyro cameraman, the hippie-ish Joshua; regular-guy Michael is along to record sound. Terror sets in on the second night when they seem to hear people circling their tent. Climax is intense and ambiguous, but the film builds up a sense of

horrific expectation that it can't quite match in its payoff.

BLAME IT ON RIO
1984, 110 mins, US Ⓥ ⊙
D: Stanley Donen **A:** Michael Caine, Joseph Bologna, Valerie Harper, Michelle Johnson, Jose Lewgoy, Demi Moore (Sherwood/20th Century-Fox)

Central premise of a secret romance between Michael Caine and the love-smitten daughter of his best friend (Joe Bologna) while the trio vacations together in torrid Rio may be adventurous comedy. Zany comedic conflict, however, is offputting, even at times nasty, in this essentially dead-ahead comedy that sacrifices charm and a light touch for too much realism. Newcomer Michelle Johnson comes off as callow and disagreeably spoiled. Director Stanley Donen gets sharp, comic performances from Caine and Bologna.

BLAME IT ON THE BELLBOY
1992, 77 mins, UK/US Ⓥ
D: Mark Herman **A:** Dudley Moore, Bryan Brown, Richard Griffiths, Andreas Katsulas, Patsy Kensit, Alison Steadman (Hollywood)

A lightweight ensemble comedy. Plot gets off to a promising start with three similarly named characters checking into a Venice hotel. Thanks to a bellboy who can't speak English, their mail gets mixed up. Realtor Dudley Moore gets a letter for hit man Bryan Brown, who gets a letter for blind-dater Richard Griffiths, who gets a letter for Moore. Problem is first-time director-scripter Mark Herman couldn't decide whether to make a breakneck farce or goofy comedy.

BLANK CHECK
1994, 93 mins, US Ⓥ ⊙
D: Rupert Wainwright **A:** Brian Bonsall, Karen Duffy, Miguel Ferrer, James Rebhorn, Tone Loc, Rick Ducommun (Walt Disney)

Blank Check is a low-yield Disney programmer with more than a wink and a nod in the direction of the *Home Alone* blockbusters. Eleven-year-old Preston Waters (Brian Bonsall) runs into fugitive criminal Quigley (Miguel Ferrer). Anxious not to arouse police interest, he gives the boy a half-completed check to pay for the damage to his bike, then drives off. Preston gleefully fills in the amount of the check $1 million, cashes it, and buys a palatial home in his neighborhood, then stocks it with high-tech games.

BLANKMAN
1994, 92 mins, US Ⓥ
D: Mike Binder A: Damon Wayans, David Alan Grier, Robin Givens, Christopher Lawford, Lynne Thigpen, Jon Polito (Columbia/Wife 'N' Kids)

Young viewers will rejoice at a comic-book fable that celebrates a self-appointed neighborhood crime fighter in the *Superman* mold. Adults, however, may find the film too goofy, too loud, and vastly uneven in humor and execution. Darryl Walker (Wayans) is an eccentric inventor who thinks he can make a difference in Metro City, IL. When crime reaches unbearable proportions, Darryl transforms himself into a mythic, vigilant hero, whom the puzzled media name Blankman. Mike Binder imbues *Blankman* with hyperactive slapstick, turning the film's assaultiveness into a comic style that is only intermittently effective or funny.

DER BLAUE ENGEL
1930, 109 mins, Germany Ⓥ ⊙
D: Josef von Sternberg A: Emil Jannings, Marlene Dietrich, Kurt Gerron, Rosa Valetti, Hans Albers, Eduard von Winterstein (UFA)

A middle-aged schoolteacher discovers that several of his pupils are hanging around the performer Lola. He falls for the singer himself. Despite the jeers of his pupils and the warnings of the principal of the school, he marries Lola. As a result, he loses his position. The teacher sinks from peddler of postcards showing his wife in seminudity to assistant in a magician's act. Dietrich as Lola has a slow-rhythmed sensuality which gets over without being in any way crude or offensive. The story is not one with strong dramatic impulse and seldom grips with suspense or moves you emotionally. It is the exceptional playing of Jannings and Dietrich, and the sensitive direction of Sternberg which put it across. [Review is of German version.]

BLAZE
1989, 108 mins, US Ⓥ ⊙
D: Ron Shelton A: Paul Newman, Lolita Davidovich, Jerry Hardin, Gailard Sartain, Jeffrey DeMunn (Touchstone/Silver Screen Partners IV)

A bawdy and audacious tale of politics and scandal, *Blaze* delivers a good love story and a brave and marvelous character turn by Paul Newman. Newman plays Louisiana governor Earl K. Long in 1959-60 during his May-December romance with famed New Orleans stripper Blaze Starr (Lolita Davidovich). Davidovich is impressive, taking the character from a clunky, overripe hillbilly teenager to a woman with her powers fully focused.
1989: Nomination: Best Cinematography

BLAZING SADDLES
1974, 93 mins, US Ⓥ ⊙ ▭
D: Mel Brooks A: Cleavon Little, Gene Wilder, Slim Pickens, David Huddleston, Mel Brooks, Madeline Kahn (Warner)

Blazing Saddles spoofs old-time westerns with an avalanche of one-liners, vaudeville routines, campy schticks, sight gags, satiric imitations, and comic anachronisms. Pic is handily stolen by Harvey Korman and Madeline Kahn is simply terrific doing a Marlene Dietrich lampoon. Little's black sheriff doesn't blend too well with Brooks's Jewish-flavored comic style. Wilder is amusingly low-key in a relatively small role.
1974: Nomination: Best Supp. Actress (Madeline Kahn), Editing, Song ("Blazing Saddles")

BLEAK MOMENTS
1972, 110 mins, UK
D: Mike Leigh A: Anne Raitt, Sarah Stephenson, Eric Allan, Joolia Cappleman, Mike Bradwell, Liz Smith (Autumn/Memorial)

A film with downbeat themes of solitude, difficulties of communication, coping with a retarded 29-year-old sister, it has enough human insight sans mawkishness or undue sentimentality to make it wryly funny, with its recognition of human foibles that gives it an edge, charm, and warmth, tempered with compassion.

DIE BLECHTROMMEL
(THE TIN DRUM)
1979, 150 mins, W. Germany/France Ⓥ
D: Volker Schlondorff A: Mario Adorf, Angela Winkler, David Bennent, Daniel Olbrychski, Katharina Thalbach, Heinz Bennent (Argos Films/Artemis/Bioskep)

This adaptation of Gunter Grass's world-renowned novel, *The Tin Drum,* is the tale of a Tiny Tim who is a Jack the Giant Killer at the same time. Even before his birth, Oskar Matzerath in his mother's womb realizes he has special gifts. One is breaking glass with his voice; another is the decision at three years of age not to grow another centimeter. Because of his stunted growth, he can crawl under tables and skirts to watch, with sardonic eye, the lies and hypocrisies about him. This is a

chronicle on the history of Germany from the beginning of this century up to 1959. Most of all, it's about that social and political phenomenon known as Nazism. As Oskar, David Bennent has the eyes and the acting talent to carry some scenes remarkably well, but he is not the insatiable wallower in sex and religious mysticism that Grass makes possible.
1979: Best Foreign Language Film

BLIND ALLEY
1939, 68 mins, US
D: Charles Vidor **A:** Chester Morris, Ralph Bellamy, Ann Dvorak, Joan Perry, Melville Cooper, Rose Stradner (Columbia)

In attempting to delve into the psychopathic reasons why a criminal carries a killer complex, *Blind Alley* holds moderate interest. Morris is aided in prison break by group of former associates, and gang winds up in weekend home of Bellamy to make prisoners of the family and guests. Setup allows mental conflict between the criminal and psychologist to generate through dramatic phases while Bellamy proceeds to uncover the subconscious basis for Morris's killing mania.

BLIND DATE
1987, 93 mins, US Ⓥ ⊙ ⊠
D: Blake Edwards **A:** Kim Basinger, Bruce Willis, John Larroquette, William Daniels, Phil Hartman, Stepanie Faracy (Tri-Star)

Bruce Willis abandons his mugging TV personality in favor of playing an animated, amiable, hardworking, ambitious financial analyst in L.A. Stuck without a date for a company function, he reluctantly agrees to ask his brother's wife's cousin (Kim Basinger) to accompany him. He's not supposed to let her drink and ignores the advice. Two sips of champagne later, she's out of control. Theme of pure mayhem works well because of chemistry between the main trio of actors, Willis, Basinger, and her spurned ex-beau (John Larroquette).

BLINDFOLD
1966, 102 mins, US ⊠
D: Philip Dunne **A:** Rock Hudson, Claudia Cardinale, Jack Warden, Guy Stockwell, Brad Dexter, Alejandro Rey (Universal/7 Pictures)

Hudson plays part of a famed NY psychologist treating a mentally disturbed scientist sought by an international ring, who becomes involved in a plot to kidnap scientist from a top-secret hideout. Film takes its title from his being blindfolded whenever he is to visit his patient. Hudson offers one of his customary light portrayals, sometimes on the cloyingly coy side, and is in for more physical action than usual. Claudia Cardinale, as the chorus-girl sister of the scientist, displays plenty of appeal.

BLIND FURY
1989, 85 mins, US Ⓥ ⊙
D: Phillip Noyce **A:** Rutger Hauer, Brandon Call, Terry O'Quinn, Lisa Blount, Meg Foster, Sho Kosugi (Tri-Star/Interscope)

Blind Fury is an action film with an amusing gimmick, toplining Rutger Hauer, as an apparently invincible blind Vietnam vet who wields a samurai sword with consummate skill. Nick Parker (Hauer) is in Miami to look up an old army buddy (Terry O'Quinn) who's in trouble with the mob in Reno. Parker's in time to prevent the kidnapping of Billy (Brandon Call), Frank's son. The rest of the film is simply a series of fights and chases as Parker heads for Reno to reunite Billy with his father.

BLIND TERROR
See: See No Evil

BLINK
1994, 106 mins, US Ⓥ ⊙ ⊠
D: Michael Apted **A:** Madeleine Stowe, Aidan Quinn, Laurie Metcalf, James Remar, Peter Friedman, Bruce A. Young (New Line)

Emma Brody (Madeleine Stowe) has recently regained her eyesight. But the coordination between what her brain registers and what she actually sees isn't quite aligned. One evening upon hearing noise in her apartment building, she goes to investigate. All she can discern is a form until the next morning, when she hallucinates a man's face. As her upstairs neighbor was murdered the night before, it doesn't take a genius to figure out what the killer might look like. Stowe simply is not good in the role of a somewhat dumb woman in jeopardy. Quinn is just barely capable of keeping a straight face confronted with his cop steeped in cliche.

BLISS
1985, 135 mins, Australia Ⓥ ⊙
D: Ray Lawrence **A:** Barry Otto, Lynette Curran, Helen Jones, Miles Buchanan, Gia Carides, Tim Robertson (Window III/ NSW Film Corp.)

Harry Joy (Barry Otto) runs an ad

agency and leads an apparently happy life. A heart attack fells him during a family gathering, and he's dead for four minutes. When he recovers, he believes he has entered hell. That's because everything seems to have changed. His loving wife (Lynette Curran) is having an open affair with his sleazy business partner (Jeff Truman); his son (Miles Buchanan) is a drug runner; his daughter (Gia Carides) is an addict who gives her brother sexual favors to get free dope; and Harry discovers, too, that his biggest client manufactures products known to cause cancer. The biggest flaw in *Bliss* is the way the novel has been adapted by its author, Peter Carey, and director Ray Lawrence. Carey and Lawrence have left nothing out; the film teems with characters.

BLISS OF MRS. BLOSSOM, THE
1968, 93 mins, UK
D: Joseph MacGrath A: Shirley MacLaine, Richard Attenborough, James Booth, Freddie Jones, William Rushton, Bob Monkhouse (Paramount)

The Bliss of Mrs. Blossom is a silly, campy, and sophisticated marital comedy, always amusing and often hilarious in impact. Shirley MacLaine stars as a wife with two husbands—Richard Attenborough, the legal and nighttime spouse, and James Booth, who lives in the attic. Script covers the laugh spectrum from throwaway verbal and sight gags through broad comedy to satirical pokes at old-fashioned film romances.

BLITHE SPIRIT
1945, 96 mins, UK Ⓥ
D: David Lean A: Rex Harrison, Constance Cummings, Kay Hammond, Margaret Rutherford, Hugh Wakefield, Joyce Carey (Two Cities/Cineguild)

Inasmuch as this is largely a photographed copy of the stage play [by Noel Coward], the camerawork is outstandingly good and helps to put across the credibility of the ghost story more effectively than the flesh-and-blood performance does. Acting honors go to Margaret Rutherford as Madame Arcati, a trance medium who makes you believe she's on the level. Kay Hammond, as dead Wife No. 1, a spoiled darling with murder in her heart for Wife No. 2, is as much a smiling menace as she is wistfully wraithlike. As the very-much-alive Wife No. 2, Constance Cummings more than holds her own. As a ghost, Cummings is not at all convincing. As Charles Condomine, twice married novel-

ist, Rex Harrison is so flawless as to merit some critics' charge of underacting.
1946: Best Special Effects

BLOB, THE
1958, 85 mins, US Ⓥ ☉
D: Irvin S. Yeaworth Jr. A: Steve McQueen, Aneta Corseaut, Earl Rowe, Olin Howlin (Paramount/Tonylyn)

A small Pennsylvania town has been plagued by teenage pranks. Hence, when high-schoolers Steve McQueen and Aneta Corseaut report that a parasitic substance from outer space has eaten the local doctor and his nurse, no one will believe them. Especially when no bodies can be found. McQueen, who's handed star billing, makes with the old college try, while Corseaut also struggles valiantly as his girlfriend. Star performers, however, are the camerawork of Thomas Spalding and Barton Sloane's special effects. Intriguing is the title number, written by Burt Bacharach and Mack David.

BLOB, THE
1988, 92 mins, US Ⓥ ☉
D: Chuck Russell A: Kevin Dillon, Shawnee Smith, Donovan Leitch, Jeffrey DeMunn, Candy Clark, Joe Seneca (Tri-Star)

A great B-movie with an A-pic budget, the Blob is back with a vengeance. Updated with awesome, no-expense-spared special effects and a feisty female hero, horrific outing should prove thoroughly satisfying for fans of the genre. Starting life as an aggressive glueball that creeps out of a fallen meteor and attacks a vagrant in the woods, the malevolent plasma grows to raging, ferocious proportions. Director Chuck Russell builds suspense slowly and carefully, devoting 30 minutes to establishing apple-pie normalcy before the first grisly strike.

BLOCKADE
1938, 73 mins, US
D: William Dieterle A: Madeleine Carroll, Henry Fonda, Leo Carrillo, John Halliday, Vladimir Sokoloff, Reginald Denny (Paramount)

Blockade is a film with a purpose—a plea against war. But it misses any claim to greatness because it pulls its punches. Modern Spain in the death grip of civil war is the background of the screenplay, an original by John Howard Lawson. He disguises the warring factions and attempts the impossible task of impersonalizing war and its helpless, starving civilian victims.

The Hays Office advised radical alterations in the original script to avoid offense to foreign powers. This is a story of romance and espionage. Madeleine Carroll is the daughter of an international agent. Henry Fonda is a farmer youth, now a soldier fighting for his land, and soon discovers that Carroll, despite all her blond beauty, is his country's enemy.

BLONDE CRAZY
1931, 78 mins, US Ⓥ ⊙
D: Roy Del Ruth **A:** James Cagney, Joan Blondell, Louis Calhern, Noel Francis, Guy Kibbee, Ray Milland (Warner)

Wise remarks, a fresh guy, and dame stuff. Quick pace and a performance by James Cagney typically Cagney. These give *Blonde Crazy* a fast start and keep it going most of the way. Strictly a petty-larceny guy is Cagney. Original yarn gives plenty of room for his customary fresh-punk characterization. Joan Blondell is Cagney's business partner. Cagney and Blondell make a natural pair. Louis Calhern uses his long experience to good effect in a class cheater part.

BLONDE FIST
1991, 100 mins, UK Ⓥ
D: Frank Clarke **A:** Margi Clarke, Carroll Baker, Ken Hutchison, Sharon Power, Angela Clarke, Lewis Bester (Blue Dolphin)

Margi Clarke packs a mean punch in *Blonde Fist* as a scrappy Liverpudlian and devoted mother who eventually wins in the boxing ring and at home. In a gritty *Thelma & Louise* meets *Rocky*, Clarke is a knockout and pic is punchy, but the complex story drags. Fight scenes are dynamically choreographed, beautifully shot, and provide pic's most engaging footage.

BLONDE IN LOVE, A
See: Jasky Jedne Plavovlasky

BLONDE SINNER
See: Yield to the Night

BLONDE VENUS
1932, 93 mins, US Ⓥ
D: Josef von Sternberg **A:** Marlene Dietrich, Herbert Marshall, Cary Grant, Dickie Moore, Gene Morgan, Robert Emmett O'Connor (Paramount)

A disappointer. Much of the blame is to be laid at director Josef von Sternberg's doorstep. In a desire to glamorously built up Marlene Dietrich he sloughs almost every other element that goes to round out a box-office production. He devotes two reels to her flight from her husband and all the drab details that went with it. Then

she's suddenly again the queen of the nightclubs, this time in Paris. Dietrich sings two numbers in that deep, throaty manner of hers. The 93 minutes are much too much considering the triteness of the basic story, a theme of mother love of the café songstress, whose child (well played by Dickie Moore, in perhaps the only convincing casting) is the sympathetic basis of it all.

BLONDIE OF THE FOLLIES
1932, 91 mins, US
D: Edmund Goulding **A:** Marion Davies, Robert Montgomery, Billie Dove, Jimmy Durante, James Gleason, ZaSu Pitts (M-G-M)

Jimmy Durante is rushed into a house-party scene for his first and only appearance after the picture has gone 70 minutes. His Barrymore-Garbo takeoff with Marion Davies easily becomes the bright spot on the picture. The story is simply the rise of two New York girls of the poor class to *Follies* girl status, their temporary enjoyment of the luxurious fancy living, and then their return to normalcy. Chief situation is love rivalry between the two girl pals, with Blondie (Davies) finally winning out. As usual, Davies is best in her few comedy chances, but on the whole this try is under par for her.

BLOOD AND SAND
1922, 110 mins, US Ⓥ ⊙ ▭
D: Fred Niblo **A:** Rudolph Valentino, Lila Lee, Nita Naldi, George Field, Walter Long, Rose Rosanova (Paramount)

Rudolph Valentino's switch to a St. Anthony type comes as a shock. The essential moral conflict of the bullfighter never gets to the surface. He is just a bewildered simpleton, which makes his gaudy clothes ridiculous. The story starts with the theme of a humble shoemaker raised to eminence as a national hero of the bullring and an idol of the people. Soon the problem is changed to "What will be the fate of a man who lives by blood and cruelty?" Then the conflict appears to be an attack on the institution of the bullfight.

BLOOD AND SAND
1941, 123 mins, US Ⓥ
D: Rouben Mamoulian **A:** Tyrone Power, Linda Darnell, Rita Hayworth, Nazimova, Anthony Quinn, John Carradine (20th Century-Fox)

Blood and Sand follows the original

[novel by Vicente Blasco Ibanez] as a straight drama of the bullfight ring. Tyrone Power is a peon kid in Seville, decidedly illiterate, and with a passion for bullfighting. As a minor-league matador, he marries Darnell and goes on to become the most famous and widely acclaimed matador of the time. Power is continually in debt, but happy with his wife until fascinated by sexy Rita Hayworth, socialite flame. Power delivers a persuasive performance. Hayworth is excellent as the vamp. Nazimova gives a corking performance as Power's mother.
1941: Best Color Cinematography
Nomination: Best Color Art Direction

BLOOD AND SAND
1989, 117 mins, Spain ⓥ
D: Javier Elorrieta **A:** Christopher Rydell, Sharon Stone, Ana Torrent, Guillermo Montesinos, Albert Vidal, Simon Andreu (Frade)

Producer Jose Frade has claimed his *Blood and Sand* is the first truly Spanish film version of Vicente Blasco Ibanez's famous novel. His picture is about as Spanish as Coke spiked with Fundador brandy. The bullfighting shown is cleansed of all blood except that shed by a couple of humans. What is left to tell of Blasco Ibanez's novel is told with plodding care and brief sex scenes between Christopher Rydell and Sharon Stone. Stone appears to be not much more than a pudgy-faced teenager with a body that one might say strips well.

BLOODBROTHERS
1978, 116 mins, US ⓥ
D: Robert Mulligan **A:** Paul Sorvino, Tony Lo Bianco, Richard Gere, Lelia Goldoni, Yvonne Wilder, Kenneth McMillan (Warner)

Bloodbrothers is an ambitious, if uneven probe into the disintegration of an Italian-American family, concerned primarily with the plight of Gere, who is trying to make one of those crucial life decisions about whether he wants to join the men on the construction girders or opt for the job that gives him real pleasure, working with small children. This pedestrian tale is placed against a background of vibrant machoism, with numerous scenes of boozing, whoring, and fighting set in the Bronx.
1978: Nomination: Best Adapted Screenplay

BLOODFIST III
FORCED TO FIGHT
1992, 88 mins, US ⓥ
D: Oley Sassone **A:** Don Wilson, Richard Roundtree, Gregory McKinney, Rick Dean, Richard Paul, John Cardone (Concorde)

This prison story is the best screen vehicle to date for kick-boxing champ Don Wilson. He's a wrongly convicted guy in the state pen who continually has to prove himself against bigger and feistier convicts. Racism is the key theme, as white and black cons are continually fighting with half-breed (half-Japanese) Wilson caught in the middle.

BLOOD FOR DRACULA
1974, 90 mins, France/Italy ⓥ ▱
D: Paul Morrissey **A:** Joe Dallesandro, Udo Kier, Vittorio De Sica, Maxime McKendry, Arno Juerging, Milena Vukotic (CC-Champion & 1/CFDC)

Paul Morrisey takes a turn at the old bloodsucker, made in Italy in English with a mixture of nationalities acting in it. Udo Kier is a youngish Dracula, in the 1930s. It seems he will die unless he gets virgin blood. So he has to leave his Transylvanian lair to go to Italy for that, since a Catholic country should have some.

BLOOD FROM THE MUMMY'S
TOMB
1971, 94 mins, UK
D: Seth Holt [Michael Carreras] **A:** Andrew Keir, Valerie Leon, James Villiers, Hugh Burden, George Coulouris, Mark Edwards (Hammer)

This polished and well-acted but rather tame Hammer horror entry revolves around an exploration group who discovered an ancient Egyptian tomb and brought relics, including the Princess Tera's mummy, home to England. The sacrilege is savagely avenged by Tera being reincarnated in the leader's beautiful daughter. Valerie Leon has the dual role of the princess and the modern miss who brings a reign of terror to a quiet London suburb.

BLOODHOUNDS OF BROADWAY
1989, 101 mins, US ⓥ ◉
D: Howard Brookner **A:** Julie Hagerty, Randy Quaid, Madonna, Jennifer Grey, Rutger Hauer, Matt Dillon (American Playhouse)

Strong character acting by an all-star cast enlivens this fluffy little piece about romance and gangsters during Prohibition

There's Harriet Mackyle (Julie Hagerty), who delivers a fine performance as a rich society babe. Randy Quaid does a satisfying job as an honorable dimwit who's madly in love with a beautiful, diamond-hungry showgirl, very adeptly played by Madonna. Matt Dillon gives a rather tepid performance as Broadway's lousiest horse player, especially in comparison with Jennifer Grey, who does a good job as an angel-faced showgirl.

BLOOD IN BLOOD OUT
1993, 174 mins, US ⓥ
D: Taylor Hackford **A:** Damian Chapa, Jesse Borrego, Benjamin Bratt, Enrique Castillo, Victor Rivers, Delroy Lindo (Hollywood Pictures)

Producer-director Taylor Hackford clearly wants this to be a major cinematic exploration of the Latino experience, from its ponderous near-three-hour length to its more-than-occasional sermonizing. Unfortunately, disjointed storytelling and uneven performances undermine those aspirations. The plot centers on three youths and follows them into their early thirties: Paco (Benjamin Bratt), a hot-tempered boxer; Cruz (Jesse Borrego), a gifted painter seemingly destined to escape the barrio; and Miklo (Damian Chapa), their half-white cousin.

BLOODLINE
1979, 116 mins, US ⓥ
D: Terence Young **A:** Audrey Hepburn, Ben Gazzara, James Mason, Irene Papas, Romy Schneider, Omar Sharif (Paramount/Geria)

Even for the never-never land of high chic melodrama the film inhabits, the tale of a woman who, unprepared, inherits control of her father's vast pharmaceutical empire contains wild implausibilities. Performers range unevenly in tone from the comic (Omar Sharif, Irene Papas, Gert Frobe) to the merely drab (James Mason, Michelle Phillips, Maurice Ronet).

BLOOD MONEY
See: Requiem for a Heavyweight

BLOOD MONEY
(US: CLINTON AND NADINE)
1988, 90 mins, UK/US ⓥ ⊙
D: Jerry Schatzberg **A:** Andy Garcia, Ellen Barkin, Morgan Freeman, Michael Lombard, John C. McGinley, Brad Sullivan (ITC)

A murder-mystery tale linked to illicit Contra fund-raising. Andy Garcia is Clinton, a parrot smuggler who stumbles onto

his brother's slaying. Nadine Powers (Ellen Barkin), a hooker on the run, is drawn reluctantly into Clinton's attempt to track down those responsible for the murders. By the time the pair become lovers, one hardly cares and problem is compounded when the story becomes bewildering as everyone is transposed suddenly to Costa Rica for the denouement.

BLOOD OATH
1990, 105 mins, Australia ⓥ ⊙
D: Stephen Wallace **A:** Bryan Brown, George Takei, Terry O'Quinn, Toshi Shioya, John Bach, Deborah Unger (Village Roadshow/Blood Oath)

Blood Oath raises questions about wartime crime and punishment. The drama, based on actual incidents, takes place on the Indonesian island of Ambon in late 1945. Ambon, site of a Japanese POW camp for Australian prisoners, was under the command of aristocratic, Oxford-educated Vice-Admiral Baron Takahashi (George Takei). Bryan Brown plays Captain Cooper, Aussie officer assigned to prosecute Takashahi and his men for war crimes. An American observer at the trial, Major Beckett (Terry O'Quinn), doesn't want Takahashi found guilty, figuring he'll be more useful in reconstructed postwar Japan.

BLOOD OF A POET
See: Le Sang d'un Poet

BLOOD OF HEROES, THE
See: The Salute of the Jugger

BLOOD ON MY HANDS
See: Kiss the Blood off My Hands

BLOOD ON THE MOON
1948, 86 mins, US ⓥ
D: Robert Wise **A:** Robert Mitchum, Barbara Bel Geddes, Robert Preston, Walter Brennan, Phyllis Thaxter (RKO)

Blood on the Moon is a terse, tightly drawn western drama. There's none of the formula approach to its storytelling. A Texas cowpoke rides into a section of range country where ranchers and settlers are battling. Broke, he hires out his gun to an old friend, who is scheming to acquire a cattle herd by promoting the feud. Robert Mitchum is the cowpoke. Barbara Bel Geddes registers strongly as the range heroine. Robert Preston plays an oily villain.

BLOOD ON THE SUN
1945, 98 mins, US ⓥ ⊙
D: Frank Lloyd **A:** James Cagney, Sylvia Sidney, Porter Hall, Robert Armstrong,

John Emery, Rosemary DeCamp (United Artists/Cagney)

Cagney portrays an American editor of a Tokyo newspaper who dares to print the story of the world-conquest plan formulated by Jap militarists. Quickly, Cagney finds himself in the midst of a dual murder committed by the Japs upon a US newspaper pal and his wife, who were leaving Japan to bring to America the document describing the world-conquest plot in detail. Cagney is the same rough-and-tumble character he's always been, ready to tell the Jap big shots off at the drop of a hat. There are a couple of overdramatic sequences, but they just add to the tension. **1945:** Best B&W Interior Decoration (Wiard B. Ihnen)

BLOOD RED
1989, 91 mins, US Ⓥ
D: Peter Masterson **A:** Eric Roberts, Giancarlo Giannini, Dennis Hopper, Burt Young, Carlin Glynn, Julia Roberts (Kettledrum)

Blood Red, a saga of oppressed Sicilian winegrowers in 19th-century California, is an unsuccessful throwback to earlier forms of filmmaking. Project was filmed in 1986, the first-time screen teaming of siblings Eric and Julia Roberts. A robust Giannini is patriarch of one of two families in Brandon, CA, and soon is warring with robber baron–railroad magnate Dennis Hopper. Roberts's scenes with real-life sister Julia, cast as his sister, are intriguing because of the visual match. She doesn't get much chance to emote, but that nascent star quality is already evident.

BLOOD RELATIVES
1978, 100 mins, France/Canada Ⓥ
D: Claude Chabrol **A:** Donald Sutherland, Stephane Audran, Micheline Lanctot, Aude Landry, Donald Pleasence, David Hemmings (Classic/Cinevideo/Filmel)

Made in Canada and based on a Yank police-precinct novel of Ed McBain, film settles down as an inspector, played with a low profile and humanity by Donald Sutherland, probes a knife killing of a teenage girl and the wounding of another girl. At first it is felt to be the work of a psychotic but then segues into a middle-class family that might have been the crucible for the gory carryings-on. French director Claude Chabrol has often used murder as a catalyst in his grim pix about upper-class French life. But here it is more psychosis, repression, and jealousy than the more absorbing social patterns of his French work.

BLOOD SIMPLE
1984, 97 mins, US Ⓥ Ⓞ
D: Joel Coen **A:** John Getz, Frances McDormand, Dan Hedaya, Samm-Art Williams, M. Emmet Walsh (River Road)

An inordinately good low-budget film noir thriller. Dan Hedaya hires a sleazy miscreant named Visser (played with appropriate malice by M. Emmet Walsh) to kill his wayward wife and her boyfriend Ray (John Getz). Walsh takes a snapshot of the lovers asleep in bed, doctors the photo to make it appear he's fulfilled the contract, and meets Hedaya to collect. Upon payment, Walsh shoots Hedaya dead in the chest. But the victim has swapped the photo and put it in the office safe before his demise, making Walsh' perfect crime not so. Final confrontation between Walsh and the lovers is outright horrific.

BLOODY MAMA
1970, 90 mins, US Ⓥ Ⓞ
D: Roger Corman **A:** Shelley Winters, Pat Hingle, Don Stroud, Diane Varsi, Bruce Dern, Robert De Niro (American International)

The story of Kate (Ma) Barker, who with her four killer sons terrorized mountain country in the Depression era, *Bloody Mama* is a pseudobiopic starring Shelley Winters in one of those all-over-the-screen performances which sometimes are labeled as bravura acting. Cast as Ma's brood are Don Stroud as the psychotic, Robert Walden as the masochistic homosexual, Robert De Niro as the drug addict, and Clint Kimbrough as the quiet boy. The best performance is that of Pat Hingle playing a wealthy businessman kidnapped for high ransom.

BLOSSOMS IN THE DUST
1941, 98 mins, US Ⓥ
D: Mervyn LeRoy **A:** Greer Garson, Walter Pidgeon, Felix Bressart, Marsha Hunt (M-G-M)

A worthy production on which much care has been showered by Mervyn LeRoy and others, but the picture fails to impress as being big. Pidgeon is the Texan who marries Edna Gladney of Wisconsin and worships her. The baby born to them dies and subsequently Pidgeon passes away suddenly after they have done some charity work for poor kids and foundlings. From there on Garson takes up the place

144

ment of unfortunate children as a lifetime work. Garson's character spans many years but does not appreciably age.
1941: Best Color Interior Decoration
Nominations: Best Picture, Actress (Greer Garson), Color Cinematography

BLOWN AWAY

1994, 121 mins, US 𝒱 ⊙ ▭

D: Stephen Hopkins **A:** Jeff Bridges, Tommy Lee Jones, Lloyd Bridges, Forest Whitaker, Suzy Amis, Caitlin Clarke (Trilogy/M-G-M)

The pyrotechnics are the stars of *Blown Away*, an overly complex, muddled thriller of politics and revenge. In need of some dynamite to dislodge an often unfathomable story, the film is just too cool and cynical. The adversaries are Jimmy Dove (Jeff Bridges), a veteran of Boston's bomb squad, and Ryan Gaerity (Tommy Lee Jones), a mad, Irish explosives expert recently escaped from Northern Ireland. In the absence of character development or depth, Bridges and Jones are reduced to a kind of posturing that borders on the embarrassing.

BLOW OUT

1981, 108 mins, US 𝒱 ⊙ ▭

D: Brian De Palma **A:** John Travolta, Nancy Allen, John Lithgow, Dennis Franz, Peter Boyden, John Aquino (Cinema 77/Geria/Filmways)

Travolta appears as a soundman working on low-budget horror films. Film turns serious with Travolta caught up in a murder and cover-up scheme when the tire of a politician's car is blown out by a rifle shot at a bridge where he is recording sounds. Saving a young woman (Nancy Allen) from drowning in the car, Travolta's fate becomes entwined with hers as he uses his professional expertise to unravel the murder mystery. With attractive leads and a stylish flair for suspense, De Palma misses sustaining involvement by his distracting allusions to prior films (ranging broadly from *Blowup* to *Touch of Evil*).

BLOW-UP

1966, 110 mins, UK 𝒱 ⊙

D: Michelangelo Antonioni **A:** Vanessa Redgrave, Sarah Miles, David Hemmings, John Castle, Jane Birkin, Gillian Hills (Bridge/M-G-M)

There may be some meaning, some commentary about life being a game, beyond what remains locked in the mind of film's creator, Michelangelo Antonioni.

But it is doubtful that the general public will get the message of this film. As a commentary on a sordid, confused side of humanity in this modern age, it's a bust. Filmed in England and Antonioni's first English-speaking production, interesting use is made of London backgrounds. Footage centers on a topflight London fashion photographer who learns of a murder through his secret lensing of a couple he sees embracing in a park. David Hemmings makes an interesting impression as the bulber, and Vanessa Redgrave, as the woman involved in the park, projects another vivid impression.
1967: Nominations: Best Director, Original Story & Screenplay

BLUE

1968, 113 mins, US ▭

D: Silvio Narizzano **A:** Terence Stamp, Joanna Pettet, Karl Malden, Ricardo Montalban, Anthony Costello, Joe De Santis (Paramount/Kettledrum)

Poor writing, dull performances, and pretentious direction waste the rugged physical beauty of the location area. Terence Stamp stars in a title role which can't amount to more than 200 words, many of them dubbed, the rest in his British accent. Basic trouble with *Blue* is that there seems to have been an attempt to make a great or definitive film. Setting is the uneasy border between Mexico and Texas, across which bandits come for looting raids.

BLUE

1993, 76 mins, UK 𝒱

D: Derek Jarman (Basilisk/Uplink/Channel 4)

This conceptual essay/meditation/memoir on the director's deteriorating condition with AIDS consists of a dense soundtrack accompanied visually by 76 minutes of a blue screen. Joined occasionally on the track by three close collaborators and backed by Simon Fisher Turner's rich score and Marvin Black's complex sound design, Jarman ponders numerous subjects and aspects of his disease. *Blue* has moments of power, but its many digressions prompt the mind to wander.

BLUE ANGEL, THE

1930, 99 mins, Germany 𝒱 ⊙

D: Josef von Sternberg **A:** Emil Jannings, Marlene Dietrich, Kurt Gerron, Rosa Valetti, Hans Albers, Karl Huszar-Puffy (UFA)

Splendid English version of a German

original [released earlier the same year]. The story is heavy, tends to drag, and holds up more on the strength of the two principals than anything else. Dietrich, as a cabaret girl of liberal morals with those continental soubrette costumes of much stocking, bare limb, and garters, is an eyeful. She seems a bit timid as regards the dialogue. This is not so when she sings. One tune carries a plaintive melody which has a tendency to linger, and Dietrich sings it better in English than in German. Emil Jannings gives a fine characterization of the circumspect schoolteacher who falls completely for the cabaret singer.

BLUE ANGEL, THE ⌑
1959, 107 mins, US ⌑
D: Edward Dmytryk **A:** Curt Jurgens, May Britt, Theodore Bikel, John Banner, Fabrizio Mioni (20th Century-Fox)

This remake is not the rocker that the Jannings-Dietrich impact made but neither Germany's Curt Jurgens nor Sweden's May Britt need be ashamed of their performances. Perhaps counting the most against them is the somewhat familiar plot motivation—the femme fatale and the destruction of the German professor who succumbs to her wiles. But the prime shortcoming is the decision to give this saga a postmidcentury topicality in 1950s West Germany.

BLUE ANGEL, THE
See: *Der Blaue Engel*

BLUEBEARD
1972, 123 mins, US ⊘
D: Edward Dmytryk **A:** Richard Burton, Raquel Welch, Joey Heatherton, Virna Lisi, Nathalie Delon, Sybil Danning (Vulcano)

Bluebeard is high camp. Richard Burton portrays title role in a modernized version of the legendary character who had a way with women—doing them in—and in dignified tread saunters through a whole phantasmagoria of murders and a veritable shower of bare bosoms to a finale that shows why he was that way, poor guy.

BLUEBEARD'S EIGHTH WIFE
1938, 83 mins, US
D: Ernst Lubitsch **A:** Claudette Colbert, Gary Cooper, Edward Everett Horton, David Niven, Elizabeth Patterson, Herman Bing (Paramount)

It's a light and sometimes bright entertainment, but gets a bit tiresome, despite its comparatively moderate running time.

Once the premise is established that Claudette Colbert wants to deflate the multimillionaire Gary Cooper, who buys his wives—seven of 'em prior to her—as he buys a fancy motorcar, making premarriage settlements with them, etc., it then becomes an always obvious farce. Atmosphere is rich and French. The Brackett-Wilder scripting is ofttimes bright but illogical and fragile.

BLUEBERRY HILL
1988, 87 mins, US ⊘
D: Strathford Hamilton **A:** Carrie Snodgress, Margaret Avery, Jennifer Rubin, Matt Lattanzi, Tommy Swerdlow (Mediacom/Prism)

Blueberry Hill is yet another small American film trying to cash in on a nostalgia craze. Pic is set in a California town in 1956. Carrie Snodgress is a woman whose husband drowned in a local creek the night their daughter Ellie was born. She has never quite recovered from his death. Local piano teacher Hattie (Margaret Avery) remembers him as a womanizing piano player. When Ellie (Jennifer Rubin)—now 16—wants to know what he was like, her piano teacher takes her to the club where he played. Best feature is the music. Avery sings fifties jazz numbers and the soundtrack features some hit songs of the era, including the title tune.

BLUE BIRD, THE
1976, 100 mins, US/USSR ⊘
D: George Cukor **A:** Elizabeth Taylor, Jane Fonda, Ava Gardner, Cicely Tyson, Robert Morley, Harry Andrews (20th Century-Fox)

Third film version of the Maurice Maeterlinck novel takes spoiled peasant children on a dream trip through a fantasy world in search of the bluebird of happiness. Elizabeth Taylor's four roles include the dominant (and dazzling) one as Light. Jane Fonda does Night, the princess of darkness, with a flair, while Ava Gardner is extremely effective as Luxury. Nobody's going to laugh in ridicule at any of it but nobody's going to be strongly moved.

BLUE CHIPS
1994, 108 mins, US ⊘ ⊙
D: William Friedkin **A:** Nick Nolte, Mary McDonnell, J. T. Walsh, Ed O'Neill, Alfre Woodard, Louis Gossett Jr. (Paramount)

The venerable all-American pastimes of greed, cheating, and winning at all costs take it on the chin in *Blue Chips*, a deafness-inducing but otherwise ho-hum would-be exposé of shady recruiting practices by college basketball programs. The combination of Nick Nolte's ranting, agitated performance as a beleaguered coach, director William Friedkin's compulsive style, and the frantic pace of the basketball action itself provides an overdose of stimulation that is more numbing than exciting.

BLUE COLLAR
1978, 110 mins, US Ⓥ ⊙
D: Paul Schrader **A:** Richard Pryor, Harvey Keitel, Yaphet Kotto, Ed Begley Jr., Harry Bellaver, George Memmoli (TAT)

A powerful, gritty, seamless profile of three automobile assembly-line workers banging their heads against the monotony and corruption that is the factory system. The film's three stars—Richard Pryor, Harvey Keitel, and Yaphet Kotto—all turn in outstanding and disciplined performances. Plot centers around the three workers' attempts to confront and battle the reality of this system. The three devise a plan to rob the union, which in the end turns into another helpless action.

BLUE DAHLIA, THE
1946, 96 mins, US
D: George Marshall **A:** Alan Ladd, Veronica Lake, William Bendix, Howard da Silva, Doris Dowling, Tom Powers (Paramount)

Playing a discharged naval flier returning home first to find his wife unfaithful, then to find her murdered and himself in hiding as the suspect, Alan Ladd does a bang-up job. Performance has a warm appeal, while in his relentless trackdown of the real criminal, Ladd has a cold, steellike quality that is potent. Ladd's path crosses Veronica Lake's, latter being separated wife of a nightclub owner who is one of the killer suspects. Scenes between Ladd and Lake are surprisingly sensitive, with an economy of dialogue and emotion doubly appealing.
1946: Nomination: Best Original Screenplay

BLUE DENIM
(UK: BLUE JEANS)
1959, 89 mins, US ▭
D: Philip Dunne **A:** Carol Lynley, Brandon de Wilde, Macdonald Carey, Marsha Hunt, Warren Berlinger, Vaughn Taylor (20th Century-Fox)

Blue Denim recounts, often movingly and intelligently, the torments of a pair of high-school lovers who are about to become unwed parents. The desperation of these babes in the basement—a 15-year-old girl and a 16-year-old boy—is further highlighted by their inability to communicate with their parents. The screenplay has been considerably watered down. The word "abortion" is never mentioned, although it is obvious what is taking place. Moreover, the ending deteriorates to cliché melodrama.

BLUE GARDENIA, THE
1953, 90 mins, US
D: Fritz Lang **A:** Anne Baxter, Richard Conte, Ann Sothern, Raymond Burr, Jeff Donnell, Nat King Cole (Warner)

A stock story and handling keep *The Blue Gardenia* from being anything more than a regulation mystery melodrama. Formula development has an occasional bright spot, mostly because Ann Sothern breathes some life into a stock character and quips. Anne Baxter is a telephone operator who believes she committed murder when she was drinking away the tears of a broken romance. Richard Conte, all-powerful newspaper columnist, falls in love with her and has to uncover the real killer.

BLUE HAWAII
1961, 103 mins, US Ⓥ ⊙ ▭
D: Norman Taurog **A:** Elvis Presley, Joan Blackman, Nancy Walters, Roland Winters, Angela Lansbury, Howard McNear (Paramount)

A handsome, picture-postcard production crammed with typical South Seas musical *hula*baloo. Plot casts Elvis Presley as the rebellious son of a pineapple tycoon who wants to make his own way in life, a project in which he succeeds after numerous romantic entanglements and misunderstandings. Romantic support is attractively dispatched by Joan Blackman and Nancy Walters.

BLUE ICE
1992, 104 mins, UK Ⓥ ⊙
D: Russell Mulcahy **A:** Michael Caine, Sean Young, Ian Holm, Alun Armstrong, Sam Kelly, Bob Hoskins (M&M)

A determinedly old-fashioned actioner that's terminally light on real thrills. Caine is Harry Anders, a retired MI6 op who's whiling away his years running a London jazz bar. When a US ambassador's wife (Sean Young) literally bumps into him at a red light, he gets drawn back into espionage when she asks him to find a former b.f. (Todd Boyce). Caine's settled, effortless performance carries the pic, but there's a lack of real electricity with Young.

BLUE IN THE FACE
1995, 89 mins, US
D: Wayne Wang, Paul Auster A: Harvey Keitel, Lou Reed, Roseanne, Michael J. Fox, Jim Jarmusch, Lily Tomlin (Blue in the Face/Miramax)

During the making of *Smoke*, director Wayne Wang and screenwriter Paul Auster apparently felt unable to include all the characters and subplots originally envisaged. Money was found to make another film. Result is a piecemeal collection of barely connected scenes and characters. It's sporadically lively and contains quite a few amusing bits and pieces. Action again centers on the Brooklyn Cigar store, which is still managed by Auggie (Harvey Keitel). Most notable newcomer is Roseanne.

BLUE JEANS
See: Blue Denim

BLUE JUICE
1995, 90 mins, UK ♥
D: Carl Prechezer A: Sean Pertwee, Catherine Zeta Jones, Steven Mackintosh, Ewan McGregor, Peter Gunn, Keith Allen (Film Four/Pandora/Skreba)

Absolutely charming, unabashedly offbeat quirky comedy about hapless surf bums stuck on the chilly Cornish coast of England. JC (Sean Pertwee) is having a hard time coming to grips with the notion that his wave-riding heroics are a thing of the past, and he's having an even tougher time dealing with his sexy girlfriend, Chloe (Catherine Zeta Jones). Three old friends show up. Dean (Ewan McGregor) is a drug-addled hipster, Josh (Steven Mackintosh) is a hot techno-music producer, and together they've kidnapped Terry (Peter Gunn), another old buddy. McGregor delivers the pic's best performance. Prechezer and coauthor's script is overloaded with finely tuned humor, and Prechezer's direction manages to strike just the right balance of yuks, watery thrills 'n spills, and heart-melting romance.

BLUE LAGOON, THE
1949, 103 mins, UK
D: Frank Launder, Sidney Gilliat A: Jean Simmons, Donald Houston, Noel Purcell, James Hayter, Cyril Cusack (Individual)

Technicolor photography of a glorious South Seas setting provides appropriate romantic background for this picturization of H. de Vere Stacpoole's novel. The story of the two children, who are shipwrecked on a South Seas island, is developed by a series of incidents rather than by a woven theme. Jean Simmons displays a sarong to advantage and Donald Houston has little more to do than show off his manly torso.

BLUE LAGOON, THE
1980, 102 mins, US ♥ ⊙
D: Randal Kleiser A: Brooke Shields, Christopher Atkins, Leo McKern, William Daniels, Elva Josephson, Glenn Kohan (Columbia)

A beautifully mounted production, a low-key love story stressing the innocent eroticism of Brooke Shields and newcomer Christopher Atkins. This is the second adaptation of the 1903 novel by Henry DeVere Stacpoole about two shipwrecked children who grow from childhood in an isolated South Seas paradise. Their romance is enhanced by Nestor Almendros' exquisite photography (and Basil Poledouris score).

1980: Nomination: Best Cinematography

BLUE LAMP, THE
1950, 82 mins, UK ♥
D: Basil Dearden A: Jack Warner, Jimmy Hanley, Dirk Bogarde, Robert Flemyng, Bernard Lee, Peggy Evans (Ealing)

Dedicated to the British police force, the story describes the postwar crime wave as seen through the eyes of the man on the beat. Jack Warner takes the part of the constable and brings to that role the typical humor associated with the London copper. Jimmy Hanley plays a raw recruit to the police force with feeling, but the best performance comes from Dirk Bogarde, who, with Patric Doonan, are the criminals.

BLUE MAX, THE
1966, 154 mins, UK ♥ ⊙ ▭
D: John Guillermin A: George Peppard, James Mason, Ursula Andress, Jeremy Kemp, Karl Michael Vogler, Anton Diffring (20th Century-Fox)

A World War I drama with some exciting aerial combat sequences helping to enliven a grounded, meller script. The hero, a lower-class climber played by George Peppard, is a heel; his adversary in the ranks of an air squadron, also for the free affections of Ursula Andress, is also a negative character, played by Jeremy Kemp. Only Karl Michael Vogler, the squadron commander, evokes any sympathy.

BLUE MURDER AT ST. TRINIAN'S
1958, 86 mins, UK ⓥ
D: Frank Launder **A:** Terry-Thomas, George Cole, Joyce Grenfell, Lionel Jeffries, Lisa Gastoni, Sabrina (British Lion)

A thin, yet complicated story line does not add up to a very satisfactory comedy film. There are all the obvious gags, with the "awful schoolgirls" of Ronald Searle's cartoons behaving like little fiends. The school is without a headmistress and the army has been called in to keep order. By cheating, the girls have won a coach trip to Rome. Trip enables Lionel Jeffries to pose as a woman, Joyce Grenfell to pose as an interpreter though actually a police woman, and Terry-Thomas to steal the film as a shady boss of a coach firm.

BLUES BROTHERS, THE
1980, 133 mins, US ⓥ ⊙
D: John Landis **A:** John Belushi, Dan Aykroyd, James Brown, Ray Charles, Carrie Fisher, Aretha Franklin (Universal)

Enacting Jake and Elwood Blues roles created for their popular concert and recording act, John Belushi and Dan Aykroyd use the slenderest of stories—attempt to raise $5,000 for their childhood parish by putting their old band back together—as an excuse to wreak havoc on the entire city of Chicago and much of the midwest. Film's greatest pleasure comes from watching the likes of James Brown, Cab Calloway, Ray Charles, and especially Aretha Franklin do their musical things. Pic plays as a spirited tribute by white boys to black musical culture, which was inspiration for the Blues Brothers act in the first place.

BLUES BROTHERS 2000
1998, 123 mins, US ⓥ ⊙
D: John Landis **A:** Dan Aykroyd, John Goodman, Joe Morton, J. Evan Bonifant, Nia Peeples, Kathleen Freeman (Universal)

Dan Aykroyd and director John Landis take a bumpy trip down memory lane in this fitfully funny follow-up to their 1980 musical-comedy extravaganza. Aykroyd reprises his signature role as Elwood Blues, who sets out to reassemble the Blues Brothers Band. He befriends Mighty Mack McTeer (John Goodman), a bartender who earns the right to replace Jake, and they take flight after they run afoul of

Russian Mafia tough guys. Landis keeps the car-crash action to a minimum. Trouble is, while restraint may be a valuable commodity in some comedies, it's hardly what audiences want or expect in a *Blues Brothers* adventure. On the plus side, the film does feature two genuine showstoppers in its second half ("John the Revelator" and "How Blue Can You Get").

BLUE SKIES
1946, 104 mins, US
D: Stuart Heisler **A:** Bing Crosby, Fred Astaire, Joan Caulfield, Billy De Wolfe, Olga San Juan, Frank Faylen (Paramount)

The cue sheet on *Blue Skies* lists 42 different Irving Berlin song items but some of them have been excised and the rest so skillfully arranged, orchestrated and presented that the nostalgic musical cavalcade doesn't pall. Fred Astaire's "Puttin 'on the Ritz" is the musical standout of the more than 30 items which have been retained. Bing Crosby is the romantic winnah throughout. Joan Caulfield is partial to the nitery troubadour (Crosby). Astaire is the suave dancing star and she's in the line of one of his shows. Astaire's romantic interest carries her along but Crosby's crooning charms her.

1946: Nominations: Best Scoring of a Dramatic Picture, Song ("You Keep Coming Back Like a Song")

BLUE SKY
1994, 101 mins, US ⓥ ⊙
D: Tony Richardson **A:** Jessica Lange, Tommy Lee Jones, Powers Boothe, Carrie Snodgress, Amy Locane, Chris O'Donnell (Orion)

Jessica Lange makes the most of an opportunity at a full-blown star turn as Carly Marshall, the wife of army scientist Hank Marshall (Tommy Lee Jones), whose irrepressible sensuality and wild spirit can't be reined in even by the military. Richardson, who died in 1991 shortly after completing the picture, mounted the action in a visually straightforward, unflashy manner, concentrating his attention on the performances. Result is very much like a solid melodrama from the 1950s. Lange has the showy role, with almost unlimited opportunities to emote and strut her stuff, which she does magnificently and with total abandon.

1994: Best Actress (Jessica Lange)

BLUE STEEL
1990, 102 mins, US ⓥ ⊙
D: Kathryn Bigelow **A:** Jamie Lee Curtis,

Ron Silver, Clancy Brown, Elizabeth Pena, Louise Fletcher, Philip Bosco (United Artists/Vestron/Lighting)

A taut, relentless thriller that hums with an electric current of outrage. Director and cowriter Kathryn Bigelow makes the most of her hook—the use of a female star (Jamie Lee Curtis) in a tough action pic—by stressing the character's vulnerability in remarkable early scenes. As rookie cop Megan Turner, Curtis is suspended after she kills an armed robber and no gun is found at the scene. The psycho bystander who picked the gun up (Ron Silver) starts commiting serial murders with bullets he's carved her name onto, and Curtis gets dragged back onto the force to help find him. Pic lacks nothing for menace and suspense, and has a frightening, explosively violent second half.

BLUE THUNDER
1983, 108 mins, US 🅥 ⊙ ▱
D: John Badham **A:** Roy Scheider, Malcolm McDowell, Warren Oates, Candy Clark, Daniel Stern, Paul Roebling (Rastar/Columbia)

Blue Thunder is a ripsnorting live-action cartoon, utterly implausible but no less enjoyable for that. Opening 15 minutes take vet L.A. police helicopter pilot Roy Scheider and rookie Daniel Stern on nocturnal rounds. Scheider is invited to a demonstration of Blue Thunder, a top-secret antiterrorist chopper. Craft has been brought to L.A. for possible use against subversives during the 1984 Olympic Games, and among those in charge of the program is cardboard villain Malcolm McDowell.
1983: Nomination: Best Editing

BLUE TIGER
1994, 87 mins, US 🅥 ⊙
D: Norberto Barba **A:** Virginia Madsen, Toru Nakamura, Dean Hallo, Ryo Ishibashi, Sal Lopez, Harry Dean Stanton (Neo Motion/First Look)

Packed with classy production values and performances that range from first-rate to standard action-pic dramatics, *Blue Tiger* is distinguished by real care to the lensing and main story, which positions Virginia Madsen and Toru Nakamura as doomed lovers caught in the cross fire of a mob battle for control of a Southern California business operation. Pic announces a first-rate directing talent in first-timer Norberto Barba.

BLUE VEIL, THE
1951, 113 mins, US
D: Curtis Bernhardt **A:** Jane Wyman, Charles Laughton, Joan Blondell, Richard Carlson, Agnes Moorehead, Don Taylor (Wald-Krasna/RKO)

Story is nothing more than a series of episodes strung together by the central character of a First World War war widow who devotes her life to children after losing her only child. Footage carries Jane Wyman through a succession of jobs as a baby nurse until, old and worn-out physically, she is given the lifetime job of caring for the offspring of one of her former charges. The episode in which she cares for Natalie Wood, daughter of fading musical actress Joan Blondell, is considerably enlivened by the pert vivacity of Blondell and her singing of two old tunes.
1951: Nominations: Best Actress (Jane Wyman), Supp. Actress (Joan Blondell)

BLUE VELVET
1986, 120 mins, US 🅥 ⊙ ▱
D: David Lynch **A:** Kyle MacLachlan, Isabella Rossellini, Dennis Hopper, Laura Dern, Hope Lange, Dean Stockwell (De Laurentiis)

Blue Velvet finds David Lynch back on familiar, strange territory. Picture takes a disturbing and at times devastating look at the ugly underside of Middle American life. Kyle MacLachlan discovers a disembodied human ear in an empty lot. He begins investigating whose ear he might have found, and ends up spying on local roadhouse chanteuse and prostie Isabella Rossellini. What he sees violent client Dennis Hopper do to sweet Laura Dern launches MacLachlan into another world, into an unfamiliar, dangerously provocative state of mind. Rossellini, dressed in lingerie or less much of the time, throws herself into this mad role with complete abandon. Hopper creates a flabbergasting portrait of unrepentant, irredeemable evil.
1986: Nomination: Best Director

BLUME IN LOVE
1973, 115 mins, US 🅥
D: Paul Mazursky **A:** George Segal, Susan Anspach, Kris Kristofferson, Marsha Mason, Shelley Winters, Paul Mazursky (Warner)

A technically well-made, but dramatically distended comedy-drama starring George Segal as a man determined to win back the affections of Susan Anspach, the wife who divorced him for infidelity. Needless time-juggling flashback, indulgent writing, lazy structure, and intrusive and pretentious social commentary blunt some fine performances. There are a few good laughs, a handful of chuckles, several smiles, and a ton of songs, some by Kris Kristofferson, who is starred as Anspach's dropout lover.

BOARDWALK
1979, 98 mins, US Ⓥ
D: Stephen Verona **A:** Ruth Gordon, Lee Strasberg, Janet Leigh, Joe Silver, Eddie Barth, Kim Delgado (Atlantic Releasing)

A small, well-wrought feature that centers on the efforts of an elderly Jewish couple to survive the barrenness and dangers of their decaying Brooklyn neighborhood. But although there's a strong emotional core (and ample talent) to its portrait of the stubbornly youthful eldsters (Lee Strasberg and Ruth Gordon), it's the film's chronicle of their mounting terrorization at the hands of a black youth gang that overrides its tone, shading the pic into a *Death Wish* finale.

BOAT, THE
See: Das Boot

BOB & CAROL & TED & ALICE
1969, 104 mins, US Ⓥ ⊙
D: Paul Mazursky **A:** Natalie Wood, Robert Culp, Elliott Gould, Dyan Cannon, Horst Ebersberg, Lee Bergere (Columbia/Frankovich)

A filmmaker (Robert Culp) and his wife (Natalie Wood) visit an institute which supposedly helps people expand their capacities for love and understanding. When our friends are back in their swank surroundings, chatting with friends Elliott Gould and wife Dyan Cannon, the comedy begins and never lets up until the final scenes when the sociological effects of this pseudoliberal thinking come into play. Cannon and Gould practically steal the film, although admittedly they have the best lines. Wood and Culp give equally fine performances. **1969: Nominations:** Best Supp. Actor (Elliott Gould), Supp. Actress (Dyan Cannon), Original Story & Screenplay, Cinematography

BOBBY DEERFIELD
1977, 124 mins, US Ⓥ ▭
D: Sydney Pollack **A:** Al Pacino, Marthe Keller, Anny Duperey, Walter McGinn, Romolo Valli, Stephan Meldegg (Columbia)

Bobby Deerfield is a brilliantly unusual love story. Al Pacino and Marthe Keller are both excellent as shallow jet-set floaters who become whole persons in their romance. Foreign location footage is lavish. Pacino plays the title character, whose interest in car racing has propelled him into international celeb status. Keller is a wealthy and elusive character, manic in her life style because of terminal illness.

BOB LE FLAMBEUR
1956, 95 mins, France Ⓥ ⊙
D: Jean-Pierre Melville **A:** Roger Duchesne, Isabelle Corey, Daniel Cauchy, Howard Vernon, Guy Decomble, Claude Cerval

Pic concerns the last job of an aging gangster who has been devoting himself to gambling until the final heist presents itself. This plods through its tale of the underworld without adding the needed fillip to make it unusual.

BOBO, THE
1967, 103 mins, US Ⓥ ⊙
D: Robert Parrish **A:** Peter Sellers, Britt Ekland, Rossano Brazzi, Adolfo Celi, Hattie Jacques, John Wells (Warner)

A clever, sophisticated, and charming farce. Peter Sellers is teamed with Britt Ekland, who plays the most beauteous, capricious, frivolous, and difficult femme in all Barcelona. Which, of course, makes all the more beguiling the challenge offered Sellers—a matador who sings, or a singer who is a half-baked torero, take your pick—of possessing her within exactly three days if he is to receive a week's engagement at the city's biggest teatro.

BOB ROBERTS
1992, 105 mins, US Ⓥ ⊙
D: Tim Robbins **A:** Tim Robbins, Giancarlo Esposito, Ray Wise, Brian Murray, Gore Vidal, Rebecca Jenkins (PolyGram/Working Title)

Both a stimulating social satire and a depressing commentary on the devolution of the US political system, caustic docudrama about a wealthy crypto-fascist folksinger who runs for US Senate showcases the impressive multiple talents of Tim Robbins as director, writer, actor, singer, and songwriter. Roberts's (Robbins) aim is to unseat longtime Pennsylvania Senator Brickley Paiste (Gore Vidal). Robbins is spookily dead-on projecting the candidate's bland confidence and homogenized middle-American personality.

BOCCACCIO '70
1962, 159 mins, Italy/France Ⓥ
D: Vittorio De Sica, Federico Fellini, Lu-

chino Visconti **A:** Sophia Loren, Luigi Giuliani, Anita Ekberg, Peppino De Filippo, Romy Schneider, Tomas Milian

Each segment was separately conceived and executed, all three being expensively mounted and lavishly lensed in Technicolor. Fellini's *The Temptation of Dr. Antonio* is a searing denunciation of hypocrisy. When a provocative poster of Anita Ekberg is set up facing his apartment, Antonio tries to fight one more battle against his concept of immorality. But he is defeated when the ebullient Ekberg comes to life and drives him berserk. *The Job* provides a complete change of pace via Luchino Visconti's elegant styling of a modern boudoir piece. Episode deals with young count (Tomas Milian) who's mixed up in a call-girl scandal and fears his wife (Romy Schneider) will divorce him. *The Raffle*, the most completely enjoyable of the lot, has Sophia Loren as the object of a raffle. The winner gets to sleep with her, and De Sica tells the tale (which has a twist ending) with a brash and earthy humor.

BODIES, REST & MOTION
1993, 93 mins, US Ⓥ ⊙
D: Michael Steinberg **A:** Phoebe Cates, Bridget Fonda, Tim Roth, Eric Stoltz (Fine Line/August)

Uncompelling but moderately engaging throughout, sharp-looking film looks at four young people coping with a malaise that seems neither easily diagnosable nor curable, taking place over one weekend mostly in a house shared by agitated, dissatisfied Tim Roth and his unfocused g.f., Bridget Fonda. In the opening scene, Roth tells former g.f. Phoebe Cates, now Fonda's best friend, that they have decided to move. However, Roth hits the road on his own, leaving the distraught Fonda alone with a pile of furniture and dope-smoking housepainter Eric Stoltz, and the new couple soon get it on.

BODY AND SOUL
1947, 101 mins, US Ⓥ ⊙
D: Robert Rossen **A:** John Garfield, Lilli Palmer, Anne Revere, Canada Lee, Hazel Brooks, William Conrad (United Artists/Enterprise)

The story concerns a youngster with a punching flair who emerges from the amateurs to ride along the knockout trail to the middleweight championship. But to get himself a crack at the title he has to sell 50 percent of himself to a big-time gambler with a penchant for making and breaking champs at will. There are a flock of loopholes in this story, but interest seldom lags. John Garfield is convincing in the lead part, and the boxing scenes look the McCoy.
1947: Best Editing
Nominations: Best Actor (John Garfield), Original Screenplay

BODY DOUBLE
1984, 109 mins, US Ⓥ ⊙
D: Brian De Palma **A:** Craig Wasson, Gregg Henry, Melanie Griffith, Deborah Shelton, Guy Boyd, Dennis Franz (Columbia/Delphi Prods II)

Brian De Palma lets all his obsessions hang out in *Body Double*. A voyeur's delight and a feminist's nightmare, sexpenser features an outrageously farfetched and flimsy plot. Pivotal murder scene occurs at about the midpoint, and it's an offensive lulu, being performed with an enormous power drill. Melanie Griffith, with punky dyed hair and teensy voice, is just right as a porno queen.

BODYGUARD, THE
1992, 129 mins, US Ⓥ ⊙
D: Mick Jackson **A:** Kevin Costner, Whitney Houston, Gary Kemp, Bill Cobbs, Ralph Waite, Michele Lamar Richards (Warner/Tig)

This Lawrence Kasdan script proves a jumbled mess with a few enjoyable moments but little continuity or flow. Those shortcomings are puzzling since the pic's core is sheer simplicity: bodyguard-for-hire Frank Farmer (Kevin Costner) takes a job protecting actress-singer Rachel Marron (Whitney Houston) and ends up falling for her. Someone is trying to kill her. The chemistry between the leads stems more from their inherent appeal than anything the story develops.
1992: Nominations: Best Song ("I Have Nothing," "Run to You")

BODYGUARD, THE
See: Yojimbo

BODY HEAT
1981, 113 mins, US Ⓥ ⊙
D: Lawrence Kasdan **A:** William Hurt, Kathleen Turner, Richard Crenna, Ted Danson, Mickey Rourke, J. A. Preston (Warner/Ladd)

Body Heat is an engrossing, mightily stylish meller in which sex and crime walk hand in hand down the path to tragedy, just like in the old days. William Hurt is a spirited but struggling lawyer whose persistent pursuit of sultry Kathleen Turner pays off in the way of a torrid affair, highly satisfying for both parties. She's the young wife of loaded middle-aged businessman Richard Crenna. Just as in *Double Indemnity* it's the dame who hatches the murder plot, with the guy finally falling into line and coming up with the ingenious way to pull it off. However familiar the elements, Kasdan has brought the drama alive by steeping it in humid, virtually oozing atmosphere.

BODY OF EVIDENCE
1993, 99 mins, US Ⓥ ⊙
D: Uli Edel **A:** Madonna, Willem Dafoe, Joe Mantegna, Anne Archer, Julianne Moore, Jurgen Prochnow (De Laurentiis)

A courtroom drama built around the charge that Madonna's body is a deadly weapon with which she fornicated a man to death, this showcase for the singerthesp as femme fatale is more silly than erotic. Defense attorney Willem Dafoe just can't say no and the pair's several sex bouts are the film's main action set pieces. Portland locations give the pic's exteriors an appealingly wet, cool feel.

BODY PARTS
1991, 88 mins, US Ⓥ ⊙ ▭
D: Eric Red **A:** Jeff Fahey, Lindsay Duncan, Kim Delaney, Brad Dourif, Zakes Mokae, Peter Murnik (Paramount)

What could have been a reasonably interesting thriller literally goes to pieces in last third, until the brain seems the most salient part missing. Jeff Fahey loses his arm in a car accident, only to have it replaced by a doctor (Lindsay Duncan) perfecting a new limb-grafting procedure. The psychologist is told that the new limb belonged to a serial killer, prompting him to wonder if the murderer's arm might be invading his own soul. Suddenly, the narrative hurriedly kicks into a slasher mode, replete with car chases, dismemberment, and unintentional, if rather vulgar, hilarity.

BODY SNATCHER, THE
1945, 70 mins, US Ⓥ ⊙
D: Robert Wise **A:** Boris Karloff, Bela Lugosi, Henry Daniell, Edith Atwater, Russell Wade, Rita Corday (RKO)

Based on a short story by Robert Louis Stevenson, *Snatcher* seldom lacks interest. Yarn deals with the traffic on dead bodies by hansom cabbie Boris Karloff. Corpses are used for study purposes in a medical school mastered by Henry Daniell. Bela Lugosi is seen briefly as a handyman. Karloff portrays his sadistic role in character-

istic style, but best performance comes from Daniell.

BODY SNATCHERS
1994, 87 mins, US Ⓥ ⊙ ▭
D: Abel Ferrara **A:** Gabrielle Anwar, Terry Kinney, Billy Wirth, Meg Tilly, Forest Whitaker, Christine Elise (Warner)

The third screen version of Jack Finney's 1954 novel *The Body Snatchers* is a tremendously exciting thriller that compares favorably with Don Siegel's classic 1956 original. Improvements include having a teenage heroine and setting the film on an Alabama military base. Gabrielle Anwar toplines as teen Marty Malone, who has moved to an army base with her EPA biologist dad (Terry Kinney), stepmom (Meg Tilly), and younger brother (Reilly Murphy). Unsettling events occur early: Anwar is accosted by a black man who warns her cryptically: "They get you when you sleep." Makeup effects eschew the genre's explicit gore, in favor of frightening tendrils snaking around the victims.

BOEING BOEING
1965, 102 mins, US
D: John Rich **A:** Tony Curtis, Jerry Lewis, Dany Saval, Christine Schmidtmer, Suzanna Leigh, Thelma Ritter (Paramount)

An excellent modern comedy. Paris-based US newsman Tony Curtis has three airline gals on a string. Curtis's cozy scheme approaches collapse when advanced design Boeing aircraft (hence, the title) augur a disastrous overlap in femme availability. Rich has also brought out a new dimension in Lewis, herein excellent in a solid comedy role as Curtis's professional rival who threatens to explode the plan. The outstanding performance is delivered by Thelma Ritter, Curtis's harried housekeeper.

BOFORS GUN, THE
1968, 105 mins, UK
D: Jack Gold **A:** Nicol Williamson, Ian Holm, David Warner, Peter Vaughan, Richard O'Callaghan, Barry Jackson (Universal)

No question of the quality of this absorbing, though downbeat military pic set in a British barracks in Germany in the mid-1950s. Clash is between David Warner as an immature, indecisive one-striper and Nicol Williamson as a half-crazy, embittered Irish rebel, alcoholic and self-tortured. Williamson, with rebellion and anger rankling inside him, sets out to humiliate the NCO and wreck his prospects of promotion.

BOILING POINT
1993, 90 mins, US/France Ⓥ ☉
D: James B. Harris A: Wesley Snipes, Dennis Hopper, Lolita Davidovich, Viggo Mortensen, Dan Hedaya, Seymour Cassel (Hexagon)

An old-fashioned police procedural, low-key and bland in the extreme. Snipes toplines as a US Treasury agent partnered with Dan Hedaya. The third T-man on their stakeout is killed by ruthless thug Viggo Mortensen, who gets away with partner Dennis Hopper before the feds can close in. Snipes is reassigned from L.A. to Newark. He holds out for one week's time to catch the killers. Because of terrific acting down to the smallest role, one's interest is maintained despite the minimalist direction and lack of story twists.

BOLERO
1984, 104 mins, US Ⓥ ☉
D: John Derek A: Bo Derek, George Kennedy, Andrea Occhipinti, Ana Obregon, Olivia D'Abo, Greg Bensen (Cannon/City)

Bolero is all about Bo Derek's determination to lose her virginity after graduating from an English boarding school. Bo ventures first to Arabia, where a sheik falls asleep in her arms. Bo moves on to Spain, where she meets handsome bullfighter Andrea Occhipinti. Ready for womanhood, Bo utters the immortal lines: "Do everything to me. Show me how I can do everything to you. Is there enough I can do for you so you can give ecstasy to me?"

BOLERO
See: Les Uns et les Autres

BONE COLLECTOR, THE
1999, 118 mins, US Ⓥ ☉ ▭
D: Phillip Noyce A: Denzel Washington, Angelina Jolie, Queen Latifah, Michael Rooker, Mike McGlone, Luis Guzman (Universal/Columbia)

The difficulties in making an action thriller out of Jeffery Deaver's bestseller *The Bone Collector* aren't entirely surmounted in Phillip Noyce's glossy adaptation. While Denzel Washington delivers a convincing central turn, suspense is compromised by paralyzed protag's physical stasis; more serious flaws lie in Angelina Jolie's credulity-straining role and a contrived climax. Brilliant NYPD criminologist Lincoln Rhyme (Washington) passes days in unhappy retirement. His former partner, Detective Sellitto (Ed O'Neill), thinks only Rhyme's uncanny skills can help find a disappeared multimillionaire and his wife. Patrol cop Amelia Donaghy (Jolie) discovers the man's corpse buried beneath subway tracks. The woman is presumed still alive, and Rhyme is able to pinpoint a likely hostage location. Clues point toward the assailant's recreation of crimes from the turn of the century.

BONFIRE OF THE VANITIES, THE
1990, 125 mins, US Ⓥ ☉ ▭
D: Brian De Palma A: Tom Hanks, Bruce Willis, Melanie Griffith, Kim Cattrall, Morgan Freeman, F. Murray Abraham (Warner)

A misfire of inanities. Wall Street maestro Sherman McCoy (Tom Hanks) is having an affair with southern bombshell Maria Ruskin (Melanie Griffith). Monkey wrench arrives in the form of an automobile mishap one night in deepest Bronx. Seemingly threatened by two black youths, Maria backs Sherman's Mercedes into one of them. When the kid falls into a coma, the rich man's status makes him an ideal scapegoat for multifarious social ills. Peter Fallow (Bruce Willis), a down-and-out alcoholic reporter, parlays the McCoy story into fame and fortune. Unfortunately, the caricatures are so crude and the revelations so unenlightening of the human condition that the satire is about as socially incisive as a *Police Academy* entry.

BONJOUR TRISTESSE
1958, 94 mins, US Ⓥ ▭
D: Otto Preminger A: Deborah Kerr, David Niven, Jean Seberg, Mylene Demongeot, Geoffrey Horne, Juliette Greco (Columbia)

In transplanting Francoise Sagan's thin book to the screen, producer-director Otto Preminger basically has stayed with her first-person tale of the amours of a middle-aged, charming, and wealthy Frenchman within both view and earshot of his daughter who, like the author at the time, is 17. Script deficiencies and awkward readings have static results. Seberg's Cecile is more suggestive of a high-school senior back home than the frisky, knowing, close friend and daughter of a roué. David Niven is properly affable as the father. Deborah Kerr is a standout talent as the artist whom Niven proposes to marry.

BONNIE AND CLYDE
1967, 111 mins, US Ⓥ ⊙
D: Arthur Penn **A:** Warren Beatty, Faye Dunaway, Michael J. Pollard, Gene Hackman, Estelle Parsons, Denver Pyle (Warner)

Warren Beatty's *Bonnie and Clyde* incongruously couples comedy with crime, in this biopic of Bonnie Parker and Clyde Barrow, a pair of Texas desperadoes during the bleak Depression days of the early 1930s. Scripters David Newman and Robert Benton have depicted these real-life characters as inept, bumbling, moronic types, and if this had been true they would have been erased in their first try. Beatty is believable at times, but his characterization lacks any consistency. Dunaway is a knockout as Bonnie Parker, registers with deep sensitivity in the love scenes, and conveys believability to her role.
1967: Best Supp. Actress (Estelle Parsons), Cinematography
Nominations: Best Picture, Director, Actor (Warren Beatty), Actress (Faye Dunaway), Supp. Actor (Gene Hackman, Michael J. Pollard), Original Story & Screenplay, Costume Design

BOOGIE NIGHTS
1997, 152 mins, US Ⓥ ⊙ ▭
D: Paul Thomas Anderson **A:** Mark Wahlberg, Burt Reynolds, Julianne Moore, John C. Reilly, Don Cheadle, Heather Graham (New Line)

Spanning the height of the disco era (1977–84), pic offers a visually stunning exploration of the adult entertainment industry, centering on a hardcore movie outfit whose members form a close-knit extended family. Story follows the rise and fall of Eddie Adams (Mark Wahlberg), a handsome, uneducated teenager lured to a promising career by Jack Horner (Burt Reynolds), a successful porn producer. As Dirk Diggler, Adams soon becomes a hot property. However, as the yarn moves into the '80s, Diggler's endless partying and enormous ego begin to interfere with his work. Pic's first hour is nothing short of brilliant, both narratively and technically. But subsequent chapters and numerous subplots and secondary characters make the saga a bit too messy for its own good. Wahlberg renders a splendid performance, Reynolds shines as the film's moral center, and the versatile Julianne Moore excels as Amber, the company's female star and surrogate mother.
1997: Nominations: Best Supp. Actor (Burt Reynolds), Supp. Actress (Julianne Moore), Original Screenplay

BOOM
1968, 112 mins, UK ▭
D: Joseph Losey **A:** Elizabeth Taylor, Richard Burton, Noel Coward, Joanna Shimkus, Michael Dunn, Romolo Valli (World Film Services/Moonlake/Universal)

The translation to film of Tennessee Williams's much-revised play *The Milk Train Doesn't Stop Here Anymore* is the uninteresting tale of a multimarried, aging shrew, played by Taylor. Burton is far more believable as a freeloading poet working the Mediterranean circuit.

BOOMERANG!
1947, 87 mins, US
D: Elia Kazan **A:** Dana Andrews, Jane Wyatt, Lee J. Cobb, Arthur Kennedy, Karl Malden, Sam Levene (20th Century-Fox)

Boomerang! is gripping, real-life melodrama, told in semidocumentary style. Lensing was done on location at Stamford, CT, the locale adding to realism. Based on a still-unsolved murder case in Bridgeport, plot is backed up with strong cast. Case on which plot is based deals with murder of a priest and how the prosecuting attorney establishes the innocence of the law's only suspect.
1947: Nomination: Best Screenplay

BOOMERANG
1992, 118 mins, US Ⓥ ⊙
D: Reginald Hudlin **A:** Eddie Murphy, Halle Berry, Robin Givens, David Alan Grier, Grace Jones, Eartha Kitt (Paramount)

Eddie Murphy straitjackets himself in an ill-fitting comedy vehicle that's desperately in need of a reality check. Murphy's credited with the high-concept story, developed by scripters as a cornball tale of comeuppance. He's a marketing exec at a New York cosmetics firm whom women find irresistible (all six female leads want to seduce him). His new departmental boss, Robin Givens, turns the tables on Murphy and treats him the way he's been treating women all his adult life. One naturalistic character in a cast of caricatures is cute subordinate Halle Berry.

BOOM TOWN
1940, 117 mins, US Ⓥ
D: Jack Conway **A:** Clark Gable, Spencer Tracy, Claudette Colbert, Hedy Lamarr, Frank Morgan, Lionel Atwill (M-G-M)

Boom Town is the tale of wildcat oil

drilling, with fortunes won and lost just as quickly as a roller coaster dips and rises. It centers around the partnership of Clark Gable and Spencer Tracy, a couple of tough, two-fisted oil drillers who know all the angles. The women will go for Gable's carefree romancing and later happy married life with Claudette Colbert, and still will be equally intrigued by the protective affection displayed by Tracy for the girl he loved but who married his partner.

BOOST, THE
1988, 95 mins, US Ⓥ ⦿
D: Harold Becker A: James Woods, Sean Young, John Kapelos, Steven Hill, Kelle Kerr, Amanda Blake (Hemdale)

A cautionary tale about a couple involved in a mutually destructive, coke-dominated lifestyle. Lenny and Linda Brown (James Woods and Sean Young) are still struggling to make ends meet when Lenny receives an extraordinary opportunity to make his fortune by selling tax shelters. Lenny suddenly finds himself deep in the hole financially, as well as hooked on the cocaine he started taking only as a boost to get him through rough times. Woods and Young are live wires, so the passion, care, and commitment the characters have for one another is palpable at all times.

DAS BOOT
(THE BOAT)
1981, 145 mins, W. Germany Ⓥ ⦿
D: Wolfgang Petersen A: Jurgen Prochnow, Arthur Grunemeyer, Klaus Wennemann, Hubertus Bengsch, Martin Semmelrogge, Bernd Tauber (Bavaria Atelier/Radiant)

The Boat is far and away the most expensive German film made since World War II, a two-hour-plus action film about the fate of a German U-boat in 1941. Everything described in the film is authentic: it's the story of a single mission in the Atlantic, from the departure of the boat from La Rochelle in Occupied France to its return to port some months later. In between, it's constantly a question of life or death, give-and-take, kill or be killed, a descent into the pit of hell with slim odds of ever returning.

BOOTS MALONE
1951, 103 mins, US Ⓥ
D: William Dieterle A: William Holden, Johnny Stewart, Stanley Clements, Basil Ruysdael, Carl Benton Reid, Ed Begley (Columbia)

Plot deals with the relationship between Johnny Stewart, a 15-year-old who loves horses, and William Holden, a jockey's agent down on his luck. Story is run off against an authentic racetrack background, drawing a good picture of the less prosperous side of racing and its hanger-ons. As producer-writer, Milton Holmes has told the story with good emotional moments and sentiment without being maudlin.

BOPHA!
1993, 121 mins, US Ⓥ ⦿
D: Morgan Freeman A: Danny Glover, Malcolm McDowell, Alfre Woodard, Marius Weyers, Maynard Eziashi, Malick Bowens (Paramount/Hall)

The theatrical directing debut of actor Morgan Freeman is a handsomely crafted, potently played drama that brings the issue of apartheid down to a visceral human dimension. Set in 1980, the story revolves around the Mangena family. Micah (Danny Glover) is the senior black police officer in his township. He takes great pride in the peace and order evident in the small community. His son, Zweli (Maynard Eziashi), is cut from a different cloth. A student, his generation is striving to make a country of majority native rule. As wife and mother, Rosie Mangena (Alfre Woodard) finds herself primarily in the role of conciliator. The only misstep comes from an all-too-familiar depiction of bigotry as embodied by McDowell.

BORDER, THE
1982, 107 mins, US Ⓥ ⦿
D: Tony Richardson A: Jack Nicholson, Harvey Keitel, Valerie Perrine, Warren Oates, Elpidia Carrillo, Shannon Wilcox (Universal/RKO)

Despite Jack Nicholson's multileveled performance, *The Border* is a surprisingly uninvolving film. Story of the personal and professional pressures on border-patrol guard Nicholson, caught between right and wrong on both fronts, becomes murky and disjointed under Tony Richardson's uninspired direction. Nicholson etches a nice guy victimized by his surroundings instead of an eccentric. He is befriended by Harvey Keitel, a fellow guard. It is their job to make sure none of the Mexicans over the border get into the US—a task to which the humane Nicholson is ill-suited.

BORDER INCIDENT

1949, 92 mins, US

D: Anthony Mann **A:** Ricardo Montalban, George Murphy, Howard da Silva, James Mitchell, Arnold Moss, Alfonso Bedoya (M-G-M)

Produced on a modest budget, pic wraps a conventional yarn within a semi-documentary casing. Film is handicapped by a screenplay which treats the important subject of illegal immigration into the US with a naive cop-and-robbers approach. Anthony Mann succeeds in imparting some tautness to the action but the pic never breaks out of its formula framework. Both George Murphy, as the US agent, and Ricardo Montalban, as the Mexican counterpart, turn in effective, hard-hitting performances in a yarn that contains no romantic angles. As the chief heavy, Howard da Silva makes a menacing smoothie.

BORDERLINE

1980, 97 mins, US ⓥ

D: Jerrold Freedman **A:** Charles Bronson, Bruno Kirby, Ed Harris, Karmin Murcelo, Michael Lerner (ITC)

This Charles Bronson vehicle tackles the profiteering in illicit Mexican immigration with workmanlike dramatic skill and a notable preference for realism over hokum. The film's big name is self-effacing almost to the point of elusiveness. As a long-serving, compassionate border patrolman, Bronson is hunched and hated virtually throughout; his face is mostly masked by heavy shadow. Newcomer Ed Harris is memorable as the frontline villain, displaying screen presence to match the star's and thus injecting a powerful sense of danger.

BORDERTOWN

1935, 80 mins, US

D: Archie Mayo **A:** Paul Muni, Bette Davis, Margaret Lindsay, Eugene Pallette, Robert Barrat, Hobart Cavanaugh (Warner)

Paul Muni is a Mexican, and does it realistically and effectively. He hitchhikes to a bordertown and becomes a power in the gambling sector. Eugene Pallette owns a joint and Muni is his bouncer, then his partner. Pallette's wife (Bette Davis) goes for Muni, who won't tumble. She kills her husband to get Muni, and he still won't play. So she tells the cops he did the murder. Finish is phony, but it can't hurt the previous good work.

BORN FREE

1966, 95 mins, UK ⓥ ☉ ▭

D: James Hill **A:** Virginia McKenna, Bill Travers, Geoffrey Keen, Peter Lukoye, Omar Chambati, Bill Godden (Open Road/High Road)

Born Free is a heartwarming story of a British couple in Africa. Gerald L. C. Copley has done a first-rate adaptation of the true story of Joy Adamson, who with hubby George involuntarily domesticated several pet lions. They kept one, Elsa, until she was fully grown and then, to save her from government-ordered zoo captivity, trained her to survive as a wild animal. The apparently childless couple are portrayed in top form by real-life married couple Virginia McKenna and Bill Travers.

1966: Best Song ("Born Free"), Original Score

BORN IN FLAMES

1983, 90 mins, US

D: Lizzie Borden **A:** Honey, Jeanne Satterfield, Adele Bertel, Becky Johnson, Pat Murphy, Kathy Bigelow (Jerome Foundation)

Lizzie Borden's 16mm independent production is impertinent, audacious, abounding in fresh, considerably untraditional ideas. On the other hand, it is disjointed, with no real characters, preachy, the script insufficiently developed, and the acting often amateurish. Situated in the near future after America has gone through a socialist revolution, the story deals with the condition of women in that new society. The film's main grace is its sense of humor, a rare quality indeed in a militant film.

BORN LOSERS

1967, 114 mins, US ⓥ

D: T. C. Frank [Tom Laughlin] **A:** Tom Laughlin, Elizabeth James, Jane Russell, Jeremy Slate, William Wellman Jr., Robert Tessier (American International)

Born Losers points up the ruthlessness of an outlaw motorcycle gang which takes over a community. Director T. C. Frank builds mounting tension and suspense and draws sock performances from his entire cast, in which Jane Russell appears as a guest star.

BORN ON THE FOURTH OF JULY

1989, 144 mins, US ⓥ ☉ ▭

D: Oliver Stone **A:** Tom Cruise, Raymond J. Barry, Caroline Kava, Kyra Sedgwick,

Willem Dafoe, Jerry Levine (Ixtlan/Universal)

Oliver Stone again shows America to itself in a way it won't forget. His collaboration with Vietnam veteran Ron Kovic to depict Kovic's odyssey from teenage true believer to wheelchair-bound soldier results in a gripping, devastating, and telling film about the Vietnam era. Stone drenches the picture in visceral reality, from the agonizing chaos of a field hospital to the dead stalemate of a Bronx veterans' hospital infested with rats, drugs, and the humiliation of lying helplessly in one's own excrement. Tom Cruise, who takes Kovic from clean-cut eager teen to impassioned long-haired activist, is stunning. Dafoe, as a disabled vet hiding out in a Mexican beach town, gives a startling, razor-sharp performance.
1989: Best Director, Editing
Nominations: Best Picture, Actor (Tom Cruise), Adapted Screenplay, Cinematography, Original Score, Sound

BORN TO DANCE
1936, 105 mins, US Ⓥ
D: Roy Del Ruth **A:** Eleanor Powell, James Stewart, Virginia Bruce, Una Merkel, Sid Silvers, Frances Langford (M-G-M)

Eleanor Powell becomes a star in her second picture. She is given an opportunity to show that she's not just a good buck dancer, but an exceptionally versatile girl. As an actress she still has not arrived, as indicated in the few occasions when this plot calls for acting. James Stewart's assignment calls for a shy youth. His singing and dancing are rather painful on their own, but he's surrounded by good people, and it's all done in a spirit of fun. It's a combination navy-backstage story, with the sailors, as usual, looking for their old girlfriends while on leave in the big town, and the understudy follows the rules by stepping into the indisposed star's part at the last moment.
1936: Nominations: Best Song ("I've Got You Under My Skin"), Dance Direction ("Swingin' the Jinx")

BORN YESTERDAY
1950, 102 mins, US Ⓥ ⊙
D: George Cukor **A:** Broderick Crawford, Judy Holliday, William Holden, Howard St. John, Frank Otto, Larry Oliver (Columbia)

The bright, biting comedy of the Garson Kanin legit hit adapts easily to film. Judy Holliday delights as she tosses off the malaprops that so aptly fit the character. William Holden is quietly effective as the newspaperman hired to coach her in social graces so she will better fit in with her junkman's ambitious plans. Broderick Crawford, as the self-made dealer in junk, comes off much less successfully.
1950: Best Actress (Judy Holliday)
Nominations: Best Picture, Director, Screenplay, B&W Costume Design

BORN YESTERDAY
1993, 101 mins, US Ⓥ ⊙
D: Luis Mandoki **A:** Melanie Griffith, John Goodman, Don Johnson, Edward Herrmann, Max Perlich, Fred Dalton Thompson (Hollywood Pictures)

Updated remake of the Pygmalion-like *Born Yesterday* arrives with a credible modern resonance. However, the attractive cast, individually strong, fails to coalesce as an ensemble. Harry Brock (John Goodman) hies to DC when the evaporation of defense contracts threatens to undo his empire. In tow is Billie Dawn (Melanie Griffith), a former showgirl with more moxie than college knowledge. Harry asks lobbyist Ed Devery (Edward Herrmann) to "smarten her up." He hires local reporter Paul Verrall (Don Johnson) to provide the Professor Higgins treatment. Screenwriter Douglas McGrath expands his source material with the latest twists on power brokering. However, he also imbues the story with a glib, sitcom breeziness that favors cuteness over content.

BORSALINO
1970, 123 mins, FRANCE/US Ⓥ
D: Jacques Deray **A:** Alain Delon, Jean-Paul Belmondo, Michel Bouquet, Catherine Rouvel, Corinne Marchand, Francoise Christophe (Adel/Paramount)

Based on the real gangster milieu of Marseilles in the 1930s, pic laces together French low-life aspects with a more probing look at organized crime in the Hollywood manner via the rise and fall of two young hoodlums. Problem is that pic is more a vehicle for its stars' personalities than a more cogent insight into French prewar organized crime. Delon is a secretive, ambitious, and cruel type, while Jean-Paul Belmondo is an easygoing, engaging hoodlum who is content with small jobs. Delon has sharp grace and poise as the handsome, more cultured member of the duo, while Belmondo displays his usual ease, good nature, but physical deadliness with aplomb.

BOSTONIANS, THE
1984, 120 mins, UK Ⓥ ⊙
D: James Ivory A: Christopher Reeve, Vanessa Redgrave, Madeleine Potter, Jessica Tandy, Nancy Marchand, Wesley Addy (Merchant Ivory)

This is a classy adaptation of a Henry James novel. From the film's opening sequence at a women's meeting in late-19th-century Boston, the dice are loaded against the feminist cause. The young Verena Tarrant offers an impassioned exposition of woman's sufferings only after being "touched" by the hands of her faith-healer father. The emotional weight of the pic is carried by the relationship that evolves between Verena (Madeleine Potter) and Olive Chancellor (Vanessa Redgrave). Latter is a mature spinster who attempts to secure her charge to the cause with a promise that she will never marry.
1984: Nominations: Best Actress (Vanessa Redgrave), Costume Design

BOSTON STRANGLER, THE
1968, 116 mins, US Ⓥ ▭
D: Richard Fleischer A: Tony Curtis, Henry Fonda, George Kennedy, Mike Kellin, Murray Hamilton (20th Century-Fox)

The Boston Strangler, based on Gerold Frank's book, emerges as a triumph of taste and restraint with a telling, low-key semidocumentary style. Henry Fonda's performance as rep of Massachusetts attorney general is excellent, from his initial dislike of the task assigned through a quiet, dogged determination to break down Tony Curtis's mental barriers.

BOTTOM OF THE BOTTLE, THE
1956, 88 mins, US ▭
D: Henry Hathaway A: Van Johnson, Joseph Cotten, Ruth Roman, Jack Carson, Margaret Hayes, Bruce Bennett (20th Century-Fox)

An escaped convict's desperate efforts to reach his wife and three children in Mexico add up to 88 minutes of melodrama. The screenplay has an emotional field day as it touches on the Cain-and-Abel relationship between brothers Van Johnson and Joseph Cotten. Former, the con who's on the lam, turns to his kin to speed his flight across the border. But Cotten, a successful lawyer-rancher, fears for his reputation. Johnson, whose yen for alcohol was indirectly responsible for his prison stretch, again becomes a victim of the bottle.

BOTTOMS UP
1934, 85 mins, US
D: David Butler A: Spencer Tracy, John Boles, Pat Paterson, Herbert Mundin, Sid Silvers, Thelma Todd (Fox)

Bottoms Up is tip-top. It's good cinematic fare from every angle, particularly the elements of comedy and plot, of which aspects most filmusicals are singularly devoid. "Pat" Paterson, a Fox importee from England, is assigned the Hollywood Cinderella role. John Boles is the film star whom she has secretly idolized. Three sympathetic sharpshooters—Spencer Tracy, Herbert Mundin, and Sid Silvers—contrive to scale the Hollywood heights. It's a personal triumph for Silvers who, while one of the script collaborators, didn't have to rely solely on the lines accorded himself for good impression.

LE BOUCHER
(THE BUTCHER)
1970, 92 mins, France Ⓥ
D: Claude Chabrol A: Stephane Audran, Jean Yanne, Antonio Passalia, Pascal Ferone, Mario Beccara, Roger Rudel (La Boetie/Euro International)

A lucid, clear style, fine narration, and expert playing make this tale of a psychopathic killer in a small French town one of Claude Chabrol's most accomplished films. But it builds suspense slowly and, perhaps, gets a bit repetitious in its denouement. The town butcher, played with direct bonhomie and brusque humanity by Jean Yanne, is enamored of the town schoolteacher, etched with warm flair and tender dedication by Chabrol's wife, Stephane Audran. The killer is shown as a fairly sympathetic character except for his sickness.

BOUDU SAUVE DES EAUX
(BOUDU SAVED FROM DROWNING)
1932, 84 mins, France Ⓥ
D: Jean Renoir A: Michel Simon, Charles Grandval, Marcelle Hainia, Jean Gehret, Max Dalban, Jean Daste (Simon-Gehret)

Jean Renoir's small-scale rites of spring has Michel Simon, as Boudu, saved from drowning. A filthy, surly, ungrateful tramp, he nearly wrecks the house and lives of his benefactors. Renoir manages to get in a few blows at the smugness of the middle-class French, the ambivalent attitudes toward sexual morality, and the less-than-heroic actions of the average human being. [Pic was reviewed on first US release, in 1967.]

BOUDU SAVED FROM DROWNING
See: Boudu Sauve des Eaux

BOULEVARD NIGHTS
1979, 102 mins, US Ⓥ

D: Michael Pressman A: Richard Yniguez, Danny De La Paz, Marta du Bois, James Victor (Warner)

The film fails to carve out a separate identity of its own, rehashing a familiar story about interfamily conflicts. The decision to film *Boulevard Nights* on location in the barrios, using a largely Hispanic cast, is admirable, but does not automatically provide a raison d'être for the pic. Authenticity is the key here, and director Michael Pressman has accurately captured the sense of despair in this community. A pat dramatic crisis wraps up the film in a depressing and inconclusive fashion.

BOUND
1996, 107 mins, US Ⓥ ⊙

D: Larry Wachowski, Andy Wachowski A: Jennifer Tilly, Gina Gershon, Joe Pantoliano, Barry Kivel, Christopher Meloni, John P. Ryan (De Laurentiis)

An attention-getting lesbians-vs.-the-mob hook merely serves as a disguise for what is just another designer thriller in *Bound,* a notably unpalatable and calculated crime piece. Novelty of having two sultry babes hook up with each other while pulling a fast one on some mobsters wears thin before becoming ludicrously contrived. Both Gershon and Tilly are initially intriguing but can't sustain interest in their superficially conceived roles. They share one passionate scene, which is covered in a single take.

BOUND & GAGGED
A LOVE STORY
1993, 94 mins, US Ⓥ ⊙

D: Daniel Appleby A: Ginger Lynn Allen, Karen Black, Chris Denton, Elizabeth Saltarrelli, Mary Ella Ross, Chris Mulkey (Cinescope)

Three disparate characters form the bizarre triangle of this black comedy. Cliff (Chris Denton) is a passive man, deeply depressed over the breakup of his marriage. His best friend, the bisexual Elizabeth (Elizabeth Saltarrelli), attempts to cheer him up by taking him on the road with her lover Leslie (Ginger Lynn Allen), an attractive blonde trapped in a bad marriage. In structure, pic approximates classical farce. In execution, however, both writing and direction suffer from the lack of crazy energy and relentless logic without which satires become square and repetitious.

BOUND FOR GLORY
1976, 147 mins, US Ⓥ ⊙

D: Hal Ashby A: David Carradine, Ronny Cox, Melinda Dillon, Gail Strickland, John Lehne, Ji-Tu Cumbuka (United Artists)

Bound for Glory is outstanding biographical cinema, not only of the late Woody Guthrie but also of the 1930s Depression era. The plot advances smoothly and sensitively through about six major phases of Guthrie's earlier life: the natural tragedy of the southwest dust bowl; Guthrie's transit to California; his exposure to the horrors in the migrant-worker valleys; his initial radio career; his political activism; finally his decision to strike out for large urban areas where his songs and experience might add some momentum to change.

1976: Best Cinematography, Original Song Score

Nominations: Best Picture, Adapted Screenplay, Costume Design, Editing

BOUNTY, THE
1984, 130 mins, US Ⓥ ▭

D: Roger Donaldson A: Mel Gibson, Anthony Hopkins, Laurence Olivier, Edward Fox, Daniel Day-Lewis, Bernard Hill (De Laurentiis)

The Bounty is an intelligent, first-rate, revisionist telling of the famous tale of Fletcher Christian's mutiny against Captain Bligh. The film is particularly distinguished by a sensational, and startlingly human performance by Anthony Hopkins as Bligh, heretofore one of history's most one-dimensional villains. This is a remake with a reason, that being the exoneration and rehabilitation of the reputation of William Bligh. The mutiny itself is here presented as a chaotic mess, with Christian nearly delirious. Bligh's subsequent 4,000-mile voyage to safety in an open boat is depicted as the amazing, arduous achievement that it was.

BOWERY, THE
1933, 92 mins, US

D: Raoul Walsh A: Wallace Beery, George Raft, Jackie Cooper, Fay Wray, Pert Kelton, George Walsh (United Artists)

Two old Bowery characters, Steve Brodie and Chuck Connors, have been dramatized to a point where the only thing that's recognizable from the record books about them are the jump from Brooklyn Bridge and Bowery lingo respectively. The important point is that as rewritten the two practically legendary characters make good entertainment. The Connors-Brodie honest rivalry over everything, from gals to fighting ability, is the story. Beery is doing *The Champ* all over again to a great extent, with Jackie Cooper again as his foil. The Cooper kid sends in another gem performance. Raft, much improved, is an okay choice as Brodie.

BOWFINGER
1999, 96 mins ⓥ ⊙
D: Frank Oz **A:** Steve Martin, Eddie Murphy, Heather Graham, Christine Baranski, Jamie Kennedy, Adam Alexi-Malle (Imagine/Universal)

Scenes of explosive hilarity punctuate *Bowfinger,* a first-time pairing of Steve Martin and Eddie Murphy. Screenwriter Martin's typically quirky premise—a down-and-out filmmaker surreptitiously shoots a feature toplining a huge star without the actor knowing it—provides a line on which to hang innumerable jokes. Linking the characters is a self-delusion that allows them to live in a state of expectant bliss. No one is more delusional than Bobby Bowfinger (Martin), a schlock producer-director who sets out to make his fortune with a sci-fi action script called *Chubby Rain.* He gets a commitment from a smarmy studio exec (a droll Robert Downey Jr.) if he can deliver action star Kit Ramsey (Murphy). A small seedy group helps him out, and the entire cast performs with verve and energy.

BOXCAR BERTHA
1972, 88 mins, US ⓥ ⊙
D: Martin Scorsese **A:** Barbara Hershey, David Carradine, Barry Primus, Bernie Casey, John Carradine (American International)

Boxcar Bertha is not much more than an excuse to slaughter a lot of people. Barbara Hershey stars in title role as a Depression wanderer. The Roger Corman production, shot on an austere budget in Arkansas area, is routinely directed by Martin Scorsese. Performances are dull. Whatever sociological, political, or dramatic motivations may once have existed in the story have been ruthlessly stripped, leaving all characters bereft of empathy or sympathy.

BOXING HELENA
1993, 107 mins, US ⓥ ⊙ ⊡
D: Jennifer Chambers Lynch **A:** Julian Sands, Sherilyn Fenn, Bill Paxton, Kurtwood Smith, Betsy Clark, Nicolette Scorsese (Main Line)

Feature debut of 24-year-old writer-director Jennifer Lynch (daughter of David) offers up Julian Sands as a top surgeon who has had a one-night stand with Sherilyn Fenn and now can't get the voluptuous sexpot out of his mind. Bitchy, condescending, and cruel, Fenn tells Sands in a hundred different ways to get lost, until a horrible accident deprives her of her legs and places her forever in the sick doctor's hands. Remainder of the warped story plays on the notion of whether one person can force another to love him through cumulative dependence, time, and the force of his own love. The thesps give it all the overheated conviction they can muster.

BOY, DID I GET A WRONG NUMBER!
1966, 98 mins, US ⓥ
D: George Marshall **A:** Bob Hope, Elke Sommer, Phyllis Diller, Cesare Danova, Marjorie Lord, Kelly Thordsen (United Artists)

Bob Hope enters the realm of near-bedroom farce as he finds a near-unclad film star on his hands in a lake cottage and his ever-loving spouse continually appearing on the scene. If the action sometimes seems to get out of hand, it really doesn't matter, for Phyllis Diller is there, too, to help him hide the delectable Elke Sommer from the missus. Hope plays his role straight for the most part, making the most of the situation. Diller is immense as the nosy domestic responsible for the majority of the funny lines that abound throughout the fast unfolding.

BOY FRIEND, THE
1971, 108 mins, UK ⓥ ⊙ ⊡
D: Ken Russell **A:** Twiggy, Christopher Gable, Max Adrian, Bryan Pringle, Murray Melvin, Glenda Jackson (M-G-M)

Ken Russell's screen translation of *The Boy Friend* is delightful entertainment, novel and engaging. Narrative revolves around the personal lives of a group of repertory players who stage an English provincial production of *The Boy Friend*

while a film director strives to catch the performance. Twiggy plays the unsophisticated young assistant stage manager suddenly thrust into top role when the star injures her ankle. (Glenda Jackson unbilled, cameos as the injured "star.") Twiggy acquits herself charmingly and professionally. She weaves a spell of her own both with her singing and dancing.
1971: Nomination: Best Adapted Score

BOY MEETS GIRL
1938, 86 mins, US
D: Lloyd Bacon **A:** James Cagney, Pat O'Brien, Marie Wilson, Ralph Bellamy, Frank McHugh, Dick Foran (Warner)

The filmization of *Boy Meets Girl* does not approximate the ripsnorting click of the play original by the Spewacks. Hollywood ribbing itself, in celluloid, sounds like a daring thing, and as the Warners have done it, it is. Director Lloyd Bacon, in fact, has out-Spewacked the dramatists in limning the madcap scenarists, as James Cagney and Pat O'Brien impersonate them. Cagney eclipses the somewhat more practical O'Brien in the buffoonery.

BOY ON A DOLPHIN
1957, 103 mins, US ▽ ▭
D: Jean Negulesco **A:** Alan Ladd, Sophia Loren, Clifton Webb, Alexis Minotis, Laurence Naismith, Jorge Mistral (20th Century-Fox)

Shot in Greece's Aegean Sea and environs, with the interiors filmed in Rome's Cinecitta Studios, *Boy on a Dolphin* develops into a chase that is a pleasant blend of archaeological research, quasi-cloak-and-dagger stuff, and earthy, primitive acquisitiveness. Ladd is the all-American-boy archaeologist; Webb the suave dastard; Loren a lustily appealing native Greek girl whose endowments fall automatically into character.
1957: Nomination: Best Scoring of a Dramatic Picture

BOYS
1996, 89 mins, US ▽ ⊙
D: Stacy Cochran **A:** Winona Ryder, Lukas Haas, Skeet Ulrich, John C. Reilly, Bill Sage, Wiley Wiggins (Interscope/PolyGram/Touchstone)

Stretched from a short story, this flat, oddly paced mystery/coming-of-age drama might have been better served sticking to that time length. Haas plays high-school senior Baker in a not-terribly-exclusive New England boys' school, bored with classes and dorky friends. A jolt of excitement arrives in the beautiful, if semiconscious, form of Ryder's mysterious, sophisticated 25-year-old, found helpless after being thrown from her horse. Baker spirits the young woman away to his dorm room, falling headlong into love and intrigue faster than you can say Holden Caulfield meets the Hardy Boys.

BOYS DON'T CRY
1999, 116 mins, US ▽ ⊙
D: Kimberly Peirce **A:** Hilary Swank, Chloe Sevigny, Peter Sarsgaard, Brendan Sexton III, Alison Folland, Alicia Goranson (Killer/Hart-Sharp)

This powerful tale of a young girl who disguises herself as a boy is anchored by two fully realized performances: Hilary Swank as the sexual misfit and Chloe Sevigny as her sensitive girlfriend. Story beings in Lincoln, NE, with the 20-year-old Brandon (Swank) getting a boyish haircut and preparing for a night out. Though warned by close friend Lonny (Matt McGrath) that "his" behavior signals big trouble, Brandon insists that her/his life is on the right track. As soon as he lays eyes on Lana (Sevigny), it's love at first sight. Turning point occurs when Brandon is thrown into the women's section of the local jail for traffic offenses and Lana comes to visit him. Brandon contends he's a case of "sexual identity crisis." With total understanding, Lana continues the affair. This first film boasts sharp cinematography and flawless acting.
1999: Best Actress (Hilary Swank)
Nomination: Best Supp. actress (Chloe Sevigny)

BOYS FROM BRAZIL, THE
1978, 123 mins, US ▽ ⊙
D: Franklin J. Schaffner **A:** Gregory Peck, Laurence Olivier, James Mason, Lilli Palmer, Uta Hagen, Denholm Elliott (Producer Circle/20th Century-Fox)

With two excellent antagonists in Gregory Peck and Laurence Olivier, *The Boys from Brazil* presents a gripping, suspenseful drama for nearly all of its two hours—then lets go at the end and falls into a heap. In a fine shift from his usual roles, Peck plays the evil Josef Mengele, a real-life character who murdered thousands of Jews, including many children, carrying out bizarre genetic experiments at Auschwitz in Poland. Olivier, slipping completely into the role of an elderly Jewish gentleman, is the Nazi hunter who brings him to bay.
1978: Nominations: Best Actor (Laurence Olivier), Editing, Original Score

BOYS FROM SYRACUSE, THE
1940, 73 mins, US
D: A. Edward Sutherland **A:** Allan Jones, Joe Penner, Martha Raye, Rosemary Lane, Charles Butterworth, Irene Hervey (Mayfair/Universal)

Writers have transformed the legiter (with a plot copped from Bill Shakespeare's *Comedy of Errors*) from a satire to plain burlesque. Martha Raye and Joe Penner are particularly outstanding in the comedy leads. Penner makes a droll slave. Raye, provided with the swell Rodgers and Hart tunes, gets good opportunity to use her pipes as well as exhibit her broad comedy style. All sorts of modernisms surround the toga-clad populace of ancient Greece. It gives plenty of opportunity for gags, and none is missed, even to the checkered chariot, with a meter.
1940: Nominations: Best B&W Art Direction, Special Effects

BOYS IN COMPANY C, THE
1978, 125 mins, US ⑲ ▭
D: Sidney J. Furie **A:** Stan Shaw, Andrew Stevens, James Canning, Michael Lembeck, Craig Wasson, Scott Hylands (Golden Harvest)

The Boys in Company C is a spotty but okay popcorn-trade drama about five young marines and how their lives were changed by duty in the Vietnam War. Stan Shaw heads the cast as a dope pusher who sees Vietnam as a major new connection, until he matures into a natural leader. Andrew Stevens, son of Stella Stevens, is a southern athlete who turns junkie in action. James Canning is an aspiring writer who records the bewildering and unnatural warfare.

BOYS IN THE BAND, THE
1970, 117 mins, US ⑲ ⊙
D: William Friedkin **A:** Kenneth Nelson, Frederick Combs, Leonard Frey, Cliff Gorman, Reuben Greene, Robert La Tourneaux (Leo/Cinema Center)

Boys in the Band drags. But despite its often tedious postulations of homosexual case histories instead of realistic dialogue, and the stagy posturing of the actors, the too literately faithful adaptation of Mart Crowley's off-Broadway swish-set piece has bitchy, backbiting humor, fascinating character studies, melodrama, and, most of all, perverse interest. As queen and host of the gay birthday party that is the film's only setting, Kenneth Nelson tells straight Peter White, it's like watching an accident, one is horrified and repulsed, but can't take his eyes away.

BOYS NEXT DOOR, THE
1985, 88 mins, US ⑲ ⊙
D: Penelope Spheeris **A:** Maxwell Caulfield, Charlie Sheen, Christopher McDonald, Hank Garrett, Patti D'Arbanville, Paul C. Dancer (New World/Republic Entertainment)

Two alienated and disturbed 18-year-olds, Roy Alston (Maxwell Caulfield) and Bo Richards (Charlie Sheen), decide to have a weekend in L.A. in which "anything goes." An eruption of violence begins with the brutal beating of a gas-station attendant. There are beatings and killings of a homosexual, a young couple, and a woman. With conventional clean-cut good looks, Caulfield and Sheen clearly resemble the title, but they fail to adequately project the angry stuff within.

BOYS' NIGHT OUT
1962, 113 mins, US
D: Michael Gordon **A:** Kim Novak, James Garner, Tony Randall, Howard Duff, Janet Blair, Anne Jeffreys (Kimco-Filmways/M-G-M)

Four grown men rent a town pad for the express purpose of sharing, one by one, an illicit evening per week with a voluptuous and accommodating blonde. Kim Novak slinks and purrs through the role of the object of all this extramarital monkeyshine. Tony Randall and Howard Morris (television funnyman in his screen bow) walk off with comedy honors.

BOYS ON THE SIDE
1995, 117 mins, US ⑲ ⊙ ▭
D: Herbert Ross **A:** Whoopi Goldberg, Mary-Louise Parker, Drew Barrymore, Matthew McConaughey, James Remar, Billy Wirth (New Regency/Hera/Warner)

Jane (Whoopi Goldberg), a semiemployed club singer, and Robin (Mary-Louise Parker), an uptight real-estate exec, meet by happenstance when they share a cross-country trip. Along the way they detour to visit Jane's friend Holly (Barrymore), who joins the twosome. The trip comes to a screeching halt when Robin falls ill and the three settle into a sort of nonnuclear family—one of the twists being that Jane, a lesbian, may have a romantic interest in her stricken roommate. Ross's direction and the stellar performances somehow create a real sense of tenderness and pathos.

BOYS' TOWN
1938, 96 mins, US Ⓥ ⊙
D: Norman Taurog A: Spencer Tracy, Mickey Rooney, Henry Hull, Leslie Fenton, Gene Reynolds, Bobs Watson (M-G-M)

The story of Father Flanagan's struggle to make a successful boys' home and then an entire community near Omaha, NB. Producers shrewdly have not made it entirely a paean of praise, but rather a realistic portrayal of Father Flanagan's untiring efforts to make something of wayward youngsters who otherwise might wind up in the electric chair. With Spencer Tracy and Mickey Rooney as the priest and the incorrigible lad, in tailor-made roles, *Boys Town* is a tearjerker of the first water. Rooney virtually takes the production away from the capable and veteran Tracy.
1938: Best Actor (Spencer Tracy), Original Story (Eleanore Griffin, Dore Schary)
Nominations: Best Picture, Director, Screenplay

BOY TEN FEET TALL, A
See: Sammy Going South

BOY WHO COULD FLY, THE
1986, 114 mins, US ⊙
D: Nick Castle A: Lucy Deakins, Jay Underwood, Bonnie Bedelia, Fred Savage, Colleen Dewhurst, Louise Fletcher (20th Century-Fox)

The Boy Who Could Fly is a well-intentioned film that deals with mental illness, suicide, and other weighty subjects and their effects on children in a general and understanding way. Story involves the special relationship between a sweet, patient teenage girl named Milly (Lucy Deakins) and her autistic neighbor Eric (Jay Underwood), who sits for hours on his roof directly across from her bedroom window with his arms outstretched as if ready to take off and fly. Deakins and Underwood handle their difficult roles with amazing grace.

BOY WHO STOLE A MILLION, THE
1961, 81 mins, UK
D: Charles Crichton A: Virgilio Texera, Maurice Reyna, Marianne Benet, Harold Kasket, Curt Christian, Bill Nagy (British Lion-Bryanston)

It's difficult to go wrong with the combo of an appealing kid, the inevitable pooch, and a chase in which the youngster's up against the world. This one is marred by some slightly uneasy dubbing and an occasional lapse into slapstick when only light comedy was needed, but overall it's a warm little piece. Mainly shot in locations in Valencia, Spain, the yarn concerns a likable youngster who finds that his taxi-driver father needs money to get his cab out of hock and decides to borrow some from the bank.

BOY WITH GREEN HAIR, THE
1948, 82 mins, US Ⓥ
D: Joseph Losey A: Pat O'Brien, Robert Ryan, Barbara Hale, Dean Stockwell, Richard Lyon, Walter Catlett (RKO)

Story is that of a war orphan who wakes to find his hair has turned green and the world turns topsy-turvy about him. Other kids jeer at him; adults are perturbed; even the kindly milkman turns against him when accused of bringing it about through his product. Through this parable about the unconscious cruelty of people to what is different, and the need for tolerance, runs another theme, that of antiwar preaching. When the boy meets children from war-orphan posters in a dream scene in the woods, and returns to annoy the townsfolk with the message that war is very bad—his green hair has thus acquired a meaning, to preach pacifism—the film hits a well-intentioned but false note.

BOYZ N THE HOOD
1991, 111 mins, US Ⓥ ⊙
D: John Singleton A: Larry Fishburne, Ice Cube, Cuba Gooding Jr., Nia Long, Morris Chestnut, Tyra Ferrell (New Deal)

Boyz N the Hood is an absorbing, smartly made dramatic encyclopedia of problems and ethics in the black community, 1991. Tale principally looks at the lives of three boys in South-Central L.A., beginning in '84 and then jumping, after a half hour, to the present, when the realities of violence hit the teens. Singleton constantly and effectively lays in the constant irritants and reminders of violence in the hood, the jets and choppers flying overhead, the ever-present dense smog, the random, easily provoked fights, the day-and-night wailing of police sirens, the nearby gunshots.
1991: Nominations: Best Director, Original Screenplay

BRADY BUNCH MOVIE, THE
1995, 88 mins, US Ⓥ ⊙
D: Betty Thomas A: Shelley Long, Gary Cole, Michael McKean, Jean Smart, Hen-

riette Mantel, Christopher Daniel Barnes (Paramount)

Two decades after their small-screen demise, the clean-cut crew is back in mythic form. Part homage, part spoof, the deft balancing act is a clever, engaging adaption—albeit culled from less-than-pedigreed source material. The Brady brood still live in a suburban split-level house and face the travails of job, home, and school. Papa Mike (Gary Cole) is hopelessly lost in a bygone era. The kids, who wear pastels, are relentlessly cute and obsessed with being popular. Mom (Shelley Long), ever smiling, is concerned about her kids without ever being less than chirpy. Into this time capsule arrives Ditmeyer (Michael McKean), an obstreperous real-estate agent who needs the Brady plot to close a massive land development deal.

BRAIN CANDY
(AKA: KIDS IN THE HALL: BRAIN CANDY)
1996, 88 mins, US Ⓥ
D: Kelly Makin **A:** David Foley, Bruce McCulloch, Kevin McDonald, Mark McKinney, Scott Thompson, Janeane Garofalo (Lakeshore/Paramount)

Television's Kids in the Hall make a relatively smooth, if offbeat, transition to the big screen with Brain Candy. The mad-scientist/corporate-heavy comedy is an odd combination of belly laughs and cerebral humor that will delight those familiar with the troupe's antics. Kids in the Hall are social satirists in an era when humor tends to be anarchic or about bowel movements. Though the story enjoys going off on tangents, it has a solid core that brings together its myriad strings.

BRAINDEAD
1992, 101 mins, New Zealand Ⓥ ⊙
D: Peter Jackson **A:** Timothy Balme, Diana Penalver, Elizabeth Moody, Ian Watkin, Brenda Kendall, Stuart Devenie (WingNut)

Kiwi gore specialist Peter Jackson goes for broke with an orgy of bad taste and splatter humor. Set in 1957, the standard zombie plot is played for laughs with a nerdy hero (Timothy Balme) whose domineering mum (Elizabeth Moody) is bitten by a rare carnivorous monkey. Mum goes rabid fast and attacks a nurse, who also becomes a zombie. The poor son locks the creatures in the cellar and tries to pacify them. Comic highlights include Balme literally reentering his mother's womb in a gore-spattered end.

BRAIN DONORS
1992, 79 mins, US Ⓥ ⊙
D: Dennis Dugan **A:** John Turturro, Bob Nelson, Mel Smith, Nancy Marchand, John Savident, George De La Pena (Paramount/Zucker)

The title Brain Donors sounds like a horror film but for those expecting a comedy, it is. Patterned after A Night at the Opera, Brain Donors badly wants to be a latter-day Marx Brothers pic. "Badly" is the key word. John Turturro is Roland T. Flakfizer, a Groucho-esque, ambulance-chasing attorney out to fleece a well-heeled and well-fed widow (Nancy Marchand). Bob Nelson and Mel Smith are his equally zany aides-de-camp, the former a clear Harpo derivative and the latter a British cabbie who at least never tries to play the piano.

BRAINSCAN
1994, 95 mins, US Ⓥ ⊙
D: John Flynn **A:** Edward Furlong, Frank Langella, T. Ryder Smith, Amy Hargreaves, Jamie Marsh, Victor Ertmanis (Roy)

Edward Furlong is well cast as a 16-year-old horror-movie fan, computer whiz, and social misfit who responds to an ad for a CD-ROM interactive virtual-reality game that promises to interface with your unconscious. Michael dreams of brutally stabbing a total stranger, then slicing off the dead man's foot. But when he wakes up, he finds the amputated foot is in his refrigerator. Once the first murder is out of the way, film becomes an exceedingly tame, only sporadically exciting thriller.

BRAIN SMASHER ...
A LOVE STORY
1993, 88 mins, US Ⓥ
D: Albert Pyun **A:** Andrew Dice Clay, Teri Hatcher, Yuji Okumoto, Deborah Van Valkenburgh, Brion James, Tim Thomerson (Kings Road)

Set in Portland, OR, pic concerns the adventures of two sisters involved in the smuggling and possession of a rare flower from China supposed to hold the secret to world domination. Constructed as clichés, the sisters' characters could not be more different: the elder (Deborah Van Valkenburgh) is a botanist, the younger (Teri Hatcher) is a model. The witless script uses the same joke over and over: the black-masked villains are continously referred to as Ninjas, despite their protests that they are Chinese, not Japanese.

BRAINSTORM
1983, 106 mins, US Ⓥ ⊙ ▭
D: Douglas Trumbull **A:** Christopher Walken, Natalie Wood, Louise Fletcher, Cliff Robertson, Jordan Christopher, Joe Dorsey (M-G-M/JF Prod.)

Brainstorm is a high-tech $18-million movie dependent on the visualization of a fascinating idea—a brain-wave device that gives characters the power to record and experience the physical, emotional, and intellectual sensations of another human being. Majority of players, including stars Christopher Walken and Wood, seem merely along for the ride. The film's acting surprise is Louise Fletcher, whose flinty, career scientist is a strong flavorful, workaholic portrait. The film offers irrefutable evidence that Natalie Wood's drowning (in Nov. 1981) did not cause the filmmakers to drastically rewrite or re-shoot scenes. Her work appears intact and, reportedly, only one scene had to be changed.

BRAINWAVES
1983, 81 mins, US Ⓥ
D: Ulli Lommel **A:** Keir Dullea, Suzanna Love, Vera Miles, Percy Rodrigues, Tony Curtis, Paul Willson (CinAmerica)

Brainwaves is a briskly told, engaging psychological thriller dealing with the sci-fi concept of transferring thought processes and memories electronically between different people. Suzanna Love toplines as a young San Francisco housewife who suffers a severe brain trauma (leaving her in a comalike trance). Her husband (Keir Dullea) and mother (Vera Miles) agree to an experimental medical procedure. Process goes awry when the donor turns out to be a murdered girl (Corinne Alphen).

BRAMBLE BUSH, THE
1960, 93 mins, US
D: Daniel Petrie **A:** Richard Burton, Barbara Rush, Jack Carson, Angie Dickinson, James Dunn, Tom Drake (Warner)

So-called mercy killing is the subject of *The Bramble Bush*, but the principals have such a brisk sex life that the subject rather gets lost in the bedclothes. Richard Burton is a young doctor who returns to his hometown to care for his best friend, Tom Drake, who is dying of Hodgkin's disease. Burton has a brief affair with Drake's wife, Barbara Rush, who becomes pregnant. Other complications include nurse Angie Dickinson's unrequited torch for Burton.

BRANDED
1950, 50 mins, US Ⓥ ⊙
D: Rudolph Mate **A:** Alan Ladd, Mona Freeman, Charles Bickford, Robert Keith, Joseph Calleia, Peter Hansen (Paramount)

Branded is a pleasing western that has a bit more plot and appeal than the average. Yarn finds Alan Ladd a no-good who figures on stealing the fortune of a cattle family by making like he's the long-lost son who was kidnapped at five. He doesn't figure, however, on falling for his sister and getting right fond of Mom and Pop. Ladd's inability to indicate successfully a transition from scoundrel to a kid with a 24-karat heart makes the story at times harder to digest than it should be.

BRANNIGAN
1975, 111 mins, UK Ⓥ ▭
D: Douglas Hickox **A:** John Wayne, Richard Attenborough, Judy Geeson, Mel Ferrer, John Vernon, Daniel Pilon (United Artists)

Okay John Wayne actioner, as a contemporary cop in London tracking down Chicago fugitive John Vernon. Richard Attenborough plays well against Wayne as an urbane Scotland Yard detective. Judy Geeson, as Wayne's policewoman escort, and Daniel Pilon, as a hired gun carrying Vernon's contract on Wayne's life, round out the principal players. Car chases, booby traps, etc. round out the formula plot turns.

BRASSED OFF
1996, 109 mins, UK Ⓥ ⊙
D: Mark Herman **A:** Pete Postlethwaite, Tara Fitzgerald, Ewan McGregor, Jim Carter, Philip Jackson, Peter Martin (Prominent/Channel 4)

There's a lot to enjoy in *Brassed Off,* but most of it is in the first half. This well-played, often very sparky dramedy about a northern English brass band composed of miners threatened with pit closure gets a bad attack of social realism in the latter stages. Film takes place during 1992, when the Conservative government launched another of its periodic programs of pit closures. Proud, stubborn Danny (Pete Postlethwaite) is determined to override his players' feelings that if the pit closes, so should the band. Movie ends up a true ensemble portrait of a community, wives included. Where it doesn't quite take flight is in its early promise of music being the defining, and elevating, force of the characters' lives.

BRASS TARGET
1978, 111 mins, US Ⓥ ⊙ ▭
D: John Hough **A:** Sophia Loren, John Cassavetes, George Kennedy, Robert Vaughn, Patrick McGoohan, Max von Sydow (M-G-M)

Brass Target, like *The Eagle Has Landed,* speculates on what might have happened to an historical figure in World War II. Writer Alvin Boretz has turned Frederick Nolan's speculative novel, *The Algonquin Project,* into a seemingly true-to-life revelation of how General George Patton actually died, not in a car accident, but at the hands of a clever paid assassin. Hough manages to interject some excitement into the action scenes, but these come few and far between. A generally competent cast is hamstrung by the material at hand.

BRAVE BULLS, THE
1951, 106 mins, US
D: Robert Rossen **A:** Mel Ferrer, Miroslava, Anthony Quinn, Eugene Iglesias, Jose Torvay (Columbia)

Columbia has a distinctive, offbeat picture in this treatment of Tom Lea's bestseller novel. There's nothing routine in the way it has been filmed, producer-director Robert Rossen apparently preferring to sacrifice some commercial values in favor of an adult handling of the story of a Mexican matador and life and death in the bull arena. Mel Ferrer has practically all of the footage and story emphasis, and dominates every bit of it.

BRAVEHEART
1995, 177 mins, US Ⓥ ⊙ ▭
D: Mel Gibson **A:** Mel Gibson, Sophie Marceau, Patrick McGoohan, Catherine McCormack, Angus McFayden, Ian Bannen (Icon/Ladd/20th Century-Fox)

A huge, bloody, and sprawling epic, Mel Gibson's second directing effort, *Braveheart,* is the sort of massive vanity piece that would be easy to disparage if it didn't essentially deliver. There are clearly elements of *Spartacus* running through the film in tone and inspiration, from the enormous battles to Gibson's William Wallace—a charismatic leader obsessed with freedom who rallies Scottish rebels against the tyrannical English king (Patrick McGoohan). The movie is not for the squeamish, demonstrating as it does in graphic detail the brutality of hand-to-hand combat—masterfully staged sequences that nevertheless become somewhat numbing after repeated exposure to all the bludgeoning and skew-

ering. McGoohan perhaps overplays his hand slightly as the villainous king. Gibson's Wallace does inspire, in both his messianic zeal and his unflinching heroism.
1995: Best Film, Best Cinematography, Best Sound Effects Editing, Best Makeup
Nominations: Director, Best Original Screenplay, Film Editing, Original Dramatic Score, Costume Design, Best Sound

BRAVE ONE, THE
1956, 100 mins, US Ⓥ ▭
D: Irving Rapper **A:** Michel Ray, Rodolfo Hoyos, Elsa Cardenas, Carlos Navarro, Joi Lansing, Fermin Rivera (RKO)

A kid's love for his pet themes this sentimentally moving story of a small Mexican boy who raises a fighting bull. The sensitive script was taken from a Robert Rich [pseudonym for blacklisted writer Dalton Trumbo] story based on an actual bullring incident that occurred in the Plaza de Toros in Barcelona in 1936 when a bull of much bravery and heart was pardoned to his young master.

BRAZIL
1944, 91 mins, US
D: Joseph Santley **A:** Tito Guizar, Virginia Bruce, Robert Livingston, Henry Da Silva, Edward Everett Horton, Roy Rogers (Republic)

With Ary Barroso, Latin-American composer who did the lilting "Brazil" song-dance number, contributing bulk of music, this is in the groove for all who like south-of-border music. Unlike too many films with Latin-American locales, this has a plot that adds up. Virginia Bruce, as author of *Why Marry a Latin?* is in Rio to get material for a book on Brazil. She's hardly given a warm welcome because of that book. Tito Guizar decides to give her an object lesson, and prove that Latins aren't such lousy lovers.
1944: Nominations: Best Scoring of a Musical Picture, Sound, Song ("Rio de Janeiro")

BRAZIL
1985, 142 mins, UK Ⓥ ⊙
D: Terry Gilliam **A:** Jonathan Pryce, Robert De Niro, Michael Palin, Kim Greist, Katherine Helmond, Ian Holm (Embassy)

Brazil offers a chillingly hilarious vision of the near future. Society is monitored by an insidious, tentacular ministry, and the film's protagonist, a diligent but unambitious civil servant, Sam Lowry—

played with vibrant comic imagination by Jonathan Pryce—becomes a victim of his own romantic delusions. He sees himself as a winged superhero, part Icarus, part Siegfried, soaring lyrically through the clouds to the tune of "Brazil," the old Xavier Cugat favorite, which as the film's ironic musical leitmotif, recurs in numerous mock variations. Robert De Niro shows delightful comic flair in a small, but succulent characterization of a proletarian superhero.
1985: Nominations: Best Original Screenplay, Art Direction

BREAKDANCE
See: Breakin'

BREAKDANCE 2
ELECTRIC BOOGALOO
See: Breakin' 2

BREAKDOWN
1997, 93 mins, US Ⓥ ⊙ ▭
D: Jonathan Mostow **A:** Kurt Russell, J. T. Walsh, Kathleen Quinlan, M. C. Gainey, Jack Noseworthy, Rex Linn (Paramount)

The fear of vast, wide-open spaces, not to mention demented redneck cowboys, fuels *Breakdown*, a tremendously tense thriller that expertly keeps tightening the screws throughout its taut running time. Jeff and Amy Taylor (Kurt Russell, Kathleen Quinlan) are on a drive moving from Massachusetts to California when they break down in a desolate part of the Southwest. They reluctantly accept an offer from truck driver Red (J. T. Walsh) to drive Amy to the nearest cafe, where she can call for assistance. When Jeff arrives at the diner, Amy isn't there and no one admits to having seen her. Russell emphasizes the reactions of a normal man to extreme events. Performance is functional, but very effective. Quinlan is off-screen most of the time, but the villains, led by the truly sinister Walsh, are all great.

BREAKER MORANT
1980, 106 mins, Australia Ⓥ ⊙
D: Bruce Beresford **A:** Edward Woodward, Jack Thompson, John Waters, Bryan Brown, Charles Tingwell, Lewis Fitz-Gerald (South Australian Film)

Harry "The Breaker" Morant (Edward Woodward) was an Englishman who went to Australia in the last century. When Britain and the Boers squared off against each other in South Africa, he volunteered. The nature of the war made prisoner taking a difficult business logistically, and the film

in no way tries to justify the killing of them. As an example to others, Morant and two other Australians were tried by court-martial. The execution sequence is profoundly affecting. Beresford then turns his audience into an unwitting jury; as a sheer exercise in manipulation, it approaches the masterful and is extremely effective.
1980: Nomination: Best Adapted Screenplay

BREAKFAST AT TIFFANY'S
1961, 115 mins, US Ⓥ ⊙
D: Blake Edwards **A:** Audrey Hepburn, George Peppard, Patricia Neal, Buddy Ebsen, Martin Balsam, Mickey Rooney (Paramount)

Out of the elusive, but curiously intoxicating Truman Capote fiction, scenarist George Axelrod has developed a surprisingly moving, stunningly visual motion picture. What makes *Tiffany's* an appealing tale is its heroine, Holly Golightly, a charming, wild, and amoral free spirit with a latent romantic streak. Axelrod's once-over-go-lightly erases the amorality and bloats the romanticism, but retains the essential spirit of the character, and, in the exciting person of Audrey Hepburn, she comes vividly to life on the screen. Henry Mancini's "Moon River," with lyrics by Johnny Mercer, is an enchanting tune.
1961: Best Song ("Moon River"), Scoring of a Dramatic Picture
Nominations: Best Actress (Audrey Hepburn), Adapted Screenplay, Color Art Direction

BREAKFAST CLUB, THE
1985, 97 mins, US Ⓥ ⊙
D: John Hughes **A:** Emilio Estevez, Judd Nelson, Molly Ringwald, Anthony Michael Hall, Ally Sheedy, Paul Gleason (A&M/Universal)

A cross section of five students—the jock, Miss Popularity, the ruffian, the nerd, and Miss Weirdo—are thrown together under adverse circumstances and cast aside all discord and unite under the sudden insight that none would be such a despicable little twit if mom or dad or both weren't so rotten. The querulous quintet are actually being forced to *spend the entire day at school on Saturday* for some previous infraction of the rules. Does director John Hughes really believe, as he writes here, that "when you grow up, your heart dies." It may. But not unless the brain has already started to rot with films like this.

BREAKFAST FOR TWO
1937, 67 mins, US
D: Alfred Santell A: Barbara Stanwyck, Herbert Marshall, Glenda Farrell, Eric Blore, Frank M. Thomas, Donald Meek (Kaufman/RKO)

Barrage of screwy situations take their cue from the efforts of a rich dame (Stanwyck) to straighten out a tippling waster (Marshall) and make him realize his responsibilities as the inheriting head of a steamship line. Also to land him as her husband. With such expert farceurs as Eric Blore and Glenda Farrell piling in to help keep things boiling, the plot gravitates from sly humor to fantastic goofiness.

BREAKFAST OF CHAMPIONS
1999, 110 mins, US Ⓥ ⊙
D: Alan Rudolph A: Bruce Willis, Albert Finney, Nick Nolte, Barbara Hershey, Glenne Headly, Lukas Haas (Buena Vista)

Breakfast of Champions is a game attempt to film Kurt Vonnegut Jr.'s 1976 satire on American greed and commercialism. Alan Rudolph's movie, a manic social-commentary comedy, fits awkwardly into today's blander Hollywood panorama. Dwayne Hoover (Bruce Willis) runs Midland City's most successful car dealership. However, Dwayne is a troubled man. His sales manager, Harry (Nick Nolte), likes to wear female undies, and his secretary Francine (Glenne Headly) is more interested in making big bucks than making her boss. Dwayne is also under investigation by the Environmental Protection Agency. Dwayne becomes convinced that the man with the solutions is Kilgore Trout (Albert Finney), a dime-store philosopher-hack. Finney, in a grouchy, hobolike role, is a major piece of miscasting. Willis and Nolte are good in the early going but are given no chance to step beyond their caricatures.

BREAK FOR FREEDOM
See: Albert, R.N.

BREAKHEART PASS
1976, 95 mins, US Ⓥ ⊙
D: Tom Gries A: Charles Bronson, Ben Johnson, Jill Ireland, Richard Crenna, Charles Durning, Ed Lauter (United Artists)

Production has Charles Bronson as a government undercover agent who trips up a gang of gunrunners, and a marvelous old steam train as setting for most of the plot. Working from a lean Alistair MacLean script (based on his own novel), director Tom Gries forges a brisk and polished cinematic tale in which the mysteries pile up as old No. 9 steams with troops and medical supplies to an army post gripped by a killer epidemic.

BREAKIN'
(UK: BREAKDANCE)
1984, 87 mins, US Ⓥ ⊙
D: Joel Silberg A: Lucinda Dickey, Adolfo Quinones, Michael Chambers, Ben Lokey, Christopher McDonald, Phineas Newborn III (Golan-Globus)

Breakin' is the first feature film entirely devoted to the breakdancing craze. Filmmakers have played it safe in focusing the action on a nice, middle-class white girl (Lucinda Dickey), whereas breakdancing is almost exclusively the domain of blacks and Latinos. Breezily entertaining on its own terms.

BREAKIN' 2
ELECTRIC BOOGALOO
1984, 94 mins, US Ⓥ ⊙
D: Sam Firstenberg A: Lucinda Dickey, Adolfo Quinones, Michael Chambers, Susie Bono, Harry Caesar, Jo de Winter (Cannon)

As a phenomenon, the hip-hop, breakdancing, sidewalk-graffiti, and rap-music culture lends itself well to a comic-book approach and to his credit director Sam Firstenberg doesn't try to interject too much reality into the picture. Ozone (Adolfo Shabba-Doo Quinones) and Turbo (Michael Boogaloo Shrimp Chambers) have turned their street-dancing talents to teaching other disadvantaged youths at a run-down community club.

BREAKING AWAY
1979, 100 mins, US Ⓥ ⊙
D: Peter Yates A: Dennis Christopher, Dennis Quaid, Daniel Stern, Jackie Earle Haley, Barbara Barrie, Robyn Douglass (20th Century-Fox)

Breaking Away is a thoroughly delightful light comedy, lifted by fine performances from Dennis Christopher and Paul Dooley. The story is nothing more than a triumph for the underdog through sports, this time cycle racing. Christopher is a heck of a bike rider with his three best friends (Quaid, Stern, and Earle) and such an adulator of Italian champions that he pretends to be Italian himself, even at home. Christopher meets pretty coed Robyn Douglass (an able film debut for her) and this ultimately brings the boys into conflict with the big men on campus that must finally be resolved in a big bike race.

1979: Best Original Screenplay **Nominations:** Best Picture, Director, Supp. Actress (Barbara Barrie), Adapted Score

BREAKING GLASS
1980, 104 mins, UK Ⓥ ⊠
D: Brian Gibson **A:** Phil Daniels, Hazel O'Connor, Jon Finch, Jonathan Pryce (Allied Stars/Film & General)

Breaking Glass presents a cynical, off-the-peg view of the postpunk record business. Cast opposite Hazel O'Connor, who's seen initially as a two-bit teenage performer, is Phil Daniels, a hustling would-be manager who teams with O'Connor. Ensuing success undermines the pair's tentative romantic partnership and, with the arrival of Jon Finch as an overly smooth-mannered producer, their professional interdependence as well.

BREAKING IN
1989, 91 mins, US Ⓥ ⊙
D: Bill Forsyth **A:** Burt Reynolds, Casey Siemaszko, Sheila Kelley, Lorraine Toussant, Albert Salmi, Harry Carey (Act III/Goldwyn)

Burt Reynolds plays a 61-year-old, graying, professional burglar with a gammy leg and the beginning of a pot-belly, in this charming buddy-caper movie. He teams up with young Mike Lefebb (Casey Siemaszko), the old-timer teaching the youngster the tricks of the trade. Reynolds plays with a relaxed charm that's wholly delightful.

BREAKING THE SOUND BARRIER
See: The Sound Barrier

BREAKING THE WAVES
1996, 159 mins, Denmark/France Ⓥ ⊠
D: Lars Von Trier **A:** Emily Watson, Stellan Skarsgard, Katrin Cartlidge, Jean-Marc Barr, Adrian Rawlins, Sandra Voe (Zentropa/La Sept)

A soaring story of love and devotion set in a remote, backward coastal village in north Scotland in the seventies, which deals with such weighty subjects as faith, sacrifice, and miracles. A sock performance from newcomer Emily Watson is the centerpiece of this distended spiritual journey. Bess (Watson), a shy, religious girl, is to marry Jan (Stellan Skarsgard), a raffish adventurer who works on a North Sea oil rig. When Jan is injured, he's confined to a hospital bed and begs Bess to entertain him by having sex with other

men and telling him about her experiences. Gradually, as her behavior becomes known, she's ostracized by the little community. The last section of the film rewards the viewer's patience with its power, and few will be unmoved by the finale.

BREAKOUT
1975, 96 mins, US Ⓥ ⊙ ⊠
D: Tom Gries **A:** Charles Bronson, Robert Duvall, Jill Ireland, John Huston, Randy Quaid, Sheree North (Persky-Bright/Vista)

Breakout is a cheap exploitation pic with Charles Bronson as a carefree aviator who rescues Robert Duvall from the Mexican prison frame-up engineered by his father-in-law, John Huston. Jill Ireland, Duvall's wife, wants him back badly. Director Tom Gries and the entire cast perform as though they all had better things to do.

BREATHLESS
1983, 100 mins, US Ⓥ ⊙
D: Jim McBride **A:** Richard Gere, Valerie Kaprisky, Art Metrano, John P. Ryan, William Tepper, Robert Dunn (Orion/Miko)

More than a little guts was required to remake such a certified film classic as Jean-Luc Godard's *Breathless*. But youthful audiences should find this update a suitably jazzy, sexy entertainment. On his way back from Las Vegas in a stolen car, Richard Gere accidentally mortally wounds a cop, then heads for the L.A. apartment of French UCLA student Valerie Kaprisky, with whom he's had just a brief fling. Gere's status as a sex star is certainly reaffirmed here. Fresh and attractive, Kaprisky does numerous scenes semiclad or less.

BREATHLESS
See: A Bout de Souffle

BREED APART, A
1984, 101 mins, US Ⓥ
D: Philippe Mora **A:** Rutger Hauer, Powers Boothe, Kathleen Turner, Donald Pleasence, John Dennis Johnston, Brion James (Hemdale/Sagittarius)

The visual splendors of North Carolina deserve top billing in *A Breed Apart*. The tale of romance and chicanery in the backwoods simply lacks reason, dramatic tension, or emotional involvement. The core of the story centers on an obsessive bird-egg collector who hires a noted climber (Powers Boothe) to illegally pilfer shells.

He must contend with their protector, a reclusive mystery man (Rutger Hauer).

BREEZY
1973, 106 mins, US
D: Clint Eastwood **A:** William Holden, Kay Lenz, Roger C. Carmel, Marj Dusay, Joan Hotchkis, Jamie Smith Jackson (Malpaso/Universal)

Clint Eastwood's third directorial effort is an okay contemporary drama about middle-aged William Holden falling for teenage Kay Lenz. Associate producer Jo Heims's script works the problem over with perhaps too much ironic, wry, or broad humor for solid impact.

BREWSTER MCCLOUD
1970, 104 mins, US Ⓥ ▭
D: Robert Altman **A:** Bud Cort, Sally Kellerman, Michael Murphy, William Windom, Shelley Duvall, Rene Auberjonois (M-G-M/Lion's Gate)

Brewster McCloud spares practically nothing in contemporary society. Literate original screenplay is a sardonic fairy tale for the times, extremely well cast and directed. Bud Cort heads the cast as a young boy, hiding in the depths of Houston's mammoth Astrodome, where he is building wings. He is, or is not, in reality a bird in human form. His guardian angel is Sally Kellerman. She can project more ladylike sensuality and emotion in a look than most actresses can in an hour.

BREWSTER'S MILLIONS
1945, 79 mins, US Ⓥ
D: Allan Dwan **A:** Dennis O'Keefe, Helen Walker, Eddie Rochester Anderson, June Havoc, Gail Patrick, Mischa Auer (Small/United Artists)

Play, first produced in 1907, remains somewhat dated despite introduction of wartime atmosphere. The young, handsome soldier finds he's inherited 8 million bucks. He's got to spend $1 million in two months, or lose the entire estate. Even with the help of a flop musical, a bankrupt banker, the stock market, the racetrack, and a spending society gal, he has trouble. *Millions* is a broad farce, of course, and gets over as such.

1945: Nomination: Best Scoring of a Dramatic Picture

BREWSTER'S MILLIONS
1985, 97 mins, US Ⓥ ⊙
D: Walter Hill **A:** Richard Pryor, John Candy, Lonette McKee, Stephen Collins, Jerry Orbach, Pat Hingle (Universal)

It's hard to believe a comedy starring Richard Pryor and John Candy is no funnier than this one is, but director Walter Hill has overwhelmed the intricate genius of each with constant background action, crowd confusions, and other endless distractions. All the frenetic motion never disguises the writers' failure to do much of distinction with the familiar story. Though Pryor plays it likably enough, he never seems particularly deserving of the fun, excitement, and brief luxury he falls into in having to spend $30 million in 30 days, much less the $300 million inheritance he stands to receive if he succeeds.

BRIDE, THE
1985, 118 mins, US Ⓥ ⊙
D: Franc Roddam **A:** Sting, Jennifer Beals, Anthony Higgins, Clancy Brown, David Rappaport, Geraldine Page (Columbia-Delphi III/Colgems)

Production departs from the host of other *Frankensteins* in its bright visual look, its lush Maurice Jarre score, its view of women, its younger characters, and its romantic scope. Pic opens with a jolting laboratory sequence, when Sting as Baron Frankenstein brings to life the gauze-wrapped Jennifer Beals as the doctor's original monster creation looks on with frothing agitation. In opting to tone down the horror aspect of the genre, producer Victor Drai and his team have created another kind of monster: a *Frankenstein* movie that's not scary.

BRIDE CAME C.O.D., THE
1941, 94 mins, US Ⓥ
D: William Keighley **A:** James Cagney, Bette Davis, Stuart Erwin, Jack Carson, Eugene Pallette, George Tobias (Warner)

In handing Davis a comedy assignment, Warners go all out in also making her the victim of continual physical and mental violence. She's dirtied up in a mine; acquires three doses of cacti needles in periodic falls; and even exposes her posterior as target for well-directed shots from Cagney's improvised slingshot. Cagney is the owner of a plane about to be repossessed by the finance company. Davis clicks strongly as the oil heiress, displaying a flair for comedy.

BRIDE COMES HOME, THE
1935, 83 mins, US
D: Wesley Ruggles **A:** Claudette Colbert, Fred MacMurray, Robert Young, William Collier Sr., Donald Meek, James Colin (Paramount)

The Bride Comes Home runs Claudette

171

Colbert and Fred MacMurray over a not-too-serious steeplechase of minor frictions and clashes. To supply the missing apex of the triangle is Robert Young, a frankly unaggressive but beaming son of $3 million. It's a made-to-measure framework for Colbert, presenting her in the always attractive position of a young lady beset by two lovers.

BRIDE FOR SALE
1949, 87 mins, US
D: William D. Russell A: Claudette Colbert, Robert Young, George Brent, Max Baer, Gus Schilling (RKO/Crest)

Colbert does glib work as a tax expert for the accounting firm conducted by Brent. She figures to find the perfect husband, with suitable bankroll, by casing the returns the firm makes out. Brent wants to keep her on the job, so enlists aid of Young to make like an eligible male, and woo the maiden. On that basis of fun, William D. Russell's direction marches the plot and the players along a broad path of antics.

BRIDE OF FRANKENSTEIN
1935, 73 mins, V ⊙
D: James Whale A: Boris Karloff, Colin Clive, Valerie Hobson, Ernest Thesiger, Elsa Lanchester, O. P. Heggie (Universal)

Perhaps a bit too much time is taken up by the monster and too little by the woman created to be his bride. Frankenstein, the monster's creator, is this time sorry and tries to crawl out, but Dr. Pretorious forces him to go into more life manufacturing, having conceived the idea of a woman to act as the monster's playmate. Karloff manages to invest the character with some subtleties of emotion that are surprisingly real and touching. Runner-up position from an acting standpoint goes to Ernest Thesiger as Dr. Pretorious, a diabolic characterization if ever there was one. Elsa Lanchester handles two assignments, being first in a preamble as author Mary Shelley and then the created woman.
1935: Nomination: Best Sound

BRIDE OF RE-ANIMATOR
1991, 97 mins, US V ⊙
D: Brian Yuzna A: Jeffrey Combs, Bruce Abbott, Claude Earl Jones, Fabiana Udenio, David Gale, Kathleen Kinmont (Wildstreet)

Fans of Re-Animator will probably dig this campy gorefest sequel. Jeffrey Combs returns in top form as H. P. Lovecraft's dotty scientist Herbert West, this time in-tent on joining the trendy club of would-be Dr. Frankensteins creating a female monster (à la Frankenhooker, Steel & Lace, Eve of Destruction). The over-the-top acting that Gordon encouraged in Re-Animator is continued here, with Combs particularly adept at the darkly comic throwaway line. Overabundance of gore will turn off mainstream viewers, however. Tall actress Kathleen Kinmont is a good choice for the monster, with her stitched-together, see-through torso.

BRIDE OF VENGEANCE
1949, 92 mins, US
D: Mitchell Leisen A: Paulette Goddard, John Lund, Macdonald Carey, Raymond Burr (Paramount)

The poisonous Borgias, who introduced the lethal Mickey Finn to early-day Italy, provide the highly romantic adventure basis for Bride of Vengeance. It's escapist material, done with a lightness that doesn't always fit its adventuring, but with enough swagger to back up the story. Title derives from Borgia role played by Paulette Goddard, who marries John Lund, head of an Italian state, to avenge the death of an earlier husband, whom she believes Lund had killed. Plot has plenty of bloodthirsty moments.

BRIDE WORE BOOTS, THE
1946, 85 mins, US
D: Irving Pichel A: Barbara Stanwyck, Robert Cummings, Diana Lynn, Patric Knowles, Robert Benchley, Natalie Wood (Paramount)

The Bride Wore Boots is never as funny as its makers intended. It is only in the final 10 minutes or so, when the story goes slapstick with a vengeance, that comedy rates a genuinely hearty response. Barbara Stanwyck and Robert Cummings are seen as married couple with divided interests. Stanwyck loves horses, in fact operates a breeding farm. Cummings is an author and hates horses. The wife hates the stuffy Civil War relics wished off on her husband by adoring Confederate Dames societies. Star trio, which has Diana Lynn as a young southern vamp, make frantic efforts to put the material over.

BRIDGE AT REMAGEN, THE
1969, 116 mins, US V ⊡
D: John Guillermin A: George Segal, Robert Vaughn, Ben Gazzara, Bradford Dillman, E. G. Marshall, Peter Van Eyck (United Artists)

The taking of a bridge provides the basis for an actionful World War II melodrama. This time out it's the Ludendorff Bridge over the Rhine in the Remagen area, scene of desperate fighting for its control by both American and German forces. Chief interest rests in the performance of George Segal, a hard-boiled American platoon leader, as he and his men attempt to accomplish the orders of their high command.

BRIDGE ON THE RIVER KWAI, THE
1957, 161 mins, UK ⓋⓄ ▭
D: David Lean **A:** William Holden, Alec Guinness, Jack Hawkins, Sessue Hayakawa, Geoffrey Horne, James Donald (Horizon)

A gripping drama, expertly put together and handled with skill in all departments, filmed against the exotic background of the steaming jungles and mountains of Ceylon. A story of the futility of war in general, the underlying message is never permitted to impede. Hayakawa is the commandant of a Japanese prison camp in which Holden, a Yank sailor posing as a commander, is a prisoner. Guinness is a British colonel who clashes immediately with Hayakawa over the latter's insistence that officers as well as men must work on the railroad bridge being built over the River Kwai. Guinness wins and then proceeds to guide his men in building a superb bridge to prove the mettle of British soldiers under any conditions. He etches an unforgettable portrait of the typical British army officer, strict, didactic, and serene in his adherence to the book.
1957: Best Picture, Director, Actor (Alec Guinness), Adapted Screenplay, Cinematography, Score, Editing
Nomination: Best Supp. Actor (Sessue Hayakawa)

BRIDGES AT TOKO-RI, THE
1955, 102 mins, US Ⓥ Ⓞ
D: Mark Robson **A:** William Holden, Grace Kelly, Fredric March, Mickey Rooney, Robert Strauss, Robert Strauss, Robert McGraw (Paramount)

James A. Michener's hard-hitting novel of the Korean conflict finds slick translation in this topflight war spectacle. Mark Robson, in his taut direction, catches the spirit of the navy and what it stood for in the Korean War. Narrative drives toward the climactic bombing by US fliers of the five bridges at Toko-Ri, which span a strategic pass in Korea's interior. Here the

story of William Holden, a reserve officer recalled to service, unfolds. March delivers a sock portrayal of the admiral. As Holden's wife, Grace Kelly is warmly sympathetic.
1955: Best Special Effects
Nomination: Best Editing

BRIDGES OF MADISON COUNTY, THE
1995, 135 mins, US Ⓥ Ⓞ
D: Clint Eastwood **A:** Clint Eastwood, Meryl Streep, Annie Corley, Victor Slezak, Jim Haynie (Amblin/Malpaso/Warner)

Clint Eastwood and Co. have performed a considerable job of alchemy, turning Robert James Waller's slender, treacly romance into a handsomely crafted, beautifully acted adult love story. Photographer Robert Kincaid stops at the farmhouse of Francesca Johnson (Meryl Streep), whose husband and two teenage kids are out of town, to ask directions to the area's photogenic covered bridges, and the two embark on a four-day fling that deeply marks both of them for the rest of their lives. It's Douglas Sirk–type women's weepie material, handled by Eastwood with the utmost tact, maturity, and restraint. The attention to detail, in both character and rural atmosphere, is superb. Onscreen together a great majority of the time, the two leads come up aces.
Nominations: Best Actress (Meryl Streep)

BRIDGE TOO FAR, A
1977, 175 mins, UK Ⓥ Ⓞ ▭
D: Richard Attenborough **A:** Dirk Bogarde, James Caan, Michael Caine, Sean Connery, Edward Fox, Elliott Gould (United Artists)

Futility and frustration are the overriding emotional elements in Joseph E. Levine's sprawling production about a 1944 attempt to expedite the end of the Second World War by an enormous paratroop operation involving a series of bridges leading to Germany. The first part of the film introduces senior officers Dirk Bogarde, Sean Connery, Gene Hackman, Michael Caine, Anthony Hopkins, and Edward Fox as the plans are outlined. Later, as operations begin, periodic appearances are made by cocky Robert Redford, wisecracking Elliott Gould, stolid Ryan O'Neal, and James Caan. Hardy Kruger, Maximilian Schell, and Wolfgang Priess represent different levels of German military thinking. Laurence Olivier and Liv

Ullmann are two Dutch residents who attend to the wounded.

BRIEF ENCOUNTER
1945, 83 mins, UK Ⓥ

D: David Lean A: Celia Johnson, Trevor Howard, Stanley Holloway, Joyce Carey, Cyril Raymond, Valentine Dyall (Cineguild)

Celia Johnson as the small-town mother whose brief encounter with a doctor, encumbered with a wife and kids, plunges her into a love affair from which she struggles vainly to escape, is terrific. Trevor Howard, as the doctor, gives a performance calculated to win the sympathy of femmes of all ages. As for the dumb husband, Cyril Raymond manages to invest the stodgy character with a lovable quality.
1946: Nominations: Best Director, Actress (Celia Johnson), Screenplay

BRIGADOON
1954, 108 mins, US Ⓥ ⊙ ▭

D: Vincente Minnelli A: Gene Kelly, Van Johnson, Cyd Charisse, Elaine Stewart, Barry Jones (M-G-M)

In transferring *Brigadoon*, a click as a Broadway musical play, to the screen, Metro has medium success. Among the more noteworthy points are the score and the stage-type settings that represent the plot's [Scottish] Highland locale, even though they are the major contribution to the feeling that this is a filmed stage show. The musical play tells of two New Yorkers who happen on Brigadoon on the one day that it is visible every 100 years. A wedding is to take place and Kelly and Van Johnson, the modern-day males, join in the fun. Particularly Kelly, who falls for Cyd Charisse heart enough to be willing to join his sweetheart in the long ago.
1954: Nomination: Best Color Costume Design, Color Art Direction, Sound

BRIGHAM YOUNG
1940, 112 mins, US

D: Henry Hathaway A: Tyrone Power, Linda Darnell, Dean Jagger, Brian Donlevy, Jane Darwell, John Carradine (20th Century-Fox)

Taking the favorable factual aspects of the trek of Mormons to the west, and combining them with well-concocted fictional ingredients, picture emerges as an epic filmization of early-American history. Through it all runs a minor romance between Tyrone Power and Linda Darnell; and a more important impress of man and wife on the parts of Young (Dean Jagger) and his first and favorite spouse, Mary Ann (Mary Astor). Jagger brings to the character of the Mormon leader a personable humanness and sympathy.

BRIGHT ANGEL
1990, 94 mins, US Ⓥ

D: Michael Fields A: Dermot Mulroney, Lili Taylor, Sam Shepard, Valerie Perrine, Sheila McCarthy, Burt Young (Hemdale-Northwood/Bright Angel)

Basically a road movie about a pair of young lovers who become involved in crime, Michael Fields's first feature as a director boasts a full cast list of near-perfect performances. The intelligent and spare screenplay is by Richard Ford. The setting is Montana. George Russell (Dermot Mulroney), 18, is attracted to Lucy (Lili Taylor). She needs to get to the Wyoming town where her brother's in prison, and George offers to drive her. Much of the film is taken up with the relationship between the naive and good-hearted George and the old-beyond-her-years Lucy as they journey to their destination, and with the characters they become involved with. Fields and Ford avoid clichés: no sex scenes (but a great deal of sexual tension); no shoot-outs (but an agonizing sequence of suspense); no neat ending.

BRIGHT LIGHTS, BIG CITY
1988, 110 mins, US Ⓥ ⊙

D: James Bridges A: Michael J. Fox, Kiefer Sutherland, Phoebe Cates, Swoosie Kurtz, Frances Sternhagen, Tracy Pollan (United Artists/Mirage)

This novel-cum-feature-film (from Jay McInerney's book) is a distinctly morose and maudlin journey tl.rough one man's destructive period of personal loss. Opening scene establishes Michael J. Fox as a lonesome barfly with a cocaine habit in the Big Apple. Fox is cast here as Jamie, a would-be writer marking time as a fact checker for literary giant *Gotham* magazine. Jamie quickly slides so badly that he's fired during a scene with editorial chief, Frances Sternhagen—an exchange that points up the benefit of placing the youthful Fox in situations with seasoned veterans.

BRIGHTON BEACH MEMOIRS
1986, 108 mins, US Ⓥ ⊙

D: Gene Saks A: Blythe Danner, Bob Dishy, Brian Dillinger, Stacey Glick, Judith Ivey, Lisa Waltz (Rastar)

The first of Neil Simon's semiautobiographical [stage] trilogy, set in 1937 in a lower-middle-class section of Brooklyn, story details assorted life crises of members of the Jerome family, hardworking moral Jews whose problems are all taken to heart by Mama Kate, played by Blythe Danner. Performances are skilled all the way through.

BRIGHTON ROCK
(US: YOUNG SCARFACE)
1948, 92 mins, UK Ⓥ
D: John Boulting **A:** Richard Attenborough, Hermione Baddeley, William Hartnell, Carol Marsh, Harcourt Williams, Nigel Stock (Boulting Brothers)

This tends to prove that Britain can turn out a gangster picture as brutal as any Hollywood had devised. Story is laid in prewar seaside resort Brighton, where two razor-slashing race gangs are feuding. It is difficult to believe that any gang that included William Hartnell could be led by Richard Attenborough. Hartnell is so much more the gangster type than Attenborough that it is obvious that an exchange of parts would have made the film more credible. Acting honors are collared by that seasoned actress Hermione Baddeley, making Ida, the concert artist, a sympathetic character.

BRIMSTONE & TREACLE
1982, 87 mins, UK Ⓥ
D: Richard Loncraine **A:** Sting, Denholm Elliott, Joan Plowright, Suzanna Hamilton, Benjamin Whitrow, Dudley Sutton (PFH/ Namara)

Strong on ambience and suggested terror, *Brimstone & Treacle* is a handsomely mounted gothic tale. Sting, rock singer from the Police, makes a strong impression in his first major film role. Playing a young drifter, Sting pretends to be a friend of Elliott's crippled daughter (Suzanna Hamilton). Elliott remains cynical but his wife (Joan Plowright) sees only his kindness and insists he stay with them overnight. Soon he's wormed his way into the troubled household. He frees Plowright of her domestic chores. He molests Hamilton, and has his eyes on money and jewels in the house. The performances, all excellent, are played slightly off-center so one never knows whether the action will darken or veer into comedy.

BRINGING OUT THE DEAD
1999, 120 mins, US Ⓥ ⊙ ▭
D: Martin Scorsese **A:** Nicolas Cage,

Patricia Arquette, John Goodman, Ving Rhames, Tom Sizemore, Marc Anthony (Rudin/ Cappa-De Fina/Paramount/ Touchstone)

Martin Scorsese teams for the fourth time with scripter Paul Schrader for *Bringing Out the Dead,* a quintessential New York tale of the occupational hazards of a paramedic, splendidly played by Nicolas Cage. Dark humor, amusing moments, visual pyrotechnics, and bravura acting make more palatable an intense movie full of gory details. Frank Pierce (Cage) is a man on the edge, an insomniac loner who works the graveyard shift and undergoes a severe spiritual crisis that may lead to self-destruction or redemption. The film follows Frank over the course of three days and three nights as he threatens to collapse from exhaustion. Each night, he teams with a different partner (John Goodman, Tom Sizemore, Ving Rhames), and his interactions with them provide the film's texture. Arquette gives a merely adequate performance as a former druggie, but rest of the cast is first-rate.

BRINGING UP BABY
1938, 102 mins, US ⊙
D: Howard Hawks **A:** Katharine Hepburn, Cary Grant, Charlie Ruggles, Barry Fitzgerald, May Robson, Walter Catlett (RKO)

This harum-scarum farce comedy, is constructed for maximum of laughs. Wacky developments include an heiress's pursuit of a zoology professor; a pet leopard, Nissa, who makes a playmate of Asta, a redoubtable Scotch terrier; an escaped wild leopard from the circus; a forgetful ex-big-game hunter; a scientifically minded brain specialist; and a tippling gardener. Hepburn is invigorating as the madcap deb. Grant performs his role to the hilt. Charlie Ruggles does wonders with a minor characterization.

BRING ME THE HEAD OF ALFREDO GARCIA
1974, 112 mins, US Ⓥ
D: Sam Peckinpah **A:** Warren Oates, Isela Vega, Gig Young, Robert Webber, Helmut Dantine, Kris Kristofferson (Optimus/ Estudios Churubosco)

Bring Me the Head of Alfredo Garcia is turgid melodrama at its worst. Warren Oates stars as an expatriate American piano-bar musician making a stab for riches in Mexico by finding the never-seen title character sought by an outraged Mexican father. Naturally the search brings unhappiness, and being a Peckinpah film, lots and lots of people get killed along the way, as well as audience interest.

BRING ON THE GIRLS
1945, 96 mins, US
D: Sidney Lanfield **A:** Veronica Lake, Sonny Tufts, Eddie Bracken, Marjorie Reynolds (Paramount)

Bring On the Girls is a lightweight musical with some sprightly tunes by Jimmy McHugh and Harold Adamson. It's the story of a young millionaire with a proclivity for becoming engaged to dames who are out only for the money. So he joins the navy, where he won't be so well known, but he becomes linked to a gold-digging ciggie girl (Veronica Lake), and thereafter the travail concerns whether or not Lake will get him.

BRITANNIA HOSPITAL
1982, 115 mins, UK ♡
D: Lindsay Anderson **A:** Leonard Rossiter, Graham Crowden, Malcolm McDowell, Joan Plowright, Jill Bennett, Marsha Hunt (EMI/General)

Britannia Hospital is a witty, unsparing exposé of British manners and mores. The film revolves around a strike at a hospital where a royal personage is expected. This gives rise to union complaints about privileges showered on monied notables when the National Health system was supposed to make medicine equally available for all. Medics' own misuse of National Health funds is pilloried in no uncertain style. Malcolm McDowell is rightly overacting as the reporter who loses his head. Leonard Rossiter copes staunchly as the beset hospital director. Marsha Hunt, Jill Bennett, and Joan Plowright do fine cameo work as nurse, doctor, and the union head.

BRITANNIA MEWS
1949, 91 mins, UK
D: Jean Negulesco **A:** Maureen O'Hara, Dana Andrews, Sybil Thorndike, Wilfrid Hyde White, Fay Compton (20th Century-Fox)

Picture tells the simple story of a girl on the better side of the street who falls in love with a drunken art teacher in the mews. By marrying him she is ostracized by her family. Production is staged almost entirely in the sordid surroundings of Britannia Mews. The only live characterization comes from Sybil Thorndike as a repulsive hag.

BRITISH AGENT
1934, 75 mins, US
D: Michael Curtiz **A:** Leslie Howard, Kay Francis, William Gargan, Philip Reed, Irving Pichel, J. Carrol Naish (First National/Warner)

A powerful yarn of espionage during the early days of the Russian Revolution. Yarn has Howard spotted in Russia, just prior to the rebellion, as the British consul general. England doesn't want the hero to butt in. But he is so determined in his belief that Russia must be kept in the war that he conducts a one-man campaign against Bolshevism. Romantic element is via Francis, cast as Lenin's secretary.

BROADCAST NEWS
1987, 131 mins, US ♡ ⊙
D: James L. Brooks **A:** William Hurt, Albert Brooks, Holly Hunter, Robert Prosky, Lois Chiles, Jack Nicholson (Gracie/20th Century-Fox)

Enormously entertaining, *Broadcast News* is an inside look at the personal and professional lives of three TV journalists. Brooks gently punctures the self-importance of his characters with a sly satirical edge. Where veteran reporter Aaron Altman (Albert Brooks) and hard-nosed producer Jane Craig (Holly Hunter) are seasoned professionals with great talent, Tom Grunick (William Hurt) is a slick ex-sportscaster who knows how to turn on the charm and seduce an audience. But is it news? his colleagues wonder. Hunter is simply superb barking out orders. As the neurotic but brilliant reporter, Brooks gives an insightful performance. As the hardest of the characters to read, Hurt does a good job keeping up the mystery.
1987: Nominations: Best Picture, Actor (William Hurt), Actress (Holly Hunter), Supp. Actor (Albert Brooks), Original Screenplay, Cinematography, Editing

BROADWAY
1929, 105 mins, US
D: Paul Fejos **A:** Glenn Tryon, Evelyn Brent, Merna Kennedy, Thomas E. Jackson, Robert Ellis, Paul Porcasi (Universal)

U paid $200,000 for the screen rights to Phil Dunning's smash. As a melodrama with music, the screenplay expands way beyond the stage production as well as in the melodramatic portion with its street scenes. U's own film players hold the leads. Glenn Tryon as the hick hoofer does nobly, discounting the singing-and-dancing. Paul Fejos directs, with much judgment, if little novelty. His work and the cutting, however, do much to make this film. The final scene is in Technicolor, giving a corking finish to a corking picture.

BROADWAY
1942, 89 mins, US
D: William A. Seiter A: George Raft, Pat O'Brien, Broderick Crawford, Janet Blair, Anne Gwynne, Marjorie Rambeau (Universal)

Universal's modernized presentation of *Broadway* could easily be the autobiography of George Raft. Picture opens with Raft wandering onto Broadway, alone; he stops at a cellar. He starts reminiscing to the old night watchman about the heyday of the spot as a cabaret during the lush Prohibition era when Raft got his start as a hoofer in the place. In addition to swift dramatic pace, provided both in script and direction, picture is studded with a group of excellent performances. Raft clicks solidly.

BROADWAY BILL
1934, 90 mins, US ⓥ
D: Frank Capra A: Warner Baxter, Myrna Loy, Walter Connolly, Helen Vinson, Douglas Dumbrille, Raymond Walburn (Columbia)

Broadway Bill has a story, a tip-top cast, and Frank Capra's direction. The troubles and jams of Dan Brooks (Baxter) as hopeful owner of a stouthearted horse, Broadway Bill, supply the action. Brooks is broke, with the entry fee unpaid and the big race a few days off. The horse gets sick, then recovers. The horse is attached for the feed bill. Brooks is jailed for fighting the sheriff. He's released just in time. The jockey is fixed by gamblers. Etcetera. Raymond Walburn is aces in the finely drawn role of a con man who touts so well he believes it himself.

BROADWAY DANNY ROSE
1984, 86 mins, US ⓥ ⊙
D: Woody Allen A: Woody Allen, Mia Farrow, Nick Apollo Forte, Milton Berle, Sandy Baron, Corbett Monica (Orion)

Broadway Danny Rose is a delectable diversion. Allen's perfect as a small-time, good-hearted Broadway talent agent, giving his all for a roster of hopeless clients. Agent's career is fondly recalled, focusing mainly on Allen's attempt to revive the career of an aging, overweight, boozing lounge singer, beautifully played by Nick Apollo Forte. One of Forte's many problems is a floozy of a girlfriend. This sunglassed bimbo is actually on screen for several minutes before most of the audience catches on that she's Mia Farrow.
1984: Nominations: Best Director, Original Screenplay

BROADWAY MELODY, THE
1929, 104 mins, US ⓥ ⊙
D: Harry Beaumont A: Anita Page, Bessie Love, Charles King, Jed Prouty, Kenneth Thomson, Edward Dillon (M-G-M)

Broadway Melody, the first screen musical, tells of a vaudeville sister team, with the older girl engaged to a song-and-dance boy in a Broadway revue. Latter goes for the kid sister, now grown up, who starts playing with one of the show's backers to stand off the boy and spare the blow to her sister. In between are the troubles of the femme team making the revue grade. Both girls, Bessie Love as the elder sister and Anita Page as the youngster, are great in their respective climaxes, especially Love. Charlie King looks as good as he plays and plants comedy lines as they should be delivered.
1928/29: Best Picture
Nominations: Best Director, Actress (Bessie Love)

BROADWAY MELODY OF 1936
1935, 102 mins, US ⓥ ⊙
D: Roy Del Ruth A: Jack Benny, Eleanor Powell, Robert Taylor, Una Merkel, Sid Silvers, Buddy Ebsen (M-G-M)

Everything revolves about Eleanor Powell, Robert Taylor and June Knight, the menace. She's the Park Avenue bankroll for a forthcoming musical comedy. Columnist Jack Benny had been building up a phony French comedienne, and so when Taylor fails to recognize his adolescent sweetheart from Albany, she (Powell) essays an accent, bizarre makeup, and goals everybody with her personality and her stepping as the pseudo-French star. Songs are all good. "Broadway Rhythm," sung by Frances Langford and with dance specialties by Powell, Nick Long Jr., Knight, and the Ebsens, is a corking creation.
1935: Best Dance Direction ("I've Got a Feeling You're Fooling")
Nominations: Best Picture, Original Story

BROADWAY MELODY OF 1938
1937, 115 mins, US ⓥ ⊙
D: Roy Del Ruth A: Robert Taylor,

Eleanor Powell, George Murphy, Binnie Barnes, Judy Garland, Sophie Tucker (M-G-M)

Much better than its predecessor of 1936, and not far behind the original 1929 *Broadway Melody*. Sophie Tucker is somewhere past 40, but when she walks on the screen something happens. Then she pushes Garland, still in her teens, into the camera foreground. Young Garland gives them "Everybody Sing." Each does numbers solo later on. Judy sings a plaint to Clark Gable's photograph which is close to great screen acting. Then, to top it off, Soph does "Your Broadway and My Broadway." Most of the rest is just filler-in between the Tucker and the Garland numbers.

BROADWAY MELODY OF 1940
1940, 102 mins, US ⓥ ⊙
D: Norman Taurog A: Fred Astaire, Eleanor Powell, George Murphy, Frank Morgan, Ian Hunter, Florence Rice (M-G-M)

Long on its display of corking dance routines and numbers by Fred Astaire, Eleanor Powell, and George Murphy, mounted against elaborate production backgrounds, *Broadway Melody of 1940* slides through at moderately satisfying entertainment. This is the first teaming of Astaire and Powell in a filmusical. The result is as to be expected, both presenting several new and applause-generating numbers. But the numbers are too many and too extended for general purposes. Murphy gains attention with a top performance as the hoofer partner of Astaire.

BROADWAY RHYTHM
1944, 115 mins, US
D: Roy Del Ruth A: George Murphy, Ginny Simms, Charles Winninger, Gloria de Haven, Lena Horne (M-G-M)

Broadway Rhythm is a typical backstage filmusical wheeled out in the usual Metro elaborate and colorful style. Displaying group of top-rank specialties and names among the entertainers, the fragile and hodge-podge yarn stops periodically while the guest stars appear. Lena Horne socks over two songs the Gershwins' "Somebody Loves Me" and "Brazilian Boogie" by Hugh Martin and Ralph Blane, and both are smartly presented for maximum effect.

BROADWAY TO HOLLYWOOD
1933, 88 mins, US
D: Willard Mack A: Alice Brady, Frank Morgan, Madge Evans, Russell Hardie, Jackie Cooper, Mickey Rooney (M-G-M)

It's all Alice Brady and Frank Morgan's picture in sterling characterizations as the original hoofing Hacketts of Tony Pastor's time and down through the years into the third generation. Madge Evans and Russell Hardie sustain the subromance interest. The third generation has Jackie Cooper as Ted III as a child, and Eddie Quillan playing the matured Ted III when he becomes an overnight Hollywood click.

BROKEN ARROW
1950, 92 mins, US ⓥ
D: Delmer Daves A: James Stewart, Jeff Chandler, Debra Paget, Basil Ruysdael, Will Geer, Joyce MacKenzie (20th Century-Fox)

Broken Arrow is a western with a little different twist—the story of the attempt of whites and Apaches to learn to live together in the Arizona of 1870. Essentially it's an appealing, sentimental Indian romance, with plenty of action. Story concerns a farsighted young frontiersman (James Stewart) who boldly plans a visit to the feared Apache leader Cochise (Jeff Chandler) to propose a truce. Meeting not only succeeds, but Stewart falls in love with an Indian maiden (Debra Paget). Both truce and troth are impeded by treachery on the part of whites and Indians.

1950: Nominations: Best Supp. Actor (Jeff Chandler), Screenplay, Color Cinematography

BROKEN ARROW
1996, 108 mins, US ⓥ ⊙ ▭
D: John Woo A: John Travolta, Christian Slater, Samantha Mathis, Delroy Lindo, Bob Gunton, Frank Whaley (20th Century-Fox)

A virtually nonstop actioner that's heavy on imaginative destruction but light on coherence and character, *Broken Arrow* doesn't score a direct hit but will still do the trick for thrill-seeking audiences. In a flat-out villainous portrayal, John Travolta continues his winning post-comeback ways as a duplicitous air-force pilot who steals two nuclear bombs. Planes, trains, boats, trucks, helicopters, Humvees—just about every mode of transportation is used as the good government guys, led by co-pilot Christian Slater and Park Ranger Samantha Mathis, try to outmaneuver the bad guys, masterminded by Travolta, before the latter lay waste to the western United States.

BROKEN BLOSSOMS OR THE YELLOW MAN AND THE GIRL
1919, 107 mins, US Ⓥ ⊙ ⊗
D: D. W. Griffith **A:** Lillian Gish, Donald Crisp, Richard Barthelmess, Edward Peil, Arthur Howard, George Beranger (Artcraft)

The story is a drama of pathos, culminating in tragedy. A pure-minded young Chinaman, reared in the beautiful teachings of Buddha, journeys to London with the altruistic idea of civilizing the white race. In London a brutish prizefighter beats his child into helplessness and she crawls away, half-dead, falling insensible into the shop of the Mongolian. He carries her to his living room above and watches over her with a love so pure as to be wholly unnatural and inconsistent. Lillian Gish as the girl, shrinking, self-effacing, timid, fearful, and wistful, has never before done anything so fine. Donald Crisp is the brutal father, as great a triumph of histrionic artistry as that registered by Gish. Yet not one whit behind these two masterful portrayals is that of Richard Barthelmess as the young Chinaman.

BROKEN HARVEST
1994, 101 mins, Ireland
D: Maurice O'Callaghan **A:** Colin Lane, Niall O'Brien, Marian Quinn, Darren McHugh, Joy Florish, Joe Jeffers (Destiny)

Part rites-of-passage movie, part meditation on the new Ireland forged from the war of Independence and subsequent civil war, *Broken Harvest* is a beautifully lensed but dramatically static pic that falls short of its aspirations. Story opens in present-day New York, where businessman Jimmy O'Leary (Pete O'Reilly) hears of the death of his mother, Catherine (Marian Quinn, sister of Aidan). The news cues a long flashback to growing up in rural West Cork during the fifties, where old tensions still linger from the anti-Brit struggles of the twenties and later divisions.

BROKEN LANCE
1954, 96 mins, US Ⓥ ▭
D: Edward Dmytryk **A:** Spencer Tracy, Robert Wagner, Jean Peters, Richard Wid-

mark, Katy Jurado, Hugh O'Brian (20th Century-Fox)

Broken Lance is top-notch western drama. Film starts with Robert Wagner's release from an Arizona prison after serving a three-year sentence. The enmity that lies between him and his three half-brothers (Richard Widmark, Hugh O'Brian, and Earl Holliman) is quickly established. Tracy is shown as a domineering cattle baron, who rules his four sons and vast empire ruthlessly. However, time is running out for him as civilization advances, and he takes the law into his own hands once too often in destroying mining property and injuring miners.
1954: Best Motion Picture Story
Nomination: Best Supp. Actress (Katy Jurado)

BRONCO BILLY
1980, 119 mins, US Ⓥ ⊙
D: Clint Eastwood **A:** Clint Eastwood, Sondra Locke, Geoffrey Lewis, Scatman Crothers, Bill McKinney, Sam Bottoms (Warner)

In the title role, Clint Eastwood plays an ex-NJ shoe salesman who has trained himself to live out a fantasy as a sharp-shooting, knife-throwing, stunt-riding cowboy. There's no place to practice it except as the leader of a run-down Wild West show touring tank towns and county fairs. Along the same highways, however, comes Sondra Locke, an arrogant spoiled heiress, and Geoffrey Lewis, delightful as the idiotic man she has just married. Bronco Billy is a caricature of many of the strong heroes whom Eastwood has played in other pix and he's obviously having a wonderful time with the satire.

BRONCO BULLFROG
1970, 86 mins, UK
D: Barney Platts-Mills **A:** Del Walker, Anne Gooding, Sam Shepherd, Roy Haywood, Freda Shepherd, Dick Philpott (British Lion)

Film is a praiseworthy attempt to show the drab environment of an area and to indicate how boredom can drive youngsters into being layabouts, petty thieves, etc. and how such trapped youngsters can develop into more hardened criminals. Through the film is woven an inarticulate, but frequently touching Romeo-and-Juliet theme, about two minors who run away from home because there is nowhere to go and nothing to do.

BRONCO BUSTER
1952, 80 mins, US Ⓥ
D: Budd Boetticher **A:** John Lund, Scott Brady, Joyce Holden, Chill Wills, Casey Tibbs (Universal-International)

A satisfying round of outdoor action thrills is provided by *Bronco Buster*. A lot of actual rodeo thrill footage is used to bolster authenticity and add interest to the development of what actually is a routine plotline. Excellent scripting and direction, however, gloss over and enliven the stock plot. John Lund and Scott Brady handle the principal male roles as rodeo and romantic rivals.

BRONENOSETS POTYOMKIN (BATTLESHIP POTEMKIN; THE POTEMKIN; CRUISER POTEMKIN)
1925, 65 mins, USSR Ⓥ ◎
D: Sergei Eisenstein **A:** Aleksandr Antonov, Vladimir Barsky, Levshin, Grigori Aleksandrov, Mikhail Gomorov (Goskino)

Scenario concerns an actual historical incident found in the czarist archives. In 1905 the armored cruiser *Potemkin* was lying off Odessa. The crew had been getting inedible rations and finally worm-ridden meat was brought on board. The sailors protested and refused to eat this. The czarist commander portioned off 10 of the sailors and ordered the marines to shoot them. After a moment of hesitancy the soldiers lowered their guns and mutiny broke out. Within a few moments all the officers had either been shot or thrown overboard. The news of the mutiny spread like wildfire through the city and the oppressed citizens, in the hope that the czarist regime was about to fall, came to pay homage at the bier. Coming from both sides of the big square and stairway leading up the hill, the Cossack troops shot down mercilessly all in the way, cripples, old men, women, and children. The direction of Sergei Eisenstein is original and powerful. There are moments in the film that will thrill even the most hardened conservative. Also, the inexorable advance of the shooting Cossacks down the steps is interesting from a rhythmic angle. [Review is of pic's first overseas showing, in Berlin in 1926.]

BRONX TALE, A
1993, 122 mins, US Ⓥ ◎
D: Robert De Niro **A:** Robert De Niro, Chazz Palminteri, Lillo Brancato, Francis Capra, Taral Hicks, Clem Caserta (Price/Tribeca)

Goodfellas with heart, *A Bronx Tale* charts the growing-up of a youngster named Calogero amidst the small-time hoods and wiseguys of the Bronx in the 1960s. The neighborhood is ruled by Sonny (Palminteri). Everything changes after nine-year-old Calogero (Francis Capra) sees Sonny shoot down a man in the street. When Calogero doesn't identify the killer to the police, Sonny takes the kid under his wing, letting him in on craps games from which he takes home more money than his bus driver father (De Niro) makes in weeks. De Niro cast himself in the script's least showy role, but he delivers some great scenes. It's also given to him to repeatedly deliver pic's theme—"The saddest thing in life is wasted talent." Palminteri is terrific as the charismatic Sonny, his quicksilver mood changes keeping everyone on their toes.

BROOD, THE
1979, 91 mins, Canada Ⓥ ◎
D: David Cronenberg **A:** Oliver Reed, Samantha Eggar, Art Hindle, Cindy Hinds, Henry Beckman, Nuala FitzGerald (Mutuelles/Elgin)

A horror entry which casts children in the role of malevolent little monsters, *The Brood* is an extremely well-made, if essentially unpleasant, shocker. Action is relatively plodding stuff, with young parent Art Hindle trying to keep his daughter away from mother Samantha Eggar, who's supposedly in psychotherapy at the posh forested retreat of analyst Oliver Reed. Unfortunately, Hindle is just too morose to enlist much sympathy, despite his plight.

BROTHER FROM ANOTHER PLANET, THE
1984, 104 mins, US Ⓥ
D: John Sayles **A:** Joe Morton, Darryl Edwards, Steve James, Leonard Jackson, Bill Cobbs, Maggie Renzi (A-Train)

John Sayles takes a turn toward offbeat fantasy in a vastly amusing but progressively erratic look at the Harlem adventures of an alien, a black E.T. Pic is essentially a series of behavioral vignettes, and many of them are genuinely delightful and inventive. Once the Brother discovers the Harlem drug scene, however, tale takes a rather unpleasant and, ultimately, confusing turn.

BROTHERHOOD, THE
1968, 96 mins, US Ⓥ ◎
D: Martin Ritt **A:** Kirk Douglas, Alex

Cord, Irene Papas, Luther Adler, Susan Strasberg, Murray Hamilton (Paramount/Bryna)

Mafia-themed story pits Kirk Douglas, as a middle-aged New Jersey syndicate chief, against Alex Cord, his ambitious younger brother, not as attuned to the curious, but rigidly structured old underworld code. Martin Ritt's top-notch direction of an excellent cast maximizes the tragedy inherent in original screenplay. Since a prologue telegraphs some tragic climax, there is not much suspense in the usual sense of the word.

BROTHERLY LOVE
See: Country Dance

BROTHERS
1977, 105 mins, US
D: Arthur Barron A: Bernie Casey, Vonetta McGee, Ron O'Neal, Renny Roker, Stu Gilliam, John Lehne (Soho)

Most favorably judged, *Brothers* is an excellent dramatization of a contemporary dispute from one angry viewpoint. It's also a cheap-shot, racist picture. Though labeled fiction, pic only makes barest effort to differ from the true story of San Quentin inmate George Jackson, whose younger brother Jonathan and a judge were killed during a wild-shoot out at the Marin County Courthouse. As seen by scripters Edward and Mildred Lewis, American prisons are torture chambers for blacks forced into them by white society.

BROTHERS IN LAW
1957, 94 mins, UK ♥
D: Roy Boulting A: Richard Attenborough, Ian Carmichael, Terry-Thomas, Jill Adams, Miles Malleson, Eric Barker (Tudor/British Lion)

The three stars in *Private's Progress* are reunited in this Roy Boulting comedy. This time it's making fun of the law, doing full justice to a laugh-loaded script. The witty and lighthearted yarn traces the experiences of a young lawyer from the day of his graduation until he achieves his first legal victory. The raw legal recruit is Ian Carmichael. He gets his chance from Terry-Thomas, a seasoned swindler with 17 appearances at the criminal court to his credit.

BROTHERS KARAMAZOV, THE
1958, 149 mins, US ♥
D: Richard Brooks A: Yul Brynner, Maria Schell, Claire Bloom, Lee J. Cobb, Richard Basehart, William Shatner (M-G-M/Avon)

Bold handling of crude unbridled passion, of violently conflicting ideas, and of earthy humor makes up *The Brothers Karamazov*. Sex and salvation are the twin obsessions of the brothers and father, and they are the two themes that are hammered relentlessly home. Lee J. Cobb is the father, a lecherous old buffoon who taunts, tantalizes, and frustrates his sons into violence, despair, and apathy. Yul Brynner is the handsome, cruel, profligate army officer, a combination of adult power and childish pleasure. They both lust after the same woman, Maria Schell as Grushenka. Brynner succeeds in making his Dmitri a hero despite the fact that every facet of his character is against it. Schell, in her American motion-picture debut, illumines her role, seemingly able to suggest innocence and depravity with the same sweet face. It is Lee J. Cobb, however, who walks or rather gallops away with the picture.
1958: Nomination: Best Supp. Actor (Lee J. Cobb)

BROTHERS RICO, THE
1957, 90 mins, US
D: Phil Karlson A: Richard Conte, Dianne Foster, Kathryn Grant, Larry Gates, James Darren, Lamont Johnson (Columbia)

Screenplay follows the efforts of a crime ring to locate one of its members who bolted after participating in a murder. Missing member's elder brother (Richard Conte), once chief accountant for the syndicate but now a reputable businessman, is recalled to find him. Phil Karlson forges hard action into unfolding of film. Performances are first-class right down the line, Conte a standout.

BROTHER SUN, SISTER MOON
1973, 121 mins, Italy/UK ♥
D: Franco Zeffirelli A: Graham Faulkner, Judi Bowker, Alec Guinness, Leigh Lawson, Kenneth Cranham, Michael Feast (Euro International/Vic)

Brother Sun, Sister Moon is a delicate, handsome quasi-fictional biography of one of the great saints of the Catholic Church, Francis of Assisi. Franco Zeffirelli has utilized a style of simple elegance, befitting both the period and the subject. Graham Faulkner makes an important film debut as Francis of Assisi. Judi Bowker, cast as a young girl who eventually sheds her materialistic existence for religious poverty, is stunningly beautiful, projecting the very essence of innocence.

1973: Nomination: Best Art Direction

BROWNING VERSION, THE
1951, 90 mins, UK Ⓥ
D: Anthony Asquith **A:** Michael Redgrave, Jean Kent, Nigel Patrick, Wilfrid Hyde White, Brian Smith, Bill Travers (Javelin)

The background of the story is an English public school with the action spanning barely 48 hours. It is the last day of term, and Andrew Crocker-Harris, an austere disciplinarian, is retiring, without a pension, because of ill health. The events leading up to the final, powerful valedictory address make up a plot which is rich in incident and human understanding. The role of the retiring master is not an easy one, but Michael Redgrave fills it with distinction. Almost matching this performance is the role of his wife, played with a mixture of callousness and coyness by Jean Kent. Nigel Patrick, in a less bombastic part than usual, chalks up another personal success as the science master.

BROWNING VERSION, THE
1994, 97 mins, UK/US Ⓥ ⊙
D: Mike Figgis **A:** Albert Finney, Greta Scacchi, Matthew Modine, Julian Sands, Michael Gambon, Ben Silverston (Percy Main/Paramount)

It's more than four decades since Michael Redgrave essayed the role of Andrew Crocker-Harris, a public school Latin teacher who's facing a forced, early retirement. Albert Finney puts his unique stamp on the role, effecting a heaviness that suggests a hard crust shielding a marshmallow center. The tragedy of this sometimes ridiculous man is multifold. His marriage to Laura (Greta Scacchi) is a sham. Her extracurricular activity is centered around Frank Hunter (Matthew Modine), the brash, well-liked Yank teaching chemistry. Ronald Harwood's adaptation has abridged the original without diluting its most potent contemporary resonances.

BRUBAKER
1980, 130 mins, US Ⓥ ⊙
D: Stuart Rosenberg **A:** Robert Redford, Yaphet Kotto, Jane Alexander, Murray Hamilton, David Keith, Morgan Freeman (20th Century-Fox)

A successfully grim and brutal drama. For the squeamish, the first half hour is rough going, indeed, as Redford is inducted into a small state prison. The prison administration is in corrupt cahoots with townspeople, leasing prisoners as slave labor; brutal trustees administer the discipline to fellow convicts, gaining good time for killing some off; minimally decent food and privileges must be bought for cash, with wormy gruel going to those who can't afford it. Just when it seems any hope is beyond these men, Redford reveals himself as the prison's new warden.

1980: Nomination: Best Original Screenplay

BRUTE FORCE
1947, 94 mins, US
D: Jules Dassin **A:** Burt Lancaster, Hume Cronyn, Charles Bickford, Yvonne De Carlo, Ann Blyth, Howard Duff (Hellinger/Universal)

A close-up on prison life and prison methods, *Brute Force* is a showmanly mixture of gangster melodramatics, sociological exposition, and sex. Yvonne De Carlo, Ann Blyth, Ella Raines, and Anita Colby are the women on the outside whose machinations, wiles, or charms accounted for their men being on the "inside." Burt Lancaster, Charles Bickford, Sam Levene, Howard Duff, Art Smith, and Jeff Corey, along with Hume Cronyn as the machinating prison captain (later warden), are the inside cast. Bristling, biting dialogue by Richard Brooks paints broad cameos as each character takes shape under existing prison life. Cronyn is diligently hateful as the arrogant, brutal captain, with his system of stool pigeons and bludgeoning methods.

BUCCANEER, THE
1958, 121 mins, US Ⓥ ⊙
D: Anthony Quinn **A:** Yul Brynner, Charlton Heston, Claire Bloom, Charles Boyer, Inger Stevens, E. G. Marshall (Paramount)

Romance is effectively brought in the Cecil B. DeMille–supervised production that focuses on the colorful historical character of Jean Lafitte. On the deficit side is a wordy script that lacks any large degree of excitement. It marks the debut of Anthony Quinn as director. It's the War of 1812 against Britain and the battle area in New Orleans. Highpoint is the land battle between Andrew Jackson's forces and the British, with Jackson aided by Lafitte's personnel and ammunition. The British, like so many toy soldiers, go down in defeat as Lafitte rules the mast. Yul Brynner is masterly as the pirate. Charlton Heston

is a hard, firm Andrew Jackson.
1958: Nomination: Best Costume Design

BUCHANAN RIDES ALONE
1958, 89 mins, US
D: Budd Boetticher **A:** Randolph Scott, Craig Stevens, Barry Kelley, Peter Whitney, Manuel Rojas, L. Q. Jones (Columbia)

Buchanan Rides Alone is an honest picture, made with skill and craftsmanship. Well-paced screenplay has Randolph Scott as a man more or less innocently involved in the problems of a frontier western border town. He befriends a young Mexican (Manuel Rojas), who kills the town bully. Scott is thrown in jail with Rojas and both are threatened with lynching. Scott gives an understated performance, taciturnity relieved by humor and warmth.

BUCK PRIVATES
1941, 82 mins, US Ⓥ ⊙
D: Arthur Lubin **A:** Lee Bowman, Alan Curtis, Bud Abbott, Lou Costello, Jane Frazee (Universal)

Geared at a zippy pace, and providing lusty and enthusiastic comedy of the broadest slapstick, *Buck Privates* is a hilarious laugh concoction. Aiding considerably is the appearance of the Andrews Sisters, who do their regularly competent harmonizing of several tuneful melodies. Abbott and Costello are inducted into the army and assigned to camp. The madcap and zany antics of Costello are displayed in numerous comedy and knockabout sequences that click for solid laughs through the timing of the gags and situations.

BUCK PRIVATES COME HOME
1947, 77 mins, US Ⓥ ⊙
D: Charles T. Barton **A:** Bud Abbott, Lou Costello, Nat Pendleton, Tom Brown, Joan Fulton (Universal-International)

Fat and thin comics romp through familiar routines with few variations. Sight gags, situations, and chases that Abbott and Costello comedies always feature are strung on a story line that has the boys smuggling a little French girl into this country upon their return from overseas. Efforts to conceal the kid are frantic fun, climaxing in a hilarious chase that is socko. Another high spot is version of the old situation wherein Costello dangles from a clothesline between two high buildings.

BUDDY BUDDY
1982, 96 mins, US Ⓥ ▭
D: Billy Wilder **A:** Jack Lemmon, Walter Matthau, Paula Prentiss, Klaus Kinski, Dana Elcar, Miles Chapin (M-G-M)

The script, based on the French Jacques Brel-Lino Ventura starrer *L'Emmerdeur,* is one of the rare Wilder projects not initiated by the director himself, and a certain lack of care and even thought permeates the effort, from script to casting to execution. Abandoned by wife Paula Prentiss, Jack Lemmon is a nebbishy failure who checks into a riverside hotel to end it all. In the next room is Walter Matthau, a stone-faced grouch and heartless hit man who's preparing to knock off a squealer. The two men's paths quickly cross, and despite Matthau's claim that "I'm nobody's friend," he allows himself to become involved in Lemmon's plight.

BUDDY HOLLY STORY, THE
1978, 113 mins, US Ⓥ ⊙
D: Steve Rash **A:** Gary Busey, Don Stroud, Charles Martin Smith, Bill Jordan, Maria Richwine, Conrad Janis (Innovisions/ECA)

The Buddy Holly Story smacks of realism in almost every respect, from the drama involving Holly and his backup band, the Crickets, to the verisimilitude of the musical numbers. Latter were recorded live, using 24 tracks, and there was no studio rerecording. It was a gamble that pays off in full, and the Holly repertoire (an extensive one) gives the pic its underlying structure. Gary Busey not only imparts the driven, perfectionist side of Holly's character, but his vocal work is excellent, as is his instrumentation.
1978: Best Adapted Score
Nominations: Best Actor (Gary Busey), Sound

DIE BUECHSE DER PANDORA (PANDORA'S BOX)
1929, 131 mins, Germany Ⓥ ⊗
D: G. W. Pabst **A:** Louise Brooks, Fritz Kortner, Franz Lederer, Carl Goetz, Alice Roberts, Gustav Diessl (Nero)

Louise Brooks, especially imported for the title role, does not pan out, due to no fault of hers. She is quite unsuited to the vamp type [Lulu, a temptress finally killed by Jack the Ripper]. Grave mistake to try to make a film of a Franz Wedekind play. Heavy vamp stuff which he wrote was already dated. G. W. Pabst, director, in an attempt to keep the whole natural and easy, succeeds merely in making it superficial and lacking in suspense or thrill.

BUFFALO BILL
1944, 90 mins, US ℗

D: William A. Wellman A: Joel McCrea, Maureen O'Hara, Linda Darnell, Thomas Mitchell, Anthony Quinn (20th Century-Fox)

Buffalo Bill is a super-western and often a tearjerker. Head-on battle between US cavalry and Cheyenne tribe at War Bonnet Gorge is the story's focal point, with Buffalo Bill, famed scout and friend of the Indian, becoming the yarn's hero in man-to-man combat with his former redskin pal. Joel McCrea makes a realistic Buffalo Bill. Maureen O'Hara, as the daughter of a senator who later weds McCrea, is satisfying. Linda Darnell, the Indian schoolteacher who loves Cody, has too little to do but does that little with charm. Thomas Mitchell is the eastern newspaperman who authors books about Buffalo Bill's fame. Per usual, a shipshape characterization.

BUFFALO BILL AND THE INDIANS OR SITTING BULL'S HISTORY LESSON
1976, 123 mins, US ℗ ▭

D: Robert Altman A: Paul Newman, Joel Grey, Kevin McCarthy, Harvey Keitel, Allan Nicholls, Geraldine Chaplin (De Laurentiis/Lion's Gate)

It appears that the idea here is to expose and debunk the Buffalo Bill legend. Film shows Paul Newman bumbling through the challenge of living up to a legend created by Burt Lancaster. The serious plot note is the determination of Sitting Bull (played very well in total silence by Frank Kaquitts) and interpreter Will Sampson not to debase history through cheap carny melodrama.

BUFFALO THE VAMPIRE SLAYER
1992, 86 mins, US ℗ ⊙

D: Fran Rubel Kuzui A: Kristy Swanson, Donald Sutherland, Paul Reubens, Rutger Hauer, Luke Perry, Michele Abrams (20th Century-Fox/Sandollar/Kuzui)

Buffy the Vampire Slayer is a bloodless comic resurrection of the undead that goes serious just when it should get wild and woolly. Blond, bouncy Buffy (Kristy Swanson) is lead cheerleader and Miss Popular in the senior class at Hemery High. A dirty old man in a long overcoat (Donald Sutherland) turns up to inform

Buffy that she is a female vampire slayer, and she passes her trial by fire with flying colors when she subdues two marauding cretins. When it becomes apparent that L.A. is under threat of a serious vampire invasion led by king Rutger Hauer, Buffy dives into an Olympian workout regimen to sharpen her skills with a stake. After biting a few teens and menacing Buffy and her would-be b.f. (Luke Perry), the vampires crash a high-school dance in a limp rehash of the big set piece in *Carrie*.

BUG
1975, 99 mins, US ℗

D: Jeannot Szwarc A: Bradford Dillman, Joanna Miles, Richard Gilliland, Jamie Smith Jackson, Alan Fudge, Jesse Vint (Paramount)

Bug concerns some mutated cockroaches liberated by an earthquake from the earth's core. Bradford Dillman, an animal scientist, gets intrigued with them, so much so that he becomes a recluse with the creatures. At the same time Dillman goes into seclusion, so does the film; its last half is largely static, and the film never revives much interest.

BUG'S LIFE, A
1998, 96 mins, US ℗ ⊙ ▭

D: John Lasseter, Andrew Stanton (Pixar/Walt Disney)

Entertaining in a very showbizzy sort of way, *A Bug's Life* is more broad based and kid friendly in its appeal than DreamWorks' more sophisticated *Antz*. A legion of ants laboriously transport food to await the arrival of their terrorizers, a gang of grasshoppers. Unfortunately, the hapless Flik (voiced by Dave Foley) knocks over the offering and the grasshoppers' big bully chief, Hopper (Kevin Spacey, oozing menace), threatens the little ones' existence unless they double their donation to the end of the season. Flik exiles himself in a search for anyone who might help. All he can find are the eccentric members of a ragtag flea circus. Story plays out at slight overlength. Colors are bold and beautiful but never gaudy; overall look is crisp, clean and invariably pretty.

BUGSY
1991, 135 mins, US ℗ ⊙

D: Barry Levinson A: Warren Beatty, Annette Bening, Harvey Keitel, Ben Kingsley, Elliott Gould, Joe Mantegna (Tri-Star/Mulholland/Baltimore)

Handsome pic about the inventor of

Las Vegas tells how Benjamin Siegel (Warren Beatty) was sent to L.A. to take over the West Coast rackets but stayed to become one of the legendary Hollywood characters of the 1940s. In James Toback's writing and Beatty's gutsy playing, Bugsy bursts out as a fully realized, psychologically complex character endowed with very human strengths and weaknesses. Unfortunately, his great love and female counterpart, Virginia Hill (Annette Bening), remains a one-dimensional and annoying stick figure. Director Barry Levinson treats this punchy, emotionally eruptive story in fluid, almost dreamy fashion, rather like a sordid fairy tale. Although ethnically wrong and lacking a street-tough attitude, Beatty gives a dynamite performance, his most vital and surprising in a long time.

1991: Best Art Direction, Costume Design **Nominations:** Best Picture, Director, Actor (Warren Beatty), Supp. Actor (Harvey Keitel, Ben Kingsley), Original Screenplay, Cinematography, Original Score

BUGSY MALONE
1976, 93 mins, UK ⊘ ⊙
D: Alan Parker **A:** Scott Baio, Jodie Foster, Florrie Dugger, John Cassisi, Martin Lev, Paul Murphy (Goodtimes)

Set in 1929 Gotham, pic is a compendium of gangster/Prohibition pic situations and clichés, played tongue-in-cheek by a splendid cast of juves, a veritable casting treasure trove. Jodie Foster is outstanding as a moll. It's a brave, funny, and winning pic which is nearly but regrettably not quite a triumph.

1976: Nomination: Best Adapted Score

BUILD MY GALLOWS HIGH
See: Out of the Past

BULLDOG BREED, THE
1960, 100 mins, UK
D: Robert Asher **A:** Norman Wisdom, Ian Hunter, David Lodge, Robert Urquhart, Edward Chapman, Eddie Byrne (Rank)

Norman Puckle (Norman Wisdom) tries to commit suicide. As in everything in life he fails horribly, is rescued, and persuaded to join the navy, where he continues to make a hash of everything. The film stands or falls by Wisdom and, though the actor, as always, seems to be trying rather too hard, his general good humor and energy carry him through the various situations entertainingly.

BULLDOG DRUMMOND
1929, 80 mins, US ⊘
D: F. Richard Jones **A:** Ronald Colman, Claud Allister, Joan Bennett, Lilyan Tashman, Lawrence Grant, Montagu Love (Goldwyn)

Entertaining picture of the highly charged thriller-meller kind, mostly because of the likable performance of Ronald Colman in his first screamer. As a picture it's intense, with the suspense often and sharply broken into for a laugh by a fop Englishman of the common stage type. Bulldog Drummond is an idler looking for excitement. He gets it by saving the grandfather of a strange young woman from an insane asylum's crooks. Lilyan Tashman is the she-devil. She takes her whiskey straight. Joan Bennett, the new lead, seems held down here, probably through inexperience.

1929/30: Nomination: Best Art Direction

BULL DURHAM
1988, 108 mins, US ⊘ ⊙
D: Ron Shelton **A:** Kevin Costner, Susan Sarandon, Tim Robbins, Trey Wilson, Robert Wuhl, Jenny Robertson (Mount/Orion)

Bull Durham is a fanciful and funny bush-league sports story whose only foul ball is its overuse of locker-room dialogue. The Durham Bulls of North Carolina endure another season of suffering the dubious distinction of being one of the losingest clubs in Carolina league history. Sent over to instruct, insult, and inspire the Bulls' bullet-fast pitcher Ebby Calvin "Nuke" LaLoosh (Tim Robbins) is embittered veteran catcher "Crash" Davis (Kevin Costner). His job is to get the cocky kid's arm on target by game time. Costner is a natural as the dyed-in-the-wool ballplayer.

1988: Nomination: Best Original Screenplay

BULLETS OR BALLOTS
1936, 68 mins, US ⊘
D: William Keighley **A:** Edward G. Robinson, Joan Blondell, Humphrey Bogart, Barton MacLane, Frank McHugh, Joseph Keen (Warner/Frank McHugh)

This is a fast, smooth-working action picture. Edward G. Robinson is Johnny Blake, a tough but honest dick. Al Kruger (Barton MacLane), obviously based on Dutch Schultz, is the racketeer king who has everything beautifully organized. MacLane is tops, with the role neatly paralleled by the work of Humphrey Bogart as a first aid and a convicing menace. Joan Blondell is dragged in as a sort of minor romance note for Robinson.

BULLETS OVER BROADWAY
1994, 99 mins, US Ⓥ ⊙
D: Woody Allen A: John Cusack, Jack Warden, Chazz Palminteri, Joe Viterelli, Jennifer Tilly, Rob Reiner (Sweetland/Miramax)

A backstage comedy bolstered by healthy shots of Prohibition gangster melodrama and romantic entanglements. David Shayne (John Cusack), a young playwright, swears he'll brook no compromise in the production of his new play. Shayne quickly changes his tune when producer Julian Marx (Jack Warden) informs him that he's found a backer with the proviso that the man's girlfriend play a prominent role. The actress, Olive Neal (Jennifer Tilly), is a goo-voiced bimbo and her only qualification is that she's the mistress of big-time mobster Nick Valenti (Joe Viterelli). Shayne must also tolerate the critical barbs of Olive's thuggish bodyguard, Cheech (Chazz Palminteri), who sits in on all rehearsals. In its mixing of showbiz and gangsters, this is a nice companion piece to Allen's *Broadway Danny Rose*, and about as amusing.
1995: Best Supp. Actress (Diane Wiest)
Nominations: Director, Supp. Actor (Chazz Palminteri), Supp. Actress (Jennifer Tilly), Original Screenplay, Art Direction, Costume Design

BULLFIGHTER AND THE LADY
1951, 87 mins, US Ⓥ ⊙
D: Budd Boetticher A: Robert Stack, Joy Page, Gilbert Roland, Virginia Grey, John Hubbard, Katy Jurado (Republic)

Use of Robert Stack as an American vacationing below the border gives an understanding insight into bullfighting. Stack falls in love with Joy Page's highborn Mexican girl. To impress her, he induces Gilbert Roland's matador idol to instruct him in the use of the cape and sword. Stack begins to feel the urge and thrill of the art, but in a careless, show-off moment, he causes Roland's death when the latter tries to save him. A particular standout is Roland. Without overplaying, he gives his matador character color and vigor, bravery without bravado, and dignity.
1951: Nomination: Best Motion Picture Story

BULLITT
1968, 113 mins, US Ⓥ ⊙
D: Peter Yates A: Steve McQueen, Robert Vaughn, Jacqueline Bisset, Don Gordon, Robert Duvall, Simon Oakland (Solar/Warner)

Conflict between police sleuthing and political expediency is the essence of *Bullitt*, an extremely well-made crime melodrama filmed in Frisco. Steve McQueen delivers a very strong performance as a detective seeking a man whom Robert Vaughn, ambitious politico, would exploit for selfish motives. Good scripting and excellent direction by Peter Yates maintain deliberately low-key but mounting suspense.
1968: Best Editing
Nomination: Best Sound

BULWORTH
1998, 107 mins, US Ⓥ ⊙
D: Warren Beatty A: Warren Beatty, Halle Berry, Don Cheadle, Oliver Platt, Paul Sorvino, Jack Warden (20th Century-Fox)

Warren Beatty's disarmingly blunt look at a U.S. senator who suddenly starts speaking the truth about the day's important issues—in rhyming rap cadences, no less—is an uncommonly smart, sharp and irreverent American picture. On the eve of the 1996 California primary, Senator Jay Bulworth (Beatty) is despondent over the hollow sound of his own voice and campaign slogans. Taking out a $10 million insurance policy, he orders a hit on himself to put him out of his misery once and for all. At an African-American church in South Central, Los Angeles the neo-con Democrat begins shocking his friendly audience with brutal remarks about why politicians ignore their promises to blacks, to a quizzical reaction from a local fox, Nina (Halle Berry). He packs Nina and two of her girlfriends into his limo and has them take him along to the wildest after-hours club in South Central. During a long, druggy night, WASPy Bulworth metamorphoses into an irreverent hip-hopper. Beatty rarely before has given the impression of having so much fun as he does here. The one insufficiently conceived character is Berry's, whose inscrutability often serves as a drain on the action.
1998: Nomination: Best Original Screenplay

BUNNY LAKE IS MISSING
1965, 107 mins, UK Ⓥ ▭
D: Otto Preminger **A:** Carol Lynley, Keir
Dullea, Laurence Olivier, Noel Coward,
Martita Hunt, Anna Massey (Columbia/
Wheel)

Preminger has achieved an entertaining, fast-paced exercise in the exploration
of a sick mind. Evelyn Piper's 1957 novel
dealt entirely with the unpredictable actions of a mother searching for her child
(real or imaginary) who had disappeared.
To this plot skeleton Preminger has added
an equally important character whose predictable actions provide the search's principal obstacles. Carol Lynley, as the
mother shoved into a state of near hysteria
almost from the beginning, is outstanding.

BUONA SERA, MRS. CAMPBELL
1968, 111 mins, Italy Ⓥ ⊙
D: Melvin Frank **A:** Gina Lollobrigida,
Shelley Winters, Phil Silvers, Peter Lawford, Telly Savalas, Janet Margolin
(United Artists/Connaught)

A very entertaining comedy about an
Italian woman who has conned three
American bed partners from World War II
into support of her and an illegitimate
daughter for more than 20 years. Lollobrigida has fooled her neighbors into believing daughter Janet Margolin was by a
deceased US Air Force pilot. However, a
reunion of the airmen, in the town where
they were based, precipitates a potential
crisis, since, in truth, the real father could
have been Silvers, Lawford, or Savalas.

'BURBS, THE
1989, 103 mins, US Ⓥ ⊙
D: Joe Dante **A:** Tom Hanks, Bruce Dern,
Carrie Fisher, Rick Ducommun, Corey
Feldman, Henry Gibson (Imagine/Universal)

Director Joe Dante funnels his decidedly cracked view of suburban life
through dark humor in The 'Burbs. The
action never strays beyond the cozy confines of the nightmarish block everyman
Ray (Tom Hanks) inhabits along with an
uproarious assemblage of wacky neighbors. Poor Ray has a week off and just
wants to spend it quietly. Instead, he's
drawn into an increasingly elaborate
sleuthing game involving the mysterious
Klopeks, who reside in a ''Munster''-
esque house rife with indications of foul
play. Hanks does a fine impersonation of
a regular guy on the verge of a nervous
breakdown.

BUREAU OF MISSING PERSONS
1933, 75 mins, US Ⓥ
D: Roy Del Ruth **A:** Bette Davis, Lewis
Stone, Pat O'Brien, Glenda Farrell, Allen
Jenkins, Ruth Donnelly (First National)

Preface mentions the large percentage
of humans who seemingly manage to drop
off the face of the earth. Lewis Stone, as
the kindly captain heading the Missing
Persons Department, is shown in sundry
cross sections how to properly pursue his
duties without working too great a hardship on any of the principals. Against
these colorful but rather disjointed details,
scenarist Robert Presnell has wisely
thrown a main romance theme involving
Bette Davis and Pat O'Brien.

BURGLAR, THE
1957, 90 mins, US
D: Paul Wendkos **A:** Dan Duryea, Jayne
Mansfield, Martha Vickers, Peter Capell,
Mickey Shaughnessy, Wendell Phillips
(Kellman)

Novel opening is a newsreel-type prologue, in which Duryea spots a necklace
he wants. Film then moves into the story,
goes through the heist of the jewels from
the mansion of a Philadelphia spiritualist,
followed by the gang's holing-up in a battered old house. Basic story idea, taken
from Goodis' novel of the same title, is
okay, but suspense and action are bypassed and sloughed while the assorted
characters go into long soliloquizing about
how they got into their various predicaments.

BURKE & WILLS
1985, 140 mins, Australia Ⓥ ⊙ ▭
D: Graeme Clifford **A:** Jack Thompson,
Nigel Havers, Greta Scacchi, Matthew
Fargher, Ralph Cotterill, Drew Forsythe
(Hoyts Edgley)

Big in scope and emotionally stimulating, this Australian pic about the doomed
1860 expedition of explorers Burke and
Wills to cross the continent and back is
satisfying entertainment despite its length
and seemingly downbeat subject. Jack
Thompson, with full beard, is an imposing
Burke, a fiery-tempered Irishman whose
determination to succeed clouds his judgment. This is one of Thompson's best performances. British actor Nigel Havers is
excellent as the scientist, Wills, stubbornly
following his friend into the unknown
while barely concealing his fears for the
outcome.

BURMESE HARP, THE
See: Biruma No Tategoto

BURNING HILLS, THE
1956, 93 mins, US Ⓥ ⌷
D: Stuart Heisler A: Tab Hunter, Natalie Wood, Skip Homeier, Eduard Franz, Earl Holliman, Claude Akins (Warner)

Tab Hunter and Natalie Wood form a team of somewhat younger stars than is customarily found in sagebrush sagas and do an okay job. Story has to do with Trace Jordan's (Hunter) efforts to avenge the death of his brother, murdered by henchmen of a big cattle baron (Ray Teal). From avenger he becomes the chased, taking off through the hills in the company of Maria Colton (Wood), Anglo-Mexican girl.

BURNING SECRET
1989, 106 mins, UK/US/W. Germany Ⓥ ⊙
D: Andrew Birkin A: Faye Dunaway, Klaus Maria Brandauer, David Eberts, Ian Richardson (NFH/CLG/BA)

Burning Secret is the intriguing story of a mother's near adultery coupled with the elegant setting of post–World War I Austria in winter. The woman is Sonya (Faye Dunaway), elegant wife of a stuffy diplomat (Ian Richardson). When their young son, who suffers severely from asthma, is sent for treatment to a sanitorium in the mountains, the mother accompanies him. The son meets Baron Alexander Maria von Hauenschild (Klaus Maria Brandauer), a charming veteran of the war. Sonya is quite willing to seize the opportunity of a passionate love affair which is only constrained by the constant presence of her innocent, inquisitive son. Although the material is a little slight, the drama works thanks to the flawless performances.

BURNT OFFERINGS
1976, 116 mins, US Ⓥ
D: Dan Curtis A: Karen Black, Oliver Reed, Burgess Meredith, Eileen Heckart, Lee H. Montgomery, Dub Taylor (PEA)

Most of the cliches of the gothic genre are encompassed in the plot about Karen Black, Oliver Reed, Bette Davis, and young Lee H. Montgomery having a weird summer after moving into a home owned by batty Burgess Meredith and Eileen Heckart. The plot is treated in mysterioso fashion but the audience can guess the ending maybe an hour before it happens.

BUSINESS AFFAIR, A
1994, 98 mins, France/UK/Germany/Spain Ⓥ
D: Charlotte Brandstrom A: Carole Bouquet, Christopher Walken, Jonathan Pryce, Sheila Hancock, Anna Manahan, Fernando Guillen Cuervo (Skouras Films)

An unremarkable contemporary dramatic comedy. Frenchwoman Kate Swallow (Carole Bouquet) works to support her adored celeb hubby, grumpy novelist Alec Bolton (Jonathan Pryce), whose creative juices aren't flowing. Vanni Corso (Christopher Walken) signs Alec to bolster the failing old London publishing firm he's bought. But when Kate submits her own first novel to Corso, Alec takes umbrage and the marriage begins to totter. Script lurches along, with the actors never seeming to inhabit their roles. Dialogue, while sometimes crude and snappy, rarely sounds spontaneous.

BUS RILEY'S BACK IN TOWN
1965, 93 mins, US
D: Harvey Hart A: Ann-Margret, Michael Parks, Janet Margolin, Brad Dexter, Jocelyn Brando, Larry Storch (Universal)

The story centers on the title character, played by newcomer Michael Parks. He tends to rely overmuch on "method" methods—the tightly-constricted gesture, the stammer, the withdrawn, hunched-shoulder, hooded-eye type of acting that is rarely effective on the wide screen. His scenes with Janet Margolin are his best, those with Ann-Margret his poorest. A simple plot—young ex-serviceman faced with succumbing to the wiles of bad girl (Ann-Margret) or meeting responsibility head-on (with implied support of good girl).

BUS STOP
1956, 96 mins, US Ⓥ ⊙ ⌷
D: Joshua Logan A: Marilyn Monroe, Don Murray, Arthur O'Connell, Betty Field, Eileen Heckart, Hope Lange (20th Century-Fox)

William Inge's rowdy play about a cowboy and a lady (sic) gets a raucous screen treatment. New face Don Murray is the exuberant young cowhand who comes to the city to win some rodeo money and learn about women. Marilyn Monroe fans will find her s.a. not so positive, but still potent, in her *Bus Stop* character, but this goes with the type of well-used saloon singer and would-be actress she portrays. Monroe comes off acceptably, even though failing to maintain any kind of consistency in the southern accent.

1956: Nomination: Best Supp. Actor (Don Murray)

BUSTER
1988, 103 mins, UK Ⓥ ⊙

D: David Green **A:** Phil Collins, Julie Walters, Larry Lamb, Stephanie Lawrence, Ellen Beaven, Michael Attwell (NFH/Movie Group/Hemdale)

Buster features a charismatic big-screen bow by popster Phil Collins in the title role. Collins gets involved in a scheme to rob a Royal Mail train, and when the gang pulls off the raid, they find themselves regarded as folk heroes. Collins, wife Walters, and daughter go into hiding, but police pressure mounts and the family is forced to go on the run to Switzerland and finally Acapulco. *Buster* can't seem to make up its mind what sort of film it is. It plays as a romantic comedy to begin with, then switches to a caper pic before ending with domestic drama.

1988: Nomination: Best Song ("Two Hearts")

BUSTER AND BILLIE
1974, 98 mins, US Ⓥ

D: Daniel Petrie **A:** Jan-Michael Vincent, Joan Goodfellow, Pamela Sue Martin, Clifton James, Robert Englund, Jessie Lee Fulton (Columbia)

Nostalgia gets another workout in *Buster and Billie*. Screenplay, conventionally directed by Daniel Petrie, has a good deal of charm and veristic detail until its romantic tale crashes in a last-reel melee of unmotivated violence. Jan-Michael Vincent and Pamela Sue Martin are the town sweethearts. The stags all get theirs from Joan Goodfellow, a rather dumpy blonde from the other side of the tracks. Vincent also pays the glumly obliging Goodfellow a visit one night, then finds himself falling in love with her.

BUSTING
1974, 91 mins, US Ⓥ

D: Peter Hyams **A:** Elliott Gould, Robert Blake, Allen Garfield, Antonio Fargas, Sid Haig, Michael Lerner (United Artists)

Elliott Gould and Robert Blake star as vagrant vice-squad detectives, the kind who in real life set law and order back decades. Production is confused, compromised, and clumsy. The plot eventually gets around to blaming nearly every criminal activity in town on a local crime lord.

Garfield, as ever an outstanding performer, brings dignity and a sense of being totally together to the part.

BUSTIN' LOOSE
1981, 94 mins, US ⊙

D: Oz Scott **A:** Richard Pryor, Cicely Tyson, Robert Christian, Alphonso Alexander, Janet Wong (Universal)

Bustin' Loose is obviously a personal project for Pryor, who produced and wrote the story, which has admirable ambitions but is also the film's greatest weakness. Still, Pryor is an infectious comedian and a master of body language, keeping the picture on the move with sheer energy. He's a bungling burglar whose parole officer forces him to go to the aid of Cicely Tyson, the director of a school for emotionally disturbed children about to close for lack of money. The prissy, prim, and dominant Tyson and vulgar, unkempt Pryor find their initial hostility turning to romance.

BUTCH AND SUNDANCE THE EARLY DAYS
1979, 110 mins, US Ⓥ ⊙

D: Richard Lester **A:** William Katt, Tom Berenger, Brian Dennehy, Peter Weller, Jeff Corey, Jill Eikenberry (20th Century-Fox/Pantheon)

This prequel doesn't match its progenitor in either casting or style. Tom Berenger and William Katt acquit themselves admirably, but they simply can't compete with the ghosts of two superstars. *Butch* is standard sagebrush material, with few of the comic misadventures that characterized the original.

1979: Nomination: Best Costume Design

BUTCH CASSIDY AND THE SUNDANCE KID
1969, 112 mins, US Ⓥ ⊙ ▭

D: George Roy Hill **A:** Paul Newman, Robert Redford, Katharine Ross, Strother Martin, Jeff Corey, Cloris Leachman (20th Century-Fox/Campanile)

Lighthearted treatment of a purportedly true story of the two badmen who made Wyoming outlaw history, film emerges as a near comedy of errors. Newman plays Butch, one of the most deadly outlaws of the west. Robert Redford portrays the Kid, wizard with a gun. Together, they make a fine team, accompanied by frequent banter. Narrative starts in Wyoming, where Butch and his gang are involved in various train holdups and pursuits by posses after

bank robberies. This leads to Butch and the Kid trying their luck in Bolivia.
1969: Best Original Story & Screenplay, Cinematography, Song ("Raindrops Keep Fallin' on My Head''), Original Score
Nominations: Best Picture, Director, Sound

BUTCHER, THE
See: Le Boucher

BUTCHER BOY, THE
1917, 30 mins, US ⊗
D: Roscoe Fatty Arbuckle **A:** Roscoe Fatty Arbuckle, Arthur Earle, Josephine Stevens, Al St. John, Buster Keaton, Agnes Neilsen (Comique)

The Comique Film Co.'s series of Arbuckle two-reelers starts off with Fatty shaking out a bag of laugh-making tricks. Arbuckle juggling with the accessories of the country store where he is an important factor, also his way of handling feminine clothes worn in his visit to the girls' boarding school, is done in such a serious, earnest way the comic effect is all the more forceful.

BUTCHER'S WIFE, THE
1991, 104 mins, US ⓥ ⊙
D: Terry Hughes **A:** Demi Moore, Jeff Daniels, George Dzundza, Mary Steenburgen, Frances McDormand, Margaret Colin (Paramount)

A gentle romantic comedy with a distinct 1940s flavor, *The Butcher's Wife* is blessed with a fine cast working from a storybook plot. Demi Moore plays a country clairvoyant whose visions of romance are answered in the surprising form of a New York butcher (George Dzundza), whom she marries immediately, returning with him to his neighborhood. Her visions immediately start to touch all those who cross her path, in the process increasingly nettling the local psychologist (Jeff Daniels), whose patients seem to need him far less as they bathe in the comfort of Moore's future gazing.

BUTLEY
1974, 129 mins, UK/US/Canada
Dir Harold Pinter **A:** Alan Bates, Jessica Tandy, Richard O'Callaghan, Susan Engel, Michael Byrne, Georgina Hale (American Express/Landau)

Alan Bates's stage triumph in Simon Gray's *Butley* has been superbly recreated on the screen. The plot basically is one horrendous day in the life of an embittered teacher, who loses his estranged wife to a lesser professional colleague, his lover to another man, and his sense of superiority over a female associate, whose lifelong book project has been accepted for publication while his lies unfinished. Jessica Tandy, a middle-aged teacher who doesn't seem to understand her modern students, is excellent.

BUTTERCUP CHAIN, THE
1970, 95 mins, UK ▭
D: Robert Ellis Miller **A:** Hywel Bennett, Leigh Taylor-Young, Jane Asher, Sven-Bertil Taube, Clive Revill, Roy Dotrice (Columbia)

The story's somewhat contrived and overglib, even superficial, but it is directed and written with sympathy and tact and acted by a small cast that could hardly be bettered. Film concerns four individualistic young people who develop as intense friendship which, during one frenzied summer, strays into dangerous ground, obviously aimed for tragedy.

BUTTERFIELD 8
1960, 109 mins, US ⓥ ⊙ ▭
D: Daniel Mann **A:** Elizabeth Taylor, Laurence Harvey, Eddie Fisher, Dina Merrill, Mildred Dunnock, Betty Field (M-G-M/Afton-Linebrook)

An extremely sexy and intimate film, but the intimacy is only skin-deep, the sex only a dominating behavior pattern. It is the tragic tale of a young woman (Elizabeth Taylor) tormented by the contradictory impulses of flesh and conscience. Victim of traumatic childhood experiences, a fatherless youth, a mother's refusal to face facts, and, most of all, her own moral irresponsibility, she drifts from one illicit affair to another until passion suddenly blossoms into love on a six-day sex spree with Laurence Harvey. The picture's major asset is Taylor. It is a torrid, stinging portrayal.
1960: Best Actress (Elizabeth Taylor)
Nomination: Best Color Cinematography

BUTTERFLIES ARE FREE
1972, 109 mins, US ⓥ
D: Milton Katselas **A:** Goldie Hawn, Edward Albert, Eileen Heckart, Michael Glasser, Mike Warren (Columbia)

Leonard Gershe's screen adaptation of his successful Broadway play is an excellent example of how to switch from one medium to another. A slight change of emphasis has resulted, moving the center of attention from the blind boy, handsomely played by Edward Albert, to the girl (Goldie Hawn). What comes over with great strength is Gershe's intimate tale of the interrelationships of three individuals. Hawn, funny and touching, is a delight throughout and Heckart gets a film role that enables her to display versatility.

1972: Best Supp. Actress (Eileen Heckart)
Nominations: Best Cinematography, Sound

BUTTERFLY
1981, 107 mins, US ⓥ ⊙
D: Matt Cimber **A:** Stacy Keach, Pia Zadora, Orson Welles, Lois Nettleton, James Franciscus, Stuart Whitman (Riklis/Par-Par)

Pia Zadora plays Kady, a nymphet who's been searching for her father (Stacy Keach) in the Nevada silver mines. She tracks him down at an abandoned mine where he is serving as a guard. The headstrong young woman brings out incestuous desires in her God-fearing father. Eventually, his inner passions overcome his honest instincts. Keach plays his role without shadings. Zadora, in her screen debut, registers well with her little-girl looks and Lolita sensuality. Orson Welles as a corrupt judge provides the film with a few comic but misplaced moments.

BUTTERFLY KISS
1995, 85 mins, UK ⓥ
D: Michael Winterbottom **A:** Amanda Plummer, Saskia Reeves, Paul Bown, Freda Dowie, Fine Time Fontayne, Des McAleer (Dan)

An often breathtakingly original weld of road movie, lesbian love story, psychodrama, and black comedy, *Butterfly Kiss* toplines Amanda Plummer and Saskia Reeves as two northerners who hook up in a macabre, realistic fairy tale of murder and romantic obsession as they travel the UK's highways. Despite director Michael Winterbottom's technical skills, confidently on display, and Frank Cottrell Boyce's street-poetic dialogue, it's the easy playing of the two leads that motors the movie. In the showier role, Plummer, sporting a thick northern English accent, dominates the early going. Reeves is seemingly outpaced at the start but finally pulls alongside Plummer with a minutely observed study of a pupil who finally becomes the master.

BWANA DEVIL
1952, 79 mins, US
D: Arch Oboler **A:** Robert Stack, Barbara Britton, Nigel Bruce, Ramsay Hill, Paul McVey (Oboler/United Artists)

The first full-length film in Natural Vision 3-D. Production is full of tricks devised to show off the process. The much-ballyhooed point of a lion seemingly leaping out of the screen into the auditorium comes off very mildly. The single gasper is the throwing of a spear by a native, which creates the illusion of coming right into the audience. With banal dialogue, stilted sequences, and impossibly directed players, Oboler tells a story, based on fact, of how two lions halt the building of a railroad in British East Africa.

BYE BYE BIRDIE
1963, 120 mins, US ⓥ ⊙ ▱
D: George Sidney **A:** Janet Leigh, Dick Van Dyke, Ann-Margret, Maureen Stapleton, Bobby Rydell, Jesse Pearson (Columbia)

Credit George Sidney with directing one of the better fun-and-frolic tune packages. Strikingly important is Ann-Margret. Singer, hoofer, and cutie pie, all wrapped up into one, she has the magnetism of early-vintage Judy Garland. Story is the wacky thing about an Elvis Presley type (Jesse Pearson) who swoons the girls no end, what with all that guitar and hipnotism. Songwriter Dick Van Dyke, trying to make time with Janet Leigh while his mother, Maureen Stapleton, interferes, also is engaged in having Presley type appear on the Ed Sullivan TV show.

1963: Nominations: Best Adapted Score, Sound

BYE BYE BRAVERMAN
1968, 94 mins, US
D: Sidney Lumet **A:** George Segal, Jack Warden, Joseph Wiseman, Sorrell Booke, Phyllis Newman, Jessica Walter (Warner/Seven Arts)

Bye Bye Braverman is a curious mixture of tasty and tasteless jokes, all at the expense of Jewish people. Pic describes, in padded vignette and travelogue transition, the hypocritical mourning of a deceased man by four alleged friends. Herbert Sargent has taken the dark comedy approach; were it black comedy, or straight comedy, it might have worked better. George Segal, Jack Warden, Joseph

Wiseman, and Sorrell Booke are the mourners.

BY HOOK OR BY CROOK
See: I Dood It

BY LOVE POSSESSED
1961, 115 mins, US ⊗

D: John Sturges **A:** Lana Turner, Efrem Zimbalist Jr., Jason Robards, George Hamilton, Susan Kohner, Barbara Bel Geddes (United Artists/Mirisch)

James Gould Cozzen's thoughtful novel has been reduced to a complex soap opera: a look into the lives of a half-dozen socially prominent, well-to-do citizens in a small eastern town. Successful lawyer (Efrem Zimbalist Jr.) finds that his perfectly ordered life is, in reality, as full of self-deception and chaos as the lives of some of his less stable friends. The latter include his law partner (Jason Robards), who, after a crippling accident, refuses the love-pity of his wife (Lana Turner), who subsequently turns to double scotches and solace with Zimbalist.

BY THE SWORD
1992, 91 mins, US ⊗ ⊙

D: Jeremy Paul Kagan **A:** F. Murray Abraham, Eric Roberts, Mia Sara, Chris Rydell, Elaine Kagan, Brett Cullen (Movie Group/Foil-Film)

Little-explored world of competitive fencing is the setting for this dramatic crowd pleaser in which F. Murray Abraham delivers a riveting performance as a complex killer, ex-con, lover, janitor, and swordsman. Pic begins in flashback, where his surreal nightmares are haunted by the trainer he skewered 20 years earlier. The dead man's son (Eric Roberts) is now an undefeated, coldhearted champ. Well-choreographed fencing scenes are used as a backdrop for the mounting tension between Roberts and his dad's murderer.

C

CABARET
1972, 124 mins, US Ⓥ ⊙
D: Bob Fosse A: Liza Minnelli, Michael York, Helmut Griem, Marisa Berenson, Fritz Wepper, Joel Grey (AA-ABC)

The film version of *Cabaret* is literate, bawdy, sophisticated, sensual, cynical, heartwarming, and disturbingly thought provoking. Bob Fosse's generally excellent direction recreates the milieu of Germany some 40 years ago. The choice of Minnelli for the part of Sally Bowles was indeed daring. Good-hearted, quasi-sophisticated amorality and hedonism are not precisely Minnelli's professional bag, and within many scenes she seems to carom from golly-gee-whiz-down-home rusticity to something closer to the mark.
1972: Best Director, Actress (Liza Minnelli), Supp. Actor (Joel Grey), Cinematography, Art Direction, Sound, Adapted Scoring, Editing
Nominations: Best Picture, Adapted Screenplay

CABIN BOY
1994, 80 mins, US Ⓥ
D: Adam Resnick A: Chris Elliott, Ritch Brinkley, James Gammon, Brian Doyle-Murray, Brion James, Russ Tamblyn (Touchstone)

Obnoxious, snide, and pointless, this ill-fated spoof carries the bonus of being as crude and gamy as the hold of an old fishing barge. Elliott plays a finishing-school snob who accidentally ends up on a schooner, the *Filthy Whore*, populated by a quintet of surly, grizzled fishermen who delight in abusing him. The ship nears an island called Hell's Bucket, which leads to several fantasy elements lifted from old Sinbad movies, from a snow beast to the six-armed dominatrix Calli (Ann Magnuson). Purposely shoddy sets and special effects only add to the mess.

CABINET OF DR. CALIGARI, THE
See: *Das Cabinett des Dr. Caligari*

DAS CABINETT DES DR. CALIGARI
(THE CABINET OF DR. CALIGARI)
1919, 69 mins, Germany Ⓥ ⊙ ⊗
D: Robert Wiene A: Werner Krauss, Conrad Veidt, Lil Dagover, Friedrich Feher (Decla)

A mystery story told in the Poe manner fairly prods the interest along at a high pace. But it is morbid. The story relates how a faker came to a fair at a small town and proceeded to enliven things by having a somnambulist, Cesare, who had been asleep for 23 years, foretell the future. The faker called himself Dr. Caligari. A murder is foretold and a series of them occur. Of first importance is the direction and cutting. This has resulted in a series of actions so perfectly dovetailed as to carry the story along at a perfect tempo. Robert Wiene has made perfect use of settings that squeeze and turn and adjust the eye, and, through the eye, the mentality. The best performance unquestionably is that given by Werner Krauss as Dr. Caligari. The unpleasant somnambulist, Cesare, is ghoulishly made evident by Conrad Veidt.

CABIN IN THE COTTON
1932, 76 mins, US
D: Michael Curtiz A: Richard Barthelmess, Dorothy Jordan, Bette Davis, Henry B. Walthall, Berton Churchill (First National)

Conflict is the feud between a southern cotton planter and tenant farmer. It's the industrial-capital-vs.-labor wrangle in another setting, and not a particularly fascinating one at that. Nub of the drama is that Marvin Blake (Barthelmess) belongs to the underdog tenant-farmer class, but is befriended by the planter and finds himself between two fires, torn by loyalty to his class and an obligation to his enemy, who also is his benefactor. Also Marvin falls in love with the naughty-naughty planter's daughter (Bette Davis).

CABIN IN THE SKY
1943, 98 mins, US Ⓥ ⊙
D: Vincente Minnelli A: Ethel Waters, Eddie Rochester Anderson, Lena Horne, Louis Armstrong, Rex Ingram (M-G-M)

The picture version is little changed from the original stage show. It still tells of Little Joe Jackson's weakness for dice, likker, and the seductive Georgia Brown, of his mortal wound in a barroom brawl, and of his six-month period of grace obtained by his eternally devoted wife, Petunia. It still shows the contest between Lucifer Jr. and the General for Little Joe's soul. The yarn appears weighed down by unimaginative handling, but Ethel Waters remains the one transcendent asset of the film *Cabin*, just as she was in the original.

1943: Nomination: Best Song ("Happiness Is a Thing Called Joe")

CABLE GUY, THE
1996, 95 mins, US ⊛ ⊙ ▭
D: Ben Stiller **A:** Jim Carrey, Matthew Broderick, Leslie Mann, Jack Black, George Segal, Diane Baker (Columbia)

Architect Steven Kovacs (Matthew Broderick) moves into a new apartment and waits for the cable-service technician to hook him up. The cable guy, Chip Douglas (Carrey), is an electronics geek who is alternately bizarre and compassionate. Steven makes the mistake of agreeing to join him on a pilgrimage to the satellite dish where all electromagnetic signals converge. It's an intriguing enough jumping-off point. But instead of a narrative progression, we are beset with a series of situations marked by mayhem. After its first surge of energy, the film goes on the blink and never recovers.

CACTUS FLOWER
1969, 103 mins, US ⊛ ⊙
D: Gene Saks **A:** Walter Matthau, Ingrid Bergman, Goldie Hawn, Jack Weston, Rick Lenz, Vito Scotti (Columbia)

Cactus Flower drags, which is probably the worst thing that can be said of a light comedy. Matthau is cast as a dentist ready to marry his young mistress, who enlists the aid of his stuffy but organized secretary. This might have worked had they found a suitable foil for him. Bergman, more believable in her role as the nurse, is too reserved and sophisticated opposite Matthau. There are some laughs, and Goldie Hawn, as the Greenwich Village kook with whom Matthau contemplates marriage, makes a credible screen debut.
1969: Best Supp. Actress (Goldie Hawn)

CADAVERI ECCELLENTI (EXQUISITE CORPSES; THE CONTEXT)
1976, 110 mins, Italy
D: Francesco Rosi **A:** Lino Ventura, Alain Cuny, Paolo Bonacelli, Marcel Bozzuffi, Tina Aumont, Max von Sydow (PEA)

Strikingly composed, well acted, with a pervasive sense of hard-to-pinpoint menace in its elliptical plot about political assassinations in Italy, production misses being a top-notch film only because of a certain dryness in the approach taken by director Francesco Rosi. Lino Ventura, playing in thoughtful but colorless fashion, is an inspector uncovering a Watergate-scope conspiracy below the surface of a series of murdered officials. The film lacks visceral excitement. Sequence involving Max von Sydow, as a fanatic official involved in the conspiracy, shows what the film could have been, giving a frightening and totally believable picture of obsessive approach to obliterating political dissent.

CADDIE
1976, 107 mins, Australia ⊛
D: Donald Crombie **A:** Helen Morse, Takis Emmanuel, Jack Thompson, Jacki Weaver, Melissa Jaffer, Ron Blanchard (Buckley)

Based on the autobiography of a Sydney barmaid who, adandoned by her husband, struggled through the Depression to bring up two children, *Caddie* is a sensitively told story of one woman's fight—not a militant, but rather one of the masses; an unsung heroine. Helen Morse, in the title role, maintains a wonderful dignity that is typical of the character's social class and aspirations. But it is in her scenes with Takis Emmanuel that Caddie's story takes on fire. Emmanuel registers power as soon as his face hits the screen.

CADDY, THE
1953, 95 mins, US ⊛
D: Norman Taurog **A:** Dean Martin, Jerry Lewis, Donna Reed, Barbara Bates, Joseph Calleia, Fred Clark (Paramount)

Dean Martin and Jerry Lewis dig a lot of divots among the fairways of *The Caddy*. Amusing romp tells how a couple of San Francisco boys, both loving golf, team for tournament play. Emphasis is on warm humor with heart. Donna Reed plays a rich society gal who sets her cap for Martin and gets him. Barbara Bates is Lewis's sweetie.
1953: Nomination: Best Song ("That's Amore")

CADDYSHACK
1980, 90 mins, US ⊛ ⊙
D: Harold Ramis **A:** Chevy Chase, Rodney Dangerfield, Bill Murray, Michael O'Keefe, Ted Knight, Cindy Morgan (Orion)

Thinly plotted shenanigans unfold against the manicured lawns and posh backdrop of a restricted country club. Stock characters include Chevy Chase as resident golf pro; club prexy and jurist Ted Knight; and Rodney Dangerfield as the personification of antisocial, nouveau riche grossness. Beyond Chase, prime lure is Bill Murray as a foul-habited, semimoronic groundskeeper, constantly aroused by the older femme golfers.

CADILLAC MAN
1990, 97 mins, US ⓥ ⊙
D: Roger Donaldson A: Robin Williams, Tim Robbins, Pamela Reed, Annabella Sciorra, Zack Norman, Fran Drescher (Orion)

Denied an opportunity to showcase his deft rapid-fire comic skills, Robin Williams produces few laughs amid wreckage of the screenplay and poorly paced direction. Only Tim Robbins gets out alive as a crazed, simpleminded, cuckolded husband who ultimately makes hostages of the womanizing Joey (Williams) and everyone else in the car dealership where he works, suspecting correctly that his wife (Annabella Sciorra) is having an affair.

CAESAR AND CLEOPATRA
1946, 135 mins, UK ⓥ
D: Gabriel Pascal A: Vivien Leigh, Claude Rains, Stewart Granger, Flora Robson, Francis L. Sullivan, Cecil Parker (Eagle Lion)

Caesar and Cleopatra is a disappointment. In spite of its prodigal magnificence, indeed in spite of its production values, such vague story interest as it has is hopelessly swamped. Claude Rains's Caesar is accurately and succinctly pinpointed by Vivien Leigh's Cleopatra when she calls him "a nice old gentleman." As for her portrayal of the queen of queens, Rains calls the turn when he tells her with justifiable incredulity that she is not Queen of Egypt, but a queen of the gypsies.
1946: Nomination: Best Color Art Direction

LA CAGE AUX FOLLES
1978, 103 mins, Italy/France ⓥ ⊙
D: Edouard Molinaro A: Ugo Tognazzi, Michel Serrault, Michel Galabru, Claire Maurier, Reni Laurent, Benny Luke (Da-Ma/Artistes Associes)

Jean Poiret's 1973 play of a middle-aged gay couple beset by problems when the 20-year-old son of one announces his marriage gets uneven film treatment. Most of the characters appear stereotyped and the familiar plotting reveals the gay duo could have easily been heterosexual or an odd couple. The film has one solid trump in Michel Serrault, who makes the more feminine member of the happy couple a very shrewd limning of outsize campy gay

attributes that avoid tastelessness. The pic revolves around fooling the parents, not letting them in on the sexual proclivities of the boy's father or his running a transvestite nitery where Serrault is the drag star.

LA CAGE AUX FOLLES II
1980, 100 mins, Italy/France ⓥ
D: Edouard Molinaro A: Ugo Tognazzi, Michel Serrault, Marcel Bozzuffi, Paola Borboni, Giovanni Vettorazzo, Michel Galabru (DaMa/Artistes Associes)

The Abbott and Costello of gaydom are back with new limp-wristed adventures. Producer Marcello Danon and his collaborators (the same as in number one) have mechanically embroiled Michel Serrault and costar Ugo Tognazzi in a dull espionage plot that lacks surprise and comic ingenuity. Almost all the comedy rests on the splendid comic talents of Serrault.

LA CAGE AUX FOLLES 3
(LA CAGE AUX FOLLES 3: THE WEDDING)
1985, 87 mins, France/Italy ⓥ
D: Georges Lautner A: Michel Serrault, Ugo Tognazzi, Antonella Interlenghi, Saverio Vallone, Benny Luke, Stephane Audran (Columbia France/DaMa)

Zaza/Albin (Michel Serrault) and Renato (Ugo Tognazzi) are alive and well, but their gay nightclub is in financial straits. Fortunately, Albin stands to inherit vast property in Scotland. Unfortunately, the will stipulates he must marry and provide an heir within 18 months. Renato, pragmatic and wily, hits on a number of schemes to goad his obstinate mate into wedlock. The poor screenplay and indifferent direction probably won't matter to those who find a full evening's entertainment in Serrault, who is always a scream, literally and figuratively.

CAGED
1950, 96 mins, US
D: John Cromwell A: Eleanor Parker, Agnes Moorehead, Ellen Corby, Hope Emerson, Jan Sterling, Jane Darwell (Warner)

Caged makes a stab at objective reporting of life in a women's prison. A grim, unrelieved study of cause and effect, it adds up to very drab entertainment. Plot provides Eleanor Parker with what is known as a meaty femme role, completely deglamorized. There are other strong portrayals among the predominantly femme cast, and the most colorful is the sadistic prison matron socked over by Hope Emerson.

1950: Nominations: Best Actress (Eleanor Parker), Supp. Actress (Hope Emerson), Story & Screenplay

CAHILL, UNITED STATES MARSHAL
1973, 103 mins, US Ⓥ ⊙ ▯

D: Andrew V. McLaglen **A:** John Wayne, Gary Grimes, George Kennedy, Neville Brand, Clay O'Brien, Marie Windsor (Batjac/Warner)

John Wayne combines the problems of fatherhood with his activities as a lawman to give different motivation from the usual western theme. Crux of the strained relationship between Wayne and his two young sons is his continued absence tracking down criminals, which leads to the boys, 17 and 12, becoming involved in a bank robbery and murder.

CAINE MUTINY, THE
1954, 123 mins, US Ⓥ ⊙

D: Edward Dmytryk **A:** Humphrey Bogart, Jose Ferrer, Van Johnson, Fred MacMurray, Robert Francis, May Wynn (Columbia)

Told on the screen as forcefully as in the Herman Wouk bestselling novel, *The Caine Mutiny* is the story of a war-weary destroyer-minesweeper and its personnel, over which presides Captain Queeg, a man beginning to crack from the strain of playing hero over the years while he hides deep his inferiority complex. Little incidents of faulty command build until, during a raging typhoon when the tired ship is in extreme danger of foundering, the executive officer relieves the captain. Scene after scene in the picture during the hour-and-a-half buildup to the court-martial stands out.

1954: Nominations: Best Picture, Actor (Humphrey Bogart), Supp. Actor (Tom Tully), Screenplay, Editing, Scoring of a Dramatic Picture, Sound

CAIRO ROAD
1950, 88 mins, UK Ⓥ

D: David Macdonald **A:** Eric Portman, Laurence Harvey, Maria Mauban, Camelia, Karel Stepanek, John Gregson (ABPC/Mayflower)

Cairo Road is a so-so thriller dealing with dope smugglers. Action takes place in Cairo, Port Said, and along the Suez. Principal characters are the chief of the Antinarcotic Bureau, suavely played by Eric Portman, and his impetuous assistant (Laurence Harvey).

CALAMITY JANE
1953, 100 mins, US Ⓥ ⊙

D: David Butler **A:** Doris Day, Howard Keel, Allyn McLerie, Philip Carey, Dick Wesson, Paul Harvey (Warner)

Giving such Wild West characters as Calamity Jane and Wild Bill Hickok a workout in a tuned-in western doubtless had strong possibilities, but Warners comes close to missing the stagecoach. Compensating factor is the total of 11 songs (music by Sammy Fain, lyrics by Paul Francis Webster) which gives the production some entertainment wallop. Doris Day works very, very hard at being Calamity and is hardly realistic at all. Howard Keel handles the Bill Hickok assignment with listless amiability.

1953: Best Song ("Secret Love")
Nominations: Best Scoring of a Musical Picture, Sound

CALENDAR GIRL
1993, 90 mins, US Ⓥ ⊙

D: John Whitesell **A:** Jason Priestley, Gabriel Olds, Jerry O'Connell, Joe Pantoliano, Steve Railsbeck, Kurt Fuller (Columbia/Parkway)

A dull, sanctimonious morality tale about the meaning of friendship and manhood. Preying on his friends' fantasy of meeting Marilyn Monroe, Roy Darpinian (Jason Priestley) talks his pals (Jerry O'Connell, Gabriel Olds) into a crazy plan: why not leave their boring Nevada town and drive to Hollywood? Chief problem is unfunny, schematic script, which consists of the boys' interminable machinations to meet Monroe.

CALIFORNIA DOLLS, THE
See: . . . All the Marbles

CALIFORNIA MAN
See: Encino Man

CALIFORNIA SPLIT
1974, 108 mins, US Ⓥ ▯

D: Robert Altman **A:** George Segal, Elliott Gould, Ann Prentiss, Gwen Welles, Edward Walsh, Joseph Walsh (Columbia)

California Split is an aimless, strung-out series of vignettes starring George Segal and Elliott Gould as compulsive gamblers. The film lacks a cohesive and reinforced sense of story direction. The pic is well cast—Segal and Gould contrast well, while Ann Prentiss and Gwen Welles play happy hookers to good effect.

CALIFORNIA SUITE
1978, 103 mins, US Ⓥ ⊙
D: Herbert Ross **A:** Alan Alda, Michael Caine, Bill Cosby, Jane Fonda, Walter Matthau, Elaine May (Columbia)

Neil Simon and Herbert Ross have gambled in radically altering *California Suite* as it appeared on stage. Instead of four separate playlets, there is now one semicohesive narrative revolving around visitors to the Beverly Hills Hotel. Alan Alda and Jane Fonda portray a divorced couple, while Michael Caine and Maggie Smith play a showbiz couple with varying sexual tastes. Walter Matthau has to explain his unwitting infidelity to spouse Elaine May, and Richard Pryor and Bill Cosby, accompanied by their wives (Gloria Gifford and Sheila Frazier), manage to turn a vacation into a series of disastrous mishaps. The technique is less than successful, veering from poignant emotionalism to broad slapstick in sudden shifts.
1978: Best Supp. Actress (Maggie Smith)
Nominations: Best Adapted Screenplay, Art Direction

CALIGULA
1979, 150 mins, Italy/US Ⓥ ⊙
D: Tinto Brass **A:** Malcolm McDowell, Teresa Ann Savoy, Helen Mirren, Peter O'Toole, John Gielgud (Penthouse/Felix)

With the biggest investment ever in porn to play with, Tinto Brass sifts through the pages of first-century Rome under syphilitic Tiberius and epileptic Caligula to demonstrate the unlimited baseness of the human condition. Such established names as John Gielgud and Peter O'Toole will have to be seen to be believed. Malcolm McDowell as the sick and/or insane emperor runs the gamut of cardboard emotions from grand guignol to hapless pathos.

CALL ME BWANA
1963, 93 mins, UK Ⓥ
D: Gordon Douglas **A:** Bob Hope, Anita Ekberg, Edie Adams, Lionel Jeffries, Percy Herbert, Arnold Palmer (Eon)

Hope has built up a phony reputation as an intrepid explorer. When an American moon-probe capsule is lost in the jungle and it's necessary to locate it before foreign powers get their thieving mitts on it, Hope is detailed for the task because of his supposed expert knowledge of the locale. Overall, there's enough fun to keep this bubbling along merrily. La Ekberg, though an unlikely Mata Hari, is a sound and decorative foil for Hope.

CALL ME GENIUS
See: The Rebel

CALL ME MADAM
1953, 114 mins, US
D: Walter Lang **A:** Ethel Merman, Donald O'Connor, Vera-Ellen, George Sanders, Billy De Wolfe, Helmut Dantine (20th Century-Fox)

A hit musical on Broadway with Ethel Merman, as Ambassador Sally Adams, the fabulous femme diplomat, representing the US in the mythical Grand Duchy of Lichtenburg. Merman still reigns in the cinematic version. Added pluses are via the widened scope and richness of the production, lush mountains, and extra trimmings for the delightful Irving Berlin score. Also, there's the fresh, inventive choreography staged by Robert Alton, with O'Connor and Vera-Ellen as a terping combo of top caliber.
1953: Best Scoring of a Musical Picture
Nomination: Best Color Costume Design

CALL ME MISTER
1951, 96 mins, US
D: Lloyd Bacon **A:** Betty Grable, Dan Dailey, Danny Thomas, Dale Robertson, Richard Boone, Jeffrey Hunter (20th Century-Fox)

Drawing but lightly on its Broadway-revue namesake for book and songs, *Call Me Mister* is smooth, easy-to-take screen entertainment. Garbed in a glowing Technicolor dress and gifted with musical-wise Betty Grable and Dan Dailey, the footage sparks along through songs, dances (staged by Busby Berkeley), and a skeleton story framework with an infectious zip.

CALL NORTHSIDE 777
1948, 111 mins, US
D: Henry Hathaway **A:** James Stewart, Richard Conte, Lee J. Cobb, Helen Walker, Betty Garde (20th Century-Fox)

Call Northside 777 registers only with a mild impact. Among the film's principal drawbacks is James Stewart's jarring and unpersuasive performance as a Chicago reporter who's assigned to dig up a human-interest angle out of an 11-year-old murder case. Based on a celebrated miscarriage of justice in 1932, the screenplay constructs a serviceable plot on the factual groundwork. Richard Conte gives an intensely sincere performance as the young Polish-American who is railroaded to jail.

CALL OF THE WILD, THE
1935, 89 mins, US
D: William A. Wellman **A:** Clark Gable, Loretta Young, Jack Oakie, Frank Conroy, Reginald Owen, Sidney Toler (20th Century)

The lionhearted dog that was Jack London's creation as the leading character of *Call of the Wild* emerges now as a stooge for a rather conventional pair of human lovebirds. Changes have made the canine classic hardly recognizable, but they have not done any damage. Clark Gable strong-and-silents himself expertly and Loretta Young is lovely and competent. But Jack Oakie has the laughs, and they land him on top. It's a story of treachery, hardship, violence, and unrequited love in Alaska, so anything that does away with sadness for a momentary giggle is highly welcome.

CALL OF THE WILD, THE
1973, 100 mins, UK/France/W. Germany/Italy/Norway/Spain ⓥ
D: Ken Annakin **A:** Charlton Heston, Raimund Harmsdorf, Michele Mercier, George Eastman, Sancho Gracia, Maria Rohm (Towers of London)

Jack London's thrilling, often-filmed tale trails a couple of roughnecks, John and Pete, on their gold-digging, mail-hopping, and booze-deal fortune hunts in Alaska's snowbound wilderness. Director Ken Annakin picked a few good actors (Charlton Heston and Italo-western hero George Eastman). But everybody appears to play merely along action line on their own and create a vacuum around themselves.

CAMELOT
1967, 179 mins, US ⓥ ⊙ ▭
D: Joshua Logan **A:** Richard Harris, Vanessa Redgrave, Franco Nero, David Hemmings, Lionel Jeffries, Estelle Winwood (Warner/Seven Arts)

While most big musicals have fine production, dazzling costumes, and all that, what gives *Camelot* special value is a central dramatic conflict that throbs with human anguish and compassion. The focus is kept on the three mentally tortured people—the cuckolded king, the cheating queen, the confused knight. Joshua Logan rates extraordinary praise for the performances he elicits from Richard Harris as King Arthur, Vanessa Redgrave as Guinevere, and Franco Nero as the knight whose idealism succumbs to passion.

1967: Best Art Direction, Adapted Scoring, Costume Design
Nominations: Best Cinematography, Sound

CAMERAMAN, THE
1928, 68 mins, US ⊗
D: Edward Sedgwick **A:** Buster Keaton, Marceline Day, Harold Goodwin, Sidney Bracy, Harry Gribbon (M-G-M)

Good laugh picture with Buster Keaton. The same old stencil about a boob that does everything wrong and cashes in finally through sheer accident. Keaton is a problem on love interest. In the present case his cowlike adoration of the heroine (Marceline Day) is used to build up sympathy as a counterirritant to his abysmal stupidity. In trying to land a job with M-G-M News, Keaton, as a tintype photographer suddenly turned cinematic, goes through a series of hoke adventures.

CAMILLA
1994, 95 mins, Canada/UK ⓥ ⊙
D: Deepa Mehta **A:** Jessica Tandy, Bridget Fonda, Elias Koteas, Maury Chaykin, Graham Greene, Hume Cronyn (Skreba/Shaftesbury)

Featuring a standout performance from Jessica Tandy in her last starring big-screen role, *Camilla* is a warm, funny road movie. Pic opens with Freda Lopez (Bridget Fonda), a frustrated singer/songwriter whose husband, Vincent (Elias Koteas), is more that a little skeptical of her musical talents. They meet Camilla Cara (Tandy), a wacky old woman prone to tall tales. Freda and Camilla, who hit it off immediately, decide to go to Toronto to catch a special performance of a Brahms concerto. Film soon turns into a May-December female-buddy pic over a series of rather improbable adventures.

CAMILLE
1921, 90 mins, US ⊗
D: Ray C. Smallwood **A:** Nazimova, Rudolph Valentino, Arthur Hoyt, Zeffie Tilbury, Edward Connelly, Patsy Ruth Miller (Nazimova/Metro)

Nazimova totally immerses her own distinct personality in that of the famed heroine. Instead of the sinuous, clinging Nazimova, she appears an actress almost newborn for the part. Second to the star is the Armand of Rudolph Valentino. There are many opportunities for obtrusiveness in the role, but he keeps it correct to the minutest detail.

CAMILLE
1927, 96 mins, US ⊗

D: Fred Niblo **A:** Norma Talmadge, Gilbert Roland, Lilyan Tashman, Maurice Costello, Harvey Clark, Alec B. Francis (Talmadge/First National)

A pretty love story that lacks the punch to make it a standout. For some reason Niblo omitted the traditional sympathy that goes with Camille's death or a pull on the heartstrings when she gives up Armand at the instigation of his father. For a demimondaine supposedly in the throes of the first and only real love of her life, Talmadge gives in much too easily. And through it all Talmadge looks beautiful. Never better, besides giving a sterling performance.

CAMILLE
1937, 108 mins, US ⊘

D: George Cukor **A:** Greta Garbo, Robert Taylor, Lionel Barrymore, Elizabeth Allan, Jessie Ralph, Henry Daniell (M-G-M)

George Cukor directs this famous play with rare skill. Robert Taylor plays with surprising assurance and ease. In all the familiar Armand scenes, Taylor holds up his end of the story with distinction. Garbo's impersonation of Marguerite Gautier is one of her best portraits. She wears striking clothes, white usually, and while she looks older than the ardent young Armand, the disparity does not work against the illusion.

1937: Nomination: Best Actress (Greta Garbo)

CAMILLE CLAUDEL
1988, 170 mins, France ⊘ ⊙ ▢

D: Bruno Nuytten **A:** Isabelle Adjani, Gerard Depardieu, Laurent Crevill, Alain Cuny, Madeleine Robinson, Katrine Boorman

Conscientious but dramatically conventional biopic about the gifted sculptress Camille Claudel, who was the muse and mistress of Auguste Rodin. Adjani throws herself into a role worthy of her abilities, giving intense relief, if not enough pathos, to a strong-willed femme artist. Depardieu, sporting a thick beard, sculpts a massive portrait of the artist as man, lover, and creator. What's missing between the two performances, however, is the evolution of feelings complicated by professional and private jealousies.

CAMPBELL'S KINGDOM
1957, 100 mins, UK

D: Ralph Thomas **A:** Dirk Bogarde, Stanley Baker, Michael Craig, Barbara Murray, James Robertson Justice, Athene Seyler (Rank)

Campbell's Kingdom is virtually a British western. It is a straightforward, virile, action-packed yarn with ample excitement and mounting drama. When Dirk Bogarde, with only six months to live, arrives in the township of Come Lucky in the Rockies to take up his grandfather's inheritance, a whole train of skulduggery is unleashed. Ruthless contractor Stanley Baker wants to flood the valley as part of a new hydroelectric scheme involving building of a new dam with inferior cement.

CAMP ON BLOOD ISLAND, THE
1958, 82 mins, UK ▢

D: Val Guest **A:** Carl Mohner, Andre Morell, Edward Underdown, Michael Goodliffe, Barbara Shelley, Michael Gwynn (Hammer)

The yarn, based on a real-life incident, takes place in a Japanese prisoner-of-war camp, ruled over by a sadistic commandant who has sworn to massacre all the British prisoners should Japan lose the war. The British officers learn on a secret radio that the war has ended, but somewhat implausibly, they manage to keep the secret from the Nips.

CANADIAN BACON
1995, 91 mins, US ⊘

D: Michael Moore **A:** Alan Alda, John Candy, Rhea Perlman, Kevin Pollak, Rip Torn, Bill Nunn (PolyGram/Propaganda)

The premise paints modern-day Americans as restless for the smell of battle. The nation's rivals, however, have all been quelled, and the president (Alan Alda) is an ineffectual peacenik. At the White House, spin doctor Stuart Smiley (Kevin Pollak) hits on the idea of a northern scapegoat. Soon phony skirmishes are being concocted to fuel tension, and the gullible—like Niagara Falls sheriff Bud Boomer (John Candy)—not only buy it, they organize their own patriotic, gun-toting forays. *Canadian Bacon* has all the makings of a funny, acidic satire. There's just enough truth in the proceedings to give the humor bite.

CANARY MURDER CASE
1929, 80 mins, US

D: Malcolm St. Clair **A:** William Powell, James Hall, Louise Brooks, Jean Arthur, Gustav von Seyffertitz, Eugene Pallette (Paramount)

Philo Vance (William Powell), detective, doesn't look at a dame without a professional motive. He's strictly a crime solver. The Canary (Louise Brooks) was a merciless little blackmailer. On the night she was murdered, she called up three rich suckers, informing them she would shortly marry Jimmy and advising them to deliver some hefty wedding gifts that evening in person. Intricacies of the motive, crime, and detection are intelligently directed.

CAN-CAN
1960, 134 mins, US Ⓥ ⊙ ▭
D: Walter Lang A: Frank Sinatra, Shirley MacLaine, Maurice Chevalier, Louis Jourdan, Juliet Prowse, Marcel Dalio (20th Century-Fox)

Can-Can is a serviceable musical. It's Las Vegas, 1960; not Montmartre, 1896. MacLaine is bouncy, outgoing, scintillating, vivacious, and appealing, but French she ain't. Sinatra is, well, Sinatra. The juxtaposition of authentic Parisians Maurice Chevalier and Louis Jourdan is jarring. The musical score has been enhanced with three Cole Porter songs not in the original Broadway musical. The dance numbers, for the most part, are the highlights of the film, particularly MacLaine's apache dance. The can-can is fun, but about as lewd and lascivious as a maypole dance.
1960: Nominations: Best Color Costume Design, Scoring of a Musical Picture

CANDIDATE, THE
1972, 109 mins, US Ⓥ ⊙
D: Michael Ritchie A: Robert Redford, Peter Boyle, Don Porter, Allen Garfield, Karen Carlson, Melvyn Douglas (Warner)

An excellent drama starring Robert Redford as a naive liberal political novice who wises up fast. The well-structured and developed screenplay takes Redford from a rural legal-assistance vocation through the temptations and tortures of mass-merchandising politics, to an upset victory over longtime California Senator Don Porter. Redford's superior acting talents are nearly all on display herein in a virtuoso performance.
1972: Best Original Story & Screenplay
Nomination: Best Sound

CANDY
1968, 123 mins, US/Italy/France
D: Christian Marquand A: Charles Aznavour, Marlon Brando, Richard Burton, James Burton, John Huston, Ewa Aulin (Selmur/Dear)

Based on a novel that was a successful satire on pornographic stories, film is at times hilarious, delightfully outrageous, silly, flat, and routine. Director Christian Marquand utilizes a Buck Henry adaptation, a very fine comedy sexpot newcomer (Ewa Aulin) and a strong cast of cameo stars and character thesps. Candy tells of the unbelievably naive and innocent sexpot heroine, whose adventures were setups for the de rigueur sexual incidents found in most pornography.

CANDYMAN
1992, 93 mins, US Ⓥ ⊙
D: Bernard Rose A: Virginia Madsen, Tony Todd, Xander Berkeley, Kasi Lemmons, Vanessa Williams, DeJuan Guy (Propaganda)

Candyman is an upper-register horror item that delivers the requisite shocks and gore but doesn't cheat or cop out. Doctoral candidate Helen Lyle (Virginia Madsen) is studying neighborhood legends and learns that Candyman, the educated, talented son of a slave, had his hand cut off and was put to death for impregnating a young upper-class woman. Lyle's investigation leads her to the site of the century-old outrage, and it doesn't take long for her to discover his gruesome lair.

CANDYMAN
FAREWELL TO THE FLESH
1995, 94 mins, US Ⓥ ⊙
D: Bill Condon A: Tony Todd, Kelly Rowan, Timothy Carhart, Veronica Cartwright, William O'Leary, Fay Hauser (Propaganda/PFE)

The avenger now resurfaces in New Orleans French Quarter in time for Mardi Gras. This time he appears to be taking a personal and lethal interest in the aristocratic Tarrant family. Dad, who believes he knows how to destroy Candyman, is first to feel the power of the merciless hook. Son Ethan (William O'Leary) is fingered for the crime and daughter Annie (Kelly Rowan) winds up delving into the legend and uncovering its dark secrets. For much of the picture, the audience is way ahead of the screen characters in guessing what comes next.

CAN HEIRONYMUS MERKIN
EVER FORGET MERCY HUMPPE
AND FIND TRUE HAPPINESS?
1969, 117 mins, UK
D: Anthony Newley A: Anthony Newley, Joan Collins, Milton Berle, George Jessel, Connie Kreski, Bruce Forsyth (Universal, Taralex)

This film is the work of Anthony New

ley, who plays an introspective film singing idol who relives his part-real, part-illusionary past in a movie within a movie, drawing on strange characters to people this past as well as lovelies who line up in wild expectancy as Heironymus plucks them one by one.

CANNERY ROW
1982, 120 mins, US Ⓥ
D: David S. Ward **A:** Nick Nolte, Debra Winger, Audra Lindley, Frank McRae, M. Emmet Walsh, Tom Mahoney (M-G-M/United Artists)

1940s tale centers mostly upon the sketchy activities of a self-employed marine biologist named Doc (Nick Nolte). Across the way stands the neighborhood bordello, into which comes mixed-up drifter girl Suzy (Debra Winger), who has eyes for Doc. The two sort of get together and break up numerous times. Nolte seems ideally cast but is hampered by incomplete nature of the part as written. Winger's winning personality and great cracking voice carry her through here, but she relies unduly on a few pat mannerisms.

CANNONBALL
(UK: CARQUAKE)
1976, 93 mins, US/Hong Kong Ⓥ
D: Paul Bartel **A:** David Carradine, Bill McKinney, Veronica Hamel, Gerrit Graham, Robert Carradine, Martin Scorsese (New World/Shaws)

Cannonball will please those who won't rest until they see every car in creation destroyed and aflame. The "sophisticated" story line puts David Carradine, Bill McKinney, and various other drivers and characters in autos in Los Angeles and promises $100,000 to the first to arrive in New York.

CANNONBALL RUN
1981, 93 mins, US Ⓥ ⊙
D: Hal Needham **A:** Burt Reynolds, Roger Moore, Farrah Fawcett, Dom DeLuise, Dean Martin, Sammy Davis Jr. (20th Century-Fox)

Film takes place in that redneck never-never land where most of the guys are beer-guzzling good ol' boys and all the gals are fabulously built tootsies. Cross-country race of the title comes off as almost entirely incidental to the star turns. Overall effect is akin to watching the troupe take a vacation.

CANNONBALL RUN II
1984, 108 mins, US Ⓥ ⊙
D: Hal Needham **A:** Burt Reynolds, Dom DeLuise, Dean Martin, Sammy Davis Jr., Telly Savalas, Shirley MacLaine (Golden Harvest/Warner)

This film is so inept that the best actor in the pic is Jilly Rizzo. But he has a great advantage: he's on screen five seconds and he doesn't have to talk. Again, a bunch of crazies, in a disparate collection of cars, are engaged in racing across the country to collect a lot of money.

CANNON FOR CORDOBA
1970, 104 mins, US ⊡
D: Paul Wendkos **A:** George Peppard, Giovanna Ralli, Raf Vallone, Pete Duel, Don Gordon, Francine York (United Artists/Mirisch)

The story is about Mex outlaws who are a source of agony to the American military. Brigadier General John J. Pershing (John Russell) dispatches his intelligence captain (George Peppard) to quell the disturbances. Peppard and a few friends conquer the army led by adversary Cordoba (Raf Vallone).

CAN SHE BAKE A CHERRY PIE?
1983, 90 mins, US Ⓥ
D: Henry Jaglom **A:** Karen Black, Michael Emil, Michael Margotta, Frances Fisher, Martin Frydberg (Jagfilm)

A talky comedy, in which the scripter-director puts his characters in a number of sitcom situations, feeds them the opening lines of their scenes, and lets them embroider the rest on their own. Characters are built very much around the personality of the two main actors, Karen Black giving a beautiful performance, and Michael Emil brings back many of the peculiarities of his part in *Sitting Ducks*.

CANTERBURY TALE, A
1944, 124 mins, UK Ⓥ
D: Michael Powell, Emeric Pressburger **A:** Eric Portman, Sheila Sim, Dennis Price, John Sweet, Charles Hawtrey, Freda Jackson (Archers)

Sincerity and simplicity shine through every foot of this oversized modern version of the Chaucer epic. Here is rare beauty. Sheila Sim is the sole femme in the story. Star of the film, Eric Portman, gives a splendid, restrained performance as a small-town justice of the peace. Four miracles occur in this story, one to each of the four principal characters.

201

CANTERVILLE GHOST, THE
1944, 95 mins, US Ⓥ

D: Jules Dassin **A:** Charles Laughton, Robert Young, Margaret O'Brien, Peter Lawford, Una O'Connor, Mike Mazurki (M-G-M)

Entertaining comedy-drama. Margaret O'Brien and Charles Laughton come through with top-notch performances. Yarn is about a 300-year-old ghost (Laughton), once walled up alive in the castle by his father because he proved a coward on the field of battle, who is looking for a kinsman to perform an act of bravery in his name so that he can be freed from his miserable existence.

CAN'T HELP SINGING
1944, 89 mins, US

D: Frank Ryan **A:** Deanna Durbin, Robert Paige, Akim Tamiroff, David Bruce (Universal)

Can't Help Singing is a bright, colorful, and gay filmusical, notable for the collection of tunes by Jerome Kern and the fine scenic mounting. Deanna Durbin's initial color starrer, and her first filmusical comedy vehicle, is set in the 1850 era, opening in Washington to introduce Durbin as the daughter of an influential senator who's determined to marry a cavalry officer. When the senator's influence ships the latter to a California post, the girl follows but never quite catches up.

CAN'T STOP THE MUSIC
1980, 118 mins, US ▭

D: Nancy Walker **A:** Valerie Perrine, Steve Guttenberg, June Havoc, Barbara Rush, Leigh Taylor-Young, the Village People (AFD/Allan Carr)

Writers have recreated the old "I know, we'll put on a show" gimmick to hinge their story on. Valerie Perrine plays the ex-model with a heart of gold. Her roommate is an aspiring pop composer (Steve Guttenberg) whom she helps. She recruits various friends (the Village People) to sing on a demo tape. Among the standout sequences is the "Y.M.C.A." number, replete with a chorus line of young males side-diving just like in an Esther Williams aquastravaganza in the 1950s.

CAPE FEAR
1962, 105 mins, US Ⓥ ⊙

D: J. Lee Thompson **A:** Gregory Peck, Robert Mitchum, Polly Bergen, Lori Martin, Martin Balsam, Telly Savalas (Universal/Melville-Talbot)

As a forthright exercise in cumulative terror, *Cape Fear* is a competent and visually polished entry. The screenplay deals with the scheme of a sadistic ex-convict (Robert Mitchum) to gain revenge against a small-town Georgia lawyer (Gregory Peck), his wife, and daughter. Mitchum has no trouble being utterly hateful. Wearing a panama fedora and cockily chomping a cigar, the menace of his visage has the look of a poised snake.

CAPE FEAR
1991, 128 mins, US Ⓥ ⊙ ▭

D: Martin Scorsese **A:** Robert De Niro, Nick Nolte, Jessica Lange, Juliette Lewis, Joe Don Baker, Illeana Douglas (Universal/Amblin)

Cape Fear is a smart and stylish remake of the 1962 suspenser. Changes, however, enrich and blacken the material, making the characters squirm physically, morally, and sexually. In maximum souped-up style, director Martin Scorsese slams through the mandatory plot mechanics with powerful short scenes, dynamic in-your-face dollies and cranes, and machine-gun editing. De Niro's Cady is a memorable nasty.

1991: Nominations: Best Actor (Robert De Niro), Supp. Actress (Juliette Lewis)

CAPONE
1975, 101 mins, US

D: Steve Carver **A:** Ben Gazzara, Susan Blakely, Harry Guardino, John Cassavetes, Sylvester Stallone, Peter Maloney (20th Century-Fox)

Capone, a somewhat crude, violent, and déjà vu actioner, focuses on Ben Gazzara as Capone, showing his brutish, casual arrogance in a climb from neighborhood punk to a Chi rackets kingpin, then his decline via an income-tax rap. Gazzara has evidently gone to great lengths to attempt a full characterization, but it's hard to shoehorn developed drama between machine-gun bullets.

CAPRICE
1967, 97 mins, US Ⓥ ▭

D: Frank Tashlin **A:** Doris Day, Richard Harris, Ray Walston, Jack Kruschen, Edward Mulhare, Michael J. Pollard (20th Century-Fox)

A timely and inventive plot—industrial espionage—is never fully developed in either writing, acting, or direction. Doris Day and Richard Harris are double-crossing double agents working, variously, for US cosmetics king Jack Kruschen, British counterpart Edward Mulhare, or Interpol. Elements of comedy, murder, satire, and psychology are blended uncertainly in the never-boiling pot.

CAPRICORN ONE
1978, 127 mins, US Ⓥ ⊙ ▭
D: Peter Hyams A: Elliott Gould, James Brolin, Brenda Vaccaro, Sam Waterston, O. J. Simpson, Hal Holbrook (Associated General)

Capricorn One begins with a workable, if cynical cinematic premise: the first manned space flight to Mars was a hoax and the American public was fooled through Hollywood gimmickry into believing that the phony landing happened. But Peter Hyams's script asks another audience—the one in the theater—to accept something far more illogical, the uncovering of the hoax by reporter Elliott Gould. The astronaut trio of James Brolin, Sam Waterston, and O. J. Simpson together add up to nothing; there's no group chemistry.

CAPTAIN BLOOD
1935, 119 mins, US Ⓥ ⊙
D: Michael Curtiz A: Errol Flynn, Olivia de Havilland, Basil Rathbone, Lionel Atwill, Ross Alexander, Guy Kibbee (Cosmopolitan/Warner)

Captain Blood, from the Rafael Sabatini novel, is a spectacle which will establish both Errol Flynn and Olivia de Havilland. It's a lavish, swashbuckling saga of the Spanish main. The engaging Flynn is the titular Peter Blood, a peer among Caribbean pirates. De Havilland is romantically beauteous as the unsympathetic plantation owner's niece. This supplies a modicum of romantic interest, although all too paltry. Lionel Atwill is sufficiently hateful as the uncle. Basil Rathbone is an effective pirate cocaptain, he and Flynn engaging in an arresting duel in the course of events.
1935: Nominations: Best Picture, Sound

CAPTAIN CAREY, U.S.A.
1950, 92 mins, US
D: Mitchell Leisen A: Alan Ladd, Wanda Hendrix, Francis Lederer, Joseph Calleia (Paramount)

Plot gets its title from Alan Ladd's OSS work in Italy during the war. Action opens during that period to establish principal characters and then deals with Ladd's return to Italy to avenge the death of a girl who had aided his war work. He finds her still alive but married, plans to return to the States until a number of mysterious doings intrigue him enough to stay.

CAPTAIN FROM CASTILE
1947, 140 mins, US
D: Henry King A: Tyrone Power, Jean Peters, Cesar Romero, Lee J. Cobb, Antonio Moreno (20th Century-Fox)

For this plume-and-saber epic of 16th-century Spanish imperial conquerors, producer and production chief have assembled a group of thespians who are cleanly tailored for the various parts. Led by Tyrone Power, who's rarely been shown to better advantage, the roster is buttressed by Cesar Romero, in a stirringly virile portrait of Cortez; Lee J. Cobb, as a fortune hunter; John Sutton, as a velvety villain; and newcomer Jean Peters, a buxom, appealing wench for the romantic byplay.
1947: Nomination: Best Scoring of a Dramatic Picture

CAPTAIN HORATIO HORNBLOWER R.N.
1951, 116 mins, UK Ⓥ ⊙
D: Raoul Walsh A: Gregory Peck, Virginia Mayo, Robert Beatty, Denis O'Dea, James Robertson Justice, Stanley Baker (Warner)

The exploits of one of Britain's greatest fictional naval adventurers have been filmed by with spectacular success. In his interpretation of the title role, Gregory Peck captures the spirit of the character and atmosphere of the period. Whether as the ruthless captain ordering a flogging as a face-saving act for a junior officer or tenderly nursing Virginia Mayo through yellow fever, he never fails to reflect the Forester character.

CAPTAIN KIDD
1945, 89 mins, US Ⓥ
D: Rowland V. Lee A: Charles Laughton, Randolph Scott, Barbara Britton, John Carradine, Gilbert Roland, John Qualen (United Artists)

Story of the late 17th century when Captain Kidd (Laughton) freebooted the Spanish Main on the route of ships from England to fabulously rich India. When the king enlists Kidd as a loyal subject of the empire to give safe escort to treasury-laden vessels belonging to the crown, Kidd's double-crossing leads him to the gallows. Laughton is capital as the ruthless brigand of the seas, ruling his equally villainous rogues with stern cruelty.

CAPTAIN KRONOS: VAMPIRE HUNTER

1974, 91 mins, UK ⓥ
D: Brian Clemens **A:** Horst Janson, John Carson, Shane Briant, Caroline Munro, John Cater, Ian Hendry (Hammer)

Captain Kronos: Vampire Hunter, as played by Horst Janson, is a prototype blond Germanic superstud caped like an operetta leading man. Kronos solves a vampire mystery with a lot of swash and buckle.

CAPTAIN NEWMAN, M.D.

1963, 126 mins, US ⓥ
D: David Miller **A:** Gregory Peck, Tony Curtis, Angie Dickinson, Eddie Albert, Bobby Darin, Robert Duvall (Universal/Brentwood/Reynard)

Captain Newman, M.D. oscillates between scenes of great dramatic impact and somewhat strained and contrived comedy of the heartwarming variety. Hero of the story is Captain Newman (Gregory Peck), chief of the neuropsychiatric ward of a wartime (1944) army hospital. Newman's treatment of three cases is illustrated. One involves a decorated corporal (Bobby Darin) who believes himself a coward. In between all of this, Newman gets his kicks in a romance with his nurse (Angie Dickinson) and by observing the antics of his number-one orderly (Tony Curtis), a glib, resourceful operator with a streak of larceny.
1963: Nominations: Best Supp. Actor (Bobby Darin), Adapted Screenplay, Sound

CAPTAINS COURAGEOUS

1937, 115 mins, US ⓥ ⊙
D: Victor Fleming **A:** Spencer Tracy, Freddie Bartholomew, Lionel Barrymore, Melvyn Douglas, Charley Grapewin, Mickey Rooney (M-G-M)

The Kipling yarn, built around a wealthy, motherless brat who accidentally lands with a cod-fishing fleet and undergoes regeneration during an enforced three months' piscatorial quest, has been given splendid production, performance, photography, and dramatic composition. Young Bartholomew's transition from a brat to a lovable child is done with convincing strokes. His performance is matched by Tracy, who doesn't seem right doing an accent and singing songs, but he, too, later gets under the skin of the character.
1937: Best Actor (Spencer Tracy)
Nominations: Best Picture, Screenplay, Editing

CAPTAINS OF THE CLOUDS

1942, 113 mins, US
D: Michael Curtiz **A:** James Cagney, Dennis Morgan, Brenda Marshall, Alan Hale, George Tobias, Reginald Gardiner (Warner)

First half depicts the adventurous and rowdy experiences of a group of freelance bush fliers of northern Canada who pilot supplies to the settlers and prospectors along the lakes and rivers of the northland, and second portion outlines their adventures as members of the Royal Canadian Air Force training schools. James Cagney holds attention throughout as the nervy, adventurous, and happy-go-lucky flying expert.

CAPTAIN'S PARADISE, THE

1953, 93 mins, UK ⓥ ⊙
D: Anthony Kimmins **A:** Alec Guinness, Yvonne De Carlo, Celia Johnson, Charles Goldner, Miles Malleson, Tutte Lemkow (London)

Alec Guinness, a ship's captain, has been in search of paradise, and eventually he finds it by having a wife in Gibraltar who satisfies his domestic yearning and a diversion in North Africa who panders to the more exotic things in life. The situation is developed with good clean fun and satire. The role of the captain is a natural for Guinness while the two women in his life are admirably portrayed by Yvonne De Carlo and Celia Johnson.

CAPTIVE

1986, 95 mins, UK/France ⓥ
D: Paul Mayersberg **A:** Irina Brook, Oliver Reed, Xavier Deluc, Corinne Decla, Hiro Arai, Nic Reding (Virgin/World Audio)

The kidnapping of a beautiful rich young girl, not for money, nor for sex, but just for the joy of doing it is the theme intricately developed in *Captive*. A trio of kidnappers—a French boy, a Japanese boy, and an English girl—imprison a rich girl. The object of the mission is a brainwashing exercise, to mold the girl to their mode of life.

CAPTIVE CITY, THE

1952, 91 mins, US
D: Robert Wise **A:** John Forsythe, Joan Camden, Harold J. Kennedy, Marjorie Crossland, Victor Sutherland, Ray Teal (Aspen/United Artists)

Tense, absorbing drama of a small town editor's fight against corruption has a documentary quality that rings with authenticity. John Forsythe and Harold J. Kennedy are co-owners of a newspaper. A local private detective discovers the existence of a big-time gambling syndicate operating with the knowledge of the city fathers, the local police, and the respectable elements of the community.

CAPTIVE HEART, THE
1946, 108 mins, UK
D: Basil Dearden A: Michael Redgrave, Rachel Kempson, Mervyn Johns, Jack Warner, Basil Radford, Gordon Jackson (Ealing)

Michael Redgrave, as a Czech fleeing from the Gestapo, takes on the identity of a dead English army officer. Even when he convinces the British, and has won freedom through repatriation, he's up against the task of squaring himself with the wife of the dead man whose identity he has assumed. That this final sequence holds one's attention says something for the writing, acting, and directing.

CAPTIVE IN THE LAND, A
1991, 96 mins, France/US/USSR Ⓥ
D: John Berry A: Sam Waterston, Alexander Potapov (Gloria/Gorky Studios/Soviet American)

A Captive in the Land is a ruggedly effective allegorical survival tale. Shot on forbidding arctic wastelands as well as in Russian studios, pic plays as a potent two-character piece about strangers forced to battle nature together. Striking opening sequence presents the crash of a Soviet military plane and rescue jump by an American (Sam Waterston). The two men set out on an arduous journey in search of possible civilization. Implicit in the personal/political exchanges is the notion that, while the American may think he's much freer than the disabled man he rescues, he's actually just as stuck as the Russian.

CAPTURE, THE
1950, 91 mins, US
D: John Sturges A: Lew Ayres, Teresa Wright, Victor Jory, Jacqueline White (RKO/Showtime)

The Capture is an offbeat drama, with psychological overtones, that plays off against the raw and rugged background of Mexican locales. Lew Ayres is fleeing the Mexican rurales, wanted on a charge of murder. A year before he had killed a fugitive, wanted for a robbery. The possibility of the man's innocence haunted him, and Ayres sought out the widow. They fall in love, are married, but his guilty conscience makes full happiness impossible. Ayres and Teresa Wright are very capable in the lead characters.

CARAVAGGIO
1986, 89 mins, UK Ⓥ
D: Derek Jarman A: Nigel Terry, Sean Bean, Garry Cooper, Spencer Leigh, Tilda Swinton, Michael Gough (BFI)

Caravaggio triumphantly rises above its financial restrictions. Pic is an imagined biopic of one of the last Renaissance painters, Michelangelo Merisi da Caravaggio (1571-1610), but the inspiration seems to be Italian film director Pier Paolo Pasolini, since both artists came from poor backgrounds and used beautiful young men from the slums in their work. Both also became involved in scandal and violence. Much of the joy of the film is to be found in the way Jarman and his team recreate the look and color of the original paintings. But film lacks a certain warmth and emotional depth.

CARAVANS
1978, 127 mins, US/Iran Ⓥ ▭
D: James Fargo A: Anthony Quinn, Michael Sarrazin, Jennifer O'Neill, Christopher Lee, Joseph Cotten, Behrooz Vosoughi (Ibex/FIDCI)

For the average viewer, the scenic scope of the film, based on James Michener's epic story, and shot entirely on locations in Iran, is so sweeping that the tale that is told is almost palatable. But barely. The film deals with the search for an American woman (Jennifer O Neill) who has married an Iranian colonel (Behrooz Vosoughi) but deserted him for a Kochi chieftain (Anthony Quinn) and has disappeared.
1978: Nomination: Best Costume Design

CARAVAN TO VACCARES
1974, 98 mins, UK/France Ⓥ
D: Geoffrey Reeve A: Charlotte Rampling, David Birney, Michel Lonsdale, Marcel Bozuffi, Michael Bryant, Manitas de Plata (Reeve/Prodis)

There's good, reliable stuff in this Alistair MacLean action-adventure item. Plot basics involve the attempt to smuggle an East European scientist out of France. Principally involved is a footloose young American (David Birney), hired to whisk the scientist onto a US-bound plane, and a pretty young British photographer (Charlotte Rampling).

CARBON COPY
1981, 92 mins, US Ⓥ ⊙ ▱
D: Michael Schultz **A:** George Segal, Susan Saint James, Denzel Washington, Jack Warden, Paul Winfield, Dick Martin (Hemdale/RKO)

Carbon Copy has business executive George Segal faced with the arrival of a long-lost and heretofore unknown son whom he describes as Hickory Bronze. Segal attempts to pass off son Denzel Washington as a social experiment in his all-white suburb, but he loses his job, credit cards, and straitlaced wife Susan Saint James throws him out of the house. Director Michael Schultz maintains a convincing balance between the film's broad humor and its genuinely poignant moments.

CARD, THE
1952, 91 mins, UK Ⓥ
D: Ronald Neame **A:** Alec Guinness, Petula Clark, Glynis Johns, Valerie Hobson, Edward Chapman, Gibb McLaughlin (British Film Makers/Rank)

The principal character in Arnold Bennett's novel *The Card*, depicting the progression of a washerwoman's son from poverty to wealth, from humble beginnings to the top of the civic tree, provides a made-to-measure part for Alec Guinness in a capital performance.
1952: Nomination: Best Sound

CARDINAL, THE
1963, 175 mins, US Ⓥ ⊙ ▱
D: Otto Preminger **A:** Tom Tryon, Carol Lynley, Romy Schneider, John Huston, Raf Vallone, John Saxon (Columbia)

The Cardinal is for most of the way superlative drama. The story concerns the development of a Rome-educated American priest who has aspirations to clerical high office. However, he experiences shattering doubt of his ability to be a good priest. Tom Tryon, who has the title role, plays it very well indeed. However, John Huston and Raf Vallone steal the picture. Both play the roles of cardinals on distinctive, captivating levels.
1963: Nominations: Best Director, Supp. Actor (John Huston), Color Cinematography, Color Costume Design, Color Art Direction, Editing

CAREER
1959, 105 mins, US
D: Joseph Anthony **A:** Dean Martin, Anthony Franciosa, Shirley MacLaine, Carolyn Jones, Joan Blackman, Robert Middleton (Paramount)

This feature centers on the ambition-driven aspiring actor. In his free time, he's out to become a star and his other roles in life are unimportant. Somewhere there must have been opportunity to get a little lighthearted. Franciosa and Martin, however somber their parts, perform convincingly. Shirley MacLaine as a producer's freewheeling daughter gets across all right, and Carolyn Jones plays it straight as an agent.
1959: Nominations: Best B&W Cinematography, B&W Costume Design, B&W Art Direction

CAREER OPPORTUNITIES
1991, 85 mins, US Ⓥ ⊙ ▱
D: Bryan Gordon **A:** Frank Whaley, Jennifer Connelly, Dermot Mulroney, Kieran Mulroney, Barry Corbin, John Candy (Universal/Hughes)

Follow-up to *Home Alone* lacks the spit-polish and magic of the blockbuster but still has plenty of absorbing characters, smart, snappy dialogue, and delightful stretches of comic foolery. Like *Home Alone,* story has a young man on his own to defend a fortress against bungling burglars, but in this case he's a 21-year-old trapped in a job he hates (night janitor at a discount store) and pitted against gun-toting hoods out to clean out, not clean up, the store.

CAREFREE
1938, 83 mins, US Ⓥ
D: Mark Sandrich **A:** Fred Astaire, Ginger Rogers, Ralph Bellamy, Luella Gear, Jack Carson, Clarence Kolb (RKO)

Fred Astaire and Ginger Rogers, with an Irving Berlin set of four good songs, delve into psychoanalysis for their script, with Astaire hypnotizing his costar Rogers, who walks to the altar, obsessed with the hypnotic suggestion that Astaire is a cad and Ralph Bellamy a nobleman, etc. Still, in the dream sequence, as result of a sedative administered by Dr. Astaire, the team does one of its best double numbers ("Color Blind" is the tune), wherein a slow-motion camera truly points up the poetry of their terpsichorean motion. Astaire's very first specialty, a golf-ball dance, gives the proceedings a fast gait, but pretty soon the story asserts its handicaps.

CAREFUL HE MIGHT HEAR YOU
1983, 116 mins, Australia ⊗ ▭
D: Carl Schultz **A:** Wendy Hughes, Robyn Nevin, Nicholas Gledhill, John Hargreaves, Geraldine Turner, Isabelle Anderson (Syme)

A completely involving emotional experience about the struggle between two sisters for custody of an eight-year-old boy, their nephew.

Story is set in the Depression in Sydney. The boy is homeless. He's taken in by a loving but impoverished aunt and uncle (Robyn Nevin and Peter Whitford). Their lives are disrupted, however, by the arrival of Vanessa, another sister, but from the moneyed side of the family, who is played, commandingly, by Wendy Hughes. She wants custody of the child.

CARETAKER, THE
1964, 105 mins, UK
D: Clive Donner **A:** Alan Bates, Donald Pleasence, Robert Shaw (Caretaker)

Harold Pinter adapted his own three-character play for the screen, but made little attempt to broaden the canvas and its stage origins are barely disguised. Donald Pleasence's standout performance as the tramp is the acting highlight, but he easily has the choicest role. Robert Shaw gives an intelligent study as the brother who offers the tramp shelter, while Alan Bates completes the stellar trio with another forceful portrayal.

CAREY TREATMENT, THE
1972, 101 mins, US ⊗ ▭
D: Blake Edwards **A:** James Coburn, Jennifer O'Neill, Pat Hingle, Skye Aubrey, Elizabeth Allen, Dan O'Herlihy (M-G-M)

The Carey Treatment stars James Coburn as a swinger-type pathologist who single-handedly solves a murder case in order to free a medic colleague from a bum rap. Written, directed, timed, paced, and cast like a feature-for-TV, the production is a serviceable release.

CARLA'S SONG
1996, 127 mins, UK/Germany/Spain ⊗ ⊙
D: Ken Loach **A:** Robert Carlyle, Oyanka Cabezas, Scott Glenn, Gary Lewis (Parallax/Channel 4/Road Movies/Tornasol)

Radical Brit filmmaker Ken Loach uses a cross-cultural love story to take a hard look at the New World Order in Central America in *Carla's Song,* set between working-class Glasgow and war-torn Nicaragua. Pic takes a stridently anti-

American stand, showing how the US government successfully used the CIA to overturn the popular democracy of the Sandinista movement and frame its enemies, the Contra guerrillas. George (Robert Carlyle) is a Glasgow bus driver when he meets Carla (Oyanka Cabezas), a Nicaraguan refugee. Film shifts register when George and Carla reach Central America and the two journey across the guerrilla-infested countryside. Carlyle turns in a sensitive humorous portrait of the free-thinking bus driver. Nicaraguan actress and dancer Cabezas has a spirited, down-to-earth beauty, but her character is noticeably underwritten.

CARLITO'S WAY
1993, 144 mins, US ⊗ ⊙ ▭
D: Brian De Palma **A:** Al Pacino, Sean Penn, Penelope Ann Miller, Luis Guzman, John Leguizamo, Viggo Mortensen (Universal/Epic)

A lively saga of the rise and fall of a Puerto Rican criminal, rich with irony and keen in its attention to detail. The great strength of David Koepp's adaptation of two books by Manhattan judge Edwin Torres is a comic strain as unexpected and unpredictable as the hair-trigger personalities of its underworld figures. Pacino plays the title role with broad strokes. Sean Penn reminds us of what we've been missing in his performance as Carlito's ambitious, amoral lawyer.

CARLTON-BROWNE OF THE F.O.
1959, 87 mins, UK ⊗
D: Jeffrey Dell, Roy Boulting **A:** Terry-Thomas, Peter Sellers, Luciana Paluzzi, Thorley Walters, Ian Bannen, Raymond Huntley (Boulting)

The F.O. in the title stands for Foreign Office and the film is a crazy peck at the indiscretions of foreign diplomacy. The pic concerns the mishaps that happen when an ex-colony of Britain's becomes news. Rich mineral deposits are indicated on the tiny island. Carlton-Browne (Terry-Thomas) is dispatched to sort things out.

CARMEN
1984, 152 mins, France/Italy ⊗ ⊙ ▭
D: Francesco Rosi **A:** Julia Migenes-Johnson, Placido Domingo, Ruggero Raimondi, Faith Esham, Jean-Philippe Lafont, Gerard Garino (Gaumont/Dassault/Opera Film)

Neorealistic opera, a lumbering cultural mammoth, overblown and graceless. Julia Migenes-Johnson is high-spirited and alluring in the title role. Placido Domingo's Don José flirts with disaster. A beautiful voice, but a uniformed lump in front of the cameras.

CARMEN JONES
1954, 105 mins, US ⊙ ▭
D: Otto Preminger **A:** Dorothy Dandridge, Harry Belafonte, Olga James, Pearl Bailey, Diahann Carroll, Roy Glenn (20th Century-Fox)

Otto Preminger has transferred the modernized, all-Negro version of opera *Carmen* to the screen with taste and imagination. Carmen is a pleasure-loving southern gal who works in a Dixie parachute factory, where Joe (José) is a member of the army regiment on guard duty. Dorothy Dandridge's performance maintains the right hedonistic note throughout.
1954: Nominations: Best Actress (Dorothy Dandridge), Scoring of a Musical Picture

CARNAL KNOWLEDGE
1971, 97 mins, US ⊙ ▭
D: Mike Nichols **A:** Jack Nicholson, Art Garfunkel, Candice Bergen, Ann-Margret, Cynthia O'Neal, Rita Moreno (Avco Embassy)

A rather superficial and limited probe of American male sexual hypocrisies. Jules Feiffer's episodic story follows for over 20 years the diverse paths of Jack Nicholson and Art Garfunkel as each tries to match his sexual fantasies with an uncooperative reality. The story pussyfoots around some underlying psychological and psychiatric hang-ups. Nicholson's compulsive stud character is the type that hates women. The film fails by avoiding confrontation with his character.
1971: Nomination: Best Supp. Actress (Ann-Margret)

CARNEGIE HALL
1947, 136 mins, US
D: Edgar G. Ulmer **A:** Marsha Hunt, William Prince, Frank McHugh, Martha O'Driscoll, Hans Yaray, Olin Downes (United Artists/Federal)

The genius of its music and of the artists who present it makes *Carnegie Hall* a quality film. On the trite side is the script, loaded with cliché dialogue and situations. Edgar G. Ulmer's direction does nothing with this part of the picture but, fortunately, the musical side is a heavy credit balance. Marsha Hunt surmounts an inane role.

CARNIVAL IN FLANDERS
See: La Kermesse Heroique

CARNIVAL OF SOULS
1962, 80 mins, US ⓥ
D: Hark Harvey **A:** Candace Hilligoss, Frances Feist, Sidney Berger, Stanley Leavitt, Art Ellison, Herk Harvey (Harcourt)

The ghost story has Candace Hilligoss a dressy blonde, and a couple of gal pals nudged off of a bridge and a watery death in the swirling river. She goes on to an eerie existence as a new organist at a Salt Lake City church. It isn't enough story to prevail, but there is a fair share of suspense and some moments of good comedy.

CARNOSAUR
1993, 82 mins, US ⓥ ⊙
D: Adam Simon **A:** Diane Ladd, Raphael Sbarge, Jennifer Runyon, Harrison Page, Clint Howard (Concorde/New Horizons)

This contemporary dino tale harks back to fifties monster epics in style and sophistication. Somewhere in the Nevada desert, genetic scientist Dr. Jane Tiptree (Diane Ladd) has cross-fertilized chicken eggs with T-Rex DNA. The result is a lethal little pecker that dines on the southwest smorgasbord of truckers and military industrial support staff.

CARNY
1980, 105 mins, US ⓥ
D: Robert Kaylor **A:** Gary Busey, Jodie Foster, Robbie Robertson, Elisha Cook, Meg Foster, Kenneth McMillan (United Artists)

Edgy tale vividly recalls, both in style and content, the poison-laden films noir of the late 1940s. Gary Busey plays a slightly demented bozo in a cage who mercilessly taunts spectators trying to dump him into water by throwing baseballs. Busey hooks up with runaway Jodie Foster. Busey is tremendous. Foster works wonders with a somewhat underwritten part.

CAROUSEL
1956, 128 mins, US ⓥ ⊙ ▭
D: Henry King **A:** Gordon MacRae, Shirley Jones, Cameron Mitchell, Barbara Ruick, Gene Lockhart, Susan Luckey (20th Century-Fox)

The stars of *Carousel* remain Rodgers and Hammerstein. The cast is uniformly attractive, from MacRae as the shiftless ne'er-do-well Billy Bigelow, to pretty Shirley Jones as Julie. Production number that precedes the gay clambake is a tribute to the ingenuity of choreographer Rod Alexander. The finale, when Julie's daughter, Louise (danced by Susan Luckey), does a number with handsome Jacques D'Amboise, is even more of a rocking production success. *Carousel* keeps elements of drama, humor, and sentiment but starts out with MacRae already dead and in heaven. His courtship and marriage are then told in flashback.

CARPETBAGGERS, THE
1964, 150 mins, US ⓥ ▱
D: Edward Dmytryk **A:** George Peppard, Alan Ladd, Bob Cummings, Martha Hyer, Elizabeth Ashley, Carroll Baker (Paramount)

The story of a ruthless, emotionally unstable chemical-aircraft-film tycoon is told in vague, often lurching manner in the scenario out of Harold Robbins's tome. George Peppard growls and glowers his way through the pivotal role, wearing one basic expression—a surly, like-it-or-lump-it look—but there is an underlying animal magnetism to this performance. The late Alan Ladd limns with conviction one of the few appealing characters—the cowboy star who ultimately restores Peppard to his senses. Carroll Baker has the flashy role of a Harlowesque sexpot, and makes the most of it.

CARQUAKE
See: Cannonball

CARRIE
1952, 118 mins, US ⓥ ⊙
D: William Wyler **A:** Laurence Olivier, Jennifer Jones, Eddie Albert, Miriam Hopkins, Basil Ruysdael, Ray Teal (Paramount)

Theodore Dreiser's novel *Sister Carrie* has been given a literal adaptation and is a somber, low-key entertainment. It is the story of a small-town girl meeting a traveling salesman and of how he becomes her "benefactor." The big love of her life, however, is the manager of a swank restaurant. Jones gives one of the bright performances of her career. For Olivier, it is a role that gives him little opportunity for shading or dramatic intensity. Eddie Albert is excellent as the traveling salesman.
1952: Nominations: Best B&W Costume Design, B&W Art Direction

CARRIE
1976, 97 mins, US ⓥ ⊙
D: Brian De Palma **A:** Sissy Spacek, Piper Laurie, Amy Irving, William Katt, Nancy Allen, John Travolta (United Artists)

Carrie is a modest but effective shock-suspense drama about a pubescent girl, her evangelical mother, and cruel schoolmates. Stephen King's novel, adapted by Lawrence D. Cohen, combines in unusual fashion a lot of offbeat story angles. Sissy Spacek heads cast in title role of an ugly-duckling-type schoolgirl. Carrie's mother is a dried-up, abandoned-wife-turned-religious freak, played superbly by Piper Laurie.
1976: Nominations: Best Actress (Sissy Spacek), Supp. Actress (Piper Laurie)

CARRIED AWAY
1996, 107 mins, US ⓥ
D: Bruno Barreto **A:** Dennis Hopper, Amy Irving, Amy Locane, Julie Harris, Gary Busey, Hal Holbrook (CineTel)

Midlife crisis forms the basis of *Carried Away*, an explicitly told tale culled from a Jim Thompson novel (*Farmer*). Anchored by a powerful performance from Dennis Hopper, it's at turns a sex comedy and a poignant drama, but the two elements never mesh. For the past six years Joseph (Hopper) has been engaged to Rosealee (Amy Irving). Joseph is exceptionally good at rationalizing why he's not quite ready to tie the knot. It's at that point that 17-year-old vixen Catherine Wheeler (Amy Locane) arrives.

CARRINGTON
1995, 120 mins, UK/France ⓥ
D: Christopher Hampton **A:** Emma Thompson, Jonathan Pryce, Steven Waddington, Samuel West, Rufus Sewell, Penelope Wilton (Gramercy/PolyGram)

This between-wars biopic of English painter Dora Carrington and her love for gay Bloomsbury Group scribe Lytton Strachey is a wobbly affair that's too dry by half and isn't helped by a badly miscast Emma Thompson in an already underwritten role. Tossing off waspish remarks with the disdain of a wannabe Oscar Wilde, Pryce simply acts Thompson (and everyone else) off the screen.

CARRINGTON, V.C.
(US: COURT MARTIAL)
1954, 105 mins, UK ⓥ
D: Anthony Asquith **A:** David Niven, Margaret Leighton, Noelle Middleton, Laurence Naismith, Clive Morton, Mark Dignam (Remus)

A wartime hero commanding an artillery battery in peacetime helps himself to army funds to advertise a grievance. His commander orders a court-martial. David Niven gives one of his best performances in recent times as the accused V.C. Some of his courtroom exchanges are dramatic high spots of the plot.

CARRY ON AGAIN DOCTOR
1969, 89 mins, UK ⓥ
D: Gerald Thomas **A:** Sidney James, Kenneth Williams, Charles Hawtrey, Jim Dale, Joan Sims, Barbara Windsor (Rank)

Carry On Again Doctor returns to a well-tilled field, with bedpans, undressed patients, discussions about symptoms, from wind to bowels, being regular dialogue fodder. This time the flimsy yarn is mainly geared around the discovery in the Beatific Islands by Jim Dale, an accident-prone young doctor, of a serum which helps girth control.

CARRY ON CABBY
1963, 91 mins, UK ⓥ
D: Gerald Thomas **A:** Sidney James, Hattie Jacques, Kenneth Connor, Charles Hawtrey, Esma Cannon, Liz Fraser (Anglo Amalgamated)

Not at first intended to be one of the *Carry On* series, the film has a rather stronger story line than usual. Sidney James is the cabby-owner of a prosperous fleet of taxicabs, but his domestic life is edgy because his wife claims he spends too much time with his beloved cabs. She sets up a rival garage called Glamcabs and decks out some shapely young women in revealing uniforms as her drivers.

CARRY ON CAMPING
1969, 88 mins, UK ⓥ
D: Gerald Thomas **A:** Sidney James, Kenneth Williams, Joan Sims, Charles Hawtrey, Terry Scott, Barbara Windsor (Rank)

Latest *Carry On* lacks a story line, however slim. Sidney James and Bernard Bresslaw plan a vacation at a nudist holiday camp at which, they hope, they will be able to break down the prim resistance of their girlfriends (Joan Sims and Dilys Laye). Camp turns out not to be nudie paradise, after all. Meanwhile, other campers are involved in their own problems, with Barbara Windsor a literal standout as an exuberant sex-mad young trollop.

CARRY ON CLEO
1964, 92 mins, US ⓥ
D: Gerald Thomas **A:** Sidney James, Kenneth Williams, Kenneth Connor, Charles Hawtrey, Joan Sims, Amanda Barrie (Anglo Amalgamated)

Intended as a parody of the expensive *Cleopatra,* this relies on the bludgeon rather than the rapier, so isn't entirely suc-

cessful in realizing its purpose. Kenneth Williams has a few twittering moments as Caesar but again irritatingly overplays. Amanda Barrie's takeoff of the Queen of the Nile gets nearer to the tongue-in-cheek sense of what filmmakers were aiming at than any of her more experienced colleagues.

CARRY ON COLUMBUS
1992, 91 mins, UK ⓥ
D: Gerald Thomas **A:** Jim Dale, Bernard Cribbins, Maureen Lipman, Peter Richardson, Alexei Sayle, Rik Mayall (Comedy House)

Columbus is the 30th in the *Carry On* series that started in 1958 with *Sergeant* and halted 20 years later with *Emmanuelle*. Vet director Gerald Thomas returns for behind-the-camera chores. Chris Columbus (Jim Dale) sets sail with a motley crew and a map in Hebrew translated by a dumb mariner (Bernard Cribbins). Losing their way, they end up in the Americas, where the natives are streetwise Indians with Brooklyn accents.

CARRY ON CONSTABLE
1960, 86 mins, UK ⓥ
D: Gerald Thomas **A:** Sidney James, Kenneth Williams, Hattie Jacques, Eric Barker, Kenneth Connor, Shirley Eaton (Anglo Amalgamated)

An anthology of police gags and situations, this concerns a flu-stricken police station which is reinforced by four fledgling cops (Kenneth Connor, Kenneth Williams, Charles Hawtrey, and Leslie Phillips). The hapless quartet distinguishes itself by rounding up, in improbable fashion, a bunch of crooks. Sidney James, a newcomer to the team, is in his usual first-class form as the sergeant who is annoyed with the recruits.

CARRY ON COWBOY
1966, 94 mins, UK ⓥ
D: Gerald Thomas **A:** Sidney James, Kenneth Williams, Jim Dale, Charles Hawtrey, Joan Sims, Angela Douglas (Anglo Amalgamated)

This Wild West spoof might well be subtitled *How the West Was Lost.* Stodge City is taken over by the Rumpo Kid (Sidney James), to the horror of Judge Burke (Kenneth Williams), who calls for a marshal to clean up the town. By error a sanitary engineer (Jim Dale) gets sent to the trouble spot, arriving on the same coach as Annie Oakley (Angela Douglas).

CARRY ON CRUISING
1962, 89 mins, UK ⓥ
D: Gerald Thomas A: Sidney James, Kenneth Williams, Kenneth Connor, Liz Fraser, Dilys Laye, Lance Percival (Anglo Amalgamated)

Sidney James is the veteran, highly improbable skipper of a Mediterranean cruising vessel. He is inflicted with five hamheaded substitutes for well-tried key men in his regular complement. They are all overanxious to please and so everything goes disastrously wrong. Jumping, familiarly, through their well-placed circus hoops are Sidney James (he glowers), Kenneth Williams (he plays archly), Kenneth Connor (he dithers), Liz Fraser (she flaunts a shapely figure), and Esma Cannon (she twitters).

CARRY ON DOCTOR
1968, 95 mins, UK ⓥ
D: Gerald Thomas A: Frankie Howerd, Sidney James, Kenneth Williams, Charles Hawtrey, Jim Dale, Barbara Windsor (Rank)

Usual unabashed mixture of double meanings, down-to-earth vulgarity, blue jokes about hypodermic syringes, etc., and slapstick situations. This time the *Carry On* team returns to hospital life for its farcical goings-on. Added zest is given by the inclusion of Frankie Howerd as a quack mind-over-matter doctor.

CARRY ON EMMANUELLE
1978, 88 mins, UK ⓥ
D: Gerald Thomas A: Suzanne Danielle, Kenneth Williams, Kenneth Connor, Jack Douglas, Joan Sims, Peter Butterworth (Cleves/National Film Trustee)

Emmanuelle, English-style, is wife to the French ambassador. She sleeps with most of London until an immigrant doctor restores hubby's priapic power and all ends happily in the embassy bedroom. The relentless phallic innuendo is as labored as makers' determination to show nothing to worry the censor. Leaden comic timing compares poorly with TV sitcoms which pic otherwise resembles in production values.

CARRY ON ENGLAND
1976, 89 mins, UK ⓥ
D: Gerald Thomas A: Kenneth Connor, Windsor Davies, Patrick Mower, Judy Geeson, Jack Douglas, Joan Sims (Rank)

Carry On England suffers from a particularly unfortunate hang-up. It's not funny! Action takes place in a mixed an-tiaircraft battery at the start of World War II. There follows 89 minutes of gags, knockabout situations, and innuendo which fall as flat as Kenneth Connor, as a bungling captain, is constantly required to do in search of belly laughs.

CARRY ON JACK
1964, 91 mins, UK ⓥ
D: Gerald Thomas A: Kenneth Williams, Bernard Cribbins, Juliet Mills, Charles Hawtrey, Donald Houston, Cecil Parker (Anglo Amalgamated)

An energetic skit on *Mutiny on the Bounty*. Only two of the resident company—Charles Hawtrey and Kenneth Williams—are on parade. Williams, playing the precious Captain Fearless, who hates the sea and violence, is in excellent form while Hawtrey plays his familiar nincompoop with ease. Only sizable femme role is played by Juliet Mills, who doesn't seem very comfortable in the robust male surroundings.

CARRY ON LOVING
1970, 90 mins, UK ⓥ
D: Gerald Thomas A: Sidney James, Kenneth Williams, Charles Hawtrey, Joan Sims, Hattie Jacques, Terry Scott (Rank)

This time the nondescript plot hovers around a phony matrimonial agency run by the plausible Sidney James and Hattie Jacques, posing as happy man and wife. Their efforts to pair off their unlikely and varied clients lead to riotous misunderstandings, sexy situations, intrigues, double-crossing, and a custard-pie finale which is rather too deliberately planned and directed to achieve full comedy effect.

CARRY ON NURSE
1959, 86 mins, UK ⓥ
D: Gerald Thomas A: Kenneth Connor, Kenneth Williams, Charles Hawtrey, Leslie Phillips, Hattie Jacques, Shirley Eaton (Anglo Amalgamated)

The humor tends to be repetitious, flirting with sex and dealing with such typical hospital subjects as bedpans, enemas, preparing patients for operations, and so on. In a long cast it is only possible to pick out Hattie Jacques, as the matron; Wilfrid Hyde White, as a suave patient; Ann Firbank, Shirley Eaton, Susan Stephen, and Diana Beaumont as pretty, efficient nurses; Joan Sims, as the blunderer; and Kenneth Connor, a pugilist-patient with a broken hand.

CARRY ON REGARDLESS
1961, 90 mins, UK ⊗
D: Gerald Thomas **A:** Sidney James, Kenneth Connor, Charles Hawtrey, Joan Sims, Kenneth Williams, Liz Fraser (Anglo Amalgamated)

The story, such as it is, has Sidney James running an agency prepared to take on any sort of job anytime. Disaster winds up every job. Typical of these are scenes which involve Kenneth Williams in taking a chimp for a walk through London, Kenneth Connor baby-sitting (the baby turns out to be a married woman), and Charles Hawtrey assisting a pugilist. Joan Sims has to demonstrate a bubble bath, Liz Fraser finds herself modeling underwear.

CARRY ON SCREAMING
1966, 97 mins, UK ⊗
D: Gerald Thomas **A:** Harry H. Corbett, Kenneth Williams, Fenella Fielding, Joan Sims, Charles Hawtrey, Jim Dale (Anglo Amalgamated)

This 12th in the successful *Carry On* series puts the skids under horror pix. Snag is that most horror films themselves teeter on parody and it is rather tough trying to burlesque a parody. Abduction of a girl by a monster starts a trail of goofy adventures as henpecked Detective Sergeant Bung (Harry H. Corbett) and his bovine assistant (Peter Butterworth) try to unravel this, the latest crime of a series. Corbett and Fenella Fielding, both debuting with the *Carry On* team, give it added strength. Corbett mugs a great deal but the role demands it and Fielding as the grisly vamp glitters with an overdone seductiveness which is often funny.

CARRY ON SERGEANT
1958, 85 mins, UK ⊗
D: Gerald Thomas **A:** William Hartnell, Bob Monkhouse, Shirley Eaton, Eric Barker, Dora Bryan, Kenneth Connor (Anglo Amalgamated)

Carry On Sergeant is an army farce exploiting practically every army gag in the book. William Hartnell is a training sergeant who is handed a bunch of rookies, which is believable only in farce. The barrack-room attorney, the young man in love, the hypochondriac malingerer, the man always out of step . . . in fact, the repertory company of trainees. Kenneth Connor steals most of the honors as the hypochondriac being chased by a love-starved army waitress, played characteristically by Dora Bryan.

CARRY ON SPYING
1964, 87 mins, UK
D: Gerald Thomas **A:** Kenneth Williams, Bernard Cribbins, Charles Hawtrey, Barbara Windsor, Eric Pohlmann, Eric Barker (Anglo Amalgamated)

The Society for Total Extinction of Non-Conforming Humans (STENCH for short) has grabbed a secret formula and the British Operational Security Headquarters (BOSH in brief) tackles the job of getting back Formula X and outwitting its archenemy, Dr. Crow. The assignment is handed to Simkins (Kenneth Williams), an agent in charge of training new spies, and three of his pupils.

Kenneth Williams's brand of camp comedy, while very funny in smallish doses, can pall when he has a lengthy chore, as here.

CARRY ON TEACHER
1959, 86 mins, UK ⊗
D: Gerald Thomas **A:** Ted Ray, Kenneth Connor, Kenneth Williams, Joan Sims, Charles Hawtrey, Hattie Jacques (Anglo Amalgamated)

Third entry in Peter Rogers's sock *Carry On* series. Ted Ray in the acting headmaster who, after 20 years, has set his heart on the headmastership of a new school in the country. Because they don't want the popular master to leave, the students start a well-planned campaign of bad behavior to influence the visiting inspectors. Some of the gags are telegraphed but the cheerful impudence with which they are dropped into the script is completely disarming.

CARRY ON UP THE JUNGLE
1970, 90 mins, UK ⊗
D: Gerald Thomas **A:** Frankie Howerd, Sidney James, Charles Hawtrey, Joan Sims, Terry Scott, Kenneth Connor (Rank)

This one is a skit about a safari in the jungle, with a parody of Tarzan thrown in for good measure. It involves the characters plunging in and out of the wrong tents mainly in search of sex, a tribe of head-hunting cannibals, another tribe of lush dames in search of men to carry on their mating industry, a sex-starved stray gorilla, and sundry other Darkest Africa situations and gags.

CARRY ON UP . . . THE KHYBER
1968, 87 mins, UK ⊗
D: Gerald Thomas **A:** Sidney James, Kenneth Williams, Charles Hawtrey, Roy Cas-

tle, Joan Sims, Bernard Bresslaw (Adder/Rank)

Up the Khyber centers on the British occupation of India in Queen Victoria's day when the local rulers suspect that the dreaded Scottish Devils in Skirts, members of the intrepid Third Foot and Mouth Regiment, actually wear drawers under their kilts. Settling of this urgent question causes considerable hoo-hah in the shape of a local uprising engineered by the local Khasi of Kalibar. Performance of Sidney James as Sir Sidney Ruff-Diamond, the bluff, vulgar British governor, is a gem.

CARRY ON VENUS
See: Carry On Jack

CARS THAT ATE PARIS, THE
1974, 91 mins, Australia Ⓥ ▭
D: Peter Weir **A:** Terry Camilleri, John Meillon, Melissa Jaffa, Kevin Miles, Max Gillies, Peter Armstrong (Australian Film Development/Royce Smeal)

Paris is a tiny Australian township with a surprising number of car accidents on its outskirts. Gradually it becomes evident that the car accidents are planned affairs. As each one occurs the townspeople swoop like vultures on the cars and retrieve any personal effects for themselves, while the doctor carries out strange experiments of his own upon the victims. At first pic seems satirical, then black comedy, degenerating into a thriller.

CARVE HER NAME WITH PRIDE
1958, 119 mins, UK Ⓥ
D: Lewis Gilbert **A:** Virginia McKenna, Paul Scofield, Jack Warner, Denise Grey, Alain Saury, Maurice Ronet (Rank)

The film pays tribute to the real-life exploits of Violette Szabo, who became a British cloak-and-dagger agent in France and won a posthumous George Cross after being tortured and executed. Part of the pic's attraction is its lack of hysteria. Virginia McKenna is top-notch. She runs the gamut of humor, charm, and toughness. By skillful playing and equally skillful makeup, McKenna's ordeal is expertly revealed.

CAR WASH
1976, 97 mins, US Ⓥ
D: Michael Schultz **A:** Franklyn Ajaye, Sully Boyar, Richard Brestoff, George Carlin, Irwin Corey, Ivan Dixon (Universal)

Car Wash uses gritty humor to polish clean the souls of a lot of likable street people. Perhaps the best known of the players is Richard Pryor, shining it on as a fancy-dressed preacher, complete with flashy car and retinue that includes the Pointer Sisters.

CASABLANCA
1942, 99 mins, US Ⓥ ⊙
D: Michael Curtiz **A:** Humphrey Bogart, Ingrid Bergman, Paul Henreid, Claude Rains, Conrad Veidt, Sydney Greenstreet (Warner)

Casablanca is pictured as a superficially gay town to which flee the monied refugees from Axis terror. There they await visas to Lisbon and then transportation to the United States. The wealthy help to allay their impatience with chemin de fer and other games at Rick's. Rick is Bogart, who has opened his fancy joint after being jilted by Bergman in Paris. Bergman turns up one evening with her husband (Paul Henreid). Henreid is leader of the underground in Europe and it is vital that he get to America. Bogart has two visas that will do the trick and the choice is between going off himself with Bergman or sending her off with Henreid. Bogart, as might be expected, is more at ease as the bitter and cynical operator of a joint than as a lover, but handles both assignments with superb finesse. Bergman, in a torn-between-love-and-duty role, lives up to her reputation as a fine actress. Henreid is well cast and does an excellent job, too.
1943: Best Picture, Director, Screenplay
Nominations: Best Actor (Humphrey Bogart), Supp. Actor (Claude Rains), B&W Cinematography, Editing, Scoring of a Dramatic Picture

CASANOVA
(FELLINI'S CASANOVA)
1976, 166 mins, Italy Ⓥ ⊙
D: Federico Fellini **A:** Donald Sutherland, Tina Aumont, Cicely Browne, Olimpia Carlisi, Adele Angela Lojodice, Margareth Clementi (PEA)

Fellini's demolition of a myth, mounted with studied virtuosity into a rambling but bigger-than-life spectacle divested, by design, of reality and emotion in portraying the legendary Venetian lover as a pathetic victim of his own vanity and virility. Tracing a continuous flux of decline from practically the opening sequence, Fellini relentlessly runs his hero into the ground for 166 minutes. Donald Sutherland gives the gallant Venetian a measure of dignity and momentarily succeeds in overcoming the mechanics of Fellini's direction.

CASBAH
1948, 93 mins, US
D: John Berry A: Yvonne De Carlo, Tony Martin, Peter Lorre, Marta Toren, Hugo Haas, Thomas Gomez (Marston/Universal)

The music is excellent, Tony Martin's singing is sock, and the Pepe le Moko story has always been good, if familiar, screen fare. That the romantic melodrama doesn't always mesh too well with the musical story makes for a distraction. Martin is good as the dashing thief whose elusive ways are the despair of the police. Major femme interest goes to Swedish newcomer Marta Toren. Peter Lorre clicks strongly as the police inspector who finally gets his man.

CASINO
1995, 177 mins, US/France ⊘ ⊙ ⊟
D: Martin Scorsese A: Robert De Niro, Sharon Stone, Joe Pesci, James Woods, Don Rickles, Alan King (Universal/Syalis/Legende)

Casino lays out how the mob controlled and ultimately lost Las Vegas. Martin Scorsese's intimate epic about money, sex, and brute force is a grandly conceived study of what happens to goodfellas from the mean streets when they outstrip their wildest dreams and achieve the pinnacle of wealth and power. The film concentrates on three central figures: Sam "Ace" Rothstein (Robert De Niro), a top gambler; Nicky Santoro (Joe Pesci), Ace's longtime best friend and impulsively violent enforcer; and Ginger McKenna (Sharon Stone), a veteran hustler. Stone lets loose with a corker of a performance as the beautiful, unstable, ultimately pathetic moll with no inner life.
1995: Nomination: Best Actress (Sharon Stone)

CASINO ROYALE
1967, 131 mins, UK/US ⊘ ⊙ ⊟
D: John Huston, Ken Hughes, Val Guest, Robert Parrish, Joseph McGrath A: Peter Sellers, Ursula Andress, David Niven, Orson Welles, Woody Allen, Joanna Pettet (Famous Artists/Columbia)

An attempt to spoof the pants off James Bond, lacking discipline and cohesion. Story line defies sane description. Sufficient to say that the original James Bond (David Niven) is persuaded back into the Secret Service to help cope with a disastrous situation.
1967: Nomination: Best Song ("The Look of Love")

CASPER
1995, 100 mins, US ⊘ ⊙
D: Brad Silberling A: Christina Ricci, Bill Pullman, Cathy Moriarty, Eric Idle, Malachi Pearson (voice), Joe Nipote (voice) (Amblin/Universal)

Another demonstration of the hazards involved turning a six-minute animated short into a big-budget movie, *Casper* skews so heavily toward children that it offers little to divert anyone over the age of eight. The movie's biggest asset is of the earthly variety. Ricci is an enchanting young actress, and whatever emotional resonance *Casper* can muster is largely to her credit.

CASQUE D'OR
1952, 95 mins, France
D: Jacques Becker A: Simone Signoret, Serge Reggiani, Claude Dauphin, Raymond Bussières, Paul Azais, Pierre Gujas (Speva/Paris)

Brisk in style and full of pictorial interest, film soberly recounts a famous turn-of-the-century love affair. Based on a true story, it recounts the love of apache moll Marie (Simone Signoret) for the honest, direct, and sympathetic Manda (Serge Reggiani). The affair is spiked by the sly, brutal Leca (Claude Dauphin), head of the mob, who wants Marie for himself. Signoret gives Marie a cynical, sensual, exciting appeal.

CASSANDRA CROSSING, THE
1977, 126 mins, US ⊘ ⊟
D: George Pan Cosmatos A: Sophia Loren, Richard Harris, Ava Gardner, Burt Lancaster, Martin Sheen, Ingrid Thulin (Associated General)

A tired, hokey, and sometimes unintentionally funny disaster film in which a trainload of disease-exposed passengers lurch to their fate. While Richard Harris, cast as a brilliant doctor, is active among those posturing leads on the train, Burt Lancaster and Ingrid Thulin hold down a command post where desperate efforts are made to isolate the train from the rest of civilization.

CASS TIMBERLANE
1947, 119 mins, US
D: George Sidney A: Spencer Tracy, Lana Turner, Zachary Scott, Tom Drake, Mary Astor, Albert Dekker (M-G-M)

A highly successful translation to the

screen of Sinclair Lewis's bookstore boff. Lana Turner is the surprise of the picture via her top performance thespically. Spencer Tracy, as a matter of fact, is made to look wooden by comparison. This is a love story all the way. Tracy, respected small-town judge, pays tender court to Turner, who's strictly out of his class socially as well as chronologically, until he wins her. She adapts herself to local society and the new life until she thinks she can stand it no more and then is off with the husband's best friend, Zachary Scott.

CAST A GIANT SHADOW
1966, 144 mins, US ⓥ ⊙
D: Melville Shavelson **A:** Kirk Douglas, Senta Berger, Angie Dickinson, Frank Sinatra, Yul Brynner, John Wayne (Mirisch/Llenroc)

Some complete fiction and fuzzy composites melodramatize the career of an American Jew who assisted in the fight for the creation of the state of Israel. Kirk Douglas stars as Colonel David ("Mickey") Marcus in a very good portrayal of a likable, adventurous soldier of fortune who cannot get used to domestic inactivity even when wife Angie Dickinson is sitting by the hearth. Unfortunately, it is found necessay to go into World War II flashbacks. John Wayne is a composite of every superior officer under whom Marcus served in those days.

CASTAWAY
1987, 118 mins, UK ⓥ ⊙
D: Nicolas Roeg **A:** Oliver Reed, Amanda Donohoe, Georgina Hale, Frances Barber (Cannon/United British Artists)

Picture this: London is cold, wet, and miserable. What else does a girl do but answer an ad from a man looking for a wife to take to a tropical island for a year? Reed gives the performance of his career as a sexually frustrated middle-aged man in search of sun and sex, and is admirably complemented by Amanda Donohoe as the determined but fickle object of his lust.

CASTLE KEEP
1969, 106 mins, US ⓥ ⊡
D: Sydney Pollack **A:** Burt Lancaster, Patrick O'Neal, Jean-Pierre Aumont, Peter Falk, Scott Wilson, Astrid Heeren (Columbia/Filmways)

Apparent efforts to insert a fresh side of war by concentrating on some of its grim humor act more as a deterrent than a booster to interest. Burt Lancaster is a realistic, one-eyed major who leads a group of eight war-weary infantrymen come to occupy a Belgian castle in 1944 in the Ardennes Forest, which becomes a haven away from war for the men, who get up to all manner of frolics.

CASTLE OF THE SPIDER'S WEB, THE
See: Kumonosu-jo

CASTLE ON THE HUDSON
(UK: YEARS WITHOUT DAYS)
1940, 76 mins, US
D: Anatole Litvak **A:** John Garfield, Ann Sheridan, Pat O'Brien, Burgess Meredith, Jerome Cowan, Henry O'Neill (Warner)

This is another in the extended series of Warners features based on Warden Lewis E. Lawes's 20,000 Years in Sing Sing. It's a routine prison melodrama. John Garfield is a tough, smart-aleck gangster who draws a 25-to-30-year stretch in Sing Sing for knocking over a jewelry store. O'Brien is okay as the warden, while Sheridan provides a strong characterization as the gangster's girl.

CASUAL SEX?
1988, 97 mins, US ⓥ ⊙
D: Genevieve Robert **A:** Lea Thompson, Victoria Jackson, Stephen Shellen, Jerry Levine, Andrew Dice Clay, Mary Gross (Jascat/Universal)

It's Lea Thompson and Victoria Jackson huffing and puffing through exercises as the excuse to meet an athletic guy who they suppose will have equally healthy attitudes about sex. With the late 1980s sensibility, their sex conversations are peppered with the girls' finding their own identities in relationships with men outside the sex act. Is it mature? Yes. Is it funny? No.

CASUALTIES OF WAR
1989, 113 mins, US ⓥ ⊙ ⊡
D: Brian De Palma **A:** Michael J. Fox, Sean Penn, Don Harvey, John C. Reilly, John Leguizamo, Thuy Thu Le (Columbia)

A powerful metaphor of the national shame that was America's orgy of destruction in Vietnam, film deals directly with the harrowing rape and murder of a Vietnamese woman by four GIs over the futile objections of the lone holdout, a cherry private played by Michael J. Fox. Casting Fox was a brilliant coup on De Palma's part, since he brings with him an image of all-American boyishness and eager-beaver conservatism. Fox's beautifully acted cowardly passivity in the face of the unthinkable challenges and implicates the viewer to examine his own conscience on the subject of Vietnam.

CAT AND THE CANARY, THE
1939, 72 mins, US Ⓥ
D: Elliott Nugent A: Bob Hope, Paulette Goddard, John Beal, Douglass Montgomery, Gale Sondergaard (Paramount)

In *Canary,* Bob Hope carries a straight dramatic characterization, with comedy quips and situations dropping into the plot naturally to accentuate the laughs. To provide chills and thrills, prospective heirs to the eccentric millionaire's fortune assemble at the bayou home of the deceased. There's the low-key lighting, eerie music, and secret passages all utilized to fullest extent to accentuate the chiller aspect of the piece. After three murders during the night, Hope solves the mystery.

CAT BALLOU
1965, 97 mins, US Ⓥ
D: Elliot Silverstein A: Jane Fonda, Lee Marvin, Michael Callan, Dwayne Hickman, Nat King Cole, Stubby Kaye (Columbia)

Cat Ballou spoofs the Old West, whose adherents take their likker neat, and emerges middlingly successful, sparked by an amusing way-out approach and some sparkling performances. A novel device has Stubby Kaye and Nat King Cole as wandering minstrels of the early west, telling the story of the goings-on via a flock of spirited and tuneful songs composed by Mack David and Jerry Livingston. Fonda delivers a lively interpretation as Cat. Lee Marvin doubles in brass, playing the gunman who shoots down her father and the legendary Kid Shelleen. In latter character, Marvin is the standout of the picture.
1965: Best Actor (Lee Marvin)
Nominations: Best Adapted Screenplay, Editing, Adapted Music Score, Song ("The Ballad of Cat Ballou")

CAT CHASER
1989, 88 mins, US Ⓥ
D: Abel Ferrara A: Peter Weller, Kelly McGillis, Charles Durning, Frederic Forrest, Tomas Milian, Juan Fernandez (Vestron/Whiskers)

Cat Chaser is another example of the difficulties of transforming a sharp and racy novel into a classy movie. Despite a fine cast and atmospheric direction by Abel Ferrara, the pic doesn't quite make the grade. Weller is fine as the intelligent,

self-contained hero, but best of all is McGillis, seemingly relishing the part of a sexually charged femme fatale. Charles Durning, as always, gives the pic a dose of class, and manages to make his manipulative killer vaguely charming.

CATCHFIRE
1991, 98 mins, US Ⓥ ⊙
D: Alan Smithee [Dennis Hopper] A: Dennis Hopper, Jodie Foster, Dean Stockwell, Vincent Price, Fred Ward, Joe Pesci (Vestron/Precision)

Quirky comedy-thriller has an L.A. artiste (Jodie Foster) accidentally witnessing a mob killing. The cops (Fred Ward, Sy Richardson) want her to talk, and the hoods (Joe Pesci, Dean Stockwell, Vincent Price) want her dead. So she dons a blond wig and an alias and goes AWOL. Top-league hit man (Dennis Hopper) runs her aground in an ad agency, possesses her for himself, and the dynamic duo set of on a weird road-movie-to-nowhere, with the mob and the law in hot pursuit.

CATCH ME A SPY
1971, 94 mins, UK/France Ⓥ
D: Dick Clement A: Kirk Douglas, Marlene Jobert, Trevor Howard, Tom Courtenay, Patrick Mower, Bernadette Lafont (Ludgate/Pleiade/Capitole)

Catch Me a Spy is a straightforward spy thriller. Gimmicks are out but the whole has been put over with tongue nicely in cheek and an impish sense of humor. Kirk Douglas, a smuggler of literary works from Iron Curtain countries, is mistaken for a spy and gets involved in tricky situations.

CATCH-22
1970, 121 mins, US Ⓥ ⊙ ▭
D: Mike Nichols A: Alan Arkin, Martin Balsam, Richard Benjamin, Art Garfunkel, Jack Gilford, Buck Henry (Paramount)

Catch-22 stumbles its way through distended burlesque and contrived stylism to its ultimate theme: antisocial nihilism. Alan Arkin heads a large cast of familiar names, playing characters scooped from Joseph Heller's famed novel by adapter Buck Henry. Low, cheap comedy mingles nervously with slick, high-fashion technical polish in a slow-boiling stew of specious philosophy and superficial characterization. A technical filmmaking brilliance plus a few effective low-comedy gags constitute the pic's assets.

CATCH US IF YOU CAN
(US: HAVING A WILD WEEKEND)
1965, 91 mins, UK/US ⓥ
D: John Boorman A: Dave Clark, Barbara Ferris, David Lodge, Robin Bailey, Yootha Joyce, David De Keyser (Anglo Amalgamated/Warner)

Apparently producer David Deutsch's idea was to try for the same success formula that made *A Hard Day's Night* more than just a film about a rock-and-roll group. He hasn't been too successful in trying to turn the Dave Clark Five into actors but has, as cinematic insurance, packed enough action into his chase film to keep older members of the audience from squirming. The musical five do eight tunes as background music.

CATERED AFFAIR, THE
1956, 92 mins, US ⓥ
D: Richard Brooks A: Bette Davis, Ernest Borgnine, Debbie Reynolds, Barry Fitzgerald, Rod Taylor, Robert Simon (M-G-M)

The Bronx bourgeoisie, represented by the Irish Hurley family, is the chief concern of this little comedy-drama. There are occasionally amusing and touching moments in the otherwise talky, mostly drab affair.

The dramatic to-do set up by the plot whirls around Ma Hurley's decision to give her daughter a catered wedding, overruling the daughter's objections and overwhelming the meager savings of taxi-driving Pa Hurley. As the mother, Bette Davis is consistent in performance, if not with her dialect, and proves a strong force to the drama side of the film.

CAT FROM OUTER SPACE, THE
1978, 103 mins, US ⓥ
D: Norman Tokar A: Ken Berry, Sandy Duncan, Harry Morgan, Roddy McDowall, McLean Stevenson, Jesse White (Walt Disney)

Cartoonist Ted Key turns to noodling over a spaceship commanded by a cat, forced to land on earth for emergency repairs. For help, the cat turns to a likable physicist, Ken Berry. Before long, Berry's girlfriend Sandy Duncan and buddy McLean Stevenson are planning to parlay the cat's extraterrestrial powers into a series of winning bets with bookie Jesse White. The fun, as usual with Disney pix, comes in the believable sight gags provided along the way.

CATHERINE THE GREAT
See: Rise of Catherine the Great

CATHY'S CHILD
1979, 89 mins, Australia
D: Donald Crombie A: Michelle Fawdon, Alan Cassell, Bryan Brown, Harry Michael, Anna Hruby, Bob Hughes (CB Films)

Cathy's Child is based on a true story in which a young Greek mother living in Sydney had her three-year-old daughter abducted by the child's father, who returned to Greece with it. Michelle Fawdon turns in a super performance as the young migrant mother. To her aid comes battered old pro journalist Wordley (Alan Cassell), who with the help of his tough young city editor forces the story onto the front page.

CAT ON A HOT TIN ROOF
1958, 108 mins, US ⓥ ⊙
D: Richard Brooks A: Elizabeth Taylor, Paul Newman, Burl Ives, Jack Carson, Judith Anderson, Madeleine Sherwood (M-G-M/Avon)

This *Cat on a Hot Tin Roof* is by no means a watered-down version, though immature dependence has replaced any hint of homosexuality. Motivations remain psychologically sound. Burl Ives, playing plantation king Big Daddy, unknowingly is dying of cancer. Big Daddy's oldest son (Jack Carson) and his obnoxious wife (Madeleine Sherwood) make capital of the problems besetting Big Daddy's favorite son (Paul Newman) and his wife (Elizabeth Taylor), he being a drunk and she being childless. It's an often gruesome, often amusing battle. Taylor has a major credit with her well-accented, perceptive interpretation of Maggie.

1958: Nominations: Best Picture, Director, Actor (Paul Newman), Actress (Elizabeth Taylor), Adapted Screenplay, Color Cinematography

CAT PEOPLE
1942, 73 mins, US ⓥ
D: Jacques Tourneur A: Simone Simon, Kent Smith, Tom Conway, Jane Randolph, Jack Holt, Alan Napier (RKO)

This is a weird drama of thrill-chill caliber, with surprise developments confined to psychology and mental reactions, rather than transformation to grotesque and marauding characters for visual impact on the audiences. Story is one of those it-might-happen dramas, if an old Serbian legend be true. Fable has it that women descendants of a certain tribe, when projected into a jealous rage, change into panthers or other members of the cat family for attack, later reverting to human form.

CAT PEOPLE
1982, 118 mins, US Ⓥ ⊙
D: Paul Schrader A: Nastassja Kinski, Malcolm McDowell, John Heard, Annette O'Toole, Ruby Dee, Ed Begley Jr. (RKO-Universal)

Paul Schrader's reworking of the 1942 *Cat People* is a super-chic erotic horror story of mixed impact. Reunited in New Orleans with her long-lost brother Malcolm McDowell, Nastassja Kinski meets zoo curator John Heard, takes a job there, and soon moves into his home. At the same time the Louisiana community is being terrorized by a big black panther. Having repressed her sexuality for a long time, Kinski finally condemns herself to repeat the pattern of her brother and ancestors. Kinski's endlessly watchable.

CAT'S EYE
1985, 93 mins, US Ⓥ ⊙
D: Lewis Teague A: Drew Barrymore, James Woods, Alan King, Kenneth McMillan, Robert Hays, Candy Clark (De Laurentiis)

Asked to do another script for Barrymore, [Stephen] King sketched out an idea about a cat who protects a young girl from a threatening troll in her bedroom wall. Unfortunately, that idea got tacked onto two other King short stories, "Quitters, Inc." and "The Ledge," lighting the fuse for the ultimate bomb. The three stories just don't connect.

CAT'S PAW, THE
1934, 101 mins, US
D: Sam Taylor A: Harold Lloyd, Una Merkel, George Barbier, Nat Pendleton, Grace Bradley, Alan Dinehart (Lloyd/Fox)

The Cat's Paw is the most adult comedy yet attempted by Harold Lloyd. Lloyd, as a missionary's son, visiting his hometown in the US after 20 years in China, is picked for a prize sap by the burg's political czars and nominated for mayor as the 1,000-to-1 shot opponent for their own man. But he surprises everybody, including himself, by winning, and the worm keeps on turning until he's cleaned up the city 100 percent.

CATTLE ANNIE AND LITTLE BRITCHES
1981, 97 mins, US
D: Lamont Johnson A: Burt Lancaster, John Savage, Rod Steiger, Scott Glenn,

Amanda Plummer, Diane Lane (Hemdale)

Cattle Annie and Little Britches is as cutesy and unmemorable as its title. Primary focus falls upon two teenage girls, the gutsy and rather reckless Amanda Plummer and the more demure Diane Lane, who aspire to become what might be called outlaw groupies. They get their chance when the Doolin-Dalton gang, headed up by an aging but still vigorous Burt Lancaster, rides into town, Plummer taking up with dashing John Savage and Lane coming under the fatherly wing of Lancaster himself.

CATTLE QUEEN OF MONTANA
1954, 88 mins, US Ⓥ
D: Allan Dwan A: Barbara Stanwyck, Ronald Reagan, Gene Evans, Lance Fuller, Anthony Caruso, Jack Elam (RKO)

There are cowboys and Indians in *Cattle Queen of Montana*, good and bad whites, peaceful and renegade Indians, and colorful Technicolor scenery, but all these ingredients fail to make the production anything more than a listless and ordinary western. In the picture's favor is an attempt to depict the problems of the redmen in fighting the encroachment on their land by the white settlers. The Indians are not all evil, scalp-hunting devils.

CAT-WOMEN OF THE MOON
1953, 64 mins, US Ⓥ
D: Arthur Hilton A: Sonny Tufts, Victor Jory, Marie Windsor, Carol Brewster, Susan Morrow, Bill Phipps (Zimbalist-Rabin)

This imaginatively conceived and produced science-fiction yarn takes the earth-to-moon premise and embellishes it with a civilization of cat women on the moon. Femmes, 2 million years ahead of Earth's civilization, very nearly wreck the Earthmen's plans to return to their home base. Carol Brewster is head of the cat women, an enticing wench, and Susan Morrow also scores as a moon femme. William Whitley's 3-D photography provides the proper eerie quality.

CAUGHT
1949, 88 mins, US Ⓥ
D: Max Ophuls A: James Mason, Barbara Bel Geddes, Robert Ryan, Ruth Brady, Curt Bois, Art Smith (Enterprise/M-G-M)

Caught is an out-and-out soap opera on film. It's the saga of the carhop who aspires to marry a millionaire. She goes to a charm school, becomes a model, and meets and marries her man. A life of riches isn't everything, so she gives it up, goes to work in the office of an East Side medico. They fall in love. The millionaire is better developed than usual in this type story. Robert Ryan plays him to the hilt.

CAVALCADE
1933, 110 mins, US
D: Frank Lloyd **A:** Diana Wynyard, Clive Brook, Una O'Connor, Herbert Mundin, Beryl Mercer, Irene Browne (Fox)

[Noel] Coward's pageant begins at the birth of the 20th century and the beginning of the Boer War. From that it swells along on through three decades, up and through the World War, and to today. Nothing of world importance is lost sight of, including the sinking of the *Titanic*. And through it all is a strong, wistful story of the growth of a family, and the clinging through years of a loving couple.
1932/33: Best Picture, Director, Interior Decoration (William S. Darling)
Nomination: Best Actress (Diana Wynyard)

CB4
1993, 86 mins, US Ⓥ ⊙
D: Tamra Davis **A:** Chris Rock, Allen Payne, Deezer D, Chris Elliott, Phil Hartman, Charlie Murphy (Universal)

This is a rap spoof attempt by a *Saturday Night Live* performer, Chris Rock. It starts promisingly enough with Ice-T and Ice Cube among the well-known rappers turning up in interview-style cameos. That tactic is soon abandoned in favor of a long flashback about how the middle-class trio (Rock, Allen Payne, and rapper Deezer D) passed themselves off as bad-ass types in order to tap into the rap audience. Tamra Davis might have really had something here had she settled on any one of the many paths the movie starts down.

C.C. AND COMPANY
1970, 94 mins, US Ⓥ
D: Seymour Robbie **A:** Joe Namath, Ann-Margret, William Smith, Jennifer Billingsley, Don Chastain, Teda Bracci (Avco Embassy/Rogallan)

Joe Namath frolics with Ann-Margret against a sordid milieu of motorbikes and an uneasy riders' commune in *C.C. and Company*. It's all put together ineffectually with one exception: Smith is impressive as the motorcyclists' guru.

CEILING ZERO
1936, 95 mins, US
D: Howard Hawks **A:** James Cagney, Pat

O'Brien, June Travis, Stuart Erwin, Barton MacLane, Henry Wadsworth (Cosmopolitan/Warner)

James Cagney reverts to the *Public Enemy* days in that he meets violent death at the finish. Up to then, as a daring and not strictly rational flier, he has been a devil with the ladies, a pilot who loses his license through irresponsible acts, and a man who is indirectly to blame for the death of a close friend. Perhaps 65 of the picture's 95 minutes unfold in the superintendent's office of a commercial airline. It's here that the exciting drama behind the business of peacetime flying is so graphically and compellingly painted.

CELEBRITY
1998, 113 mins, US Ⓥ ⊙
D: Woody Allen **A:** Kenneth Branagh, Melanie Griffith, Judy Davis, Charlize Theron, Famke Janssen, Winona Ryder (Sweetland/Miramax)

The spectacle of Kenneth Branagh and Judy Davis doing over-the-top Woody Allen impersonations creates a neurotic energy meltdown in *Celebrity*, a rehash of mostly stale Allen themes and motifs such as fame and sexual treachery. Branagh portrays Lee Simon, a feature writer doing a story on screen queen Nicole (Melanie Griffith). Thus begins Lee's desultory series of sexual escapades following his split from his wife, Robin (Judy Davis), a painfully insecure schoolteacher. Paralleling Lee's amorous misadventures is Robin's gradual blossoming under the wing of TV producer Tony Gardella (Joe Mantegna). Branagh is simply embarrassing as he flails, stammers, and gesticulates in a manner that suggests a direct imitation of Allen himself. Davis conveys too much intelligence to convince as a hopeless contemporary woman. Leonardo DiCaprio, who turns up playing a spoiled young film star throwing a tantrum in a hotel room, is entirely convincing.

CELIA
1989, 102 mins, Australia Ⓥ
D: Ann Turner **A:** Rebecca Smart, Nicholas Eadie, Maryanne Fahey, Victoria Longley, William Zappa (Seon)

Celia starts out as a likable family pic about the traumas of a sensitive nine-year-old girl growing up in a Melbourne suburb in the conservative late 1950s. It winds up as something quite different. Celia, played by Rebecca Smart, is an only child. When a national plague of rabbits results in the government calling for the handing over of all domestic bunnies, and when her beloved rabbit dies in the Melbourne Zoo, she takes a surprisingly violent revenge.

CELINE AND JULIE GO BOATING
See: Celine et Jule Vont en Bateau

CELINE ET JULIE VONT EN BATEAU
(CELINE AND JULIE GO BOATING)
1974, 190 mins, FRANCE Ⓥ
D: Jacques Rivette **A:** Juliet Berto, Dominique Labourier, Bulle Ogier, Marie-France Pisier, Barbet Schroeder (Films du Losange)

Jacques Rivette continues with his improvisatory tactics, allowing lead players to invent quite freely and also collab on the script. He mixes a modernized takeoff on *Alice in Wonderland* and a period tale of Henry James for an overindulged, overlong film that has some gemlike moments but also repetitiveness and preciosity.

CELLULOID CLOSET, THE
1995, 102 mins, US Ⓥ
D: Rob Epstein, Jeffrey Friedman (Telling Pictures/HBO)

Looking at depictions of homosexuality in mainstream American movies, documakers Rob Epstein and Jeffrey Friedman offer an immensely entertaining, galloping reflection on screen perceptions of lesbians and gay men. As the film moves systematically through each decade and trend, it shows gay visibility metamorphosing and growing. In the interviews, especially notable contributions come from Gore Vidal, Harvey Fierstein, Tom Hanks, Susan Sarandon, and novelist Armistead Maupin, who wrote the narration.

CELTIC PRIDE
1996, 90 mins, US Ⓥ
D: Tom DeCerchio **A:** Damon Wayans, Daniel Stern, Dan Aykroyd, Gail O'Grady, Adam Hendershott, Paul Guilfoyle (Hollywood)

Celtic Pride is an uneven but largely likable basketball-themed comedy. Daniel Stern and Dan Aykroyd are rabid hoop fans who yearn to see their beloved Celtics ace the NBA Finals. Seeing the hard-partying Utah Jazz team leader Lewis Scott (Damon Wayans) at a trendy nightspot, the boys at first do nothing more than try to get the star too drunk to play at the top of his game. The next morning, however, they wake up to find they kidnapped the NBA star. Wayans plays Scott with

sass and pizzazz, and is thoroughly convincing both on and off the basketball court.

CEMENT GARDEN, THE
1993, 105 mins, Germany/UK/France Ⓥ Ⓢ
D: Andrew Birkin **A:** Andrew Robertson, Charlotte Gainsbourg, Alice Coulthard, Ned Birkin, Sinead Cusack, Hanns Zischler (Neue Constantin/Laurentic/Torii)

Gallic star Charlotte Gainsbourg makes a striking English-lingo debut in a moody, dramatically uneven drama of sibling incest and teenage alienation. Pic's setting is a lone house amid a concrete wasteland. Mom (Sinead Cusack) buckles under the strain of rearing her four children. When she dies, the children start to give freer vent to their sexual confusion. The eldest, Julie (Gainsbourg), 16, plays with the incestuous infatuation of 15-year-old brother Jack (Andrew Robertson).

CENTENNIAL SUMMER
1946, 104 mins, US
D: Otto Preminger **A:** Jeanne Crain, Cornel Wilde, Linda Darnell, William Bythe, Walter Brennan, Constance Bennett (20th Century-Fox)

Centennial Summer is pleasant musical filmfare, sparked by a lilting Jerome Kern score. Film's weakness is lack of top voices to punch the numbers over. Background is the Centennial celebration held in Philadelphia during the summer of 1876. Plot projects both elderly and younger romantic complications that beset members of a Philadelphia railroading family. Papa (Walter Brennan) makes a mild play for his wife's sophisticated sister, and the two girls (Jeanne Crain, Linda Darnell) of the family both chase the same man (Cornel Wilde).

CENTRAL DO BRASIL
(CENTRAL STATION)
1998, 110 mins, Brazil/France Ⓥ Ⓢ ▱
D: Walter Salles **A:** Fernanda Montenegro, Marilia Pera, Vinicius de Oliveira, Soia Lira, Othon Bastos, Otavio Augusto (Cohn)

A sensitive art film of the old school, *Central Station* is a melancholy Brazilian road movie shot through with gently stressed cultural commentary. This handsomely crafted study of a search for family connections and personal and national hope doesn't quite manage the climactic emotional catharsis at which it aims. It's an intimate story about the troubled journey of a young boy (Vinicius de Oliveira) and an aging woman (Fernanda Montenegro) against the backdrop of a country in transition. The film drops dollops of meaning that are, if anything, rather too carefully and gingerly planted.

CENTRAL STATION
See: Central do Brasil

CENTURY
1993, 112 mins, UK ⊗ ⊙
D: Stephen Poliakoff **A:** Charles Dance, Clive Owen, Miranda Richardson, Robert Stephens, Joan Hickson, Neil Stuke (BBC/Beambright)

The dawn of a new era imbues Stephen Poliakoff's provocative *Century*. The film seamlessly incorporates such pertinent issues of turn-of-the-century England as race, religion, and sexuality. Paul (Clive Owen) emerges as the star medical researcher at a London hospital and confidant of the operation's chief, Mandry (Charles Dance). The turning point occurs when Paul defies Mandry, who he believes is purposely ignoring vital experiments developed by another doctor.

LA CEREMONIE
(A JUDGEMENT IN STONE)
1995, 109 mins, France/Germany ⊗
D: Claude Chabrol **A:** Isabelle Huppert, Sandrine Bonnaire, Jacqueline Bisset, Jean-Pierre Cassel, Virginie Ledoyen, Valentin Merlet

A character-driven tragicomic treat. The chic Catherine Lelièvre (Jacqueline Bisset) hires Sophie (Sandrine Bonnaire) to be the new live-in housekeeper at the large country estate she shares with her well-heeled husband, Georges (Jean-Pierre Cassel). Sophie's abrupt behavior eventually leads to her dismissal, but not before she's struck up a liberating friendship with Jeanne (Isabelle Huppert), an insolent live wire who runs the village post office. From the first frames, Claude Chabrol establishes an expectant atmosphere, with ample payoff in the end.

CEREMONY, THE
1963, 106 mins, US
D: Laurence Harvey **A:** Laurence Harvey, Sarah Miles, Robert Walker, John Ireland, Ross Martin, Lee Patterson (United Artists)

The dreary tale of a man (Laurence Harvey) about to be executed in a Tangier prison for a crime he did not commit, a murder that actually he'd tried to prevent but for which he is paying the supreme penalty as a kind of scapegoat. The players are all snowed under by ill-defined, unappealing roles and lack of proper direction.

CERTAIN SMILE, A
1958, 105 mins, US ▭
D: Jean Negulesco **A:** Rossano Brazzi, Joan Fontaine, Bradford Dillman, Christine Carere, Eduard Franz, Kathryn Givney (20th Century-Fox)

In the second of Francoise Sagan's novels to be filmed, once again the principal character is a young and attractive girl, only this time the shocker involves her weeklong affair with an older man. The film abounds with mouthwatering vistas of the French Riviera, which is photographed from every possible vantage point, providing an idyllic setting for the romantic goings-on between Rossano Brazzi and Christine Carere.

1958: Nominations: Best Costume Design, Art Direction, Song ("A Certain Smile")

CESAR
1936, 170 mins, France ⊗ ⊙
D: Marcel Pagnol **A:** Raimu, Pierre Fresnay, Orane Demazis, Charpin, Andre Fouche, Alida Rouffe (Pagnol)

This last of Marcel Pagnol's trilogy which started with *Marius* and continued with *Fanny* could be cut by almost half without damaging it to any extent. With *Cesar* we are faced with grown-ups who bear the scars of the lessons they have learned. Pathos caused by frustrated desires has replaced the youthful recklessness of *Marius* and the noble self-sacrificing ideals of *Fanny*. Entire story unrolls in endless dialogue, which is rendered with tremendous force and emotion by Raimu as César, the father.

C'EST ARRIVE PRES DE CHEZ VOUS
(MAN BITES DOG)
1992, 95 mins, Belgium ⊗ ⊙
D: Remy Belvaux **A:** Benoit Poelvoorde, Remy Belvaux, Andre Bonzel, Jean-Marc Chenut, Alain Oppexxi, Vincent Tavier (Artistes Anonymes)

An offbeat, darkly hilarious portrait of a freelance hit man whose every move is recorded by a documentary-film crew. Well served in black-and-white vérité-style lensing, mordant send-up of questionable newsgathering practices provides clever patter with its splatter. With evolving irony, camera crew, at first reluctant even to dine with their immoral subject, graduates to joining in on the gang rape and disembowelment of a woman in her own home. Not for the righteous or the squeamish.

CET OBSCUR OBJET DU DESIR (THAT OBSCURE OBJECT OF DESIRE)
1977, 100 mins, France/Spain Ⓥ ⊙
D: Luis Bunuel A: Fernando Rey, Carole Bouquet, Angela Molina, Julien Bertheau, Andre Weber, Milena Vukotic (Greenwich/Galaxie/In Cine)

A gemlike, almost hypnotic tale of an older man's obsession with a young woman. Loosely based on a 19th-century book by Pierre Louys, director Luis Bunuel has updated it and put a good part of the action in Paris. Bunuel decided to go back to an old idea of using two girls to play the sex object. One is willowy, lovely French actress Carole Bouquet, and the other more earthy and sensual, Hispano dancer Angela Molina. They interchange at the director's will. Fernando Rey, a Bunuel regular, is expert as the sadomasochistic rich man who falls madly for his inept new maid. Film shows desire accepting any humiliations.

CHAD HANNA
1940, 86 mins, US
D: Henry King A: Henry Fonda, Dorothy Lamour, Linda Darnell, Guy Kibbee, Jane Darwell, John Carradine (20th Century-Fox)

Chad Hanna evokes early 19th-century Americana. Chad Hanna (Henry Fonda) is a semiilliterate stable boy. Enamored of the gaudily dressed circus rider (Dorothy Lamour), he joins the small one-ringer as a roustabout, and finds Linda Darnell along as a runaway. Chad marries Darnell, and in a brief reunion with Lamour realizes he is really in love with his wife. Both script and direction handle the yarn in leisurely and rather uneventful tempo.

LE CHAGRIN ET LA PITIE
See: The Sorrow and the Pity

CHAINED HEAT
1983, 95 mins, US/W. Germany Ⓥ ⊙
D: Paul Nicolas A: Linda Blair, John Vernon, Sybil Danning, Tamara Dobson, Stella Stevens, Henry Silva (Heat/TAT/Intercontinental)

Linda Blair toplines as Carol, an innocent young girl in a California prison run by Warden Backman (John Vernon) and Captain Taylor (Stella Stevens), as

corrupt a pair as the scripters can imagine. Real power in stir is shared by statuesque Ericka (Sybil Danning) and Duchess (Tamara Dobson), lording it over the white and black prison populations, respectively. German director Paul Nicolas displays little feel for the prison genre, emphasizing archaic sex-for-voyeurs scenes.

CHAIN OF DESIRE
1993, 107 mins, US Ⓥ ⊙
D: Temistocles Lopez A: Linda Fiorentino, Grace Zabriskie, Assumpta Serna, Patrick Bauchau, Seymour Cassel, Malcolm McDowell (Distant Horizon)

A modern La Ronde played out under the shadow of AIDS, Chain of Desire is an uneven but alluringly sexy melodrama that gets better as it goes along. Set in contempo New York, mostly downtown, this version introduces a somewhat jaded, bisexual perspective to the tale, but the characters remain vibrantly alive to life's possibilities, at least where the libido is concerned.

CHAIRMAN, THE (UK: THE MOST DANGEROUS MAN IN THE WORLD)
1969, 104 mins, US Ⓥ ◻
D: J. Lee Thompson A: Gregory Peck, Anne Heywood, Arthur Hill, Alan Dobie, Conrad Yama, Zienia Merton (20th Century-Fox)

American scientist Gregory Peck, teaching at the University of London, receives a letter from his former instructor, Professor Soong Li (Keye Luke), telling him it would be impossible for Peck to visit Red China. Since Peck has no intention of visiting China, he is further mystified when the president urges him to slip into the Chinese mainland. Task of presenting the film [from a novel by Jay Richard Kennedy] on screen was stupendous, and it has been accomplished with imagination and taste.

CHALK GARDEN, THE
1964, 106 mins, UK Ⓥ
D: Ronald Neame A: Deborah Kerr, Hayley Mills, John Mills, Edith Evans, Elizabeth Sellars, Felix Aylmer (Quota Rentals)

Hayley Mills vigorously plays a 16-year-old girl, in some ways perceptive beyond her years. Her mother has remarried and her grandmother is more obsessed with her arid garden. So the confused, unhappy girl grows up in a world of fantasy and lying. Onto the scene comes a mystery woman as governess (Deborah Kerr). On

paper, this sounds like a ripe old piece of Victoriana, but curiously it works, largely because of confident, smooth performances by all concerned.
1964: Nomination: Best Supp. Actress (Edith Evans)

CHALLENGE, THE
1982, 112 mins, US Ⓥ
D: John Frankenheimer **A:** Scott Glenn, Toshiro Mifune, Donna Kei Lenz, Atsuo Nakamura, Calvin Young, Clyde Kusatsu (CBS Theatrical)

Heads seen being split or cut off in swift but bloody close-ups, along with a lot of aesthetic juxtaposition of ancient Japanese manners and architecture versus modern ditto, are the main attractions. Pitted against each other are two brothers (Toshiro Mifune and Atsuo Nakamura) and two swords of the kind that certain Japanese even today believe to have a soul of their own. Into all this is lured a young American boxing bum known only as Rick (Scott Glenn).

CHAMBER, THE
1996, 11 mins, Ⓥ ☉ ▭
D: James Foley **A:** Chris O'Donnell, Gene Hackman, Faye Dunaway, Robert Prosky, Raymond Barry, Bo Jackson (Imagine/Universal)

The Chamber is an intelligently proficient movie that works more effectively as a family drama than a legal thriller. Chris O'Donnell plays Adam Hall, who decides to represent his grandfather, Klansman Sam Cayhall (Gene Hackman). After a decade on Mississippi's death row, Sam is only 28 days away from his impending execution in "the chamber." A brief flashback reveals Sam's racist crime in 1967, when a bomb he planted caused the death of two Jewish boys, sons of a civil rights worker. What's missing in thrills and suspense is more than made up for by the intimacy of character interaction and superlative acting. Hackman dominates every scene he's in, having shed 30 pounds and sporting a credible Southern drawl. Faye Dunaway delivers a touching perf as Sam's daughter, a tortured belle.

CHAMP, THE
1931, 85 mins, US Ⓥ
D: King Vidor **A:** Wallace Beery, Jackie Cooper, Irene Rich, Roscoe Ates, Edward Brophy, Hale Hamilton (M-G-M)

A good picture, almost entirely by virtue of an inspired performance by a boy, Jackie Cooper. What also makes The *Champ* a good talker is a studied, understanding adult piece of work by the costar, Wallace Beery, and a Frances Marion original story that isn't bad for a boxing story. Beery plays a broken-down ex-heavyweight champ. He's anchored in Tijuana with his kid. In the attempts of the Champ's former wife and the boy's mother to regain her son there is some menace.
1931/32: Best Actor (Wallace Beery), Original Story
Nominations: Best Picture, Director

CHAMP, THE
1979, 121 mins, US Ⓥ ☉
D: Franco Zeffirelli **A:** Jon Voight, Faye Dunaway, Ricky Schroder, Jack Warden, Strother Martin, Joan Blondell (United Artists/M-G-M)

Walter Newman's script adroitly updates Frances Marion's original scenario, placing down-and-out boxer Jon Voight as a horse handler in Florida, accompanied by sprig Ricky Schroder. An inveterate gambler and drinker, Voight doesn't hit the comeback trail until ex-wife Faye Dunaway reappears to threaten his and Schroder's buddy-buddy relationship. Schroder projects a commendable emotional range and depth.
1979: Nomination: Best Original Score

CHAMPAGNE FOR CAESAR
1950, 99 mins, US Ⓥ ☉
D: Richard Whorf **A:** Ronald Colman, Celeste Holm, Vincent Price, Barbara Britton, Art Linkletter (United Artists)

Champagne for Caesar centers its lampooning on big-time soap companies and the quiz shows that hand out money freely to contestants. Ronald Colman plays an intellectual, a sort of walking encyclopedia, who sets out to smash such radio gimmicks and the people who sponsor them. Styles of comedy range from the quiet statement of the Colman character to the broadly burlesqued soap tycoon portrait drawn by Vincent Price.

CHAMPION
1949, 90 mins, US Ⓥ
D: Mark Robson **A:** Kirk Douglas, Marilyn Maxwell, Arthur Kennedy, Paul Stewart, Ruth Roman (Screen Plays)

Adapted from a Ring Lardner short story of the same title, *Champion* is a stark, realistic study of the boxing rackets and the degeneration of a prizefighter. Kirk Douglas is the boxer and he makes the character live. Second honors go

jointly to Arthur Kennedy, the fighter's crippled brother, and Paul Stewart as the knowing manager.
1949: Best Editing
Nominations: Best Actor (Kirk Douglas), Supp. Actor (Arthur Kennedy), Screenplay, B&W Cinematography, Scoring of a Dramatic Picture

CHAMPIONS
See: The Mighty Ducks

CHANCES ARE
1989, 108 mins, US Ⓥ ⊙
D: Emile Ardolino **A:** Cybill Shepherd, Robert Downey Jr., Ryan O'Neal, Mary Stuart Masterson, Christopher McDonald, Josef Sommer (Tri-Star)

A potentially charming premise yields only a handful of chuckles. The plot hangs on the death of Cybill Shepherd's husband, who flees heaven to be reincarnated before being inoculated to prevent a return of past-life memory. He comes back 23 years later as Robert Downey Jr. and stumbles into the life of Corinne (Shepherd), as well as that of her daughter Miranda (Mary Stuart Masterson) and former best friend Philip (Ryan O'Neal).

CHANG
1927, 70 mins, US Ⓥ ⊙ ⊗
D: Merian C. Cooper, Ernest B. Schoedsack **A:** Kru, Chantui, Nah, Ladah, Bimbo (Paramount)

Towering above all else as an animal picture is a melodramatic story of native life in the jungle. *Chang* is the first animal picture having a scenario and with just an immense jungle for the background. It carries more of a thrill than the other pictures of its sort, for the plot is fraught with danger and the ferocity of the tiger and leopards here and there is most realistic.
1927/28: Nomination: Best Artistic Quality of Production

CHANGELING, THE
1980, 107 mins, Canada Ⓥ
D: Peter Medak **A:** George C. Scott, Trish Van Devere, Melvyn Douglas, John Colicos, Jean Marsh, Barry Morse (Michaels-Drabinsky)

The Changeling is a superior haunted-house thriller. The story centers on George C. Scott, a recently widowed music professor. His new residence is an old home owned by the local historic society. After moving in, the house begins to do strange things. It turns out that the noisy spirit is a sickly young boy who was murdered at the turn of the century.

CHANGE OF SEASONS, A
1980, 102 mins, US Ⓥ
D: Richard Lang, [Noel Black] **A:** Shirley MacLaine, Anthony Hopkins, Bo Derek, Mary Beth Hurt, Michael Brandon, Ed Winter (Film Finance/Ransohoff)

It would take the genius of an Ernst Lubitsch to do justice to the incredibly tangled relationships in *A Change of Seasons*. Shirley MacLaine emerges as the most sympathetic person in the film, the wife of college professor Anthony Hopkins, whose philandering with coed Bo Derek shatters the complacency of their marriage.

CHAN IS MISSING
1982, 80 mins, US Ⓥ
D: Wayne Wang **A:** Marc Hayashi, Wood Moy, Laureen Chew, Judy Nihei, Peter Wang (Wang)

Rather roughly lensed in B&W and 16mm, tale traces the odyssey of two San Francisco Chinese taxi drivers as they search for an older partner who's vanished with their funds. Chan's relatives, local businessmen, politicos, and citizens-at-large who are interviewed by the pair constitute a fascinating and often amusing gallery of portraits of contempo Chinese-Americans.

CHANT OF JIMMIE BLACKSMITH, THE
1978, 122 mins, Australia Ⓥ ▭
D: Fred Schepisi **A:** Tommy Lewis, Freddy Reynolds, Ray Barrett, Jack Thompson, Peter Carroll, Elizabeth Alexander (Filmhouse/Australia Party)

The tale of a mulatto aborigine, raised by a Methodist minister, and torn between his people and his Christian teachings, has sweep and interesting insights into the loss of the aborigine culture and the life of a man who does not belong to either culture anymore. Tommy Lewis, a nonactor, is well utilized as Jimmie Blacksmith. The violence is instinctive, harrowing, but not exploited.

CHAPLIN
1992, 144 mins, US Ⓥ ⊙
D: Richard Attenborough **A:** Robert Downey Jr., Dan Aykroyd, Geraldine Chaplin, Kevin Dunn, Anthony Hopkins, Moira Kelly (Carolco/Canal Plus/RCS Video)

Like a stone skipping across the top of a deep, turbulent sea, *Chaplin* runs through the dramatic highs and lows in the life of the screen's foremost comic genius without stirring the water much. Epic biopic does offer the saving grace of an uncanny, truly remarkable central performance by Robert Downey Jr. and a number of lovely moments along the way. Geraldine Chaplin strongly etches her own grandmother's maternal love and incipient madness.

Nominations: Best Actor (Robert Downey Jr.), Original Score, Art Direction

CHAPMAN REPORT, THE
1962, 125 mins, US
D: George Cukor **A:** Efrem Zimbalist Jr., Shelley Winters, Jane Fonda, Claire Bloom, Glynis Johns, Ray Danton (Warner)

The Chapman Report attempts the feat of dramatically threading together the stories of four sexually unstable women who become voluntary subjects for a scientific sex survey. One (Claire Bloom) is a hopeless nympho and alcoholic. Another (Jane Fonda) suffers from fears of frigidity. The third (Glynis Johns), a kind of comedy-relief figure, is an intellectual who feels there may be more to sex than she has realized. The last (Shelley Winters) enters into a clandestine extramarital affair.

CHAPTER TWO
1979, 124 mins, US ⓥ ⊙
D: Robert Moore **A:** James Caan, Marsha Mason, Joseph Bologna, Valerie Harper, Judy Farrell, Debra Mooney (Columbia)

Chapter Two represents Neil Simon at his big-screen best. Film version of his successful and loosely autobiographical play is tender, compassionate, and gently humorous all at once, subtly concentrating on Jennie MacLaine, the actress being wooed by author Schneider, rather than on Schneider himself. Result is to downplay the unusual casting of James Caan as Schneider (the choice still pays off richly) and affords Mason the opportunity for her best-realized film work to date.

1979: Nomination: Best Actress (Marsha Mason)

CHARACTER
See: Karakter

CHARADE
1963, 113 mins, US ⓥ ⊙
D: Stanley Donen **A:** Cary Grant, Audrey Hepburn, Walter Matthau, James Coburn, Ned Glass, George Kennedy (Universal)

While vacationing at a French Alps ski resort, Audrey Hepburn meets Cary Grant

casually. Returning to Paris, she finds herself a widow, her husband having been murdered. The two stars carry the film effortlessly, with the only acting competition coming from the versatile Matthau. Fast-paced, from the pretitle shot of a body tossed from a train to the finale under a theater stage, *Charade* seldom falters (amazing, considering its almost two-hour running time). Repartee between the two stars is sometimes subtle, sometimes suggestive, sometimes satirical, but always witty.

1963: Nomination: Best Song ("Charade")

CHARGE OF THE LIGHT BRIGADE, THE
1936, 115 mins, US ⓥ ⊙
D: Michael Curtiz **A:** Errol Flynn, Olivia de Havilland, Patric Knowles, Henry Stephenson, Donald Crisp, David Niven (Warner)

Warner has turned out a magnificent production in this story based on Tennyson's immortal poem and historical facts. Foreword explains that characters and development are fictionized. The tremendous sweep of this surging charge constitutes the feature's highlight. It has been skillfully done by means of close-ups, a traveling camera shot depicting the changing pace of the horses as column after column races toward the enemy, and via some truly extraordinary process shots. Errol Flynn lives up to the promise of previous film efforts as the youthful major who sacrifices all to avenge the slaughter of his comrades.

1936: Best Assistant Director (Jack Sullivan)
Nominations: Best Score, Sound

CHARGE OF THE LIGHT BRIGADE, THE
1968, 145 mins, UK ⓥ ▷◁
D: Tony Richardson **A:** Trevor Howard, Vanessa Redgrave, John Gielgud, Harry Andrews, Jill Bennett, David Hemmings (United Artists/Woodfall)

Thanks mainly to Lord Tennyson's durable piece of doggerel, millions of people have at least a sketchy idea of the historical incident, though director Tony Richardson is more concerned with analyzing the reasons behind one of the most notorious blunders in military history. He's also intent on attacking by ridicule the class war and bigotry of the British mid-19th-century regime and the futility of the Crimean War as a whole.

CHARIOTS OF FIRE
1981, 123 mins, UK Ⓥ ☉
D: Hugh Hudson **A:** Ben Cross, Ian Charleson, Nigel Havers, Alice Krige, John Gielgud, Lindsay Anderson (Allied Stars/Enigma)

Chariots of Fire, which weaves the stories of two former British track aces who both won major events at the 1924 Paris Olympics, is about the will to win and why. Ian Charleson and Ben Cross are both exemplary as the respective super runners, Eric Liddell and Harold Abrahams, the first a Christian Scot who believes that by winning can he best honor the Lord; the latter an English Jew with a chip on the shoulder, for whom over-achieving is his ticket to acceptance in a prejudiced society.
1981: Best Picture, Original Screenplay, Score, Costume Design
Nominations: Best Director, Supp. Actor (Ian Holm), Editing

CHARLEY'S AUNT
1941, 90 mins, US
D: Archie Mayo **A:** Jack Benny, Kay Francis, Anne Baxter, Edmund Gwenn, Richard Haydn, James Ellison (20th Century-Fox)

Jack Benny playing with enthusiasm and romping merrily and crazily along the route, takes fullest advantage of laugh opportunities. Under expert direction of Archie Mayo, there's no letdown in the fast pace maintained for rollicking results. Picture closely follows the stage farce in unfolding, carrying Oxford background of 1890. Perennial student Benny is forced to masquerade as Charley's rich aunt from Brazil to provide chaperonage while Charley (Richard Haydn) and James Ellison have their girlfriends for lunch and marriage proposals.

CHARLEY VARRICK
1973, 111 mins, US Ⓥ
D: Don Siegel **A:** Walter Matthau, Joe Don Baker, Felicia Farr, Andy Robinson, John Vernon, Sheree North (Universal)

Charley Varrick is a sometimes fuzzy melodrama but so well put together that it emerges a hard-hitting actioner with a sock finale. Narrative carries the unusual twist of Walter Matthau, a small-time bank robber, trying to return his heist of a small-town New Mexico bank after later discovering his $750,000 take belongs to the Mafia and he wants none of it.

CHARLIE BUBBLES
1968, 89 mins, UK
D: Albert Finney **A:** Albert Finney, Colin Blakely, Billie Whitelaw, Liza Minnelli, Timothy Garland, Richard Pearson (Memorial)

Albert Finney stars as, and makes his directorial debut in, *Charlie Bubbles.* Comedy-drama concerns a materially successful man, fighting vainly the old ennui. Unfortunately, audiences are bound to experience the same tedium, via underplaying and limp direction.

CHARLIE CHAN AT THE OPERA
1936, 62 mins, US Ⓥ ☉
D: H. Bruce Humberstone **A:** Warner Oland, Boris Karloff, Keye Luke, Charlotte Henry, Thomas Beck, Gregory Gaye (20th Century-Fox)

Chan's interminable saga gets a shot in the arm which effectively dispels any monotony. It is the creation of a cofeature role, with Boris Karloff to play it. Being set in an opera house, the action is more complicated than in previous Chan stories. As a cross between a madman and an amnesia victim, Karloff plays a role right down his alley.

CHARLIE CHAN AT TREASURE ISLAND
1939, 72 mins, US
D: Norman Foster **A:** Sidney Toler, Cesar Romero, Pauline Moore, Sen Yung, Douglas Fowley (20th Century-Fox)

Charlie Chan bumps into a murder mystery involved with the psychic and astrological rackets, and proceeds to unravel the affair at a performance in a Treasure Island (San Francisco Fair) theater. Picture is rather slow in spots, but holds up generally to pace set by previous Chan adventures to satisfy whodunit fans.

CHARLIE CHAN CARRIES ON
1931, 69 mins, US
D: Hamilton MacFadden **A:** Warner Oland, John Garrick, Marguerite Churchill, Warren Hymer, Marjorie White, George Brent (Fox)

This story of the Honolulu detective who solves a murder mystery that baffled Scotland Yard and Europe is well directed and aptly photographed. The picture is full of wisecracks: the flippant pieces of philosophy spoken by Chan (Warner Oland) in his simple English and the more funny lingo of Warren Hymer, as the Chicago racketeer.

CHARLIE CHAN IN EGYPT
1935, 72 mins, US
D: Louis King **A:** Warner Oland, Pat Paterson, Thomas Beck, Rita Hayworth, Stepin Fetchit, James Eagles (Fox)

Story framed around Earl Derr Biggers's Chinese crime snooper taking a flier among the tombs of the pharaohs and combines a suavely sustained concept of drama and another surehanded interpretation of the central role by Warner Oland. Next to Oland's, the stand-out performance is that of James Eagles, whose superstitious fears drive him to near insanity and are brought to an end by his sudden death by a mysterious source.

CHARLIE CHAN IN LONDON
1934, 79 mins, US
D: Eugene Forde **A:** Warner Oland, Drue Leyton, Douglas Walton, Alan Mowbray, Mona Barrie, Ray Milland (Fox)

As mystery stories go, this is well above average. Although it is not by the creator of the Chan series, the tempo is so well imitated by scenarist Philip MacDonald, it would pass for an original Earl Derr Biggers composition. For Warner Oland, the Chan role now is second nature. Most of the action takes place on luxurious interior sets of a wealthy country home in England.

CHARLIE CHAN IN SHANGHAI
1935, 70 mins, US
D: James Tinling **A:** Warner Oland, Irene Hervey, Jon Hall, Russell Hicks, Keye Luke, Halliwell Hobbes (Fox)

Charlie Chan is in Shanghai this time. Strange that the Chinese detective has never been set there before, but that oversight is patched up very nicely in this film. This time he's after a gang of dope smugglers in China. Keye Luke is cast as his son and gets in some nice laughs.

CHARLIE CHAN ON BROADWAY
1937, 68 mins, US
D: Eugene Forde **A:** Warner Oland, Keye Luke, Joan Marsh, J. Edward Bromberg, Douglas Fowley, Harold Huber (20th Century-Fox)

Entry provides an opportunity for the Oriental Sherlock to perform his deductions while a guest of the NY police force. Chan uncovers the killer of two people mixed up in the big city's mob. Some of the plausible deductions lend more credibility than usual to this typical yarn.

CHARLIE CHAN'S CHANCE
1932, 73 mins, US
D: John G. Blystone **A:** Warner Oland, Alexander Kirkland, H. B. Warner, Marian Nixon, Ralph Morgan, James Kirkwood (Fox)

In solving the new mystery, Chan has the help of Inspector Fife of Scotland Yard (H. B. Warner) and Inspector Flannery of New York (James Kirkwood). But as far as really helping they're just a couple of stooges. The path to solution is studded with countless false clues and the all-important erroneous arrest of the juve love-interest team (Marian Nixon and Alexander Kirkland.

CHARLOTTE'S WEB
1973, 93 mins, US Ⓥ ⊙
D: Charles A. Nichols, Iwao Takamoto (Hanna-Barbera/Sagittarius)

A saga of a little white porker named Wilbur, petrified with fear he's fated to become a slab of tender bacon, and Charlotte, the benevolent spider who saves him from this fate through the magic weaving in her web. Based on the E. B. White children's classic, the Hanna-Barbera animated musical is heartwarming entertainment. Debbie Reynolds is heard as the voice of Charlotte, Henry Gibson as Wilbur.

CHARLY
1968, 103 mins, US Ⓥ ⊙
D: Ralph Nelson **A:** Cliff Robertson, Claire Bloom, Leon Janney, Lilia Skala, Dick Van Patton, Ed McNally (Selmur)

Charly boasts a most intriguing premise—a variation on the Pygmalion theme in which a mentally retarded "adult" grows up as the result of a brain operation. Charly merges a peculiar combination of sentimentalized documentary, romance, science fiction, and social drama. Cliff Robertson seems to overdo the external manifestations of retardation, but he is excellent in the postoperative scenes. With more help from the script he could have been a movingly tragic figure.
1968: Best Actor (Cliff Robertson)

LE CHARME DISCRET DE LA BOURGEOISIE
(THE DISCREET CHARM OF THE BOURGEOISIE)
1972, 100 mins, France/Spain/Italy Ⓥ ⊙
D: Luis Bunuel **A:** Fernando Rey, Delphine Seyrig, Stephane Audran, Jean-Pierre Cassel, Paul Frankeur, Bulle Ogier (Greenwich/Jet/Dean)

Luis Bunuel adds another fine film to

his solid record with this surrealistically oriented tale. A haughty ambassador (Fernando Rey), two fairly rich friends, and their relative come for dinner at a rich couple's home but find it is the wrong day. Going to a restaurant, they cannot eat there as the owner has just died. Dinners are interrupted by a group of soldiers on maneuvers, and terrorists breaking in and slaughtering the main characters. Each major male type has a dream that works into the fabric of the pic.
1972: Best Foreign Language Film

CHARULATA
(THE LONELY WIFE)
1964, 117 mins, India
D: Satyajit Ray **A:** Soumitra Chatterjee, Madhabi Mukherjee, Sailen Mukherjee, Shyamal Ghoshal, Geetali Roy (Bansai)
It is the style that counts as Ray unfolds his story of a successful publisher whose intelligent wife vegetates by doing embroidery. He invites his brother-in-law and wife as houseguests. Another visitor is a handsome cousin. Inevitably, the lonely wife and the handsome cousin are drawn to each other, but always maintain an appropriate degree of restraint. The period, after all, is 1879. The director keeps dialogue down to a minimum, allowing the camera to be the main storyteller.

CHASE, THE
1946, 86 mins, US ⓥ
D: Arthur Ripley **A:** Robert Cummings, Michele Morgan, Peter Lorre, Steve Cochran (United Artists)
The Chase is a meller that's taut as sprung steel for 75 minutes of its running time then slackens limply into the commonplace. Yarn concerns the attempt of a killer's wife and his chauffeur to make their getaway from his household and henchman. Steve Cochran, who plays the killer, is handsome, suave, confident, and menacing in the manner of a Humphrey Bogart.

CHASE, THE
1966, 138 mins, US ⓥ ⊙ ▭
D: Arthur Penn **A:** Marlon Brando, Jane Fonda, Robert Redford, James Fox, E. G. Marshall, Angie Dickinson (Horizon/Columbia)
Only the framework of Horton Foote's novel has been utilized by Lillian Hellman in her screenplay. She manages to provide most of the social grievances which trouble the world today. Robert Redford, as the escaped convict whose impending re-

turn to his hometown gives many of its citizens the jitters, gives the film's best performance. Jane Fonda, as Redford's wife, makes the most of the biggest female role.

CHASE, THE
1994, 88 mins, US ⓥ ⊙
D: Adam Rifkin **A:** Charlie Sheen, Kristy Swanson, Henry Rollins, Josh Mostel, Wayne Grace, Rocky Carroll (Capitol/20th Century-Fox)
An escaped convict (Charlie Sheen) kidnaps the heiress to a fortune (Kristy Swanson) and takes off for Mexico in her shiny red BMW. Virtually the rest of the action has them in that car, as the two build a grudging relationship, with the police as well as local TV stations in hot pursuit. For the most part, *The Chase* goes nowhere, wearing out its welcome with music-video techniques and an equally repetitive, percussive score.

CHASE A CROOKED SHADOW
1958, 92 mins, UK
D: Michael Anderson **A:** Richard Todd, Anne Baxter, Herbert Lom, Alexander Knox, Faith Brook (Associated Dragon/Associated British)
Chase a Crooked Shadow is a glossy, well-directed drama that has enough twists and artfully planned kicks to keep most audiences guessing. The yarn concerns Anne Baxter as an heiress who believes the plot is to drive her insane and then murder her. Final twist is a sock climax.

CHASERS
1994, 101 mins, US ⓥ ⊙
D: Dennis Hopper **A:** Tom Berenger, Erika Eleniak, William McNamara, Crispin Glover, Gary Busey, Frederic Forrest (Morgan Creek/Warner)
This mangy, dim-witted gender switch on *The Last Detail* has sultry sexpot Erika Eleniak, sentenced to 7 to 10 for assault and going AWOL. Scattered about are little morsels to keep the desperate viewer attentive: William McNamara's cockiness as hard-guy vet Tom Berenger's companion, Eleniak's incredible physique, a reasonably tasty sex scene between the two of them, some grungy southeastern-seaboard locations, and what basically amounts to cameos by an odd lot of actors.

CHATO'S LAND
1972, 100 mins, UK ⓥ
D: Michael Winner **A:** Charles Bronson, Jack Palance, Richard Basehart, James

Whitmore, Simon Oakland, Ralph Waite (Scimitar)

British producer-director Michael Winner comes up with a violence-drenched meller. Writer Gerald Wilson, adopting and-then-there-were-none theme, plots an Apache half-breed relentlessly pursued by a ragtag white posse headed by an ex-Confederate officer after the Indian has killed a white sheriff. Charles Bronson portrays the Apache Chato and Jack Palance the posse leader.

CHATTAHOOCHEE
1989, 103 mins, US ⓥ ⊙
D: Mick Jackson A: Gary Oldman, Dennis Hopper, Frances McDormand, Pamela Reed, Ned Beatty, M. Emmet Walsh (Hemdale)

Gary Oldman's bravura performance as a victimized patient in a Deep South prison hospital for the criminally insane, circa 1950s, fails to cure the film of its manifold structural and stylistic ills. The "hospital" is sort of a cross between the Turkish prison barracks of *Midnight Express,* the hard-time joint in *Brubaker* and the good ol' prison farm of *Cool Hand Luke.* Similarities to those three excellent movies end there.

CHE!
1969, 96 mins, US ⓥ ▭
D: Richard Fleischer A: Omar Sharif, Jack Palance, Cesare Danova, Robert Loggia, Woody Strode, Barbara Luna (20th Century-Fox)

Producer Sy Bartlett and director Richard Fleischer claimed to have made an "impartial, objective" film about Fidel Castro's Cuban Revolution and of subsequent events in that country. To them, Ernesto Che Guevara was an evil genius who tried to lead Castro down wrong paths, a man whose revolutionary zeal took violent turns that ignored social reality. As presented, Castro, played smokehouse by Jack Palance, is innocent not only of winning the initial revolution, but also of the deeds afterward which condemn him in many American eyes. Pic has been made in a mock-documentary style that comes out poorly.

CHEAP DETECTIVE, THE
1978, 92 mins, US ⓥ ⊙ ▭
D: Robert Moore A: Peter Falk, Ann-Margret, Eileen Brennan, Sid Caesar, Stockard Channing, James Coco (Columbia)

A hilarious and loving takeoff on all 1940s Warner Bros private-eye-and-foreign-intrigue mellers. The time is 1940, San Francisco, where clumsy gumshoe Peter Falk is accused of murdering his partner, whose wife Marsha Mason has been Falk's mistress. Madeline Kahn, with as many smart clothes changes as aliases, appears in Falk's office. She's in league with John Houseman (Sydney Greenstreet to the core), Paul Williams (Elisha Cook Jr. was never like this), and Dom DeLuise (a fat Peter Lorre) in search of ancient treasure—a dozen diamond eggs.

CHECKING OUT
1989, 93 mins, US ⓥ ⊙
D: David Leland A: Jeff Daniels, Melanie Mayron, Michael Tucker, Kathleen York, Allan Havey (HandMade/Warner)

A dreadfully unfunny one-joke black comedy about hypochondria and mortality. Jeff Daniels, as budget-airline executive Ray Macklin, witnesses the death by coronary of his irreverent best buddy Allan Havey. This trauma triggers the onset of a hysterical, fetishistic hypochondria that propels him through a series of discombobulating misadventures.

CHELSEA GIRLS, THE
1967, 210 mins, US
D: Andy Warhol A: Robert Olivio, Ondine, Mary Might, Nico, Ingrid Superstar, Mario Montez (Warhol)

The Chelsea Girls is a pointless, excruciatingly dull three and a half hours spent in the company of Andy Warhol's friends. There is no plotline. The single unifying device is that the film takes place in several rooms of a downtown hotel.

CHERRY, HARRY & RAQUEL!
1969, 71 mins, US
D: Russ Meyer A: Larissa Ely, Linda Ashton, Charles Napier, Bert Santos, Franklin H. Bolger, Astrid Lillimor (Eve/Panamint)

Film focuses on the narcotics traffic on the Mexican border, where Charles Napier is a sheriff in the pay of the drug operator. Linda Ashton plays Cherry, his girlfriend, and Larissa Ely portrays Raquel, who takes on all comers. When the two ladies of the title get tired of it all with men, they try some lesbian clinches. Flashes of nudes intersperse the unreeling every minute or so. Mebbe they're symbolic, they have no connection with the story.

CHERRY 2000
1988, 93 mins, US ⓥ ⊙
D: Steve de Jarnatt A: Melanie Griffith, David Andrews, Ben Johnson, Tim Thom-

erson, Harry Carey Jr., Pamela Gidley (ERP/Orion)

A tongue-in-cheek sci-fi action pic, *Cherry 2000*'s greatest asset is Melanie Griffith, who lifts the material whenever she's on screen. Griffith plays a tracker who lives at the edge of a desert known as the Zone. The year is 2017, and Sam Treatwell (David Andrews) seeks Johnson's help in replacing his beloved Cherry 2000, a robot sex object who suffered internal meltdown. Replacement Cherry clones are stored far out in the Zone, which is ruled over by the psychotic Lester (Tim Thomerson) and his gang. Bulk of the film consists of efforts of Johnson and Treadwell to reach the robot warehouse.

CHEYENNE AUTUMN
1964, 161 mins, US ▱
D: John Ford **A:** Richard Widmark, Carroll Baker, James Stewart, Edward G. Robinson, Karl Malden, Sal Mineo (Warner)

Cheyenne Autumn is a rambling, episodic account of a reputedly little-known historic Cheyenne Indian migration 1,500 miles through almost unbelievable hardships and dangers. Richard Widmark, in one of his hard-boiled roles, is persuasive as a cavalry captain sympathetic to the Indians. Gilbert Roland and Ricardo Montalban portray the historic Dull Knife and Little Wolf, leaders of the Cheyennes, and carry off their work with honors. James Stewart as Wyatt Earp is in strictly for laughs, not for plot motivation.
1964: Nomination: Best Color Cinematography

CHEYENNE SOCIAL CLUB, THE
1970, 103 mins, US ⓥ ▱
D: Gene Kelly **A:** James Stewart, Henry Fonda, Shirley Jones, Sue Ane Langdon, Elaine Devry, Jackie Russell (National General)

James Stewart and Henry Fonda are longtime cowpoke buddies, and when the former finds he has inherited from his brother a business in Cheyenne, the latter follows. Turns out the business is the town's pleasure dome. The story is a flimsy, one-joke affair, and Gene Kelly's direction is too sluggish to make it perk at the fast pace required to sustain momentum.

CHICAGO, CHICAGO
See: *Gaily, Gaily*

CHICAGO JOE AND THE SHOWGIRL
1990, 103 mins, UK ⓥ ☉
D: Bernard Rose **A:** Emily Lloyd, Kiefer Sutherland, Patsy Kensit, Keith Allen, Liz Fraser, Alexandra Pigg (PolyGram/Working Title)

Scripter David Yallop was inspired by the sensational Hulten/Jones murder case of 1944. The trial, which resulted in the hanging of Hulten (the only execution of a Yank by the British) and the reprieve of Jones, is passed up. Yallop instead focuses on duo's six-day London crime spree, finishing with murder of the cabbie. Problem is that Emily Lloyd fails to deliver the necessary allure, and Kiefer Sutherland is weak in playing a weak character. End result is a passionless picture.

LA CHIENNE
1931, 95 mins, France ⓥ
D: Jean Renoir **A:** Michel Simon, Janie Marese, Georges Flamant, Madeleine Berubet, Jean Gehret, Alexandre Rignault (Braunberger/Richebe)

Very cleverly made and beautifully acted. The title word is meant to apply to a prostitute who drags down a man, and the story, sordid in itself, is shown in every sordid detail relating to each one of the principals—the prostitute, her man, and the sucker. The three main characters are splendidly acted—the woman by the late Janie Marese, who died in a motor accident on the Riviera. Georges Flamant plays her man with the most true-to-life and realistic naturalness. The middle-class sucker is done by Michel Simon.

CHILD IS WAITING, A
1963, 104 mins, US ⓥ
D: John Cassavetes **A:** Burt Lancaster, Judy Garland, Gena Rowlands, Steven Hill, Bruce Ritchey (United Artists)

Producer Stanley Kramer comes up with a poignant, provocative, revealing dramatization. This time it is the subject of mentally retarded children. Burt Lancaster delivers a firm, sincere, persuasive, and unaffected performance as the professionally objective but understanding psychologist who heads the institution. Judy Garland gives a sympathetic portrayal of an overly involved teacher who comes to see the error of her obsession with the plight of one child. That child, a deeply touching borderline case, is played superbly by young Bruce Ritchey.

CHILDREN, THE

1990, 115 mins, UK/W. Germany Ⓥ

D: Tony Palmer A: Ben Kingsley, Kim Novak, Siri Neal, Geraldine Chaplin, Joe Don Baker, Karen Black (Isolde/Arbo/Film Four)

Edith Wharton's 1928 novel, *The Children*, comes to the screen as a somewhat dated enterprise. Story of a middle-aged man's infatuation with a teenage girl unfolds at a snail's pace. Ben Kingsley is Martin Boyne, a middle-aged engineer. He hopes to marry Rose Sellars (Kim Novak, looking ageless), his lifelong love. He meets a group of seven children, the oldest of which is the budding Judith (Siri Neal). The rest of the film depicts Martin's gradual emotional shift away from the demanding Rose to the guileless, appealing Judith, who appears to encourage him.

CHILDREN OF A LESSER GOD

1986, 110 mins, US Ⓥ ⊙

D: Randa Haines A: William Hurt, Marlee Matlin, Piper Laurie, Philip Bosco, Alison Gompf, John F. Cleary (Paramount)

A touching and universal love story between a deaf woman and a hearing man. At the heart of the picture is the attraction between William Hurt and Marlee Matlin. It's another seamless performance for Hurt. Matlin, who makes her professional acting debut here and is in real life hearing-impaired, as is much of the cast, is simply fresh and alive with fine shadings of expression.

1986: Best Actress (Marlee Matlin)

Nominations: Best Picture, Actor (William Hurt), Supp. Actress (Piper Laurie), Adapted Screenplay

CHILDREN OF PARADISE

See: Les Enfants du Paradis

CHILDREN OF THE CORN

1984, 93 mins, US Ⓥ

D: Fritz Kiersch A: Peter Horton, Linda Hamilton, R. G. Armstrong, John Franklin, Courtney Gains, Robby Kiger (Gatlin/Angeles)

Children of the Corn presents a normal couple, played by Peter Horton and Linda Hamilton, thrust into supernatural occurrences. Somewhere in Nebraska the couple happen on the children of the corn, a band of vicious youngsters who have murdered the adults and established a religious community worshiping a mysterious deity of the cornfields. *Children of the Corn* does have a few good scare scenes but

special effects are surprisingly disappointing.

CHILDREN OF THE CORN II
THE FINAL SACRIFICE

1993, 92 mins, US Ⓥ ⊙

D: David F. Price A: Terence Knox, Paul Scherrer, Ryan Bollman, Christie Clark, Rosalind Allen, Ned Romero (Fifth Avenue)

Coming nine years after the original, this supernatural horror sequel is a competently made but uninspired effort. Adults are again murdered in grisly fashion, some by supernatural forces (a few represented by nice visual effects reminiscent of *Wolfen*), some by the deranged kids led by Micah (Ryan Bollman). Lensing on North Carolina locations (subbing for Nebraska) is well done, with director David Price keeping the picture chugging along even when the script becomes risible.

CHILDREN OF THE DAMNED

1964, 90 mins, UK ▭

D: Anton M. Leader A: Ian Hendry, Alan Badel, Barbara Ferris, Alfred Burke, Sheila Allen, Clive Powell (M-G-M)

Like most sequels *Children of the Damned* isn't nearly as good as its predecessor, *Village of the Damned*. This time those strange, handsome parthenogenetic children are not mere invaders from the outer limits bent on occupying earth, but are actually premature samplings of man as he will be in, say, a million years.

CHILDREN'S HOUR, THE
(UK: THE LOUDEST WHISPER)

1961, 108 mins, US Ⓥ

D: William Wyler A: Audrey Hepburn, Shirley MacLaine, James Garner, Miriam Hopkins, Fay Bainter, Karen Balkin (Mirisch)

Story deals with an irresponsible, neurotic child who spreads a slanderous rumor about a lesbian relationship between the two headmistresses of the private school for girls she attends. Audrey Hepburn and Shirley MacLaine, in the leading roles, beautifully complement each other. James Garner is effective as Hepburn's betrothed, and Fay Bainter comes through with an outstanding portrayal of the impressionable grandmother who falls under the evil influence of the wicked child.

1961: Nominations: Best Supp. Actress, (Fay Bainter), B&W Cinematography, B&W Costume Design, B&W Art Direction

CHILD'S PLAY
1972, 100 mins, US

D: Sidney Lumet **A:** James Mason, Robert Preston, Beau Bridges, Ron Weyand, Charles White, David Rounds (Paramount)

A taut and suspenseful drama of a Catholic boys' school. Unfolding often carries the aspects of a chiller as mysterious malevolent forces create a reign of terror and build to a powerful climax. James Mason delivers a solid performance as a man whose hate of his fellow professor is exceeded, he says, only by Robert Preston's hate of him. Role is deeply dramatic, and Preston, in a different type of characterization, lends equal potency.

CHILD'S PLAY
1988, 87 mins, US ⓥ ⊙

D: Tom Holland **A:** Catherine Hicks, Chris Sarandon, Alex Vincent, Brad Dourif, Dinah Manoff, Tommy Swerdlow (United Artists)

Child's Play is a near miss at providing horrific thrills in a tale of a doll come to murderous life, told with a knowing tongue-in-cheek attitude. Fun withers in stretching the thin material to feature length. Director Tom Holland summons impressive technical skill in charting the preposterous story. Both Hicks and Sarandon commendably keep straight faces during these outlandish proceedings.

CHILD'S PLAY 2
1990, 85 mins, US ⓥ ⊙

D: John Lafia **A:** Alex Vincent, Jenny Agutter, Gerrit Graham, Christine Elise, Brad Dourif, Grace Zabriskie (Universal)

Child's Play 2 is another case of rehashing the few novel elements of an original to the point of utter numbness. The novelty of a smiling doll spouting expletives and crinkling his nose has long since worn off, so the filmmakers simply hammer away at walk-down-the-hallway clichés in an effort to provide the cheapest thrills. The puppet techniques are finely executed, but it's difficult after a while to take this three-foot-high version of the Terminator seriously. The adults are essentially pincushions, with about as much personality.

CHILD'S PLAY 3
1991, 89 mins, US ⓥ ⊙

D: Jack Bender **A:** Justin Whalin, Perrey Reeves, Jeremy Sylvers, Travis Fine, Dean Jacobson, Brad Dourif (Universal)

Foulmouthed killer doll Chucky returns in this noisy, mindless sequel. Fine doll effects and sporadic gore are par for the genre. Acting is good, with honors going to Andrew Robinson, amusing as the school's obsessive barber.

CHIMES AT MIDNIGHT (FALSTAFF)
1966, 113 mins, Spain/Switzerland ⓥ ⊙

D: Orson Welles **A:** Orson Welles, John Gielgud, Jeanne Moreau, Norman Rodway, Keith Baxter, Margaret Rutherford (Internacional Films Espanola/Alpine)

Pic chronicles the story of Shakespeare's Falstaff. Taken from several plays, it details the last days of Falstaff's relationship with the Prince of Wales, the future King Henry V of England. Orson Welles has tried to humanize Falstaff in dwelling on his intimations of old age. Welles himself is gigantically bloated and full of swagger that yet shows glints of lonely pride and fear of rejection under a pompous exterior. John Gielgud, on the other hand, is somber, suffering, and stately as the King Henry IV.

CHINA
1943, 78 mins, US

D: John Farrow **A:** Loretta Young, Alan Ladd, William Bendix, Philip Ahn, Iris Wong, Sen Yung (Paramount)

Alan Ladd's been trucking gasoline to the Jap armies out of Shanghai. Along the road, he is forced to take aboard group of Chinese femme university students in the charge of American instructress Loretta Young. Ladd is arrogant and unconcerned over the Jap atrocities against the Chinese, but wakes up when a Jap plane strafes his truck. Frank Butler generates authenticity in the dramatic evolution of his screenplay while director John Farrow neatly blends the human and melodramatic elements of the yarn.

CHINA BLUE
See: Crimes of Passion

CHINA DOLL
1958, 99 mins, US

D: Frank Borzage **A:** Victor Mature, Li Li-hua, Ward Bond, Bob Mathias, Johnny Desmond, Danny Chang (Romina/United Artists)

About average in its war-story telling, *China Doll* has a field day with the warmth and humor of a romance between a burly air-corps captain and a fragile Oriental beauty. It's a tale of China in 1943. Victor Mature, a lonely leader who has taken to the bottle, unknowingly purchases a young Chinese girl as a house-keeper, and she ends up carrying his child, drawing his love, and marrying him, in that order. Highlight of the picture is sumptuous femme Li Li-hua in the title role.

CHINA GATE
1957, 96 mins, US ⓥ ▭
D: Samuel Fuller A: Gene Barry, Angie Dickinson, Nat King Cole, Lee Van Cleef, Warren Hsieh, Paul Dubov (Globe/20th Century-Fox)

China Gate is an overlong but sometimes exciting story of the battle between Vietnamese and Red Chinese, told through the efforts of a small band of French Legionnaires to reach and destroy a hidden Communist munitions dump. An added exploitation turn is the casting of Nat King Cole in dual assignment of a straight role and warbling title song.

CHINA GIRL
1942, 98 mins, US
D: Henry Hathaway A: Gene Tierney, George Montgomery, Lynn Bari, Victor McLaglen (20th Century-Fox)

Plot has George Montgomery, as an American newsreel cameraman in Mandalay, falling in love with an American-educated Chinese girl (Gene Tierney). There are the usual Jap intrigue and paid spies in persons of Lynn Bari and Victor McLaglen, who try to get Montgomery into his clutches to turn over to the Japs. It's regulation stuff that has been retold many times.

CHINA GIRL
1987, 88 mins, US ⓥ ⊙
D: Abel Ferrara A: James Russo, Sari Chang, Richard Panebianco, David Caruso, Russell Wong, Joey Chin (Street Lite/Vestron)

China Girl is a masterfully directed, uncompromising drama and romance. Screenplay hypothesizes an outbreak of a gang war when a Chinese restaurant opens in Italian territory. In the midst of the battling, a beautiful Chinese teenager (Sari Chang) falls in love with a pizza-parlor gofer (Richard Panebianco). A la *West Side Story*, the adults oppose the relationship and, more to the point, the Mafia dons and Chinese elder gangsters are in cahoots to maintain peace in their bordered territory.

CHINA MOON
1994, 99 mins, US ⓥ ⊙ ▭
D: John Bailey A: Ed Harris, Madeleine

Stowe, Benicio Del Toro, Charles Dance, Patricia Healy, Tim Powell (Tig/Orion)

Ed Harris's stellar performance as the fall guy in *China Moon* elevates John Bailey's noir mystery a cut or two above the usual Hollywood thriller. Set in small-town Florida, the triangle involving Harris, a lonely homicide detective who falls for Madeleine Stowe, a beautifully seductive married woman, bears resemblance to such noir classics as *Double Indemnity* and *The Postman Always Rings Twice*. The tension in Roy Carlson's efficient, pared-down narrative derives from the complex relationship between Harris and ambitious rookie detective Benicio Del Toro, once Harris gets drawn into a murder scheme.

CHINA 9 LIBERTY 37
1978, 102 mins, Italy ⓥ ▭
D: Monte Hellman A: Fabio Testi, Warren Oates, Jenny Agutter, Sam Peckinpah, Isabel Mestres, Richard C. Adams (CEA)

An oater made in Spain with Italo backing and American and English thesps in the main roles. Fabio Testi is a gunman who runs off after having raped the wife of a gunslinger when he was sent by railroad reps to kill. But she follows him and there is love, until railroad men are sent after the gunslinger and the husband reappears with his brothers. Warren Oates is gruff as the husband, Jenny Agutter pliant as the torn wife.

CHINA SEAS
1935, 87 mins, US ⓥ
D: Tay Garnett A: Clark Gable, Jean Harlow, Wallace Beery, Rosalind Russell, Lewis Stone, Dudley Digges (M-G-M)

This is a story of love—sordid and otherwise—of piracy and violence and heroism on a passenger-boat run from Shanghai to Singapore. Clark Gable is a valiant sea captain, Wallace Beery a villainous pirate boss, and Jean Harlow a blond trollop who motivates the romance and most of the action. All do their jobs expertly. Add a running atmosphere of suspense through the picture, and there's plenty of excitement.

CHINA SKY
1945, 78 mins, US ⓥ ⊙
D: Ray Enright A: Randolph Scott, Ruth Warrick, Ellen Drew, Anthony Quinn, Carol Thurston, Philip Ahn (RKO)

Pearl Buck's novel of the tenacity of Chinese guerrillas who harass the Japanese advance, and the American medico who runs the hospital in the key Chinese village, turns out far from the spectacular production it might have been. Scripters and director are so concerned with the triangle between Randolph Scott, as the American doctor, his devoted hospital co-worker (Ruth Warrick), and his wife (Ellen Drew) that they neglect the story's movement. There finally is a bang-up battle at the end but it's too late. Warrick is superb, but her role is not sufficient to carry the whole load.

CHINA SYNDROME, THE
1979, 122 mins, US ⊙ ☉
D: James Bridges **A:** Jane Fonda, Jack Lemmon, Michael Douglas, Scott Brady, James Hampton, Peter Donat (Columbia)

A moderately compelling thriller about the potential perils of nuclear energy, whose major fault is an overweening sense of its own self-importance. Jane Fonda limns a TV anchorwoman who hires freelance cameraman Michael Douglas. While filming at a nuclear-energy plant, they witness a control-room crisis involving supervisor Jack Lemmon, which is surreptitiously lensed by Douglas. It's not until the final half hour of *China Syndrome* that its promise catches up to its punch, and the windup packs a solid wallop.
1979: Nominations: Best Actor (Jack Lemmon), Actress (Jane Fonda), Original Screenplay, Art Direction

CHINATOWN
1974, 130 mins, US ⊙ ☉ ☒
D: Roman Polanski **A:** Jack Nicholson, Faye Dunaway, John Huston, Perry Lopez, John Hillerman, Diane Ladd (Long Road/Paramount)

Chinatown is an outstanding picture. Robert Towne's complex but literate and orderly screenplay takes gumshoe Jack Nicholson on a murder manhunt all over the Los Angeles of the late 1930s, where Faye Dunaway is the wife of a dead city official. The many plot angles, including a very discreet development of incest, eventually converge in Chinatown for a climactic shoot-out which, at fadeout, will likely be papered over as a typical ghetto incident, the kind of event that respectable people never hear about. The term *Chinatown* is thus used in a cynical context and has meaning only after the film is over.
1974: Best Original Screenplay
Nominations: Best Picture, Director, Actor (Jack Nicholson), Actress (Faye Dunaway), Cinematography, Costume Design,

Art Direction, Editing, Original Dramatic Score, Sound

CHINESE CHOCOLATE
1995, 101 mins, Canada ⊙
D: Yan Cui, Qi Chang **A:** Diana Peng, Shirley Cui, Bo Z. Wang, Henry Wang, James Purcell, Fei Gao (Good Choice)

This insightful, acidic pic follows the fortunes and misfortunes of two intelligent and talented women from mainland China who relocate to Toronto. Writer-directors Yan Cui and Qi Chang take a sardonic look at life in a Westernized city where everyone seems to be on the make and where it's almost impossible not to be cheated and betrayed. Peng and Cui are fine as the two put-upon femmes who eventually turn to one another for love and happiness.

CHINESE CONNECTION, THE
See: Jingwu Men

CHISUM
1970, 110 mins, US ⊙ ☒
D: Andrew V. McLaglen **A:** John Wayne, Forrest Tucker, Christopher George, Ben Johnson, Glenn Corbett, Andrew Prine (Batjac/Warner)

John Wayne plays a rugged character set down in New Mexico Territory, circa 1878, as King of the Pecos, its greatest landholder and biggest cattle owner. Andrew J. Fenady, who scripted, has taken the events of the bloody Lincoln County cattle war which ended in 1878 to background his story. Wayne clothes his interpretation of the early-west figure with vigor and warmth.

CHITTY CHITTY BANG BANG
1968, 156 mins, UK ⊙ ⊙ ☒
D: Ken Hughes **A:** Dick Van Dyke, Sally Ann Howes, Lionel Jeffries, Gert Frobe, Anna Quayle, Benny Hill (United/Warfield)

Dick Van Dyke is starred as the widowed, absentminded, unsuccessful inventor whose children convince him to save a pioneer racing auto from destruction. Turned into a spanking and sleek vehicle by Van Dyke, car develops ability to float on water and fly. Brought into the story by this point are Sally Ann Howes and Lionel Jeffries, Van Dyke's father. Gert Frobe proceeds to kidnap auto and its inventor. He gets wrong car and wrong man, Jeffries, with result that Van Dyke, Howes, and the kids fly off on a rescue mission. The $10-million film lacks warmth. No real feeling is generated between any two characters.

1968: Nomination: Best Song ("Chitty Chitty Bang Bang")

CHLOE IN THE AFTERNOON
See: L'Amour, l'Apres-Midi

CHOICES
1981, 90 mins, US ⓥ

D: Silvio Narizzano **A:** Paul Carafotes, Victor French, Lelia Goldoni, Val Avery, Demi Moore (Oaktree)

Paul Carafotes appears to be an average high-schooler whose world consists of football and music. However, Carafotes is partially deaf and a school medical examiner rules this precludes him from playing on the football team. Carafotes resents his sudden freak status and falls in with a tough gang. *Choices* has all its sympathies in the right place and one can't help but warm to its message even if its manipulation often lacks subtlety.

CHOIRBOYS, THE
1977, 119 mins, US ⓥ

D: Robert Aldrich **A:** Charles Durning, Louis Gossett Jr., Perry King, Clyde Kusatsu, Stephen Macht, Randy Quaid (Lorimar/Airone)

When Robert Aldrich's filmmaking is good, it's very, very good; and when it's bad, it's awful. This cheap-looking ultra-raunchy alleged comedy about policemen leaves no stone unturned in its exploitation of vulgarity. Tim McIntyre is terrific in portrayal of a person audiences will come to hate.

CHOPPER CHICKS IN ZOMBIETOWN
1990, 89 mins, US ⓥ

D: Dan Hoskins **A:** Jamie Rose, Catherine Carlen, Kristina Loggia, Lycia Naff, Vicki Frederick, Gretchen Palmer (Chelsea Partners)

Chopper Chicks in Zombietown is a surprisingly funny B-movie spoof with a feminist edge. It's a classic story of bikers invading a secluded town and rattling the suspicious populace. At the same time it's another classic story: the local mad scientist is killing off citizens, reviving them as zombie slaves, and generally making the town a miserable place to live. The bikers are leather-and-chain-wearing women. Hoskins isn't able to sustain the level of lunacy and several scenes suggest the Harley-riding actresses have been asked to vamp until a funny line comes along. Still, there is a lot to laugh about, and dialogue that moviegoers will quote for days afterward.

CHORUS LINE, A
1985, 113 mins, US ⓥ ⊙ ▱

D: Richard Attenborough **A:** Michael Douglas, Terrence Mann, Alyson Reed, Cameron English, Vicki Frederick, Audrey Landers (Embassy/PolyGram)

Richard Attenborough has not solved the problem of bringing the 1975 musical *A Chorus Line* to the screen. *Chorus* often seems static and confined. Nonetheless, the director and lenser Ronnie Taylor have a fine cast, good music, and a great, popular show to work with. So if all they did was get it on film, that's not so bad. Michael Douglas is solid as the tough choreographer and Terrence Mann is good as his assistant. Audrey Landers romps delightfully through the T&A number.

1985: Nominations: Best Editing, Song ("Surprise, Surprise"), Sound

CHORUS OF DISAPPROVAL, A
1989, 100 mins, US ⓥ

D: Michael Winner **A:** Jeremy Irons, Anthony Hopkins, Prunella Scales, Jenny Seagrove, Sylvia Sims, Patsy Kensit (South Gate)

As a movie, *A Chorus of Disapproval* chugs along when Alan Ayckbourn's play raced. Jeremy Irons shines as Jones, a shy, rather nervous widower who joins the local amateur opera, which is practicing *A Beggar's Opera*. The production is directed by Dafydd Llewellyn (Anthony Hopkins), a scruffy solicitor who only really comes alive when he is directing a new play. Jones, without really trying, soon becomes a small Lothario, his actions having hilarious effects on the various members of the drama group.

CHOSEN, THE
See: Holocaust 2000

CHOSEN, THE
1981, 108 mins, US ⓥ

D: Jeremy Paul Kagan **A:** Maximilian Schell, Rod Steiger, Robby Benson, Barry Miller (Landau)

The Chosen is a first-rate adaptation of Chaim Potok's novel. Set in the latter years of World War II, the story has cultural Jew Barry Miller and orthodox Hasidic Jew Robby Benson meeting as opponents in a baseball game. To Miller, a typical American kid, Benson's Hasidic upbringing complete with 19th-century attire and long side curls makes him akin to a creature from outer space. Yet the relationship grows and Miller is asked to meet with Benson's legendary father, an orthodox rabbi portrayed by Rod Steiger. Director and writer [Edwin Gordon] do wonders with the poignant material.

LES CHOSES DE LA VIE (THE THINGS OF LIFE)
1970, 89 mins, France/Italy ⊗

D: Claude Sautet **A:** Michel Piccoli, Romy Schneider, Lea Massari, Boby Lapoint, Gerard Lartigau (Lira/Fida)

Directorial tact and visual solidity, fine, sensitive playing, and observant characterization give an engrossing tang to this familiar tale of a middle-aged man who has left his wife and grown son for a slightly younger woman. Fragmentation first shows him with his mistress, played with engaging sincerity by Romy Schneider. Michel Piccoli gives a well-regulated limning of the man, a successful architect but somehow a bit ill at ease. Claude Sautet shows a fine directorial flair for ordinary people caught up in personal decisions and dramas.

CHRISTIAN, THE
1923, 106 mins, US ⊗

D: Maurice Tourneur **A:** Richard Dix, Mae Busch, Gareth Hughes, Phyllis Haver, Cyril Chadwick, Claude Gillingwater (Goldwyn)

Here is a real picture with a corking story, a great cast, and finely produced. Hall Caine's novel is a real tale for the screen. The performance that stands out as a gem is that by Richard Dix. Next to Dix, Mae Busch is entitled to a full measure. At the same time Phyllis Haver, on the strength of the death scene alone, is entitled to all that the critics can give her in praise. The company, at least a part of it, was taken to the Isle of Man, England, and the original scenes as described by the author were utilized for the picturization.

CHRISTINE
1983, 110 mins, US ⊗ ⊙ ▢

D: John Carpenter **A:** Keith Gordon, John Stockwell, Alexandra Paul, Robert Prosky, Harry Dean Stanton, Christine Belford (Columbia/Delphi)

Christine seems like a retread. This time it's a fire-engine-red, 1958 Plymouth Fury that's possessed by the devil, and this déjà vu premise combined with the crazed vehicle format, makes *Christine* appear pretty shopworn. Christine's the object of love at first sight for misfit high-school student Keith Gordon, who restores her to her 1950s glory. Gordon also undergoes a transformation, evolving from campus klutz to Mr. Cool and acquiring the foxiest girl in the school (Alexandra Paul) in the process. But when the couple begins making out at a drive-in movie, Christine nearly knocks off Paul in a fit of romantic jealousy. Flashy auto dominates everything, its jealousy is effectively, and sometimes humorously, conveyed.

CHRISTMAS HOLIDAY
1944, 98 mins, US

D: Robert Siodmak **A:** Deanna Durbin, Gene Kelly, Dean Harens, Gale Sondergaard, Richard Whorf (Universal)

A young army lieutenant, disappointed in love, finds himself stranded in New Orleans, and meets up with another heartsick kid in a sad-faced singer at a cheap nightclub. The singer (Deanna Durbin) tells the lieutenant of her brief happy marriage to a young ne'er-do-well. As the nitery thrush, Durbin has two incidental songs.

CHRISTMAS IN JULY
1940, 67 mins, US ⊗ ⊙

D: Preston Sturges **A:** Dick Powell, Ellen Drew, Raymond Walburn, Alexander Carr, William Demarest, Ernest Truex (Paramount)

Sturges's original script details the adventures of a young romantic pair living on the East Side. Boy is victim of office joke that advises he won $25,000 in a slogan contest, even though the jury is still fighting over the winner. But he collects the check and proceeds to run up a heavy charge account before cashing the winnings, plays Santa Claus to everyone on the block, including his sweetheart, and then is presented with the payoff that it's a phony. Picture has its moments of comedy and interest, but these are interspersed too frequently by obvious and boring episodes. Dick Powell progresses as a straight lead without benefit of vocalizing.

CHRISTOPHER COLUMBUS
1949, 104 mins, UK

D: David Macdonald **A:** Fredric March, Florence Eldridge, Francis L. Sullivan, Linden Travers, Kathleen Ryan, Derek Bond (Gainsborough/Rank)

Highly dramatized version of discovery of America by Christopher Columbus, with lush Technicolor to enhance opulent settings and colorful backgrounds, turns out to be an uncertain piece of entertainment. Almost half of the footage covers the period before Columbus sets sail on his expedition. Picture really does not get under way until Columbus sails in the *Santa Maria*. How mutiny is averted and land finally sighted brings in some action. In the role of Columbus, Fredric March inevitably dominates the story.

CHRISTOPHER COLUMBUS THE DISCOVERY
1992, 120 mins, US Ⓥ ⊙ ▭
D: John Glen A: Marlon Brando, Tom Selleck, George Corraface, Rachel Ward, Robert Davi, Catherine Zeta Jones (Salkind)

Director John Glen's take on the Genoese explorer adds up to perfectly serviceable commercial entertainment. Leading man George Corraface has the diction and charisma it takes to carry off his role. Marlon Brando makes a grand Grand Inquisitor. Tom Selleck's wry turn as King Ferdinand is a pleasant surprise, although a wan Rachel Ward as Queen Isabella could use more backbone in her evangelical enthusiasm.

CHU CHIN CHOW
1934, 102 mins, UK
D: Walter Forde A: George Robey, Fritz Kortner, Anna May Wong, John Garrick, Pearl Argyle, Sydney Fairbrother (Gainsborough/Gaumont-British)

This lavish musical from the British studios is, compared to American musicals, slow. But this very slowness happens to fit this type of yarn. Story of *Chu Chin Chow* is the story of Ali Baba from the Arabian tales. George Robey is Ali Baba, the sap who became a millionaire; Anna May Wong is Zahrat, the unfaithful and vengeful slave girl; Fritz Kortner is Abu Hahan, the robber chief. All are excellent choices. John Garrick is a handsome Nural-din and has a splendid singing voice.

CHUMP AT OXFORD, A
1940, 63 mins, US Ⓥ ⊙
D: Alfred Goulding A: Stan Laurel, Oliver Hardy, James Finlayson, Forrester Harvey, Peter Cushing, Sam Lufkin (Roach/United Artists)

Stan Laurel and Oliver Hardy's farce is mildly comical without offending. Time-worn gags clutter up the earlier footage and only when Laurel and Hardy, as new initiates into Oxford, actually move into the dean's home does the action speed up.

CHUNGHING SAMLAM
1994, 103 mins, Hong Kong Ⓥ ⊙
D: Wong Kar-wai A: Brigitte Lin, Takeshi Kaneshiro, Tony Leung Chiu-wai, Faye Wang, Valerie Chow (Jet Tone)

A quicksilver magical mystery tour through the lives of a bunch of young downtown loners, hip pic is drenched in neosixties nostalgia. First story (42 minutes), set around a labyrinthine tenement building in downtown Kowloon, spins on a romantic young cop (Takeshi Kaneshiro), recently ditched by his g.f. Second, more involving story (61 minutes) centers on another young cop (Tony Leung Chiu-wai), who's the unwitting fixation of a dotty worker (Faye Wang) at Midnight Express, a fast-food joint.

CHUNG KING EXPRESS
See: Chunghing Samlam

CIAO, FEDERICO!
1970, 60 mins, US/Italy
D: Gideon Bachmann (Herbert)

Yank critic-filmmaker Gideon Bachmann, a longtime Rome resident, made this 16mm docu on Italian director Federico Fellini making *Satyricon*. Pic shows him as a chameleonlike figure. He rages, but with an underlying lack of true anger, and seems to be watching his own actions. Pic is as airy, unrevealing, but picturesque as Fellini's symbolical, circusy pix.

CIAO MANHATTAN
1973, 90 mins, US Ⓥ ⊙
D: John Palmer, David Weisman A: Edie Sedgwick, Wesley Hayes, Isabel Jewell, Paul America, Geoffrey Briggs, Tom Flye (Court)

Ciao Manhattan is Edie Sedgwick's filmed swansong—she died of acute barbiturate intoxication in 1971. Monotonous and nearly incomprehensible, *Ciao* consists chiefly of pieced-together short ends from two Sedgwick vehicles. In the last years of her life, says this intendedly antidope film, the Andy Warhol superstar took up residence at the bottom of a tented Santa Barbara pool, narcissistically surrounded by giant blowups of herself. It is here that the film dwells, and most of the nonplot consists of her drug-zonked recollections of her halcyon days.

CIMARRON
1931, 124 mins, US Ⓥ
D: Wesley Ruggles A: Richard Dix, Irene Dunne, Estelle Taylor, Nance O'Neil, William Collier Jr., Roscoe Ates (Radio)

This spectacular western holds action, sentiment, sympathy, thrills, and comedy. Two outstanders in the playing, Richard Dix and Edna May Oliver, each surpris-

ingly excellent; Dix with his straight character playing of a westerner and an Oklahoma pioneer who dies before his statue is unveiled in that state, while Oliver is nothing less than exquisite in her eccentric comedy role of a colonial dame in the wilds. Big production bits start with the land rush into Oklahoma in 1889, men on horses and in wagons racing to capture some part of the two million acres released by the government. Irene Dunne does nicely enough in a role of a loving wife and mother, which does not permit her to be much else.
1930/31: Best Picture, Adaptation, Interior Decoration (Max Ree)
Nominations: Director, Actor (Richard Dix), Actress (Irene Dunne), Cinematography

CIMARRON
1960, 151 mins, US Ⓥ ▭
D: Anthony Mann **A:** Glenn Ford, Maria Schell, Anne Baxter, Arthur O'Connell, Russ Tamblyn, Mercedes McCambridge (M-G-M)
Edna Ferber's novel of the first Oklahoma land rush (1889) shapes up in its second film translation as a good balance between rousing action and the marriage of Glenn Ford and Maria Schell as Yancey and Sabra Cravet. There are many subtle shadings in Schell's performance as she transforms over period of 25 years from adoring, lovable bride to embittered, abandoned wife, successful newspaper publisher, and bigoted mother-in-law. Ford emerges a strong and thoroughly likable adventurer-idealist as the restless rover, Yancey, who is loving and devoted after his own fashion. *Cimarron* starts off with a bang. Spectacle of thousands of land seekers straining to dash into the new territory at high noon on April 22, 1889, is masterfully handled by director Anthony Mann.
1960: Nominations: Best Art Direction, Sound

CINCINNATI KID, THE
1965, 102 mins, US Ⓥ ⊙
D: Norman Jewison **A:** Steve McQueen, Edward G. Robinson, Ann-Margret, Karl Malden, Tuesday Weld, Joan Blondell (M-G-M)
The Cincinnati Kid is the fast-moving story of a burningly ambitious young rambling-gambling man who challenges the king of stud poker to a showdown. In Steve McQueen [producer] Martin Ransohoff has the near-perfect delineator of

the title role. Edward G. Robinson is at his best in some years as the aging, ruthless Lancey Howard, champ of the poker tables for more than 30 years and determined now to defend his title against a cocksure but dangerous opponent. The card duel between the pair is dramatically developed through grueling action, building in intensity as the final and deciding hand is played.

CINDERELLA
1950, 74 mins, US Ⓥ ⊙
D: Wilfred Jackson, Hamilton Luske, Clyde Geronimi (Walt Disney)
Disney outfit makes entertainment capital out of the animal world with clever drawingboard personifications of a quartet of mice doing battle with an ornery cat. The cartoon has far more success in projecting the lower animals than in its central character, Cinderella, who is on the colorless, doll-faced side, as is the Prince Charming. The menace is supplied by the literally drawn stepmother, who's a lineal descendant of the flint-hearted, evil-eyed witch in *Snow White*. The musical numbers woven into the fantasy are generally solid.
1950: Nominations: Best Scoring of a Musical Picture, Song ("Bibbidy-Bobbidi-Boo"), Sound

CINDERELLA JONES
1946, 90 mins, US
D: Busby Berkeley **A:** Joan Leslie, Robert Alda, S. Z. Sakall, Edward Everett Horton, Elisha Cook Jr. (Warner)
Plot deals with a girl who wants to inherit $10 million but has to find a husband with a quiz-kid brain to collect. She figures an exclusively male technology institute is the proper place to find such a husband. Joan Leslie makes a delightful dumb dame who malaprops all over the place before wising up to the worth of her bandleader, both mentally and as a big hunk of man. Robert Alda gives the baton-waver role plenty of life. Tunes are not particular standouts but make for okay listening.

CINDERELLA LIBERTY
1973, 117 mins, US Ⓥ ▭
D: Mark Rydell **A:** James Caan, Marsha Mason, Kirk Calloway, Eli Wallach, Allyn Ann McLerie, Burt Young (20th Century-Fox)
Cinderella Liberty is an earthy but very touching story of a sailor's love for a prostitute. James Caan stars in an outstanding

performance, and Marsha Mason, in her second picture, is equally superb. Eli Wallach's strong featured role is that of Caan's long-ago boot-camp drill instructor, whose harsh methods provoke a fight years later.
1973: Nominations: Best Actress (Marsha Mason), Original Score, Song (''Nice to Be Around'')

CINDERFELLA
1960, 88 mins, US ⓥ
D: Frank Tashlin **A:** Jerry Lewis, Ed Wynn, Judith Anderson, Anna Marcia Alberghetti, Henry Silva, Robert Hutton (Paramount)

Jerry Lewis, who produced, stars as the male variation on Cinderella in Frank Tashlin's screenplay *Cinderfella*. There seems to have been a dearth of comic inspiration. Bits of funny business that do show instant promise is milked to extremes. Lewis depends almost exclusively on the art of cumulative mugging, but often misjudges the break-off point. Breaks for song tend to labor the issue instead of brightening the tempo. Ed Wynn is whimsical as the fairy godfather, Judith Anderson plays the wicked stepmother, Henry Silva and Robert Hutton the mercenary stepbrothers. Anna Maria Alberghetti is dazzling as the princess.

CINEMA PARADISO
See: Nuovo Cinema Paradiso

CINERAMA HOLIDAY
1955, 119 mins, US ▭
D: Robert Bendick, Philippe de Lacey (Stanley-Warner Cinerama)

The Cinerama process is seen in its second mounting. Much of the excitement remains, although there is some feeling of repeating tried-and-true pictorial effects. There is a wisp of continuity in *Holiday,* unlike the predecessor film. Betty and John Marsh of Kansas City and Beatrice and Fred Troller of Zurich do an exchange student type of act, each pair of newly-weds visiting the other's hemisphere. The second part of the show is largely made up of an extended visit to Paris.

LA CIOCIARA
(TWO WOMEN)
1961, 110 mins, Italy/France ⓥ
D: Vittorio De Sica **A:** Sophia Loren, Eleonora Brown, Jean-Paul Belmondo, Raf Vallone, Renato Salvatori, Carlo Ninchi (Champion/Marceau-Cocinor/SGC)

There is only unremitting horror and soul-trying for the mother (Sophia Loren) and her 13-year-old daughter (newcomer Eleanora Brown) as they reel from one wartime adversity to another, cresting with their marathon debauching by a band of Moroccan soldiers. It is the grim life in spades. Vittorio De Sica has directed in a way that maximizes the anguish, yet is free of melodrama. Armando Trovajoli's music is a compassionate plus.
1961: Best Actress (Sophia Loren)

CIRCLE OF DANGER
1951, 86 mins, UK
D: Jacques Tourneur **A:** Ray Milland, Patricia Roc, Marius Goring, Hugh Sinclair, Naunton Wayne, Marjorie Fielding (Coronado)

Circle of Danger is too slowly paced to build much suspense. Ray Milland is engaged in a relentless hunt to discover the circumstances behind a younger brother's death in a British commando raid during the last war. Search narrows down to a handful of men who took part in the assault with his kin.

CIRCLE OF FRIENDS
1995, 96 mins, US ⓥ ⊙
D: Pat O'Connor **A:** Chris O'Donnell, Minnie Driver, Geraldine O'Rawe, Saffron Burrows, Alan Cummings, Colin Firth (Price/Lantana)

Director Pat O'Connor brings his Irish heritage and his expertise to a familiar coming-of-age tale, set in a small Irish town in 1957. Benny (Minnie Driver) and Eve (Geraldine O'Rawe) eagerly escape the dull confines of hometown Knockglen to attend college in Dublin, where they're reunited with former mate Nan (Saffron Burrows). Tale focuses on the trio's affairs of the heart—their secrets and dreams, rites of loyalty and betrayal, punishment and redemption. Somehow the passion holds and the story's emotions survive, due in large measure to the accomplished acting. The major weight is brilliantly carried off by Driver, who moves the film along while juggling hopes, doubts, and anxieties that will ring true to adolescents experiencing first love.

CIRCLE OF LOVE
See: La Ronde

CIRCUS
1928, 70 mins, US ⓥ ⊗
D: Charles Chaplin **A:** Charles Chaplin, Allan Garcia, Merna Kennedy, Harry Crocker, Stanley Sanford, George Davis (United Artists)

In clinging to a tale of logical sequence, without the expected interpolations or detached incidents, Chaplin's *Circus* has not been equaled for speed, gags, and laughs. But it's very broad, for Chaplin makes no attempt at subtlety in this one. Pathos to a limited degree is stuck in through Chaplin attempting to protect the bareback-riding daughter of the circus owner, the father brutally abusing the girl. The tramp falls in love with her, but when the handsome new wire walker arrives, the tramp is cold. That is why Chaplin takes to practicing wire walking to rival his rival.

CIRCUS WORLD
(UK: THE MAGNIFICENT SHOWMAN)
1964, 135 mins, US/Spain 🎬 ▭

D: Henry Hathaway **A:** John Wayne, Claudia Cardinale, Rita Hayworth, Lloyd Nolan, Richard Conte, John Smith (Bronston-Midway)

Made-in-Spain wedding of spectacle and romance. The basic story is about a runaway aerialist (Rita Hayworth) who returns to watch her daughter (Claudia Cardinale) rehearsing on the lot. Hayworth looks very good and acts with warmth and authority. Wayne is the centerpole, the muscle, the virility, and the incarnate courage of this often-down-but-never-out circus. The role has been tailored to his talents and personality, a rooting-tooting-shooting figure.

CISCO PIKE
1971, 94 mins, US

D: B.W.L. Norton **A:** Gene Hackman, Karen Black, Kris Kristofferson, Harry Dean Stanton, Viva, Joy Bang (Columbia)

Kris Kristofferson makes an excellent formal acting debut as a faded and drug-busted rock star forced by corrupt cop Gene Hackman into selling marijuana. Kristofferson's screen presence is very strong. There's a look in his eyes—a combination of resignation, optimism, and torture—that sticks in the memory long after the film has ended.

CITADEL, THE
1938, 112 mins, UK 🎬

D: King Vidor **A:** Robert Donat, Rosalind Russell, Ralph Richardson, Rex Harrison, Emlyn Williams, Penelope Dudley Ward (M-G-M)

The Citadel is Metro's second British-made production. It's an effective drama based on A. J. Cronin's novel which details the adventures of a young physician (Robert Donat) who starts out with high ideals and determination to help humanity. When Welsh miners object to his research to prevent tuberculosis in the community, he goes to London, gets in with a coterie of mulcting doctors who brush aside medical ethics in their chase for money. Donat gives a most seasoned performance. Rosalind Russell turns in a sympathetic portrayal of the young wife. **1938: Nominations:** Best Picture, Director, Actor (Robert Donat), Screenplay

LA CITE DES ENFANTS PERDUS
(THE CITY OF LOST CHILDREN)
1995, 111 mins, France/Spain/Germany 🎬 ▭

D: Jean-Pierre Jeunet, Marc Caro **A:** Ron Perlman, Daniel Emilfork, Judith Vittet, Dominique Pinon, Jean-Claude Dreyfus, Genevieve Brunet (Lumiere/Canal Plus/France 3)

A vibrant, bubbling cauldron of breathtaking f/x, gross-out humor, and in-your-face imagery. Setting is a multilevel smokestack port littered with industrial detritus, rusty tankers, and the biggest collection of weirdos and humans since Tod Browning's *Freaks*. Local heavies are the Cyclops, a Nietzschean sect of one-eyed fanatics who abduct young kids for crazed, aging inventor Krank (Daniel Emilfork), who lives on a castlelike oil rig near a minefield. It's not a movie you can afford to take your eyes off for a second.

CITIZEN KANE
1941, 120 mins, US 🎬 ⊙

D: Orson Welles **A:** Orson Welles, Joseph Cotten, Ray Collins, Paul Stewart, Dorothy Comingore, Everett Sloane (RKO/Mercury)

Citizen Kane, story of a multimillion-aire newspaper publisher, political aspirant, and wielder of public opinion, is filled to the last minute with brilliant incident, unreeled in method and effects that sparkle with originality and invention. The author's conception of Kane is of a man who had every material advantage in life, but who lacked a feeling of human sympathy and tolerance. It is a story of spiritual failure. So intent is the effort to prove Kane emotionally frustrated that no allowance is made to picture him as a human being. On this account he is not wholly real. Neither he nor his associates is blessed with the slightest sense of humor. **1941:** Best Original Screenplay

Nominations: Best Picture, Director, Actor (Orson Welles), B&W Cinematography, B&W Art Direction, Editing, Scoring of a Dramatic Picture, Sound

CITIZEN'S BAND
1977, 98 mins, US Ⓥ
D: Jonathan Demme **A:** Paul Le Mat, Candy Clark, Ann Wedgeworth, Bruce McGill, Marcia Rodd, Charles Napier (Fields)

Plot peg is the truck accident of philandering husband Charles Napier, who's got Ann Wedgeworth in Dallas and Marcia Rodd in Portland, both with homes and children. The CB dialogue exemplifies the good-natured horsing around that marks those channels, at the same time demonstrating the serious emergency traffic help that often saves lives.

CITY ACROSS THE RIVER
1949, 90 mins, US
D: Maxwell Shane **A:** Stephen McNally, Thelma Ritter, Luis Van Rooten, Jeff Corey, Tony Curtis, Richard Jaeckel (Universal)

Out of Irving Shulman's grim novel *The Amboy Dukes,* Maxwell Shane has whipped together a hard-hitting and honest film on juvenile delinquency, dramatically documenting how the slums spawn crime. Against backdrops of Manhattan and Brooklyn, the film succeeds in recreating the feel and flavor of the city's streets and back alleys.

CITY BENEATH THE SEA
(UK: ONE HOUR TO DOOMSDAY)
1953, 87 mins, US
D: Budd Boetticher **A:** Robert Ryan, Mala Powers, Anthony Quinn, Suzan Ball, George Mathews, Karel Stepanek (Universal)

High romance of the pulp-fiction variety is niftily shaped in *City Beneath the Sea.* The film stages a thrilling underseas earthquake as a capper to the derring-do yarn laid in the West Indies. Scene is the historic sunken city of Port Royal, Jamaica, which went to the bottom of the Caribbean during a 1692 earthquake. Robert Ryan and Anthony Quinn team excellently as the daring divers, ever ready for the adventures offered by sunken treasure or shapely femmes. They come to Kingston, Jamaica, to dive for $1 million in gold bullion that went down with a freighter.

CITY FOR CONQUEST
1940, 105 mins, US Ⓥ
D: Anatole Litvak **A:** James Cagney, Ann Sheridan, Frank Craven, Donald Crisp,

Arthur Kennedy, Frank McHugh (Warner)

Picture is natural for Cagney, who troupes through role of an unwilling prizefighter in vigorous fashion, taking the tough breaks of partial blindness with heroic courage. It's Cagney all the way, but aided considerably by Sheridan for romance, plus two newcomers to films from the stage, Arthur Kennedy and Elia Kazan, who indicate they will stick around Hollywood some time.

CITY GIRL, THE
1984, 85 mins, US Ⓥ ⊙
D: Martha Coolidge **A:** Laura Harrington, Joe Mastroianni, Carole McGill, Peter Riegert, Jim Carrington, Lawrence Phillips (Moon)

A hard-nosed, if frequently funny look at a young woman's attempt to forge a career and self-esteem. Lead character of Anne is a young lady who, in an awfully serious way, is trying to get a foot up as a professional photographer. Joey, her sympathetic but very straight boyfriend, would rather have her fill the conventional woman's role. Most bracing aspect of Coolidge's treatment of the relatively plain material is her rigorously objective, unindulgent perspective.

CITY HALL
1996, 111 mins, US Ⓥ ⊙
D: Harold Becker **A:** Al Pacino, John Cusack, Bridget Fonda, Danny Aiello, Martin Landau, Tony Franciosa (Castle Rock/Columbia)

City Hall centers on a credible, colorful rogues' gallery of suspects within a fast-paced thriller framework. At its best, the picture conveys the visceral energy of city politics and problem solving. There are no happy endings, just reelection promises. Kevin Calhoun (John Cusack) is the deputy mayor who reveres his boss, John Pappas (Al Pacino), a passionate and fearless man of the people. At the core of this contemporary Greek tragedy is Pacino's Pappas. It's a flamboyant interpretation that reflects the character's self-aware showmanship.

CITY HEAT
1984, 97 mins, US Ⓥ ⊙
D: Richard Benjamin **A:** Clint Eastwood, Burt Reynolds, Jane Alexander, Madeline Kahn, Rip Torn, Richard Roundtree (Malpaso/Deliverance/Warner)

City Heat is an amiable but decidedly lukewarm confection geared entirely around the two star turns. Set in an unnamed city around the end of Prohibition, Clint Eastwood and Burt Reynolds were old pals in their early days as cops, but the former has taken a dim view of the latter's jump over to the private-detective business. The two stars, with tongues firmly in cheek, easily set the prevailing tone of low-keyed facetiousness.

CITY LIGHTS
1931, 87 mins, US ⓥ
D: Charles Chaplin **A:** Charles Chaplin, Virginia Cherrill, Harry Myers, Allan Garcia, Hank Mann, Florence Lee (United Artists)

It's not Chaplin's best picture, because the comedian has sacrificed speed to pathos, and plenty of it. But the British comic is still the consummate pantomimist. All through Chaplin schemes how to procure money for a blind flower girl (Virginia Cherrill). As previously, Chaplin mainly paints in broad strokes, with his most subtle maneuvering here being the sly turning of the sympathy away from the girl to himself as the picture draws to a close.

CITY LIMITS
1985, 85 mins, US ⓥ
D: Aaron Lipstadt **A:** Darrell Larson, John Stockwell, Kim Cattrall, Rae Dawn Chong, Robby Benson, James Earl Jones (Sho/Videoform)

Elements of *City Limits* fit it into the category of the postholocaust pic, but the historical disaster is a plague which has wiped out an older generation. The young survive in a condition of controlled anarchy and resist attempts to impose a centralized government. Most successful aspect of the film is its depiction of a tribal lifestyle regulated according to rules learned from comic strips. Action scenes are well executed and there's a vibrant score.

CITY OF ANGELS
1998, 117 mins, US ⓥ ⊙ ⊠
D: Brad Silberling **A:** Nicolas Cage, Meg Ryan, Andre Braugher, Dennis Franz, Colm Feore, Robin Bartlett (Atlas/Warner)

Loosely based on Wim Wenders's enchanting 1987 *Wings of Desire, City of Angels* is a superlatively crafted romantic drama that solidly stands on its own merits. Nicolas Cage, as a celestial angel, and Meg Ryan, as a pragmatic surgeon, create such blissful chemistry that they elevate the drama to a poetic level seldom reached in a mainstream movie. Seth (Cage) is a restless angel on duty in L.A., and Cassiel (Andre Braugher) is his celestial comrade who's more at ease with himself. Maggie (Ryan), an accomplished heart surgeon, loses a patient and undergoes a crisis of confidence. Seth, watching her misery, falls hard for her.

CITY OF HOPE
1991, 129 mins, US ⓥ ⊡
D: John Sayles **A:** Vincent Spano, Joe Morton, Tony LoBianco, Anthony John Denison, Barbara Williams, John Sayles (Esperanza)

John Sayles's ambitious, wide-ranging study of corruption and community in a small eastern city has a richness of theme and specificity of vision more common to serious cinema. Picture hinges on the opposite directions of two characters: Nick (Vincent Spano), disillusioned son of a well-connected builder, who has easy access to the system but only wants out of it, and Wynn (Joe Morton), a young black city councilman who's determined to work within the system.

CITY OF JOY
1992, 134 mins, UK/France ⓥ ⊙
D: Roland Joffe **A:** Patrick Swayze, Pauline Collins, Om Puri, Shabana Azmi, Art Malik, Ayesha Dharker (Lightmotive)

Impressively produced in Calcutta's teeming poverty-ridden streets and slums, Roland Joffe's noble attempt to portray the tenacity and strength of the human spirit comes off as curiously ineffectual due to predictable plotting and character evolution. Assaulted and robbed, Patrick Swayze's Dr. Max Lowe is taken to the City of Joy Self-Help School and Dispensary, presided over by a selflessly saintly British woman (Pauline Collins). Max becomes cheerleader for the dispossessed people of City of Joy in their battle against the local Mafia. Swayze gives it the old college try, but he doesn't have depth. Appealing as always, Collins has nothing but routine buttons to push as she uses all her wiles to win the doc over to her cause.

CITY OF LOST CHILDREN, THE
See: La Cite des Enfants Perdus

CITY ON FIRE
See: Lungfu Fungwan

CITY SLICKERS
1991, 112 mins, US ⓥ ⊙
D: Ron Underwood **A:** Billy Crystal, Daniel Stern, Bruno Kirby, Patricia Wettig, Helen Slater, Jack Palance (Columbia/Castle Rock)

Billy Crystal, coming to grips with the

doldrums of midlife thanks to his 39th birthday, is convinced by his wife (Patricia Wettig) and two best friends (Daniel Stern, Bruno Kirby) to take off for two weeks on a ranch driving cattle across the west. The childhood fantasy comes to life in a number of ways, perhaps foremost in the presence of gnarled trail boss Curly (Jack Palance). A series of increasingly absurd events turns the vacation into a journey of self-discovery. Crystal gets plenty of chance to crack wise while he, Stern, and Kirby engage in playful and not-so-playful banter.

1991: Best Supp. Actor (Jack Palance)

CITY SLICKERS II
THE LEGEND OF CURLY'S GOLD
1994, 116 mins, US Ⓥ ⊙
D: Paul Weiland **A:** Billy Crystal, Daniel Stern, Jon Lovitz, Jack Palance, Patricia Wettig, Bob Balaban (Castle Rock/Face/Columbia)

The lively sequel is a sure-shootin' handsome contempo oater rife with both gags and classic genre lore. Mitch (Billy Crystal) is obsessed by the notion that he just may have buried the grisled cowboy Curly (Jack Palance) a tad prematurely. So, when he stands in the mirror adjusting Curly's Stetson, providence steps in. Tucked into the lining is a map indicating the way to buried gold. The film comes alive once it heads into sagebrush territory. It hits full stride with the introduction of Duke (Jack Palance), Curly's twin brother.

CITY STREETS
1931, 83 mins, US
D: Rouben Mamoulian **A:** Gary Cooper, Sylvia Sidney, Paul Lukas, William Boyd, Guy Kibbee, Stanley Fields (Paramount)

Probably the first sophisticated treatment of a gangster picture. Story is the usual love-redeeming tale of two kids caught in a gangster vortex. Picture is lifted from mediocrity through the intelligent acting and appeal of Sylvia Sidney. Camera angles are piled on thick. Most of the time these shots serve to slow up the film and confuse.

CITY THAT NEVER SLEEPS
1953, 90 mins, US Ⓥ
D: John H. Auer **A:** Gig Young, Mala Powers, William Talman, Edward Arnold, Chill Wills, Marie Windsor (Republic)

Playing of the four cast toppers, Gig Young, a crazy, mixed-up cop; Mala Powers, a cheap saloon dancer; William Tal-

man, a magician turned hood; and Edward Arnold, suave, crooked attorney, is adequate. John L. Russell's photography makes okay use of Chicago streets and buildings for the low-key, nightlife effect required to back the melodrama.

CIVILIZATION
1916, 121 mins, US Ⓥ ⊗
D: Raymond B. West **A:** Howard Hickman, Enid Markey, Herschel Mayall, George Fisher, J. Frank Burke (Triangle/KayBee)

Master producer Thomas H. Ince was handicapped here by the limitations of C. Gardner Sullivan's scenario, designed as a strong protest against the horrors of war. The entertainment opens showing a nation suddenly plunged headlong into war by its king (Herschel Mayall), due wholly to his selfish desire for conquest. He is dependent for success upon Count Ferdinand (Howard Hickman), who has invented a submarine calculated to destroy the enemy's fleet, thus ensuring victory. The count is in love with Katheryn (Enid Markey). She belongs to a secret society, which is opposed to war. She takes him to one of the meetings and he becomes a convert. There is very little opportunity to criticize Ince's magnificent effort, but Sullivan's captions are altogether too preachy. In his effort to project pathos he slops over into bathos.

CLAIRE DOLAN
1998, 95 mins, France/US Ⓥ ⊙
D: Lodge Kerrigan **A:** Katrin Cartlidge, Vincent D'Onofrio, Colm Meaney, John Doman, Maryanne Plunkett, Miranda Stuart-Rhyne (MK2/Serene)

A rarified, emotionally distant art film, *Claire Dolan* is a rigorously controlled, occasionally arresting study of a New York prostitute's attempt to take control of her life. By imprisoning his characters within walls of mirrors, glass, chrome, plastic, and often unadorned surfaces, and by manipulating the sound mix, Kerrigan skillfully creates an intimidating, claustrophobic world. Claire (Katrin Cartlidge) devotes nearly all her waking hours to working off a large debt to mobster Roland Cain (Colm Meaney), who has known her since she was a girl. She remains bottled up emotionally and physically. A chance encounter with taxi driver Elton (Vincent D'Onofrio), shows some promise of changing that. The distance the writer-director creates between character and audience prevents Claire from sharing her inner life. D'Onofrio is appealing enough, if unassertive, and Meaney brings welcome weight and charm to his powerful character.

CLAIRE'S KNEE
See: Le Genou de Claire

CLAN OF THE CAVE BEAR, THE
1986, 98 mins, US ⓥ ⊙ ▭
D: Michael Chapman **A:** Daryl Hannah, Pamela Reed, James Remar, Thomas G. Waites, John Doolittle (Warner)

Handsomely produced on rugged Canadian exteriors, this is the story of prehistory's first feminist. Little imagination is in evidence here. A primitive language has been invented for these early humans to speak (subtitles run throughout), but nothing in their customs, habits, or attitudes proves very interesting. Daryl Hannah, at least, is a fetching and sympathetic center of attention, but emoting of the entire cast is limited to expressive grunting.
1986: Nomination: Best Makeup

CLANSMAN, THE
See: Birth of a Nation

CLARA'S HEART
1988, 108 mins, US ⓥ
D: Robert Mulligan **A:** Whoopi Goldberg, Michael Ontkean, Kathleen Quinlan, Neil Patrick Harris, Spalding Gray, Beverly Todd (MTM/Warner)

Buoyed by a beautifully measured star turn by Whoopi Goldberg and a smashing screen debut for young Neil Patrick Harris, *Clara's Heart* is a powerful, unabashedly sentimental drama. Adaptation of Joseph Olshan's novel pays attention to the values of a well-wrought character study of a noble Jamaican servant (Goldberg) and the young rich kid (Harris) she guides through adolescent rites of passage.

CLASH BY NIGHT
1952, 105 mins, US ⓥ ⊙
D: Fritz Lang **A:** Barbara Stanwyck, Paul Douglas, Robert Ryan, Marilyn Monroe, J. Carrol Naish, Keith Andes (Wald-Krasna/RKO)

A rather aimless drama of lust and passion, *Clash* captures much of the drabness of the seacoast fishing town, background of the pic, but only occasionally does the narrative's suggested intensity seep through. Barbara Stanwyck plays the returning itinerant with her customary defiance and sullenness. It is one of her better performances. Robert Ryan plays the other man with grim brutality, while Marilyn Monroe is reduced to what is tantamount to a bit role.

CLASH OF THE TITANS
1981, 118 mins, UK ⓥ ⊙
D: Desmond Davis **A:** Laurence Olivier, Harry Hamlin, Claire Bloom, Maggie Smith, Burgess Meredith, Ursula Andress (United Artists/M-G-M)

Clash of the Titans is an unbearable bore that will probably put to sleep the few adults stuck taking the kids to it. This mythical tale of Perseus, son of Zeus, and his quest for the fair Andromeda, is mired in a slew of corny dialogue and an endless array of flat, outdated special effects.

CLASS
1983, 98 mins, US ⓥ ⊙
D: Lewis John Carlino **A:** Rob Lowe, Jacqueline Bisset, Andrew McCarthy, Stuart Margolin, Cliff Robertson, John Cusack (Orion)

Class is anything but classy. About a brainy but virginal prep-school student (Andrew McCarthy) who unwittingly begins an affair with his upper-class roommate's sexy mother (Jacqueline Bisset). Lewis John Carlino's direction is frequently awkward, notably in the nudity-less sex scenes.

CLASS ACT
1992, 98 mins, US ⓥ
D: Randall Miller **A:** Christopher Reid, Christopher Martin, Karyn Parsons, Alysia Rogers, Meshach Taylor, Rick Ducommun (Warner)

This latest test for rap duo Kid 'N Play scores low on the SAT spectrum. Infused with some of the energy but not the smarts of pair's debut *House Party,* pic actually has a reasonably engaging premise that gets lost amid the too broad cartoon elements and emphasis on teen T&A. Two newcomers to a high school—one a certified genius, the other a paroled felon with a nasty reputation—swap identities, giving the nerd the tough guy's rep while replacing his counterpart among the snooty elite.

CLASS ACTION
1991, 109 mins, US ⓥ
D: Michael Apted **A:** Gene Hackman, Mary Elizabeth Mastrantonio, Colin Friels, Joanna Merlin, Larry Fishburne, Donald Moffat (20th Century-Fox/Interscope)

Winning performances by Gene Hackman and Mary Elizabeth Mastrantonio and potent direction by Michael Apted pump life into the sturdy courtroom-drama formula once again. Hackman plays Jed Ward, a, veteran civil-rights lawyer. Mastrantonio is his daughter Maggie, a ruthlessly effective corporate advocate and ladder-climber, whose disdain for her father has more to do with his amorous indiscretions than his politics. They wind up on opposite sides of a class-action suit.

CLASS OF '44
1973, 95 mins, US ⓥ ▱
D: Paul Bogart **A:** Gary Grimes, Jerry Houser, Oliver Conant, William Atherton, Sam Bottoms, Deborah Winters (Warner)

Class of '44 is an okay follow-up to *Summer of '42,* taking the three juveniles of the first film through their early college years at the end of World War II. Encoring in the lead roles are Gary Grimes, Jerry Houser, and Oliver Conant, all introduced graduating from high school. Deborah Winters is Grimes's campus sweetheart.

CLASS OF MISS MACMICHAEL, THE
1978, 100 mins, UK/US ⓥ
D: Silvio Narizzano **A:** Glenda Jackson, Oliver Reed, Michael Murphy, Rosalind Cash, John Standing, Phil Daniels (Kettledrum/Brut)

This pic is about dippy doings at a special school for unruly teenagers. Treading the usual characterizations and situations, film adds a more permissive tone in language and freewheeling sex of the students. It has Glenda Jackson adding her presence to the part of a dedicated teacher who eschews a second marriage to stay with her impossible charges. Oliver Reed overcharges his role of the martinet, hypocritical, mean principal.

CLASS OF 1984
1982, 96 mins, Canada ⓥ ⊙
D: Mark L. Lester **A:** Perry King, Timothy Van Patten, Merrie Lynn Ross, Roddy McDowall, Al Waxman, Michael J. Fox (Guerrilla High)

Class of 1984 is pure exploitation with plenty of action and a manipulative plot. The Canadian production is set at Abraham Lincoln High School in a large American city. Newcomer music teacher Perry King finds his views on education rapidly altered at the school: students are frisked for weapons, teachers carry guns, and the hallways are monitored by guards and cameras. The chief purveyors of terror are a gang led by Timothy Van Patten. King

refuses to buckle to their strong-arm tactics.

CLASS OF 1999
1990, 98 mins, US ⓥ
D: Mark L. Lester **A:** Bradley Gregg, Traci Lind, Malcolm McDowell, Stacy Keach, Pam Grier, John P. Ryan (Original/Lightning)

A follow-up to the 1982 pic *Class of 1984,* this violent exploitation film is too pretentious for its own good. The inconsistent screenplay posits high-schoolers out of control. Hamming it up as an albino megalomaniac, Stacy Keach is carrying out an experiment sending three androids reconverted from army surplus to serve as teachers at Kennedy H.S. in Seattle and whip the students into shape. John P. Ryan and Pam Grier are loads of fun as the androids.

CLASS OF NUKE 'EM HIGH
1986, 81 mins, US ⓥ ⊙
D: Richard W. Haines, Samuel Weil [Lloyd Kaufman] **A:** Janelle Brady, Gilbert Brenton, Robert Pritchard, R.I. Ryan (TNT/Troma)

Attractive couple Chrissy (Janelle Brady) and Warren (Gilbert Brenton) are exposed to a mild dose of radiation in the form of tainted reefers. First effect is to cause them to make love at a party. Next day, both go through temporary physical transformations (expanding stomachs and necks), with Chrissy emitting a small, lizardlike creature. Level of violence is extreme with slapstick overtures that are intended to be funny.

CLASS OF NUKE 'EM HIGH PART II
SUBHUMANOID MELTDOWN
1991, 95 mins, US ⓥ
D: Eric Louzil **A:** Brick Bronsky, Lisa Gaye, Leesa Rowland, Michael Kurtz, Scott Resnick, Shelby Shepard (Troma)

This unwarranted sequel is an incoherent mess. Mad-scientist Professor Holt (attractive Lisa Gaye) has created a race of drone subhumanoid workers, including beautiful Victoria (Leesa Rowland). Unfortunately, they are subject to an ailment that causes them to melt into green goo. An unfunny running gag insists on the subhumanoids having mouths where their belly buttons should be.

CLAUDIA AND DAVID
1946, 78 mins, US
D: Walter Lang **A:** Dorothy McGuire, Robert Young, Mary Astor, John Sutton,

Gail Patrick, Florence Bates (20th Century-Fox)

Strong entertainment for femme theatergoers, jammed with tears and chuckles. Dorothy McGuire makes the scatterbrained Claudia believable, and Robert Young backs her up with an equally good performance as her long-suffering husband, David. Plot generally concerns Claudia's susceptibility and strong love for her young son. Trouble starts when a phony mind-reader warns her husband he will have an accident if he takes a trip to California.

CLAUDINE
1974, 92 mins, US Ⓥ
D: John Berry A: Diahann Carroll, James Earl Jones, Lawrence Hinton-Jacobs, Tamu, David Kruger, Yvette Curtis (Third World)

Claudine is a gritty, hearty, heartful, and ruggedly tender story of contemporary urban black family life avoiding blaxploitation genre. Here we have some too real problems—Diahann Carroll as a 36-year-old mother of six trying to keep a family together without a man around; James Earl Jones as her garbage collector–boyfriend trapped in the immorality of the welfare system which encourages impropriety and discourages decency.

1974: Nomination: Best Actress (Diahnn Carroll)

CLEAN AND SOBER
1988, 124 mins, US Ⓥ ⊙
D: Glenn Gordon Caron A: Michael Keaton, Kathy Baker, Morgan Freeman, M. Emmet Walsh, Tate Donovan, Luca Bercovici (Imagine/Warner)

Covering the first 30 days of attempted recovery by middle-class cocaine addict Michael Keaton, *Sober* is sobering indeed, perhaps too grim. Keaton carries his heavy load well enough, on screen a vast majority of time. Keaton falls under the strict supervision of ex-junkie Morgan Freeman, which will do him good, but also develops a romantic interest in fellow recovering addict Kathy Baker, which won't.

CLEAN SLATE
1994, 107 mins, US Ⓥ ⊙
D: Mick Jackson A: Dana Carvey, Valeria Golino, James Earl Jones, Kevin Pollack, Michael Gambon, Michael Murphy (M-G-M)

This convoluted comedy feels like a pale follow-up to *Groundhog Day*. The clever premise—a guy suffering from a form of amnesia that causes him to forget everything when he goes to sleep—never congeals in the execution. Dana Carvey plays Pogue, a private detective who's been afflicted with this unique illness. Director Mick Jackson pulls off some amusing sequences, most of them involving a Jack Russell terrier.

CLEAR AND PRESENT DANGER
1994, 141 mins, US Ⓥ ⊙ ▭
D: Phillip Noyce A: Harrison Ford, Willem Dafoe, Anne Archer, Joaquim de Almeida, Henry Czerny, Harris Yulin (Paramount)

Jack Ryan takes on the Colombian drug cartels and some nefarious members of a duplicitous US government in the third entry in Paramount's Tom Clancy franchise. Excitement only occasionally reaches thrilling levels. Awakened to the ineffectiveness of the country's war on drugs, the prez (Donald Moffat) has Ryan (Harrison Ford), now acting CIA deputy director of intelligence due to the illness of his boss (James Earl Jones), pursue the matter, while secretly setting loose national security adviser James Cutter (Harris Yulin) and CIA hard-liner Robert Ritter (Henry Czerny) to send a paramilitary force against the drug lords. To this end, they hire CIA cowboy Clark (Willem Dafoe). The far-ranging plot isn't confusing. On an action level, pic is less highcharged than numerous other efforts of its ilk.

1994: Nominations: Sound, Sound Effects Editing

CLEO DE 5 A 7
(CLEO FROM 5 TO 7)
1961, 90 mins, FRANCE Ⓥ
D: Agnes Varda A: Corinne Marchand, Antoine Bourseiller, Dominique Davray, Dorothee Blank, Michel Legrand, Jose-Luis de Villalonga (Rome Paris)

Varda keeps alive interest in the girl and her plight (she has taken a test to determine if she has cancer). She goes to a fortune-teller, has a crying jag in public, buys a hat, sees her lover for a while, who is loath to admit any sickness she may have, visits a model friend, sees a little film comedy which buoys her up, and finally meets a soldier who helps her face up to getting the test results. Corinne Marchand is well utilized as the sick girl while others just lend silhouettes to her wanderings, except for Antoine Bourseiller's knowing portrayal of the soldier.

CLEO FROM 5 TO 7
See: Cleo de 5 a 7

CLEOPATRA
1934, 102 mins, US Ⓥ ⊙
D: Cecil B. DeMille **A:** Claudette Colbert, Warren William, Henry Wilcoxon, Gertrude Michael, Joseph Schildkraut, Ian Keith (Paramount)

Cecil B. DeMille adds nothing to his directorial rep in this one other than to again demonstrate his rare skill in the handling of mass action. Claudette Colbert's best moment is the death of Cleo. The rest of the time she's a cross between a lady of the evening and a rough soubrette in a country melodrama. It is not so much her fault as the shortcoming of the scenarists. The dialogue is made to become colloquial with disastrous results. Warren William, as Caesar, and Henry Wilcoxon, as Antony, play in the drawing-room style, and a not too select drawing room at that. Joseph Schildkraut is a fair Herod.

1934: Best Cinematography
Nominations: Best Picture, Editing, Sound, Assistant Director

CLEOPATRA
1963, 243 mins, US Ⓥ ⊙ ▭
D: Joseph L. Mankiewicz **A:** Elizabeth Taylor, Richard Burton, Rex Harrison, Roddy McDowall, Martin Landau, Hume Cronyn (20th Century-Fox/MCL-Walwa)

Cleopatra is not only a supercolossal eye-filler (the unprecedented budget shows in the physical opulence throughout), but it is also a remarkably literate cinematic recreation of an historic epoch. The film covers the 18 turbulent years leading to the foundation of the Roman Empire, from Cleopatra's first meeting with Julius Caesar until her death in defeat with Mark Antony. In the title role, Elizabeth Taylor grows to become the mature queen who matches the star's own voluptuous assurance. Rex Harrison is superb as Caesar, shrewd, vain, and wise. Richard Burton then comes to the fore in the second half. Oddly he does not seem the romantic figure expected and plot-implied. Ironically some of the weakest moments in the film are the love scenes between Liz and Dickie. The real star of *Cleopatra,* however, is Mankiewicz, who brought order out of what had been production chaos. As Caesar observes to Cleopatra, early on: "You have a way of mixing politics and passion." So does Mankiewicz.

1963: Best Color Cinematography, Color Art Direction, Special Effects, Color Costume Design
Nominations: Best Picture, Actor (Rex Harrison), Editing, Original Music Score

CLEOPATRA JONES
1973, 89 mins, US Ⓥ ▭
D: Jack Starrett **A:** Tamara Dobson, Bernie Casey, Brenda Sykes, Antonio Fargas, Bill McKinney, Shelley Winters (Warner)

Cleopatra Jones is a good programmer with the offbeat twist of having a sexy woman detective as the lead character. Tamara Dobson makes a smart starring debut as a sophisticated undercover agent working to stamp out the world drug trade. Dobson's archenemy is Shelley Winters, in vulgar characterization as a lesbian-type gang leader. The line between offbeat cameo and repulsive casting is wider than a freeway, but Winters crosses it with felicity.

CLIENT, THE
1994, 120 mins, US Ⓥ ⊙
D: Joel Schumacher **A:** Susan Sarandon, Tommy Lee Jones, Mary-Louise Parker, Anthony LaPaglia, Anthony Edwards, Ossie Davis (Warner)

The Client is a satisfactory, by-the-numbers child-in-jeopardy thriller. Overriding problem here is the basic lack of suspense. Two little brothers, Mark and Ricky Sway (Brad Renfro, David Speck), witness a man park his car, attach a hose to the exhaust pipe, and stick it through the window. Mark hears the man's secrets, which involve a US senator who was murdered by the Mob. Mark becomes the object of relentless attention on the part of fierce federal prosecutor Roy Foltrigg (Tommy Lee Jones), who hopes to use the kid's knowledge to further his own political ambitions. Mark finds a lawyer in Reggie Love (Susan Sarandon), a woman who makes up for her limited experience with unflagging tenacity and personal commitment.

1994: Nomination: Best Actress (Susan Sarandon)

CLIFFHANGER
1993, 112 mins, US Ⓥ ⊙ ▭
D: Renny Harlin **A:** Sylvester Stallone, John Lithgow, Michael Rooker, Janine Turner, Rex Linn, Caroline Goodall (Carolco/Canal Plus/Pioneer)

Cliffhanger lives up to its title as a high-octane action suspenser with thrilling vertiginous footage. Director Renny Harlin keeps the adventure coming at an

astonishing pace. What really puts this in a class of its own is the verisimilitude of the action. Despite credits to stunt and climbing doubles and the occasional process shot, there is no doubt that Stallone and other actors were really up on the sides of mountains. Tech contributions throughtout are aces.
1993: Nominations: Best Sound, Sound Editing, Visual Effects

CLINTON AND NADINE
See: Blood Money

CLIVE OF INDIA
1935, 90 mins, US
D: Richard Boleslawski **A:** Ronald Colman, Loretta Young, Colin Clive, Francis Lister, C. Aubrey Smith, Cesar Romero (20th Century)

The Black Hole of Calcutta, the battle elephants (with their gargantuan and murderous barbed armor), the famous Indian monsoons, and, of course, the basically courageous warrior, Robert Clive, and his rise from an obscure clerkship with the East India Company—all these elements of fictionized fact and glorified history are recreated here vividly for the screen. After the first three quarters of an hour or so, the plot veers to the romantic troubles besetting Clive and Margaret Maskeylne (later Lady Clive). Ronald Colman is an excellent Clive sans his familiar mustache.

CLOAK AND DAGGER
1946, 103 mins, US ⓥ
D: Fritz Lang **A:** Gary Cooper, Lilli Palmer, Robert Alda, J. Edward Bromberg, Vladimir Sokoloff, Ludwig Stossel (Warner)

This tale of the OSS and its undercover work during the war is the usual cops-and-robbers story. Fritz Lang's direction manages suspense and several top moments of gripping dramatic conflict, but otherwise fails to rise to sock levels. Gary Cooper is seen as atomic scientist drafted by OSS to get a line on Nazi atomic developments. He encounters the usual femme spy in Switzerland and romance with an Italian partisan who is assigned to aid him contact a Nazi-held scientist. Cooper fits requirements of his role, turning in his usual top-notch job.

CLOCK, THE
(UK: UNDER THE CLOCK)
1945, 90 mins, US ⓥ
D: Vincente Minnelli **A:** Judy Garland, Robert Walker, James Gleason, Keenan

Wynn, Marshall Thompson, Lucille Gleason (M-G-M)

Producer Arthur Freed and director Vincente Minnelli, the combination that scored so heavily with the Judy Garland musical *Meet Me in St. Louis,* show their versatility in this picture, which is straight drama sans any music. It's Garland's first straight dramatic role. The entire story takes place in the 48 hours that Corporal Joe Allen (Walker) is on furlough in NY City.

CLOCKERS
1995, 128 mins, US ⓥ ⊙
D: Spike Lee **A:** Harvey Keitel, John Turturro, Delroy Lindo, Mekhi Phifer, Isaiah Washington, Keith David (40 Acres & a Mule/Universal)

Spike Lee takes up the cudgel against black-on-black violence. A study of the urban dope-dealing culture and its toll on everyone who comes in contact with it, the picture has an insider's feel that is constantly undercut by the filmmaker's impulse to editorialize. As a favor to neighborhood drug kingpin Rodney (Delroy Lindo), 19-year-old Strike (Mekhi Phifer) agrees to kill a competitor. Intense veteran homicide cop Rocco Klein (Harvey Keitel) begins to hound Strike. Strike resolutely refuses to take responsibility for anything he does, but his own body is informing him of the error of his ways in the form of constant retching. Lindo oozes command and charisma as the corrupt Rodney.

CLOCKWISE
1986, 97 mins, UK ⓥ ⊙
D: Christopher Morahan **A:** John Cleese, Alison Steadman, Penelope Wilton, Stephen Moore, Joan Hickson, Sharon Maiden (Thorn EMI/Moment)

Clockwise is a somewhat uneven comic road film. John Cleese plays the headmaster of a secondary school who misses the train for a headmaster's conference. Immediately panic-struck, he seeks some other way to get to the meeting on time. The best moments depict his gradually going to pieces as he struggles to complete his journey in the company of an abducted schoolgirl (Sharon Maiden) and former girlfriend (Penelope Wilton). *Clockwise* would be a bore were it not for Cleese's comic ability.

CLOCKWORK MICE
1995, 99 mins, UK ⓥ
D: Vadim Jean **A:** Ian Hart, Catherine

Russell, Ruaidhri Conroy, Art Malik, Claire Skinner, Nigel Planer (Metrodome)

A good old-fashioned heartwarmer about a teacher and a dysfunctional teen, *Clockwork Mice* throws in the kitchen sink to embrace its humanist theme with cinematic verve. Pic is toplined by convinced playing from Ian Hart as the selfless teach, and mounted in infectious feel-good style. Setting is a fictional school for maladjusted children somewhere in rural England.

CLOCKWORK ORANGE, A
1971, 137 mins, UK ⊗
D: Stanley Kubrick A: Malcolm McDowell, Patrick Magee, Michael Bates, Miriam Carlin, Adrienne Corri, Aubrey Morris (Warner)

A Clockwork Orange is a brilliant nightmare. The film employs outrageous vulgarity, stark brutality, and some sophisticated comedy to make an opaque argument for the preservation of respect for man's free will even to do wrong. Kubrick's screenplay, based on the 1962 Anthony Burgess novel, postulates a society composed of amoral young hedonists, an older generation in retreat behind locked doors, and a police government no longer accountable to anyone or to any principles except expediency and tenure. In this world where youthful gangs control the street by night and disperse by dawn lives antihero and narrator Malcolm McDowell and his sidekicks. Their escapades include beatings, rape, and a bizarre murder.

1971: Nominations: Best Picture, Director, Adapted Screenplay, Editing

CLOSE ENCOUNTERS OF THE THIRD KIND
1977, 135 mins, US ⊗ ⊙ ▭
D: Steven Spielberg A: Richard Dreyfuss, Francois Truffaut, Teri Garr, Melinda Dillon, Cary Guffey, Bob Balaban (Columbia)

Close Encounters of the Third Kind is a daring film concept which in its special and technical effects has been superbly realized. Steven Spielberg's film climaxes in final 35 minutes with almost ethereal confrontation with life-forms from another world; the first 100 minutes, however, are somewhat redundant in exposition and irritating in tone. Story involves a series of UFO appearances witnessed by Richard Dreyfuss and Melinda Dillon and her son Cary Guffey. Concurrent with this plotline are the maneuverings of a team of military and scientific personnel in which Francois

Truffaut is a key member. There's no denying that the climax is an absolute stunner, literate in plotting, dazzling in execution, and almost reverent in tone. [In 1980 film was replaced by a 132-minute version, with extra material showing the inside of the mother ship at end. On posters, but not on prints, this was subtitled *The Special Edition*.]

1977: Best Cinematography, Special Achievment Award (sound-effects editing) **Nominations:** Best Director, Best Supp. Actress (Melinda Dillon), Art Direction, Editing, Original Score, Sound, Special Visual Effects

CLOSELY OBSERVED TRAINS
See: Ostre Sledovane Vlaky

CLOSELY WATCHED TRAINS
See: Ostre Sledovane Vlaky

CLOSE MY EYES
1991, 105 mins, UK ⊗
D: Stephen Poliakoff A: Alan Rickman, Clive Owen, Saskia Reeves, Karl Johnson, Lesley Sharp, Kate Gartside (Film Four/ Beambright)

Close My Eyes is a powerful British film about incest. The early scenes somewhat awkwardly chart the relationship between Natalie (Saskia Reeves) and her younger brother Richard (Clive Owen). Five years later Natalie is married to the wealthy Sinclair (Alan Rickman). She visits her brother in his apartment, and the hitherto unspoken passion between them erupts into a sexual encounter. Reeves and Owen give brave, strong, unstinting performances. Rickman has his best screen role to date as the pompous but kindly husband.

CLOSET LAND
1991, 93 mins, US ⊗ ⊙
D: Radha Bharadwaj A: Madeleine Stowe, Alan Rickman (Imagine)

The highly theatrical *Closet Land* addresses the horror of political torture. It's a harrowing, focused two-character piece by first-time director Radha Bharadwaj, with a man (Alan Rickman) trying to break the will of a woman (Madeleine Stowe). Despite the claustrophobic setup, a great deal occurs to hold one's interest. Rickman as interrogator is a complex, highly civilized man. Stowe is a physically captivating victim with a fierce attachment to justice. Rickman deserves a great deal of notice for his powerfully controlled, multifaceted performance. Stowe displays some flash and backbone, but not enough to make this a truly engaging match.

CLOSE TO EDEN
See: A Stranger Among Us

CLOUDED YELLOW, THE
1950, 95 mins, UK
D: Ralph Thomas **A:** Jean Simmons, Trevor Howard, Sonia Dresdel, Kenneth More, Maxwell Reed (Carillon)

Yarn describes the adventures of an ex–Secret Service agent who helps an innocent girl to escape from a murder charge. On the theory of setting a thief to catch a thief, Scotland Yard puts another secret agent on his tracks. There follows an exciting chase across England. Once the chase is on, the suspense is sustained solidly.

CZLOWIEK Z MARMARU
See: Man of Marble

CLUB, THE
1980, 99 mins, Australia ⓥ ▭
D: Bruce Beresford **A:** Jack Thompson, Graham Kennedy, Frank Wilson, Harold Hopkins, John Howard, Alan Cassell (South Australia Film/New South Wales Film)

The plot has to do with a football club and the behind-the-scenes machinations: ruthless power plays that make what takes place on the field seem relatively tame. The game plays a background role and director Bruce Beresford has shrewdly kept the thrust of his film in the hands of his main characters.

CLUB PARADISE
1986, 104 mins, US ⓥ ⊙
D: Harold Ramis **A:** Robin Williams, Peter O'Toole, Rick Moranis, Jimmy Cliff, Twiggy, Adolph Caesar (Warner)

There are enough funny skits in *Club Paradise* to make for a good hour of SCTV (Second City TV), where most of the cast is from, but too few to keep this Club Med satire afloat for 104 minutes. Robin Williams heads the cast as a disabled Chicago fireman who uses his insurance settlement to become partners with a reggae musician (Jimmy Cliff) in a seedy Caribbean club they hope to turn into a first-class resort. Williams can be a terrific actor/comedian, but the spark isn't there.

CLUE
1985, 87 mins, US ⓥ ⊙
D: Jonathan Lynn **A:** Eileen Brennan, Tim Curry, Madeline Kahn, Christopher Lloyd,

Lesley Ann Warren, Colleen Camp (Paramount)

Clue is campy, high-styled escapism. In a short 87 minutes that just zip by, the well-known board game's one-dimensional card figures like Professor Plum and others become multidimensional personalities with enough wit, neuroses, and motives to intrigue even the most adept whodunit solver. Film was released with three endings. Tim Curry plays the loquacious organizer of the evening's murder game, which takes place in a Gothic hilltop mansion in New England in 1954 during a storm (of course).

CLUELESS
1995, 97 mins, US ⓥ ⊙
D: Amy Heckerling **A:** Alicia Silverstone, Stacey Dash, Brittany Murphy, Paul Rudd, Dan Hedaya, Donald Faison (Paramount)

Clueless is a fresh, disarmingly bright, and at times explosively funny comedy well worth a trip to the mall, even if it runs out of gas. Taking her (uncredited) inspiration from Jane Austen's *Emma*, director Amy Heckerling has a dead-on ear for the updated Valley Girl dialogue with a Beverly Hills–Westside twist. Cher (Alicia Silverstone) finds there are few situations she can't talk her way out of, down to manipulating her teachers into a romance in order to mellow them out enough to get better grades. Cher's big project, however, is Tai (Brittany Murphy), a fashion victim who clearly needs a clue. She begins a wholesale makeover. Silverstone is not only adorable but possesses a real comic flair.

CLUNY BROWN
1946, 100 mins, US
D: Ernst Lubitsch **A:** Jennifer Jones, Charles Boyer, Peter Lawford, Helen Walker, Reginald Gardiner, Reginald Owen (20th Century-Fox)

Cluny Brown can be recorded as glamorizing the first of a clan: a lady plumber. And a looker, no less. The kind for whom stopped-up pipes are a pleasure. Jennifer Jones is the girl, Charles Boyer her anti-Nazi refugee vis-à-vis, Ernst Lubitsch produced and directed. *Cluny* is in the best Lubitsch tradition of subtle, punchy comedy, and his two stars make the most of it. It is a satire on British manners, with bite and relish.

COAL MINER'S DAUGHTER
1980, 125 mins, US ⓥ
D: Michael Apted **A:** Sissy Spacek,

Tommy Lee Jones, Beverly D'Angelo, Levon Helm, Phyllis Boyens, Ernest Tubb (Universal)

Coal Miner's Daughter is a thoughtful, endearing film charting the life of singer Loretta Lynn from the depths of poverty in rural Kentucky to her eventual rise to the title of "queen of country music." Thanks in large part to superb performances by Sissy Spacek and Tommy Lee Jones, film mostly avoids the sudsy atmosphere common to many showbiz tales. Both Spacek and Beverly D'Angelo, as country singer Patsy Cline, deserve a special nod for doing all of their own singing with style and accuracy.

1980: Best Actress (Sissy Spacek)
Nominations: Best Picture, Adapted Screenplay, Cinematography, Art Direction, Editing, Sound

COBB
1994, 128 mins, US Ⓥ ⊙
D: Ron Shelton **A:** Tommy Lee Jones, Robert Wuhl, Lolita Davidovich, Lou Myers, Stephen Mendillo, William Utay (Regency/Alcor/Warner)

The film is essentially the chronicle of how sports scribe Al Stump (Robert Wuhl) was summoned to the bedside of the ailing Ty Cobb (Tommy Lee Jones) to write the official bio of the Baseball Hall of Fame's first inductee. Jones plays Cobb on a Shakespearean scale, with obvious parallels between the Georgia Peach and King Lear. Wuhl is simply no match for his charismatic costar. He's a dedicated second banana, and when all else fails, he mugs.

COBRA
1986, 87 mins, US Ⓥ ⊙
D: George Pan Cosmatos **A:** Sylvester Stallone, Brigitte Nielsen, Reni Santoni, Andrew Robinson, Lee Garlington, John Herzfeld (Cannon)

Cobra is a sleek, extremely violent, and exciting police thriller. Sylvester Stallone is cast as unconventional cop Marion Cobretti, nickname Cobra, who with partner Gonzales (Reni Santoni) works the L.A. zombie squad, doing jobs no other cops will do. His low-key personality defined by his funny throwaway lines of dialogue, Stallone's Cobra is a far more ingratiating character than his recent Rocky and Rambo guises.

COBRA WOMAN
1944, 70 mins, US
D: Robert Siodmak **A:** Maria Montez, Jon Hall, Sabu, Lon Chaney (Universal)

Cobra Woman is a super-fantastic melodrama. Elaborately and colorfully mounted for constant eye appeal, and with the starring trio of Maria Montez, Jon Hall, and Sabu, picture unfolds at fast pace to concentrate on action features of the tale. Plot combines jungle-island romance with melodramatic complications, temple rituals, chases, and fights. Montez is decidedly shapely as sarong-draped native girl and dazzlingly gowned as the high priestess. She handles the dual assignment very well.

COBWEB, THE
1955, 122 mins, US ⊙ ▷
D: Vincente Minnelli **A:** Richard Widmark, Lauren Bacall, Charles Boyer, Gloria Grahame, Lillian Gish, John Kerr (M-G-M)

The neuroses of the staff and patients in a psychiatric clinic serve for drama in this filmization of William Gibson's novel. The screenplay gives a wordy account of the controversy around the hanging of a new set of drapes in the clinic's library, and the reactions of staff and patients sometimes make one wonder if the two should not be reversed. Screen newcomers Kerr and Susan Strasberg, fellow patients, are responsible for one of the few touching sequences in the film—the simple act of him looking after her on a trip to a film theater has a great deal of heart, an ingredient generally lacking in the footage.

COBWEB CASTLE
See: Kumonosu-jo

COCA-COLA KID, THE
1985, 94 mins, Australia Ⓥ ⊙
D: Dusan Makavejev **A:** Eric Roberts, Greta Scacchi, Bill Kerr, Chris Haywood, Kris McQuade, Max Gillies (Cinema Enterprises/Smart Egg)

Mix of earthy symbolism, offbeat eroticism, the picaresque, and the rough-and-tumble, social, rather unpolitical satire seems poured from a bottle that has been left uncapped overnight. Georgian Becker, played by Eric Roberts, finds the Coca-Cola dry spot on Australia's map in a remote area where a land baron (Bill Kerr, playing a Colonel Sanders look-alike) has enforced his own soda-pop monopoly on the population. The ensuing fight between two parties is complicated by a skirmish between Roberts and the local company secretary (Greta Scacchi).

COCKLESHELL HEROES
1955, 97 mins, UK Ⓥ ▱
D: Jose Ferrer **A:** Jose Ferrer, Trevor Howard, Victor Maddern, Anthony Newley, Walter Fitzgerald, Dora Bryan (Warwick/Columbia)

Operation Cockleshell was a campaign in miniature, employing only eight men of the Royal Marines who paddled four canoes into enemy waters and stuck limpet mines on Nazi boats. Actual assault is the suspense highlight of the yarn, but there's a wealth of admirably exploited incident in the buildup situations showing the volunteers in special training for this hazardous adventure.

COCKTAIL
1988, 104 mins, US Ⓥ ⊙
D: Roger Donaldson **A:** Tom Cruise, Bryan Brown, Elisabeth Shue, Lisa Banes, Laurence Luckinbill, Kelly Lynch (Touchstone/Interscope)

Tom Cruise hits Manhattan after a hitch in the army and immediately catches on as the hottest thing the uptown girls have seen in a saloon in years. Under Roger Donaldson's impeccably slick direction, film continually plays on Cruise's attractiveness, as women make goo-goo eyes at him throughout as he does his juggling act with liquor bottles, serves up drinks like a disco dancer, and charms his way through every situation.

COCOANUTS, THE
1929, 90 mins, US Ⓥ
D: Robert Florey, Joseph Santley **A:** Groucho Marx, Harpo Marx, Chico Marx, Zeppo Marx, Mary Eaton, Oscar Shaw (Paramount)

Cocoanuts is set in a Florida development hotel barren of guests. Groucho is the fast-thinking and talking boniface. Harpo does his work with craftsmanship. Chico has more of the comedy end than usually falls to this foil. Zeppo has to be straight here all of the while. Only Irving Berlin song of merit is the theme number, "When Our Dreams Come True."

COCOON
1985, 117 mins, US Ⓥ ⊙
D: Ron Howard **A:** Don Ameche, Wilford Brimley, Hume Cronyn, Brian Dennehy, Jack Gilford, Steve Guttenberg (20th Century-Fox/Zanuck-Brown)

A fountain-of-youth fable that imaginatively melds galaxy fantasy with the lives of aging mortals in a retirement home, *Cocoon* weaves a mesmerizing tale, a parable set among a pallid group of denizens shuffleboarding their twilight days away until a mysterious quartet of normal-looking visitors shows up on their Floridian shores. They are arrivals from another planet. Retirees, played by Don Ameche, Wilford Brimley, and Hume Cronyn one day discover cocoonlike shells and after a frolic in the water are soon diving in like 18-year-olds. The effect of rejuvenation on the gray people, the inevitable mania when the whole retirement hospital wants in on the public bath, and the effect of this on the plans of the visitors from outer space propel the feature toward a suspenseful, ironic conclusion.

1985: Best Supp. Actor (Don Ameche), Visual Effects

COCOON: THE RETURN
1988, 116 mins, US Ⓥ ⊙
D: Daniel Petrie **A:** Don Ameche, Wilford Brimley, Hume Cronyn, Steve Guttenberg, Maureen Stapleton, Jessica Tandy (Zanuck-Brown/20th Century-Fox)

Not altogether charmless, *Cocoon: The Return* still is far less enjoyable a seniorfolks fantasy than *Cocoon*. An overdose of bathos weighs down the sprightliness of the characters, resulting in a more maudlin than magic effort. Ameche, Gwen Verdon, and occasionally Hume Cronyn want to play funny and loose but are restrained by Daniel Petrie's direction, which too often is unfocused.

CODE OF SILENCE
1985, 101 mins, US Ⓥ ⊙
D: Andrew Davis **A:** Chuck Norris, Henry Silva, Bert Remsen, Molly Hagan, Joseph Guzaldo, Mike Genovese (Orion)

With 27 stuntmen and Chuck Norris in the credits, *Code of Silence* is a predictability cacophonous cops-and-crooks yarn that is actually quite good for the type.

UN COEUR EN HIVER
(A HEART IN WINTER)
1992, 104 mins, FRANCE Ⓥ ⊙
D: Claude Sautet **A:** Daniel Auteuil, Emmanuelle Beart, Andrea Dussolier, Elizabeth Bourgine, Myriam Boyer, Jean-Luc Bideau

Extremely subtle and intensely enjoyable, pic concentrates on Stephane (Daniel Auteuil) and Maxime (Andre Dusolier), partners in a small company that makes and repairs stringed instruments. Maxime suddenly confesses that he's in love with Camille (Emmanuelle Beart), a beautiful young violinist. Stephane's response is to ingratiate himself with the interloper, insinuating himself into her life. The picture unfolds against a background of achingly beautiful music (Maurice Ravel, under the direction of Philippe Sarde), and Beart convincingly acquits herself on the violin.

COFFY
1973, 91 mins, US 🎥 ⊙
D: Jack Hill **A:** Pam Grier, Booker Bradshaw, Robert DoQui, William Elliott, Allan Arbus, Sid Haig (American International)

Coffy is the story of a black tart, vengeance-minded, who sets out to kill everyone she holds responsible for her 11-year-old sister losing her mind from the dope habit. She blasts her victims, most of them lured into sex, with a shotgun that never misses. Pam Grier, a statuesque actress with a body she doesn't hesitate to show, is strongly cast.

COLD HEAVEN
1992, 105 mins, US 🎥 ⊙
D: Nicolas Roeg **A:** Theresa Russell, Mark Harmon, James Russo, Talia Shire, Will Patton (MCEG)

Infidelity has seldom offered as broad a canvas for torment and religious guilt as in *Cold Heaven,* a tortured study of love on the rocks that comes off like a jumbled bad dream. Theresa Russell stars as the restless wife of an unsuspecting surgeon (Mark Harmon). She gets involved with another doctor (James Russo) and plans to break things off with her husband during a Mexican business trip. Before she can do the deed, however, he's killed in a horrifying but oddly convenient boating accident. Or is he?

COLDITZ STORY, THE
1955, 97 mins, UK 🎥
D: Guy Hamilton **A:** John Mills, Eric Portman, Christopher Rhodes, Lionel Jeffries, Bryan Forbes, Ian Carmichael (Foxwell/British Lion)

Easily one of the best prisoner-of-war yarns to come from any British studio, *The Colditz Story* is a taut real-life meller. Colditz Castle was the fortress to which the German High Command sent officers who had attempted to escape from conventional prison camps. Eric Portman turns in a distinguished performance as the British colonel.

COLD ROOM, THE
1984, 92 mins, UK 🎥
D: James Dearden **A:** George Segal, Amanda Pays, Renee Soutendijk, Warren Clarke, Anthony Higgins, Ursula Howells (Jethro)

The Cold Room, a modestly intriguing psychological thriller, centers around an attractive if sulky British teenager (Amanda Pays), who joins her father (George Segal) for a vacation in (of all places) East Berlin. Spending time in her tiny room in an old-fashioned hotel, she gradually comes under the spell of another girl who lived in the same house during the war.

COLD WIND IN AUGUST, A
1961, 79 mins, US
D: Alexander Singer **A:** Lola Albright, Scott Marlowe, Herschel Bernardi, Joe De Santis, Clark Gordon, Janet Brandt (United Artists/Troy)

All the exceptional ability that went into *A Cold Wind in August* is leveled to the common denominator of its subject— a short course in the seduction, care, and feeding of a healthy 17-year-old boy by a nymphomaniacal 28-year-old stripper. This is a hormone opera of considerable quality. A factor in the film's visual impact is the extraordinarily active, inventive camerawork by Floyd Crosby.

COLLECTOR, THE
1965, 117 mins, US 🎥 ⊙
D: William Wyler **A:** Terence Stamp, Samantha Eggar, Maurice Dallimore, Mona Washbourne (Columbia)

As a character study of two persons— an inferiority-ridden young Englishman with an uncontrollable sex obsession and the young woman he abducts and holds prisoner in the cellar of his secluded farmhouse—the feature is adroitly developed and bears the stamp of class. Both Terence Stamp and Samantha Eggar turn in remarkably restrained performances under Wyler's guiding dramatic helmsmanship. Stamp makes his character of an insignificant London bank clerk entirely believable.

1965: Nominations: Best Director, Actress (Samantha Eggar), Adapted Screenplay

COLLEEN
1936, 89 mins, US
D: Alfred E. Green **A:** Dick Powell, Ruby Keeler, Jack Oakie, Joan Blondell, Hugh Herbert, Louise Fazenda (Warner)

An entertaining Dick Powell–Ruby Keeler musical romance which has greater cast than story or production strength. Story has Hugh Herbert, the eccentric, tak-

ing over a dress shop and putting Joan
Blondell in charge. Along comes Powell,
his nephew, who thinks the shop can be
made to pay. He puts Keeler in charge.
For Powell and Keeler it's the songs
mostly. Keeler has a bit the edge of it,
since she has Paul Draper, debuting on the
screen, as a dance partner, very light and
agile with the gams.

COLOR OF MONEY, THE
1986, 119 mins, US Ⓥ ⊙
D: Martin Scorsese **A:** Paul Newman,
Tom Cruise, Mary Elizabeth Mastranto-
nio, Helen Shaver, John Turturro, Bill
Cobbs (Touchstone)

Another inside look at society's outsiders from director Martin Scorsese. This
time out it's the subculture of professional
pool hustlers that consumes the screen
with a keenly observed and immaculately
crafted vision of the raw side of life. Pic
has a distinctive pulse of its own with exceptional performances by Paul Newman
and Tom Cruise. A reworking of Walter
Tevis's novel by scripter Richard Price,
The Color of Money is a continuation of
the 1961 film *The Hustler* 25 years later.
Back as Fast Eddie Felson, Paul Newman
is a self-proclaimed "student of human
moves"—a hustler. When he happens on
Vincent Lauria (Tom Cruise) in a nondescript midwest pool hall, Eddie's juices
start flowing and the endless cycle starts
again.
1986: Best Actor (Paul Newman)
Nominations: Best Supp. Actress (Mary
Elizabeth Mastrantonio), Adapted Screenplay, Art Direction

COLOR OF NIGHT
1994, 121 mins, US Ⓥ ⊙
D: Richard Rush **A:** Bruce Willis, Jane
March, Ruben Blades, Lesley Ann Warren, Scott Bakula, Brad Dourif (Holly-
wood/Cinergi)

Color of Night is a knuckleheaded
thriller. Pokey script centers upon New
York shrink Bill Capa (Bruce Willis), who
hies to L.A. after one of his patients takes
a swan dive out of his high-rise window.
His best friend, fellow head doctor Bob
Moore (Scott Bakula), is gruesomely
stabbed to death in his office. To spice
matters up, a lithe young thing named
Rose (Jane March) conveniently rear-ends
Capa one day, starting a hot affair. Motivation behind the murders is obscure at
best, and melodramatic climax is a joke.

COLOR PURPLE, THE
1985, 152 mins, US Ⓥ ⊙
D: Steven Spielberg **A:** Danny Glover,
Whoopi Goldberg, Margaret Avery, Oprah
Winfrey, Willard Pugh, Akosua Busia
(Amblin/Warner)

Steven Spielberg's turn at serious filmmaking is marred in more than one place
by overblown production that threatens to
drown in its own emotions. But there is
still much to applaud (and cry about) here.
Above all *The Color Purple* is a love story
between Celie and her sister, Nettie, from
whom she is separated at childhood, and,
later in life, between Celie and the blues
singer Shug Avery. Saving grace of the
film are the performances. As the adult
Celie, debuting Whoopi Goldberg uses her
expressive face and joyous smile to register the character's growth.
1985: Nominations: Best Picture, Actress
(Whoopi Goldberg), Supp. Actress (Margaret Avery, Oprah Winfrey), Adapted
Screenplay, Cinematography, Costume
Design, Art Direction, Original Score,
Song ("Miss Celie's Blues"), Makeup

COLORS
1988, 120 mins, US Ⓥ ⊙
D: Dennis Hopper **A:** Sean Penn, Robert
Duvall, Maria Conchita Alonso, Randy
Brooks, Grand Bush, Don Cheadle (Orion)

Colors is a solidly crafted depiction of
some current big-city horrors and succeeds
largely because of the Robert Duvall–Sean
Penn teaming as frontline cops. They're
terrific together as members of the gang
crime division of the LAPD. Plot takes
Duvall and Penn through investigation of
the latest offing of a "Blood" gang member by the rival "Crips" and shows the
police frustrations in working the case
against nearly insurmountable obstacles.

COLOSSUS OF NEW YORK, THE
1958, 70 mins, US
D: Eugene Lourie **A:** Ross Martin, Mala
Powers, Charles Herbert, Otto Kruger,
John Baragrey, Ed Wolff (Paramount)

Pretty hokey fare. The pièce de résistance is surgeon Otto Kruger's transplant
of a dead man's brain into the body of a
mechanical monster. But lacking a soul,
the mechanical man refuses to follow instructions and goes on a rampage.

COMA
1978, 113 mins, US Ⓥ ⊙
D: Michael Crichton **A:** Genevieve Bujold, Michael Douglas, Elizabeth Ashley,

Rip Torn, Richard Widmark, Lois Chiles (M-G-M)

Coma is an extremely entertaining suspense drama in the Hitchcock tradition. Director-adapter Michael Crichton neatly builds mystery and empathy around star Genevieve Bujold, a doctor who grows to suspect her superiors of deliberate surgical error. Michael Douglas also stars as her disbelieving lover.

COMANCHEROS, THE
1961, 107 mins, US ⓥ ▢
D: Michael Curtiz A: John Wayne, Stuart Whitman, Ina Balin, Nehemiah Persoff, Lee Marvin, Michael Ansara (20th Century-Fox)

A big, brash, uninhibited action western of the old school, set against the Texas of the mid-19th century, when the Comanches were on the warpath and renegade white men, or Comancheros, were aiding the Indian cause. The film relates the story of a Texas Ranger (John Wayne) and an itinerant gambler (Stuart Whitman) who team up to detect and destroy the renegade, parasitic society. Lee Marvin makes a vivid impression in a brief, but colorful role as a half-scalped, vile-tempered Comanchero agent.

COMANCHE STATION
1960, 74 mins, US ▢
D: Budd Boetticher A: Randolph Scott, Nancy Gates, Claude Akins, Skip Homeier, Richard Rust, Rand Brooks (Ranown/Columbia)

Comanche Station is by any standard a good picture. The dialogue is sparse, but colorful, and humor is not neglected. Randolph Scott plays one of those loners of the Old West, who is bringing back to her husband a settler's wife (Nancy Gates) who has been captured by Comanches. Accompanying them are a trio of bad ones, Claude Akins, Skip Homeier, and Richard Rust. Jeopardy is compounded from without by Comanches trailing the group. Charles Lawton Jr.'s camera catches some superb exteriors (there are no interior scenes at all).

COME BACK CHARLESTON BLUE
1972, 100 mins, US ⓥ
D: Mark Warren A: Godfrey Cambridge, Raymond St. Jacques, Peter De Anda, Percy Rodrigues, Jonelle Allen, Maxwell Glanville (Warner/Goldwyn)

Come Back Charleston Blue is an okay follow-up to *Cotton Comes to Harlem*, again featuring Godfrey Cambridge and Raymond St. Jacques as offbeat, comedic Harlem gumshoes. They find themselves caught between fading black drug king and mobster Maxwell Glanville, and Peter De Anda, ostensibly a successful photographer out to rid Harlem of drugs, but in reality eyeing the area for himself.

COME BACK, LITTLE SHEBA
1952, 95 mins, US ⓥ ⊙
D: Daniel Mann A: Burt Lancaster, Shirley Booth, Terry Moore, Richard Jaeckel, Philip Ober (Paramount)

The Broadway legit success *Come Back, Little Sheba* has become a potent piece of screen entertainment, faithful to the William Inge play. The story interest centers on the somewhat dull, middle-aged, and middle-class husband and wife portrayed by Lancaster and Booth. Their stodgy, routine existence is brightened when a student (Terry Moore) rents a room in their home.
1952: Best Actress (Shirley Booth)
Nominations: Best Supp. Actress (Terry Moore), Editing

COME BACK TO THE FIVE & DIME JIMMY DEAN, JIMMY DEAN
1982, 109 mins, US ⓥ ⊙
D: Robert Altman A: Sandy Dennis, Cher, Karen Black, Sudie Bond, Marta Heflin, Kathy Bates (Sandcastle 5)

Story is set in a small Texas town in 1975. Five women, who were part of a James Dean fan club, hold a 20th-anniversary reunion, in the local Woolworth's. Each offers her memories of the earlier time. The recollections are, at first, comical and innocent, but eventually the characters reveal their most painful secrets. The material is told with great emotion and Altman gets wonderful performances from his female ensemble.

COME BLOW YOUR HORN
1963, 112 mins, US ⓥ ▢
D: Bud Yorkin A: Frank Sinatra, Lee J. Cobb, Molly Picon, Barbara Rush, Jill St. John, Tony Bill (Paramount)

A superficial but diverting romp, concerned with two brothers at opposite extremities of bachelorhood, the older one (Frank Sinatra) ultimately passing into a more mature, responsible phase of life when he sees in his younger brother's (Tony Bill) sensual excesses the reflection of a ferocious personality no longer especially becoming or appealing to him. Lee J. Cobb steals the show as the explosively irascible old man forever appearing at his son's apartment when more glamorous company is expected.

1963: Nomination: Best Color Art Direction

COMEDIANS, THE
1967, 156 mins, US ▭

D: Peter Glenville **A:** Richard Burton, Elizabeth Taylor, Alec Guinness, Peter Ustinov, Paul Ford, Lillian Gish (M-G-M)

The life of people living under a despot may, indeed, be a sort of living death. Producer-director Peter Glenville's pic, scripted by Graham Greene, is a plodding, low-key, and eventually tedious melodrama. Not the least of film's flaws is the role played by Elizabeth Taylor (wife of South American ambassador Peter Ustinov), who has a recurring, deteriorating affair with hotel-owner Richard Burton.

COMEDY MAN, THE
1964, 92 mins, UK

D: Alvin Rakoff **A:** Kenneth More, Cecil Parker, Dennis Price, Billie Whitelaw, Norman Rossington, Angela Douglas (British Lion)

Douglas Hayes's lightweight novel about the struggle of a stock actor who has just passed the dangerous forties, without making the grade, hardly scratches new ground. But the authenticity and atmosphere are complete and this well-made little film recreates that atmosphere splendidly on the screen. A well-drawn performance by Kenneth More adds greatly to the entertainment value of the film.

COME FILL THE CUP
1951, 112 mins, US

D: Gordon Douglas **A:** James Cagney, Phyllis Thaxter, Raymond Massey, James Gleason, Gig Young, Selena Royle (Warner)

Warners has combined a grim study of alcoholism with a typical James Cagney drama. While Cagney scores dramatically in his study of an alcoholic, these phases haven't the commercial appeal of his later character as a reformed drunk who gets back into the newspaper game, rises to city editor, is forced to wet-nurse the publisher's nephew through a bourbon haze, and becomes involved with gangsters.

COME FLY WITH ME
1963, 107 mins, US ▭

D: Henry Levin **A:** Dolores Hart, Hugh O'Brian, Karl Boehm, Pamela Tiffin, Karl Malden, Lois Nettleton (M-G-M)

Sometimes one performance can save a picture and in *Come Fly with Me* it's an engaging and infectious one by Pamela Tiffin. Airline hostesses and their romantic pursuits provide the peg upon which William Roberts has constructed his erratic screenplay. Much of the film was shot in Paris and Vienna.

COME LIVE WITH ME
1941, 85 mins, US

D: Clarence Brown **A:** James Stewart, Hedy Lamarr, Ian Hunter, Verree Teasdale, Donald Meek, Barton MacLane (M-G-M)

It is a silly piece, never believable for a moment, and concerns itself with the beautiful young woman who meets up with the saddened young man and proposes a trick marriage in order that she may escape deportation. James Stewart tries his best to create some interest, but there are several passages where even he seems on the verge of giving up. Hedy Lamarr is quite as unhappy in her role, despite fine photographic portraiture and a little pout or two.

COMES A HORSEMAN
1978, 118 mins, US Ⓥ ▭

D: Alan J. Pakula **A:** James Caan, Jane Fonda, Jason Robards, George Grizzard, Richard Farnsworth, Jim Davis (United Artists/Chartoff-Winkler)

Comes a Horseman is so lethargic not even Jane Fonda, James Caan, and Jason Robards can bring excitement to this artificially dramatic story of a stubborn rancher who won't surrender to the local land baron. The real star of the film is a stretch of verdant land in Colorado known as the Wet Mountain Valley. The only really good part is Richard Farnsworth's Dodger. He's an altogether sympathetic character, close to the land.

1978: Nomination: Best Supp. Actress (Richard Farnsworth)

COME SEE THE PARADISE
1990, 138 mins, US Ⓥ ⊙

D: Alan Parker **A:** Dennis Quaid, Tamlyn Tomita, Sab Shimono, Shizuko Hoshi, Stan Egi, Ronald Yamamoto (20th Century-Fox)

In Alan Parker's richly mounted romantic saga of the Second World War relocation camps, the Asian-American cast is exemplary and Dennis Quaid has never been better. Noble if overlong effort depicts the love affair between the Irish-American labor activist and a woman from a well-established Japanese family ripped from its Los Angeles roots. In general,

Parker avoids most of the complexities behind the internment in favor of a broad, sentimental tale that emphasizes emotions.

COME SEPTEMBER
1961, 112 mins, US ▭
D: Robert Mulligan A: Rock Hudson, Gina Lollobrigida, Sandra Dee, Bobby Darin, Walter Slezak, Brenda de Banzie (Universal)

A rich US businessman (Rock Hudson), who ordinarily spends only the month of September at his Italian villa, abruptly puts in a July appearance to the dismay of his enterprising major domo (Walter Slezak), who has been converting the private abode into a very public hotel for 11 months out of every year. Too often, the writers seem inclined to telegraph, repeat, and pile it on. Hudson comes through with an especially jovial performance. Gina Lollobrigida need just stand there to generate sparks, but here she abets her eye-to-eye appeal with plenty of comedy savvy. Slezak is excellent.

COMFORT AND JOY
1984, 90 mins, UK ⓥ
D: Bill Forsyth A: Bill Paterson, Roberto Bernardi, Eleanor David, Clare Grogan, Patrick Malahide, Rikki Fulton (Kings Road)

Director-scripter Bill Forsyth again sets up a wacko scenario about zany, off-center characters. But after evoking much laughter over an unexpectedly funny couple living together, Forsyth abruptly switches into a more conventional plot. Pic opens with a well-dressed kleptomaniac (Eleanor David) lifting goods at a department store, followed by a man (Bill Paterson). It turns out he's her lover and aware of her stealing. David and Paterson are terrific together and almost every line between them is a joy. From the point she departs with no explanation, the pic flashes a sparky moment or two, but it doesn't reach the high spots again.

COMFORT OF STRANGERS, THE
1990, 107 mins, Italy/US ⓥ ⊙
D: Paul Schrader A: Christopher Walken, Rupert Everett, Natasha Richardson, Helen Mirren (Erre/Sovereign)

Neither the beguiling romance of Venice nor the undraped bodies of Natasha Richardson and Rupert Everett can disguise the hollowness. Among the many Venetian souls smitten by Everett's Apollonian magnetism is Robert (Christopher Walken), the grave, courtly son of an Italian diplomat. Unbeknownst to the English tourists, Walken has been photographing Everett obsessively since their arrival. The couple are easy prey for Walken's blandishments. Undermined by the script, the actors are constantly upstaged by the timeless glories of Venice.

COMING HOME
1978, 126 mins, US ⓥ ⊙
D: Hal Ashby A: Jane Fonda, Jon Voight, Bruce Dern, Robert Ginty, Penelope Milford, Robert Carradine (United Artists)

Coming Home is an excellent film which illuminates the conflicting attitudes on the Vietnam debacle from the standpoint of three participants. Gung-ho marine officer Dern goes to Vietnam while loyal wife Fonda decides to work in a veterans' hospital, where she meets high-school classmate Voight, now an embittered cripple from the war. Voight's character evolves as he and Fonda become lovers. A sex scene between the two is a masterpiece of discreet eroticism. Dern's character is the trigger for certain major events, but there remains enough exposure for him to be convincing as a career soldier disillusioned by Vietnam.
1978: Best Actor (Jon Voight), Actress (Jane Fonda), Original Screenplay
Nominations: Best Picture, Director, Supp. Actor (Bruce Dern), Supp. Actress (Penelope Milford), Editing

COMING TO AMERICA
1988, 116 mins, US ⓥ ⊙
D: John Landis A: Eddie Murphy, Arsenio Hall, John Amos, James Earl Jones, Shari Headley, Eriq LaSalle (Paramount)

Coming to America starts with a bathroom joke, quickly followed by a gag about private parts, then wanders in search of something equally original for Eddie Murphy to do for another couple of hours. It's a true test for loyal fans. Murphy has no difficulty creating a pampered young prince of Zamunda who would like a chance to live a little real life and select his own bride instead of being forced into a royal marriage of convenience. He and courtly sidekick Arsenio Hall venture to Queens to find a queen.
1988: Nominations: Best Costume Design, Makeup

COMMAND, THE
1954, 94 mins, US
D: David Butler A: Guy Madison, Joan Weldon, James Whitmore, Carl Benton

Reid, Harvey Lembeck, Ray Teal (Warner)

The first feature western under the CinemaScope label, *The Command* has a fundamentally sound cavalry-vs.-Indians plot and highly charged action footage. Guy Madison turns in a thoroughly able job of the heroics as an army medical captain unexpectedly assuming command of a cavalry troop. Story is concerned with how he improvises battle tactics to defeat attacking Indians.

COMMAND DECISION
1948, 111 mins, US Ⓥ
D: Sam Wood **A:** Clark Gable, Walter Pidgeon, Van Johnson, Brian Donlevy, Charles Bickford, John Hodiak (M-G-M)

Command Decision is a literate war drama, presented with a class touch. Clark Gable walks off with a picture in which everyone in the cast stands out. His is a believable delivery, interpreting the brigadier general who must send his men out to almost certain death with an understanding that bespeaks his sympathy with the soldier—brass or dogface.

COMMANDO
1985, 88 mins, US Ⓥ ⊙
D: Mark L. Lester **A:** Arnold Schwarzenegger, Rae Dawn Chong, Dan Hedaya, Vernon Wells, David Patrick Kelly, Alyssa Milano (Silver/20th Century-Fox)

The fetching surprise is the glancing humor between the quixotic and larky Rae Dawn Chong and the straight-faced killing machine of Arnold Schwarzenegger. Chong lights up the film like a firefly, Schwarzenegger delivers a certain light touch of his own, the result is palatable action comics.

COMMANDOS STRIKE AT DAWN, THE
1942, 100 mins, US Ⓥ
D: John Farrow **A:** Paul Muni, Anna Lee, Lillian Gish, Cedric Hardwicke, Robert Coote, Ray Collins (Columbia)

An exciting tale of the bloodless Nazi subjugation of the people of Norway and the spirit that prompts a group of Nordics to break the grip of Hitlerian despotism. Paul Muni portrays the Nordic fisherman who leads the movement and ultimately the commando expedition. His is a forthright performance, occasionally underplayed, but always ringing true.

COMMITMENTS, THE
1991, 116 mins, US/UK Ⓥ ⊙
D: Alan Parker **A:** Robert Arkins, Michael Aherne, Angeline Ball, Maria Doyle, Johnny Murphy, Andrew Strong (Beacon/First Film/Dirty Hands)

Story of a band of young Dubliners playing sixties American soul is fresh, well executed, and original. Based on the novel by Roddy Doyle, film tells the story of 21-year-old entrepreneur Jimmy Rabbitte (Robert Arkins), who envisions bringing soul music to Dublin. He pieces together a 10-piece outfit with real musical potential from among his raw or semitalented contemporaries. Constant friction among players means Jimmy spends much of his energy trying to hold the band together long enough to land at least one paying gig and pay off the rogue from whom he's more or less stolen the equipment.

1991: Nomination: Best Editing

COMO AGUA PARA CHOCOLATE (LIKE WATER FOR CHOCOLATE)
1992, 144 mins, Mexico Ⓥ ⊙
D: Alfonso Arau **A:** Lumi Cavazos, Marco Leonardi, Regine Torne John, Mario Ivan Martinez, Ada Carrasco, Claudette Maille

Strong material has been wasted by inept filmmaking. Feature suffers from an in-your-face approach to direction, with the entire story told mostly in close-up. Tita (Lumi Cavazos) is part of a family tradition where the youngest daughter is denied matrimony in order to care for her mother in her old age. When Pedro Muzquiz (Marco Leonardi) comes to ask for Tita's hand, he's offered her elder sister Rosaura, and he accepts so that he can be close to Tita, who is the cook at the hacienda. The film chronicles this sweeping, lifelong romance, an impossible love consummated only through the meals Tita prepares. She pours so much love into her quail-with-rose-petal dish that everyone at the table has an orgasm, and one of her sisters even catches on fire. [Version reviewed is director's original cut. Pic was subsequently released in Mexico at 114 mins. and in the U.S. at 106 mins.]

COMPANY BUSINESS
1991, 98 mins, US Ⓥ ⊙
D: Nicholas Meyer **A:** Gene Hackman, Mikhail Baryshnikov, Kurtwood Smith, Terry O'Quinn, Daniel Von Bargen, Oleg Rudnick (M-G-M)

This muddled comedic thriller, which asks what spies do after the cold war, has a few amusing political references but the indecisive tone scuttles the film. Gene Hackman plays a former CIA agent drafted by the company to return a former Soviet mole (Mikhail Baryshnikov) to the Soviets along with $2 million in Colombian drug booty. The swap goes bad, however, sending the two former spies racing around Europe.

COMPANY OF STRANGERS, THE
1990, 100 mins, Canada Ⓥ
D: Cynthia Scott **A:** Alice Diabo, Constance Garneau, Winifred Holden, Cissy Meddings, Mary Meigs, Catherine Roche (NFBC)

The seventh in the National Film Board of Canada series where nonactors play themselves in a fictitious setting, *The Company of Strangers* features seven elderly women marooned in an abandoned country house near an idyllic lake after their bus breaks down. A safe quiet journey becomes an adventure in survival, and in their quest for food they rediscover the hunger of youth. Pacing is slow and Hollywood-style action nonexistent. Entire story revolves around the women's lives, secrets, fears, and joys.

COMPANY OF WOLVES, THE
1984, 95 mins, UK Ⓥ ◉
D: Neil Jordan **A:** Angela Lansbury, David Warner, Stephen Rea, Tusse Silberg, Sarah Patterson, Graham Crowden (ITC/Palace)

Admirably attempting an adult approach to traditional fairy-tale material, *The Company of Wolves* nevertheless represents an uneasy marriage between old-fashioned storytelling and contemporary screen explicitness. Virtually the entire film is the dream of the gravely beautiful adolescent Sarah Patterson.

COMPETITION, THE
1980, 129 mins, US Ⓥ ◉
D: Joel Oliansky **A:** Richard Dreyfuss, Amy Irving, Lee Remick, Sam Wanamaker, Ty Henderson, James B. Sikking (Columbia/Rastar)

Richard Dreyfuss, an aging piano wunderkind, is reunited at a San Francisco music competition with Amy Irving, a less driven but more gifted young woman he had impressed briefly at an earlier festival. She tries to rekindle their attraction, but Dreyfuss is too absorbed in his music at first to respond. The film is tedious and predictable, curiously portraying music as a grim and joyless profession for these youngsters.
1980: Nominations: Best Editing, Song ("People Alone")

COMPROMISING POSITIONS
1985, 98 mins, US Ⓥ ◉
D: Frank Perry **A:** Susan Sarandon, Raul Julia, Edward Herrmann, Judith Ivey, Mary Beth Hurt, Joe Mantegna (Paramount)

Falling midway between a campy send-up of suburban-wives soap operas and a legitimate thriller, *Compromising Positions*, from the 1978 novel by Susan Isaacs, emerges as a silly little whodunit. Unlikely material, about the murder of a philandering Long Island dentist, the reactions of his many mistresses, and the official and unofficial investigations into it, has hardly been approached with a straight face. Upper-middle-class housewife Susan Sarandon undertakes some amateur sleuthing. Sarandon is, as always, highly watchable.

COMPULSION
1959, 103 mins, US ▱
D: Richard Fleischer **A:** Orson Welles, Dean Stockwell, Bradford Dillman, Diane Varsi, E. G. Marshall, Martin Milner (20th Century-Fox)

Compulsion, from Meyer Levin's novel, is almost a literal case study of the notorious Leopold-Loeb murder of Bobby Franks. The two protagonists, here called Artie and Judd, both have highly neurotic, seething minds bent on destruction as twisted proof of their superiority. That the boys have a homosexual relationship is quite clear, though the subject is not overstressed. Both come from wealthy families that spoiled them. In court, lawyer Orson Welles pleads for their life in the same idiom that Clarence Darrow used to save Nathan Leopold Jr. and Richard Loeb from the Illinois gallows.

COMPUTER WORE TENNIS SHOES, THE
1970, 90 mins, US Ⓥ
D: Robert Butler **A:** Kurt Russell, Cesar Romero, Joe Flynn, William Schallert, Alan Hewitt, Richard Bakalyan (Walt Disney)

The amusing premise of *The Computer Wore Tennis Shoes* is that of a college nonstudent who, via an electrical accident, becomes brilliant because a computer memory bank has been transferred into his brain. Good-looking production is above-average family entertainment.

COMRADES
A LANTERNIST'S ACCOUNT OF THE TOLPUDDLE MARTYRS AND WHAT BECAME OF THEM
1987, 160 mins, UK Ⓥ
D: Bill Douglas **A:** Robin Soans, William

Gaminara, Stephen Bateman, Philip Davis, Jeremy Flynn, Keith Allen (British Film Institute)

Bill Douglas has an eye for fresh detail, the rituals of rural life, and the dignity of country folk. Rarely before have the poverty, the pains, and the pleasures, the oppressiveness of the work routine, even of the weather, been so well conveyed on film. Eventually one pieces together that the Tolpuddle Martyrs, film's subject, were a small group of peasant craftsmen who dared to form a union and ask for higher wages. It's a pity that more ruthlessness in scripting and editing was not exercised.

COMRADE X
1940, 87 mins, US
D: King Vidor **A:** Clark Gable, Hedy Lamarr, Oscar Homolka, Felix Bressart, Eve Arden, Natasha Lytess (M-G-M)

Action is laid in Russia, with Clark Gable, a love-'em-and-leave-'em, elbow-bending American reporter cutting a wide swath as a carefree Lothario and outwitter of the censors in coding stories through to the outside. Felix Bressart, hotel porter, threatens exposure unless Gable gets Bressart's daughter out of the country immediately. Matter-of-fact agreement of the girl to the plan, with ritual of typical Russian marriage ceremony and her quick breakdown under Gable's embraces, sets the stage for a continual series of laugh situations before the pair finally gets out of the country.
1940: Nomination: Best Original Story

CON AIR
1997, 115 mins, US
D: Simon West **A:** Nicolas Cage, John Cusack, John Malkovich, Steve Buscemi, Ving Rhames, Colm Meaney (Touchstone)

Apart from not knowing to quit while it's ahead, *Con Air* provides quite an exciting flight prior to its crash and burn. Army ranger Cameron Poe (Nicolas Cage), unjustly imprisoned for eight years for a killing, is a man of honor. The plane on which he catches a ride home is a US Marshals Service transport with a passenger list consisting of "every creep and freak in the universe." Chief among them is Cyrus "The Virus" Grissom (John Malkovich), a certifiably insane but brilliant master criminal. The prisoners take over the plane, and on the ground, US Marshal Vince Larkin (John Cusack) does his best to keep up with what's going on in the air.

Pic sustains a number of levels of tension during the flight, but the picture deflates during the utterly overdone and needless climax-upon-a-climax.
1997: Nominations: Best Original Song ("How Do I Live"), Sound

CONAN THE BARBARIAN
1982, 129 mins, US
D: John Milius **A:** Arnold Schwarzenegger, James Earl Jones, Max von Sydow, Sandahl Bergman, Mako, Gerry Lopez (De Laurentiis)

Child Conan witnesses the brutal deaths of his father and mother at the whim of the evil Thulsa Doom (James Earl Jones). Conan Jr. grows up as a slave who eventually has the good fortune of turning into Arnold Schwarzenegger. On the road he meets up with a fellow drifter (Gerry Lopez), beautiful cohort and eventual lover Sandahl Bergman, needy king Max von Sydow, and goofy wizard Mako. The script by Milius and Oliver Stone is nothing more than a series of meaningless adventures and ambiguous references until the final expected confrontation with Jones.

CONAN THE DESTROYER
1984, 103 mins, US
D: Richard Fleischer **A:** Arnold Schwarzenegger, Grace Jones, Wilt Chamberlain, Mako, Tracey Walter, Sarah Douglas (De Laurentiis/Pressman)

Conan the Destroyer is the ideal sword-and-sorcery picture. Conan is recruited by sexy queen Sarah Douglas to accompany teenage princess Olivia D'Abo to a distant castle. Along the way, group also picks up fiery warrioress Grace Jones. As Conan, Arnold Schwarzenegger seems more animated and much funnier under Fleischer's direction than he did under John Milius in the original. Jones just about runs off with the picture. The singer throws herself into her wild woman role with complete abandon.

CONCIERGE, THE
See: For Love or Money

CONCORDE—AIRPORT '79, THE (UK: AIRPORT '80—THE CONCORDE; AKA: AIRPORT—THE CONCORDE)
1979, 123 mins, US
D: David Lowell Rich **A:** Alain Delon, Susan Blakely, Robert Wagner, Sylvia Kristel, George Kennedy, Eddie Albert (Paramount)

Unintentional comedy still seems the *Airport* series' forte, although excellent special-effects work and some decent dramatics help *Concorde* take off. Title entity is pursued by electronic missile, avoids an attack by a fighter jet, barely makes a runway landing, suffers a lost cargo door, manages a crash landing, and explodes just as its chic passengers disembark. That's all just part of a couple of days' work for pilots George Kennedy, Alain Delon, and flight engineer David Warner.

CONDEMNED OF ALTONA, THE
1963, 112 mins, Italy ▱
D: Vittorio De Sica **A:** Sophia Loren, Maximilian Schell, Fredric March, Robert Wagner, Francoise Prevost (Titanus)

Filmed on location in Hamburg, with interiors in Italy, this tale of postwar Germany, as symbolized by the members of one family, is undoubtedly anti-German. Loren creates a shudderingly magnificent portrait of a beautiful, intelligent woman just beginning to recover her dignity and self-respect from the shambles of her country's militaristic past, only to have them threatened by "secrets" of her husband's family.

CONDUCT UNBECOMING
1976, 107 mins, US ⓥ
D: Michael Anderson **A:** Michael York, Richard Attenborough, Trevor Howard, Stacy Keach, Christopher Plummer, Susannah York (Lion/Crown)

Based on a play by Barry England, this has all the ingredients of good, slightly old-fashioned courtroom drama transposed to 19th-century, British-dominated India to give it an added dimension. Basically, action centers around a secret trial by his fellow officers of a young lieutenant accused of assaulting an officer's widow. Perhaps because of his seemingly offbeat casting as a British officer, it's Stacy Keach who surprises and steals acting honors.

CONEHEADS
1993, 88 mins, US ⓥ ⊙
D: Steve Barron **A:** Dan Aykroyd, Jane Curtin, Michelle Burke, Michael McKean, Jason Alexander, Lisa Jane Persky (Paramount)

Cones phone home. Those *Saturday Night Live* cranial wonders have arrived on the big screen, and the result is a sweet, funny, anarchic pastiche that transcends the one-joke territory it inhabited on television. Aykroyd and Curtin have evolved their cartoonish TV-skit characters into figures whose robotlike demeanor just barely hides emotions sparked by human contact. As their daughter Connie, Mich-

elle Burke also proves herself to be both a face and brow to watch.

CONEY ISLAND
1943, 95 mins, US
D: Walter Lang **A:** Betty Grable, George Montgomery, Cesar Romero, Phil Silvers, Charles Winninger (20th Century-Fox)

The true Coney Island, corny, bawdy, and brash, evidently wasn't deemed sufficiently colorful for George Seaton, scripter of this film, so he just hung the title on what amounts to a 95-minute audition of Betty Grable's chassis and legs in color. Only in one musical number is Grable a boff, and that's her brown-skin takeoff of "Miss Lulu from Louisville," a pictorial review of derriere exercising.

CONFESSIONAL, THE
See: Le Confessional

LE CONFESSIONAL
(THE CONFESSIONAL)
1995, 100 mins, Canada/UK/France ⓥ
D: Robert Lepage **A:** Lothaire Bluteau, Patrick Goyette, Jean-Louis Millette, Kristin Scott Thomas, Ron Burrage, Richard Frechette (Cinemaginaire/Enigma/Cinea)

Lepage starts with the intriguing idea of setting story partly in Quebec City in 1952, where Alfred Hitchcock was lensing *I Confess*. Film contains several scenes from the Hitchcock original. Throughout, Lepage keeps viewers on their toes by cutting between events in the early fifties and 1989, when lead character Pierre Lamontagne (Lothaire Bluteau) returns to his native Quebec City for his father's funeral. Pic keeps coming back to the making of *I Confess*, as Hitchcock's assistant (Kristin Scott Thomas) negotiates with local church authorities, arranges auditions for the director, and generally fails to communicate adequately with the French-speaking locals.

CONFESSIONS OF A NAZI SPY
1939, 110 mins, US
D: Anatole Litvak **A:** Edward G. Robinson, Francis Lederer, George Sanders, Paul Lukas, Lya Lys (Warner)

Based on articles by Leon G. Turrou, former G-man, film is an adaptation of the spy trials of 1937 which resulted in the conviction of four persons. Its thesis is that espionage directed from Berlin is tied up with the German-American Bunds, their rallies and summer camps and general parading around in uniforms. The German goal is destruction of democracy. The missing motivation, anti-Semitism, is the one thing not named and ticketed.

CONFIDENTIAL AGENT
1945, 113 mins, US
D: Herman Shumlin A: Charles Boyer, Lauren Bacall, Wanda Hendrix, Peter Lorre, Katina Paxinou, George Coulouris (Warner)

Charles Boyer has given up his career to fight the fascists. He's detailed to go to England and outbid the Francoites for British coal. Secondary to this is the romance that evolves between a British coal tycoon's daughter and Boyer. Boyer, as usual, underplays to gain an effect. Lauren Bacall suffers from a monotony of voice and an uncertainty of performance. Her s.a., however, is still plenty evident.

CONFIDENTIAL REPORT
(US: MR. ARKADIN)
1955, 99 mins, France/Spain Ⓥ ⊙
D: Orson Welles A: Orson Welles, Michael Redgrave, Patricia Medina, Akim Tamiroff, Robert Arden, Paola Mori (Filmorsa)

Confidential Report is at once a fascinating (inevitably) and dismaying effort, frequently suggestive of self-parody; and indeed, in scenario and technique, it is an echo of *Kane* and that film's bravura style. Instead of newspaper tycoon Charles Foster Kane, here is Gregory Arkadin, shadow figure, arch-capitalist, graduate of a Polish white slave ring, but whose latter-day power and riches are shrouded. The mélange of darting narrative simply gets the upper hand—a case of visual virtuosity overwhelming the Arkadin parable.

CONFLICT
1945, 86 mins, US Ⓥ
D: Curtis Bernhardt A: Humphrey Bogart, Alexis Smith, Sydney Greenstreet, Rose Hobart, Charles Drake (Warner)

A convincing study of a murderer driven to revealing his crime by psychological trickery. Bogart, married to Rose Hobart, is in love with her younger sister (Alexis Smith). When his wife, aware of misplaced affection, begins to nag, Bogart plots to murder and nearly accomplishes the perfect crime. Bogart gives a heavy role convincing reading. Sydney Greenstreet is creditably restrained as the psychiatrist and family friend.

CONFORMIST, THE
See: Il Conformista

IL CONFORMISTA
(THE CONFORMIST)
1970, 108 mins, Italy/France/W. Germany Ⓥ ⊙
D: Bernardo Bertolucci A: Jean-Louis Trintignant, Stefania Sandrelli, Dominique Sanda, Enzo Tarascio, Pierre Clementi, Gastone Moschin (Mars/Marianne/Maran)

Bertolucci's free adaptation of Alberto Moravia's book *The Conformist* is the story of a coward. Marcello (Jean-Louis Trintignant) is sent to Paris by the fascist espionage organization he's joined and ordered to murder a leftist political refugee, but procrastinates, his mind riddled with doubts and fears, his body attracted by the intended victim's pretty wife. Windup is redundant, and the weakest factor in an otherwise very satisfying powerful film.

CONGO
1995, 108 mins, US Ⓥ ⊙
D: Frank Marshall A: Laura Linney, Dylan Walsh, Ernie Hudson, Tim Curry, Grant Heslov, Joe Don Baker (Paramount)

Michael Crichton's bestseller is the only ostensible star in *Congo*, so it's surprising the book doesn't receive better treatment. Dumbed down considerably, the movie is opulent and action-packed but doesn't provide the thrills or suspense those who have read it will doubtless expect. The filmmakers clearly hoped that mountain gorilla Amy—wide-eyed and marvelously expressive as realized by Stan Winston (*Jurassic Park*)—emerges as the film's star. The ape is indeed an impressive technical achievement, but she provides only a few scenes adorable enough to justify the trip.

CONGRESS DANCES
See: Der Kongress Tanzt

CONNECTICUT YANKEE, A
1931, 93 mins, US Ⓥ
D: David Butler A: Will Rogers, William Farnum, Myrna Loy, Maureen O'Sullivan, Frank Albertson, Mitchell Harris (Fox)

Opening has Will Rogers as a small-town radio store proprietor, called to a mysterious house to install a battery. An armored figure falls over, knocks Rogers out, and thence into the dream. The change back to the modern story and finish is decidedly weak. Support comes from William Farnum as King Arthur, Mitchell Harris as Merlin, the magician, and Brandon Hurst playing the menace. Myrna Loy does not do much with her femme heavy, while Maureen O'Sullivan has nothing much more than a bit.

CONNECTICUT YANKEE IN KING ARTHUR'S COURT, A
(UK: A YANKEE IN KING ARTHUR'S COURT)
1949, 106 mins, US Ⓥ ⊙
D: Tay Garnett A: Bing Crosby, Rhonda Fleming, Cedric Hardwicke, William Bendix, Henry Wilcoxon (Paramount)

Bing Crosby, songs, and color make pleasant entertainment. It's not high comedy and there's little swashbuckling, but it is pleasant. A footnote emphasizes that this latest version of Mark Twain's gentle tale of a Yankee blacksmith who's knocked on the head and awakes in King Arthur's court is adapted strictly from the book as written by the author.

CONQUEROR, THE
1956, 111 mins, US Ⓥ ▭
D: Dick Powell A: John Wayne, Susan Hayward, Pedro Armendariz, Agnes Moorehead, Thomas Gomez, William Conrad (RKO)

The viewer can sit back and thoroughly enjoy a huge, brawling, sex-and-sand actioner purporting to show how a 12th-century Mongol leader became known as Genghis Khan. The marquee value of the John Wayne–Susan Hayward teaming more than offsets any incongruity of the casting, which has him as the Mongol leader and she as the Tartar princess he captures and forcibly takes as mate.

CONQUEROR WORM, THE
See: Witchfinder General

CONQUEST
(UK: MARIE WALEWSKA)
1937, 115 mins, US Ⓥ
D: Clarence Brown A: Greta Garbo, Charles Boyer, Reginald Owen, Alan Marshall, Henry Stephenson, Leif Erickson (M-G-M)

With Greta Garbo and Charles Boyer in the characters of Marie Walewska, Polish mistress, and Napoleon Bonaparte, lover and soldier, the film is a romantic mixture of fact and fiction. Intensely emotional in spots, it is a moving and satisfying entertainment. Walewska role would seem to be a natural for Garbo. Part calls for intense feminine feeling, for coquetry and renunciation. It is not due to any shortcomings on her part, however, that the audience interest is more closely held by Boyer's Napoleon. Boyer plays the love scenes with brusque tenderness, and makes the character understood as a blazing individualist acting under reckless urges for power.
1937: Nominations: Best Actor (Charles Boyer), Art Direction

CONQUEST OF SPACE
1955, 80 mins, US Ⓥ
D: Byron Haskin A: Walter Brooke, Eric Fleming, Mickey Shaughnessy, Phil Foster, William Redfield, William Hopper (Paramount)

Plot time is the future, with the setting divided between a space station wheeling some 1,000 miles above earth and a flight from this floating base to the planet Mars. Best moments deal with a meteor hitting the space station and spilling everything before the wheel is righted, and the near crash of the rocket ship with a meteor on the trip to Mars. The rocket ship is manned by a stereotype crew. The real stars are the props and lensing.

CONQUEST OF THE PLANET OF THE APES
1972, 87 mins, US Ⓥ ▭
D: J. Lee Thompson A: Roddy McDowall, Don Murray, Ricardo Montalban, Natalie Trundy, Hari Rhodes, Severn Darden (20th Century-Fox/Apjac)

The *Planet of the Apes* series takes an angry turn in the fourth entry. The story begins about 20 years in the future, after a world epidemic has destroyed all dogs. People first had turned to apes as pets, but because of their intelligence, the apes have become servants under civil regulation of computer-age overseer Don Murray. A bloody revolt occupies the last third of the film.

CONRACK
1974, 107 mins, US Ⓥ ▭
D: Martin Ritt A: Jon Voight, Paul Winfield, Madge Sinclair, Tina Andrews, Antonio Fargas, Hume Cronyn (20th Century-Fox)

Jon Voight stars as a young southerner who treks off to an isolated South Carolina island in 1969 for a teaching post, only to find the black children there uniformly illiterate and/or retarded. Through a combination of love and pedagogical razzmatazz, he opens their eyes to the wonders of yoga, Beethoven, Babe Ruth, Ho Chi Minh, and Halloween. Few will totally resist the surefire appeal of this latest variation on Pygmalion myth.

CONSENTING ADULTS
1992, 100 mins, US ⊗ ⊙
D: Alan J. Pakula **A:** Kevin Kline, Mary Elizabeth Mastrantonio, Kevin Spacey, Rebecca Miller, Forest Whitaker, E. G. Marshall (Hollywood Pictures)

Psychotic neighbors are the latest riff on the urban paranoia theme. Most distinctive element here proves to be Kevin Spacey's over-the-top performance as the smarmy newcomer to the block, who ultimately lures his risk-aversive neighbor (Kevin Kline) into a proposed wife swap that leads to the baseball-bat murder of Spacey's wife (Rebecca Miller) as part of an elaborate insurance scam. Pic suffers from an absurdity level that somewhat undermines its chills as well as its few genuine laughs.

CONSPIRACY THEORY
1997, 135 mins, US
D: Richard Donner **A:** Mel Gibson, Julia Roberts, Patrick Stewart, Cylk Cozart (Silver/Warner)

Conspiracy Theory is a sporadically amusing but listless thriller that wears its humorous, romantic, and political components like mismatched articles of clothing. Wild-eyed New York cabbie Jerry Fletcher (Mel Gibson) rants about the diverse conspiracies being perpetrated by everyone in power and lusts for the lovely Alice Sutton (Julia Roberts) at the Justice Dept. He puts out a newsletter forwarding his theories and is interrogated by the deadly serious Dr. Jonas (Patrick Stewart). Jerry gets away, setting up the cat-and-mouse pursuit format, with Alice ricocheting between Jerry and the CIA in the remainder of the overlong film. Having done so many actioners, Donner seems to want to send up some of the genre's more tired elements.

CONSPIRATOR
1949, 83 mins, UK
D: Victor Saville **A:** Robert Taylor, Elizabeth Taylor, Robert Flemyng, Honor Blackman, Thora Hird, Wilfrid Hyde White (M-G-M)

Conspirator is a highly fanciful treatment of an obvious anti-Commie character. Major Michael Curragh, an officer in the Guards, passes on highly secret military information to "the party." The conflict, both emotional and mental, with his newly acquired young wife fails to reach the heights, and throughout the development there is neither powerful drama nor lurid melodrama. Robert Taylor gets

to grips with the starring role. Elizabeth Taylor comes out with flying colors.

CONSTANCE
1984, 103 mins, New Zealand ⊗
D: Bruce Morrison **A:** Donogh Rees, Shane Briant, Judie Douglass, Martin Vaughan, Donald MacDonald, Marc Wignall (Mirage)

A highly stylized film about a beautiful young woman living in Auckland in 1946 who dreams she is a Hollywood superstar. Constance (Donogh Rees) is given to such contrived charades as dressing as Marlene Dietrich at parties. Imported actor Shane Briant has the right air of handsome, predatory decadence as a visiting Hollywood still photographer.

CONSTANT HUSBAND, THE
1955, 88 mins, UK
D: Sidney Gilliat **A:** Rex Harrison, Margaret Leighton, Kay Kendall, Cecil Parker, Nicole Maurey, George Cole (London/British Lion)

A frothy comedy. Rex Harrison, an amnesia victim, learns, to his horror, that he has seven wives to his credit. A bigamy charge follows, but rather than face seven eager ex-spouses, he pleas in favor of jail. Harrison is thoroughly diverting as the amnesia victim. Kay Kendall, as the last of the seven wives, gives a sparkling portrayal.

CONSTANT NYMPH, THE
1928, 80 mins, UK ⊗
D: Adrian Brunel **A:** Mabel Poulton, Ivor Novello, George Heinrich, Dorothy Boyd, Frances Dable (Gainsborough)

Story is of a hoydenish group, children of a great composer who dies in his studio in the Austrian Tyrol. Later his most hoydenish daughter also dies. In between the picture dies. All of the charm of a tale of this kind has been spoiled. No attraction is left. If not the direction, it is the photography, and if neither, then the actors, excepting Ivor Novello. Mabel Poulton as Tessa, the little hoyden, who should look about 15, looks often 25, and again 35.

CONSTANT NYMPH, THE
1934, 85 mins, UK
D: Basil Dean **A:** Brian Aherne, Victoria Hopper, Peggy Blythe, Jane Baxter, Lyn Harding, Mary Clare (Gaumont-British)

Story opens in the Austrian mountains, where a slightly mad composer and his daughters live a carefree life of idyllic sweetness. There is a younger composer (Brian Aherne) and for him one of the girls (Victoria Hopper) conceives an undying passion. He marries a respectability-minded English cousin (Leonora Corbett). Ultimately he realizes he should have waited for the girl to add a year or two to her age and married her instead. It is a soft, delicate, fragile, meandering yarn, beautifully directed by Basil Dean.

CONSTANT NYMPH, THE
1943, 106 mins, US

D: Edmund Goulding **A:** Charles Boyer, Joan Fontaine, Alexis Smith, Charles Coburn, Peter Lorre, Joyce Reynolds (Warner)

A bumpy screen tale with interlay of both draggy and interesting sequences. Final event is a love triangle, with Charles Boyer the focal point for conflict betwen teenager played by Joan Fontaine and the older Alexis Smith. The stretch hits yawning periods. Script covers plenty of ground and detail, but general tightening would have helped materially.

1943: Nomination: Best Actress (Joan Fontaine)

CONTACT
1997, 150 mins, US Ⓥ ⊙ ▱

D: Robert Zemeckis **A:** Jodie Foster, Matthew McConaughey, James Woods, John Hurt, Tom Skerritt, William Fichtner (South Side Amusement/Warner)

More down-to-earth and ''realistic'' than most other Hollywood movies about an encounter with an alien intelligence, Robert Zemeckis's film places at least as much emphasis on science as on fiction, and proves quite an engrossing ride most of the way. It explores how contemporary society might react to the detection of signals from another world, and how the world might be changed by knowledge of extraterrestrials. Dr. Ellie Arroway (Jodie Foster) tunes into a broadcast emanating from the star Vega which proves to be a diagram for constructing a space capsule. The government finances the building of the enormous launch facility. Arroway gets a chance at the trip, with results that emphasize the possibility of a convergence between science and religious faith. *Contact* is not as incisive as it might have been in summarizing its concerns in nonverbal ways. Foster is excellent, very credible in her projection of innate intelligence, dedication to career, and banishment of any personal life.

1997: Nomination: Best Sound

CONTE D'ETE
(A SUMMER'S TALE)
1996, 113 mins, FRANCE Ⓥ

D: Eric Rohmer **A:** Melvil Poupaud, Amanda Langlet, Aurelia Nolin, Gwenaelle Simon (Menegoz/Films du Losange/La Sept)

A Summer's Tale is vintage Eric Rohmer, his most richly satisfying film in a number of outings, precisely and fully playing out the intimate implications of a chaste ménage à quatre. Pic intros Gaspard (Melvil Poupaud), a lean, bushy-haired kid, as he arrives for a vacation. It consists mostly of long scenes in which Gaspard and one of three girls walk along the beach talking of love, attraction, desire, their feelings about life, and other familiar Rohmer topics. The thoughts may not be profound, but they are profoundly true to life. As usual, the young thesps are appealing in their unaffectedness.

CONTEMPT
See: Le Mepris

CONTEST GIRL
See: The Beauty Jungle

CONTEXT, THE
See: Cadaveri Eccellenti

CONTINENTAL DIVIDE
1981, 103 mins, US Ⓥ ⊙

D: Michael Apted **A:** John Belushi, Blair Brown, Allen Garfield, Carlin Glynn, Tony Ganios, Val Avery (Universal/Amblin)

For a picture that you can't really believe for a second, *Continental Divide* still comes off as a reasonably engaging entertainment, thanks to some lively performances and a liberal dose of laughs throughout the script. John Belushi plays a star columnist who is sent to the Rocky Mountains to track down a crazy bird lady. At first, beauteous Blair Brown orders the interloper from her mountaintop retreat, but as his guide won't be back to fetch him for two weeks, they gradually learn to cope and, finally, love together. The problem is that these two don't seem made for each other.

CONTRABAND
(US: BLACKOUT)
1940, 91 mins, US Ⓥ

D: Michael Powell **A:** Conrad Veidt, Valerie Hobson, Hay Petrie, Joss Ambler, Raymond Lovell, Esmond Knight (British National)

As a dissertation on how to do nothing

well, film anent Britain's naval blockade earns a niche all its own. Producers have lavished their brainchild with a wealth of detail that takes care of all except one thing—imagination. This yarn of the economic war staged by the navy through its control of shipping veers from the sea to take a jaunt on espionage in London.

CONVERSATION, THE
1974, 113 mins, US Ⓥ ⊙
D: Francis Coppola **A:** Gene Hackman, John Cazale, Allen Garfield, Frederic Forrest, Cindy Williams, Harrison Ford (Paramount)

Francis Coppola's *The Conversation* stars Gene Hackman as a professional surveillance expert whose resurgent conscience involves him in murder and leads to self-destruction. What appears to be a simple case of marital infidelity suddenly shifts to a possible murder plot. A major artistic asset to the film besides script, direction and the top performances is supervising editor Walter Murch's sound collage and rerecording. Voices come in and out of aural focus in a superb tease.
1974: Nominations: Best Picture, Original Screenplay, Sound

CONVERSATION PIECE
1975, 120 mins, Italy/France Ⓥ
D: Luchino Visconti **A:** Burt Lancaster, Silvana Mangano, Helmut Berger, Claudia Marsani, Dominique Sanda, Claudia Cardinale (Rusconi/Gaumont)

Touching tale of the generation gap and the loss of life contact of an intellectual. A prof (Burt Lancaster) is addicted to collecting 18th-century British paintings of families called Conversation Pieces. Into this comes a haughty, beautiful Italian woman, her cute teenage daughter, and her rich fiancé. There is also the mother's lover, a young German (Helmut Berger). The professor gets tangled up with the young people despite himself.

CONVICTED
1950, 91 mins, US
D: Henry Levin **A:** Glenn Ford, Broderick Crawford, Millard Mitchell, Dorothy Malone, Ed Begley, Will Geer (Columbia)

Convicted isn't quite as grim a prison film as the title would indicate. It has several offbeat twists to its development. Glenn Ford is convicted of manslaughter after a man he has slugged in a barroom brawl dies. Crawford takes over as warden of the state pen and makes life more bearable for the young con.

CONVOY
1978, 110 mins, US Ⓥ ⊙ ▭
D: Sam Peckinpah **A:** Kris Kristofferson, Ali MacGraw, Ernest Borgnine, Burt Young, Madge Sinclair, Franklyn Ajaye (United Artists)

Sam Peckinpah's *Convoy* starts out as *Smokey and the Bandit,* segues into either *Moby Dick* or *Les Misérables,* and ends in the usual script confusion and disarray, the whole stew peppered with the vulgar excess of random truck crashes and miscellaneous destruction. Kris Kristofferson stars as a likable roustabout who accidentally becomes a folk hero, while Ali MacGraw recycles about three formula reactions throughout her nothing part.

COOGAN'S BLUFF
1968, 93 mins, US Ⓥ ⊙
D: Don Siegel **A:** Clint Eastwood, Lee J. Cobb, Susan Clark, Tisha Sterling, Don Stroud, Betty Field (Universal/Malpaso)

Clint Eastwood stars as a laconic, taciturn stranger, this time a deputy sheriff from Arizona sent to NY to extradite hippie Don Stroud. Lee J. Cobb, a city detective, tries to explain to Eastwood that things are done differently. Susan Clark is very good as a probation officer who falls for Eastwood.

COOKIE
1989, 93 mins, US Ⓥ ⊙
D: Susan Seidelman **A:** Peter Falk, Dianne Wiest, Emily Lloyd, Michael Gazzo, Brenda Vaccaro, Adrian Pasdar (Lorimar/Warner)

Half-baked, bland, and flat as a vanilla wafer, *Cookie* rolls out the tired marriage of comedy and organized crime to produce a disorganized mess with little nutritional or comedic value. The story gets set in motion, such as it is, when mobster Dino Capisco (Peter Falk) is released from prison after 13 years, rejoining his wife (Brenda Vaccaro), mistress (Dianne Wiest), and the headstrong daughter he had with the latter, played by Emily Lloyd. Only Wiest emerges in top form with her brassy portrayal of a weepy red-haired gun moll in the Lucille Ball mode.

COOKIE'S FORTUNE
1999, 118 mins, US Ⓥ ⊙
D: Robert Altman **A:** Glenn Close, Julianne Moore, Liv Tyler, Chris O'Donnell, Charles S. Dutton, Patricia Neal (Sandcastle 5/Elysian Dreams)

Cookie's Fortune may not be Robert Altman's best film in years, but it is certainly his most pleasurable. Distinguished by a generosity of spirit uncommon in the director's work, this is a wry melodrama about an eccentric family in a small Mississippi town. Middle-aged black man Willis (Charles S. Dutton) is caretaker for aged Jewel Mae "Cookie" Orcutt (Patricia Neal), who is still devoted to her late husband, Buck. Under way is a rehearsal for a production of *Salome,* directed by Jewel Mae's obsessive niece Camille (Glenn Close), and starring the latter's vacant younger sister, Cora (Julianne Moore). Willis goes to persuade Cora's daughter, Emma (Liv Tyler), to move in with Jewel Mae. In his absence, Jewel Mae joyfully shoots herself in order to be reunited with her beloved Buck. So begins a chain of behavior at once almost utterly absurd and yet intensely human.

COOK, THE THIEF, HIS WIFE & HER LOVER, THE
1989, 126 mins, Netherlands/France Ⓥ ⊙
D: Peter Greenaway **A:** Richard Bohringer, Michael Gambon, Helen Mirren, Alan Howard, Tim Roth, Liz Smith (Allarts/Erato/Films Inc)

Peter Greenaway's grim sense of humor and cheerful assault on all our sacred cows is evident in this new outing from the iconoclastic filmmaker. Setting is a smart restaurant where Richard, the chef (Richard Bohringer) prepares a lavish menu every night. Among his regular customers are Albert Spica (Michael Gambon), a loudmouthed, vulgar, violent gangster, and his bored, beautiful wife, Georgina (Helen Mirren). At another table each night sits Michael (Alan Howard), a quiet, diffident man. He and Georgina make eye contact, and soon they're having a series of secret rendezvous. Eventually Albert discovers his wife's infidelity and takes a typically violent revenge, triggering a more unusual retaliation from her.

COOL AND THE CRAZY, THE
1958, 78 mins, US
D: William Witney **A:** Scott Marlowe, Gigi Perreau, Dick Bakalyan, Dick Jones, Shelby Storck, Marvin J. Rosen (Imperial/American International)

The Cool and the Crazy is a low-budget exploitation item but it has the irritating itch of reality about it. Scott Marlowe plays the high-school student who drifts into pushing marijuana through his own use of the weed. He gets his classmates (Dick Bakalyan, Dick Jones, Robert Hadden, and Kenneth Plumb) to try the

stuff and almost gets them hooked, except for Bakalyan, who resists. Gigi Perreau is the nice young girl, whose good influence helps Bakalyan stay away from the marijuana.

COOLEY HIGH
1975, 107 mins, US Ⓥ ⊙
D: Michael Schultz **A:** Glynn Turman, Lawrence Hilton-Jacobs, Garrett Morris, Cynthia Davies (American International)

Cooley High is pitched as a black *American Graffiti,* and the description is apt. You don't have to be black to enjoy it immensely. The story focuses mainly on two frisky students, Glynn Turman and Lawrence Hilton-Jacobs. Girl trouble (principally charming Cynthia Davis), school trouble (with empathetic teacher Garrett Morris), and law trouble (via involvement with toughs Sherman Smith and Norman Gibson) lead the pair through experiences that range from broadly comic to deathly serious.

COOL HAND LUKE
1967, 126 mins, US Ⓥ ⊙ ▭
D: Stuart Rosenberg **A:** Paul Newman, George Kennedy, J. D. Cannon, Lou Antonio, Robert Drivas, Jo Van Fleet (Warner)

Paul Newman is Cool Hand Luke, a loner role in a film that depicts the social structure of a Dixie chain gang. Versatile and competent cast maintains interest throughout rambling exposition to a downbeat climax. Newman gives an excellent performance, assisted by a terrif supporting cast, including George Kennedy, outstanding as the unofficial leader of the cons who yields first place to Newman.
1967: Best Supp. Actor (George Kennedy).
Nominations: Best Actor (Paul Newman), Adapted Screenplay, Original Music Score

COOL RUNNINGS
1993, 97 mins, US Ⓥ ⊙
D: Jon Turteltaub **A:** Leon, Doug E. Doug, Malik Yoba, Rawle D. Lewis, John Candy, Raymond Barry (Walt Disney)

The travails and triumph of the 1988 Jamaican Olympic bobsled team deliver a highly entertaining combination in *Cool Runnings.* The offbeat, fact-based saga is enlivened by the perfect balance of humor, emotion, and insight. Unlike most sports-based films, this is one tale with universal appeal.

COOL WORLD, THE
1963, 125 mins, US Ⓥ
D: Shirley Clarke **A:** Hampton Clayton,

Yolanda Rodriguez, Carl Lee (Wiseman)

The Cool World is the world of Harlem. Elements are well blended to make this probably one of the least patronizing films ever made on Negro life in New York. Out of the crowd is picked a young teenager, Duke, whose one desire seems to be to own a gun that would give him standing in his own gang. Film alternates Duke's story with general scenes of Harlem life. The natural thesping is by a mainly nonpro cast.

COOL WORLD
1992, 102 mins, US Ⓥ ⊙
D: Ralph Bakshi **A:** Kim Basinger, Gabriel Byrne, Brad Pitt, Michele Abrams, Deirdre O'Connell, Carrie Hamilton (Paramount)

Style has seldom pummeled substance as severely as in *Cool World*, a combination funhouse ride/acid trip that will prove an ordeal for most visitors in the form of trial by animation. The comic-book premise hinges on parallel worlds—the real world and a sphere of animated characters, known as Cool World. Kim Basinger is one of the few actresses who could so convincingly breathe life into Holli, a 36-18-36 bombshell in animated form. *Cool World* is a realm with precious little humor and zero pathos, to be admired only for its brilliant synthesis of live action and animation, as well as the staggering creation of credible comic-book sets around human actors.

COP
1988, 110 mins, US Ⓥ ⊙
D: James B. Harris **A:** James Woods, Lesley Ann Warren, Charles Durning, Charles Haid, Randi Brooks, Raymond J. Barry (Atlantic/Harris-Woods)

A modestly executed, off-target police drama giving actor James Woods another outlet for his compellingly schizophrenic persona. Woods is a good LAPD cop who clearly loves his work and his eight-year-old daughter. Domestic pressures and a hard-to-crack serial murder case lead to the detective's lapses in judgment. One of the implicated is Lesley Ann Warren, a chain-smoking, feminist poet and bookshop-keeper who turns out to play a pivotal role in the murder mystery hounding Woods.

COP LAND
1997, 105 mins, US Ⓥ ⊙
D: James Mangold **A:** Sylvester Stallone, Harvey Keitel, Ray Liotta, Robert De Niro, Peter Berg, Annabella Sciorra (Woods/Miramax)

Set in a small New Jersey town just across from Manhattan, writer-director James Mangold's tale has the feel of a classic frontier Western in which the amiable sheriff is forced to wake up to the dastardly doings of the community's most prominent citizens. Garrison, NJ, a town whose population of 1,280 is composed largely of New York cops, is understandably virtually crime-free, which gives longtime sheriff Freddy Heflin (Sylvester Stallone) nothing much to do. Suspecting a cover-up, internal affairs special agent Moe Tilden (Robert De Niro) pays a visit but is unable to rouse Freddy to the stench around him. But Freddy is forced to take a stand and finally take on his enemies alone in the streets. Having put on weight to play the sluggish Freddy, Stallone shambles along in a way that emphasizes the sadness of the character.

COPS AND ROBBERSONS
1994, 93 mins, US Ⓥ ⊙
D: Michael Ritchie **A:** Chevy Chase, Jack Palance, Dianne Wiest, Robert Davi, David Barry Gray, Jason James Richter (Channel/TriStar)

The mixture of mischief and mayhem served up in this antic affair is never quite in balance. The complex setup centers on Osborn (Robert Davi), a goon involved in forgery and money laundering. The police know he's about to make a big exchange. Grizzled vet Jake Stone (Jack Palance) and partner set up their command post in the home of Norman Robberson (Chevy Chase), who lives next door to Osborn. While Robberson is the titular lead, it's really Stone who takes center stage. Palance plumbs deep inside his hard-boiled persona and extracts a rich vein of humor and pathos.

COPYCAT
1995, 123 mins, US Ⓥ ⊙ ▭
D: Jon Amiel **A:** Sigourney Weaver, Holly Hunter, Dermot Mulroney, William McNamara, Will Patton, Harry Connick Jr. (Regency/Warner)

Criminal psychologist Helen Hudson (Sigourney Weaver) points out that 90 percent of all serial killers are white males between 20 and 35 years old. One of them, in a very tense scene, nearly finishes off Hudson in a bathroom. Thirteen months later Hudson's trauma has made her so agoraphobic she can't bear to leave her apartment or return to her job. But when homicide detective M. J. Monahan (Holly Hunter) is faced with some murders that suggest a new serial killer, she pays a call on Hudson, whose interest is inevitably piqued by the kinky details of the cases. Genuine interest is generated in the main characters thanks to better-than-usual writing for this sort of piece and ultrasharp performances by the lead thesps.

CORNERED
1945, 102 mins, US Ⓥ ⊙
D: Edward Dmytryk **A:** Dick Powell, Walter Slezak, Nina Vale, Micheline Cheirel, Morris Carnovsky, Luther Adler (RKO)

It's the story of the relentless postwar hunt of a Canadian flier for the collaborationist who was responsible for the death of his French bride. Directed and played strictly for suspense and thrills, search gets under way in France, switches to Belgium, Switzerland, and then Argentina, where most of the action takes place. While all evidence points toward the death of the collaborationist, Dick Powell believes the man still alive. Finale has a definite surprise in store for audiences.

CORN IS GREEN, THE
1945, 114 mins, US Ⓥ
D: Irving Rapper **A:** Bette Davis, Nigel Bruce, John Dall, Joan Lorring, Mildred Dunnock (Warner)

The performances, not only of Bette Davis but of newcomers John Dall and Joan Lorring, together with those of Nigel Bruce and others, capture attention and admiration far and above that of the story itself. Davis, the emotional and serious-minded school mistress whose sociological ideals spur her to untiring efforts in raising the IQ of lowly Welsh mining folk, is cast in the kind of role she does well. Dall, her protégé, is much less an admirable character, though interest stays with him all the way.
1945: Nominations: Best Supp. Actor (John Dall), Supp. Actress (Joan Lorring)

CORPSE GRINDERS, THE
1971, 72 mins, US Ⓥ
D: Ted V. Mikels **A:** Sean Kenney, Monika Kelly, Sanford Mitchell, J. Byron Foster, Warren Ball, Ann Noble (Mikels)

The Corpse Grinders revolves around the grinding of stolen cadavers into canned cat food that turns a gentle pussy into a raging man-eater. Film carries enough blood to satisfy any cravings for this type

of divertissement, but it's a cheapie in every respect.

CORRINA, CORRINA
1994, 114 mins, US Ⓥ ⊙
D: Jessie Nelson **A:** Whoopi Goldberg, Ray Liotta, Tina Majorino, Wendy Crewson, Larry Miller, Erica Yohn (New Line)

Corrina, Corrina, starring Whoopi Goldberg as a perky housekeeper who brings solace and joy to a depressed fifties Jewish household, is a schmaltzy if entertaining comedy-drama. Strong chemistry between Goldberg and Ray Liotta, and a winning performance by child actress Tina Majorino, happily triumph over old-fashioned material and mediocre production values. Basing her story loosely on personal experience, writer/director Jessie Nelson examines the life of a Jewish family after the mother has suddenly died of cancer. Pic features the final performance of veteran actor Don Ameche, who plays Liotta's dying father.

CORSICAN BROTHERS, THE
1941, 111 mins, US Ⓥ
D: Gregory Ratoff **A:** Douglas Fairbanks Jr., Ruth Warrick, Akim Tamiroff, J. Carrol Naish, H. B. Warner, Henry Wilcoxon (Small/United Artists)

Dumas's story of the Corsican Brothers is widely known. Born Siamese twins of Corsican aristocracy, the babies are separated and saved from a vendetta attack that kills their parents. Twenty-one years later the twins (both portrayed by Douglas Fairbanks Jr.) are reunited, introduced, and informed of the enemy of their forebears. Swearing to avenge the murders, the two boys separate to confuse their enemy with widely separated attacks on his henchmen. Script is well set up to display the action qualities, but rather studious on the dialogue and story motivation.

COTTON CLUB, THE
1984, 127 mins, US Ⓥ ⊙
D: Francis Coppola **A:** Richard Gere, Gregory Hines, Diane Lane, Lonette McKee, Bob Hoskins, Nicolas Cage (Zoetrope)

The Cotton Club emerges as uneven and sometimes unfocused. Focus is on Dixie Dwyer (Richard Gere), a cornet player in a small Gotham club. Another thread involves club tap star Sandman Williams (Gregory Hines), who partners with his brother Clay (Maurice Hines) and has his eyes and heart set on chorus girl Lila Rose Oliver (Lonette McKee). Dramatically, Coppola and coscreenwriter William Kennedy juggle a lot of balls in the air. The parallel stories of Gere and Hines's professional rise prove more potent, thanks largely to a mixture of romance, music, and gangland involvement. Hines and McKee generate real sparks in their relationship.

1984: Nominations: Best Art Direction, Editing

COTTON COMES TO HARLEM
1970, 97 mins, US
D: Ossie Davis **A:** Godfrey Cambridge, Raymond St. Jacques, Calvin Lockhart, Judy Pace, Redd Foxx, John Anderson (United Artists)

Slam-bang, all-stops-out, comedy-action film about expatriate writer Chester Himes's two Harlem detectives, Gravedigger Jones and Coffin Ed Johnson. Godfrey Cambridge and Raymond St. Jacques are Himes's tough, rough, foulmouthed, but incorruptible policemen. Cambridge is the buffoon of the pair while St. Jacques (whose performance is easily the best in the film) is the spokesman for the Negro community. Action there is, from the opening seduction of gullible Harlem "good folks" by con-artist-cum-preacher Calvin Lockhart, to the denouement, revolving around what really happened to that $87,000 stashed away in a bale of cotton.

COUCH TRIP, THE
1988, 98 mins, US Ⓥ ⊙
D: Michael Ritchie **A:** Dan Aykroyd, Walter Matthau, Charles Grodin, David Clennon, Donna Dixon, Richard Romanus (Orion)

As an obstreperous prisoner biding his time in a loony bin, Dan Aykroyd trades places with his attending shrink, Dr. Baird (David Clennon), and moves to L.A. to fill in for radio therapist Dr. Maitlin (Charles Grodin), who is having a mental breakdown of his own. Screenplay doesn't break any new ground in suggesting there is a thin line between the certifiably crazy and certifiably sane, but it still manages some gentle jabs at the pretensions of the psychiatric profession. As a mock priest and another fringe member of society, Walter Matthau is Aykroyd's soul mate, but the connection between the men is too thinly drawn to have much meaning.

COUNSELLOR-AT-LAW
1933, 80 mins, US
D: William Wyler **A:** John Barrymore,

Bebe Daniels, Doris Kenyon, Onslow Stevens, Isabel Jewell, Melvyn Douglas (Universal)

Elmer Rice's screen adaptation of his own legit play is compelling stuff. The one flaw is in the casting of the principal role, George Simon, an East Side boy who rises to great prominence at the bar, is physically unsuited to John Barrymore, besides being a type of role that he hasn't tackled in pictures before. Barrymore's only means of conquering the role is to reshape George Simon into Barrymore. During the early moments he has a struggle on his hands, but the transformation is slowly completed. The minor characters whose lives are intertwined with Simon's in this *Grand Hotel* in a lawyer's office were largely responsible for the play's legit success. That fact has not been overlooked in the picture casting, as is evidenced by the importation of eight of the original stage players by Universal.

COUNTDOWN
1968, 101 mins, US Ⓥ ▭
D: Robert Altman **A:** James Caan, Joanna Moore, Robert Duvall, Barbara Baxley, Charles Aidman, Steve Ihnat (Warner)

Countdown, a story about a US space shot to the moon, is well developed and neatly resolved on a note of suspense. James Caan is a civilian scientist, chosen to replace military officer Robert Duvall as the moon-shot man. Added to this conflict is that between Steve Ihnat, project boss, and Charles Aidman, flight surgeon, who carry on the struggle between safety-of-life considerations and those of beating the Russians.

COUNTERPOINT
1967, 105 mins, US ▭
D: Ralph Nelson **A:** Charlton Heston, Maximilian Schell, Kathryn Hays, Leslie Nielsen, Anton Diffring, Linden Chiles (Universal)

Counterpoint is the story of an American symphony orchestra taken prisoner by the Germans during the Battle of the Bulge. Some of the incidents are contrived and characterizations of its two leads are sometimes confusing. But in the main subject has been well handled. Parts of five major music works, recorded by Los Angeles Philharmonic Orchestra, should have particular appeal for music lovers.

COUNTESS FROM HONG KONG, A
1967, 120 mins, UK
D: Charles Chaplin **A:** Marlon Brando,

Sophia Loren, Sydney Chaplin, Tippi Hedren, Patrick Cargill, Michael Medwin (Universal)

A romantic comedy. It has a nebulous plot, slim characterizations, and all the trappings of an old-fashioned bedroom farce. Sophia Loren plays a Russian emigrée countess who, after a night out on the town in Hong Kong with Marlon Brando, stows away in his cabin with the intention of getting to New York. Although the story barely taxes her acting resources, Loren adds a quality to every scene in which she appears. Brando, on the other hand, appears ill at ease.

COUNT OF MONTE CRISTO, THE
1934, 113 mins, US ⓥ
D: Rowland V. Lee **A:** Robert Donat, Elissa Landi, Louis Calhern, Sidney Blackmer, Raymond Walburn, O. P. Heggie (Reliance/United Artists)

Monte Cristo is a near-perfect blend of thrilling action and grand dialogue, both of which elements are inherent in the Alexandre Dumas original story. Robert Donat's intelligent handling of the many-sided top role hallmarks a sparkling piece of acting. Louis Calhern, Sidney Blackmer, and Raymond Walburn are the trio upon whom Cristo wreaks his vengeance.

COUNT OF MONTE CRISTO, THE
1976, 103 mins, US ⓥ ⊙
D: David Greene **A:** Richard Chamberlain, Tony Curtis, Trevor Howard, Louis Jourdan, Donald Pleasence, Kate Nelligan (ITC)

Richard Chamberlain is Edmond Dantes, the romantic young sailor railroaded to prison for 15 years. After his escape, the story gets down to his obsessive revenge against the four money- and/or power-hungry men who conspired against him. All this is developed with more sincerity than interest or dramatic originality, and with no style of its own.

COUNTRY
1984, 109 mins, US ⓥ ⊙ ▭
D: Richard Pearce **A:** Jessica Lange, Sam Shepard, Wilford Brimley, Matt Clark, Therese Graham, Levi L. Knebel (Touchstone)

Jessica Lange's pet project winds up firmly on the right track, with its basic theme of the classic struggle of the workingman against the forces of government. Lange is the focal point, essaying the mother of the family faced with losing the farm which had been in her lineage for

some 100 years. Sam Shepard—the husband—gives a quietly effective portrayal of the husband dealt a humiliating blow to his pride when the farm when the farm is fingered for liquidation.
1984: Nomination: Best Actress (Jessica Lange)

COUNTRY DANCE
(US: BROTHERLY LOVE)
1970, 112 mins, US ⓥ
D: J. Lee Thompson **A:** Peter O'Toole, Susannah York, Michael Craig, Harry Andrews, Cyril Cusack, Judy Cornwell (Windward/Keep)

Country Dance is a confusing love triangle film. Limning the decline and fall of Sir Charles Ferguson (Peter O'Toole), last scion of a noble Scottish family, there is in this descent the distasteful subject of the brother's unhealthy love for his sister (Susannah York), who has left her husband (Michael Craig) to make her home with her brother on their family estate.

COUNTRY GIRL, THE
1954, 104 mins, US ⓥ
D: George Seaton **A:** Bing Crosby, Grace Kelly, William Holden, Anthony Ross, Gene Reynolds, Jacqueline Fontaine (Paramount)

An exceptionally well-performed essay on an alcoholic song man, with Bing Crosby carrying on a bottle romance, *Country Girl* is a show-business story that has depth and movement. Adapted from the 1950 Clifford Odets play of the same title, its key player, a quondam star induced into trying a painful comeback, is a weak, lying, excessive drinker. Grace Kelly is resolute to the hilt, conveying a certain feminine strength and courage that enable her to endure the hardships of being the boozer's wife. William Holden registers in sock style as the legit director determined that Crosby can stand up to the demands of the starring role in a new play.
1954: Best Actress (Grace Kelly), Screenplay
Nominations: Best Picture, Director, Actor (Bing Crosby), B&W Cinematography, B&W Art Direction

COURAGE UNDER FIRE
1996, 115 mins, US ⓥ ⊙
D: Edward Zwick **A:** Denzel Washington, Meg Ryan, Lou Diamond Phillips, Michael Moriarty, Matt Damon, Bronson Pinchot (Davis/20th Century-Fox)

A *Rashomon*-like story about the difficulty of establishing the truth about heroism and soldiers' behavior in combat, *Courage under Fire* treats its subject with clarity and intelligence. Guilt-ridden Lieutenant Colonel Nathaniel Serling (Denzel Washington) is shuffled into a routine Pentagon job. For p.r. purposes, the White House is particularly anxious that Captain Karen Walden (Meg Ryan) receives a Medal of Honor award posthumously. Serling begins speaking to the survivors of the accident in which Walden was the pilot, and realizes that what happened was far from clear-cut. Throughout his quest for the truth, the moody, introspective Serling shuts out his wife and family and begins drinking heavily. All of Serling's predicaments are palpably and convincingly registered through Washington's probing, reserved, and sensitively drawn performance.

COURT JESTER, THE
1956, 101 mins, US ⓋⓈ ⊙

D: Norman Panama, Melvin Frank A: Danny Kaye, Glynis Johns, Basil Rathbone, Angela Lansbury, Cecil Parker, Mildred Natwick (Paramount/Dena)

Costumed swashbucklers undergo a happy spoofing. Norman Panama and Melvin Frank drag in virtually every timehonored, and timeworn, medieval drama cliché for Kaye and cast to replay for laughs via not-so-subtle treatment. A major assist comes from the Sylvia Fine–Sammy Cahn songs, of which there are five all tuned to the Kaye talent.

COURT MARTIAL
See: *Carrington, V.C.*

COURT-MARTIAL OF BILLY MITCHELL, THE
(UK: ONE-MAN MUTINY)
1955, 100 mins, US Ⓥ ⊙ ⊐

D: Otto Preminger A: Gary Cooper, Charles Bickford, Ralph Bellamy, Rod Steiger, Elizabeth Montgomery, Fred Clark (United States/Warner)

Dealing with real-life events of 1925, the picture is a real kick in the shins for the cult of blind military obedience. The picture shows Mitchell predicting the Japanese sneak attack on Pearl Harbor, and describing American vulnerability, all this 16 years before that catastrophic Sunday and in the presence of Douglas MacArthur.

1955: Nomination: Best Story & Screenplay

COURTNEY AFFAIR, THE
See: *The Courtneys of Curzon Street*

COURTNEYS OF CURZON STREET, THE
(US: THE COURTNEY AFFAIR)
1947, 120 mins, US Ⓥ

D: Herbert Wilcox A: Anna Neagle, Michael Wilding, Gladys Young, Coral Browne, Michael Medwin, Bernard Lee (British Lion)

Wilcox hasn't worried about any significant theme in this. He tells his four-generation story with smiles and tears. Michael Wilding plays the soldier son and heir of a baronet. He is in love with his mother's maid (Anna Neagle). Ignoring his mother's warning that he is risking social ostracism, he flouts tradition and marries the girl. Climax to society's persecution comes at a snobbish function with Queen Victoria. His wife has to listen to catty remarks about her lowly beginning.

COURTSHIP OF ANDY HARDY, THE
1942, 94 mins, US

D: George B. Seitz A: Lewis Stone, Mickey Rooney, Donna Reed, William Lundigan (M-G-M)

Picture is studded with laugh lines throughout. Mickey Rooney, between adolescence and manhood, successfully balances the assignment in excellent style. Judge Hardy invokes the aid of Andy to date a girl and break her of a haughty complex. Donna Reed is the girl.

COURTSHIP OF EDDIE'S FATHER, THE
1963, 118 mins, US Ⓥ ⊐

D: Vincente Minnelli A: Glenn Ford, Shirley Jones, Stella Stevens, Dina Merrill, Roberta Sherwood, Jerry Van Dyke (M-G-M/Euterpe-Venice)

Richly mounted, wittily written, and engagingly played. Glenn Ford portrays a widower who, in rearing his precocious six-and-a-half-year-old son (Ronny Howard) must take into account the future maternal preferences of the boy, whose comic-book-eye-view of candidate wives is inclined to judge statistically on the basis of bustlines and eye sockets. Never any question about Shirley Jones's credentials. Dina Merrill is an attractive loser. Stella Stevens comes on like gangbusters in her enactment of a brainy but inhibited doll from Montana.

COUSIN, COUSINE
1975, 95 mins, France Ⓥ ⊙

D: Jean-Charles Tacchella A: Marie-

Christine Barrault, Victor Lanoux, Marie-France Pisier, Guy Marchand, Ginette Garcin, Sybil Maas (Pomereu/Gaumont)

A gritty comedy of family manners that is flippant, observant, with a love story between two new cousins, both married. Players are acceptable, with Guy Marchand properly callow as the small-time Don Juan who gives up his girls to keep his wife but finds her attachment to her new cousin has grown so that she finally leaves him and their son to go off. Victor Lanoux and Marie-Christine Barrault are entrancing as the new couple, while Marie-France Pisier is shrewdly perceptive as the neurotic wife of the man.

COUSINS
1989, 110 mins, US ⓥ ⊙
D: Joel Schumacher A: Ted Danson, Isabella Rossellini, Sean Young, William Petersen, Lloyd Bridges, Norma Aleandro (Paramount)

A hugely entertaining Americanized version of the French film *Cousin, Cousine,* with nearly the same insouciant tone as the Jean-Charles Tacchella comedy of 1975. It's been spiced with a dash of 1980s social commentary and a dollop of Italian ethnic flavoring. Isabella Rossellini and Ted Danson's sappy, overly sentimental series of rendezvous are well compensated by their relatives' caustic comments, irreverent asides, and other antics at the three weddings, one funeral, and other functions all attend during the course of the picture.

COUSINS, THE
See: Les Cousins

LES COUSINS
(THE COUSINS)
1959, 103 mins, France ⓥ
D: Claude Chabrol A: Gerard Blain, Jean-Claude Brialy, Juliette Mayniel, Claude Cerval, Guy Decomble, Stephane Audran (AJYM)

Tale of a country cousin trying to make it in the big city, and destroyed in the process, gets offbeat treatment from promising new and youthful director Claude Chabrol. The country cousin, Charles (Gerard Blain), comes to stay with his worldly, decadent cousin, Paul (Jean-Claude Brialy). His attempts at love and exams fail while his indolent, debauched cousin gets all.

COVERED WAGON, THE
1923, 119 mins, US ⓥ ⊛ ⊗
D: James Cruze A: J. Warren Kerrigan,

Lois Wilson, Ernest Torrence, Charles Ogle, Alan Hale, Ethel Wales (Paramount)

The Covered Wagon is the biggest thing since Griffith made *The Birth of a Nation.* Emerson Hough, who wrote *The Covered Wagon* for *The Saturday Evening Post,* chose for his subject those pioneers who started in prairie schooners for the Pacific Coast in 1847. This particular wagon train, which has some 300 vehicles, starts for Oregon. Through it all a very pretty and simple love tale runs, as well as an element of intrigue. The big thrills are the fording of the Platte by the wagons of the train, the Indian attack, and a prairie fire.

COVER GIRL
1944, 105 mins, US ⓥ ⊙
D: Charles Vidor A: Rita Hayworth, Gene Kelly, Lee Bowman, Phil Silvers, Otto Kruger, Eve Arden (Columbia)

Plot is neatly concocted to get over idea of sudden rise to theatrical fame of Rita Hayworth as result of winning a cover-girl contest. Gene Kelly, operating the modest Brooklyn nightspot where he stages the floor shows, is in love with Hayworth, a dancer. Latter wins the contest to give the room immediate fame with the upper-crust customers from Manhattan. Dance sequences spotlighting the terping abilities of Hayworth and Kelly are expertly staged. Kelly devised his own routines for the picture. Score by Jerome Kern and Ira Gershwin, comprising seven tunes, is of high caliber.
1944: Best Score for a Musical Picture
Nominations: Best Color Cinematography, Color Art Direction, Song ("Long Ago and Far Away"), Sound

COWBOYS, THE
1972, 128 mins, US ⓥ ▭
D: Mark Rydell A: John Wayne, Roscoe Lee Browne, Bruce Dern, Colleen Dewhurst, Slim Pickens, Lonny Chapman (Sanford/Warner)

The Cowboys stars John Wayne as a tough cattleman forced to use some green teenagers to get the beef to market. Handsome, placid, and pastoral, the film is a family-type entry. The story's gentle treatment makes the length something of a hindrance to maximum enjoyment. Cast includes Colleen Dewhurst in an effective cameo as a traveling bordello madam.

CRACKERS
1984, 92 mins, US ⓥ ⊙
D: Louis Malle A: Donald Sutherland,

Jack Warden, Sean Penn, Wallace Shawn, Larry Riley, Trinidad Silva (Universal)

A mild little caper comedy with plenty of sociological overtones, *Crackers* comes as a letdown from director Louis Malle. Virtually all the action takes place within or very near a pawnshop owned by shameless profiteer Jack Warden. His buddy, Donald Sutherland, is out of work, and all but a few of the other characters make up a rainbow microcosm of today's unemployed.

CRACK IN THE MIRROR
1960, 97 mins, US ▱
D: Richard Fleischer A: Orson Welles, Juliette Greco, Bradford Dillman, Alexander Knox, Catherine Lacy, William Lucas (DFZ/20th Century-Fox)

Two parallel stories, both age-old triangle situations in which a not-so-young woman throws over her elderly lover for a much younger man. The first involves three working-class people and the second, three members of the Paris haut monde. The stories come together when the working-class dame and her young paramour are brought to trial for the murder of the older man. By casting Orson Welles as both the tyrannical old construction worker who is murdered and as the cuckolded lawyer, Juliette Greco as the mistress in both situations, and Bradford Dillman as the young laborer and the young lawyer in a hurry, producer and director have obviously intended to make some pertinent statements about guilt and the ironies of justice.

CRACK IN THE WORLD
1965, 96 mins, US
D: Andrew Marton A: Dana Andrews, Janette Scott, Kieron Moore, Alexander Knox, Peter Damon, Gary Lasdun (Paramount)

Crack in the World, distinguished principally by some startling special effects, imaginatively focuses on an ill-fated experiment to tap the unlimited energy residing within the earth's core which nearly blows up the world. Dana Andrews plays part of the scientist in charge of the operation, dying with fast cancer, and Kieron Moore his assistant. Janette Scott is Andrews's scientist-wife, actually in love with Moore.

CRACKSMAN, THE
1963, 112 mins, UK
D: Peter Graham Scott A: Charlie Drake, George Sanders, Dennis Price, Nyree Dawn Porter, Finlay Currie (Associated British)

Charlie Drake, the half-pint slapstick comedian from tele, plays an honest, little man who is the victim of fate. His problem is that he cannot resist the challenge of a lock and gets a reputation in the cooler for being the top cracksman in the business. Trouble is that most of the comedy situations are stretched too long.

CRADLE WILL ROCK
1999, 133 mins, US ▱ ▱
D: Tim Robbins A: Hank Azaria, Ruben Blades, Joan Cusack, John Cusack, Cary Elwes, Philip Baker Hall (Havoc/Touchstone)

Tim Robbins's ambitious $32 million *Cradle Will Rock* succeeds far more often than not in delivering a credible, kaleidoscopic portrait of creative and often famous individuals. Title refers to the musical drama written by Marc Blitzstein in 1936 and taken on by a 21-year-old Orson Welles and John Houseman. With the theater abruptly shut down by the authorities, the company switched to another venue where the actors, forbidden to set foot onstage, performed their roles from the auditorium. Robbins uses the *Cradle* episode as just part of a larger picture of the dynamic cultural landscape. Many perfs are splendid, particularly Cherry Jones (the Federal Theater leader), John Turturro (an actor in Welles's company), Susan Sarandon (Mussolini's beautiful emissary), Ruben Blades (Diego Rivera), Bill Murray (ventriloquist Tommy Crickshaw), and Vanessa Redgrave (arts doyenne Comtesse LaGrange).

CRAFT, THE
1996, 100 mins, US ▱
D: Andrew Fleming A: Robin Tunney, Fairuza Balk, Neve Campbell, Rachel True, Skeet Ulrich, Helen Shaver (Columbia)

A neatly crafted film that begins most promisingly as a black comedy à la *Heathers*. Story begins with the relocation of Sarah (Robin Tunney) to yet another high school, where she attracts the attention of three outsiders: white trash Nancy (Fairuza Balk), Bonnie (Neve Campbell), an insecure teenager badly scarred in a fire, and Rochelle (Rachel True), an overachiever who hides her wounds deep inside. The movie depicts, often quite sharply and humorously, the adventures of tough girls who are nonetheless determined not to let their peers back them into a corner. The revenge that Sarah and her cohorts take upon obnoxiously insensitive guys like cocky football jock Chris (Skeet Ulrich) is singularly biting. Unfortunately, yarn progressively deteriorates into a series of well-executed special effects.

CRANES ARE FLYING, THE
See: Letyat Zhuravli

CRASH
1996, 98 mins, Canada ⊘ ⊙
D: David Cronenberg **A:** James Spader, Holly Hunter, Elias Koteas, Deborah Unger, Rosanna Arquette, Peter MacNeil (Alliance)

Faithfully adapted from J. G. Ballard's 1973 cult novel and directed with precise control, this attempt to transform a fetish for automobile accidents and bodily injury into a metaphor for human adaptation to the technological age remains an exceedingly intellectual work of cold sensuality. Characters lack any meaning or connection with one another except in their pushing of sexual limits. Sex scenes are clear about what's going on, even if below-the-belt nudity is only fleeting. Nothing here is remotely a turn-on from an audience p.o.v.

CRASH DIVE
1943, 105 mins, US
D: Archie Mayo **A:** Tyrone Power, Anne Baxter, Dana Andrews, James Gleason, May Whitty, Henry Morgan (20th Century-Fox)

Salute to the submarine crews of the US Navy packs terrific wallop. Endowed with a fine cast, headed by Tyrone Power, it has been directed with consummate skill and artistry by Archie Mayo, unfolds a tense, dramatic series of undersea warfare episodes, and visually, through its excellent Technicolor treatment, is at all times highly distinctive.
1943: Best Special Effects (Fred Sersen, Roger Heman)

CRASH OF SILENCE, THE
See: Mandy

CRAWLING EYE, THE
See: The Trollenberg Terror

CRAZY IN ALABAMA
1999, 111 mins, US ⊘ ⊙ ▭
D: Antonio Banderas **A:** Melanie Griffith, David Morse, Lucas Black, Cathy Moriarty, Meat Loaf Aday, Rod Steiger (Green Moon/Columbia)

Antonio Banderas pulls off a creditable directorial debut with *Crazy in Alabama*. Yarn combines a wacky look at a southern bombshell who heads for Hollywood and a deadly-serious account of racial strife in the South, circa 1965. Lucille (Melanie Griffith), a 40-ish madcap, leaves seven kids with her mother to pursue the dream she's always put on hold. She's just killed her husband and is toting his severed head along with her. Events are seen from the p.o.v. of Lucille's 13-year-old nephew Peejoe (Lucas Black), who moves into the mortuary where Lucille's brother Dove (David Morse) works. Griffith initially seems a bit long in the tooth as a woman embarking on a Hollywood quest, but the age factor adds a touch of poignancy to her journey. Black delivers a compellingly sharp-witted teenager, and Morse is appealingly understated.

CRAZY MAMA
1975, 82 mins, US ⊘
D: Jonathan Demme **A:** Cloris Leachman, Stuart Whitman, Ann Sothern, Tisha Sterling, Jim Backus, Donn Most (New World)

Spanning nearly three decades, Cloris Leachman stars as she starts in Jerusalem, AK, 1932, when lawmen kill papa (Clint Kimbrough), making mother Ann Sothern a widow. They jump the 60-acre farm, next are in Long Beach, CA, where the pair are evicted from their beauty salon for back rent, and Leachman has a pretty, pregnant teenage daughter (Linda Pure). The three femmes, upset, steal cars and shoot their way across the US. *Crazy Mama* appears a waste of top talent in a mindless life of crime.

CRAZY PEOPLE
1990, 90 mins, US ⊘ ⊙
D: Tony Bill **A:** Dudley Moore, Daryl Hannah, Paul Reiser, Mercedes Ruehl, J. T. Walsh, David Paymer (Paramount)

Crazy People combines a hilarious dissection of advertising with a warm view of so-called insanity. Moore toplines as a burned-out adman. Under deadline pressure, he turns in campaigns that attempt an honest approach. When Moore hands in "Most of our passengers get there alive" to promote United Airlines, the film jump-cuts emphatically to Bennington Sanitarium, his new home. Director Bill envisions this loony bin as an idyllic retreat, with a natural, warm, and beautiful Daryl Hannah as Moore's nutty playmate there. The visual mismatch (she towers over the diminutive star) pays off.

CRAZY PETE
See: Pierrot le Fou

CREATURE FROM THE BLACK LAGOON
1954, 79 mins, US 🅥 ⊙
D: Jack Arnold **A:** Richard Carlson, Julie Adams, Richard Denning, Antonio Moreno, Nestor Paiva, Whit Bissell (Universal)

In the backwashes of the Amazon, a scientific expedition comes across a still-living Gill Man, half-fish, half-human. The 3-D lensing adds to the eerie effects of the underwater footage, as well as to the monster's several appearances on land. The below-water scraps between skindivers and the prehistoric thing are thrilling. Richard Carlson and Julie Adams carry off the thriller very well. As befitting the Amazonian setting, Adams appears mostly in brief shorts or swimsuits.

CREEPING UNKNOWN, THE
See: The Quatermass Experiment

CREEPSHOW
1982, 129 mins, US 🅥 ⊙
D: George A. Romero **A:** Hal Holbrook, Adrienne Barbeau, Fritz Weaver, Leslie Nielsen, Carrie Nye, E. G. Marshall (Laurel)

George Romero, collaborating with writer Stephen King, again proves his adeptness at combining thrills with tongue-in-cheek humor. He links five tales with animated bridges in the style of the comics. In "The Lonesome Death of Jordy Verrill," author King takes on the title role. He's a dull hillbilly who sees dollar signs when a meteor falls on his property. However, his fate is to turn into a plant.

CREEPSHOW 2
1987, 89 mins, US 🅥 ⊙
D: Michael Gornick **A:** Lois Chiles, George Kennedy, Dorothy Lamour, Tom Savini, Domenick John (Laurel)

Tied together with some humdrum animated sequences, three vignettes on offer obviously were produced on the absolute cheap, and are deficient in imagination and scare quotient. Whatever interest some might have in seeing George Kennedy and Dorothy Lamour is undercut by their roles as helpless vicims of a small-town robbery and double murder in the first tale.

CRIES AND WHISPERS
See: Viskningar Och Rop

CRIME AND PUNISHMENT
1935, 85 mins, US
D: Josef von Sternberg **A:** Edward Arnold, Peter Lorre, Marian Marsh, Tala Birell, Elisabeth Risdon, Douglass Dumbrille (Columbia)

The murder of the miserly pawnbroker (Mrs. Patrick Campbell in a ruthless, unsympathetic characterization) is the premeditated crime by Peter Lorre. Edward Arnold's old-fashioned police methods, combined with psychological autosuggestion and ultimate self-destruction, is the the punishment. Both contribute capital performances.

CRIME IN THE STREETS
1956, 91 mins, US
D: Don Siegel **A:** James Whitmore, John Cassavetes, Sal Mineo, Mark Rydell, Virginia Gregg, Peter Votrian (Lindbrook/Allied Artists)

Crime in the Streets sets out to be a gutsy melodrama about slum-area delinquents and, within the framework of Reginald Rose's highly contrived story, succeeds in making its shock points under Don Siegel's pat directorial handling. John Cassavetes is the bitter, unlovable young tough who leads the street rat pack. James Whitmore heads the cast as a settlement worker who does little more than observe and offer unheeded counsel.

CRIMES AND MISDEMEANORS
1989, 104 mins, US 🅥 ⊙
D: Woody Allen **A:** Martin Landau, Woody Allen, Mia Farrow, Alan Alda, Anjelica Huston, Sam Waterston (Rollins/Joffe)

Woody Allen ambitiously mixes his two favored strains of cinema, melodrama and comedy, with mixed results in *Crimes and Misdemeanours*. Two loosely linked stories here concern eye doctor Martin Landau and documentary director Allen, each facing moral dilemmas. The structural and stylistic conceit is that when Landau is onscreen, the film is dead serious, even solemn, while Allen's own appearance onscreen signals hilarious satire and priceless one-liners.

1989: Nominations: Best Director, Supp. Actor (Martin Landau), Original Screenplay

CRIMES OF DR. MABUSE, THE
See: Das Testament Des Dr. Mabuse

CRIMES OF PASSION
(AKA: CHINA BLUE)
1984, 101 mins, US Ⓥ ⊙
D: Ken Russell **A:** Kathleen Turner, Anthony Perkins, John Laughlin, Annie Potts, Bruce Davison (New World)

The provocative Kathleen Turner thuds into a wall of inanity in this dismally written, Ken Russell–directed seriocomic examination of sexual morality among American savages. Turner leads two lives. By day she is Joanna, a compulsively laboring sportswear designer. But by night she is the hottest $50-a-trick hooker in the local combat zone. Anthony Perkins has to lean on ''psycho''-somatic credentials to portray a glib, sweaty, presumably ministerial, homicidal wacko.

CRIMES OF THE FUTURE
1970, 63 mins, Canada
D: David Cronenberg **A:** Ronald Mlodzik, Jon Lidolt, Tania Zolty, Paul Mulholland, Jack Messinger, Iain Ewing (Emergent)

Cronenberg's obsession for such matters as bodily mutation and grotesque growths, aberrant medical experiments, massive plagues, and futuristic architecture are all here in a convoluted look at a future gone perverse. The world's entire female population has evidently been wiped out, and the male population has turned to various, and disappointingly tame, alternative sexual fixations. Prime symptom of the illness is Rouge's Foam, a substance which leaks from bodily orifices and is sexually exciting in its initial stage, but deadly later on.

CRIMES OF THE HEART
1986, 105 mins, US Ⓥ ⊙
D: Bruce Beresford **A:** Diane Keaton, Jessica Lange, Sissy Spacek, Sam Shepard, Tess Harper, Hurd Hatfield (Fields/Sugarman/De Laurentiis)

Thoughtfully cast, superbly acted, and masterfully written and directed, *Crimes of the Heart* is a winner. Diane Keaton, Jessica Lange, and Sissy Spacek are a delight in their roles as southern sisters attempting to come to grips with the world, themselves, and the past. The interplay between Keaton's nervously frantic Lenny, Spacek's unpredictable Babe, and Lange as the hard-living Meg is as funny as it is riveting.
1986: Nominations: Best Actress (Sissy

Spacek), Supp. Actress (Tess Harper), Adapted Screenplay

CRIMETIME
1996, 118 mins, UK/Germany Ⓥ ⊙
D: George Sluizer **A:** Stephen Baldwin, Pete Postlethwaite, Sadie Frost, Geraldine Chaplin, Karen Black, James Faulkner (Focus/Kinowelt)

Crimetime is a senseless thriller about a futuristic society in which there is no distinction between reality and its representation by the media. Toplined by a seriously miscast Stephen Baldwin and featuring a cop-out ending shamelessly lifted from Brian DePalma's *Body Double,* pic is so cynical that it ends up shooting itself in the foot. Baldwin plays Bobby, an actor catapulted to stardom when he's cast as a serial killer in a TV crime re-enactment program called *Crimetime,* and begins to immerse himself obsessively in the details of the role. George Sluizer directs in a glitzy but impersonal style.

CRIME WITHOUT PASSION
1934, 70 mins, US
D: Ben Hecht, Charles MacArthur **A:** Claude Rains, Margo, Whitney Bourne, Stanley Ridges, Paula Trueman, Esther Dale (Paramount)

This is about a great criminal lawyer, brilliant in a courtroom, but a combination egomaniac and chump in the boudoir. He's mixed up with a brunette dancer whom he'd like to shake for a blonde, but the brunette has him hooked. His profound egoism in his lovemaking dictates another procedure for airing a dame, i.e., false-evidence planting to throw suspicion of unfaithfulness upon the lady. It leads to an accidental shooting and apparent killing of the brunette in a scramble for a gun, and then the picture gets hot. Claude Rains, an expert actor, plays the lawyer with much intelligence.

CRIMINAL CODE, THE
1931, 97 mins, US Ⓥ
D: Howard Hawks **A:** Walter Huston, Phillips Holmes, Constance Cummings, Mary Doran, DeWitt Jennings, Boris Karloff (Columbia)

Walter Huston here probably turns in his best modern characterization to date as a district attorney with a daughter who becomes warden of a prison. The love theme is taken care of by the girl and a young prisoner. Plenty of action all the way, in and out of the prison yard, with the per-

formances of Huston. Phillips Holmes, and Boris Karloff always holding it together.
1930/31: Nomination: Best Adaptation

CRIMINAL LAW
1988, 117 mins, US ⓥ ⊙
D: Martin Campbell **A:** Gary Oldman, Kevin Bacon, Karen Young, Joe Don Baker, Tess Harper, Elizabeth Sheppard (Hemdale/Northwood)

A badly written and directed crime drama. Cocky lawyer Ben Chase, rendered with superb American accent and mannerisms by British Gary Oldman, pulls a sly trick out of his hat to free his wealthy, self-absorbed client Martin Thiel (Kevin Bacon). No sooner is Bacon back on the streets, however, than Oldman realizes he's unleashed a monster. The stage is set for a clumsily plotted psychological cat-and-mouse game between Oldman and Bacon.

CRIMSON KIMONO, THE
1959, 81 mins, US
D: Samuel Fuller **A:** Victoria Shaw, Glenn Corbett, James Shigeta, Anna Lee, Paul Dubov, Jaclynne Greene (Globe/Columbia)

Samuel Fuller tries to wrap up a murder mystery with an interracial romance. The mystery-melodrama part of the film gets lost during the complicated romance, and the racial-tolerance plea is cheapened by its inclusion in a film of otherwise straight action. Fuller's story has Glenn Corbett and James Shigeta as officers of the L.A. homicide squad. Corbett first falls in love with artist Victoria Shaw, then Shigeta succumbs.

CRIMSON PIRATE, THE
1952, 104 mins, UK/US ⓥ ⊙
D: Robert Siodmak **A:** Burt Lancaster, Eva Bartok, Nick Cravat, Torin Thatcher, James Hayter, Margot Grahame (Norma/Warner)

Swashbucking sea fables get a good-natured spoofing in *The Crimson Pirate*. The screen story is cloaked with a sense of humor as it pictures Lancaster, the famed Crimson Pirate, plying his trade on the high seas. Lancaster and his deaf-mute pal (Nick Cravat) sock the acrobatics required of hero and partner to a fare-thee-well under Robert Siodmak's direction.

CRIMSON TIDE
1995, 115 mins, US ⓥ ⊙ ▭
D: Tony Scott **A:** Denzel Washington, Gene Hackman, George Dzundza, Viggo Mortensen, James Gandolfini, Matt Craven (Hollywood)

A brink-of-nuclear-disaster thriller set aboard a tension-fraught US submarine, this is a boys' movie all the way. Exposition is handled with terrific dispatch, as a pseudo-CNN news report lays out the state of things in Russia, where some nationalist right-wingers initiate a civil war and grab control of a Pacific-coast nuclear base. The US sends the USS *Alabama* toward the hot zone. When an initial message ordering a nuclear attack arrives, the entire crew nervously prepares to launch World War III, even while being pursued by a rogue Russian submarine. Up to this halfway point, *Crimson Tide* is an exciting, efficient, straight-ahead thriller. But as the inevitable moment of truth arrives, is aborted, arrives again, and is once more postponed, plausibility becomes strained and the story comes to feel waterlogged.
Nominations: Film Editing, Best Sound, Best Sound Effects Editing

CRISIS
1950, 95 mins, US
D: Richard Brooks **A:** Cary Grant, Jose Ferrer, Paula Raymond, Signe Hasso, Ramon Novarro, Gilbert Roland (M-G-M)

Dictatorship versus the right of man to freedom is the theme, and the script and direction by Richard Brooks lets it get up on the soapbox too frequently. Footage kicks off with Cary Grant, a brain surgeon, and his wife (Paula Raymond) vacationing in a revolution-ridden Latin country. Grant finds the dictator-president suffering from a brain tumor and he is ordered to operate. Meantime, revolutionaries, led by Gilbert Roland, exert pressure to have the president (Jose Ferrer) die under the knife.

CRISS CROSS
1949, 87 mins, US ⓥ
D: Robert Siodmak **A:** Burt Lancaster, Yvonne De Carlo, Dan Duryea, Stephen McNally, Richard Long (Universal)

Film unreels the relentless, unswerving devotion of Burt Lancaster for his divorced wife (Yvonne De Carlo). Basically he's an honest guy in contrast to the shaky character of his ex-spouse, who has become the moll of big-time crook Dan Duryea. Caught in a rendezvous with his old flame by Duryea, Lancaster fends off the jealousy of his rival by suggesting the group pull off an armored-car holdup. Robert Siodmak's staging of the holdup scene is masterful.

CRISS CROSS
1992, 100 mins, US Ⓥ
D: Chris Menges **A:** Goldie Hawn, Arliss Howard, James Gannon, David Arnott, Keith Carradine, J. C. Quinn (M-G-M/Hawn-Sylbert)

This earnest, languid drama might have worked if it weren't so painfully obvious and slow. *Criss-Cross* deals with a boy, Chris (David Arnott), who's lost his moral compass, living with his mom (Goldie Hawn) in a run-down Key West hotel. Hawn's a waitress who turns stripper to pay the rent, while Dad (Keith Carradine, in a brief cameo) split three years earlier. Almost an hour in, the story finally stumbles into a plot as Chris discovers he's been transporting hidden cocaine from a fisherman to one of the locals.

CRITTERS
1986, 86 mins, US Ⓥ ⊙
D: Stephen Herek **A:** Dee Wallace, M. Emmet Walsh, Billy Green Bush, Scott Grimes, Nadine Van Der Velde, Terrence Mann (New Line/Sho/Smart Egg)

Critters resemble oversize hairballs and roll like tumbleweeds when prodded into action, the perfect menace for this irritatingly insipid and lightweight film which unfolds with plodding predictability and leaves few clichés unturned. Voracious Krites (a.k.a. Critters) easily escape from a maximum-security asteroid and are whizzing toward Kansas. Establish the sleepy life of farmer (yes) Brown and his wife Helen, as credibly performed by Billy Green Bush and Dee Wallace as can be expected with such material, rambunctious son Brad, and sexually budding daughter April. There's also M. Emmet Walsh as the familiar small-town sheriff.

CRITTERS 2
THE MAIN COURSE
1988, 87 mins, US Ⓥ ⊙
D: Mick Garris **A:** Scott Grimes, Liane Curtis, Don Opper, Barry Corbin, Tom Hodges (New Line/Sho/Smart Egg)

All concerned are back in small Grovers Bend, where Krites terrorized residents just two years earlier. Tip-off that they've returned is appearance of dozens and dozens of large eggs with colorful patterns on them. Outer-space bounty hunters Ug and

Lee (Terrence Mann and Roxanne Kernohan), as well as Charlie (Don Opper), are dispatched to planet Earth to obliterate the nasty little killers.

"CROCODILE" DUNDEE
1986, 102 mins, Australia Ⓥ ⊙ ⊠
D: Peter Faiman **A:** Paul Hogan, Linda Kozlowski, John Meillon, Mark Blum, Michael Lombard, David Gulpilil (Rimfire)

As the title character, Paul Hogan limns a laconic if rather dim crocodile hunter who achieves some notoriety after surviving an attack by a giant croc. New York reporter Linda Kozlowski journeys to the Northern Territory to cover the story. Rather implausibly, Kozlowski persuades Hogan to return to Gotham with her. Here he is initiated into the delights of the Big Apple. Hogan is comfortable enough playing the wry, irreverent, amiable Aussie that seems close to his own persona, and teams well with Kozlowski, who radiates lots of charm, style and spunk.
1986: Nomination: Best Original Screenplay

"CROCODILE" DUNDEE II
1988, 111 mins, US Ⓥ ⊙ ⊠
D: John Cornell **A:** Paul Hogan, Linda Kozlowski, Charles Dutton, Hechter Ubarry, John Meillon, Juan Fernandez (Rimfire/Paramount)

Too slow to constitute an adventure and too few laughs to be a comedy. Linda Kozlowski's ex-lover is killed in Colombia for taking photos of a cocaine king as he shoots one of his runners. The nefarious Rico learns the photos were sent to Kozlowski and has her kidnapped. Using outback strategy, Hogan gains entrance and frees his woman.

CROMWELL
1970, 139 mins, UK Ⓥ ⊙ ⊠
D: Ken Hughes **A:** Richard Harris, Alec Guinness, Robert Morley, Dorothy Tutin, Frank Finlay, Timothy Dalton (Allen/Columbia)

The nub is the confrontation of the two complex leading characters, Oliver Cromwell and King Charles I. Richard Harris and Alec Guinness, respectively, give powerhouse performances. Harris plays the idealistic, dedicated Cromwell with cold eyes, tortured, rasping voice, and an inflexible spirit.
1970: Best Costume Design
Nomination: Best Original Score

CROOKLYN
1994, 112 mins, US 🆅 ⊙
D: Spike Lee **A:** Alfre Woodard, Delroy Lindo, David Patrick Kelly, Zelda Harris, Carlton Williams, Sharif Rashed (40 Acres & a Mule/Universal)

Both annoying and vibrant, casually plotted and deeply personal, Spike Lee's *Crooklyn* ends up being as compelling as it is messy. Fictionalized look at the filmmaker's family life during the early 1970s is loud, grating, disorganized, and off-putting for more than half its running time, but eventually jells into an exceedingly vivid portrait of a specific household. Performances are mostly high voltage, led by Woodard as the mother understandably about to come apart at the seams.

CROSS CREEK
1983, 122 mins, US 🆅
D: Martin Ritt **A:** Mary Steenburgen, Rip Torn, Peter Coyote, Dana Hill, Alfre Woodard, Joanna Miles (Thorn-EMI)

Cross Creek, based on the memoirs of *The Yearling* author Marjorie Kinnan Rawlings, offers a sanitized vision of her early struggle to publish a novel and the Florida backwoods which inspired her prose. It's an uncompelling, yet warm tale which lightly skips over the woman's travails by illustrating a series of vignettes of rural humanity. The overall effect trivializes a life and provides little insight into the artistic process.
1983: Nominations: Best Supp. Actor (Rip Torn), Supp. Actress (Alfre Woodard), Costume Design, Original Score

CROSSED SWORDS
See: See: The Prince and the Pauper (1977)

CROSSFIRE
1947, 84 mins, US 🆅 ⊙
D: Edward Dmytryk **A:** Robert Young, Robert Mitchum, Robert Ryan, Gloria Grahame, Paul Kelly, Sam Levene (RKO)

Crossfire is a frank spotlight on anti-Semitism, a hard-hitting film whose who-dunit aspects are fundamentally incidental to the overall thesis of bigotry and race prejudice. There are three Roberts all giving capital performances. Young is unusual as the detective captain; Mitchum is the right sort of cynical GI; and Ryan a commanding personality, in this instance the bigoted soldier-killer, whose sneers and leers about Sam Levene and his tribe are all too obvious.

1947: Nominations: Best Picture, Director, Supp. Actor (Robert Ryan), Supp. Actress (Gloria Grahame), Screenplay

CROSSING DELANCEY
1988, 97 mins, US 🆅 ⊙
D: Joan Micklin Silver **A:** Amy Irving, Reizl Bozyk, Peter Riegert, Jeroen Krabbe, Sylvia Miles, Suzzy Roche (Warner)

In an unexpectedly enjoyable way, *Crossing Delancey* addresses the dilemma of how the 30-ish, attractive, successful, intelligent, and unmarried female finds a mate she can be happy with. Amy Irving works in a pretentious Manhattan bookstore. Matchmaker (Sylvia Miles) brings Irving together with an unlikely candidate, pickle maker Sam Posner (Peter Riegert). The major setups focus on Irving's torn affections between the rakish, smooth-talking charm of pulp novelist Anton Maes (Jeroen Krabbe) and earnest, straightforward, vulnerable Riegert.

CROSSING GUARD, THE
1995, 114 mins, US 🆅 ⊙
D: Sean Penn **A:** Jack Nicholson, David Morse, Anjelica Huston, Robin Wright, Piper Laurie, Richard Bradford (Miramax)

A sorrowful account of the aftermath of tragedy. Jack Nicholson plays Freddy Gale, a jeweler whose life took a seemingly irrevocable downturn following an accident in which drunk driver John Booth (David Morse) killed his seven-year-old daughter. Story picks up six years later, when Booth is released from prison and revenge-obsessed Freddy informs his ex-wife, Mary (Anjelica Huston), of his intention to kill the man. Booth looks to a sensitive painter, JoJo (Robin Wright), to help him over his crippling guilt. Much of the film plays awkwardly, its tone veering undecidedly between volatile drama and contemplative psychological study.

CROSSING THE LINE
See: The Big Man

CROSS MY HEART
1987, 90 mins, US
D: Armyan Bernstein **A:** Martin Short, Annette O'Toole, Paul Reiser, Joanna Kerns, Jessica Puscas, Lee Arenberg (Universal)

Cross My Heart wants to be both cute and incisive in its presentation of an up-to-date relationship, but proves too insipid to achieve the former and too slick to fully reach the latter goal. Conceptually ambitious, virtually the entire film is devoted to the detailing of one date over the course of a single night. In conventional terms, Martin Short and Annette O'Toole supply good characterizations.

CROSS OF IRON
1977, 130 mins, UK/W. GERMANY Ⓥ ⊙
D: Sam Peckinpah A: James Coburn, Maximilian Schell, James Mason, David Warner, Klaus Lowitsch, Roger Fritz (EMI/Rapid/Terra)

Cross of Iron more than anything else affirms director Sam Peckinpah's prowess as an action filmmaker of graphic mayhem. Told from the German viewpoint as the Wehrmacht's cream were being clobbered on the Russian front circa 1943, the production is well but conventionally cast, technically impressive, but ultimately violence-fixated.

CROSSPLOT
1969, 97 mins, UK
D: Alvin Rakoff A: Roger Moore, Martha Hyer, Claudie Lange, Alexis Kanner, Francis Matthews, Bernard Lee (United Artists/Tribune)

A thriller with a few good jokes, red herrings, a few quick genuine thrills, chases, and some mystery. It doesn't jell because the mystery is too cloudy. Motivation of most characters is indecisive and some are badly undeveloped. Roger Moore plays a debonair ad exec with a flair for his job and a roving eye for the chicks. He is not wholly convincing as a man of action.

CROSSROADS
1942, 82 mins, US
D: Jack Conway A: William Powell, Hedy Lamarr, Claire Trevor, Basil Rathbone, Felix Bressart, H. B. Warner (M-G-M)

This is a grade-A whodunit, with a superlative cast. The novel story line would do credit to an Alfred Hitchcock thriller. A prominent member of France's foreign office, William Powell is accused of having been a thief prior to a train accident in which he suffered amnesia. During the trial Basil Rathbone proves that it's a case of mistaken identity. Once freed, Powell is then harassed by Rathbone, who says that Powell was, actually, his accomplice in murder and robbery.

CROSSROADS
1986, 96 mins, US Ⓥ ⊙
D: Walter Hill A: Ralph Macchio, Joe Seneca, Jami Gertz, Joe Morton, Robert Judd, Steve Vai (Carliner/Columbia-Delphi IV)

John Fusco's screenplay makes ample use of the legend of the late bluesman Robert Johnson. Ralph Macchio, a classical-guitar student, discovers an old playing companion of Johnson's in a New York hospital. Hoping to make his reputation by finding and recording Johnson's alleged unknown 30th song, Macchio springs old Joe Seneca from the facility, and the unlikely pair hit the road for Mississippi Delta country.

CROW, THE
1994, 100 mins, US Ⓥ ⊙
D: Alex Proyas A: Brandon Lee, Ernie Hudson, Michael Wincott, David Patrick Kelly, Angel David, Rochelle Davis (Miramax)

The Crow flies high. For a while rumored to be impossible to complete due to the tragic accidental death of star Brandon Lee eight days before lensing was due to wrap, the pic that finally emerges is a seamless, pulsating, dazzlingly visual revenge fantasy. Based on James O'Barr's bold comic strip, which has generated a considerable following since he started drawing it in the early 1980s, *The Crow* centers on a dark angel who literally rises from the dead to settle matters with the gang of thugs who killed him and his fiancée on the eve of their wedding.

CROW, THE
CITY OF ANGELS
1996, 84 mins, US Ⓥ ⊙
D: Tim Pope A: Vincent Perez, Mia Kirshner, Richard Brooks, Iggy Pop, Thomas Jane, Vincent Castellanos (Pressman/Miramax-Dimension)

European hunk Vincent Perez replaces the late Brandon Lee as an avenger who returns from the dead to punish those responsible for his murder. Different hero, same m.o. And, for good measure, same makeup and costume. Imagine a punk-rock Pierrot, and you'll get the picture. While the first *Crow* was infused with all the dark, death-obsessed energy of a heavy-metal concert, *City of Angels* is a lumbering and repetitive bore. Worse, a great deal of the movie doesn't make any sense, even on the level of stylized fantasy. Overall, *City of Angels* has the look and feel of a movie that, at some point, was a good deal longer. Not necessarily better, but longer.

CROWD, THE
1928, 98 mins, US Ⓥ ⊙ ⊗
D: King Vidor **A:** Eleanor Boardman, James Murray, Bert Roach, Daniel G. Tomlinson, Dell Henderson, Lucy Beaumont (M-G-M)

A drab actionless story of ungodly length and apparently telling nothing. Superficially it reels off as an analytical insight into the life, worries, and struggles of two young, ordinary people, who marry and become parents. James Murray is the young husband and catches the spirit at times, more in looks than anything else. Both he and Eleanor Boardman have the opportunity for a big scene when seeing their child trampled by a moving truck while walking toward their home. Both parents muff the chance by a mile.
1927/28: Nominations: Best Director; Artistic Quality of Production

CROWD ROARS, THE
1932, 84 mins, US
D: Howard Hawks **A:** James Cagney, Joan Blondell, Ann Dvorak, Eric Linden, Guy Kibbee, Frank McHugh (Warner)

All auto-race pictures lead to Indianapolis, and there is no deviation from that schedule here. James Cagney's a frontrank pilot who, having added the kid brother (Eric Linden) to his crew, can't reconcile himself to having the kid on too friendly terms with the girl with whom he's been living (Ann Dvorak). To retaliate she sics her girlfriend (Joan Blondell) onto the brother, with this latter situation developing into a romance which splits the brothers.

CROWD ROARS, THE
1938, 87 mins, US
D: Richard Thorpe **A:** Robert Taylor, Edward Arnold, Frank Morgan, Maureen O'Sullivan, William Gargan, Lionel Stander (M-G-M)

Prizefighting is a rough-and-tumble racket operated by big-time gamblers with small-time ethics, according to *The Crowd Roars*, in which Robert Taylor leads with his left hand. It's exciting melodrama with plenty of ring action, some plausible romance, and several corking good characterizations, and holds to a plot about a choirboy who becomes a contender for the light-heavyweight championship.

CRUCIBLE, THE
1996, 123 mins, US Ⓥ ⊙
D: Nicholas Hytner **A:** Daniel Day-Lewis, Winona Ryder, Paul Scofield, Joan Allen, Bruce Davison, Rob Campbell (20th Centruy-Fox)

Arthur Miller's play *The Crucible* doesn't emerge onscreen with its full impact intact. This handsomely mounted tale of witch hunts, religious persecution, sexual revenge, and social hysteria in 17th-century Salem, MA, still possesses the power to stir up wrenching emotion, but neither the establishing dramatic linchpin nor the final conversion of conscience is terribly convincing. Proctor (Daniel Day-Lewis), a farmer, had an affair with young Abigail Williams (Winona Ryder) when she worked at his house, but when his wife, Elizabeth (Joan Allen), got wind of it, Abigail was tossed out. John attempts to revive the liaison, but John resolutely refuses. Abigail begins accusing other women, and the hysteria begins. Eminent Judge Danforth (Paul Scofield) arrives to lead the investigation and root out the plague of Satan. There is absolutely no apparent sexual frisson between Day-Lewis and Ryder. Allen endows the doubly wronged, weathered Elizabeth with an understated power.
1996: Nominations: Best Supp. Actress (Joan Allen), Screenplay Adaptation

CRUEL INTENTIONS
1999, 95 mins, US Ⓥ ⊙
D: Roger Kumble **A:** Sarah Michelle Gellar, Ryan Philippe, Reese Witherspoon, Selma Blair, Louise Fletcher, Joshua Jackson (Sony)

Choderlos de Laclos's notorious 1782 novel as its inspiration, *Cruel Intentions* is *Dangerous Liaisons* for the teenage crowd, nasty, profane, and wickedly entertaining for the most part. Set in Manhattan's upper-crust society during summer break, tale revolves around Kathryn Merteuil (Sarah Michelle Gellar) and Sebastian Valmont (Ryan Philippe), two wealthy stepsibs who spend their time concocting diabolical wagers. With sexual conquest as chief reward, the duo select as their new pawns the naive Cecile (Selma Blair) and the virginal Annette Hargrove (Reese Witherspoon). The first two acts provide the kind of lewd, odious fun seldom encountered in teen films. Unfortunately the last chapter is too earnest and obvious. In a significant stretch from TV's *Buffy, the Vampire Slayer,* Gellar shines as the witty, evil, and vulnerable Kathryn.

CRUEL SEA, THE
1953, 120 mins, US Ⓥ
D: Charles Frend **A:** Jack Hawkins, Don-

ald Sinden, Denholm Elliott, Stanley Baker, Virginia McKenna (Ealing)

A serious, authentic reconstruction of the battle of the Atlantic, based on Nicholas Monsarrat's bestseller. As the commentator explains, the heroes are the men, the heroines are the ships, and the villain is the cruel sea. These three elements are put into focus via the activities of a corvette which puts to sea with only one experienced officer—the captain—aboard. Their first operational duties land them in a storm, but subsequently they encounter enemy activity and are harassed by U-boats. Notable thesping comes from Jack Hawkins, who plays the captain with requisite authority.
1953: Nomination: Best Screenplay

CRUISING
1980, 106 mins, US Ⓥ
D: William Friedkin **A:** Al Pacino, Paul Sorvino, Karen Allen, Richard Cox, Don Scardino (Lorimar)

In *Cruising* writer-director William Friedkin explores the S&M life of New York City. Like any approach to the bizarre, it is fascinating for about 15 minutes. Pacino is an innocent young cop chosen to go underground in search of a killer. He ultimately zeroes in on the culprit but by now is almost as far around the bend as his prey. But that's not saying much more than the old maxim: he who lies down with dogs gets up with fleas.

CRUSADES, THE
1935, 124 mins, US
D: Cecil B. DeMille **A:** Loretta Young, Henry Wilcoxon, Ian Keith, C. Aubrey Smith, Katherine DeMille, Joseph Schildkraut (Paramount)

It's long, and the story is not up to some of Cecil B. DeMille's previous films, but the production has sweep and spectacle. DeMille patently intended his puppets to be subjugated by the generally transcendental theme of this holy war on the infidels. Only the pious wandering hermit (capably done by C. Aubrey Smith) stands out as the sole symbol of the faith in the invasion of Acre and Jerusalem. Henry Wilcoxon plays Richard the Lion-Hearted. For sheer versatility, ranging from horsemanship to boudoir, there are few players who could have done as well.
1935: Nomination: Best Cinematography

CRUSH, THE
1993, 89 mins, US Ⓥ ⊙
D: Alan Shapiro **A:** Cary Elwes, Alicia Silverstone, Jennifer Rubin, Amber Benson, Kurtwood Smith, Gwynyth Walsh (Morgan Creek)

The Crush is a by-the-numbers thriller longer on suspense than brains. Cary Elwes plays a writer who moves into the guest house of a wealthy couple and befriends their beautiful, precocious 14-year-old daughter, Darian (Alicia Silverstone). Nick (Elwes) gives in to a momentary indiscretion and kisses the girl, then watches her grow gradually more obsessed, until she starts venting her wrath. Silverstone brings the right mix of little-girl pouting and budding sensuality to a role that is, finally, a caricature.

CRY-BABY
1990, 85 mins, US Ⓥ ⊙
D: John Waters **A:** Johnny Depp, Amy Locane, Susan Tyrrell, Polly Bergen, Iggy Pop, Ricki Lake (Imagine)

John Waters's mischievous satire of the teen exploitation genre returns to the nascent days of rock-and-roll. Cry-Baby (Johnny Depp), a handsome delinquent with a perpetual tear in his eye (in memory of his criminal parents who died in the electric chair), takes the bait from a ponytailed blonde from the well-bred set (Amy Locane). There's so much commotion in the pic, with its 11 full-fledged dance numbers and elaborate production values, that one can't help but catch on that a story's missing. Depp is great as the delinquent juve.

CRY DANGER
1951, 79 mins, US Ⓥ
D: Robert Parrish **A:** Dick Powell, Rhonda Fleming, Richard Erdman, William Conrad, Regis Toomey, Jean Porter (Olympic)

Plot opens with Dick Powell returning after five years in prison, having been pardoned when new evidence turns up that clears him of a robbery rap. Powell sees the pardon as an opportunity to bring the guilty parties to justice. Robert Parrish, erstwhile film editor, makes a strong directorial bow.

CRY FREEDOM
1987, 157 mins, US Ⓥ ⊙ ▭
D: Richard Attenborough **A:** Kevin Kline, Penelope Wilton, Denzel Washington, Kevin McNally, John Thaw, Timothy West (Marble Arch/Universal)

Cry Freedom personifies the struggle of South Africa's black population against apartheid in the evolving friendship of

martyred black activist Stephen Biko and liberal white newspaper editor Donald Woods. It derives its impact less from epic scope than from the wrenching immediacy of its subject matter and the moral heroism of its appealingly played, idealistic protagonists. The singular flaw—an overemphasis in the film's final hour on the Woods family's escape to exile in England. Kline's familiar low-key screen presence serves him well in his portrayal of the strong-willed but even-tempered journalist. Washington does a remarkable job of transforming himself into the articulate and mesmerizing black nationalist leader, whose refusal to keep silent led to his death in police custody and a subsequent cover-up.
1987: Nominations: Best Original Score, Song ("Cry Freedom")

CRY HAVOC
1943, 96 mins, US
D: Richard Thorpe **A:** Margaret Sullavan, Ann Sothern, Joan Blondell, Fay Bainter, Marsha Hunt, Ella Raines (M-G-M)

Plot sets up all-femme cast with nine girls rounded up from evacuation of Manila to function as volunteers at an outland field hospital. The nine are from various fields of endeavor, including waitress Ann Sothern and former burlesque performer Joan Blondell. Best thing about the film is the capable cast tossed in for group of generally fine performances, despite the inadequacies of the plot in both suspense and movement.

CRYING GAME, THE
1992, 113 mins, US Ⓥ ⊙ ▭
D: Neil Jordan **A:** Stephen Rea, Miranda Richardson, Forest Whitaker, Jaye Davidson, Adrian Dunbar, Jim Broadbent (Palace/Channel 4)

The IRA's kidnapping in Northern Ireland of British soldier Jody (Forest Whitaker) serves as the jumping-off point for a fearlessly penetrating examination of politics, race, sexuality, and human nature. First act concerns Whitaker's countryhouse incarceration, mostly under the guard of Fergus (Stephen Rea), who develops an intense rapport with the prisoner. Fergus later escapes to London, where he finds Jody's great love, Dil (Jaye Davidson). Dil entices Fergus into a relationship that will test just how far he's willing to go for love. Whitaker's simply terrific. Rea is intriguingly handsome-homely, decisive-passive, gentle-violent. Newcomer Davidson is almost impossibly

right as the beautiful, mysterious Dil, while Richardson is equal parts fire and ice as the most resilient IRA member.
1992: Best Original Screenplay
Nominations: Best Picture, Director, Actor (Stephen Rea), Supp. Actor (Jaye Davidson), Editing

CRY IN THE DARK, A (AUSTRALIA: EVIL ANGELS)
1988, 121 mins, US Ⓥ ⊙ ▭
D: Fred Schepisi **A:** Meryl Streep, Sam Neill, Bruce Myles, Charles Tingwell, Nick Tate, Lewis Fitz-Gerald (Cannon)

One of the oddest and most illogical murder cases of modern times is recounted in intimate, incredible detail in the classy, disturbing drama *A Cry in the Dark*. The saga of Lindy Chamberlain's harassment, trial, and imprisonment for having allegedly murdered her baby daughter, when there was literally no evidence against her, was the biggest news story in Australia of the 1980s. If one didn't know who Meryl Streep is, one could easily guess Lindy was played by a fine, unknown Australian actress. Sam Neill, who here looks remarkably like the real Michael Chamberlain, well conveys the tentative strengths and very real weaknesses of a man thrust into an unimaginable situation.
1988: Nomination: Best Actress (Meryl Streep)

CRY OF THE CITY
1948, 96 mins, US
D: Robert Siodmak **A:** Victor Mature, Richard Conte, Fred Clark, Shelley Winters, Debra Paget, Hope Emerson (20th Century-Fox)

The hard-hitting suspense-of-the-chase formula is given top-notch presentation. The telling screenplay presents Victor Mature as a police lieutenant in homicide and Richard Conte as a cop killer, although both antagonists sprang from New York's Italian sector. Shelley Winters sparks small assignment of a girl who drives the killer through the New York streets.

CRYSTAL BALL, THE
1943, 80 mins, US
D: Elliott Nugent **A:** Paulette Goddard, Ray Milland, Virginia Field, William Bendix, Gladys George, Ernest Truex (United Artists)

The Crystal Ball carries a strong romantic flavor with Ray Milland and Paulette Goddard paired, while Virginia Field is the frustrated fiancée in the triangular setup. Field plays a rich widow, Goddard a stranded gal who goes to work as a shill for a shooting gallery. When the fake medium takes sick, Goddard doubles on the fortune-telling racket and nearly gets Milland into trouble by advising that he take an option on some property that the government is after.

CRY, THE BELOVED COUNTRY
(US: AFRICAN FURY)
1952, 103 mins, US Ⓥ
D: Zoltan Korda A: Canada Lee, Charles Carson, Sidney Poitier, Joyce Carey, Geoffrey Keen, Michael Goodliffe (London/British Lion)

Alan Paton's bestselling novel has been turned into an absorbing pic, the story of a simple, native Negro country preacher (Canada Lee) who goes to the big city of Johannesburg to seek a missing sister and wayward son, and who finds both in the crime-ridden, slum elements of the city. Lee's performance, restrained and underplayed, is a rich, heartwarming portrayal, dominating the film. Sidney Poitier is manly and striking as a young Negro preacher.

CRY, THE BELOVED COUNTRY
1995, 111 mins, US Ⓥ ⊙
D: Darrell James Roodt A: James Earl Jones, Richard Harris, Vusi Kunene, Leleti Khumalo, Charles S. Dutton, Eric Miyeni (Distant Horizon)

Alan Paton's novel has been remade in a markedly different style from its 1952 screen translation. New outing is considerably more majestic in scope, earnest in tone, and allegorical in style. But the low-key tone eventually works against the material. Both Jones and Harris work hard to convey their characters' innate decency, but they seem inauthentic in their surroundings.

CSILLAGOSOK, KATONAK
(THE RED AND THE WHITE)
1967, 92 mins, HUNGARY/USSR Ⓥ ▭
D: Miklos Jancso A: Andras Kozak, Krystyna Mikolajewska, Jacint Juhasz, Tatyana Konyukhova, Mikhail Kozakov, Viktor Avdushko (Mafilm/Mosfilm)

An episode in the 1918-22 civil war in Russia. Two forces fight each other: a unit of the Red Army and a group of White Guards. It seems that there is only one aim: to liquidate the other side. Jancso concentrates his message on the philosophical problem of life and death. Unknown and nameless men enter history in a given moment and after some time they step out of the scene with their death. Film is as merciless as the necessity which activates history. There is no stirring spectacle. The dialogue is limited almost to military commands. The camera moves without ceasing. This continuous movement, and the continuity of internal cutting, creates a strong tension.

CUBA
1979, 122 mins, US Ⓥ
D: Richard Lester A: Sean Connery, Brooke Adams, Jack Weston, Chris Sarandon, Denholm Elliott, Martin Balsam (United Artists)

Cuba is a hollow, pointless nondrama. Cynical and evasive about politics, pic displays uniformly unsympathetic characters enacting a vague plot amid a splendid recreation of Havana at the very end of the Batista regime. Given the worthless, motley crew seen to populate Havana—including gross American profiteer Jack Weston and cynical gentleman Denholm Elliott—political outlook would seem to be that things couldn't get much worse, and maybe Castro will be a little bit better.

CUJO
1983, 91 mins, US Ⓥ ⊙
D: Lewis Teague A: Dee Wallace, Danny Pintauro, Daniel Hugh-Kelly, Christopher Stone, Ed Lauter, Kaiulani Lee (Taft/Warner)

Although well made, this screen adaptation of Stephen King's *Cujo* emerges as a dull, uneventful entry in the horror genre. Novel about a mad dog on the rampage occupies a low place in the King canon, which is understandable if the film's stupefying predictability is an accurate reflection of the book. Except for the appealing kid played by Danny Pintauro, the characters are of little interest.

CUL-DE-SAC
1966, 111 mins, US Ⓥ
D: Roman Polanski A: Donald Pleasence, Francoise Dorleac, Lionel Stander, Jack McGowran, William Franklyn, Jacqueline Bisset (Compton)

As a study in kinky insanity, *Cul-de-Sac* creates a tingling atmosphere. Film was shot on location in and around a lonely castle on remote Holy Island off the northeast coast of Britain. Donald Pleasence is an obvious neurotic, living like a hermit with his young, bored, and flirtatious French wife (Francoise Dorleac). Suddenly two wounded gangsters on the run descend upon them. From then on it's a battle of nerves, a cat-and-mouse psychological tightrope walk. Pleasence pours some exaggerated but distinctive thesping into his pathetic role, while Lionel Stander, obviously more flamboyant, blends nicely with him.

CULPEPPER CATTLE CO., THE
1972, 92 mins, US ⊗
D: Dick Richards A: Gary Grimes, Billy "Green" Bush, Luke Askew, Bo Hopkins, Geoffrey Lewis, Wayne Sutherlin (20th Century-Fox)

An unsuccessful attempt to mount a poetic and stylistic ballet of death in the environment of a period western. Gary Grimes is featured as a teenager who matures in the course of a hard, violent, and bloody cattle drive. Billy "Green" Bush plays Culpepper, hard-bitten range boss, whose likable, easygoing, and natural manner come across as the only effective performance.

CURLY SUE
1991, 101 mins, US ⊗ ⊙
D: John Hughes A: James Belushi, Kelly Lynch, Alisan Porter, John Getz, Fred Dalton Thompson, Cameron Thor (Warner)

This predictable crowd pleaser is at heart a two-hanky affair, a mix of childish gags and shameless melodrama. Pic clearly aspires to Capraesque sentimentality: a drifting con man (James Belushi) and his adopted nine-year-old daughter (Alisan Porter) scam a corporate attorney (Kelly Lynch) and gradually win her heart, much to the chagrin of her snotty boyfriend (John Getz).

CURSE OF FRANKENSTEIN, THE
1957, 82 mins, US ⊗
D: Terence Fisher A: Peter Cushing, Christopher Lee, Hazel Court, Robert Urquhart, Valerie Gaunt, Melvyn Hayes (Hammer)

This British version of the classic shocker emphasizes the clinical details whereby the crazy scientist accumulates the odd organs with which to assemble the creature. Story is unfolded while the infamous Baron Frankenstein is awaiting execution for multiple murders he vainly protests have been committed by his man-made monster (Christopher Lee). Peter Cushing gets every inch of drama from the leading role, making almost believable the ambitious urge and diabolical accomplishment.

CURSE OF THE CAT PEOPLE, THE
1944, 70 mins, US ⊗ ⊙
D: Gunther von Fritsch, Robert Wise A: Simone Simon, Kent Smith, Jane Randolph, Ann Carter, Eve March, Elizabeth Russell (RKO)

Made as sequel to the profitable *Cat People,* having the same principals as the original chiller, this is a strange cinema stew that is apt to make audiences laugh at the wrong scenes. Plot has the offspring of the first wife of a naval architect (Kent Smith) apparently suffering from the same supernatural beliefs that brought the death of the child's mother.

CURSE OF THE MUMMY'S TOMB, THE
1964, 80 mins, UK ▭
D: Michael Carreras A: Terence Morgan, Fred Clark, Ronald Howard, Jeanne Roland, George Pastell, John Paul (Hammer)

Modest and rather slapdash horror pic. Plot hinges around the discovery of an ancient tomb in the Egyptian desert, with a curse on anybody who opens it. Murder and mayhem begins its gory trail. Terence Morgan performs smoothly enough as the villain but is too patently up to no good from the start. The liveliest performance comes from Fred Clark.

CURSE OF THE PINK PANTHER
1983, 109 mins, US ▭
D: Blake Edwards A: Ted Wass, David Niven, Robert Wagner, Herbert Lom, Capucine, Roger Moore (Titan/Edwards/United Artists)

Abetted by screen newcomer Ted Wass's flair for physical comedy, filmmaker Blake Edwards has created genuinely funny sight gags, but the film's rickety, old-hat story values waste them. Lensed simultaneously with *Trail of the Pink Panther, Curse* boasts all-new footage but virtually repeats the prior release's story line. Instead of a reporter tracking down the missing Inspector Clouseau, NY cop Clifton Sleigh (Ted Wass) is the bumbling man for the job. Format has him encountering and interviewing characters from earlier films in the series.

CURSE OF THE WEREWOLF, THE
1961, 91 mins, US ⊗
D: Terence Fisher A: Clifford Evans, Oliver Reed, Yvonne Romain, Catherine Feller, Anthony Dawson, Warren Mitchell (Hammer)

The screenplay dwells at extraordinary

length on the vile heritage responsible for the genesis of the story's monster. But this lengthy prologue sustains equal, if not greater, interest than the film's principal story, which involves the personal plight of the wolfman himself. Especially convincing characters are created by Oliver Reed as the compassionate werewolf, Clifford Evans, Anthony Dawson, Richard Wordsworth, and Martin Matthews.

CUSTER OF THE WEST
1968, 143 mins, US/Spain ▢
D: Robert Siodmak **A:** Robert Shaw, Mary Ure, Jeffrey Hunter, Ty Hardin, Charles Stanlaker, Robert Hall (Cinerama/Security)

Capable, audience-involving adventure on the visual level which doesn't rise to the epic stature but is content to résumé the facts about the 7th Cavalry without taking a coherent attitude to them. The arid, rocky Spanish vistas stand in okay for old Indian territory—especially for those not overly familiar with them. Robert Shaw gives Custer a simple forthrightness and dash that is effective, despite its naive context.

CUT ABOVE, A
See: Gross Anatomy

CUTTER AND BONE
See: Cutter's Way

CUTTER'S WAY
(AKA: CUTTER AND BONE)
1981, 105 mins, US Ⓥ ⊙
D: Ivan Passer **A:** Jeff Bridges, John Heard, Lisa Eichhorn, Ann Dusenberry, Stephen Elliott, Nina Van Pallandt (Gurian)

With any number of initially intriguing plotlines, director, and scripter never even come close to shedding light on what, if anything, this picture is really about. Jeff Bridges, John Heard, and Lisa Eichhorn all deliver exceptionally fine topline performances, but their efforts seem wasted in such a weak vehicle. Bridges limns a pretty beach-boy type. His best friend is Heard, a wildly bitter yet fiercely adventurous alcoholic who lost his leg in Vietnam. Heard is married to Eichhorn, who's also taken to the bottle but, unlike the other two, is aware that her personal world is crumbling. Unfortunately, the trio is framed in an obtuse murder mystery.

CUTTHROAT ISLAND
1995, 123 mins, US Ⓥ ⊙ ▢
D: Renny Harlin **A:** Geena Davis, Matthew Modine, Frank Langella, Maury

Chaykin, Patrick Malahide, Stan Shaw (Carolco/Forge/Studio Canal Plus/Tele-Communications)

Cutthroat Island strenuously but vainly attempts to revive the thrills of old-fashioned pirate pictures. Giving most of the swashbuckling opportunities to star Geena Davis, pic does little with its reversal of gender expectations and features a seriously mismatched romantic duo in Davis and Matthew Modine. Pic is a feast for the eyes due to Norman Garwood's lavish production design, Enrico Sabbatini's equally florid costumes, and the striking locations in Malta (doubling for 1600s Jamaica) and Thailand.

CUTTING EDGE, THE
1992, 101 mins, US Ⓥ
D: Paul Michael Glaser **A:** D. B. Sweeney, Moira Kelly, Roy Dotrice, Terry O'Quinn, Dwier Brown (M-G-M/Interscope)

This neatly formulaic romantic comedy has a sharp enough combination of teen-oriented elements and style. Pic pits frosty-tempered ice queen Kate Mosely (Moira Kelly) against brash, competitive Doug Dorsey (D. B. Sweeney), a former star of the US Olympic hockey team who approaches figure skating with great misgivings. Sport's close physical contact provides some *Dirty Dancing*–style titillation, with interest heightened by the watchable actors.

CYNARA
1932, 78 mins, US
D: King Vidor **A:** Ronald Colman, Kay Francis, Phyllis Barry, Henry Stephenson, Viva Tattersall (Goldwyn/United Artists)

Stage play has been put on the screen with beautiful balance of directness and simplicity. It has to do with gallant and likable people—Ronald Colman's very human husband, Kay Francis' glamorous wife, and the eager young London shop girl who stumbled into being the other woman without very well knowing what she was doing, and afterward paying bitterly for her wayward impulse.

CYNTHIA
1947, 97 mins, US
D: Robert Z. Leonard **A:** Elizabeth Taylor, George Murphy, S. Z. Sakall, Mary Astor, Spring Byington, Gene Lockhart (M-G-M)

Elizabeth Taylor breathes plenty of life into the title role as a sheltered young girl who has never had a date or other fun generally accepted as matter-of-fact by teenagers. Plot builds to her first romance and first high-school dance while depicting the myriad details of family life in a small town. Murphy and Astor make an excellent team to carry the adult load.

CYRANO DE BERGERAC
1950, 112 mins, US ⑳ ☉
D: Michael Gordon **A:** Jose Ferrer, Mala Powers, William Prince, Morris Carnovsky, Lloyd Corrigan (United Artists)

More stage play than motion picture. Interpreting the rhyme and prose of the play is Jose Ferrer. Film comes to the screen as an outstanding achievement in histrionics, quick with humor and sadness. The *Cyrano* plot needs little reprising. A man, made a clown by a great peninsula of a nose, supplies the love words so that another, more handsome of profile, may woo the girl to whom he has lost his heart.
1950: Best Actor (Jose Ferrer)

CYRANO DE BERGERAC
1990, 138 mins, France ⑳ ☉
D: Jean-Paul Rappeneau **A:** Gerard Depardieu, Anne Brochet, Vincent Perez, Jacques Weber, Roland Bertin, Philippe Morier-Genoud

A winner by more than a nose, *Cyrano de Bergerac* attains a near-perfect balance of verbal and visual flamboyance. Gerard Depardieu's grand performance as the facially disgraced swordsman-poet sets a new standard with which all future *Cyranos* will have to reckon. Jean-Paul Rappeneau's sumptuous ($17 million) screen adaptation of Edmond Rostand's heroic verse play has dash, lyricism, and a superb acting ensemble. Rappeneau and screenwriter Jean-Claude Carriere have opened up the play conventionally but intelli-

gently. Roxanne is played with finesse and feeling by Anne Brochet, who captures the romantic immaturity and generosity of soul.

CZLOWIEK Z MARMURU
(MAN OF MARBLE)
1977, 161 mins, Poland ⑳
D: Andrzej Wajda **A:** Jerzy Radziwilowicz, Krystyna Janda, Tadeusz Lomnicki, Jacek Lomnicki, Michal Tarkowski, Piotr Cieslak (Group X)

This epic film records two pages of history—the year 1952, the height of the Stalinization period, and the year 1976, when a revealing reassessment of the times takes place. It is the story of Mateusz Birkut, a simple, modest worker is raised to the level of a national hero without quite knowing why. Pic begins with a 24-year-old femme TV reporter, Agnieszka, greedy to tell the full story of what happened to Birkut, who has long since dropped from sight. It's her nervous search for truth that raises *Man of Marble* to a height of suspense, as in a detective thriller.

CZLOWIEK Z ZELAZA
(MAN OF IRON)
1981, 140 mins, Poland ⑳
D: Andrzej Wajda **A:** Jerzy Radziwilowicz, Krystyna Janda, Marian Opania, Irene Byrska, Boguslaw Linda, Wieslawa Kosmalska (Film Unit X/Film Polski)

Man of Iron uses the same screenplay writer, the same key actors, and the exact same thematic approach (an interview technique) employed in *Man of Marble*. Pic features the passion and determination of one of the second line of workers in the strike committee headed by Lech Walesa.

DA
1988, 102 mins, US ⊗ ⊙

D: Matt Clark **A:** Barnard Hughes, Martin Sheen, William Hickey (Dallas)

This adaptation of Hugh Leonard's autobiographical play and book *Home Before Night*, about an Irish-American playwright's journey of self-discovery from New York to his father's funeral in the Old Sod, casts a beguiling spell, thanks to the playful richness of its language and the finely knit acting. The linchpin of the affecting story is provided by Leonard's dramaturgic sleight of hand in presenting Charlie's (Sheen) dead father, Da (Hughes), and mother (Doreen Hepburn) as living, breathing temporal characters animated by the successful playwright's grief-catalyzed imagination.

DAD
1989, 117 mins, US ⊗ ⊙

D: Gary David Goldberg **A:** Jack Lemmon, Ted Danson, Olympia Dukakis, Kathy Baker, Kevin Spacey, Ethan Hawke (Amblin/Universal)

There's much that's funny, warm, and endearing about *Dad*, which deals with the familiar theme of a grown child facing his sense of duty toward an aging parent. Unfortunately, prolonged tilling of that emotional terrain and seemingly endless verbalization of feelings diminish most of what's good about the film. Ted Danson has the pivotal role of Jack Lemmon's somewhat estranged son, who moves in with his parents to ease their final days, in the process finding new meaning in his relationship with his own college-age son (Ethan Hawke).

1989: Nomination: Best Makeup

DADDY LONG LEGS
1931, 80 mins, US

D: Alfred Santell **A:** Janet Gaynor, Warner Baxter, Una Merkel, John Arledge, Claude Gillingwater Sr. (Fox)

Janet Gaynor is the orphanage drudge who suddenly rebels against the harshness of the matron. She is unceremoniously adopted by a bachelor who is also a trustee of the orphanage. She falls in love with this man, who has sent her to college unawares to her. Warner Baxter as the millionaire is an appealer here to women on a big scale.

1955: Nominations: Best Color Art Direction, Scoring of a Musical Picture, Song ("Something's Gotta Give")

DADDY LONG LEGS
1955, 126 mins, US ⊗ ⊙ ⊡

D: Jean Negulesco **A:** Fred Astaire, Leslie Caron, Terry Moore, Thelma Ritter, Fred Clark, Charlotte Austin (20th Century-Fox)

An appealing musical. Astaire was a good choice and works well as the undisciplined and friendly moneybags who develops a wanna-get-married crush on the girl he sends through college, this despite the acknowledged difference in age. And he's still the agile hoofer, although the choreography he and David Robel blueprinted doesn't require too robust a workout. Caron is beguiling all the way.

DADDY'S DYIN' . . . WHO'S GOT THE WILL?
1990, 95 mins, US ⊗ ⊙

D: Jack Fisk **A:** Beau Bridges, Beverly D'Angelo, Tess Harper, Judge Reinhold, Amy Wright, Keith Carradine (Propaganda)

Del Shores's hit play about squabbling Texas siblings is brought to the screen with panache. Shores's script presents a bittersweet family reunion, as three sisters and a brother who don't like each other convene to find out who got what in the will. Beverly D'Angelo steals scenes as the spoiled, scattered little runaround sister who's brought home a beatific California hippie-musician (Judge Reinhold) as the latest in a long line of consorts.

DA HONG DENGLONG GAO GAO GUA
(RAISE THE RED LANTERN)
1991, 122 mins, Hong Kong ⊗ ⊙

D: Zhang Yimou **A:** Gong Li, He Saifei, Ma Jingwu, Cao Cuifeng (Era)

Set in the 1920s, before the Communist revolution, film opens with a beautiful young woman tearfully agreeing to become a concubine for a wealthy master. Songlian takes her place as the youngest and most attractive of four wives. Insidious intrigue between the women immediately begins. Pacing is deliberate, but the story is still gripping and visual textures are extraordinary. Gong's presence gives the film a constant erotic charge.

DAISIES
See: Sedmikrasky

DAISY KENYON
1947, 100 mins, US
D: Otto Preminger **A:** Joan Crawford, Dana Andrews, Henry Fonda, Ruth Warrick, Peggy Ann Garner (20th Century-Fox)

Triangle, in which Dana Andrews and Henry Fonda fight it out for the love of Joan Crawford, is basically a shallow lending-library affair, but it's made to seem important by the magnetic trio's slick-smart backgrounds plus, of course, excellent direction, sophisticated dialogue, solid supporting cast, and other flashy production values.

DAISY MILLER
1974, 90 mins, US ⓥ
D: Peter Bogdanovich **A:** Cybill Shepherd, Barry Brown, Cloris Leachman, Mildred Natwick, Eileen Brennan (Paramount)

Daisy Miller is a dud. Cybill Shepherd is miscast in the title role. Frederic Raphael's adaptation of the Henry James story doesn't play. The period production by Peter Bogdanovich is handsome. But his direction and concept seem uncertain and fumbled. Supporting performances by Mildred Natwick, Eileen Brennan, and Cloris Leachman are, respectively, excellent, outstanding, and good.
1974: Nomination: Best Costume Design

DALEKS—INVASION EARTH 2150 A.D.
1966, 84 mins, UK ⓥ ▭
D: Gordon Flemyng **A:** Peter Cushing, Bernard Cribbins, Ray Brooks, Andrew Keir (Aaru)

Dr. Who, in his time-and-space machine, arrives in London in A.D. 2150 to find it ravaged after a Dalek invasion. It is all fairly naive stuff decked out with impressive scientific jargon. Peter Cushing as the professor, Jill Curzon as his niece, and Roberta Tovey as the granddaughter have learned to play it with the necessary seriousness. Bernard Cribbins as the policeman provides some amusing light relief.

DALLAS
1950, 94 mins, US
D: Stuart Heisler **A:** Gary Cooper, Ruth Roman, Steve Cochran, Raymond Massey, Leif Erickson, Barbara Payton (Warner)

Period just following the War Between the States, and the locale is Texas and the then-pioneer town of Dallas. Cooper, a southerner, rides into the territory on the prowl for three brothers, war opportunists who had destroyed his home and family in Georgia. There's a romantic triangle, plus a land-grab angle, to pad out the footage. The chases, gun battles, and other movement come across with good action.

DAMAGE
1992, 112 mins, UK/France ⓥ ⊙
D: Louis Malle **A:** Jeremy Irons, Juliette Binoche, Miranda Richardson, Rupert Graves, Ian Bannen, Leslie Caron (Skreba/NEF/Canal Plus)

A complex look at an illicit affair that ends in disaster for all concerned, *Damage* is a cold, brittle film about raging, traumatic emotions. This veddy British-feeling drama from vet French director Louis Malle proves both compelling and borderline risible, wrenching, and yet emotionally pinched. Jeremy Irons plays Stephen, a graying, very proper figure in the Tory establishment. At a boring political cocktail party, Stephen exchanges significant eye contact with his son's striking g.f., Anna Barton (Juliette Binoche), and destiny is written. At their next encounter Stephen is in Anna's pants in record time.
1992: Nomination: Best Supp. Actress (Miranda Richardson)

DAMA S SOBACHKOY
1960, 90 mins, USSR ⓥ
D: Yosif Kheifits **A:** Aleksei Batalov, Iya Savvina, Ala Chostakova, N. Alisova (Lenfilm)

A perfectly transcribed version of one of Chekhov's short stories. It concerns the Russia of the 1900s, where the upper and middle classes were bored but where propriety stifled any chance of escape. A married man (Aleksei Batalov) meets a married woman (Iya Savvina) during a stay in Yalta. They have an affair and part. He goes to see her again. She then comes to visit him in his town, but they know there is no way out of their impasse. Subtle direction evokes the inner states of the characters, and shows boredom without being boring.

DAM BUSTERS, THE
1955, 125 mins, UK ⓥ
D: Michael Anderson **A:** Richard Todd, Michael Redgrave, Ursula Jeans, Derek Farr, Patrick Barr, John Fraser (Associated British)

The story of the successful raid on the Ruhr dams, which fed the Ruhr factories and caused desolation and havoc to the German war machine. The reconstruction of the raid and the pounding of the dams is done with graphic realism. Michael Redgrave, particularly, gives a vividly human portrayal of Dr. Barnes Wallis the scientist, while Richard Todd makes a distinguished showing as Guy Gibson, the RAF commander.

1955: Nomination: Best Special Effects

DAMES
1934, 90 mins, US ⊗

D: Ray Enright, Busby Berkeley **A:** Joan Blondell, Dick Powell, Ruby Keeler, ZaSu Pitts, Guy Kibbee, Hugh Herbert (Warner)

Heavier on the comedy but lighter on the story than WB's predecessors. There are five song numbers and all amazingly well done. Busby Berkeley pyramids attention in spectacular manner, at times making 'em wide-eyed with his choreographic mating of rhythmic formations with the camera. Ruby Keeler and Dick Powell again are the romantic interest. Joan Blondell is prominent as a decorously subdued but otherwise flip chorine.

DAMIEN OMEN II
1978, 109 mins, US ⊗ ⊙ ▭

D: Don Taylor **A:** William Holden, Lee Grant, Jonathan Scott-Taylor, Robert Foxworth, Lew Ayres, Sylvia Sidney (20th Century-Fox)

Damien is 13 and has a double-personality problem, being both an Antichrist and a rather obnoxious teenager. Stoically played by Jonathan Scott-Taylor, Damien has apparently been behaving himself for the past seven years, since his uncle (William Holden) and aunt (Lee Grant) suspect nothing and love him very much. He soon gets the knack of killing people himself, with spectacular touches that top the decapitations of his tender years.

DAMNATION ALLEY
1977, 95 mins, US ⊗ ▭

D: Jack Smight **A:** Jan-Michael Vincent, George Peppard, Dominique Sanda, Paul Winfield (20th Century-Fox)

Damnation Alley is dull, stirred only occasionally by prods of special effects that only seem exciting compared to the dreariness that proceeded it. What's worse, it's dumb, depending on its stereotyped characters to do the most stupid things under the circumstances in order to keep the story moving. Jan-Michael Vincent and George Peppard are air-force officers on duty in a desert missile bunker when World War III comes.

DAMNED, THE
(US: THESE ARE THE DAMNED)
1963, 87 mins, UK ▭

D: Joseph Losey **A:** Macdonald Carey, Shirley Anne Field, Viveca Lindfors, Alexander Knox, Oliver Reed (Hammer/Swallow)

Joseph Losey's hand is so apparent that the film's considerable effectiveness must be accredited to him as must its few faults and the fearsome message it conveys. The quasi-sci-fi story centers on a group of children being exposed to radiation in preparation for the day predicted by Alexander Knox when global nuclear warfare will destroy all living things except these few.

DAMNED, THE
1969, 163 mins, Italy/W. Germany ⊗

D: Luchino Visconti **A:** Dirk Bogarde, Ingrid Thulin, Helmut Berger, Charlotte Rampling, Florinda Bolkan (Pegaso/Praesidens)

Luchino Visconti pulls out all stops to detail the progress of Nazism in the 1930s as seen via one upperclass family: they murder each other with no hesitation to achieve their ends, they have perverse sexual hang-ups, they are dope fiends, and, in film's most spectacular sequence, a mother among them sleeps with her son. Helmut Berger's progress from meek son to matricidal Nazi is clearly a superior job. Ingrid Thulin is able to handle the violent emotions required for her role as Berger's mother, although Dirk Bogarde is sometimes uncomfortable as her lover.

1969: Nominations: Best Original Story & Screenplay

DAMN THE DEFIANT!
See: H.M.S. Defiant

DAMN YANKEES
(UK: WHAT LOLA WANTS)
1958, 110 mins, US ⊗ ⊙

D: George Abbott, Stanley Donen **A:** Tab Hunter, Gwen Verdon, Ray Walston (Warner)

Story revolves around a Washington Senators fan who would give his soul for a long-ball hitter and a chance to beat the New York Yankees. Given his chance by the devil himself, the fan is whooshed into the body of a 22-year-old who proceeds to become the national hero of the national pastime in the national capital. Gwen Verdon makes a sprightly 172-year-old witch. Ray Walston, with exaggerated widow's peak and devilish red accessories, makes

a perfect comedy Satan. Hunter is sympathetic as the young baseball great, confused by all that's happening to him. Held in prominence is the Richard Adler–Jerry Ross musical score—a tuneful, storytelling assortment of gag songs and ballads.
1958: Nomination: Best Scoring of a Musical Picture

DAMSEL IN DISTRESS, A
1937, 100 mins, US/UK ⊗ ⊙
D: George Stevens **A:** Fred Astaire, George Burns, Gracie Allen, Joan Fontaine, Reginald Gardiner, Constance Collier (RKO)

It's a gay, frothy book, in a British background. Astaire is cast as the juvenile who resents the Lothario buildup endowed him by George Burns as his hyperdynamic p.a. Joan Fontaine is the titular maiden in distress. Astaire and his vet terp aide, Hermes Pan, have devised four corking dance routines. The finale is a four-minute "drum dance," Astaire's solo. Burns and Allen blend excellently, and their comedy is a standout. Gershwin songs are dandy.
1937: Best Dance Direction ("Fun House")

DANCE OF THE VAMPIRES
PARDON ME, BUT YOUR TEETH ARE IN MY NECK
(US: THE FEARLESS VAMPIRE KILLERS)
1967, 107 mins, UK ⊗ ▭
D: Roman Polanski **A:** Roman Polanski, Jack MacGowran, Alfie Bass, Jessie Robins, Sharon Tate, Ferdy Mayne (M-G-M/Cadre/Filmways)

Dance of the Vampires is a spoof on the Dracula theme. Plotline (?) deals with an old professor and his assistant who arrive at a Central Europe inn in dead of winter on a crusade to hunt down and destroy the chilling mystery figures of generations of legends, the dreaded vampires who stalk Slovania. Jack MacGowran cavorts as the nimble oldster and Polanski plays his somewhat dim-witted assistant, both up to the demands (?) of their roles.

DANCES WITH WOLVES
1990, 183 mins, US/UK ⊗ ⊙ ▭
D: Kevin Costner **A:** Kevin Costner, Mary McDonnell, Graham Greene, Rodney A. Grant, Floyd Red Crow Westerman, Tantoo Cardinal (Tig/Majestic)

In his directorial debut, Kevin Costner brings a rare degree of grace and feeling to this elegiac tale of a hero's adventure of discovery among the Sioux Indians on the pristine Dakota plains of the 1860s. Costner stars as a Union officer in the Civil War invited to choose his own post after an act of heroism. Opting for the farthest reaches of the frontier because he "wants to see it before it disappears," he discovers a culture so deeply refreshing to his spirit, compared with the detritus he's left behind, that by the time the US Army bothers to look for him, he has become a Sioux and his name is Dances with Wolves. From its three-hour length, which amazingly does not become tiresome, to its bold use of subtitled Lakota language (the Sioux tongue) for at least a third of the dialogue, it's clear the filmmakers were proceeding without regard for the rules.
1990: Best Picture, Director, Adapted Screenplay, Cinematography, Sound, Original Score, Editing
Nominations: Best Actor (Kevin Costner), Supp. Actor (Grahame Green), Supp. Actress (Mary McDonnell), Art Direction, Costume Design

DANCE WITH A STRANGER
1985, 101 mins, UK ⊗ ⊙
D: Mike Newell **A:** Miranda Richardson, Rupert Everett, Ian Holm, Matthew Carroll (First Picture/Goldcrest/NFFC)

A tale of dark passions based on a true story of the London underworld during the 1950s. Film charts the rocky course of the relationship between Ruth Ellis, a divorcée and prostitute-turned-nightclub manageress, and the upper-class dropout David Blakeley. Film ends with Ellis entering mythology as the last woman to be hanged under British law, for her shooting of Blakeley. Miranda Richardson's performance as Ruth Ellis is first-rate. Major flaw is Rupert Everett's inability to convey more about David Blakeley than that he's set to fail consistently in work and life.

DANCING CO-ED
1939, 80 mins, US
D: S. Sylvan Simon **A:** Lana Turner, Richard Carlson, Artie Shaw, Ann Rutherford, Lee Bowman (M-G-M)

This light and amusing comedy-drama with collegiate background is intended to build up Lana Turner (which it neatly accomplishes). Picture focuses attention on Richard Carlson as a juvenile lead; Ann Rutherford as something more than adolescent romance for Mickey Rooney in the *Judge Hardy* series; and highlights a fine straight performance by Leon Errol. Songs are chiefly confined to the Artie Shaw band's jive sessions, being his own arrangements of a flock of pops.

DANCING IN THE DARK
1949, 92 mins, US Ⓥ
D: Irving Reis **A:** William Powell, Mark Stevens, Betsy Drake, Adolphe Menjou (20th Century-Fox)

Plotline has William Powell, a has-been, steered into a job at 20th Century-Fox as talent scout. Studio is hot after a Broadway singing star and Powell's friendship with her father is the peg for his job. He goes to New York with studio press rep Mark Stevens to sign her up, but double-crosses the lot by signing unknown Betsy Drake. Powell's work is a great personal triumph. Drake's performance has warmth and charm. Adolphe Menjou takes off headman Zanuck to a fare-thee-well.

DANCING LADY
1933, 90 mins, US Ⓥ ⓞ
D: Robert Z. Leonard **A:** Joan Crawford, Clark Gable, Franchot Tone, May Robson, Winnie Lightner, Fred Astaire (M-G-M)

Joan Crawford's chorine days stand her in good stead to demonstrate her versatility as a song-and-dance artist. A formula backstage plot misses nothing, not even the Cinderella rise to prominence, the Park Avenue playboy (Franchot Tone), and the taciturn producer (Clark Gable) who finally succumbs to the charms of the alumna of the burleycue emporium. The dance numbers here are all well done by Sammy Lee and Eddie Prinz. Crawford works with Fred Astaire in "Let's Go Bavarian," both doing their terp stuff with commendable expertness.

DANCIN' THRU THE DARK
1990, 95 mins, UK Ⓥ
D: Mike Ockrent **A:** Claire Hackett, Con O'Neill, Angela Clarke, Mark Womack, Julia Deakin (BBC/Formost)

Shirley Valentine writer Willy Russell returns to his native Liverpool with a gritty low-budget comedy. The strong femme role is Linda (Claire Hackett), who is out on the town with friends on the night before her wedding. Unfortunately her hubbie-to-be and his friends also end up at the same nightspot. Pic is an amusingly accurate look at Liverpool lifestyles among the young and aimless, and while the transition from humor to drama is a bit uncomfortable *Dancin' thru the Dark* is ultimately satisfying and enjoyable.

DANDY IN ASPIC, A
1968, 107 mins, UK Ⓥ ⓞ ▱
D: Anthony Mann **A:** Laurence Harvey, Tom Courtenay, Mia Farrow, Harry Andrews, Lionel Stander (Columbia)

A routine, poorly titled espionage meller loaded with uninteresting, cardboard characters. Laurence Harvey, who finished pic after sudden death in Europe of producer-director Anthony Mann, and Tom Courtenay, both evidently working off pix commitments, are stiff and dull.

DANGER ISLAND
(AKA: MR. MOTO IN DANGER ISLAND)
1939, 70 mins, US
D: Herbert I. Leeds **A:** Peter Lorre, Jean Hersholt, Amanda Duff, Warren Hymer, Richard Lane, Leon Ames (20th Century-Fox)

There is a sameness about the Mr. Moto pictures, yet the plot of each new adventure is always intriguing, and the action is usually carried out in an exciting, suspenseful, and melodramatic manner. This one is also well bolstered by comedy relief, with Warren Hymer, a wrestler, becoming a self-appointed assistant to Lorre. Locale this time is Puerto Rico, where unknowns are suspected of engaging in diamond smuggling.

DANGEROUS
1935, 78 mins, US Ⓥ ⓞ
D: Alfred E. Green **A:** Bette Davis, Franchot Tone, Margaret Lindsay, Alison Skipworth, John Eldredge (Warner)

The triangle involves a successful young architect, a society girl, and an actress. The actress has been famous but has hit the skids and is soused when the architect first meets her in a cellar joint. There is a series of complications, including the reappearance of an almost forgotten husband and an automobile crash. Dialogue is adult, intelligent, and has a rhythmic beat. Davis's performance is fine on the whole. Franchot Tone is splendid as the architect.

DANGEROUS GAME
(AKA: SNAKE EYES)
1993, 107 mins, US Ⓥ ⓞ
D: Abel Ferrara **A:** Harvey Keitel, Madonna, James Russo, Nancy Ferrara, Reilly Murphy (Maverick/PentAmerica)

Filmmaker Eddie Israel (Keitel) leaves his wife and small son to fly to the coast to work on a new movie starring actors Sarah Jennings (Madonna) and Francis

Burns (James Russo) as a couple whose marriage is disintegrating. Regular Ferrara scripter Nicholas St. John has devised a screenplay in which the stresses of filming spill into private lives. *Dangerous Game* is raw, intense material, with an aura of authenticity. But despite extensive four-letter dialogue, pic plays down the sexual content, and Madonna remains clothed almost throughout. Keitel again proves he's one of the finest actors around.

DANGEROUS LIAISONS
1988, 120 mins, US ⊗ ⊙
D: Stephen Frears **A:** Glenn Close, John Malkovich, Michelle Pfeiffer, Swoosie Kurtz, Mildred Natwick, Uma Thurman (Warner)

This incisive study of sex as an arena for manipulative power games takes too long to catch fire. Choderlos de Laclos's 1782 epistolary novel expertly chronicled the cunning, cold-blooded sexual calculations of the French prerevolutionary upper class. The classic rake, Valmont (John Malkovich), is challenged by Madame Merteuil (Glenn Close) to deflower a 16-year-old virgin, Cecile de Volanges (Uma Thurman). Valmont instead proposes to seduce Madame de Tourvel (Michelle Pfeiffer), a virtuous, highly moral married woman. Glenn Close is admirably cast while the real problem is Malkovich's Valmont. This sly actor lacks the devilish charm and seductiveness one senses Valmont would need to carry off all his conquests.
1988: Best Art Direction, Adapted Screenplay, Costume Design
Nominations: Best Picture, Actress (Glenn Close), Supp. Actress (Michelle Pfeiffer), Score

DANGEROUS LIAISONS
See: Les Liaisons Dangereuses

DANGEROUSLY THEY LIVE
1942, 77 mins, US
D: Robert Florey **A:** John Garfield, Nancy Coleman, Raymond Massey, Lee Patrick (Warner)

This meller deals with Nazi spies and Bundsmen in the United States. The story starts excitingly when Nancy Coleman, a British intelligence operative, is kidnapped by German spies. Ambulance doctor John Garfield looks and acts least impressive when playing a man in white. Later he gets over with his usual expert acting.

DANGEROUS MINDS
1995, 99 mins, US ⊗ ⊙
D: John N. Smith **A:** Michelle Pfeiffer, George Dzundza, Courtney B. Vance, Robin Bartlett, Brucklin Harris, Renoly Santiago (Hollywood)

Dangerous Minds is a kid-gloves treatment of the problems in urban public schools. This earnest, sweet-natured inspirational drama almost seems like something from another, more innocent era. A dressed-down Michelle Pfeiffer plays LouAnne Johnson, an ex-marine who is immediately thrust into teaching English to some rejects from hell. Most simplistic of all, she constantly relates her teaching to the most clichéd aspects of the students' environments—drugs and violence—in an attempt to get them to relate to it. Pfeiffer tackles the part with obvious dedication, but she's thwarted by the heavy limitations of the role as written.

DANGEROUS MOONLIGHT
(US: SUICIDE SQUADRON)
1941, 90 mins, UK ⊗
D: Brian Desmond Hurst **A:** Anton Walbrook, Sally Gray, Derrick de Marney, Cecil Parker (RKO)

Plot is short on action apart from a zingy air battle in last few hundred feet. The same prosaic line is taken by Brian Desmond Hurst in directing tale of a young Polish composer with the hands of a musician and the heart of a flier. Walbrook enacts with his customary underplaying, this time almost to a point of self-suffocation. Similarly, Gray is screened for glamour that palls after too much of such footage.

DANGEROUS MOVES
See: La Diagonale du Fou

DANGEROUS WHEN WET
1953, 95 mins, US ⊗ ⊙
D: Charles Walters **A:** Esther Williams, Fernando Lamas, Jack Carson, Charlotte Greenwood, Denise Darcel (M-G-M)

A light mixture of tunes, comedy, water ballet, and Esther Williams in a bathing suit are offered. Best of the musical stints is an underwater cartoon sequence involving Williams and Tom and Jerry. Plot deals with a swimming family that falls in with Jack Carson, a salesman of a liquid vitamin, and decides to swim the English Channel en masse so they can get enough money to buy a prize bull for their Arkansas farm. Romance comes Williams's way in the person of Fernando Lamas, wealthy peddler of French champagne.

DANGEROUS WOMAN, A
1993, 101 mins, US Ⓥ ⊙
D: Stephen Gyllenhaal **A:** Debra Winger, Barbara Hershey, Gabriel Byrne, David Strathairn (Amblin/Rollercoast)

Film's main attraction is totally change-of-pace lead performance by Debra Winger. Winger has transformed herself considerably to play Martha, a pudgy, goggle-eyed nerd. Martha befriends itinerant handyman Mackey (Gabriel Byrne) and, in the first of several off-putting scenes, the two make love. When Mackey gets it on with her sexy aunt (Barbara Hershey), Martha reacts violently. The mostly leisurely pace is the trade-off for the accumulation of character detail, but the lurches into outright melodrama feel jarring.

DANGER ROUTE
1968, 92 mins, UK
D: Seth Holt **A:** Richard Johnson, Carol Lynley, Barbara Bouchet, Sylvia Syms, Diana Dors, Harry Andrews (United Artists)

Story thread focuses on Johnson, an ex-marine commando and a karate expert assigned to kill a Soviet scientist who has defected to the West. Footage abounds in such plot and counterplot that audience is uncertain as to actual happenings.

DANIEL
1983, 129 mins, US Ⓥ
D: Sidney Lumet **A:** Timothy Hutton, Mandy Patinkin, Lindsay Crouse, Ed Asner, Ellen Barkin (World Film Services)

Daniel occasionally evokes the sense of tragedy surrounding the trial and eventual execution of Julius and Ethel Rosenberg as Russian atom spies. The film flashes back and forth in time between 1967 as Daniel Isaacson (Timothy Hutton) is prodded into probing the events behind his parents' execution. Most effective portions of the film are those chronicling the parents (Lindsay Crouse in a staggeringly subtle performance as Daniel's mother, Mandy Patinkin superb as his father).

DANIEL AND THE DEVIL
See: The Devil and Daniel Webster

DANTE'S PEAK
1997, 108 mins, US Ⓥ ⊙ ▭
D: Roger Donaldson **A:** Pierce Brosnan, Linda Hamilton, Charles Hallan, Grant Heslov, Elizabeth Hoffman, Jamie Renee Smith (Pacific Western/Universal)

The effects go boom but the human story is a bust in *Dante's Peak.* Volcanologist Harry Dalton (Pierce Brosnan) is dispatched to the Pacific Northwest community of Dante's Peak and meets its comely mayor, Rachel Wando (Linda Hamilton). He's come to check out some vague activity in the dormant volcano that towers above the friendly community. At exactly the one-hour point, the old cone blows its top. The visual effects are an eyeful; the devastation is palpable and realistic. The dramatis personae are as inoffensive as they are bland.

DANTON
1983, 136 mins, France/Poland Ⓥ
D: Andrzej Wajda **A:** Gerard Depardieu, Wojciech Pszoniak, Patrice Chereau, Roger Planchon, Jacques Villeret, Angela Winkler

Danton is the first French-language film by Polish filmmaker Andrzej Wajda. Pic is a dull, plodding affair, resembling more a windy, biased history lecture than a dramatic motion picture. Gerard Depardieu is Danton: huff and puff as he may, he still looks uneasy in period costume and powdered wig, and his gestures and mannerisms are resolutely 20th century. Wojciech Pszoniak, a fine Polish actor of commanding presence, looks right as the cold, conniving Robespierre, but the dubbed voice that issues from his mouth saps his performance.

DARK ANGEL, THE
1935, 105 mins, US
D: Sidney Franklin **A:** Fredric March, Merle Oberon, Herbert Marshall, Janet Beecher, John Halliday, Henrietta Crosman (Goldwyn/United Artists)

A forthright sentimental romance. The war throws Kitty Vane (Oberon) to March as her natural romantic choice. Marshall and Oberon later berate themselves in mistaken belief they have sent March to his doom. Instead March turns up under an alias, blind and in constant dread of becoming a burden to his bride without benefit of clergy. Oberon is a revelation as a reformed vamp. Marshall and March are superb as the war-torn, love-torn boyhood chums, equally in love with Oberon.

1935: Best Interior Decoration (Richard Day)
Nomination: Best Actress (Merle Oberon)

DARK AT THE TOP OF THE STAIRS, THE
1960, 123 mins, US
D: Delbert Mann **A:** Robert Preston, Do-

rothy McGuire, Eve Arden, Angela Lansbury, Shirley Knight, Lee Kinsolving (Warner)

A poignant study of an Oklahoma family torn by internal conflicts. The film is well cast and persuasively acted. Its chief cast value lies in Robert Preston. Easily detectable is the similarity in manner and speech between his Harold Hill of *The Music Man* and Robin Flood of *Dark*. Each is a high-powered salesman, one flamboyant, the other serious. But there's a strength and an independence that's the same. Dorothy McGuire is tops as the mother caught between devotion to her children and the knowledge she must sever the cord.

1960: Nomination: Best Supp. Actress (Shirley Knight)

DARK CITY
1950, 97 mins, US ♥ ▭
D: William Dieterle A: Charlton Heston, Lizabeth Scott, Viveca Lindfors, Dean Jagger, Don DeFore, Jack Webb (Paramount)

Picture serves to introduce Charlton Heston and his film debut is impressive. Heston has turned to gambling. He and two associates trim Don DeFore in a fixed card game. DeFore hangs himself. A crazy older brother starts stalking the gamblers, intent on giving them the same kind of death suffered by DeFore. Heston takes off to Los Angeles to see DeFore's widow so that he may get a clue to the killer's appearance. Lizabeth Scott, nitery chirp and in love with Heston, gives a fine portrayal of the character.

DARK CITY
1998, 101 mins, US ♥ ⊙ ▭
D: Alex Proyas A: Rufus Sewell, Kiefer Sutherland, Jennifer Connelly, William Hurt, Richard O'Brien, Ian Richardson (Mystery Clock/New Line)

Dark City trades in such weighty themes as memory, thought control, human will, and the altering of reality, but is engaging mostly in the degree to which it sustains a visually startling alternate universe. Essentially an old film noir amnesiac yarn set in a hostile urban environment defined by late '40s noir, tale is shot through with a futuristic element that vastly increases the visual opportunities. The Strangers—lean, bald, vampire-like men with the ability to transform reality to their own purposes—have come to Earth to find a cure for their accursed mortality. Meanwhile, John Murdoch (Rufus Sewell) awakens in a hotel room with his memory gone and under suspicion in a series of murders. He has been robbed of his memory to help the Strangers try to unlock the key to the human soul. How all this is supposed to happen remains obscure, but by the final third the emphasis is on big setpieces anyway.

DARK CRYSTAL, THE
1983, 94 mins, UK ♥ ⊙
D: Jim Henson, Frank Oz (ITC)

The Dark Crystal, besides being a dazzling technological and artistic achievement by a band of talented artists and performers, presents a dark side of *Muppet* creators Jim Henson and Frank Oz. While there is plenty of humor in the film, it is actually an allegory of the triumph of good over evil, of innocence over the wicked. The outstanding character is the Aughra, an ancient one-eyed harridan of an oracle who somehow reminds one of a truly blowsy Shelley Winters.

DARK HALF, THE
1993, 122 mins, US ♥ ⊙
D: George A. Romero A: Timothy Hutton, Amy Madigan, Michael Rooker, Julie Harris, Robert Joy, Chelsea Field (Orion/Dark Half)

The writer's desk intriguingly becomes a gladiatorial arena for warring manifestations of the same personality in *The Dark Half*, a classic Jekyll-and-Hyde story. After a 1968-set prologue establishes Thad Beaumont as a precocious kid writer and a grotesque operation gives physical evidence of a twin in Thad's brain, story proper picks up in the present. Under the pseudonym George Stark, Thad (Timothy Hutton) has authored four disreputable bestsellers. When a grungy student discovers Thad's double life, Thad literally buries George Stark. But Stark begins manifesting his existence in places other than the bestseller list. The killings mount up.

DARKMAN
1990, 95 mins, US ♥ ⊙
D: Sam Raimi A: Liam Neeson, Frances McDormand, Colin Friels, Larry Drake, Nelson Mashita, Jenny Agutter (Universal/Renaissance)

Despite occasional silliness, Sam Raimi's *Darkman* has more wit, pathos, and visual flamboyance than is usual in contemporary shockers. Universal returns to its hallowed horror-film traditions with this tale of a hideously disfigured scientist

(Liam Neeson) seeking revenge on L.A. mobsters. Director Raimi, lenser Bill Pope, and production designer Randy Ser conjure up a flamboyantly expressionistic world out of downtown L.A.'s bizarre architectural mix of gleaming skyscrapers and decaying warehouses.

DARK MIRROR, THE
1946, 85 mins, US ⓥ

D: Robert Siodmak **A:** Olivia de Havilland, Lew Ayres, Thomas Mitchell, Richard Long (Universal/Inter-John)

Olivia de Havilland is cast simultaneously as a sweet, sympathetic girl and her vixenish, latently insane twin sister. A murder is committed and while one girl has been positively identified as coming out of the man's apartment on the night of the murder, the other establishes a foolproof alibi. Lew Ayres is cast in his familiar role as a medico—a specialist on identical twins. Copping thespic honors, Thomas Mitchell plays the baffled dick with a wry wit and assured bearing that carries belief.

1946: Nomination: Best Original Story

DARK OBSESSION
See: Diamond Skulls

DARK OF THE SUN
See: The Mercenaries

DARK PASSAGE
1947, 106 mins, US ⓥ ☉

D: Delmer Daves **A:** Humphrey Bogart, Lauren Bacall, Bruce Bennett, Agnes Moorehead, Tom D'Andrea, Clifton Young (Warner)

Pic is a story of a man imprisoned on circumstantial evidence for the murder of his wife, his escape from jail, and the efforts of a girl to help him. Bacall, in a simple, unglamorous pose at the start, even then has a pleasant appeal, that hypoes intensely as soon as the old, sultry makeup and sexy charm are turned on. Bogart is impressive in something of a lackluster character for him. Agnes Moorehead is sufficiently vicious as the discarded femme who turns killer, giving the film some of its most vivid moments.

DARK PAST, THE
1948, 75 mins, US ⓥ

D: Rudolph Mate **A:** William Holden, Lee J. Cobb, Nina Foch, Adele Jergens (Columbia)

An example of what psychiatry can do for a criminal is graphically shown by college prof Lee J. Cobb, who brings escaped convict William Holden to bay merely by probing into his mind to discover what impels him to be a murderer. Locale for Cobb's psychoanalysis is his own hunting lodge, where his family and several guests have been taken prisoner by Holden and his accomplices.

DARK STAR
1974, 83 mins, US ⓥ ☉

D: John Carpenter **A:** Brian Narelle, Andreijah Pahich, Carl Duniholm, Dan O'Bannon (Carpenter/Harris)

Dark Star is a limp parody of Stanley Kubrick's *2001: A Space Odyssey* that warrants attention only for some remarkably believable special effects achieved with very little money. The screenplay cloisters four astronauts together on a lengthy extraterrestrial jaunt. To pass the time, the men joke, record their diaries on videotape, take sunlamp treatments, reminisce about their past Earth lives, and play with their alien mascot (an inflated beach ball with claws).

DARK VICTORY
1939, 105 mins, US ⓥ ☉

D: Edmund Goulding **A:** Bette Davis, George Brent, Humphrey Bogart, Geraldine Fitzgerald, Ronald Reagan, Henry Travers (Warner)

Intense drama, with undercurrent of tragedy ever present, *Dark Victory* presents Bette Davis in a powerful and impressive role. Story unfolds the tragic circumstances of Davis, gay heiress, afflicted with a malignant brain tumor. A delicate operation by specialist George Brent is temporarily successful, but when the girl finally accidentally discovers her true condition, she embarks on a wild whirl of parties.

1939: Nominations: Best Picture, Actress (Bette Davis)

DARK WATERS
1944, 90 mins, US ⓥ ☉

D: Andre de Toth **A:** Merle Oberon, Franchot Tone, Thomas Mitchell, Fay Bainter, Rex Ingram (United Artists)

Merle Oberon gives one of the best portrayals of her career in the role of a young heiress beset by neuroses due to the loss of her parents. Thomas Mitchell, as the conniver intent on driving the heiress into an asylum and gaining her riches, has some poor lines to toss away before coming through with a meaty performance. Franchot Tone's portrayal of a bayou country doctor is forthright, but never too weighty.

DARK WIND, THE
1992, 109 mins, US 🕑 ⊙
D: Errol Morris A: Lou Diamond Phillips, Fred Ward, Gary Farmer, John Karlen, Lance Baker (Dark Wind/Northfork)

The Dark Wind is a good-looking version of Tony Hillerman's 1982 cult policier. Lou Diamond Phillips toplines strongly as the Navajo flatfoot. Corkscrew plot, set on an Arizona reservation divided between Navajo and Hopi, warms up gradually. Despite most of the action being purely police procedure, the combination of Phillips's mystical voice-overs, Michel Colombier's atmospheric score, and Stefan Czapsky's striking lensing of the ruddy mesa landscape keeps the mood taut.

DARLING
1965, 128 mins, UK 🕑 ⊙
D: John Schlesinger A: Julie Christie, Dirk Bogarde, Laurence Harvey, Roland Curran, Jose Villalonga (Vic)

Central character is a lovely, young, irresponsible, and completely immoral girl. Everyone calls Diana Scott (Julie Christie) "darling." She's that kind of girl—gay, good-looking, amusing company. She is married to a young, immature man, and once she has met the more sophisticated Robert (Dirk Bogarde), there is little doubt that the marriage will go on the rocks. But no sooner has she met Miles (Laurence Harvey) than she hops into bed with him. Christie almost perfectly captures the character of the immoral Diana, and very rarely misses her target.
1965: Best Actress (Julie Christie), Original Story & Screenplay, B&W Costume Design
Nominations: Best Picture, Director

DARLING LILI
1970, 139 mins, US 🕑 ▭
D: Blake Edwards A: Julie Andrews, Rock Hudson, Jeremy Kemp, Lance Percival, Michael Witney, Jacques Marin (Paramount/Geoffrey)

On its World War I canvas, the Blake Edwards presentation has comedy, adventure melodrama, aerial dogfights, spectacular production numbers, nostalgia, Julie Andrews and Rock Hudson, lush trappings, lack of a decisive hand, and smash moments. Andrews is a German spy who latches onto a relationship with Hudson, a dashing American air-squadron com-

mander. Andrews's best moments are her singing sequences.
1970: Nominations: Best Costume Design, Original Song Score, Song ("Whistling Away the Dark")

D'ARTAGNAN'S DAUGHTER
See: La Fille de D'Artagnan

D.A.R.Y.L.
1985, 99 mins, US 🕑 ▭
D: Simon Wincer A: Mary Beth Hurt, Michael McKean, Kathryn Walker, Colleen Camp, Josef Sommer, Barret Oliver (Paramount)

A young boy is taken into a foster home by the Richardsons (Mary Beth Hurt and Michael McKean). This strange young man is a robot. The film takes off in a different direction when his parents come to take Daryl (Barret Oliver) home. Home is a top-security research facility where scientists Josef Sommer and Kathryn Walker have given birth to D.A.R.Y.L. Acronym stands for Data Analyzing Robot Youth Life-form and Daryl is described as an experiment in artificial intelligence. Second half of the picture is the most farfetched and also the most fun as the young robot gets to show off some of his powers.

DATE WITH A LONELY GIRL, A
See: T. R. Baskin

DATE WITH DEATH, A
See: The High Bright Sun

DATE WITH JUDY, A
1948, 113 mins, US 🕑 ⊙
D: Richard Thorpe A: Wallace Beery, Jane Powell, Elizabeth Taylor, Carmen Miranda, Robert Stack, Scotty Beckett (M-G-M)

A Date with Judy is loaded with youthful zest. Jane Powell registers appealingly with vocals on five numbers and for her comedy antics. Plot concerns teenage love affair between Powell and Scotty Beckett which goes sour when the gal gets a crush on an older man, Robert Stack. It takes on another facet when Powell suspects her father, Wallace Beery, of a romance with Carmen Miranda, and the youngsters join forces to prevent such a folly. Beery does an ace job, and with little of his customary mugging. Elizabeth Taylor makes a talented appearance.

DAUGHTERS OF DARKNESS
1971, 87 mins, US/France 🕑
D: Harry Kumel A: Delphine Seyrig, Daniele Ouimet, John Karlen, Andrea Rau,

Paul Esser, Fons Rademakers (Gemini/Maya)

Delphine Seyrig's silver lamé presence and Harry Kumel's evocative direction make this an above-par vampire tale. Updating the old chestnut about the butch countess who remains forever young by drinking and bathing in the blood of maidens, *Daughters of Darkness* is so intentionally perverse that it often slips into impure camp, but Kumel and Seyrig hold interest by piling twists on every convention of the vampire genre.

DAVE
1993, 110 mins, US ⓥ ⊙
D: Ivan Reitman **A:** Kevin Kline, Sigourney Weaver, Frank Langella, Kevin Dunn, Ving Rhames, Ben Kingsley (Warner/Northern Lights)

Dave, the story of a run-of-the mill guy asked to stand in for a major leader who suddenly falls ill, is a delightful, buoyant new take on an old theme. In this case, the office is president of the United States, and Dave (Kevin Kline), a sometime presidential impersonator, gets drafted by White House chief of staff Bob Alexander (Frank Langella) and his communications director (Kevin Dunn). Dave also thaws the icy relationship between the president and first lady (Sigourney Weaver), providing a nifty romantic element.
1993: Nomination: Best Original Screenplay

DAVID AND BATHSHEBA
1951, 153 mins, US ⓥ ⊙
D: Henry King **A:** Gregory Peck, Susan Hayward, Raymond Massey, Kieron Moore, James Robertson Justice (20th Century-Fox)

The reign of King David projects the Old Testament in broad sweeps, depicting the obligation of David (Gregory Peck) to his subjects while at the same time spotlighting his frailties, namely his relationship with the beauteous Bathsheba (Susan Hayward). Peck is a commanding personality as the youth destined to rule Israel. His emotional reflexes are not as static as the sultry Hayward in the femme lead. Massey, as the prophet, is a dominant personality throughout.
1951: Nominations: Best Story & Screenplay, Color Cinematography, Color Costume Design, Color Art Direction, Scoring of a Dramatic Picture

DAVID AND LISA
1963, 85 mins, US ⓥ ⊙
D: Frank Perry **A:** Keir Dullea, Janet Margolin, Howard da Silva, Neva Patterson, Clifton James (Continental)

Tact, taste, insight, and forthrightness make this one of the most incisive and original films treating mental problems. A young man is brought to a mental home by his doting mother. He seems intelligent, haughty, and sophisticated. But he cannot bear to be touched by anybody. He becomes interested in the case of a schizophrenic girl called Lisa, who talks backward in rhyme and takes herself for two girls. He manages to get to her and both are aware of each other's weak spots. Keir Dullea has the knifelike, frigid presence that is right in his case of bottled-up feelings that have made him fear death and any human emotion. And Janet Margolin has the touching disorder and mute need for help required for the part of the girl.
1963: Nominations: Best Director, Adapted Screenplay

DAVID COPPERFIELD
1935, 129 mins, US ⓥ ⊙
D: George Cukor **A:** W. C. Fields, Lionel Barrymore, Freddie Bartholomew, Frank Lawton, Edna May Oliver, Roland Young (M-G-M)

Charles Dickens did not write with the idea of being dramatized. The strange charm of his characters is more important than the fidelity of his characterizations. It was almost an adventure to try to bring to the screen the expansively optimistic Micawber, but he lives again in W. C. Fields, who only once yields to his penchant for horseplay. Edna May Oliver does low comedy in the high-comedy manner and shows flashes of the underlying tenderness of Aunt Betsey. A fine performance is that of Freddie Bartholomew as the child David.
1935: Nominations: Best Picture, Editing, Assistant Director (Joseph Newman)

DAVID COPPERFIELD
1970, 118 mins, UK ⓥ
D: Delbert Mann **A:** Robin Phillips, Susan Hampshire, Edith Evans, Michael Redgrave, Ralph Richardson, Laurence Olivier (Omnibus)

Director and scriptwriter elected to tell this version of *David Copperfield* through the eyes of David as a young man. The story is jerkily and bitterly related, mainly in flashbacks, but the constant return to the brooding, self-pitying Copperfield makes for a melancholy drag. It also means that few of Dickens's wonderful array of characters get much opportunity to develop their roles. Notably, Laurence Olivier, as the schoolmaster Creakle, and Richard Attenborough, as his cringing, one-legged assistant, Tungay. Their brilliant brief appearances light up the screen in about 60 seconds flat. Then they disappear.

DAWN OF THE DEAD
(UK: ZOMBIES)
1979, 125 mins, US ⓥ ⊙
D: George A. Romero **A:** Scott Reiniger, Ken Foree, David Emge, Gaylen Ross, Tom Savini (Laurel/Cuomo-Argento)

Dawn pummels the viewer with a series of ever-more-grisly event—decapitations, shootings, knifings, flesh tearing—that make Romero's special-effects man, Tom Savini, the real star of the film—the actors are as woodenly uninteresting as the characters they play.

DAWN PATROL, THE
1930, 90 mins, US
D: Howard Hawks **A:** Richard Barthelmess, Douglas Fairbanks Jr., Neil Hamilton (First National)

Dawn Patrol finds well-bred English gentlemen running up against the grim realities of war and always remaining true to the best Oxford traditions. At the start, the air exploits are more talked about than revealed, but as the womanless chronicle unfolds, the fighting becomes more visual and less commented upon. Howard Hawks has handled his material intelligently. Camerawork is excellent throughout and the effects are vivid.

DAWN PATROL, THE
1938, 103 mins, US ⓥ
D: Edmund Goulding **A:** Errol Flynn, David Niven, Basil Rathbone, Donald Crisp, Melville Cooper, Barry Fitzgerald (Warner)

Story is reminiscent of previous yarns about the flying service at the front during the World War. Yet it is different in that it stresses the unreasonableness of the brass hats seated miles from the front who dispatched the 59th Squadron to certain death in carrying out combat assignments. Errol Flynn is Courtney, squadron flight commander. It is a character made to order for him.
1930/31: Best Original Story

DAY AT THE RACES, A
1937, 100 mins, US ⓥ ⊙
D: Sam Wood **A:** Groucho Marx, Chico Marx, Harpo Marx, Allan Jones, Maureen O'Sullivan, Margaret Dumont (M-G-M)

Surefire film fun and up to the usual parity of the madcap Marxes, even though a bit hectic in striving for jolly moments and bright quips. Obviously painstaking is the racehorse codebook sequence, a deft switch on the money-changing bit; the long-distance telephoning between the horse doctor (Groucho) and the light heavy; the midnight-rendezvous business between Groucho and Esther Muir, including the paper-handing slapstickery; the orchestra-pit hokum, which permits the standard virtuosity by Chico at the Steinway and Harpo at the harp, including a very funny breakaway piano.
1937: Nomination: Best Dance Direction ("All God's Children Got Rhythm")

DAYBREAK
1931, 73 mins, US
D: Jacques Feyder **A:** Ramon Novarro, Helen Chandler, Jean Hersholt, C. Aubrey Smith, William Bakewell, Karen Morley (M-G-M)

Lack of action works against *Daybreak,* which gets its title because the two principals stay out all night the first time they met. Although the locale is apparently in Vienna and its imperial guard, Novarro speaks with his Latin accent. The picture dies all the way through. Chandler starts wrong and never rights herself. Novarro tries the light juvenile style as the lieutenant, but it flattens at every try.

DAYBREAK
See: *Le Jour Se Leve*

DAY FOR NIGHT
See: *La Nuit Americaine*

DAY IN THE DEATH OF JOE EGG, A
1972, 108 mins, UK ⓥ
D: Peter Medak **A:** Alan Bates, Janet Suzman, Peter Bowles, Sheila Gish, Joan Hickson, Murray Melvin (Domino)

A superior black comedy-drama about a young couple trying to cope with a spastic child. Lachrymose but unsentimentalized, the gut moral issue is euthanasia. The almost surreal narrative unfolds yo-yo style from bitter or hilarious (or both) humor to emotional wrench and back again, repeatedly. Alan Bates and Janet Suzman as the couple who play games to survive their nightmare are first-rate in their sardonic despair.

DAYLIGHT
1996, 115 mins, US Ⓥ ⊙
D: Rob Cohen **A:** Sylvester Stallone, Amy Brenneman, Viggo Mortensen, Dany Hedaya, Jay O. Sanders, Karen Young (Davis-Singer/Universal)

A lower-echelon disaster thriller, *Daylight* is a noisy, technically proficient actioner about a group of people trapped in the Holland Tunnel after an explosion. Sylvester Stallone, in a familiar working-class hero role, happens to be in the right place at the right time to attempt a rescue of a cross-section of contempo New Yawkers. Unfortunately, these characters are mostly a drag to be around, making their fates a matter of relative indifference. In the film's best sequence, one that should have been truly great but isn't quite, Kit is lowered into the tunnel through a succession of giant vent fans that can be turned off only for seconds at a time.
1996: Nomination: Best Sound Effects Editing (Richard L. Anderson, David A. Whittaker)

DAY OF THE DEAD
1985, 102 mins, US Ⓥ ⊙
D: George A. Romero **A:** Lori Cardille, Terry Alexander, Joseph Pilato, Jarlath Conroy (Laurel)

Unsatisfying part three in George A. Romero's zombie saga postulates that the living dead have now taken over the world with only a handful of normal humans still alive, outnumbered by about 400,000 to one. In a claustrophobic format reminiscent of early 1950s science-fiction films, the human protagonists debate and fight among themselves in an underground missile silo while the common enemy masses topside.

DAY OF THE DOLPHIN, THE
1973, 104 mins, US Ⓥ ⊙ ▭
D: Mike Nichols **A:** George C. Scott, Trish Van Devere, Paul Sorvino, Fritz Weaver, Edward Herrmann (Avco Embassy)

Robert Merle's novel has been adapted into a screenplay which commingles creative obsession, materialism, covert espionage, and overt skulduggery. This rich mixture eventually turns to lead, but while it works it is very mind-boggling. Scott and wife Trish Van Devere are conducting advanced research into dolphins, under the sponsorship of a foundation where Fritz Weaver is a senior executive. Scott's scientific breakthrough communicating verbally with the mammals becomes the means by which Weaver and associates would blow up the yacht of the US president.
1973: Nominations: Best Original Score, Sound

DAY OF THE JACKAL, THE
1973, 141 mins, UK/France Ⓥ ⊙
D: Fred Zinnemann **A:** Edward Fox, Alan Badel, Tony Britton, Cyril Cusack, Michel Lonsdale, Delphine Seyrig (Universal)

A patient, studied, quasi-documentary translation of Frederick Forsyth's big-selling political suspense novel. Film appeals more to the intellect than the senses as it traces the detection of an assassin hired to kill French President Charles de Gaulle. The major asset of the film is that it succeeds in maintaining interest and suspense despite obvious viewer foreknowledge of the outcome.
1973: Nomination: Best Editing

DAY OF THE LOCUST, THE
1975, 144 mins, US Ⓥ ⊙
D: John Schlesinger **A:** Donald Sutherland, Karen Black, Burgess Meredith, William Atherton, Geraldine Page, Richard A. Dysart (Paramount)

Nathanael West's novel about losers on the Hollywood fringe has lost little of its verisimilitude in adaptation. The story of destined failure features Karen Black in a fine performance as an aspiring, selfish would-be starlet, the daughter of broken-down vaudevillian Burgess Meredith (a brilliant characterization). Donald Sutherland, laboring under the most striking burden of fuzzy writing, still evokes a good measure of pity as the hick whose immature love for Black is abused by her.
1975: Nominations: Best Supp. Actor (Burgess Meredith), Cinematography

DAY OF THE TRIFFIDS, THE
1963, 93 mins, UK Ⓥ ⊙ ▭
D: Steve Sekely **A:** Howard Keel, Kieron Moore, Janette Scott, Nicole Maurey, Mervyn Johns (Allied Artists)

Basically, this is a vegetarian's version of *The Birds,* a science-fiction-horror melodrama about a vile people-eater of the plant kingdom with a voracious appetite. Although riddled with script inconsistencies and irregularities, it is a more-than-adequate film of its genre. Hero of the piece is Howard Keel as a Yank seaman. Ultimately a marine biologist (Kieron Moore) stranded in a lighthouse with his wife (Janette Scott) discovers the means to dissolve and destroy the triffid.

DAYS OF HEAVEN

1978, 95 mins, US Ⓥ ⊙

D: Terrence Malick **A:** Richard Gere, Brooke Adams, Sam Shepard, Linda Manz, Robert Wilke, Stuart Margolin (OP/Paramount)

A dramatically moving and technically breathtaking American art film, one of the great cinematic achievements of the 1970s. Told through the eyes and words of an innocent but wise teenage migrant worker (Linda Manz), it traces a trio of nomads as their lives intersect with a wealthy wheat farmer. The story opens in Chicago with Richard Gere shoveling coal in a steel mill. He, his sister (Manz), and girlfriend (Brooke Adams) hit the road to find work in the fields, traveling as brother and sisters. They find employment on a farm owned by a young, wealthy Sam Shepard. The trio become entangled with Shepard when he falls in love with Adams and marries her.

1978: Best Cinematography

Nominations: Best Costume Design, Original Score, Sound

DAYS OF THUNDER

1990, 107 mins, US Ⓥ ⊙ ⊟

D: Tony Scott **A:** Tom Cruise, Robert Duvall, Nicole Kidman, Randy Quaid, Michael Rooker, Cary Elwes (Paramount)

This expensive genre film about stock-car racing has many of the elements that made the same team's *Top Gun* a blockbuster, but the producers recruited scripter Robert Towne to make more out of the story than junk food. There's the cocky but insecure young challenger (Tom Cruise) breaking into the big time, the hardened champion he's trying to unseat (Michael Rooker), the grizzled manager who dispenses fatherly wisdom (Robert Duvall), the crass promoter (Randy Quaid), and the sexy lady from outside (Nicole Kidman) who questions the point of it all. Director Tony Scott plunges the viewer into the maelstrom of stock-car racing. A highly effective blending of car-mounted camerawork and long lenses imparts documentary credibility and impact.

1990: Nomination: Best Sound

DAYS OF WINE AND ROSES

1962, 116 mins, US Ⓥ ⊙

D: Blake Edwards **A:** Jack Lemmon, Lee Remick, Charles Bickford, Jack Klugman (Warner)

J. P. Miller's grueling drama illustrates how the unquenchable lure of alcohol can conquer even love, and how marital communication cannot exist in a house divided by one-sided boozing. The wife (Lee Remick) begins to drink when her husband (Jack Lemmon), a p.r. man and two-fisted belter whose career is floundering, is dismayed by a gap in their togetherness. Upshot is the disastrous compatibility of mutual alcoholism. Lemmon gives a dynamic and chilling performance. Scenes of his collapse, particularly in the violent ward, are brutally realistic and terrifying.

1962: Best Song ("Days of Wine and Roses")

Nominations: Best Actor (Jack Lemmon), Actress (Lee Remick), B&W Costume Design, B&W Art Direction

DAY THE EARTH CAUGHT FIRE, THE

1961, 99 mins, UK Ⓥ ⊟

D: Val Guest **A:** Janet Munro, Leo McKern, Edward Judd, Bernard Braden, Michael Goodliffe, Peter Butterworth (British Lion/Pax)

Val Guest's production has a fascinating yarn, some very sound thesping, and an authentic Fleet Street (newspaper) background. By mischance, an American nuclear test at the South Pole is conducted on the same day as a Russian one at the North Pole. It first causes a sinister upheaval in the world's weather and then it is discovered that the globe has been jolted out of orbit and is racing toward the sun and annihilation. Drama of this situation is played out as a newspaper scoop. Outstanding performance comes from Leo McKern as a dependable, gruff, and understanding science reporter.

DAY THE EARTH STOOD STILL, THE

1951, 92 mins, US Ⓥ ⊙

D: Robert Wise **A:** Michael Rennie, Patricia Neal, Hugh Marlowe, Sam Jaffe, Billy Gray (20th Century-Fox)

Screenplay tells of an invasion of the earth by an eight-foot robot and an earth-like human. They have come to warn the earth's people that all other inhabited planets have banded together into a peaceful organization and that peace is being threatened by the wars of the earth people. Spaceship lands in Washington and the man, leaving the robot on guard, goes to hide among the people, to discover for himself what they are like. Michael Rennie is fine as the man from space. Patricia

Neal is attractive and competent as the widowed mother of the young boy whom he befriends and who is the first to know his secret.

DAZED AND CONFUSED
1993, 94 mins, US ⓥ ⊙
D: Richard Linklater A: Jason London, Wiley Wiggins, Sasha Jenson, Rory Cochrane, Milla Jovovich (Alphaville)

The teenage wasteland, 1976-style, of *Dazed and Confused* is smack-dab between *The Brady Bunch* and *Children of the Damned*, and it's a scary, if sometimes giddily amusing, place to visit. All the action takes place within 24 hours, as listless Austin, TX, teens endure their last day of school, making bongs in shop and cataloging every episode of *Gilligan's Island* in history, before the summer's serious business of drinking, fighting, and generally humiliating each other and themselves.

D-DAY
THE SIXTH OF JUNE
1956, 106 mins, US ⓥ ▭
D: Henry Koster A: Robert Taylor, Richard Todd, Dana Wynter, Edmond O'Brien, John Williams (20th Century-Fox)

Along with the account of the significant historical event, the picture spins an extremely moving wartime love story, distinctively performed by a fine cast. There are fine masculine performances by Robert Taylor, Richard Todd, and Edmond O'Brien, but the sensitive, tremendously compelling work by Dana Wynter gives the real point to the drama and makes the love story poignant. The plot, simply, tells of an English girl (Wynter), romantically involved with a British soldier (Todd), who meets and falls in love with a married American officer (Taylor), and how this triangle is worked out in the overwhelming upset of war. There's a bitterly ironic note to the ending.

DEAD, THE
1987, 83 mins, US ⓥ ⊙
D: John Huston A: Anjelica Huston, Donal McCann, Rachael Dowling, Cathleen Delany, Helena Carroll, Dan O'Herlihy (Vestron Zenith/Liffey)

A well-crafted miniature, this dramatization of the Joyce story directly addresses the theme of how the shades from that other world can still live in those who walk the earth. Opening hour is set exclusively in the warm Dublin town house of two spinster sisters, who every winter holiday season throw a festive party and din-

ner for their relatives and friends. Time is 1904.

The virtually all-Irish cast brings the story to life completely and believably, with Helena Carroll's bighearted Aunt Kate and Donal Donnelly's drunken Freddy Malins being special delights. Huston proves fully up to the demands of her emotionally draining monologue, and McCann simply is ideal as the thoughtful husband.
1987: Nominations: Best Adapted Screenplay, Costume Design

DEAD AGAIN
1991, 111 mins, US ⓥ ⊙
D: Kenneth Branagh A: Kenneth Branagh, Emma Thompson, Andy Garcia, Derek Jacobi, Robin Williams, Hanna Schygulla (Paramount/Mirage)

Supernatural tale of murder, hypnosis, and reincarnation involves a woman (Emma Thompson) wandering around in an amnesiac daze, tormented by memories of someone else's life. Engaging film style is buoyed by an infectious sense of fun and punctuated by wild-and-woolly character turns. Robin Williams plays a psychiatrist who's gone off the deep end, and Andy Garcia is a seedy journalist with an accent seemingly wafting in from various ports. Branagh and [then] real-life spouse Thompson, each of whom plays dual roles in past and present, are excellent thesps, but they don't make a very seductive screen couple.

DEAD CALM
1989, 96 mins, Australia ⓥ ⊙ ▭
D: Phillip Noyce A: Sam Neill, Nicole Kidman, Billy Zane (Kennedy Miller)

Though not always entirely credible, *Dead Calm* is a nail-biting suspense pic handsomely produced and inventively directed. It's basically a three-hander: a happily married couple John and Rae Ingram (Sam Neill and Nicole Kidman) have found peace alone on the Pacific on their well-equipped yacht when they're threatened by a vicious, unstable young killer, Hughie (Billy Zane). Kidman is excellent. She gives the character of Rae real tenacity and energy. Neill is good, too, as a husband who spends most of the film unable to contact his wife, and Yank newcomer Zane is suitably manic and evil as the deranged Hughie.

DEAD END
1937, 90 mins, US ⓥ ⊙
D: William Wyler A: Sylvia Sidney, Joel McCrea, Humphrey Bogart, Wendy Bar-

rie, Claire Trevor (Goldwyn/United Artists)

Producer Samuel Goldwyn has made a near-literal film translation of Sidney Kingsley's play *Dead End*, the New York stage success. The Kingsley theme is that tenements breed gangsters, and no one does anything about it. All the action is limited merely to a background setting of the river front in the East Fifties (NY). Only material plot change is to heroize the character of Dave, the student architect (Joel McCrea). Performances are uniformly fine, topped by the acting of the boy players from the New York production who seem better in the film because they do not crowd their lines so fast.
1937: Nominations: Best Picture, Supp. Actress (Claire Trevor), Cinematography, Art Direction

DEADFALL
1968, 120 mins, UK
D: Bryan Forbes **A:** Michael Caine, Eric Portman, Giovanna Ralli, Nanette Newman (Salamander)

An apparent attempt to pull off an Alfred Hitchcock suspenser, with added Freudian schleps, *Deadfall* falls dead as little more than ponderous, tedious trivia. Michael Caine is introduced in a sanitorium as a cured alcoholic; Giovanna Ralli lures him to the home she shares with husband Eric Portman, who plays a homosexual. The three principals join in a jewel heist, a 23-minute sequence which brings a halting pace to a complete stop.

DEAD FUNNY
1995, 96 mins, US ⊗
D: John Feldman **A:** Elizabeth Pena, Andrew McCarthy, Paige Turco, Blanche Baker, Allison Janney (Avondale/Movie Screen/Film Four)

Topliner Elizabeth Pena again proves her mettle by carrying this slight, quirky tale. Trouble starts when Pena returns to her Manhattan walk-up, only to find immature b.f. Reggie (McCarthy) on the kitchen table, skewered by a Samurai sword. Instead of calling the cops, confused Viv asks her pal Louise (funny Paige Turco) to come over. The women try to piece together what happened. Baffled and blotto, they're about to give up when Viv's women's group arrives for a forgotten meeting. What follows, unfortunately, lacks the manic edge that would have made the farce fly. Writer-helmer John Feldman's tight control keeps the tension high in two-handed scenes, but

when the ensembles get more complex, the steam runs out.

DEAD HEAT ON A MERRY-GO-ROUND
1966, 107 mins, US ⊗
D: Bernard Girard **A:** James Coburn, Camilla Sparv, Aldo Ray, Nina Wayne, Robert Webber (Columbia)

James Coburn has in mind the burglary of a bank at L.A. International Airport. Date set for the heist coincides with arrival of the Russian premier, when security will engage full attention of all arms of the law. What leads up to the comedy-melodrama O. Henry finale most likely was very funny in the producers' minds, but much of the action is so fragmentary and episodic that there is not sufficient exposition and the treatment goes overboard in striving for effect.

DEADLIER THAN THE MALE
1967, 98 mins, UK ▭
D: Ralph Thomas **A:** Richard Johnson, Elke Sommer, Sylva Koscina, Nigel Green, Suzanna Leigh (Rank)

There is no doubt that *Deadlier than the Male* is loaded with colorful and exciting production values. Opinion thereafter is likely to divide, however, for the film will strike some as okay dual-bill escapism, and others as overly raw and "single" entendre. Sadism, sex, and attempted sophistication mark this Bulldog Drummond pic.

DEADLINE AT DAWN
1946, 83 mins, US ⊗
D: Harold Clurman **A:** Susan Hayward, Paul Lukas, Bill Williams, Joseph Calleia, Osa Massen, Lola Lane (RKO)

Combine of playwright Clifford Odets and director Harold Clurman, two onetime NY Group Theatre stalwarts, should have produced a more plausible murder melodrama of Manhattan than this one. Film has an arty approach to an otherwise plain whodunit, and is shot through with phony bits of story and dialogue. Performances are of a mixed quality. Story concerns a naive gob (Bill Williams). A few drinks under his belt, and he remembers nothing— how he came to be one-stepping with a gal in a dime-a-dance joint, how he came to have a huge roll on him, or how the dame whose radio he fixed was murdered. A dancer (Susan Hayward) feels sympathy for him and tries to help him find the murderer.

DEADLINE U.S.A.
1952, 87 mins, US
D: Richard Brooks **A:** Humphrey Bogart, Ethel Barrymore, Kim Hunter, Ed Begley, Warren Stevens, Paul Stewart (20th Century-Fox)

Humphrey Bogart is the traditionally intrepid big-city, big-sheet editor whose responsibility to his job, his corps of 1,500 fellow workers on *The Day* (as this fictional rag is called), and his moxie is in locking horns with the No. 1 mobster is chiefly sparked when one of his news staff gets beaten up by Martin Gabel's gang. Complicating this is the projected sale of the paper by the founder-publisher's heirs. Bogart gives a convincing performance all the way, from his constantly harassed deadline existence, his personal romantic stalemate, and his guts in avenging the beating given his crime reporter.

DEADLY AFFAIR, THE
1967, 107 mins, UK ⊛
D: Sidney Lumet **A:** James Mason, Simone Signoret, Maximilian Schell, Harriet Andersson, Lynn Redgrave, Harry Andrews (Columbia/Lumet)

The Deadly Affair is based on *Call for the Dead* by John Le Carre. Shrewd and powerful development is given this tale of a British Home Office intelligence officer seeking to unravel the supposed suicide of a high Foreign Office diplomat. Mason is cast as an unromantic civil servant wed to a compulsively sexual young woman who has many affairs.

DEADLY BEES, THE
1967, 123 mins, UK ▭
D: Freddie Francis **A:** Suzanna Leigh, Frank Finlay, Guy Doleman, Catherine Finn, John Harvey, Michael Ripper (Paramount/Amicus)

The Deadly Bees is like *The Birds* only on a smaller scale. It boasts of uneven suspense, a plot long in unraveling, and some gripping cinematic moments, provided by bees in deadly pursuit. Throughout, characters show little emotional involvement, except for Leigh, who has command of all she does.

DEADLY COMPANIONS, THE
1961, 90 mins, US ⊛ ⊙ ▭
D: Sam Peckinpah **A:** Maureen O Hara, Brian Keith, Steve Cochran, Chill Wills, Strother Martin (Pathe-America)

The dramatic tale of four characters who encounter their respective moments of truth in a ghost town smack-dab in the heart of Apache country. One (Maureen O'Hara) is a dancehall woman heading for the ghost town to bury her son next to her late husband. Another is Brian Keith, whose motivation is revenge against Chill Wills, an unstable galoot with whom he has an old score to settle. Fourth member of the odd party is Steve Cochran, a gunslinger with eyes for O'Hara. An auspicious debut as director by Sam Peckinpah.

DEADLY FRIEND
1986, 99 mins, US ⊛ ⊙
D: Wes Craven **A:** Matthew Laborteaux, Kristy Swanson, Michael Sharrett, Anne Twomey, Anne Ramsey (Pan Arts/Layton)

Paul (Matthew Laborteaux) is a bit advanced for his age, having built a semi-intelligent robot named BB. One night, neighbor Richard Marcus goes a bit too far slapping his daughter (Kristy Swanson) around. Just when the doctors determine that she's brain-dead, Laborteaux steals her body and transplants BB's brain into her gray matter. That's when the fun begins. Viewers can just as easily scream as laugh through *Deadly Friend* watching the obviously made-up Swanson come back to life and walk around like a robot, crushing her enemies one by one.

DEADLY HERO
1976, 99 mins, US ⊛
D: Ivan Nagy **A:** Don Murray, Diahn Williams, James Earl Jones, Lilia Skala, George S. Irving, Treat Williams (Avco Embassy)

Deadly Hero is a neat little thriller about a psychotic NY City cop terrorizing a woman who has complained about his violent behavior in saving her from assault. If it sounds complex, it is, and the characters are drawn with believable shades of gray.

DEADLY IS THE FEMALE
See: Gun Crazy

DEADLY PURSUIT
See: Shoot to Kill

DEAD MAN
1995, 134 mins, US ⊛ ⊙
D: Jim Jarmusch **A:** Johnny Depp, Gary Farmer, Lance Henriksen, Michael Wincott, Mili Avital, Crispin Glover

Dead Man resembles a poky stroll through the Old West rather than an exciting ride. Jim Jarmusch's first period outing possesses a piquant humor and eccentric mood that brand it with the mark of one of America's most distinctive indie filmmakers, but pic's unassertiveness and considerable overlength give it a diffused impact. The almost inadvertent transformation of Johnny Depp's William Blake from a mild-mannered Ohio accountant to a notorious gunman has to do with the overwhelming force of circumstances over free will. As he has before, Depp makes for an eminently watchable, if essentially reactive, hero. Lance Henriksen is the model of a vicious western killer. Other thesps, unfortunately, are either so heavily hidden behind hair and furry costumes as to be virtually unrecognizable or seen so briefly as to not make any special use of their talents.

DEAD MAN WALKING
1995, 120 mins, US ⓥ ⊙
D: Tim Robbins A: Susan Sarandon, Sean Penn, Robert Prosky, Raymond J. Barry (Working Title/Havoc/PolyGram)

A highly intriguing drama about the complex relationship between a devout nun and a death-row convict. An intimate chamber piece for two, superbly acted by Susan Sarandon and Sean Penn, this is a mature, well-crafted movie. Inspired by true events and figures in Sister Helen Prejean's bestselling 1993 book, pic defies the conventions of both Hollywood crime melodramas and TV movies. Sans makeup, Sarandon inhabits the nun's role with powerful conviction, expressing the character's valor and vulnerability. Penn's tough yet intricate role complements Sarandon superbly.

1995: Best Actress (Susan Sarandon)
Nominations: Actor (Sean Penn), Director, Original Song ("Dead Man Walking")

DEAD MEN DON'T WEAR PLAID
1982, 89 mins, US ⓥ ⊙
D: Carl Reiner A: Steve Martin, Rachel Ward, Reni Santoni, Carl Reiner, George Gaynes (Universal/Aspen)

Lensed in black-and-white and outfitted with a straight mystery score by Miklos Rozsa and authentic 1940s costumes by Edith Head, this spoof of film noir detective yarns sees Steve Martin interacting with 18 Hollywood greats by way of intercutting of clips from some 17 old pictures. Thus, when sultry Rachel Ward enters his seedy L.A. office to discuss her father's murder, $10-per-day sleuth Martin is able to call Bogart's Philip Marlowe for assistance on the case. Ward looks sensational in period garb and is not above such Martinesque gags as removing bullets

from his wounds with her teeth or having her breasts rearranged by the hard-boiled detective.

DEAD OF NIGHT
1945, 103 mins, UK ⓥ ⊙
D: Alberto Cavalcanti, Basil Dearden, Robert Hamer, Charles Crichton A: Googie Withers, Michael Redgrave, Sally Ann Howes, Mervyn Johns, Roland Culver, Frederick Valk (Ealing)

Tightly woven script tells the story of a man summoned on business to a British estate who's shocked to find that the place and people have all been in his dreams. Other guests each tell of a strange, similarly psychic situation in which they've been involved. Best episode features Redgrave as a ventriloquist whose dummy seems imbued with a human brain and soul.

DEAD OF WINTER
1987, 100 mins, US ⓥ ⊙
D: Arthur Penn A: Mary Steenburgen, Roddy McDowall, Jan Rubes, William Russ, Mark Malone (M-G-M)

Mary Steenburgen is first-rate as the struggling actress hired to audition as a double for an actress removed from a film-in-progress because of an alleged nervous breakdown. She's taken to the isolated country estate of a psychiatrist-turned-producer where she undergoes a complete makeover until she quite uncannily resembles the stricken actress. Suspense is built artfully around her gradual realization that she's trapped with a sly shrink and his obsequious factotum, Roddy McDowall, considerably more malevolent than he first appeared.

DEAD POETS SOCIETY
1989, 128 mins, US ⓥ ⊙
D: Peter Weir A: Robin Williams, Robert Sean Leonard, Ethan Hawke, Josh Charles, Gale Hansen (Touchstone)

Pic is not so much about Robin Williams, as unconventional English teacher John Keating at a hard-line New England prep school, as it is about the youths he teaches and how the creative flames within them are kindled and then stamped out. Director Peter Weir fills the screen with a fresh gang of compelling teenagers, led by Robert Sean Leonard as outgoing Neil Perry and balanced by Ethan Hawke as deeply withdrawn Todd Anderson. Keating enters their rigidly traditional world and has them literally rip out the pages of their hidebound textbooks in favor of his

inventive didactics on the spirit of poetry. Story sings whenever Williams is on-screen. Hawke gives a haunting performance.
1989: Best Original Screenplay
Nominations: Best Picture, Director, Actor (Robin Williams)

DEAD POOL, THE
1988, 91 mins, US Ⓥ ⊙
D: Buddy Van Horn **A:** Clint Eastwood, Patricia Clarkson, Evan C. Kim, Liam Neeson, David Hunt (Malpaso/Warner)

Dirty Harry Callahan isn't the best and brightest of cops. *The Dead Pool* isn't the best and brightest of the Dirty Harry films, either. It's possible that Clint Eastwood and crew are just enjoying a bit of self-mockery with this one [the fifth in the series]. The plot has something to do with a crime lord whom Harry has dispatched to San Quentin and a psychotic film fan out to eliminate local celebrities, which includes the cop and lady friend Samantha Walker (Patricia Clarkson). In the background is a low-budget film company boringly run by Liam Neeson.

DEAD PRESIDENTS
1995, 119 mins, US Ⓥ ⊙ ⊟
D: Allen Hughes, Albert Hughes **A:** Larenz Tate, Keith David, Chris Tucker, N'Bushe Wright, Freddy Rodriguez, Rose Jackson (Underworld/Hollywood)

Mordant *Dead Presidents'* muscular engagement of weighty themes and explosive situations makes it a powerful drama, a potent social panorama from a black perspective spanning the convulsive transitional years of 1968–74. In a genteel Bronx neighborhood of 1968, the somewhat naive 18-year-old Anthony (Larenz Tate) is far from likely criminal material. His best buddies are the somewhat crazy, life-of-the-party Skip (Chris Tucker) and the unpredictable José (Freddy Rodriguez). Action jumps to the war, and pic chronicles Anthony's coming-of-age under fire. Once back home in 1973, Anthony faces the sad legacy of many Vietnam vets. Ultimately jobless and desperate, he decides to pull off a big heist. This final section, a sort of mini–*Asphalt Jungle,* feels partly like a different movie.

DEAD RECKONING
1947, 100 mins, US Ⓥ ⊙
D: John Cromwell **A:** Humphrey Bogart, Lizabeth Scott, Morris Carnovsky, William Prince, Marvin Miller (Columbia)

Humphrey Bogart's typically tense performance raises this average whodunit quite a few notches. He plays a tough ex-paratrooper captain returning home with a pal to be honored by the War Department for their achievements. When the pal jumps the DEAD train to go home instead, the perplexed captain follows to find himself enmeshed in gangland, murders, and romance. Lizabeth Scott stumbles occasionally as a nitery singer, but on the whole gives a persuasive sirenish performance.

DEAD RINGERS
1988, 115 mins, Canada Ⓥ ⊙
D: David Cronenberg **A:** Jeremy Irons, Genevieve Bujold, Heidi Von Palleske, Barbara Gordon, Shirley Douglas, Stephen Lack (Mantle Clinic II)

Dead Ringers is about identical twin gynecologists, both expertly played by Jeremy Irons, whose intense bond is fatally sliced when they both fall in love with the same internationally known actress (Genevieve Bujold). Cronenberg handles his usual fondness for gore in muted style; a brief scene has the shy twin dreaming of biting apart the skin joining Siamese twins; and the final operation, though bloody, is not lingered over.

DEAD ZONE, THE
1983, 102 mins, US Ⓥ ⊙
D: David Cronenberg **A:** Christopher Walken, Brooke Adams, Tom Skerritt, Herbert Lom, Anthony Zerbe, Martin Sheen (Dino De Laurentiis)

Joining the half-dozen shock-oriented directors who have filmed novelist Stephen King's horror and suspense yarns, David Cronenberg turns *The Dead Zone* into an accomplished psychological thriller. Focus is Johnny Smith, a shy schoolteacher who snaps out of a long coma with the questionable gift of second sight. Convincingly played by Christopher Walken, Johnny can see into anybody's past or future merely by grasping the person's hand. The dead zone seems to refer to the brain damage that enables him to change the outcome of events he sees.

DEALERS
1989, 89 mins, UK Ⓥ
D: Colin Bucksey **A:** Paul McGann, Rebecca DeMornay, Derrick O'Connor, John Castle, Paul Guilfoyle (Euston)

Dealers is a less than enthralling pic about a yuppie highflier and his glamorous mistress. Paul McGann is a dollar dealer in a London bank. To his chagrin, Mc-

Gann's boss brings in an outsider over his head, beautiful Rebecca DeMornay, the latest whiz kid in the banking business (and the boss' mistress to boot). Before long, though, McGann is romancing his rival.

DEAR BRIGITTE
1965, 100 mins, US ⓥ
D: Henry Koster A: James Stewart, Fabian, Glynis Johns, Cindy Carol, Billy Mumy, Brigitte Bardot (20th Century-Fox)

An entertaining comedy, *Dear Brigitte* focuses on poet-professor Robert Leaf, who's not only pro-humanities but very much antiscience. James Stewart is perfect in characterization of the idealistic voice in academic wilderness at mythical modern university. Complications arise when eight-year-old son Erasmus displays mathematical genius which indicates great scientific future. Yarn is lightweight, but of a sufficiently strong fiber to support a string of varied and effective comedy situations, including Erasmus's puppy love for Brigitte Bardot.

DEAREST LOVE
See: Le Souffle au Coeur

DEATH AND THE MAIDEN
1994, 103 mins, US/France/UK ⓥ
D: Roman Polanski A: Sigourney Weaver, Ben Kingsley, Stuart Wilson (Fine Line Features/New Line Cinema)

Three fine actors and a top director give a very good account of Ariel Dorfman's *Death and the Maiden* in this tense, adroit film version of the play. But as vivid and suspenseful as Roman Polanski has made this claustrophobic tale of a torture victim turning the tables on her putative tormentor, one is still left with a film in which each character represents a mouthpiece for an ideology. Cast is excellent, though having Anglo-American actors portray South Americans will bother some people. Veteran lenser Tonino Delli Colli's work indoors is superlative, as is night shooting on location.

DEATH BECOMES HER
1992, 103 mins, US ⓥ ⊙ ◉
D: Robert Zemeckis A: Meryl Streep, Bruce Willis, Goldie Hawn, Isabella Rossellini, Ian Ogilvy (Universal)

Mordant, daring, and way, way out there, *Death Becomes Her* is a very dark comedy yielding far more strange fascination than outright laughs. Robert Zemeckis' stretch of state-of-the-art special effects within a character-oriented context is a treat for somewhat specialized tastes. Long-arc script describes the epic competition between vain actress Meryl Streep and troubled author Goldie Hawn, initially for the love of superstar plastic surgeon Bruce Willis, but, more important, for the secret to eternal life and youth. Streep does an acid send-up of aging beauty queens that will be relished by devotees of showbiz and its icons. Hawn plays very well with her costar but is mostly limited to rabid vengeance.
1992: Best Visual Effects

DEATH GAME
1977, 89 mins, US ⓥ
D: Peter Traynor A: Sondra Locke, Colleen Camp, Seymour Cassel, Beth Brickell, Michael Kalmansohn, Ruth Warshawsky (Levitt-Pickman)

Two young lesbians (Sondra Locke and Colleen Camp) show up at the plush, suburban home of a San Francisco business exec (Seymour Cassel), just turned 40. After being allowed to use the telephone, pair seduce the man into a sexual threesome, and proceed to move in. Director Peter Traynor opts for the obvious both in the acting and special effects. Locke and Camp scream and lick their lips a lot.

DEATH IN A FRENCH GARDEN
See: Peril en la Demeure

DEATH IN VENICE
1971, 130 mins, Italy ⓥ ▭
D: Luchino Visconti A: Dirk Bogarde, Bjorn Andresen, Silvana Mangano, Marisa Berenson, Mark Burns (Warner)

Based on Thomas Mann's novella, *Death in Venice* could have been no easy task to translate to the screen. But Visconti and Dirk Bogarde clearly have a rapport and Bogarde gives a subtle and moving performance which fits beautifully into the atmospheric realism of Venice. Bogarde plays a German composer and conductor (made up to look very like Gustav Mahler, whose music is used for the score) who visits Venice on vacation when on the verge of a mental and physical collapse. At his hotel, he sees a young boy with his family. The lad looks to Bogarde to be the most beautiful thing he has ever seen. He follows him and watches him with a hunger which, thanks to Bogarde's performance, is clearly more intellectual and emotional than homosexual. The story has its troubles. It attempts to show how innocence can cause problems of corruption

and yet there is a pervading air over the film that is far from innocent.
1971: Nomination: Best Costume Design

DEATH OF A GUNFIGHTER
1969, 94 mins, US ⓥ
D: Allen Smithee [Robert Totten, Don Siegel] **A:** Richard Widmark, Lena Horne, John Saxon, Carroll O'Connor, David Opatoshu, Kent Smith (Universal)

Story concerns an offbeat sort of gunman, a small-town marshal with 12 killings to his credit. Script builds suspense as the council plans his departure but doesn't know how to effect it, other than to gun him down. Richard Widmark punches over title role and gives tone to the character who has always tried to run a clean town.

DEATH OF A SALESMAN
1951, 115 mins, US ⓥ
D: Laslo Benedek **A:** Fredric March, Mildred Dunnock, Kevin McCarthy, Cameron Mitchell, Howard Smith, Royal Beal (Kramer/Columbia)

Arthur Miller's Pulitzer Prize winner has been closely followed in the screen adaptation. *Salesman* starkly reveals how Willy Loman's disillusionments catch up with him, his sons, his wife Linda, of how, after 34 years selling for the same house, he is finally fired, thus bringing about his complete mental collapse. The film images Willy's memories of the past 20 years in illustrating how his desire for importance somehow became enmeshed in his confused dreams. Fredric March gives perhaps the greatest performance of his career. Mildred Dunnock is superb as Willy's wife.
1951: Nominations: Best Actor (Fredric March), Supp. Actor (Kevin McCarthy), Supp. Actress (Mildred Dunnock), B&W Cinematography, Scoring of a Dramatic Picture

DEATH ON THE NILE
1978, 140 mins, UK ⓥ ⊙
D: John Guillermin **A:** Peter Ustinov, Jane Birkin, Lois Chiles, Bette Davis, Mia Farrow, Jon Finch (EMI)

Death on the Nile is a clever, witty, well-plotted, beautifully produced, and splendidly acted screen version of Agatha Christie's mystery. It's old-fashioned stylized entertainment with a big cast and lush locations. Peter Ustinov is the fourth actor to play Belgian sleuth Hercule Poirot. When Ustinov reveals the killer in the final drawing-room scene, it comes as a complete surprise. Every one of the dozen characters floating down the Nile could have and might have murdered Lois Chiles, the arrogant millionairess.
1978: Best Costume Design

DEATH RACE 2000
1975, 78 mins, US ⓥ
D: Paul Bartel **A:** David Carradine, Simone Griffeth, Sylvester Stallone, Mary Woronov (New World)

Roger Corman's quickie production deals with ultraviolent sport in a futuristic society, in this case an annual cross-country road race with drivers scoring points by running down pedestrians. Script makes its satirical points economically, and director Paul Bartel keeps the film moving quickly.

DEATHSPORT
1978, 83 mins, US ⓥ
D: Henry Suso, Allan Arkush **A:** David Carradine, Claudia Jennings, Richard Lynch, William Smithers (New World)

Deathsport is Roger Corman's futuristic science-fiction gladiator picture, set 1,000 years into the future, where the good warriors ride horses and wield see-through sabers fighting bad guys known as Statesmen, who drive lethal motorcycles known as Death Machines. David Carradine is the quiet good guy and the best thing that can be said about his acting is that he doesn't say much. Claudia Jennings is his partner. The best thing that can be said about her performance is that she gets to take off her clothes, twice.

DEATH TAKES A HOLIDAY
1934, 79 mins, US
D: Mitchell Leisen **A:** Fredric March, Evelyn Venable, Guy Standing, Katherine Alexander, Gail Patrick, Helen Westley (Paramount)

Action of picture is laid in and around a foreign estate, the grandeur of which at times is singularly Hollywoodian. Fredric March is on top, playing Death. Wanting to take a holiday from that role, he wishes himself on a duke and his guests for three days, with death meanwhile stopping throughout the world. March turns in a skillful performance, here playing a foreigner in an accent from which there is never a break or slip. He has opposite him for main heart interest Evelyn Venable, who screens well.

DEATHTRAP
1982, 115 mins, US ⓥ
D: Sidney Lumet **A:** Michael Caine,

Christopher Reeve, Dyan Cannon, Irene Worth, Henry Jones (Warner)

Despite its intermittently amusing dialogue, *Deathtrap* comes across as a minor entertainment, cleverness of which cannot conceal its essential artificiality. Michael Caine essays a writer who was once the Neil Simon of Broadway mystery writers but has now cranked out a quartet of clinkers. Into his lap falls the manuscript of a perfect suspenser penned by unknown Christopher Reeve. Desperate for a hit, Caine invites Reeve over one evening in the guise of potential collaborator, while in fact he intends to kill him and then present the work as a new effort of his own.

DEATH WATCH
1980, 128 mins, France/W. Germany Ⓥ
⊙ ▭
D: Bertrand Tavernier **A:** Romy Schneider, Harvey Keitel, Harry Dean Stanton, Therese Liotard, Max von Sydow (Selta/ Little Bear)

The story is a throat-catcher. In a future society people die only of old age, science having almost completely banished disease. A TV producer, played with chillingly unctuous serenity by Harry Dean Stanton, hits on the idea of a program that would cover live the last days of an individual who has managed to contract a terminal illness. The proposed subject is Katherine Mortenhoe (finely played by Romy Schneider). But Katherine, after signing a contract, flees the city.

DEATH WISH
1974, 92 mins, US Ⓥ ⊙ ▭
D: Michael Winner **A:** Charles Bronson, Hope Lange, Vincent Gardenia, Steven Keats, William Redfield (Paramount/De Laurentiis)

Poisonous incitement to do-it-yourself law enforcement is the vulgar exploitation hook on which *Death Wish* is awkwardly hung. Charles Bronson stars as a husband-turned-assassin after his wife is killed and daughter raped by muggers. Plot angles are mostly overwhelmed by the easier, conventional cutting to the action, in this case one killing about every 10 minutes.

DEATH WISH II
1982, 93 mins, US Ⓥ ⊙
D: Michael Winner **A:** Charles Bronson, Jill Ireland, Vincent Gardenia, J. D. Cannon, Anthony Franciosa (Cannon/City)

Charles Bronson, as the avenging vigilante Paul Kersey, is turned loose this time on the creeps of Los Angeles and the results are every bit as revolting as in the original 1974 jackpot fantasy. What little performing style pic offers comes from Vincent Gardenia, encoring from the original edition as a NY gumshoe.

DEATH WISH III
1985, 90 mins, US Ⓥ ⊙
D: Michael Winner **A:** Charles Bronson, Deborah Raffin, Ed Lauter, Martin Balsam (Cannon)

Death Wish III adds significantly to the body count scored to date in this street-rampant series. Thrills, however, are way down due to script's failure to build motivation for Paul Kersey's latest killing spree. Attempts to justify the ensuing mass murder are perfunctory. Film opens with the butchering of an old man who turns out to be an old mate of Kersey, but there's no suggestion that the relationship was intimate. Kersey's response, like Bronson's acting, is automatonlike.

DEATH WISH IV
THE CRACKDOWN
1987, 99 mins, US Ⓥ ⊙
D: J. Lee Thompson **A:** Charles Bronson, Kay Lenz, John P. Ryan, Perry Lopez, George Dickerson (Cannon)

It's a risky business getting close to Charles Bronson. His wife, daughter, and friends have been blown away in the first three installments. Now the vigilante is back to revenge the death of his girlfriend's daughter. What raises *Death Wish IV* above the usual blowout is a semiengaging script and sure pacing by veteran action director J. Lee Thompson.

DEATH WISH V
THE FACE OF DEATH
1994, 95 mins, US Ⓥ ⊙
D: Allan A. Goldstein **A:** Charles Bronson, Lesley-Anne Down, Michael Parks, Saul Rubinek (21st Century)

Bronson, still fit and fearsome at 72, could play Kersey in his sleep. Indeed, there are one or two scenes where he appears to be doing just that. As *Death Wish* pix go, this one set in New York but filmed mostly in Toronto has a surprisingly small body count.

DECALOGUE, THE
See: Dekalog

DECAMERON NIGHTS
1953, 93 mins, UK Ⓥ
D: Hugo Fregonese **A:** Joan Fontaine, Louis Jourdan, Binnie Barnes, Joan Collins, Godfrey Tearle, Noel Purcell (Film Locations)

The producer follows the pattern of the

Boccaccio tales, with backgrounds filmed mainly on location in Spain. He has taken three of the yarns and provided a continuity link with scenes of Fiametta and her ladies at the court where the stories are retold. Joan Fontaine and Louis Jordan make an attractive and intelligent team. They translate effectively the richness of the Boccaccio tales into screen terms.

DECEIVED
1991, 103 mins, US ⓥ ⊙
D: Damian Harris **A:** Goldie Hawn, John Heard, Robin Bartlett, Ashley Peldon, Tom Irwin, Amy Wright (Touchstone)

Thrills, chills, and a convincing perf by Goldie Hawn mark this stylishly absorbing thriller. Hawn plays a New York art restoration expert who appears to be living a perfect life with her attractive career, cute kid (Ashley Peldon), and attentive, romantic husband (John Heard), who's also in the ancient-art biz. But when a forgery's discovered at the museum, fingers are pointed at Heard. Then he's killed in a car accident. Pic segues ably into thriller territory as the undead husband (corpse buried was actually a charred hitchhiker) begins haunting his former home.

DECEIVERS, THE
1988, 112 mins, US ⓥ ⊙
D: Nicholas Meyer **A:** Pierce Brosnan, Saeed Jaffrey, Shashi Kapoor, Helena Michell, Keith Michell, David Robb (Merchant Ivory)

Sumptuously produced historical action adventure tale, set in pre-Raj India circa 1825, falls short of fully developing its most interesting theme—the struggle of the rational Western psyche with the supernatural seductions of the East. Pierce Brosnan is William Savage, a resident collector for the British East India Co., who has married the commander's daughter (Helena Michell). He risks his career by setting out to prove that a series of murders are part of a horrifying conspiracy by the Thuggees—a centuries-old, pan-Indian brotherhood of evildoers who worship Kali, the goddess of destruction. Effort to depict Brosnan's spiritual struggle with dark forces is undermined by the actor's limited range and an elliptical screenplay.

DECEPTION
1946, 111 mins, US ⓥ
D: Irving Rapper **A:** Bette Davis, Claude Rains, Paul Henreid, John Abbot, Benson Fong (Warner)

A story of matrimonial lies that builds to a murder climax gives Bette Davis a potent vehicle. It's not all her show, though. Claude Rains as her elderly teacher and sponsor walks off with considerable portion of the picture in a fine display of acting ability. Plot concerns deception practiced by Davis to prevent husband Paul Henreid from discovering that she had been the mistress of Rains before her marriage. Pickup to story comes with Rains's entrance and his mad jealousy over his desertion by his mistress. To him falls juicy plums in the form of dialogue and situations that carry the story along. Music importance is emphasized by Erich Wolfgang Korngold's score and staging of orchestral numbers by LeRoy Prinz.

DECISION AT SUNDOWN
1957, 77 mins, US
D: Budd Boetticher **A:** Randolph Scott, John Carroll, Karen Steele, Valerie French, Noah Beery, Andrew Duggan (Columbia/Ranown)

Complex screenplay spans a single day in cow town of Sundown. Randolph Scott, a mysterious, revengeful gunman, rides into town. He's after unsavory local wheel John Carroll, who's slated to marry local belle Karen Steele on that day. Role is an offbeat one for Scott, but he carries off the gunman's frustrated rage very well. Carroll makes convincingly menacing heavy in the suave tradition.

DECISION BEFORE DAWN
1951, 119 mins, US
D: Anatole Litvak **A:** Richard Basehart, Gary Merrill, Oskar Werner, Hildegarde Neff, O. E. Hasse (20th Century-Fox)

Anatole Litvak gives this Second World War spy thriller a strong feeling of reality through a semidocumentary treatment, the use of mostly unknown faces, and by location lensing entirely in Germany. Oskar Werner, a sensitive Allied prisoner, volunteers to aid his captors by obtaining information behind the lines in his own country. He believes his actions will help, rather than betray, Germany. Werner's excursion is fraught with danger, and his playing and Litvak direction milk the situation for drama.
1951: Nominations: Best Picture, Editing

DECKS RAN RED, THE
1958, 97 mins, US
D: Andrew L. Stone **A:** James Mason, Dorothy Dandridge, Broderick Crawford, Stuart Whitman, Katharine Bard (M-G-M)

The Decks Ran Red is a descriptive title

for this story of an attempted mutiny at sea. Before the mutineers have been beaten down, they have spilled enough blood to make the decks sticky, if not running, with gore. The plot is a plan by Broderick Crawford and Stuart Whitman, crew members of a chartered freighter, to kill off other members of the crew, rig the ship to make it look like an abandoned derelict, and then bring it in as salvage. The story is faintly incredible at times but the picture moves swiftly and absorbingly.

LE DECLIN DE L'EMPIRE AMERICAIN (THE DECLINE OF THE AMERICAN EMPIRE)
1986, 101 mins, Canada ⊗
D: Denys Arcand A: Pierre Curzi, Remy Girard, Yves Jacques, Dominique Michel, Louise Portal, Dorothee Berryman (Image M&M/ONFC)

Behind the ironically sweeping title of Denys Arcand's film is a mordant small-scale study of private lives and sexual mores among a group of contemporary Canadian academics. Writer-director Arcand deploys a smart script, fluent technique, and a first-rate cast for this deviously sardonic comedy of carnal manners.

DECLINE AND FALL
1968, 90 mins, US
D: John Krish A: Robin Phillips, Genevieve Page, Donald Wolfit, Colin Blakely, Patience Collier, Leo McKern (20th Century-Fox)

This humorous and elegantly confected adaptation of Evelyn Waugh's first (1928) literary success makes for a witty divertissement for discriminating audiences in search of tongue-in-cheek entertainment. Pace is sprightly as we follow Paul Pennyfeather, the schoolboy who becomes teacher, then foil for a dazzling white slaver, then jailbird, until his final rebirth as, literally, a different man. Robin Phillips, in his first pic role, is excellent.

DECLINE OF THE AMERICAN EMPIRE, THE
See: Le Declin de L'Empire Americain

DECLINE OF WESTERN CIVILIZATION, THE
1981, 100 mins, US ⊗
D: Penelope Spheeris (Spheeris)

A bracing, stimulating and technically superb close-up look at the L.A. punk scene. Artistic strategy here is to combine provocative performance footage with at-home interviews with punk-group members and talks with club owners, managers, critics, and hardcore fans. Film constitutes a 100-minute total immersion in the indigenous California punk world. What comes through most strongly is purity of the rockers' dedication to their music.

DECONSTRUCTING HARRY
1997, 96 mins, US ⊗ ⊙
D: Woody Allen A: Woody Allen, Billy Crystal, Judy Davis, Demi Moore, Elisabeth Shue, Robin Williams (Doumanian/ Fine Line)

Deconstructing Harry is abrasive, lacerating, and self-revelatory. It's also very funny, most of the time. Harry Block (Allen) has a reputation as a novelist and short story writer but is unable to find the inspiration to work. He's had three wives and six shrinks (one of whom he married), plus countless lovers along the way. His latest girlfriend, Fay (Elisabeth Shue), has chosen this moment to marry Larry (Billy Crystal), Block's best friend. Meanwhile, Block's former sister-in-law (Judy Davis) is furious that in his last book he described their clandestine relationship. From the beginning, Allen establishes an edgy, disjointed style to illustrate Block's fractured way of life. With an almost constant stream of mostly funny one-liners, Block is a typical Allen protag, yet darker, sadder, more isolated, less mature.
1997: Nomination: Best Original Screenplay

DEEP, THE
1977, 124 mins, US ⊗ ⊙ ▭
D: Peter Yates A: Robert Shaw, Jacqueline Bisset, Nick Nolte, Louis Gossett, Eli Wallach (Columbia-EMI/Casablanca Filmworks)

An efficient but rather colorless film based on the Peter Benchley novel about a perilous search for treasure in the waters off Bermuda. Fully 40 percent of the film takes place underwater. Director Peter Yates keeps up the tension in a low-key way with a few shocker moments thrown in from time to time, and these scenes are more involving than the ones above the surface.
1977: Nomination: Best Sound

DEEP BLUE SEA
1999, 105 mins, US ⊗ ⊙ ▭
D: Renny Harlin A: Thomas Jane, Saffron Burrows, Samuel L. Jackson, Jacqueline McKenzie, Michael Rapaport, Stellan Skarsgard (Warner)

Powered by exceptional displays of physical filmmaking, *Deep Blue Sea* is pulled back to shore by weak plotting and weaker dialogue. Main draw is a trio of 40-foot killer sharks on the loose. Sharks are being used by marine biologist Dr. Susan McAlester (Saffron Burrows) in her experiment to wipe out Alzheimer's disease. Her corporate funder, tycoon Russell Franklin (Samuel L. Jackson), arrives at Susan's lair—a former US Navy sub base called Aquatica. Susan aims to harvest protein from the brains of the test sharks. Her shark wrangler, Carter (Thomas Jane), wrangles one of the sharks and McAlester extracts brain protein. All hell breaks loose as the seemingly subdued shark chomps off one of research partner Jim Whitlock's (Stellan Skarsgard) arms. Digitized sharks are unevenly realized, to sometimes ferocious and sometimes cartoonish effect. Jane emerges best of all with an ideal blend of brawn and charisma.

DEEP COVER
1992, 112 mins, US $\circledS$ $\odot$
D: Bill Duke **A:** Larry Fishburne, Jeff Goldblum, Victoria Dillard, Charles Martin Smith, Gregory Sierra (David-Bean)

Convoluted and mostly unconvincing as a portrait of the drug underworld, *Deep Cover* still carries some resonance due to its vivid portrait of societal decay and a heavyweight performance by Larry Fishburne. Tough, straight-arrow cop Fishburne is recruited by government drug-enforcement chief Charles Martin Smith to infiltrate the cartel of dealer Arthur Mendoza, who controls 40 percent of the L.A. cocaine market. Key behind-the-scenes contribution is Michel Colombier's superbly moody, dissonant jazz/rock score.

DEEP END
1970, 90 mins, W. Germany/US $\circledS$
D: Jerzy Skolimowski **A:** Jane Asher, John Moulder-Brown, Karl Michael Vogler, Christopher Sandford, Diana Dors (Maran/COKG/Kettledrum)

Though its main locale is a rather seamy London public bath, director Jerzy Skolimowski has avoided tawdriness by sympathy for, and awareness of, the excessive but essentially pure actions of his love-smitten boy, whose good looks make him prey for all types of women who come for their public ablutions. Skolimowski keeps the film alive with quirky incidents.

DEEP END OF THE OCEAN, THE
1999, 105 mins, US $\circledS$ $\odot$
D: Ulu Grosbard **A:** Michelle Pfeiffer, Treat Williams, Whoopi Goldberg, Jonathan Jackson, Ryan Merriman, John Kapelos (Sony)

The Deep End of the Ocean is an engaging, heart-wrenching drama. As parents forced to reexamine their values when their son disappears and, years later, returns, Michelle Pfeiffer and Treat Williams give such magnetic performances that they elevate the film way above its middlebrow proclivity for neat resolutions. Tale introduces the happily married Cappadoras: Beth (Pfeiffer) and hubby Pat (Williams), and shows the devastating effects of three-year-old Ben's vanishing on his family. Story jumps ahead nine years, when a boy named Sam (Ryan Merriman) shows up. Beth recognizes him as her lost son, but in due course Sam misses his Greek adoptive father and runs away. Ulu Grosbard's meticulous direction is impressive. Performances across the board are flawless, particularly Pfeiffer as the imperfect mother.

DEEP IMPACT
1998, 120 mins, US $\circledS$ $\odot$ $\bowtie$
D: Mimi Leder **A:** Robert Duvall, Tea Leoni, Elijah Wood, Vanessa Redgrave, Morgan Freeman, Maximilian Schell (Zanuck-Brown/DreamWorks/Paramount)

This comet-targets-Earth special effects extravaganza is spectacular enough in its cataclysmic scenes but proves far from thrilling in the downtime spent with a largely dull assortment of troubled human beings. With impact looming in a year, U.S. President Beck (a solemn Morgan Freeman) announces the news to the world. Astronauts will plant eight nukes on the comet in the hope of blowing it to smithereens. The mission proves a dismal failure, succeeding only in splitting the comet into two unequal pieces. The first big rock sends the world's biggest tidal wave breaking over the Statue of Liberty and all of Manhattan. The water effects are just the slightest bit phony looking, but they still register dramatically.

DEEPSTAR SIX
1989, 100 mins, US $\circledS$ $\odot$
D: Sean S. Cunningham **A:** Taurean Blacque, Nancy Everhard, Greg Evigan, Miguel Ferrer, Nia Peeples, Cindy Pickett (Carolco)

Tale of a sea monster attacking an ocean-bottom research team. Effect is diluted by implausibility, as creature never seems real—more like a goof on a 1950s horror-movie monster than a true threat.

DEEP THROAT
1972, 73 mins, US
D: Jerry Gerard [Gerard Damiano] A: Linda Lovelace (Vanguard)

While *Deep Throat* doesn't quite live up to its reputation as the *Ben-Hur* of porno pix, it is a superior piece which stands a head above the competition. Pic takes a tongue-in-cheek approach to conventional hetero hardcore. Plot centers on a young lady disappointed because she fails to hear bells during her repeated sex bouts with as many as 14 men at a time.

DEER HUNTER, THE
1978, 183 mins, US
D: Michael Cimino A: Robert De Niro, John Cazale, John Savage, Meryl Streep, Christopher Walken, George Dzundza (EMI)

Robert De Niro, John Cazale, John Savage, and Christopher Walken head cast as friends living in a small Pennsylvania town. They attend a Russian Orthodox wedding at the beginning of the film. Directly afterward three of them go deer hunting and soon thereafter they are to serve in Vietnam. Throughout the film various ceremonies and cultural rituals are explored, compared, and juxtaposed—the wedding, the game, and the deer hunt. It is up to the viewer to decide how these rituals fit together and it is a big comprehension demand.

1978: Best Picture, Director, Supp. Actor (Christopher Walken), Sound, Editing
Nominations: Best Actor (Robert De Niro), Supp. Actress (Meryl Streep), Original Screenplay, Cinematography

DEFECTOR, THE
1966, 108 mins, W. Germany/France
D: Raoul Levy A: Montgomery Clift, Hardy Kruger, Macha Meril, Roddy McDowall, David Opatoshu (PECF/ Rhein-Main)

The last motion picture made by Montgomery Clift prior to his death. His taut, troubled face is perfect for the role of a scientist pushed into espionage by his own country and almost erased from it by enemy agents. Most of the intellectual by-play is between Clift, as an American scientist, and Hardy Kruger, as the German-born Russian agent given the assignment of getting Clift to defect.

DEFENCE OF THE REALM
1985, 96 mins, UK
D: David Drury A: Gabriel Byrne, Greta Scacchi, Denholm Elliott, Ian Bannen, Fulton MacKay, Bill Paterson (Enigma/ NFFC/Ramk)

The state of the nation's press and the evil antics of its secret services in the nuclear age are combined in this fast-paced thriller. Script unravels a relatively uncomplicated story of events following the near crash of a nuclear bomber on an American air-force base in the English countryside. The story centers on a hack set up by the secret services.

DEFENDING YOUR LIFE
1991, 112 mins, US
D: Albert Brooks A: Albert Brooks, Meryl Streep, Rip Torn, Lee Grant, Buck Henry, Shirley MacLaine (Geffen)

Defending Your Life is an inventive and mild bit of whimsy from Albert Brooks. The former stand-up comedian has a little fun with the *Liliom* idea of being judged in a fanciful afterlife, but he doesn't carry his conceit nearly far enough. The victim is forced to watch particularly embarrassing moments from his life while listening to a torrent of vilification from the prosecutor (Lee Grant) and just a measure of defense from his cheerleader (Rip Torn). Lending all of this some meaning is Meryl Streep, the dream woman who would be the love his life if only they weren't dead.

DEFENSELESS
1991, 104 mins, US
D: Martin Campbell A: Barbara Hershey, Sam Shepard, Mary Beth Hurt, J. T. Walsh, Kellie Overbey, Sheree North (New Visions)

A murder mystery with a fine cast and wild-and-woolly story, *Defenseless* almost continuously wobbles across the line between the deliberately ambiguous and the irritatingly murky. Barbara Hershey portrays T.K., a Los Angeles attorney who, for psychological reasons that remain unexplored, has managed to make a rather spectacular mess of her life. T.K. is drawn into a web of lies when she discovers that her lover and client, Steven Seldes (the reliably snaky J. T. Walsh), is married to her long-lost college roommate Ellie (Mary Beth Hurt). Steven is later found murdered.

DEFIANT ONES, THE
1958, 97 mins, US Ⓥ ⊙
D: Stanley Kramer **A:** Tony Curtis, Sidney Poitier, Theodore Bikel, Charles McGraw, Cara Williams, Claude Akins (United Artists)

The theme of *The Defiant Ones* is that what keeps men apart is their lack of knowledge of one another. This thesis is explored in terms of a black and a white man, both convicts chained together as they make their break for freedom from a southern prison gang. The performances by Tony Curtis and Sidney Poitier are virtually flawless. Poitier captures all of the moody violence of the convict, serving time because he assaulted a white man who had insulted him. As the arrogant white man chained to a fellow convict whom he hates, Curtis delivers a true surprise performance.
1958: Best Original Story & Screenplay, B&W Cinematography
Nominations: Best Picture, Director, Actor (Tony Curtis, Sidney Poitier), Supp. Actor (Theodore Bikel), Supp. Actress (Cara Williams), Editing

DEKALOG
(THE DECALOGUE; THE TEN COMMANDMENTS)
1989, 584 mins, Poland/W. Germany Ⓥ
D: Krzysztof Kieslowski **A:** Henryk Baranowski, Aleksander Bardini, Daniel Olbrychski, Miroslaw Baka, Grazyna Szapolowska, Jerzy Stuhr (Polish TV/Sender Freies Berlin)

The 10 modern moral stories Polish director Krzysztof Kieslowski spins are inspired by the Ten Commandments. All 10 stories are placed in the same gray and depressing block of same concrete buildings in a Warsaw suburb, where university professors and taxi drivers live side by side. Leading characters in one episode emerge again, as passersby or secondary characters, in another episode. Being a pessimist at heart, Kieslowski, who cowrote all 10 scripts, unfolds a variety of human weaknesses, shows how difficult it is to conform to one commandment, let alone 10, and considers human frailty with sympathy but little hope. Kieslowski changed cameramen from film to film, not only to accommodate their schedules, but to give a slightly different look to each film.

DELICATESSEN
1991, 96 mins, France Ⓥ ⊙
D: Jean-Pierre Jeunet, Marc Caro **A:** Dominique Pinon, Marie-Laure Dougnac, Jean-Claude Dreyfus, Rufus, Ticky Holgado, Anne-Marie Pisani (Constellation/UGC/Hachette Premiere)

Beautifully textured, cleverly scripted, and eerily shot (often with a wide-angle lens making characters look even weirder), *Delicatessen* is a zany little film. In a darkly bizarre, futuristic world where food shortages have led a butcher to serve up human flesh after murdering the locals, a bumbling group of Troglodins, an underground force reminiscent of the government police in *Brazil*, are engaged in a war on cannibal crime. An excellent cast made up entirely of character actors provides a rich array of eccentrics who live in the building over the deli and the sewers used as tunnels by the Troglodins.

DELINQUENTS, THE
1989, 101 mins, Australia Ⓥ ⊙
D: Chris Thomson **A:** Kylie Minogue, Charlie Schlatter, Angela Punch-McGregor, Bruno Lawrence (Village-Roadster/Silver Lining)

The story, set in the late 1950s, about the passionate love affair of a couple of teens, is trite stuff. Lola (Kylie Minogue) and Brownie (Charlie Schlatter) live in the small town of Bundaberg in Queensland. She's still at school when they become lovers and she gets pregnant. The youngsters plan to elope, but are parted by Lola's alcoholic mother (Angela Punch-McGregor).

DELIRIOUS
1991, 96 mins, US Ⓥ ⊙
D: Tom Mankiewicz **A:** John Candy, Mariel Hemingway, Emma Samms, Raymond Burr, Robert Wagner (M-G-M/Star Partners III)

Delirious is a witless comedy about soap operas in which the estimable John Candy mugs uncomfortably through a desperately unfunny script with a plot as tediously convoluted as those it spoofs.

DELIVERANCE
1972, 109 mins, US Ⓥ ⊙ ▭
D: John Boorman **A:** Jon Voight, Burt Reynolds, Ned Beatty, Ronny Cox, Billy McKinney, James Dickey (Warner)

Deliverance can be considered a stark, uncompromising showdown between basic survival instincts and the character pretensions of a mannered and material society. Unfortunately, it can just as easily be seen as a virile, mountain-country transposition of nihilistic, specious philosophizing that exploits rather than explores

its moments of violent drama. Against the majestic setting of a river being dammed, story takes four city men out for a last weekend trip down the river. Unexpected malevolence forces each to test his personal values in order to survive. What makes for a pervading uneasiness is the implication of the story: the strongest shall survive. In the depiction of sudden, violent death, there is the rhapsodic wallowing in the deadly beauty of it all: protruding arrows, agonizing expiration, etc.
1972: Nominations: Best Picture, Director, Editing

DELTA FORCE, THE
1986, 129 mins, US Ⓥ ⊙
D: Menahem Golan **A:** Chuck Norris, Lee Marvin, Martin Balsam, Joey Bishop, Robert Forster, Lainie Kazan (Cannon)

First hour is mostly devoted to what seems to be a quite accurate rendition of the 1985 TWA Athens hijacking. From here, film is purest fantasy pitting the noble Yankees against the dirty, low-down Palestinians. Chuck Norris gets a chance to make ample use of his martial-arts skills.

DELTA FORCE 2
THE COLOMBIAN CONNECTION
1990, 105 mins, US Ⓥ ⊙
D: Aaron Norris **A:** Chuck Norris, Billy Drago, Bobby Chavez, John R. Ryan, Richard Jaeckel (Cannon)

Chuck Norris fans have all they could ask for with *Delta Force 2*. Norris and a dozen US Marines fly into the South American drug capital San Carlos, destroy half the country's cocaine production, and rub out the land's untouchable drug czar, in a cathartic blaze of exploding missiles and flying fists. Norris is a minimalist actor, rightly concentrating on the action. As the sadistic Coda, Billy Drago has a Medusa-like presence that produces shivers just from looking at him.

DEMETRIUS AND THE GLADIATORS
1954, 101 mins, US Ⓥ ⊙ ▭
D: Delmer Daves **A:** Victor Mature, Susan Hayward, Michael Rennie, Debra Paget, Anne Bancroft, Jay Robinson (20th Century-Fox)

20th-Fox's follow-up to its tremendously successful *The Robe*. Victor Mature again scores with the character of the slave. A mighty man is he battling three huge tigers in the Roman arena to satisfy the mad urges of the crazy Emperor Ca-

ligula and the wicked Messalina, dueling to the death with five of Rome's best gladiators, or making love to the same wicked temptress who has temporarily caused him to forget his God.

DEMI-PARADISE, THE
(US: ADVENTURE FOR TWO)
1943, 115 mins, UK Ⓥ
D: Anthony Asquith **A:** Laurence Olivier, Penelope Ward, Marjorie Fielding, Margaret Rutherford, Leslie Henson, Felix Aylmer (Two Cities)

Script consists of a wealth of character drawings with a thin web of a story about a young Russian engineer. He arrives in England some months before the war, with humorous misconception of the average native of Britain. It takes him some time to know the people for what they really are, with their foibles, humors, and idiosyncrasies. There is a slight love story with an English girl. Laurence Olivier, replete with Russian accent, gives a dignified and serious performance full of sincerity and repose.

LES DEMOISELLES DE ROCHEFORT
(THE YOUNG GIRLS OF ROCHEFORT)
1967, 125 mins, France Ⓥ ▭
D: Jacques Demy **A:** Catherine Deneuve, George Chakiris, Francoise Dorleac, Jacques Perrin, Gene Kelly, Danielle Darrieux (Parc/Madeleine)

Jacques Demy, writer-director, and Michel Legrand, composer, who did the successful musical *The Umbrellas of Cherbourg*, reunite for a more ambitious pic that adds dance to a tale of small-town life. It has charm, sustained human observation, mixed with catchy music, dances, and songs to come up as a tuner with grace and dynamism. Deneuve and Dorleac, real sisters, play twins with the right mixture of feminine guile, passiveness, and stubborn aggressiveness when it comes to the men they want. Darrieux is fetching as their mother; she is the only one who synced her own songs, at least in the French version. Kelly is trim, dynamic, and both brash and winning, while Chakiris has less to do. Though a fairly classic musical reminiscent of earlier Yank tuners, it has a Gallic froth, tinged with unobtrusive melancholy and character delineation.

DEMOLITION MAN

1993, 114 mins, US ⓥ ⊙ ▭

D: Marco Brambilla **A:** Sylvester Stallone, Wesley Snipes, Sandra Bullock, Nigel Hawthorne (Silver/Warner)

Demolition Man is a noisy, soulless, self-conscious pastiche that mixes elements of sci-fi, action adventure, and romance, then pours on a layer of comedy replete with Hollywood in-jokes. The screen is flushed with blue lighting, the pacing is swift, and there is a lot of montage and fast cutting. However, most of the action set pieces are poorly staged: keeping the camera too close to the fights and chases allows viewers no sense of space awareness of or where the antagonists stand in relation to each other.

DEMON KNIGHT
(AKA: TALES FROM THE CRYPT PRESENTS DEMON KNIGHT)

1995, 92 mins, US ⓥ ⊙

D: Ernest Dickerson **A:** Billy Zane, William Sadler, Jada Pinkett, Brenda Bakke, CCH Pounder, Dick Miller (Universal)

Fang-in-cheek horror thriller that likely will please fans and turn off nondevotees. Main story is a familiar but fitfully exciting supernatural tale set in and around a spectacularly seedy desert hotel. Brayker (Willian Sadler), the mysterious new guest, turns out to be the guardian of an ancient key that keeps the forces of darkness from overwhelming mankind. Trouble begins when another stranger, the charismatic Collector (Billy Zane), shows up with two local cops claiming Brayker stole the key from him. The Collector summons skeletal flesh-eating demons to help him invade the boardinghouse. Pic is neither funny enough nor scary enough to be fully satisfying as either a shocker or a spoof.

DEMON SEED

1977, 94 mins, US ⓥ ⊙ ▭

D: Donald Cammell **A:** Julie Christie, Fritz Weaver, Gerrit Graham, Berry Kroeger, Lisa Lu, Larry J. Blake (M-G-M)

Demon Seed tells of the impregnation of a female by a master computer system which seeks to perpetuate itself in human form. Julie Christie stars as the electronic Eve, along with Fritz Weaver as her scientist husband. Excellent performances and direction, from a most credible and literate screenplay, make production an intriguing achievement in storytelling.

DENNIS

See: Dennis the Menace

DENNIS THE MENACE
(UK: DENNIS)

1993, 94 mins, US ⓥ

D: Nick Castle **A:** Walter Matthau, Mason Gamble, Joan Plowright, Christopher Lloyd, Lea Thompson (Warner)

Dennis the Menace isn't really appropriate for anyone over the age of 12. Very young children may find the numbskull, by-the-numbers gags here amusing, but teens will consider this kid stuff and adults will be pained. There's no plot per se, just one lame gag after another. The one real pleasure for adults in the film comes from watching Matthau, who has reached deep into his bag of tricks to deliver a huge assortment of slow burns, simmering grimaces, delayed howls, and intolerant glances.

LA DENTELLIERE
(THE LACEMAKER)

1977, 110 mins, France/ Switzerland ⓥ ⊙

D: Claude Goretta **A:** Isabelle Huppert, Yves Beneyton, Florence Giorgetti, Anne-Marie Duringer

The film is a lacy, gentle probing of an ill-assorted couple. Isabelle Huppert is extraordinary as the childish girl living with a doting mother and working as an assistant hairdresser. On vacation she meets a young student and she makes love for the first time. They move in together in Paris but her lack of education, her inability to make contact with him, finally has him driving her out.

LE DERNIER METRO
(THE LAST METRO)

1980, 130 mins, France ⓥ

D: Francois Truffaut **A:** Catherine Deneuve, Gerard Depardieu, Jean Poiret, Heinz Bennent, Andrea Ferreol, Paulette Dubost

Francois Truffaut's 19th feature is adroit dramatic entertainment, gracefully romantic and uplifting. But it is also a fascinating chronicle of Paris life under the German Occupation—its daily terror, material deprivation, opportunism, cowardice, denunciation, as well as its quiet heroism and unexpected moments of laughter. Pic follows the difficulties of a small Paris theater struggling to stay open under the constraints of the Nazi occupants. The acting is fine down the line, with Deneuve giving one of her most accomplished performances, particularly in her scenes with Bennent, forlorn and appealing, and Depardieu, who displays vigorous range.

DERSU UZALA
1975, 137 mins, USSR/Japan Ⓥ ▯

D: Akira Kurosawa **A:** Maksim Munzuk, Yuri Solomin (Mosfilm/Toho)

Absent from the screen for two years or more, Akira Kurosawa returns as director of a heartwarming film shot entirely in eastern Siberia and on interiors in Mosfilm Studios. Film takes place at the turn of the century in eastern Siberia, where a small army detachment is surveying the unexplored forests and Taiga land. The encounter with a Siberian trapper, Dersu Uzala (Maksim Munzuk), sets the stage for an inseparable friendship between hunter and explorer Vladimir Arsenyev (Yuri Solomin) on three long and difficult survey missions.

1975: Best Foreign Language Film

DE SADE
1969, 113 mins, US/W. Germany

D: Cy Endfield **A:** Keir Dullea, Senta Berger, Lilli Palmer, Anna Massey, Sonja Ziemann, Uta Levka (American International/CCC/TransContinental)

Pseudo-biography of the young French whippersnapper whose name became a household word. Dullea's idea of a good time is to dive into a pile of nude women with his pants on, spank a few bottoms, pour wine over everybody, and howl his head off.

DESERT ATTACK
See: Ice Cold in Alex

DESERT BLOOM
1986, 104 mins, US Ⓥ ⊙

D: Eugene Corr **A:** Jon Voight, JoBeth Williams, Ellen Barkin, Allen Garfield, Annabeth Gish (Carson)

A muted, intelligently observed story of a girl's growing pains in an emotionally deprived and politically warped environment. Arid setting in question is Las Vegas, 1950, where Second World War vet Jon Voight runs a gas station and is stepfather to JoBeth Williams's three daughters. Big events in the household are the arrival of Aunt Starr (Ellen Barkin), a glamorous showgirl type, and the impending atmospheric A-bomb test, for which the entire community is preparing as if it were the Second Coming.

DESERT FOX, THE
(UK: ROMMEL—DESERT FOX)
1951, 88 mins, US Ⓥ ⊙

D: Henry Hathaway **A:** James Mason, Cedric Hardwicke, Jessica Tandy, Luther Adler, Everett Sloane, Leo G. Carroll (20th Century-Fox)

The story of Field Marshal Erwin Rommel, as biographed by Brigadier Desmond Young, comes to the screen as an episodic documentary difficult to follow or understand. A controversial angle is posed by the sympathetic pitch made for Rommel by Young, and the whitewashing given a number of Nazi military leaders previously charged with being war criminals by the British. Performances are good, with James Mason's portrait of the Desert Fox extremely able within the shadowy confines of the script.

DESERT HEARTS
1985, 93 mins, US Ⓥ ⊙

D: Donna Deitch **A:** Helen Shaver, Patricia Charbonneau, Audra Lindley, Andra Akers, Dean Butler (Goldwyn/Desert Hearts)

The plot focuses on a guest at a Nevada ranch, about to get divorced. She catches the fancy of the owner's adoptive daughter, who starts making advances, first timidly and then in a pressing fashion, until the prim, respectable East Coast intellectual has to drop her armor and face her own latent homosexuality. Since the story is placed in the 1950s, it is clear that what, by today's standards, would have been an unconventional but by no means an exceptional case, becomes an act of defiance against the accepted rules of society. Helen Shaver, playing the lead, does a most commendable job.

IL DESERTO ROSSO
(RED DESERT; THE RED DESERT)
1964, 116 mins, Italy/France Ⓥ ⊙

D: Michelangelo Antonioni **A:** Monica Vitti, Richard Harris, Carlo Chionetti, Xenia Valderi, Rita Renoir (Federiz/Francoriz)

Red Desert is on one level an untraditional study of a neurosis, on another a frightening fresco of the destructive dangers and crises implicit in present-day life. Pic tells of a woman (Monica Vitti) who desperately seeks an escape from the neurotic state of which she is conscious. Her quest for an oasis in the desert makes her seek the company of her husband's colleague, Corrado (Richard Harris), who is almost as unprepared and unwilling to assist her as is her husband. The pace is slow, objects play as important a role as humans, etc. The novelty here is color, and the director's contribution is masterful—perhaps the first time tint has been used creatively with such effect and power.

DESERT PATROL
See: Sea of Sand

DESERT RATS, THE
1953, 88 mins, US ⓥ
D: Robert Wise **A:** Richard Burton, Robert Newton, Robert Douglas, James Mason, Torin Thatcher, Chips Rafferty (20th Century-Fox)

A follow-up but not a sequel to *The Desert Fox*, the 1951 Field Marshal Rommel feature. James Mason is back to repeat his Rommel characterization, but appears only in a few scenes. Richard Burton is excellent as the British captain in charge of the Australian troops that resist attacks on Tobruk. Robert Newton figures as a drunken old schoolteacher of Burton's, whose cowardice poses a problem for the young officer.
1953: Nomination: Best Story & Screenplay

DESERT SONG, THE
1944, 90 mins, US
D: Robert Florey **A:** Dennis Morgan, Irene Manning, Bruce Cabot, Victor Francen, Lynne Overman (Warner)

In modernizing story, German agents and plans to construct new railroad in North Africa for terminus at Dakar provide motivation for Riff uprising and leadership by Dennis Morgan, an American piano player in Morocco nightspot. Irene Manning is the new singer at the café, with mutual romance developing. Despite modernization to the operetta, basic entertainment qualities are retained. Morgan is neatly cast as the Red Rider, delivering both dramatic and vocal assignments in top style. Manning capably handles the girl spot.
1944: Nomination: Best Color Art Direction

DESERT SONG, THE
1929, 125 mins, US ⓥ
D: Roy Del Ruth **A:** John Boles, Carlotta King, Louise Fazenda, Johnny Arthur, Myrna Loy (Warner)

Taking another step forward in the talking field by doing an operetta, following the story in detail and getting in the entire musical score and compositions, Warner Bros. has a winner. There is little of the romantic on the screen as the principal players were chosen more for their voices than for ability to act screen roles.

DESERT SONG, THE
1953, 110 mins, US
D: H. Bruce Humberstone **A:** Kathryn Grayson, Gordon MacRae, Steve Cochran, Raymond Massey, Dick Wesson, Allyn McLerie (Warner)

After two times around as a film vehicle, once in 1929 and again in 1943, this venerable romantic musical has just about run out of entertainment vitamins. Both story and the songs are well-worn. Latter wear their age with charm and are nicely delivered by Kathryn Grayson and Gordon MacRae. Making a pretty picture is Grayson, and she serves up her tunes well. MacRae is unbelievable as the mysterious Riff leader.

DESIGN FOR LIVING
1933, 90 mins, US
D: Ernst Lubitsch **A:** Fredric March, Gary Cooper, Miriam Hopkins, Edward Everett Horton, Franklin Pangborn, Isabel Jewell (Paramount)

Noel Coward has contributed a basic premise that's arresting—a girl and two men all of whom are very fond of each other. Edward Everett Horton, as the patient mentor of the girl, is built up here, as much by the script as his own personal histrionic ability. Miriam Hopkins's expert handling of the delicate premise which motivates the other three men is a consummate performance in every respect. She glosses over the dirt, but gets the punch over nonetheless. She confesses quite naively that she is stumped—she likes both Tom and George (Fredric March and Gary Cooper).

DESIGN FOR SCANDAL
1941, 82 mins, US
D: Norman Taurog **A:** Rosalind Russell, Walter Pidgeon, Lee Bowman, Jean Rogers, Mary Beth Hughes, Edward Arnold (M-G-M)

When ace reporter Walter Pidgeon is assigned by his alimony-burdened publisher to frame the decision-rendering female judge (Rosalind Russell), it's a cinch that the pair will eventually fall in love and the scandal plan will be tossed into the discard. Despite this obvious conclusion, story unfolds at a consistently amusing clip, held together by deft direction by Norman Taurog and a group of sterling performances.

DESIGNING WOMAN
1957, 117 mins, US Ⓥ ⌴

D: Vincente Minnelli A: Gregory Peck, Lauren Bacall, Dolores Gray, Sam Levene, Mickey Shaughnessy (M-G-M)

Runyonesque-type romp cleverly brings together the worlds of haute couture, sports (particularly boxing), show business, and the underworld. Gregory Peck, a crusading sportswriter, marries Lauren Bacall, a prominent fashion designer. Her friends are the chichi set; his cronies are fellow sports scribes and Stillman Gym characters.

DESIRE
1936, 95 mins, US Ⓥ

D: Frank Borzage A: Marlene Dietrich, Gary Cooper, John Halliday, William Frawley, Ernest Cossart (Paramount)

Desire is the first Marlene Dietrich and Gary Cooper picture since *Morocco* (1930). The two stars work unusually well as a pair. The direction is subtle and inspired, with many smart little Lubitschian touches adding to the general appeal of the yarn. Dietrich plays a jewel thief who gains possession of a valuable string of pearls. About half the footage is concerned with the efforts of Dietrich and a confederate to retrieve the pearls from Cooper, who unknowingly has become their custodian.

DESIRE & HELL AT SUNSET MOTEL
1992, 90 mins, US Ⓥ

D: Alien Castle A: Sherilyn Fenn, Whip Hubley, David Hewlett, David Johansen, Paul Bartel (Heron/Image)

The visuals are all that stand out in this low-budget sex-comedy noir set against the stylish 1950s motifs of the turquoise-and-sand Sunset Motel. Fenn, in a bombshell role and easily as photogenic as Madonna, finds a light sensual style pretty much her own, but Hubley generates no sparks as her husband.

DESIREE
1954, 110 mins, US Ⓥ ⌴

D: Henry Koster A: Marlon Brando, Jean Simmons, Merle Oberon, Michael Rennie, Cameron Mitchell, Elizabeth Sellars (20th Century-Fox)

The story of Desirée, daughter of a Marseilles silk merchant, who meets an impoverished general, Napoleon Bonaparte. They plan to marry. But Napoleon goes to Paris and there meets and weds the rich and influential Joséphine. Brando's Napoleon is arrogant, scheming, and temperamental, and yet oddly human in his failings. Jean Simmons as Desirée is lovely, innocent, and naive, as prescribed.

DESIRE ME
1947, 90 mins, US

D: [George Cukor, Mervyn LeRoy, Jack Conway] A: Greer Garson, Robert Mitchum, Richard Hart, George Zucco, Morris Ankrum (M-G-M)

A story of a wife who, after long years of faithful waiting, succumbs to lonesomeness on the eve of her supposedly dead husband's return from war. The husband kills his rival in a struggle. Locale is a small fishing village on the coast of Normandy and catches interest with colorful settings and seascapes. Flashbacks within flashbacks make plot hard to follow. Greer Garson's role requires continual emotional stress that makes for a heavy job, but she is capable. Robert Mitchum has too little footage as the husband, but he makes every scene count.

DESIRE UNDER THE ELMS
1958, 111 mins, US Ⓥ ◉

D: Delbert Mann A: Sophia Loren, Anthony Perkins, Burl Ives, Pernell Roberts (Paramount)

Desire Under the Elms is painfully slow in getting under way, the characters are never completely understandable or believable, and the ghastly plot climax of infanticide) plays with disappointingly little force. Eugene O'Neill wrote a modern version of a Greek tragedy. He chose the craggy New England of 1840 and its flinty characters with care. The casting of Sophia Loren in the role of the young (third) wife of farmer Burl Ives is a key error because it injects an alien-to-the-scene element that dislocates the drama permanently.

DESPAIR
1978, 119 mins, W. Germany Ⓥ

D: Rainer Werner Fassbinder A: Dirk Bogarde, Andrea Ferreol, Volker Spengler, Klaus Lowitsch (Bavaria Atelier/SFP/Geria)

Despite a witty, albeit theatrical, script by Tom Stoppard, prolific German director Rainer Werner Fassbinder does not quite bring off the spirited linguistic innovations, wit, and penetrating insights of Vladimir Nabokov's novel; but it is a good try. This tale of an exiled Russian in Germany in the late 1920s, who is driven to a weird murder, emerges as overlong.

DESPERADO
1995, 103 mins, US Ⓥ
D: Robert Rodriguez **A:** Antonio Banderas, Salma Hayek, Joaquim de Almeida, Cheech Marin, Steve Buscemi, Quentin Tarantino (Los Hooligans/Columbia)

Robert Rodriguez dedicates himself almost exclusively to dreaming up a hundred new ways to blow people away, to ultimately diminishing returns. The young Tex-Mex director's much-anticipated follow-up to his wildly inventive no-budget 1993 debut, *El Mariachi,* could scarcely be more dazzling on a purely visual level, but it's mortally anemic in the story, character, and thematic departments. Opening stretch is nearbrilliant in its audaciousness. A brash gringo (indie fave Steve Buscemi) struts into a Mexican dive and relates what he just saw happen at another cantina, where a mysterious stranger wiped everyone out. The stranger, of course, is El Mariachi, played by the never-more-handsome Antonio Banderas, a guitar strummer wandering the country seeking revenge for the murder of the woman he loved.

DESPERADOES, THE
1943, 85 mins, US
D: Charles Vidor **A:** Randolph Scott, Glenn Ford, Claire Trevor, Evelyn Keyes, Edgar Buchanan (Columbia)

The usual lusty and vigorous melodramatics of the early west. Randolph Scott is a sheriff in the Utah country in the 1860s, when a bank robbery is staged, and shortly after, Glenn Ford wanders into town. He's a former pal of Scott—also boyhood sweetheart of Claire Trevor, who's operating the town's hotel and gambling layout—and a fugitive with heavy coin riding on his head.

DESPERATE
1947, 73 mins, US Ⓥ
D: Anthony Mann **A:** Steve Brodie, Audrey Long, Raymond Burr, Douglas Fowley (RKO)

Desperate is a ripsnorting gangster meller. Steve Brodie, honest truck driver, becomes involved innocently in a fur-warehouse robbery and cop slaying. Picture becomes more or less a continuing flight of Brodie and his wife, Audrey Long, both from the gendarmes and the gangsters. Surprise ending gives film a lift. Anthony Mann's direction mainly stresses suspense, which is done skillfully.

DESPERATE HOURS, THE
1955, 112 mins, US Ⓥ ⊙
D: William Wyler **A:** Humphrey Bogart, Fredric March, Arthur Kennedy, Martha Scott, Dewey Martin, Gig Young (Paramount)

Desperate Hours is an expert adaptation by Joseph Hayes of his own novel about three escaped desperadoes who gunpoint their way to temporary refuge in the suburban Indianapolis home of a respectable middle-class family. This is Humphrey Bogart at his best, a tough gunman capable of murder, snarling delight with the way his captives must abide by his orders, and wise in the ways of self-preservation. Fredric March is powerful as head of the family, never before cited for bravery but now bent on protecting his family from the three intruders.

DESPERATE HOURS
1990, 105 mins, US Ⓥ ⊙
D: Michael Cimino **A:** Mickey Rourke, Anthony Hopkins, Mimi Rogers, Lindsay Crouse, Kelly Lynch, Elias Koteas (De Laurentiis)

Desperate Hours is a coldly mechanical and uninvolving remake of the 1955 Bogart pic *The Desperate Hours,* with Mickey Rourke as the hood terrorizing a suburban family. Despite being minimally updated with intensified blood and brutality on the part of the hoods and the authorities, *Desperate Hours* has no new insights to offer. The clunky script doesn't permit any vestige of humanity to Rourke, who's portrayed as a simple psycho with a low flash point. Anthony Hopkins, in the Fredric March role of the initially weak-seeming father, seems mismatched with his estranged wife, Mimi Rogers, and implausibly reckless in his defiance of Rourke.

DESPERATELY SEEKING SUSAN
1985, 104 mins, US Ⓥ ⊙
D: Susan Seidelman **A:** Rosanna Arquette, Madonna, Aidan Quinn, Mark Blum, Robert Joy, Laurie Metcalf (Orion)

Rosanna Arquette does more than her share in the pivotal part of a bored yuppie housewife who follows the personal ads, wondering about the identities behind a desperately-seeking-Susan item that runs from time to time. The ads are the way one boyfriend (Robert Joy) communicates with free-spirited Madonna between her street-life liaisons with other men. This is cause for consistent smiling and a few outright laughs, without ever building to complete comedy.

DESPERATE REMEDIES
1993, 93 mins, New Zealand ⓥ
D: Stewart Main, Peter Wells A: Jennifer Ward-Lealand, Kevin Smith, Lisa Chappell, Cliff Curtis (Wallace)

A mostly enjoyable exercise in high camp (or low kitsch). Set in the mythical colonial seaport of Hope sometime during the 19th century, where Dorothea (Jennifer Ward-Lealand), an elegantly beautiful draper, worries about her young sister, Rose (Kiri Mills), addicted to opium thanks to a liaison with the sinister Fraser (Cliff Curtis). Dorothea hires a handsome, penniless immigrant, Lawrence (Kevin Smith), to seduce Rose away from Fraser. All this is played out against a background of extravagantly stylized sets, magnificently designed costumes, and deafening opera music by Verdi and Berlioz.

DESPERATE TRAIL, THE
1994, 93 mins, US ⓥ
D: P. J. Pesce A: Sam Elliott, Craig Sheffer, Linda Fiorentino, Frank Whaley (Motion Picture Corp/Turner)

The shadows of spaghetti-western maestros Sergio Leone and Sam Peckinpah loom large over the imagery of The Desperate Trail, a new oater with a strong heroine played by Linda Fiorentino. Tale's quality and its characters never match helmer P. J. Pesce's technical savvy, speedy pacing, and thrilling shoot-outs. Fiorentino is felicitously cast as Sarah, a tough, foulmouthed woman who is being escorted by Marshall Speakes (Sam Elliott) to the nearest town, where he plans to hang her for killing a young man who was sexually abusive. It's a mouse-and-cat chase in which the roles of captor and captive are often reversed.

DESTINATION GOBI
1953, 89 mins, US ⓥ
D: Robert Wise A: Richard Widmark, Don Taylor, Casey Adams, Murvyn Vye, Darryl Hickman (20th Century-Fox)

Story of a small US Navy detachment sent to observe weather conditions in the Mongolian desert during World War II is a well-turned-out job. Screenplay has elements of excitement and choice bits of sharp humor as it focuses on the ordeals and dangers experienced by the group of sailors incongruously trying to win friends among a band of Mongols and fight off Japs in Central Asia.

DESTINATION TOKYO
1943, 133 mins, US ⓥ
D: Delmer Daves A: Cary Grant, John Garfield, Alan Hale, Dane Clark, John Ridgely, Warner Anderson (Warner)

Destination Tokyo tells of a single mission undertaken by a sub. Its destination is Tokyo. Cary Grant has never been better as the sub's skipper, underplaying the role and so setting the pace for the entire pic. Unspooling is crammed with enough excitement for possibly a couple of pictures.

DESTINY OF A MAN
See: Sudba Chelovyeka

DESTRY
1954, 95 mins, US ▭
D: George Marshall A: Audie Murphy, Mari Blanchard, Lyle Bettger, Thomas Mitchell, Edgar Buchanan, Lori Nelson (Universal)

Max Brand's soft-spoken, gunless lawman was played by Tom Mix in 1932, and by James Stewart in 1939. This time Audie Murphy tackles the role, and probably better fits the original Brand conception than his predecessors. Murphy does exceptionally well as the quiet hero who is called in to aid Thomas Mitchell, town drunk appointed sheriff in a sardonic joke, and restore law and order to the western town ruled with ruthless hand by Lyle Bettger and Edgar Buchanan.

DESTRY RIDES AGAIN
1939, 90 mins, US ⓥ ⊙
D: George Marshall A: Marlene Dietrich, James Stewart, Charles Winninger, Mischa Auer, Brian Donlevy (Universal/Realart)

Plain, good entertainment primed with action and laughs and human sentiment. This gangster fable with an early-west background revolves for the most part around the rowdy, gaudy gin mill and dance hall which Brian Donlevy operates in the frontier town of Bottle Neck. With the aid of his No. 1 entertainer (Dietrich), Donlevy cuts a wide swath cheating the townsmen at cards and working a waterhole racket until he makes the mistake of appointing the town rum pot (Charles Winniger) the local sheriff.

DETECTIVE, THE
1968, 114 mins, US Ⓥ ▭
D: Gordon Douglas **A:** Frank Sinatra, Lee Remick, Ralph Meeker, Jacqueline Bisset, Jack Klugman, Horace McMahon (20th Century-Fox)

Although extremely well cast, and fleshed out with some on-target dialogue, Abby Mann's script is strictly potboiler material. Homosexuality, police brutality, corruption in high places, and nymphomania are the peas in this literary shell game, which the admirable professional razzle-dazzle of direction, acting, and to an extent, editing, cannot sufficiently legitimize. Jack Klugman and Frank Sinatra are the only honest cops portrayed. Repeated plot digression made bearable by the fact that it involves Lee Remick explores Sinatra's unstable married life.

DETECTIVE
1985, 98 mins, France Ⓥ
D: Jean-Luc Godard **A:** Claude Brasseur, Nathalie Baye, Johnny Hallyday, Laurent Terzieff, Jean-Pierre Leaud, Alain Cuny (Sara/JLG)

Detective is a quintessential Godard pic that's more *Grand Hotel* than film noir. The plot, as much as it matters, involves four groups of people, or families whose paths intersect in the lobbies, dining rooms, and bedrooms of the Hotel Concorde in Paris. The pic is chock-full of asides, jokes, and anecdotes. Technically one of his best films, *Detective* also boasts one of his strongest casts, with everyone excellent, especially singer Hallyday as the boxing impresario.

DETECTIVE STORY
1951, 105 mins, US Ⓥ
D: William Wyler **A:** Kirk Douglas, Eleanor Parker, William Bendix, Lee Grant, Cathy O'Donnell, Joseph Wiseman (Paramount)

William Wyler has polished the legit hit by Sidney Kingsley into a cinematic gem. Even the location seldom changes from Kingsley's single set, the realistic headquarters room of the detective squad. Kirk Douglas is the tortured detective determined unswervingly to do his duty as he sees it. Hunting an illicit doctor who has been delivering illegitimate children, Douglas suddenly finds himself being vir-

tually blackmailed by the medico. Douglas's wife, long before she married him, had occasion to use the charlatan's services. The personal drama is played against a broad and entertaining mosaic of other drama, humor, and young love in the busy squad room.
1951: Nominations: Best Director, Actress (Eleanor Parker), Supp. Actress (Lee Grant), Screenplay

DETOUR
1945, 67 mins, US Ⓥ ⊙
D: Edgar G. Ulmer **A:** Tom Neal, Ann Savage, Claudia Drake, Edmund MacDonald, Tim Ryan, Esther Howard (PRC)

Detour falls short of being a sleeper because of a flat ending and its low-budgeted production mountings. Uniformly good performances and some equally good direction and dialogue keep the meller moving, however. Theme is the buffeting that man gets from the fates. Story revolves around Tom Neal as a down-and-out young pianist. Director Edgar G. Ulmer achieves some steadily mounting suspense as the pianist becomes implicated in two murders, neither of which he's committed. So he begins hitchhiking his way back east. Story is told in flashback.

DETOUR
1993, 89 mins, US Ⓥ ⊙
D: Wade Williams **A:** Tom Neal Jr., Lea Lavish, Erin McGrane, Duke Howze, Susanna Foster (Williams)

Fans of Edgar G. Ulmer's noir classic, *Detour,* are in for a disappointment: Wade Williams's low-budget remake features both laughable dialogue and inept acting. The attempt to create a period look is only intermittently successful. Like the 1945 film, the remake centers on the incredibly bad fortune of Al Roberts (Tom Neal Jr., whose father played the same part in the first *Detour*).

DEUX ANGLAISES ET LE CONTINENT
(TWO ENGLISH GIRLS; ANNE AND MURIEL)
1971, 130 mins, France Ⓥ ⊙
D: Francois Truffaut **A:** Jean-Pierre Leaud, Kika Markham, Stacey Tendeter, Sylvia Marriott, Philippe Leotard, Marie Mansart (Films du Carrosse/Cinetel)

Film is a return to the only other book by Henri Pierre Roche, author of the book Truffaut filmed as *Jules and Jim,* and reverses the triangle to have two English sisters and a young Frenchmen instead of the two thirtyish friends and an early 20th-century femme libber in *Jules*. It has Truffaut's usual charm and ease but he does not quite imbue it with the poetic flair, élan, and life force his previous pic had. Léaud does not have the elegance for his role of the dilettantish, mother-smothered young man. Markham has grace and charm as the freer sister and Tendeter the redheaded, freckled robustness of the more religious, repressed girl.

LE DEUXIEME SOUFFLE
1966, 150 mins, France

D: Jean-Pierre Melville **A:** Lino Ventura, Paul Meurisse, Raymond Pellegrin, Daniele Fabrega, Pierre Zimmer, Michel Constantin (Montaigne)

Director Jean-Pierre Melville has built a solid gangster opus influenced by some earlier American types but successfully transferred to the local milieu. It deals with a gangster who finds that there is no longer honor among thieves—or policemen, for that matter. Lino Ventura has the right weight and honesty, albeit in a criminal way, and Paul Meurisse is a smooth, competent, and ironically tongued policeman prone to use torture to extract confessions.

DEVIL AND DANIEL WEBSTER, THE
(UK: ALL THAT MONEY CAN BUY; DANIEL AND THE DEVIL)
1941, 100 mins, US Ⓥ ⊙

D: William Dieterle **A:** Edward Arnold, Walter Huston, Jane Darwell, Simone Simon, Anne Shirley, John Qualen (RKO)

The locale is New Hampshire, in 1840. The legend is about the rise, fall, and regeneration of a young farmer, Jabez Stone, who is alleged to have sold his soul to the devil for a pittance of gold and seven years of good luck. Trouble starts when Walter Huston appears on the scene via double exposure and whispers beguiling temptations into the ear of the young husband-farmer.

1941: Best Scoring of a Dramatic Picture **Nomination:** Best Actor (Walter Huston)

DEVIL AND MISS JONES, THE
1941, 92 mins, US Ⓥ

D: Sam Wood **A:** Jean Arthur, Charles Coburn, Robert Cummings, Edmund Gwenn, S. Z. Sakall, Spring Byington (RKO)

A light and fluffy tale of the richest man in the world, who loses his stern front through association with the employees of one of his enterprises—a department store. Jean Arthur is the Miss Jones of the title, a decidedly personable salesgirl who takes the elderly shoe clerk under her wing to guide him through the intricacies of store routine. Charles Coburn is the richest man who steps into the store job incognito to ferret out the leaders of a union organization. Sam Wood injects deft direction with human byplay to lift the script considerably.

1941: Nominations: Best Supp. Actor (Charles Coburn), Original Screenplay

DEVIL AT 4 O'CLOCK, THE
1961, 125 mins, US Ⓥ ⊙

D: Mervyn LeRoy **A:** Spencer Tracy, Frank Sinatra, Kerwin Mathews, Jean-Pierre Aumont, Gregoire Aslan, Barbara Luna (Columbia)

A small volcanic South Seas isle makes a colorful setting for this tale of heroism and sacrifice, but vying with interest in characterizations are the exceptional special effects of an island being blown to pieces. Story is of a priest (Spencer Tracy) who with three convicts (Frank Sinatra, Gregoire Aslan, Bernie Hamilton) saves the lives of the children in a mountaintop leper hospital by leading them through fire and lava flow to the coast and a waiting schooner after the volcano erupts and island is doomed to certain destruction. Tracy delivers one of his more colorful portrayals in his hard-drinking cleric who has lost faith in his God.

DEVIL DOLL, THE
1936, 70 mins, US Ⓥ

D: Tod Browning **A:** Lionel Barrmore, Maureen O'Sullivan, Frank Lawton, Robert Greig, Lucy Beaumont, Henry B. Walthall (M-G-M)

The premise is a scientist's discovery of a process by which all living things, including humans, can be reduced to one sixth their normal size. The director, cameraman, and art department make the most of it, but the writers' contribution is lacking in originality. Lionel Barrymore, as a framed convict named Lavond and later in the disguise of old Madam Mandelip, is a scientific Count of Monte Cristo who avenges his false imprisonment. His companion in a prison escape is the inventor of the atom-shrinking process. The inventor dies on the first night of freedom and

Barrymore carries on the great work with the man's crazy widow.

DEVIL DOLL
1964, 80 mins, UK Ⓥ
D: Lindsay Shontoff **A:** Bryant Halliday, William Sylvester, Yvonne Romain, Karel Stepanek (Gala)

This slow-paced pic never lives up to its title in the way of shocks, thrills, scares, sex, or other dividends for meller regulars. Filmed in England, its gimmick—a ventriloquist's dummy's revenge on his manipulator—has been done before and better.

DEVIL IN A BLUE DRESS
1995, 102 mins, US Ⓥ ⊙
D: Carl Franklin **A:** Denzel Washington, Tom Sizemore, Jennifer Beals, Don Cheadle, Maury Chaykin, Terry Kinney (Clinica/Mundy Lane/Tri-Star)

An engrossingly atmospheric dip into the dark waters of postwar urban intrigue, *Devil in a Blue Dress* ushers in the welcome subgenre of black noir. First screen adaptation of a Walter Mosley mystery novel featuring private detective Easy Rawlins, this navigates a complicated story of blackmail, race, and politics in confident fashion. Pic has a flavor all its own, thanks variously to its sharply observed cast of characters, astutely recreated setting, adherence to novelistic details, and solid p.o.v. Washington's performance is alert and subtle.

DEVIL IN MISS JONES, THE
1973, 74 mins, US
D: Gerard Damiano **A:** Georgina Spevlin, John Clemens, Harry Reams, Albert Gork [Gerard Damiano], Rick Livermore, Sue Flaken (Marvin/Damiano)

With *The Devil in Miss Jones,* the hardcore porno feature approaches an art form. For its genre, the pic is a sensation, marked by a technical polish that pales some Hollywood product and containing some of the most frenzied and erotic sex sequences in porno memory. A thirtyish virgin, Justine Jones (Georgina Spevlin), commits suicide and is condemned to eternal damnation. Her suicide has been the only damnable act in a lonely, despairing life, and to make herself worthy of the punishment meted out to her, Jones requests a little more time in which to experiment with and to be consumed by lust.

DEVIL IS A SISSY, THE
1936, 131 mins, US
D: W. S. Van Dyke **A:** Freddie Bartholomew, Jackie Cooper, Mickey Rooney, Ian Hunter (M-G-M)

Saga of the sidewalks of New York. The almost tragic bravery of "limey" Freddie Bartholomew to make his roughneck pals, Buck (Jackie Cooper) and Gig (Mickey Rooney), accept him into the fold as a full-fledged little denizen of the Mulberry Street sector—overlooking his polished Oxfordian diction and his French and English schooling—is perhaps, one senses, almost autobiographical in its grim determination.

DEVIL IS A WOMAN, THE
1935, 76 mins, US
D: Josef von Sternberg **A:** Marlene Dietrich, Cesar Romero, Lionel Atwill, Edward Everett Horton, Alison Skipworth (Paramount)

Josef von Sternberg both directed and photographed *The Devil Is a Woman,* working with a Pierre Louys classic, *The Woman and the Puppet,* which gives the reader a cross section of a ruthless courtesan and not much else. While *Devil* is a somewhat monotonous picture, Sternberg has given it clever photography and background. Marlene Dietrich has done the rest in playing the Louys trollop, turning in a fine performance. Story is told in a background of southern Spain during a fiesta, this permitting Sternberg some big mob scenes and color, plus music.

DEVIL MAKES THREE, THE
1952, 89 mins, US
D: Andrew Marton **A:** Gene Kelly, Pier Angeli, Richard Rober, Richard Egan, Claus Clausen, Wilfried Seyferth (M-G-M)

Postwar Germany provides the background for an interesting chase thriller. Story deals with an underground movement to revive the Nazi party and how Counterintelligence, with the aid of Gene Kelly's air-force captain, and Pier Angeli's German B-girl, puts down the aspirations of one would-be führer.

DEVIL NEVER SLEEPS, THE
See: Satan Never Sleeps

DEVIL RIDES OUT, THE
(US: THE DEVIL'S BRIDE)
1968, 95 mins, UK
D: Terence Fisher **A:** Christopher Lee, Charles Gray, Nike Arrighi, Leon Greene,

Patrick Mower, Sarah Lawson (Hammer)

Director Terence Fisher has a ball with this slice of black magic, based on the Dennis Wheatley novel. Christopher Lee is for once on the side of the goodies. As the Duc de Richleau, he and his buddy (Leon Greene) are intent on saving the soul of a young man (Patrick Mower) caught up in black magic and at the mercy of Charles Gray, chief apostle of the evil. Lee plays with his usual authority and Gray turns out another of his bland, cold essays in villainy. The weakness lies in the fact that these two rarely confront each other.

DEVILS, THE
1971, 109 mins, UK Ⓥ ▭
D: Ken Russell A: Vanessa Redgrave, Oliver Reed, Dudley Sutton, Max Adrian, Gemma Jones, Murray Melvin (Warner/Russo)

Ken Russell has taken some historical liberties in fashioning the story of Father Grandier (Oliver Reed), sensually liberated priest in 17th-century France whose virile presence and backstairs reputation cued the erotic fantasies of a humpbacked nun, Sister Jeanne (Vanessa Redgrave). When this sister's lustful ravings begin to infect other nuns in her convent, the Church brings in an exorcist (Michael Gothard) to stage circuslike public purges of the naked, foulmouthed nuns, which result in Grandie's conviction on heresy charges, his torture, and burning at the stake. Russell has spared nothing in hyping the historic events by stressing the grisly at the expense of dramatic unity.

DEVIL'S ADVOCATE, THE
1997, 144 mins, US Ⓥ ⊙ ▭
D: Taylor Hackford A: Keanu Reeves, Al Pacino, Charlize Theron, Jeffrey Jones, Judith Ivey, Connie Nielsen (Kopelson/Warner)

The Devil's Advocate is a fairly entertaining supernatural potboiler that finally bubbles over with a nearly operatic sense of absurdity and excess. Kevin Lomax (Keanu Reeves) is a dashing young attorney lured by flattery and a fat paycheck to New York City and is impressed by the extravagant offices of the law firm and, most of all, by the big boss, John Milton (Al Pacino). Before long, he believes the only wrong would lie in losing. He is assigned to one of the firm's biggest clients, a real estate tycoon (Craig T. Nelson) probably guilty of murdering his wife and

two others. Although it is not stated until deep into the picture, the trailer makes no secret that Pacino plays the devil, accentuating all this with occasional wild looks, an insinuating cackle and flicks of his tongue.

DEVIL'S BRIDE, THE
See: The Devil Rides Out

DEVIL'S BRIGADE, THE
1968, 131 mins, US Ⓥ ▭
D: Andrew V. McLaglen A: William Holden, Cliff Robertson, Vince Edwards, Andrew Prine, Claude Akins, Richard Jaeckel (United Artists)

The fusion of some US Army roughnecks and crack Canadian troops into a World War II special-forces unit certainly contained the ingredients for a strong film. But distended and stock scripting, sluggish direction, and limp pacing make an uneven combination of the worst of The Dirty Dozen and the best of What Price Glory.

DEVIL'S DISCIPLE, THE
1959, 82 mins, US/UK
D: Guy Hamilton A: Burt Lancaster, Kirk Douglas, Laurence Olivier, Janette Scott, Eva LeGallienne, Harry Andrews (Bryna/United Artists)

The Devil's Disciple by George Bernard Shaw is better than this film version would indicate to those unfamiliar with the stage original. The final third of the picture is superb Shawmanship, but the major portion preceding it is fumbling and unsatisfactory. That all is not lost may be credited almost entirely to Laurence Olivier. His character is a witty, mocking figure and mouthpiece for Shaw's wicked shafts at convention and history, in this case the American Revolution.

DEVIL'S DOORWAY
1950, 84 mins, US
D: Anthony Mann A: Robert Taylor, Louis Calhern, Paula Raymond, Marshall Thompson, Edgar Buchanan (M-G-M)

Robert Taylor is the redskin hero just after the Civil War when settlers started moving west to take over Indian lands. The whites are made the heavies and the dirty work is keynoted in Louis Calhern's character as a prejudiced, crooked attorney. Anthony Mann's direction keeps the footage moving. Actionwise, he hits some high spots, particularly Taylor's saloon fight with a gunslinger and in the mass finale clash between whites and redskins.

DEVIL'S ENVOYS, THE
See: Les Visiteurs du Soir

DEVIL'S ISLAND
1939, 62 mins, US
D: William Clemens **A:** Boris Karloff, Nedda Harrigan, James Stephenson, Adia Kuznetzoff, Rolla Gourvitch, Robert Warwick (Warner)

Just another meller of the dreaded isle down in the Caribbean. It traces the experiences of a French doctor, convicted of treason, who after arriving at Devil's Island is called upon to perform a brain operation on the commandant's daughter. The father of the girl fails to keep his promises to release him. Boris Karloff plays the lead convincingly, making himself as pathetic a character as possible.

DEVIL'S OWN, THE
1997, 110 mins, US Ⓥ ⊙ ▭
D: Alan J. Pakula **A:** Harrison Ford, Brad Pitt, Margaret Colin, Ruben Blades, Treat Williams, Natascha McElhone (Columbia)

The Devil's Own is much more interested in the moral stature and culpability of the main characters than in heavy action and thrills. By the climax, with its *Key Largo*-esque shootout on board a small boat, the film draws perilously close to conventional movie melodrama, but for the most part it concentrates on the personalities of the two men who initially bond but must ultimately face each other down in a life-and-death duel. Frankie McGuire (Brad Pitt) has become the Brits' Public Enemy No. 1, having taken out 13 soldiers and 11 cops in Ulster. He escapes to New York, where he is discreetly placed in the family home of a veteran Irish cop, Tom O'Meara (Harrison Ford). Director Alan J. Pakula has managed to maintain an admirable concentration on the central moral equation.

DEVIL'S PLAYGROUND, THE
1976, 107 mins, Australia Ⓥ
D: Fred Schepisi **A:** Arthur Dignam, Nick Tate, Simon Burke, Charles McCallum, John Frawley (Film House)

The Devil's Playground is a Roman Catholic boys boarding school where the pupils are seen at their everyday work, play, and worship. Stressed are the problems of puberty in such a community, and the evils of succumbing to self-abuse; one boy for instance is chastised for taking off his bathers while under a shower. Film,

almost like a documentary at times, has obviously been made with great sincerity.

DEVIL WITHIN HER, THE
See: I Don't Want to Be Born

DEVOTION
1946, 108 mins, US
D: Curtis Bernhardt **A:** Ida Lupino, Paul Henreid, Olivia de Havilland, Sydney Greenstreet, Arthur Kennedy, Nancy Coleman (Warner)

Plot depicts the Brontes in the village of Haworth, Yorkshire, opening in the period just before they found fame as authors. Lupino and de Havilland are expert as the two older sisters, while Nancy Coleman as the younger Anne Bronte has her moments. Greenstreet is good as Thackeray, a role that is almost a bit. Arthur Kennedy's performance as the drunken poet-painter brother of the sisters is a standout.

DIABOLIQUE
See: Les Diaboliques

DIABOLIQUE
1996, 107 mins, US Ⓥ ⊙
D: Jeremiah Chechik **A:** Sharon Stone, Isabelle Adjani, Chazz Palminteri, Kathy Bates, Spalding Gray, Shirley Knight (Morgan Creek/Warner)

A thoroughly misguided redressing of the classic 1955 French thriller. Surprisingly dull and suspenseless, given the inherent intrigue of the story, new outing coarsens every aspect of this tale of a cruel schoolmaster's wife and mistress whose conspiracy to murder him triggers an unexpected aftermath. The one element that is underplayed is a suggested sexual relationship between the two women. This is indicated several times through touches and gestures, but the emotional dynamics are too vague.

LES DIABOLIQUES
(DIABOLIQUE)
1955, 110 mins, France Ⓥ ⊙
D: Henri-Georges Clouzot **A:** Simone Signoret, Vera Clouzot, Paul Meurisse, Charles Vanel, Pierre Larquey, Michel Serrault (Filmsonor)

Although it has a few hallucinating bits of terror, the film is primarily a creaky-door type of melodrama. Its macabre aspects and lack of sympathy for the characters make this a hybrid which flounders between a blasting look at human infamy and an out-and-out contrived whodunit. A brutal headmaster of a private boy's school tyrannizes his frail, sickly wife, and has a mistress, a teacher at the school, with whom he has just broken off. The women band together and plot to kill him.

LA DIAGONALE DU FOU (DANGEROUS MOVES)
1985, 100 mins, Switzerland ⓥ
D: Richard Dembo A: Michel Piccoli, Alexandre Arbatt, Leslie Caron, Liv Ullmann, Daniel Olbrychski, Michel Aumont (Cohn)

An absorbing, if not inspired, suspense drama with a great subject, that of a championship chess showdown between a Soviet titleholder and an exiled dissident challenger. Recalling the famous Karpov-Korchnoi match of some years earlier, script by first-time director Richard Dembo has the aging Russian grand old man of chess (Michel Piccoli) travel to Geneva for a long-anticipated confrontation with a 30-year-old whippersnapper (Alexandre Arbatt), who left his homeland five years before. Dembo brings in just enough specifics of chess strategy to grab viewer interest in the contest.
1984: Best Foreign Language Film

DIAL M FOR MURDER
1954, 105 mins, US ⓥ ⊙
D: Alfred Hitchcock A: Ray Milland, Grace Kelly, Robert Cummings, John Williams, Anthony Dawson (Warner)

Dial M remains more of a filmed play than a motion picture, unfortunately revealed as a conversation piece about murder which talks up much more suspense than it actually delivers. Costarring with Ray Milland are Grace Kelly, his wife and the intended murder victim, and Robert Cummings, her lover. Milland plots his wife's death, figuring on using Anthony Dawson for the actual killing while he has an alibi established elsewhere.

DIAMOND HEAD
1962, 107 mins, US ⓥ ⊙ ▭
D: Guy Green A: Charlton Heston, Yvette Mimieux, George Chakiris, France Nuyen, James Darren (Columbia/Bresler)

Improbabilities and inconsistencies galore reside in heavy-handed screenplay about a Hawaiian agricultural tycoon hellbent on holding-that-bloodline. When the baron's (Charlton Heston) baby sister (Yvette Mimieux) defiantly announces her engagement to a full-blooded Hawaiian lad (James Darren), the battle lines are drawn. Heston etches a swaggering portrait of the bullying bigot. Mimieux is spirited as the liberal-minded sister. Darren, despite a rich tan, seems about as 100 percent Hawaiian as Paul Revere.

DIAMOND HORSESHOE
1945, 104 mins, US
D: George Seaton A: Betty Grable, Dick Haymes, Phil Silvers, William Gaxton, Margaret Dumont (20th Century-Fox)

Plot builds a solid heart story in a manner which is enough of a switch on the backstage formula to make it different. Betty Grable and Dick Haymes are costarred and this puts the crooner over solidly as a film juvenile. William Gaxton plays Haymes's father, the lead at the Horseshoe, forever squabbling with Grable, the No. 1 cheesecake. Haymes gives up medicine for a stage career, and while Grable starts out under a cloud, she emerges the noble influence to get him back to his MD studies.

DIAMONDS
1975, 106 mins, US/Israel ⓥ
D: Menahem Golan A: Robert Shaw, Richard Roundtree, Barbara Hershey, Shelley Winters (Avco Embassy/Golan-Globus)

The thin screenplay has Robert Shaw playing a jaded London aristocrat who turns diamond thief because of rivalry with his brother (also Shaw), a security expert who constructed the intricate vault in Israel where the rocks are stashed. Along on the heist are Richard Roundtree and Barbara Hershey, but no one in the cast gets much chance to develop a characterization.

DIAMONDS ARE FOREVER
1971, 119 mins, UK ⓥ ⊙ ▭
D: Guy Hamilton A: Sean Connery, Jill St. John, Charles Gray, Lana Wood, Jimmy Dean, Bruce Cabot (United Artists)

James Bond still packs a lethal wallop in all his cavortings, still manages to surround himself with scantily clad sexpots. Yet *Diamonds Are Forever* doesn't carry the same quality or flair as its many predecessors. Sean Connery is back in the role as in five previous Bond entries, and he still has his own way both with broads and deeds. One of the funniest sequences in memory focuses on Bond trying to elude the police in downtown Vegas. Up-to-the-minute-scientific-gadget use is made again when Bond steals a moon machine at a

simulated lunar testing ground in a wild drive across the Nevada desert dunes.
1971: Nomination: Best Sound

DIAMONDS FOR BREAKFAST
1968, 102 mins, UK
D: Christopher Morahan **A:** Marcello Mastroianni, Rita Tushingham, Elaine Taylor, Maggie Blye, Warren Mitchell (Paramount)

Potentially amusing, light-comedy crime idea is marred by uncertain steering by director Christopher Morahan and clashing styles of the three scripters. Comedy is never fully developed and Marcello Mastroianni, debuting in British pix, lacks his usual elegant confidence. Mastroianni is a London boutique owner who, happening to be fourth in succession to the Throne of All the Russias, hits on the idea of lifting the imperial jewels, which he figures belong to him, anyway.

DIAMOND SKULLS
(US: DARK OBSESSION)
1990, 87 mins, UK ⓥ
D: Nick Broomfield **A:** Gabriel Byrne, Amanda Donohoe, Michael Hordern, Judy Parfitt, Douglas Hodge, Sadie Frost (Film Four/British Screen)

A stylish melodrama about sex and violence among the British aristocracy, *Diamond Skulls* never quite delivers the punches it promises. Gabriel Byrne is Sir Hugo, an ex-guards officer. He has a lovely wife (the delectable Amanda Donohoe) of whom he's extremely jealous. Donohoe gives another hot performance as the elegant Virginia, whose name belies her actions. Veteran Michael Hordern is amusing as Hugo's titled father.

DIANE
1955, 110 mins, US ⓥ ▱
D: David Miller **A:** Lana Turner, Pedro Armendariz, Roger Moore, Marisa Pavan, Cedric Hardwicke, Taina Elg (M-G-M)

Metro digs back into 16th-century France for this yarn about the countess Diane de Breze, who became the most powerful woman at the court of King Henry II. Splendidly caparisoned production-wise, the first half is such old-fashioned costume drama as to draw laughs at unintended places, but picks up in interest during the later phases. Lana Turner is sympathetic in her role, and Roger Moore delivers a good account of himself as Henry, uncertain first as the callow youth

and gaining in stature after he becomes king.

DIARY OF A CHAMBERMAID
1946, 86 mins, US ⓥ
D: Jean Renoir **A:** Paulette Goddard, Burgess Meredith, Hurd Hatfield, Francis Lederer, Judith Anderson (United Artists)

Diary in its American form has not nearly the intrigue, or the color, suggested by the original French version, but it has names and an interest all its own. It is the yarn of a chambermaid who, tiring of her station in life, vows to achieve wealth whoever the man. There is Paulette Goddard, as the chambermaid with a gold glint to her orbs; Burgess Meredith, a psychopathic, aging army captain; Hurd Hatfield, the sensitive consumptive whom the girl loves; and Francis Lederer, the glowering valet-murderer.

DIARY OF A CHAMBERMAID
See: Le Journal d'Une Femme de Chambre

DIARY OF A COUNTRY PRIEST
See: Le Journal d'un Cure de Campagne

DIARY OF A HITMAN
1992, 91 mins, US ⓥ ⊙
D: Roy London **A:** Forest Whitaker, Sherilyn Fenn, Sharon Stone, Seymour Cassel, James Belushi, Lois Chiles (Continental/Vision)

Modest $2.5 million *Diary of a Hitman* transcends an unlikely scenario to offer moments of cinema well worth savoring. Hired to knock off the wife and child of a born-again commodities broker who claims his wife's a drug addict and the infant is a crack baby and not his, the reluctant killer (Forest Whitaker) breaks professional-conduct rules by conversing with the victim (Sherilyn Fenn) and discovers the broker lied. Fenn is a revelation in the substance and texture she brings to the role. Whitaker invests his beleaguered hit man with mesmerizing depth.

DIARY OF A MAD HOUSEWIFE
1970, 85 mins, US ⓥ
D: Frank Perry **A:** Richard Benjamin, Frank Langella, Carrie Snodgress, Lorraine Cullen (Universal)

An engrossing story of the disintegration of a modern loveless marriage, with Richard Benjamin and Frank Langella effectively portraying the inadequacies of husband and lover, respectively, and Carrie Snodgress as a frustrated, sensitive wife.

1970: Nomination: Best Actress (Carrie Snodgress)

DIARY OF ANNE FRANK, THE
1959, 170 mins, US ⓥ ⊙ ✉
D: George Stevens **A:** Millie Perkins, Joseph Schildkraut, Shelley Winters, Richard Beymer, Lou Jacobi, Diane Baker (20th Century-Fox)

A film of often extraordinary quality. It manages, within the framework of a tense and tragic situation, to convey the beauty of a young and inquiring spirit that soars beyond the cramped confinement of the Frank family's hideout in Nazi-occupied Amsterdam. And yet, with all its technical perfection, the inspired direction, and the sensitivity with which many of the scenes are handled, *Diary* is simply too long. There are moments when the film lags and the dialogue becomes forced. Unlike the play, the picture leaves too little to the imagination. Millie Perkins plays Anne. It is her first film role and she turns in a charming and captivating performance. It's certainly difficult to accept her as a 13-year-old, which was Anne's age at the time the Franks went into hiding.
1959: Best Supp. Actress (Shelley Winters), B&W Cinematography, B&W Art Direction
Nominations: Best Picture, Director, Supp. Actor (Ed Wynn), B&W Costume Design, Scoring of a Dramatic Picture

DICK
1999, 95 mins, US ⓥ ⊙
D: Andrew Fleming **A:** Kirsten Dunst, Michelle Williams, Jim Breuer, Will Ferrell, Dave Foley, Teri Garr (Pacific Western/Phoenix/Columbia)

Director and cowriter Andrew Fleming gleefully throws two teenybopper girls into the vortex of the Watergate scandal and extends the possibilities to outrageous extremes. Ditsy teens Betsy (Kirsten Dunst) and Arlene (Michelle Williams), while sneaking through the garage of the latter's apartment in Washington's Watergate complex one night in 1972, happen upon a certain G. Gordon Liddy (Harry Shearer) and some others up to no good. Liddy has the girls pulled in for interrogation. They meet Nixon himself (Dan Hedaya), who gives them the jobs of official White House dog walkers. If the film is devastating toward the White House crew, it is even more scathing toward Woodward and Bernstein, and this gives the picture a real charge.

DICK TRACY
1945, 61 mins, US ⓥ ⊙
D: William Berke **A:** Morgan Conway, Anne Jeffreys, Mike Mazurki, Jane Greer, Mickey Kuhn (RKO)

Chester Gould's comic strip lends itself handily to screen melodrama. Morgan Conway takes on the title role. Plot has Tracy chasing down a crazy killer tagged Splitface, so called because of a hideous scar running diagonally across his face. Mike Mazurki, as Splitface, is seeking revenge on those who sent him to prison years before, and manages to do in three victims before Tracy calls a halt.

DICK TRACY
1990, 103 mins, US ⓥ ⊙
D: Warren Beatty **A:** Warren Beatty, Charlie Korsmo, Glenne Headly, Madonna, Al Pacino, Dustin Hoffman (Touchstone)

Though it looks ravishing, Warren Beatty's longtime pet project is a curiously remote, uninvolving film. Beatty is so cool he appears frozen. Torn between Madonna's allure and the more low-key beauty and sweetness of Glenne Headly's redhead Tess Trueheart, Beatty simply sits there and mopes, occasionally rousing himself into bursts of action. A large part of what fun there is in the pic comes from the inventive character makeup by John Caglione Jr. and Doug Drexler. Al Pacino virtually runs away with the show as Tracy's nemesis, the Richard III-like hunchbacked villain Big Boy Caprice. His manic energy lifts the overall torpor.
1990: Best Art Direction, Song (''Sooner or Later''), Makeup
Nominations: Best Supp. Actor (Al Pacino), Cinematography, Costume Design, Sound

DICK TRACY'S DILEMMA
1947, 60 mins, US ⓥ ⊙
D: John Rawlins **A:** Ralph Byrd, Lyle Latell, Kay Christopher, Jack Lambert, Ian Keith, Jimmy Conlin (RKO)

This entry in RKO's Dick Tracy series draws on gruesome character of The Claw as menacing opponent of the pen-and-ink detective. Ralph Byrd is an okay Tracy. Jack Lambert gives expert study to his role as The Claw. Jimmy Conlin does an excellent character role as Sightless, pencil peddler who aids Tracy.

DICK TRACY VS. CUEBALL
1946, 62 mins, US Ⓥ ⊙
D: Gordon Douglas **A:** Morgan Conway, Anne Jeffreys, Dick Wessel (RKO)

Hot action celluloid that's bang-up and bang-bang from start to finish. Scripting is tightly welded, while top-notch direction keeps the accelerator pedal pressed to the floor throughout. Story revolves around Dick Tracy's efforts to sniff out a nest of jewel thieves. Cueball, a brutal-looking hombre who's been double-crossed by the gang, knocks off most of them himself, with Tracy left only with the job of finishing Cueball. Portrayal of Tracy by Morgan Conway is straightforward thesping. Dick Wessell makes an ominous strangler as Cueball.

DICTATOR, THE
1935, 86 mins, UK
D: Victor Saville, Alfred Santell **A:** Clive Brook, Madeleine Carroll, Emlyn Williams, Alfred Drayton, Nicholas Hannen, Helen Hays (Toeplitz)

This is one of the most lavish costume pictures that has come out of England. Clive Brook does an authoriative bit of acting, and imposes lots of femme appeal; Madeleine Carroll is attractive; Emlyn Williams is a splendid young debauchee, and Helen Hays (not the American actress) a tough old queen mother. There is humor, particularly in the earlier scenes. Trouble is with the story. It's a love tale of a beautiful queen and an ambitious young man not developed in such a way as to be really dramatic.

DIE! DIE! MY DARLING!
See: Fanatic

DIE HARD
1988, 131 mins, US Ⓥ ⊙ ▭
D: John McTiernan **A:** Bruce Willis, Alan Rickman, Alexander Godunov, Bonnie Bedelia, Reginald Vel Johnson, William Atherton (Gordon-Silver/20th Century-Fox)

Die Hard is as high tech, rock hard, and souped up as an action film can be, a suspenser pitting a lone-wolf cop against a group of terrorists that has taken over a high-rise office tower. Beefed up considerably for his role, Willis is amiable enough in the opening stretch, but overdoes the grimacing and heavy emoting later on. The cooler and more humorous he is the better. Rickman has a giddy good

time but sometimes goes over the top as the henchman.

1988: Nominations: Best Editing, Sound, Sound Effects Editing, Visual Effects

DIE HARD 2
1990, 124 mins, US Ⓥ ⊙ ▭
D: Renny Harlin **A:** Bruce Willis, Bonnie Bedelia, William Atherton, Franco Nero, William Sadler, Reginald Vel Johnson (Gordon-Silver/20th Century-Fox)

Die Hard 2 lacks the inventivenes of the original but compensates with relentless action. The film works for the most part as sheer entertainment, a full-color comic book with shoot-outs, brutal fistfights, and bloodletting aplenty. John McClane (Bruce Willis) is in DC's Dulles Airport to pick up wife Holly (Bonnie Bedelia) to spend Christmas with her folks. Unlike most domestic flights, the story takes off immediately as terrorists seize control of the airport to free a Manuel Noriegaesque foreign dictator (Franco Nero) being transported to the US.

DIE HARD
WITH A VENGANCE
1995, 128 mins, US Ⓥ ⊙ ▭
D: John McTiernan **A:** Bruce Willis, Jeremy Irons, Samuel L. Jackson, Graham Greene, Colleen Camp (Cinergi/20th Century-Fox)

An overinflated mishmash, this second *Die Hard* sequel is certainly the least accomplished of the three movies, tracing a scattered plotline that's at times virtually indecipherable. Even the premise, with Jeremy Irons as as the terrorist brother of the late Hans Gruber, the character played deliciously in the first film by Alan Rickman, doesn't provide much punch. Movie also benefits only sparingly from its *Lethal Weapon*-like rapport between Bruce Willis and a Harlem shopkeeper (portrayed by the ubiquitous Samuel L. Jackson) unwillingly drawn into the action, as their bickering eventually grows tiresome.

DIFFERENT STORY, A
1978, 106 mins, US Ⓥ
D: Paul Aaron **A:** Perry King, Meg Foster, Valerie Curtin, Peter Donat, Richard Bull (Peterson)

A Different Story certainly is. Stars Perry King and Meg Foster are excellent as a couple whose budding romance has just one problem: they are both gay. First-class production's only but serious flaw is a Henry Olek script that begins with brilliant cleverness but dissolves by fade-out into formula banality.

DIGGSTOWN
(UK: MIDNIGHT STING)
1992, 97 mins, US Ⓥ ⊙
D: Michael Ritchie **A:** James Woods, Louis Gossett Jr., Bruce Dern, Oliver Platt, Heather Graham (M-G-M/Eclectic)

Blending elements of *Rocky* and *The Sting,* this crowd-teaser mixes it up with boxing, revenge, and salty one-liners that should satisfy audiences. James Woods demonstrates his trademark intensity along with a comic flair as a just-paroled hustler who sets up a big-money boxing match pitting his ringer, Honey Roy Palmer (Louis Gossett Jr.), against any 10 men from the burg of Diggstown. Like *The Sting,* the target is truly despicable, and few can fit that description more capably than Bruce Dern, whose character stole the town from its citizens and rubs out anyone who crosses him.

DILLINGER
1973, 107 mins, US Ⓥ ⊙
D: John Milius **A:** Warren Oates, Ben Johnson, Michelle Phillips, Cloris Leachman, Harry Dean Stanton, Richard Dreyfuss (American International)

Oates is a good physical choice for role of the bank robber and killer who blazed his way to notoriety during 13 months of 1933 and 1934. Less known to the public was Melvin Purvis, the FBI man responsible for Dillinger's death in a Chicago alley, but as delineated by Ben Johnson, he is as forceful a figure. Pace is sometimes reduced during events sandwiched in between actual gunfire sequences of Dillinger's career, but there can be no criticism of Milius's ability to keep such action sequences at top heat.

LES DIMANCHES DE VILLE
D'AVRAY
(SUNDAYS AND CYBELE)
1962, 110 mins, France Ⓥ ▭
D: Serge Bourguignon **A:** Hardy Kruger, Nicole Courcel, Patricia Gozzi, Daniel Ivernel, Andre Oumansky

A basically dramatic tale of loneliness and mental difficulty is treated in a muted, dreamy style. This makes a slow but pictorially impressive film due to new director Serge Bourguignon's feeling for imagery and style. But it also leads to some preciosity. Hardy Kruger is good as the man, while Patricia Gozzi sometimes

lacks the spontaneity of childhood. In spite of a tendency to overdo effects, this platonic and spiritual Lolita-like pic marks Bourguignon as a director to be heard from.
1962: Best Foreign Language Film

DIM SUM
A LITTLE BIT OF HEART
1985, 85 mins, US Ⓥ ⊙
D: Wayne Wang **A:** Laureen Chew, Kim Chew, Victor Wong, Ida F. O. Chung, Cora Miao, John Nishio (CIM)

Dim Sum offers up a few charming observations about cultural differences among assorted generations of Chinese Americans, but the dramatic situations are so underplayed as to be mostly ineffectual. Director Wayne Wang and scripter Terrel Seltzer have focused upon the relationship between a traditional Chinese woman in her 60s and her 30-ish daughter, who unlike her brother and sister, is not yet hitched. A great deal of the sought-after humor stems from the "So when are you gonna get married?" attitudes of family friends.

DINER
1982, 110 mins, US Ⓥ ⊙
D: Barry Levinson **A:** Steve Guttenberg, Daniel Stern, Mickey Rourke, Kevin Bacon, Timothy Daly, Ellen Barkin (M-G-M/United Artists)

The year is 1959 and the diner is in Baltimore, although the action could take place in any American city. Using the diner as the proverbial street-corner hangout, Levinson centers on a close-knit group of guys in their early twenties and how their early adult lives are taking shape. In this case there's lots to worry about. Steve Guttenberg, Daniel Stern, Mickey Rourke, Kevin Bacon, Paul Reiser, and Timothy Daly are terrific as the friends, as are Ellen Barkin and Kathryn Dowling as the two females involved with different group members.
1982: Nomination: Best Original Screenplay

DINNER AT EIGHT
1933, 110 mins, US Ⓥ ⊙
D: George Cukor **A:** Marie Dressler, John Barrymore, Wallace Beery, Jean Harlow, Lionel Barrymore, Lee Tracy (M-G-M)

The story grips from beginning to end with never-relaxing tension, its somber moments relieved by lighter touches. Acting honors probably will go to Dressler and Harlow, the latter giving an astonishingly well-balanced treatment of Kitty, the canny little hussy who hooks a hard-bitten and unscrupulous millionaire and then makes him lie down and roll over. John Barrymore's playing of the has-been picture star is a stark, uncompromising treatment of a pretty thoroughgoing blackguard and ingrate. Billie Burke is eminently suited for the role of a fluttering society matron. Wallace Beery is at home as the millionaire vulgarian.

DIP HUT SEUNG HUNG
(THE KILLER)
1989, 110 mins, Hong Kong ⓥ ⊙
D: John Woo A: Chow Yun-fat, Danny Lee, Sally Yeh, Tsang Kong, Chu Kong (Film Workshop/Magnum)

This extremely violent and superbly made actioner demonstrates the tight grasp that director John Woo has on the crime meller genre, and his ability to twist the form into surprisingly satisfying shapes. *The Killer* is a buddy-buddy outing with a vengeance. Male bonding between a maverick hit man (Chow Yun-fat) and a disaffected cop (Danny Lee) is pushed to almost homoerotic extremes. The plot itself is all too familiar. The cold-blooded assassin is double-crossed by underworld bosses after knocking off a drug kingpin. The determined cop, on the outs with his superiors, has to catch his man or else.

DIPLOMATIC COURIER
1952, 98 mins, US ⓥ
D: Henry Hathaway A: Tyrone Power, Patricia Neal, Stephen McNally, Karl Malden (20th Century-Fox)

A top-notch espionage yarn based on Peter Cheyney's novel *Sinister Errand,* the script has Tyrone Power playing a diplomatic courier who is used by the counter-intelligence division to uncover the whereabouts of a missing Soviet timetable for invasion of Yugoslavia. Power is assigned to trace Hildegarde Neff, a Soviet agent, in belief she will have some clue to the mystery. Power is hampered in his work by Patricia Neal, seemingly a slightly nutty American tourist.

DIRIGIBLE
1931, 100 mins, US
D: Frank Capra A: Jack Holt, Ralph Graves, Fay Wray, Hobart Bosworth, Roscoe Karns, Clarence Muse (Columbia)

The big scene is a crack-up of the dirigible in the air; more interesting even than the explosion of the dirigible in *Hell's Angels.* The remainder of *Dirigible* is unconvincing, before or after the crack-up, the latter occurring about midway. After the crack-up comes the South Pole expedition by plane and dirigible, the latter to rescue the survivors.

DIRTY DANCING
1987, 97 mins, US ⓥ ⊙
D: Emile Ardolino A: Patrick Swayze, Jennifer Grey, Jerry Orbach, Cynthia Rhodes, Jack Weston (Vestron)

It's summer 1963 and college kids carry copies of *The Fountainhead* in their back pocket and condoms in their wallet. It's also a time for *Dirty Dancing,* and in her 17th summer, at a Borscht Belt resort, Baby Houseman (Jennifer Grey) learns how to do it in this skin-deep but inoffensive teen-throb pic designed to titillate teenage girls. Good production values, some nice dance sequences, and a likable performance by Grey make the film more than watchable.
1987: Best Song ("I've Had the Time of My Life")

DIRTY DINGUS MAGEE
1970, 90 mins, US ⓥ ▭
D: Burt Kennedy A: Frank Sinatra, George Kennedy, Anne Jackson, Lois Nettleton, Jack Elam, Michele Carey (M-G-M)

Dirty Dingus Magee emerges as a good period western comedy, covering the spectrum from satire through double entendre to low slapstick, starring Frank Sinatra and George Kennedy as double-crossing buddies.

DIRTY DOZEN, THE
1967, 149 mins, US ⓥ ⊙ ▭
D: Robert Aldrich A: Lee Marvin, Ernest Borgnine, Charles Bronson, Jim Brown, John Cassavetes, George Kennedy (M-G-M)

The Dirty Dozen is an exciting Second World War pre-D-Day drama about 12 condemned soldier-prisoners who are rehabilitated to serve with distinction. Lee Marvin heads a very strong, nearly all-male cast in an excellent performance. Marvin delivers a top performance probably because he seems at his best in a role as a sardonic authoritarian. John Cassavetes is first-rate as the tough Chicago hood who meets his match in Marvin. Charles Bronson stands out as a Polish American who, once affixing his loyalty, does not shift under even physical brutality.

1967: Best Sound Effects
Nomination: Best Supp. Actor (John Cassavetes)

DIRTY HARRY
1971, 102 mins, US ⓥ ⊙ ▭
D: Don Siegel **A:** Clint Eastwood, Harry Guardino, Reni Santoni, John Vernon, John Larch, Andy Robinson (Malpaso/Warner)

You could drive a truck through the plot holes in *Dirty Harry,* which wouldn't be so serious were the film not a specious, phony glorification of police and criminal brutality. Clint Eastwood, in the title role, is a superhero whose antics become almost satire. Strip away the philosophical garbage and all that's left is a well-made but shallow running-and-jumping meller. Don Siegel produces handsomely and directs routinely.

DIRTY MARY, CRAZY LARRY
1974, 93 mins, US ⓥ
D: John Hough **A:** Peter Fonda, Susan George, Adam Roarke, Vic Morrow, Ken Tobey, Roddy McDowall (Academy/20th Century-Fox)

Racing enthusiasts Peter Fonda and Adam Roarke steal $150,000 in order to purchase a competition sports car. Joined by sluttish Susan George, they careen around rural California with the law (demonic Vic Morrow) in pursuit. With more than a third of the footage devoted to spectacular chases and collisions, there's little time left to hint at the reasons for Fonda's increasingly unappetizing monomania.

DIRTY ROTTEN SCOUNDRELS
1988, 110 mins, US ⓥ
D: Frank Oz **A:** Steve Martin, Michael Caine, Glenne Headly, Anton Rogers, Barbara Harris (Orion)

Dirty Rotten Scoundrels is a wonderfully crafted, absolutely charming remake of the 1964 film *Bedtime Story.* In this classy version, Steve Martin and Michael Caine play the competing French Riviera con men trying to outscheme each other in consistently amusing and surprising setups.

DIRTY WEEKEND
1993, 102 mins, UK ⓥ
D: Michael Winner **A:** Lia Williams, David McCallum, Ian Richardson, Rufus Sewell, Sylvia Syms (Scimitar)

Michael Winner aims low and half-misses with *Dirty Weekend,* a jet-black genre bender of femme vengeance from the 1991 British bestseller by Helen Zahavi. Setting is Brighton, where the introverted Bella (Lia Williams) is prey to an obscene phone caller (Rufus Sewell). After an empowering visit to an Iranian fortune-teller (Ian Richardson), she brains the peeper with a hammer in his bed one night. High on the experience, she sets out on a weekend killing spree of male porkers.

DISCLOSURE
1994, 127 mins, US ⓥ ⊙ ▭
D: Barry Levinson **A:** Michael Douglas, Demi Moore, Donald Sutherland, Caroline Goodall, Dylan Baker (Baltimore/Constant/Warner)

Disclosure is polite pulp fiction, a reasonable rendition of potentially risible material. This lavishly appointed screen version of Michael Crichton's page-turner might have been even more commercial had it been more shamelessly trashy. Tom (Douglas) is fully expecting a promotion at his high-tech firm. But boss Bob Garvin (Donald Sutherland) decides to bring in outsider Meredith Johnson (Moore) for the big job. In his free-swinging single days, Tom had a hot and heavy thing with Meredith, which she seems intent upon reviving during a wine-enhanced private evening meeting. When he abruptly retreats from fully consummating the act, Meredith claims Tom sexually harassed her at their meeting.

DISCREET CHARM OF THE BOURGEOISIE, THE
See: Le Charme Discret De La Bourgeoisie

DISHONORED
1931, 91 mins, US ⓥ
D: Josef von Sternberg **A:** Marlene Dietrich, Victor McLaglen, Lew Cody, Gustav von Seyffertitz, Warner Oland, Barry Norton (Paramount)

A secret-service story. Dietrich rises above her director in this picture, as much as Sternberg smothered her while making *Morocco.* She is dominant in *Dishonored.* It is she who forces interest. Her love for the Russian rival spy (Victor McLaglen) is made quite evident at the finish.

DISHONORED LADY
1947, 86 mins, US ⓥ
D: Robert Stevenson **A:** Hedy Lamarr, Dennis O'Keefe, John Loder, Morris Car-

novsky, William Lundigan, Margaret Hamilton (United Artists)

Hedy Lamarr character is more neurotic than immoral and the film approach lessens interest and clarity. Plot still gets in shadowy implications of character's promiscuous love life, mostly through dialogue. It tells of editor of fashionable femme mag who's not getting the best out of life although apparently enjoying it. Mental desperation drives her to attempted suicide, a visit with a psychiatrist, and renunciation of old way of living.

DISORDERLY ORDERLY, THE
1964, 89 mins, US Ⓥ
D: Frank Tashlin A: Jerry Lewis, Glenda Farrell, Everett Sloane, Karen Sharpe, Kathleen Freeman, Susan Oliver (Paramount)

The Disorderly Orderly is fast and madcappish, with Lewis again playing one of the malaprop characters that seem to suit his particular talents. As the orderly, Lewis is himself almost a mental patient as he takes on all the symptoms of the individual patients in the plush sanitarium where he's employed. Glenda Farrell, cast as head of the sanitarium, displays the talent which once made her a star.

DISRAELI
1929, 90 mins, US
D: Alfred E. Green A: George Arliss, Joan Bennett, Florence Arliss, Anthony Bushell, David Torrence, Doris Lloyd (Warner)

Acting and characterization are a continuous delight, not to mention a plot that concerns the diplomatic imperative of possessing the Suez Canal. *Disraeli* without George Arliss is to shudder. The professionalism of the central figure carries and dominates both plot and conversation. Production is unstinted, sedate, and colorful, in the style of 1874.
1929/30: Best Actor (George Arliss)
Nominations: Best Picture, Writing

DISTANT DRUMS
1951, 100 mins, US Ⓥ
D: Raoul Walsh A: Gary Cooper, Mari Aldon, Richard Webb, Ray Teal, Arthur Hunnicutt (United States/Warner)

This goes back to 1840 and the Seminole War to spin an action-adventure tale grooved along conventional fiction lines. Raoul Walsh's action-wise direction makes excellent use of the standard framework most of the time to keep the film moving along at an acceptable clip. The

Florida backgrounds lend a lush, fascinating frame for a plot that covers Gary Cooper as an army captain who prefers to live in the swamps with his motherless son.

DISTANT TRUMPET, A
1964, 117 mins, US ▭
D: Raoul Walsh A: Troy Donahue, Suzanne Pleshette, Diane McBain, James Gregory, Claude Akins (Warner)

Troy Donahue enacts the role of an idealistic second lieutenant who arrives at a remote outpost in the middle of the Arizona desert and is thrust into the battle against Indian warrior War Eagle and a romantic squeeze play between Kitty (Suzanne Pleshette) and Laura (Diane McBain). The stunning location terrain of the Red Rocks area of New Mexico and Arizona's Painted Desert gives the production a tremendous pictorial lift.

DISTANT VOICES, STILL LIVES
1988, 84 mins, UK Ⓥ ⊙
D: Terence Davies A: Freda Dowie, Pete Postlethwaite, Angela Walsh, Dean Williams, Lorraine Ashbourne (BFI/Film Four)

This is the first feature film of Liverpudlian Terence Davies, obviously autobiographical, dealing with a family called Davies and their lives during the 1940s and 1950s. The film is full of singing, as the characters break into familiar songs at family gatherings or in the local pub. This isn't a film based on nostalgia, though; its very special qualities stem from the beautiful simplicity of direction, writing, and playing, and the accuracy of the incidents depicted.

DISTINGUISHED GENTLEMAN, THE
1992, 113 mins, US Ⓥ ⊙
D: Jonathan Lynn A: Eddie Murphy, Lane Smith, Sheryl Lee Ralph, Joe Don Baker, Victoria Rowell (Hollywood Pictures)

Mr. Murphy goes to Washington in *The Distinguished Gentleman,* an uneven but occasionally quite funny political satire. The movie starts with a very funny premise: what if a con man was swept into Washington by using the same name as a recently deceased congressman, playing on the notion that most people don't know if their rep is dead or alive anyway. The twist, of course, is that the biggest scams of all go on legally in Washington. However, Murphy's better nature takes over and prompts him to do the ethical thing.

DIVA
1981, 123 mins, France Ⓥ ⊙
D: Jean-Jacques Beineix **A:** Frederic Andrei, Roland Bertin, Richard Bohringer, Gerard Darmon, Wilhelmenia Wiggins Fernandez (Films Galaxie/Greenwich)

Diva is an extraordinary thriller and first film from Jean-Jacques Beineix, complex, stylish, and fast moving. The story involves a young mail courier with a passion for opera. The director dots the tale with bizarre types who continually cross each other's paths and wind up doing more harm to each other than to the young postman. The novel touches, bizarre chases and plot twists, breathtaking camerawork, and tension-filled editing make *Diva* a superior piece of entertainment.

DIVIDED HEART, THE
1954, 89 mins, UK
D: Charles Crichton **A:** Cornell Borchers, Yvonne Mitchell, Armin Dahlen, Alexander Knox, Geoffrey Keen (Ealing)

A human story taken from real life, *The Divided Heart* fails to tug the emotional heartstrings and ends up as little more than a conventional if convincing meller. Film is based on an actual story in which a blood mother claims her son, who had legally been adopted during the war by German parents. Cornell Borchers and Yvonne Mitchell give stirring performances as the two mothers involved in the dilemma.

DIVIDING LINE, THE
See: The Lawless

DIVINE MADNESS
1980, 94 mins, US Ⓥ ⊙ ▭
D: Michael Ritchie **A:** Bette Midler, The Harlettes, Irving Sudrow (Ladd)

After years of honing her act in gay baths and on concert stages, Bette Midler in 1980 committed it to film in four days at the Pasadena, CA, Civic Auditorium. Midler's monologues between songs, largely blue material familiar to devotees of her show, are uproariously funny and she delivers them with infectious physical panache. As for her voice, Midler is no Streisand, but she has a solid personality to back up her songs, and her versatility is one of her strongest assets.

DIVINE WOMAN, THE
1928, 95 mins, US ⊗
D: Victor Seastrom **A:** Greta Garbo, Lars Hanson, Lowell Sherman, Polly Moran, John Mack Brown (M-G-M)

Great Garbo is a peasant girl from Brittany. She comes to Paris to find fame as an actress. The man who brings her there is her mother's lover, played by Lowell Sherman in his best manner. She falls in love with Lucien, a private soldier, and gets him into all sorts of grief, including arrest as a deserter and prosecution for stealing a dress she admires.

DIVORCE AMERICAN STYLE
1967, 109 mins, US Ⓥ
D: Bud Yorkin **A:** Dick Van Dyke, Debbie Reynolds, Jason Robards, Jean Simmons, Van Johnson (Columbia)

Divorce American Style pokes incisive, sometimes chilling, fun at US marriage-divorce problems. Amid wow comedy situations, story depicts the breakup after 15 years of the Van Dyke–Debbie Reynolds marriage, followed by the economic tragedies exemplified by Jason Robards and Jean Simmons, caught in a vicious circle of alimony and remarriage problems.
1967: Nomination: Best Original Story & Screenplay

DIVORCEE, THE
1930, 80 mins, US Ⓥ
D: Robert Z. Leonard **A:** Norma Shearer, Chester Morris, Conrad Nagel, Robert Montgomery, Florence Eldridge (M-G-M)

In its adaptation of *Ex-Wife*, the spicy 1929 novel by Ursula Parrott, Metro has taken liberties. Norma Shearer is excellent as the ad writer who in the novel finally despairs of ever getting her husband back, but in the picture does and with a very effective, formulalike clinch for the close. Unusually fine work is contributed by Robert Montgomery, the husband's friend, who helps himself to the wife as he would to an extended cocktail.
1929/30: Best Actress (Norma Shearer)
Nominations: Best Picture, Director, Writing (John Meehan)

DIVORCE—ITALIAN STYLE
See: Divorzio all Italiana

DIVORCE OF LADY X, THE
1938, 92 mins, UK Ⓥ
D: Tim Whelan **A:** Merle Oberon, Laurence Olivier, Binnie Barnes, Ralph Richardson, Gus McNaughton (London Films)

Alexander Korda's Technicolored comedy is rich, smart entertainment, a comedy built around several situations and a wrong-identity hoax. Oberon impresses. Olivier does his role pretty well, retarded somewhat by an annoying bit of pouting business. Two key performances which sparkle are those of Ralph Richarson and Morton Selten.

DIVORZIO ALL ITALIANA (DIVORCE—ITALIAN STYLE)
1961, 108 mins, Italy
D: Pietro Germi A: Marcello Mastroianni, Daniela Rocca, Stefania Sandrelli, Leopoldo Trieste (Lux/Vides/Galatea)

Plot deals with a fed-up husband (Marcello Mastroianni) who plans several ways to get rid of his nagging wife (Daniela Rocca), finally decides to find a lover for her, spring on the couple, and shoot her dead. Skillfully written, with a penetrating, almost brutal glimpse of Sicily and its antiquated way of life, it has been directed with lagless pace and consistent incisiveness, evoking constant chuckles rather than isolated guffaws.

DIXIE
1943, 89 mins, US
D: A. Edward Sutherland A: Bing Crosby, Dorothy Lamour, Billy De Wolfe, Marjorie Reynolds, Raymond Walburn, Eddie Foy Jr. (Paramount)

Dixie is the saga of pre–Civil War minstrel man and songwriter, Daniel Decatur Emmett (Bing Crosby), who had a song in his soul and an innate showmanship which inspired what later became the standard blackface minstrel makeup. As a story it's lightweight. It's also doubtlessly a very free fictionization of Dan Emmett's career, but it's sufficient unto the purpose thereof.

D.O.A.
1950, 83 mins, US Ⓥ ⊙
D: Rudolph Mate A: Edmond O'Brien, Pamela Britton, Luther Adler, Beverly Campbell, William Chang (United Artists)

D.O.A. poses the novel twist of having a man looking for his own murderer. That offbeat idea and a strong performance by Edmond O'Brien do a lot to hold it together. But script is difficult to follow and doesn't get into its real meat until about 35 minutes of footage have passed. O'Brien is slipped deadly luminous poison in a drink, and he is told he only has a few days to live. He spends them trying to find his murderer and discover why he has been made a victim.

D.O.A.
1988, 96 mins, US Ⓥ ⊙
D: Rocky Morton, Annabel Jankel A: Dennis Quaid, Meg Ryan, Charlotte Rampling, Daniel Stern, Jane Kaczmarek,

Christopher Neame (Touchstone)

An excessively morbid and unsubtle remake of the 1949 film noir classic, D.O.A. remains unbelievable and unappealing despite a barnstorming central performance by Dennis Quaid. Quaid is diagnosed as having ingested a luminous poison, with only one to two days left to live. The protagonist who has given up on life since publishing his last novel four years back now has an obsession to live for: finding his own killer.

DOC
1971, 95 mins, US
D: Frank Perry A: Stacy Keach, Faye Dunaway, Harris Yulin, Michael Witney (United Artists)

Frank Perry attempts to remove the incrustations of myth and fantasy over the rough-hewn facts about and persons of Wyatt Earp, Doc Holliday, Kate Elder, and Tombstone. Earp (Yulin) emerges as a shifty politician of flexible motivation, by today's cynical standards a model pragmatic man of public life. His relationship with Holliday (Keach) has undertones left to the imagination (when little else is). Dunaway shakes her fashion-model fragility to become a believable frontier woman.

DOC HOLLYWOOD
1991, 103 mins, US Ⓥ ⊙
D: Michael Caton-Jones A: Michael J. Fox, Julie Warner, Barnard Hughes, Woody Harrelson, David Ogden Stiers, Bridget Fonda (Warner)

Doc Hollywood represents an attempt to rekindle the homespun humor and warmth of 1930s and 40s paeans to small-town American life. This heaped serving of recycled Capracorn has no real taste of its own, but, in its mildness and predictability, offers the reassurance of a fast-food or motel chain. Arrogant young big-city doctor Ben Stone (Michael J. Fox) on his way to L.A. and prospective riches as a plastic surgeon. Detained in Grady, SC, the quaintest li'l ol' town you ever did see, the impatient Ben is forced to perform 32 hours of community service at the local clinic for destroying the judge's white picket fence with his Porsche.

DOCK BRIEF, THE (US: TRIAL AND ERROR)
1962, 88 mins, UK
D: James Hill A: Peter Sellers, Richard Attenborough, Beryl Reid, David Lodge (M-G-M)

This offbeat, arty film gets away to a good start with the stellar pull of Peter Sellers and Richard Attenborough. Sellers plays an aging, unsuccessful barrister who gets the chance of a lifetime when briefed to defend Attenborough, a mild birdseed merchant who has murdered his wife because he wanted peace. The screenplay is a deft mixture of comedy and pathos.

DOCKS OF NEW YORK, THE
1928, 80 mins, US ♥ ⊗
D: Josef von Sternberg A: George Bancroft, Betty Compson, Baclanova, Clyde Cook, Gustav von Seyffertitz (Paramount)

Sternberg's direction is excellent, but it is in the casting that the picture falls short. Betty Compson as an elliptical-heeled frail, who is punch-drunk from life and attempts suicide, only to be rescued by Bancroft, a roughneck stoker, fails to get underneath the characterization. Bancroft as Bill Roberts, the husky, hard-drinking, two-fisted stoker, has a role that he can make roll over. Exquisite photography helps a lot.

DOC SAVAGE
THE MAN OF BRONZE
1975, 100 mins, US ♥
D: Michael Anderson A: Ron Ely, Paul Gleason, Bill Lucking, Michael Miller, Eldon Quick (Warner)

Execrable acting, dopey action sequences, and clumsy attempts at camp humor mark Doc Savage as the kind of kiddie film that gives the G rating a bad name. Ron Ely looks impressive as the blond muscleman superhero, but doesn't do much beyond flexing his muscles and flashing smiles at the group of cronies who join him on an expedition to the South American jungles to avenge his father's murder.

DOCTOR, THE
1991, 125 mins, US ♥ ⊙
D: Randa Haines A: William Hurt, Christine Lahti, Elizabeth Perkins, Mandy Patinkin, Adam Arkin (Touchstone)

The Doctor grapples powerfully with themes of mortality, compassion, social responsibility. William Hurt's perf as an emotionally constricted heart-and-lung surgeon faced with his own medical crisis is all the more moving for its rigor and restraint. Hurt's initial self-pity begins to evaporate when he enters the incandescent presence of fellow patient Elizabeth Per-

kins. Their platonic but intimate relationship becomes the film's emotional crux.

DOCTOR AT LARGE
1957, 104 mins, UK ♥
D: Ralph Thomas A: Dirk Bogarde, Muriel Pavlow, Donald Sinden, James Robertson Justice, Shirley Eaton, Michael Medwin (Rank)

This continues the adventures of the young medico who qualified in Doctor in the House and got his first appointment in Doctor at Sea. He's on a job-hunting spree and the film depicts his experiences and adventures while working for a mean provincial doctor and in a fashionable Park Lane practice. Role of the young doctor again is played by Dirk Bogarde. James Robertson Justice, who is the hospital's chief consultant, again emerges as the standout character.

DOCTOR AT SEA
1955, 93 mins, UK ♥
D: Ralph Thomas A: Dirk Bogarde, Brigitte Bardot, Brenda de Banzie, James Robertson Justice, Maurice Denham, Michael Medwin (Rank)

Sequel to Doctor in the House does not rise to the same laugh-provoking heights as its predecessor. James Robertson Justice is a gruff ship's captain on whose freighter the young medico has his first appointment at sea. Justice towers above the others and is the focal point of every scene in which he appears. Dirk Bogarde plays the medico with a pleasing quiet restraint and Brigitte Bardot has an acting talent to match her charm.

DOCTOR DOLITTLE
1967, 152 mins, US ♥ ▭
D: Richard Fleischer A: Rex Harrison, Samantha Eggar, Anthony Newley, Richard Attenborough, Peter Bull (20th Century-Fox/Apjac)

Rex Harrison, physically, is not at all the rotund original from Hugh Lofting's stories, but histrionically, he's perfect. Gentle and loving with animals, patient and kind with obtuse and very young friends, he can become a veritable holocaust when confronted with cruel and uncomprehending adults who threaten his animal world. Leslie Bricusse's adaptation retains the delightful aspects while taking considerable liberty with the plot. His mu-

sic and lyrics, while containing no smash hits, are admirably suited to the scenario.
1967: Best Song (''Talk to the Animals''), Special Visual Effects
Nominations: Best Picture, Cinematography, Art Direction, Editing, Original Music Score, Adapted Music Score, Sound

DOCTOR EHRLICH'S MAGIC BULLET
1940, 103 mins, US
D: William Dieterle **A:** Edward G. Robinson, Ruth Gordon, Otto Kruger, Donald Crisp, Maria Ouspenskaya, Albert Basserman (Warner)

Historical biography is based on the life of Paul Ehrlich, famed bacteriologist, whose most noteworthy contribution to medical science was the discovery of a cure for syphilis. Edward G. Robinson's portrayal of the famed Ehrlich is distinguished. In tracing the scientist's accomplishments, story moves through a span of about 35 years. Robinson makes the gradual transition down the years in great style.

DOCTOR FAUSTUS
1967, 92 mins, UK Ⓥ
D: Richard Burton, Nevill Coghill **A:** Richard Burton, Elizabeth Taylor, Andreas Teuber, Ian Marter (Columbia)

An oddity that records a performance by Burton that gives an insight into his prowess in classical roles. He is obviously captivated by Christopher Marlowe's 400-year-old verse, and speaks it with sonorous dignity and sense. The story concerns the medieval doctor's attempt to master all human knowledge by selling his soul to the devil, who dangles before him such delights as nights with Elizabeth Taylor, who flits through the film in various undraped poses.

DOCTOR IN THE HOUSE
1954, 92 mins, UK Ⓥ
D: Ralph Thomas **A:** Dirk Bogarde, Muriel Pavlow, Kenneth More, Donald Sinden, Kay Kendall, James Robertson Justice (Rank)

A top-drawer British comedy, particularly in the scenes featuring James Robertson Justice as a distinguished surgeon. Background to the story is the medical school of a London hospital. The new recruit to the school is Dirk Bogarde, who is taken under the protective wing of three old-timers. Kenneth More, Donald Sinden, and Donald Houston seem to have ideas

on most subjects but not how to qualify as a medico.

DOCTOR'S DILEMMA, THE
1959, 98 mins, UK
D: Anthony Asquith **A:** Leslie Caron, Dirk Bogarde, Alastair Sim, Robert Morley, Felix Aylmer, Michael Gwynn (M-G-M/Comet)

George Bernard Shaw's stringent wit still shines but his comments on the doctoring profession have lost much of their impact. *Dilemma* concerns a young woman married to an artist who is a complete bounder. But she is blinded by hero worship. He suffers from consumption, she pleads with a doctor to save his life. He thinks that he would do better to use his limited serum on a more worthwhile case. Dirk Bogarde gives a stimulating performance as the selfish young artist. Leslie Caron never suggests the strength necessary to fight the cynical doctors.

DOCTOR X
1932, 77 mins, US Ⓥ ◉
D: Michael Curtiz **A:** Lionel Atwill, Lee Tracy, Fay Wray, Preston Foster (First National)

No detail has been overlooked in providing a heavy doctor touch, plus sets of an intricate laboratory and surgical apparatus which themselves are sometimes a little gruesome. They have been well done, with the color lending much to underscore the tension. Lionel Atwill overshadows everyone as the head of a surgical research laboratory, under the roof of which several maniacal murders have been committed. As the daughter of the surgical lab's boss, Fay Wray quickly becomes involved with newspaper reporter Lee Tracy, who finally saves her from the big killer.

DOCTOR ZHIVAGO
1965, 193 mins, US Ⓥ ◉ ▭
D: David Lean **A:** Omar Sharif, Julie Christie, Tom Courtenay, Geraldine Chaplin, Rod Steiger, Alec Guinness (M-G-M)

The sweep and scope of the Russian Revolution has been captured by David Lean in *Doctor Zhivago,* frequently with soaring dramatic intensity. At the center of a universe of nine main characters is Omar Sharif as Zhivago, the sensitive man who strikes different people in different ways. To childhood sweetheart Geraldine Chaplin he is a devoted (if cheating) husband; to Julie Christie, with whom he is thrown together by war, he is a passionate lover; to Tom Courtenay, a heartless Red general, he's a symbol of the personal life which revolution has supposedly killed; to lecherous Rod Steiger he's the epitome of

rarefied selfishness; and to half brother Alex Guinness, he's a man who must be saved from himself. Sharif, largely through expressions of indignation, compassion, and tenderness, makes the character very believable.
1965: Best Adapted Screenplay, Color Cinematography, Color Art Direction, Original Musical Score, Color Costume Design
Nominations: Best Picture, Director, Supp. Actor (Tom Courtenay), Editing, Sound

DODGE CITY
1939, 100 mins, US Ⓥ ⊙
D: Michael Curtiz **A:** Errol Flynn, Olivia de Havilland, Ann Sheridan, Bruce Cabot, Frank McHugh (Warner)

Dodge City is a lusty western, packed with action, including some of the dandiest melee stuff screened; it is essentially a bad-man-and-honest-sheriff saga. Errol Flynn is a soldier of fortune, which explains his clipped English-Irish brogue as a Texas cattleman, transplanted to this Kansas frontier. Olivia de Havilland is the romance interest, and Ann Sheridan the dancehall girl.

DODSWORTH
1936, 90 mins, US Ⓥ ⊙
D: William Wyler **A:** Walter Huston, Ruth Chatterton, Paul Lukas, Mary Astor, David Niven (Goldwyn/United Artists)

Picture has a steady flow and an even dramatic wallop from zippy start to satisfying finish. Dodsworth was Walter Huston on the stage and is logically and perfectly the same actor on the screen. This is Ruth Chatterton's fanciest opportunity on the screen in a long while. Fran Dodsworth is a silly, vain, selfish, shallow kitten and in the playing of Chatterton comes to life with vividness and humanity. Mary Astor is the sympathetic other woman to whom Dodsworth ultimately turns.
1936: Best Interior Decoration (Richard Day)
Nominations: Best Picture, Director, Actor (Walter Huston), Supp. Actress (Maria Ouspenskaya), Screenplay, Sound

DOES, THE
See: Les Biches

DOG DAY AFTERNOON
1975, 130 mins, US Ⓥ ⊙
D: Sidney Lumet **A:** Al Pacino, John Cazale, Charles Durning, James Broderick, Chris Sarandon (Warner)

Based on a real life incident in NY, *Dog Day Afternoon* stars Al Pacino as the most unlikely bank robber ever to hit the screen. The holdup in question was allegedly done for the purpose of financing a sex-change operation for the male lover of one of the robbers. That incident is retained in the script, but it is just one of many key elements in a hilarious and moving story. The interactions between Pacino and other key characters are magnificently written, acted, and directed.
1975: Best Original Screenplay
Nominations: Best Picture, Director, Actor (Al Pacino), Supp. Actor (Chris Sarandon), Editing

DOGFIGHT
1991, 92 mins, US Ⓥ ⊙
D: Nancy Savoca **A:** River Phoenix, Lili Taylor, Richard Panebianco, Anthony Clark, Mitchell Whitfield, Holly Near (Warner)

An inherently repellent subject has been given surprisingly benign treatment in *Dogfight*. Title refers to a party to which a bunch of young servicemen bring the ugliest women they can find. Eddie (River Phoenix) manages to locate a candidate in young waitress Rose Fenney (Lili Taylor). The bringing together of a soldier headed for Vietnam and a future hippie on the night before President Kennedy's assassination represents a frightfully schematic screenwriting device. But Savoca underplays the character development to such an extent that the film has a muted, very modest impact.

DOGS OF WAR, THE
1980, 122 mins, UK Ⓥ ⊙
D: John Irvin **A:** Christopher Walken, Tom Berenger, Colin Blakely, Hugh Millais, Paul Freeman, JoBeth Williams (United Artists)

The Dogs of War is an intelligent and occasionally forceful treatment of a provocative but little-examined subject, that of mercenary-warrior involvement in the overthrow of a corrupt black African dictatorship. Script focuses almost exclusively on Christopher Walken, an irresponsible American who is drawn to the mercenary's loner, adventurous life.

DOG SOLDIERS
See: Who'll Stop the Rain

LA DOLCE VITA
1960, 180 mins, Italy/France Ⓥ ⊙ ▭
D: Federico Fellini **A:** Marcello Mastroianni, Yvonne Furneaux, Anouk Aimee,

Anita Ekberg, Alain Cuny, Lex Barker (RIAMA/Pathe)

High and low life in modern Rome are seen through the eyes of a reporter, Marcello (Marcello Mastroianni), whose beat brings him into contact with a world-famous film star (Anita Ekberg); with a nymphomaniac society girl (Anouk Aimee); with a false miracle; with the suicide of an intellectual (Alain Cuny) whom he's always idolized; with a debauched and tired party in a nobleman's castle; and finally, with an orgy (complete with a striptease performed by the hostess). Mastroianni is perfect in the key role of the basically good and honest boy who succumbs to the sweet life. Ekberg is a revelation as the visiting star, while Furneaux almost runs off with the picture as the reporter's instinctive, possessive mistress.

$
(UK: THE HEIST)
1971, 120 mins, US ⓥ ⊙
D: Richard Brooks **A:** Warren Beatty, Goldie Hawn, Gert Frobe, Robert Webber, Scott Brady (Columbia)

Richard Brooks wrote and directed $ with a sardonic twist to a caper plot. Bank security expert Warren Beatty, aided by friendly hooker Goldie Hawn, steal $1.5 million from three Hamburg safety-deposit boxes used by assorted criminals. An exhausting chase sequence is the ultimate destination of the production which features some good authentic locales.

DOLL'S HOUSE, A
1973, 95 mins, UK ⓥ
D: Patrick Garland **A:** Claire Bloom, Anthony Hopkins, Ralph Richardson, Denholm Elliott, Anna Massey, Edith Evans (Elkins/Freeward)

What is good here is largely what was good in the 1971 Broadway production from which pic directly derives. Film, as does play, unfolds grippingly, like a first-rate murder mystery with a cosmic consciousness. Bloom is top-notch. Her portrayal beautifully captures Nora's initial coquettishness and her emergence as an independent woman of strength and character.

DOLL'S HOUSE, A
1973, 108 mins, UK ⓥ
D: Joseph Losey **A:** Jane Fonda, David Warner, Trevor Howard, Delphine Seyrig, Edward Fox (World)

Fonda appears miscast as the Ibsen heroine who dominates this Nordic drama, lacking as she does the vibrancy, depth, and soul required to convey the transition of a fascinating character. This is otherwise a rather striking if academic achievement: physically stunning, diligently acted, told in a linear style by a man who knows his cinema, unexcitingly effective here and there.

DOLLY SISTERS, THE
1945, 114 mins, US
D: Irving Cummings **A:** Betty Grable, John Payne, June Haver, S. Z. Sakall, Reginald Gardiner (20th Century-Fox)

Regardless of biographical authenticity, this film resurrects a golden era of the theater and the international set of the early 1900s. But it's dominantly a boy-loses-and-recaptures-girl story with Betty Grable and John Payne as Harry Fox, songwriter and song-and-dance man.

DOLORES CLAIBORNE
1995, 131 mins, US ⓥ
D: Taylor Hackford **A:** Kathy Bates, Jennifer Jason Leigh, Judy Parfitt, Christopher Plummer, David Strathairn, Eric Bogosian (Castle Rock/Columbia)

Dark and grim, with a terrific central performance by Kathy Bates, pic offers more to fans of traditional melodrama than to Stephen King devotees. Accused of murdering the old woman for whom she's cared the past 22 years, Dolores is forced to confront her estranged daughter Selena (Jennifer Jason Leigh) and the mysterious death two decades earlier of her abusive husband. Dolores is a showy role, and Bates plays it to the hilt.

DOMICILE CONJUGAL
(BED AND BOARD)
1970, 104 mins, France/Italy ⓥ
D: Francois Truffaut **A:** Jean-Pierre Leaud, Claude Jade, Hiroko Berghauer, Barbara Laage, Daniel Ceccaldi (Films du Carrosse/Valoria/Fida)

Francois Truffaut carries on the adventures of one Antoine Doinel, who saw light in Truffaut's first, *The 400 Blows*, at 13. Pic traces the tribulations of early married life, a brief adulterous fling, a first child, and then settling down to married life in earnest. It is laced with little incidents, quirky characters, and incisive insights, that seem quintessentially French but that avoid chauvinism in Truffaut's gentle but never sentimental or indulgent treatment.

DOMINO KILLINGS, THE
See: The Domino Principle

DOMINO PRINCIPLE, THE
(UK: THE DOMINO KILLINGS)
1977, 97 mins, US ⓥ

D: Stanley Kramer **A:** Gene Hackman, Candice Bergen, Richard Widmark, Mickey Rooney, Edward Albert, Eli Wallach (ITC/Associated General)

A weak and tedious potboiler starring Gene Hackman as a tool of mysterious international intrigue, and a barely recognizable Candice Bergen in a brief role as his perplexed wife. Film contains a lot of physical and logistical nonsense.

DONA FLOR AND HER TWO HUSBANDS
See: Dona Flor e Seus Dois Maridos

DONA FLOR E SEUS DOIS MARIDOS
(DONA FLOR AND HER TWO HUSBANDS)
1977, 106 mins, Brazil ⓥ

D: Bruno Barreto **A:** Sonia Braga, Jose Wilker, Mauro Mendonca, Dinorah Brillanti, Nelson Xavier, Arthur Costa Filho (Barreto-Rique-Serrador)

A simplistic human comedy of manners and mores in the colorful Bahia part of Brazil in the 1940s, pic has a certain raw charm. A lovely mulatto woman marries a small-time playboy addicted to bordellos, gambling, and carousing. One day he dies during a Mardi Gras dance. She marries an exact opposite, a meticulous, unimaginative druggist. Her secret yearning for her first husband, despite his faults, has him materializing one night. Nobody but she can see him as he takes his place alongside her in bed.

DON IS DEAD, THE
1973, 115 mins, US ⓥ

D: Richard Fleischer **A:** Anthony Quinn, Frederic Forrest, Robert Forster, Al Lettieri, Angel Tompkins, Charles Cioffi (Universal)

This plodding mafiosi actioner is contrived concoction about internecine Mafia warfare with the young turks (Frederic Forrest and Robert Forster) trying to wrest control from underworld establishment represented by Don Angelo (Anthony Quinn). Even violent scenes come off as clumsy and antiseptic.

DON JUAN
1926, 100 mins, US ⓥ ⊙

D: Alan Crosland **A:** John Barrymore, Mary Astor, Estelle Taylor, Warner Oland, Montagu Love, Myrna Loy (Warner)

Several outstanders in this splendidly written, directed, and produced feature. Not alone is John Barrymore's superb playing noteworthy, but his athletics are, as well. The complete surprise is the performance of Estelle Taylor as Lucretia Borgia. Her Lucretia is a fine piece of work. The other outstanding performance is that of Mary Astor's Adriana.

DON JUAN DEMARCO
1995, 90 mins, US ⓥ ⊙

D: Jeremy Leven **A:** Marlon Brando, Johnny Depp, Faye Dunaway, Geraldine Pailhas, Bob Dishy (American Zoetrope)

Iconoclastic acting of a high order by three eccentric performers, Marlon Brando, Johnny Depp, and Faye Dunaway, is the most memorable thing about a romantic fable whose unique charm outweighs its small-scale, rather slight narrative, a modernist variation of the mythic Don Juan. Depp is cast as the world's greatest lover. But, devastated and distraught by the recent loss of his one true love, he's determined to take his life. Veteran psychiatrist Jack Mickler (Brando) miraculously succeeds in changing the desperado's mind. The episodic narrative consists of one-to-one sessions between doctor and patient.

Nominations: Original Song ("Have You Ever Really Loved a Woman?")

DONNIE BRASCO
1997, 126 mins, US ⓥ ⊙ ▭

D: Mike Newell **A:** Al Pacino, Johnny Depp, Michael Madsen, Bruno Kirby, James Russo, Anne Heche (Baltimore/Mandalay/TriStar)

Mob life receives one of its least glamorous screen portraits in *Donnie Brasco*. Al Pacino plays Lefty Ruggiero, a two-bit wiseguy who has worked as a loyal foot soldier for 30 years. He meets a young man, Donnie Brasco (Johnny Depp), who impresses him with his knowledge of jewels and his tough-guy prowess. What Lefty never knows is that his streetwise willing student is FBI agent Joseph Pistone, who is taping hours of revealing conversation and accumulates mountains of evidence. What neither the script nor Depp's performance ever attempt is an investigation into how Donnie/Joe feels about what he's doing. The film does not give him an interior voice. By contrast, Pacino unlooses an unchecked stream of visible thought and emotion. His fine work is the key to the film succeeding to the extent it does.

1997: Nomination: Best Screenplay Adaptation

DO NOT DISTURB

1965, 102 mins, US ▭

D: Ralph Levy **A:** Doris Day, Rod Taylor, Hermione Baddeley, Sergio Fantoni, Reginald Gardiner (20th Century-Fox)

Do Not Disturb is a light, entertaining comedy, set in England but filmed in Hollywood, with Doris Day teamed with a new screen hubby, Rod Taylor. Stars play extremely well together, Day as the loving, but slightly wacky wife, while Taylor is busy getting his factory into the black. Their lives diverge when Maura McGiveney becomes too much of an assistant to Taylor, and Day becomes innocently entangled with Sergio Fantoni, antique dealer and a prototype continental charmer.

DONOVAN'S REEF

1963, 104 mins, US ⓥ ◉

D: John Ford **A:** John Wayne, Lee Marvin, Jack Warden, Elizabeth Allen, Cesar Romero, Dorothy Lamour (Paramount/Ford)

Donovan's Reef, for a director of John Ford's stature, is a potboiler. John Wayne conveys an exuberance to match the mayhem, moving from fracas to fracas, facing up to a gang of toughs or a belligerent Boston beauty with equal courage. The only demand made is on his muscles. Ford brings out the ability of Elizabeth Allen, a darkling beauty. She's delightful as a Boston ice cube whose melting point is Wayne. The visual beauty of Kauai, in northern Hawaii, is captured by William Clothier's photography.

DON Q, SON OF ZORRO

1925, 110 mins, US ⓥ ⊗

D: Donald Crisp **A:** Douglas Fairbanks, Mary Astor, Jack McDonald, Donald Crisp, Warner Oland, Jean Hersholt (Elton/United Artists)

Don Q gives Fairbanks a chance to play a double role, as the youthful Don Q and as Zorro, the father of the dashing young Californian who is completing his education in Spain. His adventures there form the basis of the picture. He becomes involved with royalty, is accused of the murder of a visiting archduke, feigns suicide, almost loses the girl, but in the end emerges triumphant. Mary Astor appears to beautiful advantage in the little that she has to do.

DON'S PARTY

1976, 90 mins, Australia ⓥ

D: Bruce Beresford **A:** Ray Barrett, Claire Binney, Pat Bishop, Graeme Blundell, Jeannie Drynan (Double Head)

The eponymous get-together takes place in Australia on Election Night, 1969. The 11 characters are all friends who, save two, have assembled to cheer in a Labor-party victory. *Don's Party* is a vicious and unrelenting attack on suburbia and a harsh look at those who populate it. The entire cast turn in superlative performances.

DON'T BE A MENACE TO SOUTH CENTRAL WHILE DRINKING YOUR JUICE IN THE HOOD

1996, 88 mins, US ⓥ

D: Paris Barclay **A:** Shawn Wayans, Marlon Wayans, Tracey Cherelle Jones, Chris Spencer, Suli McCullogh (Ivory Way/Island)

Full of very obvious spoofery, and funnier in concept than in execution, this satirical film most frequently lampoons John Singleton, whose *Boyz N the Hood* provides the prototype for its fond mockery. Ashtray (Shawn Wayans) is a South Central Candide, sent to live with a father who is a model of irresponsibility. Seeking guidance, Ashtray turns to his cousin (Marlon Wayans), who carries a whole arsenal of Uzis and the like, and also keeps a Russian nuclear warhead nearby, just in case. Romantically naive, Ashtray soon loses his virginity to the lovely, poetry-writing Dashiki (Tracey Cherelle Jones), whose name supposedly is Swahili for ''doggy style.''

DON'T BOTHER TO KNOCK

1952, 76 mins, US ⓥ

D: Roy Ward Baker **A:** Richard Widmark, Marilyn Monroe, Anne Bancroft, Donna Corcoran, Jeanne Cagney, Elisha Cook Jr. (20th Century-Fox)

Marilyn Monroe gives an excellent account of herself in a strictly dramatic role, but the story of a psycho baby-sitter lacks interest. In this film she's anything but glamorous, despite her donning a negligee. Widmark doesn't appear too happy with his role. Anne Bancroft, making her screen bow, scores brightly as a torch singer.

DON'T BOTHER TO KNOCK

1961, 88 mins, UK

D: Cyril Frankel **A:** Richard Todd, Nicole Maurey, Elke Sommer, June Thorburn, Judith Anderson, Eleanor Summerfield (Associated British/Haileywood)

Story line has Richard Todd as an Edinburgh travel agent who goes off on a continental spree after quarreling with his fiancée (June Thorburn). He falls for a variety of charmers and hands out the key of his apartment to them. Having patched up his differences with his girlfriend over the phone, he returns and, of course, all the other feminine complications then arrive and take up residence. The dialogue is heavy-handed. And director Cyril Frankel has not been able to elicit performances that disguise this sorry fact.

DON'T LOOK BACK
1967, 96 mins, US ⓥ ⊙
D: D. A. Pennebaker (Leacock Pennebaker)

A cinema verité documentary of Bob Dylan's spring 1965 concert tour of Britain. Pennebaker has fashioned a relentlessly honest, brilliantly edited documentary permeated with the troubador-poet's music. During the monthlong tour, Dylan was accompanied by Joan Baez, haunted by the rival reputation of Donovan, and badgered day and night by the press, teeny-boppers, and hangers-on.

DON'T LOOK NOW
1973, 110 mins, UK/Italy ⓥ ⊙
D: Nicolas Roeg **A:** Julie Christie, Donald Sutherland, Hilary Mason, Clelia Matania, Massimo Serato (Casey/Eldorado)

This British-Italian suspenser, in which the horror gets to one almost subliminally, is superior stuff. It can be read on two levels: as simply a gripping tale of mysterious goings-on in a wintertime Venice or dealing with the supernatural and the occult as related to the established patterns of life and society. It's the fillips, introduced by director Nicolas Roeg in glimpses and flashes, that make this much more than a well-made psycho-horror thriller. Donald Sutherland is (unusually) at his most subdued, top effectiveness as the materialist who ironically becomes the victim of his refusal to believe in the intangible; Julie Christie does her best work in ages as his wife.

DON'T LOSE YOUR HEAD
1967, 90 mins, UK
D: Gerald Thomas **A:** Sidney James, Kenneth Williams, Jim Dale, Charles Hawtrey, Peter Butterworth, Joan Sims (Rank)

Don't Lose Your Head is a wild parody of *Scarlet Pimpernel* adventures in the *Carry On* mold. The film is a crazy debauch of dueling, double-crossing, and disaster. The troupers jump through their well-known hoops with agility.

DON'T MAKE WAVES
1967, 100 mins, US ⌂
D: Alexander Mackendrick **A:** Tony Curtis, Claudia Cardinale, Robert Webber, Joanna Barnes, Sharon Tate (M-G-M/Filmways-Reynard)

Don't Make Waves is a mildly amusing film that never gets off the ground as a wacky comedy. Script has a Southern California setting, mixing romance, infidelity, beach antics, and skydiving with utter confusion as Curtis plays a frantic young man and Cardinale a peppery import with an accent.

DON'T PLAY US CHEAP
1973, 104 mins, US
D: Melvin Van Peebles **A:** Esther Rolle, Avon Long, Rhetta Hughes, George Ooppee McCurn (Yeah)

Melvin Van Peebles's film offers some terrific musical numbers and an ebullient look at black culture. Van Peebles creates the atmosphere of a house party in Harlem. His fantasy premise of an imp and little devil crashing the party to spoil it out of pure meanness allows the filmmaker's militant themes to be expressed with humor and whimsy.

DON'T RAISE THE BRIDGE, LOWER THE RIVER
1968, 99 mins, UK ⓥ
D: Jerry Paris **A:** Jerry Lewis, Terry-Thomas, Jacqueline Pearce, Bernard Cribbins, Patricia Routledge (Columbia)

Mildly diverting production, filmed at Britain's Shepperton Studios, and starring Jerry Lewis as a perennial dreamer. Featured players Terry-Thomas as the typical promoter; Bernard Cribbins as a garage mechanic who doubles as a steward on unscheduled airlines; and Patricia Routledge, a man-hungry Girl Scout leader, are quite excellent.

DON'T TELL MOM THE BABYSITTER'S DEAD
1991, 105 mins, US ⓥ ⊙
D: Stephen Herek **A:** Christina Applegate, Joanna Cassidy, John Getz, Josh Charles, Keith Coogan, David Duchovny (HBO/Outlaw)

Starts with an enjoyable, if crude, black-comedy situation promised by the title, then turns into an incredibly dumb teenage girl's fantasy of making it in the business world. Christina Applegate and her four siblings are left by their ditzy vacationing mom in their suburban L.A. home with a seemingly sweet old lady baby-sitter (Eda Reiss Merin), who turns out to be a deranged Mary Poppins. Following the old lady's death from a heart attack, Applegate has to earn money to support the kids so they won't have to ask Mom to come home from Australia.

DOOM GENERATION, THE
1995, 84 mins, US
D: Gregg Araki A: James Duval, Rose McGowan, Johnathon Schaech (UGC/Teen Angst)

L.A. guerrilla filmmaker Gregg Araki proves that given a reasonable budget (less than $1 million), he can produce a stunning film with superlative production values. A nihilistic comedy about a trio of alienated youngsters, pic is bold not only in its art design, but also in its narrative and tone, a mixture of satire and horror with heavy dosage of steamy sex and macabre violence. Amy Blue (Rose McGowan), a beautiful, spoiled 17-year-old, her sweet suburban b.f., Jordan White (James Duval), and Xavier Red (Johnathon Schaech), a mysterious drifter, embark on an outlandish trip after Xavier blows off the head of a convenience-store clerk. The trio flee into a bizarre world of nightmarish violence and omnipresent danger that gets darker and darker as their odyssey progresses.

DOORS, THE
1991, 141 mins, US Ⓥ ⊙ ▭
D: Oliver Stone A: Val Kilmer, Meg Ryan, Kevin Dillon, Kyle MacLachlan, Frank Whaley, Kathleen Quinlan (Carolco/Imagine)

The Doors is another trip into 1960s hell from Oliver Stone. This $40-million look at Jim Morrison's short, wild ride through a rock-idol life is everything one expects from the filmmaker—intense, overblown, riveting, humorless, evocative, self-important, and impossible to ignore. Kilmer is convincing in the lead role, although he never allows the viewer to share any emotions. Morrison's own vocals have been skillfully augmented by Kilmer in some sequences.

DOPPELGANGER
(US: JOURNEY TO THE FAR SIDE OF THE SUN)
1969, 100 mins, UK Ⓥ
D: Robert Parrish A: Roy Thinnes, Ian Hendry, Patrick Wymark, Lynn Loring, Herbert Lom (Universal)

A story of two astronauts' trek to a hitherto undiscovered planet. Unfortu-

nately, despite some of the finest and most imaginative special effects, and sharp production values, the film is so burdened with confusing elements that it frequently fails to make sense.

DO THE RIGHT THING
1989, 120 mins, US Ⓥ ⊙
D: Spike Lee A: Danny Aiello, Ossie Davis, Ruby Dee, Richard Edson, Giancarlo Esposito, Spike Lee (40 Acres & a Mule)

Spike Lee combines a forceful statement on race relations with solid entertainment values in *Do the Right Thing*, painstakingly etching an ensemble of neighborhood characters on a Bedford Stuyvesant block in Brooklyn. Centerpiece is Danny Aiello's pizza parlor, which he runs with his sons John Turturro and Richard Edson, with Lee delivering take-out orders. On the hottest day of the summer, a myriad of contemporary issues covering personal, social, and economic matters are laid on the table in often shrill but sometimes funny confrontations.
1989: Nominations: Best Supp. Actor (Danny Aiello), Original Screenplay

DOUBLE DRAGON
1994, 95 mins, US Ⓥ ⊙
D: James Yukich A: Robert Patrick, Mark Dacascos, Scott Wolf, Kristina Malandro Wagner, Julia Nickson (Greenleaf/Imperial/Scanbox)

Even kids won't get much of a kick out this high-energy, low-IQ futuristic slugfest. Mark Dacascos and Scott Wolf play teenage brothers whose mentor (Julia Nickson) possesses half of a dragon amulet that bestows certain powers on its holder. The other half has been stolen by Koga Shuko, a power-obsessed mogul played so campily by Robert Patrick that even his bad haircut seems appropriate. Shuko spends the entire movie chasing the boys to get their half of the charm.

DOUBLE IMPACT
1991, 108 mins, US Ⓥ
D: Sheldon Lettich A: Jean-Claude Van Damme, Geoffrey Lewis, Alan Scarfe, Alonna Shaw, Philip Chan (Stone Group)

This double dose of Jean-Claude Van Damme turns on a typically lame revenge plot while dragging out unimaginatively shot action sequences until no one will give a good Van Damme. The onetime karate champ nicknamed "muscles from Brussels" apparently wanted to stretch his acting hamstring in this dual role as twins separated at six months. Van Damme uses

two looks, glowering/nasty and friendly/
bewildered, to differentiate between the
characters.

DOUBLE INDEMNITY
1944, 103 mins, US Ⓥ ⊙
D: Billy Wilder A: Fred MacMurray, Barbara Stanwyck, Edward G. Robinson, Porter Hall, Jean Heather, Tom Powers
(Paramount)

Absorbing melodrama revolves mainly
around the characterizations of Fred
MacMurray, Barbara Stanwyck, and Edward G. Robinson, the first two as lovers
and Robinson as an insurance claims agent
who balks the pair's perfect crime. Stanwyck plays the wife of an oilman, and
when MacMurray, an insurance salesman,
becomes her paramour, they sell to the
husband, fraudulently, an accidental-death
policy. They then kill him and place his
body on the railway tracks. MacMurray
has seldom given a better performance. It
is somewhat different from his usually
light roles, but is always plausible and
played with considerable restraint. Stanwyck is not as attractive as normal with
what is seemingly a blonde wig, but it's
probably part of an effort to emphasize the
brassiness of the character. Robinson, as
the infallible insurance executive quick to
determine phony claims, gives a strong
performance, too.
1944: Nominations: Best Picture, Director, Actress (Barbara Stanwyck), Screenplay, B&W Cinematography, Score of a
Dramatic Picture, Sound

DOUBLE JEOPARDY
1999, 105 mins, US Ⓥ ⊙ ▭
D: Bruce Beresford A: Tommy Lee Jones,
Ashley Judd, Bruce Greenwood, Annabeth
Gish, Roma Maffia, Davenia McFadden
(Paramount)

Double Jeopardy is single-minded and
engaging thriller storytelling without an
afterglow. Ashley Judd makes her woman
scorned an impressive star turn, sinewy,
determinedly focused, and graceful. Direction by Bruce Beresford is unassumingly
assured. After lovemaking with hubby
Nick (Bruce Greenwood) on their sailboat,
Libby (Judd) wakes in a bloodstained
bed—but no Nick. On cue, the coast guard
appears and she is convicted of murder.
Libby realizes she's been framed. She gets
paroled after six years. Parole officer
Travis (Tommy Lee Jones) can't stop her
from going back to the scene of the crime.
Jones injects every scene during a lengthy
pursuit with a wry, ironic wit.

DOUBLE LIFE, A
1947, 103 mins, US Ⓥ
D: George Cukor A: Ronald Colman,
Signe Hasso, Edmond O'Brien, Shelley
Winters, Ray Collins, Philip Loeb (Uni-
versal/Kanin)

There's murder, suspense, psychology,
Shakespeare, and romance all wrapped up
into one polished package. Plot poses an
interesting premise—that an actor takes on
some of the characteristics of the role he
is playing if the run is long. In this instance, Ronald Colman tackles Othello.
Gradually, as the play runs into a second
year, he is dominated more and more by
the character he creates on the stage. It
finally leads him to murder a chance acquaintance in the same manner as Othello
snuffs out the life of Desdemona each
night on the stage. Colman realizes on
every facet of the demanding part in a performance that is flawless. Signe Hasso, as
his stage costar and former wife, is a brilliant Desdemona and her interpretation of
the understanding ex-wife perfect.
1947: Best Actor (Ronald Colman), Score
for a Dramatic Picture
Nominations: Best Director, Original
Screenplay

DOUBLE LIFE OF VERONIQUE, THE
See: La Double Vie de Veronique

DOUBLE MAN, THE
1967, 105 mins, UK Ⓥ
D: Franklin J. Schaffner A: Yul Brynner,
Britt Ekland, Clive Revill, Anton Diffring,
David Bauer, Lloyd Nolan (Warner-Pathe/
Albion)

Intelligence agent Dan Slater (Yul
Brynner) is plunged into strange problems
when he goes to the Austrian Alps to investigate the death of his son on a ski
slope. The police write it off as an accident. Brynner suspects murder. The film
builds up an intriguing sense of tension
with the motives of various people rating
suspicion, Brynner being tailed by obvious
enemy agents and a big payoff when he is
confronted with his double.

DOUBLE TROUBLE
1967, 81 mins, US Ⓥ ⊙ ▭
D: Norman Taurog A: Elvis Presley, Annette Day, John Williams, Yvonne Romain, Chips Rafferty (M-G-M)

Double Trouble has the sketchiest of
story lines, which leaves spectator wondering what it's all about. Elvis Presley as
usual, however, gives a pretty fair account

346

of himself. He plays an American singer touring foreign discotheques. Intertwined in his travels, and femmes chasing him, are a couple of eccentric jewel thieves.

LA DOUBLE VIE DE VERONIQUE (THE DOUBLE LIFE OF VERONIQUE)
1991, 97 mins, France/Poland/Norway ⓥ ⊙

D: Krzysztof Kieslowski **A:** Irene Jacob, Philippe Volter, Sandrine Dumas, Claude Duneton, Wladyslaw Kowalski

The Double Life of Veronique will have fans of Kieslowski taking sides. Despite pic's many-splendored outbursts of filmic creativity and intense emotion, final result, about the opposite destinies of a Polish girl and a French girl who look alike and have the same name and tics, remains a head-scratching cipher with blurred edges. Pic's first third takes place in Poland in an almost perfect confluence of shots, editing, and dialogue that holds the viewer rapt. Weronika (Irene Jacob, dubbed by Anna Gronostaj) is a bubbly, happy girl whose extraordinary voice is discovered by a music teacher. She continues singing despite a dangerous heart condition. Film keeps its momentum for a little while in the French part. Veronique (also a singer) feels an inexplicable urge to quit voice training. Jacob is a sparkling newcomer who imbues both roles with an innocent but powerful magic.

DOUBLE WEDDING
1937, 87 mins, US ⓥ

D: Richard Thorpe **A:** William Powell, Myrna Loy, Florence Rice, John Beal, Jessie Ralph (M-G-M)

An outright slapstick comedy that would be funnier if it were shorter. Powell is an artist vagrant with a somewhat cock-eyed philosophy of life, which can be summed up by stating that work is for workmen of which he is not one. Loy is the proprietor of a smart-style shop and so engrossed in the problems of moneymaking and the responsibilities of rearing a younger sister that she has no time for play.

DOVE, THE
1974, 105 mins, UK ⓥ ▱

D: Charles Jarrott **A:** Joseph Bottoms, Deborah Raffin, John McLiam, Dabney Coleman, John Anderson (EMI/Peck)

Though basically a yarn about Robin Lee Graham's five-year solo trip around the world in a small sailboat, an odyssey

that provides nautical chills and thrills (as well as breathtaking scenics) aplenty, pic is also a tale of character development, plus an unpreachy lesson on ecology. Pic really takes off when hero meets the girl (played with gauche hesitation at first, but then with beauty and considerable charm by Deborah Raffin) who is to provide the driving force behind his trek and on into manhood and maturity.

DOWN AND OUT IN BEVERLY HILLS
1986, 97 mins, US ⓥ ⊙

D: Paul Mazursky **A:** Nick Nolte, Richard Dreyfuss, Bette Midler, Little Richard, Tracy Nelson, Elizabeth Pena (Touchstone)

A loving caricature of the nouveau riche (Beverly Hills variety); although it is more a comedy of manners than a well-developed story, there are enough yucks and bright moments to make it thoroughly enjoyable. Head of the household is the aptly named David Whiteman (Richard Dreyfuss). Bette Midler is the lady of the house, with their near anorexic daughter Tracy Nelson and son Evan Richards. In short, it's a household of unhappy people, and the fly (perhaps flea is more accurate) in the ointment is Nick Nolte as the bum Jerry Baskin, a disheveled and dirty street person. For the Whitemans he becomes their idealized bum, the family pet.

DOWN BY LAW
1986, 106 mins, US ⓥ

D: Jim Jarmusch **A:** Tom Waits, John Lurie, Roberto Benigni, Nicoletta Braschi, Ellen Barkin (Black Snake/Grohenberger)

Zack (Tom Waits) and Jack (John Lurie) are framed. They wind up in the slammer. Third cell mate is Roberto (Roberto Benigni), who speaks fractured English but whose naive friendliness proves contagious. After several funny scenes, the Italian proposes they escape. And so they do, out into the Louisiana swamps. The Jim Jarmusch penchant for off-the-wall characters and odd situations is very much in evidence. Benigni steals the film.

DOWNHILL RACER
1969, 101 mins, US/UK ⓥ ⊙

D: Michael Ritchie **A:** Robert Redford, Gene Hackman, Camilla Sparv, Karl Michael Vogler, Jim McMullan, Dabney Coleman (Paramount/Wildwood)

Downhill Racer is an intriguing film that balances skiing and the majesty of Alpine scenery with an absorbing story of hero Robert Redford, part of an American skiing team coached by tough Gene Hackman. A heart-in-the-throat Olympic downhill race as a finale tops everything that has gone before.

DOWN MEXICO WAY
1941, 72 mins, US Ⓥ
D: Joseph Santley **A:** Gene Autry, Smiley Burnette, Fay McKenzie, Harold Huber (Republic)

Gene Autry discovers his townfolk have been bilked out of coin supposedly aimed for picture production. Accompanied by Smiley Burnette and reformed Mexican bad man (Harold Huber), Autry trails the crooks into Mexico. Autry carries his assignment as the hero in good style, singing several songs including a couple of familiar pops in usual fashion.

DOWN TO EARTH
1947, 100 mins, US Ⓥ ⊙
D: Alexander Hall **A:** Rita Hayworth, Larry Parks, Roland Culver, James Gleason, Edward Everett Horton (Columbia)

Rita Hayworth is pictured as Terpsichore, the Greek muse of the theater. Looking down from heaven, she's unhappy over a Broadway musical about the nine muses, being done in a jazz style by producer Larry Parks. She makes a request to go down and help him so she can clean the show up. Explanation necessary to get all this across takes interminable time and all the gags which should give the yarn a bit of pepper fall flat. Hayworth does better in the vocal department and, of course is fine in the terp routines.

DOWN TO THE SEA IN SHIPS
1949, 120 mins, US Ⓥ
D: Henry Hathaway **A:** Richard Widmark, Lionel Barrymore, Dean Stockwell, Gene Lockhart, Cecil Kellaway (20th Century-Fox)

A lengthy saga of early whaling ships and the men who commanded them told with emphasis on character study rather than action. Lionel Barrymore carries off the fat part of whaling captain with fewer of the usual Barrymore tricks. Despite his youth, Dean Stockwell is a skilled thespian who more than holds his own in scenes with the adults.

DOWN WENT MCGINTY
See: The Great McGinty

DRACULA
1931, 64 mins, US Ⓥ ⊙
D: Tod Browning **A:** Bela Lugosi, Helen Chandler, Davis Manners, Dwight Frye, Edward Van Sloan (Universal)

A ghost story related with all surface seriousness and above all with a remarkably effective creepy atmosphere. Action begins in a barren mountain pass, where a spectral coach driver struggles through a miasmic mist. Story proceeds thence into a tomblike castle. In such surroundings, the sinister figure of the human vampire, the living-dead Count Dracula, who sustains life by drinking the blood of his victims, seems almost plausible. It is difficult to think of anybody who could quite match the performance of Bela Lugosi, even to the faint flavor of foreign speech that fits so neatly.

DRACULA
(US: HORROR OF DRACULA)
1958, 82 mins, UK Ⓥ
D: Terence Fisher **A:** Peter Cushing, Christopher Lee, Melissa Stribling, Michael Gough, Carol Marsh, Miles Malleson (Hammer)

Here again we have Count Dracula sleeping in a coffin by day and plying his nefarious role of a bloodsucking vampire at night. Version has its usual quota of victims before his reign of terror is ended by a fearless doctor. Peter Cushing is impressive as the painstaking scientist-doctor who solves the mystery. Christopher Lee is thoroughly gruesome as Dracula.

DRACULA
1979, 109 mins, US Ⓥ ⊙ ▭
D: John Badham **A:** Frank Langella, Laurence Olivier, Donald Pleasence, Kate Nelligan, Trevor Eve (Universal)

With its lavish retelling of an oft-told tale, this *Dracula* puts the male vamp back in vampire. Director John Badham and Frank Langella pull off a handsome, moody rendition, more romantic than menacing. Langella is the key in coming up with one more interpretation of the vampire out of hundreds previously presented. More humanly seductive, he's terrific with the ladies and the men would like him well enough if he weren't so good-looking and arrogant.

DRACULA
(AKA: BRAM STOKER'S DRACULA)
1992, 123 mins, US Ⓥ ⊙
D: Francis Coppola **A:** Gary Oldman, Winona Ryder, Anthony Hopkins, Keanu Reeves, Richard E. Grant (Columbia/American Zoetrope/Osiris)

Both the most extravagant screen telling of the oft-filmed story and the one most faithful to its literary source, this rendition sets grand romantic goals for itself that aren't fulfilled emotionally, and it is gory without being at all scary. The overarching story becomes Dracula's quest for recapturing his great love. Unfortunately, familiar plotting, Coppola's coldly magisterial style, and Gary Oldman's plain appearance in the title role combine to prevent this strategy from working in more than theory.
1992: Best Sound Effects Editing, Costume Design, Makeup
Nomination: Art Direction

DRACULA—PRINCE OF DARKNESS
1966, 90 mins, UK ▭
D: Terence Fisher **A:** Christopher Lee, Barbara Shelley, Andrew Keir, Francis Matthews, Suzan Farmer (Hammer/Seven Arts)

Four inquisitive tourists are lured to Castle Dracula, met by a sinister butler, and invited to dinner and to stay the night. The four treat this strange hospitality with incredibly bland acceptance. Christopher Lee, an old hand at the horror business, makes a latish appearance but dominates the film enough without dialogue.

DRAG NET, THE
1928, 70 mins, US ⊗
D: Josef von Sternberg **A:** George Bancroft, Evelyn Brent, William Powell, Fred Kohler, Francis MacDonald, Leslie Fenton (Paramount)

The Drag Net is cut with incredible swiftness at times, all-in action, and no sequence prolonged. Oliver H. P. Garrett, who wrote the corking story, has an interesting tale of cops vs. crooks, the latter in a gang of which William Powell is the sardonic and cynical leader. Bancroft is strong as the bulldog detective. Evelyn Brent is the girl, always acting well but not always looking so well.

DRAGNET
1954, 89 mins, US ⓥ
D: Jack Webb **A:** Jack Webb, Ben Alexander, Richard Boone, Ann Robinson, Virginia Gregg (Warner/Mark VII)

In making the transition from radio-TV to the big screen and color, this is spotty in entertainment results. As on TV, quite a bit is made of the tedium of police methods. When sticking to terse handling of facts, or in building honest emotion, such as in the splendidly done drunk scene by Virginia Gregg, grieving widow of a murdered hood, Webb brings his show off satisfactorily.

DRAGNET
1987, 106 mins, US ⓥ ⊙
D: Tom Mankiewicz **A:** Dan Aykroyd, Tom Hanks, Christopher Plummer, Harry Morgan, Alexandra Paul, Elizabeth Ashley (Universal/Applied Action)

Dragnet tries very hard to parody its 1950s TV-series progenitor but winds up more innocuous than inventive. Dan Aykroyd as Jack Webb as Sergeant Joe Friday gives the role his best but confines of the ultrastraight cop make humor difficult to sustain. Unfettered by such limits, Tom Hanks becomes the pic's winning wild card as Friday's zany sidekick, Pep Streebek.

DRAGONHEART
1996, 103 mins, US ⓥ ⊙ ▭
D: Rob Cohen **A:** Dennis Quaid, David Thewlis, Pete Postlethwaite, Dina Meyer, Julie Christie (Universal)

Freely mixing elements from Arthurian legend, *Robin Hood, Siegfried, Don Quixote,* and assorted other Anglo and Germanic myths, director Rob Cohen has pulled together a simple yarn about an itinerant dragonslayer who decides to team with his prey to rid the land of an evil ruler who has betrayed them both. Tale's poignancy stems from the fact that the fire-breathing, armor-plated, high-flying creature is the last of its kind; when he dies, dragons will have entirely passed from the earth. Everything here has been seen plenty of times before, except for the exceptionally sophisticated, wise, and well-spoken dragon, courtesy of many hands but notably those of Scott Squire's Industrial Light & Magic team.

DRAGON SEED
1944, 145 mins, US ⓥ
D: Jack Conway, Harold S. Bucquet **A:** Katharine Hepburn, Walter Huston, Aline MacMahon, Akim Tamiroff, J. Carrol Naish, Agnes Moorehead (M-G-M)

For all its two and a half hours a compelling saga. Hepburn and MacMahon and Huston are especially effective. Film traces the valley of the good earth, with its peaceful inhabitants, to whom the roar of the Japs cannons is still leagues away. But Jade (Hepburn) learns to read, and eventually Lao Er (Turhan Bey), her husband, is brought from petty marital jealousies into a full realization that their love must carry them beyond their village. They must help Free China remain free, and even the venerable Ling Tan (Huston) and his devoted wife (MacMahon) realize that turning the other cheek is no way to cope with the aggressors.

DRAGONSLAYER
1981, 108 mins, UK ⓥ ⊙ ▭
D: Matthew Robbins **A:** Peter MacNicol, Caitlin Clarke, Ralph Richardson, John Hallam (Paramount/Walt Disney)

A well-intentioned fantasy with some wonderful special effects, *Dragonslayer* falls somewhat short on continuously intriguing adventure. Technically speaking, it is an expertly mounted period piece concerning a boy's attempt to slay a fire-breathing dragon in order to save an entire kingdom. However, the story line is often tedious and the major action sequences appear much too late in the picture. The real stars (as expected) of this film are the fabulous special effects.
1981: Nomination: Best Visual Effects

DRAGON
THE BRUCE LEE STORY
1993, 121 mins, US ⓥ ⊙
D: Rob Cohen **A:** Jason Scott Lee, Lauren Holly, Robert Wagner, Nancy Kwan (Universal)

The meteoric rise and tragic death of martial-arts star Bruce Lee forms the basis of *Dragon,* an unlikely pastiche of traditional biography, Hollywood saga, and interracial romance. Director Rob Cohen, balancing disparate visual styles, keeps film pretty straightforward. Lee's metaphoric demon, visualized as a towering, faceless samurai, avoids cuteness; and the potential hokum, ranging from the spontaneous fights to the forays into the philosophy of inner strength, sidestep the high-toned silliness associated with the kung fu era.

DRAGONWYCK
1946, 100 mins, US
D: Joseph L. Mankiewicz **A:** Gene Tierney, Walter Huston, Vincent Price, Glenn Langan, Anne Revere, Jessica Tandy (20th Century-Fox)

The screenplay concerns the feudal system passed down through the generations by the old Dutch families on the Hudson. Nicholas Van Ryn has a wife and daughter whom he dislikes, and his pet anathema is his failure to have a son to carry on the baronial tradition. When a

distant relative is invited to be governess to the child, and he falls in love with her, he poisons his wife, thus leaving him free to marry the other girl. Gene Tierney plays the governess and it is one of her most sympathetic roles.

DRAUGHTSMAN'S CONTRACT, THE
1982, 108 mins, UK ⓥ ⊙
D: Peter Greenaway **A:** Anthony Higgins, Janet Suzman, Anne Louise Lambert, Hugh Fraser (BFI/Channel 4)

Though they are seemingly engaged in a comedy of manners taking place in the country home of a rich man, Herbert, the underlying viciousness of these rich denizens foreshadows coming upheavals. It is the end of the 17th century. Film has fine costumes, florid headpieces for men, and lovely surroundings on the big estate. Well lensed, with a fine limpid narration that switches from observation of this landed class to a sort of foreboding tale of murder.

DR. CYCLOPS
1940, 75 mins, US ⓥ ⊙
D: Ernest B. Schoedsack **A:** Albert Dekker, Janice Logan, Thomas Coley, Charles Halton, Victor Kilian (Paramount)

In detailing the discoveries of a madman scientist that allow him to reduce men and animals to miniature pygmies, story and direction both fail to catch and hold interest. Achieved through continual use of process and trick photography, idea gets lost in a jumble.
1940: Nomination: Best Special Effects

DREAM GIRL
1948, 83 mins, US
D: Mitchell Leisen **A:** Betty Hutton, Macdonald Carey, Patric Knowles (Paramount)

This film version of Elmer Rice's smash play has strong comedy, with a few moving scenes. The film turns the play's humor into outright comedy and sometimes into slapstick. As the self-preoccupied heroine, Betty Hutton gives one of her most skillful performances. Besides revealing her familiar vitality and drive, she underscores the comedy in the part and does reasonably well dramatically.

DREAM LOVER
1986, 104 mins, US ⓥ
D: Alan J. Pakula **A:** Kristy McNichol, Ben Masters, Paul Shenar, Justin Deas,

John McMartin, Gayle Hunnicutt (M-G-M)

Kristy McNichol is an average young lady living alone in a NY apartment. She becomes victim to an intruder (Joseph Culp), whom she stabs in the back. Was the stabbing really necessary for self-defense or did it leap out of some subconscious fury connected to her domineering father (Paul Shenar) or unfaithful lover (Justin Deas)? Only her brain knows for sure. Limps to a conclusion with no real excitement.

DREAM LOVER
1994, 103 mins, US ⊗ ⊙
D: Nicholas Kazan A: James Spader, Madchen Amick, Bess Armstrong, Frederic Lehne, Larry Miller (Propaganda/PFE)

An overly abstract mystery about the difficulty of really knowing another person and the unfathomables of amorous attachment, Dream Lover is too rarefied for a popular thriller and too dramatically hokey for an art film. Young divorced L.A. architect Ray (James Spader) manages quickly to win the favor of fashion-model-gorgeous Lena (Madchen Amick). They marry and have kids, but after a while Ray begins to imagine that his wife might not be true to or truly with him. The stakes mount quickly thereafter through accusations and admissions of indiscretions, betrayals, and overt manipulations, all leading up to legal proceedings and a climactic murder in a loony bin.

DREAM OF KINGS, A
1969, 109 mins, US ⊗
D: Daniel Mann A: Anthony Quinn, Irene Papas, Inger Stevens, Sam Levene, Val Avery (Schermer)

The adaptation of Harry Mark Petrakis's book about a larger-than-life Greek-American father, philanderer, and gambler whose dubious means of support is dispensing wisdom and wrestling instruction emerges as a warm, upbeat, artistically realized drama. It stars Anthony Quinn portraying a super mensch, the noble ethnic, and it is one of his most powerful and convincing performances.

DREAM OF PASSION, A
1978, 110 mins, Greece ⊗
D: Jules Dassin A: Melina Mercouri, Ellen Burstyn, Andreas Voutsinas (Brenfilm/Melina)

Two older women are caught up in a strange parallel. One, Melina Mercouri, is a film star who returns to her native Greece to do Medea on stage. The other, Ellen Burstyn, is an American living in Greece who has killed her three children "just as Medea did" due to her husband's flaunting of her love and needs. Pic alternates two stories as Mercouri's life and work are intertwined with her growing interest in Burstyn.

DREAMSCAPE
1984, 95 mins, US ⊗ ⊙
D: Joseph Ruben A: Dennis Quaid, Max von Sydow, Christopher Plummer, Eddie Albert, Kate Capshaw (Zupnick-Curtis)

Film centers on "dreamlinking," the psychic projection of one person's consciousness into a sleeping person's subconscious, or his dreams. If that sounds farfetched, it is. Central character Alex Garland is played with gusto by Dennis Quaid, who hooks up with Dr. Paul Novotny (Max von Sydow), who runs a dream research project.

DREAM STREET
1921, 135 mins, US ⊗ ⊗
D: D. W. Griffith A: Carol Dempster, Ralph Graves, Charles Emmett Mack, Edward Peil, Tyrone Power (Griffith/United Artists)

The theme might be set down in its briefest form as this: we are all of us made up of good and bad, and vague but strong forces at work within us give direction to the raw materials of our characters. That being the thesis, Griffith makes his meaning plain in the story of two brothers, Billy McFadden, physically weak but spiritually fine, and Spike McFadden, a physical giant with a certain arrogance and almost brutal selfishness. The players are splendid.

DREAM TEAM, THE
1989, 113 mins, US ⊗ ⊙
D: Howard Zieff A: Michael Keaton, Christopher Lloyd, Peter Boyle, Stephen Furst, Lorraine Bracco (Imagine/Universal)

The Dream Team is a hokey comedy that basically reduces mental illness to a grab bag of quirky shtick. Yet with a quartet of gifted comic actors having a field day playing loonies on the loose in Manhattan, much of that shtick is awfully funny. In an attempt to give his patients a taste of the real world, New Jersey hospital doctor Dennis Boutsikaris decides to treat four of his charges to a day game at Yankee Stadium. As soon as they hit the

Big Apple, however, the good doctor is seriously injured after witnessing a killing, and the boys are left to their own devices. Keaton is at his manic best, Lloyd prompts numerous guffaws with his impersonation of a self-serious tidiness freak, and Furst quietly impresses as the sickest and most helpless of the lot.

DREAM WIFE
1953, 99 mins, US
D: Sidney Sheldon **A:** Cary Grant, Deborah Kerr, Walter Pidgeon, Betta St. John, Eduard Franz (M-G-M)

A battle-of-the-sexes theme is used for this fairly entertaining, highly contrived piece of screen nonsense. Cary Grant, a man who wants a wife in the home, not in business, breaks with Deborah Kerr, State Department official who is too busy to have time for matrimony. Remembering a comely princess (Betta St. John) and the fact that she had been raised from birth in the art of pleasing man, Grant proposes via cable. The State Department steps in and assigns Kerr to see that her ex-fiancé sticks to protocol in his new courtship.

DIE DREIGROSCHENOPER (THE THREEPENNY OPERA)
1931, 112 mins, Germany ⓥ ⊙
D: G. W. Pabst **A:** Rudolph Forster, Carola Neher, Lotte Lenya, Ernst Busch, Valeska Gert, Fritz Rasp, Reinhold Schuenzel (Warner/Tobis/Nero)

The venerable sardonic English *Beggar's Opera* was adapted by Kurt Weill (music) and Bertolt Brecht (libretto) into *Threepenny Opera*. As directed by G. W. Pabst, picture is a successful translation of a highly stylized stage work to the realistic screen medium. The Brecht tale of the notorious cutthroat Mackie Messer ("Mack the Knife") unfolds with complete honesty and a lot of wild, hard-as-nails social satire. The relationships of Mackie with his one true love, Polly Peachum, and with the prostitute Jenny, are defined with reality and insight. This is due, not only to the performances of Rudolph Forster as Mackie, Carola Neher as Polly, and Lotte Lenya as Jenny, but, of course, to the Weill music. [Review is of a 1960 restoration.]

DRESSED TO KILL
1980, 105 mins, US ⓥ ⊙ ▭
D: Brian De Palma **A:** Michael Caine, Angie Dickinson, Nancy Allen, Keith Gordon, Dennis Franz (Filmways/Cinema 77)

Brian De Palma goes right for the audience jugular in *Dressed to Kill*, a stylish exercise in ersatz-Hitchcock suspense-terror. Despite some major structural weaknesses, the cannily manipulated combination of mystery, gore, and kinky sex adds up to a slick commercial package. The film begins with a steamy autoerotic shower scene and segues to a session between Angie Dickinson and psychiatrist Michael Caine. Matters begin in earnest when Dickinson enters an elevator and is razor-sliced to death. Dickinson is used exceptionally well as the sexually torn, quickly disposed-of heroine. Caine, until the film's internal logic breaks down, is excellent as the suave shrink.

DRESSER, THE
1983, 118 mins, UK ⓥ ⊙
D: Peter Yates **A:** Albert Finney, Tom Courtenay, Edward Fox, Zena Walker, Eileen Atkins, Michael Gough (Goldcrest/World Film Services)

Adapted by Ronald Harwood from his 1980 London comedy-drama, this is indisputably one of the best films ever made about theater. It's funny, compassionate, compelling. Finney portrays an aging, spoiled, grandiloquent actor-manager of a traditional English touring company whose dedication to his art creates chaos for those around him. The only character who can handle the old actor is his gofer-valet Norman, played with an amazing dexterity and energy by Tom Courtenay.
1983: Nominations: Best Picture, Director, Actor (Albert Finney, Tom Courtenay), Adapted Screenplay

DREYFUS
1931, 80 mins, UK
D: F. W. Kraemer, Milton Rosmer **A:** Cedric Hardwicke, Beatrix Thomson, Charles Carson, George Merritt (British International/Sudfilm)

British International, in making the picture, is understood to have followed closely to the original film, made by Sudfilm for German consumption. The Dreyfus case revolved around a framed-up treason charge against Captain Alfred Dreyfus of the French army. Treason had been committed and Dreyfus was charged, largely because he was the only Jew on the staff. Cedric Hardwicke as Dreyfus gives a fine performance; George Merritt as Zola is exceptional. Another striking performance is that of Charles Carson as Colonel Picquart.

DR. FU MANCHU
1929, 80 mins, US
D: Rowland V. Lee **A:** Warner Oland, Jean Arthur, Neil Hamilton, O. P. Heggie (Paramount)

British legation in Peking is under assault of Boxer hordes. One of the officials sends his little daughter to the protection of a friendly Chinese noble, Dr. Fu Manchu. In the ensuing attack by English troops, Fu's wife and son are slain. Whereupon the Oriental swears revenge on the white foreign devils. Years later he has brought up the white girl (Jean Arthur) left in his charge and, by putting her in a trance, has her carry out his designs. It all works up to a pip of a melodramatic climax.

DRILLER KILLER, THE
1979, 90 mins, US Ⓥ
D: Abel Ferrara **A:** Jimmy Laine [Abel Ferrara], Carolyn Marz, Baybi Day, Harry Schultz, Alan Wynroth (Navaron)

This bit of gore was undoubtedly inspired by *The Texas Chainsaw Massacre*. It's hastily shot and technically inept in every department operation. An artist finds it increasingly difficult to keep the wolf from the door. A punk rock band moves into the floor below him and the noise pushes him over the edge. When he turns into a murderer with an electric drill, he doesn't go downstairs and eliminate the band. No, he picks winos in doorways as his victims before turning to other target—his girlfriends.

DRIVE, HE SAID
1971, 95 mins, US
D: Jack Nicholson **A:** William Tepper, Karen Black, Michael Margotta, Bruce Dern, Robert Towne, Henry Jaglom (BBS)

Director Jack Nicholson seems here to be making a sort of games-people-play charade. William Tepper, as the central sports-star character of the campus convolutions, reflects the changes and protest surrounding his simplistic existence. His roommate (Michael Margotta), a Che-like student revolutionary, wants to destroy all—for he feels the draft, life around him, the war, will destroy him. Karen Black is the sensual older woman, who sexually grapples with the basketball hero. Nicholson deftly illustrates the background cynicism of big-time sports against the more obvious cynicism of college life.

DRIVER, THE
1978, 91 mins, US Ⓥ
D: Walter Hill **A:** Ryan O'Neal, Bruce Dern, Isabelle Adjani, Ronee Blakely, Matt Clark (20th Century-Fox)

By the end of *The Driver* you can almost smell rubber burning, there are so many screeching tires. This may be the first film where the star of the show isn't an actor or even a machine but a sound effect. Ryan O'Neal plays a master getaway driver who does most of his talking with his accelerator toe. Bruce Dern, departing only slightly from his maniac roles, plays an obsessed detective out to nab O'Neal.

DRIVING ME CRAZY
See: Dutch

DRIVING MISS DAISY
1989, 99 mins, US Ⓥ ⊙
D: Bruce Beresford **A:** Morgan Freeman, Jessica Tandy, Dan Aykroyd, Patti LuPone (Zanuck/Warner)

A touching exploration of 25 years of change in southern race relations (1948-73) as seen through the relationship of an elderly Jewish widow and her stalwart black chauffeur. Jessica Tandy's Daisy is a captious and lonely old stick, living a bleakly isolated widow's life in her empty old house, and her inability to keep from tyrannizing Morgan Freeman, housekeeper Esther Rolle, and other black helpers gives the film a current of bitter truth, making her gradual friendship with Freeman a hard-won achievement.
1989: Best Picture, Actress (Jessica Tandy), Adapted Screenplay, Makeup
Nominations: Best Actor (Morgan Freeman), Supp. Actor (Dan Aykroyd), Editing, Art Direction, Costume Design

DR. JEKYLL AND MR. HYDE
1932, 90 mins, US Ⓥ ⊙
D: Rouben Mamoulian **A:** Fredric March, Miriam Hopkins, Rose Hobart, Holmes Herbert, Halliwell Hobbes (Paramount)

In many passages the picture is an astonishing fine bit of interpreting a classic, but as popular fare it lacks vitality. Camera trick of changing a central figure from the handsome Fredric March into the bestial, apelike monster Hyde carries a terrific punch, but each successive use of the device weakens the hair-raising effect. March does an outstanding bit of theatrical acting. His Hyde makeup is a triumph of realized nightmare. Miriam Hopkins plays

Ivy, the London soiled dove, with a capital sense of comedy and coquetry.
1931/32: Best Actor (Fredric March) Nominations: Best Adaptation, Cinematography

DR. JEKYLL AND MR. HYDE
1941, 127 mins, US Ⓥ ⊙
D: Victor Fleming **A:** Spencer Tracy, Ingrid Bergman, Lana Turner, Ian Hunter, Donald Crisp, C. Aubrey Smith (M-G-M)

Spencer Tracy plays the dual roles with conviction. His transformations from the young physician, bent on biological and mental research as an escape from his own moral weaknesses, to the demoniac Mr. Hyde are brought about with considerably less alterations in face and stature than audiences might expect. Ingrid Bergman plays the enslaved victim of Hyde's debauches. In every scene in which the two appear, she is Tracy's equal as a strong screen personality.
1941: Nominations: Best B&W Cinematography, Editing, Scoring of a Dramatic Picture

DR. JEKYLL AND MS. HYDE
1995, 89 mins, US Ⓥ ⊙
D: David Price **A:** Sean Young, Tim Daly, Lysette Anthony, Stephen Tobolowsky, Harvey Fierstein, Polly Bergen (Rastar/Savoy)

Dr. Jekyll and Ms. Hyde is a contemporary spin in which the bad side of Jekyll (Tim Daly) is a predatory female (Sean Young) who has her sights on climbing the corporate ladder. The contempo twists provide one or two surprises, but the plot sticks pretty much to the classic, or at least the best-known film versions. Daly's easy charm and Young's full-blooded treachery go a long way to smooth over the picture's rough edges.

DR. JEKYLL AND SISTER HYDE
1971, 87 mins, UK Ⓥ
D: Roy Ward Baker **A:** Ralph Bates, Martine Beswick, Gerald Sim, Lewis Fiander, Dorothy Alison (Hammer)

Scripter Brian Clemens had the highly imaginative idea of letting Robert Louis Stevenson's 19th-century Dr. Jekyll turn into a homicidal, glamorous Sister Hyde instead of the original hairy monster. He then pinned on him/her the responsibility for the Jack the Ripper murders. Here, Jekyll, played by Ralph Bates, as male attracts the pure young miss living next door and as female (Martine Beswick) fascinates her brother. Bates and Beswick,

strong, attractive personalities, bear a strange resemblance to each other, making the transitions entirely believable.

DR. MABUSE DER SPIELER (DR. MABUSE, THE GAMBLER; THE FATAL PASSIONS)
1922, 242 mins, Germany Ⓥ ⊗
D: Fritz Lang **A:** Rudolf Klein-Rogge, Aud Egede Nissen, Gertrude Welcker, Alfred Abel, Bernhard Goetzke, Paul Richter (UCO)

The story is built around the character of Dr. Mabuse (Rudolf Klein-Rogge), the great gambler, the player with the souls of men and women. He runs an underground counterfeiting establishment, and with this money starts all his enterprises. The best moments are achieved by the conflict between Mabuse and the attorney, Von Wenk (Bernhard Goetzke), who is trying to uncover him. The film is somewhat hurt by the casting of Klein-Rogge for the title role; he is physically too small and not a clever enough actor to make one forget this.

DR. MABUSE, THE GAMBLER
See: Dr. Mabuse der Spieler

DR. NO
1962, 110 mins, UK Ⓥ ⊙
D: Terence Young **A:** Sean Connery, Ursula Andress, Joseph Wiseman, Jack Lord, Bernard Lee, Zena Marshall (United Artists/Eon)

First screen adventure of Ian Fleming's hard-hitting, fearless, imperturbable, girl-loving Secret Service Agent 007, James Bond, is an entertaining piece of tongue-in-cheek action hokum. Sean Connery excellently puts over a cool, fearless, on-the-ball, fictional secret-service guy. Terence Young directs with a pace that only occasionally lags. The hero is exposed to pretty (and sometimes treacherous) gals, a poison tarantula, a sinister crook, flamethrowers, gunshots, bloodhounds, beating up, near drowning, and plenty of other mayhem and malarkey, and comes through it all with good humor, resourcefulness, and what-have-you.

DROP DEAD DARLING
1966, 100 mins, UK
D: Ken Hughes **A:** Tony Curtis, Rosanna Schiaffino, Lionel Jeffries, Zsa Zsa Gabor, Nancy Kwan, Fenella Fielding (Seven Arts)

Pic is a silly sex comedy, as amusing at times as it is tasteless, in which Tony Curtis plays a contemporary Bluebeard.

Story attempts to make likable a character who arranges the death of his femme guardian, her sailor suitor, later his first two wives, and, unsuccessfully, Schiaffino, bride-widow of an a.k. who expires in honeymoon excitement. Withal, Curtis does a very good job, plotting with Lionel Jeffries to do in Schiaffino. Latter is by no means without acting ability, either.

DROP DEAD FRED

1991, 98 mins, US/UK Ⓥ

D: Ate De Jong A: Rik Mayall, Phoebe Cates, Marsha Mason, Tim Matheson, Carrie Fisher, Ron Eldard (PolyGram/Working Title)

Oscillating between long arid stretches, inspired explosions of slapstick, and disarming warmth, *Drop Dead Fred* is probably too slow and mushy for kids and too sporadic in its rewards for adults. Phoebe Cates stars as Elizabeth, a young wife who returns home to her domineering mother (Marsha Mason) after splitting up with her brazenly philandering husband (Tim Matheson). At home she discovers a music box that contains her long-forgotten imaginary friend, Drop Dead Fred (British comic Rik Mayall in a red Beethoven fright wig), who's been released to wreak havoc until she's having fun again.

DROP DEAD GORGEOUS

1999, 99 mins, US Ⓥ ⊙

D: Michael Patrick Jann A: Kirsten Dunst, Ellen Barkin, Allison Janney, Denise Richards, Kirstie Alley, Sam McMurray (Capella/KC Medien/New Line)

Drop Dead Gorgeous is a fitfully amusing satire that would have gained a lot of mileage from a tad more subtlety. A camera crew is hired to document a small town's participation in the 50th annual Miss American Teen Princess Pageant. Favored to win are sweet Amber (Kirsten Dunst) and scheming vixen Becky (Denise Richards). Latter is daughter to the town's richest businessman, and her mother (Kirstie Alley) is a former Teen Princess. First, one contestant dies in a threshing-machine mishap, then Becky's boyfriend, whose eyes have been straying toward Amber, experiences a fatal accident. Pic confuses satire with condescension—everyone is either stupid, venal, or perverse—and doesn't have the writing sophistication to render its more questionable jokes blackly comic. Nonetheless, fast pacing makes this a relatively pain-free, if brain-free, diversion.

DROP ZONE

1994, 101 mins, US Ⓥ ⊙ ▭

D: John Badham A: Wesley Snipes, Gary Busey, Yancy Butler, Michael Jeter, Kyle Secor (Paramount)

Pic is little more than a by-the-numbers programmer, reasonably diverting and briskly paced but thinly written and utterly predictable. Wesley Snipes gives a self-assured star performance as Pete Nessip, a US marshal who, with his brother and fellow lawman (Malcolm-Jamal Warner), is assigned guard duty for the transfer of a drug-cartel snitch (Michael Jeter). When their 747 is hijacked by alleged terrorists, the terrorists along with the snitch appear to take a fatal free fall. Pete insists the hijackers and prisoner jumped out of the plane and escaped with parachutes. While on suspension pending an FBI investigation, he goes undercover to prove his theory.

DROWNING BY NUMBERS

1988, 118 mins, UK/Netherlands Ⓥ ⊙

D: Peter Greenaway A: Bernard Hill, Joan Plowright, Juliet Stevenson, Joely Richardson, Bryan Pringle

Drowning by Numbers deals with metaphorical game playing with sex and death in the best traditions of black humor. Pic follows the darkly murderous acts of three women all named Cissie Colpitts (Joan Plowright, Juliet Stevenson, and Joely Richardson) and their friend the local coroner (Bernard Hill) and his son Smut (Jason Edwards). As an aside, Greenaway has placed the numbers 1 to 100 throughout the film (for example, 1 appears on a tree, 36 on Joely Richardson's swimsuit), yet another exercise in game playing and a challenge for the viewer to spot all the numbers.

DROWNING POOL, THE

1975, 108 mins, US ▭

D: Stuart Rosenberg A: Paul Newman, Joanne Woodward, Anthony Franciosa, Murray Hamilton, Gail Strickland, Melanie Griffith (Coleytown/Warner)

Paul Newman again assumes the Lew Harper private-eye role he first essayed in *Harper* (1966). *The Drowning Pool* is stylish, improbable, entertaining, superficial, well cast, and totally synthetic. Title derives from an offbeat and exciting climactic sequence in an abandoned mental-asylum hydrotherapy room.

DR. PHIBES RISES AGAIN

1972, 88 mins, UK ⓥ ⊙
D: Robert Fuest **A:** Vincent Price, Robert Quarry, Valli Kemp, Hugh Griffith, John Thaw (American International)

Dr. Phibes, that bizarre evil genius of *The Abominable Dr. Phibes*, is back with all his old diabolic devilry for another excusion into musical camp fantasy. Dr. Phibes rises to restore life to his wife who died many years before. Vincent Price, as Phibes, delivers one of his priceless theatric performances.

DR. SOCRATES

1935, 74 mins, US
D: William Dieterle **A:** Paul Muni, Ann Dvorak, Barton MacLane, Robert Barrat, John Eldredge (Warner)

Arriving at the tail end of the G-man-and-gangster cycle, plot stars neither the gunman nor the officer of the law, but makes both subservient to a country doctor. The young physician is adopted as the gang's medical man, and he takes a chance because he needs the money. But when the gang grabs his girl, he goes on the offensive. For an actor of Muni's caliber, the soft-spoken doc seems a minor effort.

DR. STRANGELOVE OR: HOW I LEARNED TO STOP WORRYING AND LOVE THE BOMB

1964, 102 mins, UK ⓥ ⊙
D: Stanley Kubrick **A:** Peter Sellers, George C. Scott, Sterling Hayden, Keenan Wynn, Slim Pickens, James Earl Jones (Columbia/Hawk)

Nothing would seen to be further apart than nuclear war and comedy, yet Kubrick's caper eloquently tackles a *Fail-Safe* subject with a light touch. It all begins when a Strategic Air Command general on his own initiative orders bomb-carrying planes under his command to attack Russia. From here on it's a hectic, exciting series of events, alternating between the general who has started it all, the planes en route to the USSR, and the Pentagon's war room, where the chief executive is trying his best to head off the nuclear war. It would seem no setting for comedy or satire, but the writers have accomplished this with biting, piercing dialogue and thorough characterizations. Peter Sellers is excellent, essaying a trio of roles.
1964: Nominations: Best Picture, Director, Actor (Peter Sellers), Adapted Screenplay

DR. TERROR'S HOUSE OF HORRORS

1965, 98 mins, UK ⓥ ▭
D: Freddie Francis **A:** Peter Cushing, Christopher Lee, Roy Castle, Donald Sutherland, Neil McCallum (Amicus)

Five short horror episodes, thinly linked, offer audiences several mild shudders and quite a lot of amusement. Even though occasional giggles set in, the cast sensibly plays it straight.

DRUGSTORE COWBOY

1989, 100 mins, US ⓥ ⊙
D: Gus Van Sant **A:** Matt Dillon, Kelly Lynch, James Le Gros, Heather Graham, James Remar, William Burroughs (Avenue)

No previous drug-themed film has the honesty or originality of Gus Van Sant's drama. Pic addresses the fact that people take drugs because they *enjoy them*. Set in Portland, OR, in the early 1970s, film tells of one self-confessed and completely unrepentant "drug fiend" (his own description), Bob Hughes (Matt Dillon). He robs drugstores, not for money—for drugs.

DRUM, THE

1938, 101 mins, UK ⓥ ⊙
D: Zoltan Korda **A:** Sabu, Raymond Massey, Roger Livesey, Valerie Hobson, Francis L. Sullivan (London)

An excellent machine-made suspense tale. Entire action is laid in the tribal territory of the northwest frontier of India. An elderly khan is anxious for British protection to ensure his throne for his son, Prince Axim (Sabu). Ruler's brother is fanatically anti-British, kills the old man, and the plot involves the attempt to do away with the young prince.

DRUM

1976, 100 mins, US ⓥ
Dir Steve Carver **A:** Warren Oates, Isela Vega, Ken Norton, Pam Grier, Yaphet Kotto (De Laurentiis)

Drum is a grubby follow-up to *Mandingo* [1975] that invites its own derisive audience laughter. Ham acting like you wouldn't believe, coupled with non-direction by Steve Carver and a correspondence-school script by Norman Wexler, add up to cinematic trash.

DRUM BEAT

1954, 107 mins, US ⓥ ▭
D: Delmer Daves **A:** Alan Ladd, Audrey Dalton, Marisa Pavan, Robert Keith, Rodolfo Acosta, Charles Bronson (Warner/Jaguar)

The Modoc Indian uprising on the California-Oregon border in 1869 is the basis for this Alan Ladd outdoor action starrer. Ladd is seen as a frontiersman commissioned by President Grant to negotiate a peace with the rebelling Modocs led by Captain Jack, renegade redskin forcefully played by Charles Bronson. The peace is to be effected without force of arms, which presents two-gun Ladd with quite a problem.

DRUMS
See: The Drum

DRUMS ACROSS THE RIVER
1954, 77 mins, US ▭
D: Nathan Juran A: Audie Murphy, Walter Brennan, Lyle Bettger, Lisa Gaye, Hugh O'Brian, Mara Corday (Universal)

Plenty of rough-and-ready action keeps this regulation western rolling over its course. The script has Lyle Bettger trying to open up the Ute territory and its gold deposits, closed to the whites by treaty, on one hand, and, on the other, scheming to rob the stage of a gold shipment and lay the blame at the doorstep of Audie Murphy and his dad (Walter Brennan).

DRUMS ALONG THE MOHAWK
1939, 100 mins, US Ⓥ ⊙
D: John Ford A: Claudette Colbert, Henry Fonda, Edna May Oliver, Arthur Shields, Ward Bond, John Carradine (20th Century-Fox)

Having great sweep and colorful backgrounding, with the photography unusually good, the picture is an outdoor spectacle that highly pleases the eye. The story deals with farming pioneers of the Mohawk Valley at the time of the Revolutionary War, with Indian terror and English intrigue, plus hardship, testing the stamina of the colonists. Romance of Henry Fonda and Claudette Colbert, who have married and are forging ahead to new frontiers, has pull.

1939: Nomination: Best Supp. Actress (Edna May Oliver)

DRUNKEN MASTER
See: Tsun Kun

DRUNK MONKEY IN THE TIGER'S EYES
See: Tsui Kuno

DR. WHO AND THE DALEKS
1965, 83 mins, UK Ⓥ ▭
D: Gordon Flemyng A: Peter Cushing, Roy Castle, Jennie Linden, Roberta Tovey, Barrie Ingham (Aaru)

Absentminded professor Dr. Who (Peter Cushing) has invented Tardis, a *Time And Relative Dimension In Space* machine, capable of lugging people to other worlds, in other eras. By accident, the prof, his granddaughters (Jennie Linden and Roberta Tovey), and Linden's boyfriend (Roy Castle) land on a huge, petrified planet ravaged by radiation and the quartet finds themselves in a struggle between the Daleks and the Thals.

DRY WHITE SEASON, A
1989, 97 mins, US Ⓥ ⊙
D: Euzhan Palcy A: Donald Sutherland, Winston Ntshona, Zakes Mokae, Jurgen Prochnow, Susan Sarandon, Marlon Brando (M-G-M)

A wrenching picture about South Africa that makes no compromises with feel-good entertainment values, A Dry White Season displays riveting performances and visceral style. Filmmaker Euzhan Palcy—who is black—never tempers her outrage. Set in 1976, the film moves quickly to a searing sequence in which a demonstration by black schoolchildren of Soweto is broken up with gratuitous lethal force. Naive prep-school teacher Ben du Toit (Donald Sutherland) is a basically decent man who comes to discover what he's always closed his eyes to: South African "justice and law could be described as distant cousins not on speaking terms." Those words are spoken by Ian McKenzie (Marlon Brando), rising with a world-weary magnificence to the role of a prominent human-rights attorney whose idealism has been battered into resignation.

1989: Nomination: Best Supp. Actor (Marlon Brando)

D3: THE MIGHTY DUCKS
1996, 104 mins, US Ⓥ ⊙
D: Robert Lieberman A: Emilio Estevez, Jeffrey Nordling, Joshua Jackson, David Selby, Heidi Kling, Joss Ackland (Walt Disney)

Never fear, the teen hockey sensations aren't skating on thin ice in *D3: The Mighty Ducks*. This amazingly resilient film franchise continues to be entertaining in a shamelessly manipulative way. The Ducks' achievement as international junior champs has landed them scholarships to a ritzy private school. But coach Gordon Bombay (Emilio Estevez) has passed the baton to Ted Orion (Jeffrey Nordling), a martinet, and Charlie (Joshua Jackson) has been stripped of the position of captain.

When they start losing games and the academy plans to revoke their scholarships, lawyer Bombay takes the case and reminds the school authorities about what's right and proper.

D2: THE MIGHTY DUCKS
1994, 106 mins, US ⓥ ⊙
D: Sam Weisman **A:** Emilio Estevez, Kathryn Erbe, Michael Tucker, Jan Rubes, Carsten Norgaard (Walt Disney)

Even disregarding its credibility problems, *D2* is a pretty sorry follow-up to a picture that spawned a National Hockey League franchise and enchanted the box office to the tune of $50 million. With his ongoing attempt to play in the pros again stymied by injury, Gordo (Emilio Estevez) is tipped as the ideal hockeymeister for the upcoming Junior Goodwill Games (winter edition). All he has to do is round up his old Ducks and add some new kids. But Team USA isn't really a squad, it's a collection of minorities and social causes. By the final face-off, these and other problems will be resolved.

DU BARRY WAS A LADY
1943, 96 mins, US ⓥ
D: Roy Del Ruth **A:** Red Skelton, Lucille Ball, Gene Kelly, Virginia O'Brien, Zero Mostel, Rags Ragland (M-G-M)

In adapting the script for celluloid, the studio has taken Red Skelton out of the men's room and put him in the coatroom. Otherwise it follows the general outlines of the original 1939 Broadway show: the club caddy falls for the top warbler at the spot (Lucille Ball). With the weak plot and weaker dialogue, Skelton has a tough time living up to his rep as a funnyman. Ball does a bit better, while Kelly, whose forte is terping, suffers from the histrionic and singing demands of his role and lack of opportunity to make with the feet.

DUCHESS AND THE DIRTWATER FOX, THE
1976, 104 mins, US ⓥ ▭
D: Melvin Frank **A:** George Segal, Goldie Hawn, Roy Jenson, Thayer David (20th Century-Fox)

A generally pleasant and amiable period western comedy starring George Segal as a fumbling gambler and Goldie Hawn as a singing-dancing frontier chick. Pair get involved with Roy Jenson's robber gang, Thayer David's group of Mormons, a Jewish wedding, some good gags here, some forced humor there.

DUCK SOUP
1933, 70 mins, US ⓥ ⊙
D: Leo McCarey **A:** Groucho Marx, Chico Marx, Harpo Marx, Zeppo Marx, Margaret Dumont, Louis Calhern (Paramount)

In place of the constant punning and dame chasing, *Duck Soup* has the Marxes madcapping through such bits as the old Schwartz Bros mirror routine, so well done in the hands of Groucho, Harpo, and Chico that it gathers a new and hilarious comedy momentum. Story is a mythical-kingdom burlesque that could easily have been written by a six-year-old with dust in his eyes, but it isn't so much the story as what goes with and within it. Groucho is the prime minister. For his customary dowager foil he has the high, wide, and handsome Margaret Dumont, making it perfect for him. Chico and Harpo omit their musical specialties. Zeppo is simply Zeppo.

DUCK, YOU SUCKER
See: A Fistful of Dynamite

DUDES
1987, 90 mins, US ⓥ ⊙
D: Penelope Spheeris **A:** Jon Cryer, Daniel Roebuck, Flea, Lee Ving, Catherine Mary Stewart (Vista)

Tells the story of three punked-out New Yorkers who set out for Hollywood and get attacked while camping out in Big Sky country. The humor, when intentional, is slapstick. The dialogue is hopelessly adolescent, the music incredibly loud, and the plot is dependent on a bizarre sequence of coincidences.

DUDLEY DO-RIGHT
1999, 77 mins, US ⓥ ⊙
D: Hugh Wilson **A:** Brendan Fraser, Sarah Jessica Parker, Alfred Molina, Eric Idle, Robert Prosky, Alex Rocco (David-Singer-Harris/Universal)

Dudley Do-Right does right by showcasing Brendan Fraser in the title role. Hunky actor is a dim but dashing Royal Canadian Mountie who always gets his man (with the aid of his considerably brighter horse). Dudley keeps the peace in the Canadian Rockies community of Semi-Happy Valley. But he is seriously outmatched in a duel of wits with the wicked Snidely Whiplash (Alfred Molina), who salts the local streams with stolen bullion, setting off a gold rush and transforming the valley into a garish theme park. Dudley isn't so easily beguiled, but Nell

Fenwick (Sarah Jessica Parker), Dudley's childhood sweetheart, warms to Whiplash. Fraser, with his near-beautific smile, exudes an air of blissfully naive sweetness without seeming cloyingly fey. Molina exuberantly devours the scenery as Whiplash.

DUEL
1971, 74 mins, US ⊗ ⊙
D: Steven Spielberg **A:** Dennis Weaver (Universal)

Dennis Weaver plays a salesman on his way to an appointment. He drives along a narrow highway located in a sparsely settled western locale. Along the way he passes an enormous oil-tanker rig, and later he passes it again. From then on the picture is all chase with the trucker alternately playing dangerous games with Weaver and then actually seeming to want to kill him. A clear case of absolute power corrupting absolutely. Neither Weaver nor the audience ever gets to see the face of the driver (indeed, he has no credit listing), beyond one view of his lower legs and feet and one of his hands waving Weaver on. One intrusive note is the necessity for a good deal of inner dialogue voiced over the action to indicate Weaver's feelings. [Version reviewed is the original 74-minute telemovie.]

DUEL AT DIABLO
1966, 105 mins, US ⊗
D: Ralph Nelson **A:** James Garner, Sidney Poitier, Bibi Andersson, Dennis Weaver, Bill Travers, William Redfield (United Artists)

Duel at Diablo packs enough fast action in its cavalry-Indians narrative to satisfy the most avid follower of this type of entertainment. Screenplay stars James Garner as a scout and Sidney Poitier as a former trooper who now makes his living breaking in horses for the service. Rivaling them in interest and importance, however, is Bill Travers, a cavalry lieutenant who heads the column of raw recruits to a distant fort and is attacked en route by the Apaches.

DUEL IN THE SUN
1946, 134 mins, US ⊗ ⊙
D: King Vidor **A:** Jennifer Jones, Gregory Peck, Joseph Cotten, Lionel Barrymore, Lillian Gish, Walter Huston (Selznick)

Raw, sex-laden, western pulp fiction. Plot concerns a half-breed girl who goes to live at the ranch of a Texas cattle baron. The baron's two sons fall for her, but it is the unrestrained younger one who captures her emotions. So strong is physical desire that he murders one man who wants to marry her and tries to kill the brother. Jones as the half-breed proves herself extremely capable in quieter sequences but is overly meller in others. Same is true of Peck as the virile younger Texan. Contrasting is Joseph Cotten as the older son. Role in his hands is believable and never overdrawn.
1946: Nominations: Best Actress (Jennifer Jones), Supp. Actress (Lillian Gish)

DUELLISTS, THE
1977, 95 mins, UK ⊗ ⊙
D: Ridley Scott **A:** Keith Carradine, Harvey Keitel, Cristina Raines, Edward Fox, Robert Stephens, Albert Finney (Enigma)

The Napoleonic Wars are behind the stubborn sword slashing and then pistol duels of two men caught up in their own personal vendetta. Keitel is jaunty and menancing and Carradine more determined and a bit troubled but also caught up in his strange need to prove his honor.

DUET FOR ONE
1986, 107 mins, US ⊗
D: Andrei Konchalovsky **A:** Julie Andrews, Alan Bates, Max von Sydow, Rupert Everett, Margaret Courtenay, Cathryn Harrison (Cannon)

The story of a world-class violinist who contracts multiple sclerosis and is forced to abandon her career, as long as Duet for One stays personal and specific it is a moving portrait of a life in turmoil. Film is full of lovely musical interludes, both in concert and practice, and Julie Andrews actually looks credible stroking her violin. As the philandering husband, Bates is a complex and restless soul, whose vulnerability and physical deterioration bring an added and welcome dimension to the film.

DUFFY
1968, 101 mins, UK
D: Robert Parrish **A:** James Coburn, James Mason, James Fox, Susannah York, John Alderton (Columbia)

Duffy is the story of two alienated sons stealing from their wealthy father. Weak writing and heavy-handed direction by Robert Parrish, eliciting only tepid performances, combine to snuff out much interest before the genuinely perky climax. James Mason is a cold, calculating industrialist, loathed heartily by his sons, James Fox (who needs Dad's money to pay for his hedonistic excesses) and John Alderton (who simply needs someone to rescue him from stupid blunders).

DUKE WORE JEANS, THE
1958, 90 mins, UK
D: Gerald Thomas A: Tommy Steele, June Laverick, Michael Medwin, Alan Wheatley, Eric Pohlmann (Insignia)

Tommy Steele emerges as a likable personality with acting potential. The lissome yarn has Steele playing a dual role. He is a young aristocrat who wants to evade wooing the princess of a wealthy oil monarchy mainly because he already is secretly married. When he meets a young, brash Cockney who is his exact double, he arranges for him to take his place. Opportunities are provided for Steele to sing several numbers.

DUMB AND DUMBER
1994, 106 mins, US ⓥ ⊙
D: Peter Farrelly A: Jim Carrey, Jeff Daniels, Lauren Holly, Teri Garr (MPCA)

There's not a lot of brain work involved in *Dumb and Dumber*, a flat-out celebration of stupidity, bodily functions, and pratfalls. Yet the wholeheartedness of this descent into crude and rude humor is so good-natured and precise that it's hard not to take a guilty pleasure in the exercise. Harry Dunne (Jeff Daniels) is a rather inept dog groomer. Lloyd Christmas (Jim Carrey) is a limo driver who's saving to open a worm-supply warehouse. When Mary Swanson (Lauren Holly) enters Lloyd's limo for a ride to the airport, his heart flies out the sunroof. As he pulls away, he notices that his charge has left her briefcase right in the middle of the terminal. Ever gallant, he retrieves it, but not quite in time to get it aboard Mary's flight to Aspen. It doesn't take a genius to figure where the story is going.

DUMBO
1941, 64 mins, US ⓥ ⊙
D: Ben Sharpsteen (Walt Disney)

Walt Disney returns in *Dumbo* to the formula that accounted for his original success—simple animal characterization. There's a pleasant little story, plenty of pathos mixed with the large doses of humor, a number of appealing new animal characters, lots of good music, and the usual Disney skillfulness in technique. Dumbo is a little elephant who is jeered at because of his big ears. But he is shown how to make use of his ears, they enable him to fly, and his handicap thereby becomes his greatest asset.

1941: Best Scoring of a Musical Picture
Nomination: Best Song ("Baby Mine")

DUNE
1984, 140 mins, US ⓥ ⊙ ▭
D: David Lynch A: Francesca Annis, Brad Dourif, Kyle MacLachlan, Sian Phillips, Sting, Max von Sydow (De Laurentiis)

Dune is a huge, hollow, imaginative, and cold sci-fi epic. Visually unique and teeming with incident, David Lynch's film holds the interest due to its abundant surface attractions. Set in the year 10,991, *Dune* is the story of the coming to power of a warrior savior and how he leads the lowly inhabitants of the Dune planet to victory over an evil emperor and his minions. Francesca Annis and Jurgen Prochnow make an outstandingly attractive royal couple, Sian Phillips has some mesmerizing moments as a powerful witch, Brad Dourif is effectively loony, and best of all is Kenneth McMillan, whose face is covered with grotesque growths and who floats around like the Blue Meanie come to life.

1984: Nomination: Best Sound

DUNKIRK
1958, 135 mins, UK
D: Leslie Norman A: John Mills, Bernard Lee, Richard Attenborough, Robert Urquhart, Maxine Audley (Ealing)

The story of a defeat which, miraculously, blossomed into ultimate victory because it stiffened Britain's resolve and solidarity, *Dunkirk* is a splendid near-documentary which just fails to reach magnificence. Director Leslie Norman focuses his film through the eyes of three men. John Mills, a spry Cockney corporal; Bernard Lee, a newspaper correspondent; Richard Attenborough, a civilian having an easy time. On the whole, it is an absorbing rather than an emotion-stirring film.

DUNSTON CHECKS IN
1996, 88 mins, US ⓥ
D: Ken Kwapis A: Jason Alexander, Faye Dunaway, Eric Lloyd, Rupert Everett (20th Century-Fox)

A first-class, stylish farce with a brisk pace and cool wit. Robert Grant (Jason Alexander) manages the upscale Majestic Hotel. His two boys (young Eric Lloyd, teenager Graham Sack) look upon the venerable hostelry as their private playground.

They've been warned to cool the high jinks due to the impending visit of the capricious owner (Faye Dunaway). An agent of the prestigious *Le Monde* guide is expected. He'll be traveling incognito, but the Majestic stands to be the first US hotel to earn a six-star rating. A new guest (Rupert Everett) is mistaken for the discreet inspector. He's scouting the terrain for security breaches that will allow him to practice his real vocation—thievery. He's abetted by a dexterous simian named Dunston (Sam), who's adept at second-story work.

DU RIFIFI CHEZ LES HOMMES (RIFIFI)
1955, 120 mins, France ⊙
D: Jules Dassin **A:** Jean Servais, Carl Mohner, Robert Manuel, Magali Noel (Indus/Prima/Pathe)

It took an experienced US director, Jules Dassin, who had lived in France some years, to give the French gangster pic the proper tension, mounting, and treatment. Just out of jail, the hero (Jean Servais) finds his wife living with somebody else and it prompts him to return to his old racket. A big heist of a jewelry store is planned. Then there is one brilliant bit of cinema, 30 minutes of complete silence as the gang cuts its way into the shop and carries out its mission. Dassin gives this a sharp treatment and does not neglect the Paris streets and atmosphere.

DUST DEVIL
THE FINAL CUT
1993, 108 mins, UK/US ⊛ ⊙
D: Richard Stanley **A:** Robert Burke, Chelsea Field, Zakes Mokae, John Matshikiza (Palace/Miramax)

Overflowing with ideas, visual invention, and genre references but saddled by a weak, unfocused script, *Dust Devil* is a brilliant mess. Mystical African-set slasher movie is the second feature of pop promo alum Richard Stanley. The opening 45 minutes are a tour de force of elaborate crosscutting and sustained tension as three characters compete for attention. First is a taciturn Yank (Robert Burke) hitching across country, murdering and mutilating strangers and collecting their fingers in a box. Second is black cop Ben (Zakes Mokae). Third is Wendy (Chelsea Field), a South African who walks out on her boring hubby (Rufus Swart). Story slides into focus halfway through as the trio's destinies crisscross.

DUTCH
(UK/AUSTRALIA: DRIVING ME CRAZY)
1991, 105 mins, US ⊛ ⊙
D: Peter Faiman **A:** Ed O'Neill, Ethan Randall, JoBeth Williams, Christopher McDonald (20th Century-Fox)

Writer-producer John Hughes lays in some oft-used parts, from the family holiday gathering to the travails of incompatible travelers. In this case, the focus is on Ed O'Neill as Dutch, a salt-of-the-earth guy who's volunteered to pick up his girlfriend's snotty kid, Doyle (Ethan Randall), at an elite boarding school and bring him home for Thanksgiving. Little does Dutch know what he's in for. The boy's hateful behavior is so trying that this two-character journey—even with its attendant adventures with fireworks, hookers, tacky motels, and homeless shelters—isn't all that enticing.

DUTCHMAN
1967, 55 mins, UK
D: Anthony Harvey **A:** Shirley Knight, Al Freeman. Jr. (Persson)

Dutchman is a literal filming of Le Roi Jones's 1964 off-Broadway play, pitting a white slut against a middle-class Negro youth who is, in turn, seduced, disgraced, and killed. Excellent direction and performances are enhanced by realistically grim production values. Knight, a redneck Jezebel if there ever was one, is outstanding as she deliberately debases Freeman, dragging him down from insecure middle-class status to that of an embittered, violent youth.

DYING YOUNG
1991, 105 mins, US ⊛ ⊙
D: Joel Schumacher **A:** Julia Roberts, Campbell Scott, Vincent D'Onofrio, Colleen Dewhurst, David Selby, Ellen Burstyn (20th Century-Fox/Fogwood)

In this rather thin and maudlin weeper, Campbell Scott plays an immensely wealthy young man who at 28 has been battling leukemia for 10 years. He places an ad for an attractive young lady to nurse him through the bouts of violent illness that accompany chemotherapy. Enter Roberts, who in the interest of dramatic contrast is painted as a badly dressed, uneducated street-smart type from blue-collar Oakland. For the lonely, intellectual Victor, she's raw material to be shaped in his image. Pic plays like a sentiment-soaked escapist fantasy for the bed-and-breakfast set.

DYNAMITE
1929, 128 mins, US
D: Cecil B. DeMille **A:** Conrad Nagel, Kay Johnson, Charles Bickford, Julia Faye (M-G-M)

Society picture heavily seasoned with dramatic hoke. Elaborate boudoir, bath, wild stew party, rakish Mercedes, fantastic sport carnival—they're all here, and always in the background the shadow of the People as expressed, in this instance, by a miner, whom the spoiled society bud has wed in prison on the eve of execution. All to comply with a will, leaving her millions, in order that she may buy another woman's husband. It's DeMille's first talker and Kay Johnson's debut in pictures.

E

EACH DAWN I DIE
1939, 92 mins, US ⓥ
D: William Keighley **A:** James Cagney, George Raft, Jane Bryan, George Bancroft, Victor Jory (Warner)

Cagney is kept in typical toughie surroundings, framed by unscrupulous politicians because he has uncovered their crooked work for his newspaper. Cagney is pictured as developing into a hardened prisoner. Fans will be pleasantly surprised at his restrained, skillful performance. Raft is a plausible, gripping underworld bigtimer.

EAGLE, THE
1925, 72 mins, US ⓥ ⊙ ⊗
D: Clarence Brown **A:** Rudolph Valentino, Vilma Banky, Louise Dresser, Albert Conti (Art Finance/United Artists)

Rudolph Valentino as a Russian Robin Hood of more modern times. In *The Eagle*, he really goes out and does some "he-man" stuff. Louise Dresser as the Czarina handles herself superbly. Vilma Banky makes a most charming heroine.

EAGLE AND THE HAWK, THE
1933, 74 mins, US
D: Stuart Walker, Mitchell Leisen **A:** Fredric March, Cary Grant, Jack Oakie, Carole Lombard, Guy Standing (Paramount)

Strictly a formula story of the Royal Flying Corps, the same old yarn of the man who gets fed up with the uselessness of war. He has lost observer after observer without serious injury to himself, and it breaks his morale. Yarn is adroitly told in both dialogue and action, Jack Oakie contributing some sorely needed comedy touches. March offers a finely sensitive study, acting with force, but entirely without bombast.

EAGLE HAS LANDED, THE
1977, 134 mins, UK ⓥ ⊡
D: John Sturges **A:** Michael Caine, Donald Sutherland, Robert Duvall, Jenny Agutter, Donald Pleasence, Anthony Quayle (ITC/Assoc. General)

In November 1943 Winston Churchill is due to spend a weekend at a country house in Norfolk—and the Germans propose to kidnap him there. Most perform-

ances are first-rate, with Caine thoroughly convincing as the Nazi commander. Pleasence gives a standout lifelike interpretation of Himmler.

EAGLE'S WING
1979, 104 mins, UK ⓥ ⊡
D: Anthony Harvey **A:** Martin Sheen, Sam Waterston, Harvey Keitel, Stephane Audran, Caroline Langrishe, John Castle (Rank)

Claiming to evoke "the West, the way it really was, before the myths were born," British director Anthony Harvey's poised, loving linger in the 1830s badlands of New Mexico is primarily an art film. Ostensibly a tussle for possession of a uniquely fleet white horse, the distinctly allegorical plot pits Martin Sheen as a city-bred, novice trapper against a no-longer-so-young Indian brave, played with remarkable success by Sam Waterston.

EARTH
See: Zimlya

EARTH GIRLS ARE EASY
1988, 100 mins, UK/US ⓥ ⊙ ⊡
D: Julien Temple **A:** Geena Davis, Jeff Goldblum, Julie Brown, Jim Carrey, Damon Wayans (Kestrel/Odyssey)

Ditzy, glitzy fish-out-of-water farce. Julie (Geena Davis) works as a manicurist in high-tech beauty salon operated by Candy (Julie Brown) a val-queen supreme who likes good times and good sex. Meanwhile, three aliens who look like tie-dyed werewolves are wandering around our solar system going bonkers with randiness. When their spacecraft lands in Julie's swimming pool, Julie brings this gruesome threesome to Candy's beauty parlor for a complete "makeover." They emerge as three hairless hunky dudes: the captain, Jeff Goldblum, and two flaked-out crewmen, Jim Carrey and Damon Wayans. The two val-gals and their alien "dates" take off for a weekend of L.A. nightlife.

EARTHQUAKE
1974, 122 mins, US ⓥ ⊙ ⊡
D: Mark Robson **A:** Charlton Heston, Ava Gardner, George Kennedy, Lorne Greene, Genevieve Bujold, Richard Roundtree (Universal)

An excellent dramatic exploitation extravaganza, combining brilliant special effects with a multicharacter plotline that is surprisingly above average for this type film. Large cast is headed by Charlton Heston, who comes off better than usual because he is not Superman, instead just one of the gang.

1974: Best Sound, Special Visual Effects
Nominations: Best Cinematography, Art Direction, Editing

EARTH VS. THE FLYING SAUCERS
1956, 82 mins, US ⓥ
D: Fred F. Sears **A:** Hugh Marlowe, Joan Taylor, Donald Curtis, Morris Ankrum (Columbia)

This exploitation programmer does a satisfactory job of entertaining in the science-fiction class. The technical effects created by Ray Harryhausen come off excellently, adding the required out-of-this-world visual touch to the screenplay.

EASTER PARADE
1948, 102 mins, US ⓥ ⊙
D: Charles Walters **A:** Judy Garland, Fred Astaire, Peter Lawford, Ann Miller, Jules Munshin (M-G-M)

Easter Parade is a musical with old and new Irving Berlin tunes and standout dance numbers. Astaire's standout solo is the elaborate production piece "Stepping Out with My Baby," during which he does a slow-motion dance in front of a large chorus terping in regular time. High point of comedy is reached when Astaire and Garland team for vocals and footwork on "A Couple of Swells."
1948: Best Score for a Musical Picture

EAST LYNNE
1931, 102 mins, US
D: Frank Lloyd **A:** Ann Harding, Clive Brook, Conrad Nagel, Cecilia Loftus, Beryl Mercer, O. P. Heggie (Fox)

An excellent piece of work in taking a legendary meller play and transforming it into a screen drama of strength and charm. The beauty of the cast is that they make the characters believable. All are from the stage, while the dialogue is such that it avoids petty pleasantries or overly dramatic orations. Joseph Urban's settings are sumptuous and tasteful, evidently having been given a free hand in creating the interior of a big country home. Besides which there is an elaborate Viennese café interlude, as also a certain amount of footage given over to the Franco-Prussian War and the bombarding of Paris.
1930/31: Nomination: Best Picture

EAST OF EDEN
1955, 114 mins, US ⓥ ⊙ ▭
D: Elia Kazan **A:** Julie Harris, James Dean, Raymond Massey, Burl Ives, Jo Van Fleet, Albert Dekker (Warner)

Powerfully somber dramatics have been captured from the pages of John Steinbeck's *East of Eden* and put on film by Elia Kazan. James Dean seems required to play his lead character as though he were straight out of a Marlon Brando mold, although he has a basic appeal that manages to get through to the viewer. Only the latter part of the Steinbeck novel is used in the screenplay, which picks up the principals at the time the twin sons of a lettuce farmer are graduating in the 1917 class at high school.
1955: Best Supp. Actress (Jo Van Fleet)
Nominations: Best Director, Actor (James Dean), Screenplay

EAST SIDE, WEST SIDE
1949, 104 mins, US ⓥ
D: Mervyn LeRoy **A:** Barbara Stanwyck, James Mason, Van Heflin, Ava Gardner, Cyd Charisse (M-G-M)

The yarn is one of husbandly infidelity in a New York society setting with all the trimmings. James Mason plays the cad mate who finds other women irresistible in the same way that an alcoholic can't keep from reaching for a bottle. Barbara Stanwyck is the wife done wrong, who loves him so much she can't give him up despite his widely advertised philandering. Performances throughout are convincing, with Ava Gardner probably grabbing top honors as the willful and attractive vixen.

EASY COME, EASY GO
1967, 95 mins, US ⓥ
D: John Rich **A:** Elvis Presley, Dodie Marshall, Pat Priest, Pat Harrington, Skip Ward (Paramount)

Easy Come, Easy Go stars Elvis Presley as an underwater demolitions expert who finds lost treasure. Good balance of script and songs, plus generally amusing performances by a competent, well-directed cast, add up to diverting entertainment.

EASY LIVING
1937, 88 mins, US
D: Mitchell Leisen **A:** Jean Arthur, Edward Arnold, Ray Milland, Luis Alberni, Mary Nash, Franklin Pangborn (Paramount)

Slapstick farce, incredible and without rhyme or reason, is Paramount's contribution to the cycle of goofy pictures that started with *My Man Godfrey* (1936). This one is a poor imitation, lacking spontaneity and cleverness. Screenplay by Preston Sturges is a trivia of nonsense. Mitchell

Leisen, who directs, tries to overcome the story faults with elaborate settings and Keystone gags. When the food throwing ends there is nothing left for the players to do. All semblance of probability has vanished.

EASY RIDER
1969, 94 mins, US Ⓥ ⊙
D: Dennis Hopper A: Peter Fonda, Dennis Hopper, Jack Nicholson, Robert Walker, Luana Anders, Karen Black (Pando/Raybert)

Film deals with two dropouts on a long trip from Los Angeles to New Orleans's Mardi Gras, a search for freedom thwarted by that streak of ingrained, bigoted violence in the US and their own hang-ups. Fonda exudes a groping moral force and Hopper is agitated, touching, and responsive as the sidekick, hoping for that so-called freedom their stake should give them. Jack Nicholson is excellent as an articulate alcoholic who fills in the smothered needs in a verbal way that the others feel but cannot express.
1969: Nominations: Best Supp. Actor (Jack Nicholson), Original Story & Screenplay

EASY STREET
1917, 29 mins, US ⊗
D: Charles Chaplin A: Charles Chaplin, Edna Purviance, Eric Campbell (Mutual)

Charlie Chaplin portrays a policeman assigned to "Easy Street," a narrow thoroughfare which, from the daily routine, must be the place where all the roughnecks are trained. Leader of them is Eric Campbell, whose burly bulk aptly lends itself to Chaplin's scenario. To awe the new cop, Eric bends a lamppost in half, but in that endeavor Charlie leaps on his back, shoves Eric's head through the lamp, and turns on the gas. Thus is the king of the roughs arrested. But he does not stay long in the station house, simply breaking his handcuffs and starting in search of the new copper. The roughhouse that results is pretty nearly top-class.

EASY TO LOVE
1953, 96 mins, US Ⓥ
D: Charles Walters A: Esther Williams, Van Johnson, Tony Martin, John Bromfield (M-G-M)

Metro's special knack for turning out big, splashy musicals on a lavish scale that so dazzle the eye that the story becomes negligible is exemplified in Easy to Love. The Cypress Gardens, FL, backgrounds contribute some highly scenic footage. With all the swimming, waterskiing, singing, and plush mountains maybe there just wasn't room for plot. Esther Williams, shapely and vivacious as the much-sought-after aquatic star whose only aim in life is to "hook" Van Johnson, delivers her usual cheerful performance. Van Johnson is easygoing gent who manages a good comedy line when handed one. Tony Martin does a sock stint and delivers a brace of songs in top-notch fashion. Musical numbers, created and directed by Busby Berkeley, move easily and look attractive. There are plenty of lively tunes to help brighten the proceedings.

EASY TO WED
1946, 109 mins, US
D: Edward Buzzell A: Van Johnson, Esther Williams, Lucille Ball, Keenan Wynn, Cecil Kellaway, June Lockhart (M-G-M)

Metro refurbishes the old Libeled Lady script with brilliant color, plenty of fun, and assured box-office stars. It all adds up to top-notch entertainment. Accent is on comedy with an occasional song in the new treatment. Plot concerns a newspaper faced with a libel suit by a rich playgirl and how the sheet brings in a great lover to compromise the gal so suit can be forgotten. Van Johnson as the great lover and Esther Williams, the libeled lady, team romantically and acquit themselves effectively in the plot development. Lucille Ball is a standout on the comedy end.

EAT A BOWL OF TEA
1989, 102 mins, US Ⓥ ⊙
D: Wayne Wang A: Cora Miao, Russell Wong, Victor Wong, Lee Sau-kee, Eric Tsang (American Playhouse)

Pic starts off with Wah Gay (Victor Wong) deciding to send his soldier son Ben Loy (Russel Wong) to China to marry the daughter of his best friend. Fortunately, it's love at first sight between Ben and Mei Oi (Cora Miao), and they marry and return to the States. Unfortunately, poor Ben is impotent, causing grief to his wife as well as to the couple's fathers, who eagerly want to become grandfathers. Enter Ah Song (Eric Tsang), a cheerful, rascally gambler who becomes Mei's secret lover, and who succeeds in getting her pregnant. Wah Gay tries to restore family honor by attacking Ah Song with a meat ax. Typically, the aforementioned scene is played for laughs, and indeed is the comic high point of a generally charming and amusing film.

EAT DRINK MAN WOMAN
See: Yinshi Nannu

EATING
1990, 110 mins, US
D: Henry Jaglom **A:** Lisa Richards, Mary Crosby, Gwen Welles, Nelly Alard, Frances Bergen (International Rainbow)

The ladies who lunch—and munch, breakfast, binge, dine, diet, starve, and sample—are delicious in *Eating*, but writer-director Henry Jaglom labors over the stove too long, harming a tasty soufflé. Convening a large collection of diverse friends to celebrate a three-tiered birthday party, Gwen Welles is observing her 40th, Mary Crosby her 30th, and Marlena Giovi her 50th. Gwen Welles stands out as a bitchy, backbiting bulemic.

EATING RAOUL
1982, 83 mins, US Ⓥ
D: Paul Bartel **A:** Paul Bartel, Mary Woronov, Robert Beltran, Susan Salger, Ed Begley Jr., Buck Henry (Bartel)

All poor Paul and Mary Bland want in life is enough money to buy their own restaurant. The couple live in a tacky Hollywood apartment building chock-full of all kinds of crazies. When one of the "low-lifes" tries to rape Mary, Paul kills him. Alas, the victim had all kinds of money and both Paul and Mary soon realize they have a potential answer to their financial worries. They put an ad in a local sex publication and decide to lure new "perverts" to their home. That way they can get the money for their restaurant and help clean up society in one sweeping stroke. The appeal of Paul Bartel's tongue-in-cheek approach is that he manages to remain genuinely funny and successfully tell his perverse story.

ECHO PARK
1985, 92 mins, Austria Ⓥ ⊙
D: Robert Dornhelm **A:** Susan Dey, Tom Hulce, Michael Bowen, Christopher Walker, Shirley Jo Finney, Timothy Carey (Sascha-Wien)

Although lensed on location in the Echo Park section of Los Angeles, this is another of those quite successful views of the States made by talented European directors. Wittily scripted and full of oddball twists from start to finish, *Echo Park* features three hapless people looking for the big break as they share an old-style duplex-apartment house in the run-down area of East Los Angeles. May (Susan Dey) works as a waitress while dreaming of an acting career. August (Michael Bowen), a bodybuilder from Austria, wants to become the second Arnold Schwarzenegger. Friendly pizza delivery boy Jonathan (Tom Hulce) reads books and writes poetry.

ECLIPSE, THE
See: L'Eclisse

L'ECLISSE
(THE ECLIPSE)
1962, 125 mins, Italy/France Ⓥ ⊙
D: Michelangelo Antonioni **A:** Monica Vitti, Alain Delon, Lilla Brignone, Francisco Rabal (Interopa/Cineriz/Paris)

As with all this controversial director's films, *The Eclipse* has the same exasperating pace as well as the same delving at length and in depth into the basic lack of communication between human beings. What results is a series of long silent sequences which are meaningful and powerful to those spectators who, as Antonioni has often said, are both willing and able to "work" for their enjoyment. For those who have seen *L'Avventura* and *La Notte*, *The Eclipse* makes an apt wrap-up for a telling trilogy. Vittoria (Monica Vitti) emerges from an unhappy love affair with an intellectual, Riccardo (Francisco Rabal) and almost by accident accepts the down-to-earth courtship of a young stockbroker (Alain Delon). Both fear involvement, and the melancholy finale signals another split.

ECSTASY
See: Extase

ED
1996, 94 mins, US Ⓥ
D: Bill Couturie **A:** Matt LeBlanc, Jayne Brook, Bill Cobbs, Jack Warden, Jay Caputo, Denise Cheshire (Longview/Universal)

Ed serves up a reasonable premise for a comic fantasy kidpic—a chimp good enough to play professional baseball—and has no idea what to do with it. Almost painfully modest in its ambition and accomplishment, this slow-pitch offering might tolerably amuse the under-10 crowd, but will prove borderline intolerable for everyone else. Baseball action is far outweighed by tedious scenes off the diamond. Title character is an Animatronic creation, inhabited by two actors, that seems pretty credible.

EDDIE
1996, 100 mins, US Ⓥ
D: Steve Rash **A:** Whoopi Goldberg,

Frank Langella, Dennis Farina, Richard Jenkins, Lisa Ann Walter (Hollywood)

Sports comedies are inherently predictable, but this fantasy seems especially uninspired. Whoopi Goldberg's wholehearted and likable performance, while occasionally funny, is simply not enough to lead this standard-issue programmer to victory. Goldberg plays a limousine driver and vocal basketball buff who—like all New York sports fans—thinks she knows what's best for her team, in this case the ailing New York Knicks. Enter Wild Bill Burgess, a Texas zillionaire and the team's new owner, played by a woefully miscast Frank Langella. Burgess fires his sourpuss veteran coach (Dennis Farina) and replaces him with, you guessed it, Eddie. Worst of all—given the nearly 50 NBA players who appear in the film—there aren't any good basketball scenes to speak of.

EDDIE AND THE CRUISERS
1983, 92 mins, US ⓥ ⊙
D: Martin Davidson A: Tom Berenger, Michael Pare, Joe Pantoliano, Matthew Laurance, Helen Schneider, Ellen Barkin (Aurora)

Eddie and the Cruisers is a mishmash of a film, combining elements of the ongoing nostalgia for rock music of previous decades with an unworkable and laughable mystery plotline. *Eddie* opens in strict *Citizen Kane* fashion as TV news-mag reporter Maggie Foley (Ellen Barkin) is using old clips to pitch her investigative story on the early 1960s rock group Eddie and the Cruisers. Foley interviews the lyricist–keyboard man (Tom Berenger), who is prompted to remember (in frequent flashbacks) those glory days of 1962–63. *Eddie* only comes alive during the flashbacks when John Cafferty's songs provide a showcase for the magnetic screen presences of Michael Pare and Helen Schneider.

EDDIE MACON'S RUN
1983, 95 mins, US ⓥ ⊙
D: Jeff Kanew A: Kirk Douglas, John Schneider, Lee Purcell, Leah Ayres, Lisa Dunsheath, Tom Noonan (Bregman)

Macon is an involving, enjoyable picture. Most of the credit for that, however, goes to Kirk Douglas, who brings interesting nuances to his part as the policeman in pursuit of John Schneider, and Lee Purcell as a bored but influential rich girl who gets more involved than she wants to in helping Schneider elude Douglas. Schneider ably portrays the anguish of a young husband/father wrongly sent to prison and determined to escape to rejoin his family in Mexico.

EDDY DUCHIN STORY, THE
1956, 123 mins, US ⓥ ⊙ ▭
D: George Sidney A: Tyrone Power, Kim Novak, Victoria Shaw, James Whitmore (Columbia)

Biopicturing of the career of "10 Magic Fingers" is not all the sorrow and woe that the story of Eddy Duchin might suggest. Samuel Taylor plays up humor and romance as well as the inherent hardship in his script. Key asset is Tyrone Power in the title role. He's personable and eager as he hits Gotham bent only on tapping out pop and pseudo-classical rhythms on the 88. He looks like he's genuinely thrilled with the splendors of New York and confident that his letter of introduction will land him a job with Leo Reisman's orchestra. The Novak-Power match builds tenderly. Newcomer Victoria Shaw comes across with particular effectiveness. **1956: Nominations:** Best Motion Picture Story, Color Cinematography, Scoring of a Musical Picture, Sound

EDGE, THE
1997, 117 mins, US ⓥ ⊙ ▭
D: Lee Tamahori A: Anthony Hopkins, Alec Baldwin, Elle Macpherson, Harold Perrineau, L. Q. Jones (20th Century-Fox)

Although thin character motivation and some far-fetched plotting strain credulity, for the most part *The Edge* is a tense, pleasurably visceral battle-of-wits thriller played out against a spectacular wilderness background. Billionaire Charles Morse (Anthony Hopkins) accompanies his supermodel trophy wife, Mickey (Elle Macpherson), on a photo shoot in the wilds of Alaska, along with cocky fashion photographer Robert Green (Alec Baldwin) and his assistant Stephen (Harold Perrineau). Robert and Stephen take a plane trip to more remote territory, with Charles along for the ride. The plane crashes, and the three men must formulate a strategy for survival. They manage to survive a bear attack, but Charles has no doubt the bear will track them down. Director Lee Tamahori moves things along at a muscular clip.

EDGE OF DARKNESS
1943, 120 mins, US
D: Lewis Milestone A: Errol Flynn, Ann Sheridan, Walter Huston, Judith Ander-

son, Helmut Dantine, Ruth Gordon (Warner)

The story deals with internal conditions and unrest, and, more important, the ruthlessness of the Nazis. The populace of Trollness in Norway seethe under the yoke of the Germans and finally erupt into a bloody revolt. Errol Flynn and Ann Sheridan provide the proper romantic note, plus the necessary dash as the leaders of the underground. Some of the cast's lesser-knowns eclipse them in dramatic power. Carnovsky, as an aged schoolmaster, is outstanding in a throat-catching scene when he pits his culture and kindliness against the brutish thinking of the Nazi commander, played by Helmut Dantine, who is guilty of most of the film's overacting.

EDGE OF DOOM
1950, 98 mins, US
D: Mark Robson A: Dana Andrews, Farley Granger, Joan Evans, Robert Keith, Mala Powers, Paul Stewart (RKO/Samuel Goldwyn)

A grim, relentless story, considerably offbeat, gives some distinction to *Edge of Doom*. It tells the story of a poverty-stricken boy with a mother fixation, who, after long years of caring for her, tries to give her the funeral he believes she deserves. He receives unsympathetic treatment from the parish priest and, in a rage, kills the father with a crucifix.

EDGE OF THE CITY
1957, 85 mins, US
D: Martin Ritt A: John Cassavetes, Sidney Poitier, Jack Warden, Kathleen Maguire, Ruby Dee (M-G-M)

Based on Robert Alan Arthur's teleplay *A Man Is Ten Feet Tall*, film marks a milestone in the screen presentation of an American Black. The peculiar aspect of *Edge* is that it is not dealing with the African-American problem. The protagonist is a guilt-ridden, psychologically mixed-up white youth, sensitively played by John Cassavetes. He finds employment in a New York railroad yard where he immediately is befriended by a good-natured, philosophical Negro lad (Sidney Poitier). Filmed on location in New York, the film has a real-life flavor.

EDISON, THE MAN
1940, 104 mins, US ⓥ
D: Clarence Brown A: Spencer Tracy, Rita Johnson, Lynne Overman, Charles

Coburn, Gene Lockhart, Henry Travers (M-G-M)

Sequel to *Young Tom Edison* takes up with Edison after he has gone to New York to pursue his vocation as an inventor. Action opens on the Golden Jubilee of Light banquet held in 1929, at which the now aged Edison is guest of honor. As he is being eulogized for his contributions as an inventor, the story goes back to his early manhood, his heartaches, his ambitions, the romance that came into his life, and the drama as well as lighter moments that figured in an amazing career. After Edison has brought forth the incandescent bulb after heroic struggles, the action flashes back to the banquet. Here, Spencer Tracy as an old, but benevolent Edison, makes his speech. It dwells largely on the march that science has made, emphasizing that much that man has created for the benefit of mankind also possesses the ability to turn into monsters.
1940: Nomination: Best Original Story

EDTV
1999, 122 mins, US ⓥ ⊙
D: Ron Howard A: Matthew McConaughey, Jenna Elfman, Woody Harrelson, Sally Kirkland, Martin Landau, Ellen DeGeneres (Universal)

The notion of 15 minutes of fame gets another workout in *EDtv*, a reasonably amusing look at a young man whose life becomes a popular TV show. Ron Howard's film shows how San Fran–based cable docu channel True TV initiates its round-the-clock vérité program. Program director Cynthia Topping (Ellen DeGeneres) settles on amiable doofus Ed Pekurny (Matthew McConaughey), a 31-year-old vid-store clerk. Ed's g.f., Shari (Jenna Elfman), bails on Ed when 71 percent of the public thinks she's a drag. Management engineers a romance for Ed with British sex bomb Jill (Elizabeth Hurley). It's McConaughey's picture to carry, and he manages it well; he contributes a natural zaniness that makes Ed an easy-to-take companion on the big screen and a plausible one for the small one.

EDUCATING RITA
1983, 110 mins, UK ⓥ ⊙
D: Lewis Gilbert A: Michael Caine, Julie Walters, Michael Williams, Maureen Lipman (Rank/Acorn)

Producer-director Lewis Gilbert has done a marvelous job of bringing the charming British play *Educating Rita* to the big screen. Aided greatly by an expert film adaptation by its playwright, Willy Russell, Gilbert has come up with an irresistible story about a lively, lower-class British woman hungering for an education and the rather, staid, degenerating English professor who reluctantly provides her with one. Julie Walters injects Rita with just the right mix of comedy and pathos. Michael Caine is the sadly smart, alcoholic teacher who knows the fundamentals of English literature, but long ago lost the ability to enjoy life the way his uneducated pupil does.

1983: Nominations: Best Actor (Michael Caine), Actress (Julie Walters), Adapted Screenplay

EDWARD, MY SON
1949, 112 mins, US/UK
D: George Cukor **A:** Spencer Tracy, Deborah Kerr, Ian Hunter, Mervyn Johns, Felix Aylmer, Leueen MacGrath (M-G-M)

There is never any doubt that Edward, son of the Boults, is a spoiled child as his parents rise in the social strata. Arnold Boult is the proud father whose conception of love for his offspring is to anticipate his every wish. Into the main theme is delicately woven the estrangement between Arnold and Evelyn Boult. Spencer Tracy as Arnold Boult dominates the screen with a forceful portrayal of the ambitious man who allowed nothing to stand in the way of his determination to reach the top rung of the ladder. Deborah Kerr displays remarkable ability in transforming the character of Evelyn from the demure happy young women to the embittered, drunken, and miserable wife. Ian Hunter gives a warm, understanding study of the family doctor, who is unable to hide his love for Mrs Boult.

EDWARD SCISSORHANDS
1990, 98 mins, US Ⓥ ⊙
D: Tim Burton **A:** Johnny Depp, Winona Ryder, Dianne Wiest, Anthony Michael Hall, Alan Arkin (20th Century-Fox)

Director Tim Burton takes a character as wildly unlikely as a boy whose arms end in pruning shears, and makes him the center of a delightful and delicate comic fable. Johnny Depp plays Edward, who lives in isolation in a gloomy mansion on the hill until a sunny Avon lady (Dianne Wiest) discovers him and takes him into her suburbia home and mothers him like a crippled bird. Gentle and exotic Edward becomes an instant celeb. His wistful and impossible attraction to Kim (Winona Ryder), the Avon lady's teenage daughter,

adds another level of tension. Depp gives a sensitive reading of Edward. Wiest's mother figure's a smash.

1990: Nomination: Best Makeup

EDWARD II
1991, 90 mins, UK Ⓥ
D: Derek Jarman **A:** Steven Waddington, Andrew Tiernan, Tilda Swinton, Nigel Terry, Kevin Collins, Dudley Sutton (Working Title/BBC/British Screen)

Derek Jarman comes up with a provocative and challenging adaptation of Christopher Marlowe's *Edward II*, a bio of Britain's only acknowledged gay monarch, whose preference for his lover over his queen sparked conflict with his barons and, eventually, civil war. Cutting the play to the bone, Jarman fashions the 16th-century drama into a radical attack on antigay prejudices in contempo Brit society. Drama is staged in modern dress, with contemporary police/military uniforms for the forces of repression.

ED WOOD
1994, 124 mins, US Ⓥ ⊙
D: Tim Burton **A:** Johnny Depp, Martin Landau, Sarah Jessica Parker, Patricia Arquette, Vincent D'Onofrio (Touchstone)

Tim Burton pays elaborate tribute to the maverick creative spirit in *Ed Wood*, a fanciful sweet-tempered biopic about the man often described as the worst film director of all time. Always engaging to watch and often dazzling in its imagination and technique, picture is also a bit distended, and lacking in weight at its center. Wood started gaining notoriety as an auteur of the lower depths when his beyond-bad 1950s epics *Glen or Glenda* and *Plan 9 from Outer Space* developed followings in the 1980s. Wood's other claim to fame was that he was an avid transvestite, with a particular taste for angora sweaters. Bela Lugosi (Martin Landau), the old *Dracula* star whom Wood meets by chance in Hollywood, becomes a friend and sort of spiritual mentor. Giving the story its principal weight is the Wood-Lugosi relationship, with Landau's astounding performance as the old Hungarian.

1994: Best Supp. Actor (Martin Landau), Makeup

EFFECT OF GAMMA RAYS ON MAN-IN-THE-MOON MARIGOLDS, THE
1972, 100 mins, US Ⓥ
D: Paul Newman **A:** Joanne Woodward,

Nell Potts, Roberta Wallach, Judith Lowry (20th Century-Fox)

Producer-director Paul Newman has made his finest behind-the-camera film to date in the screen version of Paul Zindel's play. As the slovenly, introverted mother of two young girls, Joanne Woodward brilliantly projects the pitiable character. Alvin Sargent's adaptation provides Woodward with a full complement of the despicable dimensions which make the focal character both a monster and an object of genuine pity.

EGG AND I, THE
1947, 108 mins, US ⓥ ⊙
D: Chester Erskine **A:** Claudette Colbert, Fred MacMurray, Marjorie Main, Percy Kilbride, Louise Allbritton, Richard Long (Universal)

This picturization of Betty MacDonald's bestselling book tampers very little with the load of amusing situations MacDonald gets herself into when her husband snaps her out of a Boston finishing school and takes her off to the modern-day frontier of the Pacific Northwest to embark on chicken farming. Claudette Colbert is appealing but not entirely believable as the city gal who accepts out of wifely love the rugged life husband Fred MacMurray lays out for her. MacMurray runs through his role in his routine, superficial fashion. Percy Kilbride and Marjorie Main, as the Kettles, the Tobacco Road–like neighbors, are high points in the film every time they're on the screen.
1947: Nomination: Best Supp. Actress (Marjorie Main)

EGYPTIAN, THE
1954, 140 mins, US ⓥ ▭
D: Michael Curtiz **A:** Edmund Purdom, Jean Simmons, Victor Mature, Gene Tierney, Michael Wilding, Peter Ustinov (20th Century-Fox)

A strange and unusual story laid against the exotic and yet harshly realistic background of the Egypt of 33 centuries ago, when there was a pharaoh who believed in one god and a physician who glimpsed a great truth and tried to live it. In the title part, Purdom makes the truth-seeking doctor a man with whom the audience can easily identify and sympathize. Jean Simmons is lovely and warm as the tavern maid. Victor Mature, as the soldier who is to become ruler, is a strong asset.
1954: Best Color Cinematography

EIGER SANCTION, THE
1975, 125 mins, US ⓥ ⊙ ▭
D: Clint Eastwood **A:** Clint Eastwood, George Kennedy, Vonetta McGee, Jack Cassidy, Thayer David (Universal/Malpaso)

The Eiger Sanction, based on the novel by Trevanian, focuses on Clint Eastwood, a retired mountain climber and hired assassin, being recalled from retirement for another lethal assignment. Pic takes its title from the leader's euphemism for assassination, to be carried out on Switzerland's Eiger Mountain during an international team's climb. Eastwood, who also directs and according to studio did his own mountain climbing, manages fine suspense.

8 1/2
1963, 140 mins, Italy ⓥ ⊙
D: Federico Fellini **A:** Marcello Mastroianni, Claudia Cardinale, Anouk Aimee, Sandra Milo, Rossella Falk, Barbara Steele (Rizzoli)

Here is the author-director picture par excellence, an exciting, stimulating, monumental creation. Basically, it is the story of a 43-year-old director's crucial visit to a health resort to cure an undetermined illness. At the spa, he is confronted with a series of crises of a personal as well as professional nature. He is about to start a major film production, but totally lacks inspiration for it. Flashbacks to his youth and flash-forwards in the form of daydreams illustrate the director's inner qualms and worries. It is a 140-minute séance on the psychiatrist's couch, in which the author turns himself inside out, confessing his innermost thoughts and problems, and finally reaching his apt conclusions. Marcello Mastroianni is excellent as the middle-aged director, often deliberately bearing an uncanny resemblance to Fellini himself. Nino Rota has penned a haunting score for the picture.
1963: Best Foreign Language Film

EIGHT MEN OUT
1988, 119 mins, US ⓥ ⊙
D: John Sayles **A:** John Cusack, Clifton James, David Strathairn, D. B. Sweeney, John Mahoney, Charlie Sheen (Orion)

Perhaps the saddest chapter in the annals of professional American sports is recounted in absorbing fashion in *Eight Men Out.* Story tells of how the 1919 Chicago White Sox threw the World Series in cahoots with professional gamblers, in what became known as the Black Sox Scandal. The most compelling figures are pitcher

Eddie Cicotte (David Strathairn), a man who feels the twin needs to ensure a financial future for his family and take revenge on his boss, and Buck Weaver (John Cusack), an innocent enthusiast who took no cash for the fix.

8MM
1999, 119 mins, US Ⓥ ⊙ ⊏
D: Joel Schumacher A: Nicolas Cage, Joaquin Phoenix, James Gandolfini, Peter Stormare, Anthony Heald, Chris Bauer (Hofflund-Polone/Columbia)

8MM is a movie that keeps jumping the gate and finally unravels all over the floor. This dark and gratuitously nasty film about a PI checking the source of a supposed ''snuff movie'' raises issues it later junks in favor of mainstream thrills and is toplined by a perf from Nicolas Cage that isn't up to the job. Cage plays Tom Welles, a surveillance specialist hired to discover the identity of a teenage girl seemingly murdered in an 8mm movie. The trail leads to L.A., where Welles meets porn-shop owner Max California (Joaquin Phoenix). Phoenix's louche, quipping performance brings a welcome touch of humor to the picture. Welles gets a break that leads to porno moviemaker Eddie Poole (James Gandolfini) and then to New York S&M specialist Dino Velvet (Peter Stormare). Cage's underwritten part changes from buttoned-down professional to screaming moral avenger in the space of a reel. Phoenix's Max is a severe loss at the two-thirds point from which the picture never recovers.

8 MILLION WAYS TO DIE
1986, 115 mins, US Ⓥ ⊙
D: Hal Ashby A: Jeff Bridges, Rosanna Arquette, Alexandra Paul, Randy Brooks, Andy Garcia (PSO)

What could have been a better film delving into complexities of one tough-but-vulnerable alcoholic sheriff out to bust a cocaine ring, instead ends up an oddly paced work that is sometimes a thriller and sometimes a love story, succeeding at neither. A former L.A. sheriff named Scudder (Jeff Bridges) comes close to death less than a handful of times while trying to dismantle a scummy Latino drug smuggler's empire and at the same time winning his girl (Rosanna Arquette).

8 SECONDS
1994, 104 mins, US Ⓥ ⊙
D: John G. Avildsen A: Luke Perry, Stephen Baldwin, James Rebhorn, Carrie Snodgress (Jersey)

8 Seconds takes a smooth, sappy ride through the life of a great bucking bull rider. Sweet, sentimental, and rose-colored to a fault, this family-oriented biopic has none of the grit, dust, and bruises that virtually define the sport in question. Luke Perry plays Lane Frost, an Oklahoma boy who became world champion bull rider in 1987 but was tragically killed in a rodeo accident two years later. Virtually all the characters in Monte Merrick's paint-by-numbers script are based on real people, which is no doubt partly responsible for the caution and reverence with which the film approaches virtually every scene.

84 CHARING CROSS ROAD
1987, 97 mins, US Ⓥ ⊙
D: David Jones A: Anne Bancroft, Anthony Hopkins, Judi Dench, Jean De Baer, Maurice Denham, Mercedes Ruehl (Brooksfilms)

An uncommonly and sweetly civilized adult romance between two transatlantic correspondents who never meet, *84 Charing Cross Road* is an appealing film on several counts, one of the most notable being Anne Bancroft's fantastic performance in the leading role. Helene Hanff's slim volume of letters between herself and a dignified antiquarian bookseller in London is the basis of the film. What began in 1949 as formal requests by the New Yorker Hanff for old books, became over a 20-year period, a warm, loving exchange of missives and gifts between her and much of the staff of the bookshop of Marks & Co.

80,000 SUSPECTS
1963, 113 mins, UK ⊏
D: Val Guest A: Claire Bloom, Richard Johnson, Yolande Donlan, Cyril Cusack, Michael Goodliffe, Mervyn Johns (Rank)

Drama concerns a city supposedly gripped by an epidemic of smallpox. Director Val Guest chose the city of Bath, and with complete cooperation from local authorities, the film has a vital authenticity. Dedicated doctor (Richard Johnson) is trying to keep together his marriage with an equally dedicated nurse (Claire Bloom). Another medico (Michael Goodliffe) despairs of saving his own marriage, and eventually becomes a key figure in the search for the ultimate germ carrier. The documentary and the fictional elements do not entirely jell. But Guest juggles adroitly enough with the problems to keep interest alert.

EL
(US: This Strange Passion)
1953, 100 mins, Mexico
D: Luis Bunuel **A:** Arturo De Cordova, Delia Garces, Luis Beristain, Aurora Walker (National)

Luis Bunuel has fashioned an absorbing melodramatic psycho pic out of *El*. Story concerns a middle-aged rich man who sweeps a beautiful young girl off her feet. He seems normal and considerate but in married life turns out to have delusions of persecution and homicidal tendencies. Arturo De Cordova is fine in delineating the breakdown of the guilt-ridden hero, while Delia Garces scores as the terrified, cornered wife.

EL CID
1961, 180 mins, US/Spain/Italy ⓥ ⊙ ⊡
D: Anthony Mann **A:** Charlton Heston, Sophia Loren, Raf Vallone, Gary Raymond, John Fraser, Genevieve Page (Bronston/Dear)

El Cid is a fast-action color-rich, corpse-strewn battle picture. The Spanish scenery is magnificent, the costumes are vivid, the chain mail and Toledo steel gear impressive. Perhaps the 11th century of art directors Veniero Colasanti and John Moore exceeds reality, but only scholars will complain of that. Action rather than acting characterizes this film. Charlton Heston's masculine personality ideally suits the title role. His powerful performance is the central arch of the narrative. Sophia Loren, as first his sweetheart and later his wife, has a relatively passive role.
1961: Nominations: Best Color Art Direction, Scoring of a Dramatic Picture, Song ("The Falcon and the Dove")

EL CONDOR
1996, 101 mins, US ⓥ
D: John Guillermin **A:** Jim Brown, Lee Van Cleef, Mariana Hill, Patrick O'Neal, Imogen Hassell, Elisha Cook Jr. (De Toth)

El Condor is Jim Brown and Lee Van Cleef in the wild west of Almeria with an army of Apaches in siege of a mountain fortress of Maximilian's Mexican treasure with enough gunplay, explosions, bloodletting, and body count for a Southeast Asian campaign. It is sex and violence, cowboys and Indians, and producer Andre de Toth and director John Guillermin have put it together with blood and guts and gusto. Brown gets the gold, which turns out to be painted lead, and Mariana Hill, who is very much the genuine article. Double-dealing, bushwhacking Van Cleef and dastardly Mexican general Patrick O'Neal in turn get theirs from Brown in the end.

EL DORADO
1967, 126 mins, US ⓥ ⊙
D: Howard Hawks **A:** John Wayne, Robert Mitchum, James Caan, Charlene Holt, Michele Carey, Ed Asner (Paramount)

Technical and artistic screen fads come and go, but nothing replaces a good story, well told. And Howard Hawks knows how to tell a good story. *El Dorado* stars John Wayne and Robert Mitchum in an excellent oater drama, laced with adroit comedy and action relief. Wayne, a hired gun, is dissuaded from working for land-grabber Ed Asner by Mitchum, a reformed gunslinger now a sharp-looking, disciplined sheriff.

ELECTION
1999, 103 mins, US ⓥ ⊙ ⊡
D: Alexander Payne **A:** Matthew Broderick, Reese Witherspoon, Chris Klein, Jessica Campbell, Mark Harelik, Phil Reeves (MTV)

Election is a dark, insidiously funny satire on the ways otherwise rational people can allow personal agendas to lead them to the point of self-destruction. Alexander Payne has delivered a caustic picture that takes on such dicey subjects as teacher-student sex, the uselessness of student government, corrupt administrators, lesbianism at girls' schools, and the ruthless cruelty of teenagers. Jim McAllister (Matthew Broderick), history and civics teacher at Carver High, can't stand Tracy, the school's Little Miss Prim, and when she announces her candidacy for the president of the student body, he secretly recruits popular jock Paul Metzler (Chris Klein) to join her on the ballot. Paul's lesbian sister, Tammy (Jessica Campbell), decides to run as well. Broderick offers up a perfect example of how the path to hell is paved with good intentions. Witherspoon is Tracy in a nifty performance.
1999: Nomination: Best Adapted Screenplay

ELECTRA GLIDE IN BLUE
1973, 106 mins, US ⓥ ⊙ ⊡
D: James William Guercio **A:** Robert Blake, Billy "Green" Bush, Mitchell Ryan, Jeannine Riley, Elisha Cook, Royal Dano (United Artists)

Director-producer James William Guercio comes on tall in a first pic about a motorcycle cop in the US west who is done in by the corruption, change, and violence about him. Robert Blake is effective as a small motorcycle cop who has a certain hard-headed dignity and feels he can help people and also wants to graduate to higher police echelons. Billy ''Green'' Bush as his slightly violent sidekick, Mitchell Ryan as a flamboyant, sadistic sheriff, Jeannine Riley as a disillusioned starlet all keep up with Blake's fine character composition.

ELECTRIC HORSEMAN, THE
1979, 120 mins, US Ⓥ ⊙ ▭
D: Sydney Pollack **A:** Robert Redford, Jane Fonda, Valerie Perrine, John Saxon, Willie Nelson (Columbia)

A moderately entertaining film, overlong, talky, and diffused. Even though Redford, as an ex-rodeo champ, and Fonda don't create the romantic sparks that might be expected, it's their dramatic professionalism that salvages *Horseman* and makes it a moving and effective film by the time the final credits roll by. Redford's attempt to liberate a prizewinning horse from an overabundance of steroids and painkilling is presumably intended as an analogy for the way the American public is force-fed consumerism from today's corporate giants.
1979: Nomination: Best Sound

ELECTRIC MAN, THE
See: Man Made Monster

ELENI
1985, 117 mins, US Ⓥ ⊙
D: Peter Yates **A:** Kate Nelligan, John Malkovich, Linda Hunt, Oliver Cotton, Ronald Pickup, Rosalie Crutchley (CBS)

Adapted from Nicholas Gage's best-selling book, pic has the most noble of intentions, but comes off as flat, tedious, and crudely biased. Screenplay cuts back and forth between events separated by 30 years. The Gage figure (John Malkovich) is assigned to the *New York Times* Athens bureau, a base from which he can investigate the events surrounding his mother's death during the civil war. Eleni, Nick's mother (Kate Nelligan), was a peasant woman in the tiny village of Lía. Portrayed as apolitical, she was forced from her home when the Communists occupied the area in the fractious period following World War II, then courageously suffered countless other indignities until being convicted as a traitor in a mock trial.

ELEPHANT BOY
1937, 81 mins, UK Ⓥ
D: Zoltan Korda, Robert Flaherty **A:** Sabu, Walter Hudd, Allan Jeayes, Wilfrid Hyde White (London)

Elephant Boy is a legendary and rather fantastic tale built around the affection that grows between a native Indian boy and his elephant, an animal which is tops as a hunter. Rudyard Kipling wrote the story under the title of *Toomai of the Elephants*. Toomai is the Indian lad whose great ambition is to be a hunter. Played by a native Indian boy named Sabu he imparts to it as much charm and näiveté as can be expected. Child has a pronounced native dialect which doesn't hurt, but many of the other characters are entirely too British to be convincing.

ELEPHANT MAN, THE
1980, 125 mins, US/UK Ⓥ ⊙ ▭
D: David Lynch **A:** Anthony Hopkins, John Hurt, Anne Bancroft, John Gielgud, Wendy Hiller, Freddie Jones (Brooksfilms)

Director David Lynch has created an eerily compelling atmosphere in recounting a hideously deformed man's perilous life in Victorian England. Hopkins is splendid in a subtly nuanced portrayal of a man torn between humanitarianism and qualms that his motives in introducing the Elephant Man to society are no better than those of the brutish carny. The centerpiece of the film, however, is the virtuoso performance by the almost unrecognizable John Hurt. Lynch commendably avoids summoning up feelings of disgust.
1980: Nominations: Best Picture, Director, Actor (John Hurt), Adapted Screenplay, Costume Design, Art Direction, Editing, Original Score

ELEPHANT WALK
1954, 102 mins, US Ⓥ
D: William Dieterle **A:** Elizabeth Taylor, Dana Andrews, Peter Finch, Abraham Sofaer (Paramount)

The novelty of the Ceylon backgrounds and pictorial beauty are recommendable points in *Elephant Walk*, an otherwise leisurely paced romantic drama. Elephants are the sympathetic heavies in this story of a bride who comes to Ceylon from England and finds her husband, the natives, and the tea plantation still under the dominance of a dead man's memory. Added to this is the always present threat that the pachyderms may eventually succeed in wrestling back from the white usurpers the trail they had used for centuries in coming down from the wilds to water.

ELEVATOR TO THE GALLOWS
See: L'Ascenseur pour L'Echafaud

11 HARROWHOUSE
1974, 95 mins, UK ⓥ ▭
D: Aram Avakian **A:** Charles Grodin, Candice Bergen, John Gielgud, Trevor Howard, James Mason, Helen Cherry (20th Century-Fox)

Charles Grodin stars in, adapted for the screen, and just about ruins *11 Harrowhouse,* a comedy caper film about a theft of billions in diamonds. Cast as a low-key diamond salesman who wreaks vengeance on the diamond establishment, Grodin messes up the film with ineffective shy-guy acting, and clobbers it with catatonic voice-over that is supposed to be funny. Trevor Howard and James Mason appear close to embarrassed in their roles.

EL MARIACHI
1992, 82 mins, US ⓥ ⊙
D: Robert Rodriguez **A:** Carlos Gallardo, Consuelo Gomez, Reinol Martinez, Peter Marquardt, Jaime De Hoyos (Los Hooligans)

Almost certainly, at $7,000, the cheapest film ever released by a major Hollywood studio, Columbia's pickup *El Mariachi* is a fresh, resourceful first feature by 24-year-old Austin filmmaker Robert Rodriguez. Spanish-lingo crime meller has a verve and cheekiness that's partly a smart wedding of such influences as Sergio Leone, George Miller, and south-of-the-border noir. Lensed in two weeks in the Mexican border town of Acuña, the pic can edify and inspire aspiring filmmakers who complain about lack of coin. Even though he shot with a handheld 16mm camera and nonsync sound, Rodriguez has put a perfectly serviceable picture up on the screen (Col paid for the 35mm blowup and Dolby sound add-on). Simple tale is that of a lone stranger in town who stirs up trouble, although in this case the newcomer is a young, hapless mariachi singer looking for a gig. Carlos Gallardo, who also cowrote and coproduced, makes for an affable mariachi.

ELMER GANTRY
1960, 146 mins, US ⓥ ⊙
D: Richard Brooks **A:** Burt Lancaster, Jean Simmons, Dean Jagger, Arthur Kennedy, Shirley Jones, Edward Andrews (United Artists)

In filming Sinclair Lewis's contentious 1927 study of a scandalous evangelist, Richard Brooks honors the spirit of Lewis's cynical commentary on circus-type primitive exhortation with pictorial imagery that is always pungent. He also has written dialogue that is frank and biting. From the standpoint of technique, this production plays like a symphony, with expertly ordered pianissimo and fortissimo story passages which build to a smashing crescendo in the cremation of Sister Sharon Falconer, an evangelist of questionable sincerity and propriety. Burt Lancaster pulls out virtually all the stops as Gantry to create a memorable characterization. He acts with such broad and eloquent flourish that a finely balanced, more subdued performance by Jean Simmons as Sister Sharon seems pale by comparison.
1960: Best Actor (Burt Lancaster), Supp. Actress (Shirley Jones), Adapted Screenplay
Nominations: Best Picture, Scoring of a Dramatic Picture

ELUSIVE PIMPERNEL, THE
1950, 109 mins, UK ⓥ
D: Michael Powell, Emeric Pressburger **A:** David Niven, Margaret Leighton, Jack Hawkins, Cyril Cusack (London)

This film version of the famed Baroness Orczy character almost robs the story of its romance, color, and thrills. It is brash, noisy, and dull. Dialogue is unusually flat and the flashes of wit expected form the suave Pimpernel are all too rare. The film shows David Niven, the "Elusive Pimpernel," disguised as an old hag, going through the army cordon with a carriage load of French nobility he has saved from the guillotine. It then goes on to relate his other exploits with members of his league. There are moments of refreshing beauty in some of the Technicolor shots. Many of the others appear unnecessarily loud and vivid. Niven is smooth, smiling, and suave, but all his efforts to lift the picture to a higher plane are unavailing. Margaret Leighton, as his French-born wife, also falls victim to this uphill fight.

ELVIRA MADIGAN
1967, 95 mins, Sweden Ⓥ ⊙
D: Bo Widerberg **A:** Pia Degermark, Thommy Berggren, Lennart Malmer, Nina Widerberg (Europa)

Based on a true story of a doomed turn-of-the-century love affair, this film opts for the poetic, timeless, and lyrical and succeeds right down the line. Softly hued color and a well-chosen background of Mozart music envelop the tale of the love affair of a young Swedish army officer of noble lineage and a young girl from a circus who is a noted tightrope walker. Pia Degermark has the luminous élan and delicacy to make her role of the girl always pleasing to the eye and revealing in her feelings. Thommy Berggren is a perfect counterpoint as the man who gives up all for love.

EMBRYO
1976, 108 mins, US Ⓥ
D: Ralph Nelson **A:** Rock Hudson, Diane Ladd, Barbara Carrera, Roddy McDowall (Cine Artists)

The story has doctor Rock Hudson grow a beautiful young woman (Barbara Carrera) in his laboratory from fetal beginnings. It's kind of *Bride of Frankenstein* tale, cast in terms of scientific mumbo jumbo, an effective blending of old and new plot elements. Hudson plays with gentleness and restraint, and Carrera's pristine fashion-model beauty is perfect for the role, but there's little feeling of genuine passion or eroticism.

EMERALD FOREST, THE
1985, 113 mins, US ⊙ ⊡
D: John Boorman **A:** Powers Boothe, Meg Foster, Charley Boorman, Dira Pass, Rui Polonah, Claudio Moreno (Embassy)

Screenplay trades on numerous enduring myths and legends about the return to nature and growing up in the wild. Powers Boothe, an American engineer and designer in Brazil, loses his young son in the wilderness and, against seemingly hopeless odds, sets out to find him. Ten years later the two finally meet up under perilous circumstances. By this time the son, played by the director's own sprog, Charley Boorman, has become well integrated into the ways of a friendly Indian tribe and has little desire to return to the outside world. Film proves engrossing and visually fascinating.

EMMA
1932, 70 mins, US
D: Clarence Brown **A:** Marie Dressler, Richard Cromwell, Jean Hersholt, Myrna Loy, John Miljan (M-G-M)

There are probably 20 actresses who would have fit the role of the old servant who spent a lifetime with the Smith family, watching the children grow up and then turn against her in her old age. But there is only one Marie Dressler, a trouper with a genius for characters of comic surface but profound pathos. The whole *Emma* affair is synthetic, in its comedy as well as in its sentiment the purest of hoke, sometimes skillfully wrought, but often far from clever in its manipulation. Dressler's acting alone gives it vitality.
1931/32: Nomination: Best Actress (Marie Dressler)

EMMA
1996, 111 mins, UK Ⓥ ⊙
D: Douglas McGrath **A:** Gwyneth Paltrow, Jeremy Northam, Toni Collete, Greta Scacchi, Alan Cumming, Juliet Stevenson (Matchmaker)

Gwyneth Paltrow shines brightly as Jane Austen's most endearing character, the disastrously self-assured matchmaker Emma Woodhouse. Emma manages to nudge Harriet Smith (Toni Collette), a simple young woman of obscure origins, into setting her sights on the smarmy Reverend Elton (Alan Cumming). Somehow, Emma hasn't noticed that the less-than-right rev is actually keen on *her*. Two other attention-getters come on the scene. Handsome, blond Frank Churchill (Ewan McGregor) never shuts up, and darkly enigmatic Jane Fairfax (Polly Walker) hardly says a word. First-time helmer and scripter Doug McGrath keeps things moving at a delirious trot without sacrificing period manners or the precision of the original language.

EMMANUELLE
1974, 105 mins, France Ⓥ
D: Just Jaeckin **A:** Sylvia Kristel, Alain Cuny, Daniel Sarky, Jeanne Colletin, Marika Green (Trinacra/Orphee)

Based on a bestselling book about the sexual liberation of a young woman, and with some production dress and the exotic locale of Bangkok, this is still softcore. Film is a series of glossy images. Kristel is acceptably ingenuous as the part-innocent, part-sex-obsessed heroine.

EMPEROR OF THE NORTH
1973, 118 mins, US ⓥ

D: Robert Aldrich **A:** Lee Marvin, Ernest Borgnine, Keith Carradine, Charles Tyner, Malcolm Atterbury, Simon Oakland (Inter-Hemisphere/20th Century-Fox)

Premise of a challenge by an easygoing tramp to ride the freight train of a sadistic conductor reputed to kill nonpaying passengers is limited in scope. The production takes its title from hobos' crowning of Lee Marvin "Emperor" for riding Ernest Borgnine's train even a mile, something no other hobo has ever accomplished. Marvin scores again in one of his uncolorful-but-commanding characterizations. Borgnine's interpretation borders on a caricature of the heavies of the past.

EMPEROR'S SHADOW, THE
See: Qin Song

EMPEROR WALTZ, THE
1948, 106 mins, US

D: Billy Wilder **A:** Bing Crosby, Joan Fontaine, Roland Culver, Lucile Watson, Richard Haydn (Paramount)

Film is a costumer laid "in the days" (sic) of Emperor Franz Joseph, and has a free-and-easy air that perfectly matches the Crosby style of natural comedy. An infectious quality surmounts the gorgeously apt trappings against which is projected the fable of an American traveling phonograph salesman and his dog who crash the court of the emperor.

L' EMPIRE DES SENS
(US: IN THE REALM OF THE SENSES; EMPIRE OF THE SENSES)
1976, 105 mins, France/Japan ⓥ

D: Nagisa Oshima **A:** Eiko Matsuda, Tatsuya Fuji, Aoi Nakajima, Yasuko Matsui (Oshima/Shibata/Argos/Oceanic/Oshima)

A topflight director working in the porno or erotic belt is still a rarity. This disturbing film, about a love that is so consuming it ultimately leads to sadomasochism and death, is one in the hands of Japanese director Nagisa Oshima. This pic's baring of sex as a means and an end, its refusal to soft-pedal either the beauty or its final harrowing results, raises it to an unusual level. The extraordinary acting of Eiko Matsuda as the obsessed girl and Tatsuya Fuji as the easygoing male are assets, as are subtle musical score, finely hued lensing, and a directorial blending of theme and image.

EMPIRE OF THE ANTS
1977, 89 mins, US ⓥ

D: Bert I. Gordon **A:** Joan Collins, Robert Lansing, John David Carson, Albert Salmi, Jacqueline Scott (American International)

The H. G. Wells–inspired exploitationer *Empire of the Ants,* is an above-average effort about ants that grow big after munching on radioactive waste. Periodic moments of good special effects are separated by reels of dramatic banality as players flounder in flimsy dialogue and under sluggish direction.

EMPIRE OF THE SENSES
See: L'Empire des Sens

EMPIRE OF THE SUN
1987, 152 mins, US ⓥ ⊙

D: Steven Spielberg **A:** Christian Bale, John Malkovich, Miranda Richardson, Nigel Havers, Leslie Phillips (Amblin/Warner)

Story of an 11-year-old boy stranded in Japanese-occupied China during World War II is based on J. G. Ballard's autobiographical 1984 novel. Jim (Christian Bale) is a proper upper-class English lad. Separated from his parents during the spectacularly staged evacuation of Shanghai, he is sent to a prison camp for the rest of the war. It is there that Jim flourishes, expending his boundless energy on creative projects and pastimes that finally land him a privileged place among the entrepreneurially minded Americans. John Malkovich's Basie, an opportunistic King Rat type, keeps threatening to become a fully developed character but never does. Other characters are complete blanks, which severely limits the emotional reverberation of the piece. It is up to young English thesp Bale to engage the viewer's interest, which he does superbly.

1987: Nominations: Best Cinematography, Costume Design, Art Direction, Editing, Original Score, Sound

EMPIRE STRIKES BACK, THE
1980, 124 mins, US ⓥ ⊙ ▭

D: Irvin Kershner **A:** Mark Hamill, Harrison Ford, Carrie Fisher, Billy Dee Williams, Frank Oz, Alec Guinness (20th Century-Fox/Lucasfilm)

The Empire Strikes Back is a worthy sequel to *Star Wars,* equal in both technical mastery and characterization, assisted again by good performances from Mark Hamill, Harrison Ford, and Carrie

Fisher. And even the ominous Darth Vader (David Prowse) is fleshed with new—and surprising—motivations. Among the new characters, Billy Dee Williams gets a good turn as a duplicitous but likable villain-ally and Frank Oz is fascinating as sort of a guru for the Force.
1980: Best Sound, Special Achievement Award (visual effects)
Nominations: Best Art Direction, Original Score

ENCHANTED APRIL
1991, 101 mins, UK ⓥ ⊙
D: Mike Newell **A:** Miranda Richardson, Joan Plowright, Josie Lawrence, Polly Walker, Michael Kitchen, Jim Broadbent (BBC)

A slim comedy of manners about Brits discovering their emotions in sunny Italy, *Enchanted April* doesn't spring many surprises. Strong cast's reliable playing is undercut by a script that dawdles over well-trod territory. Story centers on four women who rent a medieval dwelling in San Salvatore, Italy. For two of them (Miranda Richardson, Josie Lawrence), it's an excuse to get away from inattentive hubbies. Also on board are a waspish widow (Joan Plowright) and a society belle (Polly Walker). Lawrence decides to invite her husband (Alfred Molina) over, and Richardson eventually fires off a letter to hers as well. Meanwhile the house's British owner (Michael Kitchen), who'd already taken a shine to Richardson in Blighty, turns up one day.
1992: Nominations: Best Supp. Actress (Joan Plowright), Screenplay Adaptation, Costume Design

ENCHANTED COTTAGE, THE
1945, 91 mins, US ⓥ ⊙
D: John Cromwell **A:** Dorothy McGuire, Robert Young, Herbert Marshall, Mildred Natwick, Spring Byington (RKO)

Sensitive love story of a returned war veteran with ugly facial disfigurements, and the homely slavey—both self-conscious of their handicaps—is sincerely told. The girl's tender attention to the flier results in idyllic love, with each appearing beautiful to the other and pair sincerely believing that the cottage is enchanted and responsible for the transformations. McGuire turns in an outstanding performance, with Young also sharing the limelight. Herbert Marshall is excellent, while Mildred Natwick scores as the housekeeper.

1945: Nomination: Best Scoring of a Dramatic Picture

ENCINO MAN
(UK: CALIFORNIA MAN)
1992, 89 mins, US ⓥ ⊙
D: Les Mayfield **A:** Sean Astin, Brendan Fraser, Pauly Shore, Megan Ward (Hollywood Pictures)

Encino Man is a mindless would-be comedy aimed at the younger set. Low-budget quickie is insulting even within its own no-effort parameters. Incompetent screenplay dawdles over the introductions, with well over a reel elapsing before Cro-Magnon man Brendan Fraser unfreezes after turning up in a block of ice uncovered by Encino teen Sean Astin while digging a backyard swimming pool. Film is nominally a vehicle for MTV comic Shore, who flunks out on screen with his tediously unfunny patter and smaller-than-life personality.

ENCORE
1951, 89 mins, UK ⓥ
D: Pat Jackson, Anthony Pelissier, Harold French **A:** Nigel Patrick, Roland Culver, Kay Walsh, Glynis Johns, Ronald Squire, Terence Morgan (Two Cities)

A group of Somerset Maugham short stories have been collated to make a quality British film. First of the stories is "The Ant and The Grasshopper," in which Nigel Patrick is a ne'er-do-well who soaks his lawyer brother for cash until he lands a wealthy heiress. "Winter Cruise" is a light piece of a contrasting type. Kay Walsh plays a middle-aged garrulous spinster who takes a trip by cargo boat to Jamaica. "Gigolo and Gigolette" is a dramatic piece about a young vaudeville artist whose specialty is diving from an 80-foot platform into a 5-foot lake of flames.

END, THE
1978, 100 mins, US ⓥ ⊙
D: Burt Reynolds **A:** Burt Reynolds, Dom DeLuise, Sally Field, Strother Martin, David Steinberg, Joanne Woodward (United Artists)

The rather complete failure of Jerry Belson's script makes "The End" of *The End* come none too soon. Star-director Burt Reynolds, as a medically doomed sharpie, exercises and exorcises his fears while milking sympathy from everyone available. Production is a tasteless and overripe comedy that disintegrates very early into hysterical, undisciplined hamming.

ENDLESS LOVE
1981, 115 mins, US ⓥ ⊙
D: Franco Zeffirelli A: Brooke Shields, Martin Hewitt, Shirley Knight, Don Murray, Richard Kiley, Beatrice Straight (Polygram)

A cotton-candy rendition of Scott Spencer's powerful novel, *Endless Love* is a manipulative tale of a doomed romance which careens repeatedly between the credible and the ridiculous. Plot concerns the scorching love affair between a 17-year-old boy, from a social-activist Chicago family, and a 15-year-old girl. Since he's center stage most of the time, it's fortunate that newcomer Martin Hewitt registers so strongly. Brooke Shields disappears during entire center section of the film, which reduces extent to which film stands or falls by her work. One can never really tell what her responses to sex are because she's smiling all the time.
1981: Nomination: Best Song ("Endless Love")

END OF DAYS
1999, 120 mins, US ⓥ ⊙ ▭
D: Peter Hyams A: Arnold Schwarzenegger, Gabriel Byrne, Kevin Pollak, Robin Tunney, C.C.H. Pounder, Rod Steiger (Beacon/Universal)

End of Days is a middling vehicle that veers from the reasonably exciting to the risibly over-the-top. Sporting a trim beard and seemingly a shade leaner, Schwarzenegger looks great even though he's playing an alcoholic ex-cop, Jericho Cane. With four days to go before Y2K pandemonium hits, Satan (Gabriel Byrne) strides into a Manhattan restaurant and blows the place to smithereens. Rather too conveniently, Jericho figures out that there's Christine York (Robin Tunney) he's meant to protect, a 20-year-old who is supposed to give birth to the Antichrist. For this to happen, Satan must impregnate her in the hour before the new millennium. Special effects are generally groovy. It's good to see Schwarzenegger doing his thing again. Kevin Pollak proves a good sidekick for the big man, while Byrne takes barely suppressed glee in his role as the ultimate villain.

END OF INNOCENCE, THE
1990, 102 mins, US ⓥ
D: Dyan Cannon A: Dyan Cannon, John Heard, George Coe, Lola Mason, Rebecca Schaeffer, Steve Meadows (Skouras)

A moralistic drama about a woman's struggle for self-determination, *The End of Innocence* is a well-intentioned vehicle for writer-director-star Dyan Cannon. Drifting through life with no real career or focus, Stephanie (Cannon) deals with her deep unhappiness with junk food, mood pills, and marijuana. Cannon, looking remarkably good, has a field day dominating the film. But the auteur/star gets too carried away with a sense of mission here.

END OF THE AFFAIR, THE
1999, 109 mins, UK/US ⓥ ⊙
D: Neil Jordan A: Ralph Fiennes, Julianne Moore, Stephen Rea, Ian Hart, Samuel Bould, Jason Isaacs (Woolley/Columbia)

A faithful adaptation that captures the haunting spirit and religious nature of Graham Greene's 1951 novel, *The End of the Affair* unfolds as a first-person account of the liaison between a selfish novelist and the adulterous wife of a civil servant, splendidly played by Ralph Fiennes, Julianne Moore, and Stephen Rea, respectively. A passionate woman trapped in a sterile marriage, Sarah Miles (Moore) falls for Maurice Bendrix (Fiennes), a handsome young novelist, at a party given by her loyal but unexciting husband, Henry (Rea). Sarah and Bendrix begin an illicit, sexually liberating affair that lasts several years. Story jumps back and forth between the summer of 1939, when they first meet, to Sarah's sudden death, seven years later. Fiennes shines as the disenchanted and hate-ridden novelist. Sporting a spot-on English accent, Moore also excels. Jordan regular Rea plays the civil servant in dignified manner.
1999: Nominations: Best Actress (Julianne Moore), Cinematography

ENEMIES
A LOVE STORY
1989, 119 mins, US ⓥ ⊙
D: Paul Mazursky A: Ron Silver, Anjelica Huston, Lena Olin, Margaret Sophie Stein, Alan King, Paul Mazursky (Morgan Creek)

Haunting, mordantly amusing, deliciously sexy, *Enemies, a Love Story* is Paul Mazursky's triumphant adaptation of the Isaac Bashevis Singer novel about a Holocaust survivor who finds himself married to three women in 1949 New York. Ron Silver is fascinatingly enigmatic in the lead role. The character simultaneously is married to a devoted but cloddish woman (Margaret Sophie Stein), is carrying on a passionate affair with a sultry married woman (Lena Olin), and also finds himself back in the arms of his long-vanished wife (Anjelica Huston). Stein, Olin, and Huston are equally captivating. **1989: Nominations:** Best Supp. Actress (Anjelica Huston, Lena Olin), Adapted Screenplay

ENEMIES OF THE PUBLIC
See: The Public Enemy

ENEMY BELOW, THE
1957, 98 mins, ⓥ ▱
D: Dick Powell **A:** Robert Mitchum, Curt Jurgens, Al Hedison, Theodore Bikel, Kurt Kreuger (20th Century-Fox)

An engrossing tale of a chesslike duel of wits between the commanders of an American destroyer escort and a German U-boat in World War II, locked in single combat and each intent on blowing the other out of this world. Once in a while, the gallantry gets a bit thick, in the style of World War I aviation films of the twenties and thirties. To soft-soap the German side of the fight for American audiences, Jurgens is quickly established as an anti-Nazi old-line navy man, doing his sworn duty without too much enthusiasm. Mitchum is established as a veteran sub hunter who takes over a new command and has to win his crew's respect.

ENEMY FROM SPACE
See: Quatermass 2

ENEMY MINE
1985, 108 mins, US ⓥ ⊙ ▱
D: Wolfgang Petersen **A:** Dennis Quaid, Louis Gossett Jr., Brion James, Richard Marcus, (Kings Road/20th Century-Fox)

A friendship story between two disparate personalities carried to extreme lengths. Story is set up by a kind of videogame battle between the Earth forces and the warring Dracs from the distant planet of Dracon. Space pilot Willis Davidge (Dennis Quaid) is the only survivor on a desolate planet. His initial response to the half-human, half-reptilian is inbred hatred, distrust, and combativeness. Hostility soon gives way to a common goal—survival. Davidge and the Drac (Louis Gossett Jr.) peel away their outer layers and reveal two similar beings.

ENEMY OF THE PEOPLE, AN
1978, 103 mins, US ⓥ
D: George Schaefer **A:** Steve McQueen, Charles Durning, Bibi Andersson, Eric Christmas, Michael Cristofer, Richard Dysart (First Artists/Solar)

The Henrik Ibsen drama concerns a small-town doctor who discovers that his

village's new hot-springs spa is contaminated by tannery waste. He attempts to publicize the scandal, only to be declared a social outcast, his family and career ruined. Steve McQueen wanted to do the Ibsen work itself, and that was his undoing. The script isn't content to simply raise the issues. They are proclaimed in ringing tones, intensifying the preachiness of a work that is already condescending to its audience.

ENEMY OF THE STATE
1998, 127 mins, US ⓥ ⊙ ▱
D: Tony Scott **A:** Will Smith, Gene Hackman, Jon Voight, Lisa Bonet, Regina King, Stuart Wilson (Simpson-Bruckheimer/Touchstone)

Tony Scott's political thriller aspires to the level of the great '70s cycle of conspiracy-paranoia pictures. A congressman is murdered by Thomas Brian Reynolds (Jon Voight), an ambitious National Security Agency official, in a public park. A nature photographer, Zavitz (Jason Lee), has filmed the incident. Zavitz accidentally bumps into old college friend Robert Clayton Dean (Will Smith), a young hotshot attorney, and slips him the evidence. When Gene Hackman shows up as Brill, a mysterious underground information broker with a chip on his shoulder, the whole picture brightens up with much needed tension. Pic doesn't manifest the collective fears generated by the classic paranoia movies for the very reason that the zeitgeist has changed. Voight scores big as a ruthless officer, "America's ultimate guardian," who sadly realizes he may never become the agency's head.

L' ENFANT SAUVAGE (WILD CHILD)
1970, 85 mins, France ⓥ
D: Francois Truffaut **A:** Jean-Pierre Cargol, Francois Truffaut, Jean Daste, Francoise Seigner, Claude Miller (Films du Carrosse/Artistes Associes)

This is a lucid, penetrating detailing of a young doctor's attempt to civilize a retarded boy found living in the woods in southern France in the 18th century. Though based on a true case, it eschews didactics and creates a poetic, touching, and dignified relationship between the doctor and his savage charge. Director Francois Truffaut himself plays the young doctor at a deaf-and-dumb school in Paris who takes in the 11- or 12-year-old savage into his personal care. Truffaut underplays but exudes an interior tenderness and dedication. The boy is amazingly and intuitively well played by a tousled gypsy tyke named Jean-Pierre Cargol.

LES ENFANTS DU PARADIS (CHILDREN OF PARADISE)
1945, 188 mins, France ⓥ ⊙
D: Marcel Carne A: Arletty, Jean-Louis Barrault, Pierre Brasseur, Marcel Herrand, Pierre Renoir, Maria Casares (Pathe)

This ambitious French film turns out to be a strange mixture of the beautiful, the esoteric, and the downright dull. The leisurely tale centers on a mimic, Baptiste (Jean-Louis Barrault), and his passion for a demimondaine Garance (Arletty). Arletty is also pursued by a flamboyant confrere of Barrault's (Pierre Brasseur); by a sinister cutthroat (Marcel Herrand); and an aristocrat (Louis Salou). Hanging on the fringe is Nathalie (Maria Casares), hopelessly in love with Barrault. Barrault is brilliantly effective as the sensitive, lovelorn mimic. Other lead parts are sharply defined and maintained consistently in a film which is a peak of thespian artistry. [Version reviewed was a 144-min., inadequately subtitled one released in New York in 1947.]

LES ENFANTS TERRIBLES
1950, 102 mins, France
D: Jean-Pierre Melville A: Nicole Stephane, Edouard Dermithe, Renee Cosima, Jacques Bernard, Roger Gaillard (Melville)

Pic is an avant-garde treatment of an enticing psychological subject. Treatment is unorthodox, full of symbolism, and deals with the strange inner world of a strongly attached brother and sister. Jean Cocteau has written the pic and delivers the commentary, which creates a gripping, dreamlike attraction. Nicole Stephane, as the sister, is brilliant in the subtlety and neurotic strength she brings to the part. Edouard Dermithe is unsure of himself as the weak-willed brother.

ENFORCER, THE (UK: MURDER, INC.)
1951, 86 mins, US ⓥ ▭
D: Bretaigne Windust [Raoul Walsh] A: Humphrey Bogart, Zero Mostel, Ted De Corsia, Everett Sloane (United States/Warner)

Story starts with Bogart ready to crack a case on which he has worked four years; he has a witness who can pin a murder rap on the gang head. However, the witness, in fear, escapes and falls to his death.

Seeking to find some other tiny clue in the bulk of evidence, Bogart reviews the material gathered over the long years, permitting flashbacks into the past, and finally picks a single twist that gives him his lead and sets up an exciting finale. Tension builds constantly.

ENFORCER, THE
1976, 96 mins, US ⓥ ⊙
D: James Fargo A: Clint Eastwood, Tyne Daly, Harry Guardino, Bradford Dillman, John Mitchum (Warner)

The bad guys in this third installment from Dirty Harry's life include not only DeVeren Bookwalter and a group of post-Vietnam gun crazies but also his police and political superiors—like Bradford Dillman, captain of detectives, and John Crawford, whose characterization of the mayor is one of the few highlights. Tyne Daly's casting as a femme cop injects some predictable, but enjoyable, male chauvinism sparks in dialogue between her and Clint Eastwood.

ENGLAND MADE ME
1973, 100 mins, UK ⓥ
D: Peter Duffell A: Peter Finch, Michael York, Hildegard Neil, Michael Hordern, Joss Ackland (Atlantic)

England Made Me is the symbolic title for a tale of moral conflict set in prewar Germany, circa 1935. Michael York plays an innocent idealist ultimately snuffed out by the intrigues and ruthlessness that marked Nazi Germany. Superficially he runs afoul of rascally Peter Finch's great financial empire based in Germany, but his goodness is in wider conflict with the coarsened values of decadence and nihilism. Finch plays the ruthless financier with competence and physical presence while Hildegard Neil scores well as York's dominating older sister and Finch's mistress.

ENGLISHMAN WHO WENT UP A HILL BUT CAME DOWN A MOUNTAIN
1995, 99 mins, UK ⓥ ▭
D: Christopher Monger A: Hugh Grant, Tara Fitzgerald, Colm Meaney, Ian McNeice, Ian Hart (Parallax)

A flyweight, if well-crafted load of malarkey with charm to burn. The title character is Reginald Anson (Hugh Grant), a cartographer sent to Wales in 1917 to officially map out the terrain. The villagers take particular pride that the country's "first mountain" looms above them. But when Anson and colleague George Garrad

(Ian McNeice) return with news that their mountain is in fact a hill, civility becomes unusually strained. No amount of gussying-up can disguise its narrative modesty. Grant is cast effectively as a callow romantic who goes native. Tara Fitzgerald draws him out for the sake of local pride, but, not surprisingly, something more sincere evolves.

ENGLISH PATIENT, THE
1996, 162 mins, US ⓥ ⊙
D: Anthony Minghella **A:** Ralph Fiennes, Juliette Binoche, Willem Dafoe, Kristin Scott Thomas, Naveen Andrews, Colin Firth (Zaentz)

Long, involving, and rather parched emotionally, *The English Patient* is a respectable, intelligent, but less-than-stirring adaptation of Michael Ondaatje's imposingly dense and layered 1992 novel. Set against the stunning backdrops of prewar North Africa and the end of hostilities in Italy, action begins with a fiery plane crash in the desert, after which the scorched survivor (Ralph Fiennes) is tended to by Canadian nurse Hana (Juliette Binoche) in the ruins of a Tuscan monastery. In intriguing flashbacks that unfurl slowly like the opening of a scroll, the English patient's strange and ultimately traumatic tale is revealed. With its exotic, tapestry-like backgrounds, this is a picture of resplendently textured, sensuous surfaces, beginning with the sunbaked Tunisian desert. **1996:** Best Picture, Supp. Actress (Juliette Binoche), Director, Cinematography, Editing, Original Dramatic Score, Art Direction, Costume Design (Ann Roth), Sound **Nominations:** Actor (Ralph Fiennes), Actress (Kristin Scott Thomas), Screenplay Adaptation

ENIGMA
1983, 101 mins, UK/France ⓥ ⊙
D: Jeannot Szwarc **A:** Martin Sheen, Brigitte Fossey, Sam Neill, Derek Jacobi, Michael Lonsdale, Frank Finlay (Archerwest/ SFPC)

Enigma is a well-made but insufficiently exciting spy thriller which rather pleasingly emphasizes the emotional vulnerabilities of the pawns caught up in East-West intrigue. Martin Sheen ably portrays an East German refugee who is recruited by the CIA to return to East Berlin. Assignment: steal a coded microprocessor, or scrambler, from the Russians before the KGB proceeds with the assassination of five Soviet dissidents in the West.

ENORMOUS CHANGES AT THE LAST MINUTE
1983, 110 mins, US ⓥ ⊙
D: Mirra Bank, Ellen Hovde, Muffie Meyer **A:** Ellen Barkin, Kevin Bacon, Maria Tucci, Lynn Milgrim (Ordinary Lives)

Enormous Changes at the Last Minute is an enormously uneven trilogy of modern urban woman's dilemma in the precarious area of relationships with men. First vignette pits Virginia (Ellen Barkin) as a housewife with three kids who is newly deserted by her husband. In the weakest section, Faith (Lynn Milgrim) makes a trek to tell her father that she's separated from her husband. [In third seg] Alexandra (Maria Tucci) is a middle-aged, divorced, social worker who has a ludicrous affair with frenetic cabdriver/punk rocker Dennis (Kevin Bacon).

ENTER ARSENE LUPIN
1944, 72 mins, US
D: Ford Beebe **A:** Charles Korvin, Ella Raines, J. Carrol Naish, George Dolenz, Gale Sondergaard (Universal)

A slick enough combination of romance, action, and suspense offset phony, farfetched plot. Part of appeal is romantic team of Charles Korvin and Ella Raines in some torrid moments. Yarn concerns Lupin, renowned suave French thief, who robs a lady of her fabulous emerald on the Paris-Constantinople express. Gale Sondergaard is menacing enough as one of sleek, murderous cousins.

ENTERTAINER, THE
1960, 96 mins, UK ⓥ
D: Tony Richardson **A:** Laurence Olivier, Brenda de Banzie, Joan Plowright, Roger Livesey, Alan Bates, Albert Finney (Woodfall/Bryanston)

This version of John Osborne's play is raw but vital stuff, which you'll either like or loathe. The yarn is mainly a seedy character study of a broken-down, disillusioned vaude artiste, and of the various members of his family and their reactions to his problems. The stage sequences in which the third-rate comedian, Archie Rice (Laurence Olivier), has to put over some tatty material in a broken-down show, does not come over as effectively as it did on the stage. Oliver is far happier in other sequences. The way he allows his sleazy facade to slip by a twist of the

mouth, a throwaway line, or a look in the eyes is quite brilliant.
1960: Nomination: Best Actor (Laurence Olivier)

ENTERTAINER, THE
1975, 105 mins, US/Australia ⊗
D: Donald Wrye **A:** Jack Lemmon, Ray Bolger, Sada Thompson, Tyne Daly, Michael Cristofer, Annette O'Toole (Stigwood/Persky-Bright)

This basically is the John Osborne play. Setting is now America instead of England and period switched from Suez-crisis days to 1944. Jack Lemmon gives a fine performance as second-rate vaudevillian Archie Rice, desperately trying for laughs from nearly empty houses, though he is not so awful as he should be onstage.

ENTERTAINING MR. SLOANE
1970, 94 mins, UK ⊗
D: Douglas Hickox **A:** Beryl Reid, Peter McEnery, Harry Andrews, Alan Webb (Canterbury)

Based on Joe Orton's play. *Sloane* blends morbid humor, an obsession with sex, and an underlying pathos and result is interest that is always held. Beryl Reid gives a memorable study of a middle-aged, flabby, arch "nymphette," hazily pining for a lost love.

ENTER THE DRAGON
1973, 98 mins, US/Hong Kong ⊗ ⊙ ▭
D: Robert Clouse **A:** Bruce Lee, John Saxon, Jim Kelly, Shih Kien (Warner/Concord)

Enter the Dragon marks the final appearance of Bruce Lee, who died suddenly only a few weeks after he completed the film. Lee plays a James Bond-type of super-secret agent, past master in Oriental combat, who takes on the assignment of participating in brutal martial-arts competition as a cover for investigating suspected criminal activities. Lee socks over a performance seldom equaled in action. John Saxon, as an American expert drawn to the tournament, is surprisingly adept in his action scenes.

ENTER THE NINJA
1982, 99 mins, US ⊗
D: Menahem Golan **A:** Franco Nero, Susan George, Sho Kosugi, Christopher George (Cannon)

Enter the Ninja represents an unusual hybrid action film, an Italian western-type story filmed as a contemporary Japanese martial-arts action film in the Philippines. Results are pleasant though unspectacular. American ninjitsu student Cole (Franco Nero) arrives to help his old mercenary fighter buddy Landers (Alex Courtney) fight off various nasties out to steal away his plantation. Landers's tough-cookie wife (Susan George sporting a very sexy and giggly bra-less look) is on hand to help out.

ENTRAPMENT
1999, 112 mins, US ⊗ ⊙ ▭
D: Jon Amiel **A:** Sean Connery, Catherine Zeta-Jones, Ving Rhames, Will Patton, Maury Chaykin (Fountainbridge/New Regency/20th Century-Fox)

Entrapment is preposterous whimsy, a throwback to the lightweight globetrotting thrillers of the sixties. It works only as a dollop of make-believe, an opportunity to gaze at Sean Connery and Catherine Zeta-Jones pretending to enact a wary mating dance. After a Rembrandt is stolen from a New York high-rise, insurance investigator Gin Baker (Zeta-Jones), convinced that the culprit is legendary art thief Robert "Mac" MacDougal (Connery), tracks him down in London. The two plot a job together that takes the picture through its first hour, then hightail it to Malaysia, where she unveils her strategy for a stupendous computer heist—scenically located in the tallest buildings in the world, the Petronas Twin Towers in Kuala Lumpur. Action climax makes full use of the ornate tapering towers.

EQUINOX
1992, 115 mins, US ⊗ ⊙
D: Alan Rudolph **A:** Matthew Modine, Lara Flynn Boyle, Tyra Ferrell, Marisa Tomei, Kevin J. O'Connor, Lori Singer (SC Entertainment)

Equinox is one of Alan Rudolph's patently personal ensemble pieces about crisscrossing destinies. More socially minded in its depiction of a decaying society some of the characters yearn to escape, film is full of ideas and evocative scenes. Matthew Modine toplines in a double role. Henry is an awkward, nerdy chap induced to reignite a tentative romance with the lovely, painfully shy Beverly (Lara Flynn Boyle). Modine also appears as Freddy, a swaggering small-time hood who is married to Sharon (Lori Singer) and works his way up in a gang controlled by Paris (Fred Ward).

EQUUS
1977, 137 mins, US Ⓥ ⊙

D: Sidney Lumet A: Richard Burton, Peter Firth, Colin Blakely, Joan Plowright, Harry Andrews, Eileen Atkins (United Artists)

Peter Shaffer's play, which he adapted for the screen, has become under Sidney Lumet's outstanding direction a moving confrontation between a crudely mystical Peter Firth and the psychiatrist (Richard Burton), who is trying to unravel the boy's mind. The (screen) story is properly oriented to that of a suspense yarn: why did Firth blind Harry Andrews's horses? Judge Eileen Atkins wants Burton to find out.

1977: Nominations: Best Actor (Richard Burton), Supp. Actor (Peter Firth), Adapted Screenplay

ERASER
1996, 115 mins, US Ⓥ ⊙ ▭

D: Charles Russell A: Arnold Schwarzenegger, James Caan, Vanessa Williams, James Coburn (Warner)

Eraser is mid-level Arnold, a hardware-heavy, high-body-count actioner that tries to compensate for a B-movie script with advanced artillery and high-tech mayhem. Loaded with plot loopholes, implausibilities, and some phony deadlines imposed just to crank up contrived suspense, pic is punctuated with enough shootings, explosions, body puncturing, death-defying leaps, dramatic table-turning, and man-eating alligators to fill out all 15 episodes of an old Republic serial. Script centers upon Schwarzenegger's John Kruger, a government "eraser" expert at making witnesses disappear for their own safety. His new case isn't so easy: the witness in question, Lee Cullen (Vanessa Williams), has the goods on some turncoats in the defense field who plan to sell a load of top-secret super guns.

ERASERHEAD
1977, 100 mins, US Ⓥ ⊙

D: David Lynch A: Jack Nance, Charlotte Stewart, Jeanne Bates, Allen Josephs, Judith Anna Roberts, Laurel Near (AFI/Lynch)

A sickening bad-taste exercise, *Eraserhead* consists mostly of a man sitting in a room trying to figure out what to do with his horribly mutated child. Lynch keeps throwing in graphic close-ups of the piteous creature, and pulls out all gory stops in the unwatchable climax. The mind boggles to learn that Lynch labored on this pic for five years.

ERIK THE VIKING
1989, 103 mins, UK Ⓥ ⊙

D: Terry Jones A: Tim Robbins, Gary Cady, Mickey Rooney, Eartha Kitt, Terry Jones, John Cleese (Prominent)

The idea of telling the story of a Viking warrior who thought there must be more to life than rape and pillage is an amusing one, and for the most part *Erik the Viking* is an enjoyable film. American Tim Robbins is fine as the softly spoken and sensitive Erik, and especially seems to enjoy himself in the battle scenes. The film's great strength, though, is the Viking crew, which is full of wonderful characters, such as Tim McInnerny's manic Sven the Berserk, heavily disguised Antony Sher's scheming Loki, and best of all Freddie Jones's put-upon missionary.

EROICA
1958, 83 mins, Poland

D: Andrzej Munk A: Edward Dziewonski, Barbara Polomska, Leon Niemczyk, Jozef Nowak (Kadr)

Two separate stories concerned with the disillusionment of Poles in the calamitous days of 1944. First treats this theme in comic form, with the hero cast as a disenchanted volunteer trying to avoid underground training for the Warsaw uprising. More assured episode revolves around the grim joke in which a fictitious escapee from a German POW camp for Polish officers boosts the morale of his fellow prisoners.

ERRAND BOY, THE
1961, 92 mins, US Ⓥ

D: Jerry Lewis A: Jerry Lewis, Brian Donlevy, Howard McNear, Dick Wesson (Lewis/Paramount)

The Errand Boy is one of the best and funniest Jerry Lewis pictures to come along. Here Lewis is spoofing something that can stand spoofing—the pretentiousness of certain aspects of filmdom. Often he fails in development of his premises, too often he settles for the antique gag and the obvious or unfulfilled climax, but his film is a success as a whole.

ESCAPADE
1935, 93 mins, US

D: Robert Z. Leonard A: William Powell, Luise Rainer, Virginia Bruce, Frank Morgan, Reginald Owen, Mady Christians (M-G-M)

Escapade, besides being deft and amusing light comedy, is notable as the film introducing Luise Rainer to American audiences. Story concerns a sophisticated young rake (William Powell) who tumbles in love with an innocent sprite (Rainer), whose näiveté is in marked contrast to the amorous Viennese beauties who have been chasing the debonair gent. Rainer acts with her brain. Robert Leonard gives her a swell set of bell-ringing close-ups.

ESCAPE, THE
1914, 81 mins, US ⊗ ⓥ
D: D. W. Griffith **A:** Donald Crisp, Robert Harron, Blanche Sweet, Mae Marsh (Reliance)

Adapted from Paul Armstrong's stage play, the tale is hung upon one of those all-wrong families on the East Side. In this case the family consists of a father, two sisters, and a son. The film goes in the tenement house where they live to find misery, and gets nothing else. It seems foolish to waste the ability and energy of an able director of the Griffith stamp upon a scenario like *The Escape.*

ESCAPE
1930, 70 mins, UK/US
D: Basil Dean **A:** Gerald Du Maurier, Edna Best, Mabel Poulton, Madeleine Carroll, Gordon Harker, Austin Trevor (Associated Talking/RKO)

Film suffers by being made mostly with stage players, who do not generally adapt themselves to the screen. This particularly applies to Gerald Du Maurier, who overemphasizes everything. It tells how a man is sentenced to five years for killing a policeman. The prisoner, perfect English gentleman, doesn't like being treated roughly and escapes.

ESCAPE
1940, 104 mins, US
D: Mervyn LeRoy **A:** Norma Shearer, Robert Taylor, Conrad Veidt, Nazimova, Felix Bressart, Albert Basserman (M-G-M)

Escape is laid in Germany, near the Swiss border, and the action takes place soon before the start of World War II, when the secret police were terrorizing natives and foreign visitors. It is excellent, suspenseful material. Robert Taylor is the heroic young American who naively brushes against Nazi officialdom while on a search for his mother. Aid is furnished by Norma Shearer, who plays the mistress of the cultured Conrad Veidt, a German general, who tempers cruelty with love for Wagnerian music.

ESCAPE ARTIST, THE
1982, 93 mins, US ⓥ
D: Caleb Deschanel **A:** Griffin O'Neal, Raul Julia, Teri Garr, Joan Hackett, Gabriel Dell, Jackie Coogan (Zoetrope)

The Escape Artist is a muted fable about a gifted child in a never-never-land America. Treatment frequently pushes past the careful to the precious, and the quiet, odd tale never becomes more than mildly intriguing. After brash but not arrogant youth Griffin O'Neal issues a challenge to the police department that he can break out of their jail in one hour, story flips into an hour-long flashback. O'Neal imposes himself on his aunt and uncle, small-time vaudevillians, essayed by Joan Hackett and Gabriel Dell, and begins making trouble for himself and an entire midwestern town.

ESCAPE FROM ALCATRAZ
1979, 112 mins, US ⓥ ⊙
D: Don Siegel **A:** Clint Eastwood, Patrick McGoohan, Fred Ward, Roberts Blossom (Paramount/Malpaso)

From the moment Clint Eastwood walks onto The Rock, until the final title card, *Escape from Alcatraz* is relentless in establishing a mood and pace of unrelieved tension. Pic's only fault may be an ambiguous ending, tied, of course, to the historical reality of the 1962 escape. Key counterpoint to Eastwood's character comes from Patrick McGoohan as the megalomaniacal warden.

ESCAPE FROM L.A.
(AKA: JOHN CARPENTER'S ESCAPE FROM L.A.)
1996, 101 min, US ⓥ ⊙ ▭
D: John Carpenter **A:** Kurt Russell, Stacy Keach, Steve Buscemi, Valeria Golino, Peter Fonda, Pam Grier (Rysher/Paramount)

A cartoonish, cheesy and surprisingly campy apocalyptic actioner, *Escape from L.A.* is spiked with a number of funny and anarchic ideas but doesn't begin to pull them together into a coherent whole. By 2013, all the degenerates are sequestered in L.A. Island, which broke off from the mainland after an earthquake, as a means of purifying the new "moral" United States, lorded over by a Gestapo-like police force and ruled by a right-wing religious hypocrite (Cliff Robertson). But the prexy's daughter has seen through her old man, absconded with his top-secret "black box" and joined forces with gangster revolutionary Cuervo Jones (George Corraface). Former war hero and full-time bad boy Snake Plissken (Kurt Russell) is pulled out of mothballs to retrieve the black box.

ESCAPE FROM NEW YORK
1981, 99 mins, US ⓥ ⊙ ▭
D: John Carpenter A: Kurt Russell, Lee Van Cleef, Ernest Borgnine, Donald Pleasence, Isaac Hayes, Harry Dean Stanton (Avco Embassy/IFI/Goldcrest)

Although execution doesn't quite live up to the fabulous premise, *Escape from New York* is a solidly satisfying actioner. In the 1997 New York City neatly turned out by production designer Joe Alves, Manhattan is a walled, maximum-security prison inhabited by millions of felons and loonies. The president of the US has the misfortune of crash-landing on the island. Into this cesspool is sent tough criminal Kurt Russell, who is charged with extricating the prexy within 24 hours.

ESCAPE FROM THE PLANET OF THE APES
1971, 97 mins, US ⓥ ⊙ ▭
D: Don Taylor A: Roddy McDowall, Kim Hunter, Bradford Dillman, Natalie Trundy, William Windom (20th Century-Fox/Apjac)

Almost as good as the original *Planet of the Apes*, production is marked by an outstanding script, using some of the original Pierre Boulle novel characters; excellent direction by Don Taylor; and superior performances from a cast headed by encoring Roddy McDowall and Kim Hunter. After about half of the film's literate, suspenseful, delightful, and thought-provoking 97 minutes, the story emphasis segues from broad comedic antics to a rather horrifying dilemma.

ESCAPE ME NEVER
1935, 93 mins, UK
D: Paul Czinner A: Elisabeth Bergner, Hugh Sinclair, Penelope Dudley-Ward, Griffith Jones, Lyn Harding (British & Dominions/United Artists)

Escape Me Never, produced as a play in London and New York with the same star, is a well-produced film transcription of a story of moods and morbidity. Locale includes Venice, where the picture opens,

the mountains, and finally London. At the outset Elisabeth Bergner is fashioned as an impish waif of immoral cast, who instantly becomes likable in spite of her character background. Further on, by degrees, she loses a part of this charm and becomes a helpless mother and wife who is figuratively kicked around by her musician husband.

1935: Nomination: Best Actress (Elisabeth Bergner)

ESCAPE ME NEVER
1947, 101 mins, US ⓥ
D: Peter Godfrey A: Errol Flynn, Ida Lupino, Eleanor Parker, Gig Young, Reginald Deny (Warner)

Errol Flynn is given plenty of opportunity to flash the old charm. In his role of a serious composer, he turns in one of the best jobs of his career. Ida Lupino demonstrates once more her versatility as a serious actress. Story is cut sharply in half between light romance and heavy drama and therin lies its only fault of note. Chief production assist is lent by Erich Wolfgang Korngold's score, with both the ballet and theme music standout.

ESCAPE TO ATHENA
1979, 125 mins, UK ⓥ ▭
D: George Pan Cosmatos A: Roger Moore, Telly Savalas, David Niven, Claudia Cardinale, Richard Roundtree, Stefanie Powers (ITC/Grade)

Escape to Athena not only has the unabashed look of a cynical "package" but also plays like one as well. It's a joke-age wartime action retread, feeble in both humor and suspense, in which a group of Anglo-American prisoners of the Germans scramble to liberate (a) themselves and (b) some Greek art treasures.

ESCAPE TO HAPPINESS
See: Intermezzo

ESCAPE TO WITCH MOUNTAIN
1975, 97 mins, US ⓥ ⊙
D: John Hough A: Eddie Albert, Ray Milland, Donald Pleasence, Kim Richards (Walt Disney)

The two leading protagonists are a young orphaned brother and sister who are psychic. Their unusual powers lead them to an eccentric tycoon who craves a gifted clairvoyant who can make him omnipotent, arranging for their transfer to his palatial home, where they are held prisoner. Using their magical talents for an escape, they take up with an old-timer traveling in a motor home. Eddie Albert inserts just the proper type of crankiness as the camper owner, and Ray Milland properly hams the multimillionaire.

EL ESPIRITU DE LA COLMENA (THE SPIRIT OF THE BEEHIVE)
1973, 95 mins, Spain ⓥ
D: Victor Erice A: Fernando Fernan Gomez, Teresa Gimpera, Ana Torrent, Isabel Telleria (Querejeta)

This sensitive, beautifully wrought film about two small girls in a Castilian village in 1940 (just after the end of the Spanish Civil War) couldn't be more authentically Spanish in its evocation of life in the provinces; yet its suggestivity and lyricism transcend local borders. Two girls see an old Frankenstein film. They are fascinated by the scene where the small girl picks a flower and gives it to the monster. They imagine that the monster is a kind of benevolent spirit who can be invoked by saying certain words. Rest of pic shows how the two children spin a dreamworld of their own about the monster.

ET DIEU ... CREA LA FEMME (... AND GOD CREATED WOMAN; AND WOMAN ... WAS CREATED)
1957, 95 mins, France ⓥ ⊙ ▭
D: Roger Vadim A: Brigitte Bardot, Curt Jurgens, Jean-Louis Trintignant, Jeanne Marken, Isabelle Corey, Christian Marquand (IENA/UCIL/Cocinor)

Film even ran into censorship trouble in France via its emphasis on sex, and was shorn of its more intimate sensual aspects. Lagging, familiar story line is of the passion and drama which a sexy little orphan (Brigitte Bardot) inspires in three men in a Riveria port town. Bardot lacks the thespian strength to get any depth into her role here. Curt Jurgens manages to make his presence felt.

L' ETE MEURTRIER (ONE DEADLY SUMMER)
1983, 130 mins, France ⓥ
D: Jean Becker A: Isabelle Adjani, Alain Souchon, Suzanne Flon, Jenny Cleve, Francois Cluzet, Michel Galabru (SNC)

Psychological drama about a dangerously neurotic girl's obsession with a family shame. Often questionable in matters of credibility and wobbly in its dramatic conception, pic is nonetheless fairly engrossing, thanks to Isabelle Adjani, astonishing in the central role. Traumatized by her knowledge that her mother was raped

by three Italian immigrants before she was born, Adjani thinks she's on a trail of vengeance when she's courted by a young garage mechanic, whose father, now dead, was an Italian immigrant who owned a mechanical piano, the only clue to the identity of her mother's aggressors.

E.T.—THE EXTRA-TERRESTRIAL
1982, 115 mins, US ⓥ ⊙
D: Steven Spielberg A: Dee Wallace, Henry Thomas, Peter Coyote, Robert MacNaughton, Drew Barrymore (Universal)

E.T. may be the best Disney film Disney never made. Captivating, endearingly optimistic, and magical at times, Steven Spielberg's fantasy is about a stranded alien from outer space protected by three kids until it can arrange for passage home. As superlatively created by Carlo Rambaldi, the creature manages to project both a wondrous childlike quality and a sense of superior powers. It even gets to play a drunk scene, perhaps a first for screen aliens.
1982: Best Sound, Original Score, Sound, Sound Effects Editing, Visual Effects
Nominations: Best Picture, Director, Original Screenplay, Cinematography, Editing

EUREKA
1983, 129 mins, UK ⓥ
D: Nicolas Roeg A: Gene Hackman, Theresa Russell, Rutger Hauer, Jane Lapotaire, Ed Lauter, Mickey Rourke (JF Prods/Recorded Picture)

Even by modern standards, Nicolas Roeg's Eureka is an indulgent melodrama about the anticlimactic life of a greedy gold prospector after he has struck it rich. Gene Hackman performs with predictable credit as the man whose jackpot fortune only leaves him bored, surly, and suspicious of being ripped off, by one and all, family included. Theresa Russell is the girl-woman daughter who rebelliously marries a putative gigolo (Rutger Hauer) whom paranoid papa psychs as a fortune hunter.

EUREKA STOCKADE
1949, 103 mins, UK/Australia
D: Harry Watt A: Chips Rafferty, Gordon Jackson, Peter Finch, Jane Barrett, Jack Lambert (Ealing)

Eureka Stockade is staged in the middle of the 19th century when the first gold strike in Australia leads to economic chaos in the colony. Vicious taxes are imposed on the diggers, and the men themselves are hounded by the police. The gold seekers seek to impose their will by mob law, but a leader arises. If action alone could make a picture, this one would very nearly take full marks. The main weakness of the production is the low standard of acting.

EUROPA
(ZENTROPA)
1991, 114 mins, DENMARK/France/Germany ⓥ ⊙ ▭
D: Lars Von Trier **A:** Jean-Marc Barr, Barbara Sukowa, Udo Kier, Ernst Hugo, Erik Mork, Eddie Constantine (Nordisk/Obel/Mital)

Bravura film technique doesn't hide an off-putting, empty exercise in *Europa*, Lars Von Trier's rumination on war guilt in the form of a low-voltage thriller. Director works on a vast canvas with all manner of special effects to tell the Kafkaesque story of a young American, Leopold (Jean-Marc Barr), working as an apprentice railroad conductor in occupied Germany, 1945. His romance with cold, beautiful Katharina (Barbara Sukowa), daughter of the train-line owner, plays second fiddle to Leopold's surrealistic wanderings through a fantasy landscape.

EUROPEANS, THE
1979, 90 mins, UK ⓥ
D: James Ivory **A:** Lee Remick, Robin Ellis, Wesley Addy, Lisa Eichhorn, Tim Choate (Merchant-Ivory)

"The Europeans" are Americans who grew up in Europe in the mid-19th century. They come back to the US to visit rich cousins. The arrival leads to a mingling and interaction of cultures. The European cousins are Lee Remick as a mid-thirties baroness now estranged from her Austrian nobleman husband and her younger brother, a free-living portrait painter with bohemian attitudes. Director James Ivory handles this roundelay with subtlety, delivering an engaging drama.
1979: Nomination: Best Costume Design

EVE
1962, 100 mins, France/Italy
D: Joseph Losey **A:** Jeanne Moreau, Stanley Baker, Virna Lisi, Giorgio Albertazzi, James Villiers, Lisa Gastoni (Paris/Interopa)

Made by an American director in Italy using English, with French producers and French, British, and Italo actors, this is a sleek, mannered look at an affair between a cold, almost psychotic call girl and a writer, which is fraught with overtones of masochism. Picture is reminiscent of prewar Yank femme fatale films. But there is not enough character to give acceptance to the overindulgence in Jeanne Moreau as the cold-hearted harlot. Moreau speaks good English but is hampered by the overdecorated, overstylized vamp she is called on to play. Stanley Baker acquits himself acceptably as the climbing ex–coal miner.

EVEN COWGIRLS GET THE BLUES
1994, 96 mins, US ⓥ ⊙
D: Gus Van Sant **A:** Uma Thurman, John Hurt, Rain Phoenix, Noriyuki "Pat" Morita, Lorraine Bracco, Keanu Reeves (New Line)

American counterculture and early seventies values come flooding back like a peyote-induced dream in a far-out, meandering fantasy set on a ranch run by lesbians, from Tom Robbins's 1973 cult novel. Result is at best amusing; at worst, uninvolving, often confusing, and sometimes a little boring. Main character, Sissy (Uma Thurman), is a 29-year-old virgin hippie whose delicate beauty is marred only by giant, phalluslike thumbs. Sissy has a contract with the Countess (John Hurt), a prancing drag queen, to model for feminine-hygiene ads. Sissy hitches crosscountry to the Countess's Oregon beauty farm, the Rubber Rose Ranch. At the ranch, however, a pack of rebellious, unwashed cowgirls foment an uprising against the Countess and his authoritarian hireling (Angie Dickinson). [Review is of 106-min. version world-preemed at 1993 Venice fest.]

EVENING DRESS
See: Tenue de Soiree

EVENSONG
1934, 83 mins, UK
D: Victor Saville **A:** Evelyn Laye, Fritz Kortner, Emlyn Williams, Carl Esmond (Gaumont-British)

A highly absorbing and intelligently produced musical, the saga of an opera warbler whose career reaches a tragic end. Evelyn Laye is the singing lead of *Evensong*. By stages she skilfully portrays the professionally successful but tragic life of a prima donna. The music ranges from popular numbers to heavier opera. Fritz

Kortner tops the support as the diva's manager and romance slaughterer.

EVENT HORIZON
1997, 95 mins, US/UK Ⓥ ⊙ ▱
D: Paul Anderson A: Laurence Fishburne, Sam Neill, Kathleen Quinlan, Joely Richardson, Richard T. Jones, Jack Noseworthy (Golar/Impact/Paramount)

Despite acres of impressive production values, *Event Horizon* remains a muddled and curiously uninvolving sci-fi horror show. Initial promise of the offbeat premise—a rescue party finds a derelict spacecraft haunted by supernatural forces—is rapidly dissipated by routine execution and risible dialogue. Screenplay begins with the mysterious reappearance in 2047 of deep-space research vessel *Event Horizon,* which vanished somewhere beyond Neptune. Dr. William Weir (Sam Neill), who worked on the vessel's design, is eager to board the *Lewis & Clark,* a search-and-rescue ship under the demanding command of Captain Miller (Laurence Fishburne). The missing ship was testing a new form of "faster than light" propulsion that creates "an artificial black hole." Obviously, something went terribly wrong. Just how wrong becomes clear as soon as the team boards. The actors perform far beyond the call of duty, but to little avail.

EVE OF ST MARK, THE
1944, 96 mins, US
D: John M. Stahl A: Anne Baxter, William Eythe, Michael O'Shea, Vincent Price, Ruth Nelson, Ray Collins (20th Century-Fox)

Maxwell Anderson's stage hit of the 1942-43 season was a subtle flag waver. For the screen there was an inevitable elimination of some of the play's salty lines and sex implications. *St. Mark* has become a homey comedy-drama of a farmboy inductee, his family, sweetheart, and barracks comrades. It is a picture of superlative performances. William Eythe, as the farmboy inductee, has his biggest part to date, and does much with it.

EVERGREEN
1934, 92 mins, UK Ⓥ
D: Victor Saville A: Jessie Matthews, Sonnie Hale, Betty Balfour, Barry Mackay (Gaumont-British)

Jessie Matthews has the name part, which she created on the stage. The screen adaptation and dialogue are more definite and coherent. Benn Levy and Lorenz Hart wrote the original musical. Harriet Green is London's pet singing comedienne. The father of her child turns up and demands blackmail. She places the baby girl in the charge of a faithful maid and disappears. Twenty-five years later the daughter seeks a job in the chorus and is recognized by the mother's old understudy. Daughter is foisted on the public as the original Harriet Green and starred in an elaborate musical. It is the astonishingly competent performances by the principals that are most impressive.

EVERYBODY'S ALL-AMERICAN (UK: WHEN I FALL IN LOVE)
1988, 127 mins, US Ⓥ ⊙
D: Taylor Hackford A: Jessica Lange, Dennis Quaid, Timothy Hutton, John Goodman (New Visions)

Everybody's All-American has its moments, and remains watchable due to its two attractive leads, but is too predictable and not nearly incisive enough. Baton Rouge in the mid-1950s was made for the likes of dashing, easygoing, and likable Gavin (Dennis Quaid) and gorgeous blond Southern belle Babs (Jessica Lange). The couple moves comfortably into the expected environs of suburbia, a steady flow of babies, sports-themed restaurant ownership, and the like. However, the innocence of youth and the 1950s inevitably yield to the turmoil and doubt of the 1960s.

EVERYBODY SING
1938, 80 mins, US Ⓥ
D: Edwin L. Marin A: Allan Jones, Fanny Brice, Judy Garland, Reginald Owen, Billie Burke, Reginald Gardiner (M-G-M)

Everybody sings in this highly successful departure from the stereotyped filmusical. The production is a combination of straight comedy, balanced with some tuneful song interpolations. Fanny Brice scores heavily with her inimitable impersonations. The diminutive Judy Garland takes a long leap forward to stardom.

EVERYBODY WINS
1990, 97 mins, UK/US Ⓥ ⊙
D: Karel Reisz A: Debra Winger, Nick Nolte, Will Patton, Judith Ivey, Jack Warden (Recorded Picture)

Everybody Wins is a very disappointing picture. Overladen with pompous and frequently dated dialogue, Arthur Miller's script (developed from his 1982 pair of one-act plays, *Two-Way Mirror*) is essentially a routine whodunit. Nick Nolte plays an investigator and discovers a web of corruption engulfing a small Connecticut town. Winger as a schizo femme fatale copes uneasily with Miller's overblown dialogue.

EVERY DAY'S A HOLIDAY
1937, 80 mins, US
D: A. Edward Sutherland **A:** Mae West, Edmund Lowe, Charles Butterworth, Charles Winninger, Walter Catlett, Lloyd Nolan (Paramount)

By whatever standard posterity judges the acting career of Mae West, it never shall be said that she was dull. *Every Day's a Holiday,* written by herself, is a lively, innocuously bawdy, and rowdy entertainment. West's new characterization is of a Bowery girl named Peaches O'Day, one time actress of the 1890s, a con girl, with liberal views on the subject of larceny. West sways her hips and tosses her plumes in her inimitable manner. She sings a not very naughty song by Sam Coslow. Louis Armstrong leads his band in a street parade.

EVERY GIRL SHOULD BE MARRIED
1948, 85 mins, US ⓥ ⊙
D: Don Hartman **A:** Cary Grant, Franchot Tone, Diana Lynn, Betsy Drake, Alan Mowbray (RKO)

Don Hartman has fashioned a sparklingly witty comedy of modern manners which will set off a chain reaction of chuckles. Betsy Drake is the young gal set upon hooking an eligible bachelor. Accidentally bumping into Cary Grant in a drugstore, she maps an elaborate pincer strategy after studiously gathering data on his habits and habitat. When this fails, she switches to piquing Grant with jealousy, using Franchot Tone as the foil.

EVERYONE SAYS I LOVE YOU
1996, 101 mins, US ⓥ ⊙
D: Woody Allen **A:** Alan Alda, Woody Allen, Drew Barrymore, Goldie Hawn, Julia Roberts, Tim Roth (Doumanian/Sweetland)

Woody Allen's *Everyone Says I Love You* is the filmmaker's tip of the hat to movie romance, 1930s musicals and modern neurosis. This is that rare Allen outing that transcends his cozy niche and plays to the masses. The Manhattan setting is familiar, but when Holden (Edward Norton) looks adoringly into the eyes of Skylar (Drew Barrymore), he croons the bygone hit "Just You, Just Me." The story rather loosely hangs on the young lovers' impending wedding. Allen's instinct for the singing prowess of a cast dominated by performers with limited experience in the form (Alan Alda and Goldie Hawn excepted) is uncanny. Only Barrymore was ultimately dubbed by a professional. Hawn's climactic dance with Allen along the banks of the Seine is truly magical.

EVERYTHING I HAVE IS YOURS
1952, 91 mins, US
D: Robert Z. Leonard **A:** Marge Champion, Gower Champion, Dennis O'Keefe, Monica Lewis (M-G-M)

The talents of Marge and Gower Champion get a flashy showcasing. The star team is extremely likable. The plot finds the Champions opening to a smash hit on Broadway, only to discover that the gal's dizziness is caused by pregnancy. Marge Champion becomes a successful mother for the next few years while Champion continues in show business partnered with Monica Lewis.

EVERYTHING YOU ALWAYS WANTED TO KNOW ABOUT SEX BUT WERE AFRAID TO ASK
1972, 87 mins, US ⓥ ⊙
D: Woody Allen **A:** Woody Allen, John Carradine, Anthony Quayle, Tony Randall, Burt Reynolds, Gene Wilder (United Artists)

Borrowing only the title and some typically inane questions from Dr. David Reuben's oft-ingenuous but widely read overview of sexual matters, pic is divided into seven segments—blackout sketches, really—that presumably are Woody Allen's surrealistic answer to selected questions from the Reuben tome.

EVERY TIME WE SAY GOODBYE
1986, 95 mins, US ⓥ ⊙
D: Moshe Mizrahi **A:** Tom Hanks, Cristina Marsillach, Benedict Taylor (Tri-Star)

Every Time We Say Goodbye is a tale of star-crossed lovers played out against a backdrop of Jerusalem in 1942. Tom Hanks is featured as an American pilot recovering from an injury who falls in love with a girl from a traditional Sephardic Jewish family (Cristina Marsillach). Culturally rich story is aided throughout by the pic's all-Israel shoot.

EVERY WHICH WAY BUT LOOSE
1978, 119 mins, US ⓥ ⊙
D: James Fargo **A:** Clint Eastwood, Sondra Locke, Geoffrey Lewis, Beverly D'Angelo, Ruth Gordon (Malpaso/Warner)

Screenplay has Clint Eastwood as a beer-guzzling, country-music-loving truck driver who picks up spare change as a barroom brawler. When Sondra Locke, an elusive singer, takes off for Colorado, Eastwood packs his pickup truck in pursuit. There's an orangutan. His name is Clyde. He goes everywhere with Eastwood. For Eastwood fans, the essential elements are there. Lots of people get beat up, Eastwood walks tall and looks nasty, cars are crashed.

EVIL, THE
1978, 89 mins, US ⓥ
D: Gus Trikonis **A:** Richard Crenna, Joanna Pettet, Andrew Prine, Cassie Yates, Victor Buono (Rangoon)

Any satanic-oriented film that actually has the nerve to display the Wicked One in the flesh can't be all bad, and in fact, *The Evil* is quite good. Screenplay has psychologist Richard Crenna, accompanied by wife Joanna Pettet, picking up a lease on the proverbial haunted house. Throughout, there is a spirit on the loose in communication with Pettet, trying to warn her of the dangers ahead. But Crenna is a stubborn skeptic, only admitting his own helplessness in dealing with the situation when there is no other recourse. This type of psychological insight is rare in suspensers, and is a credit to both Crenna, who delivers a strong performance, and director Gus Trikonis.

EVIL ANGELS
See: A Cry in the Dark

EVIL DEAD, THE
1983, 85 mins, US ⓥ ⊙
D: Sam Raimi **A:** Bruce Campbell, Ellen Sandweiss, Betsy Baker, Hal Delrich, Sarah York (Renaissance)

The ne plus ultra of low-budget gore and shock effects. Story premise has five youngsters (in their twenties) holed up in a remote cabin where they discover a Book of the Dead. Playing the taped incantations unwittingly summons up dormant demons living in the nearby forest, which possess the youngsters in succession. While injecting considerable black humor, neophyte Detroit-based writer-director Sam Raimi maintains suspense and a nightmarish mood in between the showy outbursts of special-effects gore and graphic violence.

EVIL DEAD II
1987, 85 mins, US ⓥ ⊙
D: Sam Raimi **A:** Bruce Campbell, Sarah Berry, Dan Hicks, Kassie Wesley, Theodore Raimi (Renaissance/De Laurentiis)

More an absurdist comedy than a horror film, *Evil Dead II* is a flashy good-natured display of special effects and scare tactics so extreme they can only be taken for laughs. Action, and there's plenty, is centered around a remote cabin. It seems Professor Knowby (John Peaks) has unleashed the spirits of the dead and they want to escape limbo by claiming possession of the living. They're a remarkably protean lot and take on all sorts of imaginative and grotesque forms almost instantaneously.

EVIL OF FRANKENSTEIN, THE
1964, 84 mins, UK/US ⓥ ⊙
D: Freddie Francis **A:** Peter Cushing, Peter Woodthorpe, Duncan Lamont, Sandor Eles (Hammer/Universal)

Peter Cushing plays the baron with his usual seriousness, avoiding tongue-in-the-cheek. This time Cushing is bent on reviving the brain of one of his homemade monsters. The baron has other problems on his plate, notably a drunken, blackmailing hypnotist, a deaf-and-dumb beggar girl, the local burgomaster, and the police, but keeps a fairly stiff upper lip throughout.

EVIL UNDER THE SUN
1982, 102 mins, UK ⓥ ⊙
D: Guy Hamilton **A:** Peter Ustinov, Jane Birkin, Colin Blakely, James Mason, Diana Rigg, Maggie Smith (EMI)

Director Guy Hamilton admits to hating Agatha Christie's writing style. Apart from cutting down the number of characters, he and scripter Anthony Shaffer have also had the audacity to switch things around in the inevitable denouement scene. Poirot points right away at the guilty party, while the true suspense is put into the how's and why's that follow. But fun it is to follow this cast of English and US characters in their stay on a remote Tyrrhenian island, where a famous stage actress gives them all a good motive for doing her in. Peter Ustinov's Poirot paddles about, being demanding of staff (beeswax for his shoes) and cuisine and happy about himself.

EVITA
1996, 134 mins, US ⓥ ⊙ ▭
D: Alan Parker **A:** Madonna, Antonio Banderas, Jonathan Pryce, Jimmy Nail (Cinergi/Stigwood/Dirty Hands/Hollywood)

The long-awaited screen version of the celebrated 1978 Andrew Lloyd Webber–Tim Rice musical emerges as a stunningly crafted *object d'art* that evokes serious viewer admiration more than passionate excitement. One can only admire the finesse and resourcefulness with which Alan Parker has visualized *Evita*. As Lloyd Webber's score cascades relentlessly from one number to the next with only the scarcest of spoken dialogue to interrupt them, so do the burnished, indelible images that combine to form a stylized, highly dramatic portrait of the rise and demise of Eva Peron (Madonna), imperious first lady of fascist Argentina. By the final section, one comes to long for a little downtime, a few intimate moments. Madonna gives her all to the title role and pulls it off superbly.
1996: Best Original Song ("You Must Love Me")
Nominations: Best Cinematography, Editing, Art Direction, Sound

EXCALIBUR
1981, 140 mins, US ⓥ ⊙
D: John Boorman **A:** Nigel Terry, Nicol Williamson, Nicholas Clay, Helen Mirren, Cherie Lunghi, Corin Redgrave (Orion)

Essentially the legend of King Arthur, *Excalibur* is exquisite, a near-perfect blend of action, romance, fantasy, and philosophy, finely acted and beautifully filmed. Nicol Williamson stands out early as the wizard Merlin, at times a magician, flim-flam artist, and philosopher, always interesting.
1981: Nomination: Best Cinematography

EXECUTIONER, THE
1970, 111 mins, UK ⓥ ▭
D: Sam Wanamaker **A:** George Peppard, Joan Collins, Judy Geeson, Oscar Homolka, Charles Gray, Nigel Patrick (Schneer/Columbia)

George Peppard is a British undercover agent out to prove that a colleague is really a double agent. Supposedly a triple-cross suspenser, film just lies there, so that interest fades fast in the overexposition and redundancy.

EXECUTIVE ACTION
1973, 91 mins, US ⓥ ⊙
D: David Miller **A:** Burt Lancaster, Robert Ryan, Will Geer, Gilbert Green, John Anderson (Lewis/Wakeford-Orloff)

The open lesion known as Watergate has made more plausible the theory of an assassination conspiracy in 1963 against President John F. Kennedy. *Executive Action,* dramatized with low-key terror, is an emotional aftershock to the event. Burt Lancaster, Robert Ryan, and Will Geer star as informed men of industry and government service who concluded that JFK must be eliminated.

EXECUTIVE DECISION
1996, 132 mins, US ⓥ ⊙
D: Stuart Baird **A:** Kurt Russell, Halle Berry, John Leguizamo, Steven Seagal (Silver/Warner)

This airborne antiterrorist suspenser is a slick piece of goods with a dark sense of humor, a highly entertaining arsenal of gadgets, and a fair share of unexpected developments. At the center is Dr. David Grant (Kurt Russell), the head of a Washington, DC, antiterrorist think tank. He's enlisted into a daredevil mission when a group of Islamic militants hijack an Athens-DC flight. Antiterrorist commando Travis (Steven Seagal) assembles a crack team.

EXECUTIVE SUITE
1954, 103 mins, US ⓥ
D: Robert Wise **A:** William Holden, June Allyson, Barbara Stanwyck, Fredric March, Walter Pidgeon, Shelley Winters (M-G-M)

A dramatically interesting motion picture humanizing big business and its upper-echelon personalities. Drama is built on the efforts of the several vice-presidents to take over the top position. Eight scene-stealers vie for the star billing and each is fine. Certainly Fredric March's characterization of the controller will be remembered among the really sock delineations. So will William Holden's portrayal of the idealistic but practical young executive.
1954: Nominations: Best Supp. Actress (Nina Foch), B&W Cinematography, B&W Costume Design, B&W Art Direction

EXISTENZ
1999, 97 mins, Canada/UK ⓥ ⊙

D: David Cronenberg **A:** Jennifer Jason Leigh, Jude Law, Willem Dafoe, Ian Holm, Don McKellar, Sarah Polley

Fans of Canadian auteur David Cronenberg's more ghoulish productions are likely to be disappointed by *eXistenZ*, in which the director playfully parodies some of his past horror outings. Pic opens with a seminar in which officials of Antenna Research are about to test a new game, eXistenZ, devised by Allegra Geller (Jennifer Jason Leigh), the world's number-one game programmer. Just as the demonstration is beginning, a member of the audience opens fire, wounding Geller, who escapes with security guard Ted Pikul (Jude Law). The fugitives flee from realism fanatics and agents of Antenna's rival, Cortical Systematics. Cronenberg tosses in outrageous sexual jokes and cheerfully sadistic bloodletting, often involving strange mutant creatures. Jason Leigh enters cheerfully into the spirit of the exercise, as does Law as her unwilling collaborator. Film gets a little predictable in the later stages.

EXIT TO EDEN
1994, 113 mins, US ⓥ

D: Garry Marshall **A:** Dana Delany, Paul Mercurio, Rosie O'Donnell, Dan Aykroyd, Hector Elizondo (Savoy)

There's something essentially dishonest in *Exit to Eden* that eats away at the fabric of the picture. The mix of erotic, comic, and thriller elements diminishes whatever the original intention might have been for this mélange. The thread of the story is the track-down of Omar (Stuart Wilson), a notorious diamond smuggler, and his accomplice Nina. LAPD undercover detectives Sheila Kingston (Rosie O'Donnell) and Fred Lavery (Dan Aykroyd) have been one step away from apprehending them. The picture has the sophistication of an adolescent bathroom joke indifferently told.

EX-MRS. BRADFORD, THE
1936, 80 mins, US ⓥ ⊙

D: Stephen Roberts **A:** William Powell, Jean Arthur, James Gleason, Eric Blore, Robert Armstrong (RKO)

Another sprightly entry for the school of smart-comedy, detective mystery yarns. Teaming of Powell and Arthur, as doctor and divorced wife, is a happy one. While the romance between the pair is slowly re-vived, the whole affair is treated with smart flippancy. Much the same attitude is taken toward the doctor's tumbling efforts to solve a series of killings that has the police baffled, until they attempt to pin them on him. Here, his wife's sharp wit and impertinence help.

EXODUS
1960, 212 mins, US ⓥ ⊙ ▭

D: Otto Preminger **A:** Paul Newman, Eva Marie Saint, Ralph Richardson, Peter Lawford, Lee J. Cobb, Sal Mineo (Carlyle/Alpha/United Artists)

Transposing Leon Uris's hefty novel to the screen was not an easy task. The picture wanders frequently in attempting to bring into focus various political and personal aspirations that existed within the Jewish nationalist movement itself as well as portraying Arab opposition and the unhappy role that Great Britain played as custodian of the status quo. The romance that develops slowly between young, dedicated Hagana leader Paul Newman and Eva Marie Saint, as a widowed American, is conventional. Technically Newman gives a sound performance, but he fails to give the role warmth.

1960: Best Scoring of a Dramatic Picture
Nominations: Best Supp. Actor (Sal Mineo), Color Cinematography

EXORCIST, THE
1973, 121 mins, US ⓥ ⊙

D: William Friedkin **A:** Ellen Burstyn, Max von Sydow, Lee J. Cobb, Kitty Winn, Jack MacGowran, Linda Blair (Hoya/Warner)

William Friedkin's film of William Peter Blatty's novel *The Exorcist* is an expert telling of a supernatural horror story. The well-cast film makes credible in powerful laymen's terms the rare phenomenon of diabolic possession. Ellen Burstyn, a divorced film actress, is on location with daughter Linda Blair, the latter becoming aware of some apparent inner spiritual friend whom she calls "Captain Howdy," and their rented house now filled with strange sounds and movements. Blair's fits become genuinely vicious and destructive, provoking a shocking series of psychiatric tests. At length, Jesuit priest Max von Sydow, who has exorcised before, is sent to perform the rare rites. The climactic sequences assault the senses and the intellect with pure cinematic terror.

1973: Best Adapted Screenplay, Sound
Nominations: Best Picture, Director, Ac-

tress (Ellen Burstyn), Supp. Actor (Jason Miller), Supp. Actress (Linda Blair), Cinematography, Art Direction, Editing

EXORCIST II
THE HERETIC
1977, 117 mins, US Ⓥ
D: John Boorman A: Linda Blair, Richard Burton, Louise Fletcher, Max von Sydow, Kitty Winn, Paul Henreid (Warner)

Exorcist II is not as good as *The Exorcist*. It isn't even close. Gone now is the simple clash between Good and Evil, replaced by some goofy transcendental spiritualism. Linda Blair is back as Regan, four years older and still suffering the residual effects of her demonic possession. Another self-doubting priest (Richard Burton) is assigned to investigate the death of the old exorcist (Max von Sydow).

EXORCIST III, THE
1990, 110 mins, US Ⓥ ⊙
D: William Peter Blatty A: George C. Scott, Ed Flanders, Brad Dourif, Jason Miller, Nicol Williamson, Scott Wilson (Morgan Creek/20th Century-Fox)

It's been 15 years since Father Karras battled the Devil for the little girl and ended up dead at the bottom of the stairway. Now his old policeman friend (George C. Scott) is confronted with a series of sacrilegious murders bearing the trademarks of a killer executed about the same time the priest died. Anyway, there's a guy in chains over at the nuthouse who sometimes appears to Scott as Karras (Jason Miller) and sometimes as the executed killer (Brad Dourif), and it's all very confusing.

EXPERIMENT IN TERROR
(UK: THE GRIP OF FEAR)
1962, 123 mins, US Ⓥ
D: Blake Edwards A: Glenn Ford, Lee Remick, Stefanie Powers, Roy Poole, Ned Glass (Columbia)

The ''experiment'' is a terrifying episode in which a bank teller is forced by a psychopathic killer into embezzling $100,000 under threat of murder. She goes to the FBI. Glenn Ford and Lee Remick play the FBI agent and bank teller, respectively. For Remick it is a handsome role played with nicely modulated control. Ford has solidarity, but his role is merely that of a staunch agent doing his job well. Picture was shot extensively in San Francisco. Philip Lathrop's camera took fine advantage of known Bay City landmarks, giving the film a nice visual style.

EXPERIMENT PERILOUS
1944, 90 mins, US Ⓥ
D: Jacques Tourneur A: Hedy Lamarr, George Brent, Paul Lukas, Albert Dekker, Carl Esmond (RKO)

Plot centers around Paul Lukas's mansion in the 1903 era. The elderly Lukas has been married to the young and beautiful Hedy Lamarr for about a decade, holding her in close confinement and restraint as he would any other possession. She is continually dominated by fear of strange influences which can be felt but not seen. George Brent, a young doctor, accepts invitation to meet Lamarr and inspect the place that intrigues him. Picture carries good pace of suspense.

EXPLORERS
1985, 109 mins, US Ⓥ ⊙
D: Joe Dante A: Ethan Hawke, River Phoenix, Jason Presson, Amanda Peterson, Dick Miller (Paramount/Industrial Light & Magic)

Two young boys, a dreamer (Ethan Hawke) and a nerdy science-genius type (River Phoenix), manage to fashion a homemade spacecraft. Throughout, director Joe Dante and writer Eric Luke load the proceedings with references to sci-fiers of an earlier day, but this is nothing compared to what happens when the trio of youngsters finally take off into outer space and make contact with an alien race.

EXPOSED
1983, 100 mins, US Ⓥ
D: James Toback A: Nastassja Kinski, Rudolf Nureyev, Harvey Keitel, Ian McShane, Bibi Andersson, Ron Randell (M-G-M/United Artists)

Intelligent and illogical, beautiful and erratic, *Exposed* is a provocative, jetsetter's visit to the worlds of high fashion and international terrorism. Kinski is attending an exhibition of photos featuring her when her eye is caught by Rudolf Nureyev. After a bizarre, cat-and-mouse courtship, the inevitable big love scene arrives. Nureyev is a dedicated terrorist fighter, and when Kinski follows him to Paris, she naively becomes involved with the very forces Nureyev is intent upon wiping out.

EXPRESSO BONGO
1959, 111 mins, UK Ⓥ ⊡
D: Val Guest A: Laurence Harvey, Sylvia

Syms, Yolande Donlan, Cliff Richard (British Lion/Britannia)

Soho, with its atmosphere of sleazy stripperies, gaudy coffee bars, and frenetic teenagers, is the setting for this amusing satire. Laurence Harvey, a cheap, opportunistic promoter, picks up an amateur singer and bongo player, signs him up on a dubious contract, and boosts him to what is now regarded as stardom. Harvey gives a brashly amusing, offbeat performance. The songs are intended to spoof the whole business of pop crooning, but they come over, in Cliff Richard's larynx, as completely feasible entries in the pop market.

EXTASE
(ECSTASY)
1933, 90 mins, Czechoslovakia ⊗
D: Gustav Machaty **A:** Hedy Lamarr, André Nox, Pierre Nay, Rogoz (Elekta)

The story of Eva (Hedy Kiesler [later Lamarr]), who on her bridal night finds her husband (Rogoz) unequal to the occasion. She attempts to forget her chagrin in an active outdoor life. One day, while she is bathing, her mare runs away, carrying off her pajamas on its back. The nude Eva is rushing through the woods after her horse when a young engineer (Pierre Nay) meets her and restores both the horse and the pajamas. Soon the handsome young man awakens in Eva all the pent-up forces of her ardent nature. [Review is from the film's showing in Paris, soon after its Prague premiere.]

EXTERMINATING ANGEL, THE
See: El Angel Exterminador

EXTERMINATOR, THE
1980, 101 mins, US ⊗ ⊙
D: James Glickenhaus **A:** Christopher George, Samantha Eggar, Robert Ginty (Interstar)

An action film with little action. Listlessly paced tale of Robert Ginty deciding to avenge his war buddy, paralyzed from an encounter with a youth gang, opts for grotesque violence in a series of glum, distasteful scenes.

EXTERMINATOR 2
1984, 89 mins, US ⊗ ⊙
D: Mark Buntzman, William Sachs **A:** Robert Ginty, Mario Van Peebles, Deborah Geffner, Frankie Faison, Scott Randolph (Cannon)

A silly and tiresome revenge actioner. Reprising his title as Vietman vet Johnny Eastland, an uncomfortable Robert Ginty

is supposedly spurred into renewed vigilante action when his flashdancing girlfriend Caroline (Deborah Geffner) is murdered by all-purpose punks, led by a messianic leader ("I am the streets") X (Mario Van Peebles).

EXTRAORDINARY SEAMAN, THE
1969, 79 mins, US ▢
D: John Frankenheimer **A:** David Niven, Faye Dunaway, Alan Alda, Mickey Rooney, Jack Carter, Juano Hernandez (M-G-M)

A tepid story keel, not entirely—but almost—devoid of amusement strength, has been ballasted with padding newsreel footage and other effect to yield an unstable comedy vessel. Set in the Philippines, where three US Navy men, in flight from the Japanese, discover an urbane Niven, as a Royal Navy officer, living in uncanny nattiness aboard a beached ship. Dunaway joins the crew as Niven sets sail for Australia.

EXTREME PREJUDICE
1987, 104 mins, US ⊗ ⊙
D: Walter Hill **A:** Nick Nolte, Powers Boothe, Michael Ironside, Maria Conchita Alonso, Rip Torn (Carolco)

An amusing concoction that is frequently offbeat and at times compelling. Taut direction and editing prevail despite overstaged hyperviolence that is so gratuitous as to be farcical. Story pivots on the adversarial relationship between small-town Texas Ranger Nick Nolte and drug kingpin Powers Boothe. Originally childhood friends, they are now on opposite sides of the law and the US-Mexican border.

EXTREMITIES
1986, 90 mins, US ⊗ ⊙
D: Robert M. Young **A:** Farrah Fawcett, James Russo, Diana Scarwid, Alfre Woodard (Atlantic)

A ski-masked assailant imprisons and terrorizes Marjorie (Farrah Fawcett) in her own car. Marjorie manages to escape but the attacker knows her identity and address. Marjorie's worst nightmare comes true. She is visited at her secluded home by the man who attacked her (James Russo). Fawcett acts with a confidence and control not often seen in her screen work.

EYE FOR AN EYE, AN
1981, 106 mins, US ⊗
D: Steve Carver **A:** Chuck Norris, Chris-

topher Lee, Richard Roundtree, Mako, Rosalind Chao, Maggie Cooper (Avco Embassy/Wescom)

An Eye for an Eye is an effective martial arts actioner vehicle for Chuck Norris. Norris toplines as a San Francisco cop who quits the force and goes after revenge when his partner and partner's girlfriend are killed by drug traffickers. Aided by his former police boss, Captain Stevens (Richard Roundtree), Norris evens the accounts and takes care of the drug ring.

EYE FOR AN EYE
1995, 111 mins, US ⊗ ⊙
D: John Schlesinger A: Sally Field, Keifer Sutherland, Ed Harris, Beverly D'Angelo, Joe Mantegna (Paramount)

This muddled revenge melodrama is a B movie that somehow won the lottery and got an A-movie cast and director. Sally Field toplines to good effect as Karen McCann, the mother of a lovely teenage girl who is viciously raped and murdered by a grinning psychopath named Robert Doob (Kiefer Sutherland). Unfortunately, the psycho has a great lawyer. Karen begins to notice that in her support group for parents of murdered children, a couple of the members may be channeling their rage into retribution, prompting her to think that vigilantism may not be such a bad idea. Vet director John Schlesinger gives *Eye for an Eye* enough tension and immediacy—most of the time, at least—to make it worth a viewer's time. In most other respects, however, the screenplay is as simplistic as the worst kind of talk-radio diatribe.

EYE OF THE CAT
1969, 102 mins, US
D: David Lowell Rich A: Michael Sarrazin, Gayle Hunnicutt, Eleanor Parker, Tim Henry, Laurence Naismith (Universal)

Pic has a few good jolts, successful buildups, and good-looking people, but stilted dialogue and plot shot through with holes keep mystery at a minimum, suspense overdue. Beautician Kassia (Gayle Hunnicutt), after witnessing emphysema attack of wealthy San Francisco matron Danny (Eleanor Parker), finds Danny's runaway favorite nephew Wylie (Michael Sarrazin). Kassia plans to reestablish Wylie in the house and, after Aunt Danny changes her will in his favor, murder her and split the fortune.

EYE OF THE DEVIL
1968, 89 mins, UK
D: J. Lee Thompson A: Deborah Kerr, David Niven, Donald Pleasence, Edward Mulhare, Flora Robson, Sharon Tate (M-G-M/Filmways)

David Niven, a vineyard manor lord, is called back to his property because of another dry season. Deborah Kerr follows with his children (Suky Appleby and Robert Duncan), latter acting mysteriously at start and finish. Sharon Tate and David Hemmings loom as paper threats who speak deadpan dialogue about the goings-on. Kerr is our only touch with reality, and she tries to carry the pic, to little avail.

EYE OF THE NEEDLE
1981, 111 mins, UK ⊗ ⊙
D: Richard Marquand A: Donald Sutherland, Kate Nelligan, Ian Bannen, Christopher Cazenove (United Artists/Kings Road)

Donald Sutherland is perhaps Berlin's most reliable spy still working undetected within Britain. He makes his way to the aptly named Storm Island to rendezvous with a U-boat, waiting there to take him to Germany. Nelligan and Cazenove have resettled on the bleak outpost of civilization. Formerly a dashing pilot, the latter has become a bitter paraplegic as a result of the accident, so his beauteous wife readily responds to the mysterious stranger when he temporarily lands in their household. It's a good yarn, remindful of some of Alfred Hitchcock and Fritz Lang's wartime mellers.

EYE OF THE TIGER
1986, 90 mins, US ⊗
D: Richard C. Sarafian A: Gary Busey, Yaphet Kotto, Seymour Cassel, Bert Remsen (Scotti Bros)

Pic opens with Buck Matthews's (Busey) release from prison. A gang of motorcycle-riding drug peddlers makes a visit to Matthews's house, killing his wife, beating him up, and sending their daughter into a catatonic state. The rest of the film is about Matthews's one-man quest for vengeance, most of which is set to the pounding beat of rock music.

EYES OF LAURA MARS
1978, 104 mins, US ⊗ ⊙
D: Irvin Kershner A: Faye Dunaway, Tommy Lee Jones, Brad Dourif, René Au-

berjonois, Raul Julia (Columbia)

A very stylish thriller in search of a better ending. Faye Dunaway stars as a chic fashion photographer with mysterious and accurate premonitions about a series of murders. Tommy Lee Jones plays a police lieutenant assigned to the case and an integral element in the mystery. Especially well handled are the screen realizations of Dunaway's premonitions. They look like a blurred videotape, as she explains to Jones at one point, a conception which works well on screen.

EYES WIDE SHUT
1999, 159 mins, UK/US ⓥ ⊙
D: Stanley Kubrick **A:** Tom Cruise, Nicole Kidman, Sydney Pollack, Marie Richardson, Rade Sherbedgia, Todd Field (Hobby/Pole Star/Warner)

This intimately focused updating of Arthur Schnitzler's 1926 novella *Dream Story* remains remarkably faithful to its source while trading in familiar Kubrick concerns such as paranoia, deception, and the masks people wear. Film opens as William and Alice Harford (Tom Cruise, Nicole Kidman) prepare for a pre-Christmas New York party thrown by the wealthy Victor Ziegler (Sydney Pollack). The next evening Alice confesses the effect a handsome naval officer had on her during their recent vacation. This has a chilling effect on Bill, a medical doctor, who heads out for a long, brooding nocturnal journey that sees him become the object of a declaration of love by a dead patient's daughter (Marie Richardson), go home with a hooker (Vinessa Shaw), and attend a masked orgy. Kidman reaches a career high-water mark with the unveiling of her feelings. Cruise gives a limited, emotionally constrained performance.

EYES WITHOUT A FACE
See: Les Yeux sans Visage

EYEWITNESS
(US: SUDDEN TERROR)
1970, 95 mins, UK ⓥ
D: John Hough **A:** Mark Lester, Lionel Jeffries, Susan George, Tony Bonner, Jeremy Kemp, Peter Vaughan (EMI)

Eyewitness has its ground roots in an often-used idea. Angle of a likable kid with an imagination so vivid that unfeeling adults good-humoredly regard him as a chronic liar. Result is that when a crisis really arises no one fully believes him. Young victim is Mark Lester and it's the hook on which is hung a fairly conventional crime chase yarn.

EYEWITNESS
(UK: THE JANITOR)
1981, 102 mins, US ⓥ ⊙
D: Peter Yates **A:** William Hurt, Sigourney Weaver, Christopher Plummer, James Woods, Irene Worth, Morgan Freeman (20th Century-Fox)

Office-building janitor William Hurt on the night shift discovers a murdered body. Hurt has an obsession for newswoman Sigourney Weaver. When Weaver comes to his building to report on the murder, Hurt pretends to know something secret to prolong this unexpected encounter. That leads him into danger with assorted characters who really do know something about the murder. Weaver plays her part very well, but simply can't justify the character's actions. Consequently, the story gets more and more strained before it's resolved.

F

FABULOUS BAKER BOYS, THE
1989, 113 mins, US ⓥ ⊙
D: Steve Kloves A: Jeff Bridges, Michelle Pfeiffer, Beau Bridges, Jennifer Tilly (Gladden/Mirage)

There's nothing startlingly original about this romantic comedy of two piano-playing brothers who find an attractive young singer to give some much-needed CPR to their dying lounge act. When they're joined by sexy-surly singer Susie Diamond (Michelle Pfeiffer), it's obvious exactly where the film is headed. Jack (Jeff Bridges) and Susie are on a romantic collision course, with Frank (Beau Bridges) bound to be hurt by the explosion. The fun part is seeing it all play out, thanks to a standout cast and first-time director Steve Kloves's skill in handling them.
1989: Nominations: Best Actress (Michelle Pfeiffer), Editing, Original Score

FACE BEHIND THE MASK
1941, 69 mins, US
D: Robert Florey A: Peter Lorre, Evelyn Keyes, George E. Stone, Don Beddoe (Columbia)

Unpleasant yarn has Peter Lorre as an immigrant whose face is badly burned in a rooming-house fire. Story unfolds at deliberate pace to emphasize that a sincerely honest man is forced by unfortunate circumstances to turn to crime. Evelyn Keyes, as the blind girl who is the only one he can find to accept his love, does a good job in a role that could easily be hammed up.

FACE IN THE CROWD, A
1957, 125 mins, US ⓥ
D: Elia Kazan A: Andy Griffith, Patricia Neal, Anthony Franciosa, Walter Matthau, Lee Remick (Newtown/Warner)

A devastating commentary on hero-worship and success cults in America that exposes a beloved television personality as an unmitigated heel. Andy Griffith makes his film debut as Lonesome Rhodes, the power-mad hillbilly. As his vis-à-vis, Patricia Neal is the girl who guides Griffith to fame and fortune. Anthony Franciosa plays the unprincipled personal manager, Walter Matthau a cynical writer.

FACE OF A STRANGER
See: The Promise

FACE/OFF
1997, 138 mins, US ⓥ ⊙ ▭
D: John Woo A: John Travolta, Nicolas Cage, Joan Allen, Alessandro Nivola, Gina Gershon, Dominique Swain (Douglas-Reuther/WCG/Permut/Paramount)

A provocative premise, virtuoso direction and two dazzling lead performances go a long way toward offsetting a lack of dramatic structure and a sense of when to quit in *Face/Off*. FBI agent Sam Archer (John Travolta) is obsessed with tracking down maniacal criminal Castor Troy (Nicolas Cage). The latter is apparently blasted to smithereens by a jet engine. But he is still alive, even if comatose, and he and his demented brother, Pollux (Alessandro Nivola), have planted a nerve gas bomb that threatens to "unleash the biblical plague that L.A. deserves." Archer agrees to permit Troy's face, voice, and entire physiognomy to be transferred to his own body so he can learn the details of the heinous plot from Pollux. Gambit gives the actors a delicious opportunity to play two roles, and they make the most of it.
1997: Nomination: Best Sound Effects Editing

FACES
1968, 130 mins, US
D: John Cassavetes A: John Marley, Gena Rowlands, Lynn Carlin, Fred Draper, Seymour Cassel (Maurice McEndree)

Faces is a long, long (at least an hour too long) look at a 36-hour split-up in the 14-year marriage of a middle-class couple. As the result of tensions, inhibitions created by years of trying to adjust, and temporary clashes of personality, John Marley and his wife, played frigidly by Lynn Carlin, clash and Marley leaves the house for the temporary emotional warmth of an attractive prostitute (Gena Rowlands). An overblown opus.
1968: Nominations: Best Supp. Actor (Seymour Cassel), Supp. Actress (Lynn Carlin), Original Story & Screenplay

FACE TO FACE
1952, 89 mins, US ⓥ
D: John Brahm, Bretaigne Windust A: James Mason, Gene Lockhart, Michael Pate, Robert Preston, Marjorie Steele (Theasquare/RKO)

Two short-story classics, Joseph Conrad's "The Secret Sharer" and Stephen Crane's "The Bride Comes to Yellow Sky" have been packaged. The Conrad tale, directed by Brahm, stars James Mason and is the story of a young sea captain, taking his first command. James Agee's treatment of the Crane story, directed by Windust, has not destroyed any of the tale's essential flavor. Robert Preston is the marshal. An unregenerated old gunfighter goes on a drunken spree and waits for the marshal's return so he can have one last gun battle.

FACULTY, THE
1998, 102 mins, US Ⓥ ☉
D: Robert Rodriguez **A:** Jordana Brewster, Elijah Wood, Salma Hayek, Famke Janssen, Piper Laurie, Robert Patrick (Los Hooligans/Dimension)

The Faculty is a ripsnorting hunk of giddy, self-aware genre trash. Brainiac Casey (Elijah Wood) discovers a piece of icky tissue on the playing field that does very odd things when moistened in biology class. Then Casey and star jock Stan (Shawn Hatosy) witness something even stranger in the boys' locker room, and Casey and princessy Delilah (Jordan Brewster) narrowly survive more alarming events in the teachers' lounge. Film's pace is frantic yet so well engineered that viewer buys the notion that these students are soon the only non-"snatched" bodies left on campus. The Faculty is crafty and distinctive enough to rate full inclusion in the honor roll of Invasion of the Body Snatchers versions to date by Don Siegel, Philip Kaufman, and Abel Ferrara.

FAHRENHEIT 451
1966, 113 mins, UK Ⓥ ☉
D: Francois Truffaut **A:** Oskar Werner, Julie Christie, Cyril Cusack, Anton Diffring, Jeremy Spenser (Anglo-Enterprise Vineyard/Universal)

This excursion into science fiction has been thoughtfully directed by Francois Truffaut and there is adequate evidence of light touches to bring welcome and needed relief to a somber and scarifying subject. In author Ray Bradbury's glimpse into the future, books are considered the opiate of the people. Their possession is a crime and the state has a squad of firemen to destroy the illicit literature with flamethrowers. Fahrenheit 451, it is explained, is the temperature at which books are reduced to ashes. The yarn develops just a handful of characters, emphasizing the inevitable conflict between state and literate-minded citizens. Werner, in the difficult role of the once diffident and ambitious fireman who finally challenges authority, plays the part in low-key style that adds to the integrity of the character, and Christie is standout in dual roles.

FAIL-SAFE
1964, 112 mins, US ☉
D: Sidney Lumet **A:** Henry Fonda, Walter Matthau, Frank Overton, Dan O'Herlihy, Fritz Weaver, Larry Hagman (Columbia)

Fail-Safe is a tense and suspenseful piece of filmmaking dealing with the frightening implications of accidental nuclear warfare. It faithfully translates on the screen the power and seething drama of the Eugene Burdick–Harvey Wheeler book, capturing the full menace of a possible malfunction of the Strategic Air Command's fail-safe device, and paints a vivid canvas of an imaginary situation that conceivably could arise. Fail-Safe is a gripping narrative realistically and almost frighteningly told as the US goes all out to halt the plane carrying the bombs, even trying to shoot it down and advising the Russians of their peril and urging them to destroy the plane. Particularly dramatic are the sequences in which the president—tellingly portrayed by Henry Fonda—talks with the Russian premier over the "hot wire."

FALCON AND THE SNOWMAN, THE
1985, 131 mins, US Ⓥ ☉
D: John Schlesinger **A:** Timothy Hutton, Sean Penn, David Suchet, Lori Singer, Pat Hingle, Dorian Harewood (Hemdale)

A true story so oddly motivated it would be easily dismissed if fictional. Newspaperman Robert Lindsey wrote a book examining how an idealistic 22-year-old college dropout and a whacked-out drug pusher carried off a successful scheme to sell US secrets to the Soviets. With one working with a mind confused by addled loyalties and the other with a mind confused by chemicals, it remains hard to fathom exactly what they hoped to achieve or how they managed to progress so far toward achieving it. As the two lads, however, Timothy Hutton and Sean Penn are superb.

FALLEN ANGEL
1946, 97 mins, US
D: Otto Preminger **A:** Alice Faye, Dana Andrews, Linda Darnell, Charles Bick-

ford, Anne Revere, Bruce Cabot (20th Century-Fox)

Pic deals with a trollop (Linda Darnell) who gets a flock of guys on the string, then gets bumped off. The yarn revolves around which of her admirers committed the deed. Linked to the plot is the story's basic romantic tie-up between Alice Faye and Dana Andrews, the former as a respectable, wealthy small-town gal who is ripe for the taking, and Andrews is the guy who starts out to do the taking, even marrying her to do it, his idea being to get enough moola so he can cop the other gal. This is Faye's first straight dramatic part and she handles herself well.

FALLEN IDOL, THE
1948, 94 mins, UK Ⓥ

D: Carol Reed **A:** Ralph Richardson, Michele Morgan, Bobby Henrey, Sonia Dresdel, Jack Hawkins, Dora Bryan (London/20th Century-Fox)

A satisfying piece of intelligent entertainment based on a short story by Graham Greene. It's the story of a butler, working at a foreign embassy in London, who's in love with an embassy typist. While the lovers are together, the wife comes in and, after a hysterical row with her husband, accidentally falls and is killed. Dominating the entire theme is young Felipe, son of the ambassador, who is left in the servants' care while the parents are away. When a police investigation suggests that the wife might have been murdered, Felipe lies for all he is worth to defend the butler. There's hardly a scene in the picture in which the kid, played by Bobby Henrey, doesn't appear and he comes through like a seasoned trouper. Ralph Richardson's masterly portrayal of the butler is a gratifying piece of work.
1943: Nominations: Best Director, Screenplay

FALLING DOWN
1993, 115 mins, US Ⓥ ⊙ ▭

D: Joel Schumacher **A:** Michael Douglas, Robert Duvall, Barbara Hershey, Rachel Ticotin, Tuesday Weld, Frederic Forrest (Warner)

This at first comes across like a mean-spirited black comedy and then snowballs into a reasonably powerful portrait of social alienation. The tone is unremittingly dour, however. A laid-off defense worker, estranged from his wife and child, with a propensity for violence, Michael Douglas is a self-obsessed human powder keg heading to a home no longer his while on the verge of going off. The film provides Douglas with a real performer's showcase, and he delivers a strong, intense portrayal of a walking time bomb. Robert Duvall, as well, is at his congenial best as a henpecked burglary cop in his last day on the job.

FALLING IN LOVE
1984, 107 mins, US Ⓥ ⊙

D: Ulu Grosbard **A:** Robert De Niro, Meryl Streep, Harvey Keitel, Jane Kaczmarek, Dianne Wiest (Paramount)

Falling in Love is a polite little romance. Both De Niro, a construction engineer, and Streep, a graphic designer, have marriages which, while not unhappy, have settled into the routine. Meeting in Manhattan and on the commuter train, they are compelled to continue seeing one another, but are unsure where it's all headed.

FALLING IN LOVE AGAIN
1980, 103 mins, US Ⓥ

D: Steven Paul **A:** Elliott Gould, Susannah York, Michelle Pfeiffer, Kaye Ballard Steven Paul (OTA)

Elliott Gould is perfectly cast as Harry Lewis, a New Yorker entering middle age, recalling the good old days of his youth. On a cross-country trip by car with his family, Gould narrates flashbacks of his romance with Susannah York in the 1940s. Lewis went after and married the beautiful, "unattainable" rich girl. His hopes of career success did not materialize. Pic artfully captures the 1940s look and feel. Michelle Pfeiffer makes a strong impression as York's younger self.

FALL OF BABYLON, THE
1919, 82 mins, US d

D: D. W. Griffith **A:** Tully Marshall, Constance Talmadge, Elmer Clifton, Alfred Paget, Carl Stockdale, Seena Owen (Griffith)

The public wasn't entirely crazy about D. W. Griffith's massive production *Intolerance* when he presented it. When he pulled it out of mothballs he decided to take the Babylonian story out, of the big feature, shoot a few extra scenes to piece the story out and send it forth as *The Fall of Babylon*. He opens with a tableau that is part stage and part screen, a special small·screen to show New York, the modern Babylon, which, after a dissolve, brings the large screen and the opening scenes of the feature. The final scene of the first part is the beginning of the battle before the walls of Babylon. The second part opens in one of the halls of Babylon and here there are 12 slave girls and Margaret Fritts, a soprano. A number here, entitled "The Mountain Maid," is very pretty and a dance by the girls also helps to fill the picture nicely . Finally the fall of Babylon is accomplished and the love story that D.W. threads through the big battle scenes is brought to a fitting close with the lovers in a fond embrace.

FALL OF THE HOUSE OF USHER, THE
See: House of Usher

FALL OF THE ROMAN EMPIRE, THE
1964, 182 mins, US ⓥ ⊙ ▭
D: Anthony Mann **A:** Alec Guinness, Sophia Loren, Stephen Boyd, James Mason, Christopher Plummer, Omar Sharif (Bronston)

This made-in-Spain production is a giant-size, three-hour, sweepingly pictorial entertainment. It probably tells all that most film fans will want to know about the glory, grandeur, and greed of Rome. Marcus Aurelius (Alec Guinness) has been campaigning for years in the bleak northern frontiers of Rome. He is dying and knows it, intends to disinherit his undependable son, but neglects to do so. Stephen Boyd, a true-blue tribune, will not claim the throne but instead supports the son, his old wrestling-club chum Commodus. The entire subsequent plot swings on the failure of the noble and just emperor to assure the continued peace and prosperity of Rome. In all of which the daughter, played attractively by Sophia Loren, is a desperately unhappy witness and victim.
1964: Nomination: Best Original Music Score

FAME
1980, 134 mins, US ⓥ ⊙
D: Alan Parker **A:** Eddie Barth, Irene Cara, Paul McCrane, Laura Dean, Gene Anthony Ray, Anne Meara (M-G-M)

The idea behind Metro's *Fame* is the story of New York's venerable High School of Performing Arts. In truth, the educational institution would have none of the project. Alan Parker has come up with an exposure for some of the most talented youngsters seen on screen in years. The great strength of the film is in the school scenes—when it wanders away from the scholastic side, it loses dramatic intensity

and slows the pace. Gene Anthony Ray, plays Leroy—a superb natural dancer, but resentful of anyone trying to help, especially a white. His continuing fight with English teacher Mrs. Sherwood (Anne Meara) is the most believable plotline in the entire film.
1980: Best Song ("Fame"), Original Score
Nominations: Best Original Screenplay, Editing, Sound, Song ("Out Here on My Own")

FAME IS THE SPUR
1947, 116 mins, UK
D: Roy Boulting **A:** Michael Redgrave, Rosamund John, Bernard Miles, Carla Lehmann, Hugh Burden (Two Cities)

In 1870, Hamer Radshaw, a lad in a north country slum, dedicates his life to better the lot of his fellow workers. Attractive, he becomes a grand rabble-rouser. As a Labour member of Parliament he takes the line of least resistance, shedding old friends when necessary, making new ones if they can help, as long as it all leads to glory and power. Michael Redgrave gives a grand performance as the earnest young idealist who becomes the vain selfish politician. It is a difficult part, but he makes it wholly credible.

FAMILY AFFAIR, A
1937, 67 mins, US
D: George B. Seitz **A:** Lionel Barrymore, Cecilia Parker, Eric Linden, Mickey Rooney, Charley Grapewin, Spring Byington (M-G-M)

A Family Affair is is a triumph for Lionel Barrymore. As the honest country-town judge, and again as the family-loving father, he is in his element. Cecilia Parker and Eric Linden are successfully teamed as the youthful romantic interest. As is Mickey Rooney, as the kid, in his puppy-love affair with Margaret Marquis. Young Rooney's interpretation is true boy stuff, and good for the best laughs.

FAMILY BUSINESS
1989, 115 mins, US ⓥ ⊙
D: Sidney Lumet **A:** Sean Connery, Dustin Hoffman, Matthew Broderick, Rosana DeSoto, Janet Carroll (Regency/Gordon)

Sean Connery steals scenes as well as merchandise in an immensely charismatic turn in *Family Business,* a darkly comic tale about three generations brought together and torn apart by their common attraction to thievery. An unabashed rogue well into his sixties, Connery cuts an irresistible figure to his sheltered Ivy League grandson (Matthew Broderick), who enlists the old man's aid to carry out a high-tech robbery. Caught in the middle, literally and figuratively, is the boy's father (Dustin Hoffman), who once had the same relationship with his father and ended up doing hard time for it.

FAMILY JEWELS, THE
1965, 98 mins, US ⊗
D: Jerry Lewis A: Jerry Lewis, Sebastian Cabot, Donna Butterworth, Robert Strauss (Lewis/Paramount)

The Family Jewels puts Jerry Lewis in multiple role of contenders for guardianship of moppet and her inherited fortune. Episodic script hits some highs in satire and low comedy. The script focuses on precocious Donna Butterworth, cute nine-year-old orphan with $30 million in trust to be administered by the uncle whom she picks. Comic's tour de farce effort comes off unevenly. Standout is Lewis as screwy aviator who attempts to haul to Chi a group of five motorcycle-riding biddies. Very good satire on in-flight pix involves Anne Baxter appearing in film clip from *Sustenance*, a gag scene in which banquet guests, silverware, and food slide about with aircraft motion.

FAMILY LIFE
1972, 105 mins, UK
D: Ken Loach A: Sandy Ratcliff, Bill Dean, Grace Cave, Malcolm Tierney, Alan MacNaughton (Kestrel)

Director Ken Loach has succeeded in creating a disturbing and provocative film about a girl sinking into schizophrenia. David Mercer's succinct screenplay, Loach's probing direction, and the sensitive acting ward off the pitfalls of self-consciousness, didactics, and schematics. Sandy Ratcliff is effective as the weak but striving girl who is finally beaten by a system and misunderstanding.

FAMILY PLOT
1976, 120 mins, US ⊗ ⊙
D: Alfred Hitchcock A: Karen Black, Bruce Dern, Barbara Harris, William Devane, Ed Lauter, Cathleen Nesbitt (Universal)

Family Plot is a dazzling achievement for Alfred Hitchcock, masterfully controlling shifts from comedy to drama thoughout a highly complex plot. Witty screenplay is a model of construction, and the cast is uniformly superb. Bruce Dern and Barbara Harris are the couple who re-

ceive primary attention, a cabbie and a phony psychic trying to find the long-lost heir to the Rainbird fortune.

FAMILY VIEWING
1987, 86 mins, Canada
D: Atom Egoyan A: David Hemblen, Aidan Tierney, Gabrielle Rose, Arsinee Khanjian, Selma Keklikian (Ego)

Atom Egoyan's second feature is particularly exasperating precisely because there are streaks of filmmaking talent visible through the pretentious murk of this disjointed story about a single-minded young man and his emotionally pulverized family life. At the center of all this is college graduate Van (Aidan Tierney), who lives in a high-rise co-op with his slightly kinky father Stan (David Hemblen) and dad's provocatively flirtatious mistress Sandra (Gabrielle Rose).

FAMILY WAY, THE
1967, 114 mins, UK ⊗
D: Roy Boulting A: Hayley Mills, Avril Angers, John Comer, Hywel Bennett, John Mills, Wilfred Pickles (British Lion)

The story of an innocent young couple who marry and are unable to consummate their marriage. Hayley Mills gets away from her Disney image as the young bride, even essaying an undressed scene. Bennett is excellent as the sensitive young bridegroom. But it is the older hands who keep the film floating on a wave of fun, sentiment, and sympathy. John Mills is first-class in a character role as the bluff father who cannot understand his son. The best performance comes from Marjorie Rhodes as Mills's astute but understanding wife.

FAN, THE
1949, 79 mins, US ⊗
D: Otto Preminger A: Jeanne Crain, Madeleine Carroll, George Sanders, Martita Hunt (20th Century-Fox)

Yarn of the attractive mother who moves in 19th-century English society so as to be near her married daughter is deftly told. It shows her trying to prevent the daughter from making the same elopement mistake that she herself made only to become one of the most notorious women in Europe. Madeleine Carroll makes the young, attractive mother a vivid figure.

FAN, THE
1981, 95 mins, US ⊗ ⊙
D: Edward Bianchi A: Lauren Bacall, James Garner, Maureen Stapleton, Michael Biehn, Hector Elizondo (Paramount)

Lauren Bacall makes the film work

with a solid performance as a stage star pursued by a psychotic fan whose adoration turns to hatred. In his first major feature, Michael Biehn contributes solidly toward the picture's believability, gradually transforming his character's fantasies into a deadly delusion. James Garner is given less to do as Bacall's ex-husband.

FAN, THE
1996, 117 mins, US Ⓥ ⊙ ▭
D: Tony Scott A: Robert De Niro, Wesley Snipes, Ellen Barkin, John Leguizamo, Benicio Del Toro, Patti D'Arbanville (Scott Free/TriStar/Mandalay)

Utterly bankrupt artistically, psychologically and morally, and unconvincing from the overall concept down to the smallest detail, this would-be suspense thriller about an obsessed baseball fan's demented effort to help his favorite team and players represents ground zero from any audience p.o.v. Hardcore San Francisco Giants fan Gil Renard (Robert De Niro) is thrilled when the three-time MVP Bobby Tayburn (Wesley Snipes) joins the team. When Bobby falls into the worst slump of his career, the finger points at Juan Primo (Benicio Del Toro), who won't relinquish the number 11 uniform, which Bobby has always worn elsewhere. So it seems perfectly reasonable to Gil to murder Primo for Bobby to regain his number. De Niro's Gil is clearly an unhinged cretin from the outset, and the actor's been down this road too many times by now. Snipes's Bobby fits one's picture of an arrogant, overpaid contemporary athlete. But it's from sports and timeframe angles that the film is most preposterous.

FANATIC
(US: DIE! DIE! MY DARLING!)
1965, 97 mins, UK Ⓥ
D: Silvio Narizzano A: Tallulah Bankhead, Stefanie Powers, Peter Vaughan, Maurice Kaufmann, Yootha Joyce, Donald Sutherland (Hammer)

Melodramatic script echoes with clichés from other stories set in sinister mansions in English countryside. But it provides Tallulah Bankhead with numerous chances to display virtuosity, from sweet-tongued menace to maniacal blood lust, as religious-fanatic mother of Stefanie Powers's dead fiancé. Story line has Powers, modern miss, paying courtesy call to former fiancé's mother, only to be held prisoner while the mother tries to cleanse

her soul so she will be fit to meet the son in the hereafter.

FANCY PANTS
1950, 92 mins, US Ⓥ ⊙
D: George Marshall A: Bob Hope, Lucille Ball, Bruce Cabot, Eric Blore (Paramount)

Fancy Pants is a bright, bouncy farce. Hope is a hammy American actor masquerading as an English lord among the rough-'n-tough westerners seeking statehood, and he's forced to continue the impersonation when President Theodore Roosevelt comes a-visiting. Ball, too, is at her comedic peak in this one, matching Hope gag for gag with her uninhibited zanyisms.

FANDANGO
1985, 91 mins, US Ⓥ ⊙
D: Kevin Reynolds A: Kevin Costner, Judd Nelson, Sam Robards, Chuck Bush, Brian Cesak, Marvin J. McIntyre (Amblin/Warner)

Fandango emerges as a quite promising feature debut by writer-director Kevin Reynolds, with its feet squarely within the overused boys-coming-of-age genre but its heart betraying an appealingly anarchic, iconoclastic bent. Set in 1971, when the Vietnam War and the draft were still looming factors in students' lives, tale describes the final wild fling, or fandango, of five college roommates in Texas before splitting up to face the dreaded realities of the world at large. Despite the mildly rueful tone, pic's highlight is the comic midsection dominated by hippie pilot and certifiable space cadet Marvin J. McIntyre. Kevin Costner is a dynamic presence at the film's center.

FANFAN LA TULIPE
(FAN-FAN THE TULIP; SOLDIER IN LOVE)
1952, 104 mins, France/Italy Ⓥ
D: Christian-Jaque A: Gerard Philipe, Gina Lollobrigida, Marcel Herrand, Olivier Hussenot, Genevieve Page (Filmsonor/Ariane/Amato)

This is a rousing, good-humored costumer set in ribald 18th-century France. Done with a fine sense of parody, full of movement, chase, and swordplay, Christian-Jaque's tongue-in-cheek, slick pacing animates the antics of Fanfan (Gerard Philipe), a roguish, arrogant ladies' man who joins the king's army to escape a shotgun wedding. He and his sidekicks manage to win the war single-handed and save the sergeant's daughter, Adeline (Gina Lollobrigida), whom he loves.

FAN-FAN THE TULIP
See: Fanfan La Tulipe

FANNY
1932, 125 mins, France ⓥ ⊙
D: Marc Allegret **A:** Raimu, Pierre Fresnay, Orane Demazis, Charpin, Alida Rouffe (Pagnol)

Producer-writer Marcel Pagnol plays variations on his favorite theme of the young maid's fall from virtue into pregnancy. The story revolves around Fanny's (Orane Demazis) plight after she's deserted by her lover Marius (Pierre Fresnay), who leaves to become a sailor. Under pressure from her outraged mother (Alida Rouffe), Fanny is forced into marrying Panisse (Charpin), who's old enough to be her father. As a barkeep who's brokenhearted over his son's departure, Raimu displays his rich comic vein with a delicacy that never shatters the poignant qualities underlying his role.

FANNY
1961, 133 mins, US ⓥ
D: Joshua Logan **A:** Leslie Caron, Maurice Chevalier, Charles Boyer, Horst Buchholz, Salvatore Baccaloni, Lionel Jeffries (Warner)

Although the deep sentiment constantly threatens to lapse into the maudlin, it never quite does. Marcel Pagnol's story focuses upon four people: a thrifty waterfront bar operator (Charles Boyer); his son (Horst Buchholz), who has a yen to sail away; a fishmonger's daughter (Leslie Caron) in love with the wanderlustful lad; and an aging, wealthy widower (Maurice Chevalier), whose great wish is to add "& Son" to the sign above his shop. The contribution of cameraman Jack Cardiff is enormous, ranging from great, sweeping panoramic views of the port of Marseilles and the sea to tight, intimate shots of the faces of the principals. Old pros Boyer and Chevalier walk off with the picture.

1961: Nominations: Best Picture, Actor (Charles Boyer), Color Cinematography, Editing, Score of a Dramatic Picture

FANNY AND ALEXANDER
See: Fanny och Alexander

FANNY BY GASLIGHT
(US: MAN OF EVIL)
1944, 108 mins, UK ⓥ
D: Anthony Asquith **A:** Phyllis Calvert, James Mason, Wilfrid Lawson, Stewart Granger, Jean Kent (Gainsborough)

Unfortunately, Anthony Asquith's direction is hurt by faulty film editing and irritatingly slow tempo. The film would suffer little if all the bawdy-house sequences were removed. The main theme—the thorny path traveled by the true lovers because the man is "wellborn" while the girl is an illegitimate child, foster-fathered by the bawdy housekeeper—would be preserved for the mid-Victorian pillorying they both receive. Phyllis Calvert in the lead more than holds her own. She succeeds in portraying Fanny with girlish wistfulness and appeal.

FANNY OCH ALEXANDER
(FANNY AND ALEXANDER)
1982, 188 mins, Sweden/Germany/France ⓥ ⊙
D: Ingmar Bergman **A:** Gunn Wallgren, Allan Edwall, Ewa Froling, Bertil Guve, Pernilla Allwin, Jarl Kulle (Swedish Film Institute/STV1/Personafilm/Gaumont)

A sumptuously produced period piece that is also a rich tapestry of childhood memories and moods, fear and fancy, employing all the manners and means of cinematic theatrics from high and low comedy to darkest tragedy, with detours into the gothic, the grisly, and the gruesome. The well-to-do Ekdahl family has come together in the widow/grandmother Helena's house to celebrate Christmas of 1907. Helena (Gunn Wallgren) is a strong-willed but generous woman. She does worry, however, about her theater manager–actor son Oscar (Allan Edwall), who works too hard and is a pretty bad actor, but a good husband for Emilie (Ewa Froling) and father for their two young children Fanny and Alexander. *Fanny and Alexander* combines elegance with intimacy. Its moments of shock are surprisingly subdued (the burning to death of the bishop has a dreamlike quality), and its obvious nostalgia is tempered with the softest irony and the saltiness of home truths.

1982: Best Foreign Language Film, Costumes, Art Direction, Cinematography

FANTASIA
1940, 120 mins, US ⓥ ⊙
D: Ben Sharpsteen (sup.) (Walt Disney)

In *Fantasia*, Walt Disney enlists the assistance of Leopold Stokowski, the Philadelphia Symphony Orchestra, and Deems Taylor as screen commentator. The result of mixing all these ingredients, including his own unique approach to things theatrical, is a two-hour variety show, whose formidable range includes Mickey Mouse in the title role of Dukas's *The Sorcerer's*

Apprentice and a very lovely musical and visual interpretation of Schubert's "Ave Maria."
1941: Special Awards (use of sound, creation of a new form of visualized music)

FANTASTIC VOYAGE
1966, 100 mins, US ⓥ ⊙ ▱
D: Richard Fleischer **A:** Stephen Boyd, Raquel Welch, Edmond O'Brien, Donald Pleasence, Arthur O'Connell, Arthur Kennedy (20th Century-Fox)

Fantastic Voyage is just that. The lavish production, boasting some brilliant special effects and superior creative efforts, is an entertaining, enlightening excursion through inner space—the body of a man. An intriguing yarn about five people who undergo miniaturization for injection into the bloodstream of a scientist, action crosscuts from life-size medics to the shrunken quintet who encounter, and are endangered by, the miracles of life.
1966: Best Color Art Direction, Special Visual Effects
Nominations: Best Color Cinematography, Editing, Sound Effects

FAR AND AWAY
1992, 140 mins, US ⓥ ⊙ ▱
D: Ron Howard **A:** Tom Cruise, Nicole Kidman, Thomas Gibson, Robert Prosky, Barbara Babcock (Universal/Imagine)

Old-fashioned is the word for *Far and Away*, a timeworn tale of 19th-century immigrants making their way in the New World. Handsomely mounted and amiably performed, but leisurely and without much dramatic urgency, Howard's robust epic stars Tom Cruise and Nicole Kidman as class-crossed lovers who take nearly the entire picture to get together. Cruise's physicality is forcibly in evidence, which will not be unwelcome to his many fans. Stripped down frequently, he is genuinely impressive in the fisticuff action of pic's midsection. Heavily garbed, Kidman has the requisite grit and defiant spirit in her eyes.

FAR COUNTRY, THE
1955, 96 mins, US ⓥ ▱
D: Anthony Mann **A:** James Stewart, Ruth Roman, Corinne Calvet, Walter Brennan, John McIntire, Jay C. Flippen (Universal)

Rugged action is featured in *The Far Country* to go with its rugged outdoor scenery, and the results add up to film entertainment. A story of the far north, set back in the pioneer days when gold was luring adventurous souls to the snow country. Stewart arrives in this setting driving a herd of cattle, which he and his partner (Walter Brennan) figure to unload at fancy prices in the gold-crazy country. The partners are in trouble almost immediately, because the town of Skagway's self-styled law (John McIntire) tries to commandeer the herd. Stewart and Brennan handle their characters with the expected ease.

FAREWELL MY CONCUBINE
See: Bawang Bie Ji

FAREWELL MY LOVELY
See: Murder, My Sweet

FAREWELL, MY LOVELY
1975, 97 mins, US ⓥ
D: Dick Richards **A:** Robert Mitchum, Charlotte Rampling, John Ireland, Sylvia Miles, Jack O'Halloran, Anthony Zerbe (EK-ITC)

Farewell, My Lovely is a lethargic, vaguely campy tribute to Hollywood's private-eye mellers of the 1940s and to writer Raymond Chandler, whose Phillip Marlowe character has inspired a number of features. The plot has the cynical but humane Marlowe (Robert Mitchum) searching in seedy L.A. for the missing girlfriend of an ex-con. Mitchum seems a bit adrift here, underplaying to the point of inertia.
1975: Nomination: Best Supp. Actress (Sylvia Miles)

FAREWELL TO ARMS, A
1932, 90 mins, US ⓥ ⊙
D: Frank Borzage **A:** Gary Cooper, Helen Hayes, Adolphe Menjou, Mary Phillips, Jack La Rue (Paramount)

A Farewell to Arms is a corking flicker [from the novel by Ernest Hemingway]. Director Frank Borzage makes wholly palatable (and highly believable) the premise that a fleeting one hour's meeting behind the front with the resulting seduction (Gary Cooper and Helen Hayes) is the culmination of a love which, in another sphere, would have followed only a long span of courtship and flowers. Equally acute is the hospital situation where Hayes, as one of the nurses, violates every regulation and remains with the convalescent Cooper in his room. All this builds up to the finale, where Cooper deserts his regiment, to brave frontiers and sentinels to ultimately reach the woman. Casting Hayes was a natural. Cooper and Adolphe Menjou are aces in the two other major roles.

1932/33: Best Cinematography, Sound Recording
Nominations: Best Picture, Art Direction

FAREWELL TO ARMS, A
1957, 159 mins, US ⓥ ⊙
D: Charles Vidor A: Rock Hudson, Jennifer Jones, Vittorio De Sica, Alberto Sordi, Kurt Kasznar, Mercedes McCambridge (20th Century-Fox)

New version of the Ernest Hemingway World War I story conveys some of the Hemingway spirit that speaks of the futility of war and a desperate love that grips two strangers in its midst. But sweep and frankness alone don't make a great picture; and *Farewell* suffers from an overdose of both. Ben Hecht's often mature dialogue is also riddled with clichés, and the relationship between Rock Hudson and Jennifer Jones never takes on real dimensions. Vittorio De Sica plays the cynical Major Rinaldi with dash, and in him the Hemingway spirit comes alive with full force.
1957: Nomination: Best Supp. Actor (Vittorio De Sica)

FAREWELL TO MY CONCUBINE
See: Bawang Bie Ji

FAREWELL TO THE KING
1989, 117 mins, US ⓥ ⊙
D: John Milius A: Nick Nolte, Nigel Havers, James Fox, Marilyn Tokuda (Vestron)

The clichés are as thick as the foliage in *Farewell to the King*. Pic recycles familiar situations and stock characters in an overlong actioner that never builds to a spiritual climax. Two British army officers (Nigel Havers and Frank McRae) are parachuted into the Borneo jungle to rally the tribes against imminent Japanese invasion in the latter days of World War II. They come across a virile and fulfilled Nick Nolte, playing a freedom-loving white man who's anxious to protect his natives from the barbarities of civilization. Nolte never rises to the nobility and tragic majesty the at-first-skeptical British officers finally see in him. Havers is a sympathetic presence in an equally empty role.

FAR FROM HOME
1989, 86 mins, US ⓥ ⊙
D: Meiert Avis A: Matt Frewer, Drew Barrymore, Richard Masur, Karen Austin, Susan Tyrrell, Jennifer Tilly (Lightning/Vestron)

This poorly scripted would-be thriller is of note only as a transition film to adult roles for child actress Drew Barrymore.

Joleen (Barrymore), just turned 14, is stranded with no gas at a trailer park with her dad (Matt Frewer) on a vacation tour of national parks. A mad killer is offing people in the vicinity. With a baby face, dreamy eyes, and a *Playboy* model's body, Barrymore is sexy but ill-used by a tawdry screenplay that has her volunteering to "go for a swim" no matter how many deadly bodies pile up around her.

FAR FROM HOME
THE ADVENTURES OF YELLOW DOG
1995, 80 mins, US ⓥ ⊙
D: Phillip Borsos A: Mimi Rogers, Bruce Davison, Jesse Bradford, Tom Bower, Joel Palmer (20th Century-Fox)

The journey of a boy lost in the woods with his faithful canine is familiar territory; and while the craft is superior, the story is emotionally predictable. Set in the rugged wilderness and shores of British Columbia, the story centers on the McCormick family. Dad (Bruce Davison) runs a hauling company and son Angus (Jesse Bradford) is an industrious, inquisitive lad. Into their world arrives a golden Labrador with innate intelligence. Bradford effortlessly demonstrates an instinct, talent, and charisma no other actor of his age can equal.

FAR FROM THE MADDING CROWD
1967, 169 mins, UK ⓥ ⊙ ▭
D: John Schlesinger A: Julie Christie, Terence Stamp, Peter Finch, Alan Bates, Prunella Ransome, Fiona Walker (M-G-M)

In this case, scripter Frederic Raphael has perhaps hewn too closely to Thomas Hardy's original. It is the story of Bathsheba Everdene's multifaceted love for the three men in her life, Sergeant Troy, Gabriel Oak, and Boldwood. Julie Christie, Peter Finch, Terence Stamp, and Alan Bates are variedly handsome and have their many effective moments, but there is little they can ultimately and lastingly do to overcome the basic banality of their characters and, to a certain degree, their lines.
1967: Nomination: Best Original Music Score

FARGO
1996, 97 mins, US ⓥ ⊙
D: Joel Coen A: Steve Buscemi, William H. Macy, Peter Stormare, Harve Presnell, Frances McDormand (Working Title)

The slow unraveling of the perfect crime gone awry has long been an almost irresistible movie-thriller theme. In the darkly humorous *Fargo*, iconoclastic filmmakers Joel and Ethan Coen manage the precarious balancing act of respecting genre conventions and simultaneously pushing them to an almost surrealistic extreme. Pic is very funny stuff. Setup involves Jerry Lundegaard (William H. Macy), a financially overextended Minneapolis car salesman. He hires two lumbering ex-cons, Carl Showalter (Steve Buscemi) and Gaear Grimsrud (Peter Stormare), to kidnap his wife. After abducting Jean Lundegaard (Kristin Rudrud), the duo head for a cabin in northern Minnesota. Along the way, they're stopped by a state trooper on a seemingly minor infraction. The following morning, local police chief Marge Gunderson (Frances McDormand) wakes up with a triple homicide on her hands.

1996: Best Actress (Frances McDormand), Original Screenplay

Nominations: Best Cinematography, Best Director, Best Supp. Actor (William H. Macy)

FARMER'S DAUGHTER, THE
1947, 90 mins, US Ⓥ

D: H. C. Potter **A:** Loretta Young, Joseph Cotten, Ethel Barrymore, Charles Bickford, Harry Davenport (RKO)

The Farmer's Daughter rolls irresistibly along in a light-romantic-comedy groove. Loretta Young plays a Swedish country girl, complete with accent and rural garb, who lands a second maid's job in the mansion of Joseph Cotten and his mother, Ethel Barrymore. Latter pair are well-intentioned leaders of the local political machine, which is embroiled in a hot fight with the opposition over the election of a congressman. The country lass, being naive and frank as well as an eyeful for Cotten, openly voices her disapproval of the compromise candidate chosen by her employers. Politicking is used only as a once-over-lightly excuse for the romantic bickerings and final clinch.

1947: Best Actress (Loretta Young)

Nomination: Best Supp. Actor (Charles Bickford)

FARMER TAKES A WIFE, THE
1935, 91 mins, US Ⓥ

D: Victor Fleming **A:** Janet Gaynor, Henry Fonda, Charles Bickford, Slim Summerville, Andy Devine, Margaret Hamilton (Fox)

Too thin a plot trying to cover entirely too much area is a handicap. Molly (Janet Gaynor), cook on a canal boat, falls in love with Dan Harrow (Henry Fonda), who is driving a canal team to earn the money for the purchase of a farm. Gaynor is given a part that permits her to get away from her sometimes too sweet assignments. Fonda is youthfully manly and shows nice personality.

FARMER TAKES A WIFE, THE
1953, 80 mins, US Ⓥ

D: Henry Levin **A:** Betty Grable, Dale Robertson, Thelma Ritter, John Carroll, Eddie Foy Jr. (20th Century-Fox)

The Farmer Takes a Wife was first screened in 1935 as a straight drama and it doesn't take smoothly to the injection of songs (by Harold Arlen and Dorothy Fields) and dances, probably because the tuning is unimpressive and the terp numbers are lacking in bounce. Grable takes prettily to the Technicolor hues and the period costuming, latter being rather fancy for a canal boat cook. As the farmer turned boatman, Robertson is okay, but is out of his element in picture's musical requirements, light as they are.

FAR NORTH
1988, 90 mins, US Ⓥ ⊙

D: Sam Shepard **A:** Jessica Lange, Charles Durning, Tess Harper, Donald Moffat, Ann Wedgeworth, Patricia Arquette (Alive/Nelson)

In his film directing debut, Sam Shepard forsakes the fevered elliptical prose flights of his plays for a straightforward approach of surprising flatness and sentimentality. Bertrum (Charles Durning) is thrown from a cart by his rebellious runaway horse, and lands in the hospital obsessed with exacting revenge on the nag. His citified, unmarried pregnant daughter Kate (Jessica Lange) flies out to comfort the curmudgeon in his crisis. In what's meant to be taken as a profound gesture of filial obedience, Lange reluctantly agrees to assassinate the horse. This mystifies Lange's slightly dotty mom (Ann Wedgeworth) and outrages her fiery farmbound sister Rita (Tess Harper).

FASHIONS OF 1934
1934, 80 mins, US

D: William Dieterle, Busby Berkeley **A:** William Powell, Bette Davis, Frank McHugh, Verree Teasdale, Reginald Owen, Hugh Herbert (First National)

Fashions of 1934 may be a bit farfetched and inconsistent, but it has color, flash, dash, class, girls, and plenty of clothes. Story centers around the lives of exclusive Paris models. There's the wow feather scene wherein Busby Berkeley has combined a pageant of ostrich plumes to include a Hall of Human Harps, a Web of Dreams, and Venus and Her Galley Slaves. Berkeley again repeats the prismatic formations, dissolves, overhead shots, and other of the now established school of BB cinematerps.

FAST AND LOOSE
1930, 70 mins, US
D: Fred Newmeyer A: Miriam Hopkins, Carole Lombard, Frank Morgan, Charles Starrett (Paramount)

A frothy bit of celluloid. Hopkins is engaged to a theatric, silly-ass, and titled Englishman, while Henry Wadsworth is in love with an on-the-level chorus girl (Lombard). Hopkins seeks an out on her prospective marriage and grasps her chance when accidentally meeting Charles Starrett. Later discovery that he's merely a garage mechanic enhances the romance for her, and it's a grand mix-up when the entire family meets in a roadhouse raid.

FASTER, PUSSYCAT! KILL! KILL!
1966, 84 mins, US ⓥ
D: Russ Meyer A: Tura Satana, Haji, Lori Williams, Susan Bernard, Stuart Lancaster, Paul Trinka (Eve)

Faster, Pussycat! Kill! Kill! is a somewhat sordid, quite sexy, and very violent murder-kidnap-theft meller which includes elements of rape, lesbianism, and sadism, clothed in faddish leather and boots and equipped with sports cars. Some good performances emerge from a one-note script via very good Russ Meyer direction and his outstanding editing.

FAST LADY, THE
1963, 95 mins, UK
D: Ken Annakin A: James Robertson Justice, Stanley Baxter, Leslie Phillips, Kathleen Harrison, Julie Christie (Rank)

A thin idea is pumped up into a reasonably brisk, amusing situation comedy. Star of the film is an impressive vintage Bentley auto. Film concerns the efforts of an obstinate, overpatriotic, and gauche young Scottish civil servant to learn to drive the sports car and thus ingratiate himself with the tycoon father of a girl for whom he has fallen. Much of the humor is of the pratfall variety, but it provides predictable, easy yocks. Most hilarious, thanks to a gem of a performance by Eric

Barker, is the first driving test taken by the would-be driver (Stanley Baxter).

FAST TIMES AT RIDGEMONT HIGH
1982, 92 mins, US ⓥ
D: Amy Heckerling A: Sean Penn, Jennifer Jason Leigh, Judge Reinhold, Robert Romanus, Phoebe Cates, Ray Walston (Universal)

Cameron Crowe returned to high school after reaching voting age and chronicled his year's adventure there in a well-received book. Adapting the book now for the screen, Crowe comes up with less. Compressed to fundamentals, the high-school characters of the 1980s aren't that different from the 1950s. The nice thing is that Crowe and director Amy Heckerling have provided something pleasant to observe in all of these characters, though they really are sadly lacking in anything gripping. The really good part of *Fast Times* is Sean Penn as a spaced-out, irresponsible surfer. Similarly, Judge Reinhold is terrific as a relatively straight kid working his way through various fast-food jobs.

FAST-WALKING
1982, 115 mins, US ⓥ
D: James B. Harris A: James Woods, Tim McIntire, Kay Lenz, Robert Hooks, M. Emmet Walsh, Timothy Carey (Pickman)

A prison drama which focuses on guards rather than prisoners and which reeks of a sort of late-1960s, counterculture existentialism, pic seems oddly out of time and place. Producer-director-writer James B. Harris hasn't really pulled it all together into a meaningful finished work. James Woods a self-described redneck with little on his mind, who smokes dope even on his job as a prison guard. Woods becomes involved in two interconnecting plots brewing within the penitentiary walls. First, being engineered by his weird cousin Tim McIntire, involves the assassination of a newly arrived black militant (Robert Hooks), while the other is a competing scheme to spring Hooks.

FATAL ATTRACTION
1987, 119 mins, US ⓥ ◉
D: Adrian Lyne A: Michael Douglas, Glenn Close, Anne Archer, Fred Gwynne (Paramount)

The screws are tightened expertly in this suspenseful meller about a flipped-out femme who makes life hell for the married man who scorns her. New York attorney

Michael Douglas is happily married to the gorgeous Anne Archer and has a lovely daughter, but succumbs to Glenn Close's provocative flirtations while his wife is out of town. Douglas, in a family man role, seems warmer and more sympathetic than usual, and well conveys the evasiveness and anguish of his cornered character. Close throws herself into the physical abandon of the early reels with surprising relish, and become genuinely frightening when it comes clear she is capable of anything.

1987: Nominations: Best Picture, Director, Actress (Glenn Close), Supp. Actress (Anne Archer), Adapted Screenplay, Editing

FATAL INSTINCT
1993, 88 mins, US ⊚
D: Carl Reiner **A:** Armand Assante, Sherilyn Fenn, Kate Nelligan, Sean Young, Christopher McDonald, Tony Randall (M-G-M)

Grating send-up, which proves crude without being clever or even remotely funny, includes spoofs of *Basic Instinct, Fatal Attraction, Body Heat, Sleeping with the Enemy,* and *Cape Fear*. Armand Assante gets the thankless job of playing a cop and lawyer who busts bad guys and then defends them in court, while his wife and her lover (Kate Nelligan, Christopher McDonald) plot his death. Reiner doesn't seem to have his heart in this effort, and, with the exception of Sean Young, who plays her sex-kitten role to the hilt, neither does the cast.

FATAL PASSIONS, THE
See: Dr. Mabuse der Spieler

FAT CITY
1972, 100 mins, US ⊚
D: John Huston **A:** Stacy Keach, Jeff Bridges, Susan Tyrrell, Candy Clark (Rastar/Columbia)

John Huston takes a terse, sharp, downbeat, but compassionate look at the underside of small-town American life. It is about boxing, about failures, about part-time agricultural workers, but really about those who, in defeat, still find meaning. Huston has been blessed by a brilliantly dialogued script by Leonard Gardner from his own much-praised novel.

1972: Nomination: Best Supp. Actress (Susan Tyrrell)

FATE IS THE HUNTER
1964, 106 mins, US ▭
D: Ralph Nelson **A:** Glenn Ford, Nancy

Kwan, Rod Taylor, Suzanne Pleshette, Jane Russell (20th Century-Fox)

Realistically produced picture's greatest asset is a stirring climax. Buildup frequently plods due to lack of significant story line and situations. Production deals with the cause of a spectacular plane crash. The investigation finally centers on the dead pilot, reported to have been drinking a few hours before the tragedy. Glenn Ford as the airline's director of flight operations and old friend of the pilot (Rod Taylor) pursues his own line of inquiry.

1964: Nomination: Best B&W Cinematography

FATHER
See: Apa

FATHER
1990, 100 mins, Australia ⊚
D: John Power **A:** Max von Sydow, Carol Drinkwater, Julia Blake, Steve Jacob (Barron/Latin Quarter)

The story unfolds in Melbourne, where German-born Joe Mueller (Max von Sydow) has lived since the war. In a television program an old woman (Julia Blake) accuses Mueller of wartime atrocities. Mueller vigorously denies the charges, but winds up in an Australian court. Von Sydow is a tower of strength as the accused German who may, or may not, be guilty, while Blake is extremely touching as the accusing survivor of Nazi atrocities.

FATHER BROWN
1954, 91 mins, UK ⊚
D: Robert Hamer **A:** Alec Guinness, Joan Greenwood, Peter Finch, Cecil Parker, Bernard Lee (Columbia/Facet)

Father Brown is distinguished mainly by the excellent casting of Alec Guinness in the title role. The G. K. Chesterton stories were adapted by Thelma Schnee, who shares the credit with the director. They've fashioned a warmhearted narrative based on the exploits of the eccentric priest who sets out to outwit international crooks while the police forces of London and Paris are on his tail. Guinness's performance, good though it is, does not overshadow a first-class thesping job by Peter Finch as the international thief who likes to collect the rare treasures he cannot afford to buy.

FATHER GOOSE
1964, 115 mins, US ⊚
D: Ralph Nelson **A:** Cary Grant, Leslie

Caron, Trevor Howard, Jack Good, Sharyl Lock (Universal)

Cary Grant comes up with an about-face change of character in this World War II comedy. As a Japanese plane watcher on a deserted South Sea isle, Grant plays an unshaven bum addicted to tippling and tattered attire, a long way from the suave figure he usually projects but affording him opportunity for nutty characterization. Leslie Caron and Trevor Howard are valuable assists to plot, which brings in a flock of refugee kids.
1964: Best Original Story & Screenplay **Nominations:** Best Editing, Sound

FATHERLAND
1986, 110 mins, UK/W. Germany Ⓥ
D: Ken Loach **A:** Gerulf Pannach, Fabienne Babe, Sigfrit Steiner, Cristine Rose (Film Four/MK2/Clasart/Kestrel II)

Ken Loach has created an ambiguous yet penetrating work about two opposing cultures. Focus of the drama is Klaus Dritteman, a dissident folksinger first silenced by the East Germans, then allowed to leave quietly. He is unhappy being treated as a commodity in the West and doesn't know if he can be creative in his new environment.

FATHER OF THE BRIDE
1950, 92 mins, US Ⓥ ⊙
D: Vincente Minnelli **A:** Spencer Tracy, Joan Bennett, Elizabeth Taylor, Don Taylor (M-G-M)

Screenplay provides director Vincente Minnelli with choice situations and dialogue, sliced right from life and hoked just enough to bring out the comedy flavor. Opening shot is a daybreak scene among the debris created by a wedding reception. Weary but relieved, Spencer Tracy recounts the sorry lot of a bride's father, emotionally and financially devastating.
1950: Nominations: Best Picture, Actor (Spencer Tracy), Screenplay

FATHER OF THE BRIDE
1991, 105 mins, US Ⓥ ⊙
D: Charles Shyer **A:** Steve Martin, Diane Keaton, Kimberly Williams, Kieran Culkin, Martin Short (Touchstone)

Remake of the 1950 pic bears little resemblance to the original. Modernized version gets by more on physical shtick than verbal sparkle. Steve Martin plays the scion of a comfortable San Marino, CA, family who goes a little nuts when he learns that his beloved 22-year-old daughter (Kimberly Williams) is engaged. Beset by separation anxiety, he can't find anything right about her perfectly appealing fiancé (George Newbern) or the pricey wedding arrangements. A radiant Diane Keaton gives him first-rate support as the calm, sunny wife charged with the exhausting task of keeping up with him.

FATHER OF THE BRIDE PART II
1995, 106 mins, US Ⓥ
D: Charles Shyer **A:** Steve Martin, Diane Keaton, Martin Short, Kimberly Williams, George Newbern (Touchstone)

As holiday confections go, this breezy sequel proves pleasant enough, assuming a reasonably high tolerance for saccharine in one's diet. Steve Martin is again properly irascible as George Banks, who can't cope with the idea of his daughter becoming pregnant, prompting an amusing midlife-crisis sequence leading to an afternoon romp with his wife (Diane Keaton) that—to the shock of everyone—puts her in a family way as well.

FATHER'S DAY
1997, 98 mins, US ⊙ ⊡
D: Ivan Reitman **A:** Robin Williams, Billy Crystal, Julia Louis-Dreyfus, Nastassja Kinski, Charlie Hofheimer, Bruce Greenwood (Silver/Warner)

Robin Williams and Billy Crystal can each provoke a lot more laughs in a minute of standup than they jointly manage during the entire running time of *Father's Day*, which mechanically pushes the humor button one moment and the sentiment button the next. Combo of styles just doesn't strike the hoped-for sparks. Situation-heavy plot centers upon a scheme hatched by a long-ago girlfriend (Nastassja Kinski) of both men in which she separately informs each that he is the father of her 16-year-old son (Charlie Hofheimer), who has recently run away. Duly enchanted by the notion of fatherhood, they begin the hunt and decide to team up when they bump into each other.

FATHOM
1967, 100 mins, US ⊡
D: Leslie Martinson **A:** Anthony Franciosa, Raquel Welch, Ronald Fraser, Richard Briers, Clive Revill (20th Century-Fox)

Fathom, lensed on location in Spain to take full advantage of scenic backdrops, is a mélange of melodramatic ingredients personalized by the lush presence of Raquel Welch and highlighted by some exciting parachute scenes.

FAT MAN AND LITTLE BOY
(UK: SHADOW MAKERS)
1989, 126 mins, US ℗ ⊙ ▭
D: Roland Joffe **A:** Paul Newman, Dwight Schultz, Bonnie Bedelia, John Cusack, Laura Dern, Natasha Richardson (Light motive/Paramount)

"Fat Man" and "Little Boy" were the nicknames given to the bombs dropped over Hiroshima and Nagasaki. These names aren't mentioned by any of the characters in the film, nor do the bombings figure in the action. Film concentrates instead on General Groves (Paul Newman), the man assigned to oversee the project, and J. Robert Oppenheimer (Dwight Schultz), the brilliant scientist with far-left-to-all-out Communist connections picked to lead it. This is all well and good, except that few dramatic sparks fly.

FBI STORY, THE
1959, 149 mins, US ℗ ⊙
D: Mervyn LeRoy **A:** James Stewart, Vera Miles, Murray Hamilton, Nick Adams, Diane Jergens (Warner)

A tense, exciting film story told in human terms. The method used is to show the work of the FBI through the life of one of its agents. Stewart and his wife (Vera Miles) are torn between his dedication to his job with the FBI and his need to give his family a more rewarding life outside the bureau. The dialogue is exemplary, economical in words despite the film's length. Too, the story does not run out of plot. Stewart gives a restrained performance, wry and intelligent, completely credible as the film covers a span of about 25 years to show both the fledgling agent and the older man.

FEAR
1996, 96 mins, US ℗ ⊙ ▭
D: James Foley **A:** Mark Wahlberg, Reese Witherspoon, William Peterson, Amy Brenneman, Christopher Gray (Imagine/Universal)

In the mold of the psychological-sexual thrillers of the late eighties and early nineties, *Fear* is a gender-reversed *Fatal Attraction,* with a strong measure of *Cape Fear* thrown into the formulaic mix. In his biggest screen role to date, Mark Wahlberg plays the Glenn Close character: a sexy intruder who becomes obsessed with a naive, sexually yearning girl and in due course torments her entire family. James Foley's stylishly elegant and efficient direction is at least a notch above the material's level.

FEAR AND DESIRE
1953, 68 mins, US
D: Stanley Kubrick **A:** Frank Silvera, Kenneth Harp, Paul Mazursky, Virginia Leith (Kubrick)

Fear and Desire is a literate, unhackneyed war drama, outstanding for its fresh camera treatment and poetic dialogue. Stanley Kubrick produced, directed, photographed, and edited the film on a $100,000 shoestring budget. Film was written by 23-year-old poet Howard O. Sackler, who has confected a blend of violence and philosophy, some of it half-baked, and some of it powerfully moving. Story deals with four GIs stranded six miles behind enemy lines and what happens to their moral fibre as they try to escape.

FEAR AND LOATHING IN LAS VEGAS
1998, 119 mins, US ℗ ⊙ ▭
D: Terry Gilliam **A:** Johnny Depp, Benicio Del Toro, Craig Bierko, Ellen Barkin, Gary Busey, Cameron Diaz (Rhino/Universal)

Fear and Loathing in Las Vegas is a bad trip. Long-gestating adaptation of Hunter S. Thompson's hallucinatory 1971 gonzo tome has become an over-elaborate gross-out under Terry Gilliam's direction, a visualization of a flashpoint in the history of trendy pharmaceuticals without a story or detectable point-of-view. Cryptic narration and pop tunes of various vintages provide a fragile frame for the indulgent spree of sportswriter Raoul Duke (Johnny Depp), who drives from L.A. to Vegas with his attorney and partner-in-crime, Dr. Gonzo (Benicio Del Toro), ostensibly to cover the off-road Mint 400 motorcycle race but actually to rebel against what they see as the plastic, hypocritical nightmare of Nixon's America by becoming as wasted as possible. Numerous well-known actors make cameo appearances, but only Christina Ricci, as a somnolent teen who paints portraits of Barbra Streisand, and Ellen Barkin, as an abused, vulnerable diner waitress, stick out from the crowd.

FEAR CITY
1984, 96 mins, US ℗ ⊙
D: Abel Ferrara **A:** Tom Berenger, Billy Dee Williams, Jack Scalia, Melanie Griffith, Rossano Brazzi, Rae Dawn Chong (Zupnik/Curtis)

Fear City lives up to its title as a tough, nasty, big-league meller by throwing every element from the exploitation cookbook—gory violence, straight and gay sex, multiple murders, martial arts, raw dialogue, mobsters, drugs, and gobs of female nudity—into the pot and letting them stew. Teeming plot has B-girl talent agent Tom Berenger trying to get things started again with old flame Melanie Griffith.

FEAR EATS THE SOUL
See: Angst Essen Seele Auf

FEAR IN THE NIGHT
1947, 71 mins, US Ⓥ
D: Maxwell Shane **A:** Paul Kelly, DeForest Kelley, Ann Doran, Kay Scott, Robert Emmett Keane (Paramount)

A good psychological melodrama, unfolded at fast clip. Plot concerns young man who awakens one morning after dream that he has killed a man. Reality of dream is strengthened when he finds strange button and key in his pocket. He seeks aid from his detective brother-in-law. Paul Kelly is a believable cop who aids DeForest Kelley solve nightmare riddle.

FEAR IS THE KEY
1973, 105 mins, UK Ⓥ ▱
D: Michael Tuchner **A:** Barry Newman, Suzy Kendall, John Vernon, Dolph Sweet, Ben Kingsley, Ray McAnally (KLK/Anglo-EMI)

Sustained interest and suspense mark well-made action stuff including the obligatory auto chase routine around the highways and byways of Louisiana, where pic was shot. Barry Newman and Suzy Kendall are top-featured, he as a deep-sea salvage expert, she as an oil heiress' and kidnap victim. When Newman's wife, brother, and child are shot out of the sky while fetching a salvage cargo of priceless gems, he goes undercover in cahoots with the law to avenge the killings.

FEARLESS
1993, 116 mins, US Ⓥ ⊙
D: Peter Weir **A:** Jeff Bridges, Isabella Rossellini, Rosie Perez, Tom Hulce, John Turturro, Deirdre O'Connell (Spring Creek/Warner)

Peter Weir's distinctive study of the aftermath of a plane crash breaks apart thanks to undue symbolism and pretension, as well as a central relationship that doesn't pay off dramatically. In one of his best performances, Jeff Bridges portrays Max Klein, a man who, after walking away from a plane crash that kills his business partner and many other passengers,

enters an exalted state in which he feels that he has "passed through death" and believes that nothing can harm him.
1993: Nomination: Best Supp. Actress (Rosie Perez)

FEARLESS FRANK
See: Frank's Greatest Adventure

FEARLESS VAMPIRE KILLERS, THE
See: Dance of the Vampires

FEAR NO EVIL
1981, 99 mins, US Ⓥ
D: Frank LaLoggia **A:** Elizabeth Hoffman, Kathleen Rowe McAllen, Frank Birney, Stefan Arngrim (LaLoggia)

Though the horror genre is sated with maniacs on the menace, *Fear No Evil* stands out. Spooky and surreal, the ultimately hopeful film has its basis in religious morality. A rotten seed, born to horrified parents, grows into a menacing 17-year-old. He's a hopeless baddie consumed by the power to destroy. At Andrew/Lucifer's wicked island domain, he summons the undead and tangles with Margaret, an old woman with the power of God behind her.

FEAR STRIKES OUT
1957, 100 mins, US Ⓥ ⊙
D: Robert Mulligan **A:** Anthony Perkins, Karl Malden, Norma Moore, Adam Williams (Paramount)

Baseball is only a means to an end in this highly effective dramatization of the tragic results that can come from a father pushing his son too hard toward a goal he himself was not able to achieve. Anthony Perkins delivers a remarkably sustained performance as a sensitive young man, pushed too fast to the limits of his ability to cope with life's pressures. Karl Malden is splendid as the father who pits his own ambitions mixed up with love for his son.

FEAST OF JULY
1996, 116 mins, UK/US Ⓥ ⊙ ▱
D: Christopher Menaul **A:** Embeth Davidtz, Ben Chaplin, Tom Bell, Gemma Jones, James Purefoy, Greg Wise (Merchant Ivory/Touchstone)

This Merchant Ivory production is, as expected, visually handsome and decently acted. But it's also a stale trudge through terribly familiar territory. Turgid tale deals with a young woman (Embeth Davidtz) who is seduced and abandoned by a philandering man in late-19th-century rural England. When she is taken in by a kindly lamplighter and his wife, tragedy results when the couple's three sons all fall in love with her.

FEDORA
1978, 110 mins, W. Germany/France Ⓥ
ⓞ
D: Billy Wilder **A:** William Holden, Marthe Keller, Jose Ferrer, Hildegard Knef, Frances Sternhagen, Mario Adorf (Geria/Bavaria)

Billy Wilder goes serenely back to Hollywood treatment of itself as legend, illusion, and dream rather than reality. Neither Marthe Keller, as the once great star Fedora, nor Hildegard Knef as a crusty Polish countess and the star's keeper, have that elusive, self-absorbed, but camera-loving look that stars possessed, though they are good. Wilder's directorial flair, the fine production dress, Holden's solid presence, Michael York playing himself as a narcissistic actor, and Henry Fonda as himself, also as head of the Academy, who delivers a belated Oscar to Fedora, add some flavor to this bittersweet bow to the old star system.

FEDS
1988, 91 mins, US Ⓥ ⓞ
D: Dan Goldberg **A:** Rebecca DeMornay, Mary Gross, Ken Marshall, Fred Dalton Thompson (Warner)

Rebecca DeMornay and Mary Gross are FBI academy trainees in a buddy picture that plays more like a biddy picture. There isn't a fresh idea or a new one-liner in all of the script, an anthology of inert retreads from the *Police Academy* series and *Private Benjamin*.

FEET FIRST
1930, 93 mins, US
D: Clyde Bruckman **A:** Harold Lloyd, Robert McWade, Lillianne Leighton, Barbara Kent, Alec B. Francis (Lloyd/Paramount)

Full of Harold Lloyd gags, stunts, and tricks, all in a comedy vein, as always. Lloyd is again dangling along the front of a skyscraper building, doing his acrobatics, escaping death a dozen times, using slapstick besides, and perhaps prolonging this scene too far. Another stretch of laughs occurs where Lloyd is on a boat, without baggage or money, from Honolulu to Frisco. He falls for a girl (Barbara Kent) who is on the same boat. She thinks he is a big businessman. Lloyd's endeavor is to prevent her from discovering he is a shoe salesman.

FELLINI SATYRICON
See: Satyricon

FELLINI'S CASANOVA
See: Casanova

FELLOW TRAVELER
1990, 97 mins, UK/US Ⓥ
D: Philip Saville **A:** Ron Silver, Hart Bochner, Imogen Stubbs, Daniel J. Travanti (BFI/BBC/HBO)

The story of a blacklisted Hollywood screenwriter during the McCarthy era who is forced to Britain to find work. Pic eventually becomes rather simplistic when trying to debate the actual politics of the time. Ron Silver is convincing as the cynical writer thrown into a strange English environment, and Hart Bochner looks the handsome leading man, replete with Errol Flynn mustache. Pic is excellent at recreating the early heady days of independent TV in the UK.

FEMALE PERVERSIONS
1996, 116 mins, US Ⓥ
D: Susan Streitfeld **A:** Tilda Swinton, Amy Madigan, Karen Sillas, Laila Robins, Clancy Brown, Frances Fisher (Trans Atlantic/October/MAP)

A hardcore feminist meditation about gender and sexuality in modern life that is often academic and a bit pretentious. Tilda Swinton is perfectly cast as Eve, a bright lawyer who can't seem to control her sexual desires. She recklessly enters into a relationship with Renée (Karen Sillas), a sensitive psychiatrist. Just as Eve is facing the highest point in her life, Madelyn (Amy Madigan), her unstable sister, is experiencing her lowest, when she's arrested for shoplifting. Eve goes to rescue Madelyn and finds a super-8 film that records their mother's humiliating abuse by their father. Freudian psychiatrists will have a field day observing the sisters' struggle to gain control and power in their lives as a result of their traumatic family experience.

FEMALE TROUBLE
1975, 95 mins, US Ⓥ
D: John Waters **A:** Divine, David Lochary, Mary Vivian Pearce, Mink Stole (Dreamland/New Line)

The sordid tale of Dawn Davenport, who rises from high-school hoyden to mistress of crime before frying in the electric chair. As she climbs the ladder of success, she is raped by a stranger, gives birth to an obnoxious child who later murders the father, marries a beautician whose mother she imprisons in a birdcage before cutting

412

off her hand, and opens a nightclub act during which she guns down members of the audience. In the stellar role is Divine, a mammoth 300-pound transvestite. Camp is too elegant a word to describe it all.

FEMININE TOUCH, THE
1941, 96 mins, US
D: W. S. Van Dyke A: Rosalind Russell, Don Ameche, Kay Francis, Van Heflin, Donald Meek (M-G-M)

The Feminine Touch is important for showcasing Rosalind Russell as one of the top film comediennes. She handles the sophisticated material equally as well as the frequent excursions into slapstick. Don Ameche, as an absentminded but honest professor, can also pitch comedy. The script gives dumb football players a thorough lacing and points up the literary set as a flock of screwball lushes and predatory wolves.

UNE FEMME EST UNE FEMME
(A WOMAN IS A WOMAN)
1961, 84 mins, France/Italy
D: Jean-Luc Godard A: Anna Karina, Jean-Paul Belmondo, Jean-Claude Brialy, Nicole Paquin, Marie Dubois, Jeanne Moreau (Rome-Paris)

Jean-Luc Godard, whose use of unusual cutting, fragmented pacing, and cynical jocularity worked in his first film, *Breathless*, has now tried to apply these techniques to a situation comedy. It does not come off as well and is only intermittently bright. Too much homage to Yank musicals and comedies points up the lack of polish in this entry. A stripteaser (Anna Karina), living with a young bookseller (Jean-Claude Brialy), decides she wants a baby. She finally goes to his friend (Jean-Paul Belmondo) so that she can have her child and comes back and tells her beau, who accepts the situation.

LA FEMME INFIDELE
(UNFAITHFUL WIFE)
1969, 97 mins, France/Italy
D: Claude Chabrol A: Stephane Audran, Michel Bouquet, Maurice Ronet, Michel Duchaussoy, Guy Marly (Films La Boetie/Cinegai)

Claude Chabrol has concocted a canny film that subtly looks at a case of adultery. There is a supposedly happy suburban home with loving wife and husband and charming young son. But when the husband finds that the wife did not go to appointments she told him about, he sets a private detective on her trail who discovers she has a lover. He sees the man and plays the knowing, liberal husband. But suddenly the husband becomes angry and kills the lover. Stephane Audran is incisive as the wife, and Michel Bouquet is brilliantly right as the gentle husband. Maurice Ronet is effective as the dodgy playboy lover who still exudes charm.

LA FEMME NIKITA
See: Nikita

LA FEMME PUBLIQUE
1984, 110 mins, France
D: Andrzej Zulawski A: Francis Huster, Valerie Kaprisky, Lambert Wilson, Diane Delor, Roger Dumas (Hachette-Fox)

There's plenty of madness but little method or meaning in this tale of an inexperienced actress who lands a role in a film based on Dostoyevsky's *The Possessed,* gets bedded and then bounced out by its rabid pseudo-German director, and winds up playing a real-life role subbing as the dead girlfriend of a Czech immigrant who is manipulated by the filmmaker into committing a political assassination. Valerie Kaprisky gives her all as the aspiring thesp without much personality. Her big scenes are a series of lewd, nude convulsive dances for a voyeuristic photographer.

FENG YUE
(TEMPTRESS MOON)
1996, 130 mins, Hong Kong
D: Chen Kaige A: Leslie Cheung, Gong Li, Kevin Lin, He Saifei, Chang Shih (Tomson)

An emotionally complex look at a young gigolo's obsession with the daughter of a wealthy, decaying family, *Moon* is a visually intoxicating work. Pic's first half hour is a visual and emotional roller coaster that's among the finest work that Chen has done, with fluid use of Steadicam, resonant music, and spectacular use of light and shade by lenser Christopher Doyle. At around the one-hour mark, however, the picture starts to lose momentum. Gong rarely uncovers the heart of the role, looking a tad too old and composed for the part. Cheung, however, is excellent, moving between his confident gigolo and emotion-racked lover with ease. [In the US and UK, pic showed in a 127-min. fine cut by the director.]

FERNGULLY—
THE LAST RAINFOREST
1992, 76 mins, US
D: Bill Kroyer (FAI)

FernGully is a colorful, lively, extremely "politically correct" animated feature pitting the elfin creatures of the wild against the rapacious monsters who would destroy their habitat. Drawn in brilliantly verdant colors immediately inviting the viewer into a special world, *Ferngully* is certainly simple enough for any youngster to understand, yet is sufficiently hip around the edges to contain the sap. Robin Williams asserts his unique personality and wacky humor amazingly well in an animated context as a crazed, brain-fried bat named Batty Koda.

FERRIS BUELLER'S DAY OFF
1986, 103 mins, US ⓥ ⊙ ⊡
D: John Hughes A: Matthew Broderick, Alan Ruck, Mia Sara, Jeffrey Jones, Jennifer Grey (Paramount)

Ferris Bueller exhibits John Hughes on an off day. Paucity of invention here lays bare the total absence of plot or involving situations. The thin premise demonstrates the great lengths to which the irrepressible Ferris Bueller (Matthew Broderick) goes in order to hoodwink his parents and high-school principal into thinking he's really sick, when, in fact, all he wants to do is play hooky for a day. Picture's one saving grace is the absolutely delicious comic performance of Jeffrey Jones as the high-school principal.

FEVER PITCH
1985, 96 mins, US ⓥ
D: Richard Brooks A: Ryan O'Neal, Catherine Hicks, Giancarlo Giannini, Bridgette Andersen, Chad Everett, John Saxon (M-G-M)

Weak script, poor acting, and miscasting aside, it's the power of the subject that makes this an enjoyable ride. Writer/director Richard Brooks thoroughly researched the territory of the compulsive gambler and captures the obsession with almost a documentary eye. Unfortunately, plot is a totally unconvincing jumble and Ryan O'Neal as a sports reporter hooked on the gambling game is wooden and unsympathetic.

FEW GOOD MEN, A
1992, 138 mins, US ⓥ ⊙ ⊡
D: Rob Reiner A: Tom Cruise, Jack Nicholson, Demi Moore, Kevin Bacon, Kiefer Sutherland, Kevin Pollak (Columbia/Castle Rock)

A big-time, mainstream Hollywood movie par excellence. Expert story construction and compelling thesping and direction make all the narrative elements pay off in this exposé of peacetime military malfeasance laced with the story of a bright young lawyer's struggle to get out from under the imposing shadow of an illustrious father. Chosen to defend two young marines charged with murder is navy lawyer Lieutenant Kaffee (Tom Cruise), goaded to press further by the driven special counsel, Lieutenant Commander Joanne Galloway (Demi Moore). The showiest turn is reserved for Nicholson, and the crafty old pro makes more than the most of it. He's only got three major scenes, but they're all dynamite.
1992: Nominations: Best Picture, Supp. Actor (Jack Nicholson), Editing, Sound

FFOLKES
See: North Sea Hijack

F FOR FAKE
1975, 85 mins, France/W. Germany/Iran ⊙
D: Orson Welles, Francois Reichenbach A: Orson Welles, Oja Kodar, Joseph Cotten, Francois Reichenbach (SACI/Astrophore/Janus)

Orson Welles has reworked the docu material of Francois Reichenbach on noted art forger Elmyr De Houry, made for TV about 1968, into an intriguing, enjoyable look at illusion in general and his own, Clifford Irving's, and De Houry's dealing with it in particular. He has deftly added himself to the affair as he is seen doing some magico stints and winkingly admitting he is a charlatan.

FIDDLER ON THE ROOF
1971, 180 mins, US ⓥ ⊙ ⊡
D: Norman Jewison A: Topol, Norma Crane, Leonard Frey, Molly Picon, Paul Mann, Rosalind Harris (Mirisch/Cartier)

Sentimental in a theatrical way, romantic in the old-fashioned way, nostalgic about immigration days, affirmative of human decency, loyalty, bravery, and folk humor, here is the screen version of the long-running stage-musical smash. Pictured is the Ukrainian village of pious and tradition-ruled Jews at the point the corrupt czaristic regime was goading them to move out. Attention naturally falls on the Tevye. Topol, who played the role on the London stage, has the necessary combination of bombast and compassion, vitality and doubts. Topol sings passably, but "If I Were a Rich Man" is too serious, losing the fun.

1971: Best Cinematography, Sound, Adapted Score
Nominations: Best Picture, Director, Actor (Chaim Topol), Supp. Actor (Leonard Frey), Art Direction

FIELD, THE
1990, 110 mins, UK Ⓥ ⊙
D: Jim Sheridan **A:** Richard Harris, John Hurt, Tom Berenger, Sean Bean, Frances Tomelty, Brenda Fricker (Granada)

Superb acting and austere visual beauty are offset by a somewhat overheated screenplay in this tragic tale. Richard Harris is in the larger-than-life role of a patriarchal Irish tenant farmer with a ferocious temperament and blazing charisma. The time is the 1930s, when the memory of the great famine was fresh and feudal ways held sway in the Irish countryside. For most of his life, Bull McCabe has farmed a field belonging to a wealthy widow (Frances Tomelty), who one day decides to sell the plot. Bull is outraged. "Who would insult me by bidding for my field?" he demands at the local pub. No one but an Irish American from Boston (Tom Berenger), with a plan to pave Bull's field for an access road to lucrative limestone deposits.
1990: Nomination: Best Actor (Richard Harris)

FIELD OF DREAMS
1989, 106 mins, US Ⓥ ⊙
D: Phil Alden Robinson **A:** Kevin Costner, Amy Madigan, Gaby Hoffman, Ray Liotta, James Earl Jones, Burt Lancaster (Gordon/Universal)

Kevin Costner plays a new-age farmer who has come to Iowa's cornfields with his college sweetheart (Amy Madigan). In the fields one day he hears a celestial voice that cryptically advises: "If you build it, he will come." Costner sets out to sculpt a beautiful baseball diamond from his precious cornfield. One night his faith is rewarded: the spirit of Shoeless Joe Jackson, the most precipitously fallen of the disgraced World Series fixers, the 1919 Chicago White Sox, materializes on his ball field. In spite of a script hobbled with cloying aphorisms and shameless sentimentality, *Field of Dreams* sustains a dreamy mood in which the idea of baseball is distilled to its purest essence: a game that stands for unsullied innocence in a cruel, imperfect world.
1989: Nominations: Best Picture, Adapted Screenplay, Original Score

FIERCE CREATURES
1997, 93 mins, UK/US Ⓥ ⊙ ▭
D: Robert Young, Fred Schepisi **A:** John Cleese, Jamie Lee Curtis, Kevin Kline, Michael Palin, Ronnie Corbett, Robert Lindsay (Fish/Jersey)

It takes a stout heart to make a nonsequel sequel, but that's exactly what the makers of *A Fish Called Wanda* have done with *Fierce Creatures*. The ensemble has returned, but in new roles unrelated to the characters in the earlier pic. A London zoo is acquired by Kiwi media mogul Rod McCain (Kevin Kline). Willa Weston (Jamie Lee Curtis), recently hired by McCain's Octopus Inc., decides it would be fun to run the zoo. Ex-Hong Kong cop Rollo Lee (John Cleese), sent in to turn the operation into a profitable venture, reckons the best way is to eliminate its domesticated animals and have it stocked 100% by "fierce creatures." *Creatures* is an artful combination of high and low comedy that runs like a well-oiled machine. It's winningly character-driven, stretching but not breaking the bounds of credibility.

FIESTA
1947, 104 mins, US
D: Richard Thorpe **A:** Esther Williams, Akim Tamiroff, Ricardo Montalban, John Carroll, Mary Astor, Cyd Charisse (M-G-M)

Fiesta is an eyeful of Esther Williams. It's also pleasant if not socko film fare, "introducing a new personality, Ricardo Montalban." Leisurely the story unfolds with the birth of twins, after the famed matador (well played by Fortunio Bonanova) at first betrays his chagrin that his firstborn is a girl. But when her twin brother arrives 15 minutes later he schools the lad to follow in the bullfighter tradition, even though his penchant is for music. Eventually the "Salon Mexico" suite by Aaron Copland (brilliantly orchestrated by Johnny Green) serves as the means to project his virtuosity as a serious composer. Cyd Charisse makes a fine impression opposite Montalban, with whom she clicks in a couple of intricate native terp routines.

5TH AVE GIRL
1939, 82 mins, US Ⓥ ⊙
D: Gregory La Cava **A:** Ginger Rogers, Walter Connolly, Verree Teasdale, James Ellison, Tim Holt (RKO)

A cleverly devised comedy drama. Millionaire Walter Connolly, shunned by his family on his birthday, meets Ginger Rogers in Central Park. He hires her to pose as a gold digger and takes her to his Fifth Avenue mansion. Sock laughs are supplied by situations and surprise dialogue. Rogers, bewildered by her sudden catapult into a swank home, carries it all off with a blankness that accentuates her characterization. Connolly deftly handles the assignment of the prosperous manufacturer.

FIFTH ELEMENT, THE
1997, 127 mins, France Ⓥ ⊙ ▭
D: Luc Besson **A:** Bruce Willis, Gary Oldman, Ian Holm, Milla Jovovich, Chris Tucker, Luke Perry (Gaumont)

A misfired attempt to make an American-style sci-fi spectacular, *The Fifth Element* consists of a hodgepodge of elements that don't comfortably coalesce. In the year 2259, the Earth finds itself in the path of a huge, fiery planet that conventional weapons only make bigger and stronger. Possible salvation arrives in the form of a genetically regenerated young woman, Leeloo (Milla Jovovich), a naked, orange-haired acrobat of superhuman strength who escapes from the lab only to land in the flying taxi of New York cabby Korben Dallas (Bruce Willis). Meanwhile Zorg (Gary Oldman), overlord of all evil, is equipping some fearsome animal mercenaries for the ultimate battle, which oddly takes place on board an outer-space cruise ship that resembles a Vegas-style tropical casino. The punkish gender-crossing orientation of many of the characters looks straight out of any trendy contempo nightclub, while the score seems stuck in the hip-hop and techno-rock era.

55 DAYS AT PEKING
1963, 150 mins, US Ⓥ ⊙ ▭
D: Nicholas Ray [Andrew Marton, Guy Green] **A:** Charlton Heston, Ava Gardner, David Niven, Flora Robson, John Ireland, Leo Genn (Bronston)

Producer Samuel Bronston shows characteristic lavishness in the pictorial scope, the vivid and realistic sets, and extras by the thousands in his reproduction of the capital of Imperial China in 1900. The lensing was done in Spain, where the company built an entire city. The screenplay presumably adheres to the historical basics in its description of the violent rebellion of the "Boxers" against the major powers of the period because of their commercial exploitation of tradition-bound and unmodern China. These market-seeking nations have in their Peking outpost gallant fighting men who, although only a few hundred in number, withstand the merciless 55-day siege. David Niven is the British embassy head who stubbornly refuses to surrender, Heston is the American marine major who commands the defense.
1963: Nominations: Best Original Music Score, Song ("So Little Time")

5,000,000 YEARS TO EARTH
See: Quatermass and the Pit

52 PICK-UP
1986, 114 mins, US Ⓥ ⊙
D: John Frankenheimer **A:** Roy Scheider, Ann-Margret, Vanity, John Glover, Robert Trebor, Kelly Preston (Cannon)

52 Pick-Up is a thriller without any thrills. Although director John Frankenheimer stuffs as much action as he can into the screen adaptation of Elmore Leonard's novel, he can't hide the ridiculous plot and lifeless characters. Roy Scheider is an all-American hero, married for 23 years to the still-attractive Ann-Margret, caught in a blackmail scheme by an unlikely trio of porno operators who film him in bed with cute young Kelly Preston. Ringleader John Glover gives the role such a decadently sinister turn that he's far more interesting and lively to watch than Scheider.

FIGHT CLUB
1999, 139 mins, US Ⓥ ⊙ ▭
D: David Fincher **A:** Brad Pitt, Edward Norton, Helena Bonham Carter, Meat Loaf Aday, Jared Leto (Linson/Fox 2000/Regency)

This bold, inventive, sustained adrenaline rush of a movie about a guru who advocates brutality and mayhem plays mischievously with film conventions. David Fincher has always been attracted to dark material. In Chuck Palahniuk's novel about a cult of men who channel their pent-up physical aggression into increasingly destructive pursuits, the director has found his most disturbing subject matter yet. The story's nameless narrator (Edward Norton) meets enigmatic Tyler Durden (Brad Pitt). They get tanked together, after which a fight seals their bond and marks the beginning of a phenomenon that rapidly attracts new participants, fighting each Saturday night in a club whose members are sworn to secrecy. Performances by the leads are uniformly potent, with Norton's character demanding by far the greatest range.
1999: Nomination: Sound Effects Editing

FIGHTER SQUADRON
1948, 94 mins, US
D: Raoul Walsh **A:** Edmond O'Brien, Robert Stack, John Rodney, Tom D'Andrea, (Warner)

Picture's time of action is the tense days of 1943-44, when the US Air Force was paving the way for D-Day. It centers its story on one English-based squadron of fighter planes and pilots. The film thrives on deadly air action, and the AF combat footage that makes up a substantial part of the picture is a tingling reminder of the Second World War. Edmond O'Brien, squadron leader, stands out, and there are strong assists from Robert Stack and John Rodney as flying mates.

FIGHTING KENTUCKIAN, THE
1949, 109 mins, US ⓥ
D: George Waggner **A:** John Wayne, Vera Ralston, Philip Dorn, Oliver Hardy, Marie Windsor, Hugo Haas (Republic)

Swift-moving melodrama. A little-known bit of American history, that Congress granted four townships of land in Alabama to French officers of Napoleon's defeated armies and their families, forms the background for the story. That is until Wayne, one of the Kentucky troopers returning from the war of 1812, falls in love with Vera Ralston, daughter of French general Hugo Haas.

FIGHTING 69TH, THE
1940, 90 mins, US ⓥ
D: William Keighley **A:** James Cagney, Pat O'Brien, George Brent, Jeffrey Lynn, Alan Hale, Frank McHugh (Warner)

Based on the adventures of New York's crack Irish regiment during the First World War, *The Fighting 69th* is a vigorously melodramatic war picture. Story is a factual presentation of the 69th's war record, from training at Camp Mills through its major engagements at the front, with fictional interpolations for dramatic purposes. Cagney has a definitely unsympathetic role as the smart-aleck recruit from Brooklyn whose mental and physical fiber disintegrates under fire. His eventual regeneration through the efforts of Father Duffy (Pat O'Brien) comes too late to evoke much audience sympathy for the character. George Brent essays the role of "Wild Bill" Donovan, head of the outfit.

FIGURES IN A LANDSCAPE
1970, 95 mins, UK ▭
D: Joseph Losey **A:** Robert Shaw, Malcolm McDowell, Pamela Brown (Cinema Center)

The plight of two prisoners escaping from a relentless helicopter over "400 miles of hostile terrain" is the armature around which this yarn, which purposely never defines who the prisoners or the forces chasing them are, is spun. It is difficult to get into the characters, who always remain as elusive as the country they are traveling over is supposed to be.

FILE ON THELMA JORDON, THE
1950, 100 mins, US
D: Robert Siodmak **A:** Barbara Stanwyck, Wendell Corey, Paul Kelly, Joan Tetzel, Stanley Ridges, Richard Rober (Paramount)

Thelma Jordon unfolds as an interesting, femme-slanted melodrama, told with a lot of restrained excitement. Wendell Corey is seen as an assistant d.a., a husband and father. One night, after a quarrel with his wife Joan Tetzel, he is intrigued by the Barbara Stanwyck character. It leads him to further pursuit and a hot amour. Stanwyck is pretending to be a poor niece to her rich aunt. When the latter is killed by a housebreaker, Corey attempts to remove evidence that would point toward Stanwyck. Despite this, she is charged with murder.

LA FILLE DE D'ARTAGNAN (D'ARTAGNAN'S DAUGHTER)
1994, 125 mins, France ⓥ ⊙
D: Bertrand Tavernier **A:** Sophie Marceau, Philippe Noiret, Claude Rich, Sami Frey (CiBy 2000/Little Bear/TF1)

This is a sexy, often very funny sequel to the Alexandre Dumas classic *The Three Musketeers*. The film's strength comes from its ability to deliver the thrills 'n spills of the Errol Flynn-style actioners without being self-consciously nostalgic. Set in 1650s France, fast-paced story opens with a slave escaping from the estate of the evil Duke of Crassac (Claude Rich). The mother superior of a nearby convent gives refuge to the slave and is murdered by the duke's henchman in retaliation. Eloise (Sophie Marceau) immediately sets off for Paris hoping to enlist her famous dad, D'Artagnan (Philippe Noiret), to help seek revenge. Her aging father isn't exactly crazy about jumping back into the musketeer biz.

FILOFAX
See: Taking Care of Business

FINAL ANALYSIS
1992, 124 mins, US ⊗ ⊙
D: Phil Joanou **A:** Richard Gere, Kim Basinger, Uma Thurman, Eric Roberts (Warner)

A crackling good psychological melodrama in which star power and slick surfaces are used to potent advantage. Tantalizing double crosses mount right up to the eerie final scene. In the course of treating a patient (Uma Thurman), San Francisco psychiatrist Richard Gere takes the unusual step of meeting the young woman's older sister, who may know more about certain events in Thurman's past than the subject herself. Sis turns out to be Kim Basinger, who has no trouble overcoming his tenuous sense of professional ethics about bedding a patient's sibling. An aloof workaholic, Gere becomes hopelessly ensnared in his secret affair with Basinger.

FINAL CONFLICT, THE
1981, 108 mins, US ⊗ ⊙ ▭
D: Graham Baker **A:** Sam Neill, Rossano Brazzi, Don Gordon, Lisa Harrow (20th Century-Fox)

The last chapter in the *Omen* trilogy, which is too bad because this is the funniest one yet. This time Sam Neill plays Damien Thorn, all grown up now after killing off two nice families in the previous chapters. Fear of the orphanage, of course, never worries Damien because his real father is the devil, who only wanted him to go to the best schools, get a job, and take over the world for evil purposes. And now he has, or almost. Neill knows the only obstacle to his plan is the baby born when three stars conjoin overhead. There's also the matter of the daggers. If you remember the first two episodes, somebody or other was always trying to stab little Damien to death with the daggers.

FINAL COUNTDOWN, THE
1980, 103 mins, US ⊗ ⊙
D: Don Taylor **A:** Kirk Douglas, Martin Sheen, Katharine Ross, James Farentino, Ron O'Neal, Charles Durning (Bryna/United Artists)

The magnificent production values provided by setting the film on the world's largest nuclear-powered aircraft carrier can't transcend the predictable cleverness of plot. The liberal sympathies typical of the work of Kirk Douglas are evident in his characterization of the ship's commander whose sense of military honor will not allow him to take the opportunity provided him by a mysterious storm—his ship and crew find themselves transported back in time to Dec. 6, 1941, between Pearl Harbor and the Japanese fleet heading to destroy the American naval base.

FINAL PROGRAMME, THE (US: THE LAST DAYS OF MAN ON EARTH)
1973, 89 mins, UK ⊗ ⊙
D: Robert Fuest **A:** Jon Finch, Jenny Runacre, Hugh Griffith, Patrick Magee, Sterling Hayden, Julie Ege (Goodtimes/Gladiole)

Pic is a silly, pretentious potboiler, done in a jazzed-up style which suggests Ken Russell on an off day. Jon Finch is top-cast as a rebellious intellectual in a devastated world seeking a new messiah. Pic alternates highfalutin allegory with lowbrow facetiousness, and the film is a mishmash.

FINDERS KEEPERS
1966, 94 mins, UK ⊗
D: Sidney Hayers **A:** Cliff Richard, the Shadows, Robert Morley, Peggy Mount, Viviane Ventura, Graham Stark (Interstate/United Artists)

Story line about a minibomb dropped by accident from an American plane over Spain and subsequent attempts by various foreign "spies" to locate it could have had a good astringent and satirical tang. The theme is not only largely frittered away but is hardly suitable for a relaxed, easygoing musicomedy designed to showcase a pop group such as Cliff Richard and the Shadows. Wit gets lost, and incidents are held up, to make room for inevitable song, dance, and fiesta.

FINDERS KEEPERS
1984, 96 mins, US ⊗
D: Richard Lester **A:** Michael O'Keefe, Beverly D'Angelo, Louis Gossett Jr., Ed Lauter, Pamela Stephenson, Brian Dennehy (CBS)

Director Richard Lester returns to his pell-mell trademark and the result is maddening. Interesting cast is wasted, with bright exception of Beverly D'Angelo. Producers hang their frenetic tale of stolen money, chases, and deceptions on several characters racing up and down a train en route from California to Nebraska.

FINE AND DANDY
See: The West Point Story

FINE MADNESS, A
1966, 104 mins, US ⊗
D: Irvin Kershner **A:** Sean Connery,

Joanne Woodward, Jean Seberg, Patrick O'Neal, Colleen Dewhurst, Clive Revill (Pan Arts/Warner)

A Fine Madness is offbeat, and downbeat, in many ways. Too heavy-handed to be comedy, yet too light to be called drama, the well-mounted production depicts Sean Connery as a virile, headstrong poet, hung up in a dry spell of inspiration. He despises women in general, and to hammer home this point, all femme characters, except second wife Joanne Woodward, are shrews, battle-axes, or shallow broads. Overdue back alimony gets an outburst, eventually leading Connery to psychiatric care, alternating with a running chase from the fuzz, and climaxed by a curiously ineffective lobotomy. A lot of sophisticated throwaway dialogue is dispensed along with sight gags and slapstick.

FINE MESS, A
1986, 88 mins, US Ⓥ ⊙ ⊡
D: Blake Edwards **A:** Ted Danson, Howie Mandel, Richard Mulligan, Stuart Margolin, Maria Conchita Alonso, Paul Sorvino (BEE/Columbia-Delphi V)

Danson plays a small-time actor who overhears two crooks (Mulligan and Margolin) as they dope a horse. Before long, Danson and his buddy Mandel are being chased all over L.A. by the incompetent villains, cueing in plenty of overfamiliar car chases. *A Fine Mess* is light on plot and instead concentrates on strenuous, familiar comedy routines. Trouble is, the principal players are all quite charmless.

FINE PAIR, A
1969, 88 mins, Italy/US ⊡
D: Francesco Maselli **A:** Rock Hudson, Claudia Cardinale, Tomas Milian, Leon Askin, Ellen Corby, Walter Giller (Cinema Center)

A Fine Pair is so bogged down in contrived and confusing action that its impact is reduced to a minimum. Pic was lensed mostly in Italy. Script never rings true and Rock Hudson is called upon to enact an unconvincing character. Film opens in NY, where Claudia Cardinale claims she's been involved with an international jewel thief and she wants Hudson's help in returning a fortune in jewels stolen.

FINIAN'S RAINBOW
1968, 145 mins, US Ⓥ ⊙ ⊡
D: Francis Coppola **A:** Fred Astaire, Petula Clark, Tommy Steele, Don Francks, Keenan Wynn, Barbara Hancock (Warner)

This translation of the 1947 legituner is a light, pastoral fantasy with civil rights angles, underscored by comedy values. Film opens leisurely with Fred Astaire and Petula Clark, his daughter, on a montage tour of the US. The stars come to rest in Rainbow Valley, just as the police henchmen of racist judge Keenan Wynn are about to foreclose on property owned by vagabond Don Francks. Astaire bails out Francks, and latter's romance with Clark develops. Tommy Steele arrives as the leprechaun searching for gold which Astaire has stolen.

1968: Nominations: Best Adapted Music Score, Sound

FIRE AND ICE
1983, 81 mins, US Ⓥ ⊙
D: Ralph Bakshi (PSO)

The animation marks the film debut of America's leading exponent of heroic fantasy art, Frank Frazetta, who coproduced. Known for his classic comic-book and poster art, Frazetta works some of his famous illustrations into the film, such as his *Death Dealer* painting portraying an ax-wielding figure on horseback. Populating an Armageddon embellished with subhumans and flying dragonhawks are a blond hero, Larn; a sensuous-vulnerable dream girl in distress, Teegra; and an icy sorcerer and his willful mother, Lord Nekron and Juliana. Bakshi shot live actors first, to lay the foundation for the animation, in a process called Rotoscope.

FIRE BIRDS
(UK: WINGS OF THE APACHE)
1990, 85 mins, US Ⓥ ⊙
D: David Green **A:** Nicolas Cage, Tommy Lee Jones, Sean Young, Bert Rhine (Touchstone/Nova)

A paean to Yankee airpower, *Fire Birds* shows the US Army as a take-charge outfit able to kick the butt of those South American drug-cartel jerks. Formula script, which inevitably recalls *Top Gun*, has Nicolas Cage training to use the army's Apache aircraft while vainly trying to rekindle a romance with old flame Sean Young. Tommy Lee Jones is dead-on as the taskmaster instructor who cornily singles out Cage for rough treatment.

FIRE DOWN BELOW
1957, 116 mins, US ⊡
D: Robert Parrish **A:** Rita Hayworth, Robert Mitchum, Jack Lemmon, Herbert Lom, Bernard Lee, Anthony Newley (Warwick/Columbia)

Story: bad, bad girl (Rita Hayworth) meets youthful American, and finally agrees to marry him though warning him of her past—that of sort of a Mata Hari in Europe. Robert Mitchum, as Jack Lemmon's pal in a small fishing-and-smuggling boat operation, is vastly displeased. Hayworth is excellent. Lemmon (who takes a bow for composing the harmonica theme) shows plainly that he can handle a dramatic type role, while Mitchum contributes one of his better portrayals.

FIREFOX
1982, 137 mins, US Ⓥ ⊙ ▱
D: Clint Eastwood **A:** Clint Eastwood, Freddie Jones, David Huffman, Warren Clarke, Ronald Lacey (Warner)

Firefox is a burnout. It all sounded good on paper—Clint Eastwood, as a retired ace flier, infiltrating the Russian air force to spirit away the supposedly top-secret Firefox, a plane capable of Mach-5 speed and equipped with a thought-controlled weapons system. Despite the tense mission being depicted, there's no suspense, excitement, or thrills, and lackadaisical pacing gives viewer plenty of time to ponder the gaping implausibilities.

FIREMAN'S BALL, THE
See: Hori, Ma Panenko

FIRE OVER ENGLAND
1937, 88 mins, UK Ⓥ
D: William K. Howard **A:** Flora Robson, Raymond Massey, Leslie Banks, Laurence Olivier, Vivien Leigh (Pendennis London)

This is a handsomely mounted and forcefully dramatic glorification of Queen Bess. It projects Flora Robson in a conception of the British regent which holds the imagination. Most telling in dramatic effects are the sequences that build up to Laurence Olivier's undoing as an English spy and his subsequent escape, the queen's confronting of her coterie of exposed betrayers, and the burning of the Spanish Armada.

FIREPOWER
1979, 104 mins, UK Ⓥ
D: Michael Winner **A:** Sophia Loren, James Coburn, O. J. Simpson, Eli Wallach, Anthony Franciosa, Vincent Gardenia (ITC)

Firepower is one of those international action thrillers designed to combine a top-name cast with lots of shooting and explosions so the story can be followed regardless of whether you understand the language. Beautiful Sophia Loren believes her chemist husband was murdered at the order of Stegner (George Touliatos), a wealthy, seclusive industrialist. She persuades the Justice Department, who also wants Stegner, to put the pressure on mobster Eli Wallach to entice retired hit-man James Coburn to—get Stegner.

FIRE SALE
1977, 88 mins, US Ⓥ
D: Alan Arkin **A:** Alan Arkin, Rob Reiner, Vincent Gardenia, Anjanette Comer, Kay Medford, Barbara Dana (20th Century-Fox)

Alleged comedy is a consummately sophomoric vulgarity. Marvin Worth's production matches in crippled creativity the physical infirmities on which most of the forced and strident humor is based. Gardenia owns a dumpy department store. Sid Caesar is appropriately offensive as a veterans' hospital basket case coaxed by Gardenia into burning the store for insurance, thinking it's a World War II German installation.

FIRES ON THE PLAIN
See: Nobi

FIRESTARTER
1984, 115 mins, US Ⓥ ⊙ ▱
D: Mark L. Lester **A:** David Keith, Drew Barrymore, George C. Scott, Martin Sheen, Heather Locklear, Art Carney (De Laurentiis)

Story of a nine-year-old girl who can inflame objects and people by power of her will balances human concern of a pursued and loving father and daughter (David Keith and Drew Barrymore) against a clandestine government agency that wants to use the girl's power for nefarious ends. Pic's stars are special-effects team Mike Wood and Jeff Jarvis, whose pyrotechnics—flying fireballs, fire trenches, human balls of fire—create the film's impact.

FIRES WITHIN
1991, 86 mins, US Ⓥ ⊙ ▱
D: Gillian Armstrong **A:** Greta Scacchi, Jimmy Smits, Vincent D'Onofrio, Brit Hathaway, Luis Avalos (Pathe/M-G-M)

The timely, real-life situation involves an attractive émigré (Greta Scacchi) and her infant daughter (Brit Hathaway), among the "raft people" who continue to flee Cuba via open ocean on makeshift, floating deathtrap—hoping for landfall in the Florida Keys. They're rescued by a seaman (Vincent D'Onofrio), with whom the woman forms a romantic relationship over the next eight years. It is a cold narrative that never lingers on any situation long enough to generate either suspense or romance.

FIRM, THE
1993, 154 mins, US ⊛ ⊙
D: Sydney Pollack **A:** Tom Cruise, Jeanne Tripplehorn, Gene Hackman, Hal Holbrook, Ed Harris, Holly Hunter (Paramount/Mirage)

Tom Cruise portrays Mitch McDeere, a sought-after Harvard grad who shuns offers from big-city law offices in favor of a small, lucrative Memphis concern. Mitch's teacher-wife Abby (Jeanne Tripplehorn) smells a rat from the outset, but Mitch jumps in with the enthusiasm of a puppy, currying favor with the boss (Hal Holbrook) and lunching with mentor Avery Tolar (Gene Hackman). After two of the firm's attorneys die in a mysterious boating accident, Mitch and Avery head to the Cayman Islands to investigate. Later Mitch begins to suspect that the firm could be responsible for the deaths of four of its employees over the years. Pollack has done an ultrapro job in giving spit and polish to this star-driven, surefire commercial project.
1993: Nominations: Best Supp. Actress (Holly Hunter), Original Score

FIRST A GIRL
1935, 92 mins, UK
D: Victor Saville **A:** Jessie Matthews, Sonnie Hale, Anna Lee, Griffith Jones, Alfred Drayton (Gaumont British)

Jessie Matthews's admirers will love to see her rise from her humdrum niche in a dressmaking establishment to the giddy heights of thespian glory. She pals up with a female impersonator. He gets a wire giving him an unexpected date, which sudden loss of voice makes it impossible for him to accept. He coaches the bewildered girl and insists she take his place. Trading on the doubt concerning her sex, and carefully managed by her new partner, the act is a hit and she quickly makes a name. The starring role is a natural for Jessie Matthews, whose dancing talent is unobtrusively displayed.

FIRST BLOOD
1982, 94 mins, US ⊛ ⊙ ⊡
D: Ted Kotcheff **A:** Sylvester Stallone, Richard Crenna, Brian Dennehy, David Caruso, Jack Starrett (Orion)

Sylvester Stallone plays a former Green Beret, a "killing machine" who's

so tough, if there had been one more of him, the Viet Cong wouldn't have had a chance. Arriving unshaven at the quiet community of Hope, he winds up at the slammer. Beating up the whole station house, he escapes into the woods, commandeers an army truck and machine gun, and goes back to level the quiet little town. Supposedly, the real villain here is society itself, which invented a debacle like Vietnam and must now deal with its lingering tragedies. But *First Blood* cops out completely on that one, not even trying to find a solution to Stallone's problems.

FIRST DEADLY SIN, THE
1980, 112 mins, US ⊛ ⊙
D: Brian G. Hutton **A:** Frank Sinatra, Faye Dunaway, Brenda Vaccaro, James Whitmore, David Dukes, Martin Gabel (Kastner/Artanis/Cinema 7)

Otherwise a fairly routine and turgid crime meller, *The First Deadly Sin* commands some interest as Frank Sinatra's first film in 10 years. Plot has Sinatra latching onto an apparent series of arbitrary murders. Paralleling the crime-and-detection yarn, and slowing down the entire proceedings, are Sinatra's visits to wife Faye Dunaway, who's not recovering well from a kidney operation. As for Sinatra, this amounts to a decent performance, even if the role might have called for a more desperate attitude.

FIRST GREAT TRAIN ROBBERY, THE
(US: THE GREAT TRAIN ROBBERY)
1979, 110 mins, UK ⊛ ⊙
D: Michael Crichton **A:** Sean Connery, Donald Sutherland, Lesley-Anne Down, Wayne Sleep, Michael Elphick (United Artists/De Laurentiis)

Based on fact, the story concerns the first recorded heist from a moving train. Suave arch-criminal Sean Connery enlists Donald Sutherland and Wayne Sleep in a bid to lift a payroll of gold bars destined for the Crimea in 1855. The actual theft is ingenious. Crichton's films drag in dialogue bouts, but triumph when action takes over.

FIRST KNIGHT
1995, 132 mins, US ⊛ ⊙
D: Jerry Zucker **A:** Sean Connery, Richard Gere, Julia Ormond, Ben Cross, Liam Cunningham (Columbia)

Aside from casting Richard Gere as Lancelot, *First Knight* marches out as an agreeably intelligent, mature, and well-mounted telling of the legendary King Arthur story. On her way to take King Arthur's hand in a marriage, Guinevere (Julia Ormond) is attacked by the seethingly villainous Malagant (Ben Cross) and is saved only through the intercession of Lancelot (Gere). This Lancelot is not a courtly gentleman of the highest moral standards, but a sort of wandering samurai warrior who goes wherever his sword (or, in this case, his libido) leads him. Within moments of the rescue, Lancelot comes on strong to Guinevere, but after just one kiss, she makes him promise he'll never do that again and moves on to her appointed rendezvous with Arthur (Sean Connery) in Camelot. Literate, soberminded, and almost rigorously chaste, *First Knight* sweeps the viewer up in the doings of these impressive, larger-than-life characters. Gere's preening air of self-satisfied cockiness clashes hopelessly with the classy style displayed by the other actors. By contrast, Connery is a dream King Arthur. Ormond is a great match for him as Guinevere.

FIRST LOVE
1977, 91 mins, US ⊘
D: Joan Darling **A:** William Katt, Susan Dey, John Heard, Beverly D'Angelo, Robert Loggia, Tom Lacy (Paramount)
First Love is a sensitive and melancholy film about the impact of romance on college student William Katt when he falls for coed Susan Dey. From frame one the mood is a downer, which dampens the several nice bright moments of exuberance and telegraphs the coming climactic ambiguity.

FIRST MEN IN THE MOON
1964, 102 mins, UK ⊘ ⊙ ⊏⊐
D: Nathan Juran **A:** Edward Judd, Lionel Jeffries, Martha Hyer, Erick Chitty, Miles Malleson (BLC/Columbia)
Ray Harryhausen and his special-effects men have another high old time in this piece of science-fiction hokum filmed in Dynamation. Picture is based on H. G. Wells's novel and has been neatly updated. An aged man (Edward Judd) tells the incredible story of how he, his fiancée, and an eccentric professor actually did land on the moon. The three principals play second fiddle to the special effects and art work, which are impressive in color, construction, and animation.

FIRST MONDAY IN OCTOBER
1981, 96 mins, US ⊘ ⊙ ⊏⊐
D: Ronald Neame **A:** Walter Matthau, Jill

Clayburgh, Jan Sterling, Barnard Hughes (Paramount)
A mildly engaging talkfest in which all serious issues serve as window dressing for an almost romantic comedy. Rumpled and as likable as ever, Matthau here portrays the Supreme Court's "great dissenter," an individualistic civil libertarian. In theory he greatly welcomes the appointment of a woman, but his hair stands on end when he learns that America's first female Supreme Court justice is the arch-conservative Clayburgh.

FIRST NAME: CARMEN
See: Prenom Carmen

FIRST OF THE FEW, THE (US: SPITFIRE)
1942, 118 mins, UK ⊘
D: Leslie Howard **A:** Leslie Howard, David Niven, Rosamund John, Roland Culver (British Aviation)
In interpreting the life of R. J. Mitchell, who designed the Spitfire plane, Leslie Howard's work ranks among his finest performances. And it is an epic picture. Film portrays Mitchell's heartbreaking efforts to get his series of aircraft models accepted. His work was looked upon as too revolutionary. For sweet domestic felicity there's Rosamund John.

FIRST TIME, THE
1983, 95 mins, US ⊘
D: Charlie Loventhal **A:** Tim Choate, Krista Errickson, Marshall Efron, Wendy Fulton (New Line/Goldmine)
Dealing fictionally with Charlie Loventhal's growing-up adventures while a student at formerly all-girls school Sarah Lawrence, the comedy owes much to De Palma's freewheeling satires made in the 1960s. Charlie (Tim Choate) is an odd-man-out at college: unable to score with the pretty girls there while his black roommate Ronald (Raymond Patterson) shows off and gives him tips.

FIRST WIVES CLUB, THE
1996, 102 mins, US ⊘ ⊙
D: Hugh Wilson **A:** Goldie Hawn, Bette Midler, Diane Keaton, Maggie Smith, Sarah Jessica Parker, Dan Hedaya (Paramount)
Pic's three main characters have all recently been divorced or separated. Their spouses flew the coop for younger women and, naturally, they're mad as hell. Their brand of justice provides for a biting social comedy. The sense of anarchy recalls the zaniness of the Marx Brothers. But the

filmmakers relent with a much too tidy, wholesome conclusion that flies in the face of all that preceded it. Still, getting there is almost all the fun. Bette Midler, Goldie Hawn, and Diane Keaton are a refreshingly cohesive comedy combo. It's particularly satisfying to see Hawn making sport of her eternally youthful persona and Midler giving vent to her outsized personality. Keaton subtly keeps her co-stars from spinning into the ether.

FIRST YEAR, THE
1932, 80 mins, US
D: William K. Howard A: Janet Gaynor, Charles Farrell, Minna Gombell, Leila Bennett, Dudley Digges, Robert McWade (Fox)

Janet Gaynor and Charles Farrell in a story that's as close to perfection for them as any piece of screen writing could be. Playing house as a couple of kids in their first year of married life may not have been a romp for Gaynor or Farrell, but it looks to have been. They love each other. Their troubles are typical. They surmount the handicaps and emerge triumphant with love in their hearts and cash in the bank.

FISH CALLED WANDA, A
1988, 108 mins, US Ⓥ ⊙
D: Charles Crichton A: John Cleese, Jamie Lee Curtis, Kevin Kline, Michael Palin, Maria Aitken (M-G-M/Prominent)

Monty Pythoners John Cleese and Michael Palin get caught up in a double-crossing crime caper with a mismatched and hilarious pair of scheming Yanks, Jamie Lee Curtis and Kevin Kline. Though it is less tasteless, irreverent, and satirical than the Python pics, film still is wacky and occasionally outrageous in its own, distinctly British way. Curtis steals the show with her keen sense of comic timing and sneaky little grins and asides.
1988: Best Supp. Actor (Kevin Kline)
Nominations: Best Director, Original Screenplay

FISHER KING, THE
1991, 137 mins, US Ⓥ ⊙ ▭
D: Terry Gilliam A: Robin Williams, Jeff Bridges, Amanda Plummer, Mercedes Ruehl, Michael Jeter (Tri-Star)

The Fisher King has two actors at the top of their form, and a compelling, well-directed, and well-produced story. First-time screenwriter Richard LaGravenese's lively, detailed original script deftly delineates the top and bottom rungs of human existence in Manhattan. Jack Lucas (Jeff Bridges) is a callous, egotistical radio shock-jock who falls apart. Just as he is about to end it all, Jack is rescued by a goofy gang of derelicts led by a maniac named Parry (Robin Williams). While recovering from his suicidal state, Jack learns that Parry is obsessed with the Holy Grail, as well as with a gawky young lady Lydia (Amanda Plummer). Jack's earnest attempts to return Parry to normal life and set him up with the elusive Lydia represent his chance at personal redemption.
Nominations: Best Actor (Robin Williams), Original Screenplay, Original Score, Art Direction

F.I.S.T.
1978, 145 mins, US Ⓥ ⊙
D: Norman Jewison A: Sylvester Stallone, Rod Steiger, Peter Boyle, Melinda Dillon, Tony Lo Bianco (United Artists)

Superb telling of how a humble but idealistic young man rises to the corrupt heights of unbridled power. The first hour of the film presents the milieu of unorganized labor circa 1937. Sylvester Stallone and lifelong friend David Huffman are among the workers in Henry Wilcoxon's trucking company. They drift into organizing drivers for local union rep Richard Herd, whose assassination during a brawl triggered by management goons drives Stallone into league with Kevin Conway, a local hood. Action cuts to the late 1950s, when Stallone pushes international union leader Peter Boyle out of office by some private blackmail, only to run head-on into Rod Steiger, crusading US senator.

FISTFUL OF DOLLARS
1964, 100 mins, Italy/W. Germany/Spain Ⓥ ⊙ ▭
D: Bob Robertson [Sergio Leone] A: Clint Eastwood, Marianne Koch, Johnny Wels [Gian Maria Volonte] (Jolly/Constantin/Ocean)

A crackerjack western made in Italy and Spain by a group of Italians and an international cast, it's about a loner, Joe (Clint Eastwood), who arrives in a small southwestern settlement split by the rivalry of two families. For money, he plays both sides against the middle, eventually winning his long-standing battle with the heavy. Though there is plenty of cliché, it's handled with an all-stops-out style, vigorous use of widescreen camera, and effective juggling of close-ups and long shots. [Version reviewed was 100-minute Italian one, with Eastwood dubbed by experienced actor Enrico Maria Salerno.]

FISTFUL OF DYNAMITE, A
(AKA: DUCK, YOU SUCKER)
1972, 139 mins, Italy Ⓥ ⊙ ▭
D: Sergio Leone **A:** Rod Steiger, James Coburn, Romolo Valli, Jean Michel Antoine, Vivien Chandler (Rafran/Euro International)

Sergio Leone comes up with a tale of the Mexican revolution. Rod Steiger plays a simple bandit who wants to rob a bank in a Mexican town but instead gets mixed up in a revolution in which he has no interest. He meets Coburn, a veritable storehouse of explosives on his person, and together they become involved in the peasants' revolt.

FIST OF FURY
See: Jingwu Men

FISTS IN THE POCKET
See: I Pugni In Tasca

FISTS OF FURY
See: Tang Shan Daxiong

FITZWILLY
1967, 102 mins, US ▭
D: Delbert Mann **A:** Dick Van Dyke, Barbara Feldon, Edith Evans, John McGiver, John Fiedler (United Artists)

An okay but sluggish comedy about a butler who masterminds robberies. Potential is not realized due to generally tame direction. Dick Van Dyke is the devoted butler to Edith Evans, one of those lovable biddies who, in this case, is not at all as wealthy as she thinks. Van Dyke and crew keep planning heists in order to support her fantasies, and philanthropies.

FIVE
1951, 93 mins, US
D: Arch Oboler **A:** William Phipps, Susan Douglas, James Anderson, Charles Lampkin, Earl Lee (Oboler/Columbia)

Intriguing in theme, but depressing in its execution, *Five* ranks high in the class of out-of-the-ordinary pix. It is the story of the last five persons on earth, survivors of an atom-bomb blast which turns thriving cities into ghost towns. Principal criticism lies in its dearth of action. However, interest is sustained in suspenseful situations and convincing dialogue.

FIVE BRANDED WOMEN
1960, 100 mins, US
D: Martin Ritt **A:** Silvana Mangano, Vera Miles, Barbara Bel Geddes, Jeanne Moreau, Carla Gravina, Richard Basehart (Paramount/Laurentiis)

A grim account of the Yugoslavian partisans' fight against the invading Nazi army during World War II, the film catches the fervor of the resistance movement. The film's strength lies in Ritt's direction. If his story bogs down, he is quick to follow with a storm of action, gripping in tone and adventurous in concept. Scene by scene, the Yugoslavs are depicted as cruel, inhuman fighters who are, in fact, less sympathetic than their German enemy.

FIVE CARD STUD
1968, 101 mins, US Ⓥ
D: Henry Hathaway **A:** Dean Martin, Robert Mitchum, Inger Stevens, Roddy McDowall, Katherine Justice, Yaphet Kotto (Paramount)

Dean Martin is cast as a frontier gambler and Robert Mitchum plays a frontier parson who woos his congregation with a fast six-shooter. Script pits them against one another in the unraveling of whodunit murders, but dramatic buildup suffers through a premature disclosure of killer's identity and subsequent lessening of what should have been a more potent impact.

FIVE CORNERS
1987, 92 mins, UK Ⓥ
D: Tony Bill **A:** Jodie Foster, Tim Robbins, Todd Graff, John Turturro, Elizabeth Berridge (HandMade)

Five Corners starts out as an affectionate look back at a Bronx neighborhood circa 1964 and then about halfway through takes a darker turn into urban violence. Local no-goodnik Heinz (John Turturro) is out of jail and looking to renew his old battle with Harry (Tim Robbins) and his old longing for Linda (Jodie Foster). They are marvelously drawn parts and Robbins as the Irish working-class kid with a social conscience gets into the heart and soul of the character.

FIVE DAYS ONE SUMMER
1982, 108 mins, US Ⓥ
D: Fred Zinnemann **A:** Sean Connery, Betsy Brantley, Lambert Wilson, Jennifer Hilary, Isabel Dean, Anna Massey (Ladd/Warner)

A tale of adultery, mountain climbing, and death that is as dramatically placid as the Swiss landscape it inhabits. Seeming hale and hearty, Sean Connery plays a Scottish doctor off on an alpine vacation in 1932 with a twentyish woman he introduces as his wife. He aims to introduce her to his great sport, mountain climbing. Ultimately, it all comes down to whether or not the girl will stay or leave, and if Connery and/or the guide will survive their climb of one of the most difficult mountains in the vicinity.

FIVE EASY PIECES
1970, 96 mins, US Ⓥ ⊙
D: Bob Rafelson **A:** Jack Nicholson, Karen Black, Lois Smith, Susan Anspach, Sally Struthers (Columbia/BBS)

An absorbing, if nerve-racking, film. Jack Nicholson is first seen as a Southern California oil rigger sporting a "cracker" accent. It's clear from the beginning that he doesn't think he belongs in this environment. But only later, when he quits his job and goes back home to the state of Washington, does it become clear that his hard hat and his accent were a masquerade. Nicholson's performance is a remarkably varied and daring exploration of a complex character, equally convincing in its manic and sober aspects.
1970: Nominations: Best Picture, Actor (Jack Nicholson), Supp. Actress (Karen Black), Story & Screenplay

FIVE FINGER EXERCISE
1962, 108 mins, US
D: Daniel Mann **A:** Rosalind Russell, Jack Hawkins, Maximilian Schell, Richard Beymer, Annette Gorman (Columbia)

The title refers to the significance of five fingers operating in coordination to create harmonious music, as in a piano study for beginners. The thoroughly uncoordinated "five fingers" in this family melodrama are an uncultured, intolerant, self-made businessman-father (Hawkins), a culture-obsessed, pseudo-intellectual mother (Russell), a confused, educated, "mama's boy" son (Beymer), an animated, high-spirited daughter (Gorman), and a young German refugee (Schell), who has been employed by the family as tutor, and yearns to become a permanent part of it.

FIVE FINGERS
1952, 107 mins, US Ⓥ
D: Joseph L. Mankiewicz **A:** James Mason, Danielle Darrieux, Michael Rennie, Walter Hampden, John Wengraf (20th Century-Fox)

A good, if somewhat overlong, cloak-and-dagger thriller. Mason portrays a valet to the British ambassador in Turkey. A cold, assured character, he decides to make himself a fortune by selling Allied war plans to the Germans. His operations are moving forward without a hitch until the British begin to suspect someone within the embassy and turn Michael Rennie loose on a counterespionage job. Actual locations in Berlin, Ankara, Turkey, London, and Istanbul were used for a documentary background effect.
1952: Nominations: Best Director, Screenplay

FIVE GRAVES TO CAIRO
1943, 96 mins, US Ⓥ
D: Billy Wilder **A:** Franchot Tone, Anne Baxter, Erich von Stroheim, Peter Van Eyck, Akim Tamiroff, Fortunio Bonanova (Paramount)

Surprisingly for such a dynamic, moving vehicle, there is a minimum of actual battle stuff. Basically *Five Graves* is the story of a British corporal (Franchot Tone) who impersonates a Nazi spy to gain military information from the Germans as they sweep toward Cairo. Film affords a vivid picture of Field Marshal Rommel, Erich von Stroheim, doing a capital job.
1943: Nominations: Best B&W Cinematography, B&W Art Direction, Editing

FIVE HEARTBEATS, THE
1991, 122 mins, US Ⓥ ⊙
D: Robert Townsend **A:** Robert Townsend, Michael Wright, Leon, Harry J. Lennix, Tico Wells, Diahann Carroll (20th Century-Fox)

Convincing only in its sweet and dazzling musical sequences, this overly sincere effort otherwise misses its mark. Story begins in 1965 when fictional group the Five Heartbeats begins to emerge among other black pop groups then combining harmonies and slick choreography. Film follows the bouncing ball through the paces of every mediocre musicbiz story ever told, from talent contest to record deal to shoestring radio support tour, racism, hit single, media blitz, and superstardom.

5,000,000 YEARS TO EARTH
See: Quatermass and the Pit

FIVE STAR FINAL
1931, 85 mins, US
D: Mervyn LeRoy **A:** Edward G. Robinson, Marian Marsh, H. B. Warner, Anthony Bushell, George E. Stone, Boris Karloff (First National)

Playwright Louis Weitzenkorn's strong argument against the scandal type of tabloid newspaper makes a strong talker. Edward G. Robinson means a lot to this entertainment. It needed someone like Robinson as the managing editor. After the yellow tab, for circulation purposes, has caused two suicides by reviving a 20-year-old murder case, the picture starts to move speedily. The daughter of the unfortunate parents goes to the newspaper with a gun in her bag to ask "Why did you kill my mother?"

1931/32: Nomination: Best Picture

FIVE THOUSAND FINGERS OF DR. T., THE
1953, 89 mins, US Ⓥ ⊙
D: Roy Rowland A: Peter Lind Hayes, Mary Healy, Hans Conried, Tommy Rettig (Columbia)

The mad humor of Dr. Seuss (Ted Geisel) has been captured on film in this odd flight into chimerical fiction. Results are sometimes fascinating, more often fantastic. Tommy Rettig is the kid who would rather be out playing with his baseball and dog than learning the scales under the tutelage of Hans Conried, the Dr. Terwilliker who becomes the villain of the plot. Opening finds the youngster dreaming he is being pursued by strange creatures with butterfly nets in a land full of odd cylinders and mounds, eerie hues and fog.

1953: Nomination: Best Scoring of a Musical Picture

FIXED BAYONETS!
1951, 92 mins, US Ⓥ
D: Samuel Fuller A: Richard Basehart, Gene Evans, Michael O'Shea, Richard Hylton, Skip Homeier (20th Century-Fox)

Story revolves around a platoon left behind temporarily to fight a rearguard action for a retreating regiment in Korea. The detail is supposed to be a hand-picked group of veterans. Yet among them is a corporal (Richard Basehart) who cannot bring himself to shoot an enemy soldier. How he shakes off this fixation and ultimately assumes command of the decimated platoon is an underlying theme that pervades the whole yarn. There's a wealth of suspense in the screenplay, for until the closing minutes filmgoers are unaware whether the platoon will succeed in its mission and rejoin the regiment.

FIXER, THE
1968, 130 mins, US
D: John Frankenheimer A: Alan Bates, Dirk Bogarde, Georgia Brown, Hugh Griffith, Elizabeth Hartman, Ian Holm (M-G-M)

Much of the unfolding is in the filthy prison cell of its chief protagonist, a Jew accused of the murder of a young boy but never formally charged. Czarist Russia at the turn of the century is the period and the locality is Kiev, where a handyman is caught up in the wave of anti-Semitism. In his long suffering that follows his refusal to confess to a crime he did not commit, his case becomes known to the world. Basic character is enacted by Alan Bates in an indefinite delineation frequently baffling to the spectator.

1968: Nomination: Best Actor (Alan Bates)

FLAME AND THE ARROW, THE
1950, 89 mins, US Ⓥ ⊙
D: Jacques Tourneur A: Burt Lancaster, Virginia Mayo, Robert Douglas, Nick Cravat, Aline MacMahon (Warner/Norma-FR)

A romantic costume drama set in medieval Italy with a Robin Hood plot showing how injustice is put down under the daring leadership of a heroic mountaineer. Burt Lancaster does the latter, portraying the Arrow of the title with just the right amount of dash.

1950: Nominations: Best Color Cinematography, Scoring of a Dramatic Picture

FLAME IN THE STREETS
1961, 93 mins, UK
D: Roy Ward Baker A: John Mills, Sylvia Syms, Brenda de Banzie, Earl Cameron, Johnny Sekka, Ann Lynn (Rank)

Story, which hasn't much dramatic bounce, concerns the dilemma of a staunch trade unionist who averts a threatened factory strike over a black foreman, swaying the staff by urging that the color of a man's skin is unimportant, only to find that his daughter has fallen in love with another black man. How to reconcile his very different feelings over the two incidents is his problem. John Mills makes a convincing figure as the father. Brenda de Banzie, his wife, bitter and intolerant about black people, has two telling scenes. Sylvia Syms, the schoolmistress daughter who outrages her parents by her determination to marry a young black schoolteacher, contributes a neat performance.

FLAME OF BARBARY COAST
1945, 91 mins, US Ⓥ
D: Joseph Kane A: John Wayne, Ann Dvorak, Joseph Schildkraut, William Frawley, Virginia Grey (Republic)

A Montana cattleman comes to scoff at the pre-earthquake Barbary Coast of San Francisco and stays to like it; a "gentleman" gambler runs the most successful joint in the district until the guy from the tall grass decides to take over; and the gambler's singer-sweetheart is also the toast of the town's haut monde. The story winds a tortuous path until the earthquake breaks things up.

1945: Nominations: Best Scoring of a Dramatic Picture, Sound

FLAME OF NEW ORLEANS, THE
1941, 78 mins, US
D: Rene Clair **A:** Marlene Dietrich, Bruce Cabot, Roland Young, Anne Revere, Mischa Auer (Universal)

A very thin and familiar tale of the romantic interludes of a lady of dubious reputation a century ago. Dietrich arrives in New Orleans, determined to grab off a wealthy admirer. Roland Young is an easy victim and proposes marriage, but Bruce Cabot, tough and roving ship captain, holds a strange fascination for her. Picture is Rene Clair's first in America. He works valiantly with the flimsy material, injecting many incidental byplays that are amusing, but to meager avail.

FLAME OVER INDIA
See: North West Frontier

FLAMINGO KID, THE
1984, 100 mins, US Ⓥ ⊙
D: Garry Marshall **A:** Matt Dillon, Richard Crenna, Hector Elizondo, Jessica Walter, Molly McCarthy (ABC/Mercury)

The Flamingo Kid, set in 1963, sports amusing trappings connected with 18-year-old Matt Dillon working for a summer at the El Flamingo Beach Club in Far Rockaway, NY. At its heart, though, story has to do with the critical choices facing a youth of that age and how they will help determine the rest of his life. Dillon does a good job in his fullest, least narcissistic characterization to date.

FLAMINGO ROAD
1949, 94 mins, US Ⓥ
D: Michael Curtiz **A:** Joan Crawford, Zachary Scott, Sydney Greenstreet, David Brian, Gladys George (Warner)

A class vehicle for Joan Crawford, loaded with heartbreak, romance, and stinging violence. Yarn swivels around a deadly antagonism between Crawford and Sydney Greenstreet, a sinister small-town sheriff. Film rapidly gathers momentum after Crawford, stranded by a bankrupt sideshow company, falls in love with Zachary Scott, the sheriff's protégé.

FLAMING STAR
1960, 92 mins, US Ⓥ ⊡
D: Don Siegel **A:** Elvis Presley, Steve Forrest, Barbara Eden, Dolores Del Rio, John McIntire, Richard Jaeckel (20th Century-Fox)

The plot—half-breed hopelessly involved in war between white man and red man—is disturbingly familiar and not altogether convincing, but the film is attractively mounted and consistently diverting. Presley plays the half-breed, but lacks the facial and thespic sensitivity and projection so desperately required here. The standouts are the veterans Dolores Del Rio and John McIntire.

FLASHDANCE
1983, 96 mins, US Ⓥ ⊙
D: Adrian Lyne **A:** Jennifer Beals, Michael Nouri, Lilia Skala, Sunny Johnson, Kyle T. Heffner, Belinda Bauer (Poly-Gram/Paramount)

Watching *Flashdance* is pretty much like looking at MTV for 96 minutes. Virtually plotless, exceedingly thin on characterization, and sociologically laughable, pic at least lives up to its title by offering an anthology of extraordinarily flashy dance numbers. Appealing newcomer Jennifer Beals plays an 18-year-old come to Pittsburgh to toil in a steel mill by day and work off steam at night by performing wild, improvised dances in a local bar.

1983: Best Original Song ("Flashdance . . . What a Feeling")

Nominations: Best Cinematography, Editing, Original Song ("Maniac")

FLASH GORDON
1980, 110 mins, UK Ⓥ ⊙ ⊡
D: Mike Hodges **A:** Sam J. Jones, Melody Anderson, Topol, Max von Sydow, Ornella Muti, Brian Blessed (Universal/De Laurentiis)

The expensive new version of *Flash Gordon* is a lot more gaudy, and just as dumb, as the original series starring Buster Crabbe. Sam J. Jones in the title role has even less thespic range than Crabbe, but the badness of his performance is part of the fun. Film benefits greatly from the adroit performance of Max von Sydow as Emperor Ming.

FLATLINERS
1990, 111 mins, US Ⓥ ⊙ ⊡
D: Joel Schumacher **A:** Kiefer Sutherland, Julia Roberts, Kevin Bacon, William Baldwin, Oliver Platt, Kimberly Scott (Stonebridge/Columbia)

A cautionary tale that ends along fairly traditional horror-sci-fi lines. Daring doctor-in-training Nelson (Kiefer Sutherland) decides to make his mark on medicine by stopping his heart and brain ("flatlining," as the lack of vital signs produces a flat line on the EKG and EEG monitors) and then having himself brought back by the gifted medical students he recruits to help him. Initially angry and reluctant, the others end up totally seduced, vying with each other for the chance to go next by offering to flatline the longest. Sutherland, as always, registers real presence and pulls off a wildly demanding role, but the remarkably gifted Julia Roberts is the film's true grace note.
1990: Nomination: Best Sound Effects Editing

FLAWLESS
1999, 112 mins, US Ⓥ ⊙
D: Joel Schumacher **A:** Robert De Niro, Philip Seymour Hoffman, Barry Miller, Chris Bauer, Skipp Sudduth, Wilson Jermaine Heredia (Tribeca/M-G-M)

Joel Schumacher's *Flawless* is a small-scale, intimate serio-comedy about the unlikely camaraderie that evolves between a macho security guard and a flamboyant transvestite, played by Robert De Niro and Philip Seymour Hoffman, a movie very much grounded in the zeitgeist of the post-Stonewall era. Set on the Lower East Side, tale introduces Walt Koontz (De Niro) as a retired security guard, a proud, ultraconservative man who's set in his ways. Rusty (Hoffman), Walt's upstairs neighbor, is exactly his opposite: a street-smart drag queen who functions as a mother hen to a whole entourage of cross-dressers. De Niro is good at conveying the gradual physical and psychological transformation of a middle-aged man. Hoffman has marvelous moments but his performance lacks depth.

FLEET'S IN, THE
1942, 93 mins, US
D: Victor Schertzinger **A:** Dorothy Lamour, William Holden, Eddie Bracken, Betty Hutton, Cass Daley, Leif Erickson (Paramount)

Holden handles himself well opposite Lamour as the sailor who falls for her while the battleship crew is on furlough in Frisco. The quarrel is less with the story itself than the musical side. There are no production numbers but an overdose of vocalists, backed by the Dorsey band.

FLESH
1932, 95 mins, US
D: John Ford **A:** Wallace Beery, Karen Morley, Ricardo Cortez, Jean Hersholt (M-G-M)

Wallace Beery plays a bighearted, big-muscled, small-brained guy with lovable qualities. A wrestler, he goes chump for a faithless woman, according to pattern, and the finish is sad, only this time there's a suggestion of ultimate happiness to deaden the pain. Karen Morley is the double-crossing lady who loves her man on the side. Latter, and doing a perfect job of an 100 percent unsympathetic character, is Ricardo Cortez.

FLESH
1968, 105 mins, US
D: Paul Morrissey **A:** Joe Dallesandro, Geraldine Smith, John Christian, Maurice Bardell, Candy Darling (Warhol)

Blithely, the synopsis of Andy Warhol's opus reads: "The story of a young married couple and the efforts of the husband, Joe, to sell himself to earn money for his wife's girl friend's abortion." Paul Morrissey wrote, directed, and lensed this hapless erotica freak-out as Warhol was recuperating from gunshot wounds.

FLESH AND BLOOD
1985, 126 mins, US Ⓥ ⊙ ▭
D: Paul Verhoeven **A:** Rutger Hauer, Jennifer Jason Leigh, Tom Burlinson, Jack Thompson, Susan Tyrrell (Orion/Riverside)

Flesh and Blood is a vivid and muscular, if less than fully startling, account of lust, savagery, revenge, betrayal, and assorted other dark doings in the Middle Ages. Director Paul Verhoeven has told his tale in visceral, involving fashion, and for the amount of carnage that piles up, explicit gore is kept to a minimum.

FLESH AND BONE
1993, 124 mins, US Ⓥ ⊙
D: Steve Kloves **A:** Dennis Quaid, Meg Ryan, James Caan, Gwyneth Paltrow, Scott Wilson (Mirage/Spring Creek/Paramount)

Despite arresting images and moments, writer-director Steve Kloves doesn't quite fill the vast Texas landscapes with enough dramatic blood and muscle. Arlis (Dennis Quaid) traverses the endless highways tending to vending machines. Before long, Kay (Meg Ryan) stumbles into his life, and it's only a matter of time until they roll in the hay. An hour in, evil father, Roy (James Caan), pops up. Pic had the potential for poetic reverberations concerning futures and fates tangled across the generations. But this possibility fades in as it becomes clear that Kloves is trying to shoehorn a cute romance of tempermental opposites into an essentially somber, violent format. Gwyneth Paltrow steals every scene she's in as Caan's bad-girl sometime companion.

FLESH AND FANTASY
1943, 92 mins, US
D: Julien Duvivier **A:** Edward G. Robinson, Charles Boyer, Barbara Stanwyck, Betty Field, Robert Cummings, Thomas Mitchell (Universal)

This is a decidedly novel and unusual picture, displaying the impress on individuals of dreams, fortune-telling, and other supernatural phenomena. First episode delves into romance of Betty Field, who's become callous, bitter, and defeated through ugly features. Second episode presents Thomas Mitchell as a palmist at a socialite group. Edward G. Robinson submits to a reading, and becomes intrigued when he's told he will commit murder. Boyer shares starring honors with Barbara Stanwyck in the final episode, which predicts disaster to himself while performing as a circus high-wire artist.

FLESH AND THE DEVIL
1926, 91 mins, US Ⓥ ⊗
D: Clarence Brown **A:** John Gilbert, Greta Garbo, Lars Hanson, Barbara Kent (M-G-M)

This film is a battle between John Gilbert, starred, and Greta Garbo, featured, for honors. The story is laid in a small German or Austrian town. Two boys are at military school when the picture opens. Back home there is a ball and Lee (Gilbert), the more sophisticated of the two, dances with a girl, but fails to learn her name. Her husband walks in on them and strikes the boy, which calls for a duel. The husband is killed. The military authorities "advise" foreign service for five years for the youngster. Before going, he asks his bloodbound friend to seek out the widow and console her.

FLESH FOR FRANKENSTEIN
(US: ANDY WARHOL'S FRANKENSTEIN)
1974, 95 mins, France/Italy Ⓥ ⊙
D: Paul Morrissey **A:** Joe Dallesandro, Udo Kier, Monique Van Vooren, Arno

Juerging, Srdjan Zelenovic, Dalila Di Lazzaro (CC-Champion & 1/Ponti/Yanne/Rassam

Paul Morrissey of the Andy Warhol stable made this pic back-to-back with *Blood for Dracula*, with an added gimmick of 3-D and more skillfully direction. Morrissey plays some variations on the old Prometheus myth. He adds plenty of gore, with some dollops of sex.

FLESH GORDON
1974, 78 mins, US Ⓥ
D: Howard Ziehm, Michael Benveniste **A:** Jason Williams, Suzanne Fields, Joseph Hudgins, John Hoyt (Graffiti)

Puerile is the word for this softcore spoof of the sci-fi serials of the 1930s. Pic emerges as an expensive-looking mishmash of obvious double entendres, idiotic characterizations, and dull situations. Only compensation is flash of bawdy humor.

FLETCH
1985, 96 mins, US Ⓥ ⊙
D: Michael Ritchie **A:** Chevy Chase, Dana Wheeler-Nicholson, Tim Matheson, Joe Don Baker, Geena Davis (Universal)

What propels this contempo L.A. yarn about a dissembling newspaper columnist on the trail of a nefarious con man (Tim Matheson) is the obvious and successful byplay between Chevy Chase's sly, glib persona and the satiric brush strokes of director Michael Ritchie. Their teamwork turns an otherwise hair-pinned, anecdotal plot into a breezy, peppy frolic and a tour de force for Chase.

FLETCH LIVES
1989, 95 mins, US Ⓥ ⊙
D: Michael Ritchie **A:** Chevy Chase, Hal Holbrook, Julianne Phillips, Cleavon Little, R. Lee Ermey, Richard Libertini (Universal)

Chevy Chase is perfectly suited to playing a smirking, wisecracking, multiple-identitied reporter in *Fletch Lives*. Ridiculous and anecdotal plot that transports Chase from his beloved L.A. base to Louisiana's bayou country to take over his dead aunt's crumbling plantation works for the simple reason that Chase's sly, glib persona is in sync with Michael Ritchie's equally breezy direction.

FLIGHT OF THE DOVES
1971, 101 mins, US
D: Ralph Nelson **A:** Ron Moody, Jack Wild, Dorothy McGuire, Stanley Hollo-

way, William Rushton, Dana (Columbia)

A heartwarming, often funny, often suspenseful story of two runaway children, fleeing from a cruel stepfather (British) to their grandmother (Irish) who lives "somewhere in Ireland." Dorothy McGuire is a delight as a bright-eyed, most articulate grandmother, standing up to authority on behalf of the young runaways. With almost as many character changes as Alec Guinness had in *Kind Hearts and Coronets*, Ron Moody is so captivating that no one really believes that he won't survive.

FLIGHT OF THE INTRUDER
1991, 113 mins, US Ⓥ ⊙ ⊑
D: John Milius **A:** Danny Glover, Willem Dafoe, Brad Johnson, Rosanna Arquette, Tom Sizemore (Paramount)

The most boring Vietnam War pic since *The Green Berets* (1968) lacks the benefit of the latter's political outrageousness to spark a little interest and humor. Set mostly aboard a giant aircraft carrier, yarn unspools in 1972 while the Paris peace talks are in progress. Title refers to the A-6, a small, low-altitude bomber designed for quick in-and-out strikes. Ace of the outfit is Brad Johnson, who loses a bombardier in an elaborate credit sequence and is thereafter interested in "payback." Opportunity presents itself with the arrival of a vet bombardier (Willem Dafoe) not averse to hijinks. Johnson and Dafoe cook up a scheme to devastate People's Resistance Park in downtown Hanoi, a.k.a. SAM City, where captured US artillery is on display.

FLIGHT OF THE NAVIGATOR
1986, 90 mins, US Ⓥ ⊙
D: Randal Kleiser **A:** Joey Cramer, Veronica Cartwright, Cliff De Young, Sarah Jessica Parker, Matt Adler (Walt Disney/PSO)

Young David Freeman (Joey Cramer) vanishes from his Fort Lauderdale home only to return to the identical spot unchanged eight years later. When a sleek silver flying saucer turns up on the scene, NASA gets into the act and all roads lead to David. It seems his head has been filled with star charts and he's been serving as navigator for an exploratory ship from a distant planet. As is often the problem with extraterrestrial adventures, all life-forms are anthropomorphized with a selection of cute and cuddly creatures. There are some nifty special effects in the spacecraft sequences.

FLIGHT OF THE PHOENIX, THE
1965, 149 mins, US Ⓥ ⊙
D: Robert Aldrich **A:** James Stewart, Richard Attenborough, Peter Finch, Hardy Kruger, Ernest Borgnine, Ian Bannen (Associates & Aldrich/20th Century-Fox)

A grim, tenseful, realistic tale of a small group of men forced down on the North African desert and their desperate efforts to build a single-engine plane out of the wreckage of the twin job in which they crashed during a sandstorm. Filmic translation of the Elleston Trevor book is an often fascinating and superlative piece of filmmaking highlighted by standout performances and touches that show producer-director at his best. James Stewart, as the pilot of a desert oil company cargo-passenger plane who flies by the seat of his pants, is strongly cast in role and is strongly backed by entire cast.
1965: Nominations: Best Supp. Actor (Ian Bannen), Editing

FLIM-FLAM MAN, THE
(UK: ONE BORN EVERY MINUTE)
1967, 104 mins, US Ⓥ ⊑
D: Irvin Kershner **A:** George C. Scott, Sue Lyon, Michael Sarrazin, Harry Morgan, Jack Albertson (20th Century-Fox)

An outstanding comedy starring George C. Scott as a Dixie drifter. Michael Sarrazin, as Scott's fellow traveler, makes an impressive feature-film bow. A series of flimflams are pulled off only on people who seemingly deserve to be stiffed, thus minimizing any complaint that lawlessness is being made attractive.

FLINTSTONES, THE
1994, 92 mins, US Ⓥ ⊙
D: Brian Levant **A:** John Goodman, Elizabeth Perkins, Rick Moranis, Rosie O'Donnell, Kyle MacLachlan, Elizabeth Taylor (Hanna-Barbera/Amblin/Universal)

With all manner of friendly beasts, a super-energetic John Goodman, and a colorful supporting cast inhabiting a Bedrock that resembles a Stone Age version of Steven Spielberg suburbia, this live-action translation of the perennial cartoon favorite is a fine popcorn picture for small fry, and perfectly inoffensive for adults. Fred Flintstone (Goodman) is the happy, rock-solid workingman, thick of biceps and skull, who shockingly wins a promotion out of the rock pile and into the executive suites of Slate & Co. when his best friend, Barney Rubble (Rick Moranis), substitutes his own exam answers for Fred's. The boss (Kyle MacLachlan) and his foxy secretary (Halle Berry) easily manipulate the lazy simpleton, setting him up for a big fall as they plot to make off with ill-gotten gains.

FLIPPER
1963, 87 mins, US ⓥ
D: James B. Clark **A:** Chuck Connors, Luke Halpin, Connie Scott, Kathleen Maguire (M-G-M)

Boy meets dolphin, boy loses dolphin, boy wins dolphin. Thus substituting gill for gal, producer Ivan Tors has fashioned a serviceable little family picture that to all intents and porpoises should satisfy aquabrats everywhere. Chuck Connors limns the father firmly but agreeably, and young Halpin, in his screen bow, demonstrates keen acting instincts as the boy on a dolphin.

FLIPPER
1996, 96 mins, US ⓥ ⊙
D: Alan Shapiro **A:** Elijah Wood, Paul Hogan, Chelsea Field, Isaac Hayes, Jonathan Banks (American/Universal)

The effectively offbeat casting of Paul Hogan and some impressive underwater cinematography do much to enliven *Flipper*. In this version, Sandy, the teen hero played here by Elijah Wood, is an embittered child of divorce. And the ecologically conscious story line has Flipper battling polluters who dump toxic waste into his watery environs. Hogan takes a dry-witted and refreshingly eccentric approach to playing a stereotypical character. Wood manages to be appealing even when his character is borderline tedious.

FLIRT
1996, 84 mins, US/Germany/Japan ⓥ
D: Hal Hartley **A:** Bill Sage, Martin Donovan, Dwight Ewell, Geno Lechner, Miho Nikaidoh, Hal Hartley (True Fiction/Pandora/Nippon)

Slight but sleek, *Flirt* is still fun. Hal Hartley's three-legged set of variations on an emotional situation plays like a compressed version of his oeuvre to date. Picture gets off to a crowd-pleasing start with the first episode ("New York, February 1993," 16 mins.), the briefest and wittiest of the three. Lolling on a bed prior to leaving for Paris, Emily (Parker Posey) quizzes an offscreen lover by phone on the depth of his commitment. Bill (Bill Sage)

finally promises to make a decision when he picks her up in 90 minutes. "Berlin, October 1994" (30 mins.) initially has fun transposing the same dialogue and situations to a homosexual and German setting. For the third episode, "Tokyo, March 1995" (35 mins), Hartley lets place dictate content even more, opening with a rehearsal by a butoh mime ensemble. Out of this oblique opening emerges a similar but looser variation, with one of the dancers, the kooky Miho (Miho Nikaidoh), torn between choreographer Ozu (Toshizo Fujisawa) and departing American filmer Hal (Hartley himself).

FLIRTATION WALK
1934, 95 mins, US
D: Frank Borzage **A:** Dick Powell, Ruby Keeler, Pat O'Brien, Ross Alexander (First National)

Bright and diverting entertainment in which the musical sequences are logically worked in, albeit with the usual Hollywood flair for exaggeration. Background of West Point allows the picture to possess some snappy drill and brass-button stuff. Dick Powell, in his plebe year at the Point, plays the situations for excellent natural comedy. Ruby Keeler does not dance. She has a lot to do and does it with considerable assurance.

1934: Nomination: Best Picture

FLIRTING
1991, 96 mins, Australia ⓥ ⊙
D: John Duigan **A:** Noah Taylor, Thandie Newton, Nicole Kidman, Bartholomew Rose, Kiri Paramore (Kennedy Miller)

Miles ahead of the average teen film, this depiction of well-to-do teens in sexually segregated schools also looks obliquely at latent racism at the time of the "white Australia" policy. Events that led to the Vietnam War already were in motion. Duigan handles this material with a great deal of humor and charm, demonstrating a sharp ear for contemporary teen dialogue. A curiosity is Nicole Kidman's appearance as one of the girls'-school students.

FLIRTING WITH DISASTER
1996, 92 mins, US ⓥ ⊙
D: David O. Russell **A:** Patricia Arquette, Ben Stiller, Tea Leoni, Alan Alda, Mary Tyler Moore, George Segal (Miramax)

Most of the time a diabolically clever satire that has its way with any number of contemporary shibaoleths, this whacked-out road comedy takes any number of unexpected turns, most of them bitingly funny. Mel Coplin (Ben Stiller) is a young New York dad who decides he can't name his four-month-old son without having met his own biological parents. Mel, his moody wife Nancy (Patricia Arquette), and infant son fly to San Diego. As the trip progresses, relations between Mel and Nancy go from strained to dire, and everyone's heads are sent spinning when they arrive at the sprawling desert home of Richard and Mary Schlicting (Alan Alda, Lily Tomlin).

FLOWER DRUM SONG
1961, 133 mins, US Ⓥ ⊙ ▱
D: Henry Koster A: Nancy Kwan, James Shigeta, Juanita Hall, Jack Soo, Miyoshi Umeki, Benson Fong (Universal)

Much of the fundamental charm, grace, and novelty of Rodgers and Hammerstein's *Flower Drum Song* has been overwhelmed by sheer opulence and glamour. As a film, it emerges a curiously unaffecting, unstable, and rather undistinguished experience. The dominant issue is the clash of East-West romantic-marital customs as it affects four young people of Chinese descent living in San Francisco's Chinatown. As in most R&H enterprises, the meat is in the musical numbers. There are some bright spots in this area but even here the effect isn't overpowering.
1961: Nominations: Best Color Cinematography, Color Costume Design, Color Art Direction, Scoring of a Musical Picture, Sound

FLOWERS IN THE ATTIC
1987, 95 mins, US Ⓥ
D: Jeffrey Bloom A: Louise Fletcher, Victoria Tennant, Kristy Swanson, Jeb Stuart Adams, Ben Ganger (New World/Fries)

V. C. Andrews novel of incestuous relationships and confined childhood always has been a superb candidate for a film treatment, but director Jeffrey Bloom has squeezed the life from it. Performances are stiff and dreary. The ridiculous ending (different from the book) was one of several shot. Corinne (Victoria Tennant) takes the family—teenagers Chris (Jeb Stuart Adams) and Cathy (Kristy Swanson) and preadolescent twins Carrie (Lindsay Parker) and Cory (Ben Ganger)—and becomes gold digger deluxe, moving back to her parents' house, intent on getting reinstated into her father's will. Kids are locked into a guest room, where they are

FLUBBER
1997, 93 mins, US Ⓥ
D: Les Mayfield A: Robin Williams, Marcia Gay Harden, Christopher McDonald, Raymond Barry, Clancy Brown, Ted Levine (Great Oaks/Walt Disney)

After a slow, singularly unpromising start, this new version of *The Absent-Minded Professor* emerges as funny and frenetic family entertainment. Robin Williams is unusually subdued as Philip Brainard, an easily distracted college professor. Quite by accident, he invents Flubber—"flying rubber"—a greenish goo with a mischievous personality all its own. At times, the little critter looks like a malleable bean bag. Except for a few moments of improvisational silliness with Flubber, Williams pretty much remains in character throughout the comedy.

FLUKE
1995, 96 mins, US Ⓥ
D: Carlo Carlei A: Matthew Modine, Nancy Travis, Eric Stoltz, Max Pomeranc, Samuel L. Jackson, Ron Perlman (Rocket/M-G-M)

Intended for children as well as their parents, *Fluke,* the dramatic tale of a dog who was once a man, is strange family fare, a nonformulaic pic that tries to blend the expected magic of animal adventures with more serious ideas. Italian Carlo Carlei makes his U.S. directorial debut with a film that is stylistically excessive, flaunting his facility with the camera at the expense of simpler, more coherent storytelling, as befits children's films.

FLY, THE
1958, 94 mins, US Ⓥ ⊙ ▱
D: Kurt Neumann A: Al Hedison, Patricia Owens, Vincent Price, Herbert Marshall (20th Century-Fox)

Al Hedison plays a scientist who has invented a machine that will enable humans to travel—disintegrated—anywhere in the world at the speed of light. In experimenting on himself, however, a fly gets into the disintegration chamber. When Hedison arrives in the integration chamber, he has the head and "arm" of a fly; the fly has the head and arm of the man. One strong factor of the picture is its unusual believability. There is an appealing and poignant romance between Patricia Owens and Hedison.

FLY, THE
1986, 100 mins, US ⑰ ⊙
D: David Cronenberg **A:** Jeff Goldblum, Geena Davis, John Getz, (Brooksfilms)

Remake of the 1958 horror classic *The Fly* is not for the squeamish. Jeff Goldblum brings a quirky, common touch to the spacey-scientist role. Goldblum's got a set of teleporters that he promises will ''change the world as we know it,'' and indeed, they change his. Goldblum, in a moment of drunken jealousy, throws himself in the works. Unbeknownst to him a fly accompanies him on the journey and he starts to metamorphose. Chris Walas's design for *The Fly* is never less than visually intriguing. Cronenberg contains the action well in a limited space with a small cast.
1986: Best Makeup

FLY II, THE
1989, 105 mins, US ⑰ ⊙
D: Chris Walas **A:** Eric Stoltz, Daphne Zuniga, Lee Richardson, John Getz (Brooksfilms)

An expectedly gory and gooey but mostly plodding sequel to the 1986 hit that was a remake of the 1958 sci-fier that itself spawned two sequels. After a shock opening in which the late man-fly's son is born, slickly produced pic generates some promise as little Martin Brundle is raised in laboratory conditions. Afflicted with a dramatically accelerated life cycle, Martin by the age of five emerges fully grown in the person of Eric Stoltz. He becomes determined to perfect his father's teleportation machine.

FLY AWAY HOME
1996, 107 mins, US ⑰ ⊙
D: Carroll Ballard **A:** Jeff Daniels, Anna Paquin, Dana Delany, Terry Kinney, Holter Graham, Jeremy Ratchford (Sandollar/ Columbia)

An animal, kid, and family picture of the first order, *Fly Away Home* is an unexpectedly engrossing tale about an adolescent girl who raises a bunch of orphan goslings to maturity, then leads them on a migratory path in a homemade plane. The scenes of the flightless little birds scurrying around the Canadian farm to follow 13-year-old Amy (Anna Paquin) wherever she goes are mightily disarming. It is her endlessly resourceful dad, Thomas (Jeff Daniels), who proposes the solution of how to get the geese to migrate south. The dynamic between Daniels's artist father and Paquin's initially sullen teenager is warmly and believably conveyed.
1996: Nomination: Best Cinematography

FLY BY NIGHT
1942, 74 mins, US
D: Robert Siodmak **A:** Nancy Kelly, Richard Carlson, Albert Basserman, Martin Kosleck (Paramount)

This is one of those sinister mellers, photographed in low light tones, with a generally implausible story populated with spies, secret weapons, and nice young couples who get innocently mixed up in espionage. Nancy Kelly and Richard Carlson, as the innocents who get caught in the meshes of the spy ring, give surprisingly good performances for roles of this type.

FLYING DEUCES, THE
1939, 67 mins, US ⑰ ⊙
D: A. Edward Sutherland **A:** Stan Laurel, Oliver Hardy, Jean Parker, Reginald Gardiner (RKO)

Comedy is of early Keystone vintage with squirting water and bumps into walls used extensively to create laughs. Laurel and Hardy enlist in the Foreign Legion. Not much enthusiasm displayed for this uninspired comedy, with exception of two brief episodes. Hardy sings chorus of ''Shine On Harvest Moon'' while Laurel does some light stepping. Later, Laurel's utilization of bedsprings to play a harp solo is the picture's highlight.

FLYING DOWN TO RIO
1934, 88 mins, US ⑰ ⊙
D: Thornton Freeland, George Nicholls Jr.
A: Dolores Del Rio, Gene Raymond, Raul Roulien, Ginger Rogers, Fred Astaire (RKO)

The main point is the promise of Fred Astaire. He's distinctly likable on the screen, the mike is kind to his voice, and as a dancer he remains in a class by himself. This picture makes its bid via numbers staged by Dave Gould to Vincent Youman melodies. But *Rio*'s story lets it down. It's slow and lacks laughs. From the time of the opening melody (''Music Makes Me''—and hot) to the next number, ''Carioca,'' almost three reels elapse. It takes all that time for Gene Raymond, as a bandleader, to be enticed by Dolores Del Rio, as a South American belle, and

frame her into a plane ride to Rio de Janeiro.
1934: Nomination: Best Song ("Carioca")

FLYING LEATHERNECKS
1951, 103 mins, US Ⓥ ⊙
D: Nicholas Ray **A:** John Wayne, Robert Ryan, Don Taylor, Janis Carter, Jay C. Flippen, William Harrigan (RKO)

Story deals with a small squadron of flying leathernecks stationed in the Pacific and the frictions that develop between its commander (Wayne) and its executive officer (Ryan) when they are not busy fighting the war. This purely masculine yarn sidetracks when Wayne goes on leave to the States for time with his wife (Janis Carter) and small son.

FLYING TIGERS
1942, 96 mins, US Ⓥ ⊙
D: David Miller **A:** John Wayne, John Carroll, Anna Lee, Paul Kelly, Mae Clarke (Republic)

Based on exploits of American fliers in China who took up the cudgels against the Japs long before Pearl Harbor. Handicapped primarily by a threadbare script, production also suffers from slow pacing, while John Wayne, John Carroll, Anna Lee, and Paul Kelly are barely adequate in the major acting assignments. Some of the scenes look repetitious, the same Jap fliers apparently being shot down and killed three or four times over.
1942: Nominations: Best Scoring of a Dramatic Picture, Sound, Special Effects

FOG, THE
1980, 91 mins, US Ⓥ ⊙ ▭
D: John Carpenter **A:** Adrienne Barbeau, Hal Holbrook, Janet Leigh, Jamie Lee Curtis, John Houseman (Avco Embassy)

John Carpenter is anything but subtle in his approach to shocker material. Premise is obvious from almost the first frame, as a grizzled John Houseman tells youngsters grouped around a campfire about a foggy curse that surrounds a coastal town where a horrible shipwreck took place 100 years ago. Adrienne Barbeau makes her film debut as the husky-voiced deejay of the town's sole radio station, perched atop a lighthouse from which the title phenomenon becomes increasingly apparent.

FOLIES BERGERE
1935, 83 mins, US
D: Roy Del Ruth **A:** Maurice Chevalier, Ann Sothern, Merle Oberon, Eric Blore (20th Century/United Artists)

Maurice Chevalier handles the double assignment of Charlier, the Folies comic, and the Baron Cassini. Baron gets into a financial jam, so Charlier is hired to impersonate him while he's off to London to dig up some coin. Baron has been having marital difficulties with his wife, too, and Charlier manages to fix up both the home work and the office work for the baron. Chevalier shows that he has range as an actor. Ann Sothern as Charlier's wife sings and dances with Chevalier and makes a definite sock impression. Dance routines by Dave Gould are nifty.
1935: Best Dance Direction ("Straw Hat")

FOLLOW THAT BIRD
1985, 88 mins, US Ⓥ ⊙
D: Ken Kwapis **A:** Caroll Spinney, Jim Henson, Frank Oz, Paul Bartel, Sandra Bernhard, John Candy (Warner)

Simple premise has the slightly goofy yellow, eight-foot fowl Big Bird taken away from Sesame Street so he can grow up among a bird family named the Dodos, in Oceanview, IL. The Dodos are a bunch of loons, however, so B.B. begins the long trek back to New York on foot, while the Sesame Street gang mobilizes in assorted vehicles to find its dear friend. All turns out for the best, of course, and spicing things up along the way are Chevy Chase and Kermit the Frog as TV newscasters, Sandra Bernhard and Paul Bartel as the proprietors of a low-down roadside diner, and John Candy as a motorcycle cop.

FOLLOW THAT CAMEL
1967, 95 mins, UK Ⓥ
D: Gerald Thomas **A:** Phil Silvers, Jim Dale, Peter Butterworth, Charles Hawtrey, Kenneth Williams (Rank)

A *Carry on* foray into Foreign Legion territory, with a young hero (Jim Dale) accused of cheating at cricket, enlisting with his manservant to exculpate himself from disgrace. There he encounters Phil Silvers as a sergeant, Kenneth Williams as the German commanding officer, Charles Hawtrey as his deft adjutant, and Joan Sims as a much-cleavaged siren. The farrago climaxes in a hilarious battle at a desert fort.

FOLLOW THAT DREAM
1962, 109 mins, US Ⓥ ▭
D: Gordon Douglas **A:** Elvis Presley, Ar-

thur O'Connell, Anne Helm, Joanna Moore, Jack Kruschen, Simon Oakland (United Artists)

Elvis Presley as the hinterland's answer to the supposed advantages of formal booklarnin'. By Presley pix standards, it's above average. He portrays a sort of number-one son in a makeshift, itinerant brood of Real McCoy types who plant themselves on a strip of unclaimed Florida beach and proceed to play homesteaders while befuddled officials of city and state, welfare workers, and thugs haplessly attempt to unsquat them.

FOLLOW THE BOYS
1944, 122 mins, US ▱
D: A. Edward Sutherland **A:** George Raft, Vera Zorina, George Macready, Charles Butterworth, Regis Toomey (Universal)

Charles K. Feldman, who was prominent in Hollywood Victory Committee and allied USO Camp Shows activities, conceived the idea of glorifying the professional undertaking. The sum total is a highly entertaining film package. Thus are paraded Jeanette MacDonald, Orson Welles, Dietrich, Dinah Shore, W. C. Fields, Andrews Sisters, Artur Rubinstein, Carmen Amaya, Sophie Tucker, Delta Rhythm Boys, et al. Everybody does something, the songs running the gamut of the hit parade of three decades.

FOLLOW THE BOYS
1963, 96 mins, US ▱
D: Richard Thorpe **A:** Connie Francis, Paula Prentiss, Dany Robin, Janis Paige, Russ Tamblyn, Richard Long (M-G-M)

Youth must be served, but the service isn't very good in this lackluster romantic comedy about a group of gobs who find the same girls in every port—their faithfully itinerant wives or fiancées. It is roughly—very roughly—a sequel to *Where the Boys Are*. Heroines of the story are a group of girls dubbed "seagulls" because, like their namesakes, they are perpetually following ships. The story dwells on four such couples and illustrates, haphazardly, their togetherness difficulties.

FOLLOW THE FLEET
1936, 110 mins, US ⓥ
D: Mark Sandrich **A:** Fred Astaire, Ginger Rogers, Randolph Scott, Harriet Hilliard, Astrid Allwyn (RKO)

With Ginger Rogers again opposite, and the Irving Berlin music to dance to and sing, Astaire once more legs himself and his picture into the big-time entertain-

ment class. Imperfections in *Fleet* are confined to story. There are seven songs, which is a bit too much—all by Irving Berlin, with "Face the Music" easily the leader. Story is a double romance involving the starred duo and Harriet Hilliard–Randolph Scott. Yarn breaks them up and teams them again for the finish.

FOLLOW YOUR DREAMS
See: Independence Day

FOOL, THE
1991, 135 mins, UK ⓥ
D: Christine Edzard **A:** Derek Jacobi, Cyril Cusack, Ruth Mitchell, Paul Brooke, Corin Redgrave, John McEnery (Sands/Film Four/British Screen/Tyler

Three years after their marathon, *Little Dorrit*, husband-and-wife producers Richard Goodwin and Christine Edzard tread the same streets to lesser effect in *The Fool*. In 1857, an obscure theater clerk (Derek Jacobi) engineers a financial scam to show up the monied classes. Problems start when, posing as the carefree Sir John, he's recognized by some theater folk, and he starts taking his alter ego too seriously. Without a strong central yarn like Dickens's *Dorrit*, pic becomes a series of one-off routines by w.k. Brit thesps.

FOOL FOR LOVE
1985, 106 mins, US ⓥ ▱
D: Robert Altman **A:** Sam Shepard, Kim Basinger, Harry Dean Stanton, Randy Quaid, Martha Crawford (Cannon)

Sam Shepard's drama of intense, forbidden love in the modern west is made to seem like specious stuff filled with dramatic ideas left over from the 1950s. Eddie, a rangy, handsome cowboy, returns after a long absence to try to get back with the sexy May, with whom he has a can't-live-with-or-without-her relationship. The two shout, argue, make up, make out, split up, pout, dance around each other, and start up all over again, while an old drunk observer takes it all in. Finally, the arrival of another fellow to take May out prompts a nocturnal spilling of the beans.

FOOLISH WIVES
1922, 180 mins, US ⓥ ⊙ ⊗
D: Erich von Stroheim **A:** Erich von Stroheim, Rudolph Christians, Miss Du Pont, Maude George, Mae Busch (Universal)

Obviously intended to be a sensational sex melodrama, *Foolish Wives* is frankly salacious. Erich von Stroheim wrote the script, directed, and is the featured player. He's all over the lot every minute. His character is a Russian captain of hussars. The story starts with a flirtation between the Count (von Stroheim) and the American diplomat's wife, continues along with his obvious attempts to possess her, right under her husband's nose, and with the woman's evident liking for the count's attentions.

FOOLS OF FORTUNE
1990, 104 mins, UK Ⓥ ⊙
D: Pat O'Connor **A:** Mary Elizabeth Mastrantonio, Iain Glen, Julie Christie, Michael Kitchen, Sean T. McClory (PolyGram/Working Title)

An historical saga written with lucidity and performed with sensitivity, but tending to melodrama. The Irish war of independence is the starting point for the story of a family's destruction and the survival of an unlikely love. The Quinton family seem sheltered in their grand rural home until the British-employed soldiers, the Black and Tans, burn down the house. The only survivors of the massacre are Quinton's wife (Julie Christie), her son Willie, and their maid. Willie becomes an introspective and withdrawn young man, while his mother becomes a manic-depressive and chronic alcoholic, a role which Christie relishes.

FOOTLIGHT PARADE
1933, 102 mins, US Ⓥ ⊙
D: Lloyd Bacon, Busby Berkeley **A:** James Cagney, Joan Blondell, Ruby Keeler, Dick Powell, Guy Kibbee, Ruth Donnelly (Warner)

Footlight Parade is not as good as *42nd Street* and *Gold Diggers* but the three socko numbers here eclipse some of the preceding Busby Berkeley staging for spectacle. That water ballet, the hokum "Honeymoon Hotel" and "Shanghai Lil" are punchy and undeniable. They more than offset the lethargy of what has preceded, and sweep the spectator away.

FOOTLIGHT SERENADE
1942, 81 mins, US Ⓥ
D: Gregory Ratoff **A:** John Payne, Betty Grable, Victor Mature, Jane Wyman, Phil Silvers, James Gleason (20th Century-Fox)

New twist of minor importance has been provided for the boy-meets-girl-and-both-get-into-Broadway-show formula. Victor Mature is the champ, with the show built around him by producer James Glea-

son. His characterization is decidedly reminiscent of a heavyweight champ of the 1930s. Betty Grable gets a chorine job, while her fiancé John Payne is projected into a line of candidates for stumblebum for the champ in the show.

FOOTLOOSE
1984, 107 mins, US Ⓥ ⊙
D: Herbert Ross **A:** Kevin Bacon, Lori Singer, John Lithgow, Dianne Wiest, Christopher Penn, Sarah Jessica Parker (Paramount)

In addition to his usual directorial skill and considerable choreographic experience, Herb Ross brings to *Footloose* an adult sensibility often lacking in troubled-teen pics. To be sure, *Footloose* is mainly a youth-oriented rock picture, but with an integrated story line that works. Essential to the result is young Kevin Bacon, superb in the lead part. Bacon really just wants to get along in the small town he's been forced to move to from Chicago. Sure to complicate his life, however, is pretty Lori Singer, a sexually and otherwise confused preacher's daughter.

1984: Nominations: Best Song ("Footloose," "Let's Hear It for the Boy")

FOOTSTEPS IN THE DARK
1941, 96 mins, US
D: Lloyd Bacon **A:** Errol Flynn, Brenda Marshall, Ralph Bellamy, Alan Hale, Lee Patrick, Lucile Watson (Warner/First National)

Errol Flynn becomes a detective-book author and amateur Sherlock in his first comedy in years. Lloyd Bacon's direction furnishes the film with plenty of suspense and hokey but socko absurdities. Flynn is depicted as an investment banker, leading a double life as a writer. His search for story material takes him on nightly prowls which get him into hot water in his own home.

FOR A FEW DOLLARS MORE
1966, 130 mins, Italy/Spain/W. Germany Ⓥ ⊙ ▭
D: Sergio Leone **A:** Clint Eastwood, Lee Van Cleef, Gian Maria Volonte, Mara Krup, Luigi Pistilli, Klaus Kinski (PEA/Gonzales/Constantin)

A hard-hitting western. Story deals with a race between two bounty killers (Clint Eastwood and Lee Van Cleef) for reward money riding on head of a bandit (Gian Maria Volonte). First separately, then via a somewhat shaky and untrusting allegiance, the pair manage to set the stage for the killing of the bandido, El Indio. Script generally manages to avoid the cliché pitfalls traditional to the western. But it's principally thanks to Leone's bigger-than-life style, which combines up-front action and close-up details with a hard-hitting pace, that this acquires its impactful. [Version reviewed was Italian-language one.]

FORBIDDEN GAMES
See: Les Jeux Interdits

FORBIDDEN PLANET
1956, 98 mins, US ⊗ ⊙ ☐
D: Fred M. Wilcox A: Walter Pidgeon, Anne Francis, Leslie Nielsen, Warren Stevens, Jack Kelly, Earl Holliman (M-G-M)
Imaginative gadgets galore, plus plenty of suspense and thrills, make the production a top offering in the space-travel category. Best of all the gadgets is Robby, the Robot, and he's well used for some comedy touches. The conception of space cruisers, planet terrain, the monstrous self-operating power plant, and the terribly frightening specter that threatens the human principals in the story is weird and wonderful.
1956: Nomination: Best Special Effects

FORCE OF ARMS
1951, 98 mins, US
D: Michael Curtiz A: William Holden, Nancy Olson, Frank Lovejoy, Gene Evans (Warner)
Story uses an Italian battlefront setting as the frame for the compellingly projected romance between William Holden and Nancy Olson, a soldier and a WAC. The romance rings true and the battle action sequences are dangerously alive under the forthright staging of Michael Curtiz. Lovejoy makes his role of the friendly major a standout.

FORCE OF EVIL
1948, 78 mins, US ⊗ ⊙
D: Abraham Polonsky A: John Garfield, Beatrice Pearson, Thomas Gomez, Marie Windsor, Roy Roberts, Howland Chamberlin (M-G-M/Enterprise)
Force of Evil fails to develop the excitement hinted at in the title. Makers apparently couldn't decide on the best way to present an exposé of the numbers racket, winding up with neither fish nor fowl as far as hard-hitting racketeer meller is concerned. A poetic, almost allegorical, interpretation keeps intruding on the tougher elements of the plot. Garfield, as to be expected, comes through with a performance that gets everything out of the material furnished.

FORCE 10 FROM NAVARONE
1978, 118 mins, UK ⊗ ⊙ ▱
D: Guy Hamilton A: Robert Shaw, Harrison Ford, Edward Fox, Barbara Bach, Franco Nero, Richard Kiel (American International)
This is not a sequel to the 1961 hit Guns of Navarone, although Force 10 opens with the bang-up conclusion of the earlier exercise in World War II commando heroics. Two survivors of the spiking of the guns, British Major Mallory (now played by Robert Shaw) and demolitions expert Miller (Edward Fox) provide the link that gives some purpose to the title. Director Guy Hamilton manages over the course of almost two hours to keep his audience on edge. For a finale he has a double-whammy destruction of a giant Yugoslav dam, which sets loose forces of nature that crumble a seemingly indestructible bridge.

FOREIGN AFFAIR, A
1948, 113 mins, US
D: Billy Wilder A: Jean Arthur, Marlene Dietrich, John Lund, Millard Mitchell (Paramount)
A witty satire developed around a congressional investigation of GI morals in Germany. Much of the action is backgrounded against actual Berlin footage. The humor to which such a theme lends itself has been given a stinging bite, even though presented broadly. Jean Arthur is in a topflight characterization as a spinsterish congresswoman. The boy is John Lund, and Marlene Dietrich personifies the eternal siren as an opportunist German femme who furnishes Lund with off-duty diversion.
1948: Nominations: Best Screenplay, B&W Cinematography

FOREIGN BODY
1986, 108 mins, US/UK ⊗
D: Ronald Neame A: Victor Banerjee, Warren Mitchell, Geraldine McEwan, Denis Quilley, Amanda Donohoe, Trevor Howard (Neame/Brewer)
This variation on the ''great impostor'' plot device is still an unalloyed pleasure. Built solidly upon a fluid, comic virtuoso performance by Victor Banerjee, the pic-

aresque fable of an impoverished refugee from Calcutta faking it as a doctor to London's upper crust makes some jaunty points about racism, gullibility, and pluck.

FOREIGN CORRESPONDENT
1940, 119 mins, US Ⓥ ⊙
D: Alfred Hitchcock A: Joel McCrea, Laraine Day, Herbert Marshall, George Sanders, Albert Basserman, Edmund Gwenn (Wanger/United Artists)

Story is essentially the old cops-and-robbers. But it has a war flavor, the events taking place immediately before and at the start of World War II. Joel McCrea neatly blends the self-confidence and naïveté of the reporter-hero who knows nothing of foreign affairs, immediately runs into the tallest story a reporter can imagine—a big-league peace organization, which is operating as nothing but a spy ring. Vet Herbert Marshall as the heavy, George Sanders as McCrea's fellow reporter, 72-year-old refugee Albert Basserman as a Dutch diplomat, Edmund Gwenn as a not-to-be-trusted bodyguard, Eduardo Ciannelli as the usual hissable villain are all tops.
1940: Nominations: Best Picture, Supp. Actor (Albert Basserman), Original Screenplay, B&W Cinematography, B&W Art Direction, Special Effects

FOREVER AMBER
1947, 140 mins, US
D: Otto Preminger A: Linda Darnell, Cornel Wilde, Richard Greene, George Sanders, Jessica Tandy, Anne Revere (20th Century-Fox)

Lusty yarn is treated for what it is. Darnell runs the gamut from romantic opportunist to degraded prisoner and up again to being the king's favorite and finally a discarded mistress. In between there's a wealth of derring-do, 17th-century knavery and debauchery, the love of a good woman (Jane Ball), and the rest of a depraved court's atmosphere. It's solid escapology. Darnell manages her chameleon Amber character very well. Her blond beauty shows off well in Technicolor, and she is equally convincing when she is thrown in a pauper's jail.
1947: Nomination: Best Scoring of a Dramatic Picture

FOREVER AND A DAY
1943, 104 mins, US Ⓥ
D: Rene Clair, Edmund Goulding, Cedric Hardwicke, Frank Lloyd, Victor Saville, Robert Stevenson, Herbert Wilcox A:

Merle Oberon, Gladys Cooper, C. Aubrey Smith, Claude Rains, Anna Neagle, Ray Milland (RKO)

A sentimental romantic-adventure yarn, encompassing in cavalcade manner Britain's epochal struggles to retain the integrity of an empire and the freedom of its people. Interwoven is the quaint history of a picturesque London mansion—its illustrious builder and his descendants—built during the Napoleonic period, that withstands the ravages of time and world-shattering conflict until the days of the Nazi blitz. Some 45 name players undertook the assignment on a gratis basis. Some 21 writers and 7 accredited directors also contributed their services.

FOREVER IN LOVE
See: Pride of the Marines

FOREVER MINE
1999, 115 mins, UK/US Ⓥ ⊙ ▭
D: Paul Schrader A: Joseph Fiennes, Ray Liotta, Gretchen Mol, Vincent Laresca (Moonstar/J&M)

Paul Schrader hits a low-water mark with *Forever Mine*, a strenuously straight-faced film noir wanna-be that edges perilously close to self-parody. Yarn sports two story strands spanning 14 years. In a jet heading for New York City sits well-heeled Latino Manuel Esquema (Joseph Fiennes), his face hideously scarred and outfitted with a prosthetic hand. Back in 1974, Fiennes is Alan Riply, towel boy at an ornate Florida resort who seduces Ella (Gretchen Mol), newly married to tough guy Mark Brice (Ray Liotta), who blasts the young man in the face and leaves him for dead. Fiennes is aggressively sincere, bereft of anything resembling humor or irony. Liotta has trod his thug's ground before in more convincing fashion.

FOREVER YOUNG
1992, 102 mins, US Ⓥ ⊙
D: Steve Miner A: Mel Gibson, Jamie Lee Curtis, Elijah Wood, Isabel Glasser, George Wendt (Warner/Icon)

A big, rousing, old-fashioned romance. The action begins in 1939, as test pilot Daniel (Mel Gibson) can't bring himself to propose to Helen (Isabel Glasser), right up until the moment she walks in front of a speeding truck. Helen ends up in a coma, and the distraught Daniel volunteers for an experiment to freeze him for a year in an early test of cryogenics. Cut to 1992, when Daniel is thawed out by two mischievous 10-year-olds and moves in with one of them (Elijah Wood) and his single mom (Jamie Lee Curtis). With the army in pursuit of their long-forgotten experiment gone awry, the film takes some clever and extremely satisfying turns.

FORGET PARIS
1995, 101 mins, US Ⓥ ⊙
D: Billy Crystal A: Billy Crystal, Debra Winger, Joe Mantegna, Cynthia Stevenson, Richard Masur, Julie Kavner (Castle Rock/Face/Columbia)

Packed with a potentially unwieldy mix of shtick, bathos, sitcom-friendly slapstick, and echoes of Woody Allen's angst-ridden yuppie romances, *Forget Paris* teeters on the edge of disaster, just like the dauntless courtship that serves as the core of this comedic look at midlife love and marriage. But, amazingly, actor/cowriter/director/producer Billy Crystal manages to keep the predictable plotline and discordant elements from stymieing the pic's pull on the tear ducts and prod to the funny bone.

FORGIVEN SINNER, THE
See: Leon Morin, Pretre

FOR HEAVEN'S SAKE
1926, 58 mins, US ⊗
D: Sam Taylor A: Harold Lloyd, Jobyna Ralston, Noah Young, James Mason (Lloyd/Paramount)

Lloyd portrays a young society boy who has more money than he knows what to do with. That's the uptown angle of the picture. The downtown end has Jobyna Ralston as the daughter of a mission worker in the slums. Lloyd and the daughter meet. He falls and pulls a flock of laughs in a chase designed to round up business for the mission. The gags are so numerous that they have to be seen to be appreciated.

FOR LOVE OF IVY
1968, 101 mins, US Ⓥ
D: Daniel Mann A: Sidney Poitier, Abby Lincoln, Beau Bridges, Nan Martin, Lauri Peters, Carroll O'Connor (Palomar)

An innocuous romantic comedy. What little force the pic has stems from Sidney Poitier's clear enjoyment of a role cut from Cary Grant cloth. Simple story line is not rich in character motivation. Portier plays a lovable rogue who runs a (literally) floating crap game in the van of a truck, a gambling ploy that will probably strike even the most inveterate New York gamblers as doubtfully authentic.

1968: Nomination: Best Song ("For the Love of Ivy")

FOR LOVE OF THE GAME
1999, 137 mins, US Ⓥ ⊙ ▱
D: Sam Raimi A: Kevin Costner, Kelly Preston, John C. Reilly, Jena Malone, Brian Cox, J. K. Simmons (Beacon/Tig/Mirage/Universal)

For Love of the Game represents a modest personal comeback for star Kevin Costner, a highly uneven study of an aging vet in his swansong game in the big leagues. Pic ignores the game's grit and eccentricities in favor of a mood of valedictory romance, both for the game and for its lead characters. Billy Chapel (Costner) has his own designated catcher in Gus Sinski (John C. Reilly). Sinski's against manager Frank Perry's (J. K. Simmons) decision to pitch Chapel against the contending New York Yankees in Yankee Stadium, but Chapel's life soon gives him motivation. In a set of contrived plot moves, Chapel is stood up by his g.f. (Kelly Preston) and informed by owner Gary Wheeler (Brian Cox) that he's selling the club. Dialogue is as pat as this sounds.

FOR LOVE OR MONEY
1963, 108 mins, US
D: Michael Gordon A: Kirk Douglas, Mitzi Gaynor, Gig Young, Thelma Ritter, Julie Newmar, Leslie Parrish (Universal)

The glib, sharp scenario is seasoned with spicy spoofery of three worthy targets: motivational research, physical fitness, and modern art—and the people who practice these fads and/or professions. The wild plot has to do with a wealthy and eccentric widow's scheme to marry her three daughters off. Kirk Douglas uncorks a flair for zany comedics as the attorney-matchmaker who falls for the eldest daughter, vivaciously played by Mitzi Gaynor.

FOR LOVE OR MONEY
(UK: THE CONCIERGE)
1993, 94 mins, US Ⓥ ⊙
D: Barry Sonnenfeld A: Michael J. Fox, Gabrielle Anwar, Anthony Higgins, Michael Tucker, Bob Balaban (Imagine/Universal)

Michael J. Fox has charm to burn in *For Love or Money*. A contemporary spin on bygone romantic comedies, the tale falls short on story, however. Doug Ireland (Fox) takes on the role of head concierge at an upscale Manhattan hotel with the zeal of a Sammy Glick. What makes Doug tick is the dream of putting together the financial package for a luxury hotel. Charismatic financier Christian Hanover (Anthony Higgins) just happens to be deep into an extramarital affair with Andy (Gabrielle Anwar), the very woman for whom Doug would actually take time out in his busy schedule. Just how much crow can Doug eat for $5 million?

FOR ME AND MY GAL
1942, 104 mins, US Ⓥ ⊙
D: Busby Berkeley **A:** Judy Garland, George Murphy, Gene Kelly, Marta Eggerth, Richard Quine, Keenan Wynn (M-G-M)

Story of vaudeville troupers before and during the First World War is obvious, naive, and sentimental. It's also genuine and affectionate and lively. Picture's title is taken from the tune that brings Judy Garland and Gene Kelly together, first as vaudeville team and ultimately as a romance. It gets a sock presentation in a song-and-dance routine by them. Garland is a knockout as the warmhearted young song-and-dance girl, selling a number of the songs persuasively and getting by neatly in the hoofing routines. Kelly gives a vividly drawn portrayal of the song-and-dance man and imperfect hero.

FORMULA, THE
1980, 117 mins, US Ⓥ
D: John G. Avildsen **A:** George C. Scott, Marthe Keller, Marlon Brando, John Gielgud, Beatrice Straight (M-G-M)

A clump of sludge, impossible to understand for at least an hour before it grinds to a halt. Initial sequences solidly establish the closing hours of World War II when a German general (Richard Lynch) is entrusted with top-secret documents. But Lynch is captured by a US major (Robin Clarke), who recognizes what the secrets will be worth in the postwar world of commerce. Cut forward 35 years and Clarke is murdered in his bed. George C. Scott is called in to investigate and establishes Clarke had some mysterious dealings with oil super tycoon Marlon Brando, appearing grotesquely fat and ridiculous.
1980: Nomination: Best Cinematography

FOR PETE'S SAKE
1974, 90 mins, US Ⓥ
D: Peter Yates **A:** Barbra Streisand, Michael Sarrazin, Estelle Parsons, William Redfield, Molly Picon (Rastar/Columbia)

A flaccid, relentlessly "zany" comedy tale of a brash housewife (Barbra Streisand) married to a poor taxi driver (Michael Sarrazin). Sarrazin is given inside info about a pending meat deal. To get $3,000 necessary to invest in pork-belly futures, Streisand secretly goes to a loan shark. When she can't pay up, her "contract" is sold. Each contract sale increases the debt while allowing maximum opportunity for broad comedy shtick.

FORREST GUMP
1994, 142 mins, US Ⓥ ⊙ ⌑
D: Robert Zemeckis **A:** Tom Hanks, Robin Wright, Gary Sinise, Mykelti Williamson, Sally Field (Paramount)

A picaresque story of a simpleton's charmed odyssey through 30 years of tumultuous American history, *Forrest Gump* is whimsy with a strong cultural spine. Elegantly made and winningly acted by Tom Hanks, Robert Zemeckis' technically dazzling film will make postyuppies feel they're seeing their lives passing by on-screen. Gump narrates his story to a succession of listeners at a Savannah, GA, bus stop. Affecting a southern drawl and affable sweetness, Hanks manages to keep one intrigued and amused throughout.
1994: Best Picture, Director, Actor (Tom Hanks), Adapted Screenplay, Art Direction, Film Editing, Visual Effects
Nominations: Best Supp. Actor (Gary Sinise), Cinematography, Sound, Sound Effects Editing, Makeup, Original Score

FORSAKING ALL OTHERS
1934, 84 mins, US Ⓥ
D: W. S. Van Dyke **A:** Joan Crawford, Clark Gable, Robert Montgomery, Charles Butterworth, Billie Burke, Frances Drake (M-G-M)

The picture alternates between scintillating, gay, and sophisticated dialogue, and such hoke as a bicycle ride with Joan Crawford on Robert Montgomery's handlebars, and both (dressed in white) catapulting over a fence into a pigsty. Picture gets into gear with a sly siren (Frances Drake) copping Montgomery on the eve of his impending marriage. Crawford is literally left waiting in the church. Thereafter her wounded pride, the remorse of Montgomery, the nastiness of the scheming wife (Drake), and "big brother" Clark Gable form the guideposts of the action.

FORT APACHE
1948, 127 mins, US Ⓥ ⊙
D: John Ford **A:** John Wayne, Henry

440

Fonda, Shirley Temple, John Agar, Pedro Armendariz, Victor McLaglen (Argosy/RKO)

Mass action, humorous byplay in the western cavalry outpost, deadly suspense, and romance are masterfully combined in this production. Integrated with the tremendous action is a superb musical score by Richard Hageman. Henry Fonda is the colonel, embittered because he has been assigned to the remote fort after a brilliant war record. John Wayne makes a virile cavalry captain, wise in the way of the Indian. Shirley Temple, the colonel's daughter, perks her sequences in romance with John Agar, West Point graduate.

FORT APACHE—THE BRONX
1981, 123 mins, US ⓥ ◉
D: Daniel Petrie A: Paul Newman, Ed Asner, Ken Wahl, Danny Aiello, Rachel Ticotin, Pam Grier (Time-Life)

Driving relentlessly to make points that are almost pointless, *Fort Apache—The Bronx* is a very patchy picture, strong on dialogue and acting and exceedingly weak on story. Title is taken from the nickname for a real police station uptown, literally surrounded and often under siege from thieves, murderers, hookers, junkies, dealers. One of the cops (Danny Aiello) is a murderer himself and even the heroes (Paul Newman and Ken Wahl) aren't all that admirable in their feeble attempts to control crime in the streets.

FOR THE BOYS
1991, 145 mins, US ⓥ ◉
D: Mark Rydell A: Bette Midler, James Caan, George Segal, Patrick O'Neal, Chris Rydell (20th Century-Fox/All Girl)

Fox's song-driven wartime showbiz meller is a big, creaky balloon of a movie that lumbers along like a dirigible in a Thanksgiving parade, festooned with patriotic sentiment. Ambitious effort spans the 50-year relationship of two USO entertainers (Bette Midler and James Caan), whose song, dance, and innuendo carries them through three wars. Allegedly a "love story" between two difficult people who are each married to others, pic suffers from the couple's lack of electricity.
1991: Nomination: Best Actress (Bette Midler)

FOR THE LOVE OF BENJI
1977, 85 mins, US ⓥ
D: Joe Camp A: Patsy Garrett, Cynthia Smith, Allen Fiuzat, Ed Nelson, Art Vasil, Peter Bowles (Mulberry Square)

Only a heart of steel can resist this pooch. Item finds Benji in Greece embroiled in a tale of international espionage. Director would have audiences believe that Benji is an unwitting participant in this piece of subterfuge. But this pooch is so smart that chances are he had the plot unraveled 15 minutes after a most unmenacing villain drugged him and placed the vital info about a scientist, with a plan to turn 1 barrel of oil into 10, on his paw.

FORTRESS
1993, 89 mins, Australia/US ⓥ ◉
D: Stuart Gordon A: Christopher Lambert, Kurtwood Smith, Loryn Locklin, Lincoln Kilpatrick, Clifton Gonzales Gonzales (Village Roadshow/Davis)

Fortress is a grim, sometimes bloody, futuristic prison picture that has been well produced and directed within the limitations of a predictable, uninspired screenplay. David Copping's production design of a privately run prison of the future built 30 stories underground is the star of the film.

FORT SAGANNE
1984, 180 mins, France ⓥ ▭
D: Alain Corneau A: Gerard Depardieu, Philippe Noiret, Catherine Deneuve, Sophie Marceau, Michel Duchaussoy (Albina/Films A2/SFPC)

One of France's most expensive films is something of a throwback to the 1920s and '30s colonial sagas that thrived on local screens. Alain Corneau's film of Louis Gardel's prizewinning 1980 novel about an empire builder in the Sahara in the early years of the century is often fine in its large-scale reconstruction of a time and place and a mentality, but falters in its attempts to inscribe well-detailed characters in its widescreen canvas. Gerard Depardieu brings all his talent and presence to the role, but the immediacy of the personage is only intermittently felt. Costar Philippe Noiret is full-bloodedly excellent as the ambitious colonel seeking general's stars with his advocacy of aggressive military action in the Sahara.

FORTUNE, THE
1975, 88 mins, US ▭
D: Mike Nichols A: Jack Nicholson, Warren Beatty, Stockard Channing, Florence Stanley, Scatman Crothers (Columbia)

An occasionally enjoyable comedy trifle, starring Jack Nicholson and Warren Beatty as bumbling kidnappers of heiress Stockard Channing, who is excellent in her first major screen role. Very classy 1920s production values often merit more attention than the plot.

FORTUNE COOKIE, THE
(UK: MEET WHIPLASH WILLIE)
1966, 125 mins, US Ⓥ ⊙
D: Billy Wilder **A:** Jack Lemmon, Walter Matthau, Ron Rich, Cliff Osmond, Judi West, Lurene Tuttle (United Artists/Mirisch)

Billy Wilder presents another bittersweet comedy commentary on contemporary US mores. Generally amusing (often wildly so) but overlong, the pic is pegged on an insurance fraud in which Jack Lemmon and Walter Matthau are the conspirators. Lemmon, confined perforce to sickroom immobility (bandages, wheelchair, etc.) is saddled most of the time with the colorless image of a man vacillating with his conscience over the fraud.
1966: Best Supp. Actor (Walter Matthau)
Nominations: Best Original Story & Screenplay, B&W Cinematography, B&W Art Direction

48 HOURS
See: Went the Day Well?

48 HRS.
1982, 96 mins, US Ⓥ ⊙
D: Walter Hill **A:** Nick Nolte, Eddie Murphy, Annette O'Toole, Frank McRae, David Patrick Kelly (Paramount)

48 Hrs. is a very efficient action entertainment which serves as a showy motion-picture debut for Eddie Murphy. Pairing of Nick Nolte as a rough-and-tumble San Francisco cop and Murphy as a small-time criminal sprung for two days to help track down former associates makes for a throwback to the buddy-buddy pics of the 1970s. It's all pretty predictable stuff, but done with plenty of savvy and professionalism.

FORTY-FIRST, THE
See: Sorok Pyervi

FORTY GUNS
1957, 76 mins, US ⊡
D: Samuel Fuller **A:** Barbara Stanwyck, Barry Sullivan, Dean Jagger, John Ericson, Gene Barry, Eve Brent (20th Century-Fox)

Samuel Fuller in triple capacity of producer-scripter-director has devised a solid piece of entertainment which has femme star Barbara Stanwyck playing a ruthless Arizona ranch owner, the boss of Cochise County. Into her realm rides Barry Sullivan and his two brothers, former an ex-gunslinger now working for the US attorney general, his fame with a gun preceding him.

49TH PARALLEL
(US: THE INVADERS)
1941, 123 mins, UK Ⓥ ⊙
D: Michael Powell **A:** Leslie Howard, Raymond Massey, Laurence Olivier, Anton Walbrook, Glynis Johns, Eric Portman (Ortus)

An important and effective propaganda film. The locales depict Canadian life from an Eskimo village to a Hutterite settlement in the Canadian wheat fields. Story is the strongest possible indictment against Nazism. Plot concerns six Nazi U-boat men whose craft is blown up in the Hudson Bay straits. They reach land and commit every sort of crime up to murder in their efforts to reach the neutral territory of the US. The script of Emeric Pressburger is direct and forceful.
1942: Best Original Story
Nominations: Best Picture, Screenplay

FORTY POUNDS OF TROUBLE
1962, 106 mins, US ⊙
D: Norman Jewison **A:** Tony Curtis, Phil Silvers, Suzanne Pleshette, Claire Wilcox, Stubby Kaye (Curtis/Universal)

The troublesome 40-pounder of the title is moppet Claire Wilcox, who makes her screen debut as an orphaned youngster who gradually melts the heart of the businesslike manager of a Lake Tahoe, NV gambling resort (Tony Curtis). In the course of her conquest, she also aids the cause of husband-hunting nitery canary Suzanne Pleshette, whose romance with Curtis is complicated by the latter's relationship with his ex-wife.

42ND STREET
1933, 89 mins, US Ⓥ ⊙
D: Lloyd Bacon, Busby Berkeley **A:** Warner Baxter, Bebe Daniels, George Brent, Ruby Keeler, Guy Kibbee, Ginger Rogers (Warner)

Everything about the production rings true. It's as authentic to the initiate as the novice. There are good performances by Warner Baxter, as the neurotic showman, and Bebe Daniels as the outmoded musical-comedy ingenue. Ruby Keeler, as the unknown who comes through and registers a hit, is utterly convincing. Not the least of the total belongs to the direction by Lloyd Bacon, with Busby Berkeley an excellent aide on the terp mountings. The overhead style of camera angles, which

Berkeley introduced in the Eddie Cantor pictures and elsewhere, are further advanced.
1932/33: Nominations: Best Picture, Sound

FORTY THOUSAND HORSEMEN
1941, 100 mins, Australia ⊗
D: Charles Chauvel **A:** Grant Taylor, Betty Bryant, "Chips" Rafferty, Pat Twohill, Harvey Adams (Chauvel)

Pic portrays in sheer entertaining fashion the story of the Australian Light Horse, the famous regiment, in Palestine during World War I. Director Chauvel has with easy grace produced a telling action pic, yet carrying sufficient romance to fully satisfy the femme stubholders. The acting is top-notch, with the honors going to Betty Bryant and "Chips" Rafferty.

FOR WHOM THE BELL TOLLS
1943, 166 mins, US
D: Sam Wood **A:** Gary Cooper, Ingrid Bergman, Akim Tamiroff, Katina Paxinou, Arturo de Cordova, Vladimir Sokoloff (Paramount)

Almost three hours of running time can overdo a good thing. The saga of Roberto and Maria (Gary Cooper and Ingrid Bergman) asks for too much concentrated attention on what is basically one dramatic episode, that of blasting a crucial bridge, in order to foil the Nationalists. On a beautiful Technicolor canvas is projected an equally beautiful romance, which, perhaps, lays a little too much emphasis on the amorous phase. It's one thing to punch up boy-meets-girl sequencing, but the nature of Ernest Hemingway's bestseller, of course, was predicated on the politics of the Spanish Civil War.
1943: Best Supp. Actress (Katina Paxinou)
Nominations: Best Picture, Actor (Gary Cooper), Actress (Ingrid Bergman), Supp. Actor (Akim Tamiroff), Color Cinematography, Color Art Direction, Editing, Scoring of a Dramatic Picture

FOR YOUR EYES ONLY
1981, 127 mins, UK ⊗ ⊙ ▭
D: John Glen **A:** Roger Moore, Carole Bouquet, Topol, Jill Bennett, Lois Maxwell (United Artists/Eon)

One of the most thoroughly enjoyable of the 12 Bond pix [to date] despite absence of many of the usual ingredients in the successful 007 formula. John Glen, moving into the director's chair after long service as second-unit director and editor,

displays a fine eye. Story also benefits from presence of a truly sympathetic heroine, fetchingly portrayed by Carole Bouquet, who exhibits a humanity and emotionalism not frequently found in this sort of pop adventure.
1981: Nomination: Best Song ("For Your Eyes Only")

FOUL PLAY
1978, 116 mins, US ⊗ ⊙
D: Colin Higgins **A:** Goldie Hawn, Chevy Chase, Burgess Meredith, Rachel Roberts, Dudley Moore (Paramount)

Foul Play revives a relatively dormant film genre—the crime-suspense-romantic comedy in which low-key leading players get involved with each other while also caught up in monumental intrigue. If you think you've been through the plot before, you have: Goldie Hawn picks up undercover agent Bruce Solomon, who passes her film evidence of how heavies are going to assassinate visiting Pope Pius XIII. Chevy Chase, a detective, eventually believes Hawn's stories about attempts on her life. Car chases and theater shoot-out climax the film's 116 minutes.
1978: Nomination: Best Song ("Ready to Take a Chance Again")

FOUNTAINHEAD, THE
1949, 112 mins, US ⊗
D: King Vidor **A:** Gary Cooper, Patricia Neal, Raymond Massey, Kent Smith, Henry Hull, Robert Douglas (Warner)

The garrulous script calls for a great deal of posturing by the cast and King Vidor's direction permits much overacting where underplaying might have helped develop a better emotional feeling and a truer sense of reality. Miscast Gary Cooper has an uneasy time as an architect who is such an individualist that he dynamites a charity project when the builders alter his plans. As Cooper's costar, Patricia Neal makes a moody heroine, afraid of love or any other honest feeling. Raymond Massey is allowed to be too flamboyant as the publisher.

FOUR DAUGHTERS
1938, 90 mins, US
D: Michael Curtiz **A:** Claude Rains, May Robson, Priscilla Lane, Lola Lane, Rosemary Lane, John Garfield (Warner)

Beguiling film deals with the heart-throbs of the four talented daughters of a professor of music. Michael Curtiz's direction is both affectionate and knowing. Claude Rains is irresistibly persuasive and attractive as the father. Priscilla Lane has the best part as the youngest sister. May Robson plays the aunt in proper mother-hen fashion. As the ill-starred newcomer, Garfield plays with such tight-lipped force that for a time he threatens to throw the picture out of focus by drawing too much interest.

1938: Nominations: Best Picture, Director, Supp. Actor (John Garfield), Screenplay, Sound

FOUR FEATHERS
1929, 80 mins, US ⊗
D: Merian C. Cooper, Ernest B. Schoedsack **A:** Richard Arlen, Fay Wray, Clive Brook, William Powell, Theodore von Eltz, Noah Beery (Paramount)

The white feather is the symbol of cowardice in the British army. The principal character and subsequent hero of A. W. Mason's novel receives four white feathers. Tale is set late in the last century. *Four Feathers* is highly reminiscent of *Beau Geste*. Pictorially they are much the same.

FOUR FEATHERS, THE
1939, 130 mins, UK ⍰ ⊙
D: Zoltan Korda **A:** John Clements, Ralph Richardson, C. Aubrey Smith, June Duprez (London)

A young British officer resigns from his regiment the night before it embarks for an Egyptian campaign. Three of his pals and his fiancée hand him white feathers, indicative of cowardice. The next day he disappears. Alone and unaided in Egypt, he goes through harrowing ordeals to gain honor in their eyes.

FOUR FOR TEXAS
1963, 124 mins, US ⍰ ⊙
D: Robert Aldrich **A:** Frank Sinatra, Dean Martin, Anita Ekberg, Ursula Andress, Charles Bronson, Victor Buono (Aldrich/Warner)

A western too preoccupied with sex and romance to enthrall sagebrush-happy moppets and too unwilling to take itself seriously to sustain the attention of an adult. The screenplay is a choppy and haphazard dramatization of a feud between two soldiers of fortune (Frank Sinatra and Dean Martin) who ultimately join forces in vanquishing a treacherous banker (Victor Buono) and an irresponsible, incredibly hapless gunslinger (Charles Bronson).

FOUR FRIGHTENED PEOPLE
1934, 95 mins, US
D: Cecil B. DeMille **A:** Claudette Colbert,

Herbert Marshall, Mary Boland, William Gargan, Leo Carrillo, Tetsu Komai (Paramount)

The adventures of the quartet who are lost in the Malayan jungle are episodic and disjointed, running the gamut from stark tragedy to unbelievable farce. The De-Milleian bathtub penchant evidences itself even in the jungle, when Colbert, sans cheaters and very Eve (when a playful chimpanzee steals her clothes), emerges with plenty of s.a.

FOUR HORSEMEN OF THE APOCALYPSE, THE
1921, 130 mins, US d
D: Rex Ingram **A:** Rudolph Valentino, Alice Terry, Alan Hale, Nigel de Brulier, Jean Hersholt, Wallace Beery (Metro)

Horror stalked grinningly bold through the book of Vicente Blasco Ibanez, the greatest of the World War I romances. Ingram has mercifully treated it with distance and delicacy. This is a characteristic of the director's handling of the entire subject. It is a production of many nuances, shadings so artistic and skillful as to intrigue the mind of the spectator.

FOUR HORSEMEN OF THE APOCALYPSE, THE
1962, 153 mins, US ⍰ ▭
D: Vincente Minnelli **A:** Glenn Ford, Ingrid Thulin, Charles Boyer, Lee J. Cobb, Paul Henreid, Yvette Mimieux (M-G-M)

Although *The Four Horsemen of the Apocalypse* is a screen spectacle of dynamic artistic proportions, it gradually becomes a victim of dramatic anemia. The romantic nucleus of this tragic chronicle of a family divided and devoured by war fails to create a realistic and compassionate relationship between the lovers. Ford's performance is without warmth, without passion, without magnetism. Warmth is also missing in the performance of Ingrid Thulin. A major assist is that of Andre Previn, who has composed a tearing, soaring, emotionally affecting score.

400 BLOWS, THE
See: Les Quatre Cents Coups

FOUR IN THE MORNING
1966, 94 mins, UK
D: Anthony Simmons **A:** Ann Lynn, Brian Phelan, Judi Dench, Norman Rodway, Joe Melia (West One)

Two couples in crisis. A seemingly rootless young man picks up a singer he knows. At four in the morning they romp around the Thames's shores, steal a boat, leave it, almost touch each other emotionally, but part still uncommitted. The other couple is shown as a woman waiting for her husband, out on the town with a bachelor crony. The baby cries and exasperates her. The growing incompatibility of the couple is deftly outlined in bold, dramatic strokes.

FOUR JUST MEN, THE
(US: THE SECRET FOUR)
1939, 85 mins, UK ⊚

D: Walter Forde A: Hugh Sinclair, Griffith Jones, Francis L. Sullivan, Frank Lawton, Anna Lee, Alan Napier (Associated British)

A skilled and dramatic filmization of one of Edgar Wallace's best-known novels. Murder, sabotage, and international troublemaking form the basis of this exploit of the Four Just Men who, incognito, spend their lives breaking up dope rings and foiling plots of foreign agitators.

FOUR MUSKETEERS
THE REVENGE OF MILADY, THE
1975, 108 mins, Panama/Spain ⊚

D: Richard Lester A: Oliver Reed, Raquel Welch, Richard Chamberlain, Michael York, Frank Finlay, Christopher Lee (20th Century-Fox)

Oliver Reed, Richard Chamberlain, Frank Finlay, and Michael York joust with evil plotter Charlton Heston and evil seductress Faye Dunaway, defend fair lady queen Geraldine Chaplin, bypass imbecile King Jean Pierre Cassel, and triumph over archfiend Christopher Lee. Perhaps the film is a triumph of controlled and deliberate mediocrity, but it still closer resembles a clumsy carbon of a bad satire on the original (*The Three Musketeers*).

1975: Nomination: Best Costume Design

FOUR POSTER, THE
1953, 103 mins, US

D: Irving Reis A: Rex Harrison, Lilli Palmer (Kramer/Columbia)

Though the stars' performances are excellent, the major fault is the inability of the two characters to cope with the lack of incident. With the four-poster bed in the background as the common denominator of their marital relationship, pic traces the lives of a couple from the day the groom carries his bride across the threshold.

1953: Nomination: Best B&W Cinematography

FOUR ROOMS
1995, 102 mins, US ⊚ ⊙

D: Allison Anders, Alexandre Rockwell, Robert Rodriguez, Quentin Tarantino A: Tim Roth, Valeria Golino, Jennifer Beals, Antonio Banderas, Quentin Tarantino, Bruce Willis (A Band Apart/Miramax)

Four of America's hottest indie directors get a one-of-a-kind opportunity to display their idiosyncratic talents—and grand follies—in *Four Rooms*, a disappointing, tedious anthology of four short films, set in separate rooms of a once-grand L.A. hotel. The four stories are set in the same hotel on New Year's Eve (reportedly Rockwell's idea), with a new bellboy, Ted (Tim Roth), the only character who appears in all the segs, on the job. Roth does a cheap, inconsistent imitation of Jerry Lewis at his most neurotic.

FOUR'S A CROWD
1938, 91 mins, US

D: Michael Curtiz A: Errol Flynn, Olivia de Havilland, Rosalind Russell, Patric Knowles, Walter Connolly (Warner)

A true follower of the dizzy school of comedy. Providing much zest and spice is Walter Connolly's eccentric millionaire, whose major interest in life is his miniature electric railway system and a kennel of mastiffs that make tough going for unwanted visitors. Complications develop from Flynn's efforts to sell the hard-boiled Connolly into whitewashing his public-be-damned past by endowing a few clinical foundations. The wily public-relations counsel uses his temporary connection as managing ed of Patric Knowles's newspaper to stir up public sentiment against his proposed client.

FOUR SEASONS, THE
1981, 107 mins, US ⊚ ⊙

D: Alan Alda A: Alan Alda, Carol Burnett, Len Cariou, Sandy Dennis, Rita Moreno, Jack Weston (Universal)

A lightweight, overly contrived examination of the relationship among three couples who vacation together four times over course of story, Alan Alda's feature directorial debut is middle-brow, middle-aged material. Alda's script is particularly stingy in giving Carol Burnett and Rita Moreno anything to work with. Vivaldi background score helps lend a tony atmosphere to the proceedings.

FOUR SONS
1928, 100 mins, US d

D: John Ford A: Margaret Mann, James Hall, Earle Fox, June Collyer, George Meeker (Fox)

A profoundly moving picture of family

life in Germany during the First World War. The story is the commonplace history of a widow and her four sons. Joseph goes to America before the war, marries and has his own little delicatessen shop, and a baby is born. Then the war comes. The other three brothers go to the front and one by one are killed. There is no "war stuff," the war tragedy is enacted in the homely cottage of the lone mother. Margaret Mann's playing of the big role is a miracle of unaffected naturalness. Her Frau Bernie lives from the moment the film starts to its finish.

FOURTEEN HOURS
1951, 92 mins, US
D: Henry Hathaway A: Richard Basehart, Paul Douglas, Barbara Bel Geddes, Agnes Moorehead, Robert Keith, Grace Kelly (20th Century-Fox)

Paul Douglas is the traffic policeman who becomes a hero when his routine duties are interrupted one morning by the sight of Richard Basehart perched on a 14-story-high window ledge. Tension reaches the screaming point often as Douglas and the others try to talk Basehart back into the building while the citizens of New York make a Roman holiday of the event.
1951: Nomination: Best B&W Art Direction

1492
CONQUEST OF PARADISE
1992, 150 mins, UK/France/Spain ⓥ ⊙ ▱
D: Ridley Scott A: Gerard Depardieu, Armand Assante, Sigourney Weaver, Michael Wincott, Angela Molina, Fernando Rey (Due West/Legende/Cyrk)

All Ridley Scott's vaunted visuals can't transform 1492 from a lumbering, one-dimensional historical fresco into the complex, ambiguous character study that it strives to be. Screenwriter Roselyne Bosch offers up a humanistic pacifist driven by an enigmatic mix of motives to settle a new land. Depardieu's energy, passion, and conviction are ideal for the role, but perhaps it remains beyond him at this point to act in English in depth.

FOURTH PROTOCOL, THE
1987, 119 mins, UK ⓥ ⊙ ▱
D: John Mackenzie A: Michael Caine, Pierce Brosnan, Joanna Cassidy, Ned Beatty, Ray McAnally, Ian Richardson (Rank)

A decidedly contempo thriller, a tale of vying master spies and a chase to head off a nuclear disaster. Its edge is a fine aura of realism. Novelist Frederick Forsyth, who also was an executive producer, adapted the pic from his book. Michael Caine as a maverick counterespionage expert gives a thorough performance in a part that doesn't really stretch his abilities.

FOURTH WAR, THE
1990, 91 mins, US ⓥ ⊙
D: John Frankenheimer A: Roy Scheider, Jurgen Prochnow, Tim Reid, Lara Harris, Harry Dean Stanton (Kodiak)

A well-made cold-war thriller set on the border of Czechoslovakia and East Germany. Roy Scheider is well cast as a hard-line colonel who's caused nothing but trouble in his career and is now stationed at a post near the border by his general, Harry Dean Stanton. Scheider witnesses the murder of a fleeing defector through no-man's-land. He rightly blames the Soviet colonel (Jurgen Prochnow) for this dastardly deed and from this minor act of outrage ensues a man-to-man feud of Laurel and Hardy–like proportions.

FOUR WEDDINGS AND A FUNERAL
1994, 116 mins, UK ⓥ ⊙
D: Mike Newell A: Hugh Grant, Andie MacDowell, Kristin Scott Thomas, Simon Callow, James Fleet, Corin Redgrave (PFE/Channel 4/Working Title)

Truly beguiling romantic comedy is one of the hardest things for a modern film to pull off, but screenwriter Richard Curtis has hit just the right balance. Charles (Hugh Grant) is a charming bumbler who is very willingly seduced by another guest, the gorgeous and exceedingly accommodating American, Carrie (Andie MacDowell). Back in London, Charles blurts out his profound feelings for her even as she's heading to the altar with a wealthy older Scotsman (Corin Redgrave). A sudden death at the reception precipitates the funeral, at which the heretofore unknown diversity and depth of Charles's inner circle is revealed. The success of such lighthearted nonsense depends upon the appeal, adeptness, and timing of the cast, and it is here that the film really soars.
1994: Nominations: Best Picture, Original Screenplay

FOX, THE
1968, 110 mins, US/Canada
D: Mark Rydell A: Sandy Dennis, Keir Dullea, Anne Heywood, Glyn Morris

(Warner/Seven Arts/Motion Pictures International)

D. H. Lawrence's lesbian-themed novella is turned into a beautifully photographed, dramatically uneven Canadian-made film. Sandy Dennis and Anne Heywood are cast as lesbian lovers who have exiled themselves to a lonely farm. Arrival of Keir Dullea cues a disintegration of the femme relationship and eventual tragedy.

1968: Nomination: Best Original Music Score

FOXES

1980, 106 mins, US ⊘

D: Adrian Lyne **A:** Jodie Foster, Scott Baio, Sally Kellerman, Randy Quaid, Marilyn Kagan (United Artists/PolyGram)

Story of four teenage girls and their battles often becomes a depressing, one-sided, and melodramatic treatise on American youth. It soon becomes clear this is not the usual gaggle of girls portrayed as typical American teenagers. Cherie Currie is a stoned-out former hooker, Marilyn Kagan is an unhappy, overweight fat girl longing to shed her parents' protective shell, Kandice Stroh is a lying, confused flirt, and Jodie Foster is a levelheaded intellect.

FOXES OF HARROW, THE

1947, 115 mins, US

D: John M. Stahl **A:** Rex Harrison, Maureen O'Hara, Richard Haydn, Victor McLaglen (20th Century-Fox)

A powerful drama of an adventurer's rise to fame and fortune in New Orleans of the 19th century. Rex Harrison, the child born out of wedlock, rises to the heights in New Orleans business even though his first money is won gambling. He finally persuades Maureen O'Hara, daughter of one of New Orleans's aristocrats, to become his wife. Harrison is perfect as the suave gambler and O'Hara carries the highly dramatic scenes with surprising skill.

1947: Nomination: Best B&W Art Direction

FOX MOVIETONE FOLLIES OF 1929

1929, 80 mins, US

D: David Butler, Marcel Silver **A:** Sue Carol, David Rollins, Stepin Fetchit, Sharon Lynn, Warren Hymer (Fox)

Good entertainment all the way. The numbers, specialties, and song-and-dance stuff come through very well. One bit done in Technicolor offers a variant from

the black-and-white but achieves little itself. Sue Carol takes first honors but needs dancing lessons. Warren Hymer makes a stage manager pretty rough, tough, and nasty.

FOXY BROWN

1974, 91 mins, US ⊘

D: Jack Hill **A:** Pam Grier, Antonio Vargas, Peter Brown, Terry Carter, Kathryn Loder (American International)

Bosomy black starlet Pam Grier sets her vengeful eye on the leaders of the local vice ring (Kathryn Loder and Peter Brown). Even by the gutter-high standards of the genre, *Foxy Brown* is something of a mess. Jack Hill's screenplay has peculiar narrative gaps.

FRAMED

1947, 81 mins, US

D: Richard Wallace **A:** Glenn Ford, Janis Carter, Barry Sullivan, Edgar Buchanan, Karen Morley (Columbia)

Glenn Ford heads cast as out-of-work mining engineer who gets involved with beautiful blonde who's trying to steal $250,000. Script doesn't have too much finesse as written by Ben Maddow from Jack Patrick's story, but there's enough deftness to generate interest.

FRANCES

1982, 140 mins, US ⊘ ⊙

D: Graeme Clifford **A:** Jessica Lange, Kim Stanley, Sam Shepard, Bart Burns, Jeffrey DeMunn (EMI/Brooksfilms)

Rare to the memory is a film like *Frances* which runs 140 minutes and its star is on the screen 85 percent of the time in one intense scene after another. It's quite an accomplishment for Jessica Lange and it's too bad a better film didn't come of it. Though her troubled life made headlines around the world, Frances Farmer is still very much a mystery. The film presents her basically as a woman to be admired for standing behind her convictions regardless of the consequences. It's hard to shake the persistent feeling that she brought a lot of woe on herself.

1982: Nominations: Best Actress (Jessica Lange), Supp. Actress (Kim Stanley)

FRANKENHOOKER

1990, 90 mins, US ⊘ ⊙

D: Frank Henenlotter **A:** James Lorinz, Patty Mullen, Charlotte Helmkamp, Shirley Stoler, Louise Lasser (Shapiro Glickenhaus)

Frankenhooker is a grisly, grotesque horror comedy recommended only for the stout of heart and strong of stomach. Even by genre standards, *Frankenhooker* often is offensive in its repeated reliance on murdering, dismembering, and humiliating women for laughs. Lorinz has some inspired moments of self-absorbed craziness as Jeffrey.

FRANKENSTEIN
1931, 71 mins, US ⊗ ⊙
D: James Whale **A:** Colin Clive, Mae Clarke, John Boles, Boris Karloff, Edward Van Sloan, Dwight Frye (Universal)

Touches a new peak in horror plays and handled in production with supreme craftsmanship. Picture starts with a wallop. Midnight funeral services are in progress, with the figure of the scientist and his grotesque dwarf assistant hiding at the edge of the cemetery to steal the newly buried body. Shudder No. 2, hard on its heels occurs when Frankenstein cuts down his second dead subject from the gallows. The corpses are to be assembled into a semblance of a human body which Frankenstein seeks to galvanize into life. Laboratory sequence detailing the creation of the monster is a smashing bit of theatrical effect, taking place during a violent mountain storm. Colin Clive is a happy choice for the scientist. He plays it with force, but innocent of ranting. Boris Karloff makes a memorable figure of the bizarre monster with its indescribably terrifying face of demoniacal calm.

FRANKENSTEIN (AKA: MARY SHELLEY'S FRANKENSTEIN)
1994, 123 mins, US ⊗ ⊙
D: Kenneth Branagh **A:** Robert De Niro, Kenneth Branagh, Tom Hulce, Helena Bonham Carter, Aidan Quinn, Ian Holm (American Zoetrope/Tri-Star)

Kenneth Branagh has indeed created a monster, but not the kind he originally envisioned. A major disappointment creatively. As director/coproducer/star, he seems to overreach himself, playing every aspect at a level that's too feverish for its own good. De Niro's creature doesn't even approach the terror factor of his role in *Cape Fear,* while failing to inspire the empathy that even Boris Karloff—bolts and all—engendered. Branagh's own performance is appropriately crazed, while Carter as always proves radiant and engaging.
1994: Nomination: Best Makeup

FRANKENSTEIN CREATED WOMAN
1967, 92 mins, UK ⊗
D: Terence Fisher **A:** Peter Cushing, Susan Denberg, Thorley Walters, Robert Morris (Hammer/Seven Arts)

The good doctor, played, as usual, by Peter Cushing, dabbles as much in transmigration of souls as actual patchwork surgery, capturing the psyche of an executed young man and instilling it in the body of a drowned young woman (Denberg). The girl, originally a disfigured, shy maiden, is transformed as a beautiful femme whose touch proves très fatale when the male soul uses the female body to wreak vengeance on the trio of young wastrels responsible for his execution.

FRANKENSTEIN MEETS THE WOLF MAN
1943, 72 mins, US ⊗ ⊙
D: Roy William Neill **A:** Lon Chaney, Ilona Massey, Patric Knowles, Lionel Atwill, Bela Lugosi, Maria Ouspenskaya (Universal)

Eerie atmosphere generated right at the start, when Lon Chaney, previously killed off with the werewolf stain on him, is disinterred and returns to life. After one transformation, he winds up in a hospital to gain the sympathetic attention of medico Patric Knowles, then seeks out gypsy Maria Ouspenskaya for relief, and she takes him to the continent and the village where Frankenstein held sway. This allows Chaney to discover and revive the monster, role handled by Bela Lugosi, and from there on it's a creepy affair in grand style.

FRANKENSTEIN MUST BE DESTROYED
1969, 97 mins, UK ⊗
D: Terence Fisher **A:** Peter Cushing, Veronica Carlson, Freddie Jones, Simon Ward, Thorley Walters, Maxine Audley (Hammer)

Frankenstein's (Peter Cushing) diabolical plan is, in the cause of science, to preserve the medical knowledge of a brilliant but insane surgeon. This he'll do by murdering the medico, removing his brain, and inserting it in the body of a kidnapped man. A good enough example of its low-key type.

FRANKENSTEIN UNBOUND
1990, 85 mins, US ⊗ ⊙
D: Roger Corman **A:** John Hurt, Raul Julia, Bridget Fonda, Nick Nimble, Cathe-

rine Rabett, Catherine Corman (Mount)

A competent but uninspired riff on the venerable legend. John Hurt toplines as a mad scientist in New Los Angeles of 2031, suddenly transported to Switzerland in 1817. Out on the rampage is Frankenstein's monster, killing people until his creator fabricates a mate for him. While warring with Frankenstein and his monster, Hurt ultimately identifies with them, leading to an interesting, somber climax set in icy wastes as in Shelley's original novel. Though some of the dialogue is clutzy, acting is generally good, with top honors to Raul Julia as a thoughtful Frankenstein.

FRANKIE AND JOHNNY
1966, 87 mins, US ⊗
D: Frederick de Cordova A: Elvis Presley, Donna Douglas, Harry Morgan, Sue Ane Langdon, Nancy Kovack (Small/F&J)

Elvis all the way in a story built loosely around the classic folk song, coupled with a dozen or so tunes, pretty girls, and Technicolor. The screenplay has Elvis and Donna Douglas as entertainers on a Mississippi riverboat about 100 years ago. Elvis is Frankie, Donna is Johnny, and, as in the ageless song, they love each other. But Frankie gambles too much, losing all the time, until he finds a lucky redhead—Nellie Bly, natch—played by Nancy Kovack.

FRANKIE AND JOHNNY
1991, 118 mins, US ⊗ ⊙
D: Garry Marshall A: Al Pacino, Michelle Pfeiffer, Hector Elizondo, Nathan Lane, Kate Nelligan, Jane Morris (Paramount)

An all-star, high-gloss, feel-good romantic-feature sitcom. Amiably written and performed but fearsomely predictable, this invites audiences to indulge in watching beautiful movie stars play lonely little people struggling to find love. *Pretty Woman* director Garry Marshall sprinkles a little of his Cinderella dust on this story of an ex-con who takes a job as a short-order chef in Manhattan and instantly falls for a hardcase waitress.

FRANKIE STARLIGHT
1995, 100 mins, US ⊗
D: Michael Lindsay-Hogg A: Anne Parillaud, Matt Dillon, Gabriel Byrne, Corban Walker (Ferndale)

Offbeat tale has considerable charm on its side but lacks clear focus or intent to carry the material to a satisfying conclusion. Frank Bois (Corban Walker) is a thirty-something dwarf who walks into an

agent's office with a manuscript under his arm. His novel is the story of his youth in a small Irish village. Frank's mother, Bernadette (Anne Parillaud), arrived in Ireland illegally after the Second World War and was befriended by Jack Kelly (Gabriel Byrne), an immigration officer. Pregnant by an unkown GI, Bernadette gives birth to Frankie and mother and child are taken in by the Kelly family. In the present day, Frank struggles with his condition. He strives for normality but finds that he's denied many of the physical and emotional niceties of life.

FRANK'S GREATEST ADVENTURE (AKA: FEARLESS FRANK)
1967, 83 mins, US ▭
D: Philip Kaufman A: Jon Voight, Monique Van Vooren, Joan Darling, Severn Darden, Ben Carruthers (Jericho)

In the guise of a far-out tale of a superman and a man-made monster, gangsters and scientists, this is intended to be a disarming spoof of American myths as embodied in films. Indie pic, made in Chicago, also benefits from fine color, scope, and technical solidity. Plot has Frank (Jon Voight) awakening as a superman after apparently been slain by gangsters. Little-known players all etch neat performances.

FRANTIC
See: L'Ascenseur pour l'Echafaud

FRANTIC
1988, 120 mins, US ⊗ ⊙
D: Roman Polanski A: Harrison Ford, Emmanuelle Seigner, Betty Buckley, John Mahoney (Mount/Warner)

A thriller without much surprise, suspense, or excitement. Drama reveals director Roman Polanski's personality and enthusiasm only in brief humorous moments. Medic Harrison Ford arrives in Paris with wife Betty Buckley to deliver a paper at a conference. Buckley disappears, setting off an urgent woman hunt that takes the distraught husband to young Emmanuelle Seigner, a sleek, punky drugette and nightclubber who appears to be the only lead to the kidnappers.

FRATERNITY ROW
1977, 101 mins, US
D: Thomas J. Tobin A: Peter Fox, Gregory Harrison, Scott Newman, Nancy Morgan, Wendy Phillips, Robert Emhardt (Paramount)

A powerful film about emotional and physical violence at an eastern college frat house in 1954. Debuting director Thomas

J. Tobin handles the fresh young cast with sensitivity and avoids the thrill mongering that mars too many youth-market pix. Peter Fox is the sensitive but compromised frat pledge master who opposes Scott Newman's sadistic attitudes toward the pledges, and Gregory Harrison is the innocent one who suffers most in the hazing process.

FRAUDS
1993, 92 mins, Australia/UK Ⓥ ⊙
D: Stephan Elliott A: Phil Collins, Hugo Weaving, Josephine Byrnes, Peter Mochrie, Helen O'Connor (Live/J&M/Latent Image)

Cheerfully mixing suspense with comic-strip comedy, pic boasts a topflight performance from Phil Collins as a con-man insurance investigator with a childlike sense of humor. The home of a yuppie couple, Jonathan (Hugo Weaving) and Beth (Josephine Byrnes), is burgled; Beth shoots the masked intruder. Roland Copping (Collins) discovers that Jonathan was the burglar's accomplice and proceeds to play games with the couple. First-time director Stephan Elliott flings these disparate elements together, creating a strange and deliberately unreal world for his eccentric characters.

FREAKED
1993, 79 mins, US Ⓥ
D: Tom Stern, Alex Winter A: Alex Winter, Megan Ward, Michael Stoyanov, Randy Quaid, William Sadler, Brooke Shields (20th Century-Fox)

Freaked showcases Ted (or is it Bill?) of the *Excellent Adventure* as star, codirector, coproducer, cowriter, and conspirator. An anarchic mix of hip comedy, vague, socially correct eco politics, and overstated makeup effects, Alex Winter's pic takes a few shots at societal sacred cows but more often misses the target. The effort comes off much in the prankish manner of a student film.

FREAKS
1932, 61 mins, US Ⓥ ⊙
D: Tod Browning A: Wallace Ford, Leila Hyams, Olga Baclanova, Roscoe Ates, Harry Earles, Daisy Earles (M-G-M)

Freaks is sumptuously produced, admirably directed, and no cost was spared. But story is not sufficiently strong to get and hold the interest, partly because interest cannot easily be gained for a too fantastic romance. The plot outline is the love of a midget in a circus for a robust gymnast, her marriage with the idea of getting his fortune and putting him out of the way through poisoning, and effecting a union with the strongman of the show. The midget leads are Harry and Daisy Earles. Baclanova as the rather rowdy gymnast has several fine opportunities but at other times is handicapped by action too obvious.

FREAKY FRIDAY
1976, 95 mins, US Ⓥ ⊙
D: Gary Nelson A: Barbara Harris, Jodie Foster, John Astin, Patsy Kelly, Dick Van Patten (Walt Disney)

Certainly one of the most offbeat films Walt Disney Productions has ever made, but it isn't one of the best. A promising concept—quarreling mother and teenage daughter switch personalities for a day—has been bungled by a talky, repetitive screenplay and overbroad direction. Barbara Harris and Jodie Foster salvage some scenes through sheer behavioral charm. The film's sexual undertones are mostly hidden beneath the continual barrage of sight gags, but they are there nonetheless. This is Disney's version of *Lolita*. The film is a minefield of double meanings.

FREDDIE AS F.R.0.7.
1992, 90 mins, UK Ⓥ ⊙
D: Jon Acevski (Hollywood Road)

Yarn starts out as a never-never land fairy tale, segues rapidly to Disney-like anthropomorphism, and finally launches into a mix of James Bonderie and *Star Wars*. Plot kicks off with Freddie (voiced by Ben Kingsley) reminiscing about his origins as young Prince Frederic, turned into a frog by shape-shifting Aunt Messina (Billie Whitelaw) and saved by kindly Nessie (Phyllis Logan), the Loch Ness monster. Growing up underwater, he later relocates to Paris as Superagent F.R.0.7.

FREDDY'S DEAD
THE FINAL NIGHTMARE
1991, 90 mins, US Ⓥ ⊙
D: Rachel Talalay A: Robert Englund, Lisa Zane, Shon Greenblatt, Lezlie Deane, Yaphet Kotto (New Line)

Sixth and final edition in the *Nightmare on Elm Street* series delivers enough violence, black humor, and even a final reel in 3-D to hit pay dirt with horror-starved audiences. Tired nature of the original concept is acknowledged by a new plotline with vengeful, undead murderer Freddy Krueger (Robert Englund, again in fine form) using a young amnesiac, John

(Shon Greenblatt), to revitalize his powers and ultimately seeking his daughter (Lisa Zane) in an effort to spread his vengeance to Elm Streets worldwide.

FREEBIE AND THE BEAN
1974, 112 mins, US ⓥ ⊙ ▭
D: Richard Rush **A:** Alan Arkin, James Caan, Loretta Swit, Jack Kruschen, Mike Kellin, Valerie Harper (Warner)

Alan Arkin and James Caan as two allegedly ''funny'' lawless lawmen. Tasteless film utilized lots of stunt and action crews disturbing the peace all over San Francisco. The purported ''humor'' between the two stars largely hinges on Caan's delivery of what are nothing more than repeated racist slurs on Arkin's character's Chicano ancestry.

FREEJACK
1992, 108 mins, US ⓥ ⊙ ▭
D: Geoff Murphy **A:** Emilio Estevez, Mick Jagger, René Russo, Anthony Hopkins, Jonathan Banks, Amanda Plummer (Morgan Creek)

Employing a nightmarish vision of the year 2009 solely as a backdrop for a banal action yarn, *Freejack* has a curious list of talent (Mick Jagger and Anthony Hopkins). The primary plot—about a race-car driver (Emilio Estevez) who's plucked from a fiery death in 1991 to become a host body for the consciousness of a dying rich man—feels as superfluous as it is strained next to the other depressing evils on display. The most notable performance is that of Amanda Plummer as an abusive, gun-toting nun, providing a rare comic highlight.

FREE WILLY
1993, 111 mins, US ⓥ ⊙ ▭
D: Simon Wincer **A:** Jason James Richter, Lori Petty, Jayne Atkinson, August Schellenberg, Michael Madsen, Michael Ironside (Le Studio Canal Plus/Regency/Alcor)

An exhilarating drama of boy and nature that unabashedly pulls at the heartstrings. Jesse (Jason James Richter) is running with a gang of outsiders who are into petty theft and random vandalism. But on one outing, he's nabbed at a Portland amusement park and winds up doing community service in lieu of juvenile detention. The sullen Jesse soon becomes enthralled with Willy, a killer whale, who's the unwilling and unresponsive main attraction of the resident aquatic show. They are kindred souls.

FREE WILLY 2
THE ADVENTURE HOME
1995, 96 mins, US ⓥ ⊙ ▭
D: Dwight Little **A:** Jason James Richter, August Schellenberg, Michael Madsen, Jayne Atkinson (Canal Plus/Regency/Warner)

The continuing family saga is a swimmingly satisfying emotional yarn. The enduring strength of this unexpected franchise is its theme of family. Both the young protagonist, Jesse (Jason James Richter) and the title orca are in search of that hallowed unit. In Willy's case, the search is a literal trek obstructed by ecological dangers. Jesse learns his mother, a drug addict, is dead, and Elvis, the half brother he didn't know existed, is about to make a visit. He's also distracted by the ache of raging hormones and the proximity of a girl named Nadine. Add to all this angst an oiler gone aground and bleeding into the whale lanes off Washington State and you have *Free Willy 2* in a tightly packed nutshell. The mechanical whales rarely betray their wire-and-mesh origins.

FREE WILLY 3
THE RESCUE
1997, 86 mins, US ⓥ ⊙
D: Sam Pillsbury **A:** Jason James Richter, August Schellenberg, Annie Corley, Vincent Berry, Patrick Kilpatrick, Tasha Simms (Regency/Shuler-Donner/Warner)

Willy's latest adventure pits him and human buddy Jesse (Jason James Richter) against illegal whalers plying the seas of the Pacific Northwest. Jesse is a research assistant on a floating marine biology lab, the Noah. The mission is to find whales, rig them with a monitoring device and watch to discover what's depleting their ranks. Paralleling the Noah's activities is a tough-minded story about John Wesley (Patrick Kilpatrick), captain of an illegal poaching ship, and his preteen son, Max (Vincent Berry). The film is beautifully crafted in all departments.

FRENCH CONNECTION, THE
1971, 104 mins, US ⓥ ⊙
D: William Friedkin **A:** Gene Hackman, Fernando Rey, Roy Scheider, Tony Lo-Bianco, Marcel Bozzuffi (20th Century-Fox/D'Antoni)

Gene Hackman and Roy Scheider are very believable as two hard-nosed narcotics officers who stumble onto what turned out to be the biggest narcotics haul to date. As suave and cool as the two cops are overworked, tired, and mean, Fernando

Rey is the French mastermind of the almost perfect plan. Friedkin includes a great elevated train-automobile chase sequence that becomes almost too tense to be enjoyable, especially for New Yorkers who are familiar with such activities.

1971: Best Picture, Director, Actor (Gene Hackman), Adapted Screenplay, Editing
Nominations: Best Supp. Actor (Roy Scheider), Cinematography, Sound

FRENCH CONNECTION II
1975, 119 mins, US Ⓥ ⊚
D: John Frankenheimer **A:** Gene Hackman, Fernando Rey, Bernard Fresson, Philippe Leotard, Ed Lauter, Cathleen Nesbitt (20th-Century Fox)

Both complementary to, yet distinctly different from, *The French Connection*. Gene Hackman as Popeye Doyle goes to Marseilles in search of heroin czar Fernando Rey (also encoring from the first pic). The assignment in reality is a setup, and Hackman is duly kidnapped, drugged, and left for dead by Rey. Hackman's addiction and withdrawal sequences are terrifyingly real and make uncompromisingly clear the personal and social horror of drug abuse. Hackman's performance is another career highlight, ranging from cocky narc, Ugly American, helpless addict, humbled ego, and relentless avenger.

FRENCH DRESSING
1964, 86 mins, UK
D: Ken Russell **A:** James Booth, Roy Kinnear, Marisa Mell, Alita Naughton, Bryan Pringle (Associated British)

Gormleigh-on-Sea is one of those British holiday resorts that suffer from acute dull-itis. A bright young deckchair attendant (James Booth) cons the local entertainments manager and the mayor into running a film festival. They persuade an ambitious young French actress to be the star of the proceedings, which lead to some inevitable disasters and coy jokes, such as a total washout at the opening of a new nudist beach and a riot at a premiere. Quick cutting and speeding up of camerawork are not enough to disguise the fact that this is not a soufflé but mainly an indigestible pancake.

FRENCH KISS
1995, 111 mins, US Ⓥ ⊚ ▭
D: Lawrence Kasdan **A:** Meg Ryan, Kevin Kline, Timothy Hutton, Jean Reno, Francois Cluzet (Working Title/20th Century-Fox/PolyGram)

Meg Ryan and Kevin Kline generally outshine the material in this wispy and somewhat anachronistic romance, which has Ryan's high-strung Kate overcoming her fear of flying and winging to Paris to recapture her fiancé (Timothy Hutton) after he dumps her for another woman. Kate hooks up on the plane with Luc (Kline), an oily French thief. The two are forced into a cross-country journey that's both postcard pretty and somewhat aimless, with a shortage of laughs between the promising start and predictable finale.

FRENCH LIEUTENANT'S WOMAN, THE
1981, 127 mins, UK Ⓥ ⊚
D: Karel Reisz **A:** Meryl Streep, Jeremy Irons, David Warner, Leo McKern, Charlotte Mitchell (United Artists/Junipaer)

The film retells the story of John Fowles's epic romantic novel, set in 1867, of a strange young woman dishonored by her involvement with a French soldier and the English gentleman who finds her mystery and sadness irresistible. Simultaneously, a parallel story of the affair between the two actors portraying the central roles in a film-within-a-film unfolds onscreen. The effect of the two interwoven stories is at times irritating and confusing, but ultimately most affecting. This is due in large part to the strong performances of Meryl Streep and Jeremy Irons.

1981: Nominations: Best Actress (Meryl Streep), Adapted Screenplay, Costume Design, Art Direction, Editing

FRENCH LINE, THE
1954, 102 mins, US Ⓥ
D: Lloyd Bacon **A:** Jane Russell, Gilbert Roland, Arthur Hunnicutt, Mary McCarty, Joyce MacKenzie, Paula Corday (RKO)

Except for a four-minute, censorably costumed dance by Jane Russell, this is a rather mild, gabby, fashion parade in 3-D. The plot is the long-worked one about a rich girl who wants to be loved for herself and goes incognito as a working stiff to find the right man. Once in a while a snappy quip breaks through the long passages of verbiage that strain too hard to be smart talk. And in line with the film's principal concern, these snappy quips are bosom-conscious.

FRENCHMAN'S CREEK
1945, 113 mins, US
D: Mitchell Leisen **A:** Joan Fontaine, Arturo de Cordova, Basil Rathbone, Nigel Bruce, Cecil Kellaway (Paramount)

A 17th-century romance about the lady

and the pirate, beautifully Technicolored and lavishly mounted. The romantic pirate from France who invades the Cornish coast of England plays his role with all the musical-comedy bravado the part calls for. Joan Fontaine seeks refuge in the Cornish castle to get away from a stupid husband (Ralph Forbes) and a ducal menace. The scoundrelly servant at the Cornish retreat is actually the pirate chief's hireling, and the romance between the two is but one of a sequence of similar adventures.

1945: Best Color Art Decoration

FRENCH VAMPIRE IN AMERICA
See: Innocent Blood

FRENZY
1972, 116 mins, UK Ⓥ ⊙

D: Alfred Hitchcock **A:** Jon Finch, Barry Foster, Barbara Leigh-Hunt, Anna Massey, Alec McCowen, Vivien Merchant (Universal)

Armed with a superior script by Anthony Shaffer, an excellent cast, and a top technical crew, Alfred Hitchcock fashions a first-rate melodrama about an innocent man hunted by Scotland Yard for a series of sex-strangulation murders. Jon Finch heads the cast as something of a loser who becomes trapped by circumstantial evidence in the sordid murders of several women, including his former wife (Barbara Leigh-Hunt) and current girlfriend (Anna Massey).

FRESA Y CHOCOLATE (STRAWBERRY AND CHOCOLATE)
1994, 111 mins, Cuba/Mexico/Spain Ⓥ

D: Tomas Gutierrez Alea, Juan Carlos Tabeo **A:** Jorge Perugorria, Vladimir Cruz, Mirta Ibarra, Francisco Gattorno, Jorge Angelino (ICAIC/Imcine/Tabasco/Telemadrid/SGAE

This comedy from Cuba is a gem. Filled with malicious swipes against the Castro regime, it's a provocative but very humane comedy about sexual opposites. David (Vladimir Cruz) is a macho but naive and inexperienced youth who believes passionately in communism and the Cuban Revolution. Diego (Jorge Perugorria) is an effeminate gay instantly attracted to the handsome David, and he manages to persuade David to come to his apartment on a pretext. The homophobic David is most uneasy during this first encounter, especially when Diego prattles on about the ills of Cuban society and decides it's his duty to expose this most unrevolutionary Cuban.

1994: Nomination: Best Foreign Language Film

FRESH
1994, 112 mins, US/France Ⓥ ⊙

D: Boaz Yakin **A:** Sean Nelson, Giancarlo Esposito, Samuel L. Jackson, N'Bushe Wright, Ron Brice, Jean LaMarre (Lumiere)

Skillfully made and involving, *Fresh* is the story of one young boy's way out of the vicious circle of drug violence that defines the world in which he has grown up. In a shocking sequence, a pickup basketball game turns deadly as well-known crack dealer Jake (a very scary Jean LaMarre) shoots dead an opponent. A clear witness to the crimes, black 12-year-old Fresh (Sean Nelson) can't say anything to authorities if he wants to stay alive, but cleverly begins pitting against each other all his employers, those responsible for the violence and death all around him.

FRESH BAIT
See: L'Appat

FRESHMAN, THE
1990, 102 mins, US Ⓥ ⊙

D: Andrew Bergman **A:** Marlon Brando, Matthew Broderick, Bruno Kirby, Penelope Ann Miller, Paul Benedict, Maximilian Schell (Tri-Star)

Marlon Brando's sublime comedy performance elevates *The Freshman* from screwball comedy to a quirky niche in film history—among films that comment on cult movies. *The Godfather* is director Andrew Bergman's starting point. Incoming NYU film student Matthew Broderick is exposed not only to that Paramount film (and its sequel) but meets up with a virtual doppelgänger for Don Vito Corleone in the form of mobster Carmine Sabatini (Brando). The ornate and intentionally screwy plotline has Brando making an irresistible offer to Broderick to work for him part-time as a delivery boy.

FREUD (UK: FREUD—THE SECRET PASSION)
1962, 140 mins, US

D: John Huston **A:** Montgomery Clift, Susannah York, Larry Parks, Susan Kohner, Eric Portman (Universal)

Intricate scenario translates into dramatic, not biographical, terms the events of five key years (1885-90) in Freud's life. The drama revolves around Freud's (Montgomery Clift) treatment of a young patient (Susanna York) who has broken down mentally and physically upon the death of her father. In treating her, and relating her neuroses to his own, he is able to formulate the Oedipus-complex theory—the child's fixation on the parent of the opposite sex. The appropriately bewhiskered Clift delivers an intense, compassionate, and convincing personification of Freud.

1962: Nominations: Best Original Story & Screenplay, Original Music Score

DIE FREUDLOSE GASSE (JOYLESS STREET; STREETS OF SORROW; THE STREET OF SORROW)
1925, 96 mins, Germany ⓥ ⊙ ⊗
D: G. W. Pabst **A:** Asta Nielsen, Greta Garbo, Valeska Gert, Werner Krauss, Einar Hanson (Sofar)

Greta Garbo's role is a poor one of a rather furtive and bedraggled heroine who does not gain much sympathy. The picture's fearfully long and dull, besides being hard to follow in its complications. The central idea is good. It deals with the middle-class enmity in Europe toward the postwar social upstarts, rich war profiteers and dealers in the necessities of life who oppress the poor and become wealthy. The screen story gets them tangled up with shoddy melodrama in what one takes to be the red-light district of Vienna. The pure girl who is lured into the house of ill fame doesn't deliver much of a sensation here. Neither does the murder mystery. One solves the mystery immediately and there isn't any suspense. [Version reviewed is a toned-down 95-min. version released in the US in 1927.]

FREUD—THE SECRET PASSION
See: Freud

FRIDAY
1995, 89 mins, US ⓥ
D: F. Gary Gray **A:** Ice Cube, Chris Tucker, Nia Long, Tiny "Zeus" Lister Jr., John Witherspoon (New Line)

A crudely made, sometimes funny bit of porch-front humor from the 'hood. The South Central L.A. community on view here centers on lazybones Craig (Ice Cube), who spends the day hanging out with his fast-talking, bud-smoking buddy Smokey (Chris Tucker). What laughs there are mostly come from the reefer-puffing comedian Tucker, a lanky, rubber-faced, hyperactive near hysteric.

FRIDAY FOSTER
1975, 89 mins, US ⓥ
D: Arthur Marks **A:** Pam Grier, Yaphet Kotto, Godfrey Cambridge, Eartha Kitt, Jim Backus (American International)

Friday Foster is based on a comic strip of the same name; Pam Grier is a fearless magazine fotog, sort of a female Clark Kent, who stumbles onto a St. Valentine's Day–type massacre involving black millionaire Thalmus Rasulala and lots of political and underworld opponents mixed up on both sides. Grier has some steamy sex scenes and a lot of rugged action, though she isn't totally macho and radiates a lot of traditional feminine charm along the way.

FRIDAY THE THIRTEENTH
1933, 65 mins, UK
D: Victor Saville **A:** Sonnie Hale, Jessie Matthews, Edmund Gwenn, Max Miller, Emlyn Williams, Ralph Richardson (Gainsborough/Gaumont-British)

There's a good idea here and the execution is far from bad. It's a combination Grand Hotel and bus idea that's pretty well thought out. Opens with a bus going down a London street in a rainstorm. A crash, two people are killed and several wounded. Then the clock goes back over the day of all the passengers who were in the bus, relating the incidents that got them there at the time. All unrelated, of course. But the bus crash fixes things up all around. Cast is exceptionally good. Jessie Matthews, as the chorine, is best.

FRIDAY THE 13TH
1980, 95 mins, US ⓥ ⊙
D: Sean S. Cunningham **A:** Betsy Palmer, Adrienne King, Harry Crosby, Laurie Bartram, Robbi Morgan (Cunningham)

Low-budget in the worst sense—with no apparent talent or intelligence to offset its technical inadequacies—Friday the 13th has nothing to exploit but its title. Another teenager-in-jeopardy entry, contrived to lure the profitable Halloween audience, this one is set at a crumbling New Jersey summer camp about to be reopened for the summer. Six would-be counselors arrive to get the place ready, then are progressively dispatched by knife, hatchet, spear, and arrow.

FRIDAY THE 13TH PART II
1981, 87 mins, US ⓥ ⊙
D: Steve Miner **A:** Amy Steel, John Fu-

rey, Adrienne King, Kirsten Baker, Warrington Gillette (Paramount)

Horror fans will probably delight in seeing yet another group of sexy, teen camp counselors gruesomely executed by yet another unknown (?) assailant, but the enthusiasm will dampen once they recognize too many of the same twists and turns used in the original.

FRIDAY THE 13TH PART III
1982, 95 mins, US ⑱ ⊙ ▭
D: Steve Miner **A:** Dana Kimmell, Richard Brooker, Catherine Parks, Paul Kratka, Jeffrey Rogers, Tracie Savage (Paramount/Jason)

Terrible. This time it's Dana Kimmell who leads the gang up to evil Lake Crystal for an outing. Crazy Jason is still there, though played this time by Richard Brooker instead of Warrington Gillette. There are some dandy 3-D sequences of a yo-yo going up and down and popcorn popping.

FRIDAY THE 13TH— THE FINAL CHAPTER
1984, 91 mins, US ⑱ ⊙
D: Joseph Zito **A:** Crispin Glover, Kimberly Beck, Barbara Howard,, E. Erich Anderson, Corey Feldman, Alan Hayes (Paramount)

Opening line of film—"I don't want to scare anyone, but Jason is still out there"—is film's only laugh, aside from unintended chuckle in the credit roll for "First Aid." Everyone in sight of the lake gets it this time, except for a little boy with a fetish for masks who* slaughters the crazed Jason, and the boy's older sister (Corey Feldman and Kimberly Beck).

FRIDAY THE 13TH, PART V— A NEW BEGINNING
1985, 92 mins, US ⑱ ⊙
D: Danny Steinmann **A:** John Shepard, Melanie Kinnaman, Shavar Ross, Richard Young, Marco St. John, Juliette Cummins (Paramount)

The fifth *Friday the 13th* film reiterates a chronicle of butcherings with even less variation than its predecessors. Director Danny Steinmann does a lot with rain in this film and his conclusion is moderately well-orchestrated for maximum effect.

FRIDAY THE 13TH, PART VI
See: Jason Lives

FRIDAY THE 13TH, PART VII— THE NEW BLOOD
1988, 90 mins, US ⑱ ⊙
D: John Carl Buechler **A:** Lar Park Lincoln, Kevin Blair, Susan Blu, Terry Kiser, Susan Jennifer Sullivan (Paramount/Friday Four)

Routine screenplay introduces Tina (Lar Park Lincoln), a pretty young blonde who is under psychiatric care. Her troubled mind's eye sees tragedies before or just after they happen, and she can move objects without touching them. Tina and her mother (Susan Blu) head up to Crystal Lake for a little on-site therapy. She accidentally releases Jason from his watery grave. The rest is formula in both content and execution.

FRIDAY THE 13TH, PART VIII— JASON TAKES MANHATTAN
1989, 100 mins, US ⑱
D: Rob Hedden **A:** Jensen Daggett, Scott Reeves, Peter Mark Richman, Barbara Bingham, V. C. Dupree, Kane Hodder (Horror/Paramount)

Paramount's latest cynical excursion into sadistic violence is lifted slightly above its generic mire by the stylish efforts of debuting director Rob Hedden. The minimal variation this time in Hedden's script is to have most of the action take place on a cruise ship taking the Crystal Lake high school grads to Manhattan, where some humor naturally arises from the locals' indifference to the madman in their midst.

FRIEDA
1947, 97 mins, UK ⑱
D: Basil Dearden **A:** Mai Zetterling, David Farrar, Glynis Johns, Flora Robson, Albert Lieven (Ealing)

A thoughtful picture. Story begins in April 1945, in the bombed shell of a Polish Protestant church, when Robert (David Farrar), a British officer, marries Frieda (Mai Zetterling), a Catholic German nurse who helped him escape. She loves him, but Robert is merely repaying a debt with a British passport and a trip to his home in a small English town. Frieda gets a cool welcome. Being the sixth year of the war, and the era of flying bombs, there is natural hostility among the townspeople. Political implications constantly intruding on this tragic love story hinder it from being poignant and moving.

FRIED GREEN TOMATOES
(UK: FRIED GREEN TOMATOES AT THE WHISTLE STOP CAFE)
1991, 130 mins, US ⑱ ⊙
D: Jon Avnet **A:** Kathy Bates, Jessica Tandy, Mary Stuart Masterson, Mary-

Louise Parker, Cicely Tyson (Universal/Act III)

Celebrating the crucial, sustaining friendships between two sets of modern-day and 1930s southern femmes, pic emerges as absorbing and life-affirming quality fare, but for a story celebrating fearlessness, it's remarkably cautious. Kathy Bates plays a frumpy middle-aged southern suburbanite who finds inspiration in the tales spun by a feisty nursing-home resident (Jessica Tandy). These center on a gambling, brawling, but good-hearted rural Alabama girl (Mary Stuart Masterson), and how she almost got fingered for murder.

1991: Best Supp. Actress (Jessica Tandy)
Nomination: Best Adapted Screenplay

FRIED GREEN TOMATOES AT THE WHISTLE STOP CAFE
See: Fried Green Tomatoes

FRIENDLY PERSUASION
1956, 137 mins, US ⊙
D: William Wyler **A:** Gary Cooper, Dorothy McGuire, Anthony Perkins, Marjorie Main, Robert Middleton, Richard Eyer (Allied Artists)

The simple story of a Quaker family in Indiana back in the 1860s contains just about everything in the way of comedy and drama, suspense and action. After many warm, beguiling vignettes of family life, story works into its key dramatic point, concerning the Quaker feeling against bearing arms against a fellowman. Role of the Quaker father is glove fit for Gary Cooper and he carries it off with immense success. So does Dorothy McGuire as the mother of the family.

1956: Nominations: Best Picture, Director, Supp. Actor (Anthony Perkins), Adapted Screenplay [nominee unnamed, because of blacklist], Song ("Friendly Persuasion (Thee I Love)"), Sound

FRIENDS
1993, 109 mins, UK/France ⓥ
D: Elaine Proctor **A:** Kerry Fox, Dambisa Kente, Michele Burgers, Marius Weyers, Tertius Meintjes (Friends/Chrysalide/Rio)

The tense, divided realities of life in contemporary South Africa are vividly brought to the screen in a provocative pic. Screenplay is structured around the three titular friends, representatives of three key factions. Kerry Fox is Sophie, who comes from a privileged, white English-speaking family; Michele Burgers is Aninka, a Boer, whose family lives in a rural area;

and Dambisa Kente is Thoko, a black woman whose mother lives in a township. A major problem is that the audience is asked to take the friendship of the three women entirely on faith.

FRIENDS OF EDDIE COYLE, THE
1973, 100 mins, US ⓥ
D: Peter Yates **A:** Robert Mitchum, Peter Boyle, Richard Jordan, Steven Keats, Alex Rocco (Paramount)

A very fine film about real people on the fringes of both crime and law enforcement. Mitchum is very effective as an aging small-timer, complete with a most believable Boston-area accent (as are all the players), who retails in guns obtained from younger hotshot supplier Steven Keats. Boyle, ostensibly a bartender, is a conduit for murder contracts, criminal contacts, and, for weekly pay, tip-offs to Richard Jordan, terrific in a true "Southie" evocation of a plainsclothes narc.

FRIGHTENED CITY, THE
1961, 97 mins, UK
D: John Lemont **A:** Herbert Lom, John Gregson, Sean Connery, Alfred Marks, Yvonne Romain (Anglo-Amalgamated/Zodiac)

A conventional but brisk gangster yarn. Herbert Lom plays the brains of the crooked organization with urbane villainy and equally reliable John Gregson makes a solid, confident job of the dedicated cop. Comparative newcomer, rugged Sean Connery makes a distinct impression as an Irish crook, with an eye for the ladies. Connery combines toughness, charm, and Irish blarney.

FRIGHT NIGHT
1985, 105 mins, US ⓥ ⊙ ▭
D: Tom Holland **A:** Chris Sarandon, William Ragsdale, Amanda Bearse, Roddy McDowall, Stephen Geoffreys (Columbia/Vistar)

Director Tom Holland keeps the picture wonderfully simple and entirely believable (once the existence of vampires is accepted, of course). In a quick 105 minutes, the film simply answers the question of what would probably happen if a charming, but deadly sinister, vampire moved in next door to a likable teenager given to watching horror films on the late show. Chris Sarandon is terrific as the vampire. William Ragsdale superbly maintains due sympathy as a fairly typical youngster.

FRIGHT NIGHT PART 2
1988, 101 mins, US Ⓥ ☉ ⊡
D: Tommy Lee Wallace **A:** Roddy McDowall, William Ragsdale, Traci Lin, Julie Carmen, Russell Clark, Brian Thompson (Vista)

Pic begins with scenes from 1985's original, and continues in the same vein. Though its camp humor and goopy effects are familiar, it's better than the average schlocker. At the outset young Charley (William Ragsdale) has completed therapy and is cautiously certain he just imagined that vampire neighbor. Before long the mayhem starts all over again. This time the vampires are led by a slinky femme fatale (Julie Carmen) and include an androgynous black, a leather-jacketed hood, and a musclebound, silent type.

FRISCO KID
1935, 80 mins, US
D: Lloyd Bacon **A:** James Cagney, Margaret Lindsay, Ricardo Cortez, Lili Damita, Donald Woods, Barton MacLane (Warner)

So similar to *Barbary Coast* as to be almost its twin, *Frisco Kid* is, nevertheless, good entertainment. Vigilantes, meetings, hangings, burning of the coast, crusading newspaper, and other details are used once again. Story traces the career of Cagney from his arrival as a poor sailor through his rise to power and riches by right of might, his almost hopeless romance with a girl from the other and nicer side of the tracks, and finally his reformation.

FRISCO KID, THE
1979, 122 mins, US Ⓥ
D: Robert Aldrich **A:** Gene Wilder, Harrison Ford, Ramon Bieri, William Smith (Warner)

As Avram Belinsky, Yeshiva flunky packed off to an American rendezvous with a leaderless 1850s San Francisco congregation, Gene Wilder has his best role in years. The manic gleam featured in early Wilder pix has now turned into a mature twinkle. Excellent counterpoint is provided by Harrison Ford, as the cowboy, who proves the perfect foil for Wilder's gaffes.

FRISK
1995, 83 mins, US Ⓥ
D: Todd Verow **A:** Michael Gunther, Craig Chester, Parker Posey, Alexis Arquette, Raoul O'Connell (Industrial Eye)

An uneven but generally successful attempt to translate the work of novelist Dennis Cooper to the screen. Dennis (Michael Gunther) is attracted to envelope-pushing sexual images; he later meets a masochist, Henry (Craig Chester), he'd once seen "dead" in apparent snuff photos. Dennis becomes obsessed with a gay porn actor (Michael Stock), then succumbs to his homicidal urges—first acting alone on a hustler, then "joining forces" with a like-minded couple (James Lyons, Parker Posey). Pic's obsessive, sealed atmosphere lends Verow's slaying set pieces a real banality-of-evil queasiness.

FRITZ THE CAT
1972, 77 mins, US Ⓥ
D: Ralph Bakshi (Krantz/Cinemation)

Fritz the Cat, X-rated cartoon feature based on the characters created by Robert Crumb, is an amusing, diverting, handsomely executed poke at youthful attitudes. Production follows the title character through a series of bawdy and playpen-political encounters. Excellent animation and montage shore up a plot which has a few howls, several chuckles, and many smiles.

FROGMEN, THE
1951, 96 mins, US Ⓥ
D: Lloyd Bacon **A:** Richard Widmark, Dana Andrews, Gary Merrill, Jeffrey Hunter, Warren Stevens, Robert Wagner (20th Century-Fox)

Stress is on realism in this war action thriller kudoing the exploits of underwater demolition teams that served so effectively in the last world war. Unit commanded by Richard Widmark realistically goes about such missions as venturing to Jap-held islands to plot against underwater obstacles that would hamper beach landings, then demolishing these barricades. Story line is slight and rather commonplace. Widmark is a new commander. Noncom Dana Andrews and the other men do not understand him.

FROGS
1972, 90 mins, US Ⓥ
D: George McCowan **A:** Ray Milland, Sam Elliott, Joan Van Ark, Adam Roarke, Judy Pace (American International)

A story of nature striking back at man. Snakes, giant lizards, alligators, quicksand, frogs and toads, savage fish, granddad turtles. Action takes place on a private island in the Deep South where great-grandfather Ray Milland has gathered his family at the ancestral mansion. One by one different members of the family meet their tragic fate through violent attack. In each case it is a frightening finish.

FROKEN JULIE (MISS JULIE)
1951, 88 mins, Sweden
D: Alf Sjoberg A: Anita Bjork, Ulf Palme, Marta Doff, Anders Henrikson, Lissi Aland (Sandrews)

This is a somber study of heavy passion and conflicting social mores on an estate. Film hews close to the August Strindberg play. In the poetic, murky atmosphere, there is a ruthless battle between a highborn girl, Julie (Anita Bjork), taught by her mother to hate men, and a social-climbing valet (Ulf Palme), which ends in tragedy.

FROM DUSK TILL DAWN
1996, 107 mins, US Ⓥ ⊙
D: Robert Rodriguez A: Harvey Keitel, George Clooney, Quentin Tarantino, Juliette Lewis, Cheech Marin, Fred Williamson (A Band Apart)

A deliriously trashy, exuberantly vulgar, lavishly appointed exploitation picture, this weird combo of roadkill movie and martial-arts vampire gorefest is made to order for the stimulation of teenage boys. Written by Quentin Tarantino in 1990, two years before *Reservoir Dogs* made him a major cult figure, *Dusk* is actually two films in one, the longer first section being a brotherly variation on *Natural Born Killers,* the second coming off as a *Night of the Living Dead*–tinged offshoot of John Carpenter's 1976 low-budget classic, *Assault on Precinct 13*—a fact acknowledged by one character's T-shirt. What demands attention by a wider audience is George Clooney's instant emergence as a full-fledged movie star. What also jumps out from the opening scene is a reminder of Tarantino's indelible touch with dialogue.

FROM HERE TO ETERNITY
1953, 118 mins, US Ⓥ ⊙
D: Fred Zinnemann A: Burt Lancaster, Montgomery Clift, Deborah Kerr, Donna Reed, Frank Sinatra, Ernest Borgnine (Columbia)

The James Jones bestseller is an outstanding motion picture. The bawdy vulgarity and the outhouse vocabulary, the pros and nonpros among its easy ladies, and the slam-bang indictment of army brass have not been emasculated in the transfer to the screen. Burt Lancaster wallops the character of the professional soldier who wet-nurses a weak, pompous commanding officer and the GIs under him. Montgomery Clift, with a reputation for sensitive, three-dimensional performances, adds another to his growing list as the independent GI who refuses to join the company boxing team. Frank Sinatra scores a decided hit as a violent, likable Italo-American GI. Additional performance surprises are turned in by Deborah Kerr, the nymphomaniac wife of the faithless c.o., and Donna Reed as a hostess (sic).
1953: Best Picture, Director, Supp. Actor (Frank Sinatra), Supp. Actress (Donna Reed), Screenplay, B&W Cinematography, Sound Recording, Editing
Nominations: Best Actor (Burt Lancaster, Montgomery Clift), Actress (Deborah Kerr), B&W Costume Design, Scoring of a Dramatic Picture

FROM NOON TILL THREE
1976, 98 mins, US Ⓥ
D: Frank D. Gilroy A: Charles Bronson, Jill Ireland, Douglas V. Fowley, Stan Haze, Damon Douglas (United Artists)
An offbeat and amiable, if uneven and structurally awkward, western comedy. Frank D. Gilroy scripted his novel and directed the good-looking production. Film stars Charles Bronson as an amateur bank robber whose mistaken death supports a worldwide romantic legend, and Jill Ireland, beneficiary of the fantasy.

FROM RUSSIA WITH LOVE
1963, 110 mins, UK Ⓥ ⊙
D: Terence Young A: Sean Connery, Daniela Bianchi, Pedro Armendariz, Lotte Lenya, Robert Shaw, Bernard Lee (Eon)

A preposterous, skillful slab of hard-hitting, sexy hokum. After a slowish start, it is directed by Terence Young at zingy pace. This one has to do with Sean Connery being detailed to go to Istanbul and lift a top-secret Russian decoding machine from the embassy. Bond has a glorious slap-up fight to the death with Robert Shaw, the killer detailed to bump him off. He is hounded by a helicopter as he runs across moorland clutching the decoding machine. He beats off his pursuers in a motorboat by setting fire to the sea. He referees a fight between two jealous gypsy girls just before the encampment is invaded by the crime gang.

FROM THE TERRACE

1960, 144 mins, US ⓥ ⊙ ▱

D: Mark Robson **A:** Paul Newman, Joanne Woodward, Myrna Loy, Ina Balin, Leon Ames, Felix Aylmer (20th Century-Fox)

A study of one man's pursuit of success and money. During his climb up the Wall Street ladder, he neglects his wife, sacrifices his integrity, and unrelentingly pursues his goal. But in keeping with American popular culture, he is overcome at end by the moment of truth. Mark Robson's old-fashioned approach to the direction is no help. He has his characters speaking in sepulchral tones, particularly in the scenes between Paul Newman and Ina Balin, as if to give their conversations a world-shaking meaning. Woodward is excellent as the wife who married Newman despite the objections of her socially prominent family.

FROM THIS DAY FORWARD

1946, 96 mins, US

D: John Berry **A:** Joan Fontaine, Mark Stevens, Rosemary DeCamp, Bobby Driscoll

Plot deals with marriage of a young couple, fear for their security, the draft, and the husband's return to reestablish himself. Scenes show a soldier's mind as he goes through the red tape of government employment centers for the veteran. Joan Fontaine and Mark Stevens are the young couple. Under John Berry's direction they make real the courtship, marriage, and marital existence of the two young people.

FRONT, THE

1976, 94 mins, US ⓥ ⊙

D: Martin Ritt **A:** Woody Allen, Zero Mostel, Herschel Bernardi, Michael Murphy, Andrea Marcovicci (Columbia)

A disappointing drama about showbiz blacklisting. The offbeat casting of Woody Allen, as a perennial loser who lends his name and person to blacklisted writers, is far more showmanlike than successful. Michael Murphy, very good as an Allen chum from high-school days, gets Allen to put his name on scripts for live-TV producer Herschel Bernardi and story editor Andrea Marcovicci, latter becoming the target of Allen's emotions.

1976: Nomination: Best Original Screenplay

FRONT PAGE, THE

1931, 100 mins, US ⓥ

D: Lewis Milestone **A:** Adolphe Menjou, Pat O'Brien, Mary Brian, Edward Everett Horton, Walter Catlett, George E. Stone (Caddo/United Artists)

A very entertaining picture contained within a single setting, the press room at a courthouse. It's about newspapermen, waiting in the press room for a hanging the following morning at 7 A.M. General tenor may be taken from one of the reporters asking the sheriff if he can't advance the hanging to 5 A.M. so his story can make the first edition. Lewis Milestone's big idea appears to have been to keep it moving, and he does. A standout performance, one of three, is by Adolphe Menjou as the managing editor. Next is Mae Clarke as Molly, a prostie who is the murderer's only sympathizer. The third is Pat O'Brien as the star reporter.

1930/31: Nominations: Best Picture, Director, Actor (Adolphe Menjou)

FRONT PAGE, THE

1974, 105 mins, US ⓥ ⊙

D: Billy Wilder **A:** Jack Lemmon, Walter Matthau, Carol Burnett, Susan Sarandon, Vincent Gardenia, David Wayne (Universal)

The reteaming of Jack Lemmon and Walter Matthau, in a Billy Wilder remake of a famous 1920s-period newspaper story *The Front Page* has the slick, machine-tooled look of certain assembly line automobiles that never quite seem to work smoothly. The 1928 play by Ben Hecht and Charles MacArthur has been "liberated" from old production-code restraints. The extent of the liberation appears to be in the tedious use of undeleted expletives.

FRONT PAGE WOMAN

1935, 80 mins, US

D: Michael Curtiz **A:** Bette Davis, George Brent, June Martel, Dorothy Dare, Winifred Shaw (Warner)

This is a newspaper yarn and a completely screwy one. Lacks authenticity, but it's light and has some funny lines and situations. George Brent and Bette Davis are working for opposition papers. They're in love but always trying to outdo each other on stories. They keep topping each other on one story or another for the entire length of the film and then clinch in a truce.

F.T.W.
1994, 100 mins, US ⊗

D: Michael Karbelnikoff **A:** Mickey
Rourke, Lori Singer, Brion James, Peter
Berg, Rodney A. Grant (HKM)

Mickey Rourke does better in the rodeo
ring than in the arena of life in *F.T.W.*, a
mostly ho-hum cross between a modern
cowboy yarn and a lovers-on-the-run
crime saga. Quiet, even delicate mood set
by Rourke's performance is disrupted by
clichéd scripting and the leading characters' predictably self-destructive downward spiral.

FUGITIVE, THE
1947, 99 mins, US ⊗ ⊙

D: John Ford **A:** Henry Fonda, Dolores
Del Rio, Pedro Armendariz, J. Carrol
Naish, Leo Carrillo, Robert Armstrong
(Argosy/RKO)

Made in Mexico with Hollywood leads
and native extras, *The Fugitive* tells how
the government of one of the Mexican
states, in a ruthless drive to stamp out religion, hunts down the last remaining
priest, captures him by a cruel ruse, and
has him executed by a firing squad. The
picture is rich in atmosphere and is sincerely done, but it is slow in spots and
uneven in dramatic power. Henry Fonda is
expressive in the subdued and somewhat
static role of the priest. Dolores Del Rio is
decorative and mutely impassioned as a
devout victim of the law.

FUGITIVE, THE
1993, 127 mins, US ⊗ ⊙

D: Andrew Davis **A:** Harrison Ford,
Tommy Lee Jones, Sela Ward, Joe Pan-
toliano, Jeroen Krabbe, Julianne Moore
(Warner)

The Fugitive, inspired by the vintage
television series, is a consummate nail-
biter that never lags. It has a sympathetic
lead, a stunning antagonist, state-of-the-art
special effects, top-of-the-line craftsmanship, and a taut screenplay that breathes
life into familiar territory. Kimble (Harrison Ford) returns home to find his wife
(Sela Ward) murdered. He struggles with
a one-armed man lurking in his house. After a trial built on circumstantial evidence,
he's found guilty and sentenced to death.
Kimble escapes in the course of a show-
stopper bus-train wreck that alone is worth
the price of admission. Enter Marshal Gerard (Tommy Lee Jones) and his crack investigative team.
1993: Best Supp. Actor (Tommy Lee
Jones)

Nominations: Best Picture, Cinematography, Original Score, Sound, Sound Effects
Editing, Editing

FUGITIVE KIND, THE
1960, 119 mins, US ⊗

D: Sidney Lumet **A:** Marlon Brando,
Anna Magnani, Joanne Woodward, Maureen Stapleton, Victor Jory, R. G. Armstrong (United Artists)

Another skeleton from Tennessee Williams's seemingly inexhaustible, mixed-up
southern closet is exposed here with only
occasional flashes of cinematic power. The
combination of Marlon Brando and Anna
Magnani fails to generate the electricity
hoped for. Joanne Woodward, looking like
a battered fugitive from skid row, pops in
and out of the story to provide a distasteful
and often ludicrous extra dash of degen-
eracy.

**FUKUSHU SURE WA WARE NI ARI
(VENGEANCE IS MINE)**
1979, 128 mins, Japan ⊗ ⊙

D: Shohei Imamura **A:** Ken Ogata, Rentaro Mikuni, Chocho Miyako, Mitsuko
Baisho, Mayumi Ogawa (Imamura/Sho-
chiku)

Unfolding through multiple flashbacks,
Vengeance Is Mine is extremely violent,
sociologically probing, and packed with
incident. Inspired by real-life story of a
notorious criminal who murdered small-
time money collectors, pic is a red-hot examination of personal rage and insolence
toward society. Killer's rationale is not un-
earthed as much as his contemptuous attitude is vividly portrayed, with his lust
and brutal hostility being acted out in
equal measures.

FULL CIRCLE
1977, 98 mins, UK/Canada ⊗

D: Richard Loncraine **A:** Mia Farrow,
Keir Dullea, Tom Conti, Jill Bennett,
Robin Gammell, Cathleen Nesbitt (Fester)

Film has a fairly tight script which, in
first half at least, builds up scary tensions
nicely. There's a performance by Mia Farrow which is somewhat reminiscent of
Rosemary's Baby, and enough supernatural trappings to please those who are fascinated by the occult. Yarn uses all the old
warhorses of the genre: the creaking stairs,
the throbbing eerie music at moments of
mounting danger, a gloomy house in rainy
Kensington, the mysterious light that is
turned on and off, a seance, and the close-
up of the heroine climbing the lonely stairs
of a deserted house.

FULL METAL JACKET

1987, 116 mins, US Ⓥ ⊙

D: Stanley Kubrick **A:** Matthew Modine, Adam Baldwin, Vincent D'Onofrio, R. Lee Ermey, Dorian Harewood (Warner)

An intense, schematic, superbly made Vietnam War drama, Kubrick's picture is strikingly divided into two parts. First 44 minutes are set exclusively in a marine-corps basic-training camp, while remaining 72 minutes embrace events surrounding the 1968 Tet Offensive and skirmishing in the devastated city of Hue. Script is loaded with vivid, outrageously vulgar military vernacular that contributes heavily to the film's power. Performances by the all-male cast (save for a couple of Vietnamese hookers) are also exceptional. **1987: Nomination:** Best Adapted Screenplay

FULL MONTY, THE

1997, 91 mins, UK/US Ⓥ ⊙

D: Peter Cattaneo **A:** Robert Carlyle, Tom Wilkinson, Mark Addy, Lesley Sharp, Emily Woof, Steve Huison (Redwave/Fox Searchlight)

Bright and sassy, *The Full Monty* is a treat, a small but muscular British pic about a bunch of gawky unemployeds launching a striptease act. Among them is easygoing divorcee Gaz (Robert Carlyle), his bumbling, overweight pal Dave (Mark Addy), and their snooty ex-foreman, Gerald (Tom Wilkinson). Gaz has the idea of the three of them doing a strip act to raise some coin. They're joined by Guy (Hugo Speer), whose largest qualification is between his legs; Horse (Paul Barber), a middle-aged dancer; and the suicidal Lomper (Steve Huison). The film draws credible characters in a recognizable setting but elevates their story into crowd-pleasing fare without losing sight of the big social picture. The last few minutes of the film, as Gaz leads the lads in a full monty (a complete strip) in front of cheering women, are the stuff of standing ovations. **1997:** Best Original Comedy Score **Nominations:** Best Picture, Director, Original Screenplay

FUN

1994, 105 mins, US Ⓥ

D: Rafal Zielinski **A:** Alicia Witt, Renee Humphrey, William R. Moses, Leslie Hope, Ania Suli (Neo Modern)

Startlingly good lead performances by two new actresses give some distinction to *Fun,* an absorbing study of crime and absent values among contempo teenagers that nonetheless feels unjelled and schizophrenic. James Bosley's screenplay delineates the exceedingly brief criminal careers of Bonnie (Alicia Witt) and Hillary (Renee Humphrey), two girls who meet by chance on a California roadside, start sharing intimacies and secrets that are largely lies, and finally knock off a little old lady just for the hell of it.

FUNERAL IN BERLIN

1967, 102 mins, UK Ⓥ ⌑

D: Guy Hamilton **A:** Michael Caine, Paul Hubschmid, Oscar Homolka, Eva Renzi (Paramount/Saltzman)

Funeral in Berlin is the second presentation of the exploits of Harry Palmer, the soft-sell sleuth, this time enmeshed in Berlin counterespionage. Michael Caine encores in the role that made him a star. Excellent scripting, direction, and performances, plus colorful and realistic production, add up to surprise-filled suspense, relieved adroitly by subtle irony.

FUNHOUSE, THE

1981, 96 mins, US Ⓥ ⊙ ⌑

D: Tobe Hooper **A:** Elizabeth Berridge, Cooper Huckabee, Sylvia Miles, Largo Woodruff, William Finley, Kevin Conway (Universal)

Setup is a variation on the old dark-house premise, as four pot-smoking teens work up the nerve to spend the night in the spooky fun house of a traveling carnival. Kids witness a carny Frankenstein being serviced by, then strangling, fortune-teller Sylvia Miles, upon which malevolent barker Kevin Conway locks them in for a night of unanticipated chills and thrills. For all the elegance of photography, pic has nothing in particular up its sleeve.

FUN IN ACAPULCO

1963, 100 mins, US Ⓥ

D: Richard Thorpe **A:** Elvis Presley, Ursula Andress, Elsa Cardenas, Paul Lukas, Alejandro Rey (Paramount)

Elvis Presley fans won't be disappointed—he sings serviceable songs and wiggles a bit to boot. However, Presley is deserving of better material than has been provided in this screenplay in which he portrays an ex–trapeze catcher who has lost his nerve after a fatal mishap.

FUNNY ABOUT LOVE

1990, 101 mins, US Ⓥ ⊙

D: Leonard Nimoy **A:** Gene Wilder, Christine Lahti, Mary Stuart Masterson,

Robert Prosky, Anne Jackson, Susan Ruttan (Paramount)

A not-so-funny Gene Wilder vehicle. Tale of the "biological clock" and its winding down is told from a male point of view here. However, Wilder's problems as a would-be-daddy aren't interesting or compelling. Inability to conceive with wife Christine Lahti bogs the film down in almost clinical detail. Funniest bit has Wilder sticking ice cubes in his jockey shorts on doctor's advice to get his sperm temperature down.

FUNNY BONES
1995, 126 mins, US ⑨ ⊙
D: Peter Chelsom A: Oliver Platt, Lee Evans, Richard Griffith, Leslie Caron, Jerry Lewis, Oliver Reed (Hollywood)

Homage, memory, and unabashed zaniness infect *Funny Bones*. It is a tour de force for filmmaker Peter Chelsom, who chronicles a complex saga of vaudeville and shtick, pathos and absurdity. Tommy Fawkes (Oliver Platt) is the belligerent son of comedy icon George Fawkes (Jerry Lewis). He bombs spectacularly in Vegas with his father as a prime witness. So Tommy sets out to reinvent himself and heads out to Blackpool, England, the seaside entertainment resort where he was raised until the age of six and where his father had his first success.

FUNNY FACE
1957, 103 mins, US ⑨ ⊙
D: Stanley Donen A: Audrey Hepburn, Fred Astaire, Kay Thompson, Michel Auclair, Robert Flemyng, Suzy Parker (Paramount)

A lightly diverting, modish, Parisian-localed tintuner. This May-November pairing gives the production the benefits of Astaire's debonair style and terp accomplishments, and the sensitive acting talents of Hepburn. Hepburn plays a bookish introvert who is suddenly swept to a high, high-fashion round of Paris when she's discovered by glamour photog Astaire. Tune-wise, there are six George and Ira Gershwin numbers from the stage musical and five from producer Roger Edens and scripter Leonard Gershe.

1957: Nominations: Best Original Story & Screenplay, Cinematography, Costume Design, Art Direction

FUNNY FARM
1988, 101 mins, US ⑨
D: George Roy Hill A: Chevy Chase, Madolyn Smith, Kevin O'Morrison, Joseph Maher, Jack Gilpin (Warner)

Chevy Chase tones down his goofy shtick, moves to the country with wife Madolyn Smith, and has an occasional humorous encounter or two with the locals. As pleasant yuppie comedies go, this is about par.

FUNNY GIRL
1968, 145 mins, US ⑨ ⊙ ▭
D: William Wyler A: Barbra Streisand, Omar Sharif, Kay Medford, Anne Francis, Walter Pidgeon (Columbia/Rastar)

Barbra Streisand in her Hollywood debut makes a marked impact. The saga of the tragicomedienne Fanny Brice of the ungainly mien and manner, charmed by the suave cardsharp Nick Arnstein, is perhaps of familiar pattern, but it is to the credit of all concerned that it plays so convincingly. The durable Jule Styne–Bob Merrill songs, from the stage score, are given fuller enhancement under the flexibility of the cinematic sweep.

1968: Best Actress (Barbra Streisand)
Nominations: Best Picture, Supp. Actress (Kay Medford), Cinematography, Editing, Scoring of a Musical Picture, Song ("Funny Girl"), Sound

FUNNY LADY
1975, 136 mins, US ⑨ ⊙ ▭
D: Herbert Ross A: Barbra Streisand, James Caan, Omar Sharif, Roddy McDowall, Ben Vereen (Rastar/Columbia)

Barbra Streisand was outstanding as the younger Fanny Brice in *Funny Girl,* and in *Funny Lady* she's even better. Extremely handsome period production also stars James Caan in an excellent characterization of Billy Rose, the second major figure in Brice's personal life. The plot is partially fictionalized in its apparent main thrust of showing how Brice finally purged her first love, for gambler Nick Arnstein (Omar Sharif), but in the process lost Rose as well. Thereafter, she was prepared to go it alone, a perfect hook for first-rate dramatic climax. More than half a dozen older songs, on which Billy Rose's name appears as one of the authors, are used to good advantage.

1975: Nominations: Best Cinematography, Costume Design, Adapted Score, Song ("How Lucky Can You Get"), Sound

FUNNY THING HAPPENED ON THE WAY TO THE FORUM, A
1966, 99 mins, US Ⓥ ⊙
D: Richard Lester **A:** Zero Mostel, Phil Silvers, Buster Keaton, Jack Gilford, Michael Crawford, Annette Andre (Quadrangle/United Artists)

Will probably stand out as one of the few originals of two repetition-weary genres, the film musical comedy and the toga-cum-sandal "epic." Flip, glib, and sophisticated, yet rump-slappingly bawdy and fast-paced, *Forum* is a capricious look at the seamy underside of classical Rome through a 20th-century hipster's shades. Plot follows the efforts of a glib, con-man slave, Pseudolus (Zero Mostel), to cheat, steal or connive his freedom from a domineering mistress, Domina (Patricia Jessel), and his equally victimized master, the henpecked Senex (Michael Hordern).
1966: Best Adapted Score

FUN WITH DICK AND JANE
1977, 95 mins, US Ⓥ
D: Ted Kotcheff **A:** George Segal, Jane Fonda, Ed McMahon, Dick Gautier (Columbia)

Fun with Dick and Jane is a great comedy idea largely shot down by various bits of tastelessness, crudity, and nastiness. Stars George Segal and Jane Fonda are an upper-middle-class couple who turn to armed robbery when hubby loses his aerospace job. Fonda and Segal have all the basic comedy essentials necessary: they seem to have gotten no help from direction and/or writing in getting off the ground.

FURIES, THE
1950, 109 mins, US
D: Anthony Mann **A:** Barbara Stanwyck, Wendell Corey, Walter Huston, Judith Anderson, Gilbert Roland (Paramount)

Story is the familiar one about cattle barons and sprawling western empires. Picture was the final assignment for Walter Huston, and he brought color and a lot of punch to his role of cattle baron. Story interest falls chiefly to Barbara Stanwyck, strong-willed daughter of Huston. She swears to break the ranch, The Furies, and her father when he spitefully hangs Gilbert Roland, a Mexican friend whose family has dwelled for ages on the ranch.

FURY
1923, 116 mins, US
D: Henry King **A:** Richard Barthelmess, Tyrone Power, Pat Hartigan, Barry Macollum, Dorothy Gish (Inspiration/First National)

A great story, coupling humor with action and heart interest. The tale is laid in the Limehouse district of London and the wharves of Glasgow, with the star on board the *Lady Spray*, his father being the master of the craft. Then on shore there is revealed Dorothy Gish. She is her same flip, half-humorous, half-pathetic self she was of yore, with the first mate of the *Lady Spray* and the master's son both trying to win her. Richard Barthelmess as the boy carries with him a certain wistfulness bound to appeal.

FURY
1936, 90 mins, US Ⓥ
D: Fritz Lang **A:** Sylvia Sidney, Spencer Tracy, Walter Abel, Bruce Cabot (M-G-M)

Punchy story has been masterfully guided by the skillfull direction of the Viennese Fritz Lang. It's his first in America. Spencer Tracy gives his top performance as the upright young man until he's involved in a kidnapping mess through mistaken identity. After he escapes a necktie lynching party, the jailhouse is burned down, and legally he is dead. But somehow he manages to escape and is intent on vengeance.
1936: Nomination: Best Original Story

FURY, THE
1978, 117 mins, US Ⓥ ⊙
D: Brian De Palma **A:** Kirk Douglas, John Cassavetes, Carrie Snodgress, Charles Durning, Amy Irving (20th Century-Fox)

The Fury features Kirk Douglas and John Cassavetes as adversaries in an elaborate game of mind control. Most viewers will enjoy the razzle-dazzle of the lengthy pursuit by Douglas of son Andrew Stevens, kidnapped by Cassavetes because of his mystical powers. But apart from a few throwaway references to government agencies and psychic phenomena, there is never, anywhere, a coherent exposition of what all the running and jumping is about.

FUTURE COP
See: Trancers

FUTUREWORLD
1976, 107 mins, US Ⓥ
D: Richard T. Heffron **A:** Peter Fonda, Blythe Danner, Arthur Hill, Yul Brynner, Jim Antonio, John Ryan (American International)

Futureworld is a strong sequel to *Westworld,* in which the rebuilt pleasure dome aims at world conquest by extending the robot technology to duplicating business and political figures. Peter Fonda and Bly-the Danner come across very well as investigative reporters on a junket to help promote the theme park.

FUZZ
1972, 92 mins, US Ⓥ
D: Richard A. Colla **A:** Burt Reynolds, Jack Weston, Tom Skerritt, Yul Brynner, Raquel Welch (Filmways/Javelin)

Fuzz has an excellent screenplay by Evan Hunter, from his 87th Precinct series written under the name Ed McBain. The basic plotline is a search for a meticulous mysterious bomber, played by Yul Brynner, who keeps killing local officials. Burt Reynolds is very good, Jack Weston and James McEachin are excellent, and Tom Skerritt is outstanding as the principal quartet of detectives.

F/X
(AKA: F/X—MURDER BY ILLUSION)
1986, 106 mins, US Ⓥ ⊙
D: Robert Mandel **A:** Bryan Brown, Brian Dennehy, Diane Venora, Cliff De Young (Orion)

As contrived and plot-hole-ridden as it is, *F/X* still works quite effectively as a crowd-pleasing popcorn picture. Crackerjack film special-effects man Bryan Brown is recruited by the Justice Department to stage a phony assassination. Brown is convinced to act the role of hit man, but he finds himself a marked man, the target of both government goons and New York police. Last 80 minutes of film constitute a relentless, multifaceted chase, as Brown must rely on his wits and resourceful talents as an F/X wizard to elude and, ultimately, hunt down the baddies who set him up.

F/X 2
(AKA: FX 2—THE DEADLY ART OF ILLUSION)
1991, 109 mins, US Ⓥ ⊙
D: Richard Franklin **A:** Bryan Brown, Brian Dennehy, Rachel Ticotin, Joanna Gleason (Orion)

With all the ingenuity that went into toys and gadgetry in this five-years-removed sequel, it's a shame no one bothered to hook a brain up to the plot. Beyond the engaging leads, there's little here of what made 1986's *F/X* so entertaining as the sequel throttles a stale police-corruption setup loaded with genre clichés. The lack of an interesting villain also hurts.

G

GABLE AND LOMBARD
1976, 131 mins, US Ⓥ
D: Sidney J. Furie **A:** James Brolin, Jill Clayburgh, Allen Garfield, Red Buttons, Melanie Mayron (Universal)

A film with many major assets, not the least of which is the stunning and smashing performance of Jill Clayburgh as Carole Lombard. James Brolin manages excellently to project the necessary Clark Gable attributes while adding his own individuality to the characterization.

GABRIEL OVER THE WHITE HOUSE
1933, 83 mins, US
D: Gregory La Cava **A:** Walter Huston, Karen Morley, Franchot Tone, Arthur Byron, Dickie Moore (M-G-M/Cosmopolitan)

A mess of political tripe superlatively hoked up into a picture of strong popular possibilities. A new president (Walter Huston) is dying after an automobile smash. Divine intervention stays the hand of the reaper and brings the president back to lead the nation and the world out of the trials of depression. The resurrected president asks to be made a dictator to deal with the emergency, and when Congress refuses he declares martial law and takes control. Huston plays the part so persuasively that witnesses will be tricked into accepting its monstrous exaggerations.

GAILY, GAILY
(UK: CHICAGO, CHICAGO)
1969, 100 mins, US
D: Norman Jewison **A:** Beau Bridges, Melina Mercouri, Brian Keith, George Kennedy, Hume Cronyn, Margot Kidder (Mirisch-Cartier)

Ben Hecht's pseudo-reminiscences of a cub reporter in 1910 Chicago emerges on the screen as a lushly staged, handsomely produced, largely unfunny comedy. The very basic decision to play *Gaily, Gaily* as broadly as possible, lay it on with a trowel, divorces the film from the realities of 1910 Chicago.
1969: Nominations: Best Costume Design, Art Direction, Sound

GALAXY QUEST
1999, 104 mins, US Ⓥ ⊙ ▭
D: Dean Parisot **A:** Tim Allen, Sigourney Weaver, Alan Rickman, Tony Shalhoub, Sam Rockwell, Daryl Mitchell (DreamWorks)

A mischievously clever and slickly commercial sci-fi comedy, pic gets impressive mileage from a one-joke premise—stars of a *Star Trek*–type TV series are drafted into battling real extraterrestrial villains. A cheesy prime-time space opera called *Galaxy Quest* continues to inspire a cult following almost 20 years after its cancellation. Since his heyday as Commander Peter Quincy Taggart, in charge of the starship *Protector,* Jason Nesmith's (Tim Allen) career has been in almost total eclipse. Nesmith's overshadowed costars haven't done much either. The fun begins when Nesmith is approached by a group of extraterrestrials who assume the TV programs they've picked up from Earth are documentaries, and believe Commander Taggart and his crew are true-blue heroes who can help them defend themselves against the dreaded Sarris (Robin Sachs).

GALLIPOLI
1981, 110 mins, Australia Ⓥ ⊙ ▭
D: Peter Weir **A:** Mel Gibson, Mark Lee, Bill Kerr, Robert Grubb, Bill Hunter (Associated R&R)

Against a backdrop broader than his previous outings, Weir has fashioned what is virtually an intimate epic. A very big picture by Aussie standards, the film is all the same a finely considered story focusing closely on the relationship that builds between Frank (Mel Gibson) and Archy (Mark Lee), and how it is affected by events on the battlefield of Gallipoli.

GAMBIT
1966, 107 mins, US Ⓥ ▭
D: Ronald Neame **A:** Shirley MacLaine, Michael Caine, Herbert Lom, Roger C. Carmel, Arnold Moss, John Abbott (Universal)

A first-rate suspense comedy, cleverly scripted, expertly directed, and handsomely mounted. Sidney Carroll's original story has been adapted into a zesty laughgetter as MacLaine becomes Miss Malaprop in Caine's scheme to loot the art treasures of Mideast potentate Herbert Lom. An idealized swindle sequence lasting 27 minutes opens pic, after which the execution of the plan shifts all characterizations and sympathies.

1966: Nominations: Best Color Costume Design, Color Art Direction, Sound

GAMBLER, THE
1974, 109 mins, US ⓥ ⊙
D: Karel Reisz **A:** James Caan, Paul Sorvino, Lauren Hutton, Morris Carnovsky, Jacqueline Brookes (Paramount)

The Gambler is a compelling and effective film. James Caan is excellent and the featured players are superb. However, it is somewhat overlong in early exposition and has one climax too many. James Toback's script commingles candor and compassion, without hostility or superficial sociology or patronizing.

GAME, THE
1997, 128 mins, US/UK ⓥ ⊙ ▭
D: David Fincher **A:** Michael Douglas, Sean Penn, Deborah Kara Unger, James Rebhorn, Peter Donat, Carroll Baker (Propaganda/PolyGram)

A high-toned mind-game of a movie, this unusual dive into the world of a pastime without apparent rules generates a chilly intellectual intrigue. Michael Douglas plays Nicholas Van Orton, a fabulously wealthy San Francisco investment banker. His jumpy younger brother, Conrad (Sean Penn), turns up and offers Nicholas an entree to unusual "entertainment" courtesy of something called Consumer Recreation Services. Primed for an unusual trip, Nicholas is stunned to be informed that CRS has rejected him—merely the first of many increasingly disorienting events that turn Nicholas's life upside down and inside out. The film is limited by the material's nature as a brainy exercise and by its narrow focus; but it is more than just a technical exercise. Douglas carries the picture well.

GAME IS OVER, THE
1966, 95 mins, France/Italy ⓥ ▭
D: Roger Vadim **A:** Jane Fonda, Peter McEnery, Michel Piccoli, Tina Marquand (Marceau/Cocinor/Mega)

Updated version of an Emile Zola 19th-century novel deals with a rich financier married to a very young woman (Jane Fonda). He also has a 22-year-old son (Peter McEnery). Director Roger Vadim has a glossy style that shows the aimless life of the bored wife and the drifting son that finally results in love, only to be throttled by his weakness, which ends in the woman's breakdown.

GAME OF DEATH, A
1945, 72 mins, US
D: Robert Wise **A:** John Loder, Audrey Long, Edgar Barrier, Russell Wade, Jason Robards Sr., Russell Hicks (RKO)

Remake of *The Most Dangerous Game,* filmed by RKO in 1932. Edgar Barrier portrays a big-game hunter who has a maniacal desire to hunt humans instead. He appropriates an island, where he plots shipwrecks to bring in his human quarry. John Loder, hunter-novelist, is washed in from a wreck and soon penetrates the madman's scheme.

GAMES
1967, 100 mins, US ▭
D: Curtis Harrington **A:** Simone Signoret, James Caan, Katharine Ross, Don Stroud, Kent Smith, Estelle Winwood (Universal)

Games is a low-key suspenser with more appeal to the intellect than to the emotions. Story concerns a modern couple, Paul and Jennifer, played by James Caan and Katherine Ross, who supposedly live in a hedonistic atmosphere. Lisa (Signoret), an immigrant reduced to peddling cosmetics door-to-door, becomes a houseguest. A series of practical jokes leads to the murder of Norman (Don Stroud), and Jennifer eventually loses her mind.

GAMES, THE
1970, 97 mins, UK ⓥ
D: Michael Winner **A:** Michael Crawford, Ryan O'Neal, Charles Aznavour, Jeremy Kemp, Elaine Taylor, Stanley Baker (20th Century-Fox)

Story turns on four runners from different nations who eventually compete in a climactic 26-mile marathon in the Rome Olympic Games. Filmed in England, Italy, Austria, Czechoslovakia, Australia, and Japan, the pic is long on production values and nothing else.

GANDHI
1982, 188 mins, UK/USA/India ⓥ ⊙ ▭
D: Richard Attenborough **A:** Ben Kingsley, Candice Bergen, Edward Fox, John Gielgud, Trevor Howard, John Mills (Columbia/IFI/Goldcrest/NFDC)

The canvas upon which the turmoil of India, through its harshly won independence in 1947 from British rule, is, as depicted by Richard Attenborough, bold, sweeping, brutal; tender, loving and inspiring. He has balanced the varied emotional thrusts in expert fashion. Ben Kingsley, the British (half-Indian) actor, who portrays the Mahatma from young manhood as a lawyer in South Africa, is a physically striking Gandhi and has captured nuances in speech and movement which make it seem as though he has stepped through black-and-white newsreels into the present Technicolor reincarnation.

1982: Best Picture, Director, Actor (Ben Kingsley), Original Screenplay, Cinematography, Art Direction, Editing, Costume Design

Nominations: Best Original Score, Sound, Makeup

GANG'S ALL HERE, THE
1939, 75 mins, UK

D: Thornton Freeland **A:** Jack Buchanan, Googie Withers, Edward Everett Horton, Otto Kruger (Associated British)

Jack Buchanan plays a private detective for a large insurance company, and never takes anything seriously, even when murder. He's ably partnered with Edward Everett Horton as his brother in the farcical byplay.

GANG'S ALL HERE, THE
(UK: THE GIRLS HE LEFT BEHIND)
1943, 102 mins, US

D: Busby Berkeley **A:** Alice Faye, Carmen Miranda, Charlotte Greenwood, Eugene Pallette, Edward Everett Horton (20th Century-Fox)

A weak script is somewhat mitigated by a flock of tuneful musical numbers. Alice Faye has never been screened more fetchingly, and she still lilts a ballad for sock results. Carmen Miranda is given her fattest screen part to date, and she's a comedienne who can handle lines as well as put over her South American rhythm tunes. Phil Baker makes the most of invariably drab comedy lines, while Benny Goodman's orch is always prominently focused. Of the cast, Miranda is outstanding, and the way she kicks around the English lingo affords much of the film's comedy. Faye underplays as usual, but always clicko.

1943: Nomination: Best Color Art Direction

GANG WAR
See: Odd Man Out

GARBO TALKS
1984, 103 mins, US

D: Sidney Lumet **A:** Anne Bancroft, Ron Silver, Carrie Fisher, Catherine Hicks, Steven Hill, Hermione Gingold (United Artists)

A sweet and sour film. Packed with New York in-jokes, not everyone will appreciate its aggressive charm. But beneath its cocky exterior, picture has a bead on some very human and universal truths. Estelle Rolfe (Anne Bancroft) is a certifiable eccentric who has worshiped Garbo from afar since childhood, until the star has become woven into the fabric of her imagination. If not for Bancroft's spirited performance, Estelle would deteriorate into a caricature.

GARDEN, THE
1991, 90 mins, UK

D: Derek Jarman **A:** Derek Jarman, Tilda Swinton, Johnny Mills, Kevin Collins, Pete Lee-Wilson (Basilisk)

Derek Jarman's dense *The Garden* is a graphic look at homosexual discrimination laden with campy gestures, music, and religious dream sequences. The legacy of AIDS is alluded to powerfully. Jarman combines camera images and backdrops to juxtapose contempo England with the Passion of Christ.

GARDEN OF ALLAH, THE
1927, 96 mins, US

D: Rex Ingram **A:** Alice Terry, Ivan Petrovich, Marcel Vibert (Ingram/M-G-M)

Religious tale of a monk who leaves the monastery and hides his identity, weds, and then repent, after telling his wife of his transgression. Afterward, he returns to the monastery. Director Rex Ingram uncovered a screen bet in Ivan Petrovich, who, it is reported, was sponsored for the part by Alice Terry. His work throughout is capable. Terry does little emoting. No question that in certain passages the story becomes dull as it pauses.

GARDEN OF ALLAH
1936, 80 mins, US

D: Richard Boleslawski **A:** Marlene Dietrich, Charles Boyer, Basil Rathbone, C. Aubrey Smith, Joseph Schildkraut, John Carradine (Selznick)

Garden of Allah, sumptuously and impressively mounted by David O. Selznick, impresses in color production but is a pretty dull affair. It is optically arresting and betimes emotionally gripping, but after a spell, the spiritual significance of the Trappist monk whose earthly love cannot overcome his religious vows peters out completely. Marlene Dietrich and Charles Boyer are more than adequately competent in the leads, although sometimes slurring their lines.

1936: Special Award (color cinematography)

Nominations: Best Score, Assistant Director (Eric G. Stacey)

GARDEN OF EVIL
1954, 100 mins, US ▱

D: Henry Hathaway **A:** Gary Cooper, Susan Hayward, Richard Widmark, Hugh Marlowe, Cameron Mitchell, Rita Moreno (20th Century-Fox)

Henry Hathaway has a lot of mood setting, brooding characters, and attempts at profundity to contend with in the script. The plot has Gary Cooper, Richard Widmark, and Cameron Mitchell as three adventurers hired by Leah (Susan Hayward) to ride with her into dangerous Indian country to free her husband (Hugh Marlowe), who is trapped in a gold mine.

GARDEN OF THE FINZI-CONTINIS, THE
See: Il Giardino dei Finzi-Contini

GARDEN OF THE MOON
1938, 94 mins, US

D: Busby Berkeley **A:** Pat O'Brien, Margaret Lindsay, John Payne, Johnnie Davis, Melville Cooper, Isabel Jeans (Warner)

A bright musical, due principally to the sparkling Harry Warren and Al Dubin and Johnny Mercer tunes, an ebullient script, and the exceptionally adept direction of Busby Berkeley. It's the familiar yarn about the unknown band hired as a filler-in at a famous nitery and remaining to establish itself as a name outfit. Although not given top billing, John Payne has the leading part. As the steel-jacketed, ruthless nitery operator, Pat O'Brien gives a workmanlike performance.

GARDENS OF STONE
1987, 111 mins, US Ⓥ ⊙

D: Francis Coppola **A:** James Caan, Anjelica Huston, James Earl Jones, D. B. Sweeney, Dean Stockwell, Mary Stuart Masterson (Tri-Star)

Francis Coppola's muddled meditation on the Vietnam War seems to take its name not so much from the Arlington Memorial Cemetery, where much of the action takes place, but from the stiffness of the characters it portrays. As a two-time combat vet biding his time training young recruits for the Old Guard, the army's ceremonial unit at Fort Myer, VA, James Caan knows the war is wrong but cannot oppose it. Most contrived is Caan's affair with Anjelica Huston, who plays a reporter vehemently opposed to the war. She has enough stilted dialogue to destroy her character.

GAS, FOOD, LODGING
1992, 100 mins, US Ⓥ ⊙

D: Allison Anders **A:** Brooke Adams, Ione Skye, Fairuza Balk, James Brolin, Robert Knepper (Cineville)

Gas, Food, Lodging is filled with the kind of personal, small-scale rewards indie filmmakers seem best at delivering. Focus is on teenage Shade (Fairuza Balk) and her quest to find a man for her waitress mom, Nora (Brooke Adams), while sorting out her own romantic yearnings and dealing with her loose-living, surly-tempered older sister Trudi (Ione Skye). Rich, multilevel work is full of rueful humor, fresh, turns and small, elegant surprises.

GASLIGHT
(US: ANGEL STREET)
1940, 80 mins, UK

D: Thorold Dickinson **A:** Anton Walbrook, Diana Wynyard, Frank Pettingell, Cathleen Cordell, Robert Newton, Jimmy Hanley (British National)

Patrick Hamilton's stageplay Gaslight had considerable London success. Excellent direction by Thorold Dickinson retains all the psychological drama of the original in presenting the tale of a woman being driven steadily mad. Anton Walbrook's study of the half-insane Paul Mallen successfully avoids overplaying. Diana Wynyard brings a sympathy and understanding to her portrayal of the woman who is influenced by him into believing that she is going mad.

GASLIGHT
(UK: THE MURDER IN THORNTON SQUARE)
1944, 114 mins, US Ⓥ ⊙

D: George Cukor **A:** Charles Boyer, Ingrid Bergman, Joseph Cotten, May Whitty, Angela Lansbury (M-G-M)

Patrick Hamilton's London stage melodrama is given an exciting screen treatment. Gaslight is the story of a murderer who escaped detection for many years. He kills a famous opera singer for her jewels but is never able to uncover the baubles. Years later he marries the singer's niece so that he can continue his search for the gems in the late singer's home, which the niece has inherited and in which the newlyweds make their home.

1944: Best Actress (Ingrid Bergman), B&W Art Decoration

Nominations: Best Picture, Actor

(Charles Boyer), Supp. Actress (Angela Lansbury), Screenplay, B&W Cinematography

GAS-S-S-S, OR IT BECAME NECESSARY TO DESTROY THE WORLD IN ORDER TO SAVE IT
1970, 79 mins, US Ⓥ
D: Roger Corman **A:** Robert Corff, Elaine Giftos, Pat Patterson, George Armitage, Alex Wilson (American International)

Ostensibly about the actions of the under-25s of the world when an experimental gas kills off all those over that age, most of the screenplay is devoted to moving a group of six young people along the highways to a New Mexican commune where they've heard a "brave new world" awaits them. Obstacles appear in the form of automobile rustlers and a gang of football players who try to force them to join the team (whose motto is loot, burn, and rape).

GATHERING OF EAGLES, A
1963, 115 mins, US Ⓥ
D: Delbert Mann **A:** Rock Hudson, Rod Taylor, Mary Peach, Barry Sullivan, Kevin McCarthy, Henry Silva (Universal)

A story of the men of the Strategic Air Command, more specifically that of a wing commander (Rock Hudson) whose dedication to the task of shaping up the somewhat negligent outfit to which he is newly assigned forces him to make several unpleasant decisions that almost strain marital relations with his wife (Mary Peach) to the breaking point. Hudson invests his role with the right blend of authority and warmth. Rod Taylor creates a colorful figure as the undesirably easygoing vice-commander.

GATOR
1976, 115 mins, US Ⓥ ▭
D: Burt Reynolds **A:** Burt Reynolds, Jack Weston, Lauren Hutton, Alice Ghostley, Dub Taylor (United Artists)

This follow-up to *White Lightning* picks up Burt Reynolds as moonshiner Gator McKlusky character, now on parole. State governor can't realize political ambitions until a notorious back-water county, run by crime czar Jerry Reed, gets cleaned up. Jack Weston as Department of Justice undercover agent blackmails Reynolds into working against old pal Reed.

GATTACA
1997, 112 mins, US Ⓥ ⊙ ▭
D: Andrew Niccol **A:** Ethan Hawke, Uma Thurman, Jude Law, Gore Vidal, Alan Arkin, Loren Dean (Jersey/Columbia)

One of the first major Hollywood movies to deal with the effects of genetic engineering on human civilization, *Gattaca* is an intelligent and timely sci-fi thriller. In the near future, in a tyrannical, impersonal world, "designer people," forged in lab tubes, strive for perfection. Conceived by love, Vincent Freeman (Ethan Hawke) is labeled an In-Valid and disqualified from his lifelong dream of becoming a space navigator. With the assistance of German (Tony Shalhoub), a DNA broker who sells false identities to the genetically inferior, Vincent contacts Jerome Morrow (Jude Law), a superior specimen who, paralyzed in an accident, is willing to sell his genetic materials for cash. Film is superlatively produced, designed, and edited.
1997: Nomination: Best Art Direction

IL GATTOPARDO (THE LEOPARD)
1963, 205 mins, Italy/France Ⓥ ▭
D: Luchino Visconti **A:** Burt Lancaster, Alain Delon, Claudia Cardinale, Paolo Stoppa, Serge Reggiani (Titanus/SNPC/ SGC)

Italy's top bestseller of recent years, Giuseppe Tomasi Di Lampedusa's *The Leopard* comes to the screen in a magnificent film, munificently outfitted and splendidly acted by a large cast dominated by Burt Lancaster's standout stint in the title role. It must also be added that, at nearly 3 1/2 hours, the film is way overlong. Several sequences fail to move forward the story significantly. Director Luchino Visconti has faithfully followed the book's main outlines. Lancaster's Salina is an outstanding achievement, one which almost alone brings together the film's various threads, giving it body and provoking thought. [Version reviewed was Italian-language one, in which most actors were dubbed.]

GAUCHO, THE
1927, 102 mins, US d
D: F. Richard Jones **A:** Douglas Fairbanks, Lupe Velez, Gustav von Seyffertitz, Michael Vavitch, Nigel de Brulier, Mary Pickford (Elton/United Artists)

Doug Fairbanks is at it again. The story of *The Gaucho* is credited on the screen to Elton Thomas, but that person is none other than Doug. However, he does not hog the picture, but permits a little Mexican girl, new to films, in on the racket. This youngster is Lupe Velez, not more than 16 or 17. To please the little mountain girl, the Gaucho has a house moved from its base by 100 horses to the town he has come to take because there is an abundance of gold there. The big punch is a stampede of cattle to save the day for the Gaucho.

GAUNTLET, THE
1977, 108 mins, US Ⓥ ⊙ ⌑
D: Clint Eastwood **A:** Clint Eastwood, Sondra Locke, Pat Hingle, William Prince, Bill McKinney, Michael Cavanaugh (Warner/Malpaso)

Eastwood, a flop cop sent to extradite hooker Sondra Locke, finds they are the targets of both the underworld and law-enforcement elements tied to the Mob. Plot provides a series of narrow escapes in van rides, motorcycle rides, train rides, car rides, and climactic bus ride. Chuck Gaspar's special-effects crew destroys a house, a helicopter, and a cross-country bus as the film unfolds.

GAY CABALLERO, THE
1940, 58 mins, US
D: Otto Brower **A:** Cesar Romero, Sheila Ryan, Robert Sterling, Chris-Pin Martin (20th Century-Fox)

The Cisco Kid rides into the district with sidekick Chris-Pin Martin to find a grave marked with his name. Deciding to stick around and find out what's going on, he discovers enough plot to step in to protect a pretty girl and her father from nefarious deeds. Cesar Romero is in the familiar role of Cisco, never losing his composure in the darkest situations.

GAY DECEPTION, THE
1935, 75 mins, US
D: William Wyler **A:** Francis Lederer, Frances Dee, Benita Hume, Alan Mowbray, Lennox Pawle, Akim Tamiroff (Fox)

Smartness of direction, plus a few comedy situations, turn an ordinary Cinderella theme into pleasing light film diversion. *The Gay Deception* is so named because a prince masquerades as a hotel bellboy and makes Cindy's triumph possible. *Gay Deception* fits Francis Lederer better than anything he's done. Here he's both a bellboy and a prince. Frances Dee is excellent as Mirabel, the small-town girl who cashes $5,000 on a sweepstakes ticket and goes to New York to live like a queen.

GAY DESPERADO, THE
1936, 90 mins, US
D: Rouben Mamoulian **A:** Nino Martini, Ida Lupino, Leo Carrillo, Harold Huber,

James Blakeley (Pickford-Lasky)

This Nino Martini mesquiter is a fairly diverting Mexican western. Leo Carrillo is the bad Mexican hombre who's been influenced by US gangster pix. But Leo is a pushover for a top tenor apparently, and despite his bloodthirsty celluloid education, this small time Villa seems to take plenty from the singer (Martini). Plot is complicated by a snatch—another educational throwback at the door of the Hollywood influence on the mesa mayhemmers—and an attempt by a US hoodlum to hijack a snatch. In between all this, Martini tenors in his top-notch Me-topera style.

GAY DIVORCE, THE
See: The Gay Divorcee

GAY DIVORCEE, THE
(UK: THE GAY DIVORCE)
1934, 107 mins, US Ⓥ ⊙
D: Mark Sandrich **A:** Fred Astaire, Ginger Rogers, Alice Brady, Edward Everett Horton, Erik Rhodes, Eric Blore (RKO)

There's charm, romance, gaiety, and éclat. There's a dash of continental spice in the situation of the professional male corespondent who is to expedite Ginger Rogers's divorce. The manner in which Fred Astaire taps himself into an individual click with "Looking for a Needle in Haystack," a hoofing soliloquy in his London flat, is something which he alone could elevate and is magnificent individual artistry. "The Continental," is the smash song-and-dance hit. Cole Porter's "Night and Day," from the original show, is alone retained and worthily so, especially as Astaire interprets it. Alice Brady and Edward Everett Horton are more than just good foils. Erik Rhodes and Eric Blore, both from legit, also impress in no small manner. Terp stager Dave Gould displays considerable imagination with the dance staging.

1934: Best Song ("Continental")
Nominations: Best Picture, Art Direction, Score, Sound

GAY MRS. TREXEL, THE
See: Susan and God

GAZEBO, THE
1959, 102 mins, US Ⓥ ⌑
D: George Marshall **A:** Glenn Ford, Debbie Reynolds, Carl Reiner, John McGiver, Mabel Albertson (Avon/M-G-M)

Glenn Ford plays a television writer who is married to a Broadway star (Debbie Reynolds). Several years earlier, Reynolds posed without proper attire, and now the possessor of said photographs is blackmailing Ford. He invites the blackmailer to his home and shoots him. He hides the body on the spot where a gazebo is about to be positioned the following day. The film is nearly all Ford, and he's up to every scene, earning both sympathy and laughs as he muddles through his farcical "crime."

1959: Nomination: B&W Costume Design

GEISHA BOY, THE
1958, 95 mins, US Ⓥ
D: Frank Tashlin **A:** Jerry Lewis, Marie McDonald, Sessue Hayakawa, Barton MacLane, Suzanne Pleshette, Nobu McCarthy (Paramount)

A good Jerry Lewis comedy. Frank Tashlin, who wrote and directed, loads in wild sight and sound gags, parodies and takeoffs that relieve Lewis of some comic burden and show him in his best light. Lewis is a magician. He and his rabbit, Harry, join a USO tour of the Orient, because they can't get a job anywhere else. Lewis first tangles with the troupe's headliner (Marie McDonald); then with the army brass, represented by Barton MacLane, and finally with the Japanese themselves.

GENERAL, THE
1927, 77 mins, US Ⓥ ⊙ ⊗
D: Buster Keaton, Clyde Bruckman **A:** Buster Keaton, Marien Mack, Glen Cavender, Jim Farley, Frederick Vroom (Keaton/United Artists)

Principal comedy plot is built on that elementary bit, "the chase," but you can't continue a fight for almost an hour and expect good results. The story is a burlesque of a Civil War meller. Buster Keaton has the role of a youthful engineer on the Watern and Atlantic RR, running through Georgia, when war is declared. Ten Union daredevils steal a train in the middle of Confederate territory and start off with it, intending to burn all bridges behind them. Keaton, sore because his beloved engine has been stolen, gives chase in another locomotive. There are some corking gags in the picture, but as they are all a part of the chase, they are overshadowed.

GENERAL, THE
1998, 123 mins, Ireland Ⓥ ⊙ ▭
D: John Boorman **A:** Brendan Gleeson, Adrian Dunbar, Sean McGinley, Maria Doyle Kennedy, Angeline Ball, Jon Voight (Merlin)

Rarely has a veteran filmmaker rejuvenated his career to such startling effect as John Boorman with *The General,* a fresh-off-the-slab biopic of maverick Irish crime lord Martin Cahill that challenges and entertains the audience at a variety of levels. This movie says more about the rebellious Irish psyche than a heap of overtly political pictures. Boorman's choice of b&w and widescreen gives the film a certain distance and stylization. Pic establishes a tone of almost dreamlike unreality as Cahill (Brendan Gleeson) is gunned down outside his house. The rest of the movie is a long flashback leading up to his death, sketching his gradual rise from petty villain to local mobster, but still portraying Cahill as a likable rogue, making dummies of the local cops. Part childlike joker, part ruthless gang leader, Gleeson's Cahill is one of the screen's most memorable psychopaths.

GENERAL DIED AT DAWN, THE
1936, 98 mins, US Ⓥ
D: Lewis Milestone **A:** Gary Cooper, Madeleine Carroll, Akim Tamiroff, Dudley Digges, Porter Hall, William Frawley (Paramount)

Story is an old-fashioned piece of claptrap. It has to do with intrigue in the Far East, gunrunners, smugglers, and spies. In his first film attempt, Clifford Odets has left all that alone but has underlined Gary Cooper trying to help the downtrodden Chinese rid themselves of a money-grubbing, rapacious Chinese warlord, General Yang (Akim Tamiroff). Cooper, as the daredevil American, is at top form throughout; Tamiroff and Porter Hall, turn in exceptionally strong performances. Hall, as a sniveling, broken-down villain, handles an unusual plot beautifully.

1936: Nominations: Best Supp. Actor (Akim Tamiroff), Cinematography, Score

GENERAL'S DAUGHTER, THE
1999, 116 mins, US Ⓥ ⊙ ▭
D: Simon West **A:** John Travolta, Madeleine Stowe, James Cromwell, Timothy Hutton, Leslie Stefanson, James Woods (Paramount)

The General's Daughter is a hokey, kinky military thriller, twisty and compelling enough to hook viewers in the mood for a trashy good time. John Travolta's US Army criminal investigator Paul Brenner is enlisted to solve the murder of Captain Elisabeth Campbell (Leslie Stefanson), beautiful daughter of retiring General Campbell (James Cromwell). He's teamed with fellow Criminal Investigation Division vet Sarah Sunhill (Madeleine Stowe). Paul has 36 hours to nail the killer before the FBI moves in and the scandal goes embarrassingly public. Travolta delivers a strong performance that effectively carries the picture. Stowe gamely gets off a few shots.

GENERATION, A
See: Pokolenie

GENEVIEVE
1953, 86 mins, UK ⓥ

D: Henry Cornelius **A:** John Gregson, Dinah Sheridan, Kenneth More, Kay Kendall, Geoffrey Keen, Joyce Grenfell (Sirius)

"Genevieve" is a vintage 1904 car that has been entered for the annual London-to-Brighton rally by its enthusiastic owner (John Gregson). His wife (Dinah Sheridan) hardly shares his enthusiasm but joins him on the run and there is constant good-natured bickering between them and their friendly rival (Kenneth More) and his girlfriend (Kay Kendall). First-rate direction by Henry Cornelius keeps the camera focused almost entirely on the four principals, and rarely has a starring foursome been so consistently good.

1953: Nominations: Best Story & Screenplay, Scoring of a Dramatic Picture

GENGHIS KHAN
1965, 124 mins, US ⌒

D: Henry Levin **A:** Stephen Boyd, Omar Sharif, James Mason, Eli Wallach, Francoise Dorleac, Telly Savalas (Allen/CCC/Avala)

An introspective biopic about the Mongol chief Temujin, who unified Asia's warring tribes in the Dark Ages. Script emphasizes personal motivation rather than sweeping pageantry. Sharif does a near-excellent job in projecting with ease the zeal that propelled Temujin from bondage to a political education in China, and finally to realizing at death his dream of Mongol unity. Boyd is less successful as the brutish thorn in Sharif's side.

LE GENOU DE CLAIRE
(CLAIRE'S KNEE)
1970, 107 mins, France ⓥ ⊙

D: Eric Rohmer **A:** Jean-Claude Brialy, Aurora Cornu, Beatrice Romand, Laurence de Monaghan, Fabrice Luchini, Gerard Falconetti (Films du Losange)

With his fifth so-called moral tale, Eric Rohmer again deals in people who discuss, analyze, dissect, and worry their actions (in this case around friendship, love, and desire), but rarely indulge. Jean-Claude Brialy is a rather self-dramatizing, thirtyish young man. In France on a holiday, he meets an old friend, a Romanian woman (Aurora Cornu), who is a novelist and staying with a divorced woman and her teenage daughter, Laura (Béatrice Romand). The latter develops a crush on the visitor, which is the main hinge of the tale.

GENTLEMAN JIM
1942, 104 mins, US ⓥ ⊙

D: Raoul Walsh **A:** Errol Flynn, Alexis Smith, Jack Carson, Alan Hale, John Loder (Warner)

Warner Bros has managed to turn out a good film based on the life of James J. Corbett. In doing so, however, the scenarists have sacrificed a good deal of one of the best reputations the boxing game has ever known. On celluloid, Corbett is a "wise-guy," brash character oozing with braggadocio. In real life the heavyweight champ was a self-effacing, quiet personality so distinctly apart from the general run of mugg fighters of that day that the "gentleman" tag was a natural. All this fiction take the picture out of the biographical class and into fantasy.

GENTLEMAN'S AGREEMENT
1947, 118 mins, US ⓥ ⊙

D: Elia Kazan **A:** Gregory Peck, Dorothy McGuire, John Garfield, Celeste Holm, Anne Revere, Dean Stockwell (20th Century-Fox)

Like Laura Z. Hobson's original novel about a writer who poses as a Jew to write a magazine series on anti-Semitism, the picture is vital and stirring, memorable for numerous vivid, compelling passages. For instance, the breakfast scene, when the writer tries to explain anti-Semitism to his innocent little son, stamps the picture's urgent theme on the spectator's mind virtually at once. As Phil Green, the magazine writer, Gregory Peck gives a fine performance, with just the slight suggestion of inner vitality and turbulence.

1947: Best Picture, Director, Supp. Actress (Celeste Holm)

Nominations: Best Actor (Gregory Peck), Actress (Dorothy McGuire), Supp. Actress (Anne Revere), Screenplay, Editing

GENTLEMEN PREFER BLONDES
1953, 91 mins, US Ⓥ ⊙

D: Howard Hawks **A:** Jane Russell, Marilyn Monroe, Charles Coburn, Elliott Reid, Tommy Noonan, George Winslow (20th Century-Fox)

An attractive screen tintuner has been fashioned from the musical stage hit. Jane Russell is a standout and handles the lines and songs with a comedy flair she has previously demonstrated. Marilyn Monroe matches with a newly displayed ability to sing a song as well as point up the eye values of a scene by her presence. The big production number is "Diamonds Are a Girl's Best Friend," flashily presented by Monroe and a male line against a vivid red backdrop. Monroe, a blonde who likes diamonds, and Russell, a brunette who likes men, sail for Paris and fun. Charles Coburn is in fine form as the diamond tycoon with an eye for dames. Little George Winslow's big voice in a little body provides a comedy contrast to Monroe's little-girl voice in a big girl's body for his two scenes with her.

GENTLE SEX, THE
1943, 92 mins, UK

D: Leslie Howard **A:** Joan Gates, Joan Greenwood, Jean Gillie, Rosamund John, Lilli Palmer (Two Cities/Concanen)

Blatantly a propaganda war picture, story concerns seven girls, drawn from various grades of society, who join the ATS (women's army) and go through the routine of breaking in before being sent to different posts. At crucial moments the girls prove themselves as brave and heroic as the male contingent, and the film ends with a toast to "the women." This is spoken by an unbilled commentator. The voice is Leslie Howard's, who also directed and coproduced. Lilli Palmer, in an emotional role delicately and subtly played, has the best opportunities.

GEORGE WASHINGTON SLEPT HERE
1942, 93 mins, US Ⓥ

D: William Keighley **A:** Jack Benny, Ann Sheridan, Charles Coburn, Percy Kilbride, Hattie McDaniel, Franklin Pangborn (Warner)

The Moss Hart–George S. Kaufman play, a moderate legit hit, becomes a sock comedy on the screen under astute handling and with Jack Benny in the principal laugh role. For Benny, the part of the city fellow who unwillingly struggles through trying to make a home out of an old aban-

doned country house is rich in the sort of thing he does best.

GEORGE WHITE'S 1935 SCANDALS
1935, 83 mins, US

D: George White **A:** George White, Alice Faye, James Dunn, Ned Sparks, Lyda Roberti, Eleanor Powell (Fox)

From only one standpoint is the film worthy top-screen entertainment and that is the songs. There are six, two of them real outstanders from a tune standpoint, but all tops on lyrics. Even these numbers, however, are wasted because of poor staging. Most of the work is left to James Dunn and Alice Faye.

GEORGE WHITE'S SCANDALS
1934, 79 mins, US

D: George White, Thornton Freeland, Harry Lachman **A:** George White, Rudy Vallee, Alice Faye, Jimmy Durante, Dixie Dunbar, Adrienne Ames (Fox)

The first musical talker turned out by an important eastern legit-revue producer. George White contributes surprisingly little in the way of technique or ideas. *Scandals* follows the regulation Hollywood pattern. He not only borrows the backstage device, but weighs his production down with a dressing-room yarn that almost nullifies the picture's few meritorious moments. Alice Faye and Rudy Vallee make a pleasant team of singing leads.

GEORGE WHITE'S SCANDALS
1945, 95 mins, US Ⓥ

D: Felix Feist **A:** Joan Davis, Jack Haley, Martha Holliday, Philip Terry, Jane Greer (RKO)

The George White "Scandals" legit musicals date back to the Prohibition era, and the current picture, produced by George White, also dates back in that it is reminiscent of the backstage musicals of the early talker days. Though there are a few moments that hit home, on the whole the picture is a drawn-out affair. Joan Davis and Jack Haley try to overcome the assignments handed them, but the net result is still very negative.

GEORGIA
1995, 117 mins, France/US Ⓥ

D: Ulu Grosbard **A:** Jennifer Jason Leigh, Mare Winningham, Ted Levine, Max Perlich, John Doe, John C. Reilly (CiBy 2000)

An intense study of sibling rivalry set in the Seattle music world, *Georgia* excels in the expression of painfully unresolvable family conflicts. Performed to maximum effect by a host of topflight actors, Ulu Grosbard's strong character study is knit together by a tense subtext that underlies even the calmest moments. Coproduced by star Jennifer Jason Leigh and her mother, Barbara Turner (who wrote the script for her daughter), drama takes a pointed look at the inevitable strains in the relationship between sisters when one is a very together, happy, and successful singer and the younger one is far less talented, emotionally immature, and dependent on drugs and booze.

GEORGY GIRL
1966, 100 mins, UK ⓥ ⊙
D: Silvio Narizzano **A:** James Mason, Alan Bates, Lynn Redgrave, Charlotte Rampling, Rachel Kempson, Bill Owen (Columbia)

The role of a gawky ungainly plain Jane is a natural for Lynn Redgrave's talents, and she frequently overwhelms her costars by sheer force of personality. She's sharing a slovenly apartment with an attractive, brittle, and promiscuous girlfriend (Charlotte Rampling). Redgrave has a pushover of a part, and never misses a trick to get that extra yock, whether it's her first passionate encounter with Alan Bates or her fielding of Mason's amorous overtures.
1966: Nominations: Best Actress (Lynn Redgrave), Supp. Actor (James Mason), B&W Cinematography, Song ("Georgy Girl")

GERMANIA ANNO ZERO (GERMANY—YEAR ZERO)
1948, 73 mins, Italy ⓥ
D: Roberto Rossellini **A:** Edmund Meschke, Ernst Pittschau, Ingetraud Hintze, Franz Krueger (Tevere/Sadfilm)

Having resolved to mirror a world which has lost every moral rule, producer-director-writer Roberto Rossellini has done it in an extremely objective, cold manner, turning out more document than documentary. There are boys in it who kill their parents and then commit suicide. There are girls—but they're prostitutes. There are schoolteachers—but they're of perverted natures. All this, against the terrifying background of bombed-out Berlin. Pic isn't acted but "lived." Pro and nonpro cast play it with uniform sincerity.

GERMANY—YEAR ZERO
See: Germania Anno Zero

GERMINAL
1993, 158 mins, France/Belgium/Italy ⓥ ⊡
D: Claude Berri **A:** Renaud, Gerard Depardieu, Miou-Miou, Jean Carmet, Judith Henry, Jean-Roger Milo (Renn/France 2/DD/Alternative/Nuova Artisti Associati)

Though commendable and ambitious, Claude Berri's reverent $30-million adaptation of the 1885 Emile Zola mining saga *Germinal* is strangely flat and matter-of-fact. This earnest depiction of class struggle will be a struggle for many viewers as well. Story of the brutal conditions in Gallic coal mines in the 1870s is immediate and accessible, even to those with no prior knowledge of the book, which delineates the strained interdependence between starving miners and their well-fed overlords. Pic's major shortcoming is that characters speak of poverty and hunger but their privations are not strongly conveyed at a visual level.

GERONIMO
1962, 101 mins, US ⊡
D: Arnold Laven **A:** Chuck Connors, Kamala Devi, Ross Martin, Pat Conway, Adam West (United Artists)

The story describes the latter, leaner days of Geronimo's career, during which, denied humanitarian treatment by white supervisors on the reservation, he escaped and fled with some 50 tribesmen to Mexico, where he waged a courageous "war" against the US to focus attention on the principle of the issue—treatment of the Indian as a human being. Chuck Connors gives the film a decided lift with an impressive portrayal in the title role.

GERONIMO: AN AMERICAN LEGEND
1993, 115 mins, US ⓥ ⊙ ⊡
D: Walter Hill **A:** Jason Patric, Gene Hackman, Robert Duvall, Wes Studi, Matt Damon (Columbia)

Sad, stately, and ideologically au courant, *Geronimo* relates the final stages of the US government's subjugation of the west's native population in absorbing, detailed fashion. Picture's slightly stodgy literary quality holds it back from an even greater impact. This large-scale feature intriguingly concentrates on 1885-86, when the US Army devoted 5,000 men, or one quarter of its entire troop strength, to the effort to stamp out Indian resistance once and for all. Lieutenant Charles Gatewood (Jason Patric) takes Geronimo into custody and peacefully escorts him to Brigad-

ere General Crook (Gene Hackman), a veteran Indian fighter. Geronimo and some followers escape and head for Mexico. The army again takes up its pursuit with the aide of grizzled scout Al Sieber (Robert Duvall). Wes Studi is a rugged, commanding, admirably defiant Geronimo.
1993: Nomination: Best Sound

GERTRUD
1965, 120 mins, Denmark
D: Carl Dreyer **A:** Nina Pens Rode, Ebbe Rode, Bendt Rothe, Baard Owe, Axel Strobye (Palladium)

The heroine is a thirtyish woman who has been an opera singer. She had broken off a liaison with a poet and then married his friend. An affair with a young musician is also disappointing, since it was deep love for her but an adventure for him. Follows a look at her as an old woman who has devoted herself to a fairly solitary life of learning but has felt it was all worth it, since she had loved, even if incompatibly. Theme, with echoes of Ibsen, in its social haranguing for female independence, and Strindberg, in its focus on the difficulty in male and female understanding, lends itself admirably to Dreyer's dry but penetrating style.

GETAWAY, THE
1972, 122 mins, US Ⓥ ⊙ ▭
D: Sam Peckinpah **A:** Steve McQueen, Ali MacGraw, Ben Johnson, Sally Struthers, Al Lettieri, Slim Pickens (First Artists)

Peckinpah's particular brand of storytelling comes through in the adaptation of the Jim Thompson novel. McQueen, denied parole despite four years of good behavior, gives in to crooked politico Ben Johnson's bank-caper scheme in return for release from prison. MacGraw arranges and participates in the robbery plus the rambling escape that follows.

GETAWAY, THE
1994, 115 mins, US Ⓥ ⊙ ▭
D: Roger Donaldson **A:** Alec Baldwin, Kim Basinger, Michael Madsen, James Woods, David Morse, Jennifer Tilly (Largo/Universal)

The Getaway is a pretty good remake of a pretty good action thriller. Although the attributes and drawbacks of this well-outfitted retelling of Jim Thompson's edgy crime meller and Sam Peckinpah's gritty 1972 rendition lie in different places, the net effect of this tale of innumerable deceptions, betrayals, and double crosses is more or less the same. Peckinpah's protracted original credit sequence, within a prison surrounded by deer, was wonderful, but Donaldson has one-upped him with a startlingly fresh prologue, turning on two criminal betrayals, showing how Doc (Alec Baldwin) landed in jail. Early action also firms the characters of Doc's sharpshooting wife, Carol (Kim Basinger), and their early partner and eventual nemesis, Rudy (Michael Madsen). Plot clicks in as Doc is released from a Mexican slammer courtesy of slick crime lord Jack Benyon (James Woods), who recruits the master thief and explosives expert to head a heist of a Phoenix dog-track vault. Doc succeeds in nabbing the cash, but things go awry when a guard is killed. Baldwin fills the bill perfectly well as the smart, tenacious criminal ready to hang up his hat. Even Basinger bashers might find themselves rather taken with her gritty turn here.

GET BACK
1991, 90 mins, UK Ⓥ
D: Richard Lester **A:** Paul McCartney (Allied Filmmakers/TDK/Front Page)

A stagebound record of Paul McCartney's 1990 world tour, *Get Back* is heavy on nostalgia and light on visual zap. Sans intro or background, pic kicks off onstage and stays there for 90 minutes. Lester mostly lets the powerful songs (half Beatles classics) speak for themselves, crosscutting between fans mouthing the lyrics and Macca & Co. onstage.

GET CARTER
1971, 111 mins, UK/US Ⓥ
D: Mike Hodges **A:** Michael Caine, Ian Hendry, Britt Ekland, John Osborne, George Sewell (M-G-M)

Get Carter is a superior crime action meller. Michael Caine stars as an English hood seeking vengeance for the murder of his brother. Mike Hodges's top-notch adaptation of a Ted Lewis novel not only maintains interest but conveys with rare artistry, restraint, and clarity the many brutal, sordid, and gamy plot turns.

GET OFF MY BACK
See: Synanon

GET ON THE BUS
1996, 120 mins, US Ⓥ ⊙
D: Spike Lee **A:** Richard Belzer, DeAundre Bonds, Andre Braugher, Thomas Jefferson Byrd, Gabriel Casseus, Ossie Davis (15 Black Men/Columbia)

A bracing and often very funny dramatization of urgent sociopolitical themes,

Get on the Bus represents Spike Lee's attempt at creating a microcosm of the black male community via a cross-country trip by 20-odd Los Angeles men to the Million Man March. Filming in Super-16 in a jittery verite style that proves invigorating rather than annoying, Lee plunks the viewer down with a bunch of men preparing to board the bus in South Central L.A. Early going consists of considerable raucous good humor. When the bus breaks down, they are disgruntled to find that the driver (Richard Belzer) of their replacement vehicle is white. Later, the tone turns more serious, and what finally happens approaches theatrical melodrama with its convulsive circumstances and resulting speechifying.

GET OUT YOUR HANDKERCHIEFS
See: Preparez Vos Mouchoirs

GET SHORTY
1995, 105 mins, US ⊗ ⊙
D: Barry Sonnenfeld **A:** John Travolta, Gene Hackman, Rene Russo, Danny DeVito, Dennis Farina (Jersey/M-G-M)

A drolly offbeat look at Hollywood mores dedicated to the proposition that the best preparation for becoming a film producer is a stint in the criminal underworld, *Get Shorty* is good, sly fun. With John Travolta putting on a dazzling demonstration of what being a movie star is all about, this crafty adaptation of Elmore Leonard's filmland-set bestseller retains an appealingly quirky literary quality. Miami loan shark Chili Palmer (Travolta) arrives on the coast to collect a $150,000 gambling debt from Harry Zimm (Gene Hackman), a Z-movie producer. Seeing Zimm as his possible doorman to Hollywood, Chili pitches him an idea, and a new producing team is born. Plot mechanics play second fiddle to the smart, goofy humor generated by the collision of oddball characters. Best of all is a visit by Chili and scream queen Karen Flores (Rene Russo) to latter's ex-husband, screen superstar Martin Weir (Danny DeVito).

GETTING AWAY WITH MURDER
1996, 92 mins, US ⊗
D: Harvey Miller **A:** Dan Aykroyd, Lily Tomlin, Jack Lemmon, Bonnie Hunt (Price Entertainment/Parkway)

A distasteful lighthearted comedy about the Holocaust and an accused Nazi war criminal. Dan Aykroyd toplines as Jack Lambert, ethics professor who lives next door to Max Mueller (Jack Lemmon, with a bad German accent). Mueller is accused of being a death-camp commandant nicknamed the Beast of Berkau. Enraged that Mueller is going to be able to flee the country, Lambert poisons him. Aykroyd's bumbling Lambert looks like he should be in another film, while Lemmon and Tomlin may have hit career lows as the German father and daughter.

GETTING EVEN WITH DAD
1994, 108 mins, US ⊗ ⊙
D: Howard Deutch **A:** Macaulay Culkin, Ted Danson, Glenne Headly, Saul Rubinek, Hector Alizondo, Kathleen Wilhoite (M-G-M)

This schizophrenic comedy can't decide if it wants to be broadly farcical or fuzzily heartwarming. While it fares better on the latter front, pic doesn't succeed on either level. Macaulay Culkin plays Timmy, an 11-year-old boy dumped on the doorstep of his dad (Ted Danson), an ex-con whom he hasn't seen in years. Timmy has the bad timing to show up just when Dad is about to undertake a major theft, seeking a big enough score to go straight and buy the bakery where he works. Timmy hides his father's ill-gotten gains, forcing him to squire the kid around town in exchange for finding out where the loot.

GETTING GERTIE'S GARTER
1945, 72 mins, US
D: Allan Dwan **A:** Dennis O'Keefe, Marie McDonald, Barry Sullivan, Binnie Barnes, J. Carrol Naish, Sheila Ryan (United Artists)

The sheer frenzy of the slapstick are certain for chuckles. O'Keefe is seen as the now married scientist seeking to recover a jeweled garter he had given a pre-marriage sweetie without his wife finding out. Comedy is emphasized by the many compromising situations the search leads to and the misunderstandings that develop.

GETTING IT ON
1983, 96 mins, US ⊗ ⊙
D: William Olsen **A:** Martin Yost, Heather Kennedy, Jeff Edmond, Kathy Brickmeier, Mark Alan Ferri, Charles King Bibby (Comworld)

This North Carolina–lensed teenage comedy nimbly pumps new life into the overdone high-school-hijinks genre. Devising a video software business to earn money, high-school freshman Alex Carson (Martin Yost) uses the video equipment to record hidden footage of pretty girls.

When a friend is kicked out of school by mean principal White (Charles King Bibby), the heroes enlist the services of a friendly prostitute (Kim Saunders) to record footage of White in flagrante delicto.

GETTING IT RIGHT
1989, 102 mins, US Ⓥ ⊙
D: Randal Kleiser A: Jessie Birdsall, Helena Bonham Carter, Peter Cook, Lynn Redgrave, Jane Horrocks, John Gielgud (MCEG)

Sweet love trimphs over hollow class consciousness in a wonderful made-in-Britain sex comedy that celebrates romance in funny, quirky ways. Self-taught hairdresser Jesse Birdsall is a 31-year-old virgin still living at home. He gets yanked out one night to a trendy loft party along the Thames hosted by a socialite who dresses like a man in drag (Lynn Redgrave). Redgrave is determined to relieve the mystified Birdsall of his virginity. Helena Bonham Carter is a terrific and surprisingly convincing bulimic tramp parading as an aristocrat.

GETTING OF WISDOM, THE
1977, 100 mins, Australia Ⓥ
D: Bruce Beresford A: Susannah Fowle, Barry Humphries, John Waters, Sheila Helpmann, Pat Kennedy (Southern Cross)

A bold choice as the subject of a feature film is the story of a young girl's trials and adjustment to life in a strict, Victorian boarding school. Laura (Susannah Fowle) is strong-willed and rebellious, which creates conflicts with her peers and her teachers. The only real soul mate she finds is a senior girl (Hilary Ryan), but Laura's possessiveness drives a wedge in the relationship.

GETTING STRAIGHT
1970, 126 mins, US Ⓥ
D: Richard Rush A: Elliott Gould, Candice Bergen, Robert F. Lyons, Jeff Corey, Max Julien, Cecil Kellaway (Columbia)

A comprehensive, cynical, sympathetic, flip, touching, and hilarious story of the middle generation—those millions a bit too old for protest, a bit too young for repression. The setting is a college campus where Elliott Gould has nearly completed an education course. Bergen is his girl. Both perceive the tremendous flaws in contemporary civilization, but scorn the often-puerile methods used in protest.

GETTYSBURG
1993, 254 mins, US Ⓥ ⊙
D: Ronald F. Maxwell A: Tom Berenger,

Martin Sheen, Stephen Lang, Richard Jordan, Jeff Daniels, Sam Elliott (Turner/Neufeld-Rehme)

A 4 1/4-hour epic on the biggest battle of the Civil War, *Gettysburg* concentrates on the three days of fighting, with about 45 minutes devoted to the day before. General Robert E. Lee (Martin Sheen) believes that he can end the war with a decisive victory over federal troops by taking Gettysburg, then marching on Washington with an offer to President Lincoln of terms for peace. Thus the stage is set for a battle that would see more than 53,000 American soldiers killed, more casualties than during the entire Vietnam War. There's the sense of this being as close as an audience can come to seeing what the Battle of Gettysburg was like. Jeff Daniels walks away with the film as the mild scholar who, when tossed into battle, rises to the occasion.

GHOST
1990, 127 mins, US Ⓥ ⊙
D: Jerry Zucker A: Patrick Swayze, Demi Moore, Whoopi Goldberg, Tony Goldwyn, Rick Aviles, Vincent Schiavelli (Paramount/Koch)

Patrick Swayze and Demi Moore play Sam and Molly, a have-it-all Manhattan couple (he's a banker, she's an artist) who have just happily renovated their new TriBeCa loft when he's shot and killed by a street thug. Unknown to Molly, he's walking around as a ghost, desperate to communicate with her because she's still in danger. He stumbles upon a medium (Whoopi Goldberg) and drags her in to help him as a money-laundering and murder plot unfolds around them. *Ghost* is an odd creation—at times nearly smothering in arty somberness, at others veering into good, wacky fun.
1990: Best Supp. Actress (Whoopi Goldberg), Original Screenplay
Nominations: Best Picture, Editing, Original Score

GHOST AND MRS. MUIR, THE
1947, 103 mins, US Ⓥ ⊙
D: Joseph L. Mankiewicz A: Gene Tierney, Rex Harrison, George Sanders, Edna Best, Natalie Wood, Robert Coote (20th Century-Fox)

This is the story of a girl who falls in love with a ghost—but not an ordinary spook. It's warmly human and the out-of-this-world romance pulls audience sympathy with an infectious tug that never slackens. In his role as the lusty, seafaring

shade, Rex Harrison commands the strongest attention.
1947: Nomination: Best B&W Cinematography

GHOST AND THE DARKNESS, THE
1996, 109 mins, US Ⓥ ⊙ ▭
D: Stephen Hopkins **A:** Michael Douglas, Val Kilmer, Tom Wilkinson, John Kani, Bernard Hill, Brian McCardie (Constellation/Paramount)

A throwback to bygone historical adventures, *The Ghost and the Darkness* is a classy, high-gloss yarn, a literate and eerie true-life chiller. At the turn of the century, the British hired an army engineer, Col. John Patterson (Val Kilmer), to build a rail bridge over the Tsavo River in eastern Africa. But the challenge is considerably more difficult than he imagined. His arrival coincides with the appearance of two marauding lions who have killed more than 130 people. Director Stephen Hopkins is adroit at building tension and creating a mood of danger. He appears to favor the character of Remington (Michael Douglas), the flamboyant, garrulous American white hunter.

GHOST AT NOON
See: Le Mepris

GHOSTBUSTERS
1984, 107 mins, US Ⓥ ⊙ ▭
D: Ivan Reitman **A:** Bill Murray, Dan Aykroyd, Sigourney Weaver, Harold Ramis, Rick Moranis, Annie Potts (Columbia/Delphi)

Ghostbusters is a lavishly produced but only intermittently impressive all-star comedy lampoon of supernatural horror films. A Manhattan apartment building inhabited by beautiful Dana Barrett (Sigourney Weaver) and her nerd neighbor Louis Tully (Rick Moranis) becomes the gateway for demons from another dimension to invade the earth. To battle them come the Ghostbusters, a trio of freelance ghost catchers for hire. Aykroyd is the gung-ho scientific type, Bill Murray is faking competency and using the job to meet women, while Harold Ramis is the trio's technical expert.
1984: Nominations: Best Song ("Ghostbusters"), Visual Effects

GHOSTBUSTERS II
1989, 102 mins, US Ⓥ ⊙ ▭
D: Ivan Reitman **A:** Bill Murray, Dan Aykroyd, Sigourney Weaver, Harold Ramis, Rick Moranis (Columbia)

Kids will find the oozing slime and ghastly, ghostly apparitions to their liking and adults will enjoy the preposterously clever dialogue. In *II*, the foe is slime, a pinkish, oozing substance that has odd, selective powers—all of them (humorously) evil. Its origins have something to do with all the bad vibes generated by millions of cranky, stressed-out New Yorkers. The worse their attitude, the worse the slime problem, which is very bad indeed. Bill Murray gets the plum central role. Sigourney Weaver get to play a softie, a nice break for the actress and her admirers.

GHOST CATCHERS
1944, 67 mins, US
D: Edward F. Cline **A:** Ole Olsen, Chic Johnson, Gloria Jean, Martha O'Driscoll, Andy Devine, Leo Carrillo (Universal)

In the best Olsen and Johnson tradition, *Ghost Catchers* is a tuneful, screwy concoction, brief and zippy. The boys, with the aid of numerable stooges, join in aiding a southern family—who bought an old, haunted brownstone in the city as a showcase for the two daughters who are slated to appear at Carnegie Hall—get rid of a ghost. O&J prove they are strong laugh-getters.

GHOST GOES WEST, THE
1935, 90 mins, UK Ⓥ
D: Rene Clair **A:** Robert Donat, Jean Parker, Eugene Pallette, Elsa Lanchester (London)

Story has to do with an American who picks up a Scottish manse that has a ghost. The American buys the castle and imports it to America stone by stone, ghost and all. In Florida he sets it up again, his daughter, by way of romance, falling for the penniless heir of the castle and ghost. Robert Sherwood, in working up the story with Clair, has injected a number of hilarious sequences and some splendid dialogue. Robert Donat as the young heir and doubling as the ghost, Jean Parker as the girl, and Eugene Pallette as the father drain every possible bit of good out of their roles.

GHOST IN THE MACHINE
1993, 95 mins, US Ⓥ ⊙
D: Rachel Talalay **A:** Karen Allen, Chris Mulkey, Ted Marcoux, Wil Horneff, Jessica Walter, Rick Ducommun (20th Century-Fox)

The so-called ghost is the soul of a serial killer loose in a mainframe and adept at traveling on electrical current to mete out lethal revenge. It's an effective, if predictable, paranoid fantasy.

GHOSTS OF MISSISSIPPI
1996, 130 mins, US ⑰ ⊙ ▭
D: Rob Reiner A: Alec Baldwin, Whoopi Goldberg, James Woods, Craig T. Nelson, Susanna Thompson, Lucas Black (Castle Rock/Columbia)

Ghosts of Mississippi is history à la Hollywood that doesn't manage to be particularly vivid or exciting in recounting the chivalry of a prosecutor attempting to bring a racist assassin to justice. Tale opens with the June 1963 slaying of NAACP leader Medgar Evers (James Pickens Jr.) by Byron De La Beckwith (James Woods), an unapologetic hatemonger who goes free. A quarter-century later, a movement to reopen the case spurs the involvement of assistant d.a. Bobby De-Laughter (Alec Baldwin), who takes up the cause out of the noblest of motives, while finding inspiration in the unwavering conviction of Evers's widow, Myrlie (Whoopi Goldberg). Screenplay has no use for African-Americans who aren't martyrs or rhetorical pawns. Pic's one unarguable asset is Woods's excellent work as Beckwith. The wily old racist ends up more sympathetic than the filmmakers might have wished.
1996: Nominations: Best Supp. Actor (James Woods), Makeup (Matthew W. Mungle, Deborah La Mia Denaver)

GHOSTS . . . OF THE CIVIL DEAD
1988, 92 mins, Australia ⑰
D: John Hillcoat A: Dave Field, Mike Bishop, Chris de Rose, Nick Cave, Vincent Gil (Correctional Services/Outlaw Values)

An ambitious, confrontational feature with ruggedly explicit language and violence. Setting is a correctional institution of the near future. Film traces the events leading up to a riot and "lockdown." Drama centers around the arrival of newcomer Dave Field, who discovers a nightmare world where drug taking and gay sex are ignored by guards and where violence is the order of the day.

GHOST STORY
1981, 110 mins, US ⑰ ⊚
D: John Irvin A: Fred Astaire, Melvyn Douglas, Douglas Fairbanks Jr., John Houseman, Craig Wasson, Alice Krige (Universal)

An essentially familiar spook story. It's easy to guess early on that Fred Astaire,

Melvyn Douglas, Douglas Fairbanks Jr., and John Houseman share a dark secret that has prompted the appearance of Alice Krige in both bodily (sometimes very bodily) and ethereal forms. And whatever that secret is, they're going to pay for it. Unfortunately, film then spins backward to an extremely long reenactment of the events of long ago.

GIANT
1956, 198 mins, US ⑰ ⊙
D: George Stevens A: Elizabeth Taylor, Rock Hudson, James Dean, Carroll Baker, Mercedes McCambridge, Sal Mineo (Warner)

The picture is fairly saturated with the feeling of the vastness and the mental narrowness, the wealth and the poverty, the pride and the prejudice that make up Texas. *Giant* isn't preachy but it's a powerful indictment of the Texas superiority complex. As the shiftless, envious, bitter ranch hand who hates society, Dean delivers an outstanding portrayal.
1956: Best Director
Nominations: Best Picture, Actor (James Dean, Rock Hudson), Supp. Actress (Mercedes McCambridge), Adapted Screenplay, Color Costume Design, Color Art Direction, Editing, Scoring of a Dramatic Picture

IL GIARDINO DEI FINZI-CONTINI (THE GARDEN OF THE FINZI-CONTINIS)
1971, 103 mins, Italy/W. Germany ⑰ ⊙
D: Vittorio De Sica A: Dominique Sanda, Lino Capolicchio, Helmut Berger, Fabio Testi, Romolo Valli, Camillo Cesarei (Documento/CCC Filmkunst)

This picture is stamped with the trademark of a master of the cinema. The story is built on several layers of a time pyramid, with a base in the ominous quiet prior to World War II and the pinnacle in the deportation to the Nazi death camps of all the protagonists by the year 1943. On top stands a Jewish family, the Finzi-Continis, immensely rich, cultured, aristocratic, in the beautiful and deceptively quiet Italian town of Ferrara. They hope, in vain, that the vulgarity of fascism will not penetrate their ivory-tower world. Close to the top of the pyramid is the love story between Micol (Dominique Sanda), the daughter of the Finzi-Continis, and Giorgio (Lino Capolicchio), son of the bourgeois Jews. The screenplay is well motivated, sensitive and

slow, the dialogue terse and sparse and therefore telling.
1971: Best Foriegn Language Film

G.I. BLUES
1960, 115 mins, US ⓥ
D: Norman Taurog **A:** Elvis Presley, Juliet Prowse, Robert Ivers, Leticia Roman (Paramount)

About the creakiest "book" in musi-comedy annals has been revived as a framework within which Elvis Presley warbles 10 wobbly songs and costar Juliet Prowse steps out in a pair of flashy dances. Plot casts Presley as an all-American-boy tank gunner stationed in Germany who woos supposedly icy-hearted Prowse for what starts out as strictly mercenary reasons (if he spends the night with her, he wins a hunk of cash to help set up a nitery in the States). Needless to say, the ice melts and amor develops, only to dissolve when Prowse learns of the heely scheme.

GIDEON OF SCOTLAND YARD
See: Gideon's Day

GIDEON'S DAY
(US: GIDEON OF SCOTLAND YARD)
1958, 91 mins, UK
D: John Ford **A:** Jack Hawkins, Dianne Foster, Anna Lee, Anna Massey, Cyril Cusack, Laurence Naismith (Columbia)

One busy day in the life of a chief inspector. He accuses one of his sergeants of taking bribes. A pay snatch ties up with the killing of the sergeant in a hit-and-run car crash. A murder in Manchester has a maniac killer headed for London, and it all finishes up with a safe robbery that involves another slaying. It is a tribute to Jack Hawkins that he can hold the interest with such a run-of-the-mill character.

GIDGET
1959, 95 mins, US ⓥ ⊙ ⊡
D: Paul Wendkos **A:** Sandra Dee, Cliff Roberston, James Darren, Arthur O'Connell, Jo Morrow (Columbia)

Sandra Dee is the "gidget" of the title, being a young woman so slight in stature that she is tagged with a nickname, a contraction of girl and midget. The screenplay is played mostly out-of-doors on the ocean front west of Los Angeles. The simple plot is a contemporary restatement of the *Student Prince* theme. The surf bum Dee falls in love with (James Darren) turns out to be the respectable son of a business acquaintance of her father.

GIDGET GOES HAWAIIAN
1961, 101 mins, US ⓥ
D: Paul Wendkos **A:** James Darren, Michael Callan, Deborah Walley, Carl Reiner, Peggy Cass, Eddie Foy Jr. (Bresler/Columbia)

Those who may have been surf-bored with the Sandra Dee starrer will find even less to cheer about in this follow-up. Fortunately, it is cast with fresh and promising young people together with slick production, invigorating photography, insertion of a few musical breaks, and several witty lines of dialogue. Screenplay takes Gidget (now played by Deborah Walley) and plants her in Hawaii, complete with parents and a gang of lads vying for her affection. Walley is cute as a button and displays a versatility not matched by the equally attractive Dee in the original.

GIFT FROM HEAVEN, A
1994, 102 mins, US ⓥ
D: Jack Lucarelli **A:** Sharon Farrell, Gigi Rice, David Steen, Sarah Trigger, Gene Lythgow, Mark Ruffalo

Fine scripting and cohesive playing by a trio of female leads gives quality clout to an affecting, nuanced chamber drama of conflicting passions. Story is almost entirely set in a remote backwoods dwelling that houses a middle-aged single mother (Sharon Farrell), her simple son Charlie (Steen), and adopted daughter Messy (Gigi Rice). Arrival of pretty, naive Cousin Anna (Sarah Trigger) sets off a string of sexual and emotional firecrackers that have smoldered for years.

GIG, THE
1985, 92 mins, US ⓥ
D: Frank D. Gilroy **A:** Wayne Rogers, Cleavon Little, Andrew Duncan, Jerry Matz, Daniel Nalbach (The Gig)

A winning little film about a group of guys who try to fulfill their dream of being jazz players. Wayne Rogers has played Dixieland jazz with his five pals for their own amusement once a week since 1970. He arranges a two-week pro engagement. When their bass player George (Stan Lachow) drops out, the replacement, veteran player Marshall Wilson (Cleavon Little), causes friction in the group, because of his unfriendly personality and condescending attitude toward the upstart amateurs.

GIGI
1958, 116 mins, US ⓥ ⊙ ⊡ ⋅ ⋅
D: Vincente Minnelli **A:** Leslie Caron,

Maurice Chevalier, Louis Jourdan, Hermione Gingold, Eva Gabor, Jacques Bergerac (M-G-M)

Gigi is a naughty-but-nice romp of the hyperromantic naughty 1990s Paris-in-the-spring, in the Bois, in Maxim's, and in the boudoir. Alan Jay Lerner's libretto is tailor-made for an inspired casting job for all principals, and Fritz Loewe's tunes (to Lerner's lyrics) vie with and suggest their memorable *My Fair Lady* score. *Gigi* is a French variation, by novelist Colette, of the *Pygmalion* legend. As the character unfolds it is apparent that the hoydenish Gigi is preoccupied with a wedding ring than with casual, albeit supercharged romance. The sophistication of Maurice Chevalier (who well nigh steals the picture), Isabel Jeans, Hermione Gingold, and Eva Gabor are in contrast to the wholesomeness of the Leslie Caron–Louis Jourdan romance. Caron is completely captivating and convincing in the title role. **1958:** Best Picture, Director, Adapted Screenplay, Color Cinematography, Art Direction, Song (''Gigi''), Scoring of a Musical Picture, Editing, Costume Design

G.I. JANE
1997, 124 mins, US 🔞 ⊙ ▭
D: Ridley Scott **A:** Demi Moore, Viggo Mortensen, Anne Bancroft, Jason Beghe, Scott Wilson, Lucinda Jenney (Scott Free/Moving Pictures/Hollywood)

A bracingly gung-ho film, *G.I. Jane* is a very entertaining get-tough fantasy with political and feminist underpinnings. Far from being *Private Benjamin,* this is more like *Flashdance* in fatigues. Lieutenant Jordan O'Neil (Demi Moore), a naval intelligence officer, joins a Navy SEALs training camp in Florida, where she is quickly plunged into an astonishingly grueling series of physical ordeals. Interested in doing her no favors is the Command Master Chief (Viggo Mortensen), a tough taskmaster whose job it is to get in everyone's face. O'Neil is sent off as the leader of a simulated commando mission. Pic is as hard, polished and powerfully functional as a newly cleaned gun. Moore makes the exertion of O'Neil's will, and body, entirely believable. Doing his best to steal the film is Mortensen, terrific as the Master Chief who brings everyone to the brink.

GILDA
1946, 110 mins, US 🔞 ⊙
D: Charles Vidor **A:** Rita Hayworth, Glenn Ford, George Macready, Joseph Calleia, Steven Geray (Columbia)

Practically all the s.a. habiliments of the femme fatale have been mustered for *Gilda,* and when things get trite and frequently farfetched, somehow, at the drop of a shoulder strap, there is always Rita Hayworth to excite the filmgoer. The story is a confusion of gambling, international intrigue, and a triangle that links two gamblers and the wife of one of them. The setting is Buenos Aires. Sneaking in somehow is the subplot of a tungsten cartel operated by the husband, who also runs a swank gambling casino. A couple of Nazis are thrown in also.

GILDED LILY, THE
1935, 85 mins, US
D: Wesley Ruggles **A:** Claudette Colbert, Fred MacMurray, Ray Milland, C. Aubrey Smith, Luis Alberni, Donald Meek (Paramount)

Breezy romance, with plenty of entertainment. Fred MacMurray and Ray Milland love the girl, the one as a matter-of-fact mugg, the other as a semi-cad son of an English duke. Claudette Colbert is idealistic and romantic and falls for the Briton, but rebounds for the clinch into the arms of the unembossed Yankee.

GIMME SHELTER
1970, 90 mins, US 🔞
D: David Maysles, Albert Maysles, Charlotte Zwerin (Maysles)

16-mm documentary on 1969 Rolling Stones' US concert tour which culminated in violence and death at the Altamont Speedway in California. Lead singer Mick Jagger emerges in offstage footage as a withdrawn, almost catatonic individual totally involved in his music and virtually immune to events occurring around him. Onstage it's another matter, and *Gimme Shelter* captures that petulant omnisexuality that made many adults consider Jagger a threat to their daughters, sons, and household pets alike.

GINGERBREAD MAN, THE
1998, 115, US 🔞 ⊙
D: Robert Altman **A:** Kenneth Branagh, Embeth Davidtz, Robert Downey Jr., Daryl Hannah, Tom Berenger, Famke Janssen, Robert Duvall (Island/Enchanter/PolyGram)

Engaging enough through its first hour, this tale of deceit, manipulation, misguided lust, kidnapping, and murder down South goes astray with an excess of melodramatic implausibility as the climax approaches. Savannah lawyer Rick Magruder (Kenneth Branagh) is celebrating a court victory. After a drunken one-night stand with waitress Mallory Doss (Embeth Davidtz), Rick learns that her nut-case father Dixon (Robert Duvall) has started threatening her again. He has Dixon picked up by police and put away, but Dixon escapes from the asylum, putting the lives of everyone who conspired against him into severe jeopardy. There is a trumped-up quality to the climax that is perfunctory, and the final revelation is unsurprising.

GIRL CAN'T HELP IT, THE
1956, 96 mins, US Ⓥ ▭
D: Frank Tashlin A: Tom Ewell, Jayne Mansfield, Edmond O'Brien, Henry Jones, John Emery, Juanita Moore (20th Century-Fox)

The Girl Can't Help It is a hilarious comedy with a beat. There are so many sight gags and physical bits of business, including Jayne Mansfield and a couple of milk bottles, that males of any age will get the entertainment message. Mansfield doesn't disappoint as the sexpot who just wants to be a successful wife and mother, not a glamour queen. Edmond O'Brien, rarely seen in comedy, is completely delightful as the hammy ex-gangster who thinks his position demands that his girl be a star name. Tom Ewell scores mightily as the has-been agent.

GIRL CRAZY
1943, 97 mins, US Ⓥ ⊙
D: Norman Taurog, Busby Berkeley A: Mickey Rooney, Judy Garland, June Allyson, Nancy Walker, Gil Stratton, Rags Ragland (M-G-M)

It's to a western university that a NY newspaper publisher sends his playboy son (Mickey Rooney). Rooney puts the university on its financial feet and makes it coeducational. The girls he attracts are plenty and pretty. The story thread is light, but enough to string together the George and Ira Gershwin songs "Embraceable You," "Treat Me Rough," "Bidin' My Time," "Could You Use Me" and "Not for Me."

GIRLFRIENDS, THE
See: Les Biches

GIRLFRIENDS
1978, 86 mins, US Ⓥ
D: Claudia Weill A: Melanie Mayron, Eli Wallach, Anita Skinner, Bob Balaban, Christopher Guest, Viveca Lindfors (Cyclops)

This is a warm, emotional, and at times wise picture about friendship. Melanie Mayron is outstanding as a photographer fresh out of college maturing under the strains of professional insecurity and loneliness. Anita Skinner is Mayron's best friend. Eli Wallach portrays a rabbi for whom Mayron sometimes photographs bar mitzvahs and weddings. Bob Balaban is Mayron's slightly off-center boyfriend and Viveca Lindfors is Beatrice, owner of a Greenwich Village gallery. Each performance is a little gem.

GIRL FROM TENTH AVENUE, THE
1935, 69 mins, US
D: Alfred E. Green A: Bette Davis, Ian Hunter, Colin Clive, Alison Skipworth (First National/Warner)

Bette Davis's first starring venture allows her to go high, wide, and handsome on the emotions. She takes 'em all in a stride that saves the yarn from dying from its own befuddlement. *Girl from Tenth Avenue* is fashioned from a pattern whose every turn and twist the dullest fan can easily anticipate. A weak sister of the social set is tossed over by his Park Avenue girlfriend. The disappointed swain tries to boil his disappointment in alcohol and the girl from 10th Avenue gets him on the rebound. In time the Park Avenue Jane realizes her mistake and goes on the make for the old heart ailment.

GIRL-GETTERS, THE
See: The System

GIRL HUNTERS, THE
1963, 103 mins, UK Ⓥ ▭
D: Roy Rowland A: Mickey Spillane, Shirley Eaton, Lloyd Nolan, Hy Gardner, Scott Peters (Fellane)

A slick and entertaining adventure meller, *The Girl Hunters* also debuts author Mickey Spillane portraying his rough-and-tumble hero Mike Hammer for the first time on the screen. He turns in a credible job. Plot finds the private eye in the gutter from seven years of boozing and fretting because he believes that he sent his secretary and best gal to her doom. It develops, however, that she may still be alive and Hammer straightens out and goes in search of her, "just like the old days," as one of the characters comments.

GIRL IN A SWING, THE
1988, 117 mins, US Ⓥ ⊙
D: Gordon Hessler **A:** Meg Tilly, Rupert Frazer, Nicholas Le Prevost, Elspet Gray, Lorna Heilbron, Lynsey Baxter (Panorama)

British writer-director Gordon Hessler has turned Richard Adams's 1980 psychochiller novel *The Girl in a Swing* into a smooth, fine-looking piece of romantic-erotic entertainment with many a fine Hitchcockian touch and a rather special star turn by Meg Tilly. The recurring theme of guilt, atonement, and punishment is gently explored during the development of suspense. Tilly, in spite of a contrived Teutonic accent, is wholly convincing, whether expressing sexual abandon, poetic frailty, or fear-stricken despair.

GIRL IN EVERY PORT, A
1928, 64 mins, US ⊗
D: Howard Hawks **A:** Victor McLaglen, Robert Armstrong, Louise Brooks, Maria Casajuana, Sally Rand (Fox)

The plot deals with a Damon and Pythias friendship between two rough-and-tumble seamen. Of all the beautiful bimbos encountered by the sailors in their world travels not one is on the up-and-up, and the one (Louise Brooks) who inspires Victor McLaglen to daydream over settling down in a cottage for two is the biggest gold digger of all. The picture is a series of hoke adventures with dames and gendarmes. It holds a lot of laughs and still maintains a human note on the comrade angle.

GIRL IN EVERY PORT, A
1951, 86 mins, US Ⓥ ⊙
D: Chester Erskine **A:** Groucho Marx, Marie Wilson, William Bendix, Don DeFore, Gene Lockhart, Dee Hartford (RKO)

Chester Erskine scripted and directed the story about two sailors, Marx and Bendix, in hot water, latter having purchased a broken-down racehorse. Wilson, a gorgeous carhop, owns the twin of their horse and it is sound of limb. Some race rigging and plenty of other shenanigans crowd the footage. Marx's wisecracking dialogue and antics help the pace. Wilson, less of the dumb Dora than usual, shows to advantage, and Bendix comes over excellently.

GIRL, INTERRUPTED
1999, 127 mins, US Ⓥ ⊙
D: James Mangold **A:** Winona Ryder, Angelina Jolie, Clea Duvall, Brittany Murphy, Elisabeth Moss, Jared Leto (Red Wagon/Columbia)

Veering from the serious to the trivial and from the clinical to the lurid, James Mangold's *Girl, Interrupted* only partially conveys the spirit of its source material, Susanna Kaysen's memoir of her experience at a mental hospital in the late sixties. Confused, insecure, and baffled by the rapidly changing mores of American society, Susanna (Winona Ryder) is diagnosed with borderline personality disorder and institutionalized at Claymore Hospital. Fellow inmates include Lisa (Angelina Jolie), a charming sociopath who has spent years in the hospital; Daisy (Brittany Murphy), a pampered daddy's girl; and the sensitive Polly (Elisabeth Moss). Stealing every scene she's in, Jolie is excellent as the flamboyant, irresponsible girl who's far more instrumental than the doctors in Susanna's rehabilitation.
1999: Best Supp. Actress (Angelina Jolie)

GIRL IN THE CADILLAC
1995, 89 mins, US Ⓥ
D: Lucas Platt **A:** Erika Eleniak, William McNamara, Michael Lerner, Bud Cort, Valerie Perrine, Ed Lauter (Steinhardt Baer)

Two terrifically appealing performers, William McNamara and Erika Eleniak, occupy the center of an amiable, if also slight and derivative, variation on the perennial theme of "love on the run." Pic is loosely adapted from a Depression-era James M. Cain novella.

GIRL IN THE NEWS, THE
1940, 77 mins, UK
D: Carol Reed **A:** Margaret Lockwood, Barry K. Barnes, Emlyn Williams, Roger Livesey, Basil Radford (20th Century-Fox)

A case of murder for Scotland Yard attention. Clever directorial and script twists make the film unusually entertaining. Carol Reed has a disarming faculty of employing bits of comedy as a means of revealing important plot incidents. Emlyn Williams, in a villainous role, gets across the murderous type. Lockwood is a registered nurse who escapes from under an almost perfect net of circumstantial evidence.

GIRL NAMED TAMIKO, A
1962, 110 mins, US ⌑
D: John Sturges A: Laurence Harvey, France Nuyen, Martha Hyer, Gary Merrill, Michael Wilding, Miyoshi Umeki (Paramount)

This story of emotional conflicts in modern-day Japan is a fairly arresting work. Laurence Harvey's character is not one immediately easy to accept and this is one of the flaws. As Ivan Kalin, he's a Chinese-Russian photographer and looks, speaks, and romances like a British matinee idol. The girl of the title is France Nuyen, thoroughly enchanting as the librarian whose family adheres to the Japanese traditions while she breaks away to engage in the romance with Harvey.

GIRL OF THE GOLDEN WEST, THE
1938, 120 mins, US Ⓥ
D: Robert Z. Leonard A: Jeanette MacDonald, Nelson Eddy, Walter Pidgeon, Leo Carrillo, Buddy Ebsen (M-G-M)

This musical mustanger with Jeanette MacDonald and Nelson Eddy finds the stars hemmed in by a two-hour mélange of the great outdoors, Mexican bandits, early Spanish-Californian atmosphere, and musical boredom. MacDonald is rarely convincing as The Girl who runs the mining town's lone saloon, and Nelson Eddy is a creampuff Mexican bad man. Sigmund Romberg score allows for but two duets by the stars, "Who Are We to Say?" and "Dance with Me, My Love."

GIRL ON A MOTORCYCLE, THE (AKA: NAKED UNDER LEATHER)
1968, 91 mins, UK/France Ⓥ
D: Jack Cardiff A: Alain Delon, Marianne Faithfull, Roger Mutton, Marius Goring, Catherine Jourdan (Mid Atlantic/Ares)

A pretty young girl in a leather form-fitting getup covering her nudity rides a powerful motorcycle toward her lover after creeping out of her young husband's bed. Her ride is studded with flashbacks and even flash forwards and psychedelic inserts of torrid lovemaking. The ride gets a bit long and the film lacks a true erotic flair. But it is well lensed and has a shattering finale.

GIRLS ABOUT TOWN
1931, 80 mins, US Ⓥ
D: George Cukor A: Kay Francis, Joel McCrea, Lilyan Tashman, Eugene Pallette, Lucille Gleason (Paramount)

Kay Francis intends on going straight because she's found love with a rich rube. She's the dame with a twisted virtue. Only the boyfriend would rather marry her than take her unawares even if she's willing. There's some additional sentiment brought in between the elder of the two chumps, as played ingenuously by Eugene Pallette, and his middle-aged wife, as done by Lucile Gleason.

GIRLS! GIRLS! GIRLS!
1962, 101 mins, US Ⓥ
D: Norman Taurog A: Elvis Presley, Stella Stevens, Jeremy Slate, Laurel Goodwin, Benson Fong, Robert Strauss (Paramount)

Girls! Girls! Girls! is just that—with Elvis Presley there as the main attraction. Production puts the entertainer back into the nondramatic, purely escapist light musical vein. Hackneyed tale is of poor-boy fisherman who meets rich girl who doesn't tell him she is rich but who, naturally, falls in love with him. Most striking thing about the picture is the introduction of Laurel Goodwin. Stella Stevens, however, is wasted as a sultry torch singer.

GIRLS HE LEFT BEHIND, THE
See: The Gang's All Here

GIRLS IN UNIFORM
See: Maedchen in Uniform

GIRL 6
1996, 107 mins, US Ⓥ ⊙
D: Spike Lee A: Theresa Randle, Isaiah Washington, Spike Lee, Jenifer Lewis, Debi Mazar, Quentin Tarantino (40 Acres & a Mule/20th Century-Fox)

Despite an intriguing premise and an appealing lead performance by Theresa Randle, Spike Lee's modestly scaled look at a young actress who becomes hooked on her job as a phone-sex operator crucially lacks narrative momentum and psychological depth. Interludes detailing her indoctrination into the world of this thriving business exert an undeniable fascination. More significantly, she soon not only becomes awfully good at "phone bone," but actually gets to like it. A lot. Madonna, done up like an old tart, is in briefly as the head of a more hardcore phone service.

GIRLS TOWN
1996, 88 mins, US Ⓥ
D: Jim McKay A: Lili Taylor, Anna Grace, Brucklin Harris, Aunjanue Ellis, Ramya Pratt, Guillermo Díaz (Zalaznick)

Lili Taylor gives a superlative, gutwrenching performance in a powerfully raw, ultrarealistic drama about a trio of abused teenage girls. Jim McKay's striking feature debut reveals a sensitive grasp of the feelings of young, mostly working-class women. McKay's camera acutely observes the girls' everyday life, at or around school. It's a tribute to the film's intelligent writing and superb ensemble acting that the tale unfolds in a natural manner, without resorting to melodramatic crises or signaling blatant messages.

GIRL WITH GREEN EYES
1964, 91 mins, UK ⓥ
D: Desmond Davis **A:** Peter Finch, Rita Tushingham, Lynn Redgrave, Marie Kean, Julian Glover, T. P. McKenna (Woodfall)

Story is set in Dublin. Rita Tushingham is a quiet, withdrawn girl. Lynn Redgrave is a vivacious, gabby, good-natured colleen with a roving eye for the boys. But when the two girls casually meet a quiet, middle-aged writer (Peter Finch), the friendship that starts up is, naturally, between Tushingham and Finch. Finch does a standout job as the writer who develops a fine understanding of the problems of the girl. Tushingham is often moving, sometimes spritely, and always interesting to watch.

GIRLY
See: Mumsy, Nanny, Sonny & Girly

GIRO CITY
(US: AND NOTHING BUT THE TRUTH)
1982, 102 mins, UK ⓥ
D: Karl Francis **A:** Glenda Jackson, Jon Finch, Kenneth Colley, James Donnelly, Emrys James (Silverclam)

A British thriller which examines political corruption and media attitudes to the rot on its doorstep. Story involves a documentary filmmaker and a reporter's attempts to cover two controversial news stories. A hard-hitting and emotional core is provided by the story of a family in South Wales who take on the local council in their determination to stay on their land. Glenda Jackson and Jon Finch as filmmaker and journalist are depicted as people for whom work covers up a hollow emotional core.

GIULIETTA DEGLI SPIRITI
(JULIET OF THE SPIRITS)
1965, 148 mins, Italy ⓥ ⊙
D: Federico Fellini **A:** Giulietta Masina,

Mario Pisu, Sandra Milo, Valentina Cortese, Sylva Koscina (Federiz)

Fellini has put together an imperial-sized fantasy of physical opulence. However, the film adds up to something less than its individual parts. In the title role, Giulietta Masina (Mrs. Fellini) is at first humble and appealing as she slowly drifts into a dreamworld to escape the hard facts of a crumbling marriage. But as the Fellini fantasies grow increasingly more bizarre, there comes the realization that these are not so much the fantasies of an unhappy woman as they are those of an imaginative film director with a huge budget at his disposal. It is a nonstop show dominated by the secondary performers, particularly Sandra Milo, a female presence seen here in three roles.

GIVE A GIRL A BREAK
1953, 81 mins, US ⓥ
D: Stanley Donen **A:** Marge Champion, Gower Champion, Debbie Reynolds, Helen Wood, Bob Fosse, Kurt Kasznar (M-G-M)

The talents of a group of youthful performers are showcased in this routine tintuner. Plot twist revolves around Champion, Reynolds, and Wood competing for the lead in a show being directed by Gower Champion. This showbiz background is ample excuse to work in the songs and dances and there is a certain amount of suspense over which girl will land the role.

GIVE MY REGARDS TO BROADWAY
1948, 89 mins, US
D: Lloyd Bacon **A:** Dan Dailey, Charles Winninger, Nancy Guild, Fay Bainter, Charles Ruggles, Barbara Lawrence (20th Century-Fox)

It's a simple story about an old vaude family that lives in the hope that the Palace two-a-day will sometime be revived. Film has plenty of showbiz nostalgia. Title song, cleffed by George M. Cohan, runs through the film as its theme. Dan Dailey gets a full chance to demonstrate his amazing versatility. Winninger does one of his neatest characterizations as the old-timer who refuses to toss in the sponge, and Bainter is fine as his understanding spouse.

GIVE US THIS DAY
(US: SALT TO THE DEVIL)
1949, 120 mins, UK

D: Edward Dmytryk **A:** Sam Wanamaker, Lea Padovani, Kathleen Ryan, Bonar Colleano (Plantagenet)

The moving simplicity of the Pietro Di Donato novel *Christ in Concrete* has been brought to the screen with rare sincerity. This is one of the few occasions when British studios have embarked on a production with a New York setting. Edward Dmytryk's direction ensures faithful atmosphere. Dmytryk presents the story of Geremio, an Italian bricklayer who works as a foreman on a job which he knows to be unsafe and which culminates in tragedy. Sam Wanamaker has never been better.

GLADIATOR
1992, 98 mins, US Ⓥ ⊙

D: Rowdy Herrington **A:** Cuba Gooding Jr., James Marshall, Robert Loggia, Ossie Davis, Brian Dennehy, John Heard (Columbia/Price)

Gladiator is an exercise in audience manipulation, an interracial buddy movie. Cuba Gooding Jr. receives top billing, but the film is relentlessly centered around his white pal, James Marshall. Early reels exploit the racial tensions in a Chicago high school en route to a predictable revelation that both sets of youngsters have a common enemy, the white businessman (Brian Dennehy) who stages their illegal boxing matches.

GLASS BOTTOM BOAT, THE
1966, 110 mins, US Ⓥ ▭

D: Frank Tashlin **A:** Doris Day, Rod Taylor, Arthur Godfrey, John McGiver, Paul Lynde, Edward Andrews (M-G-M/Arwin-Reame)

An expensively mounted production given frequently to sight gags and frenzied comedy performances. Doris Day plays a conscientious public-relations staffer in a space laboratory where Rod Taylor has invented a device both the US government and the Soviets want. She becomes a spy suspect because she has a dog named Vladimir, whom she's always calling on the telephone·so its ringing will give her pet exercise when she isn't home, and because she follows a standing order that every bit of paper should be burned.

GLASS KEY, THE
1935, 77 mins, US

D: Frank Tuttle **A:** George Raft, Edward Arnold, Claire Dodd, Ray Milland, Rosalind Keith, Guinn Williams (Paramount)

This is a tale of politics which involves murder, gangsterism, and rocky romances. Performances by Raft and others are excellent, the direction is skilled, and the dialogue job leaves little to be desired, but too much has gone into the narrative that is up the alley of inconsistency. Three romances are knitted into the murder mystery, but, in the main, the romantic aspects of the picture don't impress. Raft gives a fine performance, as does Edward Arnold, playing the aspiring politician.

GLASS KEY, THE
1942, 85 mins, US Ⓥ

D: Stuart Heisler **A:** Brian Donlevy, Veronica Lake, Alan Ladd, Bonita Granville, William Bendix, Joseph Calleia (Paramount)

Parading a murder mystery amid background of politics, gambling czars, romance, and lusty action, this revised version of Dashiell Hammett's novel—originally made in 1935—is a good picture of its type. Donlevy makes the most of his role` of the political leader who fought his way up from the other side of the tracks.

GLASS MENAGERIE, THE
1950, 106 mins, US

D: Irving Rapper **A:** Jane Wyman, Kirk Douglas, Gertrude Lawrence, Arthur Kennedy (Warner)

Spotting Jane Wyman as crippled Laura, Arthur Kennedy as her compassionate brother, Gertrude Lawrence as their frowsy mother, and Kirk Douglas as the Gentleman Caller who unwittingly changes their lives, for better or worse, is a casting scoop. Familiar plot about the aging southern belle who holds her brood together in a St. Louis tenement, only to lose her son when he decides he can take her nagging no longer, unreels engrossingly.

GLASS MENAGERIE, THE
1987, 130 mins, US Ⓥ ⊙

D: Paul Newman **A:** Joanne Woodward, John Malkovich, Karen Allen, James Naughton (Cineplex Odeon)

A reverent record of Tennessee Williams's 1945 dream play, and one watches with a kind of distant dreaminess rather than an intense emotional involvement. Amanda (Joanne Woodward) is every overbearing mother more than a specific character, and she and her children are drawn in broad strokes and dark colors that keep them at a distance and contain their emotional impact. Newman has heightened this impression by framing the action at the beginning and the end with Tom (John Malkovich) returning years later to look back at the wreck of his life. But the greater victim in this world is his crippled sister Laura (Karen Allen) who is doomed to live in perpetual waiting for a gentleman caller who will never come.

GLASS MOUNTAIN, THE
1949, 97 mins, UK
D: Henry Cass **A:** Dulcie Gray, Michael Denison, Valentina Cortese, Tito Gobbi, Sebastian Shaw (Victoria)

A romantic legend of thwarted love captivates an airman who is rescued in the Italian mountain district during the war. But on his return home to his wife, obsessed with writing an operatic piece on the theme, he cannot forget the girl he left behind. When the plot breaks away from its narrow limitations and gets out among the snow and the mountains, it becomes alive and moving.

GLASS SHIELD, THE
1995, 108 mins, US/France ⊗
D: Charles Burnett **A:** Michael Boatman, Lori Petty, Ice Cube, Michael Ironside, Richard Anderson, Elliott Gould (Byrnes-Schroeder-Walker/CiBy 2000)

A powerful moral drama that tries to deal with the racism at the root of many problems in contempo American society. Writer/director Charles Burnett frames his corrosive portrait around the story of an enthusiastic black rookie cop whose tragic personal journey sees him move from being part of the solution to part of the problem. At the outset, the youthful JJ (Michael Boatman) is not exactly given a warm welcome as the first black recruit at the rough, L.A. inner-city Edgemar station. Incident that sets the dense plot in motion is the arrest of Teddy Woods (Ice Cube) at a gas station. Woods is obviously pulled over by one of the Southern Cal surfer-type cops only because he's black, but when it turns out he's got a gun hidden under his car seat, he is booked and accused of murder. Anxious to fit in and prove himself on the squad, JJ, who was also at the scene, goes along with the lie.

GLASS SLIPPER, THE
1955, 93 mins, US ⊗
D: Charles Walters **A:** Leslie Caron, Michael Wilding, Keenan Wynn, Estelle Winwood, Elsa Lanchester, Barry Jones (M-G-M)

Leslie Caron, as drab and dirty as any scullery maid could have ever been, is the Cinderella who rides to the castle on her dreams, magically whisked into an enchantingly gowned, diademed princess fit for the prince played by Michael Wilding. Wilding does not seem happily cast in his character, nor does it get over to the viewer. Where *Slipper* makes its best points is in the Bronislau Kaper score and in the ballets.

GLASS WEB, THE
1953, 81 mins, US
D: Jack Arnold **A:** Edward G. Robinson, John Forsythe, Kathleen Hughes, Marcia Henderson, Richard Denning (Universal)

Production is concerned with a TV crime show. A good cast, a satisfactory murder-mystery script and nicely valued direction by Jack Arnold make for an okay unfolding of the melodramatics. Robinson, frustrated researcher, and John Forsythe, writer, are responsible for the *Crime of the Week* TV program. Both are being taken for money by Kathleen Hughes, TV actress. The blond blackmailer is killed and her death becomes the subject of a show, with her estranged husband apparently the patsy.

GLEAMING THE CUBE
1988, 105 mins, US ⊗ ⊙
D: Graeme Clifford **A:** Christian Slater, Steven Bauer, Min Luong, Art Chudabala, Le Tuan, Richard Herd (Gladden)

A skateboarding-obsessed suburban kid (Christian Slater) goes about solving—exploitation style—the death of his adopted Vietnamese brother (Art Chudabala). Slater skateboards all over Little Saigon, going in and out of minimalls skillfully enough to elude Vietnamese hoods on his trail while conducting some Chuck Norris–inspired sleuthing. Slater is the only character who has a shading of personality. The police are inept and the mastermind villain (Richard Herd) seems to be right out of the Method acting school.

GLENGARRY GLEN ROSS
1992, 100 mins, US ⊗ ⊙ ▭
D: James Foley **A:** Al Pacino, Jack Lemmon, Alec Baldwin, Ed Harris, Alan Ar-

kin, Kevin Spacey (New Line/Zupnick-Curtis)

The theatrical roots show rather clearly in *Glengarry Glen Ross*. A superb cast acts out one of David Mamet's major works. Harsh story examines the underhanded, eventually criminal activities of the salesmen as they compete to outdo each other in hustling dubious properties to phone clients. Piece remains gripping in a way, but not in as captivating or edifying a way as it did onstage. Reasons for this have to do with the rhythms of the acting, the camera's magnification of artificial devices, and director James Foley's mite fancy approach to stagebound material.

1992: Nomination: Best Supp. Actor (Al Pacino)

GLENN MILLER STORY, THE
1954, 115 mins, US ⓥ ⊙
D: Anthony Mann **A:** James Stewart, June Allyson, Charles Drake, George Tobias, Henry Morgan, Barton MacLane (Universal)

Sentiment and swing feature in this biopic treatment on the life of the late Glenn Miller. The Miller music, heard in some 20 tunes throughout the production, is still driving, rhythmic swing at its best. Music counterpoints a tenderly projected love story, feelingly played by James Stewart and June Allyson. The first 70 minutes is given over to Miller's search for a sound in music arrangement that would be his trademark and live after him. Remaining 45 minutes cover the rocketing Miller fame, his enlisting when World War II starts, and the service band's playing for overseas troops.

1954: Best Sound Recording
Nominations: Best Story & Screenplay, Scoring of a Musical Picture

GLEN OR GLENDA
1953, 65 mins, US ⓥ
D: Edward D. Wood Jr. **A:** Bela Lugosi, Daniel Davis [Edward D. Wood Jr.], ''Tommy'' Haynes, Lyle Talbot, Dolores Fuller, Timothy Farrell (Screen Classics)

Main story concerns Glen (Daniel Davis), a man who secretly dresses in women's clothes. Other story briefly deals with Alan (''Tommy'' Haynes), who is changed into Ann by a sex-change operation (presented tastefully). Use of stock footage, cheap sets, perfunctory visuals, and recited-lecture dialogue gives the picture a phony quality. What distinguishes it are the occasional mad flights of fancy. Most involve a weird scientist, delightfully

played by Bela Lugosi in eye-popping fashion.

GLORIA
1980, 123 mins, US ⓥ ⊙
D: John Cassavetes **A:** Gena Rowlands, John Adames, Buck Henry, Julie Carmen (Columbia)

Gloria is a glorious broad perhaps pushing 40. She has been in prison but now has her nest egg and just wants to be let alone. But she has to put her neck out again, and for a precocious kid, half–Puerto Rican. Cassavetes churns out a chase film that pits Gloria and the kid against the powerful Mafia no less. Gena Rowlands is excellent.

1980: Nomination: Best Actress (Gena Rowlands)

GLORY
1989, 122 mins, US ⓥ ⊙
D: Edward Zwick **A:** Matthew Broderick, Denzel Washington, Cary Elwes, Morgan Freeman, Cliff DeYoung, Jane Alexander (Tri-Star)

A stirring and long-overdue tribute to the black soldiers who fought for the Union cause in the Civil War, *Glory* tells the story of the 54th Regiment of Massachusetts Volunteer Infantry, the first black fighting unit raised in the North during the Civil War. Matthew Broderick's Colonel Shaw, the callow youth who proved his mettle in training and leading his black soldiers, is perfectly judged. The rage caused by ill treatment is searingly incarnated in a great performance by Denzel Washington, whose combative relationship with Broderick provides the dramatic heart of the film.

1989: Best Supp. Actor (Denzel Washington), Cinematography
Nominations: Best Editing, Art Direction, Sound

GLORY GUYS, THE
1965, 111 mins, US ⓥ ▭
D: Arnold Laven **A:** Tom Tryon, Harve Presnell, Senta Berger, James Caan, Andrew Duggan, Slim Pickens (United Artists)

An entertaining US Cavalry–Indian conflict, sparked by an opportunist army general who sacrifices dedicated soldiers to his ambition. Brawling fisticuffs, comedy, and romantic triangle mark a slightly forced plot until an exciting climax. Adaptation by Sam Peckinpah of Hoffman Birney's novel *The Dice of God* finds Andrew Duggan very effective as a general again in responsible command despite prior goofs. Tryon is somewhat wooden and Presnell too refined for a frontier scout.

G-MEN
1935, 84 mins, US ⊘
D: William Keighley **A:** James Cagney, Margaret Lindsay, Ann Dvorak, Robert Armstrong, Barton MacLane, Lloyd Nolan (First National/Warner)

This is red hot off the front page. But new idea of glorifying the government gunners who wipe out the killers has nothing but a weak scenario along hackneyed lines. James Cagney is a government man. Sprinkled through and around that is just about every situation from the Dillinger–Baby Face Nelson etc. saga. The Kansas City depot massacre is paralleled, the Dillinger escape from a Chicago apartment, the Wisconsin resort roundup, the bank holdups throughout Kansas-Missouri, et al.

GO
1999, 103 mins, US ⊘ ⊙ ▭
D: Doug Liman **A:** Desmond Askew, William Fichtner, Jane Krakowski, Sarah Polley, Scott Wolf, Jay Mohr (Banner/Columbia)

Go is an overly calculated concoction that nonetheless delivers a pretty good rush. The film exerts a magnetic pull from the outset, thanks largely to the mesmerizing Sarah Polley. She plays Ronna, an L.A. checkout girl who fills in for her Brit coworker Simon (Desmond Askew) so he can holiday in Vegas. Approached by two actors (Scott Wolf, Jay Mohr) interested in scoring drugs, Ronna does business with Simon's dealer, Todd (Timothy Olyphant), but betrays him when she senses she's being set up in a sting. Todd's about to gun her down when Ronna is run over and left for dead in a ditch. Story then rewinds to follow Simon to Las Vegas, then once again to concentrate on the two actors. The combination of lively action, responsive performances, raging soundtrack, and bold widescreen visuals shoots off the screen.

GO-BETWEEN, THE
1971, 118 mins, UK ⊘ ⊙
D: Joseph Losey **A:** Julie Christie, Alan Bates, Margaret Leighton, Michael Redgrave, Michael Gough, Edward Fox (EMI)

In its glimpse of the manners and mores of the British socialites at the beginning of the century, *The Go-Between* is both fascinating and charming. It is Michael Redgrave looking back at a definitive event of his boyhood, acting as the contact (or go-between) between the daughter of the house—with whom he believes himself to be in love—and the tenant farmer, although the girl is already betrothed to a member of the aristocracy. It is the boy who has the pivotal role, and Dominic Guard, a screen newcomer, appears to play his part effortlessly.

1971: Nomination: Best Supp. Actress (Margaret Leighton)

GODFATHER, THE
1972, 175 mins, US ⊘ ⊙
D: Francis Coppola **A:** Marlon Brando, Al Pacino, James Caan, Richard Conte, Robert Duvall, Sterling Hayden (Paramount)

Film version of Mario Puzo's sprawling gangland novel best of all gives some insight into the origins and heritage of that segment of the population known off the screen (but not on it) as the Mafia or Cosa Nostra. In *The Godfather* we have the New York–New Jersey world, ruled by five ''families,'' one of them headed by Brando. This is a world where emotional ties are strong, loyalties are somewhat more flexible at times, and tempers are short. Brando does an admirable job. It is Pacino who makes the smash impression here. Initially seen as the son whom Brando wanted to go more or less straight, Pacino matures under trauma of an assassination attempt on Brando, his own double-murder revenge for that on corrupt cop Sterling Hayden and rival gangster Al Lettieri, the countervengeance murder of his Sicilian bride, and a series of other personnel readjustments.

1972: Best Picture, Actor (Marlon Brando), Adapted Screenplay
Nominations: Best Director, Supp. Actor (James Caan, Robert Duvall, Al Pacino), Music [later declared ineligible], Costume Design, Editing, Sound

GODFATHER, PART II, THE
1974, 200 mins, US ⊘ ⊙
D: Francis Coppola **A:** Al Pacino, Robert Duvall, Diane Keaton, Robert De Niro, John Cazale, Lee Strasberg (Paramount/Coppola)

Far from being a spin-off follow-up to its 1972 progenitor, *Part II* is an excellent epochal drama in its own right. Al Pacino again is outstanding as Michael Corleone, successor to crime-family leadership. The scenes alternate between Pacino's career in Nevada gambling rackets from about 1958 on and Robert De Niro's early life in Sicily and New York City. A natural break comes after 126 minutes when De Niro, involved with low-level thievery, brutally assassinates Gaston Moschin, the neighborhood crime boss, without a shred of conscience. It's the only shocking brutality in the film.

1974: Best Picture, Director, Supp. Actor (Robert De Niro), Adapted Screenplay, Art Direction, Original Score
Nominations: Best Actor (Al Pacino), Supp. Actor (Michael V. Gazzo, Lee Strasberg), Supp. Actress (Talia Shire), Costume Design

GODFATHER, PART III, THE
1990, 161 mins, US Ⓥ ⊙
D: Francis Coppola **A:** Al Pacino, Diane Keaton, Talia Shire, Andy Garcia, Eli Wallach, Joe Mantegna (Zoetrope/Paramount)

The Godfather, Part III matches its predecessors in narrative intensity, epic scope, sociopolitical analysis, physical beauty, and deep feeling for its characters and milieu. It is 1979, and Michael Corleone, having divested himself of his illegal operations, dotes on his daughter Mary (Sofia Coppola) and becomes perturbed by her affair with cousin Vincent (Andy Garcia). Vincent has been unhappily working for slumlord and old-style thug Joey Zasa (Joe Mantegna). Bad blood between the ruthless Zasa and the Corleone family mounts. After 80 minutes, the action switches to Italy. Pacino and Eli Wallach's old dons can't help begin scheming against one another. For the third time out in his career role, Pacino is magnificent. Garcia brings much-needed youth and juice to the ballsy Vincent, heir apparent to the Corleone tradition. Film's main flaw, unavoidably, is Sofia Coppola in the important, but not critical, role of Michael's daughter.

1990: Nominations: Best Picture, Director, Supp. Actor (Andy Garcia), Cinematography, Art Direction, Editing, Song ("Promise Me You'll Remember")

GOD IS MY CO-PILOT
1945, 83 mins, US
A: Dennis Morgan, Dane Clark, Raymond Massey, Alan Hale, Andrea King (Warner)

Narrative uses flashback technique to condense life of Colonel Robert Lee Scott Jr., army ace who gained fame with General Chennault's Flying Tigers. Air-fight sequences bear an authentic stamp, although studio-made. Title derives from

Scott's realization that a pilot doesn't face danger alone, and several of his real-life brushes with death sustain the belief.

GOD'S LITTLE ACRE
1958, 112 mins, US Ⓥ
D: Anthony Mann **A:** Robert Ryan, Aldo Ray, Tina Louise, Fay Spain, Buddy Hackett, Jack Lord (United Artists)

Rousing, rollicking, and ribald, God's Little Acre is a rustic revel with the kick of a Georgia mule. The production of Erskine Caldwell's novel is adult, sensitive, and intelligent. The story remains that of a Georgia farmer (Robert Ryan) who believes he can find gold on his farm. Ryan dominates the picture, as his character should. Aldo Ray, as his son-in-law, creates a moving characterization as the husband torn between his wife, sensitively played by Helen Westcott, and the voluptuous barnyard Susannah, strikingly projected by Tina Louise.

GODS MUST BE CRAZY, THE
1981, 108 mins, Botswana Ⓥ ⊙ ▭
D: Jamie Uys **A:** Marius Weyers, Sandra Prinsloo, N!xau, Louw Verwey, Jamie Uys (CAT)

A comic fable by one-man-band South African filmmaker Jamie Uys. Basic story line has Xi (N!xau), a bushman who lives deep in the Kalahari desert, setting off on a trek to destroy a Coca-Cola bottle which has caused great dissension within his tribe. Xi plans to throw the unwanted artifact of modern civilization off the edge of the world and in his trek encounters modern people.

GODS MUST BE CRAZY II, THE
1989, 99 mins, Botswana/US Ⓥ ⊙
D: Jamie Uys **A:** N!xau, Lena Farugia, Hans Strydom, Eiros, Nadies, Erick Bowen (Troskie/Weintraub)

A genial sequel to 1981 international sleeper hit The Gods Must Be Crazy that is better than its progenitor in most respects. Tongue-clicking Kalahari Bushman hero, again played by a real McCoy named N!xau, is once more unwittingly embroiled in the lunacies of civilization. First plotline has N!xau's two adorable offspring getting innocently borne away on the trailer truck of a pair of unsuspecting ivory poachers. N!xau follows the tracks and comes across two other odd couples from the nutty outside world.

GODSPELL
1973, 103 mins, US
D: David Greene **A:** Victor Garber, David

Haskell, Jerry Sroka, Lynne Thigpen, Katie Hanley (Columbia)

A youth-slanted reworking of the Gospel According to St. Matthew. Film follows original 1971 off-Broadway legit production closely. Result is that original production's appealing aspects have remained intact—a strong Stephen Schwartz score and an infectious joie de vivre conveyed by an energetic, no-name cast. So also, unfortunately, have its flaws—a relentlessly simplistic approach to the New Testament interpreted in overbearing children's-theater-style mugging.

GODZILLA
1998, 138 mins, US Ⓥ ◉
D: Roland Emmerich **A:** Matthew Broderick, Jean Reno, Maria Pitillo, Hank Azaria, Kevin Dunn, Michael Lerner (Centropolis/TriStar)

Godzilla is not so much a remake as a reinvention of the 1954 Japanese production that spawned scores of sequels, comic books, and television commercials. Dr. Niko Tatopoulos (Matthew Broderick), a biologist, is whisked to New York to help with a big problem. Broderick conveys a gee-whiz ingenuousness that is distracting at best, insipid at worst. In sharp contrast, Jean Reno offers a crafty mix of foreboding and bemusement as Philippe Roache, a French secret agent. By the time Tatopoulos and company get to Manhattan, the creature is ready to make his American debut at the Fulton Fish Market. When fully visible it resembles nothing more than a hybrid of the mother beast from *Alien* and a T-Rex from *Jurassic Park*. Godzilla designer and supervisor Patrick Tatopoulos does a bang-up job. But there is little that is charismatic about his handiwork. Size does matter, of course, but other things matter more.

GO FISH
1994, 85 mins, US Ⓥ ◉
D: Rose Troche **A:** V. S. Brodie, Guinevere Turner, T. Wendy McMillan, Migdalia Melendez (Can I Watch)

Rose Troche makes an auspicious debut as director, cowriter, and editor of a fresh, hip comedy about contemporary lifestyles within the lesbian community. The most refreshing dimension of *Go Fish* is that it's not dealing with coming out and is not burdened with the stiff, sanctimonious tone of such lesbian films as *Claire of the Moon*. The well-written comedy conveys the folklore that women share when there are no men around—sort of a current, lesbian version of Gregory La Cava's *Stage Door*. As director, Troche elicits perfectly natural performances from her mostly nonprofessional ensemble.

GO FOR BROKE!
1951, 90 mins, US Ⓥ
D: Robert Pirosh **A:** Van Johnson, Lane Nakano, George Miki, Akira Fukunaga, Ken K. Okamoto, Warner Anderson (M-G-M)

The case of the Japanese Americans who fought with honor in Italy and France during the Second World War is objectively treated. Robert Pirosh keeps his script and direction on an intimate level, projecting the story through Van Johnson, as a typical American who draws back from the thought of being assigned as a brand-new lieutenant to head a group of "Buddha-Heads," as the Nisei are known. Yarn works in quite a number of chuckles. Johnson does an excellent job of his assignment, and the heroes of the 442nd Regiment Combat Team who costar with him add to the naturalism of the production.

GOING HOME
1971, 97 mins, US ◉
A: Robert Mitchum, Brenda Vaccaro, Jan-Michael Vincent, Jason Bernard, Sally Kirkland (M-G-M)

A most unusual and intriguing melodrama about a teenage boy's vengeance against his father for the long-ago killing of his mother. Robert Mitchum in an off-beat role gives an excellent performance as the crude but sensitive father. Jan-Michael Vincent is very effective as his son. Brenda Vaccaro, as Mitchum's sweetheart, makes a catalytic role into a memorable experience.

GOING MY WAY
1944, 126 mins, US Ⓥ ◉
D: Leo McCarey **A:** Bing Crosby, Rise Stevens, Barry Fitzgerald, Gene Lockhart, Frank McHugh (Paramount)

Picture is a warm, human drama studded liberally with bright episodes and excellent characterizations accentuated by fine direction of Leo McCarey. Intimate scenes between Crosby and Fitzgerald dominate throughout, with both providing slick characterizations. Crosby plays a young priest who's assigned as assistant to crusty Fitzgerald in an East Side church saddled with burdensome mortgage that might be foreclosed by grasping Gene Lockhart. Progressive youth and staid oldster clash continually, but Crosby gradually bends Fitzgerald to his way. Crosby's song numbers include three new tunes by Johnny Burke and James Van Heusen.

1944: Best Picture, Director, Actor (Bing Crosby), Supp. Actor (Barry Fitzgerald), Original Story, Screenplay, Song ("Swinging on a Star")
Nominations: Best Actor (Barry Fitzgerald), B&W Cinematography, Editing

GOING PLACES
See: Les Valseuses

GOIN' SOUTH
1978, 101 mins, US 🅥 ⊙
D: Jack Nicholson **A:** Jack Nicholson, Mary Steenburgen, Christopher Lloyd, John Belushi, Veronica Cartwright, Danny DeVito (Paramount)

Jack Nicholson playing Gabby Hayes is interesting, even amusing at times, but Hayes was never a leading man, which *Goin' South* desperately needs. On his way to the gallows, hapless outlaw Nicholson discovers an unordinary county ordinance that would allow him to go free if picked for marriage by a maiden lady in town. Lovely young Mary Steenburgen agrees to marry the bearded, dirty horse thief. Why she should do this is never satisfactorily established.

GO INTO YOUR DANCE
1935, 92 mins, US ⊙
D: Archie Mayo **A:** Al Jolson, Ruby Keeler, Glenda Farrell, Barton MacLane, Patsy Kelly (First National/Warner)

Lavishly produced, vigorously directed, and agreeably entertaining musical picture has Al Jolson in top form, plus a nifty set of songs. Jolson plays the role of a talented actor who has broken up many a hit show by going off on bats. The star is finally barred from the musical stage. With the help of his devoted sister and a dancing girl with whom he teams up, the banished star starts his comeback via the nightclub field. Keeler is given plenty of footage for her dancing. On the hoof she's a girl who can take good care of herself, and in the histrionic moments she's carried along by Jolson's aggressive trouping.

1935: Nomination: Best Dance Direction ("Lady from Manhattan")

GOLD
1974, 118 mins, UK 🅥 ▭
D: Peter Hunt **A:** Roger Moore, Susannah York, Ray Milland, Bradford Dillman, John Gielgud (Hemdale/Avton)

An exciting motion picture lensed entirely in the South Africa locale of its well-developed narrative. Roger Moore plays a tough mine foreman unwittingly manipulated by an unscrupulous gang of financiers who want to flood the mine to raise the price of gold on the world market. Tremendous realism is accomplished in an opening tragedy of men caught in the grip of a sudden flood and later in the climactic flooding.

1974: Nomination: Best Song ("Wherever Love Takes Me")

GOLD DIGGERS OF 1933
1933, 94 mins, US 🅥 ⊙
D: Mervyn LeRoy, Busby Berkeley **A:** Warren William, Joan Blondell, Aline MacMahon, Ruby Keeler, Dick Powell, Guy Kibbee (Warner)

The real feature of *Gold Diggers of 1933* is the numbers staged by Busby Berkeley. The film's superiority to *42nd Street* lies in the greater romance interest, with a multiplicity of amorous complications wherein Warren William and Joan Blondell, and Guy Kibbee and Aline MacMahon, are paired off as subinterest to the Ruby Keeler–Dick Powell coupling. Once the numbers get going, nothing else matters. There are five impressive songs by Al Dubin and Harry Warren.

1932/33: Nomination: Best Sound

GOLD DIGGERS OF 1935
1935, 95 mins, US 🅥 ⊙ ▭
D: Busby Berkeley **A:** Dick Powell, Gloria Stuart, Adolphe Menjou, Glenda Farrell, Grant Mitchell, Alice Brady (Warner)

As in the previous *Diggers*, it's the spec that counts, but the story deficiencies are a bit more acute. Adolphe Menjou does the best job as the irascible, chiseling entrepreneur. The Al Dubin–Harry Warren songs this time miss a bit. "The Words Are in My Heart" is the waltz theme, reprised for the choreography with the baby grands—a highly effective ballet of the Steinways. "Lullaby of Broadway" is the final musical elaboration. Latter number, led by Winifred Shaw, runs overboard in footage.

1935: Best Song ("Lullaby of Broadway")
Nominations: Best Dance Direction ("Lullaby of Broadway," "The Words Are in My Heart")

GOLD DIGGERS OF 1937
1936, 101 mins, US
D: Lloyd Bacon, Busby Berkeley **A:** Dick Powell, Joan Blondell, Victor Moore,

Glenda Farrell, Lee Dixon, Osgood Perkins (Warner)

Musical opus gets moving with the advantage of a trim backstage yarn taken from *Mystery of Life*, the Broadway play by Richard Maibaum, Michael Wallach, and George Haight. Cast as a cocksure insurance salesman, Dick Powell breezes through the picture like he had been selling policies all his life. He has four outstanding songs, never overdoes them, and breaks through with his ballads at the most opportune times.

1936: Nomination: Best Dance Direction ("Love and War")

GOLD DIGGERS OF BROADWAY
1929, 105 mins, US
D: Roy Del Ruth **A:** Nancy Welford, Conway Tearle, Winnie Lightner, Ann Pennington, Lilyan Tashman, Nick Lucas (Warner)

Lots of color—Technicolor—lots of comedy, girls, songs, music, dancing, production. Somebody tossed the picture into Winnie Lightner's lap. Mugging, talking, singing, or slapsticking, she can do them all, and does in this picture. Next to Lightner in work is her comedy opposite, Albert Gran, as a gray-haired heavyweight lawyer.

GOLDEN BRAID
1990, 91 mins, Australia ⱱ
D: Paul Cox **A:** Chris Haywood, Gosia Dobrowolska, Paul Chubb, Norman Kaye, Marion Heathfield (AFC/Film Victoria)

Paul Cox has often dealt with obsession in his work, and his protagonist here, Bernard (Chris Haywood), fits well and truly into this obsessive pattern. Of Central European extraction, Bernard lives alone in a world of clocks. Bernard is also involved in an affair with Terese (Gosia Dobrowolska), wife of an unsuspecting Salvation Army major (Paul Chubb). The lovers enjoy a guilt-free relationship which cools only when Bernard is sidetracked by a new obsession: a braid of hair he discovers in a 100-year-old, supposedly Venetian, cabinet.

GOLDEN CHILD, THE
1986, 93 mins, US ⱱ ⊙
D: Michael Ritchie **A:** Eddie Murphy, Charles Dance, Charlotte Lewis, Victor Wong, J. L. Reate, Randall "Tex" Cobb (Feldman/Meeker/Murphy)

A strange hybrid of Far Eastern mysticism, treacly sentimentality, diluted reworkings of Eddie Murphy's patented

confrontation scenes across racial and cultural boundaries, and dragged-in ILM (Industrial Light & Magic) special-effects monsters, film makes no sense on any level.

GOLDENEYE
1995, 130 mins, US ⱱ ⊙ ▭
D: Martin Campbell **A:** Pierce Brosnan, Sean Bean, Izabella Scorupco, Famke Janssen, Joe Don Baker, Judi Dench (Broccoli/United Artists)

Among the better of the 17 Bonds [to-date] and a dynamic action entry in its own right, this first 007 adventure in six years breathes fresh creative and commercial life into the 33-year-old series. Pierce Brosnan makes a solid debut in the role and Ian Fleming's very midcentury secret agent has been shrewdly repositioned in the nineties. Realizing they're up against errant forces in the now unpredictable new Russia, MI6 realizes this is a job for James Bond. In St. Petersburg, Bond discovers that the shadow figure pulling the evil strings is none other than his old pal Alec, 006. Just about the only holdover from the old days is Desmond Llewelyn's Q, who again outfits Bond with a few bizarre gadgets that just happen to come in handy. Pic has a fine adversary in Bean's Alec. The stunning Famke Janssen's deliciously sadistic Xenia instantly assumes an almost unique position in the pantheon as a potential Bond girl gone very bad.

GOLDEN RENDEZVOUS
1977, 103 mins, US ⱱ
D: Ashley Lazarus **A:** Richard Harris, Ann Turkel, David Janssen, Burgess Meredith, John Vernon, Gordon Jackson (Film Trust/Okun/Golden Rendezvous)

Despite an overabundance of plot, deaths, and explosions, there's virtually nothing in this puddle of a mid-ocean thriller that wouldn't make a 12-year-old cringe in embarrassment. Pic tells the tale of the *Caribbean Star*, a combination cargo ship and floating casino, hijacked by mercenary John Vernon. First Officer Richard Harris, accompanied by Ann Turkel and Gordon Jackson, steps in to save the day.

GOLDEN VOYAGE OF SINBAD, THE
1974, 105 mins, UK ⱱ ⊙
D: Gordon Hessler **A:** John Phillip Law, Caroline Munro, Tom Baker, Douglas Wilmer, Martin Shaw, Gregoire Aslan (Columbia)

An Arabian Nightish saga told with some briskness and opulence for the childish eye, yet ultimately falling short of implied promise as an adventure spree. Ray Harryhausen encores as coproducer and special-effects collaborator. Among his creations: an animated ship's figurehead, a grotesque centaur, a many-armed religious idol and swordplay adversary, and a couple of small batlike creatures performing intelligence duty for the black artsy heavy of the piece.

GOLDFINGER
1964, 112 mins, UK Ⓥ ⊙
D: Guy Hamilton **A:** Sean Connery, Honor Blackman, Gert Frobe, Shirley Eaton, Tania Mallet, Harold Sakata (United Artists/Eon)

There's not the least sign of staleness in this third sample of the Bond 007 formula. The real business is the duel between Bond and Goldfinger. The latter plans to plant an atomic bomb in Fort Knox and thus contaminate the US hoard of the yellow stuff so that it can't be touched, and thus increase tenfold the value of his own gold, earned by hard international smuggling. Connery repeats his suave portrayal of the punch-packing Bond. Ken Adam has designed the production with a wealth of enticing invention. As Pussy Galore, Honor Blackman makes a fine, sexy partner for Bond. Gert Frobe, too, is near-perfect casting as the resourceful Goldfinger.
1964: Best Sound Effects

GOLD OF THE SEVEN SAINTS
1961, 89 mins, US
D: Gordon Douglas **A:** Clint Walker, Roger Moore, Leticia Roman, Robert Middleton, Chill Wills, Gene Evans (Warner)

A strong screenplay is the firm foundation upon which the picture remains erect and engrossing until its disappointingly shaky conclusion. Walker and Moore are cast as trapping partners who strike it rich and are chased persistently over the sprawling desert and through craggy hill country by several marauding parties who have one thing in common—total disdain for the golden rule.

GOLD RUSH, THE
1925, 120 mins, US Ⓥ ⊗
D: Charles Chaplin **A:** Charles Chaplin, Mack Swain, Tom Murray, Georgia Hale (Chaplin)

The Gold Rush is a distinct triumph for Charlie Chaplin from both the artistic and commercial standpoints. Billed as a dramatic comedy, the story carries more of a plot than the star's former offerings. Charlie is presented as a tramp prospector in the wilds of Alaska, garbed in his old familiar derby, cane, baggy pants, and shoes. Humor is the dominating force, with Chaplin reaching new heights as a comedian. Chaplin naturally carries practically the entire 10 reels of action and performs this task without difficulty.

GOLD RUSH, THE
1942, 71 mins, US Ⓥ
D: Charles Chaplin **A:** Charles Chaplin, Mack Swain, Georgia Hale, Tom Murray (United Artists)

With music and dialogue added, Charlie Chaplin's *The Gold Rush* stands the test of time. Chaplin's inimitable cane, derby, hobble, and mustache of early days still retain solid comedy for both the younger generation and older folks. Chaplin did a remarkable job in the editing, background, music, and dialogue for the new version of his greatest grosser. Original two hours of running time has been edited down to 71 minutes. All the episodes of *Gold Rush* are retained to provide strong comedy reaction of original, like the prospector's cabin marooned in the storm with Chaplin stewing the shoe when food runs out; Chaplin's own dialogue is crisply delivered, and he refers to his screen character as "The Little Fellow" throughout.
1942: Nominations: Best Scoring of a Dramatic Picture, Sound

GOLDWYN FOLLIES, THE
1938, 113 mins, US Ⓥ
D: George Marshall **A:** Adolphe Menjou, Ritz Brothers, Zorina, Kenny Baker, Andrea Leeds, Ella Logan (Goldwyn/United Artists)

The astute Samuel Goldwyn has assembled top names from grand opera, class terpsichore, music, radio, and films. The mixture, in the brilliant hues of Technicolor, turns out to be a lavish production. Four of the musical numbers were composed by the late George Gershwin, with lyrics by Ira Gershwin; Vernon Duke completed the score.
1938: Nomination: Best Score

GO NAKED IN THE WORLD
1961, 103 mins, US ▭
D: Ranald MacDougall **A:** Gina Lollobrigida, Anthony Franciosa, Ernest Borg-

nine, Luana Patten (M-G-M/Arcola)

It is Gina Lollobrigida's turn to play the trollop with the heart of gold and bank account to match. She shares an ill-fated love affair with Anthony Franciosa, rebellious son of a dominant, self-made construction tycoon (Ernest Borgnine). Screenplay adds a novel twist and a new dimension to the now classic story of hooked and hooker in that father, like son, has shared intimate relations with the girl.

GONE TO EARTH
(US: THE WILD HEART)
1950, 110 mins, UK
D: Michael Powell, Emeric Pressburger **A:** Jennifer Jones, David Farrar, Cyril Cusack, Sybil Thorndike (London/Vanguard)

A simple girl, steeped in local mysticism, when asked by her father if she will marry the first man to propose, she agrees. The first proposal is from the local parson, but after the wedding, she is induced to run away with the squire. Jones makes the character a pathetic, winsome creature. It is a genuine and at times glowing performance.

GONE WITH THE WIND
1939, 217 mins, US Ⓥ ⊙
D: Victor Fleming, [George Cukor, Sam Wood, B. Reeves Eason] **A:** Clark Gable, Vivien Leigh, Leslie Howard, Olivia de Havilland, Hattie McDaniel, Thomas Mitchell (Selznick)

One of the truly great films. The lavishness of its production, the consummate care and skill which went into its making, the assemblage of its fine cast and expert technical staff combine in a theatrical attraction completely justifying the princely investment of $3.9 million. In the desire apparently to leave nothing out, Selznick has left too much in. As in the book, the most effective portions of the saga of the destroyed South deal with human incident against the background of the War Between the States and the impact of honorable defeat to the Southern forces. Among the players, Leigh's Scarlett commands first commendation as a memorable performance, of wide versatility and effective earnestness. Gable's Rhett Butler is as close to Mitchell's conception as might be imagined. He gives a forceful impersonation. Of the other principals, de Havilland does a standout as Melanie, and Howard is convincing as the weak-charactered Ashley.
1939: Best Picture, Director, Actress (Vivien Leigh), Supp. Actress (Hattie McDaniel), Screenplay, Color Cinematography, Art Direction, Editing, Special Awards (use of color design, and use of coordinated equipment)
Nominations: Best Actor (Clark Gable), Supp. Actress (Olivia de Havilland), Original Score, Sound, Special Effects

GOODBYE CHARLIE
1964, 117 mins, US ▭
D: Vincente Minnelli **A:** Tony Curtis, Debbie Reynolds, Pat Boone, Joanna Barnes, Ellen Burstyn, Walter Matthau (Venice/20th Century-Fox)

The mildest type of entertainment. A hotshot Hollywood-writer Lothario named Charlie is thoroughly punctured by a gun-wielding Hungarian producer and is reincarnated as a luscious babe. Debbie Reynolds as the reincarnated late-departed combines the lecherous mind and mores of her former male self with a sexy exterior and newfound femininity while announcing to the world she is the writer's widow. Tony Curtis plays victim's best friend, who finds himself saddled with this reborn pal.

GOODBYE, COLUMBUS
1969, 104 mins, US Ⓥ ⊙
D: Larry Peerce **A:** Richard Benjamin, Ali MacGraw, Jack Klugman, Nan Martin, Michael Meyers (Paramount/Willow Tree)

This adaptation of Philip Roth's novella is sometimes a joy in striking a boisterous mood and otherwise handling action. Richard Benjamin as the boy, a librarian after serving in the army, and Ali MacGraw, making her screen bow as the daughter of wealthy and socially conscious parents, offer fresh portrayals seasoned with rich humor. Their romance develops swiftly after their meeting at a country-club pool.
1969: Nomination: Best Adapted Screenplay

GOODBYE GIRL, THE
1977, 110 mins, US Ⓥ ⊙
D: Herbert Ross **A:** Richard Dreyfuss, Marsha Mason, Quinn Cummings, Paul Benedict, Barbara Rhoades (M-G-M/Warner)

Richard Dreyfuss in offbeat romantic lead casting and vibrant Marsha Mason head the cast as two lovers in spite of themselves. Story peg finds Mason finding out that her ex-lover has sublet their NY pad to aspiring thesp Dreyfuss. Mason has two other problems: a precocious daughter, Quinn Cummings, and her own thirtyish age, which will prevent a successful resumption of a dancing career necessary to make ends meet.

1977: Best Actor (Richard Dreyfuss) **Nominations:** Best Picture, Actress (Marsha Mason), Supp. Actress (Quinn Cummings), Original Screenplay

GOODBYE, MR. CHIPS
1939, 110 mins, UK ⊗ ☉
D: Sam Wood **A:** Robert Donat, Greer Garson, Terry Kilburn, John Mills, Paul Heinreid (M-G-M)

A charming, quaintly sophisticated account of the life of a schoolteacher, highlighted by a remarkably fine performance from Robert Donat. Donat's range of character carries him from youth into the slightly doddering age. The romance of the schoolteacher and the girl he meets is adroitly and fascinatingly developed. Greer Garson is Katherine, who becomes Donat's wife.

1939: Best Actor (Robert Donat) **Nominations:** Best Picture, Director, Actress (Greer Garson), Screenplay, Editing, Sound

GOODBYE, MR. CHIPS
1969, 151 mins, UK ⊗ ☉ ▭
D: Herbert Ross **A:** Peter O'Toole, Petula Clark, Michael Redgrave, George Baker, Sian Phillips (M-G-M/Apjac)

M-G-M's reproduction of *Goodbye, Mr. Chips* as a big-budget musical with Peter O'Toole and Petula Clark is a sumptuous near miss that trips on its own overproduction. The scholarly, somewhat prissy and martinetish teacher who frets that his students don't like him is a total departure from O'Toole's previous roles. He creates a man of strength and dignity, whose tendency to appear ridiculous at times is endearing.

1969: Nominations: Best Actor (Peter O'Toole), Adapted Music Score

GOODBYE, NORMA JEAN
1976, 95 mins, US/Australia ⊗ ▭
D: Larry Buchanan **A:** Misty Rowe, Terrence Locke, Patch Mackenzie, Preston Hanson, Marty Zagon, Andre Philippe (Austamerican)

This is the story of Norma Jean Baker, who finds her body irresistible to men and uses it to fulfill her ambitions of becoming a movie star, Marilyn Monroe. Thesping is mostly sound, with Misty Rowe in the title role, giving a fine and sensitive performance, catching the star's own voice exactly.

GOODBYE PEOPLE, THE
1984, 104 mins, US ⊗ ☉
D: Herb Gardner **A:** Judd Hirsch, Martin Balsam, Pamela Reed, Ron Silver, Michael Tucker, Gene Saks (Coney Island)

The Goodbye People marks stage author and director Herb Gardner's first foray into film direction. Based on his late-1960s stage flop of the same name, neither time nor the transfer of media has improved the story of three eccentric losers who band together in hopes of changing their luck.

GOODBYE PORK PIE
1981, 100 mins, New Zealand ⊗
D: Geoff Murphy **A:** Kelly Johnson, Tony Barry, Claire Oberman, Shirley Gruar, Bruno Lawrence (Ama)

In *Goodbye Pork Pie, Easy Rider* meets the Keystone Kops. Following the classic road formula, a car chase covers the length of the country and it is a major plus that the pace, fun, and general mayhem do not get upstaged by the spectacular scenery. In the breathing spells between, characters that might have been ciphers—the young punk on the run, the girl hitch-hiker and others whose paths intersect the speeding car—are given human dimensions.

GOOD COMPANIONS, THE
1933, 110 mins, UK
D: Victor Saville **A:** Jessie Matthews, Edmund Gwenn, John Gielgud, Mary Glynne (Gaumont-British)

J. B. Priestley bestseller deals with a theatrical company that goes from bankruptcy to fame and fortune, helped by the stray people who flit across the canvas, the schoolmaster who writes jazz, the fading damsel who finances the show from a thirst for adventure, the little chorus girl who rises to be a great star, and so on. Characterizations are outstanding. Edmund Gwenn, as the carpenter who is really the center of the story, does the best bit of work.

GOOD COMPANIONS, THE
1957, 105 mins, UK ▭
D: J. Lee Thompson **A:** Eric Portman, Celia Johnson, Hugh Griffith, Janette Scott, John Fraser, Rachel Roberts (Associated British)

J. B. Priestley's homely and colorful yarn of a third-rate touring company makes a pedestrian musical. Much of the characterization and writing quality of the original is lost in the conventional screenplay. An old-fashioned story line, without surprise twists, is not aided by the moderate quality of the score. Janette Scott makes a refreshing and appealing showing as the concert party star with ambitions.

GOOD DIE YOUNG, THE
1954, 98 mins, UK
D: Lewis Gilbert A: Laurence Harvey, Gloria Grahame, Richard Basehart, Joan Collins, John Ireland, Stanley Baker (Romulus)

Yarn takes four characters, brought together by force of circumstances, who participate in an armed holdup and come to a sticky end, clearly to satisfy a censor's insistence that crime mustn't pay. First of the four central figures is Richard Basehart, playing an ex-GI and Korean War vet. The second is Stanley Baker, a professional boxer. Then there is John Ireland, an American airman. Finally, there is Laurence Harvey, an aristocratic English gent who conceives the holdup and talks the others into participating.

GOOD EARTH, THE
1937, 140 mins, US Ⓥ
D: Sidney Franklin A: Paul Muni, Luise Rainer, Walter Connolly, Tillie Losch, Charley Grapewin, Jessie Ralph (M-G-M)

Adaptation of the [Pearl S.] Buck novel is a tough job. The marriage of Wang and O-Lan, their raising of the family and care of their land, the drought, Wang's rise to wealth, his desertion of the farm and his taking of a second wife, his return to the farm and the earth are faithfully transcribed. There are some additions, such as the locust plague, which is a helpful contribution rather than a distraction, but the members of the House of Wang are Pearl Buck's original creations. Muni as Wang, with a great makeup, is a splendid lead. Rainer has more difficulty, since her features are not so receptive to Oriental makeup. Yet a good actress overcomes these things, and Luise Rainer is an actress.
1937: Best Actress (Luise Rainer), Cinematography
Nominations: Best Picture, Director, Editing

GOOD FAIRY, THE
1935, 98 mins, US
D: William Wyler A: Margaret Sullavan, Herbert Marshall, Frank Morgan, Reginald Owen, Alan Hale, Beulah Bondi (Universal)

Preston Sturges has translated Ferenc Molnar's dainty stage comedy to the screen, and has turned out a somewhat vociferous paraphrase. Slightly idealistic atmosphere of the original is missing, and in its place is substituted a style of comedy closely akin to slapstick.

GOODFELLAS
1990, 146 mins, US Ⓥ ◉
D: Martin Scorsese A: Robert De Niro, Ray Liotta, Joe Pesci, Lorraine Bracco, Paul Sorvino (Warner)

Simultaneously fascinating and repellent, *Goodfellas* is Martin Scorsese's colorful but dramatically unsatisfying inside look at Mafia life from 1955 to 1980 in New York City. First half of the film, introing Ray Liotta, as an Irish-Italian kid, to the Mafia milieu, is wonderful. The second half, however, doesn't develop the dramatic conflicts between the character and the milieu that are hinted at earlier. Liotta starts as a gofer for laconic neighborhood godfather Paul Sorvino, gradually coming under the tutelage of Robert De Niro, cast as a middle-aged Irish hood of considerable ruthlessness and repute. One of the film's major flaws is that De Niro, with his menacing charm, always seems more interesting than Liotta, but he isn't given enough screen time to explore the relationship fully in his supporting role.
1990: Best Supp. Actor (Joe Pesci)
Nominations: Best Picture, Director, Supp. Actress (Lorraine Bracco), Adapted Screenplay, Editing

GOOD GUYS AND THE BAD GUYS, THE
1969, 90 mins, US ⊟
D: Burt Kennedy A: Robert Mitchum, George Kennedy, David Carradine, Martin Balsam, Tina Louise, Lois Nettleton (Warners-Seven Arts)

George Kennedy plays the film mostly for comedy, and Mitchum's deadpan performance might be interpreted in same lineage. Story concerns two relics of the Old West, an aging marshal and a similarly aging outlaw far past his prime. Onetime enemies, they now combine to thwart the efforts of a band of young outlaws to rob a train.

GOOD MORNING, VIETNAM
1987, 120 mins, US Ⓥ ◉
D: Barry Levinson A: Robin Williams, Forest Whitaker, Tung Thanh Tran, Chintara Sukapatana, Bruno Kirby, J. T. Walsh (Touchstone)

After airman Adrian Cronauer (Robin Williams) blows into Saigon to be the morning man on armed-forces radio, things are never the same. On the air he's a rush of energy, perfectly mimicking everyone from Gomer Pyle to Richard Nixon as well as the working grunt in the battlefields, blasting verboten rock and roll over the airwaves while doing James Brown splits in the studio. From the start, the film bowls you over with excitement, and for those who can latch on, it's a non-stop ride.

1987: Nomination: Best Actor (Robin Williams)

GOOD MOTHER, THE
1988, 103 mins, US Ⓥ ⊙
D: Leonard Nimoy **A:** Diane Keaton, Liam Neeson, Jason Robards, Ralph Bellamy, Teresa Wright (Touchstone)

The traumatic subject matter of a child-custody fight is handled with restraint and intelligence. Well-judged script presents Anna Dunlap (Diane Keaton) as the recently divorced mother of Molly, an enthusiastic child of six. Anna is committed to her daughter above all else. Skittish and insecure where men are concerned, she nevertheless allows herself to be seduced by Leo (Liam Neeson), an iconoclastic, thoroughly charming Irish sculptor. Anna's cold ex-husband Brian (James Naughton) slaps a custody suit on her, announcing that Molly has informed him that Leo in some way molested her sexually. This is compelling stuff, and the performances are uniformly first-rate.

GOOD NEIGHBOR SAM
1964, 130 mins, US Ⓥ
D: David Swift **A:** Jack Lemmon, Romy Schneider, Edward G. Robinson, Dorothy Provine, Michael Connors, Neil Hamilton (Columbia)

Jack Lemmon's farcical flair finds amusing exposure in this situation comedy. But it is the Viennese Romy Schneider, making her first Hollywood-lensed feature, who shines the brightest. Lemmon finds himself called upon to play the ''husband'' to his next-door neighbor, who is divorced and must come up with a spouse if she is to meet the provisions of her grandfather's will in bequeathing her his $15-million estate.

GOOD SAM
1948, 114 mins, US Ⓥ
D: Leo McCarey **A:** Gary Cooper, Ann Sheridan, Ray Collins, Edmund Lowe, Joan Lorring, Ruth Roman (RKO/Rainbow)

Good Sam is a comedy whose central character, played by Gary Cooper, often slows the film's pace because of a languidness and too obviously premeditated performance in a pic that in itself is unusually long. Sam cosigns bank loans for friends who never pay up; he lends his car to neighbors without knowing actually how he's going to get to work or the children to school. Sam loves everybody. In short, everyone sponges on him. And Lu, his wife, constantly harasses Sam to get some sense. Domestication is hardly Sheridan's cinematic dish, no matter how authentic looking are her scrambled eggs. Cooper gives one of his standard performances.

GOOD SON, THE
1993, 87 mins, US Ⓥ ⊙
D: Joseph Ruben **A:** Macauley Culkin, Elijah Wood, Wendy Crewson, David Morse, Daniel Hugh Kelly, Jacqueline Brookes (20th Century-Fox)

The *Home Alone* kid as an amoral, psychotic killer? What next, Barney leveling Tokyo? This rather peculiar thriller doesn't deliver enough jolts to leave the audience screaming. The action centers around another prominent moppet, Elijah Wood, playing a young boy with some very bad luck. Not only does Mark (Wood) watch his mother die, but he's sharing a room with a prepubescent psychopath. At first, Henry (Culkin) seems only a bit eccentric, but the stunts gradually become more outrageous, until he hints that he did away with his brother and tries to off his baby sister. Culkin's cold, dispassionate performance will evoke too many laughs of the derisive kind.

GOOD, THE BAD AND THE UGLY, THE
1966, 161 mins, Italy Ⓥ ⊙ ▭
D: Sergio Leone **A:** Clint Eastwood, Eli Wallach, Lee Van Cleef, Aldo Giuffre, Mario Brega (PEA)

The Good, the Bad and the Ugly is exactly that—a curious amalgam of the visually striking, the dramatically feeble, and the offensively sadistic. Story concerns search for buried treasure by ''Good'' Eastwood, ''Ugly'' Eli Wallach, and ''Bad'' Lee Van Cleef. Unlike the earlier Leone efforts, the violence here has little of the balletic, even erotic quality. Leone's visual sense is as strong as ever, however, and his effective alternation of extreme close-ups and long shots renders much of the pic graphically electric.

GOOD WIFE, THE
1986, 92 mins, Australia Ⓥ
D: Ken Cameron **A:** Rachel Ward, Bryan Brown, Sam Neill, Steven Vidler, Jennifer

498

Claire, Bruce Barry (Laughing Kooka-burra)

A classy romantic drama set in a small Australian country town in 1939. Rachel Ward toplines as the eponymous wife who's bored with her unexciting life in this rural backwater. She's married to a burly, well-intentioned logger. Neville Gifford (Sam Neill) arrives in town. Marge becomes more and more obsessed with the handsome stranger.

GOOD WILL HUNTING
1997, 126 mins, US Ⓥ ⊙
D: Gus Van Sant **A:** Matt Damon, Robin Williams, Ben Affleck, Minnie Driver, Stellan Skarsgard, Casey Affleck (Miramax)

Gus Van Sant's emotionally involving psychological drama is a notch or two above the mainstream therapeutic sensibility of its story. This beautifully realized tale is always engaging and often quite touching. Protagonist is Will Hunting (Damon), a 20-year-old lad who works as a janitor at MIT. When professor Lambeau (Stellan Skarsgard) presents a math challenge to his students, Will solves the formula. Lambeau takes him under his wing on condition that Will begins therapy. Lambeau summons his old classmate Sean McGuire (Robin Williams), a community college instructor and therapist, and the real drama begins. Damon gives a charismatic performance in a demanding role. Williams work here is quieter, subtler and far more satisfying than in *Awakenings*.
1997: Best Supp. Actor (Robin Williams), Original Screenplay
Nominations: Best Picture, Actor (Matt Damon), Supp. Actress (Minnie Driver), Director, Editing, Original Dramatic Score, Original Song (''Miss Misery'')

GOONIES, THE
1985, 111 mins, US Ⓥ ⊡
D: Richard Donner **A:** Sean Astin, Josh Brolin, Jeff Cohen, Corey Feldman, Kerri Green, Martha Plimpton (Amblin)

Territory is typical small-town Steven Spielberg, this time a coastal community in Oregon. Story is told from the kids' point of view and takes a rather long time to be set in motion. Brothers Mikey (Sean Astin) and Brand (Josh Brolin) are joined by compulsive eater Chuck (Jeff Cohen) and mumbling Mouth (Corey Feldman). Searching through the attic, the boys uncover a pirate treasure map and begin their fairy-tale treasure hunt.

GORGEOUS HUSSY, THE
1936, 103 mins, US Ⓥ
D: Clarence Brown **A:** Joan Crawford, Robert Taylor, Lionel Barrymore, Franchot Tone, Melvyn Douglas, James Stewart (M-G-M)

Picture is primarily Lionel Barry-more's, and not particularly because the character of Andrew Jackson he portrays calls for it. His tenderness toward his backwoods wife, his rough-and-ready fighting spirit in the campaign for presidency, his opening address to Congress, his sorrow over his wife's death, and his bitter encounter with his cabinet—all are portrayed with acting acumen. Joan Crawford makes her debut in a costumer and figures in four love affairs.
1936: Nominations: Best Supp. Actress (Beulah Bondi), Cinematography

GORILLAS IN THE MIST
THE STORY OF DIAN FOSSEY
1988, 129 mins, US Ⓥ ⊙
D: Michael Apted **A:** Sigourney Weaver, Bryan Brown, Julie Harris, John Omirah Miluwi, Iain Cuthbertson (Universal/Warner)

The late anthropologist Dian Fossey devoted nearly 20 years to observing, and trying to protect, the gorillas who live in a small area in the Virunga mountain range, which extends into Rwanda. Sigourney Weaver is utterly believable and riveting in the role. Her scenes with the apes are captivating. Bryan Brown lends a nice lilt to his sympathetic interloper. Lensed high in the mountains of Rwanda, the production looks impressive.
1988: Nominations: Best Actress (Sigourney Weaver), Adapted Screenplay, Editing, Original Score, Sound

GORKY PARK
1983, 128 mins, US Ⓥ ⊙
D: Michael Apted **A:** William Hurt, Lee Marvin, Brian Dennehy, Ian Bannen, Joanna Pacula (Orion)

William Hurt is superb as a Moscow militia detective. Director Michael Apted sets Hurt up well with the discovery of three mutilated, faceless bodies in the city's Gorky Park, leading Hurt to suspect this is all the affair of the dangerous KGB and much to be avoided by plodding policemen such as himself. Very quickly, Hurt's investigation brings him into contact with Lee Marvin, a wealthy American who enjoys high privilege in important Soviet circles, obviously not simply because he's a successful trader in sables.

GOSPEL ACCORDING TO ST. MATTHEW, THE
See: Il Vangelo Secondo Matteo

GO TELL THE SPARTANS
1978, 114 mins, US Ⓥ ⊙
D: Ted Post **A:** Burt Lancaster, Craig Wasson, Jonathan Goldsmith, Marc Singer, Joe Unger (Mar Vista/Spartan)

A good war film needs heroes. But Vietnam had no heroes in the eyes of most Americans. Even a reasonably well-made and well-acted earnest effort like *Go Tell The Spartans*, set in 1964 when the US involvement was limited to "military advisers," can't overcome that disadvantage. Burt Lancaster leads a mostly untried cast. All turn in fine performances.

GOTHIC
1986, 90 mins, UK Ⓥ ⊙
D: Ken Russell **A:** Gabriel Byrne, Julian Sands, Natasha Richardson, Myriam Cyr, Timothy Spall, Andreas Wisniewski (Virgin)

Ken Russell is back to his theatrically extravagant best. Set on a stormy June night in 1816 at the Villa Diodati in Switzerland, the drug-induced excesses of the poet Byron (Gabriel Byrne) and his four guests inspire Mary Shelley to write *Frankenstein* and Dr. Polidori to write *The Vampyre*, two gothic horrror classics. Russell has made an unrelenting nightmare that is both uncomfortable and compelling to watch.

GO WEST
1925, 69 mins, US ⊗
D: Buster Keaton **A:** Buster Keaton, Kathleen Myers, Howard Truesdale (Keaton/M-G-M)

This has Buster Keaton slipping over a series of comedy stunts that cause but mild laughter. Buster gets a job as a cowhand and makes a pet of Brown Eyes, one of the milch cows in the herd. The ranch owner decides to ship 1,000 head to market and includes the cow, but when the hand tries to save her, he is paid off. A rival rancher tries to cause the shipment to be lost, but it is the comic cowhand that saves the day.

GO WEST
1940, 79 mins, US Ⓥ
D: Edward Buzzell **A:** Groucho Marx, Harpo Marx, Chico Marx, John Carroll, Diana Lewis, Walter Woolf King (M-G-M)

The three Marx Brothers ride a merry trail of laughs and broad burlesque in a speedy adventure through the sagebrush country. Groucho, Chico, and Harpo handle their assignments with zestful enthusiasm. There's a bill-changing routine in Grand Central Station, wild melee and clowning in the rolling stagecoach, a comedy safecracking episode, and the train chase for a finish that winds up with the upper-car structures dismantled by the silent Harpo to provide fuel for the engine. It's all ridiculous, but tuned for fun.

GO WEST, YOUNG MAN
1936, 80 mins, US
D: Henry Hathaway **A:** Mae West, Warren William, Randolph Scott, Lyle Talbot, Alice Brady, Isabel Jewell (Major/Paramount)

Mae West makes a rough-and-ready, very sexy character all the way through. West's swagger, the hands-on-hip business, and various devilish expressions are in almost constant evidence. In the scene in which West makes a play for Randolph Scott, the star forces him into a brief dance bit. When she pats him a bit somewhere below the shoulder blades in a rather coyish, affectionate manner, it's one of the big laughs of the feature.

GRACE OF MY HEART
1996, 116 mins, US Ⓥ ⊙
D: Allison Anders **A:** Illeana Douglas, Matt Dillon, Eric Stoltz, Bruce Davison, Patsy Kensit, John Turturro (Cappa)

Part biopic of a singer-songwriter who waits most of her career to be heard, and part paean to a golden decade of American pop music, Allison Anders's *Grace of My Heart* is an ambitious comedy-drama that is energetic and entertaining, even if it loses steam in its disharmonious final act. Illeana Douglas is an admirably unconventional choice to play gifted songwriter and singer Edna Buxton (reportedly modeled on Carole King), who leaves behind her wealthy Philadelphia family to pursue a music career. John Turturro gives credibility and a great deal of humor to music-biz manager Joel, who is presented as a work-focused, insensitive hustler. Playing a weak-willed womanizer with delusions of integrity, Eric Stoltz also scores.

GRACE QUIGLEY
See: The Ultimate Solution of Grace Quigley

GRADUATE, THE
1967, 105 mins, US Ⓥ ⊙ ▭
D: Mike Nichols **A:** Anne Bancroft, Dustin Hoffman, Katharine Ross, William

Daniels, Murray Hamilton, Elizabeth Wilson (Embassy)

A delightful, satirical comedy-drama about a young man's seduction by an older woman, and the measure of maturity he attains from the experience. Predatory Bancroft, wife of Murray Hamilton, introduces Hoffman to mechanical sex, reaction to which evolves into true love with Ross, Bancroft's daughter. Only in the final 35 minutes, as Hoffman drives up and down the L.A.-Frisco route in pursuit of Ross, does film falter in pacing.
1967: Best Director
Nominations: Best Picture, Actor (Dustin Hoffman), Actress (Anne Bancroft), Supp. Actress (Katharine Ross), Adapted Screenplay, Cinematography

GRAFFITI BRIDGE
1990, 95 mins, US Ⓥ ⊙
D: Prince **A:** Prince, Ingrid Chavez, Morris Day, Jerome Benton, Mavis Staples (Warner/Paisley Park)

Reviving the characters from Prince's 1984 hit *Purple Rain,* including a reunited Morris Day and the Time, *Graffiti Bridge* is a $7.5-million indulgence that amounts to a half-baked retread of tired MTV imagery and childish themes. That Prince wrote and directed this homage to his own creative process is evident. Mostly this amounts to a cinematic sandbox in which the Mascaraed One can play, pose, and change costumes, inviting most of his gang to join in.

LE GRAND BLEU
(THE BIG BLUE)
1988, 136 mins, France Ⓥ ⊙ ▭
D: Luc Besson **A:** Jean-Marc Barr, Jean Reno, Rosanna Arquette, Paul Shenar, Sergio Castellito (Gaumont/Films du Loup)

A waterlogged yarn about a couple of rival championship divers. Produced on a disproportionately large scale ($12-million budget, a nine-month shoot on international locations from Greece to Peru), this English-language adventure is indigently plotted and lacking in genuine dramatic and human interest. The underwater sequences, as splendidly lensed as they are, have little intrinsic suspense and quickly become repetitive. The land scenes are boring because Besson has been unable to give his characters any psychological density.

GRAND CANYON
1991, 134 mins, US Ⓥ ⊙ ▭
D: Lawrence Kasdan **A:** Danny Glover, Kevin Kline, Steve Martin, Mary McDonnell, Mary-Louise Parker, Alfre Woodard (20th Century-Fox)

Life in L.A. is the pits, according to scripters Lawrence and Meg Kasdan in their earnest, often moving, but not totally successful film. Danny Glover is given a juicy role as the moral voice of a film mourning the loss of civility in a society torn apart by the widening chasm—the Grand Canyon—between rich and poor. Kline, also very good in his more understated way, conveys the edgy uncertainty of a white liberal struggling to cope with life in a city whose police routinely terrorize angry black inhabitants. The Steve Martin character is a wicked caricature of action-pic maker Joel Silver.
1991: Nomination: Best Original Screenplay

LE GRAND CHEMIN
(THE GRAND HIGHWAY)
1987, 107 mins, France Ⓥ
D: Jean-Loup Hubert **A:** Anemone, Richard Bohringer, Antoine Hubert, Vanessa Guedj, Christine Pascal (Flach/Selena/TF1)

Le Grand Chemin is a bittersweet heartwarmer about a city boy's near-traumatic stay in the country with a childless couple. Scripted from personal memories and directed with warm restraint by Jean-Loup Hubert, production offers a good blend of pathos and humor, and excellent performances from adult and child thesps alike.

LA GRANDE ILLUSION
(US: GRAND ILLUSION)
1937, 94 mins, France Ⓥ ⊙
D: Jean Renoir **A:** Jean Gabin, Pierre Fresnay, Erich von Stroheim, Dalio, Dita Parlo, Gaston Modot (RAC)

An artistically masterful feature, the picture breathes the intimate life of warriors on both sides during the [First] World War. While the plot centers about the superhuman efforts of a group of French officers, captured in battle, to escape from prison camps, the story concerns various members of human society all juggled about by the terrific conflict. Authors and director have laid emphasis on this when two military leaders, one a shell of humanity serving as a prison keeper and the other a captured enemy officer, console and display hearty respect for each other. Pierre Fresnay is the polished aristocratic

French officer. Erich von Stroheim, cast as a German army officer, appears in one of his most sympathetic roles.

GRAND HIGHWAY, THE
See: Le Grand Chemin

GRAND HOTEL
1932, 105 mins, US ⊘ ⊙
D: Edmund Goulding **A:** Greta Garbo, John Barrymore, Joan Crawford, Wallace Beery, Lionel Barrymore, Jean Hersholt (M-G-M)

Story is many-angled in characters and incidents. First honors again go to Lionel Barrymore for an inspired performance as the soon-to-die bookkeeper. Greta Garbo gives the role of the dancer something of artificiality, risking a trace of acting swagger, sometimes stagy. Her clothes are ravishing in the well-known Garbo style. John Barrymore is back where he belongs as the down-at-heel but glamorous baron. Wallace Beery is at home in the part of the German industrialist, a grandiose but pathetic figure in his struggles with business rivals.
1931/32: Best Picture

GRAND ILLUSION
See: La Grande Illusion

LE GRAND MEAULNES (THE WANDERER)
1967, 110 mins, France ⊘ ▭
D: Jean-Gabriel Albicocco **A:** Brigitte Fossey, Jean Blaise, Alain Libolt, Alain Jean, Marcel Cuvilier (Madeleine/AWA)

A rather glossy, sentimental opus that too often uses prettiness in imagery for its own sake and a mixture of styles. Meaulnes (Jean Blaise) once met a girl at a ball but he can't find her again. He spends time searching and then gives up and goes to Paris, where he meets a girl who was the fiancée of the brother of the mysterious girl. If this sounds involved, it is. Brigitte Fossey has the right quality as the dream symbol, but the pains of adolescence, idealism, and youthful coming-of-age are somewhat lost in the maze of pretty images.

GRAND PRIX
1966, 179 mins, US ⊙ ▭
D: John Frankenheimer **A:** James Garner, Eva Marie Saint, Yves Montand, Toshiro Mifune, Brian Bedford, Jessica Walter (Douglas & Lewis/M-G-M)

The roar and whine of engines sending men and machines hurtling over the 10 top road-and-track courses of Europe, the US, and Mexico—the Grand Prix circuits—are the prime motivating forces of this action-crammed adventure interlarded with personal drama that is sometimes introspectively revealing, occasionally mundane, but generally a most serviceable framework. Frankenheimer has shrewdly varied the length and the importance of the races that figure in the film, and the overplay of running commentary on the various events, not always distinct above the roar of motors, imparts a documentary vitality. The director, moreover, frequently divides his outsized screen into sectional panels for a sort of montage interplay of reactions of the principals. There is a curious thing, however, about the characters in this screenplay. Under cold examination they are stock characters.
1966: Best Sound, Editing, Sound Effects

GRAND THEFT AUTO
1977, 89 mins, US ⊘
D: Ron Howard **A:** Ron Howard, Nancy Morgan, Marion Ross, Pete Isacksen, Barry Cahill (New World)

Grand Theft Auto is a nonstop orgy of comic destructiveness. Ron Howard has directed with a broad but amiable and well-disciplined touch in this screwball comedy about his elopement with heiress Nancy Morgan from L.A. to Las Vegas, with her father Barry Cahill and dozens of others in pursuit.

GRAPES OF WRATH, THE
1940, 129 mins, US ⊘ ⊙
D: John Ford **A:** Henry Fonda, Jane Darwell, John Carradine, Charley Grapewin, Dorris Bowdon, John Qualen (20th Century-Fox)

The Grapes of Wrath, adapted by Nunnally Johnson from John Steinbeck's bestseller, is an absorbing, tense melodrama, starkly realistic, and loaded with social and political fireworks. The film interprets the consequences of national disaster in terms of a family group—the Joads—who left their quarter section to the wind and dust and started cross-country in an overladen jalopy to the land of plenty. It is not a pleasant story, and the plight of the Joads, and hundreds of other dust-bowl refugee families, during their frantic search for work in California, is a shocking visualization of a state of affairs demanding generous humanitarian attention. Under Ford's direction a group of actors makes the characters into living people, whose frustration catches at the heart and throat. There is humor, too, but

the film as a whole scores as a gripping experience.
1940: Best Director, Supp. Actress (Jane Darwell)
Nominations: Best Picture, Actor (Henry Fonda), Screenplay, Editing, Sound

GRASS HARP, THE
1995, 107 mins, US Ⓥ
D: Charles Matthau **A:** Piper Laurie, Sissy Spacek, Walter Matthau, Sean Patrick Flannery, Nell Carter, Jack Lemmon (Matthau-Tokofsky-Davis)

Helmer Charles Matthau combines a sensitive screenplay adaptation of Truman Capote's autobiographical novel *The Grass Harp* with a wonderful ensemble cast to create a jewel of a film. Collin Fenwick, Capote's alter ego (Grayson Frick), is forced to move in with the Talbo sisters (Piper Laurie, Sissy Spacek). Laurie is the sensitive Dolly, who makes do during the Depression peddling a home remedy created in her kitchen. Dolly's sister Verena (Spacek) is a businesswoman who owns most of the stores in town. Episodic story focuses on Collin's coming-of-age, with Edward Furlong taking over as the teenage character. While no performance is off the mark, the film rises or falls on the Talbo sisters, and Laurie and Spacek are riveting.

GRASSHOPPER, THE
1970, 96 mins, US Ⓥ
D: Jerry Paris **A:** Jacqueline Bisset, Jim Brown, Joseph Cotten, Corbett Monica, Ramon Bieri (National General)

The dark side of the Hollywood story. Jacqueline Bisset is attracted by the tinsel of Las Vegas. Attractive and busty enough to make the chorus, but neither talented nor ambitious enough to go beyond, she drifts into a bad marriage, being kept by a rich old man and then into outright hustling, having run the gamut by age 22. Bisset is kept carefully within her dramatic depth by Director Jerry Paris, with unexpected outbreaks of a kooky humor.

GRASS IS GREENER, THE
1960, 105 mins, US Ⓥ ▭
D: Stanley Donen **A:** Cary Grant, Deborah Kerr, Robert Mitchum, Jean Simmons (Universal/Grandon)

A talky and generally tedious romantic exercise. A romantic triangle develops among the Earl (Cary Grant), his wife (Deborah Kerr), and a ''rip-roaring grade-A romantic'' American millionaire (Robert Mitchum), who promptly and preposterously falls in love with her, she with

him. Balance of the picture is concerned with Grant's efforts to woo his wife back to his side.

GRAY LADY DOWN
1978, 111 mins, US Ⓥ ▭
D: David Greene **A:** Charlton Heston, David Carradine, Stacy Keach, Ned Beatty, Stephen McHattie, Ronny Cox (Mirisch/Universal)

Charlton Heston is back in jeopardy. He's 60 miles off the coast of Connecticut stuck with 41 other sailors on the edge of an ocean canyon in a nuclear submarine, waiting for Stacy Keach to organize a rescue mission. Enter Carradine, a subdued navy captain and inventor of an experimental diving vessel known as the Snark, and his assistant, Beatty. They resemble a disaster movie's Laurel and Hardy. They're a nice twist.

GREASE
1978, 110 mins, US Ⓥ ⊙ ▭
D: Randal Kleiser **A:** John Travolta, Olivia Newton-John, Stockard Channing, Jeff Conaway, Eve Arden, Joan Blondell (Paramount)

Grease has got it, from the outstanding animated titles of John Wilson all the way through the rousing finale as John Travolta and Olivia Newton-John ride off into teenage happiness. Plot tracks the bumpy romantic road of Travolta and Newton-John, whose summer beach idyll sours when he feels he must revert to finger-snapping cool in the atmosphere of the high school they both wind up attending.
1978: Nomination: Best Song (''Hopelessly Devoted to You'')

GREASE 2
1982, 114 mins, US Ⓥ ⊙ ▭
D: Patricia Birch **A:** Maxwell Caulfield, Michelle Pfeiffer, Adrian Zmed, Eve Arden, Connie Stevens, Tab Hunter (Paramount)

Gorgeous Michelle Pfeiffer plays the leader of the foxy Pink Ladies. Maxwell Caulfield, fresh from England and complete with accent, is the new boy in school, and it's made clear to him that Pfeiffer is off-limits until he proves himself as a leather-clad biker. Where this film has a decided edge on its predecessor is in the staging and cutting of the musical sequences. Choreographer and director Patricia Birch has come up with some unusual settings and employs some sharp montage to give most of the songs and dances a fair amount of punch.

GREASED LIGHTNING
1977, 96 mins, US ⊗
D: Michael Schultz **A:** Richard Pryor, Beau Bridges, Pam Grier, Cleavon Little, Vincent Gardenia (Third World)

Greased Lightning is a pleasant, loose, and relaxed comedy starring Richard Pryor in an excellent characterization based on real-life racing driver Wendell Scott. Beau Bridges plays a redneck driver who helps Pryor's stolid efforts to break the color barrier in car racing. Pam Grier is wasted in a supportive-wife role.

GREAT AMERICAN BROADCAST, THE
1941, 90 mins, US ⊗
D: Archie Mayo **A:** Alice Faye, Jack Oakie, John Payne, Cesar Romero, the Four Ink Spots (20th Century-Fox)

Light and breezy, a showmanly admixture of comedy, romance, drama, and music woven around the extraordinary progress of radio broadcasting during the 1920s. Oakie tinkers with a crystal set in his room, idea-minded Payne gets enthusiastic over wireless entertainment possibilities, Faye is radio's first singing star, and Romero supplies the early coin.

GREAT BALLS OF FIRE!
1989, 108 mins, US ⊗ ⊙
D: Jim McBride **A:** Dennis Quaid, Winona Ryder, Alec Baldwin, John Doe, Stephen Tobolowsky, Trey Wilson (Orion)

A thin, cartoonish treatment of the hell-bent, musically energetic young Jerry Lee Lewis. Full-bore performance by Dennis Quaid as the kinetic piano-pumper stops at surface level, and 108 minutes of his gum-cracking smirks and cock-a-doodle-doo dandyism are hard to take.

GREAT CARUSO, THE
1951, 109 mins, US ⊗
D: Richard Thorpe **A:** Mario Lanza, Ann Blyth, Dorothy Kirsten, Jarmila Novotna, Richard Hageman, Carl Benton Reid (M-G-M)

This highly fictionalized, sentimental biog of the late, great Metropolitan Opera tenor Enrico Caruso, handsomely mounted in Technicolor, has a set of popular ingredients, including a boy-and-girl-vs.-disapproving-parent romance, the draw of Caruso's rep, glamour of the Met, a host of surefire, familiar operatic arias, and the pull of Mario Lanza. Otherwise, the film is a superficial pic, bearing little relationship to Caruso's actual story, which was a much more dramatic one than emerges here.

Lanza is handsome, personable, and has a brilliant voice. He's a lyric tenor, like Caruso; has his stocky build, his Italianate quality, and some of his flair.
1951: Best Sound Recording
Nominations: Best Color Costume Design, Scoring of a Musical Picture

GREAT CATHERINE
1968, 98 mins, UK
D: Gordon Flemyng **A:** Peter O'Toole, Zero Mostel, Jeanne Moreau, Jack Hawkins, Akim Tamiroff (Warner/Seven Arts)

Atmosphere it has, mammoth and impressive sets, Zero Mostel as a wildman like you've never seen, Peter O'Toole as a stuffy Englishman like you've never imagined, all wrapped around the amorous yearnings of Catherine of Russia. This is a souped-up version of the Russian empress's romantics, focused on her going on the make for a slightly imbecilic English light-dragoons captain. Jeanne Moreau essays Catherine with humor.

GREAT DICTATOR, THE
1940, 127 mins, US ⊗
D: Charles Chaplin **A:** Charles Chaplin, Paulette Goddard, Jack Oakie, Reginald Gardiner, Henry Daniell, Billy Gilbert (Chaplin/United Artists)

Chaplin makes no bones about his utter contempt for dictators like Hitler and Mussolini. He plays a dual role, that of a meek little Jewish barber in Tomania and the great little dictator of that country, billed as Hynkel. It's when he is playing the dictator that the comedian's voice raises its comedy content of the picture to great heights. He does various bits as a Hitler spouting a lot of double talk in what amounts to a pig-Latin version of the German tongue. Somewhat of a shock is the complete transformation of the barber when he delivers a fiery and impassioned plea for freedom and democracy. It is a peculiar and somewhat disappointing climax. Not so much action is devoted to the dictator who is Napaloni (Mussolini). Jack Oakie plays the satirized Duce to the hilt and every minute with him is socko.
1940: Nominations: Best Picture, Actor (Charles Chaplin), Supp. Actor (Jack Oakie), Original Screenplay, Original Score

GREAT ESCAPE, THE
1963, 171 mins, US ⊗ ⊙ ▭
D: John Sturges **A:** Steve McQueen, James Garner, Richard Attenborough, James Donald, Charles Bronson, Donald

Pleasence (Mirisch/United Artists)

From Paul Brickhill's true story of a remarkable mass breakout by Allied POWs during World War II, producer-director John Sturges has fashioned a motion picture that entertains, captivates, thrills, and stirs. The most provocative single impression is made by Steve McQueen as a dauntless Yank pilot. James Garner is the compound's ''scrounger,'' a traditional type in the *Stalag 17* breed of war-prison film. British thespians weigh in with some of the finest performances in the picture. Richard Attenborough is especially convincing.

1963: Nomination: Best Editing

GREATEST, THE
1977, 101 mins, US Ⓥ
D: Tom Gries **A:** Muhammad Ali, Ernest Borgnine, John Marley, Lloyd Haynes, Robert Duvall (Columbia)

Muhammad Ali is a natural performer. More to the point, starring in his own autobiopic, he brings an authority and a presence that lift John Marshall's production above some of the limitations inherent in any film bio. Intercut are actual sequences from Ali's major fights.

GREATEST SHOW ON EARTH, THE
1952, 151 mins, US Ⓥ ⊙
D: Cecil B. DeMille **A:** Betty Hutton, Cornel Wilde, Charlton Heston, Dorothy Lamour, Gloria Grahame, James Stewart (Paramount)

The Greatest Show on Earth is as apt a handle for Cecil B. DeMille's Technicolored version of the Ringling Brothers, Barnum & Bailey circus as it is for the sawdust extravaganza itself. As has come to be expected from DeMille, the story line is not what could be termed subtle. Betty Hutton is the ''queen flier'' who has a yen for Charlton Heston, the circus manager. Lad imports another aerialist, the flamboyant and debonair Sebastian (Cornel Wilde). Latter promptly falls for her and she rifts with Heston. That's quickly exploited by elephant girl Gloria Grahame, who also finds Heston a pretty attractive guy. James Stewart is pictured as a police-sought medico who never removes his clown makeup.

1952: Best Picture, Motion Picture Story
Nominations: Best Director, Color Costume Design, Editing

GREATEST STORY EVER TOLD, THE
1965, 225 mins, US Ⓥ ⊙ ▭
D: George Stevens (David Lean, Jean Negulesco) **A:** Max von Sydow, Dorothy McGuire, Robert Loggia, Claude Rains, Jose Ferrer, Charlton Heston (United Artists)

Producer-director George Stevens has elected to stick to the straight, literal, orthodox, familiar facts of the four gospels. He has scorned plot gimmicks and scanted on characterization quirks. What Stevens puts on view, overall, is panoramic cinema, cannily created backgrounds, especially the stupendous buttes of Utah. Claude Rains is standout in the opening sequence as the dying ruler of Judea. Quite properly Stevens has focused on the birth, ministry, execution, and resurrection of the Son of God. In the casting of Jesus there is occasion for compliment. The performance of the Swedish actor Max von Sydow and his English diction are ideal.

1965: Nominations: Best Color Cinematography, Color Costume Design, Color Art Direction, Original Music Score, Visual Effects

GREAT EXPECTATIONS
1946, 110 mins, UK Ⓥ
D: David Lean **A:** John Mills, Valerie Hobson, Francis L. Sullivan, Alec Guinness, Jean Simmons, Martita Hunt (Cineguild)

Only rabid Dickensians will find fault with the present adaptation, and paradoxically only lovers of Dickens will derive maximum pleasure from the film. This adaptation tells how young Pip befriends an escaped convict, who leaves Pip a fortune so he may become a gentleman with great expectations. Pip believes the unexpected fortune originated with the eccentric Miss Havisham at whose house he has met Estella, the girl he loves. So particular have the producers been to avoid offending any Dickensian and every character is drawn so precise that many of them are puppets. The film is beautiful but lacks heart. It evokes admiration but no feeling.

1947: Best B&W Cinematography, B&W Art Direction
Nominations: Best Picture, Director, Screenplay

GREAT EXPECTATIONS
1998, 111 mins, US Ⓥ ⊙ ▭
D: Alfonso Cuaron **A:** Ethan Hawke, Gwyneth Paltrow, Hank Azaria, Chris

Cooper, Anne Bancroft, Robert De Niro (20th Century-Fox)

This *Great Expectations* is something less than a pip. A fanciful and free modern-day adaptation of Charles Dickens's classic, this beautifully made production lacks the emotional depth and dramatic tension to command attention beyond the level of curiosity. Eight-year-old orphan Finn Bell, in a sleepy fishing village along the Florida coast, is accosted by an escaped convict (Robert De Niro), who coerces the boy into helping him. Finn is periodically paged to an old mansion to play with the lovely Estella, niece of the owner, Dinsmoor (Anne Bancroft). In the '80s, Finn (Ethan Hawke) and Estella (Gwyneth Paltrow) meet again and experience a highly erotic encounter, but Estella abruptly disappears. Hawke exhibits limited range as Finn. Paltrow serves up the requisite flintiness and flightiness for Estella. Bancroft's turn is colorful but predictable.

GREAT GABBO, THE
1929, 91 mins, US ⓥ
D: James Cruze **A:** Erich von Stroheim, Betty Compson, Don Douglas, Margie Kane (Meyer-Cordish)

The story is simplicity itself. Just a pair of show people—one a lovely, considerate girl and the other a ventriloquist with a hyperegotist complex. Erich von Stroheim, as the eccentric and arrogant performer who reveals a Pagliacci heart through the medium of Otto, the dummy, doubles the value of a dominant screen personality with his lines. It is the voice, frenzied and then modulated to a pianissimo, that is one of the strongest threads, carrying the interest over sequences devoted to color and stage show that would be irrelevant gaps in productions less skillfully directed and enacted.

GREAT GARRICK, THE
1937, 82 mins, US
D: James Whale **A:** Brian Aherne, Olivia de Havilland, Edward Everett Horton, Melville Cooper, Lionel Atwill, Lana Turner (Warner)

Among the distinctive features are a strictly fictional romantic comedy story around the person of David Garrick, 18th-century English actor, a production of superlative workmanship fabricated from old prints of the period, and acting by a fine cast in the flamboyant manner demanded by the script. Fact is, it should be played as a farce with speed and increasing hilar-

ity. Such, however, is not the case. James Whale's direction is geared to a slow tempo. His romantic passages between Brian Aherne and Olivia de Havilland are quite charming, but much too long.

GREAT GATSBY, THE
1949, 91 mins, US ⓥ
D: Elliott Nugent **A:** Alan Ladd, Betty Field, Macdonald Carey, Ruth Hussey, Barry Sullivan, Shelley Winters (Paramount)

F. Scott Fitzgerald's story of the roaring twenties is peopled with shallow characters and the script stresses the love story rather than the hijacking, bootlegging elements. Gatsby is a fabulous bootlegger who turns his attention to winning back a girl he lost years ago to a wealthy man. Alan Ladd handles his characterization ably, and fares better than other cast members in trying to make the surface characters come to life.

GREAT GATSBY, THE
1974, 144 mins, US ⓥ ⊙
D: Jack Clayton **A:** Robert Redford, Mia Farrow, Bruce Dern, Karen Black, Scott Wilson, Sam Waterston (Paramount)

The fascinating physical beauty of the film complements the utter shallowness of most principal characters from the F. Scott Fitzgerald novel. Robert Redford is excellent in the title role, the mysterious gentleman of humble origins and bootlegging connections; Mia Farrow is his long-lost love.
1974: Best Adapted Scoring, Costume Design

GREAT JOHN L., THE
1945, 96 mins, US
D: Frank Tuttle **A:** Greg McClure, Linda Darnell, Barbara Britton, J. M. Kerrigan, Otto Kruger, Wallace Ford (United Artists)

Dramatization of the life of boxer John L. Sullivan takes John L. from his early youth as the Boston strong boy, through his great victories, into the days of drunken disillusionment, and finally to the mature man who becomes the exponent of clean living. The real star of the film is a man who has never done anything in pictures except as an extra, Greg McClure. He not only looks the part of the Great John L, he acts the part, and grows with it.

GREAT LIE, THE
1941, 102 mins, US ⓥ ⊙
D: Edmund Goulding **A:** Bette Davis,

George Brent, Mary Astor, Hattie Mc-
Daniel, Grant Mitchell, Jerome Cowan
(Warner)

A well-rounded package of dramatic
entertainment. Story presents the situation
confronting the father of a child claimed
as her own by his wife, but in reality born
by the woman to whom he was illegally
married. Both women attempt to use the
youngster to hold the man. Davis gives a
most persuasive portrayal of the wife.
George Brent delivers a strong performance as the husband, while Mary Astor
scores notably as the case-hardened concert artist whose ambitions transcend the
motherly.

GREAT LOVER, THE
1949, 89 mins, US ⓥ
D: Alexander Hall **A:** Bob Hope, Rhonda
Fleming, Roland Young, Roland Culver
(Paramount)

Script has Hope in charge of group of
male adolescents on a European tour. That
starts the laughs. Plot then mixes in a gambler who murders his victims, a gorgeous
duchess and her cardplaying father, places
these ingredients aboard ship sailing for
the US, and then lets nature, and Hope,
carry on. Hope prances through his footage in fine style.

GREAT MAN, THE
1956, 92 mins, US ⓥ
D: Jose Ferrer **A:** Jose Ferrer, Dean Jagger, Keenan Wynn, Julie London, Joanne
Gilbert, Ed Wynn (Universal)

Film is a series of flash episodes adding
into a character study as a probing reporter
researches the background of a nationally
known and presumably revered radio figure who has died in an auto accident. The
research brings out that, away from the
mike, the late lamented was a stinker with
no scruples. The "great man" is never
seen in person. Jose Ferrer, who stars as
the reporter, collaborated on the screenplay and directed. In each function he is
extremely able.

GREAT MAN'S LADY, THE
1942, 90 mins, US
D: William A. Wellman **A:** Barbara Stanwyck, Joel McCrea, Brian Donlevy (Paramount)

Use of the trite flashback technique,
plus a tedious story of the pioneering west,
tend to slow the picture to a walk. It's a
conglomerate of the familiar story of a
woman's inspiration of a man and his ultimate achievement from a pioneer in the

west to a seat in the US Senate. It is a
story of intense drama, yet it leaves one
strangely unmoved.

**GREAT MCGINTY, THE
(UK: DOWN WENT MCGINTY)**
1940, 81 mins, US ⓥ ⊙
D: Preston Sturges **A:** Brian Donlevy,
Muriel Angelus, Akim Tamiroff, Allyn
Joslyn, William Demarest (Paramount)

Preston Sturges's story departs radically from accepted formula. His main
character is a tough, rowdy, and muscular
individual who creates more interest than
sympathy in his career as a prototype of
many political rascals of the American
scene. Brian Donlevy tells his story—a
life of crookedness and how the first honest thing he attempted chased him from
the country. When he first finds that illegal
voting brings coin, he becomes a repeater,
gets into favor of political boss (Akim
Tamiroff), and gradually rises to positions
of alderman, mayor, and finally governor.
Portrayal of Donlevy as the slightly educated political apprentice who learns the
ropes fast, and wields his fists at every opportunity, is excellent. Tamiroff clicks as
the political boss, while Muriel Angelus
provides a charming and warmful personality in the role of the politico's wife.

1940: Best Original Screenplay

GREAT MOMENT, THE
1944, 83 mins, US ⓥ
D: Preston Sturges **A:** Joel McCrea, Betty
Field, Harry Carey, William Demarest,
Franklin Pangborn, Grady Sutton (Para-
mount)

Preston Sturges brings to the screen the
compelling biography of Dr. W.T.G. Morton, who in 1844 discovered anesthesia.
The film is the story of the romance, the
trials, and the ultimate victory of a Boston
dentist, who experimented until he finally
hit upon a painless means of extracting
teeth, then passed on his discovery to the
world of medicine. Performances of Joel
McCrea and Betty Field, as well as a solid
supporting cast, are well in keeping with
the dignity of the yarn.

GREAT MOUSE DETECTIVE, THE
See: Basil, the Great Mouse Detective

GREAT MUPPET CAPER, THE
1981, 95 mins, UK ⓥ ⊙ ▱
D: Jim Henson **A:** Charles Grodin, Diana
Rigg, John Cleese, Robert Morley, Peter
Ustinov, Jack Warden (Universal/AFD)

Story hook has hapless reporters Ker-

mit, Fozzie Bear, and the Great Gonzo literally plunked down in London Town to follow up on a major jewel robbery involving fashion-world magnate Diana Rigg. Once there, Kermit mistakenly takes Miss Piggy for beautiful Lady Holiday and instantly falls in love with the rotund aspiring model. As before, much of the dialogue neatly walks the line between true wit and silly (and sometimes inside) jokes.
1981: Nomination: Best Song ("The First Time It Happens")

GREAT NORTHFIELD MINNESOTA RAID, THE
1972, 91 mins, UK Ⓥ
D: Philip Kaufman **A:** Cliff Robertson, Robert Duvall, Luke Askew, R. G. Armstrong, Dana Elcar, Donald Moffat (Universal/Robertson & Associates)

The Great Northfield Minnesota Raid—described as shedding "new light" on Cole Younger and Jesse James—may be a valiant attempt but fails to come off. Primarily, this is due to utter lack of sustained narrative, confused, and inept writing, overabundance of characters difficult for ready identification, often apparent indecision whether to make this drama or comedy, and a mishmash of irrelevant sequences. Treatment is such that characters throughout are dull fellows indeed, and picture itself is in kind.

GREAT O'MALLEY, THE
1937, 71 mins, US Ⓥ
D: William Dieterle **A:** Pat O'Brien, Sybil Jason, Humphrey Bogart, Frieda Inescort, Ann Sheridan, Donald Crisp (Warner)

One of Hollywood's pat formulas for cop pictures, but with less action than usual. It is the tough-Hibernian policeman theme, with plenty of brogue, and the eventual softening of the copper when a kid creeps into his heart. In this instance the tot is Sybil Jason, who delivers as a crippled slum child. Sybil's father (Bogart), is forced into criminal activities but later makes amends. Picture depends almost wholly on the appeal of moppet Sybil.

GREAT OUTDOORS, THE
1988, 90 mins, US Ⓥ ⊙
D: Howard Deutch **A:** Dan Aykroyd, John Candy, Stephanie Faracy, Annette Bening, Chris Young (Universal/Hughes)

John Candy stars as a sweet, slightly dopey family man who wagoneers his happy brood up from Chicago for a big-pines getaway. No sooner do they unpack than obnoxious brother-in-law Dan Aykroyd and his maladjusted family blast in uninvited to spend the week. Aykroyd's pampered wife (Annette Bening) eggs him on, while his spooky kids (twins Hilary and Rebecca Gordon) never say a word. The Aykroyd-Candy pairing is charmed. Stephanie Faracy is excellent as Candy's sweet, happy wife, and Bening is also savvy in her role.

GREAT RACE, THE
1965, 157 mins, US Ⓥ ⊙ ▭
D: Blake Edwards **A:** Jack Lemmon, Tony Curtis, Natalie Wood, Peter Falk, Keenan Wynn, Arthur O'Connell (Warner)

A big, expensive, whopping comedy extravaganza, long on slapstick and near-inspired tomfoolery whose tongue-in-cheek treatment liberally sprinkled with corn frequently garners belly laughs. A certain nostalgic flavor is achieved, both in the 1908 period of an automobile race from New York to Paris and Blake Edwards's broad borrowing from *The Prisoner of Zenda* tale and an earlier Laurel and Hardy comedy for some of his heartiest action. Characters carry an old-fashioned zest, recalling the days when it was the fashion to hiss the villain and cheer the hero. Never has there been a villain so dastardly as Jack Lemmon or a hero so whitely pure as Tony Curtis.
1965: Best Sound Effects
Nominations: Best Color Cinematography, Editing, Sound, Song ("The Sweetheart Tree")

GREAT ROCK AND ROLL SWINDLE, THE
1980, 103 mins, UK Ⓥ
D: Julien Temple **A:** Malcolm McLaren, Johnny Rotten, Sid Vicious, Steve Jones, Paul Cook, Jess Conrad (Kendon/Matrix Best/Virgin)

The Great Rock and Roll Swindle is the *Citizen Kane* of rock and roll pictures. An incredibly sophisticated, stupefyingly multilayered portrait of the 1970s phenomenon known as the Sex Pistols, unstintingly cynical pic casts a jaundiced eye at the entire pop-culture scene and, if nothing else, represents the most imaginative use of a rock group in films since the Beatles debuted in *A Hard Day's Night*.

GREAT SANTINI, THE
1980, 115 mins, US Ⓥ
D: Lewis John Carlino **A:** Robert Duvall, Blythe Danner, Michael O'Keefe, Lisa Jane Persky, Julie Anne Haddock (Orion)

Robert Duvall gives an excellent portrayal of the finest fighter pilot in the US Marines. But this isn't a war picture. Quite the contrary, it's the compellingly relevant story of a super-macho peacetime warrior with nobody to fight except himself and those who love him. As the sensitive son, Michael O'Keefe is terrific. Blythe Danner is also strong as the wife who suffers Duvall's excesses.

1980: Nominations: Best Actor (Robert Duvall), Supp. Actor (Michael O'Keefe)

GREAT SCOUT & CATHOUSE THURSDAY, THE
1976, 102 mins, US ⊗
D: Don Taylor **A:** Lee Marvin, Oliver Reed, Robert Culp, Elizabeth Ashley, Strother Martin, Kay Lenz (American International)

Up-and-down screenplay uses the plot about former partners in crime (here Lee Marvin and Indian sidekick Oliver Reed) going back to get revenge on the partner who cheated them and went respectable with the loot (Robert Culp). May-December romance between Marvin's aging cowpoke and Kay Lenz's young prostie rouses some dramatic interest, coming through the general hokiness like rays of sunshine on a smoggy day.

GREAT SMOKEY ROADBLOCK, THE
See: The Last of the Cowboys

GREAT ST. TRINIAN'S TRAIN ROBBERY, THE
1966, 94 mins, UK ⊗
D: Frank Launder, Sidney Gilliat **A:** Frankie Howerd, Reg Varney, Stratford Johns, Eric Barker, Dora Bryan, George Cole (British Lion)

Ronald Searle's little schoolgirl demons from St. Trinian's are berserk again in a yarn with a topical twist, the [1963] Great Train Robbery. Having pulled off a $7-million train robbery, a hapless gang of crooks stash the loot in a deserted country mansion. But when they go back to collect, they find the St. Trinian's school has taken over, and they are completely routed by the hockey sticks and rough stuff handed out by the little she-monsters. A great train chase is quite the funniest part of the film, having a great deal in common with the old silent slapstick technique.

GREAT TEXAS DYNAMITE CHASE, THE
1976, 90 mins, US ⊗
D: Michael Pressman **A:** Claudia Jennings, Jocelyn Jones, Johnny Crawford,

Chris Pennock, Tara Strohmeier (Yasny Talking Pictures II)

A well-made exploitation film. Claudia Jennings and Jocelyn Jones are stylish and attractive as a pair of brazen Texas bankrobbers. They use lots of dynamite along the way, but there's little bloodshed until the last part of the film, when the dominant spoof tone turns uncomfortably close to reality.

GREAT TRAIN ROBBERY, THE
See: The First Great Train Robbery

GREAT WALDO PEPPER, THE
1975, 108 mins, US ⊗ ⊙
D: George Roy Hill **A:** Robert Redford, Bo Svenson, Bo Brundin, Susan Sarandon, Geoffrey Lewis, Edward Herrman (Universal)

An uneven and unsatisfying story of anachronistic, pitiable, but misplaced heroism. Robert Redford stars as an aerial ace, unable to cope with the segue from pioneer barnstorming to big-time aviation. The film stumbles toward its fuzzy climax.

GREAT WALL, A (AKA: THE GREAT WALL IS A GREAT WALL)
1986, 97 mins, US ⊗ ⊙ ▭
D: Peter Wang **A:** Peter Wang, Sharon Iwai, Kelvin Han Yee, Li Qinqin (W&S/Nanhai)

A charming but unduly lightweight film humorously accentuates the many cultural differences between the two giant nations of the US and China, but goes out of its way to avoid dealing with politics or any other issues of substance. Peter Wang portrays a San Francisco computer executive who takes advantage of the opening up of China to visit relatives there as well as to introduce his American-born wife and son to his native land.

GREAT WALTZ, THE
1938, 107 mins, US ⊗
D: Julien Duvivier **A:** Luise Rainer, Fernand Gravet, Miliza Korjus, Hugh Herbert, Lionel Atwill (M-G-M)

A field day for music lovers plus elegant entertainment. While primarily a fanciful tale of Johann Strauss II's rise in the musical firmament, entire plot has been constructed around his outstanding works. Strauss (Fernand Gravet) marries the baker's daughter soon after his first success. His part in a short-lived revolution serves to develop romance with the opera singer Carla Donner (Miliza Korjus). It is the sudden decision to fight for her mate, after months of self-sacrifice, that takes Mrs. Strauss (Rainer) storming backstage after the successful premiere of his first opera. Besides Rainer's sterling portrayal of the adoring wife, Gravet does surprisingly well as the younger Strauss.

1938: Best Cinematography
Nominations: Best Supp. Actress (Miliza Korjus), Editing

GREAT WHITE HOPE, THE

1970, 102 mins, US ♥ ⌑
D: Martin Ritt **A:** James Earl Jones, Jane Alexander, Lou Gilbert, Joel Fluellen, Chester Morris, Robert Webber (20th Century-Fox)

In its telling of the quasi-fictionalized public life of famed black heavyweight champ, circa 1910, Jack Johnson, the film's pacing and gritty cynicism resembles the best of the old Warner Bros Depression dramas; but in the distended play-out of the fighter's tragic private life via involvement with a white woman, the picture sags.

1970: Nominations: Best Actor (James Earl Jones), Actress (Jane Alexander)

GREAT WHITE HYPE, THE

1996, 90 mins, US ♥
D: Reginald Hudlin **A:** Samuel L. Jackson, Jeff Goldblum, Peter Berg, Jon Lovitz, Cheech Marin (Altman/Berner/20th Century-Fox)

Appealing performers and sporadic moments of dead-on satiric hilarity only partly compensate for general tepidness. Set in Las Vegas, tale centers on Reverend Fred Sultan (Samuel L. Jackson), a high-spirited and gleefully devious boxing impresario who is dismayed at the meager profits brought in by his current champ (Damon Wayans). The obvious remedy is to rustle up a Caucasian contender, Terry Conklin (Peter Berg), now a luggish singer for a heavy-metal band. Despite his gruff appearance, Terry turns out to be a sweet-tempered sort who agrees to box only when assured that the fight will be used in the campaign to help the homeless. Convincing the rest of the world that Terry and the match are legit is a trickier task.

GREAT ZIEGFELD, THE

1936, 170 mins, US ♥ ⊙
D: Robert Z. Leonard **A:** William Powell, Myrna Loy, Luise Rainer, Frank Morgan, Fanny Brice, Virginia Bruce (M-G-M)

Metro emerges with a picture whose sole shortcoming is its footage. The pro-duction high mark of the numbers is "Pretty Girl" as the first-half finale. This nifty Irving Berlin tune becomes the fulcrum for one of Frank Skinner's best arrangements as Arthur Lange batons the crescendos into a mad, glittering potpourri of Saint-Saëns and Gershwin, Strauss and Verdi, beautifully blended against the Berlinesque background. William Powell's Zieggy is excellent. He endows the impersonation with all the qualities of a great entrepreneur and sentimentalist. Luise Rainer is tops of the femmes with her vivacious Anna Held.

1936: Best Picture, Actress (Luise Rainer), Dance Direction ("A Pretty Girl Is Like a Melody")
Nominations: Best Director, Original Story, Art Direction, Editing

GREED

1924, 114 mins, US ♥ ⊙ ⊗
D: Erich von Stroheim **A:** Gibson Gowland, ZaSu Pitts, Jean Hersholt, Chester Conklin (Metro-Goldwyn)

Stroheim shot 130 reels in two years. He finally cut it to 26 reels and told executives that was the best he could do. It was then taken into hand and cut to 10 reels. McTeague serves as apprenticeship with an itinerant dentist and in years after sets up an office in San Francisco. A chum brings in his cousin as a patient. McTeague falls in love with her, but before Mac and she are married, the girl wins a $5,000 lottery prize. Several years afterward, the chum, vengeful because of his failure to share in the spoils, tips off the Dentists' Society that Mac is practicing without a license. Mac then drifts from bad to worse. The picture brings to light three great character performances by Gibson Gowland as McTeague, Jean Hersholt as the chum, and ZaSu Pitts as the wife.

GREEDY

1994, 113 mins, US ♥ ⊙
D: Jonathan Lynn **A:** Michael J. Fox, Kirk Douglas, Nancy Travis, Olivia d'Abo, Ed Begley Jr. (Imagine/Universal)

The yarn centers on the McTeague brood (a cinematic reference to the protagonist of silent masterpiece *Greed* who live for the death of wheelchair-bound Uncle Joe (Kirk Douglas), a snarly, reprehensible curmudgeon. Joe barely veils his contempt for the sycophants. But the big bombshell is the arrival of Molly (Olivia d'Abo), Joe's so-called nurse. The little ace the warring clan turns up is Daniel McTeague Jr. (Michael J. Fox). Director

Jonathan Lynn knows exactly what elements to emphasize when the action moves through breakneck drawing-room comedy. But the script aims higher, embracing pathos even when the results are pure bathos.

GREEK TYCOON, THE
1978, 106 mins, US Ⓥ ▭
D: J. Lee Thompson **A:** Anthony Quinn, Jacqueline Bisset, Raf Vallone, Edward Albert, James Franciscus, Camilla Sparv (Abkco)

As a thinly disguised biopic of Aristotle Onassis and Jacqueline Kennedy Onassis—accent on thinly disguised—*The Greek Tycoon* reflects its subject. It's a trashy, opulent, vulgar, racy picture. Quinn is fabulous as Tomasis, a charming, wealthy, conniving and influential tycoon. As Liz Cassidy, Bisset capitalizes on her looks, but her accent seems off for the part and much of the acting is just posing.

GREEN BERETS, THE
1968, 141 mins, US Ⓥ ⊙ ▭
D: John Wayne, Ray Kellogg **A:** John Wayne, Ray Kellogg, David Janssen, Jim Hutton, Aldo Ray, Raymond St. Jacques (Warner/Seven Arts/Batjac)

The Green Berets, based on Robin Moore's book about US Special Forces, sheds no light on the arguments pro and con about US involvement in Vietnam. Cliché-cluttered plot structure and dialogue, wooden performances by actors playing soldiers, pedestrian direction, and lethargic editing dog this production. James Lee Barrett did the flat script, loaded with corn and cardboard.

GREEN CARD
1990, 108 mins, Australia/France Ⓥ ⊙
D: Peter Weir **A:** Gerard Depardieu, Andie MacDowell, Bebe Neuwirth, Gregg Edelman, Robert Prosky (Rio/UGC/DD/ Serif/Green Card)

A genial, nicely played romance. Gerard Depardieu is winning as a French alien who pairs up with New Yorker Andie MacDowell in a marriage of convenience in order to remain legally in the United States. Elements that might look hokey on paper—he's a freewheeling bohemian, she's an uptight prude; he's a smoker and enthusiastic carnivore, she practically faints upon exposure to a cigarette or a piece of meat—go down easily because the two leads incorporate these attitudes believably into generally well-rounded characters.

1990: Nomination: Best Original Screenplay

GREEN DOLPHIN STREET
1947, 140 mins, US Ⓥ
D: Victor Saville **A:** Lana Turner, Van Heflin, Donna Reed, Richard Hart, Edmund Gwenn, Frank Morgan (M-G-M)

Alternately localed in primitive New Zealand and one of the French channel isles (circa 1840), pic details how Lana Turner, mistaken for her sister Donna Reed, makes the perilous sea voyage to the Antipodes to marry a deserter from the British navy. Epic must primarily count on the eminent salability of earthquakes, tidal waves, and native uprisings. Its curiously unreal story offers no help.

1947: Best Special Effects
Nomination: Best B&W Cinematography, Editing, Sound

GREEN FIRE
1954, 99 mins, US ▭
D: Andrew Marton **A:** Stewart Granger, Grace Kelly, Paul Douglas, John Ericson, Murvyn Vye (M-G-M)

A good brand of action escapism is offered. The location filming in Colombia ensured fresh scenic backgrounds. The adventure end of the pic is served by the efforts of Granger to find emeralds in an old mountain mine. Romance is served through the presence of Kelly, whose coffee plantation lies at the foot of the mountain on which Granger is mining, and the attraction that springs up between these two.

GREEN FOR DANGER
1946, 91 mins, UK Ⓥ
D: Sidney Gilliat **A:** Alastair Sim, Leo Genn, Trevor Howard, Sally Gray, Rosamund John, Judy Campbell (Individual)

This whodunit has the unusual setting of an emergency wartime hospital with the operating theater as the scene of two apparently clueless murders. Alastair Sim, unconventional detective from Scotland Yard, has great fun annoying the suspects. The plot is too laboriously constructed, and the reason for the murders appears too incredible.

GREENGAGE SUMMER, THE
(US: LOSS OF INNOCENCE)
1961, 100 mins, UK
D: Lewis Gilbert **A:** Kenneth More, Danielle Darrieux, Susannah York, Jane Asher, Claude Nollier, Maurice Denham (Columbia)

Here's a stylish, warm romantic drama

set in the leisurely champagne country of France. Pic is always a delight to the eye apart from its other qualities. Story concerns four English schoolchildren, the oldest (Susannah York) being just over 16. They arrive at the hotel run by Danielle Darrieux. The children get a frigid reception, but Kenneth More, a debonair, charming, mysterious Englishman insists that they stay. He's having an affair with Miss Darrieux and she cannot resist his whims. During the long summer the atmosphere thickens. York progresses delightfully from the resentful, gawky schoolgirl to the young woman eager to live.

GREEN MANSIONS
1959, 104 mins, US ▭
D: Mel Ferrer A: Audrey Hepburn, Anthony Perkins, Lee J. Cobb, Sessue Hayakawa, Henry Silva, Nehemiah Persoff (M-G-M)

Rima (Audrey Hepburn) is a girl with unusual communion with the forest and its wildlife. She is found by Abel (Anthony Perkins) when he hides out with an Indian tribe after fleeing a political uprising. Good location work in South America is skillfully utilized, by process and editing, with backlot work. But Ferrer has been less successful in getting his characters to come alive, or in getting his audience to care about them.

GREEN MILE, THE
1999, 187 mins, US Ⓥ ⊙
D: Frank Darabont A: Tom Hanks, David Morse, Bonnie Hunt, Michael Clarke Duncan, James Cromwell, Michael Jeter (Darkwoods/Castle Rock/Warner)

The Green Mile is a powerful and meticulously crafted drama that falls short of its full potential due to excessive duration and some simplistic notions. Tale, adapted from Stephen King's bestseller, is set on death row at Cold Mountain Penitentiary in 1935 Louisiana. Head guard Paul Edgecomb (Tom Hanks) is a decent man dedicated to maintaining as much calm and dignity as possible. Behind bars are good-hearted Creole Eduard Delacroix (Michael Jeter), repentant Native American murderer Arlen Bitterbuck (Graham Greene), and John Coffey (Michael Clarke Duncan), a sweet-natured black man convicted of killing two little girls. Edgecomb becomes convinced of Coffey's innocence and of his otherworldly healing powers, leading him to try to have the inmate cure the cancer consuming the wife (Patrcia

Clarkson) of the warden (James Cromwell).

1999: Nominations: Best Picture, Best Supp. Actor (Michael Clarke Duncan), Adapted Screenplay, Sound

GREEN PASTURES, THE
1936, 93 mins, US Ⓥ
D: Marc Connelly, William Keighley A: Rex Ingram, Oscar Polk, Eddie Anderson, Frank Wilson, Abraham Gleaves (Warner)

A simple, enchanting, audience-captivating all-Negro cinematic fable. Rex Ingram's glowing personality makes for a thoroughly satisfying and convincing Lawd. It's the Harlem version of the Old Testament, as the pastor word-paints the mood of De Lawd from Genesis to Exodus and beyond. Punctuating all the biblical background are mundane references to gay fishfries, ten-cent seegars, generous fishing, and plenty of milk-and-honey for the good folks, yet it's all in fine taste and with due regard to proportions and standards of all races and creeds.

GREENWICH VILLAGE
1944, 83 mins, US
D: Walter Lang A: Carmen Miranda, Don Ameche, William Bendix, Vivian Blaine (20th Century-Fox)

Title places the locale. Time is in the early 1920s: i.e., the speakeasy era. William Bendix is the speakeasy prop, Don Ameche the tyro composer from the sticks, Carmen Miranda the joint's combination fortune-teller and entertainer, and Vivian Blaine the songstress toplining at Bendix's joint. Thin story is held together by several old songs and three new good tunes by Leo Robin–Nacio Herb Brown.

GREEN YEARS, THE
1946, 127 mins, US
D: Victor Saville A: Charles Coburn, Tom Drake, Beverly Tyler, Hume Cronyn, Gladys Cooper, Dean Stockwell (M-G-M)

Ten-year-old Stockwell is the particularly bright spot in the well-turned cast. He plays an orphan boy in this Scottish-localed story of ambitious youth and amusing old age. The oldster is Charles Coburn, as Dean's great-grandfather, a man of large heart and large desires for the native brew. While this not-so-venerable, but thoroughly enjoyable citizen is getting himself into one minor scrape after another, the youth (later played by Tom Drake) goes through the process of growing up, going to school and falling in love.

1946: Nominations: Best Supp. Actor (Charles Coburn), B&W Cinematography

GREGORY'S GIRL ♥ ⊚

1982, 91 mins, UK ♥ ⊚

D: Bill Forsyth **A:** John Gordon Sinclair, Dee Hepburn, Jake D'Arcy, Clare Grogan (Lake/NFFC/Scottish TV)

Filmmaker Bill Forsyth is concerned with young students (in particular, a soccer-team goalie, Gregory) seeking out the opposite sex. Much of the pic's peculiar fascination comes from tangential scenes, limning each character's odd obsession, be it food, girls, soccer, or just watching the traffic drive by. Main narrative thread has Gregory becoming infatuated with the cute (and athletic) new girl on his soccer team, Dorothy (Dee Hepburn), while her schoolmates delightfully maneuver him into giving the outgoing Susan (Clare Grogan) a tumble.

GREMLINS

1984, 111 mins, US ♥ ⊚

D: Joe Dante **A:** Zach Galligan, Hoyt Axton, Frances Lee McCain, Phoebe Cates, Polly Holliday, Judge Reinhold (Amblin/Warner)

In what story there is, amiable Hoyt Axton comes across a mysterious creature in Chinatown and takes it home as a Christmas present for his likable teenage son, Zach Galligan. The creature spawns a townful of evil, snarling, drooling, maniacal killer creatures who are bound to cause a lot of woe before their predictable downfall. The humans are little more than dress extras for the mechanics.

GREMLINS 2: THE NEW BATCH

1990, 105 mins, US ♥ ⊚

D: Joe Dante **A:** Zach Galligan, Phoebe Cates, John Glover, Robert Prosky, Robert Picardo, Christopher Lee (Amblin)

Joe Dante & Co. have concocted an hilarious sequel featuring equal parts creature slapstick for the small fry and satirical barbs for adults. Addition of Christopher Lee to the cast as a mad genetics-engineering scientist is a perfect touch. Hundreds of horrific gremlins are unleashed to wreak mayhem.

GREY FOX, THE

1982, 90 mins, Canada ♥ ⊚

D: Phillip Borsos **A:** Richard Farnsworth, Jackie Burroughs, Wayne Robson, Ken Pogue, Christopher Lee (Mercury)

Director Phillip Borsos approaches his material—a stagecoach robber goes to jail for 30 years and is released into an unknown world where trains have started carrying the mail—as a kind of neo-western very much in sympathy with the bandit. Richard Farnsworth's performance as the gentleman robber is one of the pic's strong points.

GREYFRIARS BOBBY

1961, 91 mins, US ♥

D: Don Chaffey **A:** Donald Crisp, Laurence Naismith, Alex Mackenzie, Kay Walsh, Andrew Cruickshank, Gordon Jackson (Walt Disney)

Greyfriars Bobby sets out to melt the heart and does it skillfully. Central character is a little Skye terrier, and this engaging little animal is quite irresistible. Story is a true one, set in and around Edinburgh some 100 years ago. It tells of an old shepherd who was buried in the little Greyfriars Kirk in Edinburgh. From the day of the funeral Bobby resolutely refused to leave his beloved master. In the end he was adopted by the entire populace of Edinburgh.

GREYSTOKE: THE LEGEND OF TARZAN, LORD OF THE APES

1984, 131 mins, US/UK ♥ ⊚

D: Hugh Hudson **A:** Ralph Richardson, Ian Holm, James Fox, Christopher Lambert, Andie MacDowell, Cheryl Campbell (Warner)

Pic adheres much more closely to the original Edgar Rice Burroughs story than have the countless previous screen tellings. While a little obligatory vine swinging is on view, this is principally the tale of the education of the seventh Earl of Greystoke, first by the family of apes, then by a Belgian explorer, and finally by the aristocracy of Britain. Christopher Lambert is a different sort of Tarzan. Tall, lean, firm, but no muscleman, he moves with great agility and mimics the apes to fine effect. Andie MacDowell smiles her way through as the eternally sympathetic Jane. **1984: Nominations:** Best Supp. Actor (Ralph Richardson), Adapted Screenplay, Makeup

GRIEF

1993, 88 mins, US ♥ ⊚ ⊡

D: Richard Glatzer **A:** Craig Chester, Jackie Beat, Illeana Douglas, Alexis Arquette, Carlton Wilborn (Grief)

The setting is offices for a TV production company. They crank out episodes of *The Love Judge,* a tacky tabloid-style syndicated series. Flashback action takes place during a workweek, framed by head writer Mark's (Craig Chester) suicide contemplation on the first anniversary of his lover's death from AIDS. Scenario starts out looking just another amusing look at behind-the-scenes Hollywood incestuousness. But the familiar satire soon develops no end of healthy wrinkles. Video-shot glimpses from the ersatz *Love Judge* series are hilarious.

GRIFTERS, THE
1990, 113 mins, US Ⓥ ⊙
D: Stephen Frears **A:** John Cusack, Anjelica Huston, Annette Bening, Pat Hingle, J. T. Walsh (Cineplex Odeon)

Jim Thompson's intriguing novel about the subculture of small-time hustlers is fashioned into a curiously uneven movie. John Cusack plays Roy Dillon, a Los Angeles con man. Roy's mother, Lilly (Anjelica Huston), gave birth at the tender age of 14, then fashioned a lucrative career as a roving racetrack bag lady, putting down bets for the Baltimore mob. Roy is ministered to by his sexy girlfriend Myra (Annette Bening). Cusack underplays Roy, making him an unbelievable wiseguy, a colorless cipher too akin to the saps he loves to fleece.
1990: Nominations: Best Director, Actress (Anjelica Huston), Supp. Actress (Annette Bening), Adapted Screenplay

GRIP OF FEAR, THE
See: Experiment in Terror

GRISSOM GANG, THE
1971, 127 mins, US Ⓥ
D: Robert Aldrich **A:** Kim Darby, Scott Wilson, Tony Musante, Irene Dailey, Robert Lansing, Connie Stevens (ABC/Associates & Aldrich)

The Grissom Gang offers no sympathy at all for the debased human beings it depicts. Rather, it treats them as the butts of a cruel joke. The action takes place in Kansas City in 1931, and concerns the kidnapping of a young heiress by an unbelievably depraved gang presided over by venomous Ma Grissom (Irene Dailey) and her cretinous son (Scott Wilson). It begins in a wash of blood, opening the same vein throughout—and the key to its debasing approach is the laughter this mayhem often provokes.

GROSS ANATOMY
(UK: A CUT ABOVE)
1989, 107 mins, US Ⓥ ⊙
D: Thom Eberhardt **A:** Matthew Modine, Daphne Zuniga, Christine Lahti, Todd Field, John Scott Clough (Touchstone)

The film follows Matthew Modine and other students through their courses, with particular focus on the anatomy lab, in which he's teamed with four classmates to work on a cadaver. Dissecting group includes his too serious roommate Todd Field; married young mother Alice Carter; the judgmental, ultrapreppy John Scott Clough; and hardworking Daphne Zuniga, who reluctantly provides love interest for Modine. *Gross* offers some nice, unexpected details and a convincing portrayal of med-school life. However, the writers came up with nothing more than stick figures and repetitive, one-note problems.

GROSSE POINTE BLANK
1997, 107 mins, US Ⓥ ⊙
D: George Armitage **A:** John Cusack, Minnie Driver, Dan Aykroyd, Alan Arkin, Joan Cusack, Jeremy Piven (Hollywood)

An artistic triumph, *Grosse Pointe Blank* is hip without being cute, and absurd in a uniquely satisfying fashion. Martin Blank (John Cusack) is a young man in crisis. He's carved out a successful career as an independent assassin, but his chief competitor, Mr. Grocer (Dan Aykroyd), wants him to become part of a union. The upcoming weekend is his 10-year high school reunion in Grosse Pointe, MI, where, coincidentally, he has to do a hit. The key to what went wrong with Blank's life rests with Debi (Minnie Driver), the prom date he stood up. Pic is foremost a romantic comedy. Its two central characters are likable. Alan Arkin is a standout as Blank's traumatized shrink, who fears there's no easy way to terminate their meetings. Giddily directed by George Armitage (*Miami Blues*, 1990), pic never falters in tone.

GROUNDHOG DAY
1993, 103 mins, US Ⓥ ⊙
D: Harold Ramis **A:** Bill Murray, Andie MacDowell, Chris Elliott, Stephen Tobolowsky, Brian Doyle-Murray (Columbia)

The premise of the romantic comedy is essentially "if you had to do it over again—and again—what would you do differently?" Bill Murray, a cynical TV weatherman, finds himself stuck in a private, repetitious hell: Groundhog Day in Punxsutawney, PA, where he has come for the annual festivities. The day begins, over and over, at 6 A.M. The situation is ripe with comic potential, but script provides more chuckles than belly laughs. Murray's weatherman is tailor-made for his smug screen persona, perhaps too much so.

GROUNDSTAR CONSPIRACY, THE
1972, 95 mins, Canada ⊛ ▭
D: Lamont Johnson **A:** George Peppard, Michael Sarrazin, Christine Belford, Cliff Potts, James Olson (Universal/Roach)

George Peppard stars as a government agent trying to break up a spy ring. Michael Sarrazin is, or is not, a traitor who worked in a super-secret lab trying to break a computer code. Spectacular locations around Vancouver, plus some excellent and offbeat music by Paul Hoffert, only partially compensate for a script that is as often routine as it is bewildering.

GROUP, THE
1966, 150 mins, US ⊛
D: Sidney Lumet **A:** Candice Bergen, Joan Hackett, Elizabeth Hartman, Shirley Knight, Joanna Pettet, Jessica Walter (Famartists/United Artists)

The principal problem in adapting Mary McCarthy's very successful college-classmates novel was to transfer its colorful characterizations and storytelling without overloading script with a mass of novelistic detail. There's little tampering with the original story line, but the film concentrates on the story of Kay (Joanna Pettet). Throughout, she and Larry Hagman, as her philandering playwright husband, have the longest roles. Biggest letdown, and doubly so because her few scenes are so effective and played so well, is the part played by Candice Bergen.

GRUMPIER OLD MEN
1995, 100 mins, US ⊛ ⊙
D: Howard Deutch **A:** Jack Lemmon, Walter Matthau, Ann-Margret, Sophia Loren, Burgess Meredith, Kevin Pollak (Lancaster Gate/Warner)

The success of this new outing isn't just the rock-solid bickering combo. The ensemble cast plays the comedy and romance to perfection. Lifelong buddies John Gustafson (Lemmon) and Max Goldberg (Matthau) continue to snipe and spar—for what other sport is there in rural Minnesota?—and pursue the legendary Catfish Hunter in the Land o' Lakes. They refrain from the game of hurling epithets only to engage in marriage plans for John's single-parent daughter, Melanie (Daryl Hannah), and Max's son Jacob (Kevin Pollak). To encounter an American film that has a true connection with characters older than 50 is refreshing. The movie has a relaxed tone that's rare but understandable.

GRUMPY OLD MEN
1993, 104 mins, US ⊛ ⊙
D: Donald Petrie **A:** Jack Lemmon, Walter Matthau, Ann-Margret, Burgess Meredith, Daryl Hannah, Kevin Pollak (Warner/Lancaster Gate)

Looking craggy and dour, Lemmon and Matthau play aging Minnesota neighbors whose decades-old feud is rekindled when they become enamored with a fetching widow, the aptly named Ariel (Ann-Margret), who moves in across the street. The film provides few big laughs before rushing to its warm, fuzzy, and overly tidy conclusion. The film doesn't truly shine, in fact, until a fabulous outtake sequence over the closing credits.

GUADALCANAL DIARY
1943, 90 mins, US ⊛
D: Lewis Seiler **A:** Preston Foster, Lloyd Nolan, William Bendix, Richard Conte, Anthony Quinn, Richard Jaeckel (20th Century-Fox)

Opening with a quiet scene aboard a transport as the marine-corps task force steams toward an as-yet-undisclosed objective, the story is narrated by an off-screen voice, fading in and out of the action sequences. All this is admirably free from bombast and chauvinistic boasting. Although the deeds of the men are heroic, the men themselves reveal no self-consciousness of heroism. Of the cast, William Bendix stands out in a juicy comedy-straight part as a tough-soft taxi driver from Brooklyn.

GUARDIAN, THE
1990, 98 mins, US ⊛ ⊙
D: William Friedkin **A:** Jenny Seagrove, Dwier Brown, Carey Lowell, Brad Hall, Miguel Ferrer (Universal)

Who knows what possessed director William Friedkin to straight-facedly tell this absurd "tree bites man" tale, but it's an impulse he should have exorcised. The scant plot involves an attractive yuppie couple (Dwier Brown, Carey Lowell) who hire a live-in nanny to take care of their infant son. The nanny (Jenny Seagrove) turns out to be some sort of evil spirit that sacrifices newborns to this big, anthropomorphic tree.

GUARDIAN ANGELS
See: Les Anges Gardiens

GUARDING TESS
1994, 96 mins, US ⊛ ⊙
D: Hugh Wilson **A:** Shirley MacLaine, Nicolas Cage, Austin Pendleton, Edward

Albert, James Rebhorn, Richard Griffiths (Channel/Tri-Star)

The premise has a young secret-service agent (Nicolas Cage) stuck in the thankless job of protecting the widow (Shirley MacLaine) of a US president. Neither truly likes the situation but they like one another, despite constant bickering and endless infractions of protocol. Aided and abetted by two charismatic performers and an underlying sweetness, the film is indeed likable. But director Hugh Wilson just skims the surface of potentially rich territory. Comedy, pathos, and thrills alternately collide, creating problems in both pacing and developing a consistent tone.

LA GUERRE DES BOUTONS (WAR OF THE BUTTONS)
1962, 95 mins, France
D: Yves Robert A: Jean Richard, Jaques Dufilho, Michel Galabru, Yvette Etievant, Martin Lartigue (Gueville)

Tale of kid warfare between the moppets of two neighboring rural towns looks at kids with the distance of grown-ups, on how cute they are, and rarely gives insight into their actions or makes a point about it all. But it is gentle, fairly refreshing, and naturally played by a group of youngsters.

LA GUERRE EST FINIE (THE WAR IS OVER)
1966, 120 mins, France/Sweden
D: Alain Resnais A: Yves Montand, Ingrid Thulin, Genevieve Bujold, Michel Piccoli, Jean Bouise, Francoise Bertin (Sofracima/Argos/Europa)

The tale of three days in the life of a refugee revolutionary (Yves Montand). He is Spanish but has been living in France since his childhood. He is part of a leftist group which still tries to control revolutionary forces in Spain. Ingrid Thulin has a luminous quality as the woman in Montand's life. Another femme, Genevieve Bujold, shows fetching young beauty and poise. Film is more a statement on a theme than a simple human tale. It succeeds on this level.

GUESS WHO'S COMING TO DINNER
1967, 108 mins, US ⊗ ⊙
D: Stanley Kramer A: Spencer Tracy, Sidney Poitier, Katharine Hepburn, Katharine Houghton, Cecil Kellaway (Columbia)

Guess Who's Coming to Dinner examines its subject matter with perception, depth, insight, humor, and feeling. The story covers 12 hours, from arrival in, and departure from, Frisco of Poitier and Katharine Houghton (Hepburn's niece, in a whammo screen debut). Tracy and Hepburn are her parents, of longtime liberal persuasion, faced with a true test of their beliefs: do they approve of their daughter marrying a Negro. Every possible interaction is explored admid comedy angles that range from drawingroom sophistication to sight gag, from bitter cynicism to telling irony.
1967: Best Actress (Katharine Hepburn), Original Story & Screenplay
Nominations: Best Picture, Director, Actor (Spencer Tracy), Supp. Actor (Cecil Kellaway), Supp. Actress (Beah Richards), Art Direction, Editing, Adapted Score

GUEST, THE
See: The Caretaker

GUEST IN THE HOUSE
1944, 117 mins, US ⊗
D: John Brahm A: Anne Baxter, Ralph Bellamy, Aline MacMahon, Ruth Warrick, Scott McKay, Marie McDonald (United Artists)

Story is about girl (Anne Baxter) who is taken into the home of a happy family at the request of a young doctor (Scott McKay). The girl becomes infatuated with the medico's older, married brother (Ralph Bellamy) and immediately proceeds to instill psychological poison, alienating one member of the family from another so that she can win the man of her choice. Production's most valuable asset, apart from its first-rate cast, is the suspense and action, which are sustained throughout once the motivation is established.

GUIDE FOR THE MARRIED MAN, A
1967, 89 mins, US ⊗ ▱
D: Gene Kelly A: Walter Matthau, Robert Morse, Inger Stevens, Sue Ane Langdon, Claire Kelly, Linda Harrison (20th Century-Fox)

Walter Matthau plays a married innocent, eager to stray under the tutelage of friend and neighbor Robert Morse. But this long-married hubby is so retarded in his immorality (it takes him 12 years to get the seven-year-itch) that he needs the entire film to have his mind made up. Guide is packed with action, pulchritude, situations, and considerable (if not quite enough) laughs.

GUILTY AS SIN
1993, 104 mins, US ⓥ ⊙
D: Sidney Lumet **A:** Rebecca DeMornay, Don Johnson, Stephen Lang, Jack Warden, Dana Ivey, Ron White (Hollywood)

It takes too long for this courtroom thriller to heat up and engage an audience. Don Johnson is effectively cast as the literal lady-killer, who's just been accused of throwing his rich wife out of a high-rise window. He's become fixated on hotshot criminal lawyer Rebecca DeMornay and uses perverse psychology to get her to take his case. Soon fearing for her very life when it becomes apparent that Johnson's killing spree is open-ended, DeMornay has detective Jack Warden gather evidence of Johnson's previous unsolved murders.

GUILTY BY SUSPICION
1991, 105 mins, US ⓥ ⊙
D: Irwin Winkler **A:** Robert De Niro, Annette Bening, George Wendt, Patricia Wettig, Sam Wanamaker, Martin Scorsese (Warner)

First writing-directing effort by vet producer Irwin Winkler squarely lays out the professional, ethical, and moral dilemmas engendered by the insidious political pressures brought to bear on filmmakers in the early 1950s. The drama comes to life only fitfully. Looking raffish and trim, De Niro perfectly conveys a charming, quiet confidence at the outset. During the extraordinary appearance before HUAC, he finally blossoms into a man of conviction and passion. The actor pulls off this last-minute transformation beautifully.

GUINEVERE
1999, 104 mins, US ⓥ ⊙
D: Audrey Wells **A:** Stephen Rea, Sarah Polley, Jean Smart, Gina Gershon, Paul Dooley, Francis Guinan (Bandeira/Millennium)

Guinevere is an emotionally sensitive and insightful look at a romance between a 20-year-old girl and a bohemian photographer more than twice her age. The film never loses sight of how the relationship is a double-edged sword for both parties. During her sister's elegant wedding party in San Francisco, pretty, blond Harper Sloane (Sarah Polley) hangs out with the wedding photographer, Connie Fitzpatrick (Stephen Rea), a shaggily attractive Irishman. Thus begins an affair that one might initially expect will be more important for Harper than for the old roué. The minute ups and downs of the relationship are wonderfully observed through Wells's of-

ten oblique dialogue. Polley and Rea are both terrific.

GULLIVER'S TRAVELS
1939, 75 mins, US ⓥ ⊙
D: Dave Fleischer (Paramount)

An excellent job of animation, audience interest, and all-around showmanship. Jonathan Swift's amusing tale introduces the inhabitants of Lilliput, on the verge of war with their neighbors because the two countries cannot agree on songs to be sung at wedding of the prince and princess. Gulliver, the giant, is discovered on the Lilliput beach one night, and the inhabitants proceed to tie him up and transport him in a creaky makeshift vehicle to the town. He remains long enough to settle the pending war. The two royal lovers capably interpret the several tuneful songs composed by Ralph Rainger and Leo Robin. Score numbers eight songs, all way above par.

GUMBALL RALLY, THE
1976, 106 mins, US ⓥ ▭
D: Chuck Bail **A:** Michael Sarrazin, Normann Burton, Gary Busey, John Durren, Susan Flannery (First Artists)

Dilettante businessman Michael Sarrazin and lifetime rival Tim McIntire are among a group of auto fanatics who periodically assemble for a cross-country race, sanctioned by nobody and psychotically opposed by policeman Normann Burton. Latter's attempts to thwart the race are supposed to remind one of Wiley Coyote's snares for the Roadrunner; the animated capers remain the more effective.

GUMSHOE
1971, 85 mins, UK ⓥ
D: Stephen Frears **A:** Albert Finney, Billie Whitelaw, Frank Finlay, Janice Rule, Carolyn Seymour (Memorial)

Gumshoe is an affectionately nostalgic and amusing tribute to the movie-fiction private-eye genre of yesteryear. Story's about a small-time Liverpool nitery emcee and would-be comedian with a buff's passion for Bogie and Dashiell Hammett who gets involved in a gun- and drug-running caper. Albert Finney is brilliant as the key figure.

GUMSHOE KID, THE
1990, 98 mins, US
D: Joseph Manduke **A:** Jay Underwood, Tracy Scoggins, Vince Edwards, Arlene Golonka, Pamela Springstein (Argus)

A charming little comedy that pays homage to the private eye genre. Jay Underwood carries the picture as a guy obsessed with Bogart who gets a job in Vince Edwards's agency. Finally assigned to a field case in surveillance, he's thrown together with femme fatale Tracy Scoggins. The two of them are on the lam for the rest of the film after Scoggins's boyfriend is nabbed by persons unknown.

GUN CRAZY
(AKA: DEADLY IS THE FEMALE)
1950, 87 mins, US Ⓥ
D: Joseph H. Lewis **A:** Peggy Cummins, John Dall, Berry Kroeger, Morris Carnovsky, Russ Tamblyn (Pioneer/United Artists)

A shoot-'em-up story of desperate love and crime. After a slow beginning, it generates considerable excitement in telling a story of a young man, fascinated by guns, who turns criminal to keep the love of a girl with no scruples. It's not a pleasant story, nor is the telling, but John Dall builds some sympathy as the male. Opposite him is Peggy Cummins, a sideshow Annie Oakley without morals.

GUNCRAZY
1992, 93 mins, US Ⓥ ⊙
D: Tamra Davis **A:** Drew Barrymore, James LeGros, Billy Drago, Joe Dallesandro, Michael Ironside, Ione Skye (Zeta)

A shoot-'em-up exploitationer with a few interesting ideas, *Guncrazy* lacks the exhilaration of a first-class lovers-on-the-run crime drama. After a promising beginning, competently made indie effort settles into a surprisingly somber mood. Drew Barrymore plays Anita, a ripe, lower-class 16-year-old who starts corresponding with an imprisoned man, Howard (James LeGros). Helping spring Howard early by finding him a job, Anita welcomes him with feverish anticipation. Gun lust begins to get the better of them, and almost by accident, they begin killing.

GUNFIGHT, A
1971, 89 mins, US Ⓥ
D: Lamont Johnson **A:** Kirk Douglas, Johnny Cash, Jane Alexander, Karen Black, Keith Carradine, Raf Vallone (Paramount)

An offbeat western drama about two aging gunfighters. Lamont Johnson's very fine direction of the ruggedly sensitive script adds up to a fine depiction in discreet allegorical form of the darker sides of human nature. First the stars decide to turn the town's unofficial speculation on the results of a shoot-out confrontation into personal profit for the survivor. Next, the pair plan the carnival duel. Finally, the event itself, with the survivor really no better off than the deceased, a fact recognized by the friends of both men.

GUNFIGHT AT THE O.K. CORRAL
1957, 122 mins, US Ⓥ ⊙
D: John Sturges **A:** Burt Lancaster, Kirk Douglas, Rhonda Fleming, Jo Van Fleet, John Ireland, Lyle Bettger (Paramount)

An absorbing yarn leading up to the gory gunfight. Burt Lancaster and Kirk Douglas enact the respective roles of Wyatt Earp and Doc Holliday, story opening in Texas when the gun-handy Dodge City marshal saves the other from a lynch mob. Action moves then to the Kansas town, where Holliday helps Earp in gunning three badmen. When the marshal heeds the plea of one of his brothers, marshal of Tombstone, for aid in handling the dangerous Clanton gang, Holliday accompanies him.
1957: Nominations: Best Editing, Sound

GUNFIGHTER, THE
1950, 84 mins, US Ⓥ ⊙
D: Henry King **A:** Gregory Peck, Helen Westcott, Millard Mitchell, Jean Parker, Karl Malden, Skip Homeier (20th Century-Fox)

A sock melodrama of the Old West. Gregory Peck perfectly portrays the title role, a man doomed to live out his span killing to keep from being killed. He gives it great sympathy and a type of rugged individualism that makes it real. Despite all the tight melodrama, the picture finds time for some leavening laughter.
1950: Nomination: Best Motion Picture Story

GUNGA DIN
1939, 120 mins, US Ⓥ ⊙
D: George Stevens **A:** Cary Grant, Victor McLaglen, Douglas Fairbanks Jr., Sam Jaffe, Joan Fontaine (RKO)

Aside from the feature's ability to tell a swiftly paced, exciting yarn about British rule in India in the 1890s, it shows Cary Grant, Victor McLaglen, and Douglas Fairbanks Jr. as a trio of happy-go-lucky British army sergeants who typify the type of hard-bitten noncoms described by Rudyard Kipling in his famed poems *Barrack Room Ballads*. Story concerns the outbreak of the Thugs, cruel religious marauders, who revolted against English troops.

GUNG HO!
1943, 88 mins, US 🅥 ▢
D: Ray Enright A: Randolph Scott, Grace McDonald, Noah Beery Jr., J. Carrol Naish, Robert Mitchum (Universal)

The story of how, out of thousands of trainees, a picked group of Marines is slated for a special mission—the first raid on Makin Island—is an at-times loosely written script. The "boot training" preliminaries to the raid are just so much of a wait, but the actual attack has its compensating and exciting moments. Scott gives one of his usually fine heroic performances.

GUNG HO
1985, 111 mins, US 🅥 ⊙
D: Ron Howard A: Michael Keaton, Gedde Watanabe, George Wendt, Mimi Rogers, John Turturro, Soh Yamamura (Paramount)

Autoworker Michael Keaton pleads with Japanese industrialists to reopen a plant in Hanleyville, PA, that's been closed by foreign competition. Soon after, the Japanese invasion begins. From the first morning of calisthenics, it's clear the American workers will not adapt well to Japanese management. The conflict between cultures is good for both a laugh and a sober thought along the way. Director Ron Howard has problems straddling the two, sometimes getting bogged down in the social significance.

GUN IN BETTY LOU'S HANDBAG, THE
1992, 89 mins, US 🅥 ⊙
D: Allan Moyle A: Penelope Ann Miller, Eric Thal, Alfre Woodard, Julianne Moore, Cathy Moriarty, William Forsythe (Touchstone/Interscope)

A clever premise that ends up being as bland as its put-upon title character. Penelope Ann Miller has the title role as a mousy librarian who seizes on a found gun (used in the motel-room slaying of an FBI informant) to shake up her pristine image and become a femme fatale. However, sadistic mobster Beaudeen (William Forsythe) fears Betty Lou possesses evidence that could convict him.

GUNMEN
1994, 90 mins, US 🅥 ⊙ ▢
D: Deran Sarafian A: Christopher Lambert, Mario Van Peebles, Denis Leary, Patrick Stewart, Kadeem Hardison, Sally Kirkland (Dimension)

A routine, vacuous actioner that tries to mix thrills with humor. Cole Parker (Mario Van Peebles), a NY special-forces agent, is sent to an unnamed South American country to confiscate the illegal gains stolen from a drug dealer who murdered his father. The adventure begins when Parker busts out of jail Dani Servigo (Christopher Lambert), an offbeat outlaw who is supposed to know the site of the huge fortune. Van Peebles's considerable acting talents are largely wasted. Lambert lacks the necessary skills to pull off what's intended as light and humorous dialogue.

GUNN
1967, 94 mins, US
D: Blake Edwards A: Craig Stevens, Laura Devon, Ed Asner, Albert Paulsen, Sherry Jackson (Paramount)

A well-made but a trifle longish programmer. There's a prologue murder of a top-dog gangster. Albert Paulsen, successor to the gangland throne, is the natural suspect. M. T. (Marion) Marshall, a seagoing madame, hires Craig Stevens to prove Paulsen guilty. Eventually, Paulsen forces Stevens to prove him innocent.

GUNS AT BATASI
1964, 102 mins, UK 🅥 ▢
D: John Guillermin A: Richard Attenborough, Jack Hawkins, Flora Robson, John Leyton, Mia Farrow, Cecil Parker (20th Century-Fox)

A strong and frequently exciting piece of work, the story of a British battalion caught in the midst of the African struggle for independence. Soldiering and politics don't mix, according to this well-developed screenplay and story which dissects the strict disciplinary attitudes that govern a true British soldier and make him retain his own individual pride in the face of unappreciative political forces.

GUNS FOR SAN SEBASTIAN
1968, 100 mins, France/Mexico/Italy ▢
D: Henri Verneuil A: Anthony Quinn, Anjanette Comer, Charles Bronson, Sam Jaffe, Silvia Pinal (M-G-M)

Anthony Quinn stars as an outcast, assumed to be a priest, in the Mexico of two centuries ago. The production, a plodding mix of religious-themed action and comedy-romance, has some good direction and battle scenes, but the very poor dubbing is hard going.

GUNS IN THE AFTERNOON
See: Ride the Wild Country

519

GUNS OF DARKNESS
1962, 102 mins, UK

D: Anthony Asquith **A:** Leslie Caron, David Niven, James Robertson Justice, David Opatoshu, Ian Hunter (Cavalcade/Associated British)

Director Anthony Asquith pursues a theme that he has explored before, that violence is sometimes necessary to achieve peace. But the film does not stand up as a psychological study. And as a pure "escape yarn," its moments of tension are only spasmodic. Film opens in a South American republic, during a revolution. The president is deposed in a swift coup and, wounded, has to take off in a hurry. David Niven, a rather boorish PRO with a British-owned plantation, elects to smuggle him across the border, for reasons which are not even clear to Niven himself. Tagging along is Niven's wife (Leslie Caron).

GUNS OF NAVARONE, THE
1961, 157 mins, UK ⓥ ⊙ ▭

D: J. Lee Thompson **A:** Gregory Peck, David Niven, Anthony Quinn, Stanley Baker, Anthony Quayle (Columbia/Open Road)

Story, adapted from Alistair MacLean's novel, is set in 1943. The Axis has virtually overrun Greece and its islands. The only chance for the worn-out garrison of 2,000 men is evacuation by sea, through a channel that is impregnably guarded by a couple of huge, radar-controlled guns on Navarone. A small bunch of saboteurs is detailed to spike these guns. The cliff-scaling sequence, a scene in which the saboteurs are rounded up by the enemy, a wonderfully directed and lensed storm segment, and the final boffo climax are just a few of the nail-biting highlights.

1961: Best Special Effects

Nominations: Best Picture, Director, Adapted Screenplay, Editing, Score of a Dramatic Picture, Sound

GUNS OF THE MAGNIFICENT SEVEN
1969, 95 mins, US ⓥ ▭

D: Paul Wendkos **A:** George Kennedy, James Whitmore, Monte Markham, Bernie Casey, Joe Don Baker (United/Mirisch)

A handy follow-up to the 1960 original *Magnificent Seven* and *Return of the Seven*. It rises above a routine story line via rugged treatment and action builds to a blazing gunplay climax. George Kennedy takes on role played by Yul Brynner in two previous films, the only remaining character of the original seven.

GURU, THE
1969, 112 mins, UK

D: James Ivory **A:** Michael York, Utpal Dutt, Madhur Jaffrey, Rita Tushingham, Aparna Sen (20th Century-Fox/Arcadia/Merchant Ivory)

A hazy study of how people can transfer their own ideas about the value or qualities of another person and in so doing miss what the person is all about. Script is never realized in concrete dramatic terms. Michael York comes to India to learn the secret of playing the sitar at the house of a master musician, Utpal Dutt. Dutt gives the film's outstanding performance. He doesn't quite understand his guest and tries, without success, to teach him the "mystic" significance of the complicated instrument and the Indian relationship between student and teacher or "guru."

GUY NAMED JOE, A
1944, 120 mins, US ⓥ

D: Victor Fleming **A:** Spencer Tracy, Irene Dunne, Van Johnson, Ward Bond, Lionel Barrymore, Esther Williams (M-G-M)

An entertaining and excellently performed picture. Tracy is cast as a squadron commander at an English base. Fulfilling a premonition felt by Dunne, he crashes on his last heroic stunt, proceeding to the land where all dead pilots go. There he meets up with The Boss, and is assigned to guide and instruct the new pilots in the earthly world. It's at this point that the serious overtones of the picture intrude themselves, with the offering of the matter-of-fact solution that "life must go on for the living" too abruptly thrust into the story's continuity.

1944: Nomination: Best Original Story

GUYS AND DOLLS
1955, 150 mins, US ⓥ ⊙ ▭

D: Joseph L. Mankiewicz **A:** Marlon Brando, Jean Simmons, Frank Sinatra, Vivian Blaine, Robert Keith, Stubby Kaye (M-G-M)

A bang-up filmusical in the top-drawer Goldwyn manner, including a resurrection of the Goldwyn Girls. The casting is good all the way. Marlon Brando and Jean Simmons (as the Salvation Army sergeant) deport themselves in inspired manner. They make believable the offbeat romance between the gambler and the spirited servant of the gospel. Vivian Blaine is capital in her original stage role. Frank Sinatra is effective.

1955: Nominations: Best Color Cinematography, Color Costume Design, Color Art Direction, Scoring of a Musical Picture

GYPSY

1962, 149 mins, US ⓥ ⊙ ▭

D: Mervyn LeRoy Anderson **A:** Rosalind Russell, Natalie Wood, Karl Malden, Paul Wallace, Ann Jilliann (Warner)

There is a certain Jane One-Note implicit in the tale of a stage mother whose egotism become something of a bore despite the canny skills of director-producer Mervyn LeRoy to contrive it otherwise. Rosalind Russell's performance as the small-time brood hen deserves commendation. It is not easy to credit Natalie Wood as a stripper, but it is interesting to watch her, under LeRoy's guidance, go through the motions in a burlesque world that is prettied up in soft focus and a kind of phony innocence.

1962: Nominations: Best Color Cinematography, Color Costume Design, Adpted Music Score

GYPSY GIRL

See: Sky West and Crooked

GYPSY MOTHS, THE

1969, 106 mins, US ⓥ

D: John Frankenheimer **A:** Burt Lancaster, Deborah Kerr, Gene Hackman, Scott Wilson, Sheree North, Bonnie Bedelia (M-G-M)

The story of three barnstorming sky divers and subsequent events when they arrive in a small Kansas town to stage their exhibition. Pairing Burt Lancaster and Deborah Kerr, stars sometimes are lost in a narrative that strives to be a tale of smoldering inner conflicts and pent-up emotions. Aside from exciting skydiving episodes, picture is a lackluster affair as far as the character relationships are concerned.

HABIT
1996, 93 mins, US
D: Larry Fessenden **A:** Larry Fessenden, Meredith Snaider, Aaron Beall, Patricia Coleman, Heather Woodbury (Glass Eye)

Another hip vampire drama set in New York's East Village, small-budget indie manages to impress with plausible scripting, first-rate performances, and an unsettling mood of mounting dread. Doing quadruple duties as writer, director, editor, and leading man, Larry Fessenden is Sam, who starts to suspect that his new lover, a mysterious beauty (Meredith Snaider), may be a vampire. *Habit* is wickedly amusing as it focuses on the perverse eroticism that is intrinsic to the vampire myth—Sam obviously is enjoying the best sex he's ever had but the pic wisely refrains from pushing the humor too far.

HACKERS
1995, 104 mins, US
D: Iain Softley **A:** Johnny Lee Miller, Angelina Jolie, Jesse Bradford, Matthew Lillard, Laurence Mason (United Artists)

A brisk little thriller about high-tech pranksters who inadvertently involve themselves in a complex embezzling plot. Script is a modestly clever reworking of a formulaic concept, pitting members of a hip teen subculture against corrupt and oppressive adults. The real villain of the piece is the Plague (Fisher Stevens), a computer security agent who is double-crossing a multinational corporation by siphoning off money to a Swiss bank account. When one of the good hackers accidentally obtains evidence of the Plague's scheme, the bad hacker tries to frame the good hackers by making them appear to be ransom-demanding terrorists.

HAIL! HAIL! ROCK 'N' ROLL
1987, 120 mins, US
D: Taylor Hackford **A:** Chuck Berry, Eric Clapton, Robert Cray, Etta James, Julian Lennon, Keith Richards (Delilah)

"If you had tried to give rock and roll another name, you might call it Chuck Berry," pronounces John Lennon in an old interview at the outset of Taylor Hackford's glowing two-hour love letter to the kingpin of rock and roll. *Hail! Hail! Rock 'n' Roll* is a joyous docu that effortlessly weaves luminary rock interviews with performance footage mostly shot at Berry's 60th-birthday bash concert at the Fox Theater in St. Louis.

HAIL THE CONQUERING HERO
1944, 101 mins, US
D: Preston Sturges **A:** Eddie Bracken, Ella Raines, William Demarest, Raymond Walburn, Freddie Steele (Paramount)

The deft hand of Preston Sturges molded this film. Yarn finds Eddie Bracken, medically discharged from the marines after only one month of service because of hay fever, befriended by six real Guadalcanal heroes. During the course of this friendship, Bracken is clothed in his old marine uniform, bodily taken back to his old hometown, where he is welcomed as a hero.

1944: Nomination: Best Original Screenplay

LA HAINE
(HATE)
1995, 97 mins, France
D: Mathieu Kassovitz **A:** Vincent Cassell, Hubert Kounde, Said Taghmaoui, Francois Leventhal, Edouarde Montoute (Lazennec/Canal Plus/La Sept)

Hard-hitting pic covers less than 24 crucial hours in the lives of three ethnically diverse friends. Relatively upbeat, hyper Said (Said Taghmaoui) is of North African heritage. Vinz (Vincent Cassel), his dense lug of a buddy, is a lower-class Jew. Their more mature friend Hubert (Hubert Kounde) is a black who conscientiously masters his emotions through boxing. The trio undergoes a subtle, then drastic change during an evening excursion to Paris.

HAIR
1979, 118 mins, US
D: Milos Forman **A:** John Savage, Treat Williams, Beverly D'Angelo, Nicholas Ray, Annie Golden (United Artists)

The story line imposed on the original musical's book has large expository gaps. These are accentuated by Milos Forman's determination to have free-form musical numbers evolve out of the tale of a draftee adopted by a bunch of New York hippies, who tune him into their uninhibited lifestyles. The spirit and élan that captivated the Vietnam protest era are long gone, and what Forman tries to make up with splash and verve fails to evoke potent nostalgia.

HAIRDRESSER'S HUSBAND, THE
See: Le Mari de la Coiffeuse

HAIRSPRAY
1988, 90 mins, US ⓥ ⊙
D: John Waters A: Sonny Bono, Ruth Brown, Divine, Colleen Fitzpatrick, Deborah Harry (Buchthal/New Line Cinema)

John Waters's appreciation for the tacky side of life is in full flower in a slight but often highly amusing diversion about integration, big girls' fashions, and music-mad teens in 1962 Baltimore. Ricki Lake, chubette daughter of Divine and Jerry Stiller, overcomes all to become queen of an afternoon teenage dance show. Divine spits out some choice bon mots while denigrating her daughter's pastime, but finally rejoicing in her success, takes Lake off for a pricelessly funny visit to Hefty Hideaway, where full-figure girls can shop to their hearts' content.

HAIRY APE, THE
1944, 90 mins, US ⓥ
D: Alfred Santell A: William Bendix, Susan Hayward, John Loder, Dorothy Comingore, Alan Napier (United Artists)

The basic character, of a ship's stoker, is particularly well portrayed by William Bendix. He imparts to it all the apelike qualities that could exist in a man in line with the Eugene O'Neill play. The script takes place in the present to furnish some wartime flavor, and opens in Lisbon, where a freighter is about to sail with a load of refugees. Love interest is injected through the central woman character, Susan Hayward, who is merely enticing John Loder, second engineer of the ship, in order to achieve her selfish aims. It is she who, revolted at the sight of Bendix, labels him a hairy ape.

HALF A SIXPENCE
1967, 148 mins, UK ⓥ ▭
D: George Sidney A: Tommy Steele, Julia Foster, Cyril Ritchard, Grover Dale, Elaine Taylor (Paramount)

As with all good musicals, the story has a simple moral—that money can be a troublesome thing. Thus Kipps is projected as a likable lad, temporarily aberrated by his coming into a fortune, and returning to the true common virtues when he loses it. The cohesive force is certainly that of Tommy Steele. His assurance is overwhelming, and he leads the terping with splendid vigor and élan. The haunting title song and the ebullient "Flash, Bang, Wallop!" remain the showstoppers.

HALF-MOON STREET
1987, 90 mins, UK/US ⓥ ⊙
D: Bob Swaim A: Sigourney Weaver, Michael Caine, Patrick Kavanagh, Keith Buckley, Nadim Sawalha (RKO/Pressman/Showtime—Movie Channel)

Script, based on Paul Theroux's thriller Dr. Slaughter, has been rendered nonsensical and incoherent by screenwriters. Weaver plays Dr. Slaughter, a scholar at the Middle East Institute in London who turns to working as an escort to supplement her paltry income. She arrives one rainy night to be the paid guest of Lord Bulbeck, played competently if uninvolvingly by Caine. Caine is somehow mixed up with Arabs in a convoluted scheme.

HALLELUJAH
1929, 109 mins, US
D: King Vidor A: Daniel L. Haynes, Nina Mae McKinney, William Fountaine, Harry Gray, Fannie Belle DeKnight, Victoria Spivey (M-G-M)

In his herculean attempt to take comedy, romance, and tragedy and blend them into a big, gripping, Negro talker, King Vidor has turned out an unusual picture from a theme that is almost as ancient as the sun. Vidor's strict adherence to realism is so effective at times it is stark and uncanny. Nina Mae McKinney as the dynamic, vivacious girl of the colored underworld, who lives by her wits and enmeshes the males by her personality, sex appeal, and dancing feet, never had a day's work before a camera. Daniel L. Haynes as Zeke, the principal male, is the big, rough, lazylike colored boy, happiest when he sings, and who loves his women.
1929/30: Nomination: Best Director

HALLELUJAH, I'M A BUM!
(UK: HALLELUJAH, I'M A TRAMP!)
1933, 83 mins, US ⓥ
D: Lewis Milestone A: Al Jolson, Madge Evans, Frank Morgan, Harry Langdon, Chester Conklin (United Artists)

An unconvincing mixture of the fictional and factional. Ultramodern realism with the playboy mayor of the city of New York and his weakness for the Central Park Casino and a pretty femme in particular (Madge Evans) is blended with such unconvincing detail as nonexisting Central Park's hobos, of which Al Jolson is the unofficial mayor. The "rhythmic dialogue" and the Lewis Milestonian method of wedding the tempo'd music to the ac-

523

tion has its moments. Cast had to talk in rhyme and rhythm rather than their accustomed dramatic prose.

HALLELUJAH, I'M A TRAMP!
See: Hallelujah, I'm a Bum!

HALLELUJAH THE HILLS
1963, 88 mins, US

D: Adolfas Mekas A: Peter H. Beard, Martin Greenbaum, Sheila Finn, Peggy Steffans (Vermont)

There is not much of a story. Two clean-cut, adventurous young American stalwarts vie for the hand of a beauteous young girl only to have her snapped up by a bearded character. Small-town life and the seasons pass in review as the two men camp out and take their turns at wooing the girl. Writer-director-editor Adolfas Mekas displays a flair for visual revelation, gags, and shenanigans that manage to keep this stimulating throughout.

HALLELUJAH TRAIL, THE
1965, 152 mins, US ⊘ ⊙ ▭

D: John Sturges A: Burt Lancaster, Lee Remick, Jim Hutton, Pamela Tiffin, Donald Pleasence, Brian Keith (United Artists)

It all begins with the burgeoning city of Denver facing the worst threat of its existence—becoming bone-dry in 10 days in the approaching winter of 1867. Thirsty miners, a worried US Cavalry, a band of whiskey-mad Sioux, a crusading temperance group, and a train of 40 wagons carrying 600 barrels of hard likker become so thoroughly involved that even the off-screen narrator has a hard time trying to keep track of them. Producer-Director John Sturges has pulled every plug in spoofing practically every western situation known to the scripter.

HALLOWEEN
1978, 93 mins, US ⊘ ⊙ ▭

D: John Carpenter A: Donald Pleasence, Jamie Lee Curtis, Nancy Loomis, P. J. Soles, Charles Cyphers, Kyle Richards (Falcon)

After a promising opening, *Halloween* becomes just another maniac-on-the-loose suspenser. However, despite the prosaic plot, director John Carpenter has timed the film's gore so that the 93-minute item is packed with enough thrills. The picture opens on Halloween night in a small midwestern town. A young boy spies his sister necking with her boyfriend. As they mount the steps for her bedroom, he slips on his Halloween mask, pulls out a butcher knife, and does some cutting. For the rest of the thriller the Hitchcockian influence remains, but the plot ambles along to a predictable conclusion.

HALLOWEEN II
1981, 92 mins, US ⊘ ⊙ ▭

D: Rick Rosenthal A: Jamie Lee Curtis, Donald Pleasence, Charles Cyphers, Dick Warlock, Jeffrey Kramer (De Laurentiis)

This uninspired version amounts to lukewarm sloppy seconds in comparison to the original film. There are, incredibly, almost never any really terrific scares in 92 minutes—just multiple shots of violence and gore that are more gruesome than anything else. The zombielike masked killer makes his way through the town slashing unsuspecting residents. It becomes difficult to care who is getting sliced or why.

HALLOWEEN III: SEASON OF THE WITCH
1982, 96 mins, US ⊘ ⊙ ▭

D: Tommy Lee Wallace A: Tom Atkins, Stacey Nelkin, Dan O'Herlihy, Ralph Strait, Michael Currie (De Laurentiis)

There's not much to say about *Halloween III* that hasn't already been said about either of the other two Halloween pics or a slew of imitators. There is the tired old cliché of a crazed toy manufacturer (in this case he makes Halloween masks), the fearless couple out to figure what's "really" going on, and plot holes big enough to shoot another film through.

HALLOWEEN IV: THE RETURN OF MICHAEL MYERS
1988, 88 mins, US ⊘ ⊙

D: Dwight H. Little A: Donald Pleasence, Ellie Cornell, Danielle Harris, George P. Wilbur (Trancas)

No-frills, workmanlike picture resurrects monster Michael Myers who escapes from a hospital to return home and wreak havoc, with the vague notion of getting to his niece Jamie (Danielle Harris). His face scarred from an earlier altercation with the monster, Donald Pleasence reprises his role as Dr. Loomis, now hell-bent on destroying the obviously unkillable Myers.

HALLOWEEN V: THE REVENGE OF MICHAEL MYERS
1989, 96 mins, US ⊘ ⊙

D: Dominique Othenin-Girard A: Donald Pleasence, Danielle Harris, Wendy Kaplan, Ellie Cornell, Donald L. Shanks (Magnum)

Pretty stupid and boring fare. The thread of a plot has the killer empathetically linked to his nine-year-old niece Jamie (Danielle Harris), who goes into a sort of epileptic seizure when she senses he's about to kill again. Meanwhile the determined Dr. Loomis (Donald Pleasence) keeps badgering the little girl to help him end his scourge.

HALLOWEEN: H20
TWENTY YEARS LATER
1998, 85 mins, US ⓥ ⊙ ▭
D: Steve Miner **A:** Jamie Lee Curtis, Adam Arkin, Josh Hartnett, Michelle Williams, Adam Hann-Byrd, Janet Leigh (Nightfall/Dimension)

While plot mechanics aren't wildly imaginative, pic nonetheless delivers requisite jolts in an above-average package. Michael Myers's sis Laurie Strode (Jamie Lee Curtis) is now live-in headmistress at an upscale SoCal boarding school, with teenage son John (Josh Hartnett) duly enrolled. Guess who's coming cross-country to visit? The majority of staff and students are on a camping trip. Plus, natch, it's Halloween. Soon Michael (Chris Durand) is slashing his way through California youth en route to his already-suspicious little sis. Director Steve Miner presses the false-scare button a few too many times early on, and script doesn't evince any special invention. Still, the scares are there. Pic belongs to Curtis, and care has been taken to make her character one credible, battle-scarred survivor.

HALLOWEEN: THE CURSE OF
MICHAEL MYERS
1995, 88 mins, US ⓥ
D: Joe Chappelle **A:** Donald Pleasence, Mitch Ryan, Marianne Hagan, Paul Rudd, Leo Geter (Nightfall)

Run-of-the-mill horror item is notable only for final appearance of the late Donald Pleasence. The masked Michael Myers (George P. Wilbur) now seems to be driven by some ancient Celtic ritual of sacrificing an entire family. The explosion of horror/slasher films in the 17 years since the first entry has made Myers's antics seem mundane.

HALLS OF MONTEZUMA
1950, 113 mins, US ⓥ ⊙
D: Lewis Milestone **A:** Richard Widmark, Jack Palance, Robert Wagner, Karl Malden, Richard Boone (20th Century-Fox)

An account of marine heroism during the fierce South Pacific fighting of the Second World War. Rather than a presentation of mass battle, film deals intimately with a small group of marines under the command of Richard Widmark and how they fulfill a mission to take Jap prisoners for questioning.

HAMBURGER HILL
1987, 110 mins, US ⓥ ⊙
D: John Irvin **A:** Anthony Barrile, Michael Patrick Boatman, Don Cheadle, Michael Dolan, Don James, Dylan McDermott (RKO/Nasatir-Carabatsos/Interaccess)

Well produced and directed with an eye to documentarylike realism and authenticity, pic centers upon a military undertaking of familiar futility during the Vietnam War. It follows a squad of 14 recruits from initial R&R through 10 days' worth of hell, as the men make 11 agonizing assaults on a heavily fortified hill. Director John Irvin makes fine use of the Philippines locations.

HAMLET
1948, 155 mins, UK ⓥ ⊙
D: Laurence Olivier **A:** Laurence Olivier, Eileen Herlie, Basil Sydney, Jean Simmons, Felix Aylmer (Rank/Two Cities)

This is picture-making at its best. Star-producer-director Laurence Olivier was the driving force behind the whole venture. Minor characters and a good deal of verse have been thrown overboard, and a four-and-a-quarter-hour play becomes a two-and-a-half-hour film. In his interpretation of Hamlet, Olivier thinks of him as nearly a great man, damned, as most people are, by lack of resolution. Special praise is due Eileen Herlie for her playing of the queen. She has made the character really live.

1948: Best Picture, Actor (Laurence Olivier), B&W Art Direction, B&W Costume Design
Nominations: Best Director, Supp. Actress (Jean Simmons), Scoring of a Dramatic Picture

HAMLET
1990, 135 mins, US ⓥ ⊙
D: Franco Zeffirelli **A:** Mel Gibson, Glenn Close, Alan Bates, Paul Scofield, Ian Holm, Helena Bonham Carter (Warner/Nelson)

Mel Gibson's best moments come in the highly physical dueling scene that climaxes the Shakespeare play. Otherwise, Mel's Hamlet is blond and Franco Zeffirelli's *Hamlet* is bland. By slicing the text virtually in half, and casting a matinee idol in the lead, the director clearly hoped to engage the masses. Performances all fall in a middle range between the competent and the lackluster. Best is probably Paul Scofield as the ghost, although Zeffirelli irritatingly cuts or pulls away from him midstream. Glenn Close brings a juicy vigor to Gertrude.

1990: Nominations: Best Art Direction, Costume Design

HAMLET
1996, 242 mins, US ⓥ ⊙ ▭
D: Kenneth Branagh **A:** Kenneth Branagh, Julie Christie, Billy Crystal, Gerard Depardieu, Charlton Heston, Derek Jacobi (Castle Rock/Columbia)

Kenneth Branagh has mounted a full-bodied, clear-headed, resplendently staged rendition of *Hamlet*. A rare unedited version of the Bard's lengthiest play, the result is the second-longest major U.S. or British feature film of all time. This yields significant artistic dividends through the revelation of normally excised or underemphasized aspects of the play. Branagh transplants the tale to the mid-to-late 19th century. The downside of his style is a literal-mindedness most evident when he makes rather forlorn attempts at poetic visual flourishes. Branagh, as a bleach-blond Hamlet, displays an energy and forcefulness that is contagious to the huge cast. At least a couple of the other actors are brilliant: Derek Jacobi as a keenly tactical and shrewd Claudius, and Richard Briers, whose Polonius is a revelation, making him a political man of tragically misguided motives.

1996: Nominations: Best Screenplay Adaptation, Original Dramatic Score, Art Direction, Costume Design

HAMMERSMITH IS OUT
1972, 108 mins, US ⓥ
D: Peter Ustinov **A:** Elizabeth Taylor, Richard Burton, Peter Ustinov, Beau Bridges, Leon Ames, George Raft (Crean)

What is, apparently, an exercise in spoofery on the part of Elizabeth Taylor, Richard Burton, and the even more energetic Peter Ustinov, starts as a variation on the Faust legend but almost immediately turns into a belabored antic. The somewhat sketchy screenplay is no more than a line on which the three principals hang their rarely inspired improvisations.

HAMMETT
1982, 94 mins, US ⓥ
D: Wim Wenders **A:** Frederic Forrest, Peter Boyle, Marilu Henner, Roy Kinnear, Sylvia Sidney (Zoetrope)

Wim Wenders' problems with this, his first Hollywood film, are many and well known. Overpolished by too many script rewrites, perhaps emasculated by massive footage scraps and belated reshoots, project (all shot on interiors) emerges as a rather suffocating film taking place in a rickety "Chinatown." Film is a sort of homage to Dashiell Hammett. Based on a fiction by Joe Gores, it has Hammett far removed from his old private-eye days and suffering from TB, eking out a precarious living with short stories penned for pulp detective magazines.

HANA-BI
1997, 103 mins, Japan ⓥ ⊙
D: Takeshi Kitano **A:** Beat Takeshi, Kayoko Kishimoto, Ren Osugi, Susumu Terajima, Tetsu Watanabe, Yuko Daike (Office Kitano/Bandai Visual/Television Tokyo/Tokyo FM)

Hana-bi is a poignant reflection on love, violence, grief, and loss. This contemplative drama about a tough ex-cop tying up the loose ends of his life is pure poetry. Detective Nishi (Takeshi Kitano) has lost his infant daughter and is about to lose his wife (Kayoko Kishimoto) to a protracted illness. He calmly carries out a plan to right some of the wrongs in his life. Having quit the force, he robs a bank singlehandedly and delivers packages of loot to a wounded colleague, a young police widow, and yakuza loan sharks, and funds a trip to give his wife one last taste of happiness—a lyrical, cleansing journey that builds to a soulful conclusion. While the nonlinear structure and constant time shifts create initial confusion, Kitano's approach is sufficiently mesmerizing to sustain interest as the plot becomes clear.

HAND, THE
1981, 104 mins, US ⓥ
D: Oliver Stone **A:** Michael Caine, Andrea Marcovicci, Viveca Lindfors, Bruce McGill, Mara Hobel, Annie McEnroe (Orion)

Premise—of an autonomous appendage wreaking havoc on anyone crossing the human it was previously attached to—has been effectively executed in many past pix. Special-visual-effects consultant Carlo Rambaldi should probably share some of the blame for the ineffectiveness of the film's villain. Cartoonist Michael Caine evokes some sympathy after he loses his hand and spends most of his time sweating and grimacing into the camera lens. It's not a pretty sight.

HANDFUL OF DUST, A
1988, 118 mins, UK ⑮
D: Charles Sturridge **A:** James Wilby, Kristin Scott Thomas, Rupert Graves, Anjelica Huston, Alec Guinness, Judi Dench (LWT/Stagescreen)

Classy stuff based on an Evelyn Waugh novel, with a high production standard but an essentially empty story. Kristin Scott Thomas as a lovely but fickle aristocrat is excellent, with an appealing fey manner. Set in Britain of the 1930s, at the beautiful country house Hetton Abbey, James Wilby and Scott Thomas and their young son seem content until the weekend visit of idle socialite Rupert Graves. Scott Thomas slips into an affair with the penniless Graves while Wilby happily wanders his estate unaware he is being cuckolded.
1988: Nomination: Best Costume Design

HANDGUN
(US: DEEP IN THE HEART)
1983, 101 mins, UK ⑮
D: Tony Garnett **A:** Karen Young, Clayton Day, Suzie Humphreys, Ben Jones (Kestrel)

Handgun takes a subject that is the stuff of exploitation and steers it toward social commentary. The result is an intelligent analysis of the political and sexual values of male society in Texas. Pic is cast in three chapters that follow the maturing of a pretty young girl who goes to the midwest to teach history. She's just too soft to counter the approaches of a macho attorney who's obsessed with guns and hunting. It's only when he decides to have his own way with her that she realizes what she's up against.

HANDGUN
1994, 90 mins, US ⑮ ⊙
D: Whitney Ransick **A:** Treat Williams, Seymour Cassel, Paul Schulze, Toby Huss, Angel Caban (Workin' Man)

Comic spin on the action/heist genre is technically uneven, but has sharp dialogue and superlative performances, particularly by Treat Williams. Wounded during a robbery that goes awry, Jack McCallister (Seymour Cassel) escapes with half a million in payroll booty, which he stashes in a locker. But as soon as the news gets around, a gallery of dubious characters, headed by McCallister's two sons, set out on a desperate hunt for the stolen cash.

Ransick's deadpan humor mixes idiosyncratic wit with laconic and cryptic dialogue.

HANDMAID'S TALE, THE
1990, 109 mins, US/W. Germany ⑱ ⊙
D: Volker Schlondorff **A:** Natasha Richardson, Robert Duvall, Faye Dunaway, Aidan Quinn, Elizabeth McGovern, Victoria Tennant (Cinecom/Bioskop)

A provocative portrait of a future totalitarian theocracy where women have lost all human rights, *Handmaid's Tale* is sci-fi from a woman's point of view. The so-called sins of late-20th-century society are blamed by the authorities as causing God's plague of infertility, requiring drastic measures to preserve the race. Natasha Richardson portrays a young mother who's rounded up by the authorities to serve as a breeder, or handmaid. Her travails unfold in Harold Pinter's uncharacteristically straightforward screenplay rather mechanically.

HANDS OF ORLAC
See: Orlacs Haende

HANDS OF THE RIPPER
1971, 85 mins, UK ⑮
D: Peter Sasdy **A:** Eric Porter, Angharad Rees, Jane Merrow, Keith Bell, Derek Godfrey, Dora Bryan (Hammer)

Hammer gives a highly intriguing twist to the Jack the Ripper murders which shook London back in the 1890s and have fascinated writers and filmmakers. Well-directed by Peter Sasdy, the tension is skillfully developed. Murders are particularly gruesome and there are shocks that will have the most hardened filmgoer sitting up.

HANDSOME SERGE
See: Le Beau Serge

HANDS OVER THE CITY
See: La Mani sulla Citta

HAND THAT ROCKS THE CRADLE, THE
1992, 110 mins, US ⑮ ⊙
D: Curtis Hanson **A:** Annabella Sciorra, Rebecca DeMornay, Matt McCoy, Ernie Hudson, Julianne Moore, Madeline Zima (Hollywood/Interscope)

Pleasant existence of pregnant Seattle housewife Claire Bartel (Annabella Sciorra) is disrupted when her new gynecologist crosses the proper boundaries during an exam. Claire files charges, upon which the doctor commits suicide. Medic's demise sends his pregnant wife into hysterics, causing her to lose her baby. Cut to six months later, and this woman (Rebecca DeMornay) turns up to offer her services as nanny to the Bartels. Helmer has obtained taut, impressive performances.

HANG 'EM HIGH
1968, 114 mins, US ⓥ ⊙
D: Ted Post **A:** Clint Eastwood, Inger Stevens, Ed Begley, Pat Hingle, Ben Johnson (United Artists/Malpaso)

A poor-made imitation of a poor Italian-made imitation of an American western. It stars Clint Eastwood as a man bent on vengeance and is an episodic, rambling tale which glorifies personal justice and mocks orderly justice. Eastwood is hanged (but not killed) by do-it-yourself vigilantes, headed by Ed Begley; district judge Pat Hingle recruits Eastwood to be a deputy marshal, and part of the job is to round up those who wronged him. Inger Stevens drifts in and out as a forced romantic interest.

HANGFIRE
1991, 89 mins, US ⓥ
D: Peter Maris **A:** Brad Davis, Kim Delaney, Jan-Michael Vincent, Ken Foree, George Kennedy, Yaphet Kotto (Krevoy-Stabler)

A tight little action thriller about a prison break that strains credibility. Character actor Lee de Broux, in a bravura performance, plays a serial killer/rapist. De Broux and his minions take over the town of Sonora and hold its fifty or so inhabitants prisoner. Local sheriff Brad Davis and his Vietnam-vet pal Ken Foree manage to defeat de Broux.

HANGING TREE, THE
1959, 106 mins, US
D: Delmer Daves **A:** Gary Cooper, Maria Schell, Karl Malden, Ben Piazza, George C. Scott (Warner)

In essence, the story follows western classic form. Gary Cooper is the mysterious stranger who drifts into a Montana gold-mining town. His first action is to rescue young Ben Piazza from a lynch-minded mob. His second is to take on the recovery of Maria Schell, a Swiss immigrant, who is ill and blinded from exposure. Stirring in these complicated relationships is the character of Karl Malden, an evil and lascivious gold prospec-

tor. There are fine performances from a good cast.
1959: Nomination: Best Song ("The Hanging Tree")

HANGIN' WITH THE HOMEBOYS
1991, 88 mins, US ⓥ ⊙
D: Joseph P. Vasquez **A:** Doug E. Doug, Mario Joyner, John Leguizamo, Nestor Serrano, Kimberly Russell (New Line)

Ensemble piece follows the misadventures of four South Bronx youths from mid-morning Friday to Saturday dawn. Willie (Doug E. Doug) is a welfare sponger. Tom (Mario Joyner) is a would-be actor. Johnny (John Leguizamo) is a shy, serious Puerto Rican supermarket stocker. Vinnie (Nestor Serrano) is a Puerto Rican who pretends to be an Italian stud. Film is infused with an aggressive and engaging street energy and plenty of humor.

HANGMEN ALSO DIE!
1943, 131 mins, US ⊙
D: Fritz Lang **A:** Brian Donlevy, Walter Brennan, Anna Lee, Gene Lockhart, Dennis O'Keefe (United Artists)

Fritz Lang succeeds with singular success in capturing the spirit of the Czech people in the face of the Nazi reign of terror. Cameraman James Wong Howe, in particular, turns in a magnificent job. Saga starts with the assassination of Heydrich, the hangman, by an appointed member of the underground (Donlevy), but the plans for his escape go awry
1943: Nominations: Best Scoring of a Dramatic Picture, Sound

HANGOVER SQUARE
1945, 77 mins, US
D: John Brahm **A:** Laird Cregar, Linda Darnell, George Sanders, Glenn Langan, Faye Marlowe, Alan Napier (20th Century-Fox)

Eerie murder melodrama of the London gaslight era is the story of a distinguished young composer-pianist with a Jekyll-Hyde personality. When he becomes overwrought, he's a madman—and his lustful forages are always succeeded by a loss of memory. Production is grade A, and so is the direction by John Brahm, with particular bows to the music score by Bernard Herrmann.

HANKY PANKY
1982, 105 mins, US ⓥ ⊙
D: Sidney Poitier **A:** Gene Wilder, Gilda Radner, Kathleen Quinlan, Richard Widmark, Robert Prosky (Columbia)

A limp romantic suspense comedy

which manages to be neither romantic, suspenseful, nor funny. Tale opens moodily with an unexplained suicide and then picks up Gene Wilder, whose short cab ride with frantic Kathleen Quinlan plunges him into a web of intrigue, obliging him to endure suspicion by the police for murder, beatings by agent Richard Widmark, and an attempt to kill him by a helicopter out in the desert.

HANNAH AND HER SISTERS
1986, 106 mins, US Ⓥ ⊙
D: Woody Allen A: Woody Allen, Michael Caine, Mia Farrow, Carrie Fisher, Barbara Hershey, Dianne Wiest (Orion)

One of Woody Allen's great films. Indeed, he makes nary a misstep from beginning to end in charting the amorous affiliations of three sisters and their men over a two-year period. Hannah, played by Mia Farrow, was formerly married to TV producer Woody Allen but is now happily wed to agent Michael Caine, who, in turn, secretly lusts after his wife's sexy sister, Barbara Hershey, the live-in mate of tormented painter Max von Sydow. The third sister (Dianne Wiest) runs a catering business with Carrie Fisher.
1986: Best Supp. Actor (Michael Caine), Supp. Actress (Dianne Wiest), Original Screenplay
Nominations: Best Picture, Director, Art Direction, Editing

HANNA'S WAR
1988, 158 mins, US Ⓥ ⊙ ▭
D: Menahem Golan A: Ellen Burstyn, Maruschka Detmers, Anthony Andrews, Donald Pleasence, David Warner (Cannon)

Hanna Senesh, a talented poet and a martyr who died in a Hungarian jail in 1944, before her 24th birthday, is a mythical figure in Israel, a symbol of gentle but determined heroism. In Menahem Golan's version, heroes and villains are easily distinguished, characters are respectfully observed and admired, or duly abhorred and discredited, and no time is spent dwelling on psychological niceties. Maruschka Detmers may not radiate the spiritual strength required by her role, but she is dedicated and often moving during the prison sequences.

HANNIBAL
1960, 103 mins, Italy/US
D: Edgar G. Ulmer A: Victor Mature, Rita Gam, Gabriele Ferzetti, Milly Vitale, Rik Battaglia (Liber/Warner)

Although this version of the noted Carthaginian general's military and romantic activities near Rome in 218 B.C. is dramatically crude and ponderously paced, it contains enough sheer spectacle, gore, and quasi-historical action to excite those still willing to meet such films on their own primitive level. Victor Mature brings physical command to the central role, but turns wooden in the romantic going, as does Rita Gam as his doomed wartime paramour.

HANNIBAL BROOKS
1969, 101 mins, UK
D: Michael Winner A: Oliver Reed, Michael J. Pollard, Karin Baal, Wolfgang Preiss, James Donald (Scimitar)

A pleasant, tame tale about a British prisoner (Oliver Reed), assigned to nursemaid an elephant in a Munich Zoo. From here, it is a short jump into attempted escapes, with the elephant in tow, across some mountain passes (à la Hannibal, hence the title) into Switzerland. The humorous vein gets sidetracked by the excursion into action and there isn't a laugh in the second half of the film. Michael J. Pollard is simply dreadful as a cocky Yank prisoner.

HANNIE CAULDER
1971, 85 mins, UK/US Ⓥ ⊙ ▭
D: Burt Kennedy A: Raquel Welch, Robert Culp, Ernest Borgnine, Strother Martin, Jack Elam, Diana Dors (Tigon/Curtwel)

Raquel Welch plays Hannie Caulder, who, having been widowed and raped by the Clemens brothers, determines to avenge these wrongs. With the aid of a bounty hunter she is soon showing that ladies shoot first and can be more deadly than the male. She is admirably supported by Ernest Borgnine as the meanest of the brothers and Robert Culp as the bounty hunter who befriends her.

HANOI HILTON
1987, 123 mins, US Ⓥ ⊙
D: Lionel Chetwynd A: Michael Moriarty, Jeffrey Jones, Paul Le Mat, Stephen Davies, Lawrence Pressman, Aki Aleong (Cannon)

A lame attempt to tell the story of US prisoners in Hoa Lo Prison, in Hanoi during the Vietnam War. Pic is a slanted view of traditional prison-camp sagas, injecting lots of hindsight and taking right-wing potshots that do a disservice to the very human drama of the subject. Michael Moriarty heads a curiously bland cast. Pic is desperately lacking side issues or subplots of interest, monotonously hammering away at the main issue of survival in the face of inhuman treatment.

HANOVER STREET
1979, 109 mins, US ⊘ ⊙ ▭
D: Peter Hyams A: Harrison Ford, Lesley-Anne Down, Christopher Plummer, Alec McCowen, Richard Masur, Patsy Kensit (Columbia)

Reasonably effective as a war film with a love-story background, it's meant to be a love story set against a war background. American flying ace David Halloran (Harrison Ford) and British hospital nurse Margaret Sellinger (Lesley-Anne Down) meet during an air raid, and fall hopelessly in love. Only when Down takes a backseat, and Ford is thrown together with her cuckolded husband, Paul, a British secret-service topper (Christopher Plummer), does *Hanover Street* manifest any vital life signs. The last third of the picture becomes a model of efficient war-film making.

HANS CHRISTIAN ANDERSEN
1952, 112 mins, US ⊘ ⊙
D: Charles Vidor A: Danny Kaye, Farley Granger, Zizi Jeanmaire, Joey Walsh, Philip Tonge, Roland Petit (Goldwyn/RKO)

A charming fairy tale about the Danish master of the childhood fantasy. Danny Kaye does a very fine job of the title role, sympathetically projecting the Andersen spirit and philosophy. No attempt at biography is made, so the imaginative production has full rein in bringing in songs and ballet numbers to round out the Andersen fairy tales told by Kaye. Socko is ''The Little Mermaid'' ballet, a spectacular display backed by the music of Franz Liszt. On the song side, the picture has Frank Loesser contributing eight songs, all given first-rate vocal treatment by Kaye.
1952: Nominations: Best Color Cinematography, Color Costume Design, Color Art Direction, Scoring of a Musical Picture, Song (''Thumbelina'')

HAPPENING, THE
1967, 101 mins, US
D: Elliot Silverstein A: Anthony Quinn, George Maharis, Michael Parks, Robert Walker, Martha Hyer, Faye Dunaway (Columbia/Horizon)

Intriguing offbeat item which, between expected laughs, seeks to offer satiric peeks at US life and values. Well-tempered plotline, with several corkscrew twists, follows the weekend hegira of four ennui-laden but debauched Miami beach bums in search of some potent stimuli. They find it, albeit accidentally, by stumbling into an unlikely kidnapping. What is bothersome about this tragi-farce is why it doesn't succeed. Newcomer Faye Dunaway, though stunning to view and essaying her role with élan, is too womanly seductive for a teenybopper role.

HAPPIEST DAYS OF YOUR LIFE, THE
1950, 81 mins, UK
D: Frank Launder A: Alastair Sim, Margaret Rutherford, Joyce Grenfell, Richard Wattis, Edward Rigby (London)

Setting is a college for boys, to which, as a result of a slip at the Ministry of Education, a girls' school is evacuated. There is no shortage of laughs, but the joke wears thin before the end. It's an ideal vehicle for Alastair Sim as the harassed headmaster, while Margaret Rutherford admirably suggests the overpowering headmistress.

HAPPIEST MILLIONAIRE, THE
1967, 164 mins, US ⊘
D: Norman Tokar A: Fred MacMurray, Tommy Steele, Greer Garson, Geraldine Page, Gladys Cooper, Hermione Baddeley (Walt Disney)

Walt Disney family comedy includes Britain's Tommy Steele in his US film debut as an Irish servant in 1916 Philadelphia. Fred MacMurray is well teamed with Greer Garson as the Philadelphia parents. Lesley Ann Warren plays the teenage daughter with charm and radiance.
1967: Nomination: Best Costume Design

HAPPILY EVER AFTER
1990, 74 mins, US
D: John Howley (Filmation)

An unauthorized sequel to the Walt Disney classic *Snow White, Happily Ever After* is a well-crafted but uninspired animated fantasy. Action picks up here with the evil queen's brother Lord Maliss (drawn to resemble Basil Rathbone and voiced with gusto by Malcolm McDowell) in a vendetta to avenge sis's death by zonking Snow White and her handsome prince. Voice casting is pic's big plus. Irene Cara warbles a catchy, uptempo song, ''Love Is the Reason,'' to bookend the film.

HAPPINESS
1998, 139 mins, US Ⓥ ⊙
D: Todd Solondz **A:** Jane Adams, Dylan Baker, Lara Flynn Boyle, Ben Gazzara, Philip Seymour Hoffman, Cynthia Stevenson (Good Machine/Killer)

Todd Solondz's *Happiness* is a disturbing black comedy about the trouble sex causes people. Joy (Jane Adams) is the non-achiever among three middle-class New Jersey sisters. Trish (Cynthia Stevenson) is a perennially perky housewife with three kids and an ultra-straight husband, Bill (Dylan Baker), a suburban shrink who counts among his patients the overweight, sexually frustrated loner Allen (Philip Seymour Hoffman). Allen is obsessed with his next-door neighbor, the glamorous, fabulously successful author Helen (Lara Flynn Boyle), the third sister. Bill develops an abnormal fascination with Johnny (Evan Silverberg), a classmate of his 11-year-old son, Billy (Rufus Read). Pic feels a bit indulgent and overextended. Nonetheless, director's control over his material is inarguable and extends uniformly over his actors.

HAPPY
1934, 80 mins, UK
D: Fred Zelnik **A:** Stanley Lupino, Laddie Cliff, Will Fyffe, Renee Gadd, Dorothy Hyson, Gus McNaughton (British International)

Stanley Lupino, Laddie Cliff, and Will Fyffe are a splendid trio of comedians. They provide the comedy for this musical mélange, which is formless but provides entertainment. Lupino and Cliff, two musicians, reside in an attic, with Fyffe as the landlord. Lupino is working on an invention, a device which, if attached to a motorcar which is stolen, will automatically yell for the police.

HAPPY BIRTHDAY, WANDA JUNE
1971, 105 mins, US
D: Mark Robson **A:** Rod Steiger, Susannah York, George Grizzard, Don Murray, William Hickey, Steven Paul (Filmakers/Sourdough/Red Lions)

Rod Steiger shines as the self-deceiving ultramasculine hero, returned from eight years in the Amazon jungle, to find that not only has his loving wife, a former pinheaded carhop (played brilliantly by Susannah York), become a level-elheaded intellectual equal but has gone to his extreme opposite in seeking another soul mate. The treatment is too irreverent to be taken seriously for a moment.

HAPPY ENDING, THE
1969, 117 mins, US Ⓥ ▭
D: Richard Brooks **A:** Jean Simmons, John Forsythe, Lloyd Bridges, Teresa Wright, Dick Shawn, Nanette Fabray (United Artists/PaxFilms)

A well-developed and acted and potentially significant "woman's movie" unfortunately drowns in Brooks's over-indulgences and overwriting. As the still-attractive but anxiously middle-aged and self-pitying matron who is financially secure but personally bankrupt, Jean Simmons gives a moving, emotionally wringing performance.
1969: Nominations: Best Actress (Jean Simmons), Song ("What Are You Doing the Rest of Your Life?")

HAPPY GO LUCKY
1943, 79 mins, US
D: Curtis Bernhardt **A:** Mary Martin, Dick Powell, Eddie Bracken, Betty Hutton, Rudy Vallee (Paramount)

Mary Martin arrives on a nameless Caribbean isle with a small b.r. amassed for the purpose of allowing her to act the wealthy lady and catch a wealthy husband in the process. Martin capably handles the ballad department, with an occasional assist from Dick Powell, while Betty Hutton, of course, is hot on the jive. They divide up six numbers by Frank Loesser and Jimmy McHugh.

HAPPY LAND
1943, 75 mins, US
D: Irving Pichel **A:** Don Ameche, Frances Dee, Harry Carey, Ann Rutherford, Richard Crane, Henry Morgan (20th Century-Fox)

The story of a typical Iowa country town and a typical family (the Marshes), their joys, disappointments, and sorrows. Plot has drugstore operator Ameche bereaved over the loss of his son, killed in naval action. Return of Gramp, his father, dead for some 25 years in the form of an apparition, is the device used to set Ameche right, since the grief-stricken father claims that the son never really lived—never had a home of his own, had not married, etc. Flashback method then traces the life of the youngster from birth.

HAPPY NEW YEAR
1987, 85 mins, US Ⓥ
D: John G. Avildsen **A:** Peter Falk, Charles Durning, Wendy Hughes, Tom Courtenay, Joan Copeland, Tracy Brooks Swope (Columbia/Delphi IV)

Crime pays off in this unpretentious

buddy picture about two middle-aged jewel thieves. Topliners Peter Falk and Charles Durning team with an easygoing charm. Film is funniest and most engrossing in the first hour or so when Falk and Durning are casing the Palm Beach branch of Harry Winston jewelers. This leads to a series of amusing encounters with the fey and smarmy jewelry-store manager Edward Sanders (expertly rendered by Tom Courtenay), who from Falk's hard-boiled honor-among-thieves perspective is a soulless money-grubber deserving the worst.

1987: Nomination: Best Makeup

HARAKIRI
See: Seppuku

HARD CONTRACT
1969, 106 mins, US ▭
D: S. Lee Pogostin **A:** James Coburn, Lee Remick, Lilli Palmer, Burgess Meredith, Patrick Magee, Sterling Hayden (20th Century-Fox)

The principle of the loner, the individual in the jungle of society, the solitary predator, is emphatically portrayed in this skillfully mounted film about the killer-for-hire (Coburn) who agrees to a hard contract to eliminate three men in Europe. Leaving the US for Torremelinos, he meets a self-indulgent jet-set quartet who bloom in the Spanish sun. Lee Remick finds herself in love with Coburn but not his profession.

HARDCORE
(UK: THE HARDCORE LIFE)
1979, 105 mins, US ⓥ ⊙
D: Paul Schrader **A:** George C. Scott, Peter Boyle, Season Hubley, Dick Sargent, Leonard Gaines (Columbia/A-Team)

George C. Scott, gives as fine a performance as he's ever done. An unventuring Calvinist, Scott lives a contented small-town Michigan life until his daughter, Ilah Davis, disappears on a trip to L.A. He hires seedy private eye Peter Boyle, who eventually finds her on film in a porno movie. Forced to watch, Scott's anguish at the sight bespeaks a clash of values still haunting the country. The easily shocked may want an exposé, or more a condemnation. The more sophisticated may grow tired of Scott's morality. But nobody's going to be bored.

HARDCORE LIFE, THE
See: Hardcore

HARD DAY'S NIGHT, A
1964, 83 mins, UK ⓥ ⊙
D: Richard Lester **A:** John Lennon, Paul McCartney, George Harrison, Ringo Starr, Wilfrid Brambell, Norman Rossington (United Artists)

A wacky, offbeat piece of filming, charged with vitality and inventiveness by director Dick Lester, slickly lensed, and put over at a fair lick. No attempt has been paid to build the Beatles up as Oliviers; they are at their best when the pic has a misleading air of off-the-cuff spontaneity. Alun Owen's screenplay attempts to portray an exaggerated 36 hours in the lives of the Beatles. But, though exaggerated, the thin story line gives a shrewd idea of the pressure and difficulties under which they work and live.

1964: Nominations: Best Story & Screenplay, Adapted Music Score

HARDER THEY FALL, THE
1956, 109 mins, US ⓥ
D: Mark Robson **A:** Humphrey Bogart, Rod Steiger, Jan Sterling, Mike Lane, Max Baer, Edward Andrews (Columbia)

Budd Schulberg's vehement novel about the fight racket is given a strong pictorial going-over. Story concerns a ruthless manager-gambler who imports a behemoth from South America, discovers he's a pugilistic cream puff, but gives him the buildup via fixed fights across the country. Humphrey Bogart is the newspaperman who goes ethically awry when his paper folds. He's glib and persuasive in promoting the boxer, and finally reveals his courage when he breaks with the racket.

1956: Nomination: Best B&W Cinematography

HARD, FAST AND BEAUTIFUL
1951, 76 mins, US
D: Ida Lupino **A:** Claire Trevor, Sally Forrest, Carleton Young, Robert Clarke (Filmakers)

An entertaining study of selfish mother love and amateur tennis. Claire Trevor socks over her character as the mother of Sally Forrest. Forrest is strong as a promising tennis player whose mother pushes and shoves her into the championship in order to ride along and soak up some of the fame and glamour that go with the top tennis brackets. Tennis-court footage is expertly interlaced with the story.

HARD TARGET
1993, 94 mins, US Ⓥ ⊙

D: John Woo **A:** Jean-Claude Van Damme, Lance Henriksen, Arnold Vosloo, Yancy Butler, Wilford Brimley (Alphaville/Renaissance/Universal)

John Woo makes his American debut with a briskly vigorous, occasionally brilliant actioner starring Jean-Claude Van Damme. However, hampered by a B script with flat, standard characters, and subjected to repeated editing of the violent sequences to win an R rating, pic doesn't bear the unique vision on display in Woo's *The Killer* and *Hard-Boiled*. Tale centers on a sadistic band of hunters who operate a profitable ''safari game'' in which the prey are homeless combat veterans. Van Damme plays a down-on-his luck merchant sailor who comes to the rescue of a young woman searching for her missing father, the latest victim.

HARD TIMES
(UK: THE STREETFIGHTER)
1975, 92 mins, US Ⓥ ⊙ ▭

D: Walter Hill **A:** Charles Bronson, James Coburn, Jill Ireland, Strother Martin, Maggie Blye (Columbia)

Charles Bronson is a mysterious stranger whose fists make money for him and small-time gambler James Coburn in illegal slugging matches. Coburn's character lacks substance; he's a likable heel one minute, an unlikable one the next. Jill Ireland is excellent in a touching performance as a down-and-out girl who has a brief affair with Bronson. The production has a very handsome mid-1930s New Orleans period flavor but the cast can't lick the script.

HARD TO HANDLE
1933, 71 mins, US

D: Mervyn LeRoy **A:** James Cagney, Mary Brian, Ruth Donnelly, Allen Jenkins, Claire Dodd, Gavin Gordon (Warner)

Plot trips a light fantastic over a series of gags. Cagney is a press agent in this one, beginning with a dance marathon, and then starting from scratch all over again when his partner kidnaps the gross. That happens in California. When reaching New York, Cagney high-pressures his way into the money, putting over a college, a reducing cream, and Florida grapefruit farmland, among other projects.

HARD TO KILL
1990, 95 mins, US Ⓥ ⊙

D: Bruce Malmuth **A:** Steven Seagal, Kelly Le Brock, Bill Sadler, Frederick Coffin, Bonnie Burroughs (Warner)

The threadbare screenplay uses a Rip van Winkle gimmick. As Mason Storm, cop Steven Seagal is nearly killed in the first reel after shooting surveillance film of corrupt politico Bill Sadler. Cop buddy Frederick Coffin hides evidence of Seagal's last-minute recovery. Seven years later Seagal comes out of his coma (sporting a laughable phony beard), uses Oriental methods of recovery, and plots his revenge. It ain't pretty, but it gets the action fans off.

HARDWARE
1990, 92 mins, UK/US Ⓥ ⊙

D: Richard Stanley **A:** Dylan McDermott, Stacey Travis, John Lynch, William Hootkins, Iggy Pop (Palace/Millimeter/Wicked)

A cacophonous, nightmarish variation on the postapocalyptic cautionary genre. After the nuclear holocaust, vast reaches of incinerated North America have been reduced to an infrared desert ravaged by guerrilla warfare and littered with cybernetic scrap heaps. Moses (Dylan McDermott) and Shades (John Lynch) are ''zone tripper'' soldiers of fortune who scavenge the corpse-strewn, irradiated wasteland for techno-detritus to blackmarket in the big city. *Hardware* becomes a black-comic exercise in F/X tour de force that's ceaselessly pushing itself over the top.

HARD WAY, THE
1991, 111 mins, US Ⓥ ⊙

D: John Badham **A:** Michael J. Fox, James Woods, Stephen Lang, Annabella Sciorra (Universal/Badham-Cohen)

Tired action-comedy formula squanders its best moments during the film's first act and wastes the nifty pairing of James Woods and Michael J. Fox. Fox is a popular star of action fluff, like *Smoking Gunn II*, who yearns for a leading role in a film ''without a Roman numeral in it.'' Determined to play a tough street cop, he decides to research the role by partnering New York cop John Moss (Woods), who's involved in hunting a lunatic serial killer (Stephen Lang). The pic degenerates into a series of random melees that will bring the buddies together.

HAREM

1985, 113 mins, France ⓥ ⊙ ▭

D: Arthur Joffe **A:** Nastassja Kinski, Ben Kingsley, Dennis Goldson, Zohra Segal, Michel Robin (Sara)

Tale concerns a fabulously wealthy Arab prince who kidnaps a beautiful young New York girl and has her brought to his desert palace, where she joins his harem. As played by Kingsley, the unscrupulous potentate turns out to be a hypersentive aesthete, trapped by tradition to maintain a way of life he doesn't believe in. The film is visually ravishing, often happily distracting the viewer from the emptiness of the script and the exasperating emptiness of the main characters.

HARLAN COUNTY, U.S.A.

1976, 103 mins, US ⓥ

D: Barbara Kopple (Cabin Creek)

A straightforward cinema verité documentary about a coal miners' strike in Kentucky. Director Barbara Kopple began the project in 1972 in Kentucky and was on hand to record the year-plus battle of coal miners at the Brookside Mine in Harlan to join the United Mine Workers.The stars of the film are the men and women of Harlan County, portrayed here not as patronized mountain folks but as human beings.

1976: Best Feature Documentary

HARLEM NIGHTS

1989, 118 mins, US ⓥ ⊙

D: Eddie Murphy **A:** Eddie Murphy, Richard Pryor, Redd Foxx, Danny Aiello, Michael Lerner (Murphy)

This blatantly excessive directorial debut for Eddie Murphy is overdone, too rarely funny, and, worst of all, boring. The film features Richard Pryor as the sage Sugar Ray to Murphy's hot-tempered Quick, who risk losing their 1930s Harlem nightclub when a corpulent crime boss (Michael Lerner) sets his sights on it. The pair hatches up a predictable scheme to turn the tables on the mobster.

1989: Nomination: Best Costume Design

HARLEY DAVIDSON AND THE MARLBORO MAN

1991, 93 mins, US ⓥ ⊙

D: Simon Wincer **A:** Mickey Rourke, Don Johnson, Chelsea Field, Daniel Baldwin, Tom Sizemore, Vanessa Williams (M-G-M/Krisjair-Laredo)

A dopey, almost poignantly bad actioner about two legends-in-their-own-minds, who bungle their way through a bank robbery on behalf of a friend, stands out only for big stars Mickey Rourke and Don Johnson. Pic scores mainly in the second-unit and stunt department, with hotly staged bike chases and an abundance of breaking glass, falling bodies, and shoot-outs.

HARLOW

1965, 107 mins, US ⓥ

D: Alex Segal **A:** Carol Lynley, Efrem Zimbalist Jr., Ginger Rogers, Barry Sullivan, Hurd Hatfield (Sargent)

This first-to-market biopic lensed in eight days in the TV-type Electronovision process is peopled with a set of characters not altogether convincing and even the star part making small impression. Carol Lynley, as the tragic, platinum-tressed queen of the 1930s, who was a sex symbol of her time, tries valiantly, but the outcome is not altogether a triumph. Hurd Hatfield in the role of the producer-writer Paul Bern, who weds the sexy blonde and then commits suicide when he discovers he's impotent, delivers a sincere performance.

HARLOW

1965, 125 mins, US ⓥ ▭

D: Gordon Douglas **A:** Carroll Baker, Martin Balsam, Red Buttons Michael Connors, Angela Lansbury, Peter Lawford (Paramount/Levine)

Second biopic of Jean Harlow is handsomely mounted. As the ill-fated Jean Harlow, Carroll Baker is a fairly reasonable facsimile, although she lacks the electric fire of the original. Several real-life characters are thinly veiled, while parts of star's mother and stepfather are importantly projected. Angela Lansbury undertakes role of Mama Jean with quiet conviction, and Raf Vallone in the Marino Bello–stepfather role also lends a persuasive presence.

HAROLD AND MAUDE

1971, 90 mins, US ⓥ ⊙

D: Hal Ashby **A:** Ruth Gordon, Bud Cort, Vivian Pickles, Cyril Cusack, Charles Tyner, Ellen Geer (Paramount)

Harold and Maude has all the fun and gaiety of a burning orphanage. Ruth Gordon heads the cast as an offensive eccentric who becomes a beacon in the life of a self-destructive rich boy, played by Bud Cort. Together they attend funerals and indulge in specious philosophizing. Director Hal Ashby's second feature is marked by a few good gags, but marred by a greater preponderance of sophomoric, overdone, and mocking humor.

HARPER
(UK: THE MOVING TARGET)
1966, 121 mins, US ⓥ ⊙ ▭
D: Jack Smight **A:** Paul Newman, Lauren Bacall, Julie Harris, Arthur Hill, Janet Leigh, Pamela Tiffin (Warner)

A contemporary mystery-comedy with Paul Newman as a sardonic private eye. Abundance of comedy and sometimes extraneous emphasis on cameo characters make for a relaxed pace and imbalanced concept, resulting in overlength and telegraphing of climax. Ross MacDonald's novel *The Moving Target*, has Newman commissioned by Lauren Bacall to find her hubby, although she has no love for either him or stepdaughter Pamela Tiffin. All principals acquit themselves admirably, particularly Winters, who makes every second count as the once-aspiring film star now on the high-calorie sauce.

HARP OF BURMA
See: Biruma No Tategoto

HARRY AND SON
1984, 117 mins, US ⓥ ⊙
D: Paul Newman **A:** Paul Newman, Robby Benson, Ellen Barkin, Wilford Brimley, Judith Ivey, Joanne Woodward (Orion)

Fuzzily conceived and indecisively executed, *Harry and Son* represents a deeply disappointing return to the director's chair for Paul Newman. Opening scenes are perhaps the strongest, as Newman gets fired from his job as a Florida construction worker. He goads his son into expanding his horizons beyond polishing cars and pretending to be a young Hemingway. Newman's character is in a position either to give up on life or make a fresh start, and perhaps film's overriding frustration is that he goes nowhere. Structurally, it's a mess.

HARRY AND THE HENDERSONS
1987, 110 mins, US ⓥ ⊙
D: William Dear **A:** John Lithgow, Melinda Dillon, Margaret Langrick, Joshua Rudoy, Kevin Peter Hall, David Suchet (Universal/Amblin)

Proof that the folks at Amblin Entertainment, a.k.a. Steven Spielberg's production company, can't keep using the same *E.T.* formula for every kiddie pic. Here, they've taken Big Foot, put him in Chewbacca's leftover *Star Wars* costume, and given him E.T.'s sweet disposition—resulting in a lobotomized hairy animal who is so wimpy, it's painful. Dad (John Lithgow) runs over the beast in the family station wagon and takes him home to Seattle. Theirs is a typical Spielberg house in the 'burbs—decorated in yuppie coziness that's soon turned topsy-turvy when Big Foot revives.
1987: Best Makeup

HARRY AND TONTO
1974, 115 mins, US ⓥ
D: Paul Mazursky **A:** Art Carney, Ellen Burstyn, Chief Dan George, Geraldine Fitzgerald, Larry Hagman, Arthur Hunnicutt (20th Century-Fox)

Harry and Tonto stars Art Carney and a trained cat, respectively, in a pleasant film about an old man who rejuvenates himself on a cross-country trek. Script is a series of good human-comedy vignettes, with the large supporting cast of many familiar names in virtual cameo roles.
1974: Best Actor (Art Carney)
Nomination: Best Original Screenplay

HARRY AND WALTER GO TO NEW YORK
1976, 120 mins, US ⓥ ▭
D: Mark Rydell **A:** James Caan, Elliott Gould, Michael Caine, Diane Keaton, Charles Durning, Lesley Ann Warren (Columbia)

An alleged period comedy about two carnival types who get involved with a big-time safecracker plus the femme leader of a radical movement. The principals' paths intertwine through miles and miles of forced comedic footage, a climactic bank heist, plus all manner of running and jumping and screaming and hollering.

HARRY IN YOUR POCKET
1973, 102 mins, US
D: Bruce Geller **A:** James Coburn, Michael Sarrazin, Trish Van Devere, Walter Pidgeon (United Artists)

Producer-director Bruce Geller invades the underworld of ''cannons'' (master pickpockets) with a fast exposé of how they operate. James Coburn and Walter Pidgeon are the experts—Coburn the cannon and Pidgeon his cocaine-sniffing associate—and Michael Sarrazin and Trish Van Devere the apprentices. Presence of Van Devere leads to romantic complications and an underlying feud between Coburn and Sarrazin.

HARVEY
1950, 103 mins, US Ⓥ ⊙
D: Henry Koster **A:** James Stewart, Josephine Hull, Peggy Dow, Charles Drake, Cecil Kellaway, Wallace Ford (Universal)

The exploits of Elwood P. Dowd, a man who successfully escaped from trying reality when his invisible six-foot rabbit pal Harvey came into his life, continually spring chuckles, often hilarity, as the footage unfolds. Stewart would seem the perfect casting for the character, so well does he convey the idea that escape from life into a pleasant half-world existence has many points in its favor. Josephine Hull, the slightly balmy aunt who wants to have Elwood committed, is immense, socking the comedy for every bit of its worth.
1950: Best Supp. Actress (Josephine Hull)
Nomination: Best Actor (James Stewart)

HARVEY GIRLS, THE
1946, 101 mins, US Ⓥ ⊙
D: George Sidney **A:** Judy Garland, John Hodiak, Ray Bolger, Angela Lansbury, Marjorie Main, Cyd Charisse (M-G-M)

A curious blend of Technicolor wild-westernism, frontier-town skullduggery, and a troupe of Harvey restaurant waitresses who deport themselves in a manner that's a cross between a sorority and a follies troupe. Judy Garland makes much of it believable and most of it acceptable.
1946: Best Song ("On the Atchison, Topeka and the Santa Fe")
Nomination: Best Scoring of a Musical Picture

HAS ANYBODY SEEN MY GAL
1952, 88 mins, US .
D: Douglas Sirk **A:** Piper Laurie, Rock Hudson, Charles Coburn, Gigi Perreau, Lynn Bari (Universal)

A rather solid piece of nostalgic entertainment is offered in this comedy-drama of the 1920s "flapper" era. Charles Coburn wallops the part of a rich old duffer who plans to leave his fortune to the family of a girl who had spurned his proposal of marriage years before. Incognito, he travels to the small Vermont town where the family lives to find out what kind of people they are. Laurie and Hudson team well as the young lovers.

HASTY HEART, THE
1949, 102 mins, US
D: Vincent Sherman **A:** Ronald Reagan, Patricia Neal, Richard Todd, Anthony Nicholls, Howard Crawford (Warner)

Background is the Second World War

and the setting is an army hospital in Burma, in a ward where six assorted soldiers sweat out their injuries while awaiting shipment home. Notable is the performance of Richard Todd in the role of the Scot who must die. Ronald Reagan plays the Yank with the exact amount of gusto such a character should have in a British outpost hospital. Patricia Neal gives feeling to her role as the nurse.
1949: Nomination: Best Actor (Richard Todd)

HATARI!
1962, 159 mins, US Ⓥ ⊙
D: Howard Hawks **A:** John Wayne, Hardy Kruger, Elsa Martinelli, Gerard Blain, Red Buttons (Paramount)

Screenplay describes at exhaustive length the methods by which a group of game catchers in Tanganyika go about catching wild animals for the zoo when not occupied at catching each other for the woo. Script lacks momentum. It never really advances toward a story goal. John Wayne heads the colorful cast assembled for this zoological field trip. The vet star plays with his customary effortless (or so it seems) authority. Germany's Hardy Kruger and French actor Gerard Blain manage, resourcefully, to pump what vigor they can muster into a pair of undernourished roles. Red Buttons and Elsa Martinelli emerge the histrionic stick-outs, Buttons with a jovial portrayal of an ex-cabbie, Martinelli as a sweet but spirited shutterbug and part-time pachydermatologist.
1962: Nomination: Best Color Cinematography

HATE
See: La Haine

HATFUL OF RAIN, A
1957, 109 mins, US ▱
D: Fred Zinnemann **A:** Eva Marie Saint, Don Murray, Anthony Franciosa, Lloyd Nolan, Henry Silva, William Hickey (20th Century-Fox)

A Hatful of Rain is more than a story of a junkie. The people involved in this web of narcotics are basically decent human beings. The story revolves about their reactions when one of them turns out to be a junkie. As the pregnant wife of a narcotics addict, Eva Marie Saint handles the emotional peaks and tender moments with sensitive understanding. Don Murray scores, too, as the likable junkie. The role of the brother is compellingly played by

Anthony Franciosa. As the widowed father, Lloyd Nolan turns in a top-notch portrayal.

1957: Nomination: Best Actor (Anthony Franciosa)

HATTER'S CASTLE
1941, 101 mins, UK
D: Lance Comfort **A:** Robert Newton, Deborah Kerr, James Mason, Emlyn Williams (Paramount)

Here is a film, if ever there was one, that is best indicative of one player's superlative performance. Robert Newton disregards tradition and enacts the featured male role without bombast or any sort of vocal pyrotechnics. The plot travels along stereotyped lines to an obvious conclusion. It is, however, artistically produced, photographed, and acted. It is the story of a strong, hard Scotsman of Gladstonian days, who rules his household with the proverbial iron rod and turns his daughter out to almost certain death in a storm on learning of her dishonor.

HAUNTED
1995, 108 mins, UK/US ⓥ
D: Lewis Gilbert **A:** Aidan Quinn, Kate Beckinsale, Anthony Andrews, John Gielgud, Anna Massey (Lumiere/Double A/American Zoetrope)

This pic version of James Herbert's bestselling spook yarn is competently helmed by veteran Lewis Gilbert. A brief prologue, set in 1905, introduces two young siblings, David and Juliet, at play in the grounds of a country house in Sussex, southern England. Juliet accidentally drowns, David feels guilty, and the plot basics are staked out. Flash-forward to 1928, when David (Quinn), who's meanwhile been raised in the States, returns to teach a course on the supernatural at a university. He's a skeptic but can't resist a letter from a dotty old nanny (Anna Massey) inviting him to a stately pile she claims is haunted.

HAUNTED HONEYMOON
1986, 82 mins, US ⓥ ⊙
D: Gene Wilder **A:** Gene Wilder, Gilda Radner, Dom DeLuise, Jonathan Pryce, Peter Vaughan (Orion)

Gene Wilder is back in the rut of sending up old film conventions in a mild farce. Title is a misnomer, since setup has radio actor Wilder taking his fiancée Gilda Radner out to his family's gloomy country estate to meet the kinfolk just before tying the knot. Clan is presided over by the tubby, genial Aunt Kate, played by Dom DeLuise, who maintains that a werewolf is on the loose in the vicinity.

HAUNTING, THE
1963, 112 mins, US ⓥ ⊙ ⊡
D: Robert Wise **A:** Julie Harris, Claire Bloom, Richard Johnson, Russ Tamblyn, Lois Maxwell, Fay Compton (Argyle/M-G-M)

After elaborately setting the audience up in anticipation of drawing some scientific conclusions about the psychic-phenomena field, the film completely dodges the issue in settling for a half-hearted melodramatic climax. The story has to do with the efforts of a small psychic research team to study the supernatural powers that seem to inhabit a 90-year-old New England house with a reputation for evil. The acting is effective all around. Davis Boulton has employed his camera with extraordinary dexterity in fashioning a visual excitement that keeps the picture alive with images of impending shock. As photographed by Boulton, the house itself is a monstrous personality, most decidedly the star of the film.

HAUNTING, THE
1999, 114 mins, US ⓥ ⊙ ⊡
D: Jan De Bont **A:** Liam Neeson, Catherine Zeta-Jones, Owen Wilson, Lili Taylor, Bruce Dern, Marian Seldes (Roth-Arnold/DreamWorks)

Extravagant technical prowess has been channeled to negligible effect in *The Haunting*, a wanna-be horror classic that turns deadly dull. No expense has been spared to rev up the low-key spookiness of Robert Wise's 1963 film version of Shirley Jackson's novel *The Haunting of Hill House*. Updating merely proves that all the money in Hollywood can't buy imagination, resourcefulness, wit, or a decent script. Researcher Dr. David Marrow (Liam Neeson) is recruiting insomniacs to test theories he has about fear and rounds up three volunteers: Nell (Lili Taylor), a withdrawn, impressionable woman; Theo (Catherine Zeta-Jones), a raffish artist and woman of the world; and Luke (Owen Wilson), a man of no particular distinction. Their few noticeable personality traits are quite irrelevant to anything that goes on. Only Taylor has something resembling a real role to play.

HAVANA
1990, 145 mins, US ⓥ ⊙
D: Sydney Pollack **A:** Robert Redford,

Lena Olin, Alan Arkin, Tomas Milian, Raul Julia, Mark Rydell (Mirage/Universal)

A notably uncompelling tale of a gringo caught up in the Cuban revolution. Robert Redford's rogue gambler character, Jack Weil, strikes a few sparks with Lena Olin's mysterious Bobby Duran and agrees to smuggle into Havana a radio that will help Castro spread his word in the capital in the waning days of 1958. Redford's eye for Olin leads him into dangerous political territory involving her wealthy left-wing husband Arturo (played suavely by an uncredited Raul Julia), a CIA spook posing as a food critic, and various military toughs.
1990: Nomination: Best Original Score

HAVANA WIDOWS
1933, 68 mins, US
D: Ray Enright **A:** Joan Blondell, Glenda Farrell, Guy Kibbee, Lyle Talbot, Allen Jenkins, Frank McHugh (First National)

Tip-top rowdy comedy. Joan Blondell and Glenda Farrell are out on the loose as gold diggers in the spicy surroundings of Havana, and Allen Jenkins is a low-comedy character. Completing the welcome package there are lively tunes, an abundance of undressed girls, and just the right amount of slapstick fun to give it climactic vigor.

HAVING A WILD WEEKEND
See: Catch Us If You Can

HAWAII
1966, 186 mins, US ⊗ ⊙ ⊡
D: George Roy Hill **A:** Julie Andrews, Max von Sydow, Richard Harris, Carroll O'Connor, Gene Hackman (Mirisch)

Based on James A. Michener's novel, which embraced centuries of history, Hawaii focuses on a critical period—1820–41—when the islands began to be commercialized, corrupted, and converted to Western ways. Superior production, acting, and direction give depth and credibility to a personal tragedy, set against the clash of two civilizations. Screenplay develops Max von Sydow's character from a young and overzealous Protestant missionary, through courtship of Julie Andrews, to their religious work in Hawaii. Richard Harris, an old beau, turns up occasionally at major plot turns. Von Sydow's outstanding performance makes his character comprehensible, if never totally sympathetic.
1966: Nominations: Best Supp. Actress

(Jocelyn Lagarde), Color Cinematography, Color Costume Design, Color Costume Design, Original Music Score, Song ("My Wishing Doll"), Sound, Visual Effects

HAWAIIANS, THE
(UK: MASTER OF THE ISLANDS)
1970, 134 mins, US ⊡
D: Tom Gries **A:** Charlton Heston, Geraldine Chaplin, John Phillip Law, Tina Chen, Alec McCowen, Mako (United Artists/Mirisch)

Charlton Heston, as the American descendant of early settlers and the only man with the vision and steadfastness to make the Hawaiian Islands one of the garden spots of the world (he's credited with introducing the pineapple as a commercial crop), is less the larger-than-life hero and more a stereotyped islander.
1970: Nomination: Best Costume Design

HAWKS
1988, 107 mins, UK ⊗
D: Robert Ellis Miller **A:** Timothy Dalton, Anthony Edwards, Janet McTeer, Camille Coduri, Connie Booth (Gibb/English/PRO)

This black comedy about terminal cancer patients escaping for one last fling stares death in the face and laughs, but takes too long to get to the punch line. Terminal bone cancer pits lawyer Bancroft (Timothy Dalton) and ex–football pro Decker (Anthony Edwards) together in a team effort to thwart their disease (and the ward nurses) with laughs, grit, and a last pilgrimage to a Dutch bordello.

HAXAN
(WITCHCRAFT THROUGH THE AGES; WITCHCRAFT)
1922, 82 mins, Sweden ⊗ ⊗
D: Benjamin Christensen **A:** Benjamin Christensen, Elisabeth Christensen, Astrid Holm, Karen Winther, Maren Pedersen (Svensk Filmindustri)

A pictorial history of black magic, of witches, of the Inquisition, and the thousand and one inhumanities of the superstition-ridden Middle Ages. Many of its scenes are unadulterated horror. The story tells how a young man lies sick. A priest passes over his body a ladle full of molten metal. This is then cooled in water, and the shape the cold metal assumes proves the patient is under the spell of a witch. An old woman beggar is accused, and a girl-wife comes under suspicion. All are hauled before the Inquisition and torture is applied. Many of the scenes are remarkable, especially those in which the girl wanders stark naked in a world of imaginative horror. [Film was reviewed from a screening in London in August 1923.]

HEAD OVER HEELS
(US: HEAD OVER HEELS IN LOVE)
1936, 84 mins, UK
D: Sonnie Hale A: Jessie Matthews, Louis Borell, Robert Flemyng, Whitney Bourne, Romney Brent (Gaumont-British)

A topsy-turvy film affair, emulating its title in more than one respect. Of the hybrid Hollywood and Elstree components, there's no disputing that outside of the star's own yeoman work, the Mack Gordon and Harry Revel songs are the most potent contributory factor. Jessie Matthews is effectively shown as a café song-and-dancer, later a radio click, and still later as a cigarette girl when the ire of the Actors' Association (for a temperamental breach) chases her from the limelight.

HEAD OVER HEELS
1979, 97 mins, US ⓥ
D: Joan Micklin Silver A: John Heard, Mary Beth Hurt, Peter Riegert, Kenneth McMillan, Gloria Grahame, Griffin Dunne (United Artists/Triple Play)

Based on Ann Beattie's novel Chilly Scenes of Winter, Joan Micklin Silver's screenplay has affable John Heard reflecting back on his happy past with Mary Beth Hurt from the wistful present. Thrust of pic has him trying to win her back from the clutches of king-sized jock Mark Metcalf. Ultimately, however, both characters rather wear out their welcome. Resolution comes off as a bit pat and conventional.

HEAD OVER HEELS IN LOVE
See: Head over Heels

H.E.A.L.T.H.
1980, 102 mins, US ▭
D: Robert Altman A: Glenda Jackson, Carol Burnett, James Garner, Lauren Bacall, Dick Cavett, Paul Dooley (Lion's Gate/20th Century-Fox)

This arch look at a Florida health-foods bash is overdrawn and thin in too many spots, but the pic is a genuinely humorous effort that affords its good cast often-seized opportunities for incisively funny performances. The convention is set in a garishly statuesque hotel, and Lauren Bacall plays a well-preserved 83-year-old health authority. Bacall's running for the presidency of the health-foods org that runs the convention, against a vaguely

masculine, cigar puffer (Glenda Jackson). Carol Burnett is first-rate as a sexually frustrated White House health emissary.

HEAR MY SONG
1992, 113 mins, UK ⓥ ⊙
D: Peter Chelsom A: Ned Beatty, Adrian Dunbar, David McCallum, Tara Fitzgerald, Shirley Anne Field, William Hootkins (Limelight)

An unabashedly romantic fantasy about a concert promoter (Adrian Dunbar). Desperate for a hit, he books a Josef Locke look-alike (William Hootkins) who seems to fill the billing as "Mr X.—Is He or Isn't He?" Legendary Irish tenor Locke fled from public view at the height of his popularity to avoid tax-evasion charges. Ned Beatty does much to stem the tide of sentiment in a tough, grounded portrayal of the real Locke. The real discovery is likely to be Fitzgerald, whose gamine charm is perfectly introduced in this old-fashioned romance.

HEAR NO EVIL
1993, 97 mins, US ⓥ ⊙
D: Robert Greenwald A: Marlee Matlin, D. B. Sweeney, Martin Sheen, John C. McGinley, Christina Carlisi (Great Movie Ventures/20th Century-Fox)

Terminally dull would-be thriller has a perfunctory story with the gimmick of a deaf damsel-in-distress grafted on uncertainly. Oscar winner Marlee Matlin's talents are wasted. Director Robert Greenwald and his scripters show little flair for suspense, nuance, or even elementary thrills. In the final reel, Matlin has a cat-and-mouse sequence trapped in a mountain lodge with the killer, her handicap (deafness) increasing her jeopardy. A clichéd climax.

HEARTACHES
1981, 83 mins, Canada ⓥ ⊙
D: Donald Shebib A: Margot Kidder, Annie Potts, Robert Carradine, Winston Rekert, George Touliatis (Rising Star)

A female buddy picture with actresses Margot Kidder and Annie Potts involved in a series of delightful misadventures in love. On her way to the big city for an abortion, Potts reluctantly teams up with Kidder. Kidder in blond wig, tight pants, and outrageous jewelry looks the part of a kook. Her foulmouthed, man-hungry character is in sharp contrast to Potts's relative innocence. However, it is basically Potts's film as the runaway wife who's tired of her husband's immature attitude.

HEARTBEAT
1946, 100 mins, US ⓥ
D: Sam Wood **A:** Ginger Rogers, Jean-Pierre Aumont, Adolphe Menjou, Melville Cooper, Basil Rathbone (RKO)

Story of a girl who becomes an apprentice in a pickpocket school, goes to an embassy ball, and finds romance after she learns how to be a lady. Jean-Pierre Aumont is interesting as the young diplomat who falls for the femme purse snatcher. Menjou is expert. Melville Cooper as a cadgering lush is good for chuckles. Basil Rathbone's professional performance furnishes laughs.

HEART BEAT
1979, 109 mins, US ⓥ
D: John Byrum **A:** Nick Nolte, Sissy Spacek, John Heard, Ray Sharkey, Ann Dusenberry, Tony Bill (Orion)

Heart Beat never manages to expand its loosely biographical tale of Jack Kerouac, Neal and Carolyn Cassady beyond a very narrow scope. Nick Nolte and Sissy Spacek, as the Cassadys, enmeshed in a love-hate relationship, are standout in a film where performances dominate. Ditto Ray Sharkey, in a manic performance as a disguised Allen Ginsberg character. John Heard struggles manfully with the Kerouac character, but writer-director John Byrum has given him few compass points on which to base a reading.

HEARTBREAK KID, THE
1972, 104 mins, US ⓥ ⊙
D: Elaine May **A:** Charles Grodin, Cybill Shepherd, Jeannie Berlin, Eddie Albert, Audra Lindley, William Prince (Palomar)

The bright, amusing saga of a young NY bridegroom whose bride's maddening idiosyncrasies freak him and he leaves her at the end of a three-day Miami honeymoon to pursue and wed another doll. Elaine May's deft direction catches all the possibilities of young romance and its tribulations in light strokes. Charles Grodin is slick and able as the fast-talking bridegroom whose patience is worn thin.
1972: Nominations: Best Supp. Actor (Eddie Albert), Supp. Actress (Jeannie Berlin)

HEARTBREAK KID, THE
1993, 97 mins, Australia ⓥ
D: Michael Jenkins **A:** Claudia Karvan, Alex Dimitriades, Steve Bastoni, Nico Lathouris, William McInnes, Doris Younane (View)

A warmhearted, liberating love story.

Set in the ethnically mixed suburbs of Melbourne, pic establishes Claudia Karvan as 22-year-old Christina, a well-educated Greek-Australian assigned to work a rowdy high school in a working-class area. Spunky 17-year-old Nick (Alex Dimitriades) makes it clear that he has the hots for his teacher and she, gradually, responds, eventually borrowing her girlfriend's apartment for secret afternoon trysts. Inevitably, the secret gets out.

HEARTBREAK RIDGE
1986, 130 mins, US ⓥ ⊙
D: Clint Eastwood **A:** Clint Eastwood, Marsha Mason, Everett McGill, Moses Gunn, Eileen Heckart, Bo Svenson (Malpaso/Weston)

Another vintage Clint Eastwood performance. Eastwood is Gunnery Sergeant Tom Highway—a man determined to teach some of today's young leathernecks how to behave like a few good men. Eastwood's stern ways inevitably prevail as his platoon is called up for emergency overseas combat.
1986: Nomination: Best Sound

HEARTBURN
1986, 108 mins, US ⓥ ⊙
D: Mike Nichols **A:** Meryl Streep, Jack Nicholson, Jeff Daniels, Maureen Stapleton, Stockard Channing, Richard Masur (Paramount)

A beautifully crafted film with flawless performances and many splendid moments, yet the overall effect is a bit disappointing. From the start Meryl Streep and Jack Nicholson are never quite a couple. He's a Washington political columnist and she's a New York food writer. They meet at a wedding. Soon they're having their own wedding. Nora Ephron adapted her own novel for the screen, which in turn borrowed heavily from her marriage with Watergate reporter Carl Bernstein. While the day-to-day details are drawn with a striking clarity, Ephron's script never goes much beyond the mannerisms of middle-class life.

HEART IN WINTER, A
See: Un Coeur en Hiver

HEART IS A LONELY HUNTER, THE
1968, 122 mins, US ⓥ
D: Robert Ellis Miller **A:** Alan Arkin, Sondra Locke, Laurinda Barrett, Stacy Keach, Chuck McCann, Cicely Tyson (Warner)

Translating to the screen the delicate if

specious tragedy of Carson McCullers's first novel was clearly not an easy matter. Nor an entirely successful one, either. *The Heart Is a Lonely Hunter* emerges as a fragmented episodic melodrama. Alan Arkin's starring performance as a deaf-and-mute loner is erratic and mannered, but supporting cast generally is on target. Story turns on Arkin and his influence on the lives of others. Pivotal character is little more than a prop, but, as rendered by Arkin, a destructive one.

1968: Nominations: Best Actor (Alan Arkin), Supp. Actress (Sondra Locke)

HEART LIKE A WHEEL
1983, 113 mins, US Ⓥ ⊙

D: Jonathan Kaplan **A:** Bonnie Bedelia, Beau Bridges, Leo Rossi, Hoyt Axton, Bill McKinney, Anthony Edwards (Aurora/20th Century-Fox)

A surprisingly fine biopic of Shirley Muldowney, the first professional female race-car driver. What could have been a routine good-ol'-gal success story has been heightened into an emotionally involving, superbly made drama. Happily married to her mechanic husband Jack and with a young son, Shirley finds her innate ability compelling her, by 1966, to enter her first pro race. Roadblocked at first by astonished, and predictably sexist, officials, Shirley proceeds to set the track record in her qualifying run, and her career is under way.

HEART OF MIDNIGHT
1988, 101 mins, US Ⓥ ⊙

D: Matthew Chapman **A:** Jennifer Jason Leigh, Peter Coyote, Gale Mayron, Sam Schacht, Denise Dummont, Frank Stallone (AG)

A twisted little sadomasochistic outing whose plot centers on Carol Rivers (Jennifer Jason Leigh), a young woman with psychological problems. She inherits property being transformed into the ''Midnight'' club. Carol moves to the building, only to find a bizarre series of rooms upstairs. They suggest that the previous owner was hosting sex parties for people of various persuasions. Carol is plunged into her own hell as a couple of workmen try to rape her. Events proceed to particularly sadistic circumstances.

HEART OF THE MATTER, THE
1953, 105 mins, UK

D: George More O'Ferrall **A:** Trevor Howard, Elizabeth Allan, Maria Schell,

Denholm Elliott, Peter Finch, Gerard Oury (British Lion/London)

The film is set in Sierra Leone during the last war, where Trevor Howard, the assistant police commissioner, is not getting along too well with his wife (Elizabeth Allan). He falls in love with a young widow (Maria Schell). Stripped of its deeper significance, the story is little more than the conventional triangle meller, but husband and wife are ardent Catholics, and divorce and remarriage cannot be contemplated. The conflict between love and religion never emerges with real conviction.

HEARTS OF FIRE
1987, 95 mins, US Ⓥ ⊙ ▭

D: Richard Marquand **A:** Bob Dylan, Rupert Everett, Fiona, Julian Glover, Ian Drury, Richie Havens (Phoenix/Lorimar)

The last film of helmer Richard Marquand fails to fire on all cylinders despite a nimble performance by the enigmatic Bob Dylan, typecast as a reclusive rock star. Dylan performs well, though he looks a mite uncomfortable during the musical numbers.

HEARTS OF THE WEST
(UK: HOLLYWOOD COWBOY)
1975, 102 mins, US Ⓥ

D: Howard Zieff **A:** Jeff Bridges, Andy Griffith, Donald Pleasence, Blythe Danner, Alan Arkin, Richard B. Schull (M-G-M)

A pleasant, amusing period comedy featuring Jeff Bridges as a cliché-quoting novice western pulp writer who is rescued by an oater quickie-film location unit. The casting is very adroit, with all principals complementing in style and charisma. The structure of the film is notable in that it tells its story in the manner of films of the 1930s.

HEARTS OF THE WORLD
1918, 117 mins, US/UK Ⓥ ⊗

D: D. W. Griffith **A:** Lillian Gish, Robert Harron, Dorothy Gish, George Fawcett, Erich von Stroheim, Noel Coward (Griffith/Artcraft)

D. W. Griffith makes his principal love story a skeleton upon which to hang a large number of brilliant war scenes, in an effort to show the horrors at close range—its effect upon the combatants and noncombatants alike. The son and daughter of two American painters who made their homes in France fall in love and are betrothed. When war is declared, the youth makes the heroic declaration that a country that is good enough to live in is worth fighting for, and joins the French army. The picture opens with scenes showing the little French village in time of peace and then goes into a depiction of the struggle with the Germans for its possession. Robert Harron as the young American is the outstanding artist of the picture.

HEAT
1995, 172 mins, US ⓥ ⊙ ▭
D: Michael Mann **A:** Al Pacino, Robert De Niro, Val Kilmer, Jon Voight, Tom Sizemore, Diane Venora (Forward Pass/ Warner)

Stunningly made and incisively acted by a large and terrific cast, Michael Mann's ambitious study of the relativity of good and evil stands apart from other films of its type by virtue of its extraordinarily rich characterizations and its thoughtful, deeply melancholic take on modern life. Mann orchestrates a sprawling tale of an obsessed, brilliantly intuitive cop (Al Pacino) hunting a superbly disciplined master criminal (Robert De Niro) across a sulfurous Los Angeles landscape. But this classic western-like structure is just the central focus for a very detailed portrait of seemingly equal forces on both sides of the law.

HEAT AND DUST
1983, 133 mins, UK ⓥ ⊙
D: James Ivory **A:** Julie Christie, Christopher Cazenove, Greta Scacchi, Julian Glover, Susan Fleetwood, Shashi Kapoor (Merchant Ivory)

Scripted from her own novel by Ruth Prawer Jhabvala, *Heat and Dust* intercuts the stories of two women and of India past and present. Julie Christie, as a distinctly modern Englishwoman researching the Indian past of a late great-aunt, is the top name, but the principal impact, partly by virtue of role, is supplied by British newcomer Greta Scacchi. Portraying the great-aunt as a young bride of scandalous behavior in colonial India, she creates an impressive study of classic underplayed well-bred English turmoil.

HEATHERS
1989, 102 mins, US ⓥ ⊙
D: Michael Lehmann **A:** Winona Ryder, Christian Slater, Shannen Doherty, Lisanne Falk, Kim Walker, Penelope Milford (Cinemarque/New World)

Daniel Waters's enormously clever screenplay blazes a trail of originality through the dead wood of the teen-comedy genre by focusing on the Heathers, the four prettiest and most popular girls at Westerburg High, three of whom are named Heather. Setting the tone for the group is founder and queen bitch Heather No. 1, who has a devastating put-down or comeback for every occasion. Heathers No. 2 and 3 get off their own zingers once in a while, while the fourth nubile beauty, Veronica (Winona Ryder), seems to have a mind of her own. She also has eyes for a rebellious-looking school newcomer (Christian Slater).

HEAT'S ON, THE
1943, 79 mins, US
D: Gregory Ratoff **A:** Mae West, Victor Moore, Lloyd Bridges, Mary Roche, Hazel Scott (Columbia)

Story of *Heat's On*, with West as the actress-siren, her hips a-swinging in a familiar manner and arms akimbo for added familiar effect, plus the affected hardboiled Westian diction, concerns the efforts of a legit producer, in love with his star, to wrest her from a rival producer after latter has been hoodwinked into believing she's been blacklisted from a reform society. West looks well but her technique somehow seems dated.

HEATWAVE
1981, 93 mins, Australia ⓥ
D: Phillip Noyce **A:** Judy Davis, Richard Moir, Chris Haywood, Bill Hunter, John Gregg (Preston Crothers/M & L)

Director Phillip Noyce projects Sydney as a cauldron in which hapless individuals are scalded by big business, organized crime, lawyers, police, and journalists, working in an unholy alliance. His chief protagonists are Richard Moir as a visionary young architect who has designed a $100-million residential complex, and Judy Davis as a radical activist in the forefront of the residents' resistance to its construction.

HEAVEN
1987, 80 mins, US ⓥ ⊙
D: Diane Keaton (Perpetual/RVF)

Diane Keaton's feature directorial debut is a small-scale, nonnarrative work using trendily shot interviews, snazzy optical effects, and loads of film clips and songs to illustrate fanciful notions of the hereafter. Close to 100 individuals, all unknown except for boxing promoter Don King, are quizzed on such matters as,

"What is heaven?" and "How do you get to heaven?"

HEAVEN AND EARTH
1993, 140 mins, US ⑮ ⊙ ▱
D: Oliver Stone **A:** Tommy Lee Jones, Joan Chen, Haing S. Ngor, Hiep Thi Le, Debbie Reynolds, Vivian Wu (Warner/Ixtlan/New Regency/Todd-AO/TAE)

The US stayed in Vietnam too long, and Oliver Stone has returned to the subject one time too many. The vessel for his latest agitated history lesson is a Vietnamese Buddhist peasant who, in the way she is soiled, dominated, exploited, raped, brutalized, colonized, transformed, and torn apart from her family, is no doubt supposed to represent Vietnam itself. Stone has taken no overt political position, and consequently adds very little to either the general discussion of Vietnam or his own.

HEAVEN CAN WAIT
1943, 112 mins, US ⑮ ⊙
D: Ernst Lubitsch **A:** Gene Tierney, Don Ameche, Charles Coburn, Marjorie Main, Laird Cregar, Louis Calhern (20th Century-Fox)

Lubitsch has endowed this production with light, amusing sophistication and heartwarming nostalgia. It opens with the deceased (Ameche) asking Satan for a passport to hell, which is not being issued unless the applicant can justify his right to it. This is followed by a recital of real and fancied misdeeds from the time the sinner discovers that, in order to get girls, a boy must have plenty of beetles for the thefting of his cousin's fiancée, whom he marries.
1943: Nominations: Best Picture, Director, Color Cinematography

HEAVEN CAN WAIT
1978, 100 mins, US ⑮ ⊙
D: Warren Beatty, Buck Henry **A:** Warren Beatty, Julie Christie, James Mason, Jack Warden, Charles Grodin, Dyan Cannon (Paramount)

Harry Segall's fantasy comedy-drama play, made in 1941 as *Here Comes Mr. Jordan*, returns in an updated, slightly more macabre treatment. Warren Beatty plays an aging football star, prematurely summoned to judgment after a traffic accident because celestial messenger (played by codirector Buck Henry) jumped the gun. This embarrasses "a heavenly supervisor" played by James Mason into permitting Beatty to inhabit temporarily another body. The only available one is that of a wealthy industrialist whose death

is plotted by floozy wife Dyan Cannon and Charles Grodin, the tycoon's nerd secretary. Script and direction provide a rich mix of visual and verbal humor.
1978: Best Art Direction
Nominations: Best Picture, Directors (Warren Beatty, Buck Henry), Actor (Warren Beatty), Supp. Actor (Jack Warden), Supp. Actress (Dyan Cannon), Adapted Screenplay, Cinematography, Original Score

HEAVEN HELP US
(UK: CATHOLIC BOYS)
1985, 104 mins, US ⑮ ⊙
D: Michael Dinner **A:** Donald Sutherland, John Heard, Andrew McCarthy, Mary Stuart Masterson, Kevin Dillon (HBO/Silver Screen Partners)

Heaven Help Us focuses upon several Catholic schoolboys, three in particular, who get into an increasing amount of trouble with the presiding priests. Andrew McCarthy, a new arrival at St. Basil's, instantly latches onto reigning outsider in his class, Malcolm Danare, a chubby egghead who is constantly picked on by school bully Kevin Dillon. Very funny in spots and wonderfully evocative of Brooklyn, circa 1965, pic suffers somewhat by dividing its attention between outrageous pranks and realistic sketches of the Catholic-school experience.

HEAVEN KNOWS, MR. ALLISON
1957, 107 mins, US ⑮ ▱
D: John Huston **A:** Deborah Kerr, Robert Mitchum (20th Century-Fox)

An intriguing yarn about a marine, marooned on a small Pacific atoll with a nun. They divide their time dodging Japs and trying to steer clear of their emotions. The film, directed by John Huston with something less than outstanding imagination, but with a good measure of humor and bravado, holds out an early promise which it doesn't keep. The high spots involve Robert Mitchum's exploits—and fantastic ones they are—when he raids the Japanese supply depot for food.
1957: Nominations: Best Actress (Deborah Kerr), Adapted Screenplay

HEAVENLY BODY, THE
1943, 90 mins, US
D: Alexander Hall **A:** William Powell, Hedy Lamarr, James Craig, Fay Bainter, Henry O'Neill, Spring Byington (M-G-M)

Yarn attempts to tell what happens when the usual triangle evolves from a situation involving Lamarr and William

Powell as the husband-wife, James Craig as an air-raid warden, and the astronomical pursuits of Powell. The crux of the story is woven around the fact that Powell works at night, as an astronomer, leaving his wife prey for prowling air-raid wardens. It may sound funny on paper, but it doesn't quite come off as expected.

HEAVENLY CREATURES
1994, 99 mins, New Zealand Ⓥ ☒
D: Peter Jackson **A:** Melanie Lynsky, Kate Winslet, Sarah Peirse, Diana Kent, Clive Merrison (WingNut/Fontana)

An exhilarating retelling of a 1950s tabloid murder, *Heavenly Creatures* combines original vision, a drop-dead command of the medium, and a successful marriage between a dazzling, kinetic techno-show and a complex, credible portrait of the out-of-control relationship between the crime's two schoolgirl perpetrators. The somewhat morose and short-on-confidence Pauline (Melanie Lynsky) is snapped out of her shell by the imperious English girl Juliet (Kate Winslet), who briskly provides her with a role model. The friendship quickly spirals to the level of passionate interdependence. Their bond falls into unclassifiable territory, being neither an innocent, misconstrued friendship, nor an acknowledged lesbian relationship.
1994: Nomination: Original Screenplay

HEAVEN ONLY KNOWS
1947, 97 mins, US
D: Albert S. Rogell **A:** Robert Cummings, Brian Donlevy, Marjorie Reynolds, Jorja Curtright (United Artists)

An amusing fantasy done in an almost straight manner to give it credibility. Story concerns an angel visiting earth to rectify a heavenly bookkeeping error. He had permitted a man to run loose without a soul. On earth, he finds the soulless creature just that. He's a ruthless killer operating a saloon in Montana. The angel's chore is to bring together the killer and the schoolmarm because, according to heaven's books, they should have been married for two years. Robert Cummings plays the visiting angel with just the right touch. Brian Donlevy, too, sparks his assignment as the man without a soul.

HEAVENS ABOVE!
1963, 118 mins, UK Ⓥ
D: John Boulting **A:** Peter Sellers, Bernard Miles, Eric Sykes, Irene Handl, Mir-

iam Karlin, Isabel Jeans (British Lion/Romulus)

The Boulting Brothers employ their favorite weapon, the rapier of ridicule. The screenplay is full of choice jokes, but the humor is often uneven. Story concerns the appointment, by a clerical error, of the Reverend John Smallwood (Peter Sellers) to a prosperous neighborhood. He shocks the district by making a Negro trashman his warden and takes a bunch of disreputable evicted gypsies into the vicarage. Sellers gives a guileful portrayal of genuine simplicity.

HEAVEN'S GATE
1980, 219 mins, US Ⓥ ☉ ☒
D: Michael Cimino **A:** Kris Kristofferson, Christopher Walken, Isabelle Huppert, Sam Waterston, John Hurt, Jeff Bridges (United Artists)

The first scenes are so energetic and beautiful that anyone who knows the saga of the $35-million epic might begin to think it was going to be worth every penny. Unfortunately the balance is so confusing, so overlong at three and a half hours and so ponderous that it fails to work at almost every level. What structure the film does have is based on the Johnson County wars, which took place in the 1890s in Wyoming. Cimino, who wrote the script himself, has simply not provided enough details for his story, leaving his audience guessing.
1981: Nomination: Best Art Direction

HEAVEN'S PRISONERS
1996, 126 mins, US/UK Ⓥ
D: Phil Joanou **A:** Alec Baldwin, Kelly Lynch, Mary Stuart Masterson, Eric Roberts, Teri Hatcher (New Line/Savoy/Rank)

However rudderless and convoluted this Cajun crime mystery becomes, picture offers Alec Baldwin one of his juicier roles. Baldwin plays Dave Robicheaux, a former cop living the quiet life of a bait-shop owner with loving wife Annie (Kelly Lynch). That life is changed forever when Dave and Annie watch a small plane crash into the Gulf and save a little Salvadoran girl. As he gets thicker and thicker into the city's criminal mire, Dave encounters more than his share of colorful, dangerous characters.

HEAVY METAL
1981, 90 mins, US
D: Gerald Potterton (Reitman-Moyer)

This technically first-rate six-segment animated anthology is an amalgam of science fiction, sword and sorcery, hip humor, violence, sex, and a smidgen of drugs. The film, which draws its title and sensibility from the adult fantasy magazine of the same name, tends to front-load its virtues. Initial segments have a boisterous blend of dynamic graphics, intriguing plot premises, and sly wit that unfortunately slide gradually downhill.

HEAVY TRAFFIC
1973, 78 mins, US Ⓥ
D: Ralph Bakshi (Film Creations/Krantz)

After their first X-rated animated feature, *Fritz the Cat,* producer Steve Krantz and writer-director Ralph Bakshi turn to "human" creatures, combining animation and live action, a blatant example of hardcore pornography. There's something to offend everyone in this melange of crudely conceived, amateurishly animated stuff.

HEDDA
1975, 104 mins, UK Ⓥ
D: Trevor Nunn **A:** Glenda Jackson, Timothy West, Peter Eyre, Jennie Linden, Patrick Stewart (Brut)

A gem, taking the Royal Shakespeare production of the Henrik Ibsen classic, complete with a fine cast headed by Glenda Jackson. It's heady stuff, nearly every line to be relished, as one watches the destructively dominant Hedda torturing her friends and relations with rapier-sharp lines and stilettolike glances.
1975: Nomination: Best Actress (Glenda Jackson)

HE GOT GAME
1998, 134 mins, US Ⓥ ⊙
D: Spike Lee **A:** Denzel Washington, Ray Allen, Milla Jovovich, Rosario Dawson, Hill Harper, Jim Brown (40 Acres & a Mule/Touchstone)

He Got Game is a contemporary basketball drama with comic overtones, centering on the turbulent relationship between a convict-father and his gifted athlete son. This vibrantly colorful film is a tad too soft at the center and is arguably the director's most mainstream movie, with Denzel Washington as the errant father desperate for forgiveness and Ray Allen, the Milwaukee Bucks basketball superstar, as his resentful son Jesus. Lee shrewdly dissects the exploitation of student athletes in the U.S. and the various dimensions of basketball—popular sport, national myth, multibillion-dollar business. Since Jesus is perceived as a "national asset" worth millions of dollars,

everybody around him wants a piece of the pie. Washington renders solid work in an uncharacteristic role. Newcomer Allen is perfectly cast as the hurting, good-natured son who needs to make peace with his father.

HEIRESS, THE
1949, 115 mins, US Ⓥ
D: William Wyler **A:** Olivia de Havilland, Montgomery Clift, Ralph Richardson, Miriam Hopkins (Paramount)

A meticulous reproduction of the Victorian scene, so faithful to its mores that it is a museum piece. Olivia de Havilland is the homely daughter of a wealthy physician. Shyness has kept her suitorless despite a sizable wealth that will be augmented when her father passes. Montgomery Clift is the first male to show her attention. Clift plays the difficult part of an ambiguous character who is more opportunist than crook in his fortune-hunting. Ralph Richardson is grand as the stern, straitlaced father.
1949: Best Actress (Olivia de Havilland), B&W Art Direction, Scoring of a Dramatic Picture, B&W Costume Design
Nominations: Best Picture, Director, Supp. Actor (Ralph Richardson), B&W Cinematography

HEIST, THE
See: $

HELEN MORGAN STORY, THE
1957, 117 mins, US ▭
D: Michael Curtiz **A:** Ann Blyth, Paul Newman, Richard Carlson, Gene Evans, Alan King, Cara Williams (Warner)

Warner's feature is little more than a tuneful soap opera, another in what appears to be a growing series of boozy biopix of showbiz greats. Morgan (Ann Blyth) comes to Chicago to seek a career. She gets her start, both professionally and romantically, with Larry (Paul Newman), a shady operator. When he comes back into her life to prey upon her friendship with attorney Wade (Richard Carlson), she takes to the bottle for solace. Director Michael Curtiz has done a good job, and the production gets added benefit from a series of hit tunes of the era, excellently sung offscreen by Gogi Grant.

HELEN OF TROY
1955, 118 mins, US ▭
D: Robert Wise **A:** Rossana Podesta, Jacques Sernas, Cedric Hardwicke, Stanley Baker, Niall MacGinnis, Robert Douglas (Warner)

The retelling of the Homeric legend, filmed in its entirety in Italy, makes lavish use of the CinemaScope screen. Like many tales of antiquity, the story is occasionally stilted. As Helen and Paris, the love-smitten Trojan prince, Warners cast two unknowns—Rossana Podesta, an exquisite Italian beauty, and Jacques Sernas, a brawny and handsome Frenchman. Visually both meet the demands of the roles. Their voices have been dubbed.

HELL AND HIGH WATER
1954, 103 mins, US ▭
D: Samuel Fuller A: Richard Widmark, Bella Darvi, Victor Francen, Cameron Mitchell, Gene Evans, David Wayne (20th Century-Fox)

CinemaScope and rip-roaring adventure mate perfectly in a highly fanciful, but mighty entertaining action feature. Plot has to do with a group of individuals who band together to thwart a scheme to start a new world war with an atomic incident. These private heroes hire Widmark, a former naval submarine officer, to command an underwater trip to the Arctic, where scientists will check reports that a Communist atomic arsenal is being built on an isolated island.
1954: Nomination: Best Special Effects

HELL BENT
1918, 77 mins, US ⊗
D: John Ford A: Harry Carey, Neva Gerber, Duke Lee, Joseph Harris (Universal)

Hell Bent was Ford's 14th film and his 9th feature. Harry Carey was Ford's most frequent early star and collaborator. Harry rides into the town of Rawhide, where he is smitten with Bess (Neva Gerber), a "good girl" forced by circumstances to work in a dance hall. B-plot mechanics take over as Harry tries to rid town of outlaws but is stymied when he learns Bess's weak-minded brother is member of gang led by Bean Ross (Joseph Harris). Film is enlivened by some of Ford's special moments.

HELL DRIVERS
1957, 108 mins, UK Ⓥ
D: Cy Endfield A: Stanley Baker, Herbert Lom, Peggy Cummins, Patrick McGoohan, Jill Ireland, Sean Connery (Aqua/Rank)

Story has to do with the rivalries of a gang of haulage truck drivers, operating between gravel pits and a construction site. Stanley Baker is an ex-convict who gets a job as one of these drivers and immediately falls foul of Patrick McGoohan, the firm's ace driver. Baker discovers that McGoohan and William Hartnell, the manager, are running a racket. The drama comes to an uneasy head when Baker's lorry is doctored. Some of the speed sequences provide some tingling thrills.

HELLER IN PINK TIGHTS
1960, 100 mins, US Ⓥ
D: George Cukor A: Sophia Loren, Anthony Quinn, Eileen Heckart, Ramon Novarro, Margaret O'Brien, Steve Forrest (Paramount)

George Cukor puts tongue in cheek to turn an ordinary story into a gaudy, old-fashioned western satire with gleeful touches of melodrama. *Heller* follows the Great Healy Dramatic and Concert Co. in two red wagons through the wilds of Wyoming. The traveling theatre is fighting for its survival, and Sophia Loren and Anthony Quinn put up a strong enough battle to make things interesting and amusing. It's when the film's plot dissolves into pure western that it becomes somewhat commonplace.

HELLGATE
1952, 87 mins, US
D: Charles Marquis Warren A: Sterling Hayden, Joan Leslie, Ward Bond, Jim Arness, Peter Coe (Commander/Lippert)

Hellgate is the old federal prison in New Mexico used long ago for the toughest offenders. Charles Marquis Warren builds a certain amount of suspense in developing escape tries by the prisoners, conflict among the convicts, and the general brutality of prison life. Sterling Hayden does an excellent job of portraying the wrongfully committed man. He's sent to Hellgate, commanded by Ward Bond, who devises numerous sadistic cruelties in an effort to make the convict try an escape so he can be legitimately killed.

HELL IN KOREA
See: A Hill in Korea

HELL IN THE PACIFIC
1968, 103 mins, US Ⓥ ▭
D: John Boorman A: Lee Marvin, Toshiro Mifune (Selmur)

Lee Marvin and Toshiro Mifune comprise the entire cast of this World War II drama, directed with an uncertain hand by John Boorman. Story takes off with the discovery by Mifune that he no longer is alone on a desolate Pacific island. Pair stalk each other, then attempt to outwit each other, finally collaborate on survival in the form of a raft. Mifune's unrestrained grunting and running about create an outdated caricature of an Oriental. Marvin has sardonic lines which resemble wisecracks, intended for onlookers.

HELL IS A CITY
1960, 98 mins, UK
D: Val Guest A: Stanley Baker, John Crawford, Donald Pleasence, Maxine Audley, Billie Whitelaw, Joseph Tomelty (Hammer)

An absorbing version of a conventional cops-and-robbers yarn. Val Guest's taut screenplay, allied to his own deft direction, has resulted in a notable film in which the characters are all vividly alive, the action constantly gripping, and the background of a provincial city put over with authenticity. Stanley Baker as a detective inspector is concerned with a dangerous escaped convict who, he suspects, will be returning to pick up the stolen jewels that sent him to the cooler. From the moment the killer (John Crawford) makes his sudden surprise entrance, suspense rarely lets up.

HELL IS FOR HEROES
1962, 90 mins, US Ⓥ ⊙
D: Don Siegel A: Steve McQueen, Bobby Darin, Fess Parker, Harry Guardino, James Coburn, Bob Newhart (Paramount)

A gripping, fast-paced, hard-hitting dramatic portrait of an interesting World War II battlefield incident. Pivotal character of the drama is a surly, rebellious, busted NCO (Steve McQueen) whose front-line courage, leadership, and keen sense of improvisation in the course of a grim and seemingly hopeless campaign to hold off a large German force backfires into a potential court-martial rap for usurping authority.

HELLO AGAIN
1987, 96 mins, US Ⓥ ⊙
D: Frank Perry A: Shelley Long, Judith Ivey, Gabriel Byrne, Corbin Bernsen, Sela Ward, Austin Pendleton (Touchstone)

Long plays Lucy Chadman, housewife who chokes to death on a chicken ball while in the occultist boutique of her sister Zelda (Judith Ivey). After much hocus-pocus, Zelda brings Lucy back from her grave a year to the day after her death. The most predictable thing that could happen does, and Lucy walks in on her husband with his gold-digging, glory-grabbing girlfriend Kim (played with nice salaciousness by Sela Ward). Scene in which Lucy

discovers the lovers is actually funny, but it's a jumping-off point into an abyss of silly plot developments.

HELLO, DOLLY!
1969, 129 mins, US Ⓥ ⊙ ▭
D: Gene Kelly A: Barbra Streisand, Walter Matthau, Michael Crawford, Louis Armstrong, Marianne McAndrew, Tommy Tune (20th Century-Fox/Chenault)

An expensive, expansive, sometimes exaggerated, sentimental, nostalgic, wholesome, pictorially opulent filmusical with the charisma of Barbra Streisand in the title role. Streisand is a unique performer, with that inborn vitality that marks great personalities. She brings her own special kind of authority. Walter Matthau is hard to accept at first, his dancing being the step-counting sort and his singing somewhat awkward. Nonetheless his experience cannot be discounted.
1969: Best Art Direction, Sound, Adapted Score for a Musical Picture
Nominations: Best Picture, Cinematography, Costume Design, Editing

HELLO, FRISCO, HELLO
1943, 90 mins, US
D: H. Bruce Humberstone A: Alice Faye, John Payne, Jack Oakie, Lynn Bari, Laird Cregar, June Havoc (20th Century-Fox)

Per usual the typical musical comedy plot is no great shakes, but nicely studded with laughs, pathos, and innumerable musical interludes. Laid in San Francisco at the turn of the century, story spots John Payne as the leader of a foursome that includes Alice Faye, Jack Oakie, and June Havoc. It's a typical tavern combo that leans on their warbling to keep a regular job in the metropolis's leading saloon. The yen of Payne to make the grade in Nob Hill society brings the usual complications.

HELLRAISER
1987, 90 mins, UK Ⓥ ⊙
D: Clive Barker A: Andrew Robinson, Clare Higgins, Ashley Laurence, Sean Chapman, Oliver Smith, Robert Hines (Film Futures)

Film concerns a dissipated adventurer who buys a sort of magic music box which is capable of providing its owner hitherto undreamed of pains and pleasures, and which ultimately causes him to be torn to shreds in a temple that transforms itself into a torture chamber. Ill-fated adventurer returns, partly decomposed, seeking human flesh and blood, which, when devoured, will enable him to regain his human form. Pic is well made, well acted, and the visual effects are generally handled with skill.

HELLRAISER II: HELLBOUND
1988, 96 mins, UK/US Ⓥ ⊙
D: Tony Randel **A:** Clare Higgins, Ashley Laurence, Kenneth Cranham, Imogen Boorman, Sean Chapman (Film Futures)

A maggotty carnival of mayhem, mutation, and dismemberment, awash in blood and recommended only for those who thrive on such junk. Helmer Tony Randel returns to the off-the-wall tale of a psychotic psychiatrist's long struggle to get the better of something called the Lament Configuration, a kind of demonic, silver-filigreed Rubik's Cube whose solution opens the transdimensional doors into a parallel world of sinful pleasure and unspeakably hellish pain.

HELLRAISER III: HELL ON EARTH
1992, 92 mins, US Ⓥ ⊙
D: Anthony Hickox **A:** Terry Farrell, Doug Bradley, Paula Marshall, Kevin Bernhardt, Ashley Laurence, Ken Carpenter (Fifth Avenue)

Well-produced effort is an effective combination of imaginative special effects with the strangeness of author Clive Barker's original conception, on which the characters are based. Terry Farrell toplines as an attractive TV newswoman summoned by the ghost of British World War I Captain Elliott Spencer. Spencer's experiments with the supernatural had unleased evil on the world in the race of the Cenobites, led by Pinhead, whose adventures were limned in the prior pics. Pinhead is back, with a strange little box that's key to sending him back to hell.

HELLRAISER: BLOODLINE
1996, 85 mins, US Ⓥ ⊙
D: Alan Smithee [Kevin Yeager] **A:** Bruce Ramsay, Valentina Vargas, Doug Bradley, Kim Myers, Christine Harnos (Dimension/Trans Atlantic)

Except for the most undiscriminating gorehound, pic is a pointless mess. The chief problem is that the films have become an excuse for grotesqueries and sadism. The focus on leather, chains, hooks, and blades makes Pinhead's world a cross between a machine shop and an S&M bar. The less said about the acting, the better.

HELL'S ANGELS
1930, 119 mins, US
D: Howard Hughes **A:** Ben Lyon, James Hall, Jean Harlow, John Darrow, Lucien Prival, Frank Clarke (Caddo)

Howard Hughes's air film is no sappy, imbecilic tale. The first half of the film builds up to a Zeppelin raid on London which runs two reels. Second half's main display is an aerial dogfight in which at least 30, maybe 40, planes simultaneously start diving and zooming at each other. Story actually opens in Munich, with Lyon trying to date every femme in town. Highly seasoned portion of the second half comes with Lyon and Hall on a spree. Hall finds Harlow half-soused and entwined with another officer in a barroom booth.
1929/30: **Nomination:** Best Cinematography (Tony Gaudio, Harry Perry)

HELL'S HIGHWAY
1932, 62 mins, US
D: Rowland Brown **A:** Richard Dix, Tom Brown, Louise Carter, Rochelle Hudson, C. Henry Gordon, Warner Richmond (Radio)

The entire action, with the exception of one scene, occurs in and around a prison camp in some southern state; the preponderance of the convict labor is Negro. The convicts have been hired to work on a new road. The contractor tells his foreman that to win a profit he must get twice as much work out of the convicts. To force their efforts, recourse is had to the lash and the sweatbox. Richard Dix is one of the convicts. His brother (Tom Brown) is sent to the gang for having shot and wounded Dix's betrayer. Dix, who is planning an escape, tries to prevent the kid from coming along. The direction is remarkably good at most points.

HELL'S ISLAND
1955, 79 mins, US
D: Phil Karlson **A:** John Payne, Mary Murphy, Francis L. Sullivan, Eduardo Noriega, Arnold Moss (Paramount)

Screenplay unfolds in the Caribbean port of Puerto Rosario, where the adventuring twirls around the search for a missing ruby. Phil Karlson gives narrative a hard glossing in his direction, occasionally letting down his pace but generally delivering a briskly told tale in which capable players lend realism to colorful characters. John Payne socks over a hard-hitting role in excellent fashion, and Mary Murphy takes on her first heavy role very competently.

HELLZAPOPPIN'
1942, 92 mins, US
D: H. C. Potter **A:** Ole Olsen, Chic Johnson, Martha Raye, Hugh Herbert, Jane Frazee, Robert Paige (Universal/Mayfair)

There's the thinnest thread of a romantic story, but it's incidental to Olsen and Johnson's stage formula for *Hellzapoppin'*. One of the picture's saving graces is the originality of its presentation of screwball comedy. The business of O&J talking from the screen to the comic projectionist (Shemp Howard) is one such detail; ditto the slide bit telling a kid in the audience, "Stinky go home," with Jane Frazee and Robert Paige interrupting a duet until Stinky finally leaves. Don Raye and Gene De Paul have contributed several nice songs for this film.
1942: Nomination: Best Song ("Pig Foote Pete")

HELP!
1965, 92 mins, UK Ⓥ ⊙
D: Richard Lester **A:** John Lennon, Paul McCartney, Ringo Starr, George Harrison, Leo McKern, Eleanor Bron (Shenson/Subafilms)

The Beatles' second effort is peppered with bright gags and situations and throwaway nonsense. Richard Lester's direction is expectedly alert and the color lensing is a delight. But there are also some frantically contrived spots and sequences that flag badly. The simple good spirits that pervaded *A Hard Day's Night* are now often smothered, as if everybody is desperately trying to outsmart themselves and be ultra-clever-clever. Nevertheless, *Help!* is a good, nimble romp with both giggles and belly laughs.

HEMINGWAY'S ADVENTURES OF A YOUNG MAN
1962, 145 mins, US ▭
D: Martin Ritt **A:** Richard Beymer, Diane Baker, Paul Newman, Ricardo Montalban, Dan Dailey, Arthur Kennedy (20th Century-Fox)

The formidable task of assembling the bits and pieces of Ernest Hemingway's autobiographical young hero, Nick Adams, and welding them into a single, substantial flesh-and-blood screen personality has nearly been accomplished. But the film has a disquieting tendency to oscillate between flashes of artistry and truth and interludes of mechanics and melodramatics. Paul Newman, almost unrecognizable behind a masterfully grotesque yet realistic makeup mask by Ben Nye, re-creates the punch-drunk Battler character. It's a colorful and compassionate acting cameo.

HENNESSY
1975, 104 mins, UK Ⓥ
D: Don Sharp **A:** Rod Steiger, Lee Remick, Richard Johnson, Trevor Howard, Eric Porter (American International)

Good suspense drama starring Rod Steiger as a man planning to blow up the British Parliament in revenge for his family's accidental death in Belfast. Richard Johnson, who wrote the intriguing original story, plays a Scotland Yard inspector.

HENRY & JUNE
1990, 136 mins, US Ⓥ ⊙
D: Philip Kaufman **A:** Fred Ward, Uma Thurman, Maria de Medeiros, Richard E. Grant, Kevin Spacey, Jean-Philippe Ecoffey (Universal/Walrus)

Story of the long-secret, passionate affair between writers Henry Miller and Anais Nin in Paris in 1931-32 will be considered liberating by some and obscene by others. The central performances of Fred Ward, as the cynical, life-loving Miller, and Maria de Medeiros, as the beautiful, insatiable Anais, splendidly fulfill the director's vision. Pic is less successful in gaining audience sympathy for these hedonists. Also, the character of June (Uma Thurman) is ill-defined.
1990: Nomination: Best Cinematography

HENRY VIII AND HIS SIX WIVES
1972, 125 mins, UK Ⓥ
D: Waris Hussein **A:** Keith Michell, Donald Pleasence, Charlotte Rampling, Jane Asher, Frances Cuka, Lynne Frederick (Anglo-EMI)

A beautifully crafted epic, pic deals almost exclusively with Henry and his succession of wives, deliberately relegating historic events to backdrops. Thanks also to a fine, tight script and sensitive but firm direction, the king acquires many more dimensions than those usually credited him. Keith Michell gives an uppercase performance all the way, through a succession of equally very believable makeup transformations.

HENRY V
1946, 127 mins, UK Ⓥ ⊙
D: Laurence Olivier **A:** Laurence Olivier, Robert Newton, Renee Asherson, Esmond Knight, Leo Genn, Felix Aylmer (Two Cities)

The color, the sets, the expanse, and the imaginative quality of the filming are

unexcelled. Henry's a British king, hardly more than a moppet, when he cons himself into believing that he ought to muscle his way into France and stake his royal claim there on the basis of ancestry. So he loads some 30,000 men and their horses and hies across the channel. There are many interesting scenes and one really exciting one—the battle. With thousands of horses, knights in armor, and longbowmen in colorful costumes, it's a Technicolor setup. Memorable for their deft humor and poignancy are both scenes in which Renee Asherson, as Princess Katharine, appears.
1946: Nominations: Best Picture, Actor (Laurence Olivier), Color Art Direction, Scoring of a Dramatic Picture

HENRY V
1989, 137 mins, UK ⓥ ⊙
D: Kenneth Branagh **A:** Kenneth Branagh, Derek Jacobi, Brian Blessed, Ian Holm, Paul Scofield, Emma Thompson (Renaissance)

A stirring, gritty, and enjoyable pic which offers a plethora of fine performances from some of the UK's brightest talents. Branagh's version is more realistic and tighter in scale, and is a contempo version of Shakespeare. Pic opens with Derek Jacobi as the chorus wandering around a film studio setting the scene. Branagh (Henry V, King of England) prepares for an invasion of France. Paul Scofield (the French king) sadly ponders his country's situation and is urged to enter in bloody battle by Michael Maloney (the Dauphin).
1989: Best Costume Design
Nominations: Best Director, Actor (Kenneth Branagh)

HENRY FOOL
1998, 141 mins, US ⓥ ⊙
D: Hal Hartley **A:** Thomas Jay Ryan, James Urbaniak, Parker Posey, Maria Porter, James Saito, Kevin Corrigan

Poetic, bawdy, contemplative, sidewrenchingly funny, and finally quite touching, *Henry Fool* is flawed only by its length. Simon Grim (James Urbaniak) is a terminally shy garbage man, sole breadwinner for his depressed mom (Maria Porter) and libidinous sister, Fay (Parker Posey). Enter Henry Fool (Thomas Jay Ryan), a mysterious bum with a gift for words who takes up residence in their basement. Henry encourages Simon to start putting any thoughts he may have on paper. The words start pouring out. Soon student journalists are interviewing Simon. Meanwhile, Henry casually seduces

Simon's mother and is revealed as a paroled con sent down for having sex with a 13-year-old. *Henry Fool* is a sly dig at the conformity of American culture; a near mini-epic on a New Jersey blue-collar family; an upbeat portrait of how the unlikeliest people can reinvent themselves; and, most Hartleyesque of all, an examination of how life deals the most unexpected hands. The pic delights in its sheer control and love of the power of words.

HENRY: PORTRAIT OF A SERIAL KILLER
1989, 83 mins, US ⓥ ⊙
D: John McNaughton **A:** Michael Rooker, Tom Towles, Tracy Arnold (Maljack)

Hard-driving, riveting pic is an unsentimental look at a sociopath as his bloody trail passes through Chicago. Story follows Henry (Michael Rooker) while he rooms with his old prison buddy Otis (Tom Towles) and Otis's sister Becky (Tracy Arnold). Film uses two strategies to keep audiences off balance. First is the use of violence, which starts off subtly but finally moves to a gory extreme. The second tactic is the use of Becky to humanize Henry. Low-budget pic looks surprisingly good, capturing the gritty feel of the characters' lives.

HER ALIBI
1989, 94 mins, US ⓥ ⊙
D: Bruce Beresford **A:** Tom Selleck, Paulina Porizkova, William Daniels, James Farentino, Hurd Hatfield (Warner)

Bestselling writer Phil Blackwood (Tom Selleck) rescues beautiful Nina (Czech-born model Pauline Porizkova) from court custody as a murder suspect. He gives her an alibi and has to take the aloof Romanian beauty out to his lush country estate while he pecks away at his new novel—about her, naturally, and his feverishly imagined version of their relationship. He soon begins to suspect she is a murderer. Mix of sexual tension, physical danger, and quirky black humor has a certain appealing buoyancy, but ultimately it's deflated by general lack of credibility.

HERBIE GOES TO MONTE CARLO
1977, 105 mins, US ⓥ
D: Vincent McEveety **A:** Dean Jones, Don Knotts, Julie Sommars, Jacques Marin, Roy Kinnear, Bernard Fox (Walt Disney)

Herbie, the spunky little Volks Beetle with a mind of his own, gets romantic buildup when he becomes a Romeo on wheels infatuated with a flirty powder-blue Lancia named Giselle, as both participate in the annual Paris-to-Monte Carlo road rally. Herbie is reunited with his original owner and driver, Dean Jones, a former second-rate racer whom he once adopted and won a flock of races for in the US.

HERBIE RIDES AGAIN
1974, 88 mins, US Ⓥ ⊙
D: Robert Stevenson **A:** Helen Hayes, Ken Berry, Stefanie Powers, John McIntire, Keenan Wynn, Huntz Hall (Walt Disney)

Disney's sequel to *The Love Bug* adds up, natch, to another fat plug for the Volkswagen "bug" as the runaway (literally) titular star. Keenan Wynn is a tycoon hellbent on putting up the tallest skyscraper yet, but the plan is frustrated and ultimately foiled by sweet little old widow lady Helen Hayes. She owns the ramshackle Victorian firehouse that stands in Wynn's greedy way, and she won't budge.

HERCULES
1983, 98 mins, Italy Ⓥ ⊙
D: Lewis Coates [Luigi Cozzi] **A:** Lou Ferrigno, Mirella D'Angelo, Sybil Danning, Ingrid Anderson, Brad Harris, Rossana Podesta (Golan-Globus)

Golan and Globus have corralled "The Incredible Lou Ferrigno" to topline in a cheesy epic that could just about be titled *Hercules in Outer Space.* Since a lumpy space suit would cover Ferrigno's mighty physique from view, the all-powerful one travels through the universe wearing nothing but his gladiatorial briefs. It is Hercules' tasks to try to rescue the Princess Cassiopea from the clutches of her evil kidnappers, and given the changing times, the muscleman doesn't have to battle cardboard monsters, but high-tech mechanical beasts made of metal, which emit deadly laser blasts from their jaws.

HERCULES
1997, 92 mins, US Ⓥ ⊙
D: John Musker, Ron Clements (Walt Disney)

Hercules is a winning tall tale, cleverly told and wonderfully voiced. Film relates how Olympian gods Zeus (voiced by Rip Torn) and Hera (Samantha Eggar) begat the ever-so-cute Hercules. Meanwhile, lord of the underworld Hades (James Woods) learns the only thing that could undo his plans to vanquish the folks on Mt. Olympus is Zeus's spawn. Zeus tells Hercules he must become a hero to be re-instated with the gods and sends him to the satyr Philoctetes (Danny DeVito), a.k.a. Phil, for grueling Rocky-style training. The source of peril is not human frailty but mythical monsters—and bad girl Megara (Susan Egan), a.k.a. Meg, forced to do Hades' bidding. The song score favors tunes that propel the story rather than focusing on character enhancement. The music itself, while serviceable, is not at all distinctive.
1997: Nomination: Best Original Song ("Go the Distance")

HERCULES RETURNS
1993, 80 mins, Australia Ⓥ
D: David Parker **A:** David Argue, Bruce Spence, Mary Coustas, Michael Carman, Brendon Suhr (Philm)

Hercules Returns follows in the footsteps of Woody Allen's *What's Up, Tiger Lily?* by completely revamping and re-voicing a bad old foreign film. David Parker has directed about 18 minutes of framing footage, but most of *Hercules Returns* consists of the revoiced film. The improvisation turns the original clinker into a hilarious romp, with Hercules now a frustrated singer sent by Zeus to perform at the Pink Parthenon nightclub, where he's offered the hand of the lovely Labia, daughter of the club's owners. She, however, prefers Testiculi and rejects Hercules to it. Film has an endearing, slapdash feel to it.

HERE COMES MR. JORDAN
1941, 93 mins, US Ⓥ ⊙
D: Alexander Hall **A:** Robert Montgomery, Evelyn Keyes, Claude Rains, Rita Johnson, Edward Everett Horton, James Gleason (Columbia)

Story humorously poses the theory of reincarnation. Robert Montgomery is an aggressive prizefighter snatched by heavenly messenger Edward Everett Horton from his earthly body, and taken to heaven for celestial registration. When it is found that Montgomery's arrival is premature, and his earthly body has already been cremated to prevent replacement, it's up to registrar Claude Rains (Mr. Jordan) to secure another suitable body.
1941: Best Original Story, Screenplay
Nominations: Best Picture, Director, Actor (Robert Montgomery), Supp. Actor (James Gleason), B&W Cinematography

HERE COMES THE GROOM
1951, 113 mins, US ⊙
D: Frank Capra **A:** Bing Crosby, Jane

Wyman, Alexis Smith, Franchot Tone, James Barton, Robert Keith (Paramount)

The merry yarn of a carefree newspaperman (Bing Crosby) who must marry within a week to be able to adopt two war orphans he has picked up during a lengthy Paris assignment. Crosby is at his casual best. Wyman is a wow as the girlfriend who makes him really work to win her. The two join on the hit-parade tune "In the Cool, Cool, Cool of the Evening," by Johnny Mercer and Hoagy Carmichael, in a socko song-and-dance session.

1951: Best Song ("In the Cool, Cool, Cool of the Evening")
Nomination: Best Motion Picture Story

HERE COMES THE NAVY
1934, 88 mins, US
D: Lloyd Bacon **A:** James Cagney, Pat O'Brien, Gloria Stuart, Frank McHugh, Dorothy Tree, Robert Barrat (Warner)

Saga of the US fleet is light on story and borders on being an elaborate newsreel, i.e., the inner workings of the gobs at maneuvers and navy life, from enlistment to war formations. The James Cagney–Pat O'Brien feud throughout the footage reminds of the Quirt-Flagg school of masculine venom. Only here Gloria Stuart is O'Brien's sister and he wants Cagney to stay away from her.
1934: Nomination: Best Picture

HERE COME THE CO-EDS
1945, 85 mins, US
D: Jean Yarbrough **A:** Bud Abbott, Lou Costello, Peggy Ryan, Martha O'Driscoll, Lon Chaney, Donald Cook (Universal)

Abbott and Costello are easily up to their high laugh standards in *Here Come the Co-eds*. Pic is helped considerably by presence of Phil Spitalny's nifty all-girl "Hour of Charm" orchestra and Peggy Ryan, who plays a typical college hepcat. *Co-eds* is smartly gagged, smoothly paced, and even the familiar routines are given new twists. Yarn shows a moss-covered, tradition-bound femme college that's stirred out of its lethargy by Abbott and Costello.

HERE COME THE GIRLS
1953, 77 mins, US ℗
D: Claude Binyon **A:** Bob Hope, Tony Martin, Arlene Dahl, Rosemary Clooney, Millard Mitchell, William Demarest (Paramount)

Bob Hope is the spark plug who keeps this film alive and kicking. The production lives up to its musical connotations and

title by using plenty of comely femmes and production numbers. Nearly every one of the eight songs forms a production piece and all of them are eye-pleasers. Hope, Tony Martin, and Rosemary Clooney are the chief song singers of the Jay Livingston–Ray Evans numbers. As a chorus boy who is made star of the show, Hope thinks it's final recognition of his talent, not knowing he's only bait to trap a slasher who carves up any admirer of Dahl's. The laughs come from Hope's inability to do any number right and his colossal conceit in believing he can do no wrong.

HER ENLISTED MAN
See: Red Salute

HERE WE GO ROUND THE MULBERRY BUSH
1968, 94 mins, UK
D: Clive Donner **A:** Barry Evans, Judy Geeson, Angela Scoular, Sheila White, Adrienne Posta, Denholm Elliott (Giant/United Artists)

A light-footed look at the teenagers with engaging performances from hitherto largely unknown youngsters, the film was made entirely on location in a new town near London. It has a nimble alertness to juve characteristics and a nice flair for comedy. The hero is a student absorbed with chasing gals but finding the hunt leaves him too often up a cul-de-sac. Barry Evans wins both sympathy and laughs as the boy. Story is spliced with Mitty-type dream bits, which give additional bite to the gap between ideal and reality.

HER HUSBAND'S AFFAIRS
1947, 84 mins, US ℗
D: S. Sylvan Simon **A:** Lucille Ball, Franchot Tone, Edward Everett Horton, Mikhail Rasumny, Gene Lockhart (Columbia)

As a comedy team, Lucille Ball and Franchot Tone excel. Tone is a slightly screwball advertising-slogan genius, while Ball is his ever-loving wife who somehow always winds up with the credit for his spectacular stunts. Motivation for much of the comedy comes from Tone's sponsorship of a screwball inventor and the products that he develops while searching for the perfect embalming fluid. Gentle fun is poked at advertising agencies and bigshot sponsors and public figures.

HER MAJESTY LOVE
1931, 75 mins, US
D: William Dieterle **A:** Marilyn Miller, Ben Lyon, W. C. Fields, Ford Sterling,

Leon Errol, Chester Conklin (First National)

Scene is laid in Berlin and a discursive opening does manage to pump up an effect of gaiety as a background for Marilyn Miller's character of a discreet barmaid who has captivated a rich young man. Scene climaxes with Ben Miller and Ben Lyon doing a tango on the cabaret dance floor, which turns out to be the picture's high point. W. C. Fields does something with the role of the girl's father, a Micawber-like character who would have counted in better surroundings.

HERO
(UK/AUSTRALIA: ACCIDENTAL HERO)
1992, 116 mins, US Ⓥ ⊙
D: Stephen Frears **A:** Dustin Hoffman, Geena Davis, Andy Garcia, Joan Cusack, Kevin J. O'Connor, Maury Chaykin (Columbia)

Muddled effort cleverly skewering media and societal fascination with heroes doesn't create compelling characters for its big-name leads. The story centers on Bernie Laplante (Dustin Hoffman), a shiftless, small-time hood who stumbles onto a plane crash and ends up saving the people aboard. A TV reporter on the plane (Geena Davis) begins a search to find the unknown hero, dubbed "the angel of Flight 104." Eventually, that title falls to John Bubber (Andy Garcia), a homeless Vietnam veteran who comes forward to claim the $1-million reward. Bubber is hailed as the next coming of Jesus and Gandhi, even as Bernie's fortunes continue to sour. Unfortunately, action tilts too heavily toward Hoffman, who simply mucks it up, seemingly playing a bad version of Ratso Rizzo had he survived events in *Midnight Cowboy*.

HEROES
1977, 113 mins, US Ⓥ
D: Jeremy Paul Kagan **A:** Henry Winkler, Sally Field, Harrison Ford, Val Avery (Universal)

Heroes is a poorly written melodrama about a troubled Vietnam veteran and a girl who helps him work out his problems. The multilocation production stars Henry Winkler, in a good though flawed performance, and Sally Field. Since the character has a history of mental malaise, the kooky bits are many and just awful.

HEROES OF TELEMARK, THE
1965, 131 mins, UK Ⓥ ▭
D: Anthony Mann **A:** Kirk Douglas, Richard Harris, Ulla Jacobsson, Michael Redgrave, Anton Diffring, Eric Porter (Benton/Rank)

Hefty, gripping, and carefully made entertainment. It's 1942 in Nazi-occupied Norway. The Germans are ahead of the Allies on atomic fission, as reports from the Norsk Hydro heavy water factory near Telemark reveal. It's the job of a tiny band of nine resistance workers to scotch the Nazi plans. Kirk Douglas, as the scientist drawn unwillingly into the exploit, and Richard Harris, as the resistance leader, turn in powerhouse performances.

HERS TO HOLD
1943, 93 mins, US
D: Frank Ryan **A:** Deanna Durbin, Joseph Cotten, Charles Winninger, Evelyn Ankers, Gus Schilling (Universal)

Deanna Durbin successfully completes transition from cinematic subdeb to young ladyhood. When rich deb Durbin coyly falls for pitches of Joseph Cotten, trifling love-and-leave-'em adventurer, he tries to get out from under when he sees that look in her eye, but his brush-off is unsuccessful and she follows him to an aircraft plant to get a job to seek him out. Four song numbers are neatly spotted along the way.

HER WEDDING NIGHT
1930, 78 mins, US
D: Frank Tuttle **A:** Clara Bow, Ralph Forbes, Charles Ruggles, Skeets Gallagher (Paramount)

Combination of jaunty comedy and a wealth of gay romance in hoke farcical setting. Clara Bow plays the racy heroine with a vigor that compensates for some of her shortcomings in voice and diction. Plot doesn't matter except that Larry (Ralph Forbes), composer of sentimental songs, persuades his friend, Bob (Skeets Gallagher), to impersonate him to escape hero-worshipping flappers. Bob goes off on a romantic spree under his pal's name, inadvertently marrying Norma (Bow) before a rural Italian magistrate.

HE SAID SHE SAID
1990, 115 mins, US Ⓥ ⊙ ▭
D: Ken Kwapis, Marisa Silver **A:** Kevin Bacon, Elizabeth Perkins, Nathan Lane, Anthony LaPaglia, Sharon Stone (Paramount)

Two awful films rolled into one. The idea of having a male and female director take separate but interlocking looks at the same love story fizzles here in the hokiest, most contrived telling imaginable. Sitcom slickness of the enterprise is established as TV news commentator team of Kevin Bacon and Elizabeth Perkins apparently breaks up on the air when she beans him with a coffee cup. Initial hour is devoted to mirthless jokes about the young hotshot's womanizing, fear of marriage, and need to feel professionally superior. Kwapis's high-gloss garishness and antic staging contrasts with the slower, more subdued approach of Silver.

HESTER STREET
1975, 90 mins, US ⓥ
D: Joan Micklin Silver **A:** Steven Keats, Carol Kane, Mel Howard, Dorrie Kavanaugh (Midwest)

Just before the turn of the century, Hester Street is a sort of mobile ghetto as Eastern European Jews pour in and go in for their Americanization before moving on. Jake sends for his wife and son but their arrival first fills him with shame at their old-world cloddishness. The wife goes another way towards becoming an American.

HE WALKED BY NIGHT
1948, 79 mins, US ⓥ
D: Alfred Werker **A:** Richard Basehart, Scott Brady, Roy Roberts, Whit Bissell (Eagle Lion)

A high-tension crime meller, supercharged with violence but sprung with finesse. Yarn is a straightforward documentary-style saga of a psychotic but brilliant killer who is tracked down through dogged detective work. Striking effects are achieved through counterpoint of the slayer's ingenuity in eluding the cops and the police efficiency in bringing him to book. High spot of the film is the final sequence, which takes place in L.A.'s storm-drainage tunnel system. Richard Basehart establishes himself as one of Hollywood's most talented finds in recent years.

HE WAS HER MAN
1934, 70 mins, US
D: Lloyd Bacon **A:** James Cagney, Joan Blondell, Victor Jory, Frank Craven (Warner)

A forthright narrative about two pieces of human flotsam. Both Blondell and Cagney turn in deftly confected performances. Plot gets its motivation from the efforts of a double-crossing cracksman (Cagney) to

escape the penalty of gang law. In his flight from the torpedoes, Cagney meets the girl (Blondell), who has just decided to call it quits with the wayfaring life she's been leading and accept a proposal of marriage from a Portuguese fisherman located 100 miles south of Frisco. Cagney elects to join the girl on her trip to the groom.

HE WHO RIDES A TIGER
1966, 103 mins, UK ⓥ ⊙
D: Charles Crichton **A:** Tom Bell, Judi Dench, Paul Rogers, Kay Walsh, Ray McAnally, Jeremy Spenser (British Lion)

Story concerns a young, nerveless cat burglar (specialty: rocks from stately homes) with a split personality. Kind to children and animals, suave, good-mannered on the one hand. But this personable young guy is equally prone to violent outbursts of impatience and hot temper. Tom Bell as the antihero has an easy style and diamond-hard personality.

HEXED
1993, 90 mins, US ⓥ
D: Alan Spencer **A:** Arye Gross, Claudia Christian, Adrienne Shelly, Ray Baker, R. Lee Ermey (Price)

Some surefire slapstick footage is about all that's funny in the stillborn comedy. Pic makes one long for the sophistication of *Police Academy* movies. Hotel desk clerk Matthew (Arye Gross) and beautiful French model and cover girl Hexina (Claudia Christian) have sex in scenes imitating *Fatal Attraction* and *Basic Instinct*, after which he finds out she's really a psychotic killer.

HICKEY & BOGGS
1972, 111 mins, US ⓥ
D: Robert Culp **A:** Bill Cosby, Robert Culp, Rosalind Cash, Carmen, Michael Moriarty·(Film Guarantors/United Artists)

Title of this Bill Cosby–Robert Culp starrer might indicate comedy, but action pairs former stars of pop *I Spy* teleseries. Dicks are employed to find a missing femme and become innocently involved in search for a $400,000 haul stolen from a Pittsburgh bank.

HIDDEN, THE
1987, 96 mins, US ⓥ ⊙
D: Jack Sholder **A:** Michael Nouri, Kyle MacLachlan, Ed O'Ross, Clu Gulager Claudia Christian (New Line/Heron)

A well-constructed thriller, directed with swift assurance, brought down by an utterly conventional sci-fi ending. L.A. homicide detective Tom Beck (Michael

Nouri) is approached by taciturn FBI agent Lloyd Gallagher (Kyle MacLachlan), who's searching for Jack DeVries (Chris Mulkey). Gallagher is unsatisfied when Beck informs him DeVries is about to die in an LA hospital, and the plot begins to unfold when the dying man force-feeds a reptilian alien down the throat of a fellow patient.

HIDDEN AGENDA
1990, 108 mins, UK Ⓥ ⊙
D: Ken Loach A: Frances McDormand, Brian Cox, Brad Dourif, Mai Zetterling (Hemdale/Initial)

A hard-hitting attack on allegedly ruthless methods of the British police in Northern Ireland. Pic is set in 1982, and Brian Cox plays Kerrigan, brought to Belfast to investigate the killings of an IRA sympathizer and an American lawyer (Brad Dourif in a tiny role). He quickly discovers the men were killed by members of the Royal Ulster Constabulary, and exposes a high-level cover-up.

HIDDEN CITY
1988, 107 mins, US Ⓥ
D: Stephen Poliakoff A: Charles Dance, Cassie Stuart, Bill Paterson, Richard E. Grant (Hidden City/Channel 4)

An overlong film with too many story lines and not enough good acting that rambles along with an air of self-importance. Charles Dance plays a statistician who gets involved with Cassie Stuart, who is obsessed with finding a mysterious piece of film that appears to have been hidden by the government. The search for fragments of the lost film takes them into a maze of tunnels underneath London.

HIDDEN FORTRESS, THE
See: Kakushi Toride No San Akunin

HIDDEN ROOM, THE
See: Obsession (1949)

HIDE IN PLAIN SIGHT
1980, 92 mins, US Ⓥ ⊟
D: James Caan A: James Caan, Jill Eikenberry, Danny Aiello, Robert Viharo, Joe Grifasi (M-G-M)

In his directorial debut, James Caan never musters the energy or emotion needed to break the unbearably slow, dismal tone. Caan is wonderfully accurate as the factory worker who becomes an innocent victim of a new witness-relocation program. Two-bit mobster Robert Viharo testifies against his cronies and the authorities relocate him, his wife (who happens to be Caan's former spouse), and her

two children by Caan to another state. The frustration of the almost hopeless search Caan attempts could have been excellent fodder for a gripping, human drama.

HIDER IN THE HOUSE
1989, 108 mins, US Ⓥ ⊙
D: Matthew Patrick A: Gary Busey, Mimi Rogers, Michael McKean, Kurt Christopher Kinder, Bruce Glover (Precision)

An intelligent, gripping, and sometimes compelling psychological thriller. Gary Busey's character, Tom Sykes, breaks into a recently renovated house and builds himself a secret space behind a false wall in the attic. His dream house also is inhabited the well-to-do Dryer family (Mimi Rogers, Michael McKean, children Kurt Christopher Kinder, and Candy Hutson). Sykes becomes obsessed with their relationships, making the family his own within his own mind. Sykes at first sees Julie Dryer as a mother figure, but he becomes increasingly focused on her. Busey gives a fine performance as the obsessed murderer and Rogers is excellent as the unknowing object of Busey's attentions.

HIGH AND DRY
See: The "Maggie"

HIGH AND THE MIGHTY, THE
1954, 147 mins, US ⊟
D: William A. Wellman A: John Wayne, Claire Trevor, Laraine Day, Robert Stack, Jan Sterling, Phil Harris (Warner/Wayne-Fellows)

A class drama, blended with mass appeal into a well-rounded show. The plot has to do with human reactions to danger as a troubled plane, carrying 22 persons, limps through stormy skies en route from Honolulu to San Francisco. Virtually every member of the large cast delivers a discerning performance.

1954: Best Score of a Dramatic Picture Nominations: Best Director, Supp. Actress (Jan Sterling, Claire Trevor), Editing, Song ("The High and the Mighty")

HIGH ANXIETY
1977, 94 mins, US Ⓥ ⊙
D: Mel Brooks A: Mel Brooks, Madeline Kahn, Cloris Leachman, Harvey Korman, Ron Carey, Howard Morris (Crossbow/20th Century-Fox)

A straight Hitchcockian send-up—homage applies as well—with highs and lows ranging from a brilliant restaging of the shower scene in Psycho to childish bathroom humor. Besides playing the role of a Harvard professor and psychiatrist with a fear of heights who takes over the Psycho-Neurotic Institute for the Very, Very Nervous, Mel Brooks dons the producer, director, and cowriter caps.

HIGH BRIGHT SUN, THE
(US: MCGUIRE, GO HOME; AKA: A DATE WITH DEATH)
1965, 114 mins, UK ⊗
D: Ralph Thomas **A:** Dirk Bogarde, George Chakiris, Susan Strasberg, Denholm Elliott, Gregoire Aslan (Rank)

Though set in Cyprus during the 1957 troubles, this sits firmly on a fence and makes virtually no attempt to analyze the troubles, the causes, or the attitudes of the cardboard characters. Susan Strasberg is visiting Cypriot friends who, unbeknownst to her, are mixed up in the local terrorist racket. She gets to know more than is good for her and is torn between loyalty to the Cypriots and to the British, as represented by an intelligence major (Dirk Bogarde) whose job it is to keep alive the unhelpful young dame for whom he has fallen.

HIGHER AND HIGHER
1943, 90 mins, US ⊗ ⊙
D: Tim Whelan **A:** Michele Morgan, Jack Haley, Frank Sinatra, Leon Errol, Victor Borge, Mel Torme (RKO)

In his first starring role on the screen, Frank Sinatra at least gets in no one's way. Though a bit stiff on occasion and not as photogenic as may be desired, he generally handles himself ably in song as well as a few brief dialogue scenes. The song-studded story is laid principally in the mansion of Leon Errol, who will have to vacate unless getting up a hunk of coin in a hurry. His valet (Jack Haley) gets the bright idea of having one of the servants (Michele Morgan) pose as Errol's daughter, and getting her married off.

HIGHER LEARNING
1995, 127 mins, US ⊗
D: John Singleton **A:** Omar Epps, Kristy Swanson, Michael Rapaport, Jennifer Connelly, Ice Cube (New Deal)

Focusing mostly on members of an incoming freshman class at fictitious Colombus University, pic takes a heightened interest in Malik (Omar Epps), a politically unformed black runner on a sports scholarship; Kristen (Kristy Swanson), a naive white girl from Orange County; and Remy (Michael Rapaport), a social misfit from Idaho. *Higher Learning* packs a fair amount of power thanks to the force of its ideas.

HIGH HOPES
1988, 112 mins, UK ⊗
D: Mike Leigh **A:** Philip Davis, Ruth Sheen, Edna Dore, Philip Jackson, Heather Tobias (Portman/Film Four/British Screen)

In the working-class London district of King's Cross, yuppies are moving into old houses, restoring them, and driving out the locals who've lived there for ages. Around these characters, Leigh builds a slight story intended to be a microcosm of today's London.

HIGHLANDER
1986, 111 mins, US ⊗ ⊙
D: Russell Mulcahy **A:** Christopher Lambert, Roxanne Hart, Clancy Brown, Sean Connery, Beatie Edney (20th Century-Fox)

Film starts out with a fantastic sword-fighting scene in the garage of Madison Square Garden and then jumps to a medieval battle between the clans set in 16th-century Scotland. Adding to the confusion in time, director Russell Mulcahy can't seem to decide from one scene to the next whether he's making a sci-fi, thriller, horror, music video, or romance—end result is a mishmash.

HIGHLANDER II: THE QUICKENING
1991, 96 mins, US ⊗ ⊙ ⊡
D: Russell Mulcahy **A:** Christopher Lambert, Sean Connery, Virginia Madsen, Michael Ironside, John C. McGinley (Davis-Panzer/El Khoury-Defait/Lam Bear)

Christopher Lambert plays immortal Connor MacLeod, who, despite his Scottish ancestry, hails from the planet Zeist. He and partner Ramirez (Sean Connery) were banished to Earth for participating in a failed rebellion. One story line involves assassins led by Michael Ironside, and the other concentrates on the disappearing ozone layer. Lambert manages to decapitate the villains arrayed against him while teaming up with attractive environmental terrorist Virginia Madsen. Connery, sporting long white hair in a ponytail, occasionally appears wielding a broadsword. *Highlander II* comes alive during the action scenes.

HIGHLANDER III: THE SORCERER
1994, 99 mins, Canada/France/UK ⊗ ⊙ ⊡

D: Andy Morahan **A:** Christopher Lambert, Mario Van Peebles, Deborah Unger, Mako, Mark Neufeld (Transfilm/Lumiere/Falling Cloud)

An unbelievably trashy meltdown of the tartan warrior franchise, *Highlander III* checks in as a breakneck, roller-coaster genre ride that's brainless fodder for undiscriminating auds. Lumbered with Lambert's largely incomprehensible accent, British video director Andy Morahan wisely keeps dialogue pared to the bone and lets his five separate units and f/x team get on with the job. Acting is video caliber.

HIGH NOON

1952, 84 mins, US Ⓥ ⊙
D: Fred Zinnemann **A:** Gary Cooper, Grace Kelly, Thomas Mitchell, Lloyd Bridges Katy Jurado (Kramer/United Artists)

A basic western formula has been combined with good characterization. The production does an excellent job of presenting a picture of a small western town and its people as they wait for a gun duel between the marshal and revenge-seeking killer, an event scheduled for high noon. The mood of the citizens, of Gary Cooper the marshal, and his bride (Grace Kelly), a Quaker who is against all violence, is aptly captured by Fred Zinnemann's direction and the graphic lensing of Floyd Crosby, which perfectly pictures the heat and dust of the sunbaked locale. Throughout the film is a hauntingly presented ballad that tells the story of the coming gun duel, tellingly sung by Tex Ritter.
1952: Best Actor (Gary Cooper), Song ("High Noon"), Scoring of a Dramatic Picture, Editing
Nominations: Best Picture, Director, Screenplay

HIGH PLAINS DRIFTER

1973, 105 mins, US Ⓥ ⊙ ◉
D: Clint Eastwood **A:** Clint Eastwood, Verna Bloom, Marianna Hill, Mitchell Ryan, Jack Ging, Stefan Gierasch (Malpaso/Universal)

A nervously humorous, self-conscious near satire on the prototype Clint Eastwood formula of the avenging mysterious stranger. Untidy patchwork script involves one of those towns with a collective guilt streak, having engineered the death-by-whipping of its honest marshal by some hoods who themselves were framed after getting out of hand. Into this setting rides Eastwood, emerging from heat waves

(among other obvious evocations of films past) as a sort of archangel of retribution.

HIGH PRESSURE

1932, 72 mins, US
D: Mervyn LeRoy **A:** William Powell, Evelyn Brent, George Sidney, Guy Kibbee Evalyn Knapp (Warner)

The phony-stock or "wallpaper" grift gets a pretty expert exposé in this yarn. William Powell does a swell job as a fast-talking and thinking promoter. Powell is first found in a speak's back room on the tail end of a five-day bender. He told his girlfriend he was going out to the drugstore for a dose of bicarbonate. The girl friend is interpreted by Evelyn Brent, who is called on to do little else than get mad at and make up with her racketeer sweetheart.

HIGH ROAD TO CHINA

1983, 120 mins, US Ⓥ ⊙
D: Brian G. Hutton **A:** Tom Selleck, Bess Armstrong, Jack Weston, Wilford Brimley, Robert Morley, Brian Blessed (Golden Harvest/Warner)

A lot of old-fashioned fun. Selleck is perfect as a grizzled, boozing biplane pilot whom 1920s flapper Bess Armstrong is forced to hire to help her find her father before he's declared dead and her inheritance is stolen. Selleck and Armstrong make a cute couple, even though their bantering, slowly developing romance is deliberately predictable throughout.

HIGH SEASON

1987, 92 mins, US Ⓥ ⊙
D: Clare Peploe **A:** Jacqueline Bisset, James Fox, Irene Papas, Sebastian Shaw, Kenneth Branagh, Robert Stephens (Hemdale)

High Season pivots around Jacqueline Bisset as a photographer and the folk she meets up with in a tiny village in Rhodes. As well as poking fun at the tourists, also thrown in are subplots about a valuable Grecian urn, an elderly Russian spy—an art-historian friend of Bisset, with overtones of Anthony Blunt—and a rebellious Greek national. Best of the cast are Kenneth Branagh and Lesley Manville as a seemingly archetypal English tourist couple.

HIGH SIERRA

1941, 100 mins, US Ⓥ ⊙
D: Raoul Walsh **A:** Humphrey Bogart, Ida Lupino, Arthur Kennedy, Joan Leslie, Henry Hull (Warner)

An action story that's partially salvaged by the fine performances of Humphrey Bogart and Ida Lupino. Throwback nature of the yarn is evident in the semiglorification of Bogart's gangster character. Story depicts him as a country boy who went wrong with John Dillinger's mob, but still retaining a soft spot for green fields and trees, a crippled girl, and a stray dog.

HIGH SOCIETY
1956, 107 mins, US Ⓥ ⊙
D: Charles Walters **A:** Bing Crosby, Grace Kelly, Frank Sinatra, Celeste Holm, John Lund, Louis Armstrong (M-G-M)

Fortified with a strong Cole Porter score, the original Philip Barry play, *The Philadelphia Story,* holds up in its transmutation from the Main Line to a Newport jazz bash. Casting of Louis Armstrong for the jazz festivities was an inspired booking also. The unfolding of the triangle almost assumes quadrangle proportions, when Sinatra (as the *Life*-mag-type feature writer), sent with Celeste Holm, almost moves in as a romantic vis-à-vis to the slightly spoiled and madcap Tracy Lord (Kelly). Crosby is her first, now ex-husband, a hip character with song-smithing predilections.
1956: Nominations: Best Motion Picture Story [withdrawn from final ballot], Scoring of a Musical Picture, Song ("True Love")

HIGH SPIRITS
1988, 97 mins, UK/US Ⓥ ⊙
D: Neil Jordan **A:** Daryl Hannah, Peter O'Toole, Steve Guttenberg, Beverly D'Angelo, Liam Neeson, Ray McAnally (Vision/Palace)

A piece of supernatural Irish whimsy with a few appealing dark underpinnings, but it still rises and falls constantly on the basis of its moment-to-moment inspirations. Elaborate physical production is set almost entirely at Castle Plunkett, a rundown Irish edifice that proprietor Peter O'Toole opens as a tourist hotel. O'Toole bills the place as a haunted castle, to this end having his staff dress up like ghouls of various persuasions. It comes as little surprise that the castle turns out to be actually haunted.

HIGH TIDE
1987, 104 mins, Australia Ⓥ ⊙
D: Gillian Armstrong **A:** Judy Davis, Jan Adele, Claudia Karvan, Colin Friels, Frankie J. Holden (FGH/SJL)

A powerful, emotional, beautifully made film which will touch the hearts of all but the very cynical. Setting is a small New South Wales coastal town where Judy Davis rents a cheap trailer by the sea. One night, when hopelessly drunk, she's helped by an adolescent girl (Claudia Karvan) who lives with her grandmother (Jan Adele) in another trailer. Davis befriends the child; only when she meets the grandmother does she realize Karvan is her own daughter whom she'd left years before.

HIGH TIME
1960, 102 mins, US ▭
D: Blake Edwards **A:** Bing Crosby, Fabian, Tuesday Weld, Nicole Maurey, Richard Beymer (Crosby/20th Century-Fox)

Pretty lightweight fare for a star of Bing Crosby's proportions. Beating on the promising premise of Crosby—51, father of two, a millionaire restaurant-chain owner—enrolling in college as a freshman and continuing through four years to graduation, film depends on individual situations and gimmicks rather than on straight story line. Crosby handles his role in his usual fashion, perfectly timing his laughs, and delivers a pair of Sammy Cahn–James Van Heusen songs.

HIGH WALL
1947, 98 mins, US
D: Curtis Bernhardt **A:** Robert Taylor, Audrey Totter, Herbert Marshall, H. B. Warner, Warner Anderson (M-G-M)

Unfolded credibly and with almost clinical attention to detail, film holds the interest in story of a man who believes he has murdered his wife during a mental blackout. Taylor scores in his role, making it believable. Audrey Totter registers strongly as a doctor.

HIGH, WIDE AND HANDSOME
1937, 110 mins, US
D: Rouben Mamoulian **A:** Irene Dunne, Randolph Scott, Dorothy Lamour, Elizabeth Patterson, Raymond Walburn, Charles Bickford (Paramount)

Film shapes up as a western, although possessed of all the elements to have made it a saga of Pennsylvania oil-well pioneering. Something went wrong on scripting and production from what was, undoubtedly, an intriguing script on paper. Film's title sounds like a musical or operetta, but it's more of a melodramatic romance, with six songs by Jerome Kern and Oscar Hammerstein II, latter also credited for the original story and the screenplay. Wherein lies the film's principal deficiency. It's a cross section of Americana tinged with too much Hollywood hokum.

HIGH WIND IN JAMAICA, A
1965, 104 mins, UK Ⓥ ▱
D: Alexander Mackendrick **A:** Anthony Quinn, James Coburn, Dennis Price, Lila Kedrova, Gert Frobe, Nigel Davenport (20th Century-Fox)

Anthony Quinn's penchant for grizzled characterization gets a colorful boost in this picturization of Richard Hughes's 1929 bestseller, which projects him as a Caribbean pirate confronted with the disturbing question of what to do with seven children who have have slipped from a ship he attacked and are found in the hold of his own craft. Quinn endows his role with a subdued humanness in which there is occasional humor. James Coburn combines humor with dramatic strength.

HILL, THE
1965, 125 mins, UK ⊙
D: Sidney Lumet **A:** Sean Connery, Harry Andrews, Ian Bannen, Alfred Lynch, Ossie Davis, Michael Redgrave (M-G-M/ Seven Arts)

A tough, uncompromising look at the inside of a British military prison in the Middle East during the last war. The screenplay puts the spotlight on a new bunch of prisoners, one of whom (Sean Connery) is a "busted" sergeant major, and a natural target for vindictive and sadistic treatment. Connery gives an intelligently restrained study, carefully avoiding forced histrionics. The juiciest role, however, is that of the prison regimental sergeant major, and Harry Andrews does a standout job.

HILL IN KOREA, A
(US: HELL IN KOREA)
1956, 81 mins, UK
D: Julian Amyes **A:** George Baker, Harry Andrews, Stanley Baker, Michael Medwin, Ronald Lewis, Stephen Boyd (Wessex/British Lion)

Story is little more than an incident, depicting the adventures of a small patrol sent to find out if a village is inhabited by the enemy. All the action, humor, and pathos centers on the mixed bunch from every walk of life, wisecracking, beefing and just plain scared. All the cast has equal opportunities to score, George Baker as the conscientious officer, Harry Andrews as the tough sergeant, and Ronald Lewis as the outsider.

HILLS HAVE EYES, THE
1978, 89 mins, US Ⓥ ⊙
D: Wes Craven **A:** Susan Lanier, Robert Houston, Virginia Vincent, Russ Grieve, Dee Wallace (Blood Relations)

Wes Craven's blood-and-bone frightener about an all-American family at the mercy of cannibal mutants is a satisfying piece of pulp. Reputedly based on 17th-century Scottish cave dwellers, these savages terrorize a strip of Californian desert in which the Carters are stranded by a snapped axle. Gratifying aspects are Craven's businesslike plotting and pacy cutting, and a script that takes more trouble over the stock characters than it needs. There are plenty of laughs, in the dialogue and in the story's disarming twists.

HILLS HAVE EYES, PART II, THE
1985, 88 mins, US/UK Ⓥ ⊙
D: Wes Craven **A:** Michael Berryman, Tamara Stafford, Kevin Blair, John Bloom (Castle Hill/Fancey/New Realm/VTC)

A lower-case follow-up by Wes Craven to his 1977 cult horror pic. Film concerns two grown-up survivors of the earlier pic. Young Bobby Carter (Robert Houston) is plagued by nightmares of the desert massacre that he survived. Ruby (Janus Blythe), a nice-gal survivor, is taking bikers to a race when they foolishly try a shortcut across the desert. From then on, it's dull, formula terror-pic clichés, with one attractive teenager after another picked off by the surviving cannibals.

HIMMEL UBER BERLIN
(WINGS OF DESIRE)
1987, 130 mins, W. Germany/France Ⓥ ⊙
D: Wim Wenders **A:** Bruno Ganz, Solveig Dommartin, Peter Falk, Otto Sander, Curt Bois (Road Movies/Argo)

This tale of angels watching over the citizens of Berlin springs from the great tradition of pics about angels involved in human affairs but is a quintessential Wenders film. Three humans are singled out. One's an old man, played by veteran Curt Bois, with memories of Berlin's shattered past. Another is Peter Falk, American movie actor in Berlin to make a pic about the Nazi era. The third is a beautiful trapeze artist (Solveig Dommartin). The angel played by Bruno Ganz begins to feel mortal when he watches the girl. Wenders invests this potentially risible material with such serenity and beauty that audiences will go along willingly with the fable.

HINDENBURG, THE
1975, 125 mins, US ⊙ ⊙ ▭
D: Robert Wise **A:** George C. Scott, Anne Bancroft, William Atherton, Roy Thinnes, Gig Young, Burgess Meredith (Universal/Filmakers)

Michael M. Mooney's nonfiction compendium of the facts and theories behind the German zeppelin's 1937 air disaster at NAS, Lakehurst, NJ, dramatized for the screen. George C. Scott stars as an air ace assigned as special security officer on the fatal Atlantic crossing. The array of characters is dealt boringly from a well-thumbed deck. William Atherton emerges as the good-guy crewman saboteur who plans to blow up the ship. It's as exciting as watching butter melt.
1975: Honorary Award (visual and sound effects)
Nominations: Best Cinematography, Art Direction, Sound

HIRED HAND, THE
1971, 90 mins, US ⓥ
D: Peter Fonda **A:** Peter Fonda, Warren Oates, Verna Bloom, Robert Pratt, Severn Darden (Pando)

An offbeat western, starring and directed by Peter Fonda, the film has a disjointed story, a largely unsympathetic hero, and an obtrusive amount of cinematic gimmickry which renders inarticulate the confused story subtleties. Warren Oates appears as Fonda's loyal and more mature friend, while Verna Bloom is Fonda's abandoned wife.

HIRELING, THE
1973, 95 mins, UK ⓥ
D: Alan Bridges **A:** Robert Shaw, Sarah Miles, Peter Egan, Elizabeth Sellars, Caroline Mortimer, Patricia Lawrence (World)

Based on a novel by L. P. Hartley set in 1923, this heavily atmospheric, painstakingly accoutred, and splendidly acted pic deals with the increasingly close relationship of a young widow (Sarah Miles) and the hired chauffeur (Robert Shaw) who drives her home after a spell in a clinic recovering from a nervous depression. Patient viewers will savor its many pluses.

HIROSHIMA, MON AMOUR
1959, 95 mins, France/Japan ⓥ
D: Alain Resnais **A:** Emmanuele Riva, Eiji Okada, Stella Dassas, Bernard Fresson (Argos/Como/Pathe Overseas/Daiei)

A noble try to make a statement on human love and the atom bomb (hardly a lovable thing), but it's too literary in conception and too cerebral in treatment. A woman (Emmanuele Riva) and a man (Eiji Okada), in a lovers' embrace, talk of Hiroshima. Then follows their realization of the impossibility of their love, since both are married. Film welds in her souvenirs of a first love during the war in France with a German soldier, his death, her breakdown, and her reacceptance of life. Director Alain Resnais directs with somber feeling and tact.

HIS BROTHER'S WIFE
1936, 91 mins, US
D: W. S. Van Dyke **A:** Barbara Stanwyck, Robert Taylor, Jean Hersholt, Joseph Calleia, John Eldredge, Samuel S. Hinds (M-G-M)

While the title telegraphs the plot, the director has cannily paced his proceedings so that the suspense values aren't militated against too much. John Eldredge is oke as the straitlaced brother Tom who, after splitting Robert Taylor and Barbara Stanwyck, is tricked into a "revenge" marriage (of the unkissed-bride type) with Stanwyck, only later to facilitate a divorce. Joseph Calleia is a restrained but sinister menace and Jean Hersholt rings the bell again with one of his kindly medico portrayals.

HIS BUTLER'S SISTER
1943, 92 mins, US
D: Frank Borzage **A:** Deanna Durbin, Pat O'Brien, Franchot Tone, Akim Tamiroff, Evelyn Ankers, Alan Mowbray (Universal)

Neatly contrived situations, consistently good pace, excellent cast, and four songs by Durbin combine to make this a top attraction of the Durbin series. Durbin hits New York to embark on a singing career through visit to older brother (Pat O'Brien), who's the butler to composer Franchot Tone. She's inducted as maid in the bachelor penthouse but fired in two days on insistence of O'Brien, afraid of losing his job if she sings to catch Tone's attention. Of course the composer becomes interested in girl.

HIS GIRL FRIDAY
1940, 92 mins, US ⓥ
D: Howard Hawks **A:** Cary Grant, Rosalind Russell, Ralph Bellamy, Gene Lockhart, Helen Mack, John Qualen (Columbia)

This is the former legit and pic smash

The Front Page. The trappings are different—even to the extent of making reporter Hildy Johnson a femme. Star-reporter Russell tells managing editor Grant, from whom she has just been divorced, that she is quitting to marry another man. Grant neither wants to see her resign nor marry again, retaining hope of a rehitching. He prevails upon her to cover story of a deluded radical charged with murder. Escape of the convicted man, his virtual falling into Russell's lap as she sits alone in the pressroom, and attempts by Grant and Russell to bottle up the story, are w.k., but still exciting.

HIS KIND OF WOMAN
1951, 120 mins, US Ⓥ
D: John Farrow A: Robert Mitchum, Jane Russell, Vincent Price, Tim Holt Charles McGraw (RKO)

Robert Mitchum, professional gambler, and Jane Russell, posing as a rich girl so she can land a husband, meet at a remote Mexican resort. Two strike plenty of sparks. The script has a deported gangster plotting to get back into the States by taking the face and identification of Mitchum. Suspense gets in some real licks when Mitchum learns he's to be killed. Much is made of Vincent Price's scenery-chewing actor character and much of it supplies relief to the film's otherwise taut development.

HIS MAJESTY O'KEEFE
1953, 89 mins, US Ⓥ
D: Byron Haskin A: Burt Lancaster, Joan Rice, Andre Morell, Abraham Sofaer, Benson Fong (Warner)

This swashbuckling South Seas adventure feature is ideally suited to Burt Lancaster's muscular heroics. The Fiji Islands location lensing is a plus factor for interest. Lancaster is seen as a daredevil Yankee intrigued by the possibilities of making a fortune off an island's copra. He battles other traders, native idleness, and superstition, becoming His Majesty O'Keefe with a beautiful Polynesian (Joan Rice) as queen.

L'HISTOIRE D'ADELE H.
(THE STORY OF ADELE H.)
1975, 97 mins, France Ⓥ ▭
D: Francois Truffaut A: Isabelle Adjani, Bruce Robinson, Sylvia Marriott, Reubin Dorey, Joseph Blatchley (Films du Carrosse/Artistes Associes)

Francois Truffaut has made a romantic period drama about a young woman destroyed by her overwhelming love for a philandering British lieutenant. She is the daughter of French writer Victor Hugo. She is looking for the lieutenant who had seduced her and whom she loved but who was looked down on by her family. She finds him but he refuses her and she sinks into madness. Truffaut has gotten an exemplary performance from Isabelle Adjani as the anguished Adèle H.

UNE HISTOIRE SIMPLE
(A SIMPLE STORY)
1978, 107 mins, France/W. Germany Ⓥ
D: Claude Sautet A: Romy Schneider, Bruno Cremer, Claude Brasseur, Roger Pigaut, Arlette Bonnard, Francine Berge (Renn/Sara/FR3/Rialto)

Quintessentially French, with its series of petty piques, sudden dramas, macho male shenanigans, and gathering femme lib, though latter is more personal than a concerted movement, pic benefits from homogeneous thesping and astute direction. Main thread of the film is Marie (Romy Schneider). She is an attractive, fortyish woman who has decided to abort a child she is bearing and drop her lover. There are little subplots alongside Schneider's march toward freedom. Schneider is radiant and effective as a woman reaching fulfillment and maturity.

LA HISTORIA OFICIAL
(THE OFFICIAL STORY)
1985, 112 mins, Argentina Ⓥ ⊙ ▭
D: Luis Puenzo A: Hector Alterio, Norma Aleandro, Chela Ruiz, Chunchuna Villafane, Hugo Arana (Historias/Progress)

A thought-provoking, indirect, yet resolute approach to the greatest Argentine tragedy of the century: the degeneration into secret genocide of the so-called ''dirty war'' against terrorism in the mid- and late-seventies. Alicia (Norma Aleandro) teaches history at a private school adhering to the official textbooks, but eventually she is impressed by the investigative, revisionist spirit of some of her pupils. Significant details lead Alicia to suspect her adopted child Gabi (Analia Castro) could be the offspring of a *desaparecida* woman. She decides to investigate, finding out her husband is linked with both the paramilitary and businessmen profiting from corruption.
1985: Best Foreign Language Film

HISTORY OF MR. POLLY, THE
1949, 94 mins, UK
D: Anthony Pelissier A: John Mills, Sally

Ann Howes, Finlay Currie, Betty Ann Davies, Edward Chapman, Megs Jenkins (Two Cities)

The story of Mr. Polly is retold simply from the time of his father's death, his inheritance and marriage, subsequent failure as a shopkeeper, and final happiness and freedom as a general handyman in a small country inn. Its success is a personal tribute to the sterling acting of John Mills. Director Anthony Pelissier has extracted every ounce of human interest from the H. G. Wells classic.

HISTORY OF THE WORLD, PART I, THE
1981, 92 mins, US ⓥ ⊙ ⌷
D: Mel Brooks A: Mel Brooks, Dom DeLuise, Madeline Kahn, Cloris Leachman, Gregory Hines, Sid Caesar (20th Century-Fox)

Boisterous cinematic vaudeville show is composed of five distinct sections: the *2001* parody "Dawn of Man, The Stone Age," featuring Brooks's acid comment on the role of the art critic, and a brief "Old Testament" bit; "The Roman Empire," the best-sustained and longest episode; *The Spanish Inquisition*, a splashy production number; "The French Revolution," a rather feeble sketch; and "Coming Attractions," which punches up the finale with the hilarious "Jews in Space" intergalactic musical action number. The one interlude that really brings down the house has Brooks working as a waiter at the Last Supper. There's something here to offend everybody, particularly the devout of all persuasions and homosexuals.

HIT!
1973, 134 mins, US ⌷
D: Sidney J. Furie A: Billy Dee Williams, Richard Pryor, Paul Hampton, Gwen Welles, Warren Kemmerling (Paramount)

Too bad that so much of the script relies on illogical plotting and heavy-handed irony, because the basic idea is excellent and many of the details are richly conceived. Billy Dee Williams plays a federal operative whose daughter dies from drug overdose. Unable to get official action that would lead to capture of the key figures in a Marseilles drug syndicate, he launches his own vendetta against the "murderers."

HIT, THE
1984, 97 mins, UK ⓥ ⊙
D: Stephen Frears A: John Hurt, Tim Roth, Laura del Sol, Terence Stamp, Bill Hunter, Fernando Rey (Central/Recorded Picture)

Director Stephen Frears and writer Peter Prince have taken a potentially familiar tale of a gangland betrayal and revenge and made something richly inventive and most entertaining. Willie Parker (Terence Stamp) fingers his fellow criminals. Ten years later Parker is living an apparently carefree existence in the Spanish countryside when four toughs kidnap him and hand him over to an experienced hit man, Braddock (John Hurt), and his novice sidekick, Myron (Tim Roth), to deliver him to the boss in Paris. It's a journey on which things keep going wrong.

HITCHER, THE
1986, 97 mins, US ⓥ ⊙ ⌷
D: Robert Harmon A: Rutger Hauer, C. Thomas Howell, Jennifer Jason Leigh, Jeffrey DeMunn (HBO/Silver Screen)

A highly unimaginative slasher that keeps the tension going with a massacre about every 15 minutes. Film proves Mom's admonition not to pick up hitchhikers, especially if they're anything like John Ryder, a psychotic and diabolical killer played with a serene coldness by Rutger Hauer.

HITLER'S CHILDREN
1943, 80 mins, US ⓥ
D: Edward Dmytryk A: Tim Holt, Bonita Granville, Kent Smith, Otto Kruger, H. B. Warner, Lloyd Corrigan (RKO)

The philosophy of Nazism and the manner in which the youth of Germany was molded to a militaristic order are forcefully brought to the screen. Tim Holt essays the leading role of the German boy who grows up to become a Gestapo officer, but cannot grow away from the childhood love he had for a girl who suffers the tortures of the Nazis.

HITLER, THE LAST TEN DAYS
1973, 108 mins, UK/Italy ⓥ ⌷
D: Ennio De Concini A: Alec Guinness, Simon Ward, Adolfo Celi, Diane Cilento, Gabriele Ferzetti, Eric Porter (Reinhardt/West)

A major fault of the film is that there's no German feeling to it. The cast, with the exception of German actress Doris Kunstmann as Eva Braun, is made up of British and Italian actors. Alec Guinness gives perhaps the best portrayal yet of Hitler. Even he, however, never conveys the fanaticism which Hitler certainly had and which he so powerfully conveyed to millions of susceptible German minds.

HITMAN, THE
1991, 95 mins, US Ⓥ ⊙
D: Aaron Norris A: Chuck Norris, Michael Parks, Al Waxman, Alberta Watson, Salim Grant (Cannon)

Chuck Norris goes to Canada in this dreary, unconvincing action vehicle which adopts a film noir visual style that masks its limited production values. Norris is in Seattle undercover as unsuspecting Italo gangster Al Waxman's No. 2 in command. Norris's assignment is to get two rival mobs to unite so that both can be nabbed. Best thing about *Hitman* is some good stuntwork.

HIT PARADE OF 1943
1943, 90 mins, US
D: Albert S. Rogell A: John Carroll, Susan Hayward, Gail Patrick, Eve Arden, Dorothy Dandridge (Republic)

Here's a little musical which is a very satisfying confection indeed. The characterization of thieving songwriter Rick Farrell, who lets talented young tunesmith Susan Hayward ghost his songs, is never wholly palatable, but John Carroll's personal charm glorifies the double-crossing, two-timing Lothario into a model swain in time for the fade-out.
1943: Nominations: Best Scoring of a Musical Picture, Song ("Change of Heart")

HIT THE DECK
1955, 112 mins, US Ⓥ ⊙ ▭
D: Roy Rowland A: Jane Powell, Tony Martin, Debbie Reynolds, Walter Pidgeon, Vic Damone, Ann Miller (M-G-M)

There's not much producer Joe Pasternak could do to refurbish the shopworn plot about three sailors on the loose, with three femmes on their mind. With the limitations, he has made it a pretty picture, replete with songs from the old footlight piece, complete with new lyrics and flashy production numbers. The vintage musical takes on its best semblance to life when Debbie Reynolds and Russ Tamblyn are lending their enthusiasm to the action.

HIT THE DUTCHMAN
1992, 118 mins, US/Russia ⓥ
D: Menahem Golan A: Bruce Nozick, Eddie Bowz, Will Kempe, Sally Kirkland, Matt Servitto, Christopher Bradley (Power/Start)

Fast-moving, splendidly trashy mobster yarn dishes up the genre goods with grind-house glee. Bruce Nozick toplines as Arthur Fleggenheimer, a cocky 24-year-old Jewish con who's freed from West Hampton pen. After literally biting the nose of Vince Coll (Christopher Bradley), he's introed to Legs Diamond (Will Kempe) and soon starts sniffing around Legs's warbler g.f. Frances Ireland (Jennifer Miller). He also adopts the name Dutch Schultz.

HIT THE ICE
1943, 81 mins, US ⓥ
D: Charles Lamont A: Bud Abbott, Lou Costello, Ginny Simms, Patric Knowles (Universal)

Abbott and Costello become mistaken for Detroit gunmen, are bystanders at the bank holdup, and head west to Sun Valley to evade arrest on suspicion. Also going west is a bank robber and his two thugs, medico Patric Knowles, nurse Elyse Knox, songstress Ginny Simms, and Johnny Long with his orchestra.

H.M. PULHAM, ESQ.
1941, 119 mins, US
D: King Vidor A: Hedy Lamarr, Robert Young, Ruth Hussey, Charles Coburn, Van Heflin (M-G-M)

Pulham (Robert Young) is of the wooldyed Boston Back Bay. Coming back from the war, he succeeds in breaking away from his family to take a job in a New York agency, where he and fellow copywriter Lamarr fall in love. She carries a torch for him for some 20 years. But Lamarr is not of Boston and refuses to take to it or give up her career. Pulham marries a family-approved gal (Ruth Hussey) and they live the conventional Hub humdrum. Major defect is the casting of Hedy Lamarr in principal femme role. It's Lamarr's Viennese accent which is jarring, although her looks and acting otherwise are tops.

H.M.S. DEFIANT
(US: DAMN THE DEFIANT!)
1962, 101 mins, UK ⓥ ⊙ ▭
D: Lewis Gilbert A: Alec Guinness, Dirk Bogarde, Anthony Quayle, Tom Bell, Maurice Denham (Columbia)

A strong naval drama about the days of the Napoleonic wars. Guinness plays the skipper of the *Defiant*, a humane man though a stern disciplinarian. Bogarde, his first lieutenant, is a sadist, anxious to jockey Guinness out of position. Belowdeck the crew, led by Quayle and Tom Bell, is plotting mutiny against the bad food, stinking living conditions, and constant floggings ordered by Bogarde.

HOBSON'S CHOICE
1954, 107 mins, UK ⓥ ⊙

D: David Lean A: Charles Laughton, John Mills, Brenda de Banzie, Daphne Anderson, Prunella Scales, Richard Wattis (British Lion/London)

There is a wealth of charm, humor, and fine characterization in David Lean's period comedy with a Lancashire setting. Laughton plays a shoemaker with three unmarried daughters. Although he richly overplays every major scene, his performance remains one of the film's highlights. Mills also makes a major contribution in his interpretation of the illiterate shoemaker's assistant. Brenda de Banzie captures top femme honors for her playing of the spirited daughter who triumphs over the ridicule of her father and sisters.

HOCUS POCUS
1993, 95 mins, US ⓥ ⊙

D: Kenny Ortega A: Bette Midler, Sarah Jessica Parker, Kathy Najimy, Omri Katz, Thora Birch (Walt Disney)

With Bette Midler and her on-screen sisters shamelessly hamming things up, it looks as if those involved in making this inoffensive flight of fantasy had more fun than anyone over 12 will have watching it. Still, the blend of witchcraft and comedy should divert kids without driving the patience of their parents to the boiling point.

HOFFA
1992, 140 mins, US ⓥ ⊙ ⊏⊐

D: Danny DeVito A: Jack Nicholson, Danny DeVito, Armand Assante, J. T. Walsh, John C. Reilly (20th Century Fox)

Hoffa presents the controversial labor leader as public icon, a man of iron, granite, and cojones who bullies his way across the union and political landscape of the midcentury all for the good of the workingman. Mainly because of Nicholson's galvanizing performance and scriptwriter David Mamet's peppery, confrontational dialogue, this is not exactly dull, but it is very dry and uninvolving. DeVito's direction tends toward the overbusy, with plenty of crane shots and imaginative but fussy scene transitions.
1992: Nominations: Best Cinematography, Makeup

HOLCROFT COVENANT, THE
1985, 112 mins, UK ⓥ ⊙

D: John Frankenheimer A: Michael Caine, Anthony Andrews, Victoria Tennant, Lilli Palmer, Mario Adorf, Michael Lonsdale (Thorn EMI)

A muddled narrative deficient in thrills or plausiblity. Film starts with the revelation to Noel Holcroft (Michael Caine) that his father left a bequest valued at over $4 billion with which the son is to make amends for the evils of Hitler's Germany. His mother (Lilli Palmer) suspects that the money is designated for the building of a new Nazi empire. Argument is supported by various deaths that happen around Holcroft. Caine just doesn't convince as a naive New Yorker.

HOLD BACK THE DAWN
1941, 114 mins, US

D: Mitchell Leisen A: Charles Boyer, Olivia de Havilland, Paulette Goddard, Victor Francen, Walter Abel, Rosemary DeCamp (Paramount)

While basically another European-refugee yarn, scenarists Charles Brackett and Billy Wilder exercised some ingenuity and imagination and Ketty Frings's original work emerges as fine celluloidia. A gigolo in Europe, Charles Boyer's washed up in Mexico and the quota laws make his entry into the United States a dream. Paulette Goddard crashed the US by marrying an American jockey, ditching him later, and she puts him wise to the simple gimmick. This sets the trap for Olivia de Havilland, a romance-hungry schoolteacher on an excursion in Mexico.
1941: Nominations: Best Picture, Actress (Olivia de Havilland), Screenplay, B&W Cinematography, B&W Art Direction, Scoring of a Dramatic Picture

HOLE, THE
See: Onibaba

HOLE, THE
See: Le Trou

HOLIDAY
1938, 93 mins, US ⓥ ⊙

D: George Cukor A: Katharine Hepburn, Cary Grant, Doris Nolan, Lew Ayres, Edward Everett Horton (Columbia)

Futility of riches is the topic. Katharine Hepburn is in her best form and type of role. Her acting is delightful and shaded with fine feeling and understanding throughout. Cary Grant plays this one straight. George Cukor brings out the best from all the players. Lew Ayres is the despondent younger brother in the wealthy family who seeks some relief from the monotony of riches by resorting to strong liquor.

1938: Nomination: Best Art Direction

HOLIDAY FOR LOVERS
1959, 103 mins, US ▭
D: Henry Levin **A:** Clifton Webb, Jane Wyman, Jill St. John, Carol Lynley, Paul Henreid, Gary Crosby (20th Century-Fox)

This is a romantic farce travelogue that plays smoothly with a good many solid laughs. The point is that daughter, not father, knows best. Clifton Webb is confronted with two daughters (Jill St. John, Carol Lynley) who are simultaneously bursting the adolescent cocoon to fall in love. The plot requires Webb and the girls' mother (Jane Wyman) to trek through South America in frustrated chaperonage. All ends happily when dense parents capitulate to siblings' wishes.

HOLIDAY INN
1942, 100 mins, US ⓥ ⊙
D: Mark Sandrich **A:** Bing Crosby, Fred Astaire, Virginia Dale, Marjorie Reynolds, Walter Abel, Louise Beavers (Paramount)

Loaded with a wealth of songs, it's meaty, not too kaleidoscopic, and yet closely knit for a compact 100 minutes of tip-top filmusical entertainment. Irving Berlin has fashioned some peach songs. Plot is a new slant on a backstage story. Frankly lazy crooner Bing Crosby has figured out there are some 15 holidays in the year and by operating a Connecticut roadhouse on those festive occasions only he can loaf the rest of the 340 days.

1942: Best Song ("White Christmas")
Nominations: Best Original Story, Scoring of a Musical Picture

HOLLYWOOD
1923, 103 mins, US ⊗
D: James Cruze **A:** Hope Drown, Luke Cosgrave, George K. Arthur, Ruby Lafayette (Paramount)

While the players proper are not well known, the majority of the better-known stars of filmdom are introduced. The list includes: Cecil B. DeMille, William S. Hart, Pola Negri, Jack Holt, Nita Naldi, Will Rogers, Ben Turpin. The cleverly conceived story concerns a pretty girl who thinks that she should be in the movies. Having nothing but beauty in her favor, she cannot get a chance; but her grandfather, being a type, is practically forced into filmwork. The grandmother and an old maid of the family are both nabbed as types and get into pictures. Every one gets into pictures but she herself.

HOLLYWOOD BOULEVARD
1976, 83 mins, US ⓥ
D: Joe Dante, Allan Arkush **A:** Candice Rialson, Mary Woronov, Rita George, Jeffrey Kramer, Dick Miller (New World)

Roger Corman's New World Pictures does as good a satire job on itself as anyone could. Candice Rialson goes to low-budget Miracle Pictures' producer Richard Doran, who turns out one a week. It seems that Mary Woronov, queen of the B-hive, doesn't like the competition from Rialson, Rita George, and Tara Strohmeier. A series of bizarre murders gradually eliminates the challengers. Intercut with the new material is a lot of older Corman footage.

HOLLYWOOD CANTEEN
1944, 124 mins, US ⓥ
D: Delmer Daves **A:** Robert Hutton, Joan Leslie, Bette Davis, John Garfield, Sydney Greenstreet, Joan Crawford (Warner)

Robert Hutton and Joan Leslie emerge as the real stars of the filmusical. They carry the story, and a human one it is, too. Hutton looks like the ideal GI Joe, back with a Purple Heart from the South Pacific, and his buddy (Dane Clark) looks the perfect Brooklynite. Story has Hutton winding up not only meeting his dream girl (Leslie) but is also the lucky winner as the millionth guest of the Hollywood Canteen.

1944: Nominations: Best Scoring of a Musical Picture, Sound, Song ("Sweet Dreams Sweetheart")

HOLLYWOOD CAVALCADE
1939, 100 mins, US
D: Irving Cummings **A:** Alice Faye, Don Ameche, J. Edward Bromberg, Alan Curtis, Stuart Erwin, Buster Keaton (20th Century-Fox)

An interesting and sentimental story of film producing in California, beginning in the pie-throwing, Keystone era of 1913, and winding up when the silent-picture days were ended. Principal novelty is the successful and amusing introduction of old-time Mack Sennett comedy routines and formula. The yarn itself relates the rise, fall, and rise again of an enthusiastic young director, played by Don Ameche. He sees a promising understudy (Alice Faye) who is substituting for the leading woman. He persuades her to make the jump to Hollywood and the films.

HOLLYWOOD CHAINSAW HOOKERS
1988, 74 mins, US ℗
D: Fred Olen Ray A: Gunnar Hansen, Linnea Quigley, Jay Richardson, Michelle Bauer (Savage Cinema)

A self-styled cult film that is entertaining for its intended fringe audience. Private dick Jay Richardson finds himself in the midst of a blood-cult ritual. Spoof goes over the edge when cult is revealed to be worshiping the chain saw, "the cosmic link by which all things are united." Pic's high point is an outrageous sequence when voluptuous Michelle Bauer, posing as a hooker, covers her Elvis wall poster with plastic as she strips to an Elvis sound-alike record and then bloodily cuts up her customer with a chain saw.

HOLLYWOOD COWBOY
See: Hearts of the West

HOLLYWOOD HOTEL
1937, 100 mins, US
D: Busby Berkeley A: Dick Powell, Rosemary Lane, Lola Lane, Ted Healy, Hugh Herbert, Glenda Farrell (Warner)

A smash musical entertainment. Hollywood film studios and broadcasting are the basis of a farcical story. Eight musical numbers are by Dick Whiting and Johnny Mercer, best of which are "I'm Like a Fish out of Water" and "Silhouetted in the Moonlight." Lane sisters, Rosemary and Lola, turn in good performances, and Ted Healy and Hugh Herbert have some very funny material. Dick Powell's song numbers are first-rate.

HOLLYWOOD HOT TUBS
1984, 102 mins, US ℗
D: Chuck Vincent A: Donna McDaniel, Michael Andrew, Paul Gunning, Katt Shea, Edy Williams (Manson International)

A very good premise simply sinks in the Hollywood hot tub. To save young Jeff from the slammer, his parents get him a job mixing plumbing with pleasure in the Hollywood hot tubs. Each half hour delivers a coupling in this not-too-funny comedy full of booze, broads, and bubbles. The final party offers look-alikes of Burt Reynolds, Lauren Bacall, and Bozo. Only the last is convincing.

HOLLYWOOD HOT TUBS 2: EDUCATING CRYSTAL
1990, 100 mins, US ℗
D: Ken Raich A: Jewel Shepard, Patrick Day, David Tiefen, Remy O'Neill, Bart Braverman (Alimar)

A well-scripted comic look at West Coast lifestyles. The Crystal of the title, Jewel Shepard, heads for business school to learn how to run her mom Remy O'Neill's hot tubs/health spa establishment. Evil Bart Braverman is conspiring to take over the business, even planning to marry O'Neill to achieve his ends. Film works due to the quirky touches of Brent Frieman's screenplay. Shepard comes into her own here in a funny and sympathetic role.

HOLLYWOOD OR BUST
1956, 94 mins, US ℗
D: Frank Tashlin A: Dean Martin, Jerry Lewis, Anita Ekberg, Pat Crowley, Maxie Rosenbloom (Paramount)

Most of this comedy caper takes place on a cross-country junket from New York, with way stops en route, including Las Vegas. Direction by Frank Tashlin scores enough comedy highspots to keep the pace fairly fast. One of the film's funniest bits comes before the title with Dean Martin introducing Jerry Lewis as different types of movie watchers. Anita Ekberg isn't have much more to do than to display what nature has wrought in the fjords of Sweden, so it's still a big part.

HOLLYWOOD REVUE
1929, 113 mins, US ☉
D: Charles Riesner A: John Gilbert, Norma Shearer, Joan Crawford, Bessie Love, Marion Davies, Buster Keaton (M-G-M)

It's a revue. No semblance of a story, and considering cast, nobody is going to care. The staging of "Singin' in the Rain" is a sweet dance melody delivered by Cliff Edwards and his uke under a sidescreen tree as the water pours down into a stage-wide pool. Individually no one stands out like Marie Dressler. Stage veteran has the one real comedy number of the picture. First of the color sequences is John Gilbert and Norma Shearer's *Romeo and Juliet,* a modern version.
1928/29: Nomination: Best Picture

HOLLYWOOD SHUFFLE
1987, 82 mins, US ℗
D: Robert Townsend A: Robert Townsend, Anne-Marie Johnson, Starletta Du-

pois, Helen Martin, Craigus R. Johnson (Conquering Unicorn)

Brimming with imagination and energy, *Hollywood Shuffle* is the kind of shoestring effort more appealing in theory than execution. Produced, directed, and cowritten by actor Robert Townsend, pic is a free-form look at the trials and tribulations of black actors trying to make it in today's Hollywood. Scattershot humor misses as much as it hits. Scenes in the actor's subconscious are dramatized onscreen. Most amusing of these is a school for black actors, run by whites, of course, where the students are trained to shuffle, jive, and generally fit the preconceived notion of what blacks are like.

HOLOCAUST 2000
(US: THE CHOSEN)
1977, 102 mins, Italy/UK ✆ ⌐

D: Alberto De Martino **A:** Kirk Douglas, Agostina Belli, Simon Ward, Anthony Quayle, Virginia McKenna, Alexander Knox (Embassy/Aston)

The conflict is between Robert Caine (Kirk Douglas), an idealist in the realm of nuclear power plants and his demon son Angelo (Simon Ward), with tenebrous plans to push Dad's project for fission power to wipe out human life. The dramatic picture-long father-son duel between Douglas with a mid-American accent and Ward with a British lilt keeps the plot in place right up to the inconclusive finale.

HOLY MATRIMONY
1943, 87 mins, US

D: John M. Stahl **A:** Monty Woolley, Gracie Fields, Laird Cregar, Una O'Connor, Alan Mowbray, Eric Blore (20th Century-Fox)

Comedy-drama themed in England at the turn of the century. Woolley is dominant throughout as Priam Farll, a painter whose fame for 25 years had mounted in England while he worked in solitude in the South Seas, accompanied only by a valet. When a command appearance is ordered by King Edward so he can be knighted, the trip back to England marks a turn of events that forms the crux for the story. Fields gives the film a highly human touch. She's a perfect mate for Woolley's cantankerous characterization.

HOLY MATRIMONY
1994, 93 mins, US ✆ ⊙

D: Leonard Nimoy **A:** Patricia Arquette, Joseph Gordon-Levitt, Armin Mueller-Stahl, Tate Donovan, John Schuck, Lois

Smith (Hollywood/Interscope/PFE)

An innocuous but problematic comedy. Bosomy sexpot Havana (Patricia Arquette) and boyfriend Peter (Tate Donovan) rob a safe and hide out at the Hutterite religious colony where Peter grew up. The vivacious, blunt-spoken Havana feels stifled by the restraints of Hutterite life—but she doesn't know where Peter has hidden the money. After Peter is killed in an accident, Havana insists on her right to remain by marrying Peter's younger brother. Trouble is, Zeke (Joseph Gordon-Levitt), is all of 12 years old. *Holy Matrimony* plays the second marriage mostly for safe, sitcom-style laughs. Arquette sparkles as Havana.

HOMAGE
1995, 96 mins, US ✆

D: Ross Kagan Marks **A:** Blythe Danner, Frank Whaley, Sheryl Lee, Danny Nucci, Bruce Davison (Skyline)

A slice of American gothic set in the desolate southwest. The psychological thriller focuses on three emotionally crippled people. The film opens with the murder of Lucy (Sheryl Lee), a sitcom actress who's returned to patch up a fractured relationship with Katherine (Blythe Danner), her widowed mother. The perp, Archie (Frank Whaley), is a mathematician working as caretaker and gardener on Katherine's ramshackle farm. The events leading up to the conclusion are related in flashback as "witnesses" provide key plot points. But the story provides no real rooting interest, and the creepiness of the material tries one's patience.

HOMBRE
1967, 119 mins, US ✆ ⊙ ⌐

D: Martin Ritt **A:** Paul Newman, Fredric March, Richard Boone, Diane Cilento, Cameron Mitchell, Martin Balsam (20th Century-Fox)

The story of an Apache-raised white boy who becomes the natural leader of a group in its fight for survival against a robber band. Paul Newman is excellent as the scorned Apache who's really white. Fredric March, essaying an Indian agent, also scores in a strong, unsympathetic—but eventually pathetic—role. Richard Boone is very powerful, yet admirably restrained as the heavy.

HOME ALONE
1990, 102 mins, US ✆ ⊙

D: Chris Columbus **A:** Macaulay Culkin, Joe Pesci, Daniel Stern, Catherine O'Hara,

John Heard, John Candy (20th Century-Fox)

The family of poor little Kevin (Macaulay Culkin) has accidentally left him behind. They're in Paris, frantically trying to reach him, and he's home alone, where a storm has knocked out the telephones, the neighbors are away for the holiday, and the houses on the street are being cleaned out by a team of burglars. Perceived by his family as a helpless, hopeless little geek, Kevin is at first delighted to be rid of them but then he realizes he's on his own to defend the place. A first-rate production, pic boasts wonderful casting, with Culkin a delight as funny, resilient Kevin.

1990: Nominations: Best Original Score, Song ("Somewhere in My Memory")

HOME ALONE 2: LOST IN NEW YORK
1992, 120 mins, US Ⓥ ⊙
D: Chris Columbus A: Macaulay Culkin, Joe Pesci, Daniel Stern, Catherine O'Hara, John Heard, Tim Curry (20th Century-Fox)

For a sequel the studio has simply remade the first movie, but with bigger pratfalls. Pic delivers on that level. Once again, Kevin (Macaulay Culkin) finds himself in the doghouse just before a family vacation, this time accidentally boarding the wrong plane and ending up in New York while the McCallister brood jets off to Florida. Under Chris Columbus's careful direction, the wide-eyed Culkin again shows his skill at being an Everykid—cutely precocious, yet still susceptible to childish whims.

HOME ALONE 3
1997, 102 mins, US Ⓥ ⊙
D: Raja Gosnell A: Alex D. Linz, Olek Krupa, Rya Kihlstedt, Lenny Von Dohlen, David Thornton, Haviland Morris (20th Century-Fox)

Home Alone 3 is essentially a remake of the first *Home Alone,* with a new young protagonist, some slightly craftier villains—and much more brutal comic mayhem. Newcomer Alex D. Linz plays Alex Pruitt, another crafty youngster who defends his suburban Chicago home from unwelcome visitors burglarizing each home on Alex's street. Alex has the chicken pox, allowing him to remain home from school and observe the activities outside his window. When the thieves finally narrow their search to Alex's home, our young hero takes matters into his own hands. While the tone is always frenetically comedic, and the mayhem bloodlessly slapsticky, some scenes are pretty rough.

HOME AT SEVEN
(US: MURDER ON MONDAY)
1952, 85 mins, UK
D: Ralph Richardson A: Ralph Richardson, Margaret Leighton, Jack Hawkins, Campbell Singer (London/British Lion)

Richardson's first attempt at direction, produced under the speedup technique of three weeks' shooting schedule after extensive rehearsals. A bank clerk loses a day in his life, and during the time he was an amnesia victim, the funds of his sports club are stolen and the steward is murdered. When the police starts its inquiries, he is soon convinced of his own guilt. Richardson directs with a straightforward competence.

HOME BEFORE DARK
1958, 137 mins, US
D: Mervyn LeRoy A: Jean Simmons, Dan O'Herlihy, Rhonda Fleming, Efrem Zimbalist Jr., Mabel Albertson (Warner)

Based on one woman's battle to regain her slipping sanity, it is a romantic melodrama of considerable power and imprint. Simmons is the wife of Dan O'Herlihy, who has ceased to love her before mental breakdown and has not changed his attitude on her recovery. Living in their home are her stepmother (Mabel Albertson) and her stepsister (Rhonda Fleming), who could drive anyone to the edge of madness. Her only real ally in the house is a stranger (Efrem Zimbalist Jr.), who is also an alien in the setting of the inbred New England college community.

HOMEBOY
1988, 112 mins, US Ⓥ ⊙
D: Michael Seresin A: Mickey Rourke, Christopher Walken, Debra Feuer, Thomas Quinn, Kevin Conway, Anthony Alda (Redbury)

Actor Mickey Rourke's decade-old pet project about a battered, burned-out small-time boxer is a sort of *Raging Bull* without horns, wallowing dully in the cliches of movieland gutter romanticism. Rourke's hero is just another inarticulate all-American lowlife. His zombielike condition doesn't prevent him from being befriended by Christopher Walken, who steals the show with a colorful portrayal of a narcissistic two-bit hoodlum.

HOMECOMING
1948, 113 mins, US
D: Mervyn LeRoy A: Clark Gable, Lana Turner, Anne Baxter, John Hodiak, Ray Collins, Gladys Cooper (M-G-M)

Gable portrays a successful surgeon, happily married, who joins the army. Three years of patching up the wounded in close association with his nurse, Turner, gradually changes the man's character from smug successfulness to an awareness of his obligations to others. The dialogue and the characters are made real by the forceful playing. There is strong sympathy for the love between Gable and Turner, even though the doctor's wife, Anne Baxter, waits at home.

HOME FOR THE HOLIDAYS
1995, 103 mins, US ⓥ ⊙
D: Jodie Foster A: Holly Hunter, Robert Downey Jr., Anne Bancroft, Charles Durning, Geraldine Chaplin, Cynthia Stevenson (Egg/PolyGram/Paramount)

Jodie Foster's second directorial effort is an affectionately drawn, multigenerational portrait of an eccentric family. Small, mostly well-observed scenes establish the many characters, who for 36 intense hours fight and reconcile, showing their simultaneously endearing and exasperating personalities. Holly Hunter's performance as a lonely woman beset by the headaches of a single mom is sincerely felt and commanding, without being truly captivating.

HOME FROM THE HILL
1960, 150 mins, US ⓥ ⊙ ⌑
D: Vincente Minnelli A: Robert Mitchum, Eleanor Parker, George Peppard, George Hamilton, Everett Sloane, Luana Patten (M-G-M)

A full-blown melodrama, high-octane in situation and characters. Setting is Texas, a town of which Robert Mitchum is not only the richest citizen but the busiest stud. The latter characteristic has iced his marriage to Eleanor Parker since the birth of their now grown son (George Hamilton). Mitchum has another son (George Peppard), born out of wedlock. Hamilton has been so marked by his parents' relationship that when he falls in love with Luana Patten, he lacks the courage to marry her. Despite the intricacies, the story plays well, due to a fine cast and Minnelli's sure-handed direction. Mitchum delivers his strongest performance in years. But it is Peppard, from the NY stage, who shines through.

HOME MOVIES
1979, 90 mins, US ⓥ ⊙
D: Brian De Palma A: Kirk Douglas, Nancy Allen, Keith Gordon, Gerrit Graham, Vincent Gardenia (SLC)

Home Movies resulted from Brian De Palma teaching students how to make films by making one with them. The story has Kirk Douglas running a cult called Star Therapy. He exhorts each pupil to ''put your name above the title'' in life. Practicing what he preaches, he has his own life continuously filmed, with himself as director and star. The sessions, filmed with a mask reducing the frame, as if by Douglas's own 16mm camera crew, are recurrently hilarious.

HOMER AND EDDIE
1989, 99 mins, US ⓥ ⊙
D: Andrei Konchalovsky A: James Belushi, Whoopi Goldberg, Karen Black, John Waters, Beah Richards (Kings Road/Borman/Cady)

This road film about a mentally deficient dishwasher and a homicidal escaped cancer patient is a downer from beginning to end. Homer, a mentally retarded dishwasher in Arizona, decides to hitchhike up to Oregon to see his father, who is dying of cancer. He meets up with wacky vagabond Eddie in an old jalopy, and soon they become pals. It is hard to feel much sympathy for these two mental patients. The image of two underprivileged people in a cruel world is rather too pat to be convincing.

HOME SWEET HOME
1914, 90 mins, US ⓥ ⊗
D: D. W. Griffith A: Henry B. Walthall, Lillian Gish, Dorothy Gish, Mae Marsh, Donald Crisp, Blanche Sweet (Reliance)

Illustrating the effect of the immortal song, together with the early life and death of the author of it, along with a story of the great good the lyric has accomplished. The first reels are devoted to John Howard Payne, showing him to have written the song in a foreign land, dying shortly after. The next episode is a western mining camp, to which comes a young easterner, who falls in love. In the third episode, a wife about to be unfaithful to her husband is stopped by the music of a violin above her apartment playing the strain.

HOMEWARD BOUND
1993, 84 mins, US ⓥ ⊙
D: Duwayne Dunham A: Robert Hays, Kim Greist, Jean Smart, Benj Thall, Ve-

ronica Lauren, Kevin Chevalia (Walt Disney)

A sprightly little entertainment that applies animation principles to live action by giving personalities to the movie's wayward dogs and cat through the clever use of the voices of Michael J. Fox, Sally Field, and Don Ameche. The plot centers on three pets, left with a family friend, who try to cross the wilderness and make it back home, encountering menaces from bears to porcupines on the way.

HOMEWARD BOUND II: LOST IN SAN FRANCISCO
1996, 88 mins, US Ⓥ ⊙
D: David R. Ellis **A:** Robert Hays, Kim Greist, Veronica Lauren, Kevin Chevalia, Benj Thall (Walt Disney)

Homeward Bound II sticks close to formula that worked so well in the original film. Michael J. Fox and Sally Field are on board again to provide voices for, respectively, Chance, an exuberant bulldog, and Sassy, a finicky cat. Ralph Waite fills in for the late Don Ameche as the voice of Shadow, the retriever. This time the claustrophobic Chance breaks free of a carrying case just before he's loaded onto the airliner carrying the family to a Canadian holiday. Sassy and Shadow follow him off the runway and onto the highway, for another incredible journey home. The matching of animals with human voices is inspired.

HOMICIDE
1991, 100 mins, US Ⓥ
D: David Mamet **A:** Joe Mantegna, William H. Macy, Natalija Nogulich, Ving Rhames, Rebecca Pidgeon (Pressman/Cinehaus)

David Mamet's first-rate writing and boldly idiosyncratic directing redeem this story of a toughened Jewish cop torn between two worlds. *Homicide* presents an urban hell in which stoic survivor Bobby Gold (Joe Mantegna) must negotiate through rotten politics, unpredictable violence, and virulent racial tension just to get through a day of police work. Gold sees a chance to regain his enthusiasm when he becomes a key player in a team effort to bring in a cop killer who's eluded the FBI. But he's callously reassigned to a routine investigation of an elderly Jewish woman shot down in her candy store in a black ghetto.

UN HOMME ET UNE FEMME (US: A MAN AND A WOMAN)
1966, 103 mins, France Ⓥ ⊙
D: Claude Lelouch **A:** Anouk Aimee, Jean-Louis Trintignant, Pierre Barouh, Valerie Lagrange, Henri Chemin, Yane Barry (Les Films 13)

Claude Lelouch has practically no story. It concerns a widow who meets a racing-car driver at the school where they board their respective offspring. He has a wife, though he seems estranged. Love blossoms but is frustrated, since she still seems too taken by the memory of her late husband. Film misses puerility and coyness by Lelouch's seeming unfettered joy in filming his scenes. Through constantly roving camera, and especially two charming actors, he redeems rough spots of repetition, archness, and a general preciosity. Music is much too saccharine and insistent.

HONDO
1953, 84 mins, US
D: John Farrow **A:** John Wayne, Geraldine Page, Michael Pate, James Arness, Rodolfo Acosta (Warner/Wayne-Fellows)

An exciting offbeat western. John Wayne arrives at the isolated ranch of Geraldine Page and her young son. Practically abandoned by her ne'er-do-well husband, she is forced to do the ranch chores by herself. Wayne accidentally kills her husband in self-defense. While the romantic attachment between Wayne and Page grows, a conflict arises over the death of her husband. Wayne scores as the silent-yet-outspoken Indian scout. Page, no glamour girl, gives a sensitive portrayal as the ranch wife.

1953: Nominations: Best Supp. Actress (Geraldine Page), Motion Picture Story (writer not eligible)

HONEY, I BLEW UP THE KID
1992, 89 mins, US Ⓥ ⊙
D: Randal Kleiser **A:** Rick Moranis, Marcia Strassman, Robert Oliveri, Daniel Shalikar, Joshua Shalikar, Lloyd Bridges (Walt Disney)

A diverting, well-crafted sequel to Disney's '89 hit *Honey, I Shrunk the Kids*. Taking its cue from 1950s sci-fi pics and inverting the shrinking gags from the original, the sequel has wacky inventor Rick Moranis accidentally blowing up his two-year-old to huge proportions. There's nothing genuinely menacing about the baby, though. Nor does *Kid* have the creepy feeling of the original. The sequel is a romp, escapism at its breeziest.

HONEY, I SHRUNK THE KIDS
1989, 86 mins, US ⓥ ⊙
D: Joe Johnston A: Rick Moranis, Matt Frewer, Marcia Strassman, Kristine Sutherland, Thomas Brown, Jared Rushton (Walt Disney)

Borrowing two good elements from two 1950s sci-fi pics, *The Incredible Shrinking Man* and *Them!*, scripters pit two sets of unfriendly neighbor kids, mistakenly shrunk to only a quarter-inch high, against what ordinarily would be benign backyard fixtures, both alive and inanimate. Pic is in the best tradition of Disney and even better than that because it is not so juvenile that adults won't be thoroughly entertained.

HONEYMOON IN VEGAS
1992, 95 mins, US ⓥ ⊙
D: Andrew Bergman A: James Caan, Nicolas Cage, Sarah Jessica Parker, Pat Morita, Anne Bancroft, Peter Boyle (Castle Rock)

Sarah Jessica Parker is the saucy, sympathetic prize in a poker game between her divorce-detective fiancé Nicolas Cage and sharkish Vegas gambler James Caan. Schoolteacher Parker has coerced NY shamus Cage into marrying her, and they take a honeymoon suite at Bally's Casino Resort during the midst of a convention of Elvis impersonators, whose presence provides hilarious running gags throughout.

HONEYMOON KILLERS, THE
1969, 115 mins, US ⓥ
D: Leonard Kastle A: Shirley Stoler, Tony LoBianco, Mary Higbee, Kip McArdle, Doris Roberts (A.I.P./Roxanne)

Made on a very low budget with care, authenticity, and attention to detail. Fernandez has disappeared from the lives of a score of women, after receiving their "dowries," when he meets Martha, but it is only when he becomes intimately involved in his life, bringing her fantastic jealousy to bear on his new targets, that murder enters the picture. There are a few lapses, but the pic goes toward its harrowing climax without losing step.

HONEY POT, THE
1967, 150 mins, UK
D: Joseph L. Mankiewicz A: Rex Harrison, Susan Hayward, Cliff Robertson, Capucine, Edie Adams, Maggie Smith (United Artists)

An elegant, sophisticated screen vehicle for more demanding tastes, vaguely drawing its inspiration from Ben Jonson's *Volpone,* film's updated plot centers around the fabulously rich Cecil Fox (Rex Harrison), who with the aid of a sometimes gigolo and secretary, William McFly (Cliff Robertson), plays a joke of sorts on three onetime mistresses by feigning grave illness and gauging their reactions as they come flocking to his bedside.

HONEYSUCKLE ROSE
1980, 119 mins, US ⓥ ⊙ ▭
D: Jerry Schatzberg A: Willie Nelson, Dyan Cannon, Amy Irving, Slim Pickens, Joey Floyd, Charles Levin (Warner)

This is not a picture for anybody who doesn't like Willie Nelson. But the picture adroitly blends his musical performances with a gently dramatic acting job in an old-fashioned love story. Picture catches Nelson when he had yet to break out with the big hit that would make him nationally famous. Dyan Cannon and Joey Floyd nicely set up Nelson's approaching conflict as the wife and son who wait affectionately at home for him to finish his periodic tours.

1980: Nomination: Best Song ("On the Road Again")

HONKY TONK
1941, 104 mins, US ⓥ
D: Jack Conway A: Clark Gable, Lana Turner, Frank Morgan, Claire Trevor, Albert Dekker, Chill Wills (M-G-M)

The major power is in the love scenes between Clark Gable and Lana Turner. Gable is a western grifter, working the three-card-monte game. He and his sidekick (Chill Wills) wind up in a gold-strike town where Gable immediately renews an acquaintanceship with Turner. She's the daughter of Frank Morgan, also a former con guy but now the justice of the peace. Gable gets Morgan under his thumb and then proceeds to take over the town.

HONKY TONK FREEWAY
1981, 107 mins, US ⓥ
D: John Schlesinger A: Beau Bridges, Hume Cronyn, Beverly D'Angelo, William Devane, Teri Garr, Geraldine Page (Universal/AFD/EMI)

The thin story line revolves around the residents of a small Florida town, Ticlaw, who are miffed that the new super-duper freeway won't have an exit for tourists to stop off and spend their money in the area. Major portion of the picture switches to the collection of people who travel the freeway and eventually (through no fault of their own) wind up in Ticlaw.

HONKYTONK MAN
1982, 122 mins, US Ⓥ ⊙
D: Clint Eastwood **A:** Clint Eastwood, Kyle Eastwood, John McIntire, Alexa Kenin, Verna Bloom, Matt Clark (Warner/Malpaso)

It seems that Clint Eastwood took great pains in telling this story of an aging, struggling country singer, but he is done in by the predictability of the script and his own limitations as a warbler. His son, Kyle, who has limited acting experience, doesn't seem to know what to do with his key role of the emerging teenager.

HONOR AMONG LOVERS
1931, 76 mins, US Ⓥ
D: Dorothy Arzner **A:** Claudette Colbert, Fredric March, Monroe Owsley, Charles Ruggles, Ginger Rogers (Paramount)

Comedy-drama. A wealthy, young, and freedom-loving businessman is nursing an impulse for one of those super-feminine screen secretaries. His offer of an apartment or a long cruise frightens her into marriage with a brokerage attaché, a weakling. The two set a pretty fast social pace for a married couple of their means and the crash comes when the husband embezzles the accounts entrusted to him, among which is that of his wife's former employer. Claudette Colbert, Fredric March, and Monroe Owsley are collectively and individually a smooth working trio.

HONORARY CONSUL, THE
(US: BEYOND THE LIMIT)
1984, 103 mins, UK Ⓥ ⊙
D: John Mackenzie **A:** Michael Caine, Richard Gere, Bob Hoskins, Elpidia Carrillo, Joaquin De Almeida, Geoffrey Palmer (World Film Services)

A weak attempt to adapt Graham Greene's 1973 novel for the screen. Strong talents on both sides of the camera haven't managed to breathe life into this intricate tale of emotional and political betrayal and result is a steady dose of tedium. First handicap is the casting of Richard Gere as the dispirited Englishman. Actor's accent only manages to stay on course when his lines consist of five words or less. Gere performs another of his seemingly obligatory postshower nude scenes here, as well as a couple of in-the-buff sex scenes with Elpidia Carrillo. Acting honors easily fall to Michael Caine as the small-time, dipsomaniacal diplomat. Bob Hoskins registers strongly as a heartless but engaging South American police chief.

HOODLUM PRIEST, THE
1961, 100 mins, US
D: Irvin Kershner **A:** Don Murray, Larry Gates, Cindi Wood, Keir Dullea (United Artists)

Biographically based on the offbeat activities of the Reverend Charles Dismas Clark, a Jesuit priest noted for his rehabilitation work with ex-cons, the screenplay pinpoints Clark's problems against the tragedy of a confused youth who pays with his life for crimes of which he is not solely responsible. Don Murray gives a vigorous, sincere performance in the title role. But the film's most moving portrayal is delivered by Keir Dullea as the doomed lad.

HOODLUM SAINT, THE
1946, 92 mins, US
D: Norman Taurog **A:** William Powell, Esther Williams, Angela Lansbury, James Gleason (M-G-M)

Drama, laid in the period just after World War I up through the 1929 stock-market crash, deals with the power of belief in St. Dismus, the good thief, to reform all hoodlums. Film gives Esther Williams a chance in something other than a musical. There's no feeling of struggle in the development of the plot, everything coming too easily to the characters—love, riches, poverty, and eventual belief in St. Dismus's power for good. Powell is his usual assured self as the opportunist, delivers a top-notch characterization.

HOOK
1991, 144 mins, US Ⓥ ⊙ ▭
D: Steven Spielberg **A:** Dustin Hoffman, Robin Williams, Julia Roberts, Bob Hoskins, Maggie Smith (Tri-Star/Amblin)

Spirited, rambunctious, often messy and undisciplined, this determined attempt to recast the Peter Pan story in contempo terms sends a modern, grown-up Peter back to Neverland to rescue his children from the clutches of the ever-vengeful Captain Hook. Peter (Robin Williams) is visited by Tinkerbell (Julia Roberts) and is transported to Neverland, where Hook (Dustin Hoffman) lords over a raucous Pirate Town from the deck of his enormous ship. Despite the cascade of wondrous special effects, massive battles between the kids and pirates, and face-offs between

Pan and Hook, the film doesn't truly take flight.

1991: Nominations: Best Art Direction, Costume Design, Song ("When You're Alone"), Makeup, Visual Effects

HOOPER
1978, 99 mins, US Ⓥ ⊙
D: Hal Needham **A:** Burt Reynolds, Jan-Michael Vincent, Sally Field, Brian Keith, John Marley, James Best (Warner/Reynolds-Gordon)

Individually, the performances in this story of three generations of Hollywood stuntmen are a delight. And Hal Needham's direction and stunt staging are wonderfully crafted. But it's the ensemble work of Burt Reynolds, Jan-Michael Vincent, Sally Field, and Brian Keith, with an able assist from Robert Klein, which boosts an otherwise pedestrian story with lots of crashes and daredevil antics into a touching and likable piece.

1978: Nomination: Best Sound

HOOSIERS
(UK: BEST SHOT)
1986, 114 mins, US Ⓥ ⊙
D: David Anspaugh **A:** Gene Hackman, Barbara Hershey, Dennis Hopper, Sheb Wooley, Fern Persons (Hemdale)

An involving tale about the unlikely success of a small-town Indiana high-school basketball team that paradoxically proves both rousing and too conventional centers around a fine performance by Gene Hackman as the coach. Dennis Hopper gets another opportunity to put in a showy turn as a local misfit.

1986: Nominations: Best Supp. Actor (Dennis Hopper), Original Score

HOPE AND GLORY
1987, 113 mins, UK Ⓥ ⊙
D: John Boorman **A:** Sarah Miles, David Hayman, Derrick O'Connor, Susan Wooldridge, Sammi Davis, Ian Bannen (Columbia)

Essentially a collection of sweetly autobiographical anecdotes of English family life during World War II. Tale is narrated from an adult perspective by Billy, an exquisite-looking nine-year-old who finds great excitement in the details of warfare. Best scenes are those with Billy center stage, and particularly those showing the unthinking callousness kids can display in the face of others' misfortune and tragedy.

1987: Nominations: Best Picture, Director, Original Screenplay, Cinematography, Art Direction

HOPSCOTCH
1980, 104 mins, US Ⓥ ⊙ ▭
D: Ronald Neame **A:** Walter Matthau, Glenda Jackson, Ned Beatty, Sam Waterston, Herbert Lom (Avco Embassy)

A high-spirited comedy which, unfortunately, reaches its peak too soon. Walter Matthau plays a CIA agent whose independent ways are too much for his finicky, double-dealing boss (Ned Beatty). So Matthau is put in charge of the files. He decides to write a book that will embarrass not only the CIA but spies in every country, making himself a target for extinction. Hiding out, Matthau takes up with Glenda Jackson. Their initial moments together serve up the same good bantering chemistry of *House Calls.*

HORI, MA PANENKO
(THE FIREMAN'S BALL; LIKE A HOUSE ON FIRE)
1967, 73 mins, Czechoslovakia/Italy Ⓥ
D: Milos Forman **A:** Vaclav Stockel, Josef Svet, Jan Vostrcil, Josef Kolb, Frantisek Debelka, Josef Sebanek (Barrandov/Ponti)

A group of elderly firemen of a small town are planning to bring off a farewell ball for their retiring director. Filmmaker Forman has cannily used a bevy of non-actors to flesh out a practically plotless vehicle, a lively, brimming comedy on human conduct and small-town life.

HORIZONS WEST
1952, 80 mins, US Ⓥ
D: Budd Boetticher **A:** Robert Ryan, Julie Adams, Rock Hudson, John McIntire, Raymond Burr (Universal)

Plot is laid in the post–War Between the States period, opening with three Texans returning to their home state. Rock Hudson and James Arness welcome a resumption of ranching, but Robert Ryan turns his attention toward easy money and a desire to build a western empire. From a rather slow start, it then becomes a session of pretentious, cliché-laden talk that even spurts of hardy action fail to enliven.

HORN BLOWS AT MIDNIGHT, THE
1945, 80 mins, US
D: Raoul Walsh **A:** Jack Benny, Alexis Smith, Guy Kibbee, Margaret Dumont, Reginald Gardiner (Warner)

Lightweight comedy that never seems able to make up its mind whether to be fantasy or broad slapstick. Jack Benny plays third trumpet in a radio-station orch. Falling asleep, Benny dreams he's an angel in heaven—and still playing third trumpet. The Big Chief, disgusted with conditions on the planet earth, dispatches Benny to Earth to destroy it. The angel is to blow his special horn promptly at midnight, the blast to do away with the earth.

HORROR CHAMBER OF DR. FAUSTUS, THE
See: Les Yeux Sans Visage

HORROR OF DRACULA
See: Dracula (1958)

HORSE FEATHERS
1932, 70 mins, US Ⓥ
D: Norman Z. McLeod A: Groucho Marx, Chico Marx, Harpo Marx, Zeppo Marx, Thelma Todd (Paramount)

The madcap Marxes, in one of their maddest screen frolics. The premise of Groucho Marx as the college prexy and his three aides and abettors putting Huxley College on the gridiron map promises much and delivers more. Zeppo is his usual straight opposite Thelma Todd as the college widow. She's a luscious eyeful and swell foil for the Marxian boudoir manhandling.

HORSEMAN ON THE ROOF, THE
See: Le Hussard sur le Toit

HORSEMEN, THE
1971, 108 mins, US Ⓥ ▭
D: John Frankenheimer A: Omar Sharif, Leigh Taylor-Young, Jack Palance, Peter Jeffrey, Mohammed Shamsi (Columbia)

A would-be epic stretched thin across Hollywood's "profound peasant" tradition. It's a misfire, despite offbeat Afghanistan locations and some bizarre action sequences. Omar Sharif, son of rural Afghanistan clan leader Jack Palance, is injured and humiliated (he thinks) in a brutal ritual soccer-type game. Sharif's leg is amputated below the knee in a remote mountain village. Back with his clan, Sharif trains hard to reestablish his honor and reputation as the greatest horseman in the area.

HORSE SOLDIERS, THE
1959, 120 mins, US Ⓥ
D: John Ford A: John Wayne, William Holden, Constance Towers, Althea Gibson, Hoot Gibson, Anna Lee (Mirisch)

This is the story of Colonel Benjamin Grierson, who, in April of 1863, was ordered to take three cavalry regiments and ride 300 miles into the heart of the Confederacy to destroy a rail link and choke off supplies. With all of Ford's skill for staging battle scenes, and his superb eye for pictorial composition, the film is extremely uneven. Also, the dramatic scenes involving John Wayne, William Holden, and newcomer Constance Towers don't come off with much conviction. William Clothier's photography is outstanding. Some of the scenes have the quality of paintings.

HORSE WHISPERER, THE
1998, 168 mins, US Ⓥ ⊙ ▭
D: Robert Redford A: Robert Redford, Kristin Scott Thomas, Sam Neill, Dianne Wiest, Scarlett Johansson, Chris Cooper (Wildwood/Touchstone)

Robert Redford has made an exquisitely crafted, morally and thematically mature picture about a modern cowboy who brings about the physical and spiritual regeneration of a teenage girl and her horse after they suffer crippling injuries. In dealing with her daughter Grace's (Scarlett Johansson) calamity, high-powered New York magazine editor Annie MacLean (Kristin Scott Thomas) decides not to have the horse Pilgrim put down. Intuiting that her daughter's recovery might be tied to that of Pilgrim's, Annie learns of a man who reputedly has a special gift with horses and heads for Montana, where the healer, Tom Booker (Redford), lives. It's almost unique in modern films for the central couple in a romance not to bed down at least once; when Annie plaintively asks, "Tom, can we have one last ride?" the hero takes her literally and saddles up a horse.

HOSPITAL, THE
1971, 103 mins, US Ⓥ
D: Arthur Hiller A: George C. Scott, Diana Rigg, Barnard Hughes, Nancy Marchand, Stephen Elliott (United Artists)

The Hospital is a civilian mis-M*A*S*H. George C. Scott stars as a NY medical center chief surgeon whose ruined personal life alternates with a daily routine of apparently inept, callous, bored, overworked, and murdered staff members. Diana Rigg is the daughter of a deranged doctor-patient whose unmasking destroys most of author Paddy Chayefsky's basic premise. The heavily sprayed-on sociological angle is that hospitals today treat patients like baggage.
1971: Best Original Story & Screenplay
Nomination: Best Actor (George C. Scott)

HOSTILE HOSTAGES
See: The Ref

HOSTSONAT
(AUTUMN SONATA)
1978, 97 mins, W. Germany/UK ⓥ ⊙
D: Ingmar Bergman A: Ingrid Bergman, Liv Ullmann, Lena Nyman, Halvar Bjork, Erland Josephson, Gunnar Bjornstrand (Personafilm/ITC)

This is the first time the Swedish director has directed Swedish actress Ingrid Bergman. It makes one wish that they had teamed up a long time ago. Ingrid Bergmann is Charlotte, a famous concert pianist who finds herself emotionally alone when her lover of many years dies. She is invited to visit her daughter, Eva (Liv Ullman), the wife of a country parson in Norway, whom she has not seen for seven years. The film deals with their reunion and the ultimate disclosure of their feelings for each other.

HOTEL
1967, 124 mins, US ⓥ
D: Richard Quine A: Rod Taylor, Catherine Spaak, Karl Malden, Melvyn Douglas, Merle Oberon, Richard Conte (Warner)

A very well-made, handsomely produced drama about the guests and management of an old hostelry which must modernize or shutter. Merle Oberon registers well as the wife of Michael Rennie, whose hit-and-run driving cues a blackmail attempt by house gumshoe Richard Conte. Karl Malden has a choice role of a key thief who is frustrated at many turns by double-crossing accomplices.

HOTEL BERLIN
1945, 98 mins, US
D: Peter Godfrey A: Helmut Dantine, Andrea King, Raymond Massey, Faye Emerson, Peter Lorre (Warner)

Grand Hotel in a 1945 Nazi setting, now known as *Hotel Berlin*. The war's already lost—or, at least, there's that defeatist aura about Hotel Berlin—and the Nazi higher-ups are packing their loot for a South American getaway. There are the periodic Allied air blitzes which chase everybody into the shelters, but otherwise it's a Grand Hotel in the lobby or on the sundry floors, but particularly in the apartments of a general (Raymond Massey), an informer (Faye Emerson), or a theater darling (Andrea King). The situations are constantly intriguing.

HOTEL IMPERIAL
1927, 67 mins, US ⊗
D: Mauritz Stiller A: Pola Negri, James Hall, George Siegmann (Paramount)

In direction and camerawork the picture stands out, but the story isn't going to give anyone a great thrill. The Hotel Imperial is located in one of the border towns of Austria-Hungary. Here a fleeing Austrian hussar is caught behind the lines of the enemy when they move into the town. Negri, as the hotel slavey, shelters him and suggests that he act as the waiter to cover himself. A Russian general makes the hotel his headquarters and falls for the girl. The waiter, in turn, loves her also and she reciprocates his feeling.

HOTEL NEW HAMPSHIRE, THE
1984, 110 mins, US ⓥ ⊙
D: Tony Richardson A: Jodie Foster, Beau Bridges, Rob Lowe, Nastassja Kinski, Wilford Brimley (Woodfall)

A fascinating, largely successful adaptation of John Irving's 1981 novel. Writer-director Tony Richardson has pulled off a remarkable stylistic tightrope act, establishing a bizarre tone of morbid whimsicality. Tale concerns an eccentric New England family that, spurred on by an ever-searching father, establishes a new hotel in locale after locale and mutates in the process. Among the unusual family members is Jodie Foster, who must endure a punishing gang rape and a prolonged fascination with one of the young men who was responsible for it.

HOTEL PARADISO
1966, 100 mins, UK ▭
D: Peter Glenville A: Alec Guinness, Gina Lollobrigida, Robert Morley, Peggy Mount, Akim Tamiroff (M-G-M)

Film version of Georges Feydeau's turn-of-the-century *L'Hôtel du Libre Échange*. Plot involves mishaps triggered by the 40-year-old "itch" of M. Boniface, played with wearily glossy perfection by Alec Guinness, for the wife of his next-door neighbor, Henri Cot, assayed with appropriate bluster by Robert Morley. Mme. Cot, adequately acted by Gina Lollobrigida, succumbs to Boniface's suggestion that they rendezvous at the Hotel Paradiso. A concatenation of endless coincidences, laboriously contrived for the better part of the film, conspire to relegate the rendezvous to farce.

HOT ENOUGH FOR JUNE
(US: AGENT 8 3/4)
1964, 98 mins, UK
D: Ralph Thomas A: Dirk Bogarde, Sylva

Koscina, Robert Morley, Leo McKern, John Le Mesurier (Rank)

A faster pace and a few more red herrings and surprise situations could have worked wonders in lifting this amiable enough spoof of espionage into a top-league comedy-thriller. Dirk Bogarde is assigned to visit a Czech factory and bring back a written message, which he guilelessly believes to be a simple commercial job. He does not know that he is now attached to the Espionage Department of the Foreign Office.

HOT MILLIONS
1968, 106 mins, UK
D: Eric Till **A:** Peter Ustinov, Maggie Smith, Karl Malden, Bob Newhart, Robert Morley, Cesar Romero (M-G-M)

Very good writing, excellent acting, zesty direction and pacing, and handsome production make this story of computer embezzlement a strong laugh-getter. Ustinov, released from prison, decides that the modern embezzler must be a computer expert. Conning his way into the good graces of Malden, head of the British wing of an American industrial conglomerate, Ustinov eventually programs into the computer three phony companies, to which large checks are sent.
1968: Nomination: Best Original Story & Screenplay

HOT ROCK, THE
(UK: HOW TO STEAL A DIAMOND IN FOUR UNEASY LESSONS)
1972, 105 mins, US Ⓥ ▢
D: Peter Yates **A:** Robert Redford, George Segal, Ron Leibman, Paul Sand, Zero Mostel, Moses Gunn (20th Century-Fox)

An offbeat crime feature. Robert Redford and George Segal head a quartet of thieves who usually miss the objective, here a famous diamond which inspired the title of the piece. Peter Yates's direction and a uniformly good cast partly overcome a William Goldman script that has many exciting and funny bits, but lacks a clear, unifying thrust.
1972: Nomination: Best Editing

HOT SHOTS!
1991, 85 mins, US Ⓥ ⊙
D: Jim Abrahams **A:** Charlie Sheen, Cary Elwes, Valeria Golino, Lloyd Bridges, Kevin Dunn, Kristy Swanson (20th Century-Fox/PAP)

Jim Abrahams tries to tap the zany *Airplane!* vein with this *Top Gun* spoof but bats far too low a percentage with the usual rapid-fire assault of numbingly stupid gags. Pic bogs down in motion picture in-jokes. Charlie Sheen is the maverick pilot competing with self-obsessed Kent (Cary Elwes). Most characters are gratingly cartoonish, especially Lloyd Bridges's way-over-the-top tin-headed admiral.

HOT SHOTS 2
See: Hot Shots! Part Deux

HOT SHOTS! PART DEUX
(AUSTRALIA: HOT SHOTS 2)
1993, 89 mins, US Ⓥ ⊙
D: Jim Abrahams **A:** Charlie Sheen, Lloyd Bridges, Valeria Golino, Richard Crenna, Brenda Bakke, Miguel Ferrer (20th Century-Fox)

A clever spoof of *Rambo* and a dozen other movies that employs the usual scattershot *Airplane!* approach but boasts a higher shooting percentage than its forebear. Charlie Sheen, with wild locks and a buffed-up physique, returns as Topper Harley, recruited by a former commander (Richard Crenna, a brilliant bit of casting due to his *Rambo* role) and a stunningly limber CIA agent (Brenda Bakke) to try to rescue US servicemen held prisoner after Desert Storm.

HOT SPOT
1941, 81 mins, US Ⓥ
D: H. Bruce Humberstone **A:** Betty Grable, Victor Mature, Carole Landis, Laird Cregar, Elisha Cook Jr. (20th Century-Fox)

A murder meller with a romantic strain of more than the ordinary strength. Mature is dogged by a detective who loses his girl when Mature takes her from obscurity and glamorizes her to the point where she wins a film contract. The murder of this girl then provides the premise for the remainder of the yarn. Betty Grable is enormously appealing as the sister of the slain girl, played by Carole Landis.

HOT SPOT, THE
1990, 120 mins, US Ⓥ ⊙
D: Dennis Hopper **A:** Don Johnson, Virginia Madsen, Jennifer Connelly, Charles Martin Smith, William Sadler (Orion)

Twisting, languorous, and very sexy thriller. As the low-key, manipulative drifter Harry Madox, Don Johnson shakes things up in a godforsaken Texas town, where his job at a used-car lot involves him with two restless women yearning to beat the heat. *The Hot Spot* seeps with atmosphere, unfolds at a deceptively relaxed pace, steadily accumulates noirish grit, then dizzily plunges into a David Lynch–like plumbing of the dark passions and nasty secrets at the heart of Main Street, USA.

HOUDINI
1953, 105 mins, US Ⓥ
D: George Marshall **A:** Tony Curtis, Janet Leigh, Torin Thatcher, Angela Clarke, Sig Ruman (Paramount)

A typical screen biography, presenting a rather fanciful version of Houdini's life. Production does well by illusions and escapes on which Houdini won his fame, using these tricks to give substance to a plot that uses a backstage formula that follows pat lines. Story spins along nicely, with occasional emphasis on drama in several of escape sequences to keep interest up. Performances of two stars are likable, although neither shows any aging in the time span that covers Houdini from 21 to death.

HOUND OF THE BASKERVILLES, THE
1939, 78 mins, US Ⓥ ⊙
D: Sidney Lanfield **A:** Richard Greene, Basil Rathbone, Nigel Bruce, Lionel Atwill, John Carradine, Wendy Barrie (20th Century-Fox)

Retains all of the suspensefully dramatic ingredients of Conan Doyle's popular adventure of Sherlock Holmes. It's a startling mystery-chiller developed along logical lines without resorting to implausible situations and overtheatrics. Doyle's tale of mystery surrounding the Baskerville castle is a familiar one. When Lionel Atwill learns that Richard Greene, heir to the estate, is marked for death, he calls in Basil Rathbone. Rathbone gives a most effective characterization of Sherlock Holmes.

HOUND OF THE BASKERVILLES, THE
1959, 88 mins, UK Ⓥ
D: Terence Fisher **A:** Peter Cushing, Andre Morell, Christopher Lee, Marla Landi, Miles Malleson, David Oxley (Hammer)

This first Sherlock Holmes pic in color takes place in the desolate setting of Dartmoor. It is difficult to fault the performance of Peter Cushing. Andre Morell is also a very good Watson—stolid, reliable and not so stupidly bovine as he is sometimes depicted. Christopher Lee has a fairly colorless role as the potential victim of the legendary hound. Terence Fisher's direction captures the eeriness of the atmosphere.

HOUNDS OF ZAROFF, THE
See: The Most Dangerous Game

HOUR OF GLORY
See: The Small Back Room

HOUR OF JUDGMENT
See: The Hour of the Pig

HOUR OF THE GUN
1967, 101 mins, US Ⓥ ⊙
D: John Sturges **A:** James Garner, Jason Robards, Robert Ryan, Albert Salmi, Charles Aidman, Steve Ihnat (United Artists/Mirisch)

A heavily populated script that traces Wyatt Earp's moral decline from an upright lawman to one bent on personal revenge. It continues the story of Earp after Gunfight at the O.K. Corral. Jason Robards and James Garner play well together, the former supplying an adroit irony in that he, an admitted gambler as much outside the law as in, becomes more moral as Garner lapses into personal vendetta. Robert Ryan is a perfect heavy.

HOUR OF THE PIG, THE (US: HOUR OF JUDGMENT; THE ADVOCATE)
1994, 115 mins, UK/France Ⓥ ⊙
D: Leslie Megahey **A:** Colin Firth, Ian Holm, Donald Pleasence, Nicol Williamson, Lysette Anthony (BBC/CiBy 2000)

A droll, deftly acted period piece based on the fact that in medieval France animals were accused of crimes and tried in court with counsel. When a band of Jewish gypsies enters the town, and their prize pig is arrested and accused of killing a young boy, exotic dark-skinned Samira (Amina Annabi) implores industrious young defense lawyer Courtois (Colin Firth) to get the pig acquitted, offering her womanly charms in exchange. Clever dialogue, laced with frank and bawdy observations, is delivered in ultradry style.

HOUSE
1986, 92 mins, US Ⓥ ⊙
D: Steve Miner **A:** William Katt, George Wendt, Robert Moll, Kay Lenz, Mary Stavin (New World)

Cornball script posits Roger Cobb (William Katt) as a successful horror novelist who moves into the spooky house where he was raised. Cobb immediately experiences odd happenings that play as hallucinations, but which the audience is supposed to believe are real. His estranged actress wife Susan (Kay Lenz) shows up, and apparently changes into a puffy monster. The monsters are fake and rubbery, better suited to a comedy than a film in search of scares.

HOUSE II: THE SECOND STORY
1987, 85 mins, US ⓥ ⊙
D: Ethan Wiley A: Arye Gross, Jonathan Stark, Royal Dano, Bill Maher, John Ratzenberger (New World)

This house isn't worth a visit. What passes for a plot has Arye Gross hear about the existence of a skull filled with jewelry, supposedly buried with the body of one of his ancestors, so he and entrepreneur pal Jonathan Stark exhume the 170-year-old corpse. The old-timer wants to have fun now that he's alive again, but an evil spirit wants that skull. Director Ethan Wiley is determined to be cute rather than scary. He intros some cuddly creatures—a baby pterodactyl, plus a critter who's a cross between a dog and a caterpillar—but they don't add anything to the pic's charm.

HOUSEBOAT
1958, 112 mins, US ⓥ ⊙
D: Melville Shavelson A: Cary Grant, Sophia Loren, Martha Hyer, Harry Guardino, Eduardo Ciannelli (Paramount/Scribe)

It's a perfect role for Cary Grant, who plays a lawyer separated from his wife and who is brought into contact with his three children, none of whom is very friendly toward him. Enter Sophia Loren, a full-blown lass with lovely knees. Grant, though he takes her for a tramp, hires her as a maid at seeing her ability to handle his children upon first meeting.

1958: Nominations: Best Original Story & Screenplay, Song ("Almost in Your Army")

HOUSE BY THE RIVER
1950, 88 mins, US
D: Fritz Lang A: Louis Hayward, Lee Bowman, Jane Wyatt, Dorothy Patrick, Ann Shoemaker (Republic/Fidelity)

A fair mystery which lacks sufficient plot twists and suspense. The film departs from the conventional whodunit in that the audience knows the identity of the murderer from the opening reel. Yarn revolves around a hack writer who strangles the maid when she rebuffs his advances. Role represents a meaty part for Louis Hayward, who essays it with such gusto that he frequently overplays.

HOUSE CALLS
1978, 98 mins, US ⓥ ⊙
D: Howard Zieff A: Walter Matthau, Glenda Jackson, Art Carney, Richard Benjamin, Candice Azzara (Universal)

A silly and uneven comedy about doctors. Walter Matthau is a newly widowed medic out to make up for lost infidelity time; Glenda Jackson, divorced from a philanderer, seeks a faithful new mate; Art Carney is a near-senile hospital chief of staff whose mistakes are supposed to be funny but come off as really nasty; Richard Benjamin is a young doctor.

HOUSEGUEST
1995, 109 mins, US ⓥ
D: Randall Miller A: Sinbad, Phil Hartman, Jeffrey Jones, Kim Greist, Stan Shaw (Hollywood)

Stand-up comic and sitcom star Sinbad is thoroughly engaging as a dreamer on the run from loan sharks. Sinbad runs into Gary Young (Hartman), an affable lawyer. Gary brings Kevin to his suburban home for a long weekend with his mildly dysfunctional family: Emily (Kim Greist), his wife, a yogurt-shop entrepreneur; Brooke (Kim Murphy), his death-obsessed daughter; Jason (Chauncey Leopardi), his insecure adolescent son; and Sarah (Talia Seider), his six-year-old and the most well-adjusted person in the family. Not surprisingly, Kevin is a big hit with everyone.

HOUSEKEEPING
1987, 116 mins, US ⓥ
D: Bill Forsyth A: Christine Lahti, Sara Walker, Andrea Burchill, Anne Pitoniak (Columbia)

Both enervating and exhilarating, Housekeeping is a very composed film about eccentric behavior, structured around the impulsive arrivals and departures of characters fundamental to the lives of two sisters in Washington State after World War II. When the girls are on the brink of adolescence, into their lives steps their long-lost aunt Sylvie (Christine Lahti). Tale then becomes that of the proverbial crazy ladies in the old house on the edge of town, but played rigorously, without sentimentality or cuteness.

HOUSE OF BAMBOO
1955, 102 mins, US ✉
D: Samuel Fuller A: Robert Ryan, Robert Stack, Shirley Yamaguchi, Cameron Mitchell, Brad Dexter, Sessue Hayakawa (20th Century-Fox)

A regulation gangster story played against a modern-day Tokyo setting. Novelty of scene and a warm, believable performance by Japanese star Shirley Yamaguchi are two of the better values in the production. The violence introduced seems hardly necessary to the melodramatic points being made. Robert Stack, required to overplay surliness by the direction, is an undercover agent out to break up the gang of renegade Yanks.

HOUSE OF CARDS
1968, 105 mins, US Ⓥ ▭
D: John Guillermin **A:** George Peppard, Inger Stevens, Orson Welles, Keith Michell, Maxine Audley (Universal)

Story has Peppard as a Yank drifter in France who falls into the job of tutor to the young son of the widow of a French general. Peppard offers a nice combo of exuberant cheek and muscle and Inger Stevens as the young widow keeps the romantic angle dangling tantalizingly. Orson Welles's flamboyance fits the role of a menacing conspirator effectively. Director John Guillermin makes the most of highspots but often cannot get the conversational and plot-laying bits off the ground.

HOUSE OF CARDS
1993, 107 mins, US
D: Michael Lessac **A:** Kathleen Turner, Tommy Lee Jones, Asha Menina, Shiloh Strong, Esther Rolle (Penta)

Well made but narrowly one-note in its concerns, drama is triggered by the fatal plunge of an archaeologist, leaving Ruth Matthews (Kathleen Turner) a widow. Ruth soon has to deal with the fact that little daughter Sally (Asha Menina) is not talking anymore. Instead, Menina emits almost deafening, rhythmic shouts when anything seems amiss to her and begins to do weird things, such as building an extraordinary tower of cards. Child psychiatrist Jake Beerlander (Tommy Lee Jones) believes she exhibits classic autistic symptoms.

HOUSE OF DOOM
See: The Black Cat

HOUSE OF DRACULA
1945, 67 mins, US Ⓥ
D: Erle C. Kenton **A:** Lon Chaney, John Carradine, Martha O'Driscoll, Lionel Atwill, Glenn Strange (Universal)

Universal has brought all of its terror figures—Dracula, the .Wolf Man, and Frankenstein's Monster—together in a nifty thriller. Plot twist has two of the

monster heavies taking a sympathetic angle. Each comes to a doctor for help in curing his strange affliction. First to appeal for help from Onslow Stevens is John Carradine, the centuries-old vampire. Next is Lon Chaney, the werewolf. The good doctor eliminates Dracula but finds he himself has acquired the bloodletting urge. In his newly acquired madness he revives Frankenstein's monster.

HOUSE OF FRANKENSTEIN
1944, 70 mins, US Ⓥ
D: Erle C. Kenton **A:** Boris Karloff, J. Carrol Naish, Lon Chaney, John Carradine, Lionel Atwill, George Zucco (Universal)

Frankenstein's Monster, Dracula, and the Wolf Man provide three-ply horror display in this chiller-diller meller. Boris Karloff is the mad scientist. He escapes from prison with deformed J. Carrol Naish, takes over a traveling chamber of horror exhibit to release the skeleton of Dracula for brief forays among the populace, and then goes to the ruins of the Frankenstein castle to secure records of former transplanting research. Lon Chaney is the Wolf Man, while John Carradine steps into the Dracula assignment.

HOUSE OF GAMES
1987, 102 mins, US Ⓥ ⊙
D: David Mamet **A:** Lindsay Crouse, Joe Mantegna, Mike Nussbaum, Lilia Skala, J. T. Walsh (Filmhaus/Orion)

Writer David Mamet's first trip behind the camera as a director is entertaining good fun, an American film noir with Hitchcockian touches and a few dead bodies along the way. Here the famous psychistrist Dr. Margaret Ford (Lindsay Crouse) allows herself to be drawn into a nest of confidence sharks. Mantegna is right on target as one of the screen's most likable baddies. *House of Games* cleverly selects its cons, explains their workings, then twists them around again, all without boring or losing the viewer.

HOUSE OF ROTHSCHILD, THE
1934, 94 mins, US
D: Alfred Werker **A:** George Arliss, Boris Karloff, Loretta Young, Robert Young, C. Aubrey Smith, Reginald Owen (Twentieth Century)

The Rothschild family, through its intimate financial connection with the Napoleonic wars, affords a meaty story. George Arliss plays the father and founder of the family, Mayer Rothschild, and when

the narrative skips 35 years, he is also the son, Nathan, head of the London branch of the banking firm. Nathan's daughter is played by Loretta Young, who never looked better. She falls in love with a Gentile English officer (Robert Young).
1934: Nomination: Best Picture

HOUSE OF STRANGERS
1949, 104 mins, US Ⓥ ⊙
D: Joseph L. Mankiewicz **A:** Edward G. Robinson, Susan Hayward, Richard Conte, Luther Adler, Paul Valentine, Efrem Zimbalist Jr. (20th Century-Fox)

Edward G. Robinson plays a New York East Side Italian banker who switches from barbering to money-lending when he discovers the high interest obtainable. Yarn deals with the hate of three of his sons for their father's unyielding nature and slave-driving tactics. The fourth son (Richard Conte), an attorney with headquarters at the bank, sticks by his father.

HOUSE OF THE SPIRITS, THE
1993, 145 mins, Germany Ⓥ ⊙ ▭
D: Bille August **A:** Jeremy Irons, Meryl Streep, Glenn Close, Winona Ryder, Antonio Banderas (Neue Constantin)

Herky-jerky meller mostly bumps from one dramatic highlight to the next. Pic charts 45 eventful years in the lives of the Trueba family in a South American country very much like Chile. Esteban Trueba (Jeremy Irons) becomes the most powerful rancher in the area, and marries Clara (Meryl Streep). Living with them at the remote hacienda is Esteban's spinster sister Ferula (Glenn Close). Jump ahead to 1963, and their daughter, the lovely 17-year-old Blanca (Winona Ryder), is in love with handsome Pedro (Antonio Banderas), the rebellious son of her father's chief ranch hand.

HOUSE OF USHER
(UK: THE FALL OF THE HOUSE OF USHER)
1960, 79 mins, US Ⓥ ▭
D: Roger Corman **A:** Vincent Price, Mark Damon, Myrna Fahey, Harry Ellerbe (American International/Alta Vista)

It's not precisely the Edgar Allan Poe short story, but it's a reasonably diverting and handsomely mounted variation without ruining the impact of the chilling climax, in which Madeline (Myrna Fahey), buried alive by her brother (Vincent Price) while under a cataleptic trance, breaks free from her living tomb. The cobweb-ridden,

fungus-infected, mist-pervaded atmosphere of cadaverous gloom has been photographed with great skill by Floyd Crosby.

HOUSE OF WAX
1953, 90 mins, US Ⓥ ⊙
D: Andre de Toth **A:** Vincent Price, Frank Lovejoy, Phyllis Kirk, Carolyn Jones, Paul Picerini, Charles Bronson (Warner)

This remake of *Mystery of the Wax Museum* (1933) is given the full 3-D treatment. Andre de Toth's direction, while uneven, is nonetheless geared it to the medium—chairs flying into the audience, cancan dancers pirouetting full into the camera, the barker's Ping-Pong ball, as a pitchman's prop, likewise shooting out at the audience, the muscular menace springing as if from the theater into the action. The stereophonic sound further assists in the illusion. Vincent Price is capital as the No. 1 menace.

HOUSE ON CARROLL STREET, THE
1988, 100 mins, US Ⓥ
D: Peter Yates **A:** Kelly McGillis, Jeff Daniels, Mandy Patinkin, Christopher Rhode, Jessica Tandy (Orion)

In this story of a sleuth trailing improbable characters involved in a ridiculous conspiracy in 1951, Kelly McGillis is the idealistic and hardly convincing political activist who collects about three clues and figures out Patinkin is smuggling Nazis in by having them take the names of dead Jews. Jeff Daniels is Ned to McGillis's Nancy Drew. He is the FBI agent who manages to come in at exactly the right moments to save her from whatever perilous predicament she is in at the time.

HOUSE ON HAUNTED HILL
1958, 75 mins, US Ⓥ ⊙
D: William Castle **A:** Vincent Price, Carol Ohmart, Richard Long, Alan Marshal, Elisha Cook Jr. (Allied Artists)

The screenplay is the one about the group of people who promise to spend the night in a haunted house. Vincent Price is offering $10,000 to anyone who lasts out the night. There is a gimmick in the plot that explains the screams, ghosts, bubbling vats of lye, and perambulating skeletons. There is some good humor in the dialogue which not only pays off well against the ghostly elements, but provides a release for laughter so it does not explode in the suspense sequences. The characters are interesting and not outlandish.

HOUSE ON HAUNTED HILL
1999, 96 mins, US Ⓥ ⊙ ▭

D: William Malone **A:** Geoffrey Rush, Famke Janssen, Taye Diggs, Peter Gallagher, Chris Kattan, Ali Larter (Dark Castle/Warner)

Given the irredeemable cheesiness of the original 1958 *House on Haunted Hill*, it's no surprise to find the new horror opus is a slicker and scarier piece of work. But it's still nothing but a gussied-up B movie. The suavely sardonic host is Stephen Price (Geoffrey Rush), multimillionaire owner-designer of amusement parks. Viewing some grisly footage of a Depression-era insane-asylum riot, Evelyn (Famke Janssen), Stephen's decadent trophy wife, demands he rent the monolithic Art Deco edifice so she can throw a birthday party there. He agrees, but replaces her guest list with his own. When he greets the invitees, however, except for Pritchett (Chris Kattan), the descendant of the asylum's original owner, he doesn't know any of these people. Evelyn didn't invite them, either.

HOUSE ON 92ND STREET, THE
1945, 83 mins, US

D: Henry Hathaway **A:** William Eythe, Lloyd Nolan, Signe Hasso, Gene Lockhart, Leo G. Carroll (20th Century-Fox)

An absorbing documentation that's frequently heavily steeped melodrama. Film ties together revelations of the vast Nazi spy system in the United States. Lloyd Nolan is the FBI inspector in charge of ferreting out the espionage on a secret formula sought by the Nazis; William Eythe is the young German-American sent to Germany by US-located Nazis (and the FBI) to learn espionage and sabotage; Signe Hasso plays a key link.
1945: Best Original Story (Charles G. Booth)

HOUSE ON TELEGRAPH HILL, THE
1951, 93 mins, US

D: Robert Wise **A:** Richard Basehart, Valentina Cortese, William Lundigan, Fay Baker, Steven Geray (20th Century-Fox)

A slow but interesting melodrama with San Francisco's quaint hill residential sections as background. Yarn starts in the femme concentration camp at Belsen. One Polish woman (Valentina Cortese) gets to America, on a dead woman's identity papers, to find she's pseudo-mother to a boy, heir to a fortune, whose guardian (Richard Basehart) is scheming to acquire the inheritance.

1951: Nomination: Best B&W Art Direction

HOUSE PARTY
1990, 100 mins, US Ⓥ ⊙

D: Reginald Hudlin **A:** Christopher Reid, Robin Harris, Christopher Martin, Martin Lawrence, Tisha Campbell (New Line)

House Party captures contemporary black teen culture in a way that's fresh, commercial, and very catchy, blending comedy, hip-hop music, and dancing in a pic that moves to a kinetic, nonstop rhythm. Rap duo Kid 'N' Play (Christopher Reid and Christopher Martin) play colleagues in rhyme, trying to get away with throwing a booming house party the night Play's parents are away and Kid is grounded by his Pop (Robin Harris) for getting in a fight at school.

HOUSE PARTY 2
1991, 94 mins, US Ⓥ ⊙

D: Doug McHenry, George Jackson **A:** Christopher Reid, Christopher Martin, Tisha Campbell, Iman, Martin Lawrence (New Line)

The crowd's the same, but the atmosphere's different in this disappointing follow-up to low-budget hit *House Party,* lacking the original's smarts and cinematic flair. Pic relies heavily on vulgarities and no-brainer plot twists. Whoopi Goldberg cameos as a nightmarish college disciplinarian in a dream scene.

HOUSE PARTY 3
1994, 93 mins, US Ⓥ ⊙

D: Eric Meza **A:** Christopher Reid, Christopher Martin, David Edwards, Angela Means, Tisha Campbell, Betty Lester (New Line)

House Party 3 should appeal only to the most ardent fans of the previous pix and Kid 'N' Play's animated TV series. New installment revolves around the engagement of Kid (Christopher Reid) to beautiful Veda (Angela Means). Kid's anxieties and fears of matrimony serve as weak glue to a loosely structured comedy composed of uninspired vignettes.

HOUSESITTER
1992, 100 mins, US Ⓥ ⊙

D: Frank Oz **A:** Steve Martin, Goldie Hawn, Dana Delany, Julie Harris, Donald Moffat (Universal/Imagine)

Tediously unfunny screwball comedy. Goldie Hawn is grating and Martin is more obnoxious than endearing. Martin's in love with wholesome Dana Delany, who refuses to marry him and move into the new architectural showcase he's built out in the countryside. Enter Hawn. After they have a one-night stand, she tracks him to the empty house. She moves in, telling everyone in town that she's his new wife, and they believe her.

HOWARD . . . A NEW BREED OF HERO
See: Howard the Duck

HOWARDS END
1992, 140 mins, UK ⊘ ⊙ ▭
D: James Ivory **A:** Anthony Hopkins, Vanessa Redgrave, Helena Bonham Carter, Emma Thompson, James Wilby (Merchant Ivory)

A most compelling drama. Ruth Wilcox (Vanessa Redgrave) on her deathbed scrawls a note bequeathing her beloved estate Howards End to Margaret Schlegel (Emma Thompson). Redgrave's aristocratic husband Henry (Anthony Hopkins) and daughter Evie (real-life daughter Jemma Redgrave) destroy the note to keep the estate in the family. Hopkins portrays an upper-crust nasty with chilling understatement. Thompson is immensely sympathetic. Helena Bonham Carter proves again that she's the best actress today at embodying the look and spirit of period roles.
1992: Best Actress (Emma Thompson), Adapted Screenplay, Art Direction
Nominations: Best Picture, Director, Supp. Actress (Vanessa Redgrave), Cinematography, Original Score, Costume Design

HOWARD THE DUCK
(UK: HOWARD . . . A NEW BREED OF HERO)
1986, 111 mins, US ⊘ ⊙
D: Willard Huyck **A:** Lea Thompson, Jeffrey Jones, Tim Robbins, Ed Gale, Chip Zien, Paul Guilfoyle (Lucasfilm)

Scripters have taken the cigar-chompin', beer-drinkin' Marvel Comics character and turned him into a wide-eyed, cutesy, midget-sized extraterrestrial. Howard encounters rock singer Beverly Switzler (Lea Thompson) after a few harrowing minutes on Earth and they become instant friends after he defends her from a couple of menacing punkers. Pic then lapses into formulaic predictability.

HOW GREEN WAS MY VALLEY
1941, 120 mins, US ⊘ ⊙
D: John Ford **A:** Walter Pidgeon, Maureen O'Hara, Donald Crisp, Roddy McDowall, Barry Fitzgerald (20th Century-Fox)

Based on a bestselling novel, this saga of Welsh coal-mining life is replete with much human interest, romance, conflict, and almost every other human emotion. Donald Crisp and Sara Allgood, as the heads of the Welsh mining family, are an inspired casting. Walter Pidgeon is excellent as the minister, Maureen O'Hara splendid as the object of his unrequited love. And, above all, there is Roddy McDowall. He's winsome, manly, and histrionically proficient in an upright, two-fisted manner.
1941: Best Picture, Director, Supp. Actor (Donald Crisp), B&W Cinematography, B&W Interior Decoration (Richard Day, Nathan Juran)
Nominations: Best Supp. Actress (Sara Allgood), Screenplay, Editing, Scoring of a Dramatic Picture, Sound

HOW I WON THE WAR
1967, 109 mins, UK ⊘ ⊙
D: Richard Lester **A:** Michael Crawford, John Lennon, Roy Kinnear, Lee Montague, Jack MacGowran, Michael Hordern (United Artists)

Patrick Ryan's novel has been adapted into a screenplay which, as directed by Richard Lester, substitutes motion for emotion, reeling for feeling, and crude slapstick for telling satire. Michael Crawford is top-featured as a gee-whiz British army officer whose unthinking ineptitude kills off all members of his unit. John Lennon, whose billing far exceeds his part, and contribution, plays one of the crew.

HOWLING, THE
1981, 91 mins, Canada ⊘ ⊙
D: Joe Dante **A:** Dee Wallace, Patrick Macnee, Dennis Dugan, Christopher Stone, Belinda Balaski, Kevin McCarthy (International/Avco Embassy)

Joe Dante's work reflects Alfred Hitchcock's insistence that terror and suspense work best when counterbalanced by a chuckle or two. There are good one-liners throughout, some delivered straight-faced. But this is supposed to be a horror film. And it definitely is in a good old-fashioned way, complete with a girl venturing out alone with a flashlight to investigate a weird noise. In large part the picture works because of the makeup effects created by Rob Bottin.

HOWLING II: YOUR SISTER IS A WEREWOLF
(UK: HOWLING II: STIRBA— WEREWOLF BITCH)
1985, 90 mins, US ⊘ ⊙
D: Philippe Mora **A:** Christopher Lee, An-

nie McEnroe, Reb Brown, Marsha A. Hunt, Sybil Danning, Ferdy Mayne (Hemdale/Granite)

A generally lackluster horror item. Tale opens with the funeral of a femme newsperson; in attendance is Christopher Lee as an expert on werewolves. He advises that the dead woman was such a creature, and is joined by her brother (Reb Brown) and colleague (Annie McEnroe) on a trip to Transylvania to destroy the werewolf queen (Sybil Danning), who is actually Lee's sister. Despite fancy editing tricks and a few touches of grim humor, suspense is woefully lacking.

HOW STELLA GOT HER GROOVE BACK
1998, 124 mins, US Ⓥ ⊙
D: Kevin Rodney Sullivan **A:** Angela Bassett, Taye Diggs, Regina King, Whoopi Goldberg, Suzzanne Douglas, Michael J. Pagan (20th Century-Fox)

Outrageously glossy and sometimes quite funny, this fantasy-driven romance about a gorgeous woman who rediscovers her sexual self in scenic Jamaica is choppy, poorly structured, and unconvincing on any number of levels. Stella (Angela Bassett) is a stunning, fit, highpowered 40-year-old San Francisco stockbroker. In other words, a totally realized woman—except, natch, for her love life. Stella takes a vacation with Delilah (Whoopi Goldberg), who encourages her friend to let herself go. Stella meets a strikingly handsome local man, Winston Shakespeare (Taye Diggs). The only problem is that Winston is only 20 years old. When she is paged to comfort the critically ill Delilah in New York, the remainder of the picture lurches awkwardly about as Winston heads for Marin County to see if there's a future with Stella. The dazzling Bassett is a delight to watch throughout, and obligingly plays second banana to Goldberg whenever the latter turns up to steal any and every scene she wants.

HOW THE WEST WAS WON
1962, 152 mins, US Ⓥ ⊙ ▭
D: Henry Hathaway, John Ford, George Marshall **A:** James Stewart, Henry Fonda, Gregory Peck, Debbie Reynolds, Richard Widmark, John Wayne (M-G-M/Cinerama)

It would be hard to imagine a subject that lends itself more strikingly to the widescreen process than this yarn of the pioneers who opened the American west. George Marshall has the credit for the buffalo stampede, started by the Indians when the railroad was moving out west. This magnificently directed sequence is as vivid as anything ever put on celluloid. Undoubtedly the highlight of Henry Hathaway's contribution is the chase of outlaws who attempt to hold up a train. John Ford's directorial stint is limited to the Civil War sequences, and there is the fullest evidence of his high professional standards.
1963: Best Original Story & Screenplay, Sound, Editing
Nominations: Best Picture, Color Cinematography, Color Costume Design, Color Art Direction, Original Music Score

HOW TO BE VERY, VERY POPULAR
1955, 89 mins, US ▭
D: Nunnally Johnson **A:** Betty Grable, Sheree North, Robert Cummings, Charles Coburn, Tommy Noonan, Fred Clark (20th Century-Fox)

Wild and wacky are dressed up considerably in eye appeal by having Betty Grable and Sheree North running through most of the footage in costumes appropriate to their striptease profession. These caperings concern two strippers who can identify the bald-headed man who guns down ecdysiast Noel Toy right in the middle of her act in a San Francisco honkytonk.

HOW TO FILL A WILD BIKINI
See: How to Stuff a Wild Bikini

HOW TO GET AHEAD IN ADVERTISING
1989, 95 mins, UK Ⓥ ⊙
D: Bruce Robinson **A:** Richard E. Grant, Rachel Ward, Richard Wilson, Jacqueline Tong, John Shrapnel (Handmade)

As a hotshot go-getter in the British equivalent of Madison Avenue, Richard E. Grant is having a problem coming up with an original campaign for a pimple cream. When a small boil breaks out on his own neck, Grant realizes the stress has become too much. The boil begins to grow—and starts to talk, giving form to all that's vile and venal in his nature. The picture would be genuinely hilarious were the subject matter not so overworked.

HOW TO MAKE AN AMERICAN QUILT
1995, 116 mins, US Ⓥ ⊙
D: Jocelyn Moorhouse **A:** Winona Ryder, Anne Bancroft, Ellen Burstyn, Kate Nel-

ligan, Jean Simmons, Alfre Woodard (Amblin/Universal)

Finn Dodd (Winona Ryder) is 26 and wrestling with a thesis on handicraft and culture and on the cusp of marriage to her carpenter boyfriend, Sam (Dermot Mulroney). Seeking a bit of breathing space, she retreats to the small Northern California town of her youth and the sanctuary of a quilting circle of family and friends. The real dilemma is that this sweet, sincere tale doesn't have a lot to tell that's novel. At best, cast members have a fleeting opportunity to display a glimmer of their talent. Still, several, including Alfre Woodard and Jean Simmons, manage to make their instants vivid.

HOW TO MARRY A MILLIONAIRE
1953, 95 mins, US ⓥ ⊙ ▭
D: Jean Negulesco A: Betty Grable, Marilyn Monroe, Lauren Bacall, David Wayne, Rory Calhoun, Cameron Mitchell (20th Century-Fox)

The plot has three girls pooling physical and monetary resources for a millionaire manhunt and the chuckles are constant. Certain for audience favor is Monroe's blonde with astigmatism who goes through life bumping into things, including men, because she thinks glasses would detract. Also captivating is Grable's Loco, a friendly, cuddly blonde. As the brains of the trio, Bacall's Schatze is a wisecracking, hard-shelled gal who gives up millions for love and gets both.
1953: Nomination: Best Color Costume Design

HOW TO MURDER YOUR WIFE
1965, 118 mins, US ⓥ
D: Richard Quine A: Jack Lemmon, Virna Lisi, Terry-Thomas, Eddie Mayehoff, Claire Trevor (Murder/United Artists)

George Axelrod's plot deals with the antics of a bachelor cartoonist, played by Jack Lemmon, who has a policy of acting out the escapades of his newsprint sleuth hero to test their credibility before actually committing them to paper. The comedian's efforts are considerable and consistent, but finesse and desire aren't enough to overcome the fact that Axelrod's script doesn't make the most of its potentially antic situations.

HOW TO SAVE A MARRIAGE AND RUIN YOUR LIFE
1968, 102 mins, US ▭
D: Fielder Cook A: Dean Martin, Stella Stevens, Eli Wallach, Anne Jackson, Betty Field, Jack Albertson (Columbia)

An amusing comedy about divorce and marital infidelity. Plot complications derive from Wallach's longtime infidelity to Jackson. Martin confuses Jackson with Stevens, latter assuming his romantic advances are legit, instead of the ruse which Martin intends.

HOW TO STEAL A DIAMOND IN FOUR UNEASY LESSONS
See: The Hot Rock

HOW TO STEAL A MILLION
1966, 127 mins, US ⓥ ▭
D: William Wyler A: Audrey Hepburn, Peter O'Toole, Eli Wallach, Hugh Griffith, Charles Boyer, Marcel Dalio (20th Century-Fox)

Plot centers on a fraud in the art world via forging "masterpieces." Audrey Hepburn's father, Hugh Griffith, is a faker of genius. She has given up trying to reform him. Peter O'Toole is a private detective who femme thinks is a burglar after she discovers him in the family home in the middle of the night apparently trying to make off with a canvas.

HOW TO STUFF A WILD BIKINI (UK: HOW TO FILL A WILD BIKINI)
1965, 90 mins, US ⓥ ▭
D: William Asher A: Annette Funicello, Dwayne Hickman, Brian Donlevy, Harvey Lembeck, Buster Keaton, Mickey Rooney (American International)

Script is hit-and-miss, twirling around a mysterious redhead suddenly appearing to fill a bikini which has been floating in midair. Frankie Avalon, on duty in Tahiti with his naval-reserve unit, enlists the services of Buster Keaton, a witch doctor, to determine whether his girlfriend back home—Annette Funicello—is being true to him. Then there's Mickey Rooney, a fast-talking press agent.

HOW TO SUCCEED IN BUSINESS WITHOUT REALLY TRYING
1967, 121 mins, US ⓥ ⊙ ▭
D: David Swift A: Robert Morse, Michele Lee, Rudy Vallee, Anthony Teague, Maureen Arthur (Mirisch)

An entertaining, straightforward filming of the legituner, featuring many thesps in their stage roles. David Swift's production is generally fast-moving in tracing the rags-to-riches rise of Robert Morse within Rudy Vallee's biz complex. Colorful production values maintain great eye appeal. Most of Frank Loesser's literate melodies

584

have been retained including "I Believe in You," "The Company Way," "Been a Long Day," and "Brotherhood of Man."

HUANG TUDI (YELLOW EARTH)
1984, 89 mins, China ⓥ
D: Chen Kaige **A:** Xue Bai, Wang Xueqi, Tan Tuo, Liu Qiang (Guangxi)

Simple story is told with considerable depth of feeling, allied to classical direction and impeccably composed images. The year is 1939, and China is at war with Japan. However, in the remote north of Shaanxi province, the war is unknown and far away. Gu Qing (Wang Xueqi), a Communist soldier, is sent to Shaanbei, partly to collect folk songs of the region, partly to influence the locals in favor of communism. He stays with a poor family—a widower, his 12-year-old daughter, Cui Qiao (Xue Bai), and 10-year-old son, Hanhan (Liu Qiang). At first they are suspicious of the stranger, but gradually he wins them over.

HUCKLEBERRY FINN
1931, 79 mins, US
D: Norman Taurog **A:** Jackie Coogan, Mitzi Green, Junior Durkin, Jackie Searl, Clara Blandick, Jane Darwell (Paramount)

It's the second Mark Twain story to be done by Paramount, first being *Tom Sawyer.* Same quartet reunite in Jackie Coogan, Junior Durkin, Mitzi Green, and Jackie Searl. Durkin is excellent throughout, overshadowing Coogan, who in spots is permitted to appear and talk in a too adult manner.

HUCKLEBERRY FINN
1939, 88 mins, US ⓥ
D: Richard Thorpe **A:** Mickey Rooney, Walter Connolly, William Frawley, Rex Ingram, Lynne Carver (M-G-M)

Picture is a fairly close adaptation of the original Mark Twain work, but has not been able to catch the rare and sparkling humor and general sincerity of the author's original. Furthermore, young Rooney seems too mature for his years. Many opportunities for comedy situations are missed. Rex Ingram gives an honest and effective characterization of the runaway slave.

HUCKSTERS, THE
1947, 110 mins, US ⓥ
D: Jack Conway **A:** Clark Gable, Deborah Kerr, Sydney Greenstreet, Adolphe Menjou, Ava Gardner, Keenan Wynn (M-G-M)

Deborah Kerr's cast as a very proper Sutton Place war hero–general's widow, with two children who go for Clark Gable, as she goes, to the extent of a quickie plane flight to his Bel Air layout, where he's cutting a new radio program for Beautee Soap, tycooned by the irascible and tyrannical Evan Llewellyn Evans. Sydney Greenstreet's portrayal of the soap despot emerges as the performance of the picture, as does Keenan Wynn as the ham ex-burlesque candy butcher gone radio comic. Gable looks trim and fit but somehow a shade too mature for the capricious role of the huckster.

HUD
1963, 113 mins, US ⓥ ⊙ 🖵
D: Martin Ritt **A:** Paul Newman, Melvyn Douglas, Patricia Neal, Brandon de Wilde, Whit Bissell (Paramount/Salem/Dover)

The new westerner is Hud (Paul Newman), noxious son of old Homer Bannon (Melvyn Douglas), pioneer Texas Panhandler who detests his offspring with a passion that persists to his bitter end. It is never clear exactly why the old man harbors such a deep-rooted, irrevocable grudge against his lad. Newman creates a virile, pernicious figure. The characteristics of old age are marvelously captured by Douglas. Another fine performance is by Brandon de Wilde as Newman's nephew. Patricia Neal comes through with a rich and powerful performance as the housekeeper.

1963: Best Actress (Patricia Neal), Supp. Actor (Melvyn Douglas), B&W Cinematography

Nominations: Best Director, Actor (Paul Newman), Adapted Screenplay, B&W Art Direction

HUDSON HAWK
1991, 95 mins, US ⓥ ⊙
D: Michael Lehmann **A:** Bruce Willis, Danny Aiello, Andie MacDowell, James Coburn, Richard E. Grant, Sandra Bernhard (Tri-Star/Silver/Ace Bone)

Ever wondered what a Three Stooges short would look like with a $40-million budget? Then meet *Hudson Hawk,* a relentlessly annoying clay duck that crashlands in a sea of wretched excess and silliness. Those willing to check their brains at the door may find sparse amusement in pic's frenzied pace. Bruce Willis plays just-released-from-prison cat burglar Hudson Hawk, who's immediately drawn into a plot to steal a bunch of Leonardo da Vinci artifacts.

HUDSUCKER PROXY, THE
1994, 111 mins, US Ⓥ ⊙
D: Joel Coen **A:** Tim Robbins, Jennifer Jason Leigh, Paul Newman, Charles Durning, John Mahoney (Warner/Silver)

One of the most inspired and technically stunning pastiches of old Hollywood pictures ever to come out of the new Hollywood. But a pastiche this $40-million production remains, with a hole in the middle where some emotion and humanity should be. Norville Barnes (Tim Robbins), straight off the bus from Muncie, IN, lands a mailroom job at the enormous Hudsucker Industries. Norville is installed as the firm's president by the cigar-chomping Machiavellian executive Sidney J. Mussberger (Paul Newman), who intends to forestall a public takeover by lowering investor confidence. But Norville surprises one and all. Plotwise, it's all been done before. But for connoisseurs of filmmaking style and technique, *Hudsucker* is a source of constant delight and occasional thrills.

HUE AND CRY
1947, 82 mins, UK Ⓥ
D: Charles Crichton **A:** Alastair Sim, Valerie White, Jack Warner, Harry Fowler (Ealing)

Story revolves around a gang of crooks who use a serial story in a kids' weekly as a means of communication. Joe Kirby, an imaginative youngster, spots this, and in spite of discouragement from his boss and an alleged detective, he perseveres, interests his pals, and brings off a great coup when boys of all ages flock to the bomb-ravaged wastes of dockland for a roundup of the criminals. Queer camera angles and shadows can add little thrill when the original material lacks it.

HUMAN CARGO
1936, 65 mins, US
D: Allan Dwan **A:** Claire Trevor, Brian Donlevy, Alan Dinehar, Ralph Morgan, Helen Troy, Rita Hayworth (20th Century-Fox)

Racket exposed and smashed in this instance is that concerned with smuggling aliens into the United States, and then blackmailing them for the rest of their lives under threat of exposure. Brian Donlevy is the ace reporter and Claire Trevor the society girl who wants to make her own living as a journalist. Rita Hayworth as a dancer who's mixed up with the gangsters is a good-looking brunette and not bad on performance.

HUMAN COMEDY, THE
1943, 119 mins, US Ⓥ
D: Clarence Brown **A:** Mickey Rooney, Frank Morgan, Fay Bainter, Ray Collins, Van Johnson, Donna Reed (M-G-M)

William Saroyan's initial original screenplay is a brilliant sketch of the basic fundamentals of the American way of life, transferred to the screen with exceptional fidelity. Rooney is the major breadwinner of his little family following departure of his older brother (Van Johnson) into the army service. Rooney shines brilliantly.
1943: Best Original Story
Nominations: Best Picture, Director, Actor (Mickey Rooney), B&W Cinematography

HUMAN CONDITION, PART I: NO GREATER LOVE, THE
See: Ningen No Joken I-II

HUMAN CONDITION, PART II: THE ROAD TO ETERNITY, THE
See: Ningen No Joken III-IV

HUMAN CONDITION, PART III: A SOLDIER'S TALE, THE
See: Ningen No Joken V-VI

HUMAN DESIRE
1954, 90 mins, US Ⓥ
D: Fritz Lang **A:** Glenn Ford, Gloria Grahame, Broderick Crawford, Edgar Buchanan (Columbia)

The audience meets some wretched characters on the railroad in this adaptation of the Emile Zola novel, *The Human Beast*. Fritz Lang, director, goes overboard in his effort to create mood. Broderick Crawford is utterly frustrated in his effort to please his wife (Gloria Grahame) and stay on an even keel with his heartless boss. Grahame is a miserable character, alternately denying and admitting she has given herself to other men. Glenn Ford dates Grahame and toys with the idea of murdering her husband.

HUMAN FACTOR, THE
1979, 115 mins, UK Ⓥ
D: Otto Preminger **A:** Richard Attenborough, John Gielgud, Derek Jacobi, Robert Morley, Ann Todd, Nicol Williamson (M-G-M/Preminger)

Graham Greene's low-key, highly absorbing 1978 novel of an aging English double agent finding himself trapped into defecting to Moscow and leaving his family behind may have seemed like ideal material for Otto Preminger's style of dispassionate ambiguity, but helmer brings little atmosphere or feeling to the delicate ticks of the story.

HUMAN JUNGLE, THE
1954, 82 mins, US

D: Joseph M. Newman **A:** Gary Merrill, Jan Sterling, Paula Raymond, Emile Meyer, Regis Toomey, Chuck Connors (Allied Artists)

A sock big-city police story packed with sex as well as violence and excitement. The politics of a metropolitan police department backdrop an almost documentary narrative which has been imaginatively directed by Joseph M. Newman with punchy overtones. Gary Merrill, a police captain, is prevailed upon to head the notorious Heights district of the city, where conditions have reached the point that no one is safe.

HUMANOIDS FROM THE DEEP
1980, 80 mins, US ⓥ

D: Barbara Peeters **A:** Doug McClure, Ann Turkel, Vic Morrow, Cindy Weintraub (New World)

Tried-and-true formula of countless sci-fiers of the 1950s is revived as gruesome, amphibious creatures rise from the ocean to stalk and destroy terrified humans. General pattern here has monsters systematically killing the guys and raping the girls. James Horner's score makes it seem that more is happening than actually takes place.

HUMORESQUE
1946, 123 mins, US ⓥ ⊙

D: Jean Negulesco **A:** Joan Crawford, John Garfield, Oscar Levant J. Carrol Naish, Joan Chandler, Tom D'Andrea (Warner)

Humoresque combines classical music and drama into a top-quality motion picture. A score of unusual excellence gives freshness to standard classics and plays as important a part as Fannie Hurst's familiar story of a violinist who rises to concert heights from the Lower East Side of New York. Principal footage goes to John Garfield as the young violinist who devotes his life to music. He turns in a distinguished, thoroughly believable performance. Joan Crawford's role is an acting part, rather than a typical femme-star assignment, and she makes the most of it.
1946: Nomination: Best Scoring of a Dramatic Picture

HUNCHBACK OF NOTRE DAME, THE
1923, 135 mins, US ⓥ ⊙ ⊗

D: Wallace Worsley **A:** Lon Chaney, Ernest Torrence, Patsy Ruth Miller, Norman Kerry, Kate Lester, Brandon Hurst (Universal Super-Jewel)

A two-hour nightmare. It's murderous, hideous, and repulsive. Lon Chaney's performance as a performance entitles him to starring honors. His misshapen figure from the hump on his back to the dead-eyed eye on his face cannot stand off his acting nor his acrobatics, nor his general work of excellence throughout this film. Patsy Ruth Miller is Esmeralda, a sweetly pretty girl carrying her troubles nicely enough for the heavy work thrust upon her.

HUNCHBACK OF NOTRE DAME, THE
1939, 115 mins, US ⓥ ⊙

D: William Dieterle **A:** Charles Laughton, Cedric Hardwicke, Maureen O'Hara, Thomas Mitchell, Edmond O'Brien (RKO)

Parading vivid and gruesome horror, with background of elaborate medieval pageantry and mob scenes, *Hunchback of Notre Dame* is a super thriller-chiller. From a strictly critical viewpoint, picture has its shortcomings. The elaborate sets and wide production sweep overshadow to a great extent the detailed dramatic motivation of the Victor Hugo tale.
1939: Nominations: Best Score, Sound

HUNCHBACK OF NOTRE DAME, THE
1957, 103 mins, US ⓥ ▭

D: Jean Delannoy **A:** Gina Lollobrigida, Anthony Quinn, Jean Danet, Alain Cuny (Allied Artists)

This version of the Victor Hugo classic, although beautifully photographed and extravagantly produced, is ponderous, often dull, and far overlength. Gina Lollobrigida appears to be somewhat miscast as a naive gypsy girl of 15th-century Paris, but occasionally displays flashes of spirit. Quinn, as the hunchbacked bell ringer of Notre Dame who saves the gypsy girl from hanging and hides her within the sanctuary of the cathedral, gives a well-etched impression of the difficult role. His makeup is not as extreme as either of the two previous incarnations.

HUNCHBACK OF NOTRE DAME, THE
1996, 86 mins, US ⓥ ⊙

D: Gary Trousdale, Kirk Wise (Walt Disney)

It's probably no surprise that the deaf, one-eyed, misshapen monster would resurface in the Disney version as a geewhiz, cuddly creature. On the other hand, it is surprising just how dark and horrific Disney's visually astonishing 34th animated feature is for most of its 86 minutes. Scripters have centered the action on the gypsy-born hunchback Quasimodo (voiced with an attractive, childlike innocence by Tom Hulce), the dashing heroic captain Phoebus (brought to sonorous life by Kevin Kline), and the beautiful gypsy dancer with whom both men fall in love, the green-eyed Esmeralda (gorgeously voiced by Demi Moore, with Heidi Mollenhauer doing the singing); and given the story a ludicrous ending. They've also given Quasi, as he's called, the inevitable Disney sidekicks, in this case three wisecracking gargoyles.

HUNGER
See: Sult

HUNGER, THE
1983, 97 mins, US Ⓥ ⊙ ▭
D: Tony Scott A: Catherine Deneuve, David Bowie, Susan Sarandon, Cliff De Young, Dan Hedaya (M-G-M/United Artists)

The Hunger is all visual and aural flash, although this modern vampire story looks so great, as do its three principal performers, and is so bizarre that it possesses a certain perverse appeal. Opening sequence provides viewers with a pretty good idea of what's in store. Catherine Deneuve and David Bowie pick up a couple of punky rock-and-rollers. Deneuve and Bowie commit a double murder in their elegantly appointed New York apartment, and the prevailing motif of sex mixed with bloody death is established.

HUNG FAN KUI
(RUMBLE IN THE BRONX)
1995, 105 mins, Hong Kong Ⓥ ⊙ ▭
D: Stanley Tong A: Jackie Chan, Anita Mui, Bill Tung, Yip Fong-wa, Bai Cheunwai (Golden Harvest)

The bod's still in shape, and the looks are still boyish, but 40-something Jackie Chan takes it a tad more gently in an enjoyable comedy-actioner whose ooh-aah moments are mostly confined to the last few reels. This NY-set update of Bruce Lee's *Return of the Dragon* lacks the sheer oomph of Chan's best pics. Pic climaxes with visual showpieces (like the supermarket being demolished and a hovercraft

run amok on the streets) that lack a human dimension, though Chan wins his usual stripes for death-defying stunts (one of which put him temporarily in a wheelchair).

HUNTED, THE
1995, 110 mins, US Ⓥ ⊙
D: J. F. Lawton A: Christopher Lambert, John Lone, Joan Chen, Yoshio Harada, Yoko Shimada, Mari Natsuki (Bregman-Baer/Davis)

Grisly yet often laughable actioner. Christopher Lambert stars as a New York businessman in Japan who happens to pick up, bed, and then witness the murder of a mysterious woman (Joan Chen) by a ninja assassin, Kinjo (John Lone). Wounded and now the target of the ninja cult, Lambert's character finds a benefactor in a samurai (Yoshio Harada) who, it turns out, wants to use the befuddled Westerner as bait to settle a centuries-old feud.

HUNTER, THE
1980, 117 mins, US Ⓥ ⊙
D: Buzz Kulik A: Steve McQueen, Eli Wallach, Kathryn Harrold, Ben Johnson (Paramount/Rastar/Mort Engelberg)

Fact that the overlong pic is based on adventures of a modern-day bounty hunter may have hampered filmmakers' imagination, as attempt to render contradictions of real-life Ralph "Papa" Thorson has made for an annoyingly unrealized and childish on-screen character. Steve McQueen may have felt that the time had come to revise his persona a bit, but what's involved here is desecration. Given star's rep since *Bullitt* as a terrific driver, someone thought it might be cute to make him a lousy one here, but seeing him crash stupidly into car after car runs the gag into the ground.

HUNT FOR RED OCTOBER, THE
1990, 137 mins, US Ⓥ ⊙ ▭
D: John McTiernan A: Sean Connery, Alec Baldwin, Scott Glenn, Sam Neill, James Earl Jones, Joss Ackland (Paramount)

A terrific adventure yarn. Tom Clancy's 1984 cold-war thriller has been thoughtfully adapted to reflect the mellowing in the US-Soviet relationship. Sean Connery is splendid as the renegade Soviet nuclearsub captain pursued by CIA analyst Alec Baldwin and the fleets of both superpowers as he heads for the coast of Maine. Baldwin's intelligent and likable performance makes his Walter Mittyish charac-

ter come alive. He's combating not only the bulk of the Soviet fleet but also the reflexive anti-Communist mentality of most pursuing on the US side—not including his wise and avuncular CIA superior James Earl Jones.
1990: Best Sound Effects Editing
Nominations: Best Editing, Sound

HUNTING PARTY, THE
1971, 108 mins, UK ⓥ
D: Don Medford **A:** Oliver Reed, Candice Bergen, Gene Hackman, Simon Oakland, Mitchell Ryan, L. Q. Jones (United Artists)

Oliver Reed (who's illiterate) and his gang, kidnap a teacher (Candice Bergen) who turns out to be the wife of the local cattle baron (Gene Hackman), who is out on a hunting party with some other millionaire friends. When he hears the news, Hackman starts a search for the gang, armed with new high-power rifles capable of killing from 800 yards. Seldom has so much fake blood been splattered for so little reason.

HUOZHE
(US: TO LIVE)
1994, 125 mins, Hong Kong ⓥ
D: Zhang Yimou **A:** Ge You, Gong Li, Niu Ben, Guo Tao, Jiang Wu, Liu Tianchi (Era)

A family drama set across 30 years of modern Chinese history, *To Live* is a well-crafted but in no way earthshaking entry in the helmer's oeuvre, topped by finely judged perfs by Gong Li and Ge You as an average couple tossed like corks in a story by civil war, revolution, and political strife. By adopting a relatively cool photographic look and distanced shooting style, Zhang rarely develops a head of steam to roll the story over the political and social changes that impinge on the characters. Result more often parades by rather than engaging the emotions for any significant period.

HURRICANE, THE
1937, 110 mins, US ⓥ ◉
D: John Ford **A:** Dorothy Lamour, Jon Hall, Mary Astor, C. Aubrey Smith, Thomas Mitchell, Raymond Massey (Goldwyn)

A scenically pretentious and colorful spectacle which has as its climax a hurricane sequence that is compellingly realistic. The force of the story does not stop with the hurricane triumph nor the brutality of prison officers, pictured as worse

than ever accredited to Devil's Island. Neither does it stop with the successful dramatic escape of the romantic lead (Jon Hall) amid frightful odds. There is also a highly emotional love story woven around Hall and Dorothy Lamour, latter playing the native girl.
1937: Best Sound Recording
Nomination: Best Score

HURRICANE
1979, 119 mins, US ⓥ
D: Jan Troell **A:** Jason Robards, Mia Farrow, Max von Sydow, Trevor Howard, Dayton Ka'ne, Timothy Bottoms (Paramount/De Laurentiis)

The storm blows fiercely but the love story doesn't match its power. Script sets the tale in eastern Samoa, circa 1920, with Jason Robards lording it over the natives on behalf of the US Navy. The female love interest is now a white woman, with Mia Farrow sailing in to see her commander father, but gradually becoming involved with the young chieftain of a nearby island (Dayton Ka'ne). The hurricane itself, which runs 25 minutes and was created entirely on location in Bora Bora, is impressive enough.

HURRICANE, THE
1999, 125 mins, US ⓥ ◉
D: Norman Jewison **A:** Denzel Washington, Vicellous Reon Shannon, Deborah Kara Unger, Liev Schreiber, John Hannah, Dan Hedaya (Azoff-Langlais/Beacon/Universal)

The Hurricane, Norman Jewison's heartfelt political drama, tells of Rubin "Hurricane" Carter, the black boxer who was wrongly convicted of triple murder and jailed for 19 years before being exonerated and released in 1985. In the lead role, Denzel Washington elevates the occasionally simplistic narrative to a touching moral exposé. Brief flashbacks recreate the 1966 killing of three people in Paterson, NJ. There follows the arrest of Carter and a young fan, John Artis (Garland Whitt). In Toronto, seven years later, a black youth named Lesra (Vicellous Reon Shannon) reads Carter's autobiography. A product of poor, illiterate parents, Lesra has been "adopted" by three Canadian students, Terry Swinton (John Hannah), Lisa Peters (Deborah Kara Unger), and Sam Chaiton (Liev Schreiber). Convinced of Carter's innocence, Lesra enlists his guardians to mount a full-time campaign for his release.
1999: Nomination: Best Actor (Denzel Washington)

HURRY SUNDOWN
1967, 146 mins, US ▭
D: Otto Preminger A: Michael Caine, Jane
Fonda, John Phillip Law, Diahann Carroll,
Faye Dunaway, Burgess Meredith (Para-
mount/Sigma)

An outstanding, tasteful, yet hard-
hitting, and handsomely produced film
about racial conflict in Georgia circa 1945.
Michael Caine leads the stars, and delivers
an excellent performance as the white social climber managing the Georgia land
holdings of wife Jane Fonda. Two tracts
block Caine's plans, those of distant relative John Phillip Law and Negro Robert
Hooks, both just-returned war vets.

**HUSBANDS: A COMEDY ABOUT
LIFE, DEATH & FREEDOM**
1970, 154 mins, US
D: John Cassavetes A: Ben Gazzara, Peter
Falk, John Cassavetes, Jenny Runacre,
Jenny Lee Wright (Columbia)

Director-writer-actor John Cassavetes,
Ben Gazzara, and Peter Falk are the "husbands," who, in the face of death, revert
to drunken, giggling, horseplaying adolescence, and, with a stunningly talented supporting cast, create and improvise a
memorably touching, human, and very
funny film. Jenny Runacre, a tall lovely
blond English girl, gives a touching performance as Cassavetes's neurotic pickup.

HUSBANDS AND WIVES
1992, 107 mins, US Ⓥ ⊙
D: Woody Allen A: Woody Allen, Judy
Davis, Mia Farrow, Sydney Pollack, Juliette Lewis, Liam Neeson (Tri-Star)

Major Woody, a richly satisfying
ensemble piece about NY neurotics falling
in and out of love. Allen creates a full-
bodied gallery of hardheaded urbanites
who more often than not operate out of
self-destructive impulses. This is definitely
his edgiest, rawest work in a good while.
Carlo Di Palma's lensing appears to be almost entirely handheld, creating a look
somewhere between early French New
Wave and cinema verité. Acting is of a
very high caliber across the board, but Davis, in a very meaty part, is incandescent,
revealing a whole new side to her on-
screen personality.
1992: Nominations: Best Supp. Actress
(Judy Davis), Original Screenplay

**HUSH ... HUSH, SWEET
CHARLOTTE**
1964, 134 mins, US Ⓥ
D: Robert Aldrich A: Bette Davis, Olivia

de Havilland, Joseph Cotten, Agnes
Moorehead, Cecil Kellaway, Mary Astor
(Associates & Aldrich/20th Century-Fox)

Robert Aldrich's follow-up (but no relation) to *What Ever Happened to Baby
Jane?* is a shocker. Bette Davis lives in
the reflection of a dreadful past, the macabre murder and mutilation of her married lover hanging over her as she
frequently confuses the past with the present. De Havilland, as her cousin, lives very
much for the present—and future—as she
attempts to soothe and rationalize with the
deeply emotional mistress of the house.
Davis's portrayal is reminiscent of Jane in
its emotional overtones, in her style of
characterization of the near-crazed former
southern belle, aided by haggard makeup
and outlandish attire. It is an outgoing performance, and she plays it to the limit.
1964: Nominations: Best Supp. Actress
(Agnes Moorehead), B&W Cinematography, B&W Costume Design, B&W Art
Direction, Editing, Original Music Score,
Song ("Hush ... Hush, Sweet Charlotte")

**LE HUSSARD SUR LE TOIT
(THE HORSEMAN ON THE ROOF)**
1995, 135 mins, France Ⓥ ⊙ ▭
D: Jean-Paul Rappeneau A: Olivier Martinez, Juliette Binoche, Isabelle Carre,
Francois Cluzet, Jean Yanne, Gerard Depardieu (Hachette Premiere)

An oddly paced journey through a
cholera-ridden Provence of the early 19th
century, *Roof* delivers an admirable re-
creation of the Romantic era. Angelo
(Olivier Martinez), an Italian officer and
mama's-boy-turned-revolutionary against
his country's Hapsburg overlords, steals
into the town of Manosque, where he's fed
by a mysterious noblewoman (Juliette
Binoche). Remainder of pic follows the
two as they effortlessly—much too effortlessly—elude or outwit all comers in their
picturesque meanderings. Binoche's restrained, decorous perf is utterly convincing. Handsome young Martinez struggles
with his unforgiving part.

HUSSY
1980, 95 mins, UK Ⓥ
D: Matthew Chapman A: Helen Mirren,
John Shea, Jenny Runacre, Murray Salem,
Paul Angelis, Patti Boulaye (Kendon)

Somewhere there's a valid love story
trying to get out. John Shea's performance
as Helen Mirren's lover, a transient American working as spotlight operator at the
London strip joint where she hosts and
hooks is mostly bland, but occasionally ef-

fective. Mirren would have come off better had she been directed toward a less ponderous conception of the role.

HUSTLE
1975, 120 mins, US ⱱ
D: Robert Aldrich **A:** Burt Reynolds, Catherine Deneuve, Ben Johnson, Paul Winfield, Eileen Brennan, Eddie Albert (Paramount/RoBurt)

Robert Aldrich's sharp-looking film reunites him with Burt Reynolds, starring here as a hardening detective trying to short-circuit the solution of a femme teenager's dope suicide because the trail may lead to Eddie Albert, a noted lawyer with many uptown and downtown connections. Reynolds is torn between his duty and his personal attraction-resistance to mistress Catherine Deneuve.

HUSTLER, THE
1961, 134 mins, US ⱱ ⊙ ⊏⊐
D: Robert Rossen **A:** Paul Newman, Jackie Gleason, Piper Laurie, George C. Scott, Myron McCormick, Murray Hamilton (20th Century-Fox)

Chief protagonist is Paul Newman, a pool shark with a compulsion to be the best of the lot—not in tournament play but in beating Chicago's big-time player (Jackie Gleason). Unfolding is far overlength, and despite the excellence of Newman's portrayal of the boozing pool hustler, the sordid aspects of overall picture are strictly downbeat. Piper Laurie establishes herself solidly as a hard-drinking floozy who lives with Newman, and George C. Scott scores as a gambler who teaches him the psychology of being a winner.

1961: Best B&W Cinematography, B&W Art Direction

Nominations: Best Picture, Director, Actor (Paul Newman), Actress (Piper Laurie), Supp. Actor (Jackie Gleason, George C. Scott [latter nom. refused]), Adapted Screenplay

I

I ACCUSE
1958, 99 mins, US/UK ▭

D: Jose Ferrer A: Jose Ferrer, Anton Walbrook, Viveca Lindfors, Leo Genn, Emlyn Williams, David Farrar (M-G-M)

This version of the drama of the Dreyfus case makes strong, if plodding, entertainment. The story concerns a Jewish staff officer of the French army who is unjustly accused of treason, found guilty through being framed to save the army's face, and condemned to life imprisonment on Devil's Island. Friends fighting to restore his tarnished honor force a retrial. Jose Ferrer takes on the heavy task of playing Dreyfus and of directing. His performance comes from the intellect rather than the heart. The court scenes are pregnant with drama, thanks to a literate screenplay by Gore Vidal.

I AM A CAMERA
1955, 98 mins, UK ⱱ

D: Henry Cornelius A: Julie Harris, Laurence Harvey, Shelley Winters, Ron Randell, Anton Diffring (Romulus)

John Van Druten's hit play, based on *The Berlin Stories* by Christopher Isherwood, is an episodic affair dealing with a young author who gets himself involved, innocently, with a crackpot girl in pre–World War II Berlin. In transferring the play to the screen, scripter John Collier hewed close to the original in dialogue and situations and the effect is always more that of a filmed stage play than a motion picture. The femmes will find more identification in the antics, even though most unconventional, of the wacky character so broadly projected by Julie Harris than the men will find with the Isherwood role played by Laurence Harvey.

I AM A FUGITIVE
See: I Am a Fugitive from a Chain Gang

I AM A FUGITIVE FROM A CHAIN GANG
(UK: I AM A FUGITIVE)
1932, 93 mins, US ⱱ

D: Mervyn LeRoy A: Paul Muni, Glenda Farrell, Helen Vinson, Noel Francis, Preston Foster (Warner)

A picture with guts. It grips with its stark realism and packs lots of punch. Paul Muni breaks away from the chain gang twice. In between he achieves success in his preferred field of engineering until a romantic angle prompts him voluntarily to surrender as the wanted fugitive, on the promise and belief he will be pardoned in 90 days. The prison board stalls that, leading into the second breakaway from the chain gang. The finale is stark in its realism. Muni turns in a pip performance.

1932/33: Nominations: Best Picture, Actor (Paul Muni), Sound

I CAN GET IT FOR YOU WHOLESALE
(UK: THIS IS MY AFFAIR)
1951, 91 mins, US

D: Michael Gordon A: Susan Hayward, Dan Dailey, George Sanders, Sam Jaffe (20th Century-Fox)

Background of New York's garment-manufacturing sector provides the setting for this adult drama. Hayward is the ambitious femme. She partners with Dailey, a hot garment salesman, and Sam Jaffe, an experienced production man, and their business grows, but not fast enough to satisfy the girl. She meets and charms Sanders, merchant prince, who offers her fame if she can break with her partners.

ICE CASTLES
1978, 113 mins, US ⱱ

D: Donald Wrye A: Lynn-Holly Johnson, Robby Benson, Colleen Dewhurst, Tom Skerritt, Jennifer Warren, David Huffman (Columbia)

Ice Castles combines a touching love story with the excitement and intense pressure of Olympic competition skating. Olympic coach Jennifer Warren propels Lyn-Holly Johnson to instant stardom as a Cinderella figure who comes out of nowhere to win the hearts of the American people. Johnson has a freak accident. Robby Benson, Johnson's boyfriend, and Tom Skerritt, her father, bring the teenager out of her shell, leading up to the inspiring ending.

1979: Nomination: Best Song ("Through the Eyes of Love")

ICE COLD IN ALEX
(US: DESERT ATTACK)
1958, 132 mins, UK ⱱ

D: J. Lee Thompson A: John Mills, Sylvia Syms, Anthony Quayle, Harry Andrews, Diane Clare, Peter Arne (Associated British)

The story of a handful of people who

drive an ambulance through the mine-ridden, enemy-occupied desert after the collapse of Tobruk in 1942. There are a nerve-strained officer who has taken to the bottle, his tough, reliable sergeant major, a couple of nurses, and a South African officer. Director J. Lee Thompson captures the stark, pitiless atmosphere of the desert superbly. The screenplay skillfully blends excitement, a hint of romance, and a fearful sense of danger.

ICE FOLLIES OF 1939
1939, 81 mins, US
D: Reinhold Schunzel A: Joan Crawford, James Stewart, Lew Ayres, Lewis Stone, Bess Ehrhardt, Lionel Stander (M-G-M)

It's the ice show and spectacle that count, chock-full of specialities and decidedly eye-appealing. Rather light story would have had trouble unfolding on its own for seven reels. Crawford marries James Stewart, and nabs a film stock contract. She gains stardom in her first picture and Stewart goes east to generate interest and backing in his Ice Follies idea.

ICE STATION ZEBRA
1968, 152 mins, US Ⓥ ⊙ ▭
D: John Sturges A: Rock Hudson, Ernest Borgnine, Patrick McGoohan, Jim Brown, Tony Bill, Lloyd Nolan (M-G-M/Filmways)

Action-adventure film, in which US and Russian forces race to recover some compromising satellite photography from a remote polar outpost. Alistair MacLean's novel adapted into a screen story is seeded with elements of intrigue, as Rock Hudson takes aboard a British secret agent, Patrick McGoohan; an expatriate, professional anti-Communist Russian, Ernest Borgnine; and an enigmatic marine-corps captain, Jim Brown.
1968: Nominations: Best Cinematography, Visual Effects

ICE STORM, THE
1997, 113 mins, US Ⓥ ⊙
D: Ang Lee A: Kevin Kline, Joan Allen, Sigourney Weaver, Christina Ricci, Jamey Sheridan (Good Machine/Fox Searchlight)

A well-observed and deftly performed examination of upper-middle-class emotional deep freeze, *The Ice Storm* is an intelligent, adult American film. Film tracks the furtive emotional adventures and transgressions of middle-aged parents and their sexually budding teenage kids in the early seventies. Paul Hood (Tobey Maguire) returns to the New Canaan, CT, home of his parents, Ben (Kevin Kline) and Elena (Joan Allen). A chill has set in on the marriage, though Ben at least tries to communicate with Paul and his precocious 14-year-old daughter, Wendy (Christina Ricci). Ben is carrying on a discreet affair with neighbor Janey Carver (Sigourney Weaver). Wendy and Janey's son Mikey (Elijah Wood) begin fooling around but are caught by Ben, who is hanging around after an assignation with Janey. Kline excels; Weaver starkly etches the boldest character of the lot.

I CONFESS
1953, 95 mins, US Ⓥ ⊙
D: Alfred Hitchcock A: Montgomery Clift, Anne Baxter, Karl Malden, Brian Aherne, O. E. Hasse (Warner)

Intriguing story idea finds a priest facing trial for a murder he didn't commit, and refusing to clear himself even though the killer had confessed to him in the sanctity of the church. Chief exponents of the melodrama are Montgomery Clift, the priest, and Anne Baxter, a married woman who still believes she is in love with him. While Hitchcock shortchanges on the expected round of suspense, he does bring out a number of topflight performances and gives the picture an interesting polish that is documentary at times.

I COULD GO ON SINGING
1963, 99 mins, US Ⓥ ⊙ ▭
D: Ronald Neame A: Judy Garland, Dirk Bogarde, Jack Klugman, Aline MacMahon, Pauline Jameson (United Artists)

Screenplay has Garland as a celebrated Yank singer who decides while in London to look up the medic with whom years ago she had an affair which culminated in the birth of a son. She now persuades the doctor to let her see the lad, and it isn't long before the true parental beans are spilled. But for some rather foggy reason, the boy elects to play it cool and keep his distance from his newfound mater. A soulful performance is etched by Garland, who gives more than she gets from the script. She also belts over four numbers as only she can belt them.

I COVER THE WATERFRONT
1933, 72 mins, US Ⓥ
D: James Cruze A: Claudette Colbert, Ben Lyon, Ernest Torrence, Hobart Cavanaugh (United Artists)

Around Ernest Torrence's Eli Kirk, a deep-sea skipper and smuggler who has few scruples, except those concerning his daughter, the scenarist has built a fable. Ben Lyon, as the reporter, has been promising a sensational expose on Kirk's activities and finally he delivers. Lyon originally intended to get Kirk through his daughter, but he falls in love, which is a cinch to see in advance, as is the finish.

I.D.
1995, 108 mins, UK/Germany ⓥ
D: Philip Davis A: Reece Dinsdale, Richard Graham, Claire Skinner, Sean Pertwee, Saskia Reeves, Warren Clarke (Parallax/Metropolis)

London bobbies come face-to-face with their own personal hell as they go undercover to root out soccer hooligans in a raw-steak drama that packs a wallop when it's on target but suffers an intermittent ID crisis of its own in the script department when it comes to delivering the psychological goods. Reece Dinsdale is excellent in his gradual transformation from clean-cut cop to long-haired troglodyte, and the copious scenes of pub drinking and tribalistic rituals of "belonging" carry an almost tangible threat of violence that's right on the money.

I DANCE ALONE
See: Stealing Beauty

I'D CLIMB THE HIGHEST MOUNTAIN
1951, 87 mins, US
D: Henry King A: Susan Hayward, William Lundigan, Rory Calhoun, Barbara Bates, Gene Lockhart, Lynn Bari (20th Century-Fox)

The plotline is strung together with a series of episodes in the life of a minister and his city-bred bride on their first duty for the church. Location of the assignment is in the red-clay hills of North Georgia, and 20th-Fox sent its cast and cameras to the actual sites, giving the picture authenticity. Hayward shines as the bride who encounters a completely strange life during her three years in the hills. William Lundigan scores as the very human minister.

IDEAL HUSBAND, AN
1947, 96 mins, UK ⓥ
D: Alexander Korda A: Paulette Goddard, Michael Wilding, Hugh Williams, Diana Wynyard, C. Aubrey Smith, Glynis Johns (British Lion)

This version of the 1895 Oscar Wilde play is given handsome mounting by Alexander Korda. Story relates how Hugh Williams, undersecretary of the Foreign Office and marked for a cabinet post, in his youth profited by selling a cabinet secret. Paulette Goddard, an adventuress, threatens him with exposure. It seems a brave experiment to cast Goddard as the adventuress. But it doesn't quite come off. Not a solitary epigram is thrown off with spontaneity, and her loveliness in gorgeous costumes is inadequate compensation.

IDEAL HUSBAND, THE
1999, 96 mins, UK ⓥ ⊙
D: Oliver Parker A: Rupert Everett, Julianne Moore, Jeremy Northam, Cate Blanchett, Minnie Driver, John Wood (Fragile/Icon/Pathe)

Oscar Wilde's legiter about emotional and political chicanery shines like a freshly minted coin in Oliver Parker's adaptation of An Ideal Husband. Textual purists may decry some of the changes Parker has made to the original, but the result is a believable milieu in which Wilde's people emerge as flawed heroes and heroines rather than just witty cynics. The film still dips in the resolution-heavy last act, with Parker not quite negotiating its changes in tone. Performances are tip-top down the line, with Rupert Everett immaculately poised as the Wilde alter ego, Lord Arthur Goring; Julianne Moore as the unflappable, scheming Laura Cheveley; Cate Blanchett making a real character out of the adoring but strong Gertrud Chiltern; and Minnie Driver bringing a slightly ditzy charm to the love-struck Mabel. Jeremy Northam may not be everyone's idea of Sir Robert Chiltern, but his softer, more human portrayal fits the movie.

IDIOT'S DELIGHT
1939, 100 mins, US ⓥ ⊙
D: Clarence Brown A: Norma Shearer, Clark Gable, Edward Arnold, Joseph Schildkraut, Burgess Meredith (M-G-M)

Gable milks his role as the small-time vaude performer, and dominates the picture throughout. His cynical yet breezy manner is a new characterization. Shearer does nobly in a part which calls for two distinct characterizations, first as the vaude trouper and later impersonating a Russian aristocrat. Antiwar angles of the play are considerably softened. Brief appearance of Burgess Meredith as the war declaimer is brilliantly handled.

IDOL, THE
1966, 109 mins, UK
D: Daniel Petrie **A:** Jennifer Jones, Michael Parks, John Leyton, Jennifer Hilary, Guy Doleman (Embassy)

An irresponsible American art student in London disbelieves in everything except himself and his own talents. He has become friendly with a young man studying to be a doctor, completely under his mother's domination. The mother, who at first takes a dislike to the brash young American, finds herself attracted to him. Characters lack much interest.

IDOLMAKER, THE
1980, 107 mins, US Ⓥ ⊙
D: Taylor Hackford **A:** Ray Sharkey, Paul Land, Olympia Dukakis, Peter Gallagher, Joe Pantoliano (United Artists)

Though it's marred by an overly melodramatic and dubious finale, *The Idolmaker* is an unusually compelling film about the music business in the late 1950s and early 1960s. It shows how teen idols were created, promoted, and discarded by entrepreneurs cynically manipulating the adolescent audience. Ray Sharkey is superb in the title role.

**I DON'T WANT TO BE BORN
(US: THE DEVIL WITHIN HER)**
1975, 90 mins, UK Ⓥ
D: Peter Sasdy **A:** Joan Collins, Eileen Atkins, Donald Pleasence, Ralph Bates, Caroline Munro (Unicapital/Rank)

This is an exceedingly stylish thriller about a satanically possessed infant, Joan Collins's abnormally strong newborn son, who inflicts scratches on cribside visitors and wreaks havoc on his room when no one is around. A frantic Collins (looking and acting splendidly) and her Italian husband, nicely played by horror vet Ralph Bates, turn to doctor Donald Pleasence for the answers, then to Bates's nun sister (Eileen Atkins, in a striking performance).

**I DOOD IT
(UK: BY HOOK OR BY CROOK)**
1943, 102 mins, US
D: Vincente Minnelli **A:** Red Skelton, Eleanor Powell, Lena Horne, Patricia Dane, Sam Levene (M-G-M)

Metro has wrapped Red Skelton and Eleanor Powell, among other names, around a popular Skelton radio phrase that's used for the film's title, and the net result is moderate entertainment. The yarn is too unbelievable, though the absurdities

fashioned for Skelton have their compensations in the actual performance.

I DREAM OF JEANIE
1952, 90 mins, US
D: Allan Dwan **A:** Ray Middleton, Bill Shirley, Muriel Lawrence, Eileen Christy, Rex Allen (Republic)

A pseudo-biopic around the life and songs of Stephen Foster gets a pretentious treatment. Foster's folksy tune-smithing is featured in 21 of his cleffings. Picture could have used a script and performances to match the singing. Bill Shirley plays Foster, tenoring ''O Susanna,'' ''Old Dog Tray,'' ''Camptown Races,'' and others. Eileen Christy is the vivacious Jeanie.

**IERI, OGGI, DOMANI
(YESTERDAY, TODAY AND TOMORROW)**
1964, 120 mins, Italy Ⓥ
D: Vittorio De Sica Armando Trovajoli **A:** Sophia Loren, Marcello Mastroianni, Aldo Giuffre, Armando Trovajoli (Ponti)

The wonders of Italy and Sophia Loren are the objects of intimate attention in this breezy, noncerebral, three-episoder directed with cinematic flair and invested with sensual gusto by Vittorio De Sica. The first episode illustrates the method by which a Neopolitan black-marketeer evades imprisonment over a seven-year span. Episode two describes the abrupt dissolution of an affair between a Milanese Rolls-Royceterer and her lover. Third item explores the adventures in Rome of a lovable prostitute, a fanciful client, and a confused young student priest.
1964: Best Foreign Language Film

IF . . .
1968, 110 mins, UK Ⓥ ⊙
D: Lindsay Anderson **A:** Malcolm McDowell, David Wood, Richard Warwick, Christine Noonan (Memorial)

Punchy, poetic pic that delves into the epic theme of youthful revolt, *if . . .* is ostensibly about a rigid tradition-ridden British private boarding school for boys from 11 to 18. The film blocks out a series of incidents that lead to a small group rebelling with mortars, machine guns, gas bombs, and pistols. The violence is symbolic and the film reflects and comments on it rather than sentimentalizing it or trying to make it realistic.

IF I HAD A MILLION
1932, 85 mins, US
D: Ernst Lubitsch, Norman Taurog, Stephen Roberts, Norman Z. McLeod, James

Cruze, William A. Seiter, H. Bruce Humberstone **A:** Gary Cooper, Charles Laughton, W. C. Fields, Charles Ruggles, George Raft, Jack Oakie (Paramount)

With so many cooks concerned, this cinematic porridge, depicting what certain individuals would do if they had $1 million, is naturally replete with a diversity of seasonings. Charlie Ruggles's sequence has about the longest footage, while Laughton's Bronx cheerio is the snappiest, and probably most effective. W. C. Fields and Alison Skipworth man a vanguard of used flivvers as the means to attack the road hogs who endanger the other motorists.

IF IT'S TUESDAY, THIS MUST BE BELGIUM
1969, 99 mins, US
D: Mel Stuart **A:** Suzanne Pleshette, Ian McShane, Mildred Natwick, Murray Hamilton (United Artists)

While main story line is based on the adventures of a polyglot pack of Yank tourists, trying to keep up with a hectic schedule, it is padded with enough sidebar items to make it a miniature *Grand Hotel* on wheels. Besides the friction caused by the inconveniences en route, there's personal friction between British guide Ian McShane and femme tourist Suzanne Pleshette.

IF I WERE KING
1938, 100 mins, US
D: Frank Lloyd **A:** Ronald Colman, Basil Rathbone, Frances Dee, Ellen Drew, C. V. France, Henry Wilcoxon (Paramount)

Paramount made a happy choice in deciding to turn out a new version of the adventures of Francois Villon. Ronald Colman's delineation of the adventurous poet-philosopher is excellent, carrying through it a verve and spontaneity for an outstanding performance. Basil Rathbone brilliantly handles the difficult assignment of the eccentric, wizened Louis XI. Preston Sturges has provided much sparkling dialogue to greatly enhance entertainment.

IF LOOKS COULD KILL
(UK: TEEN AGENT)
1991, 88 mins, US ⑲ ⊙
D: William Dear **A:** Richard Grieco, Linda Hunt, Roger Rees, Robin Bartlett, Gabrielle Anwar, Geraldine James (Warner)

Young TV star Richard Grieco barely survives silly first-film vehicle, which spoofs the James Bond formula in tiresome fashion. One-joke script runs out of gas before the halfway mark. Grieco plays a high-school student who's headed for France with his teacher (Robin Bartlett) and class. Coincidentally, a CIA spy with same name is booked on the same plane, and rest of the film stems from both villains and good-guy spooks mistaking young Grieco for a secret agent.

I FOUND STELLA PARISH
1935, 83 mins, US
D: Mervyn LeRoy **A:** Kay Francis, Ian Hunter, Paul Lukas, Sybil Jason, Jessie Ralph (Warner)

Powerful story of an actress and mother love. Kay Francis plays both a young woman and an aging, bespectacled aunt. As the Stella Parish of the London stage, she is always a cameo of film loveliness. When she becomes an aunt to her child that she may escape detection when suddenly fleeing London and a no-good American husband, who has finally caught up with her, she is shown to be an actress of much ability.

IF YOU FEEL LIKE SINGING
See: Summer Stock

IKIRU
(LIVING; TO LIVE)
1952, 143 mins, Japan ⑲ ⊙
D: Akira Kurosawa **A:** Takashi Shimura, Nobuo Kaneko, Kyoko Seki, Miki Odagiri, Makoto Kobori (Toho)

An ordinary white-collar worker (Takashi Shimura) finds he has cancer and a few months to live. He tells nobody but finds that he is really alone. He suddenly sees that his life has been dull and useless, wasted in an office from which he has not been absent in 30 years. Meeting one of his office girls (Miki Odagiri), he finds her new job, that of making toys for children, gives him a sudden goal. He pushes a needed children's playground through all the bureaucratic red tape. Kurosawa performs a tour de force in keeping a dramatic thread throughout and avoiding the mawkish.

I KNOW WHAT YOU DID LAST SUMMER
1997, 101 mins, US ⑲ ⊙ ▭
D: Jim Gillespie **A:** Jennifer Love Hewitt, Sarah Michelle Gellar, Ryan Phillippe, Freddie Prinze Jr., Muse Wats, Anne Heche (Mandalay/Columbia)

Combining familiar elements from horror staples and a few novel twists, this is a polished genre piece with superior fright elements. The setting is a North Carolina fishing community. Helen (Sarah Michelle Gellar) goes off to party with her boyfriend, Barry (Ryan Phillippe), and their friends. Driving home, they hit something in the road. As they're about to drop the body into the water, it comes to life, and a brief struggle forever cements their culpability in a murderous act. A year later, a malevolent presence disposes of Max (Johnny Galecki)—a classmate who saw the foursome at the side of the road—and goes on to terrorize Barry. Remainder of the film plays out as a cat-and-mouse game. The leads elevate their prototypes considerably. Hewitt and Prinze are particularly good, and Anne Heche is a standout as the hauntingly eviscerated sister of the hit-and-run victim.

I KNOW WHERE I'M GOING!
1945, 91 mins, UK Ⓥ
D: Michael Powell, Emeric Pressburger **A:** Wendy Hiller, Roger Livesey, Pamela Brown, Petula Clark, Nancy Price, Finlay Currie (Archers)

The tale of a girl who is sure she knows where she is going until she gets sidetracked—and likes it. She is off to the island of Mull to marry the multimillionaire boss of a great chemical combine. It is only when a gale prevents her from reaching the island and her waiting bridegroom-to-be that she finds her ambition to marry heartless, the process of disillusionment aided and abetted by her proximity to a young navy officer (Roger Livesey).

I LIKE IT LIKE THAT
1994, 105 mins, US Ⓥ ⊙
D: Darnell Martin **A:** Lauren Velez, Jon Seda, Tomas Melly, Lisa Vidal, Griffin Dunne, Rita Moreno (Think Again/Columbia)

A thick veneer of happening music, multiethnicity, tough-hood attitude, and sexual frankness gives a hip feel to what is actually an old-fashioned and conventional story of a bickering family. Debut feature by Darnell Martin, reputedly the first black American woman to write and direct a film for a Hollywood major, displays plenty of energy and a adeptness at staging scenes vividly. Mostly unknown thesps throw themselves into their roles.

I LIKE MONEY
See: Mr. Topaze

I LIVE IN GROSVENOR SQUARE (US: A YANK IN LONDON)
1945, 114 mins, UK
D: Herbert Wilcox **A:** Anna Neagle, Dean Jagger, Rex Harrison, Robert Morley (Associated British)

Story of air-corps crew sacrificing themselves to save inhabitants of an English village. Anna Neagle gives a most convincing performance. Rex Harrison as the major looks sure to impress American femmes in the service, even though the heroine jilts him.

I LIVE MY LIFE
1935, 83 mins, US
D: W. S. Van Dyke **A:** Joan Crawford, Brian Aherne, Frank Morgan, Aline MacMahon, Eric Blore, Jessie Ralph (M-G-M)

An amusing romance is backgrounded by clothes, cocktails, and butlers. The premise, as is customary with Crawford operas, is that the rich are not as good as the poor, only in this instance Crawford is on the coin side and it takes a man to trim her down. The man is an archaeologist who follows the girl from Greece to New York. Brian Aherne is aces opposite Crawford.

I'LL CRY TOMORROW
1955, 117 mins, US Ⓥ ⊙
D: Daniel Mann **A:** Susan Hayward, Richard Conte, Eddie Albert, Jo Van Fleet, Don Taylor, Margo (M-G-M)

This pulls no punches in showing a rising star's fall into alcoholic degradation that plumbs skid-row sewers before Alcoholics Anonymous provides the faith and guidance to help her up again. Susan Hayward, along with the sock of her sustained character creation, reveals pleasant pipes and song-belting ability.
1955: Best B&W Costume Design
Nominations: Best Actress (Susan Hayward), B&W Cinematography, B&W Art Direction

I'LL DO ANYTHING
1994, 115 mins, US Ⓥ ⊙
D: James L. Brooks **A:** Nick Nolte, Whittni Wright, Albert Brooks, Julie Kavner, Joely Richardson, Tracey Ullman (Columbia/Gracie)

The musical that wasn't. Brooks—having raised eyebrows initially by casting such dubious crooners as Nick Nolte and Albert Brooks—finally junked the musical numbers after test audiences voted thumbs-down, shooting new material and turning *Anything* back into a multitiered romantic comedy. Nolte plays a rarely employed actor with a six-year-old daughter (Whittni Wright). He settles for work chauffeuring around a self-obsessed, hyperkinetic producer of schlocky blockbusters (Albert Brooks)—in the process becoming entangled with a development executive (Joely Richardson).

ILLEGALLY YOURS
1988, 102 mins, US Ⓥ
D: Peter Bogdanovich A: Rob Lowe, Colleen Camp, Kenneth Mars, Harry Carey Jr. (De Laurentiis/Crescent Moon)

An embarrassingly unfunny attempt at screwball comedy. Hectic precredits sequence crudely sets up an uninteresting story of a blackmailer's murder, in which innocent Colleen Camp is arrested as the fall guy. Lowe is cast, with unbecoming glasses throughout, as a college dropout who finds himself on jury duty in Camp's case.

ILL MET BY MOONLIGHT (US: NIGHT AMBUSH)
1957, 104 mins, UK Ⓥ
D: Michael Powell, Emeric Pressburger A: Dirk Bogarde, Marius Goring, David Oxley, Cyril Cusack, Laurence Payne, Michael Gough (Rank/Archers)

In occupied Crete, two British officers, with the aid of local patriots, are given the job of kidnapping the German commander in chief and transporting him to Cairo. Dirk Bogarde turns in a satisfying performance as a British major, with David Oxley giving valuable aid as his No. 2 man. Marius Goring, as the general, is smugly confident that he'll be rescued by his own men.

I'LL NEVER FORGET WHAT'S 'IS NAME
1967, 97 mins, UK
D: Michael Winner A: Orson Welles, Oliver Reed, Carol White, Harry Andrews, Michael Hordern, Wendy Craig (Universal/Scimitar)

Story concerns a whiz kid of the advertising game (Oliver Reed), a womanizer of perpetual appetite, establishing a flightly relationship with a secretary (Carol White), who is prim at heart and takes it all seriously. Thus the theme is the aridity of fashionable achievement, and the sour smell of success is hammered home with an insistence that destroys its own claims and closes with a scene of stunning vulgarity.

ILLUSTRATED MAN, THE
1969, 103 mins, US Ⓥ ▱
D: Jack Smight A: Rod Steiger, Claire Bloom, Robert Drivas, Don Dubbins (Warner/Seven Arts)

The Illustrated Man has going for it two major aspects: a derivative Ray Bradbury story and an obtuse, time-fragmented, humanistic, allegorical morality play. Rod Steiger and Claire Bloom star in a story told in flashback and flash-forward, from a rural lakeside camp around Labor Day 1933 by wandering drifter Steiger and neighborhood boy Robert Drivas.

ILLUSTRIOUS CORPSES
See: Cadaveri Eccellenti

I LOVE A SOLDIER
1944, 106 mins, US
D: Mark Sandrich A: Paulette Goddard, Sonny Tufts, Barry Fitzgerald, Beulah Bondi (Paramount)

A lady welder (Paulette Goddard) refuses to go for a war marriage and supplements her war-effort chore by evening hostess work, entertaining soldiers just back from overseas or on the verge of going. Principal reasons for the film's weaknesses are the payoff is never in doubt, with little suspense induced, and its boy-meets-girl plot has a tedious overabundance of twists and turns.

I LOVE MELVIN
1953, 76 mins, US Ⓥ
D: Don Weis A: Donald O'Connor, Debbie Reynolds, Una Merkel, Richard Anderson, Jim Backus, Robert Taylor (M-G-M)

This is a lively, youthful musical comedy. Plot finds O'Connor a bulb carrier for Jim Backus, *Look* photog. He falls in love with Reynolds, a chorus cutie, and gives her the impression he is a photographer. She, and her family, believe the gal will make the *Look* cover. O'Connor fakes a cover but the stunt backfires. The big production number is "Saturday Afternoon before the Game," in which Reynolds plays the football and reveals every curve in a pigskin costume. The songs are by Josef Myrow and Mack Gordon.

I LOVE TROUBLE
1994, 123 mins, US Ⓥ ◉
D: Charles Shyer A: Julia Roberts, Nick Nolte, Saul Rubinek, James Rebhorn, Robert Loggia, Olympia Dukakis (Touchstone)

This ultrapolished romantic suspenser

serves up mild romance, mild suspense, and mild humor. Having one's taste in the right place is not a substitute for originality and zest, both of which are in relatively short supply in this luxuriously appointed yarn. Nick Nolte plays a Windy City columnist who is temporarily forced back onto the beat as punishment for his laziness and finds himself scooped by competing newcomer Sabrina Peterson (Julia Roberts). Story in question involves the derailment of a passenger train, which quickly builds into a case of corporate intrigue and subterfuge.

I LOVE YOU, ALICE B. TOKLAS!
1968, 92 mins, US ℗
D: Hy Averback A: Peter Sellers, Jo Van Fleet, Leigh Taylor-Young, Joyce Van Patten, David Arkin (Warner/Seven Arts)

Pic derives its prime value from an excellent screenplay. Peter Sellers, an L.A. lawyer, turns on to hippie life as an escape from conformity and hypocrisy. Later he finds out that human nature is independent of superficial environment, returns briefly to his former life, but winds up running away again. Film blasts off into orbit via top-notch acting and direction. Sellers's performance is an outstanding blend of warmth, sensitivity, disillusion, and optimism. Jo Van Feet is simply brilliant as Sellers's mother.

I LOVE YOU TO DEATH
1990, 96 mins, US ℗ ⊙
D: Lawrence Kasdan A: Kevin Kline, Tracey Ullman, Joan Plowright, River Phoenix, William Hurt, Keanu Reeves (Chestnut Hill)

A stillborn attempt at black comedy. Kevin Kline creates a stereotypical Italian restaurant owner who can't help cheating with scores of women on his frumpish wife, Tracey Ullman. Awkward script has Ullman discovering Kline in a tryst at a library and, after brief consultation with her Yugoslav mom Joan Plowright, resolving to kill him.

IMAGES
1972, 100 mins, UK ▭
D: Robert Altman A: Susannah York, Rene Auberjonois, Marcel Bozzuffi, Cathryn Harrison (Lion's Gate/Hemdale)

Robert Altman made this interior drama about a woman going through hallucinations and nearing madness in Ireland. Delving into effects of permissiveness on a hidebound, repressed nature, it also shows a probing insight into mental disorder. Susannah York has the intensity and innocence marked by strain as well as sensual underpinnings, and brings off the denouement with restraint and potency.
1972: Nomination: Best Original Score

IMAGINARY CRIMES
1994, 104 mins, US ℗
D: Anthony Drazen A: Harvey Keitel, Fairuza Balk, Kelly Lynch, Vincent D'Onofrio, Diane Baker, Chris Penn (Morgan Creek/Warner)

This teenage-girl coming-of-age story boasts some fine performances, but is weakened by an overly familiar plot. Tale opens with Sonya Weiler (Fairuza Balk) looking back on her senior year in 1962 Portland, OR. Her father, Ray (Harvey Keitel), enrolls her at an exclusive girls' school for her final year, even though it's questionable whether he will be able to pay for it. There she falls under the tutelage of a well-meaning English teacher (Vincent D'Onofrio) who encourages her writing as well as her ambitions to go to college.

I'M ALL RIGHT JACK
1959, 105 mins, UK ℗
D: John Boulting A: Ian Carmichael, Peter Sellers, Terry-Thomas, Richard Attenborough, Dennis Price, Margaret Rutherford (British Lion/Charter)

The Boulting Brothers' target is British factory life, trade unionism, and the general possibility that everybody is working for one person—himself. Ian Carmichael plays an ex-university type who wants to get an executive job in industry. Instead, he becomes the unwitting cause of a factory strike that swells to nationwide proportions. Gradually he begins to realize that he has been taken for a ride. Peter Sellers, as the chairman of the factory's union works committee, makes the film. With makeup that subtly suggests Hitler, he brings rare humor and an occasional touch of pathos to the role.

I MARRIED A COMMUNIST
(UK: THE WOMAN ON PIER 13)
1949, 72 mins, US
D: Robert Stevenson A: Laraine Day, Robert Ryan, John Agar, Thomas Gomez, Janis Carter (RKO)

Despite its heavy-sounding title, pic hews strictly to tried-and-true meller formula. Screenplay uses the simple and slightly naive device of substituting Communist for gangsters in a typical underworld yarn. Robert Ryan plays an ex-comrade who turns up in San Francisco as big-time labor-relations expert. The Commie chieftain (Thomas Gomez) reminds Ryan that he had better follow the party's directive to stir up labor trouble.

I MARRIED A MONSTER FROM OUTER SPACE
1958, 78 mins, US Ⓥ
D: Gene Fowler Jr. A: Tom Tryon, Gloria Talbott, Ken Lynch, John Eldredge, Alan Dexter (Paramount)

Screenplay deals with a race of monsters from another galaxy who secretly take over the form of some of the male townspeople. Film opens with Gloria Talbott marrying Tom Tryon, unaware the man she loves is now one of these monsters. After a year of tension she follows him one night and watches him change into his original form and enter a spaceship. Outstanding special photographic effects aid in maintaining interest.

I MARRIED A WITCH
1942, 82 mins, US Ⓥ ⊙
D: Rene Clair A: Fredric March, Veronica Lake, Robert Benchley, Susan Hayward, Cecil Kellaway, Elizabeth Patterson (United Artists)

The generally tepid story opens in 1690 in New England where a curse is laid on a Puritan and any of his descendants, the action then jumping to the present, when Fredric March, a descendant, is running for governor. He is in love with the daughter of a publisher backing him. The romance is upset and it appears that March is going to lose as a consequence of the actions taken by two departed spirits.
1942: Nomination: Best Scoring of a Dramatic Picture

I'M DANCING AS FAST AS I CAN
1982, 106 mins, US Ⓥ ⊙
D: Jack Hofsiss A: Jill Clayburgh, Nicol Williamson, Dianne Wiest, Joe Pesci, Geraldine Page (Paramount)

Crucial inability of a film to get inside a character's head spells big trouble. Result is that Jill Clayburgh's constantly center-stage character comes off as the "pill-popping dingbat" she's called at one point, rather than as a fascinating lady with a major problem. Screenplay minutely charts Clayburgh's compulsive reliance on Valium, her disastrous effort to go cold turkey, and her subsequent rehabilitation in an institution.

I MET HIM IN PARIS
1937, 85 mins, US
D: Wesley Ruggles A: Claudette Colbert, Melvyn Douglas, Robert Young, Mona Barrie, George Davis, Lee Bowman (Paramount)

One lesson in what a comedy picture ought to be. A very simple little yarn with mighty little happening—but all of it pleasantly. Story has Claudette Colbert going to Paris for a vacation on her own. She meets a couple of friendly enemies (Robert Young and Melvyn Douglas), both of whom make a play for her. Douglas is bitter and supercilious; Young is seemingly genuine and sincere, though liberal in his morals. Douglas knows Young is married and is hanging around to make Young play ball on the square. The trio go to Switzerland and much wrangling between the threesome is interspersed with snow stuff.

IMITATION OF LIFE
1934, 116 mins, US
D: John M. Stahl A: Claudette Colbert, Warren William, Louise Beavers, Fredi Washington, Rochelle Hudson (Universal)

A strong picture with an unusual plot. A young white widow (Claudette Colbert) with a baby girl goes into a business partnership with her colored maid (Louise Beavers), who also has a baby girl. Most arresting part of the picture and overshadowing the conventional romance between the late-thirtyish white widow and Warren William is the tragedy of Aunt Delilah's girl, born to a white skin and Negro blood. Picture is stolen by Beavers. She takes the whole scale of human emotions from joy to anguish and never sounds a false note.
1934: Nominations: Best Picture, Sound, Assistant Director

IMITATION OF LIFE
1959, 125 mins, US Ⓥ
D: Douglas Sirk A: Lana Turner, John Gavin, Sandra Dee, Dan O'Herlihy, Robert Alda, Susan Kohner (Universal)

Imitation of Life is a remake of Fannie Hurst's novel of the early 1930s. Lana Turner is outstanding in the pivotal role, transplanted from the original pancake-and-flour business to the American stage. This device results in the overdone busy-actress/neglected-daughter conflict, and thus the secondary plot of a fair-skinned Negress passing as white becomes the film's primary force. The relationship of the young colored girl and her mother—

played memorably by Susan Kohner and Juanita Moore—is sometimes overpowering, while the relationship of Turner and her daughter, Sandra Dee, comes to life only briefly when both are in love with same man, John Gavin.

1959: Nominations: Best Supp. Actress (Juanita Moore, Susan Kohner)

IM LAUF DER ZEIT
(KINGS OF THE ROAD)
1976, 165 mins, W. Germany ⊗

D: Wim Wenders **A:** Ruediger Vogeler, Hanns Zischler, Lisa Kreuzer, Rudolf Schuendler (Wenders)

For nearly three hours nothing much happens as two men cross the middle of Germany, but it's what they see and hear that captures attention. The charm is in the Newman-Redford types, both funny and tragic, and in the pic's improvisational character. Bruno travels along the border in a moving van that serves as a household camper; he is a projectionist who dismantles old movie equipment for sale elsewhere. Along the Elbe he meets Robert, a child psychologist running away from his women troubles. It's the beginning of a journey into the past as well as adjusting to the loneliness of the present. Pic's only drawback is its length.

IMMACULATE CONCEPTION
1992, 122 mins, UK ⊗ ⊙

D: Jamil Dehlavi **A:** James Wilby, Melissa Leo, Shabana Azmi, Zia Mohyeddin, James Cossins (Film Four/Dehlavi)

An ambitious culture-clash drama set in troubled 1988 Pakistan tries to cover too many bases. James Wilby is Alistair, a wildlife conservationist with Jewish-American spouse Hannah (Melissa Leo). Desperate to conceive a child, the couple visit a eunuch-run shrine reputed to have a cure for infertility. In fact, the eunuchs get teenager Kamal (Ronny Jhutti) to do the business with a semicomatose Hannah.

IMMEDIATE FAMILY
1989, 95 mins, US ⊗ ⊙

D: Jonathan Kaplan **A:** Glenn Close, James Woods, Mary Stuart Masterson, Kevin Dillon, Linda Darlow, Jane Greer (Columbia/Sanford-Pillsbury)

Definitely no comedy, *Immediate Family* nonetheless explodes with bursts of laughter that lighten the heartbreak of a lot of nice people tormented by their own best intentions. After 11 years of marriage, James Woods and Glenn Close are still achingly childless. After no years of marriage, young Mary Stuart Masterson and boyfriend Kevin Dillon face impending parenthood under circumstances that could wreck their chances for a happier life later. The solution, so obviously simple in a lawyer's office, is that Woods and Close adopt Masterson's baby. But first the lawyer thinks everybody should get better acquainted.

IMMIGRANT, THE
1917, 30 mins, US ⊗

D: Charles Chaplin **A:** Charles Chaplin, Eric Campbell, Edna Purviance, Henry Bergman (Mutual)

The two-reeler opens up showing Charlie leaning over a [boat's] rail apparently seasick. It develops he is fishing and lands a one-pounder in mid-ocean. Then he is seen shooting craps and going through all the gyrations of a baseball pitcher every time he "shoots the bones." The rocking and pitching of the vessel furnish unlimited opportunity for his style of comedy. There is a little heart-interest story, when he befriends a young girl and her mother who have been robbed of their small hoard.

IMMORTAL BATTALION
See: The Way Ahead

IMMORTAL BELOVED
1994, 121 mins, US ⊗ ⊙ ▭

D: Bernard Rose **A:** Gary Oldman, Jeroen Krabbe, Isabella Rossellini, Johanna Ter Steege, Barry Humphries, Valeria Golino (Icon)

An attempt to travel the *Citizen Kane* route of using a death's-door clue left by a difficult great man to penetrate his secret self. The man in question here is Ludwig van Beethoven, and the result is less than compelling due to the fragmentary telling of the story, offputting nature of the main character, and failure of the filmmakers to make their investigation seem of any particular consequence. The Rosebud here is a letter from Beethoven found soon after his death addressed to an unnamed Immortal Beloved. Beginning with the hero's death in 1827, film follows the travels throughout Middle Europe of Anton Schindler (Jeroen Krabbe), Beethoven's loyal factotum, as he pursues all his leads in the mystery.

IMMORTAL SERGEANT, THE
1943, 90 mins, US ⊗

D: John M. Stahl **A:** Henry Fonda, Maureen O'Hara, Thomas Mitchell, Allyn

Joslyn, Reginald Gardiner (20th Century-Fox)

Story is a compact drama, interestingly told, of a lost sunrise patrol on the Libyan desert, an intimate study of characters and hardships encountered. There's the sergeant (Thomas Mitchell), resourceful tactician of the last war and a most inspiring leader for the unit. It's his influence, after fatal wounding, that drives corporal Henry Fonda on with the remnants of the outfit and transforms Fonda from a self-effacing youth into a determined, confident man.

I'M NO ANGEL
1933, 87 mins, US
D: Wesley Ruggles **A:** Mae West, Cary Grant, Edward Arnold, Ralf Harolde, Russell Hopton, Gregory Ratoff (Paramount)

It's all West, plus a good directing job by Wesley Ruggles and first-rate studio production quality in all departments. Laughs are all derived from the West innuendos and the general good-natured bawdiness of the heroine, whose progress from a carnival mugg-taker to a deluxe millionaire-annexer is marked by a succession of gentlemen friends, mostly temporary and usually suckers. Every now and again West bursts into a song, generally just a chorus or a strain.

I, MOBSTER
(UK: THE MOBSTER)
1958, 80 mins, US Ⓥ ▢
D: Roger Corman **A:** Steve Cochran, Lita Milan, Robert Strauss, Celia Lovsky, Lili St. Cyr (20th Century-Fox)

I, Mobster is a well-turned-out melodrama with Steve Cochran in title role delivering a slick characterization of the rise and fall of a mobsman. Through very creditable performances, Roger Corman manages to capture the gangster feeling; in addition to Cochran outstanding portrayals are contributed by Lita Milan, as his sweetheart, Robert Strauss, socking over his henchman role after Cochran rises above him, and Celia Lovsky, as Cochran's sorely tried mother.

IMPORTANCE OF BEING EARNEST, THE
1952, 95 mins, UK Ⓥ ⊙ ⊙
D: Anthony Asquith **A:** Michael Redgrave, Edith Evans, Michael Denison, Dorothy Tutin, Margaret Rutherford, Joan Greenwood (Javelin/Two Cities)

All the charm and glossy humor of Oscar Wilde's classic comedy emerge faithfully in this British production. Michael

Redgrave brings a wealth of sincerity to the role of the earnest young man, without knowledge of his origin, whose invention of a fictitious brother leads to romantic complications.

IMPOSSIBLE OBJECT
(AKA: STORY OF A LOVE STORY)
1973, 110 mins, France
D: John Frankenheimer **A:** Alan Bates, Dominique Sanda, Evans Evans, Lea Massari, Michel Auclair, Paul Crauchet (Franco-London/Euro International)

This film is a many-pronged affair about a writer whose inventions and real life may not always be extricable. It mixes romantic drama, situation comedy, and insights into Americans or British abroad. Alan Bates is a writer, living in a country home in France with three sons and an American wife. He meets brooding but delicately sensual Dominique Sanda, who is married, in a museum, and love blossoms. Film flits lightly over the affair, the writer's embroidery on it, and sideline events that reflect on it until a sudden swerve to tragedy.

IMPOSTOR, THE
1944, 93 mins, US
D: Julien Duvivier **A:** Jean Gabin, Richard Whorf, Ellen Drew, Peter Van Eyck (Universal)

Fall of France in 1940, and subsequent formation of Free French units in Africa, forms basis for this adventure drama about the regeneration of a confirmed criminal through comradeship-in-arms. Julien Duvivier fails to generate fast enough pace to carry picture along for more than moderate attention.

IMPROMPTU
1991, 109 mins, US Ⓥ ⊙
D: James Lapine **A:** Judy Davis, Hugh Grant, Mandy Patinkin, Bernadette Peters, Julian Sands, Emma Thompson (Sovereign)

A retelling of the oft-filmed George Sand/Chopin story that's an entertaining comedy-drama. Bright playing, a bit broad at times but fitting the material, is pic's strongest suit. Aussie thesp Judy Davis plays Sand, the strong-willed author who dresses mannishly, smokes cheroots, and gets a maddening crush on composer Chopin (Hugh Grant at his most foppish). Bulk of film is lighthearted, set at the royal mansion of Emma Thompson and Anton Rodgers, where Chopin, Liszt (Julian Sands), artist Delacroix (Ralph Brown), and an uninvited George Sand show up for vacation.

IMPROPER CHANNELS
1981, 91 mins, Canada ⓥ ⊙
D: Eric Till **A:** Alan Arkin, Mariette Hartley, Sarah Stevens, Monica Parker (Paragon)

Alan Arkin puts his hapless schnook characterization to good use in *Improper Channels*. It's a screwball comedy. He's an architect, separated from his writer spouse (Mariette Hartley) and precocious five-year-old daughter (Sarah Stevens). The daughter is injured slightly in his camper and is thought to have been beaten by her father. She is bundled off by court order to an orphanage. Arkin and Hartley attempt to get her back.

IMPULSE
1984, 88 mins, US ⓥ ⊙
D: Graham Baker **A:** Tim Matheson, Meg Tilly, Hume Cronyn, John Karlen, Bill Paxton (ABC)

An ugly little picture that would play better as a comedy if it wasn't so meanspirited. Wholesome young couple Meg Tilly and Tim Matheson are called to Tilly's hometown when her mother (Lorinne Vozoff) blows her brains out. The fact that she's still alive is only the first of the implausible happenings in Sutcliffe. Matheson and Tilly encounter a seething family feud between her father (John Karlen) and her brother (Bill Paxton). Kids set Tilly's car on fire while her old friend (Amy Stryker) tells her it's not easy having children.

IMPULSE
1990, 108 mins, US ⓥ ⊙
D: Sondra Locke **A:** Theresa Russell, Jeff Fahey, George Dzundza, Alan Rosenberg, Shawn Elliott (Warner)

Theresa Russell is a beautiful undercover cop whose life is going nowhere, hence the title: she would like to break out of her rut and act on impulse like one of the prostitute or druggie personas she routinely adopts in her work. Director Locke gets high marks for the visceral, swift nature of her violent stagings. She also manages an impressively tactile sex scene that involves Russell and Fahey.

INADMISSIBLE EVIDENCE
1968, 94 mins, US
D: Anthony Page **A:** Nicol Williamson, Eleanor Fazan, Jill Bennett, Peter Sallis, Eileen Atkins (Woodfall)

As a play, the best thing about *Inad-missible Evidence* was Nicol Williamson, who brought to life the tormented, mediocre, bullying coward that John Osborne had conceived on paper. Same holds true for the screen version, in which same actor appears. There is value and insight to the film. Yet much of it is opaque and confusing. Picture is in black-and-white and it adds to the bleakness of the portrait.

IN A LONELY PLACE
1950, 92 mins, US ⓥ
D: Nicholas Ray **A:** Humphrey Bogart, Gloria Grahame, Frank Lovejoy, Robert Warwick, Jeff Donnell (Columbia/Santana)

Humphrey Bogart has a sympathetic role, though cast as one always ready to mix it with his dukes. As the screenplay scrivener who detests the potboilers, Bogart finds himself innocently suspected of a girl's slaying. Although continually kept under suspicion, he ignores the police attempt to trap him into a confession, at the same time falling for a gal neighbor.

IN & OUT
1997, 90 mins, US ⓥ ⊙
D: Frank Oz **A:** Kevin Kline, Joan Cusack, Matt Dillon, Debbie Reynolds, Tom Selleck, Bob Newhart (Paramount)

A very broad mainstream comedy, *In & Out* has more trouble than it should stretching a high-concept premise into 90 minutes of mirth. Ultra-cool young star Cameron Drake (Matt Dillon) outs his mentor to millions of viewers on a telecast, calling him "a great gay teacher." Howard Brackett (Kevin Kline) is not only not "out," he is not, he claims, even gay. True, he has passed 40 without marrying, but that's about to change with fellow schoolteacher Emily (Joan Cusack). The frenzied media descend upon cozy Greenleaf, IN, to nose out the truth. Pic is given a gratifying measure of grace by Kline's effortlessly light and dexterous performance. Aside from Dillon, who brightens every scene he's in with his hipper-than-thou 'tude, the delightful surprise here is Tom Selleck as a dirt-digging broadcaster.
1997: Nomination: Best Supp. Actress (Joan Cusack)

IN BED WITH MADONNA
See: Truth or Dare: In Bed with Madonna

INCENDIARY BLONDE
1945, 113 mins, US
D: George Marshall **A:** Betty Hutton, Ar-

turo de Cordova, Albert Dekker, Barry Fitzgerald (Paramount)

Sound musical drama based on the life of Broadway's Texas Guinan. Script picks up the Guinan career in Texas in 1909 when she first joins a Wild West show to aid her financially busted father. Her switch to Broadway musicals to escape an unhappy love affair and then desertion of the Great White Way for Hollywood are spanned more quickly. The part racketeering and Prohibition played in her life are all shown and these give dramatic wallop and tenseness to the concluding portions of the story.

INCHON
1981, 140 mins, S. Korea/US
D: Terence Young A: Laurence Olivier, Jacqueline Bisset, Ben Gazzara, Toshiro Mifune, Richard Roundtree (One Way)

A major battle of the Korean War is given a decidedly religious viewpoint via a $46 million pic from an org affiliated with the Reverend Sun Myung Moon. Laurence Olivier plays General Douglas MacArthur. Plot involves the general's orchestration of the 1950 landing at the South Korean port of Inchon by United Nations forces, with heavy emphasis on divine guidance. Olivier is convincing in his role throughout most of the saga, the only member of the cast to achieve that status. Screenplay generally treats all others as one-dimensional buffoons, giving them lines that are unintentionally laughable.

INCIDENT, THE
1967, 99 mins, US ⊛ ⊙
D: Larry Peerce A: Tony Musante, Martin Sheen, Beau Bridges, Bob Bannard, Ed McMahon, Diana Van Der Vlis (20th Century-Fox/Moned)

Strong casting, impressive direction, and generally sharp writing make The Incident a very fine episodic drama. Screenplay spotlights Tony Musante and Martin Sheen, out-for-kicks pair who terrorize 16 riders on a NY subway train. Latter include soldiers Beau Bridges and Bob Bannard, middle-class couple Ed McMahon and Diana Van Der Vlis (with child), elderly marrieds Jack Gilford and Thelma Ritter. The two toughs lay bare the weaknesses in all characters.

IN COLD BLOOD
1967, 133 mins, US ⊛ ⊙ ⊡
D: Richard Brooks A: Robert Blake, Scott Wilson, John Forsythe, Paul Stewart, Gerald S. O'Loughlin, Jeff Corey (Columbia)

Truman Capote's nonfiction novellike account of two Kansas killers becomes on-screen a probing, sensitive, tasteful, balanced, and suspenseful documentary-drama. Film has the look and sound of reality, in part from use of action locales in six states and nonpros as atmosphere players, the rest from Richard Brooks's own filmmaking professionalism. Heading the competent cast are Robert Blake and Scott Wilson, bearing a striking resemblance to the now dead Kansas drifters who, in the course of a burglary on Nov. 15, 1959, murdered four of a family.
1967: Nominations: Best Director, Adapted Screenplay, Cinematography, Original Music Score

IN COUNTRY
1989, 120 mins, US ⊛ ⊙
D: Norman Jewison A: Bruce Willis, Emily Lloyd, Joan Allen, Kevin Anderson, Judith Ivey (Warner)

A film with two stories that fail to add up to something greater: a country girl's coming-of-age, and a troubled Vietnam veteran's coming to terms with his haunting memories of war. Emily Lloyd, in a sparky performance that seizes control of the movie, plays a spirited, just-minted high-school graduate. She lives in a ramshackle house with Bruce Willis, who turns in a likable but unremarkable interpretation of her moody uncle, a veteran who has suffered lasting emotional damage from his nightmarish tour of duty in 'Nam.

INCREDIBLE JOURNEY, THE
1963, 86 mins, US ⊛
D: Fletcher Markle A: Emile Genest, John Drainie, Tommy Tweed, Sandra Scott (Walt Disney)

A live-actioner exquisitely photographed in the Canadian outdoors. A bull terrier, Siamese cat, and Labrador retriever comprise the unlikely trio of pals who, farmed out to a friend of their owners, embark on the journey—over 200 miles of treacherous terrain. They encounter crisis after crisis in what is a remarkable, nay incredible, fight to survive all sorts of adversities in their trip all the way home. The astutely guided animals steal the show.

INCREDIBLE SARAH, THE
1976, 105 mins, UK ⊛ ⊙
D: Richard Fleischer A: Glenda Jackson, Daniel Massey, Yvonne Mitchell, Douglas Wilmer, David Langton (Readers Digest)

Script, conceded in opening titles to be a "free" interpretation of Sarah Bernhardt's early years, follows the famed actress from her early halting years on the French stage, then through an initial period of fame, notoriety, and finally a youthful comeback of sorts at age 35. Glenda Jackson's versatile performance ranges from backstage, intimate situations to several lengthy excerpts from Bernhardt vehicles.

1976: Nominations: Best Costume Design, Art Direction

INCREDIBLE SHRINKING MAN, THE

1957, 81 mins, US Ⓥ ⊙

D: Jack Arnold **A:** Grant Williams, Randy Stuart, April Kent, Paul Langton, Raymond Bailey, William Schallert (Universal)

Six-footer Grant Williams and his wife (Randy Stuart) run into a fog while boating. She's below, so is untouched, but Williams gets the full force. Soon after, he finds himself shrinking and doctors decide the radioactivity in the fog has reversed his growth processes. Director Jack Arnold works up the chills for maximum effect by the time Williams is down to two inches and the family cat takes after him. The technical staff has done an outstanding job of the trick stuff.

INCREDIBLE SHRINKING WOMAN, THE

1981, 88 mins, US Ⓥ ⊙

D: Joel Schumacher **A:** Lily Tomlin, Charles Grodin, Ned Beatty, Henry Gibson, Maria Smith, Mark Blankfield (Universal)

Story of a contemporary housewife whose consistent use of chemically injected brand-name foods, soap powders, and aerosol-propelled products causes her to shrink to minuscule proportions is often strangely humorous with an underlying note of scathing social satire. Unfortunately, even Tomlin's talents begin to wear thin two thirds into the film when she's kidnapped by baddies who want to use her to formulate a serum that will reduce the size of anyone in their way.

INDAGINE SU UN CITTADINO AL DI SOPRA DI OGNI SOSPETTO (US: INVESTIGATION OF A CITIZEN ABOVE SUSPICION)

1970, 114 mins, Italy Ⓥ

D: Elio Petri **A:** Gian Maria Volonte, Florinda Bolkan, Salvo Randone, Gianni Santuccio (Vera)

Pic is dramatically effective in its obvious, stacked assault on petty dictators with a life-and-death grip over human beings. And principally because of Gian Maria Volonte's resounding performance as a homicide chief who commits a murder out of Freudian shortcomings and then deliberately points the finger of guilt at himself to prove that his power position places him above the law.

1970: Best Foreign Language Film

INDECENT PROPOSAL

1993, 117 mins, US Ⓥ ⊙

D: Adrian Lyne **A:** Robert Redford, Demi Moore, Woody Harrelson, Oliver Platt, Seymour Cassel, Billy Connolly (Paramount)

This is one of those high-concept pictures with a big windup and weak delivery. On paper, a film in which billionaire Robert Redford offers down-on-their-luck married couple Woody Harrelson and Demi Moore a cool million in exchange for one-night stand with Moore sounds surefire. On-screen, the result has little sex, goes nowhere interesting or believable in the long second hour, and sports an idiotic conclusion that looks like Test Marketing Ending No. 6. What emotional legitimacy the film does possess stems from Moore's performance, which is lively, heartfelt, and believable until the script stops letting it.

INDEPENDENCE DAY (AKA: FOLLOW YOUR DREAMS)

1983, 110 mins, US Ⓥ

D: Robert Mandel **A:** Kathleen Quinlan, David Keith, Frances Sternhagen, Cliff DeYoung, Dianne Wiest, Josef Sommer (Warner)

An unpleasant dramatic study of young people in a small southwestern town facing family problems and the perennial career decision: to stay home or trek to the big city. Unfocused screenplay centers upon two people in their twenties: Mary Ann Taylor (Kathleen Quinlan), a waitress in her dad's diner in the tiny southwestern town, and Jack Parker (David Keith), a gas-station mechanic just home after an unsuccessful stay at engineering school.

INDEPENDENCE DAY

1996, 145 mins, US ⊙ ⊡

D: Roland Emmerich **A:** Will Smith, Bill Pullman, Jeff Goldblum, Mary Mc-

Donnell, Judd Hirsch, Margaret Colin (Centropolis/20th Century-Fox)

A spectacularly scaled mix of fifties-style alien-invader science fiction, seventies disaster epics, and all-season gung-ho military actioners, this airborne leviathan features a bunch of agreeably cardboard characters saving the human race from mass extermination in a way that proves as unavoidably entertaining as it is hopelessly cornball. The magnitude of the global threat is awesomely established in the teaser opening, which shows the black mother ship, itself a quarter the size of the moon, sailing through the lunar orbit on its way to its rendezvous with Earth. In vintage disaster-pic fashion, a host of characters is sketched in. There is David (Jeff Goldblum), a New York computer genius; Captain Steven Hiller (Will Smith), a hot-dog fighter pilot; and US President Thomas J. Whitmore (Bill Pullman), a rather green national leader widely regarded as a wimp. When some helicopters are summarily blasted out of the sky by the aliens, it becomes clear that the visitors have come not for a picnic, but for a barbecue. The never-ending special effects, while massively spectacular, are not always that special, ranging from terrific computer-generated airborne battles to frankly old-fashioned-looking matte shots and model work.

INDIANA JONES AND THE LAST CRUSADE
1989, 127 mins, US ▼ ⊙ ▭
D: Steven Spielberg A: Harrison Ford, Sean Connery, Denholm Elliott, Alison Doody, John Rhys-Davies, River Phoenix (Paramount/Lucasfilm)

More cerebral than the first two Indiana Jones films, and less schmaltzy than the second, this literate adventure should entertain and enlighten kids and adults alike. The Harrison Ford–Sean Connery father-and-son team gives Last Crusade unexpected emotional depth, reminding us that real film magic is not in special effects. Witty and laconic screenplay takes Ford and Connery on a quest for a prize bigger than the Lost Ark of the Covenant—the Holy Grail. Connery is a medieval-lit prof with strong religious convictions who has spent his life assembling clues to the grail's whereabouts. Father and more intrepid archaeologist son piece them together in an around-the-world adventure, leading to a touching and mystical finale.

1989: Best Sound Effects Editing
Nomination: Best Original Score, Sound

INDIANA JONES AND THE TEMPLE OF DOOM
1984, 118 mins, US ▼ ⊙ ▭
D: Steven Spielberg A: Harrison Ford, Kate Capshaw, Ke Huy Quan, Amrish Puri, Roshan Seth, Philip Stone (Lucasfilm)

Steven Spielberg has packed even more thrills and chills into this follow-up than he did into the earlier pic, but to exhausting and numbing effect. Harrison Ford escapes from an enormous melee, coming to rest in an impoverished Indian village. Community's leader implores the ace archaeologist to retrieve a sacred, magical stone which has been stolen by malevolent neighbors. Remainder of the yarn is set in labyrinth of horrors lorded over by a pre-pubescent maharajah, where untold dangers await the heroes. What with John Williams's incessant score and the library full of sound effects, there isn't a quiet moment in the entire picture.

1984: Best Visual Effects
Nomination: Best Original Score

INDIAN FIGHTER, THE
1955, 88 mins, US ▭
D: Andre de Toth A: Kirk Douglas, Elsa Martinelli, Walter Abel, Walter Matthau, Diana Douglas, Eduard Franz (Bryna/United Artists)

This frontier actioner will satisfy the demands of the outdoor fan. Footage is inclined to get monotonous at times. Sex in the person of Elsa Martinelli and the relationship of her Indian-maid character with Kirk Douglas is a story factor and ballyhoo point. Douglas dashes about as a grinning, virile hero. His job here is to lead a wagon train through Indian country into Oregon, but he gets sidetracked from duty in wooing Martinelli long enough for some crooks to stir up trouble over Indian gold.

INDIAN IN THE CUPBOARD, THE
1995, 96 mins, US ▼ ⊙
D: Frank Oz A: Hal Scardino, Litefoot, Lindsay Crouse, Richard Jenkins, Rishi Bhat, David Keith (Kennedy-Marshall)

Based on a popular children's book, The Indian in the Cupboard never comes alive as a movie. Earnest and well intentioned, the promising concept feels stretched to feature length. Virtually no groundwork is laid before nine-year-old Omri (Hal Scardino) receives for his birthday what turns out to be a magical cupboard that can bring his action figures to life. Though the cabinet works on more extravagant items, from RoboCop to Darth Vader, he becomes enamored of a three-inch-tall Indian named Little Bear (played by recording artist Litefoot, in his acting debut).

INDIAN RUNNER, THE
1991, 126 mins, US Ⓥ ⊙
D: Sean Penn **A:** David Morse, Viggo Mortensen, Valeria Golino, Patricia Arquette, Charles Bronson, Sandy Dennis (Mount)

A tortured examination of the disintegration of a midwestern family, *The Indian Runner* is very much actors' cinema. Rambling, indulgent, and joltingly raw at times, Sean Penn's first outing as a director takes a fair amount of patience to get through but has an integrity that intermittently serves it well. Inspired by the Bruce Springsteen song ''Highway Patrolman,'' overwrought piece looks at the muted tragedy of two brothers in the late 1960s. Joe (David Morse) is a small-town Nebraska cop who tries to welcome his brother Frank (Viggo Mortensen) back into the fold after the latter returns from a stint in Vietnam, but Frank immediately takes off.

INDIAN SUMMER
1993, 97 mins, US Ⓥ ⊙ ⊏
D: Mike Binder **A:** Alan Arkin, Matt Craven, Diane Lane, Bill Paxton, Elizabeth Perkins, Vincent Spano (Touchstone/Outlaw)

Awash in romantic nostalgia for childhoods spent in summer camps, *Indian Summer* is a sentimental, TV-sitcom-like film. This *Big Chill* regrouping takes place in gorgeous Camp Tamakwa, the site of their 1972 summer. The seven returning campers include the single and increasingly desperate Jennifer (Elizabeth Perkins), Matthew and Kelly (Vincent Spano and Julie Warner), whose marriage seems in trouble, insensitive ''macho'' Jamie (Matt Craven), and his much-younger g.f. Gwen (Kimberly Williams). Presiding over the group is Unca Lou (Alan Arkin), a benevolent patriarch who has devoted his entire life to the camp.

INDISCREET
1931, 93 mins, US Ⓥ
D: Leo McCarey **A:** Gloria Swanson, Ben Lyon, Monroe Owsley, Barbara Kent, Arthur Lake (United Artists)

An original story of the musical-comedy-writing trio of DeSylva, Brown, and Henderson, film is without music of moment or quantity. As a comedy-drama it is more comedy than drama. Ben Lyon plays the light-minded but sincere author who falls for Jerry (Swanson) but won't listen about her past when she gets to the point of should-a-woman-tell.

INDISCREET
1958, 100 mins, US Ⓥ
D: Stanley Donen **A:** Cary Grant, Ingrid Bergman, Cecil Parker, Phyllis Calvert, David Kossoff (Grandon/Warner)

A beguiling love story delicately deranged by the complications of sophisticated comedy. As the successful actress who has yet to find love, Ingrid Bergman is alluring, most affectionate, and highly amusing. Grant, a rich American, also wants to find love. But the difference is he wants nothing of marriage and, to protect all concerned, advises Bergman on first meeting that he is a married man, separated, and unable to obtain a divorce.

INDISCRETION
See: Indiscretion of an American Wife

INDISCRETION OF AN AMERICAN WIFE
(UK: INDISCRETION)
1954, 63 mins, Italy/US Ⓥ
D: Vittorio De Sica **A:** Jennifer Jones, Montgomery Clift, Gino Cervi, Richard Beymer (Columbia)

An Italian-filmed feature, very consciously arty and foreign. The lensing was done in its entirety in the Stazione Termini in Rome, where the story of an American housewife (Jennifer Jones) saying farewell to her younger holiday lover (Montgomery Clift) takes place. Outside of the agonizing moments of farewells, the story's dramatic suspense pull is developed around the couple's arrest after being discovered in an extremely compromising embrace in a secluded spot. The stars give the drama a real pro try, though the character interpretations will not be liked by all.

1954: Nomination: Best B&W Costume Design

INDOCHINE
1992, 158 mins, France Ⓥ ⊙ ⊏
D: Regis Wargnier **A:** Catherine Deneuve, Vincent Perez, Linh Dan Pham, Jean Yanne, Dominique Blanc (Paradis/Generale d'Images/Bac/Orly/Cine 5)

Set during rising Communist protests in the 1930s, *Indochine* is a riveting ro-

mantic saga, thanks to Catherine Deneuve's classy performance, a sizzling story line, and eye-catching locales in Vietnam. Pic sticks close to its three main characters: a Frenchwoman who runs one of the country's biggest rubber plantations, her adopted Indochinese daughter, and the dashing French navy officer who loves each woman in quick succession. Deneuve's impeccable performance brings to life the best and worst of the French colonialism. Perez handles his fast-changing role with great sensitivity. Newcomer Pham shines as sheltered daughter and hardened revolutionary.
1993: Best Foreign Language Film

I NEVER PROMISED YOU A ROSE GARDEN
1977, 96 mins, US Ⓥ
D: Anthony Page **A:** Bibi Andersson, Kathleen Quinlan, Sylvia Sidney, Martine Bartlett, Signe Hasso, Susan Tyrrell (Fadsin/New World)

Good intentions resolve into high-minded tedium. The pic's central problem is its structure. The girl (Kathleen Quinlan) is presented at the outset as a certifiable nutto teenager. An improved mental state is a certainty, otherwise there's no film. Quinlan is an atypical young actress, who lends freshness and admirable reserve to a role that could have lapsed entirely into histrionic hysterics.
1977: Nomination: Best Adapted Screenplay

I NEVER SANG FOR MY FATHER
1970, 92 mins, US Ⓥ
D: Gilbert Cates **A:** Melvyn Douglas, Gene Hackman, Dorothy Stickney, Estelle Parsons (Columbia/Jamel)

Film version of Robert Anderson's 1968 play is distended and lacking clear point of view. Mostly the story of a middle-aged man still strung up by a family umbilical cord, the film veers awkwardly into problems of the aged. However, the performances of father Melvyn Douglas, mother Dorothy Stickney, son Gene Hackman and daughter Estelle Parsons are superb.
1970: Nominations: Best Actor (Melvyn Douglas), Supp. Actor (Gene Hackman), Adapted Screenplay

INFERNO
1953, 83 mins, US
D: Roy Ward Baker **A:** Robert Ryan, Rhonda Fleming, William Lundigan,

Larry Keating, Henry Hull (20th Century-Fox)

Technicolor and 3-D are used effectively to make this suspense melodrama a fairly entertaining entry. Playboy Carson (Robert Ryan) is left to die of thirst and a broken leg by Geraldine (Rhonda Fleming) and Duncan (William Lundigan) while on a prospecting trip. Driven by a desire to defeat their murder plot and get revenge, he finds resources within himself to conquer the burning heat, the bitter cold, and other dangers.

INFORMER, THE
1935, 91 mins, US Ⓥ Ⓒ
D: John Ford **A:** Victor McLaglen, Heather Angel, Preston Foster, Margot Grahame, Wallace Ford, Una O'Connor (RKO)

Forcefully and intelligently written, directed, and acted. Story deals with the Irish rebellion against British authority prior to 1922. Amid the rebellion-rife slums of Dublin a huge ox of a peasant, named Gypo Nolan (Victor McLaglen) is taunted by his girl for his miserable poverty and inability to provide money. Gypo, in fascinated horror at his own wickedness, deliberately turns informer on his best friend to obtain $100 reward. What makes the picture powerful is the faithful characterization of McLaglen as guided and developed by the direction of John Ford. Gypo is a blundering, pathetic fool who is not basically vicious yet is guilty of a truly foul betrayal.
1935: Best Director, Actor (Victor McLaglen), Screenplay, Score
Nominations: Best Picture, Editing

INFORMERS, THE
(US: UNDERWORLD INFORMERS)
1963, 105 mins, UK
D: Ken Annakin **A:** Nigel Patrick, Frank Finlay, Derren Nesbitt, Colin Blakely, Catherine Woodville, Maggie Whiting (Rank)

Here's a tough, hard-hitting, cops-and-robbers thriller set in London's underworld which crackles along at a brisk pace and has the smell of authenticity. Central character is Chief Inspector Johnno (Nigel Patrick), a dedicated cop at Scotland Yard. He has many contacts in the underworld and the snouts, or informers, feed him with many a juicy lead to solving a crime. But Johnno's chief insists that personal contact with informers should be out. Johnno disobeys orders.

IN GOD WE TRUST, OR, GIMME THAT PRIME TIME RELIGION
1980, 97 mins, US Ⓥ
D: Marty Feldman **A:** Marty Feldman, Peter Boyle, Louise Lasser, Wilfrid Hyde-White, Richard Pryor (Universal)

A rare achievement—acomedy with no laughs. Technically, film is a near shambles. Totally innocent monk Marty Feldman is cast out into the mean and nasty world to raise some quick cash to keep his monastery in business. He ends up on Hollywood Blvd. Object of his search is outrageous TV evangelist Armageddon T. Thunderbird (Andy Kaufman).

IN HARM'S WAY
1965, 165 mins, US Ⓥ ◻
D: Otto Preminger **A:** John Wayne, Kirk Douglas, Patricia Neal, Tom Tryon, Paula Prentiss, Henry Fonda (Sigma/Paramount)

John Wayne is in every sense the big gun of *In Harm's Way*. Without his commanding presence, chances are director-producer Otto Preminger probably could not have built the head of steam this film generates and sustains for two hours and 45 minutes. Romantic coupling of Wayne and Patricia Neal, as a navy nurse, is the most natural stroke of man and woman casting in many a year. Preminger provides, in the picture's action stretches, a highly suspenseful and, at times, shatteringly realistic account of an underdog US Navy task force boldly seeking out a Japanese group of ships. The sea-battle sequences are filmmaking at its best.
1965: Nomination: Best B&W Cinematography

INHERIT THE WIND
1960, 126 mins, US Ⓥ ◉
D: Stanley Kramer **A:** Spencer Tracy, Fredric March, Gene Kelly, Florence Eldridge, Harry Morgan (United Artists)

This is a rousing and fascinating motion picture. One suspects it needed a strong hand to restrain the forensics of Spencer Tracy and Fredric March as defense and prosecution attorneys in this drama inspired by the 1925 trial in Dayton, TN, of a young high-school teacher for daring to teach Darwin's theory of evolution. Roles of Tracy and March equal Clarence Darrow and William Jennings Bryan, who collided on evolution. March actually has the more colorful role (as Bryan), whereas Tracy has to rely solely upon his power of illusion, a most persuasive power indeed. A good measure of the film's surface bite is contributed by Gene

Kelly as a cynical Baltimore reporter (patterned after Henry L. Mencken).
1960: Nominations: Best Actor (Spencer Tracy), Adapted Screenplay, B&W Cinematography, Editing

INJI KAU
(ROUGE)
1988, 93 mins, Hong Kong Ⓥ ◉
D: Stanley Kwan **A:** Anita Mui, Leslie Cheung, Alex Man, Emily Chu, Tam Tsinhung (Golden Way)

A classy, elegant, artistic, believable, and enjoyable love story with a ghost framework. The movie is set in colorful 1900 and retells the sad story of a high-class prostitute called Flower (Anita Mui, a singer who proves that she's also a dramatic actress), who falls in love with a customer (Leslie Cheung, perfect typecasting), a spoiled, passive young man controlled by family ties. Flower dies but the young man survives. They are expected to meet in "hell'' and Flower waits for years in the spiritual dimension. When he does not come, she returns to earth to look for her lost lover.

IN-LAWS, THE
1979, 103 mins, US Ⓥ
D: Arthur Hiller **A:** Peter Falk, Alan Arkin, Richard Libertini, Nancy Dussault, Arlene Golonka, Ed Begley Jr. (Warner)

Peter Falk and Alan Arkin play an addled CIA agent and a Gotham dentist, respectively. Brought together by the impending marriage of their individual offspring (Michael Lembeck and Penny Peyser), they're quickly at each other's throat, as Falk lures Arkin into a never-ending series of improbable adventures.

IN LIKE FLINT
1967, 115 mins, US Ⓥ ◉ ◻
D: Gordon Douglas **A:** James Coburn, Lee J. Cobb, Jean Hale, Andrew Duggan, Anna Lee (20th Century-Fox)

Girls, gimmicks, girls, gags, and more girls are the essential parameters of *In Like Flint*. With James Coburn encoring as the urbane master sleuth, also harried boss Lee J. Cobb, this pic turns on a femme plot to take over the world. While the dialogue scenes tend to be a mite sluggish, pace picks up regularly with slam-bang action sequences.

IN LOVE AND WAR
1958, 107 mins, US ◻
D: Philip Dunne **A:** Robert Wagner, Dana Wynter, Jeffrey Hunter, Hope Lange, Bradford Dillman, Sheree North, France

Nuyen, Mort Sahl (20th Century-Fox)

A keen appraisal of the utility of love and the futility of war, hard-hitting in action and dialogue. Story is of the changing ideals and growing maturity of three marines in the Second World War. At the start, Jeffrey Hunter is the patriot, Robert Wagner the coward, and Bradford Dillman the intellectual who fights because he must. More than war, the tale is about love, Wagner's for Sheree North, Hunter is for Hope Lange, and Dillman for France Nuyen.

IN LOVE AND WAR
1996, 115 mins, US Ⓥ ⊙ ▭
D: Richard Attenborough **A:** Sandra Bullock, Chris O'Donnell, Mackenzie Astin, Emilio Bonucci, Ingrid Lacey, Margot Steinberg (New Line)

A pallid telling of the fleeting but indelible romance between Ernest Hemingway and his nurse in Italy during World War I, Richard Attenborough's sixth biographical drama goes through the motions of spinning a passionate love story set against a grand historical background, but doesn't get under the skin of its protagonists. Neither the script nor Attenborough's stately direction manages to take the careful, restrained romance to the emotional depths desirable in a sweeping big-screen love story, and Sandra Bullock and Chris O'Donnell lack the range and nuance to take this journey into uncharted dramatic territory. Bullock has no trouble holding viewer interest, but the true nature of her feelings for Hemingway remains somewhat unclear.

IN NAME ONLY
1939, 94 mins, US Ⓥ ⊙
D: John Cromwell **A:** Carole Lombard, Cary Grant, Kay Francis, Charles Coburn, Helen Vinson, Peggy Ann Garner (RKO)

A romantic drama of a familiar but highly poignant brand, relieved by smart comedy lines and touches. Cary Grant and Carole Lombard emerge highly impressive. Grant figures in some of the comedy relief, but Lombard is almost entirely on the romantic drama side, turning in a fine performance. As the mercenary wife, Kay Francis does well.

INNER CIRCLE, THE
1991, 134 mins, US Ⓥ
D: Andrei Konchalovsky **A:** Tom Hulce, Lolita Davidovich, Bob Hoskins, Alexandre Zbruev, Feodor Chaliapin Jr., Irina Kupchenko (Columbia)

The first Western film to shoot within the Kremlin and KGB h.q., and Andrei Konchalovsky's first Soviet-based pic in 12 years, this idiosyncratic look at the life of Stalin's personal projectionist has numerous points of interest but is too muddled and misconceived. Set in Moscow beginning in 1939 and based on a true story, this odd tale focuses on Ivan Sanshin (Tom Hulce), a groveling, pathetic projectionist for the KGB who has a kind of greatness thrust upon him when he is summarily ordered to screen a film for the supreme leader. Pic excels in glimpses of power at the top. Ultimately, however, the story proves unwieldy, with Konchalovsky unable to integrate the diverse sides of the tale and give it a proper dramatic arc.

INNERSPACE
1987, 120 mins, US Ⓥ ⊙
D: Joe Dante **A:** Dennis Quaid, Martin Short, Meg Ryan, Kevin McCarthy, Fiona Lewis, Henry Gibson (Warner/Amblin)

Hot-dog air-force flier Dennis Quaid is prepared at the outset to be shrunken and to pilot a tiny craft through the bloodstream of a laboratory rabbit. Evildoers are onto the unprecedented experiment and the syringe bearing the fearless voyager finally implants itself in the behind of Martin Short, a hapless grocery clerk. Filmmakers' ingenuity quickly begins asserting itself. As Quaid travels through different parts of the unsuspecting schnook's body and speaks to him over his radio, Short believes he's going crazy before finally accepting what's happened to him.
1987: Best Visual Effects

INNOCENCE UNPROTECTED
See: Nevinost Bez Zastite

INNOCENT, THE
1993, 107 mins, UK/Germany Ⓥ
D: John Schlesinger **A:** Isabella Rossellini, Anthony Hopkins, Campbell Scott, Ronald Nitschke, Hart Bochner (Lakehart/Sievernich/Babelsberg)

Despite a close screen translation by Ian McEwan of his own novel of intrigue, espionage, betrayal, and love, pic lacks real sense of drama. A bespectacled Campbell Scott plays Leonard Markham, a young, naive, and virginal British engineer sent to Berlin in 1955, at the height of the cold war, for reasons he does not know. His commanding officer, Lofting (Jeremy Sinden, in a spunky perf), turns Markham over to Bob Glass (Anthony Hopkins), a CIA officer overseeing a British–West German espionage project to intercept communications between East Germany and the Soviet Union. So intent is the film on its narrative purpose that it fails to build tension or suspense.

INNOCENT BLOOD
(AUSTRALIA: FRENCH VAMPIRE IN AMERICA)
1992, 113 mins, US Ⓥ ⊙
D: John Landis **A:** Anne Parillaud, Robert Loggia, Anthony LaPaglia, David Proval, Don Rickles, Chazz Palminteri (Warner)

Teens and genre fans should eat up John Landis's latest mix of horror and camp comedy. They will ''ooh'' at the various gross-out scenes and nifty special effects, ''aah'' at the film's sensuality and Anne Parillaud's easy nudity, and savor the numerous in-jokes and horror references, from cameos by other goremeister directors to clips from various late-show staples. The director benefits from a toothy performance by Robert Loggia as a Mob boss who, endowed with vampiric powers by the mysterious Marie (Parillaud), goes on a rampage.

INNOCENT BYSTANDERS
1972, 111 mins, UK
D: Peter Collinson **A:** Stanley Baker, Geraldine Chaplin, Donald Pleasence, Dana Andrews, Sue Lloyd, Warren Mitchell (Sagittarius)

A violence-packed, often confusing, but usually interesting meller of secret agents on the prowl to track down and capture a Russian scientist escaped from a Siberian prison. Scene shifts from London to NY, thence to Turkey, where major portion of action unfolds against colorful location backgrounds.

INNOCENT LIES
1995, 89 mins, UK/France Ⓥ ▭
D: Patrick Dewolf **A:** Stephen Dorff, Gabrielle Anwar, Adrian Dunbar, Sophie Aubry, Joanna Lumley (Red Umbrella/Septieme/PolyGram)

Style almost triumphs over content in an arty whodunit-cum-thriller that completely unravels in the third act but has a kind of anything-goes bravura that has to be admired. Inspired by Agatha Christie (per movie's end crawl) but not based on a specific work, film gets off to a pacey start with the death of Britisher Joe Green (Donal McCann, uncredited) near a clifftop manse ''somewhere on the French coast'' in September '38. On the next plane from Blighty comes Inspector Cross (Adrian Dunbar), bent on discovering the truth behind his best friend's apparent suicide. French helmer/coscripter Patrick Dewolf sets up a simmering atmosphere in the opening reels, but the movie falls uneasily between two stools, convincing neither as a murder mystery nor as a sexually charged meller.

INNOCENT MAN, AN
1989, 113 mins, US Ⓥ ⊙
D: Peter Yates **A:** Tom Selleck, F. Murray Abraham, Laila Robins (Touchstone/Silver Screen Partners IV)

This collection of clichés brings the prison genre to a new low. Nightmarishly structured, the film takes half hour before Tom Selleck's everyman, Jimmie Rainwood, gets wrongfully framed by two corrupt vice cops. Then he spends more than an hour in stir before he gets released to seek vengeance on the duo in one of the more absurd finales in memory.

INNOCENTS, THE
1961, 99 mins, UK ▭
D: Jack Clayton **A:** Deborah Kerr, Michael Redgrave, Peter Wyngarde, Megs Jenkins, Martin Stephens, Pamela Franklin (20th Century-Fox)

Based on Henry James's story *Turn of the Screw*, this catches an eerie, spine-chilling mood right at the start and never lets up on its grim, evil theme. Director Jack Clayton makes full use of camera angles, sharp cutting, shadows, ghost effects, and a sinister soundtrack. Deborah Kerr has a long, arduous role as a governess in charge of two apparently angelic little children in a huge country house. Gradually she finds that they are not all that they seem on the surface. Her determination to save the two moppets' corrupted souls leads up to a tragic, powerful climax.

INNOCENT SLEEP, THE
1996, 99 mins, UK Ⓥ ▭
D: Scott Michell **A:** Rupert Graves, Annabella Sciorra, Michael Gambon, Franco Nero, Graham Crowden, John Hannah (Timedial)

When Alan Terry (an effective Rupert Graves), a homeless drunk, beds down near Tower Bridge, he's got a box seat when a suave Italian (Franco Nero) oversees the execution of a fellow Italian. He discovers that the officer in charge of the investigation, Matheson (the chillingly intense Michael Gambon), was one of the killers. Terry enlists the help of a tough-as-nails Yank investigative reporter, Billie Hayman (a delightful Annabella Sciorra), who works for a London tabloid. Story builds a fair degree of suspense before the rather disappointing finale.

INN OF THE SIXTH HAPPINESS, THE
1958, 158 mins, US Ⓥ ⊙ ▭
D: Mark Robson A: Ingrid Bergman, Curt Jurgens, Robert Donat, Ronald Squire, Athene Seyler (20th Century-Fox)

Film has Ingrid Bergman as a rejected missionary in China, who gets there determinedly under her own steam. First met with hostility by the natives, she gradually wins their love and esteem. She falls in love with a Eurasian colonel, converts a powerful mandarin to Christianity, and becomes involved in the Chino-Japanese war. Finally she guides 100 children to the safety of a northern mission by leading them on an arduous journey across the rugged mountains and through enemy territory. A standout performance comes from Robert Donat as an astute yet benign mandarin.
1958: Nomination: Best Director

IN OLD ARIZONA
1929, 94 mins, US
D: Irving Cummings, Raoul Walsh A: Warner Baxter, Edmund Lowe, Dorothy Burgess, J. Farrell McDonald (Fox)

It's the first outdoor talker and a western, with a climax twist to make the story stand out from the usual hill-and-dale thesis. It has a great screen performance by Warner Baxter. That it's long and that it moves slowly is also true. Dorothy Burgess is cast as Tonia, a Mexican vixen who plays the boys across the boards and finally gets into a jam between the Cisco Kid (Baxter) and the army sergeant who is pursuing the bandit.
1928/29: Best Actor (Warner Baxter)
Nominations: Best Picture, Director, Writing, Cinematography

IN OLD CHICAGO
1938, 110 mins, US Ⓥ
D: Henry King A: Tyrone Power, Alice Faye, Don Ameche, Alice Brady, Andy Devine, Brian Donlevy (20th Century-Fox)

An elaborate and liberally budgeted entertainment, the pictorial climax is the Chicago fire of 1871. This portion envisaging mob panic, desperate efforts to stop the fire by dynamiting, etc., is highly effective. Its story is mere rehash of corrupt political mismanagement of a growing American city. But as a film entertainment it is socko. The O'Leary family plays the most important part in the story, even to the point where one of the sons is projected as mayor of the city at the time of the fire, and another is pictured as the dishonest political boss, saloonkeeper, and villain. Alice Brady and Alice Faye give the outstanding performances. Brady is Mrs. O'Leary, an honest, hardworking laundress with a pleasing Irish brogue. Faye appears as a music-hall singer.
1937: Best Supp. Actress (Alice Brady), Assistant Director (Robert Webb)
Nominations: Best Picture, Original Story, Score, Sound

IN OLD KENTUCKY
1935, 85 mins, US Ⓥ
D: George Marshall A: Will Rogers, Dorothy Wilson, Russell Hardie, Charles Sellon, Louise Henry, Esther Dale (Fox)

Will Rogers's last picture is a delightful comedy. As a foil for Rogers and excellent on his own, Bill Robinson hoofs his way to importance. The Robinson stepping also gives Rogers a chance to go on the hoof and this is built into a comedy sequence that makes the picture a honey with or without the rest of the footage.

IN SEARCH OF GREGORY
1970, 90 mins, UK/Italy
D: Peter Wood A: Julie Christie, Michael Sarrazin, John Hurt, Paola Pitagora, Roland Culver (Vic/Vera)

A superbly wrought gem about the romantic illusions people, especially would-be lovers, search for in one another, with Julie Christie ideally cast as the seeker and Michael Sarrazin as her fantasy. Christie, the daughter of a Swiss financier, is invited by Papa to attend his latest nuptials. Her real attraction is Celi's calculating description of his housequest from San Francisco, a tall, handsome "likable maniac." At the airport, she spots a giant poster of Sarrazin, an auto-ball champion, and he becomes the physical embodiment of her romantic fantasies about Gregory.

IN SEARCH OF THE CASTAWAYS
1962, 100 mins, US Ⓥ ⊙
D: Robert Stevenson A: Maurice Chevalier, Hayley Mills, George Sanders, Wilfrid Hyde White, Michael Anderson Jr., Wilfrid Brambell (Walt Disney)

A blend of every Disney trick, combining adventure and humor. A French scientist finds a note which reveals the whereabouts of Captain Grant, who mysteriously disappeared. The Frenchman and the sea captain's two children persuade a wealthy shipping owner and his son to set off for South America in search of the missing man. The party survives giant condors, jaguars, flood, lightning, crocodiles, an avalanche, an earthquake, a huge waterspout, mutiny, imprisonment by unfriendly Maoris, and an erupting volcano.

INSERTS
1975, 117 mins, UK Ⓥ
D: John Byrum **A:** Richard Dreyfuss, Jessica Harper, Stephen Davie, Veronica Cartwright, Bob Hoskins (Film & General)

Despite its British label, this is a thoroughly Yank pic that dips into nostalgia. Richard Dreyfuss is all coiled disdain as a once-great director reduced to stag pix. But it is all somewhat too surface despite allusions to Hollywood 1930s types.

INSIDE
1996, 94 mins, US
D: Arthur Penn **A:** Eric Stoltz, Nigel Hawthorne, Louis Gossett Jr., Ian Roberts, Ross Prelier (Elkins/Lo Go/Showtime)

Another antiapartheid drama largely focused on a sympathetic white protagonist, pic is a provocative if flawed chamber piece. At the outset, 30-year-old Afrikaaner Peter Martin Strydom (Eric Stoltz) already has been beaten and tortured, but as yet denies any alleged "conspiracy to commit treason, sabotage, and terrorism." Interrogating Colonel Krueger (Nigel Hawthorne) deploys a wicked array of tactics to encourage Marty's confession. Ten years later, the colonel reviews these events—under the unforgiving gaze of his own "Questioner" (Louis Gossett Jr.), investigating the former regime's human-rights crimes in a new, postapartheid era. Put in the hot seat himself for a change, the colonel remains a model of cool hypocrisy and denial—to a point. Penn, lenser Jan Weincke, and the production designers do a terrific job exploiting the claustrophobia of the central action.

INSIDE DAISY CLOVER
1965, 128 mins, US Ⓥ ⊙ ▭
D: Robert Mulligan **A:** Natalie Wood, Christopher Plummer, Robert Redford, Roddy McDowall, Ruth Gordon, Katharine Bard (Park Place/Warner)

There will be those who may claim *Inside Daisy Clover* is based on the true-life story of an actress who rose to shining blond stardom. Alan J. Pakula and Robert Mulligan focus their sights upon a teenage beach gamin who becomes a Hollywood star of the 1930s. Covering a two-year period, the outcome is at times disjointed and episodic as the title character played by Natalie Wood emerges more nebulous than definitive. Probably the outstanding parts of pic are two novel musical numbers. Wood is better than her part.

1965: Nominations: Best Supp. Actress (Ruth Gordon), Color Costume Design, Color Art Direction

INSIDE MONKEY ZETTERLAND
1992, 92 mins, US Ⓥ
D: Jefery Levy **A:** Steven Antin, Katherine Helmond, Patricia Arquette, Tate Donovan, Bo Hopkins, Sandra Bernhard (Coast Entertainment)

A charming comedy about contempo L.A. life. Although pic is populated by gay and lesbian characters, its broad canvas, humanistic vision, magnetic cast, and inspired writing extend its appeal. At the heart of scripter Steven Antin's poetic, loosely autobiographical comedy is the complex, Oedipal relationship between aspiring writer Monkey Zetterland (Antin) and his domineering Jewish mother (Katherine Helmond), a TV soap star. Pic's best sequences depict collective gatherings (Thanksgiving dinner, evenings in front of the TV) in which Monkey's friends behave like one big, extended family, expanding the conventional meaning of family life.

INSIDE MOVES
THE GUYS FROM MAX'S BAR
1980, 113 mins, US Ⓥ ⊙ ▭
D: Richard Donner **A:** John Savage, David Morse, Diana Scarwid, Harold Russell, Amy Wright, Tony Burton (AFD/Goodmark)

Inoffensive and essentially compassionate, *Inside Moves* is also a highly conventional and predictable look at handicapped citizens trying to make it in everyday life. Director focuses on the intermittently tense relationship between insecure, failed suicide John Savage and volatile David Morse. Basic plot movement has Savage, permanently hobbled after jumping off a building, gradually regaining confidence. Diana Scarwid hits the right notes as a "normal" young woman forced to confront her own limitations via the outwardly afflicted.

1980: Nomination: Best Supp. Actress (Diana Scarwid)

INSIDER, THE
1999, 157 mins, US ⓥ ⊙ ▭
D: Michael Mann A: Al Pacino, Russell Crowe, Christopher Plummer, Diane Venora, Philip Baker Hall, Lindsay Crouse (Forward Pass/Mann-Roth/Touchstone)

The impact of a challenging story boldly tackled is diminished by serious overlength and an overriding air of self-importance. The story of the unheroic scientific researcher who exposed the tobacco companies' official lies about the unhealthful nature of their product has provided director and cowriter Michael Mann with the opportunity for a dual investigation of corporate duplicity, courtesy of CBS's decision not to air its explosive interview with the whistle-blower. In the wake of CBS's cop-out, producer Lowell Bergman (Al Pacino) must battle with a smear campaign launched against Jeffrey Wigand (Russell Crowe). Crowe makes him a fascinating figure of complicated motives. Pacino invests Bergman with boundless passion for his job, but it's a one-note character.
1999: Nominations: Best Picture, Director, Best Actor (Russell Crowe), Adapted Screenplay, Cinematography, Film Editing, Sound

INSIGNIFICANCE
1985, 108 mins, UK ⓥ
D: Nicolas Roeg A: Gary Busey, Tony Curtis, Michael Emil, Theresa Russell, Will Sampson (Zenith/Recorded Picture)

A comedy set in a New York hotel room over a sweaty night in 1953, story concerns four celebrated American figures of the 1950s who, for legal reasons, are not specifically named. That's all to the good, since pic dispenses with biographical detail to focus on the nature of celebrity in cold-war America. *Insignificance* also works on a simpler level as a depiction of four people struggling against despair.

IN SOCIETY
1944, 73 mins, US
D: Jean Yarbrough A: Bud Abbott, Lou Costello, Marion Hutton, Kirby Grant (Universal)

Basic idea spots Abbott and Costello as two struggling, extra-dumb plumbers being accidentally invited to a high-society weekend soiree. Their exertions and blundering efforts to adjust themselves to new surroundings furnish the pegs on which many gags are strung. But even before

reaching Hollywood's idea of effete society, a bunch of new and old comedy routines are dusted off and whipped across deftly.

INSPECTOR CLOUSEAU
1968, 105 mins, UK ▭
D: Bud Yorkin A: Alan Arkin, Frank Finlay, Delia Boccardo, Patrick Cargill, Beryl Reid, Barry Foster (United Artists/Mirisch)

The gauche and Gallic gumshoe gets a healthy revitalization via Alan Arkin in the title role and director Bud Yorkin. Film is a lively, entertaining, and episodic story of bank robbers. Story develops to a simultaneous robbery of about a dozen Swiss banks, by a ring whose members wear face masks patterned after Clouseau. Enough momentum is sustained to hold amused interest.

INSPECTOR GADGET
1999, 77 mins, US ⓥ ⊙
D: David Kellogg A: Matthew Broderick, Rupert Everett, Joely Fisher, Michelle Trachtenberg, Andy Dick, Cheri Oteri (Walt Disney)

Inspector Gadget is a joyless and charmless disaster in which state-of-the-art special effects are squandered on pain-in-the-backside folly. Loosely based on the eighties' TV cartoon series about a bumbling bionic crime-fighter, this pic is evidently aimed at moppets with near-zero attention spans. Matthew Broderick stars as John Brown, an idealistic security guard who, all but killed by evil billionaire Sanford Scolex (Rupert Everett) and his flunky (Michael G. Hagerty), is given a new lease on life as a gizmo-enhanced cyborg and renamed Inspector Gadget. Under the direction of first-time feature helmer David Kellogg, the film careens dementedly from scene to scene. Broderick makes a game effort but overdoes the gee-whiz ingenuousness. Everett is pedestrian as the villain.

INSPIRATION
1931, 73 mins, US ⓥ ⊙
D: Clarence Brown A: Greta Garbo, Robert Montgomery, Lewis Stone, Marjorie Rambeau (M-G-M)

Replete with heavy love stuff, Garbo plays it easily and convincingly, even contributing a sparkling brief bit of light comedy. The freewheeling Parisian artist's model is introduced rather tritely as the town toast among the artistic set. She's the inspiration for the latest successful works of an artist, a sculptor, a composer, and a writer. Robert Montgomery is an excellent nice boy from the country.

INTERIORS
1978, 93 mins, US Ⓥ ⊙
D: Woody Allen **A:** Kristin Griffith, Mary Beth Hurt, Richard Jordan, Diane Keaton, E. G. Marshall, Geraldine Page (United Artists)

The film is populated by characters reacting to situations Allen has satirized so brilliantly in other pictures. Diane Keaton is a suffering poet married to Richard Jordan, a novelist overshadowed by Keaton's accomplishments and talents. Keaton has two sisters—Kristin Griffith, a television actress, and Mary Beth Hurt, the most gifted of the three, but the least directed. What would be called the film's action—like Ingmar Bergman's pictures, the movement is interior, in the mind—revolves around the relationship among the sisters and their parents, E. G. Marshall and Geraldine Page.

1978: Nominations: Best Director, Actress (Geraldine Page), Supp. Actress (Maureen Stapleton), Original Screenplay, Art Direction

INTERLUDE
1968, 113 mins, UK Ⓥ
D: Kevin Billington **A:** Oskar Werner, Barbara Ferris, Virginia Maskell, Donald Sutherland, Nora Swinburne, John Cleese (Columbia/Domino)

Oskar Werner and Barbara Ferris are the star-crossed, and star-billed, lovers in this handsome production, filmed in England. All the excitement and ecstasy, as well as the bittersweet, foredoomed disenchantment of extramarital romance are contained in the original screenplay. Strong writing, superior acting, and first-rate direction make this a powerful, personal drama. Werner plays a temperamental symphonic conductor who is interviewed by Ferris, a newspaper reporter, the story unfolding in flashback format.

INTERMEZZO
1936, 88 mins, Sweden Ⓥ ⊙
D: Gustaf Molander **A:** Gosta Ekman, Inga Tidblad, Hans Ekman, Britt Hagman, Erik Berglund, Ingrid Bergman (Svensk Filmindustri)

Intermezzo is poignant, full of pathos, and, above all, shows in Ingrid Bergman a talented, beautiful actress. Although Bergman as Anita Hoffman is outstanding,

Gosta Ekman, Sweden's veteran of the screen, is not far behind as the violin master, Holder Brandt. It is through her teaching of piano to Ann-Marie (Britt Hagman), tiny daughter of Brandt, that Anita and the violin player meet. Their friendship ripens to love. Brandt then forsakes his wife and children, leaving on a concert tour, with Anita as his accompanyist.

INTERMEZZO: A LOVE STORY
(UK: ESCAPE TO HAPPINESS)
1939, 70 mins, US Ⓥ ⊙
D: Gregory Ratoff **A:** Leslie Howard, Ingrid Bergman, Edna Best, John Halliday, Cecil Kellaway (Selznick)

An American remake of a picture turned out three years earlier in Sweden with Ingrid Bergman in the femme lead. Story structure is a love triangle involving a famed concert violinist and a young girl pianist, but the romance lacks persuasiveness. Leslie Howard, who functions as star and associate producer, is eclipsed by Bergman. Latter has charm, sincerity, and an infectious vivaciousness.

1939: Nomination: Best Score

INTERNAL AFFAIRS
1990, 117 mins, US Ⓥ ⊙
D: Mike Figgis **A:** Richard Gere, Andy Garcia, Nancy Travis, Laurie Metcalf, William Baldwin, Annabella Sciorra (Paramount)

The title is a clever double entendre, as Andy Garcia plays LAPD internal-affairs-division investigator Raymond Avila, pulled into a psychological game of chicken with quarry Dennis Peck (Richard Gere), a much-honored street cop who manipulates his position as easily as he does the people around him. While hardly new territory, director Mike Figgis wrings every ounce of tension from Henry Bean's screenplay and elicits first-rate performances from top to bottom.

INTERNATIONAL VELVET
1978, 125 mins, UK Ⓥ
D: Bryan Forbes **A:** Tatum O'Neal, Christopher Plummer, Anthony Hopkins, Nanette Newman, Peter Barkworth, Dinsdale Landen (M-G-M)

Bryan Forbes wrote, produced, and directed the sequel to *National Velvet* [1944] in such a way as to provide sentiment, excitement, and dual-level drama that should ring true with its target audience. Tatum O'Neal heads a strong cast as an orphaned teenager whose attachment to a horse leads to her own adjustment and maturity.

In the new script, the original Velvet Brown is now nearing middle age as a childless divorcée. It's Nanette Newman's good fortune to play the role, and she does so excellently.

INTERNS, THE
1962, 130 mins, US Ⓥ ⊙
D: David Swift **A:** Michael Callan, Cliff Robertson, James MacArthur, Nick Adams, Suzy Parker, Telly Savalas (Columbia)

In its apparent attempt to dramatize candidly and irreverently the process by which school-finished candidate medics manage to turn into regular doctors, the film somehow succeeds in depicting the average intern as some kind of a Hippocratic oaf. The separate stories of five interns, four male and one female, are traced alternately in a sort of razzle-dazzle style. Three of the stories are predictable from the word go and the other two are thoroughly unbelievable.

INTERSECTION
1994, 98 mins, US Ⓥ ⊙
D: Mark Rydell **A:** Richard Gere, Sharon Stone, Lolita Davidovich, Martin Landau, David Selby (Paramount)

A misguided attempt to retool a French art film as a Hollywood big-star vehicle. Claude Sautet's 1970 Les Choses de la Vie, like many French films, was more concerned with character and life's texture than with plot. This very loose adaptation, set in the bracing, gray locale of a wintry Vancouver, has trendy architect Vincent (Gere) enjoying sack time with groovy journalist Olivia (Lolita Davidovich) while working at the firm he founded with his refined wife, Sally (Stone). As the man at an emotional crossroads, Gere increasingly indulges some easy mannerisms to diminishing returns.

INTERVIEW WITH THE VAMPIRE: THE VAMPIRE CHRONICLES
1994, 122 mins, US Ⓥ ⊙
D: Neil Jordan **A:** Tom Cruise, Brad Pitt, Antonio Banderas, Stephen Rea, Christian Slater (Geffen/Warner)

Anne Rice's novel has been given an intelligent, darkly voluptuous reading, but the film also has its turgid, dialogue-heavy stretches, and the leading performances are not everything they needed to be to fully flesh out these elegant immortals. The exquisite, immaculate Louis (Brad Pitt) is ready to tell his life story into a tape recorder for an interviewer (Christian Slater). This sends the story back to 1791 Louisiana, where the 24-year-old widower Louis is singled out by the devilishly handsome, courtly Lestat (Tom Cruise). Instead of just sucking Louis's blood and killing him, Lestat gives him the gift of ageless, endless life. Their debauched bachelor existence suddenly changes with the arrival of Claudia (Kirsten Dunst), who becomes their vampire daughter and partner. Tale's second half takes Louis and Claudia to Europe, where their search for others like them leads them to the sinister Théâter des Vampires in Paris, 1870, led by the magnetic Armand (Antonio Banderas). When Banderas strides upon the stage, one suddenly witnesses the kind of compelling, charismatic presence a master vampire should have.
1994: Nominations: Art Direction, Original Score

IN THE BLEAK MIDWINTER (US: A MIDWINTER'S TALE)
1995, 98 mins, UK/US Ⓥ
D: Kenneth Branagh **A:** Michael Maloney, Richard Briers, Mark Hadfield, Nick Farrell, Gerard Horan, John Sessions (Midwinter/Castle Rock)

A "let's put on a show!" approach is brought to a provincial church production of *Hamlet* to deleterious effect. This small-scale, putatively comic meditation on the anxieties and joys of the theatrical life says nothing fresh about the artistic process and manages to be coy and grating in doing so. From the outset, it is apparent that the writer-director has decided to adopt a cutesy, antic attitude toward the obviously personal material. Pic's one becoming aspect is its modesty; lensed quickly in black-and-white on a low budget, it doesn't pretend to be anything more than it is.

IN THE COMPANY OF MEN
1997, 95 mins, US Ⓥ ⊙
D: Neil Labute **A:** Aaron Eckhart, Stacy Edwards, Matt Malloy, Mark Rector, Jason Dixie, Emily Cline (Atlantis)

Neil Labute's astonishing feature directorial debut is a dark, probing, disturbing exploration of yuppie angst and male anxieties. Pic is insightful and entertaining even when the technical aspects don't match its fluently absorbing dialogue. It centers on the complex relationship between two white-collar executives: handsome, arrogant Chad (Aaron Eckhart) and Howard (Matt Malloy), his friend from college. The two men share their frustrations in life which have left both rejected by women. Chad proposes a plan to restore their bruised egos. They plan to find an appealing woman, one susceptible enough to be lured by both of them, then brutally dash her hopes. Chad spots Christine (Stacy Edwards), a beautiful typist who turns out to be hearing-impaired, the "ideal" prey. Pic's greatest achievement is its sharply poignant dialogue which, despite the horrible consequences of the contest it describes, is also darkly amusing. In a career-making performance, Eckhart aptly embodies a 1990s yuppie.

IN THE COOL OF THE DAY
1963, 91 mins, US ▭
D: Robert Stevens **A:** Peter Finch, Jane Fonda, Angela Lansbury, Constance Cummings, Arthur Hill, Alexander Knox (M-G-M)

Production concerns a romantic encounter during a visit to Greece by an English book publisher (Peter Finch) who is taunted and tormented by a grudging, embittered, antisocial wife (Angela Lansbury), and a fragile American girl (Jane Fonda) who has been sheltered and protected to the point of absurdity by her adoring, but overly finicky husband (Arthur Hill). Finch wears one expression. It appears to be boredom, which is understandable.

IN THE FRENCH STYLE
1963, 104 mins, France/US
D: Robert Parrish **A:** Jean Seberg, Stanley Baker, Addison Powell, James Leo Herlihy, Philippe Forquet (Casana/Orsay/Columbia)

A sophisticated love story of Paris, of an American girl in love with the life not quite for her. Jean Seberg stars as the 19-year-old Chicago girl, a would-be painter who dreams of conquering the capital of art, naïve, ambitious, impressionable. Seberg brings life and brilliance to her portrayal. In Stanley Baker, the correspondent with whom she has a lingering affair, she has a first-rate costar who makes a good impression.

IN THE HEAT OF THE NIGHT
1967, 109 mins, US ⓥ ⊙
D: Norman Jewison **A:** Sidney Poitier, Rod Steiger, Warren Oates, Lee Grant, Scott Wilson, Larry Gates (Mirisch/United Artists)

An excellent Sidney Poitier performance, and an outstanding one by Rod Steiger, overcome some noteworthy flaws to make *In the Heat of the Night* an absorbing contemporary murder drama. Intriguing plot basis has Poitier as the detective on a visit to his Mississippi hometown, where a prominent industrialist is found murdered. Arrested initially on the assumption that a Negro, out late at night, must have done the deed, Poitier later is thrust into uneasy collaboration with local sheriff Steiger, a die-hard Dixie bigot.

1967: Best Picture, Actor (Rod Steiger), Adapted Screenplay, Sound, Editing
Nominations: Best Director, Sound Effects

IN THE LINE OF FIRE
1993, 128 mins, US ⓥ ⊙ ▭
D: Wolfgang Petersen **A:** Clint Eastwood, John Malkovich, Rene Russo, Dylan McDermott, Gary Cole (Columbia/Castle Rock)

A proficiently made thriller pitting Clint Eastwood's vet secret-service agent against John Malkovich's insidious assassin. Frank Horrigan (Eastwood) has been haunted by the possibility that he could have saved John F. Kennedy's life. It's this weakness that is manipulated by Mitch Leary (Malkovich), a professional assassin who makes no secret of his intention to kill the current president. Horrigan wins an assignment to cover the chief of state while he tries to nail Leary, who calls every so often to taunt him. Eastwood splendidly gives Horrigan humor, grit, and imagination. Malkovich provides a delicious villain, a true psychopath so sure of himself that he's willing to give his pursuer half a chance of catching him.

1993: Nominations: Best Supp. Actor (John Malkovich), Original Screenplay, Film Editing

IN THE MOUTH OF MADNESS
1995, 94 mins, US ⓥ ⊙ ▭
D: John Carpenter **A:** Sam Neill, Julie Carmen, Jurgen Prochnow, Charlton Heston, David Warner, John Glover (New Line)

The "what if" of *In the Mouth of Madness* posits that a famous spinner of horror novels can incite the populace to strange and hideous acts through his prose. It's a nifty idea, and director John Carpenter keeps the story moving a step ahead of the preposterous, almost to the bitter end. Enlisting the help of editor Linda Styles (Julie Carmen), crack insurance investigator

John Trent (Sam Neill) goes in search of Hobb's End, the fictional setting of the scribe's tales of the macabre. When they stumble onto the tiny New England hamlet, they know the terror that lies ahead because it's been foretold between the covers of popular past works.

IN THE NAME OF THE FATHER
1993, 132 mins, Ireland/UK/US ⓥ ⊙
D: Jim Sheridan **A:** Daniel Day-Lewis, Pete Postlethwaite, Emma Thompson, John Lynch, Corin Redgrave, Beatie Edney (Hell's Kitchen/Universal)

The real-life story of Gerry Conlon, an Irishman who spent 15 years in a British prison before his wrongful sentence was overturned. It's highly political, inflammatory, partisan, and far from comforting. Pic reaches its actorly heights in the intense, intimate scenes between Daniel Day-Lewis and Pete Postlethwaite, as the former conveys Gerry's growth in the face of deep despair and frustration while the latter reveals innate qualities previously unsuspected in the father.
1993: Nominations: Best Picture, Director, Actor (Daniel Day-Lewis), Supp. Actor (Pete Postlethwaite), Supp. Actress (Emma Thompson), Adapted Screenplay, Editing

IN THE NAVY
1941, 85 mins, US ⓥ ⊙
D: Arthur Lubin **A:** Bud Abbott, Lou Costello, Dick Powell, Claire Dodd, Andrews Sisters, Dick Foran (Universal)

Abbott and Costello continue their zany and familiar antics in nautical garb ashore and aboard a battlewagon. Dick Powell is a radio crooner fed up by continual pestering of fans. He disappears to join the navy in San Diego, where Abbott and Costello are gobs ashore. Powell delivers two tunes in effective style. Andrews Sisters handle three numbers in their usually capable, rhythmic fashion.

IN THE REALM OF THE SENSES
See: L'Empire des Sens

IN THE SPIRIT
1990, 93 mins, US ⓥ
D: Sandra Seacot **A:** Elaine May, Marlo Thomas, Jeannie Berlin, Peter Falk, Melanie Griffith, Olympia Dukakis (Running River/Castle Hill)

Elaine May and Marlo Thomas make a memorable screen odd couple in kooky black comedy. New York is a nightmare, with May moving back to Gotham from Beverly Hills with her just-fired hubby Peter Falk. She's thrown together with ditzy mystic Thomas after hiring her to redecorate an apartment. Thomas and May flee the city to hole up at Michael Emil's New Age retreat in upstate NY. Director Sandra Seacat emphasizes slapstick but also female bonding as the gals on the lam reach beyond their wacky survivalist tactics to address feminist issues.

IN THIS OUR LIFE
1942, 95 mins, US ⓥ
D: John Huston **A:** Bette Davis, Olivia de Havilland, George Brent, Dennis Morgan, Charles Coburn, Hattie McDaniel (Warner)

Story displays the ruthless and selfish personality of Bette Davis and its impress on other members of her family. She lies, cheats, and steals to gain her ends, and, when cornered, schemes her way out. As the yarn opens, she woos and steals her sister's husband, eloping with him to Baltimore. John Huston, in his second directorial assignment, provides deft delineations in the varied characters in the script.

INTIMATE WITH A STRANGER
1995, 93 mins, UK ⓥ
D: Mel Woods **A:** Roderick Mangin-Turner, Daphne Nayar, Janis Lee, Amy Tolsky, Lorelei King (Independent)

American Gigolo bumps up against *sex, lies and videotape* in a generally compelling relationships movie about a burned-out Santa Monica gigolo and his clients. Main character is Jack (producer/coscripter Roderick Mangin-Turner), a dropped-out college prof who's built a lucrative sack business servicing uptight femmes. In private, however, he's living life out of the bottom of a bottle, still scorched by former g.f. Michelle (Daphne Nayar). The movie is a showcase for a string of terrific female thumbnails, ranging from a tough career type (Ellenor Wilkinson), through a teen virgin (Janis Lee), to a Jewish wife (Amy Tolsky).

INTOLERANCE
1916, 209 mins, US ⓥ ⊙ ⊗
D: D. W. Griffith **A:** Lillian Gish, Mae Marsh, Robert Harron, Miriam Cooper, Walter Long, Tully Marshall (Wark)

Intolerance reflects much credit to the wizard director, for it required no small amount of genuine art to consistently blend actors, horses, monkeys, geese, doves, acrobats, and ballets into a film classic. Film attempts to tell four distinct stories at the same time, designed to show that intolerance in various forms has existed in all ages. Three of the examples are based upon historical fact, the fourth visualized as a modern melodrama. The ancient periods depict medieval France in the reign of Charles IX, with the horrors of massacre perpetrated by Catherine de Médicis, and Jersualem at the birth of the Christian era. The martial visualizations are confined principally to the Babylonian period (about 500 B.C.), when Belshazzar's army was defeated by the Persians. Words cannot do justice to the stupendousness of these battle scenes or feasts.

IN TOO DEEP
1990, 106 mins, Australia
D: Colin South, John Tatoulis **A:** Hugo Race, Santha Press, Rebekah Elmaloglou, John Flaus (Media World)

This moody, erotic thriller overcomes its slight narrative with its confident, bravura direction and cinematography. Atmosphere and sexual tension take pride of place over a slender plotline involving an affair between a femme jazz singer, Wendy (Santha Press), and Mack (Hugo Race), a knife-wielding young hood. Also involved is Wendy's young sister, JoJo (Rebekah Elmaloglou), a 15-year-old who gets turned on by her sister's sexual activities. Tale takes place in an Australian city (Melbourne) in the middle of summer; heat is a factor in every sense of the word.

INTO THE NIGHT
1985, 115 mins, US ⓥ ⊙
D: John Landis **A:** Jeff Goldblum, Michelle Pfeiffer, Richard Farnsworth, Irene Papas, Kathryn Harrold, Paul Mazursky (Universal)

Jeff Goldblum ambles aimlessly out to the airport, where Michelle Pfeiffer has just arrived with six smuggled emeralds. Fleeing four killers, she leaps into Goldblum's car, and from then on, it's just one misadventure and murder after another. In pursuit of the jewels are a series of cameo-plus parts handled by Irene Papas, Roger Vadim, David Bowie, and a band of Iranian zanies that includes director John Landis himself. The film itself tries sometimes too hard for laughs and at other times strains for shock. Goldblum is nonetheless enjoyable.

INTO THE SUN
1992, 100 mins, US ⓥ ⊙
D: Fritz Kiersch **A:** Anthony Michael Hall, Michael Pare, Deborah Maria Moore, Terry Kiser, Brian Haley (Trimark)

US pilot Michael Pare is assigned to show an action movie star (Anthony Michael Hall) how to portray the real thing. Pic goes over the top when real-life skirmishes in the Middle East break out, and Pare disobeys orders in taking the civilian into combat. Their derring-do, with Hall rising to the occasion, is fun if ridiculous.

INTO THE WEST
1992, 102 mins, UK/US ⓥ ⊙
D: Mike Newell **A:** Gabriel Byrne, Ellen Barkin, Ciaran Fitzgerald, Ruaidhri Conroy (Majestic/FFI/Miramax/Newcom/Little Bird)

Likable but modest pic. Gabriel Byrne is a modern-day gypsy "traveler" (hobo) in a grim, high-rise nabe of Dublin with his two kids, Tito (Ruaidhri Conroy) and Ossie (Ciaran Fitzgerald). His old father-in-law (David Kelly) captures the brats' imagination with elaborate fairy tales woven around a white horse. The law moves in and sells the white horse to a rich farmer. The kids promptly steal it back and set out for the "wild" west of Ireland, fired by grandpa's stories and cowboy movies. Byrne, joined by fellow "traveler" Kathleen (Ellen Barkin), sets out in hot pursuit.

INTRUDER, THE
1953, 84 mins, UK
D: Guy Hamilton **A:** Jack Hawkins, Hugh Williams, Michael Medwin, George Cole, Dennis Price (British Lion)

What turns a wartime hero into a post-war thief? Jack Hawkins, a former colonel of the tank regiment, returns to his home to find that a burglar has broken in. The intruder (Michael Medwin) turns out to be a former member of his regiment. The thief makes a dash for it. From there on, Hawkins is involved in a countrywide search, containing other members of the old regiment in the hopes of their leading him onto the right track. As each former soldier is contacted, the film switches into a nostalgic flashback.

INTRUDER, THE
1962, 84 mins, US ⓥ
D: Roger Corman **A:** William Shatner, Frank Maxwell, Beverley Lunsford, Rob-

ert Emhardt, Jeanne Cooper, Leo Gordon (Pathe America/Filmgroup)

Charles Beaumont's screenplay, from his novel, dramatizes the campaign instigated in a southern US town by a slick, cocky, vain, unstable merchant of hate to urge the white residents to strike back against the law of integration. The man's primary incentive is actually personal ambition. William Shatner masterfully plays the bigot.

INTRUDER IN THE DUST
1949, 87 mins, US ⓥ
D: Clarence Brown A: David Brian, Claude Jarman Jr., Juano Hernandez, Charles Kemper, Will Geer, Porter Hall (M-G-M)

Producer-director Clarence Brown took his troupe to Oxford, MS, to film the William Faulkner novel. Hanging over the story is the threat of mob violence as an old Negro, charged with murdering a white man, awaits his fate in a miserable southern jail. He refuses to speak out in his own defense to the white lawyer who believes it to be a hopeless case. There is a standout job of a proud Negro, just as bigoted in his way as the white folks, by Juano Hernandez.

INVADERS, THE
See: 49th Parallel

INVADERS FROM MARS
1953, 78 mins, US ⓥ ⊙ ⌑
D: William Cameron Menzies A: Helena Carter, Arthur Franz, Jimmy Hunt, Leif Erickson, Hillary Brooke, Morris Ankrum (20th Century-Fox)

Imaginative yarn is pegged around a typical American family. The 12-year-old son (Jimmy Hunt) awakens in a thunderstorm to observe a Martian spaceship land. His scientist-father (Leif Erickson) and mother (Hillary Brooke) investigate but return with a sinister demeanor that's in abrupt contrast to their usual cheerful attitudes. A city physician (Helena Carter) and astronomer (Arthur Franz) are convinced that an invader has landed and the country is in vital danger.

INVADERS FROM MARS
1986, 100 mins, US ⓥ ⊙
D: Tobe Hooper A: Karen Black, Hunter Carson, Timothy Bottoms, Laraine Newman, James Karen, Louise Fletcher (Cannon)

Tobe Hooper's remake is an embarrassing combination of kitsch and bore-dom. Inferior screenplay fails to bring in new ideas or provide interesting dialogue. First 45 minutes are interminably dull. Little David Gardner (Hunter Carson) sees a spaceship land one night and soon after his father George (Timothy Bottoms), biology teacher Mrs. McKeltch (Louise Fletcher), and even the police chief who investigates (Jimmy Hunt, who as a child played the lead role in the 1953 original) begin behaving out of normal character. Film finally comes alive when David wanders into Martian subterranean tunnels.

INVASION OF PRIVACY
1996, 94 mins, US ⓥ
D: Anthony Hickox A: Mili Avital, Jonathan Schaech, Naomi Campbell, David Keith, Charlotte Rampling, Tom Wright (Senator)

A stylishly directed thriller that centers on the issues of paternal rights and abortion. The story starts with a whirlwind romance between young florist Theresa (Mili Avital) and Josh (Jonathan Schaech). Theresa discovers she is pregnant, and quickly also learns that Josh is violently unbalanced. Soon Josh becomes a national cause célèbre, embraced by antiabortion crusaders, while Theresa emerges as a heartless would-be baby killer. The final stretch begins after the birth, as Josh insinuates himself into the picture via the child's nanny.

INVASION OF THE BODY SNATCHERS
1956, 80 mins, US ⓥ ⊙ ⌑
D: Don Siegel A: Kevin McCarthy, Dana Wynter, Larry Gates, King Donovan, Carolyn Jones, Whit Bissell (Allied Artists)

Tense, offbeat piece of science fiction. Narrative opens on a strange hysteria that is spreading among the populace of a small California town. Townspeople appear as strangers to their relatives and friends, while retaining their outward appearances. A weird form of plant life has descended upon the town from the skies. Tiny, this ripens into great pods and opens, from each of which emerges a "blank," the form of each man, woman, and child in the town. During their sleep, the blank drains them of all but their impulse to survive.

INVASION OF THE BODY SNATCHERS
1978, 115 mins, US ⓥ ⊙
D: Philip Kaufman A: Donald Sutherland,

Brooke Adams, Leonard Nimoy, Veronica Cartwright, Jeff Goldblum (Solofilm/United Artists)

This new version of Don Siegel's 1956 cult classic not only matches the original in horrific tone and effect, but exceeds it in both conception and execution. W. D. Richter has updated and changed the locale of Jack Finney's story to contemporary San Francisco, where Donald Sutherland is a public-health inspector, assisted by Brooke Adams. Following the blanketing of the city by spidery webs, Adams notices unusual and sudden changes in b.f. Art Hindle, who becomes emotionless and distant. Similar transformations are happening all over the city.

INVASION QUARTET
1961, 87 mins, UK
D: Jay Lewis A: Bill Travers, Spike Milligan, John Le Mesurier, Gregoire Aslan, Maurice Denham, Millicent Martin (M-G-M)

A kind of *Guns of Navarone* for laughs. The screenplay has to do with a quartet of disabled limeys so anxious to return to active duty they sneak out of a Dover hospital, cross the Channel, and proceed to blow up a long-range cannon on the coast of France. Some of the farce is pretty funny farce, and director Jay Lewis extracts every ounce of fun the script provides.

INVASION U.S.A.
1952, 73 mins, US
D: Alfred E. Green A: Gerald Mohr, Peggie Castle, Dan O'Herlihy, Robert Bice, Tom Kennedy (Columbia)

This production imaginatively poses the situation of a foreign power invading the US with atom bombs. Plot, starting out in a Gotham bar, is picked up when voice of a TV broadcaster reports that Alaska has been taken over by a huge enemy air task force. Further forces capture the state of Washington through use of atom bombs. Action then has the enemy blasting eastward. Human story is worked into this background through Gerald Mohr, a TV reporter, and others who are introduced in the bar.

INVASION U.S.A.
1985, 107 mins, US Ⓥ Ⓒ
D: Joseph Zito A: Chuck Norris, Richard Lynch, Melissa Prophet, Alexander Zale, Dehl Berti (Cannon)

A brainless plot would be almost for-

givable were it not for the perverse depiction of innocents butchered in *Invasion U.S.A.* Star Chuck Norris hits his nadir with this vicious-minded commodity. An international hoard of ruthless mercenaries invade the southeast US, turn neighbor against neighbor in selective slaughters, and are ultimately throttled by Norris's loner of a hero.

INVESTIGATION OF A CITIZEN ABOVE SUSPICION
See: Indagine su un Cittadino al di Sopra di Ogni Sospetto

INVISIBLE MAN, THE
1933, 70 mins, US Ⓥ Ⓒ
D: James Whale A: Claude Rains, Gloria Stuart, Henry Travers, William Harrigan, Una O'Connor, Holmes Herbert (Universal)

The strangest character yet created on the screen roams through *The Invisible Man*. Sometimes he is seen, dressed and bandaged up into a fantastic, eerie-looking figure, at other times he is moving through the action unseen. At the outset it is learned that a young chemist has discovered a terrible formula, including a very dangerous drug, that makes human flesh invisible. His interest had been strictly scientific, but the drug has the effect, after use, of turning him into a maniac. At about the time he starts to commit murders he is looking for the antidote to bring him back to a normal condition.

INVISIBLE MAN RETURNS, THE
1940, 81 mins, US Ⓥ
D: Joe May A: Cedric Hardwicke, Vincent Price, Nan Grey, John Sutton, Cecil Kellaway (Universal)

Stripped of the horror angles of its forerunner, *The Invisible Man Returns* is a fantastic tale of the impossible—but it maintains interest throughout. When Vincent Price is convicted of murder, medicoscientist John Sutton gives him a serum injection that makes him invisible and allows escape from prison. Sutton's brother concocted the serum, but failed to discover an antidote to prevent eventual attack of madness. While Sutton concentrates on finding a serum before his friend becomes a killing maniac, Price's invisibility allows him to uncover the real murderer.

INVITATION TO THE DANCE
1956, 93 mins, US Ⓥ
D: Gene Kelly A: Gene Kelly, Igor Yous-

kevitch, Claire Sombert, Carol Haney, Tamara Toumanova (M-G-M)

A full-length dance feature, a bold and imaginative experiment in filmmaking. Through the medium of the dance alone, producer Arthur Freed and director-choreographer-performer Gene Kelly tell three separate stories. There is no dialogue. Just ballet music, colorful costumes, and skillful photography. Standout sequence is "Ring Around the Rosy." Using the children's song and game as the tee-off, the dance story to Andre Previn's music follows the career of a bracelet as it changes hands in the perennial game of love.

IN WHICH WE SERVE
1942, 113 mins, UK 🅥

D: Noel Coward, David Lean **A:** Noel Coward, John Mills, Bernard Miles, Celia Johnson, Michael Wilding, Richard Attenborough (Two Cities)

No less than half a dozen credits for this film go to Noel Coward. And they're well earned. It is the story of a British destroyer. Only one important factor calls for criticism. It is that all the details are too prolonged. The author-producer-scriptwriter-composer and co-director gives a fine performance as the captain of the vessel. Stark realism is the keynote of the writing and depiction, with no glossing of the sacrifices constantly being made by the sailors.
1942: Special Award (outstanding production achievement by Noel Coward)
1943: Nominations: Best Picture, Original Screenplay

I OUGHT TO BE IN PICTURES
1982, 107 mins, US 🅥

D: Herbert Ross **A:** Walter Matthau, Ann-Margret, Dinah Manoff, Lance Guest, Lewis Smith (20th Century-Fox)

Neil Simon's *I Ought to Be in Pictures* is a moving family drama, peppered with the author's patented gag lines and notable for sock performances by Dinah Manoff and Walter Matthau. Film concerns a 19-year-old, spunky Brooklyn girl Libby (Dinah Manoff reprising her stage role), who hitchhikes to Los Angeles to break into films as an actress but more importantly to see her dad who left her, a brother, and mom for good 16 years earlier.

IPCRESS FILE, THE
1965, 109 mins, UK 🅥 ▭

D: Sidney J. Furie **A:** Michael Caine, Ni-

gel Green, Guy Doleman, Sue Lloyd, Gordon Jackson (Rank)

Bringing to the screen a kind of "anti-Bond" spy in the character of Harry Palmer, based on Len Deighton's novel. Palmer (Michael Caine) finds that being a secret agent is more legwork and filling in forms than inspired hunches and glamorous adventure. Present adventure concerns the steps taken to retrieve a missing boffin and does not build up to the type of suspense usually demanded of such thrillers. Sidney J. Furie's direction, allied with Otto Heller's camera, provides some striking effects. Caine's consistent underplaying adds considerably to the pull of the picture.

I.Q.
1994, 95 mins, US 🅥 ⊙ ▭

D: Fred Schepisi **A:** Tim Robbins, Meg Ryan, Walter Matthau, Lou Jacobi, Gene Saks (Paramount/Sandollar)

The conceit of this 1950s-set yarn is that the world's most famous scientist, Albert Einstein (Walter Matthau), realizes that his egghead niece is in need of some heart massaging. The promising spark occurs when the niece, Catherine (Meg Ryan), sputters into a garage and encounters mechanic Ed Walters (Tim Robbins). To win the girl for the young man, Einstein and his colleagues create an elaborate ruse that extends to refashioning Ed in tweeds and a meerschaum. A paean to movies past, *I.Q.* recalls the style and attitude of a bygone era while retaining a contemporary spirit and polish.

I REMEMBER MAMA
1948, 137 mins, US 🅥 ⊙

D: George Stevens **A:** 'rene Dunne, Barbara Bel Geddes, Oscar Homolka, Philip Dorn, Cedric Hardwicke, Edgar Bergen (RKO)

This reminiscence of growth in a San Francisco Norwegian family is related in a simple and genuine manner. It's frequently sentimental but never hokey. Irene Dunne is the central pillar of this production. Her Norwegian dialect sounds queer for the first couple of minutes but soon establishes itself solidly as a natural part of her lingo. Oscar Homolka, repeating his stage role of the uncle, contributes a massive and memorable performance. As the youngster who matures into an authoress, Barbara Bel Geddes plays a 15-year-old schoolgirl in a tour de force. Her portrait

of adolescence is sensitive, compelling, and authentic.
1948: Nominations: Best Actress (Irene Dunne), Supp. Actor (Oscar Homolka), Supp. Actress (Barbara Bel Geddes), B&W Cinematography

IRENE
1940, 104 mins, US ⓥ
D: Herbert Wilcox **A:** Anna Neagle, Ray Milland, Roland Young, Alan Marshal, May Robson, Billie Burke (Imperadio/ RKO)

Anna Neagle, as the girl who steps from the tenements to a modeling job and then into society, gives a rather spotty performance. She's too broadly Irish, for one thing, and not flattered by the camera in the first 50 minutes for another. In the color sequences she shows up much better, her red hair being especially noticeable, and is okay in one feathery dance routine and when singing "Alice Blue Gown."
1940: Nomination: Best Score

IRISHMAN, THE
1978, 108 mins, Australia ⓥ
D: Donald Crombie **A:** Michael Craig, Simon Burke, Robyn Nevin, Lou Brown, Vincent Ball, Bryan Brown (Forest Home)

The north of Queensland in the 1920s must have been much like West Texas at the turn of the century if we can believe the movies. But times are a-changing. Paddy the teamster, with his team of 20 giant Clydesdales crossing the great wide river, immediately create awe and admiration. They are such superb beasts that it is made that much easier to accept Paddy's stubbornness later when he refuses to see that his team is being superseded by the internal combustion engine. The film has great moments of emotional triumph, and at times is unabashedly sentimental, but it never descends to mawkishness.

IRMA LA DOUCE
1963, 147 mins, US ⓥ ⊙ ▭
D: Billy Wilder **A:** Jack Lemmon, Shirley MacLaine, Lou Jacobi, Herschel Bernardi (United Artists)

There are scintillating performances by Jack Lemmon and Shirley MacLaine, a batch of jovial supporting portrayals, a striking physical production, and a number of infectious comedy scenes. The hot-and-cold scenario traces the love affair of Irma (MacLaine), a proud and profitable practitioner of the oldest profession, and a young gendarme (Lemmon), who gets bounced off the force. Lemmon becomes number-one *mec*, or pimp, on the block when he knocks his predecessor's block off, thereby inheriting Irma. What hurts the film the most is its length.
1963: Best Adapted Musical Score
Nominations: Best Actress (Shirley MacLaine), Color Cinematography

IRON CURTAIN, THE
1948, 88 mins, US
D: William A. Wellman **A:** Dana Andrews, Gene Tierney, June Havoc, Berry Kroeger, Edna Best (20th Century-Fox)

A corking spy melodrama. Story is of Igor Gouzenko, former code clerk in the Soviet embassy in Ottawa. A devoted Communist when he arrives at his new post, Gouzenko is gradually aware of what it means to live without fear and, to help ensure his son's future, exposes the Soviet spy network to the world. Dana Andrews does one of his best jobs as Gouzenko.

IRON EAGLE
1986, 119 mins, US ⓥ ⊙
D: Sidney J. Furie **A:** Louis Gossett Jr., Jason Gedrick, David Suchet, Tim Thomerson, Larry B. Scott (Tri-Star)

A crackerjack fighter-pilot picture focusing on a daring rescue of a hostage. Young Jason Gedrick swings into action when word comes that pilot pop Tim Thomerson has been shot down for venturing too near the borders of the little nation defended by swarthy David Suchet. After faking the military computers into assigning two jets for their use, Gedrick persuades veteran combat pilot Louis Gossett Jr. to lead the mission and off the pair go into the wild blue yonder.

IRON EAGLE II
1988, 105 mins, Canada/Israel ⓥ ⊙
D: Sidney J. Furie **A:** Louis Gossett Jr., Mark Humphrey, Stuart Margolin, Alan Scarfe, Maury Chaykin (Alliance)

Tom Cruise look-alike Mark Humphrey is recruited by Louis Gossett Jr. (reprising his role as Chappy), who's been given a general's star as incentive to lead US and Soviet pilots on a joint mission to destroy a nuclear weapons base in an unnamed Mideast country. Pic's chief weakness is that for much of the screen time, the "joint mission" seems like just a weak premise to bring together both sides for lowbrow *Police Academy*–style antics and infighting.

IRON EAGLE III
See: Aces, Iron Eagle III

IRON EAGLE IV
1995, 95 mins, Canada ⓥ
D: Sidney J. Furie **A:** Louis Gossett Jr., Al Waxman, Jason Cadieux, Joanne Vannicola, Rachel Blanchard (Norstar)

The fourth installment of the franchise never manages to get off the runway. Louis Gossett Jr. as retired air-force General Charles "Chappy" Sinclair is now reduced to running a training center that caters exclusively to teens on the wrong side of the law. General Brad Kettle (Al Waxman) is the head bad guy, intent on dumping toxic chemicals on Cuba to test them. Some of the high-altitude stunts are reasonably entertaining, but the ground-level drama is strictly ho-hum.

IRON HAND, THE
See: Jingwu Men

IRON HORSE, THE
1924, 130 mins, US ⊗
D: John Ford **A:** George O'Brien, Madge Bellamy, Charles Edward Hull, Cyril Chadwick, Fred Kohler, J. Farrell MacDonald (Fox)

The story of the winning of the west through the linking of the Atlantic and Pacific coasts by rail. There are comedy, tragedy, and a love theme, Indians and soldiers, hordes of construction gangs, camp followers, both men and women, gamblers and dancehall girls, shooting and riding, a tremendous cattle drive, the fording of a river by a herd of beeves. John Ford puts his story over on the screen with a lot of punch.

IRON MASK, THE
1929, 95 mins, US ⓥ ⊙
D: Allan Dwan **A:** Douglas Fairbanks, Nigel de Brulier, Marguerite de la Motte, Leon Barry, Rolfe Sedan (United Artists)

Typical romantic Fairbanks picture, the sequel to Fairbanks's *Three Musketeers* (1921). Current story provides the twist of D'Artagnan going over to the Cardinal's side. It is to protect the young heir apparent, who has a twin brother whom Richelieu whisks into hiding at birth to protect the throne.

IRONWEED
1987, 144 mins, US ⓥ ⊙
D: Hector Babenco **A:** Jack Nicholson, Meryl Streep, Carroll Baker, Michael O'Keefe, Diane Venora, Fred Gwynne (Taft/Barish/Tri-Star)

Unrelentingly bleak, a film with no reason for being except its own self-importance. The story of Francis Phelan (Jack Nicholson) is loaded with elaborate expository passages trying to account for why an obviously intelligent individual has abandoned his family for a bum's life. Nicholson and Meryl Streep have approximately three scenes together, and though they clearly have a great deal of affection for each other, they are beyond passion.
1987: Nominations: Best Actor (Jack Nicholson), Actress (Meryl Streep)

IRRECONCILABLE DIFFERENCES
1984, 114 mins, US ⓥ ⊙
D: Charles Shyer **A:** Ryan O'Neal, Shelley Long, Drew Barrymore, Sam Wanamaker, Allen Garfield, Sharon Stone (Hemdale)

Irreconcilable Differences begins strongly as a human comedy about a nine-year-old who decides to take legal action to divorce her parents. Unfortunately, this premise is soon jettisoned for a rather familiar tale of a marriage turned sour as shown step-by-step. Set in the world of Hollywood writers and filmmakers, the story is also more fun for the cognoscenti than for the average filmgoer.

ISADORA
(US: THE LOVES OF ISADORA)
1969, 141 mins, UK ⓥ
D: Karel Reisz **A:** Vanessa Redgrave, John Fraser, James Fox, Jason Robards, Bessie Love (Universal)

The tragic lifelong odyssey of Isadora Duncan, whose consistent nonconformity brought her as much public success as it did personal failure, is told with a remarkable degree of excellence. The freethinking aspects of Duncan's life (unabashed out-of-wedlock affairs and births, hedonism, political idealism, naïveté, etc.), are emphasized in this sensitive, lucid, beautifully fashioned, and masterfully executed personal tragedy. Where the film falters is its length and pacing.
1969: Nomination: Best Actress (Vanessa Redgrave)

I SHALL RETURN
See: An American Guerrilla in the Philippines

I SHOT ANDY WARHOL
1996, 106 mins, US ⓥ
D: Mary Harron **A:** Lili Taylor, Jared Harris, Lothaire Bluteau, Martha Plimpton, Stephen Dorff (Playhouse Intl./Goldwyn)

The story of the radical feminist and Warhol fringe figure Valerie Solanas, who seriously wounded the artist in 1968, is an exemplary and dynamic work. Solanas (Lili Taylor) pens a subversive play which she determines only Andy Warhol (Jared Harris) can produce. But her pushy personality and guerrilla attire don't jibe with the drugged- and zoned-out Factory crowd and its taste for artifice. Warhol has Solanas excommunicated from the Factory. The main opposition is between Solanas and Warhol, the first abrasive, loud, and confrontational, the other wimpy, mildmannered, and masterfully evasive. The picture rides on Taylor's stupendous lead performance, agitated, vibrant, and resourceful.

I SHOT JESSE JAMES
1949, 81 mins, US ⊗
D: Samuel Fuller **A:** Preston Foster, Barbara Britton, John Ireland, Reed Hadley, J. Edward Bromberg (Screen Guild)

A character study of the man who felled the west's most famous outlaw with a coward's bullet. It's an interesting treatment that doesn't overlook necessary plot and action. John Ireland is the notorious Bob Ford, who dominates the story. Ireland's performance is clearly drawn and even manages to evoke a trace of sympathy.

ISHTAR
1987, 107 mins, US ⊗ ⊙ ▭
D: Elaine May **A:** Warren Beatty, Dustin Hoffman, Isabelle Adjani, Charles Grodin, Jack Weston, Tess Harper (Columbia)

Warren Beatty and Dustin Hoffman are struggling and mightily untalented songwriters-singers booked into the Chez Casablanca in Morocco. Arrival in Africa finds Beatty-Hoffman stopping in the mythical kingdom of Ishtar, with Isabelle Adjani functioning as a left-wing rebel trying to overthrow the US-backed Emir of Ishtar. Enter Charles Grodin, who upstages all involved via his savagely comical portrayal of a CIA agent. Desert sequences provide some of the film's high points as Beatty and Hoffman finally develop some genuine rapport under adverse conditions.

ISLAND, THE
1980, 114 mins, US ⊗ ⊙ ▭
D: Michael Ritchie **A:** Michael Caine, David Warner, Angela Punch McGregor,

Frank Middlemass, Don Henderson (Universal/Zanuck-Brown)

British journalist Michael Caine persuades his editor that his latest Bermuda Triangle–type ship disappearance justifies his personal research. But once the mystery is banally resolved—the island is inhabited by a tribe of buccaneers who've been inbreeding for 300 years and prey on pleasure ships—the film degenerates to a violent chase melodrama.

ISLAND AT THE TOP OF THE WORLD, THE
1974, 95 mins, US ⊗
D: Robert Stevenson **A:** David Hartman, Donald Sinden, Jacques Marin, Mako, David Gwillim, Agneta Eckemyr (Walt Disney)

Title pretty much describes pic's theme, carrying the story of four polar explorers discovering a lost land inhabited by Vikings. Script limns a rich Englishman in 1907 flying into the arctic wilderness in search of his missing son. Donald Sinden portrays the Englishman and Jacques Marin plays the French designer and captain of the balloon which figures so prominently in suspenseful action.
1974: Nomination: Best Art Direction

ISLAND IN THE SKY
1953, 108 mins, US
D: William A. Wellman **A:** John Wayne, Lloyd Nolan, Walter Abel, James Arness, Andy Devine (Warner/Wayne-Fellows)

An articulate drama of men and planes has been fashioned from Ernest K. Gann's novel. John Wayne is the pilot downed with his crew in an uncharted section of Labrador. How he holds them together during five harrowing days before rescue comes on the sixth is grippingly told. Each of the players has a chance at a big scene and delivers strongly.

ISLAND IN THE SUN
1957, 123 mins, US
D: Robert Rossen **A:** James Mason, Joan Fontaine, Dorothy Dandridge, Joan Collins, Michael Rennie, Harry Belafonte (Zanuck/20th Century-Fox)

A picture that is flat and even tedious, that hints of raw sex but stops short even of a kiss for fear it might offend, peopled by characters who appear theatrical and overdrawn. Story is about Santa Marta, an imaginary island in the British West Indies. The strongest, and dramatically the weakest, episode involves Belafonte as a rising young Negro labor leader, who greatly attracts Joan Fontaine, who is finally rejected by him in an almost embarrassingly conceived scene. Only really outstanding performance is delivered by John Williams as the police chief.

ISLAND OF DR. MOREAU, THE
1977, 98 mins, US Ⓥ ⊙
D: Don Taylor **A:** Burt Lancaster, Michael York, Nigel Davenport, Barbara Carrera, Richard Basehart, Nick Cravat (American International)

A handsome, well-acted, and involving piece of cinematic storytelling, made in the Virgin Islands. Burt Lancaster has the lead role of the renegade scientist who dabbles in forbidden eugenic experiments on a remote Pacific island, where Michael York is washed up in a shipwreck in the early days of the 20th century.

ISLAND OF DR. MOREAU, THE
1996, 95 mins, US Ⓥ ▭
D: John Frankenheimer **A:** Marlon Brando, Val Kilmer, David Thewlis, Fairuza Balk, Ron Perlman, Marco Hofschneider (Pressman/New Line)

An embarrassment for all concerned, this updated third screen version of H.G. Wells's disturbingly prophetic novel makes hash of its source and is wildly unfocused dramatically and tonally. Douglas (David Thewlis), a British UN peace negotiator stranded in the Java Sea after a plane crash, is plucked from his raft by the shady Montgomery (Val Kilmer) and taken ashore on the titular tropical isle. The great man himself is conveyed into the village of the Beast People in a vehicle resembling the Popemobile. Marlon Brando's Moreau is a most peculiar creation, almost as weird as the mongrel beasts whose genes he has fused with human ones in an attempt to forge an obedient new species. An unappetizing creature named Hyena-Swine kills him off after an hour. Thewlis is miscast as the accidental tourist. Kilmer creates no characterization whatsoever in a part that bears evidence of severe cutting.

ISLAND OF LOST SOULS
1933, 72 mins, US
D: Erle C. Kenton **A:** Charles Laughton, Bela Lugosi, Richard Arlen, Leila Hyams, Kathleen Burke (Paramount)

With such actors as Charles Laughton,

Richard Arlen, and Bela Lugosi in the cast, *Souls* is provided with a mainstay. There are undoubtedly some horror sequences which are unrivaled. Those studies of a galaxy of Dr. Moreau's 50/50 man-and-beast creations, as an example, will pique any type of mentality.

ISLANDS IN THE STREAM
1977, 105 mins, US Ⓥ ⊙ ▭
D: Franklin J. Schaffner **A:** George C. Scott, David Hemmings, Gilbert Roland, Susan Tyrrell, Claire Bloom (Paramount)

George C. Scott's semi-Hemingway pivotal character lives on a remote island, to which travel his three sons by broken marriages, as the world moves into the globe-shrinking holocaust of World War II. One can admire and follow the film without ever really getting enthusiastic about it.

1977: Nomination: Best Cinematography

ISLE OF THE DEAD
1945, 72 mins, US Ⓥ ⊙
D: Mark Robson **A:** Boris Karloff, Ellen Drew, Marc Cramer, Alan Napier, Jason Robards (RKO)

A slow conversation piece about plagues and vampires on an eerie Greek island. It's better handled and directed than most, though thriller fans will still find its lack of action a drag. Even Boris Karloff fans will note the tired way he rambles through it all.

ISN'T LIFE WONDERFUL
1924, 90 mins, US ⊗
D: D. W. Griffith **A:** Carol Dempster, Neil Hamilton, Erville Alderson, Helen Lowell, Frank Puglia, Lupino Lane (Griffith/United Artists)

The story is of the privations and struggles of a German family following the war and the collapse of the German exchange. A tale at once gripping and interesting, though heartrending and depressing. Carol Dempster and Neil Hamilton are the lovers. Dempster does work of which she may well be proud. As for Hamilton, his characterization ranks with anything that he has done in this particular line.

IS PARIS BURNING?
1966, 185 mins, US/France Ⓥ ▭
D: Rene Clement **A:** Jean-Paul Belmondo, Charles Boyer, Gert Frobe, Anthony Perkins, Simone Signoret, Orson Welles (Paramount/Seven Arts)

This spectacle traces the uprising in Paris leading to the oncoming Allies changing their plans to invade the city rather than bypass it. Underlying dilemma faces the German commander General Von Choltitz, who has been ordered to destroy Paris, if necessary or if it could not be held. The title is from Hitler's maniacal telephone demands to know if Paris was burning. Gert Frobe has the pivotal part as he plays Von Choltitz with proper despair and does not overdo the sentimental aspect of the man.

1966: Nominations: Best B&W Cinematography, B&W Art Direction

I START COUNTING
1970, 105 mins, UK Ⓥ
D: David Greene A: Jenny Agutter, Bryan Marshall, Clare Sutcliffe, Simon Ward, Lana Morris (United Artists)

Jenny Agutter plays a schoolgirl, adopted, who worships her elder "brother," who, unwittingly, has become a father figure in the household. A series of local sex crimes strikes a sinister note and from slender clues (neatly produced as red herrings) the girl suspects that her worshiped brother is the perpetrator.

I STILL KNOW WHAT YOU DID LAST SUMMER
1998, 101 mins, US Ⓥ ⊙ ▭
D: Danny Cannon A: Jennifer Love Hewitt, Freddie Prinze Jr., Brandy, Mekhi Phifer, Muse Watson, Matthew Settle (Columbia)

Follow-up to 1997's successful teens-in-jeopardy opus piles on the chills, thrills, and body count. Purists will find the pic's obviousness disappointing, but the film delivers a sufficient shock quotient. Survivor Julie James (Jennifer Love Hewitt) is attending college, still haunted by nightmares about the hook-handed killer Ben Willis (Muse Watson). Her roommate Karla (Brandy) is offered a Bahamas vacation for four. Karla invites her squeeze, Tyrell (Mekhi Phifer), and Julie calls Ray Bronson (Freddie Prinze Jr.) to join the fun. A plane and a boat ride later, they arrive in the secluded island paradise of Tower Bay. The rest runs to form. The ending leaves promise for yet another chapter. Director Danny Cannon dispenses with the barbs and social commentary in favor of visceral thrills, a prurient perspective and elaborate setpieces.

IT
1927, 64 mins, US Ⓥ ⊙ ⊗
D: Clarence Badger A: Clara Bow, Antonio Moreno, William Austin, Jacqueline Gadsdon, Julia Swayne Gordon, Gary Cooper (Paramount)

It is one of those pretty little Cinderella stories where the poor shop girl marries the wealthy owner of the big department store in which she works. Elinor Glyn makes her debut as a picture actress. Clara Bow certainly has that certain "It" for which the picture is named, and she just runs away with the film.

ITALIAN JOB, THE
1969, 100 mins, UK Ⓥ ⊙ ▭
D: Peter Collinson A: Michael Caine, Noel Coward, Benny Hill, Raf Vallone, Tony Beckley, Rossano Brazzi (Paramount/Oakhurst)

Michael Caine plays a minor crook who inherits from a dead pal (Rossano Brazzi) the idea and key plan of a heist for landing a haul of $4 million in gold ingots from a security van in Turin, Italy. Scheme involves an elaborate way of throwing the Turin traffic into a colossal, chaotic tangle on which the robbery and getaway depend. The crime is bankrolled and masterminded by Noel Coward, a top criminal, from a London jail. Coward brings all his imperturbable sense of irony and comedy to his role.

IT CAME FROM OUTER SPACE
1953, 80 mins, US Ⓥ
D: Jack Arnold A: Richard Carlson, Barbara Rush, Charles Drake, Russell Johnson, Kathleen Hughes (Universal)

Picture has been smartly fashioned to take advantage of all the tricks of science fiction and 3-D. Direction whips up an air of suspense and there is considerable atmosphere of reality created. Yarn opens with Richard Carlson, a scientist, and Barbara Rush, his schoolteacher fiancee, observing the lding of a fiery object in the Arizona desert. At first believing it is a meteor, Carlson changes his opinion when he ventures into the crater. Strange things begin to happen in the community. Townspeople disappear and their likenesses are taken over by the space visitors.

IT COULD HAPPEN TO YOU
1994, 101 mins, US Ⓥ ⊙
D: Andrew Bergman A: Nicolas Cage, Bridget Fonda, Rosie Perez, Wendell Pierce, Isaac Hayes (Tri-Star)

The simple premise has affable New York cop Charlie (Nicolas Cage) promising waitress Yvonne (Bridget Fonda) that he'll split anything he wins from the lottery with her in lieu of a tip. The ticket turns out to be a $4 million winner, and much to the chagrin of his avaricious wife, Muriel (Rosie Perez), Charlie decides to honor his pledge. What really make the film are Bergman's general restraint and the strong central performances. Cage and Fonda are extremely natural as the good-hearted lug and good-bye girl, while the squawking, raging Perez only needs to be fitted for a broomstick.

IT HAPPENED AT THE WORLD'S FAIR
1963, 105 mins, US Ⓥ ▭
D: Norman Taurog **A:** Elvis Presley, Joan O'Brien, Gary Lockwood, Vicky Tiu, Edith Atwater (M-G-M)

This is apt to be tedious going for all but the most confirmed of Presley's young admirers. The 10 tunes he sings, stacked up proportionately against the skinny story in between, seem at least three too many. Screenplay thrusts "bush pilot" Presley and sidekick Gary Lockwood into several situations, airborne and earthbound, that have a fair humor content. Most of the action takes place at the 1962 Seattle Fair and vicinity.

IT HAPPENED HERE
1964, 99 mins, UK
D: Kevin Brownlow, Andrew Mollo **A:** Pauline Murray, Sebastian Shaw, Nicolette Bernard, Bart Allison, Fiona Leland (Rath)

The story of what might have happened had England been occupied by the Germans. The action takes place in 1943. The film shows brutality on both sides. Its message is that Nazism leads to violence everywhere. Film poses the question: can Nazism only be wiped out by Nazi methods? The film is a nonprofessional feature which began as an amateur project on 16mm and remained so until financing was secured six years (!) after production had started.

IT HAPPENED IN BROOKLYN
1947, 102 mins, US Ⓥ
D: Richard Whorf **A:** Frank Sinatra, Kathryn Grayson, Peter Lawford, Jimmy Durante, Gloria Grahame (M-G-M)

Frank Sinatra's acquired the Bing Crosby knack of nonchalance. He kids himself in a couple of hilarious sequences and does a takeoff on Jimmy Durante, with Durante aiding him, that's sockeroo. Sinatra as a lonesome GI in London meets Lawford, young British nobleman. Back in Brooklyn, Sinatra returns to his old high school and meets Grayson, the music teacher, plus Durante, the school's old-time janitor. He begins falling in love with Grayson. Lawford appears and also immediately falls in love with Grayson. Interspersed in the story are a group of six new tunes from Sammy Cahn and Jule Styne.

IT HAPPENED ONE NIGHT
1934, 105 mins, US Ⓥ ◉
D: Frank Capra **A:** Clark Gable, Claudette Colbert, Walter Connolly, Roscoe Karns (Columbia)

Plot is a simple one. The headstrong but very charming daughter of a millionaire quarrels with her father and seeks to make her way to New York, with the old man raising the hue and cry. Clark Gable, who has just been fired from his Florida correspondent's job, is on the same long-distance bus. The author would have been nowhere without the deft direction of Frank Capra and the spirited and good-humored acting of the stars and practically most of their support. Claudette Colbert and Gable both play as though they really liked their characters, and therein lies much of the charm.
1934: Best Picture, Director, Actor (Clark Gable), Actress (Claudette Colbert), Adaptation

IT HAPPENED TOMORROW
1944, 84 mins, US Ⓥ
D: Rene Clair **A:** Dick Powell, Linda Darnell, Jack Oakie, Edgar Kennedy, Edward Brophy (United Artists)

A novel premise on which to spin a comedy-drama—what happens when a cub reporter gets a copy of tomorrow's newspaper. Results provide diverting escapist entertainment, with many sparkling moments and episodes along the line. Dick Powell, cub on the sheet, is befriended by the rag's veteran librarian, who, after death, hands the youth copies of the next day's paper for three successive days.
1944: Nominations: Best Scoring of a Dramatic Picture, Sound

I, THE JURY
1953, 87 mins, US
D: Harry Essex **A:** Biff Elliot, Preston Foster, Peggie Castle, Margaret Sheridan, Alan Reed, Elisha Cook Jr. (United Artists/Parklane)

Harry Essex both directed and wrote, from Mickey Spillane's novel of the same title. Hard-boiled private eye Mike Hammer traces the killer of a friend, uncovers some unsavory rackets while doing so, and then shoots down the killer at the finale. The stereo lensing by John Alton is good, and without obvious 3-D trickery. Depth treatment and the Franz Waxman score are good assists for meller mood. Biff Elliot as the sadistic Hammer does okay by the assignment; Peggie Castle, a psychiatrist, is the chief sex lure and is excellent.

I, THE JURY
1982, 109 mins, US ⓥ
D: Richard T. Heffron **A:** Armand Assante, Barbara Carrera, Laurene Landon, Alan King, Geoffrey Lewis, Paul Sorvino (American Cinema/Larco/Solofilm)

Almost 30 years after the first screen edition of Mickey Spillane's first Mike Hammer novel, the souped-up remake is hard as nails, with Armand Assante plausibly macho and ruggedly sexy as the amoral private eye who avenges the murder of his old Vietnam war buddy. Scripter Larry Cohen's plotting is swift, suitably enigmatic, and well stocked with well-stacked and well-exposed babes, of which the prime specimen is Barbara Carrera.

IT HURTS ONLY WHEN I LAUGH
See: Only When I Laugh

IT LIVES AGAIN
1978, 91 mins, US ⓥ
D: Larry Cohen **A:** Frederic Forrest, Kathleen Lloyd, John P. Ryan, John Marley, Andrew Duggan, Eddie Constantine (Warner)

In his sequel to *It's Alive*, as in the original, producer-director-writer Cohen does not show a lot of the demonic infants or explain what they really are. But whatever got into the blood of the first mom is now rampant throughout the country and they're aborning everywhere, threatening the survival of humanity. Though this is all so much silliness, Cohen effectively uses a good cast topped by Frederic Forrest and Kathleen Lloyd to build up suspense for the slashing, growling attacks by the terrible tykes.

IT'S A GIFT
1935, 73 mins, US ⓥ ⓢ
D: Norman Z. McLeod **A:** W. C. Fields, Jean Rouverol, Julian Madison, Kathleen Howard, Tammany Young, Baby LeRoy (Paramount)

Practically a comedy monologue for W. C. Fields, with little help from a number of others. No plot, no suspense; rather coarse-grained in spots, but packing a load of belly laughs for people who like that sort of humor. The plot is merely that Fields buys a California orange grove and drives the family out in the car.

IT'S ALIVE
1974, 90 mins, US ⓥ
D: Larry Cohen **A:** John Ryan, Sharon Farrell, Andrew Duggan, Guy Stockwell, Michael Ansara (Larco)

This stomach-churning little film is a ''Son of the Exorcist'' horror pic about a monstrous newborn baby who goes on a murder rampage through L.A. before being blown to smithereens in a police ambush. Bernard Herrmann's score, while not one of his most memorable, is highly effective in creating tension, but one wonders why an artist of his caliber lowered himself into such muck.

IT'S ALL HAPPENING
1963, 101 mins, UK
D: Don Sharp **A:** Tommy Steele, Michael Medwin, Angela Douglas, Jean Harvey, Bernard Bresslaw (Magna/British Lion)

The warmly exuberant personality of Tommy Steele, plus some polished, slick performances by guest top pop UK artists, solidly jacks up a lazy, old-fashioned, and flabby screenplay. Steele plays an A&R man who was brought up in an orphanage, spends every afternoon playing uncle to the kids at the home, and eventually mounts a benefit show for them. The Norman Newell–Philip Green score is the greatest aid to Steele.

IT'S ALL TRUE
1993, 85 mins, France ⓥ
D: Richard Wilson, Myron Meisel, Bill Krohn (Paramount)

After 51 years in limbo as one of the most legendary of all ''lost'' films. Orson Welles's *It's All True* finally emerges in lovingly resurrected partial form within the framework of a documentary about Welles's entire 1942 Latin American misadventure. First half hour effectively sketches the events surrounding Welles's trip to Brazil to shoot a major documentary as part of the US government's Good Neighbor Policy at the start of World War II. Nearly an hour is then devoted to the presentation of *Four Men on a Raft,* which was to have been the centerpiece of Welles's never-finished, multipart docu. The scene is set by Welles himself in excerpts from various interviews, as well as by numerous collaborators.

IT'S ALWAYS FAIR WEATHER

1955, 102 mins, US ⓥ ⊙ ⊏

D: Gene Kelly, Stanley Donen A: Gene Kelly, Dan Dailey, Cyd Charisse, Dolores Gray, Michael Kidd (M-G-M)

As well as spoofing television, *It's Always Fair Weather* takes on advertising agencies and TV commercials, and what emerges is a delightful musical satire. Gene Kelly, Dan Dailey, and Michael Kidd, a trio of former GI buddies, meet 10 years after World War II. Somehow the warm friendship that existed during the war years has deteriorated into a sour reunion as different interests have driven the buddies apart. Kelly, Dailey, and Kidd score in group routines and Kelly and Dailey have a field day in solo outings. Kelly's roller-skating routine and Dailey's drunk act at a chichi party are standouts.

1955: Nominations: Best Story & Screenplay, Scoring of a Musical Picture

IT'S A MAD MAD MAD MAD WORLD

1963, 190 mins, US ⓥ ⊙ ⊏

D: Stanley Kramer A: Spencer Tracy, Milton Berle, Sid Caesar, Mickey Rooney, Ethel Merman, Phil Silvers (United Artists)

It's a mad, mad, mad, mad picture. Being a film of extravagant proportions, even its few flaws are king-sized, but the pluses outweigh by far the minuses. It is a throwback to the wild, wacky, and wondrous time of the silent-screen comedy, a kind of Keystone Kop Kaper with modern conveniences. A group of people are given a clue by a dying man (Jimmy Durante) as to the whereabouts of a huge sum of money he has stolen and buried. Each sets out for the roughly specified site of the buried cash, breaking his back to beat the others there. An array of top-ranking comics has been rounded up, making this one of the most unorthodox and memorable casts on-screen record.

1963: Best Sound Effects

Nominations: Best Color Cinematography, Editing, Original Music Score, Song ("It's a Mad Mad Mad Mad World"), Sound

IT'S A WONDERFUL LIFE

1946, 120 mins, US ⓥ ⊙

D: Frank Capra A: James Stewart, Donna Reed, Lionel Barrymore, Thomas Mitchell, Henry Travers, Gloria Grahame (Liberty)

At 30, a small-town citizen feels he has reached the end of his rope, mentally,

morally, financially. As he contemplates suicide, heaven speeds a guardian angel, a pixieish fellow of sly humor, to teach the despondent most graphically how worthwhile his life has been. The recounting of this life is just about flawless in its tender and natural treatment. James Stewart's lead is braced by a full fan-spread of shimmering support. Donna Reed reaches full-fledged stardom. As a Scrooge-like banker, Lionel Barrymore lends a lot of luster. Thomas Mitchell especially is effective as lead's drunken uncle.

1946: Nominations: Best Picture, Director, Actor (James Stewart), Editing, Sound

IT'S A WONDERFUL WORLD

1939, 84 mins, US

D: W. S. Van Dyke A: Claudette Colbert, James Stewart, Guy Kibbee, Frances Drake, Nat Pendleton, Edgar Kennedy (M-G-M)

James Stewart, a novice private detective, is assigned to watch millionaire Ernest Truex. Latter winds up convicted of a murder. Stewart is implicated, and escapes en route to prison determined to solve the murder mystery. Kidnapping Colbert and requisitioning her car, Stewart runs through series of disguises—a Boy Scout leader, chauffeur, and actor. W. S. Van Dyke presents the yarn with good humor and a let's-have-fun attitude.

IT SHOULD HAPPEN TO YOU

1954, 86 mins, US ⓥ ⊙

D: George Cukor A: Judy Holliday, Peter Lawford, Jack Lemmon, Michael O'Shea (Columbia)

Plot is about a small-town girl who comes to the big city to make a name for herself. With her meager savings she rents a signboard on Columbus Circle and has her name emblazoned thereon. This quest for fame sets off a lot of repercussions. She becomes a television celebrity and is pursued romantically by Lawford. Also in the amatory chase is Lemmon. Holliday has a romp unto herself, and she gets major assists in the comedy from Peter Lawford and Jack Lemmon.

1954: Nomination: Best B&W Costume Design

IT SHOULDN'T HAPPEN TO A DOG

1946, 70 mins, US

D: Herbert I. Leeds A: Carole Landis, Allyn Joslyn, Margo Woode, Henry Morgan, Jean Wallace, John Ireland (20th Century-Fox)

A solid package of chuckle material.

Allyn Joslyn plays a reporter victimized by an April Fools' joke into scooping his rivals on a robbery that never took place. Stickup was allegedly performed by Carole Landis aided by the Doberman who terrorized a barkeep into forking over his receipts. Joslyn gives full sway to his talents in this pic, showing himself off as a maestro with the gag line. The dog is great.

IT'S LOVE AGAIN
1936, 83 mins, UK Ⓥ
D: Victor Saville A: Jessie Matthews, Robert Young, Sonnie Hale, Ernest Milton, Robb Wilton, Sara Allgood (Gaumont-British)

Jessie Matthews at her best. The story is about rival columnists who invent people to make exclusive news. Peter Carlton (Robert Young) invents a ''Mrs. Smythe-Smythe,'' supposedly a tiger hunter from India, pursued by a maharajah. Matthews assumes the role of the nonexistent woman to strut her stuff and possibly get an opening on the stage. She does, but gives up the impersonation when Carlton's rival senses her disguise and threatens to expose her. Matthews does a variety of dances, one a mock-Indian number in a striking, if scanty, costume. She carries her part well and sings several songs.

IT'S LOVE I'M AFTER
1937, 90 mins, US
D: Archie Mayo A: Leslie Howard, Bette Davis, Olivia de Havilland, Patric Knowles, Eric Blore (Warner)

Leslie Howard and Bette Davis are Shakespearean stars. At the conclusion of a performance, a debutante (Olivia de Havilland) gushes her infatuated adoration for Howard, who senses the prospects of an adventure. Then the girl's fiancé puts in an appearance, appeals to the more generous side of the star, and persuades him to become his weekend guest and cure the girl of her madness by behaving in a boorish manner. Scenario sparkles with witty lines, farcical situations, and just enough common sense and serious moments to balance perfectly. Bette Davis reveals a fine sense of comedy.

IT'S MY LIFE
See: Vivre Sa Vie: Film en Douze Tableux

IT'S MY PARTY
1996, 110 mins, US Ⓥ
D: Randal Kleiser A: Eric Roberts, Gregory Harrison, Lee Grant, Marlee Matlin, Paul Regina (Opala/United Artists)

Mixing comedy and drama, It's My Party is an emotionally candid chronicle of a young gay man with AIDS who decides to terminate his life while still in control of his faculties. Nick Stark (Eric Roberts) is a successful young architect engaged in a long-term relationship with Brandon (Gregory Harrison). Nick finds out that he's HIV-positive and has a short time to live. He hosts a two-day farewell party to which he invites all his friends and family members. It's My Party boasts an Altmanesque structure, but without Altman's savvy or wit. Once the core situation is established, the picture has nowhere to go.

IT'S MY TURN
1980, 91 mins, US Ⓥ ⊙
D: Claudia Weill A: Jill Clayburgh, Michael Douglas, Charles Grodin, Beverly Garland, Steven Hill, Daniel Stern (Columbia/Rastar)

Jill Clayburgh limns an offbeat but intellectually overachieving mathematics professor residing with perpetually humorous building developer Charles Grodin in Chicago. She quickly finds herself in the arms of Michael Douglas during a trip to New York. Probably the most endearing aspect here is the way action so easily moves from screwball to intellectual humor and then on to numerous emotionally touching moments.

IT'$ ONLY MONEY
1962, 84 mins
D: Frank Tashlin A: Jerry Lewis, Joan O'Brien, Zachary Scott, Jack Weston, Jesse White (York/Paramount)

Jerry Lewis is television repairman Lester March who yens to be a shamus, as is his friend Peter Flint (Jesse White). They hear about the quest for the missing scion of an electronics tycoon and set out to locate same. Turns out their quarry is none other than Lewis. Screenplay makes for a sturdy hook upon which to hang a frolicsome string of cinematic shenanigans ranging from Pearl White cliff-hanging and murderous hayhem as per Peter Lorre to the broadest burlesque on private detectiveness.

IT STARTED IN NAPLES
1960, 100 mins Ⓥ
D: Melville Shavelson A: Clark Cable, Sophia Loren, Vittorio De Sica, Marietto, Paolo Carlini (Paramount)

A frothy, frank, and irreverent comedy.

In Naples to settle the estate of his brother, recently deceased via an auto accident, lawyer Clark Gable discovers that his brother's extra-legal spouse also perished in the mishap, leaving their 10-year-old son (Marietto) in the care of the wife's sister (Sophia Loren). While debating (in and out of court and courtship) the relative merits of a Philadelphia and Neapolitan environment for the child, Gable and Loren fall in love. Gable and Loren are a surprisingly effective and compatible comedy pair. Vittorio De Sica is suave as Gable's roving-eyed, pulchritudinously influenced Italian attorney.
1960: Nomination: Best Color Art Direction

IT STARTED WITH A KISS
1959, 103 mins, US ▱
D: George Marshall **A:** Glenn Ford, Debbie Reynolds, Eva Gabor, Gustavo Rojo, Fred Clark (Arcola/M-G-M)

Highly amusing, sex-motivated study of two physically suited newlyweds getting to know each other. Glenn Ford plays an air-force sergeant, and Debbie Reynolds plays a nightclub dancer who wants to marry a millionaire, which Ford is not. After one kiss, however, she judges he's worth a million dollars, and within a few hours they are man and wife. She's convinced their marriage is solely for physical reasons, and she demands a 30-day test during which time no bed tactics will be allowed.

IT STARTED WITH EVE
1942, 90 mins, US
D: Henry Koster **A:** Deanna Durbin, Charles Laughton, Robert Cummings, Guy Kibbee (Universal)

A neatly devised romantic comedy-drama expertly tailored to the combined talents of Deanna Durbin and Charles Laughton. Laughton, crusty and cantankerous old millionaire, has the presses stopped, ready to toss his obit across the front pages. His son (Robert Cummings) suddenly arrives with his fiancée. Dying man insists on seeing the future wife and, when Cummings fails to locate her quickly, grabs a hatcheck girl (Durbin) as substitute. Miraculous recovery results from Durbin's visit.
1942: Nomination: Best Scoring of a Musical Picture

IT TAKES TWO
1995, 101 mins, US ▱
D: Andy Tennant **A:** Kirstie Alley, Steve Guttenberg, Mary-Kate Olsen, Ashley Olsen, Philip Bosco (Rysher/Warner)

Too cute for words. The hoary story line presents Amanda (Mary-Kate Olsen), a tough-talking, streetwise nine-year-old orphan, and Alyssa (Ashley Olsen), daughter of magnate and widower Roger Callaway (Steve Guttenberg), being crated off to upstate New York—Alyssa to a family estate and Amanda just across the lake at Camp Callaway for deprived kids. Each is mistaken for the other. The charm and charisma of Alley and Guttenberg keeps the film from total descent into cotton-candy sweetness.

IT! THE TERROR FROM BEYOND SPACE
1958, 68 mins, US ▱
D: Edward L. Cahn **A:** Marshall Thompson, Shawn Smith, Kim Spalding, Ann Doran, Richard Benedict, Ray Corrigan (Vogue)

"It" is a Martian by birth, a Frankenstein by instinct, and a copycat. The monster dies hard, brushing aside grenades, bullets, gas, and an atomic pile, before snorting its last snort. It's old stuff, with only a slight twist. Film starts with a disabled US rocketship on Mars. The government is of the opinion the spaceman murdered his companions. But the accused swears the nine deaths came at the hands of a strange "It"-type monster.

IVAN GROZNI
(IVAN THE TERRIBLE, PART 1)
1944, 96 mins, USSR ▱ ⊙
D: Sergei Eisenstein **A:** Nikolai Cherkasov, Lyudmila Tselikovskaya, Serafima Birman, Pavel Kadochnikov, Vsevolod Pudovkin (Central Cinema)

Despite usual good Russian photography, a powerful score, a couple of nice performances, and flashes of original direction, *Ivan the Terrible* has so much that is tiresome, has so little action, and becomes so involved that the average history student hardly will recognize this glorified Ivan. Additionally, heavy-handed propaganda slugs include bows to the common folks, the merchants and tradesmen, pleas for a strong Russia, united to face the world and halt foreign intrigue. On the credit side is a splendid score by Sergei Prokofiev, fairly good if spotty direction by Sergei Eisenstein, fine camerawork, and the superb character portrayal of Ivan by Nikolai Cherkasov.

IVAN GROZNI, II
(IVAN THE TERRIBLE, PART II: THE REVOLT OF THE BOYARS)
1958, 87 mins, USSR Ⓥ ⊙

D: Sergei Eisenstein **A:** Nikolai Cherkasov, Serafima Birman, Pavel Kadochnikov, Mikhail Zharov (Central Cinema)

Long withheld by Soviet officials, *Ivan the Terrible, Part II* is hardly an entertaining film. But it is well worth the time of students of history and the cinema. How Ivan, the first Russian czar, subdued a revolt of the boyars (members of an aristocratic order) is the story peg. In the second film, Eisenstein apparently chose to forget the party line and concentrate upon a searching character study of the czar who even killed his own son. Nikolai Cherkasov aptly conveys the tragic struggle from within that Ivan was unable to cope with.

IVANHOE
1952, 107 mins, UK Ⓥ

D: Richard Thorpe **A:** Robert Taylor, Elizabeth Taylor, Joan Fontaine, George Sanders, Emlyn Williams, Robert Douglas (M-G-M)

A great romantic adventure, mounted extravagantly and crammed with action. Robert Taylor, as Ivanhoe, is the courageous Saxon leader fighting for the liberation of King Richard from an Austrian prison and his restoration to the throne. Two women play an important part in his life. There is Rowena (Joan Fontaine), his father's ward, with whom he is in love; and Rebecca (Elizabeth Taylor), daughter of the Jew who raises the ransom money. She is in love with him.

1952: Nominations: Best Picture, Color Cinematography, Scoring of a Dramatic Picture

IVANOVO DYETSTVO
(MY NAME IS IVAN; IVAN'S CHILDHOOD)
1962, 97 mins, USSR

D: Andrei Tarkovsky **A:** Kolya Burlayev, Valentin Zubkov, Nikolai Grinko, Yevgeni Zharikov, S. Krylov (Gorky)

This is a lyrical war pic saved by Andrei Tarkovsky's obvious deep feeling for the subject. A 12-year-old boy (Kolya Burlayev) has seen his mother killed and has stayed behind to help the army by spying on the Germans. He is adopted by a captain who wants to send him off to school, but the boy rebels and comes back.

Pic details his happy thoughts of his early life and his mother. It is a measured but moving look at war through a marked child's eyes.

IVAN'S CHILDHOOD
See: Ivanovo Dyetstvo

IVAN THE TERRIBLE, PART 1
See: Ivan Grozni

IVAN THE TERRIBLE, PART II: THE REVOLT OF THE BOYARS
See: Ivan Grozni, II

I'VE HEARD THE MERMAIDS SINGING
1987, 81 mins, Canada Ⓥ ⊙

D: Patricia Rozema **A:** Sheila McCarthy, Paule Baillargeon, Ann-Marie McDonald, John Evans (Vos)

Comedy with serious undertones. Plot centers on a klutzy and innocent temporary secretary (Sheila McCarthy) at an art gallery run by an older femme who, it is established quickly on, takes a fancy to her without the secretary cottoning on. The secretary lives a fantasy life in which she flies through the air, walks on water, and actually hears mermaids singing. Those sequences are soaringly portrayed with accompanying classical music. In other off times, she observes daily life by taking photographs.

IVORY HUNTER
See: Where No Vultures Fly

IVY
1947, 98 mins, US

D: Sam Wood **A:** Joan Fontaine, Patric Knowles, Herbert Marshall, Cedric Hardwicke (Universal/Interwood)

An entry in the murderous-ladies cycle. Joan Fontaine, in the title role, portrays mercenary femme who doesn't mind murder if it will get her what she wants. Saddled with a lover and a husband, Ivy wants to be rid of both to take on a wealthy English gentleman. She poisons the husband and transfers blame to the lover.

I WAKE UP SCREAMING
1942, 81 mins, US Ⓥ

D: H. Bruce Humberstone **A:** Betty Grable, Victor Mature, Carole Landis, Laird Cregar, William Gargan, Alan Mowbray (20th Century-Fox)

A murder meller with a romantic strain of more than ordinary strength. Victor Mature plays a sports promoter who is dogged by a detective who loses his girl (Carole Landis) when Mature takes her from obscurity and glamorizes her to the point where she wins a film contract. The murder of this girl then provides the premise for the remainder of the yarn. Betty Grable is enormously appealing here as the sister of the slain girl.

I WALK ALONE
1948, 97 mins, US
D: Byron Haskin **A:** Burt Lancaster, Lizabeth Scott, Kirk Douglas, Wendell Corey, Kristine Miller (Paramount)

Tight, hard-boiled melodrama. Burt Lancaster belts over his assignment as the former jailbird who returns from prison to find the parade has passed him by and that old friends have given him the double cross. Melodrama develops as Lancaster plots to muscle in on Kirk Douglas's nitery. Lizabeth Scott holds up her end capably as nitery singer who falls for Lancaster.

I WALKED WITH A ZOMBIE
1943, 69 mins, US ⓥ ⊙
D: Jacques Tourneur **A:** Tom Conway, Frances Dee, James Ellison, Edith Barrett James Bell (RKO)

Weird yarn has two half brothers competing for the love of a girl, married to one of the pair, and their mother employing voodooism to turn the girl into a robotlike existence. With few exceptions, cast walks through the picture almost as dazed as the zombies.

I WALK THE LINE
1970, 96 mins, US ⓥ ⊡
D: John Frankenheimer **A:** Gregory Peck, Tuesday Weld, Estelle Parsons, Ralph Meeker, Charles Durning (Columbia)

Like the Johnny Cash ballads that comprise its background score, *I Walk the Line* has an authentic, somber, and gritty feel of life in the Tennessee back hills. Gregory Peck is the sheriff compromised by Tuesday Weld, moonshiner Ralph Meeker's nubile and sexually precocious daughter, and Estelle Parsons is Peck's desperate wife. Director John Frankenheimer has made a downbeat folk ballad that rings true to its people and setting.

I WANT TO GO HOME
1989, 105 mins, France ⓥ
D: Alain Resnais **A:** Adolph Green, Gerard Depardieu, Linda Lavin, Laura Benson, Micheline Presle, Geraldine Chaplin (MK2/Films A2/La Sept)

Jules Feiffer and Alain Resnais make strange bedfellows—the product of their union is this stillborn satiric comedy about an American cartoonist in Paris, played by songwriter and musical comedy veteran Adolph Green. He is making his first trip abroad, to attend an exhibition of comic-strip art. Green's real reason is to see his neurotic daughter (Laura Benson), a literature student at the Sorbonne. She has become starry-eyed before her professor Gerard Depardieu, who happens to be one of Green's most ardent admirers.

I WANT TO LIVE!
1958, 120 mins, US ⓥ
D: Robert Wise **A:** Susan Hayward, Simon Oakland, Virginia Vincent, Theodore Bikel (United Artists/Figaro)

A drama dealing with the last years and the execution of Barbara Graham (Susan Hayward), who was convicted at one time or another of prostitution, perjury, forgery, and murder. It is a damning indictment of capital punishment. There is no attempt to gloss the character of Barbara Graham, only an effort to understand it through some fine irony and pathos. The execution sequence is almost unbearable, mounting unswervingly in its intensity.
1958: Best Actress (Susan Hayward)
Nominations: Best Director, Adapted Screenplay, B&W Cinematography, Editing, Sound

I WAS A COMMUNIST FOR THE F.B.I.
1951, 82 mins, US
D: Gordon Douglas **A:** Frank Lovejoy, Dorothy Hart, Philip Carey, James Millican, Richard Webb (Warner)

Story is that of a man who, for nine years, was a member of the Commie party so he could gather information for the FBI. His informer role was made all the harder because his patriotic brothers and young son hated him for the Red taint. Excitement and suspense are set up in the many near escapes from exposure.

I WAS A MALE WAR BRIDE
(UK: YOU CAN'T SLEEP HERE)
1949, 105 mins, US
D: Howard Hawks **A:** Cary Grant, Ann Sheridan, Marion Marshall, Randy Stuart, Ken Tobey (20th Century-Fox)

Title describes the story perfectly. Cary Grant is a French army officer who, after the war, marries Ann Sheridan, playing a WAC officer. From then on it's a tale of Grant's attempts to get back to the US with his wife by joining a contingent of war brides. Picture's chief failing is that the entire production crew were apparently so intent on getting the maximum in yocks that they overlooked the necessary characterizations.

I WAS A SPY
1933, 90 mins, UK ⓥ
D: Victor Saville **A:** Madeleine Carroll, Conrad Veidt, Edmund Gwenn, Herbert Marshall, Donald Calthrop, Gerald du Maurier (Gaumont-British)

Story is based on the life of Martha Cnockhaert, a Belgian girl who was an Allied spy in the [First] World War. A reproduction of the Belgian village, where most of the action takes place, is most realistic, and the German troops of occupation, headed by Kommandant Conrad Veidt, are fine. The acting honors go to Madeleine Carroll as the fine-spirited young girl.

I WAS A TEENAGE WEREWOLF
1957, 76 mins, US ⓥ
D: Gene Fowler Jr. **A:** Michael Landon, Yvonne Lime, Whit Bissell, Tony Marshall (American International)

Only thing new about this combo teenager and science-fiction yarn is a psychiatrist's use of a problem teenager for an experiment in regression. Final reels, when the lad turns into a hairy-headed monster with drooling fangs are inclined to be played too heavily.

I WAS HAPPY HERE
(US: TIME LOST AND TIME REMEMBERED)
1966, 91 mins, UK
D: Desmond Davis **A:** Sarah Miles, Cyril Cusack, Julian Glover, Sean Caffrey, Marie Kean (Partisan)

Sarah Miles plays a girl who escapes from an Irish village to London, believing that her fisherboy sweetheart will follow her. He doesn't and Miles, lonely and unhappy in the big city, falls into a disastrous marriage with a pompous, boorish young doctor. The story is told largely in flashback, but Davis has skillfully woven the girl's thoughts and the present happenings by swift switching which mostly is sharp and pertinent.

I WAS MONTY'S DOUBLE
1958, 100 mins, UK ⓥ
D: John Guillermin **A:** John Mills, Cecil Parker, M. E. Clifton James, Michael Hordern, Marius Goring, Vera Day (Associated British)

Clifton James, a small-time stock actor, bore a startling resemblance to General Montgomery. This was used in a daring scheme devised by army intelligence to persuade the Germans that the forthcoming Allies' invasion might well take place on the North African coast. James plays both himself and Montgomery. Apart from his uncanny resemblance to Monty, James shows himself to be a resourceful actor in his own right.

I WILL ... I WILL ... FOR NOW
1976, 107 mins, US ⓥ ▭
D: Norman Panama **A:** Elliott Gould, Diane Keaton, Paul Sorvino, Victoria Principal, Robert Alda (Brut)

Passable fluff. Story finds horny Gould jealous that divorced wife Keaton has a lover, but he doesn't know it's their lawyer Sorvino. When Keaton's sister Candy Clark forms a modern contract-type marriage, pair decide to try life again under that new form, drafted with an eye to self-destruction by Sorvino.

JABBERWOCKY
1977, 100 mins, UK Ⓥ ⊙
D: Terry Gilliam A: Michael Palin, Harry H. Corbett, John Le Mesurier, Warren Mitchell, Max Wall (Umbrella/White)

Medieval farce, based on a Lewis Carroll poem, is long on jabber but short on yocks. Michael Palin is well cast as a bumpkin who threads his way through jousting knights, grubby peasants, ''drag'' nuns, and damsels both fair and plump to become the inadvertent hero who slays the vile monster menacing Max Wall's cartoon kingdom. The monster, who doesn't appear till the final minutes, is a work of inspired dark imagination.

JACK
1996, 113 mins, US Ⓥ ⊙
D: Francis Coppola A: Robin Williams, Diane Lane, Jennifer Lopez, Brian Kerwin, Fran Drescher, Bill Cosby (Zoetrope/Great Oaks/Hollywood)

Surrounded by talent but with very little to do himself, Robin Williams delivers what is probably his first altogether tiresome performance. Film has just one thing to say and says it with no sense of surprise or drama. Karen Powell (Diane Lane) gives birth to a baby boy after a 10-week pregnancy; ten years later, sprig Jack (Williams) is mentally and emotionally his own age but looks 40. Now that the folks have decided to send him to school, Jack and the real world have to come to some understanding.

JACKAL, THE
1997, 124 mins, US Ⓥ ⊙ ▭
D: Michael Caton-Jones A: Bruce Willis, Richard Gere, Sidney Poitier, Diane Venora, Tess Harper, Mathilda May (Alphaville/Mutual/Universal)

The Jackal scores as an involving high-tech thriller that occasionally hits peaks of pulsating excitement. Proficient without being genuinely inspired, this is a lavish updating of a well-known novel and film. FBI director Carter Preston (Sidney Poitier) joins the Russians in nailing an important Russian Mafia figure. In response, the criminal's brother declares war on the FBI and hires the Jackal (Bruce Willis) to take out a top American. The Jackal's solitary ways, skill with disguises and utter perfectionism make him difficult to identify. One of the few people known to have met him is IRA operative Declan Mulqueen (Richard Gere), serving a prison sentence in the US, who is persuaded to help the authorities. When the Jackal and Declan come face to face for the first time, Willis's and Gere's stares and body language do virtually all the talking before the guns start blazing. Director Michael Caton-Jones handles all the physical incident and noose-tightening quite capably.

JACK AND SARAH
1995, 110 mins, UK/France Ⓥ
D: Tim Sullivan A: Richard E. Grant, Samantha Mathis, Judi Dench, Ian McKellen, Eileen Atkins, Cherie Lunghi (Granada/PolyGram/Mainstream)

Sparky playing, a generally sharp script, and bright packaging add up to a neat little winner in the romantic comedy *Jack and Sarah*. Richard E. Grant plays Jack, a highly strung yuppie lawyer whose wife (Imogen Stubbs), dies in childbirth. Jack names the sprig after his wife, but finds nappies and notarizing don't mix. Solution? A baby-sitter. Enter Amy (Samantha Mathis), a bubbly, slightly klutzy young Yank, who moves in and an edgy friendship develops, with lotsa of complications up to fade-out.

JACK LONDON
1944, 92 mins, US Ⓥ
D: Alfred Santell A: Michael O'Shea, Susan Hayward, Osa Massen, Virginia Mayo (United Artists)

Jack London has much of the writer-adventurer's life crammed into its 92 minutes, but somewhere along the line it has missed fire. Michael O'Shea is miscast in the title role. Charmian, the author's wife, fails to appear until the film has consumed half its running time. Susan Hayward is starred in the role.
1944: Nomination: Best Scoring of a Dramatic Picture

JACKKNIFE
1989, 102 mins, US Ⓥ ⊙
D: David Jones A: Robert De Niro, Ed Harris, Kathy Baker, Charles Dutton (Kings Road/Sandollar-Schaffel)

Robert De Niro's tour de force turn as a feisty Vietnam vet fails to save a poorly scripted three-hander drama. De Niro is a burnout working as a Connecticut car repairman. He decides to get another war buddy, Dave (Ed Harris), to break out of his shell by forcing him to have a good time and remember those blocked-out adventures in 'Nam. A romance eventually blossoms between Harris's high-school-teacher sister (Kathy Baker) and De Niro (with Harris opposing the alliance). Film's central treatment of the Vietnam hangover that hamstrings Harris proves to be flat and uninvolving.

JACKPOT, THE
1950, 85 mins, US ⊘
D: Walter Lang **A:** James Stewart, Barbara Hale, Natalie Wood, James Gleason, Alan Mowbray (20th Century-Fox)

James Stewart's frenzied attempts to sell his prizes won in a radio giveaway show, to meet the Internal Revenue demands (particularly the situation wherein he's peddling a wristwatch in a bookmaker's betting room when the cops pull a raid), make for clever laugh material. Barbara Hale meets all requirements as Stewart's wife.

JACKSON COUNTY JAIL
1976, 89 mins, US ⊘
D: Michael Miller **A:** Yvette Mimieux, Tommy Lee Jones, Robert Carradine, Frederic Cook, Severn Darden (New World)

A fashionable ad woman (Yvette Mimieux) gets beaten up by juvenile hitchhikers who steal her car, leaving her stranded in some ambiguous western town where she's promptly thrown in jail on phony charges and raped by a psychotic jailkeeper. She kills the jailkeeper and is forced to go on the lam with a rowdy but caring inmate (Tommy Lee Jones). The aftereffects of the rape are handled with more care than usual, and Mimieux turns in a convincing, well-controlled performance.

JACK THE BEAR
1993, 98 mins, US ⊘ ⊙ ▭
D: Marshall Herskovitz **A:** Danny DeVito, Robert J. Steinmiller Jr., Miko Hughes, Gary Sinise, Julia Louis-Dreyfus, Reese Witherspoon (American Filmworks/Lucky Dog)

Jack the Bear concerns a boy who discovers that monsters are to be found not only on television but also in real life. A clever portrayal of eccentric fatherhood by Danny DeVito and a socko performance from young Robert J. Steinmiller Jr. as the eponymous hero are major assets. Set in suburban Oakland in 1972, film mixes comedy and horror to make its points about latent evil.

JACOB'S LADDER
1990, 113 mins, US ⊘ ⊙
D: Adrian Lyne **A:** Tim Robbins, Elizabeth Pena, Danny Aiello, Matt Craven, Ving Rhames, Macaulay Culkin (Carolco)

Jacob's Ladder means to be a harrowing thriller about a Vietnam vet (Tim Robbins) bedeviled by strange visions, but is dull, unimaginative, and pretentious. Writer Bruce Joel Rubin telegraphs his plot developments and can't resist throwing in supernatural elements that prompt giggles at the most unfortunate moments. Right from the battlefield prologue in Vietnam, where members of Robbins's battalion act strangely and throw fits, it's clear that somebody messed with their brains. His very existence denied by the Veterans Administration, Robbins thinks he's possessed, but eventually pieces together the truth with the help of his battalion buddies.

JACQUELINE SUSANN'S ONCE IS NOT ENOUGH
See: *Once Is Not Enough*

JADE
1995, 95 mins, US ⊘ ⊙
D: William Friedkin **A:** David Caruso, Linda Fiorentino, Chazz Palminteri, Michael Biehn, Richard Crenna (Paramount)

A muddled mix of sex, political corruption, and murder, *Jade* is a jigsaw puzzle that never puts all the pieces together. Director William Friedkin and writer Joe Eszterhas have traveled these streets before, as has Linda Fiorentino in her latest take on a sexy femme fatale and David Caruso in his second so-so feature outing as a leading man. The climactic sequence proves so murkily shot there's scant suspense, as it's difficult to keep track of who's doing what to whom, and the ending is cryptic and largely unsatisfying.

JAGGED EDGE
1985, 108 mins, US ⊘ ⊙
D: Richard Marquand **A:** Jeff Bridges, Glenn Close, Peter Coyote, Robert Loggia, Leigh Taylor-Young, John Dehner (Columbia)

A well-crafted, hard-boiled mystery by Joe Eszterhas, with sharp performances by murder suspect Jeff Bridges and defense attorney Glenn Close. The murder victim was a socialite and heiress. Her husband (Bridges), a very upwardly mobile San Francisco newspaper publisher, now owns his wife's fortune. Embittered by past experiences in criminal law, Close is pressed

to defend Bridges, once he convinces her of his innocence. Then she falls in love with him. Triple Oscar nominees Bridges and Close play a balancing act that is both glossy and psychologically interesting.
1985: Nomination: Best Supp. Actor (Robert Loggia)

JAILHOUSE ROCK
1957, 96 mins, US ⓥ ⊙ ▭
D: Richard Thorpe **A:** Elvis Presley, Judy Tyler, Mickey Shaughnessy, Vaughn Taylor, Dean Jones (M-G-M/Avon)

Narrative intros Presley as a hot-tempered but affable youngster who goes to prison on a manslaughter rap. In stir he's cell-mated with Mickey Shaughnessy, who teaches him his dog-eat-dog philosophy, and also some singing tricks. Released, but now embittered and cynical, he claws his way to fame in the music world, riding alike over friend and foe, even Judy Tyler, a music exploitation agent who has helped in his discovery. Singer is on for six songs, top being the title production number in a prison setting.

JAKE SPEED
1986, 100 mins, US ⓥ ⊙
D: Andrew Lane **A:** Wayne Crawford, Dennis Christopher, Karen Kopins, John Hurt, Leon Ames (New World)

A deliberately mindless adventure that keeps tongue firmly in cheek. A family is worried about their daughter's disappearance in Paris. Pop wanders in, saying they ought to hire Jake Speed, a hero of paperback thrillers, to find her. Daughter No. 2 meets Speed and his sidekick author Remo. Trio crashes the den of the international white slavers lorded over by a malicious and deliciously evil John Hurt. Speed is well played by a heavy-lidded and laconic Wayne Crawford, who talks as an old-fashioned paperback hero would—in clichés.

JAMAICA INN
1939, 99 mins, UK ⓥ
D: Alfred Hitchcock **A:** Charles Laughton, Maureen O'Hara, Emlyn Williams, Robert Newton, Basil Radford, Mervyn Johns (Mayflower)

Superb direction, excellent casting, expressive playing, and fine production offset an uneven screenplay to make *Jamaica Inn* a gripping version of the Daphne du Maurier novel. Since it's frankly a blood-'n'-thunder melodrama, the story makes no pretense at complete plausibility. Yarn concerns a gang of smugglers and ship-wreckers on the Cornish coast in the early 19th century and the district squire who is their undercover brains. Charles Laughton has a colorful, sinister part in the villainous squire with a strain of insanity.

JAMES AND THE GIANT PEACH
1996, 80 mins, US ⓥ ⊙
D: Henry Selick **A:** Joanna Lumley, Miriam Margolyes, Pete Postlethwaite, Paul Terry (Walt Disney)

Combining mesmerizing stop-motion animation with digital animation as well as live action, *James and the Giant Peach* is a delightfully demented creation that's every bit as surreal and scary as it is touching and, ultimately, uplifting. Yarn opens with a brief, live-action prologue in which young James (Paul Terry) is orphaned. He is remanded to the custody of his hideous aunts, the fat, preening Sponge (Miriam Margolyes) and the skinny, pitiless Spiker (Joanna Lumley). A mysterious Old Man (Pete Postlethwaite) gives James a bag of glowing green crocodile tongues. The boy drops some of them near a long-dead tree and immediately a peach begins growing. The live-action gives over to animation when the boy, himself now transformed into an animated figure, encounters the six bugs who will become his new family, as the peach eventually rolls down to the sea and they set sail for Gotham.

JAMES BROTHERS, THE
See: The True Story of Jesse James

JANE EYRE
1944, 97 mins, US ⓥ ⊙
D: Robert Stevenson **A:** Orson Welles, Joan Fontaine, Margaret O'Brien, Peggy Ann Garner, Agnes Moorehead, Elizabeth Taylor (20th Century-Fox)

Charlotte Bronte's Victorian novel reaches the screen in a drama that is as intense on celluloid as it is on the printed page. *Jane Eyre* is the story of a girl who secures a position as governess to the ward of one Edward Rochester, sire of an English manor house. Jane Eyre eventually falls in love with him, and he with her. When their wedding is interrupted by a man who accuses Rochester of already being married, there is divulged the secret that Rochester has kept for many years. Joan Fontaine and Orson Welles are excellent, though the latter is frequently inaudible in the slur of his lines.

JANE EYRE
1971, 110 mins, UK ⓥ
D: Delbert Mann **A:** George C. Scott, Susannah York, Ian Bannen, Jack Hawkins, Nyree Dawn Porter, Rachel Kempson (Omnibus/Sagittarius)

Charlotte Bronte's tearjerker is put over stolidly and fails to touch and move the emotions as fluently as the 1943 version with Joan Fontaine and Orson Welles. Direction and screenplay both tend to play up incident rather than characters. George C. Scott as Rochester fails to bring out the smoldering romanticism, mixed with tyranny and selfishness. Since Jane Eyre is constantly described as plain, and Susannah York patently isn't plain, credibility is strained.

JANE EYRE
1996, 112 mins, Italy/UK/France/US ⓥ
D: Franco Zeffirelli **A:** William Hurt, Charlotte Gainsbourg, Joan Plowright, Anna Paquin, Geraldine Chaplin, Billie Whitelaw (Rochester/Mediaset/RCS/Flach/Majestic/Miramax)

Zeffirelli's rendition of Charlotte Bronte's celebrated novel boasts solid craftsmanship and smart thesping from a stellar cast ably led by the vibrant Charlotte Gainsbourg. What's lacking is the spark of inspiration needed to set this costumer ahead of the pack. The tale is famous for the romance when the grown Jane (Gainsbourg) takes employment at the estate of the mysterious Rochester (William Hurt). Physically and vocally just right, Gainsbourg easily suggests the gawky, awkward duckling teetering on the edge of charm and self-confidence. As Rochester, Hurt contributes another of his quirky, idiosyncratic performances, but one that productively accents the character's inner damage and heritage of trauma. Pic's visual approach is somewhat staid and conventional.

JANITOR, THE
See: Eyewitness

JANUARY MAN, THE
1989, 97 mins, US ⓥ ⊙
D: Pat O'Connor **A:** Kevin Kline, Susan Sarandon, Mary Elizabeth Mastrantonio, Harvey Keitel, Danny Aiello, Rod Steiger (M-G-M)

Kevin Kline as an unorthodox but indispensable detective tracking a serial strangler infuses this improbable Gotham-set romantic policier with personality.

Kline is Nick Starkey, a disgraced cop summoned from exile to crack an unsolvable crime. Kline has been hung out to dry on dubious allegations of graft by his mean-spirited brother, Police Commissioner Frank Starkey (Harvey Keitel), and brutish Mayor Eamon Flynn (Rod Steiger). Kline agrees to rejoin the NYPD if he's allowed to cook dinner for Keitel's haughty, social-climbing wife Christine (Susan Sarandon). Kline also strikes sexual sparks with the mayor's daughter Bernadette (Mary Elizabeth Mastrantonio), whose friend was murdered by the break-and-enter strangler.

JAPANESE WAR BRIDE
1952, 91 mins, US
D: King Vidor **A:** Shirley Yamaguchi, Don Taylor, Cameron Mitchell, Marie Windsor, James Bell (Bernhard/20th Century-Fox)

Shirley Yamaguchi, Japanese film star, plays the title role. Her restrained personality is ingratiating. Don Taylor is good as the Korean War veteran who marries her and brings her to Salinas, CA, for a new life in an American farming community whose citizens are prejudiced. Story comes to its head when the sister-in-law spreads rumor that the child born to the couple was actually fathered by a neighboring Japanese farmer.

JASON AND THE ARGONAUTS
1963, 104 mins, UK ⓥ ⊙
D: Don Chaffey **A:** Todd Armstrong, Nancy Kovack, Gary Raymond, Laurence Naismith, Niall MacGinnis, Douglas Wilmer (Columbia)

Jason and the Argonauts stems from the Greek myth of Jason and his voyage at the helm of the Argo in search of the Golden Fleece. Among the spectacular mythological landscape and characters brought to life through the ingenuity of illusionist Ray Harryhausen are a remarkably lifelike mobile version of the colossal bronze god Talos; fluttery personifications of the bat-winged Harpies; a miniature representation of the "crashing rocks" through which Jason's vessel must cruise; a menacing version of the seven-headed Hydra; a batch of some astonishingly active skeletons who materialize out of the teeth of Hydra; and a yare replica of the Argo itself.

JASON GOES TO HELL: THE FINAL FRIDAY

1993, 88 mins, US ⓥ ⊙

D: Adam Marcus **A:** Jon D. LeMay, Kari Keegan, Kane Hodder, Steven Williams, Steven Culp, Erin Gray (New Line)

Jason goes to hell, and not a moment too soon. His descent has been far too long in coming, as the exhausted, witless ninth, allegedly final, and supposedly explanatory chapter in the popular *Friday the 13th* series makes clear. Plot, of course, is merely an excuse to see Jason julienne his way through a series of scantily clad teenage campers, stupid cops, and best of all, a sleazy tabloid-TV reporter. Tech credits, especially the grainy focus, betray the film's modest budget.

JASON LIVES: FRIDAY THE 13TH PART VI

1986, 87 mins, US ⓥ ⊙

D: Tom McLoughlin **A:** Thom Mathews, Jennifer Cooke, David Kagen, Renee Jones, Kerry Noonan (Paramount/Terror)

Jason lives, but 18 other people die in this sixth entry in *Friday the 13th* series. Body count works out to an average of one corpse every 4.83 minutes. Vivid and vigorous opening sequence has two dopey kids digging up the grave of the Masked One on a dark and stormy night to make sure he's dead. A bolt of lightning brings the insatiable killer back to life. Believing old Jason croaked for good in *Part V*, the powers-that-be in Crystal Lake refuse to believe Tommy (Thom Mathews) when he insists a new rampage has begun.

JAWS

1975, 124 mins, US ⓥ ⊙ ⌑

D: Steven Spielberg **A:** Roy Scheider, Robert Shaw, Richard Dreyfuss, Lorraine Gary, Murray Hamilton, Carl Gottlieb (Universal)

A film of consummate suspense, tension, and terror. It stars Roy Scheider as the town's police chief; Robert Shaw, absolutely magnificent as a coarse fisherman hired to locate the great white shark; and Richard Dreyfuss as a likable young scientist. The fast-moving film engenders enormous suspense as the shark attacks a succession of people; the creature is not even seen for about 82 minutes, and a subjective camera technique makes the invisibility of his earlier forays all the more excruciatingly terrifying. The final hour of the film shifts from the town to a boat where the three stars track the shark, and vice versa. John Williams's haunting score adds to the mood of impending horror.

1975: Best Sound, Original Score, Editing
Nomination: Best Picture

JAWS 2

1978, 117 mins, US ⓥ ⌑

D: Jeannot Szwarc **A:** Roy Scheider, Lorraine Gary, Murray Hamilton, Joseph Mascolo, Jeffrey Kramer, Collin Wilcox (Universal)

A worthy successor in horror, suspense, and terror to its 1975 smash progenitor. The characters of offshore island police chief Roy Scheider, loyal spouse Lorraine Gary, temporizing mayor Murray Hamilton, and gee-whiz deputy Jeffrey Kramer are used as the adult pegs for the very good screenplay. The targets of terror, and the principal focus of audience empathy, are scores of happy teenagers as evidence mounts that there's another great white shark out there in the shallow waters.

JAWS 3-D

1983, 97 mins, US ⓥ ⊙ ⌑

D: Joe Alves **A:** Dennis Quaid, Bess Armstrong, Simon MacCorkindale, Louis Gossett Jr., John Putch (Universal/Landsburg)

The *Jaws* cycle has reached its nadir with this surprisingly tepid 3-D version. Gone are Roy Scheider, the summer resort of Amity, and even the ocean. They have been replaced by Florida's Sea World, a lagoon and an undersea kingdom that entraps a 35-foot great white, and a group of young people who run the tourist sea park.

JAWS: THE REVENGE

1987, 100 mins, US ⓥ ⊙

D: Joseph Sargent **A:** Michael Caine, Lorraine Gary, Lance Guest, Mario Van Peebles, Karen Young (Universal)

Lorraine Gary nicely reprises her role as the now widowed Ellen Brody. Ellen heads down to the Bahamas to be with her son, marine biologist Michael (Lance Guest), and his family, and tries to convince him to quit his job because she's sure "it" is out to get the family. Michael Caine is Ellen's delightfully irresponsible suitor, but he doesn't get enough screen time to really develop the character. After the shark practically walks up the beach to get a bite out of the third-generation Brody (Judith Barsi), Ellen goes after "it" by herself.

JAZZ ON A SUMMER'S DAY
1959, 78 mins, US Ⓥ
D: Bert Stern

Outstanding feature-length documentary centered around the Newport Jazz Festival. It's a document of the genre, spanning most of the jazz styles and including a rich selection of top performers and material. It's Americana, and a document of its time as well via observation of audiences and the life surrounding the Newport event, not least the neatly integrated footage concerning the America's Cup yacht races.

JAZZ SINGER, THE
1927, 88 mins, US Ⓥ ⊙
D: Alan Crosland **A:** Al Jolson, May McAvoy, Warner Oland, Eugenie Besserer, William Demarest (Warner)

The combination of the religious heart-interest story and Jolson's singing "Kol Nidre" in a synagogue while his father is dying and two "Mammy" lyrics as his mother stands in the wings of the theater, and later as she sits in the first row, carries abundant power and appeal. Al Jolson, when singing, is Jolson. There are six instances of this, each running from two to three minutes. When he's without that instrumental spur, Jolson is camera-conscious. But as soon as he gets under cork the lens picks up that spark of individual personality solely identified with him.

1927/28: Special Award (pioneer talking picture)
Nominations: Best Adapted Screenplay, Engineering Effects

JAZZ SINGER, THE
1952, 106 mins, US
D: Michael Curtiz **A:** Danny Thomas, Peggy Lee, Mildred Dunnock, Eduard Franz, Tom Tully, Allyn Joslyn (Warner)

Warners' remake is still sentimental, sometimes overly so. Peggy Lee, in her first feature-film lead, sparks the song offerings in sock style, and is okay in the acting demands as a musical-comedy-record star who loves and promotes the career of a cantor's son (Danny Thomas). Latter is excellent in a sentimental part, making the most of several genuine tear-jerker sequences.

1952: Nomination: Best Scoring of a Musical Picture

JAZZ SINGER, THE
1980, 115 mins, US Ⓥ ⊙
D: Richard Fleischer [Sidney J. Furie] **A:** Neil Diamond, Laurence Olivier, Lucie Arnaz, Catlin Adams, Paul Nicholas (AFD/Leider)

This third screen version of *The Jazz Singer* asks the same question as the 1927 history maker and the 1952 update—can a nice cantor's son break with family and tradition to make it as a popular entertainer? No one's going to get sweaty palms waiting for the answer, as Samson Raphaelson's venerable chestnut lacks urgency and plausible incidental detail. Elimination of the mother character in favor of a traditional wife k.o.'s any attempt at a reprise of "Mammy."

JEAN DE FLORETTE
1986, 120 mins, France/Italy Ⓥ ⊙ ⌑
D: Claude Berri **A:** Yves Montand, Daniel Auteuil, Gerard Depardieu, Elisabeth Depardieu, Ernestine Mazurowna, Marcel Champel (Renn/Films A2/RAI-2/DD)

The first of two films that Claude Berri adapted from a two-part novel by Marcel Pagnol. Yves Montand and Daniel Auteuil play a proud, self-centered village elder and his rat-faced subintelligent nephew who covet a local piece of fertile land, its chief asset being a subterranean spring. A hunchbacked young city slicker (Gerard Depardieu) has brought his wife (Elisabeth Depardieu) and young daughter, Manon, to settle and live off the land in Rousseauist simplicity. Depardieu doesn't know about the spring, which Montand and Auteuil have blocked up. Drought, the sirocco winds, and the long desperate treks to fetch water from another spring wear down Depardieu's optimism. Berri's sympathetic work with his small cast, and his subservience to Pagnol's story and dialogue, are key factors in the film's robust dramatic appeal.

JEANNE D'ARC
(THE MESSENGER: THE STORY OF JOAN OF ARC)
1999, 148 mins, France Ⓥ ⊙ ⌑
D: Luc Besson **A:** Milla Jovovich, John Malkovich, Faye Dunaway, Dustin Hoffman, Pascal Greggory, Vincent Cassel (Gaumont)

If you're going to do Joan of Arc, it helps to have an actress to play the leading role. Although Luc Besson makes his heroine as much a neurotic teenager as a divinely driven national savior, Milla Jovovich's overwrought rantings and bug-eyed expressions make Joan seem like a possessed lunatic, by no means a young lady a presumptive king would entrust with his army. Script skirts the issue of how Joan developed a local reputation and gathered a following, but by the time she is 17 she is sufficiently known to be received by the dauphin (John Malkovich), who cannot officially become king until crowned in Rheims, which is held by the English. The battle scenes are the main reason to see the film on the big screen. Malkovich makes for a blithe and quicksilver dauphin.

JEFFERSON IN PARIS
1995, 136 mins, US Ⓥ ⊙
D: James Ivory **A:** Nick Nolte, Greta Scacchi, Jean-Pierre Aumont, Simon Callow, James Earl Jones, Michael Lonsdale (Touchstone/Merchant Ivory)

This decorous look at the great man's five years as ambassador to France in the period leading up to the French Revolution touches upon much significant history, incident, and emotion but, ironically, lacks the intrigue and drama of great fiction. The strong points of James Ivory's approach here are his attentiveness to wonderful detail, including Jefferson's passion for playing violin-piano duets with the women in his life. The downside is that Ivory's reticence makes it additionally tough for an emotionally remote figure like Jefferson to come alive on-screen.

JEFFREY
1995, 92 mins, US Ⓥ
D: Christopher Ashley **A:** Steven Weber, Michael T. Weiss, Irma St. Paule, Patrick Stewart, Robert Klein, Christine Baranski (Workin' Man/Orion)

No sooner has he gone on the sexual wagon than Jeffrey (Steven Weber) meets the man of his dreams, Steve (Michael T. Weiss), an amiable HIV-positive hunk whose initial gym workout with the hapless and horny Jeffrey is none-too-subtly infused with sexual tension. Jeffrey naturally runs scared, and much of the film follows the pursuit-rejection mating dance of the two men. Along the episodic way, Jeffrey attends a socialite's country-themed Hoedown for AIDS, a New Age revival meeting (with Sigourney Weaver as a Marianne Williamson clone), and New York's gay pride parade, where Jeffrey encounters a supremely tacky New Jersey mother (Olympia Dukakis).

JENNIFER EIGHT
1992, 124 mins, US Ⓥ ⊙
D: Bruce Robinson **A:** Andy Garcia, Uma Thurman, Lance Henriksen, Kathy Baker,

Kevin Conway, John Malkovich (Paramount)

An unusually intelligent, and unexploitative thriller, notable for avoiding most standard suspense-film contrivances. Andy Garcia toplines as a wreck of a detective who joins a small-town Northern California police force. His sister (Kathy Baker) lives there with cop hubby (Lance Henriksen), and Garcia becomes latter's partner in the search for a woman whose hand is found—in a stunningly shot nocturnal opening sequence—at a dump. Garcia postulates that the killing is just the latest in a string of murders. Next target could be Uma Thurman, who's blind like the most recent victim and was the last person to ''see'' her alive.

JENNIFER ON MY MIND
1971, 90 mins, US
D: Noel Black **A:** Michael Brandon, Tippy Walker, Lou Gilbert, Steve Vinovich, Peter Bonerz, Renee Taylor (United Artists)

A black comedy about an aimless wealthy Jewish youth who falls in love with a bored and impulsive upper-class suburban girl he meets in Venice. Story unravels through a series of flashbacks narrated by the youth, Marcus, speaking into a tape recorder as he attempts to cope with the fact that he has killed his love, Jennifer, when, in response to her painful pleading, he reluctantly injected her with heroin. This is a potpourri of disarming satire, black comedy, and poignancy that creates a strangely haunting aura.

JEOPARDY
1953, 68 mins, US
D: John Sturges **A:** Barbara Stanwyck, Barry Sullivan, Ralph Meeker, Lee Aaker (M-G-M)

An unpretentious, tightly drawn suspense melodrama. Barbara Stanwyck, Barry Sullivan, and their small son (Lee Aaker) are vacationing at a deserted Mexican beach. An accident pins Sullivan's leg under a heavy piling that falls from a rotten jetty. Knowing the rising tide will cover him within four hours, Stanwyck takes off in the family car to find either help or a rope strong enough to raise the piling. The mission is sidetracked when she comes across Ralph Meeker, a desperate escaped convict.

JEREMIAH JOHNSON
1972, 110 mins, US Ⓥ ⊙ ▭
D: Sydney Pollack **A:** Robert Redford,

Will Geer, Stefan Gierasch, Delle Bolton, Josh Albee (Warner)

Pic meticulously lays out the life of a male dropout, circa 1825, who decides to live in the Rocky Mountains as a trapper. Robert Redford, as Johnson, has a solid stamina, a fine feel for the speech of the time, giving an autodidactic flair as he sometimes comments the actions. He begins to trade with the Indians and wins the esteem of a Crow-nation chief to whom he gives a present, to find he must accept the chief's daughter in return. The film has its own force and beauty and the only carp might lie in its not always clear exposition of the humanistic spirit and freedom most of its characters are striving for.

JEREMY
1973, 90 mins, US
D: Arthur Barron A: Robby Benson, Glynnis O'Connor, Len Bari, Leonard Cimino, Ned Wilson (Kenasset/United Artists)

Jeremy, played with adolescent rumpled and bumbling charm by Robby Benson, falls for a newcomer to his school, reserved but lovely little child-woman Glynnis O'Connor. Jeremy plays the cello, loves horses. The girl, Susan, studies classical dancing. Their idyll is shattered by her father deciding to leave New York and go back to Detroit. Arthur Barron does not force things and handles this slight but glowing pic with insight.

JERK, THE
1979, 104 mins, US Ⓥ ⊙
D: Carl Reiner A: Steve Martin, Bernadette Peters, Catlin Adams, Mabel King, Richard Ward (Universal/Aspen)

An artless, nonstop barrage of off-the-wall situations, funny and unfunny jokes, generally effective and sometimes hilarious sight gags, and bawdy non sequiturs. The premise of The Jerk can be found in one of Steve Martin's more famous routines. Upon receiving the stunning news that he's the adopted, not natural, son of black parents, Martin leaves home with his dog to make his way in the world.

JERKY BOYS, THE
1995, 81 mins, US Ⓥ
D: James Melkonian A: Johnny Brennan, Kamal Ahmed, Alan Arkin, William Hickey, Alan North, Brad Sullivan (Caravan/Touchstone)

Comedy, inspired by the antics of prank phone callers Johnny Brennan and Kamal Ahmed, is a lowbrow, high-

concept item. Johnny passes himself off as a notorious Chicago hood and gets the goodfellas to believe two fugitive hit men will need their hospitality. Naturally Johnny and Kamal introduce themselves as the hit men. Johnny and Kamal pretend to be, among other things, a nightclub magician, a hotheaded gangster, a pair of roadies, and while hiding from Mafia hoods, a couple of bathroom-stall Romeos.

JERRY MAGUIRE
1996, 138 mins, US Ⓥ ⊙
D: Cameron Crowe A: Tom Cruise, Cuba Gooding Jr., Renee Zellweger, Kelly Preston, Jerry O'Connell, Jay Mohr (Gracie/TriStar)

An exceptionally tasty contempo comedic romance, Jerry Maguire runs an unusual pattern on its way to scoring an unexpected number of emotional, social, and entertaining points. Jerry Maguire (Tom Cruise) is a slick agent who handles 72 clients for L.A.-based Sports Management Intl. But in a crisis of conscience, Jerry dashes off a long memo to the company staff. His ill-advised frankness gets him fired. Jerry goes to great lengths to represent the top college draft pick, quarterback Frank Cushman (Jerry O'Connell), but when he begins to look like a loser rather than a winner, his relationship with eyes-on-the-prize fiancée Avery (Kelly Preston) hits the rocks. Cruise shows a self-deprecatory quality and humor that are new and welcome, but there is nothing he can do to prevent the scene-stealing of Cuba Gooding Jr. as a larger-than-life modern athlete with his strutting ego, showboating style and frank preference for money over the glory of the game.
1996: Best Supp. Actor (Cuba Gooding Jr.)
Nominations: Best Picture, Actor (Tom Cruise), Original Screenplay, Editing.

JERSEY GIRL
1992, 95 mins, US Ⓥ ⊙
D: David Burton Morris A: Jami Gertz, Dylan McDermott, Sheryl Lee, Joseph Mazzello, Joseph Bologna, Aida Turturro (Electric/Interscope)

Jami Gertz is the prototypical young woman from New Jersey, living with her dad Joseph Bologna (who fears her becoming an old maid) and working in a day-care center. Script's main theme is that old standby: get out of your provincial rut and blossom. Gertz takes an old-fashioned route, trying to win some young hunk (Dylan McDermott) from Manhattan.

JESSE JAMES
1939, 103 mins, US Ⓥ ⊙
D: Henry King A: Tyrone Power, Henry Fonda, Nancy Kelly, Randolph Scott, Brian Donlevy, John Carradine (20th Century-Fox)

Jesse James, notorious train and bank bandit of the late 19th century, and an important figure in the history of the midwest frontier, gets a drastic bleaching. Tyrone Power capably carries the title spot, but is pressed by Henry Fonda as his brother.

JESSICA
1962, 105 mins, US/France/Italy b
D: Jean Negulesco A: Angie Dickinson, Maurice Chevalier, Noel-Noel, Gabriele Ferzetti, Sylva Koscina, Agnes Moorehead (United Artists)

A trite, frivolous variation on the oft-exploited *Lysistrata* theme. Angie Dickinson enacts the title role of an anatomically streamlined midwife from America who unwittingly tips the Freudian scale in a small Sicilian village just by sheer sex appeal. The misguided señoritas organize a sex strike. Objective: "no babies, no midwife." Maurice Chevalier breezes through the part of village priest with that familiar sunny countenance.

JESUS CHRIST, SUPERSTAR
1973, 107 mins, US Ⓥ ⊙ ▭
D: Norman Jewison A: Ted Neeley, Carl Anderson, Yvonne Elliman, Barry Dennen, Bob Bingham, Josh Mostel (Universal)

Norman Jewison's film version of the 1969 legit stage project is both very good and very disappointing at the same time. The filming concept is that of a contemporary group of young players performing sequential production numbers in the barren desert, utitlizing sketchy props and costumes. Then something happens as Carl Anderson (outstanding as Judas in the film's best performance) finds himself, in the midst of "Damned for All Time" running away from tanks and ducking modern jet fighters. Suddenly it's *Catch-22* time, which the very moving "Last Supper" sequence can only counteract instead of contributing to a mounting dramatic impact.
1973: Nomination: Best Adapted Score

JET PILOT
1957, 112 mins, US
D: Josef von Sternberg A: John Wayne,

Janet Leigh, Jay C. Flippen, Paul Fix, Richard Rober (RKO)

Made around 1950 and kept under wraps by indie filmmaker Howard Hughes, its story has a pretty young girl as a Russian jet pilot who, on a spy mission, wings into a love match with an American airman in the United States. Questionable is the casting of Janet Leigh. The slick chick looks more at home in a bathing suit at Palm Springs than she does jockeying a Soviet MiG.

JEUX INTERDITS, LES (FORBIDDEN GAMES)
1952, 90 mins, France Ⓥ
D: Rene Clement A: Brigitte Fossey, Georges Poujouly, Lucien Hubert, Suzanne Courtal, Jacques Marin (Silver)

Film is moving, poetic idyll of the effect of the war on two moppets. Story starts with the French exodus during the war. In the midst of a strafing by the enemy, a little girl's parents and her dog are killed. She is picked up by a little farm boy, who takes her home with him. In burying the dog, they decide to make a little cemetery for animals. This leads to bloodshed between two feuding farm families. Moppets Brigitte Fossey and Georges Poujouly are brilliantly handled and give an air of spontaneity to their roles.
1952: Best Foreign Language Film

JEWEL OF THE NILE, THE
1985, 104 mins, US Ⓥ ⊙
D: Lewis Teague A: Michael Douglas, Kathleen Turner, Danny DeVito, Spiros Focas, Avner Eisenberg (20th Century-Fox)

A sequel to *Romancing the Stone*. Michael Douglas and Kathleen Turner again play off each other very well, but the story is much thinner. The main problem is the dialogue, which too often relies on the trite. Turner accepts an invitation from a sinister potentate (Spiros Focas) to accompany him and write a story about his pending ascendency as desert ruler. Left behind, Douglas runs into the excitable Danny DeVito and they become unwilling allies, again in pursuit of a jewel.

JEW SUSS
1934, 120 mins, UK
D: Lothar Mendes A: Conrad Veidt, Benita Hume, Gerald du Maurier, Pamela Ostrer, Frank Vosper, Cedric Hardwicke (Gaumont-British)

It's a spectacle of no small proportions, the saga of Jew Josef Süss-Oppenheimer, who ruthlessly achieves the economic power which permits him, a truly sensitive alumnus of the ghetto, to mingle with the Wurttemberg ducal nobility. (Locale and period is 18th century Duchy of Wurttemberg, Germany.) *Jew Süss* is all Conrad Veidt, a consummate screen artist.

JEZEBEL
1938, 100 mins, US Ⓥ ⊙
D: William Wyler **A:** Bette Davis, Henry Fonda, George Brent, Margaret Lindsay, Donald Crisp, Fay Bainter (Warner)

Against an 1852 New Orleans locale, when the dread yellow jack (yellow-fever epidemic) broke out, the astute scriveners have fashioned a rather convincing study of the flower of southern chivalry, honor, and hospitality. Detracting is the fact that Bette Davis's "Jezebel" suddenly metamorphoses into a figure of noble sacrifice and complete contriteness. William Wyler's direction draws an engrossing cross section of old southern manners and hospitality.
1938: Best Actress (Bette Davis), Supp. Actress (Fay Bainter)
Nominations: Best Picture, Cinematography, Score

JFK
1991, 189 mins, US Ⓥ ⊙ ▱
D: Oliver Stone **A:** Kevin Costner, Sissy Spacek, Joe Pesci, Tommy Lee Jones, Gary Oldman, Donald Sutherland (Warner/Regency/Canal Plus/Ixtlan)

This massive, never-boring political thriller lays out just about every shred of evidence yet uncovered for the conspiracy theory surrounding the Nov. 22, 1963, assassination of President John F. Kennedy. New Orleans d.a. Jim Garrison (Kevin Costner) begins delving into a mysterious netherworld of right-wing, anti-Castro homosexuals populated by the bewigged David Ferrie (Joe Pesci), suave businessman Clay Shaw (Tommy Lee Jones), and unpredictable hustler Willie O'Keefe (Kevin Bacon). Garrison begins to suspect that the US government's military-industrial complex initiated the killing.
1991: Best Cinematography, Editing
Nominations: Best Picture, Director, Supp. Actor (Tommy Lee Jones), Adapted Screenplay, Original Score, Sound

JIMMY HOLLYWOOD
1994, 109 mins, US Ⓥ ⊙
D: Barry Levinson **A:** Joe Pesci, Christian Slater, Victoria Abril, Jason Beghe, John Cothran Jr. (Baltimore/Paramount)

Barry Levinson's oddball attempt to mix offbeat comedy with social commentary and fringe-level character study. Jimmy (Joe Pesci) spends his time hanging out in the company of dimwit grunge puppy William (Christian Slater). Jimmy then makes an effective tape of himself as Jericho, the fearless leader of SOS (Save Our Streets), a self-appointed "watchdog of Hollywood" vigilante group. Exhilarated by the media attention, Jimmy and William don masks and catch any number of bad guys in the act.

JIMMY THE GENT
1934, 66 mins, US
D: Michael Curtiz **A:** James Cagney, Bette Davis, Alice White, Allen Jenkins, Philip Reed (Warner)

Story seems to be the first screen presentation of a plausible racket, namely, finding heirs for the fortunes lying around unclaimed in banks. Cagney is crude and primitive in his operations. The girl he is sweet on (Bette Davis) works for a gentlemanly and suave practitioneer of the same racket. Part of the fun is Cagney's trying to make a gent out of himself in emulation of the smoothie (Alan Dinehart).

JIM THORPE—ALL-AMERICAN
(UK: MAN OF BRONZE)
1951, 107 mins, US Ⓥ ⊙
D: Michael Curtiz **A:** Burt Lancaster, Charles Bickford, Steve Cochran, Phyllis Thaxter, Dick Wesson (Warner)

One of the great stories in American sports history is compellingly told. Only a few fictional liberties have been taken in telling of how Thorpe came off an Oklahoma reservation to establish himself as the greatest all-round athlete of modern times. Pic re-creates a number of events from sports history. All these Burt Lancaster has helped capture in the spirit of the grim-visaged, moody Indian. Phyllis Thaxter plays the white girl who became Thorpe's wife.

JINGLE ALL THE WAY
1996, 88 mins, US Ⓥ ⊙
D: Brian Levant **A:** Arnold Schwarzenegger, Sinbad, Phil Hartman, Rita Wilson, Robert Conrad, James Belushi (1492 Picture/20th Century-Fox)

In this highly formulaic star vehicle, Arnold Schwarzenegger gets to fly like Peter Pan, act like Superman and fulfill the kind of fantasy many kids imagine for their fathers. Slight tale centers on the desperate efforts of a workaholic father, Howard (Schwarzenegger), to get his son, Jamie (Jake Lloyd), his desired Christmas gift. The action toy Turbo Man is the season's hottest gift, sold out since Thanksgiving. Attempting to flesh out the slender material, filmmakers have Howard fight a corrupt operation, headed by a shady Santa Claus (James Belushi), who dupes Howard into buying a headless, Korean-speaking Turbo Man. Pic credits the efforts of no fewer than 60 stunt people.

JINGWU MEN
(FIST OF FURY; THE CHINESE CONNECTION; THE IRON HAND)
1972, 105 mins, Hong Kong ⓥ ▷
D: Lo Wei **A:** Bruce Lee, Nora Miao, Maria Yi, James Tien, Tien Feng (Golden Harvest)

Bruce Lee has parlayed his skill in kung fu into a profitable acting career in Hong Kong–produced features. Actioner tells of a young kung fu student who sets out to avenge the murder of his boxing master. Apart from a few tepid romantic interludes, pic focuses on a series of battles in which the fist-wielding Lee defeats anywhere from one to two dozen whimpering opponents in an Oriental paraphrase of Clint Eastwood's Ital-oaters. Lee has a good deal of aggressive boyish charm.

JINXED!
1982, 103 mins, US ⓥ
D: Don Siegel **A:** Bette Midler, Ken Wahl, Rip Torn, Val Avery, Jack Elam (M-G-M/United Artists/Jaffe)

They tried and tried to come up with a better title for *Jinxed!*, but somehow they kept returning to the only one that was fitting. The exclamation point emphasizes the totality of the disaster. Tale presents casino dealer Ken Wahl as the hapless victim of seedy gambler Rip Torn. Torn also gives grief to his small-time singer g.f. Bette Midler, who is sufficiently taken with Wahl's charms to rope him into a scheme to bump off her lover.

JOANNA
1969, 107 mins, UK ▷
D: Michael Sarne **A:** Genevieve Waite, Christian Doermer, Calvin Lockhart, Donald Sutherland (20th Century-Fox/Laughlin)

White girl loves black boy, black girl loves white boy. A sometimes funny, often tearful tale of the deflowering of a scatter-brained English girl turned loose in

wicked, wanton London. Director Michael Sarne's script contains too few hits and too many misses. The best thing about *Joanna* is the superb color photography of Walter Lassally.

JOAN OF ARC
1948, 150 mins, US ⓥ ⊙
D: Victor Fleming **A:** Ingrid Bergman, Jose Ferrer, Ward Bond, Francis L. Sullivan, Cecil Kellaway (RKO/Sierra)

A big picture in every respect. It has size, color, pageantry, a bold, historic bas-relief. It has authority, conviction, an appeal to faith, and a dedication to a cause that leaves little wanting. And then, of course, *Joan of Arc* has Ingrid Bergman and a dream supporting cast. Fleming has done an exciting job in blending the symbolism, the medieval warfront heroics, and the basic dramatic elements into a generally well-sustained whole. Bergman makes Joan a vivid albeit spiritual personality. The Technicolor is magnificent.
1948: Best Color Cinematography, Color Costume Design
Nominations: Best Actress (Ingrid Bergman), Supp. Actor (Jose Ferrer), Color Art Direction, Editing, Scoring of a Dramatic Picture

JOAN OF PARIS
1942, 93 mins, US ⓥ
D: Robert Stevenson **A:** Michele Morgan, Paul Henreid, Thomas Mitchell, Laird Cregar, May Robson (RKO)

The American screen debuts of Michele Morgan and Paul Henreid, RKO importations. Story is one of those counterespionage tales of escaping British fliers, Gestapo shadowing, and French underground. Although intriguing in first half, it gets repetitious in second section to taper off with too mild a climax without the generation of tragic note intended.

JOB, THE
See: Il Posto

JOE
1970, 107 mins, US ⓥ ⊙
D: John G. Avildsen **A:** Dennis Patrick, Peter Boyle, Susan Sarandon, Patrick McDermott, K. Callan (Cannon)

A NY ad-agency exec (Dennis Patrick) murders his daughter's junkie lover. He is found out by a hard-hat factory worker, the Joe of the title (Peter Boyle), who applauds his action as a blow struck for God and country. The two begin a class-spanning relationship which brings them nervously together in the realization that the American dream has somehow turned sour for them. Norman Wexler's script makes audience identification well nigh impossible and at the same time abstracts the questions in a way that gives the pic real importance.

1970: Nomination: Best Original Story & Screenplay

JOE KIDD
1972, 87 mins, US ⓥ ⊙ ▭
D: John Sturges **A:** Clint Eastwood, Robert Duvall, John Saxon, Don Stroud, Stella Garcia, James Wainwright (Malpaso/Universal)

Not enough identity is given Clint Eastwood in a New Mexico land struggle in which no reason is apparent for his involvement, but John Sturges's direction is sufficiently compelling to keep guns popping and bodies falling. Highlight of entire footage occurs when Eastwood and a few men run a railroad engine through the bar where some of the gunmen are holding forth and mow them down.

JOE LOUIS STORY, THE
1953, 88 mins, US ⓥ
D: Robert Gordon **A:** Coley Wallace, Paul Stewart, Hilda Simms, James Edwards, John Marley (United Artists)

A dramatic recap of the personal and ring history of the respected Negro American fighter, acted out by a predominantly colored cast headed by Coley Wallace (as the champ), the film rates high on sincerity, is alternately touching, understanding, and heart-poundingly exciting. Coley Wallace is the spitting image of Joe, from his muscular body to the expressionless face that so unexpectedly breaks out into a broad, friendly grin. He carries off the ring scenes and does well against Hilda Simms, who plays Mrs. Louis. Integration of real fight shots is excellently handled and accounts for the picture's sock appeal.

JOE MACBETH
1955, 90 mins, UK
D: Ken Hughes **A:** Paul Douglas, Ruth Roman, Bonar Colleano, Gregoire Aslan, Sidney James (Columbia)

Joe Macbeth is far removed from the famous Shakespearean character, but there is an analogy between this modern gangster story and the Bard's classic play. Although made in Britain, the film has an American setting. It is expertly staged and directed with a keen sense of tension. The plot is basically a battle for supremacy, waged by Paul Douglas, in the title role,

and egged on by his determined bride (Ruth Roman).

JOE VERSUS THE VOLCANO
1990, 102 mins, US ⓥ ⊙ ▭
D: John Patrick Shanley **A:** Tom Hanks, Meg Ryan, Lloyd Bridges, Robert Stack, Dan Hedaya, Ossie Davis (Amblin/Warner)

An overproduced, disappointing shaggy-dog comedy. Hanks is a hypochondriac and his doctor, Robert Stack, gives the hapless guy only six months to live. Coincidentally, tycoon Lloyd Bridges pops in to offer Hanks to "live like a king" for 20 days before heading for a remote Polynesian island to "die like a man," i.e., jump into an active volcano to appease the fire god. Hanks indulges himself in some rather unfunny solo bits. Ryan has fun in three personas, but they're simply revue sketches.

JOEY
1985, 95 mins, US ⓥ
D: Joseph Ellison **A:** Neill Barry, James Quinn, Elisa Heinsohn, Linda Thorson, Ellen Hammill (Rock 'n' Roll/Satori)

An intelligent, engaging pic about a youngster who's into the rock-and-roll music of the 1950s. Joey (Neill Barry), age 17, likes to play guitar the way his dad, Joe Sr. (James Quinn) used to. Joey and friends have formed a group of their own, and they win a successful audition to play backup to some of the original 1950s and 1960s groups due to appear at Radio City.

JOHN AND MARY
1969, 92 mins, US ⓥ ▭
D: Peter Yates **A:** Dustin Hoffman, Mia Farrow, Michael Tolan, Sunny Griffin, Tyne Daly (20th Century-Fox/Debrod)

A slight, indeed simple story that begins with sex and ends with love. John is selfish and self-satisfied, but Hoffman projects a screen personality which insists that more is present than is getting through the camera's eye. Mary is much more attractive, feminine, and alive. And Farrow enlarges the character sufficiently to make her worth caring about.

JOHN CARPENTER'S ESCAPE FROM L.A.
See: Escape from L.A.

JOHN CARPENTER'S VAMPIRES
See: Vampires

JOHN GRISHAM'S THE RAINMAKER
See: The Rainmaker

JOHN HUSTON AND THE DUBLINERS
1987, 60 mins, US
D: Lilyan Sievernich **A:** John Huston, Anjelica Huston, Tony Huston, Donal McCann (Liffen)

A perceptive documentary on legendary director John Huston and his working methods, shot on the set of his film *The Dead* (1987). Documaker Lilyan Sievernich (whose husband Chris is an executive producer of *The Dead*) succeeds in revealing, by interviews with Huston, his cast and crew members, plus verité footage of scenes being filmed and rehearsed, how Huston gets exactly what he wants by gentle suggestions, cajoling, and simply doing things till they come out right.

JOHNNY ALLEGRO
1949, 80 mins, US
D: Ted Tetzlaff **A:** George Raft, Nina Foch, George Macready, Will Geer (Columbia)

Typical George Raft melodrama. Plot rings in a twist or two to dress up the melodrama of an ex-gangster who is trying to go straight and who takes on a dangerous assignment from the government to help prove his good intentions. From the time Raft crosses paths with Nina Foch, wife of a big-time international agent, his life is marked with danger.

JOHNNY ANGEL
1945, 79 mins, US
D: Edwin L. Marin **A:** George Raft, Claire Trevor, Signe Hasso, Lowell Gilmore, Hoagy Carmichael (RKO)

Another maritime intrigue involving murder and lust. Raft is his invariably glowering self as a guy who really handles his mitts—and the dames—while Claire Trevor and Signe Hasso are the romantic interests. Rest of the cast is weighted down too much by the story, though Hoagy Carmichael plays the character of whimsy with tongue in cheek.

JOHNNY BELINDA
1948, 101 mins, US
D: Jean Negulesco **A:** Jane Wyman, Lew Ayres, Charles Bickford, Agnes Moorehead, Stephen McNally, Jan Sterling (Warner)

Jane Wyman portrays a mute slattern completely devoid of film glamour. It is a personal success; a socko demonstration that an artist can shape a mood and sway an audience without speaking a word. Plot essentials cover a deaf-mute girl on a barren farm in Nova Scotia. A village Romeo rapes her. She has a baby and events move forward until the deaf-mute kills her ravisher when he tries to take the baby. Jean Negulesco's direction never overplays the heartstrings, yet keeps them constantly twanging, and evidences a sympathetic instinct that is reflected in the performance.
1948: Best Actress (Jane Wyman)
Nominations: Best Picture, Director, Actor (Lew Ayres), Supp. Actor (Charles Bickford), Supp. Actress (Agnes Moorehead), Screenplay, B&W Cinematogrpahy, B&W Art Direction, Editing, Score of a Dramatic Picture, Sound

JOHNNY COME LATELY
1943, 97 mins, US ⊙
D: William K. Howard **A:** James Cagney, Grace George, Marjorie Main, Hattie McDaniel, Ed McNamara (United Artists)

James Cagney's first independent production comes through with a top-notch performance in the story of the crack tramp newspaperman, afflicted with wanderlust, who temporarily halts in his tracks to help an old lady continue publication of her newspaper and battle the crooked politico-financial forces in her town.

JOHNNY COOL
1963, 103 mins, US
D: William Asher **A:** Henry Silva, Elizabeth Montgomery, Marc Lawrence, Telly Savalas, Jim Backus, Sammy Davis Jr. (Chrislaw)

Henry Silva, as a Sicilian-born assassin, is at home as the "delivery boy of death" for deported underworld kingpin Marc Lawrence. Plot centers on Silva doing a job which takes him from Sicily to Rome, then to NY, L.A., and Las Vegas before he's finished. When a doll comes into his life and gets worked over by some hoods, he adds revenge to his baser reasons for wiping out his assorted victims.

JOHNNY DANGEROUSLY
1984, 90 mins, US ⊙
D: Amy Heckerling **A:** Michael Keaton, Joe Piscopo, Marilu Henner, Maureen Stapleton, Danny DeVito, Griffin Dunne (20th Century-Fox)

1930s gangster send-up. Deliberately overworking the Cagney mannerisms, Michael Keaton is initially good, in the title role, as is Griffin Dunne as Johnny's d.a. brother. Unfortunately, the material just gets worse and worse.

JOHNNY EAGER
1941, 106 mins, US
D: Mervyn LeRoy **A:** Robert Taylor, Lana Turner, Edward Arnold, Van Heflin, Robert Sterling (M-G-M)

Johnny Eager is an underworld meller with a few new twists to the usual trappings, but by and large it's the familiar tale of slick gangster vs. innocent rich girl. Robert Taylor, with his hair slightly ruffled to make him a rough-tough guy, drives a taxi for the benefit of the parole board while directing his underworld activities. Debutante Lana Turner falls in love with the intriguing ex-convict. After discovering his gangster activities, she holds the secret. Van Heflin, as the perpetually soused companion of Taylor, is outstanding.

JOHNNY GUITAR
1954, 111 mins, US Ⓥ ⊙
D: Nicholas Ray **A:** Joan Crawford, Sterling Hayden, Mercedes McCambridge, Scott Brady, Ernest Borgnine (Republic)

Western proves Joan Crawford should leave saddles and Levi's to someone else and stick to city lights for a background. Crawford plays Vienna, strong-willed owner of a plush gambling saloon standing alone in the wilderness of Arizona. She knows the railroad's coming through and she will build a whole new town and get rich. Opposing her is Mercedes McCambridge, bitter, frustrated leader of a nearby community. Love, hate, and violence, with little sympathy for the characters, is stirred up during the overlong film.

JOHNNY HANDSOME
1989, 95 mins, US Ⓥ ⊙
D: Walter Hill **A:** Mickey Rourke, Ellen Barkin, Elizabeth McGovern, Morgan Freeman, Forest Whitaker, Scott Wilson (Carolco/Guber-Peters)

A promising idea is gunned down by sickening violence and a downbeat ending. Born with a cleft palate and badly disfigured face, John Sedley (Rourke) has wound up a petty criminal. Kindly Dr. Resher (Forest Whitaker), a plastic surgeon, after a series of painful ops, has Johnny looking like Mickey Rourke. Johnny is allowed out of prison each day to work on the docks, where he meets pretty accountant Elizabeth McGovern. But Johnny isn't content with his new circumstances: he wants revenge for being mistreated. Rourke works hard at his character but fails to make Johnny the least bit sympathetic.

JOHNNY IN THE CLOUDS
See: The Way to the Stars

JOHNNY MNEMONIC
1995, 98 mins, CANADA Ⓥ ⊙
D: Robert Longo **A:** Keanu Reeves, Dolph Lundgren, Takeshi, Ice-T, Dina Meyer, Udo Kier (Alliance)

High-tech trash, film as video game. Set in the year 2021, when vast corporations rule the world, pic features one bit of ingenuity, its premise, which sees Johnny (Reeves) outfitted with a computer chip in his head so that he can smuggle the highly classified contents from Asia to North America. The amount of information he has taken on is enough to make his noggin explode unless he gets downloaded in short order. The long-awaited razzle-dazzle of downloading is an extended visual trip that seems intended as a modern equivalent to the stargate sequence in *2001* but comes off as so much graphic doodling. Absolutely zero human interest is generated by Reeves, who comes off as gruff, hostile, and selfish, all in one dimension.

JOHNNY O'CLOCK
1947, 95 mins, US
D: Robert Rossen **A:** Dick Powell, Evelyn Keyes, Lee J. Cobb, Ellen Drew, Nina Foch (Columbia)

This is a smart whodunit, with attention to scripting, casting and camerawork lifting it above the average. Pic has action and suspense, and certain quick touches of humor to add flavor. Ace performances by Dick Powell, as a gambling-house overseer, and Lee J. Cobb, as a police inspector, also up the rating. Plot concerns Powell's operation as a junior partner in Thomas Gomez's gambling joint, and his allure for the ladies, especially Ellen Drew, the boss's wife.

JOHNNY SUEDE
1992, 95 mins, US Ⓥ ⊙
D: Tom DiCillo **A:** Brad Pitt, Calvin Levels, Alison Moir, Catherine Keener, Tina Louise (Vega)

Taking place in an imaginary slum, Tom DiCillo's gently ironic fantasy focuses on a dreamy young man who rejects reality and, after a pair of suede shoes is literally dropped on his head, adopts the name Johnny Suede and sets out to be a pop star, using the late Ricky Nelson as his model. Brad Pitt, fresh from stealing scenes in *Thelma & Louise*, gives Johnny the right kind of innocent appeal, and the rest of the cast surround him with loving care.

JOHN PAUL JONES
1959, 126 mins, US ▭
D: John Farrow **A:** Robert Stack, Marisa Pavan, Charles Coburn, Erin O'Brien, Jean-Pierre Aumont, Bette Davis (Warner)

John Paul Jones has some spectacular sea action scenes and achieves some freshness in dealing with the Revolutionary War. But the production doesn't get much firepower into its characters. They end, as they begin, as historical personages rather than human beings. Perhaps because Jones himself was a man of action, the story gets stiff and awkward when it moves off the quarterdeck and into the drawing room. The brief appearance of Bette Davis as Catherine the Great of Russia is the cliché portrait of that vigorous empress, a woman bordering on nymphomania. Robert Stack in the title role gives a robust portrayal.

JOI-UCHI
(REBELLION; SAMURAI REBELLION)
1967, 125 mins, Japan ⊙ ▭
D: Masaki Kobayashi **A:** Toshiro Mifune, Go Kato, Tatsuya Nakadai, Michiko Otsuka, Tatsuo Matsumura (Toho/Mifune)

Written by Shinobu Hashimoto (who also wrote *Rashomon* and *Harakiri*), with music by Toru Takemitsu and directed by the man who created *Harakiri* and *Kwaidan*, this represents all the best in the Japanese period film. At the end of the 18th century, a middle-aged court official (Toshiro Mifune) discovers that the local *daimyo* (Tatsuo Matsumura) is demanding back an ex-wife (Yoko Tsukasa), who has since become married to Mifune's elder son (Go Kato). Mifune refuses. Nothing happens, except talk, for the first hour and 40 minutes, and then screen explodes into the most slashing *chambara* since *Harakiri*. The letting of blood does not purify, nor is it intended to.

JOKER IS WILD, THE
(AKA: ALL THE WAY)
1957, 124 mins, US
D: Charles Vidor **A:** Frank Sinatra, Mitzi Gaynor, Jeanne Crain, Eddie Albert, Beverly Garland, Jackie Coogan (Paramount)

The Joker Is Wild purports to be the case history of a Prohibition-era entertainer who lived through a savage attack by mobsters; loved and lost a pretty, rich girl; married a dancer whom he neglected; often was a self-pitying heel; hit the bottle

and gambled all the time; and meanwhile gagged his way to being a heavy favorite in the club-date sweepstakes. Frank Sinatra obviously couldn't be made to look like Joe E. Lewis; and Lewis's style of delivery is unique. But these are minor reservations in light of the major job Sinatra does—alternately sympathetic and pathetic, funny and sad.
1957: Best Song ("All the Way")

JOKERS, THE
1967, 94 mins, UK
D: Michael Winner **A:** Michael Crawford, Oliver Reed, Harry Andrews, James Donald, Daniel Massey, Michael Hordern (Rank Gildor-Scimitar)

Michael Crawford and Oliver Reed are two brothers, the former just expelled from still another college for a practical joke, the latter the author of that scheme. Together, they plan and execute a national outrage—theft of the Crown Jewels, with no intent to keep them, just to carry off the theft. Sight gags and underplayed British throwaway gags are interleaved neatly with the growing suspense over whether the guys will succeed.

LE JOLI MAI
1963, 180 mins, France
D: Chris Marker (Sofracima)

Film details a series of happenings, street and home interviews, plus a general panorama of Paris in May '62. Via intensive editing, people reveal themselves to give a neat look at human foibles. There are shots of riots during the Algerian fracas, an African's attitudes toward the French, stockmarket-worker outlooks, and many others. The commentary is well delivered by Yves Montand.

JOLSON SINGS AGAIN
1949, 96 mins, US ▽ ⊙
D: Henry Levin **A:** Larry Parks, Barbara Hale, William Demarest, Ludwig Donath, Bill Goodwin (Columbia)

On a broad canvas is projected Al Jolson's wartime tours under Special Services, singing from the Aleutians to the Caribbean bases until he finally contracts the serious fever that laid him low in North Africa. Barbara Hale reenacts the nurse technician from Little Rock who is now Mrs. Jolson. Larry Parks, again playing Jolson, remains an uncannily faithful impersonator of the star.
1949: Nominations: Best Story & Screenplay, Color Cinematography, Scoring of a Musical Picture

JOLSON STORY, THE
1946, 120 mins, US 🅥 ⊙
D: Alfred E. Green **A:** Larry Parks, Evelyn Keyes, William Demarest, Bill Goodwin, Ludwig Donath (Columbia)

Jolson's singing proves the big excitement for this Technicolorful film biog of the great mammy-singer's career. The yearning to sing, to give generously of himself, cued by the famed catchphrase "You ain't heard nothin' yet"; the Sunday nights at the Winter Garden; the birth of the runway as Jolson got closer to his audience; the incidental whistling in between vocalizing—all these are recaptured for the screen. It's quite apparent how Larry Parks as the mammy kid must have studied the Jolson mannerisms in black-and-white, because the vocal synchronization (with a plenitude of close-ups) defies detection.
1946: Best Sound Recording, Scoring for a Musical Picture
Nominations: Best Actor (Larry Parks), Supp. Actor (William Demarest), Color Cinematography, Editing

JONATHAN LIVINGSTON SEAGULL
1973, 114 mins, US 🅥 ▭
D: Hall Bartlett (Paramount)

Pastoral allegory, filmed with live birds and locations while some well-known players essay the vocal chores, is a combination of teenybopper psychedelics, facile moralizing, Pollyanna polemic, and superb nature photography. Though not credited, per arrangement, the vocal cast draws on many fine players. James Franciscus dubs the title bird, a nonconformist who wants to dive for fish instead of foraging in garbage like gulls always do.
1973: Nominations: Best Cinematography, Editing

JOSEPH ANDREWS
1977, 103 mins, UK 🅥
D: Tony Richardson **A:** Ann-Margret, Peter Firth, Michael Hordern, Beryl Reid, Jim Dale (Woodfall)

A tired British period piece about leching and wenching amid the high and low life of Henry Fielding's England. Tony Richardson's film is a ludicrous mix of underplayed bawdiness and sporadic vulgarity. Large cast of otherwise British players is headed by Ann-Margret, sometimes appearing grotesque in her rendition of Lady Booby, the noblewoman-with-a-past with the hots for servant Peter Firth in title role.

JOSETTE
1938, 70 mins, US 🅥
D: Allan Dwan **A:** Don Ameche, Simone Simon, Robert Young, Joan Davis, Bert Lahr (20th Century-Fox)

This is a corking good entertainment, smartly written, well directed, and deftly acted. Simone Simon is a cute little trick, pint-size alongside Don Ameche and Robert Young. These two play brothers who start out with the single thought of separating their philandering father from a cabaret singer named Josette. The real Josette fails to appear for her engagement, and Simon substitutes. The brothers, of course, start to put the pressure on the wrong girl. Ameche and Young get all the laughs obtainable from bright lines. Simon plays coyly, and sings right well two songs written by Mack Gordon and Harry Revel.

JOUR DE FETE
1949, 87 mins, France 🅥 ⊙
D: Jacques Tati **A:** Jacques Tati, Guy Decomble, Paul Frankeur, Santa Relli, Maine Vallee (Cady)

The story, which is of the thinnest, shows a French village on a holiday. There is practically no plot. Supporting cast is of very small importance compared with Jacques Tati, who does the village postman. The one thing that counts in the picture is Tati's antics, with practically no dialogue.

LE JOURNAL D'UN CURE DE CAMPAGNE
(DIARY OF A COUNTRY PRIEST)
1951, 120 mins, France 🅥 ⊙ ▭
D: Robert Bresson **A:** Claude Laydu, Nicole Maurey, Nicole Ladmirale, Marie-Monique Arkell, Jean Riveyre, Serge Bento (UGC)

A conscientious rendering of the spiritual anguish of a shy, young priest, pic is slow-moving but impressive. The priest (Claude Laydu) suffers the hostility and misunderstanding of the townspeople. Suffering from a severe stomach ailment, he subsists on bread and wine. The hostile villagers soon take him for a drunkard. Director Robert Bresson has ruthlessly stamped out any incident not in keeping with the mood and feeling of the young priest.

LE JOURNAL D'UNE FEMME DE CHAMBRE
(DIARY OF A CHAMBERMAID)
1964, 100 mins, France/Italy 🅥 ⊙
D: Luis Bunuel **A:** Jeanne Moreau, Michel

Piccoli, Georges Geret, Francoise Lugagne, Daniel Ivernel (Speva/Cine-Alliance/Filmsonor/Dear)

A look at rustic insularity in the 1920s, pic lays bare human pettiness but does it with a flair and objectivity. This makes the film funny, revealing, and, overall, quite engrossing. A bouncy, zesty, ripe 32-year-old maid (Jeanne Moreau) is on her way to a job with a landed family in the country. The maid is soon chased by the husband and also is asked to try on old-fashioned high-button boots by the father. The latter is found dead one morning, with the boots clutched in his hands. Follows the rape of an eight-year-old girl.

JOURNEY, THE
1959, 122 mins, US
D: Anatole Litvak A: Yul Brynner, Deborah Kerr, Jason Robards, Robert Morley, E. G. Marshall, Kurt Kasznar (M-G-M/Alby)

A group of passengers, American, British, French, Israeli, etc., is trapped during the 1956 Hungarian uprising. At the last checkpoint on the border, the Russian commander is Yul Brynner. He delays the party, ostensibly to verify their passports and exit permits. His reasons are not clear. One seems to be his purely whimsical desire for Western company. Another is his suspicion that one member of the party (Jason Robards) is one of the Hungarian rebel leaders. What it eventually simmers down to is a political-sexual triangle, with Brynner jealous of Deborah Kerr's attachment to Robards.

JOURNEY INTO FEAR
1943, 68 mins, US
D: Norman Foster [Orson Welles] A: Joseph Cotten, Dolores Del Rio, Ruth Warrick, Orson Welles, Agnes Moorehead, Everett Sloane (RKO/Mercury)

Joseph Cotten is the pivotal character—an American naval ordnance engineer returning to the US from Istanbul. Welles delivers an above-par characterization as the Turkish secret-police chief. Cotten is okay in the lead, despite the writers' presentation of him as a rather weakling hero throughout. Adaptation of Eric Ambler's novel was prepared by Welles and Cotten, and there's nothing new in technique or treatment.

JOURNEY OF NATTY GANN, THE
1985, 105 mins, US
D: Jeremy Paul Kagan A: Meredith Salenger, John Cusack, Ray Wise, Scatman

Crothers, Barry Miller, Lainie Kazan (Walt Disney)

More a period piece of Americana than a rousing adventure. Set in the Depression in Chicago, story has widower Saul Gann taking a job at the lumber camp out in Washington State, promising to send for daughter Natty as soon as he can. He leaves her under the auspices of a floozy hotel manager. The girl runs away and remainder of pic is her sojourn across America in search of her dad. Along the way she rescues a wolf from its captors, and he becomes her endearing traveling partner.
1985: Nomination: Best Costume Design

JOURNEY TOGETHER
1945, 95 mins, UK
D: [John Boulting] A: Edward G. Robinson, Richard Attenborough, Jack Watling, David Tomlinson, Ronald Squire, Bessie Love (RAF)

A convincing tribute to the last war aces (Yanks as well as British) and to grounded veterans of the Battle of Britain who took the rawest of raw material and made good airmen out of them. The production was written, directed, photographed, and produced by members of the RAF, some of them vets of the film biz, but all of them honest-to-God fliers. Also the cast, with four exceptions, was recruited from RAF personnel. Edward G. Robinson and Bessie Love are pros who figure in the cast.

JOURNEY TO THE CENTER OF THE EARTH
1959, 132 mins, US
D: Henry Levin A: Pat Boone, James Mason, Arlene Dahl, Diane Baker, Thayer David (20th Century-Fox)

A tongue-in-cheek approach to the Jules Verne story concerning an expedition, led by James Mason, a dedicated scientist, to the center of the earth. Among those who descend with Mason are Pat Boone, one of his students; Arlene Dahl, the widow of a Swedish geologist; and Peter Ronson, an Icelandic guide and jack-of-all-trades. The descent is filled with all kinds of dangers—underground floods, unusual winds, excessive heat, devious paths. Before reaching their goal, the intrepid explorers confront prehistoric monsters, a forest of mushrooms, a cavern of quartz crystals, and a salt vortex. Boone is given an opportunity to throw in a couple of songs.
1959: Nominations: Best Color Art Direction, Sound, Special Effects

JOURNEY TO THE FAR SIDE OF THE SUN
See: Doppelganger

LE JOUR SE LEVE (DAYBREAK)
1939, 95 mins, France ⊙
D: Marcel Carne A: Jean Gabin, Jules Berry, Arletty, Jacqueline Laurent, Mady Berry (Sigma)

The police come to arrest Jean Gabin, but he locks himself in his apartment, determined to resist. They finally close in on him at daybreak. While barricaded, Gabin reviews the events leading to his rival's violent death. The story is excellently conceived and planned. Gabin is an honest, hardworking laborer who commits a crime which is morally acceptable but which might have been avoided if the girl had made a simple explanation. Jacqueline Laurent is miscast. A girl with a more sophisticated appearance would have fit the role better. As a woman of the world, thankful for the interlude in which she was his mistress, Arletty does a realistic piece of acting. [Jules] Berry gives one of his best performances.

JOY IN THE MORNING
1965, 101 mins, US
D: Alex Segal A: Richard Chamberlain, Yvette Mimieux, Arthur Kennedy, Oscar Homolka, Joan Tetzel, Sidney Blackmer (M-G-M)

Story is of a young couple's first year of marriage at a small midwestern college in late 1920s where groom is working his way through law school. Weakness of picture lies in the treatment. There is an absence of incident and nothing is accomplished to overcome this lack through strong buildup of characterization. Richard Chamberlain seldom appears at ease as the young husband-student. Yvette Mimieux fares a little better.

JOYLESS STREET
See: Die Freudlose Gasse

JOY LUCK CLUB, THE
1993, 138 mins, US ⊙ ⊙
D: Wayne Wang A: Tsai Chin, Kieu Chinh, Lisa Lu, France Nuyen, Rosalind Chao (Hollywood)

Wayne Wang's fine adaptation of Amy Tan's No.1 fiction bestseller of 1989 is a beautifully made and acted dramatic study of trying relationships between Chinese mothers and daughters through the century. The central occasion of a festive farewell party for June (Ming-na Wen), one of

the daughters, on the eve of her departure for China, is skillfully used—like the hub of a wheel, with the individual stories its spokes. Tying things together is June's climactic trip to China, and her ultimate reunion with her lost sisters will leave millions teary-eyed at the powerful, if sentimental, fade-out.

JUAREZ
1939, 125 mins, US ⊙
D: William Dieterle A: Paul Muni, Bette Davis, Brian Aherne, Claude Rains, John Garfield, Donald Crisp (Warner)

To the distinguished list of characters he has created in films, Paul Muni adds a portrait of Benito Pablo Juarez, Mexican patriot and liberator. With the aid of Bette Davis, costarring in the tragic role of Carlota, and of Brian Aherne, giving an excellent performance as the ill-fated Maximilian, Muni again commands attention. Aherne seldom has appeared to such advantage as in this picture. His desire for fair play, his hopeless plea for Mexican unity, and the manner in which he accepts defeat and court martial provide ample reasons for sympathy.

1939: Nomination: Best Supp. Actor (Brian Aherne)

JUBAL
1956, 100 mins, US ⊙ ⊙ ⊑
D: Delmer Daves A: Glenn Ford, Ernest Borgnine, Rod Steiger, Valerie French, Felicia Farr, Charles Bronson (Columbia)

The strong point of this gripping dramatic story set in pioneer Wyoming is a constantly mounting suspense. Glenn Ford, a drifting cowpoke, runs into trouble when he takes a job on the cattle ranch operated by Ernest Borgnine. Valerie French, the rancher's amoral wife, makes an open but abortive play for him and Rod Steiger, who doesn't like to see himself replaced in her extramarital activities, plots to get even with his possible rival.

JUBILEE
1978, 103 mins, UK ⊙
D: Derek Jarman A: Jenny Runacre, Jordan, Little Nell, Linda Spurrier, Toyah Wilcox, Ian Charleson (Megalovision)

One of the most original, bold, and exciting features to have come out of Britain in the 1970s. The year is 1578. Queen Elizabeth I is transported by an angel into the future (roughly the present). Observing a renegade women's collective (a pyromaniac, a punk star, a nympho, a bent historian, etc.), Her Majesty watches as the "ladies" and their friends go about their picaresque misadventures—disrupting a café, a punk audition, a murder spree. Through this process of disemboweling the present through the evocation of the past and the anticipation of the future, Jarman unravels the nation's social history in a way that other features haven't even attempted.

JUDE
1996, 123 mins, UK ♥ ▭
D: Michael Winterbottom **A:** Christopher Eccleston, Kate Winslet, Liam Cunningham, Rachel Griffiths, June Whitfield (Revolution/PolyGram)

Young English actress Kate Winslet adds luster and energy to a bold and generally successful attempt to adapt Thomas Hardy's final novel, *Jude the Obscure*, to the big screen. Late-19th-century yarn of a country lad's attempts to better himself, and to hook the seemingly unattainable love of his life, has a vigor and freshness that minimizes the downside of Hardy's bleakest novel. Eccleston is totally convincing as the ever-patient, accepting-of-fate country lad, a generous, well-etched perf that's basically a support to the pic's real star role. The photogenic Winslet is aces.

JUDEX
1963, 95 mins, France/Italy
D: Georges Franju **A:** Channing Pollock, Francine Berge, Edith Scob, Michel Vitold, Sylva Koscina (CFF/Filmes)

Director Georges Franju has brought off a successful homage to the French film serials of the early, silent days in this tale of a super crook who rights wrongs and finally gives it all up for a girl. It does not send up this form of pic but rather captures its essential simplicity, adventurousness, and innocence. Channing Pollock, a Yank magico, has the unruffled deadpan good looks for Judex, while others fit well into their black-and-white figures.

JUDGE DREDD
1995, 96 mins, US ⊙ ▭
D: Danny Cannon **A:** Sylvester Stallone, Armande Assante, Diane Lane, Rob Schneider, Joan Chen, Max von Sydow (Cinergi/Hollywood)

A thunderous, unoriginal futuristic hardware show for teenage boys. Mega-City One, built on the former New York City, is a sprawling metropolis whose population of 65 million is threatened by teeming criminality at the street level.

Combating the anarchy are elite lawmen known as Judges, who mete out instant justice as they patrol the city on their airborne bikes. The most feared is the infamous Judge Dredd (Sylvester Stallone), an emotionless authoritarian. It's all in a day's work for Dredd until archfiend Rico (Armand Assante) escapes from the high-security Aspen Penal Colony and returns to seek revenge.

JUDGEMENT IN STONE, A
See: La Ceremonie

JUDGE PRIEST
1934, 80 mins, US ♥
D: John Ford **A:** Will Rogers, Henry B. Walthall, Tom Brown, Anita Louise, Rochelle Hudson, Berton Churchill (Fox)

Difficult, beforehand, to reconcile the idea of Irvin Cobb's *Judge Priest* with Will Rogers. Cobb's long series of stories have suggested another type: portly, slightly pompous on occasion, and somewhat lethargic in movement, and that isn't Will Rogers. But Rogers makes the old judge completely his own. Most of the comedy is contributed by Rogers and Stepin Fetchit, a natural foil to the Rogers character.

JUDGMENT AT NUREMBERG
1961, 178 mins, US ♥ ⊙
D: Stanley Kramer **A:** Spencer Tracy, Burt Lancaster, Richard Widmark, Marlene Dietrich, Maximilian Schell, Judy Garland (United Artists)

Abby Mann's drama is set in Nuremberg in 1948, the time of the Nazi war crimes trials. It deals with members of the German judiciary who served under the Nazi regime. The intense courtroom drama centers on two men: the presiding judge (Spencer Tracy), who must render a monumental decision, and the principal defendant (Burt Lancaster), at first a silent, brooding figure, but ultimately the one who rises to pinpoint the real issue and admit his guilt. Tracy delivers a performance of great intelligence and intuition. He creates a gentle, but towering, figure, compassionate but realistic, warm but objective.

1961: Best Actor (Maximilian Schell), Adapted Screenplay
Nominations: Best Picture, Director, Actor (Spencer Tracy), Supp. Actor (Montgomery Clift), Supp. Actress (Judy Garland), B&W Cinematography, B&W Costume Design, B&W Art Direction, Editing

JUDGMENT IN BERLIN

1988, 92 mins, US ⓥ ⊙
D: Leo Penn **A:** Martin Sheen, Sam Wanamaker, Max Gail, Jurgen Heinrich, Harris Yulin, Sean Penn (Bibo/January)

A quality production about an atypical defection that occurred in West Berlin in the late 1970s, made on a tight budget but with obvious care and commitment, avoiding didacticism. An East German couple traveling with a child hijack a Polish airliner headed for East Berlin, forcing the pilot to land at a West Berlin airport that serves as a US military installation. The big question is who has legal jurisdiction to prosecute the hijackers. It is decided that since they landed in US-occupied territory, a trial conducted by a US judge is the humane solution.

JUDGMENT NIGHT

1993, 109 mins, US ⓥ ⊙
D: Stephen Hopkins **A:** Emilio Estevez, Cuba Gooding Jr., Denis Leary, Stephen Dorff, Jeremy Piven (Largo/Universal)

This is an exceedingly well directed, cleverly filmed and edited, tension-filled affair. It is also a wholly preposterous, muddled, paranoid view of the inner-city nightmare, where the slightest misstep is sure to have a fateful result. The action pivots around a boys' night out in which four young men head from the suburbs to a big boxing match in downtown Chicago. En route they run into gridlock and take an offramp into a really bad neighborhood. It doesn't take much to guess what happens next.

JUDITH

1966, 105 mins, US ▭
D: Daniel Mann **A:** Sophia Loren, Peter Finch, Jack Hawkins, Hans Verner, Zharira Charifai (Paramount)

Israel in its birth pains backdrops this frequently tenseful adventure tale realistically produced in its actual locale. The production combines a moving story with interesting, unfamiliar characters. The screenplay, based on an original by Lawrence Durrell, is two-pronged: the story of Sophia Loren, as the Jewish ex-wife of a Nazi war criminal who betrayed her and sent her to Dachau, intent upon finding him and wreaking her own brand of vengeance, and the efforts of the Haganah, Israel's underground army, to capture him.

JUDITH OF BETHULIA

1914, 62 mins, US ⊗
D: D. W. Griffith **A:** Blanche Sweet, Henry B. Walthall, Robert Harron, Mae Marsh, Lillian Gish, Lionel Barrymore (Biograph)

Judith of Bethulia, in four and a half reels, founded upon the biblical tale, utilizes the services of competent players in the regular Biograph company. For the name part, Blanche Sweet; Henry Walthall for Holofernes; Robert Harron for Nathan; J. Jiquel Lanoe for the Chief Eunuch; Harry Carey for the Traitor, and so on. Fine as is the acting of the principals, the chief thing to commend is the totally wonderful handling of the mobs and the seriousness with which each super performs his individual task.

JU DOU

See: Judou

JUDOU
(JU DOU)

1990, 95 mins, Japan/China ⓥ ▭
D: Zhang Yimou, Yang Fengliang **A:** Gong Li, Li Baotian, Li Wei, Zhang Yi, Zheng Jian (Tokuma/Xi'an)

A romantic tragedy set in a mountain village in the twenties, the story centers on the house and factory of dye-maker Yang Jinshan. Yang Tianqing becomes fascinated by a pretty young woman, Judou, the old man has bought for a bride. One night, the pair become lovers. A son is eventually born. Soon after, the old man is crippled from the waist down in an accident. The lovers blatantly display their relationship in front of him, as he lies helpless. The plot has all the elements of a Hollywood melodrama of the forties and the picture is, indeed, as deliriously enjoyable as it sounds. Visually, it is extraordinary, with the splendid set of the dye factory impressively used.

JUGGERNAUT

1974, 109 mins, UK ⓥ
D: Richard Lester **A:** Richard Harris, Omar Sharif, David Hemmings, Anthony Hopkins, Shirley Knight, Ian Holm (United Artists)

Richard Harris stars as an explosives demolition expert aboard Omar Sharif's luxury liner, where several bombs have been planted. The action aboard the ship alternates with land drama, where shipline executive Ian Holm, detective Anthony Hopkins (whose wife Caroline Mortimer and children are aboard the vessel), and others attempt to locate the phantom bomber who calls himself Juggernaut in a series of telephone calls demanding a huge ransom.

JUGGLER, THE
1953, 84 mins, US
D: Edward Dmytryk A: Kirk Douglas, Milly Vitale, Paul Stewart, Joey Walsh, Alf Kjellin (Kramer/Columbia)

The Juggler deals with a man, once a famous European juggler, who has become a neurotic from his long imprisonment in Nazi concentration camps, and how he gradually comes to realize his illness and seek help from newfound friends. The storytelling fails to establish early the nature and cause of Kirk Douglas's illness and, as a result, his acts of violence create an adverse reaction, instead of gaining sympathy. Milly Vitale is very appealing as the girl Douglas meets on a kibbutz.

JUICE
1992, 96 mins, US ⊗ ⊙
D: Ernest Dickerson A: Omar Epps, Tupac Shakur, Jermaine Hopkins, Khalil Kain, Cindy Herron (Paramount)

Spike Lee cinematographer Ernest Dickerson starts off the pic promisingly, introducing a well-played quartet of New York ghetto youths and exploring their lives and frustrations. After a sudden, tragic robbery attempt, the film takes a peculiar turn into the thriller realm, as one of the teens (Tupac Shakur)—high on the ''juice'' of having killed the grocery-store clerk—begins menacing his onetime friends.

JULES AND JIM
See: Jules et Jim

JULES ET JIM
(JULES AND JIM)
1962, 105 mins, France ⊗ ⊙ ▱
D: Francois Truffaut A: Jeanne Moreau, Oskar Werner, Henri Serre, Marie Dubois, Sabine Haudepin (Carrosse/SEDIF)

Francois Truffaut has put together a tender tale that avoids mawkishness and impropriety in treating the lives of two friends who are mixed up with a woman they share. One is a Frenchman, the other an Austrian, and the girl is French. Plot covers from 1912 until about 1930. Film depends more on atmosphere, insight into characters, and emotions than on story values. Truffaut has shrewdly employed the physiques and characters of his principals sans exploiting them. Jeanne Moreau is exceptional as the headstrong girl Cathe-

rine, who never quite finds what she wants. The husband is done in a vein of rumpled honesty and dignity by Oskar Werner.

JULIA
1977, 116 mins, US ⊗ ⊙
D: Fred Zinnemann A: Jane Fonda, Vanessa Redgrave, Jason Robards, Maximilian Schell, Hal Holbrook, Meryl Streep (20th Century-Fox)

Fred Zinnemann's superbly sensitive film explores the anti-Nazi awakening in the 1930s of writer Lillian Hellman via persecution of a childhood friend, an excellent characterization by Vanessa Redgrave in title role. The period environment, brilliantly re-created in production design, costuming, and color processing, complements the topflight performances and direction. Jane Fonda and Redgrave, neither one a shrinking violet in real life, are dynamite together on the screen.

1977: Best Supp. Actor (Jason Robards), Supp. Actress (Vanessa Redgrave), Adapted Screenplay

Nominations: Best Picture, Director, Actress (Jane Fonda), Supp. Actor (Maximilian Schell), Cinematography, Costume Design, Editing, Original Score

JULIA HAS TWO LOVERS
1990, 85 mins, US ⊗
D: Bashar Shbib A: Daphna Kastner, David Duchovny, David Charles, Tim Ray, Clare Bancroft (Oneira)

While this tale of romance on the telephone has an interesting story concept, the conversation itself drags on for too long, leading to the film's uneven and frequently too slow pace. Julia (Daphna Kastner), an attractive but somewhat frustrated woman, has lived with her lover Jack (David Charles) for two years. Julia answers the phone and encounters an amicable young man, Daniel (capably played by David Duchovny). Julia soon finds herself drawn to Daniel, who apparently has dialed the wrong number.

JULIA MISBEHAVES
1948, 99 mins, US
D: Jack Conway A: Greer Garson, Walter Pidgeon, Peter Lawford, Elizabeth Taylor, Cesar Romero (M-G-M)

All forms of comedy but the subtle are used to spring the laughs that come from the frenetic antics of a middle-aged couple, long separated but bent on trying romance again. Garson is punched, doused, muddied, and tossed in her unbending process. She wears tights, takes a bubble bath, sings, and generally acquits herself like a lady out to prove she can be hoydenish when necessary. The other half of middle-aged team, Walter Pidgeon, gives away no honors. He's pitching all the time and skillfully injects just the right amount of underplaying to balance broader delivery of his partner in fun.

JULIET OF THE SPIRITS
See: Giulietta degli Spiriti

JULIUS CAESAR
1953, 121 mins, US ⊗
D: Joseph L. Mankiewicz **A:** Marlon Brando, James Mason, John Gielgud, Louis Calhern, Greer Garson, Deborah Kerr (M-G-M)

To those normally allergic to Shakespeare, this will be a surprise—a tense, melodramatic story, clearly presented, and excellently acted by one of the finest casts assembled for a film. Presented in its traditional, classic form, there is no attempt to build up the spectacle or battle scenes to gain sweep. Highlight of the film is the thesping. Every performance is a tour de force. Any fears about Marlon Brando appearing in Shakespeare are dispelled by his compelling portrayal as the revengeful Mark Antony. The entire famous funeral speech takes on a new light.
1953: Best B&W Art Direction
Nominations: Best Picture, Actor (Marlon Brando), B&W Cinematography, Scoring a Dramatic Picture

JULIUS CAESAR
1970, 117 mins, UK ⊗ ⊙ ▭
D: Stuart Burge **A:** Charlton Heston, Jason Robards, John Gielgud, Richard Johnson, Robert Vaughn, Richard Chamberlain (Commonwealth United)

This stab at Shakespeare's drama of political intrigue, corruption, ambition, envy, rhetoric, and conspiratorial cunning is disappointing. Under Stuart Burge's firm direction, the highspots are brought out effectively but the backgrounds and crowd sequences are stagy and lack the passion and abandon needed to project the star scenes. Biggest disappointment is Jason Robards's Brutus. Charlton Heston makes a praiseworthy stab at Mark Antony.

JUMANJI
1995, 104 mins, US ⊗ ⊙
D: Joe Johnston **A:** Robin Williams, Bonnie Hunt, Kirsten Dunst, Bradley Pierce, Bebe Neuwirth (Interscope/Teitler/Tri-Star)

Relying on some tried-and-true horror conventions, *Jumanji* is a grim fairy tale about a board game with supernatural powers. The film unleashes an arsenal of special effects that are dazzling to the eye but often a shock to the senses. In 1969, young Alan Parrish (Adam Hann-Byrd) discovers a buried game on a construction site. He and a friend begin to play Jumanji, a jungle-themed adventure. After Alan flings the cubes, he disappears, sucked into the vortex of the tiled diversion. The scene abruptly shifts to the present. Two youngsters dust off the seemingly innocent trifle and summon a clutch of giant mosquitoes, a man-eating lion, and a jungle wild man who turns out to be the long-absent Alan (Robin Williams). What's missing is a soul for this mechanical marvel. The script, based on a kid-lit book by Chris Van Allsburg, cozies around the primacy of the family without developing that theme.

JUMBO
(AKA: BILLY ROSE'S JUMBO)
1962, 123 mins, US ⊗ ⊙ ▭
D: Charles Walters **A:** Doris Day, Stephen Boyd, Jimmy Durante, Martha Raye, Dean Jagger, Joseph Waring (M-G-M/Euterpe-Arwin)

The showmanship of Metro has turned the combo musical and circus into a great film entertainment. Much of the Rodgers and Hart score for the 1935 legit version has been retained. Jimmy Durante is the circus owner, with Doris Day as his daughter and Martha Raye as his 14-year-awaiting fiancée. Durante plays the role as Durante. Screenplay retains only the basic circus-boy-meets-circus-girl format of Ben Hecht and Charles MacArthur's original book.
1962: Nomination: Best Adapted Music Score

JUMPING JACKS
1952, 96 mins, US
D: Norman Taurog **A:** Dean Martin, Jerry Lewis, Mona Freeman, Don DeFore, Robert Strauss, Richard Erdman (Paramount)

The situation-comedy plot is perfectly tailored to show off Jerry Lewis's uninhibited clowning and Dean Martin's pleasant straight-man chores and singing. Martin, a paratrooper, sends for his old vaude partner (Lewis) when a sourpuss general threatens to do away with the camp shows the soldiers are staging unless they are improved. Lewis has to be passed off as a regular GI, presumably for only the one performance. However, he catches the favor of the general, who orders the group to tour other camps.

JUMPIN' JACK FLASH
1986, 100 mins, US ⑳ ⊙
D: Penny Marshall A: Whoopi Goldberg, Jonathan Pryce, James Belushi, Carol Kane, Annie Potts, Peter Michael Goetz (Gordon/Silver)

A weak idea and muddled plot poorly executed not surprisingly results in a tedious film with only a few brief comic interludes from Whoopi Goldberg to redeem it. Goldberg is Terry Doolittle. Just when her life is looking most bleak along comes Jack (Jonathan Pryce). He's a British spy trapped somewhere behind the Iron Curtain who somehow, someway, taps into Goldberg's computer terminal and asks for help to escape. Goldberg is plunged into a web of intrigue.

JUNE BRIDE
1948, 96 mins, US
D: Bretaigne Windust [Raoul Walsh] A: Bette Davis, Robert Montgomery, Fay Bainter, Tom Tully, Barbara Bates (Warner)

A sometimes subtle, sometimes wacky takeoff on home magazines and human nature. Bette Davis presents a delightfully slicked-up personality as a "through with love" home-mag editor who does stereotyped articles on before-and-after houses and people. Robert Montgomery costars as a foreign correspondent assigned to aid Davis when news becomes dull in Europe. His glib handling of the assignment sharpens many a scene in the film. Both give socko interpretations.

JUNGFRUKALLAN
(THE VIRGIN SPRING)
1960, 88 mins, Sweden ⑳
D: Ingmar Bergman A: Max von Sydow, Birgitta Valberg, Birgitta Pettersson, Gunnel Lindblom, Axel Duberg (Svensk Filmindustri)

Ingmar Bergman was inspired by a 14th-century ballad of innocence, rape, murder, and revenge for this film. Karin (Birgitta Pettersson) is to make the virgin's ride to church. She encounters herdsmen in the forest, who rape her while their little brother looks on. Her father, Tore (Max von Sydow), seeks revenge, murdering the herdsmen as they sleep. He turns to God, wondering why he allowed the rape and murders. Loaded with the theme of guilt, this is an extremely powerful film. However, it lacks the human warmth of *Wild Strawberries* and the majesty of *Seventh Seal*.
1960: Best Foreign Language Film

JUNGLE BOOK
1942, 108 mins, US ⑳ ⊙ ⊐
D: Zoltan Korda A: Sabu, Joseph Calleia, John Qualen, Frank Puglia, Rosemary DeCamp (Korda)

Alexander Korda brings to the screen the diminutive East Indian player Sabu, in a film version of Rudyard Kipling's *Jungle Book*. Mowgli strayed into the jungle as a child and was brought up by a she-wolf. Mowgli's return to the native village as a grown-up youth and his subsequent adventures in civilization are handled in neither a humorous nor dramatic manner. The saga of the boy who can converse with animals is related very seriously, whereas the theme might have been better entertainment if treated in a lighter vein. The fiction takes secondary place to the highly interesting and sometimes amazing views of jungle animals in the brilliance of color photography.
1942: Nominations: Best Color Cinematography, Color Art Direction, Scoring of a Dramatic Picture, Special Effects

JUNGLE BOOK, THE
1967, 78 mins, US ⑳ ⊙
D: Wolfgang Reitherman (Walt Disney)

The Jungle Book, based on the Mowgli stories by Rudyard Kipling, was the last animated feature under Walt Disney's personal supervision before his death. Friendly panther, vocalized by Sebastian Cabot, discovers a baby boy in the jungle and deposits him for upbringing with a wolf family. At age 10, boy, looped by Clint Howard, is seen in need of shift to the human world, because man-hating tiger (George Sanders) has returned to the jungle. Encounters along the way include a friendship with a devil-may-care bear, expertly cast with the voice of Phil Harris. The standout song goes to Harris, a rhythmic "Bare Necessities," extolling the value of a simple life and credited to Terry Gilkyson.
1967: Nomination: Best Song ("Bare Necessities")

JUNGLE BOOK, THE
(AKA: RUDYARD KIPLING'S THE JUNGLE BOOK)
1994, 110 mins, US ⑳ ⊙
D: Stephen Sommers A: Jason Scott Lee,

Cary Elwes, Lena Headey, Sam Neill, John Cleese, Jason Flemyng (Walt Disney)

This *Jungle Book* seeks a more modern tone. One wonders where the movie is going before it dramatically shifts gears into a full-throttled, technically superb adventure—with more bite than most Disney live-action fare—that offers some winning moments but, ultimately, isn't as involving as it needs to be. The narrative keeps changing gears—from nature film to love story to actioner. What ultimately drives the movie is the love story, in true beauty-and-the-beast fashion. Director Stephen Sommers serves up a visual feast of beautiful animals and spectacular vistas (shot largely in Jodhpur, India).

JUNGLE FEVER
1991, 132 mins, US Ⓥ ⊙
D: Spike Lee **A:** Wesley Snipes, Annabella Sciorra, Spike Lee, Ossie Davis, Ruby Dee, John Turturro (Universal/40 Acres & a Mule)

The jungle is decidedly present but the fever is notably missing in Spike Lee's exploration of racial tensions in urban America. Lee tackles the subject of interracial romance from the unavoidable vantage point that, while things today are more open, they are also considerably more volatile and complex. Little time is actually spent with the black man and white woman whose relationship is the core of the drama. Steering clear of conventional romantic scenes once the couple gets together, Lee instead uses the affair to detonate dozens of reactive sequences, showing how the blacks and Italians close to the principals deal with the developments. Performances are all pointed and emotionally edgy. Film feels too long, but it ends powerfully.

JUNGLE FIGHTERS
See: The Long and the Short and the Tall

JUNIOR
1994, 109 mins, US Ⓥ ⊙
D: Ivan Reitman **A:** Arnold Schwarzenegger, Danny DeVito, Emma Thompson, Frank Langella, Pamela Reed (Northern Lights/Universal)

Pregnant-man comedy. What separates this straightforward chuckler from the pack is its shrewd reliance on character rather than plot, and that human dimension proves surprisingly poignant. Researchers Dr. Alex Hesse (Arnold Schwarzenegger) and Dr. Larry Arbogast (Danny DeVito) have been working on a "wonder" drug for safer pregnancies. A Canadian consortium is ready to bankroll Arbogast and the drug. What would really cement the deal is data from a human guinea pig. Arbogast fast-talks Hesse into being that test case. It's intrinsically funny to watch serious, sober scientists involved in totally goofy pursuits.

1994: Nomination: Best Original Song ("Look What Love Has Done")

JUNIOR BONNER
1972, 100 mins, US Ⓥ ⊡
D: Sam Peckinpah **A:** Steve McQueen, Robert Preston, Ida Lupino, Ben Johnson, Joe Don Baker (ABC)

The latter-day film genre of misunderstood-rodeo-drifter gets one of its best expositions. Steve McQueen stars handily in the title role. Jeb Rosebrook's original screenplay, combined with uniformly adroit casting and sensitive direction, has the virtues of solid construction and economy of dialogue. To be sure, the plot is somewhat biased in favor of the restless wanderings of McQueen, in that the alternative is a near caricature of conformity, but overall there is a good balance.

JUNIOR MISS
1945, 94 mins, US
D: George Seaton **A:** Peggy Ann Garner, Allyn Joslyn, Mona Freeman, Barbara Whiting (20th Century-Fox)

Except for the wider range of the camera, *Junior Miss* sticks to the play faithfully. George Seaton was sensible in not trying to improve upon a good thing when he did the screenplay. The cast was chosen for its appropriateness to the action involved, and Seaton knows just how to put the actors through their paces most effectively.

JUNO AND THE PAYCOCK
1930, 95 mins, UK
D: Alfred Hitchcock **A:** Sara Allgood, Edward Chapman, Maire O'Neil, Sydney Morgan, John Laurie (British International)

Cast consists almost entirely of Irish players. Edward Chapman mugs too much. Sara Allgood is a flat Juno. Three quarters of the film is just photographed stage play—excellently photographed, but slow in action. The rest moves fast, building up a swift climax of drab tragedy. The end of the play has been dropped. Irish atmosphere of the tenement life incidental to the country is well caught.

JUPITER'S DARLING
1955, 93 mins, US ⓥ ▱
D: George Sidney **A:** Esther Williams, Howard Keel, Marge Champion, Gower Champion, George Sanders, Richard Haydn (M-G-M)

As a takeoff, with satirical treatment, on costume actioners, *Jupiter's Darling* is fairly entertaining. It has Esther Williams in some outstanding swim numbers and Howard Keel's robust singing. Robert E. Sherwood's stage play *Road to Rome,* dealing with Hannibal's invasion of Rome, served as the foundation.

JURASSIC PARK
1993, 126 mins, US ⓥ ⊙
D: Steven Spielberg **A:** Sam Neill, Laura Dern, Jeff Goldblum, Richard Attenborough, Bob Peck, Martin Ferrero (Universal/Amblin)

Steven Spielberg's scary and horrific thriller may be one-dimensional and even clunky in story and characterization, but definitely delivers where it counts, in excitement, suspense, and the stupendous realization of giant reptiles. The production follows the general idea if not the letter of coscripter Michael Crichton's 1990 bestseller. Basis of this high-tech, scientifically based, up-to-date version lies in the notion that dinosaurs can be biologically engineered using fossilized dino DNA. Having accomplished this in secret, zillionaire John Hammond (Richard Attenborough) brings in a small group of experts to endorse his miracle, which is to be the world's most expensive zoo-cum-amusement park. The monsters are far more convincing than the human characters.
1993: Best Sound, Sound Editing, Visual Effects

JUROR, THE
1996, 116 mins, US ⓥ ⊙
D: Brian Gibson **A:** Demi Moore, Alec Baldwin, Joseph Gordon-Levitt, Anne Heche, James Gandolfini, Lindsay Crouse (Columbia)

A somewhat leisurely paced psychological thriller distinguished only by a kinetic, menacing performance by Alec Baldwin. Demi Moore plays Annie, a single mother targeted by the Mob to swing the jury in a murder trial, with the looming threat that a mysterious hit man (Baldwin) will kill her son (Joseph Gordon-Levitt) if

things don't work out as planned. Oozing charm and malice, Baldwin—known only as the Teacher—terrorizes Moore's character, bugging her house and endangering her child.

JURY DUTY
1995, 86 mins, US ⓥ
D: John Fortenberry **A:** Pauly Shore, Tia Carrere, Stanley Tucci, Brian Doyle-Murray, Abe Vigoda (Tri-Star/Triumph)

While the idea of dropping Pauly Shore into a courtroom setting may have possessed some promise, turning the movie into a half parody of the O. J. Simpson proceedings is utterly wrongheaded, since nothing could equal the amount of media skewering and jokes that attend[ed] the trial on a daily basis.
Beyond that, *Jury Duty* comes off like a slapdash effort of almost absurd excess, with no effort whatsoever to rein in Shore, a nonactor who comes dangerously close here to approaching the ranks of noncomics.

JUST A GIGOLO
1978, 105 mins, W. Germany ⓥ ⊙
D: David Hemmings **A:** David Bowie, Sydne Rome, Kim Novak, David Hemmings, Maria Schell, Marlene Dietrich (Leguan)

Handsomely photographed in Berlin and directed with finesse by David Hemmings, David Bowie is a Prussian war vet back from the dead who drifts from one demeaning job to another and finally into employment as a gigolo. The fascinating casting includes Marlene Dietrich and the return of Kim Novak. Sydne Rome is an appealing revelation.

JUST ANOTHER GIRL ON THE I.R.T.
1992, 92 mins, US ⓥ
D: Leslie Harris **A:** Ariyan A. Johnson, Kevin Thigpen, Ebony Jerido, Chequita Jackson, William Badget (Truth 24 fps)

Shot independently in New York on a 17-day sked, this debut effort by a young black woman filmmaker is a crude but disturbing exposé of teenage ignorance and denial about the facts of life on the streets and in the bedroom. In a raw, up-front style, writer-director Leslie Harris lays out a sad, brutal story. Chantel, 17, is an arrogant Brooklyn h.s. student who mouths off to adults, imagines she's far smarter than her classmates, and thinks nothing of dumping her regular b.f. for a hot guy with a Jeep. Determined to escape her community, she intends to finish high-school in three years and make a beeline for med school. Performances possess vigor but are on the rough side. Ariyan A. Johnson creates a very abrasive character in Chantel.

JUST BEFORE NIGHTFALL
See: Juste Avant la Nuit

JUST CAUSE
1995, 102 mins, US ⓥ ⊙ ▭
D: Arne Glimcher A: Sean Connery, Laurence Fishburne, Kate Capshaw, Blair Underwood, Ed Harris (Warner)

Just Cause ambles along for more than an hour as a perfectly respectable mystery procedural with Sean Connery's Harvard law professor as a fish out of water in the Florida backwoods gradually trying to set things right for a young man he believes was unjustly sent to death row years before. But then all hell breaks loose, with one unconvincing twist after another being thrown at the audience, to the point where all credibility and suspence are drowned irretrievably in the murk of the Everglades. Thesping is solid as long as the story retains credibility, with Connery effectively anchoring the picture. Fishburne steals most of the scenes he's in as a cop with a nasty streak.

JUSTE AVANT LA NUIT
(JUST BEFORE NIGHTFALL)
1971, 106 mins, France/Italy ⓥ
D: Claude Chabrol A: Michel Bouquet, Stephane Audran, Francois Perier, Dominique Zardi, Henri Attal (Films La Boetie/Cinemar)

Michel Bouquet starts with killing his best friend's wife, who had been his mistress. Then pic deals with his attempts at living with this deed. In the background are shrewdly concocted visual ideas and events that reflect on his dilemma. His middle-aged accountant absconds with funds due a young girl. There is a rat in his ornate house which is finally seen trapped, to counterpoint his own state. Chabrol shows a mixed attitude toward his upper-class types, which both condemns and seems to understand their seeming class outlooks, problems, and intimations of crack-ups.

JUST FOR YOU
1952, 95 mins, US
D: Elliott Nugent A: Bing Crosby, Jane Wyman, Ethel Barrymore, Robert Arthur, Natalie Wood, Cora Witherspoon (Paramount)

Musical has a rousing, melodic score,

by Harry Warren and Leo Robin, and a logical story of how a Broadway producer almost loses the affections of his teenage boy and girl because he's been too intent upon his own career to take note of his motherless children's activities. Crosby and Wyman turn in bang-up performances as the producer and his musicomedy star, respectively.

JUSTINE
1969, 117 mins, US ⓥ ▭
D: George Cukor A: Anouk Aimee, Dirk Bogarde, John Vernon, Anna Karina, Philippe Noiret, Michael York (20th Century-Fox)

Difficulties and hazards involved in compressing four novels into a single film are obvious. Based upon Lawrence Durrell's novel *Justine* and three other volumes comprising author's *Alexandria Quartet*, the plottage is particularly difficult to follow. While the story rivets on Anouk Aimee as the Egyptian Jewess, a prostitute wed to one of her country's most powerful financiers, there is such a multiplicity of elements and forms of love as to prove overly burdensome for the screen.

JUST LIKE A WOMAN
1992, 106 mins, UK ⓥ ⊙
D: Christopher Monger A: Julie Walters, Adrian Pasdar, Paul Freeman, Gordon Kennedy, Ian Redford (Rank/LWT/Zenith)

Except for Edward D. Wood's notorious *Glen or Glenda*, which wasn't intentionally amusing, *Just Like a Woman* is the funniest plea for tolerance of transvestites ever made. Adrian Pasdar seems to have it all: a rewarding job, a wife, two children, and all the lacy underwear a crossdresser could want. His world comes crashing down when his wife, finding some unfamiliar panties at home, figures her husband is unfaithful and kicks him out. Pasdar moves into a rooming house operated by Julie Walters, cast as a divorcée longing for excitement.

JUST ONE OF THE GUYS
1985, 100 mins, US ⓥ ⊙
D: Lisa Gottlieb A: Joyce Hyser, Clayton Rohner, Billy Jacoby, William Zabka, Toni Hudson, Sherilyn Fenn (Summa/Triton)

Popular and tenacious high-school girl passing herself off as a boy at a rival campus serves as a deceptive cover for this comedy that's really about what it's like to be an outsider in the rigid teenage caste system. Joyce Hyser, affecting a lower register, a short haircut, and a subtle swagger, is not totally convincing as a boy because she's too pretty and too chic.

J.W. COOP
1971, 112 mins, US
D: Cliff Robertson **A:** Cliff Robertson, Geraldine Page, Cristina Ferrare, R. G. Armstrong, John Crawford (Columbia)

An engaging yarn that follows the reorientation of a rodeo rider after spending 10 years in jail for passing a bum check and fighting with a sheriff. Cliff Robertson, who stars, produced, directed, and scripted, has fashioned a strong, believable character study of a professional rider who finds he must not only adjust to radically altered American attitudes, but also to the rodeo circuit, which has taken on a big-business air that is alien to him.

KAFKA
1991, 98 mins, US ⓥ ⊙
D: Steven Soderbergh **A:** Jeremy Irons, Theresa Russell, Joel Grey, Ian Holm, Jeroen Krabbe, Alec Guinness (Baltimore/Renn-Pricel)

Defiantly not a biopic, outing places the literary world's first alienated man in a sinister Prague, c. 1919, echoing author's fictional universe. But the story ultimately feels too conventional, and the portrait of the artist too shallow to stand as a compelling or convincing evocation of a complex mind. Kafka (Jeremy Irons) is introduced to a group of anarchists by a coworker (Theresa Russell) and increasingly drawn into a maze of intrigue. The villain of the piece is not named Dr. Murnau (Ian Holm) for nothing. The old-world setting and exaggerated visual style readily recall German Expressionism.

KAGEMUSHA
(THE SHADOW WARRIOR)
1980, 179 mins, Japan/US ⓥ ▭
D: Akira Kurosawa **A:** Tatsuya Nakadai, Tsutomu Yamazaki, Kenichi Hagiwara, Kota Yui, Hideji Otaki (Toho/Kurosawa/20th Century-Fox)

A sweeping epic of the clan wars in 16th-century Japan. A clan leader, Shingen Takeda, uses doubles to take his place. His younger brother, his usual double, finds a petty thief who looks exactly like Takeda and he is taken on as a new *kagemusha*. When Takeda dies, the thief is groomed to replace him for three years, per Takeda's last wishes. The double, tutored by the brother, gains dignity and even convinces Takeda's family that he is the real leader. Tatsuya Nakadai is extraordinary as the leader and his double. Kurosawa, at 70, shows himself young indeed in the impressive handling of this historical drama.

KAIDAN
(KWAIDAN)
1964, 164 mins, Japan ⓥ ⊙ ▭
D: Masaki Kobayashi **A:** Rentaro Mikuni, Michiyo Aratama, Keiko Kishi, Tatsuya Nakadai, Katsuo Nakamura (Ninjin Club)

Film is visually and physically stunning but its three tales of the supernatural are more intellectual than visceral. First story has a poor samurai leaving his wife to join a ruling clan and to marry again. But his love stays with his first wife and her image haunts him constantly. Second tale is about a blind monk, taken by a spirit to unfold his story of a famous sea battle to the place where the clan was destroyed. Third deals with a man who sees a reflection of someone in a cup of tea and drinks it. He has swallowed the man's soul and is then haunted by him.

KAKUSHI TORIDE NO SAN AKUNIN
(THE HIDDEN FORTRESS)
1958, 137 mins, Japan ⓥ ⊙ ▭
D: Akira Kurosawa **A:** Toshiro Mifune, Kamatari Fujiwara, Minoru Chiaki, Eiko Miyoshi, Takashi Shimura (Toho)

A long, interesting, humor-laden picture of medieval Japan, story concerns efforts of a beaten warlord (Toshiro Mifune) to sneak his defeated princess (Misa Uehara) out of enemy territory, where their hidden fortress is situated, into a friendly province with the family's gold. They're aided and distracted, alternately, by two greedy yokels (Minoru Chiaki and Kamatari Fujiwara) who stumble on the gold and their hiding place.

KALEIDOSCOPE
(AKA: THE BANK BREAKERS)
1966, 102 mins, UK/US
D: Jack Smight **A:** Warren Beatty, Susannah York, Clive Revill, Eric Porter, Murray Melvin (Winkast/Warner)

An entertaining comedy suspenser, the production has some eye-catching mod clothing styles, inventive direction, and other values that sustain the simple story line. The original screenplay turns on the exploits of Warren Beatty as he etches hidden markings on cards, wins big at various continental casinos, and, via an affair with Susannah York, comes under o.o. of her dad, Scotland Yard inspector Clive Revill.

KALIFORNIA
1993, 117 mins, US ⓥ ▭
D: Dominic Sena **A:** Brad Pitt, Juliette Lewis, David Duchovny, Michelle Forbes, Sierra Pecheur (PFE/Propaganda)

The fascination with the homicidal urge and the inability to recognize it in ourselves and others provides the chilling core of this road movie. Though somewhat overplayed and coy about its destination, the film packs a wallop. Writer Brian Kessler (David Duchovny) concocts a cross-country tour of nefarious murder sites to collect info augmented by photos shot by girlfriend Carrie Laughlin (Michelle Forbes). The film crosscuts between the relatively mundane lives of the yuppish Pittsburgh couple and scenes of Early Grace (Brad Pitt) with the bedraggled, naive Adele Corners (Juliette Lewis), portraying a white-trash, trailer-park life in which fragile circumstances tend to erupt into unpleasantness.

KAMERADSCHAFT
1931, 87 mins, Germany
D: G. W. Pabst **A:** Ernst Busch, Georges Charlia, Alexander Granach, Elizabeth Wendt, Fritz Kampers (Nero)

A mining catastrophe in the hands of an able director, G. W. Pabst. Story is based upon the disaster at Courrières, on the German-French border, in which several hundred French miners were imprisoned underground and freed by their German colleagues. Pabst has made it a powerful recounting and accentuates more the happenings than the men.

KANAL
(THEY LOVED LIFE)
1957, 97 mins, Poland ⊗
D: Andrzej Wajda **A:** Wienczyslaw Glinski, Teresa Izewska, Tadeusz Janczar, Emil Karewicz, Wladyslaw Sheybal (Kadr)

Hallucinating pic, depicting the last days of the Polish resistance in Warsaw, is not for the squeamish. It takes a company of partisans and deftly blocks out their characters, and then follows their nightmarish descent into the sewers to escape the Germans. Here mass heroism and the utter horror of war are made explicit.

KANGAROO
1986, 108 mins, Australia ⊗ ▭
D: Tim Burstall **A:** Colin Friels, Judy Davis, John Walton, Julie Nihill, Hugh Keays-Byrne (Naked Country)

Kangaroo was written in 1922 by D. H. Lawrence after a brief visit to Australia. A serious, literary pic, handsomely produced and boasting a very strong cast, it opens in Cornwall, England, in 1916, establishing the problems that Lawrence (Colin Friels)—called Somers in the book and film—and his German-born wife, Harriet (Judy Davis), experience during the war. Setting then shifts to Sydney in 1922 as the couple settle into a house next to Jack and Vicky Calcott. Jack is secretly involved with a society of returned soldiers training to fight an expected socialist revolution. Somers is courted both by socialist leader Struthers and by the dangerously charming "Kangeroo," a sexually ambivalent fascist.

KANSAS CITY
1996, 115 mins, France/US ⊗
D: Robert Altman **A:** Jennifer Jason Leigh, Miranda Richardson, Harry Belafonte, Michael Murphy, Steve Buscemi (CiBy 2000/Sandcastle 5)

Although it focuses upon two very off-center white female characters, Robert Altman's period-drenched meller basks in the glory of the 1930s black jazz, and the music furnishes a flavorsome distraction even when the narrative riffs onto some weird sidings. Blondie O'Hara (Jennifer Jason Leigh) hopes that kidnapping Carolyn Stilton (Miranda Richardson), the socialite wife of Democratic-party bigwig Henry Stilton (Michael Murphy), will somehow get her back her husband, two-bit hood Johnny O'Hara (Dermot Mulroney), who's disappeared. Blondie is played by Leigh at her most eccentric, sketching an ill-educated floozy with plenty of illusions and bad teeth. Richardson plays with great subtlety and finesse. Belafonte invests his slick gangster with a harsh toughness never before seen from the actor.

KANSAS CITY BOMBER
1972, 99 mins, US ⊗
D: Jerrold Freedman **A:** Raquel Welch, Kevin McCarthy, Helena Kallianiotes, Norman Alden, Jeanne Cooper, Jodie Foster (M-G-M)

A gutsy, sensitive, and comprehensive look at the barbaric world of the roller derby. Raquel Welch, who did a lot of her own skating, is most credible as the beauteous but tough star for whom team owner Kevin McCarthy has big plans. A fake grudge fight moves her from KC to Portland, where McCarthy is building his team for a profitable sale. At the same time Welch is torn between her professional life and her two fatherless children.

KANSAS CITY CONFIDENTIAL
(UK: THE SECRET FOUR)
1952, 98 mins, US ⊗
D: Phil Karlson **A:** John Payne, Coleen Gray, Preston Foster, Lee Van Cleef, Neville Brand, Jack Elam (Edward Small/ United Artists)

Mastermind of a holdup on a Kansas City bank is former police captain Preston

Foster. Heist is executed successfully but police seize ex-con John Payne as a prime suspect. Cleared later, Payne hunts down the gang whom he suspects of framing him. With exception of the denouement, director Phil Karlson reins his cast in a grim atmosphere that develops momentum through succeeding reels.

KARAKTER
(CHARACTER)
1997, 120 mins, Netherlands Ⓥ ⊙
D: Mike van Diem **A:** Fedja van Huet, Jan Decleir, Betty Schuurman, Victor Low, Tamar van den Dop, Hans Kesting (First Floor)

A lushly mounted historical drama about a young man's lifelong struggle with his cruel, powerful father, *Character* boasts a rich evocation of twenties Holland, solid thesping and assured, dynamic handling by debuting helmer Mike van Diem. A young lawyer named Katadreuffe (Fedja van Huet) is arrested for the murder of an important and feared citizen, bailiff Dreverhaven (Jan Decleir), who also happens to be his father. Flashbacks give the accused's version of events. Katadreuffe's mother, Joba (Betty Schuurman), was Dreverhaven's maid and gave in to his advances only once. The fleeting liaison gave her a son. The boy grew into an adolescent aching to make something of himself. He took out a business loan that turned disastrous, thanks to the influence of his father in revenge for Joba's rejection of marriage. *Character* feels overloaded with incident and shaped by a world view more literary than cinematic. Even so, pic has loads to recommend it and is extremely impressive for its grand scale and vivid period textures.
1997: Best Foreign Language Film

KARATE KID, THE
1984, 126 mins, US Ⓥ ⊙
D: John G. Avildsen **A:** Ralph Macchio, Noriyuki "Pat" Morita, Elisabeth Shue, Martin Kove, Randee Heller (Columbia)

Daniel (Ralph Macchio) and his mother (Randee Heller) move to Southern California. Daniel encounters the attacks of his schoolmates and he is well established as an underdog. Enter Mr. Miyagi (Noriyuki "Pat" Morita), the mysterious maintenance man who takes Daniel under his wing. Daniel wants Miyagi to teach him how to defend himself, but the old man resists until Daniel learns that karate is a discipline of the heart and mind, of the spirit, not of vengeance and revenge.

1984: **Nomination:** Best Supp. Actor (Noriyuki "Pat" Morita)

KARATE KID PART II, THE
1986, 113 mins, US Ⓥ ⊙
D: John G. Avildsen **A:** Ralph Macchio, Noriyuki "Pat" Morita, Nobu McCarthy, Danny Kamekona, Yuji Okumoto (Columbia)

Film literally picks up where the 1984 one left off, with spunky teen Ralph Macchio winning a karate contest against nogood ruffians. Informed that his father is gravely ill, Noriyuki "Pat" Morita heads back to his native Okinawa, with Macchio in tow. His father, who soon dies, turns out to be the last of Morita's concerns. Anyone over the age of 18 is liable to start fidgeting when Macchio dominates the action, but then viewers beyond that advanced age are irrelevant with this film.
1986: **Nomination:** Best Song ("Glory of Love")

KARATE KID PART III, THE
1989, 111 mins, US Ⓥ ⊙
D: John G. Avildsen **A:** Ralph Macchio, Noriyuki "Pat" Morita, Robyn Lively, Thomas Ian Griffith, Martin Kove (Columbia)

A particularly dim-witted film that will likely spell the death of the series. The only remarkable things about it are that Ralph Macchio still looks young enough to play a 17-year-old and that Noriyuki "Pat" Morita can still milk some charm from his character by mumbling sage Miyagi-isms about things like life and tree roots, despite their utter inanity this time around.

KEEP, THE
1983, 96 mins, UK/US Ⓥ ⊙ ▭
D: Michael Mann **A:** Scott Glenn, Alberta Watson, Jurgen Prochnow, Robert Prosky, Gabriel Byrne, Ian McKellen (Paramount)

Buried deep within *The Keep*'s mysterious exterior lies that chilling Hollywood question: how do these dogs get made? Some Germans have arrived at a small Romanian village, unaware and unafraid that the keep where they will be headquartered has an uneasy history. Their commander (Jurgen Prochnow) is a nice guy despite his job with the Wehrmacht and it's hardly his fault that his troops are gradually being eaten alive and blown apart by an unseen force that moves smokily through the keep.

KEEP 'EM FLYING
1941, 86 mins, US ⓥ ⊙
D: Arthur Lubin A: Bud Abbott, Lou Costello, Martha Raye, Carol Bruce, Dick Foran (Universal)

Interwoven with typical A&C byplay are a plentiful supply of physical thrill action and three songs. It's all thrown together in a loose mélange to showcase the two comics. Opening in a carnival to allow Abbott and Costello to display some knockabout routines, picture swings to a nightclub and then to the prep school for army fliers. The comedy pair are stooges for stunt flier Dick Foran, and when he ditches the carny, pair go along with him to the flying school to become flunkies around the place.

KEEP SMILING
1938, 91 mins, UK
D: Monty Banks A: Gracie Fields, Roger Livesey, Mary Maguire, Peter Coke, Jack Donohue, Hay Petrie (20th Century-Fox)

Carefully prepared with an eye to establishing the topflight British star Gracie Fields in the US, results are meritorious, a fast-moving filmusical with several songs delivered in crackerjack style by Fields. Story concerns show troupe headed by Fields, which gets stranded; beds in at farm of girl's grandfather; luckily acquires a bus for a tour; and winds up for a two-year engagement at a pavilion near Brighton.

KELLY'S HEROES
1970, 148 mins, US ⓥ ⊙ ⊡
D: Brian G. Hutton A: Clint Eastwood, Telly Savalas, Don Rickles, Carroll O'Connor, Donald Sutherland (M-G-M)

Clint Eastwood, Telly Savalas, Don Rickles, and Donald Sutherland are among the stars cast as lovable roughnecks who decide to steal $16 million in gold bullion; it belongs to the Germans, so that's okay. Nearly satirical in its overall effect, plot caroms between cliché dogface antics, detailed and gratuitous violence, caper melodramatics, and outrageous anachronism.

KENNEL MURDER CASE, THE
1933, 73 mins, US ⓥ
D: Michael Curtiz A: William Powell, Mary Astor, Eugene Pallette, Ralph Morgan (Warner)

Philo Vance comes back to the screen in the hands of William Powell, unraveling a murder mystery in an interesting and entertaining manner. Again Eugene Pallette is with the master detective as the snap-judgment cop, most of the comedy relief issuing via his character. The title relates to a kennel club on Long Island, various members of which are concerned in the story in addition to the two who are murdered, brothers. Vance himself is a dog fancier as well as master murder unraveler.

KENTUCKIAN, THE
1955, 103 mins, US ⓥ ⊡
D: Burt Lancaster A: Burt Lancaster, Dianne Foster, Diana Lynn, John McIntire, Walter Matthau, John Carradine (United Artists)

The rather simple story of a pioneer father, his son, and their dream of new lands is the basis for this adventure-drama. The footage is long and often slow, with the really high spots of action rather scattered. Burt Lancaster takes on the added chore of director for the production. He does a fairly competent first job of handling most everyone but himself.

KENTUCKY FRIED MOVIE, THE
1977, 90 mins, US ⓥ
D: John Landis A: Donald Sutherland, George Lazenby, Henry Gibson, Bill Bixby (Kentucky Fried Theatre)

The Kentucky Fried Movie boasts excellent production values and some genuine wit, though a few of the sketches are tasteless. Some of the appeal of this kind of material is purely juvenile, but there is also a more substantial undertone in using satire of TV and films as a means of satirizing American cultural values.

LA KERMESSE HEROIQUE
(CARNIVAL IN FLANDERS)
1935, 95 mins, France
D: Jacques Feyder A: Françoise Rosay, Jean Murat, Alerme, Louis Jouvet (Tobis)

Plot unfolds the tale of a Flanders village, peopled by rather timid males, visited by a regiment of Spanish soldiers. Recalling the brutal treatment visited on other towns by Spain's military forces in the past, the male gentry decide to play dead. This is literal in the case of the burgomaster, and it furnishes some of the richest farcical scenes as he feigns death, lying in state. His robust wife rallies the women of the town, prepares a royal welcome for the duke and his men, and showers the Spaniards with hospitality.

KES
1970, 112 mins, UK ⓥ
D: Ken Loach A: David Bradley, Colin Welland, Freddie Fletcher, Lynne Perrie,

Brian Glover (Woodfall/Kestrel)

Film tells of a lad in a drab Yorkshire village with a permissive mum and a drunken, bullying brother. He goes to a school where the kids are also bullies and the teaching staff mainly a bunch of aggressive, unsympathetic, impatient robots. Then he finds a baby kestrel (a small falcon) on the moors. He determines to train the kestrel to fly and from then on he's obsessed with his new interest, which gives him his first purpose in life. Simply, the filmmakers have brought the background of the boy's life vividly into reality and turned the spotlight on this black side of British education and home life.

KEY, THE
1934, 82 mins, US
D: Michael Curtiz **A:** William Powell, Edna Best, Colin Clive, Hobart Cavanaugh, Halliwell Hobbes (Warner)

Setting is the Irish revolution of 1920 in which the marauding Black-and-Tan troops, the street-sniping patriots, and the phantom-moving Michael Collins combined to make a gory, tumultuous time of it. Only a minor part of the color and dynamic drama has been captured. But there is enough pulsing sweep to the background episodes to overcome the vapidity of a formula triangle—husband (Colin Clive), wife (Edna Best), and returned lover (William Powell)—to give the film an above-average rating.

KEY, THE
1958, 134 mins, UK Ⓥ ⊙ ⊡
D: Carol Reed **A:** William Holden, Sophia Loren, Trevor Howard, Oscar Homolka, Kieron Moore (Open Road/Columbia)

A wartime yarn, with William Holden and Trevor Howard as commanders of tugs engaged in convoy rescue duty. This highly hazardous chore provides some standout thrills which alone make the pic great entertainment. Holden finds his old buddy Howard sharing an apartment with a beautiful Swiss refugee, played with dignity and sensitive understanding by Sophia Loren. She identifies both these men with her dead fiancé. When Howard is killed, Holden uses the spare key that Howard has given him to keep the apartment among tug men.

KEY LARGO
1948, 100 mins, US Ⓥ ⊙
D: John Huston **A:** Humphrey Bogart, Edward G. Robinson, Lauren Bacall, Lionel Barrymore, Claire Trevor (Warner)

A tense film thriller. Atmosphere of the deadly, still heat of the Key West locale, the threat of a hurricane, and the menace of merciless gangsters make the suspense seem real, and Huston's direction stresses the mood of anticipation. Humphrey Bogart is a veteran, stopping off at Key Largo to visit the family of a buddy killed in the war. He finds the run-down hotel taken over by gangsters. Kept prisoners over a long day and night, during which a hurricane strikes, the best and the worst is brought out in the characters.
1948: Best Supp. Actress (Claire Trevor)

KEYS OF THE KINGDOM, THE
1945, 137 mins, US Ⓥ
D: John M. Stahl **A:** Gregory Peck, Thomas Mitchell, Vincent Price, Roddy McDowall, Edmund Gwenn, Cedric Hardwicke (20th Century-Fox)

A cavalcade of a priest's life, played excellently by Gregory Peck, what transcends all the cinemation is the impact of tolerance, service, faith, and godliness. When the monsignor (Cedric Hardwicke) visits the aged, limping, and poor father (Peck), he departs with humility and a new respect after he reads the good father's journal, first learning of unrequited love (in youth) and later of unselfish devotion, self-punishing denials, and unswerving fealty to his mission of more than a half century.
1945: Nominations: Best Actor (Gregory Peck), B&W Cinematography, B&W Art Direction, Scoring of a Dramatic Picture

KEY TO THE CITY
1950, 100 mins, US
D: George Sidney **A:** Clark Gable, Loretta Young, Marilyn Maxwell, Frank Morgan (M-G-M)

A noisy, wisecracking comedy telling of a quickie romance that is bred at a mayors' convention in San Francisco. Clark Gable is the honest mayor of a Northern California city. Story brings Loretta Young, the equally honest mayor from New England, into antagonistic contact. Together they strike sparks despite character opposites, become involved in unwelcome adventures that keep them in and out of jail, and find love on the fog-shrouded Telegraph Hill.

KHARTOUM
1966, 134 mins, UK Ⓥ ⊙ ⊡
D: Basil Dearden **A:** Charlton Heston, Laurence Olivier, Richard Johnson, Ralph

667

Richardson, Alexander Knox (United Artists)

The historical drama depicts the events leading up to the savage death of General Charles Gordon, famed British soldier, as he sought to mobilize public opinion against the threat of a religious-political leader who would conquer the Arab world. Heston delivers an accomplished performance as Gordon. Olivier, playing the Mahdi, is excellent in creating audience terror of a zealot while projecting respect and compassion for his equally religious adversary.

1966: Nomination: Best Original Story & Screenplay

KICKBOXER
1989, 105 mins, US Ⓥ ⊙
D: Mark DiSalle, David Worth **A:** Jean-Claude Van Damme, Denis Alexio, Dennis Chan, Tong Po, Haskell Anderson (Kings Road)

Pic opens with Dennis Alexio (Eric Sloane) being crowned world kickboxing champion, watched by his younger brother, Jean-Claude Van Damme. The duo head off to Thailand to take on the originators of kickboxing. Alexio fights, and is crippled by top Thai fighter Tong Po, leaving Van Damme to swear revenge. Much of *Kickboxer* is macho nonsense, full of cliché characters and risible dialogue, though the fight scenes—choreographed by Van Damme—are well-handled.

KID, THE
1921, 80 mins, US Ⓥ ⊗
D: Charles Chaplin, Charles Riesner **A:** Charles Chaplin, Jackie Coogan, Edna Purviance, Carl Miller, Chuck Reisner (Chaplin/First National)

In this, Chaplin is less of the buffoon and more of the actor. But his comedy is all there and there is not a dull moment once the comedian comes into the picture. Film also will touch their hearts and win sympathy, not only for the star, but for his leading woman, and little Jackie Coogan.

KID BROTHER, THE
1927, 83 mins, US ⊗
D: Ted Wilde **A:** Harold Lloyd, Jobyna Ralston, Walter James, Leo Willis, Olin Francis (Lloyd/Paramount)

Harold Lloyd has clicked again with about as gaggy a gag picture as he has ever done. It is just a series of gags, one following the other, some funny and others funnier. Lloyd is the youngest son of a family of three boys who live with their father, a widower. When Dad finds out that a medicine show has made a pitch and that the boy has given them a license, he orders the youngster to go down and close up the show. Jobyna Ralston plays opposite Lloyd as the little medicine-show girl and handles herself perfectly.

KID FOR TWO FARTHINGS, A
1955, 96 mins, UK Ⓥ
D: Carol Reed **A:** Celia Johnson, Diana Dors, David Kossoff, Brenda de Banzie, Joe Robinson (London)

Carol Reed has extracted a great deal of charm from a series of cameos set in the Jewish quarter of London and around the famed Petticoat Lane. He uses color for the first time in his career with telling effect and, within the framework of the setting, has achieved all that could have been expected. David Kossoff gives a performance as the trouser maker (with an unusual bent toward philosophy) that is a model of sincerity. Diana Dors plays her part as a blond popsie with complete conviction.

KID FROM BROOKLYN, THE
1946, 114 mins, US Ⓥ ⊙
D: Norman Z. McLeod **A:** Danny Kaye, Virginia Mayo, Vera-Ellen, Steve Cochran, Eve Arden, Lionel Stander (Goldwyn)

Based on the old Harold Lloyd starrer *The Milky Way*, the film is aimed straight at the belly laughs and emerges as a lush mixture of comedy, music, and gals. Danny Kaye clicks with his unique mugging, song stylizing, and antics, but still packs in plenty of the wistful appeal. Story has Kaye as a mild-mannered milkman who gets involved with a prizefight gang when he accidentally knocks out the current middleweight champ. With the champ's publicity shot to pieces, his manager decides to capitalize on the situation by building Kaye into a contender and then cleaning up on the title bout.

KID GALAHAD
1937, 100 mins, US Ⓥ
D: Michael Curtiz **A:** Edward G. Robinson, Bette Davis, Humphrey Bogart, Wayne Morris, Jane Bryan, Harry Carey (Warner)

One of the oldest stories in pictures—the grooming of a heavyweight champion—has been done again with good results. Also more than the usual amount of romance for a slugfest. This allows room for Bette Davis to moon over the clean kid from the farm, and for the fight manager's convent-bred sister to also fall in love with him. But essentially it's the story of the kid's manager (Edward G. Robinson), who maneuvers to match the bellhop-pugilist (Wayne Morris) in order to pay off the grudge he holds for a felonious fellow manager (Humphrey Bogart).

KID GALAHAD
1962, 95 mins, US ⓥ
D: Phil Karlson A: Elvis Presley, Gig Young, Lola Albright, Joan Blackman, Charles Bronson (United Artists)

Two of the screen's most salable staples are united. One is Elvis Presley. The other is the hackneyed yarn about the wholesome, greenhorn kid who wanders into training camp, KOs with one mighty right the hardest belter on the premises, gets an instant nickname, and proceeds to score a string of victories en route to the inevitable big fight in which the fix is on. Presley's acting resources are limited. It is, however, a surprisingly paunchy Presley in this film, and the added avoirdupois is not especially becoming. Elvis sings some half-dozen songs.

KID GLOVE KILLER
1942, 76 mins, US
D: Fred Zinnemann A: Van Heflin, Marsha Hunt, Lee Bowman, Samuel S. Hinds (M-G-M)

One of those moderately budgeted programmers that rise far above the level intended. Van Heflin's skillful timing and delivery of lines hold interest in many sequences that might easily have crumbled in less capable hands. Story unfolds a compact and interesting drama of political corruption, and the experiences of a scientific criminologist in getting a test-tube solution to the murder of the mayor.

KID MILLIONS
1934, 90 mins, US ⓥ
D: Roy Del Ruth A: Eddie Cantor, Ann Sothern, Ethel Merman, George Murphy (Goldwyn)

Another Samuel Goldwyn–Eddie Cantor musical-comedy extravaganza and again strong entertainment. An ice-cream-factory number in Technicolor is one of the finest jobs of tint work yet turned out and the handling of the colors, mass movements, and girls creates a flaming crescendo for the production. Story works up to an Egyptian comedy sequence, with harem, mummy, torture chamber, and underground wealth as elements.

KIDNAPPED
1948, 81 mins, US
D: William Beaudine A: Roddy McDowall, Sue England, Dan O'Herlihy, Roland Winters, Jeff Corey (Monogram)

Robert Louis Stevenson's swashbuckler of feuding Scots and foul play in the 18th century has lost a lot of its punch in the screen adaptation. The Stevenson classic concerns a young Scot who comes to claim an inheritance from his uncle. Latter has him kidnapped and shipped off to slavery but lad is saved by a political adventurer.

KIDNAPPED
1960, 97 mins, US ⓥ ⊙
D: Robert Stevenson A: Peter Finch, James MacArthur, Bernard Lee, Niall MacGinnis, John Laurie, Peter O'Toole (Walt Disney)

Walt Disney's live-action feature is a faithful re-creation of the Robert Louis Stevenson classic. The film itself is sluggish because its story line is not clear enough and does not arouse any great anxiety or excitement in the spectator. James MacArthur plays the young 18th-century Scottish boy cheated of his inheritance by a conniving uncle. The boy is kidnapped by a cruel shipmaster to be sold as an indentured servant in the Carolinas. He escapes through the aid of a dashing fellow Scotsman (Peter Finch).

KIDNAPPED
1972, 100 mins, UK ⓥ ▭
D: Delbert Mann A: Michael Caine, Trevor Howard, Jack Hawkins, Donald Pleasence, Lawrence Douglas (Omnibus)

Combination of Robert Louis Stevenson's *Kidnapped* and its lesser-known sequel results in an intriguing adventure piece set against that period in Scottish history when the English were trying to take over that country's rule. Michael Caine plays the swashbuckling character of Alan Breck, who embodies the spirit of the bloody but unbowed Highlanders. Delbert Mann's direction catches the proper flavor of the times.

KIDS
1995, 90 mins, US ⓥ
D: Larry Clark A: Leo Fitzpatrick, Justin Pierce, Chloe Sevigny, Sarah Henderson, Rosario Dawson (Miramax/The Guys Upstairs)

Celebrated photographer Larry Clark's first feature is bluntly about sex, drugs, and irresponsibility. From the opening scene, which unflinchingly observes the cocky Telly (Leo Fitzpatrick) talking a sweet blonde (Sarah Henderson) into surrendering her virginity to him, the film takes a direct, nonjudgmental view of what it's presenting. It would seem that Clark and young screenwriter Harmony Korine intend the film as a truthful depiction of urban kids today, with a cautionary overlay about the wages of blatant disregard for safe sex. More of a gray area is the extent to which the picture seems voyeuristic and exploitative of its young subjects.

KIDS IN THE HALL: BRAIN CANDY
See: Brain Candy

KIKUJIRO
See: Kikujiro No Natsu

KIKUJIRO NO NATSU (KIKUJIRO)
1999, 122 mins, Japan Ⓥ ⊙

D: Takeshi Kitano **A:** Beat Takeshi, Yusuke Sekiguchi, Kayoko Kishimoto, Yuko Daike, Kazuko Yoshiyuki, Beat Kiyoshi (Bandai Visual/Tokyo FM/Nippon Herald/Office Kitano)

A complete departure from the lyrical violence of his gangster films, Takeshi Kitano's *Kikujiro* is a disappointment. The film displays many of the inventive visual touches that distinguished Kitano's previous work, but its treacly mix of emotional manipulation and klutzy comedy makes it hard to digest. Film centers on lonely nine-year-old Masao (Yusuke Sekiguchi), who lives with his grandmother. Told that his father died in a car accident and that the mother he has never known lives in a distant town, Masao sets off to find her. His unlikely traveling companion is Kikujiro (Kitano, aka Beat Takeshi), a smart-mouthed goon instructed to accompany the boy. Kitano plays Kikujiro as an overgrown delinquent, uncovering a more sensitive side as his bond with Masao grows.

KILL
1971, 102 mins, France/Spain/Italy/ W. Germany

D: Romain Gary **A:** Stephen Boyd, Jean Seberg, James Mason, Curt Jurgens, Daniel Emilfork (Procinex/Barnabe/Este/ ICAR/Geissler)

Novelist Romain Gary decides to play this as out-and-out melodrama, even camp, to give a rather strong message that boils down to murdering all those involved in drug dealing. James Mason is an Interpol inspector involved in the drug racket. Sent on a trip to the Orient, he does not want to take his wife (Seberg), but she goes on ahead of him and gets involved with a kidnapping, murdered people in her car, and some cliffhanging adventures played à la Pearl White before daylight finds her okay.

KILLER, THE
See: Dip Hut Seung Hung

KILLER
1994, 95 mins, US Ⓥ ⊙

D: Mark Malone **A:** Anthony LaPaglia, Mimi Rogers, Matt Craven, Peter Boyle, Monika Schnarre (Keystone)

Equal parts fresh observation and strained contrivance, pic features a mesmerizing central performance by Anthony LaPaglia as a nihilistic hit man. Mike (LaPaglia) is the ultimate pro, supplying efficient services for big bucks. Real suspense begins when Mick is assigned a rather unusual duty: killing Fiona (Rogers), a mysterious femme who's not only expecting him but is willing to be murdered.

KILLER: A JOURNAL OF MURDER
1996, 90 mins, US Ⓥ

D: Tim Metcalfe **A:** James Woods, Robert Sean Leonard, Ellen Greene, Cara Buono, Steve Forrest (Ixtlan/Spelling)

A disturbing prison drama about the unlikely relationship between a self-proclaimed reprobate, who may have been America's first serial killer, and a conscientious guard seeking the man's redemption. Oliver Stone's production features top-notch performances by James Woods, as the remorseless criminal, and Robert Sean Leonard, as the liberal guard.

KILLER ELITE, THE
1975, 122 mins, US Ⓥ ⊙ ▭

D: Sam Peckinpah **A:** James Caan, Robert Duvall, Arthur Hill, Bo Hopkins, Mako, Gig Young (Exeter/Persky-Bright/United Artists)

An okay Sam Peckinpah actioner starring James Caan and Robert Duvall as two modern mercenaries who wind up stalking each other in a boringly complex double-cross plot. Street shoot-outs, car chases, and a climactic facedown resolve many of the convoluted plot turns.

KILLER MCCOY
1947, 103 mins, US

D: Roy Rowland **A:** Mickey Rooney, Brian Donlevy, Ann Blyth, James Dunn, Tom Tully, Sam Levene (M-G-M)

A fast action melodrama to introduce Mickey Rooney to adult roles. Sentimental hoke is mixed with prize-ring action. Rooney makes much of his tailor-made assignment in the title role. He's a tough kid who comes up to ring prominence after accidentally killing his friend, the ex-champ, who had started him on the road up. There's nothing that's very original with the story, but scripting by Frederick Hazlitt Brennan has given it realistic dialogue that pays off.

KILLERS, THE
1946, 103 mins, US
D: Robert Siodmak A: Burt Lancaster, Ava Gardner, Edmond O'Brien, Albert Dekker, Sam Levene, William Conrad (Universal/Hellinger)

Taken from Ernest Hemingway's story, picture is a hard-hitting example of forthright melodrama. Plot opens with Lancaster's murder in a small town. Insurance investigator O'Brien tries to piece together events that will prove the murder has more significance than appears on the surface. Story has many flashbacks, told when O'Brien interviews characters in Lancaster's past, but it is all pieced together neatly for sustained drive and mood, finishing with exposé of a colossal double cross.
1946: Nominations: Best Director, Screenplay, Editing, Scoring of a Dramatic Picture

KILLERS, THE
1964, 95 mins, US Ⓥ ⊙
D: Don Siegel A: Lee Marvin, Angie Dickinson, John Cassavetes, Ronald Reagan, Clu Gulager, Claude Akins (Universal)

Scenario is similar in basic structural respects, but different in character and plot specifics from Mark Hellinger's 1946 vintage elaboration on Hemingway's concise short story. In this version, the "hero" (John Cassavetes) is a racing-car driver, which provides the background for some flashy track scenes. Ronald Reagan fails to crash convincingly through his good-guy image in his portrayal of a ruthless crook.

KILLER'S KISS
1955, 67 mins, US Ⓥ
D: Stanley Kubrick A: Frank Silvera, Jamie Smith, Irene Kane, Jerry Jarret, Mike Dana (Minotaur)

Stanley Kubrick turned out *Killer's Kiss* on the proverbial shoestring. Not only did he coproduce but he directed, photo-graphed, and edited from his own screenplay and original story. Familiar plot of boy-meets-girl finds small-time fighter Jamie Smith striking up a romance with taxi dancer Irene Kane. Kubrick's low-key lensing occasionally catches the flavor of the seamy side of Gotham life. His scenes of tawdry Broadway, gloomy tenements, and grotesque brick-and-stone structures that make up Manhattan's lower East Side loft district help offset the script's deficiencies.

KILLING, THE
1956, 84 mins, US Ⓥ ⊙
D: Stanley Kubrick A: Sterling Hayden, Coleen Gray, Marie Windsor, Elisha Cook, Vince Edwards, Jay C. Flippen (Harris-Kubrick)

This story of a $2-million racetrack holdup and steps leading up to the robbery, occasionally told in a documentary style that at first tends to be somewhat confusing, soon settles into a tense and suspenseful vein which carries through to an unexpected and ironic windup. Sterling Hayden, an ex-con, masterminds the plan which includes five men. Stanley Kubrick's direction of his own script is tight and fast-paced, a quality Lucien Ballard's top photography matches to lend particular fluidity of movement.

KILLING DAD
1989, 93 mins, UK Ⓥ ⊙
D: Michael Austin A: Denholm Elliott, Julie Walters, Richard E. Grant, Anna Massey, Laura del Sol (Scottish TV/British Screen)

Black humor does not come off. Nathy (Denholm Elliott), who left home 23 years ago claiming he was going to buy some cigarettes, wants to come home, but the news doesn't please his son, Alistair Berg (Richard E. Grant), who enjoys a peaceful existence with his mother. He travels to Southend, on the coast, checks into the same faded hotel as his father, with the plan to kill Elliott. What he finds is an unreformed character who gets drunk, lies, and "borrows" money, and lives with Judith (Julie Walters). The acting is all first-rate.

KILLING FIELDS, THE
1984, 141 mins, UK Ⓥ ⊙
D: Roland Joffe A: Sam Waterston, Haing S. Ngor, John Malkovich, Julian Sands, Craig T. Nelson, Bill Patterson (Enigma/Goldcrest/IFI)

A story of perseverance and survival in hell on earth, *The Killing Fields* represents

an admirable, if not entirely successful, attempt to bring alive the horror story that is the recent history of Cambodia. Film is designed as a story of friendship. The intent and outward trappings are all impressively in place, but at its heart there's something missing. Action begins in 1973, with Schanberg (Sam Waterston) arriving in Cambodia and being assisted in his reporting by Dith Pran (Haing S. Ngor), an educated, exceedingly loyal native. Through a stupendous effort, and at great risk to his own existence, Dith Pran manages to save the lives of Schanberg and some colleagues after their capture by the victorious Khmer Rouge two years later.
1984: Best Supp. Actor (Haing S. Ngor), Cinematography, Editing
Nominations: Best Picture, Director, Actor (Sam Waterston), Adapted Screenplay

KILLING OF A CHINESE BOOKIE, THE
1976, 135 mins, US
D: John Cassavetes **A:** Ben Gazzara, Timothy Carey, Azizi Johari, Meade Roberts, Seymour Cassel (Faces)

Cassavetes challenges a Hollywood cliché: that technology is so advanced even the worst films usually look good. With ease, he proves that an awful film can look even worse. Ben Gazzara gets into hock with the Mob, which asks him to erase the debt by knocking off an elderly Chinese bookie. Gazzara picks up a stomach wound of his own, which is soon forgotten in the thrill of more aimless improvisation with girls and gangsters.

KILLING OF ANGEL STREET, THE
1981, 101 mins, Australia
D: Donald Crombie **A:** Liz Alexander, John Hargreaves, Alexander Archdale, Reg Lye, Gordon McDougall (Forest Home/AFC)

Feature is a powerful, hard-hitting, and provocative story about corruption permeating the highest levels of society. The eponymous Angel Street consists of a row of old but charming terrace houses on the shores of Sydney Harbor. An outwardly respectable development company wants to buy the homes, raze them, and erect high-rise apartments.

KILLING OF SISTER GEORGE, THE
1968, 138 mins, US Ⓥ
D: Robert Aldrich **A:** Beryl Reid, Susannah York, Coral Browne, Ronald Fraser,

Patricia Medina (Palomar/Associates & Aldrich)

Frank Marcus's legiter, adapted by Lukas Heller, describes the erosion of a longtime lesbian affair between Beryl Reid—by day, the bleeding-heart heroine of a British TV sudser; by night, gin-guzzling dominant lover—and Susannah York. Breakup is cued by decision to write Reid out of her key TV role, as executed with relish by Coral Browne, a broadcast exec who catches York's eye. Director Robert Aldrich has achieved the look and feel of a made-in-Britain pic, although most of it was shot near downtown L.A.

KILLING ZOE
1994, 96 mins, US Ⓥ ⊙
D: Roger Avary **A:** Eric Stoltz, Jean-Hugues Anglade, Julie Delpy, Gary Kemp, Bruce Ramsay (Davis)

Vivid thriller finds recently released con Zed (Eric Stoltz) arriving in Paris to do a "job" for a friend. His specialty is cracking safes, and Eric (Jean-Hugues Anglade), the mastermind, has selected a particularly difficult one for him. Zed takes some long-overdue R&R with a Parisian professional named Zoe (Julie Delpy). The bank siege is a botch from the word go. Obviously an aficionado of the genre, Avary culls from some classics and twists the material into a new form.

KILL ME AGAIN
1989, 96 mins, UK/US Ⓥ ⊙
D: John Dahl **A:** Val Kilmer, Joanne Whalley-Kilmer, Michael Madsen, Jonathan Gries, Michael Greene, Bibi Besch (PolyGram/Propaganda/ITC)

A thoroughly professional little entertainment. Set in contemporary Nevada, pic gets off to a fast start with a small-time con couple (Michael Madsen, Joanne Whalley-Kilmer) scoring big when they cop a suitcase full of cash from a pair of Mafia bagmen. The antiheroine beans her beau with a rock and takes off for a round of fast living in Reno. She asks a seedy detective, Jack (Val Kilmer), to fake her murder. He's well prepared for the round of murders, double crosses, and escapes that make up the film's last half.

KILL-OFF, THE
1989, 95 mins, US Ⓥ
D: Maggie Greenwald **A:** Loretta Gross, Andrew Lee Barrett, Jackson Sims, Steve Monroe, Cathy Haase (Filmworld)

A rigorous, well-acted adaptation of a hard-boiled novel by Jim Thompson, with an unrelentingly grim view of human nature. Loretta Gross gives a strong performance as an acid-tongued gossipmonger hated by almost everyone in her little community. Things come to a head when folks decide to get rid of her, including her husband (Steve Monroe), a slow-witted fellow whose new girlfriend (Cathy Haase) plots against his wife.

KIM
1950, 112 mins, US Ⓥ
D: Victor Saville **A:** Errol Flynn, Dean Stockwell, Paul Lukas, Robert Douglas, Thomas Gomez, Cecil Kellaway (M-G-M)

Story of youthful adventure in India does have its appealing moments, particularly when young Dean Stockwell is onscreen—a young orphan who plays at being a native and encounters derring-do adventures while aiding British intelligence ferret out a dastardly czarist Russian plot to seize India. Errol Flynn is the star, playing with flamboyant gusto the wily and amorous horse trader who aids the government and Kim.

KINDERGARTEN COP
1990, 110 mins, US Ⓥ ◉
D: Ivan Reitman **A:** Arnold Schwarzenegger, Penelope Ann Miller, Pamela Reed, Linda Hunt, Carroll Baker (Universal)

A mishmash of violence, psychodrama, and lukewarm kiddie comedy. Schwarzenegger plays a stoic, unfriendly L.A. cop obsessed with putting away a murderous drug dealer (Richard Tyson). He needs the testimony of Tyson's ex-wife. Plan is for Schwarzenegger's goofy gal-pal partner (Pamela Reed) to infiltrate the kindergarten as a teacher and figure out which kid is Tyson's, but Schwarzenegger has to report for the job. It's supposed to be wildly funny to have this grim, musclebound control freak confronted with five-year-olds he can't intimidate, but it isn't.

KIND HEARTS AND CORONETS
1949, 106 mins, UK Ⓥ ◉
D: Robert Hamer **A:** Dennis Price, Alec Guinness, Valerie Hobson, Joan Greenwood, Miles Malleson (Ealing)

Story of the far-removed heir to the Dukedom of Chalfont who disposes of all the obstacles to his accession to the title and subsequently finds himself tried for a murder of which he is innocent may appear to be somewhat absurd. But translation to a screen comedy has been effected with a mature wit. Greatest individual acting triumph is scored by Alec Guinness, who

plays in turn all the members of the ancestral family.

KIND LADY
1935, 70 mins, US
D: George B. Seitz **A:** Aline MacMahon, Basil Rathbone, Mary Carlisle, Frank Albertson, Dudley Digges (M-G-M)

Implausible basic idea has been made digestible by skillful direction. Viewers are asked to believe that an English lady, disappointed in her love affairs, would invite a strange man, his wife and baby in as guests of her palatial home while it is rather apparent that he is up to no good. To adapt herself to the character of an Englishwoman was no mean job, but MacMahon does it with skill. Rathbone makes a suave villain.

KIND OF LOVING, A
1962, 112 mins, UK Ⓥ
D: John Schlesinger **A:** Alan Bates, June Ritchie, Thora Hird, James Bolam, Leonard Rossiter (Anglo-Amalgamated)

The screenplay is set in a Lancashire industrial town and tells the bittersweet yarn of a young draftsman who is attracted to a typist. It is a physical attraction that he cannot resist. She, on the other hand, has a deeper feeling for him. The fumbling romance proceeds, often hurtfully, often poignantly. The inevitable happens. She becomes pregnant and he grudgingly marries her. Schlesinger handles this film with a sharp documentary eye, but does not forget that he is unfolding a piece of fiction.

KING AND COUNTRY
1964, 88 mins, UK
D: Joseph Losey **A:** Dirk Bogarde, Tom Courtenay, Leo McKern, Barry Foster, James Villiers (BHE)

The story of Private Hamp, a deserter from the battlefront in World War I, is a highly sensitive and emotional drama. Hamp is sent back to his unit to face court-martial. The job of defending the private goes to Dirk Bogarde, a typically arrogant officer who accepts the assignment because it is his duty to do so. He responds to Hamp's beguiling simplicity and honesty, coming to the inevitable conclusion that he was not responsible for his actions. Tom Courtenay gives a compelling performance as a simpleminded soldier, unable to accept the fact that he has committed a heinous crime.

KING AND I, THE
1956, 133 mins, US Ⓥ ◉ ◺
D: Walter Lang **A:** Deborah Kerr, Yul

Brynner, Rita Moreno, Martin Benson, Rex Thompson (20th Century-Fox)

A pictorially exquisite, musically exciting, and dramatically satisfying motion picture. As the Victorian Englishwoman who comes to Siam to teach Western manners and English to the royal household, Deborah Kerr gives one of her finest performances. She handles the role of Mrs. Anna with charm and understanding and, when necessary, the right sense of comedy. As the brusque, petulant, awkwardly kind despot confused by the conflicts of Far Eastern and Western cultures, Yul Brynner gives an effective, many-shaded reading.
1956: Best Actor (Yul Brynner), Color Art Direction, Sound Recording, Scoring of a Musical Picture, Color Costume Design
Nominations: Best Picture, Director, Actress (Deborah Kerr), Color Cinematography, Color Art Direction

KING AND THE CHORUS GIRL, THE
1937, 95 mins, US
D: Mervyn LeRoy **A:** Fernand Gravet, Joan Blondell, Edward Everett Horton, Alan Mowbray, Jane Wyman (Warner)

A romantic comedy, silly but funny. Gravet is wholly engaging as the bored ex-monarch, and Joan Blondell is capital as the American chorine in the Folies Bergère. Entire background is Paris. Edward Everett Horton is at his droll best as the king's buffer.

KING CREOLE
1958, 116 mins, US Ⓥ
D: Michael Curtiz **A:** Elvis Presley, Carolyn Jones, Walter Matthau, Dolores Hart, Dean Jagger, Vic Morrow (Paramount)

Elvis Presley is a high-school youth who is prevented from graduating by his attempts to take care of his weak-willed father and the density of his schoolteachers. He gets involved in a minor theft but thereafter goes straight when given a chance to perform in a saloon. Presley sings 13 new songs and shows himself to be a surprisingly sympathetic and believable actor on occasion. He also does some very pleasant, soft and melodious singing. Carolyn Jones contributes a strong and bitter portrait of a good girl gone wrong, moving and pathetic.

KING DAVID
1985, 114 mins, US Ⓥ ⊙ ▭
D: Bruce Beresford **A:** Richard Gere, Edward Woodward, Denis Quilley, Niall Buggy, Jack Klaff, Cherie Lunghi (Paramount)

An intensely literal telling of familiar portions of the saga of Israel's first two rulers, more historical in approach than religious. Richard Gere is of little help in the title role. Granted, he could have been truly awful (which he isn't), but he doesn't seem comfortable, either. There's a lot of history here, brought to life with good period film work and performances are generally fine.

KINGDOM OF THE SPIDERS
1977, 94 mins, US Ⓥ
D: John Cardos **A:** William Shatner, Tiffany Bolling, Woody Strode, Lieux Dressler, Altovise Davis (Dimension)

Though hardly original, *Kingdom of the Spiders* creates its creeps and scares with care, accomplishing exactly what it sets out to do. On paper, the picture sounds like most of many predecessors: likable scientist William Shatner, helped by beautiful, but capable woman scientist, Tiffany Bolling, finds something amiss among the tarantulas of Arizona. Their problem: stop the little beasties before they eat the world.

KING IN NEW YORK, A
1957, 105 mins, UK Ⓥ
D: Charles Chaplin **A:** Charles Chaplin, Dawn Addams, Oliver Johnston, Maxine Audley, Harry Green, Michael Chaplin (Archway)

Charles Chaplin's first British offering is a tepid disappointment. Tilting against American TV is fair game and while doing this Chaplin contributes some shrewd, funny observations on a vulnerable theme. But when he sets his sights on the problem of Communism and un-American activities, the jester's mask drops. He loses objectivity and stands revealed as an embittered man.

KING KONG
1933, 100 mins, US Ⓥ ⊙
D: Ernest B. Schoedsack, Merian C. Cooper **A:** Fay Wray, Robert Armstrong, Bruce Cabot, Frank Reicher, Sam Hardy, Noble Johnson (RKO)

Highly imaginative and super-goofy yarn is mostly about a 50-foot ape who goes for a five-foot blonde. After the audience becomes used to the machinelike movements and other mechanical flaws in the gigantic animals on view, and becomes accustomed to the phony atmosphere, they may commence to feel the film's power.

The technicians' two big moments arrive in the island jungle, where Kong and other prehistoric creatures reign, and in New York, where Kong goes on a bender. Fay Wray is the blonde who's chased by Kong, grabbed twice, but finally saved. It's a film-long screaming session for her, too much for any actress and any audience. A gripping and fitting musical score and some impressive sound effects rate with the scenery and mechanism in providing *Kong* with its technical excellence.

KING KONG
1976, 134 mins, US 𝒱 ⊙ ▱
D: John Guillermin **A:** Jeff Bridges, Charles Grodin, Jessica Lange, John Rudolph, René Auberjonois, Julius Harris (Paramount)

Faithful in substantial degree not only to the letter but also the spirit of the 1933 classic for RKO, this version neatly balances superb special effects with solid dramatic credibility. Rick Baker is acknowledged for his "special contributions" to the Kong character; this means that Baker did virtually all of the perfectly matched and expertly sized close-ups, in which the beast's range of emotions emerges with telling effect.
1976: Honorary Award (visual effects)
Nominations: Best Cinematography, Sound

KING KONG LIVES
1986, 105 mins, US 𝒱 ⊙
D: John Guillermin **A:** Brian Kerwin, Linda Hamilton, John Ashton, Peter Michael Goetz, Frank Maraden (De Laurentiis)

The giant ape is stunningly revealed to be breathing via life-support systems, with Linda Hamilton heading a surgical team preparing to give him an artificial heart. Brian Kerwin enters from far-off Borneo, where he has stumbled on a female Kong. He delivers her to the Hamilton group so her blood can be used for the heart-transplant operation. Meantime, the proximity of the two Kongs prompts these primates to discover what comes naturally. Mindless chase then proceeds pell-mell for the rest of the film, with the army in hot pursuit.

KING OF COMEDY, THE
1983, 101 mins, US 𝒱 ⊙
D: Martin Scorsese **A:** Robert De Niro, Jerry Lewis, Diahnne Abbott, Sandra Bernhard, Shelley Hack, Tony Randall (20th Century-Fox)

The King of Comedy is a royal disappointment. To be sure, Robert De Niro turns in another virtuoso performance for Martin Scorsese, just as in their four previous efforts. But once again—and even more so—they come up with a character that it's hard to spend time with. Even worse, the characters—in fact, all the characters—stand for nothing.

KING OF JAZZ, THE
1930, 98 mins, US 𝒱
D: J. Murray Anderson **A:** Paul Whiteman and His Band, John Boles, Laura La Plante, Jeanette Loff (Universal)

The millions who never heard the great Paul Whiteman band play George Gershwin's *Rhapsody in Blue* won't hear it here, either. J. Murray Anderson sees fit to scramble it up with "production." It's all busted to pieces. Nothing here counts excepting Whiteman, his band, and the finale, "The Melting Pot." This is an elaborately produced number, in the same manner that Anderson or Ziegfeld would have put it on in a stage show.
1929/30: Best Interior Decoration (Herman Rosse)

KING OF KINGS, THE
1927, 155 mins, US 𝒱 ⊗
D: Cecil B. DeMille **A:** H. B. Warner, Dorothy Cumming, Ernest Torrence, Joseph Schildkraut, James Neill, Jacqueline Logan (DeMille/PDC)

Tremendous is *The King of Kings*—tremendous in its lesson, in the daring of its picturization, and in its biggest scene, the Crucifixion of Christ. Technicolor is employed in two sections. In scenes such as the Last Supper, the seduction of Judas by the Romans to betray the Christ, the healing miracles, the driving out of the evil spirits from Mary, or the carrying of the Cross by Jesus, there is a naturalness that is entrancing. And the acting is no less.

KING OF KINGS
1961, 168 mins, US/Spain 𝒱 ⊙ ▱
D: Nicholas Ray [Charles Walters] **A:** Jeffrey Hunter, Hurd Hatfield, Ron Randell, Harry Guardino, Rip Torn, Frank Thring (M-G-M/Bronston)

King of Kings wisely substitutes characterizations for orgies. Director Nicholas Ray has brooded long and wisely upon the meaning of his meanings, has planted plenty of symbols along the path, yet avoided the banalities of religious calendar art. The sweep of the story is rich in melodrama, action, battle, and clash. But author Philip Yordan astutely uses the bloodthirsty Jewish patriots, unable to think except in terms of violence, as telling counterpoint to the Messiah's love-one-another creed. Jeffrey Hunter's blue orbs and auburn bob (wig, of course) are strikingly pictorial.

KING OF MARVIN GARDENS, THE
1972, 103 mins, US
D: Bob Rafelson A: Jack Nicholson, Bruce Dern, Ellen Burstyn, Julia Anne Robinson, Scatman Crothers (BBS/Columbia)

Tale centers on the relationship between two brothers—the older (Bruce Dern) a self-deceiving wheeler-dealer, flanked by two chippies (Ellen Burstyn and Julia Anne Robinson); the younger (Jack Nicholson) a self-effacing FM-radio monologist who allows himself to be seduced by his brother's bravura lifestyle. For all the artistic and intellectual shortcomings, there are sufficient moments of demonstrable talent that suggest what Rafelson could have achieved with better material.

KING OF NEW YORK
1990, 103 mins, Italy ✪
D: Abel Ferrara A: Christopher Walken, David Caruso, Larry Fishburne, Victor Argo, Wesley Snipes (Reteitalia/Scena/Caminito)

Christopher Walken, a fresh-out-of-prison gangster, vows to take over Gotham's $1-billion-plus drug industry. With his mainly black henchmen, he blows away leading Colombian, Italian, and Chinese kingpins and soon sets up shop as the King of New York. Director Abel Ferrara has an ominous view of New York as a place where deadly violence can erupt instantaneously. Also impressive are large-scale set pieces, including a climax shot in Times Square, as well as a balletic orgy of bloodletting.

KING OF THE HILL
1993, 102 mins, US ✪ ▭
D: Steven Soderbergh A: Jesse Bradford, Jeroen Krabbé, Lisa Eichhorn, Karen Allen, Spalding Gray, Elizabeth McGovern (Wildwood/Bona Fide)

Drawing upon A. E. Hotchner's 1972 book about his St. Louis childhood, Soderbergh creates a vibrant picture of the Middle American social fabric while maintaining sharp focus on the changing fortunes of 12-year-old Aaron Kurlander (Jesse Bradford) and his disintegrating family, living in the seedy Empire Hotel in a working-class section. All the characters are indelibly drawn, a brilliant gallery of types from all social levels. But the film wouldn't work nearly so well without Bradford. His Aaron is an exemplar of the limitless potential that can exist in children before they are damaged, limited, or brought down.

KING OF THE KHYBER RIFLES
1953, 100 mins, US ▭
D: Henry King A: Tyrone Power, Terry Moore, Michael Rennie, John Justin, Guy Rolfe (20th Century-Fox)

Picture is laid in the India of 1857 when British colonial troops were having trouble with Afridi tribesmen. The male heroics are played with a stiff-lipped, stout-fellowish Britishism perfectly appropriate to the characters. Power is a good hero, Moore attractively handles the heroine unabashedly pursuing her man. Rennie is excellent as the commanding general and Rolfe does another of his top-notch villains.

KING OF THE TURF
1939, 88 mins, US
D: Alfred E. Green A: Adolphe Menjou, Roger Daniel, Dolores Costello, Walter Abel, William Demarest (United Artists)

Adolphe Menjou is tops as the former horseman turned bum who, through the inspiration of a boy, recovers the position he once held in turfdom as a stable owner. The lad (Roger Daniel), badly bitten by the racing bug, has run away from home to become a stable boy. The many touching angles of the story and the plot reach a climax when the father turns against him as a means of forcing him to return to his mother.

KING, QUEEN, KNAVE
1972, 92 mins, W. Germany/US ✪
D: Jerzy Skolimowski A: David Niven, Gina Lollobrigida, John Moulder Brown, Mario Adorf, Carl Fox-Duering (Maran/Wolper)

An intermittently funny black comedy about first love, avariciousness, and, underneath, a subversive look at economic booms and human relations in the upper classes. A gauche young orphan is invited, by an uncle he has never seen, to Germany. The blundering boy likes his easy-going uncle, David Niven, but is smitten by his sexy aunt Gina Lollobrigida, who first decides to seduce the boy and then have him kill her husband to inherit the fortune.

KING RALPH
1991, 97 mins, US Ⓥ ⊙
D: David S. Ward **A:** John Goodman, Peter O'Toole, John Hurt, Camille Coduri, Richard Griffiths, Leslie Phillips (Universal/Mirage/Jbro)

Crowned with John Goodman's lovable loutishness and a regally droll performance by Peter O'Toole, *King Ralph* doesn't carry much weight in the story department, though the wispy premise is handled with a blend of sprightly comedy and sappy romance. Britain's entire royal family dies, resulting in a boorish American nightclub entertainer becoming king. After that, it's a basic fish-out-of-water tale, with King Ralph (Goodman) adjusting to the perks and constraints of nobility.

KING RAT
1965, 134 mins, US Ⓥ ⊙
D: Bryan Forbes **A:** George Segal, Tom Courtenay, James Fox, Patrick O'Neal, Denholm Elliott, John Mills (Coleytown/Columbia)

A grim, downbeat, and often raw prison-camp drama has some fine characterizations and direction, backed by stark, realistic, and solid production values, which offset in part its overlength and some script softness. George Segal does an excellent job as US Corporal King, the "Rat," a con artist who manipulates the meager goods and characters of other prisoners, most of whom have higher military rank.

1965: Nominations: Best B&W Cinematography, B&W Art Direction

KING RICHARD AND THE CRUSADERS
1954, 113 mins, US Ⓥ ⊟
D: David Butler **A:** Rex Harrison, Virginia Mayo, George Sanders, Laurence Harvey, Robert Douglas, Michael Pate (Warner)

The Talisman, Walter Scott's classic about the third Crusade, gets the full spectacle treatment in this entry. It details the efforts of Christian nations, under the leadership of England's King Richard, to gain the Holy Grail from the Mohammedans. In addition to the fighting wiles of the crafty Muslims, King Richard must contend with the sinister ambitions of some of his entourage, and these rivalries almost doom the crusade. The script is especially good in its dialogue, particularly that handed to Rex Harrison.

KINGS GO FORTH
1958, 109 mins, US Ⓥ
D: Delmer Daves **A:** Frank Sinatra, Tony Curtis, Natalie Wood, Leora Dana, Karl Swenson (United Artists)

The year is late 1944, and the American 7th Army has the job of cleaning out pockets of German resistance in the south of France. Natalie Wood—an American living in France—is of mixed blood, her mother being white and her (dead) father having been a Negro. This revelation is the key to Wood's romantic entanglements. Sinatra meets Wood and falls in love with her. She in turn falls in love with Curtis. Sinatra, the rough-tough soldier, creates sympathy by underplaying the role. Wood looks pretty, but that's just all. Curtis has experience acting the heel, and he does a repeat. He's best when acting the charm boy.

KINGS OF THE ROAD
See: Im Lauf der Zeit

KINGS OF THE SUN
1963, 108 mins, US ⊟
D: J. Lee Thompson **A:** Yul Brynner, George Chakiris, Shirley Anne Field, Richard Basehart, Brad Dexter (Mirisch)

The story of a young Mayan king (George Chakiris), the leader (Yul Brynner) of a not-so-savage tribe that comes to the ultimate defense of the Mayans, and a Mayan maiden (Shirley Anne Field). Brynner easily steals the show with his sinewy authority, masculinity, and catlike grace. Chakiris is adequate, although he lacks the epic, heroic stature with which the role might have been filled. Field is an attractive pivot for the romantic story. Others of importance include Richard Basehart as a high priest.

KING SOLOMON'S MINES
1937, 80 mins, UK Ⓥ
D: Robert Stevenson **A:** Paul Robeson, Cedric Hardwicke, Roland Young, John Loder, Anna Lee (Gaumont-British)

With all the dramatic moments of H. Rider Haggard's adventure yarn, and production values reaching high and spectacular standards, here is a slab of genuine adventure decked in finely done, realistic African settings. Robeson is a fine, impressive figure as the native carrier proved to be a king, and puts on a proud dignity that his frequent lapses into rolling song cannot bring down. Hardwicke is excellent as a tough white hunter, and Roland Young puts in his lively vein of comedy to excellent effect.

KING SOLOMON'S MINES
1950, 102 mins, US ⓥ ⊙

D: Compton Bennett, Andrew Marton A: Stewart Granger, Deborah Kerr, Richard Carlson, Hugo Haas (M-G-M)

King Solomon's Mines has been filmed against an authentic African background, lending an extremely realistic air to the H. Rider Haggard classic novel of a dangerous safari and discovery of a legendary mine full of King Solomon's treasure. The standout sequence is the animal stampede. Stewart Granger scores strongly as the African hunter who takes Deborah Kerr and her brother (Richard Carlson) on the dangerous search for her missing husband.
1950: Best Color Cinematography, Editing
Nomination: Best Picture

KING SOLOMON'S MINES
1985, 100 mins, US ⓥ ⊙ ▱

D: J. Lee Thompson A: Richard Chamberlain, Sharon Stone, Herbert Lom, John Rhys-Davies, Ken Gampu (Cannon)

King Solomon's Mines is often clumsy about logic, making the action hopelessly cartoonish. It has an unrelenting pace with no variation that ultimately becomes tedious. Neither the camp humor nor the romance between Richard Chamberlain as the African adventurer Allan Quatermain and heroine-in-distress Sharon Stone breaks the monotony of the action.

KING'S PIRATE, THE
1967, 100 mins, US

D: Don Weis A: Doug McClure, Jill St. John, Guy Stockwell, Mary Ann Mobley, Kurt Kasznar (Universal)

Madagascar, circa 1700, backdrops a screenplay that twirls around efforts of the British to halt piracy of the rich trade route to India. Doug McClure, playing a colonial American, volunteers to silence the guns of the pirate port of Diego Suarez. If the plot and dialogue creak a bit, ingredients are still there to suffice as an okay buccaneer yarn if the spectator doesn't take it too seriously.

KING'S ROW
1941, 127 mins, US ⓥ ⊙

D: Sam Wood A: Ann Sheridan, Robert Cummings, Ronald Reagan, Betty Field, Charles Coburn, Claude Rains (Warner)

Henry Bellamann's widely read novel of small-town life at the turn of the century becomes an impressive and occasionally inspiring, though overlong picture, opening with the childhood of the five leading characters. Narration then jumps 10 years, as the hero begins studying medicine. Concluding portion includes the hero's return from studying in Vienna, his beginnings as a pioneer psychiatrist, his treatment and saving of his boyhood friend, and his romance with a new resident of the town.
1942: Nominations: Best Picture, Director, B&W Cinematography

KIPPS
1941, 112 mins, UK ⓥ

D: Carol Reed A: Michael Redgrave, Diana Wynyard, Phyllis Calvert, Michael Wilding, Arthur Riscoe (20th Century-Fox)

Any effort to give impetus or sharpness to this late-Victorian yarn isn't discernible. Playing throughout is impressive in creating the leeches and well-wishers who descend on Kipps, an illiterate department-store clerk, when a fat legacy is dropped in his lap. The sap—and there's no other word for him—undergoes only partial metamorphosis as a gent, eventually sloughing off the new clique for his longtime sweetheart, a servant. Michael Redgrave is believable as the hick; Phyllis Calvert as the peachy domestic; Diana Wynyard as the tony milady for whom the lower-case Kipps almost sells his heart.

KISMET
1944, 100 mins, US

D: William Dieterle [Stanley Donen] A: Ronald Colman, Marlene Dietrich, James Craig, Edward Arnold, Florence Bates (M-G-M)

The sheer mystic fantasy of Baghdad and its royal pomp and splendor remain acceptable escapism. Colman, the king of beggars, is impressive as the phony prince. Dietrich's terp specialty and getup is out of the dream book, but boffo.
1944: Nominations: Best Color Cinematography, Color Art Direction, Sound, Scoring of a Dramatic Picture

KISMET
1955, 112 mins, US ⓥ ⊙ ▱

D: Vincente Minnelli A: Howard Keel, Ann Blyth, Dolores Gray, Vic Damone, Monty Woolley, Sebastian Cabot (M-G-M)

Opulent escapism is what *Kismet* has to sell. Howard Keel is the big entertainment factor, and in somewhat lesser degree, so is Dolores Gray. Without these two, there would be very few minutes that could be counted as really good fun. Robust in voice and physique, Keel injects just the right amount of tongue-in-cheek into his role of Baghdad rogué. The Baghdad fable tells of how the supposedly magical powers of street poet Keel are commandered by the scheming wazir to advance his own power.

KISS, THE
1929, 62 mins, US ⓥ ⊙ ⊗
D: Jacques Feyder A: Greta Garbo, Conrad Nagel, Anders Randolf, Holmes Herbert, Lew Ayres (M-G-M)

The Kiss is one of Greta Garbo's best. Few actresses could weather the series of close-ups required of Garbo in this one. Pierre, the juvenile admirer of Irene, is essayed superbly by Lew Ayres. The title is introduced in the climax when Irene is found in the wild embrace of the lad. Anders Randolf is exceptionally fine as the infuriated husband returning unexpectedly. Action is laid in France.

KISS, THE
1988, 101 mins, US ⓥ ⊙
D: Pen Densham A: Nicholas Kilbertus, Joanna Pacula, Meredith Salenger, Mimi Kuzyk (Tri-Star/Astral/Trilogy)

Kernel of a decent story, of an evil woman (Joanna Pacula) who passes on her powers via a kiss, is never fleshed out in the script. If the setups were hokier, they might have been funny. There's a chilling enough moment when the first devastating kiss is bestowed on the younger version of Pacula (Priscilla Mouzakiotis), but when the action moves back to present-day suburbia, whatever suspense is foretold dissipates quickly.

KISS BEFORE DYING, A
1956, 94 mins, US ▭
D: Gerd Oswald A: Robert Wagner, Jeffrey Hunter, Joanne Woodward, Virginia Leith, Mary Astor, George Macready (Crown/United Artists)

This multiple-murder story is an offbeat sort of film. Robert Wagner portraying a calculating youth who learns that his college sweetheart (Joanne Woodward) is expecting a baby, a circumstance that means she'll be disinherited by her wealthy father and his plans to latch onto the family fortune ruined. He pushes her to her death from the top of a building, and since no one knows they've been dat-

ing (hard for the spectator to swallow), Wagner is in the clear.

KISS BEFORE DYING, A
1991, 95 mins, US ⓥ ⊙
D: James Dearden A: Matt Dillon, Sean Young, Max von Sydow, James Russo, Diane Ladd (Initial)

This update on the pulpy 1956 thriller is a real clunker. A brooding, wounded nobody (Matt Dillon), obsessed with the fortunes of the local industrial magnate (Max von Sydow), gets involved with the magnate's daughter, Dory (Sean Young), but throws her over (a ledge, that is) when he learns she is pregnant. He then gets involved with her twin, social worker Ellen (Young again), eventually marrying her and getting a job as right-hand man to von Sydow. The only problem is Ellen's relentless interest in her sister's unsolved murder. Young, in a blandly uncommitted perf, connects not at all with Dillon's hunky young beau.

KISSIN' COUSINS
1964, 96 mins, US ⓥ ▭
D: Gene Nelson A: Elvis Presley, Arthur O'Connell, Glenda Farrell, Jack Albertson, Pam Austin (M-G-M/Four Leaf)

This Elvis Presley concoction is a pretty dreary effort concerned with the US government attempting to establish an ICBM base on land owned by an obstinate hillbilly clan. The air force sends in a lieutenant (Presley) who is kin to the stubborn critters, among whom is his look-alike cousin (Elvis in a blond wig, no less). Histrionically, Presley does as well as possible under the circumstances. He also sings eight songs.

KISS ME AGAIN
1925, 67 mins, US ⊗
D: Ernst Lubitsch A: Marie Prévost, Monte Blue, John Roche, Clara Bow, Willard Louis (Warner)

The story is decidedly Parisian in its flavor. The Fleurys are married, the husband is a businessman, the wife is somewhat fond of music, and Maurice, the musician, is fond of the wife. This brings about a flirtation, and finally the husband decides that he will not stand in the way of his wife's happiness, so he arranges for a divorce, with his wife to receive his home and half his fortune. But the wife in reality loves her husband and wants him back. It is the touch of arranging for the divorce evidence that creates much laughter. It is well acted, delightfully directed, and edited without a wasted foot of film.

KISS ME DEADLY
1955, 105 mins, US Ⓥ ⊙
D: Robert Aldrich **A:** Ralph Meeker, Albert Dekker, Paul Stewart, Wesley Addy, Maxine Cooper, Cloris Leachman (Parklane)

Ralph Meeker takes on Mike Hammer and as the surly, hit-first, ask-questions-later shamus turns in a job that is acceptable, even if he seems to go soft in a few sequences. From the time Hammer picks up a half-naked blonde on a lonely highway, he's in for trouble. The girl is killed and he nearly so in an arranged accident. This gets his curiosity aroused and he sets about trying to unravel the puzzle.

KISS ME GOODBYE
1982, 101 mins, US Ⓥ
D: Robert Mulligan **A:** Sally Field, James Caan, Jeff Bridges, Paul Dooley, Claire Trevor, Mildred Natwick (Boardwalk/Sugarman/Barish/20th Century-Fox)

Tale begins with Sally Field starting her life up again after the death, three years earlier, of her talented theatrical hubby (James Caan). Field has decided to marry Egyptologist Jeff Bridges. Caan's ghost decides to join Field back in the apartment, making possible all sorts of "zany" scenes, such as having Caan talk to his former wife while Bridges tries to make love to her. Almost all the alleged humor stems from Field relating to Caan, whom no one else can hear or see, while she tries to engage in everyday activities.

KISS ME KATE
1953, 109 mins, US Ⓥ ⊙
D: George Sidney **A:** Kathryn Grayson, Howard Keel, Ann Miller, Keenan Wynn, Bobby Van, James Whitmore (M-G-M)

Shakespeare's *Taming of the Shrew* done over in eminently satisfying fashion via a collaboration of superior song, dance, and comedy talents. *Kate* unfolds smoothly all the way as it goes back and forth from the backstage story to the play within the play and works in the numerous—and brilliant—Cole Porter tunes. Howard Keel is a dynamic male lead, in complete command of the acting role and registering superbly with the songs. Kathryn Grayson is fiery and thoroughly engaging as Kate.
1953: Nomination: Best Scoring of a Dramatic Picture

KISS ME, STUPID
1964, 126 mins, US Ⓥ ⊙ ☐
D: Billy Wilder **A:** Dean Martin, Kim Novak, Ray Walston, Felicia Farr, Cliff Osmond (Phalanx/Minsch)

Kiss Me, Stupid is not likely to corrupt any sensible audience. But there is a cheapness and more than a fair share of crudeness about the humor of a contrived double adultery situation. Wilder has directed with frontal assault rather than suggestive finesse the means by which Walston and Osmond, a pair of amateur songwriters in a Nevada waystop called Climax, contrive to bag girl-crazy star Martin and sell him on their ditties. Idea is to make Martin stay overnight in Walston's house, get latter's wife out of the way by creating a domestic crisis, and substitute a floozy (Novak) from a tavern as wife for a night.

KISS OF DEATH
1947, 98 mins, US Ⓥ
D: Henry Hathaway **A:** Victor Mature, Brian Donlevy, Coleen Gray, Richard Widmark, Karl Malden, Mildred Dunnock (20th Century-Fox)

Story of an ex-convict who sacrifices himself to gangster guns to save his wife and two small daughters. Henry Hathaway's real-life slant on direction brings the picture close to authentic tragedy. Victor Mature, as the ex-convict, does some of his best work. The acting sensation of the piece is Richard Widmark, as the dim-wit, blood-lusty killer.
1947: Nominations: Best Supp. Actor (Richard Widmark), Original Story

KISS OF DEATH
1995, 101 mins, US Ⓥ ⊙
D: Barbet Schroeder **A:** David Caruso, Samuel L. Jackson, Nicolas Cage, Helen Hunt, Stanley Tucci (20th Century-Fox)

A very loose and "contemporized" remake, *Kiss of Death* is a crackling thriller that feels unusually attuned to its low-life characters. Pic is most noteworthy for Nicolas Cage's amazing turn as a colossally tough hood. Jimmy Kilmartin (David Caruso) is an ex-con rigorously walking the straight and narrow with his wife, Bev (Helen Hunt), and baby daughter. When Jimmy lands back in the slammer, he agrees to help persistent assistant d.a. Frank Zioli (Stanley Tucci) nail the criminal king Little Junior (Cage), by taping incriminating conversations while wired with a mike.

KISS OF THE SPIDER WOMAN

1985, 119 mins, US/Brazil ⓥ ⊙

D: Hector Babenco **A:** William Hurt, Raul Julia, Sonia Braga, José Lewgoy, Nuno Leal Maia (SugarLoaf/HB Filmes)

Drama centers upon the relationship between cell mates in a South American prison. Molina, played by William Hurt, is an effeminate gay locked up for having molested a young boy, while Valentin, played by Raul Julia, is a journalist in for a long term due to his radical political activities under a fascist regime. Some will find Hurt mesmerizing, others artificially low-key. By contrast, Julia delivers a very strong, straightforward, and believable performance.

1985: Best Actor (William Hurt)
Nominations: Best Picture, Director, Adapted Screenplay

KISS THE BLOOD OFF MY HANDS (UK: BLOOD ON MY HANDS)

1948, 79 mins, US

D: Norman Foster **A:** Joan Fontaine, Burt Lancaster, Robert Newton, Lewis L. Russell, Jay Novello (Universal)

Intensely moody melodrama concerns an uprooted vet of the Second World War whose life is shattered after he accidentally kills a man in a London pub. Lancaster delivers a convincing and sympathetic portrayal. Fontaine performs with sensitivity and sincerity. Newton is properly oily and detestable.

KISS THE BOYS GOODBYE

1941, 83 mins, US

D: Victor Schertzinger **A:** Mary Martin, Don Ameche, Oscar Levant, Jerome Cowan, Raymond Walburn (Paramount)

Light, humorous, and breezy piece of entertainment effectively showcases the acting and vocal talents of Mary Martin. Clare Boothe's play was a satire on the search for the Scarlett to portray the lead in *Gone with the Wind*. For picture purposes, the lead sought is a southern beauty for a Broadway show to be produced by Jerome Cowan, angeled by Raymond Walburn, and staged by Don Ameche. Publicity stunt sends Ameche and composer Oscar Levant on tour of the south.

KISS THE GIRLS

1997, 120 mins, US ⓥ ⊙ ▭

D: Gary Fleder **A:** Morgan Freeman, Ashley Judd, Cary Elwes, Tony Goldwyn, Jay O. Sanders, Brian Cox (Brown-Wizan/Paramount)

Kiss the Girls is a derivative but fairly effective *Seven* knock-off, right down to its casting of Morgan Freeman as a shrewd detective pursuing a crafty and kinky serial killer—who is all too obvious from the very beginning. Dr. Alex Cross (Freeman), a forensic pathologist on the Washington, D.C., police force, zips down to Durham, NC, when his niece Naomi goes missing. Eight women have recently disappeared, and local policemen have found just two bodies, each tied to a tree and sexually ravaged. A local doctor, Kate McTiernan (Ashley Judd) is abducted and strapped down in a dungeonlike cell. She manages to escape and is able to confirm Alex's suspicions: the perpetrator is a man dedicated to maintaining a "harem" of strong-willed women who have to submit to his demands. Freeman invests this project with more class and dignity than it deserves.

KISS TOMORROW GOODBYE

1950, 102 mins, US ⓥ ⊙

D: Gordon Douglas **A:** James Cagney, Barbara Payton, Helena Carter, Ward Bond, Luther Adler (Warner)

Yarn opens with the trial of an assorted bunch of heavies and then quickly segues into a flashback to tell how circumstances put them in the courtroom. Flashback kicks off with a jailbreak, and the pace doesn't slow down as it takes James Cagney through a series of murders, robberies, and romantic episodes. Barbara Payton impresses as the girl who first falls victim to his tough fascination. Helena Carter is very good as a bored rich girl.

KITCHEN TOTO, THE

1987, 95 mins, UK ⓥ ⊙

D: Harry Hook **A:** Bob Peck, Phyllis Logan, Edwin Mahinda, Kirsten Hughes, Robert Urquhart, Edward Judd (British Screen/Film Four/Skreba)

Pic unfolds in 1950 when the British were facing attacks from a Kikuyu terrorist group known as Mau Mau. Bob Peck plays a regional police officer in charge of a small force of native Africans. When Mau Mau murder a black priest, Peck agrees to take in the dead man's young son (Edwin Mahinda) as his "kitchen toto," or houseboy. Story unfolds from the perspective of this alert, intelligent youngster, who's torn between his tribal feelings and the loyalties he has both to his murdered father and to the British who have been kind to him.

KITTEN WITH A WHIP
1964, 82 mins, US
D: Douglas Heyes **A:** Ann-Margret, John Forsythe, Peter Brown, Patricia Barry, Richard Anderson (Universal)

Contrived plot carries an unpleasant theme. A vicious femme juvenile-hall escapee (Ann-Margret) breaks into the home of a politically ambitious family man, whose wife is out of town, and refuses to leave. She threatens him with scandal should he call the police; then calls in a couple of strong-arm associates who take over the house and keep owner a virtual prisoner. Action is burdened with frequent uncalled-for violence. Ann-Margret plays the unsympathetic lead with a display of over-acting and John Forsythe fares little better as her victim.

KITTY
1945, 103 mins, US
D: Mitchell Leisen **A:** Paulette Goddard, Ray Milland, Patric Knowles, Reginald Owen, Cecil Kellaway (Paramount)

Plot tells of an 18th-century easy lady who rose from the London slums to high position in court society—a society that was no better than that from which she rose; it only dressed better. Paulette Goddard credibly depicts Kitty in the various phases of the slum girl's rise in station. Ray Milland has the more difficult task of keeping the unpleasant, foppish character of Sir Hugh Marcy, Kitty's beloved, consistent and does well by it. Reginald Owen and Cecil Kellaway deliver character gems.

KITTY AND THE BAGMAN
1982, 95 mins, Australia ⊗ ⊡
D: Donald Crombie **A:** Liddy Clark, John Stanton, Val Lehman, Gerard Maguire, Collette Mann (Forest Home)

A light, frothy bag of entertainment set in Sydney during the naughty 1920s, pic veers wildly from serious drama to a zany spoofing of the underworld genre. Yarn revolves around two waterfront crime queens, their pimps and beaux and "bagmen." Latter are corrupt police go-betweens. Kitty, wonderfully and zestfully portrayed by Liddy Clark, rises from an innocent young bride arriving at the end of World War I, to the owner of a no-holds-barred niterie.

KITTY FOYLE
THE NATURAL HISTORY OF A WOMAN
1940, 105 mins, US ⊗ ⊙
D: Sam Wood **A:** Ginger Rogers, Dennis Morgan, James Craig, Eduardo Ciannelli, Gladys Cooper (RKO)

The romantic life of a white-collar girl—her happiness and heartbreaks and final decision for lifelong happiness. Picture unfolds in retrospect from the time the girl is forced to choose between two men—one she madly loves, but cannot marry, and the other waiting at church. Despite its episodic, and at times, vaguely defined motivation, picture on whole is a poignant and dramatic portrait of a typical Cinderella girl's love story. Ginger Rogers provides a strong dramatic portrayal in the title role.

1940: Best Actress (Ginger Rogers)
Nominations: Best Picture, Director, Screenplay, Sound

KLANSMAN, THE
1974, 112 mins, US ⊗
D: Terence Young **A:** Lee Marvin, Richard Burton, Cameron Mitchell, Lola Falana, Luciana Paluzzi, David Huddleston (Paramount)

Miserable film stars Lee Marvin as a Dixie sheriff with lots of unoriginal, cliché racial trouble on his hands, and Richard Burton as an unpopular landowner in a performance as phony as his southern accent. There's not a shred of quality, dignity, relevance, or impact in this yahoo-oriented bunk.

KLONDIKE ANNIE
1936, 78 mins, US
D: Raoul Walsh **A:** Mae West, Victor McLaglen, Philip Reed, Harold Huber, Lucille Gleason, Helen Jerome Eddy (Paramount)

This one is again Mae West with the usual arsenal of wisecracks. That is no longer enough. Scene is the early 1890s, the time of the Klondike rush. West kills her Chinese paramour and flees to Alaska for safety. This projects her into the story as a prostie and a murderess. West plays it always in the same key and is handicapped by having to wear rather dowdy dresses in about half the footage.

KLUTE
1971, 114 mins, US ⊗ ⊙ ⊡
D: Alan J. Pakula **A:** Jane Fonda, Donald Sutherland, Charles Cioffi, Roy Scheider, Rita Gam (Warner)

Despite a host of terminal flaws, *Klute* is notable for presenting Jane Fonda as a much-matured actress in a role which demands that she make interesting an emotionally unstable prostitute. The film is a

suspenser without much suspense. The film's wanderings through the sordid side of urban life come across more as titillation than logical dramatic exposition. The only rewarding element is Fonda's performance.
1971: Best Actress (Jane Fonda)
Nomination: Best Original Story & Screenplay

KNACK . . . AND HOW TO GET IT, THE
1965, 84 mins, UK
D: Richard Lester **A:** Rita Tushingham, Ray Brooks, Michael Crawford, Donal Donnelly, John Bluthal (Woodfall)

There is quite a knack in the art of making it successfully with girls. And that about sums up the plot of this offbeat production. The expert exponent of the knack is played by Ray Brooks, and the immediate target is Rita Tushingham, a young girl just up from the country. The other two characters are both young men being instructed in how to acquire the knack from the master. As Michael Crawford plays a schoolteacher, it is a neat trick to cut into schoolroom lessons and hear him speaking the same dialogue used by Brooks to his two friends.

KNICKERBOCKER HOLIDAY
1944, 85 mins, US ⓥ
D: Harry Joe Brown **A:** Nelson Eddy, Charles Coburn, Constance Dowling, Shelley Winters, Percy Kilbride, Chester Conklin (United Artists)

A comedy set to music, film is laid in old New Amsterdam of Peter Stuyvesant's day. It deals with a gay, singing, but fighting newspaper publisher who fights for freedom in the colony and relief for the oppressed from conniving politicians. He crosses the path of the crafty, humorous Governor Stuyvesant in his political and newspaper crusading and also in his desire to wed the daughter of a politician. Film has nine songs, five more than the Broadway show.

KNIFE IN THE WATER
See: Noz W Wodzie

KNIGHTRIDERS
1981, 145 mins, US ⓥ
D: George A. Romero **A:** Ed Harris, Gary Lahti, Tom Savini, Amy Ingersoll, Christine Forrest (Laurel)

A potentially exciting concept—that of modern-day knights jousting on motorcycles—is all that's good. Otherwise, George A. Romero's homage to the Ar-

thurian ideal falls flat in all departments. Premise is that of an itinerant troupe devoted to ancient principles that stages Renaissance fairs featuring bloodless jousts. All Romero can come up with in the way of drama over the next two-plus hours is the spectacle of invidious, greedy big-city promoters and agents preying upon the group, with the pure, idealistic King Arthur figure going off to sulk when several of his men are seduced by the notion of becoming media stars.

KNIGHTS OF THE ROUND TABLE
1953, 115 mins, US/UK ⓥ ⊙ ▭
D: Richard Thorpe **A:** Ava Gardner, Mel Ferrer, Anne Crawford, Stanley Baker, Felix Aylmer (M-G-M)

A dynamic interpretation of Thomas Malory's classic *Morte d'Arthur*. The action is fierce as the gallant Lancelot fights for his king, and armies of lancers are pitted against each other in combat to the death. The story has dramatic movement—it could easily have come off stiltedly under less skillful handling—as the knight's love for his queen nearly causes the death of both. Robert Taylor's right at home with derring-do heroics. Not apparently so at home is Ava Gardner. The role of the lovely Guinevere calls for more projected warmth.
1953: Nominations: Best Color Art Direction, Sound

KNIGHT WITHOUT ARMOUR
1937, 108 mins, UK ⓥ
D: Jacques Feyder **A:** Marlene Dietrich, Robert Donat, Irene Vanburgh, Herbert Lomas, Austin Trevor (London)

A labored effort to keep this picture neutral on the subject of the Russian Revolution finally completely overshadows the simple love story intertwining Marlene Dietrich and Robert Donat. Story reveals Donat as a young British secret-service agent who becomes a Red to achieve his purpose. He's sent to Siberia just before the outbreak of the [First] World War and returns after the revolution as an assistant commissar. He rescues Dietrich's countess from execution.

K-9
1989, 102 mins, US ⓥ ▭
D: Rod Daniel **A:** James Belushi, Mel Harris, Kevin Tighe, Ed O'Neill, Jerry Lee (Gordon/Universal)

The mismatched-buddy-cop picture has literally and perhaps inevitably gone to the dogs, and the only notable thing about *K-9* is that it managed to dig up the idiotic premise first. A flimsy plot deals with the cop (Belushi) trying to break a drug case, an unwanted partner (Jerry Lee, a gifted German shepherd) being foisted on him, and the grudging respect that develops between the two during the course of a series of shoot-outs, brawls, and sight gags.

KNOCK ON ANY DOOR
1949, 98 mins, US Ⓥ ⊙
D: Nicholas Ray **A:** Humphrey Bogart, John Derek, George Macready (Santana)

An eloquent document on juvenile delinquency, its cause and effect, has been fashioned. John Derek is the bad boy of the picture. Story opens when the youth, arrested for the wanton killing of a cop, calls on lawyer Humphrey Bogart to defend him. Bogart, himself a slums product who rose above it, reluctantly takes the case after being convinced Derek, no matter how bad, is innocent. Nicholas Ray gives the film a hard, taut pace that compels complete attention.

KNUTE ROCKNE—ALL AMERICAN
1940, 97 mins, US Ⓥ
D: Lloyd Bacon **A:** Pat O'Brien, Gale Page, Ronald Reagan, Donald Crisp, Albert Basserman (Warner)

Highlights in the colorful life of one of the most prominent figures in the world of football are woven into a biographical film drama that carries both inspirational and dramatic appeal on a wide scale. Picture is studded with familiar incidents in Rockne's life. Through it all runs the theme of Rockne's whole purpose in life—molding boys under his care to become good Americans. Pat O'Brien delivers a fine characterization of the immortal Rockne.

KOLYA
1996, 105 mins, UK/Czech Ⓥ ⊙
D: Jan Sverak **A:** Zdenek Sverak, Andrej Chalimon, Libuse Safrankova, Ondrez Vetchy, Stella Zazvorkova, Ladislav Smoljak (Portobello/Sverak)

Unfolding toward the end of Communist rule in what was then Czechoslovakia, *Kolya* is a bittersweet comedy-drama about a cherubic Russian tyke and a middle-aged cynic thrown together by circumstance. Pic balances heartwarming sentiment with gentle humor and observations. Virtuoso cellist Frantisek Louka (Zdenek Sverak) hits hard times and agrees to wed Nadezda (Irena Livanova),

a young Russian woman seeking Czech citizenship. Nadezda disappears to West Germany, leaving her five-year-old son, Kolya (Andrej Chalimon), with his grandmother. When she is rushed to hospital, Kolya is dumped on Frantisek's doorstep. The script makes some ironic points on conflicting Czech attitudes toward Russia. But this is essentially a two-handed drama, the components of which are familiar but no less touching.
1996: Best Foreign-Language Film

KONGRESS TANZT, DER (CONGRESS DANCES)
1931, 95 mins, Germany
D: Erik Charell **A:** Lilian Harvey, Willy Fritsch, Otto Wallburg, Conrad Veidt, Lil Dagover, Alfred Abel (UFA)

A revue more than a story. Erik Charell offers grace, taste, and a light hand. Plot is rather thin and goes back to the time of the Congress of Vienna, 1814, when all princes, kings, and diplomats assembled to confer about the fate of Europe, and Emperor Napoleon. But the Austrian prime minister arranges festivities and dances in order to divert the gentlemen from the actual questions and the political events. The Russian czar (Willy Fritsch), especially, seems dangerous to him and he sends two ladies so that he will not trouble about the negotiations. The czar is wiser, he has a double take his place at the official festivities. However, he falls in love with one of these women, a Viennese glove maker (Lilian Harvey).

KORHINTA (MERRY-GO-ROUND)
1956, 100 mins, Hungary
D: Zoltan Fabri **A:** Bela Barsi, Manyi Kiss, Mari Torocsik, Imre Soos, Adam Szirtes, Antal Farkas (Mafilm)

This is mainly the tale of two lovers separated by social conventions and politics who finally assert themselvs and their love. It has a human, sentimental quality, never descending to mawkishness. Scenes of the lovers first meeting on a fairground swing, a brilliantly mounted dance scene when the young lover makes his desires evident in a long dance with the girl (a masterful piece of cinema), and the treatment of characterization, combine to make this a fine pic.

KOTCH
1971, 113 mins, US Ⓥ
D: Jack Lemmon **A:** Walter Matthau,

Deborah Winters, Felicia Farr, Charles Aidman (ABC Pictures)

A great film in several ways: Jack Lemmon's outstanding directorial debut; Walter Matthau's terrific performance as an unwanted elderly parent who befriends a pregnant teenager; John Paxton's superior adaptation of Katharine Topkins's novel, and a top-notch supporting cast. This heartwarming, human comedy will leave audiences fully nourished, whereas they should be left a bit starved for more.
1971: Nominations: Best Actor (Walter Matthau), Editing, Song ("Life Is What You Make It"), Sound

KOYAANISQATSI
1982, 87 mins, US Ⓥ ⊙
D: Godfrey Reggio (IRE)

At first awe-inspiring with its sweeping aerial wilderness photography, it becomes depressing when the phone lines, factories, and nuke plants spring up. The pic then runs the risk of boring audiences with shot after glossy shot of man's commercial hack job on the land and his resulting misery. The viewer is relentlessly bombarded with images reminiscent of the Hopi Indian title, meaning "crazy life," while Philip Glass's tantalizing but dirgelike score drones on.

KRAKATOA, EAST OF JAVA
1969, 135 mins, US Ⓥ ⊑
D: Bernard L. Kowalski **A:** Maximilian Schell, Diane Baker, Brian Keith, Barbara Werle, Sal Mineo, Rossano Brazzi (ABC/Cinerama)

Krakatoa plods through a search for a sunken treasure on a boat that contains a score of one-dimensional characters. In the background is a rumbling and warning that a big volcano near where they are going, Krakatoa, may erupt again, but the captain scoffs that it has been quiet for 200 years.
1969: Nomination: Best Visual Effects

KRAMER VS. KRAMER
1979, 105 mins, US ⊙
D: Robert Benton **A:** Dustin Hoffman, Meryl Streep, Justin Henry, Jane Alexander, Howard Duff, JoBeth Williams (Columbia)

A perceptive, touching, intelligent film about the dissolution of the family unit. A highly effective technique of short, poignant scenes brings home the message that no one escapes unscarred from the trauma of separation. Meryl Streep breaks with up-and-coming ad exec Dustin Hoffman

and tyke Justin Henry to find her own role in life. Hoffman is thus left with a six-year-old son and begins a process of "parenting" that is both humorous and affecting.
1979: Best Picture, Director, Actor (Dustin Hoffman), Supp. Actress (Meryl Streep), Adapted Screenplay
Nominations: Best Supp. Actor (Justin Henry), Supp. Actress (Jane Alexander), Cinematography, Editing

KRAYS, THE
1990, 119 mins, UK Ⓥ ⊙
D: Peter Medak **A:** Billie Whitelaw, Tom Bell, Gary Kemp, Martin Kemp, Susan Fleetwood (Parkfield/Fugitive)

A chilling, if somewhat monotonous, biopic charting the rise and fall of two prominent hoods in 1950-60s London, Cockney lads whose psychosexual warping leads them into ultraviolence. Screenwriter Philip Ridley deftly explores the cynical amorality of the us-vs.-them lower-class milieu, and the destructive effect of smothering mom Billie Whitelaw (in a superb performance) on her sociopathic twins, while virtually ignoring the standard cops-and-robbers dramaturgy of gangster films.

KREMLIN LETTER, THE
1970, 118 mins, US ⊑
D: John Huston **A:** Bibi Andersson, Richard Boone, Nigel Green, Dean Jagger, Max von Sydow, Orson Welles (20th Century-Fox)

An American official sends a letter about China to the Kremlin and it must be gotten back because of its explosiveness and lack of authorization. It is an engagingly photographed piece of business. Max von Sydow is a political strong man within the Russian regime. Ex–US Navy officer Patrick O'Neal has the job of salvaging the Kremlin Letter. But Russia, in the person of Richard Boone, would also like to retrieve the document.

KRIEMHILD'S REVENGE
See: Die Nibelungen

KRONOS
1957, 78 mins, US Ⓥ ⊙ ⊑
D: Kurt Neumann **A:** Jeff Morrow, Barbara Lawrence, John Emery, George O'Hanlon, Morris Ankrum (Regal)

A well-made, moderate-budget science-fictioner which boasts quality special effects that would do credit to a much-higher-budgeted film. Script tells of the efforts of a people from outer space to capture Earth's energy. To do this, they send an accumulator to Earth, which is directed in its movement by the head of a great American lab, whose brain has been seized by a higher intelligence from space.

KROTKI FILM O MILOSCI
See: Dekalog

KROTKI FILM O ZABIJANIU
See: Dekalog

KRULL
1983, 117 mins, US Ⓥ ⊙ ▭
D: Peter Yates A: Ken Marshall, Lysette Anthony, Freddie Jones, Francesca Annis, Alun Armstrong (Columbia)

Collection of action set pieces never jells into an absorbing narrative. Plot is as old as the art of storytelling itself. Young Prince Colwyn (Ken Marshall) falls heir to a besieged kingdom, but must survive a Ulysses-scaled series of tests on the way to rescuing his beautiful bride from the clutches of the Beast, whose army of slayers imperils his journey every step of the way. Crucial to Colwyn's quest is his recovery of the glaive, a razor-tipped, spinning boomerang that will enable him to combat the Beast.

K2
1991, 111 mins, UK/US Ⓥ ⊙
D: Franc Roddam A: Michael Biehn, Matt Craven, Raymond J. Barry, Hiroshi Fujioka, Patricia Charbonneau (Trans Pacific)

The buddy movie hits the Himalayas in an entertaining enough mountain-climbing saga. Story rapidly sets up two main characters: yuppy, womanizing Seattle lawyer Biehn and gentler, married-with-child professor Craven. When a US climbing group loses two of its members, Biehn and Craven take their place for the big one—an attempt on K2, the world's second highest peak and a w.k. engorger of climbers. Both thesps perform far better than the script deserves.

KUFFS
1992, 101 mins, US Ⓥ ⊙
D: Bruce A. Evans A: Christian Slater, Tony Goldwyn, Milla Jovovich, Bruce Boxleitner, Troy Evans (De Laurentiis)

Christian Slater's energy fails to carry a mishmash cop comedy very reminiscent of several Eddie Murphy films. Film veers from ultraviolence to slapstick comedy in an arbitrary and irritating fashion. Slater is the fish out of water this time, inheriting his murdered brother's police protection business. Avenging brother Bruce Box-

leitner's death is an utterly conventional quest, but the few laughs along the way are the film's raison d'être.

KUMONOSU-JO
(THRONE OF BLOOD; THE CASTLE OF THE SPIDER'S WEB; COBWEB CASTLE)
1957, 105 mins, Japan Ⓥ ⊙
D: Akira Kurosawa A: Toshiro Mifune, Isuzu Yamada, Minoru Chiaki, Takashi Shimura (Toho)

This Japanese adaptation of Shakespeare's *Macbeth* is all motion picture, an achievement of mood and photographic invention. Yet little but the embellished plot skeleton of Shakespeare's masterpiece survives. Leading Japanese actor Toshiro Mifune gives a ranting, raving, rooting, tooting performance in the central role. Isuzu Yamada is calm, cool, collected, and appropriately despicable as Lady M.

KUNDUN
1997, 134 mins, US Ⓥ ⊙ ▭
D: Martin Scorsese A: Tenzin Thuthob Tsarong, Gyurme Tethong, Tulku Jamyang Kunga Tenzin, Tenzin Yeshi Paichang, Tencho Gyalpo, Tsewang Migyur Khangsar (Cappa-De Fina/Touchstone)

Martin Scorsese's haunting meditation on the early life of the Dalai Lama is one from the heart, a majestic spectacle of images and sounds. But pic is bogged down by a routine screenplay that fails to provide a fresh perspective on Tibet's culture. Story begins in 1933 with the death of the 13th Dalai Lama and the search for a successor. It's told from the subjective point of view of the child destined to become the new Dalai Lama. At the end of World War II, he is confronted with China's aggressive campaign to convince the world that Tibet belongs to China. In 1949, Mao Zedong (Robert Lin) ruthlessly enforces tight military control over Tibet. Last section depicts the Chinese massacre of innocent Tibetans and the Dalai Lama's exile. The weakest sequences are the meetings between the Dalai Lama and Chairman Mao. In a performance that borders camp, the Chinese leader comes across as a monstrous caricature. Ultimately, *Kundun* emerges as a movie that's hypnotic without being truly compelling and sensuously stunning but not illuminating.
1997: Nominations: Best Cinematography, Original Dramatic Score, Art Direction, Costume Design

KVARTERET KORPEN
(RAVEN'S END)
1963, 100 mins, Sweden
D: Bo Widerberg **A:** Thommy Berggren, Keve Hjelm, Emy Storm, Ingvar Hirdwall (Europa)

This tender, well-observed pic about the coming-of-age of a young man in the Sweden of the thirties is slow and relies on a muted series of scenes to build to its moments of truth. A young writer tries to break out and finally does. In the process, the first rays of worker determination and the need to raise the level of the poverty-stricken sections of the population are well limned.

KWAIDAN
See: Kaidan

LA BAMBA
1987, 108 mins, US Ⓥ ⊙
D: Luis Valdez A: Lou Diamond Phillips, Esai Morales, Rosana De Soto, Elizabeth Peña, Danielle von Zerneck (New Visions)

There haven't been too many people who died at age 17 who have warranted the biopic treatment, but 1950s rock-and-roller Ritchie Valens proves a worthy exception. For anyone to achieve his dreams by 17 is close to miraculous. It was even more so for Valens, who, less than two years before his death, was a Mexican-American fruitpicker named Ricardo Valenzuela living in a tent. In Lou Diamond Phillips's sympathetic turn, Valens comes across as a very fine young man. Rosana De Soto scores as his tireless mother, and Elizabeth Peña has numerous dramatic moments as Bob's (Ritchie's brother) distraught mate.

LA BOHEME
1926, 101 mins, US ⊗
D: King Vidor A: Lillian Gish, John Gilbert, Renee Adoree, Edward Everett Horton, Roy D'Arcy (MGM)

The American representatives of the Milan music publisher who holds the rights to all of the Puccini works would not permit the utilization of that composer's score. William Axt wrote an entirely original accompaniment. The girls are going to go crazy over Jack Gilbert as Rodolphe, the lover, and the boys will like Mimi as played by Lillian Gish, although she gives a rather watered-milk characterization.

LABYRINTH
1986, 101 mins, US Ⓥ ⊙ ▭
D: Jim Henson A: David Bowie, Jennifer Connelly, Toby Froud, Shelley Thompson, Christopher Malcolm (Henson/Lucasfilm)

An array of bizarre creatures and David Bowie can't save Labyrinth from being a crashing bore. Characters created by Jim Henson and his team become annoying rather than endearing. Story soon loses its way and never comes close to archetypal myths and fears of great fairy tales. Instead it's an unconvincing coming-of-age saga.

LACEMAKER, THE
See: La Dentelliere

LACOMBE LUCIEN
1974, 136 mins, France/Italy/W. Germany
D: Louis Malle A: Pierre Blaise, Aurore Clement, Holger Lowenadler, Thérèse Giehse, Stéphane Bouy (NEF/UPF/Vides/Hallelujah)

Film looks at a young farm boy, 17, who drifts into the French gestapo by ignorance rather than intent. Pic displays the banality of evil and refrains from didactics or heroics. Lucien Lacombe, played with a remarkable flair by nonactor Pierre Blaise, wants to join the resistance (it is 1944) but is refused, and when dragged into the local French gestapo quarters, he gives away the head of the resistance. He takes pride in his act, while seemingly unaffected by the torture, decadence, and hysteria he sees around him. Pic is expertly directed and acted.

L.A. CONFIDENTIAL
1997, 136 mins, US Ⓥ ⊙ ▭
D: Curtis Hanson A: Kevin Spacey, Russell Crowe, Guy Pearce, James Cromwell, David Strathairn, Kim Basinger (Regency/Warner)

Drenched in the tawdry glamor of Hollywood in the early fifties, L.A. Confidential is an irresistible treat with enough narrative twists and memorable characters for a half dozen films. Sgt. Jack Vincennes (Kevin Spacey) gets plenty of mileage out of arresting celebs and acting as unofficial adviser on the Badge of Honor TV show. Bud White (Russell Crowe) is a rough, quick-tempered cop. Ed Exley (Guy Pearce) is a ruthlessly honest, college-educated young officer. A massacre at the Nite Owl Coffee Shop leaves six victims in its wake. White and Exley are thrown onto a collision course when it appears there may be more to the case than meets the eye. Intrigue and tension mount steadily in ways that are complicated but not confusing. Aussie actors Crowe and Pearce are dynamite. Spacey is aces as the somewhat older homicide veteran who relishes his status as a "real Hollywood" cop. Kim Basinger's vulnerable whore inspires her best screen work in quite some time. Working deeply within film noir territory, Hanson resists overdoing self-conscious stylistics, telling the story in superbly chosen settings that convey a pungent sense of a virtually vanished L.A.
1997: Best Actress (Kim Basinger), Screenplay Adaptation

Nominations: Best Picture, Director, Cinematography, Editing, Original Dramatic Score, Art Direction, Sound

LADIES' MAN, THE
1961, 106 mins, US ⓥ ⊙
D: Jerry Lewis **A:** Jerry Lewis, Helen Traubel, Kathleen Freeman, Hope Holiday, Lynn Ross (Paramount)

The slight plot concerns a girl-shy goof who becomes the houseboy in a sort of palatial girlatorium. Primarily the plot is little more than a limp excuse for a series of anything-goes slapstick sequences and sight gags punctuated by an occasional song or dance, an occasional romantic interlude, and a lethal dose of the star's homely philosophy. Lewis will try anything for a laugh. When he hits, it's a belly laugh. But too often he misses. The odd characteristic of this picture, and of many of Lewis's pictures, is its close resemblance to the style of an animated cartoon.

LADRI DI BICICLETTE
(US: THE BICYCLE THIEF;
BICYCLE THIEVES)
1948, 90 mins, Italy ⓥ ⊙
D: Vittorio De Sica **A:** Lamberto Maggiorani, Lianella Carrell, Enzo Staiola, Elena Altieri, Vittorio Antonucci (PDS)

Made with a cast of principals who were picked up in Rome's streets and had never before faced a camera, and with a story incredible in its simplicity, the picture is a pure exercise in directorial virtuosity. The beauty of it, however, is that this is never apparent. On the surface it is about nothing more than the theft of a bicycle from one of the army of unemployed in postwar Rome and his efforts to recover the vehicle, necessary to his job in a city where jobs are scarce. He sets out with his young son to find the bike. As the son Bruno, Enzo Staiola is the star of the film, if it has one. His funny face, serious but urchinlike manner, and ability to win laughs with the minor troubles he gets himself into rank him as a top moppet performer.
1949: Best Foreign Language Film

LADY AND THE TRAMP
1955, 75 mins, US ⓥ ⊙ ⊙
D: Hamilton Luske, Clyde Geronimi, Wilfred Jackson (Walt Disney)

The first animated feature in CinemaScope is a delight for the juveniles and lots of fun for adults. This time out the producer turned to members of the canine world and each of these hounds of

Disneyville reflects astute drawing-board know-how and richly humorous invention. The songs by Peggy Lee and Sonny Burke figure importantly, too.

LADY BE GOOD
1941, 110 mins, US ⓥ
D: Norman Z. McLeod **A:** Eleanor Powell, Ann Sothern, Robert Young, John Carroll, Red Skelton (M-G-M)

The picture looks as though director Norman Z. McLeod was given a time allotment to fill, no matter how, and he did. While confused, the story pattern is familiar—that of a crack songwriting team splitting up and becoming individually unsuccessful until resuming their partnership. In this instance it's the case of ex-waitress Ann Sothern and composer Robert Young.
1941: Best Song ("The Last Time I Saw Paris")

LADYBIRD, LADYBIRD
1994, 102 mins, UK ⓥ ⊙
D: Ken Loach **A:** Crissy Rock, Vladimir Vega, Ray Winstone, Sandie Lavelle, Mauricio Venegas (Parallax/Film Four)

A tough, steam-rolling, semi-verité look at a (non) family life in 1990s Britain through the eyes of a battered but ballsy unmarried mother caught between her own willfulness and an intrusive nanny state. Pic is propelled by a natural, gutsy performance by newcomer Crissy Rock. In tone and content, Loach hasn't directed anything this emotionally powerful since his earlier work of the 1960s and early 1970s. Based on a true story, pic has Maggie (Rock), a tough Liverpudlian mother of four, meeting gentle Paraguayan Jorge (Vladimir Vega) in a London bar where she sings. Loach progressively tightens the screws as the authorities take her baby girl into care, Jorge gets heat from the immigration authorities after his visa expires, and the relationship comes under strain as Maggie's insecurities resurface.

LADYBUGS
1992, 90 mins, US ⓥ ⊙
D: Sidney J. Furie **A:** Rodney Dangerfield, Jackee, Jonathan Brandis, Ilene Graff, Vinessa Shaw (Paramount/Ruddy & Morgan)

A klutzy would-be comedy about a girls' soccer team, *Ladybugs* is sexist, homophobic, and woefully unfunny to boot. As a salesman for a Colorado tycoon (Tom Parks), Rodney Dangerfield is put in charge of a soccer team. His bright idea for turning them into winners is to have his fiancée's son join the team in drag.

LADY CAROLINE LAMB ✉
1972, 122 mins, UK/Italy Ⓥ ▱
D: Robert Bolt A: Sarah Miles, Jon Finch, Robert Chamberlain, John Mills, Margaret Leighton, Pamela Brown (Anglo-EMI/Pulsar/Vides)

If it's a lushly, unabashedly romantic—yet tastefully executed—tale that you relish, then *Lady Caroline Lamb* is your likely cup of tea. For his first stint behind the camera, Robert Bolt comes up with a period piece. His tragic heroine, a controversial freethinker of the early British 1800s, has obvious parallels in present-day femme emancipation. Sarah Miles shines in a tailored role.

LADY CHATTERLEY'S LOVER
1981, 105 mins, France/UK Ⓥ ⊙
D: Just Jaeckin A: Sylvia Kristel, Shane Briant, Nicholas Clay, Ann Mitchell, Elizabeth Spriggs (Producteurs Associes/Cannon)

A cop-out adaptation of D. H. Lawrence's onetime scandalous literary hymn to human sexuality. It's coy and superficial, worth little as erotic fare and not considerably more as sentimental drama. The sex scenes are all the more unmoving because the surrounding story and characters are inadequately realized. Lady Chatterley (Sylvia Kristel) is the wife of an English aristocrat totally paralyzed from the waist down. Starved for carnal affection, she becomes the lover of Chatterley's gamekeeper.

LADY EVE, THE
1941, 90 mins, US Ⓥ
D: Preston Sturges A: Henry Fonda, Barbara Stanwyck, Charles Coburn, Eugene Pallette, William Demarest, Eric Blore (Paramount)

Third writer-director effort of Preston Sturges is laugh entertainment of top proportions with its combo of slick situations, spontaneous dialogue, and a few slapstick falls tossed in for good measure. Basically, story is the age-old tale of Eve snagging Adam, but dressed up with continually infectious fun and good humor. Barbara Stanwyck is girl-lure of trio of confidence operators. She's determined, quick-witted, resourceful, and personable. Henry Fonda is a serious young millionaire, a cinch pushover for girl's advances on the boat—but pair fall in love. Sturges provides numerous sparkling situations in his direction

and keeps picture moving at a merry pace.
1941: Nomination: Best Original Story

LADY FOR A DAY
1933, 93 mins, US Ⓥ
D: Frank Capra A: Warren William, May Robson, Guy Kibbee, Glenda Farrell, Walter Connolly (Columbia)

Lady for a Day asks the spectator to believe in the improbable. It's Hans Christian Andersen stuff written by a hard-boiled journalist and transferred to the screen by trick-wise Hollywoodites. Warren William is the superstitious gambler for whom Apple Annie is a good-luck omen. It is he who stage manages the gigantic make-believe, whereby the shoddy peddler of apples becomes a "lady for a day," to preserve her finely reared daughter's illusions that her mother is a society somebody.
1932/33: Nominations: Best Picture, Director, Actress (May Robson), Adaptation

LADY FROM SHANGHAI, THE
1948, 86 mins, US Ⓥ ⊙
D: Orson Welles A: Rita Hayworth, Orson Welles, Everett Sloane, Ted De Corsia, Glenn Anders (Columbia)

Script is wordy and full of holes which need the plug of taut storytelling and more forthright action. Rambling style used by Orson Welles has occasional flashes of imagination, particularly in the tricky backgrounds he uses to unfold the yarn, but effects, while good on their own, are distracting to the murder plot. Contributing to the stylized effect stressed by Welles is the photography, which features artful compositions entirely in keeping with the production mood. Welles uses an Irish brogue and others portray erratic characters with little reality. Hayworth isn't called on to do much more than look beautiful. Best break for players goes to Everett Sloane, and he gives a credible interpretation of the crippled criminal attorney.

LADY GAMBLES, THE
1949, 98 mins, US
D: Michael Gordon A: Barbara Stanwyck, Robert Preston, Stephen McNally, Edith Barrett, Leif Erickson (Universal)

An entry in the psychiatric sweepstakes—this time of a gal who becomes a gambling addict because of a guilt complex. Story meanders too long for top results. Barbara Stanwyck is the lady who gambles and the role is practically a tour de force for her, giving her numerous opportunities for emotions, ranging from humor to hysterics. Standout in the film is Stephen McNally, as the professional gambler who takes her under his wing.

LADY HAMILTON
See: That Hamilton Woman

LADYHAWKE
1985, 124 mins, US ⓥ ⊙ ▭
D: Richard Donner **A:** Matthew Broderick, Rutger Hauer, Michelle Pfeiffer, Leo McKern, John Wood (Warner/20th Century-Fox)

A very likable, very well-made fairy tale. Handsome Rutger Hauer is well cast as the dark and moody knight who travels with a hawk by day. Lovely Michelle Pfeiffer is perfect as the enchanting beauty who appears by night, always in the vicinity of a vicious but protective wolf. As readers of one or more variations of this legend will instantly recognize, Pfeiffer is the hawk and Hauer the wolf, each changing form as the sun rises and sets, former lovers cursed to never humanly share the clock together.

LADY ICE
1973, 93 mins, US ⓥ
D: Tom Gries **A:** Donald Sutherland, Jennifer O'Neill, Robert Duvall, Patrick Magee (Tomorrow)

A routine programmer, the handsomely lensed actioner pits jewel thieves against an insurance-company private eye (Sutherland) in recovery of $3 million in ice from a Chicago holdup. O'Neill turns out to be the lady in charge of the caper. The rather thin plot is made up of numerous chases, a bit of violence, and long, dull passages of Sutherland trying to make it with the lady criminal.

LADY IN A CAGE
1964, 94 mins, US ⓥ
D: Walter Grauman **A:** Olivia de Havilland, Ann Sothern, Jeff Corey, James Caan, Jennifer Billingsley, Rafael Campos (Paramount)

There's not a single redeeming character or characteristic to producer Luther Davis's sensationalistically vulgar screenplay. Had the basic premise—of an invalid woman (Olivia de Havilland) trapped in her private home elevator when the power is cut off—been developed simply, neatly, and realistically, gripping dramatic entertainment might have ensued. But Davis has infested the woman's house with a scummy assortment of characters: a delirious wino (Jeff Corey), a plump prostitute

(Ann Sothern), and three vicious young hoodlums (James Caan, Jennifer Billingsley, and Rafael Campos). De Havilland gives one of those ranting, raving, wild-eyed performances often thought of as Academy Award–oriented.

LADY IN CEMENT
1968, 93 mins, US ⓥ ▭
D: Gordon Douglas **A:** Frank Sinatra, Raquel Welch, Richard Conte, Martin Gabel, Lainie Kazan (20th Century-Fox)

Follow-up to *Tony Rome* stars Frank Sinatra as a Miami private eye on the trail of people in whom there couldn't be less interest. Raquel Welch adds her limited, but beauteous contribution, and Dan Blocker is excellent as a sympathetic heavy.

LADY IN RED, THE
1979, 93 mins, US ⓥ ⊙
D: Lewis Teague **A:** Pamela Sue Martin, Robert Conrad, Louise Fletcher, Christopher Lloyd, Robert Hogan (New World)

With her sights vaguely set on Hollywood, farm girl Pamela Sue Martin heads first for Chicago, where one mishap after another lands her in prison, then in the employ of classy madam Louise Fletcher. Lewis Teague guides his large cast reasonably well through John Sayles's craftsmanlike script.

LADY IN THE DARK
1944, 100 mins, US
D: Mitchell Leisen **A:** Ginger Rogers, Ray Milland, Jon Hall, Warner Baxter, Barry Sullivan, Mischa Auer (Paramount)

Produced on a lavish scale against backgrounds of a glittering character with costuming that fills the eye, *Lady in the Dark* is at the outset a technically superior piece of craftsmanship based on the Broadway stage hit by Moss Hart, with music by Kurt Weill and lyrics by Ira Gershwin. Ginger Rogers plays the editor of a fashion magazine who, realizing she's on the edge of a nervous breakdown, finally places herself in the hands of a psychoanalyst.

1944: Nominations: Best Color Cinematography, Color Art Direction, Scoring of a Musical Picture

LADY IN THE LAKE
1947, 103 mins, US ⓥ
D: Robert Montgomery **A:** Robert Montgomery, Audrey Totter, Lloyd Nolan, Tom Tully, Leon Ames (M-G-M)

Lady in the Lake employs a novel method of telling the story, in which the camera itself is the protagonist, playing the lead role from the subjective viewpoint of star Robert Montgomery. Idea comes off excellently, transferring what otherwise would have been a fair whodunit into socko screen fare. Camera thus gets bashed by the villains, hits back in turn, smokes cigarettes, makes love, and, in one of the most suspenseful sequences, drives a car in a hair-raising race that ends in a crash. Montgomery plays private detective Philip Marlowe, who's dealt into a couple of murders when he tries to sell a story based on his experiences to a horror-story mag.

LADY IN WHITE
1988, 112 mins, US Ⓥ ⊙
D: Frank LaLoggia **A:** Lukas Haas, Len Cariou, Alex Rocco, Katherine Helmond, Jason Presson (New Century/Vista)

A superb supernatural horror film. At the center is big-eyed Lukas Haas, the youngest boy of a loving and earthy Italian family that is headed by his widowed dad, Angelo (Alex Rocco). On Halloween night, his school chums lock him in his classroom cloakroom, where he is visited by those who wouldn't ordinarily be there—the ghost of a young girl about his age and a masked man searching for something in the heating grate. As the mystery unravels, it is revealed how they are connected.

LADY IS WILLING, THE
1942, 93 mins, US
D: Mitchell Leisen **A:** Marlene Dietrich, Fred MacMurray, Aline MacMahon, Arline Judge, Stanley Ridges (Columbia/Feldman Group)

A racy and sophisticated marital comedy that carries a good share of amusement for adult audiences. Picture carries light and breezy tempo in the first portion, with adoration of cute baby as motivating factor in holding interest. An inconclusive finish, with the oldy situation of an emergency operation necessary to save the child's life, and the pendulum-swinging problem of life-and-death crisis, allows the tale to sluff off with elemental formula convenience.

LADY JANE
1986, 142 mins, UK/US Ⓥ ⊙
D: Trevor Nunn **A:** Helena Bonham Carter, Cary Elwes, John Wood, Michael Hordern, Jill Bennett, Jane Lapotaire (Paramount)

A tragic historical romance tinged with a strong 1960s feeling. In 1553, some extraordinary maneuverings brought to the English throne the scholarly but unprepared 15-year-old Lady Jane Grey. Lady Jane's parents and the Duke of Northumberland scheme to force a marriage between Jane and the latter's dissolute 17-year-old son, Guilford Dudley, to keep Britain free of the pope's influence. Pic belongs squarely within the traditions of good taste and literate dialogue one associates with the British cinema. Performances are all top-drawer, beginning with newcomer Helena Bonham Carter in the title role.

LADY KILLER
1933, 67 mins, US Ⓥ ⊙
D: Roy Del Ruth **A:** James Cagney, Mae Clarke, Leslie Fenton, Margaret Lindsay, Henry O'Neill (Warner)

Whole picture goes on a rampage with the you-be-damned personality that Cagney has so assiduously developed. Cagney plays an underworld crook who by accident crashes a Hollywood studio and earns his way to picture fame. Crook angle is handled with a cheerful style of humor and there is a certain spirit about the Cagney character, played in his energetic way that carries its own persuasive charm. Comedy is first-rate. Mae Clarke does extremely well as the gang girl.

LADYKILLERS, THE
1955, 96 mins, UK Ⓥ
D: Alexander Mackendrick **A:** Alec Guinness, Cecil Parker, Herbert Lom, Peter Sellers, Katie Johnson, Danny Green (Ealing)

This is an amusing piece of hokum, being a parody of American gangsterdom interwoven with whimsy and exaggeration that makes it more of a macabre farce. Alec Guinness sinks his personality almost to the level of anonymity. Basic idea of thieves making a frail old lady an unwitting accomplice in their schemes is carried out in ludicrous and often tense situations.
1956: Nomination: Best Original Screenplay

LADY L
1965, 124 mins, US/Italy ▭
D: Peter Ustinov **A:** Sophia Loren, Paul Newman, David Niven, Claude Dauphin, Philippe Noiret, Michel Piccoli (M-G-M/Ponti)

Story, set in Paris and Switzerland at the turn of the century, has Loren as an aging, allegedly aristocratic mystery woman recounting her life story for the benefit of a biographer (Cecil Parker). David Niven is immaculately debonair and wittily amusing, but Paul Newman is not happily cast—his role calling out for the dependable mixture of solidity and lightness. Ustinov weighs in with a choice cameo as the doddering Prince Otto.

LADY OF BURLESQUE
(UK: STRIPTEASE LADY)
1943, 89 mins, US Ⓥ
D: William A. Wellman A: Barbara Stanwyck, Michael O'Shea, J. Edward Bromberg, Iris Adrian, Marion Martin (United Artists)

Although based on Gypsy Rose Lee's novel *G-String Murders,* story plows an obvious straight line in generating the whodunit angles, and two gal burlesque performers are knocked off in succession before the culprit is disclosed. But gallant trouping by Barbara Stanwyck, colorful background provided by Stromberg, and speedy direction by William Wellman carry picture through for good entertainment for general audiences.
1943: Nomination: Best Scoring of a Dramatic Picture

LADY ON A TRAIN
1945, 96 mins, US
D: Charles David A: Deanna Durbin, Ralph Bellamy, Edward Everett Horton, Dan Duryea, George Coulouris, Allen Jenkins (Universal)

A mystery comedy containing plenty of fun for both whodunit and laugh fans. Deanna Durbin sings three tunes as well as handling herself excellently in the comedy role. Actress is seen as a murder-mystery addict who witnesses a murder from her train window while arriving in Grand Central Station. Police discount her story and she turns to David Bruce, mystery writer, for help.
1945: Nomination: Best Sound

LADY OSCAR
1979, 122 mins, Japan Ⓥ
D: Jacques Demy A: Catriona Maccoll, Barry Stokes, Christina Bohm, Jonas Bergstrom, Terence Budd, Constance Chapman (Kitty Music)

Jacques Demy has given this international project an opulent, disarming naïveté in keeping with its adaptation from a very popular Japanese comic strip, also a stage show in Japan. Story takes place in 19th-century France, where a girl is brought up like a boy by her noble martinet father fed up with a long line of girls.

She becomes the bodyguard of Marie Antoinette, and wears a man's uniform and is known as Oscar. The housekeeper's son loves her but she sees him only as a brother. This is to change as France heads for revolution. Shooting on actual location in Versailles is an asset.

LADY SINGS THE BLUES
1972, 144 mins, US Ⓥ ⊙ ▭
D: Sidney J. Furie A: Diana Ross, Billy Dee Williams, Richard Pryor, James Callahan, Paul Hampton (Paramount)

Individual opinions about this film may vary markedly, depending on a person's age, knowledge of jazz tradition and feeling for it, and how one wishes to regard the late Billie Holiday as both a force and a victim of her times. Although the film serves as a very good screen-debut vehicle for Diana Ross, it still requires a severe gritting of teeth to overlook the truncations, telescoping, and omissions. Holiday's personal romantic life herein is restricted to Billy Dee Williams as Louis McKay, her third husband. Richard Pryor registers strongly as her longtime piano-playing friend.
1972: Nominations: Best Actress (Diana Ross), Original Story & Screenplay, Costume Design, Art Direction, Adapted Score

LADY'S MORALS, A
1930, 86 mins, US
D: Sidney Franklin A: Grace Moore, Reginald Denny, Wallace Beery, Jobyna Howland (Cosmopolitan/M-G-M)

A costume play that rises above traditional handicaps. The picture is full of brilliant touches and has some fine pictorial backgrounds. It has one serious defect. The romantic story is finished many hundreds of feet before the actual conclusion. Paul (Reginald Denny), a young composer, is in love with Jenny Lind (Grace Moore) and pursues her from place to place, at length making an impression on the songstress by his persistency. Chief of picture's assets is Moore, an actress of indescribable charm. Denny is a revelation in his part.

LADY VANISHES, THE
1938, 96 mins, UK Ⓥ ⊙ ▭
D: Alfred Hitchcock A: Margaret Lockwood, Michael Redgrave, Paul Lukas, May Whitty, Cecil Parker, Linden Travers (Gainsborough/Gaumont-British)

An elderly English governess, homeward bound, disappears from a transcontinental train, and a young girl, who says she recently received a blow on the head, is confronted by numerous other passengers who say they never saw the governess. This becomes so persistent the girl finally thinks she has gone nuts. The story is sometimes eerie and eventually melodramatic, but it's all so well done as to make for intense interest.

LADY VANISHES, THE
1979, 99 mins, UK Ⓥ ⊙
D: Anthony Page **A:** Elliott Gould, Cybill Shepherd, Angela Lansbury, Herbert Lom, Ian Carmichael, Arthur Lowe (Hammer)

A midatlantic mishmash with some moderately amusing moments but no cohesive style. Cybill Shepherd as a madcap Yank heiress and Elliott Gould as a *Life*-mag photographer foil a political conspiracy aboard a train outbound from prewar Germany. Alfred Hitchcock's original version, circa 1938, had pretty much everything the remake doesn't.

LADY WINDERMERE'S FAN
1925, 79 mins, US ⊗
D: Ernst Lubitsch **A:** Ronald Colman, Irene Rich, May McAvoy, Bert Lytell (Warner)

The tempo of this Oscar Wilde play is not that which Lubitsch can most effectively handle. Farce is his forte, and here they gave him a comedy-drama which is in reality almost melodrama and expect him to be at his best. He is good, but far from at his best. Beautifully cast in so far as the five leading players are concerned, well acted by them, and with clever touches of the director's art furnished by Lubitsch.

LADY WITHOUT PASSPORT, A
1950, 72 mins, US
D: Joseph H. Lewis **A:** Hedy Lamarr, John Hodiak, James Craig, George Macready, Steven Geray (M-G-M)

Hedy Lamarr is the lady of the title. Lingering in Cuba, she is used by an undercover immigration agent to set up a trap for the smuggling ring operated by George Macready. A complication is the romantic development between the lady and the agent. Footage lensed in Cuba helps to supply an authentic touch.

LADY WITH THE DOG, THE
See: *Dama S Sobachkoy*

LADY WITH THE LAMP, THE
1951, 110 mins, UK
D: Herbert Wilcox **A:** Anna Neagle, Michael Wilding, Gladys Young, Felix Aylmer, Sybil Thorndike (Wilcox-Neagle/British Lion)

Anna Neagle's characterization of Florence Nightingale is a sincerely moving study. The story opens shortly before the Crimean War when Nightingale, with a training in nursing, refuses to be a member of the leisure class into which she was born, but insists on continuing her work. The minister of war, a steadfast believer in Nightingale's theories, gets her to organize a band of nurses to tend the wounded at Scutari. Michael Wilding is not too happily cast as Sidney Herbert, war minister. The strong featureed cast includes Felix Aylmer with an exceptionally good study of Lord Palmerston.

LADY WITH THE LITTLE DOG, THE
See: *Dama S Sobachkoy*

LAIR OF THE WHITE WORM, THE
1989, 93 mins, UK Ⓥ ⊙
D: Ken Russell **A:** Amanda Donohoe, Hugh Grant, Catherine Oxenberg, Sammi Davis, Peter Capaldi, Stratton Johns (White Lair/Vestron)

Adapted from a tale by Bram Stoker, creator of Dracula, *Lair*, a rollicking, terrifying, postpsychedlic head trip, features a fangy vampiress of unmatched erotic allure. Donohoe as the vampire seductress projects a beguiling sexuality that should suck the resistance out of all but the most cold-blooded critics. She is also hilarious, a characteristic shared by everyone and everything in *The Lair of the White Worm*.

LAKE PLACID
1999, 82 mins, US Ⓥ ⊙ ▭
D: Steve Miner **A:** Bill Pullman, Bridget Fonda, Oliver Platt, Brendan Gleeson, Betty White, David Lewis (Rocking Chair/Phoenix/Fox 2000)

This is a lamer-than-lame attempt at stirring up the summer movie scene with a scary creature-in-the-depths scenario. It seriously lacks a genuine third act containing the kind of roller-coaster thrills expected from vet horror helmer Steve Miner. In a glassy lake in Maine a diver is chomped in half. Boston paleontologist Kelly Scott (Bridget Fonda) studies a tooth extracted from the diver's torso and finds it to be "ancient." Soon Fish-and-Game studmuffin Jack Wells (Bill Pullman) must contend with a fresh wave of attacks by the creature, which turns out to be a 30-foot crocodile that has managed to swim from its warm natural habitat in Asia.

Whatever attracted the fine cast to the script is now gone, as they all search desperately for their characters.

LA LUNA
1979, 145 mins, Italy
D: Bernardo Bertolucci **A:** Jill Clayburgh, Matthew Barry, Renato Salvatori, Tomas Milian, Fred Gwynne (20th Century-Fox/Fiction)

The saga is of Jill Clayburgh as Yank lyric star afflicted with professional neuroses, fading pipes, a son on drugs, and a close-to-incest mother-son development. Sudden death of singer's spouse and decision to resume singing in Italy, with son Joe accompanying, moves the scene to Rome where the mother-son cleft takes over from Verdi appearances. Clayburgh is hard-pressed to sustain the melodramatics.

LAMBADA
1990, 98 mins, US
D: Joel Silberg **A:** J. Eddie Peck, Melora Hardin, Shabba-Doo, Ricky Paull Goldin (Cannon)

Eddie Peck plays the Beverly Hills teacher by day, East L.A. lambada dancer by night, his sculpted dancer's physique straining the credibility of this most unlikely of teen-fantasy scenarios. He forgoes evenings at home with his wife and son to motorbike over to the lambada club, where he teaches math in the back room to a gang of east-side dropouts. The dancing occupies little screen time compared with the sudsy intrigue sexually precocious Sandy (Melora Hardin) stirs up on the school front.

LAMERICA
1994, 125 mins, Italy/France
D: Gianni Amelio **A:** Enrico Lo Verso, Michele Placido, Carmelo Di Mazzarelli, Piro Milkani (CGG Tiger/Arena)

Gino, an apprentice swindler, comes to Albania with the more experienced Fiore (Michele Placido) to buy a shoe factory they never intend to run. Their get-rich-quick scheme is to cash in on Italian government aid to Albania's devastated post-Communist economy, but first they need to find a local puppet company president. The choice falls on 80-year-old Spiro (nonpro Carmelo Di Mazzarelli), a helpless senior who has been driven mad by 20 years of hard labor in the Communist prisons. The story takes its first turn when Spiro disappears. Gino's angry search for the old man is a frightening descent into the world of no-way-out poverty. Pic's uncompromising scorn for the two exploiters is matched by its hellish vision of a starving nation desperately searching for an escape hatch.

LANA IN LOVE
1991, 85 mins, Canada
D: Bashar Shbib **A:** Daphna Kastner, Clark Gregg, Susan Eyton-Jones, Ivan E. Roth, Michael Gillis, Cheryl Platt (Oneira)

An amusing tale of mistaken identities quickly falls apart as Daphna Kastner's shrill voice belittles love interest Marty, stifling both their budding romance and pic. Legit thesp Clark Gregg makes an impressive screen debut as the plumber Marty who arrives at the wrong address. Lana is waiting for a podiatrist and assumes Marty is her mystery man.

LANCELOT AND GUINEVERE (US: SWORD OF LANCELOT)
1963, 116 mins, UK
D: Cornel Wilde **A:** Cornel Wilde, Jean Wallace, Brian Aherne, George Baker, John Longden (Emblem/Universal)

This version of the much-told tale of King Arthur and the Knights of the Round Table is an elaborately mounted production that generates fair amounts of interest and excitement when the fighting's going on but barely rises above the routine in telling the legend. It's Cornel Wilde most of the way, he having coproduced, directed, and costarred with his wife, Jean Wallace, latter making a beautiful Guinevere.

LAND AND FREEDOM
1995, 106 mins, UK/Spain/Germany
D: Ken Loach **A:** Ian Hart, Rosana Pastor, Iciar Bollain, Tom Gilroy, Marc Martinez (Parallax/Messidor/Road Movies)

Film follows a Liverpudlian to the Republican trenches and political treachery of the Spanish Civil War. Despite a slight windiness in its political discussions, pic's superb performances, gentle humor, human warmth, action sequences, and beautifully teased-out love story should make this one of the must-see art movies of the year. Loach's real triumph is to get the viewer rooting for characters in a conflict that, for most, is as remote as the Trojan War.

LAND BEFORE TIME, THE
1988, 66 mins, US
D: Don Bluth (Sullivan-Bluth/Amblin)

Sure, kids like dinosaurs, but beyond that, premise doesn't find far to go. Story is about Littlefoot (Gabriel Damon), an innocent dinosaur tyke who gets separated from his family and after a perilous journey finds them again in a new land. Idea develops that surviving in a changing environment depends on achieving unity among the species. For the most part, pic is about as engaging as what's found on Saturday-morning TV.

LANDLORD, THE
1970, 112 mins, US
D: Hal Ashby A: Beau Bridges, Lee Grant, Diana Sands, Pearl Bailey, Louis Gossett (United Artists/Mirisch)

Beau Bridges heads the uniformly excellent cast as a bored rich youth who buys a black ghetto apartment building and learns something about life. Bridges and his economically secure family are played off and against the black tenants. Then, Bridges's sexual encounter with married Diana Sands results in a mixed-race baby and a confrontation with some hard facts of life.
1970: Nomination: Best Supp. Actress (Lee Grant)

LAND OF THE PHARAOHS
1955, 103 mins, US ⓥ ⊙ ▭
D: Howard Hawks A: Jack Hawkins, Joan Collins, Dewey Martin, Alexis Minotis, James Robertson Justice (Continental/Warner)

Egypt of 5,000 years ago comes to life in a tremendous film spectacle. Audience is constantly overwhelmed with cast of thousands, tremendously sized settings, or the surging background score by Dimitri Tiomkin. The story tells of a great pharaoh, ably played by Jack Hawkins, who for 30 years drives his people to build a pyramid in which his body and treasure shall rest secure forevermore, and of a woman, portrayed by Joan Collins, who conspires to win his kingdom and riches for herself.

LAND THAT TIME FORGOT, THE
1975, 91 mins, UK ⓥ
D: Kevin Connor A: Doug McClure, John McEnery, Susan Penhaligon, Keith Barron (American International)

The "land" in question is an uncharted island, icy on the outside and smoldering within, that's populated with all sorts of big critters. This island of Caprona is reached by a German submarine which torpedoes and sinks the ship. The survivors, led by Doug McClure, come aboard and capture the sub. The sub is lost in the Ant-

arctic. Luckily, they spot Caprona. Somebody identifies the problem immediately. "This can't be. These creatures have been extinct for millions of years."

LAND UNKNOWN, THE
1957, 78 mins, US ⓥ ▭
D: Virgil Vogel A: Jock Mahoney, Shawn Smith, William Reynolds, Henry Brandon, Douglas R. Kennedy (Universal)

This imaginative science-fictioner recounts adventures of a helicopter party forced down in area untouched by the Ice Age, going back to the Mesozoic era, a setting that provides thrills as party fights against such creatures as a giant Tyrannosaurus rex and a swimming elasmosaurus. Stark realism is afforded through the remarkable smooth and lifelike movement of these creatures, special effected by Fred Knoth, Orien Ernest, and Jack Kevan.

LASER MAN, THE
1988, 92 mins, US/Hong Kong ⓥ
D: Peter Wang A: Marc Hayashi, Maryann Urbano, Tony Leung, Peter Wang, Joan Copeland (Wang/Film Workshop)

A quirky, cross-cultural, high-tech comedy about serious matters. Self-consciously implausible story concerning the manipulation of a laser expert by big business serves as a pegboard on which Wang hangs any number of amusing observations about the the Melting Pot, 1988, particularly where Chinese Americans are concerned. Unfortunately, the plotting is not always hospitable to the engagingly flippant tone Wang mostly maintains.

LASKY JEDNE PLAVOVLASKY (US: LOVES OF A BLONDE; A BLONDE IN LOVE)
1965, 85 mins, Czechoslovakia ⓥ ⊙
D: Milos Forman A: Hana Brejchova, Vladimir Pucholt, Vladimir Mensik, Antonin Blazejovsky, Jiri Hruby (Barrandov)

This is a lightweight item with plenty of charm to overcome the basic fragility of its plot. Boy meets girl at a dance organized for factory workers. Couple falls in love and eventually goes to bed, where the usual promises are exchanged. The day after, each returns to work, but the gal believes the boy and tracks him down at his surprised parents' home. Humorous observations on the human scene appear to be Forman's forte.

LASSIE
1994, 92 mins, US ⓥ
D: Daniel Petrie A: Thomas Guiry, Helen Slater, Jon Tenney, Brittany Boyd, Fred-

eric Forrest, Richard Farnsworth (Broadway/Paramount)

New telling is a well-wrought, affecting adventure, thanks to the steady hand of vet helmsman Daniel Petrie and a sensitive, insightful screenplay that focuses on the human drama while providing a long leash to the famed collie's canine charisma, cunning, and athletic prowess. This *Lassie* is classy. Strongest appeal lies in the sharply observed and emotionally rich portrayal of a family confronting challenges together. Contractor Steve Turner (Jon Tenney) decides to move his family from Baltimore to the ancestral country home of his late wife, in the Shenandoah Valley. On the way to their old Virginia home, a spry four-pawed friend named Lassie leaps into their car and their lives, and helps them face the challenges of living on the land.

LASSIE COME HOME
1943, 90 mins, US ⍟ ⊙
D: Fred M. Wilcox **A:** Roddy McDowall, Donald Crisp, May Whitty, Edmund Gwenn, Elsa Lanchester, Elizabeth Taylor (M-G-M)

Nice entertainment enhanced by color photography and good scenic shots. Lassie, a beautiful collie, is given a great deal of camera attention and is docile, if not extraordinarily trained. Her Yorkshire owner (Donald Crisp) sells her to the lord of the manor, thus depriving his son (Roddy McDowall) of his bosom companion. The dog escapes a couple of times to rejoin McDowall, then finally makes a trek of hundreds of miles from Scotland to England to get back to the kid.

LASSITER
1984, 100 mins, US ⍟ ⊙
D: Roger Young **A:** Tom Selleck, Jane Seymour, Lauren Hutton, Bob Hoskins, Ed Lauter (Golden Harvest)

Set in London in 1934, part caper picture, part intrigue story. Nick Lassiter (Tom Selleck) is an elegant jewel thief who is blackmailed by a coalition of the FBI and English police to liberate $10 million in Nazi diamonds passing through London. The diamonds are to be transported out of London by none other than Lauren Hutton, playing German agent Countess Kari von Fursten. Hutton is totally unbelievable with her Germanic accent and evil habits.

LAST ACTION HERO
1993, 130 mins, US ⍟ ⊙ ⊡
D: John McTiernan **A:** Arnold Schwarzenegger, F. Murray Abraham, Art Carney, Charles Dance, Anthony Quinn (Columbia/Oak)

A joyless, soulless mishmash of fantasy, industry in-jokes, self-referential parody, film-buff gags, and too-big action set pieces. Arnold Schwarzenegger plays indestructible screen superhero Jack Slater. Little 11-year-old Danny Madigan (Austin O'Brien) is invited by projectionist friend Nick (Robert Prosky) to a private screening of Slater's latest picture. Nick presents Danny with a golden magic ticket with which Danny passes into the world on-screen. Benedict (Charles Dance), sinister triggerman of a mobster (Anthony Quinn), comes into possession of the magic ticket and takes his evil ways into the "real" world of Times Square, followed by Danny and Slater, who is dismayed to discover that violence can actually hurt and that his entire life has been lived in movies. It's all heavy, empty, and exceptionally noisy. Jabbering incessantly and always badgering his hero, O'Brien delivers a one-note performance.

LAST AMERICAN HERO, THE
1973, 95 mins, US ⍟ ⊡
D: Lamont Johnson **A:** Jeff Bridges, Valerie Perrine, Geraldine Fitzgerald, Ned Beatty, Art Lund, Gary Busey (20th Century-Fox)

After a fumbling start, *The Last American Hero* settles into some good, gritty, family Americana, with Jeff Bridges excellent as a flamboyant auto racer determined to succeed on his own terms and right a wrong to his father, played expertly by Art Lund. Between the script, Lamont Johnson's sure direction, and the excellent performances, all but the early choppy scenes add up to a well-told story.

LAST ANGRY MAN, THE
1959, 100 mins, US ⍟
D: Daniel Mann **A:** Paul Muni, David Wayne, Betsy Palmer, Luther Adler, Joby Baker (Columbia)

As pungent and indelible as Brooklyn on a hot summer afternoon, the film is taken from Gerald Green's bestselling novel about a Jewish doctor. The conflict arises from the lifetime of selfless service by the doctor (Paul Muni) juxtaposed to the commercial demands of contemporary television. Television wants to exploit the

Jewish doctor. Muni gives a superlative performance.
1959: Nominations: Best Actor (Paul Muni), B&W Art Direction

LAST BOY SCOUT, THE
1991, 105 mins, US Ⓥ ⊙ ▭
D: Tony Scott **A:** Bruce Willis, Damon Wayans, Chelsea Field, Noble Willingham, Taylor Negron, Danielle Harris (Geffen/Silver)

There's nothing special about this entertaining if mindless shoot-'em-up other than an ample supply of amusing juvenile put-downs and elaborate action sequences. Equipped with a persona suited to his gifts, Bruce Willis limns a former secret-service agent whose devotion to justice (accounting for pic's title) put him out on the street scrounging for work as a sleazy p.i. The plot is a haze of barely connected story lines about political corruption, pro football, gambling, infidelity, and blackmail—a sort of poor man's *The Big Sleep,* but here all the questions are answered by another car chase, smashing someone in the face, or shooting someone in the forehead.

LAST COMMAND, THE
1928, 90 mins, US Ⓥ ⊕
D: Josef von Sternberg **A:** Emil Jannings, Evelyn Brent, William Powell, Nicholas Soussanin (Paramount)

Russia in the early days of the revolution. Emil Jannings is the commander in chief of the czar's armies in the field. The general, overthrown by the revolutionists, drifts to Hollywood, to become a $7.50-a-day extra waiting for a call. A Russian picture director recognizes a photo of the general as the same who whipped him in Russia in 1914, when the director then was a starving actor-revolutionist. They make him a general again, at $7.50 daily, with many studio scenes, to lead a movie army of Russians. Herman Mankiewicz's titles are no small part of the interest, always perfectly placed and phrased.
1927/28: Best Actor (Emil Jennings)
Nominations: Best Picture, Original Story

LAST DANCE
1996, 103 mins, US Ⓥ
D: Bruce Beresford **A:** Sharon Stone, Rob Morrow, Randy Quaid, Peter Gallagher, Jack Thompson (Touchstone)

Respectably crafted on most levels, this pic about an unrepentant death row femme whose case is taken up by a clemency-board rookie never resonates at any deep emotional level and completely blows what kudos it's acquired in the final reel. Pic's center of conscience is young Rick Hayes (Rob Morrow). With shortish red hair, a tattoo on the back of her hand, a passable southern accent, and blue prison duds, Stone gives her part a decent shot, with no obvious Oscar grandstanding. Morrow is blandish.

LAST DAYS OF CHEZ NOUS, THE
1992, 96 mins, Australia Ⓥ ⊙
D: Gillian Armstrong **A:** Lisa Harrow, Bruno Ganz, Kerry Fox, Miranda Otto, Bill Hunter (Chapman/AFFC)

This postfeminist drama about two sisters involved with the same man is beautifully acted and crafted, despite some script problems. Fortyish Beth (Lisa Harrow) works hard as a writer, bosses people around, lacks emotion, and finds it difficult to "be part of a couple," which is hard on her French husband, J.P. (Bruno Ganz). Beth's daughter by her first marriage, Annie (Miranda Otto), is a gangly teen on the brink of her first love affair. Everyone gets along until the return from overseas of Vicki (Kerry Fox), Beth's younger sister.

LAST DAYS OF DISCO, THE
1998, 113 mins, US Ⓥ ⊕
D: Whit Stillman **A:** Chloe Sevigny, Kate Beckinsale, Chris Eigeman, Matt Keeslar, Mackenzie Astin, Matthew Ross (Castle Rock/Westerly)

The good times don't exactly roll in *The Last Days of Disco,* which is as interesting to watch for its serious disjunction between style and content as for its cute cast and fabulous soundtrack. Whit Stillman's stiff directorial approach ill suits the sensual ambience of the club scene so intently depicted, and the characters seem to have walked through the wrong door to turn up in this flamboyant druggie scene. One September in the early 1980s, a bunch of friends converge on the hottest disco in New York. Nervous young ad exec, Jimmy (Mackenzie Astin), is embarrassed that he can't get two dorky clients in, although club assistant manager pal Des (Chris Eigeman) often helps him slip in the back door. Beautiful and well dressed, Charlotte (Kate Beckinsale) and Alice (Chloe Sevigny) have no such trouble. The harried Des seems to be in the midst of a sexual identity crisis. Part of the film's dislocation stems from the gay and druggie environment being foregrounded dramatically by sexually constipated preppies who engage in defensive debates as to whether they qualify as yuppies.

LAST DAYS OF MAN ON EARTH, THE
See: The Final Programme

LAST DAYS OF POMPEII, THE
1935, 96 mins, US Ⓥ
D: Ernest B. Schoedsack **A:** Preston Foster, Basil Rathbone, David Holt, Alan Hale, Louis Calhern (RKO)

A spectacle picture, full of action, and holds a good tempo throughout. What is presented is a behind-the-scenes of Roman politics and commerce, both of which are shown as smeared with corruption and intrigue. Basil Rathbone comes very close to stealing the picture with his playing of Pontius Pilate. Preston Foster carries through from the boyish blacksmith of the opening sequence to the rich man who sees his beloved son face probable death in the arena (just before the volcano erupts). On the way he is a gladiator, slave trader, horse stealer, and general tough guy.

LAST DETAIL, THE
1973, 103 mins, US Ⓥ ⊙
D: Hal Ashby **A:** Jack Nicholson, Otis Young, Randy Quaid, Clifton James, Michael Moriarty, Carol Kane (Columbia)

A salty, bawdy, hilarious, and very touching story about two career sailors escorting to a naval prison a dumb boot sentenced for petty thievery. Jack Nicholson is outstanding at the head of a superb cast. Robert Towne's outstanding adaptation of Darryl Ponicsan's novel has caught the flavor of noncombat military life. The dialogue vulgarisms are simply part of the eternal environment of men in uniform.
1973: Nominations: Best Actor (Jack Nicholson), Supp. Actor (Randy Quaid), Adapted Screenplay

LAST EMBRACE
1979, 103 mins, US Ⓥ
D: Jonathan Demme **A:** Roy Scheider, Janet Margolin, Christopher Walken, Sam Levene, John Glover (United Artists)

Director Jonathan Demme proves conclusively that he can handle a strictly commercial assignment, while embellishing it with the creative touches that mark a first-rate filmmaker. *Last Embrace* tells of a government agent being phased out after a nervous breakdown. Roy Scheider is the paranoid subject of more attention than he'd prefer, especially when it comes from

Janet Margolin, a wigged-out grad student. The Hitchcock references are frequent.

LAST EMPEROR, THE
1987, 160 mins, UK/Italy Ⓥ ⊙ ▭
D: Bernardo Bertolucci **A:** John Lone, Joan Chen, Peter O'Toole, Ying Ruocheng, Victor Wong (Thomas/Columbia)

A film of unique, quite unsurpassed visual splendor, *The Last Emperor* makes for a fascinating trip to another world, but for the most part also proves as remote and untouchable as its subject, the last imperial ruler of China. A prodigious production in every respect, Bernardo Bertolucci's film is an exquisitely painted mural of 20th-century Chinese history as seen from the point of view of Pu Yi, a hereditary leader who never knew his people. John Lone, who plays Pu Yi from age 18 to 62, naturally dominates the picture with his carefully judged, unshowy delineation of a sometimes arrogant, often weak man. Joan Chen is exquisite and sad as his principal wife, who almost literally fades away, and Peter O'Toole, as Lone's tutor, doesn't really have that much to do but act intelligently concerned for the emperor's well-being.
1987: Best Picture, Director, Adapted Screenplay, Cinematography, Art Direction, Sound, Original Score, Editing, Costume Design

LAST EXIT TO BROOKLYN
1989, 102 mins, W. Germany Ⓥ ⊙
D: Uli Edel **A:** Stephen Lang, Jennifer Jason Leigh, Burt Young, Peter Dobson, Jerry Orbach (Neue Constantin/Bavaria/Allied)

A bleak tour of urban hell, production of Hubert Selby Jr.'s controversial 1964 novel doesn't hold a scalpel to the lacerating torrential prose that made the book so cringingly urgent. Director Uli Edel lacks that fundamental gift of empathy that would make these damned souls more than just figures under a cinematic microscope. Action is set in a working-class section of Brooklyn in 1952, close by the navy yards where young Americans are embarking for the Korean War. One of the protagonists is Stephen Lang, a venal married shop steward who has been dipping into the union till to subsidize his first homosexual affair. Other major character is a tawdry, hard-drinking teen hooker named Tralala (Jennifer Jason Leigh), who lures unsuspecting bar-hopping servicemen to a back lot where they are mugged and robbed.

LAST FLIGHT, THE
1931, 80 mins, US
D: William Dieterle A: Richard Barthelmess, David Manners, John Mack Brown, Helen Chandler, Elliot Nugent (Warner)

As a sensitively neurotic, sometime goofy, sometimes dumb, but always good-looking Nikki, Helen Chandler can take a bow even though her mutterings in this film may be hard to savvy for the Mob. Film opens with a thrill and a tear to suit the femmes, who see Barthelmess and David Manners coming down in a plane and then in a hospital. Before the picture unwinds much further, the two are grown into four, all as handsome, shattered airmen wandering aimlessly against life in sensitive and temperamental progress. Direction was successful in keeping the shell-shocked side of the permanently wounded airmen continuously before the audience. The cast acts uniformly good with Barthelmess highlighting and Chandler fitting right in.

LAST GOOD TIME, THE
1994, 90 mins, US Ⓥ
D: Bob Balaban A: Armin Mueller-Stahl, Maureen Stapleton, Lionel Stander, Olivia D'Abo (Apogee)

Armin Mueller-Stahl delivers a towering performance in an unusually poignant, finely observed comedy-drama. Mueller-Stahl plays Joseph Kopple, an elegant 70-year-old widower who still clings to the memories of his beautiful wife. One evening, Joseph witnesses a nasty fight between a young couple upstairs, which ends with Charlotte (Olivia D'Abo) being kicked out of the apartment by boyfriend Eddie (Adrian Pasdar). The freezing Charlotte has no place to go, so Joseph takes her in and gradually they develop a strange friendship. Director Bob Balaban succeeds in steering away from sentimental melodrama.

LAST HARD MEN, THE
1976, 103 mins, US Ⓥ ▭
D: Andrew V. McLaglen A: Charlton Heston, James Coburn, Barbara Hershey, Jorge Rivero, Michael Parks (20th Century-Fox)

Charlton Heston and James Coburn are both fine as a retired lawman and his half-Indian nemesis matching their wits in 1909 Arizona. Coburn escapes from a Yuma prison gang to wreak carefully planned revenge on Heston, who killed his wife years ago in a scattershot shoot-out. Recruiting a motley gang, Coburn lures the anxious Heston out of Tucson by kidnapping and molesting his daughter (Barbara Hershey).

LAST HURRAH, THE
1958, 121 mins, US Ⓥ ◉
D: John Ford A: Spencer Tracy, Jeffrey Hunter, Dianne Foster, Pat O'Brien, Basil Rathbone, James Gleason (Columbia)

Spencer Tracy makes the most of the meaty role of the shrewd politician of the "dominantly Irish-American" metropolis in New England (unmistakably Boston but not Boston). Tracy's resourcefulness makes for a series of memorable scenes. Jeffrey Hunter is the shrewd mayor's favored nephew, who perceives the old codger's humaneness.

LAST MAN STANDING
1996, 100 mins, US Ⓥ ◉ ▭
D: Walter Hill A: Bruce Willis, Christopher Walken, Bruce Dern, Alexandra Powers, David Patrick Kelly, William Sanderson (Lone Wolf/New Line)

Bruce Willis's one-note performance and monotonous plotting doom Walter Hill's combination Western and gangster pic, despite the director's typically virile staging of numerous gun battles. Plot is based on Kuroswa's classic *Yojimbo*. Hill updates the action to the dusty one-horse Texas border town of Jericho during Prohibition. John Smith (Willis) is a big-city guy en route to Mexico. Jericho has been taken over by rival bootleg gangs who run booze across the border. The local sheriff (Bruce Dern) has given up trying to impose law and order. Fine actors like Bruce Dern and especially Christopher Walken as a sinister, scarred sidekick, are given far too little to do.

LAST MARRIED COUPLE IN AMERICA, THE
1980, 103 mins, US Ⓥ
D: Gilbert Cates A: George Segal, Natalie Wood, Richard Benjamin, Dom DeLuise, Valerie Harper (Universal)

Script offers not a single new idea about divorce in suburbia and doesn't even develop the clichés well. Wood plays the nice pretty lady who wants a happy, faithful marriage to George Segal, who plays the nice, handsome husband befuddled by the world around him. Richard Benjamin is the neurotic modern male and Dom DeLuise the likable, nutty fat guy, while Valerie Harper is essentially Rhoda running rampant, tresses turned blond from the sheer excitement of it all.

LAST METRO, THE
See: Le Dernier Metro

LAST MOVIE, THE
1971, 110 mins, US ⓥ
D: Dennis Hopper **A:** Dennis Hopper, Stella Garcia, Sam Fuller, Peter Fonda, Julie Adams, Kris Kristofferson (Universal)

The narrative fluidity and use myths to make a statement on youth, so effective in Dennis Hopper's *Easy Rider,* are here overdone and film suffers from a multiplicity of themes, ideas, and its fragmented style with flash-forwards intertwined. Film begins with Hopper wandering all bloody among Peruvian Indians playing at filmmaking with cameras, booms, etc., made of rattan. Then a scene from the film shot there, a gun battle with horses falling and men bloodied. Sam Fuller plays a nononsense director with aplomb in these scenes. Hopper has the canteen, plays stuntman, and stays on with a native girl.

LAST OF ENGLAND, THE
1987, 87 mins, UK/W. Germany ⓥ
D: Derek Jarman **A:** Tilda Swinton, Spencer Leigh, Spring, Gay Gaynor, Matthew Hawkins (British Screen/Film Four/ZDF/Anglo-International)

The avant-garde helmer returns with a blatantly personal vision that combines documentary-style footage of ruined streets, home movies, and a segment with glimpses of a screen story. All is filmed and linked abstractly, but without the glimmer of plot or narrative line.

LAST OF MRS. CHEYNEY, THE
1929, 94 mins, US
D: Sidney Franklin **A:** Norma Shearer, Basil Rathbone, George Barraud, Herbert Bunston, Hedda Hopper (M-G-M)

Whole story is sentimental, a deftly manipulated version of the bunk about the good girl drawn into associations with a band of crooks, getting herself accepted into society so they can prey upon the rich, the girl all the time retaining the chaste and delicate spirit of a nun. Norma Shearer does extremely well with the heroine.

LAST OF MRS. CHEYNEY, THE
1937, 95 mins, US ⓥ
D: Richard Boleslawski **A:** Joan Crawford, William Powell, Robert Montgomery, Frank Morgan, Jessie Ralph, Nigel Bruce (M-G-M)

This is Richard Boleslawski's postmortem release. Another director wound up the perfunctory details, but Boleslawski gets, and merits, the sole directorial bill-ing. His hand is evident in a number of fine scenes, pacing this society-crook comedy-drama with effective contrasts of suspense and laughs. Scenes that are outstanding are made so by a rare combination of pace, scripting, and direction. The sequence, for example, where the snooty English household is wondering what will happen to the crooks (Joan Crawford and her accomplice, William Powell) is a double broadside in deft comedy painting.

LAST OF SHEILA, THE
1973, 120 mins, US ⓥ
D: Herbert Ross **A:** Richard Benjamin, Dyan Cannon, James Coburn, Joan Hackett, James Mason, Raquel Welch (Warner)

A major disappointment—simply a confused and cluttered demi *Sleuth,* grossly overwritten and underplayed. The plot is self-indulgent camp at its most deadly. The *Sheila* of the title is the luxury yacht named after the late wife of a Hollywood producer (James Coburn) killed by a hit-and-run driver shortly after exiting a party. A year later Coburn asks six of those party guests on Riviera cruise aboard the *Sheila.* On board, Coburn initiates a game in which each guest is given a card indicating a secret which is to be discovered by the others. Since one of the cards reads "I am a hit-and-run driver," the mystery concerns the person responsible for Sheila's demise.

LAST OF THE COWBOYS, THE
(US: THE GREAT SMOKEY
ROADBLOCK)
1977, 100 mins, US ⓥ
D: John Leone **A:** Henry Fonda, Eileen Brennan, Robert Englund, Austin Pendelton, Susan Sarandon, Melanie Mayron (Mar Vista/Preminger)

Film shrewdly plays on Henry Fonda's moral force as an aging, ailing truck driver who has had his big truck taken from him when he got behind in payments. He steals the truck and sets out to make one last run across the US. His final haul turns out to be six young prosties working for an old flame, played with gusto by Eileen Brennan. This touching pic is neatly paced, zesty, and manages to pay homage to the old-time Hollywood films without satirizing them.

LAST OF THE FINEST, THE
1990, 106 mins, US ⓥ ⊙
D: John Mackenzie **A:** Brian Dennehy, Joe Pantoliano, Jeff Fahey, Bill Paxton, Deborra-Lee Furness (Davis/Orion)

The Last of the Finest belongs to a rarely attempted brand of pastiche film. The central characters are Brian Dennehy and his band of dedicated cops who tumble upon a bunch of corrupt characters (who parallel the Iran-Contra protagonists) while working on a drug bust. Despite the deficiencies of a script that unwisely mixes tongue-in-cheek elements with soapbox messages, Scottish director John Mackenzie keeps the pic moving and enjoyable on a strictly thriller level.

LAST OF THE MOHICANS, THE
1936, 91 mins, US Ⓥ
D: George B. Seitz A: Randolph Scott, Binnie Barnes, Heather Angel, Henry Wilcoxon, Bruce Cabot (United Artists)

The James Fenimore Cooper novel is transferred to the screen with surprising fidelity. Hawkeye, the colonial scout, is set up as the typical American frontiersman of that day, willing to aid the British, but first interested in defending courageous colonists. Picture is hardly 15 minutes before the first brush with the cruel Huron Indian tribe. From then it is a series of carefully conceived and deftly executed climaxes, starting with the siege and surrender of the fort. Randolph Scott gives a virile interpretation as the scout. Henry Wilcoxon, as the snobbish British major, vies for honors on the male side.
1936: Nomination: Best Assistant Director (Clem Beauchamp)

LAST OF THE MOHICANS, THE
1992, 122 mins, US Ⓥ ⊙ ▭
D: Michael Mann A: Daniel Day-Lewis, Madeleine Stowe, Jodhi May, Russell Means, Eric Schweig, Steven Waddington (20th Century-Fox)

Adventure tale of life in the British colonies in America is a great ode to freedom and self-determination played out against codes of honor and loyalty, c. 1757. Lensed in South Carolina, pic blends pure adventure with a compelling central romance. Lean and intense, with a dashing mane of hair, Day-Lewis brings his usual concentration to the role of the courageous woodsman at one with nature. He and Stowe spark a convincing attraction arising from shared ideals and piqued by the excitement of life-and-death ordeals. Well-staged battle sequences are brutal and bloody.
1992: Best Sound

LAST OF THE RED HOT LOVERS
1972, 98 mins, US Ⓥ ⊙
D: Gene Saks A: Alan Arkin, Sally Kellerman, Paula Prentiss, Renee Taylor (Paramount)

A funny motion picture. Every husband who ever let his eye wander will empathize with Barney Cashman—happily married for 22 years, trying to make it, "just once," with another gal—and suffer with his repeated failures. Alan Arkin, a very funny man with some personal mannerisms that don't always fit the role, makes good use of all of them here, even those nervous eyes.

L.A. STORY
1991, 95 mins, US Ⓥ ⊙
D: Mick Jackson A: Steve Martin, Victoria Tennant, Richard E. Grant, Marilu Henner, Sarah Jessica Parker (Carolco/Indieprod/LA Films)

Goofy and sweet, *L.A. Story* constitutes Steve Martin's satiric valentine to his hometown and a pretty funny comedy in the bargain. Martin is in typically nutty form as an L.A. TV meteorologist who doesn't hestitate to take the weekends off since the weather isn't bound to change. What he can't predict, however, is the lightning bolt that hits him in the form of Brit journalist Victoria Tennant. Despite the frantic style, the feeling behind Martin's view of life and love in L.A. comes through, helped by the seductively adoring treatment of Tennant (actually Martin's wife).

LAST PICTURE SHOW, THE
1971, 118 mins, US Ⓥ ⊙
D: Peter Bogdanovich A: Timothy Bottoms, Jeff Bridges, Cybill Shepherd, Ben Johnson, Cloris Leachman, Ellen Burstyn (BBS)

Timothy Bottoms and Jeff Bridges portray the pair of youths. Bridges is the high-school hero, more aggressive; Bottoms is the more sensitive, hence the more lonely, of the pair. The boys grow a bit, some good people die, a few more secrets are revealed, and another "nothing" decade has passed. Bridges, spurned by his girl, joins the army; Bottoms matures a bit. Not much else happens. The best, most solid, most moving performances in the film are given by Ben Johnson as Sam the Lion, the owner of the picture show and pool room, and Cloris Leachman as the football coach's wife, who introduces Bottoms to sex. Peter Bogdanovich elected to shoot the film in black-and-white, artistically appropriate for the dust-blown, tired little community.

1971: Best Supp. Actor (Ben Johnson), Supp. Actress (Cloris Leachman)

Nominations: Best Picture, Director, Supp. Actor (Jeff Bridges), Supp. Actress (Ellen Burstyn), Adapted Screenplay, Cinematography

LAST REMAKE OF BEAU GESTE, THE

1977, 84 mins, US Ⓥ

D: Marty Feldman **A:** Ann-Margret, Marty Feldman, Michael York, Peter Ustinov, James Earl Jones, Trevor Howard (Universal)

An often hilarious, if uneven, spoof of Foreign Legion adventure films. An excellent cast, top to bottom, gets the most out of the stronger scenes, and carries the weaker ones. Feldman stars as the ugly-duckling brother of Michael York (as Beau Geste). Feldman joins York in the desert, where sadistic Peter Ustinov and bumbling Roy Kinnear run the garrison for urbane Henry Gibson, in the character of the Legion general.

LAST RITES

1987, 103 mins, US Ⓥ ◉

D: Donald P. Bellisario **A:** Tom Berenger, Daphne Zuniga, Chick Vennera, Anne Twomey, Dane Clark, Paul Dooley (M-G-M)

Startling opening scene has an elegant woman gun down a mobster. The woman (Daphne Zuniga) escapes and eventually comes under the protection of Father Michael Pace (Tom Berenger), a young priest in New York. The rugged holy man finds himself having erotic dreams about the saucy young thing in his bed, and finally spirits her south of the border to shed her pursuers. Donald P. Bellisario stages much of the action vividly, but it's just not very convincing. Berenger's casting was probably a mistake.

LAST RUN, THE

1971, 92 mins, US Ⓥ ▭

D: Richard Fleischer **A:** George C. Scott, Tony Musante, Trish Van Devere, Colleen Dewhurst (M-G-M)

A suspense melodrama with a set of criminal characters to keep action lively, its story line is so blurred by unexplained elements that it emerges as little more than an ordinary actioner. George C. Scott gives certain authority to a hard-hitting role. He plays a retired American mobster who once drove for criminals in fast get-aways. He returns to activity after nine years to aid an escaped con and whisk him across the Spanish border into France.

LAST SEDUCTION, THE

1994, 109 mins, US Ⓥ ◉

D: John Dahl **A:** Linda Fiorentino, Peter Berg, Bill Pullman, J. T. Walsh, Bill Nunn (ITC)

Well-paced, cleverly written, and quite diabolical thriller. Linda Fiorentino toplines as one of the screen's most formidable femmes fatales ever in a sexy and polished performance. Bridget Gregory (Fiorentino) is an intelligent NY insurance exec who has conned her medic husband,Clay (Bill Pullman),into doing a dangerous but lucrative drug deal. Bridget rewards him by simply ankling with the money, heading for Chicago. Fiorentino is quite wonderful as the diabolical Bridget, who uses her beauty and her body to get what she wants without qualms.

LAST STARFIGHTER, THE

1984, 100 mins, US Ⓥ

D: Nick Castle **A:** Lance Guest, Robert Preston, Dan O'Herlihy, Catherine Mary Stewart, Barbara Bosson (Universal/Lorimar)

Director Nick Castle and writer Jonathan Betuel have done something so simple it's almost awe-inspiring: they've taken a very human story and accented it with sci-fi special effects, rather than the other way around. Lance Guest is a teenager with a talent for a lone video game. When he breaks the record for destroying alien invaders, Guest not only excites the whole trailer park, he attracts a visit from Robert Preston.

LAST SUMMER

1969, 97 mins, US Ⓥ

D: Frank Perry **A:** Barbara Hershey, Richard Thomas, Bruce Davison, Cathy Burns, Ralph Waite (Allied Artists/Alsid)

A solid insight into a quartet during a summer that also has fine acting and sensitive direction and writing. The boys are expertly played by Bruce Davison and Richard Thomas, and Cathy Burns is engaging and touching as the lonely, homely little girl, drawn to those more emancipated friends, but finally appalled by their cowardice and cruelty, only to be the victim of their pent-up inarticulate needs.

1969: Nomination: Best Supp. Actress (Cathy Burns)

LAST SUMMER IN THE HAMPTONS
1995, 105 mins, US
D: Henry Jaglom A: Victoria Foyt, Viveca Lindfors, Jon Robin Baitz, Melissa Leo, Martha Plimpton (Jagtoria)

A mildly amusing comedy of manners. Story concerns three generations of a large, narcissistic theatrical family, headed by powerful matriarch Helena (Viveca Lindfors). The usual comic and not-so-comic shenanigans are exacerbated by the arrival of Oona (Victoria Foyt), a young Hollywood star whose unexpected visit wreaks havoc on almost every member of the family. Most of the film consists of intimate encounters in which the characters bare their hearts and reveal their dreams and frustrations. After 40 minutes or so, pic begins to lose steam and become repetitious.

LAST SUPPER, THE
1995, 92 mins, US ♥
D: Stacy Title A: Cameron Diaz, Ron Eldard, Annabeth Gish, Jonathan Penner, Courtney B. Vance (Vault)

In a brilliant opening sequence, five graduate students engage in a lively discussion with Zac (Bill Paxton). The proceedings heat up when the ultrapatriotic right-winger voices his racist views. Zac begins a physical fight, which unexpectedly ends with his own death. Once the quintet's initial shock and dismay pass, they decide to embark upon a crusade, ridding society of its most deplorable members. *The Last Supper* aims to be at once a black comedy, à la *Arsenic and Old Lace*, and a political critique of the 1990s, but ultimately it's too ambitious for its own good. After the first reel, the narrative becomes increasingly schematic—and a bit tiresome.

LAST TANGO IN PARIS
1972, 130 mins, Italy/France ♥ ⊙
D: Bernardo Bertolucci A: Marlon Brando, Maria Schneider, Maria Michi, Jean-Pierre Léaud, Massimo Girotti, Catherine Allegret (PEA/Artistes Associes)

Brando plays an aging lothario trailing the debris of a failed life. Pic opens on the day of his wife's suicide when the distraught Brando meets a young girl (Maria Schneider) while both are inspecting a vacant apartment. After a sudden, almost savage sexual encounter, Brando proposes that they meet on a regular basis. Brando insists that no names or personal information be exchanged, that the affair re-

main purely carnal. Plot has all the ingredients of a 1940s meller. Bertolucci uses it to explore the psyche of a man at the end of his emotional and sexual tether and at the same time to investigate on the most primitive level the chemistry of romantic love.
1973: Nominations: Best Director, Actor (Marlon Brando)

LAST TEMPTATION OF CHRIST, THE
1988, 164 mins, US ♥ ⊙
D: Martin Scorsese A: Willem Dafoe, Harvey Keitel, Barbara Hershey, Harry Dean Stanton, David Bowie, Verna Bloom (Universal/Cineplex Odeon)

A film of challenging ideas, and not salacious provocations, a powerful and very modern reinterpretation of Jesus as a man racked with anguish and doubt concerning his appointed role in life. Blondish and blue-eyed in the Anglo-Saxon tradition, Willem Dafoe offers an utterly compelling reading of his character. Harvey Keitel puts across Judas's fierceness and loyalty. Barbara Hershey, adorned with tattoos, is an extremely physical, impassioned Mary Magdalene. One could have used more of David Bowie's subdued, rational Pontius Pilate.
1988: Nomination: Best Director

LAST TIME I SAW PARIS, THE
1954, 116 mins, US ♥
D: Richard Brooks A: Elizabeth Taylor, Van Johnson, Walter Pidgeon, Donna Reed, Eva Gabor, Kurt Kasznar (M-G-M)

An engrossing romantic drama. F. Scott Fitzgerald's short story ''Babylon Revisited'' was updated and revised as the basis for the potent screenplay. Plot is laid in Paris in the reckless, gay period that followed V-E Day of World War II. There, Johnson meets and marries Taylor and starts a struggling existence as a daytime reporter for a news service and would-be author at night. Even the faith of his wife cannot balance the frustration he feels after too many rejection slips.

LAST TRAIL, THE
1927, 53 mins, US ⊗
D: Lewis Seiler A: Tom Mix, Carmelita Geraghty, William Davidson, Jerry the Giant (Fox)

In this one there is a free-for-all stagecoach race replete with thrills and spills. Tom Mix has Jerry the Giant, a cute youngster, working with him almost throughout the picture. Carmelita Geraghty is his leading woman and she more than makes good. Mix, as Tom Dane, gets a note from his old friend Joe Pascal, the sheriff at Carson City. The stage line, which is carrying the gold, has been repeatedly robbed until the sheriff decides to drive the stage through to the railroad with a guard.

LAST TRAIN FROM GUN HILL
1959, 94 mins, US ⓥ
D: John Sturges A: Kirk Douglas, Anthony Quinn, Carolyn Jones, Earl Holliman, Brad Dexter (Paramount/Bryna)

A top western that plays for almost pure action. Kirk Douglas's Indian wife is raped and killed by two young brutes (Earl Holliman and Brian Hutton). Douglas, marshal of the town of Pauley, finds a clue that leads him to the neighboring community of Gun Hill. He discovers his fugitive (Holliman) is the son of his old friend (Anthony Quinn). His problem is how to get Holliman away to justice on that "last train," with Quinn and his hired gun hands determined to thwart him. Douglas and Quinn, by performances in depth, give the film the inevitability of tragedy.

LAST TYCOON, THE
1976, 122 mins, US ⓥ ⊙
D: Elia Kazan A: Robert De Niro, Tony Curtis, Robert Mitchum, Jeanne Moreau, Jack Nicholson, Donald Pleasence (Paramount)

A handsome and lethargic film, based on F. Scott Fitzgerald's unfinished Hollywood novel of the 1930s, as adapted by Harold Pinter. Elia Kazan's direction seems unfocused though craftsmanlike. Robert De Niro's performance as the inscrutable boywonder of films is mildly intriguing.
1976: Nomination: Best Art Direction

LAST UNICORN, THE
1982, 84 mins, US ⓥ
D: Arthur Rankin Jr., Jules Bass (Rankin-Bass/ ITC)

A rare example of an animated kids' pic in which the script and vocal performances outshine the visuals. Continuing thread is the search of the fabled last unicorn, in this case a beautiful white mare. However vapid the unicorn may appear to the eye, Mia Farrow's voice brings a moving plaintive quality to the character that sees the entire film through. Alan Arkin also scores as the bumbling magician, as do Christopher Lee as the evil king and,

in a showstopping turn, Paul Frees as a peg-legged, eye-patched cat.

LAST VALLEY, THE
1971, 125 mins, UK/US ⓥ ⊡
D: James Clavell A: Michael Caine, Omar Sharif, Florinda Bolkan, Nigel Davenport, Per Oscarsson, Arthur O'Connell (ABC/Season)

A disappointing 17th-century period melodrama, too literal in historical detail to suggest artfully the allegory intended and, paradoxically, too allegorical to make clear the actual reality of the Thirty Years War. Sharif, neither peasant nor nobleman, is fleeing the ravages of war and finds a valley still spared from devastation. Caine, hard-bitten leader of mercenaries, also discovers the locale. At Sharif's urging, Caine decides to live in peace for the winter with the residents, headed by Nigel Davenport, and an uneasy truce develops.

LAST WAGON, THE
1956, 98 mins, US ⊡
D: Delmer Daves A: Richard Widmark, Felicia Farr, Susan Kohner, Tommy Rettig, George Mathews (20th Century-Fox)

The mounting menace of Indian attack as the survivors of a wagon-train massacre make their way through hostile Apache country provides stirring motivation for this excellent production. Its suspenseful plot and rugged characterization by Richard Widmark as a Comanche-reared white man are admirably backdropped by the magnificent northern Arizona scenery. Under Delmer Daves's shrewd direction, film comes off as an interesting enterprise far off the beaten path of routine westerns.

LAST WALTZ, THE
1978, 115 mins, US ⓥ
D: Martin Scorsese A: Bob Dylan, Joni Mitchell, Neil Diamond, Van Morrison, Eric Clapton, The Band (United Artists)

An outstanding rock documentary of the last concert by The Band on Thanksgiving 1976 in San Francisco. The Band performs 12 numbers and backs up guest artists on another dozen. They include Ronnie Hawkins, Dr. John, Neil Young, the Staples, Neil Diamond, Joni Mitchell, Paul Butterfield, Muddy Waters, Eric Clapton, Emmylou Harris, Van Morrison, Bob Dylan, Ringo Starr, and Ron Wood.

LAST WAVE, THE
1977, 106 mins, Australia ⓥ
D: Peter Weir A: Richard Chamberlain, Olivia Hamnett, David Gulpilil, Frederick

Parslow, Nandjiwarra Amagula (Ayer/SAFC/AFC)

Australian director Peter Weir's film about the possibility of a tidal wave that may destroy the country or the world. Richard Chamberlain is highly effective as a young lawyer caught up in a case of an Aborigine murdered by some townfolk. Film builds, and though it sometimes falters in narrative, picks up again as Chamberlain turns out to be a sort of psychic member of a mysterious people who supposedly came to Australia long ago and disappeared.

LAST WILL OF DR. MABUSE, THE
See: Das Testament Des Dr. Mabuse

LAST WINTER, THE
1990, 103 mins, Canada
D: Aaron Kim Johnston **A:** Gerard Parkes, Joshua Murray, David Ferry, Wanda Cannon (Rode/Aaron)

This vivid, imaginative tale of a Manitoba farm boy's coming-of-age captures a uniquely Canadian heartland experience. Writer-director Aaron Kim Johnson has crafted a tribute to his childhood in a tale seen through the eyes of 10-year-old Will (Joshua Murray) as he resists his family's move to the city. Will creates a fantasy shield between himself and reality, hallucinating a white horse named Winter, who charges across the farmland bearing some mysterious message.

LAST YEAR AT MARIENBAD
See: L'Annee Derniere a Marienbad

LATE SHOW, THE
1977, 94 mins, US ⊗ ◉
D: Robert Benton **A:** Art Carney, Lily Tomlin, Bill Macy, Eugene Roche, Joanna Cassidy, John Considine (Warner)

Art Carney and Lily Tomlin make an arresting screen duo in a tribute to the private-eye yarns of the 1940s. Carney plays Duff, an aging private detective. When his onetime partner is murdered, Carney, in the best Sam Spade tradition, vows to get the killer. The trail begins with Tomlin, whose stolen cat Duff had been hired to find. Top-heavy plot unwinds with the usual potboiler ingredients—blackmail, murder, philandering wives, and doublecross.
1977: Nomination: Best Original Screenplay

LATIN LOVERS
1953, 104 mins, US
D: Mervyn LeRoy **A:** Lana Turner, Ricardo Montalban, John Lund, Louis Calhern, Jean Hagen, Beulah Bondi (M-G-M)

Plot problem confronting Lana Turner, a girl with $37 million, is to make sure the man she marries is interested in something more than her money. She can't be sure of John Lund, even though he has $48 million, and Ricardo Montalban is well-off, but not in the millionaire class by any means. Payoff of the complications takes place in Brazil, the romantic spot to which she has followed Lund and where she meets Montalban.

LAUGHING POLICEMAN, THE
1973, 111 mins, US ⊗
D: Stuart Rosenberg **A:** Walter Matthau, Bruce Dern, Lou Gossett, Albert Paulsen (20th Century-Fox)

After an extremely overdone prologue of violent mass murder on a bus, The Laughing Policeman becomes a handsomely made manhunt actioner, starring Walter Matthau and Bruce Dern in excellent performances as two San Francisco detectives assigned to the case. Lack of clear motive, disparity in backgrounds of all the dead people, and absence of clues sends detective lieutenant Anthony Zerbe up the wall in frustration. Matthau's character is developed and played with low-key irony. Dern is superbly cast as a callous cop.

LAUGHTER
1930, 85 mins, US
D: Harry D'Arrast **A:** Nancy Carroll, Fredric March, Frank Morgan, Glenn Anders, Diane Ellis (Paramount)

Laughter has its drama in a suicide and again in a girl's desire to leave wealth, to gamble with the irresponsible composer she fell in love with in Paris, just before her marriage, to go to gaiety and mingle with laughs. The girl is Nancy Carroll and the composer March. Hugely enjoyable entertainment, with plenty of comedy.

LAUGHTER IN PARADISE
1951, 94 mins, UK
D: Mario Zampi **A:** Alastair Sim, Fay Compton, Guy Middleton, George Cole, Beatrice Campbell, Audrey Hepburn (Associated British)

Producer-director Mario Zampi very nearly succeeds in bringing off an outstanding comedy. Plot describes what happens after a practical joker leaves $140,000 to each of four relatives provided they fulfill certain stipulated conditions. A cousin (Alastair Sim), who secretly writes trashy thrillers, has to get himself sentenced to 28 days in jail. The plum comedy part is undoubtedly Sim's, his endeavors to land in jail being loaded with chuckles.

LAUGHTER IN THE DARK
1969, 101 mins, UK/France
D: Tony Richardson **A:** Nicol Williamson, Anna Karina, Jean-Claude Drouot, Sheila Burrell, Sian Phillips, Kate O'Toole (Gershwin-Kastner/Marceau/Woodfall)

Fascinating attempt to transpose the Nabokov novel to the screen. The intricate story centers on a wealthy, titled young art dealer, Edward (Nicol Williamson), who is attracted to usherette Margot (Anna Karina), continues to return to the theater where she works, and finally arranges to meet her. Richardson's direction ranges from brilliantly evocative to confusing.

LAURA
1944, 88 mins, US Ⓥ ☉
D: Otto Preminger **A:** Gene Tierney, Dana Andrews, Clifton Webb, Vincent Price, Judith Anderson (20th Century-Fox)

The film's deceptively leisurely pace at the start, and its light, careless air, only heighten the suspense. Situations neatly dovetail and are always credible. Developments, surprising as they come, are logical. The dialogue is honest, real, and adult. The yarn concerns an attractive femme art executive who has been brutally murdered in her New York apartment, and the attempts of a police lieutenant to solve the case. Clifton Webb makes a debonair critic-columnist. Dana Andrews's intelligent, reticent performance as the lieutenant gives the lie to detectives as caricatures.
1944: Best B&W Cinematography
Nominations: Best Director, Supp. Actor (Clifton Webb), Screenplay, B&W Art Direction

LAVENDER HILL MOB, THE
1951, 81 mins, UK Ⓥ ☉
D: Charles Crichton **A:** Alec Guinness, Stanley Holloway, Sidney James, Alfie Bass, Marjorie Fielding, Ronald Adam (Ealing)

Ealing clicks with another comedy winner. Story is notable for allowing Alec Guinness to play another of his w.k. character roles. This time, he is the timid escort of bullion from the refineries to the vaults. With three accomplices, he plans the perfect crime. Bullion worth over £1 million is made into souvenir models of the Eiffel Tower and shipped to France.

Stanley Holloway is an excellent aide, while the two professional crooks in the gang (Sidney James and Alfie Bass) complete the quartet with an abundance of Cockney humor.
1952: Best Story & Screenplay
Nomination: Best Actor (Alec Guinness)

LAW AND DISORDER
1958, 76 mins, UK Ⓥ
D: Charles Crichton **A:** Michael Redgrave, Robert Morley, Ronald Squire, George Coulouris, Joan Hickson, Lionel Jeffries (Hotspur)

A highly amusing offbeat comedy that notches guffaws and giggles with disarming ease. Michael Redgrave is a con man who does rather well financially in his racket even though Robert Morley, a strict and pompous judge, is constantly sending him to the cooler. His only problem is to keep his profession away from his young son, who grows up in the belief that his dad is a missionary away for long stretches in far-off lands.

LAWLESS, THE
(UK: THE DIVIDING LINE)
1950, 81 mins, US
D: Joseph Losey **A:** Macdonald Carey, Gail Russell, Lalo Rios, Maurice Jara, Lee Patrick (Paramount)

Racial tolerance gets a working-over in a hard-hitting drama, equipped with action and fast pace. Plot concerns itself with so-called fruit tramps who make a skimpy living harvesting California's various crops. They are scorned by the whites and subjected to physical abuse by bullies. Macdonald Carey strides easily through his assignment as the editor who takes up the cudgels for justice.

LAWLESS BREED, THE
1952, 83 mins, US
D: Raoul Walsh **A:** Rock Hudson, Julie Adams, Mary Castle, John McIntire, Hugh O'Brian, Dennis Weaver (Universal)

Early-west gunman John Wesley Hardin has his life put on film. The plot unfolds episodically and swiftly, telling how Hardin earned his reputation as a killer after getting his first victim in self-defense, goes on the lam from the law and vengeance-seeking kinfolk, is forced into more killings, loses his sweetheart (Mary Castle) to a posse's bullets, and acquires a new one in Julie Adams, the girl who later becomes his wife. Rock Hudson does a very good job as the main character.

LAWMAN
1971, 98 mins, UK
D: Michael Winner **A:** Burt Lancaster, Robert Ryan, Lee J. Cobb, Sheree North, Joseph Wiseman, Robert Duvall (Scimitar)

Burt Lancaster plays a marshal so dedicated that he is inflexible and even arrogant in his intepretation of the law. He rides into a nearby town to pick up a bunch of locals who, on a drunken spree, were responsible for the death of an old man. Point of the story is just how far a man can compromise with his conscience and whether the end justifies the means. Lancaster, as usual, is a highly convincing marshal, tough and taciturn. Ryan is also excellent as the faded, weak marshal with only memories. But it's Cobb who quietly steals the film as the local boss who is no ruthless villain.

LAWNMOWER MAN, THE
1992, 105 mins, US Ⓥ ⊙
D: Brett Leonard **A:** Jeff Fahey, Pierce Brosnan, Jenny Wright, Mark Bringleson, Geoffrey Lewis, Jeremy Slate (Allied Vision/Lane Pringle)

Loosely adapted from Stephen King, story has a mentally retarded gardener's assistant (Jeff Fahey) becoming the guinea pig for a scientist (Pierce Brosnan) experimenting with "virtual reality." The concept involves creating a computer simulation that seems real to nearly all the senses. As Fahey's intelligence improves, he begins to rebel against those who have been abusing him. The stunning visuals for the virtual-reality sequences really put *The Lawnmower Man* over. The computer animation doesn't necessarily break new ground, but it marks the first time it has been so well integrated into a live-action story.

LAWNMOWER MAN 2: BEYOND CYBERSPACE
1996, 93 mins, US Ⓥ ⊙
D: Farhad Mann **A:** Patrick Bergin, Matt Frewer, Austin O'Brien, Ely Pouget, Kevin Conway (New Line/Allied Entertainments)

Serviceable sci-fi actioner. Matt Frewer replaces Jeff Fahey as Jobe. Evil corporate interests have brought Jobe back to create a global network linking all computers that will be impossible to escape. Representing the forces of good are a group of kids led by Peter (Austin O'Brien, repeating his role from the first movie) and Dr. Benjamin Trace (Patrick Bergin). Frewer and Bergin's performances make the film

work. Pic is handsome throughout, the integration of live actors with the virtual sets seamless.

LAW OF DESIRE, THE
See: Lay Ley del Deseo

LAWRENCE OF ARABIA
1962, 222 mins, UK Ⓥ ⊙ ▱
D: David Lean **A:** Peter O'Toole, Alec Guinness, Anthony Quinn, Jack Hawkins, Omar Sharif, Anthony Quayle (Horizon)

King-size adventure yarn. Authentic desert locations, a stellar cast, and an intriguing subject combine to put this into the blockbuster league. Robert Bolt's well-written screenplay does not tell the audience anything much new about Lawrence of Arabia, nor does it offer any opinion or theory about the character of this man or the motivation for his actions. So he remains a legendary figure and a shadowy one. Story line concerns Lawrence as a young intelligence officer in Cairo in 1916. British intelligence is watching the Arab revolt against the Turks with interest. Lawrence (Peter O'Toole) is seconded to observe the revolt. He sets out to find Prince Feisal, top man of the revolt. Lawrence is given the task of helping the Arabs to achieve independence and he becomes a kind of desert Scarlet Pimpernel. He is captured by the Turks, tortured, and emerges a shaken, broken, and disillusioned man. Yet still he takes on the job of leading a force to Damascus. Lean and cameraman F. A. Young have brought out the loneliness and pitiless torment of the desert with an artistic use of color and with almost every frame superbly mounted. Maurice Jarre's musical score always contributes to the mood of the film. Peter O'Toole does a striking job with the complicated and heavy role of Lawrence. **1962:** Best Picture, Director, Color Cinematography, Color Art Direction, Sound, Original Music Score, Editing
Nominations: Best Actor (Peter O'Toole), Supp. Actor (Omar Sharif), Adapted Screenplay

LAWYER MAN
1932, 68 mins, US
D: William Dieterle **A:** William Powell, Joan Blondell, Helen Vinson, Alan Dinehart (Warner)

William Powell is the entire picture as an East Side New York attorney, but Joan Blondell as his secretary is the wrong type opposite him. The two don't seem to stack up right together. Quite a number of good laughs permeate the action, but there's little in the way of courtroom stuff. Most of what happens in courtrooms is covered by flashes of newspaper headlines. David Landau stands out as the political boss who traps the lawyer in a blackmail stunt in order to gain control of him, only to pay for it dearly in the end.

LEAGUE OF GENTLEMEN, THE
1960, 116 mins, UK ⊘
D: Basil Dearden **A:** Jack Hawkins, Nigel Patrick, Roger Livesey, Richard Attenborough, Bryan Forbes, Kieron Moore (Allied Film Makers)

Hawkins, disgruntled at being axed from the army he has faithfully served for many years, decides to have a go at a bank robbery. He picks up the idea from an American thriller and recruits seven broke and shady ex-officers, all experts in their own line in the army. Forbes has written a strong, witty screenplay from John Boland's novel. The eight members of the gang all give smooth, plausible performances, with Hawkins and Patrick, as his second in command, having the meatiest roles.

LEAGUE OF THEIR OWN, A
1992, 128 mins, US ⊘ ⊙ ▭
D: Penny Marshall **A:** Tom Hanks, Geena Davis, Madonna, Lori Petty, Jon Lovitz (Parkway/Columbia)

A comic look at the first season of the women's baseball league in 1943, film benefits from a fresh, unusual subject, the joy of baseball being played by women having the time of their lives, and a wonderful central performance by Geena Davis. Downside includes contrived plotting, obvious comedy and heart-tugging, some hammy thesping, and a general hokiness. Adding a little testosterone to the recipe is Tom Hanks, a former big-league star who sees life from so deep in the bottle that he virtually sleeps through practice and the initial games.

LEAP OF FAITH
1992, 108 mins, US ⊘ ⊙
D: Richard Pearce **A:** Steve Martin, Debra Winger, Lolita Davidovich, Liam Neeson, Lukas Haas, Meat Loaf (Paramount)

Steve Martin gives a showy but sober performance as a phony faith healer. The film waffles as to what it's about, never embarking on a full-scale indictment of charlatans and TV ministries and never unabashedly embracing any higher power, despite its cryptic ending. Minister Jonas

Nightingale's (Martin) traveling motorcade is forced to make an unscheduled stopover in a small, depressed Kansas town. Martin's assistant (Debra Winger) becomes enamored with the local sheriff (Liam Neeson) while the ersatz preacher gets entangled with a pretty waitress (Lolita Davidovich) and her crippled brother (Lukas Haas).

LEARNING TREE, THE
1969, 106 mins, US ⊘ ▭
D: Gordon Parks **A:** Kyle Johnson, Alex Clarke, Estelle Evans, Dana Elcar (Warner/Seven Arts)

Sentimental, sometimes awkward, but ultimately moving film about the growing-up of a black teenager in rural Kansas during the 1920s is, apparently, the first film financed by a major company to be directed by a Negro. The worst moments occur when director Gordon Parks interpolates small sermonettes. Also, the film cannot quite carry the large helping of melodrama which occurs near the end.

LEATHER BOYS, THE
1964, 108 mins, UK ⊘ ▭
D: Sidney J. Furie **A:** Rita Tushingham, Colin Campbell, Dudley Sutton, Gladys Henson, Betty Marsden (British Lion/Garrick)

Main theme is the doomed marriage of a couple of immature kids. Reggie (Colin Campbell), who spends a riotous leisure as a motorcyclist, hitches up with Dot (Rita Tushingham). The crack-up comes when Dot turns out an incompetent wife. Reggie takes up with a "buddy" called Peter (Dudley Sutton). Despite Pete's insistent affection, his reluctance to associate with girls, and his housekeeping ability, Reggie does not wise up to the fact that he's a homosexual. As the audience gets the drift early, this somewhat punctures the plot. Virtues of the pic lie in Sidney Furie's direction and in the two male performances.

LEAVE ALL FAIR
1985, 88 mins, New Zealand
D: John Reid **A:** John Gielgud, Jane Birkin, Feodor Atkine, Simon Ward (Pacific/Goldeneye/Challenge)

Lensed entirely in France, this elegiac story about the husband of New Zealand writer Katherine Mansfield, who died in 1922, is a sober, affecting experience. John Gielgud, playing another elderly man of letters, returns to France to meet his publisher (Feodor Atkine). The trip brings back memories of his life with Mansfield

(Jane Birkin), memories made more painful when he meets Atkine's mistress, Marie (also played by Birkin), who not only resembles his long-dead wife, but is also a New Zealander.

LEAVE HER TO HEAVEN
1945, 110 mins, US ⊙
D: John M. Stahl **A:** Gene Tierney, Cornel Wilde, Jeanne Crain, Vincent Price, Ray Collins (20th Century-Fox)

Sumptuous Technicolor mounting and a highly exploitable story lend considerable importance to *Leave Her to Heaven* that it might not have had otherwise. Script hasn't been as forcefully interpreted by the leads as it could have been. Essentially woman's story tells of a girl (Gene Tierney) whose possessive jealousy smothered her father and destroyed her husband's love.
1945: Best Color Cinematography
Nominations: Best Actress (Gene Tierney), Color Art Direction, Sound

LEAVING LAS VEGAS
1995, 112 mins, US ⓥ ⊙
D: Mike Figgis **A:** Nicolas Cage, Elisabeth Shue, Julian Sands, Richard Lewis, Valeria Golino (United Artists/Lumiere)

Nicolas Cage assays a character who's sinking deeper into depression and alcoholism. The film pulls no punches, takes no prisoners, and flies in the face of feel-good pictures. Ben Sanderson (Cage) heads for the gambling capital, puts himself on an allowance, and contends that he'll be able to drink himself to death in four to five weeks. Every conceivable cliché is turned on its head. Story evolves into a two-character piece in which he's partnered with Sera (Elisabeth Shue), a prostitute. She's attracted to his vulnerability, and he agrees to move in with her on condition she never asks him to stop drinking. The two performers are attractive without pushing it. Figgis's score is a visceral treat.
1995: Best Actor (Nicolas Cage)
Nominations: Best Actress (Elisabeth Shue), Director, Screenplay Adaptation

LEAVING NORMAL
1992, 110 mins, US ⓥ ⊙
D: Edward Zwick **A:** Christine Lahti, Meg Tilly, Patrika Darbo, Lenny Von Dohlen, Maury Chaykin (Universal/Mirage)

Cocktail waitress Christine Lahti and battered housewife Meg Tilly are headed from the small western town of Normal to Alaska, where Lahti will claim her inherited home and land. First they stop off to visit Tilly's relatives in Portland and get an eyeful of the dreaded "perfect homemaker" existence (nicely caricatured by Eve Gordon as a sister). After Lahti's car breaks down, they get a ride from friendly truckers Maury Chaykin and Lenny Von Dohlen. Lahti's distrust of all men nips this relationship in the bud, but Tilly is determined to pursue Von Dohlen someday. Director Edward Zwick uses optical effects, matte shots, and other fantasy touches from the outset to avoid realism in depicting the women's fanciful saga.

LA LECTRICE
(US: THE READER)
1988, 100 mins, France ⓥ
D: Michel Deville **A:** Miou-Miou, Christian Ruche, Maria Casarès, Patrick Chesnais, Marianne Denicourt (Elefilm/AAA/TSF/Cine-5)

Stylish frothy "light read" of a film recounts the adventures of a young woman who rents her services as a professional reader to bourgeois clients ill-disposed to doing their own page-turning. Michel Deville has fashioned an elegant entertainment with humor, irony, eroticism. Miou-Miou is the engaging heroine.

LEFT-HANDED GUN, THE
1958, 105 mins, US ⓥ
D: Arthur Penn **A:** Paul Newman, Lita Milan, Hurd Hatfield, James Congdon, James Best, John Dehner (Warner/Haroll)

Another look at Billy the Kid. In this version he's Billy, the crazy, mixed-up Kid. The picture is a smart and exciting western paced by Paul Newman's intense portrayal. Scripter Leslie Stevens emphasizes the youthful nature of the desperado by giving him two equally young companions, James Best and James Congdon. The three team after Newman's mentor, cattleman Colin Keith-Johnston, is shot by a crooked officer of the law. Newman is determined to avenge the cattleman's death. The best parts of the film are the moments of hysterical excitement as the three young desperadoes roughhouse with each other as feckless as any innocent boys and in the next instant turn to deadly killing without flicking a curly eyelash.

LEFT HAND OF GOD, THE
1955, 87 mins, US ⓥ ▭
D: Edward Dmytryk **A:** Humphrey Bogart, Gene Tierney, Lee J. Cobb, Agnes Moorehead, E. G. Marshall, Carl Benton Reid (20th Century-Fox)

The film is somewhat provocative, in that its central character is a man who masquerades as a priest. Carrying on this deception is Yank flier Humphrey Bogart, who believes it to be the sole way he can escape as prisoner of Chinese warlord Lee J. Cobb. The drama and suspense aren't to be found in whether the flier escapes from China but in the soul-searching to which he subjects himself in continuing the masquerade.

LEGACY, THE
1979, 100 mins, US $\circledV$
D: Richard Marquand **A:** Katharine Ross, Sam Elliott, Hildegard Neil, Roger Daltrey, John Standing, Charles Gray (Universal/Turman-Foster)

Using the hoary convention of stranding a young couple in the mansion of a reclusive millionaire whose guests are progressively bumped off in an assortment of gruesome ways, *The Legacy* tries for an added dimension of satanic possession, but winds up a tame, suspenseless victim of its own lack of imagination.

LEGAL EAGLES
1986, 114 mins, US $\circledV$ $\odot$ $\boxdot$
D: Ivan Reitman **A:** Robert Redford, Debra Winger, Daryl Hannah, Brian Dennehy, Terence Stamp, Steven Hill (Northern Lights)

Loss of intrigue with a scattered plot involving art fraud and murder is made up for by often witty, albeit lightweight dialogue led by the ever-boyish star Robert Redford. Lavish production opens with charmer Redford as one of the d.a.'s office's winningest attorneys, Tom Logan, assigned to prosecute the daughter of a famous artist. He faces Laura Kelly (Debra Winger), a court-appointed defense attorney known for daffy courtroom antics to get her clients off.

LEGEND
1986, 94 mins, US $\circledV$ $\odot$ $\boxdot$
D: Ridley Scott **A:** Tom Cruise, Mia Sara, Tim Curry, David Bennett, Alice Playten, Billy Barty (Legend/20th Century-Fox)

Legend is a fairy tale produced on a grand scale, set in some timeless world and peopled with fairies, elves, and goblins, plus a spectacularly satisfying Satan. At the same time the basic premise is alarmingly thin, a compendium of any number of ancient fairy tales. Kids of all ages should be entranced by the magnificent makeup effects of Rob Bottin and his crew, from the smallest elves to the giant

Darkness. The latter is unquestionably the most impressive depiction of Satan ever brought to the screen. Tim Curry plays him majestically.
1956: Nomination: Best Makeup

LEGEND OF HELL HOUSE, THE
1973, 94 mins, UK/US $\circledV$ $\odot$
D: John Hough **A:** Pamela Franklin, Roddy McDowall, Clive Revill, Gayle Hunnicutt, Roland Culver (Academy/20th Century-Fox)

Richard Matheson's scripting of his novel *Hell House* builds into an exceptionally realistic and suspenseful tale of psychic phenomena. John Hough's direction maintains this spirit as his cast of characters arrive at the deserted Hell House with an assignment from its present tycoon owner to learn the truth about survival after death, a secret he believes the house with its terrifying history may hold. Shock value is an important element as audience literally feels the unseen power that exists in the house.

LEGEND OF LYLAH CLARE, THE
1968, 127 mins, US
D: Robert Aldrich **A:** Kim Novak, Peter Finch, Ernest Borgnine, Milton Selzer, Rossella Falk, Coral Browne (M-G-M/Associates & Aldrich)

Script spotlights the making of a film about Lylah Clare, a world-famous pic star who died sometime before under mysterious circumstances. Her onetime producer-discoverer wants to revive the Clare legend via a biopic, and succeeds in convincing Lewis Zarkan, the director who made her, to coach look-alike Elsa Brinkman into capturing the departed star's mannerisms. Kim Novak brings off her dual role as Elsa-Lylah well. Peter Finch is very good as the director.

LEGENDS OF THE FALL
1994, 134 mins, US $\circledV$ $\odot$
D: Edward Zwick **A:** Brad Pitt, Anthony Hopkins, Aidan Quinn, Julia Ormond, Henry Thomas (Tri-Star/Bedford Falls/Pangaea)

The story focuses on the three sons of retired cavalry officer William Ludlow (Anthony Hopkins). As the spring thaw of 1913 arrives, the youngest son, Samuel (Henry Thomas), returns with his fiancée, Susannah Finncannon (Julia Ormond). His older brothers have taken over key areas of the ranch business. Alfred (Aidan Quinn) is a sort of operating manager and Tristan (Brad Pitt) is the barely housebro-

ken head wrangler. The film escapes the abyss of melodrama and sentimentality. Zwick imbues the story with an easy, poetic quality that mostly sidesteps the precious. The actors, working as an ensemble, are near perfect in the service of the material.
1994: Best Cinematography
Nominations: Best Art Direction, Sound

LEI DO MAIS FRACO, A
(US: PIXOTE; SURVIVAL OF THE WEAKEST)
1981, 130 mins, Brazil Ⓥ
D: Hector Babenco **A:** Fernando Ramos Da Silva, Jorge Juliano, Gilberto Moura, Marilia Pera (Babenco/Embrafilme)

A trenchant, uncompromising look at Brazilian juvenile delinquents, *Pixote* is a social exposé of the first order. Although milieu of the urban jungle is sordid and situation depicted seems beyond hope even for the most idealistic reformers, director Hector Babenco has made this tragic drama come vividly, even excitingly, alive through the extraordinary performances of his nonprofessional cast of slum youngsters. Tale's primary focus is on Pixote, an abandoned boy with an oddly haunting face.

LE MANS
1971, 108 mins, US Ⓥ ▭
D: Lee H. Katzin [John Sturges] **A:** Steve McQueen, Siegfried Rauch, Elga Andersen (Solar/Cinema Center)

Marked by some spectacular car-racing footage, *Le Mans* is a successful attempt to escape the potboiler level of prior films on same subject. The solution was to establish a documentary mood. Steve McQueen stars (and races). The spare script finds McQueen returning to compete in the famed car race a year after he has been injured. Elga Andersen, wife of a driver killed in the same accident, also returns, somewhat the worse for emotional wear. Siegfried Rauch is McQueen's continuing rival in racing competition.

LEMON DROP KID, THE
1951, 91 mins, US Ⓥ Ⓞ
D: Sidney Lanfield **A:** Bob Hope, Marilyn Maxwell, Lloyd Nolan, Jane Darwell, Fred Clark (Paramount/Hope)

The Lemon Drop Kid is neither true Damon Runyon, from whose short story of the same title it was adapted, nor is it very funny Bob Hope. His comedy style, particularly his wisecracks, not only destroys the Runyonesque sentimental flavor but actually pulls the props from under the inherent humor of the story.

LEMON POPSICLE
1978, 100 mins, Israel Ⓥ
D: Boaz Davidson **A:** Yiftach Katzur, Anat Atzmon, Jonathan Segal, Zachi Noy (Noah)

Tel Aviv in the late 1950s. Three youths have only girls on their mind, while the hit parade on the radio (Elvis Presley) reflects their own emotional engagement in the world. The schoolboy romance has a funnier side to it. It's in the search for an initial sexual experience—first with a middle-age nympho to whom one boy delivers ice, then with a prostitute who gives them the crabs—both handled with appropriate gags to put the scenes over.

LENIN IN OCTOBER
See: Lyenin V Oktyabrye

LENNY
1974, 111 mins, US Ⓥ Ⓞ
D: Bob Fosse **A:** Dustin Hoffman, Valerie Perrine, Jan Miner, Stanley Beck, Gary Morton (United Artists)

Lenny Bruce was one of the precursors of social upheaval, and like most pioneers, he got clobbered for his foresight. Bob Fosse's remarkable film version of Julian Barry's legit play stars Dustin Hoffman in an outstanding performance. Production was photographed in black-and-white, lending not only a slight period look but also capturing the grit and the sweat, as well as the private and public tortures of its principal character.
1974: Nominations: Best Picture, Director, Actor (Dustin Hoffman), Actress (Valerie Perrine), Adapted Screenplay, Cinematography

LEON
(US: THE PROFESSIONAL)
1994, 106 mins, France Ⓥ Ⓞ ▭
D: Luc Besson **A:** Jean Reno, Gary Oldman, Natalie Portman, Danny Aiello, Peter Appel (Gaumont/Dauphin)

Shooting entirely in English, Besson delivers a naive fairy tale splattered with blood. Mathilda (Natalie Portman), a bright but abused 12-year-old truant, returns from the grocery store to find that corrupt cop Stansfield (Gary Oldman) and his trigger-happy crew have used her entire family for target practice. Mathilda is reluctantly taken in by her towering and taciturn neighbor, Leon (Jean Reno), a self-described "cleaner" (Bessonian slang for "hit man"). The ambitious, only mildly bereaved waif thinks that's "cool" and begs 40-ish Leon to teach her his trade. The mismatched couple bonds, and the formerly invincible hit man becomes vulnerable.

LEON MORIN, PRETRE
(US: LEON MORIN, PRIEST; THE FORGIVEN SINNER)
1961, 114 mins, France

D: Jean-Pierre Melville A: Jean-Paul Belmondo, Emmanuele Riva, Irene Tunc, Nicole Mirel, Monique Bertho, Patricia Gozzi (Rome Paris)

Tale of a young agnostic woman's conversion to Catholicism and her physical love for a priest during the Nazi occupation of France is handled with tact and talent. Jean-Paul Belmondo displays a reserve and understanding of his role as progressive young priest. Emmanuele Riva gives the role an intensity that is acceptable in spite of some overdone personal tics and mannerisms.

LEON MORIN, PRIEST
See: Leon Morin, Pretre

LEON THE PIG FARMER
1993, 103 mins, UK Ⓥ ⊙

D: Vadim Jean, Gary Sinyor A: Mark Frankel, Janet Suzman, Brian Glover, Connie Booth, David de Keyser, Maryam D'Abo (Leon the Pig Farmer)

A good-humored riff on Jewish-gentile stereotypes. Sitcom elements and British scatological humor keep peeking through the comic fabric. Opening has Leon (Mark Frankel) finding he and his brothers are actually the products of artificial insemination, as Dad has a low sperm count. His real father is gentile pig farmer Chadwick (Brian Glover) up north in the wilds of Yorkshire. Surprised but delighted, Chadwick and his wife (Connie Booth) go 200 percent Jewish to make Leon feel at home. Twist comes when Leon, helping out on the farm, accidentally injects a pig with sheep's semen, producing the world's first kosher porker.

LEOPARD, THE
See: Il Gattopardi

LEOPARD MAN, THE
1943, 65 mins, US Ⓥ ⊙

D: Jacques Tourneur A: Dennis O'Keefe, Margo, Jean Brooks, Isabel Jewell, James Bell (RKO)

Dennis O'Keefe is press agent for a New Mexican nitery and rents a tame black leopard for a publicity stunt which backfires when the cat escapes and a girl is presumably killed by the fugitive. Yarn then spins through regulation eerie channels with two other strange murders—one in the timeworn setting of a cemetery and windstorm combined. O'Keefe and Margo stick around long enough to trip the real culprit in time for the fade-out.

LEO THE LAST
1970, 103 mins, UK

D: John Boorman A: Marcello Mastroianni, Billie Whitelaw, Calvin Lockhart, Glenna Forster-Jones, Vladek Sheybal (United Artists)

An absurd satire on dethroned European royalty with a neorealistic view of the London ghetto. Marcello Mastroianni, the last of his line, lives in exile in a magnificent London town house at the end of a cul-de-sac in a black ghetto area. There is a grotesquely hilarious scene of a mass nude water therapy.

LES GIRLS
1957, 114 mins, US Ⓥ ⊙ ⊠

D: George Cukor A: Gene Kelly, Mitzi Gaynor, Kay Kendall, Taina Elg, Jacques Bergerac, Leslie Phillips (M-G-M)

An exceptionally tasty musical morsel, the story of a song-and-dance team made up of Gene Kelly and Mitzi Gaynor, Kay Kendall, and Taina Elg. Known as "Barry Nichols and Les Girls," they are a popular continental act. Many years after the act has broken up, Kendall has written a book of reminiscences that lands her in a London court, the defendant in a libel suit brought by Elg. A series of flashbacks provides the setting for a number of Cole Porter tunes and dances brightly staged by Jack Cole. Porter created seven new songs for the picture.
1957: Best Costume Design
Nominations: Best Art Direction, Sound

LES MISERABLES
1934, 265 mins, France

D: Raymond Bernard A: Harry Bauer, Charles Vanel, Charles Dullin, Jean Servais, Odette Florelle (Pathe/Natan)

The great Harry Baur supports this epic with a power strangely comparable to that of the Jean Valjean he plays. Baer is powerful, disciplined, and moving in the lead role, while other lead and supporting players are far better than average. Raymond Bernard's sharp direction is constantly in evidence. Story is still essentially a moral essay, with Valjean the reformed criminal who becomes the embodiment of good under the constant flagellation of a scrupulous conscience. Vanel, as Javert, the police inspector who constantly haunts Valjean, is excellent; Dullin plays a scurrilous innkeeper.

[Above review is of a (poorly) subtitled 209-min. version released in the US in December 1946.]

LES MISERABLES
1935, 109 mins, US Ⓥ ⊙

D: Richard Boleslawski A: Fredric March, Charles Laughton, Cedric Hardwicke, Rochelle Hudson, John Beal, Frances Drake (20th Century)

Les Miserables will satisfy the most exacting Victor Hugo followers, and at the same time please those looking only for entertainment. Fredric March makes the screen Jean Valjean a living version of the panegyrical character. He is the same persecuted, pursued, pitiable, but always admirable man that all readers of the book must visualize. Side by side with March, throughout the picture, is Charles Laughton, as Javert, the cop. His performance is much more on the quiet side, but equally powerful and always believable.

1935: Nominations: Best Picture, Cinematography, Editing, Assistant Director (Eric Stacey)

LES MISERABLES
1952, 105 mins, US

D: Lewis Milestone A: Michael Rennie, Debra Paget, Robert Newton, Edmund Gwenn, Sylvia Sidney, Cameron Mitchell (20th Century-Fox)

In the first episode, when Valjean is sentenced to 10 years as a galley slave for stealing a loaf of bread, director Lewis Milestone permits the players to cry out flamboyantly against such injustice and the stark miseries of a prison ship existence. The film actually gets going when Valjean, released under parole, becomes a successful pottery owner. He aids Sylvia Sidney, a poor, dying woman, and takes in her daughter (Debra Paget). Rennie does exceptionally well with his role.

LES MISERABLES
1958, 217 mins, France ⊠

D: Jean-Paul le Chanois A: Jean Gabin, Bernard Blier, Bourvil, Daniele Delorme, Gianni Esposito, Serge Reggiani (Pathe/PAC)

This pic, taken from the Victor Hugo novel, with plenty of stars and production values, follows the monumental book too closely. Main strength is Jean Gabin's thesping of Jean Valjean, the man who served 20 years for stealing a crust of bread and then devoted himself to a lifetime of good due to a priest's kindness. The implacable policeman Javert is well played by Bernard Blier. Bourvil is standout as the avaricious enemy of Valjean. In all, the pic is an overdrawn, plodding odyssey.

LES MISERABLES
1982, 187 mins, France Ⓥ ⊠

D: Robert Hossein A: Lino Ventura, Michel Bouquet, Evelyne Bouix, Christiane Jean, Jean Carmet (GEF/SFPC/TF1/DD)

A handsomely produced, but dramatically denatured adaptation of the famous Victor Hugo novel, inhibited by a solemn sense of high purpose. The antimelodramatic style is better-suited to Ventura's dignified, if unmoving, Jean Valjean (though he glosses several crucial dramatic beats), and to Michel Bouquet's ramrod-rigid Javert, who speaks softly and carries a big stick. Two veterans glow briefly: Louis Seigner, as Monseigneur Myriel, and Fernand Ledoux, as a crabby royalist guardian.

LES MISERABLES
1995, 177 mins, France Ⓥ ⊙ ⊠

D: Claude Lelouch A: Jean-Paul Belmondo, Michel Boujenah, Alessandra Martines, Annie Girardot, Philippe Léotard (Les Films 13/TF1)

Hugely ambitious in both theme and scope and brimming with sheer delight in the medium, Claude Lelouch's three-hour *Les Misérables* is the summation of ideas and obsessions the helmer has pursued with increasing complexity during the past 15 years. Taking characters and themes from Victor Hugo's 1862 novel and recycling them through the sieve of key events in the first half of the current century, this is the mightiest of Lelouch's humanist hymns. There is no need to know the Hugo original beyond its broadest outlines: an average guy, imprisoned for a peccadillo, rebuilds his life but is dogged by an obsessive nemesis. Lelouch's saga kicks off with a New Year's ball welcoming in the 20th century, flashes forward to 1931 and 1942, and moves on through the D-Day invasion, the euphoria of the Allied victory (cf. *Bolero*), to the eventual reunion of the main characters in a joyous, end-piece waltz. Jean-Paul Belmondo gives one of the finest perfs of his career, his rubbery, weather-beaten physiognomy moving from moments of interior drama to cheerful optimism with surprising ease.

LESS THAN ZERO
1987, 98 mins, US Ⓥ ⊙
D: Marek Kanievska **A:** Andrew McCarthy, Jami Gertz, Robert Downey Jr., James Spader, Tony Bill (20th Century-Fox)

If it's possible, *Less Than Zero* is even more specious and shallow than the Bret Easton Ellis book it is based on. There's a story somewhere tracking the dissipated lifestyles of the super-rich, super-hip kids and their L.A. haunts. Drugs take over Julian (Robert Downey Jr.), Clay (Andrew McCarthy) avoids the scene by attending an eastern college, and his g.f. Blair (Jami Gertz) loses her identity, which was never much to begin with. This is where they are at the beginning of the film—and pretty much where they are at the end.

LETHAL WEAPON
1987, 110 mins, US Ⓥ ⊙
D: Richard Donner **A:** Mel Gibson, Danny Glover, Gary Busey, Mitchell Ryan, Tom Atkins (Warner/Silver)

A film teetering on the brink of absurdity when it gets serious, but thanks to its unrelenting energy and insistent drive, it never quite falls. Danny Glover is a family-man detective who gets an unwanted partner in the possibly psychotic Mel Gibson. Story is on the back burner as the two men square off against each other, more as adversaries than partners. A plot slowly unfolds involving a massive drug-smuggling operation. Ultimately the common ground for Glover and Gibson is staying alive as the film attempts to shift its buddy story to the battlefields of L.A.
1987: Nomination: Best Sound

LETHAL WEAPON 2
1989, 113 mins, US Ⓥ ⊙ ⊡
D: Richard Donner **A:** Mel Gibson, Danny Glover, Joe Pesci, Joss Ackland, Derrick O'Connor, Patsy Kensit (Warner/Silver)

Loaded with the usual elements, *Lethal Weapon 2* benefits from a consistency of tone that was lacking in the first film. This time, screenwriter and director have wisely trained their sights on humor and the considerable charm of Mel Gibson and Danny Glover's on-screen rapport. They've also dreamed up particularly nasty villains and incorporated enough chases and shoot-outs to hold the attention of a hyperactive nine-year-old.

LETHAL WEAPON 3
1992, 118 mins, US Ⓥ ⊙ ⊡
D: Richard Donner **A:** Mel Gibson, Danny Glover, Joe Pesci, Rene Russo, Stuart Wilson (Warner/Silver)

The recipe again works here, producing a pic that's really more about moments—comic or thrilling—than any sort of cohesive whole. The plot hinges on a wispy premise about an ex-cop (Stuart Wilson) providing confiscated guns to gangs. This time, the emotional focus is on Danny Glover's Roger Murtaugh, who counts down the days to his retirement. Murtaugh and gonzo partner Martin Riggs (Mel Gibson) stumble onto the gun racket, bringing them into contact with high-kicking investigator Lorna Cole (Rene Russo).

LETHAL WEAPON 4
1998, 127 mins, US Ⓥ ⊡
D: Richard Donner **A:** Mel Gibson, Danny Glover, Joe Pesci, Rene Russo, Chris Rock, Jet Li (Silver/Warner)

The quintessence of the buddy cop pic, *Lethal Weapon 4* is big on action, playful banter and just enough plot to keep our attention from wandering. It matters little that the film is rife with non sequiturs, nonsense and nihilistic violence, because its heroes are so darn buoyant and charming. Riggs (Mel Gibson) is about to be a papa, courtesy of Internal Affairs officer Lorna Cole (Rene Russo), and Murtaugh (Danny Glover) is on the cusp of grandfatherhood. Adding to the humor mix is Leo Getz (Joe Pesci), who's now a private detective, and Lee Butters (Chris Rock), a cop with an attitude. A group of Chinese triad members in L.A. are smuggling in families from the mainland, directed by martial arts master and triad leader Wah Sing Ku (Jet Li). Series vet director Richard Donner deftly effects a dazzling freeway chase and a well-choreographed duel-to-the-death sequence.

LET HIM HAVE IT
1991, 115 mins, UK Ⓥ ⊙
D: Peter Medak **A:** Chris Eccleston, Paul Reynolds, Tom Courtenay, Tom Bell, Eileen Atkins (Vivid)

Let Him Have It takes one of the most controversial murder trials in postwar Brit history and comes up with a powerful mix of social conscience and solid entertainment. Pic reconstructs the events leading to the 1952 shoot-out between local cops and cocky, gun-crazy Chris Craig. At age 16, Craig was legally too young to be hanged, so his 19-year-old partner, Derek

Bentley, went to the gallows instead. Pic studiously avoids a docu approach. The dramatic focus begins and ends on a tragic figure of Bentley (Chris Eccleston), an epileptic with the mental age of an 11-year-old.

LET IT BE
1970, 80 mins, UK ⊘

D: Michael Lindsay-Hogg A: Paul McCartney, John Lennon, George Harrison, Ringo Starr, Yoko Ono (Apple)

As a 16mm cinema verité of four rock musicians in a studio jamming a bit, trying to get their music together, clowning and rapping a little, and finally doing a brief concert, *Let It Be* is a relatively innocuous, unimaginative piece of film. But the musicians are the Beatles. Through the studio session, Lennon's wife, Yoko Ono, is always present. The Beatles' past togetherness, the chummy camaraderie, the quickness to seize on a line and build a series of gags, is no longer there. The film finally settles into a studio concert with "Two of Us" and Paul McCartney's "Let It Be." Then the concert moves onto a London roof.

LET'S DANCE
1950, 111 mins, US ⊘ ⊙

D: Norman Z. McLeod A: Fred Astaire, Betty Hutton, Roland Young, Lucile Watson (Paramount)

A light concoction of story, songs, and dances, sprinkled with humor, that is generally acceptable as escapist filmfare. Plot kicks off with a prologue showing Betty Hutton and Fred Astaire entertaining troops in England. She reveals to him her marriage to a flier. Story picks up five years later with Hutton's extrovert character being subdued in the straitlaced environs of a Back Bay Boston mansion, home of her husband, killed in the war. She rebels and steals away in the night with her small son to return to show business.

LET'S DO IT AGAIN
1975, 112 mins, US ⊘

D: Sidney Poitier A: Sidney Poitier, Bill Cosby, Calvin Lockhart, John Amos, Jimmie Walker, Ossie Davis (Warner)

Sidney Poitier, who has a mysterious hex power, and Bill Cosby, whose versatility herein seems as great as that of Peter Sellers, hie to New Orleans to parlay a bankroll into big winnings for their lodge, presided over by a patriarchal Ossie Davis. With wives Lee Chamberlin and Denise Nicholas in tow, the pair confound old-time gangster John Amos and new-wave hood Calvin Lockhart. The film could have been a nightmare of lethargy, but it's a good mixture of broad comedy.

LET'S FACE IT
1943, 76 mins, US

D: Sidney Lanfield A: Bob Hope, Betty Hutton, ZaSu Pitts, Eve Arden (Paramount)

The yarn is about a wacky soldier, who, with two pals, gets involved with three a.k. dames figuring to get revenge on their philandering husbands by hiring soldiers as consorts. Bob Hope, a master at fast vaudeville timing of comedy material, and Betty Hutton, glamorized to an unprecedented degree for a hoydenish singer, are an okay romantic team.

LET'S GET HARRY
1986, 107 mins, US ⊘ ⊙

D: Alan Smithee [Stuart Rosenberg] A: Michael Schoeffling, Tom Wilson, Glenn Frey, Gary Busey, Robert Duvall, Ben Johnson (Tri-Star/Delphi IV & V)

A well-made but utterly routine action picture, worth catching for two excellent (as usual) support performances by Robert Duvall and Gary Busey. It's the trite concept of a group of young guys, led by Michael Shoeffling, deciding to take matters into their own hands to go to Colombia to rescue Schoeffling's brother, Harry (Mark Harmon), kidnapped along with the US ambassador (Bruce Gray) by terrorists. Picture follows rigidly the clichés of this mini-genre, such as the old-hand mercenary (Robert Duvall) who takes the youngsters under his wing.

LET'S MAKE IT LEGAL
1951, 77 mins, US ⊘

D: Richard Sale A: Claudette Colbert, Macdonald Carey, Zachary Scott, Barbara Bates, Robert Wagner, Marilyn Monroe (20th Century-Fox)

A frothy comedy package about a middle-aged couple's divorce and their eventual reconciliation. Gags and mildly amusing situations abound in the script, but they're never genuinely effective. After 20 years of varying bliss, Claudette Colbert and Macdonald Carey call it quits. Just when the final decree becomes effective, Zachary Scott comes on the scene. An old beau of Colbert's, he still has the fire of conquest burning in him. Carey rises to meet the competition.

LET'S MAKE LOVE
1960, 118 mins, US ⓋⒸ
D: George Cukor **A:** Marilyn Monroe, Yves Montand, Tony Randall, Frankie Vaughan, Wilfrid Hyde-White (20th Century-Fox)

The entire film has taken something not too original (the Cinderella theme) and dressed it up like new. Monroe is a sheer delight in the tailor-made role of an off-Broadway actress who wants to better herself intellectually (she is going to night school to study geography), but she also has a uniquely talented costar in Yves Montand. Latter gives a sock performance, full of both heart and humor, as the richest man in the world who wants to find a woman who'll love him for himself alone. Whenever the story threatens to intrude with tedium, there's a knockout Cole Porter musical number.
1960: Nomination: Best Scoring of a Musical Picture

LETTER, THE
1940, 95 mins, US Ⓥ
D: William Wyler **A:** Bette Davis, Herbert Marshall, James Stephenson, Gale Sondergaard (Warner)

Essentially a mystery, film opens with Bette Davis shooting a man dead as he runs from her plantation house. The question mark from there to the climax is why? She explains to her planter-husband (Herbert Marshall) and an attorney friend (James Stephenson) that the murdered man had made advances toward her. It's evident that she's not telling the truth. Davis's frigidity at times seems to go even beyond the characterization. Marshall never falters. Virtually stealing thesp honors in the pic, however, is Stephenson as the attorney, while Sondergaard is the perfect masklike threat. The music by Max Steiner is particularly noteworthy.
1940: Nominations: Best Picture, Director, Actress (Bette Davis), Supp. Actor (James Stephenson), B&W Cinematography, Editing, Original Score

LETTER FROM AN UNKNOWN WOMAN
1948, 84 mins, US Ⓥ
D: Max Ophuls **A:** Joan Fontaine, Louis Jourdan, Mady Christians, Marcel Journet, Art Smith (Rampart/Universal)

Joan Fontaine and Louis Jourdan both turn in splendid performances in difficult parts that could easily have been overplayed. The mounting has an artistic flavor that captures the atmosphere of early-day

Vienna and has been beautifully photographed. Film is endowed with little touches that give it warmth and heart while the tragic tale is being unfolded. It concerns a young girl who falls in love with a neighbor, a concert pianist. Years later she again meets her only love but he fails to remember. Story is told as he reads a letter from the girl, written after the second meeting.

LETTER TO BREZHNEV
1985, 95 mins, UK Ⓥ
D: Chris Bernard **A:** Alexandra Pigg, Alfred Molina, Peter Firth, Margi Clarke, Tracy Lea (Yeardream/Film Four/Palace)

This is a farce, penned with wit and acted with appropriate deadpan honesty. Picture a Russian ship docking in Liverpool. Two sailors go ashore for a night on the town, both primed with Beatles folklore and one speaking enough English to get them both by with the lasses in a dance hall. Elaine, the Liverpool innocent, meets Peter, the Russian romantic from the Black Sea. They fall in love at first sight. When they part, the naive Elaine finds it unfair that the world's political stage should prove a hindrance to their ever seeing each other again. So she writes a letter to Brezhnev—and gets an answer.

LETTER TO THREE WIVES, A
1948, 108 mins, US Ⓥ
D: Joseph L. Mankiewicz **A:** Jeanne Crain, Linda Darnell, Ann Sothern, Kirk Douglas, Paul Douglas, Barbara Lawrence (20th Century-Fox)

Idea has three young housewives all jealous of the same she-wolf who grew up with their husbands. The "other woman" addresses a letter to all three wives explaining that she has run away with one of their spouses but without identifying which one. The audience is then given a chance to figure out which one it is, before a surprise denouement explains all. Legit actor Paul Douglas's role is that of a big, blustering, but slightly dumb tycoon and he really gives it a ride with some neat character shading. Rest of the cast is equally good.
1949: Best Director, Screenplay
Nomination: Best Picture

LET THE GOOD TIMES ROLL
1973, 99 mins, US Ⓒ
D: Sid Levin, Robert Abel **A:** Chuck Berry, Little Richard, Fats Domino, Chubby Checker, Bo Diddley, the Shirelles (Metromedia)

A smash recreation of 1950s rock-and-roll frenzy, a moving and exciting nostalgia trip. The production focuses on two rock-and-roll revival concerts, personalizes the 33 musical numbers with penetrating backstage views of the performers, and underpins the whole with astutely chosen film and video clips and stills of the decade. In a group consisting of such 1950s giants as Fats Domino, Chubby Checker, the Shirelles, Bill Haley and the Comets, the Five Satins, the Coasters, Danny and the Juniors, and the Bobby Comstock Rock & Roll Band, best of all is Little Richard, that pompadoured teenage screamer who affects the next best thing to drag for his frenetic workouts with an equally hysteric audience.

LETYAT ZHURAVLI
(US: THE CRANES ARE FLYING)
1957, 90 mins, USSR ⊗
D: Mikhail Kalatozov **A:** Tatyana Samoilova, Aleksei Batalov, Vasili Merkuryev, A. Shvorin, S. Kharitonova (Mosfilm)

A moving tale of a tender love affair shattered by the war. Its bravura is sometimes too flashy, but the sensitivity of portrayals lifts this overcontrived plot to a poignant level. Virile, sometimes overboard direction nonetheless brings out intelligent acting by Tatyana Samoilova and Aleksei Batalov.

LEVIATHAN
1989, 98 mins, US ⊗ ⊙ ▱
D: George Pan Cosmatos **A:** Peter Weller, Richard Crenna, Amanda Pays, Daniel Stern, Ernie Hudson (De Laurentiis/Gordon/M-G-M)

Breed an *Alien* with *Thing*, marinate in salt water, and you get *Leviathan*. It's a soggy recycling of gruesome monster attacks unleashed upon a crew of macho men and women confined within a far-flung scientific outpost. Shot on elaborate sets in Rome, pic boasts impressive production design by Ron Cobb.

LA LEY DEL DESEO
(US: THE LAW OF DESIRE)
1987, 101 mins, Spain ⊗ ⊙
D: Pedro Almodovar **A:** Eusebio Poncela, Carmen Maura, Antonio Banderas, Miguel Molina (El Deseo/Laurenfilm)

Spain's master of pop and pastiche, Pedro Almodovar, turns his talents here to a gay love triangle, with extraneous touches of fantasy, farce, and camp humor. Pic also has a certain outrageous look to it which makes the antics more palatable.

Convoluted story concerns a famous film director, Pablo (Eusebio Poncela), and his way-out sister, Tina (Carmen Maura). Pablo is madly in love with Juan (Miguel Molina), who works in an outdoor bar in Andalucia. The third part of the triangle, Antonio (Antonio Banderas), falls deeply in love with the director, and ultimately decides to get rid of his competitor, Juan, by pushing him off a cliff.

LES LIAISONS DANGEREUSES
(US: DANGEROUS LIAISONS)
1960, 108 mins, France ⊗
D: Roger Vadim **A:** Gérard Philipe, Jeanne Moreau, Jeanne Valérie, Annette Vadim, Jean-Louis Trintignant (Marceau/Cocinor)

Based on an 18th-century classic, updated pic is a glossy study of an immoral couple who get their comeuppance. A young diplomat (Gérard Philipe) and his wife (Jeanne Moreau) have found a perfect harmony. He allows her to have all the affairs she wants and she helps him in his conquests. Both seem content until love comes into this completely immoral household to bring on tragedy. Philipe plays the eternal Don Juan in a pasty way and rarely elicits an understanding of his character and drive. But Moreau is perfect as the catlike, steely wife.

LIANNA
1983, 110 mins, US ⊗
D: John Sayles **A:** Linda Griffiths, Jane Hallaren, Jon DeVries, Jo Henderson, Jesse Solomon, John Sayles (Winwood)

John Sayles again uses a keen intelligence and finely tuned ear to tackle the nature of friendship and loving. Story of a 33-year-old woman (Linda Griffiths), saddled with an arrogant and unsupportive professor-husband (John DeVries) who constricts her life until she finds herself falling in love, for the first time, with a woman teacher (Jane Hallaren). Particularly well-drawn are her doubly hurt husband's sense of sexual betrayal, the half-formed understandings of her children, and the ambivalence of once-close women friends.

LIBEL
1959, 100 mins, UK ⊗
D: Anthony Asquith **A:** Dirk Bogarde, Olivia de Havilland, Paul Massie, Robert Morley, Wilfrid Hyde-White, Richard Wattis (M-G-M)

A stylish and attention-holding film. The idea is simple enough. Is Sir Mark

Loddon (Dirk Bogarde), owner of one of the stately homes of England, really Loddon or an unscrupulous imposter, as alleged by a wartime comrade? A young Canadian airman is convinced that he is really Frank Welney, a small-part actor. The three were in prison camp together and he is confident that Loddon was killed during a prison break. Bogarde carries much of the onus since he plays both Loddon (during the war and at the time of the trial) and Welney. He does a standout job, suggesting the difference in the two characters remarkably well.

1959: Nomination: Best Sound

LIBELED LADY
1936, 85 mins, US Ⓥ ⊙
D: Jack Conway **A:** Jean Harlow, William Powell, Myrna Loy, Spencer Tracy, Walter Connolly (M-G-M)

Even though *Libeled Lady* goes overboard on plot and its pace snags badly in several spots, Metro has brought in a sockeroo of a comedy. Powell, as the troubleshooter for a newspaper, undertakes to frame a young millionairess and thereby compel her to drop a $5-million libel suit. The expected occurs; he falls in love with her. Concerned with Powell in the frame are Tracy, managing editor of the sheet, and the latter's fiancée (Harlow). Latter frequently steals the picture when the opportunities for cutting loose fall her way.

1936: Nomination: Best Picture

LIBERATION OF L. B. JONES, THE
1970, 102 mins, US Ⓥ
D: William Wyler **A:** Lee J. Cobb, Anthony Zerbe, Roscoe Lee Browne, Lola Falana, Lee Majors, Barbara Hershey (Columbia)

This story of a glossed-over Negro's murder by a Dixie policeman is, unfortunately, not much more than an interracial sexploitation film. The well-structured plot finds lawyer Cobb trying to avoid an open-court revelation that a white married cop is a Negro woman's lover.

LIBERTY HEIGHTS
1999, 127 mins, US Ⓥ ⊙
D: Barry Levinson **A:** Adrien Brody, Ben Foster, Orlando Jones, Bebe Neuwirth, Joe Mantegna, Rebekah Johnson (Baltimore/Spring Creek/Warner)

Barry Levinson goes deep with *Liberty Heights*, his fourth "Baltimore picture," and the result is a grand slam. Film pinpoints a moment in the mid-fifties when previously partitioned segments of society began gingerly mixing and influencing each other. In the Kurtzman family, grown-ups live by the motto "If they're not Jewish, they're 'the other kind.' " This attitude is not heeded by the two boys, college student Van (Adrien Brody) and high-schooler Ben (Ben Foster). Van falls hard for blond, blue-eyed goddess Dubbie (Carolyn Murphy), while Ben pursues an ardent friendship with Sylvia (Rebekah Johnson), the first black student in his class. Levinson asserts story's human grounding in resolutions that are bittersweet, properly scaled, and historically prescient.

LICENSE TO KILL
1989, 133 mins, UK Ⓥ ⊙ ▭
D: John Glen **A:** Timothy Dalton, Carey Lowell, Robert Davi, Talisa Soto, Anthony Zerbe (United Artists/Eon)

The James Bond production team has found its second wind with a cocktail of high-octane action, spectacle and drama. Dalton plays 007 with a vigor and physicality that harks back to the earliest Bond pics, letting full-bloodied actions speak louder than words. The thrills-and-spills chases are superbly orchestrated as pic spins at breakneck speed through its south Florida and Central American locations. Bond survives a series of underwater and midair stunt sequences that are above par for the series.

LIEBELEI
1933, 83 mins, Germany
D: Max Ophuls **A:** Magda Schneider, Wolfgang Liebeneiner, Luise Ullrich, Gustaf Gruendgens, Willy Eichberger (Elite)

Arthur Schnitzler's play is the simple little story of two lieutenants picking up two sweet little Vienna girls. With the elder and more experienced couple it's just a gay, harmless love affair; with the other two (not yet out of their teens) it develops into deep love. The film treatment has succeeded in preserving most of the play's flavor, adding a good amount of comedy, music, and background.

LIEBESTRAUM
1991, 102 mins, US Ⓥ ⊙
D: Mike Figgis **A:** Kevin Anderson, Pamela Gidley, Bill Pullman, Kim Novak, Catherine Hicks (M-G-M/Initial)

Pic is set in a grimy town hoping for an economic turnaround via demolition of a defunct department store and the construction of a shopping mall. The town continues to have repercussions of a murder that took place 30 years earlier (and shown during the opening credits). Figgis gets good use of his Binghamton, NY, locations, including the old building that's the focus of much of the film. Problem here is the confused script, which doesn't seem to have a point.

LIES MY FATHER TOLD ME
1975, 103 mins, Canada ⓥ
D: Jan Kadar **A:** Yossi Yadin, Len Birman, Marilyn Lightstone, Jeffrey Lynas, Ted Allan (Pentimento/Pentacle VIII)

Set in Montreal in the 1920s, film centers on an emotional relationship between a young boy, portrayed by newcomer Jeffrey Lynas, and his aged, peddler grandfather, played by Israeli actor Yossi Yadin. Threatening this relationship at all times is the boy's hard luck, no-talent father (Len Birman), and his long-suffering mother (Marilyn Lightstone). An absorbing nostalgic trip, powerful but never pushy.
1975: Nomination: Best Original Screenplay

LIEUTENANT WORE SKIRTS, THE
1956, 98 mins, US ▭
D: Frank Tashlin **A:** Tom Ewell, Sheree North, Rita Moreno, Rick Jason, Les Tremayne (20th Century-Fox)

Amusing comedy affair. Tom Ewell's an aging World War II hero now a TV writer, and Sheree North, his wife, is an ex-WAC considerably younger. The comedy of errors tees off when she rejoins the service because he is recalled. However, he's rejected, and then dejected because she likes her uniform. From then on comedy hinges on his efforts to get her discharged.

LIFE
1999, 108 mins, US ⓥ ◉
D: Ted Demme **A:** Eddie Murphy, Martin Lawrence, Obba Babatunde, Ned Beatty, Bernie Mac, Miguel A. Nunez Jr. (Imagine/Universal)

Covering 55 years in the lives of two bickering convicts bonded by a miscarriage of justice and inextinguishable hope, *Life* careens from decade to decade, and from relative dramatic realism to frequent hilarity, in often winning fashion. Yarn starts in 1932 Harlem, where fast-talking hustler Ray Gibson (Eddie Murphy) and aspiring bank teller Claude Banks (Martin Lawrence) incur debts to a bootlegger. To pay it off the pair drive south to pick up a load of moonshine, are framed for murder by the venal local sheriff, and sentenced to life. All along, the two men cling to the idea that they'll escape one day. Murphy's rude, live-wire personality is turned on to strong comic effect. Lawrence provides a fine foil, but his anger doesn't go deep enough.
1999: Nomination: Best Makeup

LIFE AND DEATH OF COLONEL BLIMP, THE
1943, 163 mins, UK ⓥ ◉
D: Michael Powell, Emeric Pressburger **A:** Roger Livesey, Deborah Kerr, Anton Walbrook, Roland Culver, Albert Lieven (Archers/Independent)

A clear, continuous unreeling of events in the life of an English military man, from the Boer War, through World War I, and up to the completion of the training and equipment of England's home guard. Story revolves around an officer (Clive Candy) who has spent all his life in the army and still feels the German people as a whole are decent human beings, and that they're only tools of their warlords. The role of Candy is spasmodically well enacted by Roger Livesey. More generous praise should go to Anton Walbrook as an Uhlan officer. Deborah Kerr contributes attractively as the feminine lead in three separate characters. Title is based on the symbolic figure of the old-time English officers who have been axed.

LIFE AND TIMES OF JUDGE ROY BEAN, THE
1972, 120 mins, US ⓥ
D: John Huston **A:** Paul Newman, Victoria Principal, Anthony Perkins, Ned Beatty, John Huston, Ava Gardner (First Artists)

Two-hour running time is not fleshed out with anything more than scenic vignettes, with an Alan and Marilyn Bergman–lyricked tune and Maurice Jarre's music sometimes attempting honest spoofing of westerns, and sometimes trying to play the story historically straight. The overkill and the underdone do it in. Newman is good as Bean, injecting charm into the character along with the rough exterior.
1972: Nomination: Best Song ("Marmalade, Molasses and Honey")

LIFE AT THE TOP
1965, 118 mins, UK
D: Ted Kotcheff **A:** Laurence Harvey,

Jean Simmons, Honor Blackman, Michael Craig, Donald Wolfit, Robert Morley (Romulus)

Some of the gloss of *Room at the Top* rubs off on this follow-up, but the film lacks both the motivation and rare subtlety that elevated its predecessor. It continues the story of the young, designing opportunist who rose to the top in society and business, but at loss of his self-respect. Having enjoyed the position he sought for a decade, he is even more aware of the necessity of clinging to his ideals and tries to do something about a life he has found empty. Laurence Harvey continues in the mood of his character in *Room*. Jean Simmons as his wife has a rather unsympathetic character.

LIFE BEGINS
1932, 71 mins, US
D: James Flood, Elliott Nugent **A:** Loretta Young, Eric Linden, Aline MacMahon, Glenda Farrell, Vivienne Osborne (Warner)

A good picture, a woman's picture, different, and on the serious side. The theme is childbirth, with the entire locale a hospital and the story particularly concerned with a cross section of probably any maternity ward. Aline MacMahon, as the ever efficient nurse, Glenda Farrell, and Eric Linden comprise the performing highlights.

LIFE BEGINS IN COLLEGE
1937, 90 mins, US
D: William A. Seiter **A:** Ritz Brothers, Joan Davis, Tony Martin, Gloria Stuart, Fred Stone (20th Century-Fox)

The frères Ritz first appear as student tailors with a record of seven years in school and seven on the football bench. Then they're seen in a madcap rumba specialty; as newly rich undergrads bracing the dean for a favor; as footballers who help the enemy more than their teammates; as an Indian burlesque troupe; and then as hokum Spirit of '76 boys. Outside of the Ritz Brothers, Nat Pendleton's interpretation of the Indian grid star is standout, and Joan Davis, especially excellent in that goofy Indian powwow song and dance.

LIFEBOAT
1944, 86 mins, US ⊘ ⊙
D: Alfred Hitchcock **A:** Tallulah Bankhead, William Bendix, Walter Slezak, John Hodiak, Hume Cronyn, Canada Lee (20th Century-Fox)

John Steinbeck's devastating indictment of the nature of Nazi bestiality emerges as powerful adult motion-picture fare. The picture is based on an original idea of director Alfred Hitchcock. It's a lusty, robust story about a group of survivors from a ship sunk by a U-boat. One by one the survivors find precarious refuge on the lifeboat. Finally they pick up a survivor from the German U-boat. He is first tolerated and then welcomed into their midst. And he repays their trust and confidence with murderous treachery. Walter Slezak, as the German, comes through with a terrific delineation.

1944: Nominations: Best Director, Original Story, B&W Cinematography

LIFEFORCE
1985, 101 mins, US ⊘ ⊙ ▭
D: Tobe Hooper **A:** Steve Railsback, Peter Firth, Frank Finlay, Mathilda May, Patrick Stewart (Cannon)

Yank and British space travelers discover seemingly human remains. The astronauts don't make it back but the humanoids do, and one of them, Space Girl (Mathilda May), is possessed of special talents, which include a form of electroshock vampirism and the ability to inhabit other bodies. Pic descends into subpar Agatha Christie territory, as fanatical inspector Peter Firth and surviving astronaut Steve Railsback scour the countryside for the deadly Space Girl.

LIFE FOR RUTH
(US: WALK IN THE SHADOW)
1962, 91 mins, UK
D: Basil Dearden **A:** Michael Craig, Patrick McGoohan, Janet Munro, Paul Rogers, Megs Jenkins, Frank Finlay (Allied Film Makers)

Eight-year-old daughter of an honest workingman (Michael Craig) is gravely ill. Only a blood transfusion can save her. Because of his strict religious principles, the father adamantly refuses, and the child dies. The doctor (Patrick McGoohan) who urged the transfusion is so irate that he gets the father tried for manslaughter. This is good telling stuff for drama and it poses questions about religion, the law, conscience, marital relationship with intelligence and conviction.

LIFEGUARD
1976, 96 mins, US ⦵
D: Daniel Petrie **A:** Sam Elliott, Anne Archer, Stephen Young, Parker Stevenson, Kathleen Quinlan (Paramount)

An unsatisfying film, of uncertain focus about a 30-ish guy who doesn't yet seem to know what he wants. Script takes Sam Elliott through another Southern California beach summer as a career lifeguard, encountering the usual string of offbeat characters found in the type of made-for-TV feature which this project resembles.

LIFE IS CHEAP... BUT TOILET PAPER IS EXPENSIVE
1990, 90 mins, US ⦵
D: Wayne Wang, Spencer Nakasako **A:** Spencer Nakasako, Cora Miao, Victor Wong, John K. Chan (Far East Stars)

Audaciously stylish and visually mesmerizing, *Life Is Cheap* aims to evoke the uncertain mood of Hong Kong as viewed from the perspective of an Asian-American naif. Screenwriter-star Spencer Nakasako is a stable hand from San Francisco who has agreed to act as a courier for a Triad, the Chinese Mafia, in return for an all-expenses-paid sojourn in Hong Kong. He wants to see the legendary port before its takeover by China. Wang skewers the lofty notion of Chinese self-superiority by populating his film with a widely variegated gallery of funny and flawed characters.

LIFE IS SWEET
1991, 102 mins, UK ⦵ ⊙
D: Mike Leigh **A:** Alison Steadman, Jim Broadbent, Timothy Spall, Claire Skinner, Jane Horrocks, David Thewlis (Thin Man)

Mike Leigh's third pic is a highly sympathetic comedy, embroidered by a superb performance from helmer's wife, Alison Steadman. Steadman is ideally cast as a suburban housewife and mother who sells baby clothes, supports her husband (Jim Broadbent), and attempts to look after her teen twin daughters (one a plumber, the other an anorexic rebel). She is a survivor, who helps others survive, too.

LIFE LESS ORDINARY, A
1997, 103 mins, UK ⦵ ⊙
D: Danny Boyle **A:** Ewan McGregor, Cameron Diaz, Holly Hunter, Delroy Lindo, Ian Holm, Stanley Tucci (Figment/PolyGram)

After *Shallow Grave* and *Trainspotting*, the Brit trio of helmer Danny Boyle, producer Andrew Macdonald and writer John Hodge hit major speed bumps. This offbeat comedy-romancer is a pleasant enough ride but has too many ideas in the script to satisfy at any emotional level. Part kooky romance, part screwball comedy, part quirky fantasy and part Roadrunner cartoon, it has everything except an involving story line and characters. Celine (Cameron Diaz) is a businessman's pampered daughter, while Robert (Ewan McGregor) works as a janitor in her dad's corporation. When Robert is pinkslipped, he storms into the office of Celine's dad (Ian Holm) and kidnaps her at gunpoint. The twist is that Celine hates her father and, realizing Robert is no threat, schools the klutzy Scot in bargaining techniques. The humor is very British in tone (Hodge originally intended to set the story in the UK and France) and sounds more natural in McGregor's mouth than in Diaz's.

LIFE OF BRIAN
1979, 93 mins, UK ⦵ ⊙
D: Terry Jones **A:** Terry Jones, Michael Palin, John Cleese, Eric Idle, Spike Milligan, George Harrison (Warner/Orion)

Monty Python's utterly irreverent tale of a reluctant messiah whose impact proved somewhat less pervasive than that of his contemporary Jesus Christ is just as wacky and imaginative as their earlier film outings. Film was shot using stunning Tunisian locales. Tone of the film is set by such scenes as a version of the Sermon on the Mount in which spectators shout out that they can't hear what's being said and start fighting among themselves.

LIFE OF EMILE ZOLA, THE
1937, 123 mins, US ⦵
D: William Dieterle **A:** Paul Muni, Gloria Holden, Gale Sondergaard, Joseph Schildkraut, Robert Warwick (Warner)

A vibrant, tense, and emotional story about the man who fought a nation with his pen and successfully championed the cause of the exiled Captain Alfred Dreyfus. With Paul Muni in the title role, supported by distinguished players, the film is finely made. Dreyfus was banished by court-martial after conspiracy charges that he betrayed military secrets to Germany. Although the release of Dreyfus is made the principal dramatic incident of the picture, the development of the character and career of Zola remains dominant.
1937: Best Picture, Supp. Actor (Joseph Schildkraut), Screenplay

Nominations: Best Director, Actor (Paul Muni), Original Story, Score, Sound, Assistant Director (Russ Saunders)

LIFE OF HER OWN, A
1950, 106 mins, US
D: George Cukor **A:** Lana Turner, Ray Milland, Tom Ewell, Louis Calhern, Jean Hagen (M-G-M)

A true-confession type of yarn concerned with a big-city romance between a married man and a beautiful model. Lana Turner is believable as the model. Since the entire story is pointed to the distaff side, Ray Milland's role suffers as the man, married to a crippled wife, who goes off the deep end for the model.

LIFE STINKS
1991, 95 mins, US Ⓥ ⊙
D: Mel Brooks **A:** Mel Brooks, Lesley Ann Warren, Jeffrey Tambor, Stuart Pankin, Howard Morris, Rudy De Luca (Brooksfilms)

A fitfully funny vaudeville caricature about life on skid row. Premise of a rich man who chooses to live among the poor for a spell feels sorely undeveloped, and suffers from the usual gross effects and exaggerations. Some effective bug-eyed, freewheeling comedy is scattered throughout, much of it descending to the Three Stooges level of sophistication. But distressingly little is done with the vast possibilities offered by the setting and the characters populating it.

LIFE WITH FATHER
1947, 118 mins, US Ⓥ
D: Michael Curtiz **A:** Irene Dunne, William Powell, Elizabeth Taylor, Edmund Gwenn, ZaSu Pitts (Warner)

Irene Dunne and William Powell have captured to a considerable extent the charm of the play by Howard Lindsay and Russel Crouse. The major humor of the story, based on Father's eccentric characteristics and Mother's continual mollifying of his tantrums, is still evident in the pic. The Day children are not as effectively projected as in the play, but this, too, has been shrouded by the lesser intimacy of the pic.
1947: Nominations: Best Actor (William Powell), Color Cinematography, Color Art Direction, Scoring of a Dramatic Picture

LIFE WITH MIKEY
1993, 91 mins, US Ⓥ ⊙
D: James Lapine **A:** Michael J. Fox, Christina Vidal, Nathan Lane, Cyndi Lauper, David Huddleston (Touchstone)

Michael Chapman (Fox) was once the star of his own sitcom. Unfortunately, he topped out at age 15, and now suffers from a serious case of Peter Pan–itis. Then a streetwise 10-year-old (newcomer Christina Vidal) steals Michael's wallet and puts on a Meryl Streep–quality performance when caught. She quickly lands a major commercial gig and moves in with Michael. This is all very stock, predictable stuff, but director James Lapine and writer/co-producer Marc Lawrence bring an easy charm to most of the proceedings. Fox turns in an extremely likable, believable performance.

LIFT, THE
See: De Lift

DE LIFT
(US: THE LIFT)
1983, 99 mins, Netherlands Ⓥ
D: Dick Maas **A:** Huub Stapel, Willeke van Ammelrooy, Josine van Dalsum (Sigma)

Humor from charcoal gray to pitch-black, fine suspense, murders and thrills, and all of it without gratuitous gore combine for a jaunty entertainment. Hero is an elevator maintenance man, Felix (Huub Stapel). The antihero is the elevator itself—an eccentric, malign, office-building conveyance whose passengers either suffocate, are decapitated by the doors, or dumped down the shaft. The vexed maintenance man finally gets to the bottom of the mystery.

LIFT TO THE SCAFFOLD
See: L'Ascenseur pour L'Echafaud

LIGHT AT THE EDGE OF THE WORLD, THE
1971, 120 mins, US Ⓥ ⊡
D: Kevin Billington **A:** Kirk Douglas, Yul Brynner, Samantha Eggar, Jean-Claude Drouot, Fernando Rey, Renato Salvatori (National General)

Good action-adventure escapism. The stars are Kirk Douglas, who produced on Spanish locations, as the sole survivor on an island captured by pirate Yul Brynner, with Samantha Eggar as a shipwrecked hostage.

LIGHTHORSEMEN, THE
1987, 128 mins, Australia Ⓥ ⊡
D: Simon Wincer **A:** Jon Blake, Peter Phelps, Tony Bonner, Bill Kerr, Anthony Andrews (RKO/Picture Show)

Toward the end of this epic about Aussie cavalry fighting in the Middle East in 1917, there's a tremendously exciting and spectacular 14-minute sequence in which soldiers of the Light Horse charge on German/Turkish–occupied Beersheba. It's a pity writer and coproducer Ian Jones couldn't come up with a more substantial story line to build around his terrific climax. Main story involves four friends (Jon Blake, John Walton, Tim McKenzie, Gary Sweet) who are members of the Australian cavalry, chaffing because the British, who have overall command of Allied troops in the area, misuse the cavalry time and again.

LIGHT IN THE DARKNESS
See: Pokolenie

LIGHT IN THE PIAZZA
1962, 102 mins, US ▭
D: Guy Green A: Olivia de Havilland, Rossano Brazzi, Yvette Mimieux, George Hamilton, Barry Sullivan (M-G-M)

Discerningly cast and deftly executed in the intoxicatingly visual environments of Rome and Florence, film is an interesting touching drama. Concise and graceful screenplay examines the odd plight of a beautiful, wealthy 26-year-old American girl (Yvette Mimieux) who has been left with a permanent 10-year-old mentality. It is, too, the story of her mother's (Olivia de Havilland) dilemma—whether to commit the girl to an institution or pave the way for the girl's marriage to a well-to-do young Florentine fellow (George Hamilton) by concealing knowledge of the child's retarded intelligence.

LIGHT OF DAY
1987, 107 mins, US ⓥ ⓞ
D: Paul Schrader A: Michael J. Fox, Gena Rowlands, Joan Jett, Michael McKean, Thomas G. Waites (Taft/Barish)

A tortured family melodrama with a rock-and-roll beat. Renegade daughter Patti Rasnick (Joan Jett) and her younger brother, Joe (Michael J. Fox), play in a talented but routine bar band that performs in taverns around Ohio. Director Paul Schrader, who also wrote the screenplay, has spread enough guilt around this family to fill a book. Jett has a four-year-old son (Billy Sullivan) but won't tell anyone who the father is. She hates her mother (Gena Rowlands) despite Mom's attempts to show her God's way. With the passive father (Jason Miller) and the dutiful son (Fox), this could be anyfamily USA as written by Eugene O'Neill.

LIGHTSHIP, THE
1985, 89 mins, US ⓥ
D: Jerzy Skolimowski A: Robert Duvall, Klaus Maria Brandauer, Tom Bower, Robert Costanzo, William Forsythe (CBS)

The setting is the only seaworthy lightship left, and it's on this precarious wreck that everything takes place. The other major plus is the acting duel between Robert Duvall and Klaus Maria Brandauer, both with thespian styles of their own and in direct contrast to each other. As a psychological thriller, *The Lightship* has its tense moments, but the narrative line takes so many detours that the problem is trying to figure out the non sequiturs as they surface out of nowhere.

LIGHT SLEEPER
1992, 100 mins, US ⓥ ⓞ
D: Paul Schrader A: Willem Dafoe, Susan Sarandon, Dana Delaney, David Clennon, Mary Beth Hurt (Seven Arts)

Paul Schrader has created a pointed companion piece to his earlier portraits of lonely outcasts (*Taxi Driver*, *American Gigolo*). Contemplative and violent by turns, this quasi-thriller about a longtime drug dealer leaving the business has a great deal to recommend it but could have been significantly better. A former heavy user himself, LeTour (Willem Dafoe) has long worked as a drug delivery boy for Ann (Susan Sarandon). He runs into the love of his life, Marianne (Dana Delaney), who has gone clean with difficulty and now wants nothing to do with him. A superb Dafoe contributes crucially to the degree of success the film achieves.

LIGHTS OF NEW YORK
1928, 57 mins, US
D: Bryan Foy A: Helene Costello, Cullen Landis, Gladys Brockwell, Mary Carr, Wheeler Oakman, Eugene Pallette (Warner)

This picture got pretty billing in Warners describing it as "the first 100 percent all-talking picture." Every character speaks, more or less. But it's not an expensively made picture in appearance, either in sets or cast. It's underworld, starting in a small town and moving to a nightclub on the Giddy Wild Way. There are bootleggers and gunmen, cops and muggs, the latter a couple of simps falling for con men back home in a hotel about

724

twice the size of the town—from the looks of the set. Helene Costello, in the fem lead, is a total loss. For talkers she had better go to school right away.

LIKE A HOUSE ON FIRE
See: Hori, Ma Panenko

LIKE WATER FOR CHOCOLATE
See: Como Agua Para Chocolate

LI'L ABNER
1959, 113 mins, US ⊗
D: Melvin Frank A: Peter Palmer, Leslie Parrish, Stubby Kaye, Howard St. John, Julie Newmar, Stella Stevens (Paramount)

The Norman Panama–Melvin Frank filmization of their Broadway hit is lively, colorful, and tuneful. Congress plans to use L'il Abner's hometown of Dogpatch for an atom-bomb testing ground, it being the most worthless locale in the US. Dogpatchers must prove the town has some value so it will be spared. The item found is Mammy Yokum's Yokumberry Tonic, a stimulant to health and wealth and romance. The songs, by Gene De Paul and Johnny Mercer, are breezy and amusing. DeeDee Wood's dances, based on Michael Kidd's stage choreography, have considerable dazzle. Stubby Kaye creates the most fun with a brisk portrayal of Marryin' Sam.
1959: Nomination: Best Scoring of a Dramatic Picture

LILAC TIME
1928, 100 mins, US
D: George Fitzmaurice A: Colleen Moore, Gary Cooper, Burr McIntosh, George Cooper, Edward Dillon, Kathryn McGuire (First National)

The story has elements recalling *Wings* in the air and *Seventh Heaven* in the closing scenes of the romantic portion. The romance is laid on thick, at times too thick. Worked into the air battle is the Red Ace of Germany, a famous flier of the First World War. Picture throws too much work on the girl. Colleen Moore never misses on the light or heavy side. Nevertheless her tribulations or those of the fliers and her captain lover never raise a lump. Gary Cooper readily falls into the role as the captain.

LILI
1953, 80 mins, US ⊗
D: Charles Walters A: Leslie Caron, Mel Ferrer, Jean-Pierre Aumont, Zsa Zsa Gabor, Kurt Kasznar, Amanda Blake (M-G-M)

Leslie Caron is a young French orphan who turns to a fascinating carnival magician, Jean-Pierre Aumont, for help. He's a Gallic wolf, but Lili's naive, 16-year-old innocence is too much for him, so he brushes her off with a waitress job with the show. Mel Ferrer, a puppeteer, uses his little friends to woo her from her sorrow. The impromptu performance is so successful, Ferrer makes it part of the act. Gruff and moody in his dealings with the girl, the puppet master actually loves her and is jealous over her continuing infatuation for Aumont. Caron's metamorphosis from the forlorn little ugly duckling to a pixie-faced, attractive young lady is well handled.
1953: Best Scoring of a Dramatic Picture
Nominations: Best Director, Actress (Leslie Caron), Screenplay, Color Cinematography, Color Art Direction

LILIES OF THE FIELD
1963, 94 mins, US ⊗
D: Ralph Nelson A: Sidney Poitier, Lilia Skala, Lisa Mann, Stanley Adams (Rainbow/United Artists)

Made on a modest budget and filmed on location in Arizona, *Lilies* reveals Sidney Poitier as an actor with a sharp sense of humor. He is a journeyman laborer who meets his match in five members of a holy order. As the mother superior sets eyes on Poitier, she is convinced that God has answered her prayers and sent a strong healthy man to fix the roof of their farmhouse. Many factors combine in the overall success of the film, notably the restrained direction by Ralph Nelson, a thoroughly competent screenplay by James Poe, and, of course, Poitier's standout performance.
1963: Best Actor (Sidney Poitier)
Nominations: Best Picture, Supp. Actress (Lilia Skala), Adapted Screenplay, B&W Cinematography

LILITH
1964, 110 mins, US ⊗
D: Robert Rossen A: Warren Beatty, Jean Seberg, Peter Fonda, Kim Hunter, Jessica Walter, Gene Hackman (Centaur)

The story of a young man who becomes an occupational therapist in a private mental institution where patients share three conditions—schizophrenia, wealth, and uncommon intelligence: Warren Beatty undertakes lead role with a hesitation jarring to the watcher. As he finds himself falling in love with Jean Seberg, a fragile girl who lives in her own dream-world and wants love, the change of character from normal to sexually obsessed never carries conviction.

LIMBO
1972, 111 mins, US
D: Mark Robson A: Kate Jackson, Katherine Justice, Stuart Margolin, Hazel Medina, Kathleen Nolan (Filmakers/Omaha-Orange)

An excellent melodrama about three wives whose husbands are missing or imprisoned in Vietnam. An outstanding script, terrific performances by a cast of relatively new players, and Robson's finest direction in years add up to solid emotional impact. Framework of the plot is a ride the three principal wives take to an airport where one man is returning.

LIMELIGHT
1936, 80 mins, UK
D: Herbert Wilcox A: Anna Neagle, Arthur Tracy, Ellis Jeffreys, Tilly Losch, Alexander Field (Wilcox/GFD)

The highspots of this picture are its graceful dancing and Arthur Tracy's fine voice. Anna Neagle is natural in the role of an ambitious chorus girl who dries up completely when her big moment comes. There is too much repetition; too much flashing back to the same stage set and recurrence of song scenes. But withal there is an air of sincerity that makes the story pleasing, if not epoch-making. Tilly Losch graces a few scenes of exotic dancing, with Robinson and Martin responsible for some charming and graceful steps.

LIMELIGHT
1952, 135 mins, US
D: Charles Chaplin A: Charles Chaplin, Claire Bloom, Nigel Bruce, Buster Keaton, Sydney Chaplin, Norman Lloyd (Celebrated/United Artists)

Charlie Chaplin's production is probably derivative of his personal career over the years. Its backdrop is the British stage. Departing from most forms of Hollywood stereotype, the film has a flavor all its own in the sincere quality of the story anent the onetime great vaudemime and his rescue of a femme ballet student from a suicide attempt and subsequently from great mental depression. The British music-hall milieu of 1914 and the third-rate rooming house, where a good deal of the story unfolds, come through as honest reproductions.

1972 [sic]: Best Original Score

LIMEY, THE
1999, 90 mins, US
D: Steven Soderbergh A: Terence Stamp, Peter Fonda, Lesley Ann Warren, Luis Guzman, Barry Newman, Joe Dallesandro (Artisan)

Steven Soderbergh's crime picture positions two icons of sixties cinema, the very British Terence Stamp and the very American Peter Fonda, as enemies in what's basically a routine revenge thriller. After nine years behind bars, Wilson (Stamp) arrives in L.A. to unravel the death of his daughter Jenny, who was involved with Valentine (Fonda), an affluent record producer. Meeting Elaine (a splendid Lesley Ann Warren), an actress who knew Jenny, Wilson has to face his irresponsible conduct as a father. Narrative resembles a western, in which two aging criminals must come to terms with their own identity—and mortality. The film proceeds as a series of setpieces that don't build much continuity or excitement.

LINEUP, THE
1958, 85 mins, US
D: Don Siegel A: Eli Wallach, Robert Keith, Warner Anderson, Richard Jaeckel, Mary LaRoche (Columbia)

A moderately exciting melodrama based on dope smuggling in San Francisco, but short on action until the final, well-plotted and photographed climax. The action centers around the attempt by a narcotics gang to get the heroin it has planted abroad in the possession of travelers debarking in San Francisco. Eli Wallach heads the gang's pickup squad, aided by brains Robert Keith and driver Richard Jaeckel.

LINK
1986, 103 mins, UK
D: Richard Franklin A: Terence Stamp, Elisabeth Shue, Steven Pinner, Richard Garnett (Thorn EMI)

You know right off the film is in trouble when the chimpanzees outperform their human counterparts. Film plods along for almost an hour at an isolated English coastal manor house where preeminent primatologist Dr. Steven Phillip (Terence Stamp) conducts rudimentary experiments on a handful of chimps. The chimps' malevolent ringleader, Link, takes over the lead from the first time he is seen as the tuxedoed butler—even though he never utters a word.

LIONHEART
1987, 104 mins, US ⓥ ⊙

D: Franklin J. Schaffner **A:** Eric Stoltz, Gabriel Byrne, Nicola Cowper, Dexter Fletcher, Deborah Barrymore, Nicholas Clay (Taliafilm II/Orion)

The Children's Crusade of the 12th century is the subject of a flaccid, limp kiddie adventure yarn with little of its intended grand epic sweep realized. The story concerns bands of medieval tykes who set out to search for the elusive King Richard II on his quest to recapture the Holy Land from the Muslims.

LION IN WINTER, THE
1968, 135 mins, UK ⓥ ⊙ ⊟

D: Anthony Harvey **A:** Peter O'Toole, Katharine Hepburn, Jane Merrow, John Castle, Timothy Dalton, Anthony Hopkins (Avco Embassy/Haworth)

The Lion in Winter, based on James Goldman's play (1966) about treachery in the family of England's King Henry II, is an intense, fierce, personal drama. Goldman has blended in his absorbing screenplay elements of love, hate, frustration, fulfillment, ambition, and greed. O'Toole scores a bull's-eye as the king, while Hepburn's performance is amazing.

1968: Best Actress (Katharine Hepburn), Adapted Screenplay, Original Score
Nominations: Best Picture, Director, Actor (Peter O'Toole), Costume Design

LION IS IN THE STREETS, A
1953, 87 mins, US ⓥ

D: Raoul Walsh **A:** James Cagney, Barbara Hale, Anne Francis, Warner Anderson, John McIntire, Jeanne Cagney (Warner)

Just an average drama of a man's political ambitions. James Cagney plays the swamp peddler who tries to ride into the governor's mansion by making a crusade of the plight of poor sharecroppers. The portrayal has an occasional strength, but mostly is a stylized performance done with an inconsistent southern dialect that rarely holds through a complete line of dialogue. Barbara Hale is sweet and charming as the schoolteacher who marries him.

LION KING, THE
1994, 87 mins, US ⓥ ⊙

D: Roger Allens, Rob Minkoff (Walt Disney)

Set off by some of the richest imagery the studio's animators have produced and held together by a timeless coming-of-age

tale, The Lion King marks a dazzling—and unexpectedly daring—addition to the Disney canon, abetted by a marvelous cast of star voices and songs by Elton John and Tim Rice tending toward huge, sonorous choral numbers. As the sun rises over the African jungle, the animals gather—as the anthemlike "Circle of Life" builds to a roaring crescendo. Mufasa (voiced by James Earl Jones), the Lion King, and his Queen, Sarabi (Madge Sinclair), look on approvingly as the mystical baboon Rafiki (Robert Guillaume) presents their cub, Simba (Jonathan Taylor Thomas), as the future Lion King, while Zazu the hornbill (a hilarious Rowan Atkinson) flits about. But there's a shadow on the festivities—Mufasa's brother, Scar (Jeremy Irons), who begins his campaign to kill off his competition for the throne.

1994: Best Original Score, Original Song ("Can You Feel the Love Tonight")
Nominations: Best Original Song ("Circle of Life," "Hakuna Matata")

LION OF THE DESERT
1981, 162 mins, Libya/UK ⓥ ⊟

D: Moustapha Akkad **A:** Anthony Quinn, Oliver Reed, Rod Steiger, John Gielgud, Irene Papas, Raf Vallone (Falcon International)

A very well-produced, frequently stirring war film about a Libyan anticolonial hero. Functional script concentrates on the Italians' efforts in 1929–31 to conquer Libya. Mussolini (Rod Steiger in two effective scenes as the strutting fascist leader) sends his general Graziani (Oliver Reed) to put down the Bedouins led by Omar Mukhtar (Anthony Quinn), a whitebearded old teacher and freedom fighter. While never explicit, the overtones of the Bedouins' desire for international recognition, Mukhtar's insistence that confiscated lands must be returned, and other militant dialogue emphasize parallels with today's Palestinians.

LIONS LOVE
1969, 115 mins, US

D: Agnes Varda **A:** Viva, Gerome Ragni, James Rado, Shirley Clarke, Carlos Clarens (Raab)

Occupying a Hollywood house Viva, Gerome Ragni and James Rado are actors in love. Into this ménage à trois comes filmmaker Shirley Clarke to make a movie. These four plus assorted producers, actors, children, and film buffs play themselves in facsimiles of their real lives. Director Agnes Varda presents her fascination with the banal myth and mania that is Southern California. The result is a pleasant, sometimes humorous blend of style and technique that ultimately is unsuccessful.

LIPSTICK
1976, 89 mins, US ✇ ⊚
D: Lamont Johnson A: Margaux Hemingway, Chris Sarandon, Perry King, Anne Bancroft, Mariel Hemingway (Paramount/ De Laurentiis)

Lipstick has pretensions to being an intelligent treatment of the tragedy of female rape. David Rayfiel's script tells how high-fashion model Margaux Hemingway is brutally assaulted by mild-mannered music teacher Chris Sarandon. The early-on rape sequence is really the dramatic highlight. Somehow one just knows that society's procedures will degrade the rape victim and that the ending of the film will contrive some opportunity for partially justified violence.

LIQUIDATOR, THE
1966, 104 mins, UK ✇ ⊡
D: Jack Cardiff A: Rod Taylor, Trevor Howard, Jill St. John, Wilfrid Hyde-White, David Tomlinson, Akim Tamiroff (M-G-M)

This spy yarn features Boysie Oakes, a creation of John Gardner, a vulnerable sort of guy who hates killing. An ex-sergeant who accidentally saves Trevor Howard's life, he is conned into joining the service by Howard (Security's No. 2). He compromises by hiring a professional killer to do the dirty work for him, an angle that has promise as a film plot. But this fairly quickly gets sidetracked when Oakes takes "No. 2's" lush secretary for a dirty weekend on the Riviera. The vulnerable Oakes is played with plenty of charm and guts by Taylor.

LIQUID SKY
1982, 118 mins, US ✇ ⊚
D: Slava Tsukerman A: Anne Carlisle, Paula Sheppard, Susan Doukas, Otto Von Wernherr, Bob Brady, Elaine Grove (Z Films)

Created by Russian émigrés living in New York, *Liquid Sky* is an odd, yet generally pleasing mixture of punk rock, science fiction, and black humor. Story centers on Anne Carlisle, a new-wave fashion model. A pie-plate-sized flying saucer takes up residence in the neighborhood. The creature proceeds to eliminate Carlisle's lovers as they reach orgasm. Carlisle assumes she's developed some strange curse.

LISBON
1956, 90 mins, US ✇ ⊡
D: Ray Milland A: Ray Milland, Maureen O'Hara, Claude Rains, Yvonne Furneaux, Francis Lederer, Percy Marmont (Republic)

Lisbon makes a colorful setting for this tale of nefarious adventure among the international intrigue set. Republic's anamorphic Naturama process and Trucolor go a long way toward visual impressiveness. Ray Milland stars, produces, and directs. As a smooth, romantically inclined American amusing himself with smuggling operations, his trouping comes off very well. As a production, the picture could have used a little sharper overseeing of story material.

LISTEN, DARLING
1938, 72 mins, US ✇
D: Edwin L. Marin A: Judy Garland, Freddie Bartholomew, Mary Astor, Walter Pidgeon, Scotty Beckett (M-G-M)

Handicapped by an illogical and unconvincing story, effort of Metro to team Judy Garland and Freddie Bartholomew is a lightweight offering that has little aside from three good song numbers handled capably by Garland. When Mary Astor considers marriage to ensure security of her two children (Garland and Scotty Beckett), Bartholomew steps in to assist Garland to prevent such a move.

LIST OF ADRIAN MESSENGER, THE
1963, 98 mins, US ✇
D: John Huston A: George C. Scott, Dana Wynter, Clive Brook, Gladys Cooper, Herbert Marshall (Universal)

The story of efforts to nab a killer who has ingeniously murdered 11 men who represent obstacles to his goal—the acquisition of a huge fortune to which he will become heir as soon as he eliminates the 12th obstacle, the 12-year-old grandson of his aged uncle, the wealthy Marquis of Gleneyre. The film hums along smoothly and captivatingly until the killer shows up at the estate of the marquis. Here the story begins to fall apart. An even more damaging miscue is the utilization of stars who are hidden behind facial disguises in fundamentally inconsequential roles. Of the five stars who "guest," Kirk Douglas has the major assignment and carries it off colorfully and credibly. The others are Tony Curtis, Burt Lancaster, Robert Mitchum, and Frank Sinatra.

LISZTOMANIA
1975, 104 mins, UK Ⓥ ⊙ ⊏

D: Ken Russell A: Roger Daltrey, Sara Kestelman, Paul Nicholas, Fiona Lewis, Veronica Quilligan, Ringo Starr (Goodtimes)

Ken Russell's *Lisztomania* combines his customary zany and bawdy artfulness with a style close to *Tommy*. Liszt is depicted as somewhat of a self-indulgent professional hustler, whose added ambition of unifying Germany lends the kind of "meaningful commitment" so often necessary to put over otherwise mediocre pop music.

LITTLE ANNIE ROONEY
1925, 95 mins, US Ⓥ ⊙ ⊗

D: William Beaudine A: Mary Pickford, William Haines, Walter James, Hugh Fay (Pickford/United Artists)

Mary Pickford is again a smudgy-faced gamin of the streets. She's dirty hands, dirty face, and all that sort of thing. It is a New York story of the two children of Rooney the cop. Mary is the daughter, who is about 12, and her brother is around 18 or so. The kids of the neighborhood taunt Mary with "Little Annie Rooney Is My Sweetheart" and she starts a battle, part of the gang being lined up with her and part against her.

LITTLE BIG MAN
1970, 147 mins, US Ⓥ ⊙ ⊏

D: Arthur Penn A: Dustin Hoffman, Faye Dunaway, Martin Balsam, Richard Mulligan, Chief Dan George (Hiller-Stockbridge/Cinema Center)

A sort of vaudeville show, framed in fictional biography, loaded with sketches of varying degrees of serious and burlesque humor, and climaxed by the Indian victory over General George A. Custer at Little Big Horn in 1876. The story strand is Dustin Hoffman's long life (he is over 120 at prologue and epilogue brackets), especially his years as an adopted Indian who witnessed Custer's megalomaniacal massacre attempt that backfired.

1970: Nomination: Best Supp. Actor (Chief Dan George)

LITTLE BUDDHA
1993, 140 mins, UK/France Ⓥ ⊙

D: Bernardo Bertolucci A: Keanu Reeves, Chris Isaak, Bridget Fonda, Alex Wiesendanger, Ying Ruocheng (Recorded Pictures/CiBy 2000)

A visually stunning but dramatically underwhelming attempt to forge a bridge between ancient Eastern religion and modern Western life, as the double narrative is awkwardly structured and never comes into sharp focus. Modern story sees the aged, august Lama Norbu (Ying Ruocheng) traveling from the Himalaya kingdom of Bhutan to Seattle in search of the reincarnation of his order's revered late teacher. Path leads to Dean and Lisa Konrad (Chris Isaak, Bridget Fonda), whose energetic son, Jesse (Alex Wiesendanger), is the suspected enlightened one. Jesse is told of the life of Siddhartha (a strikingly darkened Keanu Reeves), a handsome prince who abandoned his charmed existence to live in poverty and search for the true path.

LITTLE CAESAR
1931, 77 mins, US Ⓥ ⊙

D: Mervyn LeRoy A: Edward G. Robinson, Douglas Fairbanks Jr., Glenda Farrell, Sidney Blackmer, Thomas Jackson, Ralph Ince (Warner)

There are enough killings herein to fill the quota for an old time cowboy-Indian thriller. And one tough mugg, in the title part, who is tough all the way from the start, when he's a bum with ambition, to the finish, when he's a bum again, but a dead one. For a performance as "Little Caesar" no director could ask for more than Edward G. Robinson's contribution. Here, no matter what he has to say, he's entirely convincing. Young Douglas Fairbanks is splendid as the gunman's friend. Mervyn LeRoy, directing, had a good yarn to start with and gives it plenty of pace besides astute handling.

1930/31: Nomination: Best Adapted Screenplay

LITTLE COLONEL, THE
1935, 80 mins, US Ⓥ ⊙

D: David Butler A: Shirley Temple, Lionel Barrymore, Evelyn Venable, John Lodge, Sidney Blackmer (Fox)

Skillful hokum. A southern colonel (Lionel Barrymore) is embittered when his daughter (Evelyn Venable) elopes with a Northerner. The wife is forced to return with her small daughter (Shirley Temple). Of course, the child is the means of patching everything up, finale taking the form of a "pink party" photographed in Technicolor. It's a gingerbread fade-out for a film loaded with sweetness and light. Bill Robinson, vet colored hoofer from vaudeville, grabs standout attention here. He plays the kindly and aging family butler. A strong point for the film is the youngster doing Robinson's stair dance with him. Dressed in the bustled costumes of the 1880s, the diminutive miss is a fetching, beautiful, and amiable infant. Her acting range remains surprising.

LITTLE DARLINGS
1980, 92 mins, US Ⓥ ▭
D: Ronald F. Maxwell **A:** Tatum O'Neal, Kristy McNichol, Matt Dillon, Armand Assante, Krista Errickson (Paramount)

Little Darlings makes an honest effort to deal with the sexual stirrings of two teenage girls. Tatum O'Neal and Kristy McNichol are both excellent as virgins of widely different social backgrounds who meet at summer camp. O'Neal is a sheltered rich girl and McNichol the poor, streetwise urchin, but their different upbringings do not release their shared hesitancy about making love for the first time.

LITTLE DORRIT
1987, 360 mins, UK Ⓥ
D: Christine Edzard **A:** Alec Guinness, Derek Jacobi, Cyril Cusack, Sarah Pickering, Joan Greenwood, Max Wall (Sands/Cannon)

A remarkable achievement. For writer-director Christine Edzard the epic project [from the novel by Charles Dickens] was obviously a labor of love, and what she has accomplished on a small budget is astounding. The project is in fact two films, each three hours long, with the latter being virtually a remake of the former. A large cast of uniformly excellent British actors is topped off by quite brilliant portrayals by Alec Guinness as William Dorrit and Derek Jacobi as Arthur Clennam. The style of showing virtually the same story through two people allows charming reinterpretations of certain scenes, and presents a more fully rounded piece than usually found in the cinema.
1988: Nominations: Best Supp. Actor (Alec Guinness), Adapted Screenplay

LITTLE DRUMMER GIRL, THE
1984, 130 mins, US Ⓥ ⊙
D: George Roy Hill **A:** Diane Keaton, Yorgo Voyagis, Klaus Kinski, Sami Frey, Michael Cristofer, David Suchet (Pan Arts)

A disappointingly flat film of one of John Le Carré's top novels. Diane Keaton plays the role of Charlie. A team of Israeli operatives, led by the supremely self-confident Klaus Kinski, recruits her in Greece, breaks down her Arab sympathies, and eventually puts her in place as an ideal agent. Keaton's loud, pushy, erratic showbiz character isn't all that easy to warm up to.

LITTLE FAUSS AND BIG HALSY
1970, 98 mins, US Ⓥ ▭
D: Sidney J. Furie **A:** Robert Redford, Michael J. Pollard, Lauren Hutton, Noah Beery, Lucille Benson (Paramount)

An uneven, sluggish story of two motorcycle racers—Robert Redford playing a callous heel and Michael J. Pollard as a put-upon sidekick who eventually (in modified finale) surpasses his fallen idol. Hampered by a thin screenplay, film is padded further by often pretentious direction by Sidney J. Furie.

LITTLE FOXES, THE
1941, 115 mins, US Ⓥ ⊙
D: William Wyler **A:** Bette Davis, Herbert Marshall, Teresa Wright, Richard Carlson, Patricia Collinge, Dan Duryea (RKO/Goldwyn)

From starring Bette Davis down the line to the bit roles portrayed by minor Negroes the acting is well nigh flawless. The story is about the Hubbard family of the Deep South—as mercenary a foursome as has ever emerged from fact or fiction. In this picture Davis murders her husband, played by Herbert Marshall, but with the unique weapon of disinterest. When Marshall, in the throes of a heart attack, crashes a bottle of medicine that can save his life, Davis sits by and watches him do a dying swan. Marshall turns in one of his top performances in the exacting portrayal of a suffering, dying man. On top of the smooth pace, Wyler has handled every detail with an acutely dramatic touch.
1941: Nominations: Best Picture, Actress (Bette Davis), Supp. Actress (Patricia Collinge, Teresa Wright), Screenplay, B&W Art Direction, Editing, Scoring of a Dramatic Picture

LITTLE GIANTS
1994, 105 mins, US Ⓥ ⊙
D: Duwayne Dunham **A:** Rick Moranis, Ed O'Neill, John Madden, Shawna Waldron, Mary Ellen Trainor (Amblin/Warner)

Rick Moranis heads the fine cast as Danny O'Shea, a small-town single father who wants to help his tomboyish daughter,

Becky (Shawna Waldron)—and maybe upstage Kevin (Ed O'Neill), his cocky older brother—by coaching a team of kids who have been rejected by Kevin for the town's Pop Warner junior team. Story is pat and predictable as Danny whips his team into shape for a big practice game against his brother's Cowboys team. On the other hand, pic is never less than engaging, and often manages to be genuinely amusing.

LITTLE GIRL WHO LIVES DOWN THE LANE, THE
1977, 91 mins, Canada/France ⊘ ⊙ ▭
D: Nicholas Gessner **A:** Jodie Foster, Martin Sheen, Alexis Smith, Mort Shuman, Scott Jacoby (ICL/Filmel)

This film, about a homicidal orphan girl, is farfetched nonsense with precious little to appease shriek freaks. Laird Koenig's screenplay from his novel is riddled with unsuspended disbelief—coincidences, gimmicks. Jodie Foster plays an all-alone sangfroid little liar of 13 going on 23 who isn't about to let herself be pushed around or dominated by crummy grown-ups. Martin Sheen plays a sicko with a thing for little girls who harasses the kid. Foster's poise is impressive enough as the cool, calculating adolescent with a passion for Chopin records. But it's a one-note character.

LITTLE HUT, THE
1957, 90 mins, US
D: Mark Robson **A:** Ava Gardner, Stewart Granger, David Niven, Walter Chiari, Finlay Currie (Herbson/M-G-M)

Sex is incessantly hinted at in this saucy triangle which keeps husband and wife intact for the moral code. Government business has left Stewart Granger with little time to practice the arts of a husband, so Gardner turns to hubby's best friend (David Niven) for companionship. Transfer this situation to a deserted tropical isle after a shipwreck, feed the principals a stimulating seafood diet, mostly oysters, and something has to give.

LITTLE LORD FAUNTLEROY
1921, 120 mins, US ⊗
D: Alfred E. Green, Jack Pickford **A:** Mary Pickford, Claude Gillingwater, Joseph Dowling, James Marcus, Rose Dione (Pickford/United Artists)

A perfect Pickford picture. It exploits the star in dual roles, one of them one of the immortal and classic boy parts of all times. Mary Pickford shows a versatility

as the blue-blooded and somber mother and the blue-blooded but mischievous kid that is almost startling. She meets herself many times in double exposures, and she is taller than herself and different from herself, and incredibly true to each.

LITTLE LORD FAUNTLEROY
1936, 98 mins, US ⊘
D: John Cromwell **A:** C. Aubrey Smith, Freddie Bartholomew, Dolores Costello Barrymore, Henry Stephenson, Guy Kibbee, Mickey Rooney (Selznick/United Artists)

A theme as prissy as *Fauntleroy*, where the earl-to-be calls his mother "Dearest," might have proved quite hazardous in anything but the most expert hands. As Hugh Walpole adapts it, John Cromwell directs it, and a sterling cast troupes it—all under Selznick's keen aegis—it's very palatable cinematic fare. Young Freddie Bartholomew is capital in the title role and Dolores Costello Barrymore, marking her film comeback as "Dearest," his young and widowed mother, are an ideal coupling in the two principal roles. C. Aubrey Smith as the gruff and grumpy earl well nigh steals the picture. Henry Stephenson as the English barrister is on a par in a role that calls for much restraint.

LITTLE MALCOLM AND HIS STRUGGLE AGAINST THE EUNUCHS
1974, 112 mins, UK
D: Stuart Cooper **A:** John Hurt, John McEnery, Raymond Platt, Rosalind Ayres, David Warner (Apple)

A frequently hilarious, generally thought-provoking and sobering, beautifully acted, but a trifle overlong and repetitious film of uncertain destination. On one level, story dealing with a carefully plotted sham uprising by a trio of students draws laughs in its Mitty-ish mock evocations of sociopolitical tirades, while subsurface, the conclusions drawn are frightening, as evidenced in the climactic scene of useless violence against a girl.

LITTLE MAN TATE
1991, 99 mins, US ⊘ ⊙
D: Jodie Foster **A:** Jodie Foster, Dianne Wiest, Adam Hann-Byrd, Harry Connick Jr., David Pierce (Orion)

Jodie Foster makes an appealing, if modest, directorial debut with this nicely observed tale of a year in the life of a seven-year-old genius. An accomplished painter, poet, and pianist in addition to being a math wizard, Fred Tate (Adam Hann-Byrd) comes to the attention of wealthy Jane Grierson (Dianne Wiest), a child psychologist and teacher of the gifted. Fred moves in with her and strikes up an engaging relationship with a somewhat older math genius named Damon (memorably impersonated by P. J. Ochlan). Most of the film's emotional power lies in the open, alert, eager-to-please face of Hann-Byrd, making his acting debut. Film never really gets inside Fred's head, but it neatly sketches the external aspects of his predicament.

LITTLE MERMAID, THE
1989, 82 mins, US ⊗ ⊙
D: John Musker, Ron Clements (Walt Disney)

Borrowing liberally from the studio's classics, *The Little Mermaid* may represent Disney's best animated feature since the underrated *Sleeping Beauty* in 1959. The source material is a Hans Christian Andersen tale. The mermaid princess Ariel (voiced by newcomer Jodi Benson) lives in her sea-lord father Triton's (Kenneth Mars) undersea kingdom but yearns for a life above. The animation proves lush and fluid, augmented by the use of shadow and light as elements like fire, sun, and water illuminate the characters. Key contributions are made by lyricist Howard Ashman (who coproduced with Musker) and composer Alan Menken, whose songs frequently begin slowly but build in cleverness and intensity.
1989: Best Song ("Under the Sea"), Original Score
Nomination: Best Song ("Kiss the Girl")

LITTLE MISS BROADWAY
1938, 70 mins, US ⊗
D: Irving Cummings **A:** Shirley Temple, George Murphy, Jimmy Durante, Phyllis Brooks, Edna May Oliver, George Barbier (20th Century-Fox)

With Jimmy Durante, George Murphy, Edna May Oliver, George Barbier, Donald Meek, and El Brendel in featured roles, something approaching hilarity is expected. The result is far short of the promise. Shirley is an orphan discharged into the care of an uncle (Edward Ellis) who manages a theatrical hotel near Broadway. Edna May Oliver, who owns the building, is annoyed by the constant rehearsing of the acts and decides to close the place by demanding immediate payment of past due rent. Her nephew (George Murphy)

intercedes at the behest of Shirley Temple, but the issue finds its way to court.

LITTLE MISS MARKER
1980, 103 mins, US ⊗
D: Walter Bernstein **A:** Walter Matthau, Julie Andrews, Tony Curtis, Sara Stimson, Bob Newhart (Universal)

There is something irresistible about Damon Runyon's story of a darling little girl left in the care of colorfully kind gamblers. If ever there was an actor who should play "Sorrowful Jones," it's Walter Matthau, and Bob Newhart should have been a wonderful "Regret," while Tony Curtis could have been a respectable antagonist. But they are all flat in their parts. Even worse, Julie Andrews is woefully miscast with her British accent. The only really decent thing about the picture is little Sara Stimson.

LITTLE MURDERS
1971, 110 mins, US ⊗
D: Alan Arkin **A:** Elliott Gould, Marcia Rodd, Vincent Gardenia, Elizabeth Wilson, Donald Sutherland, Alan Arkin (20th Century-Fox)

Alan Arkin, making a most impressive directorial debut, has made a film that is not only funny but devastating in its emotional impact. Arkin's actors play very broadly, just at the edge of the caricatures they are in Jules Feiffer's screenplay. But they fill in the outlines with such a wealth of human detail that it's impossible not to identify with them. Elliott Gould plays a photographer who was successful until he began to "lose the people" in his pictures. Into his life comes Marcia Rodd, a girl who would like to mold him into "a strong, vital, self-assured man." Then the world gets in the way, and Feiffer once and for all stops being the amiably satiric cartoonist, and hurtles toward a painful conclusion.

LITTLE NIGHT MUSIC, A
1977, 124 mins, Austria/US/W. Germany ⊗ ⊙
D: Hal Prince **A:** Elizabeth Taylor, Diana Rigg, Len Cariou, Hermione Gingold, Lesley-Anne Down (Sascha-Wien/Kastner)

An elegant-looking, period romantic charade. There is one sprightly number as the assorted characters set out for a country dinner that will resolve their complicated love problems. There is a noted promiscuous actress ready to settle down with a steady man and her teenage daughter, a staid lawyer with a young wife of

18 whose marriage has yet to be consummated, plus his son and a fiery army lieutenant, lover of the actress, and his jealous but submissive wife. Uneven and sometimes slow, pic has good looks.
1977: Best Adapted Scoring
Nomination: Best Costume Design

LITTLE NIKITA
(UK: THE SLEEPERS)
1988, 98 mins, US Ⓥ ⊙
D: Richard Benjamin **A:** Sidney Poitier, River Phoenix, Richard Jenkins, Caroline Kava, Richard Bradford (Columbia)

An unsatisfying execution of a clever premise—a teen's traumatic discovery that his parents are Soviet spies. Film opens strongly as parallel story lines unfold and audience is drawn in by the need to decipher the link between the mission of a Soviet agent and an all-American family in the mythical San Diego suburb of Fountain Grove. Poised at the juncture of these developments is FBI agent Sidney Poitier, whose natural intensity seems just right for the role.

LITTLE ODESSA
1994, 98 mins, US Ⓥ ▱
D: James Gray **A:** Tim Roth, Edward Furlong, Moira Kelly, Vanessa Redgrave, Maximilian Schell, Paul Guilfoyle (New Line/Addis-Wechsler)

A somberly explosive family tragedy. Contracted to erase an Iranian jeweler, Brooklyn-bred hit man Joshua Shapira (Tim Roth) returns reluctantly to his childhood neighborhood. Word of his arrival reaches his kid brother, Reuben (Edward Furlong), who eagerly tracks him down. While he lays plans for the hit, he almost indifferently rekindles something approaching romance with hardened neighborhood girl Alla (Moira Kelly). Roth appears as a man who, in many ways, is already dead, yet he makes the character resonantly sympathetic. Kelly also makes an indelible impression during her brief screen time. But perhaps the most striking is Furlong, whose intense gaze and fragile grace push his character under the audience's skin without artifice.

LITTLE PRINCE, THE
1974, 88 mins, UK Ⓥ ⊙
D: Stanley Donen **A:** Richard Kiley, Steven Warner, Bob Fosse, Gene Wilder, Joss Ackland, Clive Revill (Paramount)

Handsome production plus excellent photography and effects cannot obscure the limited artistic achievement of *The Lit-* *tle Prince.* Alan Jay Lerner's adaptation of the book by Antoine de Saint-Exupéry is flat and his lyrics are unmemorable, as are Frederick Loewe's melodies. Richard Kiley is cast as the child-man, and Steven Warner is the man-child, who ruminate on the meaning of a good life.
1974: Nominations: Best Adapted Score, Song ("Little Prince")

LITTLE PRINCESS, THE
1939, 95 mins, US Ⓥ ⊙
D: Walter Lang **A:** Shirley Temple, Richard Greene, Anita Louise, Ian Hunter (20th Century-Fox)

Shirley Temple appears in Technicolor for the first time, cast as Sara Crewe. Her father (Ian Hunter) goes off to war with the Boers and leaves the youngster in Mary Nash's school. Shirley is immediately dubbed "The Little Princess" because of her regal bearing and attitude. When word comes that her father has died, Shirley is made a galley slave by Nash, who mistreats her in every way possible.

LITTLE PRINCESS, A
1995, 97 mins, US Ⓥ ⊙
D: Alfonso Cuaron **A:** Eleanor Bron, Liam Cunningham, Liesel Matthews, Rusty Schwimmer, Vanessa Lee Chester (Baltimore/Warner)

An astonishing work of studio artifice, *A Little Princess* is that rarest of creations, a children's film that plays equally well to kids and adults, an exquisite, perfectly played serious fantasy that movingly stresses the importance of magic and the imagination in the scheme of life. Ten-year-old Sara Crewe (Liesel Matthews) is the daughter of a loving British army captain. When the war calls Captain Crewe (Liam Cunningham), he enrolls Sara at Miss Minchin's School for Girls. Sara quickly wins over many of the girls by introducing an element of excitement and adventure into their strictly regimented lives. When Captain Crewe is reported killed, the stern Miss Minchin (Eleanor Bron) strips her of all privileges. Performances could scarcely be improved upon.
1995: Nominations: Best Cinematography, Art Direction

LITTLE RASCALS, THE
1994, 82 mins, US Ⓥ
D: Penelope Spheeris **A:** Travis Tedford, Bug Hall, Brittany Ashton Holmes, Kevin Jamal Woods, Zachary Mabry, Ross Elliot Bagley (Universal/King World)

Those who grew up watching *The Lit-*

tle Rascals on murky UHF TV stations may well be intrigued by the idea of introducing their kids to this full-color, big-screen version. Rather conventional plot has love-smitten Alfalfa (Bug Hall) violating the rules of the all-male He-Man Woman-Haters Club by wooing the decidedly feminine Darla (cherubic Brittany Ashton Holmes). This irks his pal, Spanky (Travis Tedford), and inadvertently results in the destruction of their clubhouse.

LITTLE ROMANCE, A
1979, 108 mins, US/France ⓥ ⊙ ▭
D: George Roy Hill A: Laurence Olivier, Arthur Hill, Sally Kellerman, Diane Lane, Broderick Crawford (Orion/Pan Arts/Trinacra)

Scripter Allan Burns has craftily kept the point of view of the youngsters, Diane Lane and Thelonious Bernard, while the adults, with certain exceptions, are seen as suitably grotesque and ridiculous, giving *Romance* a crest of humor on which to ride. Fulcrum in script is the beneficent boulevardier, limned by Laurence Olivier. The prototypical lovable scoundrel, Olivier hams it up unmercifully.
1979: Best Original Score
Nomination: Best Adapted Screenplay

LITTLE SHOP OF HORRORS, THE
1961, 70 mins, US ⓥ ⊙
D: Roger Corman A: Jonathan Haze, Jackie Joseph, Mel Welles, Myrtle Vail, Jack Nicholson (FilmGroup)

A serviceful parody of a typical screen horror number. *Little Shop of Horrors* is kind of one big sick joke, but it's essentially harmless and good-natured. The plot concerns a young, goofy florist's assistant who creates a talking, bloodsucking, man-eating plant, then feeds it several customers from skid row before sacrificing himself to the horticultural gods. Horticulturalists and vegetarians will love it.

LITTLE SHOP OF HORRORS
1986, 88 mins, US ⓥ ⊙
D: Frank Oz A: Rick Moranis, Ellen Greene, Vincent Gardenia, Steve Martin, James Belushi, John Candy (Warner/Geffen)

A fractured, funny production transported rather reluctantly from the stage to the screen. Almost nothing is left besides the setting and story outline from the 1961 Roger Corman film that inspired the 1982 stage musical. Through a chain of events just silly enough to be fun, Seymour (Rick

Moranis) becomes the proud owner of Audrey II, a rare breed of plant that makes him famous and his boss (Vincent Gardenia) prosperous. Audrey II develops an insatiable appetite for human flesh.
1986: Nominations: Best Song ("Mean Green Mother from Outer Space"), Visual Effects

LITTLEST REBEL, THE
1935, 70 mins, US ⓥ
D: David Butler A: Shirley Temple, John Boles, Jack Holt, Karen Morley, Bill Robinson, Guinn Williams (20th Century-Fox)

A good Shirley Temple picture. The Civil War emerges as a misunderstanding among kindly gentlemen with eminently happy slaves and a cute little girl who sings and dances through the story. War brings successive losses culminating in the death of the mother (Karen Morley). Bill Robinson and the child again dance. Robinson is once more the trusty family butler who guards little missy.

LITTLE WOMEN
1933, 117 mins, US ⓥ
D: George Cukor A: Katharine Hepburn, Joan Bennett, Paul Lukas, Frances Dee, Jean Parker, Edna May Oliver (RKO)

A profoundly moving history of youth. Katharine Hepburn as Jo creates a new and stunningly vivid character; strips the Victorian hoyden of her syrupy goody-goodiness; and endows the role with awkwardly engaging youthful energy. Story is full of tearfully sentimental passages, but they are managed with beautiful restraint. A notable company of standard screen names supports the star.
1932/33: Best Adaptation
Nominations: Best Picture, Director

LITTLE WOMEN
1949, 121 mins, US ⓥ ⊙
D: Mervyn LeRoy A: June Allyson, Peter Lawford, Margaret O'Brien, Elizabeth Taylor, Janet Leigh, Rossano Brazzi (M-G-M)

Unstinting remake of Louisa May Alcott's old-lace classic of a quartet of daughters and their strivings in Civil War years. The tender story, with its frank and unashamed assault on the emotions, still has its effective moments when the sentiment doesn't grow a little too thick. Playing Jo, June Allyson's thesping dominates the film. As Beth, the youngest of the group, Margaret O'Brien is peculiarly subdued except for one touching scene. Elizabeth Taylor and Janet Leigh neatly

counterfoil Allyson's irrepressible cavortings.
1949: Best Color Art Direction
Nomination: Best Color Cinematography

LITTLE WOMEN
1994, 118 mins, US Ⓥ ⓥ ⊙
D: Gillian Armstrong **A:** Winona Ryder, Gabriel Byrne, Trini Alvarado, Samantha Mathis, Susan Sarandon, Eric Stoltz (Columbia/Di Novi)

This outstanding version of Louisa May Alcott's perennial surpasses even the best previous rendition, George Cukor's 1933 outing starring Katharine Hepburn. The four March "little women" are Meg (Trini Alvarado), Jo (Winona Ryder), Beth (Claire Danes), and Amy (initially Kirsten Dunst, then Samantha Mathis), presided over by their mother, Marmee (Susan Sarandon), while their father is off fighting in the Union Army. Armstrong paces her scenes at about half the speed that Cukor did, and they are all the better for it in terms of emotional resonance. Performances by the actresses are all at least very good. Film has a splendid period look.
1994: Nominations: Best Actress (Winona Ryder), Costume Design, Original Score

LIVE AND LET DIE
1973, 121 mins, UK Ⓥ ⊙ ▷
D: Guy Hamilton **A:** Roger Moore, Yaphet Kotto, Jane Seymour, Clifton James, Julius W. Harris, Geoffrey Holder (United Artists/Eon)

The eighth Cubby Broccoli–Harry Saltzman film based on Ian Fleming's James Bond introduces Roger Moore as an okay replacement for Sean Connery. Here Bond's assigned to ferret out mysterious goings-on involving Yaphet Kotto, diplomat from a Caribbean-island nation who in disguise also is a big-time criminal. The comic-book plot meanders through a series of hardware production numbers. These include some voodoo ceremonies; a hilarious airplane-vs.-auto pursuit scene; a double-decker bus escape; and a climactic inland waterway powerboat chase. Killer sharks, poisonous snakes, and man-eating crocodiles also fail to deter Bond.
1973: Nomination: Best Song ("Live and Let Die")

LIVE FOR LIFE
See: Vivre pour Vivre

LIVE NOW PAY LATER
1962, 104 mins, UK
D: Jay Lewis **A:** Ian Hendry, June Ritchie,
John Gregson, Liz Fraser, Geoffrey Keen (Woodlands)

Screenplay has many amusing moments, but overall it is untidy. Ian Hendry plays a smart aleck, philandering, double-crossing tallyman who, with two illegitimate babies to his discredit, still finds that the easiest way to bluff his femme patrons into getting hocked up to their eyebrows in installment buying is via the boudoir. The character has a certain brash, breezy assurance, but no charm. And that's the way Hendry plays it, to the point of irritation. June Ritchie can do little in this cardboard role of wronged young mistress.

LIVES OF A BENGAL LANCER, THE
1935, 110 mins, US Ⓥ
D: Henry Hathaway **A:** Gary Cooper, Franchot Tone, Richard Cromwell, Guy Standing, C. Aubrey Smith, Akim Tamiroff (Paramount)

A sweeping, thrilling military narrative in Britain's desert badlands. There is a stirring emotional conflict between father and son, the former a traditional British commander with whom discipline and loyalty to the service come first, and the boy rebelling against his father's cold-blooded attitude. Gary Cooper and Franchot Tone, as a pair of reconnoitering officers, provide the story with its dynamite. Story concerns their rescue of the colonel's son after the latter's disillusionment over his father's reception of him makes him a setup for capture by a warring native chieftain.
1935: Best Assistant Directors (Clem Beauchamp, Paul Wing)
Nominations: Best Picture, Director, Screenplay, Art Direction, Editing, Sound

LIVING
See: Ikiru

LIVING DAYLIGHTS, THE
1987, 130 mins, UK Ⓥ ⊙ ▷
D: John Glen **A:** Timothy Dalton, Maryam D'Abo, Jeroen Krabbe, Joe Don Baker, John Rhys-Davies (United Artists/Eon)

Timothy Dalton, the fourth Bond, registers beautifully on all key counts of charm, machismo, sensitivity, and technique. He's abetted by material that's a healthy cut above the series norm of superhero fantasy. There's a more mature story of its kind, too, this one about a phony KGB defector involved in gunrunning and a fraternal assassination plot. There are even some relatively touching moments of romantic contact between Dalton and lead femme Maryam D'Abo as Czech concert cellist.

LIVING FREE
1972, 90 mins, UK ⓥ
D: Jack Couffer **A:** Nigel Davenport, Susan Hampshire, Geoffrey Keen, Edward Judd (Open Road/Highroad)

The same loving care that characterized *Born Free* is evident in the sequel. Sensitive screenplay, based on the Joy Adamson book of her and her gamewarden-husband's efforts to assure that the cubs, following the death of their mother, shall live free and not be sent to a zoo, often carries a dramatic pitch. Possibly the most remarkable facet of picture is the animal photography of the cubs and other beasts that the couple encounter.

LOCAL HERO
1983, 111 mins, UK ⓥ ⊙
D: Bill Forsyth **A:** Burt Lancaster, Peter Riegert, Fulton MacKay, Denis Lawson, Peter Capaldi (Enigma/Goldcrest)

While modest in intent and gentle in feel, *Local Hero* is loaded with wry, off-beat humor. Basic story has Peter Riegert, rising young executive in an enormous Houston oil firm, sent to Scotland to clinch a deal to buy up an entire village, where the company intends to construct a new oil refinery. Local Scots can hardly wait to sign away their town, so strong is the smell of money in the air. Back in Houston, oil magnate Burt Lancaster is more concerned with his prodding, sadistic psychiatrist and his obsessive hobby of astronomy.

LOCH NESS
1996, 101 mins, UK ⓥ ⊙ ▭
D: John Henderson **A:** Ted Danson, Joely Richardson, Ian Holm, Kirsty Graham, Harris Yulin (Working Title)

Ted Danson goes beastie-hunting in an old-fashioned family pic with feel-good to spare. Okay playing by Danson, an excellent perf by Joely Richardson, and a big-hearted score by Trevor Jones elevate a basically modest picture into medium-size family fare. Danson plays once-renowned L.A. zoologist Jonathan Dempsey. His boss (Harris Yulin) makes him an offer he can't refuse: disprove once and for all that the Loch Ness Monster exists. Unwillingly, Dempsey hightails it to the Highlands. Finding a room in a small hotel run by feisty single mom Laura MacFeteridge (Richardson), Dempsey sets out scanning

the giant loch. Pic starts to develop its own low-key charm as the Danson and Richardson characters strike up a cautious relationship.

LOCKET, THE
1947, 83 mins, US ⓥ
D: John Brahm **A:** Laraine Day, Brian Aherne, Robert Mitchum, Gene Raymond, Ricardo Cortez, Sharyn Moffet (RKO)

A case history of a warped mind and its effect on the lives of those it touches intimately. Vehicle is a strong one for Laraine Day and she does much with the role of Nancy, a girl with an abnormal obsession that wrecks the lives of four men who love her. Story carries the flashback technique to greater lengths than generally employed. The writing by Sheridan Gibney displays an understanding of the subject matter and proves a solid basis for the able performances achieved by John Brahm's direction.

LOCK UP
1989, 105 mins, US ⓥ ⊙
D: John Flynn **A:** Sylvester Stallone, Donald Sutherland, John Amos, Sonny Landham, Tom Sizemore (White Eagle/Carolco)

Lock Up is made in the same, simplistic vein as most other Sylvester Stallone pics. Emotional guy that he is, Stallone couldn't wait for his six-month prison term to be up because in the meantime his foster father may die, so he escapes to see him one last time. It seems his coldhearted warden (Donald Sutherland) wouldn't allow him a supervised furlough to make the trip. The rest of the film is Stallone trying to survive "hell" that Sutherland, as the Devil, has diabolically allowed to run amok.

LOCK UP YOUR DAUGHTERS!
1969, 102 mins, UK ⓥ
D: Peter Coe **A:** Christopher Plummer, Susannah York, Glynis Johns, Ian Bannen, Tom Bell (Columbia/Domino)

Much of the wit and satire in this portrait of the permissive morals and the corruptive decay of the 18th century is blunted, making it a noisy, bawdy, slapstick yarn. It centers around the romantic entanglements of three wenches and their sailors, which, after many misfortunes, complications, and misunderstandings, land practically everybody in court.

LODGER, THE
(US: THE PHANTOM FIEND)
1932, 85 mins, UK
D: Maurice Elvey **A:** Ivor Novello, Eliz-

abeth Allan, Jack Hawkins, A. W. Baskcomb, Peter Gawthorne (Twickenham)

Despite its subject of Jack the Ripper, this is an eerie, absorbing story without being morbid. Running parallel with the narration of the frightful murders is a sweet love story. Ivor Novello plays a sensitive musician with a sorrow so great he is unable to confide in anyone. Elizabeth Allan's depiction of a working girl carried off her feet is a fine piece of acting.

LODGER, THE
1944, 84 mins, US ⊘
D: John Brahm **A:** Merle Oberon, George Sanders, Laird Cregar, Cedric Hardwicke, Sara Allgood (20th Century-Fox)

With a pat cast, keen direction, and tight scripting, 20th-Fox has an absorbing and, at times, spine-tingling drama concocted from Marie Belloc Lowndes's novel *The Lodger*. It's a super chiller-diller in its picturization of a Scotland Yard manhunt for London's Jack the Ripper. Director John Brahm and scripter Barre Lyndon make it as much a psychological study of the half-crazed ''Lodger'' (Laird Cregar). Laird Cregar gives an impressive performance.

LOGAN'S RUN
1976, 118 mins, US ⊘ ⊙ ▭
D: Michael Anderson **A:** Michael York, Richard Jordan, Jenny Agutter, Roscoe Lee Browne, Farrah Fawcett, Michael Anderson Jr. (M-G-M)

A rewarding futuristic film that appeals both as spectacular-looking escapist adventure as well as intelligent drama. Heading the cast are Michael York and Richard Jordan, two members of a security guard force that supervises the life of a domed-in hedonistic civilization all composed of persons under the age of 30.
1976: Honorary Award (visual effects)
Nominations: Best Cinematography, Art Direction

LOLA
1961, 90 mins, France/Italy ⊘ ▭
D: Jacques Demy **A:** Anouk Aimee, Marc Michel, Elina Labourdette, Alan Scott, Annie Dupéreux (Rome Paris)

A young man meets an old flame who dances in a club and has halfhearted affairs with Yank sailors while waiting for her first lover and father of her illegitimate son to come back. The boy falls for her again but up pops her old lover for a wry, happy ending. Anouk Aimee has a pathetic quality as the dancer, while Marc

Michel is properly aimless as the boy. Lensing has the proper gray quality for this pleasant, unusual pic.

LOLA MONTES
1956, 110 mins, France/W. Germany ⊘ ⊙ ▭
D: Max Ophuls **A:** Martine Carol, Peter Ustinov, Anton Walbrook, Oskar Werner, Ivan Desny (Gamma/Florida/Union)

A lush color vehicle, relating the life story of a 19th-century courtesan. Treatment of the lady of easy virtue's life is done via flashbacks while she is being exhibited in a strangely stylized circus somewhere in America. Martine Carol, as Lola Montes, lacks the depth needed. She looks good but never seems to display the temperament required. Peter Ustinov has little acting to do but registers as the ringmaster who narrates the round of Lola's life. Anton Walbrook is fine as the king.

LOLITA
1962, 152 mins, US ⊘ ⊙
D: Stanley Kubrick **A:** James Mason, Shelley Winters, Peter Sellers, Sue Lyon, Gary Cockrell (M-G-M)

Vladimir Nabokov's witty, grotesque novel is, in its film version, like a bee from which the stinger has been removed. It still buzzes with a sort of promising irreverence, but it lacks the power to shock and, eventually, makes very little point either as comedy or satire. The result is an occasionally amusing but shapeless film about a middle-aged professor who comes to no good end through his involvement with a well-developed teenager. James Mason has never been better than he is as erudite Humbert Humbert. Peter Sellers gets a chance to run through several hilarious changes of character. Sue Lyon makes an auspicious film debut as the deceitful child-woman who'd just as soon go to a movie as romp in the hay.
1962: Nomination: Best Adapted Screenplay

LOLITA
1997, 137 mins, US/France ⊘ ⊙
D: Adrian Lyne **A:** Jeremy Irons, Melanie Griffith, Frank Langella, Dominique Swain, Suzanne Shepherd, Keith Reddin (Kassar/Pathe)

Adrian Lyne's *Lolita* is neither as irredeemable nor as morally shocking as its ''untouchable'' status would suggest. But after an intriguing opening stretch, and despite Jeremy Irons's potent lead performance, the film becomes repetitive, flat and often dull. Second screen version of Vladimir Nabokov's scabrous but ironic satire on love depicts Lolita (Dominique Swain) as a knowing manipulator and seductress and her ardent adult lover as a helpless, frequently pitiable victim. Adaptation generally sticks much closer to the novel than Stanley Kubrick's 1962 version. Lyne establishes a light, ironic tone, milking laughs out of Humbert Humbert's dumbstruck surrender to passion. But problems arise when the director succumbs to the urge to make an Adrian Lyne Film, with gratuitous art-directional flourishes and aggressive techno-gloss. Swain takes the role in stride but is more bratty than sensual. Sex scenes are fairly chaste, implying more than they show.

LOLLY-MADONNA WAR, THE
See: Lolly-Madonna XXX

LOLLY-MADONNA XXX
(UK: THE LOLLY-MADONNA WAR)
1973, 105 mins, US ▭
D: Richard C. Sarafian **A:** Rod Steiger, Robert Ryan, Jeff Bridges, Scott Wilson, Katherine Squire (M-G-M)

Sue Grafton's novel *The Lolly-Madonna War* has been handsomely and sensitively filmed. Excellent performances abound by older and younger players in a mountain-country clan feud story which mixes extraordinary human compassion with raw but discreet violence. Rod Steiger heads one clan, which also includes Katherine Squire in outstanding performance as his wife.. The opposition clan is headed by Robert Ryan, with Tresa Hughes also outstanding as his wife. A land dispute has brought the families to the edge of violence. Trigger for the explosion is a fake postcard signed by a nonexistent, apparent bride-to-be named Lolly-Madonna.

LONDON BELONGS TO ME
1948, 112 mins, UK
D: Sidney Gilliat **A:** Richard Attenborough, Alastair Sim, Fay Compton, Stephen Murray, Susan Shaw (Individual/Rank)

Plot depicts the struggles and hopes of a group of ordinary people. All lead a humdrum existence until a young lad gets involved in a murder and is sentenced to death. Without warning, and in questionable taste, the tempo changes and the organizing of a petition to save the life of the boy is treated as something meant to be hilariously funny. Top honors go to Richard Attenborough, living the part of the flashy youngster, and Alistair Sim, who just can't miss as a fake medium.

LONDON BY NIGHT
1937, 70 mins, US
D: William Thiele **A:** George Murphy, Rita Johnson, Virginia Field, Leo G. Carroll, George Zucco (M-G-M)

Meritorious melodrama Among the virtues of the picture is the skillful manner in which suspense is sustained. Suspicion is pointed in various interesting directions and one of the novelties of the plot is that two murders were of imaginary victims. George Murphy acquits himself creditably as a romantic lead, while Rita Johnson digs herself deeply into audience favor in a role that calls for less work.

LONDON KILLS ME
1991, 107 mins, UK ▽ ⊙
D: Hanif Kureishi **A:** Justin Chadwick, Steven Mackintosh, Emer McCourt, Roshan Seth, Fiona Shaw, Brad Dourif (Polygram/Working Title)

Flabby slice of London street life among pushers and hustlers drags itself across the screen for 107 minutes and collapses in a dramatic mess on the sidewalk. Main character is the Candide-like Clint (Justin Chadwick), who hangs out with a group led by small-time dealer Muffdiver (Steven Mackintosh). To raise the cash for a job in a swank local eatery, Clint joins in Muffdiver's plans to go big time and helps himself to latter's hidden stash. What was obviously meant as an ironic look at lost souls in 1990s London rapidly blurs into a string of undramatic incidents.

LONELINESS OF THE LONG-DISTANCE RUNNER, THE
1962, 104 mins, UK ▽ ⊙
D: Tony Richardson **A:** Tom Courtenay, Michael Redgrave, James Bolam, Avis Bunnage, Alec McCowen, Julia Foster (Woodfall)

It is difficult to conjure up much sympathy for the young "hero" who comes out as a disturbed young layabout (he seems thoroughly to deserve his fate of landing in Borstal, the corrective establishment for British juve delinquents). Yet the performance of Tom Courtenay and the imaginative, if sometimes overfussy, direction of Tony Richardson, plus some standout lensing by Walter Lassally make this a worthwhile pic. Courtenay is selected to represent Borstal in a long-distance race against a public school team. It is the ambition of the rather pompous, stuffy governor (Michael Redgrave) to win the cup for Borstal.

LONELY ARE THE BRAVE
1962, 107 mins, US ⓥ ⊙ ▭
D: David Miller A: Kirk Douglas, Gena Rowlands, Walter Matthau, Michael Kane, Carroll O'Connor, George Kennedy (Universal/Joel)

Often touching, and well served by its performances and photography, *Lonely Are the Brave* ultimately blurs its focus on the loner fenced in and bemused by the encroachments and paradoxes of civilization. Its makers have settled for surface instead of substance. As the loner, Douglas is extremely likable and understands his part within its limitations, as written. Most beguiling performance is turned in by Walter Matthau as the laconic and harassed sheriff.

LONELY GUY, THE
1984, 90 mins, US ⓥ ⊙
D: Arthur Hiller A: Steve Martin, Charles Grodin, Judith Ivey, Steven Lawrence, Robyn Douglass, Merv Griffin (Universal)

Derived from a comic tome by Bruce Jay Friedman, premise has Steve Martin bounced by sexpot girlfriend, Robyn Douglass, and thereby banished to the world of Lonely Guys. He meets and commiserates with fellow LG Charles Grodin. Martin's trademark wacky humor is fitfully in evidence, but seems much more repressed than usual in order to fit into the relatively realistic world of single working people.

LONELY HEARTS
1982, 95 mins, Australia ⓥ ⊙
D: Paul Cox A: Wendy Hughes, Norman Kaye, Jon Finlayson, Julia Blake (Adams-Packer)

Norman Kaye plays Peter, a nervous, vapid character who is so weak he nearly recedes into the woodwork. Wendy Hughes is Patricia, dowdy, sexually repressed, and smothered by her parents. They meet and through a dating service after his mother dies, and embark on possibly the world's longest and dreariest courtship. Both Kaye and Hughes struggle to make their characters interesting or engaging.

LONELY PASSION OF JUDITH HEARNE, THE
1987, 110 mins, UK ⓥ
D: Jack Clayton A: Maggie Smith, Bob Hoskins, Wendy Hiller, Marie Kean, Prunella Scales (HandMade/United British Artists)

An ensemble of sterling performances highlights an intelligent, carefully crafted adaptation of Brian Moore's well-regarded first novel. Film's centerpiece is Maggie Smith's exceptionally detailed portrait of a middle-aged Irish spinster who tragically deludes herself into imagining herself involved in a great romance. She takes a liking to her landlady's brother, James (Bob Hoskins), a widower recently returned from 30 years in New York, and begins stepping out with him. Hoskins, laying a brash New York accent over a hint of the Irish, brings great energy and creative bluster to the irrepressible dreamer who has been instilled with Yankee get-up-and-go.

LONELY WOMAN, THE
See: Viaggio in Italia

LONE STAR
1996, 134 mins, US ⓥ ⊙ ▭
D: John Sayles A: Chris Cooper, Elizabeth Peña, Joe Morton, Ron Canada, Clifton James, Kris Kristofferson (Rio Dulce/Castle Rock)

A richly textured and thoroughly engrossing drama that ranks with indie filmmaker John Sayles's finest work. This time he focuses on a small Texas border town where the sins of fathers continue to haunt sons. Chris Cooper is Sam Deeds, the taciturn but easygoing sheriff of Frontera. The locals still swap stories about the fateful night 40 years ago when his father, Buddy Deeds (Matthew McConaughey), ran his corrupt predecessor, Charlie Wade (Kris Kristofferson), out of town. Skeletal remains are uncovered and identified as those of Charlie Wade. Sam suspects his father killed the villain, and begins to question Buddy's friends and associates. The more he digs into his father's past, the more he learns about himself.

LONE WOLF MCQUADE
1983, 107 mins, US ⓥ
D: Steve Carver A: Chuck Norris, David Carradine, Barbara Carrera, Leon Isaac Kennedy, L. Q. Jones (1818 Production/Orion)

Every conceivable type of portable weapon on the world market is tried out by the macho warriors on both sides of the law in this modern western, which pits Texas Ranger Chuck Norris and his cohorts against multifarious baddies who like to play rough. Opening sequence makes it clear that film's primary source of inspiration is Sergio Leone.

LONG AGO TOMORROW
See: The Raging Moon

LONG AND THE SHORT AND THE TALL, THE
(US: JUNGLE FIGHTERS)
1961, 105 mins, UK Ⓥ
D: Leslie Norman A: Richard Todd, Laurence Harvey, Richard Harris, Ronald Fraser, David McCallum, John Meillon (Associated British)

Film's set in the Far East jungle during the Japanese campaign. A small patrol led by a sergeant (Richard Todd) is cut off from the rest of the troops. Suddenly "sparks" makes radio contact and jabbering Japanese voices nearby cause them to realize that they're in a spot. A lone Japanese scout moves into their position and Todd insists that they must get him back to base alive as a source of information. The remainder want to bump him off with the solitary, surprise exception of a loudmouthed and brash private (Laurence Harvey). Standout performance comes from Harvey.

LONG DAY CLOSES, THE
1992, 83 mins, UK Ⓥ ⊙
D: Terence Davies A: Marjorie Yates, Leigh McCormack, Anthony Watson, Nicholas Lamont, Ayse Owens, Tina Malone (BFI/Film Four)

A technically elaborate, dryly witty moodpiece centered on a shy young daydreamer in mid-1950s working-class Liverpool, with a free-form ride down the helmer's memory lane of family, friends, Catholicism, and cinema. Central character is Bud (movingly limned by 13-year-old newcomer Leigh McCormack), a shy loner who finds escape from the grayness of Britain in movie theaters. There's little resolution in conventional terms: Davies simply builds a kaleidoscope out of memory fragments and shakes it every which way in a series of visual vignettes.

LONG DAY'S DYING, THE
1968, 93 mins, UK ▭
D: Peter Collinson A: David Hemmings, Tom Bell, Tony Beckley, Alan Dobie (Paramount)

The Long Day's Dying is a bore. In tracing the steps of three British soldiers and their German captive during a single day of weary trekking through the Euro-

pean countryside, it adds nothing in the way of insight or impact to the dreary platitudes of countless previous antiwar pix. No sympathy or interest is developed for any of the men. Fact that all four players register little beyond grim impassivity hardly lightens the pace of this lethargic film.

LONG DAY'S JOURNEY INTO NIGHT
1962, 176 mins, US Ⓥ
D: Sidney Lumet A: Katharine Hepburn, Ralph Richardson, Jason Robards, Dean Stockwell (Landau)

This is an excellent film adaption of Eugene O'Neill's lengthy stage work. It takes a family through the probing of themselves, their relations, and their relative reasons for acting as they do. It all develops when the mother one day begins to sink back to drug addiction. Katharine Hepburn's beautifully boned face mirrors her anguish and needs. She makes the role of the mother breathtaking and intensely moving. Ralph Richardson brings his authority to the part of the miserly father. Jason Robards has flair and insight as the tortured older brother, while Dean Stockwell is effective as the younger brother.
1962: Nomination: Best Actress (Katharine Hepburn)

LONG DUEL, THE
1967, 115 mins, UK ▭
D: Ken Annakin A: Yul Brynner, Trevor Howard, Harry Andrews, Andrew Keir, Charlotte Rampling (Rank)

This is an ambitious actioner which has plenty of punch. But the yarn, though based on fact, unfolds with little conviction and is repeatedly bogged down by labored dialogue and characterization. Story is set on the Indian northwest frontier during the 1920s. Trevor Howard, an idealistic police officer, is ordered to track down the Bhanta tribe leader (Yul Brynner), who is trying to lead his people from the bondage of the British. Howard recognizes Brynner as a fellow idealist and an enemy to respect.

LONGEST DAY, THE
1962, 180 mins, US Ⓥ ⊙ ▭
D: Ken Annakin, Andrew Marton, Bernhard Wicki A: John Wayne, Robert Mitchum, Henry Fonda, Robert Ryan, Richard Todd, Richard Burton (Zanuck/20th Century-Fox)

Solid and stunning war epic details the first day of the D-Day landings by the Allies on June 6, 1944. The savage fury and sound of war are ably caught on film. It emerges as a sort of grand-scale semifictionalized documentary concerning the overall logistics needed for this incredible invasion. The use of over 43 actual star names in bit and pivotal spots helps keep up the aura of fictionalized documentary. But it is the action, time and place, and the actual machinery of war that are the things. The battles ably take their places among some of the best ever put on the screen.

1962: Best B&W Cinematography, Special Effects

Nominations: Best Picture, B&W Art Direction, Editing

LONGEST YARD, THE
(UK: THE MEAN MACHINE)
1974, 121 mins, US ⓥ ⊙
D: Robert Aldrich A: Burt Reynolds, Eddie Albert, Ed Lauter, Michael Conrad, Bernadette Peters (Paramount/Long Road)

An outstanding action drama, combining the brutish excitement of football competition with the brutalities of contemporary prison life. Burt Reynolds asserts his genuine star power, here as a former football pro forced to field a team under blackmail of warden Eddie Albert. This is quality action drama, in which brute force is fully motivated and therefore totally acceptable.

1974: Nomination: Best Editing

LONG GOODBYE, THE
1973, 112 mins, US ⓥ ⊙ ⊟
D: Robert Altman A: Elliott Gould, Nina Van Pallandt, Sterling Hayden, Henry Gibson, Mark Rydell (United Artists)

Robert Altman's film version of Raymond Chandler's novel is an uneven mixture of insider satire on the gumshoe film genre, gratuitous brutality, and sledgehammer whimsy. Herein, the Philip Marlowe character becomes embroiled in a Malibu murder, stolen money, the apparent death of his best friend, and a compounded double cross. No longer the sardonic idealist, Marlowe has become part Walter Mitty. Elliott Gould keeps a low dramatic profile throughout as a passive catalyst.

LONG GOOD FRIDAY, THE
1981, 114 mins, UK ⓥ
D: John Mackenzie A: Bob Hoskins, Helen Mirren, Eddie Constantine, Dave King, Pierce Brosnan (Calendar/Black Lion)

In many respects a conventional thriller set in London's underworld, *The Long Good Friday* is much more densely plotted and intelligently scripted than most such yarns. Bob Hoskins displays natural, and sizable, big-screen presence in the anchor role of a gangland boss faced with a series of seemingly gratuitous reprisals by unknown ill-wishers against his waterfront empire. Visual style is too stolid to lend due gut impact.

LONG GRAY LINE, THE
1955, 135 mins, US ⊟
D: John Ford A: Tyrone Power, Maureen O'Hara, Robert Francis, Ward Bond, Donald Crisp (Columbia)

A standout drama on West Point. For Tyrone Power the role of Marty Maher, Irishman through whose eyes the story is told, is a memorable one. Maureen O'Hara brings to the role of Maher's wife her Irish beauty and seldom-displayed acting ability. Both are very fine. Production is based on the autobiography of Maher's 50 years at the Point. Story oscillates between unashamed sniffles and warm chuckles, Ford not being afraid to bring a tear or stick in a laugh.

LONG HOT SUMMER, THE
1958, 115 mins, US ⓥ ⊟
D: Martin Ritt A: Paul Newman, Joanne Woodward, Anthony Franciosa, Orson Welles, Lee Remick, Angela Lansbury (Wald/20th Century-Fox)

A simmering story of life in the Deep South, steamy with sex and laced with violence and bawdy humor. A young Mississippi redneck (Paul Newman) has a reputation for settling his grudges by setting fire to the property of those he opposes. This notoriety follows him when he drifts into the town owned and operated by Orson Welles, a gargantuan character who has reduced the town to sniveling peonage. Welles senses immediately in Newman a fellow predator and they set to trying to outdo each other in villainy and connivance.

LONG KISS GOODNIGHT, THE
1996, 120 mins, US ⓥ ⊙ ⊟
D: Renny Harlin A: Geena Davis, Samuel L. Jackson, Patrick Malahide, Craig Bierko, Brian Cox, David Morse (Forge/New Line)

A violent and fantastic actioner, *The Long Kiss Goodnight* has a jokey good time with its outlandish pyrotechnics and offbeat character interplay. Samantha Caine (Geena Davis) seems the ideal mom in a New England small town. But she turns out to have been a highly trained government assassin in her previous life, which she can't remember due to an amnesiac block. Samantha hooks up with low-rent detective and ex-jailbird Mitch (Samuel L. Jackson) to seek the truth, threatened every step of the way by government hit man Timothy (Craig Bierko) and his treacherous intelligence chief, Perkins (Patrick Malahide). Davis fits the bill of a smart, tough capable femme operative as well as anyone could. Playing a lifelong loser with a lively sense of humor, Jackson lightens the proceedings in a welcome manner.

LONG NIGHT, THE
1947, 97 mins, US
D: Anatole Litvak **A:** Henry Fonda, Barbara Bel Geddes, Vincent Price, Ann Dvorak, Elisha Cook Jr. (RKO)

A sullen brooding film about vet of World War II who goes on killing spree when his girl takes up with another guy. There's some good, challenging writing that indicts a society in which a guy can kill legally in war and get it in the neck if he does it in peace. Brilliant thesping jobs are turned in by Henry Fonda, Barbara Bel Geddes (making her film bow), Vincent Price, and others, but picture is too grim.

LONG PANTS
1927, 70 mins, US ⊗
D: Frank Capra **A:** Harry Langdon, Gladys Brockwell, Al Roscoe, Alma Bennett, Priscilla Bonner, Frankie Darro (Langdon/First National)

A bit of a letdown for Harry Langdon. It hasn't the popular laughing quality of his other full-length productions, principally because the sympathetic element is overdeveloped at the expense of the gags and the stunts that made *The Strong Man* a riot. By anybody else the picture would be hailed as a great production.

LONG RIDERS, THE
1980, 100 mins, US ⓥ ⊙
D: Walter Hill **A:** David Carradine, Keith Carradine, Stacy Keach, James Keach, Dennis Quaid, Randy Quaid (United Artists)

The Long Riders is striking in several ways, not the least of which being the casting of actor brothers as historical outlaw kin, but narrative is episodic in the extreme. Yarn opens in bang-up fashion with a bank robbery, after which triggerhappy Dennis Quaid is kicked out of the Younger-James-Miller gang for needlessly

murdering a man during stickup. Director Walter Hill resolutely refuses to investigate the psychology or motivations of his characters, explaining away men's life of banditry as a "habit" acquired in wake of the Civil War.

LONG SHADOW, THE
1992, 89 mins, US/Hungary/Israel ⓥ
D: Vilmos Zsigmond **A:** Michael York, Liv Ullmann, Oded Teomi, Ava Haddad, Babi Neeman (Prolitera)

Lush lensing and some eye-filling Israeli locations can't rescue a trite semimeller sabotaged by the blah script and some dubious casting. Michael York toplines weakly as a Hungarian Jew working out an Oedipus-Schmoedipus complex on a trip to the Holy Land. Directorial bow by Oscar-winning Magyar cinematographer Vilmos Zsigmond is strictly in-flight fare.

LONG SHIPS, THE
1964, 124 mins, UK/Yugoslavia ⓥ ⋈
D: Jack Cardiff **A:** Richard Widmark, Sidney Poitier, Russ Tamblyn, Rosanna Schiaffino, Beba Loncar, Oscar Homolka (Columbia/Warwick/Avala)

Any attempt to put this into the epic class falls down because of a hodgepodge of a story line, a mixture of styles, and insufficient character development. Throughout there's a great deal of noise and the entire experience is a very long drag. Film concerns the rivalry of the Vikings and the Moors in search of a legendary Golden Bell containing "half the gold in the world." Leaders of the rival factions are Richard Widmark, an adventurous Viking con man, who plays strictly tongue in cheek, and Sidney Poitier, dignified, ruthless top man of the Moors. In contrast to Widmark, he seeks to take the film seriously. The clash in styles between these two is a minor disaster.

LONGTIME COMPANION
1990, 96 mins, US ⓥ
D: Norman René **A:** Bruce Davison, Campbell Scott, Stephen Caffrey, Mark Lamos, Mary-Louise Parker (American Playhouse)

The first feature film to tell the story of how AIDS devastated and transformed the gay community is simply an excellent film, with a graceful, often humorous script and affecting performances. Story begins during the carefree pre-AIDS party days on Fire Island, where Willy (Campbell Scott) and Fuzzy (Stephen Caffrey)

meet. A year later Willy's best friend John (Dermont Mulroney) becomes violently ill and dies. It's only the beginning. One by one, this community of actors, writers, and lawyers is affected.
1990: Nomination: Best Supp. Actor (Bruce Davison)

LONG VOYAGE HOME, THE
1940, 105 mins, US Ⓥ ⊙
D: John Ford **A:** John Wayne, Thomas Mitchell, Ian Hunter, Barry Fitzgerald, Wilfred Lawson, Mildred Natwick (Argosy)

Combining dramatic content of four Eugene O'Neill one-act plays, John Ford pilots adventures of a tramp steamer from the West Indies to an American port, and then across the Atlantic with cargo of high explosives. Picture is typically Fordian, his direction accentuating characterizations and adventures of the voyage. There's plenty of dialogue and action in the crew's quarters, with Thomas Mitchell, the accepted leader of the group. Mitchell hits a high mark in the seaman's character—two-fisted, domineering, and still kindly and loyal to his pals. John Wayne's role is submerged among the sailor characters.
1940: Nominations: Best Picture, Screenplay, B&W Cinematography, Editing, Original Score

LONG WALK HOME, THE
1990, 97 mins, US Ⓥ ⊙
D: Richard Pearce **A:** Sissy Spacek, Whoopi Goldberg, Dwight Schultz, Ving Rhames, Dylan Baker (New Visions)

Set in Montgomery, AL, during the 1955 civil-rights bus boycott, *The Long Walk Home* is an effectively mounted drama about the human impact of changing times on two families, with sturdy performances by Sissy Spacek as an upper-crust white housewife and Whoopi Goldberg as her maid. The film resists the temptation to succumb to sentimentality and offers believable characterizations in the context of its time and place.

LOOK BACK IN ANGER
1959, 115 mins, UK Ⓥ
D: Tony Richardson **A:** Richard Burton, Claire Bloom, Mary Ure, Edith Evans, Gary Raymond, Donald Pleasence (Woodfall)

Tony Richardson has lost the heart and the throb that made the play an adventure. The film simultaneously impresses and depresses. In the play, Jimmy Porter was a rebel—but a mixed-up weakling of a rebel. In the film, as played by Richard Burton, he is an arrogant young man who thinks the world owes him something. It is not his fault that the role gives him little opportunity for variety. Mary Ure as the downtrodden, degraded young wife is first-class.

LOOKER
1981, 94 mins, US Ⓥ ⊙ ☐
D: Michael Crichton **A:** Albert Finney, James Coburn, Susan Dey, Leigh Taylor-Young, Darryl Hickman (Ladd/Warner)

Writer-director Michael Crichton has used interesting material, public manipulation by computer-generated TV commercials, to create a silly and unconvincing contempo sci-fi thriller. Albert Finney heads the cast as a plastic surgeon being set up as the fall guy in a string of murders of beautiful models. He teams with model Cindy (Susan Dey) to track down the real killers, with Cindy infiltrating a suspicious research institute run by Jennifer Long (Leigh Taylor-Young), part of the conglomerate headed by John Reston (James Coburn).

LOOKING FOR MR. GOODBAR
1977, 135 mins, US Ⓥ ⊙
D: Richard Brooks **A:** Diane Keaton, Tuesday Weld, William Atherton, Richard Kiley, Richard Gere, Tom Berenger (Paramount)

Writer-director Richard Brooks manifests his ability to catch accurately both the tone and subtlety of characters in the most repellent environments—in this case the desperate search for personal identity in the dreary and self-defeating world of compulsive sex and dope. Diane Keaton's performance as the good/bad girl is excellent. At its best, the film, through Tuesday Weld's great performance as Keaton's sister, suggests dimly some alternatives.
1977: Nominations: Best Supp. Actress (Tuesday Weld), Cinematography

LOOKING FOR RICHARD
1996, 109 mins, US Ⓥ
D: Al Pacino **A:** Al Pacino, Harris Yulin, Penelope Allen, Alec Baldwin, Kevin Spacey, Estelle Parsons (Jam)

High-spirited and infectiously energetic, Al Pacino's *Looking for Richard* is a master class in Shakespeare and acting conducted by an uncommonly passionate and delightful teacher. Ranging from New York's streets to the reconstructed Globe Theatre in London, Pacino is the voluble, mercurial center of a film that ingeniously interweaves commentary on Shakespeare with analysis of, rehearsals for, and key segments from *Richard III* on film. What starts as history lessons and rehearsals has, by its end, left behind all intellectual props and achieved a magnificent emotional force.

LOOKING GLASS WAR, THE
1970, 106 mins, UK Ⓥ ▢
D: Frank Pierson **A:** Christopher Jones, Pia Degermark, Ralph Richardson, Paul Rogers, Anthony Hopkins, Susan George (Columbia/Frankovich)

Jones, a ship-jumping Polish seaman, is recruited by Richardson and Rogers, two old hands in British espionage, to enter East Germany to verify some missile sites. Anthony Hopkins, a younger undercover agent, is a key character. Based on the John Le Carré novel about cold-war espionage, Pierson's adaptation has some superior dialogue and structuring.

LOOKIN' TO GET OUT
1982, 104 mins, US Ⓥ
D: Hal Ashby **A:** Jon Voight, Ann-Margret, Burt Young, Bert Remsen, Jude Farese (Northstar International/Lorimar)

An ill-conceived vehicle for actor (and cowriter) Jon Voight to showcase his character comedy talents. Alex (Jon Voight) and Jerry (Burt Young) flee to Las Vegas to escape thugs Harry (Jude Farese) and Joey (Allen Keller), whose $10,000 Alex has dropped in a poker game. Duo set up shop in the *Dr. Zhivago* suite of the M-G-M Grand Hotel and use a false identity to obtain unlimited credit from the casino. Occasionally amusing, picture often has the feel of being improvised. Interplay between Voight and Young is the film's raison d'être.

LOOKS AND SMILES
1983, 104 mins, UK
D: Ken Loach **A:** Graham Green, Carolyn Nicholson, Tony Pitts, Phil Askham, Cilla Mason (Black Lion/Kestrel/MK2)

Somber but dramatically right tale of teenagers running into unemployment and broken families in a northern industrial town. The three protagonists are played by nonpros, and very well, too. The film certainly has a feel for its characters, and place, helped by a sharply dramatic use of B&W lensing which fits the milieu and theme.

LOOK WHO'S TALKING
1989, 90 mins, US Ⓥ ◉
D: Amy Heckerling **A:** John Travolta, Kirstie Alley, Olympia Dukakis, George Segal, Bruce Willis (Tri-Star/MCEG)

Like a stand-up comic pouring "flop-sweat," this ill-conceived comedy about an infant whose thoughts are given voice by actor Bruce Willis palpitates with desperation. *Look Who's Voice-Overing* would be a far more appropriate moniker, as Willis isn't heard by the film's other characters. Kirstie Alley does the best she can as the child's mother.

LOOK WHO'S TALKING NOW
1993, 97 mins, US Ⓥ ◉
D: Tom Ropelewski **A:** John Travolta, Kirstie Alley, Olympia Dukakis, Lysette Anthony, David Gallagher (Tri-Star)

Once again, pic derives yuks from wisecracking inner monologues of non-talking characters. First it was the baby boy, then the baby girl. Now it's the dogs. What's next, the refrigerator? Still, scripters find droll if not witty voices in Danny DeVito's street-smart mutt and Diane Keaton's prissy poodle.

LOOK WHO'S TALKING TOO
1990, 81 mins, US Ⓥ ◉
D: Amy Heckerling **A:** John Travolta, Kirstie Alley, Olympia Dukakis, Elias Koteas, Neal Israel (Tri-Star)

This vulgar sequel to 1989's sleeper hit looks like a rush job. Filmmaker Amy Heckerling overemphasizes toilet humor and expletives to make the film appealing mainly to adolescents. Unwed mom Alley and cabbie John Travolta are married for the sequel, with her cute son, Mikey, metamorphosed into Lorne Sussman, still voice-overed as precocious by Bruce Willis. First mutual arrival is undeniably cute Megan Milner, unfortunately voiced over by Roseanne Barr. Comedienne gets a couple of laughs but is generally dull, leaving Willis to again carry the load in the gag department with well-read quips.

LOOPHOLE
1981, 105 mins, UK Ⓥ
D: John Quested **A:** Albert Finney, Martin Sheen, Susannah York, Colin Blakely, Jonathan Pryce, Robert Morley (Brent Walker)

A clever plan to knock off a rich London bank is about the only thing that works. Caper, filmed in and around the British capital, squanders some fine talent on a trite, low-voltage script. Albert Finney as the mastermind of the heist, and Martin Sheen as an honest architect who lends the gang his talents, perform okay with little room to flex their histrionic skills.

LOOSE CANNONS
1990, 93 mins, US ⓥ ⓞ
D: Bob Clark **A:** Gene Hackman, Dan Aykroyd, Dom DeLuise, Ronny Cox, Nancy Travis (Tri-Star)

Dan Aykroyd's dexterous multipersonality shtick is the only redeeming feature of this chase-heavy comedy. Plot involves gruesome murders, a secret 45-year-old porno film, a candidate for the chancellorship of West Germany, and a horde of Uzi-brandishing neo-Nazis. All of that is irrelevant to the main plot, which pairs the gruff Mac (Gene Hackman) with Ellis (Aykroyd)—recently (and apparently prematurely) reactivated after suffering a nervous breakdown that causes him to lapse into multiple personalities.

LOOSE CONNECTIONS
1983, 99 mins, UK ⓥ
D: Richard Eyre **A:** Stephen Rea, Lindsay Duncan, Jan Niklas, Carole Harrison, Gary Olsen (Umbrella/Greenpoint)

Sally (Lindsay Duncan) has built a Jeep to drive from London to a feminist conference in Munich. She takes out a newspaper ad for a fellow driver, seeking a female nonsmoking vegetarian who speaks German and knows something about car engines. The only applicant is Harry (Stephen Rea), who claims to fill all the requirements except sex, and furthermore claims he's gay. Needless to say, Harry's a liar. The trip to Munich is one comic disaster after another. It's a film of continual quiet chuckles.

LOOSE ENDS
1975, 103 mins, US
D: David Burton Morris **A:** Chris Mulkey, John Jenkins, Linda Jenkins, Bobby Jenkins, Irv Fink (American Eagle/Fat Chance)

Many American nonachievers, zonked by dreams of unattainable affluence and adventure, could probably relate to the had-it-up-to-here despair expressed in *Loose Ends*, low-budget art film written, directed, and produced by the husband-wife team of David Burton Morris and Victoria Wozniak. But while working-class frustration of the three principals is well delineated, the picture fails to develop much identification with, or empathy for, the trapped participants.

LOOT
1970, 101 mins, UK ⓥ
D: Silvio Narizzano **A:** Richard Attenborough, Lee Remick, Hywel Bennett, Roy Holder, Milo O'Shea, Dick Emery (British Lion)

Joe Orton's macabre black comedy has transferred uneasily to the screen. Nevertheless, it has enough speed, inventiveness, and sharp, acid, irreverent comedy to satisfy many. Hywel Bennett and Roy Holder blow a bank and hide the loot in the coffin of Holder's mother, who has conveniently died. But there's no room for the cash and the corpse, so the poor woman's hidden in the lavatory. The hotel belonging to Holder's father (Milo O'Shea) becomes a bedlam of frenzied rushing around, complicated by the arrival of an eccentric, pompous, and venal inspector (Richard Attenborough) and Lee Remick, as a gold-digging sexpot of a private nurse.

LORD JIM
1965, 154 mins, UK/US ⓥ ▭
D: Richard Brooks **A:** Peter O'Toole, James Mason, Curt Jurgens, Jack Hawkins, Eli Wallach, Daliah Lavi (Columbia/Keep)

Many may be disappointed with Richard Brooks's handling of the Joseph Conrad novel. The story concerns a young merchant seaman. In a moment of cowardice he deserts his ship during a storm and his life is dogged throughout by remorse and an urge to redeem himself. Brooks has teetered between making it a full-blooded, no-holds-barred adventure yarn and the fascinating psychological study that Conrad wrote. O'Toole, though a fine, handsome figure of a man, goes through the film practically expressionless and the audience sees little of the character's introspection and soul-searching.

LORD LOVE A DUCK
1966, 105 mins, US
D: George Axelrod **A:** Roddy McDowall, Tuesday Weld, Lola Albright, Martin West, Ruth Gordon (Charleston/United Artists)

Film is packed with laughs, often of the truest anatomical kind, and there is a veneer of sophistication which keeps showing despite the most outlandish goings-on. The characters are developed brightly along zany lines, topped by Roddy McDowall as a Svengali-type high-school student leader who pulls the strings on the destiny of Tuesday Weld, an ingenuish-type sexpot whose philosophy is wrapped up in her words "Everybody's got to love me.'' Scoring almost spectacularly is Lola Albright as Weld's mother, a cocktail bar ''bunny'' who commits suicide when she thinks she's ruined her daughter's chances for marriage.

LORD OF ILLUSIONS
1995, 108 mins, US Ⓥ ⊙
D: Clive Barker **A:** Scott Bakula, Kevin J. O'Connor, Famke Janssen, Vincent Schiavelli, Barry Del Sherman (Seraphim/United Artists)

Horror novelist and filmmaker Clive Barker has toned down the full-bore gore of his earlier directorial efforts. Even so, there's still enough gruesome stuff here to delight genre fans and unsettle everybody else. *Lord* features Scott Bakula as Harry D'Amour, a New York–based p.i. who periodically encounters the supernatural in his work. While on a routine case in L.A., D'Amour runs across cultists who want to revive their spiritual leader. Bakula's virile good looks, low-key humor, and matter-of-fact authority make him an engaging Everyman.

LORD OF THE FLIES
1963, 90 mins, UK Ⓥ
D: Peter Brook **A:** James Aubrey, Tom Chapin, Hugh Emwards, Roger Elwin (Two Arts)

The theme of young boys reverting to savagery when marooned on a deserted island has its moments of truth, but this pic rates as a near miss on many counts. Evacuation in some future war has a group of youngsters surviving an air crash on a tropical island. They meet, and one boy is elected chief, but with dissent from another. Latter says his group will become hunters and they are soon drawing blood from some wild pigs and recounting tales of a monster on the island. The last-named is a dead paratrooper swaying on a ledge. But soon the hunting group goes completely native and persecutes and even exterminates those of the other group.

LORD OF THE FLIES
1990, 90 mins, US Ⓥ ⊙
D: Harry Hook **A:** Balthazar Getty, Chris Furth, Danuel Pipoly, Badgett Dale, Edward Taft (Jack's Camp/Signal Hill)

The notion that the story of civilized boys reverting to savagery on a desert isle would be improved by shooting in color and substituting American actors for British child thesps is an odd one indeed. Director Harry Hook's literal, unimaginative visual approach makes the tale seem mundane and tedious. The flat screenplay makes all the boys seem like dullards and does little to help differentiate the cast members.

LORD OF THE RINGS, THE
1978, 131 mins, US Ⓥ
D: Ralph Bakshi (Fantasy)

Unquestionably, Bakshi has perfected some outstanding pen-and-ink effects while translating faithfully a portion of J.R.R. Tolkien's trilogy. But in his concentration on craft and duty to the original story—both admirable in themselves—Bakshi overlooks the uninitiated completely. Quite simply, those who do not know the characters of Middle Earth going in will not know them coming out.'

LORDS OF DISCIPLINE, THE
1983, 102 mins, US Ⓥ ⊙
D: Franc Roddam **A:** David Keith, Robert Prosky, G. D. Spradlin, Barbara Babcock, Michael Biehn (Paramount)

A military school Watergate saga laced with heavy doses of sadism, racism, and macho bullying. Designed as an exposé of the corruption to be found within the hallowed walls of a venerable American institution, pic wants to have it both ways. Set around 1964, drama follows cadet David Keith through his senior year at the Carolina Military Institute. As far as the new recruits are concerned, the poop hits the fan on ''hell night.'' One boy dies, which leads outsider-type Keith onto the existence of The Ten, a secret society to ferret out undesirables.

LORDS OF FLATBUSH, THE
1974, 86 mins, US Ⓥ ⊙
D: Stephen Verona, Martin Davidson **A:** Perry King, Sylvester Stallone, Henry Winkler, Paul Mace, Susan Blakely (Columbia)

Perry King and Sylvester Stallone play a couple of would-be toughies who occasionally leave their pals for some dating. Stallone's romancing leads to getting his pal (Maria Smith) pregnant, and King to getting the final brush-off from the femme (Susan Blakely) he pursues. Not too much finesse distinguishes the script, which carries neither warmth nor particular interest for the various characters.

LORENZO'S OIL
1992, 135 mins, US Ⓥ ⊙
D: George Miller **A:** Nick Nolte, Susan Sarandon, Peter Ustinov, Kathleen Wilhoite, Zack O'Malley Greenburg (Universal)

As grueling a medical case study as

any audience would ever want to sit through. A true-life story brought to the screen intelligently and with passionate motivation, pic details in a very precise way how a couple raced time to save the life of their young son after he contracted a rare, always fatal disease. Among the irritants is an acting style that is generally cranked up to full throttle or beyond. Susan Sarandon convincingly conveys a fierceness and tenacity that is almost frightening. The character never lets up, and neither does the film.

1992: Nomination: Best Actress (Susan Sarandon), Original Screenplay

LORNA
1965, 78 mins, US

D: Russ Meyer **A:** Lorna Maitland, Mark Bradley, James Rucker, Hal Hooper, James Griffith (Eve)

A sort of sex morality play, *Lorna* is Russ Meyer's first serious effort after six nudie pix. Story concerns Lorna Maitland as the buxom wife of James Rucker, a handsome young clod who works at a salt mine. Mark Bradley, escaped con and vicious killer, encounters Maitland in the fields with predictable results, after which she takes him home for encores.

LORNA DOONE
1934, 100 mins, UK

D: Basil Dean **A:** Victoria Hopper, John Loder, Mary Clare, Frank Cellier, George Curzon (Associated Talking)

Not a bad effort to make an artistic picture out of a novel that is generally rated among British classics. But it lacks drama and grip. Story on which the film is based tells how a famous family of rebels, the Doones, live in a Somerset valley, the terror of surrounding farms and settlements. A boy, John Ridd, sees his father killed by the outlaws, and he grows up seeking vengeance, only to fall in love with the Doone daughter, Lorna.

LORNA DOONE
1951, 82 mins, US

D: Phil Karlson **A:** Barbara Hale, Richard Greene, Carl Benton Reid, William Bishop, Ron Randell, Sean McClory (Columbia)

This freely adapted film version of Richard D. Blackmore's classic is a mixture of action and romance against the outdoor beauties of rural England (as location-filmed in Yosemite) back in the days of Charles II. It depicts the uprising of poor villagers and farmers, under the leadership of John Ridd (Richard Greene), against the oppression of an arrogant, titled family that ruthlessly rules its lands. Barbara Hale and Richard Greene take to the period garb and settings neatly.

LOSERS, THE
1970, 95 mins, US ⓥ

D: Jack Starrett **A:** William Smith, Bernie Hamilton, Adam Roarke, Daniel Kemp, Houston Savage (Fanfare)

The Philippines is supposed to pass, on the screen, as Vietnam. The viewer is asked to believe that a contingent of motorcycle bums would be hired by the US to rescue a CIA agent, held prisoner in Cambodia by the North Vietnamese or Red Chinese. The script is so inane, with not even a feeble attempt at logic, that what are intended as serious moments come off as funny. Some of the acting is excellent.

LOSING ISAIAH
1995, 106 mins, US ⓥ

D: Stephen Gyllenhaal **A:** Jessica Lange, Halle Berry, David Strathairn, Cuba Gooding Jr., Samuel L. Jackson (Paramount)

A grimly serious, issue-oriented drama of custody battles between birth and adoptive parents. Chicago ghetto fringe dweller Khaila Richards (Halle Berry) leaves her little boy in a trash heap in her haste to score another hit of crack. The tot is taken home by social worker Margaret Lewin (Jessica Lange). By the time he's a toddler, little Isaiah (four-year-old Marc John Jefferies) has been officially adopted. A lawyer (Samuel L. Jackson) tells Khaila she has a good case for asserting her maternal rights, and the battle is on. Despite its problem-picture format and lack of character depth, film manages to pack a punch due to its subject and many intense scenes of emotional anguish.

LOSIN' IT
1983, 104 mins, US ⓥ ⊙

D: Curtis Hanson **A:** Tom Cruise, Jackie Earle Haley, John Stockwell, Shelley Long, Hector Elias (Embassy)

There are only so many ways to show teenagers not having sex. But director Curtis Hanson makes a commendable effort with a rather obvious story about three teenage boys who head for a wild weekend in Tijuana, hoping to trade hard cash for manly experience. They are accompanied by wimpy John P. Navin Jr., because he has the necessary cash to make the trip possible. And along the way they pick up crazy—but nice—Shelley Long, on the lam from her husband. This doesn't sound like much and it isn't, but the picture is a solid credit for all involved.

LOSS OF INNOCENCE
See: The Greengage Summer

LOST ANGEL
1944, 91 mins, US
D: Roy Rowland **A:** Margaret O'Brien, James Craig, Marsha Hunt, Keenan Wynn (M-G-M)

Lost Angel reveals Margaret O'Brien as a foundling picked up by scientists as the subject for experiment in human behavior. A genius at the age of six, the human element, however, has been overlooked. But then a police reporter (James Craig) is assigned to check on the prodigy, and the rest chiefly concerns a rehabilitation to her innate child consciousness with Craig as her tutor. Roy Rowland intelligently directs the moppet, and his ability to keep the more implausible moments down to a minimum is worthy of note.

LOST ANGELS
(AKA: THE ROAD HOME)
1989, 116 mins, US ⊙ ⊙ ▭
D: Hugh Hudson **A:** Donald Sutherland, Adam Horovitz, Amy Locane, Don Bloomfield (Orion)

Wannabe *Rebel Without a Cause* update tries to be a serious exploration of throwaway middle-class teens in the San Fernando Valley, but despite some gripping moments it's often clichéd and incoherent. Adam Horovitz of the Beastie Boys rap band has a sympathetic presence but not enough to do as the troubled lead. Sutherland brings subtlety to his occasional scenes as a scruffy shrink who has enough emotional problems to be empathetic.

LOST BOYS, THE
1987, 92 mins, US ⊙ ⊙ ▭
D: Joel Schumacher **A:** Jason Patric, Corey Haim, Dianne Wiest, Barnard Hughes, Kiefer Sutherland (Warner)

A horrifically dreadful vampire teen-sploitation entry that daringly advances the theory that all those missing teens pictured on garbage bags and milk cartons are actually the victims of bloodsucking bikers. It all ends in a colossal battle with bats, punks, froth, spears, and blood flying through the air in a frenzy of nonsensical action.

LOST COMMAND
1966, 129 mins, US ⊙ ▭
D: Mark Robson **A:** Anthony Quinn, Alain Delon, George Segal, Michèle Morgan, Maurice Ronet, Claudia Cardinale (Columbia)

A good action-melodrama about some French paratroopers who survive France's humiliation and defeat in Southeast Asia, only to be sent to rebellious Algeria. Production has enough pace, action, and exterior eye appeal to overcome a sometimes routine script. Anthony Quinn heads the players as the gruff, lowborn soldier who has risen to field-grade rank. Alain Delon is the sensitive, quiet but effective assistant. Maurice Ronet is brutal, sadistic, and callous, yet with enough fighting effectiveness to be needed in battle.

LOST HIGHWAY
1997, 135 mins, France/US ⊙ ⊙ ▭
D: David Lynch **A:** Bill Pullman, Patricia Arquette, Balthazar Getty, Robert Blake, Natasha Gregson Wagner, Richard Pryor (CiBy 2000/Asymetrical)

Lost Highway is a mysterious, ultra-Lynchian exercise in Designer Noir involving weird crimes, bizarre sex, freakish characters, social unease and fully warranted paranoia. But there remains a nagging sense of a work not completely achieved. Tenor sax player Fred (Bill Pullman) and his wife, Renee (Patricia Arquette), see their life destroyed through a disturbing series of events. Fred is convicted of first-degree murder and sentenced to the electric chair. In a great jump into the unexplainable, a young man named Pete (Balthazar Getty) is suddenly occupying Fred's cell, only to emerge and work as a garage mechanic for a wheelchair-bound boss, Arnie (Richard Pryor). These narrative strategies create intentional mysteries for which there are no answers, making this a dream-film that will leave its partisans attempting to puzzle it out and non-fans out in the cold. Dramatically, film verges on the lethargic at times.

LOST HORIZON
1937, 125 mins, US ⊙ ⊙
D: Frank Capra **A:** Ronald Colman, Edward Everett Horton, H. B. Warner, Jane Wyatt, Sam Jaffe, Margo (Columbia)

Audiences will be carried away by the histrionic illusion, skill, and general Hollywood legerdemain which so effectively capture the best elements in this saga of Shangri-la. Ronald Colman, with fine restraint, conveys the metamorphosis of the foreign diplomat falling in with the Arcadian idyll that he beholds in the Valley of the Blue Moon. Sam Jaffe is capital as the priest who first founded Shangri-la some 300 years ago—a Methuselah who is still alive, thanks to the Utopian philosophy of the community he has nurtured. The valley's philosophy of moderation in work, food, drink, pleasure, acquisition, and all other earthly wants is cannily scripted for audience appeal.

1937: Best Interior Decoration (Stephen Goosson), Editing

Nominations: Best Picture, Supp. Actor (H. B. Warner), Score, Sound, Assistant Director (C. C. Coleman Jr.)

LOST HORIZON
1973, 150 mins, US ⊙ ▭
D: Charles Jarrott **A:** Peter Finch, Liv Ullmann, Sally Kellerman, George Kennedy, Michael York, Olivia Hussey (Columbia)

The form of producer Ross Hunter's lavish updated adaptation is that of filmed operetta in three acts, superbly mounted. Peter Finch heads the cast as Conway, an international statesman selected by high lama Charles Boyer to succeed to rule of Shangri-la, where the world's wisdom is being preserved against the foreseen Apocalypse. Sir John Gielgud is the high lama's chief aide, who reveals the mystery of the place to Finch.

LOST IN A HAREM
1944, 88 mins, US ⊗
D: Charles Riesner **A:** Bud Abbott, Lou Costello, Marilyn Maxwell, John Conte (M-G-M)

Good standard fare for Abbott and Costello fans. The film has some neat production numbers built around appearances of Jimmy Dorsey and his orchestra. Story has to do with a mystical eastern land ruled by a sheik who has defrauded his nephew of the throne. Nephew (John Conte) hires Abbott and Costello, a stranded American troupe's magic act, to regain his kingdom by stealing some magic rings his uncle wears.

LOST IN AMERICA
1985, 91 mins, US ⊗
D: Albert Brooks **A:** Albert Brooks, Julie Hagerty, Garry Marshall, Art Frankel, Michael Greene (Geffen)

Film opens on Albert Brooks and wife, Julie Hagerty, in bed on eve of their move to a $450,000 house. Brooks glides into his boss's office only to hear that he's be-

ing transferred to New York. He quits his job and convinces his wife to quit her personnel job. The pair will liquidate their assets, buy a Winnebago, and head across America. Brooks, who directed and cowrote with Monica Johnson, is irrepressible but always very human.

LOST IN SPACE
1998, 131 mins, US ⊗ ⊙ ▭
D: Stephen Hopkins **A:** William Hurt, Mimi Rogers, Heather Graham, Lacey Chabert, Jack Johnson, Gary Oldman (Prelude/New Line)

Pic provides one hour's decent, eye-filling ride, then crashes and burns amid some of the worst writing since scenarist/producer Akiva Goldsman's last effort, *Batman & Robin*. Goldsman and director Stephen Hopkins don't overtly parody the material. But the writer just can't stop forcing his characters to parrot the lamest possible wisecracks, and an effort to inject contemporary relevance by making the Space Family Robinsons a stock dysfunctional unit plays even worse than it sounds. It's 2058 and life on this planet is running out of time. The United Global Space Force sends Prof. John Robinson (William Hurt) and his family to a faraway colony to help prepare mankind for its "offshore" future. Bad guys hire veteran spy Dr. Smith (Gary Oldman) to sabotage the mission, but strand him on the vessel whose destruction he's already programmed. Hopkins delivers satisfying spectacle on a moment-to-moment basis but no sense of overall structure or pacing.

LOST IN YONKERS
1993, 112 mins, US ⊗ ⊙
D: Martha Coolidge **A:** Richard Dreyfuss, Mercedes Ruehl, Irene Worth, Brad Stoll, David Strathairn (Columbia/Rastar)

A carefully rendered, ultimately unexciting screen version of Neil Simon's play. Story, set in the summer of '42, begins as Eddie Krunitz (Jack Laufer) attempts to deposit his two sons with his mother. The two boys, 15-year-old Jay and Arty, two years younger, are bright, presentable, well-behaved kids, and much of the pleasure of the film lies in watching the alert, bright-eyed perfomances of Brad Stoll and Mike Damus. Still, they are susceptible to the brash appeal of their uncle Louie (Richard Dreyfuss), a small-time hood. The film seems bound by its theatrical origins in the way everything is stated and spelled out.

LOST PATROL, THE
1934, 74 mins, US Ⓥ

D: John Ford **A:** Victor McLaglen, Boris Karloff, Wallace Ford, Reginald Denny, J. M. Kerrigan (RKO)

All of the action takes place in the Mesopotamian desert during the campaign of the English against militant Arabs in 1917. A patrol, lost after the commanding officer has been killed, discovers an oasis where one by one the men either die or are bumped off by Arabs, until Victor McLaglen is the last. McLaglen turns in a good job. As a Bible nut, Boris Karloff gives a fine account of himself.
1934: Nomination: Best Score

LOST SQUADRON, THE
1932, 80 mins, US Ⓥ ◉

D: George Archainbaud **A:** Richard Dix, Mary Astor, Erich von Stroheim, Dorothy Jordan, Joel McCrea, Robert Armstrong (RKO)

Squadron glorifies the cinematic stunt flier. The "behind the scenes" of an aerial film production is the best appeal *Squadron* has. Erich von Stroheim plays the role of a domineering, militaristic Prussian film director who is a martinet on location, callous to all else but the box-office effect of his celluloid production. Action takes Richard Dix, Joel McCrea, Robert Armstrong, and Hugh Herbert from an aviation corps right after the war to Hollywood as stunt fliers (Dick Grace, Art Gobel, Leo Nomis, and Frank Clark get the billing for the actual aerial stunting).

LOST WEEKEND, THE
1945, 104 mins, US ◉

D: Billy Wilder **A:** Ray Milland, Jane Wyman, Howard da Silva, Philip Terry, Doris Dowling, Frank Faylen (Paramount)

This psychiatric study of an alcoholic is an unusual picture. It is intense, morbid—and thrilling. Ray Milland has certainly given no better performance in his career. Jane Wyman is the girl, Philip Terry the brother. They help make the story overshadow the characters. The entire cast, in fact, contributes notably. And that goes especially for Howard da Silva as the bartender. Billy Wilder's direction is always certain, always conscious that the characters not overstate the situations.
1945: Best Picture, Director, Actor (Ray Milland), Screenplay
Nominations: Best B&W Cinematography, Editing, Scoring of a Dramatic Picture

LOST WORLD, THE
1960, 97 mins, US ▱

D: Irwin Allen **A:** Michael Rennie, Jill St. John, David Hedison, Claude Rains, Fernando Lamas, Richard Haydn (20th Century-Fox)

Venturing into the headwaters of the Amazon are Claude Rains, overly affected as Professor Challenger; Michael Rennie, a bit wooden as a playboy; Jill St. John, ill at ease as an adventuress; David Hedison, bland as a newsman-photog; and Fernando Lamas, unconvincing as a Latin guitar player and helicopter operator. The dinosaurs are exceptionally lifelike (although they resemble horned toads and alligators more than dinosaurs) and the violent volcanic scenery (like hot, bubbling chili sauce) and lush vegetation form backdrops that are more interesting and impressive than the action taking place in front of them.

LOST WORLD, THE
JURASSIC PARK
1997, 134 mins, US Ⓥ ◉

D: Steven Spielberg **A:** Jeff Goldblum, Julianne Moore, Pete Postlethwaite, Arliss Howard, Richard Attenborough, Vince Vaughn (Amblin/Universal)

The good news is that the dinosaur creations are even better, credible, breathtaking and frightening. As for the rest, every department pales by comparison. The premise is that on Site B, the island locale where the prehistoric animals were engineered and shipped off to the failed theme park, the dinos have been thriving unmonitored. A small expedition arrives to chronicle the progress. A second, much larger team comes for less honorable pursuits—to capture a selection of bygone species for a San Diego park. Underneath the technical virtuosity is a standard chase film, and director Steven Spielberg does little to elevate it dramatically. The film moves at a breathless clip that almost makes one forget the thinness of the plot.
1997: Nomination: Best Visual Effects

LOUDEST WHISPER, THE
See: The Children's Hour

LOUISIANA PURCHASE
1941, 95 mins, US

D: Irving Cummings **A:** Bob Hope, Vera Zorina, Victor Moore, Irene Bordoni, Dona Drake (Paramount)

Louisiana Purchase comes to the screen an almost literal translation from the stage. Victor Moore's Senator Logan-berry, who single-handedly invades the political bayous of graft-besmirched Louisiana, is the highspot of the comedy, due in considerable measure to the teamwork of his support, including the irrepressible Bob Hope. Latter plays it straight when the script demands.

LOUISIANA STORY
1948, 77 mins, US ⓥ

D: Robert Flaherty A: Joseph Boudreaux, Lionel Le Blanc, Mrs. E. Bienvenu, Frank Hardy, C. T. Guedry (Lopert Films)

Documentary-type film, told almost purely in camera terms, has a slender, appealing story, moments of agonizing suspense, vivid atmosphere, and superlative photography. Filmed entirely in the bayou country of Louisiana, the picture tells of a Cajun boy and his parents, who live by hunting and fishing in the alligator-infested swamps and streams, and of the oil-drilling crew that brings its huge derrick to sink a well.

1948: Nomination: Best Motion Picture Story

LOULOU
1980, 110 mins, France ⓥ

D: Maurice Pialat A: Isabelle Huppert, Gérard Depardieu, Guy Marchand, Humbert Balsan, Christian Boucher (Gaumont/Action)

Maurice Pialat deals with a fringe semidelinquent colossus (Gérard Depardieu) and a frail but headstrong middle-class girl (Isabelle Huppert). Depardieu leads her in the looting of a warehouse of electronic goods, he gets stabbed in a bar fight over a girl, and she gets pregnant. Pialat was attempting to revive the French prewar poetic, naturalistic dramas, But he has eschewed their romanticism and added sharp modern language and an acceptance of conditions with perhaps a possibility of changing them.

LOVE
See: Szerelem

LOVE
1927, 84 mins, US ⓥ ⊗

D: Edmund Goulding A: Greta Garbo, John Gilbert, George Fawcett, Emily Fitzroy, Philippe De Lacy (M-G-M)

What is there to tell about the Tolstoy story *Anna Karenina*? Its locale is Russia in the time of the czars. Anna (Greta Garbo) has a husband and a young son; Vronsky (John Gilbert), a military heritage and a desire for Anna. There are rich interiors, appropriate exteriors, and an ex-cellent officers' steeplechase to get the action figuratively off of a couch for a while. When all is said and done, *Love* is a cinch because it has Gilbert and Garbo.

LOVE AFFAIR
1939, 87 mins, US ⓥ

D: Leo McCarey A: Irene Dunne, Charles Boyer, Maria Ouspenskaya, Lee Bowman, Astrid Allwyn (RKO)

First half is best described as romantic comedy, while second portion switches to drama with comedy. Aboard boat sailing to New York, Charles Boyer starts a flirtation with Irene Dunne. He is engaged to Astrid Allwyn, and she to Lee Bowman. They separate with pact to meet six months later. While on her way to keep tryst, Dunne is injured. Faced with life of a cripple, girl refuses to contact Boyer to explain. Dunne is excellent. Boyer is particularly effective as the modern Casanova. Maria Ouspenskaya provides a warmly sympathetic portrayal as Boyer's grandmother in Madeira.

1939: Nominations: Best Picture, Actress (Irene Dunne), Supp. Actress (Maria Ouspenskaya), Original Story, Art Direction

LOVE AFFAIR
1994, 108 mins, US ⓥ ⊙

D: Glenn Gordon Caron A: Warren Beatty, Annette Bening, Katharine Hepburn, Garry Shandling, Chloe Webb, Pierce Brosnan (Mulholland/Warner)

The appeal of this *Love Affair* is only skin-deep. This third rendition of a perennial sentimental favorite is easy on the eyes and has its share of beguiling moments in the early going, but crucially lacks a compelling climax and any sense of urgency in its storytelling. Warren Beatty and Annette Bening as jet-setters, already engaged to others, become irresistibly attracted to each other and, after an intense tryst, resolve to meet at the top of the Empire State Building in three months if they are serious about each other. There is the curiosity of seeing Katharine Hepburn on the big screen in a major film for the first time in 13 years. Beatty has fun with his own image here, but in a mild and innocuous way. Bening is enchantingly vivacious and sparkling, a fine match in looks, wit, and sophistication with her leading man.

LOVE AND BULLETS
1979, 95 mins, UK ⓥ ▭

D: Stuart Rosenberg A: Charles Bronson, Rod Steiger, Jill Ireland, Strother Martin,

Bradford Dillman (ITC/Grade)

Slowly and predictably, script plots Charles Bronson's mission, on behalf of the FBI, to pick up a mobster's moll (Jill Ireland) who's gotten separated from her paramour and is presumed to be a mine of incriminating information. Rod Steiger's performance as the effete Mafia boss is tantalizing. So, too, is the emergent love affair between Bronson and Ireland, her comic talent largely starved for lack of material.

LOVE AND DEATH
1975, 85 mins, US Ⓥ ⊙
D: Woody Allen A: Woody Allen, Diane Keaton (United Artists)

Woody Allen and Diane Keaton invade the land and spirit of Anton Chekhov. *Love and Death* is another mile-a-minute visual-verbal whirl by the two comedy talents, this time through czarist Russia in the days of the Napoleonic Wars. Allen's script traces his bumbling adventures with distant cousin Keaton, latter outstanding as a prim lady of both philosophical and sexual bent. Between malaprop battlefield heroics and metaphysical deliberations, Allen eventually combines with Keaton in an assassination attempt on Napoleon himself.

LOVE AND HUMAN REMAINS
1993, 98 mins, Canada Ⓥ ⊙
D: Denys Arcand A: Thomas Gibson, Ruth Marshall, Cameron Bancroft, Mia Kirshner, Joanne Vannicola, Matthew Ferguson (Max/Atlantis)

A bawdy and spirited comedy about a group of mostly 30-ish urbanites trying to get a grip on their sexuality and place in the world. Lead character is David (Thomas Gibson), a charismatic, devilishly good-looking young lothario. David lives with Candy (Ruth Marshall), a former g.f. whose disenchantment with men makes her susceptible to the avid attentions of cute lesbian Jerri (Joanne Vannicola). Another friend is Benita (Mia Kirshner), a young S&M specialist who, in one extreme and hilarious case, calls upon David to help her out. Weighing too heavily on the story is a backdrop of serial murders of young women.

LOVE AND MONEY
1982, 90 mins, US
D: James Toback A: Ray Sharkey, Ornella Muti, Klaus Kinski, Armand Assante, King Vidor (Lorimar/Paramount)

Arresting romantic suspense film that fails to ignite. Ray Sharkey toplines as Byron Levin, a case of arrested development. He comes out of his robotlike shell upon meeting the beautiful Catherine (Ornella Muti), young wife of multinational business magnate Stockheinz (Klaus Kinski). Following an intense romance with Catherine, Levin becomes involved in an international plot masterminded by Stockheinz.

LOVE AND OTHER CATASTROPHES
1996, 76 mins, Australia Ⓥ
D: Emma-Kate Croghan A: Matt Day, Matthew Dyktynski, Alice Garner, Frances O'Connor, Radha Mitchell, Suzi Dougherty (Screwball Five/Beyond)

A fast, funny excursion into the world of college students in the mid-nineties, boosted by a terrific ensemble of five engaging young thesps. Visually, pic is rough at the edges and looks as though it was made on the run, but it makes up in sheer likability what it lacks in production values.

LOVE AND PAIN AND THE WHOLE DAMN THING
1973, 110 mins, US
D: Alan J. Pakula A: Maggie Smith, Timothy Bottoms, Jaime de Mora y Aragon, Emiliano Redondo, Charles Baxter (Columbia)

A modest, affecting romantic comedy about two mismatched neurotics stumbling into love during a Spanish tour. The shy, asthmatic son of a professor, Timothy Bottoms joins a tourist bus, where he is seated next to Maggie Smith, a jumpy lady of middle age. They explore the countryside and gradually accept a warmth and companionship that leads to a believable affair. But pic succumbs to a fatal attack of *Love* Story-itis, and goes down for the count.

LOVE AT FIRST BITE
1979, 96 mins, US Ⓥ ⊙
D: Stan Dragoti A: George Hamilton, Susan Saint James, Richard Benjamin, Dick Shawn, Arte Johnson (American International)

"What would happen if" Dracula was victimized by life in modern New York City? It's a fun notion and George Hamilton makes it work. He's funny just to watch. Story evicts Dracula from his Transylvania castle and takes him in pursuit of Susan Saint James, a fashion model he loves from an old photo. Hamilton's coffin is naturally misrouted by the airline, winding up in a black funeral home.

LOVE AT LARGE
1990, 97 mins, US 𝒱 ⊙
D: Alan Rudolph A: Tom Berenger, Elizabeth Perkins, Anne Archer, Ted Levine, Annette O'Toole, Kate Capshaw (Orion)

A tongue-in-cheek take on the gumshoe genre that mostly seeks to explore the perplexing possibilities of love. Wealthy and idle Dolan (Anne Archer) hires rumpled cheap detective Harry Dobbs (Tom Berenger) to trail a lover she underdescribes. Berenger picks the wrong guy and ends up pursuing a quarry far more interesting—this one's not only married, he's got two separate families. Meanwhile, he's being followed by novice detective Stella (Elizabeth Perkins), who's been hired by his girlfriend, Doris (Ann Magnuson).

LOVE BEFORE BREAKFAST
1936, 65 mins, US
D: Walter Lang A: Carole Lombard, Preston Foster, Janet Beecher, Cesar Romero, Betty Lawford (Universal)

A society girl (Carole Lombard) loves a boy, and is in turn loved by a wealthy big business man. Latter gives the boy a job in Japan to get him out of the way so he can go to town with the lady, lavish her with gifts, and win her over. He does, after 65 minutes. In fact, he wins her sooner than that, only the lady won't admit it. Lombard wears some stunning clothes and conducts herself competently.

LOVE BUG, THE
1969, 108 mins, US 𝒱 ⊙
D: Robert Stevenson A: Dean Jones, Michele Lee, David Tomlinson, Buddy Hackett (Walt Disney)

Because Dean Jones, a second-rate racing driver, objects to David Tomlinson, a wealthy but stuffy racer, kicking it, a little car—a Volkswagen—adopts Jones and wins a flock of races for him. For sheer inventiveness of situation and the charm that such an idea projects, *The Love Bug* rates as one of the better entries of the Disney organization. Treatment is light and imaginative, and Herbie gradually takes on all the attributes of a human.

LOVE CHILD
1982, 97 mins, US 𝒱
D: Larry Peerce A: Amy Madigan, Beau Bridges, Mackenzie Phillips, Albert Salmi, Joanna Merlin (Ladd/Warner)

A tasteful and sincere filmization of young Ohioan Terry Jean Moore's battle to have and keep her baby (fathered by a guard) while serving a 20-year robbery term in Broward Correctional Institution in Florida. Script emphasizes Moore's self-reform as catalyzed by her awareness of the baby growing inside her and the new responsibility it represents. Amy Madigan is excellent in the physically demanding central role.

LOVE CRAZY
1941, 97 mins, US 𝒱
D: Jack Conway A: William Powell, Myrna Loy, Gail Patrick, Jack Carson, Florence Bates (M-G-M)

William Powell and Myrna Loy romp merrily through another marital comedy. It's the happily married pair's fourth anniversary, and they plan to repeat happenings of their wedding night, but mother-in-law arrives to send plans awry. Meeting of Powell with a former flame (Gail Patrick) prompts jealousy, separation, and plans for a divorce. To gain time, in endeavor to reconcile with his wife, Powell simulates insanity and returns home to masquerade as his sister.

LOVE CRIMES
1992, 85 mins, US 𝒱
D: Lizzie Borden A: Sean Young, Patrick Bergin, Arnetia Walker, James Read, Ron Orbach (Sovereign)

A poorly constructed thriller suffering from a bad lead performance by Sean Young, as a mannishly styled Atlanta assistant district attorney. She becomes obsessed with women's charges against a con man (Patrick Bergin) posing as a famous fashion photographer. He picks up plain-looking women, snaps seminude Polaroids, sexually dominates them, and then robs them. Young travels to Savannah to capture Bergin herself.

LOVED ONE, THE
1965, 119 mins, US 𝒱
D: Tony Richardson A: Robert Morse, Anjanette Comer, Jonathan Winters, Rod Steiger, James Coburn, John Gielgud (M-G-M)

Poor taste is prominent in the Terry Southern–Christopher Isherwood script, based on Evelyn Waugh's scathing 1948 satire. Most of the subtlety is lost in an episodic screenplay bearing only a wavering story line and given often to sight gags. Story centers around the pomp and ceremony attendant upon the daily operation of a posh mortuary and the idea (not in the book) of the sanctimonious owner of a Southern California cemetery of orbiting cadavers into space so he can convert to a senior citizens' paradise for additional profit.

LOVE FIELD
1992, 104 mins, US Ⓥ ⊙
D: Jonathan Kaplan **A:** Michelle Pfeiffer, Dennis Haysbert, Stephanie McFadden, Brian Kerwin, Louise Latham (Orion)

A sincere, not fully realized 1960s drama that is yet another variation on the "where were you when you heard JFK was shot" theme. Lurene Hallett (Michelle Pfeiffer), a rather dim Dallas hairdresser with a 100-watt platinum coif, imagines a kinship with Jacqueline Kennedy, since both lost infant children. Lurene hops a Greyhound north to attend the state funeral. On board she meets and gradually befriends a "Negro" man, Paul (Dennis Haysbert), with something to hide.
1992: Nomination: Best Actress (Michelle Pfeiffer)

LOVE HAPPY
1949, 91 mins, US Ⓥ ⊙
D: David Miller **A:** Groucho Marx, Harpo Marx, Chico Marx, Ilona Massey, Vera-Ellen, Raymond Burr (United Artists)

The story, such as it is, deals with a chase for a priceless necklace. Involved are a private eye (Groucho Marx), a blond continental (Ilona Massey), a mute klepto (Harpo), plus a shoestring musicomedy troupe whom Harpo feeds. The major portion of the film centers around Harpo and there are a number of his pantomimic scenes. Some of it is too obviously contrived but plenty laugh provoking nonetheless.

LOVE HAS MANY FACES
1965, 104 mins, US Ⓥ
D: Alexander Singer **A:** Lana Turner, Cliff Robertson, Hugh O'Brian, Ruth Roman, Stefanie Powers, Virginia Grey (Bresler/Columbia)

High life among American beach bums in Acapulco is lavishly dramatized. Turner portrays a millionairess surrounded by moochers—including her husband, Robertson—and desperately striving for unfound happiness in her own particular brandy-swilling world. Narrative concerns the love affairs—the many faces of love—at the glamorous resort.

LOVE IN THE AFTERNOON
1957, 126 mins, US Ⓥ
D: Billy Wilder **A:** Gary Cooper, Audrey Hepburn, Maurice Chevalier, John Mc-Giver (Allied Artists)

It is all about romance before nightfall, in Paris, with Audrey Hepburn and Gary Cooper as the participants. Under Billy Wilder's alternately sensitive, mirthful, and loving-care direction, and with Maurice Chevalier turning in a captivating performance as a private detective, the production holds enchantment and delight in substantial quantity. It's in Chevalier's files that his daughter, the lovely, wistful Hepburn, comes upon knowledge of Cooper's international conquests, runs to him with the warning that his current passion (Madame X) has a husband (Mr. X) bent on murder, and finds herself a candidate for one of her own father's file cards.

LOVE IS A BALL
1963, 113 mins, US ⌑
D: David Swift **A:** Glenn Ford, Hope Lange, Charles Boyer, Ricardo Montalban, Telly Savalas, Ulla Jacobson (Oxford Gold Medal/United Artists)

Love Is a Ball is an airy fairy tale thrust into cinematicomedic orbit by the devious new campaign of a mercenary cupid who designs carefully tailored affairs between his prefabricated "clients" and the most eligible heiresses of the world. But heiress Hope Lange is a shoo-in to fall not for Ricardo Montalban, who is the graduate of fearless Eros Charles Boyer's school for husbands, but for Glenn Ford, who has been planted by Boyer as chauffeur in Hope's household to drive her swiftly into the clutches of his prized pupil. The scenario on the whole plays to advantage, and the actors bat it out expertly.

LOVE IS A MANY-SPLENDORED THING
1955, 102 mins, US Ⓥ ⊙ ⌑
D: Henry King **A:** William Holden, Jennifer Jones, Torin Thatcher, Isobel Elsom, Virginia Grey (20th Century-Fox)

William Holden as the American correspondent, and Jennifer Jones as the Eurasian doctor, make a romantic team of great appeal. This is something of a tearjerker, to be sure, but an awfully well-made one. Since Elliott (Holden) is married and his wife won't give him a divorce, marriage is impossible. Director Henry King and lenser Leon Shamroy do a magnificent job in utilizing the Hong Kong backgrounds. Holden is restrained and completely believable. Jones is pure delight in a very difficult part.
1955: Best Color Costume Design, Song

("Love Is a Many-Splendored Thing"), Scoring of a Dramatic Picture

Nominations: Best Picture, Actress (Jennifer Jones), Color Cinematography, Color Art Direction, Sound

LOVE IS A RACKET
1932, 74 mins, US

D: William A. Wellman **A:** Douglas Fairbanks Jr., Ann Dvorak, Frances Dee, Lee Tracy, Lyle Talbot (Warner)

A shrewdly wrought comedy-drama blending the newspaper locale and gangland. Douglas Fairbanks does a nice job in his role of a quiet but sophisticated go-getting newspaper columnist. Ann Dvorak makes a light part stand out, and Lee Tracy is a tower of strength on the comedy side.

LOVE LAUGHS AT ANDY HARDY
1946, 93 mins, US Ⓥ

D: Willis Goldbeck **A:** Mickey Rooney, Lewis Stone, Bonita Granville, Fay Holden (M-G-M)

This pic doesn't vary much from the basic formula used in the numerous predecessors in the Hardy family saga, but why should it? Bowing to the fact that Rooney is growing older, if no larger, story line pushes him to the brink of a marital plunge. Back from the wars, Andy picks up his academic career as a college freshman and falls badly for Bonita Granville, who trips him up by marrying someone else. Heartbroken, Andy is set to pack up for exile in South America until he's diverted back to normal by the chili wiles of Lina Romay, a south-of-the-border chick.

LOVE LETTERS
1945, 101 mins, US

D: William Dieterle **A:** Jennifer Jones, Joseph Cotten, Ann Richards, Gladys Cooper, Anita Louise (Paramount)

Warm and appealing, sentimental and emotional, it's the yarn of two British army officers, one of whom writes beautiful love letters for his friend to the latter's fiancée in England. The girl falls in love with the letters, and in turn with the man she thinks has written them. The friend marries the girl, and she soon learns it wasn't he who wrote the letters. Jennifer Jones gives to the part of the girl an elfin quality that at times reaches sheer brilliance. Joseph Cotten, as the writer of the letters, gives a fine, quietly restrained characterization.

LOVE LETTERS
1983, 98 mins, US Ⓥ ⊙

D: Amy Jones **A:** Jamie Lee Curtis, James Keach, Amy Madigan, Bud Cort, Matt Clark (New World)

A fine intimate drama. Although in no way intended to seem typical, Jamie Lee Curtis is seen living a life that is certainly shared by many young contempo women. Suddenly, barely past ago 40, Curtis's mother dies, and the daughter discovers a collection of old letters that reveal the secret love of her mother's life, a love that can stand as a pure ideal to Curtis.

LOVELY TO LOOK AT
1952, 101 mins, US Ⓥ ⊙

D: Mervyn LeRoy **A:** Kathryn Grayson, Howard Keel, Red Skelton, Marge Champion, Gower Champion, Ann Miller (M-G-M)

A pleasant round of light musical-comedy entertainment in this remake of *Roberta*. Kathryn Grayson and Howard Keel for songs; Red Skelton for comedy; Marge and Gower Champion and Ann Miller for terps. All deliver expertly. Score has 10 tunes cleffed by Jerome Kern, including the standard "Smoke Gets in Your Eyes."

LOVELY WAY TO DIE, A
(UK: A LOVELY WAY TO GO)
1968, 103 mins, US

D: David Lowell Rich **A:** Kirk Douglas, Sylva Koscina, Eli Wallach, Kenneth Haigh, Sharon Farrell (Universal)

This is the kind of hard-hitting polished murder-mystery meller that Kirk Douglas can play in his sleep. Cast with the cool, aloof Sylva Koscina and Eli Wallach, the screenplay is crisp and tangy, though the plotline wavers at a few spots. Douglas is hired by Wallach, a shrewd homespun attorney, to protect Koscina, being defended by Wallach on a rap of murdering her husband. As a male bodyguard Douglas is intrigued by the girl. As an ex-cop he's intrigued by the murder mystery.

LOVELY WAY TO GO, A
See: A Lovely Way to Die

LOVE ME OR LEAVE ME
1955, 122 mins, US Ⓥ ⊙ ▭

D: Charles Vidor **A:** Doris Day, James Cagney, Cameron Mitchell, Robert Keith, Tom Tully (M-G-M)

The offbeat aspects of the strange real-life relationship of Ruth Etting and "Colonel" Moe (here called Martin) Snyder have been caught with an honesty and realism that borders on creating mixed emotions. In short, Doris Day as Etting is so consumed by ambition as to blot out the wicked nature of "The Gimp," so ably played by James Cagney. His impersonation of the clubfooted Chicago hoodlum and muscle man is the Cagney of gangster pictures of the early 1930s—hard-bitten, cruel, sadistic, and unrelenting. Musically there's almost too much, but Day does uncork a flock of socko standards, and two good new ones. It's a rich canvas of the Roaring Twenties with gutsy and excellent performances.

LOVE ME TENDER
1956, 94 mins, US ⓥ ▱
D: Robert D. Webb **A:** Richard Egan, Debra Paget, Elvis Presley, Robert Middleton, Neville Brand (20th Century-Fox)

Appraising Presley as an actor, he ain't. Not that it makes much difference. There are four songs, and lotsa Presley wriggles thrown in for good measure. Story line centers on Presley, the youngest of four brothers, who stayed on their Texas farm while the older three are away fighting the Yankees. The older brother (Richard Egan) left a gal (Debra Paget), and when word comes that he's been killed, she weds Presley. When the three boys come home, it's hard to keep Egan down on the farm because he's still in love with Paget.

LOVE ME TONIGHT
1932, 90 mins, US
D: Rouben Mamoulian **A:** Maurice Chevalier, Jeanette MacDonald, Charles Ruggles, Charles Butterworth, Myrna Loy, C. Aubrey Smith (Paramount)

Musical-comedy frolic gives Jeanette MacDonald an excellent opportunity for quiet comedy playing, which she rises charmingly to meet. Story has to do with Maurice Chevalier, a Paris tailor, going to a great French castle to collect a bill, and being introduced as Baron Courtelin and held as an honored guest to keep his mission secret. Fun of the situation arises from the presence of the lively young Parisian commoner among a crowd of fossilized old nobles of both sexes. Musical numbers are as amusing for once in their lyrics as they are attractive in their melodies, and are blended in smoothly with the action.

LOVE ON THE DOLE
1941, 99 mins, UK ⓥ
D: John Baxter **A:** Deborah Kerr, Clifford Evans, Geoffrey Hibbert (British National)

Drab tale of near matrimony during the Depression. North Country town and its poverty are authentically caught in atmosphere and sets. John Baxter's direction skillfully builds episode upon episode as he drives for that final decision of the wench, Sally, to trek self and family out of the relief mire via the primrose path. Deborah Kerr is satisfactorily hard as Sally; Clifford Evans's Larry shows understanding of the role of the labor crusader out for a better deal in life.

LOVE ON THE RUN
1936, 70 mins, US
D: W. S. Van Dyke **A:** Joan Crawford, Clark Gable, Franchot Tone, Reginald Owen, Mona Barrie, Donald Meek (M-G-M)

Crowded with ludicrous situations, considerable action, and popular gagging, the film is lightweight and synthetic. Story pits Franchot Tone and Clark Gable as rival scribes. Gable, as usual outwitting the slower-moving Tone, promises to fill the void in the life of Joan Crawford, the abused heiress, who has deserted a titled fortune seeker at the altar. The newspaperman sees the makings of a great series of articles depicting the rich femme's reactions to real romance.

LOVE PARADE, THE
1929, 107 mins, US
D: Ernst Lubitsch **A:** Maurice Chevalier, Jeanette MacDonald, Lupino Lane, Lillian Roth, Eugene Pallette (Paramount)

Paramount's first original screen operetta production is a fine, near-grand entertainment. The philandering Chevalier, brought back to Sylvania, ruled by MacDonald, because of his scandalous affairs as a military attaché in France's capital, must, in accepting marriage to the queen, keep his fingers out of all matters of state and be subject to her commands.
1929/30: Nominations: Best Picture, Director, Actor (Maurice Chevalier), Cinematography, Art Direction, Sound

LOVER, THE
1992, 110 mins, France/UK ⓥ ⊙
D: Jean-Jacques Annaud **A:** Jane March, Tony Leung, Frédérique Meininger, Arnaud Giovaninetti, Melvil Poupaud (Renn/Films AZ/Burrill)

Sophisticated adaptation of Marguerite Duras's bestselling memoir about her love affair as a 15-year-old with a rich, older Chinese man lacks the distinctive voice and ambience of the book, but the abundant sex—softcore and tasteful—and the splendid sets make up for the film's banal

style. Jane March pouts to perfection but does not convey the jaded spirit of the girl. Tony Leung is excellent as the shiftless scion whose love for the girl makes him emotionally naked and vulnerable.
1992: Nomination: Best Cinematography

LOVER COME BACK
1961, 107 mins, US ⓥ
D: Delbert Mann **A:** Rock Hudson, Doris Day, Tony Randall, Edie Adams, Jack Oakie (Universal)

This is a funny, most-of-the-time engaging, smartly produced farce. Hudson and Day are rival Madison Avenue ad account people. He deceives her into thinking he's a scientist working on an actually nonexistent product called VIP. She undertakes to wrest the VIP account from the masquerading Hudson. He meanwhile is trying to maneuver her into romantic conquest. Tony Randall draws yocks consistently as head of an agency.
1961: Nomination: Best Original Story & Screenplay

LOVERS, THE
See: Les Amants

LOVERS AND OTHER STRANGERS
1970, 104 mins, US ⓥ
D: Cy Howard **A:** Bea Arthur, Bonnie Bedelia, Michael Brandon, Richard Castellano, Robert Dishy, Harry Guardino (ABC)

Tells in a delightful way of the marriage of a young couple who have been making it on the sly for over a year. Bonnie Bedelia and Michael Brandon have their own lifestyle, which rubs against but does not destroy relations with their respective parents. Gig Young and Cloris Leachman are her folks, while Richard Castellano and Bea Arthur are his. Screenplay is essentially a string of intercut vignettes about the young couple's relatives.
1970: Best Song ("For All We Know")
Nominations: Best Supp. Actor (Richard Castellano), Adapted Screenplay

LOVE SERENADE
1996, 101 mins, Australia ⓥ ▭
D: Shirley Barrett **A:** Miranda Otto, Rebecca Frith, George Shevtsov, John Alansu (Chapman)

Oblique vision of love and sex in an isolated Australian town is full of delights. Vicki-Ann (Rebecca Frith) runs a hair salon. Her kid sister, 20-year-old Dimity (Miranda Otto), spends her days aimlessly riding around on her bicycle; in the evening, she works as a waitress. Ken Sherry

(George Shevtsov) drives into town. A child of the hippie era now well into middle age, Sherry seduces both sisters. The filmmaker has a wry, offbeat sense of humor, and a delight in the foibles and eccentricities of her characters.

LOVESICK
1983, 95 mins, US ⓥ ◉
D: Marshall Brickman **A:** Dudley Moore, Elizabeth McGovern, Alec Guinness, John Huston, Alan King (Ladd/Warner)

An engaging idea—Dudley Moore as a successful, married shrink who becomes obsessed with a beautiful patient (Elizabeth McGovern)—is rendered inoperable by Marshall Brickman's witless script and uninspired direction. Perhaps most descriptive of the script's desperation is the inclusion of Sigmund Freud, who mystically materializes in the person of Alec Guinness whenever Moore seeks professional help.

LOVES OF A BLONDE
See: Lasky Jedne Plavovlasky

LOVES OF ISADORA, THE
See: Isadora

LOVES OF JOANNA GODDEN, THE
1947, 91 mins, UK
D: Charles Frend **A:** Googie Withers, Jean Kent, John McCallum, Derek Bond, Chips Rafferty (Ealing)

As a record of sheep farming in a corner of England in 1905, this picture may have its points. But as a story of a high-spirited, lovely young woman who inherits a farm and is expected to marry and let her husband do the job, the picture falls short of its intentions. Joanna (Googie Withers), impetuous and self-willed, is bequeathed one of the leading farms. She outrages the countryside by running the farm herself and sends her young sister, Ellen (Jean Kent), to a finishing school, from which the girl returns an accomplished gold digger.

LOVE STORY
1970, 99 mins, US ⓥ ◉
D: Arthur Hiller **A:** Ali MacGraw, Ryan O'Neal, John Marley, Ray Milland, Russell Nype (Paramount)

An excellent film propelled by the best-selling Erich Segal novel written from the original screenplay. Ali MacGraw is a girl of poor origins who has worked her way to high academic status; Ryan O'Neal, restive in his identity, but at the outset just another rich man's athletic-oriented son at the old family college, develops true man-

liness through his love for her, through their marriage and the severe challenge of her terminal illness.
1970: Best Original Score
Nominations: Best Picture, Director, Actor (Ryan O'Neal), Actress (Ali MacGraw), Supp. Actor (John Marley), Original Story & Screenplay

LOVE STREAMS
1984, 136 mins, US Ⓥ
D: John Cassavetes **A:** Gena Rowlands, John Cassavetes, Diahnne Abbott, Seymour Cassel, Margaret Abbott (Cannon)

One of John Cassavetes's best in some time, emotionally potent, technically assured, and often brilliantly insightful. Robert Harmon (Cassavetes) is a successful writer currently researching the subject of love for sale on a firsthand basis. Intercut is Sarah Lawson's (Gena Rowlands) story—an emotionally erratic woman proceeding through a divorce and custody case.

LOVE THAT BRUTE
1950, 85 mins, US
D: Alexander Hall **A:** Paul Douglas, Jean Peters, Cesar Romero, Keenan Wynn, Joan Davis (20th Century-Fox)

Parody of the Chicago gangster era, circa 1928. Without stopping for plausibility, it races through a series of screwball situations. Paul Douglas, a not-too-bright but bighearted gangster, falls for a country gal (Jean Peters), and in order to give her a governess job inside his house, he pretends to be a widower with a couple of kids. Douglas's auditioning of a juve hoodlum (Peter Price) to play his son is one of the pic's highspots.

LOVE WALTZ, THE
1930, 70 mins, Germany
D: Wilhelm Thiele **A:** Lilian Harvey, John Batten, Georg Alexander (UFA)

The all-English dialogue version of this UFA talker errs somewhat in starting off as snappy comedy and ending up as the usual Ruritanian romance, being much more entertaining first half than in the final reels. Story tells how a bored youngster rivets himself on an equally bored archduke, who is due to get engaged to an even more bored princess. Lilian Harvey isn't photographed to the best advantage and John Batten hasn't much difficulty in getting honors among the leads, although Georg Alexander's duke is nicely rounded off.

LOVE WITH THE PROPER STRANGER
1963, 102 mins, US Ⓥ ⊙
D: Robert Mulligan **A:** Natalie Wood, Steve McQueen, Edie Adams, Herschel Bernardi, Tom Bosley (Paramount)

Picture describes the curious love affair that evolves between a freedom-loving freelance musician (Steve McQueen) and a sheltered girl (Natalie Wood) when she becomes pregnant following their one-night stand. Wood plays her role with a convincing mixture of feminine sweetness and emotional turbulence. McQueen displays an especially keen sense of timing. Although he's probably the most unlikely Italian around, he is an appealing figure nevertheless.
1963: Nominations: Best Actress (Natalie Wood), Original Story & Screenplay, B&W Cinematography, B&W Costume Design, B&W Art Direction

LOVING
1970, 89 mins, US Ⓥ
D: Irvin Kershner **A:** George Segal, Eva Marie Saint, Sterling Hayden, Keenan Wynn, Nancie Phillips (Columbia)

A good story about marriage crack-ups among the 40-ish set in suburbia is handicapped by a protagonist who, while not supposed to be sympathetic, isn't even interesting in his selfishness and immaturity. George Segal is the character, an aging commercial artist. Eva Marie Saint is quite outstanding as the slightly nagging but steadfast wife.

LOVING COUPLES
1980, 97 mins, US Ⓥ
D: Jack Smight **A:** Shirley MacLaine, James Coburn, Susan Sarandon, Sally Kellerman, Stephen Collins (20th Century-Fox)

Young stud Stephen Collins tries to put the make on Shirley MacLaine. Not too long after, he gets it. She's not getting much attention from her doctor husband (James Coburn) who learns of her affair from Collins's friend (Susan Sarandon). And they, in turn, fall into a motel bed. It's all fun and sexual games. Direction by Jack Smight is assured and never lags.

LOVING YOU
1957, 101 mins, US Ⓥ ⊙
D: Hal Kanter **A:** Elvis Presley, Lizabeth Scott, Wendell Corey, Dolores Hart, James Gleason (Paramount)

Elvis Presley's second screen appearance is a simple story, in which he can shout out his rhythms, bang away at his guitar, and perform the strange, knee-bending, hip-swinging contortions that are his trademark. Story has Presley picked up by Lizabeth Scott, a publicity girl touring with a hillbilly band on a whistle-stop tour. She gets Wendell Corey, the leader of the outfit, to take on Presley, and they stunt him into a rock-and-roll personality.

LOVIN' MOLLY
1974, 98 mins, US
D: Sidney Lumet **A:** Anthony Perkins, Beau Bridges, Blythe Danner, Edward Binns, Susan Sarandon (Columbia)

Misguided, heavy-handed attempt to span 40 years in the lives of three Texas rustics opens in 1925 and sets up the situation in which two farmboy friends (Anthony Perkins, Beau Bridges) wage amicable war for the affections of a liberated earth mother (Blythe Danner). Jumping to 1945 with a voice-over bridge, Danner has been married and widowed, bearing two children by a married Perkins and still-bachelor Bridges. Pic's final section takes place in 1964 as the three find their time running out.

L-SHAPED ROOM, THE
1962, 142 mins, UK ⊗
D: Bryan Forbes **A:** Leslie Caron, Tom Bell, Brock Peters, Cicely Courtneidge, Bernard Lee (Romulus)

Bryan Forbes's screenplay and his tactful, sensitive direction create a tender study in loneliness and frustrated love. Yarn concerns a girl (Leslie Caron) from provincial France who, in London, has a brief affair resulting in pregnancy. Rejecting the idea of an abortion, she decides to live it out on her own. And, in the loneliness of her L-shaped room in a seedy tenement, she finds a new hope and purpose in life through meeting others who, in various ways, suffer their own loneliness and frustration.
1963: Nomination: Best Actress (Leslie Caron)

L.627
1992, 145 mins, France ⊗
D: Bertrand Tavernier **A:** Didier Bézace, Jean-Paul Comart, Charlotte Kady, Jean-Roger Milo, Nils Tavernier (Little Bear/Sarde)

An impassioned look inside the day-to-day activities of a small branch of the Paris drug squad. Protagonist is Lulu (Didier Bézace), a dedicated cop posted to a drug squad run by Dodo (Jean-Claude

Comart), a racist with a sick sense of humor, and the attractive Marie (Charlotte Kady), who copes amazingly well with her difficult job. They are underequipped, underpaid, overworked—and they make a lot of mistakes. Yet there's a camaraderie here, and many, like Lulu, are determined against all odds to get the drug dealers off the streets. Title refers to a French drug law.

LUCK OF GINGER COFFEY, THE
1964, 100 mins, US/Canada
D: Irvin Kershner **A:** Robert Shaw, Mary Ure, Liam Redmond, Tom Harvey, Libby McClintock (Roth)

A well-turned-out drama based on a Brian Moore novel. A married couple have found the going in Montreal rough since they arrived from Dublin six months before. Shaw plays his brash Irishman with sincerity and Ure lends credibility to the wife.

LUCKY JIM
1957, 95 mins, UK ⊗
D: John Boulting **A:** Ian Carmichael, Terry-Thomas, Hugh Griffith, Sharon Acker, Clive Morton (Charter/British Lion)

Kingsley Amis's novel has been built up into a farcical comedy. Even though the comedy situations loom up with inevitable precision, they are still irresistible. Ian Carmichael as a junior history lecturer at a British university in the sticks becomes disastrously involved in such serious college goings-on as a ceremonial lecture on "Merrie England" and a procession to honor the new university chancellor. Carmichael is a deft light-comedy performer who proves that he also can take hold of a character and make him believable.

LUCKY LADY
1975, 177 mins, US
D: Stanley Donen **A:** Gene Hackman, Liza Minnelli, Burt Reynolds, Geoffrey Lewis, Robby Benson (20th Century-Fox)

What appears to have been conceived as a madcap Prohibition-era action comedy, combined with an amusing romantic ménage, emerges as forced hokum. Burt Reynolds, a gringo on the lam in Mexico, figures he can assume the dual role of major smuggler and lover of Liza Minnelli when her husband dies. Gene Hackman, also on the run, assumes a leadership role and the trio begin running hooch.

LUCKY LUCIANO
1973, 113 mins, Italy/France ⓥ
D: Francesco Rosi **A:** Gian Maria Volonte, Rod Steiger, Charles Siragusa, Edmond O'Brien, Vincent Gardenia, Charles Cioffi (Vides/La Boetie)

Rosi takes crime kingpin Lucky Luciano as his main clinical study, objective enough throughout to question his own facts, legendary accusations, and hearsay. Crime action is condensed in first few reels in sharply paced scenes and montage escalating Luciano to the Mafia throne, his arrest and conviction in the mid-1930s, with his deportation to Italy after serving 9 years of a 30- to 50-year prison term.

LUCKY ME
1954, 99 mins, US ⓥ ⊙ ⊏⊐
D: Jack Donohue **A:** Doris Day, Robert Cummings, Phil Silvers, Eddie Foy Jr., Martha Hyer (Warner)

A tissue of tired, often tiresome gags and situations without redeeming imagination or originality. The songs by Sammy Fain and Paul Francis Webster are only so-so listening. A tab show headed by Hap (Phil Silvers) is stranded in Miami Beach and Hap, Candy (Doris Day), Duke (Eddie Foy Jr.), and Flo (Nancy Walker) are working out their debts in the kitchen of a swank hotel. Stopping at the hotel is Dick (Robert Cummings), successful songsmith who is about to stage his own musical if Lorraine's (Martha Hyer) oil-rich Texan dad (Bill Goodwin) turns angel.

LUDWIG
1973, 186 mins, Italy/France/W. Germany ⊙ ⊏⊐
D: Luchino Visconti **A:** Helmut Berger, Romy Schneider, Trevor Howard, Silvana Mangano, Gert Fröbe (Mega/Cinetel/Divina)

As his third project based on German history and personages, Luchino Visconti chose King Ludwig II (Helmut Berger), the so-called "mad" monarch of Bavaria. *Ludwig* bears the Visconti stamp of dazzling, tasteful opulence and an operatic style. Major phases of Ludwig's life include his patronage of composer Richard Wagner, portrayed effectively by Trevor Howard. Wagner's last original piano composition is performed publicly for first time herein.
1973: Nomination: Best Costume Design

LULLABY OF BROADWAY
1951, 91 mins, US ⓥ ⊙
D: David Butler **A:** Doris Day, Gene Nelson, S. Z. Sakall, Billy De Wolfe, Gladys George, Florence Bates (Warner)

Mounted in gorgeous Technicolor, and displaying the song-and-dance talents of costars Doris Day and Gene Nelson, *Lullaby of Broadway* has a solid comedy story line, deft direction, and a capable cast. Most of the tunes are hits of the previous two decades. Story has Day returning to meet her mother (Gladys George), former stage headliner who hit the skids due to drink. Girl arrives at supposed mansion of her mother, and is taken in tow by Billy De Wolfe and Anne Triola, two at-liberty vaudevillians working as butler and maid.

LUNATIC, THE
1992, 93 mins, US ⓥ
D: Lol Crème **A:** Julie T. Wallace, Paul Campbell, Reggie Carter, Carl Bradshaw, Winston Stona (Island)

Novelist-scripter Anthony C. Winkler turns a colorful phrase but billboards all his themes unsubtly in this Jamaican-lensed tale of an innocent black lad Aloysius (Paul Campbell in a winning interpretation) who talks to flora and fauna. Everyone brands him a lunatic, but visiting German photographer Inga (British thesp Julie T. Wallace) makes him her love slave. Soon a ménage à trois is set up when she takes a fancy to a butcher (Carl Bradshaw).

LA LUNE DANS LE CANIVEAU (US: THE MOON IN THE GUTTER)
1983, 137 mins, France/Italy ⓥ ⊏⊐
D: Jean-Jacques Beineix **A:** Gerard Depardieu, Nastassja Kinski, Victoria Abril, Vittorio Mezzogiorno, Dominique Pinon (Gaumont/TF1/Opera)

A love-cum-whodunit comedy featuring frames to hang worthily in any museum of photography, some good acting, some stagy acting, plus a plot and dialogue that together constitute a catalog of all the favorite corny twists and mouthings of yesterday's popular films and novels. None of this works even as tongue-in-cheek satire. Jean-Jacques Beineix has based his script on a murder novel by David Goodis. He has a big, solid longshoreman, Gerard (played with muted strength by Gerard Depardieu), continuing a restless search for the rapist who caused his adult kid sister to commit suicide. Film goes on to have a couple of endings, or new beginnings maybe. But most audiences will by then have ceased to care long ago.

LUNGFU FUNGWAN
(US: CITY ON FIRE)
1987, 104 mins, Hong Kong ⓥ ⊙
D: Ringo Lam **A:** Chow Yun-Fat, Sun Yueh, Danny Lee, Carrie Ng, Roy Cheung (Cinema City)

Highly animated, fast-moving entertainment. The bloody death of an undercover policeman gets the Royal Hong Kong Police in a complex situation. Chow (Chow Yun-Fat) is recruited for the mission of penetrating the gangsters. He poses as a sly wheeler-dealer of guns for hire. Chow is introduced to Fu (Danny Lee), sort of lieutenant of the syndicate. Fu is a cautious man and puts Chow to various character tests to assure that security is maintained. In the process, a male bonding is developed between the two supposedly gutter-type characters.

LUSH LIFE
1994, 104 mins, US ⓥ ⊙
D: Michael Elias **A:** Jeff Goldblum, Forest Whitaker, Kathy Baker, Tracey Needham, Lois Chiles (Showtime/Chanticleer)

The free-floating world of the NY session musician forms a richly textured background to a moving celebration of friendship and the joy of music-making, lit up by sympathetic ensemble playing from leads Jeff Goldblum, Forest Whitaker, and Kathy Baker. When Whitaker, who's been getting headaches from his high notes, finds he has a malignant brain tumor and only weeks to live, the trio's tight relationship is put to the test.

LUST FOR LIFE
1956, 122 mins, US ⓥ ⊙ ▭
D: Vincente Minnelli **A:** Kirk Douglas, Anthony Quinn, James Donald, Pamela Brown, Everett Sloane (M-G-M)

Basically a faithful portrait of van Gogh, *Lust for Life* is unexciting. Lensed in Holland and France, it is largely conversation plus expert tint photography, and both on a high level. Kirk Douglas plays with undeniable understanding of the artist, conveying the frustrations which beset van Gogh. But somehow the measure of sympathy that should be engendered for the genius who was to turn insane is not realized.
1956: Best Supp. Actor (Anthony Quinn)
Nominations: Best Actor (Kirk Douglas), Adapted Screenplay, Color Art Direction

LUST IN THE DUST
1984, 87 mins, US ⓥ ⊙
D: Paul Bartel **A:** Tab Hunter, Divine, Lainie Kazan, Geoffrey Lewis, Henry Silva, Cesar Romero (Fox Run)

A saucy, irreverent, quite funny send-up of the western. Prevailing attitude is established immediately via some florid narration and the sight of the outsized Divine making his way across the desert in full drag on a donkey. Picture is Divine's for the taking, and take it he does with a vibrant, inventive comic performance.

LUSTY MEN, THE
1952, 112 mins, US ⓥ ⊙
D: Nicholas Ray **A:** Susan Hayward, Robert Mitchum, Arthur Kennedy, Arthur Hunnicutt (Wald-Krasna/RKO)

Robert Mitchum is a faded rodeo champion. Returning broke to the tumble-down ranch where he spent his boyhood, he finds the property desired by Arthur Kennedy, poor cowpoke, and his wife (Susan Hayward). Tales of Mitchum's past glory light a fire under Kennedy, who sees a chance at quick realization of his ranch-owning yen via rodeoing prizes. A somewhat slow starter is kept playing with growing interest under Nicholas Ray's firm direction.

LUV
1967, 93 mins, US ⓥ ⊙ ▭
D: Clive Donner **A:** Jack Lemmon, Peter Falk, Elaine May, Nina Wayne, Eddie Mayehoff (Columbia)

Much of the humor is forced, proving that a sophisticated stage comedy isn't always ideal fare for the screen. Opening on Manhattan Bridge, where Jack Lemmon, a self-proclaimed failure, is about to commit suicide, story takes form as Peter Falk, a self-proclaimed success, comes along and saves him. Falk takes him home to meet his wife, whom he immediately tries to palm off on Lemmon so he can get a divorce and marry the girl of his dreams.

LYDIA
1941, 103 mins, US ⓥ
D: Julien Duvivier **A:** Merle Oberon, Edna May Oliver, Alan Marshal, Joseph Cotten, Sara Allgood (Korda)

Lydia displays the life span of a woman from 20 to 60, and her torching for a lover whose promises and memories are forgotten 35 years later. Loved by three men of various standings—football hero, famous doctor, and blind musical genius—she holds in her heart through the years the brief, but hot, romance with a seafarer lover. Merle Oberon turns in an excellent performance. Makeup for the span of years is particularly excellent.

1941: Nomination: Best Scoring of a Dramatic Picture

LYDIA BAILEY
1952, 89 mins, US

D: Jean Negulesco **A:** Dale Robertson, Anne Francis, Charles Korvin, William Marshall (20th Century-Fox)

A lush tale of period adventure, action, and romance. In 1802, Haiti is an armed camp swarming with plotters and counter-plotters. Into this atmosphere comes Dale Robertson, a young American attorney whose mission is to secure the signature of Lydia Bailey (Anne Francis) to settle an estate.

LYENIN V OKTYABRYE
(US: LENIN IN OCTOBER)
1937, 92 mins, USSR

D: Mikhail Romm, Dmitri Vasiliev **A:** Boris Shchukin, Nikolai Okhlopkov, Vasili Vanin, I. Golshtab (Mosfilm)

Lenin in October could be Lenin at any other time and still be a highly interesting production. Pic deals out reams of comedy, suspense, drama, and assorted histrionics. Boris Shchukin's characterization of Lenin is an excellent performance.

M

M

1931, 114 mins, Germany ⓥ ⊙

D: Fritz Lang **A:** Peter Lorre, Ellen Widmann, Inge Landgut, Gustav Gruendgens, Fritz Gnass (Nero)

An extraordinary, good, impressive, and strong talker. *M* is the sign of recognition of a child's murderer who is sought by the police and an underworld organization. Peter Lorre does unusually well as the murderer, changing from human despair to bestial lust. It is most gripping when he pleads for human treatment and understanding for his pathological tendencies.

M

1951, 88 mins, US ⓥ ⊙

D: Joseph Losey **A:** David Wayne, Luther Adler, Howard da Silva, Martin Gabel, Raymond Burr, Glenn Anders (Columbia)

M is a remake of picture produced in Germany in 1931. Principal change is its shift in locale, presumably to California. David Wayne, as the killer of small children, is effective and convincing. Luther Adler, as a drunken lawyer member of a gangster mob, turns in an outstanding performance, as do Martin Gabel, the gang leader, and Howard da Silva and Steve Brodie as police officials. Joseph Losey's direction has captured the gruesome theme skilfully.

MAC

1992, 117 mins, US ⓥ

D: John Turturro **A:** John Turturro, Michael Badalucco, Carl Capotorto, Katherine Borowitz, Ellen Barkin (Macfilms)

John Turturro's intense, offbeat personality as an actor comes through equally clearly in his directorial debut. A tribute to the notion of craftsmen loving their work, as well as an expression of quirky humor among three Italian-American brothers, pic is appealing in an idiosyncratic way. Performances are sharp, led by Turturro's own as the headstrong leader of the clan. Michael Badalucco and Carl Capotorto are both distinctive and entirely complementary as the brothers, and Katherine Borowitz, as Turturro's wife, and Ellen Barkin, as a suburban beatnik, are vibrant as the main women on hand.

MACAO

1952, 81 mins, US ⓥ ⊙

D: Josef von Sternberg, [Nicholas Ray] **A:** Robert Mitchum, Jane Russell, William Bendix, Thomas Gomez, Gloria Grahame, Brad Dexter (RKO)

Macao contains the cliché elements of adventure, romance, and intrigue, and is set in the Portuguese colony south of Hong Kong. It opens with the arrival of three Americans—Russell, a cynical, wisecracking chirper; Mitchum, an ex-GI running away from a minor shooting scrape; and William Bendix, a detective entrusted with the job of bringing back to the States Brad Dexter, local gambling kingpin.

MACARONI

1985, 104 mins, Italy ⓥ ⊙

D: Ettore Scola **A:** Jack Lemmon, Marcello Mastroianni, Daria Nicolodi, Isa Danieli, Maria Luisa Santella (Filmauro/Massfilm)

A mild comedy drama. Lemmon toplines as Bob Traven, visiting Naples. It's his first time back since 1946 when, as a GI, he was stationed there. An acquaintance from that period, Antonio Jasiello (Marcello Mastroianni) takes the at-first-unwilling (too busy) American around town to meet the family and friends. Jasiello has been surreptitiously writing letters using Traven's name over the years to his own sister Maria, who had a brief romance in 1946 with the American. She's long since been married and now has adult grandchildren. Relying too heavily on its two stars, at first abrasive adversaries but later best of friends, *Macaroni* rarely achieves the comedic heights of director Ettore Scola's previous work.

MACARTHUR

1977, 128 mins, US ⓥ ⊙

D: Joseph Sargent **A:** Gregory Peck, Ed Flanders, Dan O'Herlihy, Marj Dusay, Sandy Kenyon (Universal/Zanuck-Brown)

MacArthur is as good a film as could be made, considering the truly appalling egomania of its subject. Film stars Gregory Peck in an excellent and remarkable characterization. Screenplay depicts the public aspects of Douglas MacArthur's life from Corregidor in 1942 to dismissal a decade later in the midst of the Korean War, all framed between segments of his farewell address to West Point cadets.

MACBETH
1948, 106 mins, US ⓥ ⊙
D: Orson Welles A: Orson Welles,
Jeanette Nolan, Dan O'Herlihy, Roddy
McDowall, Edgar Barrier, Alan Napier
(Republic/Mercury)

Welles's idea of Shakespeare is such a
personalized version. Mood is as dour as
the Scottish moors and crags that background the plot. Film is crammed with
scenery-chewing theatrics in the best
Shakespearean manner with Welles dominating practically every bit of footage.
Only a few of the Bard's best lines are
audible. The rest are lost in strained, dia-
lectic gibbering that is only sound, not
prose. A: best, Shakespeare dialogue requires close attention; but even intense
concentration can't make intelligible the
reading by Welles and others in the cast.

MACBETH
1972, 140 mins, UK ⓥ ⊙ ⌑
D: Roman Polanski A: Jon Finch, Francesca Annis, Martin Shaw, Nicholas
Selby, John Stride (Playboy)

Macbeth receives a most handsome
treatment by Roman Polanski and artistic
adviser Kenneth Tynan. The film is traditional in the sense that there are no forced
sociological overtones, no Freudianisms,
and no pop-art formula-epic "production
numbers." The prominent surrounding
characters have been cast and directed
with the same care. In such heady surroundings, Francesca Annis as Lady Macbeth often pales in impact, and Finch as
Macbeth completely fades in effectiveness. Both seem almost to be of another
time and place: she closer to Sherwood
Forest and pampered gentility; he, almost
a 20th-century drawing room psychotic.

MACHINE-GUN KELLY
1958, 84 mins, US ⓥ ⌑
D: Roger Corman A: Charles Bronson,
Susan Cabot, Morey Amsterdam, Jack
Lambert, Connie Gilchrist (American-
International)

A first-rate little picture out of the depressing but intriguing account of a badman's downfall. Charles Bronson plays
Kelly, shown as an undersized sadist who
grows an extra foot or so as soon as he
gets a submachine gun tucked under his
arm. His exploits, proceeding from penny-
ante robbery to big-time kidnapping, are
adroitly and swiftly shown. Bronson gives
a brooding, taut performance. Gerald Fried
has done a fine progressive jazz score.

MACKENNA'S GOLD
1969, 128 mins, US ⓥ ⌑
D: J. Lee Thompson A: Gregory Peck,
Omar Sharif, Telly Savalas, Julie Newmar,
Camilla Sparv, Keenan Wynn (Highroad/
Columbia)

A standard western. Mackenna (Gregory Peck) has memorized a map, now destroyed, which will lead to a canyon of
gold. The young Apache warriors want the
gold to support them in their fight against
the white men. The Mexican bandit Colorado (Omar Sharif) wants the gold so he
can emigrate to Paris and become a gentleman.

MACKINTOSH MAN, THE
1973, 98 mins, UK ⓥ
D: John Huston A: Paul Newman, Dominique Sanda, James Mason, Harry Andrews, Ian Bannen, Michael Hordern
(Warner)

A tame tale of British espionage and
counterespionage, starring Paul Newman
as a planted assassin, James Mason as a
cynical right-wing politician in reality a
spy, and Dominique Sanda as a semiro-
mantic interest. There's a whole lot of
nothing going on here.

MACOMBER AFFAIR, THE
1947, 89 mins, US
D: Zoltan Korda A: Gregory Peck, Robert
Preston, Joan Bennett, Reginald Denny
(United Artists)

The Macomber Affair, with an African-
hunt background, isn't particularly pleasant in content, even though action often is
exciting and elements of suspense frequently hop up the spectator. Robert Preston enacts role of Francis Macomber, a
rich American with an unhappy wife (Joan
Bennett), who arrives at Nairobi and hires
Gregory Peck, a white hunter, to take him
lion hunting. On the safari, Macomber
can't stand up under a lion charge and his
wife sees him turn coward. Thereafter,
Macomber broods over his shame and his
wife falls for the hunter.

MAD ABOUT MUSIC
1938, 98 mins, US
D: Norman Taurog A: Deanna Durbin,
Herbert Marshall, Arthur Treacher, Gail
Patrick, William Frawley (Universal)

A genuine and enthralling, if somewhat
obvious story. So as not to risk her popularity as a glamour girl, a beauteous widowed film star hides her 14-year-old
daughter away in a Swiss boarding school.
When the other girls talk about their par-

ents, the youngster imposes on a vacationing British composer to pretend to be her legendary father. Deanna Durbin has acquired more varied technique before the camera, without losing her ingenuous charm or her luminous screen personality. As the adopted-by-surprise father, Herbert Marshall plays with unaccustomed warmth.

1938: Nominations: Best Original Story, Cinematography, Art Direction, Score

MADAME BOVARY
1949, 114 mins, US Ⓥ ⊙
D: Vincente Minnelli **A:** Jennifer Jones, James Mason, Van Heflin, Louis Jourdan, Christopher Kent, Gene Lockhart (M-G-M)

As a character study, *Madame Bovary* is interesting to watch, but hard to feel. Jennifer Jones is the daring Madame Bovary, a greedy woman so anxious to better her position in life that sin and crime do not shock her moral values. Jones answers to every demand of direction and script. Van Heflin portrays her doctor husband, an essentially weak man. James Mason is excellent as the author Gustave Flaubert.

1949: Nomination: Best B&W Art Direction

MADAME CURIE
1943, 125 mins, US Ⓥ
D: Mervyn LeRoy **A:** Greer Garson, Walter Pidgeon, Robert Walker, Van Johnson, Margaret O'Brien, Henry Travers (M-G-M)

Every inch a great picture. While the events leading up to the discovery of radium and the fame it brought Madame Curie are of the greatest underlying importance to the picture as entertainment, it's the love story that dominates all the way. Thus, this is not just the saga of a great scientist or just a story of test tubes and laboratories. It throws Greer Garson and Walter Pidgeon together immediately after the opening, and as the romance between them ripens, it gathers terrific momentum.

1943: Nominations: Best Picture, Actor (Walter Pidgeon), Actress (Greer Garson), B&W Cinematography, B&W Art Direction, Scoring of a Dramatic Picture, Sound

MADAME DE . . .
1953, 105 mins, France
D: Max Ophuls **A:** Charles Boyer, Danielle Darrieux, Vittorio De Sica, Jean Debucourt, Lea De Leo (Franco-London)

Max Ophuls has created a delicate, half-toned study of turn-of-the-century manners and love. Slight story concerns a general's wife who sells a pair of earrings when she needs the money. The earrings become the motif to keep the plot moving as the general buys them back from the jeweler and gives them to his mistress. The girl loses them, and they are picked up by a diplomat who becomes enamored of the general's wife. Danielle Darrieux is fine as the lovely, shallow lady whose indiscretions lead to a tragedy. Charles Boyer and Vittorio De Sica are the rivals, and underplay their roles to fit in with the general style of the piece.

MADAME DUBARRY
1934, 75 mins, US
D: William Dieterle **A:** Dolores Del Rio, Reginald Owen, Victor Jory, Osgood Perkins, Verree Teasdale, Anita Louise (Warner)

A Hollywood idea of Versailles. Under William Dieterle's directorial aegis, the decadent court of Louis XV becomes even more so in its broad well-nigh travesty version of the comtesse's influence on the doddering Louie. Dolores Del Rio's Dubarry is rarely believable. It's a theatrical conception eclipsed by the performances of Reginald Owen, who is capital as the senile Louie, and Victory Jory as d'Aiguillon. In its tinsel, costuming, and general pretentiousness, it's more musical comedy than history.

MADAME ROSA
See: La Vie Devant Soi

MADAME SOUSATZKA
1988, 122 mins, UK/US Ⓥ ⊙
D: John Schlesinger **A:** Shirley MacLaine, Navin Chowdhry, Peggy Ashcroft, Twiggy, Leigh Lawson (Sousatzka/Cineplex Odeon)

Although essentially a rather old-fashioned British pic, *Madame Sousatzka* is filled with pleasures, not the least of them being Shirley MacLaine's effervescent performance. Setting is London, where middle-aged Mme. Sousatzka teaches piano to only the most gifted students. She insists her pupils not only learn to play, but also to live the kind of traditional cultured lifestyle which she herself does. Her latest protégé is a 15-year-old Indian youth, Manek (Navin Chowdhry). All their scenes have great charm, with the piano playing effectively handled.

MADAME X
1929, 95 mins, US
D: Lionel Barrymore **A:** Ruth Chatterton,
Lewis Stone, Raymond Hackett, Ullric
Haupt, Sidney Toler (M-G-M)

This is Lionel Barrymore's first full-
length directorial effort on a talker.
Barrymore excels in the minor bits and
roles. The two big moments are Jacqueline
killing her small-time blackmailing companion to prevent her son discovering
what a horror his mother has become; the
other the famous trial scene. Chatterton
has not a flaw in her performance or
makeup.
1928/29: Nominations: Best Director,
Actress (Ruth Chatterton)

MADAME X
1937, 75 mins, US
D: Sam Wood **A:** Gladys George, John
Beal, Warren William, Reginald Owen,
Henry Daniell (M-G-M)

This is a reverent handling of the
Alexandre Bisson play, chosen to demonstrate the dramatic and emotional talent
of Gladys George. It's a quiet, comforting
sniffle. George's performance is effective,
and her characterization of the tipsy, defeated, and maudlin old woman is faithful
and moving. John Beal has the prize spot
of Raymond, youthful public defender of
his mother, whose identity is unknown to
him.

MADAME X
1966, 99 mins, US ⓥ
D: David Lowell Rich **A:** Lana Turner,
John Forsythe, Ricardo Montalban, Bur-
gess Meredith, Constance Bennett, Keir
Dullea (Universal/Hunter)

Latest time out for Alexandre Bisson's
now classic 1909 drama of mother love is
an emotional, sometimes exhausting, and
occasionally corny picture. Lana Turner
takes on the difficult assignment of the
frustrated mother, turning in what many
will regard as her most rewarding portrayal. Producer Ross Hunter draws generally on the original plot but has changed
the locale from Paris to the US for pic's
opening and climax. Constance Bennett, in
her last film appearance before her death,
endows the mother-in-law role with quiet
dignity and strength.

MAD AT THE MOON
1992, 97 mins, US ⓥ
D: Martin Donovan **A:** Mary Stuart Masterson, Hart Bochner, Fionnula Flanagan,

Cec Verrell, Daphne Zuniga (Jaffe/Spec-
tacor)

Miscasting and klutzy plot development take the shine out of a Wild West
amour fou movie that sprouts hairs halfway and turns into a werewolf pic. The
main problems here are accepting topliner
Mary Stuart Masterson as a 25-year-old
virgin and figuring out a story line that
takes a left turn 50 minutes in. Pic works
best when no one's talking and director
Martin Donovan can stoke up the atmosphere via sound, music, and images
alone.

MAD DOG AND GLORY
1993, 96 mins, US ⓥ ⊙
D: John McNaughton **A:** Robert De Niro,
Uma Thurman, Bill Murray, David Caruso, Kathy Baker (Universal)

A pleasurably offbeat picture that manages the rare trick of being both charming
and edgy. Amusing premise—a poor
schmo saves a gangster's life and is given
a beautiful woman for a week as thanks—
ends up taking on unexpected dramatic
and romantic dimensions, and leads are
played to the hilt by its stellar trio. With
the aid of the exceptional actors, the story
takes on a resonance and emotional urgency that aren't initially indicated.

MADE FOR EACH OTHER
1939, 90 mins, US
D: John Cromwell **A:** Carole Lombard,
James Stewart, Charles Coburn, Lucile
Watson (United Artists)

This is an exquisitely played, deeply
moving combination of young love, sharp
clean-cut humor, and tearjerker that provides Carole Lombard with virtually her
first straight dramatic role. She makes the
newlywed Jane Mason a sincere young
wife who struggles valiantly through all
obstacles to save her newborn baby and
make her husband amount to something.

MADE IN AMERICA
1993, 110 mins, US ⓥ ⊙
D: Richard Benjamin **A:** Whoopi Goldberg, Ted Danson, Will Smith, Nia Long,
Jennifer Tilly (Stonebridge/Kalola/Mil-
chan)

The plot has Zora (Nia Long), a high-
school honors student, discovering her
mother, Sarah (Whoopi Goldberg), conceived her after her father's death using a
donor from a sperm bank. Zora finds the
name of Hal Jackson (Ted Danson)—a car
salesman who turns out to be white. Hostile toward each other at first, an unlikely

relationship develops between Hal and Sarah. The action suddenly veers into a heavy-handed, semiserious mode that doesn't mesh with the screwball opening. If there's chemistry between Danson and Goldberg, it's certainly not allowed to unfold adequately.

MADE IN HEAVEN
1987, 103 mins, US Ⓥ ⊙
D: Alan Rudolph **A:** Timothy Hutton, Kelly McGillis, Maureen Stapleton, Don Murray, Ellen Barkin, Debra Winger (Lorimar)

A gentle comedy. Mike Shea (Timothy Hutton) is a nice small-town boy who dies and goes to heaven. There he meets the solicitous Annie (Kelly McGillis), with whom he falls in love. Before Mike and Annie can establish a valid union, she is sent to do her stint on Earth. He is granted 30 years to find his love again down below. If Hutton and McGillis are likable, it is mostly through their own personalities that this quality comes out.

MADE IN PARIS
1966, 103 mins, US ⊏⊐
D: Boris Sagal **A:** Ann-Margret, Louis Jourdan, Richard Crenna, Edie Adams, Chad Everett, John McGiver (Euterpe/M-G-M)

A Parisian setting and some snazzy femme costumes provide the major props for this otherwise weak and formula comedy programmer. Sexy plot overtones are too protracted in scripting, and become boring via heavy-handed direction. Ann-Margret and Louis Jourdan top the list of adequate players.

MADEMOISELLE
1967, 100 mins, UK/France
D: Tony Richardson **A:** Jeanne Moreau, Ettore Manni, Keith Skinner, Jeanne Beretta (United Artists/Woodfall/Procinex)

Coproduction mixes Tony Richardson's freewheeling style and the script of the controversial French writer-playwright Jean Genet. A small French farming town is the locale. Story is about an arsonist who is terrorizing the people. A poisoned drinking well, and opened irrigation ditches which flood the farms, finally lead the populace to form a lynching mob. The ingrained suspicion regarding a foreigner makes an Italian woodcutter (Ettore Manni) the scapegoat. Moreau's presence manages to make her schoolmarm character quite plausible in revealing her lurking lusts.

MAD GAME, THE
1933, 73 mins, US
D: Irving Cummings **A:** Spencer Tracy, Claire Trevor, Ralph Morgan, J. Carrol Naish, John Miljan (Fox)

Entertaining film and first of the gangster pictures to deal with kidnapping. Film would be better if it didn't take so long to reach the plot. That's where Tracy, in prison, convinces the warden he can serve society and the government better as a detective than as a prisoner behind bars. Perhaps farfetched, but the picture unrolls fast from that point. Claire Trevor impels an exciting interest. About the best portrayal of a newspaper gal which the studios have submitted.

MADIGAN
1968, 101 mins, US Ⓥ ⊏⊐
D: Don Siegel **A:** Richard Widmark, Henry Fonda, Inger Stevens, Harry Guardino, James Whitmore, Susan Clark (Universal)

Pic gets away to a flying start, with Richard Widmark as a dedicated cop and sidekick Harry Guardino bursting into a sleazy bedroom to pick up a wanted killer for questioning. Momentarily distracted by the nude broad in the room, Widmark and Guardino are taken off guard and the psychopathic killer, played with menacing hysteria by Steve Ihnat, goes on the lam. Cops are given 72 hours to pick him up. This is a good solid big-city adventure yarn with Widmark at his best.

MAD LOVE
1935, 67 mins, US Ⓥ
D: Karl Freund **A:** Peter Lorre, Frances Drake, Colin Clive, Ted Healy, Sarah Padden (M-G-M)

Ideal starring material for Peter Lorre, making his first appearance in a Hollywood-milled product. However, the results are disappointing. Main character, in the hands of Lorre, is that of a surgeonscientist with sadistic tendencies. Lorre buys a statue of an actress and idolizes it, refusing to recognize that she is in love with her husband, a distinguished pianist (Orlac). When the latter is injured in a train wreck and his hands have to be amputated, the doctor grafts on the mitts of a murderer who has just been guillotined.

MAD LOVE
1995, 95 mins, US Ⓥ
D: Antonia Bird **A:** Chris O'Donnell, Drew Barrymore, Matthew Lillard, Richard Chaim, Joan Allen (Touchstone)

Whatever else is wrong with *Mad*

Love, yet another variation on *amour fou* and love on the run, the sensual acting of its charismatic leads, Chris O'Donnell and Drew Barrymore, is beyond reproach. Matt is a serious young man, preparing for a college career. It's clear that he's never been in love—and is still a virgin. As soon as he lays his eyes on the beautiful Casey, a free, uninhibited spirit who's precisely his opposite, Matt becomes captivated, willing to abandon everything he's worked for to pursue a liaison. The movie gains momentum in its second part, effectively capturing the spontaneous, combustible intensity of Matt and Casey's love.

MAD MAX
1979, 90 mins, Australia Ⓥ ⊙ ▭
D: George Miller **A:** Mel Gibson, Joanne Samuel, Hugh Keays-Byrne, Steve Bisley, Roger Ward (Roadshow)

An all-stops-out, fast-moving exploitation pic. The plot is extremely simple. A few years from now (opening title), the Australian countryside is terrorized by marauders. Mad Max is one of the fastest and most ruthless of the cops of the future. When the Toecutter's gang kills his wife and child, he dons his leather uniform to hunt them down. The film belongs to the director, cameraman, and stunt artists.

MAD MAX 2
(US: THE ROAD WARRIOR)
1981, 94 mins, Australia Ⓥ ⊙ ▭
D: George Miller **A:** Mel Gibson, Bruce Spence, Mike Preston, Emil Minty, Max Phipps (Kennedy Miller)

Uncomplicated plot has Max (Mel Gibson), a futuristic version of the western gunslinger, reluctantly throwing in his lot with a communal group whose life-support system is a rudimentary refinery in the desert (he needs the gas). The climactic chase has Max at the wheel of a super-tanker in a desperate flight. It's a dazzling demolition derby, as men and machines collide and disintegrate, featuring very fine stunt work and special effects.

MAD MAX BEYOND THUNDERDOME
1985, 106 mins, Australia Ⓥ ⊙ ▭
D: George Miller, George Ogilvie **A:** Mel Gibson, Tina Turner, Angelo Rossitto, Helen Buday, Bruce Spence, Frank Thring (Kennedy Miller)

The third in the series. Gibson has to confront Tina Turner, the improbably named Aunty, mistress of Bartertown, a bizarre bazaar where anything up to and including human lives is traded as the only form of commerce in the postapocalyptic world. Turner throws him a challenge: engage in a fight to the death with a giant known as the Blaster (Paul Larsson) in the Thunderdome, a geometric arena that serves as a kind of futuristic Roman Colosseum.

MADNESS OF KING GEORGE, THE
1994, 107 mins, US Ⓥ ⊙
D: Nicholas Hytner **A:** Nigel Hawthorne, Helen Mirren, Ian Holm, Rupert Everett, Rupert Graves, Amanda Donohoe (Samuel Goldwyn/Close Call)

Nicholas Hytner makes a stunning screen directorial debut in Alan Bennett's comic-tragic drama of the tormented king who almost lost his mind. The tale begins in 1788, with King George III (Nigel Hawthorne) a vibrant, robust leader, almost 30 years into his reign. He's happily married to his devoted Queen Charlotte (Helen Mirren), who has borne him 15 children. The king's veneer of respectability is shattered in a series of brief scenes that disclose his "darker side," as he spews obscenities at the queen or sexually assaults her attractive mistress of the robes (Amanda Donohoe). Through his increasingly irrational conduct, it soon becomes evident that the king is ill. Hawthorne brings to his complex part a strong screen presence, light self-mockery, and pathos that set divergent moods throughout the film.
1994: Best Art Direction
Nominations: Best Actor (Nigel Hawthorne), Supp. Actress (Helen Mirren), Adapted Screenplay

MAD ROOM, THE
1969, 93 mins, US
D: Bernard Girard **A:** Shelley Winters, Stella Stevens, Barbara Sammeth, Michael Burns, Skip Ward (Columbia)

Weak story that pretends to be a psycho-suspense yarn. Screenplay is based on the 1940 play *Ladies in Retirement*. Shelley Winters, surrounded by an able cast, thin plot, good color, and some magnificent scenery on and near Vancouver Island, is the better part of the pic. Barbara Sammeth and Michael Burns, playing brother and sister recently released from a mental institution, are the focus of the story, which is long on melodramatics.

MADWOMAN OF CHAILLOT, THE
1969, 142 mins, US Ⓥ ⊙
D: Bryan Forbes A: Katharine Hepburn, Richard Chamberlain, Yul Brynner, Margaret Leighton, John Gavin, Giulietta Masina (Warner/Seven Arts)

Story of struggle between good and evil becomes audience's struggle against tedium. Margaret Leighton with her imaginary dog and Giulietta Masina with her imaginary amours ricochet around the Chaillot district of Paris sharing a phantom world of the past with Katharine Hepburn. Film doesn't come off. Hepburn fails to capture the fantasy spirit of the countess. Her performance suffers because of indecision.

MAEDCHEN IN UNIFORM
(US: GIRLS IN UNIFORM)
1931, 90 mins, Germany Ⓥ
D: Leontine Sagan A: Emilia Unda, Dorothea Wieck, Hedwig Schlichter, Hertha Thiele (Deutsche)

A whispering campaign managed to get started to the effect that the picture has to do with the subject of mannish femmes. The film is merely an overlong and sometimes dull psychological study of a schoolgirl's crush on her teacher. The picture is very arty and dry. It's poignant and clearly outlined, with the last reel actually exciting. But so slow, so painstaking.

"MAGGIE," THE
(US: HIGH AND DRY)
1954, 93 mins, UK Ⓥ
D: Alexander Mackendrick A: Paul Douglas, Alex Mackenzie, James Copeland, Abe Barker, Hubert Gregg (Ealing)

One of the small coastal colliers that ply in Scottish waters provides the main setting for this Ealing comedy. The yarn has been subtly written as a piece of gentle and casual humor. The skipper of the Maggie is a crafty old sailor, short of cash to make his little coaster seaworthy. By a little smart practice he gets a contract to transport a valuable cargo, but when a hustling American executive realizes what has happened, he planes from London to Scotland to get his goods transferred to another vessel.

MAGIC
1978, 106 mins, US Ⓥ ⊙
D: Richard Attenborough A: Anthony Hopkins, Ann-Margret, Burgess Meredith, Ed Lauter (20th Century-Fox)

The premise is that of a dummy slowly taking over the personality of its ventriloquist master. In adapting his own bestseller, William Goldman has opted for an atmospheric thriller, a mood director Richard Attenborough fleshes out to its fullest. The dilemma of Magic is that the results never live up to the standards established in the film's opening half hour. Magic becomes disappointingly transparent. Goldman has Hopkins becoming involved in the standard love triangle that inevitably leads to disaster for all parties concerned.

MAGIC BOX, THE
1951, 118 mins, UK
D: John Boulting A: Robert Donat, Margaret Johnston, Maria Schell, Robert Beatty, James Kenney, Bernard Miles (Festival/ British Lion)

Biopic of William Friese-Greene, the British motion-picture pioneer, is charged with real-life drama. The script pinpoints all the major triumphs and tragedies, from his youthful beginnings as a photographer's assistant, to his death in 1921 at a film-industry meeting with only the price of a cinema ticket in his pocket. The selection of Robert Donat as Friese-Greene is an excellent one. Mention must be made of a fine cameo from Laurence Olivier as a policeman who is the first to see the inventor's moving picture.

MAGIC CHRISTIAN, THE
1969, 95 mins, UK Ⓥ ⊙
D: Joseph McGrath A: Peter Sellers, Ringo Starr, Richard Attenborough, Christopher Lee, Raquel Welch, Laurence Harvey (Commonwealth United/Grand)

A spotty, uneven satire (from the novel by Terry Southern) with a number of good yocks, but insufficient sustained wit or related action. Sellers gives a very bright and stylish performance as the posh Sir Guy Grand, richest man in the world, who adopts a young hobo (Ringo Starr) and then sets out to prove to him man's venality. Ringo Starr's effort to project himself as a non-Beatle actor is a distinct nonevent.

MAGIC TOWN
1947, 103 mins, US Ⓥ
D: William A. Wellman A: James Stewart, Jane Wyman, Kent Smith, Ned Sparks, Wallace Ford (RKO)

James Stewart plays an enterprising researcher who plans to get rich quickly with what he calls his "mathematical miracle" method—finding one small town that thinks as the nation does, and by polling it constantly on various issues have a cross section of American opinion at very small cost. He finds the town in Grandview. Posing as an insurance salesman planning to settle there, Stewart upsets plans a young newspaper editor (Jane Wyman) has for improving the place with a new civic center.

MAGNIFICENT AMBERSONS, THE
1942, 88 mins, US Ⓥ ⊙
D: Orson Welles A: Joseph Cotten, Dolores Costello, Anne Baxter, Tim Holt, Agnes Moorehead, Ray Collins (RKO/Mercury)

Orson Welles devotes 9,000 feet of film to a spoiled brat who grows up as a spoiled, spiteful young man. This film hasn't a single moment of contrast; it piles on and on a tale of woe, but without once striking at least a true chord of sentiment. Welles comes up with a few more tricks in the direction of the dialogue. He plays heavily on the dramatic impact of a whisper, and on the threatened or actual hysterics of a frustrated woman as played by Agnes Moorehead.
1942: Nominations: Best Picture, Supp. Actress (Agnes Moorehead), B&W Cinematography, B&W Art Direction

MAGNIFICENT DOLL
1946, 93 mins, US
D: Frank Borzage A: Ginger Rogers, David Niven, Burgess Meredith, Stephen McNally, Peggy Wood (Universal/Hallmark)

Dolly Madison has always been considered one of the most colorful figures in this country's early history and her true life story would probably have been a natural for films. It's difficult to understand why such obvious fiction has been subsituted as having Aaron Burr, with a crush on Dolly, give up his claims to the presidency just because Dolly talked him out of it. Picture's chief graces result from the fine work of the cast. Ginger Rogers gives expert handling to the title role.

MAGNIFICENT OBSESSION
1935, 110 mins, US
D: John M. Stahl A: Irene Dunne, Robert Taylor, Charles Butterworth, Betty Furness, Ralph Morgan (Universal)

With its metaphysical theme of godliness and faith, the spiritual background of *Magnificent* is magnificent. It's patent that Irene Dunne and Robert Taylor, costarred, must clinch for the finale, even though it was a drunken mishap by the wastrel (Taylor) which had something to do with the death of the venerable Dr. Hudson. Dunne is the widow of Dr. Hudson, and Taylor's ultimate reformation is achieved because of the romantic attachment for her.

MAGNIFICENT OBSESSION
1954, 107 mins, US Ⓥ ⊟
D: Douglas Sirk A: Jane Wyman, Rock Hudson, Barbara Rush, Agnes Moorehead, Otto Kruger (Universal)

The same inspirational appeal that marked the 1935 making of Lloyd C. Douglas's bestseller is again caught in this version. It is a sensitive treatment of faith told in terms of moving, human drama which packs emotional impact. Hudson is the rich playboy responsible for Wyman's blindness who renounces his past existence to devote himself to study and work, hoping as a surgeon to cure her.
1954: Nomination: Best Actress (Jane Wyman)

MAGNIFICENT SEVEN, THE
See: Shichinin No Samurai

MAGNIFICENT SEVEN
1960, 128 mins, US Ⓥ ⊙ ⊟
D: John Sturges A: Yul Brynner, Eli Wallach, Steve McQueen, Horst Buchholz, Charles Bronson, Robert Vaughan, Brad Dexter, James Coburn (United Artists)

Until the women and children arrive on the scene, this is a western with lots of bite and tang and old-fashioned abandon. The last third is a long and cluttered anticlimax. Odd foundation for the able screenplay is the Japanese film *Seven Samurai*. The plot, as adapted, is simple and compelling. A Mexican village is at the mercy of a bandit (Eli Wallach), whose recurrent "visits" with his huge band of outlaws strip the meek peasant people of the fruits of their labors. They hire seven American gunslingers for the obvious purpose.
1960: Nomination: Best Scoring of a Dramatic Picture

MAGNIFICENT SHOWMAN, THE
See: Circus World

MAGNIFICENT YANKEE, THE
1950, 89 mins, US
D: John Sturges A: Louis Calhern, Ann Harding, Philip Ober, Ian Wolfe, Eduard Franz, Jimmy Lydon (M-G-M)

The life of Justice Oliver Wendell Holmes. Louis Calhern makes of the Supreme Court judge a robust, living character. Holmes, with his lifelong friend and associate justice, Louis D. Brandeis (Eduard Franz), at his side, battles his way through many of the legal cases that won him the tag of "The Great Dissenter" and revealed the two of them as the most progressive judges on the High Court bench during that time.

MAGNOLIA
1999, 188 mins, US Ⓥ ⊙ ▭
D: Paul Thomas Anderson **A:** Jason Robards, Julianne Moore, Tom Cruise, Philip Seymour Hoffman, John C. Reilly, Melora Walters (Sellar-Ghoulardi/New Line)

Set in the San Fernando Valley area of L.A. and ambitious in its scope and operatic style, *Magnolia* features a superlative ensemble in a meditation on urban alienation highly in tune with the zeitgeist. Dying patriarch Earl Partridge (Jason Robards) cheated on his first wife and walked out on her, leaving their son, Frank Mackey (Tom Cruise), to nurse her through terminal cancer. Earl is married to the much younger Linda (Julianne Moore), who can't deal with his impending death. He's tended by Phil (Philip Seymour Hoffman), a devoted nurse who's emotionally involved with Earl. Meanwhile Jim Kurring (John C. Reilly), a religious cop, is tentatively courting Claudia (Melora Walters), a high-strung woman addicted to drugs and loud music.
1999: Nominations: Best Supp. Actor (Tom Cruise), Original Screenplay, Original song ("Save Me")

MAGNUM FORCE
1973, 122 mins, US Ⓥ ⊙ ▭
D: Ted Post **A:** Clint Eastwood, Hal Holbrook, Mitchell Ryan, Felton Perry, David Soul (Malpaso/Warner)

An intriguing follow-up to *Dirty Harry* in that nonconformist Frisco detective Clint Eastwood is faced with tracking down a band of vigilante cops headed by Hal Holbrook, his nominal superior and career nemesis. The story contains the usual surfeit of human massacre for the yahoo trade, as well as a few actual thoughts.

MAGUS, THE
1969, 117 mins, UK ▭
D: Guy Green **A:** Michael Caine, Anthony Quinn, Candice Bergen, Anna Karina, Paul Stassino (20th Century-Fox/Blazer)

An esoteric, talky, slowly developing, sensitively executed, and somewhat dull film. Adapted by John Fowles from his novel, the production is a black fantasy-drama of self-realization. Caine is an English teacher dispatched to a Greek island

as replacement for a suicide. On the island, he meets Quinn, who is a mystic, or a wealthy spiritual hedonist playing God, or a film producer, or a recluse.

MAHLER
1974, 115 mins, UK Ⓥ
D: Ken Russell **A:** Robert Powell, Georgina Hale, Richard Morant, Lee Montague, Rosalie Crutchley (Goodtimes)

Another maddening meeting of Russellian extremes, brilliant and irritating, inventive and banal, tasteful and tasteless, exciting and disappointing. Flashbacks during composer Gustav Mahler's 1911 train ride to a Vienna deathbed give us glimpses of oppressed youth, childhood memories, early frustrations, a conversion from Judaism, his constant obsession with death, and so on.

MAIN EVENT, THE
1979, 112 mins, US Ⓥ
D: Howard Zieff **A:** Barbra Streisand, Ryan O'Neal, Paul Sand, Patti D'Arbanville, Rory Calhoun (Warner/First Artists/Barwood)

Situation of a bankrupt perfume queen left with a sore-handed fighter as her only asset has comic potential. Streisand is the garrulous yenta, after the passive and resistant Ryan O'Neal to resume his championship form. Zieff has chosen to emphasize sexual innuendo and result is a low-blow effort that evokes more titters than guffaws. Romantic aspects are also blunted, until a final seduction scene instigated by Streisand that gives the pic its only resonance.

MAJOR AND THE MINOR, THE
1942, 100 mins, US
D: Billy Wilder **A:** Ginger Rogers, Ray Milland, Diana Lynn, Robert Benchley, Rita Johnson (Paramount)

A sparkling and effervescing piece of farce-comedy. Ginger Rogers, disillusioned by New York, decides to head back home to Iowa. Her savings are not sufficient for ticket, she dolls up as a youngster under 12 to ride for half rate. But complications arise that throw her into compartment of Ray Milland, major at a boys' military academy, and into the school for a three-day layover.

MAJOR BARBARA
1941, 113 mins, UK Ⓥ
D: Gabriel Pascal [Harold French, David Lean] **A:** Wendy Hiller, Rex Harrison, Robert Morley, Robert Newton, Emlyn Williams, Deborah Kerr (Pascal)

Adapted from an old Shaw play, circa

1905, it still carries the lightning thrusts of Shavian caustic satire at any and all levels of society. The script, prepared by Shaw, closely follows his original. Wendy Hiller, daughter of a multimillionaire, sincerely works to save souls as the Salvation Army major in the Limehouse slums. Hiller is suddenly disillusioned in the Army soul-saving when heavy financial aid is gladly accepted from her munitions-making father and a rich distiller.

MAJOR DUNDEE
1965, 134 mins, US Ⓥ ▢
D: Sam Peckinpah **A:** Charlton Heston, Richard Harris, Jim Hutton, James Coburn, Michael Anderson Jr., Senta Berger (Columbia)

What started out as a straight story line—a troop of US Cavalry chasing a murderous Apache and his band into Mexico to rescue three kidnapped white children and avenge an Indian massacre—devolves into a series of subplots and tedious, poorly edited footage in which much of the continuity is lost. Sam Peckinpah's direction of individual scenes is mostly vigorous, but he cannot overcome the weakness of screenplay. Charlton Heston delivers one of his regulation hefty portrayals and gets solid backing from a cast headed by Richard Harris as the rebel captain.

MAJORITY OF ONE, A
1961, 156 mins, US
D: Mervyn LeRoy **A:** Rosalind Russell, Alec Guinness, Ray Danton, Madlyn Rhue, Mae Questel (Warner)

Brew of schmaltz and sukiyaki is an outstanding film. Russell's Yiddish hex-cent, though at times it sounds like what it is—a Christian imitating a Jew—is close enough to the genuine article. Guinness becomes Japanese through physical suggestion and masterful elocution. Ray Danton play Russell's son-in-law, who paves the way for the unusual romance between middle-class Brooklyn widow and wealthy, influential Tokyo widower.

MAJOR LEAGUE
1989, 107 mins, US Ⓥ ⊙
D: David S. Ward **A:** Tom Berenger, Charlie Sheen, Corbin Bernsen, Margaret Whitton, Rene Russo (Morgan Creek/Mirage)

R-rated baseball comedy. Though the plot turns are mostly predictable, they are executed with wit and style. There's a lot of rooting interest for the audience in the sad sacks cynically assembled by new In-dians owner Margaret Whitton with the secret hope that they'll draw so poorly that she'll be able to break the stadium lease and head for Miami. Naturally, when the guys get wind of this maneuver, they recover their lost pride. The cast is a fine ensemble, leading off with Tom Berenger as the battered, world-weary catcher and Charlie Sheen as the juve-delinquent pitcher.

MAJOR LEAGUE II
1994, 104 mins, US Ⓥ ⊙
D: David S. Ward **A:** Charlie Sheen, Tom Berenger, Corbin Bernsen, Dennis Haysbert, James Gammon (Morgan Creek/Warner)

A singularly unfunny, dramatically tepid follow-up, with the second season imposing a straitjacket structure that's in direct opposition to the inspired chaos of the original. Apart from an emotional ninth-inning surge, this is one yarn that unravels into a heap of plot strands all too quickly. While the original was a true ensemble piece, *Major League II* places its dominant emphasis on Sheen's character.

MAJOR PAYNE
1995, 97 mins, US Ⓥ ⊙
D: Nick Castle **A:** Damon Wayans, Karyn Parsons, Bill Hickey, Michael Ironside, Albert Hall (Wife 'n' Kids/Universal)

The private war of Major Benson Payne (Damon Wayans) is that he's a modern-day military anachronism. A natural-born killing machine, his pleasure in an era bereft of enemies is a pain to the marine corps. The clash of hard-nosed marine training and youthful antics are the grist of the film's comedy. Wayans remains an odd choice for family-film stardom. His rude brand of humor is largely muted here, and when he slyly reveals it, the effect is jarring.

MAKE MINE MINK
1960, 101 mins, UK Ⓥ
D: Robert Asher **A:** Terry-Thomas, Athene Seyler, Hattie Jacques, Billie Whitelaw, Jack Hedley (Rank)

Plot concerns the blundering excursions into crime of a bunch of amateurs, lifting valuable furs and devoting the loot to charity. Dame Beatrice Appleby's (Athene Seyler) "gang" consists of Albert (Terry-Thomas), a retired officer who plans the raids, a daffy spinster (Elspeth Duxbury), and Nanette (Hattie Jacques), a heavyweight teacher of deportment. The humor is episodic.

MAKE MINE MUSIC
1946, 75 mins, US
D: Jack Kinney, Clyde Geronimi, Hamilton Luske, Bob Cormack, Josh Meador (RKO/Disney)

Walt Disney treat—10 items pieced together in one "musical fantasy"—tees off with an interesting cinematurgical treatment of "The Martins and the Coys." This gives way to a clever visualization of Sergey Prokofiev's *Peter and the Wolf* in rich hues with some fine new Disney characters. And the finale, "The Whale Who Wanted to Sing at the Met," is as imaginative a conceit as Disney ever essayed. Willie the Whale, fished out of the briny, runs the gamut of familiar operatic excerpts.

MAKE WAY FOR TOMORROW
1937, 91 mins, US
D: Leo McCarey **A:** Victor Moore, Beulah Bondi, Fay Bainter, Thomas Mitchell (Paramount)

Leo McCarey has firmly etched the dilemma in which an elderly married couple find themselves when they lose their old dwelling place and their five grown-up children are nonreceptive. He keeps audience interest focused on old Lucy Cooper and Pa Cooper as they are separated. Victor Moore as Pa Cooper makes the biggest impression in the lighter, more whimsical moments. Beulah Bondi, as the aged Lucy is standout from the viewpoint of clever character work and makeup. Fay Bainter does splendidly as the wife of one of the sons to whose house the mother goes to live.

MAKING IT
See: Les Valseuses

MAKING LOVE
1982, 111 mins, US ⊘
D: Arthur Hiller **A:** Michael Ontkean, Kate Jackson, Harry Hamlin, Wendy Hiller, Arthur Hill, Nancy Olson (20th Century-Fox/Indie)

This homosexual-themed domestic drama of a married man's "coming out" stands up well on all counts, emerging as an absorbing tale. First half hour presents Michael Ontkean and Kate Jackson as a successful young L.A. couple. Then Ontkean meets Harry Hamlin, a gay writer. Ontkean takes the plunge with Hamlin and finds he likes it, so much so that he quickly knows his marriage is finished.

MAKING MR. RIGHT
1987, 95 mins, US ⊘ ⊙
D: Susan Seidelman **A:** John Malkovich, Ann Magnuson, Glenne Headly, Ben Masters, Laurie Metcalf, Hart Bochner (Orion/Barry & Enright)

Desperately unfunny romance between an android and a new-wave "image consultant." The actors nearly suffocate delivering stiff dialogue, with jokes that are bad or vulgar (or both) in scenes that reek of contrivance. Scripters have taken Frankenstein and turned him into Frankie Stone (Ann Magnuson). She's a very unlikely whiz-bang publicist who practically moves in with an android and his creator (John Malkovich in both roles) to get the best handle on how to sell the invention to the American public before he's launched into space.

MAKIOKA SISTERS, THE
See: Sasame Yuki

MALAYA
1949, 95 mins, US
D: Richard Thorpe **A:** Spencer Tracy, James Stewart, Valentina Cortese, Sydney Greenstreet, John Hodiak, Lionel Barrymore (M-G-M)

Pulp-fiction adventure yarn tied to the government's need to obtain rubber during the war. James Stewart plays a roaming newspaper reporter who promises to steal rubber for his government, which supplies him with ships for transporting and gold for bribing. He effects the release from prison of Spencer Tracy to aid in the daring adventure. Tracy and Stewart are at home in their toughie roles.

MALCOLM X
1992, 201 mins, US ⊘ ⊙
D: Spike Lee **A:** Denzel Washington, Angela Bassett, Albert Hall, Al Freeman Jr., Delroy Lindo, Spike Lee (Warner/40 Acres & a Mule)

Spike Lee has made a disappointingly conventional and sluggish film in *Malcolm X*. The pic comes up short in several departments, notably in pacing and in giving a strong sense of why this man became a legend. This is one long sit. Despite Denzel Washington's forceful, magnetic, multilayered lead performance, the film only clicks sporadically.
1992: Nominations: Best Actor (Denzel Washington), Costume Design

MALE AND FEMALE
1919, 107 mins, US ⊗
D: Cecil B. DeMille **A:** Thomas Meighan,

Gloria Swanson, Lila Lee, Bebe Daniels, Theodore Roberts, Raymond Hatton (Paramount)

Cecil B. DeMille's picturization of J. M. Barrie's play *The Admirable Crichton* is impressive. The cast is a pippin and Thomas Meighan does good work. Gloria Swanson and Lila Lee divide the women honors of the piece. Swanson plays the role of Lady Mary, while Lee is the little slavey, Tweeny. The former appears to advantage in both the London and the desert-island scenes, looking beautiful at all times, and especially so as she slips into the sunken bath.

MALICE
1993, 107 mins, US Ⓥ ⊙
D: Harold Becker A: Alec Baldwin, Nicole Kidman, Bill Pullman, Bebe Neuwirth, George C. Scott, Anne Bancroft (Columbia/Castle Rock)

The immaculately crafted *Malice* is a virtual scrapbook of elements borrowed from other suspense pics, but no less enjoyable for being so familiar. The film starts slowly, with college dean Andy (Bill Pullman) concerned over the mysterious rapist who's attacked several students and worrying about the mysterious abdominal pains plaguing his wife, Tracy (Nicole Kidman). Enter polished, self-assured surgeon Jed (Alec Baldwin). The pic shifts into high gear when Baldwin performs emergency surgery on Kidman, which kicks off a series of revelations, plot reversals, and character twists.

MALLRATS
1995, 95 mins, US Ⓥ
D: Kevin Smith A: Shannen Doherty, Jeremy London, Jason Lee, Claire Forlani, Michael Rooker (Alphaville)

Writer-director Kevin Smith takes aim at hangin' at the shopping arcade. While admittedly ragged and ribald, it's a picture with an innate charm and honesty. Peeling away the contempo trappings, it's still basically an old-fashioned boy-loses-girl saga and how he proceeds to get her back. In fact, it's two boys who are best friends losing girlfriends on the same day.

MALTA STORY
1953, 103 mins, UK Ⓥ
D: Brian Desmond Hurst A: Alec Guinness, Jack Hawkins, Anthony Steel, Muriel Pavlow, Flora Robson, Renée Asherson (Rank)

This is an epic story of the courage and endurance of the people and defenders of the island of Malta, handled in grimly realistic but not overdramatic style. Alec Guinness plays a camera reconnaissance pilot stranded in Malta. Jack Hawkins is the air officer in command who stands helplessly by while his airfields are blasted night and day. Bulk of the acting laurels go to Guinness, who here forsakes his chameleonlike whimsicality for the shy diffident charm of an inexperienced lover.

MALTESE FALCON, THE
1931, 80 mins, US Ⓥ
D: Roy Del Ruth A: Bebe Daniels, Ricardo Cortez, Dudley Digges, Una Merkel, Thelma Todd (Warner)

With a naturally nonchalant although extremely odd private detective in Ricardo Cortez, director Roy Del Ruth takes his audience out of the screen-story rut for a series of surprise incidents and a totally different finis. The mystery element is so flung about that not until the last reel or so does the most studious follower know who did any of the killings. Meantime a number of clever gags happen through Sam Spade in disarming people, then apologizing; taking money and then having it taken from him; making love one minute and turning the girl over to the police the next.

MALTESE FALCON, THE
1941, 100 mins, US Ⓥ
D: John Huston A: Humphrey Bogart, Mary Astor, Peter Lorre, Sydney Greenstreet, Barton MacLane, Gladys George (Warner)

This is one of the best examples of actionful and suspenseful melodramatic storytelling in cinematic form. Unfolding a most intriguing and entertaining murder mystery, picture displays outstanding excellence in writing, direction, acting, and editing. Humphrey Bogart gives an attention-arresting portrayal that not only dominates the proceedings throughout but is the major motivation in all but a few minor scenes. Mary Astor skillfully etches the role of an adventuress. Sydney Greenstreet scores heavily in his first screen appearance.

1941: Nominations: Best Picture, Supp. Actor (Sydney Greenstreet), Screenplay

MAMBO
1954, 94 mins, Italy/US Ⓥ
D: Robert Rossen A: Silvana Mangano, Michael Rennie, Vittorio Gassman, Shelley Winters, Katherine Dunham, Eduardo Ciannelli (Ponti-De Laurentiis/Paramount)

Story is near soap opera, and involves the trials of a girl who wants to be a dancer. She is torn between the pure love for a dying prince and the passionate embraces of an adventurer. For a while Giovanna (Silvana Mangano) is happy with the dance group led by Tony (Shelley Winters), and soon becomes star of the show. But despite her success on returning to her home town of Venice, she falls once more under the adventurer's (Vittorio Gassman) spell while turning down a marriage proposal by the prince (Michael Rennie).

MAMBO KINGS, THE
1992, 101 mins, US Ⓥ ⊙

D: Arne Glimcher A: Armand Assante, Antonio Banderas, Cathy Moriarty, Maruschka Detmers, Desi Arnaz Jr., Roscoe Lee Browne (Warner)

Ambitious, old-fashioned Hollywood film lovingly re-creates the Latino ambience of its Pulitzer Prize–winning source material. With impeccable period sets and costumes and striking cinematography, pic beautifully evokes 1950s New York. Oscar Hijuelos's novel is pared down to its essential story about the rise and fall of two Cuban immigrant musicians. Assante makes a likable skirt chaser and later conveys Cesar's downward spiral with great economy. But he occasionally slips into a New York accent and never sounds anything like brother, Antonio Banderas, a Spanish actor in Pedro Aldomovar's films. As the tormented Nestor, Banderas gives a sensitive performance.
1992: Nomination: Best Song ("Beautiful Maria of My Soul")

MAME
1974, 132 mins, US Ⓥ ⊙ ⊡

D: Gene Saks A: Lucille Ball, Robert Preston, Beatrice Arthur, Kirby Furlong, Bruce Davison (Warner/ABC)

The Lucille Ball reincarnation of *Mame* is a fantasy of the good old days of Prohibition, the Depression and the world travel folders. The narrative pretty much follows the familiar sequence of events. Mame goes down with the market in 1929, tackles show business, then clerking, is rescued by the romantic Beauregard, and spends the rest of her life traveling. A comedy with songs, not a musical comedy, per se, this *Mame* climaxes with its foxhunting number in Georgia.

MAMMY
1930, 83 mins, US ⊙

D: Michael Curtiz A: Al Jolson, Lois Moran, Louise Dresser, Lowell Sherman, Hobart Bosworth (Warner)

A lively picture with Al Jolson singing new and old songs, including among the Irving Berlin new numbers a couple of melodious hits. Here is a minstrel show on the stage and on the street—the parade, the blacking up in the dressing room, and the semicircle with its white-face interlocutor, songs by the quartet, jokes by the end men, and dancing. The one section where Technicolor is employed is on the extended semicircle minstrel scene.

MAN, THE
1972, 93 mins, US

D: Joseph Sargent A: James Earl Jones, Martin Balsam, Burgess Meredith, Lew Ayres, William Windom, Barbara Rush (ABC Circle)

Compelling and sometimes explosive adaptation of the Irving Wallace bestseller. James Earl Jones portrays the black man who ascends unexpectedly and without precedent to the presidency of the United States through the rules of succession. Jones delivers an honest, forceful characterization of the president who accepts his fate with humility.

MAN ALONE, A
1955, 95 mins, US Ⓥ

D: Ray Milland A: Ray Milland, Mary Murphy, Ward Bond, Raymond Burr, Lee Van Cleef (Republic)

Western suspense, combined with action and drama. Ray Milland turns director and acquits himself fairly well. Quarantined in her Arizona desert-town home where her father, the sheriff (Ward Bond), is ill with yellow fever, Nadine Corrigan (Mary Murphy) finds the house has become sanctuary for a notorious gunman Wes Steele (Milland), being hunted by a lynch mob. A drama of love and regeneration is developed, leading eventually to the exposure of the guilty parties.

MAN AND A WOMAN, A
See: Un Homme et une Femme

MAN AND HIS MATE
See: One Million B.C.

MAN BETWEEN, THE
1953, 101 mins, UK

D: Carol Reed A: James Mason, Claire Bloom, Hildegarde Neff, Geoffrey Toone (London)

Carol Reed picks war-torn Berlin for a story of political intrigue. Atmosphere is created almost from the opening shot, although it takes some time for the plot of sinister intrigue to emerge clearly. It is virtually a battle of wits between East and West, with the Red Zone police striving to end the trafficking of human bodies into the Western Zone. The plot is woven around Claire Bloom, an English girl, who comes to spend a holiday, and James Mason, an East Berliner who rescues her after she is mistakenly picked up by Red police.

MAN BITES DOG
See: C'est Arrive pres de Chez Vous

MAN CALLED HORSE, A
1970, 114 mins, US Ⓥ ▱
D: Elliot Silverstein **A:** Richard Harris, Judith Anderson, Jean Gascon, Manu Tupou, Dub Taylor (Cinema Center)

A Man Called Horse is said to be an authentic depiction of American Indian life in the Dakota territory of about 1820. Authentic it may be, but an absorbing film drama it is not. Durango-lensed production stars Richard Harris as an English nobleman captured by the Sioux. Captivity segues to understanding and finally to tribal membership.

MANCHURIAN CANDIDATE, THE
1962, 126 mins, US Ⓥ ⊙
D: John Frankenheimer **A:** Frank Sinatra, Laurence Harvey, Janet Leigh, Angela Lansbury, Henry Silva (United Artists)

George Axelrod and John Frankenheimer's jazzy, hip screen translation of Richard Condon's bestselling novel works in all departments. Its story of the tracking down of a brainwashed Korean War "hero" being used as the key figure in an elaborate Communist plot to take over the US government is, on the surface, one of the wildest fabrications any author has ever tried to palm off on a gullible public. But the fascinating thing is that, from uncertain premise to shattering conclusion, one does not question plausibility—the events being rooted in their own cinematic reality.

1962: Nominations: Best Supp. Actress (Angela Lansbury), Editing

MANDALAY
1934, 65 mins, US
D: Michael Curtiz **A:** Kay Francis, Lyle Talbot, Ricardo Cortez, Warner Oland, Ruth Donnelly (Warner)

Kay Francis is a girl of doubtful past, present, and future who eventually casts her lot with an outcast doctor. Much of the action occurs on a boat bound from Rangoon for Mandalay. Earlier sequences are in the former seaport, where the heroine

has been forced into a life of doubtful purity when her gunrunner boyfriend takes a powder. This portion of the story isn't as convincing as it might be.

MANDINGO
1975, 126 mins, US Ⓥ ⊙
D: Richard Fleischer **A:** James Mason, Susan George, Percy King, Richard Ward, Brenda Sykes (Paramount)

Embarrassing and crude film that wallows in every cliché of the slave-based white society in the pre–Civil War South. The cornball adaptation is exceeded in banality only by the performances of James Mason, slave-breeder father of son Percy King, who in turn develops what passes for genuine affection for Brenda Sykes, while wife, Susan George, descends into revenge with Ken Norton, stud slave.

MANDY
(US: THE CRASH OF SILENCE)
1952, 92 mins, UK
D: Alexander Mackendrick **A:** Phyllis Calvert, Jack Hawkins, Terence Morgan, Mandy Miller, Godfrey Tearle (Ealing)

Central character is a young child who was born deaf and is, inevitably, dumb. Against a background of parental disagreement, the plot traces the methods used in teaching youngsters the art of lip-reading and expression. The dominating performance comes from little Mandy Miller in the title role. The best adult performance comes from Jack Hawkins, who makes the headmaster a vital and sincere character.

MAN FOR ALL SEASONS, A
1966, 120 mins, UK Ⓥ ⊙
D: Fred Zinnemann **A:** Paul Scofield, Wendy Hiller, Leo McKern, Robert Shaw, Orson Welles, Susannah York (Highland/Columbia)

Fred Zinnemann has blended all filmmaking elements into an excellent, handsome, and stirring film. Robert Bolt adapted his 1960 play, a timeless, personal conflict based on the 16th-century politico-religious situation between adulterous King Henry VIII and Catholic Sir Thomas More. Paul Scofield delivers an excellent performance as More, respected barrister, judge, and chancellor. Faced with mounting pressure to endorse publicly the royal marriage of Henry VIII to Anne Boleyn, More outfoxed his adversaries until "perjury" was used to justify a sentence of death. Robert Shaw is also excellent as the king, giving full exposi-

tion in limited footage to the character.
1966: Best Picture, Director, Actor (Paul Scofield), Adapted Screenplay, Color Cinematography, Color Costume Design
Nominations: Best Supp. Actor (Robert Shaw), Supp. Actress (Wendy Hiller)

MAN FRIDAY
1975, 115 mins, UK Ⓥ ▭
D: Jack Gold **A:** Peter O'Toole, Richard Roundtree, Peter Cellier, Christopher Cabot (Keep/ABC/ITC)

Variation of Daniel Defoe's classic has Crusoe (Peter O'Toole) discovering his Friday (Richard Roundtree) after the shipwrecked mariner has brutally shot and killed the black's companions. O'Toole's Crusoe proceeds to indoctrinate the "savage," with missionary zeal, into the manners and mores of Western society. Slowly, however, Friday begins to question him, his theories and teachings, soon in effect himself becoming the teacher of newer, freer, more open-minded ideas and ideals.

MAN FROM HONG KONG, THE
1975, 99 mins, Hong Kong/Australia Ⓥ ▭
D: Brian Trenchard-Smith **A:** Jimmy Wang Yu, George Lazenby, Ros Spiers, Hugh Keays-Byrne, Roger Ward (Golden Harvest/Movie)

A Hong Kong policeman (Wang Yu) is sent to Australia to extradite a Chinese courier who works for an international drug syndicate. Wang, though lacking the charisma of the late Bruce Lee, does have an aura of realism about him. George Lazenby does little for his image by appearing as a heavy Mr. Big. The Hong Kong–Australian James Bond hybrid comes off well for a kung fu pic.

MAN FROM LARAMIE, THE
1955, 102 mins, US Ⓥ
D: Anthony Mann **A:** James Stewart, Arthur Kennedy, Donald Crisp, Cathy O'Donnell, Alex Nicol, Aline MacMahon (Columbia)

The plot concerns the search by James Stewart for the man guilty of selling repeating rifles to an Apache tribe. The rifles had been used to wipe out a small cavalry patrol to which Stewart's younger brother had been attached, so there is a motive of personal vengeance. Violence gets into the act early and repeats with regularity as Stewart's trail crosses that of a number of warped sadistic characters.

MAN FROM PLANET X, THE
1951, 70 mins, US
D: Edgar G. Ulmer **A:** Robert Clarke, Margaret Field, Raymond Bond, William Schallert, Roy Engel (Mid-Century)

Two scientists, the daughter of one, and a newspaperman are on a small Scottish island to observe a strange planet swinging close to the earth. The girl accidentally sees a weird creature from outer space. They take the superior being in, try to communicate with him, but one of the scientists, seeing a chance to control the world, upsets the plans. Edgar Ulmer's direction builds a strong mood and the suspense is sustained.

MAN FROM SNOWY RIVER, THE
1982, 102 mins, Australia Ⓥ ◉
D: George Miller **A:** Kirk Douglas, Jack Thompson, Tom Burlinson, Sigrid Thornton, Lorraine Bayly (Edgley/Cambridge)

A rattling-good adventure story, inspired by a legendary poem, filmed in spectacularly rugged terrain in the Great Dividing Ranges in Victoria. Kirk Douglas plays two brothers who have had a terrible falling-out. While one brother, the wealthy autocratic landowner, fits him like a glove, the actor is less believable as Spur, a gruff, grizzled, out-of-luck prospector.

MAN FROM THE ALAMO, THE
1953, 79 mins, US Ⓥ
D: Budd Boetticher **A:** Glenn Ford, Julie Adams, Chill Wills, Hugh O'Brian, Victor Jory (Universal)

This basic outdoor feature has a rousing climax, good performances, and beautifully photographed outdoor values. Plot is hung on the supposed escape of one man (Ford) from the Alamo before its valiant defenders fell to Santa Ana's forces. He finds his own and the other families wiped out by renegades posing as Mexican soldiers, is branded a coward for deserting the fort, and spends the rest of the footage proving himself and getting revenge.

MANHANDLED
1924, 77 mins, US ⊗
D: Allan Dwan **A:** Gloria Swanson, Tom Moore, Frank Morgan, Lilyan Tashman, Ian Keith (Paramount)

A typical hick salesgirl in the basement of a department store, one of those tough, gum-chewing slang slingers, manages to climb out of the cellar into the bohemian set through the efforts of an author who wishes to make an experiment and pulls her out of the place and introduces her to artists, sculptors, and a gown creator. Gloria Swanson reveals unsuspected qualities as an actress. Tom Moore plays the young mechanic hero and handles it very well.

MANHATTAN
1979, 96 mins, US ⓥ ⊙ ▱
D: Woody Allen **A:** Woody Allen, Diane Keaton, Michael Murphy, Mariel Hemingway, Meryl Streep, Anne Byrne (United Artists)

Woody Allen has, in black-and-white, captured the inner beauty that lurks behind the outer layer of dirt and grime in Manhattan. The core of the story revolves around Allen as Isaac Davis, an unfulfilled television writer and his best friends, Yale and Emily. Isaac has lately taken up with Tracy (Mariel Hemingway), a gorgeous 17-year-old, but the age difference is becoming too much of an obstacle for him. He meets Yale's girlfriend, Mary, a fast-talking, pseudo-intellectual, expertly played by Diane Keaton, to whom he is instantly attracted.
1979: Nominations: Best Supp. Actress (Mariel Hemingway), Original Screenplay

MANHATTAN MELODRAMA
1934, 93 mins, US ⓥ ⊙
D: W. S. Van Dyke **A:** Clark Gable, William Powell, Myrna Loy, Leo Carrillo, Nat Pendleton, Mickey Rooney (Cosmopolitan/M-G-M)

Apart from the Clark Gable–William Powell stellar duo and Myrna Loy, who does an excellent job as the principal femme, the story is replete with punchy popularly appealing ingredients. The fast, crisp, intelligent dialogue further enhances it. There are a couple of spots where perhaps Gable as the too suave hoodlum is glorified a bit, but there are also many offsetting peeches by Powell as the DA as he charges the jury to remember that there's no longer public sympathy with bootleggers.
1934: Best Original Story

MANHATTAN MURDER MYSTERY
1993, 105 mins, US ⓥ ⊙
D: Woody Allen **A:** Alan Alda, Woody Allen, Anjelica Huston, Diane Keaton (Tri-Star)

Light, insubstantial, and utterly devoid of the heavier themes Woody Allen has grappled with in most of his recent outings, this confection keeps the chuckles coming. It resembles nothing so much as the goofy backstage murder mellers of the 1930s, complete with vanishing corpses, high-society settings, bickering leads, and self-consciously theatrical denouement. Allen and Keaton play Larry and Carol Lipton, a long-married pair whose next-door neighbors are Paul and Lillian House (Jerry Adler, Lynn Cohen). Suddenly Lillian drops dead of a heart attack. Carol becomes obsessed with the idea that Paul murdered his wife.

MANHATTAN PROJECT, THE
1986, 117 mins, US ⓥ ⊙
D: Marshall Brickman **A:** John Lithgow, Christopher Collet, Cynthia Nixon, Jill Eikenberry, John Mahoney (Gladden)

Warm, comedy-laced doomsday story has 16-year-old student Paul Stevens (Christopher Collet) tumbling to the fact that the new scientist in town, Dr. Mathewson (John Lithgow), is working with plutonium in what fronts as a pharmaceutical-research installation. While Mathewson is romancing Stevens's mom (Jill Eikenberry), the genius kid is plotting with his helpful girlfriend, Jenny (Cynthia Nixon), to steal a canister of plutonium. Their goal: to expose the danger of the secret nuclear plant placed in their community.

MAN HUNT
1941, 100 mins, US
D: Fritz Lang **A:** Walter Pidgeon, Joan Bennett, George Sanders, John Carradine, Roddy McDowall (20th Century-Fox)

Geoffrey Household's tale of an English big-game hunter who invades the precincts of Berchtesgaden to draw a bead on Hitler with an unloaded rifle; his capture and torture by the gestapo; escape and return to England and further hounding by German agents; and final dropping back into Germany with a rifle for a future crack at Hitler, fails to sustain adventurous excitement on screen. Fritz Lang's direction maintains excellent suspense in the first half.

MANHUNTER
1986, 119 mins, US ⓥ ⊙ ▱
D: Michael Mann **A:** William Petersen, Kim Greist, Joan Allen, Brian Cox, Dennis Farina, Tom Noonan (De Laurentiis/Roth)

An unpleasantly gripping thriller that rubs one's nose in a sick criminal mentality for two hours. An FBI agent (William Petersen) is summoned from retirement to work on a particularly perplexing case. Petersen's excellent deductive talents are due, in large measure, to his tendency to deeply enter the minds of killers, to begin thinking like them. This trick takes the film into interesting Hitchcockian guilt-transference territory and Mann's grip on his material is tight and sure. Director is at all times preoccupied by visual chic.

MANIAC COP
1988, 85 mins, US Ⓥ
D: William Lustig A: Tom Atkins, Bruce Campbell, Laurene Landon, Richard Roundtree, William Smith, Sheree North (Shapiro Glickenhaus)

A disappointing thriller that wastes an oddball premise and offbeat point of view. Gimmicky approach has the novelty of all leading characters (male and female) working for the police force. A maniac dressed in police blues is terrorizing New Yorkers and the investigator on the case, Lieutenant McCrae (no-nonsense Tom Atkins), is convinced the killer is really a cop.

MANIAC COP 2
1990, 88 mins, US Ⓥ
D: William Lustig A: Robert Davi, Claudia Christian, Michael Lerner, Bruce Campbell, Laurene Landon (Movie House Sales/Fadd)

A thinking man's exploitation film, improving on the 1988 original. This time the title character Cordell (Robert Z'Dar), a framed cop killed in prison, is resurrected as a disfigured supernatural character stalking the streets of Manhattan. With director William Lustig creating a brooding, morbid atmosphere akin to classical film noir, pic benefits from producer-writer Larry Cohen's extremely dark humor. Time and again the cop-monster shows up at a crime scene and violently aids the criminal rather than the victim.

MAN I KILLED, THE
1932, 77 mins, US
D: Ernst Lubitsch A: Lionel Barrymore, Nancy Carroll, Phillips Holmes, Lucien Littlefield, ZaSu Pitts (Paramount)

This is a hard and somber theme to digest. Telling of the young Frenchman whose conscience drives him to the home of the German boy he killed in the war, the picture is particularly noteworthy for a superb performance by Lionel Barrymore as the bereaved German father. Phillips Holmes is not a happy choice for the mentally tortured soldier. Yet his performance is not without its good points.

MAN I MARRIED, THE
1940, 76 mins, US
D: Irving Pichel A: Joan Bennett, Francis Lederer, Lloyd Nolan, Anna Sten, Maria Ouspenskaya (20th Century-Fox)

A powerful dramatic presentation of the Nazi regime in Germany in 1938. Story sends American-born Joan Bennett to Europe with her husband (Francis Lederer). He becomes a follower of Hitler. Hypnotized to a fanatical stage, Lederer declares he will divorce his wife in Germany, and their son must remain with him. His wife gradually awakens to the suffering imposed on opponents of Hitler's regimentation, and the elimination of individual liberties.

MAN IN A COCKED HAT
See: Carlton-Browne of the F.O.

MAN IN THE GRAY FLANNEL SUIT, THE
1956, 152 mins, US Ⓥ ▭
D: Nunnally Johnson A: Gregory Peck, Jennifer Jones, Fredric March, Marisa Pavan, Lee J. Cobb, Ann Harding (20th Century-Fox)

This is the story of an American who gets a chance to become a big shot and turns it down because he realizes that he's a nine-to-five man to whom family means more than success. It's also the story of a man with a conscience, who had a love affair in Rome that resulted in a child. Gregory Peck is handsome and appealing, if not always convincing. It is only really in the sequences with Marisa Pavan, who plays his Italian love, that he takes on warmth. As his wife, Jennifer Jones allows almost no feeling of any real relationship between her and Peck.

MAN IN THE IRON MASK, THE
1939, 110 mins, US Ⓥ
D: James Whale A: Louis Hayward, Joan Bennett, Joseph Schildkraut, Alan Hale, Warren William (United Artists/Small)

Alexander Dumas's classic is a highly entertaining adventure melodrama. D'Artagnan and the Three Musketeers reappear as stalwart supporters of Philippe, twin brother of Louis XIV, who is tossed into the Bastille with a fiendishly designed locked iron mask. Louis Hayward, carrying the dual role of the arrogant Louis XIV and the vigorously self-assured Philippe, gives one of the finest dual characterizations of the screen.
1939: Nomination: Best Original Score

MAN IN THE IRON MASK, THE

1998, 132 mins, US ✆ ⊙

D: Randall Wallace **A:** Leonardo DiCaprio, Jeremy Irons, John Malkovich, Gerard Depardieu, Gabriel Byrne, Anne Parillaud (United Artists/M-G-M)

Leonardo DiCaprio delivers a wonderful double star turn in *The Man in the Iron Mask.* An unusually sober and serious-minded telling of Alexandre Dumas's classic tale, this handsome costumer is routinely made and comes up rather short in boisterous excitement. Story centers on a barbarous king of France, his noble twin brother and the aging musketeers. Tone remains uncertain for the first reel or two, and the unmeshed accents of the American, English, Irish, and French thesps help pic to dig itself further into a hole. DiCaprio almost single-handedly hoists the film above ground, and the pull of high-level intrigue and melodrama take hold. Debut director Randall Wallace's essential seriousness adds unexpected weight to the work's central themes. Most of all, however, the actors make the film a pleasure to watch.

MAN IN THE MOON, THE

1991, 99 mins, US ✆ ⊟

D: Robert Mulligan **A:** Sam Waterston, Tess Harper, Gail Strickland, Reese Witherspoon, Jason London (M-G-M)

Bucolic coming-of-age story set in 1957 Louisiana follows Reese Witherspoon, a 14-year-old envious of her college-bound sister (Emily Warfield). Jason London becomes friendly with Witherspoon against his better judgment. Inevitable conflict arises when London meets the older sister, and he quickly relegates Witherspoon to the status of kid sister. Unfortunately, vet director Mulligan and tyro screenwriter Jenny Wingfield could not come up with a dramatic resolution to this triangle, and resort to a melodramatic device. Cinematography of Freddie Francis catches the summer light and warmth important to the story.

MAN IN THE WHITE SUIT, THE

1951, 97 mins, UK ✆ ⊙

D: Alexander Mackendrick **A:** Alec Guinness, Joan Greenwood, Cecil Parker, Michael Gough, Ernest Thesiger (Ealing)

A young research scientist invents a cloth that is everlasting and dirt resisting. The textile industry sees the danger signal and tries to buy him out, but he outwits them. Particular tribute must be paid to the sound-effects department. The bubbly sound of liquids passing through specially prepared contraptions in the lab is one of the most effective running gags seen in a British film. Alec Guinness's interpretation of the little research worker is warm, understanding, and always sympathetic.

1952: Nomination: Best Screenplay

LA MANI SULLA CITTA
(US: HANDS OVER THE CITY)

1963, 105 mins, Italy

D: Francesco Rosi **A:** Rod Steiger, Guido Alberti, Salvo Randone, Marcello Cannavale (Galatea)

Rod Steiger, as city councilman Nottola, is out for a 5,000 percent profit on a remote suburban area he's just bought. Pic shows how he and his party colleagues maneuver the deal by secret alliances and other crooked methods, against the opposition of left-wing elements in the city council. Film contains a very direct criticism of Italian government laissez-faire in real-life scandals of a similar nature. Characters have little human depth, but are almost purely symbolic pawns repping various political tendencies.

MANITOU, THE

1978, 104 mins, US ✆ ⊟

D: William Girdler **A:** Tony Curtis, Michael Ansara, Susan Strasberg, Stella Stevens, Burgess Meredith (Avco Embassy/Weist-Simon)

This time the demon is a 400-year-old American Indian medicine man. He's a little devil in the literal sense, thanks to overexposure to X rays, which have shriveled him into a three-foot-tall redskin monster. Until he makes a rather dramatic entrance onto the floor of a hospital bedroom, he can be found growing as a fetus on Susan Strasberg's upper back. Tony Curtis plays a charlatan of the supernatural, reading tarot cards for rich old ladies. Only Burgess Meredith as a befuddled professor of anthropology has any fun with his part.

MAN MADE MONSTER
(UK: THE ELECTRIC MAN)

1941, 89 mins, US

D: George Waggner **A:** Lionel Atwill, Lon Chaney Jr., Anne Nagel, Frank Albertson (Universal)

A shocker that's in the groove for the horror fans. Weird events resulting from a mad scientist's lab experiments in transforming a normal human being into a monster controlled by electrical impulses could have been made mawkish. Sincere portrayals plus alert direction and deft photography span several implausible pit-falls.

MANNEQUIN
1938, 92 mins, US ⓥ

D: Frank Borzage A: Joan Crawford, Spencer Tracy, Alan Curtis, Ralph Morgan, Mary Phillips (M-G-M)

A down-to-earth story, interestingly related, excellently directed, and splendidly acted. The story is the old standby plot of the girl of the tenements who forces herself from her environment and climbs in the world. Curtis is the ne'er-do-well and gives a properly villainous performance. Tracy, as a self-made tugboat capitalist, has his serious moments. But the film is primarily director Frank Borzage's. Without the atmosphere he creates and the movement of his characters through believable situations, *Mannequin* would be routine entertainment.

1938: Nomination: Best Song ("Always and Always")

MANNEQUIN
1987, 89 mins, US ⓥ ⊙

D: Michael Gottlieb A: Andrew McCarthy, Kim Cattrall, Estelle Getty, G. W. Bailey, James Spader (Gladden)

As stiff and spiritless as its title suggests. Night work makes strange bedfellows of Andrew McCarthy, an aspiring artist working as a model maker, and Hollywood (Meshach Taylor), the flamboyant near transvestite who dresses store windows, and of McCarthy and Emmy (Cattrall), his mannequin. She comes alive when they're alone together, but reverts back to her cold self if anyone else appears.

1987: Nomination: Best Song ("Nothing's Gonna Stop Us Now")

MANNEQUIN ON THE MOVE
1991, 95 mins, US ⓥ ⊙

D: Stewart Raffill A: Kristy Swanson, William Ragsdale, Terry Kiser, Stuart Pankin, Meshach Taylor (Gladden)

It took four writers to struggle with another idea of why a mannequin would come to life in a department store and what would happen if she did. Their solution: the dummy (Kristy Swanson) is actually a Bavarian peasant girl hexed 1,000 years ago to prevent her marriage to the prince. As part of a promotion, the legendary statue is displayed at a Philadelphia store under the care of William Ragsdale, who's the spitting image of the prince, and jealous eye of Count Terry Kiser, a spit-

on descendant of the sorcerer who bewitched her.

MAN OF AFRICA
1954, 73 mins, UK

D: Cyril Frankel A: Violet Mukabureza, Frederick Bijurenda, Mattayo Bukwirwa, Butensa, Seperiera Mpambara (Group Three)

Struggle for existence of a native tribe is leisurely told in a semidocumentary filmed in the more remote parts of Uganda. Picture eschews the hokey aspects found in most films lensed in "darkest Africa," but is often languorous to the point of becoming dull. In depicting the migration of a tribe to virgin country after the fertility of their homeland has been exhausted, producer John Grierson has seen fit to include a romance between a clerk-turned-farmer and a native belle.

MAN OF ARAN
1934, 75 mins, UK ⓥ

D: Robert Flaherty A: Colman "Tiger" King, Maggie Dirrane, Michael Dillane (Gainsborough/Gaumont-British)

Central characters are not actors, but natives of the barren, sea-beaten islands off the western coast of Ireland, where this picture takes place. The sea is the villain and the quest for food the plot of this peasants-among-peasants picture, which rates high artistically. There is practically no dialogue except short sentences of warning, advice, comment on the hazards of shark hunting.

MAN OF A THOUSAND FACES
1957, 122 mins, US ▭

D: Joseph Pevney A: James Cagney, Dorothy Malone, Jane Greer, Jim Backus, Robert J. Evans, Marjorie Rambeau (Universal)

The title stems from the billing given Lon Chaney, who was born of deaf-and-dumb parents, an important emotional factor in his motivations. Screenplay ranges song-and-dance vaudeville days, two marriages, the birth of his son, early struggles as a Hollywood extra, eventual rise to stardom, and tragic death. As Chaney, James Cagney has immersed himself so completely in the role that it is difficult to spot any Cagney mannerisms. Bud Westmore deserves special mention for the excellent makeup jobs on the various characters portrayed by Chaney.

1957: Nomination: Best Original Story & Screenplay

MAN OF BRONZE
See: Jim Thorpe—All-American

MAN OF EVIL
See: Fanny by Gaslight

MAN OF FLOWERS
1983, 93 mins, Australia ⓥ ⊙
D: Paul Cox A: Norman Kaye, Alyson
Best, Chris Haywood, Sarah Walker, Bob
Ellis (Flowers)

Film, flickering between realism and
fantasy, follows the progress of Bremer, a
rich naive eccentric (Norman Kaye),
whose inherited wealth both protects him
from the coldness of the outside world and
isolates him from its warmth. He is co-
cooned in a childlike innocence, dwelling
on the sexual exploration of his boyhood.
Kaye delivers a wonderful, understated
performance.

MAN OF IRON
See: Czlowiekz Zelaza

MAN OF LA MANCHA
1972, 129 mins, US ⓥ ⊙ ⊟
D: Arthur Hiller A: Peter O'Toole, Sophia
Loren, James Coco, Harry Andrews, John
Castle (United Artists/PEA)

Man of La Mancha, produced in the
style of the musical play from which it
was adapted, is the fanciful tale of Don
Quixote, that fictional Middle Ages lunatic
living in a fantasy world of chivalry long-
since past. The production is more a vehicle for music than for narrative. Peter
O'Toole persuasively brings to life the demented would-be knight.
1972: Nomination: Best Adapted Score

MAN OF MARBLE
See: Czlowiek z Marmuru

MAN OF NO IMPORTANCE, A
1995, 98 mins, UK ⓥ
D: Suri Krishnamma A: Albert Finney,
Brenda Fricker, Michael Gambon, Tara
Fitzgerald, Rufus Sewell (Little Bird/
Majestic/Newcomm/BBC)

Deception is the key element in the
early-1960s, Dublin-set *A Man of No Importance*. While it initially reveals itself as
a larkish, romantic ode to a bygone time,
it evolves darker tones and comes perilously close to full-bore tragedy by
fade-out. Unquestionably, the emotional
roller-coaster ride is kept under control by
another full-blooded performance by Albert Finney. He's a fiftysomething bus
conductor with a glint of the poet. He's
been toying with the idea of staging Oscar
Wilde's *Salome* when Adele Rice (Tara

Fitzgerald) climbs aboard—his idealized
vision of the temptress.

MAN OF THE HOUSE
1995, 96 mins, US ⓥ ⊙
D: James Orr A: Chevy Chase, Farrah
Fawcett, Jonathan Taylor Thomas, George
Wendt, David Shiner (Walt Disney/All
Girls)

Jonathan Taylor Thomas is stuck playing a character so bratty at first that adults
may wonder why someone hasn't throttled
the kid, his wry one-liners notwithstanding. The simple premise has Jack Sturges
(Chevy Chase), a district attorney, trying
to win over Ben (Thomas), the young son
of the woman he plans to marry (Farrah
Fawcett). Abandoned by his real dad and
therefore wary of potential suitors, Ben
schemes to get Jack out of the picture. The
gags at best approach the level of a standard sitcom.

MAN OF THE WEST
1958, 100 mins, US ⓥ ⊟
D: Anthony Mann A: Gary Cooper, Julie
London, Lee J. Cobb, Arthur O'Connell,
Jack Lord (United Artists/Mirisch)

Gary Cooper, a reformed gunman now
a respected citizen entrusted with the savings of his community, is robbed of the
money by members of his old gang. Superficially, the story is simply the account
of Cooper's efforts to free himself, Julie
London, and Arthur O'Connell from the
outlaws. It is given dimension by the fact
that to do this he must revert to the savagery he has foresworn. Cooper gives a
characteristically virile performance.

MAN ON A TIGHTROPE
1953, 105 mins, US
D: Elia Kazan A: Fredric March, Terry
Moore, Gloria Grahame, Cameron Mitch-
ell, Adolphe Menjou, Richard Boone (20th
Century-Fox)

Fredric March maneuvers his one-ring
circus from Czechoslovakia into freedom.
Director Elia Kazan limns his characters
with proper mood and shade, as the red
tape of the Reds becomes mountingly ob-
structive. The bold manner in which the
circus, in full calliope style, parades right
by the auxiliary frontier guards and plans
its diversion tactics for escape into the
American zone is plausibly staged by Kazan. Much of this footage was shot in Austria and Germany.

MANON DES SOURCES
1953, 222 mins, France
D: Marcel Pagnol A: Jacqueline Pagnol,

Raymond Pellegrin, Rellys, Henri Poupon, Robert Vattier (Pagnol)

Manon contains the best and worst of Pagnol. On the debit side is the mediocre technical quality, the indifference to classical notions of direction, and a major miscasting. Manon, the wild solitary shepherdess, is played by the filmmaker's wife, whose artificial manner and diction never suggest an orphan who's grown up in the Provençal hills. Yet the film is buoyed by its other vivid characterizations and the nonstop verve of Pagnol's dialogue. [Pic was reviewed at the first showing of the uncut version, in October 1988.]

MANON DES SOURCES
(US: MANON OF THE SPRING)
1986, 113 mins, France /Italy Ⓥ ⊙ ▱
D: Claude Berri **A:** Yves Montand, Daniel Auteuil, Emmanuelle Beart, Hippolyte Girardot, Elisabeth Depardieu (Renn/Films A2/DD/RAI-2)

Manon des Sources is the poignant, but more dramatically wobbly, follow-up to *Jean de Florette*. Manon, the hunchback's daughter, grown into a beautiful young woman who now lives in the hills as a reclusive shepherdess, learns the treachery that brought about her father's death and exacts vengeance on Yves Montand, Daniel Auteuil, and the village. Auteuil is again superb as the ratty unmalicious nephew, Ugolin. Berri is unable to overcome the inherent feebleness of the Manon character, here played ineffectually by the lovely and talented Emmanuelle Beart.

MAN ON FIRE
1957, 95 mins, US
D: Ranald MacDougall **A:** Bing Crosby, Inger Stevens, Mary Fickett, E. G. Marshall (M-G-M)

As a father embroiled in a harsh custody battle with his ex-wife, Bing Crosby gives an appealing and sensitive performance. Crosby is determined to maintain the custody of his young son at any cost. Not only is he motivated by a sincere love for his child, but by his own hurt feelings and bitterness about his wife having left him to marry another man. Inger Stevens, as a femme lawyer, is particularly appealing as she nurses Crosby through his vicious and embittered moods.

MANON OF THE SPRING
See: Manon des Sources

MAN ON THE MOON
1999, 118 mins, US Ⓥ ⊙ ▱
D: Milos Forman **A:** Jim Carrey, Danny DeVito, Courtney Love, Paul Giamatti, Vincent Schiavelli, Peter Bonerz (Jersey/Cinehaus/Mutual/Universal)

Film portrays Andy Kaufman (Jim Carrey), who made his name in the TV series *Taxi* and died in 1984 of cancer at the age of 35. But the impression is of a hopeless neurotic of little discernible talent other than for making those around him miserable. Hollywood agent George Shapiro (Danny DeVito) takes him on and gets him a *Saturday Night Live* gig, followed by the offer to join *Taxi*. Kaufman is seen as a highly disruptive prima donna, bereft of true personal connections until he meets Lynne Margulies (Courtney Love), who eventually moves in with him. But even this relationship has a shaky foundation. Carrey unerringly captures the quirkiness and disquieting vacantness of the man he's portraying, but psychological penetration is essentially impossible in Kaufman's case.

MANPOWER
1941, 100 mins, US
D: Raoul Walsh **A:** Edward G. Robinson, Marlene Dietrich, George Raft, Alan Hale, Frank McHugh, Eve Arden (Warner)

Raft and Robinson are buddies in a construction and maintenance crew for power lines, and when Robinson is burned by a high-tension wire, Raft is made foreman. Dietrich works in a clip joint. Raft tabs her immediately, but Robinson falls in love with her for quick marriage. First third of the picture displays racy action and spicy dialogue for maximum attention, and then drifts into formula triangle dramatics.

MAN-PROOF
1937, 80 mins, US
D: Richard Thorpe **A:** Myrna Loy, Franchot Tone, Rosalind Russell, Walter Pidgeon, Rita Johnson, Ruth Hussey (M-G-M)

Smartly produced, well-directed, and excellently acted society comedy-drama. Myrna Loy plays a young woman who is handed a message that the man she loves (Walter Pidgeon) is to marry one of her rich girlfriends (Rosalind Russell) and the couple invite her to be a bridesmaid. It's a shock, but she is a thoroughbred and she hides her disappointment and resentment. Thereafter the story recounts the thoughts and actions of a girl on the rebound from a thwarted love affair.

MAN'S CASTLE

1933, 75 mins, US

D: Frank Borzage **A:** Spencer Tracy, Loretta Young, Marjorie Rambeau, Glenda Farrell, Walter Connolly, Arthur Hohl (Columbia)

Spencer Tracy is cast in his most distasteful role. It's a story of a worthless mug who rudely picks up a homeless girl and transports her to a shantytown, where he and other no-goods reside. The story attempts to justify it all by reformation of the callous, smart-cracking hero via marriage to the girl when she is about to become a mother. Loretta Young does a noble job as the little girl who stands nearly everything.

MAN'S FAVORITE SPORT?

1964, 120 mins, US ⓥ

D: Howard Hawks **A:** Rock Hudson, Paula Prentiss, Maria Perschy, John McGiver, Charlene Holt, Roscoe Karns (Universal)

The comically ripe premise: what happens when a celebrated piscatorial authority and fishing equipment salesman who doesn't know how to fish is suddenly ordered by his unaware boss to compete in a fishing tournament? For a while the adventures of this angler (Rock Hudson) romp along with a kind of breezy charm. But then, poof, the fish story begins to sag under the weight of its bulky romantic midsection and lumbers along tediously and repetitiously to a long-overdue conclusion.

MANSFIELD PARK

1999, 110 mins, UK/US ⓥ ⊙

D: Patricia Rozema **A:** Embeth Davidtz, Jonny Lee Miller, Alessandro Nivola, Frances O'Connor, Harold Pinter, Lindsay Duncan (Miramax HAL/BBC)

This picture should have been called *Patricia Rozema's Mansfield Park*. It certainly isn't Jane Austen's. Pic reinterprets the central character, Fanny Price, as a cross between Austen herself and a tomboyish proto-feminist, throws in some gratuitous lesbian *frissons*, and adopts a knowing, politically correct attitude to the society portrayed. Ten-year-old Fanny (Hannah Taylor Gordon) is sent to live with her mother's sisters (Lindsay Duncan, Sheila Gish) at the sprawling country mansion Mansfield Park. The grown-up Fanny (Frances O'Connor) turns out to be a passionate amateur writer, experienced horsewoman, and wearer of tomboyish

garb. Aussie actress O'Connor is excellent. As her fumbling vis-à-vis, Edmund, Jonny Lee Miller is variable, with the dialogue not always sitting easily in his modern mouth.

MANTRAP

1926, 68 mins, US ⊗

D: Victor Fleming **A:** Ernest Torrence, Clara Bow, Percy Marmont, Eugene Pallette (Paramount)

Clara Bow just walks away with the picture from the moment she steps into camera range. As a fast-working, slang-slinging manicurist from a swell barbershop in Minneapolis, who marries the big hick from the Canadian wilds, she is fitted just like a glove. The picture itself is a wow for laughs, action, and corking titles.

MAN TROUBLE

1992, 100 mins, US ⓥ ⊙

D: Bob Rafelson **A:** Jack Nicholson, Ellen Barkin, Harry Dean Stanton, Beverly D'Angelo, Michael McKean (Penta/American Filmworks/Budding Grove)

An insultingly trivial star vehicle. Jack Nicholson portrays a dog trainer who meets opera singer Ellen Barkin when she needs a guard dog. Scripter Carole Eastman drags in several pointless subplots. Main one concerns Beverly D'Angelo, who's penned a tell-all book about her relationship with reclusive billionaire Harry Dean Stanton. None of this adds up to entertainment or even momentarily involving escapism. Instead there's strenuously overacted comic set pieces, most of which fail.

MA NUIT CHEZ MAUD
(US: MY NIGHT AT MAUD'S)

1969, 110 mins, France ⓥ

D: Eric Rohmer **A:** Jean-Louis Trintignant, Francoise Fabian, Marie-Christine Barrault, Antoine Vitez, Anne Dubot (Losange/FFP/Simar/Carrosse/Gueville/Renn/Pleiade/Deux-Mondes)

A 34-year-old engineer (Jean-Louis Trintignant) runs into an old friend, a schoolteacher, who invites him to dinner at the home of his mistress, Maud (Francoise Fabian), a divorcée. The friend gets drunk and leaves them alone. Maud is a sensuous woman, but the engineer fends off her verbal and physical advances. A confirmed Catholic, he can no longer make love for its own sake. This moralistic fable is refined, knowing, and has a rich mixture of wit and revealing content.

MAN WHO CAME BACK, THE
See: Swamp Water

MAN WHO CAME TO DINNER, THE
1942, 112 mins, US ⓥ
D: William Keighley A: Bette Davis, Ann Sheridan, Monty Woolley, Jimmy Durante (Warner)

Monty Woolley is the bearded writer who is inveigled to dinner at a home in a small Ohio town where he happens to be lecturing and slips on the front steps. He's confined to a wheelchair there for three weeks and with his witty insults, domineering talk, and meddling in the affairs of his secretary and of the family with whom he is staying, brings havoc upon all.

MAN WHO FELL TO EARTH, THE
1976, 140 mins, UK ⓥ ⊙ ▭
D: Nicolas Roeg A: David Bowie, Candy Clark, Rip Torn, Buck Henry, Bernie Casey (British Lion)

David Bowie descends to Earth from another planet to secure water supply for the folks at home. It's a story that must be seen and not told, so rich is it in subplots mirroring the "pure" spaceman's reaction to a corrupt environment. In fact, pic is perhaps too cluttered with themes. Visually and aurally, it's stunning stuff throughout, and Bowie's choice as the ethereal visitor is inspired.

MAN WHO HAD POWER OVER WOMEN, THE
1970, 89 mins, UK ⓥ
D: John Krish A: Rod Taylor, Carol White, James Booth, Penelope Horner, Charles Korvin, Alexandra Stewart (Kettledrum)

Sex comedy, done in lively enough fashion, strays into more serious territory trying to show up the hollowness behind the tinselly pop world. Rod Taylor plays a disenchanted talent exec in an agency. His chilly wife (Penelope Horner) walks out and Taylor moves in temporarily with his best friend and colleague (James Booth), and latter's wife (Carol White), in whose arms Taylor finds solace.

MAN WHO HAUNTED HIMSELF, THE
1970, 94 mins, UK ⓥ
D: Basil Dearden A: Roger Moore, Hildegard Neil, Alastair Mackenzie, Hugh Mackenzie, Thorley Walters (Associated British)

Roger Moore plays a businessman guilty of reckless, out-of-character driving. From the moment of his recovery, he seems to be in two places at once. He apparently indulges in sharp business practice. He is apparently having an affair with a girl he has only once met. Has he an unscrupulous double? Or is it all a figment of his imagination? These add up to a tense riddle.

MAN WHO KNEW TOO MUCH, THE
1935, 74 mins, UK ⓥ ⊙
D: Alfred Hitchcock A: Leslie Banks, Edna Best, Peter Lorre, Frank Vosper, Hugh Wakefield, Nova Pilbeam (Gaumont-British)

An unusually fine dramatic story with a lot of melodramatic suspense. Starts at a party in St. Moritz. A man is shot during a dance. He whispers to a friend that there's a message in a brush in his bathroom. Friend realizes the dying man was in the secret service and gets the message. Before he can communicate with the police, he is handed a note saying his daughter has been kidnapped and will be killed if he talks. Acting is splendid most all of the way. Peter Lorre's work stands out again. He's the gang chief.

MAN WHO KNEW TOO MUCH, THE
1956, 119 mins, US ⓥ ⊙
D: Alfred Hitchcock A: James Stewart, Doris Day, Brenda de Banzie, Bernard Miles, Daniel Gelin (Paramount))

Good thriller. Hitchcock backstops his mystery in the colorful locales of Marrakesh in French Morocco and in London. While drawing the footage out a bit long, he still keeps suspense working at all times. Hitchcock did the same pic under the same title back in 1935. James Stewart's characterization is matched by the dramatic work contributed by Doris Day as his wife. Both draw vivid portraits of tortured parents when their son is kidnapped.
1956: Best Song ("Qué Sera, Sera (Whatever Will Be, Will Be)")

MAN WHO LOVED CAT DANCING, THE
1973, 114 mins, US ⓥ ▭
D: Richard C. Sarafian A: Burt Reynolds, Sarah Miles, Lee J. Cobb, Jack Warden, George Hamilton, Bo Hopkins (M-G-M)

Supposedly a period western told from a woman's viewpoint, pic emerges as a steamy, turgid meller, uneven in dramatic focus and development. Sarah Miles, fleeing from husband, George Hamilton, accidentally witnesses a train robbery and is virtually kidnapped by the gang. Role calls less for acting ability than a willingness to be dragged, beaten, stomped on, and abused in a variety of ways.

MAN WHO LOVED WOMEN, THE
1983, 110 mins, US ⊗
D: Blake Edwards A: Burt Reynolds, Julie Andrews, Kim Basinger, Marilu Henner, Barry Corbin, Cynthia Sikes (Columbia)

Truly woeful, reeking of production-line, big-star filmmaking and nothing else. Once again, Burt Reynolds appears as the irresistible, yet sensitive, modern man in search of something fulfilling in his life. Had not director Blake Edwards been fooling around with an "American extension" of Francois Truffaut's 1977 film of the same title, there probably was a better picture contained here in Reynolds's one really amusing sojourn into a bemused, adulterous affair with Kim Basinger.

MAN WHO NEVER WAS, THE
1956, 103 mins, UK ⊗ ▢ ▭
D: Ronald Neame A: Clifton Webb, Gloria Grahame, Robert Flemyng, Josephine Griffin, Stephen Boyd, Andre Morell (20th Century-Fox)

Of all the fantastic stories to come out of World War II, the use by British naval intelligence of a corpse to deceive the Germans about the planned invasion of Sicily undoubtedly outfictions fiction. The role of Montagu, the "master planner," is distinctly offbeat for Clifton Webb, and on the whole, he handles it competently. Josephine Griffin, a British newcomer, is completely believable.

MAN WHO SHOT LIBERTY VALANCE, THE
1962, 123 mins, US ⊗ ⊙
D: John Ford A: John Wayne, James Stewart, Vera Miles, Lee Marvin, Edmond O'Brien, Andy Devine (Paramount)

Entertaining and emotionally involving western falls distinctly shy of its innate story potential. Stewart, as a dude eastern attorney forging idealistically into lawless western territory, is promptly greeted by the sadistic brutality of Valance (Lee Marvin), a killer who owes his allegiance to the vested interests of wealthy cattlemen opposed to statehood, law, and order. The audience instantly senses that Stewart did

not fire the fatal shot that gives him his reputation and destines him for political fame. Had the body of the film (it is told in flashback) ended at this maximum point, it would have been a taut, cumulative study of the irony of heroic destiny.
1962: Nomination: Best B&W Costume Design

MAN WHO WATCHED TRAINS GO BY, THE
(US: THE PARIS EXPRESS)
1952, 80 mins, UK ⊗
D: Harold French A: Claude Rains, Marta Toren, Marius Goring, Anouk Aimée, Herbert Lom, Ferdy Mayne (Stross/Shaftel)

While it varies from the original Georges Simenon novel, this keeps to essentially the same main character. Claude Rains, loyal chief clerk to a firm of Dutch merchants, turns when he discovers his boss is running off with the firm's money. He takes the cash himself and goes to Paris, where he is involved in a series of implausible but exciting adventures. Rains plays the main role of the chief clerk with quiet, dignified restraint.

MAN WHO WOULD BE KING, THE
1975, 129 mins, US ⊗ ⊙ ▭
D: John Huston A: Sean Connery, Michael Caine, Christopher Plummer, Saeed Jaffrey, Shakira Caine (Columbia/Allied Artists)

Tale of action and adventure is a too-broad comedy, mostly due to the poor performance of Michael Caine. As a loudmouth braggart and former soldier in the Indian army, Caine joins forces with another veteran (Sean Connery) to make their fortunes in a mountain land beyond Afghanistan. Connery, in the title role, gives a generally credible, but not very sympathetic, portrayal. The most redeeming aspect of the film is the performance of Christopher Plummer as Rudyard Kipling.
1975: Nominations: Best Adapted Screenplay, Costume Design, Art Direction, Editing

MAN WITH A MILLION
See: The Million Pound Note

MAN WITH BOGART'S FACE, THE
1980, 106 mins, US ⊗
D: Robert Day A: Robert Sacchi, Franco Nero, Michelle Phillips, Olivia Hussey, Herbert Lom, Misty Rowe (20th Century-Fox)

Clearly and intentionally the picture is a gimmick. Bogart look-alike Robert Sacchi plays Bogart as Bogart himself might have portrayed private eye Sam Marlow, always relating incidents and personalities to stars and films of yesteryear. Producer Andrew J. Fenady, whose script is based on his own novel, has sprinkled his involved plot with a continuous flow of laugh lines. It adds up to a lot of fun.

MAN WITHIN, THE
(US: THE SMUGGLERS)
1947, 86 mins, UK
D: Bernard Knowles A: Michael Redgrave, Jean Kent, Joan Greenwood, Richard Attenborough, Francis L. Sullivan (Gainsborough)

This adaptation of Graham Greene's novel has much to commend it. Most glaring fault is amount of talk used. Most mature performance comes from Redgrave, who plays a gentleman smuggler with a sure touch. Attenborough, as the coward who finds courage, has his moments, but Joan Greenwood as Attenborough's real love is somewhat handicapped by a slow genuine Sussex dialect. Jean Kent is alarmingly modern as an 1820 vamp.

MAN WITHOUT A FACE, THE
1993, 114 mins, US ⓥ ⊙ ▭
D: Mel Gibson A: Mel Gibson, Nick Stahl, Margaret Whitton, Fay Masterson, Gaby Hoffmann, Geoffrey Lewis (Icon/Warner)

Mel Gibson's directing debut reinforces his status as a genuinely fine actor. Twelve-year-old Chuck (fine newcomer Nick Stahl) lives in a Maine coastal village with his uninterested mother (Margaret Whitton) and two difficult half sisters. Chuck dreams of getting into his late father's old military academy. Needing a tutor, he enlists the aid of Mr. McLeod (Gibson), a gruff, mysterious recluse whose teaching career was ended by an accident that scarred him and took the life of one of his students.

MAN WITHOUT A STAR
1955, 89 mins, US ⓥ ▭
D: King Vidor A: Kirk Douglas, Jeanne Crain, William Campbell, Claire Trevor, Richard Boone (Universal)

Kirk Douglas, in the title role, takes easily to the saddle as a tumbleweed cowpoke who has a way with a six-gun or the ladies. William Campbell scores as the young greenhorn who learns his cowboy-

ing from Douglas and about the wrong kind of women from Jeanne Crain. The plot is basic western in this setup of open versus fenced land, but writing variations keep it fresh and the action high as things move towards the climax.

MAN WITH THE DEADLY LENS, THE
See: Wrong Is Right

MAN WITH THE GOLDEN ARM, THE
1955, 119 mins, US ⓥ
D: Otto Preminger A: Frank Sinatra, Eleanor Parker, Kim Novak, Arnold Stang, Darren McGavin, Robert Strauss (Carlyle/United Artists)

Focuses on addiction to narcotics. Clinical in its probing of the agonies, this is a gripping, fascinating film, performed with marked conviction by Frank Sinatra as the drug slave. Sinatra returns to squalid Chicago haunts after six months in hospital where he was "cured" of his addiction. Eleanor Parker is a pathetic figure as his wife, pretending to be chair-ridden. Novel titles are by Saul Bass, and the music by Elmer Bernstein deftly sets the mood.
1955: Nominations: Best Actor (Frank Sinatra), B&W Art Direction, Scoring of a Dramatic Picture

MAN WITH THE GOLDEN GUN, THE
1974, 123 mins, UK ⓥ ⊙ ▭
D: Guy Hamilton A: Roger Moore, Christopher Lee, Britt Ekland, Maud Adams, Herve Villechaize, Clifton James (United Artists/Eon)

Screenwriters' mission this ninth time around was to give the James Bond character more maturity, fewer gadgetry gimmicks, and more humor. Story diverts Bond from tracking down a missing solar-energy scientist toward locating mysterious international hit man (Christopher Lee), who uses tailor-made gold bullets on his contract victims. To nobody's surprise, Lee has the solar-energy apparatus installed on his Hong Kong–area island hideaway. Bond finds some fade-out sack time for Britt Ekland, the local British intelligence charmer.

MAN WITH THE GREEN CARNATION, THE
See: The Trials of Oscar Wilde

MAN WITH THE X-RAY EYES, THE
See: X

MAN WITH TWO BRAINS, THE
1983, 93 mins, US Ⓥ ⊙

D: Carl Reiner **A:** Steven Martin, Kathleen Turner, David Warner, Paul Benedict, Richard Brestoff (Aspen/Warner)

Kathleen Turner proves to be a master at withholding her sexual favors from her frustrated husband, ace neurosurgeon Steve Martin, who decides to take her on a honeymoon to Vienna in an attempt to thaw her out. While there, Martin visits the lab of colleague David Warner and meets the love of his life, a charming woman and marvelous conversationalist who also happens to be a disembodied brain suspended in a jar. Too much of the film seems devoted to frantic overkill to compensate for general lack of belly laughs and top-notch inspiration.

MAN, WOMAN AND CHILD
1983, 99 mins, US Ⓥ

D: Dick Richards **A:** Martin Sheen, Blythe Danner, Sebastian Dungan, Arlene McIntyre, Missy Francis, David Hemmings (Paramount)

Sweetly dramatic picture unfortunately reaches so hard for sobs at the end that all logic is suspended. Martin Sheen is superb as a happily married husband of Blythe Danner. Trouble arrives with news that a brief fling of the past in France (seen in flashback with Nathalie Nell) has caused a problem for the present. Nell has been killed in an accident, leaving a son for Sheen that he never knew about. For Sheen, the only decent thing to do is confess all to Danner and invite the boy to the US.

MANXMAN, THE
1929, 98 mins, UK Ⓥ ⊗

D: Alfred Hitchcock **A:** Carl Brisson, Malcolm Keen, Anny Ondra, Randle Ayrton, Clare Greet (British International)

All there is to the story is Pete, a fisherman, having Philip, an attorney, for a buddy; Pete being in love with Kate; getting the cold mitt from her father because he is poor, and going abroad to make money, leaving Kate in care of Philip. Pete is said to be dead. Then he turns up and Philip persuades Kate her duty is to marry Pete. More is actually gotten out of it by direction and sharply defined characterization than there is in the story. There's a fair amount of suspense in the scenes between Pete and Kate arising out of the concealed parentage of the baby.

MAP OF THE HUMAN HEART
1993, 106 mins, UK/Australia/France/Canada Ⓥ ⊙ ▭

D: Vincent Ward **A:** Jason Scott Lee, Robert Joamie, Anne Parillaud, Patrick Bergin, John Cusack, Jeanne Moreau (Working Title/Ward/Ariane/Sunrise)

An immensely ambitious and audacious love story spanning 30 years and two continents. Much of it is set and filmed above the Arctic Circle in northern Canada, providing breathtaking icescapes. In 1931, a vintage aircraft lands on the ice near an Innuit Eskimo village, bringing with it dashing Brit, Walter Russell (Patrick Bergin). He befriends Avik (Robert Joamie), a cheerful young Innuit, who later forms a close friendship with a half-French Canadian, half-Indian girl, Albertine (Annie Galipeau). Ten years later, in 1941, Russell returns to the Arctic on a mission to track down a German U-boat and meets Avik (Jason Scott Lee) again. Hearing that Albertine (Anne Parillaud) is in Europe, Avik enlists in the Canadian air force. [Version reviewed was 126-minute "work in progress" shown at Cannes in May 1992.]

MARATHON MAN
1976, 125 mins, US Ⓥ ⊙

D: John Schlesinger **A:** Dustin Hoffman, Laurence Olivier, Roy Scheider, William Devane, Marthe Keller, Fritz Weaver (Paramount)

Film spends half of its length getting some basic plot pieces fitted and moving. By which time it's asking a lot if anybody still cares why Dustin Hoffman's brother Roy Scheider is a mysterious globe-trotter; why Laurence Olivier as an ex-Nazi disguises his appearance to leave a jungle hideaway to go to NY; why the memory of Hoffman's dishonored professor-father, a victim of the McCarthy era, relates to anything. Hoffman is stuck in the role of a bewildered man-in-the-middle about whom bodies fall like flies.

1976: Nomination: Best Supp. Actor (Laurence Olivier)

MARAT/SADE
See: The Persecution and Assassination of Jean-Paul Marat as Performed by the Inmates of the Asylum of Charenton under the Direction of the Marquis de Sade

MARCH OR DIE
1977, 106 mins, US ⊗

D: Dick Richards **A:** Gene Hackman, Terence Hill [Mario Girotti], Max von Sydow, Catherine Deneuve, Ian Holm, Jack O'Halloran (ITC-Associated General)

This Foreign Legion adventure caper has lots of actionful battle scenes, a few squeamish torture scenes, and beautiful photography. Terence Hill shows a tongue-in-cheek approach to his role that allows him to dominate every scene he's in. Biggest disappointment is the "acting" of Gene Hackman, who walks listlessly through the major role of a washed-out West Pointer who has given 16 years of his life to the Legion.

MARE NOSTRUM
1926, 113 mins, US

D: Rex Ingram **A:** Alice Terry, Antonio Moreno, Alex Nova (MGM)

War stuff from a naval angle and not too potent in the telling. The woman in the case, Freya (Alice Terry), is a German spy, and the man, Ulysses (Antonio Moreno), a Spanish sea captain who deserts his home for her. Few will deny that Ingram has turned out a picturesque gem. Barcelona, Pompeii, Naples, Marseilles—they're all there. But landscapes can't and don't make a picture which runs just five minutes short of two hours.

MARGARET'S MUSEUM
1995, 114 mins, Canada/UK ⊗

D: Mort Ransen **A:** Helena Bonham Carter, Clive Russell, Craig Olejnik, Kate Nelligan, Kenneth Welsh, Andrea Morris (Ranfilm/Imagex/TeleAction/Skyline)

Featuring a remarkable performance from Helena Bonham Carter, *Margaret's Museum* is an emotionally charged story about one woman's fight against the tyranny of the coal mine in her tiny Nova Scotia community. The script takes a witheringly tough stance on the deadly toll exacted by life—and death—in the coal mines. The title refers to the shrine that Margaret MacNeil (Bonham Carter) builds to commemorate her dead family members—which features various body parts preserved in all their gore.

MARIA'S LOVERS
1984, 100 mins, US ⊗ ⊙

D: Andrei Konchalovsky **A:** Nastassja Kinski, John Savage, Robert Mitchum, Keith Carradine, Bud Cort (Cannon)

A turbulent, quite particularized period romance about the sometime lack of synchronization of love and sex. Vet John Savage, who survived a Japanese prison camp, is terribly glad to be home in small-town Pennsylvania. His grizzled father Robert Mitchum gives Savage an understated welcome, and latter then has the misfortune of dropping by the home of his great love, Nastassja Kinski, just as she turns up in the grasp of another soldier, Vincent Spano.

LE MARI DE LA COIFFEUSE (US: THE HAIRDRESSER'S HUSBAND)
1990, 80 mins, France ⊗ ⊙ ▭

D: Patrice Leconte **A:** Jean Rochefort, Anna Galiena, Roland Bertin, Maurice Chevit, Philippe Clevenot (Lambart/TF1)

Another of director Patrice Leconte's original, hypnotic efforts about sexual longing and romantic obsession. Delicate and stylish, it's the story of a man who fulfills his childhood dream of marrying a lady hairdresser. Passionately in love, the lady barber frequently questions how long love will last. Jean Rochefort is outstanding as the man obsessed. Anna Galiena, who has a beautiful model-type presence, is a dream come true as his lovely wife.

MARIE
1985, 112 mins, US ⊗ ▭

D: Roger Donaldson **A:** Sissy Spacek, Jeff Daniels, Keith Szarabajka, Morgan Freeman, Fred Thompson (De Laurentiis)

Powerfully made political melodrama vitiated only by the relative familiarity of the exposé, little-person-vs.-the-establishment framework. Sissy Spacek adds another excellent characterization to her credits.

Spacek and her small kids leave home after she is brutalized by her husband. After educating herself further, she is appointed chairman of the parole board for the state of Tennessee. Ostensible friend Jeff Daniels, a close aide of Governor Blanton, frequently comes to Spacek with overt suggestions that they speed through the parole of certain individuals.

MARIE ANTOINETTE
1938, 160 mins, US ⊗ ⊙

D: W. S. Van Dyke **A:** Norma Shearer, Tyrone Power, John Barrymore, Robert Morley, Anita Louise, Joseph Schildkraut (M-G-M)

Produced on a scale of incomparable splendor and extravagance, *Marie Antoinette* approaches real greatness as cinematic historical literature. What is related on the screen is a brilliant, historic tragedy—the crushing of the French monarchy by revolution and terror. Norma Shearer's performance is lifted by skillful portrayal of physical and mental transitions through a score of years. Her moments of ardor with Ferson (Tyrone Power) are tender and believable. Robert Morley, who plays the vacillating King Louis XVI, creates sympathy and understanding for a dullard and misfit.

1938: Nominations: Best Actress (Norma Shearer), Supp. Actor (Robert Morley), Art Direction, Original Score

MARIE WALEWSKA
See: Conquest

MARIUS
1931, 127 mins, France Ⓥ
D: Alexander Korda A: Raimu, Pierre Fresnay, Orane Demazis, Charpin, Alida Rouffe (Paramount-Joinville)

Made from a popular legit hit [by Marcel Pagnol], and acted by the same cast, the screen version shows the call of the sea acting on the son, Marius (Pierre Fresnay), of an innkeeper, César (Raimu), whose sweetheart, Fanny (Orane Demazis), aids him to satisfy his craving for travel, despite his having seduced her. It's a very clever mixture of gags peculiar to the Marseilles locale, and of pathos created by the girl's self-sacrifice.

MARJORIE MORNINGSTAR
1958, 125 mins, US Ⓥ
D: Irving Rapper A: Gene Kelly, Natalie Wood, Claire Trevor, Everett Sloane, Ed Wynn (Warner/Beachwold)

Natalie Wood gives a glowing and touching performance as the title heroine. When Marjorie changes her name from Morgenstern to Morningstar, she unwittingly cuts herself off from her Jewish background and plunges without support into a world of no visible connections and even less stability. She falls in love with Gene Kelly, one of those fascinating men of small talent who flourish on the theatrical fringe of Broadway. He has changed his name, too, and the resulting rootlessness has left him uneasy and unsatisfied, although he never truly understands why.

1958: Nomination: Best Song ("A Very Precious Love")

MARKED FOR DEATH
1990, 94 mins, US Ⓥ ⊙
D: Dwight H. Little A: Steven Seagal, Basil Wallace, Keith David, Tom Wright, Joanna Pacula (Victor & Grais)

This dim-witted revenge yarn is the simplest of showcases for Steven Seagal—an extremely compelling action presence with his brutal martial-arts fighting style, imposing size, and nasty demeanor. It would be hard to imagine a more straightforward plot: former Drug Enforcement Agency troubleshooter Hatcher (Seagal) crosses a group of Jamaican drug dealers who mark him and his family for death. Naturally, he has to kill the leader to protect his loved ones.

MARKED WOMAN
1937, 96 mins, US Ⓥ ⊙
D: Lloyd Bacon A: Bette Davis, Humphrey Bogart, Isabel Jewell, Eduardo Ciannelli, Lola Lane, Jane Bryan (Warner)

A hard-hitting yarn of five girls working for a vice lady. They are hostesses in an elaborate clip joint, with Bette Davis the only one with any intention of eventually breaking away. Entanglement, and death, of her kid sister at the hands of Vanning, the boss, arouses her and the four other girls to become witnesses in the trial which washes him up. Davis's performance is rife with subtleties of expression and gesture. Humphrey Bogart as the prosecuting attorney is capable.

MARK OF ZORRO, THE
1940, 93 mins, US ▭
D: Rouben Mamoulian A: Tyrone Power, Linda Darnell, Basil Rathbone, Gale Sondergaard, Eugene Pallette, J. Edward Bromberg (20th Century-Fox)

The colorful background, detailing Los Angeles as little more than a pueblo settlement under the Spanish flag, is utilized for some thrilling melodramatics. Despite its obvious formula of hooded Robin Hood who terrorizes the tax-biting officials of the district to finally triumph for the peons and caballeros, picture holds plenty of entertainment. Power is plenty heroic and sincere in his mission. Sword duel between Power and Rathbone, running about two minutes, is a dramatic highlight.

1940: Nomination: Best Original Score

MARLOWE
1969, 95 mins, US Ⓥ
D: Paul Bogart A: James Garner, Gayle Hunnicutt, Carroll O'Connor, Rita Moreno, Bruce Lee (Katzka-Berne/Cherokee)

Plodding, unsure piece of so-called

sleuthing in which James Garner can never make up his mind whether to play it for comedy or hard-boil. Garner as the private eye is hired by a girl from Kansas to find her missing brother, then finds himself involved in a maze in which he's as mystified as the spectator.

MARNIE
1964, 130 mins, US Ⓥ ⊙
D: Alfred Hitchcock A: Tippi Hedren, Sean Connery, Diane Baker, Martin Gabel, Bruce Dern (Universal)

The character study of a thief and a liar—but what makes her tick remains clouded even after a climax reckoned to be shocking but somewhat missing its point. Hedren is recognized by her new employer, book publisher Connery, as the girl who stole $10,000 from a business associate, and rather than turn her in, he marries her. Balance of tale dwells on husband's efforts to ferret out mystery of why she recoils from the touch of any man—himself included—and why other terrors seem to overcome her. Hedren lends credibility to a part never sympathetic.

MAROC 7
1967, 91 mins, UK Ⓥ ▱
D: Gerry O'Hara A: Gene Barry, Cyd Charisse, Elsa Martinelli, Leslie Phillips, Denholm Elliott, Alexandra Stewart (Cyclone/Rank)

Story has Cyd Charisse as a sophisticated editress of a fashionable magazine. Her frequent trips abroad with a photographic team and a bunch of leggy models are ostensibly for magazine layouts, but actually are a front for daring jewel robberies. Suspecting this, special cop Gene Barry poses as a thief, and forces Charisse to let him tag along on her latest trip to Morocco. Cinemagoers will often be in doubt as to whether the characters are goodies or baddies and the answer never offers much of a kick. The genuine Moroccan backgrounds give a colorful zest to the action.

MAROONED
1969, 134 mins, US Ⓥ ▱
D: John Sturges A: Gregory Peck, Richard Crenna, David Janssen, James Franciscus, Gene Hackman, Lee Grant (Columbia)

What happens when a lunar rocket fails to fire for reentry to Earth's gravity? The men on such a capsule become lost in space. Such is the situation presented in this gripping drama, a superbly crafted, taut, and a technological cliff-hanger. The production's major flaw is a hokey old-fashioned Hollywood Renfrew-to-the-rescue climax that is dramatically, logically, and technologically unconvincing.

1969: Best Special Visual Effects
Nominations: Best Cinematography, Sound

MARRIAGE-GO-ROUND, THE
1960, 98 mins, US ▱
D: Walter Lang A: Susan Hayward, James Mason, Julie Newmar, Robert Paige (20th Century-Fox)

Rather tame and tedious film rotates laboriously around one joke—the idea that an amorous Amazonian doll from Sweden would match endowments, gene for gene, with a brilliant cultural anthropology professor from the US. Since the prof is a happily married monogamist, Miss Sweden's forward pass is intercepted right in the shadow of the goal (i.e., bed) posts. In the role of the professor, James Mason is competent. Susan Hayward does exceptionally well in the role of the wife. The intimacy of larger-than-life celluloid reveals a queen-sized heap of overacting from Julie Newmar as the blond bombshell.

MARRIAGE OF A YOUNG STOCKBROKER, THE
1971, 95 mins, US Ⓥ
D: Lawrence Turman A: Richard Benjamin, Joanna Shimkus, Elizabeth Ashley, Adam West, Tiffany Bolling (20th Century-Fox)

Richard Benjamin as a dull husband and Joanna Shimkus as his equally confused wife have an all-too-true marital blandness, disrupted by his predilection for eyeing girls. The hang-up is nowhere near criminal; in fact it's rather innocent. But Shimkus has had it, and packs off to Pasadena, where barracuda sister Elizabeth Ashley, who already has emasculated hubby Adam West, begins stage-managing a divorce. The varying elements of farce and satire in the genuine marital tragedy in progress are neatly interwoven.

MARRIED TO IT
1992, 110 mins, US Ⓥ ⊙
D: Arthur Hiller A: Beau Bridges, Stockard Channing, Robert Sean Leonard, Mary Stuart Masterson, Cybill Shepherd, Ron Silver (Orion/Three Pair)

Story brings together three couples

who gain perspective on their relationships through the course of their friendship. Problem here is one can never figure out why they're friends. Pic's most effective scenes are the knockdown fights about emotional issues.

MARRIED TO THE MOB
1988, 103 mins, US ⓥ ⊙

D: Jonathan Demme **A:** Michelle Pfeiffer, Matthew Modine, Dean Stockwell, Mercedes Ruehl, Alec Baldwin, Joan Cusack (Mysterious Arts/Orion)

Fresh, colorful, and inventive offbeat entertainment. Story line's basic trajectory has unhappy suburban housewife Michelle Pfeiffer taking the opportunity presented by the sudden death of her husband, who happens to have been a middle-level gangster, to escape the limitations of her past and forge a new life for herself and her son in New York City. The enormous cast is a total delight, starting with Pfeiffer, with hair dyed dark, a New York accent, and a continuously nervous edge. Matthew Modine proves winning as the seemingly inept FBI functionary, and Dean Stockwell is a hoot as the unflappable gangland boss. **1988: Nomination:** Best Supp. Actor (Dean Stockwell)

MARRYING KIND, THE
1952, 92 mins, US

D: George Cukor **A:** Judy Holliday, Aldo Ray, Madge Kennedy, Sheila Bond, Mickey Shaughnessy (Columbia)

A mélange of marital errors. The plot gets under way in a divorce court with a kindly judge, beautifully played by Madge Kennedy, former silent-screen name, trying to effect a reconciliation between Holliday and Ray, through talking out their troubles and misunderstandings. Footage then becomes a series of dialogue-laden flashbacks.

MARRYING MAN, THE
(UK/AUSTRALIA: TOO HOT TO HANDLE)
1991, 115 mins, US ⓥ ⊙

D: Jerry Rees **A:** Kim Basinger, Alec Baldwin, Robert Loggia, Elisabeth Shue, Armand Assante (Hollywood/Silver Screen Partners IV)

A stillborn romantic comedy of staggering ineptitude. Author Neil Simon reportedly disowned this film. An awkward flashback structure tells of egotistical toothpaste heir Alec Baldwin falling in love with chanteuse Kim Basinger on an outing to Las Vegas in 1948 with his buddies. Baldwin is forced into a shotgun wedding with Basinger by Armand Assante as Bugsy Siegel, Basinger's main man. Key plot point is that this is Bugsy's "revenge" for catching Baldwin in the sack with his g.f. Also unbelievable are the duo's several breakups and remarriages.

MARS ATTACKS!
1996, 103 mins, US ⓥ ⊙ ▱

D: Tim Burton **A:** Jack Nicholson, Glenn Close, Annette Bening, Pierce Brosnan, Danny DeVito, Martin Short (Warner)

A goofy cultural artifact, Tim Burton's *Mars Attacks!* is a cult sci-fi comedy miscast as an elaborate, all-star studio extravaganza. As the world awaits the Martians' landing, a gung-ho general (Rod Steiger) and the first lady (Glenn Close) urge the prez (Jack Nicholson) to nuke the visitors, while a pipe-smoking scientific advisor (Pierce Brosnan) assures everyone of the Martians' undoubted goodwill. When the big day arrives, the Martian spokesthing assures the crowd that they come in peace—and then abruptly leads its cohorts in deep-frying the assembled humans with ray guns. Script by British playwright Jonathan Gems, who worked closely with Burton in developing the story line, serves up any number of sweetly subversive scenes. But the picture is lacking in the uproarious humor that might well have ensued from the material. Computer-generated creatures interact with utter precision with the human actors.

MARTIN
1978, 95 mins, US ⓥ ⊙

D: George A. Romero **A:** John Amplas, Lincoln Maazel, Christine Forrest, Elayne Nadeau, Tom Savini (Braddock/Laurel)

Title character is a supposed 84-year-old vampire whose youthful visage has survived his escape from Romania through his contemporary journey to Braddock, Pa. This urban vampire kills not with his teeth, but with prepackaged razor blades. Romero has inserted some sepia-toned flashback scenes of Martin in Romania that are extraordinarily evocative, and his direction of the victimization scenes shows a definite flair for suspense.

MARTY
1955, 93 mins, US ⓥ ⊙

D: Delbert Mann **A:** Ernest Borgnine, Betsy Blair, Esther Minciotti, Augusta

Ciolli, Karen Steele (Hecht-Lancaster/United Artists)

Based on Paddy Chayefsky's teleplay, and screenplayed by the author, *Marty*'s a warm, human, sometimes sentimental, and an enjoyable experience. Basically, it's the story of a boy and girl, both of whom consider themselves misfits in that they are unable to attract members of the opposite sex. The boy is sensitively played by Ernest Borgnine and the girl is beautifully played by Betsy Blair. Chayefsky has caught the full flavor of bachelor existence in a Bronx Italian neighborhood.

1955: Best Picture, Director, Actor (Ernest Borgnine), Screenplay

Nominations: Best Supp. Actor (Joe Mantell), Supp. Actress (Betsy Blair), B&W Cinematography, B&W Art Direction

MARUSA NO ONNA (US: A TAXING WOMAN)

1987, 127 mins, Japan ⓥ ⊙

D: Juzo Itami **A:** Nobuko Miyamoto, Tsutomu Yamazaki, Masahiko Tsugawa, Hideo Murato, Shuji Otaki (Itami/New Century)

The taxing woman of the title is a tax inspector, but she is also taxing since she never tires or lets go of her prey once she has set her sights on him. The victim, in this case, is a hood operating adult motels and crooked real-estate deals. The heroine's running duel with the hood holds plenty of twists and surprises, as new plots and tricks for beating the tax rap are introduced and one by one unveiled by the law.

MARVIN'S ROOM

1996, 98 mins, US ⓥ ⊙

D: Jerry Zaks **A:** Meryl Streep, Leonardo DiCaprio, Diane Keaton, Robert De Niro, Hume Cronyn, Gwen Verdon (Tribeca/Miramax)

The most interesting aspect of *Marvin's Room* is observing Diane Keaton, Meryl Streep, and Leonardo DiCaprio submerge their idiosyncratic talents and personas in an effort to portray ordinary individuals. Bessie (Keaton) is a middle-aged woman in Orlando, FL, taking care of her dying father, Marvin (Hume Cronyn), and eccentric aunt (Gwen Verdon). Her younger sister, Lee (Streep), is a tough divorcee, raising rebellious Hank (DiCaprio) and quieter brother Charlie (Hal Scardino). A reunion of sorts is forced upon the sisters when Bessie is diagnosed with leukemia by Dr. Wally (Robert De Niro). Truly collaborating, Keaton and Streep render brilliant performances. The rest of the cast is flawless.

1996: Nomination: Best Actress (Diane Keaton)

MARY OF SCOTLAND

1936, 123 mins, US ⓥ ⊙

D: John Ford **A:** Katharine Hepburn, Fredric March, Florence Eldridge, Douglas Walton, John Carradine (RKO)

On the face of it, Katharine Hepburn would seem to be the wrong choice for the character of the Scots queen. She is nowhere as hard as she should be, she nowhere shows the strength of courage and decision that the schoolbooks talk of. And that is all in the film's favor because it humanizes it all. Fredric March as Hepburn's vis-à-vis, the swashbuckling Bothwell, is a natural and excellent choice. Florence Eldridge as Elizabeth, again a questionable choice from a strict historical standpoint, also turns in such a fine acting job as to convince quite definitely of the wisdom of it.

MARY POPPINS

1964, 140 mins, US ⓥ ⊙

D: Robert Stevenson **A:** Julie Andrews, Dick Van Dyke, David Tomlinson, Glynis Johns, Hermione Baddeley, Ed Wynn (Walt Disney)

Disney has gone all-out in his dream-world rendition of a magical Engish nanny who one day arrives on the East Wind and takes over the household of a very proper London banker. Besides changing the lives of everyone therein, she introduces his two young children to wonders possible only in fantasy. Julie Andrews's first appearance on the screen is a triumph and she performs as easily as she sings. Van Dyke, as the happy-go-lucky jack-of-all-trades, scores heavily, the part permitting him to showcase his wide range of talents.

1964: Best Actress (Julie Andrews), Song ("Chim-Chim-Cher-ee"), Original Musical Scoring, Editing, Visual Efects

Nominations: Best Picture, Director, Adapted Screenplay, Color Cinematography, Color Costume Design, Color Art Direction, Adapted Music Score, Sound

MARY, QUEEN OF SCOTS

1972, 128 mins, UK ▭

D: Charles Jarrott **A:** Vanessa Redgrave, Glenda Jackson, Patrick McGoohan, Timothy Dalton, Nigel Davenport, Trevor Howard (Universal)

Mary Stuart (Vanessa Redgrave) emerges as a romantic, immature, but idealistic young woman. Elizabeth (Glenda Jackson) had a well-oiled machine of intrigue. The result of such a dramatic imbalance renders Redgrave's character that of a storm-tossed waif, while Jackson benefits from a far more well-defined character. The face-to-face confrontations between the two women are said to be historically inaccurate. The script almost has to have one, and these brief climactic encounters are electric.

1971: Nominations: Best Actress (Vanessa Redgrave), Costume Design, Art Direction, Original Score, Sound

MARY REILLY
1996, 108 mins, US ⊗
D: Stephen Frears **A:** Julia Roberts, John Malkovich, George Cole, Michael Gambon, Glenn Close (Tri-Star)

Attempting a gothic-romance slant on the legend of Jekyll and Hyde, *Mary Reilly* has plenty of production polish but little of the dramatic force and erotic spark needed to vivify a tale of the famous split personality (John Malkovich) and his young chambermaid (Julia Roberts). Roberts tries hard and manages a convincing plaintiveness, but a plain Jane is hardly her strong suit, and she gets little help from Malkovich.

MARY SHELLEY'S FRANKENSTEIN
See: Frankenstein (1994)

M*A*S*H
1970, 116 mins, US ⊗ ⊙ ▭
D: Robert Altman **A:** Donald Sutherland, Elliott Gould, Tom Skerritt, Sally Kellerman, Jo Ann Pflug, Robert Duvall (20th Century-Fox/Aspen)

A Mobile Army Surgical Hospital (MASH), two minutes from bloody battles on the 38th Parallel of Korea, is an improbable setting for a comedy, even a stomach-churning, gory, often tasteless, but frequently funny black comedy. Elliott Gould, Donald Sutherland, and Tom Skerritt head an extremely effective, low-keyed cast of players whose skillful subtlety eventually rescue an indecisive union of script and technique.

1970: Best Adapted Screenplay
Nominations: Best Picture, Director, Supp. Actress (Sally Kellerman), Editing

MASK
1985, 120 mins, US ⊗ ⊙
D: Peter Bogdanovich **A:** Cher, Sam Elliott, Eric Stoltz, Estelle Getty, Richard Dysart, Laura Dern (Universal)

Based on a true story, *Mask* is alive with the rhythms and textures of a unique life. Rocky Dennis (Eric Stoltz) is a 16-year-old afflicted with a rare bone disease which has ballooned his head to twice its normal size and cast the shadow of an early death over him. Rocky is one of those rare individuals who has a vitality and gift for life and the emphasis here is not on dying, but living. The irony of the title is that his feelings are exposed far more than is customary and his experiences are intensified rather than dulled.

1985: Best Makeup

MASK, THE
1994, 101 mins, US ⊗ ⊙
D: Charles Russell **A:** Jim Carrey, Cameron Diaz, Peter Riegert, Peter Greene, Amy Yasbeck (New Line)

Offbeat romantic adventure showcase for the talents of Jim Carrey is adroitly directed, viscerally and visually dynamic, and just plain fun. Dejected sap Carrey spies what he thinks is a body floating in the river. He dives into the polluted waters only to discover a carved face mask. When he tries on the relic, drab mild-mannered Stanley morphs into a confident whirlwind of color. The dazzling special effects come as close as humanly possible to replicating the mayhem and invention of forties Warner Bros cartoons. The title character literally bounces off walls, and when he spies his dream girl Tina Carlyle (Cameron Diaz), his jaw puts a dent in the floorboards.

1994: Nomination: Best Visual Effects

MASK OF DIMITRIOS, THE
1944, 96 mins, US
D: Jean Negulesco **A:** Sydney Greenstreet, Zachary Scott, Faye Emerson, Peter Lorre, Victor Francen (Warner)

Dimitrios, which traces the yearlong international criminal career of one Dimitrios Makropoulos (played by Zachary Scott), has the benefit of a good cast headed by Sydney Greenstreet and Peter Lorre, but it is mostly a conversational piece that too frequently suggests action in the dialogue when, actually, the film itself practically has none.

MASK OF FU MANCHU, THE
1932, 66 mins, US
D: Charles Brabin **A:** Boris Karloff, Lewis Stone, Karen Morley, Charles Starrett, Myrna Loy, Jean Hersholt (M-G-M)

Fu Manchu's latest mission is discovery of the tomb of Genghis Khan. Possession of the mask and sword of Genghis would give Fu the leadership of the East. Then he could lead his subjects on to victory in the Western world, with ultimate extermination of the white race which he fanatically despises. So that Fu doesn't get to the late Genghis's paraphernalia first, Scotland Yard dispatches a museum expedition to the spot. After that it's a contest over the tomb's contents. Everybody is handicapped by the story and situations.

MASK OF ZORRO, THE
1998, 136 mins, US Ⓥ ⊙ ▭
D: Martin Campbell **A:** Antonio Banderas, Anthony Hopkins, Catherine Zeta-Jones, Stuart Wilson, Matt Letscher, Maury Chaykin (Amblin/TriStar)

The return of the legendary swordsman is well served by a grandly mounted production in the classic style. Pic lacks the snap and concision that would have made it bang-up entertainment, but it's closer in spirit to a vintage Errol Flynn or Tyrone Power swashbuckler than anything that's come out of Hollywood in quite some time. Pic favors dashing adventure, dramatic and political intrigue, well-motivated characters, and romance between mightily attractive leads. Zorro is the aristocratic Don Diego de la Vega (Anthony Hopkins). Outgoing Spanish governor Montero (Stuart Wilson) kidnaps Elena and throws Don Diego into a dungeon. Twenty years later, Montero is back with a devious scheme to buy Alta California. Now old and gray, Don Diego recruits an outlaw, Alejandro Murrieta (Antonio Banderas), and teaches him everything he knows as the reincarnation of Zorro.

MASQUE OF THE RED DEATH, THE
1964, 86 mins, UK Ⓥ ⊙ ▭
D: Roger Corman **A:** Vincent Price, Hazel Court, Jane Asher, David Weston, Patrick Magee, Nigel Green (Anglo Amalgamated)

Vincent Price is the very essence of evil, albeit charming when need be, and as film progresses the dark workings of his mind are stressed, tortuously intent on evil as a follower of the devil. He plays Prince Prospero, a tyrannical power in Spain in the Middle Ages, who seizes a young girl and tries to make her choose between him saving the life of her beloved or her father, even as the Red Death is killing off most of his impoverished serfs.

MASQUERADE
1965, 102 mins, UK
D: Basil Dearden **A:** Cliff Robertson, Jack Hawkins, Marisa Mell, Christopher Witty, Bill Fraser, Michel Piccoli (United Artists)

Clever, tongue-in-cheek spoof of cloak-and-dagger yarns involves kidnapping, disguised identity, macabre doings in a travelling circus, a mysterious Spanish girl, and escape from an eerie castle. The British Foreign Office hires Jack Hawkins and Cliff Robertson for a daring mission. Hawkins is an ex–war colonel and hero. Robertson is an American soldier of fortune who is down on his luck. Their job is to abduct the young heir to the throne of a Near East state.

MASQUERADE
1988, 91 mins, US Ⓥ ⊙
D: Bob Swaim **A:** Rob Lowe, Meg Tilly, Doug Savant, Kim Cattrall, John Glover (M-G-M/Levy)

A beautiful backdrop and dreamy settings aren't enough to compensate for uninvolving characters caught in an unsuspenseful scheme. Meg Tilly's womanizing, drunkard stepfather (John Glover) is in on a plot with Rob Lowe, who, unbeknownst to her, is intent upon securing her hand in marriage so that he and his buddy will be set for life. Lowe is a rake, the cocky captain of a racing boat while at the same time making it with the boat owner's much-younger wife (Kim Cattrall). Tilly's just out of a Catholic women's college, innocent and apparently chaste.

MASSACRE IN ROME
1973, 103 mins, Italy Ⓥ
D: George Pan Cosmatos **A:** Richard Burton, Marcello Mastroianni, Leo McKern, John Steiner (Champion)

Massacre in Rome depends on its dramatic documentary flavor for a number of spellbinding sequences and its polemical shafts at Vatican reticence in resisting the massacre of 300 Italian hostages in reprisal for a partisan assault on a German storm-troop detachment in Rome. Richard Burton as German security forces commander Colonel Kappler gets a richer role than his superiors and subordinates.

MASTER GUNFIGHTER, THE
1975, 121 mins, US ⊐
D: Frank Laughlin [Tom Laughlin] A: Tom Laughlin, Ron O'Neal, Lincoln Kilpatrick, GeoAnn Sosa, Barbara Carrera, Victor Campos (Billy Jack)

A curious blend of amateurish plotting and slick production values, film also presents an ambiguous moral attitude toward the Old West. The oater alternates sermonizing with gunfights and sword fights. The Laughlin character talks like a liberal but behaves like a reactionary, and therein lies the confusion. It's a throwback to an earlier age of swashbuckling, but the blend with contemporary bleeding-heart attitudes makes the film seem hypocritical.

MASTER OF BALLANTRAE, THE
1953, 88 mins, US ⓥ
D: William Keighley A: Errol Flynn, Roger Livesey, Anthony Steel, Beatrice Campbell, Yvonne Furneaux, Felix Aylmer (Warner)

Robert Louis Stevenson's novel provides a tailor-made vehicle for Errol Flynn. Picture was filmed mostly in Scotland, and the backgrounds are a colorful addition to the period values and escapism. Flynn's customary heroics are brought off with debonair dispatch, whether it's wooing the girls, dueling, or engaging in mass battle. He's seen as Jamie Durrisdeer, heir to the Scottish estate of Ballantrae, who joins a Stuart rebellion against the King of England, becomes a fugitive after the rebels are put down, and flees to the West Indies.

MASTER OF THE ISLANDS
See: The Hawaiians

MASTER RACE, THE
1944, 94 mins, US ⓥ
D: Herbert J. Biberman A: George Coulouris, Osa Massen, Stanley Ridges, Lloyd Bridges, Nancy Gates, Morris Carnovsky (RKO)

Picture opens with brief clips of the D-Day invasion of June 6, and then swings to headquarters of George Coulouris, member of the German general staff. Latter tells assemblage of German officers that the war is lost and they are to proceed according to individual instructions to points designated. Their purpose: create dissension among the peoples of the liberated countries and further destroy Europe so that the self-styled master race can again rise to rule the continent.

MASTERS OF THE UNIVERSE
1987, 106 mins, US ⓥ ⊙
D: Gary Goddard A: Dolph Lundgren, Frank Langella, Meg Foster, Billy Barty, Courteney Cox (Cannon)

All elements are of epic proportions in this *Conan–Star Wars* hybrid rip-off, based on the bestselling line of children's toys. Epitome of Good takes on Epitome of Evil for nothing less than the future of the Universe, and the result is a colossal bore. Dolph Lundgren's He-Man is an impressive physical specimen, the ultimate warrior epitomizing all that is good and defending the honor of inhabitants of the planet Eternia. On the dark side is the hideously made-up Frank Langella, as Skeletor. Makeup and costuming are universally good, special effects uninspiring.

MATADOR
1986, 102 mins, Spain ⓥ ⊙
D: Pedro Almodovar A: Assumpta Serna, Antonio Banderas, Nacho Martinez, Eva Cobo, Carmen Maura (Iberoamericana)

Angel (Antonio Banderas), an emotionally repressed 21-year-old who lives with his conservative harridan of a mother, secretly attends the bullfighting school of Diego (Nacho Martinez), a gored-into-retirement ex–champion matador with the sexual appetite of a lusty bull. Diego supplements his relationship with the gorgeous but vacuous fashion model Eva (Eva Cobo) with diversionary flings, hardcore bondage porn and "snuff" videos, and, as it transpires, the occasional murder of pretty girls. Almodovar unfolds his convoluted plot with zigzagging surrealism and a careening, sordidly erotic energy that effectively undermines the culturally institutionalized repression targeted by the filmmaker.

MATA HARI
1931, 90 mins, US ⓥ
D: George Fitzmaurice A: Greta Garbo, Ramon Novarro, Lionel Barrymore, Lewis Stone, C. Henry Gordon, Karen Morley (M-G-M)

Though Garbo is sexy and hot in a less subtle way this time, and though the plot goes about as far as it can in situation warmth, the story presents nothing sensational. Its few attempts at power are old style and all have been used before in similar trite spy stories. Garbo does a polite cooch to Oriental music as a starter. The finish is a neatly masked strip with Greta's back to the lens. Two other torrid moments later in the running are given to Garbo and Novarro. Both times they turn out the lights. Barrymore, as a broken general who loses his honor and finally his life through the glamorous Mata Hari, succeeds in inserting a punch in his moments of despair.

MATCHMAKER, THE
1958, 100 mins, US ⊗ ⊙
D: Joseph Anthony A: Shirley Booth, Anthony Perkins, Shirley MacLaine, Paul Ford, Robert Morse, Wallace Ford (Paramount)

Based on the Thornton Wilder Broadway hit; Shirley Booth takes the role of "marriage counselor," dominating character in this yarn of 1884. Its period action permits added opportunity for laughs, some of the belly genre. The screenplay catches every nuance of the situation of the widowed Booth ostensibly seeking a wife for the grasping Yonkers merchant (Paul Ford) while adroitly plotting to capture him for her own. Use of "asides" by various principals, speaking directly into the camera, peppers the action.

MATEWAN
1987, 130 mins, US ⊗ ⊙
D: John Sayles A: Chris Cooper, Will Oldham, Mary McDonnell, Bob Gunton, James Earl Jones, Kevin Tighe (Cinecom/Film Gallery/Red Dog)

A heartfelt, straight-ahead tale of labor organizing in the coal mines of West Virginia in 1920 that runs its course like a train coming down the track. Among the memorable characters is Joe Kenehan (Chris Cooper), a young union organizer who comes to Matewan to buck the bosses. Of the townfolk, 16-year-old Danny (Will Oldham) is already a righteous preacher and a seasoned union man who passionately takes up the workingman's struggle. Director John Sayles adds some texture to the mix by throwing in Italian immigrants and black migrant workers who become converted to the union side.
1987: Nomination: Best Cinematography

MATINEE
1993, 99 mins, US ⊗ ⊙
D: Joe Dante A: John Goodman, Cathy Moriarty, Simon Fenton, Omri Katz, Lisa Jakub (Universal/Renfield)

Joe Dante lovingly re-creates the monster pics of his youth in an okay film geared toward buffs that should have been much better. The real-life fears of the 1962 Cuban missile crisis interact with the artificial fears of a horror film premiering at a Key West movie house. Believably cast as a huckster/showman modeled after producer-director William Castle, John Goodman is previewing his new monster pic *Mant!* ("Half Man, Half Ant, All Terror!"). Film-in-a-film is a very accurate, hilarious black-and-white pastiche. Yet Dante lets his own film lapse into the excruciating clichés of both the "good teen" romances and the j.d. sagas of the fifties.

MATING GAME, THE
1959, 97 mins, US ▭
D: George Marshall A: Debbie Reynolds, Tony Randall, Paul Douglas, Fred Clark, Una Merkel (M-G-M)

Tony Randall plays a tax agent assigned to investigate the Maryland farm family headed by Paul Douglas and Una Merkel. Douglas gets Randall predictably drunk, and Randall is predictably smitten with one of the Douglas-Merkel offspring, hoydenish Debbie Reynolds. Most of this is foreseeable farce, and much of it is done with allusions to sex, of both the human and animal variety. Reynolds is very good. Randall, somewhat uncomfortable as a straight actor, is brilliant in his comedy scenes.

MATING SEASON, THE
1951, 101 mins, US
D: Mitchell Leisen A: Gene Tierney, John Lund, Miriam Hopkins, Thelma Ritter, Jan Sterling (Paramount)

Nominal stars are Gene Tierney and John Lund, but it is Thelma Ritter who glitters the brightest, having been given the pivotal character and choicest lines. Bolstering the comedy considerably is the fact laughs are not based on situations that are too farfetched, even though a plot springboard that finds a mother-in-law taking a maid's job in the home of her new daughter would seem to come under that heading. Scripters make it all seem perfectly logical, and the playing and direction strengthen that effect.
1951: Nomination: Best Supp. Actress (Thelma Ritter)

MATRIX, THE
1999, 136 mins, US ⊗ ⊙ ▭
D: Andy Wachowski, Larry Wachowski

A: Keanu Reeves, Laurence Fishburne, Carrie-Anne Moss, Hugo Weaving, Gloria Foster, Joe Pantoliano (Silver/Warner)

The Matrix offers an eye-popping but incoherent extravaganza of morphing and superhuman martial arts. A slacker-style software expert (Keanu Reeves) is led to the mysterious Morpheus (Laurence Fishburne), a cult leader who tells the recruit that he is The One, the savior, from 2,000 years in the future. The underground city of Zion, the last bastion of humankind, awaits The One to disrupt the Matrix, a power field controlled by humanoid computers that have created a ''virtual'' world fed by laboratory-controlled human energy. Cybertronically reconstituted and renamed Neo, the software expert is ready to do battle with the evil forces. The script never really gets on track, winding up in a muddle of showdowns, deaths, and resurrections that follow no rules.

1999: Film Editing, Sound, Sound Effects Editing, Visual Effects

MATTER OF INNOCENCE, A
See: Pretty Polly

MATTER OF LIFE AND DEATH, A (US: STAIRWAY TO HEAVEN)
1946, 104 mins, UK

D: Michael Powell, Emeric Pressburger **A:** David Niven, Kim Hunter, Marius Goring, Roger Livesey, Raymond Massey (Archers)

Like other Powell-Pressburger pictures, the striving to appear intellectual is much too apparent. Story is set in this world (graced with Technicolor) and the Other World (relegated to dye monochrome) as it exists in the mind of an airman whose imagination has been affected by concussion. Returning from a bomber expedition, squadron leader David Niven is shot up. Miraculously, he falls into the sea and is washed ashore apparently unhurt. In the Other World, there's much bother. Owing to delinquency of Heavenly Conductor Marius Goring, Niven has failed to check in, and Goring is dispatched to this world to persuade Niven to take his rightful place and balance the heavenly books.

MAURICE
1987, 140 mins, UK ⓋⓄ

D: James Ivory **A:** James Wilby, Hugh Grant, Rupert Graves, Denholm Elliott, Simon Callow, Billie Whitelaw (Merchant-Ivory)

Based on a posthumously published novel by E. M. Forster, this is a well-crafted pic on the theme of homosexuality. Maurice Hall (James Wilby) is seen attending Cambridge, where he meets handsome Clive Durham (Hugh Grant). Durham falls in love with him, and though resisting at first, Maurice later reciprocates, all on a platonic level. Maurice finally physically consummates his homosexual inclination with Durham's young gamekeeper Alec Scudder (Rupert Graves). Wilby gives a workmanlike performance, adequate to the role but never soaring. He is far outshadowed by a superlative supporting cast.

1987: Nomination: Best Costume Design

MAUSOLEUM
1983, 96 mins, US Ⓥ

D: Michael Dugan **A:** Marjoe Gortner, Bobbie Bresee, Normann Burton, Maurice Sherbanee, Laura Hippe (Western International)

An engaging minor film concerning demonic possession. Bobbie Bresee toplines as Susan Farrell, a 30-year-old woman who has been possessed by a demon at age 10. Twenty years after, the demon has finally taken over, going on a killing spree that arouses the suspicions of her husband, Oliver (Marjoe Gortner). Friend and psychiatrist Dr. Andrews (Norman Burton) is enlisted to help Susan, and ultimately bests the demon.

MAVERICK
1994, 129 mins, US ⓋⓄ ▢

D: Richard Donner **A:** Mel Gibson, Jodie Foster, James Garner, Graham Greene, James Coburn, Alfred Molina (Icon/Warner)

This exuberant western is a crowd pleaser that remains faithful to the genre while having a roaring good time sending up its conventions. The original *Maverick* was a popular television staple with James Garner. In its new big-screen incarnation, Mel Gibson takes up the mantle with glee. Jodie Foster as a sometimes treacherous temptress, Garner as a seasoned lawman, and a rogues' gallery of characters are along for the ride. Director Richard Donner serves it all up as one rollicking piece of dumb fun. But thanks to a keen, comical script by William Goldman and a sterling cast, it's smart dumb fun.

1994: Nomination: Costume Design

MAX DUGAN RETURNS
1983, 98 mins, US Ⓥ

D: Herbert Ross **A:** Marsha Mason, Jason Robards, Donald Sutherland, Matthew Broderick, Dody Goodman (20th Century-Fox)

A consistently happy comedic fable. Struggling to raise a 15-year-old son (Matthew Broderick) on a meagre teacher's salary, widow Marsha Mason maintains a wonderful attitude as life generally never quite works. Broderick is a good kid who accepts her poor-but-honest morality very well. In addition, there's a budding romance with Donald Sutherland, an exceptionally intelligent detective. Out of a dark night, however, returns Max Dugan (Jason Robards), the father who abandoned Mason when she was nine years old.

MAXIE
1985, 90 mins, US Ⓥ ⊙
D: Paul Aaron **A:** Glenn Close, Mandy Patinkin, Ruth Gordon, Barnard Hughes, Valerie Curtin (Orion/Aurora)

As forgettable as it is well meaning, *Maxie* represents a stab at an old-fashioned sort of romantic fantasy, the story of a dead person returning to inhabit the body of a living soul. Such is what happens to Close, the normal, cheerful wife of book specialist Patinkin. She has some very good comic moments, but Close may be too down-to-earth an actress for foolishness of this kind. Ruth Gordon, in her last film role, contributes another of her patented nutty-neighbor turns.

MAXIMUM OVERDRIVE
1986, 97 mins, US Ⓥ ⊙
D: Stephen King **A:** Emilio Estevez, Pat Hingle, Laura Harrington, Yeardley Smith, Ellen McElduff (De Laurentiis)

Master manipulator Stephen King, making his directoral debut from his own script, fails to create a convincing enough environment to make the kind of nonsense he's offering here believable or fun. He starts out with a small-town idyll soon disrupted by a mindless revolt of trucks. Truck stop is run as if it were a feudal fiefdom, complete with arsenal, by redneck despot Pat Hingle, who gives an amusing performance as a true screen swine.

MAXIMUM RISK
1996, 100 mins, US Ⓥ ⊙ ▭
D: Jean-Claude Van Damme, Natasha Henstridge, Zach Grenier, Jean-Hugues Anglade, Paul Ben-Victor, Frank Senger (Birnbaum-Diamant/Columbia)

Maximum Risk is a visceral delight that refuses to be deterred by niceties of plot or character consistency and prefers sweat to emotion. Alain Moreau (Jean-Claude Van Damme), a Frenchman discovers his deceased twin brother was New York City resident Mikhail Suverov. Assuming his brother's identity, he heads for the Big

Apple's Little Odessa. The good news is that Mikhail has a stunningly attractive girlfriend (Natasha Henstridge), but the bad news is that both the local Russian Mafia and corrupt FBI agents want him dead. Director Ringo Lam's U.S. studio debut looks like a high-gloss version of the potboilers he made in Hong Kong. If newcomer Henstridge has dramatic qualities, they will have to be discovered in another movie.

MAYERLING
1968, 140 mins, UK/France Ⓥ ▭
D: Terence Young **A:** Omar Sharif, Catherine Deneuve, James Mason, Ava Gardner, James Robertson Justice, Genevieve Page (Winchester/Corona)

Film misfires through a flattish script and uninspired performances by two leads, Omar Sharif and Catherine Deneuve. The political background—the always shaky Austrian throne, the students' violent protests, court intrigue—is introduced promisingly at the beginning, but later gets swamped in the romantic story, which is protracted, humorless, often hesitant and plodding.

MAYTIME
1937, 132 mins, US Ⓥ
D: Robert Z. Leonard **A:** Jeanette MacDonald, Nelson Eddy, John Barrymore, Herman Bing, Tom Brown, Lynne Carver (M-G-M)

Maytime has so many fine qualities that its length, occasional lapses into the superfluous, and betimes dull interludes will be acceptable. The vocal pièce de résistance, of course, is the Sigmund Romberg waltz ballad "Will You Remember?" perhaps better known as "Sweetheart, Sweetheart." It's chiefly MacDonald's picture. She looks her best in the Napoleonic period costumes, and is charming in her makeup as the venerable old lady, with a slightly mysterious past. Eddy carries through the worthy impression made by this pair in their past operetta successes. His robust baritone again nicely balances MacDonald's soprano.

1937: Nominations: Best Score, Sound

M. BUTTERFLY
1993, 100 mins, US Ⓥ ⊙
D: David Cronenberg **A:** Jeremy Irons, John Lone, Ian Richardson, Annabel Leventon, Shizuko Hoshi, Richard McMillan (Geffen/Warner)

Inspired by the true story of a French diplomat in China who conducted an 18-year affair with a native man he always thought was a woman, this butterfly just doesn't fly, due to lack of chemistry and heat on the part of the two leads. Irons's sang froid and dissolute air don't work for the role, and all the effort in the world can't prevent Lone from looking like a man in drag.

McBAIN
1991, 102 mins, US Ⓥ ⊙
D: James Glickenhaus **A:** Christopher Walken, Maria Conchita Alonso, Michael Ironside, Steve James, Jay Patterson (Shapiro Glickenhaus)

Silly action film. Prologue has Chick Vennera and fellow soldiers rescuing POW Christopher Walken on the day the Vietnam War ended in 1973, so Walken owes him one. When Vennera is killed in an abortive coup of the Colombian government 18 years later, Walken agrees to help Vennera's sister (Maria Conchita Alonso) overthrow the drug-cartel-run dictatorship there and let the common people come to power. Cartoonish action is amusing but never gripping. Walken appears awkward and bored.

McCABE AND MRS. MILLER
1971, 121 mins, US Ⓥ ⊙ ⊐
D: Robert Altman **A:** Warren Beatty, Julie Christie, René Auberjonois, William Devane, Shelley Duvall, Keith Carradine (Warner)

A period story about a small northwest mountain village where stars Warren Beatty and Julie Christie run the bordello, the production suffers from overlength; also a serious effort at moody photography that backfires into pretentiousness; plus a diffused comedy-drama plotline that is repeatedly shoved aside in favor of bawdiness. Beatty seems either miscast or misdirected. His own youthful looks cannot be concealed by a beard, makeup, a grunting voice, and jerky physical movements. Christie, on the other hand, is excellent.
1971: Nomination: Best Actress (Julie Christie)

McGUIRE, GO HOME!
See: The High Bright Sun

McHALE'S NAVY
1964, 93 mins, US
D: Edward J. Montagne **A:** Ernest Borgnine, Joe Flynn, Tim Conway, Carl Ballantine, George Kennedy (Universal)

One wonders how America won the war in the Pacific, if the exploits of Lieutenant Commander Quinton McHale and his PT-boat crew were typical of that dark period in US history. Like its original TV counterpart, action here depends upon outlandish situations in which McHale and his crew, who do things the "McHale" way first and the navy's way second, get involved. In the present case, it's getting out of debt.

MCKENZIE BREAK, THE
1970, 106 mins, US Ⓥ
D: Lamont Johnson **A:** Brian Keith, Helmut Griem, Ian Hendry, Patrick O'Connell, Caroline Mortimer (United Artists)

A taut, classically crafted World War II POW escape drama with an original twist. This time it is the Germans, a corps of crack U-boat officers, led by Helmut Griem, breaking out of a camp in Scotland. An imaginative, intelligent script, crackling direction, and strong, three-dimension portrayals by Griem and Brian Keith, as a British intelligence officer trying to outguess and outmaneuver the Nazi, transform the film into a tense personal duel that maintains its suspense until the final frames.

McLINTOCK!
1963, 127 mins, US ⊐
D: Andrew V. McLaglen **A:** John Wayne, Maureen O'Hara, Yvonne De Carlo, Patrick Wayne, Stefanie Powers (Batjac/United Artists)

A John Wayne western. The style of the production is forked-tongue-in-cheek. Nucleus of yarn is the marital duel between Wayne, straight-shooting, rough-and-tumble, high-living, hard-drinking cattle baron, and Maureen O'Hara, who has more reservations than a Comanche real-estate agent. Wayne is in his element, or home, home on the Waynge.

MCQ
1974, 115 mins, US Ⓥ ⊙ ⊐
D: John Sturges **A:** John Wayne, Eddie Albert, Diana Muldaur, Colleen Dewhurst, Clu Gulager, Al Lettieri (Batjac/Warner)

Good contemporary crime actioner filmed entirely in Seattle, with John Wayne discovering that his slain buddy was a member of a crooked police ring stealing dope evidence. Featured as an aging bar waitress from whom Wayne obtains evidence, Colleen Dewhurst is outstanding in her two scenes.

MCVICAR
1980, 111 mins, UK Ⓥ ⊙
D: Tom Clegg **A:** Roger Daltrey, Adam Faith, Cheryl Campbell, Brian Hall, Ian

Hendry (Curbishley-Baird/The Who)

A conscientious reconstruction of several crucial months in the life of John McVicar, who escaped from the high-security wing of an English prison where he was serving eight years for robbery with violence. Roger Daltrey projects a disquieting mix of danger and vulnerability.

ME AND MY GAL
1932, 79 mins, US
D: Raoul Walsh **A:** Spencer Tracy, Joan Bennett, Marion Burns, George Walsh (Fox)

A story about a cop, the waitress he finally marries, and the girl's sister who gets tangled up with a rodman. That's about all. Spencer Tracy makes a good cop. Joan Bennett doesn't make as good a hard-boiled waitress, but she gets by with it. Picture is not altogether a dud through having some comedy.

ME AND MY GAL
1942, 94 mins, US
D: Busby Berkeley **A:** Judy Garland, George Murphy, Gene Kelly, Richard Quine, Horace McNally (M-G-M)

Story of vaudeville troupers before and during the First World War is obvious, nave, and sentimental. It's also genuine and affectionate and lively. Garland is a knockout as the warmhearted young song-and-dance girl, giving a tender, affecting dramatic performance. Kelly gives a vividly drawn portrayal of the song-and-dance man and imperfect hero.

MEAN MACHINE, THE
See: The Longest Yard

MEAN SEASON, THE
1985, 103 mins, US ⓥ ⊙ ▭
D: Phillip Borsos **A:** Kurt Russell, Mariel Hemingway, Richard Jordan, Richard Masur, Richard Bradford (Orion)

Pic establishes solid Florida heat and humidity as the ''mean'' background to a series of murders that perversely link together the killer (Richard Jordan) and a Miami police reporter (Kurt Russell). Jordan is at his shrewdly crazed best, anchoring the movie with a felt terror. Russell plays a reporter who gets swept away with all the national hype he's getting as the only man who can talk to the killer.

MEAN STREETS
1973, 110 mins, US ⓥ ⊙
D: Martin Scorsese **A:** Robert De Niro, Harvey Keitel, David Proval, Amy Rob-

inson, Cesare Danova (TPS/Warner)

In essence, *Mean Streets* is an updated, downtown version of *Marty* (1955), with small-time criminality replacing those long stretches of beer drinking in a Bronx bar. Four aging adolescents, all in their mid-20s but still inclined toward prankish irresponsibility, float among the lower-class denizens of Manhattan's Little Italy, struggling to make a living out of loan-sharking, the numbers game, and bartending. Scorsese is exceptionally good at guiding his largely unknown cast to near-flawless re-creations of types. Outstanding in this regard is De Niro.

MEATBALLS
1979, 92 mins, Canada ⓥ ⊙
D: Ivan Reitman **A:** Bill Murray, Harvey Atkin, Kate Lynch, Russ Banham, Kristine DeBell (Paramount)

It's difficult to come up with a more clichéd situation than a summer camp, where all the characters and plot turns are readily imaginable. That makes director Ivan Reitman's accomplishment all the more noteworthy. Scripters have managed to gloss over the stereotypes and come up with a smooth-running narrative that makes the camp high jinks part of an overall human mosaic. No one is unduly belittled or mocked, and *Meatballs* is without the usual grossness and cynicism of many contempo comedy pix.

MECHANIC, THE
1972, 100 mins, US ⓥ ⊙
D: Michael Winner **A:** Charles Bronson, Keenan Wynn, Jan-Michael Vincent, Jill Ireland, Frank de Kova (United Artists)

A mechanic, in underworld parlance, is a highly skilled contract killer. Possibilities of limning such a character are realistically pointed up in this action-drenched gangster yarn burdened with an overly contrived plot. Bronson plays the son of a former gang leader cut down in his prime, left a fortune, but still associated with crime as a hired executioner.

MEDICINE MAN
1992, 106 mins, US ⓥ ⊙ ▭
D: John McTiernan **A:** Sean Connery, Lorraine Bracco, Jose Wilker, Rodolfo De Alexandre, Angelo Barra Moreira (Hollywood/Cinergi)

An indelicate attempt to create some *African Queen*–style magic while curing cancer and saving the rain forests in the bargain, this jumbo-budget two-character piece suffers from a very weak script and a lethal job of miscasting. Ponytailed and bearded, Sean Connery portrays a maverick biochemist who's been working in the Amazon for six years when his sponsoring company sends a researcher to check up on him. She is played by Lorraine Bracco, whose manner is so abrasive that it's a wonder Connery doesn't just toss her to the crocodiles.

MEDITERRANEO
1991, 105 mins, Italy ⓥ ⊙

D: Gabriele Salvatores **A:** Diego Abatantuono, Claudio Bigalli, Giuseppe Cederna, Claudio Bisio, Gigio Alberti (Pentafilm/AMA)

Eight Italian soldiers are sent to garrison a remote, strategically unimportant Greek island during World War II. As they adapt to island life, the delicate comic moments stay just on the right side of schlocky: one soldier mourns his beloved donkey, a burly boy falls quietly in love with the sergeant, two brothers and a shepherdess have a sexually spiritual ménage à trois, and the group underdog and the local prositute undergo a little courtship. The pic is rich in affectionate new slants on old Italo emblems like soccer, sex, and snappy dressing. The ensemble work of the performers and crew give this pic much of its buoyancy.
1991: Best Foreign Language Film

MEDIUM, THE
1951, 85 mins, US ⓥ

D: Gian-Carlo Menotti **A:** Marie Powers, Anna Maria Alberghetti, Leo Coleman, Belva Kibler, Beverly Dame (Transfilm)

An impressive pic that it is stark modern opera, all in song or recitative. Menotti filmed the opus in Rome, utilizing Marie Powers and Leo Coleman from the original legit cast, and the 15-year-old Italian coloratura find, Anna Maria Alberghetti, in her film debut, for the third principal. Menotti is too fond of the camera, and too intent on trick angles and effects. He overworks the close-ups. But he comes up with some nifty shots that dovetail with the bizarre opus. Story is that of a shabby medium, Madame Flora (Powers), living with her daughter Monica (Alberghetti), and Toby, a mute gypsy waif they adopted (Coleman), and the séances they hold for gullible clients.
1950: Nomination: Best Scoring of a Musical Picture

MEDIUM COOL
1969, 110 mins, US ⓥ

D: Haskell Wexler **A:** Robert Forster, Verna Bloom, Peter Bonerz, Marianna Hill, Harold Blankenship (Paramount/H&J)

Photographed in Chicago against the clamor and violence of the 1968 Democratic National Convention, where cast principals were on their own as they made their way through the crowds and police lines. Buildup to these later sequences frequently is confusing and motives difficult to fathom. Director mixes "reality" with the "theatrical," his two chief protagonists a realistic TV newsreel cameraman and a young hillbilly mother come to Chicago with her young son.

MEDUSA TOUCH, THE
1978, 110 mins, UK/France ⓥ

D: Jack Gold **A:** Richard Burton, Lino Ventura, Lee Remick, Harry Andrews, Marie-Christine Barrault, Michael Hordern (ITC/Coatesgold)

John Morlar (Richard Burton) is attacked by an unknown intruder who bashes in his skull. Why? The man didn't seem to have a single enemy. Inspector Brunel is puzzled. Why a French detective instead of British? Apparently due to French financial participation in this film. In any case, it allows Lino Ventura to make his British film debut and very good he is. It turns out that Morlar is not dead at all. His mind is fighting a desperate battle to survive.

MEETING VENUS
1991, 117 mins, UK ⓥ ⊙

D: Istvan Szabo **A:** Glenn Close, Niels Arestrup, Erland Josephson, Moscu Alcalay, Macha Meril (Enigma)

Glenn Close hits the high notes as a cool diva, but romantic comedy set in a strife-torn Paris opera house is knocked on the head by a central love story that's dumb and uninvolving. Yarn opens in sprightly style with Budapest conductor (Niels Arestrup) flying in for a production of Wagner's *Tannhauser* at the fictional Opera Europa. After being introduced to polyglot staff, he soon realizes that "here you can be misunderstood in six languages." Things start to go wrong when the Close-Arestrup affair gets serious.

MEET JOE BLACK
1998, 180 mins, US ⓥ ⊙

D: Martin Brest **A:** Brad Pitt, Anthony Hopkins, Claire Forlani, Jake Weber, Marcia Gay Harden, Jeffey Tambor (City Light/Universal)

This thoroughly over-elaborated whimsy dawdles disractedly in delineating one man's confrontation with death, in the person of a handsome young stranger who assumes human form for a few days and falls in love along the way. New York media tycoon William Parrish (Anthony Hopkins) suffers a heart seizure. Death materializes in the guise of a visitor by the name of Joe Black (Brad Pitt), who informs the older man he can buy some time by acting as his guide to all things earthly. William's daughter Susan (Claire Forlani) is determined to figure out who the mystery man is, and sure enough she maneuvers him into her arms. Hopkins plays with tremendous verve and sympathy, but the character seems impossibly idealized. Looking dashing and slightly impish, Pitt's Joe Black is an odd egg indeed.

MEET JOHN DOE
1941, 129 mins, US Ⓥ ⊙
D: Frank Capra A: Gary Cooper, Barbara Stanwyck, Edward Arnold, Walter Brennan, Spring Byington, James Gleason (Capra/Warner)

Picture tells the story of the rehabilitation of a tramp ex–baseball player who assents to the role of a puppet social reformer in the hands of a young newspaperwoman. The heroine invents a fictitious John Doe as author of a letter of protest against the prevailing injustices of a political and social system which permits hunger and idleness. He declares he will commit suicide on Christmas Eve in expiation for the sins of society. The synthetic fabric of the story is the weakness of the production, despite the magnificence of the superstructure.

1941: Nomination: Best Original Story

MEET ME AFTER THE SHOW
1951, 86 mins, US
D: Richard Sale A: Betty Grable, Macdonald Carey, Rory Calhoun, Eddie Albert, Fred Clark (20th Century-Fox)

Top-notch escapist musical entertainment. A star-producer, husband-wife team breaks up because the missus suspects that hubby is chasing other gals. As the supposedly wronged wife, Grable feigns amnesia and goes back to the cheap nightclub where hubby Macdonald Carey had first discovered her. Carey and Eddie Albert, longtime suitor of Grable, pursue her, and plenty of comedy touches are poured on for laughs as they try to protect her from

a sea-loving nature boy, neatly portrayed by Rory Calhoun,and bring back her memory.

MEET ME AT THE FAIR
1952, 87 mins, US
D: Douglas Sirk A: Dan Dailey, Diana Lynn, Chet Allen, Scatman Crothers, Hugh O'Brian, Carole Mathews (Universal)

The production has a period flavor featuring nostalgia and schmaltz against a 1904 setting. The old-fashioned drama revolves around an orphan kid who runs away from a grim institution, takes up with a medicine man, with his new friend charged with kidnapping. Best in the musical department is Carole Mathews doing ''Bill Bailey'' and the title number. Dailey is very likable as the medicine man.

MEET ME IN ST. LOUIS
1944, 118 mins, US Ⓥ ⊙
D: Vincente Minnelli A: Judy Garland, Margaret O'Brien, Mary Astor, Lucille Bremer, Tom Drake, Marjorie Main (M-G-M)

It's the time of the St. Louis fair, hence the title song, and everything that makes for the happy existence of a typical American family is skillfully panoramaed. Seasonal pastorals, from summer into the next spring, take the Smith clan through their appealing little problems. Judy Garland's plaint about ''The Boy Next Door'' (played by Tom Drake); the Paul Jones dance routine to the tune of ''Skip to My Lou''; the holiday ''Have Yourself a Merry Christmas''; and the ''Trolley Song,'' en route to the fairgrounds, are four socko musical highlights. Garland achieves true stature with her deeply understanding performance, while her sisterly running mate, Lucille Bremer, likewise makes excellent impact.

1944: Nominations: Best Color Cinematograhy, Scoring of a Musical Picture, Song (''The Trolley Song'')

MEET THE APPLEGATES
(AUSTRALIA: THE APPLEGATES)
1991, 82 mins, US Ⓥ ⊙
D: Michael Lehmann A: Ed Begley Jr., Stockard Channing, Cami Cooper, Bobby Jacoby, Dabney Coleman (New World)

In a bid to save the Brazilian rain forest, a family of giant beetles is sent to infiltrate American society and blow up a nuclear power station as a warning. Chameleonlike, they assume the form of humans, and become the average America family. Surrounded by temptations in a community-minded town in Ohio, the family soon degenerates. Such a wacky premise could derail easily, but Lehmann handles it with humor and paces it well. Scenes of the Applegates becoming bugs (usually with disastrous consequences) are cleverly done.

MEET WHIPLASH WILLIE
See: The Fortune Cookie

MELANCHOLIA
1989, 87 mins, UK/W. Germany Ⓥ
D: Andi Engel **A:** Jeroen Krabbé, Susannah York, Ulrich Wildgruber, Jane Gurnett, Kate Hardie (BFI/Lichtblick)

Stimulating contemporary thriller about an idealist from the 1960s who decides to take violent action in support of his long-submerged beliefs. Jeroen Krabbé plays a German, Keller, long resident in London. He is aroused from his inertia by a phone call asking him to assassinate a Chilean torturer Vargas, currently visiting London. The film raises questions about the use of violence to prevent further violence, and about the passivity of idealists. It doesn't play as a straight commercial thriller, but as a serious pic exploring provocative themes with intelligence.

MELODY
1971, 103 mins, UK Ⓥ
D: Waris Hussein **A:** Jack Wild, Mark Lester, Tracy Hyde, Sheila Steafel, Roy Kinnear (Hemdale/Sagittarius)

The story of a couple of 10-year-olds who fall in love and want to get married. Mark Lester and Tracy Hyde are the very young lovers forthrightly present their marriage plans to their parents and teachers. Screenwriter Alan Parker and director Waris Hussein are to be congratulated for attempting something that—whatever its surface strains on credulity—is a lot closer to what kids are about than the mush they're usually served at matinees. The acting by the adults is intentionally exaggerated, as if seen through the kids' eyes, and the young people, for the most part, are both natural and appealing.

MELODY OF LIFE
See: Symphony of Six Million

MELVIN AND HOWARD
1980, 93 mins, US Ⓥ
D: Jonathan Demme **A:** Paul Le Mat, Jason Robards, Mary Steenburgen, Michael J. Pollard, Dabney Coleman, Gloria Grahame (Universal)

Fable about the elusiveness of the American Dream is a richly textured, highly individualistic look at Melvin Dummar, a man in over his head both before and after becoming the beneficiary of $156 million via Howard Hughes's so-called Mormon will. Despite Jason Robards's amusing portrait of Hughes as a grizzled old coot, pic takes a while to generate a full head of steam.

1980: Best Supp. Actress (Mary Steenburgen), Original Screenplay
Nomination: Best Supp. Actor (Jason Robards)

MEMOIRS OF AN INVISIBLE MAN
1992, 99 mins, US Ⓥ ⊙ ☐
D: John Carpenter **A:** Chevy Chase, Daryl Hannah, Sam Neill, Michael McKean, Stephen Tobolowsky (Warner/Cornelius)

Main problem with this mildly entertaining special-effects showcase proves as transparent as its title character—namely that Chevy Chase, who can only play Chevy Chase, lacks leading-man qualities necessary to make this sort of Hitchcockian man-in-peril scenario work. Director and a trio of screenwriters go the espionage route with a comedy twist, but the film fails to satisfy fully on either level.

MEMOIRS OF A SURVIVOR
1981, 117 mins, UK Ⓥ
D: David Gladwell **A:** Julie Christie, Christopher Guard, Leonie Mellinger, Debbie Hutchins, Nigel Hawthorne (EMI/Memorial/NFFC)

Julie Christie's D, an attractive middle-aged woman living alone in the midst of chaos, dreams of a Victorian time and can go through a wall to witness events. A little girl, maybe her, is seen in the rich, gilded interiors adroitly given a candle-light feeling by lenser Walter Lassally. But reality is grim. A teenage girl is moved in with D and she takes care of her. The girl becomes involved with a young man trying to help vagrant children, living in an abandoned subway station. They have already killed one of his helpers and cannibalized others.

MEMPHIS BELLE
1990, 106 mins, UK Ⓥ ⊙
D: Michael Caton-Jones **A:** Matthew Modine, Eric Stoltz, Tate Donovan, D. B. Sweeney, David Strathairn, John Lithgow (Enigma)

Offering a romanticized view of heroism drawn from the Hollywood war epic, pic's subject is the 25th and final mission of the *Memphis Belle,* the most celebrated of the US Air Force B-17 bombers. The plane flew 24 perfect missions, and its 25th became part of a massive p.r. drive to boost war-bond sales and morale. The plane and its team are sent to Germany to drop one last load, setting the scene for suspense, tension, terror, and a fitting celebration when all return safe and (almost) sound.

MEN, THE
1950, 85 mins, US ⓥ
D: Fred Zinnemann A: Marlon Brando, Teresa Wright, Everett Sloane, Jack Webb, Richard Erdman (United Artists)

The difficult cinematic subject of paraplegics, treated expertly, becomes sensitive, moving, and yet entertaining and earthy-humored. From the opening shot, a tensely played battle scene where Lieutenant Wilozek (Marlon Brando) suffers his crushing wound, film maintains its pace and interest. Thereafter, it centers on the overwhelming problems of paralyzed vets who must be convinced that their wounds are incurable and that they must yet fight their way to a useful existence. Brando, who film-debuts as Wilozek, fails to deliver the necessary sensitivity and inner warmth.
1950: Nomination: Best Story & Screenplay

MENAGE
See: Tenue de Soiree

ME, NATALIE
1969, 110 mins, US
D: Fred Coe A: Patty Duke, James Farentino, Martin Balsam, Elsa Lanchester, Salome Jens (Cinema Center)

Sensitive, often-poignant drama painted with a light touch of an ugly duckling trying to find her place in the scheme of things. Patty Duke, in title role, delivers a warm, roundly developed characterization of a girl who all her life has tried to be pretty, and is keenly aware she isn't nor ever will be. As the mother, Nancy Marchand delivers a tremendous performance.

MEN DON'T LEAVE
1990, 113 mins, US ⓥ ⊙
D: Paul Brickman A: Jessica Lange, Chris O'Donnell, Charlie Corsmo, Arliss Howard, Joan Cusack (Geffen/Warner)

Quietly moving tale of a widow (Jessica Lange) and her struggle to support her two sons in shabby Baltimore surroundings. The title misleadingly suggests a feminist tract, not the warmhearted comedy-drama this pic becomes. The film's dramatic heart is a sequence showing Lange, after losing her job in a blowup with restaurant boss Kathy Bates, descending into a catatonic state and refusing to leave her bed for days as the apartment turns into a quiet vision of hell. It's a scary piece of acting by Lange, beautifully directed by Brickman, and it turns a somewhat meandering film into a memorable emotional experience.

MENG LONG GUO JIANG
(US: THE WAY OF THE DRAGON;
WAY OF THE DRAGON; RETURN
OF THE DRAGON)
1972, 100 mins, Hong Kong ⓥ ▭
D: Bruce Lee A: Bruce Lee, Nora Miao, Chuck Norris, Marisa Longo, Robert Wall, Whong In-sik (Golden Harvest/Concord)

Written and directed by Chinese chopsocky superstar Bruce Lee and filmed both in Hong Kong and Rome, film is noteworthy more for the martial arts action than for narrative. Highlight is the exciting climax as Lee and an international karate champ (Chuck Norris) hired by the gangsters battle it out on one of the upper levels of the Colosseum.

MEN IN BLACK
1997, 98 mins, US ⓥ ⊙
D: Barry Sonnenfeld A: Tommy Lee Jones, Will Smith, Linda Fiorentino, Vincent D'Onofrio, Rip Torn, Tony Shalhoub (Amblin)

A witty and sometimes surreal sci-fi comedy, *Men in Black* is a wild knuckleball of a movie that keeps dancing in and out of the strike zone. The fabulous first half-hour could scarcely be more droll in establishing how top-secret INS Division 6 combats the aliens that walk covertly among us. For a while, the film is a rare example of successful mainstream surrealism, with bizarre sights presented as part of the landscape. Unfortunately, it doesn't manage to sustain this level of inventiveness, going soft around the middle as new partners agent K (Tommy Lee Jones) and J (Will Smith) set out on their cases. Director Barry Sonnenfeld is ever-alert to the unusual comic touch that can enliven the material, although the story could have been sustained better with more character development.
1997: Best Makeup (Rick Baker, David LeRoy Anderson)
Nominations: Best Original Comedy Score, Art Direction

MEN IN HER LIFE, THE
1941, 89 mins, US
D: Gregory Ratoff A: Loretta Young, Conrad Veidt, Dean Jagger, Otto Kruger, Ann Todd (Columbia)

Details the intensive training required to bring a ballet dancer to stardom—and her love life along the way. Loretta Young comes under the stern hand of elderly ballet master Conrad Veidt, marrying him in appreciation after a sensational debut. After Veidt's death, she marries shipping magnate Dean Jagger, and honeymoon tour of Europe finds her forgetting the stage life. But she returns to dancing after separation, and bears a daughter (Ann Todd). Gregory Ratoff generates strong sympathy in the latter reels with the mother-love heart tugs for the absent child.

1941: Nomination: Best Sound

MEN IN WAR
1957, 102 mins, US Ⓥ
D: Anthony Mann A: Robert Ryan, Aldo Ray, Robert Keith, Philip Pine, Vic Morrow, Nehemiah Persoff (Security/United Artists)

A two-fisted account of what happens to an infantry platoon in Korea is told with a general air of excitement, tension, and action. Robert Ryan, battle-weary lieutenant trying to get the remnants of his platoon back to battalion headquarters, and Aldo Ray, hostile, disrespectful sergeant from another company trying to get his combat-shocked colonel to safety, each score strongly. Film stands out from the usual war pic in its intelligent use of music.

MEN IN WHITE
1934, 81 mins, UK
D: Richard Boleslawski A: Clark Gable, Myrna Loy, Jean Hersholt, Elizabeth Allen, Otto Kruger (M-G-M)

The story is familiar—a surgeon gives his best energy to his profession and thus irritates the woman he is to marry, who suggests that she is rich enough to permit him to adapt his office hours to their social engagements. Eventually, she is led to realize the importance of the work. The story permits Clark Gable to disclose a tenderness wholly foreign to the rough stuff he often does. Myrna Loy is an excellent choice as his society admirer.

MEN OF BOYS TOWN
1941, 107 mins, US Ⓥ
D: Norman Taurog A: Spencer Tracy, Mickey Rooney, Lee J. Cobb, Larry Nunn, Bobs Watson (M-G-M)

Like its predecessor *Boys Town,* this one carries socko entertainment, including plenty of tear-jerking and sentimental episodes to blur the eyes of the most callous, and spotlighting the life work of Father Edward J. Flanagan in his enterprise devoted to rehabilitation of wayward boys. Spencer Tracy again presents a sincere and human portrayal of the priest. Story introduces Larry Nunn into the institution. Kid is bitter because of a crippled back sustained in a reform-school beating, and Mickey Rooney heads a group of boys to try to make him laugh again. The kindly Father Flanagan and a dog do the trick.

MEN OF TWO WORLDS
(US: WITCH DOCTOR)
1946, 109 mins, UK Ⓥ
D: Thorold Dickinson A: Eric Portman, Phyllis Calvert, Orlando Martins, Robert Adams (Two Cities)

This ambitious production is honest, dull, and in Technicolor. It states the case for a scientific treatment of sleeping sickness among the African tribes as opposed to witchcraft and superstition. But it is a statement of the obvious. Randall, the district commissioner, plans to evacuate an African village to save the inhabitants from the man-killing tsetse fly. Kisenga, a noble savage, takes Randall's side, but the power of black magic in the hands of the local witch doctor, Magole (played with remarkable force by Orlando Martins), is too much for him.

MEN'S CLUB, THE
1986, 100 mins, US Ⓥ ⊙
D: Peter Medak A: Roy Scheider, Frank Langella, Harvey Keitel, Treat Williams, Richard Jordan (Atlantic)

Film is a distasteful piece of work that displays the worst in men. Production is as tired as the material. Pic plays like a stage play, so static is Peter Medak's direction. A group of friends nearing age 40 get together and for most of the film's 100 minutes the camera is on their heads talking. Leader of the group is Cavanaugh (Roy Scheider), supposedly a retired baseball star who looks too unhealthy to have ever played anything more strenuous than cards.

MEN WITHOUT WOMEN
1930, 76 mins, US
D: John Ford A: Kenneth MacKenna,

Frank Albertson, Paul Page, Warren Hymer (Fox)

Film opens in Shanghai with a shore party of American gobs going whoopee. Back to the ship, some great views of a sub streaking out to sea at night in clouds of black smoke and weird light and water reflections. Sub is run down in a collision and goes to the bottom in 90 feet of water with all escape cut off, and here begins the sledgehammer situation that lasts to the finish. Finale is a whopping bit of flagwaving.

MEN WITH WINGS
1938, 102 mins, US
D: William A. Wellman **A:** Fred MacMurray, Ray Milland, Louise Campbell, Andy Devine, Lynne Overman, Porter Hall (Paramount)

Story begins with the beginning of aviation. In first scene, the three kids of the picture, who grow up into Fred MacMurray, Ray Milland, and Louise Campbell, are charmingly pictured trying to fly with a kite, successful as it happens. Action progresses through various stages, ending with MacMurray leaving his wife (Campbell) and baby again for the Sino-Jap War. Milland as disappointed suitor but faithful friend plays his part with fine restraint, understanding, and poise.

MEPHISTO
1981, 146 mins, Hungary/W. Germany Ⓥ
D: Istvan Szabo **A:** Klaus Maria Brandauer, Krystyna Janda, Ildiko Bansagi, Karin Boyd, Rolf Hoppe (Objektiv/Durniok)

Mephisto details a provincial actor's climb to fame before and during the Nazi period. Klaus Maria Brandauer is extraordinary as this flamboyant actor. When the Nazis come to power, his wife leaves but he stays. He eventually becomes head of the National Theater, where he begins to subvert classic figures to Nazi outlooks. The sadistic culture minister takes him to the 1936 Olympic stadium and makes him run around with spotlights trained on him. It is a brilliantly dramatic epiphany regarding the corruption of power.
1981: Best Foreign Language Film

MEPHISTO WALTZ, THE
1971, 115 mins, US Ⓥ
D: Paul Wendkos **A:** Alan Alda, Jacqueline Bisset, Barbara Parkins, Bradford Dillman, William Windom, Curt Jurgens (20th Century-Fox/QM)

Pic follows the antics of a deranged concert pianist (Curt Jurgens) dying of leukemia, whose lust for Alda's daughter (Barbara Parkins) and devotion to devil worship destroy the marriage of writer Alan Alda and Jacqueline Bisset. To revive his sexual prowess, Jurgens has Alda killed, then assumes his body. Main fault is a tired script with more than a full quota of arch, laughable dialogue, spouted with relish by performers struggling to keep their heads above water.

LE MEPRIS
(US: CONTEMPT; GHOST AT NOON)
1963, 100 mins, France/Italy Ⓥ ⊙ ▭
D: Jean-Luc Godard **A:** Brigitte Bardot, Jack Palance, Fritz Lang, Michel Piccoli, Georgia Moll, Jean-Luc Godard (Rome Paris/Concordia/Champion)

Crossing Brigitte Bardot with an arty, personal director, ex–New Waver Jean-Luc Godard, was not a bad idea. Bardot appears, at last, as an actress in her own right. Slim tale has Bardot married to a hack scriptwriter called in by an egotistical American producer to rewrite scenes on an epic he is making in Italy, with Fritz Lang himself directing. Film details her sudden intimations of contempt for her husband. Though full of inside film talk, grandiloquent phrasings, sudden sharp ellipses, or quick repeat montage scenes of early incidents to make a point, film has a decisive visual flair that lays bare the figures.

MERCENARIES, THE
(US: DARK OF THE SUN)
1968, 106 mins, UK ⊙
D: Jack Cardiff **A:** Rod Taylor, Yvette Mimieux, Peter Garsten, Jim Brown, Kenneth More, Andre Morell (M-G-M)

Based on a Congo uprising, this is a raw adventure yarn with some glib philosophizing that skates superficially over the points of view of the cynical mercenaries and the patriotic Congolese. Rod Taylor plays a hard-bitten mercenary major who's prepared to sweat through any task, however dirty, providing his fee is okay. Jim Brown brings some dignity and interest to the role of the Congolese native.

MERMAIDS
1990, 111 mins, US Ⓥ ⊙
D: Richard Benjamin **A:** Cher, Bob Hoskins, Winona Ryder, Michael Schoeffling, Christina Ricci (Orion)

Set in the early 1960s, *Mermaids* begins rousingly, introducing flamboyant Mrs. Flax (Cher) and her two daughters:

confused Charlotte (Winona Ryder), 15, who is obsessed with Catholicism, and Kate (Christina Ricci), 9, who's obsessed with swimming. Constantly on the move due to mother's vagabond ways, they soon relocate to a small New England town that brings with it new romantic entanglements. The delightful Ryder is really the star. Cher is also fine as the cavalier, self-centered mom, an equally amusing if less sympathetic character.

MERRILL'S MARAUDERS
1962, 98 mins, US ⓥ ▭
D: Samuel Fuller **A:** Jeff Chandler, Ty Hardin, Peter Brown, Andrew Duggan, Claude Akins (United States)

Jeff Chandler's last role, as Brigadier General Frank Merrill, is one of his best. The rugged, gray-thatched Chandler portrays one of World War II's most colorful personalities with a proper blend of military doggedness and personal humanity. Screenplay balances battle scenes with character-establishing vignettes and gives the subject-hero a closer contact with his men through playing his story against the background of their daily activities.

MERRILY WE LIVE
1938, 90 mins, US
D: Norman Z. McLeod **A:** Constance Bennett, Brian Aherne, Billie Burke, Alan Mowbray, Patsy Kelly, Ann Dvorak (Favorite/M-G-M)

Most of the fun comes from a fine performance by Billie Burke, who plays a scatterbrain wife and mother in a family of irresponsibles. Burke has a weakness for helping worthless humanity. Brian Aherne is welcomed to the fold. It happens he isn't a tramp at all, but a writer who forgot to shave. In his calm and self-possessed manner, he begins to bring some order to the confusion in which the Kilbourne family lives.
1938: Nominations: Best Supp. Actress (Billie Burke), Cinematography, Art Direction, Sound, Song ("Merrily We Live")

MERRY ANDREW
1958, 103 mins, US ▭
D: Michael Kidd **A:** Danny Kaye, Pier Angeli, Baccaloni, Noel Purcell, Robert Coote, Patricia Cutts (M-G-M)

Merry Andrew has a happy-go-chuckly attitude and some smart musical numbers set up by standout music and lyrics. Danny Kaye is anything but merry in the opening sequences. He is an instructor in a stuffy British boys' school, presided over by his martinet father (Noel Purcell) and engaged to cool and detached Patricia Cutts. Via his vocation (archaeology), he gets mixed up with a family circus presided over by papa Baccaloni and featuring daughter Pier Angeli. This gives Kaye an opportunity to slap on the clown makeup and do several turns with handy circus props.

MERRY CHRISTMAS, MR. LAWRENCE
1983, 122 mins, UK ⓥ
D: Nagisa Oshima **A:** David Bowie, Tom Conti, Ryuichi Sakamoto, Takeshi, Jack Thompson (Recorded Picture)

This thinking man's version of *The Bridge on the River Kwai* makes no concessions to the more obvious commercial requirements, unless it is the selection of David Bowie, the pop star, for the leading dramatic role. The strongest points of the script are the philosophical and emotional implications, brought up in a careful and intricate comparison between Orient and Occident on every possible level. Set in a Japanese prisoner-of-war camp in Java, the plot has a Japanese captain, Yonoi (Ryuichi Sakamoto), trying to impose his own ideas of discipline, honor, order, and obedience, in a clash with a British major, Celliers (Bowie), who represents the diametrically opposed train of thought.

MERRY-GO-ROUND
See: Korhinta

MERRY WIDOW, THE
1925, 107 mins, US ⊗
D: Erich von Stroheim **A:** Mae Murray, John Gilbert, Roy D'Arcy, Josephine Crowell, George Fawcett, Tully Marshall (M-G-M)

Erich von Stroheim turns out Mae Murray in the most gorgeous production she has yet had. Von Stroheim has eliminated a number of captions by symbolizing. Distinct images are the freezing of rain upon a window to denote the passing of time, a royal funeral suggested through a corps of muffled drums descending a long flight of stairs, and the brilliant silhouetting of gems adorning Murray to the exclusion of her face and figure when gazed upon by the mercenary prince.

MERRY WIDOW, THE
1934, 110 mins, US ⓥ
D: Ernst Lubitsch **A:** Maurice Chevalier, Jeanette MacDonald, Edward Everett Horton, Una Merkel, George Barbier (M-G-M)

Ernst Lubitsch has here brought the genre of operetta to the level of popular taste. Two or three new airs have been added, but the music still stands pat on Lehar—smartly so. Maurice Chevalier and Jeanette MacDonald both are aces as Danilo and Sonia.
1934: Best Interior Decoration (Cedric Gibbons, Frederic Hope)

MESMER
1994, 107 mins, Germany/Canada/UK
D: Roger Spottiswoode **A:** Alan Rickman, Amanda Ooms, Gillian Barge, Jan Rubes, David Hemben (Levergreen/Babelsberg/ Accent/ Mayfair)

Biography is the least of concerns in the film, which focuses on a few short years in the life of the 18th-century medical radical who ventured into such areas as hypnosis and harmonics before they had names. The drama and humor come from the threat he poses to the establishment. Mesmer truly has the esteemed Viennese doctors working overtime to explain away his success. Rickman effects an eerie, otherworldly quality in his role. Ooms is a striking presence in her first major English-speaking film.

MESSAGE, THE
(US: MOHAMMED, MESSENGER OF GOD)
1976, 179 mins, UK ⓥ
D: Moustapha Akkad **A:** Anthony Quinn, Irene Papas, Michael Ansara, Johnny Sekka, Michael Forest (Filmco)

Saga of the birth of the Islamic religion bears favorable comparison as a religious epic. The action snowballs from underground cell meetings by followers of Mohammad, through brutal harassment, expulsion from Mecca, pitched battles in the desert, and the final conquering pilgrimage back to Mecca. Throughout the narrative, there is uncommon respect for the mind and the eye. Ultimately it's a triumph for Akkad, who welded a logistically sprawling epic into coherence.

MESSENGER, THE
THE STORY OF JOAN OF ARC
See: Jeanne D'arc

METEOR
1979, 103 mins, US ⓥ ▭
D: Ronald Neame **A:** Sean Connery, Natalie Wood, Karl Malden, Brian Keith, Martin Landau, Trevor Howard (American International)

Meteor really combines several disasters in one continuous cinematic bummer.

Along with the threat of a five-mile-wide asteroid speeding toward earth, with smaller splinters preceding it, there's an avalanche, an earthquake, a tidal wave, and a giant mud bath. Inevitably, topliners Sean Connery as an American scientist, Brian Keith as his Soviet counterpart, and Natalie Wood as the translator in between them take a backseat to the effects.
1979: Nomination: Best Sound

METEOR MAN, THE
1993, 99 mins, US ⓥ ⊙
D: Robert Townsend **A:** Robert Townsend, Marla Gibbs, Robert Griffin, Robert Guillaume, James Earl Jones (Tinsel Townsend)

Set in Washington, DC, yarn centers on schoolteacher and aspiring musician Jefferson Reed (Townsend). An advocate of nonviolence and flight in the face of danger, Jeff walks into the path of a falling meteor fragment, and when he awakens, realizes that he's gained super powers. The idea of a street-smart though awkward superhuman crime fighter ought to have been a rich mine from which to excavate laughs. But Townsend seems strangely out of place in this milieu. His characters are stereotypes culled from two decades of television viewing.

METROPOLIS
1927, 107 mins, Germany ⓥ ⊙ ⊗
D: Fritz Lang **A:** Alfred Abel, Gustav Froelich, Rudolf Klein-Rogge, Theodor Loos, Heinrich George, Brigitte Helm (UFA)

The scene is laid 100 years in the future, in the mighty city of Metropolis, a magnified New York. It is ruled by a millionaire, who lives in the upper city and whose son falls in love with a girl of the workers, who lives below in the city of the toilers. This girl is preaching goodwill to the workers in the catacombs below the city. An inventor has discovered a way to make artificial human beings, and at the request of the millionaire gives a creation of his form of the girl. She preaches destruction to the workers. Too bad that so much really artistic work was wasted on this manufactured story. Brigitte Helm, in the leading feminine role, is a find.

METROPOLITAN
1990, 98 mins, US ⓥ ⊙
D: Whit Stillman **A:** Carolyn Farina, Edward Clements, Christopher Eigeman, Taylor Nichols (Westerley)

Filmmaker Whit Stillman makes a strikingly original debut with a glib, ironic

portrait of the vulnerable young heirs to Manhattan's disappearing debutante scene. Story centers on a set of East Side friends who drag into their number a newcomer, Tom (Edward Clements), who openly disapproves of them but nonetheless shows up every night for private gatherings after black-tie parties and dances. A self-serious but insensitive young man, Tom inspires the first-time love of Audrey (Carolyn Farina). Tom repeatedly humiliates her as he continues to pursue an old flame, Serena (Elizabeth Thompson).
1990: Nomination: Best Original Screenplay

M. HIRE
See: Monsieur Hire

MIAMI BLUES
1990, 99 mins, US Ⓥ ⊙
D: George Armitage **A:** Alec Baldwin, Fred Ward, Jennifer Jason Leigh, Nora Dunn, Charles Napier (Orion/Tristes Tropiques)

This quirky and sometimes brutally funny film strings together terrific moments but never takes a point of view. Junior (Alec Baldwin) blows into town, initiates a crime spree with a homicide detective's stolen badge, and settles down with a simpleminded hooker named Susie (Jennifer Jason Leigh). The sense that Junior can go off at any time, and the explosive and graphic bursts of violence, create tension throughout.

MIAMI RHAPSODY
1995, 95 mins, US Ⓥ
D: David Frankel **A:** Sarah Jessica Parker, Gil Bellows, Antonio Banderas, Mia Farrow, Paul Mazursky, Kevin Pollak (Hollywood)

Very Woody Allen-ish comedy about the amorous travails of a family of neurotics. Light, effervescent, and exceedingly colorful, film offers no new insight into the human condition but glosses over it in beguilingly entertaining fashion. Like any self-respecting neurotic, Gwyn (Sarah Jessica Parker) has as many reasons not to get married as she does to proceed, but still agrees to become engaged to her b.f. Matt (Gil Bellows). However, at the wedding of her promiscuous younger sister, Leslie (Carla Gugino), to football hunk Jeff (Bo Eason), Gwyn's father, Vic (Paul Mazursky), confides to her that he suspects that her mother, Nina (Mia Farrow), is having an affair. Sexy and funny, caustic and vulnerable, Sarah Jessica Parker carries the pic in the zingy manner of the best comediennes.

MICHAEL
1996, 105 mins, US Ⓥ ⊙
D: Nora Ephron **A:** John Travolta, Andie MacDowell, William Hurt, Bob Hoskins, Robert Pastorelli, Jean Stapleton (Alphaville/Turner)

John Travolta's charismatic screen presence is the only element that propels *Michael* over its rough narrative spots and scattered direction. Travolta plays a heaven-sent angel who brings joy, love, and redemption to a team of cynical and frustrated tabloid journalists. When rumor of an angel's existence reaches a sleazy tabloid, down-on-his luck journalist Frank Quinlan (William Hurt) senses a front-page scoop and tracks the story along with Huey Driscoll (Robert Pastorelli), another troubled reporter, and Dorothy Winters (Andie MacDowell), a mysterious woman who claims to be an "angel expert." *Michael* is at once underwritten and overwritten. Rowdy, slapdash, and unevenly directed, the movie is basically a collection of episodes tied together with a flimsy string.

MICHAEL COLLINS
1996, 132 mins, US Ⓥ ⊙
D: Neil Jordan **A:** Liam Neeson, Aidan Quinn, Stephen Rea, Alan Rickman, Julia Roberts, Ian Hart (Geffen/Warner)

Such is its catalog of violence, vendettas, betrayals, vengeance, assassinations, and insidious factionalism that *Michael Collins* comes off as political history writ in the mode of the gangster film. Staggeringly well made, the film is a highly thought-out rendition of a difficult and, by now, obscure political struggle. To a surprising degree, Neil Jordan has made this a film of tremedous action, incident and momentum. Michael Collins (Liam Neeson) was a mysterious figure who, after the failed Easter Rising of 1916, realized that conventional fighting against the British was doomed to failure. Instead, he raised the Irish Volunteers, who staged stunning ambushes on the Brits occupying Ireland. Neeson is a compulsive dynamo as Collins, with the actor seizing his part with passion and boldness.

MICKEY
1918, 90 mins, US ⊗
D: F. Richard Jones **A:** Mabel Normand, Wheeler Oakman, Lew Cody, Minta Durfee (Normand/Sennett)

Mickey and Mabel Normand are one

and the same. With all her tomboy pranks and cutting up, she is a wonderful little actress. Mickey lives with her uncle and his squaw housekeeper. He is working a mine and they are not even prosperous, but they are a happy trio. But Mickey's life in the wild and woolly west comes to an end when her uncle receives an invitation to send her east to some relations. She goes there, but when these folks learn Mickey has no money, they put her to work. As a domestic, she is a rank failure and disrupts the whole household. The whole production breezes along, with action every minute.

MICKEY BLUE EYES
1999, 103 mins, UK/US ⊛ ⊙
D: Kelly Makin **A:** Hugh Grant, James Caan, Jeanne Tripplehorn, Burt Young, James Fox, Joe Viterelli (Simian/Castle Rock)

Mickey Blue Eyes provides Hugh Grant with an excellent vehicle. He plays Michael Felgate, a proper English auctioneer enamored of a schoolteacher, Gina (Jeanne Tripplehorn), who happens to be a Mafia princess. When he proposes, she's terrified he'll be sucked into the family business. Her uncle Vito "The Butcher" Graziosi (Burt Young) has plans to implicate the auctioneer in a money-laundering scheme. Grant's part fits him like a custom-tailored Italian suit. James Caan is a fine foil as his prospective father-in-law, and Young makes an impressively intimidating, tight-lipped crime boss. Tripplehorn doesn't get to do much other than look dejected, disapproving, or disappointed.

MICKEY ONE
1965, 93 mins, US ⊛ ⊙
D: Arthur Penn **A:** Warren Beatty, Hurd Hatfield, Alexandra Stewart, Teddy Hart, Jeff Corey, Franchot Tone (Florin/Tatira/Columbia)

Mickey One could be described as a study in regeneration, but the screenplay is overloaded with symbolic gestures that obscure the main objectives of the plot. Title character is a onetime top nitery comic. In a bid to get away from his past and start afresh, he assumes the identity of a Pole whose name is conveniently abbreviated to Mickey One and rediscovers the art of wowing an audience. Warren Beatty gives a commanding, though highly mannered, performance.

MICKI & MAUDE
1984, 118 mins, US ⊛ ⊙ ▭
D: Blake Edwards **A:** Dudley Moore, Amy Irving, Ann Reinking, Richard Mulligan, George Gaynes, Wallace Shawn (Columbia-Delphi III/BEE)

A hilarious farce. Dudley Moore is in top antic form, and Amy Irving has never been better. Debuting screenwriter Jonathan Reynolds has constructed a farce of simple, classical proportions about a man who accidentally gets his wife and new girlfriend pregnant at virtually the same time.

MIDDLE-AGE CRAZY
1980, 89 mins, Canada ⊛
D: John Trent **A:** Bruce Dern, Ann-Margret, Graham Jarvis, Helen Hughes (20th Century-Fox/Tormont)

Bobby Lee (Bruce Dern) is a successful building contractor on the verge of his 40th birthday. He is getting hung up on his milestone date as a result of his wife's persistence that he's still the old stud she married. Constant reminders from friends and family on his dependability eventually drive him to change his style. Dern is equally convincing dressed in three-piece suits or denim and boots. Ann-Margret as his wife is also outstanding.

MIDDLE-AGE SPREAD
1979, 94 mins, New Zealand
D: John Reid **A:** Grant Tilly, Donna Akersten, Dorothy McKegg, Bridget Armstrong, Bevan Wilson (Endeavour/NZ Film Commission)

Middle Age Spread centers on Colin (Grant Tilly), a college teacher whose promotion to principal coincides with a number of personal crises. Not least are a widening girth and a tentative first-and-last affair with a much younger colleague (Donna Akersten). At a dinner party he hosts, with his increasingly sexually disinterested wife, Elizabeth (Dorothy McKegg), the morality and values of their tight-knit circle of friends are played out with deadly accuracy.

MIDNIGHT
1939, 92 mins, US
D: Mitchell Leisen **A:** Claudette Colbert, Don Ameche, John Barrymore, Francis Lederer, Mary Astor (Paramount)

Story is a slender thread on which to tie series of adventures of a stranded showgirl in Paris. After a flirtation with Don Ameche, Claudette Colbert crashes a musicale and poses as a countess. This leads to job for John Barrymore, in which she is to attract the amorous attentions of Francis Lederer away from Barrymore's wife, Mary Astor.

MIDNIGHT COWBOY
1969, 119 mins, US Ⓥ ⊙
D: John Schlesinger **A:** Dustin Hoffman, Jon Voight, Sylvia Miles, John McGiver, Brenda Vaccaro (United Artists)

The sometimes amusing but essentially sordid saga of a male prostitute in Manhattan. Dustin Hoffman is cast as gimp-legged, always unshaven, cough-racked petty chiseler who at first exploits and then befriends the stupid boy hustler from Texas. The title role is played by Jon Voight. The film is full of unnice people from bad environments. It is obsessed with mercenary sex and haunted by memories of cruel group ravishments. Indignity is endemic.
1969: Best Picture, Director, Adapted Screenplay
Nominations: Best Actor (Dustin Hoffman, Jon Voight), Supp. Actress (Sylvia Miles), Editing

MIDNIGHT EXPRESS
1978, 120 mins, UK Ⓥ ⊙
D: Alan Parker **A:** Brad Davis, Randy Quaid, John Hurt, Bo Hopkins, Paul Smith, Mike Kellin (Casablanca)

Sordid and ostensibly true story about a young American busted for smuggling hash in Turkey and his subsequent harsh imprisonment and later escape. Cast, direction, and production are all very good, but it's difficult to sort out the proper empathies from the muddled and moralizing screenplay which, in true Anglo-American fashion, wrings hands over alien cultures as though our civilization is absolutely perfect. The script loads up sympathy for Davis, also fellow convicts Randy Quaid (a psycho character), John Hurt (a hard doper), and Norbert Weisser (playing the obligatory gay inmate), by making the prison authorities even more worse.
1978: Best Adapted Screenplay, Original Score
Nominations: Best Picture, Director, Supp. Actor (John Hurt), Editing

MIDNIGHT IN THE GARDEN OF GOOD AND EVIL
1997, 155 mins, US Ⓥ ⊙
D: Clint Eastwood **A:** Kevin Spacey, John Cusack, Jack Thompson, Alison Eastwood, Irma P. Hall, Paul Hipp (Malpaso/Warner)

Midnight in the Garden of Good and Evil is an outstanding lean film trapped in a fat film's body. Clint Eastwood's film about a sensational murder case in genteel, eccentric old Savannah, GA, vividly captures the atmosphere and presents memorable characters. But the picture's sprawling structure and exceedingly leisurely pace finally weigh too heavily on its virtues. Author John Kelso (John Cusack) checks into Savannah to report on the glittering Christmas party to be given by leading society figure Jim Williams (Kevin Spacey). In the wee hours, Williams shoots and kills his violence-prone houseboy and lover, Billy Hanson (Jude Law). As Kelso switches from society reporter to chronicler of crime, the less reputable portion of Savannah's colorful social strata is revealed. Performances are mostly aces, beginning with Spacey's Williams, oozing with savoir-faire, urban confidence, silken wit and a vaguely sinister charm.

MIDNIGHT LACE
1960, 108 mins, US Ⓥ
D: David Miller **A:** Doris Day, Rex Harrison, John Gavin, Myrna Loy, Roddy McDowall, Herbert Marshall (Universal)

Doris Day is victimized by what seems to be a crank on the telephone. Informed by a nagging, mysterious, persistent caller that her life is in jeopardy, she works herself into such a lather that others, Scotland Yard included, begin to believe her obsession is the myth of a neglected wife (husband Rex Harrison is constantly preoccupied with business matters). Among the chief suspects are John Gavin, a construction-gang foreman; Roddy McDowall, a spoiled young punk; and Herbert Marshall, treasurer in Harrison's firm. The effervescent Day sets some sort of record here for frightened gasps. Director David Miller adds a few pleasant little humorous touches and generally makes the most of an uninspired yarn.

MIDNIGHT MAN, THE
1974, 117 mins, US
D: Roland Kibbee, Burt Lancaster **A:** Burt Lancaster, Susan Clark, Cameron Mitchell, Morgan Woodward, Harris Yulin, Joan Lorring (Universal)

Burt Lancaster stars as a paroled ex-cop stumbling into a series of small-town murders. With Roland Kibbee, Lancaster adapted, produced, and directed on some refreshingly different locations in South Carolina. The cluttered plot's twists and turns get tiring after 117 minutes, but the violence highlights are well motivated and discreetly executed.

MIDNIGHT RUN
1988, 122 mins, US Ⓥ ⊙
D: Martin Brest **A:** Robert De Niro, Charles Grodin, Yaphet Kotto, John Ashton, Dennis Farina (City Lights)

Robert De Niro shows he can be as wonderful in a comic role as he is in a serious one. Pair him, a gruff ex-cop and bounty hunter, with straight man Charles Grodin, his captive, and the result is one of the most entertaining, best-executed, original road pictures *ever*. *Midnight Run* is more than a string of well-done gags peppered by verbal sparring between a reluctant twosome; it is a terrifically developed script full of inventive, humorous twists made even funnier by wonderfully realized secondary characters.

MIDNIGHT STING
See: Diggstown

MIDSUMMER NIGHT'S DREAM, A
1935, 132 mins, US Ⓥ ⊙
D: Max Reinhardt, William Dieterle **A:** James Cagney, Olivia de Havilland, Mickey Rooney, Victor Jory, Joe E. Brown, Dick Powell (Warner)

Question of whether a Shakespearean play can be successfully produced on a lavish scale for the films is affirmatively answered by this commendable effort. The familiar story of *A Midsummer Night's Dream*, half of which is laid in a make-believe land of elves and fairies, is right up the film alley technically. The fantasy, the ballets of the Oberon and Titania cohorts, and the characters in the eerie sequences are convincing and illusion compelling. Film is replete with enchanting scenes, beautifully photographed and charmingly presented. All Shakespearean devotees will be pleased at the soothing treatment given to the Mendelssohn score. There are some outstanding performances, notably by Victor Jory as Oberon.
1935: Best Cinematography, Editing
Nomination: Best Picture

MIDSUMMER NIGHT'S DREAM, A
1999, 116 mins, US Ⓥ ⊙ ▱
D: Michael Hoffman **A:** Kevin Kline, Michelle Pfeiffer, Rupert Everett, Stanley Tucci, Calista Flockhart, Anna Friel (Fox Searchlight/Regency)

A Midsummer Night's Dream is a whimsical, intermittently enjoyable, but decidedly unmagical version of the Bard's wild romantic comedy. Preparations for the wedding of Duke Theseus (David Strathairn) and Hippolyta (Sophie Marceau) are under way. Hermia (Anna Friel) is promised to Demetrius (Christian Bale), but she loves Lysander (Dominic West) and plans to elope with him. Her best friend, Helena (Calista Flockhart), who is in love with Demetrius, knows of the plot. Bound for the same forest is a band of amateur players, of whom Bottom the Weaver (Kevin Kline) is the most dilettante. The forest is home of the fairies, where the trickster Puck (Stanley Tucci) administers a love potion that causes the participants to change and mix their partners. Bottom becomes a pawn in the games of the fairies' king and queen, Oberon and Titania (Rupert Everett, Michelle Pfeiffer). Overall, the Brits give more resonant performances.

MIDSUMMER NIGHT'S SEX COMEDY, A
1982, 88 mins, US Ⓥ
D: Woody Allen **A:** Woody Allen, Mia Farrow, Jose Ferrer, Julie Hagerty, Tony Roberts, Mary Steenburgen (Orion)

A pleasant disappointment, pleasant because Woody Allen gets all the laughs he goes for in a visually charming, sweetly paced picture, a disappointment because he doesn't go for more. The time is the turn of the century, the place a lovely old farmhouse. Here, Wall Street stockbroker Allen spends his spare time inventing odd devices and trying to bed his own wife (Mary Steenburgen), who has turned cold. Arriving for a visit are Steenburgen's cousin Jose Ferrer, a stuffy, pedantic scholar, and his bride-to-be (Mia Farrow); Allen's best friend, who else but Tony Roberts, an amorous physician and his current short-term fling (Julie Hagerty).

MIDWAY
(UK: BATTLE OF MIDWAY)
1976, 132 mins, US Ⓥ ⊙
D: Jack Smight **A:** Charlton Heston, Henry Fonda, James Coburn, Glenn Ford, Hal Holbrook, Toshiro Mifune (Mirisch)

The June 1942 sea-air battle off Midway Island was a turning point in World War II. However, the combat was the usual hysterical jumble of noise, explosion, and violent death. *Midway* tries to combine both aspects but succumbs to the confusion. Henry Fonda's performance as Pacific Fleet Commander Chester W. Nimitz towers over everything else.

MIGHTY APHRODITE

1995, 95 mins, US Ⓥ ⊙

D: Woody Allen A: Woody Allen, Helena Bonham Carter, Mira Sorvino, Michael Rapaport, F. Murray Abraham, Claire Bloom (Sweetland/Miramax)

Zippy, frothy confection emerges as agreeable middle-range Woody, dominated by a striking performance from Mira Sorvino as a sweet-tempered hooker. After a surprising opening with a mock Greek chorus, Allen's middle-aged Lenny fulminates to his wife, Amanda (Helena Bonham Carter), against the idea of adopting children. Before the viewer can recover from the autobiographical implications of this tirade, Lenny and Amanda are bringing home an adopted infant son. A few years down the line, Lenny is so impressed with his son that he decides the kid's real mom must be some kind of genius. With a little stealth, Lenny is able to track his prey, and encounters an incredibly statuesque bimbo whose amiable nature prevails over her notable life scars.

1995: Best Supporting Actress (Mira Sorvino)

Nomination: Best Original Screenplay

MIGHTY BARNUM, THE

1934, 87 mins, US

D: Walter Lang A: Wallace Beery, Adolphe Menjou, Virginia Bruce, Rochelle Hudson, Janet Beecher, Tammany Young (Twentieth)

P. T. Barnum's life, the things he did, and the things that were done to him up to the time of the inspiration for the circus that was to become Barnum & Bailey, proves engrossing if not sensational screen entertainment. The story turns back 100 years to the time when Barnum was operating a general store in New York. Barnum (Wallace Beery) signs up Joyce Heth (Lucille La Verne), supposed nursemaid to George Washington, who's later exposed as a fake. Then Barnum puts Zorro, the bearded lady (May Boley), on display but Zorro then double-crosses him. Barnum tries again, this time his show becoming so successful with Tom Thumb (George Brasno) and his little midget wife (Olive Brasno) that Barnum decides to bring singer Jenny Lind into the act (Virginia Bruce). His romance with the singer causes P.T. to neglect his museum of freaks as well as his wife.

MIGHTY DUCKS, THE
(UK/AUSTRALIA: CHAMPIONS)

1992, 101 mins, US Ⓥ ⊙

D: Stephen Herek A: Emilio Estevez, Joss Ackland, Lane Smith, Heidi Kling, Josef Sommer (Walt Disney)

A formulaic pic meant for children but actually focusing on a yuppie's struggle for redemption. Emilio Estevez stars as an arrogant Minneapolis lawyer who gets nailed on drunk-driving charges. His boss cuts a deal for him to do community service instead of suffering the humiliation of court. Once Estevez meets the undisciplined, street-wise kids he must shape into a winning peewee hockey team, pic becomes predictable and mighty preachy.

MIGHTY JOE YOUNG

1949, 88 mins, US Ⓥ ⊙

D: Ernest B. Schoedsack A: Terry Moore, Ben Johnson, Robert Armstrong, Frank McHugh, Regis Toomey (Arko/RKO)

Film is fun to laugh at and with, loaded with incredible corn, plenty of humor, and a robot gorilla who becomes a genuine hero. The technical skill of the large staff of experts gives the robot life. Plot deals with a gorilla, raised in the African jungle by a young girl. Both the girl and the giant ape are happy until a safari headed by Broadway producer Robert Armstrong arrives in the jungle. Armstrong immediately sees the possibilities of the ape and the girl.

1949: Best Special Effects

MIGHTY JOE YOUNG

1998, 114 mins, US Ⓥ ⊙ ▭

D: Ron Underwood A: Charlize Theron, Bill Paxton, Rade Serbedzija, Peter Firth, David Paymer, Regina King (Walt Disney)

Mighty Joe Young is wholesome, well-crafted family fare like Hollywood used to make, about an oversized African gorilla out of his element in urban America. Scientist Dr. Ruth Young (Linda Purl) and her young daughter Jill (Mika Boorem) are studying the behavior of a family of apes in Tanzania. Among the gorillas is young Joe, whose rare genetic mutation makes him grow faster than his peers. Years later, the adult Jill (Charlize Theron) and Joe live in peace and seclusion on their mountain. Scientist Gregg O'Hara (Bill Paxton) stumbles onto evidence of Joe and persuades Jill to move the gorilla to a California wildlife preserve, where Joe escapes and roams through Hollywood, terrorizing dumbstruck throngs. There's not a lot to be said for the acting, since the humans play second banana to the gorilla throughout.

MIGHTY MORPHIN POWER RANGERS: THE MOVIE
1995, 95 mins, US ⓥ ⊙
D: Bryan Spicer **A:** Karan Ashley, Johnny Yong Bosch, Steve Cardenas, Jason David Frank, Amy Jo Johnson (Saban/Toei)

Sci-fi adventure pic is much slicker than its small-screen counterpart. The Rangers are six teenage martial artists who moonlight as superheroes when they're not attending high school in Angel Grove, USA. The rubber bogeymen—and the rubber bogeymen—are lifted intact from a Japanese TV series, giving the show an undeniably amusing air of low-rent tackiness. The special effects in the movie, shot in Australia, are a great deal more special. High point is a battle with two huge, brightly metallic insect creatures that thrash downtown Angel Grove. On just about every other level, however, the pic plays like an elongated version of a 30-minute episode. Dialogue is as corny as Kansas in August. The photogenic young actors are, well, sincere.

MIKE'S MURDER
1984, 97 mins, US ⓥ
D: James Bridges **A:** Debra Winger, Mark Keyloun, Darrell Larson, Brooke Alderson, Paul Winfield (Skyeway/Ladd)

An intriguing, if not entirely successful, suspenser and paranoid mood piece. Mark Keyloun's Mike is a casual, off-and-on-again lover of Debra Winger. He's a tennis teacher who earns additional dough as a small-time drug dealer. Keyloun is killed and Winger, a modestly successful bank employee, spurns friends' advice and begins investigating the realities of Mike's world, meeting some of his lawless friends and ultimately being threatened.

MIKEY AND NICKY
1976, 119 mins, US ⓥ
D: Elaine May **A:** Peter Falk, John Cassavetes, Ned Beatty, Rose Arrick, William Hickey (Paramount)

Peter Falk and John Cassavetes star as two old friends whose relationship is falling apart. Cassavetes is a low-level criminal marked for extinction by gang lord Sanford Meisner, who employs Ned Beatty as hit man. Cassavetes calls Falk to help him, though neither Cassavetes nor the audience is certain that Falk isn't part of the rubout strategy. That's the superficial hook on which hangs the real story of human relationships and mutual abuse.

MILAGRO BEANFIELD WAR, THE
1988, 117 mins, US ⓥ ⊙
D: Robert Redford **A:** Ruben Blades, Richard Bradford, Sonia Braga, Julie Carmen, John Heard, Melanie Griffith (Universal)

A charming, fanciful little fable built around weighty issues concerning the environment, the preservation of a cultural heritage and the rights of citizens versus the might of the dollar. Redford and company have put a quirky twist on the material, investing it with a quasi-mystical aspect as well as some raw comedy. Set in modern-day New Mexico, tale is set in motion when impoverished farmer Joe Mondrago (Chick Vennera) improperly diverts some water from a main irrigation channel onto his own modest plot of land in order to start up a beanfield.
1988: Best Original Score

MILDRED PIERCE
1945, 109 mins, US ⓥ ⊙
D: Michael Curtiz **A:** Joan Crawford, Jack Carson, Zachary Scott, Eve Arden, Ann Blyth, Bruce Bennett (Warner)

The story of a woman's sacrifices for a no-good daughter, told in flashback as Mildred Pierce is being questioned by police about the murder of her second husband. Character goes back to the time she separated from her first husband and how she struggled to fulfill her ambitions for her children. Joan Crawford reaches a peak of her acting career in this pic. Ann Blyth, as the daughter, scores dramatically in her first genuine acting assignment. Zachary Scott makes the most of his character.
1945: Best Actress (Joan Crawford)
Nominations: Best Picture, Supp. Actress (Eve Arden, Ann Blyth), Screenplay, B&W Cinematography

MILK MONEY
1994, 108 mins, US ⓥ
D: Richard Benjamin **A:** Melanie Griffith, Ed Harris, Michael Patrick Carter, Malcolm McDowell, Anne Heche (Paramount/Kennedy-Marshall)

With a tip of the hat to the performers, this is a misguided comedy with Hall of Shame pedigree. Three boys on the cusp of puberty raid their piggy banks and sell their vintage comic books to head for the big city to pay to see a real live naked lady. The naifs fall right into an urban scam but are saved from robbery at gunpoint by a good-hearted prostitute, V (Melanie Griffith). The film is obvious, loud, mean-spirited, and has its mind in the gutter.

MILKY WAY, THE
1936, 80 mins, US Ⓥ ⊙
D: Leo McCarey A: Harold Lloyd, Adolphe Menjou, Verree Teasdale, Helen Mack, William Gargan, George Barbier (Paramount)

A good laff picture. The role of the timid milk-wagon route man who is catapulted into pugilistic fame and fortune is almost made to order for Lloyd and he plays it to the hilt. Adolphe Menjou is his usual capital self as the harassed fight manager who finds himself with a dead herring on his hands when middleweight champ William Gargan gets the headline razz. This results in Lloyd's buildup as The Killer.

MILLENNIUM
1989, 108 mins, US Ⓥ ⊙
D: Michael Anderson A: Kris Kristofferson, Cheryl Ladd, Daniel J. Travanti, Robert Joy, Lloyd Bochner (Gladden)

Millennium tries hard to combine sci-fi special effects and a love story, but unfortunately neither are convincing. Bill Smith (Kris Kristofferson) meets Louise Baltimore (Cheryl Ladd), leader of a commando unit of women from 1,000 years in the future. The complicated pic involves movement through time, the search for the powerful "stunner" and the future civilization's efforts to continue. Kristofferson gives the film his best shot and breathes some life into the tired lines, while Ladd sports many outfits and wacky hairstyles but lacks real passion.

MILLER'S CROSSING
1990, 114 mins, US Ⓥ ⊙
D: Joel Coen A: Gabriel Byrne, Albert Finney, Marcia Gay Harden, Jon Polito, John Turturro (Circle/Pedas-Barenholtz-Durkin)

Substance is here in spades, along with the twisted, brilliantly controlled style on which filmmakers Joel and Ethan Coen made a name. Story unspools in an eastern city in the 1930s where gangster Johnny Caspar (Jon Polito) wants approval from the city's political boss, Leo (Albert Finney), to rub out Bernie Bernbaum (John Turturro). But Leo's fallen in love with Bernie's sister, Verna (Marcia Gay Harden), who wants Bernie protected. Leo's

cool, brainy aide-de-camp Tom (Gabriel Byrne) sees that Leo is making a big mistake, and it's up to Tom to save him as his empire begins to crumble. Rarely does a screen hero of Tom's gritty dimensions come along, and Irishman Byrne brings him gracefully and profoundly to life. Also outstanding is Finney as the bighearted political fixer.

LE MILLION
1931, 85 mins, France Ⓥ
D: Rene Clair A: Annabella, Rene Lefebvre, Constantin Stroesco, Paul Ollivier, Vanda Greville (Tobis)

Story of an impecunious painter in love with a girl in the opera ballet is fanciful, with no attempt at probability, but is highly entertaining. Director Rene Clair has a new trick of having a tune with lyrics applying to a certain thought played during appropriate silent sequences. There is a song about remorse, or a song about helplessness, sung when the principals are in appropriate situations, but without the principals singing themselves.

MILLIONAIRE FOR CHRISTY, A
1951, 90 mins, US
D: George Marshall A: Fred MacMurray, Eleanor Parker, Richard Carlson, Una Merkel, Raymond Greenleaf (Thor/20th Century-Fox)

Eleanor Parker, as poor legal secretary, is sent to notify Fred MacMurray, a syrupy radio philosopher, that he has inherited $2 million. Parker makes a pitch for MacMurray without knowing he is on the brink of marriage. When the best man (Richard Carlson) walks out on the wedding, the knotting is postponed while MacMurray chases him, taking along an unwilling Parker. Director George Marshall has staged a wow scene involving a big wave that dashes the principals around.

MILLIONAIRESS, THE
1960, 90 mins, UK Ⓥ ▭
D: Anthony Asquith A: Sophia Loren, Peter Sellers, Alastair Sim, Vittorio De Sica, Dennis Price (20th Century-Fox)

This stylized pic has Sophia Loren at her most radiant, wearing a series of stunning Balmain gowns. George Bernard Shaw's Shavianisms on morality, riches and human relationship retain much of their edge. Anthony Asquith breaks up the pic with enough hilarious situations to keep the film from getting tedious. The yarn concerns a beautiful, spoiled young heiress who can't find love. She sets her cap for a dedicated Indian doctor runing a poor-man's clinic. He's scared of her money and power. Sellers plays the doctor straight, apart from an offbeat accent, but he still manages to bring in some typical comedy touches.

MILLION DOLLAR MERMAID
1952, 115 mins, US Ⓥ
D: Mervyn LeRoy **A:** Esther Williams, Victor Mature, Walter Pidgeon, David Brian, Donna Corcoran (M-G-M)

This is a gaudy, conventional biopic based on the career of Australian swimmer Annette Kellerman. Toppers of the flashy acquatics are the fountain and smoke numbers, imaginatively staged by Busby Berkeley and boldly splashed with Technicolor hues. Film opens with Kellerman (Esther Williams) as a crippled child in Australia who heals her leg in taking up swimming. She heads for London, attracts the attention of Victor Mature, a sports promoter, who brings her to America.
1952: Nomination: Best Color Cinematography

MILLION POUND NOTE, THE (US: MAN WITH A MILLION)
1954, 92 mins, UK Ⓥ
D: Ronald Neame **A:** Gregory Peck, Jane Griffiths, Ronald Squire, Joyce Grenfell, Reginald Beckwith, Maurice Denham (Group)

Mark Twain's classic story makes gentle screen satire. With Edwardian settings providing a fascinating background, the yarn suffers from the protracted exploitation of one basic joke. The plot is based on a bet between two brothers (Ronald Squire and Wilfrid Hyde White) that a man with a million-pound banknote in his possession could live on the fat of the land for a month without having to break into it. The guinea pig for their wager is Gregory Peck, a penniless American stranded in London.

MILLIONS LIKE US
1943, 103 mins, UK
D: Frank Launder, Sidney Gilliat **A:** Eric Portman, Patricia Roc, Gordon Jackson, Anne Crawford, Basil Radford, Naunton Wayne (Gainsborough)

Film is designed as patriotic propaganda on the UK front, minus flag waving and such-like. Eric Portman has a relatively small part, but gives to it a dignified and intelligent portrayal. The outstanding roles are Patricia Roc and Gordon Jack-

son—she a factory worker, and he a young airman. Their lovemaking is crudely simple, but so sincere as to lift it out of the commonplace.

MIMIC
1997, 105 mins, US Ⓥ ⊙
D: Guillermo Del Toro **A:** Mira Sorvino, Jeremy Northam, Josh Brolin, Giancarlo Giannini, Charles S. Dutton, F. Murray Abraham (Dimension)

Mimic is a dark, dank and drippy sci-fi shocker that threatens to become something unusual before trailing off into ridiculousness. Gifted young scientist Susan Tyler (Mira Sorvino) introduces a new breed of insect into the city to eliminate the cockroaches that she has determined are spreading a terrible disease through Manhattan. Three years later, however, the roaches come home to roost. Various unsuspecting victims are gobbled up by the hungry, hard-shelled predators, which have the ability to transform themselves into human-like form. Remainder of the picture is mostly set in the dingy bowels of the subway, as Susan tries to turn the tables on the lip-smacking beasts. Mexican director Guillermo Del Toro clearly knows his way around the camera, but the shadowy eeriness winds up being just dull. Special insect effects are accomplished enough, if fleeting.

MIND BENDERS, THE
1963, 101 mins, UK
D: Basil Dearden **A:** Dirk Bogarde, Mary Ure, John Clements, Michael Bryant, Wendy Craig, Edward Fox (Anglo-Amalgamated/Novus)

James Kennaway's original screenplay finds the peg for its bizarre plot in "reduction of sensation" experiments. By eliminating a subject's various senses by submerging him in an isolation tank a shortcut to brainwashing is achieved. Suicide of elderly scientist Harold Goldblatt prompts an investigation to determine whether military security has been violated. Clements suspects Goldblatt has turned traitor. The scientist's associate, Dirk Bogarde, blames Goldblatt's death on the experiments. Bogarde voluntarily submits to isolation to prove his theory. Under Basil Dearden's firm direction, the cast absorbingly captures suspense and gruesome space-age qualities.

MINISTRY OF FEAR
1945, 84 mins, US
D: Fritz Lang **A:** Ray Milland, Marjorie

Reynolds, Dan Duryea, Carl Esmond, Hillary Brooke (Paramount)

Pic starts out to be a humdinger, and continues that way for the most part, but when the roundup of the spy gang gets under way the situation becomes drawn out and elementary. Ray Milland is tossed into the midst of a spy chase when he is drawn to the crowds at a British fair and wins a cake by guessing its weight. The cake contains a capsule which one of the spies is to have delivered to other enemy agents.

MINIVER STORY, THE
1950, 104 mins, UK/US
D: H. C. Potter **A:** Greer Garson, Walter Pidgeon, John Hodiak, Leo Genn, Cathy O'Donnell, Peter Finch (M-G-M)

Opening with a strangely pallid reproduction of London on VE day, Mrs. Miniver has just come from a doctor, realizes she has not long to live and bravely determines to keep the news from her family. Chief laurels go to Greer Garson who, even with the unmistakable signs of illness and mental stress, makes feasible the husband's claim that she looks as lovely as ever.

MINNIE AND MOSKOWITZ
1971, 114 mins, US
D: John Cassavetes **A:** Gena Rowlands, Seymour Cassel, Val Avery, Timothy Carey, Katherine Cassavetes, John Cassavetes (Faces Music/Universal)

An oppressive and irritating film in which a shrill and numbing hysteria of acting and direction soon kills any empathy for the loneliness of the main characters. John Cassavetes wrote and directed in his now-familiar home-movie improvisational and indulgent style. Cassavetes has laid on with a trowel the borderline psychosis. The principals live on the knife-edge of breakdown.

MIRACLE, THE
1959, 121 mins, US ▢
D: Irving Rapper **A:** Carroll Baker, Roger Moore, Walter Slezak, Vittorio Gassman, Katina Paxinou (Warner)

Spectacle, though laid in the 19th century, is a "biblical" subject with the elements and approach of such films. Carroll Baker is a postulant at a Spanish convent when she falls in love with Roger Moore, a soldier. When she leaves the convent to follow Moore, the statue of the Virgin in the chapel comes down from its pedestal and assumes the form of the postulant.

And Baker is off on various adventures. It is not exactly clear what "The Miracle" is supposed to do, other than give Baker a chance to gallivant about Europe in a variety of costumes.

MIRACLE, THE
1991, 96 mins, UK Ⓥ ⊙
D: Neil Jordan **A:** Beverly D'Angelo, Donal McCann, Niall Byrne, Lorraine Pilkington, J. G. Devlin (Palace/Promenade)

Irish writer-director Neil Jordan returns to his home turf with uneven results. Jimmy (Niall Byrne) is a musician and a dreamer who spends much of his time in the company of Rose (Lorraine Pilkington). Rose would like their relationship to become more intimate. Jimmy never knew his mother and lives with his father (Donal McCann), a drunken musician. One day his eye is caught by an attractive American woman (Beverly D'Angelo). He fantasizes a romantic liasion with her, but there are no prizes for guessing that she's really his long-lost mother. Like everything else in the film, the incest theme is tentatively handled.

MIRACLE CAN HAPPEN, A
See: On Our Merry Way

MIRACLE IN MILAN
See: Miracolo a Milano

MIRACLE IN SOHO
1957, 98 mins, UK Ⓥ
D: Julian Amyes **A:** John Gregson, Belinda Lee, Cyril Cusack, Rosalie Crutchley, Ian Bannen, Billie Whitelaw (Rank)

A rather slow-moving sentimental yarn has been woven around the polyglot population in central London's Soho. A small side street of shops and cafés has been shut down for road repairs and Mike, one of the working gang, gets involved with an Italian family about to emigrate to Canada. The younger girl falls for Mike's charm, and stays behind, only to find he doesn't want her. John Gregson never seems quite at home in rough clothes but makes a likable personality of the roving Romeo, and Belinda Lee is simple and naive as the anglicized Italian girl in love with him.

MIRACLE OF LIFE, THE
See: Our Daily Bread

MIRACLE OF MORGAN'S CREEK, THE
1944, 101 mins, US Ⓥ
D: Preston Sturges **A:** Eddie Bracken,

Betty Hutton, Diana Lynn, William Demarest, Brian Donlevy, Akim Tamiroff (Paramount)

The miracle, as director Preston Sturges terms it, is the birth to Eddie Bracken and Betty Hutton of a set of sextuplets. Directed in the satirical Sturges vein, the story makes much of characterization and somewhat wacky comedy, plus some slapstick, with excellent photography figuring throughout. The Sturges manner of handling crowds and various miscellaneous characters who are almost nothing more than flashes in the picture, such as the small-town attorney and the justice of the peace, contribute enormously to the enjoyment derived. Bracken is a small-town bank clerk who yearns to get into uniform and is madly in love with Hutton. After getting out to an all-night party with soldiers, the latter wakes up to remember that she married a serviceman, but can't recall the name, what the spouse looked like, or anything except that they didn't give their right names.

1944: Nomination: Best Original Screenplay

MIRACLE ON 34TH STREET
(UK: THE BIG HEART)
1947, 95 mins, US Ⓥ ⊙

D: George Seaton **A:** Maureen O'Hara, John Payne, Edmund Gwenn, Gene Lockhart, Natalie Wood, Thelma Ritter (20th Century-Fox)

Story poses question of just how valid is the belief in Santa Claus. Edmund Gwenn, old man's home inmate, becomes Santa at Macy's department store, events pile up that make it necessary to actually prove he is the McCoy and not a slightly touched old gent. Gwenn has no doubt that he's the real article. Film is an actor's holiday, providing any number of choice roles that are played to the hilt. Edmund Gwenn's Santa Claus performance will be thoroughly enjoyed by all.

1947: Best Supp. Actor (Edmund Gwenn), Original Story, Screenplay
Nomination: Best Picture

MIRACLE ON 34TH STREET
1994, 114 mins, US Ⓥ Ⓥ ⊙

D: Les Mayfield **A:** Richard Attenborough, Elizabeth Perkins, Dylan McDermott, Mara Wilson, Robert Prosky, J. T. Walsh (Hughes/20th Century-Fox)

There's no lack of Santa mentality in the remake of the Christmas chestnut. Minor and subtle tampering with the 1947 vintage holiday yarn proves both an asset and a hindrance. Kriss Kringle (Richard Attenborough) becomes the department store Santa. Not only does he resemble the yuletide icon, he genuinely loves children and embodies the spirit of giving. And, oh yes, he just happens to be the real McCoy, so he says. The trouble is that there are still folks who refuse to recognize the obvious. Not only is Attenborough the embodiment of decency, he's having a crackling good time bringing the character to earth.

MIRACLE WOMAN, THE
1931, 90 mins, US

D: Frank Capra **A:** Barbara Stanwyck, David Manners, Sam Hardy, Beryl Mercer, Russell Hopton (Columbia)

Film has two unusual aspects. One is its basic theme of an exposé on evangelism. The other is a punch sequence at the opening, perhaps the strongest scene the feature possesses. Frank Capra traces the girl through her exhortatory racket to the thrill finish of a tabernacle blaze which, from the mob standpoint, has been exceedingly well handled. Barbara Stanwyck's performance here is splended, with plenty of fire balanced by undertones of instinctive character softness and mood as she slowly falls in love with a blind boy who becomes one of her ardent followers.

MIRACLE WORKER, THE
1962, 106 mins, US Ⓥ

D: Arthur Penn **A:** Anne Bancroft, Patty Duke, Victor Jory, Inga Swenson, Andrew Prine (United Artists)

Production was directed by Arthur Penn, who staged the legit version, and stars Anne Bancroft and Patty Duke in the roles they introduced to Broadway. William Gibson's screenplay relates the story of the young Helen Keller and how, through the dedication, perseverance and courage of her teacher, Annie Sullivan, she establishes a means of communication with the world she cannot see or hear. Where the picture really excels, outside of its inherent story values, is in the realm of photographic technique. The measured dissolves, focal shifts and lighting and filtering enrich the production considerably.

1962: Best Actress (Anne Bancroft), Supp. Actress (Patty Duke)
Nominations: Best Director, Adapted Screenplay, B&W Costume Design

MIRACOLO A MILANO
(US: MIRACLE IN MILAN)
1951, 100 mins, Italy Ⓥ ⊙

D: Vittorio De Sica **A:** Emma Gramatica, Francesco Golisano, Paolo Stoppa, Brunella Bovo, Anna Carena (De Sica/ENIC)

An intellectual fairy tale, film tells the story of Toto (Francesco Golisano), an orphan boy who joins a colony of beggars in a shack village on the outskirts of Milan. When the rich owner of the land discovers oil under the village and tries to evict the beggars, Toto helps fight them off with the aid of a miraculous dove given him for his good qualities by a friendly fairy. The opening sequences, the foster mother's funeral, Toto's arrival at the beggar village, the tramps' fight for heat on a cold wintry day, the innocent love of Toto and his girl, are among many superb moments. The sharp satire of the oil-greedy industrialist is handled in a broader, perhaps exaggerated manner, and pic is liberally sprinkled with intelligent humor, much of it ironic.

MIRAGE
1965, 108 mins, US Ⓥ

D: Edward Dmytryk **A:** Gregory Peck, Diane Baker, Walter Matthau, Kevin McCarthy, Jack Weston, Leif Erickson (Universal)

Mirage starts as a mystery, unfolds as a mystery, ends as a mystery. There are moments of stiff action and suspense but plot is as confusing as it is overly contrived. Gregory Peck stars as an amnesiac trying to learn why he is the target for assassins. Edward Dmytryk keeps a tight rein on pace and manages vigorous movement in individual sequences, but cannot overcome script deficiencies. Peck makes the most of what's offered him as a brooding man trying to save his life.

MIRANDA
1948, 80 mins, UK

D: Ken Annakin **A:** Glynis Johns, Googie Withers, Griffith Jones, John McCallum, Margaret Rutherford, David Tomlinson (Gainsborough)

Planning a holiday alone in Cornwall, a doctor is dragged out of his fishing boat to the sea bottom by Miranda, a lovely mermaid. Price for return to his home and wife is that he takes Miranda to London. Everything is rightly played for laughs and Glynis Johns makes the mermaid an attractive and almost credible creature.

MIRROR CRACK'D, THE
1981, 105 mins, UK Ⓥ ⊙

D: Guy Hamilton **A:** Angela Lansbury, Elizabeth Taylor, Kim Novak, Rock Hudson, Geraldine Chaplin, Tony Curtis (EMI)

A nostalgic throwback to the genteel British murder mystery pix of the 1950s. Though Angela Lansbury is top billed in the role of Agatha Christie's famed sleuth Jane Marple, the central part really is Elizabeth Taylor's, with her most genuinely affecting dramatic performance in years as a film star attempting a comeback following an extended nervous breakdown. Taylor has an uproarious good time as she trades bitchy insults with Kim Novak.

MIRROR HAS TWO FACES, THE
1996, 126 mins, US Ⓥ

D: Barbra Streisand **A:** Barbra Streisand, Jeff Bridges, Pierce Brosnan, George Segal, Mimi Rogers, Lauren Bacall (Milchan-Barwood/TriStar)

The Mirror Has Two Faces is a vanity production of the first order. A staggeringly obsessive expression of the importance of appearances and being adored, Barbra Streisand's third directorial outing is an old-fashioned wish-fulfillment romantic comedy directed and performed in the broadest possible manner. Hunky university prof Gregory (Jeff Bridges) feels so desperate for a meaningful relationship not based on sex that he places a personals ad. He ends up on a "date" with fellow prof Rose Morgan (Streisand), who lives with her hovering mother (Lauren Bacall). Gregory proposes they get married, with no sex in the equation to mess things up. After he leaves on a European book tour, Rose has a complete makeover. When he returns, she tells him their old deal is off. Bacall snaps out the one-liners with consummate skill. But ultimately, of course, it is Streisand who is the subject of the director's uninterrupted gaze.

1996: Nominations: Best Supp. Actress (Lauren Bacall), Original Song ("I Finally Found Someone")

MISERY
1990, 107 mins, US Ⓥ ⊙

D: Rob Reiner **A:** James Caan, Kathy Bates, Frances Sternhagen, Richard Farnsworth, Lauren Bacall (Castle Rock/Nelson)

A very obvious gothic thriller, a functional adaptation of the Stephen King bestseller. Misery is the name of the 19th-

century heroine of a series of gothic romances penned by James Caan. His car crashes and Kathy Bates digs him out of the snow and wreckage. A plump former nurse, she fixes up his severely injured legs and virtually holds him prisoner, incommunicado, for the rest of the film. Key plot gimmick is that Caan's killed off the profitable but hack-work Misery character, an act that turns adoring fan Bates against him and sets in motion her obsession that he resurrect the fictional character.
1990: Best Actress (Kathy Bates)

MISFITS, THE
1961, 124 mins, US Ⓥ ⊙
D: John Huston **A:** Clark Gable, Marilyn Monroe, Montgomery Clift, Thelma Ritter, Eli Wallach (United Artists)

Clark Gable essays the role of a self-sufficient Nevada cowboy. Into his life ambles a woman (Marilyn Monroe) possessed of an almost uncanny degree of humanitarian compassion. Their relationship matures smoothly enough until Gable goes mustanging, a ritual in which wild, ''misfit'' mustangs are rudely roped into captivity. Revolted by what she regards as cruel and mercenary, Monroe, with the aid of yet another misfit, rodeo performer Montgomery Clift, strives to free the captive horses. The film is somewhat uneven in pace and not entirely sound in dramatic structure. Character development is choppy in several instances.

MISHIMA
A LIFE IN FOUR CHAPTERS
1985, 120 mins, US Ⓥ
D: Paul Schrader **A:** Ken Ogata, Kenji Sawada, Yasosuke Bando, Toshiyuki Nagashima (Zoetrope/Filmlink)

A boldly conceived, intelligent and consistently absorbing study of the Japanese writer and political iconoclast's life, work and death. The most famous of contemporary Japanese novelists to Westerners, Yukio Mishima became forever notorious in 1970 when he entered a military garrison in Tokyo, ''captured'' a general, delivered an impassioned speech to an assembly and then committed *seppuku* (ritual suicide). Director Paul Schrader and collaborators have opted to combine relatively realistic treatment of some aspects of Mishima's life, particularly his final day, with highly stylized renditions of assorted semiautobiographical literary works in an effort to convey key points about the man's personality and credos.

MISS FIRECRACKER
1989, 102 mins, US Ⓥ ⊙
D: Thomas Schlamme **A:** Holly Hunter, Mary Steenburgen, Tim Robbins, Alfre Woodard, Scott Glenn, Trey Wilson (Corsair)

Holly Hunter reprises her stage role as Carnelle, a former goodtime girl whose dream is to win the local Miss Firecracker contest in her hometown of Yazoo City, MS. *Miss Firecracker* is peopled with oddball characters, notably Tim Robbins as Steenburgen's free-spirit brother and Alfre Woodard as the black seamstress assigned to fabricate Carnelle's contest costume. Putting the show over with a bang is Hunter, the epitome of energy in a tailor-made feisty role.

MISSING
1982, 122 mins, US Ⓥ ⊙
D: Constantin Costa-Gavras **A:** Jack Lemmon, Sissy Spacek, Melanie Mayron, John Shea, Charles Cioffi, David Clennon (Universal)

Although the country in question is never named, the subject here is unequivocally that of US involvement in the 1973 military coup in Allende's Chile. Drama presents John Shea and Sissy Spacek as a vaguely counterculturish couple living in Santiago. When Shea inexplicably disappears and Spacek can get nowhere in locating him, his father (Jack Lemmon) flies down to get heavy with US government officials. Real jolt of the picture derives from the premise that, when pressed, the US government places the interests of business above those of individual citizens.
1982: Best Adapted Screenplay
Nominations: Best Picture, Actor (Jack Lemmon), Actress (Sissy Spacek)

MISSING IN ACTION
1984, 101 mins, US Ⓥ ⊙
D: Joseph Zito **A:** Chuck Norris, M. Emmet Walsh, Lenore Kasdorf, James Hong, David Tress (Cannon)

With the Philippines filling in for Vietnam jungles, with Chuck Norris kicking and firing away, with a likable sidekick in the black-marketeering figure of M. Emmet Walsh, and with a touch of nudity in sordid Bangkok bars, writer and director have marshaled a formula pic with a particularly jingoistic slant: even though the war is long over, the Commies in Vietnam still deserve the smack of a bullet.

MISSION, THE
1986, 125 mins, UK ⓥ ⊙ ⌑
D: Roland Joffe **A:** Robert De Niro, Jeremy Irons, Ray McAnally, Liam Neeson, Aidan Quinn, Ronald Pickup (Goldcrest/Kingsmere/Enigma)

Spectacular scenery and an extraordinary high degree of production values can't conceal serious flaws. The script is based on an intriguing historical incident in mid-18th-century South America, pitting avaricious colonialists against the Jesuits. The fundamental problem is that the script is cardboard thin, pinning labels on its characters and arbitrarily shoving them into stances to make plot points. The two principal actors, Robert De Niro and Jeremy Irons, work hard to animate their parts, but there is little to do. *The Mission* is probably the first film in which De Niro gives a bland, uninteresting performance.
1986: Best Cinematography
Nominations: Best Picture, Director, Costume Design, Art Direction, Editing, Original Score

MISSIONARY, THE
1983, 90 mins, UK ⓥ ⌑
D: Richard Loncraine **A:** Michael Palin, Maggie Smith, Trevor Howard, Denholm Elliott, Michael Hordern, Graham Crowden (HandMade)

Turn-of-the-century English gentry targeted in *The Missionary* remains good for laughs, especially in the hands of the talented Michael Palin. But Palin's script meanders wastefully across three separate story possibilities, never making full use of any of them. As the Anglican title character called home to England, Palin has a brief encounter on the boat with her ladyship Maggie Smith. But the reverend's mind is on marriage to his childhood sweetheart (Phoebe Nicholls). Once in London, Palin is to start a slum mission for "fallen women." And here comes Smith with the seed money Palin needs, provided he's friendly in return.

MISSION IMPOSSIBLE
1996, 110 mins, US ⓥ ⊙ ⌑
D: Brian De Palma **A:** Tom Cruise, Jon Voight, Emmanuelle Beart, Henry Czerny, Jean Reno, Ving Rhames (Paramount)

Mission Impossible just might be the most dour sexless piece of escapism in memory. Cruise stars as Ethan Hunt, a hotshot member of an elite, unnamed US intelligence group. A former Russian spy is planning the theft of a computer disk containing the true identities of the world's top undercover agents, and the team's mission is to interrupt the crime. Suffice it to say that everything goes wrong, with only Cruise's Hunt and Emmanuelle Beart's Claire surviving. With Hunt alive his own agency decides that he must be a mole. Cruise's character spends the bulk of the film running from his former cohorts. More often than not, the various twists and turns are less ingenious than simply confusing.

MISSION TO MOSCOW
1943, 123 mins, US
D: Michael Curtiz **A:** Walter Huston, Ann Harding, Oscar Homolka, Gene Lockhart, Eleanor Parker, Helmut Dantine (Warner)

Hollywood's initial effort at living history is of a highly intellectual nature. Real names are used throughout—Roosevelt, Churchill, Stalin, Davies, Litvinov, et al. and the casting is aimed for physical likeness to the person portrayed. The jolting realism of the likenesses is far from the least of the picture's interesting aspects. Film follows pretty much in chronological order from the time of Roosevelt's appointment of the progressively minded, capitalist-corporation lawyer Joseph E. Davies to the post of ambassador to Russia.
1943: Nomination: Best B&W Art Direction

MISSISSIPPI
1935, 80 mins, US
D: A. Edward Sutherland **A:** Bing Crosby, W. C. Fields, Joan Bennett, Queenie Smith, Gail Patrick (Paramount)

Paramount obviously couldn't make up its mind what it wanted to do with this film; it's rambling and hokey. For a few moments it's sheer farce, for a few moments it's romance. And it never jells. W. C. Fields works hard throughout the film, giving it whatever entertainment value it has. All three numbers are slow, dreamy tunes for Crosby to sing.

MISSISSIPPI BURNING
1988, 125 mins, US ⓥ ⊙
D: Alan Parker **A:** Gene Hackman, Willem Dafoe, Frances McDormand, Brad Dourif, R. Lee Ermey (Orion)

Though its credibility is undermined by a fanciful ending, *Mississippi Burning*

captures much of the truth in its telling of the impact of a 1964 FBI probe into the murders of three civil rights workers. Story follows the FBI men (Gene Hackman and Willem Dafoe) who've been sent down to Jessup, MS, to investigate the disappearance of three voter activists, one black and two white Jews. The two run into resistance from both the guilty parties and the blacks, who've been terrorized into silence. Dafoe gives a disciplined and noteworthy portrayal, but it's Hackman who steals the picture.
1988: Best Cinematography
Nominations: Best Picture, Director, Actor (Gene Hackman), Supp. Actress (Frances McDormand), Editing, Sound

MISSISSIPPI GAMBLER, THE
1953, 99 mins, US
D: Rudolph Mate **A:** Tyrone Power, Piper Laurie, Julie Adams, John McIntire, Paul Cavanaugh (Universal)

Opening finds Tyrone Power ready to start a career as an honest-dealing riverboat gambler. As he is ready to take off for the trip to New Orleans, dockside incidents team him with John McIntire, a card dealer, and acquaint him with Piper Laurie, spitfire southern belle, and her brother (John Baer). Power carries off the romantic requirements with ease, looks good in his fencing scenes, and otherwise takes good care of what action he is given.

MISSISSIPPI MASALA
1992, 118 mins, US ⊙
D: Mira Nair **A:** Denzel Washington, Sarita Choudhury, Roshan Seth, Sharmila Tagore, Charles S. Dutton (Cinecom/Mirabi)

Indian director Mira Nair's tragicomedy is less passionate and disturbing than many US pics dealing with race relations. The dramatic opening, set in Uganda in 1972, shows a middle-class Indian family forced to leave when Idi Amin takes power. Story jumps to present-day Mississippi, where the family has settled. There's a minor traffic accident involving a white redneck, black youth Demetrius (Denzel Washington), and Indian girl Mina (Sarita Choudhury). Mina and Demetrius are attracted to each other right away. Washington and Choudhury carry the film smoothly and agreeably.

MISS JULIE
See: Froken Julie

MISSOURI BREAKS, THE
1976, 126 mins, US ⊙
D: Arthur Penn **A:** Marlon Brando, Jack Nicholson, Kathleen Lloyd, Randy Quaid, Frederic Forrest, Harry Dean Stanton (United Artists)

The environment is the Montana headlands of the Missouri River, where pioneer John McLiam is pretty well master of the territory. Enter Jack Nicholson, leader of the area's horse thieves. Finally comes Marlon Brando, hired gun, engaged by McLiam to ferret out the Nicholson gang. *The Missouri Breaks* leaves a depressing sense of waste. As a film achievement it's corned beef and ham hash.

MISS SADIE THOMPSON
1953, 90 mins, US ⊙ ⊙
D: Curtis Bernhardt **A:** Rita Hayworth, Jose Ferrer, Aldo Ray, Russell Collins, Peggy Converse, Charles Bronson (Columbia/Beckworth)

Rain, the stage play which John Colton made from W. Somerset Maugham's story about sex, sin, and salvation, is back for a third try as a motion picture, fancied up with 3-D and Technicolor. The lensing having been done in Hawaii, the presentation has a lush tropical look. In this treatment, Sadie is a shady lady chased out of a Honolulu bawdy house by Davidson, a man determined to keep sin out of the islands. Rita Hayworth catches the feel of the title character well, even to deglamorizing makeup, costuming, and photography. Less effective is Jose Ferrer's Alfred Davidson, no longer a missionary bigot but a straight layman bigot.
1953: Nomination: Best Song ("Blue Pacific Blues")

MISS TATLOCK'S MILLIONS
1948, 99 mins, US
D: Richard Haydn **A:** John Lund, Wanda Hendrix, Barry Fitzgerald, Monty Woolley, Robert Stack (Paramount)

Plot concerns a screwball family and the idiot heir to millions, with a number of tangential ramifications that keep the fun pot boiling. John Lund and Wanda Hendrix team brightly in the principal roles and film receives major assists from Barry Fitzgerald, Monty Woolley, Ilka Chase and others. In addition to directing, Haydn cuts himself in for a very funny bit as an eccentric lawyer, using the name of Richard Rancyd.

MISTER FROST

1990, 104 mins, France/UK 🎥 ⊙

D: Philippe Setbon **A:** Jeff Goldblum, Alan Bates, Kathy Baker, Roland Girand, Jean-Pierre Cassel, Daniel Gelin (Hugo/AAA)

Tepid thriller about a mass murderer who claims to be the devil himself. Most of the story is set in a clinic "somewere in Europe" where Jeff Goldblum tells lady psychiatrist Kathy Baker, Yes, he's Satan in person, and he's fuming mad because modern psychiatry has cheated him out of authorship in 20th-century evil. Now he wants to make a comeback and has chosen Baker as his agent.

MISTER MOSES

1965, 115 mins, US ▭

D: Ronald Neame **A:** Robert Mitchum, Carroll Baker, Ian Bannen, Alexander Knox, Raymond St. Jacques, Orlando Martins (United Artists)

The biblical Moses, in a manner, has been updated for this Frank Ross production, switching the plot to an American diamond smuggler leading an African tribe to a promised land. Director Ronald Neame has taken every advantage of fascinating African terrain for his unusual adventure yarn from Max Catto's novel.

MISTER QUILP

1975, 117 mins, UK

D: Michael Tuchner **A:** Anthony Newley, David Hemmings, David Warner, Michael Hordern, Paul Rogers, Jill Bennett (Avco Embassy)

Sprightly musical version of Charles Dickens's *The Old Curiosity Shop*. Anthony Newley, a corrupt lender in league with fringe lawyer David Warner and the latter's sister Jill Bennett, harasses shop owner Michael Hordern and granddaughter Sarah Jane Varley, both rescued in time by arrival of Paul Rogers, Hordern's wealthy long-lost brother.

MISTER ROBERTS

1955, 120 mins, US 🎥 ▭

D: John Ford, Mervyn LeRoy **A:** Henry Fonda, James Cagney, William Powell, Jack Lemmon, Betsy Palmer (Orange/Warner)

Henry Fonda, who scored on the stage in the title role, repeats in the picture as the cargo officer who resented not being in the thick of the fighting in the Pacific during World War II. James Cagney is simply great as the captain of the ship.

William Powell tackles the role of ship's doctor with an easy assurance that makes it stand out, and Jack Lemmon is a big hit as Ensign Pulver.

1955: Best Supp. Actor (Jack Lemmon)
Nominations: Best Picture, Sound

MISUNDERSTOOD

1984, 91 mins, US 🎥

D: Jerry Schatzberg **A:** Gene Hackman, Henry Thomas, Rip Torn, Huckleberry Fox, Susan Anspach (Accent/Keith Barish)

Somber and largely unsentimental study of a rift and ultimate reconciliation between father and son, is a "remake and adaptation" of Luigi Comencini's 1967 Italian pic *Incompreso*. New version places former postwar black-marketeer and now shipping magnate Gene Hackman in a palatial home in Tunisia. His wife has just died, and Hackman has a tough time breaking the news to his seven- or eight-year-old son, Henry Thomas.

MITT LIV SOM HUND
(US: MY LIFE AS A DOG)

1985, 100 mins, Sweden 🎥

D: Lasse Hallstrom **A:** Anton Glanzelius, Anki Liden, Tomas von Bromssen, Manfred Serner, Melinda Kinnaman (Svensk Filmindustri)

An exquisite look at childhood. Ingemar Johansson has a hard time adjusting to the atmosphere of his beloved mother's house. She is bedridden with a terminal illness, but also given to temper tantrums. When his mother eventually dies, Ingemar finds elbowroom for his mischief when settling permanently with his soccer-playing, glassblower uncle, an amiable prankster himself, in a cozily tolerant household of no-nonsense love and happiness. Getting down on his knees to bark turns out to be the boy's best means of getting around various moments of crisis. Otherwise, he is endowed with a charm so obvious that nobody can quite help loving him.

MI VIDA LOCA

1993, 95 mins, US 🎥

D: Allison Anders **A:** Angel Aviles, Seidy Lopez, Jacob Vargas, Marlo Marron, Nelida Lopez (Cineville/HBO/Odyssey)

A portrait of young Latino women in the Los Angeles barrios. Dramatically fuzzy and very flat visually and in performance, this slice-of-life look at the gang culture focuses on two gang girls, Sad Girl (Angel Aviles) and Mousie (Seidy Lopez), lifelong friends who nearly come to blows after discovering they have been sharing the same man. Anders's staging of scenes is listless and unimaginative. The actresses' range seems limited at best.

MIXED BLOOD
(UK: COCAINE)
1984, 97 mins, US ⊚
D: Paul Morrissey A: Marilia Pera, Richard Ulacia, Linda Kerridge, Geraldine Smith, Angel David (Sef Saellite)

A tale of rival youth gangs tied into the city's drug scene, *Mixed Blood* paints a colorful story of kingdom building, corruption, and revenge. Adopting an overblown style of performance, the picture maintains an edgy quality where one is often wondering whether to laugh or shudder at the proceedings.

MIXED NUTS
1994, 97 mins, US Ⓥ ⊚
D: Nora Ephron A: Steve Martin, Madeline Kahn, Robert Klein, Anthony LaPaglia, Juliette Lewis, Rob Reiner (Tri-Star)

The holiday spirit goes into life-threatening cardiac arrest with this Christmas-themed comedy. Philip (Steve Martin) operates the Venice, CA, help line, Lifesavers. In fact, the crew manning the phones could stand a little bit of counseling. Blanch Munchnik (Madeline Kahn) is a tart-tongued widow and Catherine (Rita Wilson) is repressed. There's a parade of weirdos on the line and in the office. Director/coscripter Nora Ephron pitches the humor at a cacophonous level and displays the comedic equivalent of two left feet in evolving an absurdist, slapstick yarn.

MOANA
1926, 69 mins, US Ⓥ ⊚ ⊗
D: Robert Flaherty (Paramount)

A magnified travel film. The Flahertys have delved into the southern climes for their subject matter. A subtitle states that the men lingered with the Samoans for two years in order to win the confidence of the tribe and get the inside native stuff. The spearing of fish, the capture of a giant turtle in the water by two swimmers, and the riding of the breakers by a home-made skiff provide the major "action" scenes.

MOB, THE
1951, 87 mins, US
D: Robert Parrish A: Broderick Crawford, Betty Buehler, Richard Kiley, Neville Brand, Ernest Borgnine (Columbia)

Broderick Crawford is fine as a cop who poses as a hood to overthrow racketeers who've been shaking down dockworkers on the waterfront. Fistfights, gunfire, and some salty dialogue and sexy interludes involving Crawford with Lynne Baggett enliven the proceedings considerably.

MO' BETTER BLUES
1990, 127 mins, US Ⓥ ⊚
D: Spike Lee A: Denzel Washington, Spike Lee, Wesley Snipes, Joie Lee, Cynda Williams, Giancarlo Esposito (40 Acres and a Mule/Universal)

Personal rather than social issues come to the fore in a Spike Lee personality piece dressed in jazz trappings. More focused on the sexual dilemmas of its main character than on musical themes, contempo tale stars Denzel Washington as Bleek Gilliam, a self-absorbed New York horn player who leads a jazz quintet on a roll at a trendy Manhattan club. Joie Lee and Cynda Williams play the women who compete for Bleek's attention. If *Mo' Better* is soft in the center, the characters in and around the band and the nightclub provide winning entertainment.

MOBSTER, THE
See: I, Mobster

MOBSTERS
1991, 104 mins, US Ⓥ ⊚
D: Michael Karbelnikoff A: Christian Slater, Patrick Dempsey, Richard Grieco, F. Murray Abraham, Lara Flynn Boyle, Anthony Quinn (Universal)

Seemingly can't-miss premise of teen-heartthrob gangsters gets lost in self-important direction, a shoddy script, and muddled storytelling. The narrative is amazingly confused in light of its simplicity: two Italian and two Jewish kids from the ghetto team up in the 1920s and get into organized crime, gradually finding themselves caught between two dons. True highlights come from its longer-toothed characters, with Anthony Quinn's lusty portrayal of Don Masseria and F. Murray Abraham as the Yiddish-spouting no-goodnik, Arnold Rothstein.

MOBY DICK
1956, 116 mins, UK Ⓥ ⊚
D: John Huston A: Gregory Peck, Richard Basehart, Leo Genn, Harry Andrews, Orson Welles (Moulin/Warner)

Moby Dick is interesting more often

than exciting, faithful to the time and text more than great theatrical entertainment. Essentially it is a chase picture and yet not escaping the sameness and repetitiousness which often dulls the chase formula. Gregory Peck wears a stump leg made of the jaw of a whale and he lives only to kill the greatest whale of all, the white-hided super-monster, Moby Dick, the one which had chewed off his leg. Peck's Ahab is not very "elemental." Peck often seems understated and much too gentlemanly for a man supposedly consumed by insane fury.

MODEL SHOP
1969, 90 mins, US
D: Jacques Demy **A:** Anouk Aimee, Gary Lockwood, Alexandra Hay, Carol Cole, Severn Darden (Columbia)

French filmmaker Jacques Demy brings a fresh look at L.A. and American youth. And it is a work of love in its attitude toward the city and its characters. Demy can be sentimental, sans bathos or mawkishness, and comes up with a day in the life of a 26-year-old youthful drifter whose one romantic interlude is a step in coping with his life.

MODERN ROMANCE
1981, 93 mins, US Ⓥ ⊙
D: Albert Brooks **A:** Albert Brooks, Kathryn Harrold, Bruno Kirby, Jane Hallaren, James L. Brooks, George Kennedy (Columbia)

Star, director, and cowriter Albert Brooks plays a nice-enough young fellow who cannot make a permanent commitment to his girlfriend, sympathetically portrayed by the beautiful and talented Kathryn Harrold. At first, he dumps her, then immediately regrets it and goes crazy trying to get her back. Succeeding in that, he starts aggravating her with jealousies. Many scenes play far beyond the laughs they're worth. One thing Brooks does well, however, is pepper the bit parts with interesting characters who all have a point to make, most particularly Bruno Kirby as his best friend.

MODERNS, THE
1988, 126 mins, US Ⓥ ⊙
D: Alan Rudolph **A:** Keith Carradine, Linda Fiorentino, John Lone, Wallace Shawn, Genevieve Bujold, Geraldine Chaplin (Alive/Nelson)

The artistic world of Paris in the 1920s comes to life as if in a lustrous dream in a romantic's lush vision of a group of expatriate Americans at a time and place of some of the century's most tumultuous creative activity. There is Nick Hart (Keith Carradine) who, at 33, is viewed suspiciously for not having made it yet as an artist. Oiseau (Wallace Shawn), a gossip columnist; Bertram Stone (John Lone), an elegant, rich, philistine art dealer; his wife, Rachel (Linda Fiorentino), with whom Nick has a past and, he hopes, a future; and Hemingway himself (Kevin J. O'Connor), who amusingly careens through the action in varying states of inebriation, trying out titles for a new book.

MODERN TIMES
1936, 85 mins, US Ⓥ
D: Charles Chaplin **A:** Charles Chaplin, Paulette Goddard, Henry Bergman, Chester Conklin, Hank Mann (United Artists)

As a cinematic entertainment Chaplin's first picture since *City Lights* (1931) is wholesomely funny. The pathos of the machine worker who suffers temporary derangement, as he tightens the bolts on a factory treadmill to a clocklike tempo, gives way to a series of similarly winning situations. In each the victim of circumstance meets temporary frustration, almost inevitably resulting in a ride in Black Maria. When finally achieving what promises to be a semblance of economic security the menace, in the form of the law, enters to arrest Paulette Goddard as a refugee vagrant. Goddard, a winsome waif attired almost throughout in short, ragged dress, registers handily.

MODESTY BLAISE
1966, 118 mins, UK Ⓥ
D: Joseph Losey **A:** Monica Vitti, Terence Stamp, Dirk Bogarde, Harry Andrews, Michael Craig (Janni)

One of the nuttiest, screwiest pictures ever made. Not merely a spy spoof, based on a book and a comic strip about a femme James Bond type, the colorful production gives the horse laugh to many different film plots and styles. Wacky screenplay propels Blaise, played by Monica Vitti, into a British government espionage scheme. Heading the opposition is Dirk Bogarde, an effete international criminal, while Vitti is aided by longtime sidekick, bed-hopping Terence Stamp.

DIE MOERDER SIND UNTER UNS (US: THE MURDERERS ARE AMONGST US)
1946, 80 mins, Germany
D: Wolfgang Staudte **A:** Hildegard Knef,

Wilhelm Borchert, Arno Paulsen, Robert Forsch, Albert Johann (Defa)

This first postwar German production is a serious film concerned with the knotty problem of the individual German's guilt for Nazism. While not fully successful, either as drama or ideology, film is marked by superb camera and montage technique recalling some of the first-rate German productions before the Nazi era. Framed against the ruins of Berlin, story is concerned with a young medico haunted into drunkenness by the memory of mass executions which were ordered by his captain in Poland. When the doctor once again meets the captain, now a kindly family man, he determines to kill the war criminal.

MOGAMBO
1953, 115 mins, US ⊛
D: John Ford A: Clark Gable, Ava Gardner, Grace Kelly, Donald Sinden, Laurence Naismith (M-G-M)

The lure of the jungle and romance get a sizzling workout in a socko package of entertainment, crammed with sexy two-fisted adventure. Romantic conflict boils up between the principals during a safari into gorilla country, where an anthropologist and his wife plan to do research. Clark Gable is the great white hunter leading the party. Gardner is the girl on the prowl for a man, and who has now settled on Gable. To get him she has to offset the sweeter charms of Grace Kelly, the wife, who also has become smitten with the Gable masculinity and is ready to walk out on Donald Sinden, the unexciting anthropologist.
1953: Nominations: Best Actress (Ava Gardner), Supp. Actress (Grace Kelly)

MOLL FLANDERS
1996, 123 mins, US ⊛ ◉ ⊨
D: Pen Densham A: Robin Wright, Morgan Freeman, Stockard Channing, John Lynch, Brenda Fricker (Trilogy/M-G-M)

Writer-director Densham uses Daniel Defoe's 1722 novel as only the most basic of blueprints to fashion a picaresque tale, by turns romantic and gritty, of a fiercely intelligent woman forever at odds with her lowly station in 18th-century London. Robin Wright holds together the film's swinging moods, her Moll moving from youthful exuberance to despair and, reawakened by love, on to something between resignation and hope. She's convincing at every turn.

MOLLY AND ME
1945, 76 mins, US ⊛
D: Lewis Seiler A: Gracie Fields, Monty Woolley, Roddy McDowall, Reginald Gardiner (20th Century-Fox)

Inauspicious title cloaks a pleasant comedy-drama. Story, with an English locale, opens with a jobless music hall entertainer (Fields) taking job as a housekeeper. She revitalizes a gloomy household, discharges a parasitical group of thieving servants, makes the place seem like home to the motherless boy, and finally brings about an understanding between father and son.

MOLLY MAGUIRES, THE
1970, 124 mins, US ⊛ ⊨
D: Martin Ritt A: Sean Connery, Richard Harris, Samantha Eggar, Frank Finlay, Anthony Zerbe (Paramount/Tamm)

The Molly Maguires, based on a Pennsylvania coal miners' rebellion of the late 19th century, is occasionally brilliant. Story is primarily that of Harris, hired by the mine owners to infiltrate the workers' ranks. Connery is a rebel leader. Eggar appears occasionally for some light romantic interludes with Harris.
1970: Nomination: Best Art Direction

MOM AND DAD SAVE THE WORLD
1992, 88 mins, US ⊛ ◉
D: Greg Beeman A: Teri Garr, Jeffrey Jones, Jon Lovitz, Thalmus Rasulala, Wallace Shawn, Eric Idle (Warner/HBO)

Little kids will find some infantile laughs in this silly sci-fi comedy. Teri Garr and Jeffrey Jones gamely struggle with inane dialogue as a California couple transported to a tacky-looking "planet of idiots." With garish color, goofy-looking creatures in rubbery costumes, and sets parodying old Flash Gordon serials, pic flaunts its modest budget with engaging candor. Basic trouble is with dumbness jokes stretched too far.

MOMENT BY MOMENT
1978, 105 mins, US
D: Jane Wagner A: Lily Tomlin, John Travolta, Andra Akers, Bert Kramer, Debra Feuer (Universal)

What seemed like inspired casting on paper, the teaming of John Travolta and Lily Tomlin, fails badly in execution. Improbable story is of a Beverly Hills chic housewife whose marriage has gone sour, and who meets up with an insecure young drifter, with whom she has an affair. Tomlin never varies her nasal monotone, nor her imperturbable exterior. It's a one-note performance that frustrates the entire picture. Not helping matters is the banal script, which has cliché piled atop cliché, and dialogue that evokes embarrassing laughter.

MOMENTS
1975, 92 mins, UK
D: Peter Crane **A:** Keith Michell, Angharad Rees, Bill Fraser, Jeanette Sterke, Donald Hewlett (Pemini)

Sincere and often moving film probes into man's loneliness and the dead-end meaninglessness of a middle-aged accountant (Keith Michell) who, after 20 years at his job and after the death of his wife and children in a car crash, decides to put an end to his life. Relationship between him and a young, flighty, and vivacious girl (Angharad Rees) who temporarily prevents him from carrying out his project is touchingly told.

MOMENT TO MOMENT
1966, 108 mins, US
D: Mervyn LeRoy **A:** Jean Seberg, Honor Blackman, Sean Garrison, Arthur Hill, Gregoire Aslan (Universal/Le Roy)

Mild suspense story blending a wife's infidelity and amnesia doesn't entirely jell for several reasons, mainly thin scripting, weak acting, and Mervyn LeRoy's too-leisurely pace. Jean Seberg lacks dimension as the wife, even allowing for the script. In early scenes, an overly passive limning—which suggests jaded boredom instead of a well-adjusted spouse in a single fall from grace—robs the role of most sympathy.

MOMMIE DEAREST
1981, 129 mins, US Ⓥ ⊙
D: Frank Perry **A:** Faye Dunaway, Diana Scarwid, Steve Forrest, Howard da Silva, Jocelyn Brando (Paramount)

This is Faye Dunaway as Joan Crawford and the results are, well, screen history. Dunaway does not chew scenery. Dunaway starts neatly at each corner of the set in every scene and swallows it whole, costars and all. Director Frank Perry's portrait here is sorry indeed, 129 minutes with a very pathetic and unpleasant individual. The story is familiar: self-centered, insecure, and pressured movie queen adopts two babies for both love and personal aggrandizement. Growing up, the

kids are battered between luxurious pampering and abuse, never finding real affection with mother, who finally dies and cuts them out of the will, reaching beyond the grave for final revenge.

MO' MONEY
1992, 89 mins, US Ⓥ ⊙
D: Peter Macdonald **A:** Damon Wayans, Marlon Wayans, Stacey Dish, Joe Santos, John Diehl (Columbia/Wife 'n' Kids)

Damon Wayans and his younger brother, Marlon, make a terrific comedy team in *Mo' Money*. Damon casts himself as a ne'er-do-well street punk who sets a poor role model for younger brother (Marlon). To pursue a lovely romantic interest (Stacey Dash), Damon gets a job in the mailroom for her credit card company. Soon the Wayanses have cooked up a scam using uncanceled credit cards to finance a shopping spree.

MONA LISA
1986, 104 mins, UK Ⓥ ⊙
D: Neil Jordan **A:** Bob Hoskins, Cathy Tyson, Michael Caine, Robbie Coltrane, Kate Hardie, Sammi Davis (HandMade/Palace)

The couple at the center of this wide and wayward romantic thriller are about as odd as you could find anywhere. George (Bob Hoskins), short in stature as well as intellect, is just out of prison. Simone (Cathy Tyson) is a tall, slender black whore who plies the poshest London hotels for her up-market trade. George gets a job driving Simone to her various assignations and finds himself falling in love with her. What follows is a pic that skillfully combines comedy and thriller, romance and sleaze.
1986: Nomination: Best Actor (Bob Hoskins)

MONDO CANE
1962, 105 mins, Italy Ⓥ ⊙
D: Gualtiero Jacopetti, Paolo Cavara, Franco Prosperi (Cineriz)

Various themes pop up along the way through this impressive, hard-hitting documentary feature, notably the cruel treatment inflicted on animals, including the human species. Vehicle is impressive on many counts: first, the material found on a round-the-world hunt; second, the juxtaposition of the various elements, sequences, and themes in order to provoke the viewer; third, the adult commentary which, in its original Italian version, manages glibness, irony, and satire without overdoing it.

MONEY FOR NOTHING
1993, 100 mins, US Ⓥ ⊙ ▭
D: Ramon Menendez **A:** John Cusack, Debi Mazar, Michael Madsen, Benicio Del Toro, Michael Rapaport, Maury Chaykin (Hollywood)

A predominantly serious film about a subject matter that seems rife with humor—an uneven true story about an out-of-work longshoreman who finds $1.2 million lying in the street. Joey (John Cusack) finds a bundle of money that has fallen out of an armored car, and he starts dreaming of the good life. Unfortunately, his ill-advised use of the cash creates an easy trail for a local detective (Michael Madsen) to follow, while Joey gets in deeper and deeper over his head by trying to launder the loot through the mob.

MONEY PIT, THE
1986, 91 mins, US Ⓥ ⊙
D: Richard Benjamin **A:** Shelley Long, Tom Hanks, Alexander Godunov, Maureen Stapleton, Joe Mantegna, Philip Bosco (Amblin)

The Money Pit is simply the pits. Shortly after the starring couple has bought a beautiful old house which quickly shows itself to be at the point of total disrepair, Tom Hanks says to Shelley Long, "It's a lemon, honey, let's face it." There is really very little else to be said about this gruesomely unfunny comedy.

MONEY TRAIN
1995, 110 mins, US Ⓥ ⊙
D: Joseph Ruben **A:** Wesley Snipes, Woody Harrelson, Jennifer Lopez, Robert Blake, Chris Cooper (Peters/Columbia)

In a wrinkle fabricated by some packaging agent, Wesley Snipes and Woody Harrelson play foster brothers (there are plenty of jokes about the lack of a resemblance) who work as New York City transit cops. John (Snipes) is protective of Charlie (Harrelson), a free spirit who gets himself indebted to the mob in a high-stakes poker game and keeps aggravating their obsessive boss, Patterson (wildly overplayed by Robert Blake). The script features a few laughs but plenty of completely inane and hackneyed dialogue. Pic's saving grace is Snipes.

MONEY TRAP, THE
1966, 91 mins, US ▭
D: Burt Kennedy **A:** Glenn Ford, Elke Sommer, Rita Hayworth, Ricardo Montalban, Joseph Cotten (M-G-M)

Adaptation of a Lionel White novel has the kernel of a good drama about a contemporary problem, that of an underpaid gumshoe dazzled into dishonesty by the riches of the criminals whom he encounters. Nearly all interest in this angle is snuffed out by extraneous, unbelievable subplots. Specifically, Glenn Ford is the cop, husband of Elke Sommer. They live in a splashy pad made possible by her father's will and stocks. When the stocks plummet, hard times loom.

MONKEY BUSINESS
1931, 78 mins, US Ⓥ ⊙
D: Norman Z. McLeod **A:** Groucho Marx, Harpo Marx, Chico Marx, Zeppo Marx, Thelma Todd (Paramount)

The usual Marx madhouse. It starts with the foursome as stowaways on a class liner, and switches to shore as the quartet evenly divide up to become bodyguards for a couple of racketeers. Leads to the kidnaping of one gangster's daughter (Ruth Hall) from a masquerade ball, with the finish a free-for-all between Zeppo (the youngest) and the heavy in a barn as Groucho gags his way from rafter to rafter and in and out of the hay. Harpo's main sequence is a mix-up in a Punch and Judy show evolving from a chase, while Groucho is always slipping through his double-meaning quips—Thelma Todd, a consistent eyeful, the subject of these cracks.

MONKEY BUSINESS
1952, 97 mins, US Ⓥ ⊙
D: Howard Hawks **A:** Cary Grant, Ginger Rogers, Charles Coburn, Marilyn Monroe, Hugh Marlowe (20th Century-Fox)

Attempt to draw out a thin, familiar slapstick idea isn't carried off. Story has Cary Grant as a research chemist using monkeys in his lab for elixir-of-youth experiments. Ginger Rogers is his amiable wife. One of the lab monkeys mixes up an assortment of chemical ingredients, dumps the concoction into the watercooler. First Grant, then Rogers, drink from the cooler, and immediately get teenage notions, emotions and symptoms. Marilyn Monroe appears as a nitwit secretary.

MONKEYS, GO HOME!
1967, 101 mins, US Ⓥ
D: Andrew V. McLaglen **A:** Maurice Chevalier, Dean Jones, Yvette Mimieux, Bernard Woringer (Walt Disney)

Set in France but filmed completely in Walt Disney's Studio, *Monkeys, Go Home* is an amusing comedy-romance in which Dean Jones, heir to an olive farm, provokes political and romantic complications when he decides to use chimpanzee labor. Maurice Chevalier heads the cast as a village priest. Film has the usual professional Disney blend of children, animals, humor, and charm.

MONKEY SHINES
1988, 115 mins, US Ⓥ ⊙
D: George A. Romero A: Jason Beghe, John Pankow, Melanie Parker, Joyce Van Patten (Orion)

Befuddled story about a man constrained from the neck down told by a director confused from the neck up. Jason Beghe starts out as a very virile, able-bodied young man. An accident robs Beghe of all physical ability below his jawline, leaving him despondently dependent on an array of technology. Beghe's best friend John Pankow, a yuppie mad scientist, volunteers one of his highly intelligent, chemically dependent capuchins to be trained to serve as Beghe's companion and helper. For a while, this all works beautifully. Until something dreadful happens.

MONKEY TROUBLE
1994, 95 mins, US Ⓥ ⊙
D: Franco Amurri A: ''Finster,'' Thora Birch, Harvey Keitel, Mimi Rogers, Christopher McDonald (New Line/Scott-Main)

Starring an adorably cute capuchin monkey, which performs magnificent tricks, *Monkey Trouble* is a touching children's adventure that belongs among the great animal movies. Nine-year-old Eva Gregory (Birch) desperately wants a pet. Opportunity knocks when Shorty Kohn (Harvey Keitel), a gypsy hustler, loses a capuchin monkey trained to entertain and lift the wallets and jewelry of the crowds along Venice Beach's boardwalk.

MON ONCLE
(US: MY UNCLE)
1958, 120 mins, France/Italy Ⓥ ⊙
D: Jacques Tati A: Jacques Tati, Jean-Pierre Zola, Alain Becourt, Adrienne Servanti, Lucien Fregis (Specta/Gray/Alter/Centauro)

Tati's film has inventiveness, gags, warmth, and a ''poetic'' approach to satire. Tati has built it via comic juxtaposition of two ways of life—his, as the eccentric, independent uncle, alongside a supermodern, hygienic, materialistic brother-in-law. Antiseptic house of Hulot's (Tati) relatives operates a myriad of time-saving but noisy electronic gadgets. Tati is the catalyst who unintentionally creates havoc. He wins over his nephew whose parents have no time for him and who is only really happy during the wonderful escapades with his uncle.
1958: Best Foreign Language Film

MONSIEUR BEAUCAIRE
1946, 90 mins, US
D: George Marshall A: Bob Hope, Joan Caulfield, Patric Knowles, Cecil Kellaway (Paramount)

Frantic, screwballish version of Booth Tarkington's costume novel about a court barber forced to impersonate royalty has plenty of giggles and a few solidly premised laughs. Bob Hope plays the French barber, Beaucaire, with all stops out, waltzes through trying situations and varied romances with a bravado that is his particular forte. It's all fun, but could have been even more so if treated with a bit less broadness.

MONSIEUR HIRE
(US: M. HIRE)
1989, 79 mins, France Ⓥ ⊙ ▭
D: Patrice Leconte A: Michel Blanc, Sandrine Bonnaire, Luc Thuillier, Andre Wilms (Cinea/Hachette Premiere/FR3)

Michel Blanc, the bald, diminutive funnyman, plays it utterly straight in an unconvincing adaptation of a 1933 novel by Georges Simenon. M. Hire's transfixed by the attractive young woman Alice (Sandrine Bonnaire) who lives across the courtyard and who doesn't believe in curtains. When Alice realizes she is being watched, she begins coming on to the lovesick voyeur who offers to take her abroad, away from her sordid life. Blanc does a creditable if not credible job as M. Hire in a dour, no-nonsense performance. Bonnaire gives some ambiguities and touching shadings to the two-faced girl.

MONSIEUR VERDOUX
1947, 122 mins, US Ⓥ
D: Charles Chaplin A: Charles Chaplin, Martha Raye, Isobel Elsom, Marilyn Nash, Irving Bacon, William Frawley (United Artists)

Comedy based on the characterization of a modern Parisian Bluebeard treads dangerous shoals indeed. Even if the accent were more effective, the fundamentals are unsound when it's revealed that Chaplin has been driven to marrying and murdering middling mesdames in order to provide for his ailing wife and their son of 10 years' marriage. Chaplin's endeavor to get his "common man" ideology into the film militates against its comedy values. Point is that depressions in the economy force us into being ruthless villains and murderers, despite the fact we are actually kind and sympathetic.

1947: Nomination: Best Original Screenplay

MONSIGNOR
1982, 122 mins, US ⓥ
D: Frank Perry **A:** Christopher Reeve, Genevieve Bujold, Fernando Rey, Jason Miller, Adolfo Celi (20th Century-Fox/Yablans)

Lots of potential for a rare, absorbing, behind-the-scenes look at the Vatican is totally blown. Constructed as a scene-by-scene exposé of all sorts of nefarious goings-on in post–Second World War Rome, the self-serious pic teeters on the brink of being an all-out hoot through much of its running time. It's amazing that screenwriters didn't spot the most gaping fundamental flaw here, namely the lack of any convincing explanation why Christopher Reeve's character became a priest in the first place.

MONSTER IN A BOX
1991, 88 mins, UK ⓥ
D: Nick Broomfield **A:** Spalding Gray (Blair)

Spalding Gray struts his anecdotal stuff once again. Titular "Monster" is Gray's 1,800-page autobiography, *Impossible Vacation*. Starting his peregrinations in 1987, Gray recounts how celeb status after *Swimming to Cambodia* gave him plenty of excuses to procrastinate. The easy laughs come at the start: East Coaster Gray's barbed comments on Tinseltown, where execs invite him to "idea lunches." Subsequent divertissements include AIDS hysteria in New York, a flying saucer project for HBO, and taking *Swimming* to the Moscow fest.

MONTE CARLO
1930, 93 mins, US
D: Ernst Lubitsch **A:** Jack Buchanan, Jeanette MacDonald, ZaSu Pitts, Claud Allister (Paramount)

If it were not for Jeanette MacDonald there would be no picture, this despite the disappointing direction of Ernst Lubitsch and the talker debut of England's Jack Buchanan, just the usual sort of juve with closely plastered down hair. A count, to meet an unknown countess, maneuvers to get her hairdresser's job, which he does. Then he wins, he says, 200,000 francs to take her out of Monte Carlo hock. About that time, as they both see *Monsieur Beaucaire* in different boxes at the theater, she surmises he isn't a hairdresser. It needs 90 minutes of film to unravel that.

MONTE WALSH
1970, 99 mins, US ⓥ ▭
D: William A. Fraker **A:** Lee Marvin, Jeanne Moreau, Jack Palance, Mitch Ryan, Jim Davis (Cinema Center)

A listless, wandering story of the old American West, which takes too long to get moving. Lee Marvin stars as a taciturn roughneck whose tragic romance with Jeanne Moreau comes across as irrelevant digression in a confused story. The basic feeble theme is what happened to prototype pioneers when Eastern money bought up ranches and began operating long-distance.

MONTH IN THE COUNTRY, A
1987, 96 mins, UK ⓥ ⓞ
D: Pat O'Connor **A:** Colin Firth, Kenneth Branagh, Natasha Richardson, Patrick Malahide, Richard Vernon (Euston)

Gentle but moving pic about two men recovering from the horrors of World War I during an idyllic summer in remote rolling English countryside. Birkin (Colin Firth), arriving at the remote Yorkshire village of Oxgodby to uncover a medieval wall painting in the local church, meets Moon (Kenneth Branagh), who is excavating a grave outside the churchyard. Birkin falls in love with the wife (Natasha Richardson) of an unfriendly local vicar, but never lets on to her about his passion, while the Branagh character turns out to be a homosexual.

MONTY PYTHON AND THE HOLY GRAIL
1975, 89 mins, UK ⓥ ⓞ
D: Terry Gilliam, Terry Jones **A:** Graham Chapman, John Cleese, Terry Gilliam, Eric Idle, Terry Jones, Michael Palin (Python)

Monty Python's Flying Circus send-up of Arthurian legend, performed in whimsical fashion with Graham Chapman an effective straight man as King Arthur.

Running gags include lack of horses for Arthur and his men, and a lackey clicking coconuts together to make suitable hoof noises as the men trot along. The extravagantly gruesome fight scenes, including one which ends with a man having all four limbs severed, will get laughs from some and make others squirm.

MONTY PYTHON'S LIFE OF BRIAN
See: Life of Brian

MONTY PYTHON'S THE MEANING OF LIFE
1983, 103 mins, UK ⑱ ⊙

D: Terry Jones **A:** Graham Chapman, John Cleese, Terry Gilliam, Eric Idle, Terry Jones, Michael Palin (HandMade)

Gross, silly, caustic, tasteless and obnoxious are all adjectives that alternately apply to *Monty Python's The Meaning of Life*, though probably the most appropriate description would simply be funny. Tracing the human existence from birth through death, the group touches on such areas as religion, education, marriage, sex, and war in a way it was no doubt never taught in school or in the home.

MOON AND SIXPENCE, THE
1943, 89 mins, US ⑱

D: Albert Lewin **A:** George Sanders, Herbert Marshall, Doris Dudley, Steven Geray, Eric Blore, Florence Bates (United Artists)

Somerset Maugham's widely read novel has been made into an intriguing, distinctive screen vehicle. The story of an English stockbroker who won fame as a painter, only just before his death, at times is reminiscent of *Citizen Kane*. George Sanders makes the strange life of the struggling artist live, and it's his outstanding screen role to date. The episodes in the distant island of Tahiti are rich in tropical flavor.

1943: Nomination: Best Scoring of a Dramatic Picture

MOONFLEET
1955, 86 mins, US ⑱ ⊙ ▭

D: Fritz Lang **A:** Stewart Granger, George Sanders, Joan Greenwood, Viveca Lindfors, Jon Whiteley, Liliane Montevecchi (M-G-M)

Costumed action, well spiced with loose ladies and dashing rakehells, is offered. Stewart Granger was a good choice for the dubious hero of the story, a high-living dandy who heads a gang of murderous smugglers headquartering in the English coastal village of Moonfleet. Later, it reminds of *Treasure Island* a bit when Granger and a small boy go through some highly imaginative adventures.

MOON IN THE GUTTER, THE
See: La Lune dans le Caniveau

MOON IS DOWN, THE
1943, 90 mins, US ⑱

D: Irving Pichel **A:** Cedric Hardwicke, Henry Travers, Lee J. Cobb, Peter Van Eyck (20th Century-Fox)

Story of Norway's invasion and resulting undercover uprising becomes the fight of inhabitants to survive in all conquered lands. There's the punishing of obdurate citizens, the executions to halt sabotage, and dropping of dynamite by 'chute to help this program with blasting of rail lines, bridges, radio, etc., finally bringing the mass hanging of top village officials. Director Pichel also plays an innkeeper bit and proves he's still a polished screen performer.

MOONLIGHT AND VALENTINO
1995, 104 mins, US ⑱

D: David Anspaugh **A:** Elizabeth Perkins, Whoopi Goldberg, Gwyneth Paltrow, Kathleen Turner, Jon Bon Jovi, Peter Coyote (Working Title)

Sharply observed, if a tad too earnest, comedy-drama with terrific female cast headed by a superlative Elizabeth Perkins. Story revolves around Rebecca Lott (Perkins), a happily married woman whose husband is hit by a car. Shellshocked and disoriented, she stubbornly refuses at first to acknowledge the W word (widow) to her eccentric best friend, Sylvie (Whoopi Goldberg). Rebecca's support group includes Lucy (Gwyneth Paltrow), her neurotic, virginal younger sister, and Alberta (Kathleen Turner), their overbearing former stepmother. Things begin to change in pic's second part, when, as a birthday present for Rebecca, Alberta hires a sexy house painter (Jon Bon Jovi) to "spruce up her siding."

MOONLIGHTING
1982, 97 mins, UK ⑱ ⊙

D: Jerzy Skolimowski **A:** Jeremy Irons, Eugene Lipinski, Jiri Stanislaw, Eugeniusz Haczkiewicz (White)

Four Poles are sent to London by their boss, who owns a house there, to fix it up. They go off a week before military law is declared. The four are headed by Jeremy

Irons, who is the only one who can speak English. The crew want to finish, buy things for their family, and go home. Irons pushes the work but then finds out about the military coup. He decides to keep it from the others. Film is inventive, though anecdotal.

MOONLIGHT SONATA
1937, 90 mins, UK ⊗
D: Lothar Mendes **A:** Ignace Jan Paderewski, Charles Farrell, Marie Tempest, Barbara Green, Eric Portman (Pall Mall)

Charming love story woven round the central personality of the world-famous pianist, Paderewski. Locale is Sweden, where Charles Farrell, agent for a country estate, declares his love for Ingrid, granddaughter of the baroness, by whom he is employed. Forced landing by a passenger plane brings into the household three men, one of them Paderewski. Of the aged maestro there can be no criticism; they wished to weave a story around him, and artistically and unpretentiously they have succeeded.

MOON OVER PARADOR
1988, 105 mins, US ⊗ ⊙
D: Paul Mazursky **A:** Richard Dreyfuss, Raul Julia, Sonia Braga, Jonathan Winters, Fernando Rey, Sammy Davis Jr. (Universal)

Paul Mazursky's elaborate farce has moments of true hilarity emerging only fitfully from a ponderous production. Pic has Richard Dreyfuss well cast as a stage and film actor on a location shoot in Parador. He's given an offer he can't refuse by police chief Raul Julia to impersonate the just-deceased dictator. Dreyfuss reluctantly adopts the role, but soon takes on the new persona in earnest after being coached by the dictator's sexy mistress Madonna (Sonia Braga in a flamboyant, delicious turn).

MOONRAKER
1979, 126 mins, UK ⊗ ⊙ ▭
D: Lewis Gilbert **A:** Roger Moore, Lois Chiles, Michael Lonsdale, Richard Kiel, Bernard Lee (United Artists/Eon)

Roger Moore clearly has adapted the James Bond character to himself and serves well as the wisecracking, incredibly daring, and irresistible hero. The main problem this time is the outer-space setting, which somehow dilutes the mammoth monstrosity that 007 must save the world from. One more big mother ship hovering over Earth becomes just another model intercut with elaborate interiors. The visual effects, stunt work, and other technical contributions all work together expertly to make the most preposterous notions believable.
1979: Nomination: Best Visual Effects

MOON-SPINNERS, THE
1964, 118 mins, UK ⊗
D: James Neilson **A:** Hayley Mills, Eli Wallach, Peter McEnery, Joan Greenwood, Irene Papas, Pola Negri (Walt Disney)

With a mixture of American, English, and Greek talents, engaged in a silly but zestful tale, told against some photogenic landscapes, *The Moon-Spinners* naturally concentrates on Hayley Mills. Two English females (Mills and Joan Greenwood) become involved in a jewel-theft adventure that concerns the Moon-Spinners, the Cretan inn where they're staying. The intrigue includes an odd but colorful assortment of local types headed by Eli Wallach, a most hissable villain, his sister (Irene Papas), and a young, mysterious Englishman (Peter McEnery).

MOONSTRUCK
1987, 102 mins, US ⊗ ⊙
D: Norman Jewison **A:** Cher, Nicolas Cage, Vincent Gardenia, Olympia Dukakis, Danny Aiello (M-G-M)

A mostly appetizing blend of comedy and drama. Leads Cher and Nicolas Cage are both solid and appealing, but it's the pic's older lovers—especially the splendidly controlled Olympia Dukakis—who give *Moonstruck* its endearing spirit. Cher is Loretta Castorini, a vaguely dour, superstitious widow who accepts a wedding proposal from the altogether unprepossessing Johnny Cammareri (Tony Aiello). Loretta, resigned to accepting mediocrity for the sake of security, receives a shock upon meeting his kid brother. Cage's Ronny is a brooding, vital, angry, barely contained force haunted by his past.
1987: Best Actress (Cher), Supp. Actress (Olympia Dukakis), Original Screenplay
Nominations: Best Picture, Director, Supp. Actor (Vincent Gardenia)

MOONTIDE
1942, 94 mins, US
D: Archie Mayo **A:** Jean Gabin, Ida Lupino, Thomas Mitchell, Claude Rains, Jerome Cowan (20th Century-Fox)

Jean Gabin, known as an earthy player

in France, is given just that type of role in *Moontide*. He's an itinerant dockworker who for years hasn't had a home and is chiefly interested in getting drunk. Until, that is, he rescues from the surf a hash-house waitress (Ida Lupino) intent on killing herself. *Moontide* is a series of incidents. The total effect is one of slowness and lack of suspense.
1942: Nomination: Best B&W Cinematography

MOONWALKER
1988, 93 mins, US ⓥ ⊙
D: Colin Chivers, Jerry Kramer, Will Vinton, Jim Blashfield **A:** Michael Jackson, Sean Lennon, Kellie Parker, Brandon Adams, Joe Pesci (Lorimar)

Moonwalker—also the title of a Michael Jackson autobiography—seems unsure of what it was supposed to be. At the center of the pic is the *Smooth Criminal* segment, a musical/dramatic piece full of dancing, schmaltzy kids, sci-fi effects and blazing machine guns [directed by Colin Chilvers, based on a story by Jackson]. Around it are really just numerous Jackson music videos with little or no linkage. Although quite enjoyable the whole affair does not make for a structured or professional movie.

MOON ZERO TWO
1969, 100 mins, UK ⓥ
D: Roy Ward Baker **A:** James Olson, Catherine Schell, Warren Mitchell, Adrienne Corri, Bernard Bresslaw (Hammer)

Moon Zero Two never makes up its mind whether it is a spoof or a straightforward space-adventure yarn. Overall it's a fairly dull experience, despite some capable artwork and special effects. Olson is a melancholy hero. Mitchell plays with tongue in cheek.

MORE
1969, 115 mins, Luxembourg
D: Barbet Schroeder **A:** Mimsy Farmer, Klaus Grunberg, Heinz Engelmann (Jet/Two World)

In his first pic director Barbet Schroeder shows an insight into youths, be they American or Europeans, who have been labeled everything from beatnik to yippie. He gives a feeling of how it is sans didactics or obviousness. Drug taking is a part of it in this tale of a youth from Germany destroyed by it. Mimsy Farmer reveals a potent personality and gives her role a tension, inner hurt, and alienation.

MORE AMERICAN GRAFFITI
1979, 111 mins, US ⓥ ⊙ ▢
D: B.W.L. Norton **A:** Candy Clark, Bo Hopkins, Ron Howard, Scott Glenn, Paul Le Mat, Charles Martin Smith (Universal/Lucasfilm)

More American Graffiti may be one of the most innovative and ambitious films of the last five years, but by no means is it one of the most successful. Writer-director B.W.L. Norton overloads the sequel with four wholly different cinematic styles to carry forward the lives of *American Graffiti*'s original cast. The flirtation with split-screen, anamorphic, 16-mm, and 1:85 screen sizes does not justify itself in terms of the film's content.

MORE THAN A MIRACLE
1967, 102 mins, Italy/France
D: Francesco Rosi **A:** Sophia Loren, Omar Sharif, Dolores Del Rio, Georges Wilson, Leslie French (M-G-M)

Real curiosity, labeled in production notes as a "fairy tale for adults," tells a Cinderella story, with some heavy-handed anticlericalism and antimonarchism thrown in. The script defeats itself in part by going too far into reality. Omar Sharif, therefore, is not only handsome but arrogant, wilful, brutal to his servants; also the beautiful Sophia Loren, looking a bit uneasy and out of place in peasant weeds, eventually berates Sharif publicly for oppression of the lower classes.

MORE THE MERRIER, THE
1943, 101 mins, US ⓥ ⊙
D: George Stevens **A:** Jean Arthur, Joel McCrea, Charles Coburn, Richard Gaines (Columbia)

Sparkling and effervescing piece of entertainment is one of the most spontaneous farce-comedies of the wartime era. Although Jean Arthur and Joel McCrea carry the romantic interest, Charles Coburn walks off with the honors. Coburn arrives in wartime Washington and sublets half interest in Miss Arthur's minute apartment, and when he finds the girl without a boyfriend, conveniently picks up McCrea to become partner in his share of the housing layout. Naturally complications ensue in hilarious fashion.
1943: Best Supp. Actor (Charles Coburn)
Nominations: Best Picture, Director, Actress (Jean Arthur), Original Story, Screenplay

MORE THINGS CHANGE, THE
1986, 95 mins, Australia
D: Robyn Nevin **A:** Judy Morris, Barry Otto, Victoria Longley, Lewis Fitz-Gerald (Syme)

Universally topical film about a modern marriage, told with humor and insight, is also splendidly acted. Connie (Judy Morris) and Lex (Barry Otto) have purchased a small farm two hours' drive from the city, but until the farm is self-sufficient one of them has to keep working. A live-in baby-sitter is the answer, and Connie engages Geraldine (Victoria Longley). The viewer's expectations are, naturally, that Lex and Geraldine will have an affair, but Moya Wood's sharp screenplay is much more subtle than that.

MORGAN!
See: A Suitable Case for Treatment

MORGAN (A SUITABLE CASE FOR TREATMENT)
See: A Suitable Case for Treatment

MORITURI
(US/UK: THE SABOTEUR—CODE NAME "MORITURI")
1965, 118 mins, US Ⓥ
D: Bernhard Wicki **A:** Marlon Brando, Yul Brynner, Janet Margolin, Trevor Howard, Hans Christian Blech (20th Century-Fox)

Second World War sea drama carries strong suspense at times and a brooding menace that communicates to the spectator. Action takes place aboard a German blockade runner with a cargo of 7,000 tons of indispensable crude rubber for the Nazis, which the Allies also want. British put a man on the freighter with orders to disarm explosive charges by which the captain would scuttle his ship rather than allow capture. Both Brando and Brynner contribute hard-hitting performances, Brando as the saboteur and Brynner as captain.
1965: Nominations: Best B&W Cinematography, B&W Costume Design

MORNING AFTER, THE
1986, 103 mins, US Ⓥ ⊙
D: Sidney Lumet **A:** Jane Fonda, Jeff Bridges, Raul Julia, Diane Salinger, Richard Foronjy (Lorimar/American Filmworks)

Overwrought and implausible, *The Morning After* is a dramatic situation in search of a thriller plot. Jane Fonda stars as a boozy, washed-up actress who wakes up one morning next to a man with a dagger in his heart, and her efforts to cope with the dilemma are neither terribly suspenseful nor entertaining.
1986: Nomination: Best Actress (Jane Fonda)

MORNING GLORY Ⓥ
1933, 70 mins, US Ⓥ ⊙
D: Lowell Sherman **A:** Katharine Hepburn, Douglas Fairbanks Jr., Adolphe Menjou, C. Aubrey Smith, Don Alvarado (RKO)

Katharine Hepburn provides a strong performance. This one is heavy on legit class and lacks action and sustained conflict. Story is at great pains to build up the charming character of a well-bred, utterly innocent country girl who comes to Broadway seeking footlight fame. No sooner is the figure built to completeness than the hapless little Cinderella is dragged through the mud of backstage casual amours. This happens less than midway of the footage, and thereafter the grip of an engaging story relaxes fatally. The fate of this bedraggled Cinderella becomes a matter of indifference.
1932/33: Best Actress (Katharine Hepburn)

MORNING GLORY
1993, 95 mins, US Ⓥ ⊙
D: Steven Stern **A:** Christopher Reeve, Deborah Raffin, Lloyd Bochner, Nina Foch, Helen Shaver, J. T. Walsh (Dove Audio)

Weak scripting and a choppy, uninspired narrative turn the Depression-era yarn into a garbled collection of predictable soap opera scenes. Christopher Reeve as down-and-out ex-con Will Parker answers a newspaper classified ad for a husband. Recently widowed Elly Dinsmore (Deborah Raffin) is not looking for love, just someone to share the chores. Then, as if imported from a different pic, sheriff Reese Goodloe (J. T. Walsh) roughs up Parker and local floozy Lula Peaks (Helen Shaver) pesters him with seduction attempts.

MOROCCO
1930, 90 mins, US Ⓥ ⊙
D: Josef von Sternberg **A:** Gary Cooper, Marlene Dietrich, Adolphe Menjou, Ullrich Haupt (Paramount)

Marlene Dietrich has few opportunities in her first American talker. There's nothing to the picture, except what Josef von

Sternberg gives it in direction, and that's giving it more than it's got. The story is given a terrific kick early, when Dietrich arrives in Morocco to star in the concert hall. The first evening of her appearance she gives the key to her home to a legionnaire, Cooper. After that the rest is apple sauce, even to her joining the female followers of the troops to keep near her soldier.

1930/31: Nominations: Best Director, Actress (Marlene Dietrich), Cinematography, Art Direction

MORTAL KOMBAT
1995, 101 mins, US Ⓥ ⊙
D: Paul Anderson **A:** Robin Shou, Linden Ashby, Bridgette Wilson, Cary-Hiroyuki Tagawa, Christopher Lambert (Threshold/New Line)

The novel twists in this martial arts action-adventure are superb technical and visual effects, a tongue-in-cheek script, and performers who can convey its mocking tone without stooping to the obvious. The action revolves around a rather unusual tournament of champions. One side consists of the human league and the other is repped by the dark, unworldly forces of evil sorcerer Shang Tsung (Cary-Hiroyuki Tagawa). The latter group includes characters who can turn into serpents, throw spitballs of lethal ice, or simply tower two stories high with four arms, each with the strength to crush iron. But the best of the flesh-and-blood crew are better than their seemingly impossible adversaries, thanks to superior intellect, an ability to adapt, and the watchful tutelage of good sorcerer Rayden (Christopher Lambert).

MORTAL PASSIONS
1989, 98 mins, US Ⓥ ⊙
D: Andrew Lane **A:** Zach Galligan, Michael Bowen, Krista Errickson, Luca Bercovici, Sheila Kelley, David Warner (Gibraltar)

Delightfully silly beneath its earnestness, *Mortal Passions* revels in the amoral, murderous frustrations of a beautiful young wife (Krista Errickson) doing her best to bed and bounty any and all of the men in her life. There is absolutely nothing predictable about this wonderful group of loonies, and director Andrew Lane never lets slip where he and the tightly wrapped script are taking them.

MORTAL STORM, THE
1940, 100 mins, US
D: Frank Borzage **A:** Margaret Sullavan, James Stewart, Robert Young, Frank Morgan, Robert Stack, Bonita Granville (M-G-M)

A combination of entertainment and democratic preachment. The locale is Germany, 1933. Through the lives of the members of the family of a university professor there is revealed the soul-crushing effect of Nazi regimentation. Sons turn from their parents, friends become deadly enemies, innocent elders are tossed into concentration camps. James Stewart is the courageous individualist who refuses to join the Nazi party, and Robert Young is the heavy. Frank Morgan draws a fine characterization of the non-Aryan professor.

MORTAL THOUGHTS
1991, 104 mins, US Ⓥ ⊙
D: Alan Rudolph **A:** Demi Moore, Glenne Headly, Bruce Willis, John Pankow, Harvey Keitel (Columbia/New Visions/Polar)

Two gals make a murderous mess of a bad situation. Played straight and for sympathy, tale of dark retaliation goes astray early on, despite the promise created at the outset by imaginative, energetic production and appealing performances. Demi Moore and Glenne Headly play lifelong friends who run a blue-collar New Jersey beauty shop and remain closer to each other than to their husbands. Small wonder, since Moore's husband (John Pankow) is a boorish salesman, and Headley's wed to a thoroughly despicable, abusive lout (Bruce Willis).

MOSCOW DOES NOT BELIEVE IN TEARS
See: Moskva Slezam Ne Verit

MOSCOW NIGHTS
1935, 77 mins, UK Ⓥ
D: Anthony Asquith **A:** Harry Baur, Laurence Olivier, Penelope Dudley-Ward, Athene Seyler, Hay Petrie (Denham/London)

A triumph for director Anthony Asquith in that no book could give you a more vivid spectacle of things as they existed in Russia in 1916. A handsome young Russian officer (Laurence Olivier) is carried into a hospital in a delirious condition from war wounds. Upon regaining consciousness he discovers a celestial-looking Red Cross nurse in the person of

Penelope Dudley-Ward, and falls hard. She is, however, engaged to a middle-aged war profiteer played by Harry Baur, who brings to the role a dominance that always falls short of being repellent. This is Olivier's first big opportunity, and he takes advantage of it to the full.

MOSCOW ON THE HUDSON
1984, 115 mins, US ⓥ ⊙
D: Paul Mazursky A: Robin Williams, Maria Conchita Alonso, Cleavant Derricks, Alejandro Rey, Savely Kramarov (Columbia)

Sweet, beautifully performed picture would be in a lot of trouble without a superbly sensitive portrayal by Robin Williams of a gentle Russian circus musician who makes a sudden decision to defect while visiting the US. Williams thus becomes one more in a flood of immigrants who still are discovering virtues that those already here many times forget. The entire film is full of performers working way beyond the material.

MOSES
1975, 140 mins, UK/Italy ⓥ
D: Gianfranco De Bosio A: Burt Lancaster, Anthony Quayle, Ingrid Thulin, Irene Papas, Mariangela Melato, William Lancaster (ITC/RAI)

Moses is another attempt at compressing a big slice of biblical drama, and the inevitable result is superficial storytelling. The film was impressively photographed in Israel and has Burt Lancaster in a restrained portrayal as the patriarch of the ancient Hebrews who leads them from Egyptian bondage to the promised land. Feature was "inspired" by the TV miniseries *Moses, the Lawgiver*. Besides recutting, the theatrical edition supposedly contains much footage not included in the TV version.

MOSKVA SLEZAM NE VERIT (US: MOSCOW DOES NOT BELIEVE IN TEARS)
1980, 145 mins, USSR ⓥ
D: Vladimir Menshov A: Vera Alentova, Irina Muravyova, Raisa Ryazanova, Natalya Vavilova, Aleksei Batalov (Mosfilm)

Three girls come to Moscow from the country to find new lives and challenges. Men outweigh politics and their work in factories. One ends up with an illegitimate child, another does not marry, and one has a good simple marriage. Film is engagingly played and directed with ease. Perhaps a bit reminiscent of American romantic comedies of the 1930s, but without their more dynamic pacing, bite, and tongue-in-cheek innocence.
1980: Best Foreign-Language Film

MOSQUITO COAST, THE
1986, 117 mins, US ⓥ ⊙
D: Peter Weir A: Harrison Ford, Helen Mirren, River Phoenix, Jadrien Steele, Hilary Gordon, Rebecca Gordon (Warner)

It is hard to believe that a film as beautiful as *The Mosquito Coast* can also be so bleak, but therein lies its power and undoing. It starts out as a film about idealism and possibilities, but takes a dark turn and winds up questioning the very values it so powerfully presents. There's a stunning performance by Harrison Ford with firstrate filmmaking by Peter Weir. Ford's Allie Fox rants and raves against prepackaged, mass-consumed American culture, and packs up his wife and four kids and moves them to a remote Caribbean island.

MOSS ROSE
1947, 82 mins, US
D: Gregory Ratoff A: Peggy Cummins, Victor Mature, Ethel Barrymore, Vincent Price, Margo Woode (20th Century-Fox)

Good whodunit run off against background of early-day England that provides effective setting for theme of destructive mother love. Gregory Ratoff's direction lends considerable flavor to the period melodramatics. Cummins is unusually interesting: English pronunciation, at first broad and then becoming more educated, is a trick she uses to develop character of music-hall girl who uses her knowledge of murder to satisfy a childhood desire. Mature handles his somber character of a well-bred Englishman expertly.

MOST DANGEROUS GAME, THE (UK: THE HOUNDS OF ZAROFF)
1932, 61 mins, US ⓥ
D: Ernest B. Schoedsack, Irving Pichel A: Joel McCrea, Fay Wray, Leslie Banks, Robert Armstrong, Steve Clemento, Noble Johnson (RKO)

Fantastic would-be thriller whose efforts at horrifying are not very effective. A crazy Russian count (Leslie Banks), who derives more pleasure from hunting human beings than lions and tigers, operates alone on a deserted tropical isle, using shipwreck victims for game. When he gets 'em he fattens 'em up. The routine then is to send them out with a few hours' start.

It's a foregone cinch that Joel McCrea, as a big game hunter tossed into the count's trap, will hand the manhunter a trimming. Banks grabs everything worth grabbing among performance honors.

MOST DANGEROUS MAN IN THE WORLD, THE
See: The Chairman

MOTHER, JUGS & SPEED
1976, 95 mins, US ✌ ⬚
D: Peter Yates **A:** Raquel Welch, Bill Cosby, Harvey Keitel, Allen Garfield, Larry Hagman, L. Q. Jones (20th Century-Fox)

The three titular characters are Bill Cosby, Raquel Welch, and Harvey Keitel, all very pleasant in their roles as ambulance drivers. Their easygoing camaraderie, which provides a strong role for Welch, allows for many good behavioral moments. The film remains oddly appealing despite its serious flaws—in many ways it's an accurate reflection of what really goes on in hustling ambulance outfits.

MOTHER LODE
1982, 101 mins, US ✌
D: Charlton Heston **A:** Charlton Heston, Nick Mancuso, Kim Basinger, John Marley (Agamemnon)

As the title indicates, the consuming issue in *Mother Lode* is a search for gold. The picture is not without shortcomings, but is long on good performances, charismatic people in the three principal roles, compelling outdoor aerial sequences in British Columbia, and high-level suspense throughout. The role of Silas McGee, the disreputable Scottish miner trying to protect his great secret find, is a switch to villainy for Charlton Heston, but he relishes the role and even makes a creditable pass at a thick Scottish brogue.

MOTHER'S BOYS
1994, 95 mins, US ✌ ◉
D: Yves Simoneau **A:** Jamie Lee Curtis, Peter Gallagher, Joanne Whalley-Kilmer, Vanessa Redgrave, Luke Edwards (Miramax/Dimension)

Elegant style and amiable cast can't conceal the silliness of an unsuspenseful variation of the yuppie-in-peril thriller. Set in L.A., story begins as Jude (Jamie Lee Curtis), an attractive woman who deserted her husband (Peter Gallagher) and three sons, suddenly returns, determined to win back her family. When begging forgiveness and other "charming" strategies fail,

Jude resorts to manipulating eldest son, Kes (Luke Edwards). Film has an uninteresting beginning, an exploitative middle that actually cheats by genre standards, and a ludicrous climax that is borderline laughable.

MOTHER WORE TIGHTS
1947, 107 mins, US
D: Walter Lang **A:** Betty Grable, Dan Dailey, Mona Freeman, Connie Marshall, Vanessa Brown, Sara Allgood (20th Century-Fox)

A familiarly styled Technicolor musical opus on the life and times of a song-and-dance team that knocked around the vaude circuits about the century's turn. Musical is severely limited by its long and mediocre score of tunes which are presented without any visual imaginative touches. Numerous hoofing sequences featuring Betty Grable and Dan Dailey also fail to rate the heavy accent put on them by the footage. Chief drawback, however, is the rambling story and a script which pulls out all the stops in its use of clichés and sentimentalism.

1947: Best Scoring for a Musical Picture
Nominations: Best Color Cinematography, Song ("You Do")

MOTOR PSYCHO
1965, 73 mins, US
D: Russ Meyer **A:** Stephen Oliver, Haji, Alex Rocco, Holle K. Winters, Joseph Cellini (Eve)

A violent Russ Meyer production concerning three young bums on a rape-murder spree in a California desert town. Slick, well made, and initially absorbing, it features sex angles which kill the credibility of a script which itself is long on loose ends and short on moral compensation. Meyer's direction is good, while his interesting and crisp camera work is excellent.

MOUCHETTE
1967, 85 mins, France
D: Robert Bresson **A:** Nadine Nortier, Jean-Claude Guilbert, Maria Cardinal, Paul Herbert, Jean Vimenet (Argos/Parc)

A 14-year-old girl, a drudge in an impoverished alcoholic peasant family, is the heroine of this brilliant film. Her sullen defiance, her failure to connect with life, and a final opting out via suicide are treated with clear and uncluttered insight. Everyday incidents take on an almost spiritual intensity in Bresson's controlled and incisive direction and handling of the players. Nadine Nortier has the animal ferocity and gentleness needed for the role.

MOULIN ROUGE
1928, 90 mins, UK ⊗
D: E. A. Dupont A: Olga Tschechowa, Eve Gray, Jean Bradin, George Treville, Marcel Vibert (British International)

Well done, but overlong. It's a love complication with the young man falling for his fiancée's mother, the leading lady of the Moulin Rouge revue. Its principals are interesting personalities, notably Olga Tschechowa, who resembles Pola Negri but with more humor. Some of the back-stage stuff is done exceptionally well—better, in fact, than the usual Hollywood efforts to reproduce convincingly a musical stage show.

MOULIN ROUGE
1952, 118 mins, UK Ⓥ ⊙
D: John Huston A: Jose Ferrer, Colette Marchand, Suzanne Flon, Zsa Zsa Gabor, Christopher Lee (Romulus)

Jose Ferrer endows with conviction the part of Toulouse-Lautrec, the cultured, gifted artist of Paris in the 1880s whose glaring deformity repulses the women whom he constantly seeks. The cancan ribaldry, the frank depiction of streetwalkers, the smoky atmosphere of Parisian bistro life—they come through in exciting pictorial terms. And the Technicolor tinting captures the flamboyant aura of Montmartre. But overall, the production requires some dramatic explosiveness. The story unfolds in a constantly minor-key tone.
1952: Best Color Art Direction, Color Costume Design
Nominations: Best Picture, Director, Actor (Jose Ferrer), Supp. Actress (Colette Marchand), Editing

MOUNTAIN MEN, THE
1980, 102 mins, US Ⓥ ▱
D: Richard Lang A: Charlton Heston, Brian Keith, Victoria Racimo, Seymour Cassel, John Glover (Columbia)

Lethargic wilderness pic. Screenplay by star's son Fraser Clarke Heston is loaded with vulgarities that seem excessive for the genre, and scene after scene dwells on bloody hand-to-hand battles between Indians and the grizzled trappers played by Heston and sidekick Brian Keith. Film takes ages to drag from one plot development to another, though the Indian battles occur with sufficient regularity to keep the audience from snoozing.

MOUNTAINS OF THE MOON
1990, 135 mins, US Ⓥ ⊙
D: Bob Rafelson A: Patrick Bergin, Iain Glen, Fiona Shaw, Richard E. Grant, Peter Vaughan, Anna Massey (Carolco/Indieprod)

An outstanding adventure film, adapted from William Harrison's book *Burton and Speke* and the journals of 19th-century explorers Richard Burton and John Hanning Speke. Without sacrificing the historical context this pic provides deeply felt performances and refreshing, offbeat humor. Starting in 1854, pic documents duo's ill-fated first two expeditions to Africa, climaxing with Speke's discovery of what became named Lake Victoria, the true source of the Nile. As Speke, Scots actor Iain Glen creates sympathy for a wayward character.

MOURIR A MADRID
See: To Die in Madrid

MOURNING BECOMES ELECTRA
1947, 173 mins, US Ⓥ ⊙
D: Dudley Nichols A: Rosalind Russell, Michael Redgrave, Raymond Massey, Katina Paxinou, Leo Genn, Kirk Douglas (RKO)

Eugene O'Neill's post–Civil War version of the ancient Greek classic was at best "good for those who like that sort of thing." Unfortunately, the picture—although still laden with tense drama—lacks much of the impact of the play. It is every bit as unrelenting in its detailing of family tragedy, brought on by the warping effect of Puritan conscience in conflict with human emotion, as was the play. Even the distorted Oedipal relationships are unflaggingly handled. Performances are uniformly good, although they never rise beyond the drama that is inherent in the situations themselves. Outstanding are Raymond Massey and Henry Hull, the latter in the secondary role of an aged retainer.
1947: Nominations: Best Actor (Michael Redgrave), Actress (Rosalind Russell)

MOUSE THAT ROARED, THE
1959, 83 mins, UK Ⓥ
D: Jack Arnold A: Peter Sellers, Jean Seberg, David Kossoff, William Hartnell, Leo McKern, Macdonald Parke (Open Road/Columbia)

A comedy in the old Ealing tradition.

The Grand Duchy of Grand Fenwick, the world's smallest country, relies for its existence on the export of a local wine to the US. When California bottles a cheaper, inferior imitation, Grand Fenwick is on the verge of going broke. So the prime minister hits on the wily scheme of going to war against America, on the grounds that the loser in any war is invariably on the receiving end of hefty financial handouts from the winners. Peter Sellers plays three roles in the film. He is the Grand Duchess Gloriana, the prime minister, and also the hapless field marshal who upsets the prime minister's plans.

MOVE OVER, DARLING
1963, 103 mins, US ▭
D: Michael Gordon A: Doris Day, James Garner, Polly Bergen, Chuck Connors, Thelma Ritter, Fred Clark (20th Century-Fox)

Something old, something new, something borrowed, something blue is the nature of *Move Over, Darling*, a reproduction of the 1940 romantic comedy *My Favorite Wife*. The "old" is the basic yarn about the guy who remarries after his first wife is thought to have perished only to have his first wife turn up alive and kicking. The "new" are the chiefly lackluster embellishments tagged on. The "borrowed," to cite one example, is a telephone sequence that owes more than a little something to Shelley Berman. The "blue" isn't of a really offensive nature. Doris Day and James Garner play it to the hilt, comically, dramatically, and last but not least (particularly in the case of the former), athletically. What is missing in their portrayals is a light touch.

MOVIE MOVIE
1978, 105 mins, US ⊗
D: Stanley Donen A: George C. Scott, Barbara Harris, Eli Wallach, Trish Van Devere, Red Buttons (Warner)

Clumsy attempt to spoof the kind of film fare encountered in pic houses of the 1930s and 1940s. The idea, patronizing in its conception, is a flatout embarrassment in its execution. The overlong, 105-minute feature is split into a black-and-white sendup of those boxing sagas where the slum youth fueled by earnest ambition gets catapulted to fame and riches; a satire of a coming attractions trailer; and finally, a shot-in-color takeoff of the making of a Flo Ziegfeld–type Broadway musical.

MOVING TARGET, THE
See: Harper

MR. AND MRS. BRIDGE
1990, 124 mins, US ⊗ ⊙
D: James Ivory A: Paul Newman, Joanne Woodward, Robert Sean Leonard, Kyra Sedgwick, Blythe Danner, Simon Callow (Cineplex Odeon/Merchant-Ivory/Halmi)

An affecting study of an uppercrust Midwestern family in the late 1930s. The screenplay presents a series of highly dramatic scenes in the lives of stuffy Kansas City lawyer Walter Bridge and his wife, India. Central theme of India Bridge's gradual realization that her life has been crushed in her husband's shadow is strongly conveyed by Woodward in the role. Casting of hubby Newman as her husband resonates in their intimate scenes. Kyra Sedgwick is smashing as the Bridges' bohemian daughter.
1990: Nomination: Best Actress (Joanna Woodward)

MR. AND MRS. SMITH
1941, 90 mins, US ⊗ ⊙
D: Alfred Hitchcock A: Carole Lombard, Robert Montgomery, Gene Raymond, Jack Carson, Philip Merivale (RKO)

Carole Lombard and Robert Montgomery are teamed successfully here in a light and gay marital farce, with accent on the laugh side through generation of continual bickering of the pair. Advised that their three-year-old marriage is void because of legal technicalities, Mrs. Smith tosses Mr. Smith out of the house. Then the yarn develops into a run-around—with Mr. making continual stabs to recapture his wife, while his law partner, (Gene Raymond) is a ready victim of her advances aimed at inspiring jealousy. Alfred Hitchcock pilots the story in a straight farcical groove.

MR. ARKADIN
See: Confidential Report

MR. ASHTON WAS INDISCREET
See: The Senator Was Indiscreet

MR. BASEBALL
1992, 109 mins, US ⊗ ⊙ ▭
D: Fred Schepisi A: Tom Selleck, Ken Takakura, Aya Takanashi, Dennis Haysbert, Toshi Shioya (Walt Disney/Outlaw)

A tame look at cultural differences. Given the central character of Jack Elliot (Tom Selleck), former Yankee World Series MVP who's traded off to Japan, there's only one direction in which the story can go, and it does, as if by prescription: he arrives in Nagoya to play for the Chunichi Dragons, hates it, looks down on all these little men who play such a safe, conformist brand of baseball, bristles at his stern manager, then finally starts getting it together. Selleck is utterly believable as the star, but even his broad shoulders can't carry the weight of the entire pic. All the Japanese remain one-dimensional.

MR. BILLION
1977, 91 mins, US Ⓥ
D: Jonathan Kaplan A: Terence Hill [Mario Girotti], Valerie Perrine, Jackie Gleason, Slim Pickens, William Redfield, Chill Wills (Pantheon)

Terence Hill is charming as an Italian mechanic who inherits a fortune and has a hell of a time getting to Frisco in time to claim it. Valerie Perrine and Jackie Gleason are among those who try to fleece the innocent of his loot. There are many loose ends in the plot, and some choppy sequences, but the pic is brisk enjoyment.

MR. BLANDINGS BUILDS HIS DREAM HOUSE
1948, 93 mins, US Ⓥ ⊙
D: H. C. Potter A: Cary Grant, Myrna Loy, Melvyn Douglas, Reginald Denny, Jason Robards (Selznick/RKO)

Eric Hodgins's novel of the trials and tribulations of the Blandings, while building their dream house, read a lot funnier than it filmed. Script gets completely out of hand when unnecessary jealousy twist is introduced. Grant is up to his usual standard as Blandings, getting the best from the material, and Myrna Loy comes through with another of her screen wife assignments nicely. Melvyn Douglas, the lawyer friend of the family, gives it a tongue-in-cheek treatment.

MR. DEEDS GOES TO TOWN
1936, 115 mins, US Ⓥ ⊙
D: Frank Capra A: Gary Cooper, Jean Arthur, George Bancroft, Lionel Stander, Douglass Dumbrille, Raymond Walburn (Columbia)

With a sometimes too-thin structure, the players and director Frank Capra have contrived to convert *Deeds* into fairly sturdy substance. The farce is good-humored and the trouping and production workmanlike, but there are some lapses in midriff that cause considerable uncertainty. Deeds is a guy who plays a tuba in bed, slides down banisters, decides to give away his $20 million just like that, after

John Wray in a theatrical hokum bit waves a gun at him, fortified with a quasicomunistic plea. Combined with some of the other lines and business accorded the male topper, audience credulity, despite the general lightness of the theme, becomes strained.
1936: Best Director
Nominations: Best Picture, Actor (Gary Cooper), Screenplay, Sound

MR. DESTINY
1990, 105 mins, US Ⓥ ⊙
D: James Orr A: James Belushi, Linda Hamilton, Michael Caine, Jon Lovitz, Hart Bochner, René Russo (Touchstone/Silver Screen Partners IV)

A heavy-handed, by-the-numbers fantasy about an ordinary Joe who thinks his life would have been different if he'd connected with that all-important pitch in a high school baseball game. James Belushi plays working stiff Larry Burrows, who on his depressing 35th birthday stumbles into a bar where a mysterious, twinkly-eyed barman (Michael Caine) serves him up a "spilled milk" elixir that sends him spinning back in time to take another swat at that baseball.

MR. HOBBS TAKES A VACATION
1962, 115 mins, US ⊙
D: Henry Koster A: James Stewart, Maureen O'Hara, Fabian, John Saxon, Reginald Gardiner, Marie Wilson (20th Century-Fox)

Togetherness, all-American family style, is given a gently irreverent poke in the ribs. Hobbs (James Stewart) is a St. Louis banker who has the misfortune to spend his vacation at the seashore with 10 other members of his immediate family, setting up a series of situations roughly designed to illustrate the pitfalls of that grand old Yankee institution, the family reunion. The picture has its staunchest ally in Stewart, whose acting instincts are so remarkably keen that he can instill amusement into scenes that otherwise threaten to fall flat. Some of the others in the cast, endowed with less intuitive gifts for light comedy, do not fare as well.

MR. HOLLAND'S OPUS
1995, 142 mins, US Ⓥ ⊙ ⊡
D: Stephen Merek A: Richard Dreyfuss, Glenne Headly, Jay Thomas, Olympia Dukakis, W. H. Macy (Interscope/PolyGram/Hollywood)

An idealized tribute to a charismatic

teacher who has devoted his entire life to music appreciation, *Mr. Holland's Opus* has the same old-fashioned texture as *Goodbye, Mr. Chips*. Covering 1965 to the present, tale concerns Glenn Holland (Richard Dreyfuss), a passionate composer who believes that his true calling is to write one memorable piece of music. Over the course of his life, however, Holland becomes a reluctant hero, a man who fulfills himself not at the piano but at the blackboard. While Stephen Herek's film has an epic arc embracing the era's major political events (Vietnam, Nixon's resignation) and cultural traumas (John Lennon's assassination), it lacks epic vision. The narrative unfolds as a catalogue of familiar, often clichéd episodes. Dreyfuss acquits himself with a sensitive, honorable performance.

1995: Nomination: Best Actor (Richard Dreyfuss)

MR. HULOT'S HOLIDAY
See: Les Vacances de Monsieur Hulot

MR. JOHNSON
1990, 103 mins, US Ⓥ
D: Bruce Beresford **A:** Maynard Eziashi, Pierce Brosnan, Edward Woodward, Beatie Edney, Denis Quilley (Fitzgerald)

Ponderous but well-made film suffers from a slow, marginally involving story line. Pic's foremost discovery is Nigerian actor Maynard Eziashi as a young African obsessed with British mores, resourcefully working outside the rigid limits of his colonial clerkship. Johnson uses that knack to help his boss, Rudbeck (Pierce Brosnan), build a road connecting their small outpost to the outside world, though his consistent circumvention of proper channels eventually proves his downfall.

MR. JONES
1993, 112 mins, US Ⓥ ⊙
D: Mike Figgis **A:** Richard Gere, Lena Olin, Anne Bancroft, Tom Irwin, Delroy Lindo (Rastar/Tri-Star)

Mixing therapy and romance is a no-no in real life, and it proves problematic as well as the subject of *Mr. Jones*. A high-energy performance by Richard Gere and an intensely brooding one from Lena Olin engage attentive viewer interest, but the stars are forced to overcompensate for a rather slow pace and lack of plot. Gere gets carted away as a loony, diagnosed as a bipolar manic depressive. But he's soon released, against the wishes of Dr. Libbie

Bowen (Olin), who thinks the guy poses a real threat, particularly to himself. With nothing else going on, the screenwriters have doctor and patient fall in love.

MR. LUCKY
1943, 94 mins, US Ⓥ ⊙
D: H. C. Potter **A:** Cary Grant, Laraine Day, Charles Bickford, Gladys Cooper, Henry Stephenson (RKO)

Cary Grant is a resourceful and opportunist gambling operator, figuring on outfitting his outlawed gaming ship for a trip to Havana. But coin and draft registration balk his departure. Pursuing society heiress Laraine Day, he lands as a member of the war relief agency. Picture carries an authentic ring to operations of bigtime gamblers.

MR. MAJESTYK
1974, 104 mins, US Ⓥ
D: Richard Fleischer **A:** Charles Bronson, Al Lettieri, Linda Cristal, Lee Purcell, Alejandro Rey (Mirisch)

Mr. Majestyk makes a first-reel pretense of dealing with the thorny subject of migrant Chicano farm laborers, but social relevance is soon clobbered by the usual Charles Bronson heroics, here mechanically navigated by director Richard Fleischer. Bronson, in a boringly stoic performance, plays a melon grower whose fair labor practices are rewarded with a trumped-up assault charge that lands him in jail.

MR. MOM
1983, 91 mins, US Ⓥ ⊙
D: Stan Dragoti **A:** Michael Keaton, Teri Garr, Frederick Koehler, Taliesin Jaffe, Courtney and Brittany White, Christopher Lloyd (Sherwood/20th Century-Fox)

The comic talents of Michael Keaton and Teri Garr are largely wasted in an unoriginal romantic comedy where breadwinner-husband and homemaker wife switch roles. Keaton, close to perfection as the husband and father depressed by unemployment but always a sport with his family, especially shines here in some more dramatic moments with his children. Garr, as always, is a delight to watch.

MR. MOTO IN DANGER ISLAND
See: Danger Island

MR. MOTO'S GAMBLE
1938, 71 mins, US
D: James Tinling **A:** Peter Lorre, Keye Luke, Dick Baldwin, Lynn Bari, Douglas Fowley (20th Century-Fox)

Romance and comedy are well interwoven as Moto (Peter Lorre) solves a ring murder. Moto runs a school for sleuths. While attending a fight, one of the ring contestants is killed in action. Moto's chief assistants are his two unwittingly funny pupils, Wellington (Maxie Rosenbloom), and Lee Chan, son of Charlie Chan (Keye Luke).

MR. MOTO'S LAST WARNING
1939, 71 mins, US Ⓥ
D: Norman Foster A: Peter Lorre, Ricardo Cortez, Virginia Field, John Carradine, George Sanders, Joan Carol (20th Century-Fox)

One of the better Moto pictures, cast in a colorful Egyptian background. Strong supporting cast is chiefly notable for excellent comeback by Ricardo Cortez. Posing as a vaudeville ventriloquist, Cortez plots to blow up the French fleet as it steams into Port Said for maneuvers. Lorre, working as a Japanese shopkeeper, survives several attempts on his life, but ultimately frustrates the plot.

MR. MOTO TAKES A CHANCE
1938, 57 mins, US
D: Norman Foster A: Peter Lorre, Rochelle Hudson, Robert Kent, J. Edward Romberg, Chick Chandler (20th Century-Fox)

Picture, which concerns the activities of two government secret agents, has trapdoors, poison air guns, hidden passages, machine guns, carrier pigeons, bolo knives, and a generous assortment of jungle beasts. There are too many hairbreadth escapes and uncanny accomplishments for a regulation feature. It all smacks of serial style. Film also is weakened because it gives Peter Lorre few chances. Instead, the plot has him double as a mysterious, wrinkled priest, adding further mystification and little to the yarn.

MR. MOTO TAKES A VACATION
1939, 65 mins, US
D: Norman Foster A: Peter Lorre, Joseph Schildkraut, Lionel Atwill, Virginia Field, John King (20th Century-Fox)

A very weak effort, full of incongruities in both story development and direction. Peter Lorre, with regulation Moto calm assurance, does the best he can with material at hand. Moto follows the supposed crown of the Queen of Sheba from its discovery in Egyptian diggings until arrival in a San Francisco museum.

Motivation is conveniently set up for jewel thieves to go after the sparklers. Story unfolds in unconvincing manner, action swinging in and out of dark alleys and passages, winding up in darkened museum to generate mysterious and unrecognizable figures sneaking around to further confuse onlookers.

MR. MUSIC
1950, 110 mins, US
D: Richard Haydn A: Bing Crosby, Nancy Olson, Charles Coburn, Ruth Hussey, Robert Stack, Tom Ewell (Paramount)

A variation of a backstage musical, utilizing a lazy songsmith as the central figure. Nancy Olson is the serious-minded undergraduate turned secretary who gets Crosby back into harness as a songwriter instead of running off to the golf course, hobnobbing with bookies, and the like. The utilization of Peggy Lee, the Champions (Gower and Marge), Groucho Marx, the Merry Macs, and Dorothy Kirsten gives the unfolding a proper lift in the right spots.

MR. NANNY
1993, 84 mins, US Ⓥ ◉
D: Michael Gottlieb A: Terry "Hulk" Hogan, Sherman Hemsley, Austin Pendleton, Robert Gorman, Madeline Zima (New Line)

Comedy-actioner that should entertain the under-12 and couch potato sets. Excuse for a plot has "Hulk" Hogan as an ex-grappler whiling away days fishing in Florida. He reluctantly takes a job as bodyguard to computer tycoon Austin Pendleton. Twist is that Hogan, who loathes kids, has in reality been hired to protect Pendleton's brats (Robert Gorman, Madeline Zima), as well as double as nanny. The anklebiters have been targeted for kidnapping by a psycho loon (David Johansen).

MR. NORTH
1988, 92 mins, US Ⓥ ◉
D: Danny Huston A: Anthony Edwards, Robert Mitchum, Lauren Bacall, Harry Dean Stanton, Anjelica Huston, Mary Stuart Masterson (Heritage/Goldwyn)

Woefully flat affair which even a stellar cast cannot bring to life. Fanciful yarn has Theophilus North, a bright Yale graduate, arriving in the seaside bastion of old money and extravagance and making his way in society by magically curing the rich of what ails them, and charming them to boot. All of this doesn't go down too well with the pillar of the local medical community, who drags the shining fellow into court. Anthony Edwards gives it a reasonable try in the leading role.

MR. SATURDAY NIGHT
1992, 119 mins, US Ⓥ ⊙
D: Billy Crystal **A:** Billy Crystal, David Paymer, Julie Warner, Helen Hunt, Jerry Orbach, Ron Silver (Castle Rock/Face)

By turns relentlessly jokey and shamelessly schmaltzy, Billy Crystal's directorial debut charts a sometimes unpleasant funnyman's long career in choppy, two-dimensional fashion, but delivers enough laughs and heart tugging. Flashbacks reveal that the stubborn comic was usually his own worst enemy, deliberately undercutting himself with his superiors and letting his emotions get the better of him. Other than his career, the only thing of enduring importance to Buddy is his relationship with his brother, Stan, a gentle, kind soul (David Paymer, in a standout performance).
1992: Nomination: Best Supp. Actor (David Paymer)

MRS. BROWN
1997, 103 mins, UK Ⓥ ⊙
D: John Madden **A:** Judi Dench, Billy Connolly, Geoffrey Palmer, Anthony Sher, Gerard Butler, Richard Pasco (Ecosse/BBC)

Mrs. Brown is a sensitive, richly detailed drama about the complex and intimate friendship Queen Victoria developed with her loyal servant John Brown. The story begins in 1864, with Victoria (Judi Dench) still mourning her beloved husband and mentor, Albert. Enter Scottish servant Brown (Billy Connolly), the Queen's loyal hunting guide. Down-to-earth and with no regard for protocol, Brown causes immediate upheaval in the court. Rumors of an affair begin to scandalize British society. Director John Madden employs an unobtrusive style that serves the drama effectively and allows his gifted thesps to develop highly modulated characterizations.
1997: Nominations: Best Actress (Judi Dench), Makeup

MRS. DOUBTFIRE
1993, 125 mins, US Ⓥ ⊙ ▭
D: Chris Columbus **A:** Robin Williams, Sally Field, Pierce Brosnan, Harvey Fierstein, Polly Holliday (20th Century-Fox/Blue Wolf)

Williams plays a flaky, unemployed actor Daniel who botches his son's birthday party and ends up getting tossed out by his wife (Sally Field). Limited to weekly visitation, Daniel and his brother (Harvey Fierstein), a gay makeup artist, hatch the plan of having him masquerade as a matronly nanny—the better to steal precious hours with his three adorable moppets. The pic does reveal occasional inspiration in terms of sharp dialogue and in scenes of well-choreographed slapstick lunacy, among them a crowning scene in which Daniel/Mrs. Doubtfire fulfills two dinner engagements at the same time. That said, *Mrs. Doubtfire*'s warm-fuzzy aspects prove a bit much.
1993: Best Makeup

MR. SKEFFINGTON
1944, 126 mins, US Ⓥ ⊙
D: Vincent Sherman **A:** Bette Davis, Claude Rains, Walter Abel, Richard Waring, George Coulouris (Warner)

Not only another triumph for Bette Davis but also a picture of terrific strength. The dialogue ranges from the smart to the trenchantly dramatic in limning the life of the woman who lived for her beauty but found that it wasn't of a lasting character. Davis, playing the coquettish daughter of a once-wealthy family, progresses to around 50 years when suddenly aging badly as result of illness. Opposite Davis is the able Claude Rains, the successful Wall Street tycoon who goes blind and also prematurely ages as result of several years spent in a Nazi concentration camp.
1944: Nominations: Best Actor (Claude Rains), Actress (Bette Davis)

MRS. MIKE
1949, 98 mins, US
D: Louis King **A:** Dick Powell, Evelyn Keyes, J. M. Kerrigan, Angela Clarke (United Artists/Regal)

The story of a Boston girl who married a mountie and goes into the wilderness of Canada's Northwest Territories to live. Evelyn Keyes particularly shines in the title role with a portrayal that has excellent emotional depth and just the right touch of humor. Dick Powell is fine as the conscientious mountie. The emotional gamut abounds in childbirth, epidemics, amputation, and death.

MRS. MINIVER
1942, 133 mins, US Ⓥ ⊙
D: William Wyler **A:** Greer Garson, Walter Pidgeon, Teresa Wright, May Whitty, Reginald Owen, Henry Wilcoxon (M-G-M)

A poignant story of the joys and sorrows, the humor and pathos of middle-class family life in wartime England. When Mrs. Miniver's husband is summoned from his bed at 2:00 A.M. to help rescue the legions of Dunkirk, when her son flies out across the Channel each night, when she frightenedly captures a sick and starving German pilot who bears resemblance to her own boy, *Mrs. Miniver* truly brings the war into one's own family. Greer Garson, with her knee-weakening smile, and Walter Pidgeon, almost equally personable, are the Minivers. Scarcely less engaging or capable are young Teresa Wright as their daughter-in-law, and Richard Ney in the difficult role of their son.
1942: Best Picture, Director, Actress (Greer Garson), Supp. Actress (Teresa Wright), Screenplay, B&W Cinematography
Nominations: Best Actor (Walter Pidgeon), Supp. Actor (Henry Travers), Supp. Actress (May Whitty), Editing, Sound, Special Effects

MR. SMITH GOES TO WASHINGTON
1939, 126 mins, US Ⓥ ⊙
D: Frank Capra **A:** Jean Arthur, James Stewart, Claude Rains, Edward Arnold, Thomas Mitchell, Guy Kibbee (Columbia)

Frank Capra never attempts to expose political skullduggery on a wide scale. He selects one state political machine and after displaying its power and ruthlessness, proceeds to tear it to pieces. Stewart is a most happy choice for the title role, delivering sincerity to a difficult part that introduces him as a self-conscious idealist, but a stalwart fighter when faced with a battle to overcome the ruthles political machine of his own state. Jean Arthur is excellent as the wisely cynical senatorial secretary who knows the political ropes of Washington.
1939: Best Original Story
Nominations: Best Picture, Director, Actor (James Stewart), Supp. Actor (Harry Carey), Screenplay, Art Direction, Editing, Score, Sound

MRS. MUNCK
1995, 90 mins, US Ⓥ
D: Diane Ladd **A:** Diane Ladd, Bruce Dern, Kelly Preston, Shelley Winters, Jim Walton (Viacom)

Screen veteran Diane Ladd's helming bow is a campily claustrophobic two-hander about lost love and misperceived intentions that wears out its welcome after a bouncy start. Ladd, who also scripted, toplines as the recently widowed title character, now ready for a new lodger. Rose Munck's selection of her wheelchair-bound father-in-law is not as sensible as it seems. You see, her relatives don't realize she had a lengthy affair with mean old Mr. Leary (Ladd ex, Bruce Dern). Few viewers will be thrilled by this attempt to blend the macabre with slapstick violence and earnest psychological melodrama.

MRS. PARKER AND THE VICIOUS CIRCLE
1994, 123 mins, US Ⓥ ⊙
D: Alan Rudolph **A:** Jennifer Jason Leigh, Matthew Broderick, Campbell Scott, Peter Gallagher, Jennifer Beals (Altman)

A striking performance by Jennifer Jason Leigh provides the centerpiece for a highly absorbing but naggingly patchy look at the acerbic writer Dorothy Parker and her cohorts at the legendary Algonquin Round Table. Contrast between the sadness and disappointment in Parker's personal and creative life, and the exhilaration of important friendships and glittering social swirl, gives this film its poignance. Her husband, Eddie (Andrew McCarthy), reveals himself to be a morphine addict, and hardly Dorothy's match upstairs. At *Vanity Fair,* she and the other writers, including Robert Benchley (Campbell Scott) wear their salaries around their necks to protest their measly wages, and she is soon fired. Dorothy launches into a passionate affair with rakish newspaperman Charles MacArthur (Matthew Broderick). At the heart of the picture is the intense but carefully platonic friendship between Mrs. Parker and Mr. Benchley, as they nearly always call each other.

MRS. PARKINGTON
1944, 123 mins, US
D: Tay Garnett **A:** Greer Garson, Walter Pidgeon, Edward Arnold, Agnes Moorehead, Peter Lawford, Dan Duryea (M-G-M)

Film version of Louis Bromfield's

novel is an absorbing and warm presentation of the history of an American empire builder. Story covers period from 1875 to 1938. Garson is presented at opening as the grand old lady and head of the family and its huge fortune. History of the founder of the fortune, Walter Pidgeon, is developed via series of numerous extended flashbacks as reminiscences of the old lady.

MRS. SOFFEL
1984, 110 mins, US ⓥ
D: Gillian Armstrong **A:** Diane Keaton, Mel Gibson, Matthew Modine, Edward Herrmann, Trini Alvarado (M-G-M)

The potential for a moving, tragic love story is clearly there, but *Mrs. Soffel* proves distressingly dull for most of its running time. True story is set in Pittsburgh in 1901, and has Diane Keaton as the wife of Allegheny County Prison warden, Edward Herrmann. She quickly takes a special interest in two cons on Death Row, brothers Mel Gibson and Matthew Modine. Defying all reason, Keaton helps the brothers escape.

MRS. WINTERBOURNE
1996, 104 mins, US ⓥ
D: Richard Benjamin **A:** Shirley MacLaine, Ricki Lake, Brendan Fraser, Miguel Sandoval, Loren Dean (A & M)

Sappy, old-fashioned, and predictable vehicle for actress-turned-talk-maven-turned-actress-again Ricki Lake delivers requisite warmth but few laughs. Striving for a fairy-tale tone, story centers on Connie Doyle (Lake), a down-on-her-luck young woman wrongly believed to be the widow of a young man who was an heir to the Winterbourne family fortune. Most of the laughs come courtesy of MacLaine's ailing Grace, who can't resist cigarettes or booze, and her loyal butler, Paco (Sandoval).

MR. TOPAZE
(US: I LIKE MONEY)
1961, 95 mins, UK
D: Peter Sellers **A:** Peter Sellers, Nadia Gray, Herbert Lom, Leo McKern, Martita Hunt, Billie Whitelaw (20th Century-Fox/De Grunwald)

Peter Sellers plays a kindly, dedicated, and very poor schoolmaster in a little French town. When he refuses to compromise over a pupil's report to satisfy the child's rich, influential grandmother he is fired by the arrogant headmaster. The gullible Sellers is soft-talked into becoming the front for a swindling business man, finds that he has been a pawn, but by then has discovered the wicked ways of the world. The early stages are crammed with sly humor.

MR. WONDERFUL
1993, 98 mins, US ⓥ ⊙
D: Anthony Minghella **A:** Matt Dillon, Annabella Sciorra, Mary-Louise Parker, William Hurt, Vincent D'Onofrio, David Barry Gray (Goldwyn)

This charming, almost sedate little romantic comedy offers an appealing array of characters lacking a villain or heavy—just a lot of well-meaning folks stumbling their way through life, trying to find a soulmate. The hook centers on the efforts of blue-collar worker Gus (Matt Dillon) to marry off his ex-wife, Leonora (Annabella Sciorra), as a means of escaping his alimony payments, only to rekindle his feelings for her in the process. What sets the pic apart is the richness of its characters and the top-to-bottom strength of its cast.

MR. WRONG
1996, 96 mins, US ⓥ ⊙
D: Nick Castle **A:** Ellen DeGeneres, Bill Pullman, Joan Cusack, Dean Stockwell, Joan Plowright (Mandeville/Touchstone)

Saga of how the perfect mate evolves into the date from hell has an underlying darkness. Martha Alston (DeGeneres), the thirty-something producer of a morning chat show, is the victim of parental pressure. It's time for Martha to settle down with a nice guy. Whitman Crawford (Bill Pullman) looks like Gary Cooper and acts like a dreamboat. Martha cannot believe her luck. Still, it doesn't take long for the cracks in the plaster to emerge. Whit's idea of fun is shoplifting—and, to prove his love, he'd literally snap off a finger. For Martha, the final straw is when she's taken to meet Mrs. Crawford (Joan Plowright), who grants her approval, based on criteria more commonly applied to horse breeding.

MS. 45
(AKA: ANGEL OF VENGEANCE)
1981, 84 mins, US ⓥ ⊙
D: Abel Ferrara **A:** Zoe Tamerlis, Steve Singer, Darlene Stuto, Jack Thibeau, Peter Yellen (Rochelle/Navaron)

Crisply told tale deals with a mute, stunningly attractive young woman worker (Zoe Tamerlis) who is traumatized one night by (1) being raped in an alley on the way home and then (2) raped a second time by a burglar waiting in her apartment. Killing the burglar in self-defense, she takes his gun and embarks on a vendetta of shooting down lecherous males.

MUCH ADO ABOUT NOTHING
1993, 110 mins, UK/US Ⓥ ⊙
D: Kenneth Branagh **A:** Kenneth Branagh, Michael Keaton, Robert Sean Leonard, Keanu Reeves, Emma Thompson, Denzel Washington (Renaissance/Goldwyn)

A spirited, winningly acted rendition of one of the Bard's most popular comedies, continuously enjoyable from its action-filled opening to the dazzling final shot. Only real drawback is pic's visual quality, which is unaccountably undistinguished, even ugly, especially considering the sun-drenched Tuscan location. Branagh and Thompson bring appealing intelligence and verbal snap to their sparring. Looking almost as weird as in *Beetlejuice*, Michael Keaton delivers a very alert, surprising turn as the malapropping constable Dogberry.

MUDLARK, THE
1950, 98 mins, UK Ⓥ
D: Jean Negulesco **A:** Irene Dunne, Alec Guinness, Andrew Ray, Beatrice Campbell, Anthony Steel, Finlay Currie (20th Century-Fox)

The adventures of the young mudlark—a waif who picks up scraps left on the mud reaches of the Thames—who goes to Windsor in the hope of seeing Queen Victoria, make an appealing and tender yarn. Prime minister Disraeli (Alec Guinness) uses the mudlark incident to win the sympathy of Parliament for reform legislation, as well as persuading the queen to come out of her retirement.
1950: Nomination: Best B&W Costume Design

MUI DU DU XANH
(US: THE SCENT OF GREEN PAPAYA)
1993, 104 mins, France Ⓥ
D: Tran Anh Hung **A:** Tran Nu Yen-Khe, Lu Man San, Truong Thi Loc, Nguyen Anh Hoa, Vuong Hoa Hoi (Lazennec/SFP/La Sept)

An exquisite exploration of a Vietnamese servant girl's private world in '50s Saigon, striking feature bow by 30-year-old helmer Tran Anh Hung was entirely shot in a studio outside Paris. First hour, set in 1951, limns the everyday chores and small joys of Mui (Tran Nu Yen-Khe), a peasant girl engaged by a family headed by a feckless, spendthrift father. Pic's second seg, 10 years later, finds the family on hard times and Mui, now a true beauty, is sent to work at the house of Khuyen, a talented classical pianist. It's a film of small events, often quietly humorous, that builds to a moving but undogmatic portrait of quiet female strength.
1993: Nomination: Best Foreign Language Film

MUJERES AL BORDE DE UN ATAQUE DE NERVIOS
(US: WOMEN ON THE VERGE OF A NERVOUS BREAKDOWN)
1988, 87 mins, Spain Ⓥ ⊙
D: Pedro Almodovar **A:** Carmen Maura, Antonio Banderas, Fernando Guillen, Julieta Serrano, Maria Barranco (El Deseo/Lauren)

The dilemma of a woman on the verge of a nervous breakdown after breaking up with a married man is fascinatingly treated in a comic vein. Central character is Pepa, superbly played by Carmen Maura. Using mostly the interior of her apartment as the scenario of the action, Almodovar introduces her zany girlfriend, then the son of the man who has jilted Pepa, his outraged wife, a second girlfriend, two policemen, a distaff lawyer, and a gay taxi driver.

MULAN
1998, 88 mins, US Ⓥ ⊙
D: Barry Cook, Tony Bancroft (Walt Disney)

Mulan plays out as a rich dramatic tapestry lightly stained by some strained comedy, rigorous political correctness and more adherence to Disney formula than should have been the case. With the marauding Huns invading the country, Mulan (Ming-Na Wen, sung by Lea Salonga) dresses herself as a man and joins a motley crew of recruits commanded by dashing young captain Shang (B. D. Wong, sung by Donny Osmond). Mulan saves the day, but when she is unmasked in victory's wake, she is spared only because she has saved Shang's life. The Huns rise again, challenging the ostracized Mulan to ever greater feats of bravery. From a design point of view, *Mulan* is constantly stimulating. Jerry Goldsmith's scoring brings the drama to life much as it would a live-action film. The standard comic and kid-friendly elements, notably the cutesy animals, seem incongruous. There is a feeling of how every last plot turn, line and gesture has been weighed for its full dramatic, ideological and cultural impact.

MULHOLLAND FALLS
1996, 107 mins, US Ⓥ ⊙
D: Lee Tamahori **A:** Nick Nolte, Melanie Griffith, Chazz Palminteri, Michael Madsen, Chris Penn, Treat Williams (M-G-M)

This sex-and-corruption-drenched mystery meller about a big official cover-up in postwar L.A. simply feels underachieved. Subject of a real-life bunch of elite cops called the Hat Squad, four tough guys in the LAPD known for their sartorial elegance, would appear to possess strong screen potential. Opening scene has group's bulldog leader Max Hoover (Nick Nolte) and his boys (Chazz Palminteri, Michael Madsen, Chris Penn) busting up a mob party and dumping one of them down a ravine off the avenue of the title. Hoover shortly becomes sidetracked by a professional crisis. The body of beautiful young Allison Pond (Jennifer Connelly) is found. Some home movies feature, among other things, the late young lady in some frisky sex play with Hoover. Trail in the case eventually leads to a desert military base active in A-bomb tests, as the top brass there, nutty genius General Timms (John Malkovich), also was involved with the busy Miss Pond.

MUMMY, THE
1933, 63 mins, US Ⓥ ⊙
D: Karl Freund **A:** Boris Karloff, Zita Johann, David Manners, Edward Van Sloan, Arthur Byron (Universal)

The first starring film for Boris Karloff. Revival of the mummy comes comparatively early in the running time. The transformation of Karloff's Im-Ho-Tep from a claylike figure in a coffin to a living thing is the highlight. The sequence in the museum with Im-Ho planning to kill Helen Grosvenor, of Egyptian heritage, to revive her ancient state, is too stagey. The mustiness of the tombs excavated is also over-suggestive of the Hollywood set.

MUMMY, THE
1999, 124 mins, US Ⓥ ⊙ ▭
D: Stephen Sommers **A:** Brendan Fraser, Rachel Weisz, John Hannah, Arnold Vosloo, Kevin J. O'Connor, Jonathan Hyde (Alphaville/Universal)

The Mummy tries to have it both ways, by sending up the adventure genre for laughs while going for shocks, but finds the sand slipping through its fingers on both counts. Story is set in the mid-twenties. Yank soldier-explorer Rick O'Connell (Brendan Fraser) is rescued from the noose by Evelyn (Rachel Weisz), a librarian who pals around with her maladroit brother (John Hannah). They set out down the Nile for Hamunaptra, the legendary burial site of priest Imhotep, the location of which only Rick knows. This being the age of CGI, one can be assured that the mummy will assume numerous different forms. Fraser is ideal for the swashbuckling leading role, but like the film itself never finds the proper serio-comic pitch. Buffoonery hardly seems like Weisz's natural domain.

1999: Nomination: Sound

MUMSY, NANNY, SONNY AND GIRLY
(US: GIRLY)
1970, 101 mins, UK Ⓥ
D: Freddie Francis **A:** Michael Bryant, Ursula Howells, Pat Heywood, Howard Trevor, Vanessa Howard (Fitsroy)

An offbeat, low-key horror melo-drama—a macabre combo of Disney and Hammer films, in which a lady, her maid, and two kids kidnap and murder unsuspecting males. Story is set in a country estate populated by mumsy Ursula Howells, nanny Pat Heywood, sonny Howard Trevor and girly Vanessa Howard. It's a quaint family, mannered in the niceties of civilized living, except that they get their kicks from kidnapping stray males.

MUPPET CHRISTMAS CAROL, THE
1992, 85 mins, US Ⓥ ⊙
D: Brian Henson **A:** Michael Caine, Dave Goelz, Steve Whitmire, Jerry Nelson, Frank Oz (Walt Disney/Henson)

This adaptation of Charles Dickens's Christmas classic is not as enchanting or amusing as the previous entries in the Muppet series. But nothing can really diminish the late Jim Henson's irresistibly appealing characters. Michael Caine is perfectly cast as the nasty Scrooge, though his role is too dominant. Muppets take the other roles: Kermit the Frog (Steve Whitmire) becomes abused bookkeeper Bob Cratchit, Miss Piggy (Frank Oz) his wife, Emily, and the Great Gonzo (Dave Goelz) is transformed into Dickens himself.

MUPPET MOVIE, THE
1979, 98 mins, US Ⓥ ⊙
D: James Frawley **A:** Jim Hanson, Frank

Oz, Charles Durning, Austin Pendleton, Scott Walker (ITC/Henson)

Jim Henson, Muppet originator, and Frank Oz, creative consultant, have abandoned the successful format of their vidshow, and inserted their creations into a well-crafted combo of musical comedy and fantasy adventure. Result is a muppet update of *The Wizard of Oz,* with Kermit the Frog leading a motley Muppet troupe on the asphalt road to Hollywood. Script incorporates the zingy one-liners and bad puns that have become the teleseries' trademark.

1979: Nominations: Best Adapted Score, Song ("The Rainbow Connection")

MUPPETS FROM SPACE

1999, 88 mins, US Ⓥ ⊙
D: Tim Hill **A:** Jeffrey Tambor, F. Murray Abraham, Rob Schneider, Josh Charles, Ray Liotta, David Arquette (Henson/Columbia)

The sixth full-length feature to showcase Jim Henson's immensely popular puppets is a modestly clever comedy. Bent-beaked Gonzo (voiced by Dave Goelz) begins to receive cryptic messages and snaps to the idea that maybe he's the offspring of extraterrestrials. When Miss Piggy lands a job at a TV station, she uses Gonzo as her stepping-stone to replace a superstar reporter (Andie MacDowell) as the host of a "reality" series titled *UFO Mania.* Gonzo's on-air appearance attracts the attention of K. Edgar Singer (Jeffrey Tambor), chief of a government agency charged with capturing and dissecting alien visitors. Gonzo is suitably engaging in his first starring role, while roommate Rizzo the Rat provides wiseguy comic relief. Kermit remains, as always, serenely graceful under pressure.

MUPPETS TAKE MANHATTAN, THE

1984, 94 mins, US Ⓥ ⊙
D: Frank Oz **A:** Jim Henson, Frank Oz, Dave Goelz, Steve Whitmire, Richard Hunt, Jerry Nelson (Tri-Star/Delphi II)

A genuinely fun confection of old-fashioned entertainment. Feature poses a hypothetical story of Kermit the Frog penning a successful senior variety show, *Manhattan Melodies,* and deciding to take it to Broadway. A hit show will enable him to marry his sweetheart, Miss Piggy, but the Muppets find it difficult to find backing and split up to various towns, working at odd jobs to support themselves.

1984: Nomination: Best Original Song Score

MUPPET TREASURE ISLAND

1996, 99 mins, US Ⓥ ⊙
D: Brian Henson **A:** Tim Curry, Steve Whitmire, Frank Oz, Billy Connolly (Henson/Disney)

This pirate adventure is a rollicking musical reworking of the Robert Louis Stevenson classic. The blustery Billy Bones (Billy Connolly) spins yet again the saga of a fabulous treasure buried on a remote island. Bones's last act is to give the Hawkins lad the treasure map. Jim hightails it with tavern coworkers Gonzo the Great and Rizzo the Rat in search of a ship to take him to the remote atoll. Kermit the Frog (performed by Steve Whitmire) essays the role of Captain Smollett, the skipper of the ship. Aboard, and pivotal, is the seemingly decent, salt-of-the-earth John Silver (Tim Curry).

MURDER

1930, 110 mins, UK Ⓥ
D: Alfred Hitchcock **A:** Herbert Marshall, Norah Baring, Phyllis Konstam, Edward Chapman, Miles Mander (British International)

A girl is convicted of murder on circumstantial evidence and sentenced to death. One of the jurymen, an actor, sets to work to solve the crime. Well photographed and mounted, it contains all the gadgets of the pet Alfred Hitchcock technique, from quick cutting to skillful dialogue blending. Long episodes have clever satirical values as attacks on the conventional and lower-class English.

MURDER AT 1600

1997, 107 mins, US Ⓥ ⊙ ▭
D: Dwight Little **A:** Wesley Snipes, Diane Lane, Daniel Benzali, Dennis Miller, Alan Alda, Ronny Cox (Warner)

Murder at 1600 is a trashy movie that's intermittently intriguing and enjoyable on its own terms. D.C. homicide detective Harlan Regis (Wesley Snipes) is called to investigate the murder of Carla (Mary Moore), a young, beautiful secretary whose body is found in a White House bathroom. Regis is assisted by a laconic Secret Service agent, Nina Chance (Diane Lane), ordered by her supervisor, ultra-tough Nick Spikings (Daniel Benzali), to wrap up the case as quickly and quietly as possible. Murder mystery unfolds in the midst of a global political crisis. President Jack Neil (Ronny Cox) hesitates to take aggressive action against North Korea, which holds hostage some American soldiers. What makes the film involving in its first hour is a thick, multilayered plot, but the last act turns the yarn into a routine, wildly implausible actioner. Snipes lends a sarcastic edge to his character, whose one-liners provide useful comic relief.

MURDER AT THE VANITIES
1934, 95 mins, US ⓥ
D: Mitchell Leisen **A:** Carl Brisson, Victor McLaglen, Jack Oakie, Kitty Carlisle, Gertrude Michael, Gail Patrick (Paramount)

Herein they mix up the elements of a musical show and a murder mystery, with effective comedy to flavor, and come out with 95 minutes of entertainment that should genuinely satisfy. Victor McLaglen is in charge of the investigation of a couple murders that tax his limited detective prescience. McLaglen shares with Jack Oakie the comedy burden and for each it's a strike. Picture serves to bring out Carl Brisson, Danish actor. In addition to having an ingratiating personality and photographing well, he sells his songs for good results.

MURDER BY CONTRACT
1958, 80 mins, US
D: Irving Lerner **A:** Vince Edwards, Phillip Pine, Herschel Bernardi, Caprice Toriel, Michael Granger (Orbit)

The story of a paid killer. Interest centers around Claude (Vince Edwards), an unemotional executioner who takes on a major assignment in Los Angeles after handling several eastern commitments with speed and dispatch. His victim here is a woman. A standout music score by Perry Botkin, using only a guitar which he plays to perfection, gives fine atmospheric backing.

MURDER BY DEATH
1976, 94 mins, US ⓥ ⊚
D: Robert Moore **A:** Eileen Brennan, Peter Sellers, James Coco, Peter Falk, Alec Guinness, David Niven (Columbia)

Very good silly-funny Neil Simon satirical comedy, with a super all-star cast cavorting as recognizable pulp fiction detectives gathered at the home of Truman Capote, wealthy hedonist fed up with contrived gumshoe plots.

MURDER BY DECREE
1980, 120 mins, UK/Canada ⓥ ⊙
D: Bob Clark **A:** Christopher Plummer, James Mason, Donald Sutherland, Gene-

vieve Bujold, David Hemmings, Susan Clark (Ambassador/CFDC/Famous Players)

Probably the best Sherlock Holmes film since the inimitable pairing of Basil Rathbone and Nigel Bruce. The film's charm derives mainly from John Hopkins's literal, deadpan script that makes no attempt either to mock or contemporize Sir Arthur Conan Doyle's literary creation. Holmes and Watson are not called in to help solve a series of murders linked to Jack the Ripper. Anthony Quayle, as the new topper at Scotland Yard, has his reasons for excluding them, as does Inspector David Hemmings.

MURDERERS ARE AMONGST US, THE
See: Die Moerder Sind unter Uns

MURDERERS' ROW
1966, 108 mins, US ⓥ
D: Henry Levin **A:** Dean Martin, Ann-Margret, Karl Malden, Camilla Sparv, James Gregory (Meadway-Claude/Columbia)

Sequel to the successful *The Silencers*. This time out, Dean Martin's secret agent has to trek to the Riviera to catch that bad old Karl Malden, who's about to blow up Washington with a secret beam. Whenever the viewer begins to take things seriously, Levin cuts back to a laugh (or Martin ripping off Ann-Margret's miniskirt, which contains an explosive, and hurling it at a wall decorated with Frank Sinatra's picture).

MURDER, HE SAYS
1945, 89 mins, US
D: George Marshall **A:** Fred MacMurray, Helen Walker, Marjorie Main, Porter Hall (Paramount)

This one tosses logic out the window and devotes itself to broad slapstick. MacMurray is the Trotter Poll man, sent into a mountain district to find out what has happened to previous Trotterites collecting rural data. It seems they have done okay until approaching the Fleagles, who don't like strangers and calmly bump them off. Continuous chases, fights, etc., keep the issues in a mad shambles. Marjorie Main finds role of Ma Fleagle little different from her usual uncouth blowsy parts.

MURDER, INC.
See: The Enforcer (1951)

MURDER, INC.
1960, 103 mins, US ▭
D: Burt Balaban, Stuart Rosenberg **A:**

Stuart Whitman, May Britt, Henry Morgan, Peter Falk, Sarah Vaughan (20th Century-Fox)

Professional killers of the crime syndicate headed by Albert Anastasia and Louis "Lepke" Buchalter were a scourge in the Depression era. They later became known as Murder, Inc. The script recounts how Lepke and the syndicate shook down the garment district, trucking business, and sundry other legitimate enterprises through goon squads and hired killers. With the possible exception of Peter Falk's portrayal of killer Abe Reles, scarcely any of the cast's performances could be rated as dynamic.

1960: Nomination: Best Supp. Actor (Peter Falk)

MURDER IN THE CATHEDRAL
1952, 140 mins, UK
D: George Hoellering **A:** John Groser, Alexander Gauge, David Ward, George Woodbridge, Basil Burton, T. S. Eliot (Hoellering)

T. S. Eliot's legit play *Murder in the Cathedral* has been turned into a moving but very ponderous film. Story of the life of Thomas Becket, the martyred Archbishop of Canterbury, unfolds too statically in the picture form. Eliot scripted this from his own play, but failed to add sufficient movement.

MURDER IN THE FIRST
1995, 122 mins, US ⊗ ⊙
D: Marc Rocco **A:** Christian Slater, Kevin Bacon, Gary Oldman, Embeth Davidtz, Bill Macy, Brad Dourif (Studio Canal Plus/Warner)

A terrific true story, a good script, some potent performances and overly fancy, show-off direction combine to mostly strong effect in tale of a convict's hellacious punishment in solitary on Alcatraz in the late 1930s and a young attorney's attempt to expose the unspeakable conditions within America's most famous prison. Gary Oldman makes a strong showing in his few scenes as the fastidious but sadistic associate warden. Alcatraz locations and outstanding production design give a strong sense of time and place.

MURDER IN THORNTON SQUARE, THE
See: Gaslight (1944)

MURDER MOST FOUL
1964, 90 mins, UK ⊗
D: George Pollock **A:** Margaret Rutherford, Ron Moody, Charles Tingwell, Andrew Cruickshank, Dennis Price, Francesca Annis (M-G-M)

Margaret Rutherford brings considerable assurance to the third Agatha Christie thriller to cast the doughty old-timer in the role of Miss Marple, the eccentric amateur sleuth. Miss Marple is the lone member of a murder jury who holds out for acquittal. She proceeds to unsnarl the case and prove herself far more professional than the investigating police.

MURDER, MY SWEET
(UK: FAREWELL MY LOVELY)
1945, 92 mins, US ⊗
D: Edward Dmytryk **A:** Dick Powell, Claire Trevor, Anne Shirley, Otto Kruger, Mike Mazurki, Miles Mander (RKO)

Taut thriller, about a private detective enmeshed with a gang of blackmailers, is as smart as it is gripping. Story begins with a private dick hired by an ex-convict to find his one-time girlfriend. Dick Powell is a surprise as the hard-boiled copper. The portrayal is potent and convincing. Claire Trevor is as dramatic as the predatory femme.

MURDER ON MONDAY
See: Home at Seven

MURDER ON THE ORIENT EXPRESS
1974, 127 mins, UK ⊗ ⊙
D: Sidney Lumet **A:** Albert Finney, Lauren Bacall, Ingrid Bergman, Sean Connery, Vanessa Redgrave, Richard Widmark (EMI)

Agatha Christie's 1934 Hercule Poirot novel has been filmed in a bygone film style as some treasure out of a time capsule. Albert Finney is outstanding as Poirot, his makeup, wardrobe, and performance a blend of topflight theater. The mysterious death of Richard Widmark triggers Finney's investigation at the behest of Martin Balsam, a railroad executive who hopes the crime can be solved before the snowbound train is reached by rescuers

1974: Best Supp. Actress (Ingrid Bergman)
Nominations: Best Actor (Albert Finney), Adapted Screenplay, Cinematography, Costume Design, Original Dramatic Score

MURDER SHE SAID
1961, 86 mins, UK ⊗
D: George Pollock **A:** Margaret Rutherford, Arthur Kennedy, Muriel Pavlow, James Robertson Justice, Thorley Walters (M-G-M)

Somewhat unconvincing whodunit. In adaptation of the Agatha Christie novel, *4:50 from Paddington*, Margaret Rutherford witnesses a murder transpiring in the compartment of a passing train. Since the police do not believe her story, and being an avid reader of mystery fiction, she takes it upon herself to solve the case.

MURDERS IN THE RUE MORGUE
1932, 60 mins, US Ⓥ
D: Robert Florey A: Bela Lugosi, Sidney Fox, Leon Ames, Bert Roach, Brandon Hurst, Noble Johnson (Universal)

Edgar Allan Poe wouldn't recognize his story. This version's hero is a young medical student who mixes romance with science. The cast's other scientist, a loony Dr. Mirakle played in Bela Lugosi's customary fantastic manner, is an evolution bug who seeks to prove a vague fact by mixing the blood of his captive gorilla with that of Parisian women. The murders—three real and one almost—are results of his fiendish transfusions.

MURIEL
OU LE TEMPS D'UN RETOUR
1963, 120 mins, France Ⓥ
D: Alain Resnais A: Delphine Seyrig, Jean-Pierre Kerien, Nita Klein, Jean-Baptiste Thierre, Claude Sainval (Argos/Alpha/Pleiade/Eclair/Dear)

A fortyish woman invites an old lover to come to see her. He appears accompanied by a 20-year-old mistress whom he passes off as his niece. There can be no denying Resnais's brilliance in his rapid cutting, which replaces camera movement, plus maintenance of a mood and knowing use of color. Delphine Seyrig etches a mannered but acceptable portrait of the almost spinsterish widow who cannot cope with herself or her memories.

MURIEL'S WEDDING
1994, 105 mins, Australia/France Ⓥ
D: P. J. Hogan A: Toni Collette, Bill Hunter, Rachel Griffiths, Jeanie Drynan, Gennie Nevinson Brice (House & Moorhouse/CiBy 2000)

Aesthetically crude ugly-duckling fantasy establishes poor Muriel (Toni Collette) as, in her own words, "stupid, fat, and useless." After a vacation where the overweight 22-year-old high school dropout hooks up with g.f. Rhonda (Rachel Griffiths) to do a lip-synched Abba routine in a club, the young ladies move to Sydney. Muriel fulfills at least the externals of her fantasy by marrying a hunky South African swimmer. Most of the action is played for broad laughs. The humor is base and often cruel, making fun of people's looks and ineptitude.

MURMUR OF THE HEART
See: Le Souffle au Coeur

MURPHY'S LAW
1986, 100 mins, US Ⓥ ⊙
D: J. Lee Thompson A: Charles Bronson, Kathleen Wilhoite, Carrie Snodgress, Robert F. Lyons, Angel Tompkins (Cannon)

Very violent urban crime meller is tiresome but too filled with extreme incident to be boring. Title character (played by Charles Bronson) is a tough loner whose main companion in life is his flask now that his wife has left him. Murphy's life is shaken up when the ex-wife and numerous others around him are mowed down. Booked for the crimes, he clears his name by tracking down killer Carrie Snodgress.

MURPHY'S ROMANCE
1985, 107 mins, US Ⓥ
D: Martin Ritt A: Sally Field, James Garner, Corey Haim, Dennis Burkley, Georgann Johnson (Columbia)

This sweet and homey picture, which casts two very decent actors in two very decent roles, falls far short of compelling filmmaking. Field plays a divorced mother who is determined to make a living as a horse trainer on a desolate piece of property on the outskirts of a one-street town in rural Arizona. She meets Murphy, a widower who is the town's pharmacist. He takes a liking to her almost immediately, but her ne'er-do-well former husband, Brian Kerwin, rides back into her life.
1985: Nominations: Best Actor (James Garner), Cinematography

MURPHY'S WAR
1971, 108 mins, UK Ⓥ ▭
D: Peter Yates A: Peter O'Toole, Sian Phillips, Philippe Noiret, Horst Janson, John Hallam (Dimitri de Grunwald)

Wartime anecdote shot mainly in a remote uncomfortable part of Venezuela's Orinoco River. A German U-boat torpedoes an armed merchantman. O'Toole, one of the ship's aviation mechanics, is rescued by a French oil engineer (Philippe Noiret) who takes O'Toole to a nearby Quaker mission where he's nursed by the missionary-nurse, played by Sian Phillips. Another survivor pleads with O'Toole to find his wrecked plane and keep it out of enemy hands. He has a better idea. He decides to patch it up and blow the submarine to the high heavens.

MUSCLE BEACH PARTY
1964, 94 mins, US ⓥ ⊙ ▭
D: William Asher **A:** Frankie Avalon, Annette Funicello, Luciana Paluzzi, John Ashley, Don Rickles, Jody McCrea (American International)

Follow-up to *Beach Party*. The novelty of surfing has worn off, leaving in its wake little more than a conventional teenage-geared romantic farce with songs. The clash of three factions at a beach site sets off the romantic, comedic, and musical fireworks. At one end is a group of youthful surfers. At another is a band of Atlasian musclemen. Catalyst is a wealthy, fickle contessa. Peter Lorre puts in an unbilled appearance.

MUSIC BOX
1989, 123 mins, US ⓥ ⊙ ▭
D: Constantin Costa-Gavras **A:** Jessica Lange, Armin Mueller-Stahl, Frederic Forrest, Donald Moffat, Lukas Haas (Carolco)

Jessica Lange plays a Chicago defense attorney who must defend her own father (Armin Mueller-Stahl), accused of having committed war crimes during World War II. Slowly losing her conviction as to his innocence, Lange's character pulls out all the stops to try to exonerate her dad. Even the film's accounts of Holocaust atrocities prove for the most part strangely unaffecting under Joe Eszterhas's limp dialogue and Costa-Gavras's stodgy direction, which relies on a concussive score to try to create tension where there is none.
1989: Nomination: Best Actress (Jessica Lange)

MUSIC LOVERS, THE
1971, 122 mins, UK ⓥ ▭
D: Ken Russell **A:** Richard Chamberlain, Glenda Jackson, Max Adrian, Christopher Gable, Izabella Telezynska (United Artists)

There is frequently a thin line between genius and madness. By going over that line and unduly emphasizing the mad and the perverse in their biopic of the 19th-century Russian composer Peter Ilyich Tchaikovsky, producer-director Ken Russell and scripter Melvyn Bragg lose their audience. The result is a motion picture that is frequently dramatically and visually stunning but more often tedious and grotesque. Richard Chamberlain, bushy

bearded and eyes constantly brimming with tears, plays the homosexual, irrationally romantic composer, and Glenda Jackson the neurotic trollop he tragically marries.

MUSIC MAN, THE
1962, 151 mins, US ⓥ ⊙ ▭
D: Morton DaCosta **A:** Robert Preston, Shirley Jones, Buddy Hackett, Hermione Gingold, Paul Ford (Warner)

Handsomely dressed and ultimately endearing supermusical. Call this a triumph, perhaps a classic, of corn, small-town nostalgia, and American love of a parade. DaCosta's use of several of the original Broadway cast players is thoroughly vindicated. Paul Ford is wonderfully fatuous as the bumptious mayor. Pert Kelton shines with warmth and humanity as the heroine's earthy mother. For the title role, Warner might have secured bigger screen names but it is impossible to imagine any of them matching Robert Preston's authority, backed by 883 stage performances.
1962: Best Adapted Music Score
Nominations: Best Picture, Color Costume Design, Color Art Direction, Editing, Sound

MUSIC OF CHANCE, THE
1993, 98 mins, US ⓥ ⊙
D: Philip Haas **A:** James Spader, Mandy Patinkin, M. Emmet Walsh, Charles Durning, Joel Grey (IRS-Transatlantic/American Playhouse)

An auspicious feature debut for documentary filmmaker Philip Haas is ultimately more of an intellectual tease. Mandy Patinkin offers a lift to a bloodied drifter (James Spader). Spader convinces him to put up $10,000 for a poker game with two rich pushovers. The pair proceed to the splendid country estate of Charles Durning and Joel Grey. After initial success, Spader's luck turns and he and Patinkin are forced to agree to work off their debt by reconstructing a medieval stone wall, a job estimated to take 50 days.

MUSIC OF THE HEART
1999, 124 mins, US ⓥ ⊙
D: Wes Craven **A:** Meryl Streep, Aidan Quinn, Angela Bassett, Cloris Leachman, Gloria Estefan, Josh Pais (Craven/Maddalena/Miramax)

Horrormeister Wes Craven makes an abrupt U-turn with *Music of the Heart*, a gloriously sentimental true-life drama about a deserted wife who makes a fresh start in life by teaching violin to under-privileged kids in East Harlem. Pic is not for cynics. In 1988, music-loving navy wife Roberta Guaspari (Meryl Streep) is dumped by her husband. Traumatized, the middle-class Roberta is forced to reenter the workforce and engineers an introduction to Janet Williams (Angela Bassett), principal of a school in East Harlem. Roberta proposes she teach violin. Though warned that most of the kids have attention spans that don't go past do-re-mi, Roberta nevertheless perseveres.

1999: Nominations: Best actress (Meryl Streep), Original Song ("Music of My Heart")

MUTINY ON THE BOUNTY
1935, 132 mins, US ⓥ ⊙
D: Frank Lloyd **A:** Clark Gable, Charles Laughton, Franchot Tone, Dudley Digges, Donald Crisp, Movita (M-G-M)

This one is Hollywood at its very best. First hour or so of the film leads up, step by step, to the mutiny, with a flexible "story" backgrounding some thrilling views of seamanship on a British man-o'-war in the early 18th century, and the cruel Captain Bligh's inhuman treatment of his sailors. Bligh, through the cruelties he performs and due to the faithful portrait drawn by Charles Laughton, is as despicable a character as has ever heavied across a screen. Gable, as brave Fletcher Christian, fills the doc's prescription to the letter.

1935: Best Picture
Nominations: Best Director, Actor (Clark Gable, Charles Laughton, Franchot Tone), Screenplay, Editing, Score

MUTINY ON THE BOUNTY
1962, 185 mins, US ⓥ ⊙ ▭
D: Lewis Milestone, [Marlon Brando, Carol Reed] **A:** Marlon Brando, Trevor Howard, Richard Harris, Hugh Griffith, Richard Haydn, Tarita (M-G-M/Arcola)

Physically superlative entertainment may be somewhat short of genuine dramatic greatness, but it is often overwhelmingly spectacular. Marlon Brando as Fletcher Christian and Trevor Howard as Captain Bligh etch their own brilliant entries in the *Bounty*'s log. Director Lewis Milestone has come up with some terrific scenes, from opening a man's back by laying on the whip to fighting wind, cold, snow, rain, towering seas, and a murderous, runaway cask in the hold. This is a superb blending of direction, photography, and special effects artistry.

1962: Nominations: Best Picture, Color Cinematography, Color Art Direction, Editing, Original Music Score, Song ("Follow Me"), Special Effects

MUTTERS COURAGE
(US: MY MOTHER'S COURAGE)
1996, 88 mins, Germany/UK/Austria ▭
D: Michael Verhoeven **A:** Pauline Collins, Ulrich Tukur, Natalie Morse, Heirbert Sasse, Robert Giggenbach (Sentana/Little Bird/Wega)

German filmmaker Michael Verhoeven returns to the subject of the Holocaust. Based on writer George Tabori's recollection of his Jewish mother's plight in Nazi-held Budapest of 1944, it's an odd vignette of the war, one day in the life of Elsa Tabori (Pauline Collins). A woman who's boundlessly chipper, she is told she is among the Jews to be deported to some unknown destination. But the logical arc and oft-told tragic scenario do not occur, and Elsa Tabori became a hero virtually by default.

MY BEAUTIFUL LAUNDRETTE
1985, 97 mins, UK ⓥ ⊙
D: Stephen Frears **A:** Daniel Day Lewis, Gordon Warnecke, Saeed Jaffrey, Roshan Seth, Shirley Anne Field (Working Title/SAF/Channel Four)

Tale of profiteering Pakistani capitalists making a fortune in an impoverished London. Focus is on two youths, friends from school days. Johnny is a working-class white whose punkish mates are members of the National Front. Omar lives with his left-leaning widower father. Omar and Johnny convert a rundown laundrette into a veritable palace. A repressed love blossoms between Omar and Johnny, adding tension to the already volatile racial situation.

1986: Nomination: Best Original Screenplay

MY BEST FRIEND'S WEDDING
1997, 105 mins, US ⓥ ⊙ ▭
D: P. J. Hogan **A:** Julia Roberts, Dermot Mulroney, Cameron Diaz, Rupert Everett, Philip Bosco, M. Emmet Walsh (Predawn/TriStar)

Anchored by skilled comedienne Julia Roberts, this skewed variation on jealousy and the wrong woman doing battle in the aisles is a winning balance of the familiar and the novel. Julianne (Roberts) believes her former lover Michael (Dermot Mulroney), is about to propose marriage. But Michael has been smitten by heiress Kimmy (Cameron Diaz) and wants Julianne to attend the wedding party in Chicago. Julianne plans to break it up by hook or by crook. Kimmy would appear to be no match for Julianne's devices. She's unworldly, vulnerable and sincere. However, every plot to demean the imminent bride backfires. While the film has its antic moments, it's far more sober-minded than the usual film of this ilk. Roberts's character is commanding yet out of control. Diaz is a performer with a powerful physical presence that runs counter to a chameleonlike emotional range. And Rupert Everett, as Roberts's gay editor, makes great sport of it when she pretends they're engaged to make Michael jealous.

1997: Nomination: Best Original Comedy Score

MY BEST GIRL
1927, 64 mins, US Ⓥ ⊗
D: Sam Taylor **A:** Mary Pickford, Charles "Buddy" Rogers, Sunshine Hart, Lucien Littlefield, Carmelita Geraghty (Pickford/ United Artists)

Mary is the brains and character of an incompetent, shiftless, but well-meaning family. The stock girl in the five-and-ten, she falls in love with a new clerk, not knowing he is the son of the owner. The boy is betrothed to a society miss, but the father insists he makes some sort of a showing in the store before engagement is announced. Charles Rogers overcomes his good looks with a display of naturalistic humanness. Pickford is her usual sweet and likable self.

MY BLUE HEAVEN
1950, 96 mins, US
D: Henry Koster **A:** Betty Grable, Dan Dailey, David Wayne, Jane Wyatt, Mitzi Gaynor (20th Century-Fox)

Yarn has Betty Grable and Dan Dailey trying to adopt a baby, scripters getting into considerable detail on both the legal and illegal sides of the adoption business. While Grable and Dailey offer their capable standard brands of song-and-dance, the real eye-catcher of the pic is a lush brunette youngster making her initial screen appearance. She's Mitzi Gaynor. She's long on terping and vocalizing.

MY BLUE HEAVEN
1990, 95 mins, US Ⓥ ⊙
D: Herbert Ross **A:** Steve Martin, Rick

Moranis, Joan Cusack, Melanie Mayron, Carol Kane (Hawn-Sylbert/Warner)

Steve Martin and Rick Moranis do the mismatched-pair-o'-guys shtick in a lighthearted fairy tale. But the fish-out-of-water premise isn't funny enough to sustain a whole picture. Moranis plays Barney Coopersmith, a stiff-necked FBI agent who's assigned to settle mobster Martin into a new life as part of a government witness-protection program. Life in a brand-new subdivision is too placid for Vinnie, who immediately starts getting involved in illegal mischief.

MY BODYGUARD
1980, 97 mins, US Ⓥ
D: Tony Bill **A:** Chris Makepeace, Adam Baldwin, Matt Dillon, Ruth Gordon, John Houseman, Craig Richard Nelson (20th Century-Fox/Simon/Market Street)

In his directorial debut, Tony Bill assembles a truly remarkable cast of youngsters with little or no previous acting experience. Chris Makepeace is superb as the slightly built kid coming anew to a Chicago high school dominated by extortionist gang leader Matt Dillon, also terrific in his part. Adam Baldwin is a standoffish, uncommunicative brute rumored to be a psychotic weirdo who has killed cops and other kids. Dillon and gang use the rumors to demand payment from smaller fellows for "protection" from Baldwin.

MY BOYFRIEND'S BACK
1993, 84 mins, US ⊙
D: Bob Balaban **A:** Andrew Lowery, Traci Lind, Danny Zorn, Edward Herrmann, Mary Beth Hurt, Austin Pendleton (Touchstone)

Idiotic offbeat comedy about an obsessive teenage love. Missy (Traci Lind), the most attractive and desirable girl of her class, has a b.f. (Matthew Fox), but is obsessively pursued by Johnny Dingle (Andrew Lowery), a shy, daydreaming classmate. Dingle stages a robbery at the convenience store where Missy is working so he can save her life. But the ill-conceived caper backfires and he loses his life. The relentless Dingle then comes back from the dead—as a frail and decaying zombie.

MY BRILLIANT CAREER
1979, 98 mins, Australia Ⓥ ▭
D: Gillian Armstrong **A:** Judy Davis, Sam Neill, Wendy Hughes, Robert Grubb, Pat Kennedy (New South Wales/ GUO)

This Australian film is a charming look at 19th-century rural days in general and the stirrings of self-realization and feminine liberation in the persona of a headstrong young girl who wants to go her own way. Judy Davis is fine as an ugly duckling who blossoms into an independent writer and refuses to give in to the ritual and place reserved for women at the time which was, namely, marriage.

1980: Nomination: Best Costume Design

MY CHAUFFEUR
1986, 97 mins, US ⓥ ⊙

D: David Beaird **A:** Deborah Foreman, Sam J. Jones, Sean McClory, E. G. Marshall (Crown)

David Beaird avowedly set out to imitate the screwball comedies of the 1930s and 1940s and has succeeded admirably, thanks to adorably spunky Deborah Foreman and her stuffy foil, Sam J. Jones. Summoned mysteriously by a millionaire limo company owner (E. G. Marshall), Foreman takes a job as a driver, much to the objections of chauvinistic chauffeurs who want to maintain their male-dominated domain. She gets the impossible assignments including Jones, a spoiled, domineering industrialist who is, unknown to her, Marshall's son.

MY COUSIN RACHEL
1952, 98 mins, US

D: Henry Koster **A:** Olivia de Havilland, Richard Burton, Audrey Dalton, Ronald Squire, George Dolenz (20th Century-Fox)

A dark, moody melodrama has been fashioned from Daphne du Maurier's best-seller. Olivia de Havilland endows the title role with commanding histrionics. Richard Burton creates a strong impression. The story, set in early 19th-century England, tells of a young man with a deep affection for the foster father who had raised him. When the foster father marries a distant cousin, the young man receives letters that indicate his beloved relative is being poisoned by the bride.

1952: Nominations: Best Supp. Actor (Richard Burton), B&W Cinematography, B&W Costume Design, B&W Art Direction

MY COUSIN VINNY
1992, 119 mins, US ⓥ ⊙

D: Jonathan Lynn **A:** Joe Pesci, Ralph Macchio, Marisa Tomei, Mitchell Whitfield, Fred Gwynne (20th Century-Fox)

Joe Pesci puts in a lovable underdog turn as a hopelessly inept lawyer battling to prove himself in his first case. Tale has coarse Brooklynite Pesci called upon by family members to help his college-age cousin Bill (Ralph Macchio) out of a jam. The lawyer and his mouthy but beautiful girlfriend, Lisa (Marisa Tomei), must go to Alabama. Pic's running joke is that Vinny can't stay awake in court. Tomei, sashaying through the proceedings as kind of a sexy hood ornament, creates a buoyant chemistry with her combative b.f.

1992: Best Supp. Actress (Marisa Tomei)

MY DARLING CLEMENTINE
1946, 97 mins, US ⊙

D: John Ford **A:** Henry Fonda, Linda Darnell, Victor Mature, Walter Brennan, Cathy Downs (20th Century-Fox)

Trademark of John Ford's direction is clearly stamped on the film with its shadowy lights, softly contrasted moods, and measured pace, but a tendency is discernible toward stylization for stylization's sake. Major boost to the film is given by the simple, sincere performance of Henry Fonda. Script doesn't afford him many chances for dramatic action, but Fonda, as a boomtown marshal, pulls the reins taut on his part, charging the role and the pic with more excitement than it really has. Victor Mature registers nicely as a Boston aristocrat turned gambler and killer.

MY DINNER WITH ANDRE
1981, 110 mins, US ⓥ ⊙

D: Louis Malle **A:** Wallace Shawn, Andre Gregory (Andre)

Something of a film stunt, consisting almost entirely of a conversation over dinner between two theatrical acquaintances. Shawn, a cherubic figure roughly playing himself as a sometime playwright and actor, is the audience surrogate. Somewhat apprehensive, he has dinner at a posh restaurant with Andre, portrayed also semiautobiographically by theater director Andre Gregory. What ensues is an overlong but mainly captivating conversation, consisting largely of stream-of-consciousness monologues by Gregory.

MY FAIR LADY
1964, 170 mins, US ⓥ ⊙ ▭

D: George Cukor **A:** Audrey Hepburn, Rex Harrison, Stanley Holloway, Wilfrid Hyde White, Gladys Cooper, Jeremy Brett (Warner)

The great long-run stage musical made by Lerner and Loewe out of the wit of

Bernard Shaw's play *Pygmalion* has been transformed into a stunningly effective screen entertainment. Rex Harrison's performance and Cecil Beaton's design of costumes, scenery, and production are the two powerhouse contributions. This is a man-bullies-girl plot with story novelty. An unorthodox musical without a kiss, the audience travels to total involvement with characters and situation on the rails of sharp dialogue and business. The deft segues of dialogue into lyric are superb, especially in the case of Harrison.

1964: Best Picture, Director, Actor (Rex Harrison), Color Cinematography, Color Art Direction, Sound, Adapted Musical Scoring, Color Costume Design

Nominations: Best Supp. Actor (Stanley Holloway), Supp. Actress (Gladys Cooper), Adapted Screenplay, Editing

MY FATHER, THE HERO
1994, 90 mins, US/France ⑫ ⊙
D: Steve Miner **A:** Gerard Depardieu, Katherine Heigl, Dalton James, Lauren Hutton, Faith Prince (Touchstone/Cite/ Film Par Film/DD)

Gerard Depardieu reprises a role he played in a 1991 French feature, *Mon pere, ce heros,* for a US version. He stars as an absentee father who takes his willful, resentful 14-year-old daughter, Nicole (Katherine Heigl), on a tropical vacation, only to have her concoct a lie about Dad being her lover to impress a slightly older boy (Dalton James). That simple premise provides a fertile planting ground for comedy, as word of the liaison spreads among the hotel's increasingly outraged vacationers and staff, who view the oblivious André (Depardieu) as the worst sort of dirty old man.

MY FAVORITE BLONDE
1942, 78 mins, US
D: Sidney Lanfield **A:** Bob Hope, Madeleine Carroll, Gale Sondergaard (Paramount)

Madeleine Carroll is ideally cast as a British agent who involves vaudevillian Bob Hope into a helter-skelter coast-to-coast hop from Broadway to Hollywood. The blend of a secret scorpion (containing the revised flying orders for a convoy of Lockheed bombers headed for Britain) with the wacky semibackstage atmosphere, an al fresco plumbers' picnic, Nazi spies, etc., has been well kneaded.

MY FAVORITE BRUNETTE
1947, 87 mins, US ⑫ ⊙
D: Elliott Nugent **A:** Bob Hope, Dorothy Lamour, Peter Lorre, Lon Chaney, John Hoyt, Reginald Denny (Paramount/Hope)

Hope, a condemned murderer being groomed for the gas chamber, relates his tale of woe. When Hope's next-door neighbor, a private eye, leaves town requesting Hope to tend his office, the comic's usual pot of trouble rises to a simmer. He tangles with Lamour in a fantastic snarl involving a mysterious map (concealed by Hope in a drinking cup container) and Lamour's missing uncle who's been snatched by a gang headed by Peter Lorre.

MY FAVORITE SPY
1951, 93 mins, US
D: Norman Z. McLeod **A:** Bob Hope, Hedy Lamarr, Francis L. Sullivan, Arnold Moss, John Archer (Paramount)

Hope, as a burly comic, is talked into doubling for an international spy so the US government can get hold of plans for a pilotless plane. Dispatched to Tangiers, the masquerading Hope is met by Lamarr, another spy employed by a rival government agent (Francis L. Sullivan). From here on, the script involves the comic in a wild and woolly free-for-all of danger, escape, lovely girls, and chase.

MY FAVORITE WIFE
1940, 88 mins, US ⑫ ⊙
D: Garson Kanin **A:** Irene Dunne, Cary Grant, Randolph Scott, Gail Patrick, Ann Shoemaker, Scotty Beckett (RKO)

Irene Dunne and Cary Grant pick up the thread of marital comedy at about the point where they left off in *The Awful Truth*. With these two stars working again with Leo McCarey, a surefire laughing film is guaranteed. Dunne turns up at home after seven years' absence from her husband and two small children. She was shipwrecked and returns on the day her husband has remarried.

1940: Nominations: Best Original Story, B&W Art Direction, Original Score

MY FAVORITE YEAR
1982, 92 mins, US ⑫ ⊙
D: Richard Benjamin **A:** Peter O'Toole, Mark Linn-Baker, Jessica Harper, Joseph Bologna, Bill Macy (Brooksfilms/Gruskoff)

An enjoyable romp through the early days of television. Looking exquisitely ravaged, O'Toole portrays a legendary Hollywood star in the Errol Flynn mold who, in 1954, the year of the title, agrees to make his TV debut on *The Comedy Cavalcade*. O'Toole is put in the hands of young comedy writer Mark Linn-Baker for safekeeping, latter's sole responsibility being to keep his idol sober enough to make it through the performance a few days later.

1982: Nomination: Best Actor (Peter O'Toole)

MY FIRST WIFE
1984, 95 mins, Australia ⓥ
D: Paul Cox **A:** John Hargreaves, Wendy Hughes, Lucy Angwin, Anna Jemison, David Cameron, Charles Tingwell (Dofine)

A lacerating, emotionally exhausting drama about a marriage breakup, *My First Wife* manages to breathe new life into familiar material. Director Paul Cox and coscripter Bob Ellis ring a few changes. This 10-year marriage is collapsing because the wife (Wendy Hughes), not the husband (John Hargreaves), is having an affair, and it's the husband who desperately wants her back, willing to forgive and forget everything if only she'll return to him. Pic rings utterly true, with no false sentimentality, no firm ending.

MY FOOLISH HEART
1949, 98 mins, US ⓥ
D: Mark Robson **A:** Dana Andrews, Susan Hayward, Kent Smith, Lois Wheeler, Jessie Royce Landis, Robert Keith (Goldwyn)

Among the better romantic films with a script that is honest and loaded with dialogue that is alive. Plotting opens in 1949, and finds Susan Hayward at the tail end of an unhappy wartime marriage with Kent Smith. The sight of an old gown arouses memories and takes her back to 1941 when she was enfolded in romance with Dana Andrews. Hayward's performance is a gem, displaying a positive talent for capturing reality.

1949: Nominations: Best Actress (Susan Hayward), Song ("My Foolish Heart")

MY FORBIDDEN PAST
1951, 71 mins, US
D: Robert Stevenson **A:** Robert Mitchum, Ava Gardner, Melvyn Douglas, Lucile Watson, Janis Carter (RKO)

This drama hasn't much in the way of strong entertainment. It's a period piece, laid in early New Orleans, that makes

much to-do about bloodlines and first-family snobbery, with a few s.a. tidbits thrown in for exploitation. Ava Gardner physically lives up to title implications, but her role is obvious and never socks enough to be believable. Robert Mitchum, as a young medical professor whom she wants, is required only to deliver a wooden performance, but his personality does give it some lift.

MY FRIEND FLICKA
1943, 89 mins, US ⓥ
D: Harold Schuster **A:** Roddy McDowall, Preston Foster, Rita Johnson, Jeff Corey, James Bell (20th Century-Fox)

Essentially it's the story of a daydreaming youngster's longing for a colt of his own, the boy's complete transformation once his rancher father fulfills his desire, and the trials and tribulations in taming and nursing the filly back to health. Fine color photography, capable performances by Roddy McDowall, Preston Foster, Rita Johnson and, of course, the magnificent horses, are assets.

MY GAL SAL
1942, 101 mins, US
D: Irving Cummings **A:** Rita Hayworth, Victor Mature, Carole Landis, John Sutton, Phil Silvers, James Gleason (20th Century-Fox)

Theodore Dreiser's biography of his songwriting brother, Paul Dresser, parades a number of popular tunes of the 1890s to round out a fairly entertaining piece of filmusical entertainment. Dresser's life is far from sugar-coated in its cinematic unreeling. Young Paul (Victor Mature) runs away from home to pursue a musical career. After a short stretch as entertainer with a cheap medicine show, and an intimate association with Carole Landis, he finally tosses over the small-time for a whirl at the big town of New York.

1942: Best Color Art Direction
Nomination: Best Scoring of a Musical Picture

MY GEISHA
1962, 119 mins, US ⓥ ⌑
D: Jack Cardiff **A:** Shirley MacLaine, Yves Montand, Edward G. Robinson, Robert Cummings, Yoko Tani (Paramount/Sachiko)

Although hampered by an implausible one-joke premise and a tendency to fluctuate uneasily between comedy and drama, the picture has been richly and elaborately produced on location in Japan. An American film actress (Shirley MacLaine) blithely executes a monumental practical joke on her insecure director-husband (Yves Montand) by masquerading as a geisha to win the part of Madame Butterfly in his arty production of same in Japan. MacLaine skillfully submerges her unpredictably gregarious personality into that of the dainty, tranquil gesisha.

1962: Nomination: Best Color Costume Design

MY GIRL
1991, 102 mins, US ⓥ ⊚
D: Howard Zieff **A:** Dan Aykroyd, Jamie Lee Curtis, Macaulay Culkin, Anna Chlumsky, Richard Masur, Griffin Dunne (Imagine)

The widower mortician (Dan Aykroyd) takes barely a passing interest in the doings of his daughter, Vada (Anna Chlumsky). Things change around the funeral home when Dad hires a sexy hippie (Jamie Lee Curtis) to apply makeup to cadavers. Vada spends most of her time with an engaging neighbor (Macaulay Culkin), and although a bit young for a real romance, the two experience their first kiss together. It's a rough summer for an 11-year-old, but director Howard Zieff paints it in the manner of a watercolor of a youthful idyll.

MY GIRL 2
1994, 99 mins, US ⓥ ⊚
D: Howard Zieff **A:** Dan Aykroyd, Jamie Lee Curtis, Anna Chlumsky, Austin O'Brien, Richard Masur (Imagine/Columbia)

Pleasant, painless, and, as sequels go, genuinely ambitious in its efforts to be a continuation rather than just a retread. Precocious Vada (Anna Chlumsky), now 13, still lives with her father, Harry (Dan Aykroyd), operator of the town's funeral parlor. Harry has married g.f. and co-worker Shelly (Jamie Lee Curtis). After a leisurely paced but amiable start, *My Girl 2* moves to Los Angeles, where Vada wants to research her mother's past for a school project.

MY HEROES HAVE ALWAYS BEEN COWBOYS
1991, 106 mins, US ⓥ
D: Stuart Rosenberg **A:** Scott Glenn, Kate Capshaw, Ben Johnson, Balthazar Getty, Tess Harper, Gary Busey (Gaylord-Poll)

A predictable tale of an aging, aching cowpoke's shot at redemption. It's Scott Glenn's turn out of the gate, playing H. D. Dalton, who returns to his family in Oklahoma. His father, Jesse (Ben Johnson), has been moved to an old folks' home by sister Cheryl (Tess Harper) and brother-in-law Clint (Gary Busey). H. D.'s former girlfriend Jolie (Kate Capshaw) has lost her husband and is faced with raising two children alone. When Jesse is injured, pressure mounts on H. D. to make some big bucks fast.

MY HUSTLER
1967, 79 mins, US
D: Chuck Wein, Andy Warhol **A:** Paul America, Ed Hood, John McDermott, Genevieve Charbon, Joseph Campbell (Warhol)

For all the technical blunders, *My Hustler* possesses some narrative fascination for those with sufficiently strong stomachs and/or psyches. A young boy, hired for the weekend by a wealthy homo, is fought over by the aging deviate, a girl from next door, and another hustler well past his prime. What makes the film morbidly absorbing is the detail with which gay life is documented. About a third of the dialogue is muffled, and lip sync is off for most of the film.

MY LEARNED FRIEND
1943, 80 mins, UK ⓥ
D: Basil Dearden **A:** Will Hay, Claude Hulbert, Mervyn Johns (Ealing)

An amusing vehicle for Will Hay. A released convict has it in for Hay, a disbarred lawyer, for failing to save him from a forgery sentence, and implies he intends rubbing out six people responsible for his incarceration, from the judge down to Hay himself. Highlight is a chase to prevent Big Ben from striking 12, when a mechanical device set by the unhinged avenger will blow up the House of Lords.

MY LEFT FOOT
THE STORY OF CHRISTY BROWN
1989, 98 mins, UK ⓥ ⊚
D: Jim Sheridan **A:** Daniel Day-Lewis, Ray McAnally, Brenda Fricker, Ruth McCabe, Fiona Shaw, Cyril Cusack (Granada)

The warm, romantic, and moving true story of a remarkable man: the Irish writer and painter Christy Brown born with cerebral palsy into an impoverished family. A brilliant performance by Daniel Day-Lewis and a fine supporting cast lifts it from mildly sentimental to excellent. *My*

Left Foot is not a sad film. In fact, there is a great deal of humor in Day-Lewis's Brown.
1989: Best Actor (Daniel Day-Lewis), Best Supp. Actress (Brenda Fricker)
Nominations: Best Picture, Director, Adapted Screenplay

MY LIFE
1993, 114 mins, US ⓥ ⊙
D: Bruce Joel Rubin **A:** Michael Keaton, Nicole Kidman, Bradley Whitford, Queen Latifah, Haing S. Ngor (Columbia)

Emotional, spiritual odyssey centered on a man confronting terminal cancer and, coincidentally, the birth of his first child, tugs shamelessly at the heartstrings. A videotape is being prepared by Bob Jones (Michael Keaton) for his unborn child. His wife (Nicole Kidman) gently cajoles him into seeing a healer (Haing S. Ngor), and it is at these sessions that he begins to get in touch with what's really ailing him: his roots. Keaton gives a textured performance that goes a long way to smooth the narrative's rough edges.

MY LIFE AS A DOG
See: Mitt Liv Som Hund

MY LIFE TO LIVE
See: Vivre Sa Vie
Film en Douze Tableux

MY LITTLE CHICKADEE
1940, 83 mins, US ⊙
D: Edward Cline **A:** Mae West, W. C. Fields, Joseph Calleia, Dick Foran, Ruth Donnelly, Magaret Hamilton (Universal)

Mae West teamed with W. C. Fields for a hefty package of lusty humor. The familiar Westian swagger, drawl, wisecracks, and innuendos are all included, likewise the typical Fields routines and quick-triggered comments. Sequences in which the pair work together are reduced to a minimum. Meeting Fields, whom she believes rich, aboard the train, West promotes a fake marriage ceremony. Pair hit the next frontier settlement, where Fields is inducted into job of sheriff, and West tosses her charms around rather freely.

MY MAN GODFREY
1936, 93 mins, US ⓥ
D: Gregory La Cava **A:** William Powell, Carole Lombard, Alice Brady, Gail Patrick, Eugene Pallette, Alan Mowbray (Universal)

William Powell and Carole Lombard are pleasantly teamed in this splendidly produced comedy. Lombard's whole family, with the exception of the old man, seem to have been dropped on their respective heads when young. Into this punchy society tribe walks Powell, a former social light himself who had gone on the bum over a woman and is trying to become a man once more in butler's livery. He straightens out the family, as well as himself.
1936: Nominations: Best Director, Actor (William Powell), Actress (Carole Lombard), Supp. Actor (Mischa Auer), Supp. Actress (Alice Brady), Screenplay

MY MAN GODFREY
1957, 92 mins, US ▭
D: Henry Koster **A:** June Allyson, David Niven, Jessie Royce Landis, Robert Keith, Eva Gabor, Martha Hyer (Universal)

Updated version of *My Man Godfrey* (1936) is a pretty well turned out comedy with June Allyson and David Niven recreating the original Carole Lombard–William Powell star roles. Ross Hunter's production of the butler to an eccentric New York family of wealth who helps straighten them out, meanwhile recipient of the affections of the younger daughter, manages to pack plenty of lusty humor in the fast 92 minutes. Where film misses is in the Niven character of butler. The screenplay drags him in by the heels in too fabricated a character. Jessie Royce Landis as the wacky society mother registers a definite hit.

MY MOTHER'S COURAGE
See: Mutters Courage

MY NAME IS IVAN
See: Ivanovo Dyetstvo)

MY NAME IS JULIA ROSS
1945, 64 mins, US
D: Joseph H. Lewis **A:** Nina Foch, May Whitty, George Macready, Roland Varno, Doris Lloyd (Columbia)

Mystery melodrama with a psychological twist runs only 64 minutes but it's fast and packed with tense action throughout. Story is of gal hired fraudulently as secretary to wealthy English dowager. Purpose of hiring is to impose a murder scheme in which the dowager's son is implicated. Whitty gives creditable performance; so does Macready as her son.

MY NIGHT AT MAUD'S
See: Ma Nuit chez Maud

MY OWN PRIVATE IDAHO
1991, 102 mins, US ⑰ ⊙
D: Gus Van Sant **A:** River Phoenix, Keanu Reeves, James Russo, William Richert, Rodney Harvey (New Line)

One of those ambitious, overreaching disappointments that is more interesting than some more conservative successes. Mike (River Phoenix) is a sex-for-hire boy, a sensitive but raw youth who will go both ways but has the unfortunate habit of passing out on the job. Mike's cohort and soon-to-be best friend is Scott (Keanu Reeves). The wealthy son of Portland's mayor, Scott is clearly hanging with the boys as an act of teenage rebellion against his family. For a story about two gay hustlers, film deals very little with sex.

MY PAL GUS
1952, 83 mins, US
D: Robert Parrish **A:** Richard Widmark, Joanne Dru, Audrey Totter, George Winslow (20th Century-Fox)

Richard Widmark is too busy to devote much time to his small son. As a result, the kid is a problem child in the progressive school operated by Joanne Dru. Little Winslow takes to the teacher, and so does dad, when Audrey Totter, Widmark's ex-wife, appears on the scene. Widmark is very good as the tough, rags-to-riches father, showing both good comedy feeling as well as the more touchingly dramatic flavor required in the final scenes.

MYRA BRECKINRIDGE
1970, 94 mins, US ⑰ ▭
D: Michael Sarne **A:** Mae West, John Huston, Raquel Welch, Rex Reed, Farrah Fawcett, Roger C. Carmel (20th Century-Fox)

The film version of Gore Vidal's Hollywood-themed transsexual satire starts off promisingly, but after a couple of reels plunges straight downhill under the weight of artless direction. As a lecherous female agent, Mae West, after an absence from the screen of over 26 years, provides some funny moments. John Huston, as drama school promoter Buck Loner, is good, while title-roled Raquel Welch—like the film, good at the beginning—has been let down as story progresses.

MY REPUTATION
1946, 93 mins, US
D: Curtis Bernhardt **A:** Barbara Stanwyck, George Brent, Eve Arden, Warner Anderson (Warner)

Story emphasis is on psychological conflict rather than action. It attempts to picture the dilemma in the mind of an attractive young widow (Barbara Stanwyck) as she balances the demands of community and family convention against her desire to live her life as she sees it—namely, an affair with a rather attractive wolf in wolf's clothing. Unfortunately, the script fails to demonstrate the deftness which is necessary to present a conflict like this.

MY SISTER EILEEN
1942, 97 mins, US ⊙
D: Alexander Hall **A:** Rosalind Russell, Brian Aherne, Janet Blair, Richard Quine, June Havoc, Jeff Donnell (Columbia)

Pacing is fast and smooth, with constant use of sight gags and comedy situations. Most of the action takes place in a Greenwich Village basement studio apartment, with a crescendo of exaggerated events breaking out near and in the place. Rosalind Russell's performance as authoress Ruth is an effective blend of curtness and warmth.

1942: Nomination: Best Actress (Rosalind Russell)

MY SISTER EILEEN
1955, 106 mins, US ⊙ ▭
D: Richard Quine **A:** Janet Leigh, Jack Lemmon, Betty Garrett, Bob Fosse, Kurt Kasznar (Columbia)

Scripters have turned out a simplified filmusical, in that the tunes and dances come naturally to situations and are not overly staged. Thus, the problems that befall two sisters from Ohio, who come to New York to seek fame as a writer and actress respectively, play naturally, even with some broadening for comedy. Two major assets are Betty Garrett and Jack Lemmon. Seconding this pair are Janet Leigh, very attractive as the little sister, and Bob Fosse, the shy soda jerk.

MY SIX CONVICTS
1952, 104 mins, US
D: Hugo Fregonese **A:** Millard Mitchell, Gilbert Roland, John Beal, Marshall Thompson, Alf Kjellin, Henry Morgan (Kramer/Columbia)

The experiences of a prison psychologist come to the screen as mighty satisfying entertainment. The film makes humans of the imprisoned men, and deals with them with whimsical humor and intelligent understanding. Picture gets under way with the arrival at prison of John Beal, who is to establish, on trial, a psychological system for rehabilitating convicts. It's not until Millard Mitchell's safecracker decides to try out the new doc that Beal is able to get going.

MY STEPMOTHER IS AN ALIEN
1988, 108 mins, US ⓥ ⊙
D: Richard Benjamin A: Dan Aykroyd, Kim Basinger, Jon Lovitz, Alyson Hannigan, Joseph Maher (Weintraub)

A failed attempt to mix many of the film genres associated with the ''alien'' idea into a sprightly romp. Dan Aykroyd, as a rumpled, overweight widower scientist, foils one of his own experiments, which results in a signal reaching a planet in peril. Soon after, two aliens come in the form of Kim Basinger in a slinky red sheath dress with an alien-buddy-mentor (the snake, voice courtesy of Ann Prentiss) hiding in her purse.

MYSTERIOUS ISLAND
1962, 100 mins, UK ⓥ ⊙
D: Cy Endfield A: Michael Craig, Joan Greenwood, Michael Callan, Gary Merrill, Herbert Lom (Columbia)

Film illustrates the strange plight that befalls three Union soldiers, a newspaperman, and a rebel who, in 1865, land on an island in the remote South Seas, where they encounter 1) a giant crab, 2) a giant bird, 3) two lovely shipwrecked British ladies of average proportions, 4) a giant bee, 5) a band of cutthroat pirates, 6) Captain Nemo's inoperative sub, 7) Captain Nemo. Photographically it is noteworthy for the Super-dynamation process and special visual effects by Ray Harryhausen.

MYSTERIOUS LADY, THE
1928, 83 mins, US ⓥ ⊗
D: Fred Niblo A: Greta Garbo, Conrad Nagel, Gustav von Seyffertitz, Edward Connelly, Richard Alexander (M-G-M)

Secret service story involving a Russian female spy and an Austrian officer. Using up 83 minutes to unload this yarn is ridiculous. Productionally it is very nice. Court balls, hundreds of uniforms, big interiors, and beneath the surface much intrigue. Garbo is capable of better work.

MYSTERIOUS MR. MOTO
1938, 61 mins, US
D: Norman Foster A: Peter Lorre, Mary Maguire, Henry Wilcoxon, Erik Rhodes, Leon Ames (20th Century-Fox)

This time Mr. Moto (Peter Lorre) of the oily tongue and suave detection traps a gang of international murderers under circumstances that even baffle a beleaguered Scotland Yard. He escapes from traps laid for him, from flocks of hoodlums, from gunfire, and from wet feet, or a head cold. The story is hackneyed and the dialogue isn't brilliant but the vital element in pictures of this kind, action, is in evidence in abundance.

MYSTERY OF THE WAX MUSEUM, THE
1933, 78 mins, US ⓥ ⊙
D: Michael Curtiz A: Lionel Atwill, Fay Wray, Glenda Farrell, Frank McHugh (Warner)

Technicolor horror-mystery production with a loose and unconvincing story. Atwill is the maniacal custodian of the London wax museum whose fanatic enterprise with his transplanted museum on American soil leads Farrell, as the sob sister, to unearth this weird yarn.

MYSTERY SCIENCE THEATER 3000: THE MOVIE
1996, 73 mins, US ⓥ
D: Jim Mallon A: Michael J. Nelson, Trace Beaulieu, Kevin Murphy, Jim Mallon, John Brady (Best Brains)

Just like the cable TV series that spawned it, this is cheap, silly fun, a barrage of one-liners aimed at a risible old picture by one human and two robots who constitute an on-screen audience. The creators actually picked a moderately revered and amply budgeted one, Universal's 1955 release *This Island Earth*. The threesome are constantly on view in silhouette along the bottom of the screen, needling it mercilessly throughout. Humor ranges from lots of mild gay innuendo about the male characters' ''real'' relationship to comments on the cheesy special effects and even inside industry jokes.

MYSTERY TRAIN
1989, 113 mins, US ⓥ ⊙
D: Jim Jarmusch A: Masatoshi Nagase, Youki Kudoh, Nicoletta Braschi, Elisabeth Bracco, Joe Strummer (JVC/MTI)

A three-episode pic handled by indie writer-director Jim Jarmusch in his usual playful, minimalist style. It could be almost dubbed *Memphis Stories*, as this is Jarmusch's tribute to the city of Elvis and other musical greats. Characteristically, the director explores the crumbling, decaying edges of the city through the eyes of foreigners: Japanese teenagers, an Italian widow, and a British punk.

MYSTIC PIZZA
1988, 104 mins, US ⓥ ⊙
D: Donald Petrie **A:** Annabeth Gish, Julia Roberts, Lili Taylor, Vincent D'Onofrio, William R. Moses (Goldwyn)

Deftly told coming-of-age story about three young femmes as they explore their different destinies, mostly through romance; it's genuine and moving. Title refers to a pizza parlor in Mystic, CT, where three best friends, two of them sisters, are working the summer after high-school graduation. Jojo (Lili Taylor) apparently is headed for marriage to high school sweetheart Bill (Vincent D'Onofrio). Daisy (Julia Roberts) is a vamp who's after the good life and knows how to use her looks, while Kat (Annabeth Gish) is headed for college.

MY UNCLE
See: Mon Oncle

N

NADINE
1987, 83 mins, US $\mathbb{V}$ ⊙
D: Robert Benton A: Jeff Bridges, Kim Basinger, Rip Torn, Gwen Verdon, Glenne Headly (Tri-Star/Delphi Premier)

An innocuous soufflé. Recipe of screw-ball comedy and small-town thriller fails to jell. Jeff Bridges and Kim Basinger are husband and wife on the verge of divorce drawn together again by a killing. Basinger witnesses the murder of two-bit photographer Raymond Escobar (Jerry Stiller). Local mobster Buford Pope (Rip Torn) is the only truly interesting character here and the film comes alive when he's on the screen.

NADJA
1994, 95 mins, US
D: Michael Almereyda A: Suzy Amis, Galaxy Craze, Martin Donovan, Peter Fonda, Elina Lowensohn (Kino Link)

Vampires stalk the netherworld of downtown New York, a lovely idea for a film that's been beautifully executed but slips too far off its narrative tracks to get where it wants to go. Low budgeter is stunningly lensed in a mixture of black-and-white 35mm and Pixelvision and featuring one of the sexiest female vampires ever to bare her teeth onscreen, the darkly mysterious, extravagantly beautiful Nadja (Elina Lowensohn).

NAKED
1993, 131 mins, UK $\mathbb{V}$
D: Mike Leigh A: David Thewlis, Lesley Sharp, Katrin Cartlidge, Greg Cruttwell, Claire Skinner (Thin Man/Film Four)

A Stygian comedy on nineties London social angst, shot through with sudden, psychotic mood shifts, from comedy to violence to, finally, a strangely moving love story. An unemployed philosopher-bum, Johnny (David Thewlis), has fled south from Manchester and initially stays with former g.f. Louise (Lesley Sharp). After bedding his loopy flat mate, punkette Sophie (Katrin Cartlidge), he suddenly ups and leaves on a weird nocturnal odyssey on the streets of London. Dialogue is four-letter stuff all the way.

NAKED AND THE DEAD, THE
1958, 131 mins, US $\mathbb{V}$ ⌑
D: Raoul Walsh A: Aldo Ray, Cliff Robertson, Raymond Massey, Lili St. Cyr, Barbara Nichols, Richard Jaeckel (RKO)

The film bears little more than surface resemblance to the hard-hitting Norman Mailer novel of the same title. It becomes just another war picture, weighed with some tedious dialogue sporadically lifted from the book. Aldo Ray plays the frustrated, bitter, and sadistic Sergeant Croft with gusto and certain raw power. As the playboy whom the general picks as his aide, Cliff Robertson turns in a slick performance.

NAKED CITY, THE
1948, 94 mins, US
D: Jules Dassin A: Barry Fitzgerald, Howard Duff, Dorothy Hart, Don Taylor, Ted De Corsia (Universal)

A boldly fashioned yarn about a blond beaut's mysterious murder in an apartment house. There are no props. A Manhattan police station scene was photographed in the police station; a Lower East Side cops-and-robbers chase was actually filmed in the locale; the ghetto and its pushcarts were caught in all their realism. Barry Fitzgerald, in playing the police lieutenant of the homicide squad, strides through the role with tongue in cheek.
1948: Best B&W Cinematography, Editing
Nomination: Best Motion Picture Story

NAKED EARTH, THE
1958, 96 mins, UK ⌑
D: Vincent Sherman A: Richard Todd, Juliette Greco, Finlay Currie, John Kitzmiller, Laurence Naismith (Fox/Foray)

Thoroughly well made film that peeks into the heart of Africa and comes out with a captivating actress in Juliette Greco. It also presents a twinkling performance by Richard Todd and an excellent photographic record of a bird picking the teeth of a crocodile. Tale is set in a forsaken section of the darkest continent at the end of the 19th century. Todd, an Irishman looking for new wealth, treks to the African hinterlands to launch a farming effort. Bad luck with his plants pushes Todd into the gloomy rivers to stalk the treacherous crocodiles for their valued skins.

NAKED EDGE, THE
1961, 99 mins, US
D: Michael Anderson A: Gary Cooper, Deborah Kerr, Eric Portman, Diane Cil-

ento, Hermione Gingold, Peter Cushing (United Artists/Pennebaker-Baroda)

Neatly constructed, thoroughly professional suspense meller casts Gary Cooper as a businessman living in London. When a blackmailer (Eric Portman) accuses her husband of murder, Deborah Kerr remembers that Cooper had been the key prosecution witness at the murder trial and had come into a lot of money quite suddenly. The lady's further investigations confirm her suspicions.

NAKED EYE, THE
1957, 71 mins, US
D: Louis Clyde Stoumen, W. S. Van Dyke (Camera Eye)

A film about the fun and art of photography. Millions of shutterbugs also will find it an engrossing 71 minutes of what can be done with photography, both from the examples of the artists shown and from the equally outstanding production-photography job done by Louis Clyde Stoumen.

NAKED GUN
FROM THE FILES OF POLICE
SQUAD!, THE
1988, 85 mins, US ⓥ ⊙
D: David Zucker A: Leslie Nielsen, George Kennedy, Priscilla Presley, Ricardo Montalban, O. J. Simpson (Paramount)

Crass, broad, irreverent, wacky fun—and absolutely hilarious from beginning to end. Leslie Nielsen is the clumsy detective and George Kennedy his straight sidekick who wreaks havoc in the streets of L.A. trying to connect shipping magnate and socialite Ricardo Montalban with heroin smuggling. Scintilla of a plot weaves in an inspired bit of nonsense with Queen Elizabeth II lookalike Jeannette Charles as the target for assassination plus a May-December romance between Nielsen and vapid-acting Priscilla Presley.

NAKED GUN 2 1/2
THE SMELL OF FEAR, THE
1991, 85 mins, US ⓥ ⊙
D: David Zucker A: Leslie Nielsen, Priscilla Presley, George Kennedy, O. J. Simpson, Robert Goulet, Richard Griffiths (Paramount)

The Naked Gun 2 1/2 is at least two-and-a-half times less funny than its hilarious 1988 progenitor. Clothesline plot has bad guy Robert Goulet kidnaping the president's wheelchair-bound energy czar and replacing him with a lookalike. Case sees

Lieutenant Frank Drebin (Leslie Nielsen) catching up with his erstwhile inamorata (Priscilla Presley). Pair communes soulfully over a potter's wheel in a send-up of Ghost.

NAKED GUN 33 1/3
THE FINAL INSULT
1994, 82 mins, US ⓥ ⊙
D: Peter Segal A: Leslie Nielsen, Priscilla Presley, George Kennedy, O. J. Simpson, Fred Ward, Kathleen Freeman (Paramount)

Third spin of The Naked Gun is loaded with the usual barrage of irreverent, politically incorrect, and virtually nonstop gags. Police squad detective Frank Drebin (Leslie Nielsen) goes undercover to bunk up with a terrorist (Fred Ward) and the terrorist's mob, including his snarling mother (Kathleen Freeman) and bombshell girlfriend (supermodel Anna Nicole Smith). By now Nielsen, Priscilla Presley, and the other regs can virtually mail in their performances, which give shameless mugging a good name.

NAKED JUNGLE, THE
1954, 95 mins, US ⓥ ⊙
D: Byron Haskin A: Eleanor Parker, Charlton Heston, Abraham Sofaer, William Conrad, Douglas Fowley (Paramount)

Interesting feature mixes in jungle adventure with a science-fiction touch. A mail-order bride comes from New Orleans to bed with a man who has spent 15 years hewing a profitable plantation and palatial home out of the jungles of South America. As the conflict of this marital situation moves forward to a not-unexpected climax, the dread soldier ants organize in a purposeful march and descend on the plantation.

NAKED KISS, THE
1965, 90 mins, US ⊙
D: Samuel Fuller A: Constance Towers, Anthony Eisley, Michael Dante, Virginia Grey, Patsy Kelly (Allied Artists/Firks)

Good programmer, about a prostie trying the straight route, is primarily a vehicle for Constance Towers. Hooker angles and sex perversion plot windup are handled with care, alternating with handicapped children ''good works'' theme.

NAKED LUNCH
1991, 115 mins, Canada/UK ⓥ ⊙
D: David Cronenberg A: Peter Weller, Judy Davis, Ian Holm, Julian Sands, Roy Scheider (Thomas)

William S. Burroughs's notorious, and

notoriously unfilmable, novel has landed in the right hands. David Cronenberg has come up with a fascinating, demanding, mordantly funny picture. William Lee (Peter Weller), an insect exterminator in New York City circa 1953, lives in quiet squalor with his wife (Judy Davis). Breaking into a hallucinatory state, Lee escapes to an imaginatively demented rendition of Tangier heavily populated by artist addicts, homosexuals, and secret agents.

NAKED PREY, THE
1966, 86 mins, US Ⓥ ⊙ ▭
D: Cornel Wilde **A:** Cornel Wilde, Gert Van Der Berg, Ken Gampu, Patrick Mynhardt (Theodora/Persson)

Filmed entirely in South Africa, told with virtually no dialogue, the basic story is set in the bush country of a century ago, where safari manager Cornel Wilde and party are captured by natives. All save Wilde are tortured in some explicit footage that is not for the squeamish, while he is given a chance to survive—providing he can exist while eluding some dedicated pursuers.
1966: Nomination: Best Original Story & Screenplay

NAKED RUNNER, THE
1967, 104 mins, UK Ⓥ ▭
D: Sidney J. Furie **A:** Frank Sinatra, Peter Vaughan, Derren Nesbitt, Nadia Gray (Warner/Sinatra)

A dullsville script, based on premise that British Intelligence cannot assign one of its own to murder a defector to Russia. Instead, Frank Sinatra, a Second World War spy now a businessman-widower, is dragooned into service, and by events, deliberately staged, is goaded into killing the defector. Not only British Intelligence, but anybody's intelligence, is likely to be affronted by this potboiler.

NAKED SPUR, THE
1953, 91 mins, US Ⓥ
D: Anthony Mann **A:** James Stewart, Janet Leigh, Robert Ryan, Ralph Meeker, Millard Mitchell (M-G-M)

Taut outdoor melodrama deals with the violence to which greed spurs the oddly assorted characters caught up in the story. James Stewart is after Robert Ryan, an outlaw killer, so he can collect a $5,000 reward and start a ranch. As he corners the killer in the mountains after a long, arduous chase, he is joined by Millard Mitchell, an old prospector, and Ralph Meeker, who has just been dishonorably discharged

from the Union army. They aid in the capture and determine to share in the reward, so it is a party at cross-purposes that starts the long trek back.
1953: Nomination: Best Story & Screenplay

NAKED TANGO
1990, 93 mins, US Ⓥ
D: Leonard Schrader **A:** Vincent D'Onofrio, Mathilda May, Esai Morales, Fernando Rey, Cipe Lincovsky (Sugarloaf/Gotan)

Tango equals sex equals death in writer-director Leonard Schrader's fatally dark exploration of the 1920s tango underworld. French actress Mathilda May as Stephanie trades identities with a waif and learns she is now Alma, a Polish mail-order bride. Her future husband proves to be the handsome young Zico (Esai Morales), a gangster who runs a tango bordello with his mercenary mother (Cipe Lincovsky) and brutal "tango king" brother, Cholo (Vincent D'Onofrio).

NAKED UNDER LEATHER
See: The Girl on a Motorcycle

NAME OF THE ROSE, THE
1986, 130 mins, W. Germany/Italy/France Ⓥ ⊙
D: Jean-Jacques Annaud **A:** Sean Connery, F. Murray Abraham, Christian Slater, Michel Lonsdale, Ron Perlman (Neue Constantin/Cristaldifilm/Ariane/ZDF)

A sorrowfully mediocre screen version of Umberto Eco's novel, confusingly written and sluggishly staged. Fourteenth-century tale has English Franciscan monk Sean Connery and novice Christian Slater arriving at an Italian abbey for a conclave. After a series of murders Connery undertakes an investigation of the deaths while more delegates continue to arrive. Connery's performance, along with some tantalizing E. M. Escher–style labyrinths in the interior of the abbey, are about the only blessings.

NANA
1934, 87 mins, US
D: Dorothy Arzner **A:** Anna Sten, Phillips Holmes, Lionel Atwill, Richard Bennett, Mae Clarke, Muriel Kirkland (Goldwyn/United Artists)

Sam Goldwyn brilliantly launches a new star in a not-so-brilliant vehicle. Anna Sten has beauty, glamour, charm, histrionic ability (although there are a couple of moments which seemed a bit beyond her), and s.a. The script is a very free adaptation of Emile Zola's famous novel. Much care is evident to make it as circumspect as possible and yet maintain its color and allure, which is the basis of this transition of a Parisian gamine to music hall heights.

NANCY GOES TO RIO
1950, 99 mins, US
D: Robert Z. Leonard A: Jane Powell, Ann Sothern, Barry Sullivan, Carmen Miranda, Louis Calhern (M-G-M)

All that a light, glittering musical should be. Plot setup for the melange of song and dance deals with the theatrical family of Ann Sothern. Mom goes to Rio to rest and study a new play. Daughter is chosen for the play, and dashes to Rio to tell of her good fortune. She finds Sothern set on doing the show and holds off her own good news long enough for some side-bar complications to come to a boil.

NANNY, THE
1965, 93 mins, UK ⓥ
D: Seth Holt A: Bette Davis, Wendy Craig, Jill Bennett, James Villiers, William Dix, Pamela Franklin (Hammer)

It's not necessary to be an astute student to guess that Bette Davis, as a middle-aged Mary Poppins in a fairly fraught household, will eventually be up to no good. But the balance of power between Davis, posing as a devoted nanny, and William Dix, as a knowing youngster who hates Davis's innards, is so skillfully portrayed as to make *The Nanny* a superior psycho-thriller.

NANOOK OF THE NORTH
1922, 55 mins, US ⓥ
D: Robert Flaherty (Revillon Freres)

The granddaddy (or the Eskimo equivalent) of all documentaries and widely extolled as the classic in its field. Despite the comparatively primitive technique and the natural difficulties of shooting a film in the frozen Hudson Bay wastelands, every minute of *Nanook* lives up to its reputation. Yarn holds tremendous interest in detailing the life of an Eskimo family through the seasons of the year. [Reviewed in 1947.]

NAPOLEON
1927, 300 mins, France ⓥ ⊙ ▭
D: Abel Gance A: Albert Dieudonné, Abel Gance, Antonin Artaud, Gina Manes, Daniel Burret (Westi/Société Generale des Films)

Superproduction by Abel Gance deals with the earlier life of Napoléon Bona-

parte, particularly episodes of the French Revolution. The triple screen, whereby (in certain portions of the picture for war scenes) the screen is increased to thrice the ordinary size caused a sensation. The extended vision is obtained by projecting three reels on three screens, the pictures synchronizing. Albert Dieudonné in the title role is excellent. A special score by Arthur Honegger accompanies.

NARAYAMA BUSHI-KO (US: THE BALLAD OF NARAYAMA)
1958, 98 mins, Japan ▭
D: Keisuke Kinoshita A: Kinuyo Tanaka, Teiji Takahashi, Yuko Mochizuki, Seiji Miyaguchi, Yunosuke Ito (Shochiko)

Distasteful story and slow pace are basic strikes against pic, despite moments of great poetry and top acting by all concerned, and especially by Kinuyo Tanaka. Plot concerns a 69-year-old widow (Tanaka) who must find a wife for her son before the law of the land forces her to the hills to die on reaching the age of 70. When all is done and her great-grandchild is on the way, her son reluctantly carries her up the mountain to her peaceful death in the snow. Theme of hunger also permeates entire pic.

NARAYAMA BUSHI-KO (US: THE BALLAD OF NARAYAMA)
1983, 130 mins, Japan
D: Shohei Imamura A: Ken Ogata, Sumiko Sakamoto, Takeshiro Aki, Seiji Kurasaki, Junko Takada (Toei/Imamura)

Excellently crafted, strongly acted and directed, and well shot. Focus is on the now-past Japanese custom of taking their elderly to the mountains to die: in this case, a determined 69-year-old woman, portrayed convincingly by actress Sumiko Sakamoto, 47, who puts her own family in order and, though healthy, demands to be left on the mountain well before she becomes infirm. Her eldest son protests, but leaves her to the elements.

NARROW MARGIN, THE
1952, 71 mins, US ⓥ ⊙
D: Richard Fleischer A: Charles McGraw, Marie Windsor, Jacqueline White, Gordon Gebert, Queenie Leonard (RKO)

Two Los Angeles detectives (Charles McGraw and Don Beddoe) are sent to Chicago to escort the widow of a racketeer to the coast for testimony before the grand jury. Beddoe is killed and McGraw starts back with Marie Windsor, closely pursued by gangsters who want to keep the widow from testifying. Chase makes for some excitement aboard the train as McGraw keeps outwitting the crooks.

1952: Nomination: Best Motion Picture Story

NARROW MARGIN

1990, 97 mins, US Ⓥ ⊙ ▭
D: Peter Hyams **A:** Gene Hackman, Anne Archer, James B. Sikking, J. T. Walsh, M. Emmet Walsh (Carolco)

Spectacular stunt work and Canadian locations punch up the train thriller but remake is too cool and remote to grab the viewer. Basic plotline is retained. Gene Hackman plays a deputy d.a. delivering key witness Anne Archer to testify against gangster Harris Yulin. Hackman's teammate, cop M. Emmet Walsh, is killed leaving Hackman and Archer to flee to a train headed across Canada and to play cat-and-mouse with the thugs (led by evil James B. Sikking) who've boarded the train to eliminate them.

NASHVILLE

1975, 157 mins, US Ⓥ ⊙ ▭
D: Robert Altman **A:** Ned Beatty, Karen Black, Keith Carradine, Geraldine Chaplin, Shelley Duvall, Henry Gibson (Paramount/ABC)

One of the most ambitious, and more artistically successful, backstage musical dramas is strung on the plot thread of a prepresidential campaign in which 24 principal characters are followed over a few days in the country music capital of America. Outstanding are Henry Gibson, as a respected music vet; Ronee Blakely, in a great film debut as a country-and-western femme star on the brink of nervous collapse; Gwen Welles, as a pitiably untalented waitress.

1975: Best Song ("I'm Easy")
Nominations: Best Picture, Director, Supp. Actress (Ronee Blakely, Lily Tomlin)

NASTY HABITS

1976, 98 mins, UK Ⓥ
D: Michael Lindsay-Hogg **A:** Glenda Jackson, Melina Mercouri, Geraldine Page, Sandy Dennis, Anne Jackson, Anne Meara (Bowden)

A witty, intelligent screenplay leaves no doubts that this is the Watergate circus transposed to a convent. It's all about the battle for power in a Philly convent which pits establishment against young lib "outsiders" who want a change. Glenda Jackson is superb, making her role as the scheming climber unerringly her own. Only one actress nearly bests her: Edith Evans in a memorable cameo, the actress's last stint.

NATIONAL LAMPOON'S ANIMAL HOUSE

1978, 109 mins, US Ⓥ ⊙
D: John Landis **A:** John Belushi, Tom Matheson, John Vernon, Verna Bloom, Tom Hulce, Donald Sutherland (Universal)

Readers of the *National Lampoon* may find this a somewhat soft-pedaled parody of college campus life circa 1962. However, there's enough bite and bawdiness to provide lots of smiles and several broad guffaws. Writers have concocted a pre-Vietnam college confrontation between a scruffy fraternity and high-elegant campus society. Interspersed in the new faces are John Vernon as a corrupt dean; Verna Bloom, Vernon's swinging wife; Cesare Danova, the Mafioso-type mayor; Donald Sutherland as the superhip young professor.

NATIONAL LAMPOON'S CHRISTMAS VACATION

1989, 97 mins, US Ⓥ ⊙
D: Jeremiah Chechik **A:** Chevy Chase, Beverly D'Angelo, Randy Quaid, Diane Ladd, John Randolph, E. G. Marshall (Warner/Hughes)

Solid family fare with plenty of yocks is Chevy Chase and brood doing what they do best. Despite the title, which links it to previous pics in the rambling *Vacation* series, this third entry is firmly rooted at the Griswold family homestead, where Clark Griswold (Chase) is engaged in a typical overreaching attempt to give his family a perfect, old-fashioned Christmas.

NATIONAL LAMPOON'S CLASS REUNION

1982, 84 mins, US Ⓥ ⊙
D: Michael Miller **A:** Gerrit Graham, Michael Lerner, Fred McCarren, Miriam Flynn, Stephen Furst (ABC)

Reunion gets sidetracked almost immediately thanks to a harebrained lunatic-on-the-loose plot in which the 1972 graduating class's high school is turned into the semblance of a haunted house. Motley crew here includes former wise-acre Gerrit Graham, a snooty yacht salesman; Fred McCarren, a do-gooder that no one can remember; Miriam Flynn, a Little Miss Prim.

NATIONAL LAMPOON'S EUROPEAN VACATION

1985, 94 mins, US ⑫ ⊙

D: Amy Heckerling **A:** Chevy Chase, Beverly D'Angelo, Jason Lively, Dana Hill, Eric Idle, Victor Lanoux (Warner)

Story of a frenetic, chaotic tour of the Old World, with Chevy Chase and Beverly D'Angelo reprising their roles as determined vacationers, is graceless and only intermittently lit up by lunacy and satire. As the characters cartwheel through London, Paris, Italy, and Germany, director Amy Heckerling gets carried away with physical humor while letting her American tourists grow tiresome and predictable.

NATIONAL LAMPOON'S LOADED WEAPON 1

1993, 83 mins, US ⑫ ⊙

D: Gene Quintano **A:** Emilio Estevez, Samuel L. Jackson, Jon Lovitz, Tim Curry, Kathy Ireland, William Shatner (New Line)

This would-be comedy is very short on laughs. Premise is spoofing Richard Donner's three *Lethal Weapon* movies right down to copying their logo. Ostensible plotline has evil general William Shatner (allowed to ham it up disturbingly) and goofy-accented henchman Tim Curry in a scheme involving cocaine and Girl Scout cookies.

NATIONAL LAMPOON'S SENIOR TRIP

1995, 91 mins, US ⑫

D: Kelly Makin **A:** Matt Frewer, Valerie Mahaffey, Lawrence Dane, Tommy Chong, Jeremy Renner (Alliance)

Witless item involves a bunch of seniors in an Ohio high school whose detention assignment is to write a letter to the president of the United States about why the educational system has failed. The president invites the kids to Washington. A manipulative senator (Lawrence Dane) sees the moronic teens' arrival as an opportunity to embarrass his political rival. Matt Frewer, as the principal, manages to flesh out his character to two dimensions; most of the cast are simply playing one-joke stick figures.

NATIONAL LAMPOON'S VACATION

1983, 96 mins, US ⑫ ⊙

D: Harold Ramis **A:** Chevy Chase, Beverly D'Angelo, Anthony Michael Hall,

Imogene Coca, Randy Quaid, John Candy (Warner)

An enjoyable trip through familiar comedy landscapes. Chevy Chase is perfectly mated with Beverly D'Angelo as an average suburban couple setting out to spend their annual two-week furlough. Despite home-computer planning, this trip is naturally going to be a disaster. No matter how bad this journey gets, Chase perseveres in treating each day as a delight.

NATIONAL VELVET

1944, 125 mins, US ⑫ ⊙

D: Clarence Brown **A:** Mickey Rooney, Donald Crisp, Elizabeth Taylor, Anne Revere, Angela Lansbury (M-G-M)

A horse picture with wide general appeal. Backgrounded in England, it tells of a former jockey (Mickey Rooney) who plans to steal from a family. But their 11-year-old daughter, Velvet, softens him. Velvet is nuts about horses. When a neighbor raffles off an unmanageable brute he's unable to handle she wins it on tickets paid for by Rooney. Nag is entered in the greatest race in England, the Grand National Sweepstakes. Story is told with warmth and understanding.

1945: Best Supp. Actress (Anne Revere), Editing

Nominations: Best Director, Color Cinematography, Color Art Direction

NATURAL, THE

1984, 134 mins, US ⑫ ⊙

D: Barry Levinson **A:** Robert Redford, Robert Duvall, Glenn Close, Kim Basinger, Wilford Brimley, Barbara Hershey (Tri-Star)

An impeccably made, but quite strange, fable about success and failure in America. Robert Redford plays an aging rookie who takes the baseball world by storm in one season. While remaining faithful to Bernard Malamud's 1952 novel in many regards, scenarists have drastically altered some major elements. Film has become the story of the redemption of a born athlete whose life didn't unfold as anticipated. The female characters schematically and simplistically stand for the archaic angel-whore syndrome.

1984: Nominations: Best Supp. Actress (Glenn Close), Cinematography, Art Direction, Original Score

NATURAL BORN KILLERS

1994, 116 mins, US ⑫ ⊙

D: Oliver Stone **A:** Woody Harrelson, Juliette Lewis, Robert Downey Jr., Tommy

Lee Jones, Rodney Dangerfield (Ixtlan/New Regency/Warner)

A scabrous look at a society that promotes murderers as pop culture icons, as well as a scathing indictment of a mass media establishment that caters to and profits from such star-making, this is Oliver Stone's most exciting work to date from a filmmaking point of view. Mickey (Woody Harrelson) and Mallory (Juliette Lewis) kill for the sake of their great love for each other, they say, and the film's psychological ambitions never get much deeper than that. The sheer amount of carnage is numbingly enormous, even though its stylized, sometimes even cartoonlike, quality makes the killing much less shocking than in more realistic contexts.

NAUGHTY BUT NICE
1939, 90 mins, US
D: Ray Enright A: Ann Sheridan, Dick Powell, Gale Page, Helen Broderick (Warner)

Naughty but Nice has a good quota of laughs. Powell finds himself a commercial songsmith, especially when partnered with Gale Page's lyrics. Sheridan is the slight menace here, a mike siren who would break up the songwriting team. An insidious rum drink is a plot essential. Mistaken for lemonade, it sends the staid Powell into high jinks and front-page notoriety as a let's-tear-the-joint-down kid.

NAUGHTY MARIETTA
1935, 105 mins, US ⓥ ⊙
D: W. S. Van Dyke A: Jeanette MacDonald, Nelson Eddy, Frank Morgan, Elsa Lanchester (M-G-M)

Adaptation of the Victor Herbert operetta tells of a group of girls sailing to Louisiana to find husbands and build up that colony. The princess (MacDonald) escapes from the aged suitor her tyrannical uncle has selected. In New Orleans she falls in love with the captain of the mercenaries (Eddy). The comedy being insufficient to sustain this much footage, with no especially exciting action, provides serious handicaps. Although Marietta may have been naughty in 1910, if she's still naughty it's her secret. MacDonald sings particularly well. Eddy reveals a splendid and powerful baritone.

1935: Best Sound Recording
Nomination: Best Picture

NAVIGATOR, THE
1924, 60 mins, US ⊗
D: Donald Crisp, Buster Keaton A: Buster Keaton, Kathryn McGuire, Frederick Vroom (Metro-Goldwyn)

The story has Keaton unknowingly board a deserted steamship. The girl is also caught on board with no chance of a return to land. The entire action practically takes place on the ship, with the girl (Kathryn McGuire) and Keaton the only figures. There's an abundance of funny business in connection with Keaton's going overboard to fix a propeller shaft and a thrill has been inserted through the comedian getting mixed up with a devil fish.

NAVIGATOR, THE
A MEDIAEVAL ODYSSEY
1988, 93 mins, Australia/New Zealand ⓥ
D: Vincent Ward A: Bruce Lyons, Chris Haywood, Hamish McFarlane, Marshall Napier, Noel Appleby (Arenafilm/NZ Film Investment Corp)

The Navigator is remarkable because of its absorbing story that links medieval fears and fortunes to our times, while confirming director Vincent Ward as an original talent. The story begins in Cumbria in 1348, the year of the Black Death. Young Griffin (Hamish McFarlane) is haunted by a dream about a journey. When his brother (Bruce Lyons) returns to the village with tales of impending doom, the two set out on the journey fired by Griffin's prophetic dream. It takes them to a city of the late 1980s and on a mission against time if their village is to be saved.

NAVY LARK, THE
1959, 82 mins, UK ▭
D: Gordon Parry A: Cecil Parker, Ronald Shiner, Leslie Phillips, Elvi Hale, Nicholas Phipps (20th Century-Fox)

The oldie about a "forgotten" naval base off the South Coast of Britain. They're having a high old time feathering their nests with illicit smuggling and other rackets. Suddenly higher authority decides that the unit is redundant and chaos breaks out as they scheme to avoid being posted elsewhere. Only occasionally does the comedy creak. Some skilled performers hold the fort.

NAVY SEALS
1990, 113 mins, US ⓥ ⊙
D: Lewis Teague A: Charlie Sheen, Michael Biehn, Joanne Whalley-Kilmer, Rick Rossovich, Bill Paxton (Orion) ·

Nifty performances make this routine action flick better than it probably has a right to be. Playing to the Rambo mentality by focusing on an elite naval-attack group kicking tail around the globe, the film won't be a favorite of peaceniks or any Arab antidefamation leagues.

NAZARIN
1959, 94 mins, Mexico ⓥ ⊙
D: Luis Bunuel **A:** Francisco Rabal, Marga Lopez, Rita Macedo, Jesus Fernandez (Ponce)

A priest unfrocks himself and takes to the road to live on alms. He is followed in his pilgrimage by a prostitute and a woman who has been left by a lover. Film details their wanderings and attempts to help humanity and their constant rebuffs until the priest realizes one must love humanity first before one can be a human being or a priest. Director Luis Bunuel's mastery of his theme and subject make this an unusual offbeater.

NEAR DARK
1987, 95 mins, US ⓥ ⊙
D: Kathryn Bigelow **A:** Adrian Pasdar, Jenny Wright, Lance Henriksen, Bill Paxton (De Laurentiis)

A new look in vampire films. Nervous, edgy opening has sharp young cowboy Adrian Pasdar hooking up with Jenny Wright, a good-looking new girl in town not averse to some nocturnal roistering as long as she gets home by dawn. Wright soon welcomes Pasdar into her "family," a bunch of real low-down boys and girls that hibernates by day, but at night scours the vacant landscapes in search of prey.

NECESSARY ROUGHNESS
1991, 108 mins, US ⓥ
D: Stan Dragoti **A:** Scott Bakula, Hector Elizondo, Robert Loggia, Harley Jane Kozak, Larry Miller (Paramount)

This gridiron comedy piles up clichés. Seemingly unable to settle on a single-wing hackneyed story line, the filmmakers float at least three—a 34-year-old quarterback seeks to belatedly claim his college glory days, a female kicker joins a football team, and a team of "real" students is assembled after a major college program is disbanded for recruiting violations—but basically settle on the former, with Scott Bakula carrying the ball.

NECRONOMICON
1994, 96 mins, US ⓥ ⊙
D: Brian Yuzna, Christophe Gans, Shu Kaneko **A:** Jeffrey Combs, Bruce Payne, David Warner, Bess Meyer, Millie Perkins (Davis)

Three-parter (plus wraparound) drawn from the deep well of H. P. Lovecraft is

diverting but uneven. Yuzna helms the fanciful wraparound (*The Library*), in which H. P. (Jeffrey Combs) visits a library where resides a copy of the Necronomicon that contains "the very secrets of the universe." H. P. jots down notes for stories. Segue to first seg (*The Drowned*), a *House of Usher*-like variation. Set in Boston, *The Cold* centers on an aggressive reporter (Gary Graham, twitchy) researching a spate of killings. *Whispers* follows a feisty female cop (Signy Coleman) who is drawn into a pit full of monsters. Best of the bunch is the most serious, *The Drowned*, in which French director Christophe Gans finds more modern equivalents of the Roger Corman legacy.

NED KELLY
1970, 101 mins, UK ⓥ
D: Tony Richardson **A:** Mick Jagger, Diane Craig, Clarissa Kaye, Frank Thring (Woodfall)

Ned Kelly is a film to which one applies the damning word "interesting." In the 1870s Australia was a brutal frontier, settled by Irish, English, and Scots convicts and their descendants. Unable to exist otherwise, Kelly and the other Irishmen turn to rustling. Given whiskers, Mick Jagger's gaunt, tough pop hero face takes on a classic hard-bitten frontier look that is totally believable for the role. However he has no one to play to. Jagger's Clyde has no Bonnie, his Sundance Kid has no Butch Cassidy.

NEEDFUL THINGS
1993, 120 mins, US ⓥ ⊙
D: Fraser C. Heston **A:** Max von Sydow, Ed Harris, Bonnie Bedelia, Amanda Plummer, J. T. Walsh (Castle Rock/Columbia)

Fatherly-looking Leland Gaunt (Max von Sydow) is the proprietor of a new shop providing objects to the town's residents in exchange for each doing him 'a favor." Gaunt successfully uses those prankish deeds to set the good people homicidally at each other's throats. Only the town sheriff (Ed Harris) seems to realize something is rotten in the state of Maine, while even his fiancée (Bonnie Bedelia) falls under Gaunt's promise-fulfilling spell. Heston employs a too-slow buildup to an explosion of mayhem that incorporates gruesome violence with awkward attempts at dark humor.

NEGOTIATOR, THE
1998, 138 mins, US ⓥ ⊙ ▭
D: F. Gary Gray **A:** Samuel L. Jackson,

Kevin Spacey, David Morse, Ron Rifkin, John Spencer, J. T. Walsh (Regency/Mandeville/New Regency/Warner)

The teaming of Samuel L. Jackson and Kevin Spacey, in perfectly fitting roles that call for a battle of wits and wills, proves to be the best element of *The Negotiator*. Pic is slightly impaired by an overlong, overbaked production. The partner of Danny Roman (Jackson), top hostage negotiator of the Chicago police force, is assassinated minutes before he was due to disclose vital info about embezzlement within their department. Roman becomes prime suspect and resorts to a desperate gambit: he takes his nemesis, Inspector Terence Niebaum (J. T. Walsh), two assistants and Commander Frost (Ron Rifkin) hostage. Roman demands that Chris Sabian (Spacey), a respected negotiator from another precinct, be brought in to mediate. As the cover-up reaches further into the upper echelons, it's only a matter of time before the two negotiators join forces. Jackson and Spacey rise to the occasion and excel without outshining one another.

NEGRO SOLDIER, THE
1944, 42 mins, US
D: Frank Capra A: Carlton Moss (War Department)

A two-fisted plea for tolerance, told simply, honestly, and conscientiously. Carlton Moss, Negro author, scripted and plays the leading role of the pastor. Facts are presented about the role of the Negro soldier, from Crispus Attucks, mulatto hero of the Boston Massacre in 1770, to Robert Brooks, first American soldier to die in World War II. But the main part deals with his activities during the Second World War. An enlisted man is picked up and followed through basic training, additional fundamentals, and through actual combat.

NEIGHBORS
1981, 94 mins, US
D: John G. Avildsen A: John Belushi, Kathryn Walker, Cathy Moriarty, Dan Aykroyd (Columbia)

Story focuses on staid suburbanite John Belushi slowly being driven crazy by his new, nutsy neighbors—a dyed-blond goon Dan Aykroyd and his smooth, sexually scintillating wife, Cathy Moriarty. They take over his car, his bank account, his house, and even his family while making it seem like Belushi is a stick-in-the mud poor sport for not going along with it. Belushi and Aykroyd make the picture work.

When they hit the comedic mark, nothing else seems to matter.

NELL
1994, 113 mins, US
D: Michael Apted A: Jodie Foster, Liam Neeson, Natasha Richardson, Richard Libertini, Nick Searcy (Egg/20th Century-Fox)

Nell seems rather too aware of its studied artfulness and sensitivity. Nell (Jodie Foster) is left alone in a remote lakeside cabin when her mother dies. She speaks in a unique way due to her mother's stroke-induced speech impediments. Nell is fortunate in being found by an independent-minded doctor, Jerome Lovell (Liam Neeson). Psychologist Paula Olsen (Natasha Richardson) turns up to do her own monitoring of Nell's behavior. Foster's performance relies in great measure upon techniques of movement, dance, and mime.
1994: Nomination: Best Actress (Jodie Foster)

NELL GWYN
1935, 85 mins, UK
D: Herbert Wilcox A: Anna Neagle, Cedric Hardwicke, Jeanne De Casalis, Lawrence Anderson, Miles Malleson, Esme Percy (British & Dominions/United Artists)

A generally unsympathetic saga of a 17th-century music-hall trollop who captured the fancy of King Charles II, besting the Duchess of Portsmouth (capably played by Jeanne De Casalis), the king's favorite until he sees Nell. The backgrounds contribute not a little charm; also more than a little dullness. That goes for the stilted dialogue. Cedric Hardwicke, as King Charles, lends to his assignment the necessary regal poise and dignity. Anna Neagle's hoydenish personality fits her role.

NELLY AND MONSIEUR ARNAUD
(US: NELLY & MR. ARNAUD)
1995, 105 mins, France/Italy/Germany
D: Claude Sautet A: Emmanuelle Beart, Michel Serrault, Jean-Hugues Anglade, Charles Berling, Daniele Lebrun, Michael Lonsdale (Sarde/TF1/Cecchi Gori/Prokino)

Emmanuelle Beart plays Nelly, 25, who meets the emotionally remote but gentlemanly Arnaud (Serrault), a retired magistrate who offers Nelly work as a typist at his apartment office. By distilling the pair's relationship into a series of conversations, mostly in Arnaud's apartment, Sautet studiously avoids the expected course of a May-December romance. Sautet is more interested in the what-could-have-happened than the what-actually-has. Beart proves surprisingly touching in the pic's key emotional moments.

NELLY AND MR. ARNAUD
See: Nelly and Monsieur Arnaud

NELSON AFFAIR, THE
See: Bequest to the Nation

NEON BIBLE, THE
1995, 92 mins, US/UK Ⓥ ▭
D: Terence Davies **A:** Gena Rowlands, Jacob Tierney, Diana Scarwid, Drake Bell, Denis Leary (Miramax/Channel 4/Scala)

A beautifully crafted but thin and self-conscious tale about a dysfunctional family in rural Georgia in the 1940s. For about the first half hour, Davies and his superb creative team weave a potent spell. The gliding camera, the use of popular songs of the era, the disarming performances, and the elegant direction all combine to exert a distinctive magic. But, starting with a poorly staged revival meeting sequence, things start to go wrong; Davies's grip slackens, and the artifice overwhelms the perilously slim story line.

NEPTUNE FACTOR, THE
1973, 98 mins, Canada Ⓥ ▭
D: Daniel Petrie **A:** Ben Gazzara, Yvette Mimieux, Walter Pidgeon, Ernest Borgnine (Quadrant/Bellevue-Pathe)

Undersea sci-fi potboiler loaded with interesting technology and kindergarten plotting has a dull script, dreary direction, and a cast of familiar names for whom audiences may feel some embarrassment. Script traces the rescue of some underwater scientists whose sea-bottom lab is hurled into an ocean crevasse by an earthquake.

NEPTUNE'S DAUGHTER
1949, 92 mins, US Ⓥ
D: Edward Buzzell **A:** Esther Williams, Red Skelton, Ricardo Montalban, Betty Garrett, Keenan Wynn, Xavier Cugat (M-G-M)

Neat concoction of breezy, light entertainment combines comedy, songs, and dances into an amusing froth. Williams's bathing beauty and Skelton's comedy make for a pleasing combination that does much to get over the pleasant, but fluffy, story. Top tune of the Frank Loesser score is "Baby, It's Cold Outside,"

dueted by Williams and Ricardo Montalban, and, for comedy, by Skelton and Garrett.
1949: Best Song ("Baby It's Cold Outside")

NET, THE
1995, 112 mins, US Ⓥ ⊙
D: Irwin Winkler **A:** Sandra Bullock, Jeremy Northam, Dennis Miller, Diane Baker, Wendy Gazelle (Columbia)

A reasonably suspenseful thriller trades effectively on time-tested female-in-jeopardy gambits. Sandra Bullock plays Angela Bennett, a cuddly computer nerd. On the eve of her vacation, a colleague sends her a new program through which she is strangely able to access some highly restricted government files. Angela heads off to Mexico, where she meets a British hacker, Jack Devlin (Jeremy Northam). But it soon develops that he's more interested in her unique diskette than in her mind or body.

NETWORK
1976, 121 mins, US Ⓥ ⊙
D: Sidney Lumet **A:** Faye Dunaway, William Holden, Peter Finch, Robert Duvall, Wesley Addy, Ned Beatty (M-G-M/UA)

This is a bawdy, stops-out, no-holds-barred story of a TV network that will, quite literally, do anything to get an audience. Peter Finch, the passé evening-news anchorman is about to get the heave. To the dismay of all, Finch announces his own axing, becoming an instant character. Finch's on-air freakout suggests to Faye Dunaway that she turn the news into a gross entertainment package. It works, of course.
1976: Best Actor (Peter Finch), Actress (Faye Dunaway), Supp. Actress (Beatrice Straight), Original Screenplay
Nominations: Best Picture, Director, Actor (William Holden), Supp. Actor (Ned Beatty), Cinematography, Editing

NEVADA SMITH
1966, 131 mins, US Ⓥ ⊙ ▭
D: Henry Hathaway **A:** Steve McQueen, Karl Malden, Brian Keith, Arthur Kennedy, Suzanne Pleshette, Raf Vallone (Paramount/Embassy/Solar)

Yarn is centered on the Nevada Smith character who acted as guardian to Jonas Cord Jr., the youthful antihero of *Carpetbaggers*. Steve McQueen is the young half-Indian boy whose parents are brutally murdered by Karl Malden, Arthur Kennedy, and Martin Landau. Vowing revenge, McQueen sets off to kill them all. Brian Keith plays the elder Jonas Cord, then an itinerant gunsmith, who befriends the greenhorn. Henry Hathaway's uneven direction alternates jarring, overbearing fisticuffs with exterior footage as spectacular in some cases as it is dull in others.

NEVER A DULL MOMENT
1943, 60 mins, US
D: Edward Lilley **A:** Harry Ritz, Al Ritz, Jimmy Ritz, Frances Langford, Mary Beth Hughes (Universal)

Familiar story is used principally as background for the Ritzes' shenanigans, variety numbers and Langford's neat warbling. Ritz brothers pose as Chicago mobsters, taking jobs at a NY nightclub under the impression they've been hired on their vaude rep as "the Three Funny Bunnies." When they learn that Mary Beth Hughes is a femme pickpocket hired by the nitery operator to pass the stolen jewels to them, the whacky trio attempts to duck out. Romance concerns the nightclub singer (Frances Langford) and a socialite.

NEVER A DULL MOMENT
1950, 89 mins, US ⓥ ⊚
D: George Marshall **A:** Irene Dunne, Fred MacMurray, William Demarest, Andy Devine, Gigi Perreau, Natalie Wood (RKO)

Never a Dull Moment doesn't always live up to its title in telling the story of a smooth femme songwriter who falls in love with a western rancher and goes to his impoverished acreage to make a home. George Marshall's direction is a great help in selling the physical business that goes with the comedy, and where scripting isn't strong he still manages chuckles for the average audience.

NEVER CRY WOLF
1983, 105 mins, US ⓥ ⊚
D: Carroll Ballard **A:** Charles Martin Smith, Brian Dennehy, Zachary Ittimangnaq, Samson Jorah, Hugh Webster (Walt Disney)

A story about the white wolves in the Arctic. Biologist Tyler (Charles Martin Smith) is investigating whether the predatory wolf is responsible for the gradual disappearance of the caribou herds. A friendly but reticent Eskimo (Zachary Ittimangnaq) happens to the helpless biologist's stakeout in the dead of winter to rescue him. Then begins the study of the white wolf. The most praise goes to the imagery of this poetic fiction-documentary. Yet the magic

of the film is in that quaint comic performance rendered by thesp Smith.

NEVERENDING STORY, THE
1984, 94 mins, W. Germany ⓥ ⊚ ⌖
D: Wolfgang Petersen **A:** Noah Hathaway, Barret Oliver, Tami Stronach, Moses Gunn, Patricia Hayes, Sydney Bromley (Neue Constantin)

A marvelously realized flight of pure fantasy opens with a little boy, Bastian (Barret Oliver), borrowing a strange-looking book. Book depicts a world known as Fantasia, threatened by an advancing force called The Nothing (represented by storms) which is gradually destroying all. To save Fantasia, an ailing empress (Tami Stronach) sends for a young warrior from among the plains people, Atreyu (Noah Hathaway) to go on a quest to find a cure for her illness.

NEVERENDING STORY II THE NEXT CHAPTER, THE
1990, 89 mins, Germany/US ⓥ ⊚ ⌖
D: George Miller **A:** Jonathan Brandis, Kenny Morrison, Clarissa Burt, Alexandra Johnes, Martin Umbach (Geissler/Scriba/Deyhle/Warner)

Part II utilizes a whole new cast (except for Thomas Hill, reprising as Koreander the bookseller) to depict adventures in the imaginary world of Fantasia. Main innovation is that young hero Bastian joins his fantasy counterpart Atreyu in a heroic trek in search of the childlike empress locked in her Ivory Tower in Fantasia, rather than just reading about her. Another improvement is the inclusion of a delicious villainess, dark beauty Clarissa Burt as Xayide.

NEVERENDING STORY III, THE
1994, 95 mins, German ⓥ
D: Peter Macdonald **A:** Jason James Richter, Melody Kay, Freddie Jones, Jack Black, Ryan Bollman (CineVox/Babelsberg/Geissler)

A charmless, desperate reworking of the franchise throws over the magical charm of the 1984 original and darker fantasy of the 1990 sequel for a semihip yarn patched together by a marketing committee. Bastian (Jason James Richter) is bullied at school by a bunch of senior punks called the Nasties. Bastian wishes himself back into the dream world of Fantasia, courtesy of Jim Henson's Creature Shop. But when the Nasties get a hold of the tome and start filling it with their own warped imagination, Fantasia starts to crumble. Fantasia's child empress (now the shapely Julie Cox) begs him to get the book back.

NEVER GIVE AN INCH
See: Sometimes a Great Notion

NEVER GIVE A SUCKER AN EVEN BREAK
(UK: WHAT A MAN)
1941, 70 mins, US Ⓥ ⊙
D: Edward Cline **A:** W. C. Fields, Gloria Jean, Margaret Dumont, Susan Miller, Franklin Pangborn (Universal)

W. C. Fields parades his droll satire and broad comedy in this takeoff on eccentricities of filmmaking—from the original story by Fields under nom de plume of Otis Criblecoblis. Picture is studded with Fieldsian satire and cracks—many funny and several that slipped by the blue-pencil squad. Byplay and reference to hard liquor is prominent throughout.

NEVER LET ME GO
1953, 94 mins, UK/US Ⓥ
D: Delmer Daves **A:** Clark Gable, Gene Tierney, Bernard Miles, Richard Haydn, Belita, Kenneth More (Metro-British)

Clark Gable plays an American newspaperman who weds a Russian ballerina (Gene Tierney), but is forced to leave her behind in Moscow. Back in Washington, he tries his hand at wire-pulling without success, and finally comes to London to tackle Molotov, who is attending a four-power conference. Plot reeks of implausibility, but this is compensated by bold direction, nimble scripting and lively performances and there is suspense and action in good measure.

NEVER LOVE A STRANGER
1958, 91 mins, US Ⓥ
D: Robert Stevens **A:** John Drew Barrymore, Lita Milan, Robert Bray, Steve McQueen, R. G. Armstrong (Allied Artists)

This New York location melodrama is ineptly, unprofessionally done, especially in its handling of such volatile subjects as race and religion. John Drew Barrymore plays a young man raised in a Catholic orphanage who discovers that his parents were Jewish. Already involved with hoodlum elements and feeling rejection by the orphanage, young Barrymore takes the final plunge into the gangster world.

NEVER ON SUNDAY
See: Pote Tin Kyriaki

NEVER SAY NEVER AGAIN
1983, 137 mins, US Ⓥ ⊙ ⌨
D: Irvin Kershner **A:** Sean Connery, Klaus Maria Brandauer, Max von Sydow, Barbara Carrera, Kim Basinger, Alec McCowen (Taliafilm)

After a 12-year hiatus, Sean Connery is back in action as James Bond. The new entry marks something of a retreat from the farfetched technology of many of the later Bonds in favor of intrigue and romance. Although not acknowledged, pic is roughly a remake of the 1965 *Thunderball*. World-threatening organization SPECTRE manages to steal two US cruise missiles and announces it will detonate their nuclear warheads in strategic areas unless ransom demands are met. Klaus Maria Brandauer makes one of the best Bond opponents since very early in the series. And Connery's in fine form and still very much looking the part.

NEVER SO FEW
1959, 126 mins, US Ⓥ ⊙ ⌨
D: John Sturges **A:** Frank Sinatra, Gina Lollobrigida, Peter Lawford, Steve McQueen, Richard Johnson, Paul Henreid (Canterbury/M-G-M)

Individual scenes and sequences play with verve and excitement. It is only when the relation of the scenes is evaluated, and their cumulative effect considered, that the threads begin to unravel like an old, worn sock. The locale is Burma during World War II. Frank Sinatra is the ruggedly individualistic commander of a small task force, the bulk of which is made up of native Kachin troops. He is idolized by them and his Occidental troops. Chief action of the film has Sinatra leading a foray against a Japanese position near the Chinese border.

NEVER TAKE SWEETS FROM A STRANGER
1960, 81 mins, UK
D: Cyril Frankel **A:** Gwen Watford, Patrick Allen, Felix Aylmer, Niall MacGinnis, Alison Leggatt (Hammer)

The yarn, set in Canada, deals with a senile, psychopathic pervert (Felix Aylmer). When he persuades two innocent little girls to dance naked in front of him in exchange for candy, the English parents of one of them decide to take him to court. Unfortunately, they do not realize that he is the local big shot, the man who has helped to build the Canadian town to its prosperity and power. Aylmer, who doesn't utter a word throughout the film, gives a terrifying acute study of crumbling evil.

NEVER TALK TO STRANGERS
1995, 86 mins, US ⊛
D: Peter Hall A: Rebecca De Mornay, Antonio Banderas, Dennis Miller, Len Cariou, Harry Dean Stanton (Alliance)

A reasonably entertaining but largely uninspired erotic thriller. Cool criminal psychiatrist Dr. Sarah Taylor (De Mornay) bumps into mysterious-but-attractive stranger Toni Ramirez (Banderas) in the supermarket wine aisle. Before you can say Cabernet Sauvignon, the shy, distrustful shrink is off tasting wine at the suitably spooky loft of the self-described "surveillance consultant." After Taylor's upstairs neighbor Cliff (Dennis Miller) gets clobbered with a lead pipe, the identity of the stalker is revealed in a surprise ending that will severely stretch the credulity of most viewers.

NEVER TOO LATE
1965, 104 mins, US ▱
D: Bud Yorkin A: Paul Ford, Connie Stevens, Maureen O'Sullivan, Jim Hutton, Jane Wyatt, Lloyd Nolan (Tandem/Warner)

Paul Ford and Maureen O'Sullivan are smartly reteamed in their Broadway roles of small-town Massachusetts parents, settled in middle-aged habits until wife's increasing fatigue is diagnosed as pregnancy. O'Sullivan looks great and handles light comedy with a warm, gracious flair. Ford carries the pic as the flustered father-to-be, saddled with the sly grins of neighbors, the incompetency of son-in-law, Jim Hutton, and the domestic bumblings of daughter, Connie Stevens.

NEVINOST BEZ ZASTITE
(US: INNOCENCE UNPROTECTED)
1968, 78 mins, Yugoslavia ⊛
D: Dusan Makavejev A: Dragoljub Aleksic, Ana Miloslavljevic, Vera Jovanovic, Bratoljub Grigorijevic, Ivan Zivkovic (Avala)

A curious mixture of facts and fiction, newsreel footage, the remainder being from an old privately made film of 1942 vintage. Acrobat Dragoljub Aleksic made the film about himself and a comely if sad orphan, Nada (Ana Milosavljevic) in occupied Belgrade. Director Dusan Makavejev searched for the acrobat and then put the old feature pic together via a documentary-type framework. Also, he added color to the old pic. The outcome is both amusing and interesting.

NEW ADVENTURES OF DON JUAN, THE
See: Adventures of Don Juan

NEW ADVENTURES OF TARZAN, THE
1935, 71 mins, US ⊛
D: Edward Kull, W. F. McGaugh A: Herman Brix, Ula Holt, Frank Baker, Dale Walsh, Don Castello (Burroughs-Tarzan)

Despite skillful cutting job, this picture, taken from 12-episode serial, remains of serial caliber. Adventures take Tarzan into Guatemalan jungles in search of a missing friend, winding up in a mad dash for a lost goddess filled with valuable gems. Then the animal stuff with the hero triumphant. Battle with natives is closest thing to realism in pic. Herman Brix is an athletic Tarzan who struggles manfully with absurdities of the dialogue.

NEW AGE, THE
1994, 110 mins, US ⊛
D: Michael Tolkin A: Peter Weller, Judy Davis, Patrick Bauchau, Corbin Bernsen, Jonathan Hadary (Warner/Regency/Alcor/Ixtlan)

Michael Tolkin's film gets all dressed up but doesn't quite know where to go. Peppy opening scenes have upscale L.A. denizens Peter and Katherine Witner (Weller, Davis) losing big-buck jobs. As their lives collapse around them, the two seek salvation elsewhere; Katherine in New Age spirituality, Peter tentatively in the kinky club scene and ultimately in phone sales.

NEW BABYLON, THE
See: Novi Vavilon

NEW CENTURIONS, THE
(UK: PRECINCT 45—LOS ANGELES POLICE)
1972, 103 mins, US ⊛ ⊚
D: Richard Fleischer A: George C. Scott, Stacy Keach, Jane Alexander, Scott Wilson, Rosalind Cash (Columbia)

Somewhat unsatisfying film largely avoids any real confrontation with the gray areas of citizen-police interactions which are at the seat of unrest. George C. Scott dominates the first 76 minutes, starring as the old-time cop. He sees nothing wrong in applying some pragmatic justice at the street level; at the same time, he is obviously blind to the realization that laws are contemporary reflections of transient attitudes which every few generations undergo a major flushing out. After Scott retires from the force the film falls off in impact.

NEW JACK CITY
1991, 97 mins, US Ⓥ ⊙
D: Mario Van Peebles **A:** Wesley Snipes, Ice-T, Mario Van Peebles, Allen Payne, Judd Nelson (Jackson-McHenry)

Filmmakers pull off a provocative, pulsating update on gangster pics with this action-laden epic. Strongest element is the anger and disgust directed squarely at drug dealers. Pic presents the fictional story of Nino Brown (Wesley Snipes), who in 1986 foresees the potential of crack and by 1989 has built an empire around it. After Nino takes over an apartment building, brutally ejecting the tenants, police detective Stone (played by the director) recruits undercover cops Scotty (rap artist Ice-T) and Peretti (Judd Nelson) to bring him in.

NEW JERSEY DRIVE
1995, 95 mins, US
D: Nick Gomez **A:** Sharron Corley, Gabriel Casseus, Saul Stein, Gwen McGee, Andre Moore (40 Acres and a Mule)

As an in-your-face evocation of what it's like to be young and living in an urban combat zone, *New Jersey Drive* could scarcely be more vivid and immediate. At the same time, lack of a discernible point of view on this out-of-control lawlessness and mayhem until the final minutes leaves the viewer nowhere to put one's concerns or sympathies. At the center of things is Jason (Sharron Corley), a black teenager who mostly follows the lead of a shaven-headed wise guy named Midget (Gabriel Casseus). The conflict between the local hoods and the cops escalates into a war neither side can win.

NEW LEAF, A
1971, 102 mins, US Ⓥ
D: Elaine May **A:** Walter Matthau, Elaine May, Jack Weston, George Rose, William Redfield, James Coco (Paramount)

It's sophisticated and funny, adroitly put together for the most part. Matthau is the marriage-aloof middle-ager who has to come upon a rich wife to sustain himself. Rich wife turns out to be unglamorous May. The director and cosmetician have made May about as sexy as an Alsophilia Grahamicus, which is a new leaf she has cultivated in her role as botanist. A new leaf is also something that Matthau turns over because after he weds May he de-

cides, rather than kill her, to take care of her.

NEW LIFE, A
1988, 104 mins, US Ⓥ ⊙
D: Alan Alda **A:** Alan Alda, Ann-Margret, Hal Linden, Veronica Hamel, John Shea (Paramount)

Perhaps trying to break his image as the most conscientiously nice guy of the latter half of the 20th century, Alan Alda has tried to give himself an edge in *A New Life*. As the newly divorced Steve Giardino, he is loud, obnoxious, neurotic, argumentative, and manic. After some 20 years of marriage, New Yorkers Alda and Ann-Margret decide to call it quits. Alda's screenplay follows the two equally as each endures the predictably excruciating blind dates, singles parties, and match-ups.

NEWS BOYS, THE
See: Newsies

NEWSFRONT
1978, 110 mins, Australia Ⓥ ⊙
D: Phillip Noyce **A:** Bill Hunter, Gerard Kennedy, Angela Punch, Wendy Hughes, Chris Hayward (Palm Beach)

Set in an historically turbulent period for Australia (1949–56), *Newsfront* deals with the lives of movie newsreel cameramen and uses the events in which they are involved as a sort of microcosmic view of how, in a very short period of time, the country underwent remarkable sociopolitical change. Plot concerns the rivalry between two competing newsreel companies: Len works for the plodding, traditionally valued, Aussie-owned Cinetone, and ambitious brother Frank (Gerard Kennedy) has left them to run the go-ahead, pushy, Yank-owned Newsco.

NEWSIES
(UK: THE NEWS BOYS)
1992, 121 mins, US Ⓥ ⊙ ▭
D: Kenny Ortega **A:** Christian Bale, David Moscow, Luke Edwards, Ann-Margret, Robert Duvall (Walt Disney)

Newsies was made with care and affection by choreographer-turned-director Kenny Ortega. But the writers have created cardboard cutouts instead of flesh-and-blood characters. Lyrics here are relentlessly banal and unmemorable. Cast has pleasant but ordinary voices. Christian Bale plays the leader of the newsboys' walk-out against the penny-pinching Pulitzer (bearded Robert Duvall). He's a charismatic figure, with a compelling blend of brashness and vulnerability. Duvall is a cartoon figure of ranting hard-heartedness. Ann-Margret's Jenny Lind–like thrush is shoehorned into the film to provide s.a. in a male-dominated story.

NEW YEAR'S DAY
1989, 89 mins, US Ⓥ
D: Henry Jaglom **A:** Maggie Jakobson, Gwen Welles, Melanie Winter, Henry Jaglom, Milos Forman, Michael Emil (International Rainbow)

New Year's Day is notable for introducing a luminous new actress, Maggie Jakobson. Jaglom stars as a depressed obsessive who returns to New York in the midst of a midlife crisis. Arriving on New Year's morning, Jaglom finds his apartment occupied by three young ladies who thought they had until the end of the day to vacate the premises. Instead of booting them out, Jaglom immediately imposes himself upon their most personal concerns.

NEW YORK CONFIDENTIAL
1955, 87 mins, US
D: Russell Rouse **A:** Broderick Crawford, Richard Conte, Marilyn Maxwell, Anne Bancroft, J. Carrol Naish (Warner)

Tough melodrama relies more on logical development for effect than on bare-knuckles action. Story tells of the rise of Richard Conte, ambitious triggerman, in the big syndicate said to control all crime. Conte does a topnotch job of making a cold-blooded killer seem real and Broderick Crawford is good as the chairman of the crime board, as is Marilyn Maxwell as his girlfriend. Anne Bancroft scores with a standout performance of Crawford's unhappy daughter.

NEW YORK, NEW YORK
1977, 153 mins, US Ⓥ Ⓞ
D: Martin Scorsese **A:** Liza Minnelli, Robert De Niro, Lionel Stander, Barry Primus, Mary Kay Place (United Artists)

Taking Liza Minnelli and Robert De Niro from their first meeting after VJ Day, film proceeds slowly and deliberately through their struggle to make it as a band singer and saxophonist and as a marriage in which her voice is early acclaimed while his music is ahead of its time. In a final burst from old Hollywood, Minnelli tears into the title song and it's a wowser.

NEW YORK STORIES
1989, 123 mins, US Ⓥ Ⓞ
D: Martin Scorsese, Francis Coppola, Woody Allen **A:** Nick Nolte, Rosanna Arquette, Heather McComb, Talia Shire, Woody Allen, Mia Farrow (Touchstone)

Scorsese's *Life Lessons* gets things off to a pulsating start, as Nestor Almendros's camera darts, swoops, and circles around Nick Nolte and Rosanna Arquette as they face the end of an intense romantic entanglement. At 33 minutes, Coppola's *Life without Zoe* is not nearly short enough. Vignette is a wispy urban fairy tale about a 12-year-old girl who basically lives alone at the ritzy Sherry Netherland Hotel. Woody Allen salvages matters rather nicely with *Oedipus Wrecks*. When Allen takes shiksa girlfriend, Mia Farrow, home for dinner, he winces as mama assails him for choosing a blond with three kids.

NEXT KARATE KID, THE
1994, 104 mins, US Ⓥ Ⓞ
D: Christopher Cain **A:** Noriyuki "Pat" Morita, Hilary Swank, Michael Ironside, Constance Towers, Chris Conrad (Columbia)

A troubled teenage girl is transformed from bratty rebel into confident martial artist. Having witnessed Julie's swift reflexes in averting a near-accident, wise Mr. Miyagi, played again by Noriyuki "Pat" Morita, embarks on a low-key mission to rescue the floundering 17-year-old via karate. Wholesome apprenticeship tale has its scattered moments of humor and insight but lacks sustained verve. There's not much karate action compared with previous three pix.

NEXT MAN, THE
1976, 108 mins, US Ⓥ
D: Richard C. Sarafian **A:** Sean Connery, Cornelia Sharpe, Albert Paulsen, Adolfo Celi, Marco St. John (Artists Entertainment)

More a slick travesty with political overtones than the cynical suspense meller it was designed to be. Sean Connery plays a peace-mongering Saudi Arabian diplomat, dispatched to the UN to plead a case for Israeli cooperation. For such arrant revisionism he is plagued by a network of Arab terrorists in whose employ is a beautiful, wealthy playgirl, friskily portrayed by Cornelia Sharpe.

NEXT OF KIN
1989, 108 mins, US Ⓥ Ⓞ
D: John Irvin **A:** Patrick Swayze, Liam Neeson, Adam Baldwin, Helen Hunt, Andreas Katsulas, Michael J. Pollard (Lorimar/Warner)

Bill Paxton, a Kentucky boy from the hills now working in Chicago, is ruthlessly murdered by mafia enforcer Adam Baldwin. Paxton's older brother, Patrick Swayze, is a Chicago cop determined to find the killer. Interfering with Swayze's efforts is the old-fashioned eye-for-an-eye vengeance demanded by eldest brother, Liam Neeson. Picture climaxes with an elaborate war in a Chicago cemetery between Baldwin's mafiosi and Neeson's Kentucky kin, matching automatic weaponry with primitive (but reliable) crossbows, hatchets, snakes, and knives.

NEXT STOP, GREENWICH VILLAGE
1976, 111 mins, US Ⓥ
D: Paul Mazursky **A:** Lenny Baker, Shelley Winters, Ellen Greene, Lois Smith, Christopher Walken (20th Century-Fox)

A very beautiful motion picture. Lenny Baker heads the cast in an excellent depiction of a young Brooklyn boy aiming for an acting career; quite naturally, pop Mike Kellin and mom Shelley Winters have their doubts. Baker's new life centers around a group of arresting people: Ellen Greene, his girl; Christopher Walken; lothario-playwright; Dori Brenner, the type of girl who hides her sensitivities in kookiness; Antonio Fargas, the gay equivalent of Brenner's character, and so on.

NEXT VOICE YOU HEAR . . . , THE
1950, 82 mins, US
D: William A. Wellman **A:** James Whitmore, Nancy Davis, Gary Gray, Lillian Bronson, Art Smith, Tom D'Andrea (M-G-M)

Unusual picture experience, beautifully handled in the understanding writing, direction, and playing. Footage carries a hearty load of warm, earthy humor that adds to the potency of the storytelling. James Whitmore and Nancy Davis are average Americans, living a quiet life. They have a son (Gary Gray) and another child is on the way. One night a voice suddenly speaks out from the radio, a voice that is heard all over the world. William A. Wellman's direction turns scene after scene into actual slices of life. Davis's obvious pregnancy, the little bits of business between her and Whitmore, and with young Gray, ring true.

NIAGARA
1953, 89 mins, US Ⓥ ⊙
D: Henry Hathaway **A:** Marilyn Monroe, Joseph Cotten, Jean Peters, Casey Adams, Denis O'Dea (20th Century-Fox)

A morbid, clichéd expedition into lust and murder. Marilyn Monroe is vacationing at the falls with hubby, Joseph Cotten. His eye-filling blond wife deliberately goes out of her way to irritate him. She has a clandestine affair in progress with Richard Allan. A plot of Monroe and Allan to kill Cotten backfires when the latter shoves his attacker over the falls. The camera lingers on Monroe's sensuous lips, roves over her slip-clad figure and accurately etches the outlines of her derriere as she weaves down a street to a rendezvous with her lover. As a contrast to the beauty of the female form is another kind of nature's beauty—that of the falls. The natural phenomena have been magnificently photographed on location.

DIE NIBELUNGEN KRIEMHILDS RACHE (US: KRIEMHILD'S REVENGE; THE SHE DEVIL)
1924, 97 mins, Germany Ⓥ ⊙ ⊗
D: Fritz Lang **A:** Margarethe Schoen, Rudolf Klein Rogge, Rudolf Rittner, Hans Adalbert von Schlettow (Decla-Bioscop)

This sequel to *Siegfried* is a partial rehash and follow-up. The formerly beautiful Kriemhild is not as comely, physically as well as mentally overcome with the desire for vengeance. To advance her purpose Kriemhild weds the distorted Attila, King of the Huns. As queen of that domain she avenges the death of her beloved Siegfried. The typical fantastic settings are notable and look like a lot of money.

DIE NIBELUNGEN SIEGFRIEDS TOD (US: SIEGFRIED)
1924, 110 mins, Germany Ⓥ ⊙ ⊗
D: Fritz Lang **A:** Paul Richter, Margarethe Schoen, Hanna Ralph, Bernhard Goetzke, Theodor Loos (Decla-Bioscop)

Two-sectioned film, centered about the Nibelungen legends. Not a single scene in the whole 16 reels was taken outdoors; all exteriors were built and photographed in a studio. Even the Germans had to admit that, as a whole, they found it rather boresome. Siegfried, the son of King Siegmund of the Netherlands, forges a sword and sets out to win Kriemhild of Burgundy, of whose beauty he has heard tell. On the way he kills a dragon, in whose blood he bathes himself, thus making himself unwoundable. The star is unquestionably Otto Hunte, who designed the scenery, and was brilliantly supported by the photography of Karl Hoffmann. Lang's direction is consistent, and achieves plasticity, dignity, and very nearly power.

NICE GIRL LIKE ME, A
1969, 90 mins, UK ⊕

D: Desmond Davis **A:** Barbara Ferris, Harry Andrews, Gladys Cooper, Bill Hinnant, James Villiers (Partisan/Levine)

Candida (Barbara Ferris) escapes two gorgon aunts to go to Paris to study languages. Her first tutor is a young student and, after a brief idyllic affair, she is pregnant. She kids her aunts that she is minding the babe for a friend and nips off to Venice to continue her linguistic ''studies.'' There, a hip young American picks her up and, pronto, she's carrying a second child. Screenplay is light and gently amusing and director Davis keeps the film on a nonserious yet perceptive level. Ferris is a pleasantly attractive combo of intelligent approach and charm.

NICHOLAS AND ALEXANDRA
1971, 185 mins, UK ⊕ ⊙ ▭

D: Franklin J. Schaffner **A:** Michael Jayston, Janet Suzman, Harry Andrews, Irene Worth, Jack Hawkins, Laurence Olivier (Columbia)

Sam Spiegel comes up with a rarity, the intimate epic, in telling the fascinating story of the downfall of the Romanovs. Scripter James Goldman (with an assist from Edward Bond) has provided literate, sparse dialogue in fashioning a crystal-clear picture of a confused and confusing period. Certainly, there's a feel here for tragically opposed worlds both heading blindly on a collision course toward the inevitable bloody clash. Michael Jayston makes a most believable Nicholas, while Janet Suzman is also just right in the perhaps more difficult role of the empress.
1971: Best Art Direction, Costume Design **Nominations:** Best Picture, Actress (Janet Suzman), Cinematography, Orignal Music Score

NICHOLAS NICKLEBY
1947, 108 mins, UK ⊕

D: Alberto Cavalcanti **A:** Derek Bond, Cedric Hardwicke, Sally Ann Howes, Sybil Thorndike, Stanley Holloway (Ealing)

The 52 characters of this Dickens classic prove too much for the scriptwriter. The screenplay is more in the nature of a condensation into a series of scenes. And that's the way it appears on the screen. Nicholas's adventures with the Crummles family has an old ham actor grandly played by Stanley Holloway. The stage

scenes are amusing, but they do little to further the main story and, as an interlude, they slow up what action there might be. Scenes in Dotheboys Hall are slovenly, untidy, and cramped. Derek Bond brings manly grace to the title role, but betrays inexperience.

NICKELODEON
1976, 121 mins, US ⊕

D: Peter Bogdanovich **A:** Ryan O'Neal, Burt Reynolds, Tatum O'Neal, Brian Keith, Stella Stevens, John Ritter (Columbia)

Okay comedy-drama about the early days of motion pictures. Story begins with a group of barnstorming filmmakers in the prefeature film era, later segues to the adolescence of the industry. Stars include Ryan O'Neal, struggling lawyer who literally stumbles into directing; Burt Reynolds, roustabout who becomes a leading man; Tatum O'Neal, enterprising California country girl; Brian Keith, composite pioneer mogul; and Stella Stevens as an early leading lady.

NICK OF TIME
1995, 89 mins, US ⊕

D: John Badham **A:** Johnny Depp, Christopher Walken, Charles S. Dutton, Peter Strauss, Gloria Reuben (Paramount)

Using real time as its gimmick, this okay but undistinguished thriller takes a simple Hitchcockian premise and milks things about as well as it can, given its confines, before a rather silly and abrupt conclusion. Pic features Johnny Depp as recently widowed father Gene Watson, arbitrarily drafted to kill the governor of California by a shady man (Christopher Walken) who takes his young daughter as hostage. The challenge: carry out the act in 90 minutes or his daughter dies. Depp tries his hand at an everyday Joe with solid results. Walken brings trademark venom to his role.

NICO
See: Above the Law

NIGHT, THE
See: La Notte

NIGHT AMBUSH
See: Ill Met by Moonlight

NIGHT AND DAY
1946, 120 mins, US ⊕

D: Michael Curtiz **A:** Cary Grant, Alexis Smith, Monty Woolley, Jane Wyman, Dorothy Malone, Mary Martin (Warner)

Filmusical, based on the career of Cole

Porter. Here's a guy to whom nothing more exciting happens than that he's born to millions and stays in a "rut" for the rest of his career by making more money. The plot, per se, therefore is static on analysis but paradoxically it emerges into a surprisingly interesting unfolding. A real-life ambulance driver in World War I, Porter is shown with the French Army. Alexis Smith plays the nurse whom he marries. And thereafter, save for a fall off a spirited steed, which caused Porter much real-life suffering, the footage is a succession of hit shows and hit songs.

1946: Nomination: Best Scoring of a Musical Picture

NIGHT AND THE CITY
1950, 96 mins, UK/US
D: Jules Dassin **A:** Richard Widmark, Gene Tierney, Googie Withers, Hugh Marlowe, Francis L. Sullivan, Herbert Lom (20th Century-Fox)

An exciting, suspenseful melodrama, produced in London, which is the story of a double-crossing heel who finally gets his just desserts. In this role, Richard Widmark scores a definite hit. Jules Dassin, in his direction, manages extraordinarily interesting backgrounds, realistically filmed to create a feeling both of suspense and mounting menace.

NIGHT AND THE CITY
1992, 98 mins, US Ⓥ ⊙
D: Irwin Winkler **A:** Robert De Niro, Jessica Lange, Cliff Gorman, Alan King, Jack Warden, Eli Wallach (Penta/Tribeca)

A skilled, if not entirely psychologically convincing, remake of the 1950 film noir classic of the same name. Lively performances, pungent NYC atmosphere, and abundance of dramatic incident keep this story of an irrepressible low-life hustler ripping along. Playing a frenetic, wired character right up his alley, Robert De Niro stars as Harry Fabian, a longtime ambulance-chasing lawyer who conceives the big-time scheme to promote "the return of people's boxing" with a night of fights featuring sharp locals. But boxing promoter Boom Boom Grossman (Alan King), a genial tough guy, doesn't take kindly to Harry horning in.

NIGHT AT THE OPERA, A
1935, 93 mins, US Ⓥ ⊙
D: Sam Wood **A:** Groucho Marx, Harpo Marx, Chico Marx, Kitty Carlisle, Sig Ruman, Allan Jones (M-G-M)

Story is a rather serious grand opera satire in which the comics conspire to get a pair of Italian singers a break over here. Groucho and Chico in a contract-tearing bit, the Marxes with O'Connor in a bed-switching idea, and a chase finale in the opera house are other dynamite comedy sequences, along with a corking buildup by Groucho while riding to his room on a trunk. The backstage finish, with Harpo doing a Tarzan on the fly ropes, contains more action than the Marxes usually go in for, but it relieves the strictly verbal comedy and provides a sock exit.

NIGHTBREED
1990, 99 mins, US Ⓥ ⊙
D: Clive Barker **A:** Craig Sheffer, Anne Bobby, David Cronenberg, Charles Haid (Morgan Creek)

A mess. The last survivors of shape-shifters (legendary monsters including vampires and werewolves) are huddled below ground in a tiny Canadian cemetery, trying to avoid final extinction. Hero Craig Sheffer is plagued by nightmares and heads there in hopes of becoming a monster, while his nutty shrink (revered Canadian director David Cronenberg) is on a messianic mission to destroy the undead critters. Pic presents unrelated sequences of gore and slashing until the ridiculously overproduced finale.

NIGHTCOMERS, THE
1972, 96 mins, UK Ⓥ ⊙
D: Michael Winner **A:** Marlon Brando, Stephanie Beacham, Thora Hird, Verna Harvey, Harry Andrews (Scimitar)

Inspired by characters in Henry James's *The Turn of the Screw*, one of those atmosphere-drenched thrillers in which a semblance of surface decorum and respectability hides a multitude of aberrations beneath. Two recently orphaned children live alone on a British country estate with their nurse, a housekeeper and a gardener, Quint. It's the last-named (played by Brando) who fascinates the boy and girl to such a degree that his instinctive actions, mysterious manners, home-spun philosophizing becomes their (only) guide and lifeline.

NIGHT CROSSING
1981, 106 mins, UK Ⓥ
D: Delbert Mann **A:** John Hurt, Jean Alexander, Glynnis O'Connor, Beau Bridges, Ian Bannen, Kay Walsh (Walt Disney)

There's plenty of drama hiding in this tale of two families' daring escape from

East to West Germany by homemade hot-air balloon, but this Disney production can't find much of it. Unbelievable mix of actors from different nations is forced to deliver one bad line after another.

NIGHT FLIGHT
1933, 89 mins, US

D: Clarence Brown **A:** John Barrymore, Helen Hayes, Clark Gable, Lionel Barrymore, Robert Montgomery, Myrna Loy (M-G-M)

It's a competently done saga of commercial flying. The woman's angle comes from the mental stress on behalf of their menfolk, who are braving the aerial elements, and the heart tug is the necessity of speed to hasten serum across a continent to a stricken city suffering an epidemic of infantile paralysis. As a story it's all rather simple but the veracity of detail and the other elements entailed make it an outstanding production.

NIGHT HAS A THOUSAND EYES
1948, 80 mins, US

D: John Farrow **A:** Edward G. Robinson, Gail Russell, John Lund, Virginia Bruce, William Demarest (Paramount)

Suspense is the dominating element in this thriller, which follows a man who can foresee the future. Told in flashback form, story starts with Gail Russell about to commit suicide by jumping from a trestle onto a track in front of onrushing train, in terror after having been told by Edward G. Robinson, the diviner, that she will meet a violent death within a few days.

NIGHTHAWKS
1981, 99 mins, US Ⓥ ⊙

D: Bruce Malmuth **A:** Sylvester Stallone, Billy Dee Williams, Rutger Hauer, Lyndsay Wagner, Persis Khambatta, Nigel Davenport (Universal)

An exciting cops-and-killers yarn with Sylvester Stallone to root for and cold-blooded Rutger Hauer to hate. While Stallone is doing his best to rid Gotham's streets of riffraff, Hauer is introduced in London as one of the most wanted and most murderous terrorists in the world. Hauer comes to NY accompanied by equally evil Persis Khambatta and pursued by Nigel Davenport, a terrorist expert from Interpol who recruits the assistance of Stallone and Williams. Though there's never much doubt how the duel will end, the climax is nonetheless surprising and totally satisfying, topping the energy of the previous pursuit.

NIGHT IN CASABLANCA, A
1946, 85 mins, US Ⓥ

D: Archie Mayo **A:** Groucho Marx, Harpo Marx, Chico Marx, Lisette Verea, Charles Drake (United Artists)

This isn't the best the Marx brothers have made but it's a pretty funny farce. Postwar Nazi intrigue in Casablanca is the theme with loot cached in the Hotel Casablanca. When three of the hotel's managers get bumped off in rapid succession, Groucho gets the nod. Chico runs the Yellow Camel Company and Harpo is his mute pal who later breaks the bank in the hotel's casino and stumbles on the Nazi gold through a mishap with the lift. Against the desert background of French provincial political bungling and Nazi chicanery the Marxes get off some effective comedy, and some of it not so.

NIGHTMARE
1964, 83 mins, UK ⌑

D: Freddie Francis **A:** David Knight, Moira Redmond, Brenda Bruce, Jennie Linden (Hammer)

Best features of this highly contrived chiller is the direction and lensing of the atmosphere of a house where eerie things happen. Jennie Linden is convinced that she may have inherited a streak of madness. She is taken from school to her home where she is apparently safely guarded by her young guardian (David Knight) and a nurse (Moira Redmond). But Knight and Redmond are clandestine lovers. Their attempts to prey on the mind of the girl are elaborately worked out.

NIGHTMARE ALLEY
1947, 110 mins, US

D: Edmund Goulding **A:** Tyrone Power, Joan Blondell, Coleen Gray, Helen Walker, Ian Keith, Mike Mazurki (20th Century-Fox)

Harsh, brutal story deals with the roughest phases of carnival life and showmanship. Tyrone Power is Stan Carlisle, reform school graduate, who works his way from carney roustabout to big-time mentalist and finally to important swindling in the spook racket. Ruthless and unscrupulous, he uses the women in his life to further his advancement, stepping on them as he climbs. Most vivid of these is Joan Blondell as the girl he works for the secrets of the mind-reading act.

NIGHTMARE BEFORE CHRISTMAS, THE
See: Tim Burton's The Nightmare Before Christmas

NIGHTMARE ON ELM STREET, A

1984, 91 mins, US Ⓥ ⊙

D: Wes Craven A: John Saxon, Ronee Blakley, Heather Langenkamp, Amanda Wyss, Johnny Depp, Robert Englund (New Line/Media Home/Smart Egg)

A highly imaginative horror film. Teenagers in a Los Angeles neighborhood are sharing common nightmares about being chased and killed by a disfigured bum in a slouch hat who has knives for fingernails. With original special effects, the nightmares are merging into reality, as teens are killed under inexplicable circumstances. Writer-director Wes Craven tantalizingly merges dreams with the ensuing wake-up reality but fails to tie up his thematic threads satisfyingly at the conclusion.

NIGHTMARE ON ELM STREET, PART 2, A
FREDDY'S REVENGE

1985, 84 mins, US Ⓥ ⊙

D: Jack Sholder A: Mark Patton, Kim Myers, Robert Rusler, Clu Gulager, Hope Lange, Robert Englund (New Line/Heron/Smart Egg)

Follow-up to Wes Craven's 1984 hit is a well-made though familiar reworking of demonic horror material. A teenage boy Jesse Walsh (Mark Patton) is experiencing the traumatic nightmares previously suffered by a young girl. The slouch-hatted, disfigured monster Freddy (Robert Englund), long steel fingernails affixed, is attempting to possess Walsh's body in order to kill the local kids once more, and, judging from the film's body count, is quite successful.

NIGHTMARE ON ELM STREET 3, A
DREAM WARRIORS

1987, 96 mins, US Ⓥ

D: Chuck Russell A: Heather Langenkamp, Patricia Arquette, Larry Fishburne, Priscilla Pointer, Craig Wasson, Robert Englund (New Line/Heron/Smart Egg)

Heather Langenkamp, young heroine of the first film in the series, returns as an intern assigned to the ward of seven nightmare-plagued teens under the care of medicos Priscilla Pointer (instantly hissable) and Craig Wasson (decidedly miscast). Pic is mainly focused on the violent special-effects outbursts of Freddy Krueger (ably limned under heavy makeup by Robert Englund), the child murderer's de-

mon spirit who seeks revenge on Langenkamp and the other Elm Street kids for the sins of their parents.

NIGHTMARE ON ELM STREET 4, A
THE DREAM MASTER

1988, 93 mins, US ⊙

D: Renny Harlin A: Robert Englund, Lisa Wilcox, Rodney Eastman, Danny Hassel, Andras Jones (New Line/Heron/Smart Egg)

Imaginative special effects highlight the fourth entry in the series. As before, Freddy's out for revenge on the kids of Elm Street for their parents' having murdered him. A clever plot has him rapidly (and unexpectedly) dispensing with the surviving kids, only to extend his mayhem to their friends. Robert Englund is delightful as Freddy, delivering his gag lines with relish and making the grisly proceedings funny.

NIGHTMARE ON ELM STREET, A
THE DREAM CHILD

1989, 89 mins, US Ⓥ ⊙

D: Stephen Hopkins A: Robert Englund, Lisa Wilcox, Kelly Jo Winter, Danny Hassel, Erika Anderson (New Line/Heron/Smart Egg)

Fifth edition of the hit series is a poorly constructed special effects showcase. Alice (Lisa Wilcox) learns that the vengeful monster Freddy Krueger (steady Robert Englund) is now preying on her friends, materializing through the dreams of the fetus she's carrying. New title character is Jacob (Whitby Hertford), 10-year-old dream child who represents what Alice's child will become and is the focus of her war with Freddy.

NIGHT MOVES

1975, 99 mins, US Ⓥ

D: Arthur Penn A: Gene Hackman, Jennifer Warren, Edward Binns, Susan Clark, James Woods, Melanie Griffith (Hiller-Layton/Warner)

A paradox: a suspenseless suspenser, very well cast with players who lend sustained interest to largely synthetic theatrical characters. Minor L.A. detective Hackman, hired to find runaway teenager Melanie Griffith, becomes enmeshed in the Florida smuggling operations of John Crawford (Griffith's stepfather), whose classy mistress, Jennifer Warren, indirectly helps Hackman's own reconciliation with wife, Clark, herself dallying out of loneliness with Harris Yulin.

NIGHT MUST FALL
1964, 99 mins, UK
D: Karel Reisz **A:** Albert Finney, Susan Hampshire, Mona Washbourne, Sheila Hancock, Michael Medwin (M-G-M)

Artfully composed and strikingly photographed, this British-manufactured shock-suspense thriller makes up, to some degree, in cinematic flamboyance what it lacks in dramatic tidiness and conviction. Albert Finney's performance as the cunning madman is vivid and explosive. Yet Finney's thespic thunder is often stolen by Mona Washbourne's masterful delineation of the lonely "invalid" who becomes his victim.

NIGHT NURSE
1931, 73 mins, US Ⓥ ⊙
D: William A. Wellman **A:** Barbara Stanwyck, Ben Lyon, Joan Blondell, Charlotte Merriam, Charles Winninger, Clark Gable (Warner)

A conglomeration of exaggerations, often bordering on serial dramatics. The two nurses are a couple of pretty, well-baked femmes when they start, and thereby cut short their chances for sympathy. Clark Gable goes through socking everybody, including Stanwyck. What legitimate performances crop up in the footage seem to belong to Joan Blondell and Charlie Winninger as the hospital head. Stanwyck plays her dance-hall type of a girl on one note throughout and is shy of shading to lend her performance some color.

NIGHT OF THE COMET
1984, 95 mins, US Ⓥ
D: Thom Eberhardt **A:** Robert Beltran, Catherine Mary Stewart, Kelli Maroney, Sharon Farrell, Mary Woronov, Geoffrey Lewis (Atlantic)

Successful pastiche of numerous science-fiction films, executed with an entertaining, tongue-in-cheek flair that compensates for its absence in originality. When nearly everyone is out watching the arrival of a comet, a few lucky people are indoors protected by steel walls from the comet's deadly rays. Baddies are scientists led by Geoffrey Lewis and Mary Woronov. They're rounding up unaffected survivors, draining them of their blood to perform tests to come up with a serum before they gradually turn into disfigured monsters. As resourceful sisters, Catherine Mary Stewart and Kelli Maroney are de-

lightful, providing, respectively, a believably feisty battler who can beat up monsters and a new, improved Valley girl.

NIGHT OF THE FOLLOWING DAY, THE
1969, 93 mins, UK
D: Hubert Cornfield **A:** Marlon Brando, Richard Boone, Rita Moreno, Pamela Franklin (Universal/Gina)

Intriguing, offbeat kidnap drama soon shifts emphasis to delineating the freaked-out characters of its principals, and ends abruptly on a cop-out note. Lionel White's book, *The Snatchers*, has been adapted into a rambling stew of deliberate and accidental black comedy and melodrama. Pamela Franklin is the prop focal character, a young woman kidnapped for ransom.

NIGHT OF THE GENERALS
1967, 148 mins, UK/France Ⓥ ⊙ ⌑
D: Anatole Litvak **A:** Peter O'Toole, Omar Sharif, Tom Courtenay, Donald Pleasence, Charles Gray, Joanna Pettet (Columbia/Horizon)

With an important theme about the nature of guilt and the promise of a teasing battle of wits, this is an interesting feature that lets the tension run slack. Plot opens in Nazi-occupied Warsaw in 1942, with a prostie being brutally murdered, the killer wearing the uniform of a German general. Major Grau (Omar Sharif), the Military Intelligence man in charge of the hunt, establishes that only three brass hats could have committed the crime. One is Tanz (Peter O'Toole), a ruthless and devoted Nazi who destroys a quarter of Warsaw as an exercise in discipline. The performance by O'Toole lacks the firm savagery Tanz seems to require.

NIGHT OF THE HUNTER, THE
1955, 93 mins, US Ⓥ ⊙
D: Charles Laughton **A:** Robert Mitchum, Shelley Winters, Lillian Gish, Billy Chapin, Peter Graves, James Gleason (Gregory/United Artists)

The relentless terror of Davis Grubb's novel got away. Completed product, bewitching at times, loses sustained drive via too many offbeat touches that have a misty effect. Robert Mitchum intermittently shows some depth in his interpretation of the preacher but in instances where he's crazed with lust for the money, there's barely adequate conviction.

NIGHT OF THE IGUANA, THE
1964, 117 mins, US ⓥ

D: John Huston **A:** Richard Burton, Ava Gardner, Deborah Kerr, Sue Lyon, Grayson Hall (Seven Arts/M-G-M)

Unfoldment takes place mainly in a ramshackle Mexican seacoast hotel where Burton, an unfrocked minister and now guide of a cheap bus tour, takes refuge from a group of complaining American schoolteachers. Frankness in dealing with his emotional problems as first he is pursued by a young sexpot in the party, then his involvement with the aggressive, man-hungry hotel owner and a sensitive, itinerant artist traveling with her 97-year-old grandfather, produces compassionate undertones finely realized. Burton has stature as he progresses to the point of a near-mental crack-up. Gardner, in the earthy role of the proprietress, is a gutsy figure. Kerr lends warm conviction as a helpless creature yet endowed with certain innate strength.

1964: Best B&W Costume Design
Nominations: Best Supp. Actress (Grayson Hall), B&W Cinematography, B&W Art Direction

NIGHT OF THE JUGGLER
1980, 100 mins, US ⓥ

D: Robert Butler **A:** James Brolin, Cliff Gorman, Richard Castellano, Abby Bluestone, Dan Hedaya, Julie Carmen (Columbia)

A relentlessly preposterous picture that never gives its cast a chance to overcome director Robert Butler's passion for mindless action. This is supposed to be the story of James Brolin's frantic pursuit of a kidnapper who grabs his daughter and takes off with her in a car. But who cares, if the performers are never allowed to make the characters come true?

NIGHT OF THE LIVING DEAD
1968, 90 mins, US ⓥ ⊙

D: George A. Romero **A:** Judith O'Dea, Russell Streiner, Duane Jones, Karl Hardman, Keith Wayne (Image Ten)

Although pic's basic premise is repellent—recently dead bodies are resurrected and begin killing human beings in order to eat their flesh—it is in execution that the film distastefully excels. No brutalizing stone is left unturned. The rest of the pic is amateurism of the first order. Pittsburgh-based director George A. Romero appears incapable of contriving a single graceful setup, and his cast is uniformly poor.

NIGHT OF THE LIVING DEAD
1990, 89 mins, US ⓥ ⊙

D: Tom Savani **A:** Tony Wood, Patricia Tallman, Tom Towles, McKee Anderson, William Butler, Katie Finnerman (21st Century)

The original producers of *Night of the Living Dead* have remade their own cult classic in a crass bit of cinematic grave robbing. The story faithfully follows the original except for the bonehead decision to replace the ending with a "meaningful" twist that reeks of pretentiousness. The plot still involves seven people trapped in a farmhouse fending off hordes of walking corpses intent on devouring them.

NIGHT ON EARTH
1992, 130 mins, US ⓥ ⊙

D: Jim Jarmusch **A:** Winona Ryder, Gena Rowlands, Giancarlo Esposito, Armin Mueller-Stahl, Beatrice Dalle, Roberto Benigni (JVC/Locus Solus)

Jim Jarmusch covers in five separate segments his favorite theme of lonely people interacting but ultimately facing the great void alone. Opening L.A. segment is pic's weakest, as tomboyish cabbie Winona Ryder is matched against her patrician passenger Gena Rowlands. Contrasting with this is a powerful finale, set in Helsinki with Matti Pellonpaa genuinely moving as a cabbie pouring out his tragic story to a trio of drunken guys. En route to this somber finish, Jarmusch provides ebullient comedy in the hilarious and unlikely team of Giancarlo Esposito and Armin Mueller-Stahl in New York as well as a goofy, all-stops-out monologue by Roberto Benigni as a Roman cabbie. Filming in the languages of each city results in a feature about 60 percent English subtitled.

NIGHT ON THE TOWN, A
See: Adventures in Babysitting

NIGHT PASSAGE
1957, 90 mins, US ▭

D: James Neilson **A:** James Stewart, Audie Murphy, Dan Duryea, Dianne Foster, Elaine Stewart, Brandon de Wilde (Universal)

Taut, well-made, and sometimes fascinating western. Borden Chase has fashioned a script around two brothers—James Stewart, decent, upright; Audie Murphy, wild, a deadly gunman. Pic was lensed in the Durango-Silverton region of Colorado. Plot carries a railroad-building backdrop. Both stars deliver sound portrayals, Murphy making up in color Stewart's greater footage. Dan Duryea is immense as outlaw chief who isn't quite certain whether he can outdraw Murphy, a wizard with a gun.

NIGHT PEOPLE
1954, 93 mins, US ▭
D: Nunnally Johnson A: Gregory Peck, Broderick Crawford, Anita Bjork, Rita Gam, Walter Abel, Buddy Ebsen (20th Century-Fox)

Topnotch, exciting cloak-and-dagger thriller, modernly paced and with a contemporary feel, which tells of the kidnaping of a young American soldier and how a CIC officer manages to get him back safely to the western zone by being quicker witted than the GI's captors and their agents. Peck plays the colonel and how he brings off the rescue makes for plenty of suspense-laden and credibly conceived footage.

NIGHT PORTER, THE
1974, 115 mins, US/Italy ⓥ ⊙
D: Liliana Cavani A: Dirk Bogarde, Charlotte Rampling, Philippe Leroy, Gabriele Ferzetti, Isa Miranda (United Artists)

Liliana Cavani deals with the ambivalent relationship between a concentration camp victim (Charlotte Rampling) and her torturer-lover (Dirk Bogarde) in a strange, brooding tale. They meet accidentally, but the past and a group of still-ardent Nazis force them to revert to their camp relationship. Bogarde treads intelligently through his role of an unbalanced man.

NIGHT SHIFT
1982, 105 mins, US ⓥ ⊙
D: Ron Howard A: Henry Winkler, Michael Keaton, Shelley Long, Gina Hecht, Pat Corley (Ladd)

Nerdy Henry Winkler is a meek attendant at the city morgue who must work the night shift with Looney Tune Michael Keaton—the type of guy who talks nonstop as he blasts rock songs on the radio while dancing up and down the aisles. Winkler befriends Shelley Long, the perennial "nice-girl hooker" who happens to have just lost her pimp. It's not long before Winkler and Keaton devise a scheme to act as pimps for Long using the morgue as a base of operation. Director Ron Howard and screenwriters Lowell Ganz and Babaloo Mandel are bent on giving the audience a good time.

NIGHT THE PROWLER, THE
1978, 90 mins, Australia
D: Jim Sharman A: Ruth Cracknell, John Frawley, Kerry Walker, John Derum, Maggie Kirkpatrick (Chariot)

A young woman (Kerry Walker) moves into adulthood as an overweight, sullen, neurotic, and ill-mannered daughter of a couple of middle-class stereotypes. She fakes (or misinterprets) a visit from a prowler—in her version—with rape in mind. She goes through a series of increasingly demoralizing changes, finally emerging as a leather-clad night prowler on her own.

NIGHT THEY RAIDED MINSKY'S, THE
1968, 100 mins, US ⓥ
D: William Friedkin A: Jason Robards, Britt Ekland, Norman Wisdom, Forrest Tucker, Harry Andrews, Joseph Wiseman (United Artists/Tandem)

Norman Lear's period peek at a peculiarly American form of entertainment—burlesque—is most successful in its art direction and nostalgic recapturing of New York's Lower East Side during its most hoydenish period. So easily does Norman Wisdom dominate the many scenes he's in that the other cast members suffer by comparison, particularly leading man Jason Robards, who's cast as the top banana in the Minsky burlesque theater.

NIGHT TIDE
1961, 85 mins, US ⓥ
D: Curtis Harrington A: Dennis Hopper, Linda Lawson, Gavin Muir, Luana Anders (American International/Filmgroup-Virgo)

Curtis Harrington, one-time avant-garde filmmaker, mixes a love affair with the supernatural. If Harrington displays a good flair for narration and mounting, his feel for mood, suspense, and atmospherics is not too highly developed. A sailor meets a girl who works as a mermaid in a sideshow on the amusement pier. It develops into love but there is a strangeness in her comportment. Her guardian tells the sailor that she is really a mermaid. Dennis Hopper is acceptably bewildered by his plight while Linda Lawson has the exotic looks for the psychotic siren.

NIGHT TO REMEMBER, A
1958, 123 mins, UK ⓥ
D: Roy Ward Baker A: Kenneth More, Honor Blackman, Anthony Bushell, Jill Dixon, Jane Downs, Michael Goodliffe (Rank)

Producer William MacQuitty and director Roy [Ward] Baker have done an honest job in putting the tragic sinking of the *Titanic* in 1912 on the screen with an impressive, almost documentary flavor. The film takes only 37 minutes less than the time of the actual disaster. The errors and confusion which played a part in the drama are brought out with no whitewashing. Although many of the passengers and crew come vividly to life, there has been no attempt to hang a fictional story on any of them. Dialogue is natural, devoid of undue sentimentality and without needless humor dragged in for light relief. The main problem here is that the story is too familiar to most people for there to be any element of suspense.

NIGHT TRAIN TO MUNICH
1940, 95 mins, UK ⊘
D: Carol Reed **A:** Margaret Lockwood, Rex Harrison, Paul Henreid, Basil Radford, Naunton Wayne (Gaumont-British)

Story opens in the tense days of August 1939 with a Nazi espionage agent in London capturing two Czechs, an aged armorplate inventor and his pretty daughter. A British Secret Service operative follows them to Berlin and escapes with them into Switzerland. Yarn is not only told without a single letdown but it actually continues to pile up suspense to a nerve-clutching pitch. The headlong chase and escape at the end is a time-tested melodramatic device superbly handled. Lockwood is an appealing heroine and her performance is direct and persuasive. Rex Harrison is properly suave as the ubiquitous British operative, while Paul Henreid is rightly cold as the treacherous Gestapo agent, Radford and Wayne repeat their goofy Britisher performances of *Lady Vanishes* and again click. There are countless touches of atmosphere and comedy that add immeasurable flavor and zest to the picture.

NIGHT UNTO NIGHT
1949, 84 mins, US
D: Don Siegel **A:** Ronald Reagan, Viveca Lindfors, Broderick Crawford, Rosemary DeCamp (Warner)

Night unto Night ventures into a dramatic theme rarely more than hinted at on the screen—epilepsy. Picture's major strength comes from the performance of Viveca Lindfors, but it is not enough to carry the film. Plot brings together a young man, who has just learned he is suffering from epilepsy, and a woman, still grieving over the loss of her husband.

NIGHT WARNING
1983, 94 mins, US ⊘
D: William Asher **A:** Jimmy McNichol, Susan Tyrrell, Bo Svenson, Marcia Lewis, Julia Duffy, Britt Leach (S2D Associates/Royal American)

A fine psychological horror film. As the maniacally possessive aunt and guardian of a 17-year-old boy, Susan Tyrrell gives a tour-de-force performance. Billy (Jimmy McNichol) is a basketball player at high school who has been brought up by his aunt Cheryl (Tyrrell). The film's horror content begins (replete with slow-motion violence and plenty of blood) when she kills a young TV repairman after failing to seduce him. Cop on the case, Detective Carlson (Bo Svenson) makes Billy the prime suspect instead of his aunt.

NIGHT WATCH
1973, 105 mins, UK ⊘
D: Brian G. Hutton **A:** Elizabeth Taylor, Laurence Harvey, Billie Whitelaw, Robert Lang, Tony Britton (Brut)

Average stage play turned into a better-than-average film. Astute direction and an improved cast more than help. Elizabeth Taylor dominates the doings. Director Brian G. Hutton makes the most of the suggested violence in the film and that is where it remains, suggested, until a brouhaha among the film's three principals at the end. The biggest demand on credibility is believing that anyone would want to leave the beautiful Taylor. It suggests madness on the part of husband Laurence Harvey (first-rate in the role).

NIGHT WE NEVER MET, THE
1993, 99 mins, US ⊙
D: Warren Leight **A:** Matthew Broderick, Annabella Sciorra, Kevin Anderson, Jeanne Tripplehorn, Justine Bateman (Miramax)

A quintessential New York movie takes a novel premise—time-sharing a Greenwich Village apartment by days of the week—and develops it in fits and starts. Hissable yuppie Kevin Anderson is behind the scheme, wanting two nights out a week with his buddies while living with patrician fiancée, Justine Bateman. One customer is Matthew Broderick, moping over losing his girlfriend (Jeanne Tripplehorn). Third tenant is housewife Annabella Sciorra, who uses it to get away from her dense husband (Michael Mantell). Unfortunately, it's not really so much an ensemble piece as a film of alternating casts or vignettes.

NIJINSKY
1980, 125 mins, UK ⊙

D: Herbert Ross A: Alan Bates, George De La Pena, Leslie Browne, Alan Badel, Janet Suzman (Hera)

Male-to-male romantic tragedy takes the form of a broad flashback covering only two critical years (1912–13) in the young dancer's early twenties. Beginning with his mentor-lover Sergei Diaghilev (Alan Bates), the period charts Nijinsky's gradual allegiance to a wealthy homosexual patron—brilliantly etched by Alan Badel; and the successful attempt of Hungarian aristocrat Romola de Pulsky (Leslie Browne) to catch Nijinsky on his briefly heterosexual rebound from Diaghilev. George De La Pena has the intensity and ambiguous sexual aura to make him a credible Nijinsky.

NIKITA
(US: LA FEMME NIKITA)
1990, 115 mins, France/Italy ⊙ ⊙ ⊡

D: Luc Besson A: Anne Parillaud, Jean-Hugues Anglade, Tcheky Karyo, Jeanne Moreau, Jean Reno (Gaumont/Tiger)

An absurd, shrill, ultraviolent but soft-centered urban thriller about a pretty, young, cop-killing junkie who's reeducated as a crack secret service agent, with license to kill. Anne Parillaud does her frenetic best to make Nikita something resembling a human being, but she remains a totally uninteresting figment of Besson's blinkered movieland imagination. Jeanne Moreau provides a touch of class in a small role as over-the-hill agent who tutors Parillaud in feminine graces. Jean Reno plays a killer with stone-faced parodic panache.

NIL BY MOUTH
1997, 128 mins, UK ⊙

D: Gary Oldman A: Ray Winstone, Kathy Burke, Charlie Creed-Miles, Laila Morse, Edna Dore, Chrissie Cotterill (SE8 Group)

Rough, tough but with an underlying generosity toward its characters, Gary Oldman's *Nil by Mouth* is an impressive writing-helming debut, a perf-driven portrait of a dysfunctional London working-class family. Raymond (Ray Winstone) is the brutish, foul-mouthed husband of Val (Kathy Burke) and brother-in-law of young Billy (Charlie Creed-Miles), with whom he has an edgy relationship. Also around are Val and Billy's mother (Laila Morse) and grandmother (Edna Dore). When Raymond kicks Billy out, the young kid, who has a drug habit, is forced to survive outside the family circle. In a fit of jealousy, Raymond savagely beats the pregnant Val, prompting a show of female solidarity. Winstone, a former boxer, dominates the film with an intensely focused performance. Though the movie stands on its performances, Oldman has wrapped them in an edgy directorial style that alternates between hand-held, *vérité* lensing, and moments of remarkable stillness.

NINE 1/2 WEEKS
1986, 113 mins, US ⊙ ⊙

D: Adrian Lyne A: Mickey Rourke, Kim Basinger, Margaret Whitton, David Margulies, Karen Young (PSO/Kimmel/Barish/Jonesfilm/Galactic/Triple Ajaxxx)

The film is about the crazy, overwhelming attachment a successful Wall Street type and a beautiful art gallery employee have to one another, and nothing else. The virtual absence of anything interesting happening between them—like plausible attraction, exotic, amazing sex, or, God forbid, good dialogue—leaves one great big hole on the screen for two hours. Mickey Rourke is less than totally convincing as a big businessman, but Kim Basinger manages to retain a certain dignity.

NINE HOURS TO RAMA
1963, 125 mins, US ⊡

D: Mark Robson A: Horst Buchholz, Jose Ferrer, Valerie Gearon, Don Borisenko, Robert Morley (20th Century-Fox)

At the core, this dramatization of circumstances surrounding the assassination of Mahatma Gandhi is an achievement of insight and impact. As the perpetrator, Horst Buchholz delivers a performance of intensity and conviction. Jose Ferrer is excellent as a conscientious police superintendent guarding Gandhi against disheartening odds. An astonishingly accurate personification of the latter is etched by J. S. Casshyap. The story falls down in its development and clarification of certain secondary characters, among them the assassin's unwilling accomplice (Don Borisenko), a baffling Indian politico (Robert Morley), and an impulsive prostitute (Diane Baker).

NINE LIVES OF FRITZ THE CAT, THE
1974, 76 mins, US ⊙

D: Robert Taylor (American International)

Fritz the Cat is back again. The synthetic troublemaker and dilettante revolutionary was a trifle anachronistic when he first hit the screens in 1972. He is even more so in *The Nine Lives of Fritz the Cat*. The animated production utilizes several random flashback and flash-forward sequences within the framework of Fritz being chewed out by his wife and lapsing into reveries.

NINE MONTHS
1995, 102 mins, US Ⓥ ⊙
D: Chris Columbus **A:** Hugh Grant, Julianne Moore, Tom Arnold, Joan Cusack, Jeff Goldblum, Robin Williams (1492/20th Century-Fox)

An innocuously funny, audience-pleasing comedy very much tailored around the cuddly charm and boyish good looks of Hugh Grant. Grant stars as a breezy young man who's got it all—red Porsche, San Francisco apartment with a bay view and a lovely girlfriend of five years, Rebecca Taylor (Julianne Moore). When Rebecca announces she's pregnant, Samuel runs his fancy car off the road in shock. Unable to summon the nerve to tell his beloved he simply doesn't want the kid, Samuel starts suffering from discarded-mate/praying mantis nightmares. Grant does lay on the mugging and facial contortions a bit thick at times, but his debonair manner and appealing personality do a lot to put the film over.

1984
.1956, 90 mins, UK
D: Michael Anderson **A:** Michael Redgrave, Edmond O'Brien, Jan Sterling, David Kossoff, Mervyn Johns, Donald Pleasence (Holiday/Associated British)

A sinister glimpse of the future as envisaged by George Orwell, *1984* is a grim, depressing picture. London, the setting for the story, is the capital of Oceania and is run by a ruthless regime, the heads of which are members of the inner party while their supporters are in the outer party. There are ministries of Love and Thought, antisex leagues and record divisions where the speeches of the great are rewritten from time to time to suit the needs of contemporary events. The story is built around the illegal romance of two members of the outer party.

NINETEEN EIGHTY-FOUR
1984, 120 mins, UK Ⓥ ⊙
D: Michael Radford **A:** John Hurt, Richard Burton, Suzanna Hamilton, Cyril Cusack, Gregor Fisher (Virgin/Umbrella)

This unremitting downer introduces no touches of comedy or facile sensationalism to soften a harsh depiction of life under a totalitarian system as imagined by George Orwell in 1948. Richard Burton is splendid as inner-party official O'Brien. Ironically, his swan-song performance as the deceptively gentle spur to Winston Smith's "thought-crimes," and then as the all-knowing interrogator who takes on the attributes of a father figure to the helpless man, is something new in Burton's repertoire.

1941
1979, 118 mins, US Ⓥ ⊙ ▭
D: Steven Spielberg **A:** Dan Aykroyd, Ned Beatty, John Belushi, Toshiro Mifune, Nancy Allen, Robert Stack (Universal/Columbia/A-Team)

Billed as a comedy spectacle, *1941* is long on spectacle but short on comedy—an exceedingly entertaining, fast-moving revision of 1940s war hysteria in Los Angeles spawned by the bombing of Pearl Harbor. Dan Aykroyd is very impressive in his feature debut as the serious army sergeant, but John Belushi turns in a snarling, obnoxious performance. Real cast standouts are Bobby DiCicco, who spends the pic wrestling pretty Diane Kay away from horny soldier Treat Williams; Robert Stack as a bemused general; Nancy Allen as the airborne inamorata of Tim Matheson; Wendie Jo Sperber as a frustrated femme; and Joseph P. Flaherty as a croony forties emcee.

1979: Nominations: Best Cinematography, Sound, Visual Effects

1900
See: Novecento

1969
1988, 90 mins, US Ⓥ ⊙
D: Ernest Thompson **A:** Robert Downey Jr., Kiefer Sutherland, Bruce Dern, Mariette Hartley, Winona Ryder, Joanna Cassidy (Atlantic)

One of the murkiest reflections on the Vietnam War era yet, notwithstanding good performances all around and bright packaging of Kiefer Sutherland and Robert Downey Jr. in the leads.

Director-screenwriter Ernest Thompson (*On Golden Pond*) has a wonderful feel for the relationships. It's only when it comes time to deliver a screen-size story that things go goofy. College students and best pals Scott (Sutherland) and Ralph (Downey) hit the road in a psychedelic van to taste America in their last "summer of innocence."

9/30/55
(AKA: SEPTEMBER 30, 1955)
1977, 101 mins, US ⊙ ▭
D: James Bridges **A:** Richard Thomas, Susan Tyrrell, Deborah Benson, Lisa Blount, Tom Hulce, Dennis Quaid (Universal)

Title is the date of the car-crash death of James Dean, and James Bridges's original script tells of the impact on Richard Thomas, starring in an excellent performance as a small-town Arkansas college kid whose life is permanently transformed by the incident. Thomas helps commemorate Dean's demise with booze and mock-occult mysticism, leading to a prank on other students.

NINE TO FIVE
1980, 110 mins, US Ⓥ ⊙
D: Colin Higgins **A:** Jane Fonda, Lily Tomlin, Dolly Parton, Dabney Coleman, Sterling Hayden, Elizabeth Wilson (IPC/ 20th Century-Fox)

This picture is a lot of fun. Story concerns a group of office workers (Lily Tomlin, the all-knowing manager who trained the boss but can't get promoted; Jane Fonda, the befuddled newcomer; and Dolly Parton, the alluring personal secretary) who band together to seek revenge on the man who is making their professional lives miserable. Tomlin comes off best in the most appealing role as the smart yet underappreciated glue in the office cement.
1980: Nomination: Best Song ("Nine to Five")

99 AND 44/100% DEAD
1974, 97 mins, US Ⓥ ▭
D: John Frankenheimer **A:** Richard Harris, Edmond O'Brien, Bradford Dillman, Ann Turkel, Constance Ford, Chuck Connors (20th Century-Fox)

Director John Frankenheimer struggles with Robert Dillon's sophomoric, repulsive screenplay about gang warfare, but pyrrhic victory eludes him. Hired killer Richard Harris enters a mythical, futuristic city and hunts down mob kingpin Bradford Dillman for rival gangster Edmond O'Brien's peace of mind. For a short while Dillon seems to have parody on his mind. Unfortunately, Dillon has neither the wit nor the invention to sustain this tone for more than a few reels.

NINGEN NO JOKEN I-II
(US: THE HUMAN CONDITION;
THE HUMAN CONDITION, PART I:
NO GREATER LOVE)
1959, 208 mins, Japan Ⓥ ▭
D: Masaki Kobayashi **A:** Tatsuya Nakadai, Michiyo Aratama, So Yamamura, Eitaro Ozawa, Akira Ishihama (Shochiku)

Picture's main claim to fame is that it's the first to be seen on this side that portrays the Japanese war machine as seen by Japanese. The drama is candid and stark; unfortunately, it is also lightly motivated, overlong, and haphazardly edited. Story is set in 1943 with southern Manchuria as its locale. Protagonist is an idealistic young Japanese, Kaji (Tatsuya Nakadai), who takes a post as a labor overseer at an isolated mine to escape army service. Troubles arise when the guy tries to improve the lot of the labor force and objects to the treatment given to 600 Chinese POWs who are brought in to dig. [Version reviewed was a 138-min. one for US release in 1959.]

NINGEN NO JOKEN III-IV
(US: THE HUMAN CONDITION,
PART II: THE ROAD TO
ETERNITY)
1960, 181 mins, Japan Ⓥ ▭
D: Masaki Kobayashi **A:** Tatsuya Nakadai, Michiyo Aratama, Keiji Sada, Hideo Kisho, Jun Tatara (Shochiku)

This is the second part of Masaki Kobayashi's great and monumental trilogy concerning the dilemma of a young Japanese who is forced to play a part in war, yet is the loser whichever side he takes. The mentality of the Imperial Army of Japan, the brutalities and stupidities of army life, the way men act when facing violent death, and the way men are reduced to bestiality by killing and primitive treatment, are the elements which make this slow-moving tragedy so compelling and piercing.

NINGEN NO JOKEN V-VI
(US: THE HUMAN CONDITION,
PART III: A SOLDIER'S PRAYER)
1961, 190 mins, Japan Ⓥ ▭
D: Masaki Kobayashi **A:** Tatsuya Nakadai, Michiyo Aratama, Taketoshi Naito, Keijiro Morozumi, Yusuke Kawazu (Shochiku)

A Soldier's Prayer shows the final disillusionment in the three-year agony of the simple Japanese soldier who endures much, only to end by losing everything. Sick and weary, Kagi (Tatsuya Nakadai) gives himself up to the Russians, under the impression that the conquerors will surely dispense a more humane rule than the Imperial Japanese Army. But once again his illusions are shattered. If there is any weakness in the writing or playing of the part of Kagi, it is that he seems to lack spiritual motivation.

NINJA III
THE DOMINATION
1984, 95 mins, US Ⓥ

D: Sam Firstenberg **A:** Sho Kosugi, Lucinda Dickey, Jordan Bennett, David Chung, Dale Ishimoto (Cannon)

With Ninja III producers reunite members of the team that made their second entry in the martial arts series about the more deadly cousins of the samurai. The new outing into the never-never land of the world's trickiest controlled violence is done with quite a twist. The twist has several quite humorous aspects, the least of which being that most of the ninja action is performed by a woman (Lucinda Dickey).

NINOTCHKA
1939, 111 mins, US Ⓥ ⊙

D: Ernst Lubitsch **A:** Greta Garbo, Melvyn Douglas, Bela Lugosi, Sig Ruman, Felix Bressart (M-G-M)

Selection of Ernst Lubitsch to pilot Garbo in her first light performance in pictures proves a bull's-eye. The punchy and humorous jabs directed at the Russian political system and representatives, and the contrast of Bolshevik receptiveness to capitalistic luxuries and customs, are displayed in farcical vein. Three Russian trade representatives arrive in Paris to dispose of royal jewels "legally confiscated." Playboy Melvyn Douglas, intent on cutting himself in for part of the jewel sale, is confronted by special envoy Garbo who arrives to speed the transactions. Douglas gets romantic, while Garbo treats love as a biological problem.

1939: Nominations: Best Picture, Actress (Greta Garbo), Original Story, Screenplay

NINTH CONFIGURATION, THE
1980, 105 mins, US Ⓥ ⊙

D: William Peter Blatty **A:** Stacy Keach, Scott Wilson, Jason Miller, Neville Brand, Moses Gunn, Robert Loggia (Warner)

Stacy Keach limns an army colonel who has been brought Stateside to play psychiatrist to a compound of disturbed military men. From the beginning it's apparent Keach is infinitely more disturbed

than any of the men he is supposed to be treating, making the actor's monotone, robotlike state unbearably grating on the nerves only minutes after his appearance.

NINTH GATE, THE
1999, 127 mins, France/Spain Ⓥ ⊙ ⊟

D: Roman Polanski **A:** Johnny Depp, Frank Langella, Lena Olin, Emmanuelle Seigner, Barbara Jefford, Jack Taylor (RP/Orly/TF1/Kino Vision/Origen)

Roman Polanski's The Ninth Gate is a sardonic detective thriller peppered with carefully crafted pleasures. Its giddy, ironic tone may throw viewers expecting a scary movie. Powerful New Yorker Boris Balkan (Frank Langella), hell-bent on completing his collection of rare books concerning Lucifer, commissions ambitious young broker Dean Corso (Johnny Depp) to track down two special tomes. Meanwhile, the recently widowed Liana Telfer (Lena Olin) doesn't know that her late spouse sold one of only three known copies of The Nine Gates of the Kingdom of Shadows to a fellow collector the day before. As a street-smart American able to beat erudite Europeans at their own game, Depp is a good choice. Olin does her determined-hellcat routine with gusto, Langella convinces even in pic's loonier moments, and Shakespearean vet Barbara Jefford is terrific as a baroness in Paris.

NIXON
1995, 190 mins, US Ⓥ ⊙ ⊟

D: Oliver Stone **A:** Anthony Hopkins, Joan Allen, Powers Boothe, Ed Harris, Bob Hoskins, E. G. Marshall (Illusion/Cinergi/Hollywood)

Nixon far overstays its welcome. Beginning with the cause and effect of Watergate, pic slides back in time to Nixon's loss to JFK in the 1960 election, and finally back to 1925, with young Dick Nixon in Whittier. Storytelling jumps around willy-nilly in the early going. On it goes, through Nixon's dubious Cuban criminal connections that led to his links with the Watergate plumbers, his complicity with J. Edgar Hoover, and his winning the presidency on the promise of ending the Vietnam War. Anthony Hopkins is physically and vocally just not entirely convincing. Joan Allen gives her Pat Nixon a surprising dimensionality and often touching humanity.

1995: Nominations: Best Actor (Anthony Hopkins), Supporting Actress (Joan Allen), Original Screenplay, Original Dramatic Score

NOAH'S ARK
THE STORY OF THE DELUGE
1928, 135 mins, US
D: Michael Curtiz **A:** Dolores Costello, George O'Brien, Noah Beery, Guinn Williams, Myrna Loy (Warner)

The Warner staff show everything conceivable under the sun—mobs, mobs, and mobs; Niagaras of water; train wreck; war aplenty; crashes; deluges and everything. Nothing is missed from way back when folks thought that praying to the real God instead of Jehovah was the right thing until Noah got the message from above that it was not. Talk does not enter into the picture until after the first 35 minutes. It starts with a love scene between George O'Brien and Dolores Costello. The Costello voice hurts the impression made by her silent acting.

NOBI
(US: FIRES ON THE PLAIN)
1959, 100 mins, Japan ⓥ ▭
D: Kon Ichikawa **A:** Eiji Funakoshi, Mantaro Ushio, Yoshihiro Hamaguchi, Osamu Takizawa, Mickey Curtis (Daiei)

One of the most searing comments on war yet made. Story covers the defeat of the Imperial Japanese Army during the Philippine campaign in the last World War. A ragged remnant is warned that the Americans will slaughter them, and so start a trek through the jungles to the sea. It is all seen through the eyes of one tubercular Japanese soldier whose approaching death has put him above it all. He manages to maintain a semblance of humanity to keep him from sinking to the cannibalism of many of his fellow soldiers.

NOBODY LIVES FOREVER
1946, 100 mins, US
D: Jean Negulesco **A:** John Garfield, Geraldine Fitzgerald, Walter Brennan, Faye Emerson, George Coulouris (Warner)

The old gangster reformation theme. John Garfield is seen as a drafted mobster, intent on a long vacation from war duties, who is talked into taking a wealthy widow for a large slice of her inheritance. The gangster falls for the gal he's trying to take. John Garfield's performance gives the picture a considerable lift.

NOBODY RUNS FOREVER
(US: THE HIGH COMMISSIONER)
1968, 101 mins, UK ⓥ
D: Ralph Thomas **A:** Rod Taylor, Christopher Plummer, Lilli Palmer, Camilla Sparv, Daliah Lavi (Rank)

Undemanding melodrama with political undertones. Rod Taylor is an Australian police officer sent to London to arrest the Australian High Commissioner on a charge of murdering his first wife. The commissioner (Christopher Plummer) is holding peace talks in London and courteously, but obstinately, refuses to go back to Australia until his mission is completed. Taylor becomes reluctantly involved as bodyguard and the job becomes trickier as he becomes more convinced that the commissioner is not guilty.

NOBODY'S FOOL
1986, 107 mins, US ⓥ ⊙
D: Evelyn Purcell **A:** Rosanna Arquette, Eric Roberts, Mare Winningham, Jim Youngs, Louise Fletcher (Island/Katz-Denny)

Kookiness without real comedy, romance without magic. Rosanna Arquette, a small-town western girl, attends dutifully to her burned-out mother and bratty younger brother as she tries to forget the public shame she endured when she impulsively stabbed her old beau in a restaurant. Eric Roberts, the lighting technician with a visiting theatrical troupe, begins quietly noticing her.

NOBODY'S FOOL
1994, 110 mins, US ⓥ ⊙
D: Robert Benton **A:** Paul Newman, Jessica Tandy, Bruce Willis, Melanie Griffith, Dylan Walsh (Paramount/Cinehaus)

A gentle, flavorsome story of a loose-knit dysfunctional family whose members essentially include every glimpsed citizen of a small New York town. Fronted by a splendid performance from Paul Newman as a spirited man who has made nothing of his life, Robert Benton's character-driven film is sprinkled with small pleasures. Playing 10 years younger than his real age with no problem, Newman delivers one of his most engaging performances in years, the sort of old coot to be found in every small town. In her second-to-last role, Tandy has some ominous initial lines, saying "I've got a feeling God's creeping in on me. I've got a feeling this is the year he'll lower the boom." Willis delivers a tangy turn.

1994: Nominations: Actor (Paul Newman), Adapted Screenplay

NOBODY WAVED GOODBYE
1964, 80 mins, Canada
D: Don Owen **A:** Peter Kastner, Julie Biggs, Claude Rae, Toby Tarnow, Charmion King (National Film Board of Canada)

This is a simple story, simply told, about a couple of Toronto juves, the boy typically smart-alecky, the girl attractive, decent, and naive. From truancy and petty offenses, the road is downhill until by fadeout the young couple is split, the girl pregnant, and the boy having to decide whether to go back and face the music for theft while there's still time to rehabilitate himself. Peter Kastner and Julie Biggs are naturally charming enough to get away with momentary lapses in their performance.

NOCTURNE
1946, 86 mins, US Ⓥ ⊙
D: Edwin L. Marin **A:** George Raft, Lynn Bari, Virginia Huston (RKO)

Detective thriller with action and suspense plentiful and hard-bitten mood of story. George Raft is seen as hard-boiled detective lieutenant whose stubbornness leads to uncovering a murder previously tagged a suicide. He gives his usual, slow-paced, tough touch to assignment to make it thoroughly effective.

NOISES OFF
1992, 104 mins, US Ⓥ ⊙
D: Peter Bogdanovich **A:** Carol Burnett, Michael Caine, Denholm Elliott, Julie Hagerty, Marilu Henner, Christopher Reeve (Touchstone/Amblin)

Michael Frayn's play centered on a theatrical company bumbling through the British provinces in a silly sex comedy, *Nothing On.* In Marty Kaplan's smart adaptation, the company is an American troupe working toward a New York opening. Action is framed—and the acts are divided—by director Michael Caine fretting outside a Broadway theater during the opening-night performance. Bogdanovich has judged his approach to the material astutely, resisting impulses toward comic overkill.

NOMADS
1985, 100 mins, US Ⓥ
D: John McTiernan **A:** Pierce Brosnan, Lesley-Anne Down, Anna-Maria Montecelli, Adam Ant, Hector Mercado (PSO/Kastner/Cinema 7)

Nomads avoids the more obvious ripped-guts devices in favor of dramatic visual scares. Everything seems to come naturally in a tale that even has the supernatural ring true. Pierce Brosnan plays a French anthropologist who intends to settle in L.A. with his wife (Anna-Maria Montecelli), when flesh-and-blood (seemingly) evil spirits of nomads he once studied materialize to haunt him.

NO MAN OF HER OWN
1932, 75 mins, US Ⓥ ⊙
D: Wesley Ruggles **A:** Clark Gable, Carole Lombard, Dorothy Mackaill, Grant Mitchell, Elizabeth Patterson (Paramount)

Gable is a swank card gyp who hits the trail heavy for the women. Gable was under loan to Paramount for this one, his first away from the Metro apron strings. Story revolves around a crooked gambler who marries a small-town girl on a bet and finally does time in order to clear the mud off his feet for her.

NO MAN OF HER OWN
1950, 97 mins, US
D: Mitchell Leisen **A:** Barbara Stanwyck, John Lund, Phyllis Thaxter, Lyle Bettger, Jane Cowl (Paramount)

Combines an adult love story with melodrama, and is altogether satisfying screen dramatics. Barbara Stanwyck does a beautiful job of portraying a girl who has been kicked out by her lover after becoming pregnant. She takes advantage of a train accident to assume the identity of a fellow passenger killed in the wreck and moves in with the latter's in-laws to assure her son a home. John Lund wraps up his role as the man who falls in love with a girl he believes to be the widow of his dead brother.

NO MAN'S LAND
1987, 106 mins, US Ⓥ ⊙
D: Peter Werner **A:** Charlie Sheen, D. B. Sweeney, Randy Quaid, Lara Harris, Bill Duke (Orion)

Stylish thriller about a lower-class rookie cop becoming caught up in the fast-lane high life of the filthy-rich car thief he's assigned to nail. Charlie Sheen and D. B. Sweeney are both extremely effective as two young men, barely into their twenties, whose diametrically opposed backgrounds make for a dynamic and ultimately deadly relationship. A little joy-riding and partying with the handsome, crafty Sheen easily seduces Sweeney into taking a softer view of illegal activity. He comes to like Sheen a lot and, further-more, gets sexually involved with the lat-ter's beautiful sister (Lara Harris).

NO MERCY
1986, 105 mins, US Ⓥ ⊙
D: Richard Pearce **A:** Richard Gere, Kim Basinger, Jeroen Krabbe, George Dzundza, William Atherton (Tri-Star Del-phi IV & V)

Despite some graphically brutal vio-lence and a fair bit of "too-cool" police jargon, *No Mercy* turns out to be a step above most other films in this blooming genre of lone-cop-turned-vigilante stories. Eddie Jillette (Richard Gere) and his part-ner, Joe Collins (Gary Basaraba), go un-dercover. Collins is murdered brutally. Jillette has only one lead in tracking his partner's murder, a mysterious blond (Kim Basinger).

NONE BUT THE BRAVE
1965, 105 mins, US/Japan Ⓥ ⊙ ▭
D: Frank Sinatra **A:** Frank Sinatra, Clint Walker, Tommy Sands, Bill Dexter, Tony Bill (Artanis/Tokyo Eiga-Toho)

Frank Sinatra makes his directorial bow and is responsible for some good ef-fects in maintaining a suspenseful pace. The compact and mostly tense screenplay tells its story through the eyes of a Japa-nese lieutenant, commanding a small de-tachment of troops forgotten on an uncharted South Pacific island where an American plane carrying US Marines crash lands. A truce is arranged after Si-natra, as a pharmacist's mate, amputates the leg of one of the Japanese soldiers wounded in a skirmish with the Ameri-cans.

NONE BUT THE LONELY HEART
1944, 110 mins, US Ⓥ
D: Clifford Odets **A:** Cary Grant, Ethel Barrymore, Barry Fitzgerald, June Duprez, Jane Wyatt, Dan Duryea (RKO)

With the sotto voce accent on any so-cial significance, *Heart* emerges as a med-ley of simple romance in London's East End, interspersed with a little melodrama. Cary Grant starts as a shiftless cockney who lets his struggling mother (Ethel Bar-rymore) fend for herself with her small secondhand shop until a pawnbroker friend (well underplayed by Konstantin Shayne) tips him off that his mother is dy-ing of cancer.
1944: Best Supp. Actress (Ethel Barry-more)

Nominations: Best Actor (Cary Grant), Editing, Scoring of a Dramatic Picture

NO, NO, NANETTE
1940, 96 mins, US
D: Herbert Wilcox **A:** Anna Neagle, Rich-ard Carlson, Victor Mature, Roland Young, Helen Broderick, ZaSu Pitts (Suf-folk/RKO Radio)

In making a film version of the 1925 Broadway hit, Herbert Wilcox saves all the book but very little of the music. Anna Neagle, as the little Miss Fix-It who sparks the film, is passable. Yarn finds Young a gay oldster with a penchant for making people happy, particularly pretty girls, by promising them help to get ahead in their fields. Neagle as Young's niece, sets about getting each of the femmes the things they wants, thus keeping from Young's wife the sordid details.

NOOSE HANGS HIGH, THE
1948, 77 mins, US
D: Charles Barton **A:** Lou Costello, Bud Abbott, Cathy Downs, Joseph Calleia, Leon Errol (Eagle Lion)

The Noose Hangs High gives Abbott and Costello full opportunity to display their fine slapstick art. Pic kicks off with window-washing setup that has the boys fumbling on a high window ledge. From there it moves into a mistaken-identity theme, involving comics with gambling syndicate and a missing $50,000 bet.

NORA PRENTISS
1947, 110 mins, US
D: Vincent Sherman **A:** Ann Sheridan, Kent Smith, Bruce Bennett, Robert Alda, Rosemary DeCamp (Warner)

Nora Prentiss is an overlong melo-drama, never quite believable. Ann Sher-idan makes much of her role but the production has unsympathetic slant for leads and a lack of smoothness. Yarn con-cerns a stuffy, middle-aged doctor who falls in love with a nightclub singer. To follow his love to New York, the doctor fakes death, destroying the body of a pa-tient and assuming the latter's identity. Later he's arrested for killing himself.

NORMA RAE
1979, 113 mins, US Ⓥ ⊙ ▭
D: Martin Ritt **A:** Sally Field, Beau Bridges, Ron Leibman, Pat Hingle, Gail Strickland (20th Century-Fox)

That rare entity, an intelligent film with heart, updating the traditional management-labor struggles to a sharp contemporary setting. Now the battle is being waged in southern textile mills, where the din of the machinery is virtually unbearable, and workers either go deaf or suffer the consumptive effects of "brown lung" disease. Ron Leibman arrives on the scene as a New York–based labor organizer, who picks Sally Field as his most likely convert. This unlikely pairing of Jewish radicalism and southern conservatism is made real and touching by the individual performances of Leibman and Field.

1979: Best Actress (Sally Field), Song ("It Goes Like This")
Nominations: Best Picture, Adapted Screenplay

EL NORTE
(US: THE NORTH)
1983, 139 mins, US Ⓥ
D: Gregory Nava A: Zaide Silvia Gutierrez, David Villalpando, Ernest Gomez Cruz, Alicia del Lago (American Playhouse/Independent)

Three-part film is beautifully lensed and comes across as a kind of giant Renaissance canvas. The Guatemalan seg introduces a closely knit family in a picturesque setting, but the paradise is deceiving. The 1982 military coup has led to a wave of political violence and terror, whereupon some 200,000 Guatemalans have sought refuge in Mexico or elsewhere "to the north." The Mexican seg deals with a brother and sister in search of a contact who might help them to cross the border illegally into California. This is the strongest of the three parts. The American seg finds the brother and sister living as Mexican illegals in Los Angeles.

NORTH, THE
See: El Norte

NORTH
1994, 88 mins, US Ⓥ
D: Rob Reiner A: Elijah Wood, Bruce Willis, Jon Lovitz, Matthew McCurley, Alan Arkin, Dan Aykroyd (Castle Rock)

Shaggy-dog tale. The single-named title character (Elijah Wood) is the perfect preteen, but his interaction with work-obsessed parents (Jason Alexander, Julia Louis-Dreyfus) is increasingly having a negative impact on his psyche. He meets a man dressed in an Easter bunny suit (Bruce Willis) who listens to his problem. An eccentric judge (Alan Arkin) rules that North must reconcile with his family or find suitable new parents within two months, otherwise he will be sent to an orphanage. The boy travels the globe in his quest.

NORTH BY NORTHWEST
1959, 136 mins, UK Ⓥ ☉
D: Alfred Hitchcock A: Cary Grant, Eva Marie Saint, James Mason, Jessie Royce Landis, Leo G. Carroll, Martin Landau (M-G-M)

The Alfred Hitchcock mixture—suspense, intrigue, comedy, humor—has seldom been served up so delectably. Cary Grant is a Madison Avenue man-about-Manhattan, sleekly handsome, carelessly twice-divorced, debonair as a cigarette ad. He's mistaken for a US intelligence agent by a pack of foreign agents headed by James Mason. The complications are staggering but they play like an Olympic version of a three-legged race. Grant's problem is to avoid getting knocked off by Mason's gang without tipping them that he is a classic case of the innocent bystander. The case is serious, but Hitchcock's macabre sense of humor and instinct for romantic byplay never allows it to stay grim for too long.

1959: Nominations: Best Original Story & Screenplay, Color Art Direction, Editing

NORTH DALLAS FORTY
1979, 119 mins, US Ⓥ ▭
D: Ted Kotcheff A: Nick Nolte, Mac Davis, Charles Durning, Dabney Coleman, Dayle Haddon, Bo Svenson (Paramount)

A most realistic, hard-hitting, and perceptive look at the seamy side of pro football. What distinguishes this screen adaptation of Peter Gent's bestseller is the exploration of a human dimension almost never seen in sports pix. And in large measure, that success is due to a bravura performance in the lead role by Nick Nolte. Ted Kotcheff has perfectly captured the locker-room intensity and postgame letdown that never shows up on the tube.

NORTHERN PURSUIT
1943, 93 mins, US Ⓥ
D: Raoul Walsh A: Errol Flynn, Julie Bishop, Helmut Dantine, John Ridgely, Gene Lockhart (Warner)

Yarn pits Errol Flynn as a heroic mountie against Nazi flyer Helmut Dantine, who's been dropped in the Hudson Bay region by a sub for a war mission in Canada. Snow-blanketed North is a fresh background for staging a Nazi spy chase, and full advantage is taken to blend the scenery with the dramatics.

NORTH SEA HIJACK
(US: FFOLKES)
1980, 99 mins, UK Ⓥ
D: Andrew V. McLaglen A: Roger Moore, James Mason, Anthony Perkins, Michael Parks (Universal)

A misogynist but dedicated frogman, whose private crew of frogmen are the only seeming rescuers of a hijacked supply ship, Roger Moore is ably supported by James Mason as a by-the-book admiral.

NORTH STAR, THE
1943, 105 mins, US Ⓥ
D: Lewis Milestone A: Anne Baxter, Dana Andrews, Walter Huston, Walter Brennan, Farley Granger, Erich von Stroheim (RKO)

Samuel Goldwyn as the producer and Lillian Hellman, the writer, team to tell of the Nazi invasion of the Soviet. The early parts of the film are almost always colorful in depicting the simple life of the villagers around whom this story revolves, but it's a question of too premeditatedly setting the stage of a simple, peace-loving people who, through the bestiality of the enemy, are driven to an heroic defense that must, in time, become legendary. For this is the story of the Soviet people as seen through the eyes of a small village.
1943: Nominations: Best Original Screenplay, B&W Cinematography, B&W Art Direction, Scoring of a Dramatic Picture, Sound, Special Effects

NORTH TO ALASKA
1960, 122 mins, US Ⓥ ⊙ ▭
D: Henry Hathaway A: John Wayne, Stewart Granger, Ernie Kovacs, Fabian, Capucine, Mickey Shaughnessy (20th Century-Fox)

Good-humored, old-fashioned, no-holds-barred, all-stops-out northern, a kind of rowdy second cousin to a not-very-adult western, must be accepted in absolutely the right spirit to be fully appreciated. The three brawls are classics of the cinematic art of make-believe pugilistics. It's the story of the successful Alaskan gold prospector who transports a girl from Seattle north to Alaska for his lovesick partner, then proceeds to fall in love with her, she with him. Wayne and Ernie Kovacs share comedy honors.

NORTHWEST FRONTIER
(US: FLAME OVER INDIA)
1959, 129 mins, UK Ⓥ ▭
D: J. Lee Thompson A: Kenneth More, Lauren Bacall, Herbert Lom, Wilfrid Hyde White, I. S. Johar, Ursula Jeans (Rank)

Ageless chase yarn, transferred from the prairie to the sun-baked plains of India, and done with a spectacular flourish. Time is the turn of the century when the English still held sway in India. Kenneth More plays an officer ordered to take a boy prince to safety in the teeth of Moslems. In company with an assorted group, More makes his getaway from a besieged citadel in a makeshift coach drawn by a worn-out locomotive.

NORTHWEST MOUNTED POLICE
1940, 125 mins, US
D: Cecil B. DeMille, Arthur Rosson, Eric Stacey A: Gary Cooper, Madeleine Carroll, Preston Foster, Paulette Goddard, Robert Preston, George Bancroft (Paramount)

The story is founded upon an incident of insurrection and bloodshed which took place in and around Regina in 1885, when Canadian troops finally subdued settlers' discontent and revolt. Gary Cooper, Texan Ranger in search of a murderer, finds himself in the middle of gunplay before the end of the second reel. Preston Foster as the sergeant-leader of the redcoats gets the better of Cooper in the contest for Madeleine Carroll. Foster has the girl and Cooper has George Bancroft, the heavy, tied up with his lariat and on his way back home.
1940: Best Editing
Nominations: Best Color Cinematography, Color Art Direction, Original Score, Sound

NORTHWEST PASSAGE
1940, 125 mins, US Ⓥ ⊙
D: King Vidor A: Spencer Tracy, Robert Young, Walter Brennan, Ruth Hussey, Nat Pendleton (M-G-M)

Fine epic adventure covers one expedition through upper New York State to the St. Lawrence territory where the village of a hostile tribe is wiped out. Spencer Tracy is brilliantly impressive as the dominating and driving leader of Rogers' Rangers, a band of 160 trained settlers inducted into service to clean up the hostile tribes to make homes and families safe. Robert Young, as the Harvardian who joins the Rangers to sketch Indians, turns in a fine performance. Walter Brennan provides a typically fine characterization as the friend of Young.
1940: Nomination: Best Color Cinematography

NOSFERATU
See: *Nosferatu: Eine Symphonie des Grauens*

NOSFERATU EINE SYMPHONIE DES GRAUENS
(US: NOSFERATU; NOSFERATU THE VAMPIRE)
1922, 70 mins, Germany ⓥ ⊚ ⊗
D: F. W. Murnau **A:** Max Schreck, Alexander Granach, Gustav von Wangenheim, Greta Schroeder, Karl Schnell (Parana)

Story is claimed to have been inspired by *Dracula*. Action details the forages of a nobleman who is dead yet alive, making nighttime raids on human beings and compelling them to become subservient to him by sucking the blood from their necks, often plaguing them to death. His especial delight is a pretty woman. Murnau is a master artisan demonstrating not only a knowledge of the subtler side of directing but in photography. Max Schreck as the vampire is an able pantomimist and works clocklike, his makeup suggesting everything that's goose pimply.

NOSFERATU THE VAMPIRE
See: *Nosferatu*

NO SMALL AFFAIR
1984, 102 mins, US ⓥ ⊚
D: Jerry Schatzberg **A:** Jon Cryer, Demi Moore, George Wendt, Peter Frechette, Elizabeth Daily (Columbia-Delphi II)

An okay coming-of-age romance in which the believability of the leading characters far outweighs that of many of the situations in which the script places them. Jon Cryer as a 16-year-old snaps a shot of a sharp-looking gal (Demi Moore) and finds her singing in a seedy North Beach night spot. He spends his entire lifesavings and gets her photo placed on top of 175 SF taxicabs.

NOSTRADAMUS
1995, 118 mins, UK/Germany ⓥ
D: Roger Christian **A:** Tcheky Karyo, F. Murray Abraham, Rutger Hauer, Amanda Plummer, Julia Ormond (Allied Entertainments/Vereinigte)

A gaudy tableau on an epic scale, *Nostradamus* is a disappointingly conventional biopic about the noted medieval scholar/prophet. Designed as a monument, this costume drama exhibits most of the sorrows of international productions: a rambling narrative, anachronistic language, and an unsuccessful blend of accents and acting styles. In the lead, handsome French thesp Tcheky Karyo acquits himself with a decent performance. Of the large international cast, Rutger Hauer is effective as a mad monk, F. Murray Abraham is for once effectively cast as the hero's mentor, and Amanda Plummer is so weird as Catherine de Medici that her lines almost sound campy.

NOT AS A STRANGER
1955, 135 mins, US
D: Stanley Kramer **A:** Olivia de Havilland, Robert Mitchum, Frank Sinatra, Gloria Grahame, Broderick Crawford, Charles Bickford (United Artists)

Producer Stanley Kramer took Morton Thompson's bestselling novel of a young doctor as the occasion of his own directorial debut. Charles Bickford comes near to stealing the picture. Gloria Grahame, as a neurotic widow with lots of money, also stands out. Frank Sinatra comes close to doing a little picture stealing. Robert Mitchum is poker-faced from start to finish.
1955: Nomination: Best Sound

NOTHING BUT THE BEST
1964, 99 mins, UK
D: Clive Donner **A:** Alan Bates, Denholm Elliott, Harry Andrews, Millicent Martin (Domino/Anglo Amalgamated)

This stylish British comedy is the story of an ambitious young man of humble background who is excited by the glitter of money, business power, and an entry into the fascinating world of hunt balls, Ascot, smart restaurants, shooting, hunting, fishin' and the rest of the trappings, and lies, bluffs, smiles, cheats, loves, and smooth-talks his way to marrying the boss's daughter, and doesn't stop at murder en route. Alan Bates, showing a previously unexplored vein of comedy, is first-class as the dubious hero.

NOTHING BUT TROUBLE
1944, 69 mins, US
D: Sam Taylor **A:** Stan Laurel, Oliver Hardy, Mary Boland, Philip Merivale, Henry O'Neill (M-G-M)

In the Depression era, Laurel and Hardy, descendants of a long line of cooks and butlers, are seeking employment against great odds. When convinced there isn't a job to be had in America, they hit on a tour of foreign lands. Same situation obtains there, and they return to America in the lush era of employment. They are grabbed by Mary Boland, social climber, to handle chores at a dinner in honor of the boy regent of a mythical kingdom.

NOTHING BUT TROUBLE
1991, 94 mins, US Ⓥ ⊙
D: Dan Aykroyd **A:** Chevy Chase, Dan Aykroyd, John Candy, Demi Moore (Warner/Applied Action)

Premise had potential: a faceless drive-through town seems to have no resident except the cop who miraculously appears to pinch unsuspecting drivers. The story turns into an extended maze with Chevy Chase and Demi Moore as the principal targets running through one tepid peril after another, while mouthing banal wisecracks.

NOTHING LASTS FOREVER
1984, 82 mins, US
D: Tom Schiller **A:** Zach Galligan, Apollonia van Ravenstein, Lauren Tom, Dan Aykroyd, Paul Rogers, Bill Murray (Broadway)

Forever is a film in black-and-white (with brief color sequences) mishmash of film styles of the 1940s, 1950s, and 1960s, with old newsreel clips, some from old films, plenty of panoramas and aerials of New York City, and surely one of the oddest love stories extant. A comedy (perhaps) with few laughs: the love story (and problems) of Adam Beckett, well played by Zach Galligan, is the only unifying cord evident. Beckett wants to be an artist in some future New York City that is ruled by the Port Authority, an institution that calls everyone to work, tells them when to stop, and regulates the influx of artists. He has a brief love affair with artsy Mara Hofmeier (Apollonia van Ravenstein). He inadvertently gets on a bus that turns out to be a Lunar cruiser, taking shoppers to the moon. . . .

NOTHING PERSONAL
1995, 86 mins, UK Ⓥ
D: Thaddeus O'Sullivan **A:** Ian Hart, John Lynch, James Frain, Michael Gambon, Gary Lydon (Little Bird/Channel 4)

An uncompromising depiction of the cult of sectarian violence, totally riveting drama is set in Belfast 20 years ago. A Loyalist (i.e., pro-British) paramilitary group is effectively run by the hotheaded Ginger (Ian Hart), a fanatical bigot for whom the only good Catholic is a dead one. The fanatical Protestants are contrasted with a Catholic, Liam Kelly (John Lynch), who deplores the violence. Filmed on location in Dublin, pic has a totally authentic feel.

NOTHING SACRED
1937, 75 mins, US Ⓥ ⊙
D: William A. Wellman **A:** Carole Lombard, Fredric March, Charles Winninger, Walter Connolly, Sig Ruman (Selznick)

A village beauty becomes the center of a fantastic newspaper circulation stunt which justifies itself in the belief, unfounded, that the girl has only a short time to live. Fredric March does the reporter behind the dizzy ride given Carole Lombard by a sucker-victimized New York which thinks she already has one foot in the grave. Walter Connolly bristles with importance from a comedy viewpoint as March's publisher-boss.

NO TIME FOR COMEDY
1940, 98 mins, US
D: William Keighley **A:** James Stewart, Rosalind Russell, Genevieve Tobin, Charles Ruggles, Louise Beavers (Warner)

Stewart is top-notch in the characterization of the boyish playwright from the sticks who writes a play in which Russell is being starred on Broadway. The author is needed to make revisions, which for the first time brings him to the big city. He and Russell just naturally get entangled and enter on domestic bliss. Stewart authors four comedy successes in four years when enter the villainess (Genevieve Tobin). She convinces him he's wasting time on comedy when he could be doing great plays and he not only turns out a tragedy—in more ways than one—but thinks he has fallen for Tobin. Combined with a deftness for handling comedy and a class type of beauty which is plenty well demonstrated right here, Russell emerges as a player of unusual dignity and authority.

NO TIME FOR LOVE
1944, 83 mins, US
D: Mitchell Leisen **A:** Claudette Colbert, Fred MacMurray, Ilka Chase, Ruth Havoc, Richard Haydn (Paramount)

Story concerns a famous femme photographer for a national picture magazine (Colbert), and the complications that evolve when, on an assignment to lens a tunnel construction project, she meets up with a sandhog (MacMurray). From there on the basic story is pretty much pretense, but the laughs come fast, and the performances by Colbert and MacMurray are capital.
1944: Nomination: Best B&W Art Direction

NOTORIOUS

1946, 101 mins, US ⓥ ⊙

D: Alfred Hitchcock **A:** Cary Grant, Ingrid Bergman, Claude Rains, Louis Calhern, Reinhold Schunzel (RKO)

Production and directorial skill of Alfred Hitchcock combine with a suspenseful story and excellent performances to make *Notorious* forceful entertainment. Story deals with espionage, the picture opening in Miami in the spring of 1946. Bergman's father has been convicted as a German spy. Yarn shifts quickly to Rio de Janeiro, where Bergman, known to be a loyal American, unlike her father, is pressed into the American intelligence service with a view to getting the goods on a local group of German exiles under suspicion. Inducted into espionage through Cary Grant, an American agent with whom she is assigned to work. Bergman, because she loves Grant, doesn't want to go through with an assignment to feign love for Claude Rains, head of the Brazilian Nazi group.

1946: Nominations: Best Supp. Actor (Claude Rains), Original Screenplay

NOTORIOUS GENTLEMAN

See: The Rake's Progress

NOTORIOUS LANDLADY, THE

1962, 127 mins, US

D: Richard Quine **A:** Kim Novak, Jack Lemmon, Fred Astaire, Lionel Jeffries, Estelle Winwood (Columbia)

Comedy-suspense melodrama is neither sound enough as a mystery nor consistently merry enough as a comedy. Screenplay deals with the plight of a Yankee foreign diplomat (Jack Lemmon) newly arrived from London, who becomes implicated in some confusing homicidal shenanigans involving his landlady (Kim Novak). Seems the landlady is suspected of having done in her husband, who has disappeared. In the midst of the budding Novak-Lemmon romance, the "dead" hubby shows up, only to be plugged for real by his wife.

NO TREES IN THE STREET

1959, 98 mins, UK

D: J. Lee Thompson **A:** Sylvia Syms, Herbert Lom, Ronald Howard, Stanley Holloway, Joan Miller (Associated British)

A seamy slice of life in a London slum 20 years ago. Film is played on a violently strident note. The slim story line shows how the various larger-than-life characters face up to the challenge of the street. Syl-via Syms gives a moving performance as the gentle girl who refuses to marry the cheap racketeer just to escape. Lom, as the opportunist who dominates the street, is sufficiently suave and unpleasant. Stanley Holloway is a bookmaker's tout with the cheerful philosophy that the world's gone mad.

LA NOTTE
(US: THE NIGHT)

1961, 125 mins, Italy/France ⓥ

D: Michelangelo Antonioni **A:** Marcello Mastroianni, Jeanne Moreau, Monica Vitti, Bernhard Wicki (Nepi/Silva/Sofitedip)

After 10 years of marriage, a popular writer and his wife begin to realize their affair is nearing breaking point. She's bored, has had an extramarital fling with a family friend who has just died suddenly, leaving her even more despondent. Pic covers one day and a night. And when dawn breaks up the party which the couple is attending, habit, fear, loneliness, and sorrow bring them together again in one last desperate act of love. Jeanne Moreau walks off with acting honors in a carefully modulated, masterful performance as the wife. Slow pace fits the mood admirably.

NOTTING HILL

1999, 123 mins, UK ⓥ ⊙ ▭

D: Roger Michell **A:** Julia Roberts, Hugh Grant, Hugh Bonneville, Emma Chambers, James Dreyfus, Rhys Ifans (Notting Hill/PolyGram)

Notting Hill, the second outing of scripter Richard Curtis, producer Duncan Kenworthy, and actor Hugh-Grant, has buckets to spare of engaging charm—plus a cast that delivers when the chips are down. Toplined in style by Grant and Julia Roberts, this is a romantic comedy about a shy London bookseller who falls for a Hollywood megastar. Unspectacular life of William Thacker (Grant) changes one day when Anna Scott (Roberts), the planet's most famous actress, walks in and buys a book. Only after more coincidental meetings, spread over a year and a half, does the on-off relationship resolve itself. A crucial late-on line, heartbreakingly delivered by Roberts, unlocks a reservoir of emotion that powers the movie to its cliffhanger ending.

NOT WITH MY WIFE, YOU DON'T!

1966, 118 mins, US

D: Norman Panama **A:** Tony Curtis, Virna

Lisi, George C. Scott, Carroll O'Connor (Warner)

Story sets up Tony Curtis and George C. Scott as old Korean conflict buddies whose rivalry for Virna Lisi is renewed when Scott discovers that Curtis won her by subterfuge. The amusing premise is thoroughly held together via an unending string of top comedy situations, including domestic squabbles, flashback, and an outstanding takeoff on foreign pix.

NOT WITHOUT MY DAUGHTER
1991, 114 mins, US Ⓥ ⊙
D: Brian Gilbert A: Sally Field, Alfred Molina, Sheila Rosenthal, Roshan Seth, Sarah Badel (Pathe/Ufland)

True story of Betty Mahmoody is a harrowing one by any standard. Married to Iranian doctor Moody who has lived in the US for 20 years, she reluctantly agrees to accompany him back to Teheran to visit his family, only to be told that he has decided to remain in Iran. As related in the by-the-numbers screenplay Iran turns Moody into an intolerant monster. Not only is Betty restricted to the home but she can't use the phone, has her passport taken away, and is told that her daughter will be raised as a Muslim. Sally Field has the stage to herself to engage the audience's sympathy, and this she does with an earnest, suitably emotional performance.

NOVECENTO
(US: 1900)
1976, 320 mins, Italy/France/W. Germany Ⓥ ⊙
D: Bernardo Bertolucci A: Burt Lancaster, Robert De Niro, Sterling Hayden, Gerard Depardieu, Dominique Sanda, Stefania Sandrelli (PEA/Artistes Associes/Artemis)

Spine of Bertolucci's ambitious generational canvas is the dialectical interlock of two families—landowners and sharecroppers—from 1900 to Italy's liberation in 1945. Bertolucci introduces a patriarchal landowner, Alfredo Berlinghieri (Burt Lancaster) and an equally sturdy family head, Leo Dalco (Sterling Hayden). Berlinghieri and Falco polarize the intricate genealogies, the social chasms, and the human overlap in a lyric opening, ripe with Bertolucci nostalgia for the magical naturalism and folk culture of his Emilia region at the turn of the century. Awkward then deepening friendship of the two grandsons, Alfredo (Robert De Niro) and Olmo (Gerard Depardieu), opens an arc that spans the entire film. [Paramount re-

leased a 248-min. English version in the US.]

NOVEMBER MEN, THE
1993, 98 mins, US Ⓥ ⊙
D: Paul Williams A: P. W. Williams [Paul Williams], James Andronica, Leslie Bevis, Beau Starr, Rod Ellis (Rohd House/Sun Lion)

Ultimate in conspiratorial presidential assassination films works well as both thriller and black comedy. The filmmaking is wild and unconventional, as befits the subject matter. Noted cineaste Arthur Gwenlyn (Williams) is mad as hell that there hasn't been an assassin from the left in recent American history. In the months leading up to the 1992 US elections, he rolls up his sleeves, mortgages the house, and adopts guerrilla tactics to get his little epic off the ground. Up to the very last moment, one remains unsure whether the movie's assassination script is only a movie or some horrible extreme of ego and dementia.

NOVI VAVILON
(US: THE NEW BABYLON)
1929, 110 mins, USSR ⊗
D: Grigori Kozintsev, Leonid Trauberg A: Yelena Kuzmina, Pyotr Sobolevsky, D. Gutman, Sophie Magarill, Sergei Gerasimov (Sovkino)

This film has only the vestige of continuity. Faces, feet, mud, singers, soldiers, and guns are projected time and again. Babylon is described in the subtitles as the name of a department store. The owner (D. Gutman) is allowed plenty of footage in which to sip liquor monotonously or adjust his top hat. Nearest line to the story is an extemporaneous romance suddenly springing up between the soldier Jean and a salesgirl. Picture claims it follows episodically events in the Franco-Prussian war and Commune activities in 1871.

NOW AND FOREVER
1934, 83 mins, US
D: Henry Hathaway A: Gary Cooper, Carole Lombard, Shirley Temple, Guy Standing, Charlotte Granville (Paramount)

Now and Forever has Shirley Temple. It also has Gary Cooper and Carole Lombard, who almost make the unbelievable romantic crook yarn ring true. It's another version of *Little Miss Marker,* the Temple child being Cooper's offspring by a former marriage. His impossibly supercilious socialite in-laws want to keep the child away from the roving renegade of a father's influence and he sees a $75,000 bankroll in that. Only Cooper forgets his hunger for economic wherewithal and resumes practical custody of the baby.

NOW AND THEN
1995, 96 mins, US Ⓥ
D: Lesli Linka Glatter **A:** Christina Ricci, Thora Birch, Gaby Hoffmann, Ashleigh Aston Moore, Demi Moore, Rosie O'Donnell (Moving Pictures)

Formulaic comedy-drama about teens coming of age in 1970 has the novelty of being mostly about girls rather than boys. Grown-up stars Moore, Melanie Griffith, Rosie O'Donnell, and Rita Wilson do little more than provide marquee allure in brief bookending scenes that add little to rest of the pic. For the most part, *Now and Then* is a showcase for four fine actresses in their early teens: Christina Ricci (*Casper*), Thora Birch (*Patriot Games*), Gaby Hoffmann (*Sleepless in Seattle*), and newcomer Ashleigh Aston Moore (no relation to Demi). They winningly play 12-year-old best friends who share confidences and misadventures during the summer of 1970.

NO WAY OUT
1950, 106 mins, US
D: Joseph L. Mankiewicz **A:** Richard Widmark, Linda Darnell, Stephen McNally, Sidney Poitier, Joanne Smith (20th Century-Fox)

Race riot hysteria is the theme of the original script. Story is told with words rather than action. The racial question is forcibly raised when two hoodlum brothers are injured in a gunfight. The Negro doctor takes over and one of the brothers dies during examination. The other brother, slum bred with all the prejudices of such an environment, charges the doctor with murder. Equally prejudiced, a group of Negroes turns on the hoods. Richard Widmark's work as the vindictive brother is exaggerated just enough.
1950: Nomination: Best Story & Screenplay

NO WAY OUT
1987, 116 mins, US Ⓥ ⊙ ▭
D: Roger Donaldson **A:** Kevin Costner, Gene Hackman, Sean Young, Will Patton, Howard Duff, George Dzundza (Orion)

Effective updating and revamping of the 1948 film noir classic *The Big Clock* is set primarily in the Pentagon, with heroic Kevin Costner cast as a lieutenant commander assigned to the secretary of defense (Gene Hackman). Costner has a torrid love affair with good-time girl Sean Young, ended when she is murdered by her other lover, Hackman. Costner recognizes his boss in the shadows but Hackman sees only an unidentified figure. Hackman starts a cover-up to find the unidentified man he saw leaving the apartment. Costner is put in charge of the top-security investigation to catch himself.

NO WAY TO TREAT A LADY
1968, 108 mins, US Ⓥ
D: Jack Smight **A:** Rod Steiger, Lee Remick, George Segal, Eileen Heckart, Murray Hamilton, Michael Dunn (Paramount)

Entertaining suspense film neatly laced with mordant humor. Plotline casts Rod Steiger as a psychotic theatrical entrepreneur who takes to strangling drab middle-aged women as a means of working out his hangups over his dead mother. He employs a variety of disguises, accents, and mannerisms for each murder. Steiger relishes the multiple aspect of his part, and audiences should equally relish his droll impersonations.

NOW BARABBAS WAS A ROBBER
1949, 87 mins, UK
D: Gordon Parry **A:** Richard Greene, Cedric Hardwicke, Kathleen Harrison, Ronald Howard, Richard Burton (Warner)

The odd assortment of men who make up a prison community are the central characters. The pic rarely moves outside its prison setting but the gloomy atmosphere is frequently relieved by human touches from the guards and inmates. The film is focused on a number of the prisoners with an occasional flashback to indicate how they landed inside.

NOWHERE TO RUN
1993, 94 mins, US Ⓥ ⊙
D: Robert Harmon **A:** Jean-Claude Van Damme, Rosanna Arquette, Kieran Culkin, Ted Levine, Joss Ackland (Columbia)

Action hero Jean-Claude Van Damme takes a career step backward in a relentlessly corny and shamelessly derivative vehicle with its central loner role modeled after the Alan Ladd classic *Shane*. Van Damme is a bankrobber who hides out on Rosanna Arquette's farm. She's a widow (the major plot change from *Shane*) with two young kids, pressured by evil land developer Joss Ackland to sell her homestead.

NOW, VOYAGER

1942, 117 mins, US ⓥ ⊙
D: Irving Rapper A: Bette Davis, Paul Henreid, Claude Rains, Bonita Granville, Gladys Cooper, Ilka Chase (Warner)

Voyager affords Bette Davis one of her superlative acting roles, that of a neurotic spinster fighting to free herself from the shackles of a tyrannical mother. The first scenes show Davis as dowdy, plump, and possessed of a phobia that fairly cries for the ministrations of a psychiatrist. Treatment by the doctor, played by Claude Rains, transforms the patient into a glamorous, modish, attractive woman who soon finds herself, after long being starved for love. The yarn's major love crisis focuses on Davis and Paul Henreid, the latter unable to upset the conventions of a complicated marital life.

1942: Best Score for a Dramatic Picture
Nominations: Best Actress (Bette Davis), Supp. Actress (Gladys Cooper)

NOW YOU SEE HIM, NOW YOU DON'T

1972, 88 mins, US ⓥ
D: Robert Butler A: Kurt Russell, Cesar Romero, Joe Flynn, Jim Backus, William Windom (Walt Disney)

Discovery of a fluid that makes people and objects invisible provides the inventive plot peg for uproarious golf games and car chase sequences involving students, professors, police, and criminals. Kurt Russell is a college student who accidentally discovers the invisible potion.

NOZ W WODZIE
(US: KNIFE IN THE WATER)

1962, 95 mins, Poland ⓥ
D: Roman Polanski A: Leon Niemczyk, Jolanta Umecka, Zygmunt Malanowicz (Kamera)

Lively and inventive little pic. A couple driving along a deserted road to the sea almost run over a young man. The driver is a self-absorbed husband, the woman his pretty, irritated young wife, and the hitchhiker a teenager. The husband, out of sheer patronizing goodwill, invites them to come sailing on their boat. Pic is then concerned with the subtle battle of personalities between the men and the wife's amused onlooking. For a first pic, director Roman Polanski shows a flair for simple character revelation and wit.

LA NUIT AMERICAINE
(US: DAY FOR NIGHT)

1973, 120 mins, France/Italy ⓥ ⊙
D: Francois Truffaut A: Jacqueline Bisset, Valentina Cortese, Dani, Alexandra Stewart, Jean-Pierre Aumont, Jean-Pierre Leaud (Films du Carrosse/PECF/PIC)

Francois Truffaut turns to filmmaking itself for his story. From the first day's shooting to the last, he mixes comedy and intimations of drama but keeps it mainly a love letter to the cinematic art, more pointedly commercial films. Here are loving observations, charming if familiar characterizations, and an ease in intertwining the story and the film within the story. Wittily, and avoiding any undue whimsy or self-indulgence, Truffaut plays the director of the film under way and makes it clear that this is his life's love.

1973: Best Foreign Language Film

NUN AND THE BANDIT, THE

1992, 92 mins, Australia ⓥ
D: Paul Cox A: Gosia Dobrowolska, Chris Haywood, Victoria Eagger, Charlotte Hughes Haywood, Norman Kaye (Illumination/Film Victoria/AFFC)

Aussie auteur Paul Cox has updated E. L. Grant's kidnap thriller, playing down the thriller elements in favor of a brittle character study. Michael Shanley (Chris Haywood) devises an impromptu, harebrained scheme to hold a rich man's young granddaughter (Charlotte Hughes Haywood) for ransom. The child is snatched when she is with her aunt, Sister Lucy (Gosia Dobrowolska), a Polish nun. The bulk of the film plays as a two-hander between the frightened, unworldly nun and the strange "bandit" who refuses to rape his victim but demands that she "be nice" to him.

NUNS ON THE RUN

1990, 90 mins, UK ⓥ ⊙
D: Jonathan Lynn A: Eric Idle, Robbie Coltrane, Camille Coduri, Janet Suzman, Doris Hare (HandMade)

Eric Idle and Robbie Coltrane are motivated by fear for their lives to dress in women's garb. New pic has rival British and Chinese gangs trying to recover two suitcases full of illicit cash. Idle and Coltrane make a wonderful pair of dumbbells, both in and out of their habits. Both are oddly believable as nuns, even while writer-director Jonathan Lynn mines all the expected comic benefits of drag humor.

NUN'S STORY, THE
1959, 149 mins, US Ⓥ ⊙
D: Fred Zinnemann **A:** Audrey Hepburn, Peter Finch, Edith Evans, Peggy Ashcroft, Dean Jagger, Mildred Dunnock (Warner)

Fred Zinnemann's production is a soaring and luminous film. Audrey Hepburn has her most demanding film role, and she gives her finest performance. Despite the seriousness of the underlying theme, *The Nun's Story* has the elements of absorbing drama, pathos, humor, and a gallery of memorable scenes and characters. The struggle is that of a young Belgian woman (Hepburn), to be a successful member of an order of cloistered nuns. Although the story is confined chiefly to three convents, in Belgium and the Congo, the struggle is fierce. Hepburn, attempting to be something she is not, is ground fine in the process.

1959: Nominations: Best Picture, Director, Actress (Audrey Hepburn), Adapted Screenplay, Color Cinematography, Scoring of a Dramatic Picture, Sound

NUOVO CINEMA PARADISO (US: CINEMA PARADISO)
1988, 155 mins, Italy/France Ⓥ ⊙
D: Giuseppe Tornatore **A:** Philippe Noiret, Salvatore Cascio, Marco Leonardi, Jacques Perrin, Brigitte Fossey (Cristaldi / Films Ariane)

Colorful, sentimental film about a marvelous Sicilian village and a boy who loves the movies divides into three parts, corresponding to the three ages of cineaste-hero Salvatore. As an adorable 10-year-old moppet (first-timer Salvatore Cascio), the boy sneaks into the parochial Paradise Cinema to watch a priest (Leopoldo Trieste) snip out all the kissing scenes. He worms his way into the heart of crusty peasant projectionist Alfredo (a well-balanced Philippe Noiret). Second part shows Salvatore as a teenager in love with a blond banker's daughter (Agnese Nano). Last, and least satisfying, is Salvatore as white-haired Jacques Perrin, now a famous (what else?) film director.
1988: Best Foreign Language Film

NUTS
1987, 116 mins, US Ⓥ ⊙
D: Martin Ritt **A:** Barbra Streisand, Richard Dreyfuss, Maureen Stapleton, Karl Malden, Eli Wallach, Robert Webber (Barwood/Ritt)

Nuts presents a premise weighted down by portentous performances. Issue of society's right to judge someone's sanity and the subjectivity of mental health is not only trite but dated. As Claudia Draper, an upper-crust kid who has gone off the deep end into prostitution, Barbra Streisand is flamboyantly, eccentrically crazy in a way that implies she is just a spirited woman society is trying to crush. After she is arrested for killing her high-priced trick, it is Richard Dreyfuss's job as Streisand's reluctant public defender to convince a preliminary hearing that Streisand is mentally competent enough to stand trial with little help from her and against her parents' wishes.

NUTTY PROFESSOR, THE
1963, 107 mins, US Ⓥ ⊙
D: Jerry Lewis **A:** Jerry Lewis, Stella Stevens, Del Moore, Kathleen Freeman, Howard Morris (Paramount/Lewis)

The Nutty Professor is only fitfully funny. Too often the film bogs down in pointless, irrelevant, or repetitious business. The star is cast as a meek, homely, accident-prone chemistry prof who concocts a potion that transforms him into a handsome, cocky, obnoxiously vain "cool cat" type. Stella Stevens, who portrays the professor's student admirer, is not only gorgeous, she is a very gifted actress.

NUTTY PROFESSOR, THE
1996, 95 mins, US Ⓥ ⊙
D: Tom Shadyac **A:** Eddie Murphy, Jada Pinkett, James Coburn, Larry Miller, Davé Chappelle (Imagine/Universal)

Eddie Murphy's reworking of Jerry Lewis's 1963 film *The Nutty Professor* is an apt and comic update of the Jekyll/Hyde formula. Sherman Klump (Murphy) is a good-hearted, slightly absentminded tub of lard conducting molecular research experiments at a fictional university. His goal is to find a solution that will make you thin. But the sedentary life that is his custom gets shaken with the arrival of Carla (Jada Pinkett), a comely grad student impressed by his work and seemingly undaunted by his girth. Pinkett demonstrates that her range ranks her among the most versatile young performers in movies.

O

OBCHOD NA KORZE
(UK: THE SHOP ON MAIN STREET; A SHOP ON THE HIGH STREET)
1964, 125 mins, Czechoslovakia Ⓥ Ⓞ
D: Jan Kadar, Elmar Klos **A:** Jozef Kroner, Frantisek Zvarik, Ida Kaminska, Hanna Slivkova (Barrandov)

Racism is looked at deeply and provocatively. During the last World War, a small town in Slovakia was turned into a crucible fascist state by the Nazis. A mean little man who harbors a resentment against the local Nazis is given the right to take over the store of an old Jewish woman. She has lost her husband in the last war and all that is left is this little dry-goods shop. When the deportations start she is somehow forgotten and he decides he will hide her.
1965: Best Foreign Language Film

OBJECTIVE, BURMA!
1945, 142 mins, US Ⓥ
D: Raoul Walsh **A:** Errol Flynn, Henry Hull, William Prince, James Brown, George Tobias (Warner)

Yarn deals with a paratroop contingent dropped behind the Japanese lines in Burma to destroy a radar station. While returning to a designated spot to be picked up by planes they're overtaken by Japs. Then follows a series of exciting experiences by the troopers against overwhelming odds. Flynn gives a quietly restrained performance as the contingent's leader.
1945: Nominations: Best Original Story, Editing, Scoring of a Dramatic Picture

OBJECT OF BEAUTY, THE
1991, 101 mins, US/UK Ⓥ
D: Michael Lindsay-Hogg **A:** John Malkovich, Andie MacDowell, Lolita Davidovich, Rudi Davies, Joss Ackland, Bill Paterson (Avenue/BBC)

Throwback to the romantic comedies of swinging London cinema lacks the punch of the best of that late 1960s genre. John Malkovich toplines as a ne'er-do-well holed up in a swank hotel with mate Andie MacDowell. Plot concerns a small Henry Moore figurine that MacDowell received from estranged hubbie, Peter Riegert, as a present and which Malkovich desperately wants to sell or use for an insurance scam to cover his hotel tab and business reverses.

OBLONG BOX, THE
1969, 91 mins, UK Ⓥ Ⓞ
D: Gordon Hessler **A:** Vincent Price, Christopher Lee, Alastair Williamson, Hilary Dwyer (American-International)

This 13th Edgar Allan Poe entry turned out by AIP is the tale of a man, terribly mutilated by African savages, kept chained by his brother (Vincent Price) in a gloomy 19th-century English manor house, his escape, and embarkation upon a series of murders. Price as usual overacts, but it is an art here to fit the mood and piece and as usual Price is good in his part.

OBSESSION
(US: THE HIDDEN ROOM)
1949, 96 mins, UK Ⓥ ▭
D: Edward Dmytryk **A:** Robert Newton, Sally Gray, Naunton Wayne, Phil Brown (Rank/Independent Sovereign)

Powerful suspense is the keynote of Edward Dymtryk's first British directional effort. A doctor plans the perfect murder of his wife's American lover. First the victim is confined in chains and the intention is to keep him alive while the hue and cry is on. If suspicion should fall on the doctor he could always produce the missing person. Naunton Wayne's nonchalant manner as the Yard superintendent deserves particular praise.

OBSESSION
1976, 98 mins, US Ⓥ Ⓞ
D: Brian De Palma **A:** Cliff Robertson, Genevieve Bujold, John Lithgow, Sylvia "Kuumba" Williams (Columbia)

A complex but comprehensible mix of treachery, torment, and selfishness. Robertson is haunted with guilt for the death of wife, Bujold, and child, Wanda Blackman, both kidnapped. Sixteen years later, on a trip abroad, he sees a lookalike to Bujold, and gets swept away with this new girl. Robertson's low-key performance is as crucial to the manifold surprise impact as Bujold's versatile, sensual, and effervescent charisma.
1976: Nomination: Best Original Score

O. C. AND STIGGS
1987, 109 mins, US Ⓥ
D: Robert Altman **A:** Daniel H. Jenkins, Neill Barry, Paul Dooley, Jane Curtin, Ray Walston, Dennis Hopper (M-G-M/UA)

An anarchistic jab at the insurance business and any other American institution that happens to be handy. Plot has something to do with O. C. (Daniel H. Jenkins) and Stiggs's (Neill Barry) efforts to extract a pound of flesh from Arizona insurance magnate Randall Schwab (Paul Dooley) in revenge for canceling the old-age insurance of O. C.'s grandfather (Ray Walston). In spite of the shortcomings and tedium, there are moments when it becomes evident there is a vision and talent behind all the nonsense.

OCEAN'S ELEVEN
1960, 127 mins, US ⓥ ▱
D: Lewis Milestone **A:** Frank Sinatra, Dean Martin, Sammy Davis Jr., Peter Lawford, Angie Dickinson, Richard Conte (Warner)

Although basically a no-nonsense piece about the efforts of 11 ex-war buddies to make off with a multimillion-dollar loot from five Vegas hotels, the film is frequently one resonant wisecrack away from turning into a musical comedy. Laboring under the handicaps of a contrived script, an uncertain approach, and personalities in essence playing themselves, the production never quite makes its point, but romps along merrily unconcerned that it doesn't.

OCTAGON, THE
1980, 103 mins, US ⓥ ⊙
D: Eric Karson **A:** Chuck Norris, Karen Carlson, Lee Van Cleef, Tadashi Yamashita, Carol Bagdasarian, Art Hindle (American Cinema)

A bizarre plot involving the ninja cult of Oriental assassins with international terrorism provides plenty of chances for Chuck Norris and other martial arts experts to do their stuff, and pic has a nicely stylized look with excellent lensing and music.

OCTOBER
See: Oktyabr

OCTOBER MAN, THE
1947, 93 mins, UK ⓥ
D: Roy Ward Baker **A:** John Mills, Joan Greenwood, Edward Chapman, Kay Walsh, Joyce Carey, Felix Aylmer (Two Cities)

A study of the conflict in the mind of a mentally sick man, not absolutely certain that he hasn't committed murder. John Mills suffers from a brain injury and develops suicidal tendencies. Molly, a fashion model (Kay Walsh), is found murdered and Jim is suspected. From then on it is the police versus Jim until he tracks down the murderer. The dialogue is

taut and adult, and the direction is imaginative. For a suspense pic the tempo sometimes lacks pace.

OCTOPUSSY
1983, 130 mins, UK ⓥ ⊙ ▱
D: John Glen **A:** Roger Moore, Maud Adams, Louis Jourdan, Kristina Wayborn, Kabir Bedi (Eon/United Artists)

Story line concerns a scheme by hawkish Russian general Orlov (Steven Berkoff) to launch a first-strike attack against the NATO countries in Europe. Orlov is aided in his plan by a beautiful smuggler Octopussy (Maud Adams), her underling Kamal (Louis Jourdan), and exquisite assistant Magda (Kristina Wayborn). James Bond (Roger Moore, in his sixth entry) is set on their trail, which takes Bond to India (lensed in sumptuous travelog shots). Film's high points are the spectacular aerial stuntwork marking both the precredits teaser and extremely dangerous-looking climax.

ODD ANGRY SHOT, THE
1979, 90 mins, Australia ⓥ
D: Tom Jeffrey **A:** Graham Kennedy, John Hargreaves, John Jarratt, Bryan Brown (Samson)

Australia's involvement in the Vietnam War created a political and moral dichotomy in the country. The film concentrates on a group of Aussie volunteers rather more bawdy than the Americans as depicted in *The Deer Hunter*. It is the same futile war, but what Jeffrey has expressed faithfully is the pragmatism and essential hope-of-survival of the troops on the ground. There is no agonizing political or moral message.

ODD COUPLE, THE
1968, 105 mins, US ⓥ ⊙ ▱
D: Gene Saks **A:** Jack Lemmon, Walter Matthau, John Fiedler, Herb Edelman, David Sheiner (Paramount)

The poignant laughs inherent in the rooming together of two men whose marriages are on the rocks. As the hypochondriac, domesticated, and about-to-be-divorced Felix, Lemmon is excellent. Matthau also hits the bull's-eye in a superior characterization.
1968: Nominations: Best Adapted Screenplay, Editing

ODD MAN OUT
(US: GANG WAR)
1947, 116 mins, UK ⓥ ⊙
D: Carol Reed **A:** James Mason, Robert

Newton, Robert Beatty, Kathleen Ryan, Cyril Cusack (Two Cities)

Accent is on Art with a capital A. Story is set in a city in Northern Ireland. Johnnie, leader of an organization, has broken jail. During a holdup to obtain funds, he accidentally kills a man, and is badly wounded himself. For Mason two thirds of the film is silent. From the moment he is wounded he has few lines and has to drag himself along. It is hardly his fault that, in this passive character, he is less effective than he could be.

1947: Nomination: Best Editing

ODDS AGAINST TOMORROW
1959, 96 mins, US
D: Robert Wise **A:** Harry Belafonte, Robert Ryan, Shelley Winters, Ed Begley, Gloria Grahame (HarBel/United Artists)

On one level, a taut crime melodrama. On another, an allegory about racism, greed, and man's propensity for self-destruction. Not altogether successful in the second category, it still succeeds on its first. Harry Belafonte, Robert Ryan, and Ed Begley plan to rob a bank. An ill-matched trio, their optimistic plans are dependent on the closest teamwork. Director Robert Wise has drawn fine performances. It is the most sustained acting Belafonte has done. Ryan makes the flesh crawl as the fanatical bigot. Begley turns in a superb study of a foolish, befuddled man.

ODESSA FILE, THE
1974, 128 mins, UK/W. Germany ⓥ ⊙ ⌑
D: Ronald Neame **A:** Jon Voight, Maximilian Schell, Maria Schell, Mary Tamm, Derek Jacobi (Columbia)

An excellent filmization of Frederick Forsyth's novel of a reporter who tracks down former Nazi SS officers still undetected in 1960s Germany. Jon Voight's accidental reading of the diary of a suicide leads to his attempted infiltration of Odessa, a secret network of SS veterans who have maintained their cover in diverse positions in postwar commerce and government.

ODE TO BILLY JOE
1976, 105 mins, US ⓥ
D: Max Baer **A:** Robby Benson, Glynnis O'Connor, Joan Hotchkis, Sandy McPeak, James Best (Warner)

Superbly sensitive period romantic tragedy, based on Bobbie Gentry's 1967 hit song lyric. Robby Benson is excellent as Billy Joe McAllister, and Glynnis

O'Connor is outstanding as his Juliet. The puppy love affair unfolds smoothly as it is interwoven with family, church, work, and community functions, all of which establish the people as real, loving folk and create a magnificent dramatic environment.

ODETTE
1950, 123 mins, UK
D: Herbert Wilcox **A:** Anna Neagle, Trevor Howard, Marius Goring, Peter Ustinov, Bernard Lee (British Lion)

The film recaptures all the essential details of Odette's adventures as a secret agent in France during the last war. Anna Neagle puts all she's got into the playing of Odette. Trevor Howard gives a smooth and confident interpretation of the British agent whom she subsequently marries. Marius Goring plays the counterespionage officer with a genuine conviction, while Peter Ustinov gives one of his best performances as the secret radio operator.

OEDIPUS THE KING
1968, 97 mins, UK
D: Philip Saville **A:** Christopher Plummer, Orson Welles, Lilli Palmer, Richard Johnson, Cyril Cusack (Rank/Crossroads)

This version of Sophocles' play deals fairly superficially with the bare bones of the tragic story of the king, dragged down to degradation after having discovered that, unwittingly, he has murdered his father and married and had children by his mother. Christopher Plummer as Oedipus gives a sterling performance. Orson Welles is unusually subdued, but all the more effective, as Tiresias, the blind prophet of doom.

OF A THOUSAND DELIGHTS
See: Vaghe Stelle Dell'Orsa

OFF BEAT
1986, 92 mins, US ⓥ ⊙
D: Michael Dinner **A:** Judge Reinhold, Meg Tilly, Harvey Keitel, Cleavant Derricks, Joe Mantegna, John Turturro (Touchstone)

Except for Cleavant Derricks, who shows a natural comedic talent playing a cop, cast seem so conscientious about trying to be funny, they forget to lighten up. Judge Reinhold, a library clerk, agrees to replace Derricks in the chorus line at the annual police benefit dance auditions, where he falls instantly for a cute little policewoman (Meg Tilly). To keep up the charade for Tilly, he ends up in uniform more often than he should and unwittingly gets himself involved in a few incidents.

OFFENCE, THE
1973, 112 mins, US/UK Ⓥ
D: Sidney Lumet A: Sean Connery, Trevor Howard, Vivien Merchant, Ian Bannen, Derek Newark, Peter Bowles (United Artists/Tantallon)

There's a powerful confrontation of authority and accused between police sergeant Sean Connery and suspected child molester Ian Bannen. This often cold and dreary tale is about the self-realization of a veteran police officer that his own mind contains much of the evil with which he is confronted daily. It is not long before accuser becomes the accused. However, the lengthy lead-up to this important scene is played against dreary backgrounds and with colorless people.

OFFICER AND A GENTLEMAN, AN
1982, 126 mins, US Ⓥ ⊙
D: Taylor Hackford A: Richard Gere, Debra Winger, Louis Gossett Jr., David Keith, Lisa Blount (Lorimar)

Rarely does a film come along with so many finely drawn characters to care about. *Officer* belongs to Louis Gossett Jr., who takes a near-cliché role of the tough, unrelenting drill instructor and makes him a sympathetic hero. Pic is a bit muddled, via flashback, in setting up Richard Gere's motives for going into the training. On leave, Gere meets Debra Winger. It's another fetching little slut role for Winger and she makes the most of it.
1982: Best Supp. Actor (Louis Gossett Jr.), Original Song ("Up Where We Belong")
Nominations: Best Actress (Debra Winger), Original Screenplay, Editing, Original Score

OFFICIAL STORY, THE
See: La Historia Oficial

OFF LIMITS
1953, 87 mins, US Ⓥ
D: George Marshall A: Bob Hope, Mickey Rooney, Marilyn Maxwell, Eddie Mayehoff, Jack Dempsey (Paramount)

Bob Hope's brash, smart-aleck comedy is turned loose on the army. Hope is his boastful self as manager-trainer of Stanley Clements, lightweight fighter. When Clements is drafted, Hope's gangster partners make him enlist to watch over the fighter. Mickey Rooney enters the picture as a draftee eager to have Hope make him into a fighter.

OFF LIMITS
(UK: SAIGON)
1988, 102 mins, US Ⓥ ⊙
D: Christopher Crowe A: Willem Dafoe, Gregory Hines, Fred Ward, Amanda Pays, Scott Glenn (20th Century-Fox)

Well-crafted story explores the underbelly of 1968 Saigon well enough as two undercover detectives (Willem Dafoe, Gregory Hines) go about to solve a string of prostitute murders by a high-ranking army officer. While the plot and characterizations are well worked out, what this production lacks is enough pizzazz to distinguish it from others of this genre.

OFFRET
(US: THE SACRIFICE)
1986, 150 mins, Sweden/France Ⓥ ⊙
D: Andrei Tarkovsky A: Erland Josephson, Susan Fleetwood, Allan Edwall, Sven Wolter, Gudrun Gisladottir (SFI/Argos)

The Sacrifice takes place in and around a house on the desolate coastal plains of a Swedish island. Film concerns a middle-aged intellectual, Alexander (Erland Josephson), whose birthday dinner is interrupted by what is obviously the nuclear Big Bang, although it is seen rather than heard. A mailman (Allan Edwall) advises him to go sleep with a local witch and use her innocence to seek atonement for the sins of mankind. All Tarkovsky's pet images and sounds are emulated to heighten film's aesthetic values.

OF HUMAN BONDAGE
1934, 83 mins, US Ⓥ ⊙
D: John Cromwell A: Leslie Howard, Bette Davis, Frances Dee, Kay Johnson, Reginald Denny (Radio)

Basically, it's an obvious and familiar theme The unrequited love of the art-medical student, inhibited and clubfooted, commands respect and sympathy. But the feeling grows that he's pretty much of a clunk to go the hard way he does for the strumpet who treats him so shabbily. Perhaps Bette Davis is to blame. She plays her free-'n'-easy vamp too well, so that it negates any audience sympathy for the gentle Leslie Howard.

OF HUMAN BONDAGE
1946, 100 mins, US
D: Edmund Goulding A: Eleanor Parker, Paul Henreid, Alexis Smith, Edmund Gwenn, Janis Paige (Warner)

Somerset Maugham story has been given excellent period mounting to fit early London background, is well played and directed in individual sequences, but lacks overall smoothness. Three femmes represent various loves that enter the life of Henreid, frustrated artist, but major interest is concentrated on character played by Parker and how she affects Henreid's happiness. Parker's work is excellent, as is Henreid's depiction of the self-pitying cripple.

OF HUMAN BONDAGE
1964, 98 mins, UK ⓥ
D: Ken Hughes, Henry Hathaway **A:** Kim Novak, Laurence Harvey, Robert Morley, Siobhan McKenna, Roger Livesey (Seven Arts/M-G-M)

This perceptive but highly introspective yarn by Somerset Maugham may seem a hard-to-take slab of period meller. A medical student very conscious of his clubfoot becomes a doctor in London's East End despite being totally besotted with the tawdry charms of a promiscuous waitress. Harvey plays the role in such a stiff, martyred manner as to forfeit any sympathy. Novak gamely tackles a wide range of emotions.

OF HUMAN HEARTS
1938, 100 mins, US
D: Clarence Brown **A:** Walter Huston, James Stewart, Beulah Bondi, Guy Kibbee, Charles Coburn (M-G-M)

Frontier life in a village on the banks of the Ohio River in the days preceding the Civil War is the background against which Clarence Brown tells the story of a mother's sacrifice for the career of an ungrateful son. Walter Huston is the zealous circuit-riding preacher. Beulah Bondi is the wife and mother, and she shades the transitions of age with convincing acting. Gene Reynolds first appears as the son, a role played by James Stewart in the later scenes. Chief cause for disappointment with the film is its slow pace, and the defeatist mood of the story.
1938: Nomination: Best Supp. Actress (Beulah Bondi)

OF MICE AND MEN
1939, 104 mins, US ⓥ
D: Lewis Milestone **A:** Burgess Meredith, Lon Chaney Jr., Betty Field, Charles Bickford, Roman Bohnen (Roach/United Artists)

Picture retains all of the forceful and poignant drama of John Steinbeck's original play and novel, in presenting the strange palship and eventual tragedy of the two California ranch itinerants. George's strange wardship of the half-wit Lennie possessed of Herculean strength is never quite explained—in fact he wonders himself just why. George keeps Lennie close to him always—continually fearful that the simpleton will kill someone with his brute power. Lon Chaney Jr. dominates throughout with a fine portrayal of the childlike giant.
1939: Nominations: Best Picture, Original Score, Sound

OF MICE AND MEN
1992, 110 mins, US ⓥ
D: Gary Sinise **A:** John Malkovich, Gary Sinise, Ray Walston, Casey Siemaszko, Sherilyn Fenn (M-G-M)

Well mounted and very traditional, *Of Mice and Men* honorably serves John Steinbeck's classic story of two Depression-era drifters without bringing anything new to it. George (Sinise) is a quick-witted man of few but well-chosen words with no family or money to his name. His only charge is Lennie (Malkovich), a lumbering simpleton who has the mind of a child but the strength of an ox. Dramatic gears start turning when belligerent farm boss son, Curley (Casey Siemaszko), starts picking on Lennie.

OH DAD, POOR DAD, MAMMA'S HUNG YOU IN THE CLOSET, AND I'M FEELIN' SO SAD
1967, 86 mins, US ⓥ
D: Richard Quine **A:** Rosalind Russell, Robert Morse, Barbara Harris, Hugh Griffith, Jonathan Winters, Lionel Jeffries (Paramount)

Producers have labored mightily to bring forth a mouse. Rosalind Russell is the emasculating mother of Robert Morse, sired by Jonathan Winters, who is dead but stuffed and carried around by his widow as she and son travel about. Barbara Harris is the nymphet chippie who puts the make on Morse so successfully that he kills her in a psycho substitution for his ma. Hugh Griffith is an aging lecher eyed by Russell as her next victim.

O. HENRY'S FULL HOUSE
1952, 116 mins, US
D: Henry Hathaway, Howard Hawks, Henry King, Henry Koster, Jean Negulesco **A:** Charles Laughton, Marilyn Monroe, Richard Widmark, Anne Baxter, Fred Allen, Jeanne Crain (20th Century-Fox)

This ties together five of O. Henry's classics into a full house of entertainment that has something for all tastes. *The Cop and the Anthem* gets the quintet off to an enjoyable 19-minute start as Charles Laughton milks the fat part of the gentleman bum who tries to get arrested so he can spend the winter months in a warm jail. Picture closes with a choice little account of that tender story of young love, *The Gift of the Magi*, splendidly trouped by Jeanne Crain and Farley Granger.

OH! FOR A MAN
See: Will Success Spoil Rock Hunter?

OH, GOD!
1977, 97 mins, US ⊗
D: Carl Reiner A: George Burns, John Denver, Teri Garr, Donald Pleasence, Ralph Bellamy, William Daniels (Warner)

Oh, God! is a hilarious film that benefits from the brilliant teaming of George Burns, as the Almighty in human form, and John Denver, sensational in his screen debut as a supermarket assistant manager who finds himself a suburban Moses. Teri Garr is excellent as Denver's perplexed but loyal wife.
1977: Nomination: Best Adapted Screenplay

OH, GOD! BOOK II
1980, 94 mins, US ⊗
D: Gilbert Cates A: George Burns, Suzanne Pleshette, David Birney, Louanne, Howard Duff (Warner)

Not a sequel to the hit 1977 release but rather an alternate approach to the same basic premise. Bland, unstimulating film has a pleasant moppet (Louanne) meeting God (Burns) in the lounge of a Chinese restaurant. It seems that Burns has decided to enlist a child "with belief in things you can't see" to remind people that God is still around. Since Louanne's dad (David Birney) is an adman, she sets out to concoct a slogan that will "make God a household name."

OH, GOD! YOU DEVIL
1984, 96 mins, US ⊗ ⊙
D: Paul Bogart A: George Burns, Ted Wass, Ron Silver, Roxanne Hart, Eugene Roche, Robert Desiderio (Warner)

After two turns as an amusing Supreme Being, George Burns proves to be an equally diverting demon. Struggling musician Ted Wass is desperate for the break that will bring happiness. Bad Burns picks up Wass's wail and a deal is soon struck. Burns switches him with an already reigning rock star (Robert Desiderio) whose own pact with the devil has run out. By the time Burns as God heeds Wass's plea for salvation, it's almost too much for even Him to iron out satisfactorily.

OH, MR. PORTER!
1937, 84 mins, UK ⊗
D: Marcel Varnel A: Will Hay, Moore Marriott, Graham Moffatt, Dennis Wyndham (Gainsborough)

A railway comedy, reminiscent of *The Ghost Train* (1931), written around the comic personality of Will Hay, supported by his very "aged" and very "young" foils. An amiable misfit is sent as a last resort to a tiny village in Ireland as stationmaster. Finding a decrepit clerk and fat-boy porter the only occupants of the station, where no train ever stops, the newcomer tries to convert the ramshackle dump into something worthy of his dignity.

O.H.M.S.
(US: YOU'RE IN THE ARMY NOW)
1937, 87 mins, UK
D: Raoul Walsh A: Wallace Ford, John Mills, Anna Lee, Grace Bradley, Frank Cellier (Gaumont-British)

Not much to get excited about. Narrative poses Wallace Ford as a petty American racketeer who flees to England. There he turns to the army as a hideout, enlisting as from Canada. With occasional touches of humor, picture relates his doings as a recruit, adding romance to the proceedings. Picture goes melodramatic for the final reel.

OH . . . ROSALINDA!!
1955, 101 mins, UK ▭
D: Michael Powell, Emeric Pressburger A: Michael Redgrave, Mel Ferrer, Anton Walbrook, Dennis Price, Anthony Quayle, Ludmilla Tcherina (ABPC)

The story of *Die Fledermaus* is brought up to date and set in Vienna under the control of the four occupying powers. It is a lavish production, highly diverting and spectacular. Michael Redgrave has an adequate lightness of touch as the Gallic philanderer. Tcherina shows more of her person than her personality as his gay wife, with her role attractively sung by Sari Barabas. Mel Ferrer is dashing as the persistent American wooer, and Anthony Quayle supplies the requisite somber touch to the character of the Russian officer.

OH! WHAT A LOVELY WAR
1969, 144 mins, UK ⊗ ▭
D: Richard Attenborough A: Ralph Rich-

ardson, Laurence Olivier, John Gielgud, John Mills, Michael Redgrave, Vanessa Redgrave (Paramount/Accord)

Satire on war, in which the songs are an integral part of the message, never relies on violence. Sudden, brutal death in combat is omitted and far more effectively, is rammed home by the symbol of poppies for each death. The film brilliantly pinpoints the collective stupidity that made such a holocaust possible. The familiar wartime songs, sentiment, humor, and satire are all incorporated, but Attenborough has never allowed any to stretch a mood beyond its capacity.

OIL FOR THE LAMPS OF CHINA
1935, 110 mins, US
D: Mervyn LeRoy **A:** Pat O'Brien, Josephine Hutchinson, Jean Muir, Lyle Talbot, Donald Crisp (Cosmopolitan/Warner)

A choppy, long, and sometimes confused yarn is laid practically entirely in China. Alice Tisdale Hobart's original was an indictment of a great oil company for its subjugation of its employees. Film switches that around to a man's blind struggle against mistreatment, dishonesty in officials, personal misfortune, and rank deception on the part of his officers, with nothing more than faith in "the company" as his wand.

OKLAHOMA!
1955, 142 mins, US ⊗ ⊙ ☐
D: Fred Zinnemann **A:** Gordon MacRae, Gloria Grahame, Gene Nelson, Charlotte Greenwood, Shirley Jones, Rod Steiger (Magna)

The innovating musical comedy magic that Richard Rodgers and Oscar Hammerstein II created has been captured and, in some details, expanded in the film version. The tunes ring out with undiminished delight. The characters pulsate with spirit. The Agnes De Mille choreography makes the play literally leap. The wide screen used for the Todd-AO process adds visual grandeur. Gordon MacRae as Curly, and Shirley Jones as Laurey make a bright, romantic pair.
1955: Best Sound Recording, Scoring of a Musical Picture
Nominations: Best Color Cinematography, Editing

OKLAHOMA CRUDE
1973, 108 mins, US ⊗ ☐
D: Stanley Kramer **A:** George C. Scott, Faye Dunaway, John Mills, Jack Palance, Rafael Campos (Columbia)

Dramatically choppy potboiler about oil wildcatting in 1913. Faye Dunaway plays a bitter woman determined to bring in an oil well on her own. John Mills, aiming to help her out after years of parental abandonment, recruits George C. Scott from the hobo jungles. The three of them joust with Jack Palance, snarling provocateur of the oil trust that wants Dunaway's property.

OKTYABR
(US: OCTOBER; TEN DAYS THAT SHOOK THE WORLD)
1928, 115 mins, USSR ⊗ ⊙ ⊗
D: Sergei Eisenstein, Grigori Alexandrov **A:** Vasili Nikandrov, N. Popov, Boris Livanov, Eduard Tisse (Sovkino)

Eisenstein's classic evocation of the Bolshevik revolution has been criticized for its lack of clarity and often idiosyncratic interpretation of the major events. For all its incoherence, *October* carries the spectator on a tidal wave of stunning imagery. Eisenstein's often playful experiments in intellectual montage are not always his forte here. Though the famous satiric passage on Prime Minister Kerensky's symbolic rise to power in the provincial government still is cinematically sharp, other sequences are long-winded and hermetic. [Version reviewed was shown on pic's 50th anniversary.]

OLD ACQUAINTANCE
1943, 110 mins, US
D: Vincent Sherman **A:** Bette Davis, Miriam Hopkins, Gig Young, John Loder, Dolores Moran (Warner)

Bette Davis and Miriam Hopkins were schoolgirl chums. With former leaving hometown to carve literary career, while latter settles to happy marriage to John Loder, Davis returns for lecture and finds her with child and writer of hot sexy novels. Eight years later, Hopkins is a successful pop novelist and hits New York with Loder and daughter for opening of Davis's play. Latter sees impending breakup of marriage and tries to prevent it, even though Loder tells of his walkout and real love for her. John Van Druten and Lenore Coffee have devised fine script, deftly molding it to particular dramatic talents of Hopkins-Davis.

OLD BOYFRIENDS
1979, 103 mins, US ⊗ ⊙
D: Joan Tewkesbury **A:** Talia Shire, Richard Jordan, Keith Carradine, John Belushi,

John Houseman, Buck Henry (Avco Embassy)

The premise is an intriguing and universal one, the fantasy of revisiting lovers out of an individual's past. The femme (Talia Shire) is a clinical psychologist who roots into her past after a failed suicide attempt. Shire's odyssey takes her across America to old beaux including her college sweetheart (Richard Jordan), high school romance (John Belushi) and first adolescent love (Keith Carradine). The experience proves to be disquieting.

OLD DARK HOUSE, THE
1932, 74 mins, US
D: James Whale A: Boris Karloff, Melvyn Douglas, Charles Laughton, Gloria Stuart, Lillian Bond, Ernest Thesiger (Universal)

It has all the elements for horror and thriller exploitation, including a mad brute butler (Boris Karloff), insanity, ghosts in the family closets, sex, romance, not to mention the titular setting in a storm-torn Welsh mountain retreat. Among the performances, Karloff with a characteristically un-drawing-room physical getup, by no means impresses as a sissy by stature, demeanor, and surliness. Gloria Stuart gives excellent account of herself, although that extreme decolletage is rather uncalled for considering the locale. Charles Laughton turns in one of his usually top-hole performances as the Lancashire knight.

OLD DRACULA
See: Vampira

OLD ENOUGH
1984, 91 mins, US Ⓥ
D: Marisa Silver A: Sarah Boyd, Rainbow Harvest, Neill Barry, Danny Aiello, Susan Kingsley (Silverfilm)

Tale of friendship has just the right balance of humor and insight. Story centers on 12-year-old Lonnie Sloan (Sarah Boyd) from an upper-class New York City family and slightly older Karen Bruckner (Rainbow Harvest) from blue-collar background. Both are at important emotional turning points when they meet on the street of the widely divergent economic neighborhood. It is an easily understandable attraction of opposites. Boyd and Harvest have burden of carrying the film, which they accomplish with ease.

OLD FASHIONED WAY, THE
1934, 69 mins, US
D: William Beaudine A: W. C. Fields, Joe Morrison, Judith Allen, Jan Duggan, Nora Cecil, Baby LeRoy (Paramount)

Made to order for W. C. Fields and permitting him to do his old cigar-box juggling among other things, The Old Fashioned Way is light comedy material that will please the Fields followers. A repertoire troupe of the days when The Drunkard and East Lynne were big draws serves as the background and the small town of Bellefontaine, Ohio, is the locale. It is here that the Great McGonigle, who heads the rep company, runs into all kinds of difficulties, most of them of a financial origin.

OLD GRINGO
1989, 119 mins, US Ⓥ ⊙
D: Luis Puenzo A: Jane Fonda, Gregory Peck, Jimmy Smits, Patricio Contreras, Jenny Gago (Fonda/Columbia)

Jane Fonda, in the plum role of fortyish spinster on the run Harriet Winslow, is swept up by accident in the Mexican Revolution and swept off her feet by a charismatic general. A rakish Jimmy Smits as General Arroyo is superbly cast. He conveys the cocksure yet sensitive machismo and motivations of his character's torment between the revolution he lives and the woman he loves. As the embittered, sardonic journalist Ambrose Bierce, Gregory Peck has found a role that suits him to a T.

OLD MAID, THE
1939, 92 mins, US Ⓥ ⊙
D: Edmund Goulding A: Bette Davis, Miriam Hopkins, George Brent, Donald Crisp, Jane Bryan, James Stephenson (Warner)

Film is stagey, somber, and generally confusing fare. Story opens during the Civil War days. Miriam Hopkins loves George Brent, but, when he fails to return after two years, prepares to marry rich James Stephenson. Brent arrives on the wedding day and is comforted by Bette Davis. Brent goes to war and is killed, leaving Davis with a child. Davis provides a strong portrayal in the title role. Hopkins provides a strong contrast as the motherly matron.

OLD MAN AND THE SEA, THE
1958, 86 mins, US
D: John Sturges A: Spencer Tracy, Felipe Pazos, Harry Bellaver (Warner)

Ernest Hemingway's introspective one-episode novelette is virtually a one-character film, the spotlight being almost continuously on Spencer Tracy as the old Cuban fisherman who meets his final test

in his tremendous struggle with the huge marlin. The picture has power, vitality, and sharp excitement as it depicts the grueling contest between man and fish. It is exquisitely photographed and skillfully directed. It captures the dignity and the stubbornness of the old man, and it is tender in his final defeat. And yet it isn't a completely satisfying picture. There are long and arid stretches, when it seems as if producer and director were merely trying to fill time.
1958: Best Scoring of a Dramatic Picture
Nominations: Best Actor (Spencer Tracy), Color Cinematography

OLD YELLER
1957, 83 mins, US ⓥ ⊙
D: Robert Stevenson **A:** Dorothy McGuire, Fess Parker, Tommy Kirk, Kevin Corcoran, Chuck Connors (Walt Disney)

Disney flair for taking a homely subject and building a heartwarming film is again aptly demonstrated in this moving story set in 1869 of a Texas frontier family and an old yeller dog. This is a careful blending of fun, laughter, love, adventure, and tragedy.

OLEANNA
1994, 89 mins, US ⓥ
D: David Mamet **A:** William H. Macy, Debra Eisenstadt (Bay Kinescope)

David Mamet's *Oleanna* is a tale of sexual tension in the workplace (here, academia) in which a common situation is propelled into the stuff of tragedy. Mamet's first act finds a professor, John (William H. Macy), in conference with Carol (Debra Eisenstadt), a failing student. He spends more time grappling with her inability to comprehend than he should. In the second act, John has asked Carol to his office. She's made accusations of sexual harrassment against him. John's not guilty of anything. Mamet makes that very clear—too clear, in fact, leaving little dramatic ambiguity. With an obvious villain in Carol, the subject of sexual harrassment gets hopelessly lost. Eisenstadt is shrill as Carol. Macy fares little better in a part that largely demands a lot of preening.

OLIVER!
1968, 140 mins, UK ⓥ ⊙ ▭
D: Carol Reed **A:** Ron Moody, Shani Wallis, Oliver Reed, Harry Secombe, Mark Lester, Jack Wild (Columbia/Romulus)

A bright, shiny, heartwarming musical, packed with songs and lively production high spots. Lionel Bart's stage musical hit is adroitly opened out. Mark Lester is a frail Oliver, with a tremulous, piping singing voice, but he's vigorous and mischievous enough, and is sufficiently dewy eyed and angelic to captivate the audience. Major honors go to a diminutive 15-year-old, Jack Wild, who plays the Artful Dodger with knowing cunning and impudent self-confidence.
1968: Best Picture, Director, Art Direction, Sound, Scoring of a Musical Picture, Honorary Award (Onna White, for choreography)
Nominations: Best Actor (Ron Moody), Supp. Actor (Jack Wild), Adapted Screenplay, Cinematography, Costume Design, Editing

OLIVER'S STORY
1978, 92 mins, US ⓥ
D: John Korty **A:** Ryan O'Neal, Candice Bergen, Nicola Pagett, Edward Binns, Ray Milland (Paramount)

Love Story is a tough act to follow, but *Oliver's Story* manages to hold its own. Ryan O'Neal, working as a lawyer in a prestigious New York firm, is burdened by a sense of despair and loneliness, along with a liberal dose of self-pity. Enter Candice Bergen as the Bonwit heir in Bonwit Teller, the flip side in looks and disposition to the Jenny character created by Ali MacGraw. The most moving segments come from a few brief scenes between O'Neal and Ray Milland, who encores as his wealthy banker father.

OLIVER TWIST
1948, 116 mins, UK ⓥ ⊙
D: David Lean **A:** Robert Newton, Alec Guinness, Kay Walsh, Francis L. Sullivan, John Howard Davies, Anthony Newley (Cineguild)

A superb achievement. The child Oliver has the wistful air of the typical Dickens waif and heads almost faultless casting. Camerawork is on an exceptionally high level. Opening shots of a storm-swept sky and heavy clouds give an eerie quality that immediately grips the imagination. Alec Guinness gives a revoltingly faithful portrait of Fagin. Robert Newton is a natural for the brutish Sikes and gets every ounce out of his opportunities.

O LUCKY MAN!
1973, 176 mins, UK ⓥ
D: Lindsay Anderson **A:** Malcolm McDowell, Ralph Richardson, Rachel Rob-

erts, Arthur Lowe, Helen Mirren (Memorial/SAM)

No less than an epic look at society is created in Lindsay Anderson's third and most provocative film. It is in the form of a human comedy on a perky, ambitious, but conformist young man using society's ways to get to the top. Malcolm McDowell is first a salesman, then guinea pig to science, assistant to a great business tycoon, railroaded to prison as a fall guy, converted to near saintliness, almost martyred, and then returned to conformism by an almost mystical reaching of understanding through a Zen Buddhist–like happening. The music and songs of Alan Price also add by underlining and counterpointing the action.

LOS OLVIDADOS (US: THE YOUNG AND THE DAMNED)
1950, 88 mins, Mexico Ⓥ
D: Luis Bunuel **A:** Alfonso Mejia, Roberto Cobo, Estela Inda, Miguel Inclan, Efrain Arauz (Ultramar)

Film is an objective, unrelenting close-up of life among some delinquents in a Mexican slum. Boys are presented as a group who grow up without any moral conceptions or responsibilities. Film offers no hope except in sweeping social changes. Bunuel has filled his pic with such symbols as a terrifying blind man, donkeys bearing dead bodies, and bloody battles.

OMAR KHAYYAM
1957, 101 mins, US
D: William Dieterle **A:** Cornel Wilde, Michael Rennie, Debra Paget, Raymond Massey, John Derek, Yma Sumac (Paramount)

Static cumbersomeness of some sets of the romantic love duets between Cornel Wilde and Debra Paget flaw this spectacular; but well-staged battle and court intrigue sequences speed up the pace and hold interest. Script sets forth Omar (Wilde) as poet, lover, scholar, scientist, and court counselor—all in one. Romance between Omar and wife (Paget) of the ruling Shah (Raymond Massey) is woven against intrigue in court and the machinations of the murderous and mysterious Eastern cult of Assassins.

OMEGA MAN, THE
1971, 98 mins, US Ⓥ ▭
D: Boris Sagal **A:** Charlton Heston, An-

thony Zerbe, Rosalind Cash, Paul Koslo, Lincoln Kilpatrick (Warner)

An extremely literate science-fiction drama starring Charlton Heston as the only survivor of a worldwide bacteriological war, circa 1975. Thrust of the well-written story is Heston's running battle with deranged survivors headed by Anthony Zerbe.

OMEN, THE
1976, 111 mins, US Ⓥ ⊙ ▭
D: Richard Donner **A:** Gregory Peck, Lee Remick, David Warner, Billie Whitelaw, Harvey Stephens (20th Century-Fox)

Suspenser starring Gregory Peck and Lee Remick as the unwitting parents of the anti-Christ. Direction is taut. Players all are strong. Peck, well cast as a career American ambassador, is convinced by Italian priest Martin Benson to substitute another hospital baby for the one wife Remick lost in childbirth. Five years later, strange things begin to happen. At various points, portents of Satanism emerge, underscored (or, rather, overscored) by Jerry Goldsmith's heavy music.
1976: Best Original Score
Nomination: Best Song ("Ave Satani")

ON A CLEAR DAY YOU CAN SEE FOREVER
1970, 129 mins, US Ⓥ ⊙ ▭
D: Vincente Minnelli **A:** Barbra Streisand, Yves Montand, Bob Newhart, Larry Blyden, Simon Oakland, Jack Nicholson (Paramount)

The story line, without the gimmick of reincarnation, is pure soap suds. Barbra Streisand is a chain smoker. To stop smoking before an important dinner, she crashes a medical school class in hypnotism taught by Yves Montand. He accidentally discovers that she has extra sensory perception. Under hypnosis, she becomes an aristocratic femme fatale with whom Montand falls in love.

ONCE AROUND
1991, 114 mins, US Ⓥ ⊙
D: Lasse Hallstrom **A:** Richard Dreyfuss, Holly Hunter, Danny Aiello, Laura San Giacomo, Gena Rowlands (Universal/Cinecom)

Intelligently engaging domestic comedy-drama keenly delineates how a woman finding happiness with a man paradoxically involves the serious deterioration of relations within her close-knit family. Rebuffed by her b.f., Hunter flees chilly Boston for the Caribbean, where she instantly is swept off her feet by irrepressible, vulgar, tireless, wealthy condominium salesman Richard Dreyfuss. Brightest strategy is forcing the viewer to experience Hunter's family's acceptance of Dreyfuss. His sheer relentlessness darkens the mood and thickens the complexity of the situation.

ONCE A THIEF
1965, 106 mins, US ▢
D: Ralph Nelson **A:** Alain Delon, Ann-Margret, Van Heflin, Jack Palance, John Davis Chandler (M-G-M)

Once a Thief packs both violence and young married love in unfoldment of its theme, aptly titled, about an ex-con trying to go straight, but constantly harassed by a vengeful cop. Delon is first-rate. Heflin, as Delon's nemesis, effectively plays the relentless police officer, and Palance, with less footage, similarly scores.

ONCE IN PARIS
1978, 100 mins, US ⓥ
D: Frank D. Gilroy **A:** Wayne Rogers, Gayle Hunnicutt, Jack Lenoir, Philippe March, Tanya Lopert (Gilroy)

A highly personalized tale of a rough-around-the-edges Yank screenwriter's relationship with a worldly chauffeur and a beauteous British aristocrat, developed in subtle, believable, intelligent, and often humorous fashion. Shot entirely in Paris, with a French crew, the pic gets maximum mileage from its three principals: Wayne Rogers, Gayle Hunnicutt, and Jack Lenoir.

ONCE IS NOT ENOUGH
(AKA: JACQUELINE SUSANN'S ONCE IS NOT ENOUGH)
1975, 121 mins, US ⓥ ▢
D: Guy Green **A:** Kirk Douglas, Alexis Smith, David Janssen, George Hamilton, Melina Mercouri (Paramount)

Tame potboiler. Kirk Douglas heads as a fading film producer devoted to daughter Deborah Raffin, so much so that he marries wealthy Alexis Smith to pay for the daughter's lifestyle. Opulent production credits put the shallow dramaturgy even more to shame. Henry Mancini's lush romantic score is appropriate.
1975: Nomination: Best Supp. Actress (Brenda Vaccaro)

ONCE MORE, MY DARLING
1949, 92 mins, US
D: Robert Montgomery **A:** Robert Montgomery, Ann Blyth, Jane Cowl, Lillian Randolph (Universal/Neptune)

As director and star, Robert Montgomery gives the picture deft direction and first-class comedy playing. Montgomery is seen as an attorney-actor who is called up from his inactive army reserve status to woo a young heiress (Ann Blyth) and track down the man who has given her several pieces of "liberated" Nazi jewelry. Blyth shows a bent for comedy and tickles viewers with her furious wooing of the man who was supposed to make the romantic pitch.

ONCE MORE, WITH FEELING
1960, 92 mins, US
D: Stanley Donen **A:** Yul Brynner, Kay Kendall, Geoffrey Toone, Maxwell Shaw, Gregory Ratoff, Mervyn Johns (Columbia)

A smart, perfectly cast comedy. Kay Kendall died less than three months after *Once More* was completed. Her eyes clouded with tears, Kendall blows a kiss in her final scene, the sentiment seeming peculiarly prophetic. However, the picture of the actress through the rest of the film is one of life and of a spirited performer. As a pompous sympathy conductor with a love of fine music that surpasses his participation in mundane existence, Yul Brynner has strength and humor, adeptly playing sly appeal against defiant arrogance. Together, he and Kendall make an overwhelming screen couple.

ONCE UPON A CRIME
1992, 94 mins, US ⓥ ⊙
D: Eugene Levy **A:** John Candy, James Belushi, Cybill Shepherd, Sean Young, Ornella Muti (De Laurentiis)

A group of US stars chews its way through Italy and France in search of a movie. The action is fittingly spurred along by a dog, as an out-of-work actor (Richard Lewis) and just-jilted woman (Sean Young) find a stray dachshund and trek from Rome to Monte Carlo to collect the $5,000 reward for its return. But the pair find the dog's owner murdered and get implicated in the crime, as do a compulsive gambler (John Candy), a too-ugly American (James Belushi), and his neglected wife (Cybill Shepherd).

ONCE UPON A HONEYMOON
1942, 116 mins, US ⓥ ⊙
D: Leo McCarey **A:** Ginger Rogers, Cary Grant, Walter Slezak, Albert Dekker, Albert Basserman (RKO)

Story picks up Ginger Rogers as a naive gold digger and former stripper from Flatbush in Vienna on the eve of her wedding to influential Nazi (Walter Slezak). Cary Grant, American war correspondent, meets her and falls in love, following the honeymooning couple through Eastern Europe until he convinces Rogers that her husband is Hitler's henchman.

ONCE UPON A TIME IN AMERICA
1984, 227 mins, US Ⓥ ⊙
D: Sergio Leone **A:** Robert De Niro, James Woods, Elizabeth McGovern, Treat Williams, Tuesday Weld, Burt Young (Ladd)

A disappointment of considerable proportions. Sprawling saga of Jewish gangsters over the decades is surprisingly deficient in clarity and purpose, as well as excitement and narrative involvement. Pic opens with a series of extraordinary violent episodes. It's 1933 and some hoods knock off a girlfriend and some cohorts of ''Noodles'' (Robert De Niro), while trying to track down the man himself. Then, action shifts to 1968, when the aging De Niro (superior makeup job) returns to New York after a 35-year absence and reunites with a childhood pal, Fat Moe (Larry Rapp). De Niro is clearly on a mission relating to his past.

ONCE UPON A TIME IN THE WEST
1969, 165 mins, Italy/US Ⓥ ⊙ ▭
D: Sergio Leone **A:** Henry Fonda, Claudia Cardinale, Jason Robards, Charles Bronson, Gabriele Ferzetti, Lionel Stander (Paramount/Rafran/San Marco)

Henry Fonda and Jason Robards relish each screen minute as the heavies, and Charles Bronson plays Clint Eastwood's ''man with no name'' role. Leone's story focuses on the various reactions of four people—the three male leads, plus Claudia Cardinale, extremely effective as a fancy lady from New Orleans—to the idea of garnering extreme wealth via ownership of a crucial water town on the route of the transcontinental railroad. The paradoxical but honest ''fun'' aspect of Leone's previous preoccupation with elaborately stylized violence is here unconvincingly asking for consideration in a new ''moral'' light.

ONCE WERE WARRIORS
1994, 99 mins, New Zealand Ⓥ
D: Lee Tamahori **A:** Rena Owen, Temuera Morrison, Mamaengaroa Kerr-Bell, Julian ''Sonny'' Arahanga, Taungaroa Emile (Communicado)

The barren lives of members of an ur-

ban Maori family are rigorously exposed in this rugged and painful picture. First-time director Lee Tamahori has done a marvelous job in depicting the day-to-day horror of the Heke family, which is held together only by its women, the sorely tried Beth and her eldest daughter, 16-year-old Grace. Beth comes from a noble Maori family, who disapproved of her marriage to Jake Heke some 18 years earlier. Pic would be unrelentingly downbeat if not for the magnetic performances of the lead players and for the fact that, despite the drinking and violence, the relationship between Beth and Jake is, against the odds, a warm one.

ON DANGEROUS GROUND
1951, 82 mins, US Ⓥ ⊙
D: Nicholas Ray **A:** Ida Lupino, Robert Ryan, Ward Bond, Charles Kemper, Anthony Ross (RKO)

Lack of definition in characters is chief flaw. There's not much Robert Ryan can do with the character of a cop made tough by the types with whom he is brought into contact, nor does Ida Lupino have much opportunity as a blind girl who presumably softens Ryan's character. Ray manages to inject an occasional bit of excitement into the yarn, and had the psychotic touches been elimated in the script, film could have qualified as okay, even if grim, melodrama.

ON DEADLY GROUND
1994, 101 mins, US Ⓥ ⊙ ▭
D: Steven Seagal **A:** Steven Seagal, Michael Caine, Joan Chen, John C. McGinley, R. Lee Ermey (Warner)

This filigree thriller with eco trappings and a decibel and body count that strains mind and matter is a vanity production parading as a social statement. It nonetheless has enough sound, fury, and flash to satisfy the action crowd who have propped up Steven Seagal's career. Seagal is a Red Adair-style troubleshooter and fire quasher for Aegis Oil Company in Alaska. After imploding one fire, he comes to the alarming discovery that it was preventable. The greed of chairman Michael Jennings (Michael Caine) is responsible for the orders to install substandard equipment. Soon Seagal is in mortal combat with the forces of evil from the corporate world.

ONE BORN EVERY MINUTE
See: The Flim-Flam Man

ONE DAY IN THE LIFE OF IVAN DENISOVICH

1972, 100 mins, UK/Norway ⊗ ⊙
D: Caspar Wrede **A:** Tom Courtenay, Espen Skjonberg, James Maxwell, Alfred Burke, Eric Thompson (Group W/Norsk)

Life chronicles a "good" day for Ivan Denisovich, a prisoner in the eighth year of a 10-year sentence at a Siberian labor camp. The day is filled with small victories over the system. Sincerity (and austerity) of the production, lensed expertly under fierce conditions in Norway by Sven Nykvist, cannot compensate for Caspar Wrede's lackluster direction and a script so sparse it almost seems nonexistent. Courtenay captures a mix of wiliness and childlike enthusiasm that is consistently convincing.

ONE DEADLY SUMMER

See: L'Ete Meurtrier

ONE-EYED JACKS

1961, 141 mins, US ⊗ ⊙
D: Marlon Brando **A:** Marlon Brando, Karl Malden, Pina Pellicer, Katy Jurado, Ben Johnson, Slim Pickens (Paramount/Pennebaker)

The brooding, deliberate tale of a young man (Marlon Brando) consumed by a passion for revenge after he is betrayed by an accomplice (Karl Malden) in a bank robbery. His vengeful campaign leads him to the town of Monterey, where Malden has attained respectability and the position of sheriff, but romantic entanglements with Malden's stepdaughter (Pina Pellicer) persuade Brando to abandon his intention until the irresistibility of circumstance and Malden's own irrepressible will to snuff out the living evidence of his guilt draws the two men into a showdown.

1961: Nomination: Best Color Cinematography

ONE FALSE MOVE

1991, 105 mins, US ⊗ ⊙
D: Carl Franklin **A:** Bill Paxton, Cynda Williams, Billy Bob Thornton, Michael Beach, Jim Metzler (IRS Media)

Offbeat scenario features an attractive young woman (Cynda Williams), who's fallen into very bad company in L.A. Her b.f. (Billy Bob Thornton) and his accomplice (Michael Beach), both vicious killers, are after a big cache of cash and cocaine. They hit the road for Houston, where they plan to off-load the drugs on a dealer. Also on the itinerary is a promised trip to small-town Arkansas to visit the baby Williams left behind. Working for the most part in straightforward style, director Carl Franklin achieves considerable suspense by pitting the frailties of each party against the other.

ONE FINE DAY

1996, 108 mins, US ⊗ ⊙
D: Michael Hoffman **A:** Michelle Pfeiffer, George Clooney, Mae Whitman, Alex D. Linz, Charles Durning, Ellen Greene (Fox 2000/20th Century-Fox)

One Fine Day is the pretty ideal baby-boomer romance, made with breezy insouciance and performed with consummate flair. Melanie (Michelle Pfeiffer) and Jack (George Clooney) "meet cute" and are antagonistic from the outset. Divorced Jack, a hard-hitting columnist, is in charge of his five-year-old daughter (Mae Whitman). Same-aged Sammy (Alex D. Linz), (classmate of Jack's daughter) and son of divorced architect Melanie, misses a school trip on a ferry. Thus, the two parents are stuck with their kids for the day. Jack is in the middle of an erupting City Hall controversy. Melanie has a major presentation to make. With accident-prone Sammy causing a succession of disasters, his defiant mother finally agrees to let the egotistical Jack help her out a bit. By fade-out, pic conveys a sweet quality that mostly overrides the time-squeezed contrivances of the plotting.

ONE FLEW OVER THE CUCKOO'S NEST

1975, 133 mins, US ⊗ ⊙
D: Milos Forman **A:** Jack Nicholson, Louise Fletcher, William Redfield, Dean Brooks, Scatman Crothers, Danny DeVito (Fantasy)

One Flew over the Cuckoo's Nest is brilliant cinema theater. Jack Nicholson stars in an outstanding characterization of asylum antihero McMurphy, and Milos Forman's direction of a superbly cast film is equally meritorious. The film traces the havoc wrecked in Louise Fletcher's zombie-run mental ward when Nicholson (either an illness faker or a free spirit) displays a kind of leadership that neither Fletcher nor the system can handle.

1975: Best Picture, Director, Actor (Jack Nicholson), Actress (Louise Fletcher), Adapted Screenplay
Nominations: Best Supp. Actor (Brad Dourif), Cinematography, Editing, Original Score

ONE FOOT IN HEAVEN
1941, 106 mins, US
D: Irving Rapper **A:** Fredric March, Martha Scott, Beulah Bondi, Gene Lockhart, Harry Davenport (Warner)

A warm and human preachment for godliness. Spence (Fredric March) comes to religion through listening to an evangelist. He takes his fiancée (Martha Scott) from her opulent Canadian home to his first parish in an Iowa mudroad town. This is the beginning of a trek through similar parishes with the Spences undergoing various privations. They raise three children, likably played by Frankie Thomas, Elisabeth Fraser, and Casey Johnson. March and Scott are both splendid in their roles.
1941: Nomination: Best Picture

ONE FROM THE HEART
1982, 101 mins, US Ⓥ ⊙
D: Francis Ford Coppola **A:** Frederic Forrest, Teri Garr, Nastassja Kinski, Raul Julia, Lainie Kazan, Harry Dean Stanton (Zoetrope)

A hybrid musical romantic fantasy, lavishing giddy heights of visual imagination and technical brilliance onto a wafer-thin story of true love turned sour, then sweet. Set against an intentionally artificial fantasy version of Las Vegas, the film quite simply plots the breakup, separate dalliances, and eventual happy ending of a pair of five-year lovers (Frederic Forrest and Teri Garr) over the course of a single Independence Day. He meets a sultry, exotic circus girl (Nastassja Kinski); she's swept away by a suave Latino singing waiter (Raul Julia).
1982: Nomination: Best Original Song Score

ONE GOOD COP
1991, 105 mins, US Ⓥ ⊙
D: Heywood Gould **A:** Michael Keaton, Rene Russo, Anthony LaPaglia, Kevin Conway, Rachel Ticotin, Tony Plana (Hollywood/Silver Screen Partners IV)

Michael Keaton plays a staunchly decent cop who's as close to his longtime partner (Anthony LaPaglia) as he is to his fashion designer wife (Rene Russo). When widowed LaPaglia gets killed, Keaton and Russo take in his three orphaned little girls. But the authorities seem rather eager to take them away and Keaton's crowded digs can't accommodate a family, so he winds up on a wrong-side-of-the-law stunt to come up with enough money to be a hero at home. The skill with which the writer-director works the audience into the

palm of his hand makes this a crowd pleaser.

ONE HOUR TO DOOMSDAY
See: City Beneath the Sea

ONE HOUR WITH YOU
1932, 75 mins, US
D: Ernst Lubitsch **A:** Maurice Chevalier, Jeanette MacDonald, Genevieve Tobin, Charles Ruggles, Roland Young (Paramount)

Chevalier periodically interrupts the romantic sequence to come downscreen for a close-up to intimately address the "ladies and gentlemen" as to his amorous problems. It starts first with the opening scene in the Bois de Boulogne of Paris where Chevalier and his bride (Jeanette MacDonald) of three years are caught necking. The gendarme won't believe it's legal so they retire to their home where, in a boudoir scene, Chevalier interrupts just in time for that first aside to tell the audience that they really are married. Genevieve Tobin in an obvious "make" role completes the triangle. Jeanette MacDonald is a superb complement to the star, intelligently getting her song lyrics over in a quiet, chatty manner.
1931/32: Nomination: Best Picture

ONE HUNDRED AND ONE DALMATIANS
1961, 79 mins, US Ⓥ
D: Wolfgang Reitherman, Hamilton Luske, Clyde Geronimi (Walt Disney)

While not as indelibly enchanting or inspired as some of the studio's most unforgettable animated endeavors, this is nonetheless a painstaking creative effort. Even the most hardened, dogmatic pooch detester is likely to be amused by several passages in this story. Yarn, based on the book by Dodie Smith, is set in London and concerned with the efforts of Blighty's four-legged population to rescue 99 dognapped pups from the clutches of one Cruella De Vill, a chic up-to-date personification of the classic witch.

101 DALMATIANS
1996, 103 mins, US Ⓥ ⊙ ▭
D: Stephen Herek **A:** Glenn Close, Jeff Daniels, Joely Richardson, Joan Plowright, Hugh Laurie, Mark Williams (Great Oaks/Walt Disney)

Glenn Close and the lead dogs are great, but a key conceptual decision prevents Disney's live-action *101 Dalmatians* from being the cat's meow. The attraction between the Dalmatians of American computer game designer Roger (Jeff Daniels) and Brit fashion designer Anita (Joely Richardson) brings their masters into instantaneous marriage. Canine lovebirds Pongo and Perdy are soon expecting, as are their human counterparts. Anita's boss, fearsome fashion-world diva Cruella DeVill (Glenn Close) is more intrigued by the prospect of some little doggies for an authentic Dalmatian coat. The pups are kidnapped and spirited to a distant old mansion, where 84 other Dalmatians await a cruel fate. Where the film misses its biggest bet is in depriving the animals of the voices they had in the 1961 animated version. In the post-*Babe* era, the dogs could have been given the same capacity for verbal expression, but, alas, they just bark, whimper and growl.

ONE HUNDRED MEN AND A GIRL
1937, 85 mins, US
D: Henry Koster **A:** Deanna Durbin, Adolphe Menjou, Alice Brady, Eugene Pallette, Mischa Auer, Leopold Stokowski (Universal)

Deanna Durbin is a bright, luminous star in her second picture. Universal wisely gives her excellent support in Leopold Stokowski, director of the Philadelphia Symphony Orchestra, who plays a lengthy film role with surprising ease and conviction, and Adolphe Menjou, in a role quite different from his usual type of part. The "hundred men" of the title are members of a symphony orchestra of unemployed musicians whom Durbin is organizing and managing. Idea is that the unemployed artists in order to get sponsorship for a radio contract must obtain a conductor with an outstanding name of wide radio appeal.
1937: Best Score
Nomination: Best Picture, Original Story, Editing, Sound

ONE IN A MILLION
1936, 92 mins, US
D: Sidney Lanfield **A:** Sonja Henie, Adolphe Menjou, Jean Hersholt, Ned Sparks, Don Ameche, Ritz brothers. (20th Century-Fox)

A very entertaining, adroitly mixed concoction of romance, music, comedy, and skating introduces to film audiences Olympic figure-skating champion Sonja Henie. A sweet demeanor, engaging personality, an intriguing Scandinavian accent, and an abundance of poise are among her assets. In *One in a Million* Henie wears the skates a good part of the

time, giving various exhibitions that are Pavlovaesque on frozen water.

ONE IS A LONELY NUMBER
1972, 97 mins, US V
D: Mel Stuart **A:** Trish Van Devere, Monte Markham, Janet Leigh, Melvyn Douglas, Jane Elliot (M-G-M)

An excellent contemporary drama about the big and little problems affecting a divorced woman. Trish Van Devere is forced into self-reliance for the first time in her life. It isn't always easy. But Van Devere does get help, principally from the kindness of old store-keeper Melvyn Douglas; professional man hater Janet Leigh; Jane Elliot, the heroine's best friend; and Maurice Argent, manager of the neighborhood swimming pool where she finds employment. Van Devere, strikingly beautiful, projects a credible warmth, depth of character, and a great deal of ladylike sensuality.

ONE MAN MUTINY
See: The Court-Martial of Billy Mitchell

ONE MILLION B.C.
(UK: MAN AND HIS MATE)
1940, 80 mins, US V ⊙
D: Hal Roach, Hal Roach Jr. **A:** Victor Mature, Carole Landis, Lon Chaney Jr., John Hubbard, Nigel de Brulier (Roach/United Artists)

One Million B.C. looks something like A.D. 1910; it's that corny. Except for the strange-sounding grunts and monosyllabic dialogue, it is also another silent. There isn't much sense to the action nor much interest in the characters. Majority of the animals fail to impress but the fight between a couple of lizards, magnified into great size, is exciting and well photographed. The ease with which some of the monsters are destroyed by man is a big laugh, notably the way one is subdued with a fishing spear. Knocking off a giant iguana is another audience snicker. The story, pretty thin, relates to the way common dangers serve to wash up hostilities between the Rock and Shell clans.
1940: Nominations: Best Original Score, Special Effects

ONE MILLION YEARS B.C.
1966, 100 mins, UK V
D: Don Chaffey **A:** Raquel Welch, John Richardson, Percy Herbert, Robert Brown, Martine Beswick (Hammer)

Biggest novelty gimmick is that dialogue is minimal, consisting almost entirely of grunts. Raquel Welch here gets little opportunity to prove herself an actress but she is certainly there in the looks department. Don Chaffey does a reliable job directorially, but leans heavily on the ingenious special effects in the shape of prehistoric animals and a striking earthquake dreamed up by Ray Harryhausen. Simple idea of the film is of the earth as a barren, hostile place, one million years B.C., inhabitated by two tribes, the aggressive Rock People and the more intelligent, gentler Shell People.

ONE NIGHT OF LOVE
1934, 98 mins, US ⓥ ⊙
D: Victor Schertzinger A: Grace Moore, Tullio Carminati, Lyle Talbot, Mona Barrie, Jessie Ralph, Luis Alberni (Columbia)

Basically an operatic film. It's the fact that the film is human and down to earth that helps most. Even the operatic excerpts have all been carefully picked for popular appeal. A singer (Grace Moore) fails to win a radio contest so goes to Europe on her own, has usual student struggles, sings in a café, is discovered by Tullio Carminati, a great singing teacher. He drives her, mesmerizes her, makes her into a star. She falls in love with him, and is jealous of another girl singer.
1934: Best Score, Sound Recording
Nominations: Best Picture, Director, Actress (Grace Moore), Editing

ONE NIGHT STAND
1984, 94 mins, Australia ⓥ
D: John Duigan A: Tyler Coppin, Cassandra Delaney, Jay Hackett, Saskia Post, Midnight Oil (Edgley)

It's New Year's Eve on a hot summer night in Sydney. Nuclear war has broken out in Europe and North America, and bombs have already dropped on US facilities in Australia: everyone is warned to stay where they are. Thus begins a long, long night. Pic builds inexorably to a truly shattering climax, yet doesn't rely on special effects or histrionics.

ONE NIGHT STAND
1995, 92 mins, US ⓥ
D: Talia Shire A: Ally Sheedy, A. Martinez, Frederic Forrest, Don Novello, Diane Salinger (Concorde/New Horizons)

An intriguing exploration of the sexuality of a lonely and frustrated woman eventually develops into a banal and familiar thriller involving murder and incest. Commercial designer "Micky" Sanderson (Ally Sheedy) allows herself to be picked up by a complete stranger (A. Martinez)

for a hot night of sex. Next morning, Micky wakes up alone in an empty apartment. She becomes obsessed with finding her dream lover again. Sheedy is fine in a gutsy portrayal.

ONE NIGHT STAND
1997, 102 mins, US ⓥ ⊙
D: Mike Figgis A: Wesley Snipes, Nastassja Kinski, Ming-Na Wen, Robert Downey Jr., Kyle MacLachlan, Amanda Donohoe (Red Mullet/New Line)

As fluid, loose and seductive as the languid jazz riffs with which Mike Figgis underscores its moods, *One Night Stand* is a complex, almost existential take on relationships and reassessing life choices. Tryst of the title takes place with successful Los Angeles–based commercials director Max (Wesley Snipes) is in New York on a job and meets Karen (Nastassja Kinski). Returning to L.A. the next morning, Max squirms guiltily in front of his wife, Mimi (Ming-Na Wen). Profoundly altered by the New York experience, Max begins to pull back from the soullessness of his job and shallow social circle. He returns to New York a year later, now accompanied by Mimi, and unexpectedly meets Karen. Conclusion feels wrong in its neat symmetry, but this is the work of a filmmaker firmly in control and not afraid to take risks. Snipes has rarely been better: his sleek masculinity is arrestingly paired with the dreamy poise of Kinski. Interestingly, no issue is made of the interracial dynamics.

ONE OF OUR AIRCRAFT IS MISSING
1942, 100 mins, UK ⓥ
D: Michael Powell A: Godfrey Tearle, Eric Portman, Hugh Williams, Bernard Miles, Pamela Brown (British National)

A bomber is returning from a raid on Stuttgart when it is hit. Over Holland the crew are compelled to bale out, landing in Dutch (occupied) territory, where the people protect them and give them disguises. A lot of Dutch people are recruited as natives of Holland, all of them excellent, not to mention Hay Petrie as the burgomaster.
1942: Nominations: Best Original Screenplay, Special Effects

ONE ON ONE
1977, 98 mins, US ⓥ
D: Lamont Johnson A: Robby Benson, Annette O'Toole, G. D. Spradlin, Gail Strickland, Melanie Griffith (Warner)

A trite and disappointing little film

about a Los Angeles college basketball player. It follows the formula about the underdog-turned-hero but fails to ignite the emotions. Robby Benson's awkward performance slows down the film badly and makes it hard to empathize with him. It's unbelievable that this nebbish would be pursued by such mature and attractive women as Annette O'Toole and Gail Strickland.

ONE POTATO, TWO POTATO
1964, 102 mins, US
D: Larry Peerce A: Barbara Barrie, Bernie Hamilton, Richard Mulligan, Marti Merika (Cinema V/Weston-Bowalco)

Tender, tactful look at miscegenation that speaks in human rather than polemic terms. It deals with a seemingly well-adjusted young Negro office worker who meets a young white divorcée who has a little girl. Their idyll grows slowly and gently as both react on normal planes with the color no apparent problem. Then along comes the woman's first husband, who demands the custody of the little girl. A sympathetic judge locates the girl in a good home, since he feels that as long as prejudice exists the little girl's life could be touched by it.
1964: Nomination: Best Original Story & Screenplay

ONE SPY TOO MANY
1966, 101 mins, US
D: Joseph Sargent A: Robert Vaughn, David McCallum, Rip Torn, Dorothy Provine, Leo G. Carroll (Arena/M-G-M)

Expanded from a Man from U.N.C.L.E. TV two-parter, One Spy Too Many zips along at a jazzy spy thriller pace. Action and gadgetry are hung on a slender plot. Alexander, played by Rip Torn, hoists from the US Army biological warfare division a tankful of its secret "will gas." International espionage agents Robert Vaughn and David McCallum begin to pursue Alexander and are joined in their efforts by his wife (Dorothy Provine).

ONE TOUCH OF VENUS
1948, 81 mins, US Ⓥ ◉
D: William A. Seiter A: Robert Walker, Ava Gardner, Dick Haymes, Eve Arden, Olga San Juan, Tom Conway (Universal)

Pleasant comedy fantasy. Ava Gardner steps into the top ranks as the goddess Venus. Hers is a sock impression, bountifully physical and alluring, delivered with a delightfully sly instinct for comedy. Plot covers the romantic adventures of a department store window dresser (Robert Walker), who kisses a statue of Venus and brings her to life for 24 hours. Walker delivers a gifted comedy performance. Eve Arden, the store owner's glib secretary, gives another of her punchy deliveries. Musical high spots please the ear and best is "Speak Low", from the original Kurt Weill–Ogden Nash score, reprised several times.

ONE, TWO, THREE
1961, 115 mins, US Ⓥ ◉ ⌑
D: Billy Wilder A: James Cagney, Horst Buchholz, Pamela Tiffin, Arlene Francis, Lilo Pulver, Howard St. John (Mirisch)

Fast-paced, high-pitched, hard-hitting, lighthearted farce crammed with topical gags and spiced with satirical overtones. Story is so furiously quick-witted that some of its wit gets snarled and smothered in overlap. But total experience packs a considerable wallop. James Cagney is the chief exec of Coca-Cola's West Berlin plant whose ambitious promotion plans are jeopardized when he becomes temporary guardian of his Stateside superior's wild and vacuous daughter. Cagney proves himself an expert farceur with a glib, full-throttled characterization.
1961: Nomination: Best B&W Cinematography

ONE WAY PENDULUM
1965, 90 mins, UK
D: Peter Yates A: Eric Sykes, George Cole, Julia Foster, Jonathan Miller, Peggy Mount, Mona Washbourne (Woodfall)

What there is of a plot deals with an eccentric British family. Papa (Eric Sykes) seeks change from his humdrum existence by erecting a do-it-yourself replica of the Old Bailey in his living room; the mother (Alison Leggatt) engages a charwoman (Peggy Mount) not to clean but to eat the family's leftovers. Nearly rational is daughter (Julia Foster), whose only concern is that her arms don't reach her knees. Peter Yates directs with a technique that treats comedy as deadly serious.

ONE WILD NIGHT
See: Career Opportunities

ONE WOMAN'S STORY
See: The Passionate Friends

ON GOLDEN POND
1981, 109 mins, US Ⓥ ◉
D: Mark Rydell A: Katharine Hepburn, Henry Fonda, Jane Fonda, Dabney Cole-

man, Doug McKeon (Universal/ITC/IPC)

Without question, these are major, meaty roles for Katharine Hepburn and Henry Fonda. The fact that Ernest Thompson's 1978 play backs away from the dramatic fireworks that might have been tends to mute the overall impact of the piece, but sufficient pleasures remain. Fonda and Hepburn arrive at their New England cottage to spend their 48th summer together. He's approaching his 80th birthday and his mostly intentional rudeness and irascibility make life difficult for others in his vicinity. Along come daughter, Jane Fonda, future son-in-law, Dabney Coleman, and latter's son, Doug McKeon. Jane is clearly still terrified of her dad, suffering from lingering feelings of neglect and inferiority.
1981: Best Actor (Henry Fonda), Actress (Katharine Hepburn), Adapted Screenplay **Nominations:** Best Picture, Director, Supp. Actress (Jane Fonda), Cinematography, Editing, Score, Sound

ON HER MAJESTY'S SECRET SERVICE
1969, 139 mins, UK Ⓥ ⊙ ▭
D: Peter Hunt **A:** George Lazenby, Diana Rigg, Telly Savalas, Ilse Steppat, Gabriele Ferzetti, Bernard Lee (United Artists)

Film of breakneck physical excitement and stunning visual attractions in which George Lazenby replaced Sean Connery as James Bond. Lazenby is pleasant, capable, and attractive in the role, but he doesn't have the latter's physique, voice, and saturnine, virile looks. Telly Savalas is experimenting with biological warfare to take over the world. Bond finds his true love, Diana Rigg, coolly beautiful, intelligent, sardonic.

ONIBABA
(US: THE HOLE)
1965, 103 mins, Japan
D: Kaneto Shindo **A:** Nobuko Otowa, Jitsuko Yoshimura, Kei Sato, Jukichi Uno, Taiji Tonomura (Kindai/Tokyo)

Too often a pot-pourri of ravenous eating and blatant sex. Basic plot shows an elderly woman and her daughter-in-law during the civil wars of 16th-century Japan. They live among the reeds. When wounded, exhausted warriors wander in, the women kill them. The victims are stripped of their weapons and clothing, which they sell in return for food. Nobuko Otowa is superb as the older woman, while Jitsuko Yoshimura contributes an excellent characterization as the daughter-in-law.

ONION FIELD, THE
1979, 122 mins, US Ⓥ ⊙
D: Harold Becker **A:** John Savage, James Woods, Ted Danson, Ronny Cox, Franklyn Seales (Avco Embassy/Black Marble)

Highly detailed dramatization of a true case deals with death and guilt, and the manipulation of the judicial system to pervert justice. Set in 1963, two plainclothes cops stop a couple of suspicious-looking punks in a car. One of the bad guys pulls a gun and the cops are disarmed and kidnapped. They are taken to an onion field miles away and one is brutally murdered. The second makes his escape. The two killers are quickly arrested but each claims the other did the killing.

ONLY ANGELS HAVE WINGS
1939, 120 mins, US Ⓥ
D: Howard Hawks **A:** Cary Grant, Jean Arthur, Richard Barthelmess, Rita Hayworth, Thomas Mitchell, Sig Ruman (Columbia)

Cary Grant is boss of the kindly Dutchman's decrepit airline. Jean Arthur is an American showgirl en route to Panama. Subplot has Richard Barthelmess coming on the scene with Rita Hayworth as his wife. Baranca is the basic setting of this subtropical aviation romance where treacherous mountain crags, capricious rainstorms, and the like do their utmost to worst the mail plane service. The Grant-Arthur cynicism and tough romance are kept at a high standard.
1939: Nomination: Best Special Effects

ONLY GAME IN TOWN, THE
1970, 113 mins, US Ⓥ
D: George Stevens **A:** Elizabeth Taylor, Warren Beatty, Charles Braswell, Hank Henry (20th Century-Fox)

A rather mixed blessing. Elizabeth Taylor and Warren Beatty star as two Vegas drifters who find love with each other. Beatty delivers an engaging performance as a gambling addict, working off his debts as a saloon pianist. Frank D. Gilroy's script permits both stars to shine in solo and ensemble moments of hope, despair, recrimination, and sardonic humor. But the drama develops too sluggishly.

ONLY THE LONELY
1991, 102 mins, US Ⓥ ⊙
D: Chris Columbus **A:** John Candy, Maureen O'Hara, Ally Sheedy, Kevin Dunn,

Milo O'Shea, Anthony Quinn (20th Century-Fox/Hughes)

A charming and well-observed romantic comedy about a single Chicago cop (John Candy) trying to break free from his smothering Irish mom (Maureen O'Hara, in her welcome return to the screen after 20 years). Performances are delightfully true and never descend into bathos or cheap sentiment. O'Hara uses her native Dublin accent and her feistiest nononsense style to convey the mean-spirited, bigoted personality of Rose Muldoon. Candy is a sweet-natured fellow who yearns for something more out of life but is afraid to ask for it. When he meets a shy mortuary cosmetician (Ally Sheedy), Candy begins to assert himself in ways that drive his mother to new lows of tart-tongued nastiness.

ONLY THE VALIANT
1951, 104 mins, US ⓥ ⊙
D: Gordon Douglas A: Gregory Peck, Barbara Payton, Ward Bond, Gig Young, Lon Chaney Jr., Neville Brand (Cagney/Warner)

In this cavalry yarn unfolding in the wild Apache country of the old West, Gregory Peck plays a martinet, an army captain who lives strictly by the rule book; consequently, although regarded as a fine soldier he is greatly disliked by his men. Plot revolves around his leading a detachment of men to an outpost that guards the only pass by which the Apaches can cross the mountain.

ONLY TWO CAN PLAY
1962, 106 mins, UK ⓥ
D: Sidney Gilliat A: Peter Sellers, Mai Zetterling, Virginia Maskell, Richard Attenborough (British Lion)

Film never fully decides whether it is supposed to be light comedy, farce, or satire. But it remains a cheerful piece of nonsense with some saucy dialogue and situations capably exploited by Sellers and his colleagues. He is a member of the staff of a Welsh public library, a white-collar job. He is fed up and frustrated with the eternal prospect of living in a shabby apartment with a dispirited wife, two awful kids, peeling wallpaper, erratic plumbing, and a dragon of a landlady. Into his drab life floats the bored, sexy young wife of a local bigwig and she makes a play for Sellers.

ONLY WHEN I LARF
1968, 103 mins, UK
D: Basil Dearden A: David Hemmings, Richard Attenborough, Alexandra Stewart, Nicholas Pennell, Terence Alexander (Paramount)

A pleasant little joke. Filmed in London, New York, and Beirut, it has Richard Attenborough, David Hemmings, and Alexandra Stewart as a con trio. Situation arises whereby Attenborough and Hemmings fall out and seek to double-cross each other. The whole film has Attenborough at his considerable comedy best. Hemmings is equally effective as the discontented young whiz-kid lieutenant, and Stewart manages to look both efficient and sexy.

ONLY WHEN I LAUGH
(UK: IT HURTS ONLY WHEN I LAUGH)
1981, 120 mins, US ⓥ ⊙
D: Glenn Jordan A: Marsha Mason, Kristy McNichol, James Coco, Joan Hackett, David Dukes, Kevin Bacon (Columbia)

Patrons expecting a skin-deep laugh fest may be surprised at the unusually somber shadows and heavy dramatics that make their way into this tale, though abundant humor still shines through. Marsha Mason delivers a bravura performance as a divorced actress who returns from a drying-out session at an alcoholic clinic to face a revitalized career both on the legit boards and as a mother to her long-estranged, 17-year-old daughter, well played here by Kristy McNichol. Core of the film is McNichol's attempt to reestablish a full-time relationship with her mother.
1981: Nominations: Best Actress (Marsha Mason), Supp. Actor (James Coco), Supp. Actress (Joan Hackett)

ONLY YESTERDAY
1933, 105 mins, US
D: John M. Stahl A: Margaret Sullavan, John Boles, Edna May Oliver, Billie Burke, Benita Hume, Reginald Denny (Universal)

Introducing to the screen Margaret Sullavan, trained in legit, this picture is as auspicious a launching as could be asked by any performer. It is the irony of the heroine's life to be twice seduced by the same man but not recognized by him. A lapse of 12 years has wiped the man's memory clean but to the woman, in her middle thirties, her love for the man is as pristine as when she first surrendered. The lad with the faulty memory is John Boles, a tenor who turns out to be a dependable dramatic leading man.

ONLY YOU
1994, 108 mins, US Ⓥ ⊙
D: Norman Jewison **A:** Marisa Tomei, Robert Downey Jr., Bonnie Hunt, Joaquim De Almeida, Fisher Stevens (Tri-Star/Yorktown)

A puff of romantic comedy set in a storybook Italy. As a child, Faith is informed by both a Ouija board and a fortune-teller that her man of destiny will be named Damon Bradley. Fourteen years later, Faith (Marisa Tomei), a Pittsburgh schoolteacher, is set to marry straight-and-narrow podiatrist Dwayne (John Benjamin Hickey) when an old friend of Dwayne's calls in his regrets for not being able to attend the wedding, since he's leaving for Venice that very day. Oh, yes, his name is Damon Bradley. Tomei comes on a little strong for some tastes, but her enthusiasm and ordinary-gal quality will get most viewers rooting for her. Downey is spirited and winning in one of the more conventional roles he's played to date.

ON MOONLIGHT BAY
1951, 94 mins, US
D: Roy Del Ruth **A:** Doris Day, Gordon MacRae, Jack Smith, Leon Ames, Rosemary DeCamp, Mary Wickes (Warner)

Nostalgic comedy-romance of the 1915–17 period. Doris Day is seen as the 18-year-old tomboyish daughter of Leon Ames and Rosemary DeCamp and the sister of puckish kid brother, Billy Gray. Day transitions from tomboy to dating miss when she meets Gordon MacRae after papa has moved his family to a new neighborhood, and the plot carries the principals through typical involvements, romantic and family, before pop finally consents to a marriage.

ON MY WAY TO THE CRUSADES, I MET A GIRL WHO . . .
1968, 93 mins, Italy/US
D: Pasquale Festa Campanile **A:** Tony Curtis, Monica Vitti, Nino Castelnuovo, Hugh Griffith, John Richardson (Julia/Warner/Seven Arts)

There's plenty of entertainment in this release. Set in the Middle Ages, when bumpkin-type provincial noble Guerrando (Tony Curtis) is knighted to become a crusade draftee. He gets a castle, the tax-collecting concession, and the right to have affairs with all eligible soft-bosomed

femininity in his fief. Only holdout is Boccadoro (Golden Lips) played by Monica Vitti, an emancipated forest wench. Director fluctuates between classy ribald satire and stock burlesque.

ON OUR MERRY WAY
(AKA: A MIRACLE CAN HAPPEN)
1948, 107 mins, US
D: King Vidor, Leslie Fenton **A:** Burgess Meredith, Paulette Goddard, Fred MacMurray, James Stewart, Dorothy Lamour, Henry Fonda (United Artists)

The fact that this attempt at whimsy doesn't always come off is incidental; just look at the cast! The film is divided in episodic sequences when an inquiring reporter seeks to have answered the question of how a child influenced the lives of a group of selected adults. Meredith responds capitally to the mood of the character he plays, being given more of a chance to do so than any of the other stars.

ON THE AVENUE
1937, 90 mins, US Ⓥ
D: Roy Del Ruth **A:** Dick Powell, Madeleine Carroll, Alice Faye, Ritz brothers, Alan Mowbray (20th Century-Fox)

On the Avenue is no sock but has attractive personalities. It needs, however, all the tuneful support it can get from the Irving Berlin score. *Avenue* tells of Powell starring in his own revue, which satirizes "the richest girl in the world" (Carroll). In pique, she eventually buys up the entire production just to jazz up a romantic (stage) scene for Powell.

ON THE BEACH
1959, 134 mins, US Ⓥ
D: Stanley Kramer **A:** Gregory Peck, Ava Gardner, Fred Astaire, Anthony Perkins, Donna Anderson (United Artists)

Solid film of considerable emotional, as well as cerebral, content. But the final impact is as heavy as a leaden shroud. Gregory Peck is a US submarine commander. He and his men have been spared the atomic destruction because their vessel was submerged when the bombs went off. The locale is Australia and the time is 1964. It is only a matter of time before the radiation hits the continent and its people die as the rest of the world has died. All the personal stories are well presented. The trouble is that it is almost impossible to care with the implicit question ever-present—do they live? Fred Astaire, in his first straight dramatic role, attracts considerable attention.

1959: Nominations: Best Editing, Scoring of a Dramatic Picture

ON THE BLACK HILL
1988, 116 mins, UK ⓥ
D: Andrew Grieve **A:** Mike Gwilym, Robert Gwilym, Bob Peck, Gemma Jones (BFI/Film Four/British Screen)

A low-budget drama about Welsh hill farmers may not sound broadly appealing, but *On the Black Hill* is a remarkably moving and entertaining film offering a fascinating view of life in the border country between Wales and England. Pic follows the Jones family from 1895–1980, but mainly centers around twin brothers (played by brothers Mike and Robert Gwilym). It is through their inseparability, and the traumas and humor that inspires, that the story is told.

ON THE RIVIERA
1951, 89 mins, US ⓥ
D: Walter Lang **A:** Danny Kaye, Gene Tierney, Corinne Calvet, Marcel Dalio, Sig Ruman (20th Century-Fox)

Danny Kaye is an American entertainer working the Riviera with his French girlfriend (Corinne Calvet). Kaye is called in to double for French aviation hero at an important party from which the latter had been called by business. Gene Tierney is the beautiful wife of the flier and is wise to the impersonation, but the glib script introduces enough complications so that before the evening is over she's not sure. Full range of the Kaye talent is used, both in the music-comedy divisions and in straight performance.

ON THE TOWN
1949, 97 mins, US ⓥ ⊙
D: Gene Kelly, Stanley Donen **A:** Gene Kelly, Frank Sinatra, Betty Garrett, Ann Miller, Jules Munshin, Vera-Ellen (M-G-M)

Gene Kelly, Frank Sinatra, and Jules Munshin are the three sailors on a 24-hour leave in New York. Betty Garrett, Ann Miller, and Vera-Ellen are the three femmes who wind up with the navy. Picture is crammed with songs and dance numbers. Picture kicks off and ends with "New York, New York." Tune is used in the beginning as a musical backing for a montage of three curious sailors prowling the city's points of interest. It gets the film off to a fascinating start and the style and pacing is continued.

1949: Best Scoring of a Musical Picture

ON THE WATERFRONT
1954, 108 mins, US ⓥ ⊙
D: Elia Kazan **A:** Marlon Brando, Karl Malden, Lee J. Cobb, Rod Steiger, Eva Marie Saint (Columbia/Horizon)

Longshore labor scandals serve as the takeoff point for a flight into fictionalized violence concerning the terroristic rule of a dock union over its coarse and rough, but subdued, members. Marlon Brando puts on a spectacular show, giving a fascinating, multifaceted performance as the uneducated dock walloper and former pug, who is basically a softie with a special affection for his rooftop covey of pigeons and a neighborhood girl back from school. Eva Marie Saint has enough spirit to escape listlessness in her characterization.

1954: Best Picture, Director, Actor (Marlon Brando), Supp. Actress (Eva Marie Saint), Story & Screenplay, B&W Cinematography, B&W Art Direction, Editing **Nominations:** Best Supp. Actor (Lee J. Cobb, Carl Malden, Rod Steiger), Scoring of a Dramatic Picture

OPEN CITY
See: Roma, Citta Aperta

OPENING NIGHT
1978, 144 mins, US
D: John Cassavetes **A:** Gena Rowlands, Ben Gazzara, John Cassavetes, Joan Blondell, Paul Stewart, Zohra Lampert (Faces)

John Cassavetes, the cinematic poet of middle-class inner turmoil, explores the angst-ridden world of a famous actress on the brink of breakdown. Preparing a difficult role in a Broadway play, she witnesses the accidental death of a devoted fan, a traumatic event that causes her to reexamine her personal and professional relationships. Gena Rowlands turns in a virtuoso performance as the actress.

OPERATION CROSSBOW
1965, 118 mins, US ⓥ ▭
D: Michael Anderson **A:** Sophia Loren, George Peppard, Trevor Howard, John Mills, Tom Courtenay, Richard Johnson (M-G-M)

A sometimes suspenseful war melodrama. George Peppard plays the chief protagonist in this rambling tale of a British espionage mission, whose members impersonate German scientists believed dead, sent to locate and transmit information on the underground installation where

Nazis are working on their deadly project of long-range rockets.

OPERATION PETTICOAT
1959, 124 mins, US Ⓥ ⊙
D: Blake Edwards A: Cary Grant, Tony Curtis, Joan O'Brien, Dina Merrill, Gene Evans, Arthur O'Connell (Granart/Universal)

Operation Petticoat has no more weight than a sackful of feathers, but it has a lot of laughs. The time is December 1941, and the locale is the Philippines. Grant is the commander of a wheezy old submarine. The sub takes on as passengers five army nurses, a couple of Filipino families (including expectant mothers), and a goat. Grant is a living lesson in getting laughs without lines. Most of the gags play off him. Curtis is a splendid foil, and his different style of playing meshes easily with Grant's.
1959: Nomination: Best Original Story & Screenplay

OPERATION UNDERCOVER
See: *Report to the Commissioner*

OPPORTUNITY KNOCKS
1990, 105 mins, US Ⓥ ⊙
D: Donald Petrie A: Dana Carvey, Robert Loggia, Todd Graff, Julia Campbell, Milo O'Shea (Imagine/Brad Grey/Melendandri-Gordon)

Television and standup comic Dana Carvey's deft mimicry and physical comedy are used to the max but pic's routine venture into action and romance genres subtracts from the laughs. Carvey and con accomplice Todd Graff break, enter, and take up residence in a luxurious suburban house. Carvey is mistaken for a house-sitting friend by the mother of the house's owner (Doris Belack). Carvey starts a "love con" with Julia Campbell, the earthy doctor daughter of Belack and Robert Loggia.

OPTIMISTS OF NINE ELMS, THE (US: THE OPTIMISTS)
1974, 110 mins, UK Ⓥ
D: Anthony Simmons A: Peter Sellers, Donna Mullane, John Chaffey, David Daker (Cheetah/Sagittarius)

Peter Sellers, playing an aging vaudevillian whose meager income derives from sidewalk minstreling, tentatively befriends an 11-year-old girl and her 6-year-old brother, opening their eyes to a world of magical dreams while they offer him the blessing of human contact. Even at its worst *The Optimists* is acceptable family fare, and for much of its first 80 minutes it engagingly achieves a sense of fantasy.

ORCA
1977, 92 mins, US Ⓥ ⊙ ▭
D: Michael Anderson A: Richard Harris, Charlotte Rampling, Will Sampson, Bo Derek, Keenan Wynn (De Laurentiis)

Orca is man-versus-beast nonsense. Some fine special effects and underwater camera work are plowed under in dumb storytelling. Richard Harris is a shark-hunting seafarer who incurs the enmity of a superintelligent whale after harpooning the whale's pregnant mate.

ORDINARY PEOPLE
1980, 123 mins, US Ⓥ ⊙
D: Robert Redford A: Donald Sutherland, Mary Tyler Moore, Judd Hirsch, Timothy Hutton, Elizabeth McGovern, M. Emmet Walsh (Paramount/Wildwood)

A powerfully intimate domestic drama. While not ultimately downbeat or despairing, tale of a disturbed boy's precarious tightrope walk through his teens is played out with tremendous seriousness. Dilemma is of a youth who has recently attempted suicide in remorse for not having saved his older brother from drowning.
1980: Best Picture, Director, Supp. Actor (Timothy Hutton), Adapted Screenplay
Nominations: Best Actress (Mary Tyler Moore), Supp. Actor (Judd Hirsch)

ORFEU NEGRO (US: BLACK ORPHEUS)
1959, 100 mins, France Ⓥ ⊙
D: Marcel Camus A: Breno Mello, Marpessa Dawn, Lea Garcia, Lourdes De Oliveira, Adhemar Da Silva (Gordine)

With a background of the pulsating, colorful Rio carnival in Brazil, a reenactment of the Orpheus legend is executed in this vehicle. This time they are Negroes and there is a clever transposition of the tragedy to modern times. Eurydice (Marpessa Dawn) is pursued by man trying to kill her after she turned him down. She meets Orpheus, a streetcar conductor who is engaged to another girl. They fall in love but she is killed inadvertently by Orpheus.
1959: Best Foreign Language Film

ORGANIZATION, THE
1971, 105 mins, US Ⓥ
D: Don Medford A: Sidney Poitier, Barbara McNair, Gerald S. O'Loughlin, Sheree North, Allen Garfield (United Artists)

Sidney Poitier is back for third time

around as Virgil Tibbs, the San Francisco homicide lieutenant, faced this time with combatting a worldwide dope syndicate. Pic's opening is a heist of a furniture factory—front for crime ring—and seizure of heroin by a group of young people taking law into their own hands to try to halt the drug sale that has been ruining lives. Tibbs is assigned the case when the murdered body of the factory manager is found.

ORIGINAL GANGSTAS
1996, 98 mins, US ⓥ
D: Larry Cohen A: Fred Williamson, Jim Brown, Pam Grier, Paul Winfield, Richard Roundtree, Ron O'Neal (Po'Boy/Orion)

A return to the so-called blaxploitation pics of the 1970s. Eschewing parody, this two-fisted urban gang drama kicks off with a basketball hustle that goes sour. The gang shoots the wrong shopkeeper—he's the papa of John Bookman (Williamson). Bookman enlists his former buddies to help him quell the terror. There's a sense of elation as law is tossed aside in favor of justice.

ORLACS HAENDE
(US: HANDS OF ORLAC)
1925, 80 mins, Austria ⓥ ⊗
D: Robert Wiene A: Conrad Veidt, Alexandra Sorina, Fritz Strassny, Paul Askenas, Fritz Kortner (Pan)

Were it not for Conrad Veidt's masterly characterization, *The Hands of Orlac* would be an absurd fantasy in the old-time mystery-thriller class. As the musician who learns that the hands he lost in a train wreck have been replaced by hands transplanted from a man guillotined for a murder, Veidt keeps his audience highly tensed in spots.

ORLANDO
1993, 93 mins, UK/Russia/Italy/France/Netherlands ⓥ ⊙
D: Sally Potter A: Tilda Swinton, Billy Zane, Lothaire Bluteau, John Wood, Charlotte Valandrey, Quentin Crisp (Adventure/Lenfilm/Mikado/Rio/Sigma)

Exciting, wonderfully witty entertainment with glorious settings and costumes. Virginia Woolf's 1928 novel is structured around the intriguing notion of a character who lived for 400 years, changing sex in the course of time. Orlando is a youth who, in 1600, becomes the favorite of the aging queen Elizabeth I and lives to tell the tale well into the 20th century. Though she's really too feminine to pass for a man

in pic's first half, Swinton is extraordinary as the eponymous Orlando.
1993: Nominations: Best Art Direction, Costume Design

ORPHANS
1987, 120 mins, US ⓥ ⊙
D: Alan J. Pakula A: Albert Finney, Matthew Modine, Kevin Anderson, John Kellogg (Lorimar)

The inherent dramatic insularity of Lyle Kessler's play about two urban outcast brothers and the Mephistophelian gangster who transforms their hermetic world is driven by the inspired energies of its principal cast. Treat (Matthew Modine) and Phillip (Kevin Anderson) live in isolated squalor. Treat is a violent sociopath. Phillip is a recluse. Control of self and one's destiny is the gospel of Harold (Albert Finney), a hard-drinking mobster who offers these destitute marginals an opportunity for big money and a spiffy new life.

ORPHANS OF THE STORM
1921, 170 mins, US ⓥ ⓓ
D: D. W. Griffith A: Lillian Gish, Dorothy Gish, Joseph Schildkraut, Frank Losee, Katherine Emmett (Griffith/United Artists)

D. W. Griffith has tossed two orphans onto the tempestuous sea of the French Revolution and uses the ride-to-the-rescue for a finale, with an orphan under the guillotine and "Danton five miles away." The plot carries the two orphan girls, one blind, into Paris. Dorothy Gish is the blind girl, and this step from comedienne roles into a role of unlimited emotional possibilities reveals new capabilities in the less famous of the two Gish girls.

ORPHEE
(US: ORPHEUS)
1950, 95 mins, France ⓥ ⊙
D: Jean Cocteau A: Jean Marais, Marie Dea, Francois Perier, Maria Casares, Juliette Greco, Edward Dhermitte (Palais Royal)

Pic is a highly personalized, modernistic production, a poetic interpretation of the Orpheus myth transposed to modern times. The modern Orpheus is a Left Bank poet (Jean Marais) envied by his fellow writers. He becomes enamored of a strange princess depicted as Death (Maria Casares). From then on, the plot follows the general Orpheus fable.

OSCAR, THE
1966, 122 mins, US ⓥ
D: Russell Rouse A: Stephen Boyd, Elke Sommer, Milton Berle, Eleanor Parker, Jo-

seph Cotten, Jill St. John (Greene-Rouse)

This is the story of a vicious, bitter, first-class heel who rises to stardom on the blood of those close to him. Without a single redeeming quality, part played by Stephen Boyd is unsympathetic virtually from opening shots. Milton Berle switches to dramatic role as a top Hollywood agent, and Tony Bennett, the singer, portrays a straight character, Boyd's longtime friend victimized by the star in his battle for success.
1966: Nominations: Best Color Costume Design, Color Art Direction

OSCAR
1991, 109 mins, US ⊘ ⊙
D: John Landis **A:** Sylvester Stallone, Ornella Muti, Don Ameche, Peter Riegert, Tim Curry, Vincent Spano (Touchstone)

An intermittently amusing throwback to gangster comedies of the 1930s. Manic proceedings unfold on the morning when legendary hood Angelo "Snaps" Provolone (Stallone) will officially go straight by entering the banking business. Snaps is rudely awakened by his young accountant (Vincent Spano), who needs a big raise so he can afford to marry the gangster's daughter (Marisa Tomei). This sets in motion a domestic tempest. Stallone does no more than a serviceable job in getting across the humor.

OSCAR AND LUCINDA
1997, 132 mins, Australia/US ⊘ ⊙ ▭
D: Gillian Armstrong **A:** Ralph Fiennes, Cate Blanchett, Ciaran Hinds, Tom Wilkinson, Richard Roxburgh, Clive Russell (Dalton/Fox Searchlight)

Oscar and Lucinda is a truly poetic movie, a Victorian-era romance revolving around two eccentric soulmates, reckless dreamers and gamblers. Pic's first part is too literary, relying heavily on voiceover narration. Film gains momentum when Oscar goes to Oxford to train as a minister. His fateful meeting with Lucinda takes place on board ship, en route to become a missionary in the Australian outback. Their unusual relationship inevitably leads to scandal and controversy. Ralph Fiennes renders an astoundingly nuanced performance. Newcomer Cate Blanchett also excels as the fiery, self-reliant female industrialist.
1997: Nomination: Best Costume Design

OSCAR WILDE
1960, 98 mins, UK
D: Gregory Ratoff **A:** Robert Morley, Phyllis Calvert, John Neville, Ralph Richardson, Dennis Price, Alexander Knox (Vantage)

Story of the poet-playwright-wit whose tragic downfall on homosexual charges was a scandal in Victorian times. The literate screenplay draws heavily on both Wilde's own epigrams and wisecracks but also on the actual documented evidence in the two celebrated court cases. Robert Morley looks perhaps a little too old for the role of Oscar Wilde but he gives a very shrewd performance, not only in the rich relish with which he delivers Wilde's bon mots but also in the almost frighteningly pathetic way in which he crumbles and wilts in the dock.

OSSESSIONE
1942, 140 mins, Italy ⊘ ⊙
D: Luchino Visconti **A:** Clara Calamai, Massimo Girotti, Juan De Landa, Dhia Cristiani, Elio Marcuzzo (ICI)

This film, based on James M. Cain's novel *The Postman Always Rings Twice*, emerges a grim tale that rings true in character. Visconti has made this essentially Yank hardboiled tale completely Italian by unfolding it without any recourse to suspense or glibness. The original story line is followed as a tramp falls for the young wife of an old tavern keeper. This leads to their murdering him, and they turn to distrusting each other to a final ironic climax.

OSTERMAN WEEKEND, THE
1983, 102 mins, US ⊘ ⊙
D: Sam Peckinpah **A:** Rutger Hauer, John Hurt, Craig T. Nelson, Dennis Hopper, Chris Sarandon, Burt Lancaster (Davis-Panzer/20th Century-Fox)

A competent, professional, but thoroughly impersonal meller. CIA chief Burt Lancaster recruits operative John Hurt to convince TV journalist Rutger Hauer that several of his closest friends are actually Soviet agents. After Hurt has equipped the California ranch house with sophisticated surveillance gear, Hauer warily bids welcome to his pals. They get wind of Hauer's suspicions of them, and the domestic situation rapidly deteriorates.

OSTRE SLEDOVANE VLAKY (US: CLOSELY WATCHED TRAINS; UK: CLOSELY OBSERVED TRAINS)
1966, 92 mins, Czechoslovakia ⊘ ⊙
D: Jiri Menzel **A:** Vaclav Neckar, Jitka Bendova, Vladimir Valenta, Libuse Havelkova (Barrandov)

Without being vulgar or tasteless, this

Czech production mixes comedy, drama, and the most delicate love sequences against the background of the German occupation and the Czech resistance during the last days of WWII. The locale is a small railway station somewhere in Bohemia. The old stationmaster is mainly concerned with his small cattle; the adjunct's main interest is the opposite sex; the apprentice Hrma is still rather shy when it comes to making love to a girl. But he's eventually given practice by an attractive female resistance fighter.
1967: Best Foreign Language Film

OTAC NA SLUZBENOM PUTU (US: WHEN FATHER WAS AWAY ON BUSINESS)
1985, 135 mins, Yugoslavia ⓥ
D: Emir Kusturica **A:** Moreno De Bartolli, Miki Manojlovic, Mirjana Karanovic (Forum)

Set in Sarajevo following Tito's break with Stalin, pic is seen through the eyes of six-year-old Malik (Moreno De Bartolli), and it's his rather witty commentary on events that sets the tone of this finely etched tragicomedy. Malik sees his father Mesa (Miki Manojlovic) always away on business trips, but what he doesn't know (until the final scenes) is that he's a lusty Lothario with a yen for the girls. A girlfriend of the father turns her erstwhile lover over to the local police inspector during a fit of jealousy. Mesa is packed off to the salt mines, so to speak.

OTHELLO
1952, 91 mins, Morocco
D: Orson Welles **A:** Orson Welles, Micheal MacLiammoir, Suzanne Cloutier, Robert Coote, Hilton Edwards, Fay Compton (Mercury)

An impressive rendering of the Shakespearean tragedy. After the marriage of Othello and Desdemona, the film takes a firm dramatic line and crescendos as the warped Iago brings on the ensuing tragic results. Micheal MacLiammoir is good as Iago. Orson Welles gives the tortured Moor depth and stature. Standout scenes are the murder of Roderigo in a Moroccan bath as the chase weaves through the steamy air and ends in general skewering and mayhem.

OTHELLO
1995, 124 mins, US/UK ⓥ ⊙
D: Oliver Parker **A:** Laurence Fishburne, Irene Jacob, Kenneth Branagh, Nathaniel Parker, Michael Maloney (Dakota/Imminent/Castle Rock/Columbia)

A pared-down, straightforward, respectable screen version of the Bard. Laurence Fishburne grapples successfully with its eloquent language and churning emotions. With the text slashed nearly in half, this Othello comes off as an elemental tale of passion, jealousy, treachery, and murder, with few adornments, shot in straight-ahead style on Italian locations. Irene Jacob, while a lovely object of Othello's desire, simply can't get her mouth around the Elizabethan dialogue. Passionate scenes between Othello and Desdemona are rather hotter than usual.

OTHER, THE
1972, 108 mins, US ⓥ
D: Robert Mulligan **A:** Uta Hagen, Diana Muldaur, Chris Udvarnoky, Martin Udvarnoky, Norma Connolly (20th Century-Fox)

This occult shocker is an outstanding example of topflight writing and dialogue, enhanced to full fruition by a knowing director. On a farm in 1935 a tragedy-stricken family is plagued further with a series of deaths. The story unfolds around, and from the viewpoint of, Diana Muldaur's two young identical-twin sons, expertly played by 10-year-olds Chris and Martin Udvarnoky. Martin is aloof, introverted, and a downbeat influence on Chris, whose more normal juvenile attributes and fantasies are nurtured lovingly by Hagen.

OTHER PEOPLE'S MONEY
1991, 101 mins, US ⓥ ⊙
D: Norman Jewison **A:** Danny DeVito, Gregory Peck, Penelope Ann Miller, Piper Laurie, Dean Jones (Warner/Yorktown)

Danny DeVito does a very entertaining star turn as big-time Wall Street operator Lawrence Garfield (DeVito), who sets his sights on a venerable old company run by folksy "Jorgy" Jorgenson (Gregory Peck). Jorgy is convinced to call in Kate Sullivan (Penelope Ann Miller), a sharp young lawyer. Constant maneuvers and one-upsmanship ploys constitute good, peppery drama, and the strongly etched settings provide a vivid backdrop for this drama of capitalistic conflict.

OTHER SIDE OF MIDNIGHT, THE
1977, 165 mins, US ⓥ
D: Charles Jarrott **A:** Marie-France Pisier, John Beck, Susan Sarandon, Raf Vallone, Clu Gulager, Christian Marquand (20th Century-Fox)

Marie-France Pisier sleeps her way up to international film star status, all the while paying out money to follow John Beck. Beck meanwhile marries Susan Sarandon before going off to the Pacific theater of war. Pisier fixes it so Beck has to turn to work abroad, hiring on as her pilot so she can degrade him.

1977: Nomination: Best Costume Design

OTHER SIDE OF THE MOUNTAIN, THE
(UK: WINDOW IN THE SKY)
1975, 101 mins, US ⊗
D: Larry Peerce **A:** Marilyn Hassett, Beau Bridges, Belinda J. Montgomery, Nan Martin, Dabney Coleman (Universal/Film-ways)

This is a heartwarming love story—the true-life tale of a desperately injured 19-year-old girl skier with such love for life she beats her way back to a future of hope. Film is a standout in every department—perfect casting, fine acting, sensitive direction, imaginative photography, and general overall production all combining to give unusual strength to subject matter.

1975: Nomination: Best Song ("Richard's Window")

OTLEY
1969, 90 mins, UK ⊗
D: Dick Clement **A:** Tom Courtenay, Romy Schneider, Alan Badel, James Villiers, Leonard Rossiter (Columbia)

Otley focuses on exploits of bumbling "everyman type" thrust into the espionage game. Story line is pegged around Tom Courtenay unfortuitously present at an acquaintance's London flat when the latter is bumped off. In seeking to avoid heroics as well as the pitfalls of parody, the film has an uneasy lack of a point of view and fails to focus viewer's attention on any particular character or plotline philosophy.

OUR DAILY BREAD
(UK: THE MIRACLE OF LIFE)
1934, 74 mins, US ⊗ ⊙
D: King Vidor **A:** Karen Morley, Tom Keene, John Qualen, Barbara Pepper (Viking/United Artists)

Story deals with a throng of unemployed who take up squatter rights on an abandoned farm and turn it into a thriving collective project. On the way they have various difficulties, chiefly from drought. It's a glorification of human will power driving man beyond ordinary feats of endurance. Primitive, forceful, real, and moving.

OUR DANCING DAUGHTERS
1928, 86 mins, US ⊗
D: Harry Beaumont **A:** Joan Crawford, John Mack Brown, Dorothy Sebastian, Anita Page, Nils Asther (M-G-M/Cosmopolitan)

This jazz epic is sumptuously mounted, gets plenty of playing from three girls, and is sufficiently physically teasing. Story marries off the juvenile to the scheming flapper before he gets back to the frank and daring but honest heroine. Joan Crawford and Anita Page seesaw for cast honors. The boyishly figured Crawford has seldom looked better than in this one. Page is given her major spot down next to closing in a lengthy drunken sequence.

OUR GIRL FRIDAY
(US: THE ADVENTURES OF SADIE)
1953, 88 mins, UK
D: Noel Langley **A:** Joan Collins, George Cole, Kenneth More, Robertson Hare, Hermione Gingold, Hattie Jacques (Renown)

After a collision at sea, Joan Collins finds herself on a desert island with George Cole, a journalist; Kenneth More, a ship's stoker; and Robertson Hare, an insufferable professor. For the sake of harmony, the three men make a pact not to make a pass at the girl, but two of them, Cole and Hare, rapidly succumb to her charms. The story has its moments of fun but the dialogue is often flat and forced.

OUR HOSPITALITY
1923, 81 mins, US ⊗ ⊙ ⊗
D: Buster Keaton, John G. Blystone **A:** Buster Keaton, Natalie Talmadge, Buster Keaton Jr., Joseph Keaton (Schenck/Metro)

A comedy masterpiece about as serious a subject as a feud—between the McKays and Canfields. William McKay (Buster Keaton) meets Virginia Canfield (Natalie Talmadge Keaton). Unknown to each other, the girl invites him to her house for dinner. Her two brothers and father have sworn to kill him, but their Southern code of hospitality will not allow them to kill him in the house. The usual low comedy and slapstick have been modified and woven into a consistent story that is as funny as it is entertaining.

OUR MAN FLINT
1966, 107 mins, US ⊗ ⊙ ▱
D: Daniel Mann **A:** James Coburn, Lee J.

Cobb, Gila Golan, Edward Mulhare, Benson Fong (20th Century-Fox)

Dazzling, action-jammed swashbuckling spoof of Ian Fleming's valiant counterspy, given more tools and gimmicks to pursue his craft as he tracks down the perpetrators of a diabolical scheme to take over the world. James Coburn takes on the task of being surrounded by exotically undraped beauts and facing dangers that would try any man. But he comes through unscathed, helped by a dandy little specially designed lighter that has 83 separate uses. Lee J. Cobb has a field day as the exasperated head who cannot keep Flint in line.

OUR MAN IN HAVANA
1960, 111 mins, UK ◻

D: Carol Reed A: Alec Guinness, Burl Ives, Maureen O'Hara, Ernie Kovacs, Noel Coward, Ralph Richardson (Columbia)

Shot mainly in colorful Cuba, polished, diverting entertainment is brilliant in its comedy but falls apart toward the end when undertones of drama, tragedy, and message crop up. Story concerns a mild-mannered vacuum-cleaner salesman in Havana persuaded to become a member of the British secret service. To hold down his job, he is forced to invent mythical subagents and concoct highly imaginative, fictitious reports, which he sends back to London. They are taken so seriously that two assistants are sent to help him, and the web of innocent deceit that he has spun gradually mounts up to sinister and dramatic consequences.

OUR MOTHER'S HOUSE
1967, 104 mins, UK/US

D: Jack Clayton A: Dirk Bogarde, Margaret Brooks, Pamela Franklin, Louis Sheldon Williams, Mark Lester (Heron/M-G-M)

A film about seven destitute moppets, not to be considered in any way a kiddie pic. After the death of their long-ailing mother (Annette Carell), she is buried in the backyard, eldest child Margaret Brooks imposing her belief on others that this will eliminate orphanage fears. Dirk Bogarde stars in an excellent performance as their long-lost legal father.

OUR RELATIONS
1936, 72 mins, US ◐ ⊙

D: Harry Lachman A: Stan Laurel, Oliver Hardy, Betty Healy, Daphne Pollard, Sidney Toler, James Finlayson (Roach/M-G-M)

Laurel and Hardy get plenty of chances to talk and the dialogue handed them is considerably above par. Picture is full of deft gags, with the slapstick routine nicely contrasted with the saner moments. Most of mix-ups involve instances of mistaken identity, with the twin brothers of Laurel and Hardy wandering into situations that obviously contain dynamite for the unsuspecting victims. Outstanding sequences are the phone booth episode with three men packed in, and the climactic one where the two clowns sway along the dock with their feet embedded in cement forms.

OUR TOWN
1940, 89 mins, US ◐

D: Sam Wood A: William Holden, Martha Scott, Fay Bainter, Beulah Bondi, Thomas Mitchell, Frank Craven (Lesser/United Artists)

Divided into three periods, 1901, 1904, and 1913, the film version of Thornton Wilder's play is a plain and homey exposition of life, romance, marriage, and death in the New Hampshire town. More explicitly, it concerns the intimacies of two families, the adolescent and matured romance and married life of a boy and girl. Martha Scott delivers a sincerely warm portrayal as the girl, displaying a wealth of ability and personality. William Holden is fine as the boy.

1940: Nominations: Best Picture, Actress (Martha Scott), B&W Art Direction, Original Score, Sound

OUR WIFE
1941, 92 mins, US

D: John M. Stahl A: Melvyn Douglas, Ruth Hussey, Ellen Drew, Charles Coburn, John Hubbard (Columbia)

Composer-musician Melvyn Douglas, drowning sorrows of his recent unhappy marriage, meets Ruth Hussey; her father, Charles Coburn; and brother, John Hubbard, on a cruise off Panama. When they accept his offer to use his Long Island home while they are in New York, Douglas quickly falls in love with Hussey. Her companionship inspires him to compose a concerto, which is performed to acclaim. His divorced wife decides to regain him. Stahl's direction proceeds at a bumpy pace at times, while in other sections he zips along at a good speed.

OUTBREAK
1995, 127 mins, US ⊗ ⊙
D: Wolfgang Petersen **A:** Dustin Hoffman, Rene Russo, Morgan Freeman, Kevin Spacey, Cuba Gooding Jr., Donald Sutherland (Warner)

Smashing opening sequence shows the ravaging effects of a mystery virus on a mercenary camp in Zaire in 1967. Jump to the present, and when another instance of such a devastating plague is detected in a Zairian village, ace army medic Colonel Sam Daniels (Dustin Hoffman) is sent in. In a breathless, disturbingly credible stretch of narrative, pic indelibly shows how the virus's "host," an African monkey, is captured in the jungle, transported by a sailor to San Francisco and, ultimately, released into the Californean wild. Director Wolfgang Petersen demonstrates a smooth stylistic savvy that keeps the film highly absorbing from beginning to end.

OUTCAST OF THE ISLANDS
1952, 102 mins, UK
D: Carol Reed **A:** Ralph Richardson, Trevor Howard, Robert Morley, Kerima, Wendy Hiller, George Coulouris (London/British Lion)

Picture is based on the Joseph Conrad story, but the screenplay fails to capture the authentic atmosphere of the Far East in which the story is set. The outcast is played by Trevor Howard. The film concentrates on developing his shifting character as a man without honor, without principle, and without friends, yet having a devouring passion for a native girl.

OUTFIT, THE
1973, 102 mins, US ⊗
D: John Flynn **A:** Robert Duvall, Karen Black, Joe Don Baker, Robert Ryan, Timothy Carey, Richard Jaeckel (M-G-M)

In *The Outfit* two outside-the-law characters, stylishly handled by Robert Duvall and Joe Don Baker, drive off into the credits laughing gleefully. In their wake they leave countless stiffs, including crime-syndicate topper Robert Ryan, Duvall's girlfriend (Karen Black), and a batch of other broken-boned, face-smashed individuals who were caught up in pair's vengeance-motivated assault on organized crime. John Flynn keeps the pace extremely fast and engaging.

OUT FOR JUSTICE
1991, 91 mins, US ⊗ ▭
D: John Flynn **A:** Steven Seagal, William

Forsyth, Jerry Orbach, Jo Champa, Shareen Mitchell (Warner)

Out for Justice harbors an incredibly simple vengeance plot loaded with enough macho sadism to satiate the action genre's bloodthirsty fans. Steven Seagal plays an Italian cop pursuing the murderous, drugged-out Richie (William Forsythe), dispatching his henchmen in brutal encounters. Stuntwork is first-rate, and Seagal remains a convincing action figure.

OUTLAND
1981, 109 mins, US ⊗ ⊙ ▭
D: Peter Hyams **A:** Sean Connery, Peter Boyle, Frances Sternhagen, Kika Markham, James B. Sikking (Warner/Ladd)

Outland is something akin to *High Noon* in outer space, a simple good guys–bad guys yarn set in the future on a volcanic moon of Jupiter. The film emerges as a tight, intriguing old-fashioned drama that gives audiences a hero worth rooting for. Newly arrived marshal Sean Connery finds out that miners are growing crazy due to an amphetamine that makes them produce more but eventually destroys their brains. It doesn't take long to figure out that the manager who runs the colony's operations (Peter Boyle) is involved in supplying the drug.
1981: Nomination: Best Sound

OUTLAW, THE
1943, 124 mins, US ⊗ ⊙
D: Howard Hughes **A:** Jack Buetel, Jane Russell, Thomas Mitchell, Walter Huston (Howard Hughes)

Beyond sex attraction of Jane Russell's frankly displayed charms, picture, according to accepted screen entertainment standards, falls short. Slowness is not so much a matter of length as a lack of tempo in individual scenes. This variation of the checkered career of Billy the Kid has the outlaw joining forces with legendary Doc Holliday, played by Walter Huston, to escape the pursuing Sheriff Pat Garrett (Thomas Mitchell). Mixing strangely into the kid's life is Rio, a Latin charmer, portrayed by Russell.

OUTLAW BLUES
1977, 100 mins, US ⊗
D: Richard T. Heffron **A:** Peter Fonda, Susan Saint James, John Crawford, James Callahan, Michael Lerner (Warner)

Script takes Peter Fonda from prison, where he has developed a musical ability, to Texas in pursuit of James Callahan, country and western singer who has stolen the title song from Fonda. Accidental shooting of Callahan in a scuffle launches a manhunt for Fonda. The film revolves into a series of chases, interleaved with some okay songs which Fonda is said to have sung himself. Story opts for the laughs and smiles which come easily in abundance.

OUTLAW JOSEY WALES, THE
1976, 135 mins, US Ⓥ ⊙ ▭
D: Clint Eastwood **A:** Clint Eastwood, Chief Dan George, Sondra Locke, Bill McKinney, John Vernon, Paula Trueman (Warner)

Clint Eastwood is a Civil War–era farmer whose family is murdered by brigands led by Bill McKinney; Vernon is a fellow counterguerrilla who is tricked into surrendering his men; George is an old Indian whom Eastwood encounters on the long trail of retribution. Eastwood's character meanders through the Middle West, disposing of antagonists by the dozen aided at times by George; Sam Bottoms; romantic interest Sondra Locke; latter's granny, Paula Trueman and others.
1976: Nomination: Best Original Score

OUT OF AFRICA
1985, 150 mins, US Ⓥ ⊙
D: Sydney Pollack **A:** Meryl Streep, Robert Redford, Klaus Maria Brandauer, Michael Kitchen, Malick Bowens, Joseph Thiaka (Universal)

At two and a half hours, *Out of Africa* certainly makes a leisurely start into its story. Just short of boredom, however, the picture picks up pace and becomes a sensitive, enveloping romantic tragedy. *Africa* is the story of Isak Dinesen, who wrote of her experiences in Kenya. Though Dinesen remembered it lovingly, hers was not a happy experience. Pic opens in 1914. With one landscape after another, Pollack and lenser David Watkin prove repeatedly, however, why she should love the land so, but at almost travelogue drag. Eventually, Streep and husband, Klaus Maria Brandauer, split, leaving an opening for Redford to move in. True love follows, but not happiness.
1985: Best Picture, Director, Adapted Screenplay, Cinematography, Art Direction, Sound, Original Score
Nominations: Best Actress (Meryl Streep), Supp. Actor (Klaus Maria Brandauer), Costume Design, Editing

OUT OF SEASON
1975, 90 mins, UK Ⓥ
D: Alan Bridges **A:** Vanessa Redgrave, Cliff Robertson, Susan George, Edward Evans, Frank Jarvis (EMI/Lorimar)

Though basic plot is that old chestnut about the dark stranger returning—after 20 years away—to visit an isolated hotel in an English seaside town, its handling is expert enough to avoid most of the pitfalls of the genre. And so is the acting. This ping-pong match of the affections often has the suspense of a whodunit as audience tries to guess next move by the entangled mother-daughter-lover trio.

OUT OF SIGHT
1998, 122 mins, US Ⓥ ⊙
D: Steven Soderbergh **A:** George Clooney, Jennifer Lopez, Ving Rhames, Don Cheadle, Dennis Farina, Albert Brooks (Jersey/Universal)

A sly, sexy, vastly entertaining film version of Elmore Leonard's playful novel, this reflexively witty crime caper boasts the sort of bright, snappy dialogue that's rarely heard in a mainstream picture. Jack Foley (George Clooney) is an ex-con about to perform another bank robbery. A dead car battery leads to his imprisonment in Florida. It just happens that deputy federal marshal Karen Sisco (Jennifer Lopez) is on the premises when his prison break occurs. The mismatched Foley and Sisco (held hostage) begin their courtship in the tight space of the getaway car's trunk, where they share their love for movies. It's obvious that their paths will crisscross and their fates will intertwine. The densely rich yarn is more character-driven than plot-driven. Not since *Boogie Nights* has a Hollywood movie had so many characters and seemed so perfectly cast.

OUT OF THE BLUE
1980, 94 mins, Canada Ⓥ
D: Dennis Hopper **A:** Linda Manz, Sharon Farrell, Dennis Hopper, Raymond Burr (Robson Street)

Linda Manz has tart authority as a streetwise 15-year-old. She had been in a terrible accident while driving with Hopper, her father, who plowed into a school bus, killing many of the kids. Hopper has been sentenced to five years in prison. He has become a hero to his daughter, who has fantasized the late Elvis Presley into another hero. Dramatically economical, pic captures urban overcrowding, personal problems, and violence but sans excess.

OUT OF THE PAST
(UK: BUILD MY GALLOWS HIGH)
1947, 95 mins, US Ⓥ ⊙

D: Jacques Tourneur **A:** Robert Mitchum, Jane Greer, Kirk Douglas, Rhonda Fleming, Richard Webb (RKO)

Hard-boiled melodrama, strong on characterization, pays close attention to mood development, achieving realistic flavor that is further emphasized by real-life settings and topnotch lensing. Plot depicts Robert Mitchum as a former private detective whose past catches up with him. Hired by a gangster to find a girl who had decamped with $40,000 after shooting the crook, Mitchum crosses her path in Acapulco, falls for her himself, and they flee the gangster together.

OUT-OF-TOWNERS, THE
1970, 97 mins, US Ⓥ ⊙

D: Arthur Hiller **A:** Jack Lemmon, Sandy Dennis, Sandy Baron, Anne Meara, Robert Nichols, Ann Prestiss (Paramount/Jalem)

The Out-of-Towners is a total delight. Neil Simon's first modern original screen comedy stars Jack Lemmon and Sandy Dennis, an Ohio couple who come to NY on one of those expense-paid executive-suite job interviews and become disillusioned with big-city life, New York style. Dennis and Lemmon are superb in comedy characterizations.

OUT-OF-TOWNERS, THE
1999, 92 mins, US Ⓥ

D: Sam Weisman **A:** Steve Martin, Goldie Hawn, Mark McKinney, John Cleese, Oliver Hudson (Paramount)

Warmer and rowdier than its 1970 predecessor, Sam Weisman's remake of *The Out-of-Towners* is an amusing comedy that showcases first-rate comic thesping by Steve Martin and Goldie Hawn. Screenwriter Marc Lawrence puts his own imprint on the material, changing the overall tone of the story and offering a more affectionate view of Manhattan. Martin and Hawn play Henry and Nancy Clark, a long-married couple forced to cope with empty nest blues. Henry is newly unemployed, a fact he has concealed from Nancy when he's beckoned to New York for a job interview. The remake is aggressively upbeat and indicates that the quality of life has drastically improved since 1970.

OUTRAGE
1950, 79 mins, US

D: Ida Lupino **A:** Mala Powers, Tod Andrews, Robert Clarke, Raymond Bond, Lilian Hamilton, Rita Lupino (RKO/Filmakers)

Rape and its effect on the victim and her loved ones set up the melodramatic plot. However, the film is more focused on the events that transpire afterward. Mala Powers impresses as the victim. Ida Lupino directed from a script written with Collier Young and Malvin Wald, coproducers. Her handling of the earlier sequences packs a hefty punch.

OUTRAGE, THE
1964, 95 mins, US Ⓥ ▭

D: Martin Ritt **A:** Paul Newman, Laurence Harvey, Claire Bloom, Edward G. Robinson, William Shatner, Howard da Silva (M-G-M)

The Outrage is adapted from the Broadway play *Rashomon*, which in turn was based on Kurosawa's Japanese film of the same name. It is the story of a killing of a southern gentleman and the rape of his wife by a bloodthirsty bandit, told through the eyes of the three protagonists and then by a disinterested eyewitness, each version differing. Newman as the violent and passionate killer plays his colorful character with a flourish and heavy accent. Bloom has her gamut during the four versions of her ravishment, running from pure innocence to her demand to the outlaw to kill her husband so she can go with her new lover. She delivers strongly, turning smoothly from drama to comedy.

OUTRAGEOUS FORTUNE
1987, 100 mins, US Ⓥ ⊙

D: Arthur Hiller **A:** Shelley Long, Bette Midler, Peter Coyote, Robert Prosky, John Schuck (Touchstone/Interscope)

Well-crafted, old-fashioned entertainment, a traditional buddy film that has substituted women. The main plot device is that the two heroines are sleeping with the same man (Peter Coyote). The film takes off as a chase picture with the girls following Coyote to New Mexico to demand a decision. They're not the only ones looking for him. It seems the CIA is hot on his trail, as is the KGB.

OUTRIDERS, THE
1950, 93 mins, US

D: Roy Rowland **A:** Joel McCrea, Arlene Dahl, Barry Sullivan, Claude Jarman Jr.,

James Whitmore, Ramon Novarro (M-G-M)

Sturdy meat for the action fan. Joel McCrea, Barry Sullivan, and James Whitmore are Confederate soldiers dispatched to New Mexico to figure an angle to lead a wagon train of gold slated for the Yanks into an ambush. Roy Rowland's direction packs a wallop. Some scenes are alive with tingling suspense, such as the crossing of a raging river at high flood.

OUTSIDER, THE
1979, 128 mins, US
D: Tony Luraschi **A:** Craig Wasson, Sterling Hayden, Patricia Quinn, Niall O'Brien, T. P. McKenna, Ray McAnally (Paramount/Cinematic Arts)

The Outsider represents the first attempt to get into the minds and motives at work on one of the longest-fought terrorist campaigns of the times—through an intelligent fictional story with an Irish setting. A measure of the effectiveness of Craig Wasson's performance, as a young Irish-American inflamed to join the IRA, is that by the time he finally leaves Ireland as a disillusioned fugitive he looks—without artifice—10 years older.

OUTSIDERS, THE
1983, 91 mins, US ⊛ ⊙ ▭
D: Francis Ford Coppola **A:** C. Thomas Howell, Matt Dillon, Ralph Macchio, Patrick Swayze, Rob Lowe, Emilio Estevez (Zoetrope)

A well-acted and crafted but highly conventional film based on S. E. Hinton's popular youth novel. C. Thomas Howell and his buddies (Matt Dillon and Ralph Macchio) have an unpleasant confrontation with the Socs, rival gang from the well-heeled part of town. When the Socs attack Howell and Macchio, latter ends up killing a boy to save his friend, and the two flee to a hideaway in an abandoned rural church. It is during this midsection that the film starts coming to life, largely due to the integrity of the performances by Howell and Macchio.

OUTWARD BOUND
1930, 83 mins, US
D: Robert Milton **A:** Leslie Howard, Douglas Fairbanks Jr., Beryl Mercer, Dudley Digges, Helen Chandler (Warner)

The story is that allegorical theme of going before an examiner (Dudley Digges) in heaven. The boy and the girl—"half-ways" held between death and life—are neither sinners nor saints in the full sense. But they sought death and carry their secret along with a suspense that's worthy of the production and the theme.

OVERBOARD
1987, 112 mins, US ⊛ ⊙
D: Garry Marshall **A:** Goldie Hawn, Kurt Russell, Edward Herrmann, Katherine Helmond, Roddy McDowall (M-G-M)

An uninspiring, unsophisticated attempt at an updated screwball comedy. Only element that occasionally lifts pic is the redoubtable Goldie Hawn, who gives a gem of a performance. Hawn plays Joanna Stayton, a millionaire wife who decides it's time to have her yacht's closet remodeled. She fires Kurt Russell as carpenter Dean Proffitt. Joanna falls off the boat and washes back on shore with a nasty case of amnesia. Proffitt devises a scheme to claim her as his wife.

OVERLANDERS, THE
1946, 91 mins, UK/Australia ⊛
D: Harry Watt **A:** Chips Rafferty, John Nugent Hayward, Daphne Campbell, Jean Blue (Ealing)

Across 2,000 miles of heat and dust, drovers battled with 500,000 head of cattle to get them out of reach of a probable Jap landing. Story begins in 1942 at the tiny town of Wyndham, where meatpacking works are destroyed, personnel evacuated, and Chips Rafferty, boss cattle drover, is told to shoot 1,000 head of prime beasts. He decides instead to overland them across 2,000 miles of tough going. Epic trip lasts 15 months, and the adventures are graphic.

OVERLORD
1975, 85 mins, UK ⊛
D: Stuart Cooper **A:** Brian Stirner, Davyd Harries, Nicholas Ball, Julie Neesam, Sam Sewell (Imperial War Museum)

Overlord concentrates on a British youngster's World War II blitz-time induction into the army, his brief training period, and his early D-day death. Pic has a lovely reminiscent feel for its period and the deceptively peaceful at-home backdrop to the war in the buildup phase to the Allied invasion of the Continent. Youth's indoctrination is very skillfully melded with real footage.

OVER THE BROOKLYN BRIDGE
1984, 106 mins, US ⊛
D: Menahem Golan **A:** Elliott Gould, Margaux Hemingway, Sid Caesar, Burt

Young, Shelley Winters, Carol Kane (City)

A warm and pleasant romance, short on laughs but very effective. Elliott Gould stars as Alby Sherman, owner of a Brooklyn eatery who dreams of buying a posh restaurant on the East Side in midtown Manhattan. His love affair with an aristocratic Catholic girl from Philadelphia (Margaux Hemingway) raises the ire of his Jewish family. Sid Caesar is very funny as a man who tries to run everyone else's lives for them.

OVER THE TOP
1987, 93 mins, US Ⓥ ⊙ ▭
D: Menahem Golan **A:** Sylvester Stallone, Robert Loggia, Susan Blakely, Rick Zumwalt, David Mendenhall (Cannon)

Sylvester Stallone, as a down-on-his-luck trucker, appears out of the blue to fetch his son when the latter graduates from military academy. Absent from both the kid's and mama Susan Blakely's lives for years, Stallone proposes a get-to-know-you truck ride back home to Los Angeles. Little Michael (David Mendenhall) doesn't make things especially easy for his papa, his military rigidity and formality providing a formidable barrier. Stallone is sincere and soulful as a "father who messed up pretty bad" and Mendenhall is a likable tyke.

OWL AND THE PUSSYCAT, THE
1970, 98 mins, US Ⓥ ⊙ ▭
D: Herbert Ross **A:** Barbra Streisand, George Segal, Robert Klein, Allen Garfield, Roz Kelly (Columbia)

A zany, laugh-filled story of two modern NY kooks who find love at the end of trail of hilarious incidents. Streisand is a casual hooker, who first confronts Segal after he has finked on her activities to building superintendent Jacques Sandulescu. One of her old scores turns out to be Segal's intended father-in-law, but that plot turn blows up his affair and leads into the excellent climax we have been waiting for.

OX-BOW INCIDENT, THE
1943, 75 mins, US ⊙
D: William A. Wellman **A:** Henry Fonda, Dana Andrews, Mary Beth Hughes, Anthony Quinn, Jane Darwell (20th Century-Fox)

A brutal close-up of a Nevada necktie party. Western opus follows the escapades of two cowboys, played by Henry Fonda and Henry Morgan, tossed into the turmoil aroused by the report of a cattleman's slaying by rustlers. A posse is formed to get the culprits and handle them western style. Remainder of story concerns efforts of the few law-abiding gentry to halt the lynching. Fonda measures up to star rating, as one of the few level-headed cowhands.

1943: Nomination: Best Picture

OXFORD BLUES
1984, 93 mins, UK/US Ⓥ ⊙
D: Robert Boris **A:** Rob Lowe, Ally Sheedy, Amanda Pays, Julian Sands, Alan Howard (Winkast/M-G-M)

Though source material is M-G-M's 1938 *A Yank at Oxford*, treatment is decidedly modern. Director-writer Robert Boris fails to establish a consistent tone to make his fairy-tale story believable. Nick's reason for going to England is not to crew and certainly not for an education, but to chase his dream girl, aristocrat covergirl Lady Victoria (Amanda Pays). Lowe is suitably nasty as the streetwise Nick in a way that often passes for charm in films like this.

PACIFIC HEIGHTS
1990, 102 mins, US Ⓥ ⊙
D: John Schlesinger A: Melanie Griffith,
Matthew Modine, Michael Keaton, Mako,
Nobu McCarthy, Laurie Metcalf (Morgan
Creek)

The specter of a menace who invades
one's home turf and can't be ousted is universally disturbing, and director John
Schlesinger goes all out to make this
creepy thriller-chiller as unsettling as it
needs to be. Story has home buyers Patty
(Melanie Griffith) and Drake (Matthew
Modine) restoring a Victorian house,
counting on the income from two apartments to meet the mortgage. The studio
falls to reptilian Michael Keaton, who
plays the system to his advantage, finally
provoking Modine into attacking him so
he can go after his assets with a lawsuit.
But pic loses its grip when it tips over into
psycho-chiller territory.

PACIFIC PALISADES
1990, 94 mins, France
D: Bernard Schmitt A: Sophie Marceau,
Adam Coleman Howard, Anne Curry, Virginia Capers, Toni Basil (BVF/Sandor)

Marceau is a dissatisfied Parisian waitress who heads for L.A. on a bum job offer and finds herself living alone. She's
quickly exasperated and bored. Then she
gets involved with the Canadian boyfriend
(Adam Coleman Howard) of a Yank actress she initially was to have flown in
with. Despite the platitudes and plot inconsistencies, film is charmingly acted by
Marceau in her first (mostly) English-lingo
role.

PACK, THE
1977, 99 mins, US Ⓥ
D: Robert Clouse A: Joe Don Baker,
Hope Alexander-Willis, Richard B. Shull,
R. G. Armstrong, Ned Wertimer (Warner)

Well-made and discreetly violent story
of a pack of wild dogs menacing residents
of a remote island. Joe Don Baker stars as
a marine biologist who leads the humans'
defense. Strong story peg is habit of summer vacationers to abandon pets, but in
this case, the stranded mutts band together
in ferocious attack on people.

PACKAGE, THE
1989, 108 mins, US Ⓥ ⊙
D: Andrew Davis A: Gene Hackman,
Joanna Cassidy, Tommy Lee Jones, John
Heard, Dennis Franz, Pam Grier (Orion)

Smartly written, sharply played, and directed at a cracking pace that never sacrifices clarity for speed, The Package is an
enormously satisfying political thriller.
Poised and professional as ever, Gene
Hackman is perfectly cast as a career army
officer, escorting a troublesome soldier
(Tommy Lee Jones) Stateside to stand
trial. When this "package" (the military
term for the person being delivered) takes
a powder, Hackman visits the man's estranged wife—and soon realizes the package is posing as someone he's not.

PACK UP YOUR TROUBLES
1932, 70 mins, US Ⓥ
D: George Marshall, Raymond McCarey
A: Stan Laurel, Oliver Hardy, Donald
Dillaway, Jacquie Lyn, James Finlayson
(M-G-M)

Seventy minutes of slapstick is a tall
order for Laurel and Hardy and they hardly fill it. It's one of those hokum war
farces with the numbskull Laurel and
Hardy jazzing up the army as hapless
rookies.

PAD (AND HOW TO USE IT), THE
1966, 86 mins, US
D: Brian G. Hutton A: Brian Bedford, Julie Sommars, James Farentino, Edy Williams, Nick Navarro (Universal)

The Private Ear, which made up one
half of the Peter Shaffer play, The Private
Ear and the Public Eye, was a short but
observant look at loneliness and the
aborted effort of one shy male to communicate with the opposite sex. Screen
adaptation, thanks almost entirely to Shaffer's original dialogue and the recreation
by Brian Bedford of the shy young man
he played in the New York production, recaptures much of the humor, compassion,
and wisdom of the legit production.

PADRE PADRONE
1977, 114 mins, Italy Ⓥ
D: Paolo Taviani, Vittorio Taviani A:
Omero Antonutti, Saverio Marioni, Mar-
cella Michelangeli, Fabrizio Forte (RAI/
Cinema Srl)

This little low-budget film for TV is a
probe of unusual dimension into the de-
formation of young Sardinians compelled
by local economics and the mysteries of

genealogy to sacrifice childhood and adolescence as sheepherders in the high country. Around the initiation of a seven-year-old boy into the lonely life of sheepherder until his triumphant rift at the age of 20 with a remarkably overbearing father-patriarch (Omero Antonutti), the Taviani brothers have for the most part succeeded in adapting a miniature epic.

PAGEMASTER, THE
1994, 75 mins, US ⓥ ⊙
D: Joe Johnston, Maurice Hunt **A:** Macaulay Culkin, Christopher Lloyd, Ed Begley Jr., Mel Harris (20th Century-Fox)

The simplest of childhood fantasies, the story begins in the world of live action before our chronically frightened hero, Richard (Macaulay Culkin), with the help of a mysterious librarian (Christopher Lloyd), gets transported into an animated world where fictional characters come to life. The problem is that after introducing these characters—Captain Ahab, Long John Silver, Dr. Jekyll/Mr. Hyde, etc.—the filmmakers don't have anything to do with them, other than the sort of madcap chase with Mr. Hyde that feels plucked from an old Bugs Bunny cartoon.

PAGE MISS GLORY
1935, 92 mins, US
D: Mervyn LeRoy **A:** Marion Davies, Pat O'Brien, Dick Powell, Mary Astor, Patsy Kelly (Cosmopolitan/Warner)

Marion Davies is the hotel chambermaid catapulted into being "Down Glory," the mythical composite beauty who cops a contest. Pat O'Brien and Frank McHugh are the broken-down promoters who engineer the photographic combo girl into a $2,500 cash prize and a flock of offers. Davies does well by her generous comedy opportunities. Dick Powell is well nigh wasted, virtually dragged in for his "Page Miss Glory" title song duet with the star.

PAINTED VEIL, THE
1934, 83 mins, US ⓥ
D: Richard Boleslawski **A:** Greta Garbo, Herbert Marshall, George Brent, Warner Oland, Jean Hersholt, Beulah Bondi (M-G-M)

A bad picture, clumsy, dull and long-winded. Yarn has Greta Garbo as the daughter of a Viennese professor (Jean Hersholt). A doctor in China (Herbert Marshall) asks her to marry him and she does, largely, it's indicated, because she wants to see China. She meets George Brent. He flatters her for a while, then manages to get in a kiss. Hubby Marshall finds out, so he goes to clear up a bad cholera plague and drags her along. Garbo doesn't get much chance to emote. Acting honors really go to Marshall.

PAINT YOUR WAGON
1969, 166 mins, US ⓥ ⊙ ▭
D: Joshua Logan **A:** Lee Marvin, Clint Eastwood, Jean Seberg, Ray Walston, Harve Presnell (Paramount)

Paint Your Wagon is the tale of a gold-mining town in California in the 1840s. Main story centers around Lee Marvin; his pardner, Clint Eastwood; and Marvin's wife (Jean Seberg). What the film (from the 1951 Lerner and Loewe Broadway musical) lacks in a skimpy story line it makes up in the music and expert choreography. The actors used their own voices, which are pleasant enough and add to the note of authenticity.
1969: Nomination: Best Adapted Music Score

PAISA
(US: PAISAN)
1946, 124 mins, Italy ⓥ
D: Roberto Rossellini **A:** Carmela Sazio, Dots Johnson, Maria Michi, Harriet White, Bill Tubbs (OFI/FFP/Capitani)

Paisan (meaning "fellow countryman") comprises six episodes as Yank and British troops battle their way northward to push the Nazis out of Sicily and Italy. Most of the film's quality must be credited to young Italian writer-director-producer Roberto Rossellini's feeling for people and his ability to put them in an atmosphere of reality. Rome sequence is the best of the lot. A prostitute (Maria Michi) picks up a GI (Gar Moore) and takes him to her room. He lies on her bed too drunk to do anything but babble of the fresh, sweet girl who befriended him with a drink of water when his tank burst into the city six months earlier. In Florence, there's a chase by an American nurse and a partisan through German lines. It's more tense and breathtaking than any staged by maestro Alfred Hitchcock himself.

PAISAN
See: Paisa

PAJAMA GAME, THE
1957, 101 mins, US ⓥ ⊙ ▭
D: George Abbott, Stanley Donen **A:** Doris Day, John Raitt, Carol Haney, Eddie Foy Jr., Reta Shaw, Barbara Nichols (Warner)

Romantic conflict between pajama factory superintendent John Raitt and grievance committee chairman Doris Day. Raitt is properly serious as the earnest factory executive and earnestly smitten with the blond and beauteous Day. Day, always authoritative with a song, makes her chore even a shade more believable than Raitt.

PAJAMA PARTY
1964, 82 mins, US ⊗ ▭
D: Don Weis A: Tommy Kirk, Annette Funicello, Elsa Lanchester, Jody McCrea, Buster Keaton, Dorothy Lamour (American International)

Exuberance of youth fires the action, which twirls around a personable young Martian—Tommy Kirk—arriving on earth during a swimming party tossed by an eccentric wealthy widow (Elsa Lanchester). He immediately falls for Annette Funicello, girlfriend of widow's lug nephew (Jody McCrea).

PALEFACE, THE
1948, 91 mins, US ⊗ ⊙
D: Norman Z. McLeod A: Bob Hope, Jane Russell, Robert Armstrong, Iris Adrian (Paramount)

Smart-aleck travesty on the West, told with considerable humor and bright gags. Hope isn't all the film has to sell. There's Jane Russell as Calamity Jane, that rough, tough gal of the open West whose work as a government agent causes Hope's troubles, but whose guns save him from harm and give him his hero reputation. She makes an able sparring partner for the Hope antics, and is a sharp eyeful in Technicolor. "Buttons and Bows" is top tune of the score's three pop numbers.
1948: Best Song ("Buttons and Bows")

PALE RIDER
1985, 115 mins, US ⊗ ⊙ ▭
D: Clint Eastwood A: Clint Eastwood, Michael Moriarty, Carrie Snodgress, Christopher Penn, Richard Dysart, Richard Kiel (Malpaso/Warner)

As he did in his Sergio Leone trilogy, Clint Eastwood portrays a nameless drifter, here called Preacher, who descends into the middle of a struggle between some poor, independent gold prospectors and a big company intent upon raping the beautiful land for all it's worth. Preach pulls the threatened community together and inspires them to fight for their rights to the land. It's all been seen before, but Eastwood serves it up with authority, fine craftsmanship, and a frequent sense of fun.

PAL JOEY
1957, 112 mins, US ⊗ ⊙
D: George Sidney A: Rita Hayworth, Frank Sinatra, Kim Novak, Barbara Nichols, Bobby Sherwood, Hank Henry (Columbia/Essex-Sidney)

Strong, funny entertainment. Dorothy Kingsley's screenplay, from John O'Hara's book, is skillful rewriting, with colorful characters and solid story built around the Richard Rodgers and Lorenz Hart songs. Frank Sinatra is almost ideal as the irreverent, freewheeling, glib Joey. Point might be made, though, that it's hard to figure why all the mice fall for this rat. Hayworth, no longer the ingenue, moves with authority as Joey's sponsor and does the "Zip" song visuals in such fiery, amusing style as to rate an encore. Standout of the score is "Lady Is a Tramp." It's a wham arrangement and Sinatra gives it powerhouse delivery.
1957: Nominations: Best Costume Design, Art Direction, Editing, Sound Recording

PALLBEARER, THE
1996, 97 mins, US ⊗ ⊙
D: Matt Reeves A: David Schwimmer, Gwyneth Paltrow, Michael Rapaport, Toni Collette, Carol Kane (Miramax)

Aside from its blatant appropriation of themes, situations, and even shots from The Graduate, The Pallbearer is a passably entertaining seriocomedy about the dawning of adulthood for some, uh, graduates who don't quite know what to do with their lives. Appealing performances by David Schwimmer and Gwyneth Paltrow go a long way toward putting over this very slightly offbeat tale of twentysomethings trying to find their way.

PALM BEACH STORY, THE
1942, 96 mins, US ⊗ ⊙
D: Preston Sturges A: Claudette Colbert, Joel McCrea, Mary Astor, Rudy Vallee, William Demarest, Sig Arno (Paramount)

This Preston Sturges production is packed with delightful absurdities. Claudette Colbert comes through with one of her best light comedy interpretations as the slightly screwball wife who, after seeing husband, Joel McCrea, out of debt, suddenly decides to seek a divorce, adventure, and a bankroll for the husband she leaves behind. Tongue-in-cheek spoofing of the idle rich attains hilarious proportions where Rudy Vallee proposes to the errant wife and later woos her by singing to her to the accompaniment of a privately hired symphony orchestra. McCrea plays it straight, for the most part, as the husband intent on winning his wife back.

PANDORA AND THE FLYING DUTCHMAN
1951, 122 mins, UK
D: Albert Lewin **A:** James Mason, Ava Gardner, Nigel Patrick, Sheila Sim, Marius Goring (Kaufman/Lewin)

Albert Lewin produced, directed, and did the story and script, keeping this film on an almost unrelieved level of somber depression. James Mason plays the Dutchman of the title, a sea captain who, back in the 17th century, had been condemned to sail the oceans of the world until he found a woman willing to die for love. When this miracle occurs, his soul can find salvation. Ava Gardner fares less distinctively as the girl who falls in love with this restless shade. Standout quality of the production is Jack Cardiff's color photography.

PANDORA'S BOX
See: Die Bueschse der Pandora

PANIC IN NEEDLE PARK, THE
1971, 110 mins, US ⓥ
D: Jerry Schatzberg **A:** Al Pacino, Kitty Winn, Alan Vint, Richard Bright, Kiel Martin (20th Century-Fox)

A total triumph. Gritty, gutsy, compelling, and vivid to the point of revulsion, it is an overpowering tragedy about urban drug addiction. Director Jerry Schatzberg in only his second film becomes a major talent, while Al Pacino and Kitty Winn are terrific as a heroin-doomed couple.

PANIC IN THE CITY
1968, 96 mins, US
D: Eddie Davis **A:** Howard Duff, Linda Cristal, Stephen McNally, Nehemiah Persoff, Anne Jeffries (United)

Panic in the City posits that a Communist operative in the US, acting independently of his Russian superiors, should be able to collect the material to construct an atomic bomb in Los Angeles. The panic of the title never really happens thanks to the ingenious efforts of Howard Duff, an agent of the National Bureau of Investigation. It's all done perfunctorily and without any real distinction.

PANIC IN THE STREETS
1950, 92 mins, US ⓥ
D: Elia Kazan **A:** Richard Widmark, Paul Douglas, Barbara Bel Geddes, Jack Palance, Zero Mostel (20th Century-Fox)

This is an above-average chase meller.

Tightly scripted and directed, it concerns the successful attempts to capture a couple of criminals, who are germ carriers, in order to prevent a plague and panic in a large city. The plague angle is somewhat incidental to the cops-and-bandits theme. There is vivid action, nice human touches, and some bizarre moments. Jack Palance gives a sharp performance.
1950: Best Motion Picture Story

PANIC IN YEAR ZERO
1962, 92 mins, US ▭
D: Ray Milland **A:** Ray Milland, Jean Hagen, Frankie Avalon, Mary Mitchel, Joan Freeman (American-International)

The aftermath of a nuclear attack is the subject pursued by this serious, sobering, and engrossing film. A family unit of four—father, mother, and two teenaged children—is followed here in the wake of a series of initial nuclear blasts destroying Los Angeles and four other major US cities. The family is followed to an isolated cave in the hills where, thanks to the father's negative ingenuity, it remains until it is safe to come out.

PANTHER
1995, 124 mins, US ⓥ
D: Mario Van Peebles **A:** Kadeem Hardison, Bokeem Woodbine, Joe Don Baker, Courtney B. Vance, Tyrin Turner (PolyGram/Working Title)

Fictionalized telling of some incidents in the life of the Black Panthers, represents a gloss on history for the ennobling benefit of its protagonists. Simplified when it should be complex, and sanitized when moral ambiguity doesn't suit its ideological agenda, this film is motivated by a desire to nail the FBI for its relentless efforts to destabilize and destroy the Panthers. The tale's central character is Judge (Kadeem Hardison), a young man in his early twenties who witnesses the police oppression of blacks and begins siding with firebrands. But Judge is tagged early on by local authorities as someone they can squeeze for help in their attempt to infiltrate the group. Judge ends up as the classic man in the middle.

PAPER, THE
1994, 110 mins, US ⓥ ⊙
D: Ron Howard **A:** Michael Keaton, Robert Duvall, Glenn Close, Marisa Tomei, Randy Quaid, Jason Robards (Imagine/Universal)

A rambunctious look at a day in the life of a struggling New York tabloid, *The Pa-*

per is Paddy Chayefsky lite. With every member of the all-star staff battling personal-life crises as they race to put the next edition to bed, Ron Howard's pacy meller can't help but generate a fair share of humor, excitement, and involvement, even if it veers off the tracks in the final reels with some contrived, over-the-top theatrics. Howard is handsomely helped by his uniformly talented actors, all of whom snap out the lines, good and bad, like the crafty pros they are, even if they aren't hitting any unfamiliar notes.

1994: Nomination: Best Original Song ("Make Up Your Mind")

PAPER CHASE, THE
1973, 111 mins, US ⊗ ⊙
D: James Bridges **A:** Timothy Bottoms, Lindsay Wagner, John Houseman, Edward Herrmann (20th Century-Fox)

The Paper Chase has some great performances, literate screenwriting, sensitive direction, and handsome production. The tale of a young law school student, confused by his professional calling vs. his inner evolution as a human being, seems timeless yet dated, too narrowly defined for broad audience empathy, and too often a series of sideways-moving (though entertaining) thespian declamations. John Houseman is outstanding as a hard-nosed but urbane law professor.

1973: Best Supp. Actor (John Houseman)
Nominations: Best Adapted Screenplay, Sound

PAPER HEARTS
1993, 90 mins, US ⊗ ⊙
D: Rod McCall **A:** Sally Kirkland, James Brolin, Pamela Gidley, Kris Kristofferson, Laura Johnson, Michael Moore (King-Moonstone)

A modest, sensitive, and often touching family drama that poignantly dissects the effects of a dissolving marriage. Sally Kirkland stars as Jenny Stevenson, an attractive, middle-aged woman separated from her scoundrel womanizer of a husband, Henry (James Brolin), who left her a mountain of debts. Jenny tries to hold on to the house she inherited, now on the verge of foreclosure. The family's disparate members reunite for one stormy and fateful weekend, during which Kirkland's youngest daughter (Renée Estevez) gets married. Regrettably, the big climactic scene is overly melodramatic.

PAPERHOUSE
1989, 92 mins, UK ⊗ ⊙
D: Bernard Rose **A:** Charlotte Burke, Ben Cross, Glenne Headly, Elliott Spears, Gemma Jones (Working Title)

Paperhouse is the thinking person's *A Nightmare on Elm Street*, a riveting fantasy film. Anna (Charlotte Burke), psychologically disturbed, has become a discipline problem at school. She faints and finds herself by a strange house on a cliff top, a house similar to one she'd earlier drawn on paper. Gradually she discovers that as she embellishes the drawing, she can enter the house in her dreams. There's no violence in this film, but there's considerable suspense and tension. Crucial to the film's success is a superb soundtrack, with a strong music score, but also heightened sound effects of great impact.

PAPER MASK
1990, 118 mins, UK ⊗ ⊙
D: Christopher Morahan **A:** Paul McGann, Amanda Donohoe, Frederick Treves, Tom Wilkinson, Barbara Leigh-Hunt (Film Four/Granada/British Screen)

Christopher Morahan's taut suspense thriller, from John Collee's novel about a young man who gets away with posing as an emergency-room doctor in a British hospital, raises provocative questions about human pretense and the ruses of professional survival. Pic focuses on a dissatisfied hospital worker, Matthew (Paul McGann), who seizes the chance to assume the identity of a promising young doctor after the other man dies in a car crash.

PAPER MOON
1973, 101 mins, US ⊗ ⊙
D: Peter Bogdanovich **A:** Ryan O'Neal, Tatum O'Neal, Madeline Kahn, John Hillerman, P. J. Johnson, Randy Quaid (Directors/Paramount/Saticoy)

Ryan O'Neal stars as a likable con artist in the Depression Midwest, and his real-life daughter, Tatum O'Neal, is outstanding as his nine-year-old partner in flimflam. Prominent among the large cast is Madeline Kahn, excellent as a carny stripper who captivates Ryan O'Neal. Tatum O'Neal makes a sensational screen debut.

1973: Best Supp. Actress (Tatum O'Neal)
Nominations: Best Supp. Actress (Madeline Kahn), Adapted Screenplay, Sound

PAPER TIGER
1975, 101 mins, UK ⓥ ⊙
D: Ken Annakin **A:** David Niven, Toshiro Mifune, Hardy Kruger, Ando, Jeff Corey, Irene Tsu (Shalako/Maclean)

Paper Tiger recalls the plots of vintage Shirley Temple vehicles in its cutesy relationship between English tutor David Niven and an 11-year-old Japanese moppet (Ando), kidnapped together during turmoil in Southeast Asia. Ando, like Temple, is dimpled, plucky, clever, and more resourceful than any of the adults in the story. He has a fresh, engaging personality, and it isn't his fault the camera moons over him at every opportunity.

PAPILLON
1973, 150 mins, US ⓥ ⊙ ▱
D: Franklin J. Schaffner **A:** Steve McQueen, Dustin Hoffman, Victor Jory, Don Gordon, Anthony Zerbe (Allied Artists)

Henri Charriere's story of confinement in, and escape from, the infamous French Guiana prison colony was that of an ordeal. So is film version. For 150 uninterrupted minutes, the mood is one of despair, brutality, and little hope. The script is very good within its limitations, but there is insufficient identification with the main characters. Steve McQueen, for example, says he has been framed for murdering a pimp; we do not see the injustice occur, hence have insufficient empathy.
1973: Nomination: Best Original Score

PARADINE CASE, THE
1947, 131 mins, US ⓥ
D: Alfred Hitchcock **A:** Gregory Peck, Ann Todd, Charles Laughton, Charles Coburn, Louis Jourdan, Alida Valli (RKO/Selznick)

Plot concerns murder of a blind man by his wife so she can marry her lover. Her attorney, believing in her not-guilty plea, fights for her life. Himself infatuated with his client, the barrister plots and schemes to defeat justice but as dramatic events are brought out the truth is revealed. Charles Laughton gives a revealing portrait of a gross, lustful nobleman who presides at the trial. Alfred Hitchcock's penchant for suspense, unusual atmosphere and development get full play. As the barrister who defends Alida Valli, Gregory Peck answers every demand of a demanding role.
1947: Nomination: Best Supp. Actress (Ethel Barrymore)

PARADISE
1991, 110 mins, US ⓥ ⊙
D: Mary Agnes Donoghue **A:** Melanie Griffith, Don Johnson, Elijah Wood, Thora Birch, Louise Latham (Touchstone)

Writer Mary Agnes Donoghue debuts as a film director with her careful adaptation of a 1987 French drama *Le grand chemin*. Story focuses on 10-year-old Elijah Wood, sent by his pregnant mom (Eve Gordon) to spend a school vacation in the sleepy town of Paradise. Melanie Griffith and husband, Don Johnson, who are mysteriously cold to each other, take care of the boy. The boy is befriended by nine-year-old Thora Birch, and film gently follows their pranks and adventures in an idyllic natural setting. Johnson and Griffith are deglamorized for their character roles and are convincing as a rustic, unsophisticated couple.

PARADISE ALLEY
1978, 107 mins, US ⓥ ⊙
D: Sylvester Stallone **A:** Sylvester Stallone, Kevin Conway, Anne Archer, Armand Assante, Lee Canalito (Force Ten/Universal)

Set in New York's Hell's Kitchen area during the 1940s, it tells the uplifting tale of three brothers, played by Sylvester Stallone, Armand Assante, and Lee Canalito, and how they literally wrestle their way out of the ghetto. It's an upbeat, funny, nostalgic film populated by colorful characters, memorable more for their individual moments than for their parts in the larger story.

PARADISE FOR THREE
1938, 75 mins, US
D: Edward Buzzell **A:** Frank Morgan, Robert Young, Mary Astor, Edna May Oliver, Reginald Owen (M-G-M)

Genuinely funny farce recounts the adventures of a prosperous Continental soap manufacturer (Frank Morgan) who wins a prize in his own radio slogan contest and proceeds to sneak a fortnight's vacation under an assumed name in a mountain winter resort. He gets into some comical scrapes, including a breach-of-promise suit. Mary Astor is the adventuress who becomes the nemesis of the multimillionaire.

PARADISE, HAWAIIAN STYLE
1966, 87 mins, US ⓥ
D: Michael Moore **A:** Elvis Presley, Suzanna Leigh, James Shigeta, Donna Butter-

worth, Marianna Hill, Irene Tsu (Paramount)

Gaily garbed and flowing musical. Presley plays an airplane pilot with girl trouble, who loses one job after another when he becomes innocently embroiled. His troubles continue after he and James Shigeta team up for inter-island ferrying, with usual romantic entanglements, fights, and outbursts of song.

PARADISE LAGOON
See: The Admirable Crichton

PARALLAX VIEW, THE
1974, 102 mins, US ⊘ ▭
D: Alan J. Pakula A: Warren Beatty, Hume Cronyn, William Daniels, Paula Prentiss, Anthony Zerbe, Kenneth Mars (Paramount/Gus)

The adaptation of Loren Singer's novel follows news hawk Warren Beatty in his discovery of a security organization (called the Parallax Corp) that deliberately seeks out social misfits, dispatched by clients to murder political figures of various persuasions. The story begins with the murder of Senator Bill Joyce, followed by the official investigation, after which many witnesses begin to die. Paula Prentiss, very good as a prototype TV news hen, before her mysterious death.

PARAMOUNT ON PARADE
1930, 101 mins, US
D: Dorothy Arzner, Victor Heerman, Ernst Lubitsch, A. Edward Sutherland, Otto Brower, Edwin H. Knopf, Lothar Mendes, Edmund Goulding, Rowland V. Lee, Victor Schertzinger, Frank Tuttle A: Maurice Chevalier, Jean Arthur, Gary Cooper, Clara Bow, Jack Oakie, George Bancroft (Paramount)

Interspersed throughout the 20 numbers are 11 songs, the work of 13 writers. Technicolor is used in seven of the numbers. Even with all the competition Maurice Chevalier comes through in first place. He is featured in three numbers and in two of these renders the song hits of the production. Jack Oakie and Zelma O'Neal do a tapping special, in a gym. Clara Bow, in sailor garb, does her regular on the navy.

PARANOIAC
1963, 80 mins, UK ⊙ ▭
D: Freddie Francis A: Janette Scott, Oliver Reed, Liliane Brousse, Alexander Davion, Maurice Denham (Hammer)

Suspenseful and smartly paced opus is a reworking of the imposter-heir swindle bit in which someone poses as a long-lost member of a family who just happens to turn up in time to claim a tidy inheritance. Oliver Reed plays the scheming brother with demonic skill, blending bits of spoiled brat and sneaky madman for a menacing portrayal. Janette Scott is pretty and disarming as the sister and emotes credibly. Alexander Davion makes a fine baddie-turned-hero, thesping with ease and believability.

LES PARAPLUIES DE CHERBOURG
(US: THE UMBRELLAS OF CHERBOURG)
1964, 95 mins, France/W. Germany ⊘
D: Jacques Demy A: Catherine Deneuve, Nino Castelnuovo, Anne Vernon, Marc Michel, Ellen Farmer (Parc/Madeleine/Beta)

It takes nerve to make a pic in which all dialogue is sung. Director-writer Jacques Demy went to the port town of Cherbourg to make this simple tale of a boy and girl in love. He is depicted leaving for the army, with said girl pregnant, and she giving in to her mother's blandishments and marrying a well-heeled suitor. He comes back and finally marries a childhood friend and they see each other briefly one Christmas night. Seemingly banal and sentimental on the surface, Demy has avoided these aspects by tasteful handling and the right balance in emotion, compassion, and narrative. Michel Legrand has supplied a richly tuneful score.

PARASITE
1982, 85 mins, US ⊘ ▭
D: Charles Band A: Robert Glaudini, Demi Moore, Luca Bercovici, James Davidson, Al Fann, Vivian Blaine (Embassy)

Tale has a skimpy sci-fi peg of scientist Dr. Paul Dean (Robert Glaudini) attempting to neutralize a strain of parasite. Morbid premise is that the large, wormlike parasite is in his abdomen growing while he studies another specimen. Pic's raison d'être is a set of frightening mechanical and sculpted monster makeup effects by Stan Winston. Convincing gore and sudden plunges at the camera are enhanced by Stereo Vision 3-D filming. Otherwise *Parasite* is a test of patience for all but the fanatical followers of horror cheapies.

PARASITE MURDERS, THE
See: Shivers

PAR-DELA LES NUAGES
(US: BEYOND THE CLOUDS)
1996, 104 mins, France/Italy/Germany
D: Michelangelo Antonioni, Wim Wenders **A:** John Malkovich, Kim Rossi Stuart, Ines Sastre, Sophie Marceau, Fanny Ardant, Peter Weller (Sunshine/Cine. B/France 3/Cecchi Gori/Road Movies)

Beyond the Clouds might be the most intimate, personal film Michelangelo Antonioni has made, but it may also be his least significant, his first feature in 13 years after a stroke in 1985. Production, laced with a top-drawer cast of Euro thesps, is a leaky boat whose slow artiness is more sleep-inducing than insightful. The body of Tonio Guerra's screenplay is directed by Antonioni and is based on four short-short stories from Antonioni's book *That Bowling Alley on the Tiber River.* [Version reviewed was a 113-min. "last work print" previewed at the 1995 Venice Film Festival.]

PARDON MY PAST
1945, 89 mins, US
D: Leslie Fenton **A:** Fred MacMurray, Marguerite Chapman, Akim Tamiroff, William Demarest, Rita Johnson (Columbia/Mutual)

A top-notch comedy of mistaken identity and frustration. Fred MacMurray and William Demarest are just-discharged GIs enroute to Wisconsin to start a mink farm with their service savings. MacMurray is mistaken for a rich playboy by a gambler who tries to collect an old debt. MacMurray's dual role is deftly handled so that the two characters he portrays never actually meet on the screen. Dry wit and dumbness of the Demarest character are also good for many a chuckle.

PARDON MY SARONG
1942, 83 mins, US
D: Erle C. Kenton **A:** Bud Abbott, Lou Costello, Virginia Bruce, Lionel Atwill, Robert Paige, William Demarest (Universal/Mayfair)

Abbott and Costello starrer is one continual chase, with the boys displaying their familiar routines and antics for plenty of laughs en route. In addition, picture has six song numbers. Chase gets away right at the opening, with the two comics heading west in a Chicago municipal bus bound for the coast. Gags and routines are dropped plentifully along the route, until boys switch to a sailing yacht. This lands them on a South Sea island as locale for further horseplay.

PARDON US
1931, 56 mins, US ⓥ ⊙
D: James Parrott **A:** Stan Laurel, Oliver Hardy, Walter Long, James Finlayson, June Marlowe (Roach/M-G-M)

A two-reel idea on a six-reel frame with the usual strain resulting. Opening is an excellent piece of comedy business. Boys are jotting down a recipe outside a malt and hop store. They decide to make some beer. Laurel's idea is to sell what they don't drink. In the next scene they're being waltzed into jail. Second-best laugh comes pretty early and nothing else that follows deserves to be in the same scenario. This is when the two attempt to get comfortable in a single upper berth in the cell.

PARENTHOOD
1989, 124 mins, US ⓥ ⊙
D: Ron Howard **A:** Steve Martin, Mary Steenburgen, Dianne Wiest, Jason Robards, Rick Moranis, Tom Hulce (Imagine/Universal)

An ambitious, keenly observed, and often very funny look at one of life's most daunting passages, *Parenthood*'s master stroke is that it offers the points of view of everyone in an extended and wildly diverse middle-class family. At its center is overanxious dad Steve Martin and Mary Steenburgen, his better-adjusted wife. Rick Moranis is the yuppie extreme. Dianne Wiest is a divorcée and working mother. Jason Robards is the acidic patriarch of the family forced to take another shot at fatherhood late in life when his ne'er-do-well 27-year-old son (Tom Hulce) moves back in.

1989: Nominations: Best Supp. Actress (Dianne Wiest), Song ("I Love to See You Smile")

PARENTS
1989, 82 mins, US ⓥ ⊙
D: Bob Balaban **A:** Randy Quaid, Mary Beth Hurt, Sandy Dennis, Bryan Madorsky, Juno Mills-Cockell (Vestron)

Your typical anthropological analysis of cannibalism in 1950s suburbia. Dad (Randy Quaid) lords it over little Michael (Bryan Madorsky) while Mom (Mary Beth Hurt) mostly busies herself in the kitchen. Michael suffers from recurring nightmares, and is sent to see the in-house psychologist-social worker (Sandy Dennis). It's pretty clear to the viewer early on that Mom and Dad are up to something very nasty, so it's only a matter of time, quite laboriously spent, until the folks attempt to indoctrinate little Michael in their peculiar tastes. While the potential for considerable black comedy exists, the laughs never come.

PARENT TRAP, THE
1961, 129 mins, US Ⓥ ⊙
D: David Swift **A:** Hayley Mills, Maureen O'Hara, Brian Keith, Charles Ruggles, Una Merkel, Leo G. Carroll (Walt Disney)

Screenplay describes the nimble-witted method by which identical twin sisters (both played by Mills) succeed in reuniting their estranged parents after a 14-year separation during which the sisters were parted, unbeknownst to them, in opposite parental camps. Mills seems to have an instinctive sense of comedy and an uncanny ability to react in just the right manner. Overshadowed, but outstanding in his own right, is Brian Keith as the father. Maureen O'Hara's durable beauty makes the mother an extremely attractive character.
1961: Nominations: Best Editing, Sound

PARIS BELONGS TO US
See: Paris Nous Appartient

PARIS BLUES
1961, 98 mins, US Ⓥ
D: Martin Ritt **A:** Paul Newman, Joanne Woodward, Sidney Poitier, Louis Armstrong, Diahann Carroll, Serge Reggiani (Pennebaker/Diane)

Within a snappy, flashy veneer is an undernourished romantic drama of a rather traditional screen school. The screenplay relates the romantic experiences of two expatriate US jazz musicians (Paul Newman and Sidney Poitier) and two American girls (Joanne Woodward and Diahann Carroll) on a two-week vacation fling in Paris. The men fall in love with the girls, then must weigh their philosophies and careers against their amour. The film is notable for Duke Ellington's moody, stimulating jazz score. Louis Armstrong is on hand for one flamboyant interlude of hot jazz.
1961: Nomination: Best Scoring of a Musical Picture

PARIS BY NIGHT
1989, 101 mins, UK Ⓥ
D: David Hare **A:** Charlotte Rampling, Michael Gambon, Robert Hardy, Iain Glen, Jane Asher (British Screen/Zenith/Film Four/Greenpoint-Pressman)

A handsomely produced, rather cold drama about the fall of a femme politician. Clara Paige, a high-profile, pro-Thatcher Tory politico and member of the European Parliament, finds other people's lives more

attractive than her own. Her husband, Gerald (an MP), is a drunk she's come to despise. On a high-level trip to Paris she meets with a young British businessman, Wallace, and starts an affair with him. Hare handles it all with dry, often witty, precision, but with a slightly academic style.

PARIS CALLING
1941, 93 mins, US
D: Edwin L. Marin **A:** Elisabeth Bergner, Randolph Scott, Basil Rathbone, Gale Sondergaard, Lee J. Cobb (Universal)

Smash spy melodrama with Bergner as the wealthy Frenchwoman who serves her country as an underground operative. The romance between her and Scott, a Texan serving in the RAF, is kept warm without losing the main plot thread—activity of the French loyalists working underground and in league with Great Britain. Director Edwin Marin builds powerful suspense, first as the Texan RAF husky evades capture and later when Bergner extricates herself from carefully laid traps of the Nazis.

PARIS EXPRESS
See: The Man Who Watched Trains Go By

PARIS NOUS APPARTIENT
(US: PARIS BELONGS TO US)
1960, 140 mins, France
D: Jacques Rivette **A:** Betty Schneider, Gianni Esposito, Francoise Prevost, Daniel Crohem, Jean-Claude Brialy (AJYM/Carrosse)

This uses a vague suspense theme and budding love story around a tale of a supposedly perking world totalitarian takeover by some sort of secret organization. This turns out to be a fiction in the mind of a psychotic American ex-journalist who had to leave the US for political reasons. All this is overblown, making it pretentious, slow-moving, and fairly confused. It takes much too long to tell its overcomplicated story.

PARIS, TEXAS
1984, 150 mins, W. Germany/France Ⓥ ⊙
D: Wim Wenders **A:** Harry Dean Stanton, Nastassja Kinski, Dean Stockwell, Aurore Clement, Bernhard Wicki (Road/Argos)

Pic is the story of a man, Travis, wandering aimlessly along the Texas-Mexican border. Travis's brother in Los Angeles, Walt, took in the hero's boy four years ago when the mother literally left him on their doorstep. Travis decides to win back the love of his son. Once he has done so, the pair's then off to Houston to find the missing mother. Dean Stockwell as Walt is a standout.

PARIS TROUT
1991, 100 mins, US Ⓥ ⊙
D: Stephen Gyllenhaal **A:** Dennis Hopper, Barbara Hershey, Ed Harris, Ray McKinnon, Tina Lifford (Viacom)

Pete Dexter's haunting novel about an unspeakable crime in a simple southern town circa 1949 is brought masterfully to life in a mesmerizing, morbidly fascinating tale. Trouble begins when a young black man (Eric Ware) signs a note to buy a used car from Trout (Hopper). When the worthless car is wrecked the same day, he declares he won't pay. Hopper, beefy and aged for the role and sporting a clipped redneck haircut, gives an extraordinary portrayal of a tortured madman. Hershey is marvelous as the compassionate spouse.

PARIS WHEN IT SIZZLES
1964, 108 mins, US Ⓥ
D: Richard Quine **A:** William Holden, Audrey Hepburn, Gregoire Aslan, Raymond Bussieres, Christian Duvaleix (Paramount)

Paris When It Sizzles fizzles. Marshmallow-weight hokum is concerned with the evolution of a romantic relationship between a somewhat broken-down, middle-aged screenwriter (William Holden) and his Tessie the Typist, an adorable Givenchy wench also known as Audrey Hepburn. Their affair is more or less paralleled in the creative ramblings of Holden's mind as he dreams up an artificial cloak-and-dagger screenplay. The basic error in this film seems to be the artificiality of the shell in which the take-offs are encased.

PARRISH
1961, 140 mins, US
D: Delmer Daves **A:** Troy Donahue, Claudette Colbert, Karl Malden, Dean Jagger, Connie Stevens, Diane McBain (Warner)

A long, plodding account of man versus monopoly in Connecticut's tobacco game. Troy Donahue essays the title role of a poor young man who challenges the dynasty of mighty land baron Karl Malden. A number of romantic entanglements crop up to complicate this basic conflict. Then there is the supreme complication: Malden's marriage to Donahue's mother (Claudette Colbert).

PARTING GLANCES
1986, 90 mins, US Ⓥ
D: Bill Sherwood **A:** Richard Ganoung, John Bolger, Steve Buscemi, Adam Nathan (Rondo)

Parting Glances is bracingly forthright and believable in its presentation of an all-gay world within contempo New York City. Set within a 24-hour period, Bill Sherwood's highly sophisticated pic centers around a series of farewell events for Robert (John Bolger), good-looking boyfriend of ultrayuppie Michael (Richard Ganoung). Film indulges in no special pleading, merely regarding AIDS as another fact of gay life.

PARTNERS
1976, 96 mins, Canada Ⓥ
D: Don Owen **A:** Denholm Elliott, Hollis McLaren, Michael Margotta, Lee Broker, Judith Gault (Clearwater)

Love story played off against a background of unscrupulous methods used by an American firm interested in buying out a large Canadian pulp-and-paper firm. Don Owen brings it off with elan and a few mystifying moments along the way. A thief and dope smuggler, played with macho vigor by Michael Margotta, gets romantically and sexually involved with the daughter of the pulp-and-paper firm's owner.

PARTNERS
1982, 93 mins, US Ⓥ
D: James Burrows **A:** Ryan O'Neal, John Hurt, Kenneth McMillan, Robyn Douglass, Jay Robinson, Denise Galik (Paramount)

Production ultimately runs one very tired joke into the ground. Essentially, this is the story of straight, macho detective Ryan O'Neal and closeted gay police office clerk John Hurt—an odd pair forced by their superior to go undercover and pose as a homosexual couple in order to trap the murderer of a male model.

PARTY, THE
1968, 98 mins, US Ⓥ ⊡ ▭
D: Blake Edwards **A:** Peter Sellers, Claudine Longet, Marge Champion, Steve Franken (United Artists)

The one-joke script, told in laudable, if unsuccessful, attempt to emulate silent pix technique, is dotted with comedy ranging from drawing-room repartee to, literally, bathroom vulgarity. Peter Sellers is a disaster-prone foreign thesp who fouls up an important Bengal Lancer–type film location. His outraged producer (Gavin MacLeod) blackballs him to studio chief J. Edward McKinley, but, in a mix-up, Sellers gets invited to a party at McKinley's home.

PARTY GIRL
1958, 99 mins, US Ⓥ ⊙ ▭
D: Nicholas Ray A: Robert Taylor, Cyd Charisse, Lee J. Cobb, John Ireland, Claire Kelly, Corey Allen (Euterpe/M-G-M)

Melodrama of gangster days in Chicago, played straight. Robert Taylor plays a crippled lawyer, mouthpiece for gangster boss Lee J. Cobb. Taylor uses his disability to play on the sympathies of juries. He begins to be disturbed about his way of life when he meets Cyd Charisse, a dancer at a nightclub who picks up a little money occasionally at parties. Taylor sees he cannot censure Charisse for making money out of the mobs when he is doing the same thing himself. Taylor's breaking point comes when he is called to defend a psychopath mobster (Corey Allen).

PARTY'S OVER, THE
1965, 94 mins, UK
D: Guy Hamilton A: Oliver Reed, Clifford David, Ann Lynn, Catherine Woodville, Eddie Albert (Tricastle)

Tawdry yarn concerns a young American girl, daughter of a tycoon, who comes to London and gets involved with a group of young Chelsea layabouts known as the Pack, a disillusioned bunch that lives only for kicks. Eventually the girl disappears after one of the wildest parties, and is found dead. How she met her death, the events leading up to it and immediately after, all merge into a pseudopsychological and phony finale.

PASCALI'S ISLAND
1989, 104 mins, UK Ⓥ ⊙
D: James Dearden A: Ben Kingsley, Charles Dance, Helen Mirren, George Murcell, Sheila Allen (Avenue/Initial)

Mildly exotic British pic that looms as too languid and remote to make much impact. Kingsley plays Pascali, a seedy little Turkish spy filled with self-importance. Sexually ambivalent, he carries a half-hearted torch for a comely, middle-aged Austrian painter, Lydia (Helen Mirren). Enter Charles Dance as a bronzed British adventurer planning to loot the island of its ancient treasures. Before long he's involved in an affair with Lydia, observed by the frustrated and jealous Pascali.

PASSAGE TO INDIA, A
1985, 163 mins, UK Ⓥ ⊙
D: David Lean A: Judy Davis, Victor Banerjee, Peggy Ashcroft, James Fox, Alec Guinness, Nigel Havers (Columbia/HBO)

An impeccably faithful, beautifully played, and occasionally languorous adaptation of E. M. Forster's classic novel about the clash of East and West in colonial India. Tale is set in 1928. A young woman, Judy Davis, is taken from England to India. Intelligent and well brought up, Davis chafes at the limitations and acute snobbery of the ruling British community. Breaking the general rule against racial intermingling, local medic Victor Banerjee invites the ladies to the nearby Marabar caves, an excursion which ends in tragedy when a bloodied Davis returns to accuse Banerjee of having attempted to rape her.
1984: Best Supp. Actress (Peggy Ashcroft), Original Score
Nominations: Best Picture, Director, Actress (Judy Davis), Adapted Screenplay, Cinematography, Costume Design, Art Direction, Editing, Sound

PASSAGE TO MARSEILLE
1944, 110 mins, US Ⓥ
D: Michael Curtiz A: Humphrey Bogart, Michele Morgan, Claude Rains, Sydney Greenstreet, Peter Lorre (Warner)

Yarn, dedicated to the fighting French, unwinds in a series of flashbacks, as related by a French liaison officer (Claude Rains). A ship he was on picked up a group of men in a lifeboat in the Atlantic, escaped prisoners from Devil's Island who wish to return to France to fight for their country. The wireless crackles with the news of French surrender to the Nazis. The captain of the ship (Victor Francen) secretly orders its course changed toward England, but not before the fascist wireless operator radios the ship's position to a German patrol bomber. Humphrey Bogart gives a forthright performance as one of the escaped convicts. But Rains captures practically all the acting honors in a film filled with good acting.

PASSENGER, THE
1975, 123 mins, US Ⓥ ▭
D: Michelangelo Antonioni A: Jack Nicholson, Maria Schneider, Jenny Runacre, Ian Hendry (M-G-M)

Jack Nicholson plays a seasoned TV newsman, adjusted to established limits yet conscious of his inadequacy in probing through the grim truth. Death of a British adventurer in a small North African hotel becomes a last chance for the newsman to scrap his own anguished identity and take on the mission of the dead man. His new probe becomes a showdown with the merciless revolutionary currents and countercurrents in today's world.

PASSENGER 57
1993, 83 mins, US Ⓥ ⊙
D: Kevin Hooks A: Wesley Snipes, Bruce Payne, Tom Sizemore, Alex Datcher, Elizabeth Hurley (Warner)

Reasonably saucy action tale runs out of gas before landing. With his henchmen disguised as crew members, Bruce Payne seizes a jet, murdering FBI agents and pilot. That leaves it to newly hired airline security expert Wesley Snipes (cutting his teeth as a big-time action hero) to try to stop them. Payne's hissable villain contributes greatly to maintaining the film's intensity.

PASSION
1982, 87 mins, France/Switzerland Ⓥ
D: Jean-Luc Godard A: Hanna Schygulla, Michel Piccoli, Isabelle Huppert, Jerzy Radziwilowicz, Laszlo Szabo (Sara/Sonimage/Films A2/Film & Video)

A return to Jean-Luc Godard's talky, quirky films where dialogue often vied with commentary. As is usual, both are irritating, but good visual ideas abound if taken at face value. There is a video film being made which imitates great paintings and old myths. Everybody has trouble but Godard insists the plan should work. Godard's visuals are fine, as usual, but whether it will grip new audiences is chancy. However, Godard does not care and goes his way.

PASSIONATE FRIENDS, THE
(US: ONE WOMAN'S STORY)
1949, 91 mins, UK
D: David Lean A: Ann Todd, Claude Rains, Trevor Howard, Betty Ann Davies, Isabel Dean (Cineguild)

Polished acting, masterly direction, and an excellent script put *The Passionate Friends* in the top rank of class British productions. Ann Todd rises to new heights as the girl who forswears love for security and wealth. Claude Rains, in the role of the banker husband, is a model of competence, and Trevor Howard brings vigor and polish to the part of the lover.

PASSIONATE PLUMBER, THE
1932, 73 mins, US
D: Edward Sedgwick A: Buster Keaton,

Jimmy Durante, Irene Purcell, Polly Moran, Gilbert Roland, Mona Maris (M-G-M)

Nonsensical slapstick story derived somehow from Frederick Lonsdale's *Her Cardboard Lover*. The cast and the laughs are constantly obliged to fight the plot and motives; unfortunately the plot wins the battle. While Durante and Keaton are cross-firing for laughs the rest is momentarily laid aside, and when the chief laugh grabbers return to the theme, they don't mix.

LE PASSION DE JEANNE D'ARC
(US: THE PASSION OF JOAN OF ARC)
1928, 114 mins, France ⊙ ⊗
D: Carl Dreyer A: Maria Falconetti, Eugene Silvain, Antonin Artaud, Maurice Schutz, Michel Simon (SGF)

A deadly tiresome picture that merely makes an attempt to narrate without sound or dialogue an allegedly written recorded trial in the 15th or 16th century of Joan of Arc for witchery, leading to her condemnation and burning at the stake. In appearance, Joan is at all times immobile in countenance and always staring into the camera when she isn't washing tears off her face.

PASSION FISH
1992, 134 mins, US Ⓥ ⊙
D: John Sayles A: Mary McDonnell, Alfre Woodard, David Strathairn, Vondie Curtis-Hall, Sheila Kelley (Atchafalaya)

A sympathetic if somewhat deliberate and overlong intimate study of two women emerging from their protective shells. Mary McDonnell plays May-Alice, a TV soap star paralyzed from the waist down in an accident. She installs herself in the deserted family home in Louisiana's Cajun country and nastily rejects a succession of nurses until Chantelle (Alfre Woodard) comes along. May-Alice sinks into a daily grind of drinking and nonstop TV watching. Chantelle soon forces her employer to shape up. But Chantelle is fighting demons of her own.
1992: Nominations: Best Actress (Mary McDonnell), Original Screenplay

PASSION OF JOAN OF ARC, THE
See: Le Passion de Jeanne D'Arc

PASSOVER PLOT, THE
1976, 108 mins, US/Israel Ⓥ
D: Michael Campus A: Harry Andrews, Hugh Griffith, Zalman King, Donald

Pleasence, Scott Wilson, Dan Ades (Atlas/Golan-Globus)

Disappointing film, based on Hugh J. Schonfield's revisionist 1960s book on the life of Jesus Christ, drains the vitality out of the Christ story through verbiage and overacting. Zalman King's Jesus (or Yeshua, the Hebraic name used in the book and film) is an angry young man with little of the warmth and folk humor the character displays in the Bible texts. Far from seeming disrespectful, the film errs on the side of excessive respect.
1976: Nomination: Best Costume Design

PASSPORT TO FAME
See: The Whole Town's Talking

PASSPORT TO PIMLICO
1949, 84 mins, UK ⊘
D: Henry Cornelius **A:** Stanley Holloway, Barbara Murray, Raymond Huntley, Paul Dupuis, Hermione Baddeley (Ealing)

Sustained, lightweight comedy scoring a continual succession of laughs. An unexploded wartime bomb in a London street goes off and reveals ancient documents that make the territory part of the duchy of Burgundy. Ration cards are joyfully torn up and customs barriers are put up by British. The theme is related with a genuine sense of satire and clean, honest humor.
1949: Nomination: Best Story & Screenplay

PASSWORD IS COURAGE, THE
1962, 116 mins, UK ⊟
D: Andrew L. Stone **A:** Dirk Bogarde, Maria Perschy, Alfred Lynch, Nigel Stock, Reginald Beckwith (M-G-M)

Screenplay has pumped into its untidy 116 minutes an overdose of slapstick humor. What could have been a telling tribute to a character of guts and initiative lacks conviction. Sergeant Major Charles Coward (Dirk Bogarde) becomes a prisoner of war dedicated to sabotaging and humiliating his German captors. As senior soldier in Stalag 8B, he rallies the other men to escape so that they can get back to fighting the Nazis. Bogarde gives a performance that is never less than competent, but never much more.

PAT AND MIKE
1952, 94 mins, US ⊘ ⊙
D: George Cukor **A:** Spencer Tracy, Katharine Hepburn, Aldo Ray, William Ching, George Mathews (M-G-M)

The smooth-working team of Spencer Tracy and Katharine Hepburn spark the fun in *Pat and Mike*. Hepburn is quite believable as a femme athlete taken under the wing of promoter Tracy. Film settles down to a series of laugh sequences of training, exhibitions, and cross-country tours in which Hepburn proves to be a star. Tracy is given some choice lines in the script and makes much of them in an easy, throwaway style.
1952: Nomination: Best Story & Screenplay

PATCH OF BLUE, A
1965, 105 mins, US ⊘ ⊟
D: Guy Green **A:** Sidney Poitier, Shelley Winters, Elizabeth Hartman, Wallace Ford, Ivan Dixon (M-G-M/Berman)

Touching contemporary melodrama, relieved at times by generally effective humor, about a blind white girl from a dreary home rehabilitated by a Negro. Film has very good scripting plus excellent direction and performances, including an exceptional screen debut by Elizabeth Hartman as the gal. Shelley Winters is very good as Hartman's sleazy mother.
1965: Best Supp. Actress (Shelley Winters)
Nominations: Best Actress (Elizabeth Hartman), B&W Cinematography, B&W Art Direction, Original Music Score

PATERNITY
1981, 94 mins, US ⊘ ⊙
D: David Steinberg **A:** Burt Reynolds, Beverly D'Angelo, Paul Dooley, Elizabeth Ashley, Lauren Hutton (Paramount)

There are several funny bits in a harmless enough romantic comedy that strangely has its strongest laughs in its least important scenes. But the basic story of a successful 44-year-old man who decides to fulfill his desire for fatherhood through a pact with a woman to have his child never comes across with much punch. While Reynolds and D'Angelo make a nice enough onscreen couple, they just don't provide the sparks needed to light up a romantic comedy.

PAT GARRETT AND BILLY THE KID
1973, 106 mins, US ⊙ ⊟ ⊙
D: Sam Peckinpah **A:** James Coburn, Kris Kristofferson, Bob Dylan, Richard Jaeckel, Katy Jurado, Jason Robards (M-G-M)

"It feels like times have changed," mutters James Coburn as gunman-turned-sheriff Pat Garrett, now hot on the trail of erstwhile buddy, Billy the Kid (Kris Kristofferson). Coburn offers more of his smiles as testimony to the wizardry of old West dentistry, while Kristofferson ambles through his role with solid charm. Neither conveys the psychological tension felt between the two men whose lives diverge after years of camaraderie.

PATHER PANCHALI
1955, 112 mins, India ⓥ ⊙
D: Satyajit Ray **A:** Kanu Bannerjee, Karuna Bannerjee, Subir Bannerjee, Uma Das Gupta (State of West Bengal)

Film poetically and lyrically unfolds a tender but penetrating tale of coming of age in India, a land of poverty but also of spiritual hope. Two adolescents, a boy and his sister, grow in this atmosphere. The treatment of old age is one of the most profound ever seen on the screen. An old woman lives and dies among the budding children with a dignity and beauty that counterpoints the growth and experiences of the children. Acting, lensing, and all other aspects are masterfully orchestrated by Ray into a document on life in India.

PATHS OF GLORY
1957, 87 mins, US ⓥ ⊙
D: Stanley Kubrick **A:** Kirk Douglas, Ralph Meeker, Adolphe Menjou, George Macready, Wayne Morris, Richard Anderson (Bryna/Harris-Kubrick/United Artists)

Starkly realistic recital of French army politics in 1916 during World War I. Story revolves around decision of the General Staff for a military unit commanded by George Macready, a general of the old school, to take an objective held for two years by the Germans. Knowing full well the impossibility of such an assault, the general nevertheless orders Kirk Douglas, colonel in command of the regiment, to make the suicidal attempt. Stanley Kubrick in his taut direction catches the spirit of war with fine realism. Douglas scores heavily in his realization that his is a losing battle against the system, and Macready socks over what may be regarded his most effective role to date.

PATRICK
1978, 110 mins, Australia ⓥ
D: Richard Franklin **A:** Susan Penhaligon, Robert Helpmann, Rod Mullinar, Bruce Barry, Julia Blake (Australian International)

Patrick, having done away with mom and her lover, is next seen in a state of chronic, advanced—and, we're told—irreversible catatonic reaction. Kathy Jac-

quard (Susan Penhaligon) returns to nursing to support herself. She's given Patrick to watch over. The patient falls in love with his nurse, which would be okay if he only had tonsillitis and was normal: Patrick is polyplegic and homicidal and possessed of this really terrific sixth sense which he uses spitefully. The inert (and uncredited) lead creates an incredible menace.

PATRICK THE GREAT
1945, 86 mins, US ⓥ
D: Frank Ryan **A:** Donald O'Connor, Peggy Ryan, Frances Dee, Eve Arden (Universal)

Donald O'Connor and Peggy Ryan as a song-and-dance team with romantic ups and downs help mightily to make *Patrick the Great* a diverting musical. The story is built around Donald Cook, a musical comedy star, and young O'Connor as his stagestruck son, plus Ryan who, in addition to having theatrical ambitions, is also plenty sweet on O'Connor.

PATRIOT, THE
1928, 108 mins, US
D: Ernst Lubitsch **A:** Emil Jannings, Lewis Stone, Florence Vidor, Neil Hamilton, Vera Voronina (Paramount)

Many elements combine to give *The Patriot* a valid claim to greatness. The magnificent performance of Emil Jannings as the mad czar Paul alone. Time is the late 18th century, and locale the richly picturesque atmosphere of the Russian court under Czar Paul, the insane emperor of all the Russias. Surrounded by murderous plots, the only creature the madman trusts is his minister of war, Count Pahlen (Lewis Stone). The role of Pahlen is really the star part, and it is only Jannings's genius that holds up the character of the czar. Stone gives a balanced and polished performance. Sound effects are managed inconspicuously. There is no dialogue.
1928/29: Best Writing
Nominations: Best Picture, Director, Actor (Lewis Stone), Art Direction

PATRIOT GAMES
1992, 116 mins, US ⓥ ⊙ ▭
D: Phillip Noyce **A:** Harrison Ford, Anne Archer, Patrick Bergin, Sean Bean, James Fox (Paramount)

Mindless, morally repugnant, and ineptly directed to boot, *Patriot Games* is a shoddy follow-up to Par's 1990 hit *The Hunt for Red October*. The ultraviolent, fascistic, blatantly anti-Irish film stars a dour Harrison Ford. A visit to London with his family places him in the middle of an attack on a high British official (James Fox) by what Ford later identifies as "some ultraviolent faction of the IRA." His rescue of Fox and killing of one attacker makes him the quarry of a vengeful, ice-blooded IRA man (Sean Bean).

PATSY, THE
1928, 64 mins, US ⊗
D: King Vidor **A:** Marion Davies, Orville Caldwell, Marie Dressler, Del Henderson, Lawrence Gray, Jane Winton (M-G-M)

A dandy laugh picture. Marion Davies does some really great comedy work. Many of the laughs come from the subtitles. Efforts of a younger girl to attract the attention of the man who is courting her sister form the basis of the comedy. Davies does a series of imitations of Pola Negri, Mae Murray, and Lillian Gish that are great and reveal her as a skillful comic.

PATSY, THE
1964, 100 mins, US ⓥ ⊙
D: Jerry Lewis **A:** Jerry Lewis, Ina Balin, Everett Sloane, Phil Harris, Keenan Wynn, Peter Lorre (Paramount)

Premise of a group of film professionals—a producer, director, writer-gagman, press agent, and secretary—who have lost their star in a plane disaster and find another meal ticket by grabbing a hotel bellboy and building him to stardom, lacks development—which might have made a better comedy. Jerry Lewis also directs in the part, and as the patsy of this pack of hangers-on he indulges in his usual mugging and clowning, good for guffaws and enough nonsensical anticking to appeal to juve audiences especially.

PATTI ROCKS
1987, 87 mins, US ⓥ
D: David Burton Morris **A:** Chris Mulkey, John Jenkins, Karen Landry (Film Dallas)

An often bitingly humorous exposé of the male ego accomplished dramatically in one night, quintessential American independent production is a very good one. Billy (Chris Mulkey), a working stiff into his thirties with a wife and two kids, shanghais his old buddy Eddie (John Jenkins) to drive with him to a distant town to help him tell a woman he's "knocked up" that she ought to have an abortion. Eddie ends up sitting in the passenger seat for hours as Billy delivers a torrential monologue of ever-escalating sexual boasts and fantasies. Unknown thesps are not charismatic, but are vividly believable.

PATTON
1970, 170 mins, US ⓥ ⊙ ▭
D: Franklin J. Schaffner **A:** George C. Scott, Karl Malden, Michael Bates, Karl Michael Vogler, Edward Binns, Lawrence Dobkin (20th Century-Fox)

War is hell, and *Patton* is one hell of a war picture. George C. Scott's title-role performance is outstanding. Film begins in North Africa, just before General George S. Patton Jr. takes over command in 1943 of an American component of an Anglo-American unit decimated by German attack. It ends after the surrender of Germany, and Patton's relief from an occupation command because of embarrassing statements contrary to civilian and Allied policy.
1970: Best Picture, Director, Actor (George C. Scott, declined award), Original Story & Screenplay, Art Direction, Sound, Editing
Nominations: Best Cinematography, Original Score, Visual Effects

PATTY HEARST
1988, 108 mins, US ⓥ
D: Paul Schrader **A:** Natasha Richardson, William Forsythe, Ving Rhames, Frances Fisher (Atlantic/Zenith)

Frequently wrapped in surrealistic stylization, film manages only to tell Hearst's side of her kidnapping ordeal. Stuffed into a closet and blindfolded for nearly 50 days, Hearst is subjected to verbal abuse by the deranged band of self-styled revolutionaries that called themselves the Symbionese Liberation Army. In portraying Hearst, Natasha Richardson manages to convey all the sympathy clearly intended.

PAWNBROKER, THE
1965, 112 mins, US ⓥ ⊙
D: Sidney Lumet **A:** Rod Steiger, Geraldine Fitzgerald, Brock Peters, Thelma Oliver, Jaime Sanchez (Landau/Allied Artists)

A painstakingly etched portrait of a man who survived the living hell of a Nazi concentration camp and runs a pawnshop in Harlem. Rod Steiger plays the embittered pawnbroker. He has lost his faith in God, the arts and sciences, he has no discriminatory feelings against white or colored man, but regards them all as human scum. There is little plot in the regular sense, but a series of episodes spanning just a few days of the present, which recall

many harrowing experiences of the past. The pic is dominated by Steiger. He knows most of the tricks of the trade, and puts them to good use.
1965: Nomination: Best Actor (Rod Steiger)

PAYBACK
1999, 110 mins, US Ⓥ ⊙ ▭
D: Brian Helgeland A: Mel Gibson, Gregg Henry, Maria Bello, Deborah Kara Unger, David Paymer, Bill Duke (Icon/Paramount)

Payback is such a loose reworking of John Boorman's dazzling 1967 noir, *Point Blank,* that it hardly qualifies as a remake. Yarn is moved from Alcatraz and Los Angeles to Chicago's urban jungle. Porter (Mel Gibson) and partner Val (Gregg Henry) engage in a heist. Val steals Porter's share and his druggie wife, Lynn (Deborah Kara Unger), and shoots Porter. Porter is reborn with one obsessive motivation: retribution. The film vacillates between the dark and sinister and the comic and whimsical, with funny one-liners that change the morbid, metaphysical tone of the story. Reflecting the zeitgeist, *Payback* is more graphically violent than *Point Blank.*

PAYMENT ON DEMAND
1951, 90 mins, US
D: Curtis Bernhardt A: Bette Davis, Barry Sullivan, Jane Cowl, Kent Taylor, Betty Lynn, Frances Dee (Skirball-Manning/RKO)

Bette Davis is in top form. Her interpretation of the overly ambitious wife has great believability. The part of the husband, who stuns Davis with the announcement that he wants a divorce, is the sympathetic role, and Barry Sullivan handles it neatly and with a quiet dignity.

PCU
1994, 79 mins, US Ⓥ ⊙
D: Hart Bochner A: Jeremy Piven, Chris Young, Jon Favreau, David Spade, Jessica Walter (20th Century-Fox)

A boisterous if not uproariously funny look at political correctness as it afflicts a campus divided into so many protest groups that students have no time to attend classes. At the center is a coed gang whose anarchic leader, Droz (Jeremy Piven), encourages any form of offensive and bizarre behavior. Into this chaos arrives Tom (Chris Young), a handsome prefreshman unprepared for life on the treacherous campus.

PEACEMAKER
1990, 90 mins, US Ⓥ ⊙
D: Kevin S. Tenney A: Robert Forster, Lance Edwards, Hilary Shephard, Bert Remsen (Gibraltar/Mentone)

An unexpected gem, a sci-fi action thriller that really delivers the goods. Inventive plot is a tale of two humanoid aliens (Robert Forster and Lance Edwards) who crash-land on Earth. One is an intergalactic serial killer, the other a police officer, or peacemaker. A simple setup, except for one complication: both claim to be the cop. *Peacemaker* is a stunt extravaganza, a nonstop, fast-paced assemblage of chases, shootouts, and explosions building to an impressive climax. Pic has a big-budget look throughout.

PEACEMAKER, THE
1997, 123 mins, US Ⓥ ⊙ ▭
D: Mimi Leder A: George Clooney, Nicole Kidman, Marcel Iures, Alexander Baluev, Rene Medvesek, Gary Werntz (DreamWorks)

This is an uncommonly dour action thriller that offers a very limited political, emotional and dramatic view. Nine nuclear weapons are stolen from a Bosnian train. Thrust together to piece things out are scientist Dr. Julia Kelly (Nicole Kidman) and U.S. Army Special Forces Lt. Col. Thomas Devoe (George Clooney). One of the stolen bombs has already disappeared, which sends the heroes to New York City. The finale is reasonably impressive but ends with a hackneyed race with time to prevent a nuclear holocaust. Script alternates between information conveyance and shouted commands. Clooney and Kidman are mainly asked to keep moving.

LA PEAU DOUCE
(US: SOFT SKIN; UK: SILKEN SKIN)
1964, 118 mins, France Ⓥ ⊙
D: Francois Truffaut A: Jean Desailly, Francoise Dorleac, Nelly Benedetti, Daniel Ceccaldi, Jean Lanier (Films du Carrosse/SEDIF)

Film details the matter-of-fact home life of a semisuccessful highbrow magazine editor and lecturer who one day becomes enamored of an airline hostess. Truffaut shows that he can make a solidly carpentered film like anybody else. There are some irrepressibly witty scenes. Francoise Dorleac has the right feckless quality for the girl, while Jean Desailly has the reserve and phlegmatic qualities of a supposedly set man who succumbs to the flesh. Nelly Benedetti is more unclear as the seemingly settled housewife.

PEEPER
1975, 87 mins, US ▭
D: Peter Hyams A: Michael Caine, Natalie Wood, Kitty Winn, Thayer David, Liam Dunn, Dorothy Adams (20th Century-Fox)

Limp spoof of a 1940s private-eye film stars Michael Caine as a fumbling gumshoe and Natalie Wood as a member of a mysterious wealthy family. Story gets under way with Michael Constantine hiring Caine to find his long-lost daughter so she will get his money. But comic assassins Timothy Agoglia Carey and Don Calfa keep popping up doing bad numbers on people.

PEEPING TOM
1960, 109 mins, UK ⓥ
D: Michael Powell A: Karl Boehm, Moira Shearer, Anna Massey, Maxine Audley, Shirley Anne Field (Anglo-Amalgamated/Powell)

Stripped of its color and some excellent photography plus imaginative direction by Michael Powell, the plot would have emerged as a shoddy yarn. Story concerns a young man who, as a boy, was used as a guinea pig by his father, a noted professor studying the symptoms of fear. The boy grows up to become an insane killer obsessed with the desire to photograph the terror on the faces of his victims as he kills them. He also has an unhealthy craving for peeping at young lovers, hence the title. This mixed-up young man is played rather stolidly by Karl Boehm. The standout feature of *Peeping Tom* is some fascinating photography by Otto Heller.

PEE-WEE'S BIG ADVENTURE
1985, 90 mins, US ⓥ ⊙
D: Tim Burton A: Pee-Wee Herman [Paul Reubens], Elizabeth Daily, Mark Holton, Diane Salinger, Judd Omen (Aspen/Shapiro)

Pee-Wee wakes up in a children's bedroom full of incredible toys, slides down a fire-stationlike brass pole, materializing in his trademark tight suit with white shoes and red bow tie, proceeds to make a breakfast à la Rube Goldberg, and winds up in a front yard that looks like a children's farm. It's a delicious bit, remarkably drawing for adult viewers the joys and frustrations of being a kid. Rest of narrative deals with Pee-Wee's unstoppable pursuit of his prized lost bicycle, a rambling kidvidlike spoof.

PEGGY SUE GOT MARRIED
1986, 104 mins, US ⓥ ⊙
D: Francis Ford Coppola A: Kathleen Turner, Nicolas Cage, Barry Miller, Catherine Hicks, Joan Allen (Rastar/Tri-Star Delphi IV & V)

A nice mix of sap and sass for Peggy Sue's (Kathleen Turner) character, a melancholy mother of two facing divorce who finds herself revived as an 18-year-old high school senior of the class of 1960. She realizes she's returned to her youth with all the knowledge and experience learned as an adult, quickly figuring out that she can alter the course of her future life by changing certain crucial decisions she made as a teenager.

1986: Nominations: Best Actress (Kathleen Turner), Cinematography, Costume Design

PEG O' MY HEART
1923, 106 mins, US ⊗
D: King Vidor A: Laurette Taylor, Mahlon Hamilton, Russell Simpson, Ethel Grey Terry, Nigel Barrie (Metro)

Laurette Taylor does a unique piece of work here. New to the camera, she looks 20 and acts 16 with an exquisite grace that is memorable. Except for her deft and dainty comedy, the picture might be pretty tepid. Production has some exquisite settings, authentic scenic background taken abroad, and interiors done in the best form.

PEKING EXPRESS
1951, 85 mins, US
D: William Dieterle A: Joseph Cotten, Corinne Calvet, Edmund Gwenn, Marvin Miller, Benson Fong (Paramount)

An excellent coating of intrigue and action provides enough thriller melodramatics to satisfy action-minded audiences. Aboard the Peking Express on a run between Shanghai and Peking are Joseph Cotten, UN doctor; Corinne Calvet, adventuress and old flame of Cotten's; Edmund Gwenn, a priest; Marvin Miller, black market operator; and Benson Fong, rabid Commie newspaperman. Action becomes rapid when Miller has his bandits seize the train and the principal passengers to hold as hostages.

PELICAN BRIEF, THE
1993, 141 mins, US ⓥ ⊙ ▭
D: Alan J. Pakula A: Julia Roberts, Denzel Washington, Sam Shepard, John

Heard, James B. Sikking (Warner)

Taut, intelligent thriller that succeeds on almost every level. Julia Roberts is sensational as law-student-on-the-run Darby Shaw, and Denzel Washington proves her equal in a laudable example of color-blind casting. The story opens with two Supreme Court justices murdered on the same night. Twenty-four-year-old law student Darby drafts a brief detailing an obscure case that could provide inspiration for the dual murders. Darby's professor boyfriend, Thomas Callahan (Sam Shepard) passes the brief along to a friend at the FBI (John Heard). When Thomas's car explodes, the game of cats-and-mouse is on—with both the government and the perpetrators pursuing Darby.

PELLE EROBREREN
(US: PELLE THE CONQUEROR)
1987, 160 mins, Denmark/Sweden Ⓥ ⊙
D: Bille August A: Max von Sydow, Pelle Hvenegaard, Erik Paske, Bjorne Granath, Axel Strobye (Holst/Svensk Filmindustri)

A feature film of epic proportions and a relentlessly unsentimental look at life among the haves and, primarily, the have-nots on a big turn-of-the-century farm. Lasse, an elderly and widowed farmer (Max von Sydow), and his young son, Pelle (Pelle Hvenegaard), join a boatload of immigrants to escape from impoverished rural Sweden to the Land of Plenty of their dreams, Denmark's Baltic island of Bornholm. Lasse comes to terms with a life of near-slavery as the lowliest tender of the farm's cows, while Pelle casts off his chains and sets out, in time-honored style (a lone figure crossing the snowy fields), to conquer the world.
1988: Best Foreign Language Film

PELLE THE CONQUEROR
See: Pelle Erobreren

PENDULUM
1969, 101 mins, US Ⓥ ⊙
D: George Schaefer A: George Peppard, Jean Seberg, Richard Kiley, Charles McGraw, Madeleine Sherwood, Robert F. Lyons (Columbia)

Although the end result is a somewhat routine crime meller, *Pendulum* attacks head-on the issue of individual liberties under the US Constitution versus society as a whole. An excellent basic plot has been weakened by potboiler elements. George Peppard is a police hero who is suspected of the murder of his wife (Jean Seberg) and becomes a victim of a society

that while mouthing the principle that an accused is innocent until he's proven guilty, tends to think along reverse lines.

PENELOPE
1966, 94 mins, US ▭
D: Arthur Hiller A: Natalie Wood, Ian Bannen, Dick Shawn, Peter Falk, Jonathan Winters, Lila Kedrova (M-G-M)

One of those bright, delightfully wacky comedies. Script gives full sway to the story of a young wife whose hobby is larceny. Film opens with a little old lady holding up a bank and getting away with $60,000 a few hours after bank's official opening. She turns out to be Natalie Wood, married to the bank's president (Ian Bannen). Peter Falk socks over his role as police lieutenant assigned to the bank case.

PENITENTIARY
1979, 99 mins, US Ⓥ
D: Jamaa Fanaka A: Leon Isaac Kennedy, Thommy Pollard, Hazel Spears, Badja Djola, Gloria Delaney (Gross)

Circumstantial evidence lands lanky, streetwise Leon Isaac Kennedy in prison. Balance of power in his cellblock, largely inhabited by blacks, is dictated by brute force. The realities of prison life are rendered with extreme believability, and a welcome lack of preachiness or liberal posturing.

PENNIES FROM HEAVEN
1981, 107 mins, US Ⓥ ⊙
D: Herbert Ross A: Steve Martin, Bernadette Peters, Christopher Walken, Jessica Harper, Tommy Rall, John McMartin (M-G-M/Hera)

Steve Martin, in Depression-ridden Chicago, is a sheet-music salesman, whose "real" life consists of one squalid little scene after another: he makes virginal schoolteacher Bernadette Peters pregnant, after which she becomes a streetwalker. Worked into this lugubrious, neo-Brechtian tragedy are more than a dozen musical numbers of grave opulence. Purpose is to illustrate the idealism and innocence to which Martin presumably aspires, with the vivid contrast between the sunny escapism of 1930s song lyrics and the somber dispiritedness of the era from whence they came.
1981: Nominations: Best Adapted Screenplay, Costume Design, Sound

PENNY SERENADE
1941, 110 mins, US Ⓥ
D: George Stevens A: Irene Dunne, Cary

Grant, Beulah Bondi, Edgar Buchanan, Ann Doran (Columbia)

Irene Dunne and Cary Grant adopt a six weeks' old baby and raise her until she is six, when she dies after a brief illness. Then they adopt a boy of two. The telling of it occupies nearly two hours, in the course of which there are tenderness, heartthrob, comedy, and good, old-fashioned, gulping tears. Half a dozen times the yarn approaches the saccharine, only to be turned back into sound, human comedy-drama.

1941: Nomination: Best Actor (Cary Grant)

PENTHOUSE
1933, 90 mins, US
D: W. S. Van Dyke A: Warner Baxter, Myrna Loy, Charles Butterworth, Mae Clarke, Phillips Holmes (M-G-M)

It's a sugarcoated gang story. Development has capital comedy incident and some of the most likable characters of underworld pictures. Action revolves around a rich lawyer with a taste for criminal cases—the gangster he saves from the chair, and the girl who appears to help him clear a society friend framed in a killing by a rival gang chief.

PENTHOUSE, THE
1967, 90 mins, UK
D: Peter Collinson A: Suzy Kendall, Terence Morgan, Tony Beckley, Norman Rodway, Martine Beswick (Tahiti-Twickenham/Compton)

Story finds hero and heroine trapped in an isolated apartment with a pair of deranged hoodlums alternating physical and mental bouts of sadism as they break down the couple's resistance. The quality of the lines and the subtle yet powerful impact of their content, plus the superbly controlled delivery by the cast, make this a compelling—if at times inevitably distasteful—glimpse at some of the seamier characteristics of the human being.

PEOPLE AGAINST O'HARA, THE
1951, 101 mins, US
D: John Sturges A: Spencer Tracy, Pat O'Brien, Diana Lynn, John Hodiak, Eduardo Ciannelli (M-G-M)

A basically good idea for a film melodrama is cluttered up with too many unnecessary side twists and turns, and the presentation is uncomfortably overlong. Plot premise finds Spencer Tracy, practicing civil law after pressure of criminal cases had driven him to the bottle, taking on the defense of James Arness, a young man charged with murder. Arness is convicted, but Tracy does not give up.

PEOPLE THAT TIME FORGOT, THE
1977, 90 mins, US ⓥ
D: Kevin Connor A: Patrick Wayne, Doug McClure, Sarah Douglas, Dana Gillespie, Thorley Walters (American International)

Story of a small party seeking a marooned World War I naval hero north of the ice barrier in the Arctic. Special effects predominate as group is attacked by a giant pterodactyl and encounter all manner of hair-raising beasties and erupting fire.

PEOPLE UNDER THE STAIRS, THE
1991, 102 mins, US ⓥ ⊙
D: Wes Craven A: Brandon Adams, Everett McGill, Wendy Robie, A. J. Langer, Ving Rhames (Alive)

A pretense of social responsibility and most of the necessary tension get lost in a combination of excessive gore and over-the-top perfs. Writer-director Wes Craven sneaks in a post–Reagan-era message about haves and have-nots by making his hero a 13-year-old ghetto kid. Pic's still an old-style haunted-house film with spooky couple Everett McGill and Wendy Robie terrorizing their teen daughter (A. J. Langer) and keeping a horde of ashen youths locked in the basement.

PEOPLE VS. LARRY FLYNT, THE
1996, 127 mins, US ⓥ ⊙ ⊡
D: Milos Forman A: Woody Harrelson, Courtney Love, Edward Norton, James Cromwell, Crispin Glover, James Carville (Ixtlan/Columbia)

Picture uses the shenanigans and occasional serious gestures of an unabashed pornographer to serve up a roller-coaster ride across the sociopolitical landscape from the anything-goes irreverence of the early seventies to the hypocritical self-righteousness of the Reagan years. The film also tells a poignant love story. It sketches the rise to riches of Kentucky backwoods boy Larry Flynt (Woody Harrelson) with *Hustler* magazine. While running sleazy Cincinnati strip clubs, he takes up with one of his dancers, Althea (rock star Courtney Love), who stands by him through the years despite his insane provocations. Flynt is gunned down outside a Georgia courthouse, which paralyzes him from the waist down. He rebounds with his battle with Moral Majority leader Jerry Falwell (Richard Paul). Harrelson gives a quite agreeable lead performance. But Love is the revelation here in an impulsive, nakedly emotional, quicksilver turn.

PEOPLE WILL TALK
1951, 109 mins, US
D: Joseph L. Mankiewicz **A:** Cary Grant, Jeanne Crain, Finlay Currie, Hume Cronyn, Walter Slezak (20th Century-Fox)

Cary Grant, doctor facing charges of conduct unbecoming to his profession, finds time to become interested in medical student Jeanne Crain when she faints. He discovers she is pregnant, but when she tries to commit suicide, he proclaims the diagnosis a mistake and marries her. Climax is hung on Grant's trial by the college board, and its more serious touches are carefully leavened with a lightness that makes it more effective.

PEPE LE MOKO
1937, 90 mins, France ⓥ
D: Julien Duvivier **A:** Jean Gabin, Mireille Balin, Line Noro, Lucas Gridoux, Charpin (Paris)

Fugitive from the law takes refuge in Casablanca's native quarter to head a huge theft ring, only to kill himself because he cannot leave with the white woman with whom he is in love. Role is Jean Gabin's meat, and he masticates it well. Support, headed by Mireille Balin and Line Noro, is of high standard, while the simple story is directed with dexterity, to make the whole a commendable finished product, but the scissors could have been used a bit more severely.

PEREZ FAMILY, THE
1995, 112 mins, US ⓥ ⊙
D: Mira Nair **A:** Marisa Tomei, Alfred Molina, Anjelica Huston, Chazz Palminteri, Trini Alvarado (Samuel Goldwyn)

An enormously likable ensemble struggles hard to give the proper color, texture, and mood to Mira Nair's seriocomic exploration of Cuban immigrants in Miami. Juan Raul Perez (Alfred Molina) has patiently endured hard prison life by dreaming about a reunion with his wife, Carmela (Anjelica Huston), who's had to raise their daughter, Teresa (Trini Alvarado), alone in Miami. Finally on board a boat to the promised land, Juan meets Dottie Perez (Marisa Tomei), a spunky prostitute. The immigration authorities erroneously list Juan and Dottie, who have the same surname, as a married couple. An indefatigable survivor, Dottie takes advantage of Juan's frustration, realizing that if they want to stay in America they'll have to become a family.

PERFECT
1985, 120 mins, US ⓥ ⊙ ☐
D: James Bridges **A:** John Travolta, Jamie Lee Curtis, Anne De Salvo, Marilu Henner, Laraine Newman (Columbia/Delphi III)

Perfect pretends to be an old-fashioned love story dressed up in leotards, but more than anything else, it's a film about physical attraction. Set in the world of journalism, pic is guilty of the sins it condemns—superficiality, manipulation, and smugness. Jamie Lee Curtis is an aerobics instructor who was burned by a reporter and must be thawed out before she can enter into a relationship with star Travolta. John Travolta is the heat, but before she can accept him, he must prove himself a decent fellow, something the film never really succeeds in doing.

PERFECT COUPLE, A
1979, 110 mins, US ☐
D: Robert Altman **A:** Paul Dooley, Marta Heflin, Titos Vandis, Belita Moreno, Henry Gibson (20th Century-Fox/Lion's Gate)

Immensely likable in some parts, and a complete turn-off in others. Alex Theodopoulos (Paul Dooley), imprisoned in a suffocating, Old World Greek clan, and Sheila Shea (Marta Heflin), an elfin singer locked into a rock group/commune, have an on-again, off-again relationship complicated by both families.

PERFECT FRIDAY
1970, 94 mins, UK ⓥ
D: Peter Hall **A:** Ursula Andress, David Warner, Stanley Baker, Patience Collier, T. P. McKenna (Sunnymede)

Ursula Andress, Stanley Baker, and David Warner form a triangle of totally amoral thieves in a charming, ingenious, and sexy bank job, tightly masterminded to the split second by director Peter Hall. The gorgeously undressed Andress spends a great deal of the footage at maximum exposure, but also demonstrates a flair for low-key comedy. Warner is superb as the foppish young lord.

PERFECT MURDER, A
1998, 105 mins, US ⓥ ⊙
D: Andrew Davis **A:** Michael Douglas, Gwyneth Paltrow, Viggo Mortensen, David Suchet, Sarita Choudhury, Constance Towers (Kopelson/Warner)

A Perfect Murder, based on the play

and subsequent Hitchcock film *Dial M for Murder*, freely adapts a lesser work by the master and only proves that even that minor bygone film is superior to a high gloss, misconceived modernization. Emily (Gwyneth Paltrow), married to commodities trader Stephen Taylor (Michael Douglas) is entangled with bohemian painter David Shaw (Viggo Mortensen). Stephen confronts David with a dossier that includes jail time and a series of past scams. He'll forgive and forget if David will murder Emily. Pic, however, fails to create a rooting interest for a character or situation. Once David agrees to the conspiracy, he's lost our sympathy. Stephen lacks even the passion of jealousy, driven solely by the allure of Emily's gelt. Emily's vulnerability wears thin as she habitually fails to grasp the obvious. What's chiefly out of kilter is the pic's leaden seriousness.

PERFECT STRANGERS
1945, 100 mins, US
D: Alexander Korda **A:** Robert Donat, Deborah Kerr, Glynis Johns, Ann Todd, Roland Culver (London)

A young worker and his suburban wife find themselves respectively in the Royal Navy and the Wrens with the war's outbreak. Both benefit physically and mentally from the change. Donat shaves his moustache: Deborah Kerr puts on lipstick. Neither expects to like the other when they meet again, but they do. It's the type of yarn that offers many possibilities of drama and situation, but all have been missed.

PERFECT STRANGERS
1950, 87 mins, US ⓥ
D: Bretaigne Windust **A:** Ginger Rogers, Dennis Morgan, Thelma Ritter, Margalo Gillmore (Warner)

The stars are spotted as jurors in a murder trial. Dennis Morgan is a married man with two children, Ginger Rogers a divorcée. They fall in love. Margalo Gillmore, whose husband has deserted her, holds out for the death sentence because the accused had asked his wife for a divorce before she was pushed, or fell, from a cliff. Suspense mounts neatly, hand in glove with the love story, to a gripping climax.

PERFECT WORLD, A
1993, 137 mins, US ⓥ ⊙ ▭
D: Clint Eastwood **A:** Kevin Costner, Clint Eastwood, Laura Dern, T. J. Lowther, Keith Szarabajka (Warner/Malpaso)

A somber, subtly nuanced study of an escaped con's complex relationship with an abducted boy carries a bit too much narrative flab for its own good. Story centers on Butch Haynes (Costner), a lifelong loser toughened up by many years in the pen. Butch and his nasty partner, Terry (Keith Szarabajka), break out of the joint, commandeer a car, and make off with seven-year-old Phillip Perry (T. J. Lowther) as a hostage. Quickly taking up the chase is Texas Ranger Red Garnett (Eastwood), a seasoned, instinctive pro who gets saddled with an unwanted contingent of manhunters, including Laura Dern's state criminologist and Bradley Whitford's odious sharpshooter.

PERFORMANCE
1971, 102 mins, UK ⓥ ⊙
D: Donald Cammell, Nicolas Roeg **A:** James Fox, Mick Jagger, Anita Pallenberg, Michele Breton, Ann Sidney (Goodtimes/Warner)

Crime meller laced with needless, boring sadism and dull, turn-off sex angles. Fox is a hood who finally gets the heat put on him; he hides in a house owned by Jagger, entrenched in freaky atmosphere with Pallenberg and Michele Breton. Fox finally is found out, there's a phony sadness to the climax, and it all runs out after a too-long 102 minutes.

PERIL
See: Peril en la Demeure

PERIL EN LA DEMEURE
(US: PERIL; UK: DEATH IN A FRENCH GARDEN)
1985, 100 mins, France ⓥ ⊙
D: Michel Deville **A:** Christophe Malavoy, Nicole Garcia, Michel Piccoli, Anemone, Richard Bohringer (Gaumont/Elefilm/TF1)

Sleek drama of eroticism and murder intrigues by its camera virtuosity, cryptic dialogue, and shadowy characterizations. Christophe Malavoy is David, a guitar instructor hired by Julia and Graham Tombsthay (Nicole Garcia, Michel Piccoli), to give lessons to their teenage daughter. The latter (Anais Jeanneret) is seemingly attracted to Malavoy, but mother is quicker on the sexual draw and beds the young man in no time. David drifts on the erotic currents. A new element comes in the form of Daniel, a professional killer (Richard Bohringer), who saves David from a mugger and befriends him, apparently out of homosexual impulse.

PERILS OF PAULINE, THE
1947, 93 mins, US ✪
D: George Marshall **A:** Betty Hutton, John Lund, Constance Collier, William Demarest, Billy De Wolfe (Paramount)

Betty Hutton is tiptop in the title role, giving distinction to antics of early picture making and four bright tunes. It's a fun fest for the actress and she makes the most of it. Screenplay purports to show how Pearl White, early-day serial queen, got her start in silent films. Scripters carry her from a New York sweatshop to a traveling stock company and then into pictures. Romance angle is the only apparent hoke factor in script but it, too, blends·well with overall high entertainment level.
1947: Nomination: Best Song ("I Wish I Didn't Love You So")

PERIOD OF ADJUSTMENT
1962, 112 mins, US ▭
D: George Roy Hill **A:** Anthony Franciosa, Jane Fonda, Jim Hutton, Lois Nettleton, John McGiver (M-G-M)

Period of Adjustment is lowercase Tennessee Williams, but it also illustrates that lowercase Williams is superior to the upper case of most modern playwrights. Jane Fonda–Jim Hutton and Lois Nettleton–Anthony Franciosa are two teams whose emotional instability is explored. The togetherness of the first couple—newlyweds—is threatened by the insecurity of the afflicted groom. Relations of the second pair are impaired by in-law interference—coupled with the wife's accurate knowledge that she was wed for money, not love. Doesn't sound very funny, but there are spurts and flashes of good fun, both in dialogue and situation.
1962: Nomination: Best B&W Art Direction

PERMANENT RECORD
1988, 91 mins, US ✪ ●
D: Marisa Silver **A:** Alan Boyce, Keanu Reeves, Michelle Meyrink, Jennifer Rubin, Pamela Gidley (Paramount)

A look at how a bunch of high schoolers try to deal with the suicide of their class's most promising member, pic is populated by profoundly unrewarding characters doing and saying utterly uninteresting things. Shocking event forces everyone to face their own insecurity and vulnerability, but it is especially painful to Chris, David's best friend. Chris's gradual

coming to grips with his sense of self gives the film its only point of interest, largely due to Keanu Reeves's performance. All the girls are vapid dips.

PERSECUTION
1974, 92 mins, UK ✪
D: Don Chaffey **A:** Lana Turner, Ralph Bates, Trevor Howard, Olga Georges-Picot, Suzan Farmer, Patrick Allen (Tyburn)

In this British-made gothic suspenser, Lana Turner toplines as a sick-in-the-head mother who has killed her husband and goes on to blight her bastard son's life, ultimately seeing that his child and marriage are destroyed before she herself ends up an ironic corpse. It's all heavy with Freudian symbols. The old-fashioned meller is riddled with ho-hum and sometimes laughably trite scripting. Also, very tame in the shock horror department.

PERSECUTION AND ASSASSINATION OF JEAN-PAUL MARAT AS PERFORMED BY THE INMATES OF THE ASYLUM OF CHARENTON UNDER THE DIRECTION OF THE MARQUIS DE SADE, THE
(AKA: MARAT/SADE)
1967, 115 mins, UK/US ◉
D: Peter Brook **A:** Ian Richardson, Patrick Magee, Glenda Jackson, Clifford Rose, Michael Williams, Susan Williamson (Marat Sade/United Artists)

As a theatrical production, the Royal Shakespeare Company's version of Peter Weiss's play has elements to make it impressive and stunning, also horrific and repellent. As a film directed and acted by the same director and cast, the result is somewhat less powerful. Ostensibly a play within a play, written by de Sade, the story centers on the murder of the revolutionary leader Jean-Paul Marat by Charlotte Corday. The action, however, is hysterically performed by the inmates until their excitation reaches an intolerable pitch, and each segment of the action is periodically aborted by lengthy arguments between the paranoiac Marat and the egomaniacal de Sade.

PERSONA
1966, 84 mins, Sweden ✪
D: Ingmar Bergman **A:** Bibi Andersson, Liv Ullmann, Margaretha Krook, Gunnar Bjornstrand (Svensk Filmindustri)

There is no denying the absorbing theme and the perfection in direction, acting, editing, and lensing. Pic is hypnotic in its first part, as stark black-and-white imagery tells of a noted actress who has suddenly stopped dead during a performance of a Greek tragedy and has refused to talk since. She is tended by a nurse and they are finally sent off to a beach island house together under orders of a psychiatrist. Bergman has come up with probably one of his most masterful films technically and in conception, but also one of his most difficult ones.

PERSONAL BEST
1982, 122 mins, US Ⓥ

D: Robert Towne **A:** Mariel Hemingway, Scott Glenn, Patrice Donnelly, Kenny Moore, Luana Anders (Geffen/Warner)

Personal Best offers audiences a lot to like in solid characterizations, plus some shock that is a Robert Towne trademark. What they probably won't share, however, is his tedious fascination with physical perfection. At his best, Towne handily overcomes the surface distractions of a lesbian relationship between two track stars (Mariel Hemingway and Patrice Donnelly). Towne's sensitive pen creates two entirely believable characters in search of affection. Towne is equally adept at drawing the two male characters, Scott Glenn as tough, domineering coach, and Kenny Moore, an ex-Olympic jock.

PERSONAL PROPERTY
1937, 88 mins, US

D: W. S. Van Dyke **A:** Jean Harlow, Robert Taylor, Reginald Owen, Una O'Connor, Henrietta Crossman (M-G-M)

A good two-reel farce padded rather too thinly into a feature. Taylor gets himself the job of a sheriff's officer and moves into Harlow's London house as custodian of her person and her possessions. The idea is that she resents his presence. He stays around a couple of days—and nights. The picture is about what doesn't happen.

PERSONALS, THE
1982, 90 mins, US Ⓥ ⊙

D: Peter Markle **A:** Bill Schoppert, Karen Landry, Paul Elding, Michael Laskin, Vicki Dakil (New World)

A terrific little picture. Story really isn't all that profound, but it's told with sincerity and humor. Bill Schoppert is a true discovery as an average, balding, career-minded, and funny fellow whose equally nice wife feels neglected and leaves him for another man. Reluctantly tossed back into the singles world. Schoppert resorts to placing a personal ad in a newspaper.

PERSONAL SERVICES
1987, 105 mins, UK Ⓥ ⊙

D: Terry Jones **A:** Julie Walters, Alec McCowen, Shirley Stelfox, Danny Schiller, Tim Woodward (British Screen/Zenith)

Pic about sex is remarkably unerotic. It deals with society's two-faced attitude toward sex for sale in a humorous but essentially sad way, and is excellently acted and directed. Pic tells the story of the transition of Christine Painter (a dominating performance by Julie Walters) from waitress to madam of Britain's most pleasant brothel, where the perversions are served up with a cooked breakfast and a cup of tea to follow. She looks after the aged and infirm along with eminent clients, none of whom has a kink her girls can't cater to.

PETE KELLY'S BLUES
1955, 95 mins, US Ⓥ ⊙ ☆

D: Jack Webb **A:** Jack Webb, Janet Leigh, Edmond O'Brien, Peggy Lee, Andy Devine, Lee Marvin (Mark VII/Warner)

Melodramatic story catches the mood of the Prohibition era. Jack Webb enacts a cornet player in a 1927 Kansas City speakeasy. Mostly it develops as a gangster picture (without the cops) with a Dixieland accompaniment. Plot has to do with the move-in into the band field by Edmond O'Brien, small-time bootlegger-racketeer, and the abortive efforts at resistance made by Webb to protect his small outfit. Webb's understatement of his character is good and Peggy Lee scores a personal hit with her portrayal of a fading singer taken to the bottle.

1955: Nomination: Best Supp. Actress (Peggy Lee)

PETE 'N' TILLIE
1972, 100 mins, US Ⓥ ⊟

D: Martin Ritt **A:** Walter Matthau, Carol Burnett, Geraldine Page, Barry Nelson, Rene Auberjonois (Universal)

A generally beautiful, touching, and discreetly sentimental drama-with-comedy, starring Walter Matthau and Carol Burnett as two lonely near-middle-agers whose courtship, marriage, breakup, and reunion are told with compassion.

1977: Nominations: Best Supp. Actress (Geraldine Page), Adapted Screenplay

PETER IBBETSON
1935, 83 mins, US

D: Henry Hathaway **A:** Gary Cooper, Ann

Harding, John Halliday, Ida Lupino, Douglass Dumbrille, Doris Lloyd (Paramount)

Picture gains so much weight in beauty and serenity that it almost outweighs the incredibility of the story. Casting is not of the happiest. Gary Cooper was never meant to be a dreamy lovesick boy. When he tells the Duchess of Towers that she can't have things the way she wants them but the way he wants them, he's fine. When he lies dying in a stinking jail and dreams of wandering in Elysian lanes with his sweetheart—he's just not believable. Ann Harding, on the other hand, as the duchess, is splendid.

1935: Nomination: Best Score

PETER PAN
1953, 76 mins, US Ⓥ ⊙
D: Hamilton Luske, Clyde Geronimi, Wilfred Jackson (Walt Disney)

James M. Barrie's childhood fantasy is a feature cartoon of enchanting quality. The Barrie plot deals familiarly with a little boy (Peter Pan) who refused to grow up, preferring to remain a pixie in Never-Never Land, and a little girl (Wendy) under paternal orders to pass into young ladyhood. The voice of young Bobby Driscoll, and cartoon animation in his likeness, sell the Peter Pan character. Equally good are the voices of Kathryn Beaumont as Wendy; Hans Conried as the villainous Hook and the exasperated father, Mr. Darling; and Bill Thompson as the fawning Smee.

PETERSEN
1974, 103 mins, Australia Ⓥ
D: Tim Burstall **A:** Jack Thompson, Jacki Weaver, Joey Hohenfels, Amanda Hunt, George Mallaby (Hexagon)

Tony Petersen (Jack Thompson) is an ex-electrician at university in pursuit of an arts degree. Women find Petersen irresistible, and the attraction is mutual. He even actively participates in a public-sex-act protest by the University Women's Liberationists. Plotwise pic is not too strong but has several meaningful meanderings. It contains some of playwright David Williamson's best writing yet.

PETER'S FRIENDS
1992, 100 mins, UK/US Ⓥ ⊙
D: Kenneth Branagh **A:** Kenneth Branagh, Emma Thompson, Stephen Fry, Hugh Laurie, Rita Rudner, Imelda Staunton (Renaissance/Channel 4/Goldwyn)

Kenneth Branagh's third feature is a sometimes funny, often cloying entertainment. Script confines the action almost entirely to the country estate of Peter (Stephen Fry), a witty, charmingly dissolute young aristocrat who invites his college theatrical friends for a New Year's reunion. Playing an insecure egotist and fitness freak who secretly raids the fridge, cowriter Rita Rudner has given herself a lion's share of the good bits and she carries off the Joan Collins–ish role in high style. As her tag-along hubby who has deserted the UK for L.A., Branagh is slyly humorous, but a hollow character.

PETE'S DRAGON
1977, 134 mins, US Ⓥ ⊙
D: Don Chaffey **A:** Helen Reddy, Jim Dale, Mickey Rooney, Red Buttons, Shelley Winters (Walt Disney)

Enchanting and humane fable introduces a most lovable animal star (albeit an animated one). The headliner has been created with love and care by Disney animators headed by Ken Anderson and Don Blyth. Elliott, the dumpy, clumsy, 12-foot-tall mumbling dragon with the ability to go instantly invisible and the misfortune of setting the idyllic Maine town of Passamaquoddy even further back into the early 20th century, is a triumph.

1977: Nominations: Best Adapted Score, Song ("Candle on the Water")

PETRIFIED FOREST, THE
1936, 75 mins, US Ⓥ ⊙
D: Archie L. Mayo **A:** Leslie Howard, Bette Davis, Humphrey Bogart, Genevieve Tobin, Joseph Sawyer (Warner)

The picture sticks closely to the legit script by Robert E. Sherwood. Playing the roles they created in the stage version are Leslie Howard and Humphrey Bogart— the former a soul-broken, disillusioned author, seeking to find some new significance in living, and the latter a killer, harried and surrounded by pursuers, revealing in his last moments a bewildered desperation that is not far removed from that of the writer. The scenes in which the desperado holds court, as he awaits his own doom, over the group in the little Arizona gas station–barbecue stand are packed with skillfully etched drama and embroidered with appropriate touches of comedy.

PET SEMATARY
1989, 102 mins, US Ⓥ ⊙
D: Mary Lambert **A:** Dale Midkiff, Fred

Gwynne, Denise Crosby, Brad Greenquist (Paramount)

Pet Sematary marks the first time Stephen King has adapted his own book for the screen, and the result is undead schlock dulled by a slasher-film mentality—squandering its chilling and fertile source material. King appears in a cameo as a minister presiding over a funeral.

PET SEMATARY TWO
1992, 100 mins, US Ⓥ ⊙
D: Mary Lambert **A:** Edward Furlong, Anthony Edwards, Clancy Brown, Jared Rushton, Darlanne Fluegel, Lisa Waltz (Paramount)

Pet Sematary Two is about 50 percent better than its predecessor, which is to say it's not very good at all. The latest incarnation relies more on gore than genuine chills and is sorely lacking in subtlety. The story opens with the accidental death of an actress (Darlanne Fluegel) in front of her teenage son (Edward Furlong). Jeff (Furlong) befriends another boy (Jason McGuire) whose tyrannical stepfather (Clancy Brown) guns down the kid's dog. Duo take the beast to the "pet sematary," an ancient Indian burial ground rumored to revive the dead, subsequently repeating the process on the stepfather and setting up the inevitable question about tempting the forces of nature by awakening Mom.

PETTICOAT PIRATES
1961, 87 mins, UK Ⓥ
D: David Macdonald **A:** Charlie Drake, Anne Heywood, Cecil Parker, Maxine Audley, Thorley Walters (Associated British)

Film has a flimsy, screwball, but acceptable theme for a comedy-farce. Wren Officer Anne Heywood and the 150 girls under her command maintain the right to serve at sea in warships. When the plan is turned down by the authorities they raid a frigate and set off to sea. These goings-on are mainly an excuse for pocket-sized television comedian Charlie Drake to masquerade as a Wren and for the main decks of the frigate to be turned into a sun-bathing parade, with the girls stripped down to their scanties.

PETULIA
1968, 103 mins, UK Ⓥ
D: Richard Lester **A:** Julie Christie, George C. Scott, Richard Chamberlain, Arthur Hill, Shirley Knight, Pippa Scott (Petersham-Wagner)

Excellent romantic drama turns on the hectic, sometimes ecstatic affair between Christie, unhappy wife of sadistically weak Richard Chamberlain, and Scott, just divorced from Shirley Knight and currently squiring Pippa Scott. Scott's performance, in the face of a plot and film structure that could have relegated him to a reactive posture, is excellent. The natural emphasis is on Christie, who turns in a vital, versatile performance.

PEYTON PLACE
1957, 166 mins, US Ⓥ ⊗
D: Mark Robson **A:** Lana Turner, Hope Lange, Lee Philips, Lloyd Nolan, Arthur Kennedy, Russ Tamblyn (20th Century-Fox)

Every one of the performers delivers a top-notch portrayal. Performance of Diane Varsi particularly is a standout as the rebellious teenager Allison, eager to learn about life and numbed by the discovery that she is an illegitimate child. Also in top form in a difficult role is Hope Lange, stepdaughter of the school's drunken caretaker. As Varsi's mother, Lana Turner looks elegant and registers strongly.
1957: Nominations: Best Picture, Director, Actress (Lana Turner), Supp. Actor (Arthur Kennedy, Russ Tamblyn), Supp. Actress (Hope Lange, Diana Varsi), Adapted Screenplay, Cinematography

PHANTASM
1979, 90 mins, US Ⓥ ⊙
D: Don Coscarelli **A:** Michael Baldwin, Bill Thornbury, Reggie Bannister, Kathy Lester (Avco Embassy)

Thirteen-year-old Mike Pearson (Michael Baldwin) disobeys his older brother's orders not to attend a funeral. Mike hides in the bushes and happens to eye the villainous tall man (Angus Scrimm) loading the casket into a car. Once inside the mausoleum, the fun begins, with Mike treated to a quite grisly murder courtesy of a futuristic flying silver sphere and the wrath of the tall man, who doesn't cotton to the kid's curiosity. Strong point of the feature is that it's played for both horror and laughs.

PHANTASM II
1988, 90 mins, US Ⓥ ⊙
D: Don Coscarelli **A:** James Le Gros, Reggie Bannister, Angus Scrimm, Paula Irvine, Samantha Phillips (Universal)

Utterly unredeeming, full-gore sequel to the original nine years earlier. The special-effects horrors run amok here, with slimy, hissing apparitions constantly erupting from the bodies of the afflicted. Story involves the morbid obsessions of two psychically connected teens, Mike (James Le Gros) and Liz (Paula Irvine). The pair are tortured in their dreams by the Tall Man (Angus Scrimm), who wreaks evil via flying spheres that carve up people's faces.

PHANTOM, THE
1996, 100 mins, US Ⓥ ⊙ ⌑
D: Simon Wincer **A:** Billy Zane, Kirsty Swanson, Treat Williams, Catherine Zeta Jones, James Remar (Village Roadshow)

While it hardly stands to vanquish the celluloid incarnations of Superman and Batman, this version of an older cartoon crusader's exploits does have a pleasingly astute sense of its place in the great scheme of things pulp. Pic brings a light touch to appealingly old-fashioned action material. Story opens with four fedora-wearing thugs braving the jungle to steal a mysterious metal skull. The Phantom (Billy Zane) swoops in to thwart the heist. Master criminal Xander Drax (Treat Williams) has been trying to acquire the legendary Skulls of Touganda, which supposedly have magical powers when united. Like much of the surrounding film, Zane's masked hero is unapologetically two-dimensional, and he's nicely matched by Swanson's Girl Scout of a heroine. The baddies come across more vividly. The standouts here are Remar Jones and, especially, Williams.

PHANTOM LADY
1944, 83 mins, US
D: Robert Siodmak **A:** Franchot Tone, Ella Raines, Alan Curtis, Elisha Cook Jr. (Universal)

Expertly contrived, suspenseful mystery meller rolls through a maze of episodes to allow a femme amateur detective to unravel a strange murder. Plot has Alan Curtis picking up a strange woman in a bar. During the evening his wife is murdered, and he is convicted on circumstantial evidence when he cannot find or identify his woman companion of the night. While Curtis is facing execution, secretary Ella Raines embarks on sleuthing tour to find the woman.

PHANTOM OF THE OPERA, THE
1925, 101 mins, US Ⓥ ⊙ ⊗
D: Rupert Julian **A:** Lon Chaney, Mary Philbin, Norman Kerry, Arthur Edmund Carewe, Gibson Gowland, John Sainpolis (Universal)

It's not a bad film from a technical viewpoint, revolving around the terrifying of all inmates of the Grand Opera House in Paris by a criminally insane mind (Lon Chaney) behind a hideous face. The understudy (Mary Philbin) whom the Phantom cherishes is twice abducted by the Phantom to his cellar retreat, and the finish is built up by the pulling of levers, concealed buttons, etc. to make active secret doors, heat chambers, flooding passages, and other appropriate devices. However, the kick of the picture is in the unmasking of the Phantom by the girl. It's a wallop.

PHANTOM OF THE OPERA
1943, 92 mins, US Ⓥ ⊙
D: Arthur Lubin **A:** Claude Rains, Nelson Eddy, Susanna Foster, Jane Farrar, Hume Cronyn, J. Edward Bromberg (Universal)

Far more of a musical than a chiller, story is about the mad musician who haunts the opera house and kills off all those who are in his protegée's way toward becoming the headliner. Nelson Eddy, Susanna Foster, and Jane Farrar (niece of operatic star Geraldine Farrar) score individually in singing roles. Outstanding performance is turned in by Claude Rains as the musician who grows into a homicidal maniac.
1943: Best Color Cinematography, Color Art Direction
Nominations: Best Scoring of a Musical Picture, Sound

PHANTOM OF THE OPERA, THE
1962, 84 mins, UK Ⓥ ⊙
D: Terence Fisher **A:** Herbert Lom, Heather Sears, Thorley Walters, Michael Gough, Edward De Souza (Hammer)

Herbert Lom somewhat precariously follows in the macabre footsteps of Lon Chaney and Claude Rains. Switched to a London Opera House background, lushed up in color, with a new character, a dwarf rather confusingly brought in to supplement the sinister activities of the Phantom, it still provides a fair measure of goose pimples to combat some potential unwanted yocks.

PHANTOM OF THE OPERA, THE
1989, 90 mins, US Ⓥ ⊙
D: Dwight H. Little **A:** Robert Englund, Jill Schoelen, Alex Hyde-White, Bill Nighy, Stephanie Lawrence (21st Century)

Opening in contemporary New York, this *Phantom* starts with its heroine being hit on the head by a sandbag and mentally transported back to the mid-19th century for the bulk of the plot. Set in London, rather than the Paris of Phantom tradition, this rendition seems faithful in broad outline to the original, save for the fact that its tragic antihero is a Jack the Ripper–style maniac. Running about encased in makeup that makes him appear a kind of Jack Palance gone to seed, Robert England is his usual broad self.

PHANTOM OF THE PARADISE
1974, 91 mins, US ⓥ ⊙
D: Brian De Palma **A:** Paul Williams, William Finley, Jessica Harper, Gerrit Graham (Pressman-Williams/20th Century-Fox)

A very good horror comedy-drama about a disfigured musician haunting a rock palace. The story takes novice songwriter William Finley through the despair of being ripped off by Paul Williams (excellent as a composite rock entrepreneur mogul), framed into prison, disfigured by an accident, and nearly betrayed anew by Williams. Part of Phantom Finley's motivation is his distant love of Jessica Harper, whom he wants to sing his music in Williams's rock cantata production.
1974: Nomination: Best Adapted Score

PHANTOM OF THE RUE MORGUE
1954, 83 mins, US
D: Roy Del Ruth **A:** Karl Malden, Claude Dauphin, Patricia Medina, Steve Forrest, Allyn McLerie, Veola Vonn (Warner)

The horror in *Phantom of the Rue Morgue* is more to be taken lightly than seriously. Malden is the mad scientist who has his trained ape destroy all pretty girls who spurn him. After Allyn McLerie, Veola Vonn, and Dolores Dorn have died violent deaths, the rather stupid police inspector played by Dauphin figures Forrest, young professor of psychology, is the guilty party. The 3-D color lensing by J. Peverell Marley puts the turn-of-the-century Paris scenes on display to full advantage.

PHANTOM PRESIDENT, THE
1932, 78 mins, US
D: Norman Taurog **A:** George M. Cohan, Claudette Colbert, Jimmy Durante, George Barbier, Sidney Toler (Paramount)

Political satire holding a full share of laughs has Cohan playing a dual role. As T. K. Blair he's the colorless banker whom his party would make president but fears it can't because of his lack of personality. In playing Peter Varney, the medicine-show man, Cohan is unquestionably happier with circumstances bringing

about his substituting for Blair during the pre-election campaign. Meanwhile there's Durante as Varney's helper who by the simple expedient of adapting his medicine show technique to the occasion stampedes his pal into the nomination. It's the high action mark of the film, done in rhythm and lyrics with the assembled delegates acting as the chorus.

PHAR LAP
1983, 118 mins, Australia ⓥ ▭
D: Simon Wincer **A:** Tom Burlinson, Martin Vaughan, Judy Morris, Ron Leibman, Celia de Burgh (Edgley)

Phar Lap was a champion Australian racehorse, a legend in his own lifetime, who met a mysterious death in California in 1932. Tom Burlinson is very effective as the shy stable boy. Martin Vaughan is impressive as the grimly determined trainer, as is Celia de Burgh, luminous as his loyal but neglected wife. Ron Leibman practically walks away with the picture as Davis, the smooth American horse owner.

PHASE IV
1974, 93 mins, US ⓥ ⊙
D: Saul Bass **A:** Nigel Davenport, Michael Murphy, Lynne Frederick, Alan Gifford, Robert Henderson (Alced)

This one's another in the Hollywood cycle of films based on every kind of creature enlarged by radiation. In *Phase IV*, the ants are it. A couple of scientists (Nigel Davenport and Michael Murphy) set up an elaborate outpost in the desert to find out what the ants are up to and why. Joining them as an ant attack refugee, Lynne Frederick only adds to the confusion. Cinematically, the ants are never very menacing.

PHENIX CITY STORY, THE
1955, 87 mins, US
D: Phil Karlson **A:** John McIntire, Richard Kiley, Kathryn Grant, Edward Andrews, Biff McGuire (Allied Artists/Bischoff)

Vice, southern style, gets the exposé treatment. There's quite a bit of violence. The downfall of Phenix City sin is woven around the return of Richard Kiley with wife and two children to find his hometown still living up to its wicked reputation. Kiley plays John Patterson, the son of the murdered candidate, who was elected to the attorney general post by an aroused citizenry after the death of the father, ably depicted by John McIntire. Edward Andrews plays Rhett Tanner, a menacing, entirely believable crime czar.

Picture was lensed almost entirely in the actual locale.

PHENOMENON
1996, 124 mins, US Ⓥ ⊙ ▭
D: Jon Turteltaub A: John Travolta, Kyra Sedgwick, Forest Whitaker, Jeffrey DeMunn, Robert Duvall, Richard Kiley (Touchstone)

The notion that human beings use something like just 10 percent of their brain capacity provides the springboard for a movie that lives up to a similar fraction of its potential. The premise, of a simple man who suddenly finds himself endowed with exceptional mental powers, generates some undeniable interest, with John Travolta's sympathetic performance as an everyman transformed into a latter-day Einstein. Sedgwick is classy as the wary object of his affections, and Whitaker and (as a local doctor) Robert Duvall warmly fill out the emotional aspects of their decent, friendly characters.

PHFFFT
1954, 91 mins, US Ⓥ
D: Mark Robson A: Judy Holliday, Jack Lemmon, Jack Carson, Kim Novak, Luella Gear (Columbia)

Phffft is a lightweight farce running from bed to verse. Judy Holliday and Jack Lemmon are the married couple whose bickering leads to the great divide of Reno. Each seeks to put the newly found freedom to exciting use. Kim Novak gets across a zesty show as an accessible blond out to cure Lemmon of the postconnubial blues. Jack Carson, as a bachelor wont to boast of his success in freewheeling romance, registers colorfully.

PHILADELPHIA
1993, 122 mins, US Ⓥ ⊙
D: Jonathan Demme A: Tom Hanks, Denzel Washington, Jason Robards, Mary Steenburgen, Antonio Banderas (Tri-Star/Clinica Estetico)

This extremely well-made message picture about tolerance, justice, and discrimination is pitched at mainstream audiences, befitting its position as the first major Hollywood film to directly tackle the disease of AIDS. Intelligent but too neatly worked out in its political and melodramatic details, pic is fronted by a dynamite lead performance from Tom Hanks. Hanks stars as Andrew Beckett, a rising young attorney at a powerful Philadelphia law firm. But as soon as he displays the first visible signs of AIDS, he's fired by the firm over a bit of alleged incompetence, but Andrew knows he was dismissed because of his illness. Determined to spend the rest of his life, if necessary, fighting this gross injustice, Andrew, in desperation, is finally able to recruit Joe Miller (Denzel Washington), a somewhat flashy lawyer, as his attorney. Hanks makes it all hang together in a performance that constantly connects on the most basic human level.

1993: Best Actor (Tom Hanks), Original Song ("Streets of Philadelphia")
Nominations: Best Original Screenplay, Makeup, Song ("Philadelphia")

PHILADELPHIA EXPERIMENT, THE
1984, 102 mins, US Ⓥ
D: Stewart Raffill A: Michael Pare, Nancy Allen, Eric Christmas, Bobby Di Cicco, Louise Latham (New World/Cinema Group)

An adequate sci-fi yarn. In 1943, Michael Pare and Bobby Di Cicco are sailors at the center of a secret radar experiment that goes awry, throwing them into 1984. Befriended in the future by Nancy Allen, the pair obviously are a bit bemused at their surroundings before Di Cicco fades again into the past, leaving Pare to develop a romance with Allen.

PHILADELPHIA STORY, THE
1940, 112 mins, US Ⓥ ⊙
D: George Cukor A: Cary Grant, Katharine Hepburn, James Stewart, Ruth Hussey, John Howard, Roland Young (M-G-M)

It's Katharine Hepburn's picture, but pushing hard is little Virginia Weidler, the kid sister, who has as twinkly an eye and a quip as fast as a blinker light. Ruth Hussey is another from whom director George Cukor has milked maximum results. As for Cary Grant, James Stewart, and Roland Young, there's little to be said that their reputation hasn't established. Hepburn, divorced from Grant, a bit of rather useless uppercrust like herself, is about to marry a stuffed-bosom man of the people (Howard). Grant, to keep publisher Henry Daniell from running a scandalous piece about Hepburn's father (John Halliday), agrees to get a reporter and photog into the Hepburn household preceding and during the wedding. Stewart and Hussey are assigned, and Grant, whose position as ex-husband is rather unique in the mansion, manages to get them in under a pretext.

1940: Best Actor (James Stewart), Screenplay
Nominations: Best Picture, Director, Ac-

tress (Katharine Hepburn), Supp. Actress (Ruth Hussey)

PHONE CALL FROM A STRANGER
1952, 96 mins, US ⓥ
D: Jean Negulesco **A:** Shelley Winters, Gary Merrill, Michael Rennie, Keenan Wynn, Bette Davis (20th Century-Fox)

A solidly based dramatic story idea has been brought off with a reasonable amount of success. Plot concerns the survivor of an airplane crash who decides to call on the families of three people with whom he had become friends during the air trip that led up to the tragedy.

PHYSICAL EVIDENCE
1989, 99 mins, US ⓥ ⊙
D: Michael Crichton **A:** Burt Reynolds, Theresa Russell, Ned Beatty, Kay Lenz, Ted McGinley (Columbia)

Burt Reynolds plays the lead suspect in a murder investigation. His case is given to an assertive debutante (Theresa Russell) working in the public defender's office, whose obsession with the case begins to wreak havoc on her relationship with her fiancé stockbroker (Ted McGinley). The film is so choppily assembled none of the various clues and innumerable suspects ever seem to lead anywhere.

PIANO, THE
1993, 120 mins, Australia/France ⓥ ⊙
D: Jane Campion **A:** Holly Hunter, Harvey Keitel, Sam Neill, Ana Paquin, Kerry Walker (Chapman/Ciby 2000)

Jane Campion's fourth feature is a visually sumptuous and tactile tale of adultery set during the early European colonization of New Zealand, with Harvey Keitel daringly cast in the role of a passionately romantic lover, and Holly Hunter a knockout as a woman physically unable to articulate her feelings. Ada McGrath (Hunter) can hear, and can communicate in sign language through her young daughter, Fiona (Ana Paquin), but she can't talk. Apart from her child, Ada's most treasured possession is her piano.
1993: Best Actress (Holly Hunter), Supp. Actress (Anna Paquin), Original Screenplay
Nominations: Best Picture, Director, Cinematography, Costume Design, Film Editing

PICCADILLY
1929, 92 mins, UK
D: E. A. Dupont **A:** Gilda Gray, Jameson Thomas, Anna May Wong, King Ho Chang, Cyril Ritchard, Charles Laughton (British International)

This Arnold Bennett story is set in a cabaret in Piccadilly. The owner of the class joint digs up a dancer from the scullery. It's Anna May Wong. In the cabaret are a couple of ballroom dancers, with Gilda Gray one of them. Business commences to fade and the proprietor remembers the girl downstairs, calls her up and dresses her up, then falls for her. The audience apparently sees Gray shoot Wong.

PICKLE, THE
1993, 103 mins, US ⓥ
D: Paul Mazursky **A:** Danny Aiello, Dyan Cannon, Clotilde Courau, Shelley Winters, Barry Miller (Columbia)

The Pickle is a vegetarian turkey. Self-indulgent story about a depressed, dispirited, middle-aged film director aims for comedy and poignance that never come, and feels wearily disenchanted and out of touch. Harry Stone (Danny Aiello) has made a string of flops and is suffering convulsions of remorse over having sold out for the first time in his career.

PICK-UP ARTIST, THE
1987, 81 mins, US ⓥ ⊙
D: James Toback **A:** Molly Ringwald, Robert Downey Jr., Dennis Hopper, Danny Aiello, Mildred Dunnock, Harvey Keitel (20th Century-Fox)

As long as this film sticks to what its title suggests, *The Pick-Up Artist* is a tolerably amusing comedy. But as soon as the compulsive skirt-chaser gets hooked on one girl, James Toback's portrait of a one-track mind becomes bogged down in unconvincing plot mechanics. Opening reels possess considerable buoyancy and zip, as make-out king Robert Downey Jr. cruises the streets of New York trying out his shtick on every pretty woman who crosses his path. Downey hits on Ringwald and quickly scores in his convertible, but predictably becomes intrigued by her apparent lack of interest in seeing him again.

PICKUP ON SOUTH STREET
1953, 80 mins, US ⓥ
D: Samuel Fuller **A:** Richard Widmark, Jean Peters, Thelma Ritter, Murvyn Vye, Richard Kiley, Willis Bouchey (20th Century-Fox)

If *Pickup on South Street* makes any point at all, it's that there is nothing really wrong with pickpockets, as long as they don't play footsie with Communist spies.

Since this is at best a thin theme, *Pickup* for the most part falls flat on its face and borders on presumably unintended comedy. Story has Richard Widmark picking Jean Peters's purse in the subway. In the wallet he lifts are films of a secret chemical formula obtained by a Commie spy ring. Widmark's act is observed by two federal agents who are shadowing Peters. Latter is instructed to trace Widmark and get back the film.

1953: Nomination: Best Supp. Actress (Thelma Ritter)

PICKWICK PAPERS, THE
1952, 109 mins, UK ⓥ

D: Noel Langley **A:** James Hayter, James Donald, Nigel Patrick, Kathleen Harrison, Joyce Grenfell, Donald Wolfit (Langley-Minter/Renown)

The adventures of Mr. Pickwick (James Hayter) and his henchmen have been deftly adapted for the screen. The picture follows the members of the Pickwick Club on their encounter with Mr. Jingle (Nigel Patrick), the unscrupulous ne'er-do-well; the famous literary fancy-dress breakfast; the engagement of Sam Weller (Harry Fowler); the breach-of-promise suit brought against Mr. Pickwick. In manner and appearance Hayter gives the impression of being the genuine article.

PICNIC
1955, 115 mins, US ⓥ ⊙ ▭

D: Joshua Logan **A:** William Holden, Rosalind Russell, Kim Novak, Betty Field, Susan Strasberg, Cliff Robertson (Columbia)

The story of a robust and shiftless show-off who, looking up an old college chum in a small town in Kansas, sets off various emotional responses among the small group of local inhabitants he encounters. William Holden is the drifter, giving a forceful interpretation all the way. Kim Novak is the town's No. 1 looker, and an emotional blank until Holden proves an awakening force. Rosalind Russell, spinster schoolteacher, is a standout.

1955: Best Color Art Direction, Editing.
Nominations: Best Picture, Director, Supp. Actor (Arthur O'Connell), Scoring of a Dramatic Picture

PICNIC AT HANGING ROCK
1975, 115 mins, Australia ⓥ ⊙

D: Peter Weir **A:** Rachel Roberts, Dominic Guard, Vivian Gray, Helen Morse, Kirsty Child (SAFC)

In 1900 some schoolgirls picnic at Hanging Rock. Four girls venture forth on their own; one, Edith, falls asleep and wakes to find the other three are climbing higher. The police are called to make an unsuccessful search. Visually it probably is one of the most beautiful pix ever seen, with Aussie flora and fauna and wonderful blue skies.

PICTURE OF DORIAN GRAY, THE
1945, 107 mins, US ⓥ ⊙

D: Albert Lewin **A:** George Sanders, Hurd Hatfield, Donna Reed, Angela Lansbury, Peter Lawford (M-G-M)

The morbid theme of the Oscar Wilde story is built around Gray: his contempt for the painting that was made of him, the fears of not retaining youth and, of course, the unregenerate depths to which Gray sinks. Hurd Hatfield plays pretty-boy Gray with little feeling, as apparently intended. As a cheap music hall vocalist, Angela Lansbury registers strongly and very sympathetically.

1945: Best B&W Cinematography
Nominations: Best Supp. Actress (Angela Lansbury), B&W Art Direction

PICTURE SHOW MAN, THE
1977, 99 mins, Australia

D: John Power **A:** Rod Taylor, John Meillon, John Ewart, Harold Hopkins, Patrick Cargill (Limelight)

The story of an itinerant purveyor of motion picture entertainment in the country areas of Australia in the 1920s, it's cute without being cloying, and episodic without being disjointed. Rod Taylor's portrayal of the heavy is definitely light-weight.

PICTURE SNATCHER
1933, 70 mins, US

D: Lloyd Bacon **A:** James Cagney, Ralph Bellamy, Patricia Ellis, Alice White, Ralf Harolde (Warner)

James Cagney is a reformed hoodlum just out of stir. His yen to work on a newspaper finds him getting impossible pictures for a scurilous tab. Among the highlights are lensing a Sing-Sing execution via an ankle-strapped miniature camera. Dominating it all is Cagney. He takes full advantage of the fly, crisp lines and situations, and a couple of the situation are not Sunday school. It's all sex stuff. A moll and a double-dealing sob sister are the femme pursuers, while Cagney is chasing the honest cop's daughter. It's a punchy, meaty yarn, properly peppered with topical highlights that never permit things to sag.

PIED PIPER, THE
1972, 90 mins, UK ⓥ
D: Jacques Demy **A:** Jack Wild, Donald Pleasence, John Hurt, Donovan, Michael Hordern, Roy Kinnear (Sagittarius/Goodtimes)

In recreating the story of the minstrel who leads the rats out of Hamelin, but then leads its children away when the politicians fail to keep a promise, the writers started with one of folklore's greatest presold subjects. However, the script seems more a series of broad, arch, low-comedy vignettes without a clear emphasis.

PIERROT LE FOU
(US: CRAZY PETE)
1965, 110 mins, France/Italy ⓥ ⊙ ▭
D: Jean-Luc Godard **A:** Jean-Paul Belmondo, Anna Karina, Dirk Sanders, Raymond Devos, Graziella Galvani (Rome Paris/SNCC)

A bored young man (Jean-Paul Belmondo) married to a rich woman goes off with the baby-sitter (Anna Karina) after a boring party. A dead man is found in her flat and they are soon on the run. After an idyllic time at the seashore, they get bored and hit the road and live by stealing. There is brilliant use of color in spots to mark the mood. There are also some seemingly spontaneous scenes of the two living off the land that are topflight Godard. But there is too much padding, and interspersed songs and fabricated scenes make up a compendium of all his stylistic tricks rather than a more coherent offbeater.

PIGEON THAT TOOK ROME, THE
1962, 101 mins, US ▭
D: Melville Shavelson **A:** Charlton Heston, Elsa Martinelli, Harry Guardino, Salvatore Baccaloni, Brian Donlevy (Paramount)

This is a good-fun comedy and there's no incongruity in the fact that the setting is authentic-looking World War II Italy. Charlton Heston's an American infantry officer assigned to a cloak-and-dagger role in Rome before the Nazis decide to leave and the Yanks walk in. It comes to be that homing pigeons represent his contact with the Allies.
1962: Nomination: Best B&W Art Direction

PILGRIMAGE
1933, 90 mins, US
D: John Ford **A:** Henrietta Crosman,

Heather Angel, Norman Foster, Marian Nixon, Lucille La Verne (Fox)

Story deals with the selfishness of mother love, but works out a new twist. Opening passages deal with the mother and her fatherless boy working an Arkansas farm. She's determined to hold her son to the farm and when the boy determines to marry the girl of his choice, she gives him up to the World War I draft board. When he's killed in action and the girl has a child, the old woman remains as unyielding and grim in her grief. Henrietta Crosman plays the mother under wraps, leaving the impression of a reserve of power and vitality.

PILLOW BOOK, THE
1996, 123 mins, UK/Netherlands/France
D: Peter Greenaway **A:** Vivian Wu, Ewan McGregor, Yghi Oida, Ken Ogata, Hideko Yoshida (Woodline/Kasander & Wigman/Alpha)

Iconoclastic British helmer Peter Greenaway's fascination with the most arcane reaches of the world's art and literature is on full display in the dense yet enormously impressive *The Pillow Book*, uniquely bold and arresting depiction of exotic erotica, with inventive visual design and slow but inexorably logical plot development. Pic revolves around the erotic adventures of a young Japanese woman, Nagiko (played as an adult by Vivian Wu). Nagiko's birthdays are celebrated in a highly ritualized manner as her father (Ken Ogata), an impoverished writer and expert calligrapher, writes a sensuous birthday greeting on her face with brush and ink.

PILLOW TALK
1959, 105 mins, US ⓥ ▭
D: Michael Gordon **A:** Rock Hudson, Doris Day, Tony Randall, Thelma Ritter, Nick Adams (Arwin/Universal)

Sleekly sophisticated production deals chiefly with s-e-x. The principals seem to spend considerable time in bed or talking about what goes on in bed, but the beds they occupy are always occupied singly. There's more talk than action, natch. The plot (slight) is based on the notion that a telephone shortage puts Doris Day and Rock Hudson on a party line. Hudson is here a sophisticated man about town. Day displays a brace of smart Jean Louis gowns, and delivers crisply.
1959: Best Story & Screenplay
Nominations: Best Actress (Doris Day),

Supp. Actress (Thelma Ritter), Color Art Direction, Scoring of a Dramatic Picture

PINK FLAMINGOS
1974, 95 mins, US ⓥ
D: John Waters **A:** Divine, David Lochary, Mink Stole, Mary Vivian Pearce, Edith Massey (Dreamland)

Divine is a 300-pound drag queen of grotesque proportions who holds the title "the filthiest person in the world." Vying for the title are Connie and Raymond Marble, who kidnap girls, impregnate them, and sell the children to lesbian couples in order to finance "an inner-city heroin ring" catering to high school students. One of the most vile, stupid, and repulsive films ever made.

PINK FLOYD THE WALL
1982, 99 mins, UK ⓥ ▭
D: Alan Parker **A:** Bob Geldof, Christine Hargreaves, James Laurenson, Bob Hoskins (M-G-M/United Artists/Tin Blue)

This $12 million production is not a concert film but an eye-popping dramatization of an audio story line. Being a visual translation of a so-called "concept" album, pic works extremely well in carrying over the somber tone of the LP. The music is the core of the film, vocals subbing for the usual film dialogue. But there's little need for dialogue, since the visual treats offered by animation director Gerald Scarfe and photography director Peter Biziou tell the story. Powerful performance of Boomtown Rats lead singer Bob Geldof works to the pic's overall believability, despite its fantasy aura.

PINK PANTHER, THE
1964, 115 mins, US ⓥ ▭ ⊙
D: Blake Edwards **A:** David Niven, Peter Sellers, Robert Wagner, Capucine, Claudia Cardinale, Brenda de Banzie (Mirisch/GE)

Intensely funny. The yocks are almost entirely the responsibility of Peter Sellers as a clumsy cop who can hardly move a foot without smashing a vase, or open a door without hitting himself on the head. The Panther is a priceless jewel owned by the Indian princess Dala (Claudia Cardinale), vacationing in the Swiss ski resort of Cortina. The other principals are introduced in their various habitats, before they converge on the princess and her jewel.
1964: Nomination: Best Original Music Score

PINK PANTHER STRIKES AGAIN, THE
1976, 103 mins, UK ⓥ ⊙ ▭
D: Blake Edwards **A:** Peter Sellers, Herbert Lom, Colin Blakely, Leonard Rossiter, Lesley-Anne Down, Burt Kwouk (United Artists)

Hilarious film about the further misadventures of Peter Sellers as Inspector Clouseau. Herbert Lom, Clouseau's nemesis in the police bureau, has had his character expanded into a Professor Moriarty–type fiend, which works just fine. This time around, Lom is introduced nearly cured of his nervous collapse. But Sellers has assumed Lom's old chief inspector job, and when Lom escapes, Sellers is assigned to the case.
1976: Nomination: Best Song ("Come to Me")

PINK STRING AND SEALING WAX
1945, 93 mins, UK
D: Robert Hamer **A:** Mervyn Johns, Mary Merrall, Gordon Jackson, Sally Ann Howes, Googie Withers, Catherine Lacey (Ealing)

Bringing the England of the Victorian period to life is the best thing *Pink String and Sealing Wax* accomplishes. The black, high-necked, rustling Sunday-best bombazines that the churchgoing women wear contrast violently with the billowing cleavages of the bad women. The unrelenting tyranny of the lord and master of the respectable family is offset by the free-and-easy beatings-up the naughty gals receive at the hands of Cagney-ish husbands and sweethearts. In giving this side of English life, the picture is tops.

PINKY
1949, 102 mins, US ⓥ
D: Elia Kazan **A:** Jeanne Crain, Ethel Barrymore, Ethel Waters, William Lundigan (20th Century-Fox)

Pinky is the tag hung by Negroes on a member of their own race who is light skinned enough to pass for white. Jeanne Crain had passed herself off as ofay while studying in Boston. When she returns to her grandmother (Ethel Waters) in the south, the scripters have her quickly reveal herself as Negro. That's what leads to the complications, romantic and dramatic. Crain brings proper dignity and sincerity to her role, although she's not always convincing.
1949: Nominations: Best Actress (Jeanne Crain), Supp. Actress (Ethel Barrymore, Ethel Waters)

PINOCCHIO

1940, 87 mins, US Ⓥ ⊙

D: Ben Sharpsteen, Hamilton Luske (Walt Disney/RKO)

A substantial piece of entertainment for young and old. Both animation and photography are vastly improved over Walt Disney's first cartoon feature, *Snow White*. Jiminy, the witty, resourceful, and effervescing cricket, introduces the old woodcarver, Geppetto, and his workshop. Place abounds with musical clocks and gadgets, pet kitten and goldfish—and the puppet whom he names Pinocchio. Geppetto's wish for a son is granted when the blue fairy appears and provides life for the puppet; with Jiminy Cricket appointed guardian of the latter's conscience. Pinocchio soon encounters villainous characters and his impetuous curiosity gets him into a series of escapades. Cartoon characterization of Pinocchio is delightful, with his boyish antics and pranks maintaining constant interest.

1940: Best Song ("When You Wish upon a Star"), Original Score

PIN UP GIRL

1944, 85 mins, US Ⓥ ⊙

D: H. Bruce Humberstone **A:** Betty Grable, John Harvey, Martha Raye, Joe E. Brown (20th Century-Fox)

Escapist filmusical's all very pleasing and pleasant. The plot—Missouri gal crashes welcome-home party of war hero (John Harvey) in NYC nightclub—brooks no examination. Betty Grable is almost trapped in her gate-crashing, when she poses as a musical comedy actress, mounts the rostrum pronto, and Charlie Spivak picks up the music cue and it all comes out all right. Just like that! Joe E. Brown as the café proprietor and Martha Raye as his jealous star carry the low comedy.

PIRANHA

1978, 92 mins, US Ⓥ

D: Joe Dante **A:** Bradford Dillman, Heather Menzies, Kevin McCarthy, Keenan Wynn, Dick Miller, Barbara Steele (New World)

Since the title characters in *Piranha* are never actually seen (there's lots of speeded-up nibbling, but no close-ups of the deadly Brazilian river munchers), the pic utilizes a lot of red dye in the water, and an auditory effect for the gnawing that sounds like an air-conditioner on the fritz. What is different about *Piranha* is the unusual number of victims. Not only is the requisite slew of cameo performers dispatched quickly (Keenan Wynn, Kevin McCarthy, Bruce Gordon), but an entire campful of schoolchildren, and a holiday crowd at a lakeside resort get chomped. This is one film where the fish win.

PIRANHA II
THE SPAWNING
(US: PIRANHA 2: FLYING KILLERS)

1983, 95 mins, Italy Ⓥ ⊙

D: James Cameron **A:** Tricia O'Neil, Steve Marachuk, Lance Henriksen, Ricky G. Paul, Ted Richert (Chako)

Routine monster film, unrelated to Joe Dante's 1978 *Piranha*. Idiotic premise has US government genetic engineering experiments creating a deadly form of grunions (hinted at being used in the Vietnam War). A missing canister of fertile eggs of these mutant fish (called piranha for horror fans' sake) turns up in the Caribbean resort of Club Elysium, and the beasties start chewing up vacationers. Special effects experts come up with convincing gore for the victims, but the monsters are laughably phony.

PIRATE, THE

1948, 101 mins, US Ⓥ ⊙

D: Vincente Minnelli **A:** Judy Garland, Gene Kelly, Walter Slezak, Gladys Cooper, Reginald Owen, George Zucco (M-G-M)

Escapist film fare's an eye and ear treat of light musical entertainment, garbing its amusing antics, catchy songs, and able terping in brilliant color. Gene Kelly and Judy Garland team delightfully. The Cole Porter score is loaded with tunes that get over to the ear and the foot. Picture tells of the cloistered Latin girl about to fulfill an arranged wedding when she meets a traveling troupe of entertainers headed by Kelly.

1948: Nomination: Best Scoring of a Dramatic Picture

PIRATES

1986, 124 mins, France/Tunisia Ⓥ ▭

D: Roman Polanski **A:** Walter Matthau, Damien Thomas, Richard Pearson, Cris Campion, Charlotte Lewis (Carthago/Accent-Cominco)

A decidedly underwhelming comedy adventure. Walter Matthau essays the central role of Captain Thomas Bartholomew Red, a peg-legged British pirate captain with plenty of Long John Silver in his manner. Captured by Don Alfonso (Damien Thomas), captain of the Spanish galleon *Neptune*, Red causes the *Neptune's* crew to mutiny, takes the niece (Charlotte Lewis) of the governor of Maracaibo hos-

tage, and steals a golden Aztec throne from the Spaniards.
1986: Nomination: Best Costume Design

PIRATES OF PENZANCE, THE
1983, 112 mins, US Ⓥ ⊙ ⊡
D: Wilford Leach **A:** Kevin Kline, Angela Lansbury, Linda Ronstadt, George Rose, Rex Smith (Pressman/Universal)

Gilbert and Sullivan's durable *The Pirates of Penzance* has been turned into an elaborate screen musical by basically the same hands responsible for Joseph Papp's smash New York Shakespeare Festival and Broadway stage production, and result is a delight. Simple tale has orphan Rex Smith leaving, upon turning 21, the band of pirates with whom he's been raised. Upon hitting land, he encounters eight sisters and becomes smitten with one of them, Linda Ronstadt.

PIT AND THE PENDULUM
1961, 85 mins, US Ⓥ ⊡
D: Roger Corman **A:** Vincent Price, John Kerr, Barbara Steele, Luana Anders, Antony Carbone (American International)

Elaboration of the short Poe classic about bloodletting in 16th-century Spain is a physically stylish, imaginatively photographed horror film, though needlessly corny in many spots. Scriptwriter Richard Matheson has contrived a plot involving an ill-fated nobleman slowly losing his mind because he thinks he accidentally buried his wife alive. The last portion of the film builds to genuine excitement in a reverse twist ending that might well have pleased Poe himself.

PLACE FOR LOVERS, A
1969, 88 mins, Italy/France
D: Vittorio De Sica **A:** Faye Dunaway, Marcello Mastroianni, Caroline Mortimer (M-G-M/Ponti-Cohn)

This romantic drama comes out at times as somewhat sudsy and flabby. But with Vittorio De Sica's direction, the eye-pleasing atmosphere of the Italian Alps, and Marcello Mastroianni and Faye Dunaway a good team as a pair of ill-starred lovers, there's enough pull. Dunaway arrives to stay at a deserted elegant villa near Venice. She phones Mastroianni and he hotfoots it to the villa. Without quite understanding what gives, he is in the sack with Dunaway before the night's out.

PLACE IN THE SUN, A
1951, 118 mins, US Ⓥ ⊙
D: George Stevens **A:** Montgomery Clift, Elizabeth Taylor, Shelley Winters, Anne Revere, Fred Clark, Raymond Burr (Paramount)

Theodore Dreiser's much-discussed novel of the 1920s, *An American Tragedy,* is transposed to the screen for the second time. Montgomery Clift, Shelley Winters, and Elizabeth Taylor give wonderfully shaded and poignant performances. Tale is of a poor and lonely boy and girl who find comfort in each other. Unhappily, while the girl progresses to real love of the boy, he finds love elsewhere in a wealthy lass of a social set to which he'd like to become a part. His first attachment is not easily broken off, however, because the girl discovers herself pregnant.
1951: Best Director, Screenplay, B&W Cinematography, Scoring of a Dramatic Picture, Editing, B&W Costume Design
Nominations: Best Picture, Actor (Montgomery Clift), Actress (Shelley Winters)

PLACES IN THE HEART
1984, 102 mins, US Ⓥ ⊙
D: Robert Benton **A:** Sally Field, Lindsay Crouse, Ed Harris, Amy Madigan, John Malkovich, Danny Glover (Tri-Star)

A loving, reflective homage to his hometown by writer-director Robert Benton. He creates a full tapestry of life in Waxahachie, Texas, circa 1935, but filmgoers may find his understated naturalistic approach lacking in dramatic punch. Sally Field is solid in the lead role as a widowed mother. Nestor Almendros's photography radiates a lived-in autumnal light.
1984: Best Actress (Sally Field), Original Screenplay
Nominations: Best Picture, Director, Actor (John Malkovich), Supp. Actress (Lindsay Crouse), Costume Design

PLAGUE OF THE ZOMBIES, THE
1966, 90 mins, UK Ⓥ
D: John Gilling **A:** André Morell, Diane Clare, John Carson, Brook Williams, Alexander Davion, Jacqueline Pearce (Hammer/Seven Arts)

A well-made horror programmer about strange happenings a century ago in a small town on the moors. Script brings André Morell, a distinguished medical professor, to the boondocks town where a dozen people have died mysteriously, and local squire John Carson won't permit autopsies.

PLAINSMAN, THE
1937, 112 mins, US ⓋⓄ
D: Cecil B. DeMille A: Gary Cooper, Jean Arthur, James Ellison, Charles Bickford, Helen Burgess, Porter Hall (Paramount)

A big and a good western. It's cowboys and Indians on a broad, sweeping scale. Gary Cooper is Hickok, Jean Arthur is Calamity Jane, and James Ellison is a rather aggrandized Buffalo Bill. The spec appeal is in the redskin warfare. The sequence with the near burning-at-the-stake of Hickok in Yellow Hand's camp is tingling and the soldiers' holding out for several days against an almost overwhelming horde of Comanches, with some corking charging-through-the-water action, is another.

PLANES, TRAINS AND AUTOMOBILES
1987, 93 mins, US ⓋⓄ
D: John Hughes A: Steve Martin, John Candy, Laila Robins, Michael McKean, Kevin Bacon (Paramount)

An effective nightmare-as-comedy. Disaster-prone duo of Steve Martin and John Candy repeatedly recall a contemporary Laurel and Hardy as they agonizingly try to make their way from New York to Chicago by various modes of transport. Tale throws together Martin, an ad exec, and Candy, a shower curtain ring salesman, as they head home from Manhattan to their respective homes in Chicago two days before Thanksgiving.

PLANET OF THE APES
1968, 112 mins, US ⓋⓄ▣
D: Franklin J. Schaffner A: Charlton Heston, Roddy McDowall, Kim Hunter, Maurice Evans, James Whitmore, Linda Harrison (Apjac/20th Century-Fox)

Sociopolitical allegory, cast in the mold of futuristic science fiction, is an intriguing blend of chilling satire, a sometimes ludicrous juxtaposition of human and ape mores, optimism and pessimism. Charlton Heston, leader of an aborted space shot that propels his crew 20 centuries ahead of Earth, is a cynical man who eventually has thrust upon him the burden of reasserting man's superiority over all other animals.
1968: Honorary Award (John Chambers, for makeup design)
Nominations: Best Costume Design, Original Music Score

PLATINUM BLONDE
1931, 82 mins, US
D: Frank Capra A: Loretta Young, Robert Williams, Jean Harlow, Louise Closser Hale, Donald Dillaway, Reginald Owen (Columbia)

It's entertaining, has a lot of light, pleasing comedy, and carries a cast that's tops. Robert Williams is a very likable character as a reporter who marries himself off to a snobbish society frail, and he plays it like a champ. Always displaying a fine screen presence and manner, Williams quickly ingratiates himself.

PLATOON
1986, 120 mins, US ⓋⓄ
D: Oliver Stone A: Tom Berenger, Willem Dafoe, Charlie Sheen, Forest Whitaker, John C. McGinley, Kevin Dillon (Hemdale)

An intense but artistically distanced study of infantry life during the Vietnam War. Writer-director Oliver Stone seeks to immerse the audience totally in the nightmare of the United States's misguided adventure, and manages to do so in a number of very effective scenes. Willem Dafoe comes close to stealing the picture as the sympathetic sergeant whose drugged state may even heighten his sensitivity to the insanity around him.
1986: Best Picture, Director, Sound, Editing
Nominations: Best Supp. Actor (Tom Berenger, Willem Dafoe), Original Screenplay, Cinematography

PLAYBOYS, THE
1992, 110 mins, US Ⓥ
D: Gillies MacKinnon A: Albert Finney, Aidan Quinn, Robin Wright, Milo O'Shea, Niamh Cusack (Goldwyn)

Story concerns an Irish lass (Wright) in 1957 who's shamed by her fellow townsfolk for being an unwed mother. A new love enters her life with the arrival of Milo O'Shea's troupe of traveling actors, The Playboys. Newest thesp in the company (Aidan Quinn) immediately impresses Wright and eventually beds her. Fly in the ointment is the local constable (Albert Finney) who has always been in love with Wright and explodes into violence.

PLAY DIRTY
1969, 117 mins, UK ▭
D: André de Toth A: Michael Caine, Nigel Davenport, Nigel Green, Harry Andrews (United/Lowndes)

Michael Caine is cast as an inexperienced British Army captain, detailed to lead reluctantly a small band of mercenaries into the desert to dispose of a vital enemy fuel dump. Caine plays with an often tired and flat lack of expression that doesn't pump much blood into the dialogue or action. He comes out second best to Nigel Davenport, a resourceful rogue with style.

PLAYER, THE
1992, 123 mins, US ⓥ ⊙
D: Robert Altman A: Tim Robbins, Greta Scacchi, Fred Ward, Whoopi Goldberg, Peter Gallagher, Vincent D'Onofrio (Avenue)

Mercilessly satiric yet good-natured, this is quite possibly the most resonant Hollywood saga since the days of *Sunset Boulevard* and *The Bad and the Beautiful*. Plot hinges on a series of threatening postcards received by hotshot studio executive Griffin Mill (Tim Robbins) from an ignored screenwriter. Mill tracks down the man he suspects of being the sender and, in a fit of anger, accidentally kills him. The postcards keep coming, but Mill initiates a romance with his victim's sexy girlfriend, June (Greta Scacchi), then maneuvers brilliantly on a film project that provides *The Player* with its showstopping capper. Center screen throughout, Robbins is superb as Mill.
1992: Nomination: Best Director, Screenplay Adaptation, Editing

PLAYERS
1979, 120 mins, US ⓥ
D: Anthony Harvey A: Ali MacGraw, Dean-Paul Martin, Maximilian Schell, Pancho Gonzalez, Steve Guttenberg (Paramount)

Another love story in disguise, this time backgrounded against the tennis world, *Players* is disqualified by exec producer Arnold Schulman's wobbly script, a simpering performance by Ali MacGraw, and a preponderance of tennis footage. Only ace in *Players* is casting of Dean-Paul Martin, who, in his first film role proves highly believable in both his tennis and dramatic scenes.

PLAY IT AGAIN, SAM
1972, 84 mins, US ⓥ ⊙
D: Herbert Ross A: Woody Allen, Diane Keaton, Tony Roberts, Jerry Lacy, Susan Anspach (Paramount/Apjac)

Woody Allen's 1969 legit comedy-starrer has become 84 minutes of fragile fun on the screen. Allen's adaptation showcases his self-deprecating, and sometimes erratic, comedy personality. Ditched by wife, Susan Anspach, who cannot stand his vicarious living of old Humphrey Bogart films, Allen is consoled by Diane Keaton and Tony Roberts, to the point that Keaton begins to fall for Allen. Jerry Lacy is most effective as the Bogart phantom who drops in from time to time.

PLAYMAKER
1994, 88 mins, US ⓥ
D: Yuri Zeltser A: Colin Firth, Jennifer Rubin, John Getz, Jeff Perry (Odyssey/Steinhardt Baer-Samuelson)

An every-which-way script takes the heat out of *Playmaker*, part erotic thriller, part psychodrama, part old-fashioned murder mystery that can't make up its mind which direction it's headed, despite good chemistry between leads Colin Firth and Jennifer Rubin, and smart-looking direction by Yuri Zeltser.

PLAY MISTY FOR ME
1971, 102 mins, US ⓥ
D: Clint Eastwood A: Clint Eastwood, Jessica Walter, Donna Mills, John Larch, Don Siegel (Universal/Malpaso)

An often fascinating suspenser about psychotic Jessica Walter, whose deranged infatuation for Eastwood leads her to commit murder. For that 80 percent of the film that constitutes the story, the structure and dialogue create a mood of nervous terror that the other 20 percent nearly blows away. Walter gives a superior performance as an unusual woman whose eccentricities are killing.

PLAY TIME
1967, 145 mins, France ⓥ
D: Jacques Tati A: Jacques Tati, Barbara Dennek, Georges Montant, John Abbey, Reinhardt Kolldehoff, Yves Barsacq (Specta)

Jacques Tati has come up with a big-scale comedy about people (mainly tourists) in the growing new metal-and-glass cities that resemble each other. Pic takes to the 70 mm process with an extraordinary impressionistic outdoor set of a new Paris, and is an observant romp during a one-day stay of a group of tourists. Tati builds meticulous gags founded on a gentle, anarchic individualism that is always sympathetic, personal, and, above all, funny and constantly inventive. Dialogue is just functional.

PLAZA SUITE
1971, 114 mins, US ⓥ ⊙
D: Arthur Hiller A: Walter Matthau, Maureen Stapleton, Barbara Harris, Lee Grant (Paramount)

Neil Simon's excellent adaptation of

his 1968 Broadway hit stars Walter Matthau in three strong characterizations of comedy-in-depth, teamed separately with Maureen Stapleton, Lee Grant, and Barbara Harris. Film opens with a sketch featuring Stapleton as a nervous suburban wife who has taken her bridal suite at NYC's Plaza Hotel while the paint dries at home. Hubby Matthau is a cool, jaded mate. Middle episode is lecherous farce, as Hollywood producer Matthau puts the make on Harris, a flame of 15 years past. Final 37 minutes involve father-of-the-bride Matthau, trying to coax frightened daughter, Jenny Sullivan, out of a locked hotel bathroom and into marriage to Thomas Carey.

PLEASE DON'T EAT THE DAISIES
1960, 111 mins, US ⓥ ⌨
D: Charles Walters A: Doris Day, David Niven, Janis Paige, Spring Byington, Richard Haydn, Patsy Kelly (M-G-M)

A light and frothy comedy based on the adventures of Doris Day and David Niven after he turns to newspaper drama criticking during which they buy a monstrosity in the country—70 miles from Broadway—where Day takes on community life while trying to modernize and make their new home livable. Janis Paige enters scene as a Broadway actress whom Niven pans in his very first review.

PLEASURE OF HIS COMPANY, THE
1961, 114 mins, US
D: George Seaton A: Fred Astaire, Debbie Reynolds, Lilli Palmer, Tab Hunter, Gary Merrill, Charles Ruggles (Paramount)

Fred Astaire plays the prodigal, middle-aged playboy papa who returns after a 15–20 year absence to visit his wealthy ex-wife (Lilli Palmer) and daughter (Debbie Reynolds) just prior to the latter's wedding. Balance of the film consists of a contest of sorts in which Astaire more or less vies with his daughter's fiancé for her affection over the protestations of the shrewd, knowing Palmer and the vexations of her present husband. Palmer's reactions are responsible for the picture's strongest comedy wallops.

PLEASURE SEEKERS, THE
1964, 106 mins, US ⌨
D: Jean Negulesco A: Ann-Margret, Tony Franciosa, Carol Lynley, Gardner McKay, Pamela Tiffin, Gene Tierney (20th Century-Fox)

Three Coins in the Fountain is back in new dress. Background has been switched to Madrid from Rome, but the basic plot structure fashioned around the romantic adventures of three American girls residing there still provides a happy story line under the direction of Jean Negulesco, who also helmed *Fountain*. Trio of young femme charmers—Ann-Margret, Carol Lynley, and Pamela Tiffin—spice the events. Foiling for them romantically are Tony Franciosa, Gardner McKay, and André Lawrence, and for complications Brian Keith. There is the added plus of Ann-Margret warbling four songs.

PLENTY
1985, 124 mins, US/UK ⓥ ⊙ ⌨
D: Fred Schepisi A: Meryl Streep, Charles Dance, Tracey Ullman, John Gielgud, Sting, Ian McKellen (RKO/Pressman)

Absorbing and fastidiously made adaptation of David Hare's acclaimed play comes off as cold and ultimately unaffecting. Hare charts the growing social malaise of Western Europe and, specifically, Great Britain, in the years following World War II. He does this through the character of Susan Traherne, a difficult, unsettled, neurotic young woman who moves from idealism to frustration and madness in her passage through a succession of bleak political and personal events.

PLOT AGAINST HARRY, THE
1989, 80 mins, US ⊙
D: Michael Roemer A: Martin Priest, Ben Lang, Henry Nemo (King Screen)

The Plot Against Harry is hilarious and often poignant. Shot in 1969, black-and-white pic is a sociological fossil of manners, mores, and life in the 1960s. Harry Plotnick (Martin Priest), a Jewish numbers racketeer, gets released from prison. His loyal schlemiel assistant, Max, makes him realize the world has changed, and blacks and Hispanics now have dibs on his area. In a farcical accident, Harry hits the rear end of a car carrying his ex-wife, Kay, and his ex-brother-in-law, Leo, and wife. As the story unfolds, Harry is faced with a new world and the gnawing lures of the solid middle-class family life that he's always eschewed.

PLOUGH AND THE STARS, THE
1937, 72 mins, US
D: John Ford A: Barbara Stanwyck, Preston Foster, Barry Fitzgerald, Denis O'Dea, Arthur Shields, Una O'Conner (RKO)

Story is an account of the Irish rebellion in 1916. So many changes have been made in adapting this Sean O'Casey play that the tragic original has been modified into a romantic melodrama. Primarily the screen version is a woman's starring picture calling for an actress of considerably more gifts than Barbara Stanwyck here possesses. The opening shows the struggle and grief in a young bride's heart when her husband is selected by the citizen army to be the commandant of the fighting forces in Dublin. She has no interest in the uprising to free Ireland. Her world is her home.

PLOUGHMAN'S LUNCH, THE
1983, 100 mins, US ⊗

D: Richard Eyre **A:** Jonathan Pryce, Tim Curry, Rosemary Harris, Frank Finlay, Bill Paterson (Greenpoint/Goldcrest/ White)

Pic is set in the heartland of bourgeois England among its media creators and academic pontificators. The film evidently springs from its author Ian McEwan's heart in characterizing the radio journalist played by Jonathan Pryce as lacking in virtue and understanding. His sins include political convictions that blow with the wind; neglect of a dying mother; leading on an older woman; and a fruitless infatuation with the TV researcher played by Charlie Dore. Film reaches an astonishing climax during the Conservative party conference, where crew and cast filmed undercover.

PLYMOUTH ADVENTURE
1952, 104 mins, US

D: Clarence Brown **A:** Spencer Tracy, Gene Tierney, Van Johnson, Leo Genn, Lloyd Bridges, Dawn Adams (M-G-M)

Metro has made the story of the Mayflower's perilous voyage to America a large-scale sea spectacle. The production, ably executed, puts more emphasis on the voyage itself and the attendant dangers than on developing the characters into flesh-and-blood people. To Spencer Tracy falls the chore of enacting Captain Christopher Jones, the tough, earthy master of the Mayflower.

1952: Best Special Effects

POCAHONTAS
1995, 87 mins, US ⊗ ⊙

D: Mike Gabriel, Eric Goldberg (Walt Disney)

Disney's 33rd animated feature, and its first drawn, so to speak, from an actual historic figure, hooks from the start. Pocahontas's father, the chief, wants her to marry the tribe's bravest warrior, but she's holding out for someone a little more exciting. Excitement arrives in the form of John Smith, an adventurer. For Smith and Pocahontas, it's pretty much love at first sight. He's ruggedly blond, and, as if that's not enough, he comes with Mel Gibson's voice. She is equally blessed, not only with beauty but with the singing voice of Judy Kuhn. The Disney artists have created a vivid palette for the picture. The colors are intense and play with nature. The forests and mountains are majestically rendered, and some effects—sunlight through the forests, the falling water—are stunning.

1995: Best Original Musical or Comedy Score

Nominations: Best Original Song ("Colors of the Wind")

POCKETFUL OF MIRACLES
1961, 136 mins, US ⊗ ⊙ ▭

D: Frank Capra **A:** Glenn Ford, Bette Davis, Hope Lange, Arthur O'Connell, Peter Falk, Edward Everett Horton (Franton)

Based on the 1933 *Lady for a Day*, which was also directed by Frank Capra, it has to do with an impoverished applevender (Bette Davis) who would have her long-lost daughter (Ann-Margret) believe that she is a lady of means. This is simple enough when the daughter is on the other side of the globe, but when she comes trotting over for a look-see, mama is in trouble. Enter mama's favorite apple polisher, influential Dave the Dude (Glenn Ford), who hastily sets up an elaborate masquerade with the aid of a horde of typical 1930s Runyonesque hoodlums who are as hard as nails on the surface, but all whipped cream on the inside. The picture seems too long, considering that there's never any doubt as to the outcome, and it's also too lethargic, but there are sporadic compensations of line and situation that reward the patience.

1961: Nomination: Best Supp. Actor (Peter Falk), Color Costume Design, Song ("Pocketful of Miracles")

POETIC JUSTICE
1993, 110 mins, US ⊗ ⊙

D: John Singleton **A:** Janet Jackson, Tupac Shakur, Regina King, Joe Torry, Tyra Ferrell (Columbia)

John Singleton's follow-up to *Boyz 'n' the Hood* and the screen debut of Janet Jackson is a hermetic inner-city love story

elevated by resonant social commentary. Justice (Jackson) has cut herself off from the world outside the beauty salon where she works. Lucky (Tupac Shakur) attempts to break the ice with brittle consequences. Things finally get into gear when Justice's planned trip from South Central L.A. to Oakland is fouled up. Her friend Iesha (Regina King) arranges a last-minute ride with Chicago (Joe Torry) and his buddy from work. The pal turns out to be Lucky.
1993: Nomination: Best Song ("Again")

POINT BLANK
1967, 92 mins, US Ⓥ ▭
D: John Boorman **A:** Lee Marvin, Angie Dickinson, Keenan Wynn, Carroll O'Connor, John Vernon, Sharon Acker (M-G-M)

A violent, dynamic, thinly scripted film. Lee Marvin stars as a double-crossed thief seeking vengeance, only to find he has again been used. Britisher John Boorman's first Hollywood pic is a textbook in brutality and a superior exercise in cinematic virtuosity. The futility of revenge is exemplified by the cyclic pattern of Marvin's movements, and Boorman's frequent cuts to the past overmake the point.

POINT BREAK
1991, 122 mins, US Ⓥ ⊙ ▭
D: Kathryn Bigelow **A:** Patrick Swayze, Keanu Reeves, Gary Busey, Lori Petty, John McGinley (Largo)

A harebrained wild ride through big surf and bad vibes, *Point Break* acts like a huge, nasty wave, picking up viewers for a few major thrills but ultimately grinding them into the sand via overkill and absurdity. Keanu Reeves plays a 25-year-old ex-footballer turned FBI agent who is assigned to penetrate the southern California surf culture in search of some highly successful bank robbers. Director Kathryn Bigelow affects a hyperkinetic, agitated visual style that generates plenty of excitement.

POINT OF NO RETURN
1993, 109 mins, US Ⓥ ⊙ ▭
D: John Badham **A:** Bridget Fonda, Gabriel Byrne, Dermot Mulroney, Miguel Ferrer, Anne Bancroft, Harvey Keitel (Warner)

For those who saw Luc Besson's high-tech thriller *Nikita*, about a female criminal transformed into a government assassin, this soulless, efficiently slavish remake is almost like watching it all over again. But the premise remains a strong hook on which to peg a taut, straight-line action narrative. Sentenced to death for killing a cop in a robbery, a young drug-addicted punk (Bridget Fonda), here named Maggie, is given a chance to live, under the supervision of an agent named Bob (Gabriel Byrne). Ending is a shade more upbeat and conventional than the French version. Fonda acquits herself admirably in all departments.

POISON
1991, 85 mins, US Ⓥ
D: Todd Haynes **A:** Edith Meeks, Millie White, Larry Maxwell, Susan Norman, Scott Renderer (Bronze Eye)

Todd Haynes's *Poison* is a conceptually bold, stylistically audacious first feature. Point of departure is the works of the late French writer Jean Genet. Haynes has composed three distinctive stories that constitute case studies of antisocial aberrations, shot them in three strikingly different styles, and intercut them in surprisingly successful ways. *Hero* takes up the case of a seven-year-old boy who, in blandest suburbia, murders his father. The vastly effective *Horror* relates the sad story of a scientist who isolates the source of human sex drive. *Homo* scrutinizes an obsessive relationship between a hardened criminal and a new arrival in a 1940s French prison.

POISON IVY
1992, 89 mins, US Ⓥ ⊙ ◉
D: Katt Shea Ruben **A:** Tom Skerritt, Drew Barrymore, Sara Gilbert, Cheryl Ladd, Alan Stock (New Line)

Drew Barrymore is Ivy, a tarty-looking high schooler living in Sylvie's (Sara Gilbert) opulent Hollywood Hills home with dad (Tom Skerritt), a recovering alcoholic with a decided Humbert Humbert bent, and mom (Cheryl Ladd), who is slowly expiring from emphysema. Methodically, the blond siren conquers not only all the family members but the dog as well. Suicide, hints of lesbianism, murder, staged accidents, and every other applicable melodramatic contrivance is dragged in. Unfortunate thesps take it all very seriously.

POKEMON
THE FIRST MOVIE
MEWTWO STRIKES BACK
1999, 75 mins, Japan/US Ⓥ ⊙
D: Kunihiko Yuyama (Pikachu Project '98/Shogakukan/Kids WB!)

This anime saga about a boy named Ash Ketchum and his mission to become the world's greatest Pokemon master is a bloated and epic-sized departure from the subversive humor of the massively popular Japanese TV show. Scientists discover that their efforts to bioengineer the rarest Pokemon of all, Mew, have created a monster—Mewtwo. Mysterious "mistress of the greatest number-one trainer" invites Ash and friends to remote New Island, but number-one trainer reveals himself to be Mewtwo. Little does Mewtwo know, though, that the rare Mew is heading for the New Island lair. The only new visual elements include a certain sepulchral darkness in key scenes and digitized backgrounds that don't match the foreground art.

POKOLENIE
(US/UK: A GENERATION)
1955, 90 mins, Poland Ⓥ
D: Andrzej Wajda **A:** Tadeusz Lomnicki, Urszula Modrzynska, Tadeusz Janczar, Janusz Paluszkiewicz, Roman Polanski (WFF)

Story concerns a youth during the occupation of Poland in the last World War who comes to adulthood through love and adversity. Members of the old Polski governmental underground here are treated mainly as gangster types, with the Communists more humane and active. Wajda's feeling for the period and heroism weld this so well it becomes a moving tale of youth in crisis.

POLICE
1985, 113 mins, France Ⓥ
D: Maurice Pialat **A:** Gerard Depardieu, Sophie Marceau, Richard Anconina, Pascale Rocard, Sandrine Bonnaire (Gaumont/TF1)

Pialat subverts the mainstream thriller genre for a personal film that deliberately works against conventional expectations. He ruthlessly strips everything down to a deliberately anticlimactic study of an ill-fated romance between a cop and a drug dealer's girlfriend. Gerard Depardieu gives a superb, buttressing performance as the flic, whose boisterous, macho manner hides an abyss of mediocrity and desperate loneliness.

POLICE ACADEMY
1984, 95 mins, US Ⓥ ☉
D: Hugh Wilson **A:** Steve Guttenberg, G. W. Bailey, George Gaynes, Michael Winslow, Kim Cattrall (Warner/Ladd)

Harmless, innocent poke at authority that does find a fresh background in a police academy. Marion Ramsey as a timid-voiced trainee is fine in the film's most vivid female part. Through it all, Steve Guttenberg is a likable rogue in a role that's too unflappable to set off any sparks.

POLICE ACADEMY 2
THEIR FIRST ASSIGNMENT
1985, 87 mins, US Ⓥ ☉
D: Jerry Paris **A:** Steve Guttenberg, Bubba Smith, David Graf, Michael Winslow, Marion Ramsey (Warner/Ladd)

Follow-up features much of the original's cast. Only actor to get any mileage out of this one is series newcomer, Art Metrano, as an ambitious lieutenant bent upon taking over the department. With the recruits assigned to saving the neighborhood from the grasp of marauding punks, Metrano does everything he can to make them fail, whereupon they exact some faintly amusing revenge upon him.

POLICE ACADEMY 3
BACK IN TRAINING
1986, 82 mins, US Ⓥ ☉
D: Jerry Paris **A:** Steve Guttenberg, Bubba Smith, David Graf, Michael Winslow, Marion Ramsey (Warner)

Cast of cartoon misfits is still basically intact and if *Police Academy 3* has any charm it's in the good-natured dopiness of these people. Leading the charge for the third time is Steve Guttenberg. His role as the cute straight man seems a bit abbreviated, with the comic burden spread out among the cast. Plot has something to do with one of the two rival police academies being shut down by the penny-pinching governor (Ed Nelson).

POLICE ACADEMY 4
CITIZENS ON PATROL
1987, 87 mins, US Ⓥ ☉
D: Jim Drake **A:** Steve Guttenberg, Bubba Smith, Michael Winslow, David Graf, Sharon Stone (Warner)

Police Academy 4 carries the banner of tasteless humor raised in the first three installments to new heights of insipidness. As usual, Steve Guttenberg leads the proceedings as Mahoney, the cute cop. Instead of just resembling a puppy dog, he actually imitates one at one point. Plot, such as it is, has something to do with Commandant Lassard's (George Gaynes) Citizens on Patrol program and attempts by archrival Captain Harris (G. W. Bailey) to make him look bad.

POLICE ACADEMY 5
ASSIGNMENT: MIAMI BEACH
1988, 90 mins, US ⓥ ⊙
D: Alan Myerson **A:** Matt McCoy, Janet Jones, George Gaynes, G. W. Bailey, Rene Auberjonois, Bubba Smith (Warner)

Miami field trip only brings a pastel backdrop to the insipid infighting of the boobs in blue. The jokes are all on Captain Harris (G. W. Bailey) as he makes a disastrous attempt to unseat Commandant Lassard (George Gaynes), aging leader of this dunce-cap police academy, by pulling out a mandatory retirement clause. Lassard's last act is to address a Miami police convention, which gives his graduates an excuse to follow him there for some surfside antics.

POLICE ACADEMY 6
CITY UNDER SIEGE
1989, 83 mins, US ⓥ ⊙
D: Peter Bonerz **A:** Bubba Smith, David Graf, Michael Winslow, Leslie Easterbrook, Marion Ramsey (Warner)

Commandant Lassard (George Gaynes) and his crack team are assigned to stop a wave of robberies, much to the chagrin of the cartoonish Captain Harris (G. W. Bailey). Rarely has a film cried out so desperately for a laughtrack.

POLICE ACADEMY
MISSION TO MOSCOW
1994, 83 mins, US ⓥ
D: Alan Metter **A:** George Gaynes, Michael Winslow, David Graf, Leslie Easterbrook, Christopher Lee (Warner)

Seventh *Police Academy* stanza, with the gang taking on the Moscow mafia, is an inept, geriatric romp that's for completists only.

POLICE STORY 4
FIRST STRIKE
1996, 110 mins, HONG KONG ⓥ ⊙ ⊟
D: Stanley Tong **A:** Jackie Chan, Jackson Lou, Annie Wu, Bill Tung, Yuri Petrov (Golden Harvest)

Enlisted by the CIA, Jackie (Chan) is sent undercover to Ukraine to keep tabs on a woman (Nonna Grishajeva) acting as go-between in the transfer of nuclear secrets. The Russian winter offers ample opportunity for 007-style chase on skis. There's also an extended, tongue-in-cheek homage to *Jaws* and *Thunderball*, with sharks and assassins in an underwater ballet. There's also plenty of Chan's signature acrobatic martial-arts wizardry to satisfy fans.

POLLYANNA
1960, 133 mins, US ⓥ ⊙
D: David Swift **A:** Jane Wyman, Hayley Mills, Richard Egan, Karl Malden, Nancy Olson, Adolphe Menjou (Walt Disney)

That the incredibly confectionery pre–World War I character emerges normal and believably lovable is a tribute to Hayley Mills's ability and to writer-director David Swift's sane sensible approach to the familiar character from Eleanor H. Porter's novel. *Pollyanna* is the tale of the little 12-year-old girl who plays the "glad game" so well that she's soon got everyone she knows playing it.
1960: Honorary Award (Hayley Mills)

POLTERGEIST
1982, 114 mins, US ⓥ ⊙ ⊟
D: Tobe Hooper **A:** Craig T. Nelson, JoBeth Williams, Beatrice Straight, Dominique Dunne, Oliver Robins (M-G-M/United Artists)

The subject is interesting, a persistent parapsychological phenomenon that defies scientific explanation, yet refuses to go away. But producer Steven Spielberg and the director don't really care. They're fully content to demonstrate how well they can create the physical manifestations, plus a lot of standard sideshow horrors. Craig T. Nelson and JoBeth Williams are the parents in a suburban development. When the furniture starts to fly around the room and the big tree in the yard gets hungry for the kids nobody ever seems to notice. Here you have a house in the middle of the street going berserk in Dolby stereo and nobody calls the cops.
1982: Nominations: Best Original Score, Sound Effects Editing, Visual Effects

POLTERGEIST II
THE OTHER SIDE
1986, 90 mins, US ⓥ ⊙ ⊟
D: Brian Gibson **A:** JoBeth Williams, Craig T. Nelson, Heather O'Rourke, Oliver Robins, Zelda Rubinstein (M-G-M)

It's another horrifying house party at the Freelings' in *Poltergeist II*. Sequel finds the poor Freeling family a year later penniless and slightly crazed. Scripters have the focus of evil in human form, in the perfectly cast, since deceased, Julian Beck. Juiciest moments revolve around Craig Nelson playing a soppy drunk, a lustful husband (again to the warm JoBeth Williams), a loving father, and a ghoulie-spewing monster.
1986: Nomination: Best Visual Effects

POLTERGEIST III
1988, 97 mins, US Ⓥ ⊙
D: Gary Sherman A: Tom Skerritt, Nancy Allen, Heather O'Rourke, Zelda Rubinstein, Lara Flynn Boyle (M-G-M)

Poor little Carol Anne (the late Heather O'Rourke) has had to move again. Her parents have shipped her off to live with her aunt and uncle (Nancy Allen and Tom Skerritt) in a brand-new Chicago high-rise. No sooner does Carol Anne move in than the mirrors start to crack and icebergs begin to form, not to mention the noise in her bedroom and the smoke that follows her down the hallway. Director/cowriter Gary Sherman demonstrates absolutely no interest in whether this film ever has a modicum of meaning as he rushes from one special effect to another.

POLYESTER
1981, 94 mins, US Ⓥ
D: John Waters A: Divine, Tab Hunter, Edith Massey, Mary Garlington, David Samson, Stiv Bators (New Line)

Fitfully amusing comedy of not-so-ordinary people. Transvestite thesp Divine never steps out of character essaying the role of a housewife stuck with horrid children (Mary Garlington and Ken King), an unsympathetic husband (David Samson), and a truly evil mother (Joni Ruth White). Camp followers may enjoy Divine's eye-rolling reactions but to the uninitiated most scenes play as overacted melodrama. With nudity and explicit sex and violence absent, *Polyester* strains for a marketing gimmick by introducing Odorama, a scratch-and-sniff card handed out to the viewer, keyed manually to numbers flashed on the screen periodically during the film.

PONTIAC MOON
1994, 107 mins, US Ⓥ ⊙
D: Peter Medak A: Ted Danson, Mary Steenburgen, Ryan Todd, Eric Schweig, Cathy Moriarty (Paramount)

Sincere but tedious road movie. Katherine (Mary Steenburgen) hasn't ventured outside the house for seven years, and her husband, Washington (Ted Danson), an eccentric teacher, fears her phobias may be extending to their 11-year-old son (Ryan Todd), who isn't even allowed to ride in a car. Seizing on the immenent moon landing to create "one perfect act," Washington decides to take the boy and his vintage Pontiac the 1,776 miles (no doubt additional symbolism regarding his declaration of independance) to Spires of the Moon National Park, which would push the car's mileage to 238,857—equaling the distance between the earth and the moon.

PONY EXPRESS, THE
1925, 110 mins, US ⊗
D: James Cruze A: Betty Compson, Ricardo Cortez, Ernest Torrence, Wallace Beery, George Bancroft (Paramount)

Plot concerns the machinations of Senator Glen of California, and his attempt to establish an empire of that state and Sonora, Mexico. To this end, he plots to have the new Pony Express system "fixed" at Julesberg, MS, so that any political news from the East that would have a bearing on his plans might be delayed. Production has been careful and elaborate, but the scenario and story are weak. The film has its moments, but 110 minutes of running time is long.

POOKIE
See: The Sterile Cuckoo

POOL OF LONDON
1951, 85 mins, UK
D: Basil Dearden A: Bonar Colleano, Susan Shaw, Renee Asherson, Earl Cameron, Moira Lister (Ealing)

Story spans just 48 hours when a cargo ship is in the London docks. The plot goes off at various tangents before finally converging on the basic dramatic theme of a manhunt following a holdup, murder, and jewel robbery. The central character, played by Bonar Colleano, is an over-confident, overexuberant seaman tempted by a gang of jewel thieves. While the main story is being developed, the film traces the warm attachment of the Negro seaman for a white girl. Although tastefully done, it has no bearing on the plot.

POOR COW
1967, 101 mins, UK Ⓥ
D: Ken Loach A: Carol White, Terence Stamp, John Bindon, Kate Williams, Queenie Watts, Malcolm McDowell (Vic/Anglo Amalgamated)

A portrait of Joy, who has married a brutal crook (John Bindon) and, after he is nabbed by the cops, shacks up with another thief (Terence Stamp), a gentler type. The incidents of the plot are an excuse for an examination of promiscuous Joy. Kenneth Loach uses an improvisatory technique in all this, and it largely works. Carol White scores with a flow of varied emotion.

POPE JOAN
1972, 101 mins, UK Ⓥ ▭
D: Michael Anderson A: Liv Ullmann, Trevor Howard, Lesley-Anne Down, Franco Nero, Olivia de Havilland, Maximilian Schell (Columbia/Big City)

Pope Joan deals with a female head of the Roman Catholic Church. The story is told as the ancient prototype of a modern female evangelist. She's ''adopted'' in more ways than one by an artist-monk who eventually takes her to Greece as a male. They eventually wind up in Rome where they street preaching brings her to the attention of Leo XII, who takes her on as a papal secretary, raises her to cardinal, and eventually his successor.

POPE MUST DIE, THE
(US: THE POPE MUST DIET)
1991, 97 mins, UK Ⓥ
D: Peter Richardson A: Robbie Coltrane, Beverly D'Angelo, Herbert Lom, Paul Bartel, Salvatore Cascio (Palace/British Screen)

Breezy satire of mob pictures and religious pics. Scots comic Robbie Coltrane toplines as a priest who doubles as a car mechanic and rock musician in a rural Italian orphanage. When the pope kicks it in Rome, Father Dave Albinizi's name comes up thanks to a clerical error, and next thing he's riding around in the popemobile and dispensing blessings.

POPE MUST DIET, THE
See: The Pope Must Die

POPE OF GREENWICH VILLAGE, THE
1984, 120 mins, US Ⓥ ⊙
D: Stuart Rosenberg A: Eric Roberts, Mickey Rourke, Daryl Hannah, Geraldine Page, Kenneth McMillan, Tony Musante (United Artists)

Set in Manhattan's Italian community, an offbeat slice-of-life tale of small-time guys involved in big trouble. Charlie (Mickey Rourke) is a supervisor in a restaurant where Paulie (Eric Roberts) works as a waiter. Both are heavily in debt and headed nowhere. Fired from their jobs, they seek a way out via a crime caper.
1984: Nominations: Best Supp. Actress (Geraldine Page)

POPEYE
1980, 114 mins, US Ⓥ ⊙ ▭
D: Robert Altman A: Robin Williams, Shelley Duvall, Ray Walston, Paul L. Smith, Paul Dooley, Linda Hunt (Paramount/Walt Disney)

Popeye is far, far better than it might have been. To the eye, Robin Williams is terrifically transposed into the squinting sailor with the bulging arms. But to the ear, his mutterings are not always comprehensible. Shelley Duvall makes a delightful Olive Oyl, and Paul L. Smith a perfectly jealous Bluto.

POPI
1969, 115 mins, US Ⓥ
D: Arthur Hiller A: Alan Arkin, Rita Moreno, Miguel Alejandro, Ruben Figueroa (United Artists)

Alan Arkin is cast as a Puerto Rican father, living in Spanish Harlem, whose fantastic plan to improve the lot of his two small sons backfires. Arkin is given too much free rein for his very personal style, and is sometimes guilty of working a scene, meant to be poignant or even dramatic, for a laugh, which he usually gets.

POPIOL I DIAMENT
(US: ASHES AND DIAMONDS)
1958, 106 mins, Poland Ⓥ
D: Andrzej Wajda A: Zbigniew Cybulski, Ewa Krzyzewska, Adam Pawlikowski, Waclaw Zastrzezynski, Bogumil Kobiela (Kadr)

Taut thriller has a heavier theme of the futility of killing and violence. It concerns two men told to kill a top Communist on the last day of the war. They represent the prewar Polski ruling forces. Film details the eventual murder and the ironic death of the murderer. Director is masterly in composing atmosphere and gets fine performances, especially from Zbigniew Cybulski as the erratic young killer. But it is somewhat overdone in expressionistic bravura.

POPPY
1936, 75 mins, US
D: A. Edward Sutherland A: W. C. Fields, Rochelle Hudson, Richard Cromwell, Lynne Overman (Paramount)

There's one thing that W. C. Fields will never be, and that's unfunny. He could get laughs with Hamlet's soliloquy, which is just about what he does in Poppy. The role of Professor Eustace McGargle, carnival guy, shell-game operator, medicine man, and beloved rogue, is a setup for Fields. The juvenile romance by Richard Cromwell and Rochelle Hudson is just a series of interruptions between the Fields comedy business.

PORGY AND BESS
1959, 136 mins, US ▱
D: Otto Preminger A: Sidney Poitier, Dorothy Dandridge, Sammy Davis Jr., Pearl Bailey, Brock Peters, Diahann Carroll (Columbia)

Porgy and Bess retains most of the virtues and some of the libretto traits of the folk opera melodrama of a 1905 Charleston waterfront slum. Sidney Poitier makes his character thoroughly believable though when he opens his voice to sing it is Robert McPherrin. Bess, the incompletely regenerate floozie, is Dorothy Dandridge, but the voice is Adele Addison. (Neither voice gets screen credit.) The love affair of this oddly assorted pair has considerable humanity though Dandridge is perhaps too "refined" to be quite convincing.
1959: Best Scoring of a Musical
Nominations: Best Color Cinematography, Color Costume Design, Sound

PORK CHOP HILL
1959, 97 mins, US ⊗ ⊙
D: Lewis Milestone A: Gregory Peck, Harry Guardino, Rip Torn, George Peppard, Woody Strode (United Artists/Melville)

Grim, utterly realistic story drives home both the irony of war and the courage men can summon to die in a cause that they don't understand and for an objective that they know to be totally irrelevant. King Company, commanded by Gregory Peck as Lieutenant Joe Clemons, is ordered to take Pork Chop Hill from the Chinese Reds. The time is the Korean War, and the irony of the situation is that (1) armistice negotiations are virtually concluded, and (2) Pork Chop Hill has absolutely no tactical importance. It must be taken simply because its loss means a loss of face on the part of the Americans in the eyes of the Communist negotiators.

PORKY'S
1981, 94 mins, Canada ⊗ ⊙
D: Bob Clark A: Dan Monahan, Mark Herrier, Wyatt Knight, Kim Cattrall, Alex Karras, Susan Clark (Simon/Astral Bellevue/Pathe)

Locker-room humor reaches new heights (depths) here. Young Florida boys are itching to score and title refers to a redneck establishment out in the Everglades known for its available women. After being embarrassingly turned away on their first visit, the boys return to wreak havoc on the joint, proving once and for all that violence will result when the sex drive is repressed.

PORKY'S II THE NEXT DAY
1983, 95 mins, US ⊗ ⊙
D: Bob Clark A: Dan Monahan, Mark Herrier, Wyatt Knight, Roger Wilson, Cyril O'Reilly (Simon-Reeves-Landsburg/Astral Bellevue/Pathe)

Bill Wiley's bigoted Reverend Bubba Flavel makes a crusade out of shutting down the school's Shakespeare festival due to the lewdness he finds strewn throughout the Bard's work. Enlisted in his cause is the ample girls' gym teacher Miss Balbricker and the local contingent of the Ku Klux Klan, who are each the victims of two of the film's three "big scenes." Director Bob Clark has not allowed success to lead him astray into the dreaded realm of good taste.

PORTE DES LILAS
1957, 95 mins, France/Italy
D: Rene Clair A: Pierre Brasseur, Georges Brassens, Henri Vidal, Dany Carrel, Raymond Bussieres (Filmsonor/Cinetel/Seca/Rizzoli)

Rene Clair has come up with a light tale that wavers between comedy and drama, making a slight, fragile pic. A genial good-for-nothing drunkard (Pierre Brasseur) gets saddled with a gangster (Henri Vidal) who has just killed three people. The killer stays on until he is discovered by a clever young girl (Dany Carrel). The gangster woos and wins her and tries to get her to steal money from her father.

PORTNOY'S COMPLAINT
1972, 101 mins, US ⊗ ▱
D: Ernest Lehman A: Richard Benjamin, Karen Black, Lee Grant, Jeannie Berlin, Jill Clayburgh (Warner/Chenault)

Besides adapting the Philip Roth novel into a lucid, balanced, and moral screenplay, and producing handsomely on various locations, Ernest Lehman makes an excellent directorial debut. Richard Benjamin heads an outstanding cast. Alexander Portnoy's hang-up derives from heterosexual masturbation fantasies, and the first 44 minutes constitute the slaphappy, kinky exposition of his development. But what the story then pulls an audience into is the inevitable consequence.

PORTRAIT OF A LADY, THE
1996, 144 mins, US/UK ⊗ ⊙ ▱
D: Jane Campion A: Nicole Kidman, John

Malkovich, Barbara Hershey, Mary-Louise Parker, Martin Donovan, Shelley Winters (Propaganda/PolyGram)

Jane Campion's *The Portrait of a Lady,* emerges as a literary adaptation of intelligence, beauty and concentrated artistry, but it's emotionally remote and dramatically problematic. The beautiful 23-year-old Isabel Archer (Nicole Kidman) rejects the idea of marriage out of hand and acquires a vast fortune that allows her to live as she likes. But when she places herself in a cage through marriage to a manipulative, spirit-sapping man (John Malkovich), her life, as well as the film, loses definition and clarity, leaving the viewer perplexed by the story's arc and ultimate point. Kidman is everything one could ask for as Isabel—bright, alert, optimistic. Malkovich's quirks and hard-to-read behavior work well for the deceptive Osmond.

PORTRAIT OF JENNIE
1948, 86 mins, US Ⓥ
D: William Dieterle **A:** Joseph Cotten, Jennifer Jones, Ethel Barrymore, David Wayne, Lillian Gish, Cecil Kellaway (RKO/Selznick)

An unusual, ethereal romance between two generations is told with style, taste, and dignity. The work of an artist living in New York in the 1930s lacks depth and it is only when he meets a strange child in the park one day that inspiration to paint people comes. The next time she appears he sees her as a girl just entering her teens. Her growth moves into college years and then as a graduate while he, meantime, is discovering she is a person who has been dead for years. Jennifer Jones's performance is standout.
1948: Best Special Effects.
Nomination: Best B&W Cinematography

POSEIDON ADVENTURE, THE
1972, 117 mins, US Ⓥ ⊙ ▭
D: Ronald Neame **A:** Gene Hackman, Ernest Borgnine, Red Buttons, Carol Lynley, Roddy McDowall, Stella Stevens (20th Century-Fox)

Highly imaginative and lustily produced meller socks over the dramatic struggle of 10 passengers to save themselves after an ocean liner capsizes when struck by a mammoth tidal wave created by a submarine earthquake. Chief protagonist is played by Gene Hackman, as a free-talking minister who keeps his cool and assumes leadership.
1972: Best Song (''The Morning After''),

Honorary Award (special visual effects)
Nominations: Best Supp. Actress (Shelley Winters), Cinematography, Costume Design, Art Direction, Editing, Original Score, Sound

POSSE
1975, 92 mins, US Ⓥ ⊙ ▭
D: Kirk Douglas **A:** Kirk Douglas, Bruce Dern, Bo Hopkins, James Stacy, Luke Askew (Paramount/Bryna)

Posse is a good western, with Kirk Douglas as a cynical US Marshal who eventually stumbles on his own political ambitions while tracking thief Bruce Dern under a strident law-and-order platform.

POSSE
1993, 109 mins, US/UK Ⓥ ⊙
D: Mario Van Peebles **A:** Mario Van Peebles, Stephen Baldwin, Charles Lane, Tiny Lister Jr., Billy Zane (PolyGram/Working Title)

Begin with a reliable pursuit-and-revenge plotline, lay on a Sergio Leone look and flashback structure, stir in some John Ford community values and Sam Peckinpah violence, tag *The Magnificent Seven* on at the end and paint it black, and you've got *Posse.* Eventful script packs in enough confrontations, fights, and shootouts for several films, which will keep action fans happy.

POSSESSED
1947, 108 mins, US Ⓥ ⊙
D: Curtis Bernhardt **A:** Joan Crawford, Van Heflin, Raymond Massey, Geraldine Brooks (Warner)

Joan Crawford cops all thesping honors in this production with a virtuoso performance as a frustrated woman ridden into madness by a guilt-obsessed mind. Film vacillates between being a cold clinical analysis of a mental crack-up and a highly surcharged melodramatic vehicle for Crawford's histrionics. Heflin's part of a footloose engineer who romances his ladies with one eye on the railroad schedule is drawn with equal sharpness. By sheer power of personal wit, however, Heflin infuses his role with charm and degree of credibility despite a lack of clear motivation for his behavior.
1947: Nomination: Best Actress (Joan Crawford)

POSSESSION
1981, 127 mins, France/W. Germany Ⓥ
D: Andrzej Zulawski **A:** Isabelle Adjani, Sam Neill, Heinz Bennent, Margit Carstensen (Oliane/Marianne/Soma)

Possession starts on a hysterical note, stays there, and surpasses it as the film progresses. There are excesses on all fronts: in supposedly ordinary married life and then occult happenings, intricate political skulduggery with the infamous Berlin Wall as background—they all abound in this horror-cum-political-cum-psychological tale. Adjani is game as she plays a deranged, obsessed woman in high gear throughout.

POSSESSION OF JOEL DELANEY, THE
1972, 105 mins, UK Ⓥ
D: Waris Hussein **A:** Shirley MacLaine, Michael Hordern, Edmundo Rivera Alvarez, Robert Burr, Miriam Colon (ITC)

Unusual occult thriller centers on a chic East Side society divorcée (Shirley MacLaine) who harbors an inordinate affection for her brother, Joel (Perry King), and attempts to save him when he is possessed by the spirit of a Puerto Rican friend fond of ritual beheadings.

POSTCARDS FROM THE EDGE
1990, 101 mins, US Ⓥ ⊙
D: Mike Nichols **A:** Meryl Streep, Shirley MacLaine, Dennis Quaid, Gene Hackman, Richard Dreyfuss, Rob Reiner (Columbia)

Mike Nichols's film of Carrie Fisher's novel packs a fair amount of emotional wallop in its dark-hued comic take on a chemically dependent Hollywood mother and daughter (Shirley MacLaine and Meryl Streep). Streep's tour through Hollywood hell is signposted with many recognizable, on-target types: predatory macho creep (Dennis Quaid), sleazy business manager (Gary Morton), oafish producer (Rob Reiner), airheaded and roundheeled actress (Annette Bening) and sternly paternalistic director (Gene Hackman).
1990: Nominations: Best Actress (Meryl Streep), Song ("I'm Checkin' Out")

IL POSTINO
(US: THE POSTMAN)
1995, 116 mins, Italy Ⓥ ⊙
D: Michael Radford **A:** Massimo Troisi, Philippe Noiret, Maria Grazia, Cucinotta, Linda Moretti (CG Group Tiger-Pentafilm/Esterno Mediteraraneo/Blue Dahlia)

Late Italo actor Massimo Troisi bows out with an affecting performance in a sad-sweet tale of a simple Mediterranean islander whose life is forever changed by his friendship with an exiled Chilean poet. It's Troisi's show but, with little assistance

from Radford's by-the-numbers direction, and a script that starts to become very diffused halfway through, the bottom line is that it's a performance in a vacuum.
1995: Nominations: Best Film, Director, Actor (Massimo Troisi), Screenplay Adaptation, Original Dramatic Score

POSTMAN, THE
See: Il Postino

POSTMAN, THE
1997, 177 mins, US Ⓥ ⊙ ▭
D: Kevin Costner **A:** Kevin Costner, Will Patton, Larenz Tate, Olivia Williams, James Russo, Daniel von Bargen (Tig/Warner)

A passionately expressed vision of what the United States was and is meant to be, *The Postman* is a rare epic film that is actually about something, stressing the overriding importance of community. Set in 2013 in the wake of a devastating war in which most of the US is wiped out, the film comes to feel more like a Western than anything else. Kevin Costner's solitary wayfarer comes across an abandoned old mail Jeep, puts on the uniform he finds there and, at a small town called Pineview, announces he is to deliver 15-year-old mail in his role as representative of the restored United States. The Postman wins over the skittish citizens simply because they need to believe in something, and he is forced into the role of a reluctant leader who represents the rebirth of the nation's democratic pinciples. Pic has an undeniable streak of vanity but, despite the missteps, is played with general conviction.

POSTMAN ALWAYS RINGS TWICE, THE
1946, 110 mins, US Ⓥ ⊙
D: Tay Garnett **A:** Lana Turner, John Garfield, Cecil Kellaway, Hume Cronyn, Audrey Totter, Leon Ames (M-G-M)

Lana Turner, as the sexy blond murderess, and John Garfield, as the footloose vagabond whose lust for the girl made him stop at nothing, each give to the assignments the best of their talents. Development of the characters makes Tay Garnett's direction seem slowly paced during first part of the picture, but this establishment was necessary to give the speed and punch to the uncompromising evil that transpires. The script is a rather faithful translation of James M. Cain's story of a boy and girl who murder the girl's husband, live through terror, and eventually make payment for their crime.

POSTMAN ALWAYS RINGS TWICE, THE

1981, 123 mins, US ⱱ ⊙

D: Bob Rafelson **A:** Jack Nicholson, Jessica Lange, John Colicos, Anjelica Huston, Christopher Lloyd (Northstar/Lorimar)

Cain's yarn is essentially a morality tale of a Depression drifter who comes to work for a beautiful young woman and her older Greek husband. Falling madly in lust, they murder the old man, escape justice, and then get their desserts in an ironical twist at the end. In the key roles, Nicholson and Lange are excellent, as is Michael Lerner as their defense attorney.

IL POSTO
(US: THE JOB; THE SOUND OF TRUMPETS)

1961, 105 mins, Italy

D: Ermanno Olmi **A:** Sandro Panzeri, Loredana Detto, Tullio Kezich, Mara Revel, Bice Melegari (The 24 Horses)

This is a little jewel of a picture made as his first feature effort by Ermanno Olmi. Players are all nonprofessional but they and other facets of pic form a winning combo. A youngster has just finished school and leaves his town for the big city to seek a job. After an exam, at which he meets a young girl to whom he takes a teenage fancy, they are both admitted. He serves a period of apprenticeship, then finally is seated at a desk of his own. Plot is deceptively simple, but every frame of pic is rich with shadings and nuances.

POT CARRIERS, THE

1962, 84 mins, UK

D: Peter Graham Scott **A:** Ronald Fraser, Paul Massie, Carol Lesley, Dennis Price, Davy Kaye (Associated British)

This lively slice of life in jail is a moderately unpretentious job but it shrewdly captures the atmosphere of the locale, neatly blends comedy and drama, and offers some sharp playing, biggest impact being made by Ronald Fraser as the trusty who is the kingpin among the fiddlers. Paul Massie is a likable, straightforward hero.

POTEMKIN, THE

See: Bronenosets "Potyomkin"

POTE TIN KYRIAKI
(US: NEVER ON SUNDAY)

1960, 97 mins, Greece ⱱ

D: Jules Dassin **A:** Melina Mercouri, Jules Dassin, Georges Foundas, Titos Vandis, Mitsos Liguisos (Melina/Lopert)

Philosophical romp about an intellectual but prudish American who tries to reform a jolly Greek prostitute. Pic serves to establish Greek actress Melina Mercouri who has a temperament that comes over well. Yank director Jules Dassin also wrote and plays the American. The racy, jangling music score, with local instruments, the bouzoukis, is also an asset. Film is mainly in English with some Greek bits.

POWDER

1995, 111 mins, US ⱱ

D: Victor Salva **A:** Mary Steenburgen, Sean Patrick Flanery, Lance Hendriksen, Jeff Goldblum, Brandon Smith (Hollywood)

By turns affecting and annoying, *Powder* is a sentimental sci-fi drama that features some fine performances, an imaginative premise, and a couple of go-for-broke emotional scenes. But the muddled script plays like a first draft, the continuity is jagged, and the climax is a cop-out of sappy mysticism. Small-town Texas sheriff Barnum (Lance Henriksen), investigating an elderly man's fatal heart attack, discovers the dead man's grandson, Powder (Sean Patrick Flanery), a hairless, white-skinned teenager. It turns out Powder has highly evolved mental powers, to the point where he can read—and transmit—the thoughts of others.

POWER, THE

1968, 108 mins, US ▭

D: Byron Haskin **A:** George Hamilton, Suzanne Pleshette, Richard Carlson, Yvonne De Carlo, Earl Holliman, Arthur O'Connell (M-G-M)

What started out as an ingenious, imaginative sci-fi premise developed into a confusing maze of cloudy characters, motivations, and events in its development. Screenplay is set among a group of scientists engaged in human endurance research. It is discovered that one among them has a superintelligence, possibly a mind of the next level of evolution, so strong it controls the others' minds. As murder starts, George Hamilton, one of the scientists, undertakes to learn the identity of the Power, while himself a suspect by the police.

POWER

1986, 111 mins, US ⱱ ⊙

D: Sidney Lumet **A:** Richard Gere, Julie Christie, Gene Hackman, Kate Capshaw,

Denzel Washington, E. G. Marshall (Lorimar/Polar)

Not so much about power as about p.r., this facile treatment of big-time politics and media, featuring Richard Gere as an amoral image maker, revolves around the unstartling premise that modern politicians and their campaigns are calculatedly packaged for TV. In spite of relentless jet-propelled location hopping that helps to stave off boredom, *Power* never gets airborne.

POWER AND THE GLORY, THE
1933, 73 mins, US
D: William K. Howard **A:** Spencer Tracy, Colleen Moore, Ralph Morgan, Helen Vinson, Clifford Jones (Fox)

Production is unique through its "narratage" style of cinematurgy. Its treatment has been consummately developed by director William K. Howard and scenarist Preston Sturges. Film starts with its ending—the ecclesiastic services for the dead. Showing the finale of the life span of your central character is something that is by no means easy to offset. And that's where the "narratage" comes in. Morgan is the narrator, detailing the highlights in the career of his friend (Tracy) who, even in death, is much maligned. Morgan undertakes to show that Tracy, who fought his way up from an ignorant, unschooled track walker to the presidency of railroads, and a tycoon of industry, was not the bad egg everybody painted. It's well done in every respect. Casting right down the line is punchy for performance.

POWER OF ONE, THE
1992, 111 mins, US ⑨ ⊙
D: John G. Avildsen **A:** Stephen Dorff, Armin Mueller-Stahl, Morgan Freeman, John Gielgud, Maria Marais (Regency/Canal Plus/Alcor)

A captivating and inspiring tale of a boy's journey to courage amid searing injustice often gives way to scenes of intense violence. In 1930s Zimbabwe, young white P. K. is sent to a boarding school. Dignified black prisoner Geel Piet (Morgan Freeman) molds P. K. into a boxing champion and spreads word among the hundreds of other black prisoners that he's the legendary Rainmaker, come to make peace. As P. K. grows up (played admirably at age 18 by Californian Stephen Dorff), he decides to fulfill that destiny, defying the brutally racist regime.

POWER OF THE PRESS
1928, 62 mins, US ⊗
D: Frank Capra **A:** Douglas Fairbanks Jr., Jobyna Ralston, Robert Edeson, Mildred Harris, Dell Henderson (Columbia)

Exciting and insistently engaging melodrama with a light touch. Having by his story ruined the virtuous candidate of a mayoralty election and disgraced the daughter, a young reporter (Douglas Fairbanks Jr.) goes after the hidden aspects of the scandal and ends by exposing the whole kaboodle. Fairbanks in ease and confidence belies his age and takes after his famous pop, never an introvert in the matter of self-assurance.

PRAGUE
1992, 88 mins, UK/France
D: Ian Sellar **A:** Alan Cumming, Sandrine Bonnaire, Bruno Ganz (BBC/Constellation/Young/UGC/Hachette Premiere)

This leisurely paced lightweight effort for scripter/helmer Ian Sellar comes across like a collection of ideas rather than an accomplished and vital picture. On his maiden journey to Prague, young Alexander (Alan Cumming) arrives from the UK in search of newsreel film supposedly stored at Czech film archives. Alex knows exactly what he's looking for but has not anticipated the sluggish serendipity of the archive and its two key employees, Elena (Sandrine Bonnaire) and Josef (Bruno Ganz).

PRAYER FOR THE DYING, A
1988, 107 mins, UK/US ⑨ ⊙
D: Mike Hodges **A:** Mickey Rourke, Bob Hoskins, Alan Bates, Sammi Davis, Liam Neeson (PFD/Goldwyn)

Disappointing thriller adapted from Jack Higgins's novel. Mickey Rourke, styled with red hair and Irish brogue, portrays Martin Fallon, an IRA hitman who sees the light and flees to London. He reluctantly agrees to carry out a mob hit for gangster Jack Meehan (Alan Bates), but the killing is witnessed by priest Father Da Costa (Bob Hoskins). Fallon confesses the murder to the priest, who refuses to identify Fallon to the police.

PREACHER'S WIFE, THE
1996, 124 mins, US ⑨ ⊙
D: Penny Marshall **A:** Denzel Washington, Whitney Houston, Courtney Vance, Gregory Hines, Justin Pierre Edmund, Jenifer Lewis (Goldwyn/Touchstone)

The Preacher's Wife, is a likable, modern musical fairy tale. The Rev. Henry

Biggs (Courtney Vance) is in the throes of a crisis of confidence. He asks for divine intervention, and help is sent in the form of a handsome angel named Dudley (Denzel Washington). Pic remains rooted in sentiments from another era, but there still are plenty of timeless and modern elements for director Penny Marshall to explore. As the rev's wife, Julia (Whitney Houston), remains more a presence than an actress, but she is extremely commanding all the same. Both male leads are exceptionally strong. Although some of Marshall's pacing and structure is a tad inelegant, camerawork and production design are pristine.
1996: Nomination: Best Original Musical Score

PRECINT 45—LOS ANGELES POLICE
See: The New Centurions

PREDATOR
1987, 107 mins, US Ⓥ ⊙
D: John McTiernan **A:** Arnold Schwarzenegger, Carl Weathers, Elpidia Carrillo, Bill Duke, Jesse Ventura (20th Century-Fox)

A slightly above-average actioner tries to compensate for tissue-thin plot with ever-more-grisly death sequences and impressive special effects. Arnold Schwarzenegger plays Dutch, the leader of a military rescue team that works for allied governments. Called into a US hot spot somewhere in South America, he encounters old buddy Dillon (Carl Weathers), who now works for the CIA. The unit starts to get decimated in increasingly garish fashion by an otherworldly Predator. Enemy is a nasty, formidable foe with laser powers.
1987: Nomination: Best Visual Effects

PREDATOR 2
1990, 108 mins, US Ⓥ ⊙
D: Stephen Hopkins **A:** Danny Glover, Gary Busey, Ruben Blades, Maria Conchita Alonso, Bill Paxton (20th Century-Fox)

While the film doesn't achieve the same thrills of the final 45 minutes of *Predator* in terms of overall excitement, it outdoes its first safari in start-to-finish hysteria. The setting is Los Angeles, 1997, where outgunned cops face hordes of assorted drug dealers who rule the streets. Danny Glover heads a dedicated, ethnically mixed group of cops who are more than a little confused as the drug dealers

start turning up dead in droves. Centerpiece is, again, a massive alien gifted with strange weaponry and camouflage abilities.

PRELUDE TO A KISS
1992, 106 mins, US Ⓥ ⊙
D: Norman Rene **A:** Alec Baldwin, Meg Ryan, Kathy Bates, Ned Beatty, Patty Duke (20th Century-Fox)

Peter (Baldwin) and Rita (Meg Ryan) tie the knot at a lovely lakeside ceremony that turns curious with the arrival of a mysterious old man who asks to kiss the bride. Strangely drawn to the oldster, Rita agrees, then scarely knows what hit her. During their Jamaica honeymoon, Rita doesn't seem at all like her old self. She flees back to her parents, leaving Peter to track down the old man whose ailing body now contains his wife's personality, and then to effect a retransference. Overarching theme has to do with the spiritual prevailing over the physical, of the primacy of love no matter what the temporal obstacles.

PRELUDE TO WAR
1943, 53 mins, US
D: Frank Capra (US War Department)

First in the series of seven *Why We Fight* films produced for the US War Department by Lieutenant Colonel Frank Capra, of the Special Service Division, Army Service Forces, *Prelude to War* was originally intended for exclusive use in the army's orientation courses. In piecing together the collection of clips—many of them released for the first time—giving the causes and events leading up to the present conflict, Capra has turned out a forceful, dramatic, and ofttimes spectacular presentation. Particularly stirring is a marching sequence showing how, almost from infancy, the youth of Germany, Italy, and Japan were being trained, drilled, and regimented.

PRENOM CARMEN
(US: FIRST NAME: CARMEN)
1983, 85 mins, France Ⓥ
D: Jean-Luc Godard **A:** Maruschka Detmers, Jacques Bonnaffe, Myriem Roussel, Christophe Odent, Jean-Luc Godard (Sara/JLG)

Film has no Bizet, but the title character is rather a gypsy, attached to a group of terrorists, working for an unnamed cause. Having held up a bank, Carmen (Maruschka Detmers) starts what develops into a love affair with the young cop, Joseph (Jacques Bonnaffe), who tried to stop her from getting away. There is, on the whole, more crude humor and less poetical-political philosophy than in most of Godard's earlier works.

PREPAREZ VOS MOUCHOIRS (US: GET OUT YOUR HANDKERCHIEFS)
1977, 108 mins, France Ⓥ ⊙
D: Bertrand Blier **A:** Gerard Depardieu, Patrick Dewaere, Carole Laure, Riton, Michel Serrault, Eleonore Hirt (Ariane/CAPAC)

A rather bizarre mixture of gritty comedy, satire, and delving into female status makes this a literary film. Gerard Depardieu insists he loves his pretty but vacant-looking wife enough to give her to another man. He talks a bespectacled young man (Patrick Dewaere) into going with his wife. The wife (lovely Canadian thesp Carole Laure) accepts. The three go off to a summer camp run by Dewaere where Laure warms to a 13-year-old kid and lets him sleep with her. The boy manages to tap her need for a child.
1978: Best Foreign Language Film

PRESENTING LILY MARS
1943, 106 mins, US Ⓥ
D: Norman Taurog **A:** Judy Garland, Van Heflin, Fay Bainter, Marta Eggerth, Richard Carlson (M-G-M)

Stage Cinderella yarn supplies minor switches to regulation formula. Garland, an aspiring and stagestruck youngster, attempts to catch attention of producer Van Heflin in a small Indiana town. She makes a pest of herself for 40 minutes of the running time until she follows him into New York, gets a job in his new show, and eventually falls in love with the producer. Garland delivers in her usual effective style, putting across her numbers in top fashion.

PRESIDENT'S ANALYST, THE
1967, 103 mins, US Ⓥ ▭
D: Theodore J. Flicker **A:** James Coburn, Godfrey Cambridge, Severn Darden, Joan Delaney (Paramount/Panpiper)

Inventive story peg—James Coburn starring as the personal analyst to the president of the US—is fleshed out with hilarious incidents that zero in on, and hit, their targets. William Daniels scores as an upper-middle-class compulsive liberal. Barry McGuire and Jill Banner are hippies, and Banner's sex scene with Coburn is a comedy highlight in which several foreign and domestic spies kill each other off as they plot Coburn's demise.

PRESIDENT'S LADY, THE
1953, 96 mins, US Ⓥ
D: Henry Levin **A:** Susan Hayward, Charlton Heston, John McIntire, Fay Bainter (20th Century-Fox)

Lady covers more than 40 years in the life of Andrew Jackson, the seventh president of the United States. It covers the period when the young Tennessee lawyer is attorney general, through his battles with the Indians. It is the story of Jackson being forced to fight his way up the political ladder with the stigma of adultery plaguing him along the way. Charlton Heston supplies a forthright steely-eyed portrayal. Susan Hayward gives the pic a simple, sustained performance in addition to physical beauty.
1953: Nominations: Best B&W Costume Design, B&W Art Direction

PRESIDIO, THE
1988, 97 mins, US Ⓥ ⊙ ▭
D: Peter Hyams **A:** Sean Connery, Mark Harmon, Meg Ryan, Jack Warden, Mark Blum (Paramount)

Sean Connery and Mark Harmon go head-to-head as an army provost marshal and a San Francisco cop who clash jurisdictions and styles in the investigation of an MP's murder. Naturally, there's a back story—they'd locked horns earlier when Connery was Harmon's c.o. in the military—and a complication—Harmon gets involved with Connery's frisky and equally willful daughter (Meg Ryan). Tug-of-war for dominance among the trio provides the interest in an otherwise ordinary crime story.

PRESUMED INNOCENT
1990, 127 mins, US Ⓥ ⊙ ▭
D: Alan J. Pakula **A:** Harrison Ford, Brian Dennehy, Raul Julia, Bonnie Bedelia, Paul Winfield, Greta Scacchi (Mirage/Warner)

Presumed Innocent is a demanding, disturbing javelin of a courtroom murder mystery. Deputy prosecutor and family man Rusty Sabich (Harrison Ford) learns his beautiful colleague Carolyn Polhemus (Greta Scacchi) has been brutally murdered. Forced to lead the investigation by his longtime boss Raymond Horgan (Brian Dennehy), Sabich can scarcely admit he'd had an affair with the dead attorney. Before long Sabich is embroiled in a grand jury investigation that spurs his politically frightened boss to turn on him. Ford, in a very mature, subtle, low-key performance, pulls off the difficult feat of making it impossible to be sure whether Sabich did the deed or not until pic's astonishing denouement.

PRET-A-PORTER
See: Ready to Wear

PRETTY BABY
1978, 109 mins, US ⓥ ⊙
D: Louis Malle **A:** Keith Carradine, Susan Sarandon, Brooke Shields, Frances Faye, Antonio Fargas (Paramount)

Offbeat depiction of life in New Orleans's Storyville red-light district circa 1917, as experienced by a lifelong resident—a 12-year-old girl. The film is handsome, the players nearly all effective, but the story highlights are confined within a narrow range of ho-hum dramatization. Susan Sarandon is one of the girls who has given birth to a child, in this case Brooke Shields, who gives either an extraordinarily subtle or else a totally perplexed performance as a preteenager whose entire world is that of the brothel.
1978: Nomination: Best Adapted Score

PRETTY BOY FLOYD
1960, 96 mins, US
D: Herbert J. Leder **A:** John Ericson, Barry Newman, Joan Harvey, Carl York, Phil Kenneally (Le-Sac)

This is a grim, almost sadistic reworking of the tale of the Oklahoma farm boy who won fame and ill fortune in the early 1930s. It points a glib moral (crime does not pay) without ever presenting anything more than a few superficial reasons for the phenomenon that Pretty Boy Floyd represented. Script says Floyd had a bad temper and was ignorant. Period. John Ericson does a good job in the role and is backed by a competent group of New York actors, few of whom have been on the screen before.

PRETTY IN PINK
1986, 96 mins, US ⓥ ⊙
D: Howard Deutch **A:** Molly Ringwald, Harry Dean Stanton, Jon Cryer, Andrew McCarthy, Annie Potts, James Spader (Paramount)

Rather intelligent (if not terribly original) look at adolescent insecurities. Molly Ringwald is the proverbial pretty girl from the wrong side of the tracks, called to a motherless life with down-on-his-luck dad (Harry Dean Stanton) and the misfortune to have to attend high school where the rich kids lord it over the poor. That's enough to make any young lady insecure, even before the wealthy nice guy (Andrew McCarthy) asks her to the senior prom.

PRETTY MAIDS ALL IN A ROW
1971, 95 mins, US
D: Roger Vadim **A:** Rock Hudson, Angie Dickinson, Telly Savalas, John David Carson, Roddy McDowall, Keenan Wynn (M-G-M)

Roger Vadim's first US-made film is apparently intended as a sort of genteel black murder-sex comedy. Rock Hudson stars as a married high-school guidance counselor who gets to know his girl students in the academic and biblical sense, and eventually has to kill several to keep them quiet. Whatever substance was in the original or screen concept has been plowed under, leaving only superficial, one-joke results.

PRETTY POISON
1968, 89 mins, US ⓥ
D: Noel Black **A:** Anthony Perkins, Tuesday Weld, Beverly Garland, John Randolph, Dick O'Neill (20th Century-Fox)

An attempt at low-key psychological terror. Anthony Perkins is a disobedient parolee from confinement for arson-murder. Main body of the story, all shot on location in Massachusetts, concerns his playacting and sexual playing with Weld, restless daughter of the widowed Beverly Garland. From an innocent-looking teenager, Weld progresses to a cold, pathological killer and betrayor.

PRETTY POLLY
(US: A MATTER OF INNOCENCE)
1967, 102 mins, UK
D: Guy Green **A:** Hayley Mills, Trevor Howard, Shashi Kapoor, Brenda de Banzie, Dick Patterson (Universal)

Hayley Mills (as Polly) goes on vacation with a rich, disagreeable aunt to Singapore. Frumpish, bespectacled, and lumpily dressed, Polly is encouraged by an Indian acting as guide and helpmate to have her hair done, exchange her glasses for contact lenses, and indulge in a riot of makeup. She emerges as a siren. The script goes all out for sentiment, and, on its undemanding level, achieves it.

PRETTY WOMAN
1990, 117 mins, US ⓥ ⊙
D: Garry Marshall **A:** Richard Gere, Julia Roberts, Ralph Bellamy, Jason Alexander, Laura San Giacomo, Hector Elizondo (Touchstone)

Formula screenplay owes plenty to

Pygmalion, Cinderella, and *The Owl and the Pussycat* in limning a fairy tale of a prostitute with a heart of gold who mellows a stuffy businessman. Corporate raider Richard Gere is unconvincingly thrown together with streetwalker Julia Roberts when he seeks directions to Beverly Hills. Seducing this reluctant john, she's improbably hired by Gere to spend the week with him as escort since he's split up with his girlfriend. Film blossoms along with Roberts, when she embarks on a massively entertaining shopping adventure on Rodeo Drive. Roberts handles the transition from coarse and gawky to glamorous with aplomb.
1990: Nomination: Best Actress (Julia Roberts)

PRICK UP YOUR EARS
1987, 108 mins, UK Ⓥ ⊙
D: Stephen Frears **A:** Gary Oldman, Alfred Molina, Vanessa Redgrave, Wallace Shawn, Julie Walters, Frances Barber (Civilhand/Zenith)

Though selling itself as a biography of controversial young British playwright Joe Orton, who was murdered in 1967, *Prick Up Your Ears* actually says very little about Orton the author, but deals almost totally with his relationship with Kenneth Halliwell, his lover and bludgeon killer. Gary Oldman is excellent as Orton, right down to remarkable resemblance, while Alfred Molina creates both an amusing and tormented Halliwell. Vanessa Redgrave takes top honors, though, as a compassionate and benign agent.

PRIDE AND PREJUDICE
1940, 117 mins, US Ⓥ
D: Robert Z. Leonard **A:** Greer Garson, Laurence Olivier, Mary Boland, Edna May Oliver, Edmund Gwenn, Maureen O'Sullivan (M-G-M)

M-G-M reaches into the remote corners of the library bookshelf for this old-time novel about English society and the vicissitudes of a British mother faced with the task of marrying off five daughters in a limited market. *Pride and Prejudice* was written by Jane Austen in 1793. As a film it possesses little of general interest, except as a co starring vehicle for Greer Garson and Laurence Olivier. Elizabeth Bennet (Garson), eldest of the eligible sisters, is trimmed to fit into a yarn about a family, rather than about an unusual and courageous girl. Olivier appears very unhappy in the role of Darcy, rich young bachelor, who is first spurned and then

forgiven for his boorishness, conceit, and bad manners.
1940: Best B&W Interior Decoration

PRIDE AND THE PASSION, THE
1957, 132 mins, US Ⓥ
D: Stanley Kramer **A:** Cary Grant, Frank Sinatra, Sophia Loren, Theodore Bikel (United Artists)

Powerful production about the Spanish "citizens' army" that went to battle against the French in 1810. It is the story of the band of guerrillas who come upon an oversized cannon that is abandoned by the retreating Spanish Army. All things revolve around the huge weapon; it becomes symbolic of the spirit and courage of the Spanish patriots and their leader (Frank Sinatra). Their ally is Cary Grant, a British naval officer assigned to retrieve the gun for use against Napoleon's forces. Sophia Loren is Sinatra's sultry and inflammable mistress with beaucoup accent on the décolletage.

PRIDE OF THE MARINES
(US/UK: FOREVER IN LOVE)
1945, 119 mins, US
D: Delmer Daves **A:** John Garfield, Eleanor Parker, Dane Clark, Ann Doran, Rosemary DeCamp (Warner)

The simple story of Al Schmid, real-life marine hero of Guadalcanal, is a heart-tugging, sentimentally heroic tale. John Garfield, as the brittle Schmid, ex-machinist now marine hero, albeit blinded, gives a vividly histrionic performance. He is buoyed plenty by Dane Clark and Anthony Caruso, with Eleanor Parker as the No. 1 femme.
1945: Nomination: Best Screenplay

PRIDE OF THE YANKEES, THE
1942, 120 mins, US Ⓥ ⊙
D: Sam Wood **A:** Gary Cooper, Teresa Wright, Babe Ruth, Walter Brennan, Dan Duryea (RKO/Goldwyn)

Stirring epitaph on Lou Gehrig. For baseball and nonbaseball fan alike, this sentimental, romantic saga of the NY kid who rose to the baseball heights and later met such a tragic end is well worth seeing. Gary Cooper makes his Gehrig look and sound believable. He's depicted for what he was, a quiet, plodding personality who strived for and achieved perfection in his profession.
1942: Best Editing
Nominations: Best Picture, Actor (Gary Cooper), Actress (Teresa Wright), Original Story, Screenplay, B&W Cinematog-

raphy, B&W Art Direction, Scoring of a Dramatic Picture, Sound, Special Effects

PRIEST
1995, 105 mins, UK ⊚
D: Antonia Bird **A:** Linus Roache, Tom Wilkinson, Cathy Tyson, James Ellis, Robert Carlyle (BBC)

An absolutely riveting slice-of-life drama. Father Greg (Linus Roache), a young priest brimming with lofty ideals, is in for a rude shock when he arrives in a tough, inner-city Liverpool parish. There's his colleague Father Matthew (Tom Wilkinson), openly breaking his vows of celibacy and living with a woman. The young priest's naive sense of right and wrong soon begins to come apart at the seams. One night, he heads out to a local gay bar. Roache will turn heads with his intense performance in a difficult role, and the rest of the cast get the job done with gritty flair. Liverpool writer Jimmy McGovern's script is refreshingly down-to-earth, and it's his willingness to generate laughs from even the direst situations that makes the pic so accessible.

PRIEST OF LOVE
1981, 125 mins, UK ⊚
D: Christopher Miles **A:** Ian McKellen, Janet Suzman, Ava Gardner, Penelope Keith, Jorge Rivero, John Gielgud (Milesian)

An impressively mounted and acted biopic dealing with the later years in the life of author D. H. Lawrence opens in 1924 with Lawrence (Ian McKellen); wife, Frieda (Janet Suzman), and their friend Dorothy Brett (Penelope Keith) enroute to Taos, New Mexico, for a self-imposed exile. Key scenes involve the fearless duo pushing relentlessly for the truth in a sexual manifesto in literature and tasteful scenes indicating his bisexuality and relentless selfishness in inviting Dorothy to bed and then spurning her suddenly. McKellen gives a bravura performance, all the more remarkable for its avoidance of easy empathy.

PRIMAL FEAR
1996, 129 mins, US ⊚ ⊙
D: Gregory Hoblit **A:** Richard Gere, Laura Linney, John Mahoney, Alfre Woodard, Frances McDormand, Edward Norton (Paramount)

A densely plotted, talky murder-case drama with some well-placed twists, crammed with critical insights into the complicity, hypocrisy, and compromises of big-city ruling elites and the selfishly misguided motives of celebrity attorneys, slickly produced film has plenty to say, but does so a bit insistently and obviously. Richard Gere plays Martin Vail, a hot-shot Chicago lawyer who used to work for the state. When the popular archbishop of Chicago is gruesomely butchered in his bedroom, and one of his altar boys, Aaron (Edward Norton), a shy, former street kid, is instantly picked up fleeing, blood soaked, from the scene, Vail volunteers to represent him.

PRIMARY COLORS
1998, 143 mins, US ⊚ ⊙ ▭
D: Mike Nichols **A:** John Travolta, Emma Thompson, Billy Bob Thornton, Kathy Bates, Adrian Lester, Maura Tierney (Universal/Mutual)

Frequently funny, wonderfully performed and gratifyingly blunt in its assessment of what it takes to get to the top in modern American politics, pic also lacks something crucial at its center that prevents it from being an entirely credible portrait of the first Clinton presidential campaign. Opening scenes are near-brilliant in their precise focus and nuanced layering. Gov. Jack Stanton (John Travolta), from an unspecified southern state, convinces the skeptical Henry Burton (Adrian Lester) to become his deputy campaign manager. Invaluable to Stanton are his attractive and bracingly frank wife, Susan (Emma Thompson), and his close adviser Richard Jemmons (Billy Bob Thornton), who bluntly identifies his boss's Achilles' heel: "The woman thing, that's the killer." Director Mike Nichols reinforces his central theme in varied and subtle ways. But because Travolta so uncannily impersonates the real president, one is also forcibly reminded of what is missing from his characterization—intellectual distinction, the Rhodes Scholar side to the man.

PRIME CUT
1972, 86 mins, US ⊚ ▭
D: Michael Ritchie **A:** Lee Marvin, Gene Hackman, Angel Tompkins, Gregory Walcott, Sissy Spacek (Cinema Center)

Another contemporary underworld bloodletting, which is drawn, quartered, and ground according to an overused recipe for hash. Lee Marvin and Gene Hackman provide the dressing along with the scenery of Calgary. Writer Robert Dillon sends collection-agent Marvin to Eddie Egan, a Chi gangster who no longer is get-

ting his cut from Hackman, a Kansas cattle
king who also deals in dope and girls,
among whom are Sissy Spacek and Janit
Baldwin.

PRIME OF MISS JEAN BRODIE, THE
1969, 116 mins, UK ⊛
D: Ronald Neame A: Maggie Smith, Rob-
ert Stephens, Pamela Franklin, Gordon
Jackson, Celia Johnson (20th Century-
Fox)

The story, set in 1930s Edinburgh,
treats in a tenderly savage way the decline
of an age-resisting schoolmarm who lives
too vicariously through a select group of
prodigy-stooges. The telling involves elements of warm humor, biting sarcasm,
pity, contempt, betrayal, and despair.
Smith's performance is a triumph.
1969: Best Actress (Maggie Smith)
Nomination: Best Song (''Jean'')

PRINCE AND THE PAUPER, THE
1937, 115 mins, US ⊛
D: William Keighley A: Errol Flynn,
Claude Rains, Henry Stephenson, Billy
Mauch, Bobby Mauch (Warner)

Of all his stories, Mark Twain loved
best *The Prince and the Pauper*. Produced
with sincerity and lavishness, this is a costume picture minus any romance whatsoever. In this film are the Mauch twins. It's
the story of the Tudor prince who exchanges places with a beggar boy, and regains his throne on Coronation Day
through the heroism of a dashing soldier
of fortune. The Mauch boys play their
contrasting parts with earnestness if not
too much skill.

PRINCE AND THE PAUPER, THE (US: CROSSED SWORDS)
1977, 121 mins, UK ⊛ .
D: Richard Fleischer A: Oliver Reed, Raquel Welch, Mark Lester, Ernest Borgnine, George C. Scott, Rex Harrison
(Salkind)

Some of the irony and wit of Mark
Twain's original fable about an English
prince's switch with his poor lookalike has
been lost or subdued, but this edition still
makes for satisfactory entertainment. Mark
Lester as the prince trades identities with
Lester the pauper and is then launched into
an odyssey around medieval England,
finding a land of wretched poor and persecuted. As the pauper, meantime, he
breathes a refreshing humanity into the
court of ruthless King Henry.

PRINCE AND THE SHOWGIRL, THE
1957, 117 mins, US ⊛
D: Laurence Olivier A: Marilyn Monroe,
Laurence Olivier, Sybil Thorndike, Richard Wattis, Jeremy Spenser (Monroe/War-
ner)

A generally pleasant comedy, but the
pace is leisurely. The story takes place in
London in 1911 at the time of the coronation of King George V. Laurence Olivier and his entourage come to London for
the ceremonies. The regent's roving eye
alights on Monroe and the British Foreign
Office, apprehensive of the delicate balance of power in the Balkan area, makes
a determined effort to give the regent what
he wants. Olivier's performance is flawless. The part of the seemingly naive
showgirl is just right for Monroe; she
shows a real sense of comedy and can
command a laugh with her walk or with
an expression.

PRINCE JACK
1984, 100 mins, US ⊛
D: Bert Lovitt A: Robert Hogan, James F.
Kelly, Kenneth Mars, Lloyd Nolan, Cameron Mitchell (LMF)

An ambiguous little indie mock documentary about key events and private encounters during the Kennedy years. The
ambiguity lies in writer-director Bert Lovitt's wavering between depicting Jack
Kennedy as a tough wheeler-dealer and a
politician of the grandest vision. Toward
the end, the Cuban missile crisis is solved
with Martin Luther King as a go-between.
The only thoroughly likable and almost
all-around popular guy in this feature,
King is played with cool and quiet charm
by Robert Guillaume.

PRINCE OF DARKNESS
1987, 101 mins, US ⊛ ⊙ ▭
D: John Carpenter A: Donald Pleasence,
Jameson Parker, Victor Wong, Lisa
Blount, Dennis Dun (Alive/Universal)

The great Satan doesn't just reside in
man's heart of darkness. Instead he lives
in an opposite dimension, and manifests
himself in this world in . . . bugs. That's
about the extent of the horror that John
Carpenter conjures up. Carpenter spends
so much time turning the screws on the
next scare that he completely forsakes his
actors, who are already stranded with a
shoddy script.

PRINCE OF EGYPT, THE
1998, 97 mins, US Ⓥ ⊙
D: Brenda Chapman, Steve Hickner, Simon Wells (DreamWorks)

Far more than a cartoon rendering of a much-beloved Bible story, *The Prince of Egypt* proves to be an outstanding artistic achievement. Rich in historic and character detail and full of eye-popping tableaux, this new spin on the Moses saga admirably refuses to play down to little ones—there are no talking camels. Like an abbreviated, considerably less vulgar version of the story Cecil B. DeMille filmed twice, pic opens masterfully with an eight-minute musical prologue establishing the majesty and ruthlessness of ancient Egypt. Pharaoh (Patrick Stewart) reminds Rameses (Ralph Fiennes) of his duties as divine successor, and Moses (Val Kilmer), after a chance meeting with his slave sister, Miriam (Sandra Bullock), begins to question his own lineage. The burning bush and parting of the Red Sea don't disappoint. Even more impressive is the plague-and-pestilence sequence. At 97 minutes, pic is longer than most animated features, but darn-near brisk next to DeMille's nearly four-hour extravaganza.

PRINCE OF FOXES
1949, 107 mins, US Ⓥ
D: Henry King **A:** Tyrone Power, Orson Welles, Wanda Hendrix, Everett Sloane, Katina Paxinou (20th Century-Fox)

Fictional incident in the history of the Italian Renaissance general Cesare Borgia too often is slow and plodding in its exposition and execution. The episode, despite its 16th-century background, has been conceived and executed in true Capone and Chicago tradition. As the murderous Cesare, Orson Welles is alternately glowering, reposing, and diabolical. Tyrone Power plays Orsini, who assumes the mantle of nobility to achieve social stature and ultimately bests Borgia.
1949: Nominations: Best B&W Cinematography, B&W Costume Design

PRINCE OF PLAYERS
1955, 102 mins, US ▭
D: Philip Dunne **A:** Richard Burton, Maggie McNamara, John Derek, Raymond Massey, Charles Bickford (20th Century-Fox)

Pic tells a powerfully dramatic story of a great American actor of the past—Edwin Booth—and weaves into its narrative also the tragic tale of Booth's brother, John Wilkes, who gained fame and infamy by assassinating Lincoln. There are excerpts, staged with skill and acted masterfully, from *Richard III, Romeo and Juliet, Hamlet* and *King Lear*. In the part of Booth, Richard Burton onstage and off etches a portrayal that stands out with its fire and strength.

PRINCE OF THE CITY
1981, 167 mins, US Ⓥ ⊙
D: Sidney Lumet **A:** Treat Williams, Jerry Orbach, Bob Balaban, Lindsay Crouse, James Tolkan (Warner/Orion)

Concentrated, unrelievedly serious, and cerebrally involving film, exhaustively detailing the true-life saga of a Gotham detective who turned Justice Department informer to eke out widespread corruption in his special investigating unit during the 1960s. Treat Williams is outstanding as the young gung-ho cop who is courted by federal investigators and finds himself on a conscience-wracking approach-avoidance track that finally leads him to accept the informant role.
1981: Nomination: Best Adapted Screenplay

PRINCE OF TIDES, THE
1991, 132 mins, US Ⓥ ⊙
D: Barbra Streisand **A:** Nick Nolte, Barbra Streisand, Blythe Danner, Kate Nelligan, Jeroen Krabbe, Melinda Dillon (Columbia/Barwood-Longfellow)

A deeply moving exploration of the tangled emotions of a dysfunctional Southern family, this lovingly crafted (though unevenly scripted) film centers on Nick Nolte's performance of a lifetime. Bringing her usual strengths of character to her role as Nolte's psychiatrist/lover, Barbra Streisand marks every frame with the intensity and care of a filmmaker committed to heartfelt, unashamed emotional involvement with her characters.
1991: Nominations: Best Picture, Actor (Nick Nolte), Supp. Actress (Kate Nelligan), Adapted Screenplay, Cinematography, Original Score, Art Direction

PRINCESS AND THE PIRATE, THE
1944, 92 mins, US Ⓥ ⊙
D: David Butler **A:** Bob Hope, Virginia Mayo, Walter Brennan, Walter Slezak, Victor McLaglen, Hugo Haas (RKO/Goldwyn)

Virginia Mayo is the princess, on the lam because she loves a commoner, and Victor McLaglen is the buccaneer of another century who steers his course to capture the beautiful princess. Bob Hope is cast as the 18th-century small-timer who does a protean act—"The Great Sylvester, Man of Seven Faces"—and is admittedly a coward. He wants nought of pirates, whereas the beauteous princess, who is also brave in the face of direst danger, bolsters him throughout.

PRINCESS BRIDE, THE
1987, 98 mins, US Ⓥ ⊙
D: Rob Reiner A: Cary Elwes, Mandy Patinkin, Chris Sarandon, Christopher Guest, Robin Wright, Peter Falk (Act III/20th Century-Fox)

Postmodern fairy tale that challenges and affirms the conventions of a genre that may not be flexible enough to support such horseplay. It also doesn't help that Cary Elwes and Robin Wright as the loving couple are nearly comatose and inspire little passion from each other, or the audience. Mandy Patinkin especially is a joy to watch and the film comes to life when his longhaired, scruffy cavalier is on screen.
1987: Nomination: Best Song ("Storybook Love")

PRINCESS CARABOO
1994, 96 mins, US/UK Ⓥ
D: Michael Austin A: Phoebe Cates, Jim Broadbent, Wendy Hughes, Kevin Kline, John Lithgow, Stephen Rea (Beacon/Longfellow/Artisan)

Based on a true story, the romantic comedy about a Pacific island princess in 1817 England who may not be for real could be considered Merchant Ivory Lite. The great costumes and sets are more substantial than the plot and characters. Princess Caraboo (Phoebe Cates) shows up in a country village unable to speak or write English, but slowly conveys a story of her kidnapping from a royal household and her swimming for safety from a pirate ship. Gutch (Stephen Rea), a local reporter, is suspicious of the princess even as he finds himself falling in love.

PRINCESS O'ROURKE
1943, 92 mins, US
D: Norman Krasna A: Olivia de Havilland, Robert Cummings, Charles Coburn, Jack Carson, Jane Wyman (Warner)

A spritely, effervescing, and laugh-explosive comedy-romance. Norman Krasna provides numerous humorous and novel twists to the tale of an American who falls in love with a girl after a whirlwind romance, and then discovers she's a refugee princess of European royalty. After approval for marriage has been given to cement relations of the two countries, the boy balks at renouncing his American citizenship. Olivia de Havilland shines brightly as the girl, with Robert Cummings getting equal prominence for excellent portrayal of the airline pilot.

PRINCE VALIANT
1954, 100 mins, US Ⓥ ▱
D: Henry Hathaway A: James Mason, Janet Leigh, Robert Wagner, Debra Paget, Sterling Hayden, Victor McLaglen (20th Century-Fox)

The cartoon strip hero comes to the screen as a good offering for fans who dote on the fanciful derring-do of the Arthurian period. Heading the star list is James Mason, who plays Sir Brack, pretender to King Arthur's throne. His dirty work is excellent, whether thinking up ambushes for Robert Wagner, in the title role, or engaging the young hero in joust or broadsword combat. The way Wagner and Mason have at each other in the climaxing duel puts a top-notch action capper on the tale.

PRISON
1988, 102 mins, US Ⓥ ⊙
D: Renny Harlin A: Lane Smith, Viggo Mortensen, Chelsea Field, Andre De Shields, Lincoln Kilpatrick (Empire)

Rough penal pic with its special-effects-laden horror story. In 1964 guard Ethan Sharpe (Lane Smith) watched an innocent man fry in the electric chair. Sharpe, now a warden, is appointed to the prison's helm despite recurrent nightmares brought on by a guilty conscience. The wronged convict's evil spirit is mad enough to eliminate a few of the new guards and inmates.

PRISONER, THE
1955, 94 mins, UK Ⓥ
D: Peter Glenville A: Alec Guinness, Jack Hawkins, Wilfrid Lawson, Jeannette Sterke, Ronald Lewis (Columbia)

Closely following the Bridget Boland play, this British filmization retains the essentials of this stark and dramatic narrative with Alec Guinness repeating his original role of the cardinal held on a phony charge of treason. The flawless performance by Guinness is matched by a superb portrayal by Jack Hawkins. But both of these stars find their equal in Wilfrid Lawson's interpretation of the jailor.

PRISONER OF SECOND AVENUE, THE

1974, 98 mins, US ⊗ ▭

D: Melvin Frank **A:** Jack Lemmon, Anne Bancroft, Gene Saks, Elizabeth Wilson, Florence Stanley (Warner)

Neil Simon's play *The Prisoner of Second Avenue* has Jack Lemmon and Anne Bancroft as a harried urban couple. The film is more of a drama with comedy, for the personal problems as well as the environmental challenges aren't really funny, and even some of the humor is forced and strident. Atop the couple's problems in their apartment comes Lemmon's axing after many years on the job.

PRISONER OF SHARK ISLAND, THE

1936, 95 mins, US ⊗

D: John Ford **A:** Warner Baxter, Gloria Stuart, Claude Gillingwater, Arthur Byron, Harry Carey (20th Century-Fox)

Warner Baxter as Dr. Samuel A. Mudd, "America's Jean Valjean" of the post–Civil War hysteria, turns in a capital performance as the titular prisoner of "America's Devil's Island." The saga of Dr. Mudd is founded on fact. Baxter's woes start when he unknowingly sets the broken leg of John Wilkes Booth, Lincoln's assassin. Accused of conspiracy in the crime, he is court-martialed and, of eight codefendants, three are hung and Dr. Mudd is among those committed to Shark Island for life. John Carradine stands out as a new face among especially sinister heavies, a highly effective villain.

PRISONER OF ZENDA, THE

1922, 130 mins, US ⊗

D: Rex Ingram **A:** Lewis Stone, Alice Terry, Robert Edeson, Stuart Holmes, Barbara La Marr (Metro)

To say that Rex Ingram and a remarkably good company of screen players have made the very utmost of the possibilities of Anthony Hope's novel about sums up this venture. It is the kind of romance that never stales—fresh, genuine, simple, and wholesome. Another bit of finesse is the choice of the hero and heroine, in Lewis Stone, who makes no pretense to Apollo-like beauty, and Alice Terry who makes a Princess Flavia of surpassing blond loveliness in her regal robes.

PRISONER OF ZENDA, THE

1937, 100 mins, US ⊗

D: John Cromwell **A:** Ronald Colman, Madeleine Carroll, Douglas Fairbanks Jr., Mary Astor, David Niven, Raymond Massey (Selznick/United Artists)

Hokum of the 24-carat variety; a piece of sheer romantic nonsense about a mythical European kingdom; a struggle for possession of a throne between a dissolute true heir and an ambitious stepbrother with larcenous inclinations; a lovely blond princess; a swashbuckling duke who bends with the political wind; and a young Englishman, on his annual outing, who is persuaded to impersonate the king. It's a close race between Colman and Fairbanks Jr. for top acting honors. Best femme part is the scheming Antoinette, which Mary Astor is inclined to underplay.

1937: Nomination: Best Art Direction, Score

PRISONER OF ZENDA, THE

1952, 100 mins, US ⊗

D: Richard Thorpe **A:** Stewart Granger, Deborah Kerr, James Mason, Louis Calhern, Jane Greer, Lewis Stone (M-G-M)

Fanciers of costumed swashbucklers will find this remake a likable version. This time it wears Technicolor dress. Stewart Granger, dueling as the Englishman and the king he impersonates, gives the roles the proper amount of dashing heroics. Opposite him is Deborah Kerr, the lovely princess, and her looks and ability to wear period gowns are just what the part requires. James Mason makes a rather likable heavy.

PRIVATE AFFAIRS OF BEL AMI, THE

1947, 110 mins, US ⊗

D: Albert Lewin **A:** George Sanders, Angela Lansbury, Ann Dvorak, Frances Dee, John Carradine (Loew-Lewin)

A scrubbed-face version of the complete scoundrel depicted in Guy de Maupassant's novel. The title character pays for his sins by being killed in a duel that he brought on himself, in strict compliance with the Production Code's "crime doesn't pay" edict. Prosties, who had a feature part in the story, emerge as dancers of questionable character. Entire tempo of the story is slow paced. Director Albert Lewin's script builds up little sympathy for George Sanders, the Bel Ami of the piece, who climbs to the top of Paris social and political circles in the 1880s over the broken hearts of five women. Sanders plays it with the correct hammy touch, emoting with de Maupassant epigrams for sock effect. Angela Lansbury is beauteous and competent as the young widow with whom he's probably in love all the time.

PRIVATE BENJAMIN
1980, 109 mins, US ⊗ ⊙
D: Howard Zieff **A:** Goldie Hawn, Eileen Brennan, Armand Assante, Sam Wanamaker, Harry Dean Stanton, Robert Webber (Warner/Meyers-Shyler-Miller)

Goldie Hawn's venture in producing her own film is actually a double feature—one is a frequently funny tale of an innocent who is conned into joining the US Army and her adventures therein; the other deals with the same innocent's personality problems as a Jewish princess with only an intermittent chuckle to help out. The star's not so gifted that she can carry a heavy load of indifferent material on her own two little shoulders, without considerable sagging.
1980: Nominations: Best Actress (Goldie Hawn), Supp. Actress (Eileen Brennan), Original Screenplay

PRIVATE FILES OF J. EDGAR HOOVER, THE
1977, 112 mins, US ⊗
D: Larry Cohen **A:** Broderick Crawford, Jose Ferrer, Michael Parks, Ronee Blakely, Rip Torn, Celeste Holm (Larco)

According to Larry Cohen, who wrote, produced, and directed this look at America's top cop, J. Edgar Hoover was a public relations gimmick. As a vindictive, puritanical paranoid he shipped agents off to Knoxville for reading *Playboy* magazine. Privately, he was a mama's boy and a homosexual who got his jollies by sitting in the dark with a bottle of bourbon and a tape recorder playing the sounds of a powerful government official's hotel liaisons. As Hoover, the jowly Crawford turns in a fine performance. However, the remainder of the performances, starting with Michael Parks's Robert Kennedy, are grotesque attempts to mimic well-known public officials.

PRIVATE FUNCTION, A
1984, 93 mins, UK ⊗
D: Malcolm Mowbray **A:** Michael Palin, Maggie Smith, Liz Smith, Denholm Elliott, Richard Griffiths (HandMade)

Pic is set in 1947, at a time of national rejoicing over a royal wedding and hardship caused by food rationing. Plot evolves out of a plan hatched by a group of town notables to fatten up a secret pig for festive devouring on the wedding night. Central characters are a husband and wife team played by Maggie Smith and Michael Palin. She's a bullying wife anxious to reach the social highspots in the Yorkshire village where he works as a foot doctor.

PRIVATE LESSONS
1981, 87 mins, US ⊗ ⊙
D: Alan Myerson, [James Fargo] **A:** Sylvia Kristel, Howard Hesseman, Ron Foster, Eric Brown, Pamela Bryant, Ed Begley Jr. (Jensen Farley)

A novelty comedy limning an adolescent boy's introduction to sex via his worldly European housekeeper, picture has a sustained air of amorality quite unusual for US films. Story is set at a ritzy mansion in idyllic Arizona during summer vacation, with premise of Mr. Fillmore (Ron Foster) leaving orders that his beautiful housekeeper (Sylvia Kristel) initiate his 15-year-old son, Philly (Eric Brown), to sex before he returns from a business trip. *Private Lessons* should satisfy general audiences with its diversions of frequent nudity, softcore sex, dominant rock music score, and gags.

PRIVATE LIFE OF DON JUAN, THE
1934, 89 mins, UK ⊗
D: Alexander Korda **A:** Douglas Fairbanks, Merle Oberon, Binnie Barnes, Joan Gardner, Benita Hume, Barry Mackay (London/United Artists)

Douglas Fairbanks's prime portrayal is as the antiquated knight who is finally disillusioned as the arch-heartbreaker when he must bow to his years and recognize that his amorous porch-climbing career is finis. But the film holds more than that. There are many fine lights and shadings that convey the fact that the susceptible Seville femmes, who were not loath to two-timing their senors, had glorified Don Juan into an almost mythical figure.

PRIVATE LIFE OF HELEN OF TROY, THE
1927, 87 mins, US ⊗
D: Alexander Korda **A:** Maria Corda, Lewis Stone, Ricardo Cortez, George Fawcett, Alice White (First National)

Helen is all comedy. Satirizing ancient myth in general and Helen's affairs particularly, the titles are topical, while the music is mainly based on pop dance tunes. The film kids the husband-wife complex throughout, the king, following the conquest of Troy, making a beeline for Helen's dressmaker to destroy the shop.

Meanwhile, he has been trying to go fishing since nine o'clock.

1927/28: Nomination: Best Engineering Effects

PRIVATE LIFE OF HENRY VIII, THE

1933, 96 mins, UK Ⓥ ⊙

D: Alexander Korda **A:** Charles Laughton, Binnie Barnes, Merle Oberon, Elsa Lanchester, Wendy Barrie, Robert Donat (London)

Unquestionably the perfect pick for the part, it must also be said that Charles Laughton is aided no little by the script, more generous to the character of Henry VIII than most of his biographers. The corpulent ruler is here made rather a jolly old soul and, for those who may have forgotten, it can be said that he had six wives, of whom the picture concerns itself with five. A couple are inclined to beat about the royal bush, so they thereby lose their heads for being promiscuous.

1932/33: Best Actor (Charles Laughton) **Nomination:** Best Picture

PRIVATE LIFE OF SHERLOCK HOLMES, THE

1970, 125 mins, UK Ⓥ ⊙ ▭

D: Billy Wilder **A:** Robert Stephens, Colin Blakely, Genevieve Page, Christopher Lee, Tomara Toumanova, Clive Revill (Mirisch/United Artists)

Billy Wilder's enterprise is a strange one because of its shift in directions from quite good satire to straight spy stuff. Robert Stephens is the detective consultant, the man from Baker Street who fakes a story about his being not all masculine to duck out on an assignment from a Russian ballerina. But is he really faking? Stephens plays Sherlock in rather gay fashion under Wilder's tongue-in-cheek direction. Colin Blakely is Dr. John H. Watson, a performer who plays it broad and bright. The dialogue is crisp and amusing, Wilder and I.A.L. Diamond having a way with such matters.

PRIVATE LIVES

1931, 82 mins, US

D: Sidney Franklin **A:** Norma Shearer, Robert Montgomery, Reginald Denny, Una Merkel, Jean Hersholt (M-G-M)

Sidney Franklin has followed the Noel Coward play closely. Both Norma Shearer and Robert Montgomery capably handle themselves as the divorced couple who again run away together the night of their honeymoons with their newly acquired better halves. Both having tempestuous natures, their lovemaking and quarreling is equally violent and the warfare is apt to start any time.

PRIVATE LIVES OF ELIZABETH AND ESSEX, THE

1939, 106 mins, US Ⓥ

D: Michael Curtiz **A:** Bette Davis, Errol Flynn, Olivia de Havilland, Vincent Price, Donald Crisp (Warner)

Bette Davis dominates a lavishly produced historical drama at every turn as Elizabeth, virgin queen of England. Story details the intimate May-and-December love affair of youthful Lord Essex (Errol Flynn) and matronly Queen Elizabeth. Both are headstrong and stubborn; each is ambitious to rule England.

1939: Nominations: Best Color Cinematography, Color Art Direction, Score, Sound, Special Effects

PRIVATE NAVY OF SGT. O'FARRELL, THE

1968, 92 mins, US

D: Frank Tashlin **A:** Bob Hope, Phyllis Diller, Jeffrey Hunter, Mylene Demongeot, Gina Lollobrigida, Mako (NAHO)

An okay but crudely plotted comedy set in World War II has Bob Hope as one of these stock all-knowing, all-wise paternal noncoms, herein looking out for the morale of his troops. Site is a South Pacific island, around which the war and the action have detoured. Seems a cargo ship loaded with beer has been torpedoed, and Hope fears a dip in morale unless the booze is found.

PRIVATE POTTER

1963, 89 mins, UK

D: Caspar Wrede **A:** Tom Courtenay, James Maxwell, Ralph Michael, Brewster Mason, Ronald Fraser (M-G-M)

This film is an egghead pic that doesn't quite come off. Tom Courtenay plays an inexperienced young soldier who screams in terror while tracking down a terrorist leader on a Mediterranean island. As a result, the mission misfires and a colleague is killed. The young soldier excuses himself with the plea that he saw a vision of God. Question that arises is whether he is to be court-martialed for cowardice or whether, in fact, he did have this religious experience. The young soldier's character is never clearly defined and the film eventually flounders in speculation and conjecture.

PRIVATE'S PROGRESS
1956, 102 mins, UK ⓥ
D: John Boulting **A:** Richard Attenborough, Dennis Price, Terry-Thomas, Ian Carmichael, Peter Jones, William Hartnell (Charter/British Lion)

As a lighthearted satire on British army life during the last war, *Private's Progress* has moments of sheer joy based on real authenticity. But it is not content to rest on satire alone and introduces an unreal melodramatic adventure, which robs the story of much of its charm. The basic comedy, however, derives from the depiction of the typical misfit into the army way of life. Ian Carmichael is shown as the earnest university student who interrupts his studies to join the forces. He is a lamentable failure.

PRIVATE WORLDS
1935, 84 mins, US
D: Gregory La Cava **A:** Claudette Colbert, Charles Boyer, Joan Bennett, Joel McCrea, Helen Vinson (Paramount)

Set against a morbid background, that of a mental hospital where psychiatrists Claudette Colbert, Charley Boyer, and Joel McCrea are thrown together, *Private Worlds* emphasizes the romanticism and the melodramatics. Colbert manifests her usual restraint and intelligently gets across the spirit of her own little "private world"—that of nurturing a romance with a shadow of the past, a boy who lost his life in the war. Charles Boyer's private world has been the shielding of his murderess-sister (capably played by Helen Vinson). Joel McCrea's unintentional neglect of his domestic life is similarly depicted in intelligent vein. Joan Bennett as his wife is at her dramatic best.

PRIVILEGE
1967, 103 mins, UK ⓥ
D: Peter Watkins **A:** Paul Jones, Jean Shrimpton, Mark London, William Job (Rank-Universal/World-Film/Memorial)

Privilege cannot make up its mind whether it's a crusading film for the intelligentsia or a snide with-it comedy. A coalition government encourages the violence of the act of pop idol Steve Shorter (Jones) as a means of guiding the violence of Britain's youth into controllable channels. Then, cynically, it's decided that his image must be changed and he is exploited by the Church as a kind of godlike hot gospeler. The best angles of the pic are those that turn a cynical and only too accurate searchlight on the pop music scene.

PRIZE, THE
1963, 135 mins, US ⓥ ▭
D: Mark Robson **A:** Paul Newman, Edward G. Robinson, Elke Sommer, Diane Baker, Micheline Presle (M-G-M/Roxbury)

Stockholm during Nobel week is the setting. Seven selected prizewinners convene to receive the award. The man from literature (Paul Newman) senses something amiss in the behavior and physique of the man from physics (Edward G. Robinson). *The Prize* is a suspense melodrama played for laughs. Newman tackles his task with sufficient vivacity to keep an audience concerned for his welfare and amused by his antics. Robinson achieves a persuasive degree of contrast in his dual role.

PRIZE OF ARMS, A
1962, 105 mins, UK
D: Cliff Owen **A:** Stanley Baker, Helmut Schmid, Tom Bell, Tom Adams (RLC/British Lion)

Stanley Baker plays an ex-army captain who has been cashiered. He has dreamed up a perfect plan for revenge (and to get rich), enlisting the help of Helmut Schmid, an explosives expert, and Tom Bell, a daring but edgy young man. Baker realizes that when troops are on the move abroad they have to take money with them. The trio plans to hijack the dough while the forces are preparing to go abroad at the time of the Suez crisis. Baker, Schmid, and Bell play the three leads confidently, with Baker particularly on the ball in the type of harsh tough part that he plays so often and so well.

PRIZE OF GOLD, A
1955, 96 mins, UK
D: Mark Robson **A:** Richard Widmark, Mai Zetterling, Nigel Patrick, George Cole, Donald Wolfit (Warwick/ Columbia)

Taut suspense thriller unfolds against vividly interesting Berlin-London backgrounds, detailing the hijacking of gold bullion being air transported from Berlin to London. The writing lays a good foundation for the climaxing action, switching from lightly humorous handling in the first half to tight excitement in the latter half. Mark Robson's direction projects it all strongly with the aid of the top-notch cast.

PRIZZI'S HONOR
1985, 129 mins, US ⓥ ⊙
D: John Huston **A:** Jack Nicholson, Kathleen Turner, Robert Loggia, William

Hickey, John Randolph, Anjelica Huston (ABC)

Plot centers on the tragicomedy that results when a hit man for a powerful crime family (Jack Nicholson) falls hard for a svelte blond (Kathleen Turner) who turns out to be his female counterpart in hired killings. Anjelica Huston is the black sheep of the powerful clan who maneuvers the plot in insidious ways, all of them tied to the fact that she harbors a lost love for Nicholson.

1985: Best Supp. Actress (Anjelica Huston)

Nominations: Best Picture, Director, Actor (Jack Nicholson), Supp. Actor (William Hickey), Adapted Screenplay, Costume Design, Editing

PROBLEM CHILD
1990, 81 mins, US Ⓥ ⊙

D: Dennis Dugan **A:** John Ritter, Jack Warden, Michael Oliver, Gilbert Gottfried, Amy Yasbeck (Imagine)

Unbelievable mess. John Ritter and Amy Yasbeck play a yuppie couple suckered into adopting round-faced Junior (Michael Oliver), a child repulsive enough to make nuns cheer when he's taken from their care. The major subplot has Junior becoming pen pals with a serial killer (Michael Richards). The most offensive character is Yasbeck's shrill, status-conscious wife.

PROBLEM CHILD 2
1991, 91 mins, US Ⓥ

D: Brian Levant **A:** John Ritter, Michael Oliver, Jack Warden, Laraine Newman, Amy Yasbeck, Ivyann Schwan (Universal/Imagine)

At times this poor version of a sitcom seems written by five-year-olds for five-year-olds, so much so that one suspects its script was fingerpainted. Junior (Michael Oliver) grapples with his fear of losing his adopted dad (John Ritter) by reverting to various revolting if not terribly funny habits. A second "problem child" (Ivyann Schwan) teams up with Junior to try to bring his lonely dad together with her sheepish mom (Amy Yasbeck). Oliver remains an annoying child actor who mugs constantly.

PROCES DE JEANNE D'ARC (US: THE TRIAL OF JOAN OF ARC)
1962, 65 mins, France

D: Robert Bresson **A:** Florence Carrez, Jean-Claude Fourneau, Marc Jacquier,

Roger Honorat, Jean Gillibert (Delahaie)

Joan of Arc is judged again in this austere version of the trial and burning of the 15th-century French saint. Director-author Robert Bresson has relied on trial and rehabilitation transcripts. Vehicle relies on the play of questions and answers, done mainly in medium shots, to achieve an insight into Joan of Arc (Florence Carrez) character. Using nonactors, there are no false dramatics.

PRODIGAL, THE
1955, 117 mins, US Ⓥ ⊙ ▱

D: Richard Thorpe **A:** Lana Turner, Edmund Purdom, Louis Calhern, Audrey Dalton, Neville Brand, Taina Elg (M-G-M)

Treatment of the parable of the Prodigal Son (from Luke XV) is a large-scale spectacle. End result, however, is only fair entertainment. With rather empty characters to portray, the performances by Lana Turner, as the high priestess; Edmund Purdom, the prodigal; Louis Calhern, the high priest of Baal; and most of the others in the huge cast are hollow and generally uninteresting. Almost the only note of character warmth is to be found in the romance between the mute runaway slave (James Mitchell) and the high priestess slave (Taina Elg).

PRODUCERS, THE
1968, 100 mins, US Ⓥ ⊙

D: Mel Brooks **A:** Zero Mostel, Gene Wilder, Kenneth Mars, Estelle Winwood, Dick Shawn (Embassy)

Mel Brooks has turned a funny idea into a slapstick film, thanks to the performers, particularly Zero Mostel. Playing a Broadway producer of flops who survives (barely) by suckering little old ladies, he teams with an emotionally retarded accountant (Gene Wilder). By selling 25,000 percent of production, they figure to be rich when it flops. For the twist, the musical comedy *Springtime for Hitler,* penned by a shell-shocked Nazi, is a smash.

1968: Best Original Story & Screenplay

Nomination: Best Supp. Actor (Gene Wilder)

PROFESSIONAL, THE
See: Leon

PROFESSIONALS, THE
1966, 116 mins, US Ⓥ ⊙ ▱

D: Richard Brooks **A:** Burt Lancaster, Lee Marvin, Robert Ryan, Jack Palance, Claudia Cardinale, Ralph Bellamy (Columbia)

Well-made actioner, set in 1917 on the Mexican-US border, depicts the strategy of Lee Marvin and cohorts, sent by gringo Ralph Bellamy into the political turmoil of Mexico to rescue his missing wife, Claudia Cardinale, known to be secreted in the brigand village of Jack Palance. Lancaster is the most dynamic of the crew, as a light-hearted but two-fisted fighter.

1966: Nominations: Best Director, Adapted Screenplay, Color Cinematography

PROGRAM, THE
PROJECTED MAN, THE
1967, 77 mins, UK ⊡

D: Ian Curteis **A:** Mary Peach, Bryant Haliday, Norman Wooland, Ronald Allen, Derek Farr (MLC/Compton)

Professor Steiner (Bryant Haliday), whose experiments involve converting objects to energy and re-forming them elsewhere, is told the project will be dismantled. Anxious to continue, he attempts to project himself into a visiting scientist's living room but an accident causes him to miss target, become facially disfigured and possessed with an electrical charge that is fatal on contact. Happily, the characters do not fall prey to the usual clichés. Deformed scientist Steiner is "angry" but not "insane," and retains his human personality, killing only from fear or sense of justice.

PROJECT X
1987, 108 mins, US Ⓥ ◉

D: Jonathan Kaplan **A:** Matthew Broderick, Helen Hunt, Bill Sadler, Johnny Ray McGhee, Jonathan Stark (20th Century-Fox)

The ultimate film for monkey lovers. Matthew Broderick plays a wayward air force pilot sent to play zookeeper at the Strategic Weapons Research Center, where intelligent chimps are trained for top secret and, it transpires, fatal experiments involving the effects of radiation. Brightest of the little hairy ones is Virgil. When Virgil is put on the line, Broderick feels compelled to act and end the seemingly needless experiments. The director has covered the monkeys' actions with loving care and skillful attention, which cannot have been easy.

PROMISE, THE
(AKA: FACE OF A STRANGER)
1979, 97 mins, US Ⓥ ⊡

D: Gilbert Cates **A:** Kathleen Quinlan, Stephen Collins, Beatrice Straight, Laurence Luckin, Michael O'Hare (Universal)

Romantic melodrama has to do with a buried necklace and the promise of undying love and faith in each other made by a young architectural student and a girl student. The girl is severely injured in an auto accident and the boy is unconscious for some time, during which his mother persuades the girl to undergo some very expensive plastic surgery and seek a new life elsewhere. She tells her son the girl is dead.

1979: Nomination: Best Song ("I'll Never Say Goodbye")

PROMISED LAND
(AKA: YOUNG HEARTS)
1988, 100 mins, US Ⓥ ◉

D: Michael Hoffman **A:** Jason Gedrick, Kiefer Sutherland, Meg Ryan, Tracy Pollan, Googy Gress (Wildwood/Oxford)

Drama about aimless Middle American lives covers familiar, unexciting ground as it looks at four thoroughly unremarkable young people. A cattle prod would have been a useful tool on the set, as the actors show boundless earnestness and little energy except for Meg Ryan, whose role calls for her to be dangerously wild and reckless in a sexy, silly way, something she manages just fine.

PROMISE HER ANYTHING
1966, 96 mins, UK/US

D: Arthur Hiller **A:** Warren Beatty, Leslie Caron, Bob Cummings, Keenan Wynn, Hermione Gingold, Lionel Stander (Seven Arts/Stark)

Light, refreshing comedy-romance, set in Greenwich Village but filmed in England. Leslie Caron, with a precocious baby boy but no hubby, hopes to connect with her employer, child psychologist Bob Cummings who, in private life, abhors moppets. Caron's neighbor (Warren Beatty) wants her, although he is careful to conceal his profession—making mail-order nudie films.

PROMISES IN THE DARK
1979, 115 mins, US Ⓥ

D: Jerome Hellman **A:** Marsha Mason, Kathleen Beller, Ned Beatty, Susan Clark, Michael Brandon (Orion)

An admirable attempt to focus attention on the death of a young cancer victim. Major problem remains not the promises physician Marcia Mason makes to her terminally ill patient (Kathleen Beller) but the premise itself. No matter how well acted (and thesping here is superior) or mounted, a story that spends two hours watching a pretty young girl expire is just not most people's idea of a good time.

PROM NIGHT
1980, 91 mins, US ⓥ ⊙
D: Paul Lynch **A:** Leslie Nielsen, Jamie Lee Curtis, Casey Stevens, Eddie Benton (Simcom)

Borrowing shamelessly from *Carrie* and any number of gruesome exploitation pics, the film manages to score a few horrific points amid a number of sagging moments. It opens with the falling death of a 10-year-old girl brought on by unmerciful teasing on the part of four of her peers. It's six years later and prom night for the surviving kiddies and each is slated to meet an unsavory fate due to past exploits—unbeknownst to anyone.

PROMOTER, THE
See: The Card

PROOF
1991, 86 mins, Australia ⓥ
D: Jocelyn Moorhouse **A:** Hugo Weaving, Genevieve Picot, Russell Crowe, Heather Mitchell, Jeffrey Walker (House and Moorhouse)

An intriguing psychological drama is structured around the contradictory character of a blind photographer, required to rely on the information of others, and what if those people don't tell the truth? In his thirties, Martin lives alone, his only company a seeing-eye dog and Celia (Genevieve Picot), the young woman who comes to clean his house and do his shopping. She has become infatuated with Martin, but he keeps her firmly at arm's length. Enter Andy (Russell Crowe), a guileless young man. Celia decides to get at Martin through Andy.

PROPHECY
1979, 102 mins, US ⓥ ▱
D: John Frankenheimer **A:** Talia Shire, Robert Foxworth, Armand Assante, Richard Dysart, Victoria Racimo (Paramount)

A frightening monster movie that people could laugh at for generations to come, complete with your basic big scary thing, cardboard characters, and a story so stupid it's irresistible. Once again, the real villain is Careless Mankind. Only this time, it isn't Atomic Fallout that's creating giant ants and killer cockroaches but Industrial Pollution.

PROSPERO'S BOOKS
1991, 124 mins, UK/France ⓥ
D: Peter Greenaway **A:** John Gielgud, Michael Clark, Michel Blanc, Roland Josephson, Tom Bell (Allarts/Cinea/Camera/Penta)

The playwright's tale is presented basically intact, but Peter Greenaway's underlying gambit is to make Prospero (John Gielgud) the author of his own story. Through the use of exquisite calligraphy, the old man's writing is made vivid on the screen, and the device opens the way for Gielgud himself to supply the voices for many of the supporting characters. Shot entirely indoors in Amsterdam, the production is stunning from every physical point of view. Michael Nyman's score plays a major part in the effectiveness.

PROTECTOR, THE
1985, 95 mins, US ⓥ ⊙
D: James Glickenhaus **A:** Jackie Chan, Danny Aiello, Roy Chiao, Victor Arnold, Kim Bass (Golden Harvest/Warner)

Jackie Chan and Danny Aiello head for Hong Kong to track down a drug kingpin who has kidnapped the daughter of the Kingpin's estranged business partner. A furious barroom shoot-out at the outset is immediately followed by a speedboat chase in New York Harbor that rivals James Bond pictures for elaborate thrills. What also puts matters on the right track is the tongue-in-cheek humor running throughout.

PROTOCOL
1984, 96 mins, US ⓥ ⊙
D: Herbert Ross **A:** Goldie Hawn, Chris Sarandon, Richard Romanus, Andre Gregory, Gail Strickland (Warner)

Goldie Hawn's insistence on Saying Something Important takes a lot of the zip out of *Protocol,* but the light comedy still has its moments for the forgiving. Here she's a sweet, unsophisticated cocktail waitress hurdled into the unfamiliar world of Washington diplomacy and Mideast travail. Hawn's main adversary is Gail Strickland as a devious, plotting protocol officer.

PROUD ONES, THE
1956, 94 mins, US ▱
D: Robert D. Webb **A:** Robert Ryan, Virginia Mayo, Jeffrey Hunter, Robert Middleton, Walter Brennan, Arthur O'Connell (20th Century-Fox)

A credible story with excellent dramatic values, direction that sharpens them and builds suspense, and strong performances by an able cast are among the entertainment assets of this outdoor drama.

Robert Ryan, Jeffrey Hunter, and Robert Middleton are the male cast toppers. Playing a marshal who knows his business, a young man who has not yet determined where he is going, and a gambling saloon operator, respectively, the trio responds exactly right to Robert D. Webb's forceful direction. Virginia Mayo gives the pic a performance asset as the girl who loves the marshal.

PROUD REBEL, THE
1958, 100 mins, US ⓥ
D: Michael Curtiz A: Alan Ladd, Olivia de Havilland, Dean Jagger, David Ladd, Cecil Kellaway, John Carradine (Buena Vista)

Warmth of a father's love and faith, and the devotion of a boy for his dog, are the standout ingredients of this suspenseful and fast-action post–Civil War yarn. David Ladd, star's 11-year-old son, plays Alan Ladd's boy in the pic. Youngster has been shocked mute when he saw his mother killed and his home destroyed by fire, and it's Alan Ladd's dogged wandering of the land to find a doctor who can cure his son that motivates plot.

PROVIDENCE
1977, 110 mins, France ⓥ
D: Alain Resnais A: Dirk Bogarde, Ellen Burstyn, John Gielgud, David Warner, Elaine Stritch (Action/SFP)

Riveting pictorially, pic offers dense insights into the flights of imagination of a supposedly dying writer of perhaps some faddish fame. The style is impeccable as the film sashays from the novelist's feverish, drunken ramblings about his new novel, putting his family into it, and commenting on them. John Gielgud's mellifluous and impassioned delivery as the writer is extraordinary, as is Dirk Bogarde's performance as the son, a cold, internally wounded man who cannot show emotion.

PROWLER, THE
1951, 92 mins, US
D: Joseph Losey A: Van Heflin, Evelyn Keyes, John Maxwell, Katherine Warren, Emerson Treacy (Horizon/Eagle)

Combination of illicit love, murder, and premarital relations makes a bawdy, daring story. Van Heflin makes the most of an unsympathetic role, that of a cop who steals the love of a woman (Evelyn Keyes) who had called the police when she saw a prowler. Keyes also has an un-

sympathetic part, as a gal wooed and won by Heflin behind her husband's back.

PRUDENCE AND THE PILL
1968, 92 mins, UK
D: Fielder Cook A: Deborah Kerr, David Niven, Judy Geeson, David Dundas, Vickery Turner (20th Century-Fox)

Deborah Kerr and David Niven team as a couple who wind up married to others. Film is little more than a one-joke script— the secret switching of birth-control pills so that the wrong people get pregnant— and to the credit of the pic, this is not a tasteless recurring incident.

PSYCHO
1960, 109 mins, US ⓥ ⊙
D: Alfred Hitchcock A: Anthony Perkins, Janet Leigh, Vera Miles, John Gavin, Martin Balsam (Paramount)

Alfred Hitchcock is up to his clavicle in whimsicality and apparently had the time of his life in putting together *Psycho*. He's gotten in gore, in the form of a couple of graphically depicted knife murders, a story that's far-out in Freudian motivations, and occasional little amusing plot items that suggest the whole thing is not to be taken seriously. Anthony Perkins is the young man who doesn't get enough "exorcise" of that other inner being. Among the victims are Janet Leigh and Martin Balsam, as a private eye who winds up in the same swamp in which Leigh's body also is deposited.

1960: Nominations: Best Director, Supp. Actress (Janet Leigh), B&W Cinematography, B&W Art Direction

PSYCHO
1998, 109 mins, US ⓥ ⊙
D: Gus Van Sant A: Vince Vaughn, Anne Heche, Julianne Moore, Viggo Mortensen, William H. Macy, Robert Forster (Imagine/Universal)

A faithful-unto-slavish remake of the 1960 Hitchcock classic, pic contains nothing to outrage or offend partisans of the original, nor does it stand to add much to their appreciation. And as for introducing a new generation to the granddaddy of all slasher films, forget about it. This *Psycho* is a "scene by scene" restaging in which many shots of the original, especially the most famous and striking, are copied. The color reduces the dream-like mood as well as the visual rigor of Hitchcock's design. Van Sant restages the most famous scene, the shower knife-murder, with slightly more nudity and realism and at what seems like a slightly more protracted length. Vince Vaughn's awkwardness as Norman only proves the extraordinary skill and subtlety of Anthony Perkins's work for Hitchcock. Anne Heche ends up a pale, vapid, slightly vulgar shadow of Janet Leigh's brilliant, hard-edged original. Two bright spots in the cast are William H. Macy, whose Arbogast has presence, dimension and believable quirkiness, and Robert Forster, who does a surprisingly good job in the thankless role of the psychiatrist.

PSYCHO II
1983, 113 mins, US Ⓥ Ⓞ
D: Richard Franklin A: Anthony Perkins, Vera Miles, Meg Tilly, Robert Loggia, Dennis Franz (Universal/Oak Industries)

Psycho II is an impressive, 23-years-after follow-up to Alfred Hitchcock's suspense classic. New story, set 22 years later, has Norman Bates (Anthony Perkins) released from a mental institution on the petition of his psychiatrist, Dr. Raymond (Robert Loggia). Securing a job as cook's assistant at a local diner, Bates is befriended by a young waitress, Mary (Meg Tilly). A series of mysterious murders ensue, beginning with the killing of the obnoxious manager Toomey (Dennis Franz), who has turned the Bates-family business into a hot-sheets motel.

PSYCHO III
1986, 96 mins, US Ⓥ Ⓞ
D: Anthony Perkins A: Anthony Perkins, Diana Scarwid, Jeff Fahey, Roberta Maxwell, Hugh Gillin (Universal)

A few amusing little notions are stretched to the point of diminishing returns. Opening sequence is a full-fledged homage to *Vertigo* and helps set the comic, in-joke tone. Unhappy novice Diana Scarwid is all set to jump from a church bell tower but one of the nuns falls to her death instead. Scarwid flees in distress, is given a ride through the desert by aspiring musician Jeff Fahey, and where should the unlikely and unsuspecting duo wind up but the Bates Motel. Main pleasure of the picture stems from Anthony Perkins's amusing performance.

PSYCHOMANIA
1964, 90 mins, US
D: Richard L. Hilliard A: Lee Philips, Shepperd Strudwick, James Farentino, Jean Hale, Sylvia Miles (Emerson)

Low-budget, well-done shocker with a tightly knit plot and a believable surprise ending. Lee Philips does a fine acting job as the karate-expert artist who gets involved in a pair of bizarre murders. Shepperd Strudwick and James Farentino are believable as a lawyer and a tough motorcycle hood, respectively.

PSYCH-OUT
1968, 88 mins, US Ⓥ Ⓞ
D: Richard Rush A: Susan Strasberg, Dean Stockwell, Jack Nicholson, Bruce Dern, Henry Jaglom (American International)

An above-average programmer about San Francisco hippies. Thin story line is sufficient as the vehicle for a series of incidents, including drug-induced hallucinations, all directed in excellent fashion by Richard Rush. Script follows Susan Strasberg on her search for far-out brother, Bruce Dern. Dean Stockwell is a disenchanted hippie, while Jack Nicholson is a swinger tending toward a romantic interest in Strasberg.

PUBERTY BLUES
1981, 97 mins, Australia Ⓥ ▭
D: Bruce Beresford A: Nell Schofield, Jad Capelja, Geoff Rhoe, Tony Hughes, Sandy Paul (Limelight)

Leisurely, entertaining tale about a group of teenagers fumbling, fighting, and fretting their way through adolescence. Set in the middle-class suburb of one of Sydney's southern beaches, the story focuses on Debbie and Sue, two fairly average girls. When Debbie fears she is pregnant, her boyfriend, Garry, cannot cope; he seeks refuge in heroin and dies of an overdose. To offset the bleakness, the pic is laced with Debbie's witty observations and humorous interludes.

PUBLIC ACCESS
1993, 89 mins, US Ⓥ Ⓞ
D: Bryan Singer A: Ron Marquette, Dina Brooks, Burt Williams, Larry Maxwell, Charles Kavanaugh (Cinemabeam/Tokuma)

This very low-budget study of malaise lurking beneath the tranquil surface of a typical small American town bounces around some provocative ideas, but is vague about key story points, motivation, and overriding theme. Handsome, flinty, and disconcertingly creepy, Whiley Pritcher (Ron Marquette) rents a room in the sleepy community of Brewster and immediately takes airtime on the local public-access channel, where he poses the simple question "What's wrong with

Brewster?'' Polite, smiling, and affable in public, Whiley allows neither other characters nor the audience behind his steely persona.

PUBLIC ENEMY, THE
(UK: ENEMIES OF THE PUBLIC)
1931, 83 mins, US Ⓥ ⊙
D: William A. Wellman A: James Cagney, Edward Woods, Donald Cook, Joan Blondell, Jean Harlow, Beryl Mercer (Warner)

There's no lace on this picture. It's raw and brutal. It's lowbrow material given such workmanship as to make it highbrow. To square everything there's a foreword and postscript moralizing on the gangster as a menace to the public welfare. Pushing a grapefruit into the face of a moll (Mae Clarke) with whom he's fed up, socking another fellow on the chin for inducing him to spend the night with the gal while he's drunk, and spitting a mouthful of beer into the face of a speakeasy proprietor for using a rival's product are a few samples of James Cagney's deportment as Tom, a tough in modern gangster's dress.
1930/31: Nomination: Best Original Story

PUBLIC EYE, THE
1992, 98 mins, US Ⓥ ⊙
D: Howard Franklin A: Joe Pesci, Barbara Hershey, Stanley Tucci, Jerry Adler, Jared Harris (Universal)

A down-and-dirty subject gets the velvet-glove treatment. Playing a 1940s tabloid crime photographer (based on w.k. shutterbug Weegee) who yearns for respectability and a little love, Joe Pesci creates an involving character, but almost everything is muted and moody where it should be bold and brash. Pic approaches physical beauty of a Coen brothers or David Cronenberg film. Unfortunately, this is entirely counterproductive to the style that would have been appropriate for the tabloid subject matter.

PUBLIC HERO NO. 1
1935, 91 mins, US
D: J. Walter Ruben A: Lionel Barrymore, Jean Arthur, Chester Morris, Joseph Calleia, Paul Kelly, Lewis Stone (M-G-M)

Rates with the best of the G-men pictures. Legit recruit Joseph Calleia does a consummate job as the arch-menace into whose confidence the G-man has wormed himself. Action opens fast and tense on the plotting and successful execution of a prison break. It's all part of the scheme to get Sonny (Calleia) out of confinement in order that Chester Morris (pseudo-convict, and coconspirator with Calleia in the break) might ferret out the Purple Gang's retreat. That's the first indication that Morris is a fed.

I PUGNI IN TASCA
(US: FISTS IN THE POCKET)
1965, 105 mins, Italy
D: Marco Bellocchio A: Lou Castel, Paola Pitagora, Marino Mase, Liliana Gerace, Pier Luigi Troglio (Doria)

A provincial family with some money lives in a big house. Two brothers are epileptic, the mother is blind, the sister acts much more childish than her age (early 20s), and one normal, older brother runs this strange household. Director Marco Bellocchio displays expert tact in first laying out this inbred sickly family in their unrestrained daily lives. Film is photographed with sharp definition, with acting extremely well balanced to keep it from falling into the merely clinical or shocking.

PULP
1972, 95 mins, UK Ⓥ
D: Mike Hodges A: Michael Caine, Mickey Rooney, Lionel Stander, Lizabeth Scott, Nadia Cassini, Dennis Price (Three Michaels/United Artists)

A crime fictionalist (Michael Caine) reluctantly enters the reality of his own fantasies in Pulp, a reasonably entertaining piece of rococo recall, at its best as visual camp. Caine is hired by a faded screen tough guy (Mickey Rooney) to ghost his memoir, and the plot thereafter hinges on a scandal in the star's past involving elements of the local shady set. They fear Rooney means to spill the beans in his book, hence they contract his murder. Caine is naturally compelled not to turn tail but to see the mystery and danger through.

PULP FICTION
1994, 153 mins, US Ⓥ ⊙ ▭
D: Quentin Tarantino A: John Travolta, Samuel L. Jackson, Uma Thurman, Harvey Keitel, Tim Roth, Amanda Plummer (A Band Apart/Jersey)

A spectacularly entertaining piece of pop culture, pic begins in a coffee shop, with a young couple (Tim Roth, Amanda Plummer) deciding to hold up the place. Next sequence, two hit men (John Travolta, Samuel L. Jackson) bump off some kids who didn't play straight with crime

lord Marsellus (Ving Rhames). Vincent (John Travolta), as a courtesy, takes his boss's statuesque wife, Mia (a dark-haired Uma Thurman), out for an amazing outing to a giant 1950s-themed restaurant/club. An hour in, pic becomes even more audacious, as Tarantino leads the audience deeper into uncharted territory with Bruce Willis as a boxer on the run for his life. Some of the earlier characters begin to drop back into the story, and a grand design starts falling into place.
1994: Original Screenplay
Nominations: Best Picture, Director, Actor (John Travolta), Supp. Actor (Samuel L. Jackson), Supp. Actress (Uma Thurman), Film Editing

PUMPING IRON
1977, 85 mins, US ⓥ ⊙
D: George Butler, Robert Fiore **A:** Arnold Schwarzenegger, Lou Ferrigno, Matty Ferrigno, Ken Waller, Franco Columbu (Cinema 5)

The most fascinating aspect of this film is the dedicated training that turns average-built young men (frequently they refer to themselves as weaklings in their early youth) into superbly created physical edifices. The film, while spotlighting Arnold Schwarzenegger, also deals with other competitors, preparing for the Mr. Universe and Mr. Olympia contests.

PUMPING IRON II: THE WOMEN
1985, 107 mins, US ⓥ ⊙
D: George Butler **A:** Lori Bowen, Carla Dunlap, Bev Francis, Rachel McLish, Kris Alexander (Pumping Iron/White Mountain)

This enjoyable documentary on the subculture of women's bodybuilding could have been better had director George Butler tempered his penchant for camera's-eye detachment with some analytical and repertorial sweat. Although he succeeds fairly well in exploiting the inherent drama of the 1983 Caesars Palace World Cup Championship for women bodybuilders, Butler is too content to let the alluring amazons speak for themselves on the film's central question: what is femininity and how far can women go in liberating themselves from stereotypes before confronting immovable cultural resistance?

PUMPKIN EATER, THE
1964, 118 mins, UK
D: Jack Clayton **A:** Anne Bancroft, Peter Finch, James Mason, Cedric Hardwicke,

Richard Johnson, Eric Porter (Columbia/Romulus)

Story of a shattered marriage. Anne Bancroft plays the mother of several young children who leaves her second husband to marry Peter Finch, a scriptwriter. As he succeeds in his work, so she becomes aware of his increasing infidelities and she becomes a case for psychiatric treatment. The role may sound conventional enough, but Bancroft adds a depth and understanding that put it on a higher plane. James Mason plays a deceived husband with a sinister, malevolent bitterness, to provide one of the acting highlights of the picture.
1964: Nomination: Best Actress (Anne Bancroft)

PUMP UP THE VOLUME
1990, 105 mins, US/Canada ⓥ ⊙
D: Allan Moyle **A:** Christian Slater, Samantha Mathis, Ellen Greene, Scott Paulin, Cheryl Pollack, Annie Ross (New Line/SC Entertainment)

Story about a shy high-school student who galvanizes an Arizona suburb with a rebellious pirate radio show has rambunctious energy and defiant attitude. Christian Slater is first-rate as a student who feels trapped and disconnected in a suburban "whitebread land" where "everything is sold out." Slater's rebellious late-night broadcasts soon make him a hero and stir up the dormant anger of other alienated kids. But one night his talk-radio antics go out of control.

PUNCH AND JUDY MAN, THE
1963, 96 mins, UK
D: Jeremy Summers **A:** Tony Hancock, Sylvia Syms, Ronald Fraser, Barbara Murray, John Le Mesurier, Hugh Lloyd (Macconkey)

Tony Hancock's second film produces many amusing sequences, but story line is too slight. Result is a series of spasmodic incidents which Hancock has, largely, to carry on his own personality. Hancock plays a Punch-and-Judy man at a seaside resort that is ruled over by a snobbish mayor. Hancock's marriage is foundering, since he fights the snobbery while his social-climbing wife (Sylvia Syms) is anxious for him to mend his ways so that she can move into the local big league. Climax is the gala held to celebrate the 60th anniversary of the resort.

PUNCHLINE
1988, 128 mins, US Ⓥ ⊙
D: David Seltzer A: Sally Field, Tom Hanks, John Goodman, Mark Rydell, Kim Greist (Columbia)

Punchline is not a comedy. It's an uneven melodrama in which Tom Hanks exhibits flashes of brilliance as a caustically tongued stand-up comic in a strange, undefinable romance with protégée Sally Field. Pic opens up the unfunny backstage world of stand-up comics by zeroing in on two very different people—Hanks as a failing medical student who derives his humor from his experiences with cadavers and other things, and Field as a Jersey hausfrau and achingly bad novice comic.

PUNISHER, THE
1990, 90 mins, US/Australia Ⓥ ⊙
D: Mark Goldblatt A: Dolph Lundgren, Louis Gossett Jr., Jeroen Krabbe, Kim Miyori, Bryan Marshall (New World)

With origins in a Marvel Comics character, *The Punisher* is, as might be expected, two-dimensional. The Punisher has killed 125 people before the film even begins, and the ensuing 90 minutes are crammed with slaughters of every conceivable kind. Story involves an ex-cop whose wife and children were murdered by the Mafia in New York. For five years he's been killing the various heads of the mob families in nonstop vengeance. Dolph Lundgren breezes through the B-grade plot with tongue firmly placed in cheek.

PUNISHMENT PARK
1971, 88 mins, US
D: Peter Watkins A: Paul Alelyanes, Carmen Argenziano, Stan Armsted, Harold Beaulieu, Jim Bohan (Francoise)

Escalation of Asian wars is presupposed with the increase of antiwar propaganda and demonstrations of draft evaders. Rebels are given the choice of serving penal sentences or a three-day endurance test in Punishment Park. The rules are that ''corrective groups'' are given three days to reach, on foot, an American flag 57 miles away. They are allowed two to three hours' start, after which the national guard hounds them out. If they manage to reach the flag in the allotted time, they will be given their freedom.

PUPPET ON A CHAIN
1971, 98 mins, UK Ⓥ
D: Geoffrey Reeve A: Sven-Bertil Taube, Barbara Parkins, Alexander Knox, Patrick Allen, Vladek Sheybal (Unger)

This could be remembered as the film with the speedboat chase. Don Sharp, who was engaged specially to direct this sequence, has in no way spared the boats as the hero relentlessly pursues the villain through the canals of Amsterdam. Regrettably the standard of this sequence is not reflected in the rest of the film. Sven-Bertil Taube plays a US narcotics agent seeking a drug syndicate in Amsterdam. Alistair MacLean scripted his own story, but he has created little sympathy for the characters.

PURE COUNTRY
1992, 112 mins, US Ⓥ
D: Christopher Cain A: George Strait, Lesley Ann Warren, Isabel Glasser, Kyle Chandler, Rory Calhoun (Warner/Weintraub)

An effective vehicle for amiable country star George Strait. Screenplay mingles corn with knowing satire of the hollowness of stardom, but the heartfelt romantic chemistry between Strait and Texas ranch gal Isabel Glasser carries the day.

PURE HELL OF ST. TRINIAN'S, THE
1960, 94 mins, UK Ⓥ
D: Frank Launder A: Cecil Parker, Joyce Grenfell, George Cole, Thorley Walters, Irene Handl, Eric Barker (Hallmark/Tudor)

Ronald Searle's familiar cartoon characters come to life in a St. Trinian's School romp well up to standard. Current yarn gets off to a flying start with the girls burning down the school and being brought to trial at the Old Bailey. But to the horror of the police and the Ministry of Education they are acquitted. A strange professor who offers to start a new St. Trinian's turns out to be a dubious character mixed up with a racket for supplying glamour girls to an Oriental emir as wives for his numerous sons.

PURPLE HEART, THE
1944, 90 mins, US Ⓥ
D: Lewis Milestone A: Dana Andrews, Richard Conte, Farley Granger, Sam Levene (20th Century-Fox)

The celluloid version of the tragic events that followed the capture of eight of the American fliers who bombed Tokyo is an intensely moving piece, spellbinding though gory at times, gripping and suspenseful for the most part. Scenes depicting, by inference, the tortures that the American boys were subjected to strike home with terrific impact. The story is about the fliers on trial before a Jap civil court on a murder rap, charged with purposely bombing and machine-gunning Jap civilians.

PURPLE HEARTS
1984, 115 mins, US Ⓥ ⊠
D: Sidney J. Furie A: Ken Wahl, Cheryl Ladd, Stephen Lee, David Harris, Cyril O'Reilly (Ladd)

A systematically simple love story set against the Vietnam War, with the action largely overwhelming the romantic time-outs. Ken Wahl is a handsome, young, and dedicated doctor in Vietnam, where he meets a beautiful young and dedicated nurse (Cheryl Ladd). They fall in love. Between kisses, they assure each other that they hope one day to return Stateside and do medical good together forever.

PURPLE PLAIN, THE
1954, 100 mins, UK
D: Robert Parrish A: Gregory Peck, Win Min Than, Bernard Lee, Maurice Denham, Lyndon Brook (Two Cities)

A fine dramatic vehicle set in the Burmese jungle in the last days of the [Second World] war. Peck has crashed his plane in mountainous terrain held by the Japs while on a flight with his navigator (Lyndon Brook) and a fellow officer (Maurice Denham). The entire incident concentrates on their attempts to get out, with Peck in an obstinate mood and insisting that they should not wait by the wreckage for help but should try to reach water.

PURPLE RAIN
1984, 104 mins, US Ⓥ ⊙
D: Albert Magnoli A: Prince, Apollonia Kotero, Morris Day, Olga Karlatos, Clarence Williams III (Warner/Purple)

Playing a character rooted in his own background, and surrounded by the real-life members of his Minneapolis-based musical "family," rock star Prince makes an impressive feature-film debut in a rousing contemporary addition to the classic backstage musical genre.
1984: Best Original Song Score

PURPLE ROSE OF CAIRO, THE
1985, 82 mins, US Ⓥ ⊙
D: Woody Allen A: Mia Farrow, Jeff Daniels, Danny Aiello, Dianne Wiest, Van Johnson (Orion)

Tale is a light, almost frivolous treatment of a serious theme. For all its situational goofiness, pic is a tragedy, and it's too bad Allen didn't build up the characters and drama sufficiently to give some weight to his concerns. Allen introduces Depression-era waitress Mia Farrow, a hopeless film buff who spends all her free time seeing films over and over again, until Tom Baxter (Jeff Daniels), a character in fictional epic *The Purple Rose of Cairo* stops the action, starts speaking to Farrow directly from the screen, and steps out of the film and asks to be shown something of real life.
1985: Nomination: Best Original Screenplay

PURSUED
1947, 100 mins, US Ⓥ
D: Raoul Walsh A: Teresa Wright, Robert Mitchum, Judith Anderson, Dean Jagger, Harry Carey Jr. (Warner/United States)

Potent frontier-days western-film fare. Standout in picture is suspense generated by the original script and Raoul Walsh's direction. There are psychological elements in the script, depicting the hate that drives through a man's life and forces him into unwanted dangers. Robert Mitchum is the victim of that hate, made to kill and fear because of an old family feud. His role fits him naturally and he makes it entirely believable. Teresa Wright upholds the femme lead with another of her honest, sincere portrayals.

PURSUIT OF D. B. COOPER, THE
1981, 100 mins, US Ⓥ
D: Roger Spottiswoode A: Robert Duvall, Treat Williams, Kathryn Harrold, Ed Flanders, R. G. Armstrong (PolyGram/Universal)

D. B. Cooper—whoever he really was—did indeed excite the nation by taking over a jet with a fake bomb, demanding $200,000, and then parachuting out the back door, never to be seen again. That tale could still make an exciting picture. Unfortunately, director and writer choose to invent a totally specious yarn that begins with Treat Williams leaping from the plane. Williams drops by the homestead to gather up his suffering wife (Kathryn Harrold) to escape with him. The resulting endless chases have the cinematic value of a laundry dryer.

PURSUIT OF THE GRAF SPEE
See: The Battle of the River Plate

PUSHING TIN
1999, 124 mins, US Ⓥ ⊙ ⊠
D: Mike Newell A: John Cusack, Billy

Bob Thornton, Cate Blanchett, Angelina Jolie, Vicki Lewis, Jake Weber (Linson/Regency/Fox 2000)

Pushing Tin, a punchy and involving look at the seemingly crazed fraternity of NY air-traffic controllers, benefits from its peek at a fresh milieu and from fine character detailing by the four leading players. Unfortunately, story's tension climaxes a half hour before the film is over. Nick Falzone (John Cusack) is the self-styled ace of the team, and Russell Bell (Billy Bob Thornton) a new arrival from out west whose Zen-like cool unnerves Nick. Nick's wife, Connie (Cate Blanchett), dabbles in classes to improve herself. Russell's voluptuous young wife, Mary (Angelina Jolie), has a weakness for booze. Nick takes advantage of her drunken vulnerability. The tension among the four is sustained until Nick is undone at home by Connie learning the truth, and at the office by Russell becoming a media hero. The biggest surprise is Blanchett, who adds more layers to her performance than anyone else.

PUSSYCAT ALLEY
See: The World Ten Times Over

PUTNEY SWOPE
1969, 84 mins, US Ⓥ
D: Robert Downey **A:** Stanley Gottlieb, Allen Garfield, Arnold Johnson, Laura Greene, Ramon Gordon (Herold)

What happens when black militants take over a large Manhattan advertising agency is the basis for a comic satire on black racial identity and the dollar sign on the American altar of success. The situations include political caricature, but disappointedly nothing much beyond marginal interest occurs. The comedy is only intermittently funny and the satire is mostly shallow and obvious.

PUZZLE OF A DOWNFALL CHILD
1970, 104 mins, US
D: Jerry Schatzberg **A:** Faye Dunaway, Barry Primus, Viveca Lindfors, Barry Morse, Roy Scheider (Universal)

Faye Dunaway stars as a confused high-fashion model with severe emotional problems, most never resolved. Unfortunately, the film is marked by cinema verité chic, though Dunaway makes the most of a tour de force opportunity. Plot takes a riches-to-rags course, Dunaway entering as the latest hot model, insecure in frustrating relationships with photographer Barry Primus and well-to-do Roy Scheider.

PYGMALION
1938, 96 mins, UK Ⓥ ⊙
D: Anthony Asquith, Leslie Howard **A:** Wendy Hiller, Leslie Howard, Wilfrid Lawson, Marie Lohr, Jean Cadell (Pascal)

Smartly produced, this does an excellent job of transcribing George Bernard Shaw, retaining all the key lines and giving freshness to the theme. Leslie Howard's performance is vital and at times dominating. Wendy Hiller never loses sight of the fact that she is playing a guttersnipe on whom culture has been imposed; even in the final argument the Cockney is always peeping through the veneer. Wilfred Lawson's Doolittle is only a shadow of the part G.B.S. wrote, but he presents a thoroughly enjoyable old reprobate.

1938: Best Adaptation, Screenplay (George Bernard Shaw)
Nominations: Best Picture, Actor (Leslie Howard), Actress (Wendy Hiller)

PYROMANIAC'S LOVE STORY, A
1995, 94 mins, US Ⓥ
D: Joshua Brand **A:** William Baldwin, John Leguizamo, Sadie Frost, Erika Eleniak, Michael Lerner, Joan Plowright (Hollywood)

A modern-day fairy tale with a bemused appreciation of romantic love, blazing passions, and other human follies. Plot revolves around a mysterious fire that razes a bakery in a multiethnic, inner-city neighborhood. Pastry boy Sergio Cuccio (John Leguizamo) quickly learns the real culprit is the hot-blooded, mood-swinging son of a successful businessman. Mr. Lumpke (an unbilled Richard Crenna) offers Sergio $25,000 to take the rap for his son, Garet (William Baldwin). Sergio seriously considers the deal, as it will enable him to see the world with the young woman of his dreams, Hattie (Sadie Frost), a spirited waitress with a serious case of wanderlust.

Q

Q
(UK: Q—THE WINGED SERPENT;
AKA: THE WINGED SERPENT)
1982, 92 mins, US Ⓥ
D: Larry Cohen **A:** Michael Moriarty,
Candy Clark, David Carradine, Richard
Roundtree, Lee Louis (Larco)

Larry Cohen's tale of a religious bird
of prey terrorizing New York City has its wit,
style, and an above-average script for the
genre. Story centers on Michael Moriarty,
an ex-junkie who takes refuge in the
Chrysler Building's summit, where he
stumbles onto the title character's lair,
complete with a large unhatched egg. The
green bird has been having a merry feed
of workmen and apartment dwellers in the
city's high-rises.

Q&A
1990, 132 mins, US Ⓥ ⊙
D: Sidney Lumet **A:** Nick Nolte, Timothy
Hutton, Armand Assante, Patrick O'Neal,
Lee Richardson (Regency/Odyssey)

Hard-hitting thriller takes on weighty
topics of racism and corruption in the New
York City justice system, opening with
cop Nick Nolte ruthlessly killing a Latino
drug dealer and then intimidating witnesses on the scene. New assistant d.a.
Timothy Hutton is summoned to do a routine investigation, writing up a Q&A with
Nolte and other principal players. Nolte is
outstanding, bringing utter conviction to
the stream of racist and sexist epithets that
pour from his good-ol'-boy lips.

QIN SONG
(US: THE EMPEROR'S SHADOW)
1996, 116 mins, Hong Kong/China Ⓥ ⊙
D: Zhou Xiaowen **A:** Jiang Wen, Ge You,
Xu Qing, Ge Zhijun, Wang Qingxiang
(Ocean/Xi'an)

Chinese costumers finally come of age
with a gorgeously accoutred, bleeding
chunk of history with a script and performances that are for once masters rather
than slaves of the setting. Teaming for the
first time two of the mainland's biggest
male stars in the yarn of a ruthless reaper
who meets his match in a wily court musician, the pic belatedly establishes
middle-generation helmer Zhou Xiaowen
as a formidable talent in Sino cinema.

QIUJU DA GUANSI
(US: THE STORY OF QIU JU)
1992, 99 mins, Hong Kong Ⓥ
D: Zhang Yimou **A:** Gong Li, Lei Kesheng, Ge Zhijun, Liu Peiqi (Sil-Metropole)

Zhang Yimou's first contempo story
has a mesmerizing quality able to hook audiences from beginning to end. Gong Li
forgoes glamour to play a round, pregnant
peasant, Qiu Ju. Her young husband (Liu
Peiqi) is laid up after a fight with the village head (Lei Kesheng) in which he received a debilitating kick in the groin. Qiu
Ju makes up her mind that the village chief
must apologize; this the old man refuses
to do. Qiu Ju embarks on a series of pil-
grimages to get justice done.

Q PLANES
1939, 82 mins, UK
D: Tim Whelan **A:** Laurence Olivier,
Ralph Richardson, Valerie Hobson (Har-
efield/London)

Q Planes is an aviation picture, but not
heavy on heroics. Even in the final rescue
sequence, there is a refreshing tongue-in-
cheek attitude. The acting honors go—and
at a gallop—to Ralph Richardson, playing
a Scotland Yard eccentric. Plot concerns
the use of a salvage ship anchored at sea
to capture army airplanes on their test
flights. All of the crew speak with German
accents and little doubt is left as to who
the villains are.

Q—THE WINGED SERPENT
See: Q

QUADROPHENIA
1979, 120 mins, UK Ⓥ ⊙
D: Franc Roddam **A:** Phil Daniels, Mark
Wingett, Toyah Wilcox, Sting, Leslie Ash
(The Who)

Set in 1963, when rival image cults
among young Britishers led to a wave of
crowd fights in normally staid seaside resorts, the picture plots the plight of one
pill-popping, fashion-mad "mod" who
abandons himself completely to the gang
identity. It's a tribute to helmer Franc
Roddam's simple, restrained direction that
the downbeat ending, when the jobless,
exhausted kid is left in the advanced state
of schizophrenia implied by the title, succeeds in being climactic.

QUAI DES ORFEVRES
1947, 110 mins, France
D: Henri-Georges Clouzot **A:** Louis Jouvet, Simone Renant, Bernard Blier, Suzy
Delair, Pierre Larquey (Majestic)

Outstanding detective meller. The murder on which the investigation hangs is but an excuse for the story, which combines a character study of a show-business couple and detective work most realistically staged in authentic sets of police headquarters. Jouvet does his part of the poor but honest detective with his usual peculiar mannerisms, but in exemplary manner. Bernard Blier, as the weak husband whom jealousy makes a potential murderer, brings out everything in the character.

QUALITY STREET
1937, 84 mins, US Ⓥ ⊙
D: George Stevens **A:** Katharine Hepburn, Franchot Tone, Eric Blore, Fay Bainter, Joan Fontaine (RKO)

Incredibly romantic and farcical, the idea of a 30-year-old woman deceiving her sweetheart into believing she is her own niece of 16 was tough going for the horse-and-buggy patrons of 1901. The men in the cast, headed by Franchot Tone, are soldiers in England's army which smashed Napoleon. Working from a script possessing neither imagination nor ingenuity, George Stevens is limited in his direction.
1937: Nomination: Best Score

QUARE FELLOW, THE
1962, 90 mins, UK
D: Arthur Dreifuss **A:** Patrick McGoohan, Sylvia Syms, Walter Macken, Harry Brogan, Dermot Kelly (British Lion)

Based on Brendan Behan's play, this is an all-out protest against capital punishment. It is shot entirely in a Dublin prison and on location. Patrick McGoohan is a jail warder with lofty ideals. Two men are awaiting the noose. One is reprieved but hangs himself. That shakes McGoohan. He meets the young wife (Sylvia Syms) of the other murderer and his convictions totter still more when he hears precisely what caused her husband to murder his brother. Mostly, though, he is influenced by a veteran warder (Walter Macken), who believes that capital punishment is often a worse crime than the original offense.

QUARTET
1948, 120 mins, UK Ⓥ
D: Ken Annakin, Arthur Crabtree, Harold French, Ralph Smart **A:** Basil Radford, Naunton Wayne, Dirk Bogarde, George Cole, Cecil Parker, Nora Swinburne (Rank/Gainsborough)

Of the four stories that make up the film, the first and last are the most intriguing. "The Facts of Life" is a superbly told piece about a 19-year-old who disregards his father's advice on his first trip to Monte Carlo and outwits an obvious adventuress, and "The Colonel's Lady" is a delightful yarn of a colonel's wife (Nora Swinburne) who causes much embarrassment to her husband (Cecil Parker) by the publication of a book of verse purporting to describe her romantic experiences.

QUARTET
1981, 100 mins, UK/France Ⓥ
D: James Ivory **A:** Alan Bates, Maggie Smith, Isabelle Adjani, Anthony Higgins, Pierre Clementi (Merchant Ivory/Lyric)

An elegant tale of a pretty, innocent, but resilient woman set in the Paris of the late 1920s. Director James Ivory takes his usual aloofly observant distance and the film's love triangle loses some drastic impetus. Isabelle Adjani is alone and penniless. A noted English agent, played by Alan Bates with massive solemnity, asks her to move in with him and his wife, an edgy, middle-aged painter limned with asperity by Maggie Smith.

QUATERMASS AND THE PIT
(AKA: 5,000,000 YEARS TO EARTH)
1968, 98 mins, UK
D: Roy Ward Baker **A:** James Donald, Andrew Keir, Barbara Shelley, Julian Glover, Duncan Lamont (Hammer)

A long-dormant tribe from Mars, accidentally liberated by a London excavation, forms a good story peg, but routine, somewhat distended development blunts impact. Nigel Kneale's script again turns on the Professor Quatermass character, essayed by Andrew Keir, when a scientist (James Donald) discovers skeletons in a London subway expansion. Evil demons, brain waves, and sketchy visions of a dying Mars civilization, plus some great special-effects work, provide plot complications.

QUATERMASS EXPERIMENT, THE
(AKA: THE CREEPING UNKNOWN)
1955, 81 mins, UK Ⓥ
D: Val Guest **A:** Brian Donlevy, Jack Warner, Richard Wordsworth, David King-Wood, Gordon Jackson, Lionel Jeffries (Hammer)

An extravagant piece of science fiction. Despite its obvious horror angles, production is crammed with incident and suspense. Brian Donlevy (in the title role) is the scientist who designs a new rocket that is sent into space with three men on board. It crash-lands in a small English village, with only one survivor. The mystery is what happened to the other two who have disappeared without trace.

QUATERMASS 2
(AKA: ENEMY FROM SPACE)
1957, 84 mins, UK Ⓥ ⊙
D: Val Guest A: Brian Donlevy, John Longden, Sidney James, Bryan Forbes, William Franklyn, Vera Day (Hammer)

Brian Donlevy stars as a scientist engaged in interplanetary research. He suddenly stumbles upon a hush-hush government project on the moorlands, where it's announced that synthetic food is being produced, but actually operations are being directed by an enemy from space, working to take over the earth. Yarn unfolds in fine confusion. Special effects are imaginative.

LES QUATRE CENTS COUPS
(US: THE 400 BLOWS)
1959, 98 mins, France Ⓥ ⊙ ▱
D: François Truffaut A: Jean-Pierre Léaud, Claire Maurier, Albert Remy, Guy Décomble, Patrick Auffay (Carrosse/SEDIF)

Offbeat pic gets deep into the life of a 12-year-old boy, his disorientation with school and parents, and his final commitment to, and escape from, an institution. It eschews conventional blames and emerges an engaging, moving film. Young director François Truffaut still lacks form and polish but emerges an important new director here.

QUEEN CHRISTINA
1933, 100 mins, US Ⓥ ⊙
D: Rouben Mamoulian A: Greta Garbo, John Gilbert, Ian Keith, Lewis Stone, Elizabeth Young, C. Aubrey Smith (M-G-M)

Chief fault with Christina is its lethargy. It is slow and ofttimes stilted. This is perhaps good cinematic motivation to establish the contrast between the queen, who has been reared as a boy to succeed to the Swedish throne, and the episode in the wayside inn where she shares her room with the new Spanish envoy (John Gilbert), who had mistaken her for a flip Nordic youth. Garbo's performance is too often apace of the script's lethargy, but her regal impression is convincing, which counts for plenty.

QUEEN KELLY
1929, 96 mins, US Ⓥ ⊙
D: Erich von Stroheim A: Gloria Swanson, Seena Owen, Walter Byron, Wilhelm

von Brincken, Madge Hunt (Gloria/United Artists)

Undertaken at the behest of Gloria Swanson, film was in production less than three months when Swanson, finally fed up with her director's excesses, told financier Joseph Kennedy to shut it down. Since Queen Kelly was shot in sequence, what exists of it plays very smoothly and coherently up through its arbitrary, but dramatically valid, conclusion. Set in the sort of fin de siècle Ruritanian principality, tale presents the mad young Queen Regina (Seena Owen) forcing the playboy Prince Wolfram (Walter Byron) into a royal marriage. Far from resigned to a life of amorous activity, Wolfram encounters a troup of convent girls and, in a legendary scene, meets Kitty Kelly (Gloria Swanson). [Version reviewed is a reconstruction in 1985.]

QUEEN MARGOT
See: La Reine Margot

QUEEN OF OUTER SPACE
1958, 80 mins, US ▱
D: Edward Bernds A: Zsa Zsa Gabor, Eric Fleming, Laurie Mitchell, Paul Birch, Barbara Darrow (Allied Artists)

Good-natured attempt to put some honest sex into science fiction. The year is 1985, and Eric Fleming, Patrick Waltz, and Dave Willock are in charge of a spaceship checking on a satellite space station. Taken prisoner by a malignant queen (Laurie Mitchell), they are rescued by a promasculine group headed by Zsa Zsa Gabor. The cast is predominantly feminine and attractively garbed in the brief raiment that appears to be customary on other planets.

QUEEN OF SPADES, THE
1949, 95 mins, UK Ⓥ
D: Thorold Dickinson A: Anton Walbrook, Edith Evans, Yvonne Mitchell, Ronald Howard (Associated British Pathe)

Opulence of imperial Russia at the beginning of the 19th century provides a colorful background for this filmization of Alexander Pushkin's short story. Central character is a captain of the engineers. He cannot afford to gamble but is prepared to stake his all on a secret formula believed to have been passed on to a certain countess. Outstanding performance comes from Edith Evans. Her interpretation of the old grotesque countess is almost terrifying in its realism.

QUENTIN DURWARD
(UK: THE ADVENTURES OF QUENTIN DURWARD)
1955, 101 mins, US ▱

D: Richard Thorpe **A:** Robert Taylor, Kay Kendall, Robert Morley, George Cole, Alec Clunes (M-G-M)

This lively film version of Walter Scott's *Quentin Durward* finds knighthood again in bloom with enough dash and costumer derring-do to make fans of swashbucklers happy. Robert Taylor's been dispatched to France from Scotland to look over a prospective bride for his aged uncle. He falls in love with the lady himself, but nobly remembers his mission. Robert Morley stands out as the scheming Louis XI who will resort to any unscrupulous act to keep peace in France.

QUERELLE
1982, 120 mins, W. Germany/France
Ⓥ ▱

D: Rainer Werner Fassbinder **A:** Brad Davis, Franco Nero, Jeanne Moreau, Laurent Malet, Hanno Poschl (Planet/Gaumont)

The last film of Rainer Werner Fassbinder is, unfortunately, disappointing. His attempt to put the mystical homosexual world of French writer Jean Genet on film is ultimately tedious. There is curio value in this strange tale of a young sailor, Querelle, who fascinates all who come in contact with him but who seems more absorbed in himself.

QUEST, THE
1996, 103 mins, US Ⓥ ⊙

D: Jean-Claude Van Damme **A:** Jean-Claude Van Damme, Roger Moore, James Remar, Janet Gunn, Jack McGee (Touchstone)

Self-consciously old-fashioned swashbuckling adventure. Van Damme plays Chris Dubois, an honest, idealistic street criminal who embarks on an odyssey of self-discovery that literally spans the globe, from the slums of New York City to the mysterious magic of Tibet's Lost City. Having choreographed his own battles and stunts for years, Van Damme's move into the director's chair is not a surprising development. Framed by a contempo prologue and epilogue, *The Quest* is not badly directed or executed.

QUEST FOR FIRE
1981, 97 mins, France/Canada Ⓥ ⊙ ▱

D: Jean-Jacques Annaud **A:** Everett McGill, Rae Dawn Chong, Ron Perlman, Namer El Kadi, Gary Schwartz (ICC/Belstar/Stephan)

An engaging prehistoric yarn that happily never degenerates into a club-and-lion-skin spin-off of *Star Wars* and resolutely refuses to bludgeon the viewer with facile or gratuitous effects. Three warriors of a primitive homo sapiens tribe are sent out to find a source of fire after their old pilot lights are extinguished during an attack by a group of unneighborly Neanderthals. After numerous adventures they find a fire among a cannibal tribe, but also learn how to produce it when they are led to an advanced human community by a young girl whom they've saved from the cannibals.

1982: Best Makeup

QUICK AND THE DEAD, THE
1995, 105 mins, US Ⓥ ⊙

D: Sam Raimi **A:** Sharon Stone, Gene Hackman, Russell Crowe, Leonardo DiCaprio, Tobin Bell (IndieProd/Tri-Star)

The bloodthirsty spirit of the Roman circus invades the Old West in an ill-flavored concoction that tastes like warmed-over spaghetti. The stylistic flourishes mark this as an elaborate tribute to the late Sergio Leone. But *The Quick and the Dead* feels utterly unauthentic from the moment Sharon Stone rides into the hellhole called Redemption and signs up to take part in an annual tournament in which the town's citizens basically kill each other off in a series of gun duels. Presiding over this slaughter like a mad emperor is Herod (Gene Hackman), who not only rules the town but, as the territory's fastest gun, wins the competition every year. Among the many putting their lives on the line are the Kid (Leonardo DiCaprio), a cocksure teenager who may be Herod's son.

QUICK CHANGE
1990, 88 mins, US Ⓥ ⊙

D: Howard Franklin, Bill Murray **A:** Bill Murray, Geena Davis, Randy Quaid, Jason Robards, Bob Elliott (Warner/Devoted)

Bill Murray delivers a smart, sardonic, and very funny valentine to the rotten Apple. He plays a fed-up New Yorker who enlists his girlfriend (Geena Davis) and lifelong pal (Randy Quaid) in a bank heist so they can get outta town. Holdup sets off a carnival of police and crowd reaction in the New York streets, but none of it flaps the dynamite-rigged Murray.

QUICK MILLIONS
1931, 69 mins, US
D: Rowland Brown **A:** Spencer Tracy, Marguerite Churchill, Sally Eilers, Robert Burns, John Wray, Warner Richmond (Fox)

A gangster story written down to the bone and directed for everything it contains. Story concerns a tough truck driver, with ideas, who climbs to the top, even socially, through forcing contractors into the right corner, only to topple from his throne at the hands of rival gangsters after being turned down by a girl, a contractor's daughter. Spencer Tracy is excellent.

QUIET AMERICAN, THE
1958, 120 mins, US
D: Joseph L. Mankiewicz **A:** Audie Murphy, Michael Redgrave, Claude Dauphin, Giorgia Moll, Kerima, Bruce Cabot (United Artists/Figaro)

Overlong, overdialogued adaptation of Graham Greene's bitter and cynical book. Story follows the line of the book, but with the all-important difference that the character of the American, played without much depth by Audie Murphy, has been drained of meaning, giving the whole picture a pro-American slant. Murphy here doesn't represent the US government, but merely works for a private US aid mission. In other words, his ideas of a Third Force standing between Communism and French colonialism are his own. Michael Redgrave's moody portrayal of the neurotic aging Britisher hiding personal anxieties under a mask of cynicism makes the whole thing worthwhile.

QUIET DAYS IN CLICHY
1970, 100 mins, Denmark
D: Jens-Jorgen Thorsen **A:** Louise White, Paul Valjean, Wayne John Rodda, Ulla Lemvigh-Muller (SBA)

This is a true-to-the-letter retelling of Henry Miller's memoir about Montmartre life, with very little food and many, many women. Paul Valjean looks like the popular image of Henry Miller, easygoing, nice, lecherous, hungry, and full of fun. Louise White, Ulla Lemvigh-Muller, and Susanne Krage bring off the rather spectacular achievement of making the audience remember their faces as well as their bodies.

QUIET EARTH, THE
1985, 100 mins, New Zealand Ⓥ ⊙
D: Geoff Murphy **A:** Bruno Lawrence, Al-

ison Routledge, Peter Smith (Cinepro/Pillsbury)

Scientist Zac Hobson (Bruno Lawrence) wakes to discover he is alone in the world. A global top-secret energy project he has been working on has malfunctioned and altered the fabric of the universe. He finds two other survivors—a woman Joanne (Alison Routledge) and a man Api (Peter Smith). The emotions unleashed by this trio propels the story, which has an intriguing mystical dimension, to a shattering conclusion.

QUIET MAN, THE
1952, 129 mins, US Ⓥ ⊙
D: John Ford **A:** John Wayne, Maureen O'Hara, Victor McLaglen, Barry Fitzgerald, Ward Bond, Mildred Natwick (Argosy/Republic)

John Ford took cast and cameras to Ireland to film this robust romantic drama. Wayne is the quiet man of the title, returning to the land of his birth. Wayne buys the cottage where he was born, immediately arousing the ire of Victor McLaglen, a well-to-do farmer who wanted the property himself. His next mistake is to fall for Maureen O'Hara, McLaglen's sister. Custom decrees the brother must give consent to marriage, so Wayne's suit is hopeless until newly made friends are able to trick McLaglen long enough to get the ceremony over with.
1952: Best Director, Color Cinematography
Nominations: Best Picture, Supp. Actor (Victor McLaglen), Screenplay, Color Art Direction, Sound

QUIET ROOM, THE
1996, 91 mins, Australia/Italy Ⓥ
D: Rolf de Heer **A:** Celine O'Leary, Paul Blackwell, Chloe Ferguson, Phoebe Ferguson (Vertigo/Fandango)

Rolf de Heer's audacious film takes the viewer into the mind of a seven-year-old girl whose parents are separating. Heer's acute insights into a child's mentality and speech patterns, his bold visual design, and the quite amazing performance of Chloe Ferguson, his young protagonist, will rivet audiences. The entire film is seen from the child's perspective; the viewer is given no information other than that available to her.

QUIGLEY DOWN UNDER
1990, 119 mins, US Ⓥ ⊙ ⊙
D: Simon Wincer **A:** Tom Selleck, Laura San Giacomo, Alan Rickman, Chris Hay-

wood, Ron Haddrick (M-G-M/Pathe)

An exquisitely crafted, rousing western made in Oz. Tom Selleck is in the title role as a sharpshooter from the American west who answers villain Alan Rickman's ad and heads to Fremantle in western Australia. Quigley is informed that he's been hired to kill Aborigines with his longrange, custom-made rifle as part of Rickman's campaign of genocide, encouraged by the local authorities. Selleck's violent response to the request begins a vendetta in which Rickman has him left for dead in the middle of nowhere.

QUILLER MEMORANDUM, THE
1966, 103 mins, UK ⊛ ▭
D: Michael Anderson **A:** George Segal, Alec Guinness, Max von Sydow, Senta Berger, George Sanders, Robert Helpmann (Rank)

Set largely on location in West Berlin, film has George Segal replacing a British agent who has come to a sticky end at the hands of a new infiltrating group of Nazis. His job is to locate their headquarters. He does this in a lone-wolf way. Segal plays Quiller with a laconic but likable detachment. Alec Guinness never misses a trick as the cold, witty fish in charge of Berlin sector investigations. Max von Sydow plays the Nazi chief quietly but with highcamp menace.

QUINTET
1979, 118 mins, US ⊛
D: Robert Altman **A:** Paul Newman, Vittorio Gassman, Fernando Rey, Bibi Andersson, Brigitte Fossey, Nina Van Pallandt (Lion's Gate)

Here's another one for Robert Altman's inner circle. In one of the few obvious points about the picture, the title refers to a game popular in some future city (Montreal?) that's slowly dying in a new Ice Age. Though the finer details are anybody's guess, the game involves five players trying to eliminate each other, plus a sixth who comes late to the board. Before it's over, there have been two bloody throat slashings, a hand bursting open in a fire, and one vigorous stabbing.

QUIZ SHOW
1994, 130 mins, US ⊛ ⊙
D: Robert Redford **A:** John Turturro, Rob Morrow, Ralph Fiennes, Paul Scofield,

David Paymer (Wildwood/Baltimore/Hollywood)

A national scandal is smoothly dramatized against the lively backdrop of fifties television and the vibrant New York City of the era. If the film lacks an edge of excitement and daring, the story still proves strongly engrossing. Set in 1958, pic sweeps the viewer into a live broadcast of the NBC game show *Twenty-One*. King of *Twenty-One* is Herbie Stempel (John Turturro), a brainy, ill-mannered Jewish grad student. The show's producer, Dan Enright (David Paymer), asks Stempel to take a dive for a large fee, thus allowing the handsome, brilliant, patrician Charles Van Doren (Ralph Fiennes), to be crowned. Van Doren goes along with the ruse, persuaded that it's been done that way all along and no one will ever know. But shadowing it all is young Dick Goodwin (Rob Morrow), a similarly bright Harvard grad.

1994: Nominations: Best Picture, Director, Supp. Actor (Paul Scofield), Adapted Screenplay

QUO VADIS
1951, 171 mins, US ⊛
D: Mervyn LeRoy **A:** Robert Taylor, Deborah Kerr, Leo Genn, Peter Ustinov, Finlay Currie (M-G-M)

Quo Vadis is a super-spectacle in all respects. Quibbling about the story line, some of the players' wooden performances in contrast to the scenery chewing of Peter Ustinov (Nero) are part and parcel of the genre. The contrast is sharp in that Leo Genn's slick underplaying makes Ustinov's sybarite conception of Nero that much more·out of focus with realities. High points in the production include the Circus of Nero, the profligate court scenes, the marching armies, the racing chariots, the burning of Rome, the shackled captives under Roman rule, the pagan ceremonies, the secret Christian meetings, the gladiators unto the death, and the climax as the Christian martyrs face the unleashed lions in the great circus.

1951: Nominations: Best Picture, Supp. Actor (Leo Genn, Peter Ustinov), Color Cinematography, Color Costume Design, Color Art Direction, Editing, Scoring of a Dramatic Picture

RABID
1977, 91 mins, Canada ⑲

D: David Cronenberg A: Marilyn Chambers, Frank Moore, Joe Silver, Howard Ryshpan, Patricia Gage (Cinema Entertainment)

Here is an extremely violent, sometimes nauseating picture about a young woman affected with rabies, running around Montreal infecting others. Marilyn Chambers, the Ivory-Snow-girl-turned-porno-film-actress, plays the infected one—sort of a cross between Typhoid Mary with rabies and a vampire.

RACE WITH THE DEVIL
1975, 88 mins, US ⑲

D: Jack Starrett A: Peter Fonda, Warren Oates, Loretta Swit, Lara Parker, R. G. Armstrong (20th Century-Fox)

A follow-up to *Dirty Mary, Crazy Larry,* this meller includes the requisite road chases and other hyped-up thrills, some of them slickly executed by director Jack Starrett. Otherwise the production is a sloppy, cynical blend of secondhand plot elements. Patchwork screenplay also uses story elements from horror pix as it pits vacationing Peter Fonda, Warren Oates, and their wives Lara Parker and Loretta Swit against a horde of rampaging satanists in the Texas backwoods.

RACHEL AND THE STRANGER
1948, 92 mins, US ⑲ ⊙

D: Norman Foster A: Loretta Young, William Holden, Robert Mitchum, Gary Gray, Tom Tully (RKO)

Mood of the picture is pleasant but is so even that interest isn't too strong. Single incident of excitement is a socko Indian raid on a settler's homestead. A pioneer (William Holden) buys a bride (Loretta Young) to do the chores and teach niceties of life to his motherless son. The bride is only a servant until a hunter (Robert Mitchum) appears and makes a play for her.

RACHEL PAPERS, THE
1989, 95 mins, UK ⑲

D: Damian Harris A: Dexter Fletcher, Ione Skye, Jonathan Pryce, James Spader, Bill Patterson, Michael Gambon (Initial/Longfellow)

Charles Highway is a 19-year-old with no money problems who maps out his sexual conquests via his desktop. He meets beautiful American Rachel Noyce, also 19. After a bit of frustration, they have a steamy, passionate affair, of which he tires all too soon. They part. End of story. Dexter Fletcher is rather too self-conscious and makes Charles a less-than-endearing hero. Ione Skye as Rachel gives a glowingly sensual performance.

RACHEL, RACHEL
1968, 101 mins, US ⑲

D: Paul Newman A: Joanne Woodward, James Olson, Kate Harrington, Estelle Parsons, Donald Moffatt (Warner/Seven Arts)

A low-key melodrama starring Joanne Woodward as a spinster awakening to life. Produced austerely by Paul Newman, who also directs, offbeat film moves too slowly to an upbeat, ironic climax. Screenplay not only conveys the tedium of Woodward's adult life but also, unfortunately, takes its time in so doing. Direction is awkward. Were Woodward not there, film could have been a shambles.

1968: Nominations: Best Picture, Actress (Joanne Woodward), Supp. Actress (Estelle Parsons), Adapted Screenplay

RACING WITH THE MOON
1984, 108 mins, US ⑲

D: Richard Benjamin A: Sean Penn, Elizabeth McGovern, Nicolas Cage, John Karlen, Rutanya Alda (Paramount)

A sweet, likable film. Time is 1942, and Penn and his rowdy buddy Nicolas Cage have just a few weeks left until they join the marines. Penn becomes dazzled by a new face (McGovern) whom he takes to be a rich girl. Cage, a wrong-side-of-the-tracks type, gets his g.f. pregnant. Penn forces himself to enlist McGovern's help in raising $150 for an abortion for his friend's gal. First-time scenarist Steven Kloves has created two nice leading characters, nicely essayed by Penn and McGovern.

RACKET, THE
1928, 70 mins, US ⊗

D: Lewis Milestone A: Thomas Meighan, Marie Prevost, Louis Wolheim, George Stone, Skeets Gallagher (Paramount/Caddo)

Thomas Meighan has his best role in years as Captain McQuigg, and Louis Wolheim, as Nick Scarsi, adds to a screen rep that has already labeled him the best

character heavy. *The Racket* grips your interest from the first shot to the last, and never drags for a second. It's another tale of the underworld, a battle of wills and cunning between an honest copper and a gorilla who has the town in his lap.
1927/28: Nomination: Best Picture

RACKET, THE
1951, 89 mins, US 🟅 ⊙
D: John Cromwell **A:** Robert Mitchum, Lizabeth Scott, Robert Ryan, William Talman, Ray Collins (RKO)

Robert Mitchum is the honest police captain pitted against Robert Ryan, the mobster, and both dominate the picture with forceful credible performances. Development is enlivened with some solid thriller sequences, such as a rooftop fight between Mitchum and a gunman, careening autos and crashes, and gunplay between the forces of good and evil.

RADIO DAYS
1987, 85 mins, US 🟅 ⊙
D: Woody Allen **A:** Mia Farrow, Seth Green, Julie Kavner, Josh Mostel, Michael Tucker, Dianne Wiest (Orion)

Although lacking the bite and depth of his best work, *Radio Days* is one of Woody Allen's most purely entertaining pictures. It's a visual monologue of bits and pieces from the glory days of radio and the people who were tuned in. Set at the start of World War II, it's a world of aunts and uncles all living on top of each other and the magical events and people, real and imagined, that forever shape one's young imagination.
1987: Nominations: Best Original Screenplay, Art Direction

RADIO FLYER
1992, 113 mins, US 🟅 ⊙ ▭
D: Richard Donner **A:** Lorraine Bracco, John Heard, Adam Baldwin, Elijah Wood, Ben Johnson, Tom Hanks (Columbia/Stonebridge)

Radio Flyer is a film one would like to like more. Underdeveloped screenplay is sometimes moving but too often distant and literal-minded. Film builds a quiet sense of dread as two boys spend as little time as possible in a home that has become a purgatory. Elijah Wood, the older, has a believable mixture of strength and timidity in his attempts to protect Joseph Mazzello from the (mostly offscreen) beatings by their drunken stepfather (Adam Baldwin). Mazzello, terrific as Baldwin's stoic victim, gives the film much of its intermittent emotional power.

RADIOLAND MURDERS
1994, 108 mins, US 🟅 ⊙
D: Mel Smith **A:** Brian Benben, Mary Stuart Masterson, Ned Beatty, George Burns, Scott Michael Campbell (Lucasfilm/Universal)

Billed as a "romantic mystery-comedy," set in 1939, all the action takes place during the debut night of a new radio network. Various staffers turn up dead, each time preceded by a cackling, "Shadow"-like voice coming from somewhere in the building. For the most part, *Radioland* feels like a theme-park ride without an exit—rolling out a nonstop barrage of stale sight gags and snappy repartee that's both cliché-ridden and sorely lacking in snap.

RAFFERTY AND THE GOLD DUST TWINS
1975, 91 mins, US 🟅 ▭
D: Dick Richards **A:** Alan Arkin, Sally Kellerman, Mackenzie Phillips, Alex Rocco, Charles Martin Smith (Warner)

Sterile comedy-drama. Alan Arkin stars as a loutish bumbler, fraudulently kidnapped by Sally Kellerman and teenager Mackenzie Phillips, who lead him into an odyssey through many lower-class southwest locations. Arkin's stereotyped Everyman clod meshes awkwardly with spaced-out Kellerman's formula characterization, thereby throwing interest by default to Phillips.

RAFFLES
1930, 70 mins, US
D: Harry D'Arrast, George Fitzmaurice **A:** Ronald Colman, Kay Francis, David Torrence, Frances Dade, Alison Skipworth (Goldwyn)

The essence of interest is a rascal so captivating that you are pleased to see him emerge triumphant, though guilty, from his brush with Scotland Yard. Picture version capitalizes such instinctive feeling, by actually having the defeated Inspector K. MacKenzie take his final trimming with a philosophical grin.
1929/30: Nomination: Best Sound

RAFFLES
1939, 70 mins, US
D: Sam Wood, William Wyler **A:** David Niven, Olivia de Havilland, May Whitty, Dudley Digges, Douglas Walton, Lionel Pape (Goldwyn)

Script concentrates on cat-and-mouse

byplay between Scotland Yard inspector Mackenzie (Douglas Digges) and the elusive cracksman (David Niven), with the romantic interludes of minor importance. Present version lacks the sparkle and good humor of the original with Colman. The E. W. Hornung tale has moments of interest and suspense in its present telling, but overall is able to generate only slight reaction for a familiar yarn. Niven is adequate as Raffles.

RAGE
1966, 103 mins, US/Mexico ⊗ ▱
D: Gilberto Gazcon A: Glenn Ford, Stella Stevens, David Reynoso, Armando Silvestre, Ariadna Wellter (Schenck/Jalisco)

Glenn Ford plays a guilt-ridden physician. His base of operations is a construction camp practically in the wilderness. Nipped by his pet dog, he finds later it has rabies, and figures he has only about 48 hours to reach a medical center where he may be treated. With Stevens, a hooker who has been in the camp, he races through desert and mountain. Good suspense is worked up in situation and writer-director Gilberto Gazcon maintains mood realistically.

RAGE
1972, 99 mins, US ⊗
D: George C. Scott A: George C. Scott, Richard Basehart, Martin Sheen, Barnard Hughes, Nicolas Beauvy (Warner/Weintraub)

A sluggish, tired, and tiring melodrama, starring George C. Scott, in his directorial debut, as a father wreaking vengeance for the death of his son after a chemical-warfare experimental accident. The story resolution becomes a shambles as Scott begins killing and blowing up installations.

RAGE IN HARLEM, A
1991, 108 mins, US ⊗ ⊙
D: Bill Duke A: Forest Whitaker, Gregory Hines, Robin Givens, Zakes Mokae, Danny Glover (Palace/Miramax)

Director Bill Duke has brought a stylish sheen to A Rage in Harlem, but his mix of comedy and violence in the Chester Himes period crime tale is dubious. Many will be turned off by the excessive bloodshed, but the fine cast keeps the pic watchable. Coproducer Forest Whitaker, as an innocent mortuary accountant sucked into a plot involving stolen gold transported to 1956 Harlem from Mississippi, provides

amiable but overdone antics in the lead role.

RAGE OF PARIS, THE
1938, 75 mins, US ⊗
D: Henry Koster A: Danielle Darrieux, Douglas Fairbanks Jr., Mischa Auer, Louis Hayward, Helen Broderick (Universal)

Universal successfully launches Danielle Darrieux, young French star of unusual beauty and charm. Nothing more exacting is required than to play a light comedy role in one of those adjacent-bedroom farces. Story is about a French girl having difficulty finding a model's job in New York. Helen Broderick, older and experienced in the ways of life and men, and Mischa Auer, hotel headwaiter, connive a campaign to get the young woman a rich husband. Louis Hayward is the object of their conspiracy, but Douglas Fairbanks Jr. interferes.

RAGE TO LIVE, A
1965, 101 mins, US ▱
D: Walter Grauman A: Suzanne Pleshette, Bradford Dillman, Ben Gazzara, Peter Graves, James Gregory (Mirisch/United Artists)

Nympho heroine goes from man to man amid corny dialogue and inept direction which combine to smother all thesps.
1965: Nomination: Best B&W Costume Design

RAGGEDY MAN
1981, 94 mins, US ⊗ ⊙
D: Jack Fisk A: Sissy Spacek, Eric Roberts, Sam Shepard, William Sanderson, Henry Thomas (Universal)

Sissy Spacek plays a spunky divorcée, struggling to raise two young boys as a small-town telephone operator tied to the switchboard in her house. The setting is Texas in 1944. Enter sailor Eric Roberts in a rainstorm, knocking on the door to use the phone. After a night on the porch, Roberts spends a warmhearted day with Spacek and the lads (Henry Thomas and Carey Hollis Jr.). Gradually, warmth turns to heat in Spacek's bed.

RAGGEDY RAWNEY, THE
1988, 102 mins, UK ⊗
D: Bob Hoskins A: Bob Hoskins, Dexter Fletcher, Zoe Nathanson, Dave Hill, Zoe Wanamaker (HandMade)

Bob Hoskins brings to the screen an insightful perspective on the horrors suffered by the innocent amid warfare. Heading an ensemble cast as Darky, he plays the gritty leader of a gypsylike band of refugees on the run from a war purposely set in an unspecified period somewhere in Europe. A young soldier named Tom (Dexter Fletcher) deserts. By the time he catches up with Darky, et al, Tom is deemed to be a "rawney"—a person who is half-mad and half-magical.

RAGING BULL
1980, 119 mins, US ⓥ ⊙

D: Martin Scorsese A: Robert De Niro, Cathy Moriarty, Joe Pesci, Frank Vincent, Nicholas Colasanto (United Artists)

Martin Scorsese makes pictures about the kinds of people you wouldn't want to know. In his mostly B&W biopic of middleweight boxing champ Jake La Motta, Robert De Niro is one of the most repugnant and unlikable screen protagonists in some time. But the boxing sequences are possibly the best ever filmed, and the film captures the intensity of a boxer's life with considerable force. Aside from the customary genre plot of a boxer selling out to the Mob, what seems to be on the minds of Scorsese and his screenwriters is an exploration of an extreme form of Catholic sadomasochism.

1980: Best Actor (Robert De Niro), Editing

Nominations: Best Picture, Director, Supp. Actor (Joe Pesci), Supp. Actress (Cathy Moriarty), Cinematography, Sound

RAGING MOON, THE
(AKA: LONG AGO TOMORROW)
1971, 110 mins, UK ⓥ

D: Bryan Forbes A: Malcolm McDowell, Nanette Newman, Georgia Brown, Bernard Lee, Michael Flanders (M-G-M/EMI)

Tender love story woven round a delicate situation has some good tangy dialogue and some funny situations. The young hero is injured in a football match and lands up in a home for cripples. He's surly, resentful, and a pain to the rest of the inmates. But at the home he falls in love with a girl who has been wheelchaired for six years. Malcolm McDowell handles the two or three facets of the hero with strong facility. Nanette Newman has a stunning warmth and radiance.

RAGMAN'S DAUGHTER, THE
1972, 94 mins, UK

D: Harold Becker A: Simon Rouse, Victoria Tennant, Patrick O'Connell, Leslie Sands, Rita Howard (Penelope/Harpoon)

Slow-paced but poignant pic based on an Alan Sillitoe novel captures both the lyricism and grime of the Nottingham area. Carefully avoiding the pitfalls of the motorcycle-thug genre, director Harold Becker weaves a bittersweet love affair between a petty teenage thief and the daughter of a wealthy rag dealer. Touches of humor and implied social comment, plus imaginative location lensing, give a ring of authenticity and honesty.

RAGTIME
1981, 155 mins, US ⓥ ⊙ ⊠ ⊐

D: Milos Forman A: James Cagney, Brad Dourif, Elizabeth McGovern, Pat O'Brien, Donald O'Connor, Mandy Patinkin (Paramount/De Laurentiis)

The page-turning joys of E. L. Doctorow's bestseller have been realized almost completely in Milos Forman's superbly crafted screen adaptation. The film charts the syncopated social forces that truly ushered in 20th-century America by pivoting them around a nameless upper-crust family unexpectedly caught up in the maelstrom. Overriding focus of the film is on the travails of a fictional black ragtime pianist (Howard E. Rollins), whose common-law wife (Debbie Allen) is taken in by The Family after she abandons her newborn child in their garden.

1981: Nominations: Best Supp. Actor (Howard E. Rollins), Supp. Actress (Elizabeth McGovern), Adapted Screenplay, Cinematography, Costume Design, Art Direction, Score, Song ("One More Hour")

RAIDERS OF THE LOST ARK
1981, 115 mins, US ⓥ ⊙ ⊐

D: Steven Spielberg A: Harrison Ford, Karen Allen, Denholm Elliott, Paul Freeman, Ronald Lacey (Paramount)

Crackerjack fantasy-adventure, steeped in an exotic atmosphere of lost civilizations, mystical talismans, gritty mercenary adventurers, Nazi archvillians, and ingenious death at every turn, is largely patterned on the serials of the 1930s, with a large dollop of Edgar Rice Burroughs. Indiana Jones (Harrison Ford), an archaeologist and university professor, is approached by US intelligence agents who tell him that the Nazis are rumored to have discovered the location of the Lost Ark of the Covenant (where the broken 10 Commandments were sealed). The ark is assumed to contain an awesome destructive power. Ford's mission is to beat the Germans to the ark.

RAINMAKER, THE
(AKA: JOHN GRISHAM'S THE RAINMAKER)
1997, 135 mins, US Ⓥ ⊙ ▭

D: Francis Ford Coppola **A:** Matt Damon, Claire Danes, Jon Voight, Mary Kay Place, Mickey Rourke, Danny DeVito (Constellation/Paramount)

As carefully constructed, handsomely crafted and flavorsomely acted as a top-of-the-line production from Hollywood's studio era, this story of a young Southern lawyer taking on an evil insurance giant exerts an almost irresistible David and Goliath appeal, climaxing inevitably in a courtroom scene. Memphis law school grad Rudy Baylor (Matt Damon) goes to work for the aptly named Bruiser Stone (Mickey Rourke), a slimy operator. From Bruiser's shameless leg man Deck Schifflet (Danny DeVito), Rudy learns the basics of ambulance-chasing. He also meets Dot Black (Mary Kay Place), whose son Donny Ray (Johnny Whitworth) is dying of leukemia. Their insurance company has rejected all eight attempts to secure coverage for Donny Ray's care. At the slightest threat of being taken to court, the insurance company's slick lawyer, Leo F. Drummond (Jon Voight), offers to settle. Coppola seems bent on leavening the melodrama with as many laughs as possible, and they are generally honest and well-earned.

RANDOM HEARTS
1999, 133 mins, US Ⓥ ⊙

D: Sydney Pollack **A:** Harrison Ford, Kristin Scott Thomas, Charles S. Dutton, Bonnie Hunt, Dennis Haysbert, Sydney Pollack (Rastar/Mirage/Columbia)

An ideal rainy-day matinee for well-to-do ladies of a certain age, Sydney Pollack's immaculately crafted anachronism is about the retroactive discovery of adultery. Sergeant Dutch Van Den Broeck (Harrison Ford) of the Washington, DC, police force, lives in suburban comfort with a beautiful wife. When Dutch hears of the crash of a Miami-bound airliner, he thinks nothing of it. Similarly, Kay Chandler (Kristin Scott Thomas), a patrician congresswoman from New Hampshire, has no idea that her husband was headed for Florida. When Kay joins Dutch in a visit to Miami to observe the setting for what they've learned was a long-term affair between their mates, the media picks up the scent. It's all very adult, serious, and legitimate; it's also laborious, remote, and strangely uninvolving for the audience.

RANSOM!
1956, 101 mins, US Ⓥ

D: Alex Segal **A:** Glenn Ford, Donna Reed, Leslie Nielsen, Juano Hernandez, Robert Keith, Richard Gaines (Nayfack/M-G-M)

This kidnap melodrama has a quota of tension-arousing scenes—a couple of which are really potent. A happy family's small son is kidnapped and held for $500,000 ransom. The father can and does raise the money, as he's a prosperous industrialist. But the switch comes when he decides not to pay the ransom and goes on television to tell the watching kidnapper that the ransom is to become blood money for the kidnapper's capture—dead or alive—if the child's not returned unharmed. Glenn Ford is splendid as the father, a role that takes full advantage of his talent for projection. Most of the other players seem at odds with the characters they play. One exception is Juano Hernandez's understanding butler. His big scene is when he comforts the father while the latter wonders if his decision was the right one after it is believed the boy is dead.

RANSOM
1996, 120 mins, US Ⓥ ⊙

D: Ron Howard **A:** Mel Gibson, Rene Russo, Gary Sinise, Delroy Lindo, Lili Taylor, Liev Schreiber (Grazer-Rudin/Touchstone)

A crackerjack thriller with some unusually tasty plot twists, *Ransom* pays plenty of entertaining dividends. A self-made airline boss, Tom Mullen (Mel Gibson) has settled into Upper East Side comfort and respectability with his wife, Kate (Rene Russo), and son, Sean (Brawley Nolte). On an outing in Central Park, nine-year-old Sean vanishes. Tom is contacted with a demand for $2 million. Ringleader is a renegade cop (Gary Sinise), whose knowledge of technology and police techniques is so complete that he can thwart all attempts to trace him. Tom goes on television, withdraws the ransom and offers it instead as bounty for the head of the kidnapper. Picture's most intriguing subtext lies in the fact that the rich, sympathetic leads are played by big movie stars, while the villains are largely portrayed by icons of the low-budget independent cinema. Are the filmmakers trying to tell us something?

REBECCA
1940, 130 mins, US ⑫ ⊙
D: Alfred Hitchcock A: Laurence Olivier, Joan Fontaine, George Sanders, Judith Anderson, Nigel Bruce (Selznick/United Artists)

Picture is noteworthy for its literal translation of Daphne du Maurier's novel to the screen, presenting all of the somberness and drama of the book. Alfred Hitchcock pilots his first American production with exceptional understanding of the motivation and story mood. Laurence Olivier provides an impressive portrayal as the master of Manderley, unable to throw off the memory of his tragic first marriage. Joan Fontaine is excellent as his second wife, carrying through the transition of a sweet and vivacious bride to that of a bewildered woman struggling to understand the tragedy.
1940: Best Picture, B&W Cinematography
Nominations: Best Director, Actor (Laurence Olivier), Actress (Joan Fontaine), Supp. Actress (Judith Anderson), Screenplay, B&W Art Direction, Editing, Original Score, Special Effects

REBECCA OF SUNNYBROOK FARM
1917, 74 mins, US ⊙ ⊗
D: Marshall Neilan A: Mary Pickford, Eugene O'Brien, Helen Jerome Eddy, Charles Ogle, Marjorie Daw (Artcraft)

The story is of Rebecca, a member of a large family, who is sent to the home of her aunts for rearing, ultimately inheriting their estate, and, incidentally, marrying the finest young man in the town. Mary Pickford plays as she has never played before, varying lights and shades to elicit the major interest, tearful at one moment and laughing the next. Her support is flawless, including many artists of repute.

REBECCA OF SUNNYBROOK FARM
1938, 80 mins, US ⑫ ⊙
D: Allan Dwan A: Shirley Temple, Randolph Scott, Jack Haley, Gloria Stuart, Helen Westley, Bill Robinson (20th Century-Fox)

Shirley Temple proves she's a great little artist in this one. The rest of it is synthetic and disappointing. The story is about a talented stage child who wins a broadcasting moppet contest, then is lost to the advertising agency in the shuffle and rediscovered at Aunt Mirandy's farm. The supporting characters, mostly unsympath-

etic, overdrawn, and exaggerated, are familiar types.

REBECCA'S DAUGHTERS
1992, 94 mins, Germany/UK ⑫
D: Karl Francis A: Peter O'Toole, Paul Rhys, Joely Richardson, Keith Allen, Simon Dormandy (Astralma Erste/Rebecca's Daughters/Delta)

Peter O'Toole goes way over the top and stays there in an irresistible period romp about Welsh peasants taking on the English taxmen. Set in southern Wales in 1843, yarn opens with Anthony Raine (Paul Rhys) returning from service in India. He gets wise to the peasants' problems, including a tollgate tax levied by drunken lord of the manor (O'Toole). He's soon leading a hit squad of yokels in drag who turn the tables on a snotty English captain (Simon Dormandy) in nocturnal raids.

REBEL, THE
(US: CALL ME GENIUS)
1961, 105 mins, UK
D: Robert Day A: Tony Hancock, George Sanders, Paul Massie, Margit Saad, Gregoire Aslan, Irene Handl (Associated British)

Tony Hancock's TV writers, Alan Simpson and Ray Galton, scripted this, and they knew their man's idiosyncrasies intimately. Here, he is a downtrodden London city clerk with a yen to be a sculptor. Unfortunately, he's very unskilled. Eventually, he throws up his job and sets up shop as an existentialist painter in Paris. He talks himself into being accepted on the Left Bank as the leader of a new movement in art.

REBELLION
See: Joi-uchi

REBEL WITHOUT A CAUSE
1955, 111 mins, US ⑫ ⊙ ▭
D: Nicholas Ray A: James Dean, Natalie Wood, Corey Allen, Sal Mineo, Dennis Hopper, Jim Backus (Warner)

Here is a fairly exciting, suspenseful and provocative, if also occasionally farfetched melodrama of unhappy youth on another delinquency kick. Although essentially intent upon action, director Nicholas Ray, who sketched the basic story, does bring out redeeming touches of human warmth. There is a better-than-average-for-a-psychological-thriller explanation of the core of confusion in the child. James Dean is very effective as a boy groping for adjustment.
1955: Nominations: Best Supp. Actor

(Sal Mineo), Supp. Actress (Natalie Wood), Motion Picture Story

RECKLESS
1935, 95 mins, US ⑰
D: Victor Fleming A: Jean Harlow, William Powell, Franchot Tone, May Robson, Rosalind Russell, Mickey Rooney (M-G-M)

A hodgepodge of melodrama, backstage story, and quasi-musical. From the moment the infatuated Franchot Tone buys out the whole evening's performance and sops up champagne in the audience while solo-appreciating the performance, up until the elopement, which culminates in his suicide, it's ever make-believe. William Powell is an equally vague character. Instead of a torcher, Jean Harlow is a dancer, yet for the climatic situation she's the fulcrum of a dramatic song number.

RECKLESS
1995, 91 mins, US ⑰
D: Norman Rene A: Mia Farrow, Scott Glenn, Mary Louise Parker, Tony Goldwyn, Eileen Brennan, Stephen Dorff (Goldwyn)

This twisted fairy tale is a grossly misfired entertainment. One magical Christmas Eve, Rachel (Mia Farrow) is told by her repentant husband, Tom (Tony Goldwyn), that the noise downstairs isn't Santa but a contract killer. He pushes her out the window, and in flight she hooks up with Lloyd (Scott Glenn) and his crippled, mute companion, Pooty (Mary Louise Parker). Filmed as if it were a make-believe world, pic's heightened sense of unreality only serves to remind of film's stage origins.

RECKLESS KELLY
1993, 94 mins, Australia ⑰ ⊙
D: Yahoo Serious A: Yahoo Serious, Melora Hardin, Alexei Sayle, Hugo Weaving, Kathleen Freeman (Serious)

Australian comic Yahoo Serious's second outing is full of ideas and nonsense but short on geniune laughs and zest. Starting from the engaging premise that the spirit of Australia's legendary outlaw Ned Kelly (1855–80) lives on in one of his descendants, Serious puts the new Ned Kelly (himself) and family on an island paradise.

RECKLESS MOMENT, THE
1949, 81 mins, US
D: Max Ophuls A: James Mason, Joan Bennett, Geraldine Brooks, Henry O'Neill, Shepperd Strudwick (Columbia)

Plot wrings out suspense in its concern with a mother who becomes involved in murder and blackmail to save her daughter from the consequences of a romance with an unsavory older man. James Mason's ability as an actor makes his assignment as a blackmailer very substantial and Joan Bennett shows up exceptionally well in a part that is tinged with coldness despite the fact it deals with a mother's concern.

RECKONING, THE
1970, 109 mins, UK
D: Jack Gold A: Nicol Williamson, Rachel Roberts, Ann Bell, Zena Walker, Paul Rogers (Columbia)

The story of a ruthless man who rises from a Liverpool slum to the upper strata of cutthroat big business in London is interesting in its treatment and for Nicol Williamson's performance in a hard-hitting role. Rachel Roberts is realistic as a married woman Williamson picks up at a wrestling match the night his father dies.

RED AND THE WHITE, THE
See: Csillagosok, Katonak

RED BADGE OF COURAGE, THE
1951, 68 mins, US ⑰
D: John Huston A: Audie Murphy, Bill Mauldin, John Dierkes, Royal Dano, Arthur Hunnicutt, Douglas Dick (M-G-M)

This is a curiously moody, arty psychological study of the birth of a fighting man from a frightened boy, as chronicled in Stephen Crane's novel. Pic follows two figures during the days of the War Between the States. They are Audie Murphy, the youth who goes into his first battle afraid but emerges a man, and Bill Mauldin, on whom the same fears and misgivings have less powerful impact.

RED BEARD
See: Akahige

RED DANUBE, THE
1950, 119 mins, US
D: George Sidney A: Walter Pidgeon, Ethel Barrymore, Peter Lawford, Angela Lansbury, Janet Leigh, Louis Calhern (M-G-M)

Metro aims a haymaker at Soviet repatriation methods in Europe and general Communist ideology, but the punch lands short of the mark. Film might have been rescued by a more winning portrayal of its prodemocratic forces. But Walter Pidgeon, who limns a British army colonel engaged in fulfilling the Western allies' commitment to repatriate forcibly all refugees from Russia, is hamstrung for too many reels by callous and blundering do-

ings. His adjutant, Peter Lawford, is depicted as a peculiarly capricious character. Chief pawn is a ballerina (Janet Leigh) beloved by Lawford.
1950: Nomination: Best B&W Art Director

RED DAWN
1984, 114 mins, US Ⓥ ⊙
D: John Milius **A:** Patrick Swayze, C. Thomas Howell, Ron O'Neal, William Smith, Powers Booth, Charlie Sheen (United Artists/Valkyrie)
Red Dawn charges off to an exciting start as a war picture and then gets all confused in moralistic hard-winging, finally sinking in the sunset. Sometime in the future, Soviet and Cuban forces bomb launch a conventional invasion across the southern and northwest borders. *Dawn* takes place entirely in a small town taken by surprise by paratroopers. Grabbing food and weapons on the run, a band of teens led by Patrick Swayze and C. Thomas Howell makes it to the nearby mountains as the massacre continues below.

RED DESERT
See: Il Deserto Rosso

RED DUST
1932, 83 mins, US Ⓥ
D: Victor Fleming **A:** Clark Gable, Jean Harlow, Gene Raymond, Mary Astor, Donald Crisp, Tully Marshall (M-G-M)
Familiar hot-love-in-the-isolated-tropics theme. This time it's a rubber plantation in Indochina, bossed by Clark Gable. Jean Harlow is the Sadie Thompson of the territory. Enter Gene Raymond and Mary Astor on Raymond's initial engineering assignment. Gable makes a play for Astor and it looks like the young husband will have his ideals shattered.

RED-HEADED WOMAN
1932, 74 mins, US Ⓥ
D: Jack Conway **A:** Jean Harlow, Chester Morris, Lewis Stone, Leila Hyams, Una Merkel, Henry Stephenson (M-G-M)
Jean Harlow gives an electric performance. Heroine (Harlow) is a home wrecker, a vicious vamp and a destroyer of peace, and the wages of sin in her case are paid in the final close-up in strange and wonderful coin. Picture is handled with a curious blending of bluntness and subtlety. Some of the ''vamping'' sequences, and there are plenty of them, are torrid. But the overall effect is conveyed with a great deal of fancy skating over very thin ice and its very candor is disarming.

RED HEAT
1988, 103 mins, US Ⓥ ⊙
D: Walter Hill **A:** Arnold Schwarzenegger, James Belushi, Peter Boyle, Ed O'Ross, Larry Fishburne, Gina Gershon (Carolco/Lone Wolf/Oak)
Film establishes the notion that one of the prices the East will pay for opening up is an increase in the Western disease of drug dealing. A particularly loathsome practitioner, Viktor (Ed O'Ross), manages to slip through the fingers of the Red Army's top enforcer (guess who) and heads for Chicago. In full uniform, Arnold Schwarzenegger arrives at O'Hare Airport, where he is greeted by two working stiffs from the Chicago Police Department, James Belushi and Richard Bright. Belushi is assigned to keep tabs on the terminator as the latter tracks down Viktor.

RED HOUSE, THE
1947, 100 mins, US Ⓥ
D: Delmer Daves **A:** Edward G. Robinson, Lon McCallister, Judith Anderson, Allene Roberts, Julie London, Rory Calhoun (United Artists)
Interesting psychological thriller has too slow a pace, so that the paucity of incident and action stands out sharply. Robinson is cast as a farmer, living with a sister and an adopted daughter, withdrawn from the community by his strange, gloomy moods. Part of his property is a wooded area to which no one can go. A young hired hand is intrigued by the wooded area, and enters it, to meet with several mishaps.

RED LINE 7000
1965, 118 mins, US Ⓥ
D: Howard Hawks **A:** James Caan, Laura Devon, Gail Hire, Charlene Holt, John Robert Crawford, Marianna Hill (Paramount)
Script, based on a story by director Howard Hawks, centers on three sets of characters as they go about their racing and lovemaking. Trio of racers are members of a team operating out of Daytona, FL, their individual lives uncomplicated until three femmes fall in love with them. In a thrilling climax, one of the drivers, overcome with jealousy, causes another to crash. Hawks is on safe ground while his cameras are focused on race action. His troubles lie in limning his various characters in their more intimate moments.

RED PLANET MARS
1952, 87 mins, US
D: Harry Horner **A:** Peter Graves, Andrea King, Walter Sande, Marvin Miller, Willis Bouchey (Melaby/United Artists)

Despite its title, *Red Planet Mars* takes place on terra firma, sans spaceships, cosmic rays, or space cadets. Pic's main theme deals with a scientist (Peter Graves) who has managed to achieve radio contact with Mars. Messages from the planet cause all sorts of havoc on Earth. Despite the hokum dished out, the actors turn in creditable performances.

RED PONY, THE
1949, 89 mins, US ⓥ ⊙
D: Lewis Milestone **A:** Myrna Loy, Robert Mitchum, Louis Calhern, Shepperd Strudwick, Peter Miles, Margaret Hamilton (Republic/Feldman-Milestone)

Lewis Milestone's filmization of a novelette by John Steinbeck has been pieced together with taste and fidelity. Boy-and-pony theme owes much of its compassion and winning graces to a sensitive performance by Peter Miles. As the hired man, Robert Mitchum underscores a likable role. Neither Myrna Loy nor Shepperd Strudwick is as satisfactory as the boy's parents.

RED RIVER
1948, 126 mins, US ⓥ ⊙
D: Howard Hawks, Arthur Rosson **A:** John Wayne, Montgomery Clift, Joanne Dru, Walter Brennan, Coleen Gray, John Ireland (Monterey)

Howard Hawks gives a masterful interpretation to a story of the opening of the Chisholm Trail, over which Texas cattle were moved to Abilene to meet the railroad. Also important is the introduction of Montgomery Clift. Clift brings to the role of Matthew Garth a sympathetic personality that invites audience response. Picture realistically depicts trail hardships; the heat, sweat, dust, storm, and marauding Indians that bore down on the pioneers. Neither has Hawks overlooked sex, exponents being Joanne Dru and Coleen Gray.
1948: Nominations: Best Motion Picture Story, Editing

RED ROCK WEST
1993, 97 mins, US ⊙
D: John Dahl **A:** Nicolas Cage, Dennis Hopper, Lara Flynn Boyle, J. T. Walsh, Timothy Carhart (PFE/Propaganda)

Wry thriller with a keen edge is a sprightly, likable noirish yarn. Centered on a case of mistaken identity, the internecine plot becomes progressively more complex without losing its sense of fun. Essentially a bumbler, Michael (Nicolas Cage) finds himself in a nest of vipers and only through dumb luck manages to elude getting bitten.

REDS
1981, 200 mins, US ⓥ ⊙
D: Warren Beatty **A:** Warren Beatty, Diane Keaton, Jerzy Kosinski, Jack Nicholson, Maureen Stapleton, Edward Herrmann (Paramount)

Courageous and uncompromising attempt to meld a high-level sociopolitical drama of ideas with an intense love story is ultimately too ponderous. More than just the story of American journalist-activist John Reed's stormy romantic career with writer Louise Bryant, a kinetic affair backdropped by pre–World War I radicalism and the Russian Revolution, the film is also, to its eventual detriment, structured as a Marxist history lesson. *Reds* bites off more than an audience can comfortably chew. As director, Beatty has harnessed considerable intensity into individual confrontations but curiously fails to give the film an overall emotional progression.
1981: Best Director, Supp. Actress (Maureen Stapleton), Cinematography
Nominations: Best Picture, Actor (Warren Beatty), Actress (Diane Keaton), Supp. Actor (Jack Nicholson), Original Screenplay, Costume Design, Art Direction, Editing, Sound

RED SALUTE
(AKA: RUNAWAY DAUGHTER; HER ENLISTED MAN; ARMS AND THE GIRL)
1935, 77 mins, US
D: Sidney Lanfield **A:** Barbara Stanwyck, Robert Young, Hardie Albright, Ruth Donnelly, Cliff Edwards (Reliance)

Stripped of its anti-Red angle, *Red Salute* resolves itself down to a weak takeoff of *It Happened One Night*. While it is studded here and there with pungent humor, after the first few rounds, the rough, wisecracking exchange between Barbara Stanwyck and Robert Young begins to pall. Moral film seeks to convey concerns the agitation against war by student groups on various college campuses. Into this topical idea is woven the story of a young radical orator (Hardie Albright) who is loved by a general's daughter (Stanwyck), the efforts of her father to keep them apart, and the new romance that comes into her life (Young).

RED SCORPION
1989, 102 mins, US ⓥ ⊙
D: Joseph Zito **A:** Dolph Lundgren, M. Emmet Walsh, Al White, T. P. McKenna, Carmen Argenziano (Shapiro Glickenhaus)

Dull, below-average action pic, lensed in Swaziland, has Scandinavian star Dolph Lundgren playing a Russian special-services officer. Under the guidance of a knowing, mystical bushman, Lundgren realizes the commies are oppressing the Africans. Anticlimax has this Nordic giant leading the otherwise defeated rebels to defeat the combined Russian/Cuban might. Lundgren provides little more than sustained beefcake.

RED SHOES, THE
1948, 134 mins, UK ⓥ ⊙
D: Michael Powell, Emeric Pressburger **A:** Anton Walbrook, Marius Goring, Moira Shearer, Leonide Massine, Robert Helpmann, Ludmilla Tcherina (Archers)

For the first 60 minutes, this is a commonplace backstage melodrama, in which temperamental ballerinas replace the more conventional showgirls. Then a superb ballet of ''The Red Shoes,'' based on a Hans Andersen fairy tale, is staged with breathtaking beauty. Then the melodrama resumes, story being about the love of a ballerina for a young composer, thus incurring the severe displeasure of the ruthless guiding genius of the ballet company. Although the story may be trite, there are many compensations, notably the flawless performance of Anton Walbrook. Shearer, a glamorous redhead, shows that she can act as well as dance, while Marius Goring plays the young composer with enthusiasm.
1948: Best Color Art Direction, Score for a Dramatic Picture
Nominations: Best Picture, Motion Picture Story, Editing

RED SONJA
1985, 89 mins, US ⓥ ⊙ ▭
D: Richard Fleischer **A:** Brigitte Nielsen, Arnold Schwarzenegger, Sandahl Bergman, Paul Smith, Ronald Lacey (De Laurentiis/Famous)

Return to those olden days when women were women and the menfolk stood around with funny hats on until called forth to be whacked at. Except, of course, for Arnold Schwarzenegger, who has just enough muscles to make him useful to the ladies, but not enough brains to make him a bother, except that he talks too much. Nielsen does think it's kind of cute when he wades into 80 guys and wastes them in an effort to impress her.

RED SUN
1971, 115 mins, France ⓥ
D: Terence Young **A:** Charles Bronson, Ursula Andress, Toshiro Mifune, Alain Delon, Capucine (Corona/Oceania)

East is East and West is West, but the twain meet in this actionful oater. Mifune is a Samurai accompanying the Japanese ambassador in a mid-19th-century trek to deliver a jeweled, golden sword to the US president. On the way the train is held up by Bronson and Delon, but the latter double-crosses Bronson and also kills a samurai friend of Mifune and takes the sword. Mifune's code requires he find the sword and kill Delon.

RED TENT, THE
1971, 121 mins, Italy/USSR ⓥ ⊙
D: Mikhail Kalatozov **A:** Sean Connery, Claudia Cardinale, Hardy Kruger, Peter Finch, Massimo Girotti (Vides/Mosfilm)

This first Italo-Russian coproduction deals with the 1928 rescue of an Italian polar expedition stranded by a dirigible crash. Some spectacularly beautiful arctic footage, plus an exciting personal story of survival, make the production compelling and suspenseful. Peter Finch plays General Nobile, an Italian arctic explorer who is lost in the North Atlantic wastes. Years later his nightmares about the incident summon up phantoms of those involved with him.

REF, THE
(UK: HOSTILE HOSTAGES)
1994, 93 mins, US ⓥ ⊙
D: Ted Demme **A:** Denis Leary, Judy Davis, Kevin Spacey, Robert J. Steinmiller Jr., Glynis Johns (Touchstone)

The Ref mines a few laughs from the case of a high-strung cat burglar named Gus (Denis Leary) who, after a bungled second-story job on Christmas Eve, grabs Connecticut yuppie couple Caroline (Judy Davis) and Lloyd (Kevin Spacey) as hostages while he plots his escape. The plot-driving problem is that these are two of the most grating, unrelentingly angry neurotics one could find. Gus essentially becomes hostage to their bickering.

REFLECTING SKIN, THE
1990, 93 mins, UK ⓥ

D: Philip Ridley **A:** Viggo Mortensen, Lindsay Duncan, Jeremy Cooper, Sheila Moore, Duncan Fraser (Fugitive)

Pretentious essay into the grotesque. The script's abnormal situations and morbid characters pall quickly and leave little more than a bad aftertaste. Set in grassroots America of the 1950s (film was shot in Canada), story describes how a young boy persecutes and catalyzes the death of a young widow whom he thinks is a vampire with bloodthirsty aims on his elder brother.

REFLECTIONS IN A GOLDEN EYE
1967, 109 mins, US ⓥ ⊙ ▭

D: John Huston **A:** Elizabeth Taylor, Marlon Brando, Brian Keith, Julie Harris, Robert Forster (Warner/Seven Arts)

Carson McCullers's novel about a latent homosexual US Army officer in the pre–Second World War period, has been turned into a pretentious melodrama. Brando, the latent homosexual, struts about and mugs, his Dixie dialect often incoherent. Taylor, a practicing heterosexual—practicing with Brian Keith—is appropriately unaware of her husband's torment. Her dialect also obscures some vital plot points. Brian Keith is superb as the rationalizing and insensitive middle-class hypocrite.

REFLECTIONS ON A CRIME
1994, 96 mins, US ⓥ

D: Jon Purdy **A:** Mimi Rogers, Billy Zane, John Terry, Kurt Fuller, Lee Garlington (Concorde/Saban)

A full-bore star turn by Mimi Rogers, playing a glamorous killer about to take the chair, is the main selling point for this slickly made, intellectually empty character study. Sharp style on a mini-budget and uncompromising seriousness lend some distinction.

REFORM SCHOOL GIRLS
1986, 94 mins, US ⓥ ⊙

D: Tom deSimone **A:** Linda Carol, Wendy O. Williams, Pat Ast, Sybil Danning, Charlotte McGinnis (New World)

Reform School Girls don't have it so bad. For one thing, they don't have to wear uniforms—or much else for that matter. They talk dirty, play dirty, and are allowed to take long, long showers. Busty Wendy O. Williams, who made a name for herself as the head-banging lead singer of the rock group the Plasmatics, continues her trashy theatrics here as a leather-clad lesbian who reigns terror over the other girls serving time.

REGARDING HENRY
1991, 107 mins, US ⓥ ⊙

D: Mike Nichols **A:** Harrison Ford, Annette Bening, Bill Nunn, Mikki Allen, Donald Moffat (Paramount)

A subtle emotional journey is impeccably orchestrated by director Mike Nichols and acutely well acted. The controlling, intolerant Henry Turner (Harrison Ford), who steps out of his Manhattan brownstone late one night for a pack of Merits only to become the victim of mindless, hysterical violence, is certainly not the same man who has to be coaxed back home from the hospital after a lengthy rehabilitation. Henry has to start from scratch to regain such basic skills as reading, taking a walk, or making love to his wife. The grace of the script by 23-year-old Jeffrey Abrams is that it doesn't contrive a practical alternative for Henry. The change in his character is story enough.

LA REGLE DU JEU
(US: THE RULES OF THE GAME)
1939, 113 mins, France ⓥ ⊙

D: Jean Renoir **A:** Nora Gregor, Jean Renoir, Dalio, Roland Toutain, Paulette Dubost, Gaston Modot (NEF)

Jean Renoir, who directs, wrote the scenario and dialogue, and takes a leading role, has made a common error: he attempts to crowd too many ideas into 80 minutes of film fare, resulting in confusion. Also weak is Nora Gregor, the former Princess Starhemberg, whose accent is far from pleasing and her acting stilted. Tale concerns transatlantic flyer Andre Jurieu (Roland Toutain), who confesses to his buddy, Octave (Jean Renoir), that he's frantically in love with the Marquise (Gregor). Whimsical Octave wants to see the love affair carried out to its denouement and arranges for a hunting party at the Marquis's (Dalio) chateau. [Renoir's original 113-min. version was cut before release to 100 mins., and in the furor after release to 80 mins. Version reviewed is the latter, just prior to the pic's withdrawal.]

REINCARNATION OF PETER PROUD, THE
1975, 104 mins, US ⓥ ⊙

D: J. Lee Thompson **A:** Michael Sarrazin, Jennifer O'Neill, Margot Kidder, Cornelia

Sharpe, Paul Hecht (American International)

Embodies all the thrills of Max Ehrlich's bestseller, plus an outstandingly rich performance from Margot Kidder. Only weakness still is story's sudden and unsatisfactory ending. Michael Sarrazin realizes that some unknown person is within him. Tracing scenes from his dreams, he ventures to small Massachusetts town where Kidder had murdered philandering husband. Sarrazin is best in contending with the semi-incestuous love affair that develops between him and Jennifer O'Neill.

LA REINE MARGOT
(US: QUEEN MARGOT)
1955, 125 mins, France/Italy
D: Jean Dreville **A:** Jeanne Moreau, Armando Francioli, Francoise Rosay, Henri Genes, Daniel Ceccaldi, Louis de Funes (Vendome/Lux)

Historical fresco concerns the impetuous Margot (Jeanne Moreau), who is married to a Huguenot prince (Andre Versini) in order to form a bulwark for the king and ward off trouble. A handsome count stumbles into Margot's boudoir. It is, of course, love after the first fright. Then intrigue builds. Massacre has its share of bloodiness, with the nudity and love scenes not sparing the anatomy.

LA REINE MARGOT
(US: QUEEN MARGOT)
1994, 161 mins, France/Germany/Italy ♥ ⊙
D: Patrice Chereau **A:** Isabelle Adjani, Daniel Auteuil, Jean-Hughes Anglade, Vincent Perez, Virna Lisi, Dominique Blanc (Renn/France 2/DA/NEF/Degeto/WMG/RCS)

Aspires to the mantle of Shakespearean tragedy but plays more like bad Grand Guignol theater. Sprawling, bloody costumer about the dastardly deeds of 16th-century French royalty is a frenzy of religious conflict, personal betrayal, raw passion, and enough killing for all three parts of *The Godfather*. Celebrated theater and opera director Patrice Chereau plays the swirling action to the highest balcony, encouraging his actors to emote and gesticulate without restraint. The focus is almost exclusively on the carnage rather than on understanding it.

REIVERS, THE
1969, 107 mins, US ♥ ▭
D: Mark Rydell **A:** Steve McQueen,

Sharon Farrell, Rupert Crosse, Mitch Vogel, Clifton James, Will Geer (Duo)

Adaptation of William Faulkner's last novel is a nice bawdy film about a winsome 11-year-old in turn-of-the-century Mississippi who gets himself cut up in a Memphis bordello defending the good name of a lovely professional lady. Mitch Vogel, as the kid, is appealing, subtle, and sensitive. He is led astray by the family handy Steve McQueen, who gives a lively ribald characterization. Rupert Crosse is a humorously lighthearted but sardonically mocking dude.

1969: Nominations: Best Supp. Actor (Rupert Crosse), Original Music Score

REKOPIS ZNALEZIONY W
SARAGOSSIE
(US: THE SARAGOSSA
MANUSCRIPT)
1964, 175 mins, Poland
D: Wojciech J. Has **A:** Zbigniew Cybulski, Slawomir Lindner, Franciszek Pieczka, Barbara Krafftowna, Leon Niemczyk (Kamera)

Adult costumer follows a young Spanish captain into a series of adventures while reason and magic strive for his soul. Though filled with the trappings of 18th-century Spain, much derring-do, and exotic and occult adventures, its appeal is more intellectual than swashbuckling. Film's main appeal is its expert stylization, imaginative period recreations, and gutsy playing by a big cast, with bouncy and valorous Zbigniew Cybulski as the man on the quest. [Version reviewed is the complete one shown at the 1965 Venice fest. Outside Poland, pic is generally available in a 124-min. version.]

RELENTLESS
1989, 92 mins, US ♥ ⊙
D: William Lustig **A:** Judd Nelson, Robert Loggia, Leo Rossi, Meg Foster, Patrick O'Bryan (Cinetel)

A riveting, splendidly acted suspense thriller. Phil Alden Robinson's fresh and invigorating script strikes a careful balance in focusing not just on maniacal killer Judd Nelson's murderous escapades but also on dedicated cop Leo Rossi and his supportive wife Meg Foster. Director William Lustig keeps the screws tightened for an exciting, sometimes scary ride, while allowing for considerable warmth to be generated in the idiosyncratic family scenes involving Rossi, Foster, and their young son.

RELUCTANT DEBUTANTE, THE
1958, 96 mins, US ♥ ▭
D: Vincente Minnelli A: Rex Harrison, Kay Kendall, John Saxon, Sandra Dee, Angela Lansbury (M-G-M/Avon)

Refreshing and prettily dressed version of the William Douglas Home stage trifle is the story of London's social "season," a time when bright and not-too-bright 17-year-olds make their debuts in society. Rex Harrison and Kay Kendall, as newly married on-screen as off, invite his American daughter (by a former marriage) for a British visit that results in the girl's coming out socially. As played by Sandra Dee, the teenager is bored with English stiffs but falls madly for an American drummer (John Saxon). It's Kendall's picture, and she grabs it with a single wink. She's flighty and well meaning, snobbish and lovable.

RELUCTANT DRAGON, THE
1941, 73 mins, US
D: Alfred Werker, Hamilton Luske A: Robert Benchley, Frances Gifford, Buddy Pepper, Nana Bryant, Claud Allister (Walt Disney)

Film is a trip through the Disney plant interspersed with cartoon shorts. In his stumbling through the plant, Robert Benchley (and the audience) sees some eight operations in the making of cartoons, plus three full shorts and hunks of a number of other Disney features in work, notably *Bambi*. Cartoons include "Baby Weems," "How to Ride a Horse," and "The Reluctant Dragon." Many of the performers in the live-action portions are Disney employees doing their actual jobs.

REMAINS OF THE DAY, THE
1993, 135 mins, US/UK ♥ ⊚ ▭
D: James Ivory A: Anthony Hopkins, Emma Thompson, James Fox, Christopher Reeve, Peter Vaughan, Hugh Grant (Columbia/Merchant Ivory)

This curious, cloistered piece, which examines the life of a very proper English butler who sacrifices anything resembling a personal life in total dedication to his master's needs, is continuously absorbing, but lacks the emotional resonance that would have made it completely satisfying, despite top performances from Anthony Hopkins and Emma Thompson. Story begins with the aging butler Stevens (Hopkins) traveling across Britain to see his former coworker Miss Kenton (Thompson). Stevens's employer at the palatial Darlington Hall is now an American ex-congressman, Mr. Lewis (Christopher Reeve), and in the course of his journey, Stevens recalls life at the great estate during the 1930s.
1993: Nominations: Best Picture, Director, Actor (Anthony Hopkins), Actress (Emma Thompson), Original Score, Adapted Screenplay, Art Direction, Costume Design

REMBRANDT
1936, 85 mins, US ♥
D: Alexander Korda A: Charles Laughton, Gertrude Lawrence, Elsa Lanchester, Edward Chapman, Roger Livesey (London)

An idealized film biography of the life of the famous painter. Story begins at the height of Rembrandt's fame, and carries on to his solitary, poverty-stricken old age. It was an inspiration to film many of the scenes with a suggestion of the lighting for which Rembrandt is famous in his paintings. Charles Laughton is far from satisfactory. The only tragic things in his life are the deaths of his two wives. On neither occasion does Laughton express the overwhelming sorrow the story calls for.

REMEMBER MY NAME
1978, 95 mins, US
D: Alan Rudolph A: Geraldine Chaplin, Anthony Perkins, Moses Gunn, Berry Berenson, Jeff Goldblum (Lion's Gate)

An incomprehensible mélange of striking imagery, obscure dialogue, a powerful score, and a script that doesn't know how to go from A to B. Anthony Perkins is a construction worker married to Berry Berenson. Geraldine Chaplin arrives on the scene and begins a petty harassment of the couple, which gradually turns more sinister. Film might have induced some interest as a moderate chiller with emotional undertones. In Rudolph's infuriatingly oblique style, however, it becomes an irritating and puzzling affair that insults, rather than teases, the viewer.

REMEMBER THE DAY
1941, 95 mins, US
D: Henry King A: Claudette Colbert, John Payne, John Shepperd, Anne Revere (20th Century-Fox)

A warmly human drama. Story is slightly reminiscent of *Goodbye, Mr Chips*. Here, it's a femme schoolteacher who holds the spotlight; but there's still the neat admixture of happiness and semitragedy in her involvement in a brief romance that upsets the puppy-love adoration of a teenage pupil she has helped.

REMEMBER THE NIGHT
1940, 93 mins, US
D: Mitchell Leisen A: Barbara Stanwyck, Fred MacMurray, Beulah Bondi, Elizabeth Patterson, Sterling Holloway (Paramount)

Preston Sturges's original screenplay is a tale of a girl crook (Barbara Stanwyck) who becomes enmeshed with the law after lifting a bracelet. Deputy district attorney Fred MacMurray is assigned to prosecute, even though he plans to leave for Christmas holidays with his mother in Indiana. When the girl has to remain in jail in the interim, MacMurray suffers pangs of conscience and gets her out on bail. When he finds her home is also in Indiana, he takes her along on the trip. Stanwyck turns in a fine performance. MacMurray is impressive as the serious-minded prosecutor, but loosens up for the comedy stretches.

REMODELING HER HUSBAND
1920, 65 mins, US ⊗
D: Lillian Gish A: Dorothy Gish, James Rennie, Marie Burke, Downing Clarke, Frank Kingdon (New Art/Paramount)

This feature will be liked by film fans through the exquisite comedy Dorothy Gish offers. The picture seems to be a real Gish family affair, with Dorothy starring and Lillian directing. But Lillian does not qualify as a particularly strong directress in this production. The story may have had something to do with that. It is not a world-beater, but with the action that Dorothy supplies it gets by with laughs.

REMO: UNARMED AND DANGEROUS
See: Remo Williams: The Adventure Begins

REMO WILLIAMS: THE ADVENTURE BEGINS (UK: REMO: UNARMED AND DANGEROUS)
1985, 121 mins, US Ⓥ ⊙
D: Guy Hamilton A: Fred Ward, Joel Grey, Wilford Brimley, J. A. Preston, Charles Cioffi (Orion)

Poor man's James Bond never seems to know where it's going and, when the smoke has cleared, doesn't seem to have gotten there either. Williams (Fred Ward) is a cop recruited for some secret government agency (headed by Wilford Brimley). What levity occurs in the film is mostly reserved for the section in which Remo is placed under the tutelage of the

last living master of the Korean martial art Sinanju. Charles Cioffi as an arms manufacturer is a cardboard heavy surrounded by bumbling bad guys.
1985: Nomination: Best Makeup

RENAISSANCE MAN
1994, 129 mins, US Ⓥ ⊙
D: Penny Marshall A: Danny DeVito, Gregory Hines, James Remar, Cliff Robertson, Lillo Brancato Jr. (Cinergi-Parkway/Touchstone)

This bittersweet comedy needed a clearer focus, or a more ruthless hand in the editing room. DeVito plays Bill Rago, an advertising executive forced to take a temporary gig teaching a group of army underachievers. Rago stumbles onto the idea of teaching the kids Shakespeare, gradually winning them over and becoming involved in their various hard-luck stories. DeVito is such an engaging character that the film generates its share of laughs, and the eight recruits with fresh faces bring an inordinate amount of energy to the project.

RENDEZVOUS
1935, 96 mins, US
D: William K. Howard A: William Powell, Rosalind Russell, Binnie Barnes, Lionel Atwill, Cesar Romero (M-G-M)

Chill-and-chuckle play scoring a bull's-eye. William Powell is puzzle editor of a Washington newspaper who quits to enlist in the army. The day before he leaves he meets Rosalind Russell, whose uncle is one of the undersecretaries of war. Love develops in the speedy fashion of those times and she persuades her uncle that Powell will be more useful in decoding messages than in shooting at the enemy. The comedy is cleverly worked into the action.

RENEGADES
1989, 106 mins, US Ⓥ ⊙
D: Jack Sholder A: Kiefer Sutherland, Lou Diamond Phillips, Jami Gertz, Rob Knepper, Bill Smitrovich (Morgan Creek/Interscope)

Pic offers some roller-coaster thrills thanks to Jack Sholder's full-throttle direction but ultimately exhausts itself with unrelenting bedlam. Kiefer Sutherland plays Buster, an undercover cop chasing a baddie who's stolen $2 million in diamonds. In the process, Marino (Rob Knepper) kills the brother of Hank (Lou Diamond Phillips) and makes off with an ancient spear, an artifact sacred to their Lakota Indian tribe. Phillips must recover it to satisfy his father, throwing him together with Sutherland.

RENT-A-COP
1988, 95 mins, US Ⓥ ⊙
D: Jerry London **A:** Burt Reynolds, Liza Minnelli, James Remar, Richard Masur, Dionne Warwick (Kings Road)

Cheesy little crime thriller. Reynolds, a cop suspected of being crooked, is bounced from the force. He gets work as a ''rent-a-cop,'' undercover (dressed as a Santa Claus) in a department store. Liza Minnelli, as a Chicago hooker, attaches herself to him for protection. Reynolds looks bored and is boring here, with an ill-fitting toupee. Minnelli is a lot of fun as the flamboyant prostie.

REPLACEMENT KILLERS, THE
1998, 86 mins, US Ⓥ ⊙
D: Antoine Fuqua **A:** Chow Yun-Fat, Mira Sorvino, Michael Rooker, Jurgen Prochnow, Kenneth Tsang, Til Schweiger (Brillstein-Grey/WCG/Columbia)

A Westernization of the Hong Kong movies of Chow Yun-Fat, this mechanical effort is studied rather than heartfelt. Chow is John Lee, a hired gun with a debt to Manhattan-Asian crime czar Terence Wei (Kenneth Tsang). His mission is to murder the seven-year-old boy of the cop (Michael Rooker) responsible for the death of Wei's son during a botched drug transaction. A crisis of conscience prevents John from pulling the trigger. He contacts master forger Meg Coburn (Mira Sorvino) for a phoney passport. But Wei's trigger men descend, and Lee and Coburn begin their long flight through New York. First-time feature director Antoine Fuqua has obviously studied every slo-mo sequence and violently choreographed ballet of blood Hong Kong has served up in recent years. The performances, too, have a rote quality.

REPO MAN
1984, 94 mins, US Ⓥ ⊙
D: Alex Cox **A:** Harry Dean Stanton, Emilio Estevez, Olivia Barash, Tracey Walter, Vonetta McGee (Edge City)

Pic has the type of unerring energy that leaves audiences breathless and entertained. Title refers to the people who repossess cars from those behind on their payments. The initial plot thrust involves Otto Maddox (Estevez) and Bud (Harry Dean Stanton), the veteran repo man who teaches him the ropes. However, these are certainly tame facets as a story of alien invaders evolves. Stanton turns in yet another indelible portrait of a seamy lowlife, while Estevez registers as a charismatic and talented actor.

REPORT TO THE COMMISSIONER (UK: OPERATION UNDERCOVER)
1975, 112 mins, US Ⓥ
D: Milton Katselas **A:** Michael Moriarty, Yaphet Kotto, Susan Blakely, Hector Elizondo, William Devane, Richard Gere (United Artists)

Superb suspense drama of the tragic complexities of law enforcement tells why Michael Moriarty, an idealistic new detective, is being harassed to provide an alibi for the death of Susan Blakely, an undercover narc killed accidentally in the pad she shares with big-time dealer Tony King. Richard Gere is very good as a small-time pimp.

REPOSSESSED
1990, 84 mins, US Ⓥ ⊙
D: Bob Logan **A:** Linda Blair, Ned Beatty, Leslie Nielsen, Anthony Starke, Lana Schwab (New Line)

Nonstop silliness keeps this frightless spoof of *The Exorcist* entertaining enough to make an undemanding audience happy. Linda Blair, her teeth and hair encrusted with green gunk, once again plays the devil's host. Leslie Nielsen plays the priest pulled out of retirement to battle Satan. This time the rematch is staged on national TV.

REPULSION
1965, 104 mins, UK Ⓥ
D: Roman Polanski **A:** Catherine Deneuve, Ian Hendry, John Fraser, Patrick Wymark, Yvonne Furneaux (Compton/Tekli)

A classy, truly horrific psychological drama in which Roman Polanski draws out a remarkable performance from Catherine Deneuve. Deneuve is a youngster working in a beauty shop, a deliberately sharp contrast to the drab apartment she shares with her flighty elder sister. The girl is sexually repressed, deeply attracted to men, but at the same time loathing them. Her daydreaming grows into erotic sexual fantasies, and when her sister and boyfriend leave her for a few days, her loneliness and imagination take hold and insanity sets in.

REQUIEM FOR A HEAVYWEIGHT (UK: BLOOD MONEY)

1962, 85 mins, US

D: Ralph Nelson **A:** Anthony Quinn, Jackie Gleason, Mickey Rooney, Julie Harris, Cassius Clay (Columbia)

Rod Serling's poignant portrait of the sunset of a prizefighter packs considerable punch as a character study. Quinn's punchy, inarticulate behemoth is so painfully natural that one winces when he feels pain, whether to his body or his feelings. Gleason is amazingly fine. He's weak, crafty, shiftly, and still a little pathetic. Mickey Rooney, hampered with some bad makeup, is warm and sympathetic as Army, the trainer.

RESCUERS, THE

1977, 76 mins, US ♥

D: Wolfgang Reitherman, John Lounsbery, Art Stevens (Walt Disney)

Four years of work were invested on this production and the expense, care, and expertise show. Admirably simple story is about two mice (voiced by Bob Newhart and Eva Gabor) who embark on a quest to rescue a kidnapped orphan girl (Michelle Stacy) from the clutches of an evil witch (Geraldine Page). There's real terror in the story, and in the gothic setting of the swamp where the girl is held captive; the maudlin pitfalls of the plot are avoided through deft use of humor, and the plucky character of the young captive.

1977: Nomination: Best Song ("Someone's Waiting For You")

RESCUERS DOWN UNDER, THE

1990, 74 mins, US ♥ ⊙

D: Hendel Butoy, Mike Gabriel (Walt Disney)

Sort-of sequel to the 1977 hit *The Rescuers*. The mediocre story hinges on a little boy who inexplicably cavorts with animals in Dolittle-esque fashion, including a huge golden eagle, a species apparently indigenous to the Aussie Outback. The bird is the prey of an evil hunter, McLeach (voiced by George C. Scott), who kidnaps the boy, resulting in a round-the-world call for those fearless mice of the Rescue Aid Society to come a-runnin'.

RESERVOIR DOGS

1992, 105 mins, US ♥ ⊙ ⊡

D: Quentin Tarantino **A:** Harvey Keitel, Tim Roth, Michael Madsen, Chris Penn, Steve Buscemi, Lawrence Tierney (Live America)

Show-off piece of filmmaking is an intense, bloody, in-your-face crime drama about a botched robbery and its aftermath, colorfully written in vulgar gangster vernacular and well played by a terrific cast. Strikingly shot and funny opening scene has eight criminals at breakfast arguing about the true meaning of Madonna's "Like a Virgin." Script fractures very cleverly into an intricate flashback structure that mixes the postrobbery mess with telling character and plot details from the planning stages. Tarantino's complex plot construction works very well, relieving the warehouse setting's claustrophobia.

RESTLESS YEARS, THE

1958, 86 mins, US ⊡

D: Helmut Kautner **A:** John Saxon, Sandra Dee, Teresa Wright, James Whitmore, Luana Patten, Margaret Lindsay (Universal)

A touching account of adolescence. In almost the first line of dialogue, Sandra Dee is described as an illegitimate child. Her problems arise out of this and the fact that her unwed mother (Teresa Wright) has never recovered from the desertion by the father. The girl begins to grow up when a new boy in town (John Saxon) meets her and falls in love. His life is complicated by his luckless father (James Whitmore).

RESTORATION

1995, 118 mins, US ♥ ⊙

D: Michael Hoffman **A:** Robert Downey Jr., Sam Neill, David Thewlis, Polly Walker, Meg Ryan, Ian McKellen (Segue/Avenue/Miramax)

Resplendent in its evocation of teeming, gaudy, plague-stricken 17th-century England, sweeping yet intimate drama boasts an exemplary cast headed by Robert Downey Jr., who does bravura work as a wastrel physician who devotes more passion to whoring than to his patients. Merivel (Downey) finds himself a favored courtier of King Charles II (Sam Neill). When the king bids him, as a ruse, to marry the royal mistress but not, under any circumstances, fall in love with her, Merivel approaches a precipice. And falls.

1995: Best Art Direction, Best Costume Design.

RESURRECTION

1980, 103 mins, US ♥

D: Daniel Petrie **A:** Ellen Burstyn, Sam Shepard, Richard Farnsworth, Roberts Blossom (Universal)

Unusual supernatural drama about a

faith healer gives Ellen Burstyn a shot at a tour de force performance, but never comes into strong enough focus dramatically or philosophically. She begins as a housewife who gives her husband a sports car, only to have it cause his death in a crash which leaves her legs paralyzed. She discovers that her close brush with death has given her the power of healing by the laying on of hands.

1980: Nominations: Best Actress (Ellen Burstyn), Supp. Actress (Eva Le Gallienne)

RETREAT, HELL!
1952, 94 mins, US Ⓥ
D: Joseph H. Lewis A: Frank Lovejoy, Richard Carlson, Russ Tamblyn, Anita Louise, Ned Young (United States/Warner)

Top-notch war drama blending some celluloid rah-rah with tense action. Film has a personal element, detailing the broader battle action through its effect on cast principals such as Frank Lovejoy, battalion commander; Richard Carlson, a "retread" captain from World War II; Russ Tamblyn, youthful enlistee; and Ned Young, a marine regular.

RETURN FROM THE ASHES
1965, 108 mins, UK ▭
D: J. Lee Thompson A: Maximilian Schell, Samantha Eggar, Ingrid Thulin, Herbert Lom, Talitha Pol (Mirisch)

The screenplay builds around a plot for the perfect murder by an unscrupulous Polish chess master married to one woman and in love with her stepdaughter. Set in Paris at the close of the Second World War, when the wife, a Jewess, returns from tortured internment in Dachau to find her husband living with the younger woman. Plot concerns the Pole's passion for money. Maximilian Schell delivers strongly in a blackhearted role.

RETURN FROM WITCH MOUNTAIN
1978, 93 mins, US Ⓥ
D: John Hough A: Bette Davis, Christopher Lee, Kim Richards, Ike Eisenmann, Jack Soo (Walt Disney)

Kim Richards and Ike Eisenmann reprise their roles from *Escape to Witch Mountain* (1975) as sister and brother from another world, this time back on Earth for a vacation. Siblings get a quick test of their psychic powers as mad scientist Christopher Lee and accomplice Bette Davis are testing their mind-control

device on henchman Anthony James—when Eisenmann saves James from falling off a building by antigravity display, Lee sees the youngster as his meal ticket to world power. Film is basically a chase caper.

RETURN OF A MAN CALLED HORSE, THE
1976, 125 mins, US Ⓥ ▭
D: Irvin Kershner A: Richard Harris, Gale Sondergaard, Geoffrey Lewis, Bill Lucking, Jorge Luke (United Artists)

A visually stunning sequel, again starring Richard Harris as an English nobleman who this time returns to the American west to save his adopted Indian tribe from extinction. Film is handsome, leisurely, placid to the point of being predictable, but dotted with some action highlights; in particular, Harris encores a physical torture ritual, explicit enough to drive some audiences to the concession stand.

RETURN OF DR. FU MANCHU, THE
1930, 73 mins, US
D: Rowland V. Lee A: Warner Oland, Neil Hamilton, Jean Arthur, O. P. Heggie, Evelyn Hall (Paramount)

Another chapter in the lurid melodramatic series from the detective stories by Sax Rohmer. As a picture, it's absurd. Fu Manchu (Warner Oland) having been apparently killed in the previous picture, it became necessary to bring him to life again in an elaborate Chinese funeral. The archdemon escapes from his own coffin by a spring door and the story becomes a checker game between the wily Celestial and the super detective, Nayland Smith (O. P. Heggie).

RETURN OF FRANK JAMES, THE
1940, 92 mins, US Ⓥ ⊙
D: Fritz Lang A: Henry Fonda, Gene Tierney, Jackie Cooper, John Carradine, J. Edward Bromberg (20th Century-Fox)

Jesse James was murdered by those cowards, the Ford brothers. Jesse's older brother, Frank, returns to even the score, but it's pretty slow stuff in the telling. Henry Fonda, underplaying Frank in typical quiet style, is impressive; John Carradine is a duly hissable villain as Bob Ford.

RETURN OF SWAMP THING, THE
1989, 88 mins, US Ⓥ ⊙
D: Jim Wynorski A: Louis Jourdan, Heather Locklear, Sarah Douglas, Dick Durock, Ace Mask (Lightyear)

Scientific hokum without the fun. Second attempt to film the DC Comics character will disappoint all but the youngest critters. They may be entertained by watching crossbred creatures squirm helplessly or buy into the Swamp Thing's (Dick Durock) instant love for Heather Locklear. He's a plant; she's a vegetarian. Pic is set against a backdrop of evil where Dr. Arcane (Louis Jourdan) has a mutant lab inhabited by failed experiments as he tries to discover the genetic equivalent of the Fountain of Youth.

RETURN OF THE DRAGON
See: Meng Long Guo Jiang

RETURN OF THE FLY
1959, 78 mins, Ⓥ Ⓒ ▭
D: Edward L. Bernds **A:** Vincent Price, Brett Halsey, John Sutton, David Frankham, Dan Seymour (20th Century-Fox)

Sequel's amateurishly contrived plot picks up at the death of the inventor's widow, who had been acquitted of murdering him. Vincent Price, the only actor carried over from the original, explains to the inventor's now-grown son, played by Brett Halsey, the plot of the other picture. What follows is one unmotivated episode after another, loosely tied to the notion that the son, in following in his father's footsteps, will come to the same bad end.

RETURN OF THE JEDI
1983, 133 mins, US Ⓥ Ⓒ ▭
D: Richard Marquand **A:** Mark Hamill, Harrison Ford, Carrie Fisher, Billy Dee Williams, Anthony Daniels, Peter Mayhew (Lucasfilm/20th Century-Fox)

Jedi is the conclusion of the middle trilogy of George Lucas's planned nine-parter and suffers a lot in comparison to the initial *Star Wars*, when all was fresh. The basic dramatic hook this time is Mark Hamill's quest to discover the true identity of menacing Darth Vader, while resisting the evil intents of the Emperor (Ian McDiarmid). Hamill is not enough of a dramatic actor to carry the plot load here. Harrison Ford is given little to do but react to special effects. But Lucas and director Richard Marquand have overwhelmed these performer flaws with a truly amazing array of creatures, old and new, plus the familiar space hardware.
1983: Best Special Visual Effects
Nominations: Best Art Direction, Original Score, Sound, Sound Editing

RETURN OF THE LIVING DEAD, THE
1985, 90 mins, US Ⓥ Ⓒ
D: Dan O'Bannon **A:** Clu Gulager, James Karen, Don Calfa, Thom Mathews, Beverly Randolph (Hemdale/Fox)

It's the same old story, as unusually vigorous, athletic zombies besiege the motley bunch of human beings holed up in the vicinity and eat the brains of anyone they get their hands on. Director Dan O'Bannon deserves considerable credit for creating a terrifically funny first half hour of exposition.

RETURN OF THE LIVING DEAD PART II
1988, 89 mins, US Ⓥ Ⓒ
D: Ken Weiderhorn **A:** James Karen, Thom Mathews, Michael Kenworthy, Marsha Dietlein, Dana Ashbrook (Greenfox/Lorimar)

Comedy/horror flick is neither scary nor funny and adds salt in the wound with an obnoxious soundtrack of grating rock music. This time a canister falls off an army truck. A weird fog spews from the container, awakening a ghoul who is packed inside as neatly as tuna fish. As the fog spreads, it is a call to arms for the occupants of a cemetery, unleashing a throng of decaying cadavers.

RETURN OF THE LIVING DEAD III
1993, 97 mins, US Ⓥ Ⓒ
D: Brian Yuzna **A:** Mindy Clarke, J. Trevor Edmond, Kent McCord, Sarah Douglas, James T. Callahan (Trimark)

Playing it straight, sans humor, tale begins with two attractive lovebirds, Curt (J. Trevor Edmond) and Julie (Mindy Clarke), sneaking into his father's army research lab, where experiments are conducted with a chemical capable of bringing the dead back to life. When Julie dies in a tragic motorcycle accident, the heartbroken Curt is determined to keep her alive by exposing her to the "magical" chemical.

RETURN OF THE MUSKETEERS, THE
1989, 94 mins, UK/France/Spain Ⓥ
D: Richard Lester **A:** Michael York, Oliver Reed, Frank Finlay, C. Thomas Howell, Richard Chamberlain, Kim Cattrall (Burrill/Filmdebroc/Cine 5/Iberoamericana)

In 1974, Richard Lester boosted his career with *The Three Musketeers* and its sequel, *The Four Musketeers*, lavish swashbucklers with a comic touch. His attempt at a comeback is, sadly, a stillborn event which stands as tired as its reassembled cast. King Charles is dead, and his son Louis, a 10-year-old, reigns with his mother (a reprise by Geraldine Chaplin). D'Artagnan (Michael York) is assigned to bring together his three former comrades to fight for the queen and cardinal. There follows a complicated plot involving a failed attempt to rescue King Charles I of England from execution.

RETURN OF THE PINK PANTHER, THE
1975, 115 mins, UK Ⓥ ⊙ ▭
D: Blake Edwards A: Peter Sellers, Christopher Plummer, Catherine Schell, Herbert Lom, Gregoire Aslan (United Artists)

Peter Sellers is reestablished as the bane of the existence of chief detective Herbert Lom, who is forced to reinstate Sellers when the Pink Panther diamond is stolen from its native museum. Suspicion falls on Christopher Plummer, ostensibly retired phantom jewel thief who decides he must catch the real culprit to save himself. Catherine Schell plays Plummer's wife. All hands seem to be having a ball, especially Schell, whose unabashed amusement at Clouseau's seduction attempts often matches the audience's hilarity.

RETURN OF THE SECAUCUS 7
1980, 110 mins, US Ⓥ
D: John Sayles A: Mark Arnott, Gordon Clapp, Maggie Cousineau, Brian Johnston, Adam LeFevre, John Sayles (Salsipuedes)

John Sayles has fashioned an admirable postmortem of the 1960s student left. Drama is set at eight-year reunion of seven student activists who were arrested together in Secaucus, NJ, on their way to a Washington demonstration. Film is virtually wall-to-wall talk, all of it interesting and much of it rather witty.

RETURN OF THE SEVEN
1966, 95 mins, US Ⓥ ▭
D: Burt Kennedy A: Yul Brynner, Robert Fuller, Julian Mateos, Warren Oates, Claude Akins (Mirisch)

Unsatisfactory follow-up to The Magnificent Seven, filmed in Spain. Yul Brynner, sole holdover thesp, stars. Dreary screenplay reunites Brynner and two other members of the Sturges septet—Robert Fuller evidently in the old Steve McQueen part, and Julian Mateos filling the former Horst Buchholz role—when the latter is dragooned by Emilio Fernandez, psychotic Mexican rancher who enslaves local farmers to rebuild a village.

RETURN OF THE SOLDIER, THE
1982, 102 mins, UK Ⓥ
D: Alan Bridges A: Julie Christie, Alan Bates, Glenda Jackson, Ann-Margret, Ian Holm, Frank Finlay (Brent Walker)

Alan Bates comes home from World War I with shell shock and is partly amnesiac. He does not remember his wife (Julie Christie) but does recall a lower-class girl (Glenda Jackson) he loved as a young man and his doting cousin (Ann-Margret). It is more quaint than anything else and fails to find the depth in these people.

RETURN OF THE TEXAS CHAINSAW MASSACRE, THE
1995, 102 mins, US Ⓥ
D: Kim Henkel A: Renee Zellweger, Matthew McConaughey, Robert Jacks, Tony Perenski, Joe Stevens (Return)

Not so much a sequel as an unofficial remake, Return manages the difficult feat of being genuinely scary and sharply self-satirical all at once. Jenny (Renee Zellweger) and three friends wind up terrorized by Vilmer (Matthew McConaughey). Jenny seeks refuge in the secluded office of Darla (Tony Perenski), a voluptuous, silicone-enhanced real-estate agent. Unfortunately, Darla is in league with Vilmer. Even more unfortunately, both Darla and Vilmer are in league with Leatherface (Robert Jacks), the chain-saw-wielding maniac.

RETURN TO OZ
1985, 110 mins, US Ⓥ ⊙
D: Walter Murch A: Nicol Williamson, Jean Marsh, Fairuza Balk, Piper Laurie, Matt Clark (Walt Disney/Silver Screen Partners II)

An astonishingly somber, melancholy, and, sadly, unengaging telling of little Dorothy's second voyage to the Emerald City employs an amusement park full of imaginative characters and special effects, but a heaviness of tone and absence of narrative drive prevent the flights of fancy from getting off the ground. Dorothy discovers the Yellow Brick Road in disrepair, the Emerald City in ruins, and her companions from the previous trip turned to stone. Along the way, as before, she accumulates some helpful friends.
1985: Nomination: Best Visual Effects

RETURN TO PARADISE
1953, 90 mins, US

D: Mark Robson **A:** Gary Cooper, Roberta Haynes, Barry Jones, Moira MacDonald (Aspen)

The simplicity of authentic Samoan settings provides a strong, appealing background for this leisurely, idyllic, romantic drama. Gary Cooper portrays a soldier of fortune taking his ease in the unhurried life of the island paradises. A beauty attracts his attention to set the romance of the piece. For conflict there is the domination of the natives by a missionary who has forgotten the Bible teaches more than hellfire and damnation. Cooper's easygoing, understated style of histrionics is just right for the character.

RETURN TO PEYTON PLACE
1961, 123 mins, US ⓥ ▢

D: Jose Ferrer **A:** Carol Lynley, Jeff Chandler, Eleanor Parker, Mary Astor, Tuesday Weld (20th Century-Fox)

High-class soap opera preserves the nature of Grace Metalious's novel, alternately building three related story veins: (1) Carol Lynley's, as the tyro novelist whose close-to-home fiction produces civic repercussions; (2) Tuesday Weld's, as the girl whose past misfortunes are soothed when Lynley's book sheds new light; and (3) Mary Astor's, as a superpossessive mother who attempts to wreck the marriage of her son. The lovely Lynley does a thoroughly capable job, but veteran Astor walks off with the picture.

RETURN TO THE BLUE LAGOON
1991, 100 mins, US ⓥ

D: William A. Graham **A:** Milla Jovovich, Brian Krause, Lisa Pelikan, Courtney Phillips, Garette Patrick Ratcliff (Columbia/Price)

Pointless spin-off of the 1980 hit has the original's leading characters found dead in a tiny boat along with their young son, who has survived the journey in fine shape. But the tyke is soon put out to sea again to escape an outbreak of cholera and, along with straitlaced American Lisa Pelikan and her little daughter, washes up on the same tropical island his parents inhabited. The budding beauties hit adolescence and assume the bodies of international model Milla Jovovich and TV hunk Brian Krause.

REUBEN, REUBEN
1983, 101 mins, US ⓥ

D: Robert Ellis Miller **A:** Tom Conti, Kelly McGillis, Roberts Blossom, Cynthia Harris, E. Katherine Kerr (20th Century-Fox/Taft Entertainment)

About a leching, alcoholic Scottish poet making the New England campus circuit, film is exceptionally literate, with lines that carom with wit from the superb adaptation by Julius J. Epstein of a 1964 Peter De Vries novel. Kelly McGillis becomes the all-consuming obsession of Tom Conti as he lurches from one bottle and bed to another. The film is a tour de force act for Conti.
1983: Nominations: Best Actor (Tom Conti), Adapted Screenplay

REUNION
1942, 101 mins, US

D: Jules Dassin **A:** Joan Crawford, John Wayne, Philip Dorn, Reginald Owen, Albert Basserman (M-G-M)

Story opens just prior to move-in of the Germans to Paris, with rich playgirl Crawford engaged to French patriot and arms manufacturer Philip Dorn. On fall of the city, girl discovers that her intended is co-operating to the fullest with the Nazis. Disillusioned, she hides John Wayne, who has eluded the gestapo, and gradually falls in love with him. Direction lacks smoothness in pace, and dwells too long in many spots on character development and minor incidents.

REUNION
1989, 110 mins, France/W. Germany/UK ⓥ

D: Jerry Schatzberg **A:** Jason Robards, Christian Anholt, Samuel West, Francoise Fabian, Barbara Jefford (Ariane/FR3/NEF/Vertriebs/CLG/Tac/Arbo/Maran)

This enormously impressive film ranks as one of the best of countless pics dealing with the rise of Nazism in Germany in the early 1930s. Based on Fred Uhlman's autobiographical novel, drama is set in Stuttgart in 1933 and deals with the growing friendship between two schoolboys: Hans (Christian Anholt), son of a Jewish doctor and World War I vet who, till now, was considered a pillar of the community; and the aristocratic Konrad (Samuel West), who's led a sheltered life, taught by private tutors, and who finds himself stimulated by the intelligent, sensitive Hans. Gradually, as the year progresses, the fascist movement takes hold.

REVENGE
1990, 124 mins, US ⓥ ⊙ ▢

D: Tony Scott **A:** Kevin Costner, Anthony

Quinn, Madeleine Stowe, Sally Kirkland, James Gammon (New World/Rastar)

Contempo tale of a doomed love triangle in lawless Mexico has a romantic sweep and elemental power that ultimately transcend its flaws. Cochran (Kevin Costner) heads down to Puerto Vallarta for recreation at the home of a wealthy sportsman friend Tibey (Anthony Quinn) and is smitten with his host's unhappy wife Miryea (Madeleine Stowe). Despite his friend's graciousness and reputation as a cold-blooded killer, Cochran takes the suicide plunge into passion, running off with Miryea for a sexual idyll.

REVENGE OF FRANKENSTEIN, THE
1958, 89 mins, UK ⓥ
D: Terence Fisher **A:** Peter Cushing, Francis Matthews, Eunice Gayson, Michael Gwynn, Lionel Jeffries (Hammer)

Frankenstein is again collecting bits of bone and tissue, muscle and blood, to put together a man of his creation. Again he succeeds, but again something goes wrong and his creature—through brain damage—becomes a cannibal, slavering blood and saliva. The production is a rich one. The screenplay is well plotted.

REVENGE OF THE CREATURE
1955, 82 mins, US ▭
D: Jack Arnold **A:** John Agar, Lori Nelson, John Bromfield, Robert P. Williams, Nestor Paiva (Universal)

Sequel to *Creature from the Black Lagoon* is a routine shocker that doesn't get much of a boost from 3-D treatment. The fellow who plays the scaly monster in the film certainly rates top billing. Expertly made up, he's the only one who looks and acts believable. Fact that he only roars and has no speaking lines helps since the script is hardly on the expert side.

REVENGE OF THE NERDS
1984, 90 mins, US ⓥ ⊙
D: Jeff Kanew **A:** Robert Carradine, Anthony Edwards, Ted McGinley, Bernie Casey (Interscope)

Simpleminded romp about a group of freshmen outcasts doesn't qualify for the dean's list, but shows more than enough smarts to deserve passing grades. The nerds suffer constant humiliations from the older students and ultimately decide to fight back. Led by hometown buddies Lewis (Robert Carradine) and Gilbert (Anthony Edwards), they rent a house and form their own frat.

REVENGE OF THE NINJA
1983, 88 mins, US ⓥ
D: Sam Firstenberg **A:** Sho Kosugi, Keith Vitali, Virgil Frye, Arthur Roberts, Mario Gallo (Cannon)

Entertaining martial-arts actioner, following up *Enter the Ninja* (1981). Cho Osaki (Sho Kosugi), with his child and its grandma, runs a gallery featuring imported Japanese dolls, which unbeknownst to him is a front for heroin smuggling run by his pal Braden (Arthur Roberts). Braden kills granny, kidnaps the child Kane (Kane Kosugi), and later kills Osaki's best friend, martial-arts expert Dave Hatcher (Keith Vitali). Fine fight choreography by Kosugi keeps the film cooking.

REVENGE OF THE PINK PANTHER
1978, 98 mins, US ⓥ ⊙ ▭
D: Blake Edwards **A:** Peter Sellers, Herbert Lom, Dyan Cannon, Robert Webber, Burt Kwouk (United Artists)

This time out Sellers tracks down an international drug ring. Herbert Lom encores as Sellers's nemesis and Dyan Cannon is delightful as the resourceful discarded mistress of dope smuggler Robert Webber. The screenplay is an embarrassment of riches: Sellers, faithful servant Burt Kwouk, Lom, Cannon, etc., are too much for a simple story line. The result is that the plot roams all over the map, in totality adding up to less than the parts.

REVERSAL OF FORTUNE
1990, 120 mins, US ⓥ
D: Barbet Schroeder **A:** Jeremy Irons, Glenn Close, Ron Silver, Anabella Sciorra, Uta Hagen (Warner/Shochiku Fuji/Sovereign)

Reversal of Fortune turns the sensational Claus von Bulow case into a riveting film. The story of the Newport society figure's trial, conviction, and acquittal on appeal for the attempted murder of his wealthy wife is presented here in an absorbing, complex mosaic. Jeremy Irons gives a memorable performance as the inscrutable European blueblood emigre. Cast in perfect opposition is Ron Silver, seizing with dynamic gusto the role of a career as von Bulow's passionately idealistic but streetwise defense attorney. Glenn Close is typically excellent in the smaller but pivotal role of Sunny von Bulow.
1990: Best Actor (Jeremy Irons)
Nominations: Best Director, Adapted Screenplay

REVOLUTION
1986, 125 mins, UK/Norway Ⓥ ⊙ ▭
D: Hugh Hudson A: Al Pacino, Donald
Sutherland, Nastassja Kinski, Joan Plowright, Annie Lennox (Goldcrest/Viking)

Watching *Revolution* is a little like visiting a museum—it looks good without really being alive. The film doesn't tell a
story so much as it uses characters to illustrate what the American Revolution has
come to mean. While intimate story of
Tom Dobb (Al Pacino) and his son Ned
(Dexter Fletcher, Sid Owen as young Ned)
and Tom's love for renegade aristocrat
Daisy McConnahay (Nastassja Kinski) is
full of holes, the larger canvas is staged
beautifully.

REWARD, THE
1965, 91 mins, US ▭
D: Serge Bourguignon A: Max von Sydow, Yvette Mimieux, Efrem Zimbalist
Jr., Gilbert Roland, Emilio Fernandez (Ar-
cola/20th Century-Fox)

The reward for a fugitive and its effects
on a group thrown together by fate comprise the theme of this moody, somewhat
uneven, desert meller. Crop duster Max
von Sydow crash-lands in a boondocks
Mexican town coincident with the passing
through of Efrem Zimbalist Jr., on the lam
from a murder rap and accompanied by
Yvette Mimieux. Sydow cues police inspector Gilbert Roland to the price on
Zimbalist's head, and the slow chase is on,
leading to uneventful and unresisted capture.

RHAPSODY IN BLUE
1945, 130 mins, US Ⓥ ⊙
D: Irving Rapper A: Robert Alda, Joan
Leslie, Alexis Smith, Charles Coburn, Oscar Levant, Albert Basserman (Warner)

The years have certainly been kind to
George Gershwin's music, and the glib interplay of names such as Otto Kahn, Jas-
cha Heifetz, Maurice Ravel, Walter
Damrosch, and Rachmaninoff (all of
whom are impersonated) lend conviction
to the basic yarn of the New York East
Side boy whose musical genius was to
sweep the world. Robert Alda plays
Gershwin and makes him believable. Herbert Rudley as Ira Gershwin looks startlingly like the famed lyricist brother of
the composer. Oscar Levant as Oscar Levant can't miss, and he doesn't here.
1945: Nominations: Best Scoring of a
Musical Picture, Sound

RHINESTONE
1984, 111 mins, US Ⓥ ⊙ ▭
D: Bob Clark A: Sylvester Stallone, Dolly
Parton, Richard Farnsworth, Ron Leibman, Tim Thomerson (20th Century-Fox)

Effortlessly living up to its title,
Rhinestone is as artificial and synthetic a
concoction as has ever made its way to the
screen. Directed in low-down, good-
spirited vulgar fashion, film is a genuine
oddball. Sylvester Stallone's character,
that of a Gotham cabbie whom singer
Dolly Parton bets she can turn into a convincing country crooner in two weeks'
time, is like no one ever encountered on
Earth before.

RICH AND FAMOUS
1981, 117 mins, US Ⓥ ⊙
D: George Cukor A: Jacqueline Bisset,
Candice Bergen, Meg Ryan, David Selby,
Hart Bochner (M-G-M)

An absorbing drama of some notable
qualities, the greatest of which is a gutsy
and fascinating performance by Jacqueline
Bisset. Tale delineating the friendship of
two smart, creative ladies over a period of
two decades makes for a "woman's picture" in the best sense of the term. Plot
dynamics of Gerald Ayres's imaginative
updating of John Van Druten's 1940 play
Old Acquaintance rather closely follow
those of solid 1943 film version.

RICHARD III
1955, 160 mins, UK Ⓥ
D: Laurence Olivier, Anthony Bushell A:
Laurence Olivier, John Gielgud, Claire
Bloom, Ralph Richardson, Alec Clunes,
Stanley Baker (London)

The Bard pulled no punches in his
dramatization of *Richard III*, and Laurence
Olivier's filmization likewise portrays him
as a ruthless and unscrupulous character.
The murder of his brother Clarence (John
Gielgud), the betrayal of his cousin Buckingham (Ralph Richardson), the suffoca-
tion of the princes in the Tower are among
the unscrupulous steps in the path of Richard's crowning, which are staged with lurid, melodramatic conviction. Running
Olivier's performance a very close second
is Richardson's scheming Buckingham.
1956: Nomination: Best Actor (Laurence
Olivier)

RICHARD III
1996, 105 mins, UK/US Ⓥ ⊙ ▭
D: Richard Loncraine A: Ian McKellen,
Annette Bening, Jim Broadbent, Robert
Downey Jr., Nigel Hawthorne, Kristen

Scott Thomas (First Look/United Artists)

Spirited acting, machine-gun pacing, and ominous Art Deco settings combine to rousing effect in this *Richard III*. Adapting an acclaimed British stage production, director Richard Loncraine and star Ian McKellen do the Bard a favor by transferring his most celebrated royal thug from the Middle Ages to the no-less-blood-soaked 1930s. Loncraine and McKellen have condensed Shakespeare's second-longest play, yet the cutting is so intelligently done that it both aids the pace and sometimes makes meanings and character relationships clearer than they are in Olivier's celebrated 1955 movie, which is longer by fifty-five minutes. McKellen's Richard is less the Machiavellian monster of some versions and more the craftiest of organization men. A vivid, finely honed characterization, it receives top-notch support.

1995: Nominations: Best Art Direction, Costume Design

RICHARD PRYOR—HERE AND NOW
1983, 94 mins, US ⊽

D: Richard Pryor **A:** Richard Pryor (Columbia/Indigo)

Pryor's third concert film is a mixture of the ones done before and after the fire that almost killed him. Drug-free and still grateful for a second chance, Pryor remains much more mellow, but less self-examining and contemplative than in *Live on the Sunset Strip* (1982). Some of the hostility and bite have returned, though well under control. On top of the laughs, he also displays a deepening sympathy for those doomed by substances.

RICHARD PRYOR LIVE ON THE SUNSET STRIP
1982, 82 mins, US ⊽

D: Joe Layton **A:** Richard Pryor (Columbia/Rastar)

Richard Pryor's stand-up routine was captured on film in two nights at the Palladium in 1981. After a number of roles in successful pictures, he brings an acting ability to his stage routine that enhances his well-established talent for caricature. What this allows him to do is pull the audience into moments of genuine emotion, then clobber them suddenly with a hilarious switch. By far the best comes with a candid discussion of his drug addiction that culminates in the freebase explosion that almost killed him.

RICHIE RICH
1994, 95 mins, US ⊽ ☉

D: Donald Petrie **A:** Macaulay Culkin, John Larroquette, Edward Herrmann, Jonathan Hyde, Christine Ebersole (Silver/Warner)

Decently crafted but oddly charmless, *Richie Rich* isn't likely to jump-start the fading superstardom of aging child star Macaulay Culkin. Based on the popular Harvey comic books (and subsequent cartoon spin-offs), pic casts Culkin in the title role as the world's richest 12-year-old. Richie is able to find some working-class kids to pal around with. His new buddies prove to be valuable allies when Lawrence Van Dough (John Larroquette), a Rich Industries executive, attempts a hostile takeover of the Rich fortune.

RICH IN LOVE
1993, 105 mins, US ⊽ ☉

D: Bruce Beresford **A:** Albert Finney, Jill Clayburgh, Kathryn Erbe, Kyle MacLachlan, Piper Laurie, Ethan Hawke (M-G-M/Zanuck)

The creative team that brought *Driving Miss Daisy* to the screen fails to conjure up similar magic. Despite a luminous performance by Kathryn Erbe, the story of a South Carolina teen's coming-of-age in a dysfunctional family seems overly familiar and dramatically diffuse. Is it a story about the shattering effect of divorce on Erbe and her aimless, recently retired father (Albert Finney)? Not really, since they eventually adapt quite well to life without mom (Jill Clayburgh), who briefly pops in and out of the film without making much of an impression.

RICOCHET
1991, 97 mins, US ⊽ ☉ ▭

D: Russell Mulcahy **A:** Denzel Washington, John Lithgow, Ice T, Kevin Pollak, Lindsay Wagner (HBO/Silver)

A taut, twisty urban suspenser powered by the spring-loaded performance of Denzel Washington in his first major action role, film has a nasty streak and a tendency toward implausible excess. Washington plays an ambitious young cop who nails a vicious hit man (John Lithgow). The killer watches the gifted cop become district attorney and acquire a loving family and a promising political future. When Lithgow finally breaks out of jail, he's armed with a diabolical plan to wreak havoc on everything his nemesis has attained. Pic threatens to become truly absorbing as Lithgow's brilliant revenge scheme unfolds, but soon abandons cleverness in favor of spectacle.

RIDE 'EM COWBOY
1942, 84 mins, US
D: Arthur Lubin A: Bud Abbott, Lou Costello, Dick Foran, Anne Gwynne, John Mack Brown (Universal)

Typical Abbott and Costello film fare whose title and background of a dude ranch out west are only props for the usual broadly burlesqued antics of the pair. The two comics are picked up in New York as a couple of peanut-and-hot-dog vendors at a rodeo show and are quickly shunted west to join up as cowhands on a dude ranch.

RIDE IN THE WHIRLWIND
1966, 82 mins, US ⓥ ⊙
D: Monte Hellman A: Cameron Mitchell, Jack Nicholson, Millie Perkins, Katherine Squire, Harry Dean Stanton (Proteus)

A flat, woodenly acted western with mild suspense that never grabs. Jack Nicholson's script is little more than a promising plotline rather than a fully developed scenario. A trio of uncommunicative saddle tramps—Nicholson, Cameron Mitchell, Tom Filer—stumble on a motley gang holed up in a mountain shack after a stagecoach robbery. They find themselves surrounded by a posse of vigilantes that is going to string them up first and ask questions later.

RIDE LONESOME
1959, 74 mins, US ⊟
D: Budd Boetticher A: Randolph Scott, Karen Steele, Pernell Roberts, James Best, Lee Van Cleef, James Coburn (Ranown/Columbia)

Ride Lonesome has Randolph Scott as a bounty hunter whose interest in a young murderer (James Best) seems to be solely the money he will collect. Along the way, he picks up a young widow (Karen Steele) and two feckless outlaws (Pernell Roberts and James Coburn). Soon Best's brother (Lee Van Cleef) is trailing them, intent on rescuing Best. Scriptwriter Burt Kennedy has used genuine speech of the frontier and some humor to give the screenplay additional interest where the pursuit portions necessarily lag.

RIDE THE HIGH COUNTRY
(UK: GUNS IN THE AFTERNOON)
1962, 94 mins, US ⓥ ⊙ ⊟
D: Sam Peckinpah A: Randolph Scott, Joel McCrea, Mariette Hartley, Edgar Buchanan, Ron Starr, Warren Oates (M-G-M)

Scott and McCrea play their ages in roles that could well be extensions of characters each has played in countless earlier films. They are quick-triggered ex-lawmen reduced to taking jobs as guards for a gold shipment. They engage in one last battle—over a woman and involving a youth who epitomizes their own youth. Sam Peckinpah's direction gives N. B. Stone Jr.'s script a measure beyond its adequacy, instilling bright moments of sharp humor and an overall significant empathetic flavor.

RIDE, VAQUERO
1953, 91 mins, US
D: John Farrow A: Robert Taylor, Ava Gardner, Howard Keel, Anthony Quinn, Kurt Kasznar, Jack Elam (M-G-M)

Locale is a territory under the thumb of outlaw gangs controlled by Anthony Quinn and his lieutenant (Robert Taylor). When Howard Keel tries to found a cattle empire and brings in settlers, the outlaws fight back, knowing they will be through if civilization comes to the land. Keel brings Ava Gardner, his bride, to his new homestead, only to find it a smoking ruin. Taylor is very good in selling the quiet menace of his character, and Quinn stands out as the flamboyant outlaw leader.

RIDE WITH THE DEVIL
1999, 138 mins, US ⓥ ⊙ ⊟
D: Ang Lee A: Skeet Ulrich, Tobey Maguire, Jewel, Jeffrey Wright, Simon Baker, Jonathan Rhys Meyers (Good Machine/Universal)

Impressing once again with the diversity of his choices of subject matter and milieu, director Ang Lee has made a brutal but sensitively observed film about the fringes of the Civil War along the Missouri-Kansas border. Jack Bull Chiles (Skeet Ulrich) is a product of old-style Southern life. His close friend Jake Roedel (Tobey Maguire) is the son of a poor German immigrant. Among their colleagues are confident leader Black John (James Caviezel), mistrustful psychotic Pitt Mackeson (Jonathan Rhys Meyers), and young gentleman George Clyde (Simon Baker). When the men hole up for winter, a self-possessed widow, Sue Lee (Jewel), brings them provisions and Jack initiates a romance with her. Intelligent script pays gratifying attention to linguistic niceties. On the downside, story slows as the men retreat increasingly from the action.

RIDICULE
1996, 102 mins, France ⊗ ▢
D: Patrice Leconte **A:** Charles Berling, Jean Rochefort, Fanny Ardant, Judith Godreche, Bernard Giraudeau (Epithete/ Cinea/France 3)

Resplendent and intelligent from start to finish, *Ridicule* strikes a winning balance between humor and heart as it pillories an era in France (the court of Louis XVI, circa 1780) when wit was the most valuable currency and a man's fortune and reputation could be made or undone on the strength of a single remark. Engineer Gregoire Ponceludon de Malavoy (Charles Berling) is baron of an estate where the peasants are dropping (literally) like flies, felled by diseases that breed in the murderous swamps. Gregoire sets out from the provinces to plead his case at Versailles. Berling fits the bill as the Candide-like interloper who is both attracted to and repelled by the heady, elitist atmosphere at court.

RIDING HIGH
1943, 89 mins, US
D: George Marshall **A:** Dorothy Lamour, Dick Powell, Victor Moore, Cass Daley (Paramount)

Lots of ingredients for a b.o. musical are in this one, and George Marshall makes the most of a rather flimsy framework. An ex-burlesque principal (Dorothy Lamour) lands back at her father's ill-fated silver mine out in Arizona when her show folds. She finds that mining engineer Dick Powell is also back after trying unsuccessfully to sell stock in the same mine. Lamour takes a job at the elaborate Dude Ranch cabaret, run by Cass Daley, in order to help her dad.

RIFF-RAFF
1992, 92 mins, UK ⊗
D: Ken Loach **A:** Robert Carlyle, Emer McCourt, Jimmy Coleman, Ricky Tomlinson, Willie Ross (Parallax/Film Four)

Sprightly ensemble comedy is strong on yocks and easy to digest. Stevie (Robert Carlyle), a young Glaswegian, has come south and gotten a job converting a closed-down hospital into luxury apartments. His coworkers are from all over. They're breaking every regulation in the book and running scams on the side. Home is a squat in a dingy council block. After Stevie meets Susan (Emer McCourt), a drifter from Belfast, they move in together and make a go of it in the big city. Story yo-yos between their fragile relationship and the shenanigans on the building site.

RIFIFI
See: Du Rififi Chez les Hommes

RIGHT CROSS
1950, 89 mins, US
D: John Sturges **A:** June Allyson, Dick Powell, Ricardo Montalban, Lionel Barrymore (M-G-M)

Ricardo Montalban portrays a champion prizefighter who carries a chip on his shoulder because he is a Mexican. There's a neat shift of the social problem, the persecution being Montalban's own and not the result of any prejudice from those he terms the "gringos." June Allyson is Montalban's manager, carrying on for her crippled dad (Lionel Barrymore). A breezy style brightens up the drama and makes it good entertainment.

RIGHT STUFF, THE
1983, 193 mins, US ⊗
D: Philip Kaufman **A:** Sam Shepard, Scott Glenn, Ed Harris, Dennis Quaid, Fred Ward, Barbara Hershey (Ladd Company)

This big-scale look at the development of the US space program and its pioneering aviators is full of beauty, intelligence, and excitement. Tale spans 16 years, from ace test pilot Chuck Yeager's breaking of the sound barrier over the California desert to Vice-President Johnson's welcoming of the astronauts to their new home in Houston with an enormous barbecue inside the Astrodome. Emblematic figure here is Yeager, played by a taciturn Sam Shepard, the embodiment of "the right stuff," that ineffable quality which separates the men from the boys, so to speak.
1983: Best Original Score, Editing, Sound, Sound Editing
Nominations: Best Picture, Supp. Actor (Sam Shepard), Cinematography, Art Direction

RIKKY AND PETE
1988, 101 mins, Australia ⊗ ⊙
D: Nadia Tass **A:** Stephen Kearney, Nina Landis, Tetchie Agbayani, Bill Hunter, Bruce Spence (United Artists/Cascade)

Film has a clutch of potentially interesting characters and a promising story line, but the characters are inadequately developed and the plotting doesn't live up to expectations. Pete is an inventor in Melbourne. His sister, Rikky, is tired of her latest beau and of singing in a bar. They take off for the Outback. Stephen Kearney gives Pete plenty of raffish charm, and

Nina Landis has a warm personality as Rikky.

RING, THE
1927, 106 mins, UK ⊘ ⊗
D: Alfred Hitchcock **A:** Carl Brisson, Lillian Hall-Davies, Ian Hunter, Forrester Harvey, Gordon Harker (B.I.P.)

At last, the performance of the long-deferred "promise" of Alfred Hitchcock. Carl Brisson is overshadowed by the acting of the heavy, Ian Hunter. He is a first-rate film actor with an engaging he-man personality. Gordon Harker, on the screen for the first time, nearly steals this one as a hard-boiled cynical trainer. His sense of screen comedy is acute and restrained at the same time. Hitchcock gets more out of Lillian Hall-Davies than any continental director.

RING, THE
1952, 79 mins, US ⊘
D: Kurt Neumann **A:** Gerald Mohr, Rita Moreno, Lalo Rios, Robert Arthur, Robert Osterloh, Jack Elam (King Bros/United Artists)

Efforts of a young boxer to fight his way up from preliminaries to main-bout stature provides a sock setting for a well-spun yarn of discrimination against the Mexican-Americans. Cast is headed by Gerald Mohr as the manager, Lalo Rios as the boxer, and Rita Moreno.

RING OF BRIGHT WATER
1969, 107 mins, UK ⊘
D: Jack Couffer **A:** Bill Travers, Virginia McKenna, Roddy McMillan, Jameson Clark (Palomar)

An engaging film about an otter. Story concerns a London civil servant, anxious to get out of the rat race to write. He makes his decision when he acquires Mij, a young otter, as a pet. So he and Mij depart for a lonely coastal village in the Highlands. Travers and McKenna unselfishly subdue their performances to the star demands of the lolloping young rascal, Mij.

RING OF SPIES
1964, 90 mins, UK
D: Robert Tronson **A:** Bernard Lee, William Sylvester, Margaret Tyzack, David Kossoff (British Lion)

In 1961, British spies were sentenced for their part in the Portland Spy Case. This film presents a realistic documentary of the surface events leading up to the uncovering of the spies. Henry Houghton (Bernard Lee) is transferred to records at the Portland Underwater Weapons Establishment. With a chip on his shoulder and a desire for easy money, he is readily blackmailed into borrowing secret documents. He inveigles a respectable spinster who is in charge of the safe keys, to help him.

RINGS ON HER FINGERS
1942, 85 mins, US ⊘
D: Rouben Mamoulian **A:** Henry Fonda, Gene Tierney, Laird Cregar, Spring Byington (20th Century-Fox)

Lightweight film tumbles and stumbles along in boresome fashion to emerge as misfit entertainment. Gene Tierney is a store clerk plucked by confidence operators Laird Cregar and Spring Byington for a whirl as cute decoy for their shakedowns of rich victims. Henry Fonda, an accountant vacationing in California with savings of $15,000 to buy a sailboat, gets caught in the net and clipped.

RIO BRAVO
1959, 140 mins, US ⊘ ⊙
D: Howard Hawks **A:** John Wayne, Dean Martin, Ricky Nelson, Angie Dickinson, Walter Brennan (Armada)

A big, brawling western. Wayne, a fast-shooting sheriff, is clubbed, another man knocked out, and a third man murdered. Plot thereafter revolves around Wayne's attempts to hold the murderer, brother of the most powerful rancher in the area, until the arrival some days hence of the US marshal. He's up against the rancher utilizing gunman tactics to free the jailed killer. Producer-director Howard Hawks makes handsome use of force in logically unraveling his hard-hitting narrative, creating suspense at times and occasionally inserting lighter moments to give variety.

RIO CONCHOS
1964, 105 mins, US ⊘ ▭
D: Gordon Douglas **A:** Richard Boone, Stuart Whitman, Anthony Franciosa, Wende Wagner, Warner Anderson, Edmond O'Brien (20th Century-Fox)

Big, action-packed slam-bang western, with as tough a set of characters as ever rode the sage, is adventure at its best. Script limns the quest of four men for 2,000 stolen repeating rifles that a group of former Confederate soldiers have been running to the Apaches. Quartet is composed of Stuart Whitman, a cavalry captain; Richard Boone, an ex-Reb who hates Apaches; Tony Franciosa, a Mexican gigolo-type killer; and Jim Brown, a cavalry corporal. Their destination is the camp of a demented Confederate gunrunner (Edmond O'Brien) who wants vengeance on the North for the South's defeat.

RIO GRANDE
1950, 105 mins, US Ⓥ
D: John Ford A: John Wayne, Maureen O'Hara, Ben Johnson, Claude Jarman Jr., Harry Carey Jr., Victor McLaglen (Republic/Argosy)

Outdoor action at its best, delivered in the John Ford manner. John Wayne is a lonely man, fighting Indians in the west. To his fort comes his young son, Claude Jarman Jr., whom he has not seen in 15 years, and Maureen O'Hara, Wayne's estranged wife, determined to take the son back.

RIO LOBO
1970, 114 mins, US Ⓥ ⊙
D: Howard Hawks A: John Wayne, Jorge Rivero, Jennifer O'Neill, Jack Elam, Chris Mitchum (Malabar/Cinema Center)

In the Civil War, Wayne is a Union colonel who keeps losing army gold shipments to Confederate guerrillas led by Jorge Rivero and Chris Mitchum. He captures them, but they won't tell him who the traitors are who have been tipping them off about the gold. Hawks's direction is as listless as the plot.

RIO RITA
1929, 135 mins, US
D: Luther Reed A: Bebe Daniels, John Boles, Bert Wheeler, Robert Woolsey, Dorothy Lee (RKO)

Adapted from Ziegfeld's stage *Rio Rita*, picture is in black-and-white except for the ballroom portion, handsomely colored by Technicolor. Bebe Daniels hogs the talker, although John Boles as the ranger captain is entitled to a word of credit, both for a splendid canned voice and his playing. In comedy it's Bert Wheeler first, with Robert Woolsey next, while Dorothy Lee stands second to Daniels. The story is that of a captain of the Texas Rangers seeking a bandit over the border and falling in love, with the attendant incidents, sometimes melodramatic.

RIO RITA
1942, 91 mins, US Ⓥ
D: S. Sylvan Simon A: Bud Abbott, Lou Costello, Kathryn Grayson, John Carroll, Tom Conway (M-G-M)

Script relies principally on a Nazi espionage story. Abbott and Costello, along with hero John Carroll, save the day in the nick. Director has spaced the A&C nonsensities with a good sense of timing to properly break up the hoke. So far as the former Ziegfeld stage musical is concerned, Metro uses nothing but the original title song and the "Rangers" number.

RIOT
1968, 96 mins, US
D: Buzz Kulik A: Jim Brown, Gene Hackman, Mike Kellin, Gerald S. O'Loughlin, Ben Carruthers (Paramount)

Good prison programmer produced with authenticity inside Arizona state prison. Jim Brown and Gene Hackman are leaders of a convict revolt which paralyzes prison routine and unleashes some violent passions. Brown's immensely strong screen presence is manifest. Hackman gives the best performance as an equivocating, cynical manipulator of crowd psychology.

RIOT IN CELL BLOCK 11
1954, 80 mins, US Ⓥ
D: Don Siegel A: Neville Brand, Emile Meyer, Frank Faylen, Leo Gordon, Robert Osterloh (Allied Artists)

Hard-hitting, suspenseful prison thriller deals with a riot, how it started and why, what was done to halt it, and the capitulations on both sides. The points for reform made in the Wanger production cover overcrowding housing, poor food, the mingling of mentally well and mentally sick prisoners, and the character-corroding idleness of men caged in cell blocks. A standout performance is given by Emile Meyer, the warden who understands the prisoners' problems.

RISE OF CATHERINE THE GREAT, THE
(AKA: CATHERINE THE GREAT)
1934, 95 mins, UK Ⓥ ⊙
D: Paul Czinner A: Douglas Fairbanks Jr., Elisabeth Bergner, Flora Robson, Gerald du Maurier, Irene Vanbrugh (London)

Elisabeth Bergner charms as she progresses and is altogether believable as the minor German princess summoned to Russia by the Empress Elizabeth to wed her erratic nephew, the Grand Duke Peter, sometimes called Peter the Impossible. The throne needs an heir. Bergner's scene with the dying empress (Flora Robson) is a gem of expert playing by both women and there are other highlights particularly a banquet sequence, which stand out. Fairbanks's performance as the fuming Peter is one of the best he has ever given.

RISING SUN
1993, 129 mins, US Ⓥ ⊙
D: Philip Kaufman **A:** Sean Connery, Wesley Snipes, Harvey Keitel, Cary-Hiroyuki Tagawa, Mako (20th Century-Fox/Walrus)

A thriller spurred by the murder of a white party girl at the opening of a Japanese office tower in Los Angeles. Lieutenant Web Smith (Wesley Snipes) is advised to bring with him Detective John Connor (Sean Connery), who is so expert on the Japanese that he is suspected of having been co-opted by them. Structure tiresomely flip-flops investigative scenes with interludes of the men driving through the wet night as Connor imparts his wisdom to his less experienced partner. Snipes seems lax and unfocused here. Connery brings plenty of authoritative, fatherly appeal to the role, issuing sage aphorisms.

RISKY BUSINESS
1983, 96 mins, US Ⓥ ⊙
D: Paul Brickman **A:** Tom Cruise, Rebecca DeMornay, Curtis Armstrong, Bronson Pinchot, Raphael Sbarge (Geffen)

High-schooler Tom Cruise meets sharp-looking hooker Rebecca DeMornay. She shacks up in Cruise's splendid home while his parents are out of town and, since he's anxious to prove himself as a Future Enterpriser in one of his school's more blatantly greed-oriented programs, convinces him to make the house into a bordello for one night. Not only is Cruise rewarded financially, it gets him into Princeton to boot.

RITA, SUE AND BOB TOO
1987, 95 mins, UK Ⓥ ⊙
D: Alan Clarke **A:** Michelle Holmes, Siobhan Finneran, George Costigan, Lesley Sharp (Film Four/Umbrella/British Screen)

Sad-funny comedy about sex and life in the Yorkshire city of Bradford. In the opening sequence, Bob, a real estate agent, gives schoolgirls Rita and Sue a lift home, but stops off first on the moors above the city and proposes sex with them. The girls are agreeable, with Sue taking the first turn on the reclining seat in Bob's Rover. Immediately screenwriter Andrea Dunbar injects a completely convincing mixture of raunchy comedy and sadness.

RITZ, THE
1976, 90 mins, US Ⓥ
D: Richard Lester **A:** Jack Weston, Rita Moreno, Jerry Stiller, Kaye Ballard, F. Murray Abraham (Warner)

Terrence McNally adapted his 1975 play about assorted mistaken identities and hang-ups in a NY gay steambath. Story has Weston fingered for rubout by dying father-in-law George Coulouris. Escaping from the midwest, Weston heads for a notorious Gotham gay bath, figuring that avenging brother-in-law Jerry Stiller will never find him. Classic farce construction provides the expected physical action.

RIVER, THE
1938, 30 mins, US
D: Pare Lorentz (Farm Security Administration)

Documentary pic seeks to tell the story of the Mississippi River, its sources, its majestic course, its destination, its uses and abuse by heedless man, and its relentless retaliation. It skips from fact to fact, argument to argument, but doesn't quite weave a perfect pattern. Film's score, blended from symphonic sources, ballads, spirituals, and original compositions, highlights the film dramatically. Narrative is vividly effective, being a composite of the straight forward and the poetic.

RIVER, THE
1951, 99 mins, India/US Ⓥ ⊙
D: Jean Renoir **A:** Nora Swinburne, Esmond Knight, Arthur Shields, Thomas E. Breen, Adrienne Corri (Oriental-International/United Artists)

Life on the Ganges River in west Bengal. It is a distinctive story of adolescent love, with a philosophy that life flows on just as the river. It is ablaze with vivid, contrasting colors. But one never feels the real India and rather suspects that this is a highly glamorized version. The story tells how the life of a British family is interrupted by the appearance of one Captain John on a visit to a neighbor. Two young teenagers fall as madly in love with the captain, who lost a leg in the last war, as their newly awakened emotions will allow.

RIVER, THE
1984, 122 mins, US Ⓥ ⊙
D: Mark Rydell **A:** Mel Gibson, Sissy Spacek, Shane Bailey, Becky Jo Lynch, Scott Glenn (Universal)

Pic puts fundamental American values to the test in a society that has come unglued. Setting the tone is the Garvey family battling the floodwaters of the river to save their farm. Farmers are forced to sell off their land with hungry-wolf businessman Joe Wade (Scott Glenn) waiting to pick up the pieces.

1984: Nominations: Best Actress (Sissy Spacek), Cinematography, Original Score, Sound, Special Achievement Award (Sound Effects Editing)

RIVER OF GRASS
1994, 75 mins, US Ⓥ

D: Kelly Reichardt **A:** Lisa Bowman, Larry Fessenden, Dick Russell (Plan B)

Outlaw-lovers-on-the-run saga, in which the leads don't commit a crime, fall in love, or ever hit the road, is a modern, ennui-laden film noir turned inside out and filmed in bright colors under the Florida sun. A bored housewife, Cozy (Lisa Bowman) meets Lee (Larry Fessenden), who still lives at home at 29 and whose ambition is to "just drink." Lee has come into possession of a gun. When Cozy accidentally fires the weapon, she and Lee believe they've shot a black man and bolt to a motel. Bowman and Fessenden occasionally generate some deadpan humor but generally make for lackluster centers of attention.

RIVER OF NO RETURN
1954, 90 mins, US Ⓥ ⊙ ▭

D: Otto Preminger **A:** Robert Mitchum, Marilyn Monroe, Rory Calhoun, Tommy Rettig, Murvyn Vye (20th Century-Fox)

Mitchum and Rettig, playing father and son, pull Monroe and Calhoun from a river that races by their wilderness farm. Calhoun is trying to get to a settlement to file a gold claim he has won dishonestly at cards and Monroe is along because she expects to marry him. Calhoun steals Mitchum's horse and gun and rides off, leaving the others to the mercy of warring Indians. Man, woman, and boy take to the river on a raft to escape the redskins. The competition between scenic splendors of the Jasper and Banff National Parks and entertainment values finds the former finishing slightly ahead.

RIVER RUNS THROUGH IT, A
1992, 123 mins, US Ⓥ ⊙

D: Robert Redford **A:** Craig Sheffer, Brad Pitt, Tom Skerritt, Brenda Blethyn, Emily Lloyd (Columbia)

Skilled, careful adaptation of a much-admired story is a convincing trip back in time to a virtually vanished American

west, as well as a nicely observed family study. The film traces Norman Maclean's relationship with his wilder, younger brother, Paul, in Montana against the backdrop of fly-fishing, used as a metaphor for achieving a state of grace in life. With the showiest role, Brad Pitt shines, his smoldering James Dean-ish looks and recklessness encompassing both Paul's charm and doom.

1992: Best Cinematography
Nominations: Best Screenplay Adaptation, Original Score

RIVER'S EDGE
1986, 99 mins, US Ⓥ ⊙ ▭

D: Tim Hunter **A:** Crispin Glover, Keanu Reeves, Ione Skye, David Roebuck, Dennis Hopper (Hemdale)

Unusually downbeat and depressing youth pic. The setting is a small town, presumably in Oregon. Pic opens with 12-year-old Tim destroying his kid sister's doll and then spotting high-schooler Samson sitting on a riverbank with the naked body of a girl he's just murdered. Tim's reaction is to steal a couple of cans of beer for the killer. But the kids are really nice at heart, the film seems to be saying. They have to cope with broken homes and the threat of the Bomb, otherwise they wouldn't be so hopeless.

RIVER WILD, THE
1994, 111 mins, US Ⓥ ⊙ ▭

D: Curtis Hanson **A:** Meryl Streep, Kevin Bacon, David Strathairn, Joseph Mazzello, John C. Reilly (Turman-Foster/Universal)

The characters and the audience take a wild ride in a tense, sharply made thriller about a family held hostage during a river-rafting vacation. Pic marks a career watershed for Meryl Streep, outstanding as a buff white-water rafter who has it all over the men around her. Production materials state that Streep did 90 percent of the rapids work herself, but film makes it look as though she did it all. Kevin Bacon proves insidiously effective as a boyish baddie, and John C. Reilly's white-trash sidekick reps the film's most forceful reminder of its closest precursor, *Deliverance*.

ROAD GAMES
1981, 100 mins, Australia Ⓥ ▭

D: Richard Franklin **A:** Stacy Keach, Jamie Lee Curtis, Marion Edward, Grant Page (Quest)

Above-average suspenser concerns an offbeat truck driver who winds up stalking a murderer. Stacy Keach's characterization of the amusing, poetry-spouting man is particularly endearing, but the film builds all too effectively to a rather disappointing climax. Jamie Lee Curtis appears midway through as an heiress hitchhiker who befriends Keach while looking for some diversion from everyday life.

ROAD HOME, THE
See: Lost Angels

ROAD HOUSE
1948, 95 mins, US ⓥ
D: Jean Negulesco **A:** Ida Lupino, Cornel Wilde, Celeste Holm, Richard Widmark (20th Century-Fox)

Yarn constructs a love triangle with an arrestingly psychotic twist supplied by Richard Widmark. Film finally bogs down in a lack of incident until a climactic shot-in-the-arm revives interest. Ida Lupino plays a warbler who finds herself in the middle between Widmark and Cornel Wilde. Widmark, the roadhouse operator, has a powerful yen for the singer but she prefers his general manager, Wilde. Lupino's standout performance is highlighted by her first-rate handling of a brace of blues numbers.

ROAD HOUSE
1989, 114 mins, US ⓥ ⊙
D: Rowdy Herrington **A:** Patrick Swayze, Kelly Lynch, Sam Elliott, Ben Gazzara, Marshall Teague (United Artists/Silver)

Ill-conceived and unevenly executed, pic essentially is a western, but its vigilante justice, lawlessness, and wanton violence feel ludicrous in a modern setting. A club owner (Kevin Tighe) recruits Dalton (Patrick Swayze) to clean up his bar, which is frequented by lowlifes and bikers. At first, Dalton avoids fighting when possible yet carries a big rep—including the label of having killed a man.

ROAD TO BALI
1952, 91 mins, US ⓥ
D: Hal Walker **A:** Bob Hope, Bing Crosby, Dorothy Lamour, Murvyn Vye, Peter Coe (Paramount)

Bing Crosby, Bob Hope, and Dorothy Lamour are back again in another of Paramount's highway sagas, with nonsensical amusement its only destination. Five songs are wrapped up in the production. Needing a job, Crosby and Hope hire out to Murvyn Vye, a South Seas island prince, as divers, sail for Vye's homeland, and meet Princess Lamour, which is excuse enough

for her to sing "Moonflowers," later reprised as the finale tune.

ROAD TO GLORY, THE
1936, 103 mins, US ▭
D: Howard Hawks **A:** Fredric March, Warner Baxter, June Lang, Lionel Barrymore, Gregory Ratoff (20th Century-Fox)

Fredric March, Warner Baxter, and June Lang constitute a war-front triangle. Barrymore is the veteran soldier who refuses to be sent back of the lines by his son (Baxter), chief in command, and who forms a sympathetic alliance with March, a French lieutenant. As romantic war stuff, film is a bit too obvious and stylized, but the highly competent production treatment elevates it to big-league company.

ROAD TO HONG KONG, THE
1962, 91 mins, UK/US ⓥ
D: Norman Panama **A:** Bing Crosby, Bob Hope, Joan Collins, Dorothy Lamour, Robert Morley (United Artists/Melnor)

The seventh *Road* comedy, after a lapse of seven years, takes the boys on a haphazard trip to a planet called Plutonius, though this only happens as a climax to some hilarious adventures in Ceylon and Hong Kong. Plot involves Crosby and Hope as a couple of flop vaudevillians who turn con men. Somewhere along the line, Hope loses his memory and that leads them to involvement with a mysterious spy (Joan Collins), a secret formula, and a wacky bunch of thugs led by Robert Morley. Peter Sellers plays a native medico and it is a brilliantly funny cameo.

ROAD TO MOROCCO
1942, 83 mins, US ⓥ
D: David Butler **A:** Bing Crosby, Bob Hope, Dorothy Lamour, Anthony Quinn, Vladimir Sokoloff (Paramount)

Bubbling spontaneous entertainment without a semblance of sanity; an uproarious patchwork of gags, old situations, and a blitzlike laugh pace that never lets up for a moment. It's Bing Crosby and Bob Hope at their best, with Dorothy Lamour, as usual, the pivotal point for their romantic pitch. The story's absurdities are predicated on Crosby and Hope as shipwrecked stowaways cast ashore on the coast of North Africa.
1942: Nominations: Best Original Screenplay, Sound

ROAD TO RIO
1947, 100 mins, US ⓥ
D: Norman Z. McLeod **A:** Bing Crosby, Bob Hope, Dorothy Lamour, Gale Son-

dergaard, Frank Faylen (Paramount)

Bing Crosby and Bob Hope repeat their slaphappy characters. Opening establishes the boys, as usual, in trouble and broke. When they set a circus on fire, pair escape by taking refuge on a ship heading for Rio. It doesn't take them long to discover a damsel in distress (Dorothy Lamour) and action centers around their efforts to save her from a wicked aunt and a forced marriage.
1947: Nomination: Best Scoring of a Musical Picture

ROAD TO SINGAPORE
1940, 84 mins, US ⓥ
D: Victor Schertzinger **A:** Bing Crosby, Dorothy Lamour, Bob Hope, Charles Coburn, Anthony Quinn, Jerry Colonna (Paramount)

Initial teaming of Bing Crosby and Bob Hope provides foundation for good comedy of rapid-fire order, swinging along at a zippy pace. Story is a light framework on which to drape the situations for Crosby and Hope, with Dorothy Lamour providing decorative character as a native gal in saronglike trappings. Crosby is the adventurous son of a shipping magnate, who ships to the South Seas with sailor-buddy Hope. Lamour moves in with the pair, and from there on it's a happy mixture of both making passes at the native beauty while they struggle to raise the necessary coin to live in comfort on the island.

ROAD TO UTOPIA
1946, 90 mins, US ⓥ ⊙
D: Hal Walker **A:** Bing Crosby, Bob Hope, Dorothy Lamour, Robert Benchley, Hillary Brooke (Paramount)

Action is laid in the Klondike of the Gold Rush days. On their way there, scrubbing decks because they'd lost their money, Crosby and Hope come upon a map leading to a rich gold mine. It had been stolen from Lamour's father by two of the toughest badmen of Alaska. Lamour goes to the Klondike in search of them.
1946: Nomination: Best Original Screenplay

ROAD TO WELLVILLE, THE
1994, 120 mins, US ⓥ ⊙
D: Alan Parker **A:** Anthony Hopkins, Bridget Fonda, Matthew Broderick, John Cusack, Lara Flynn Boyle (Dirty Hands/Beacon/Columbia)

Satire of health fanaticism in turn-of-the-century America is a curiosity of the first order. Amusing without being particularly funny, and not especially involving in terms of its characters or melodrama, Alan Parker's unzipped cereal comedy is more something to gape at in wonderment. Physically resplendent picture takes a comical look at the shenanigans perpetrated in the name of good health at the Battle Creek Sanitarium, circa 1907. Founded by the Seventh Day Adventists, the impeccably appointed lakeside spa has become the personal laboratory of Dr. John Harvey Kellogg (Anthony Hopkins), who thunders on to his affluent clients about the evils of meat, smoking, alcohol, and sex, and the virtues of Bulgarian yogurt and frequent enemas.

ROAD TO ZANZIBAR
1941, 89 mins, US ⓥ
D: Victor Schertzinger **A:** Bing Crosby, Bob Hope, Dorothy Lamour, Una Merkel, Eric Blore (Paramount)

Paramount's second coupling of Bing Crosby, Bob Hope, and Dorothy Lamour has sufficient comedy situations and dialogue between its male stars, but it lacks the compactness and spontaneity of its predecessor. Crosby-Hope combo are stranded in South Africa, with Crosby the creator of freak sideshow acts for Hope to perform. With his saved passage money back to the States, Crosby buys a diamond mine, which is quickly sold by Hope for profit. Then pair start out on strange safari with Lamour and Una Merkel, pair of Brooklyn entertainers, pursuing a millionaire hunter.

ROAD WARRIOR, THE
See: Mad Max 2

ROAR
1981, 102 mins, US ⌑
D: Noel Marshall **A:** Tippi Hedren, Noel Marshall, John Marshall, Melanie Griffith, Jerry Marshall (Marshall)

The noble intentions of director-writer-producer Noel Marshall and his actress-wife Tippi Hedren shine through the faults and shortcomings of their 11-year, $17-million project—touted as the most disaster-plagued pic in Hollywood history. Here is a passionate plea for the preservation of African wildlife meshed with an adventure-horror tale which aims to be a kind of *Jaws* of the jungle. If it seems at times more like *Born Free* gone berserk, such are the risks of planting the cast in the bush (actually the Marshalls' ranch in Soledad Canyon in California), surrounded by 150 untrained lions, leopards, tigers, cheetahs, and other big cats, not to mention several large and ill-tempered elephants.

ROARING TWENTIES, THE
1939, 106 mins, US Ⓥ ⊙
D: Raoul Walsh **A:** James Cagney, Humphrey Bogart, Priscilla Lane, Gladys George, Paul Kelly (Warner)

This is a partially true gangster melodrama from the pen of Mark Hellinger. As a seasoned Broadway columnist, Hellinger had intimate knowledge of the El Fay, the Del Fey, and the Guinan clubs, and the Texas Guinan–Larry Fay operation thereof. He has thinly disguised them as the central figures of this yarn, in a good many instances spilling some inside facts, but the blow-off (for the sake of better picture entertainment) is certainly fictionized.

ROBBERY
1967, 114 mins, UK Ⓥ
D: Peter Yates **A:** Stanley Baker, Joanna Pettet, James Booth, Frank Finlay, Barry Foster (Oakhurst)

This precision-tooled suspense thriller turns many of the traditional ingredients that usually go into this kind of film inside out and manages to come up with a tight, well-paced, highly entertaining pic. Peter Yates directs with a sense of authenticity and detail which make the viewer both detached and increasingly curious concerning the various incidents involved in blueprinting and executing the robbery of 3 million from a British mail train.

ROBBERY UNDER ARMS
1957, 99 mins, UK Ⓥ
D: Jack Lee **A:** Peter Finch, Ronald Lewis, Laurence Naismith, Maureen Swanson, David McCallum, Jill Ireland (Rank)

Set in Australia of a 100 years earlier, the story has Peter Finch as Captain Starlight, a virile, likable rogue who runs a gang of bushrangers. In search of adventure, Ronald Lewis and David McCallum join the gang which includes their father. Direction splendidly captures the Australian atmosphere. Lenser Harry Waxman fills the screen with sweeping camerawork, suggesting the vastness of the Australian canvas.

ROBE, THE
1953, 135 mins, US Ⓥ ⊙ ▭
D: Henry Koster **A:** Richard Burton, Jean Simmons, Victor Mature, Michael Rennie, Jay Robinson, Dean Jagger (20th Century-Fox)

A big picture in every sense of the word. One magnificent scene after another, under the anamorphic CinemaScope technique, unveils the splendor that was Rome and the turbulence that was Jerusalem at the time of Christ on Calvary. The homespun robe worn by Jesus is the symbol of Richard Burton's conversion when the Roman tribune realizes he carried out the crucifixion of a holy man at Pontius Pilate's orders. Victor Mature is the Greek slave for whom Burton outbid the corrupt Caligula (Jay Robinson), the Roman prince regent.
1953: Best Color Art Direction, Color Costume Design
Nominations: Best Picture, Actor (Richard Burton), Color Cinematography

ROBERTA
1935, 105 mins, US Ⓥ ⊙
D: William A. Seiter **A:** Irene Dunne, Fred Astaire, Ginger Rogers, Randolph Scott, Helen Westley (RKO)

Musical picture-making at its best—fast, smart, good-looking, and tuneful. When not dancing, Fred Astaire is trying for laughs, and he can handle light comedy with the best of them. In Ginger Rogers, Astaire has an ideal partner. Rogers holds her own in the stepping numbers, which is something when dancing with Astaire. Irene Dunne looks like a million and sings like just as much. Jerome Kern's "Smoke Gets in Your Eyes" is good enough to rate its preferred spot in the picture's score.

ROBIN AND MARIAN
1976, 106 mins, UK Ⓥ
D: Richard Lester **A:** Sean Connery, Audrey Hepburn, Robert Shaw, Richard Harris, Nicol Williamson, Denholm Elliott (Columbia/Rastar)

A disappointing and embarrassing film. The incompatible blend of tongue-in-cheek comedy, adventure, and romance gives the Robin Hood–revisited film the grace and energy of a geriatric discotheque. Sean Connery's Robin and Nicol Williamson's Little John return to England after Harris's King Richard dies abroad; Robert Shaw's Sheriff of Nottingham is still in office; Audrey Hepburn's Marian has retired to a nunnery.

ROBIN & THE SEVEN HOODS
1964, 123 mins, US Ⓥ ⊙ ▭
D: Gordon Douglas **A:** Frank Sinatra,

Dean Martin, Sammy Davis Jr., Peter Falk, Bing Crosby, Barbara Rush (Warner/P-C)

Spoof on gangster pix of bygone days. The daffy doings of Chicago's hoodlums during the Prohibition era in a battle for leadership of the rackets backdrops action which usually is on the slightly wacky side. Scripter takes the legend of Robin Hood and his merrie men and retailors it loosely to the frolickings of Sinatra and his pack. In some measure the parallel is successful, at least as a premise for the plot, as Sinatra, as Robbo, the good-hearted hood, takes from the rich to give to the poor.

1964: Nominations: Best Adapted Musical Score, Song ("My Kind of Town")

ROBIN HOOD
1922, 120 mins, US 🅥 ⊗
D: Allan Dwan **A:** Douglas Fairbanks, Wallace Beery, Sam De Grasse, Enid Bennett, Paul Dickey (Fairbanks/United Artists)

Production just misses being great through a slow, long opening in the days of Richard the Lion-Hearted and his First Crusade. The prettiness of the sets of Robin Hood's lair in Sherwood Forest; the picturesqueness of his band of outlaws who were for their king and against his villainous brother, Prince John; the breadth of the settings; the stunts by Douglas Fairbanks when he gets going; the superb supporting cast; the castle—that's *Robin Hood* and why it is a good picture. It holds you tense in the Robin Hood portion and lets you down badly when it's about Richard.

ROBIN HOOD
1991, 104 mins, UK/US 🅥 ⊙
D: John Irvin **A:** Patrick Bergin, Uma Thurman, Jurgen Prochnow, Edward Fox, Jeroen Krabbe (Working Title/20th Century-Fox)

This awkwardly depicted *Robin Hood* has nobleman Robert Hode (Patrick Bergin) giving spoils to the poor as an afterthought. Having already turned to crime, he thinks the gesture could be just the one to protect his hide. The one wrinkle that does work is Uma Thurman's scrappy, sexy Maid Marian, a woman who battles alongside the men. The lack of major action sequences is surprising in light of the résumés of director John Irvin and exec producer John McTiernan. [Version reviewed was the 180-min. telemovie broadcast on US TV May 13, 1991.]

ROBIN HOOD: MEN IN TIGHTS
1993, 102 mins, US 🅥 ⊙
D: Mel Brooks **A:** Cary Elwes, Richard Lewis, Roger Rees, Amy Yasbeck, Tracey Ullman, Mel Brooks (Brooksfilms/20th Century-Fox)

Pic marks a return to the wild, anarchic scatological comedies that made Mel Brooks a marquee name around the world. Friar Tuck has been reinvented for Brooks to play as Rabbi Tuckman, and the characters include a black foreign-exchange student and plenty of anachronistic modern references. The manic ensemble is grounded by Elwes's virtually straight-faced interpretation of Robin with a glib assuredness that hits the target dead center. Rather slier is Yasbeck's Marian, who gets great comic effect from being the girl too good to be true.

ROBIN HOOD: PRINCE OF THIEVES
1991, 138 mins, US 🅥 ⊙
D: Kevin Reynolds **A:** Kevin Costner, Morgan Freeman, Mary Elizabeth Mastrantonio, Christian Slater, Alan Rickman, Sean Connery (Morgan Creek)

Kevin Costner's *Robin Hood* is a Robin of wood. Murky and uninspired, this $50-million rendition bears evidence of the rushed and unpleasant production circumstances that were much reported upon. At the same time this seriously intended, more realistically motivated revision of the Robin myth may have diminished the hero, but it hasn't destroyed him. The best that can be said for Costner's performance is that it is pleasant. Looking beautiful and sporting an accent that comes and goes, Mary Elizabeth Mastrantonio makes a sprightly, appropriately feisty Marian. As the sheriff, Rickman goes way over the top, emoting with facial and vocal leers. It's a relief whenever this resourceful thesp is on-screen, such is the energy and brio he brings to the proceedings.

1991: Nomination: Best Original Song ("(Everything I Do) I Do It For You")

ROBOCOP
1987, 103 mins, US 🅥 ⊙
D: Paul Verhoeven **A:** Peter Weller, Nancy Allen, Ronny Cox, Kurtwood Smith, Dan O'Herlihy (Davison)

A comic-book movie that's definitely not for kids, welding extreme violence with four-letter words and tempered with gut-level humor and technical wizardry. In the not-too-distant future there are three

organizations inextricably wound into Detroit's anarchical society—the police, a band of sadistic hoodlums, and a multinational conglomerate that has a contract with the city to run the police force. Police officer Murphy (Peter Weller) is blown to bits just at the time the multinational is ready to develop a prototype cyborg—half man, half machine programmed to be an indestructible cop. Thus Weller becomes RoboCop, unleashed to fell the human scum he encounters.
1987: Special Award (Sound Effects Editing)
Nominations: Best Editing, Sound

ROBOCOP 2
1990, 118 mins, US Ⓥ ⊚
D: Irvin Kershner **A:** Peter Weller, Nancy Allen, Dan O'Herlihy, Belinda Bauer, Tom Noonan (Orion/Tobor)

This ultraviolent, nihilistic sequel has enough technical dazzle to impress hardware fans, but no one told filmmakers that less is more. The future is represented by a crumbling Detroit dominated by Dan O'Herlihy's company. He's set to foreclose on loans and literally take possession of Motown. Standing in his way is drug magnate/user Tom Noonan. Peter Weller as RoboCop must defeat both factions. Noonan is reconstituted as RoboCop 2 for the film's final half hour of great special effects as an end in themselves.

ROBOCOP 3
1993, 104 mins, US Ⓥ ⊚
D: Fred Dekker **A:** Robert John Burke, Nancy Allen, Rip Torn, John Castle, Jill Hennessy (Universal)

This latest widget off the *RoboCop* assembly line is a bit better than the first sequel, which amounts to damnation with faint praise. Limiting the gore, but not the carnage, pic remains a cluttered, nasty exercise. Robert John Burke replaces Peter Weller in the title role of the murdered cop who returns as a crime-fighting cyborg. This time ubiquitous conglomerate OCP is trying to evict poor tenants from a run-down neighborhood to erect Delta City, a pet project of tycoon villain Kanemitsu (Mako). The series' enduring stars remain Rob Bottin's knockout RoboCop suit and Basil Poledouris' musical score.

ROBOT MONSTER
1953, 62 mins, US Ⓥ ⊚
D: Phil Tucker **A:** George Nader, Claudia Barrett, Selena Royle, Gregory Moffett, John Mylong (Three Dimensional)

The Tru-Stereo Process (3-D) utilized here is easy on the eyes, coming across clearly at all times. To the picture's credit, no 3-D gimmicks were employed. Yarn here concerns the last six people on Earth—all pitted against a mechanical monster called Ro-Man, sent from another planet.

ROB ROY
(AKA: ROB ROY, THE HIGHLAND ROGUE)
1953, 81 mins, UK Ⓥ
D: Harold French **A:** Richard Todd, Glynis Johns, James Robertson Justice, Michael Gough, Finlay Currie (Walt Disney)

History has been conveniently romanticized to provide a boisterous and rollicking epic of the revolt of the Scottish clans against the English monarchy. Central character is played by Richard Todd, who takes the part of the adventurous Rob Roy MacGregor with a surprise virility. It is he who leads the clan against the redcoats. The misty highlands have been effectively photographed and the overall background provides the right touch of atmosphere.

ROB ROY
1995, 139 mins, US Ⓥ ⊚ ▭
D: Michael Caton-Jones **A:** Liam Neeson, Jessica Lange, John Hurt, Tim Roth, Eric Stoltz (Talisman/United Artists)

An old-fashioned epic about honor, righteousness, and fidelity, pic comes fully to life only when it is portraying outright treachery and venality. This handsome look at a Scottish legend is a fair way too solemn, wooden, and dour for its own good. When Rob Roy (Liam Neeson) falls victim to the evil scheming Killearn (Brian Cox) and Cunningham (Tim Roth), the latter a foppish, obsequious British opportunist, the humorlessly dashing Scot becomes the object of a pointedly violent manhunt. Hero makes no end of high-minded speeches about the importance of honor and the sanctity of his word, and these quickly become wearisome. By contrast, the scenes involving Roth's unctuous Cunningham are a wild delight.
1995: Nomination: Best Supp. Actor (Tim Roth)

ROB ROY, THE HIGHLAND ROGUE
See: Rob Roy

ROCCO AND HIS BROTHERS
See: Rocco e I Suoi Fratelli

ROCCO E I SUOI FRATELLI
(US: ROCCO AND HIS BROTHERS)
1960, 180 mins, Italy/France ⓥ ⊙
D: Luchino Visconti **A:** Alain Delon, Renato Salvatori, Annie Girardot, Katina Paxinou, Claudia Cardinale (Titanus/Marceau/Cocinor)

Plot deals with a south Italian family's trek to the big northern city of Milan, where it intends to start a new life, and of its slow disintegration. It's plotted in the form of an epic poem, each stanza dedicated to a member of the group. Rocco is the all-good brother who falls for the same girl, Nadia, a prostitute, as his brother Simone. He reluctantly gives her up, but the affair ends tragically. Other brothers break off and live honest lives on their own, while Rocco is tormented by the tragedy and wishes only to return to the land where he was born. The impact of the main story line, aided by the sensitive, expertly guided playing of Alain Delon as Rocco, Annie Girardot as the prostie, and Renato Salvatori as Simone, is great.

ROCK, THE
1996, 136 mins, US ⓥ ⊙ ▭
D: Michael Bay **A:** Sean Connery, Nicolas Cage, Ed Harris, Michael Biehn, William Forsythe (Hollywood)

Pic is inescapably entertaining, a high-octane, kick-butt actioner that dresses up a farfetched premise with topflight actors and an ultraslick package. The yarn has its share of gaping holes and jaw-dropping improbabilities, but director Michael Bay sweeps them all aside with his never-take-a-breath pacing. Brigadier General Hummel (Ed Harris) absconds with a bunch of rockets, takes 81 hostages from a tour group on Alcatraz, and promises to launch the missiles on the Bay Area unless Washington forks over $100 million. The only man who can save the day is John Patrick Mason (Sean Connery), a former SAS operative who is compelled to lead a team of navy SEALs underwater to Alcatraz, with FBI biochemical weapons expert Stanley Goodspeed (Nicolas Cage).

ROCK AROUND THE CLOCK
1956, 76 mins, US ⓥ
D: Fred F. Sears **A:** Bill Haley and the Comets, the Platters, Tony Martinez and His Band, Freddie Bell and His Bellboys, Alan Freed, Lisa Gaye (Clover/Columbia)

Film takes off to a bouncy little beat and never lets up for 76 minutes of foot-patting entertainment. Bill Haley and the Comets set the beat with nine of their rec-

ord favorites, including the title tune, ''Razzle Dazzle,'' ''Happy Baby,'' ''See You Later, Alligator,'' and others. Direction keeps interest going with a story that tells how a band manager finds the Haley Comets in the mountains and brings dancing back to ballrooms throughout the country.

ROCKETEER
See: The Rocketeer

ROCKETEER, THE
(UK: ROCKETEER; AUSTRALIA: THE ADVENTURES OF THE ROCKETEER)
1991, 108 mins, US ⓥ ⊙ ▭
D: Joe Johnston **A:** Bill Campbell, Jennifer Connelly, Alan Arkin, Timothy Dalton, Paul Sorvino, Ed Lauter (Walt Disney/Gordon)

Based on a comic unveiled in 1981, this adventure fantasy puts a shiny polish on familiar elements: airborne hero, damsel in distress, Nazi villains, 1930s Hollywood glamour, and dazzling special effects. Object of intense interest is a portable rocket pack which, if strapped to one's back, can send its wearer zipping around almost as fast, if not as quietly, as Superman. The invention makes its way into the hands of ace pilot Bill Campbell, but it's coveted by a dashing star of swashbuckling films who also happens to be a dedicated Nazi (Timothy Dalton). Although he has hired thugs to recover the priceless device, Dalton has his own ideas about getting at Campbell through his gorgeous g.f. (Jennifer Connelly).

ROCKING HORSE WINNER, THE
1949, 96 mins, UK ⓥ
D: Anthony Pelissier **A:** Valerie Hobson, John Howard Davies, Ronald Squire, John Mills, Hugh Sinclair (Two Cities)

The story of an extravagant mother as seen through the eyes of a sensitive child. How to raise the cash to bring the family out of debt and anxiety is the problem preying on the youngster's mind. Then, gradually, the boy realizes he has a facility for picking winners in horse races. John Howard Davies plays the sensitive lad with a skill and sincerity that would do credit to a seasoned trouper.

ROCK, PRETTY BABY
1956, 89 mins, US ⓥ
D: Richard Bartlett **A:** Sal Mineo, John Saxon, Luana Patten, Edward C. Platt, Fay Wray, Rod McKuen (Universal)

Universal liberally sprinkled this entry

with rock-and-roll tunes, offering a total of 17 musical numbers. No juvenile delinquency is involved. The youngsters come from fairly well-to-do parents and live in nice neighborhoods. Saxon, as an 18-year-old high-school senior, wants to follow a career in music and become a bandleader. His father—a physician—wants his son to follow in his footsteps. That's the basic conflict.

ROCKY

1976, 119 mins, US ⓥ ⊙

D: John G. Avildsen **A:** Sylvester Stallone, Talia Shire, Burt Young, Carl Weathers, Burgess Meredith, Thayer David (United Artists)

Sylvester Stallone stars in his own screenplay about a minor local boxer who gets a chance to fight a heavyweight championship bout. Stallone's title character is that of a near loser, a punchy reject scorned by gym owner Burgess Meredith, patronized by local loan shark Joe Spinell, rebuffed by plain-Jane Talia Shire, whose brother, Burt Young, keeps engineering a romantic match.

1976: Best Picture, Director, Editing **Nominations:** Best Actor (Sylvester Stallone), Actress (Talia Shire), Supp. Actor (Burgess Meredith, Burt Young), Story & Screenplay, Best Song ("Gonna Fly Now"), Sound

ROCKY II

1979, 119 mins, US ⓥ ⊙

D: Sylvester Stallone **A:** Sylvester Stallone, Talia Shire, Burt Young, Carl Weathers, Burgess Meredith (United Artists)

In its boxing and training scenes, *Rocky II* packs much of the punch of the original, complete with an exciting pugilistic finale that's even better than its predecessor. However, in an attempt to tell a new story—that of Rocky's adjustment to near success and an attempt to lead a nonboxing life—the picture takes on a murky quality.

ROCKY III

1982, 99 mins, US ⓥ ⊙

D: Sylvester Stallone **A:** Sylvester Stallone, Carl Weathers, Mr. T, Talia Shire, Burt Young, Burgess Meredith (United Artists)

Revisiting the champ three years after the big victory, we find him and wife Talia Shire happily married with a son, a big house, lots of money, and media attention after successfully defending his title 10 times. But Clubber Lang, menacingly and beautifully played by Mr. T, is also tough and hungry for a title shot. Stallone insists on proving himself and quickly goes down for the count under T's hammering. It's obvious now that Stallone has never been a very skilled boxer. But Carl Weathers steps in to teach and train him, if Stallone can work up the will.

1982: Nomination: Best Original Song ("Eye of the Tiger")

ROCKY IV

1985, 91 mins, US ⓥ ⊙

D: Sylvester Stallone **A:** Sylvester Stallone, Talia Shire, Burt Young, Carl Weathers, Brigitte Nielsen, Dolph Lundgren (United Artists)

Sylvester Stallone is really sloughing it off shamelessly, but it's still impossible not to root for old Rocky Balboa to get up off the canvas and whup that bully one more time. Beyond its visceral appeal, *Rocky IV* is truly the worst of the lot, though Stallone himself is more personable in this one and that helps. Dolph Lundgren is the most contrived opponent yet, an almost inhuman giant fighting machine created in Russian physical-fitness labs.

ROCKY V

1990, 104 mins, US ⓥ ⊙

D: John G. Avildsen **A:** Sylvester Stallone, Talia Shire, Burt Young, Sage Stallone, Burgess Meredith, Tommy Morrison (United Artists)

Stallone again scripted and positively goes wild with clichés here: Rocky left broke by mismanagement of his fortune, a Don King–like promoter (Richard Gant) pressuring Rocky to fight again, strained relations between Rocky and his son (real-life son Sage) because of Rocky's tutelage of a young boxer (Tommy Morrison) who ultimately turns on him. The central problem is that Rocky suffers brain damage from his various beatings in the ring, making it risky for him ever to fight again. Bill Conti's score remains the series' greatest asset.

ROCKY HORROR PICTURE SHOW, THE

1975, 100 mins, UK ⓥ

D: Jim Sharman **A:** Tim Curry, Susan Sarandon, Barry Bostwick, Richard O'Brien, Jonathan Adams (White/20th Century-Fox)

Adapted from a rock stage musical of same title set in a spooky castle deep in the heart of Ohio. Into it on a rain-swept night stumble affianced Janet and Brad, wholesome straights, finding the earthy lair of some weirdos from the planet Transylvania. Chief freak therein is the bisexual Frank N. Furter, played with relish by Tim Curry. Most of the jokes that might have seemed jolly fun on stage now appear obvious and even flat. The sparkle's gone.

ROGER AND ME
1989, 90 mins, US Ⓥ ⊙
D: Michael Moore (Dog Eat Dog)

Cheeky and smart indictment of General Motors for closing its truck plant in Flint, MI, throwing 30,000 employees out of work, and, as a result, leaving many neighborhoods abandoned. Michael Moore, a Flint native, wants GM chairman Roger Smith to see the human tragedy caused by the plant closing. Pic is one-sided, for sure, but Moore makes no pretense otherwise. The irony of the title pervades the piece.

ROLLERBALL
1975, 129 mins, US Ⓥ ⊙
D: Norman Jewison **A:** James Caan, John Houseman, Maud Adams, John Beck, Moses Gunn (United Artists)

Norman Jewison's sensational futuristic drama about a world of corporate states stars James Caan in an excellent performance as a famed athlete who fights for his identity and free will. The year is 2018, and the world has been regrouped politically into six conglomerate cartels. There is total material tranquillity: no wars, no poverty, no unrest—and no personal free will and no God. The ingenious way of ventilating human nature's residual aggression is the world sport of rollerball, a combination of roller derby, motorcycle racing, and basketball, where violent death is part of the entertainment.

ROLLERCOASTER
1977, 119 mins, US Ⓥ ▭
D: James Goldstone **A:** George Segal, Richard Widmark, Timothy Bottoms, Henry Fonda, Harry Guardino, Susan Strasberg (Universal)

Timothy Bottoms is a subdued maniac with a plan to blackmail $1 million from a group of amusement-park owners. Bottoms and the man trying to outsmart him (George Segal) are adversaries who develop a mutual respect and, in a sense, a rapport. Pic's taut opening 20 minutes depict the major catastrophe—bombing of a roller-coaster track and the subsequent de-

railing of the cars. The roller-coaster rides are the picture's highlights and they are fabulous.

ROLLING THUNDER
1977, 99 mins, US Ⓥ ⊙
D: John Flynn **A:** William Devane, Tommy Lee Jones, Linda Haynes, Lisa Richards, Dabney Coleman (AIP)

Excellent cast performs well, but not well enough, and story is strong, but not strong enough. In sum, it neither rolls nor thunders. Script follows an embittered loner to a bloody conclusion. After eight years of torture as a prisoner of war, William Devane returns to a hero's welcome, except at home, where wife Lisa Richards has fallen in love with his friend Lawrason Driscoll. But neither the good nor the ill has much impact on Devane, who left all emotion behind in the prison camp.

ROLLOVER
1981, 118 mins, US Ⓥ ▭
D: Alan J. Pakula **A:** Jane Fonda, Kris Kristofferson, Hume Cronyn, Josef Sommer, Bob Gunton (Orion/Warner)

Fundamentally disappointing political-romantic thriller set in the rarefied world of international high finance. Jane Fonda plays a former film star whose corporate-big-wheel husband is mysteriously murdered. Bank troubleshooter Kris Kristofferson is called in, quickly begins consoling the widow by night as well as by day, and soon accompanies her to Saudi Arabia to firm a deal for venture capital. Pakula's previously displayed expertise at conveying pervasive paranoia triggered by massive conspiracies at high levels is perfectly in tune with the story's aims. But there's a certain lack of reality, cued in part by numerous melodramatic contrivances.

ROMA, CITTA APERTA
(US: OPEN CITY; ROME, OPEN CITY)
1945, 100 mins, Italy Ⓥ
D: Roberto Rossellini **A:** Vito Annichiarico, Nando Bruno, Aldo Fabrizi, Harry Feist, Anna Magnani (Excelsa)

Human, credible story set during the German occupation of Rome. Climax to series of intrigues and adventures of the "little people" in getting money and information and other assistance to the underground comes during a raid. Gestapo agents carry off the key underground leader and shoot his girl. There is a nasty torture scene at prison. This much of the film is standard hero-and-villain stuff. But what makes picture good is the story of other characters involved in the tragedy. Aldo Fabrizi does superb job of portraying the understanding priest who inspires the hero with courage in the final ordeal.

ROMANCE
1930, 76 mins, US ⓥ
D: Clarence Brown A: Greta Garbo, Lewis Stone, Gavin Gordon, Elliott Nugent (M-G-M)

When Garbo gargles on the low ones, it's hard to accept her as the operatic high soprano an offscreen singer presents her to be, but the picture is Garbo all the way. Director uses her very nicely in a part that might have easily been overacted. A French opera star with a past falls in love with a holy and wealthy young American preacher—in America. Her rep is generally known, but the boy love laughs that off. The uncle of the good girl the preacher-boy is to wed himself the French woman's ex-master.

ROMANCE OF A HORSETHIEF
1971, 101 mins, US
D: Abraham Polonsky A: Yul Brynner, Eli Wallach, Jane Birkin, Oliver Tobias, Lainie Kazan, Serge Gainsbourg (Allied Artists)

A large cast and extensive location shooting can't salvage a lifeless script made even flatter by Abraham Polonsky's derivative direction. Set in Poland (but shot in Yugoslavia), pic centers on a small rural community of Jewish peasants who live off the ofttimes illegal horse trade. Town is ruled by Cossack-in-exile Stoloff (Yul Brynner), who maintains a love-hate relationship with its residents, including horse thief Kifke (Eli Wallach), his madam ladylove Estusha (Lainie Kazan), and his protégé Zanvill (Oliver Tobias). When the town's horses are commandeered by Stoloff in the name of Czar Nicholas, the people begin to stir under his oppressive boot.

ROMANCING THE STONE
1984, 105 mins, US ⓥ ⌑
D: Robert Zemeckis A: Michael Douglas, Kathleen Turner, Danny DeVito, Zack Norman, Alfonso Arau (El Corazon/20th Century-Fox)

Living alone with her cat, Kathleen Turner writes romantic novels. She receives a package mailed from South America just ahead of her sister's phone call that she's been kidnapped and will die if Turner doesn't deliver the contents of the package south of the border as soon as possible. Turner is guaranteed that her drab existence is about to be transformed— probably by a man, preferably handsome and adventurous. Sure enough, Michael Douglas pops out of the jungle. The expected complications are supplied by the kidnappers, Danny DeVito and Zack Norman.
1984: Nomination: Best Editing

ROMAN HOLIDAY
1953, 118 mins, US ⓥ ⊙
D: William Wyler A: Gregory Peck, Audrey Hepburn, Eddie Albert, Hartley Power, Harcourt Williams (Paramount)

Romantic comedy-drama is the Graustarkian fable in modern dress, plus the Cinderella theme in reverse. Wyler times the chuckles with a never-flagging pace, puts heart into the laughs, endows the footage with some boff bits of business, and points up some tender, poignant scenes in using the smart script and the cast to the utmost advantage. A princess rebels against the goodwill tour she is making of Europe after arriving in Rome. Her adventures with Peck, in the role of an American newspaperman, are natural and amusing.
1953: Best Actress (Audrey Hepburn), Motion Picture Story [awarded to Ian McLellan Hunter, in place of blacklisted Dalton Trumbo], B&W Costume Design (Edith Head)
Nominations: Best Picture, Director, Supp. Actor (Eddie Albert), Screenplay, B&W Cinematography, B&W Art Direction, Editing

ROMANOFF AND JULIET
1961, 103 mins, US ⌑
D: Peter Ustinov A: Peter Ustinov, Sandra Dee, John Gavin, Akim Tamiroff, Suzanne Cloutier (Universal)

Ustinov's performance as the general of Concordia, a tiny mock republic feverishly wooed by Russia and the US to solicit its vital UN vote, is a beautiful blend of outrageous mugging and sly comment. When he's on, the picture's at its best. Sandra Dee and John Gavin costar as daughter and son of the US and Russian ambassadors to Concordia, whose romance and marriage ultimately blots out the political crisis, representing Ustinov's love-and-laughter platform for harmonious international relations.

ROMAN SCANDALS

1933, 93 mins, US ⓥ

D: Frank Tuttle, Busby Berkeley A: Eddie Cantor, Ruth Etting, Gloria Stuart, David Manners, Verree Teasdale, Edward Arnold (Goldwyn/United Artists)

Comedy highspots and moments of exotic beauty in production retrieve a sometimes ineffective Eddie Cantor vehicle. Subject matter is the hokiest kind of hoke. Best of the bits has Cantor as the Roman emperor's food taster trying to stall off the queen's plot to poison her royal spouse and struggling at the same time with a stubborn attack of hiccups. Hilarity of Cantor's buffoonery lies in the dignity of the stately surroundings of the Roman court and the straight playing of the supporting cast. Long sequence in a swank Roman women's bath is the elaborate preparation for one of the song numbers, ''Keep Young and Beautiful,'' which gets a remarkably intricate buildup for the Cantor rendering in blackface.

ROMAN SPRING OF MRS. STONE, THE

1962, 103 mins, UK ⓥ

D: Jose Quintero A: Vivien Leigh, Warren Beatty, Coral Browne, Jill St. John, Lotte Lenya (Warner)

Vivien Leigh portrays a lonely, uncertain ex-actress who has given up her profession and her past to settle in Rome following the sudden death of her wealthy husband. Leigh has the misfortune to fall in love with her ''young man'' (Warren Beatty), who convincingly feigns amour. Leigh gives an expressive, interesting delineation. Beatty gives a fairly convincing characterization of the young, mercenary punk-gigolo.

1962: Nomination: Best Supp. Actress (Lotte Lenya)

ROMANTIC ENGLISHWOMAN, THE

1975, 115 mins, UK/France ⓥ

D: Joseph Losey A: Glenda Jackson, Michael Caine, Helmut Berger, Beatrice Normand, Nathalie Delon, Michel Lonsdale (DIAL/Meric-Matalon)

Glenda Jackson is off to the German bath and gambling site of Baden-Baden at the start of the pic. There she notices Helmut Berger, who is noted as smuggling in heroin. In Britain the husband, Michael Caine, invites him to stay. Eventually she and Berger are caught necking by Caine. Pic remains disappointing in its cocktail of satire, intrigue, and romantic comedy-drama that do not quite jell.

ROME EXPRESS

1932, 94 mins, UK

D: Walter Forde A: Conrad Veidt, Esther Ralston, Joan Barry, Cedric Hardwicke, Frank Vosper, Hugh Williams (Gaumont-British)

Story is set on a train that travels out of Paris. Veidt and Hugh Williams are adventurers chasing Donald Calthrop, who double-crossed them after stealing a famous painting. Also on the train are Joan Barry and Harold Huth, married but not traveling with their legal mates; Esther Ralston, a film star, and her manager, Finlay Currie; Cedric Hardwicke, a philanthropist, and his secretary (Eliot Makeham); and Vosper, head of the French police. Theft, murder, and explanation unravel before the train ends its run.

ROMEO AND JULIET

1936, 130 mins, US ⓥ

D: George Cukor A: Norma Shearer, Leslie Howard, John Barrymore, Edna May Oliver, Basil Rathbone, C. Aubrey Smith (M-G-M)

Faithful and not too imaginative translation to the screen of the William Shakespeare play. Norma Shearer never conveys the impression that she is getting a great kick out of the part, and her restraint aids her portrayal of a child of 14. The famous balcony love scene with Leslie Howard is played sincerely and beautifully. Shearer makes the final tragic moments of the play convincing and moving. Against her childlike figure, Howard and Ralph Forbes, rival suitors, appear years her senior. Howard's Romeo is a forthright young man of considerable determination, rather than a headstrong, impassioned young lover. But what illusion is lost in looks, Howard adequately makes up for in speech. After a rather hesitant beginning John Barrymore makes a real, live person out of Mercutio.

1936: Nominations: Best Picture, Actress (Norma Shearer), Supp. Actor (Basil Rathbone), Art Direction

ROMEO AND JULIET

1968, 152 mins, Italy/UK ⓥ ⊙

D: Franco Zeffirelli A: Olivia Hussey, Leonard Whiting, Milo O'Shea, Michael York, John McEnery (Verona/De Laurentiis/British Home Entertainment)

Shot entirely in Italy, director Franco Zeffirelli has conjured up a very good eyeful, with splendid use of color in costumes and backgrounds. Neither Olivia Hussey nor Leonard Whiting has the experience, looks, or vital personality to rise to the pinnacles of the star-cross'd lovers. Dramatic highlights are stilted and much of the verse flat to the ear. Rarely will audiences be moved to throat-gulping by the plight of the young couple.

1968: Best Cinematography, Costume Design

Nominations: Best Picture, Director (Danilo Donati)

ROMEO + JULIET
(AKA: WILLIAM SHAKESPEARE'S ROMEO + JULIET)
1996, 120 mins, US ⊙ ⊙ ▭

D: Baz Luhrmann **A:** Leonardo DiCaprio, Claire Danes, Brian Dennehy, John Leguizamo, Pete Postlethwaite, Paul Sorvino (Bazmark/20th Century-Fox)

The most aggressively modern, assertively trendy adaptation of Shakespeare ever filmed, this version transports the Montagues and Capulets to Verona Beach and a violent contemporary world dominated by designer guns, customized cars and incessant music. Result is simultaneously striking and silly. Although arresting in spots, it falls far short of bringing out the full values of the play, and doesn't approach the emotional resonance of Franco Zeffirelli's 1968 screen version. Playing Romeo, Leonardo DiCaprio brings youthful energy to the role and gets his speeches out without undue embarrassment but, unlike with Claire Danes, they don't seem second-nature to him. Her Juliet is the picture of youthful purity, spontaneity and romantic readiness. Her scenes stand as a welcome relief from the unrelenting cacophony of the rest of the picture.

ROMEO IS BLEEDING
1993, 108 mins, US ⊙ ⊙

D: Peter Medak **A:** Gary Oldman, Lena Olin, Annabella Sciorra, Juliette Lewis, Roy Scheider, Will Patton (PFE/Working Title)

This heavy dose of ultraviolent neo-noir gives Gary Oldman a face-first trip through the gutter, but the plotting eventually goes so far over the top that pic flirts with inventing a new genre of film noir camp. Oldman's New York police sergeant, Jack Grimaldi, does his job on the organized crimes task force while accepting payoffs from the Mob. Mona Demarkov (Lena Olin) has been nabbed after wiping out some feds and a government witness. Grimaldi is entrusted with guarding her at a safe house, but she's got him disarmed and sexually compromised before the feds even arrive to pick her up. One of pic's prime motives would seem to be the creation of the most astoundingly, memorably vicious and sexy female villain in movie history.

ROME, OPEN CITY
See: Roma, Citta Aperta

ROMMEL—DESERT FOX
See: The Desert Fox

ROMPER STOMPER
1992, 92 mins, Australia ⊙ ⊙

D: Geoffrey Wright **A:** Russell Crowe, Daniel Pollock, Jacqueline McKenzie, Alex Scott, Leigh Russell (Seon)

A Clockwork Orange without the intellect. In many ways genuinely appalling, pic centers on a gang of moronic neo-Nazi skinheads who regularly do battle with Melbourne's Vietnamese community. Russell Crowe gives a powerful performance as skinhead leader Hando, a brute with a veneer of charm whose bible is Mein Kampf.

ROMY AND MICHELE'S HIGH SCHOOL REUNION
1997, 91 mins, US ⊙ ⊙

D: David Mirkin **A:** Mira Sorvino, Lisa Kudrow, Janeane Garofalo, Alan Cumming, Julia Campbell, Mia Cottet (Touchstone)

Pic looks like a peroxided Clueless wannabe straggling along to the party two years after it's over. Desperately uncertain in tone and able to generate only sporadic laughs, pic decks out its meager story of revenge and comeuppance with a vulgar, flashy shimmer. Best friends since high school, Romy (Mira Sorvino) and Michele (Lisa Kudrow) are virtual caricatures of Hollywood bimbos. Due to return to Tucson for their tenth high-school reunion, the deluded dolls furiously work out, try to score boyfriends and, in Michele's case, find a job, before realizing they can just pretend they've got same. They pass themselves off as the fabulously rich inventors of Post-its, a deception uncovered by the class cynic and curmudgeon (Janeane Garofalo). Sorvino and Kudrow get off some good, blank takes and the occasional dumb line readings. Garofalo lets loose with some zingers that put her at the head of the class.

LA RONDE
1950, 109 mins, France ♥
D: Max Ophuls **A:** Anton Walbrook, Simone Signoret, Serge Reggiani, Simone Simon, Daniel Gelin, Danielle Darrieux (Gordine)

A raconteur leads the audience through a series of affairs by a group of people, the plethora of situations making the pic ponderous. First character is a streetwalker who meets a soldier for a brief moment and then he is called back to the barracks. The soldier next meets a lovely chambermaid whom he loves and leaves. The raconteur then leads her into an adventure with a sensitive young student. The student in turn has an affair with a married woman. It goes on and on, but that is the basic format of the yarn. Ophuls has used a dearth of close-ups, brilliant decor playing a vital part. There is much filming through carved glass, linen, silks, and mirrors to create the aura of romance.

LA RONDE
(US: CIRCLE OF LOVE)
1964, 110 mins, France ♥ ▭
D: Roger Vadim **A:** Jean-Claude Brialy, Jane Fonda, Anna Karina, Catherine Spaak, Marie Dubois (Paris/Interopa)

An almost classic French film, insouciant, elegant, witty, and on track in its series of seductions as love is handed from one character to another until the round is completed when the last meets the first. Roger Vadim's direction stresses the cluttered and cozy decors of the era. His treatment of love is almost modest, to give this a sort of comedic air rather than an ironic undertone. Jane Fonda is especially beguiling and deceptively naive as the philandering wife.

RONIN
1998, 118 mins, US ♥ ⊙ ▭
D: John Frankenheimer **A:** Robert De Niro, Jean Reno, Natascha McElhone, Stellan Skarsgard, Sean Bean, Michael Lonsdale (FGM/United Artists)

Even though the characters are virtual cut-outs and the story is without much meaning or resonance, *Ronin* offers enough potent action, intriguing shifting loyalties and scenic French locations to hold interest. Sam (Robert De Niro) arrives at a seedy Montmartre bar, where Irish ringleader Deidre (Natascha McElhone) presides over a meeting about an ambush to retrieve a mysterious briefcase from some criminals. Gang consists of American expert strategist Sam, French coordinator Vincent (Jean Reno), German electronics and surveillance whiz Gregor (Stellan Skarsgard), Yank driver Larry (Skipp Sudduth), and British weapons advisor Spence (Sean Bean). The first major setpiece, a nocturnal face-off by the Seine that erupts into a huge shoot-out, is excitingly handled, whereupon the action shifts to the South of France. De Niro and Gallic star Reno are well matched, with the weight of having seen and done it all showing everywhere on their faces. Title refers to the 47 ronin of Japanese legend, samurai who became solitary agents wandering the land after their leader was killed.

ROOKIE, THE
1990, 121 mins, US ♥ ⊙ ▭
D: Clint Eastwood **A:** Clint Eastwood, Charlie Sheen, Raul Julia, Sonia Braga, Tom Skerritt, Lara Flynn Boyle (Malpaso/Warner)

Overlong, sadistic, and stale even by the conventions of the buddy-pic genre, Clint Eastwood's film is actually *Dirty Harry 51/2*, since Eastwood's tough-as-nails cop Nick Pulovski could just as easily be named Harry Callahan, his penchant for breaking in partners (and getting them killed) is a holdover from Harry's first three patrols. This time, however, the troubles lie in partner Charlie Sheen, a rich kid working out childhood guilt and hostility against his parents by playing policeman. Pair pursues a stolen-car ring operated by ruthless thief Raul Julia and sweaty henchwoman Sonia Braga.

ROOKIE OF THE YEAR
1993, 103 mins, US ♥ ⊙
D: Daniel Stern **A:** Gary Busey, Albert Hall, Amy Morton, Dan Hedeya, Eddie Bracken (20th Century-Fox)

Film aspires to be a pint-sized "It's a Wonderful Field of Dreams," and largely succeeds in minor-league fashion. Preteen Henry Rowengarter (Thomas Ian Nicholas) is your typical enthusiastic baseball-playing Chicago kid. Henry fails to notice a loose baseball in his path, falling with a thud and breaking his arm. Months later, when his cast is removed, Henry discovers his tendons have tightened, allowing him to hurl a ball faster than a speeding bullet. Circumstance brings this to the attention of his beloved Chicago Cubs. Soon the peewee player is on his way to delivering his franchise a berth in the World Series.

ROOM AT THE TOP
1959, 117 mins, UK Ⓥ

D: Jack Clayton **A:** Laurence Harvey, Simone Signoret, Heather Sears, Donald Wolfit, Donald Houston, Hermione Baddeley (Remus)

An adult, human picture enhanced by subtle, intelligent direction from first-timer Jack Clayton and a batch of top-notch performances. Laurence Harvey takes a job in the local government offices of a North Country town. He is an alert young man with a chip on his shoulder because of his humble background. He quickly finds that the small town is virtually controlled by a self-made millionaire and sets his cap for the millionaire's daughter. At the same time he is irresistibly drawn to an unhappily married Frenchwoman (Simone Signoret).

1959: Best Actress (Simone Signoret), Adapted Screenplay

Nominations: Best Picture, Director, Actor (Laurence Harvey), Supp. Actress (Hermione Baddeley)

ROOM FOR ONE MORE
1952, 97 mins, US

D: Norman Taurog **A:** Cary Grant, Betsy Drake, George Winslow, Iris Mann, Clifford Tatum Jr. (Warner)

A happy combination of good humor and warm drama. Cary Grant and Betsy Drake make a smart star team to head up this story of a real-life couple who open hearts and home to unfortunate children. Themselves Mr. and Mrs., Grant and Drake spark the film with the humor it needs without neglecting honest tugs at the heart.

ROOMMATES
1995, 108 mins, US Ⓥ ⊙

D: Peter Yates **A:** Peter Falk, D. B. Sweeney, Julianne Moore, Jan Rubes, Ellen Burstyn (Interscope/PFE/Hollywood)

An exceedingly mild story of the emotional tug-of-war between a lovably cantankerous old codger and the grandson he raises to maturity, agreeably humorous at times and less squishily sentimental than it might have been. The main attraction is Falk's old-age performance. With bald pate, trim mustache, and leathery skin, the actor looks a bit like a diminutive version of Brando's elderly Godfather.

1995: Nomination: Best Makeup

ROOM SERVICE
1938, 76 mins, US Ⓥ ⊙

D: William A. Seiter **A:** Groucho Marx, Chico Marx, Harpo Marx, Lucille Ball, Ann Miller, Frank Albertson (RKO)

Room Service with the Marx Brothers will satisfy on the laugh score. There may be captious ones who'll miss (1) Groucho's standard rasslin' with a femme via-à-vis; (2) Harpo's harp solo; (3) Chico's equally standard pianology. But the Marxes have a more staple story structure upon which to hang their buffoonery. Cliff Dunstan is the distrait hotel manager who has permitted the shoestring impresario (Groucho Marx) to camp a stranded troupe of 22 in his hostelry and run up a $1,200 tab.

ROOM WITH A VIEW, A
1986, 115 mins, UK Ⓥ ⊙

D: James Ivory **A:** Maggie Smith, Helena Bonham Carter, Denholm Elliott, Julian Sands, Daniel Day-Lewis (Merchant-Ivory/Goldcrest)

A thoroughly entertaining adaptation of novelist E. M. Forster's comedy of manners about the Edwardian English upper class at home and abroad, distinguished by superb ensemble acting, intelligent writing, and stunning design. Set in 1907, film moves between a pensione in Florence, Italy, where an English lady, Lucy Honeychurch (Helena Bonham Carter), is traveling on the type of horizon-broadening tour that was the prerogative of her class, chaperoned by her fussy aunt Charlotte (Maggie Smith), and the insular Surrey countryside where she lives with her mother (Rosemary Leach).

1986: Best Adapted Screenplay, Art Direction, Costume Design

Nominations: Best Picture, Director, Supp. Actor (Denholm Elliott), Supp. Actress (Maggie Smith), Cinematography

ROOSTER COGBURN
1975, 107 mins, US Ⓥ ⊙ ▭

D: Stuart Millar **A:** John Wayne, Katharine Hepburn, Anthony Zerbe, Richard Jordan, John McIntire, Strother Martin (Universal)

The title is based on the character from *True Grit.* Spinster Hepburn and Indian lad Richard Romancito join reinstated marshal Wayne to track down the bad guys. A little artfulness, a little creativity, a little subtlety could work wonders. Like Hepburn and Wayne not doing a frontier version of *The Bickersons.* Like not shoehorning *The African Queen* plotline into this script.

ROOSTERS
1993, 93 mins, US ⊘
D: Robert M. Young A: Edward James
Olmos, Sonia Braga, Maria Conchita
Alonso, Danny Nucci, Sarah Lassez
(American Playhouse/WMG)

Centering on a classic father-son conflict, *Roosters* is an absorbing family
drama marked by Freudian symbolism and
the fatalism of a Greek tragedy. Superb
acting, particularly by Sonia Braga, almost
makes up for the lack of sustained dramatic interest and some rough shifts between the film's realistic scenes and its
more poetic ones. Narrative, set in the
southwest, begins with the coming home
of Gallo Morales (Edward James Olmos),
a legendary breeder of fighting cocks, after
seven years in prison. His return is anxiously anticipated by his wife, Juana
(Braga), 20-year-old son Hector (Danny
Nucci), and adolescent daughter Angela
(Sarah Lassez).

ROOTS OF HEAVEN, THE
1958, 130 mins, US ▭
D: John Huston A: Errol Flynn, Juliette
Greco, Trevor Howard, Eddie Albert, Or-
son Welles, Herbert Lom (20th Century-
Fox)

The Roots of Heaven has striking pictorial aspects, some exciting performances, and builds to a pulsating climax of
absorbing tension. Unfortunately, these
plus factors almost all come in the second
half of the picture. The locale of the
screenplay, from Romain Gary's novel, is
French Equatorial Africa. Trevor Howard
is launching a campaign to save the elephants of Africa. Howard gets only two
signatures. One is from Errol Flynn, an alcoholic British ex-officer, and the other is
from Juliette Greco, a prostitute. So Howard decides on a campaign of harassment
of the hunters.

ROPE
1948, 80 mins, US ⊘ ⊙
D: Alfred Hitchcock A: James Stewart,
John Dall, Farley Granger, Cedric Hardwicke, Constance Collier (Transatlantic)

Focus is on a thrill murder, done for no
reason but to satisfy a sadistic urge and
intellectual vanity. Action takes place
within an hour-and-a-half period and the
film footage nearly duplicates the span,
being 80 minutes. It is entirely confined to
the murder apartment. James Stewart, as
the ex-professor who first senses the guilt
of his former pupils, does a commanding
job. John Dall stands out as the egocentric

who masterminds the killing and ghoulish
wake. Equally good is Farley Granger as
the weakling partner in crime.

ROSALIE
1937, 123 mins, US ⊘
D: W. S. Van Dyke A: Nelson Eddy,
Eleanor Powell, Frank Morgan, Edna May
Oliver, Ray Bolger, Ilona Massey (M-G-
M)

Nelson Eddy is a West Point cadet-
baritone; Eleanor Powell, a dancing Balkan princess; Frank Morgan and Edna
May Oliver, amusing musical comedy
king and queen; and a light operetta story.
It is in the festival scenes in the Balkan
capital that Rosalie really shows its cinematic girth. There are hundreds of dancers,
thousands of costumed extras, and innumerable others. In the midst of this ensemble Powell does an acrobatic tap atop
some massive drums. Cole Porter has written new music and lyrics. Ray Bolger is
the real discovery in the pic. His humor is
clean, unforced, and spontaneous.

ROSARY MURDERS, THE
1987, 105 mins, US ⊘ ⊙
D: Fred Walton A: Donald Sutherland,
Charles Durning, Josef Sommer, Belinda
Bauer, James Murtaugh (First Take)

A string of a half-dozen murders, victims being nuns and priests in a Detroit
parish, is lacking in suspense or dramatic
buildup. A priest turns sleuth after the
murderer drops a few clues to him in the
confessional. As a man of the cloth, latter
can't tip off the police or probable victims
because of his secrecy vows.

ROSE, THE
1979, 134 mins, US ⊘ ⊙ ▭
D: Mark Rydell A: Bette Midler, Alan
Bates, Frederic Forrest, Harry Dean Stanton, David Keith (20th Century-Fox)

While there are certainly similarities to
the tragic story of Janis Joplin, *The Rose*
emerges as its own self-contained tale.
The screenwriters dwell solely on the
downward career spiral of Bette Midler's
character. Result is an ultrarealistic look at
the infusion of money, sex, drugs, and
booze in the simple process of singing a
song, a chore Midler does faultlessly in
several excellent concert sequences.
1979: Nominations: Best Actress (Bette
Midler), Supp. Actor (Frederic Forrest),
Editing, Sound

ROSEBUD
1975, 126 mins, US ▭
D: Otto Preminger A: Peter O'Toole,

Richard Attenborough, Cliff Gorman, Claude Dauphin, Peter Lawford (United Artists)

Political-tumult story, involving Palestine Liberation Organization terrorist kidnapping, is a bland and unexciting film. Peter O'Toole heads the cast as a Briton, secret-agenting for the US, who sorts out the crisis. O'Toole's is among the few strong performances, but that isn't saying much.

ROSELAND
1977, 103 mins, US ⓥ

D: James Ivory A: Teresa Wright, Lou Jacobi, Christopher Walken, Louise Kirtland, Geraldine Chaplin (Merchant-Ivory)

There is romance to the notion that our buildings will outlast us. That is the emotional underpinning of *Roseland,* a clean, well-lighted ballroom of New York's West Side. Standout is Lilia Skala, playing an elderly German woman. Tale of a gigolo, nicely crafted by Christopher Walken, concerns his failure to separate himself from Joan Copeland, excellent in her portrayal of a lonely and dying woman.

ROSE-MARIE
1936, 110 mins, US ⓥ ⊙

D: W. S. Van Dyke A: Jeanette MacDonald, Nelson Eddy, James Stewart, Reginald Owen, Allan Jones, Alan Mowbray (M-G-M)

There is a wholly satisfying blend of sophisticated behind-the-opera-scenes temperament with the great-outdoors stuff that comprises much of the ensuing footage as Eddy pursues MacDonald's scapegrace-brother. The classic "Indian Love Call" as it reechoes through the woodlands means more than it ever did in its stage original. Eddy's balladeering of the titular "Rose-Marie" as he paddles MacDonald on the trek for the escaped criminal (her brother) is likewise enhanced.

ROSE MARIE
1954, 106 mins, US ▭

D: Mervyn LeRoy A: Ann Blyth, Howard Keel, Fernando Lamas, Bert Lahr, Marjorie Main (M-G-M)

The views of the forests, the lakes, and the mountains are breathtaking. Unfortunately, operetta plot of yesteryear is sweet and occasionally sad, but with little substance. Fine-looking leads Ann Blyth, Howard Keel, and Fernando Lamas fail to instill much verve or enthusiasm to the proceedings. Marjorie Main and Bert Lahr provide some welcome comedy relief.

Blyth is seen as the backwoods French-Canadian gal who has to choose between Howard Keel, the Mountie, and Lamas, "the ornery but no killer" trapper.

ROSEMARY'S BABY
1968, 134 mins, US ⓥ ⊙

D: Roman Polanski A: Mia Farrow, John Cassavetes, Ruth Gordon, Sidney Blackmer, Maurice Evans, Ralph Bellamy (Paramount)

Excellent film version of Ira Levin's diabolical chiller novel holds attention without explicit violence or gore. Mia Farrow and John Cassavetes, a likable young married couple, take a flat in a run-down New York building. Ralph Bellamy, an obstetrician, prescribes some strange prenatal nourishment for Farrow. The near climax—Farrow has been drugged so as to conceive by Satan—and the final wallop make for genuine cliff-hanger interest. Farrow's performance is outstanding.

1968: Best Supp. Actress (Ruth Gordon)
Nomination: Best Adapted Screenplay

ROSENCRANTZ AND GUILDENSTERN ARE DEAD
1991, 118 mins, UK ⓥ ⊙

D: Tom Stoppard A: Garry Oldman, Tim Roth, Richard Dreyfuss, Iain Glen, Joanna Roth (Brandenberg)

Tom Stoppard takes two marginal characters from Shakespeare's *Hamlet* and places them at the center of a comedy-drama, while the major characters of the play—Hamlet, Ophelia, Claudius, and the rest—are only part of the background. Stoppard's 1967 play has been seen as a mixture of Samuel Beckett and Shakespeare, but on film, the two protagonists come across as a mixture of Abbott and Costello and Laurel and Hardy. There's also a touch of Monty Python. Gary Oldman and Tim Roth are splendid.

ROSE OF WASHINGTON SQUARE
1939, 90 mins, US

D: Gregory Ratoff A: Tyrone Power, Alice Faye, Al Jolson, William Frawley, Joyce Compton (20th Century-Fox)

It's not much of a filmusical—primarily a story deficiency. Al Jolson is the altruistic patron of the beauteous and talented Alice Faye. She in turn is stuck on the wrong-guy character played by Tyrone Power.

ROSE TATTOO, THE
1955, 117 mins, US ⓥ ⊙

D: Daniel Mann A: Anna Magnani, Burt

Lancaster, Marisa Pavan, Ben Cooper, Jo Van Fleet (Paramount)

The Rose Tattoo creates a realistic Italiano atmosphere in the bayou country of the south. Anna Magnani is spellbinding as the signora content with the memory of the fidelity of her husband until she discovers he had a blond on the side before his death. The characters inspire little sympathy. Magnani has animalistic drive and no beauty. Burt Lancaster, as the village idiot by inheritance, takes on a role bordering on the absurd.
1955: Best Actress (Anna Magnani), B&W Cinematography, B&W Art Direction
Nominations: Best Picture, Supp. Actress (Marisa Pavan), B&W Costume Design, Editing, Scoring of a Dramatic Picture

ROTTEN TO THE CORE
1965, 89 mins, UK ▭
D: John Boulting **A:** Anton Rodgers, Eric Sykes, Charlotte Rampling, Ian Bannen, Avis Bunnage (BLC/Boulting)

Big-time crime is the main target of the Boulting Brothers' latest piece of satirical joshing. But the Boultings' knives are less sharp than customary. Idea hinges on the appeal of Prime Minister Harold Wilson to adapt scientific methods to 1965 big business and industry. And this the Boultings have applied to the activities of a gang of crooks whose young boss (Anton Rodgers) has set his beady eye on hijacking an army payroll.

ROUGE
See: Inji Kau

ROUGH CUT
1980, 112 mins, US Ⓥ ⊙ ▭
D: Don Siegel **A:** Burt Reynolds, Lesley-Anne Down, David Niven, Patrick Magee, Timothy West (Paramount)

Undistinctive, frothy romantic comedy. Love match of Burt Reynolds and Lesley-Anne Down works only in selected spots and frame of the story, intrigue over a $30-million diamond heist, is hard-pressed to sustain interest. Problem seems to lie in much of the dialogue, which comes across as both wooden and contrived.

ROUGH NIGHT IN JERICHO
1967, 102 mins, US ▭
D: Arnold Laven **A:** Dean Martin, George Peppard, Jean Simmons, John McIntire, Slim Pickens (Universal)

Most unusual aspect is offbeat casting of Dean Martin as a heavy without a single redeeming quality. George Peppard is the hero. Both are embroiled in a bloody and violent western. Peppard becomes involved in the affairs of the town of Jericho—and Martin—when he arrives with John McIntire, onetime marshal under whom he once served. Latter has come to help Jean Simmons save her stage line, coveted by Martin, who also wants its femme owner.

ROUNDERS
1998, 120 mins, US Ⓥ ⊙ ▭
D: John Dahl **A:** Matt Damon, Edward Norton, John Turturro, Gretchen Mol, Famke Janssen, John Malkovich (Spanky/Miramax)

Intermittently engaging but dramatically slack, this tale of a law student's discovery of his true calling as a world-class poker player is more interesting around the edges than it is at its core. College boy Mike McDermott (Matt Damon) loses his life savings in a poker game against a crafty Russian hood, Teddy KGB (John Malkovich). Nine months later, Mike's g.f. Jo (Gretchen Mol) is alarmed by the release from prison of Worm (Edward Norton), Mike's wise-ass friend who she suspects will lead her mate astray once again. Worm owes some heavies $15,000 and is obliged to fork over the money in five days or else. Mike and Worm go on a sleepless binge of games that concludes with a showdown with Teddy KGB. Malkovich has a grand old time hamming it up as the thickly accented Russian card master. Unfortunately, the writers didn't give their leading character any emotional dimension or compelling characteristics, and the big card games don't convey the expected tension and excitement.

'ROUND MIDNIGHT
1986, 133 mins, France/US Ⓥ ⊙ ▭
D: Bertrand Tavernier **A:** Dexter Gordon, Francois Cluzet, Gabrielle Haker, Sandra Reaves-Phillips, John Berry, Martin Scorsese (Little Bear/PECF/Warner)

Gallic director Bertrand Tavernier pays a moving dramatic tribute to the great black musicians who lived and performed in Paris in the late 1950s. Screenplay dramatizes the friendship between an aging jazz saxophonist and a passionate young French admirer who is ready to make personal sacrifices to help his idol. Tavernier cast a nonprofessional in the central role, the 63-year-old jazz veteran Dexter Gordon, who fills the part of the world-weary artist with his own jagged warmth.

1986: Best Original Score
Nomination: Best Actor (Dexter Gordon)

ROXANNE
1987, 107 mins, US Ⓥ ⊙ ▭
D: Fred Schepisi A: Steve Martin, Daryl
Hannah, Rick Rossovich, Shelley Duvall,
Michael J. Pollard, Damon Wayans, Fred
Willard (Columbia/Melnick/LA Films)

A reworking of Edmond Rostand's
play *Cyrano de Bergerac,* the only reason
to see the film is for a few bits of inspired
nonsense by Steve Martin as the nosy
lover. The central plot device of the play,
in which a true love writes letters to help
another suitor, is here adapted to a small
ski community where Martin, called CB,
is fire chief. Roxanne (Daryl Hannah) is
out of her clothes and locked out of her
house. When CB comes to the rescue, it's
love at first sight, but his enlarged probos-
cis disqualifies him as a serious suitor, or
so he thinks.

ROXIE HART
1942, 72 mins, US
D: William A. Wellman A: Ginger Rogers, Adolphe Menjou, George Montgomery, Lynne Overman, Nigel Bruce (20th
Century-Fox)

Ginger Rogers is the girl who stands
trial for murder committed by her husband, after getting buildup on publicity
values by cynical crime reporter Lynne
Overman. Banner-lined all over town,
Roxie becomes an enthusiastic stooge for
the press, court, and slick mouthpiece
(Adolphe Menjou). Ginger Rogers does
well as the tough girl dazzled by the sudden attention, but seems to overdo her
characterization at several points. Menjou
is excellent as the criminal mouthpiece.

ROYAL FLASH
1975, 121 mins, UK Ⓥ
D: Richard Lester A: Malcolm McDowell,
Alan Bates, Florinda Bolkan, Oliver Reed,
Britt Ekland, Lionel Jeffries (20th
Century-Fox)

Royal Flash is a royal pain. Richard
Lester's formula period-comedy style
achieves its customary levels of posturing
silliness. Malcolm McDowell falls in with
Florinda Bolkan, playing Lola Montez, alienating Oliver Reed's Otto von Bismarck.
The latter, with accomplice Alan Bates
and hit men Lionel Jeffries and Tom Bell,
force McDowell to impersonate a Prussian
nobleman for purposes of marriage to
duchess Britt Ekland. Complex political,

sexual, and survival strategies lurch the
plot forward.

ROYAL HUNT OF THE SUN, THE
1969, 121 mins, UK ▭
D: Irving Lerner A: Robert Shaw, Christopher Plummer, Nigel Davenport, Michael Craig, Leonard Whiting, Andrew
Keir (Rank)

Based on Peter Shaffer's rich, imaginative play, film is striking in many ways,
visually and verbally. Story concerns General Francisco Pizarro, Spanish soldier of
fortune who, for the third time, penetrates
Peru, the Land of the Sun, in search of the
Kingdom of Gold. Shaw powerfully portrays the conquistador and his varying and
complicated moods. Plummer is particularly outstanding in the tricky role of King
Atahualpa.

ROYAL SCANDAL, A
1945, 94 mins, US
D: Otto Preminger A: Tallulah Bankhead,
Charles Coburn, Anne Baxter, William
Eythe, Vincent Price (20th Century-Fox)

Highly hilarious comedy with superb
performances by Tallulah Bankhead and
Charles Coburn, in particular, and the wit
of the original play by Lajos Biro and
Melchior Lengyel. Producer Ernst Lubitsch and director Otto Preminger have
neatly interwoven court intrigue with
Catherine the Great's w.k. amorous proclivities.

ROYAL WEDDING
(UK: WEDDING BELLS)
1951, 93 mins, US Ⓥ ⊙
D: Stanley Donen A: Fred Astaire, Jane
Powell, Peter Lawford, Sarah Churchill,
Keenan Wynn (M-G-M)

This is an engaging concoction of
songs and dances in a standard musical
framework. Two of the numbers almost
carry the picture by themselves: Astaire's
solo dance on a ceiling, upside-down, and
the teaming with Powell in a sort of
Frankie-and-Johnny-apache-hepcat presentation. Light plot sees Astaire and
Powell as a brother-sister team of Broadway musical stars. They go to London to
open their show. Astaire falls in love with
Sarah Churchill, show hoofer, and Powell
catches the love bug from Peter Lawford,
an English lord-romeo.
1951: Nomination: Best Song ("Too Late
Now")

R.P.M. (REVOLUTIONS PER MINUTE)

1970, 92 mins, US ⓥ
D: Stanley Kramer **A:** Anthony Quinn, Ann-Margret, Gary Lockwood, Paul Winfield (Columbia)

This campus-crisis meller slowly spins its improbable wheels to the climactic production number involving a student riot. Anthony Quinn is introduced as a 53-year-old professor, risen to his post from Spanish Harlem and popular with his students. At the outset, the current college head has thrown in the towel as students have occupied the administration building, housing a big computer. Gary Lockwood, along with Paul Winfield, are the radical student leaders.

RUBY

1977, 84 mins, US ⓥ
D: Curtis Harrington **A:** Piper Laurie, Stuart Whitman, Roger Davis, Janit Baldwin (Dimension/Krantz)

In the cookbook school of filmmaking, *Ruby* is strictly leftovers. Begin with a hunk of the occult. Add a cup of 1950s nostalgia, some hard-boiled detective, a dash of camp from old horror movies, and sprinkle with violence. Piper Laurie is the wife of a big-time mobster. She owns a drive-in staffed by "associates" of her dead husband. He was gunned down 16 years ago, but his spirit is back to haunt the drive-in.

RUBY

1992, 110 mins, US ⓥ ⊙
D: John Mackenzie **A:** Danny Aiello, Sherilyn Fenn, Arliss Howard, Tobin Bell, David Duchovny, Richard C. Sarafian (PolyGram/Propaganda)

Danny Aiello and Sherilyn Fenn's earnest, first-rate performances can't overcome strewed story elements of this otherwise well-put-together drama. Highly fictionalized bio of the club owner and small-time hood who killed Lee Harvey Oswald points a finger at organized crime and rogue elements within the CIA as the parties responsible for bringing Camelot to a crashing end.

RUBY CAIRO

1993, 110 mins, US/Japan ⓥ ⊙
D: Graeme Clifford **A:** Andie MacDowell, Liam Neeson, Viggo Mortensen, Jack Thompson, Jeff Corey (Kadokawa)

Old-fashioned Yank-in-Europe mystery-adventure squanders an interesting cast. Too bad everyone forgot to pack a script along with their passports and sunscreen. MacDowell plays the wife of Viggo Mortensen, who runs an aircraft salvage company. Realizing he's done a runner, she sets off tracking him down. The trail leads from Panama and the Bahamas to Berlin, Athens, and Cairo, where with the help of food-aid worker Liam Neeson she uncovers a scam smuggling a chemical for making poison gas inside grain shipments.

RUBY GENTRY

1952, 82 mins, US ⓥ
D: King Vidor **A:** Jennifer Jones, Charlton Heston, Karl Malden, Tom Tully, James Anderson (Bernhard-Vidor/20th Century-Fox)

This is a story of fleshy passions in the tidewater country of North Carolina with neither Jennifer Jones nor Charlton Heston gaining any sympathy in their characters. Story starts with the animal attraction between Jones, from the wrong side of the tracks, and Heston, purse-poor southern gent who for marriage chooses Phyllis Avery's wealthy, properly bred girl so he can rebuild his family fortunes. Jones goes through much of the footage in skintight Levi's, of which she and careful camera angles and lighting make the most.

RUBY IN PARADISE

1993, 115 mins, US ⓥ
D: Victor Nunez **A:** Ashley Judd, Todd Field, Bentley Mitchum, Allison Dean, Dorothy Lyman (Full Crew/Say Yeah)

A wonderfully expressive character study, exhibiting a thoughtfulness and concern for real life rare in American cinema. Ashley Judd manages to rivet one's attention even when she is doing nothing. Showing her escape from small-town Tennessee, tale lands Ruby in a tourist town on Florida's "redneck Riviera." Ruby sleeps with Ricky (Bentley Mitchum), who ranks himself the local roué, but later develops a more meaningful romance with Mike (Todd Field), a smart biker who works in the local tree nursery.

RUDYARD KIPLING'S THE JUNGLE BOOK

See: The Jungle Book

RUGGLES OF RED GAP

1923, 89 mins, US ⊗
D: James Cruze **A:** Edward Everett Horton, Ernest Torrence, Lois Wilson, Fritzi Ridgeway, Louise Dresser (Paramount)

Here is a great comedy novel made into a delightful feature picture. Ernest Torrance's Cousin Egbert is a gem, a bit of comic characterization that hasn't a suspicion of clowning. Edward Horton's Ruggles is a fitting companion piece. This most British of British valets is almost as good fun in the film as he was in the book. Ruggles is as far from the familiar comic picture of the English valet as could be. He is actually a likable human being.

RUGGLES OF RED GAP
1935, 90 mins, US Ⓥ
D: Leo McCarey **A:** Charles Laughton, Mary Boland, Charles Ruggles, ZaSu Pitts, Roland Young (Paramount)

Leo McCarey has turned out a fast and furiously funny film. Story plants Elmer (Charlie Ruggles) and his wife (Mary Boland) in Paris. They play poker with the Earl of Burnstead (Roland Young) and win his butler, Ruggles (Charles Laughton). They take him back to Red Gap, state of Washington. Laughton turns in a performance that's not satire; it's not a pathological character study. Just plain comedy.

1935: Nomination: Best Picture

RULES OF THE GAME, THE
See: La Regle du Jeu

RULING CLASS, THE
1972, 154 mins, UK Ⓥ ⊙
D: Peter Medak **A:** Peter O'Toole, Alastair Sim, Arthur Lowe, Harry Andrews, Coral Browne (Keep)

Peter Barnes's amusing but hard-hitting script plays well in recounting the rise of the allegedly insane 14th Earl of Gurney, who believes he's J.C. and whose family wants him back in the nuthouse—once he's fathered the child through which they hope to get their hands back on the estate the earl has unexpectedly inherited. Pic avoids usual message film pitfalls in coming across almost throughout with amusing tongue-in-cheek finesse alternating with hilarious stretches.

1972: Nomination: Best Actor (Peter O'Toole)

RUMBLE FISH
1983, 94 mins, US Ⓥ
D: Francis Coppola **A:** Matt Dillon, Mickey Rourke, Diane Lane, Dennis Hopper, Diana Scarwid (Zoetrope)

Another Francis Coppola picture that's overwrought and overthought. Beautifully photographed in black-and-white by Stephen H. Burum, the picture really doesn't need all the excessive symbolism Coppola tries to cram into it. For those who want it, however, *Fish* is another able examination of teenage alienation, centered around two brothers. One, Matt Dillon, is a young tough inspired to no good purposes by an older brother, Mickey Rourke, now a bit of an addled eccentric, though remaining a hero to neighborhood thugs.

RUMBLE IN THE BRONX
See: Hung Fan Kui

RUNAWAY
1984, 100 mins, US Ⓥ ⊙ ▭
D: Michael Crichton **A:** Tom Selleck, Cynthia Rhodes, Gene Simmons, Kirstie Alley, Stan Shaw (Tri-Star/Delphi III)

Tom Selleck, with a cop's short haircut and playing a workaday stiff who's afraid of heights, cuts a more accessible figure than in prior pictures. However, this robotic nightmare is so trite that the story seems lifted from Marvel Comics, with heat-seeking bullets and a villain so bad he would be fun if the film wasn't telling us to take this near-futuristic adventure with a straight face.

RUNAWAY BRIDE
1999, 116 mins, US Ⓥ ⊙ ▭
D: Garry Marshall **A:** Julia Roberts, Richard Gere, Joan Cusack, Hector Elizondo, Rita Wilson, Paul Dooley (Interscope/ Paramount/Touchstone)

Julia Roberts, Richard Gere, and director Garry Marshall score with *Runaway Bride*, an ultracommercial mainstream romantic comedy that delivers all the laughs it intends to. Journalist Ike Graham (Gere) heads for Hale, MD, to get the full story about a woman with the habit of leaving fiancés at the altar. Approaching her fourth attempted wedding, to high-school sports coach Bob (Christopher Meloni), Maggie Carpenter (Roberts) is none too happy to have Ike cozying up to her father (Paul Dooley). At pic's halfway point, Maggie agrees to cooperate with the writer, which leads to prolonged proximity, which in turn leads to the unavoidable recognition of mutual attraction. Roberts has a perfect role in Maggie. She can be goofy, sporty, or amorous with ease. Gere drops the preening, posing, self-satisfied air he affects when he's the biggest star in a picture.

RUNAWAY DAUGHTER
See: Red Salute

RUNAWAY TRAIN
1985, 111 mins, US Ⓥ ⊙
D: Andrei Konchalovsky **A:** Jon Voight, Eric Roberts, Rebecca DeMornay, Kyle T.

Heffner, John P. Ryan (Cannon/Northbrook)

A most exciting action epic is fundamentally serious enough to work strongly on numerous levels. An exercise in relentless, severe tension, tale follows two escaped cons as they become inadvertent passengers on some diesel units that run out of control through the Alaskan wilderness. Jon Voight brilliantly portrays a two-time loser determined never to return to prison after his third breakout. Younger con Eric Roberts impressively manages to hold his own.
1985: Nominations: Best Actor (Jon Voight), Supp. Actor (Eric Roberts), Editing

RUN FOR THE SUN
1956, 98 mins, US ▭
D: Roy Boulting **A:** Richard Widmark, Trevor Howard, Jane Greer, Peter Van Eyck, Carlos Henning (Russ-Field)

Film is a chase feature in practically all phases. Jane Greer, news mag staffer, comes to Mexico to find Richard Widmark, writer-adventurer. She falls for her quarry and then the plane in which they are flying crashes in the jungle. The couple is rescued by Trevor Howard and Peter Van Eyck, a mysterious pair. When Widmark discovers their true identities as war criminals hiding out, it becomes a murderous game through the jungle.

RUNNERS
1983, 110 mins, UK ⊙
D: Charles Sturridge **A:** James Fox, Jane Asher, Kate Hardie, Robert Lang, Eileen O'Brien (Hanstoll/Goldcrest)

There are a lot of interesting ideas in *Runners*, but they're never really shaped into a coherent film. The meandering plot follows a father, played by James Fox, who searches for his daughter long after everyone else, including his wife, has given up. Tracking her down to a car-hire firm, rather than some perverse religious sect as he had expected, he is horrified at her reluctance to return.

RUNNER STUMBLES, THE
1979, 99 mins, US ⊙
D: Stanley Kramer **A:** Dick Van Dyke, Kathleen Quinlan, Maureen Stapleton, Ray Bolger, Tammy Grimes, Beau Bridges (Stanley Kramer)

Based on an actual case in 1927 in which a priest was accused of killing a nun, subject matter is celibacy in the Catholic Church. At times, it appears like the best of the old-fashioned 1940s tearjerkers complete with overly lush sound track. The film is paced by fine performances, especially Van Dyke as Father Rivard, Quinlan as Sister Rita, and Maureen Stapleton as Van Dyke's housekeeper.

RUNNING MAN, THE
1963, 103 mins, UK ▭
D: Carol Reed **A:** Laurence Harvey, Lee Remick, Alan Bates, Felix Aylmer, Eleanor Summerfield (Columbia)

The story is not exactly new. But Carol Reed makes it holding entertainment. Film opens with a memorial service for Laurence Harvey, believed drowned. Solemnly his wife (Lee Remick) accepts the sympathy of friends. But soon Harvey turns up, larger than life, and sets in motion their plan to collect $140,000. The claim goes through and the wife joins Harvey in Spain. Harvey has a role that suits him admirably. Bates, in the less flashy role of an insurance agent, is a most effective contrast to the flamboyance of Harvey.

RUNNING MAN, THE
1987, 101 mins, US ⊘ ⊙
D: Paul Michael Glaser **A:** Arnold Schwarzenegger, Maria Conchita Alonso, Richard Dawson, Yaphet Kotto, Jim Brown (Tri-Star/Taft/Barish/HBO)

Pic opens in 2017 when the world, following a financial collapse, is run by a police state. Arnold Schwarzenegger is Ben Richards, a helicopter pilot who disobeys orders to fire on unarmed people during an L.A. food riot. Producer-host of popular TV gameshow *The Running Man* Damon Killian (Richard Dawson) orders Richards up as his next contestant and he is duly captured and made a runner in this lethal (and fixed) gladiatorial contest for the masses. Format works only on a pure action level.

RUNNING ON EMPTY
1988, 116 mins, US ⊘ ⊙
D: Sidney Lumet **A:** Christine Lahti, River Phoenix, Judd Hirsch, Martha Plimpton, L. M. Kit Carson (Lorimar/Double Play)

A complex, turbulent tale successfully operates as study of the primacy of the family unit, an anguished teen romance, a coming-of-age story, and a look at what happened to some political radicals a generation later. Arthur and Annie Pope (Judd Hirsch and Christine Lahti) have been on the FBI's most-wanted list since bombing a university defense research installation, an act that blinded a janitor. Their life since then has required them to be as unobtrusively middle-class as possible. Son Danny (River Phoenix), now 17, is quickly recognized by the local music teacher as an exceptionally promising pianist. Danny slowly commences an edgy but potent first love with Lorna (Martha Plimpton).

1988: Nominations: Best Supp. Actor (River Phoenix), Original Screenplay

RUNNING SCARED
1986, 106 mins, US ⓥ ⊙ ▱
D: Peter Hyams **A:** Gregory Hines, Billy Crystal, Steven Bauer, Darlanne Fleugel, Jimmy Smits (M-G-M/Turman-Foster)

An ultrahip cop picture, shot in gritty style. Gregory Hines and Billy Crystal are undercover cops who risk their necks by the hour without a hint of fear, chase women together at night, and feel smugly superior to their cohorts in the force. Hines and Crystal are concerned particularly with aborting the career of aspiring Spanish godfather Jimmy Smits. Nonstop banter between the two stars is rowdy, intimate, natural, and often very funny. Hyams keeps most of it fresh, including the action ending, staged within the cavernous, glass-enclosed Illinois State Building.

RUN OF THE ARROW
1957, 86 mins, US ⓥ ▱
D: Samuel Fuller **A:** Rod Steiger, Sarita Montiel, Brian Keith, Ralph Meeker, Jay C. Flippen, Charles Bronson (RKO/Globe)

Yankee-hating southerner goes west after the Civil War to join the Sioux in their uprising against the US. Slow in takeoff, action becomes pretty rough at times. Forceful use is made of Indians and their attacks on the whites to give unusual color to feature. Steiger is never sympathetic and character itself is not clearly defined, though actor endows his character with vigor.

RUN SILENT, RUN DEEP
1958, 93 mins, US ⓥ
D: Robert Wise **A:** Clark Gable, Burt Lancaster, Jack Warden, Brad Dexter, Nick Cravat (United Artists/Hecht-Hill-Lancaster)

A taut, exciting drama of submarine warfare during the Second World War. Clark Gable is seen as a submarine commander with a single-minded purpose—to seek out and destroy a Japanese destroyer he holds responsible for sinking his previous sub. His dedication leads to charges of cowardice and incompetency which result in what seems like a "mutiny" on the part of Burt Lancaster, his tough executive officer.

RUN WILD, RUN FREE
1969, 100 mins, UK
D: Richard C. Sarafian **A:** John Mills, Sylvia Syms, Bernard Miles, Mark Lester, Gordon Jackson (Irving Allen)

This sensible and sensitive film is handled with care and obvious affection. Young Lester registers an excellent performance as an introverted, psychosomatically mute lad growing up on the moors of England. Lester's meeting with a wild, white colt concurrent with his initial acquaintance with moorman Mills, a retired army colonel, provides a setup for interaction between the three that is basis for the film.

RUSH
1991, 120 mins, US ⓥ ⊙
D: Lili Fini Zanuck **A:** Jason Patric, Jennifer Jason Leigh, Sam Elliott, Max Perlich, Gregg Allman (Zanuck)

Head-swiveling directorial debut of Lili Fini Zanuck lays out a tough masculine scenario in a way that is always emotionally riveting. A bearded Jason Patric stars as Jim, an earthy, direct, Texas narcotics cop who sees a spark in rookie Kirsten (Jennifer Jason Leigh). Kirsten soon finds Jim has a disturbing way of getting too involved in his work. Kirsten tries to draw the line, but she's already too emotionally involved with Jim, who's become her lover, and the strange, secret, and intoxicating rituals of drug buys and the underworld.

RUSH HOUR
1998, 98 mins, US ⓥ ⊙
D: Brett Ratner **A:** Jackie Chan, Chris Tucker, Tom Wilkinson, Elizabeth Pena, Philip Baker Hall, Mark Rolston (New Line)

Jackie Chan scores his biggest American-produced hit with *Rush Hour*, a formulaic but raucously entertaining action comedy that comes equipped with the additional marquee lure of up-and-comer Chris Tucker. Tucker's manic, motor-mouth style of comedy is an effective counterbalance to Chan's rapid-fire acrobatics. Maverick Detective James Carter

(Tucker) yearns to join the FBI and thinks he's gotten a big break when he's assigned to the bureau for a major case. But the feds simply want Carter to "baby-sit" Hong Kong supercop Det.-Insp. Lee (Chan), who has flown to L.A. to help his old friend the Chinese consul (Tzi Ma) recover his abducted 11-year-old daughter (Julia Hsu). Ratner gives the two leads ample opportunity to bouce humorously off each other. A peroxided Ken Leung provides silken menace as Sang, the chief kidnapper. Chan and vet stunt coordinator Terry Leonard choreograph some full-throttle action sequences to keep the party lively.

RUSH TO JUDGMENT
1967, 122 mins, US
D: Emile de Antonio (Impact Films/Judgment)

Lawyer Mark Lane, whose "brief for the defense" of Lee Harvey Oswald was in the No. 1 nonfiction bestseller position for several months, converts his material into a film of the same name. For many it will seem a convincing pic, opening up severe doubts about the thoroughness and even integrity of the Warren Commission's [investigation into the assassination of President Kennedy].

RUSSIA HOUSE, THE
1990, 123 mins, US ⓥ ⊙ ▭
D: Fred Schepisi A: Sean Connery, Michelle Pfeiffer, Roy Scheider, James Fox, Klaus Maria Brandauer, Ken Russell (Pathe)

John le Carré's glasnost-era espionage novel has been turned into intelligent adult entertainment. Sean Connery plays Barley Blair, a boozy, iconoclastic London publisher to whom a highly sensitive manuscript is sent via a Moscow book editor named Katya (Michelle Pfeiffer). The text, authored by a leading physicist, purports to lay out the facts about Soviet nuclear capabilities. Blair is sent to Moscow to meet the writer, the mysterious Dante (Klaus Maria Brandauer), determine his reliability, and put more questions to him. His intermediary is the beautiful Katya, with whom he falls in love.

RUSSIANS ARE COMING! THE RUSSIANS ARE COMING!, THE
1966, 124 mins, US ⓥ ⊙ ▭
D: Norman Jewison A: Carl Reiner, Eva Marie Saint, Alan Arkin, Brian Keith, Jonathan Winters (Mirisch/United Artist)

Outstanding cold-war comedy. Basically, story concerns aftermath of an accidental grounding on a mythical Massachusetts island of a Russian sub by overly curious skipper Theodore Bikel, who sends Alan Arkin ashore in charge of a landing party to get a towing boat. The wild antics which follow center around sheriff Brian Keith, sole resident who manages to keep cool except when arguing with Paul Ford, firebrand civil-defense chief (self-appointed), who arms himself to repel the "invasion" with a sword and an American Legion cap.
1966: Nominations: Best Picture, Actor (Alan Arkin), Adapted Screenplay, Editing

RUTHLESS
1948, 104 mins, US ⓥ
D: Edgar G. Ulmer A: Zachary Scott, Louis Hayward, Diana Lynn, Sydney Greenstreet, Lucille Bremer, Martha Vickers (Producing Artists)

Despite a sextet of name players, *Ruthless* is a victim of clichéd and outmoded direction and of weary dialogue to which no actor could do justice. Practically the entire yarn stems from the mental reflections of Louis Hayward, onetime partner of powerful financier Zachary Scott. Early sequences show how Scott moved from a poor environment to a position of prestige and wealth by a "what makes Zachary run" technique. Picture boils down to a character study of Scott.

RUTHLESS PEOPLE
1986, 93 mins, US ⓥ ⊙
D: Jim Abrahams, David Zucker, Jerry Zucker A: Danny DeVito, Bette Midler, Judge Reinhold, Helen Slater, Bill Pullman (Touchstone)

Hilariously venal comedy is about a kidnapped harridan whose rich husband won't pay for her return. Impoverished couple Judge Reinhold and Helen Slater kidnap Bel-Air princess Bette Midler because her mercenary husband, played by Danny DeVito, has ripped off Slater's design for spandex miniskirts. There is much, much more to it than that, as screenwriter Dale Launer cleverly builds twist upon complication.

RYAN'S DAUGHTER
1970, 194 mins, UK ⓥ ⊙ ▭
D: David Lean A: Robert Mitchum, Trevor Howard, Sarah Miles, Christopher Jones, John Mills (M-G-M/Faraway)

David Lean achieves to a marked degree the daring and obvious goal of intimate romantic tragedy along the rugged geographical and political landscape of 1916 Ireland. Robert Mitchum gives a stolid performance as a schoolteacher to whom Sarah Miles pours out her conception of love. United in marriage, pair never achieve a full sexual-spiritual union—he is 20 years her senior, she is immature. Arrival of shell-shocked Christopher Jones to take over the British occupation garrison cues an illicit affair.

1970: Best Supp. Actor (John Mills), Cinematography

Nominations: Best Actress (Sarah Miles), Sound

SABOTAGE
1936, 76 mins, UK 🅥 ⊙
D: Alfred Hitchcock **A:** Sylvia Sydney, Oscar Homolka, Desmond Tester, John Loder, Joyce Barbour (Gaumont-British)

Competent and experienced hand of the director is apparent throughout this production. But the plot is more or less obscure. It revolves around a secret organization that hires people to plant bombs in crowded sections of London, but the reason for their desire to systematically blow up innocent persons is not made clear. Film thus just misses being great.

SABOTEUR
1942, 100 mins, US 🅥 ⊙
D: Alfred Hitchcock **A:** Priscilla Lane, Robert Cummings, Norman Lloyd, Otto Kruger (Universal)

Saboteur is a little too self-consciously Hitchcock. Its succession of incredible climaxes, its mounting tautness and suspense, its mood of terror and impending doom could have been achieved by no one else. Norman Lloyd is genuinely plausible as the ferretlike culprit who sets an airplane factory on fire. Robert Cummings lacks variation in his performance of the thickheaded, unjustly accused worker who crosses the continent to expose the plotters and clear himself.

SABOTEUR, CODE NAME—"MORITURI", THE
See: Morituri

SABRINA
(UK: SABRINA FAIR)
1954, 112 mins, US 🅥 ⊙
D: Billy Wilder **A:** Humphrey Bogart, Audrey Hepburn, William Holden, Walter Hampden, John Williams, Martha Hyer (Paramount)

A slick blend of heart and chuckles makes *Sabrina* a sock romantic comedy. Basically, the plot's principal business is to get Audrey Hepburn, daughter of a chauffeur in service to an enormously wealthy family, paired off with the right man. She's always been in love with playboy William Holden, but ends up with Humphrey Bogart, the austere, businessman brother. Bogart is sock as the tycoon with no time for gals until he tries to get

Hepburn's mind off Holden. Hepburn again demonstrates a winning talent for being "Miss Cinderella."
1954: Best B&W Costume Design
Nominations: Best Director, Actress (Audrey Hepburn), Screenplay, B&W Cinematography, B&W Art Direction, Costume Design (Edith Head)

SABRINA
1995, 127 mins, US 🅥 ⊙
D: Sydney Pollack **A:** Harrison Ford, Julia Ormond, Greg Kinnear, John Wood, Nancy Marchand, Richard Crenna (Mirage/Sandollar/Paramount)

This new *Sabrina* is more fizzle than fizz. Sydney Pollack and his writers have uncomfortably tilted this Cinderella story of a young woman's romantic blossoming toward being the tale of a workaholic tycoon's midlife crisis, to less-than-scintillating results. Julia Ormond's Sabrina not only doesn't come close to Hepburn's, but is singularly colorless, dour, and lacking in inner spark.
1995: Nominations: Original Musical or Comedy Score, Original Song ("Moonlight")

SABRINA FAIR
See: Sabrina

SACRIFICE, THE
See: Offret

SADDLE THE WIND
1958, 84 mins, US ▱
D: Robert Parrish **A:** Robert Taylor, Julie London, John Cassavetes, Donald Crisp, Charles McGraw (M-G-M)

Tale of compulsive evil against the magnificent location backgrounds of the Colorado Rockies. Taylor plays a retired gunman farming the lush valley presided over by Donald Crisp, patriarchal landowner who has given Taylor his chance to forswear violence and bring up his orphaned, much-younger brother, John Cassavetes. But Cassavetes is one of those young men to whom a gun is more exciting than a beautiful woman. Cassavetes has a tendency to be rather mannered, but his intensity gives great conviction.

SADIE MCKEE
1934, 90 mins, US 🅥
D: Clarence Brown **A:** Joan Crawford, Gene Raymond, Franchot Tone, Edward Arnold, Esther Ralston (M-G-M)

Sadie McKee is the Cinderella theme all over again, the story of the housemaid (Joan Crawford) who marries the boss of the manor, but not until he comes humbly to her, and after she has experienced turbulent affairs with two others. The playing is expert throughout, so much so that in its realism the film perhaps makes the star suffer a bit, particularly at the hands of Edward Arnold, whose bluff, constantly inebriated performance almost steals the picture.

SADIE THOMPSON
1928, 94 mins, US Ⓥ ⊛

D: Raoul Walsh **A:** Lionel Barrymore, Gloria Swanson, Blanche Friderici, Raoul Walsh, Charles Lane (United Artists)

Program credits make no reference to *Rain* the play, the picture having been adapted from the ''original story'' by W. Somerset Maugham. Sadie's costume, her struggle to articulate above and over a wad of rum, and her familiarity with the marines is sufficient to establish her character at the beginning. But there's likely to be a wide difference of opinion on Gloria Swanson's interpretation of the role. The scene in which Hamilton enters Sadie's room during the night is not more than barely hinted at, finishing with Lionel Barrymore standing at the door.
1927/28: Nominations: Best Actress (Gloria Swanson), Cinematography

SAFE PLACE, A
1971, 94 mins, US

D: Henry Jaglom **A:** Tuesday Weld, Orson Welles, Jack Nicholson, Philip Proctor, Gwen Welles (BBS/Columbia)

Tuesday Weld is the childlike woman in whose silly pussycat consciousness the backward, forward, now-it's-now, now-it-isn't-now action takes place. In her one clear decision she is casually cruel to the young man (Philip Proctor) who adores her while receptive to the curiously charming stud played by Jack Nicholson. Weld has many scenes in a park with an itinerant magician. Of the many weirdo roles played in his time by Orson Welles, this may be the prize example. All this deliberate experimentation puts a heavy burden upon the viewer.

SAFETY LAST
1923, 77 mins, US Ⓥ ⊛

D: Fred Newmeyer, Sam Taylor **A:** Harold Lloyd, Mildred Davis, Bill Strother, Noah Young, Westcott B. Clarke (Roach)

This Harold Lloyd high-class low comedy has thrills as well as guffaws. It leads up to big shrieks through Lloyd apparently climbing the outside wall to the top or

12th floor of a building. The comedy business of the department store where Lloyd is a clerk nearly equals the remainder.

SAHARA
1943, 85 mins, US Ⓥ ⊙ ▭

D: Zoltan Korda **A:** Humphrey Bogart, Bruce Bennett, Lloyd Bridges, Rex Ingram, J. Carrol Naish, Dan Duryea (Columbia)

Story displays Libyan desert fighting in 1942, with Bogart heading his 28-ton tank south in drive to regain the British lines. He picks up six Allied stragglers, including Sudenese soldier Rex Ingram with latter's Italian prisoner, J. Carrol Naish; and a downed Nazi pilot (Kurt Krueger). Bogart reaches a water hole which provides a trickle but enough to sustain the group. Nazi motorized battalion also heads for the water supply. Script is packed with pithy dialogue, lusty action and suspense, and logically and well-devised situations.
1943: Nominations: Best Supp. Actor (J. Carrol Naish), B&W Cinematography, Sound

SAHARA
1983, 104 mins, US Ⓥ

D: Andrew V. McLaglen **A:** Brooke Shields, Lambert Wilson, Horst Buchholz, John Rhys-Davies, John Mills (Cannon)

Old-fashioned B-grade romantic adventure is lamentably low on excitement, laughs, and passion. Brooke Shields promises her dying daddy that she'll win the world's toughest endurance rally driving the car he designed. After the race starts, she's captured by Arab thug John Rhys-Davies. Handsome sheik Lambert Wilson saves her from his clutches.

SAIGON
See: Off Limits

SAIGON
1948, 93 mins, US

D: Leslie Fenton **A:** Alan Ladd, Veronica Lake, Wally Cassell, Douglas Dick, Morris Carnovsky (Paramount)

Alan Ladd fans and other followers of high adventure will like saga of three ex-army fliers who go adventuring in Saigon with a beautiful blond. There's a load of menacing and mysterious characters, a plane crash, a jungle boatride, and lushly backgrounded Saigon to point up action and intrigue before finale.

SAILOR BEWARE
1951, 104 mins, US

D: Hal Walker **A:** Dean Martin, Jerry

Lewis, Corinne Calvet, Marion Marshall, Robert Strauss (Paramount)

Martin and Lewis set out to scuttle the navy. There's the usual round of scenes depicting navy training, plus a television broadcast involving the comics and screaming femmes, and other incidents that set up the sailors' bets that Lewis can't kiss Calvet, nitery entertainer, when their submarine reaches Honolulu. Marion Marshall is a WAVE who has struck a spark with Lewis because she uses no makeup to which the comic is allergic.

SAILOR FROM GIBRALTAR, THE
1967, 89 mins, UK
D: Tony Richardson A: Jeanne Moreau, Ian Bannen, Vanessa Redgrave, Zia Moyheddin, Hugh Griffith, Orson Welles (Lopert Pictures)

A Britisher (Ian Bannen) and his mistress (Vanessa Redgrave) are on an Italian holiday. She's still hungry for him but he can't stand her but isn't brave enough to send her away. When a mysterious woman (Jeanne Moreau) crosses their path, his greed (both sexual and practical) provides the impetus to ditch his mistress and make a fast pass at the yachtswoman.

SAILOR'S RETURN, THE
1978, 112 mins, UK
D: Jack Gold A: Tom Bell, Shope Shodeinde, Mick Ford, Paola Dionisotti, Clive Swift (Ariel/NFFC)

Set in the early reign of Queen Victoria, story is about a sailor who returns home to England with a bride from the black kingdom of Dahomey in West Africa. It's her dowry, a treasure of pearls, that sets them up in business with an inn for thirsty passersby in a lush English countryside. But her color and the presence of a black son set them off from intolerant neighbors, despite some support from friends in the area.

SAILOR TAKES A WIFE, THE
1946, 92 mins, US
D: Richard Whorf A: Robert Walker, June Allyson, Hume Cronyn, Audrey Totter, Eddie "Rochester" Anderson (M-G-M)

Robert Walker and June Allyson make the antics and complications around which the plot revolves delightful. Plot deals with a sailor and a girl who meet and marry, all in one evening, and subsequent efforts to adjust themselves to marital status. Bride's first disappointment comes when her husband is discharged almost imme-

diately, leaving her with a civilian instead of the hero she expected.

SAILOR WHO FELL FROM GRACE WITH THE SEA, THE
1976, 104 mins, UK ⊠
D: Lewis John Carlino A: Sarah Miles, Kris Kristofferson, Jonathan Kahn, Margo Cunningham, Earl Rhodes (Avco Embassy)

The prime problem with *Sailor* is trying to transfer decidedly Oriental ideas about honor, order, and death into an English countryside. Yukio Mishima's novel was about a Japanese widow who falls in love with a sailor. At first attracted to the sailor as an honorable symbol, her 13-year-old son defends him before his gang of idealistic schoolmates. But when the sailor leaves the sea to marry, the boy and his gang feel betrayed. On film, the story won't settle down with these upper-class young English lads.

SAINT, THE
1997, 116 mins, US Ⓥ ⊙ ⊠
D: Phillip Noyce A: Val Kilmer, Elisabeth Shue, Rade Serbedzija, Valery Nikolaev, Henry Goodman, Alun Armstrong (Paramount)

A generic suspenser that becomes increasingly hard to swallow, *The Saint* comes off more as a pallid imitation of *Mission: Impossible* than as anything resembling the further adventures of Leslie Charteris's charming rogue. In Moscow, Simon Templar (Val Kilmer) steals a microchip important to Ivan Tretiak (Rade Serbedzija), a blowhard nationalist and Mafia-style billionaire. In England, Templar is induced by Tretiak to nab a breakthrough formula for cold-fusion developed by Yank scientist Dr. Emma Russell (Elisabeth Shue). He seduces the smart-but-vulnerable genius. The second hour descends into routine cat-and-mouse stuff as the Russian baddies chase the breathless couple all over Moscow. Kilmer's Saint is mostly a cipher. Shue may be a vision, but she is not a vision one readily believes has solved the daunting challenge of cold fusion.

SAINT IN LONDON, THE
1939, 72 mins, UK Ⓥ
D: John Paddy Carstairs A: George Sanders, Sally Gray, David Burns, Athene Seyler, Henry Oscar (RKO)

This is a workmanlike job. The Saint aids Scotland Yard in rounding up a gang that's ready to foist upon the public $5-

million worth of banknotes printed in England for a continental country.

SAINT IN NEW YORK, THE
1938, 72 mins, US Ⓥ
D: Ben Holmes A: Louis Hayward, Kay Sutton, Sig Ruman, Jonathan Hale, Jack Carson (RKO)

A rugged gangster melodrama, highly fantastic in plot but intriguing, has been skillfully shaped from the Leslie Charteris novel about a modern Robin Hood whose dish is rubbing out baddies. It makes no pretentions to being more than a B picture. To some extent, Louis Hayward has too much the appearance of a college freshman to suggest that his exploits could be anything but imaginative.

SAINT JACK
1979, 112 mins, US Ⓥ
D: Peter Bogdanovich A: Ben Gazzara, Denholm Elliott, James Villiers, Joss Ackland, Rodney Bewes (New World/Playboy/Shoals Creek-Copa de Oro)

Shot entirely on location in Singapore, the film is extremely well crafted, finely acted, and conjures up a positively intriguing milieu. Based on Paul Theroux's novel, it is set in 1971, putting its exclusive focus on Gazzara, an expatriate US hustler type who uses the cover of a local provision broker to operate a freelance prostitution ring.

SAINT JOAN
1957, 110 mins, US Ⓥ
D: Otto Preminger A: Jean Seberg, Richard Widmark, Richard Todd, Anton Walbrook, John Gielgud (United Artists)

Preminger showed courage when he decided to film G. B. Shaw's Saint Joan and to star an unknown in the role. Jean Seberg makes a sincere effort, but her performance rarely rises above the level of the Iowa prairie. Seberg is helped most by her appealing looks. But Shaw's Joan is more than just an innocent country maiden. In vivid contrast, Preminger surrounds her with a supporting cast that performs brilliantly. Graham Greene wrote the screenplay.

SALAAM BOMBAY
1988, 113 mins, India Ⓥ ⊙
D: Mira Nair A: Shafik Syed, Sarfuddin Qurassi, Raju Barnad, Raghubir Yadav, Nana Patekar (Mirabai)

About kids living on the sidewalks of Bombay utilizing their wits, the story revolves around a young boy, Krishna. As he carries tea in a slum for pimps and prostitutes, sleeping on a pile of rubble, and learning the ways of the street and the means to survive, innocence gradually is beaten out of him. Director tells her story efficiently. She indulges in some melodramatic explorations, however, dangerously verging on a romanticized Oriental tearjerker mood.

LE SALAIRE DE LA PEUR
(US: THE WAGES OF FEAR)
1953, 155 mins, France/Italy Ⓥ ⊙
D: Henri-Georges Clouzot A: Yves Montand, Charles Vanel, Peter Van Eyck, William Tubbs, Vera Clouzot, Fulco Lulli (CICC/Filmsonor/Vera/Fono Roma)

A harrowing odyssey of four derelicts inching two trucks loaded with nitroglycerine over a tortuous terrain puts this in the strong-meat department with a downbeat theme of fear and its manifestations. Story shows a group of foreign tramps huddled in a small tropical village suffering from heat and boredom, and plotting some means of getting out. A chance offers itself because an American oil company wants two trucks loaded with explosives driven to a well fire.

SALLY IN OUR ALLEY
1931, 77 mins, UK
D: Maurice Elvey A: Gracie Fields, Ian Hunter, Florence Desmond, Fred Groves, Gibb McLaughlin (Associated Talking Pictures/Radio)

Gracie Fields doesn't exactly suggest sufficient sympathy to hold the romantic lead, but her eccentric singing and dialect-gagging records well. Story tells how a Lancashire girl refuses to marry because her boyfriend is reported killed in the war, although actually he isn't dead but pretends to be because he's crippled. She makes a hit serving and singing in a coffee shop.

SALLY, IRENE AND MARY
1925, 58 mins, US ⊗
D: Edmund Goulding A: Constance Bennett, Joan Crawford, Sally O'Neill, William Haines (M-G-M)

Rather trashy chorus-girl stuff doesn't ring true. Sally is the "kept woman" of the trio; Irene can't make up her mind whether to choose a "chaser" or a boy with honorable intentions, and Mary is the innocent miss who nearly loses Sally her deluxe flat when the latter's moneyman takes a tumble in her favor. Constance Bennett gives the one genuine performance in the picture as Sally, and suffers because of an unsympathetic role.

SALLY, IRENE AND MARY
1938, 86 mins, US
D: William A. Seiter **A:** Alice Faye, Tony Martin, Fred Allen, Jimmy Durante, Gregory Ratoff, Joan Davis (20th Century-Fox)

Another in the Darryl F. Zanuck formula of vaudscreen musicals, skillfully blending the variety components and dovetailing them into an amiable entertainment. Fred Allen foils with and for Jimmy Durante, both proving an effective team throughout with a running-gag sequence. It's the vocal prowess of Tony Martin and Alice Faye, the romance interest here, that does much to sustain the interest.

SALLY OF THE SAWDUST
1925, 104 mins, US ⊗ ⊗
D: D. W. Griffith **A:** Carol Dempster, W. C. Fields, Alfred Lunt, Erville Alderson (Griffith/United Artists)

D. W. Griffith is down to common picture making in this one. It is strange to witness a Griffith film directed by him in a straight manner. W. C. Fields screams his screen debut as a film funny man. Sally is an orphan, her mother a gentlewoman from New England, having married a theatrical man against her parents' wishes. When her mother dies, Professor McGargle (Fields) takes charge of Sally, bringing her up as his daughter with the girl unaware of her parentage.

SALOME
1922, 75 mins, US ⊗
D: Charles Bryant **A:** Nazimova, Rose Dione, Mitchell Lewis, Nigel de Brulier (Nazimova/Allied)

Highly fantastic *Salome* is far from the *Salome* Oscar Wilde penned. The picture is done with a decidedly modernistic touch. It is very pretty as to lighting, setting, and photography, but there ends about all that can be said in praise. *Nazimova in Facial Expressions,* with Salome as the background, would have been much better billing for the picture.

SALOME
1953, 102 mins, US ⊗
D: William Dieterle **A:** Rita Hayworth, Stewart Granger, Judith Anderson, Cedric Hardwicke, Alan Badel, Charles Laughton (Columbia/Beckworth)

The story and screenplay change and embroider the biblical tale of the girl who danced for King Herod and caused the beheading of John the Baptist. It is a vehicle especially slanted for Rita Hayworth. Opening finds Salome, Herod's stepdaughter, banished from Rome because Caesar's nephew wants to marry her. During the trip back to Galilee, she vents her spite against all Romans on Commander Claudius, played by Stewart Granger, even though they are attracted to each other. When Hayworth injects excellent dramatic values and wears the clinging Roman costumes to advantage. Her dance, staged by Valerie Bettis, packs plenty of s.a.

SALT OF THE EARTH
1954, 94 mins, US ⊗ ⊙
D: Herbert J. Biberman **A:** Rosaura Revueltas, Juan Chacon, Will Geer, David Wolfe, Mervin Williams, David Sarvis (Independent/International Union of Mine, Mill & Smelter Worker)

Salt of the Earth is a good, highly dramatic, and emotion-charged piece of work that tells its story straight. It is, however, a propaganda picture which belongs in union halls rather than theaters. In a bitter tale that Michael Wilson has concocted and the large cast acts it out with a conviction that obviously didn't require much prompting. The story concerns Mexican miners in a small New Mexican mining community, Zinc Town. A series of mine accidents prompts a strike. The company attempts to break it via acts of intimidation that include arrest and brutality.

SALT ON OUR SKIN
1993, 110 mins, Germany/France/Canada ⊗ ⊙
D: Andrew Birkin **A:** Greta Scacchi, Vincent D'Onofrio, Anais Jenneret, Petra Berndt, Claudine Auger (Constantin)

Old-fashioned weepie about mismatched lovers whose rare, passionate encounters over 30 years make both their lives worth living. Shortly after discovering true ecstasy in Vincent D'Onofrio's arms in the late 1950s, Scacchi discovers Camus, Sartre, and—bingo!—Simone de Beauvoir's *The Second Sex.* When D'Onofrio proposes, Scacchi assures him it could never work: she's a restless intellectual, he's a hunky fisherman, and a future cannot be built on sex alone. They part but end up trysting every so often.

SALT TO THE DEVIL
See: Give Us This Day

SALUTE OF THE JUGGER, THE (AKA: THE BLOOD OF HEROES)
1989, 102 mins, Australia ⊗
D: David Peoples **A:** Rutger Hauer, Joan

Chen, Vincent D'Onofrio, Anna Katarina, Delroy Lindo (Kings Road)

Murky, familiar screenplay about a band of wandering "juggers." They're futuristic gladiators, led by the deeply scarred Sallow (Rutger Hauer), who was once a member of the League, the ruling elite, but who was banished over a misdemeanor. Now Sallow is determined to challenge the League's juggers and regain his position. Plot development is slim. Much of running time is given over to the game itself, which seems to have no rules except that the winning team places the skull of a dog atop a pointed stick.

SALVADOR
1986, 123 mins, US Ⓥ ⊙
D: Oliver Stone A: James Woods, James Belushi, Michael Murphy, John Savage, Elpidia Carrillo (Hemdale)

Tale of American photojournalist Richard Boyle's adventures in strife-torn Central America is as raw, difficult, compelling, unreasonable, reckless, and vivid as its protagonist. James Woods portrays the real-life Boyle, who shanghais fun-loving buddy James Belushi for the long drive down to (El) Salvador, where Woods has left behind a native girlfriend and where he thinks he might be able to pick up some freelance work.
1986: Nominations: Best Actor (James Woods), Original Screenplay

SALVATORE GIULIANO
1961, 125 mins, Italy
D: Francesco Rosi A: Salvo Randone, Frank Wolff, Federico Zardi, Pietro Cammarata (Lux/Vides/Galatea)

An outstanding film has been fashioned by Francesco Rosi using the story of Sicilian bandit Giuliano as a pretext for a historical, political, and social document of its times (the late 1940s and early 1950s), and of the island setting (Sicily) which made it possible. Tale is told in flashback, beginning with a graphic reenactment of Giuliano's death (shot by his best friend, then again by the police, who claimed credit for the deed), and the ending when still another gang member, who betrayed, is shot during a recent Sicilian night.

SAME TIME, NEXT YEAR
1978, 119 mins, US Ⓥ ⊙
D: Robert Mulligan A: Ellen Burstyn, Alan Alda, Ivan Bonar (Universal)

The picture opens in 1951 at a resort in California. Burstyn, a 24-year-old housewife, and Alda, a 27-year-old accountant, have a fling. The next morning they realize that while they're both happily married, with six children between them, they're in love. They make a pact to meet at the same resort every year, which is just what they do. It's nice to see a film about two people who like each other this deeply.
1978: Nominations: Best Actress (Ellen Burstyn), Adapted Screenplay, Cinematography, Song ("The Last Time I Felt Like This")

SAMMA NO AJI
(US: AN AUTUMN AFTERNOON)
1962, 113 mins, Japan
D: Yasujiro Ozu A: Shima Iwashita, Shinichiro Mikami, Keiji Sata, Mariko Okada, Nobuo Nakamura, Chishu Ryu (Shochiku)

Screenplay tells the story of a bourgeois widower's adjustment to coming old age, the departure of his children into marriage, and the changes in a society which has apparently been very good to him. It's a gentle, nostalgic view of life which director Yasujiro Ozu draws. The picture is nicely acted throughout, and does have its comic and affecting moments.

SAMMY AND ROSIE GET LAID
1987, 100 mins, UK Ⓥ ⊙
D: Stephen Frears A: Shashi Kapoor, Frances Barber, Claire Bloom, Ayub Khan Din, Roland Gift (Working Title)

Pic brings the force of an accelerated cinematic attack to bear upon its complex thematic juxtaposition of sexual warfare, cross-cultural dislocation, racism, and the ruthlessness of power. Sammy (Ayub Khan Din), the hedonistic, thoroughly English son of a prominent Pakistani politician, lives in a dangerous and decaying black neighborhood with his wife Rosie (Frances Barber), a sexually adventurous feminist journalist. Change enters their lives with the arrival of Rafi (Shashi Kapoor), Sammy's long-lost father who has been forced to flee his political enemies in Pakistan.

SAMMY GOING SOUTH
(AKA: A BOY TEN FEET TALL)
1963, 128 mins, UK ▭
D: Alexander Mackendrick A: Edward G. Robinson, Fergus McClelland, Constance Cummings, Harry H. Corbett, Paul Stassino (British Lion/Bryanston Seven Arts)

Pic is based on an uneasy, incredible idea. A 10-year-old youngster (Fergus McClelland) is orphaned when his parents are killed in an air raid during the Suez crisis. In a blur he remembers that he has an Aunt Jane in Durban and that Durban is in the south. So he sets out, armed only with a toy compass. Not until he meets up with a grizzled old diamond smuggler (Edward G. Robinson) does the film flicker into some spark of human interest. The old man and the moppet strike up a splendid friendship.

LE SAMOURAI
(US: THE SAMURAI)
1967, 105 mins, France/Italy
D: Jean-Pierre Melville **A:** Alain Delon, Nathalie Delon, Cathy Rosier, Francois Perier (Filmel/Borderie/TCP/Fida

Melville uses an American book about a hired killer and transposes it to France for a curiously hybrid pic. It is intermittently successful. Without a true French gangster core that would breed this sort of automaton killer, Melville tries to compare him to the Japanese samurai dedicated to military codes. Alain Delon has the empty agate eyes, cold demeanor, and implacable presence for the glacial killer who manages to spark love in a part-time kept woman, and becomes the prey of a dedicated, unswerving police inspector.

SAMSON AND DELILAH
1950, 120 mins, US Ⓥ ⊙
D: Cecil B. DeMille **A:** Hedy Lamarr, Victor Mature, George Sanders, Angela Lansbury, Henry Wilcoxon (Paramount)

Cecil B. DeMille has again dipped into the Bible for his material, made appropriately dramatic revisions in the original, and turned up with a DeMille-size smash. Victor Mature fits neatly into the role of the handsome but dumb hulk of muscle that both the Bible and DeMille make of the Samson character. Hedy Lamarr never has been more eye-filling and makes of Delilah a convincing minx.

1950: Best Color Art Direction, Color Costume Design (Edith Head)

Nominations: Best Color Cinematography, Scoring of a Dramatic Picture, Special Effects

SAMURAI, THE
See: Le Samourai

SAMURAI REBELLION
See: Joi-uchi

SAN ANTONIO
1945, 110 mins, US Ⓥ
D: David Butler **A:** Errol Flynn, Alexis Smith, S. Z. Sakall, Victor Francen, Paul Kelly (Warner)

Here's a western in the old, old tradition in which one lone, honest hombre defeats the hordes of evil gathered in San Antonio (Texas). Errol Flynn looks and acts right handsome as that hero. Paul Kelly and Victor Francen earn their villainous hisses.

SAND CASTLE, THE
1961, 70 mins, US
D: Jerome Hill **A:** Barrie Cardwell, Laurie Cardwell, George Dunham, Erica Speyer (De Rochemont/Noel)

A little boy and his sister (Barrie and Laurie Cardwell) start the day's activities as their mother leaves them on the beach to play. Slowly but in ever-increasing numbers, other people begin to arrive. Oblivious to them all, the boy starts to build a large sand castle in the shape of a fort, helped by his sister, who fetches driftwood and shells. The others gather 'round and admire his work. There is no dialogue, only incidental and amusing conversation. Nothing is overstated and none of the characters is overdrawn or derivative. The mood is always one of gentleness, charm, and tranquillity.

SAN DEMETRIO–LONDON
1943, 93 mins, UK
D: Charles Frend **A:** Walter Fitzgerald, Mervyn Johns, Ralph Michael, Robert Beatty, Gordon Jackson (Ealing)

Epic tale of the British Merchant Marine omits the customary cast of characters in the screen credits. Thus does it emphasize the genuineness of the personalities concerned in the unfolding of a gripping drama. If the chief engineer—who performs miracles in the half-flooded, fireswept engine room by not only restarting the engines, but by cooking a pailful of potatoes in live steam from a leaking valve—is not a c.e. in real life, it really doesn't make any difference. And this goes for all of them, from the bosun to the kid apprentice whose first voyage it is.

SANDERS OF THE RIVER
1935, 98 mins, UK Ⓥ
D: Zoltan Korda **A:** Paul Robeson, Leslie Banks, Nina Mae McKinney, Robert Cochrane, Martin Walker (London/United Artists)

Leslie Banks and Paul Robeson carry the greater part of this tale of a British commissioner who rules an African sector through commanding both fear and respect. Sanders (Banks) makes a minor chief of Bosambo (Robeson), an engaging fugitive from prison, revealing the excellence of his judgment of men. Mofolabo, known as "the old king," is in an inaccessible section of the district and gives much trouble. Robeson gets two of the songs, with the third, a lullaby, going to Nina Mae McKinney.

SANDLOT, THE
1993, 101 mins, US Ⓥ ⊙ ▭
D: David Mickey Evans **A:** Tom Guiry, Mike Vitar, Patrick Renna, Chauncey Leopardi, Karen Allen, James Earl Jones (20th Century-Fox)

Yet another wallow in the coming-of-age stakes circa 1962. Sweet and sincere, the film is also remarkably shallow, rife with incident and slim on substance. Scotty Smalls (Tom Guiry) arrives in some quiet piece of Americana and is recruited into the neighborhood's ad hoc baseball team. Scotty's mentor is Benny Rodriguez (Mike Vitar), the most charismatic and best player on the block. Running beneath the surface is the promise of some cataclysmic event.

SAND PEBBLES, THE
1966, 193 mins, US Ⓥ ▭
D: Robert Wise **A:** Steve McQueen, Richard Attenborough, Richard Crenna, Candice Bergen, Mako (Argyle/Solar/20th Century-Fox)

Out of the 1926 political and military turmoil in China, Robert Wise has created a sensitive, personal drama, set against a background of old style US Navy gunboat diplomacy. Steve McQueen looks and acts the part he plays so well—that of a machinist's mate with nine years of navy service. Richard Attenborough likewise is authentic as the gunboat captain. The major drawback to the film as a whole is a surfeit of exposition, mainly in the second half.
1966: Nominations: Best Picture, Actor (Steve McQueen), Supp. Actor (Mako), Color Cinematography, Color Art Direction, Editing, Original Music Score, Sound

SANDPIPER, THE
1965, 115 mins, US Ⓥ ▭
D: Vincente Minnelli **A:** Elizabeth Taylor, Richard Burton, Eva Marie Saint, Charles Bronson, Robert Webber (M-G-M/Filmways)

The story of a passing affair, between an unwed nonconformist and a married Episcopalian minister who is headmaster of a private boys' school attended by femme's nine-year-old son, is trite and often ponderous in its philosophizing by the two principals, and picture is further burdened by lack of any fresh approach.
1965: Best Song ("The Shadow of Your Smile")

SANDRA
See: Vaghe Stelle Dell'Orsa

SANDS OF IWO JIMA
1949, 110 mins, US Ⓥ ⊙
D: Allan Dwan **A:** John Wayne, John Agar, Adele Mara, Forrest Tucker, Wally Cassell (Republic)

This is a vast saga of a marine platoon whose history is traced from its early combat training through its storming of Iwo Jima's beaches to the historic flag-raising episode atop the sandy atoll. It falls short of greatness because of its sentimental core and its superficial commentary on the war. John Wayne draws a powerful portrait of a soldier with the job of making plain joes into murdering machines.
1949: Nominations: Best Actor (John Wayne), Motion Picture Story, Editing, Sound

SANDS OF THE KALAHARI
1965, 119 mins, UK ▭
D: Cy Endfield **A:** Stuart Whitman, Stanley Baker, Susannah York, Harry Andrews, Nigel Davenport (Paramount/Levine)

A planeload of assorted types crashes in the desert and the rest of the film deals with their efforts to survive. Susannah York, as the only female, gets plenty of exposure. Stuart Whitman, a gun-happy survivalist, and Stanley Baker, a nondescript loser, are the only main characters. Entertainment, pure and simple, was evidently what the filmmakers aimed for and that's the target they hit.

SANDWICH MAN, THE
1966, 95 mins, UK Ⓥ
D: Robert Hartford-Davis **A:** Michael Bentine, Dora Bryan, Harry H. Corbett, Bernard Cribbins, Diana Dors (Titan)

Michael Bentine, who wrote the screenplay with the director, seeks to give a picture of London and some of the way-out, curious behavior of its inhabitants through the eyes of a sandwich-board man who, wandering the streets, has a load of opportunity of observing, and of getting implicated. Not a bad idea, and filmed on location entirely, it gives director and cameraman Peter Newbrook a swell chance of bringing London to life.

SAN FRANCISCO
1936, 115 mins, US Ⓥ ⊙
D: W. S. Van Dyke A: Clark Gable, Jean-ette MacDonald, Spencer Tracy, Jack Holt, Jessie Ralph (M-G-M)

An earthquake, noisy and terrifying, is film's forte. Quake occurs after more than an hour, and up to then the picture is distinguished chiefly for its corking cast and super-fine production. Story basically follows the outline traced previously by Warner's *Frisco Kid* and Goldwyn's *Barbary Coast*. Gable is "king" of the Barbary Coast, and like his predecessors, his reformation is the essence of the plot. As Blackie Norton, he operates a prosperous gambling joint and beer garden. The closest friend of this godless soul is a priest, who doesn't try to reform Blackie but always hopes for the best.
1936: Best Sound Recording
Nominations: Best Director, Actor (Spencer Tracy), Original Story, Assistant Director (Joseph Newman)

LE SANG D'UN POETE
(US: BLOOD OF A POET)
1932, 60 mins, France
D: Jean Cocteau A: Lee Miller, Pauline Carton, Odette Talazac, Enrique Rivero, Jean Desbordes (Vicomte de Nouailles)

Director-writer Jean Cocteau is a Parisian poet, artist, and author, one of the finest. He has been called "a mad genius." No sense to try and explain what happens in this picture. It's all silent footage with Cocteau personally explaining the action (in French) in words that are just as meaningless as the action itself.

SANJURO
See: Tsubaki Sanjuro

SAN QUENTIN
1937, 70 mins, US
D: Lloyd Bacon A: Pat O'Brien, Humphrey Bogart, Ann Sheridan, Barton MacLane, Joseph Sawyer, Veda Ann Borg (Warner Bros.)

Stark, authentic-looking prison melodrama that misses being big entertainment because of a love story that is none too strong and a plot that is only moderately forceful. Various scenes were made in and around the San Quentin pen. Romantic leads are Pat O'Brien and Ann Sheridan, while the girl's brother is Humphrey Bogart, a tough convict.

SAN QUENTIN
1946, 66 mins, US
D: Gordon Douglas A: Lawrence Tierney, Barton MacLane, Harry Shannon, Marian Carr, Carol Forman (RKO)

Plot frames its melodramatics around efforts of Harry Shannon, San Quentin warden, to keep his prisoners' welfare league going in the face of opposition. Taking a group of prisoners to San Francisco to speak to a newspaper club, Shannon is wounded and others killed when a supposedly reformed inmate arranges an escape. To clear the warden's plan and make life better for majority of prisoners, Tierney goes on a manhunt for Barton MacLane, the killer.

SANSHO DAYU
(US: SANSHO THE BAILIFF; THE BAILIFF)
1954, 120 mins, Japan Ⓥ
D: Kenji Mizoguchi A: Kinuyo Tanaka, Kyoko Kagawa, Eitaro Shindo, Yoshiaki Hanayagi, Ichiro Sugai (Daiei)

This elegant film, set in 11th-century Japan, tells the story of a noble mother and her two children who are separated by river pirates. The latter sell the children to a tyrant, and the mother to a brothel. Film builds up a fine, well-ordered story as the children grow up but never forget their mother. Legend, adventure, and poetry fuse to make this engrossing, if overlong, film material.

SANSHO THE BAILIFF
See: Sansho Dayu

SANTA CLAUS
1985, 112 mins, US Ⓥ ⊙ ▭
D: Jeannot Szwarc A: David Huddleston, Dudley Moore, John Lithgow, Judy Cornwell, Christian Fitzpatrick (Salkind/Santa Claus)

A film for children of all ages that will probably skew best toward infancy or senility. David Huddleston is a perfect Claus, first introduced several centuries ago as a woodcutter who delights in distributing Christmas gifts to village children. Wondrously, Mr. and Mrs. Claus awake to discover they are at the North Pole, where their arrival is excitedly hailed by elves led by Dudley Moore.

SANTA CLAUSE, THE
1994, 97 mins, US Ⓥ ⊙
D: John Pasquin A: Tim Allen, Judge Reinhold, Wendy Crewson, Eric Lloyd, Peter Boyle (Outlaw/Hollywood)

The hapless hero is ad exec Scott Calvin (Tim Allen), divorced from his wife and doing the split-custody holiday scene with son Charlie (Eric Lloyd). Except this year, a clatter arises from the roof, and when Scott investigates, he startles a red-suited gent who falls with a thud. That's when he passes along his card and Scott reluctantly dons the costume and, with Charlie, climbs aboard the Reindeermobile, grabs the list, and goes to work. When he wakes up the following morning in his suburban bed, he assumes the events of the previous night were all a dream. The humor centers on characters' reactions to the preposterous premise. Laura (Wendy Crewson), the ex-spouse, and her cloying new mate (Judge Reinhold), have the court suspend Santa dad's visitation rights.

SANTA FE TRAIL
1940, 110 mins, US Ⓥ ⊙ ▭
D: Michael Curtiz **A:** Errol Flynn, Olivia de Havilland, Raymond Massey, Ronald Reagan, Van Heflin (Warner)

Thrilling saga of hard-bitten US army officers' fight to wipe out John Brown's marauding crew of Kansas abolition days. Newly made army officers Jeb Stuart (Errol Flynn) and George Custer (Ronald Reagan), assigned to guard a freight caravan, have a bloody encounter with Brown and his renegade crew. The whole army troop is assigned the task of capturing him. Some historians may find fault with the way John Brown is pictured as a fanatic, religious zealot. However, this is tempered, with references to his basic ideas on slavery in US being sound. Raymond Massey makes the John Brown role the film's outstanding characterization.

SAPPHIRE
1959, 92 mins, UK Ⓥ
D: Basil Dearden **A:** Nigel Patrick, Yvonne Mitchell, Michael Craig, Paul Massie, Earl Cameron (Rank)

Well-knit pic showing how the police patiently track down a murderer, though obviously inspired by 1958's outbreak of color-bar riots in London and Nottingham, adds up merely to another whodunit. Nigel Patrick is fine as a suave, polite but ruthlessly efficient cop. Michael Craig, his assistant, is equally good as a less tolerant man who loathes colored people. But perhaps the best performance is that of Earl Cameron as an intelligent, tolerant Negro doctor, brother of the slain girl.

SARABAND
See: Saraband for Dead Lovers

SARABAND FOR DEAD LOVERS (AKA: SARABAND)
1948, 96 mins, UK
D: Basil Dearden, Michael Relph **A:** Stewart Granger, Joan Greenwood, Flora Robson, Francoise Rosay, Anthony Quayle (Ealing)

Colorful production, magnificent settings and costumes enhanced by unobtrusive use of Technicolor, and a powerful melodramatic story of court intrigue in the House of Hanover in the early 18th century, add up to a first-rate piece of hokum entertainment. Film tells the poignant story of the unhappy Princess Dorothea, compelled to marry against her will the uncouth Prince Louis to strengthen his title to the kingship of England. Joan Greenwood is charming and colorful as Dorothea. Flora Robson is merciless as the arch-intriguer at the court.
1949: Nomination: Best Color Art Direction

SARAFINA!
1992, 115 mins, South Africa Ⓥ
D: Darrell James Roodt **A:** Leleti Khumalo, Whoopi Goldberg, Miriam Makeba, John Kani (Distant Horizon/Ideal)

Powerfully lensed on location in Soweto, emotionally and politically impassioned piece effectively registers the antiapartheid movement's anger and hope in an infectious musical context. The beautiful Sarafina, who idolizes Nelson Mandela, sees a fellow student she may fancy shot dead by police, participates in the rioting following the shooting of more blacks, takes part in the torching of a black officer who works for the whites, and is tortured in prison. Terrific songs by Ngema and Hugh Masekela propel the work at a fine clip and are exceedingly well performed and staged.

SARAGOSSA MANUSCRIPT, THE
See: Rekopis Znaleziony W Saragossie

SARATOGA
1937, 90 mins, US
D: Jack Conway **A:** Jean Harlow, Clark Gable, Lionel Barrymore, Frank Morgan, Walter Pidgeon (M-G-M)

Glamorous comedy-drama about the Thoroughbreds and the men and women who follow the horses around the circuit. Gable plays a bookmaker in a breezy manner. Harlow is the daughter of a family that has bred and raced horses for generations. She takes her small inheritance and wagers on the horses in an effort to win enough to repurchase the family breeding farm from Gable. Harlow's performance is among her best. She has several rowdy comedy passages with Gable which are excellently done.

SARATOGA TRUNK
1943, 135 mins, US
D: Sam Wood A: Gary Cooper, Ingrid Bergman, Flora Robson, Jerry Austin, Florence Bates (Warner)

Story has color, romance, adventure, and not a little s.a. Ingrid Bergman is the beautiful albeit calculating Creole, and Gary Cooper is very effective in the plausible role of a droll, gamblin' Texan who has the romantic hex on her. Flora Robson is capitally cast as her body servant and Jerry Austin does a bang-up job as the dwarf who, with the mulatto servant, makes a strange entourage. The 1875 period, and the New Orleans and Saratoga locales, combine into a moving story.
1946: Nomination: Best Supp. Actress (Flora Robson)

SASAME YUKI
(US: THE MAKIOKA SISTERS)
1983, 140 mins, Japan ⓥ
D: Kon Ichikawa A: Keiko Kishi, Yoshiko Sakuma, Sayuri Yoshinaga, Yuko Kotegawa, Juzo Itami (Toho)

This rambling family epic makes for an elegant view of life in Japan a half century ago. There is rich opportunity for ensemble acting—and it's done to perfection in Ichikawa's hands.

SASOM I EN SPEGEL
(US: THROUGH A GLASS DARKLY)
1961, 89 mins, Sweden ⓥ
D: Ingmar Bergman A: Harriet Andersson, Gunnar Bjornstrand, Max von Sydow, Lars Passgard (Svensk Filmindustri)

Pic deals with four members of a family who are estranged through their inability to express feelings for each other. The action is limited to 24 hours. The time is the nightless Scandinavian summer and the setting is an isolated island in the Baltic. Not a pleasant film, it is a great one. Karin (Harriet Andersson) is suffering from a mental ailment. She seeks the security of her childhood, the love of her father, David (Gunnar Bjornstrand), and her 17-year-old brother, Fredrick (Lars Passgard). She turns further and further away from her husband Martin (Max von Sydow).
1961: Best Foreign Language Film

SATAN BUG, THE
1965, 114 mins, US ⓥ ▭
D: John Sturges A: George Maharis, Richard Basehart, Anne Francis, Dana Andrews, Ed Asner (Mirisch-Kappa)

Superior suspense melodrama. The scientist who develops the deadly virus known as the Satan Bug, so lethal it can cause instant death over great areas, is murdered and flasks containing the liquid mysteriously spirited out of the lab. George Maharis is a former army intelligence officer recalled to find the virus before it can be put to the use threatened by a millionaire paranoiac who masterminded the theft.

SATAN MET A LADY
1936, 74 mins, US ⓥ
D: William Dieterle A: Bette Davis, Warren William, Alison Skipworth, Arthur Treacher, Winifred Shaw (Warner)

Inferior remake of *The Maltese Falcon.* Among items changed are the names of the characters as well as a few of the characters themselves. The plaster bird is now a ram's horn. There's hardly any mystery in this version. The comedy isn't strong enough to fill the bill. William tries hard to be gay as the eccentric private cop and his performance is all that keeps the picture moving in many lagging moments.

SATAN NEVER SLEEPS
(UK: THE DEVIL NEVER SLEEPS)
1962, 133 mins, US ▭
D: Leo McCarey A: William Holden, Clifton Webb, France Nuyen, Athene Seyler, Weaver Lee (20th Century-Fox)

China in its critical year of 1949 is the setting, from a novel by Pearl S. Buck. Cornered in this moment of transition to Communism are two Catholic priests, played by Clifton Webb and William Holden, the latter adoringly but hopelessly pursued by a Chinese maiden (France Nuyen). The priests are soon imprisoned by the local People's party leader (Weaver Lee), who also rapes the girl.

SATURDAY NIGHT AND SUNDAY MORNING
1960, 89 mins, UK ⓥ
D: Karel Reisz A: Albert Finney, Shirley Anne Field, Rachel Roberts, Hylda Baker, Norman Rossington (Woodfall/Bryanston)

This is a good, absorbing, but not very likable film. The hero is a Nottingham factory worker who refuses to conform. He hates all authority but protests so blunderingly. In his spare time—Saturday night and Sunday morning (and a couple of evenings)—he comes into his own. Liquor and women. Albert Finney, in his first major screen performance, handles scenes of belligerence and one or two love scenes with complete confidence and is equally effective in quieter moments. On a par is the performance of Rachel Roberts as the married woman carrying on a hopeless affair with him.

SATURDAY NIGHT FEVER
1977, 119 mins, US ℣ ⊙
D: John Badham A: John Travolta, Karen Lynn Gorney, Barry Miller, Joseph Cali, Bruce Ornstein (Paramount)

John Travolta stars as an amiably inarticulate NY kid who comes to life only in a disco environment. Coloring-book plotlines give Travolta a bad home life (Val Bisoglio's father is an ethnic horror story), a formula gang of buddies, an available "bad" girl (Donna Pescow), an elusive "good" girl (Karen Lynn Gorney), plus lots of opportunity to boogie on the dance floor and make out in automobile backseats.
1977: Nomination: Best Actor (John Travolta)

SATURDAY NIGHT OUT
1964, 96 mins, UK
D: Robert Hartford-Davis A: Heather Sears, Bernard Lee, Erica Remberg, Colin Campbell, Francesca Annis (Compton Tekli)

Several sailors in the merchant navy descend on London with 15 hours' shore leave and the film depicts their brief adventures. Since most of the folks involved are concerned mainly with the delights of dames and drink, the results are predictable and the gals-and-guzzle routine palls.

SATURDAY'S CHILDREN
1940, 97 mins, US
D: Vincent Sherman A: John Garfield, Anne Shirley, Claude Rains, Roscoe Karns, Lee Patrick (Warner)

John Garfield delivers impressively as Rims Rosson, a slow-thinking youth who devises impractical inventions and is tricked into marriage. Anne Shirley is excellent as Bobby Halevy, the romantic girl and wife. Claude Rains is strong in the support as girl's plodding and sympathetically understanding father. Couple soon find the marital struggle tough when she loses her job and his income is inadequate.

SATURN 3
1980, 88 mins, UK ℣ ⊙
D: Stanley Donen A: Farrah Fawcett, Kirk Douglas, Harvey Keitel, Ed Bishop (Grade-Kastner)

Somewhere in deepest, darkest space, Kirk Douglas and Farrah Fawcett jog around through a space station. Harvey Keitel builds Hector, the mad robot, whose tubes and hubcaps develop goose bumps for Farrah. Best scene in the entire effort is Hector's resurrection after he has been dismantled for being randy. The parts find each other and reconnect, which is more than this film does. Douglas is sprightly, but he has to handle some pretty awful lines in this Martin Amis script.

SATYRICON
(AKA: FELLINI SATYRICON)
1969, 138 mins, Italy/France ℣ ⊙
D: Federico Fellini A: Martin Potter, Hiram Keller, Max Born, Capucine, Alain Cuny, Lucia Bose (PEA/Artistes Associes)

Federico Fellini presents an incredible frescolike vision of Rome's social structure 2,000 years ago in which survival and pleasure were man's sole motivating forces. The adventures of two young student vagabonds Encolpio (Martin Potter) and Ascilto (Hiram Keller)—both infatuated with a young boy, Gitone (Max Born)—constitute the bare continuity for a hallucinating view of Roman life.

SAVAGE, THE
1953, 95 mins, US
D: George Marshall A: Charlton Heston, Susan Morrow, Peter Hanson, Joan Taylor, Richard Rober (Paramount)

This tale of Indian fighting travels in fairly devious circles to relate a standard story. Charlton Heston plays Warbonnet, a white lad who has been brought up as an Indian. His major problem comes when he has to choose on which side he'll fight in the impending war between the paleface and the Indians.

SAVAGE EYE, THE
1959, 68 mins, US
D: Ben Maddow, Sidney Meyers, Joseph Strick A: Barbara Baxley, Herschel Bernardi, Jean Hidey (City)

Fascinating and uncompromising semidocumentary impressively put together as an obvious labor of love. Story of a divorced woman's attempts to readjust to a single life affords an excellent opportunity to dissect some frightening and depressing panoramas of modern existence. Portions of the film feature, among other things, the detailed horror of a nose-bobbing operation, the bloodthirsty behavior of men and women at boxing and wrestling matches, a detailed and critically observed striptease sequence, a cruelly fascinating sequence shot during a faith-healing service, and a harrowing and nightmarish bit depicting a pervert's party.

SAVAGE INNOCENTS, THE
1960, 111 mins, UK/Italy/US Ⓥ ▱
D: Nicholas Ray **A:** Anthony Quinn, Yoko Tani, Marie Jang, Francis De Wolff, Peter O'Toole (Rank/Appia/Paramount)

Film is for long sessions a documentary of life in the Eskimo belt. The story line is simple. It concerns a powerful, good-humored hunter (Quinn) who spends the early stages of the film deciding which of two young women he wishes to make his wife. Second half becomes melodrama when he accidentally murders a missionary. The memorable moments are those of Quinn hunting down foxes, bears, seals, walruses, and the majesty of the bleak wastes, the ice, the storms, and primitive living conditions. The human element doesn't come off quite so well.

SAVAGE MESSIAH
1972, 100 mins, UK
D: Ken Russell **A:** Dorothy Tutin, Scott Antony, Helen Mirren, Lindsay Kemp, Michael Gough, John Justin (Russfilm/M-G-M)

Offbeat in subject matter (the platonic yet deeply affectionate love of an extroverted young French sculptor, Henri Gaudier, for an introverted older woman, set early in this century), pic shows that the British director has lost none of his filmic impudence. A potentially introverted tale is played broadly and with considerable panache, especially in having the artist portrayed as a physically strong and agile extrovert, and young to boot. A virtual unknown in his first pic role, Scott Antony rises beautifully to the challenge. More expected, but enjoyable nevertheless, is Dorothy Tutin's astute and measured delivery as the object of the sculptor's affection.

SAVAGES
1973, 105 mins, US Ⓥ
D: James Ivory **A:** Louis J. Stadlen, Anne Francine, Thayer David, Susan Blakely, Salome Jens (Angelika/Merchant-Ivory)

Members of a primitive tribe are lured by the appearance of a rolling croquet ball to an old deserted mansion where they dress in clothes and take on "civilized" societal behavior, only to return to the forest and their primitive ways the following morning. The playing has flair and grace. No denying an almost hypnotic charm and fascination in this offbeat, insouciant look at mankind and its climb to civilization and fall.

SAVAGE STREETS
1984, 93 mins, US Ⓥ ⊙
D: Danny Steinmann **A:** Linda Blair, John Vernon, Robert Dryer, Johnny Venocur, Sal Landi (Savage Street)

Linda Blair toplines as an L.A. girl who turns vigilante when her mute younger sister (Linnea Quigley) is brutally gang-raped by a local gang of toughs. Pic unfolds as a tough update of the juvenile-delinquency B pictures of the 1950s. Blair emerges as a tawdry, delightfully trashy sweater girl.

SAVE THE TIGER
1973, 99 mins, US Ⓥ ⊙
D: John G. Avildsen **A:** Jack Lemmon, Jack Gilford, Laurie Heineman, Normann Burton, Thayer David (Filmways)

Pic ostensibly lays bare the crass materialism of the age. Producer-writer Steve Shagan's script stars Jack Lemmon in an offbeat casting as a pitiable businessman trapped in his own life. Partnered with Jack Gilford in the garment business, Lemmon finds his finances so strapped that he decides to hire a professional arsonist to have what used to be called a "successful fire" in one of his factories. This trauma occurs on fashion-show day, when lecherous out-of-town buyer Norman Burton demands some call-girl kinkiness and has a coronary attack.
1973: Best Actor (Jack Lemmon)
Nominations: Best Supp. Actor (Jack Gilford), Original Story & Screenplay

SAVING GRACE
1986, 112 mins, US Ⓥ ⊙ ▱
D: Robert M. Young **A:** Tom Conti, Fernando Rey, Erland Josephson, Giancarlo Giannini, Donald Hewlett (Embassy)

This may be the first comedy ever about a pope running away from office—for a short, private spree in the country among the real people whose shepherd he is supposed to be, sans the bureaucratic interference of the Vatican hierarchy. Tom Conti may be a little young and literally too light on his feet to play a pope, but he is too good an actor not to make the best of it.

SAVING PRIVATE RYAN
1998, 169 mins, US Ⓥ ⊙
D: Steven Spielberg **A:** Tom Hanks, Edward Burns, Tom Sizemore, Adam Goldberg, Matt Damon, Dennis Farina (Amblin/DreamWorks/Paramount)

Steven Spielberg's World War II drama is a vivid, realistic and bloody portrait of armed conflict, as well as an intimate drama about a handful of men on a mission of debatable value. Pic drops the audience into the midst of the first GIs to hit Omaha Beach on June 6, 1944. Capt. John Miller (Tom Hanks) and his squad are finally able to take one of the enemy's concrete pillboxes on top of the bluff. Nonstop action lasts 24 minutes, every one of them infinitely more intense than anything in *The Longest Day*. Squad is ordered to locate a certain private, James Ryan, whose three brothers have all recently been killed in combat. Even if the story is irksome in its contrived nature, the film packs a heavy emotional punch as the tenuousness of life and the abruptness of loss assert themselves. Cinematographer Janusz Kaminski has desaturated the color in a way that emphasizes the pale greens of the uniforms and landscapes, blue-grays of the water and skies, and flesh tones; in this context, the red of the blood always jumps out.
1998: Best Director, Editing, Sound, Sound Effects Editing, Cinematography
Nominations: Best Picture, Actor (Tom Hanks), Art Direction/Set Decoration, Makeup, Original Dramatic Score, Original Screenplay

SAY ANYTHING
1989, 100 mins, US Ⓥ ⊙
D: Cameron Crowe **A:** John Cusack, Ione Skye, John Mahoney, Lili Taylor, Lois Chiles (20th Century-Fox/Gracie)

Appealing tale elicits a few laughs, plenty of smiles, and some genuine feeling. On the eve of high-school graduation, bright but unremarkable student John Cusack decides he's just got to go out with "Miss Priss" (Ione Skye). Skye is headed for studies in England on a fellowship. Cusack starts a friendship that slowly grows into something more. Conflict rears its head in a conventional way when Skye becomes torn between leaving for England and staying with her boyfriend.

SAY IT WITH SONGS
1929, 93 mins, US
D: Lloyd Bacon **A:** Al Jolson, Davey Lee, Marian Nixon, Holmes Herbert, John Bowers (Warner)

A marked advancement for Al Jolson as a screen player. Jolson is happily cast as a radio singer. The story has him married, with a son, Davey Lee. The station announcer tries to make Marian Nixon, the wife. The radio singer lets him have it and gets life for manslaughter. Al sings seven songs in all, four by DeSylva, Brown, and Henderson.

SAYONARA
1957, 147 mins, US Ⓥ ▭
D: Joshua Logan **A:** Marlon Brando, Red Buttons, Ricardo Montalban, Patricia Owens, Martha Scott, James Garner (Warner)

Amid the tenderness and the tensions of a romantic drama, picture puts across the notion that human relations transcend race barriers. Marlon Brando, as Major Gruver, the Korean War air ace, is wholly convincing as the race-conscious southerner whose humanity finally leads him to rebel against army-imposed prejudice. Upset because Airman Joe Kelly, played by Red Buttons, wants to marry a Japanese (Miyoshi Umeki), Brando meets a beautiful Japanese actress-dancer (Miiko Taka) and gradually falls deeply in love with her. When Buttons and his wife, in desperation, commit suicide, Brando realizes that regardless of the consequences, he must marry Taka.
1957: Best Supp. Actor (Red Buttons), Supp. Actress (Miyoshi Umeki), Art Direction, Sound
Nominations: Best Picture, Director, Actor (Marlon Brando), Adapted Screenplay, Cinematography, Editing

SCALPHUNTERS, THE
1968, 102 mins, US Ⓥ ▭
D: Sydney Pollack **A:** Burt Lancaster, Shelley Winters, Telly Savalas, Ossie Davis, Dabney Coleman (United Artists)

A satirical, slapstick, intellectual drama, laced with civil rights overtones, and loaded with recurring action scenes, story top-casts Lancaster as a fur trapper, robbed of his skins by Indian chief Armando Silvestre, who swaps cultured Negro ex-slave Ossie Davis. Telly Savalas heads a crew of scalp hunters, with Winters as mistress to Savalas. Lancaster and Davis pursue the scalp hunters.

SCAMP, THE
1957, 88 mins, UK
D: Wolf Rilla **A:** Richard Attenborough, Terence Morgan, Dorothy Alison, Jill Adams, Colin Petersen, Geoffrey Keen (Minter)

Run-of-the-mill domestic drama has a touch too much of sentimentality and many situations are implausible. Richard Attenborough, a schoolmaster, and his doctor-wife befriend a youngster (Colin Petersen). His father, a drunken vaudeville actor, leaves his son with Attenborough and his wife, who try to show the kid a new way of life. But the authorities order that he should be returned to his father, who has returned from tour with a new wife. No praise can be too high for Petersen as the 10-year-old scamp. Here is a natural.

SCANDAL
1989, 114 mins, UK ⓥ ⊙
D: Michael Caton-Jones **A:** John Hurt, Joanne Whalley-Kilmer, Bridget Fonda, Ian McKellen, Leslie Phillips, Britt Ekland (Palace)

In 1963, the sensational revelations that a good-time girl had been having affairs with a British cabinet minister and a Soviet naval attaché shocked the UK. *Scandal* reexamines the controversy. Man-about-town Stephen Ward (John Hurt) meets young showgirl Christine Keeler (Joanne Whalley-Kilmer) and decides to transform her into a glamorous sophisticate. Ward is delighted when Soviet naval attaché Ivanov (Jeroen Krabbe) takes a shine to Whalley-Kilmer, though at the same time cabinet minister John Profumo (Ian McKellen), the secretary of state for war, falls for her.

SCANDAL AT SCOURIE
1953, 89 mins, US
D: Jean Negulesco **A:** Greer Garson, Walter Pidgeon, Donna Corcoran, Agnes Moorehead (M-G-M)

Plot, laid in Canada, is a gentle tale of a young Catholic orphan who wins the hearts of a childless Protestant couple and the community, but not without causing plenty of commotion that makes for chuckles, drama, and tears.

SCANNERS
1981, 102 mins, Canada ⓥ ⊙
D: David Cronenberg **A:** Stephen Lack, Jennifer O'Neill, Patrick McGoohan, Michael Ironside (Filmplan)

Film offers at least one literally eye-popping moment and another that can only be called mind-blowing. Not readily distinguished from normal humans, scanners are telepathic curiosities who are able to zap people and things at will. There are good scanners and bad scanners and one, Stephen Lack, who is in between finds himself recruited to infiltrate the evil group. Lack of any rooting interest vitiates any possible suspense and highly elegant visual style works against much shock value. Ending is also a bit puzzling.

SCARAMOUCHE
1923, 132 mins, US ⊗
D: Rex Ingram **A:** Ramon Novarro, Alice Terry, Lewis Stone, Lloyd Ingraham, Julia Swayne Gordon (Metro)

Scaramouche tells of a youth in love with a titled lady, also sought by a marquis who holds domination over that portion of France. The boy sees his chum murdered in a duel by the marquis. The story then carries the boy through the various stages of French history up to the breaking of the revolution in Paris. Navarro's performance has a sincere boyishness coupled with natural good looks. Alice Terry not only is beautiful in the white wig and gowns of the period, but gives a capable performance.

SCARAMOUCHE
1952, 115 mins, US ⓥ ⊙
D: George Sidney **A:** Stewart Granger, Eleanor Parker, Janet Leigh, Mel Ferrer, Nina Foch (M-G-M)

Version of *Scaramouche* never seems to be quite certain whether it is a costume adventure or a satire on one. The highly complex Sabatini plot has been greatly simplified. Granger is a brash young man determined to avenge the death of a friend at the hand of nobleman Mel Ferrer, the best swordsman in France. Granger discovers Janet Leigh is not his sister, so he can grab her, and the marquis is really his brother. That leaves everyone mildly happy except Eleanor Parker, who, when last seen, is being hauled into a bedroom by Napoleon.

SCARECROW
1973, 112 mins, US ⓥ ▭
D: Jerry Schatzberg **A:** Gene Hackman, Al Pacino, Dorothy Tristan, Ann Wedgeworth, Eileen Brennan (Warner)

Periodically interesting but ultimately unsatisfying character study of two modern drifters. Hackman and Pacino meet in the California countryside. The former is gruff, eccentric, crude, and volatile. The latter is likable, weak, but sufficiently put together to return to Detroit to the wife and child he abandoned years earlier. In their travels, pair encounter several extremely well-cast characters.

SCARECROW, THE
1982, 87 mins, New Zealand
D: Sam Pillsbury A: Jonathan Smith, Daniel McLaren, Stephen Taylor, Des Kelly, Tracy Mann, John Carradine (Oasis/NZNFU)

A kind of hillbilly gothic thriller of the impact on a small New Zealand country township, circa 1953, of the quintessential evil stranger, embodied by the smooth-talking itinerant sideshow magician and hypnotist, Salter. The central role of Salter is given the full saturnine treatment by John Carradine, abetted by ominous lighting and sound effects at every turn.

SCARED STIFF
1953, 106 mins, US Ⓥ
D: George Marshall A: Dean Martin, Jerry Lewis, Lizabeth Scott, Carmen Miranda, Dorothy Malone (Paramount)

Dean Martin and Jerry Lewis provide a freewheeling round of slapstick hilarity on a lonely, zombie-haunted island off the coast of Cuba. Martin, a cabaret singer, and his awkward chum (Lewis) get mixed up with a gangster's girl (Dorothy Malone) and, in fleeing a gangland ride, meet up with Lizabeth Scott, hieress to the island. M&L decide to go along with her as protection against mysterious men who are attempting to keep her from claiming her inheritance.

SCARFACE
1932, 90 mins, US Ⓥ ⊙ ▭
D: Howard Hawks A: Paul Muni, Ann Dvorak, Karen Morley, George Raft, Boris Karloff, Osgood Perkins (Hughes/United Artists)

Pic contains more cruelty than any of its gangster-picture predecessors, but there's a squarer for every killing. The blows are always softened by judicial preachments and sad endings for the sinners. Plot traces the rise of Scarface from the position of bodyguard for an early district beer baron to the booze chief of the whole city. Along the way he overthrows his employer and later has him slain. He even cops the boss's girl. She's a wicked blond with a love for gunmen and gunfire, and she of all the gang is left unpunished at the finish.

SCARFACE
1983, 170 mins, US Ⓥ ⊙
D: Brian De Palma A: Al Pacino, Steven Bauer, Michelle Pfeiffer, Mary Elizabeth Mastrantonio, Robert Loggia, F. Murray Abraham (Universal)

A grandiose modern morality play, excessive, broad, and operatic at times, film's origins lie in the 1932 production directed by Howard Hawks. Contours of the saga are very similar as the nearly three-hour effort charts the rise and fall of an ambitious young thug who for a while becomes the biggest shot in gangsterdom, but ultimately is just too dumb to stay at the top. Performances are all extremely effective, with Pacino leading the way. Michelle Pfeiffer does well with a basically one-dimensional role as blond WASP goddess.

SCARLET BUCCANEER, THE
See: Swashbuckler

SCARLET EMPRESS, THE
1934, 104 mins, US
D: Josef von Sternberg A: Marlene Dietrich, John Lodge, Sam Jaffe, Louise Dresser, Maria Sieber, C. Aubrey Smith (Paramount)

Josef von Sternberg becomes so enamoured of the pomp and flash values that he subjugates everything else to them. That he succeeds as well as he does is a tribute to his artistic genius and his amazingly visual sense. Marlene Dietrich has never been as beautiful. Again and again she is photographed in close-ups, under veils, and behind thin mesh curtains, and always breathtakingly. But never is she allowed to become really alive and vital. She is as though enchanted by the immense sets through which she stalks. Film claims to be based on a diary of Catherine II, which, perhaps, forgives its choppiness and episodic quality.

SCARLET LETTER, THE
1926, 98 mins, US ⊗
D: Victor Seastrom A: Lillian Gish, Lars Hanson, Henry B. Walthall, Karl Dane (MGM)

Lillian Gish makes of Hester Prynne—the little English Puritan maid who, through the wishes of her father, married before coming to America a man she did not love, expecting him to follow after—a really sympathetic character. Hester and the Reverend Dimmesdale, her Puritan lover, receive all the sympathy of the audience, but particularly through the toll that the little heroine is compelled to pay for loving. Lars Hanson plays the male lead with a great deal of finesse.

SCARLET LETTER, THE
1995, 135 mins, US ⓥ ⊙ ▢
D: Roland Joffe **A:** Demi Moore, Gary Oldman, Robert Duvall, Robert Prosky, Edward Hardwicke, Joan Plowright (Lightmotive/Allied Stars/Cinergi/Moving Pictures)

This borderline campy look at the Puritans is a politically correct melodrama with sex on the brain. As lugubriously and lubriciously directed by Roland Joffe, pic's first act is basically devoted to the headstrong Hester Prynne (Demi Moore) and Gary Oldman's repressed romantic reverend casting furtive looks at each other until they can't stand it any longer, while the remainder shows them suffering the extensive repercussions of their one night of passion. A very nineties take on a 1660s tale written in 1850, as a picture of early colonial life it's about as convincing as *Pocahontas*. Moore obviously connects with the frank, mind-of-her-own aspect of Hester Prynne and makes a respectable account of the character on that basis.

SCARLET PIMPERNEL, THE
1934, 98 mins, UK ⓥ ⊙
D: Harold Young **A:** Leslie Howard, Merle Oberon, Raymond Massey, Nigel Bruce, Joan Gardner (London)

An intriguing adaptation of a noted novel. As the Scarlet Pimpernel, an English nobleman who seeks to rescue the aristocrats of France from Robespierre's guillotine, Howard essays what amounts to a dual role. At home a foppish, affected clotheshorse; abroad, a gallant adventurer playing a dangerous game. With the story in his favor, Howard has the acting edge all the way. As Chauvelin, the villain of the piece, Raymond Massey turns in a gem of a performance.

SCARLET STREET
1945, 96 mins, US ⓥ
D: Fritz Lang **A:** Edward G. Robinson, Joan Bennett, Dan Duryea, Margaret Lindsay, Rosalind Ivan (Universal/Diana)

Fritz Lang ably projects the sordid tale of the romance between a Milquetoast character and a gold-digging blond. Edward G. Robinson is the mild cashier and amateur painter whose love for Joan Bennett leads him to embezzlement, murder,

and disgrace. Two stars turn in top work to keep the interest high, and Dan Duryea's portrayal of the crafty and crooked opportunist whom Bennett loves is a standout in furthering the melodrama.

SCENE OF THE CRIME
1949, 91 mins, US ⓥ
D: Roy Rowland **A:** Van Johnson, Arlene Dahl, Gloria de Haven, Norman Lloyd (M-G-M)

Taut, tough, and often relentless picture of the backroom activities of a detective team on the hunt for a murderer has its serious limitations via a generous dose of cinematic clichés and a story that periodically sacrifices clarity for pace. Los Angeles plainclothes lieutenant (Van Johnson) tracks the killers of a fellow cop regardless of where the chips may fall. Adding bone and grist to the story are important revelations of how Johnson lives.

SCENES FROM A MALL
1991, 87 mins, US ⓥ ⊙
D: Paul Mazursky **A:** Bette Midler, Woody Allen, Bill Irwin, Daren Firestone, Paul Mazursky (Touchstone/Silver Screen Partners IV)

Paul Mazursky's 14th film as director is a cozy, insular middle-aged marital comedy that's about as deep and rewarding as a day of mall cruising. Talents of Bette Midler and Woody Allen seem misspent in roles as cuddly but squabbling spouses. He's a successful sports lawyer; she's a psychologist who's written a high-concept book on how to renew a marriage. They head for the Beverly Center mall to spend their 16th anniversary indulging their every whim.

SCENES FROM THE CLASS STRUGGLE IN BEVERLY HILLS
1989, 102 mins, US ⓥ ⊙
D: Paul Bartel **A:** Jacqueline Bisset, Ray Sharkey, Robert Beltran, Mary Woronov, Ed Begley Jr. (North Street)

A lewd delight. In top form here, director Paul Bartel brings a breezy, sophisticated touch to this utterly outrageous sex farce and thereby renders charming even the most scabrous moments. Script is structured in the manner of a classical French farce, and features more seductions and coitus interruptus than a season of soap operas.

SCENT OF A WOMAN
1992, 157 mins, US ⓥ ⊙
D: Martin Brest **A:** Al Pacino, Chris

O'Donnell, James Rebhorn, Gabrielle Anwar, Philip S. Hoffman (Universal/City Light)

Of note for Al Pacino's theatrical, virtuoso star turn as a blind ex-military officer, film indulgently stretches a modest conceit well past the breaking point. Script takes the p.o.v. of teenager Charlie Simms (Chris O'Donnell), a straight-arrow student obliged to earn a few bucks by caring for a sightless lieutenant colonel (Pacino) whose family is leaving for the long weekend. Frank Slade is a feisty, combative, irascible, remarkably insightful character who whisks the reluctant Charlie to New York, where he intends to savor some of his favorite things one last time.
1992: Best Actor (Al Pacino)
Nominations: Best Picture, Director, Screenplay Adaptation

SCENT OF GREEN PAPAYA, THE
See: Mui Du Du Xanh

SCENT OF MYSTERY
1960, 125 mins, US ▭
D: Jack Cardiff **A:** Denholm Elliott, Peter Lorre, Paul Lukas, Peter Arne, Leo McKern (Todd)

Pic is carefully planned to synchronize scents with action in the film. In Smell-O-Vision, odors are piped via plastic tubing to individual seats, the scents being triggered automatically by signals on the film's soundtrack. Among the smells that clicked were those involving the perfume of the mystery girl in the film, tobacco, baked bread, coffee, lavender, and peppermint. The picture—with or without the smells—is fun. Denholm Elliott, a very proper Englishman on Spanish holiday, stumbles through the cities and countryside as a self-appointed protector of a damsel in distress accompanied by a philosophical taxi driver, neatly portrayed by Peter Lorre.

SCHINDLER'S LIST
1993, 195 mins, US ⓥ ⊙
D: Steven Spielberg **A:** Liam Neeson, Ben Kingsley, Ralph Fiennes, Caroline Goodall, Jonathan Sagalle, Embeth Davidtz (Amblin/Universal)

This searing historical and biographical drama, about a Nazi industrialist who saved some 1,100 Jews from certain death in the concentration camps, evinces an artistic rigor and unsentimental intelligence unlike anything Spielberg has demonstrated before. Despite its 3 1/4-hour

length, the film moves forward with great urgency and is not a minute too long. The performances from the enormous cast are impeccable. In a superlative performance, Neeson makes Schindler a fascinating but highly ambiguous figure. The extraordinary Fiennes creates an indelible character in Goeth, as evil as any Nazi presented on-screen over the past 50 years, but considerably more complex and human than most. Shot mostly on location in Poland, the picture captures in exceptional detail the nightmare world of 50 years earlier. Black-and-white lensing by Janusz Kaminsk is outstanding.
1993: Best Picture, Director, Screenplay Adaptation, Cinematography, Film Editing, Original Score, Art Direction
Nominations: Best Actor (Liam Neeson), Supp. Actor (Ralph Fiennes), Costume Design, Sound, Makeup

SCHIZOPOLIS
1996, 99 mins, US
D: Steven Soderbergh **A:** Steven Soderbergh, Betsy Brantley, David Jensen (Point 406)

Satire and critique of modern life is so scattershot in its aim and techniques that it misses the mark more often than it hits. Pic is a real head-scratcher that so insistently jumps all over the place that it becomes impossible to pinpoint its intent. Pic starts out as an apparent satire of, and attack on, Scientology-like organizations. Focus then veers to the annoying antics of a weird exterminator whose aggressively promiscuous activities remain utterly unfathomable. Along the way, characters begin speaking in different forms of gibberish. Technically, film is a hodgepodge that doesn't attempt to gloss over its made-on-the-run quality

SCHOOL DAZE
1988, 120 mins, US ⓥ ⊙
D: Spike Lee **A:** Larry Fishburne, Giancarlo Esposito, Tisha Campbell, Kyme, Joe Seneca, Spike Lee (40 Acres & a Mule/Columbia)

A loosely connected series of musical set pieces exploring the experience of blackness at an all-black university, film is a hybrid of forms and styles that never comes together in a coherent whole. Surprising, too, is the almost dour tone of the film. Story, such as it is, focuses on the conflict between the militant activists on campus and the good-time boys of Gamma Phi Gamma fraternity, which comes to a head during homecoming week. Leading the freshman pledges and begging for acceptance is the diminutive Half-Pint (Spike Lee). Making life miserable for Half-Pint is his pledge master Julian Eaves (Giancarlo Esposito).

SCHOOL FOR SCOUNDRELS, OR HOW TO WIN WITHOUT ACTUALLY CHEATING
1960, 94 mins, UK ⊗
D: Robert Hamer **A:** Ian Carmichael, Terry-Thomas, Alastair Sim, Janette Scott, Dennis Price, Peter Jones (Guardsman)

The gentle art of getting and remaining "one up" on the next fellow, so painstakingly chronicled by British humorist Stephen Potter in his series of books, is engagingly translated to the screen in this delicate English comedy. Ian Carmichael is a delight as the pitifully inept wretch who undergoes metamorphosis at Alastair Sim's finishing school for social misfits, and Terry-Thomas masterfully plummets from one-up to one-down as his exasperated victim. Janette Scott, a fresh, natural beauty, charmingly plays the object of their attention.

SCIUSCIA (US: SHOESHINE; SHOESHINE BOYS)
1946, 105 mins, Italy ⊗
D: Vittorio De Sica **A:** Rinaldo Smordoni, Franco Interlenghi, Carlo Ortensi, Aniello Mele (Alfa)

Two bootblacks are the principal characters, the film showing their change from honest lads into bitter juvenile gangsters. Producers used real shoeshine boys, and the absence of experienced actors works out okay. Scenes in Rome's jail emphasize the need for drastic reforms.

SCORCHERS
1992, 88 mins, UK ⊗ ⊙
D: David Beaird **A:** Emily Lloyd, Jennifer Tilly, Leland Crooke, Faye Dunaway, James Earl Jones, Denholm Elliott (Goldcrest)

Writer-director David Beaird's beguiling stage play about a bawdy, rollicking wedding night in the Louisiana bayou makes an uneven transfer to film. Emily Lloyd plays a nervous 20-year-old virgin bride whose Cajun-wedding-night jitters are exacerbated by the community's lusty interest in the goings-on. Jennifer Tilly plays a preacher's daughter who can't get her husband to prefer her to the town whore (Faye Dunaway).

SCORPIO
1973, 114 mins, US ⊗
D: Michael Winner **A:** Burt Lancaster, Alain Delon, Paul Scofield, Gayle Hunnicutt, J. D. Cannon (Scimitar/United Artists)

Scorpio might have been an acceptable action programmer if its narrative were clearer, its dialogue less "cultured," and its visuals more straightforward. Ultimately, pic settles down into the usual is-he-or-isn't-he-a-double-agent gimmick, with CIA-blackmailed Alain Delon pursuing supposed Soviet defector Burt Lancaster from Washington to Europe.

SCOTT JOPLIN
1977, 96 mins, US
D: Jeremy Paul Kagan **A:** Billy Dee Williams, Clifton Davis, Margaret Avery, Eubie Blake, Godfrey Cambridge (Motown/Universal)

Biopic starring Billy Dee Williams, originally intended for TV, is buoyant fun for the first half but then becomes a harrowing ordeal when Joplin learns he has syphilis. He turns into a desperate wreck, forsaking his popular ragtime tunes to write an opera, *Treemonisha*, which wasn't performed until 1975.

SCOTT OF THE ANTARCTIC
1948, 111 mins, US ⊗
D: Charles Frend **A:** John Mills, Harold Warrender, Derek Bond, Reginald Beckwith, James Robertson Justice (Ealing)

Pic's greatest asset is the superb casting of John Mills in the title role. Scott's discovery that he has been beaten in the race to the South Pole should be a piece of poignant and moving drama. Although depicted with fidelity, the agonies of the explorers on their homeward trek are not adequately dramatized, with the result that the audience isn't emotionally affected.

SCOUNDREL, THE
1935, 75 mins, US
D: Ben Hecht, Charles MacArthur **A:** Noel Coward, Julie Haydon, Stanley Ridges, Martha Sleeper, Hope Williams, Ernest Cossart (Paramount)

The film is something of an audible novel. Beaucoup dialogue and much palaver, with a minimum of action. It's a talky, slow exposition for the first three reels or so, all tending to indicate what a rat Anthony Mallare (Noel Coward), publisher, is. Coward meets destruction when an equally self-centered, cynical individual (Hope Williams) treats him in kind, and he thus becomes the victim of a plane wreck.
1935: Nomination: Best Original Story

SCOUT, THE

1994, 101 mins, US V ⊙

D: Michael Ritchie A: Albert Brooks, Brendan Fraser, Dianne Wiest, Lane Smith, Anne Twomey (20th Century-Fox)

Baseball fans won't get their needed fix with this virtually baseball-free baseball movie—an odd hybrid of broad comedy and a darker undercurrent of psychological drama. The film is about a down-on-his-luck talent scout, Al (Albert Brooks), who discovers in the inner wilds of Mexico Steve Nebraska (Brendan Fraser), a fireball-throwing, ambidextrous dream come true.

SCREAM

1996, 110 mins, US V ⊙ ⊏⊐

D: Wes Craven A: Neve Campbell, David Arquette, Courteney Cox, Matthew Lillard, Skeet Ulrich, Drew Barrymore (Woods/Dimension)

Director Wes Craven is on familiar turf with *Scream*. The setting is a small town, the protagonists are teens and there's a psychotic killer on the prowl. Next on the maniac's list is Sidney Prescott (Neve Campbell), whose mother was murdered by a similar-style fiend a year earlier. Aggressive tabloid television reporter Gale Weathers (Courteney Cox) believes it's the same killer. Though the material is more intelligent than the norm and has an unusual third-act twist, it also employs some very clunky stereotypes. The sleepy hamlet is populated by callous teens and ineffectual adults. The kids can quote chapter and verse from *Halloween Prom Night* and Craven's *Nightmare on Elm Street* to explain the killer's gestalt. Craven displays a fascination with blurring the lines between reality and film. But *Scream* merely ponders copycat murders, something that occurs more often onscreen than in dozing towns.

SCREAM 2

1997, 120 mins, US V ⊙ ⊏⊐

D: David Arquette A: David Arquette, Neve Campbell, Courteney Cox, Sarah Michelle Gellar, Jamie Kennedy, Laurie Metcalf (Konrad/Dimension)

The filmmakers have been ultradiligent about keeping the second outing on course. This sequel is visceral, witty and appropriately redundant. Story relocates to Windsor College in small-town Ohio. Sidney (Neve Campbell) and Randy (Jamie Kennedy) are students attempting to escape the notoriety created by the previous year's tabloid-sensation murder and may-

hem, now turned into a movie. At the premiere, a young couple become the first victims of a copycat killer. Sidney is thrown back into the limelight, and former deputy Dewey (David Arquette) flies cross-country to protect the imperiled young woman. The house-of-mirrors structure has a more chilling underlying message about the consequences of confusing artifice with the real thing. The killer tells his intended victims that his legal defense will be that he was corrupted by violent images from movies and other popular media.

SCREAM OF STONE

1991, 105 mins, Germany/France/Canada V

D: Werner Herzog A: Vittorio Mezzogiorno, Mathilda May, Stefan Glowacz, Brad Dourif, Donald Sutherland (SERA/Molecule/Stock)

Clumsy prologue introduces two champion climbers. Martin (Vittorio Mezzogiorno) is a young hotshot. Roger (Stefan Glowacz), an older man, scoffs at Martin as a mere "acrobat." Roger accepts a challenge to climb what he regards as the toughest peak in the world, a needlelike peak in Patagonia that he has tried and failed to conquer twice before. While film does feature some spectacular mountain photography, the dramatic and psychological aspects remain so obscure as to become silly.

SCREWBALLS

1983, 90 mins, US V

D: Rafal Zielinski A: Peter Keleghan, Lynda Speciale, Alan Daveau, Kent Deuters, Jason Warren (New World)

This compendium of horny high-school jokes set in 1965 is full of youthful exuberance and proves utterly painless to watch. Five guys dedicate themselves to depurifying homecoming queen Purity Busch, evidently the only female virgin left at the school.

SCROOGE

1970, 118 mins, US V ⊙ ⊏⊐

D: Ronald Neame A: Albert Finney, Alec Guinness, Edith Evans, Kenneth More, Laurence Naismith (Cinema Center/Waterbury)

A most delightful film in every way. Albert Finney's remarkable performance in the title role; Leslie Bricusse's fluid adaptation of the Charles Dickens classic *A Christmas Carol,* plus his unobtrusive complementary music and lyrics; and

Ronald Neame's delicately controlled direction, which conveys, but does not force, all the inherent warmth, humor, and sentimentality.
1970: Nominations: Best Costume Design, Art Direction, Song Score, Song ("Thank You Very Much")

SCROOGED
1988, 101 mins, US ⓥ ⊙
D: Richard Donner **A:** Bill Murray, Karen Allen, John Forsythe, John Glover, Carol Kane, Robert Mitchum (Paramount)

Appallingly unfunny comedy is a vivid illustration of the fact that money can't buy you laughs. This updating of Dickens's *A Christmas Carol* into the world of cutthroat network television is, one episode apart, able to generate only a few mild chuckles. Scrooge here is an utterly venal network chief. Unfortunately, things ring false from the start because Bill Murray's cruelty seems very arbitrary, unfunny, and ultimately unconvincing. Murray's network, IBC, is preparing to broadcast a live version of *A Christmas Carol* (with, in a good bit, Buddy Hackett as Scrooge), so it is against this backdrop that Murray's own journey through his past and toward his personal salvation takes place.
1988: Nomination: Best Makeup

SCUM
1979, 96 mins, UK ⓥ
D: Alan Clarke **A:** Ray Winstone, Mick Ford, John Judd, Phil Daniels (Boyd's)

Given that *Scum,* a relentlessly brutal slice of British reform-school life, is strongly directed and acted with admirable conviction, it is a pity that the hard-hitting screenplay is more passionate tract than powerful entertainment. Its appeal could have been wider if the basic point—that a youth penitentiary can kill, not cure—had been made through more investigative character study, instead of via a catalog of horrific events.

SEA CHASE, THE
1955, 116 mins, US ⓥ ⊙ ▭
D: John Farrow **A:** John Wayne, Lana Turner, David Farrar, Lyle Bettger, Tab Hunter (Warner)

Producer-director John Farrow and scripters turn a rather neat trick in making a chase picture without the suspenseful excitement of a chase, albeit based on Andrew Geer's novel of the pursuit of a nondescript German freighter from Australia to the North Sea by the British navy.

There is a romance woven in, between John Wayne, a German sea captain who despises Nazism but is determined to bring his ship home, and Lana Turner, a Nazi spy and adventuress who has been no more than the term implies.

SEA GULL, THE
1968, 141 mins, UK
D: Sidney Lumet **A:** James Mason, Vanessa Redgrave, Simone Signoret, David Warner, Harry Andrews, Denholm Elliott (Warner/Seven Arts)

Sensitive, well-made, and abstractly interesting period pic. Downbeat eternal verities—frustration, unrequited love, etc.—are projected admirably by a cast featuring James Mason, Simone Signoret (both in memorable performances), Vanessa Redgrave, and David Warner. The deliberate adherence to the Chekhov's script necessarily retains the somewhat old-fashioned character motivations and plot structures. Director Sidney Lumet has created an appropriately somber mood.

SEA HAWK, THE
1924, 129 mins, US ⊗
D: Frank Lloyd **A:** Milton Sills, Enid Bennett, Lloyd Hughes, Wallace MacDonald, Marc MacDermott (First National)

This picture has no end of entertainment value. All of the punch of Sabatini's writings has been brought to the screen. There's action aplenty. It starts in the first reel and holds true to the last minute. Milton Sills comes into his own in this production. *The Sea Hawk* cost around $800,000. The properties used alone cost $135,000. The picture looks it.

SEA HAWK, THE
1940, 127 mins, US ⓥ ⊙
D: Michael Curtiz **A:** Errol Flynn, Brenda Marshall, Claude Rains, Flora Robson, Donald Crisp (Warner)

The Sea Hawk retains all of the bold and swashbuckling adventure and excitement of its 1923 predecessor. But the screenplay is expanded to include endless episodes of court intrigue during the reign of Queen Elizabeth that tend to diminish the epic sweep of the high-seas dramatics. Story traces the adventures of the piratical sea fighter (Errol Flynn), commander of a British sailing ship that preys on Spanish commerce in the late 16th century. Colorful and exciting sea battle at the start, when Flynn's ship attacks and sinks the galleon of the Spanish ambassador, comes too early and is never topped by any succeeding sequences.

1940: Nominations: Best B&W Art Direction, Score, Sound, Special Effects

SEANCE ON A WET AFTERNOON
1964, 116 mins, UK ⊗

D: Bryan Forbes **A:** Kim Stanley, Richard Attenborough, Nanette Newman, Patrick Magee (Beaver)

A medium of dubious authenticity inveigles her spouse into a nutty plan to "borrow" a child, make out it has been kidnapped, collect the ransom loot, and wait for the story to pump up to front-page sensation. Then she aims to hold a séance and reveal clues that will enable the cops to find the child unharmed. The film throughout is pitched in somber key. The dankness of the house in which medium's shabby machinations evolve is well caught. Though Kim Stanley is exciting to watch, she is much Method. Attenborough is her weak, loving, and downtrodden husband. Here is a splendid piece of trouping which rings true throughout.

1964: Nomination: Best Actress (Kim Stanley)

SEA OF GRASS, THE
1947, 122 mins, US ⊗

D: Elia Kazan **A:** Spencer Tracy, Katharine Hepburn, Robert Walker, Melvyn Douglas, Phyllis Thaxter (M-G-M)

Drama of the New Mexico prairie lands is built around the traditional American feud between cattlemen and farmers. Katharine Hepburn is a cultured St. Louis belle who goes to New Mexico to marry range baron Spencer Tracy. His attachment is so great for the "sea of grass" that he has no understanding of his wife's feeling for the farm families whom he is forcing to starvation by illegally keeping them from the land. Melvyn Douglas, as a lawyer and judge, not only has a feeling for the farmers, but for Hepburn as well, and a natural amity grows between them. There's never a surprise. Likewise, the clichéd dialogue is frequently hard to accept.

SEA OF LOVE
1989, 112 mins, US ⊗ ⊙

D: Harold Becker **A:** Al Pacino, Ellen Barkin, John Goodman, Michael Rooker, William Hickey (Universal)

Suspenseful film noir boasts a superlative performance by Al Pacino as a burned-out Gotham cop. Handsome production benefits from a witty screenplay limning the bittersweet tale of a 20-year veteran NYC cop (Pacino) assigned to track down a serial killer of men who've made dates through the personal columns. Ellen Barkin appears as one of the suspects, but Pacino is smitten with her and crucially decides not to get her fingerprints for analysis. Pic builds some hair-raising twists and turns as the evidence mounts pointing to her guilt, climaxing in a surprising revelation.

SEA OF SAND
(AKA: DESERT PATROL)
1958, 97 mins, UK

D: Guy Green **A:** Richard Attenborough, John Gregson, Michael Craig, Vincent Ball, Percy Herbert (Tempean)

Routine war adventure, with excellent all-around acting and taut direction by Guy Green, deals with the Long Range Desert Group on the eve of Alamein. Y Patrol is given the arduous task of blowing up one of the Nazis' biggest oil dumps. Mission accomplished, the nine men fight their way back to base.

SEARCH, THE
1948, 105 mins, US ⊗

D: Fred Zinnemann **A:** Montgomery Clift, Aline MacMahon, Jarmila Novotna, Ewart G. Morrison, Wendell Corey (M-G-M)

This simple film was made principally in and around the rubbled remains of Nuremberg. A Czech mother and a nine-year-old boy are separated. The lad lives among the rubble until hunger tempts him close enough to a GI for the soldier to catch him. The four professionals in the cast are Montgomery Clift, as the GI, making his film debut; Aline MacMahon, as the camp official; Jarmila Novotna, Metropolitan Opera singer who plays the mother; and Wendell Corey.

1948: Best Motion Picture Story, Special Award (Ivan Jandl)

Nominations: Best Director, Actor (Montgomery Clift), Screenplay

SEARCH AND DESTROY
1995, 90 mins, US ⊗

D: David Salle **A:** Griffin Dunne, Illeana Douglas, Dennis Hopper, Christopher Walken, John Turturro, Rosanna Arquette (New Image)

Visual artist David Salle's eagerly awaited premiere aspires to be an inventive black comedy of the absurd, but instead is a disappointing film with few bright moments and many more tedious ones. Griffin Dunne plays Martin Mirkhein, an ambitious Florida businessman who stumbles on the philosophy of Dr. Luther Waxling (Dennis Hopper), a self-help guru. Martin flies to Dallas to propose making a movie out of the guru's best-seller. But his initial attempts to meet Waxling are rebuffed by his assistant, Roger (Ethan Hawke), and his sexy receptionist, Marie (Illeana Douglas). Martin and Marie eventually elope to New York to pursue his obsessive dream. From then on, pic is structured as a madcap fantasy (with horror and violence) that throws Martin in one catastrophe after another.

SEARCHERS, THE
1956, 119 mins, US Ⓥ ⊙
D: John Ford **A:** John Wayne, Jeffrey Hunter, Vera Miles, Ward Bond, Natalie Wood, Hank Worden (Whitney/Warner)

A western on the grand scale—eye-filling and impressive. Yet there is a feeling that it could have been so much more. Overlong and repetitious, there are subtleties in the basically simple story that are not adequately explained. There are, however, some fine vignettes of frontier life. The picture involves a long, arduous trek through primitive country by two men in search of a nine-year-old girl kidnapped by hostile Comanche Indians. Wayne, the uncle of the girl, is a bitter, taciturn individual who feels the girl has been defiled by the Indians during her years with them and is determined to kill her. His partner in the search is Jeffrey Hunter, who is also involved in labored attempts at comic relief. Wayne is fine in the role of hard-bitten, misunderstood, and mysterious searcher.
1956: Nominations: Best Editing, Original Musical Score

SEARCH FOR PARADISE
1957, 120 mins, US ▭
D: Otto Lang **A:** Lowell Thomas, James S. Parker, Christopher Young (Cinerama)

The fourth Cinerama sticks almost slavishly to established formulae. Once more strange lands are "seen" by two selected "tourists," this time a make-believe air-force major (Christopher Young) and sergeant (James S. Parker). The several stops are all way stations en route to Nepal. The picture centers upon the approach to and environs of the Himalayas, world's greatest peaks, truthfully described as a region of mystery, mysticism, and Communist intrigue. The visit to Nepal is a genuine peep into dazzling fantasy and a true coup for Cinerama.

SEARCHING FOR BOBBY FISCHER
1993, 110 mins, US Ⓥ ⊙
D: Steven Zaillian **A:** Joe Mantegna, Max Pomeranc, Joan Allen, Ben Kingsley, Laurence Fishburne (Mirage/Paramount)

Based on a true story, pic focuses on Josh Waitzkin (Max Pomeranc), a relatively normal seven-year-old who possesses a stunning aptitude for chess. His father, Fred (Joe Mantegna), takes him to a chess coach (Ben Kingsley), who says that Josh could well be the second coming of Bobby Fischer, the legendary former chess champ. *Searching* is at its best when exploring the tension between wanting to develop a child's abilities and allowing him to remain a child.
1993: Nomination: Best Cinematography

SEARCHING WIND, THE
1946, 107 mins, US
D: William Dieterle **A:** Robert Young, Sylvia Sidney, Ann Richards, Dudley Digges, Albert Basserman (Paramount)

A searching indictment of the once-weak-willed, liberal appeasement policy of the US, pic is story of a bewildered diplomat, stationed in Europe to report the significance of changing events to the US State Department, who fails to see importance of a fascist takeover in Italy, the rise of Nazism in Germany, the Munich agreement, etc. Tied up with the political is a personal story, the diplomat's marriage to the wrong woman and his constant love for the newspaper woman he should have wed. Robert Young plays the diplomat with an honest sense of bewilderment.

SEA WOLF, THE
1941, 98 mins, US Ⓥ
D: Michael Curtiz **A:** Edward G. Robinson, Ida Lupino, John Garfield, Alexander Knox, Gene Lockhart, Barry Fitzgerald (Warner)

Jack London's famous hell ship sails for another voyage. Edward G. Robinson steps into the role of the callous and inhuman skipper, Wolf Larsen. John Garfield signs on to the sailing schooner to escape the law. Ida Lupino (also a fugitive) and the mild-mannered novelist (Alexander Knox) are rescued from a sinking ferryboat in San Francisco Bay. Robinson takes fiendish delight in breaking the spirits of his crew and unwilling passengers. Robinson provides plenty of vigor and two-fisted energy to the actor-proof role of Larsen, and at times is overdirected.

SEA WOLVES, THE: THE LAST CHARGE OF THE CALCUTTA LIGHT HORSE

1980, 120 mins, US ⊗

D: Andrew V. McLaglen A: Gregory Peck, Roger Moore, David Niven, Trevor Howard, Barbara Kellermann, Patrick Macnee (Lorimar)

Sea Wolves is unabashed flag-waving, a salute to the Calcutta Light Horse, a part-time regiment whose membership consisted mainly of colonial business types way past draft age but recruited as volunteers for the destruction of three German freighters interned in coastal waters off the then-neutral Portuguese colony of Goa. Gregory Peck's a Britisher in this one, but the affected accent won't fool anyone. He and Roger Moore are regular army. The stiff-uppered civvy retreads, headed by David Niven, include Trevor Howard and Patrick Macnee.

SEBASTIAN

1968, 100 mins, UK ⊗

D: David Greene A: Dirk Bogarde, Susannah York, Lilli Palmer, John Gielgud, Janet Munro, Ronald Fraser (Paramount/ Maccius)

Moderately entertaining cold-war comedy-drama depicts Dirk Bogarde as a daffy genius in cryptography. Susannah York, a new recruit to the code force, breaks down his romantic reserve. Lilli Palmer, as a politically suspect coder, and John Gielgud, an intelligence chief, add luster. Janet Munro scores very well as a boozy fading pop singer who, with Ronald Fraser, attempts to compromise Bogarde's security clearance. Despite all the plus elements, film wanders about in its unfolding.

SECOND BEST

1994, 105 mins, UK/US ⊗

D: Chris Menges

A: William Hurt, Chris Cleary Miles, Keith Allen, Prunella Scales, Jane Horrocks, John Hurt (Fron/Regency/Alcor)

Acutely felt story revolves around the deprived emotional lives of 10-year-old James (Chris Cleary Miles) and the 42-year-old man who would adopt him, Graham Holt (William Hurt). A rumpled, withdrawn village postmaster, Graham has never had a significant emotional contact or sexual experience, but now has the sudden impulse to adopt a boy, which would be the first assertive thing he's done in his life. A seemingly unlikely choice to play an unworldly Welshman, Hurt lets his in-

wardness work to great benefit and creates a completely convincing and often touching characterization.

SECONDS

1966, 108 mins, US

D: John Frankenheimer A: Rock Hudson, Salome Jens, John Randolph, Will Geer, Jeff Corey (Joel/Frankenheimer/Paramount)

A middle-aged man has lost contact with his wife. His only daughter is married and gone. Even his work, which was his mainstay in life, seems to pall. He is told he can be redone surgically to become a young man and start life over again. He decides to go through with it and after surgery wakes up as Rock Hudson. Film does not quite come off as a thriller, sci-fi adventure, or philosophical fable.

SECRET AGENT

1936, 83 mins, UK ⊗ ⊙

D: Alfred Hitchcock A: Madeleine Carroll, Peter Lorre, John Gielgud, Robert Young, Percy Marmont (Gaumont-British)

Pic rates as good spy entertainment, suave storytelling, and, in one particular case, brilliant characterization. This is the role of the "Mexican," a hired killer played by Peter Lorre. Director Alfred Hitchcock has done well at adding deftly humorous details to the tale's grim theme, appropriate romantic interplay, and some swell outdoor photography. Gielgud is assigned to Switzerland to prevent a German spy from getting back into pro-German territory. To do the actual killing, Lorre, a Mexican with a juvenile sense of fun, is sent along. Gielgud finds that Carroll had been matched with him for the job, with the pair to pose as man and wife.

SECRET BEYOND THE DOOR

1947, 98 mins, US ⊗

D: Fritz Lang A: Joan Bennett, Michael Redgrave, Anne Revere, Barbara O'Neil (Universal/Diana)

Film is arty, with almost surrealistic treatment in camera angles, storytelling mood, and suspense, as producer-director Fritz Lang hammers over his thrill points. Costarring with Bennett is Michael Redgrave. He disappoints as the man with an antiwoman complex who nearly murders his wife before finding out what his trouble is.

SECRET CEREMONY

1968, 109 mins, UK ⊗

D: Joseph Losey A: Elizabeth Taylor, Mia Farrow, Robert Mitchum, Peggy Ashcroft,

Pamela Brown (Universal/WFS)

Robert Mitchum is featured in this macabre tale of mistaken identity, psychological and sexual needs, suicide, and murder. Mia Farrow, playing a wealthy, demented, and incest-prone nympho, appears to have kidnapped Elizabeth Taylor, in the role of an aging prostitute. As things turn out, Taylor does not mind being mistaken for Farrow's deceased mother; instead, she gradually, but fitfully, eases into the child's desired mold.

SECRET COMMAND
1944, 81 mins, US
D: A. Edward Sutherland A: Pat O'Brien, Carole Landis, Chester Morris, Ruth Warrick (Columbia/Terneen)

Lusty melodrama of counterespionage. Naval intelligence gets wind of Nazi sabotage plans at a large shipyard, and Pat O'Brien as a secret agent is sent in to get a job. He starts as a pilebuck on shift bossed by brother Chester Morris.

SECRET FOUR, THE
See: The Four Just Men

SECRET FOUR, THE
See: Kansas City Confidential

SECRET GARDEN, THE
1949, 92 mins, US ⓥ
D: Fred M. Wilcox A: Margaret O'Brien, Herbert Marshall, Dean Stockwell, Brian Roper, Gladys Cooper, Elsa Lanchester (M-G-M)

Margaret O'Brien is an orphan come to live with her uncle (Herbert Marshall). He has turned against the world in bitterness. He has a son (Dean Stockwell) who suffers from a paralysis of the legs. Among Marshall's quirks is a phobia about anyone going into the garden. O'Brien secretly nurtures the neglected flowers and plants back to beauty. The production throughout is on a lavish scale. Unfortunately, the performances do not equal it.

SECRET GARDEN, THE
1993, 101 mins, US ⓥ ⊙
D: Agnieszka Holland A: Kate Maberly, Heydon Prowse, Andrew Knott, Maggie Smith, Laura Crossley (Warner/American Zoetrope)

Children's classic executed to near perfection. Ten-year-old orphan Mary Lennox (Kate Maberly) is sent to live in the gloomy Yorkshire mansion of her reclusive uncle, Lord Craven (John Lynch). Craven ignores both Mary and his crippled son, Colin (Heydon Prowse). Mary soon becomes intrigued by a secret garden. In league with down-to-earth local boy Dickon (Andrew Knott), she begins nurturing the unkempt garden. Using all British thesps of proper age (unlike the earlier Hollywood version, which seemed cast too old), Polish-born director Agnieszka Holland displays an unerring instinct for obtaining truthful performances from child actors.

SECRET HEART, THE
1946, 97 mins, US
D: Robert Z. Leonard A: Claudette Colbert, June Allyson, Walter Pidgeon, Lionel Barrymore, Robert Sterling (M-G-M)

Tale of a young girl with a father fixation. A college-age girl, an excellent pianist, is in love with the memory of her father, who taught her to play. Her only interest is to shut out the rest of the world by locking herself in a room and playing for him. In a role that's a far cry from her usual song-and-dance parts, June Allyson gives out with what's undoubtedly the best emoting of her career. Claudette Colbert is fine as the young widow, with her flair for comedy helping to lighten the film's heavy mood.

SECRET LIFE OF AN AMERICAN WIFE, THE
1968, 93 mins, US ⓥ
D: George Axelrod A: Walter Matthau, Anne Jackson, Patrick O'Neal, Edy Williams (20th Century-Fox/Charlton)

Basic idea, which sometimes takes on the aspect of a French romp, takes a comedy look at sex in the person of a 34-year-old Connecticut wife who thinks she's gone to pot and lost all her appeal. Overall the tale is amusing. Even when such a past master at comedy as Walter Matthau, in role of a top film star on whom Anne Jackson tries her wiles, enters, the focus is on her.

SECRET LIFE OF WALTER MITTY, THE
1947, 108 mins, US ⓥ ⊙
D: Norman Z. McLeod A: Danny Kaye, Virginia Mayo, Boris Karloff, Fay Bainter, Ann Rutherford, Florence Bates (RKO/Goldwyn)

Thurber's conception of Mitty was of an inconsequential fellow to whom nothing—but nothing—ever happened. The picture builds a spy plot around Mitty that is more fantastic than even his wildest dream. Mitty's fantasies carry him through sessions as a sea captain taking his schooner through a storm, a surgeon performing a next-to-impossible operation, an RAF pilot, a Mississippi gambler, a cowpuncher, and a hat designer. They're all well loaded with satire, as is the real-life plot with pure slapstick.

SECRET OF BLOOD ISLAND, THE
1965, 84 mins, US ⓥ
D: Quentin Lawrence **A:** Barbara Shelley, Jack Hedley, Charles Tingwell, Bill Owen, Lee Montague (Hammer)

A British female agent is shot down near a Jap prison camp in Malaya. The prisoners hide her and eventually help her to escape. Barbara Shelley manages to fool the Jap guards into thinking she's just another male prisoner much more easily than she does the audience.

SECRET OF MY SUCCESS, THE
1965, 112 mins, UK ▭
D: Andrew L. Stone **A:** Shirley Jones, Stella Stevens, Honor Blackman, James Booth, Lionel Jeffries (M-G-M)

What might have been a bright, little British comedy turns out to be neither comedy nor melodrama. Three almost separate yarns are employed to trace the rise of a lowly English town constable to position of ruler in a mythical Latin American country. A sharp maneuver by his mother wins Booth the job of liaison officer to the president of Guanduria. By helping Shirley Jones, who is secretly plotting a revolution, he winds up as new ruler of this country.

SECRET OF MY SUCCESS, THE
1987, 110 mins, US ⓥ ◉
D: Herbert Ross **A:** Michael J. Fox, Helen Slater, Richard Jordan, Margaret Whitton, John Pankow (Rastar)

Bedroom farce with a leaden touch, a corporate comedy without teeth, does have Michael J. Fox in a winning performance as a likable hick out to hit the big time in New York. Fresh off the bus from Kansas, Brantley Foster (Fox) doesn't want to return until he has a penthouse, Jacuzzi, a beautiful girlfriend, and a private jet. After he lands a job in the mailroom of an anonymous NY corporation, his big chance comes when he takes over an abandoned office and sets himself up as a young exec.

SECRET OF NIMH, THE
1982, 82 mins, US ⓥ ◉
D: Don Bluth (M-G-M/United Artists)

Richly animated and skillfully structured film created by former Disney animators Don Bluth, Gary Goldman, and John Pomeroy. A mother mouse (voiced by Elizabeth Hartman) is trying to find a new home for her brood before the old one is destroyed by spring plowing. Her task is complicated by the severe illness of a son, too sick to move. On the light side there's the comedy of Dom DeLuise as a clumsy crow who tries to help. At the worst are a pack of rats led for good and ill by Derek Jacobi, Peter Strauss, and Paul Shenar.

SECRET OF ROAN INISH, THE
1994, 103 mins, US ⓥ ◉
D: John Sayles **A:** Mick Lalley, Eileen Colgan, John Lynch, Jeni Courtney, Richard Sheridan (Jones Entertainment)

Plucky 10-year-old Fiona (Jeni Courtney) is shipped off to her grandparents' coastal home in post–World War II County Donegal. Strange sights pique her curiosity. She finally convinces grandfolk (Mick Lally, Eileen Colgan) to row out to Roan Inish, the nearby island home they've abandoned, in hopes of solving the puzzle of her infant brother Jamie. Film captures hardscrabble life of this remote fishing culture, but low-key direction and somber lensing could use more leavening touches to help script's fantastic side take flight.

SECRET OF SANTA VITTORIA, THE
1969, 134 mins, US ▭
D: Stanley Kramer **A:** Anthony Quinn, Anna Magnani, Virna Lisi, Hardy Kruger, Sergio Franchi (United Artists)

Carrying charm, suspense, romance, the production offers Anthony Quinn at his seasoned best, a plot, and unfolding that holds the spectator. The people of a hill town in northern Italy are suddenly thrown into shock when told that a detachment of the retreating German army is to confiscate all their wine, their very lifeblood.

SECRET PEOPLE
1952, 96 mins, UK
D: Thorold Dickinson **A:** Valentina Cortese, Serge Reggiani, Charles Goldner, Audrey Hepburn, Athene Seyler (Ealing)

Hackneyed story of political agents working against a tyrannical dictator is dressed up with all the familiar clichés to make a dull and rather confusing offering. Audrey Hepburn, in a minor role, combines beauty with skill, particularly in two dance sequences.

SECRET PLACES
1984, 96 mins, UK ⓥ
D: Zelda Barron **A:** Marie-Therese Relin, Tara MacGowran, Claudine Auger, Jenny Agutter, Cassie Stuart (Skreba/Virgin)

Pleasing evocation of schoolgirl life in England during World War II recounts the initially hostile response of a group of adolescents to the enrollment of a German refugee in their all-girl school. Gradually her exotically winning ways and intelligence secure her inclusion in the select circle that gathers in "secret places." Things turn sour when a girl's father is killed in battle.

SECRET POLICEMAN'S BALL, THE
1980, 91 mins, UK ⓥ ⊙
D: Roger Graef **A:** John Cleese, Peter Cook, Eleanor Bron, Pete Townshend, Rowan Atkinson, Michael Palin (Document/Amnesty International)

Film record of the 1979 Amnesty International benefit show. John Cleese, Michael Palin and Terry Jones of the *Monty Python* team appear in various sketches; guitarist Pete Townshend plays acoustic versions of a couple of the Who's repertoire, joined on one by classical picker John Williams; Billy Connolly, Clive James, and Eleanor Bron, among others, contribute solo spots. All gave their services free.

SECRET POLICEMAN'S OTHER BALL, THE
1982, 99 mins, UK ⓥ ⊙
D: Julien Temple **A:** Rowan Atkinson, Alan Bennett, John Cleese, Billy Connolly, Victoria Wood, Eric Clapton (Amnesty International)

Second filmed record of biannual Amnesty International fund-raiser in London is a thoroughly entertaining concert pic. As irreverent and clever as its title, show boasts comic talents from *Monty Python, Beyond the Fringe,* and *Not the Nine O'Clock News* and therefore does require a taste for British humor. Particularly hilarious are a quiz-show takeoff in which the moderator gets the correct answers mixed up, and a deadpan, coming-out-of-the-closet sexual confession by Alan Bennett.

SECRET RAPTURE, THE
1994, 96 mins, US ⓥ ⊙
D: Howard Davies **A:** Juliet Stevenson, Joanne Whalley-Kilmer, Penelope Wilton,

Neil Pearson, Alan Howard, Robert Stephens (Channel 4/Greenpoint)

Broad family melodrama is a fitfully successful adaptation (by the author) of the David Hare play. Isobel (Juliet Stevenson), whose father has recently died, is torn apart when she discovers her bereavement for the dead man isolates her from friends and family. Hare's screenplay delineates with frightening precision and alarming logic the machinations that bring the principals to the breaking point. But the story is never satisfyingly resolved. Stevenson effects a powerful, strident, and unpleasant pose that ultimately works against the material.

SECRETS AND LIES
1996, 142 mins, France/UK ⓥ
D: Mike Leigh **A:** Timothy Spall, Brenda Blethyn, Phyllis Logan, Marianne Jean-Baptiste, Claire Rushbrook (CiBy 2000/Thin Man/Channel 4)

Mike Leigh's first film in three years is a return to his less stygian style of dysfunctional dramatic comedy, but painted on a far more ambitious and serious canvas. *Secrets and Lies* is unquestionably a finely observed, deeply felt work. Pic yo-yos between sequences of interior drama and classic observational humor, with the emphasis on the former. Film opens with the funeral of the adoptive parents of a young black woman, Hortense (Marianne Jean-Baptiste), an optometrist with a yuppie-ish London lifestyle. Plot driver is Hortense's decision, now that she's sans family, to discover her birth parents, not least when it emerges that her biological mother may have been white.

SECRET WAR OF HARRY FRIGG, THE
1968, 110 mins, US ⓥ ▭
D: Jack Smight **A:** Paul Newman, Sylva Koscina, Tom Bosley, Andrew Duggan, John Williams (Universal/Albion)

Amusing World War II comedy starring Paul Newman as a dumb army private sent to rescue five Axis-held Allied generals. Newman plays a perennial goof-off, who achieves a measure of self-confidence and maturity under pressure. Sympathy is with him all the way.

SECRET WAYS, THE
1961, 112 mins, US
D: Phil Karlson **A:** Richard Widmark, Sonja Ziemann, Charles Regnier, Walter Rilla, Howard Vernon, Senta Berger (Universal)

Ludicrous, imitative, unintentional parody of dozens of cloak-and-dagger pictures amounts to a sort of poor man's *Third Man*. Widmark stars as an American adventurer-for-hire who hires out to rescue a noted scholar from behind the Iron Curtain in Hungary.

SEDMIKRASKY
(US: DAISIES)
1966, 75 mins, Czechoslovakia
D: Vera Chytilova **A:** Jitka Cerhova, Ivana Karbanova, Julius Albert (Barrandov)

Two zany young teenage girls are the focus of this extremely funny, witty, and expertly fashioned film. The gals seem to live on men, do not work, and have no ties with society. Director Vera Chytilova presents them as engaging but futile rebels or misfits who can never seem to fit into life. Chytilova-harks back to early silent comedies and displays a remarkable control of filmic language, special effects, and rhythm and sight gags.

SEDUCTION OF JOE TYNAN, THE
1979, 107 mins, US Ⓥ ⊙
D: Jerry Schatzberg **A:** Alan Alda, Barbara Harris, Meryl Streep, Rip Torn, Melvyn Douglas (Universal)

Adroitly combining humor and intimate drama, *Joe Tynan* joins list of exemplary Washington-set pix. In large part, the credit goes to Alan Alda, whose portrayal in the title role is no less complex and multifaceted than his screenplay. Joe Tynan is a familiar political figure: the young, handsome liberal senator who rides upward on the coattails of a few big media victories. As Alda's intelligent and frustrated wife, Barbara Harris gives the performance of her career.

SEE NO EVIL
(UK: BLIND TERROR)
1971, 87 mins, US Ⓥ ⊙
D: Richard Fleischer **A:** Mia Farrow, Dorothy Alison, Robin Bailey, Diane Grayson, Brian Rawlinson (Filmways)

Script has Mia Farrow recuperating from a blinding accident at the home of Robin Bailey, his wife, and daughter. A young punk slays the household while Farrow is out riding. Extremely good suspense is maintained as Farrow discovers the senseless murders, then outwits the murderer. Farrow's lengthy travails become rather heavy on the meller side; all that's missing is for her to be trapped on an ice floe. Still, her performance as a blind girl is very convincing.

SEE NO EVIL, HEAR NO EVIL
1989, 103 mins, US ⊙
D: Arthur Hiller **A:** Richard Pryor, Gene Wilder, Joan Severance, Kevin Spacey, Anthony Zerbe (Tri-Star)

Broadly played, occasionally crass, funny physical comedy. How the blind Pryor ends up working for the deaf Wilder at a Manhattan lobby newsstand really is inconsequential, since neither their first encounter, nor anything that follows, is believable for a minute. While Wilder's back is turned, a customer is shot in the back. The cops arrive and, in predictable fashion, arrest the only suspects around, the two numbskulls who couldn't possibly coordinate anything, much less a murder.

SEE YOU IN THE MORNING
1989, 119 mins, US Ⓥ ⊙
D: Alan J. Pakula **A:** Jeff Bridges, Alice Krige, Farrah Fawcett, Drew Barrymore, Lukas Haas, Macaulay Culkin (Lorimar)

Pakula produced, wrote, and directed the semiautobiographical story of a man torn between two families and two marriages. Jeff Bridges is a psychiatrist who tries to fit in with his new life with second wife Beth (Alice Krige) and her two kids, while remaining the most decent of dads to his own two kids. Their mother is played by Farrah Fawcett. As dull as this sounds, it's even more boring to watch. Pakula tried too hard to make this into a romantic comedy.

SEIZE THE DAY
1986, 93 mins, US Ⓥ ⊙
D: Fielder Cook **A:** Robin Williams, Jerry Stiller, Joseph Wiseman, Glenne Headly, William Hickey, Tony Roberts (Learning in Focus)

First film based upon a Saul Bellow novel can boast of earnest performances and intent, but is swamped in obviousness and the broadness of its brush strokes. Having lost his job as a salesman, disappointed his girlfriend, and allowed himself to be bled dry by his estranged wife, Tommy (Robin Williams in a "serious" starring role), who's pushing 40, returns to New York City to appeal to his father in an attempt at a new start. Tommy finds heartlessness everywhere he turns.

SEMI-TOUGH
1977, 107 mins, US Ⓥ ⊙
D: Michael Ritchie **A:** Burt Reynolds, Kris Kristofferson, Jill Clayburgh, Robert

Preston, Roger E. Mosley (United Artists)

Film begins as a bawdy and lively romantic comedy about slaphappy pro football players, then slows down to a too-inside put-down of contemporary self-help programs. Pals Reynolds and Kristofferson are members of a flashy team owned by eccentric Robert Preston, whose daughter (Clayburgh) roommates with the two guys. She tilts romantically toward Kristofferson, whose personality has become more assured after undergoing training by Bert Convy.

SENATOR WAS INDISCREET, THE (UK: MR. ASHTON WAS INDISCREET)
1947, 86 mins, US ℗
D: George S. Kaufman **A:** William Powell, Ella Raines, Arleen Whelan, Charles D. Brown, Peter Lind Hayes, Myrna Loy (Universal)

Fast-moving bit of fluff about a flannel-mouth Solon whose presidential aspirations become complicated when he loses an incriminating diary wherein he had recorded every step taken by his political backers in the past 30 days. Powell does a fine job as the stuffy dimwit of a senator. Charles D. Brown does a capital job as the bullying political boss. Ella Raines is the newspaper gal who rightly suspects Arleen Whelan got away with the diary as a favor to her beau, who, too, has political ambitions in opposition to the senator.

SENDER, THE
1983, 91 mins, US ℗ ⊙
D: Roger Christian **A:** Kathryn Harrold, Zeljko Ivanek, Shirley Knight, Paul Freeman, Sean Hewitt (Paramount)

A superbly crafted modern horror picture, credibly using telepathic communication as its premise for creating nightmarish situations. Screenplay concerns a suicidal young amnesiac (Zeljko Ivanek). He establishes a telepathic link with his psychiatrist Gail Farmer (Kathryn Harrold), causing her to experience involuntarily his violent nightmares. The "sender" cannot control his telepathic powers, and when Dr. Denman (Paul Freeman), Farmer's superior, subjects him to shock treatment and surgical experiments, he sends telepathic images of horror which disrupt the entire hospital.

SEND ME NO FLOWERS
1964, 100 mins, US ℗
D: Norman Jewison **A:** Rock Hudson,

Doris Day, Tony Randall, Paul Lynde, Edward Andrews (Universal)

Thin story line romps around Hudson, a hypochondriac, overhearing his doctor discussing the fatal symptoms of another patient and believing them to be his own. He sets about trying to find a suitable man to take his place as Day's husband. Tony Randall plays his next-door neighbor, who takes his friend's expected fate even harder than the soon-to-be-deceased and goes on a three-day drunk.

SENSATIONS OF 1945
1944, 85 mins, US ℗
D: Andrew L. Stone **A:** Eleanor Powell, Dennis O'Keefe, C. Aubrey Smith, Eugene Pallette, Mimi Forsythe (United Artists)

Eleanor Powell is the ambidextrous musicomedy dancer turned p.a. whose imagination cooks up spectacular ideas calling for lavish showmanship and Miss Fixit technique. It's to producer-director Andrew L. Stone's credit that he has been able to jell the Woody Herman and Cab Calloway bands, the specialties of W. C. Fields (too brief), Sophie Tucker's two dandy numbers (with Teddy Shapiro omnipotently at the Steinway), and the crack boogie-woogieing of Dorothy Donegan.

SENSE AND SENSIBILITY
1995, 135 mins, US ℗ ⊙
D: Ang Lee **A:** Emma Thompson, Alan Rickman, Kate Winslet, Hugh Grant, James Fleet, Harriet Walter (Mirage/Columbia)

This shrewd, highly humorous adaptation reps the first screenplay written by actress Emma Thompson, while this is the first entirely non-Chinese picture directed by Taiwanese helmer Ang Lee. Deftly setting the stage in late 18th-century rural England, pic briskly delineates the suddenly reduced circumstances of widow Dashwood (Gemma Jones) and her three lovely daughters. Eldest daughter Elinor (Thompson) is the sensible one, widely regarded as an incipient spinster. Middle daughter Marianne (Kate Winslet), in her late teens, is quite the opposite, a reckless romantic. Little sister Margaret (Emile Francois) is an 11-year-old tomboy. The wealthy, brooding, middle-aged Colonel Brandon (Alan Rickman) comes to call, but Marianne finds her romantic dreams come to life in the person of the dashing John Willoughby (Greg Wise).

1995: Best Screenplay Adaptation
Nominations: Best Picture, Actress

(Emma Thompson), Best Supporting Actress (Kate Winslet), Cinematography, Original Dramatic Score, Costume Design

SENSO
(US: THE WANTON CONTESSA)
1954, 122 mins, Italy ⓥ
D: Luchino Visconti **A:** Alida Valli, Farley Granger, Massimo Girotti, Heinz Moog, Christian Marquand (Lux)

An elegant, expensively produced, period love story, set back in the Italian 1860s, and a stylist delight, film was originally shot with an English sound track, with dialogue by Tennessee Williams and Paul Bowles. Story, in which married Venetian countess Lidia (Alida Valli) falls for young Austrian officer Franz Mahler (Farley Granger), is intertwined with historical-political events of the period. Valli falls more and more in love with her officer while his interest is more financial than real. Luchino Visconti's direction of Valli and Granger, his care for detail and backdrop atmosphere, for lighting and color, costumes and decor, his handling of the sweeping battle scenes help keep a shaky story together and give the film class.

SENTINEL, THE
1977, 91 mins, US ⓥ
D: Michael Winner **A:** Chris Sarandon, Cristina Raines, Martin Balsam, John Carradine, Jose Ferrer, Ava Gardner (Universal)

A grubby, grotesque excursion into religioso psychodrama, notable for uniformly poor performances by a large cast of familiar names and direction that is hysterical and heavy-handed. The story is based on the familiar device of taking some innocent (in this case, Cristina Raines, whose performance is miserable), confronted with kooky situations and characters. The only clear concept is that the innocent seems to be losing mental control.

SEPARATE LIVES
1995, 101 mins, US ⓥ
D: David Madden **A:** James Belushi, Linda Hamilton, Vera Miles, Elisabeth Moss, Drew Snyder (Interscope/Trimark)

Thinly plotted and tiresomely formulaic drama. Hamilton plays Lauren Porter, a demure psychology professor who occasionally turns into Lena, her promiscuous, sexy alter ego. Fearing she may have killed someone during one of her split-personality perambulations, she seeks help

from Tom Beckwith (Belushi), an ex-cop-turned-psych-student.

SEPARATE TABLES
1958, 98 mins, US ⓥ
D: Delbert Mann **A:** Rita Hayworth, Deborah Kerr, David Niven, Wendy Hiller, Burt Lancaster, Gladys Cooper (United Artists/Hecht-Hill-Lancaster)

Story is a character study of a group of residents of a small British seaside town. The majority of the residents are tortured by psychological problems and unhappy pasts. As a phony major, David Niven gives one of the best performances of his career. Deborah Kerr is excellent as a plain, shy girl. As a writer hurt by life, Lancaster turns in a shaded performance. Hayworth is equally good as his former wife. Hiller is the efficient manager of the hotel who finds her romance with Lancaster shattered on the arrival of his attractive and fashionable ex-wife.
1958: Best Actor (David Niven), Supp. Actress (Wendy Hiller)
Nominations: Best Picture, Actress (Deborah Kerr), Adapted Screenplay, B&W Cinematography, Scoring of a Dramatic Picture

SEPPUKU
(US: HARAKIRI)
1962, 135 mins, Japan ☐
D: Masaki Kobayashi **A:** Tatsuya Nakadai, Akira Ishihama, Shima Iwashita, Tetsuro Tamba, Rentaro Mikuni (Shochiku)

This stunning film is a somber tragedy and a powerful indictment of militarism and fanatical political systems and beliefs. In 17th century Japan, a powerful centralizing shogun breaks up various self-sufficient clans and creates a flock of rootless ronins, samurai sans masters, who roam the countryside. Some threaten to commit harakiri. One clan feels this is against the idealistic military code of the samurai. When a young man comes begging, they decide to force him to perform the act, with a wooden blade.

SEPTEMBER
1987, 82 mins, US ⓥ ⊙
D: Woody Allen **A:** Denholm Elliott, Dianne Wiest, Mia Farrow, Elaine Stritch, Jack Warden (Orion)

September sees Woody Allen in a compellingly melancholy mood. Set entirely within the lovely Vermont country home of Mia Farrow at summer's end, tale is constructed around a pattern of unrequited, mismatched infatuations that drive the high-strung, intellectual characters to distraction. Neighbor Denholm Elliott loves Farrow, Farrow is a goner for guest-house occupant Sam Waterston, and Waterston is nuts for Farrow's best friend Dianne Wiest, who is married. Also visiting are Farrow's mother, a former screen star and great beauty played by Elaine Stritch, and the latter's husband, physicist Jack Warden.

SEPTEMBER AFFAIR
1950, 91 mins, US ⊛ ⊙
D: William Dieterle **A:** Joan Fontaine, Joseph Cotten, Francoise Rosay, Jessica Tandy, Fortunio Bonanova (Paramount)

Joan Fontaine, pianist, and Joseph Cotten, an engineer, are on the same plane. Engine trouble forces the plane down in Naples. Both go sightseeing. They return to the airport just in time to see their plane roaring away overhead. More sightseeing together to Pompeii and Capri. They discover that the plane crashed and that they are reported dead. They decide that since the world no longer believes they exist, they will start a new life together.

SEPTEMBER 30, 1955
See: 9/30/55

SERGEANT, THE
1968, 107 mins, US
D: John Flynn **A:** Rod Steiger, John Phillip Law, Ludmila Mikael, Frank Latimore (Warner/Seven Arts)

A five-minute prologue establishes Rod Steiger as a hero during the 1944 liberation of France. The heroic deed included the strangling of a helpless, disarmed German soldier. His death grip on the younger man betrays a latent homosexuality. Time shifts to 1952, with Steiger reporting as first sergeant at a US base in rural France. He works to shape up the slovenly unit. Practically dragooned into the company office, John Phillip Law falls increasingly under the thrall of Steiger. Story threads are strongly woven, through Dennis Murphy's fine adaptation of his book as well as Flynn's incisive direction.

SERGEANT RUTLEDGE
(AKA: THE TRIAL OF SERGEANT RUTLEDGE)
1960, 111 mins, US
D: John Ford **A:** Jeffrey Hunter, Constance Towers, Billie Burke, Woody Strode, Juano Hernandez (Warner)

Pic deals with racial prejudice in the post–Civil War era. Ford expertly blends the action-pictorial and the story elements to create lively physical excitement as well as sustained suspense about the fate of a Negro trooper who is accused of rape and double murder. As the giant-sized Negro first sergeant, Woody Strode gives an unusually versatile performance.

SERGEANTS 3
1962, 113 mins, US ⊠
D: John Sturges **A:** Frank Sinatra, Dean Martin, Sammy Davis Jr., Peter Lawford (United Artists)

Sergeants 3 is warmed-over *Gunga Din,* a westernized version of that screen epic, with American-style Indians and Vegas-style soldiers of fortune. The emphasis here is tongue-in-cheek, with serious overtones. The "Big Three" of Sinatra, Martin, and Lawford reenact the parts played in the original by Cary Grant, Victor McLaglen, and Douglas Fairbanks Jr. Martin seems by far the most animated and comfortable, Sinatra and Lawford coming off a trifle too businesslike for the irreverent, look-ma-we're-cavalrymen approach.

SERGEANT YORK
1941, 134 mins, US ⊛
D: Howard Hawks **A:** Gary Cooper, Walter Brennan, Joan Leslie, Ward Bond, Margaret Wycherly (Warner)

For more than 20 years Sergeant York refused the necessary cooperation to make a film of his heroism on October 8, 1918, when he single-handedly killed 20 Germans and compelled the surrender of 132 of the enemy. For Gary Cooper, the role is made to order. He convincingly portrays the youthful backwoodsman, unruly as a youth, who in time gains mastery over his wildness. The romantic passages played with Joan Leslie are tender and human. But Cooper is best, perhaps, in the scenes of early camp training when his marksmanship, learned in the woods, attracts attention.

1941: Best Actor (Gary Cooper), Editing **Nominations:** Best Picture, Director, Supp. Actor (Walter Brennan), Supp. Actress (Margaret Wycherly), Original Screenplay, B&W Cinematography, B&W Art Direction, Scoring of a Dramatic Picture, Sound

SERIAL MOM
1994, 93 mins, US ⊛ ⊙
D: John Waters **A:** Kathleen Turner, Sam Waterston, Ricki Lake, Matthew Lillard, Mary Jo Catlett (Polar)

John Waters's latest exposé is almost

endearing in its cheeky irreverence, but also rather mild and scattershot in its satiric marksmanship. To all outward appearances, Baltimore hausfrau Beverly Sutphin (Kathleen Turner) is an endlessly supportive wife to dentist Eugene (Sam Waterston), college-student daughter Misty (Ricki Lake), who has extensive boy problems, and high-schooler son Chip (Matthew Lillard), a gore-film junkie. As soon as they all leave for the day, however, Beverly jumps into action. By the time she's arrested and charged with murder, she has killed six people. Turner turns in a game, rambunctious star performance that hits the right note between satire and seriousness.

SERIOUS CHARGE
1959, 105 mins, UK
D: Terence Young **A:** Anthony Quayle, Sarah Churchill, Andrew Ray, Irene Browne, Cliff Richard (Eros)
The plausible situation takes place in a small British town. A new vicar arrives. A young good-looking bachelor, athletic, sincere, keen, he comes up against a vindictive teenager who leads a local gang of small-time hoodlums. The kid frames the vicar by alleging a homo attack. Anthony Quayle's well-rounded portrayal of the vicar is sympathetic and gripping. Andrew Ray is a typical, credible juve delinquent. Cliff Richard sings a trio of useful beat songs.

SERPENT AND THE RAINBOW, THE
1988, 98 mins, US Ⓥ ⊙
D: Wes Craven **A:** Bill Pullman, Cathy Tyson, Zakes Mokae, Paul Winfield, Michael Gough (Universal)
Better-than-average supernatural tale is intriguingly eerie as long as it explores the secrets of voodoo in a lush Haitian setting alive with mysteries of the spirit. In Haiti, psychiatrist Marielle Celine (Cathy Tyson) is battling the cumulative effects of deep-rooted black magic, religion, and everyday mental illness. Opposing her are the reactionary political and supernatural forces of police chief Dargent Peytraud, played with evil zeal by Zakes Mokae.

SERPENT OF THE NILE
1953, 81 mins, US
D: William Castle **A:** Rhonda Fleming, William Lundigan, Raymond Burr, Michael Ansara, Julie Newmar (Columbia)
Producer Sam Katzman dusts off some incidents in the life and loves of Cleopatra

for mediocre results. Yarn has Raymond Burr, as Mark Antony, proposing an alliance between Rome and wealthy Egypt, which is ruled by Rhonda Fleming as Cleopatra. She schemes to eliminate Burr and place herself on the throne of Rome. Her plan, however, is nipped by William Lundigan, Burr's lieutenant, who brings the Roman legions to Alexandria. Fleming fails to impress as the Egyptian beauty, primarily due to the stilted dialogue.

SERPENT'S EGG, THE
1977, 120 mins, W. Germany/US Ⓥ
D: Ingmar Bergman **A:** Liv Ullmann, David Carradine, Gert Frobe, Heinz Bennent, James Whitmore (Rialto/De Laurentiis)
Ingmar Bergman's first English-language feature lacks both the strength and depth of his major work. By going international, the master comes perilously close to becoming shallow as well. Production designer Rolf Zehetbauer has recreated a Berlin of a poverty-ridden, fear-stricken early 1920s that is much more than paint-deep. Bergman makes his actors, with one fatal exception (David Carradime), work their individualities into the grandest of ensemble playing.

SERPICO
1973, 129 mins, US Ⓥ ⊙
D: Sidney Lumet **A:** Al Pacino, John Randolph, Jack Kehoe, Biff McGuire, Cornelia Sharpe (De Laurentiis/Artists Entertainment)
Serpico is based on the actual experiences of an honest NY policeman who helped expose corruption. Sidney Lumet's direction adeptly combines gritty action and thought-provoking comment. Pacino dominates the entire film. His personal torment is vividly detailed, manifested first in the breakup of an affair with Cornelia Sharpe and later, much more terribly, in the wreck of his love for Barbara Eda-Young.
1973: Nominations: Best Actor (Al Pacino), Adapted Screenplay

SERVANT, THE
1963, 117 mins, UK Ⓥ
D: Joseph Losey **A:** Dirk Bogarde, Sarah Miles, Wendy Craig, James Fox, Catherine Lacey (Springbok)
The Servant is for the most part strong dramatic fare, though the atmosphere and tension is not fully sustained. Harold Pinter's screenplay based on the Robin Maugham novel is distinguished by its literacy and sharp incisive dialogue. Dirk

Bogarde plays a manservant who is hired by a young and elegant man about town to run a house in a fashionable part of London, and who, almost imperceptibly, begins to dominate his master. The relationship of master and servant, with its underlying suggestion of homosexuality, is sensitively handled.

SET-UP, THE
1949, 72 mins, US Ⓥ
D: Robert Wise **A:** Robert Ryan, Audrey Totter, George Tobias, Alan Baxter, Percy Helton (RKO)

Compact and suspenseful, boxing film shows the seamier side of the fight racket. It throws the spotlight on 35-year-old washed-up heavyweight (Robert Ryan). Feeling that it's his lucky night, he wades through a four-rounder to kayo his opponent and spoil a match that had been fixed. Under Robert Wise's skillful direction, the assorted ringside audience "types" give an added luster of realism. Dressing-room hangers-on, rubdown boys, and other pugs on the bill also come in for scalpellike scrutiny.

SEVEN
1995, 127 mins, US Ⓥ ⊙ ▭
D: David Fincher **A:** Brad Pitt, Morgan Freeman, Gwyneth Paltrow, Kevin Spacey, R. Lee Ermey, Richard Roundtree (New Line)

An intensely claustrophobic, gut-wrenching thriller about two policemen's desperate efforts to stop an ingenious serial killer whose work is inspired by the seven deadly sins, this weirdly off-kilter suspenser goes well beyond the usual police procedural or killer-on-a-rampage yarn due to a fine script, striking craftsmanship, and a masterful performance by Morgan Freeman. Feature cuts against most expectations for this sort of genre piece: it's not a buddy picture; the murders themselves are not actually depicted; and the usual gritty big-city realism has been replaced by a highly stylized, borderline-arty visual conception that greatly cranks up the psychological and physical intensity of the drama, by first-time screenwriter Andrew Kevin Walker. Virtuoso French cinematographer Darius Khondji and production designer Arthur Max have sculpted a dark, murky world, parts of which are illuminated only by flashlight and much of the rest of which is suffused in a pea-soup green that defies penetration.
1995: Nomination: Film Editing

SEVEN BRIDES FOR SEVEN BROTHERS
1954, 102 mins, US Ⓥ ⊙ ▭
D: Stanley Donen **A:** Howard Keel, Jane Powell, Jeff Richards, Russ Tamblyn, Tommy Rall (M-G-M)

Happy, hand-clapping, foot-stomping country type of musical with eight songs, all of which jibe perfectly. Howard Keel's robust baritone and Jane Powell's lilting soprano make their songs extremely listenable. A real standout is the acrobatic hoedown staged around a barn-raising shindig, during which six of the title's seven brothers vie in love rivalry with the town boys for the favor of the mountain belles. The brothers are all good, with Russ Tamblyn standing out in particular for performance and his dance work.
1954: Best Scoring of a Musical Picture
Nominations: Best Picture, Screenplay, Color Cinematography, Editing

SEVEN DAYS IN MAY
1964, 120 mins, US Ⓥ ⊙
D: John Frankenheimer **A:** Burt Lancaster, Kirk Douglas, Fredric March, Ava Gardner, Edmond O'Brien, Martin Balsam (Seven Arts/Joel)

Strikingly dramatic, realistic, and provocative film undertakes the proposition that extremists could reach the point where they'd try to uproot the present form of government. Such a man is General James M. Scott, played with authority by Burt Lancaster. He's a member of the joint chiefs of staff, burning with patriotic fervor and seeking to "save" the country from the perils of a just-signed nuclear pact with Russia. He enlists the support of fellow chiefs. The performances are excellent down the line, under the taut and penetrating directorial guidance of John Frankenheimer. Kirk Douglas is masterfully cool and matter-of-fact as Scott's aide, utterly devoted until he comes to be suspicious.
1964: Nominations: Best Supp. Actor (Edmond O'Brien), B&W Art Direction

SEVEN DAYS TO NOON
1950, 94 mins, UK
D: Roy Boulting, John Boulting **A:** Barry Jones, Olive Sloane, Andre Morell, Joan Hickson (London/Boulting)

Focal point of the plot is an ultimatum sent to the prime minister by an atomic scientist who becomes mentally deranged because his work is being used for destruction, not for mankind's benefit. He warns that unless atom bomb production

ceases by noon the following Sunday, he will, himself, blow up all of London with a bomb he has stolen. Barry Jones's interpretation of the scientist is intelligent.
1951: Best Motion Picture Story

711 OCEAN DRIVE
1950, 102 mins, US
D: Joseph M. Newman **A:** Edmond O'Brien, Joanne Dru, Donald Porter, Otto Kruger, Dorothy Patrick (Columbia)

Story concerns a telephone worker (Edmond O'Brien) with a knack for electrons who joins a syndicate and expands its operations with his inventions. When the syndicate chief is killed, O'Brien takes charge of the organization and runs into the opposition of an eastern syndicate. Joseph M. Newman's direction keeps action at a fast pace.

SEVEN LITTLE FOYS, THE
1955, 92 mins, US ⓥ
D: Melville Shavelson **A:** Bob Hope, James Cagney, Milly Vitale, Angela Clarke, George Tobias (Paramount)

Bob Hope abandons the buffoon to go straight actor in biopicturing Eddie Foy, song-and-dance man of the vaudeville age. Milly Vitale does a fine job of portraying the Italian ballerina who marries Foy. Their hit-and-miss life together is told with heart. A standout sequence is the appearance of James Cagney as George M. Cohan. He and Hope turn in some mighty slick hoofing.
1955: Nomination: Best Story & Screenplay

SEVEN MINUTES, THE
1971, 115 mins, US ⓥ
D: Russ Meyer **A:** Wayne Maunder, Marianne McAndrew, Philip Carey, Edy Williams, Jay C. Flippen, Lyle Bettger (20th Century-Fox)

Large cast is headed by Wayne Maunder, attorney for bookstore owner busted by vice cop Charles Drake. Philip Carey, excellent as a d.a., is egged on by J. C. Flippen, a behind-the-scenes king-maker, to prosecute John Sarno for brutally raping Yvonne D'Angers, though sadist Billy Durkin was really to blame. Meyer's artistic eye remains most sure in composition and pacing. As usual, all femme castings are knockouts, including Edy Williams (Mrs. Meyer).

SEVEN NIGHTS IN JAPAN
1976, 104 mins, UK/France ⓥ
D: Lewis Gilbert **A:** Michael York, Hidemi Aoki, Charles Gray, Ann Lonnberg, Eleonore Hirt, James Villiers (EMI/Paramount)

Beautifully photographed pastiche bears little true resemblance to the enigmatic life of bustling Tokyo, where it was lensed. Simplistic plot details the implausible romance between a royal prince (Michael York) who is serving as a naval officer, and a petite Japanese bus guide (Hidemi Aoki), whom he meets when his ship visits Japan. Script is sadly lacking in humor and pace and the story line can only be labeled corny and unreal.

SEVEN-PER-CENT SOLUTION, THE
1976, 113 mins, UK ⓥ ⊙
D: Herbert Ross **A:** Alan Arkin, Vanessa Redgrave, Robert Duvall, Nicol Williamson, Laurence Olivier, Joel Grey (Universal)

Producer-director Herbert Ross and writer Nicholas Meyer, adapting his novel, have fashioned a most classy period crime drama. The concept is terrific, in that Sherlock Holmes (Nicol Williamson), while a patient of Sigmund Freud (Alan Arkin), becomes his analyst's partner as both apply their specialized abilities in the parallel solution of a kidnap crime. Simultaneously, there is resolved Holmes's own childhood trauma, which has motivated his lifelong enmity toward Professor Moriarty.
1976: Nominations: Best Adapted Screenplay, Costume Design

SEVEN SAMURAI, THE
See: Shichinin No Samurai

SEVEN SAMURAI
See: Shichinin No Samurai

SEVENTH CROSS, THE
1944, 111 mins, US ⓥ
D: Fred Zinnemann **A:** Spencer Tracy, Signe Hasso, Hume Cronyn, Jessica Tandy, Agnes Moorehead, George Macready (M-G-M)

The story of seven men who escape from a concentration camp. The camp's commandant has ordered seven trees stripped and crosses nailed to them. It is his plan, as each fugitive is caught, to pinion him to a cross and let him die of exposure. This becomes the story of the seventh cross—the one that was never occupied. Spencer Tracy, as usual, underplays and gives one of his invariably creditable portrayals.
1944: Nomination: Best Supp. Actor (Hume Cronyn)

7TH DAWN, THE

1964, 123 mins, UK
D: Lewis Gilbert A: William Holden, Susannah York, Capucine, Tetsuro Tamba, Allan Cuthbertson (United Artists)

Pivotal characters in the film, set in the Malayan jungle, circa 1945, each represent an allegorical type, a fact that leads to some rather predictable problems and solutions. William Holden handles himself in credible fashion as a major local landowner involved in the new politics because of his old-time friendship for the leader of the Red terrorists, played by Tetsuro Tamba. Holden is further involved because of his mistress, a Malayan loyalist portrayed by Capucine.

7TH HEAVEN

1927, 115 mins, US ⊗
D: Frank Borzage A: Janet Gaynor, Charles Farrell, Ben Bard, David Butler, Marie Mosquini (Fox)

A great big romantic, gripping, and red-blooded story told in a straight-from-the-shoulder way. Borzage has made a real star out of Janet Gaynor overnight. There is not more than 2,500 feet of actual warfare in the film. Balance of the story is romance.
1927/28: Best Director, Actress (Janet Gaynor), Adaptation
Nominations: Best Picture, Interior Direction

SEVENTH HEAVEN

1937, 100 mins, US
D: Henry King A: Simone Simon, James Stewart, Jean Hersholt, Gregory Ratoff, Gale Sondergaard, J. Edward Bromberg (20th Century-Fox)

Tenderness of this Austin Strong play has been retained in a fine film production. Picture is a remake dating back to 1927 as a film and 1922 as a Broadway legit entry. Simone Simon's is a mixed, and at times disturbing, performance. Frequent impression is that she's uncertain of the character. She is a pretty Diane, and not so much the beaten, bewildered, cringing slavey. There are several scenes brilliantly mixed for poignancy and humor. Major credit for this is due James Stewart's firm grasp of his role and to Henry King's direction. Little of war is woven into the narrative, nor are the armistice-celebration scenes too obtrusive.

SEVENTH SEAL, THE

See: Det Sjunde Inseglet

SEVENTH VEIL, THE

1945, 94 mins, UK ⊗
D: Compton Bennett A: James Mason, Ann Todd, Herbert Lom, Albert Lieven (Sydney Box/Ortus)

Apart from the engrossing story (of the merciless discipline to which a sensitive teenage, orphan is subjected by a grim bachelor guardian) as it surges swiftly to its tremendous climax, there is a feast of harmony by the London Symphony Orchestra, accompanying an unidentified piano virtuoso—ostensibly Todd.
1946: Best Original Screenplay

SEVENTH VICTIM, THE

1943, 71 mins, US ⊗
D: Mark Robson A: Kim Hunter, Tom Conway, Isabel Jewell, Jean Brooks, Evelyn Brent (RKO)

A particularly poor script is the basis for the ills besetting this mystery melodrama. Even the occasional good performance can't offset this minor dualer about a strange Greenwich Village coterie.

7TH VOYAGE OF SINBAD, THE

1958, 89 mins, US ⊗ ⊙
D: Nathan Juran A: Kerwin Mathews, Kathryn Grant, Richard Eyer, Torin Thatcher, Danny Green (Morningside/Columbia)

Just about every trick in the book—including one called Dynamation, i.e., the animation of assorted monsters, vultures, skeletons, etc.—has been used to bring a vivid sort of realism to the various and terrifying hazards that Sinbad encounters on his voyage and in his battle with Sokurah the magician. Add to this a love story, interrupted when the Princess Parisa is shrunk to inch size by the magician, and what emerges is a bright, noisy package. Ray Harryhausen, responsible for visual effects, emerges as the hero of this piece.

SEVEN-UPS, THE

1973, 103 mins, US ⊗ ⊙
D: Philip D'Antoni A: Roy Scheider, Victor Arnold, Jerry Leon, Ken Kercheval, Tony Lo Bianco (20th Century-Fox)

Serviceable dualer about some underground cops who get caught in a series of gangland kidnappings features, at midpoint, a complicated and extravagant car chase which must have taxed the ingenuity of the director and that of stunt coordinator Bill Hickman. Roy Scheider heads an okay cast in a fair script.

7 WOMEN
1965, 88 mins, US ⊙ ⊡
D: John Ford **A:** Anne Bancroft, Sue Lyon, Margaret Leighton, Flora Robson, Mildred Dunnock, Eddie Albert (M-G-M)

Run-of-the-mill story of an isolated American mission in North China whose serenity is rudely shattered by a ravaging Mongolian barbarian and his band of cutthroats. Production is set in 1935 and takes its title from the seven femmes trapped in mission and subjected to gross indignities. John Ford manages regulation treatment.

7 WONDERS OF THE WORLD
1956, 120 mins, US ⊡
D: Ted Tetzlaff, Andrew Marton, Tay Garnett, Paul Mantz, Walter Thompson (Stanley Warner/Cinerama)

While the titular *7 Wonders of the World* might be pointed to captiously as a misnomer, [this third Cinerama production] is a resourceful kickoff for an airlift from Manhattan through 32 countries in 120 minutes. The Sphinx and the Pyramids are pointed to as the sole remainders of the seven ancient wonders and the unfolding is a modern odyssey.

SEVEN YEAR ITCH, THE
1955, 105 mins, US ⓥ ⊙ ⊡
D: Billy Wilder **A:** Marilyn Monroe, Tom Ewell, Evelyn Keyes, Sonny Tufts, Robert Strauss, Victor Moore (20th Century-Fox)

Film version of George Axelrod's play concerns only the fantasies, and omits the acts, of the summer bachelor, who remains totally, if unbelievably, chaste. Laughs come thick and fast. The performance of Marilyn Monroe is baby-dollish as the dumb-but-sweet number upstairs who attracts the eye of the guy, seven years married and restless, whose wife and child have gone off for the summer. The acting kudos belongs to Tom Ewell, a practiced farceur and pantomimist.

SEVEN YEARS IN TIBET
1997, 139 mins, US ⓥ ⊙ ⊡
D: Jean-Jacques Annaud **A:** Brad Pitt, David Thewlis, B. D. Wong, Mako, Danny Denzongpa, Victor Wong (Reperage/Vanguard-Applecross/Mandalay/TriStar)

Brad Pitt climbs many mountains and meets the young Dalai Lama, but doesn't carry the audience with him for much of the odyssey. Pic asks auds to identify with a ruthlessly self-absorbed member of the Nazi Party, and the script rarely hits the heights of eloquence or poetry needed. Brad Pitt's Harrer remains a somewhat cold, one-dimensional cipher prior to finally meeting the young Dalai Lama. It's only then that the picture starts to tread solid ground. In 1939, the blond, Aryan-looking Harrer sets out to conquer Nanga Parbat peak, but not until the fall of 1942 does he reach the closed kingdom of Tibet. Emotional clout is largely thanks to the scenes between Harrer and Kundun, the boy Dalai Lama (Bhutanese actor Jamyang Jamtsho Wangchuk), which have zest and some welcome humor. But often you just long for the pic to cut loose from the ethnography and correct attitudes and go with the drama in old Hollywood style.

SEVERED HEAD, A
1971, 98 mins, UK
D: Dick Clement **A:** Lee Remick, Richard Attenborough, Ian Holm, Claire Bloom, Jennie Linden, Clive Revill (Winkast)

This is a very upper-class and intellectually snobbish film about "civilized copulation." It's based on Iris Murdoch's novel. It's the writing, direction, and acting that gives it stylish panache. The mattress merry-go-round has a great game of musical chairs among its cast. Ian Holm plays a wine taster, with a mistress played by Jennie Linden. Holm's wife (Lee Remick), a predatory nympho, is having an affair with her husband's best friend, psychologist Richard Attenborough, who is also sexually involved with his sister, Claire Bloom.

SEX AND THE SINGLE GIRL
1964, 114 mins, US ⓥ ⊙
D: Richard Quine **A:** Tony Curtis, Natalie Wood, Henry Fonda, Lauren Bacall, Mel Ferrer, Edward Everett Horton (Quine-Reynard/Warner)

Natalie Wood is Dr. Helen Brown of International Institute of Advanced Marital and Pre-Marital Studies, who is target of scandal-mag editor Tony Curtis, bent on exposing her to be 23-year-old virgin without background for advising single girls about sex. Curtis poses as his neighbor, Henry Fonda, who has monumental wife trouble, and goes to Wood for advice. Inevitably, they fall for one another, with Wood ignorant of Curtis's identity as ogre out to ruin her career. As usual in this type of farce, male and female leads have fewer comic lines than supporting players. Edward Everett Horton shines as boss of Curtis's mag.

SEX, LIES AND VIDEOTAPE
1989, 101 mins, US ⓥ ⊙

D: Steven Soderbergh **A:** James Spader, Andie MacDowell, Peter Gallagher, Laura San Giacomo (Outlaw)

Sexy, nuanced, beautifully controlled examination of how a quartet of people are defined by their erotic impulses and inhibitions. Opening intercuts the embarrassed therapy confessions of young wife Andie MacDowell with the impending arrival in town of James Spader, a chum of MacDowell's handsome husband (Peter Gallagher). Given MacDowell's admissions that she and Gallagher are no longer having sex, it would seem that Spader is walking into a potentially provocative situation. He drops a bombshell by revealing that he is impotent. Meanwhile Gallagher has been conducting a secret affair with his wife's sexy wild sister (Laura San Giacomo).

1989: Nomination: Best Original Screenplay

SEXTETTE
1978, 91 mins, US ⓥ

D: Ken Hughes **A:** Mae West, Timothy Dalton, Dom DeLuise, Tony Curtis, Ringo Starr, George Hamilton (Briggs-Sullivan)

Mostly unfunny musical comedy. The screenplay, based on a play by Mae West, concerns a sexy Hollywood movie star who has married a young British nobleman. It's her sixth marriage, and in the course of attempting to consummate the liaison, she's interrupted by numbers four and five, fans, newspapermen, Rona Barrett, an American gymnastic team, and a group of international diplomats. West is on screen for most of the film, mostly attempting Mae West imitations and lipsynching a series of undistinguished musical numbers. It's an embarrassing attempt at camp from the lady who helped invent the word.

S.F.W.
1995, 92 mins, US ⓥ

D: Jefery Levy **A:** Stephen Dorff, Reese Witherspoon, Jake Busey, Joey Lauren Adams, Pamela Gidley (Gramercy)

Satirical spin through America's fascination with celebrities, no matter how empty or facile, tries hard to juice up a subject that feels done to death. When suburban teen buddies Cliff Spab (Stephen Dorff) and Joe Dice (Jack Noseworthy) zip into their local convenience store, waiting inside is a group of video camera–wielding terrorists who hold the two boys and three other customers hostage. The gang demands that TV networks broadcast the tapes they're creating, but the lack of a political or financial explanation for their actions is only one of several key weaknesses. Pic focuses on the aftereffects of what turns into a 36-day ordeal.

SGT. BILKO
1996, 94 mins, US ⓥ ⊙

D: Jonathan Lynn **A:** Steve Martin, Dan Aykroyd, Phil Hartman, Glenne Headly, Daryl Mitchell (Imagine/Universal)

Even Steve Martin back in his wild-and-crazy mode can't breathe much life into a somewhat unlikely candidate for translation from the TV sitcom vaults to the big screen. The plot has Bilko's nemesis, Major Thorn (Phil Hartman), coming to the base, seeking revenge on Bilko for a past indiscretion that nearly scuttled his career. Another thread finds Bilko trying to win over a strait laced new addition to the unit, Wally (Daryl Mitchell). *Bilko* simply misfires on too many of its gags, often seeking to mask its deficiencies with a frenetic energy that's difficult even for Martin to maintain.

SGT. PEPPER'S LONELY HEARTS CLUB BAND
1978, 111 mins, US ⓥ ⊙ ▭

D: Michael Schultz **A:** Peter Frampton, Barry Gibb, Robin Gibb, Maurice Gibb, Frankie Howerd (Universal)

Pepper will attract some grown-up flower children of the 1960s who will soon find the film to be a totally bubblegum-and-cotton-candy mélange of garish fantasy and narcissism. The production crams nearly 30 songs, largely by the Beatles, into newly recorded versions tailored for stars Peter Frampton and the Bee Gees. Plot has Frampton as the grandson of the earlier Sergeant Pepper who carries on the family band tradition with a modern sound, in partnership with the Bee Gees. Story introduces a lot of freakish characters out to steal the band's instruments.

SHADOW, THE
1994, 107 mins, US ⓥ ⊙

D: Russell Mulcahy **A:** Alec Baldwin, John Lone, Penelope Ann Miller, Peter Boyle, Ian McKellen, Tim Curry (Universal)

Although clearly trying to mine the *Batman* lode, down to its impressive production design, somber tone, and occasional flashes of high camp, *The Shadow*—which enjoyed its greatest success in radio in the thirties after being created in pulp novels—lacks the same visceral appeal. The heart of the story involves a comic-book nemesis, Shiwan Khan (John Lone), a descendant of Genghis Khan who possesses the same mental powers as the Shadow. Baldwin turns in a sturdy central performance, managing to bring some dimension and self-effacing humor to his role. Lone provides a shrewd and formidable adversary.

SHADOWLANDS
1994, 130 mins, UK/US ⓥ ⊙ ▭
D: Richard Attenborough **A:** Anthony Hopkins, Debra Winger, Edward Hardwicke, Michael Denison, John Wood (Shadowlands/Spelling)

Anthony Hopkins delivers a towering performance in a touching, somewhat fictionalized account of a late-in-life love between eminent English writer and scholar C. S. Lewis and Joy Gresham, an American poet. Set in the early 1950s, it's a quiet, pensive tale of two eccentric individuals whose personae, lifestyles, and cultures couldn't have been more different. Up to the last reel, the film resists sentimentality, but then it succumbs to a level of slow, old-fashioned—even heavy-handed—melodrama that negates its earlier matter-of-fact tone.
1993: Nominations: Best Actress (Debra Winger), Adapted Screenplay

SHADOW MAKERS
See: Fat Man and Little Boy

SHADOW OF A DOUBT
1943, 106 mins, US ⓥ ⊙
D: Alfred Hitchcock **A:** Joseph Cotten, Teresa Wright, Macdonald Carey, Henry Travers, Patricia Collinge, Hume Cronyn (Skirball/Universal)

Hitchcock poses a study in contrasts when the world-wise adventurer (Joseph Cotten) eludes police in Philadelphia to journey to his sister's home and family in the small California town of Santa Rosa. His deb-age niece (Teresa Wright) is not only named young Charlie after her uncle, but knows there's a mental contact somewhere along the line. Amid the typical small-town family life, she intuitively feels that Cotten has a guilty conscience, and finally ties the ends together to cast suspicion on him as a murderer and fugitive.
1943: Nomination: Best Original Story

SHADOW OF THE THIN MAN
1941, 97 mins, US ⓥ
D: W. S. Van Dyke **A:** William Powell, Myrna Loy, Barry Nelson, Donna Reed, Sam Levene (M-G-M)

Much of the farcical flavor that characterized the earlier *Thin Man* films is reclaimed in the new picture. William Powell and Myrna Loy get a great deal of fun from their first appearance as parents of a four-year-old son, who has a way of asking embarrassing questions. For excitement the couple find themselves in the middle of an investigation into racetrack gambling, in the course of which there are three homicides, half a dozen suspects, and a bit of gunplay.

SHADOW OF THE WOLF
1993, 112 mins, Canada/France ⓥ ▭
D: Jacques Dorfmann **A:** Lou Diamond Phillips, Toshiro Mifune, Jennifer Tilly, Donald Sutherland (Vision)

Story, circa 1935, of survival, revenge, and murder in the frozen north has all the subtlety of a silent-movie serial. Reportedly the costliest Canadian production ever, tale relates the maturation of a young Inuit Eskimo hunter (Lou Diamond Phillips) who, out of violent hatred for whites, is banished by his shaman father, impetuously kills a trader, and, in company with the local beauty, forges a difficult life on the tundra. Unfortunately, the film borders on the laughable throughout due to dialogue that erases the distinction between simple and simpleminded.

SHADOWS
1961, 84 mins, US
D: John Cassavetes **A:** Lelia Goldoni, Ben Carruthers, Tony Ray, Hugh Hurd, Rupert Crosse (McEndree-Cassel)

First made in 16mm as an exercise in improvisation by a group of actors directed by John Cassavetes, *Shadows* was then filled out and blown up to 35mm. A brother and sister who look white have a brother who is completely Negro. The film dwells on the dramatic interludes in their lives and the inevitable race problems. Nothing rings false. Though the narrative is rambling, it strikes solid truths and dimension in showing people living and reacting in a manner that is dictated from within rather than forced on them by a script.

SHADOWS AND FOG
1992, 86 mins, US ⓥ ⊙
D: Woody Allen **A:** Woody Allen, Mia Farrow, John Malkovich, Madonna, Donald Pleasence, Jodie Foster (Orion)

Exquisitely shot in black-and-white,

Woody Allen's *Shadows and Fog* is a sweet homage to German expressionist filmmaking and a nod to the content of socially responsible tales since narrative film began. Allen's fans will regard this as a nice try that falls short. Helmer throws in some Kafka (Allen's persecuted character is never sure what he's supposed to do), some evil (there's a killer on the loose, casting shadows in the fog), a spunky counterbalancing force (Mia Farrow), and a little magic.

SHADOW WARRIOR, THE
See: Kagemusha

SHAFT
1971, 98 mins, US ⓥ
D: Gordon Parks **A:** Richard Roundtree, Moses Gunn, Gwenn Mitchell, Christopher St. John, Charles Cioffi (M-G-M)

Take a formula private-eye plot, update it with all-black environment, lace with contemporary standards of on- and off-screen violence, and the result is *Shaft*. It is directed with a subtle feel for both the grit and the humanity of the script. Ernest Tidyman's novel, adapted by himself and John D. F. Black, concerns the kidnap by the Mafia of Sherri Brewer, daughter of Harlem underworld boss Moses Gunn. Richard Roundtree, as a black Sam Spade, is hired by Gunn to find her.
1971: Best Song ("Theme from *Shaft*")
Nomination: Best Original Score

SHAFT IN AFRICA
1973, 112 mins, US ⓥ ▭
D: John Guillermin **A:** Richard Roundtree, Frank Finlay, Vonetta McGee, Neda Arneric, Debebe Eshetu (M-G-M)

Third pic in the series takes a new story telling direction which gets it out of the well-plowed inner-city ghetto rut. Richard Roundtree again stars as the black private eye, now infiltrating an Africa-to-Europe slave-smuggling ring. Script, from the Ernest Tidyman character trove, is surprisingly good.

SHAFT'S BIG SCORE
1972, 105 mins, US ⓥ ▭
D: Gordon Parks **A:** Richard Roundtree, Moses Gunn, Joseph Mascolo, Julius W. Harris (M-G-M)

Richard Roundtree again heads the cast as a swinging black private eye. Script finds Roundtree trapped in the double-dealings of Wally Taylor, who has killed partner Robert Kya-Hill for money. Moses Gunn is again excellent as a black mobster, and Joseph Mascolo is a white mob-

ster eyeing Taylor's territory for a move-in. The first *Shaft* had a running-scared excitement not only in the characters, but also throughout the whole picture. The new film seems more self-conscious, contrived, ambitious, and sluggish.

SHAG
1988, 100 mins, UK/US ⓥ ⊙
D: Zelda Barron **A:** Phoebe Cates, Scott Coffey, Bridget Fonda, Annabeth Gish, Page Hannah (Palace/Hemdale)

As a dance flick, *Shag* suffers from an unexciting dance style and so-so choreography but compensates with a fine young cast and likable story. Pic, set in South Carolina in 1963, opens with three girls, Page Hannah, Annabeth Gish, and Bridget Fonda, picking up pal Phoebe Cates for her last summer fling before she marries dull Tyrone Power Jr. They head for Myrtle Beach and the Sun Fun Festival, full of boys, beer, a beauty parade, and shagging. The four female leads are excellent, though it is Fonda who exudes confidence and star quality.

SHAGGY D.A., THE
1976, 91 mins, US ⓥ
D: Robert Stevenson **A:** Dean Jones, Tim Conway, Suzanne Pleshette, Keenan Wynn, Dick Van Patten (Walt Disney)

In *The Shaggy Dog*, teenager Tommy Kirk came into possession of a magical ring which periodically changed him into a sheepdog. Here, in script drawn from the same material, fledgling d.a. candidate Dean Jones suffers the same fate. Most of the brisk film is physical comedy as Jones tries to escape embarrassing situations and outwit villainous d.a. Keenan Wynn.

SHAGGY DOG, THE
1959, 101 mins, US ⓥ ⊙
D: Charles T. Barton **A:** Fred MacMurray, Jean Hagen, Tommy Kirk, Annette Funicello, Tim Considine, Kevin Corcoran (Walt Disney)

Fred MacMurray plays the father of the two boys, Tommy Kirk and Kevin Corcoran. MacMurray himself is a mailman physically allergic to dogs. Young Kirk accidentally transforms himself into a large, shaggy sheepdog when he comes into possession of a spell-casting ring. When MacMurray has a good line, he shows that he has few peers in this special field of comedy. Jean Hagen, as his wife, is pretty and pleasant, while the two boys handle their comedy nicely.

SHAKE HANDS WITH THE DEVIL
1959, 104 mins, US
D: Michael Anderson **A:** James Cagney, Don Murray, Dana Wynter, Glynis Johns, Michael Redgrave, Sybil Thorndike (United Artists/Pennebaker)

Against a background of the 1921 Irish Rebellion, Cagney is a professor of medicine at a Dublin university, and Murray, an American veteran of World War I, is his student. Cagney is also a "commandant" of the underground, and wants to continue the terror when the leader of the Irish independence movement (Michael Redgrave) works out a treaty with the British. The principals, paced by Cagney, are interesting but seem posed against the Irish background rather than part of it.

SHAKESPEARE IN LOVE
1998, 122 mins, US Ⓥ ⊙
D: John Madden **A:** Joseph Fiennes, Gwyneth Paltrow, Geoffrey Rush, Judi Dench, Simon Callow, Colin Firth (Bedford Falls/Miramax/Universal)

With *Shakespeare in Love,* director John Madden does for adults what Baz Luhrmann did for teens in *Romeo + Juliet*—he makes Shakespeare accessible, entertaining and fun for modern audiences. Shakespeare (Joseph Fiennes) has writer's block and needs a muse to unlock his creative abilities. When he falls for the lovely Viola De Lesseps (Gwyneth Paltrow), his passion is released, and his ineptly-titled *Romeo and Ethel, the Pirate's Daughter* becomes *Romeo and Juliet.* But Viola is betrothed to the insufferable Lord Wessex (Colin Firth), and that union has been sanctioned by Queen Elizabeth (Judi Dench). Paltrow has a luminosity that makes Viola irresistible, and RSC-trained Fiennes endows Shakespeare with a likable humanity and romantic charm. The supporting cast is a dream; Madden keeps them together with the skill of a veteran, finding opportunities to let almost every actor shine.
1998: Best Picture, Actress (Gwyneth Paltrow), Supp. Actress (Judi Dench), Art Direction, Costume Design, Original Musical or Comedy Score, Original Screenplay
Nominations: Best Cinematography, Director, Editing, Makeup, Sound, Supp. Actor (Geoffrey Rush)

SHAKESPEARE WALLAH
1965, 125 mins, India/US Ⓥ
D: James Ivory **A:** Shashi Kapoor, Felicity Kendal, Geoffrey Kendal, Laura Liddell, Madhur Jaffrey (Merchant Ivory)

English-language production is the story of a touring theatrical company specializing in Shakespearean production which has seen better days. Founders Tony and Carla Buckingham (Geoffrey Kendal and Laura Liddell) are totally dedicated, and expect the same from all around, particularly from their daughter Lizzie. Some of the Shakespearean excerpts could advantageously be cut. Nevertheless, there is a naive charm to the production.

SHALAKO
1968, 118 mins, UK Ⓥ ⊏
D: Edward Dmytryk **A:** Sean Connery, Brigitte Bardot, Peter Van Eyck, Stephen Boyd, Honor Blackman, Jack Hawkins (Kingston/Palomar)

Nineteenth-century story of an aristocratic, "dude" hunting safari from Europe which is led into Apache territory by its double-crossing "white" hunter and given a hard time by the redskins. Shalako (Sean Connery) rescues one of them (Brigitte Bardot) from Indians and has to pit his wits and resources, not only against the Apaches but against members of the expedition, before he manages to save the party from complete destruction. Intriguing are the relationships between members of the hunting party.

SHALLOW GRAVE
1994, 91 mins, UK Ⓥ
D: Danny Boyle **A:** Kerry Fox, Christopher Eccleston, Ewan McGregor, Keith Allen, Ken Stott (Figment/Film Four)

Tar-black comedy zings along on a wave of visual and scripting inventiveness. Story, set in modern-day Scotland, revolves around a trio of unlikely friends sharing an apartment. Juliet (Kerry Fox) is a seemingly levelheaded nurse; David (Christopher Eccleston), a studiously boring accountant; and Alex (Ewan McGregor), a wild-side journalist. Hugo (Keith Allen) takes up residence but is found dead in bed, along with a suitcase stuffed with money. The trio decides to chop up the cadaver, bury the bits, and keep the loot—a sequence that sets the tone for the pic's several grisly comic set pieces.

SHALL WE DANCE?
1937, 101 mins, US Ⓥ ⊙
D: Mark Sandrich **A:** Fred Astaire, Ginger Rogers, Edward Everett Horton, Eric Blore, Ketti Gallian (RKO)

Seventh in the Astaire-Rogers series is a standout. All six songs have been nicely spotted with no attempt to overplay any of them. Nor is there a bad ditty in the batch. Basically the story is of a ballet dancer (Astaire) who would rather be a hoofer. Romantically the script ties him into a complicated affinity with Ginger Rogers, who is a musical-comedy star. The rumors of their marriage grow to such proportion it forces them to secretly wed with the understanding of an immediate divorce.

1937: Nomination: Best Song ("They Can't Take That Away from Me")

SHAMPOO
1975, 109 mins, US Ⓥ ⊙

D: Hal Ashby **A:** Warren Beatty, Julie Christie, Goldie Hawn, Lee Grant, Jack Warden, Tony Bill (Columbia)

Late-1960s story about the ultimate emotional sterility and unhappiness of a swinger emerges as a mixed farcical achievement. Warren Beatty is a Beverly Hills hairdresser who turns onto all his customers, including Lee Grant, bored wife of Jack Warden (latter in turn keeping Julie Christie on the side), while Beatty's current top trick is Goldie Hawn. All the excellent creative components do not add up to a whole. Warden's performance is outstanding. Hawn's excellent delineation of a bubbly young actress has a solid undertone of sensitivity.

1975: Best Supp. Actress (Lee Grant)
Nominations: Best Supp. Actor (Jack Warden), Original Screenplay, Art Direction

SHAMUS
1973, 98 mins, US Ⓥ ⊙

D: Buzz Kulik **A:** Burt Reynolds, Dyan Cannon, John Ryan, Joe Santos, Georgio Tozzi (Columbia/Weitman)

Confusing, hard-biting meller. Burt Reynolds plays a rough-hewn and alert character who has turned to private investigation in his tough Brooklyn neighborhood. He's called in by a multimillionaire to ferret out the identity of the person who bumped off a man who stole a fortune in diamonds owned by a tycoon.

SHANE
1953, 118 mins, US Ⓥ ⊙

D: George Stevens **A:** Alan Ladd, Jean Arthur, Van Heflin, Brandon de Wilde, Jack Palance, Ben Johnson (Paramount)

A western ranking with some of the select few that have become classics. Plot is laid in early Wyoming, where a group of farmer-settlers have taken land formerly held by a cattle baron. Latter resents this intrusion. His fight is against Heflin chiefly, who is the driving force that keeps the frightened farmers together. Just when it seems the cattleman may eventually have his way, a stranger, known only as Shane, rides on to Heflin's homestead, is taken in, and becomes one of the settlers, as he tries to forget his previous life with a gun. Wyoming's scenic splendors against which the story is filmed are breathtaking.

1953: Best Color Cinematography
Nominations: Best Picture, Director, Supp. Actor (Brandon de Wilde, Jack Palance), Screenplay

SHANGHAI EXPRESS
1932, 80 mins, US

D: Josef von Sternberg **A:** Marlene Dietrich, Clive Brook, Anna May Wong, Warner Oland, Eugene Pallette (Paramount)

As to plot structure and dialogue, *Shanghai Express* runs much too close to old meller and serial themes to command real attention. The finished product is an example of what can be done with a personality and photogenic face such as Marlene Dietrich possesses to circumvent a trashy story. The script relates how the heroine, China's most famed white prostitute, meets her former English fiancé (Clive Brook) on board train. Warner Oland, rebel leader, has the train held up and in looking for a hostage he picks Brook. To save Brook's eyes being burned from his head, Shanghai Lily promises to become mistress of the revolutionary.

1931/32: Best Cinematography
Nominations: Best Picture, Director

SHANGHAI GESTURE, THE
1942, 97 mins, US Ⓥ ⊙

D: Josef von Sternberg **A:** Gene Tierney, Victor Mature, Ona Munson, Walter Huston, Albert Basserman (Arnold)

Rather dull and hazy drama of the Orient. Mother Gin Sling (Ona Munson) is the operating brains of a gambling casino. When property in the district is bought up by Walter Huston, English financier, and the mother is told to fold, she goes out to get the goods on her enemy in typical Oriental fashion. Result is Gin Sling's manipulation of Huston's daughter (Gene Tierney) and his rebuttal that the girl she has ruined is actually her daughter.

1942: Nominations: Best B&W Art Direction, Scoring of a Dramatic Picture

SHANGHAI SURPRISE
1986, 97 mins, UK/US Ⓥ

D: Jim Goddard **A:** Sean Penn, Madonna, Paul Freeman, Richard Griffiths (M-G-M/Handmade/Vista)

Tale is a phony, thoroughgoing concoction. A missionary (Madonna) enlists the services of a down-and-outer (Sean Penn) to help her track down a supply of opium that disappeared a year before, in 1937, during the Japanese occupation of China. Penn seems game and has energy, while Madonna can't for a moment disguise that her character makes no sense at all.

SHANGHAI TRIAD
See: Yao a Yao Yao Dao Waipo Qiao

SHARKY'S MACHINE
1981, 119 mins, US Ⓥ ⊙
D: Burt Reynolds **A:** Burt Reynolds, Vittorio Gassman, Rachel Ward, Brian Keith, Charles Durning, Earl Holliman (Deliverance/Orion)

Directing himself, Burt Reynolds has combined his own macho personality with what's popularly called mindless violence. Reynolds is "Sharky" and the "machine" is police parlance for a team of fellow cops working with him. They have been relegated to unchallenging assignments, mainly in the cesspool of the vice squad. But a hooker's murder brings Reynolds within sniffing distance of big-time shenanigans.

SHATTERED
1991, 98 mins, US Ⓥ ⊙
D: Wolfgang Petersen **A:** Tom Berenger, Bob Hoskins, Greta Scacchi, Joanne Whalley-Kilmer, Corbin Bernsen (Capella/Connexion/Geissler)

Farfetched thriller about unlikable characters aspires to Hitchcockian suspense and surprise, but the parade of hokey implausibilities puts the viewer off. A devastating car wreck leaves real-estate developer (Tom Berenger) a disfigured mess, although his wife (Greta Scacchi) escapes virtually unscathed. Although plastic surgery restores his good looks, husband's memory is a blank. Enter a private detective (Bob Hoskins) to help Berenger figure everything out. The ever-gorgeous Scacchi has the meatiest role, that of a scheming liar accustomed to getting her way.

SHAWSHANK REDEMPTION, THE
1994, 142 mins, US Ⓥ ⊙ ▭
D: Frank Darabont **A:** Tim Robbins, Morgan Freeman, Bob Gunton, William Sadler, Clancy Brown, James Whitmore (Castle Rock/Columbia)

There's a painstaking exactness to this film that is both laudable and exhausting. The 19 years that the protagonist spends behind prison walls is a term shared by the audience. The saga begins in 1947, when bank vice-president Andy Dufresne (Tim Robbins) lands in Shawshank Prison with two concurrent life sentences. The chronicle is related in voice-over by "Red" (Morgan Freeman), a lifer who marvels at the new man's tenacity, knowing intrinsically that Andy is different and that he likes him, quirks and all. Central to the film's success is a riveting, unfussy performance from Robbins. Freeman has the showier role, allowing him a grace and dignity that come naturally.

1994: Nominations: Best Picture, Actor (Morgan Freeman), Adapted Screenplay, Cinematography, Film Editing, Sound, Original Score

SHE
1935, 96 mins, US ⊙
D: Irving Pichel, Lansing C. Holden **A:** Helen Gahagan, Randolph Scott, Helen Mack, Nigel Bruce, Gustav von Seyffertitz (RKO)

In the bowels of the earth is the mythical land of Kor. Its she-monster ruler (Helen Gahagan) has the gift and the curse of eternal life. All these hundreds of years she has been waiting for her lover to come back reincarnated. Meanwhile the embalmed corpse of the original lover (whom she killed in a jealous tantrum) lies in state until his counterpart, a grandson 15 generations removed (Randolph Scott), shows up. The ceremonials, bacchanals, ballets, and executions provide the materials for a psychopathic pipe dream. Some of the sequences are stunning, merging sound effects, camera angles, imaginative costuming, socky choreography. On the performance end, Cahagan cops honors.

SHE
1965, 104 mins, UK ▭
D: Robert Day **A:** Ursula Andress, Peter Cushing, Bernard Cribbins, John Richardson, Christopher Lee, Andre Morell (Seven Arts/Hammer)

Fourth filming of H. Rider Haggard's fantasy adds color and widescreen to special effects, all of which help overcome a basic plot no film scripter has yet licked. Ursula Andress is the immortal She, cold-blooded queen of a lost kingdom who pines for return of the lover she murdered eons ago. It turns out that John Richardson is the look-alike lover. Andress's role calls for sincere warmth as a woman in love, also brutal cruelty as queen, and she convinces.

SHE DEVIL, THE
See: Die Nibelungen: Kriemhilds Rache

SHE-DEVIL
1989, 99 mins, US Ⓥ ⊙
D: Susan Seidelman A: Meryl Streep, Roseanne Barr, Ed Begley Jr., Linda Hunt, Sylvia Miles (Orion)

Dark and gleeful revenge saga offers a unique heroine in Ruth Patchett (Roseanne Barr), a dumpy but dedicated housewife afflicted with a conspicuous facial mole. When her uninterested husband (Ed Begley Jr.) strays into the arms of a fabulously wealthy and affected romance novelist (Meryl Streep), Barr clicks into an inspired attack mode. The casting is a real coup, with Barr going her everywoman TV persona one better by breaking the big-screen heroine mold, and Streep blowing away any notion that she can't be funny.

SHE DONE HIM WRONG
1933, 65 mins, US Ⓥ
D: Lowell Sherman A: Mae West, Cary Grant, Owen Moore, Gilbert Roland, Noah Beery Sr. (Paramount)

A few highlights in the career of Diamond Lou, née Lil. Director restrains Mae West from going too far. White-slavery angle is thinly disguised, with the girls instead shipped to Frisco to pick pockets. The swan bed is in, but for a flash only, with West doing her stuff on the chaise longue in this version. West gets all the lens gravy and full figure most of the time.
1932/33: Nomination: Best Picture

SHEENA
1984, 117 mins, US Ⓥ ⊙ ▱
D: John Guillermin A: Tanya Roberts, Ted Wass, Donovan Scott, Elizabeth of Toro, France Zobda (Columbia)

There are plenty of laughs to be had, but it's impossible to tell how many of them were intentional. Attempt to install this 1930s jungle heroine in the pantheon of the contempo adventure icons fails to find a consistent tone. Orphaned in deepest Africa, much like Tarzan, a blond-tressed Sheena is raised by a remote, noble tribe and appears to be the fulfillment of a prophecy concerning a mysterious lady who will protect it in dire times. Pleasing as Roberts's statuesque physique may be, it's eye-popping in a PG-rated film to see her indulge in an *au naturel* waterfall shower, or conduct an extended dialogue scene totally in the buff. Result is a T&A kidpic.

SHEIK, THE
1921, 100 mins, US Ⓥ ⊗
D: George Melford A: Agnes Ayres, Rudolph Valentino, Adolphe Menjou, Walter Long, Lucien Littlefield (Paramount)

Edith M. Hull's novel, preposterous and ridiculous as it was, won out because it dealt with every caged woman's desire to be caught up in a love clasp by some he-man. Lady Diana has gone alone into the desert when a native guide only to be captured by a young sheik and he detains her in his palace of a tent, and that is all. The acting could not be worse than the story, but it is bad enough. Valentino is revealed as a player without resource. He depicts the fundamental emotions of the Arabian sheik chiefly by showing his teeth and rolling his eyes, while Agnes Ayres looks too matronly.

SHELF LIFE
1993, 83 mins, US Ⓥ
D: Paul Bartel A: O-Lan Jones, Andrea Stein, Jim Turner, Paul Bartel, Justin Houchin, Shelby Lindley

Sprightly, compact, and quickly paced, *Shelf Life* is a nifty little allegorical number about secondhand life in a fallout shelter where two sisters and their brother have spent nearly their entire lives. With the skeletons of Mom and Pop lying nearby, Tina, Pam, and Scotty, now well into their 30s, go through the motions of real life as they have learned it from TV, which they have managed to receive uninterrupted over the years.

SHE'LL BE WEARING PINK PAJAMAS
1985, 90 mins, UK Ⓥ
D: John Goldschmidt A: Julie Walters, Anthony Higgins, Jane Evers, Janet Henfrey, Paula Jacobs (Film Four/Pink Pajamas)

About a group of British women from mixed backgrounds on an outdoor survival course. Intimate discussions take place as the women ford streams, climb mountains, canoe, swing on ropes, or go on a marathon hike. There's one man around (Anthony Higgins), but he's almost an intrusion. Standout is Julie Walters as a bouncy type who proves surprisingly weak in the crunch.

SHELTERING SKY, THE
1990, 137 mins, UK/Italy Ⓥ ⊙ ▱
D: Bernardo Bertolucci A: John Malkovich, Debra Winger, Campbell Scott, Jill Bennett, Timothy Spall (Thomas)

Paul Bowles's classic 1949 novel of a journey into emptiness has been visualized with intense beauty. But those who haven't read the book will be left bewildered. John Malkovich and Debra Winger play Port and Kit Moresby, Americans traveling without destination or itinerary in postwar North Africa. Their 10-year marriage is unraveling while their opportunistic companion, Tunner (Campbell Scott), looks on. Pic boils down to the existential love story between Kit and Port, who are groping through the ruins of their infidelities toward whatever is left between them when all is lost.

SHENANDOAH
1965, 105 mins, US $\circledV$ $\odot$
D: Andrew V. McLaglen A: James Stewart, Doug McClure, Glenn Corbett, Patrick Wayne, Rosemary Forsyth, Katharine Ross (Universal)

During the Civil War, Stewart, a prosperous Virginia farmer, has raised his family of six sons and one daughter to be entirely self-contained. Not believing in slavery, he wants no part in a war based upon it, providing the conflict does not touch either his land or his family. When his youngest, a 16-year-old boy, is captured as a Reb by Unionists, the farmer makes the war his own business. Stewart endows his grizzled role with warm conviction.
1965: Nomination: Best Sound

SHERIFF OF FRACTURED JAW, THE
1958, 100 mins, UK $\circledV$ $\square$
D: Raoul Walsh A: Kenneth More, Jayne Mansfield, Robert Morley, Ronald Squire, Bruce Cabot (20th Century-Fox)

The starring combo of Jayne Mansfield and Kenneth More merge like bacon and eggs, and the result is a wave of yocks. Raoul Walsh directs this cheerful skit about the wild, woolly west with vigor and pace. Yarn starts off in London. More has inherited a fading gunsmith business. He decides that the Wild West's the place to sell his guns. It's not long before he becomes involved with Injuns, two warring sets of cowboys, and with Mansfield, the pistol-packing boss of a saloon. He is conned into becoming the sheriff of the one-horse town of Fractured Jaw.

SHERLOCK JR.
1924, 48 mins, US $\otimes$
D: Buster Keaton A: Buster Keaton, Kath-ryn McGuire, Ward Crane, Joseph Keaton (Keaton/Metro)

This Buster Keaton feature-length comedy is about as unfunny as a hospital operating room. There is one piece of business that is worthy of comment—where Buster as a motion-picture machine operator in a dream scene walks out of the booth and into the action that is taking place on the screen of the picture that he is projecting. That is clever. The rest is bunk.

SHE'S GOTTA HAVE IT
1986, 100 mins, US $\circledV$ $\odot$
D: Spike Lee A: Tracy Camilla Johns, Redmond Hicks, John Terrell, Spike Lee, Raye Dowell, Joie Lee (40 Acres & a Mule)

All the elements of an interesting yarn are implicit here—save one: a compelling central figure (played by Tracy Camilla Johns). The young woman is, clearly, trying to find herself. She juggles three beaux, fends off a lesbian's overtures, and consults a shrink to determine if she's promiscuous or merely a lady with normal sexual appetites.

SHE'S HAVING A BABY
1988, 106 mins, US $\circledV$ $\odot$
D: John Hughes A: Kevin Bacon, Elizabeth McGovern, Alec Baldwin, Isabel Lorca, William Windom (Paramount)

An oddly uneven and quasi-serious look into the angst of the early years of a contemporary marriage. Kevin Bacon ties the knot with teenage sweetheart Kristy (Elizabeth McGovern) and begins to fantasize about what he's going to be missing out on as a married man. It soon becomes evident why Bacon is endlessly dreaming: take away his imaginings and his home life is dull indeed. McGovern is so uncomplicated and unabashedly adoring toward her husband, it gets one wondering what such a bright guy is doing with her.

SHE'S OUT OF CONTROL
1989, 95 mins, US $\circledV$ $\odot$
D: Stan Dragoti A: Tony Danza, Catherine Hicks, Ami Dolenz, Wallace Shawn, Dick O'Neill (Weintraub)

Despite some funny scenes, sitcomish treatment of a father's anxiety over his teenage daughter's budding sexuality is mostly shallow and uneven. The widowed g.m. of a rock radio station, Tony Danza freaks out when his g.f. Catherine Hicks decides to transform his daughter Ami Dolenz from a studious wallflower into an airheaded sexpot. After a shaky opening, film picks up some wit and steam when Danza begins consulting a shrink, played with his customary sly intelligence by Wallace Shawn.

SHE'S THE ONE
1996, 96 mins, US Ⓥ ⊙ ⊡
D: Edward Burns **A:** Jennifer Aniston, Maxine Bahns, Edward Burns, Cameron Diaz, John Mahoney, Mike McGlone (Good Machine/Marlboro Road Gang)

She's the One, Ed Burns's romantic comedy has charm to burn. Mickey Fitzpatrick (Burns) is an emotionally fried cab driver who marries Hope (Maxine Bahns) after a couple of days of whirlwind romance. Mickey's brother, Francis (Mike McGlone), married childhood sweetheart, Rene (Jennifer Aniston), got a respectable job on Wall Street and has the driving need to compete with and best Mickey. The battleground between the brothers is represented by Heather (Cameron Diaz), who was supposed to wed Mickey and is carrying on an affair with Francis. Burns is a natural-born filmmaker. There's no sign of artifice in his style. The picture is also blessed with a uniformly strong cast, but it's the filmmaker himself who emerges as the most significant screen presence, assured and centered.

SHE WORE A YELLOW RIBBON
1949, 103 mins, US Ⓥ ⊙
D: John Ford **A:** John Wayne, Joanne Dru, John Agar, Ben Johnson, Victor McLaglen, Mildred Natwick (RKO/Argosy)

Western meller done in the best John Ford manner. Drama of an undermanned US Cavalry post far out in the Indian country is centered on a veteran captain about to retire. It develops into a saga of the cavalry, its hard-bitten men, loyal wives, and usual intrigues. The tale moves along easily as it shows how the troop surmounts the Indian peril. Wayne wears well in a somewhat older characterization. He makes the officer an understanding, two-fisted guy without overdoing it. Victor McLaglen gives the production tremendous lift as the whiskey-nipping noncom.
1949: Best Color Cinematography

SHICHININ NO SAMURAI
(US: THE SEVEN SAMURAI; SEVEN SAMURAI; THE MAGNIFICENT SEVEN)
1954, 200 mins, Japan Ⓥ ⊙
D: Akira Kurosawa **A:** Takashi Shimura, Toshiro Mifune, Yoshio Inaba, Seiji Miyaguchi, Minoru Chiaki (Toho)

High adventure and excitement are stamped all over this film about seven Samurai warriors who save a little village from annihilation at the hands of bandits in 15th-century Japan. Besides the well-manned battle scenes, the pic has a good feeling for characterization and time. It is primarily a man's film, with the brief romantic interludes also done with taste. Toshiro Mifune as the bold, harebrained, but courageous warrior dominates the picture.

SHINE
1996, 105 mins, Australia Ⓥ
D: Scott Hicks **A:** Geoffrey Rush, Armin Mueller-Stahl, Noah Taylor, Lynn Redgrave, John Gielgud, Googie Withers (Momentum)

An unconventional biopic about a brilliant young pianist who is driven to the edge of madness by his monstrously protective father and, as an adult, finds unexpected redemption thanks to an astonishingly understanding woman. Hicks and Sardi have tackled tricky material here: their Australian protagonist, David Helfgott, is very much alive and has a growing rep as an unconventional concert pianist in parts of Europe. His extraordinary life is intelligently charted here. The real-life Helfgott plays the piano for his screen counterparts.
1996: Best Actor (Geoffrey Rush)
Nominations: Best Picture, Director, Supp. Actor (Armin Mueller-Stahl), Screenplay, Editing, Music

SHINING, THE
1980, 146 mins, US Ⓥ ⊙
D: Stanley Kubrick **A:** Jack Nicholson, Shelley Duvall, Danny Lloyd, Scatman Crothers, Barry Nelson, Anne Jackson (Warner)

Stanley Kubrick has teamed with jumpy Jack Nicholson to destroy all that was so terrifying about Stephen King's bestseller. King took a fundamental horror formula—an innocent family marooned in an evil dwelling with a grim history—and built layers of ingenious terror upon it. The father is gradually possessed by the demonic, desolate hotel. But Kubrick sees things his own way, throwing 90 percent of King's creation out. The crazier Nicholson gets, the more idiotic he looks. Shelley Duvall transforms the warm sympathetic wife of the book into a simpering, semiretarded hysteric. [Pic was cut to 142 minutes by Kubrick soon after the premiere.]

SHINING HOUR, THE
1938, 75 mins, US
D: Frank Borzage A: Joan Crawford, Margaret Sullavan, Robert Young, Melvyn Douglas, Fay Bainter (M-G-M)

The familiar theme of a widely publicized showgirl who tosses over her career for a conservative blueblood, with later complications when his family resents her intrusion into their life, is an okay premise. But after sympathy is built up for the girl and her problems, she accepts the amorous advances of her brother-in-law, and story goes haywire and winds up in unhappy status of too many heavies with no heroine. Basic trouble with the production lies in confusing script. Story keeps on pretty well-defined track until the latter half, when it falls apart entirely.

SHINING THROUGH
1992, 132 mins, US ⓥ ⊙ ▱
D: David Seltzer A: Michael Douglas, Melanie Griffith, Liam Neeson, Joely Richardson, John Gielgud (20th Century-Fox)

An old-fashioned women's picture, this oddly titled melodrama turns out to be little more than a big, brassy Hallmark card with a World War II backdrop, combining shameless romance with predictable spy intrigue. Melanie Griffith plays a half-Jewish, half-Irish woman who goes to work for a mysterious attorney (Michael Douglas) who turns out to be a spy for the US government. The two become lovers, and despite his reluctance, she is ultimately sent to Berlin, as a spy, infiltrating the house of a German honcho (Liam Neeson).

SHIP OF FOOLS
1965, 148 mins, US ⓥ ⊙
D: Stanley Kramer A: Vivien Leigh, Simone Signoret, Jose Ferrer, Lee Marvin, Oskar Werner, Elizabeth Ashley (Columbia)

As screen entertainment, *Ship of Fools* is intelligent and eminently satisfying most of the time. The human cargo aboard the German ship *Vera* sailing from Vera Cruz to Bremerhaven (1933) is a cross section of humanity. All of the principals give strong performances, from the aggressive interpretation by Jose Ferrer as a loathsome disciple of the emerging Hitlerian new order to Vivien Leigh as a fading American divorcée who gets her kicks out of leading on admirers and throwing cold water on their burning desires.

1965: Best B&W Cinematography, B&W Art Direction

Nominations: Best Picture, Actor (Oskar Werner), Actress (Simone Signoret), Supp. Actor (Michael Dunn), Adapted Screenplay, B&W Costume Design

SHIP WAS LOADED, THE
See: Carry On Admiral

SHIPWRECK
See: The Sea Gypsies

SHIRLEY VALENTINE
1989, 108 mins, UK ⓥ ⊙
D: Lewis Gilbert A: Pauline Collins, Tom Conti, Alison Steadman, Julia McKenzie, Joanna Lumley (Paramount)

Uneven but generally delightful romantic comedy has as its lead the irresistible Pauline Collins. Collins *is* Shirley Valentine, the perfect match of actress and character. Tom Conti is barely recognizable playing a very convincing swarthy Greek tavern keeper whose specialty is the romantic sail to a secluded cove.

1989: Nominations: Best Actress (Pauline Collins), Song ("The Girl Who Used to Be Me")

SHIVERS
(AKA: THEY CAME FROM WITHIN; THE PARASITE MURDERS)
1975, 88 mins, Canada ⓥ
D: David Cronenberg A: Paul Hampton, Joe Silver, Lynn Lowry, Alan Migicovsky, Barbara Steele (DAL/Reitman)

Low-budget Canadian production is a silly but moderately effective chiller about creeping parasites that systematically (and comically) "infect" an entire high-rise population with nothing less than sexual hysteria. The star of the movie is special effects and makeup man Joe Blasco, whose bloody, disgusting-looking crawlers are seen climbing out of people's throats as well as high-rise plumbing.

SHOCK CORRIDOR
1963, 101 mins, US ⓥ ⊙
D: Samuel Fuller A: Peter Breck, Constance Towers, Gene Evans, James Best, Larry Tucker (Allied Artists)

Samuel Fuller's thin plot has a newspaperman (Peter Breck) contriving, with the aid of a psychiatrist no less, to get himself committed to a mental ward in order to identify a murderer known only to the inmates and whom the police have been unable to detect. Within all this lurks three points about Americana, each embodied in characters the fourth-estater encounters in the hospital. But all these points go for naught because the film is dominated by sex and shock superficialities. Among the grueling passages are a striptease and an attack on the hero in a locked room by half a dozen nymphos.

SHOCKER
1989, 110 mins, US Ⓥ ⊙
D: Wes Craven **A:** Michael Murphy, Peter Berg, Mitch Pileggi, Cami Cooper, Dr. Timothy Leary (Alive/Universal)

Pic seems a potential winner, an almost unbearably suspenseful, stylish, and blood-drenched ride. As it continues, however, the camp aspects simply give way to the ridiculous. The obtuse story has Horace Pinker (Mitch Pileggi) slaying the foster family of Jonathan (Peter Berg) who ''sees'' the events in a prescient dream that indicates he's linked to the murderer. That leads the police to Pinker's door, and he's caught and executed. But Horace lives on after the execution as a disembodied malevolent spirit.

SHOCKPROOF
1949, 78 mins, US
D: Douglas Sirk **A:** Cornel Wilde, Patricia Knight, John Baragrey, Howard St. John (Columbia)

Plot deals with probationary work, with Cornel Wilde as one of the officers in the local bureau. A paroled murderess, Patricia Knight, is assigned to his care, and story is based on what happens to him and the girl when love moves into their lives. Situations come together with pat coincidences that don't make for credibility.

SHOCK TO THE SYSTEM, A
1990, 87 mins, US Ⓥ ⊙
D: Jan Egleson **A:** Michael Caine, Elizabeth McGovern, Peter Riegert, Swoosie Kurtz, Will Patton (Corsair)

Very dark comedy about escaping the current rat race via murder. Unsympathetic, poorly motivated central character and flat direction nullify Michael Caine's reliable thesping. Caine is cast as a Britisher working for a NY firm who's passed over for the post of marketing-department head. Upstart Peter Riegert (way too sympathetic for the role) gets the job instead and starts throwing his weight around. After doing away with wife Swoosie Kurtz, Caine blows up Riegert (and obnoxious assistant Philip Moon) on his sailboat.

SHOESHINE
See: Sciuscia

SHOESHINE BOYS
See: Sciuscia

SHOES OF THE FISHERMAN, THE
1968, 162 mins, US Ⓥ ▭
D: Michael Anderson **A:** Anthony Quinn, Laurence Olivier, Oskar Werner, David Janssen, Vittorio De Sica (M-G-M)

Anthony Quinn plays a future pope of Russian extraction who would, if necessary, strip the Roman Catholic Church of its material wealth in order to avoid nuclear world war. Occasionally awkward script structure and dialogue, and overall sluggish pacing, do not substantially blunt the impact of the basic story (from Morris L. West's novel), as interpreted by an excellent international cast.

1968: Nominations: Best Art Direction, Original Music Score

SHOGUN
1981, 150 mins, US Ⓥ ⊙
D: Jerry London **A:** Richard Chamberlain, Toshiro Mifune, Yoko Shimada, Alan Badel, Michael Hordern (Paramount)

East meets West in a period clash of swords and culture, but with scarcely the wit, style, dramatic tension, or plausibility to justify a running time of 150 tiresome minutes for this spin-off from the eight-hour TV miniseries. Richard Chamberlain and Toshiro Mifune are top-featured in this bilingual (and subtitled) tale of 17th-century Japanese political intrigue, the former as a shipwrecked Englishman, the latter as one of the tribal chieftains vying for the title and power of shogun, or supreme godfather. The whole shebang was lensed on locations in Japan.

SHOOT FIRST
1953, 88 mins, UK
D: Robert Parrish **A:** Joel McCrea, Evelyn Keyes, Herbert Lom, Roland Culver, Marius Goring, Frank Lawton (United Artists)

Screenplay has Joel McCrea stumbling into the role of a British counterspy, aiding Herbert Lom, a real cloak-and-dagger character. Foreign agents plan to fly in a spy on McCrea's farm, and McCrea, his wife (Evelyn Keyes), and Lom greet the plane and smuggle off the spy, posing as his English confederates. Plan is to get to London, have the foreign spy meet his contact, and then arrest the pair. But the real agents, led by Marius Goring, along with the police, who want McCrea on suspicion of murder, make a chase out of it that doesn't let up in suspense until the last minute. Inventive direction keeps the story moving at a rapid pace.

SHOOTING PARTY, THE
1984, 106 mins, UK ⓥ
D: Alan Bridges **A:** Edward Fox, Cheryl Campbell, James Mason, Dorothy Tutin, John Gielgud (Reeve)

Handsome historical homage to the proprieties and values of pre–First World War landed aristocracy in England revolves around a holiday spent on an estate in 1913, as an era ends. James Mason as Sir Randolph is as world-weary as he is tired of his genuinely tiresome guests. John Gielgud eclipses the gentry as a pamphleteering defender of animal rights, opposed to slaughter as amusement.

SHOOTIST, THE
1976, 99 mins, US ⓥ ⊙
D: Don Siegel **A:** John Wayne, Lauren Bacall, Ron Howard, Bill McKinney, James Stewart, Richard Boone (De Laurentiis)

One of John Wayne's towering achievements. Don Siegel's terrific film is simply beautiful, and beautifully simple, in its quiet, elegant, and sensitive telling of the last days of a dying gunfighter at the turn of the century. Wayne and Lauren Bacall are both outstanding.

1976: Nomination: Best Art Direction

SHOOT THE MOON
1982, 124 mins, US ⓥ
D: Alan Parker **A:** Albert Finney, Diane Keaton, Karen Allen, Peter Weller, Dana Hill (M-G-M)

A grim drama of marital collapse proves disturbing and irritating by turns. Noisy pic belongs almost entirely to top-lined Albert Finney and Diane Keaton, who play affluent serious writer and housewife, respectively, and parents of four girls. First act is devoted to couple hitting absolute rock bottom, with nothing to do but for Finney to walk out into the arms of g.f. Karen Allen. Finney is a walking time bomb, exploding horrendously on one occasion before the climax when he beats his most troublesome daughter. Stripped of most of her charm, Keaton is more erratic.

SHOOT THE PIANIST
See: Tirez sur le Pianiste

SHOOT THE PIANO PLAYER
See: Tirez sur le Pianiste

SHOOT TO KILL
(UK: DEADLY PURSUIT)
1988, 110 mins, US ⓥ ⊙
D: Roger Spottiswoode **A:** Sidney Poitier, Tom Berenger, Kirstie Alley, Clancy Brown, Richard Masur, Andrew Robinson (Touchstone/Silver Screen Partners III)

Everybody, including the audience, gets a good workout in a rugged, involving manhunt adventure. Sidney Poitier is a veteran FBI man forced to engage the services of tough backwoodsman Tom Berenger to lead him up into the mountains to apprehend the villain before he makes it over the border into Canada. A self-styled macho hermit, Berenger considers Poitier a cityfied softy incapable of making it in the mountains. This sets up a clichéd enmity between the two men that one knows will have to be broken down. Poitier's directness and easiness on the screen are refreshing. Berenger solidly fills the bill as the confident mountain man. British Columbia locations give the film tremendous scenic impact.

SHOP AROUND THE CORNER, THE
1940, 97 mins, US ⓥ ⊙
D: Ernst Lubitsch **A:** Margaret Sullavan, James Stewart, Frank Morgan, Joseph Schildkraut, Felix Bressart (M-G-M)

Although picture carries the indelible stamp of Ernst Lubitsch at his best in generating humor and human interest, it carries further to impress via the outstanding characterizations by Margaret Sullavan and James Stewart in the starring spots. Sullavan's portrayal is light and fluffy—in contrast to the seriousness of Stewart in both business and romance. Practically all of the action takes place in a small shop. Stewart, senior clerk, corresponds with a girl (Sullavan) through a newspaper ad, and takes the affair with the unknown very seriously. Sullavan arrives to apply for a job and is hired. From that point on it's an intimate tale of the store and its workers.

SHOP ON MAIN STREET, THE
See: Obchod Na Korze

SHOP ON THE HIGH STREET, A
See: Obchod Na Korze

SHOPPING
1994, 106 mins, UK ⓥ ⊙
D: Paul Anderson **A:** Sadie Frost, Jude Law, Sean Pertwee, Fraser James, Marianne Faithfull, Sean Bean (Impact/Film Four)

All-style, no-content actioner is as

blank-minded as its vapidly rebellious leading characters. Set in a vaguely futuristic Britain exclusively populated by valueless kids and fascistic police, this slick, sleek, and empty joyless ride is immediately unhinged by its lack of credible forces of opposition; there's nothing colliding here except cars.

SHOPWORN ANGEL, THE
1928, 80 mins, US
D: Richard Wallace **A:** Nancy Carroll, Gary Cooper, Paul Lukas (Paramount)

A glamorous gem, stirring, finely drawn, and beautifully presented. Nancy Carroll and Gary Cooper contribute excellent work. Both seem natural and lifelike. As the showgirl Daisy living with the worldly sophisticate (Paul Lukas), Carroll's hard, smart, and strong-willed. The soldier boy, William Tyler (Cooper), is from Texas where he never saw a showgirl or a skyscraper firsthand. He bumps into Daisy accidentally, is driven to camp in her limousine, and then brags to the gang. She later weakens enough to get the soldier out of the mess. Only two dialogue sequences in the picture, both highly effective.

SHOPWORN ANGEL, THE
1938, 85 mins, US
D: H. C. Potter **A:** Margaret Sullavan, James Stewart, Walter Pidgeon, Hattie McDaniel, Alan Curtis (M-G-M)

This remake is still the wartime yarn about the crafty Broadway chorine who meets a Texas rookie on his way to France and, when he falls for her, marries him rather than disillusion him. The present version seems a softer one and as a result less absorbing. Instead of the cool schemer played by Nancy Carroll, the chorine is now generous and warmhearted. The girl's lover is no longer the menace of the earlier version, but is now the typical Walter Pidgeon man-who-doesn't-get-the-girl. Margaret Sullavan's playing is pliant, has depth and eloquence. James Stewart is a natural enough rookie.

SHORT CIRCUIT
1986, 98 mins, US Ⓥ ⊙ ▭
D: John Badham **A:** Ally Sheedy, Steve Guttenberg, Fisher Stevens, Austin Pendleton, Brian McNamara (Tri-Star/PSO)

Hip, sexless sci-fi send-up features a Defense Department robot who comes "alive" to become a pop-talking peacenik. Robot lands on top of a natural-foods catering truck and under the influence of

its sweet but tough animal-loving owner, Stephanie (Ally Sheedy). Scripters get credit for some terrific dialogue that would have been a lot less disarming if not for the winsome robot and Sheedy's affection for it.

SHORT CIRCUIT 2
1988, 110 mins, US Ⓥ ⊙
D: Kenneth Johnson **A:** Fisher Stevens, Michael McKean, Cynthia Gibb, Jack Weston, Tim Blaney (Turman-Foster/Tri-Star)

Mild and meek follow-up has an uncomplicated sweetness. "Johnny Five" makes his way to the Big City, where protector Fisher Stevens struggles to make ends meet hawking toy models of his mechanical wonder on the street. Cutie-pie store employee Cynthia Gibb orders 1,000 of the little buggers for the Christmas season. Underhanded banker Jack Weston has some other ideas for the tireless automaton, scheming to press it into service stealing some priceless jewels from a safe-deposit box.

SHORT CUTS
1993, 184 mins, US Ⓥ ⊙ ▭
D: Robert Altman **A:** Andie MacDowell, Tim Robbins, Chris Penn, Julianne Moore, Anne Archer, Jack Lemmon (Avenue/Spelling)

Exploding 10 of Raymond Carver's spare stories onto the screen with startling imagination, Robert Altman has made his most complex and full-bodied human comedy since *Nashville*. Crisscrossing 22 significant characters, this is a bemused contemplation of the unaccountable way people behave when fate deals them unexpected hands, embracing everything from slapstick comedy to devastating tragedy. Editor Geraldine Peroni has done a stupendous job juggling the story lines, never losing sight of one for too long, and expertly judging when to resume another.
1993: Nomination: Best Director

SHORT CUT TO HELL
1957, 89 mins, US
D: James Cagney **A:** Robert Ivers, Georgann Johnson, William Bishop, Jacques Aubuchon (Paramount)

Updated version of the 1942 *This Gun for Hire* comes off as a crackling melodrama. James Cagney socks over his helming and gives part plenty of meaning. Pair of unknowns, Robert Ivers and Georgann Johnson, handle themselves expertly.

Yarn is motivated by the search of Ivers, a ruthless young gunman, for the man who has paid him off in stolen money for two murders. Police have the numbers of the bills, which makes it impossible for gun to pass them. He picks up Johnson, girlfriend of William Bishop, detective in charge of the murders, and forcibly keeps her with him.

SHORT FILM ABOUT KILLING, A
See: Dekalog

SHORT FILM ABOUT LOVE, A
See: Dekalog

SHOT IN THE DARK, A
1964, 103 mins, US Ⓥ ⊙ ▭
D: Blake Edwards **A:** Peter Sellers, Elke Sommer, Herbert Lom, George Sanders, Graham Stark (Mirisch/United Artists)

"Give me 10 men like Clouseau, and I could destroy the world!" his superior exclaims in despair, summing up the character played by Sellers, sent to investigate a murder in the château of a millionaire outside Paris. His investigations revolve about chief suspect Elke Sommer, a French maid, whom the dick is convinced is innocent. The chores takes him to a nudist camp, a tour of Parisian nightclubs, where dead bodies are left in his wake, and to his apartment, where one of the funniest seduction scenes ever filmed unfolds to the tune of three in a bed and an exploding time bomb.

SHOULDER ARMS
1918, 36 mins, US ⊗
D: Charles Chaplin **A:** Charles Chaplin, Edna Purviance, Sydney Chaplin, Loyal Underwood, Henry Bergman (First National)

Shoulder Arms includes much more action than generally found in a Chaplin comedy. With Chaplin in uniform without his derby hat and cane, it says that Charlie Chaplin is a great film comedian. At the opening Chaplin is the most awkward member of an awkward drilling squad. At the finish he captures the kaiser, crown prince, and Hindenburg. Chaplin's camouflage as a small tree, during which he runs through a wood, is one of the best and most original pieces of comedy work ever put on a screen.

SHOUT, THE
1978, 87 mins, UK Ⓥ
D: Jerzy Skolimowski **A:** Alan Bates, Susannah York, John Hurt, Robert Stephens, Tim Curry (Recorded Picture)

Alan Bates, a tramplike figure, accosts a man (John Hurt) outside a church one day. Bates gets invited to dinner and stays. He tells strange tales of how he lived with Australian Aborigines, killed his own children, and learned how to cast various spells, especially a shout that can kill. Hurt is an electronic-music composer and his work counterpoints Bates's shout in a way. The story builds as the listener becomes apprehensive. It crescendos as Bates, in the tale, reduces the wife to his whims.

SHOUT
1991, 89 mins, US Ⓥ ⊙
D: Jeffrey Hornaday **A:** John Travolta, James Walters, Heather Graham, Richard Jordan, Linda Fiorentino (Universal)

Nineteen-fifties rock-and-roll fantasy winds up sorely out of tune. Set in an isolated hamlet on the Texas plains, film purports to be about the liberating effect of the birth of rock-and-roll, but as producers have not secured rights to any signature songs of that era, musical mix sounds wildly inauthentic. Tale is about a home for wayward and orphaned boys. Kid with the worst attitude (James Walters) clashes with the grim and heavy-handed headmaster (Richard Jordan). Along comes a music teacher (John Travolta), who indoctrinates the boys in the forbidden pleasures of rock-and-roll. It's the kind of hokey scenario that would fly only if aided by a camp sense of humor or the promise of a good musical number about to break out, and neither of these is present.

SHOUT AT THE DEVIL
1976, 147 mins, UK Ⓥ ⊙ ▭
D: Peter Hunt **A:** Lee Marvin, Roger Moore, Barbara Parkins, Ian Holm (Hemdale)

A nice sprawling, basic, gutsy, and unsophisticated film concerning an attempt to put permanently out of action a crippled World War I German battle cruiser. Exotic tropical settings, man-eating crocodiles, air and sea combat, shipwreck, big-game hunting, natives on a rampage, ticking time bombs, rape and fire, malaria, they're all there and then some. The oddball opposites-attract relationship between Lee Marvin and Roger Moore generally works very well.

SHOW BOAT
1936, 110 mins, US Ⓥ ⊙
D: James Whale **A:** Irene Dunne, Allan

Jones, Charles Winninger, Paul Robeson, Helen Morgan (Universal)

Basic tender romance between Magnolia (Irene Dunne) and Gaylord Ravenal (Allan Jones), romantic wastrel of the Mississippi riverbanks, has been most effectively projected by this reproduction of the classic Edna Ferber–Oscar Hammerstein II–Jerome Kern operetta. The now classic songs, "Make Believe," "Ol' Man River," "Can't Help Lovin' That Man," "Why Do I Love You," "Bill," and "You Are Love," as the duet thematic, have been retained, and three new numbers, all in a novelty vein, have been added. Dunne and Jones are superb. Robeson's "Ol' Man River" is perhaps the single song highlight, although some may be captious a bit over the camera angles illustrating "totin' the bales" and "landing in jail."

SHOW BOAT
1951, 107 mins, US ♥ ⊙
D: George Sidney **A:** Kathryn Grayson, Howard Keel, Ava Gardner, Joe E. Brown, Marge Champion, Gower Champion (M-G-M)

There are a few changes in this latest film version, the first in color. "Ol' Man River," "Make Believe," "Why Do I Love You," "You Are Love," "My Bill," and "Can't Help Lovin' That Man" are Kern tunes that lose nothing in the passing of the years. With voices of such ableness as Kathryn Grayson and Howard Keel's to sing them, they capture the ear and tear at the emotions. Grayson is a most able Magnolia, the innocent showboat girl who runs off with the dashing gambler (Keel), finds her marriage wrecked by his love of lady chance, goes back to the showboat to have her child and then reconciles with the wandering mate after a few years.
1951: Nominations: Best Color Cinematography, Scoring of a Musical Picture

SHOWDOWN IN LITTLE TOKYO
1991, 76 mins, US ♥
D: Mark L. Lester **A:** Dolph Lundgren, Brandon Lee, Cary-Hiroyuki Tagawa, Tia Carrere, Toshiro Obata (Warner)

Story is all by-the-numbers revenge stuff, although screenplay skips a lot of numbers, the better to focus on nonstop and generally unimaginative action sequences. The Japanese Mafia (yakuza) provide the cardboard-cutout villains for the good guys to knock over. Dolph Lundgren plays a raised-in-Japan supercop.

Brandon Lee (son of Bruce Lee) is his preppy, comic-relief Eurasian partner.

SHOWGIRLS
1995, 131 mins, US ♥ ⊙ ▭
D: Paul Verhoeven **A:** Elizabeth Berkley, Kyle MacLachlan, Gina Gershon, Robert Davi, Alan Rachins (United Artists/Chargeurs/Carolco)

The sensibility of the film perfectly matches that of its Vegas milieu. Impossibly vulgar, tawdry, and coarse, this much-touted major-studio splash into NC-17 waters is akin to being keelhauled through a cesspool, with sharks swimming alongside. Pic wobbles between the risible and the merely unconvincing throughout. For all the time spent backstage, no effort is made to convey a credible or detailed picture of the lives of the (mostly) women who populate this world. Worse is that with the exception of the film's two black characters, everyone in the picture is a selfish, heartless, unsympathetic user. Gershon has a little fun with her queen-of-the-fleshpot role. Tech contributions are suitably gaudy and ostentatious.

SHOW PEOPLE
1928, 63 mins, US ♥ ▭
D: King Vidor **A:** Marion Davies, William Haines, Dell Henderson, Paul Ralli, Tenen Holtz (M-G-M)

Pic has laughs, studio atmosphere galore, intimate glimpses of various stars, considerable Hollywood geography, and just enough sense and plausibility to hold it together. Marion Davies is obviously mimicking the peculiar pucker of the lips identified with Mae Murray, former M-G-M star. However, at other times the story suggests the career of Gloria Swanson, particularly with emphasis upon the custard-pie gal becoming an emotional actress. Bebe Daniels is also suggested.

SHUTTERED ROOM, THE
1966, 99 mins, UK ♥
D: David Greene **A:** Gig Young, Carol Lynley, Oliver Reed, Flora Robson, William Devlin (Seven Arts)

With a good quota of shudders and a neat suggestion of evil throughout, this is an efficient entry in a somewhat old-fashioned vein of melodrama. Susannah Kelton (Carol Lynley) has inherited an old millhouse on a remote island, and turns up there with husband Mike (Gig Young). There's a mad dame locked up in an upper story. Ethan (Oliver Reed), who heads a mischievous gang of layabouts, surveys her with a morose and lascivious eye.

SHY PEOPLE
1987, 118 mins, US 📼 ⊙ ▭
D: Andrei Konchalovsky **A:** Jill Clayburgh, Barbara Hershey, Martha Plimpton, Merritt Butrick, John Philbin (Cannon)

Jill Clayburgh is totally in her element as a spoiled middle-aged woman trying to cope with her too-hip daughter (Martha Plimpton). They are soon out of their element, though, when they travel to Louisiana. What they find is Ruth Sullivan (Barbara Hershey), the matriarch of a family of three sons, one of whom is kept in a cage and another retarded, plus a pregnant daughter (Mare Winningham). Konchalovsky and cinematographer Chris Menges offer a slow and seductive descent into this world of alligators and primordial beauty.

SIBLING RIVALRY
1990, 88 mins, US 📼 ⊙
D: Carl Reiner **A:** Kirstie Alley, Bill Pullman, Carrie Fisher, Jami Gertz, Scott Bakula (Castle Rock/Nelson)

Kirstie Alley's adulterous hop in the sack with mystery hunk Sam Elliott results in his death by heart attack. What follows involves weird vertical-blinds salesman Bill Pullman as her black-sheep younger brother. Pullman and Alley are united in crime after Pullman thinks *he* accidentally killed Elliott with his vertical-blinds equipment. Both he and Alley attempt to cover up the fatality as a suicide. Carl Reiner directs swiftly and efficiently, getting maximum yocks out of borderline vulgar content.

SICILIAN, THE
1987, 115 mins, US 📼 ⊙ ▭
D: Michael Cimino **A:** Christopher Lambert, Terence Stamp, Joss Ackland, John Turturro, Barbara Sukowa, Ray McAnally (Gladden/Beckerman)

Botched telling of the life of postwar outlaw leader Salvatore Giuliano. Cimino seems to be aiming for an operatic telling of the short career of the violent 20th-century folk hero, but falls into an uncomfortable middle ground between European artfulness and stock Hollywood conventions. In the lead, Christopher Lambert betrays little inner conflict or sense of thought, and simply does not make Giuliano interesting.

SID AND NANCY
1986, 111 mins, UK 📼 ⊙
D: Alex Cox **A:** Gary Oldman, Chloe Webb, David Hayman, Drew Schofield, Debby Bishop (Embassy/Zenith/Initial)

The definitive pic on the punk phenomenon. The sad, sordid story of Sid Vicious, a lead member of the Sex Pistols, and his relationship with his American girlfriend, Nancy Spungen, is presented by Alex Cox without flinching. Authenticity is the film's major asset. It's a world of drugs and booze, with sex lagging behind in interest for the most part. But grim as much of the film is, it's not without humor. Gary Oldman fits the part like a glove. Chloe Webb doesn't spare her looks as the ravaged, shrill Nancy. Both actors are beyond praise.

SIDDHARTHA
1972, 95 mins, US ▭
D: Conrad Rooks **A:** Shashi Kapoor, Simi Garewal, Romesh Sharma, Pincho Kapoor, Zul Vellani (Lotus)

Pic, based on the 1922 book by Hermann Hesse, takes place 2,500 years ago in India. It is about a well-to-do young Brahman who feels he must leave home and find himself and also echoes a man questing for nirvana in a confused society. Rooks has chosen to give this a surface elegance which sometimes robs the film of its needed earthiness and sensuality in its love angle and more robustness in detailing the vagaries of social aspects and values at the time.

SIDEKICKS
1993, 100 mins, US 📼 ⊙
D: Aaron Norris **A:** Chuck Norris, Beau Bridges, Jonathan Brandis, Mako, Julia Nickson-Soul (Gallery)

Daydreaming teen (Jonathan Brandis), an asthmatic outsider, seeks refuge in heroic fantasies where he is the brave and resourceful sidekick of his favorite action-movie hero (Chuck Norris). Film is peppered with moderately clever daydream sequences modeled after (and featuring brief excerpts from) Norris movies. Coached by the sage uncle (Mako) of his only compassionate teacher (Julia Nickson-Soul), Brandis quickly picks up enough martial-arts skill to compete in a karate tournament.

SIEGE, THE
1998, 116 mins, US 📼 ⊙ ▭
D: Edward Zwick **A:** Denzel Washington, Annette Bening, Bruce Willis, Tony Shal-

houb, Sami Bouajila, David Proval (20th Century-Fox)

A potentially provocative idea is played out to diminishing returns in *The Siege*. Edward Zwick's attempt to extend recent history into a hypothetical nightmare scenario descends into stock action and cartoon-like confrontations. First act has some crackle and pop, as FBI Terrorism Task Force chief Anthony Hubbard (Denzel Washington) mobilizes his Gotham-based team to get to the bottom of an Arab bomb threat. When a massive explosion at a Broadway theater wipes out scores of Manhattan culturati, Washington demands action, and Gen. William Devereaux (Bruce Willis) heads the massive force deployed on the New York streets when the president declares martial law. The Arabs, who are strictly cardboard cutouts, are bad enough, but Willis's tough-guy general single-handedly changes the character of the film from an ambitious, serious-minded thriller to a one-dimensional ''my cojones are bigger than yours'' bazooka-fest.

SIEGE OF SIDNEY STREET, THE
1960, 93 mins, UK ▭
D: Robert S. Baker, Monty Berman **A:** Donald Sinden, Nicole Maurey, Kieron Moore, Peter Wyngarde, Leonard Sachs (Mid-Century)

Quite a lively version of a celebrated incident when a gang of Russians brought out the police and the army before they could be smoked out of their hideout in Sidney Street. The East End of London in 1911 is vividly brought to life. Peter Wyngarde gives an alert, strong portrayal of the quiet but ruthless top gangster.

SIEGFRIED
See: Die Nibelungen: Siegfrieds Tod

SIESTA
1987, 97 mins, US/UK ⓥ
D: Mary Lambert **A:** Ellen Barkin, Gabriel Byrne, Julian Sands, Isabella Rossellini, Martin Sheen, Jodie Foster (Lorimar/Siren/Palace)

Told in a fragmented, time-jumping style, this subjective, hallucinatory recollection of a five-day descent into hell sustains intense interest throughout, to a great extent because of Ellen Barkin's extravagantly fine performance in the leading role. In its elaborate, jigsaw-puzzle way, film tells of how Barkin, a daredevil sky diver, impulsively leaves her home and husband in Death Valley for a quick trip to Spain to find the man she still loves, trapeze artist Gabriel Byrne.

SIGN OF THE CROSS, THE
1932, 115 mins, US
D: Cecil B. DeMille **A:** Fredric March, Claudette Colbert, Elissa Landi, Charles Laughton, Ian Keith (Paramount)

Religion triumphant over paganism. And the soul is stronger than the flesh. Religion gets the breaks, even though its followers all get killed in this picture. It's altogether a moral victory. Only one exceptional performance is registered. That's Laughton's as Nero, the degenerate emperor and musical pyromaniac as Rome burns. Most of the last half is taken up with a bloody festival staged by crazy Caesar in the arena. With utmost subtlety and a minimum of effort, he manages to get over his queer character before his first appearance is a minute old. Claudette Colbert, Elissa Landi, Fredric March, and Ian Keith are called upon chiefly to look their parts, and they manage. Frequently some badly written and often silly dialogue holds them down.

1932/33: Nomination: Best Cinematography

SIGN OF THE PAGAN
1954, 91 mins, US ▭
D: Douglas Sirk **A:** Jeff Chandler, Jack Palance, Ludmilla Tcherina, Rita Gam, Jeff Morrow (Universal)

Plot deals with Attila the Hun, the Scourge of God, and his sweep across Europe some 1,500 years ago. Particularly noteworthy is the treatment of the barbarian in writing and direction, and the manner in which Jack Palance interprets the character. Instead of a straight, all-evil person, he is a human being with some good here and there to shade and make understandable the bad. Representing good in the plot is Jeff Chandler, centurion made a general by his princess, Ludmilla Tcherina, to fight off Attila's advancing hordes.

SIGN O' THE TIMES
1987, 85 mins, US ⓥ
D: Prince (Cavallo Ruffalo & Fragnoli)

Shot on location at a music hall in Rotterdam and at the musician's studio in Minnesota, *Sign o' the Times* is a filmed treatment of Prince's touring show of 14 songs from his hit LP of the same name. Defiantly carnal in the face of AIDS-era safe sexiness, the Prince revue is set in a film noir fantasy zone where the come-hither blinking of gaudy neon honky-tonk signs flashes over an idealized back-alley netherworld. There, strong-willed, Nautilus-sinewed, lascivious women—lissome gladiatrixes of rock-and-roll blood sport—challenge the sexual imperatives of Princely machismo.

SILENCE, THE
See: Tystnaden

SILENCE OF THE LAMBS, THE
1991, 118 mins, US ⊗ ⊙
D: Jonathan Demme **A:** Jodie Foster, Anthony Hopkins, Scott Glenn, Ted Levine, Brooke Smith (Orion/Strong Heart)

Young FBI recruit Clarice Starling (Jodie Foster) seeks the help of the American prison system's No. 1 resident monster in fashioning a psychological profile of a killer. Dr. Hannibal Lecter (Anthony Hopkins) gives Starling clues as to the killer's identity in exchange for details about her past. Just as it seems the noose is tightening around the killer, Lecter, in a remarkably fine suspense sequence, manages an unthinkable escape. Hopkins, helped by some highly dramatic lighting, makes the role the personification of brilliant, hypnotic evil, and the screen jolts with electricity whenever he is on.
1991: Best Picture, Director, Actor (Anthony Hopkins), Actress (Jodie Foster), Adapted Screenplay
Nominations: Best Editing, Sound

SILENCERS, THE
1966, 103 mins, US ⊗
D: Phil Karlson **A:** Dean Martin, Stella Stevens, Daliah Lavi, Victor Buono, Arthur O'Connell, Cyd Charisse (Meadway/Claude)

Dean Martin—as Matt Helm, ace of the American counterespionage agency, ICE—succeeds in a kind of lover-boy way in taking his place up there with such stalwarts as Sean Connery, James Coburn, and David Niven. Plot focuses on a Chinese agent (Victor Buono) who masterminds a ring that plans to divert a US missile so it will destroy Alamogordo, NM, thus creating wide devastation and atomic fallout leading perhaps to global war. All Matt Helm has to do is halt this catastrophe.

SILENT ENEMY, THE
1958, 112 mins, UK ⊗
D: William Fairchild **A:** Laurence Harvey, Dawn Addams, Michael Craig, John Clements, Gianna Maria Canale (Romulus)

Smooth, impressive drama, done without heroics but with excitement, tells the remarkable story of a young naval bomb-disposal officer. Laurence Harvey arrives in Gibraltar in 1941 to tackle the Italian menace that is striking successfully at key shipping in the area. Without permission, Harvey and Michael Craig, one of the seamen, slip across to Spain and discover that the enemy base is in an interned Italian ship. The hull has been converted so that the frogmen can come and go underwater without being seen. The remarkable underwater scenes give this polished film a sock rival.

SILENT FALL
1994, 100 mins, US ⊗
D: Bruce Beresford **A:** Richard Dreyfuss, Linda Hamilton, John Lithgow, J. T. Walsh, Liv Tyler (Morgan Creek/Warner)

An awkward synthesis of autism as a clinical problem and family abuse as a social issue, *Silent Fall* is a well-crafted murder mystery that unfortunately is short on excitement and genuine suspense. Richard Dreyfuss plays Jake Rainer, a psychiatrist forced out of his profession when a bizarre double murder occurs. There are two witnesses: Tim Warden (Ben Faulkner), an autistic nine-year-old boy, and his overly protective sister (Liv Tyler). It's only when the stern Dr. Harlinger (John Lithgow) subjects Tim to his notorious authoritarian treatment that Jake takes the child under his wing. After an hour or so, pic changes gears and turns into a rather conventional thriller.

SILENT MOVIE
1976, 86 mins, US ⊗ ⊙
D: Mel Brooks **A:** Mel Brooks, Marty Feldman, Dom DeLuise, Bernadette Peters, Sid Caesar (20th Century-Fox)

It took a lot of chutzpah for Mel Brooks to make a film with only one word of dialogue in an almost nonstop parade of sight gags. Brooks, Marty Feldman, and Dom DeLuise head the cast as a has-been director and his zany cronies, conning studio chief Sid Caesar into making their silent film as a desperate ploy to prevent takeover of the studio by the Engulf & Devour conglomerate. Parallels with realities are drolly satiric.

SILENT PARTNER, THE
1979, 103 mins, Canada ⊗ ⊙
D: Daryl Duke **A:** Susannah York, Christopher Plummer, Elliott Gould, Celine Lomez, John Candy (EMC)

Christopher Plummer plays the villain

in for a change—a bank robber. The story has Elliott Gould, a teller in a branch office, get suspicious when it is the Christmas season and the bank is filled with shoppers. The robber hits and Gould's alertness inspires him to hide $50,000 in a lunch box with the police believing that the robber has all the loot.

SILENT PLAYGROUND, THE
1964, 75 mins, UK
D: Stanley Goulder **A:** Roland Curram, Bernard Archard, Jean Anderson (Focus/British Lion)

The story concerns a mentally retarded youth who hands out highly colored barbiturate tablets to youngsters in a cinema matinee queue. End of show finds a number of unconscious children slumped in their seats. All are dangerously ill. Then begins the police hunt for the donor of the tablets. Writer-director Stanley Goulder's screenplay is taut, economical, and natural in dialogue, and his direction is unfussy and alert.

SILENT RAGE
1982, 100 mins, US ⊗ ⊙
D: Michael Miller **A:** Chuck Norris, Ron Silver, Steven Keats, Toni Kalem, William Finley (Unger/Topkick)

Combination horror–kung fu–oater–woman-in-peril–mad-scientist film with more unintentional laughs than possible in the space of 100 minutes. A crazy young man chops a woman and another man to death. Chuck Norris (the sheriff) catches him but the guy is shot by some over-anxious law enforcers. One of the hospital surgeons has been working on a formula. All he needs is a human guinea pig. Now we have a murderer who is not only crazy but indestructible.

SILENT RUNNING
1972, 89 mins, US ⊗ ⊙
D: Douglas Trumbull **A:** Bruce Dern, Cliff Potts, Ron Rifkin, Jesse Vint (Universal)

Film depends on excellent special effects and the appreciation of a literate but broadly entertaining script. Those highlights are virtually wiped out by the crucial miscasting of Bruce Dern. As a result, the production often teeters on the edge of the ludicrous. Dern and three clod companions man a space vehicle. Dern kills his three shipmates and goes deeper into space. His only companions are two small robots, whose lifelike qualities are rather touching.

SILENT TONGUE
1993, 106 mins, France/US ⊗ ⊙ ▭
D: Sam Shepard **A:** Alan Bates, Richard Harris, Dermot Mulroney, River Phoenix, Sheila Tousey (Canal Plus/Belbo/Alive)

Sam Shepard transplants a couple of his famously dysfunctional families to the Old West in a bizarre, meandering, and finally maddening mystic-oater with characters literally haunted by the ghosts of those they wronged. The dialogue is mostly rambling and unmemorable and, in the case of Bates and his brogue-tinted blustering, indecipherable.

SILENT TOUCH, THE
1993, 100 mins, UK/Poland/Denmark ⊗ ⊙
D: Krzysztof Zanussi **A:** Max von Sydow, Lothaire Bluteau, Sarah Miles, Sofie Grabol, Aleksander Bardini (Forstater/Tor/Metronome)

Max von Sydow delivers a definitive performance as a silenced classical-music composer and Holocaust survivor who reblossoms from a miserable old drinker into a meticulous artist when Stefan (Lothaire Bluteau) arrives as "guardian angel." Casting is superb, though Sarah Miles's stiff delivery (in the wife role) is pic's drawback.

SILKEN SKIN
See: La Peau Douce

SILK STOCKINGS
1957, 117 mins, US ⊗ ⊙ ▭
D: Rouben Mamoulian **A:** Fred Astaire, Cyd Charisse, Janis Paige, Peter Lorre, Jules Munshin (M-G-M)

Silk Stockings has Fred Astaire and Cyd Charisse, the music of Cole Porter, and comes off as a top-grade musical version of Metro's 1939 *Ninotchka*. Astaire enacts an American film producer in Paris who falls for the beautiful commie when she arrives from Moscow to check on the activities of three Russian commissars. Janis Paige shares top honors with the stars for a knock-'em-dead type of performance, and commissar trio Peter Lorre, Jules Munshin, and Joseph Buloff are immense.

SILKWOOD
1983, 128 mins, US ⊗ ⊙
D: Mike Nichols **A:** Meryl Streep, Kurt Russell, Cher, Craig T. Nelson, Diana Scarwid, Fred Ward (ABC)

Very fine biographical drama concerns Karen Silkwood, a nuclear-materials factory worker who mysteriously died just before she was going to blow the whistle on her company's presumed slipshod methods and cover-ups. A low-down, spunky, and seemingly uneducated southern gal, Silkwood works long hours at a tedious job which presents the constant threat of radiation contamination. She finds herself increasingly at odds with management after she becomes involved with a union committee fighting decertification of the union at the plant.

1983: Nominations: Best Director, Actress (Meryl Streep), Supp. Actress (Cher), Original Screenplay, Editing

SILVERADO
1985, 132 mins, US Ⓥ ⊙ ▭
D: Lawrence Kasdan **A:** Kevin Kline, Scott Glenn, Kevin Costner, Danny Glover, John Cleese, Rosanna Arquette (Columbia)

Film strikes an uneasy balance between the intimate and naturalistic with concerns that are classical and universal. Real rewards are in the visuals, and rarely has the west appeared so alive, yet unlike what one carries in his mind's eye. Drifters Paden (Kevin Kline) and Emmett (Scott Glenn) follow their destiny to Silverado. Along the way they meet up with Glenn's gun-happy brother Jake (Kevin Costner), whom they break from a jail guarded by Sheriff Langston (John Cleese). Modern element in the stew is introduction of Danny Glover, an itinerant black. On the other side of the fence is archvillain Cobb, sheriff of Silverado (Brian Dennehy).

1985: Best Original Score, Sound

SILVER BEARS
1978, 113 mins, US Ⓥ
D: Ivan Passer **A:** Michael Caine, Cybill Shepherd, Louis Jourdan, Stephane Audran, Tom Smothers, David Warner (Columbia)

Michael Caine goes to Switzerland to set up a bank for mobster Martin Balsam, with the help of swindler Louis Jourdan. Caine and Jourdan get involved with Stephane Audran and David Warner's swindle involving silver-mines in Iran. Unceasingly cynical, the film lacks a single sympathetic character. Everybody lies; everybody swindles; and all the bad guys—and girl—win in the end.

SILVER CHALICE, THE
1954, 142 mins, US Ⓥ ▭
D: Victor Saville **A:** Virginia Mayo, Pier Angeli, Jack Palance, Paul Newman, Natalie Wood, Joseph Wiseman (Warner)

The picture introduces Paul Newman. Helping his debut is Pier Angeli, and it is their scenes together that add warmth to what might otherwise have been a cold spectacle. The plot portrays the struggle of Christians to save for the future the cup from which Christ drank at the Last Supper. On the side of the Christians is a Greek sculptor, played by Newman, who is fashioning a silver chalice to hold the religious symbol. On the side of evil are the decadent Romans and Simon, the magician, played by Jack Palance, who wants to use the destruction of the cup to further his own rise to power.

1954: Nominations: Best Color Cinematography, Scoring of a Dramatic Picture

SILVER CITY
1984, 101 mins, Australia Ⓥ ▭
D: Sophia Turkiewicz **A:** Gosia Dobrowolska, Ivar Kants, Anna Jemison, Steve Bisley (Limelight)

A passionate love story set against a background of postwar European emigration to Australia. Vibrant new actress Gosia Dobrowolska plays Nina, a young Polish girl who arrives, bereaved and alone, in Australia in 1948 and becomes one of thousands of citizens of so-called Silver City, a migrant camp outside Sydney. There she meets a fellow Pole and falls in love with him, although he's married to one of her best friends.

SILVER DREAM RACER
1980, 111 mins, UK Ⓥ ▭
D: David Wickes **A:** David Essex, Beau Bridges, Cristina Raines, Harry H. Corbett, Diane Keen (Rank)

It's about motorcycle racing. But among all the biking footage in a yarn about a "revolutionary" prototype that challenges and, natch, licks all world championship comers, there's not one memorable shot of the machine in action. The film's action sequences prove generally disappointing. Pop star David Essex is a natural as the ingenuous-looking Cockney fellow. Beau Bridges is fine as the loudmouthed American Goliath against whom David pits his derided British mount.

SILVER STREAK
1976, 113 mins, US Ⓥ ⊙
D: Arthur Hiller **A:** Gene Wilder, Jill Clayburgh, Richard Pryor, Patrick McGoohan, Ned Beatty (20th Century-Fox)

Okay adventure comedy starring Gene Wilder on the lam from crooked art

thieves aboard a transcontinental train. Only when Pryor enters the film is there some long-overdue snap and zest.
1976: Nomination: Best Sound

SIMPLE MEN
1992, 106 mins, US/UK ⓥ
D: Hal Hartley **A:** Robert Burke, William Sage, Karen Sillas, Elina Lowensohn, Martin Donovan (Zenith/American Playhouse/True Fiction)

A beautifully realized American art film. Tale of two brothers' search for their renegade father, and the major life change one of them experiences, possesses exceptional literary and cinematic qualities, as well as emotional resonance new for the director. Thesps are a constant pleasure to watch. No matter how arbitrary or bizarre some of Hartley's ploys seem at first, pic is so carefully constructed that they all resurface to pay off in the end.

SIMPLE STORY, A
See: Une Histoire Simple

SIMPLE TWIST OF FATE, A
1994, 106 mins, US
D: Gillies MacKinnon **A:** Steve Martin, Gabriel Byrne, Laura Linney, Catharine O'Hara (Touchstone)

The pairing of Steve Martin and 19th-century novelist George Eliot betrays no telltale clashing of sensibilities. Martin leavens the material—inspired by *Silas Marner*—somewhat, but this is a faithful, heartfelt, somber piece about family and responsibility. Pic's twist involves the proverbial child abandoned at the doorstep. Dour, reclusive furniture maker Michael McCann (Martin) finds meaning in his life through his care of an infant girl. The baby's biological dad is John Newland (Gabriel Byrne), the wealthiest man in the county, who is primed for a political career. Eventually, he goes to court to win back custody in a bitterly contested trial.

SINBAD AND THE EYE OF THE TIGER
1977, 112 mins, US ⓥ ⊙
D: Sam Wanamaker **A:** Patrick Wayne, Taryn Power, Margaret Whiting, Jane Seymour, Patrick Troughton (Columbia)

The plot takes Patrick Wayne, as Sinbad, on a quest to free a prince (Damien Thomas) from the spell of evil sorceress Margaret Whiting. Thomas has quite a dilemma, in that he's turned into a baboon and is fast losing all vestiges of human behavior. The scenes are hammy beyond belief. When the fantasy creatures have

center stage, the film is enjoyable to watch. Such beasties as skeletons, a giant bee, and an outsized walrus are marvelously vivified by Ray Harryhausen.

SINBAD THE SAILOR
1947, 116 mins, US ⓥ ⊙
D: Richard Wallace **A:** Douglas Fairbanks Jr., Maureen O'Hara, Walter Slezak, Anthony Quinn, Jane Greer (RKO)

Douglas Fairbanks Jr. matches do-and-dare antics of his father to make Sinbad a dashing fictional hero. Maureen O'Hara lends shapely presence as the heroine. Story concerns Sinbad's mythical eighth adventure, wherein he seeks a fabulously rich island and the love of an Arabian Nights beauty. Major production fault is that dialogue and main story points are obscure, making it difficult to follow the plot.

SINCE YOU WENT AWAY
1944, 158 mins, US ⓥ ⊙
D: John Cromwell **A:** Claudette Colbert, Jennifer Jones, Joseph Cotten, Shirley Temple, Monty Woolley, Robert Walker (Selznick)

A heartwarming panorama of human emotions, reflecting the usual wartime frailties of the thoughtless and the chiseler, the confusion and uncertainty of young ideals and young love, all of it projected against a background of utterly captivating home love and life in the wholesome American manner. Claudette Colbert is the attractive, understanding mother of Jennifer Jones, 17, and Shirley Temple, in her earliest teens, all of whom adore their absent husband and father, a captain off to the wars.
1944: Best Score for a Dramatic Picture
Nominations: Best Picture, Actress (Claudette Colbert), Supp. Actor (Monty Woolley), Supp. Actress (Jennifer Jones), B&W Cinematography, B&W Art Direction, Editing, Special Effects

SINFUL DAVEY
1969, 95 mins, UK
D: John Huston **A:** John Hurt, Pamela Franklin, Nigel Davenport, Ronald Fraser, Robert Morley, Anjelica Huston (Mirisch)

Bland, lethargic period comedy is about a 19th-century teenage highwayman. A competent cast and a good screenplay are shot down by the clubfooted, forced direction of John Huston, who seems to think that comedy is chatter, alternating with pratfall running and jumping.

SING, BOY, SING
1936, 90 mins, US
D: Sidney Lanfield **A:** Alice Faye, Adolphe Menjou, Gregory Ratoff, Ted Healy, Patsy Kelly (20th Century-Fox)

Ritz Brothers, long in vaude, make their debut in this musical. They are a riot. Ritzes are cast as performers, as are Alice Faye, Ted Healy, Patsy Kelly, and Tony Martin. Adolphe Menjou plays an actor with a Shakespearean complex and a lust for liquor. He is obviously doing a caricature of John Barrymore.

SINGER NOT THE SONG, THE
1961, 132 mins, UK ♥
D: Roy Ward Baker **A:** Dirk Bogarde, John Mills, Mylene Demongeot, Laurence Naismith, Eric Pohlmann, John Bentley (Rank)

Mills is a dedicated Roman Catholic priest who comes to the tiny community of Quantana, Mexico, to replace an older priest who is worn out from battling with bandits led by Anacleto (Bogarde). To intimidate the newcomer, Bogarde's gang sets out on a series of murders by the alphabetical method. Priest Mills, resolutely deciding to break Bogarde's power, shows a struggle in which the two gain mutual respect, though their religious opinions clash badly. Mills and Bogarde have some excellent acting encounters, though their accents, like those of many others, strike odd notes in the Mexican atmosphere.

SINGING FOOL, THE
1928, 105 mins, US
D: Lloyd Bacon **A:** Al Jolson, Betty Bronson, Josephine Dunn, Reed Howes, Edward Martindel (Warner/Vitaphone)

There are seven songs sung by Al Jolson, with one, "Sonny Boy," plugged as the theme number, sung by Jolson at three different points. Jolson is a singing waiter and Dunn the soubrette. Jolson goes for the blond, but she tells him she's off any waiter, even after he has written a song for her that she won't read. So he sings it to her on the floor. It is "It All Depends on You." A Broadway producer is in the joint. That's it.

SINGING NUN, THE
1966, 96 mins, US ▭
D: Henry Koster **A:** Debbie Reynolds, Ricardo Montalban, Greer Garson, Agnes Moorehead, Chad Everett, Katharine Ross (M-G-M)

Designed to cash in on the story of the Belgian nun Soeur Sourire and her song "Dominique," slight and frequently slow-moving production unfolds mostly in the small Samaritan House, in a slum section of Brussels, where the nun carries on her work with children. In this role, Debbie Reynolds expertly warbles a dozen numbers to her own guitar accompaniment, some nine of the songs composed by the Belgian sister.

1966: Nomination: Best Adapted Musical Score

SINGIN' IN THE RAIN
1952, 102 mins, US ♥ ☉
D: Gene Kelly, Stanley Donen **A:** Gene Kelly, Donald O'Connor, Debbie Reynolds, Jean Hagen, Millard Mitchell, Cyd Charisse (M-G-M)

Musical has pace, humor, and good spirits aplenty, in a breezy, good-natured spoof at the film industry. The 1927 era, with advent of the talkies, lends itself to some hilarious slapstick. Story has Gene Kelly and Jean Hagen as a team of romantic-film favorites of the silents, and the studio's problem of translating their popularity to the talkies because of Hagen's high-pitched, squeaky voice. Kelly's dancing is standout. O'Connor has the film's highspot with a solo number, "Make 'em Laugh."

1952: Nominations: Best Supp. Actress (Jean Hagen), Scoring of a Musical Picture

SINGLES
1992, 99 mins, US ♥ ☉
D: Cameron Crowe **A:** Bridget Fonda, Campbell Scott, Kyra Sedgwick, Sheila Kelley, Jim True, Matt Dillon (Atkinson-Knickerbocker/Warner)

There's no shortage of tender moments in this comedy about young adults in a Seattle apartment building. Linda (superbly played by Kyra Sedgwick) becomes the link between the audience and parallel comedies, including her budding love story with honest, earnest, cool dude Steve (Campbell Scott). Bridget Fonda turns in a stunning performance as dipsy Janet, in love with hopelessly bad guitar player Cliff (Matt Dillon, doing a great job as a brain-dead, self-centered, second-rate musician).

SINGLE WHITE FEMALE
1992, 107 mins, US ♥ ☉
D: Barbet Schroeder **A:** Bridget Fonda, Jennifer Jason Leigh, Steven Weber, Peter Friedman (Columbia)

Calculated attempt to cross an acutely

observed character study with a slasher pic feels like two different movies in one. Smart, upwardly mobile designer/software expert Bridget Fonda takes waify Jennifer Jason Leigh in to share her attractive Upper West Side flat. The ways in which Leigh tries to nicely insinuate herself remain beautifully observed and psychologically true. But pic gradually tilts in the direction of a production-line thriller. Both Fonda and Leigh play with an ease and unselfconsciousness that are bracingly refreshing.

SINK THE BISMARCK
1960, 97 mins, UK ⓥ ⊙ ▭
D: Lewis Gilbert **A:** Kenneth More, Dana Wynter, Carl Mohner, Laurence Naismith, Maurice Denham (20th Century-Fox)

First-rate film re-creation of a thrilling historical event concentrates almost entirely on three playing areas: the subterranean London headquarters of the British admiralty, where the battle is plotted and directed; aboard the Germans' "unsinkable" battleship, the *Bismarck;* and on board the various British vessels called into pursuit of the Nazi raider. Kenneth More plays the British captain who directs the battle with his customary and effective taciturnity.

SIN OF HAROLD DIDDLEBOCK, THE
1947, 90 mins, US ⓥ
D: Preston Sturges **A:** Harold Lloyd, Raymond Walburn, Franklin Pangborn, Margaret Hamilton, Edgar Kennedy (California)

Film segues from an actual sequence from Lloyd's *The Freshman,* made in 1923, to Raymond Walburn, as head of a top ad agency, promising Lloyd a job for having won the game. Lloyd takes the job after graduation but is forgotten for 22 years. Walburn finally remembers him long enough to fire him—which is where the fun starts. One sequence, in which Lloyd dangles from a leash 80 stories above the sidewalk, with the other end of the leash tied to a nervous lion, is standout.

SINS OF RACHEL CADE, THE
1960, 123 mins, US
D: Gordon Douglas **A:** Angie Dickinson, Peter Finch, Roger Moore, Errol John, Woody Strode, Juano Hernandez (Warner)

Nothing very novel or enlightening occurs in this production about a spinster missionary. Chief conflict is the heroine's (Angie Dickinson) emotional turmoil as her religious principles clash with her sexual impulses. Arriving in the Congo, she dramatically persuades the region's "left wing" element to adopt the Christian philosophy, but has a deuce of a time practicing what she has been preaching when a handsome RAF doctor (Roger Moore) arrives.

SIRENS
1994, 94 mins, Australia/UK ⓥ ⊙
D: John Duigan **A:** Hugh Grant, Tara Fitzgerald, Sam Neill, Elle Macpherson, Portia de Rossi (Samson/Radclyffe/Sirens)

A deliciously sexy and hedonistic comedy of morals and manners. In the early 1930s, artist Norman Lindsay (Sam Neill) became embroiled in a controversy over an etching, *The Crucified Venus.* The Reverend Anthony Campion (Hugh Grant) journeys to Lindsay's home in the Blue Mountains to convince him the painting must be removed. Campion and his young, naive wife, Estella (Tara Fitzgerald), arrive to find the unrepentant artist living with his wife/model, Rose (Pamela Rabe), and three models. Sheela (Elle Macpherson) and Pru (Kate Fischer) enjoy flaunting their frequent nudity, while the younger and shyer Giddy (Portia de Rossi) refuses to disrobe. Director-writer John Duigan injects plenty of humor into this sensual saga.

SIROCCO
1951, 98 mins, US ⓥ ⊙
D: Curtis Bernhardt **A:** Humphrey Bogart, Marta Toren, Lee J. Cobb, Everett Sloane, Zero Mostel (Santana)

The year is 1925 and in the war between French occupation troops and the Syrians in Damascus, Humphrey Bogart is a gunrunner, constantly keeping ahead of the French intelligence commanded by Lee J. Cobb. He goes on the make for Marta Toren, a girl who is being kept by Cobb. She sees a chance to escape to Cairo, but Cobb outsmarts the fleeing pair, and forces Bogart to establish contact with the Syrian leader so Cobb can try to negotiate a truce.

SISTER ACT
1992, 100 mins, US ⓥ ⊙
D: Emile Ardolino **A:** Whoopi Goldberg, Maggie Smith, Kathy Najimy, Wendy Makkena, Mary Wickes, Harvey Keitel (Touchstone)

Blessed with the from-on-high concept

of Whoopi Goldberg bringing rock-and-roll to a nuns' chorus, this infectious little throwaway has a warmhearted story and engaging premise. Goldberg plays a Reno lounge singer who witnesses a murder by her mobster b.f. Vince (Harvey Keitel). The detective (Bill Nunn) trying to bust Vince pops her into a San Francisco convent for safekeeping, where onetime Catholic-school girl promptly outrages the mother superior (Maggie Smith).

SISTER ACT 2: BACK IN THE HABIT
1993, 106 mins, US Ⓥ ⊙
D: Bill Duke **A:** Whoopi Goldberg, Kathy Najimy, Barnard Hughes, Mary Wickes, James Coburn, Maggie Smith (Touchstone)

Two trips to the convent is one too many. Suffering a bad case of sequelitis, this *Sister Act* follow-up is too formulaic and frequently pauses to sermonize at the expense of entertaining. The action opens with Deloris (Whoopi Goldberg) headlining in Vegas. Almost immediately, however, she's doing the nun thing again at the request of the mother superior (Maggie Smith), who needs help reaching her young flock. The lone menace this time around is rather pallid, coming in the form of an officious administrator (James Coburn) intent on closing the school.

SISTERS
See: Some Girls

SISTERS, THE
1938, 95 mins, US
D: Anatole Litvak **A:** Errol Flynn, Bette Davis, Anita Louise, Ian Hunter, Donald Crisp (Warner)

Totally different marriages of three sisters, daughters of a small Montana-town druggist, are clearly set out, their wedded lives often taking the happy sisters close to the brink of matrimonial smashup but always managing to surmount trying difficulties. Most of the interest centers on Louise (Bette Davis) who elopes with Frank Medlin (Errol Flynn). Davis turns in one of her most scintillating performances. Flynn's happy-go-lucky reporter is a vivid portrayal.

SISTERS
1973, 92 mins, US Ⓥ
D: Brian De Palma **A:** Margot Kidder, Jennifer Salt, Charles Durning, William Finley, Lisle Wilson (American International)

A good psychological murder melo-drama, starring Margot Kidder as the schizoid half of Siamese twins, and Jennifer Salt as a news hen driven to terror in her investigation of a bloody murder. Brian De Palma's direction emphasizes exploitation values which do not fully mask script weakness.

SITTING DUCKS
1979, 90 mins, US Ⓥ
D: Henry Jaglom **A:** Michael Emil, Zack Norman, Patrice Townsend, Richard Romanus, Henry Jaglom (Sunny Side Up)

Rather loopy story provides a framework for several fabulous character riffs and to give a little momentum to any number of enjoyable crazy situations. Two small-time hustlers make off with loot from a gambling syndicate and drive down the eastern seaboard. Hyped-up pair, acted in a marvel of improvisational style by Michael Emil and Zack Norman, meet up with two young ladies who hitch on for the wild ride.

SITTING PRETTY
1933, 80 mins, US
D: Harry Joe Brown **A:** Jack Oakie, Jack Haley, Ginger Rogers, Thelma Todd, Gregory Ratoff, Lew Cody (Paramount)

Jack Oakie and Jack Haley as a songwriting team in New York are told to go west by Mack Gordon, who plays a music publisher in the film and, with Harry Revel, wrote the score. Ginger Rogers slips in as a kindhearted lunch-wagon proprietress whom the boys happen to touch while hitchhiking westward. Oakie's again the fresh guy who goes swellheaded from success. Rogers is hemmed in by story limitations, but she looks good.

SITTING TARGET
1972, 93 mins, UK Ⓥ
D: Douglas Hickox **A:** Oliver Reed, Jill St. John, Ian McShane, Edward Woodward, Frank Finlay, Freddie Jones (M-G-M)

Story of a British prison break by a hardened convict to kill the wife he believes unfaithful has been recounted with no holds barred. The escape of Oliver Reed and two other cons is spectacularly depicted. Jill St. John becomes the sitting target.

SIX DAYS SEVEN NIGHTS
1998, 101 mins, US Ⓥ ✉
D: Ivan Reitman **A:** Harrison Ford, Anne Heche, David Schwimmer, Jacqueline Obradors, Temuera Morrison, Allison Janney (Northern Lights/Touchstone)

A passable romantic comedy, this old-fashioned popcorn picture is agreeably breezy and colorful, but lacks pizazz and star chemistry. Harrison Ford plays a South Pacific cargo pilot, Quinn Harris, who becomes stranded on a deserted island with a neurotic, high-powered New York magazine editor, Robin Monroe (Anne Heche). Just when it appears that she's too irremediably urban to cope with the Robinson Crusoe lifestyle, she starts coming around, pitching in to prove herself to Quinn. Ford and Heche make a tolerable team—decent enough company for the quick, bouncy ride the film provides. There are too many shots in which the sky has obviously been computer enhanced, and the film is almost quaint in the way the artificiality of studio-shot scenes contrasts with location work.

SIX DEGREES OF SEPARATION
1993, 111 mins, US ⓥ ⊙ ⊡
D: Fred Schepisi **A:** Stockard Channing, Will Smith, Donald Sutherland, Ian McKellen, Mary Beth Hurt, Bruce Davison (Maiden Movies/New Regency/M-G-M)

The Kittredges (Stockard Channing, Donald Sutherland), chic Fifth Avenue folk, have an incredible story to relate about a young black man who arrived at their doorstep late one evening bleeding from a knife wound. Identifying himself as Paul (Will Smith), a friend and classmate of their children at Harvard, he enters their life for a moment. Posing as the son of Sidney Poitier, he captivates the couple and a visiting friend (Ian McKellen). Next morning Paul flees. The Kittredges simply must get to the root of why anyone would go to such elaborate lengths to create such an elegant ruse for no tangible profit. Pic is in essence an examination of artifice. On that level it has few equals.
1993: Nomination: Best Actress (Stockard Channing)

SIXTEEN CANDLES
1984, 93 mins, US ⓥ ⊙
D: John Hughes **A:** Molly Ringwald, Anthony Michael Hall, Michael Schoeffling, Paul Dooley, Justin Henry (Universal)

Teen comedy about the miseries of a girl turning 16 turns out to be an amiable, rather Goldilocked film. For the girls, there's Molly Ringwald, engaging and credible as the film's angst-ridden centerpiece. For the boys, there's a bright, funny performance by Anthony Michael Hall, a hip freshman wimp. There's also a darkly handsome heartbreak kid (Michael

Schoeffling), a merciful brisk pace, some quick humor, and a solid music track.

SIXTH AND MAIN
1977, 103 mins, US
D: Christopher Cain **A:** Leslie Nielsen, Roddy McDowall, Beverly Garland, Leo Penn (National Cinema)

Very professionally made low-budgeter succeeds to a great extent in exploring the emotions underneath the skin of the cliché skid-row character. Plot takes Beverly Garland, a slumming literary type, to downtown L.A. to absorb atmosphere for a book. She stumbles onto Leslie Nielsen, who hardly ever speaks but lives in a junked trailer full of promising manuscripts.

SIXTH SENSE, THE
1999, 107 mins, US ⓥ ⊙
D: M. Night Shyamalan **A:** Bruce Willis, Toni Collette, Olivia Williams, Haley Joel Osment, Donnie Wahlberg, Glenn Fitzgerald (Spyglass/Hollywood)

A terrific last-minute twist goes a fair way toward redeeming *The Sixth Sense*, a mostly ponderous tale of paranormal communication. Prologue has the Philadelphia home of child psychologist Dr. Malcolm Crowe (Bruce Willis) and his wife, Anna (Olivia Williams) broken into by a mental case (Donnie Wahlberg), who shoots Malcolm before turning the gun on himself. The following autumn, Malcolm takes an interest in the case of eight-year-old Cole Sear (Haley Joel Osment), who is capable of seeing and hearing the dead. Writer-director M. Night Shyamalan keeps the dramatic temperature low throughout, making mood and state of mind the content of the film but resulting in a lot of downtime. Osment is the standout here with his straight-faced intelligence. Willis is at his most subdued.
1999: Nominations: Best Picture, Director, Supp. Actor (Haley Joel Osment), Supp. Actress (Toni Collette), Original Screenplay, Film Editing

633 SQUADRON
1964, 94 mins, UK ⓥ ⊡
D: Walter Grauman **A:** Cliff Robertson, George Chakiris, Maria Perschy, Harry Andrews, Donald Houston (Mirisch)

Spectacular achievement is a technically explosive depiction of an RAF unit's successful but costly mission to demolish an almost impregnable Nazi rocket-fuel installation in Norway. Unfortunately, the characters are somewhat shallowly drawn and fall into rather familiar war-story molds and behavior patterns.

SIX WEEKS
1982, 107 mins, US Ⓥ ⊙ ▭
D: Tony Bill A: Dudley Moore, Mary Tyler Moore, Katherine Healy, Shannon Wilcox, Bill Calvert (PolyGram/Universal)

Unabashed tearjerker for the most part takes place in the rarefied, monied atmosphere of upper-class L.A. and NY as leukemia-stricken Katherine Healy is the 12-year-old daughter of cosmetics tycoon Mary Tyler Moore and has had all the advantages in life, except for a father. Daddy figure comes along in the person of California congressional candidate Dudley Moore. He chucks everything for a whirlwind weekend in Gotham, where he "miraculously" manages to get ballet-addict Healy cast in a children's production of *The Nutcracker.*

DET SJUNDE INSEGLET (US: THE SEVENTH SEAL)
1957, 95 mins, Sweden Ⓥ ⊙
D: Ingmar Bergman A: Max von Sydow, Gunnar Bjornstrand, Bengt Ekerot, Nils Poppe, Bibi Andersson (Svensk Filmindustri)

Director-writer Ingmar Bergman has a morality play in this tale of a returning crusader in the 14th century who keeps Death at bay, via a chess game, while he tries to find out the meaning of life. The knight (Max von Sydow) comes back to his home, which is in the grip of the black plague. The re-creation of medieval times is evocative in its bawdiness, superstition, cruelty, and humanity. Characters abound with vitality, and Bergman wraps this into an absorbing film.

SKIDOO
1968, 97 mins, US ▭
D: Otto Preminger A: Jackie Gleason, Carol Channing, Frankie Avalon, Fred Clark, Frank Gorshin (Sigma/Paramount)

Dreary, unfunny attempt at contemporary comedy in which allegedly lovable, old-time gangster types are foiled by hippies. Jackie Gleason and Carol Channing are respectable marrieds, long since retired from their gang. Plot starts to shuffle along when Cesar Romero and Frankie Avalon, reps of a syndicate headed by Groucho Marx, insist Gleason does one more torpedo job. Mark this time is old pal Mickey Rooney, living rather nicely in prison and about to spill the beans to politically motivated crime crusader Peter Lawford.

SKIN DEEP
1978, 103 mins, New Zealand Ⓥ
D: Geoff Steven A: Jim Macfarlane, Ken Blackburn, Alan Jervis, Grant Tilly, Bill Johnson (Phase Three)

Soberly paced but absorbing tale of a small country town making its bid, via a publicity campaign, to attract tourists and industry. When a masseuse is imported from the nearest big city and Vic's Gym becomes a massage parlor and sauna, the inevitable happens. Many local males are anxious to try the parlor-style sex that previously they had only read about, and the respectable matrons pressure the police to shutter the den of vice.

SKIN DEEP
1989, 101 mins, US Ⓥ ⊙
D: Blake Edwards A: John Ritter, Vincent Gardenia, Alyson Reed, Joel Brooks, Julianne Phillips (Morgan Creek/BECO)

Blake Edwards centers again on the trials and tribulations of his favorite kind of character—the charming, womanizing sot. He freshens up his trademark formula by satirizing safe sex. John Ritter is a dissipated writer with writer's block who is always to be found with a drink in his hand and an eye on a potential sexual conquest. Ritter gets his due in any number of silly and embarrassing situations which he handles with nearly perfect comic timing.

SKIN GAME, THE
1931, 85 mins, UK Ⓥ
D: Alfred Hitchcock A: Edmund Gwenn, Jill Esmond, John Longden, C. V. France, Frank Lawton (BIP)

With Alfred Hitchcock its director, more was expected. The story appears to be run through in a straight style closely following John Galsworthy's London stage hit. Story is of a retired Englishman who sold his estate to a Scotsman. The buyer broke his word not to eject tenants on the estate and not to further build on a factory site. To assert the family's moral rights and enforce the verbal obligation, the wife connives to uncover the past of the Scotsman's daughter-in-law.

SKIPPY
1931, 85 mins, US
D: Norman Taurog A: Jackie Cooper, Robert Coogan, Mitzi Green, Jackie Searl, Willard Robertson (Paramount)

All credit to the kid players, director Taurog, and the adapters for making a newspaper comic strip readable and moving in scenario form. Skippy (Jackie Coo-

per) is so sorely depressed over the death of his poor-kid pal's dog that he goes up to his bed to cry. When Skippy's father gives him the promised bike to ease his sorrow, Skippy trades it for a dog. Sooky (Robert Coogan) already had gotten a new mutt meanwhile, making it a bad deal for Skippy, but Skippy's father makes the ending happy. Cooper's playing could not be improved upon. The small and young Coogan boy is cute in every sense.
1930/31: Best Director
Nominations: Best Picture, Actor (Jackie Cooper), Adapted Screenplay, Writing (Joseph L. Mankiewicz, Sam Mintz)

SKIP TRACER
1977, 93 mins, Canada
D: Zale Dalen **A:** David Petersen (Highlights/CFDC)

Account of the methods of persons employed to recover automobiles, television sets, furniture, or whatever on which the time-purchase buyers have defaulted. David Petersen is the poker-faced epitome of a hard-hearted, alibi-contemptuous sleuth. There is a slow pace and a lack of action, but the film involves the viewer.

SKIRTS AHOY!
1952, 109 mins, US Ⓥ
D: Sidney Lanfield **A:** Esther Williams, Joan Evans, Vivian Blaine, Barry Sullivan, Keefe Brasselle (M-G-M)

Three femmes join the WAVES, after varied romantic troubles. Plot is an adequate support for the typical musical-comedy material most of the time, with seven tunes by Ralph Blane and Harry Warren. Femme trio is made up of Esther Williams as a rich girl who left her groom at the altar; Vivian Blaine, shopgirl; and Joan Evans, deserted at the altar by a hesitant fiancé. Williams has two okay swim numbers.

SKYJACKED
1972, 100 mins, US ▭
D: John Guillermin **A:** Charlton Heston, Yvette Mimieux, James Brolin, Claude Akins, Jeanne Crain, Susan Dey (M-G-M)

Charlton Heston and Yvette Mimieux star as. pilot and stewardess of a jetliner seized by James Brolin. Heston is a most effective leader as the plane captain suddenly faced with a lipstick-scrawled demand for a course change to Anchorage, AK, where Claude Akins as a ground controller heightens the suspense of a delicate landing maneuver.

SKYLARK
1941, 92 mins, US
D: Mark Sandrich **A:** Claudette Colbert, Ray Milland, Brian Aherne, Binnie Barnes (Paramount)

Posing the problem of a wife who finds that her husband is absorbed in business and taking his marital relations for granted, *Skylark* proceeds to develop a sparkling farce. Claudette Colbert's performance of the wife is of high merit, and Ray Milland is top-notch as the business-absorbed executive; Brian Aherne catches attention as the suave "other man."

SKY RIDERS
1976, 91 mins, US Ⓥ ▭
D: Douglas Hickox **A:** James Coburn, Susannah York, Robert Culp, Charles Aznavour, Zou Zou (20th Century-Fox)

Hang-gliding stunts provide most of the interest. The political-terrorism story line is a familiar one and the screenplay is synthetic formula stuff, but the stunt work is good. The simple plot has pilot James Coburn masterminding the rescue of Susannah York and her two children after bungling police operation led by Charles Aznavour doesn't produce results.

SKY WEST AND CROOKED
(AKA: GYPSY GIRL)
1966, 102 mins, UK Ⓥ
D: John Mills **A:** Hayley Mills, Ian McShane, Laurence Naismith, Geoffrey Bayldon, Annette Crosbie (Rank)

It's a family affair with Hayley Mills starring, papa John Mills doing his first directorial stint, and his wife Mary (who writes professionally as Mary Hayley Bell), sharing the screenplay with John Prebble from her own story. Hayley Mills portrays a village girl who is a misfit. The adults tolerantly regard her as slightly idiotic, with her morbid obsession with death. This naive yarn is rescued from bathos by the evident sincerity of both star and director and by a very convincing portrayal of village life.

SLACKER
1991, 97 mins, US Ⓥ
D: Richard Linklater **A:** Richard Linklater, Mark James, Stella Weir, John Slate, Louis Mackey (Detour)

One of the freshest independent films to come along in some time. Title refers to a new species of beatnik or hippie that has some humor and wants to be committed to some ideal. People on display are nearly all white and in their 20s. There's the young man (director Richard Linklater himself) who regales a diffident cabdriver with his theories of alternate realities. He notices a woman who has been run over, whereupon the action switches to the woman's disturbed son. And so it goes with a population consisting of political-conspiracy freaks, out-of-work musicians, car fanatics, anarchists, idle girls, would-be philosophers, and proselytizers of many persuasions.

SLAM DANCE
1987, 99 mins, US/UK ⊗

D: Wayne Wang **A:** Tom Hulce, Mary Elizabeth Mastrantonio, Virginia Madsen, Millie Perkins, Adam Ant, Harry Dean Stanton (Island/Zenith/Sho)

Slam Dance is like junk food. It's brightly packaged, looks good, and satisfies the hunger for entertainment, but it isn't terribly nourishing or well made. Tom Hulce is underground cartoonist C. C. Drood, the kind of man who never lets a little thing like marriage stand in the way of a good time or a hot romance with the beautiful and mysterious Yolande (Virginia Madsen). Only one day Yolande turns up dead and Drood's the prime suspect. What holds the film together is Hulce's loosey-goosey performance which sets the tempo for the action.

SLAP SHOT
1977, 123 mins, US ⊗ ⊙

D: George Roy Hill **A:** Paul Newman, Strother Martin, Michael Ontkean, Jennifer Warren, Lindsay Crouse (Universal)

Like the character played by Paul Newman in the pic, director George Roy Hill is ambivalent on the subject of violence in professional ice hockey. Half the time Hill invites the audience to get off on the mayhem, the other half of the time he decries it. Interspersed with the roughhouse rink action are scenes delineating the confused sexual liaisons of Newman and the others.

SLAUGHTERHOUSE FIVE
1972, 104 mins, US ⊗ ⊙

D: George Roy Hill **A:** Michael Sacks, Ron Leibman, Eugene Roche, Sharon Gans, Valerie Perrine (Universal/Vanadas)

Mechanically slick, dramatically sterile commentary about World War II and afterward, as seen through the eyes of a boob Everyman. Arch achievement emphasizes the diffused cant to the detriment of characterizations, which are stiff, unsympathetic, and skin-deep. Michael Sacks plays Billy Pilgrim, the luckless loser who always seems to be in the wrong place at the wrong time.

SLAUGHTER ON TENTH AVENUE
1957, 103 mins, US

D: Arnold Laven **A:** Richard Egan, Jan Sterling, Dan Duryea, Julie Adams, Walter Matthau, Charles McGraw (Universal)

The title of Richard Rodgers's ballet music is effectively employed for a hard-hitting and commendable film about racketeering on the New York waterfront. The story presents Richard Egan as Keating, a young assistant DA. Mickey Shaughnessy, an honest longshoreman, is shot because of his efforts to eliminate the gangster elements from the docks. Shaughnessy, his wife (Jan Sterling), and his supporters follow the underworld code of not revealing the identity of the triggermen. However, Keating is persistent.

SLAVE SHIP
1937, 90 mins, US

D: Tay Garnett **A:** Warner Baxter, Wallace Beery, Elizabeth Allan, Mickey Rooney, George Sanders, Jane Darwell (20th Century-Fox)

While a lot of the acting and motivation reeks of the phony, *Slave Ship* is so effectively mounted and shot through with action that it stands up. As a couple of the last of the slave runners, Warner Baxter and Wallace Beery move along elementary grooves, the former going from one tight spot to another, and the latter playing his dumb, sentimental scalawag to the hilt. Most of the action is laid aboard the barque *Albatross*. The ship comes into the ownership of Baxter, who, with Beery as his first mate and partner, puts her in the trade of smuggling slaves from Africa to America.

SLEEPER
1973, 88 mins, US ⊗ ⊙

D: Woody Allen **A:** Woody Allen, Diane Keaton, John Beck, Mary Gregory, Don Keefer (United Artists)

A nutty futuristic comedy, with Allen brought back to life 200 years hence to find himself a wanted man in a totally regulated society. Diane Keaton again plays his foil, and both are hilarious. The Dixieland music score is just one more delightful non sequitur. The film is loaded with throwaway literacy and broad slapstick, and while it fumbles the end, the parade of verbal and visual amusement is pleasant as long as it lasts.

SLEEPERS

1996, 152 mins, US 🔊 ⊙ ▭

D: Barry Levinson **A:** Kevin Bacon, Robert De Niro, Dustin Hoffman, Jason Patric, Brad Pitt, Minnie Driver (Propaganda/Baltimore/PolyGram)

Sleepers is shrewdly packaged to appeal to a mass audience, though its revenge theme carries a questionable message. Four Hell's Kitchen teenagers—Shakes, Michael, John and Tommy—have their lives irreparably changed in the summer of '67, when a thoughtless incident involving a quick-tempered Greek hot-dog vendor results in a near-fatal accident. The boys are sentenced to a Dickensian hellhole, where chief guard Nokes (Kevin Bacon) proves to be a sadistic pedophile. In the fall of 1981, Shakes (Jason Patric) is now a journalist and Michael (Brad Pitt) an assistant d.a., while John (Ron Eldard) and Tommy (Billy Crudup) are streetsmart drug dealers and killers. Revenge theme kicks in when John and Tommy happen across Nokes. The assumption is that because the crimes against the four youths were truly terrible, the avenging of those crimes outside the legal system is perfectly in order.

1996: Nomination: Best Original Score

SLEEPERS, THE

See: Little Nikita

SLEEPING BEAUTY

1959, 75 mins, US 🔊 ⊙ ▭

D: Clyde Geronimi (Walt Disney)

Adapted from the Charles Perrault version of the fairy tale, film is no surprise in its familiar outlines. Mary Costa's rich and expressive voice for the title character gives substance and strength to it. The music is an adaptation of Tchaikovsky's *Sleeping Beauty* ballet. Bill Shirley, as the prince, contributes some good vocal work. His cartoon character is considerably more masculine than Disney heroes usually are. Disney gives credit to more than 70 contributors. Eric Larson, Wolfgang Reitherman, and Les Clark were the sequence directors.

1959: Nomination: Best Scoring of a Musical Picture

SLEEPING CITY, THE

1950, 85 mins, US

D: George Sherman **A:** Richard Conte, Coleen Gray, Richard Taber, Peggy Dow, Alex Nicol (Universal)

Sleeping City tells of two deaths in which a hospital is involved. Both victims are interns. Both, because of meager wages that all interns receive, are forced to steal narcotics from the hospital stocks and sell them to pay off gambling debts. Both have become linked with an unknown bookmaker. Conte plays a member of the police confidential squad who is planted in the hospital as an intern to uncover the mystery.

SLEEPING DOGS

1977, 107 mins, New Zealand 🔊

D: Roger Donaldson **A:** Sam Neill, Bernard Kearns, Nevan Rowe, Ian Mune, Ian Watkin (Aardvark)

Film has sharp directional flair evident, particularly in the action segments, taut performances by the large cast, and a handsome technical gloss. The script is less successful. Set in New Zealand of the near future, political thriller sees the small democracy taken over by the rightist party in power. Overnight a police state is set up, and a counterrevolutionary force of freedomfighters starts hitting back. Sam Neill projects the right intensity for a man caught up in an Orwellian nightmare.

SLEEPING WITH THE ENEMY

1991, 98 mins, US 🔊 ⊙

D: Joseph Ruben **A:** Julia Roberts, Patrick Bergin, Kevin Anderson, Elizabeth Lawrence, Kyle Secor (20th Century-Fox)

A chilling look at marital abuse gives way to a streamlined thriller. Laura (Roberts) appears to be a perfect doll wife dwelling in an isolated beach manse with successful financial consultant Martin (Patrick Bergin). In fact, he's an overbearing control freak. One night she slips off a sailboat during a storm and swims ashore while her husband believes she's drowned. Soon after Laura is ensconced in an idyllic college town, the menacing Martin is on the trail. Roberts is terrific in a layered part. Bergin is chillingly twisted.

SLEEPLESS IN SEATTLE

1993, 104 mins, US

D: Nora Ephron **A:** Tom Hanks, Meg Ryan, Bill Pullman, Ross Malinger, Rosie O'Donnell (Tri-Star)

Shamelessly romantic comedy delivers ample warmth and some explosively funny moments. Sam (Tom Hanks) is still grieving over the death of his wife when his son Jonah (Ross Malinger) phones a late-night radio call-in show saying he thinks the solution is for Dad to remarry. Sam reluctantly gets on the line and ends up spilling his guts. Among those listening is Annie (Meg Ryan), a just-engaged newspaper reporter. She finds herself increasingly obsessed with "Sleepless in Seattle," Sam's on-air handle. Since the big question isn't "if," but "when" and "how," the film loses considerable momentum about two thirds through before rallying for a heart-tugging finale.

1993: Nominations: Best Original Screenplay, Song ("A Wink and a Smile")

SLEEP, MY LOVE
1948, 94 mins, US
D: Douglas Sirk **A:** Claudette Colbert, Robert Cummings, Don Ameche, Hazel Brooks, George Coulouris (United Artists)

Basic story is the familiar one of the man who wants to kill off his wealthy wife so he can marry the sex trollop. Development, however, brings in some new angles. Claudette Colbert is the healthy, wealthy wife who is being stealthily drugged by husband Don Ameche. Under drugged hypnosis, she is made to do strange things that indicate a mental crackup.

SLEEPWALKERS
1992, 91 mins, US Ⓥ ⊙
D: Mick Garris **A:** Brian Krause, Madchen Amick, Alice Krige, Jim Haynie, Cindy Pickett (Ion/Victor & Grais)

New approach to the vampire legend is an idiotic horror potboiler. Brian Krause and mom Alice Krige are incestuous monsters called Sleepwalkers who survive by draining the life force from virgin girls. Stephen King's screenplay has no internal logic and relies wholly on stupid gimmicks like the monsters' ability to become invisible and their vulnerability to cats.

SLEEP WITH ME
1994, 85 mins, US Ⓥ
D: Rory Kelly **A:** Eric Stoltz, Meg Tilly, Craig Sheffer, Todd Field, Susan Traylor, Quentin Tarantino (Castleberg/August)

Group portrait of twentysomethings in romantic disarray slowly gathers interest. Script is structured around several large-scale social events—some parties, a dinner, and a couple of poker games—each of which was written by a different writer. A hilarious recurring riff by Quentin Tarantino, in which he delivers a convoluted but coherent interpretation of *Top Gun* as a gay film, packs more punch than anything else in the picture.

SLEEPY HOLLOW
1999, 105 mins, US Ⓥ ⊙
D: Tim Burton **A:** Johnny Depp, Christina Ricci, Miranda Richardson, Michael Gambon, Casper Van Dien, Jeffrey Jones (Rudin/American Zoetrope/Mandalay/Paramount)

Tim Burton's *Sleepy Hollow* is an entertainingly eccentric horror tale that envelopes the audience in a dreamy and bloody nightmare. Washington Irving's classic story has been radically reconceived to maximize the mayhem. In 1799, NYC constable Ichabod Crane (Johnny Depp) is sent on a two-day journey up the river to investigate three grisly beheadings near Sleepy Hollow, a mostly Dutch community haunted by a violent past. Welcomed at the home of the village's richest citizen, Baltus Van Tassel (Michael Gambon), Ichabod hears of the Hessian Horseman (Christopher Walken), a German mercenary who slew settlers on behalf of the English during the Revolutionary War before being killed himself. Tousled, obstinate, and resolute in his rationalism, Depp is engaging as the thoughtful outsider who takes on the literal demon of an insular community.

1999: Art Direction
Nominations: Cinematography, Costume Design

SLENDER THREAD, THE
1965, 98 mins, US
D: Sydney Pollack **A:** Sidney Poitier, Anne Bancroft, Telly Savalas, Steven Hill, Ed Asner (Athene/Paramount)

As a showy vehicle for talents of Sidney Poitier and Anne Bancroft, the production offers mounting tension, but could have been improved through more lucid writing. Story is of a distraught woman who has taken an overdose of barbiturates and phones a clinic. Film takes its title from the telephone line, which suddenly becomes a slender thread that Poitier, a college-student volunteer who answers femme's call, must not break if he is to save her life.

1965: Nominations: Best B&W Costume Design, B&W Art Direction

SLEUTH
1973, 138 mins, UK Ⓥ ⊙
D: Joseph L. Mankiewicz **A:** Laurence Olivier, Michael Caine (Palomar/20th Century Fox)

Anthony Shaffer's topnotch screenplay of his legit hit provides Laurence Olivier and especially Michael Caine with two of their best roles. Olivier is outstanding as the famed mystery novelist and society figure who is galled at the prospect of losing his wife to Caine. Latter is sensational as the hairdresser who eventually proves himself worthy of playing the game of cat and mouse with which Olivier seeks to avenge his honor.

1972: Nominations: Best Director, Actor (Michael Caine, Lawrence Olivier), Original Score

SLIDING DOORS
1998, 108 mins, UK/US ⓥ ⊙

D: Peter Howitt **A:** Gwyneth Paltrow, John Hannah, John Lynch, Jeanne Tripplehorn, Zara Turner, Douglas McFerran (Mirage/Miramax/Paramount)

Sliding Doors is a frothy, lightweight romantic comedy that strives to seem richer and more complex than it really is. Helen (Paltrow) is fired from her job, mugged by a purse-snatcher and deceived by her live-in boyfriend, Gerry (John Lynch). But the latter turn of events is one Helen sees only in an alternative reality triggered when the sliding doors of a subway car close on her. Picture plays out on parallel tracks: what might have happened had she made the train—or not. Either Helen arrives home early to find Gerry in the sack with his former g.f., Lydia (Jeanne Tripplehorn), or she vaguely suspects he is cheating on her based on odd hints. Picture is built around Paltrow, who very nearly shines as a young career woman caught up short by professional and personal setbacks. Her pain at being betrayed is gradually offset by the amorous attentions of James (John Hannah), whom the actor makes almost impossibly charming and tactful.

SLING BLADE
1996, 136 mins, US ⓥ ⊙

D: Billy Bob Thornton **A:** Billy Bob Thornton, Dwight Yoakam, J. T. Walsh, John Ritter, Lucas Black, Natalie Canderday (Shooting Gallery)

A slowly accruing character study of Southern misfits that possesses the remorseless inevitability of a Greek tragedy, *Sling Blade* makes a forceful but uneven cut. This talented directorial debut by actor-writer Billy Bob Thornton has its effectiveness diluted by serious overlength and a monotonous, unmodulated tone. A patient in a mental hospital, Karl Childers (Thornton), due to be released, tells how when he was about 12 he hacked up a neighbor and his own mother who were

having sex. Karl takes up residence with an unhappy young boy (Lucas Black) and his widowed mother, Linda (Natalie Canderday). Here he comes into contact with another outcast, Vaughan (John Ritter), as well as Linda's boyfriend (country singer Dwight Yoakam). Slowly, the gears of Thornton's script start to turn toward its inexorable climax.

SLIPPER AND THE ROSE: THE STORY OF CINDERELLA, THE
1976, 146 mins, UK ⓥ ▭

D: Bryan Forbes **A:** Richard Chamberlain, Gemma Craven, Annette Crosbie, Edith Evans, Michael Hordern (Paradine)

What script has managed to do so surprisingly well is first of all to modernize the classic Cinderella tale, making it entertaining and (almost) believable for adults while preserving basic pattern and texture of the original for the youngsters. Richard Chamberlain makes a believable, feet-on-the-ground Prince, Gemma Craven is a pretty and very effective Cinderella.

1977: Nomination: Best Adapted Score, Song

SLIPSTREAM
1989, 101 mins, UK ⓥ

D: Steven Lisberger **A:** Mark Hamill, Bob Peck, Bill Paxton, Kitty Aldridge, Ben Kingsley, F. Murray Abraham (Entertainment)

British-made sci-fi adventure romp seems to be offering some kind of ecological message; the film's version of Earth is a place ruined by pollution with the planet washed clean by a river of wind called the "Slipstream." Lawman Mark Hamill and partner Kitty Aldridge capture Bob Peck, wanted for murder. When adventurer Bill Paxton discovers there is a price on Peck's head, he snatches him and makes his escape down the Slipstream. Strong points are the stunning locations (Turkey and the Yorkshire moors), the performances by Hamill and Aldridge, plus impressive aircraft and technical effects.

SLITHER
1973, 98 mins, US ⓥ

D: Howard Zieff **A:** James Caan, Peter Boyle, Sally Kellerman, Louise Lasser, Allen Garfield (M-G-M)

W. D. Richter's first produced script is a smash achievement in structure and dialogue. James Caan is superb as a likable paroled car thief whose incidental friendship with Richard B. Shull, an embezzler, leads him into contact with a bizarre set of characters, some in search of a concealed fortune, others determined to thwart the treasure hunt. The characters road-run over the countryside, where a couple of ominous black vans and several ordinary-looking businessmen create a mood of latent terror.

SLIVER
1993, 106 mins, US ⓥ ⊙ ▱
D: Phillip Noyce **A:** Sharon Stone, William Baldwin, Tom Berenger, Polly Walker, Colleen Camp, Martin Landau (Paramount)

Cold, inaccessible yarn about murder and voyeurism is too leisurely about getting where it needs to go and doesn't fully develop what should be its core: a just-divorced woman (Sharon Stone) drawn into a kinky, voyeuristic relationship with mysterious younger man (William Baldwin). Carly (Stone) is a book editor who moves into a new building and catches the eye of both Zeke (Baldwin), a computer whiz, and Jack (Tom Berenger), a burned-out writer who comes on strong right away. Carly discovers Zeke owns the building, has each unit wired with intrusive video cameras, and that there's been a series of murders there.

SLOW DANCING IN THE BIG CITY
1978, 101 mins, US
D: John G. Avildsen **A:** Paul Sorvino, Anne Ditchburn, Nicolas Coster, Anita Dangler, Hector Jaime Mercado (United Artists)

A simple boy-meets-girl tale, or in this case, dancer meets columnist. Anne Ditchburn, a lovely dancer and choreographer, meets Paul Sorvino, the columnist. Sorvino's just terrific here. A number of dancing scenes featuring Ditchburn—performances, rehearsals, and a solo on the roof of a Manhattan apartment—are among the production's high points. Second genuinely touching plot concerns a young ghetto kid Sorvino is writing about and his struggle to overcome the harsh city. Somewhere on the cutting-room floor probably is a fine film.

SLUMBER PARTY MASSACRE
(UK: SLUMBER PARTY MURDERS)
1982, 84 mins, US ⓥ
D: Amy Jones **A:** Michele Michaels, Robin Stille, Michael Villela, Andre Honore (Santa Fe)

Entertaining terror thriller concerns high-school girls having a sleep-over party, with ''let's scare 'em'' antics by the boyfriends. Meanwhile, a mad killer is in the vicinity, wasting kids of both sexes in bloody fashion with a portable drill and various wicked knives. Helmer Amy Jones develops some very stylish sequences.

SLUMBER PARTY MURDERS
See: Slumber Party Massacre

SMALL BACK ROOM, THE
(AKA: HOUR OF GLORY)
1949, 106 mins, UK
D: Michael Powell, Emeric Pressburger **A:** David Farrar, Kathleen Byron, Jack Hawkins, Cyril Cusack, Michael Gough, Leslie Banks (London/Archers)

Central character is Sammy Rice, scientist and research worker, whose lame foot has made him a complex individual. Although becoming extremely unpopular by his frank and adverse comments on a new type of antitank gun, he redeems himself by dismantling a booby bomb which is the enemy's latest secret weapon. Latter scene is handled to extract every ounce of suspense.

SMALLEST SHOW ON EARTH, THE
(AKA: BIG TIME OPERATORS)
1957, 81 mins, UK ⓥ
D: Basil Dearden **A:** Bill Travers, Virginia McKenna, Leslie Phillips, Peter Sellers, Margaret Rutherford, Bernard Miles (British Lion)

A shrewd and bright comedy around a small, derelict picture house inherited by a young struggling writer. The theater is adjacent to the mainline railroad station. The staff comprises three ancients—Margaret Rutherford, who played the piano in the silent days, but now sits at the cash desk; Peter Sellers, the projectionist with a weakness for whiskey; and Bernard Miles, a doorman and general handyman. The film is loaded with delightful touches, and there's one prolonged laughter sequence when the projectionist is on a drinking bout and Bill Travers takes over the booth.

SMALL FACES
1996, 102 mins, UK ⓥ
D: Gillies MacKinnon **A:** Claire Higgins, Iain Robertson, Joseph McFadden, J. S. Duffy (Skyline/BBC)

The violent flip side to the swinging sixties is captured to powerful effect in a drama of restless hormones and teen confusion. Setting is Glasgow, 1968, where widow Lorna MacLean (Claire Higgins, good in a shaded performance) has her hands full with her three teenage kids: screwed-up Bobby (J. S. Duffy), who runs with the gang led by thug Charlie Sloan (Gerry Sweeney); sensitive Alan (Joseph McFadden), who just wants to go to art school; and 13-year-old midget Lex (Iain Robertson), who gets drawn into the escalating violence that's the only escape valve for tenement youths in the north.

SMALL TOWN GIRL
1936, 95 mins, US
D: William A. Wellman A: Janet Gaynor, Robert Taylor, Binnie Barnes, Lewis Stone, James Stewart (M-G-M)

Romance with nice comedy sequences gives a few neat twists to the ancient plot of the obscure Cinderella who marries into the wealthy family. Gaynor displays considerable authority in her performance. Taylor looks like the dames like him to look, and he acts like the boys can okay him.

1953: Nomination: Best Song ("My Flaming Heart")

SMALL TOWN GIRL
1953, 93 mins, US ⓥ
D: Leslie Kardos A: Jane Powell, Farley Granger, Ann Miller, S. Z. Sakall, Bobby Van (M-G-M)

An engaging round of light musical comedy has a plot with just enough substance to hold the attention without wearing. Jane Powell and Farley Granger are the chief exponents of young love and both carry a major portion of the entertainment to excellent results. Young Bobby Van in a song-dance-comedy spot that impresses the most. Shapely Ann Miller exposes her gams in two hot production pieces as well.

SMALL TOWN IN TEXAS, A
1976, 95 mins, US ⓥ
D: Jack Starrett A: Timothy Bottoms, Susan George, Bo Hopkins, Art Hindle, John Karlen (CoCaCo)

Plot picks up Timothy Bottoms en route home from a prison stretch to reunite with girlfriend Susan George and their out-of-wedlock son, also to contemplate revenge on Bo Hopkins, who busted him on a pot charge and is now involved with George. The film jettisons believability to concentrate on stunt crashes and explosions. Bo Hopkins does an excellent job of conveying the sheriff's unsettling mixture of boyish charm and viciousness.

SMALL WORLD OF SAMMY LEE, THE
1963, 107 mins, UK
D: Ken Hughes A: Anthony Newley, Julia Foster, Robert Stephens, Wilfrid Brambell, Warren Mitchell (British Lion/Bryanston Seven Arts)

A sharp, snide commentary on the sleazy side of Soho emerges as a first-class vehicle for Anthony Newley. Newley is the smart-aleck emcee of a shabby strippery. Between churning out tired, near-blue gags and introducing the peelers, he is an inveterate poker and horse player. The story consists entirely of his efforts to raise $840 in five hours to pay off a gangster-bookie who is threatening to cut him up. Hughes's uninhibited screenplay is incisive and tart while his direction has deft assurance.

SMASHING TIME
1967, 96 mins, UK
D: Desmond Davis A: Rita Tushingham, Lynn Redgrave, Michael York, Anna Quayle, Ian Carmichael (Paramount/Solmur)

Rita Tushingham and Lynn Redgrave are a pair of girls from the north of England who go to London. Femmes play Laurel and Hardy characters, Tushingham as the bewildered Stan, Redgrave the aggressive Oliver. George Melly's original screenplay might be the further misadventures of the Hollywood comics in change-of-sex garb. Extensive use is made of a swinging London background, with many of its characters, particularly the fey.

SMASH PALACE
1981, 100 mins, New Zealand ⓥ ⊙
D: Roger Donaldson A: Bruno Lawrence, Anna Jemison, Greer Robson, Keith Aberdein (Aadvark)

A thoroughly remarkable drama about a marital breakup which erupts into an impulsive kidnapping of a child by its father and a totally believable escalation to the brink of tragedy. The eponymous location is a vast junkyard of cars, established by Al Shaw's father, and now the pannier of hope for Al, a former Grand Prix driver, returned to a remote New Zealand country town with a pregnant French wife.

SMILE
1975, 113 mins, US ⓥ
D: Michael Ritchie A: Bruce Dern, Barbara Feldon, Michael Kidd, Geoffrey Lewis, Colleen Camp (United Artists)

Hilarious but ultimately shallow put-down of teenage beauty contests. Script depicts the climactic days of a statewide beauty competition, where a group of adolescent girls gets caught up in the mélange of mercantilism, boosterism, and backstage politics attendant to such tribal rites. Excellent performances come from Bruce Dern, a compulsively upbeat small-town mobile-home dealer and chief judge of the contest, and Michael Kidd, imported big-time choreographer whose career is in a slump.

SMILES OF A SUMMER NIGHT
See: Sommarnattens Leende

SMILING LIEUTENANT, THE
1931, 88 mins, US
D: Ernst Lubitsch **A:** Maurice Chevalier, Claudette Colbert, Miriam Hopkins, Charles Ruggles (Paramount)

Story is a pert yarn of free morals and makes no attempt to be otherwise. Maurice Chevalier steals Claudette Colbert, a violinist, from Charles Ruggles. She moves in and stays until the officer becomes embroiled with Miriam Hopkins as the unsophisticated and plain but willing princess whom he has to marry. Thereafter it's something of a contest to lure the lieutenant into the princess' chamber. Film's real weakness is in the disappointing Oscar Straus score of four numbers.
1931/32: Nomination: Best Picture

SMILIN' THROUGH
1932, 96 mins, US
D: Sidney Franklin **A:** Norma Shearer, Fredric March, Leslie Howard, O. P. Heggie, Ralph Forbes (M-G-M)

Norma Shearer reveals a fine feeling for this old-fashioned but perennial romantic role. Story is about as sentimental as it could be without spilling over, and the trick of using current slang in the love scenes serves to emphasize by its very nonchalance the depth of the feeling. Many sequences are a bit overdone, for no good reason save that of pictorial effect, and the episode of the tragic wedding is held a fatal instant too long.
1932/33: Nomination: Best Picture

SMOKE
1995, 112 mins, US
D: Wayne Wang **A:** William Hurt, Harvey Keitel, Harold Perrineau Jr., Forest Whitaker, Victor Argo (Miramax/Nippon/Smoke)

There's plenty of smoke but not a great deal of fire in *Smoke,* which unites the talent of director Wayne Wang and cult novelist Paul Auster, who provides his first original screenplay. Episodic pic is pleasant but insubstantial. Most of the 15 or so characters in the film hang out at the Brooklyn Cigar Store, which is managed by Auggie Wren (Harvey Keitel). Pic is divided into five chapters. Chapter one features William Hurt as a novelist saved from being hit by a truck by the intervention of a black teenager who calls himself Rashid (Harold Perrineau Jr.). Paul is so grateful he offers the boy accommodation for a couple of nights. Hurt gives another subdued performance, but it's Keitel, extremely relaxed as Auggie, who gives the film most of its charm.

SMOKEY AND THE BANDIT
1977, 96 mins, US ⓥ ⊙
D: Hal Needham **A:** Burt Reynolds, Sally Field, Jerry Reed, Jackie Gleason (Universal/Rastar)

The plot is simple: rich father-son team of blowhards Pat McCormick and Paul Williams offer a reward if Reynolds will truck a load of beer from Texas to Georgia; Reynolds and buddy Reed race to meet the deadline: Field complicates matters as a not-yet bride who flees beau Mike Henry, son of outraged Gleason, who then chases them all across the southeast. There is a parade of roadside set pieces involving many different ways to crash cars. Field is the hottest element in the film.

SMOKEY AND THE BANDIT II
1980, 101 mins, US ⓥ ⊙
D: Hal Needham **A:** Burt Reynolds, Jackie Gleason, Sally Field, Dom DeLuise, Jerry Reed (Universal/Rastar)

Stale sequel seems to be evidence of going through the motions for money instead of fun. Here, Reynolds is hired to haul a pregnant elephant to the Republican Convention. The heavy reliance on elephant gags quite literally slows down the film.

SMOKEY AND THE BANDIT III
1983, 88 mins, US ⓥ ⊙ ▢
D: Dick Lowry **A:** Jackie Gleason, Paul Williams, Pat McCormick, Jerry Reed, Mike Henry (Universal)

Filmmakers have wisely returned to the nonstop car-chasing destruction derby of the first movie. But the sense of fun in that original is missing and the countless smashups and near misses are orchestrated randomly. Result is a patchwork of arbitrary mayhem as Jackie Gleason's sheriff, who tires of retirement in Florida, pursues Jerry Reed and sidekick Colleen Camp through the south.

SMOKING/NO SMOKING
1993, 135 mins, France ⓥ ◉
D: Alain Resnais **A:** Sabine Azema, Pierre Arditi (Arena/Camera One/France 2 Cinema)

Smoking and *No Smoking* light up the screen and rev up the intellect. In having the vision and audacity to compress Alan Ayckbourn's variation-loaded octet of plays into two freestanding but richly complementary feature films, Alain Resnais may have made the first self-regulating interactive movie. The ingenious premise is to eavesdrop on the lives, loves, aspirations, and disappointments of nine characters (all played by Sabine Azema and Pierre Arditi). Each film flows from a similar opening sequence: faculty wife Celia Teasdale goes onto the terrace, eyes a pack of cigarettes, and (according to pic's title) either lights up or doesn't. At about the 55-minute point, after recounting one story straight, each pic then asks "what if?" and explores a parallel universe peopled by the same characters.

SMUGGLERS, THE
See: The Man Within

SMULTRONSTALLET
(US: WILD STRAWBERRIES)
1957, 90 mins, Sweden ⓥ ◉
D: Ingmar Bergman **A:** Victor Sjostrom, Bibi Andersson, Ingrid Thulin, Gunnar Bjornstrand (Svensk Filmindustri)

Grim drama deals with an old man (Victor Sjostrom) who is on his way to get an honorary doctorate degree after 50 years as a doctor. He is accompanied by his daughter-in-law (Ingrid Thulin). The trip becomes a reliving of the old man's life as he realizes he led an empty life due to his stuffiness, egotism, and inability to really love and feel. Nightmares, dreams, and reminiscences are expertly blended as space and time are broken to work on the various levels of the man's thoughts.

SNAKE EYES
1998, 99 mins, US ⓥ ◉ ▭
D: Brian De Palma **A:** Nicolas Cage, Gary Sinise, John Heard, Carla Gugino, Stan Shaw, Kevin Dunn (DeBart)

Snake Eyes is snakebit. After a razzle-dazzle opening, this hyperactive thriller about a corrupt cop's investigation of a political assassination devolves into a mere excuse for a stylistic exercise by director Brian De Palma. Atlantic City homicide Det. Rick Santoro (Nicolas Cage) takes a stadium ringside seat next to his boyhood friend, navy commander Kevin Dunne (Gary Sinise) and watches the first round of the title fight, which concludes with a sniper shooting of the US secretary of defense, who was sitting in the row behind Santoro. Although Dunne manages to nail the apparent assassin, Santoro has the stadium doors locked in hopes of finding other suspects among the 14,000 fight fans. His suspicions are aroused when a videotape replay reveals that the champ went down after a phantom punch. Cage supplies beaucoup energy, but his hustler-cop character provides little else in which he can invest his talent. Sinise wears an increasingly grim demeanor in a part that comes to make no sense.

SNAKE EYES
See: Dangerous Game

SNAKE PIT, THE
1948, 107 mins, US
D: Anatole Litvak **A:** Olivia de Havilland, Mark Stevens, Leo Genn, Celeste Holm, Leif Erickson (20th Century-Fox)

Picture probes the subject of mental illness with a razor-sharp forthrightness. Olivia de Havilland is a young bride who goes insane and is committed to an institution for treatment. An understanding medico (Leo Genn) uses kindness and knowledge of mental ills to restore her. De Havilland's performance is top gauge. Genn goes about his part of the doctor with a quietness that gives it strength and Mark Stevens is excellent as De Havilland's husband.
1948: Best Sound Recording
Nominations: Best Picture, Director, Actress (Olivia de Havilland), Screenplay, Scoring of a Dramatic Picture

SNEAKERS
1992, 125 mins, US ⓥ ◉
D: Phil Alden Robinson **A:** Robert Redford, Dan Aykroyd, Ben Kingsley, Mary McDonnell, River Phoenix, Sidney Poitier (Universal)

Slick, hip, liberal, high-tech, all-star buddy spy comic-caper pic serves up a breezy good time. Film gets off to a good start demonstrating the skill of Redford's company in cracking security systems. His gang of fun-loving experts sports a full complement of shady backgrounds: Sidney Poitier was fired from the CIA, Dan Aykroyd is an ex-con, David Strathairn is a blind wiretapping and audio expert, and River Phoenix changed his school grades by computer. Two alleged agents from the top-secret National Security Agency enlist Redford's services to recover a mysterious black box that turns out to contain a device that can penetrate the computer systems of vital services.

SNIPER
1993, 98 mins, US Ⓥ ⊙
D: Luis Llosa **A:** Tom Berenger, Billy Zane, J. T. Walsh, Aden Young, Ken Radley (Baltimore/Tri-Star)

An expertly directed psychological thriller is undermined by underdeveloped characters and pedestrian dialogue. Tom Berenger essays a marine sniper in Panama. Pic quickly establishes sniping as a lonely profession shunned even by other gung-ho marines. He's accompanied by an ambitious young Washington bureaucrat, Richard Miller (Billy Zane), who is so green he doesn't really need camouflage. The hostile interplay between the emotionally detached veteran and the cocky youngster is strictly textbook, as is their eventual male bonding.

SNOOPY, COME HOME
1972, 80 mins, US Ⓥ ⊙
D: Bill Melendez (Melendez)

Second cartoon feature based upon Charles M. Schulz's cartoon creations focuses most attention on the independent beagle who is the despair of his master, Charlie Brown. Schulz has written the story of the adventures of Snoopy as he leaves home to try to find Lila, his original owner, who writes from the hospital that she needs him.

SNOWS OF KILIMANJARO, THE
1952, 113 mins, US Ⓥ
D: Henry King **A:** Gregory Peck, Susan Hayward, Ava Gardner, Hildegarde Neff, Leo G. Carroll (20th Century-Fox)

The script broadens the 1927 Ernest Hemingway short story considerably without losing the Hemingway penchant for the mysticism behind his virile characters and lusty situations. Gregory Peck delivers with gusto the character of the writer who lies dangerously ill at the base of Kilimanjaro, highest mountain in Africa, and re-

lives what he believes is a misspent life. Susan Hayward is splendid in the less colorful role of Peck's wife.
1952: Nominations: Best Color Cinematography, Color Art Direction

SNOW WHITE AND THE SEVEN DWARFS
1937, 80 mins, US Ⓥ
D: David Hand (Disney/RKO)

Walt Disney's seven reels of animated cartoon in Technicolor unfold an absorbingly interesting and, at times, thrilling entertainment. More than two years and $1 million were required by the Disney staff to complete the film. The opening shows the cover of Grimms' book of tales. Soon all the characters assume lifelike personalities. Snow White is the embodiment of girlish sweetness and kindness. The queen is a vampish brunette, of homicidal instincts, who consorts with black magic and underworld forces of evil. And the seven little dwarfs, Doc, Grumpy, Dopey, Sleepy, Happy, Sneezy, and Bashful, are the embodiments of their name tags, a merry crew of masculine frailities.
1938: Special Award (significant screen innovation)
1937: Nomination: Best Score

SOAPDISH
1991, 95 mins, US Ⓥ ⊙
D: Michael Hoffman **A:** Sally Field, Kevin Kline, Robert Downey Jr., Cathy Moriarty, Whoopi Goldberg, Elizabeth Shue (Paramount)

Sally Field and Kevin Kline play a feuding pair of soap-opera stars in this broad but amiable send-up of daytime TV. Field, the reigning "queen of misery" on the sudser *The Sun Also Sets,* is going to pieces emotionally. Amazonian harpy Cathy Moriarty is scheming to take over the show by using her sexual wiles to convince the slimy producer (Robert Downey Jr.) to have Field's character destroy her popularity. To drive Field even more off the edge, Downey surprises her by bringing back her long-ago flame, Kevin Kline, whom she had thrown off the show. Field works hard and shows an expert sense of comic timing. Kline is utterly marvelous as a sort of low-rent John Barrymore type. Moriarty is a scream.

S.O.B.
1981, 121 mins, US Ⓥ ⊙ ▭
D: Blake Edwards **A:** Julie Andrews, William Holden, Robert Webber, Larry Hag-

man, Robert Preston, Robert Vaughn (Paramount/Lorimar)

One of the most vitriolic—though only occasionally hilarious—attacks on the Tinseltown mentality ever, spinning the chronicle of a producer (Richard Mulligan) whose latest $30 million musical extravaganza is hailed as the b.o. turkey of the century, relegating him to has-been status overnight. Mulligan tries several failed variations on the suicide route until a mid-orgy epiphany tells him to cut and reshoot the G-rated failure as an opulent softcore porno fantasy.

SO BIG
1953, 101 mins, US
D: Robert Wise **A:** Jane Wyman, Sterling Hayden, Nancy Olson, Steve Forrest, Martha Hyer (Warner)

So Big is big and sprawling, covering a period of some 25 years. Wyman is superb in transition from the young girl with the aristocratic background to the widow of a Dutch truck farmer. She takes poverty, backbreaking farmwork, widowhood, and disappointment serenely, philosophically, and with dignity. Sterling Hayden scores as the unlearned, rugged, yet gentle farmer who wins the schoolteacher.

SOCIETY
1989, 99 mins, US ⓥ ⊙
D: Brian Yuzna **A:** Billy Warlock, Devin Devasquez, Evan Richards, Ben Meyerson, Connie Danese (Wild Street)

Extremely pretentious, obnoxious horror film that unsuccessfully attempts to introduce kinky sexual elements into extravagant makeup effects. Sole bright spot is a very sexy turn by former *Playboy* magazine model Devin Devasquez.

SO DARK THE NIGHT
1946, 71 mins, US
D: Joseph H. Lewis **A:** Steven Geray, Micheline Cheirel, Eugene Borden, Ann Codee, Egon Brecher (Columbia)

Around the frail structure of a story about a schizophrenic Paris police inspector who becomes an insane killer at night, a tight combination of direction, camerawork, and musical scoring produce a series of isolated visual effects that are subtle and moving to an unusual degree. Settings for the pic, which unfolds in an obscure French village, are outstanding for their density and accuracy of detail.

SODOM AND GOMORRAH
1962, 153 mins, Italy ⓥ ⊙ ⊨
D: Robert Aldrich **A:** Stewart Granger, Pier Angeli, Stanley Baker, Anouk Aimee, Rossana Podesta, Claudia Mori (20th Century-Fox/Titanus)

Film has many of the faults of the biblical epic, but many good qualities. Story concerns Lot's pilgrimage to the Valley of Jordan with the Hebrews. They are involved in a bitter clash between the Helamites, who covet the wealth of Sodom and Gomorrah, two cesspools of depravity, ruled over by the cold, beautiful, unscrupulous Queen Bera. Stewart Granger makes a distinguished, solemn, and sincere figure of Lot, and Stanley Baker, as the treacherous Prince of Sodom, is sufficiently sneaky.

SO FINE
1981, 91 mins, US ⓥ
D: Andrew Bergman **A:** Ryan O'Neal, Jack Warden, Mariangela Melato, Richard Kiel, Fred Gwynne (Warner)

So Fine is quite all right. Ryan O'Neal is an English professor implausibly recruited into his father Jack Warden's dressmaking firm upon the demand of Big Eddie, played by the seven-foot, two-inch Richard Kiel. Latter's petite wife, Mariangela Melato, quickly corrals O'Neal into the sack (while Kiel's in it, too, no less) and in his best bumbling manner, O'Neal inadvertently hits upon a new fashion discovery—skintight jeans with see-through behinds. It all ends up in a slapstick, amateur-hour operatic production of Verdi's *Otello*.

SOFT SKIN
See: La Peau Douce

SOFT TOP HARD SHOULDER
1993, 93 mins, UK ⓥ ⊨
D: Stefan Schwartz **A:** Peter Capaldi, Elaine Collins, Frances Barber, Simon Callow, Phyllis Logan, Richard Wilson (Gruber Bros./Road Movies)

Gavin Bellini (scripter Peter Capaldi) is a crazy Italo-Scot in London. He learns he has 36 hours to make it to his father's surprise 60th-birthday party in Glasgow if he's to collect a chunk of family money. Hitting the highways in a bronchial old auto, he quickly meets kooky hitchhiker Yvonne (Elaine Collins). Rest of pic follows the familiar route of the pair's love-hate relationship, stopovers, and breakdowns, capped by a happy ending.

SO I MARRIED AN AXE MURDERER
1993, 93 mins, US Ⓥ ⊙
D: Thomas Schlamme **A:** Mike Myers, Nancy Travis, Anthony LaPaglia, Amanda Plummer, Brenda Fricker, Charles Grodin (Tri-Star)

Don't expect to see gobs of gore. Comedy is a hip slice of life about the dilemma of marital commitment with just a pinch of Hitchcock providing the cutting edge. The San Francisco–set yarn finds poet Charlie Mackenzie (Mike Myers) glibly fashioning a verse concerning his umpteenth failed relationship. His eye catches Harriet Michaels (Nancy Travis), a butcher at the not-too-elegant Meats of the World. Quicker than you can say ''hae ya got any haggis?'' they are kindred souls. But Charlie begins to believe that Harriet might be an uncaught husband killer.

SOLARIS
See: Solyaris

SOLDIER BLUE
1970, 112 mins, US Ⓥ ▭
D: Ralph Nelson **A:** Candice Bergen, Peter Strauss, Donald Pleasence, John Anderson, Jorge Rivero (Avco Embassy)

Screenplay deals with the attempt of US soldier Honus Gant (Peter Strauss), the ''soldier blue'' of the title, and a white woman who was captured by Indians two years before (Candice Bergen) to stay alive until they can reach an army outpost. The climax of the film makes the army the complete villain and the Cheyennes the complete innocents. The seeming handful of warriors are quickly wiped out, the women raped, children mutilated and, in many cases, murdered. It would appear obvious that director Ralph Nelson is trying to correlate this allegedly historical incident with more contemporary events.

SOLDIER IN LOVE
See: Fanfan La Tulipe

SOLDIER IN THE RAIN
1963, 87 mins, US Ⓥ
D: Ralph Nelson **A:** Jackie Gleason, Steve McQueen, Tuesday Weld, Tony Bill, Tom Poston, Ed Nelson (Allied Artists/Cedars-Solar)

One might classify this film as a fairy tale in khaki. The screenplay, from a novel by William Goldman, relates the bittersweet tale of two modern army buddies—a smooth-operating master sergeant (Jackie Gleason) and his hero-worshiping protégé (Steve McQueen), a supply sergeant who is about to return to civvies and hopes Gleason will join him in private enterprise on the outside. Mirth is only spasmodic and is snowed under by a sentimental approach that misfires. Tuesday Weld's convincing portrait of the classic dizzy blond as a teenager is a standout.

SOLDIER OF FORTUNE
1955, 94 mins, US Ⓥ ▭
D: Edward Dmytryk **A:** Clark Gable, Susan Hayward, Michael Rennie, Gene Barry, Tom Tully (20th Century-Fox)

Clark Gable and Susan Hayward team advantageously in this thriller about mystery and intrigue in the Orient. When Hayward's husband (Gene Barry) disappears on a photographic trip into Red China, she comes to Hong Kong to start a search for him. With British authorities and others no help, her path leads to Gable, soldier of fortune reaping just that with some smuggling enterprises. Standout photography by Leo Tover takes the audience on an intriguing tour of Hong Kong and its points of interest.

SOLDIER'S STORY, A
1984, 101 mins, US Ⓥ ⊙
D: Norman Jewison **A:** Howard E. Rollins Jr., Adolph Caesar, Dennis Lipscomb, Art Evans, Denzel Washington (Caldix)

Taut, gripping film features brilliant ensemble acting, excellent production values, a crackling script, fine direction, and a liberal political message. Howard Rollins Jr. plays a prideful black army attorney called into Fort Neal, LA, to investigate the murder of Sergeant Waters (Adolph Caesar). Rollins's arrival at this holding tank for black soldiers is cause for racial strife on both sides of the fence—the white officers are contemptuous and the black soldiers are proud.

1984: Nominations: Best Picture, Supp. Actor (Adolph Caesar), Adapted Screenplay

SOLDIERS THREE
1951, 91 mins, US
D: Tay Garnett **A:** Stewart Granger, Walter Pidgeon, David Niven, Robert Newton, Cyril Cusack (M-G-M)

A string of incidents involving three soldiers (Stewart Granger, Robert Newton, and Cyril Cusack) in India. Trio's off-limits antics, such as drunken brawling, add to the hot water in which their colonel (Walter Pidgeon) finds himself and do nothing to calm the colonel's aide (David Niven). Granger is very likable in his comedy role, and his two cohorts do their full share in getting laughs.

SOLID GOLD CADILLAC, THE
1956, 99 mins, US
D: Richard Quine **A:** Judy Holliday, Paul Douglas, Fred Clark, John Williams, Neva Patterson, Ralph Dumke (Columbia)

Satire on minority-stockholder gadfly treatment of vested interests and pompous executives makes for hilarity. It's a broad treatment of big corporation board members who get their comeuppance from a femme who owns only 10 shares of common in the company. As the dizzy blond with some native, and naive, common sense, Holliday is a delight.
1956: Best B&W Costume Design

SOL MADRID
1968, 90 mins, US ☐
D: Brian G. Hutton **A:** David McCallum, Stella Stevens, Telly Savalas, Rip Torn, Pat Hingle, Ricardo Montalban (M-G-M)

Hard-hitting action compensates for certain confusing story elements, and plotting is sufficiently exciting and suspenseful to maintain interest. Direction is a potent assist to film's unfolding, in which David McCallum takes on the Mafia and drug smuggling across the Mexican border. Hutton, who draws strong performances from entire cast, specializes here in legitimately premised violence and hits a torrid pace.

SOLOMON AND SHEBA
1959, 141 mins, US ⊗ ⊙ ☐
D: King Vidor **A:** Yul Brynner, Gina Lollobrigida, George Sanders, Marisa Pavan, David Farrar, Harry Andrews (United Artists)

The story concerns the clash between Solomon and his brother Adonijah when King David crowns the poet-philosopher instead of the warrior. From then on it's political intrigue, with Egypt conniving with Sheba to bring down Israel, which is flourishing under the wise rule of Solomon, and the treacherous manner in which the Queen of Sheba undermines Solomon but falls in love with him in the process. The fascinating clash between the two brothers is only spasmodically developed and, inevitably, plays second fiddle to the relationship between the queen and her infatuated target. Often what should have been a moving, gripping romance turns out to be little more than an affair between a couple of people at the local golf club. There are some magnificent production scenes. Lollobrigida not only looks stunning but shows the queen to be a woman of intelligence.

SO LONG AT THE FAIR
1950, 84 mins, UK
D: Terence Fisher, Antony Darnborough **A:** Jean Simmons, Dirk Bogarde, David Tomlinson, Honor Blackman, Cathleen Nesbitt, Felix Aylmer (Gainsborough/Rank)

Setting for a good workmanlike British thriller is the Paris exhibition of 1889. Vicky Barton (Jean Simmons) arrives in Paris with her brother (David Tomlinson). The brother disappears. At the hotel they insist that the girl came alone and both the British consul and the chief of police find it hard to accept her story. Dirk Bogarde displays a keen determination as the young artist who helps her unravel the mystery.

SOLYARIS
(US: SOLARIS)
1972, 168 mins, USSR ⊗ ☐
D: Andrei Tarkovsky **A:** Natalya Bondarchuk, Juri Jaarvet, Donatas Banionis, Anatoli Solonitsyn, Vladislav Dvoryetsky (Mosfilm)

Andrei Tarkovsky spins a strange, slow, but absorbing parable on life and love in the guise of a sci-fi theme. Pic seems to take place in a near future when there is a space station around a strange planet called Solaris, made up of viscous swirling waters, like an ocean but lensed to suggest an oozing mixture of sea and sky, which leads to apparent hallucinations by those up there. Solaris, in fact, may be a thinking mass which creates humans from man's secret needs or desires.

SOMEBODY LOVES ME
1952, 97 mins, US
D: Irving Brecher **A:** Betty Hutton, Ralph Meeker, Robert Keith, Adele Jergens, Billy Bird (Paramount)

Suggested by the careers of Blossom Seeley and her husband, Benny Fields, the semibiopic treatment flows along conventional lines, highlighted by Betty Hutton's vivacity, song-selling talents and the memorable tunes of another era. The Seeley career is picked up in a Barbary Coast spot as the 1906 earthquake hits San Francisco. Then comes a try at vaude, her World War I work, and Broadway success.

SOMEBODY TO LOVE
1994, 103 mins, US ⓥ
D: Alexandre Rockwell **A:** Rosie Perez,
Harvey Keitel, Anthony Quinn, Michael
DeLorenzo, Steve Buscemi, Sam Fuller
(Lumiere)

Rosie Perez shines as a spunky Latino
taxi dancer with showbiz in her eyes, but
she's too often a lone beacon in a dramatically foggy and curiously unaffecting
pic. Despite some treasurable moments,
and a largely reliable cast, pic rarely fires
on more than one cylinder at a time. Rockwell wrote the main role of a dollar-a-
dance babe in a tacky L.A. club with Perez
in mind. Mercedes (Perez) spends her days
being rejected at casting calls. Her lover,
Harry (Harvey Keitel), also from the East
Coast, is a passed-over star who's going
through mid-age career and marital crises.
Enter Ernesto (Michael DeLorenzo) a
dewy-eyed Latin kid who falls for Mercedes at the dance club and starts
following her around like a faithful dog.

SOMEBODY UP THERE LIKES ME
1956, 112 mins, US ⓥ
D: Robert Wise **A:** Paul Newman, Pier
Angeli, Everett Sloane, Eileen Heckart,
Sal Mineo (M-G-M)

Superbly done, frank, and revealing
film probe of Rocky Graziano, the East
Side punk who overcame a lawless beginning to win respect and become middle
weight champion of the world. Paul Newman's talent is large and flexible, revealing
an approach to the Graziano character that
scores tremendously. When Norma Unger,
played with beautiful sensitivity by Pier
Angeli, comes into his life, the audience
is pulling for him to shake off the past,
and literally cheering him on in that potently staged championship match with
Tony Zale.
1956: Best B&W Cinematography, B&W
Art Direction
Nomination: Best Editing

SOME CAME RUNNING
1958, 137 mins, US ⓥ ⊙ ▭
D: Vincente Minnelli **A:** Frank Sinatra,
Dean Martin, Shirley MacLaine, Martha
Hyer, Arthur Kennedy, Nancy Gates (M-
G-M)

The story is pure melodrama, despite
the intention of the original novel's author,
James Jones, to invest in with greater stature. But the integrity with which the film
is handled lifts it at times to tragedy. Frank
Sinatra is an ex-serviceman and ex-

novelist who returns to his hometown, unconscious on a bus. Accompanying him is
Shirley MacLaine, who is generally unwitting but never unwilling, a good-
natured tart with no pretensions. Sinatra
can't stand his brother (Arthur Kennedy)
or the brother's wife (Leora Dana), but he
falls deeply in love with a friend of theirs
(Martha Hyer). He meets a pal (Dean Martin) who becomes an ally, and he becomes
involved in the personal life of his niece
(Betty Lou Keim).
1958: Nominations: Best Actress (Shirley
MacLaine), Supp. Actor (Arthur Kennedy), Supp. Actress (Martha Hyer), Costume Design, Song ("To Love and Be
Loved")

SOME GIRLS
(UK: SISTERS)
1988, 94 mins, US ⓥ
D: Michael Hoffman **A:** Patrick Dempsey,
Florinda Bolkan, Jennifer Connelly, Lance
Edwards, Lila Kedrova (Oxford/Wild-
wood)

Cross-cultural teen sex farce with some
good moments hinges on the deadpan
comic timing of Patrick Dempsey, who
plays Michael, an American student invited by his college sweetheart Gabby
(Jennifer Connelly) to spend Christmas
with her family in Quebec City. The ar-
chitecturally stately city is presented as a
snow-covered fairyland in the eyes of the
Yank visitor. Gabby informs Michael that
she doesn't love him anymore and that
sleeping arrangements will be separate.
Fortunately for Michael, Gabby has two
fetching sisters (Sheila Kelley, Ashley
Greenfield) each of whom shows more
than a passing interest in him.

SOME KIND OF HERO
1982, 97 mins, US ⓥ ⊙
D: Michael Pressman **A:** Richard Pryor,
Margot Kidder, Ray Sharkey, Ronny Cox,
Lynne Moody (Paramount)

Richard Pryor's performance is truly a
class piece of acting, playing a likable
enough fellow who loses everything but
his sense of humor during five years in a
Vietnamese prison camp. During this tenure, he establishes a loving friendship with
hot-tempered POW Ray Sharkey. When
Sharkey becomes deathly ill, Pryor signs
a denunciation of US activities in the war
to get the North Vietnamese to provide
proper medical attention. Action then
shifts to Pryor's return to the US, where
the act comes back to haunt him.

SOME KIND OF WONDERFUL
1987, 93 mins, US Ⓥ ⊙
D: Howard Deutch **A:** Eric Stoltz, Mary Stuart Masterson, Lea Thompson, Craig Sheffer, John Ashton (Paramount)

Simple, lovely, and thoughtful teenage story occasionally shines due to fine characterizations and lucid dialogue. Film centers on high-school senior Eric Stoltz, who is struggling so hard to develop his artistic talent while juggling school, part-time work as a car mechanic, and the distraction of the immensely popular Lea Thompson that he can't quite pick up on the emotions of Mary Stuart Masterson, whom he dismisses early on as just a tomboy friend. Masterson is so adept and appealing in her role that she becomes the most interesting character of all.

SOME LIKE IT HOT
1959, 105 mins, US Ⓥ ⊙
D: Billy Wilder **A:** Marilyn Monroe, Tony Curtis, Jack Lemmon, George Raft, Pat O'Brien, Joe E. Brown (Ashton/Mirisch)

Wacky, clever, farcical comedy starts off like a firecracker and keeps on throwing off lively sparks till the very end. Tony Curtis and Jack Lemmon witness the St. Valentine's Day massacre and "escape" into the anonymity of a girl band by dressing up as feminine musicians. This leads to the obvious complications, particularly since Curtis meets Marilyn Monroe (ukulele player, vocalist, and gin addict) and falls for her. Lemmon, in turn, is propositioned by an addlebrained millionaire (Joe E. Brown). Marilyn has never looked better. Her performance has a deliciously naive quality. It's a toss-up whether Curtis beats out Lemmon or whether it goes the other way round. Both are excellent. The Wilder touch is indelible. If the action is funny, the lines are there to match it.
1959: Best B&W Costume Design
Nominations: Best Director, Actor (Jack Lemmon), Adapted Screenplay, B&W Cinematography, B&W Art Direction

SOME MOTHER'S SON
1996, 112 mins, Ireland/US Ⓥ
D: Terry George **A:** Helen Mirren, Fionnula Flanagan, Aidan Gillen, David O'Hara, John Lynch (Hell's Kitchen/Castle Rock)

The troubles in Northern Ireland are given yet another spin in a film that takes the point of view of the mothers whose IRA-affiliated sons were jailed by the British. This emotional perspective is designed to transcend mundane political details, but the fact remains that the action is dominated by domestic violence, prison life, and a prolonged hunger strike. The directorial debut of Terry George, coscenarist of *In the Name of the Father* with present cowriter and producer Jim Sheridan, doesn't come within hailing distance of its predecessor artistically or commercially.

SOMEONE ELSE'S AMERICA
1995, 96 mins, France/UK/Germany Ⓥ
D: Goran Paskaljevic **A:** Tom Conti, Miki Manojlovic, Mana Casares, Zorka Manojlovic, Sergej Trifunovic (Mact/Intrinsica/Lichtblick)

This fairy-tale-like study of a friendship between two Euro bozos in Brooklyn is a charmer on every level. Bayo (Miki Manojlovic) is a Montenegran illegal in NY who does construction gigs and works as a cleaner at the scuzzy Brooklyn bar of Alonso (Tom Conti), a shifty-eyed Spaniard who lives with his blind mother. Bayo also shares a room atop Alonso's bar with his pet rooster. Unknown to Bayo, his young daughter Savka (Andjela Stojkovic) is seriously ill back home in the mountains of Montenegro, so the whole family decides to emigrate illegally to the US to join the paterfamilias. Though the film centers on the volatile friendship between Alonso and Bayo, it's very much an ensemble piece. Director Goran Paskaljevic's view of his characters is alert to their shortcomings, but film is done with a twinkle in the eye.

SOMEONE TO LOVE
1987, 109 mins, US Ⓥ ⊙
D: Henry Jaglom **A:** Orson Welles, Henry Jaglom, Andrea Marcovicci, Michael Emil, Sally Kellerman, Oja Kodar (Rainbow)

Jaglom plays himself, a director so frustrated at his girlfriend Andrea Marcovicci's unwillingness to settle down he decides to devote an entire feature to what he perceives as a general malaise of his generation. Without revealing his intentions, Jaglom invites many friends to a St. Valentine's Day party who are somewhat taken aback by their host's desire to scrutinize their innermost feelings and insecurities with a camera, and some bow out. Pic is blessed with an almost overwhelming final screen appearance by Orson Welles.

SOMEONE TO WATCH OVER ME
1987, 106 mins, US Ⓥ ⊙
D: Ridley Scott **A:** Tom Berenger, Mimi Rogers, Lorraine Bracco, Jerry Orbach, John Rubinstein (Columbia)

Stylish and romantic police thriller manages, through the sleek direction of Ridley Scott and persuasive ensemble performances, to triumph over several hard-to-swallow plot developments. Tom Berenger portrays a happily married NY cop assigned to protect socialite Claire Gregory (Mimi Rogers), witness to a brutal murder. Berenger carries the film handily, utterly convincing as the working-class stiff out of his element accompanying Rogers through her elegant apartment and posh parties. Rogers is alluring as the romantic interest, while wife, Lorraine Bracco, is fully sympathetic and easily has the viewer siding against the two leads during their hanky-panky segments.

SOME PEOPLE
1962, 93 mins, UK
D: Clive Donner **A:** Kenneth More, Ray Brooks, Annika Wills, Angela Douglas, David Hemmings (Anglo Amalgamated)

The pic is set in the industrial town of Bristol. Three lads, part of a gang of ton-up motorcyclists, are banned from driving. Out of sheer boredom, they become potential young hoods. Luckily, they become involved with Kenneth More, playing a voluntary church choirmaster. He gives them the opportunity of rehearsing their rock-and-roll combo. More handles the role of the sympathetic choirmaster with his usual, easy charm. Ray Brooks, David Andrews, and David Hemmings play the three main teenagers with authority.

SOMETHING FOR THE BOYS
1944, 87 mins, US
D: Lewis Seiler **A:** Carmen Miranda, Michael O'Shea, Vivian Blaine, Phil Silvers, Perry Como, Sheila Ryan (20th Century-Fox)

Screen adaptation of the musical play includes various amusing situations, but the story does not have particular punch in dialogue or otherwise. Also, the comedy values are somewhat spotty. Carmen Miranda, Vivian Blaine, and Phil Silvers are the three cousins who fall heir to the old plantation, only to learn that they are poorer by having acquired the debt-laden property. They get an idea to make it a home for army wives, and raise money through putting on shows to repair and maintain it.

SOMETHING TO SING ABOUT
1937, 90 mins, US/UK Ⓥ ⊙
D: Victor Schertzinger **A:** James Cagney, Evelyn Daw, William Frawley, Mona Barrie, Gene Lockhart (Grand National)

James Cagney's second independently produced film is a first-class comedy with music. He sings, dances, and plays a romantic juvenile. Having been a song-and-dance man originally, he does that well. Hero is a bandleader from a New York café who is beguiled to take a fling at picture acting. There is the overnight sensational screen success, but the consequences are amusing and farcical. Newcomer Evelyn Daw sings four numbers and makes a good impression.

SOMETHING TO TALK ABOUT
1995, 106 mins, US Ⓥ ⊙
D: Lasse Hallström **A:** Julia Roberts, Dennis Quaid, Robert Duvall, Gena Rowlands, Kyra Sedgwick (Spring Creek/Warner)

Star-driven comic take on the wages of infidelity. An affluent young wife and mother, Grace (Julia Roberts), is frantic, scattered, and absentminded, the southern version of neurotic. She's quick to react when she spots her husband, Eddie (Dennis Quaid), making out on the street with a flashy blond. None of this sits well with her dad, Wyly King (Robert Duvall), the wealthy owner of a horse-breeding spread, where he lives with his compliant wife, Georgia (Gena Rowlands), and saucy second daughter, Emma Rae (Kyra Sedgwick). Sedgwick's uninhibited Emma Rae has all the best lines. By the time the picture winds its way back to resolving Grace and Eddie's domestic dilemma, it has nothing more original to say on the subject than that only time and a forgiving attitude can mend such wounds.

SOMETHING WICKED THIS WAY COMES
1983, 94 mins, US Ⓥ ⊙
D: Jack Clayton **A:** Jason Robards, Jonathan Pryce, Diane Ladd, Pam Grier, Royal Dano (Walt Disney/Bryna)

Film version of Ray Bradbury's popular novel must be chalked up as something of a disappointment. Two young boys are intrigued by a mysterious carnival troupe. By day, fairgrounds seem innocent enough, but by night they possess a strange allure which leads local inhabitants to fall victim to their deepest desires. Thanks to the diabolical talents of carnival leader Mr. Dark (Jonathan Pryce), these wishes can be granted, but at the price of becoming a member of the traveling freak show. Mr. Dark decides that little Will and Jim would make excellent recruits and pursues them vigilantly until the apocalyptic finale.

SOMETHING WILD
1986, 113 mins, US ⓥ ⊙
D: Jonathan Demme A: Jeff Daniels, Melanie Griffith, Ray Liotta, Margaret Colin, Tracey Walter (Religioso Primitiva)

This offbeat thriller is about an unlikely couple on the run. Super-yuppie Jeff Daniels is picked up by hot number Melanie Griffith at a luncheonette, driven out to New Jersey, and, before he knows what's happening, is handcuffed to a bed and ravished by this crazy lady. Everything changes at her high-school reunion, however, as Griffith's ex-con husband makes an unexpected appearance and proceeds to change the couple's joyride into a nightmare. Griffith is provocative enough, but falls a little short in putting across all the aspects of this complicated woman.

SOMETIMES A GREAT NOTION (UK: NEVER GIVE AN INCH)
1971, 114 mins, US ⓥ ▭
D: Paul Newman A: Paul Newman, Henry Fonda, Lee Remick, Michael Sarrazin, Richard Jaeckel (Universal)

A good, if plot-sprawling, outdoor action film set in northwest lumber country, about a family of individualists fighting a town and a union. Paul Newman directed, produced, and stars as the crown prince to family patriarch Henry Fonda. Adaptation of Ken Kesey's novel tries to balance the intellectual angles—Fonda's rigorous adherence to a principle, Newman's unending follow-through after disaster, and Michael Sarrazin's transformation from a self-indulgent dropout. The result is rather good—a sort of contemporary ''western'' in the timber territory.
1971: Nominations: Best Supp. Actor (Richard Jaeckel), Song (''All His Children'')

SOMEWHERE I'LL FIND YOU
1942, 107 mins, US
D: Wesley Ruggles A: Clark Gable, Lana Turner, Robert Sterling, Patricia Dane, Lee Patrick (M-G-M)

Lana Turner is a sexy, torchy, clinging blond. Clark Gable has seemingly always made the same impress on women. Tossing them both together, even if surrounding their clinches with but a specious story, provides an extremely potent brew. At the finish, when Gable—a go-getting foreign correspondent for a NY daily—is dictating the story of the fall of Bataan peninsula, the story seems to merely await the final showdown with Turner.

SOMEWHERE IN EUROPE
See: Valahol Europaban

SOMEWHERE IN TIME
1980, 103 mins, US ⓥ ⊙
D: Jeannot Szwarc A: Christopher Reeve, Jane Seymour, Christopher Plummer, Teresa Wright, Bill Erwin (Universal/Rastar)

Charming, witty, passionate romantic drama, about a love transcending space and time, is an old-fashioned film in the best sense of that term. In the finely wrought screenplay by veteran fantasy writer Richard Matheson, Christopher Reeve is a young Chicago playwright who becomes mysteriously fascinated by a 1912 photo of a stage actress (Jane Seymour). He is drawn to a hotel on Mackinac Island in Michigan, where it is learned that they actually did meet and have an affair at the time the photo was taken.
1971: Nomination: Best Costume Design

SOMMARNATTENS LEENDE (US: SMILES OF A SUMMER NIGHT)
1955, 108 mins, Sweden ⓥ ⊙
D: Ingmar Bergman A: Eva Dahlbeck, Ulla Jacobsson, Harriet Andersson, Margit Carlqvist, Jarl Kulle (Svensk Filmindustri)

Offbeat Swedish comedy of manners and passions has an unusual lusty comedy manner. It details how a group of badly assorted couples are straightened out one summer night, influenced by a strange elixir that makes people do what they want. Clever, and at times ribald, it has a too ponderous a touch to really light up the comedic aspects of this slightly overlong affair.

SOMMERSBY
1993, 112 mins, US ⓥ ⊙ ▭
D: Jon Amiel A: Richard Gere, Jodie Foster, Bill Pullman, James Earl Jones, William Windom (Warner/Canal Plus/Regency/Alcor)

One of those rare occasions when the Americanization of a foreign property (here *The Return of Martin Guerre*) works as well as the original. The missing-in-action and presumed dead Jack Sommersby (Gere) suddenly reappears after the end of the Civil War and attempts to start life anew with his wife, Laurel (Foster), and young son. He returns a new man, as tender and committed to his wife as he had once been distant and cruel. Naturally, this arouses suspicion about his identity. The movie keeps the question beautifully unresolved. Foster is a compelling actress, but Gere comes close to stealing the picture.

SONG IS BORN, A
1948, 112 mins, US ⊘
D: Howard Hawks A: Danny Kaye, Virginia Mayo, Benny Goodman, Hugh Herbert, Steve Cochran, Louis Armstrong (RKO/Goldwyn)

Remake of *Ball of Fire* (1941) presents a group of professors compiling a history of music. When Danny Kaye is working with them, the picture is standout entertainment. Last half, though, in which they get a semi-brush-off as Kaye becomes involved with a group of gangsters, drags by comparison. Script makes good use of the various musicians involved as Kaye tours Broadway niteries to get an idea of swing and jazz.

SONG OF BERNADETTE, THE
1943, 158 mins, US ⊘ ◉
D: Henry King A: Jennifer Jones, Charles Bickford, Gladys Cooper, Vincent Price, Lee J. Cobb, Anne Revere (20th Century-Fox)

Warming and intimate narrative of godly visitation on the young girl of Lourdes which led to establishment of the shrine at Lourdes. Jennifer Jones, in title role, delivers an inspirationally sensitive and arresting performance. Despite the deeply religious tone of the dramatic narrative, theme is handled with utmost taste and reverence.
1943: Best Actress (Jennifer Jones), B&W Cinematography, B&W Interior Decoration, Score for a Dramatic Picture
Nominations: Best Picture, Director, Supp. Actor (Charles Bickford), Supp. Actress (Gladys Cooper, Anne Revere), Screenplay, Editing, Sound

SONG OF CEYLON
1935, 39 mins, UK
D: Basil Wright (Ceylon Tea Production Board)

This four-reel travelogue on Ceylon attempts to dig down deep and cinematically explain the country and its people in more thorough manner than customarily encountered. The fancy and at times fantastic treatment will largely mystify audiences.

SONG OF LOVE
1947, 117 mins, US ⊘
D: Clarence Brown A: Katharine Hepburn, Paul Henreid, Robert Walker, Henry Daniell, Leo G. Carroll (M-G-M)

Story of the lives, loves, and music of Robert and Clara Schumann and Johannes Brahms has a good cast, entertaining tale, and the usual top Metro production mountings. Picture offers a gold mine of thesping opportunities to its three stars, Katharine Hepburn, Paul Henreid, and Robert Walker, all of whom play it to the hilt. All three, moreover, show a surprising adeptness at the pianistics which is highly necessary despite the fact that Artur Rubinstein ghosted for them all.

SONG OF NORWAY
1970, 138 mins, US ⊘ ⊏
D: Andrew L. Stone A: Toralv Maurstad, Florence Henderson, Christina Schollin, Harry Secombe, Robert Morley, Edward G. Robinson (ABC)

Production and staging, the Robert Wright–George Forrest music and lyrics based on Norwegian composer Edvard Grieg's music, and widescreen photography make a magnificent motion picture. Unfortunately, screenplay imparts a frequently banal, two-dimensional note featuring a wooden performance by Norwegian actor Toralv Maurstad as Grieg.

SONG OF SCHEHERAZADE
1947, 105 mins, US
D: Walter Reisch A: Yvonne De Carlo, Brian Donlevy, Jean-Pierre Aumont, Eve Arden, Philip Reed (Universal)

The music of Rimsky-Korsakov and eye value of brilliant color give this pic entertainment elements not otherwise found in the fluffy, ineptly directed and played story. Score contains 10 Rimsky-Korsakov tunes, ably adapted to the screen by Miklos Rozsa. Jean-Pierre Aumont plays the young composer. Yvonne De Carlo is the Spanish dancer with whom he falls in love during the week's adventuring. Brian Donlevy does a chain-smoking captain of the training ship who tries to make his students the pride of the Russian navy.

SONG OF SONGS

1933, 83 mins, US

D: Rouben Mamoulian **A:** Marlene Dietrich, Brian Aherne, Lionel Atwill, Alison Skipworth, Hardie Albright (Paramount)

Marlene Dietrich is glamorous. She's an eyeful, but she has nothing but directorial artistry to augment her innate qualities. There are long stretches of dreary talk and tedious detail until the obvious is attained. The unsophisticated maiden, the artist, and the craven colonel are a cinch formula, especially if the artist is Brian Aherne. Lionel Atwill makes the German colonel a lecherous a.k. character.

SONG OF THE ISLANDS

1942, 73 mins, US Ⓥ ⊙

D: Walter Lang **A:** Betty Grable, Victor Mature, Jack Oakie, Thomas Mitchell (20th Century-Fox)

Spontaneous and breezy mixture of comedy, song, dance, and romance—set in Hawaiian atmosphere. Betty Grable is the daughter of Thomas Mitchell, philosophical Irish beachcomber, who owns a portion of a small island in the Hawaiian group and treats the natives with consideration. Victor Mature sails in and immediately romance gets under way. Liberal potions of surefire comedy are supplied by Jack Oakie, who has a field day in byplay with buxom native maid (Hilo Hattie).

SONG O' MY HEART

1930, 85 mins, US Ⓥ

D: Frank Borzage **A:** John McCormack, Maureen O'Sullivan, John Garrick, J. M. Kerrigan, Alice Joyce (Fox)

Fox has molded what might easily have become so much sentimental sop into a charming background for the Irish tenor John McCormack, singing 11 songs. The script draws him as a prominent singer in his native land with an unsuccessful love affair, the subject of which, Mary, has wed elsewhere by command. The buildup to the "I Hear You Calling Me" climax comes when Mary dies and a cable so informs McCormack's accompanist as the tenor is in the midst of an American concert.

SONG TO REMEMBER, A

1945, 110 mins, US Ⓥ ⊙

D: Charles Vidor **A:** Paul Muni, Merle Oberon, Cornel Wilde, Stephen Bekassy, George Coulouris, Sig Arno (Columbia)

Plot introduces Polish composer Frederic Chopin as a prodigy at 11, with Paul Muni the old music master who recognizes his genius. When 22, the student and teacher flee to Paris after Chopin refuses to perform for the Russian governor. Young Franz Liszt befriends the newcomer and is directly responsible for getting him recognition. Cornel Wilde is spotlighted as Chopin and establishes himself as a screen personality.

1945: Nominations: Best Actor (Cornel Wilde), Original Story, Color Cinematography, Editing, Scoring of a Musical Picture, Sound

SONG WITHOUT END

1960, 145 mins, US ▢

D: Charles Vidor, George Cukor **A:** Dirk Bogarde, Capucine, Genevieve Page, Patricia Morison, Martita Hunt (Columbia)

Pic dramatizes the story of pianist-composer Franz Liszt, depicted as a man tragically embroiled in overlapping romantic, religious, and professional conflicts. His relations with the opposite sex are stormy, illicit, and ill-fated. Discarding the irreligious mother of his two children, he discovers happiness and the germ of artistic fulfillment during his affair with the devout wife of a Russian prince, only to have it dissolve abruptly on the eve of their wedding. The film is a feast of sight and sound.

1960: Best Scoring of a Musical Picture

SONGWRITER

1984, 94 mins, US Ⓥ ⊙

D: Alan Rudolph **A:** Willie Nelson, Kris Kristofferson, Melinda Dillon, Rip Torn, Lesley Ann Warren, Richard C. Sarafian (Tri-Star)

Good-natured film that rolls along on the strength of attitudes and poses long ago established outside the picture by its stars, Willie Nelson and Kris Kristofferson, basically playing themselves disguised as fictional characters. Doc Jenkins is the saint of country music. Luckily Nelson has enough of a screen presence to support his sanctification. As Blackie Buck, Kristofferson is the outlaw with a heart of gold who will probably never grow up.

1984: Nomination: Best Original Song Score

SON OF DRACULA

1943, 79 mins, US Ⓥ ⊙

D: Robert Siodmak **A:** Lon Chaney, Robert Paige, Louise Allbritton, Evelyn Ankers, J. Edward Bromberg (Universal)

Plot, in detailing the legendary transformation of humans to vampire form at night, ships Dracula's son (Lon Chaney) to a small town where Louise Allbritton is an occult follower. There's the usual lonely manse with surrounding woods, and killings by the night-flying vampire to arouse the countryside.

SON OF FRANKENSTEIN
1939, 94 mins, US Ⓥ ⊙

D: Rowland V. Lee **A:** Basil Rathbone, Boris Karloff, Bela Lugosi, Lionel Atwill, Josephine Hutchinson (Universal)

Boris Karloff's man-made monster is revived in the castle of Frankenstein. Basil Rathbone, son of the scientist-creator, returns from America to the family estate, becomes intrigued with the dormant ogre, and revives him with idea of changing the brute nature within. Bela Lugosi is the mad cripple who guides the monster on murder forays. Lionel Atwill is prominent as village inspector of police.

SON OF FURY: THE STORY OF BENJAMIN BLAKE
1942, 98 mins, US Ⓥ

D: John Cromwell **A:** Tyrone Power, Gene Tierney, George Sanders, Frances Farmer, Roddy McDowall, Elsa Lanchester (20th Century-Fox)

Set in England during the reign of King George III, the story is that of Benjamin Blake (Tyrone Power) who undergoes great hardships in an attempt to establish the birthright that had been snatched from him nefariously by a scheming uncle of the upper crust. Generally the story commands rapt attention and emerges as sound, compelling entertainment.

SON OF KONG, THE
1933, 69 mins, US Ⓥ ⊙

D: Ernest B. Schoedsack **A:** Robert Armstrong, Helen Mack, Frank Reicher, John Marston (RKO)

Story is concerned mostly in building up the explorer's return to the island of prehistoric animals, which cuts down the trick stuff to perhaps less than 25 percent of the total footage. His pop was one tough hombre, but young Kong is lots more friendly. The explorer saves him from destruction in quicksand, so he proceeds to reciprocate. He wrassles and kayoes some bad eggs among the beasts of the Stone Age jungle while protecting the visiting mortals. Junior is a comparative

shrimp, standing a mere 25 feet or so, but he can handle himself in a scrap.

SON OF LASSIE
1945, 100 mins, US

D: S. Sylvan Simon **A:** Peter Lawford, Donald Crisp, June Lockhart, Nigel Bruce, Nils Asther, Leon Ames (M-G-M)

Lassie's son, Laddie, follows his young master into the war and a high-adventure trek across Nazi-occupied countries back to England after their plane is shot down. Suspense elements hit high peaks at times, offsetting the sticky sentiment, and flamboyant adventures carry sufficient interest to move film along.

SON OF PALEFACE
1952, 95 mins, US Ⓥ ⊙

D: Frank Tashlin **A:** Bob Hope, Jane Russell, Roy Rogers, Bill Williams (Paramount)

A freewheeling, often hilarious, rambunctious follow-up to *The Paleface*. Plot finds Roy Rogers and Lloyd Corrigan, government agents, assigned to running down "The Torch," a bandit. The job is complicated by the appearance of Hope, the Harvard-grad son of the late Paleface Potter. The agents decide to use him to confirm their suspicions that Jane Russell, the amorous keeper of the Dirty Shame Saloon, is the leader of the robbers.

1952: Nomination: Best Song ("Am I in Love?")

SON OF THE PINK PANTHER
1993, 93 mins, US Ⓥ ⊙ ▱

D: Blake Edwards **A:** Roberto Benigni, Herbert Lom, Claudia Cardinale, Debrah Farentino (United Artists)

The eighth episode in the series that began in 1964. Starring Italian comedian Roberto Benigni as the new bumbling inspector, it is a tired pastiche of recycled sketches and gags. Benigni's vast talents are underutilized.

SON OF THE SHEIK, THE
1926, 70 mins, US Ⓥ ⊙ ⊗

D: George Fitzmaurice **A:** Rudolph Valentino, Vilma Banky, George Fawcett, Montagu Love, Agnes Ayres (Feature/United Artists)

In *The Son of the Sheik*, Rudolph Valentino not only is the dashing youth of the Arabian plains but he also plays his father, the sheik. Naturally, the "son" is the predominant character, and in this role Valentino wins new laurels. Sequel is best described as an interesting study in psychology, showing how a son of the desert inherited the love, passions, and hate of his father.

SONS AND LOVERS
1960, 99 mins, UK ⌐

D: Jack Cardiff A: Trevor Howard, Dean Stockwell, Wendy Hiller, Mary Ure, Heather Sears (20th Century-Fox)

A well-made and conscientious adaptation of D. H. Lawrence's famed novel. Against the background of the grimy mining village is unfolded the story of a miner's son with promising artistic talents who is caught up in continual conflict between his forthright father and possessive mother. He sacrifices a chance to study art in London, gives up the local farm girl he loves, and eventually becomes entangled with a married woman separated from her husband. Easily the outstanding feature of the production is the powerful performance by Trevor Howard as the miner.

1960: Best B&W Cinematography
Nominations: Best Picture, Director, Actor (Trevor Howard), Supp. Actress (Mary Ure), Adapted Screenplay, B&W Art Direction

SONS OF KATIE ELDER, THE
1965, 120 mins, US ⓥ ⊙ ⌐

D: Henry Hathaway A: John Wayne, Dean Martin, Martha Hyer, Michael Anderson Jr., Earl Holliman (Paramount)

John Wayne, a notorious gunslinger, and Dean Martin, a gambler, return to their Texas home to attend their mother's funeral. Two stars are joined by Earl Holliman and Michael Anderson Jr., latter the kid brother, in family setup. Drama takes form as the brothers decide to stay long enough to learn who murdered their father six months previously. Wayne delivers one of his customary rugged portrayals, a little old, perhaps, to have such a young brother as Anderson. Martin plays his part with a little more humor than the others.

SONS OF THE DESERT
1934, 68 mins, US ⓥ ⊙

D: William A. Seiter A: Stan Laurel, Oliver Hardy, Charlie Chase, Mae Busch, Dorothy Christy, Lucien Littlefield (Roach/M-G-M)

This appears to be a blowup of a two-reel comedy, *We Faw Down*. In the original the comedians used a visit to a vaudeville theater as an alibi for their dalliance. In the longer version it's a trip to a lodge convention, with a supposed voyage to Honolulu as a cover. They return home to find that the steamer on which they were supposed to have sailed, foundered. About the only injection of novelty is a slick bit in which Laurel hysterically breaks down and tells the truth. Which gets him a Japanese dressing gown and permission to smoke cigarettes, while Hardy is on the receiving end of the family china and tinware.

SOPHIE'S CHOICE
1982, 157 mins, US ⓥ ⊙

D: Alan J. Pakula A: Meryl Streep, Kevin Kline, Peter MacNicol, Rita Karin, Stephen D. Newman (ITC)

Handsome, doggedly faithful, and astoundingly tedious adaptation of William Styron's bestseller. Set in 1947, tale has young aspiring writer Stingo (Peter MacNicol) taking a room in a house in which also dwell Sophie (Meryl Streep), a Polish former Catholic, and her exuberant Jewish lover (Kevin Kline). After 90 minutes, film flips into a half-hour, subtitled, sepiatoned flashback to portray Sophie's tenure as secretary to the commanding officer at Auschwitz. Streep, Kline, and MacNicol never coalesce into the close, warm trio called for by the story.

1982: Best Actress (Meryl Streep)
Nominations: Best Screenplay Adaptation, Cinematography, Costume Design, Original Score

SO PROUDLY WE HAIL
1943, 126 mins, US

D: Mark Sandrich A: Claudette Colbert, Paulette Goddard, Veronica Lake, George Reeves, Barbara Britton, Sonny Tufts (Paramount)

Saga of the war-front nurse and her heroism under fire. Background is story of how a group of brave American Nightingales came through the hellfire to Australia and thence back to Blighty. With Claudette Colbert rapidly sinking physically, the saga of their travail pitches to the situation where, out of the past, a love letter from her officer-lover finally brings her back on the road to recovery. Sonny Tufts walks off with the picture every time he's on.

1943: Nomination: Best Supp. Actress (Paulette Goddard), Original Screenplay, B&W Cinematography, Special Effects

SORCERER
(UK: WAGES OF FEAR)
1977, 121 mins, US Ⓥ ⊙
D: William Friedkin **A:** Roy Scheider, Bruno Cremer, Francisco Rabal, Amidou, Ramon Bieri (Universal/Paramount)

Painstaking, admirable, but mostly distant and uninvolving suspenser based on the French classic *The Wages of Fear*. Friedkin vividly renders the experience of several men driving trucks loaded with nitro through the South American jungle, yet the characters are basically functional. "Sorcerer" is merely the name of one of the trucks. The story has a strong existential feeling, desperate men staking their lives on a suicidal mission because they have no other way of making a living. But the film fails to bring them alive as people.
1977: Nomination: Best Sound

SORCERERS, THE
1967, 86 mins, UK Ⓥ
D: Michael Reeves **A:** Boris Karloff, Catherine Lacey, Ian Ogilvy, Elizabeth Ercy, Susan George (Tigon)

Boris Karloff brings his familiar adroit horror touch to the role of an aging somewhat nutty ex-stage mesmerist. Karloff persuades Ian Ogilvy, a feckless youth, to become the subject for his experiments to benefit mankind. But Karloff's wife, motivated by greed, insists that the lad should work for their benefit.

SOROK PYERVI
(US: THE FORTY-FIRST)
1956, 90 mins, USSR
D: Grigori Chukhrai **A:** Isolda Izvitskaya, Oleg Strizhenov, Nikolai Kryuchkov (Mosfilm)

Extremely well-made adventure-love opus which has an interesting mood and story despite the propaganda line. A female sharpshooter, taking back a White Russian prisoner during the revolution, is marooned on a desert isle with him. They fall in love, only to have it end in tragedy when she shoots him rather than be rescued by czarist soldiers searching for him.

SORROW AND THE PITY, THE
See: Le Chagrin et la Pitie

SORROWS OF SATAN, THE
1926, 117 mins, US ⊗
D: D. W. Griffith **A:** Adolphe Menjou, Ricardo Cortez, Carol Dempster, Lya De Putti (Paramount)

D. W. Griffith symbolizes good and evil, meanwhile out-DeMille-ing DeMille in sets and bacchanalian revels, plus liberal suggestiveness. Picture is overshadowed in story and cast by its superb photography. After the ruined young lady (Carol Dempster) comes the enticing of the poor lover (Ricardo Cortez) to the upper social stratum by Satan (Adolphe Menjou), and later a broad display of passion by Lya De Putti when she figuratively strips her soul.

SORRY, WRONG NUMBER
1948, 89 mins, US Ⓥ
D: Anatole Litvak **A:** Barbara Stanwyck, Burt Lancaster, Ann Richards, Wendell Corey (Wallis/Paramount)

Real chiller deals with an invalid femme who overhears a murder scheme through crossed telephone lines. She gradually comes to realize that it is her own death that is planned. Barbara Stanwyck plays her role almost entirely in bed. Her reading is sock, the actress giving an interpretation that makes the neurotic, selfish woman understandable. Same touch is used by Burt Lancaster to make audiences see through the role of the invalid's husband and how he came to plot her death.
1948: Nomination: Best Actress (Barbara Stanwyck)

S.O.S. ICEBERG
1933, 77 mins, US/Germany
D: Tay Garnett **A:** Rod La Rocque, Leni Reifenstahl, Sepp Rist, Gibson Gowland (Universal)

Made chiefly in Greenland. A young scientist seeks to recover the records of the ill-fated Wegener expedition. He achieves his purpose with the aid of three experienced ice men, and his financial backer. They are marooned on an iceberg. The hero's wife, a noted flier, goes to the rescue and crashes against the berg in landing. The finest acting is contributed by Gibson Gowland. Leni Reifenstahl supplies the alleged love interest while otherwise serving only to impede the story.

SO THIS IS PARIS
1926, 80 mins, US ⊗
D: Ernst Lubitsch **A:** Monte Blue, Patsy Ruth Miller, Lilyan Tashman, Andre Beranger, Myrna Loy (Warner)

A highly laughable farce with the laughs heavy on situations, and humorous captions added to make an excellent total. The story develops several angles in complications with two married couples living opposite each other drawn into a mass of lies and deceptions. Hardly anything is foretold nor can it be guessed at.

LE SOUFFLE AU COEUR
(US: MURMUR OF THE HEART; DEAREST LOVE)
1971, 118 mins, France/Italy Ⓥ ⊙
D: Louis Malle A: Lea Massari, Daniel Gelin, Michele Lonsdale, Benoit Ferreux (NEF/Marianne/Vides)

Film is quintessentially French in its look at the awakening sexuality of a 14-year-old boy who likes to pass himself off as 15. Suffering from a heart murmur, he is sent to a spa with his young mother, who, he knows, has a young lover. This leads eventually to a sort of love bout with his mother, which is to be a secret between them and never repeated. Benoit Ferreux has the vulnerability, warmth, and witty outlook that give his young protagonist a human and recognizable quality. His mother is excellently drawn by Lea Massari, whose need for freedom will not allow her to give way to a demanding suitor.

SOUL MAN
1986, 101 mins, US Ⓥ ⊙
D: Steve Miner A: C. Thomas Howell, Arye Gross, Rae Dawn Chong, James Earl Jones, Leslie Nielsen (Balcour/Tisch)

This social farce is excellently written, fast paced, and intelligently directed. Film consistently engages via fablelike tale of a white man (C. Thomas Howell) darkening his skin in order to win a law-school scholarship intended for a black, producing a comedic review of the state of America's racist attitudes.

SOULS AT SEA
1937, 90 mins, US
D: Henry Hathaway A: Gary Cooper, George Raft, Frances Dee, Henry Wilcoxon, Harry Carey (Paramount)

A good picture, second in cycle of slave-ship films. Narrative opens with a courtroom trial and flashes back to recount the saga of Gary Cooper and George Raft as adventurous seamen, the latter frankly a slave trader, but Cooper of finer and seemingly nobler antecedents. Human touch when little Virginia Weidler capsizes the kerosene lamp which fires the packet from Liverpool to Philadelphia is vividly translated to the audience.

SOUND AND THE FURY, THE
1959, 115 mins, US ▭
D: Martin Ritt A: Yul Brynner, Joanne Woodward, Margaret Leighton, Stuart Whitman, Ethel Waters, Jack Warden (20th Century-Fox)

A mature, provocative, and sensitively executed study of the decadent remnants of an erstwhile eminent family of a small southern town, from the William Faulkner novel. The Compsons are a weak alcoholic and a mute idiot (John Beal and Jack Warden) and a sister (Margaret Leighton) who has a long history of promiscuity. Stepson (Yul Brynner) rules as master over a decrepit estate and his wretched second hand relatives. Subject to his control also is Joanne Woodward, cast as Leighton's youthful, illegitimate daughter. A Negro-servant family, headed by Ethel Waters, completes the cast of residents.

SOUND BARRIER, THE
(AKA: BREAKING THE SOUND BARRIER)
1952, 118 mins, UK Ⓥ
D: David Lean A: Ralph Richardson, Ann Todd, Nigel Patrick, John Justin, Dinah Sheridan (London/British Lion)

Topflight British offering. The visionary in the film is superbly played by Ralph Richardson. His ambition to make the first faster-than-sound plane has brought him nothing but grief and disaster. He sees his only son killed on his first solo try; he accepts the estrangement of his daughter (Ann Todd) when his son-in-law (Nigel Patrick) crashes. David Lean's direction is bold and imaginative.
1952: Best Sound Recording
Nomination: Best Story & Screenplay

SOUNDER
1972, 105 mins, US Ⓥ ⊙ ▭
D: Martin Ritt A: Cicely Tyson, Paul Winfield, Kevin Hooks, Carmen Mathews, Taj Mahal (20th Century Fox)

Outstanding film depicts the struggles of a poor black sharecropper family in the Depression era. Kevin Hooks is excellent as the eldest son who assumes the challenges of manhood when his father (Paul Winfield) is sentenced to a year at hard labor for stealing some food for his family. Winfield is a smash in combining youth and mature virility into a figure of parental authority and parental love. His scenes with Hooks are magnificent, as are his interactions with Cicely Tyson as his wife.
1972: Nominations: Best Picture, Actor (Paul Winfield), Actress (Cicely Tyson), Adapted Screenplay

SOUND OF MUSIC, THE
1965, 173 mins, US ⊗ ⊙ ⊡

D: Robert Wise **A:** Julie Andrews, Christopher Plummer, Eleanor Parker, Richard Haydn, Peggy Wood (20th Century-Fox)

The magic and charm of the Rodgers-Hammerstein-Lindsay-Crouse 1959 stage hit are sharply blended in this filmic translation. Production is a warmly pulsating, captivating drama set to the most imaginative use of the lilting R&H tunes. For the story of the Von Trapp family singers, of the events leading up to their becoming a top concert attraction just prior to the Second World War, and their flight from Nazi Austria, Wise went to the actual locale, Salzburg, limning his action in the scenic Bavarian Alps. Andrews endows her role of the governess with fine feeling and a sense of balance.
1965: Best Picture, Director, Sound, Adapted Musical Scoring, Editing
Nominations: Best Actress (Julie Andrews), Supp. Actress (Peggy Wood), Color Cinematography, Color Art Direction, Color Costume Design

SOUND OF TRUMPETS, THE
See: Il Posto

SOURSWEET
1989, 110 mins, UK ⊗

D: Mike Newell **A:** Sylvia Chang, Danny Dun, Jodi Long, Soon-Teck Oh (First/British Screen/Zenith)

An aptly titled charmer about a Chinese family living in a dismal suburb of London. Pic sympathetically explores the insidious ways in which Chinese emigrants have to adapt to life in Britain after moving to London from Hong Kong. It's the small details that are most significant. The way a little boy discovers at school that the Chinese way of fighting, taught to him by his mother, is considered unfair. Or the way traditional Chinese customs give way in the face of British culture and lifestyle; french fries replace noodles.

SOUS LES TOITS DE PARIS
1930, 86 mins, France

D: Rene Clair **A:** Albert Prejean, Pola Illery, Gaston Modot, Edmond Greville, Paul Ollivier (Tobis)

A boy loves a girl. He is sent to jail for a short time. When he comes back he finds she has fallen in love with his best friend. They shake hands all around. Practically nothing else of importance happens, and yet the director has managed to wind to-

gether a film that holds and never lags. Clair permits only occasional sequences with conversation. But the acting, the score, and sound effects allow for perfect understanding of the action. Albert Prejean does an excellent piece of acting as the boy, and Pola Illery is as good as the girl.

SOUTH CENTRAL
1992, 99 mins, US ⊗

D: Steve Anderson **A:** Glenn Plummer, Byron Keith Minns, Lexie D. Bigham, Vincent Craig Dupree, LaRita Shelby (Warner/Ixtlan)

As a cautionary tale about the nihilistic life of street gangs, pic speaks eloquently to black kids desperately in need of straight talk. A profoundly moving story of a father's attempt to save his son from his own mistakes, film has performances by Glenn Plummer and young Christian Coleman that will touch any viewer.

SOUTHERN COMFORT
1981, 100 mins, US ⊗ ⊙

D: Walter Hill **A:** Keith Carradine, Powers Boothe, Fred Ward, Franklyn Seales, Peter Coyote (20th Century-Fox)

Arresting visual exercise and a tautly told suspenser about men out of their depths in the Louisiana swamps. Traditional themes of group camaraderie and mutual support are turned inside out. Set in 1973, tale presents nine national-guard members, weekend soldiers, heading out into the bayou for practice maneuvers. They make the mistake of appropriating some canoes belonging to local Cajuns, and when the densest of the group commits the lunacy of firing (blanks) at some native pursuers, the ill-prepared unit finds itself in a virtual state of war.

SOUTHERNER, THE
1945, 91 mins, US ⊗

D: Jean Renoir **A:** Zachary Scott, Betty Field, Beulah Bondi, Percy Kilbride, J. Carrol Naish, Charles Kemper (Producing Artists)

There is something distressing about the lives of the soil's human migrants, and all the squalor that one associates with their condition is brought to *The Southerner*. This is the story of Sam and Nona, and their struggle to cultivate the rich earth of their midwest farm. It is a farm beset by liabilities, of which lack of money and food are no small factors. Their home is a patchwork of sagging planks and misguided faith.

1945: Nominations: Best Director, Scoring of a Dramatic Picture, Sound

SOUTH PACIFIC
1958, 163 mins, US Ⓥ ⊙ ▭
D: Joshua Logan **A:** Rossano Brazzi, Mitzi Gaynor, John Kerr, Ray Walston, Juanita Hall, France Nuyen (20th Century-Fox/South Pacific Enterprises/Magna)

Compelling entertainment. The songs, perennial favorites, are mated to a sturdy James A. Michener story. John Kerr is the right romantic vis-à-vis for Eurasian beauty France Nuyen. Mitzi Gaynor is uneven in her overall impact. She is in her prime with ''Honey Bun'' in that captivating misfit sailor's uniform, and she is properly gay and buoyant and believable in ''Wonderful Guy.'' In other sequences she is conventional. Rossano Brazzi is properly serious of mien and earnest in his love protestations. The seabees are forthrightly dame-hungry; and there is enough cheesecake among the nurses corps to decorate the beachhead. The treatment of ''Nothing Like a Dame'' is standout. From ''Some Enchanted Evening'' to ''My Girl Back Home,'' it's a surefire Rodgers and Hammerstein score.
1958: Best Sound
Nominations: Best Color Cinematography, Scoring of a Musical Picture

SOUTH PARK
BIGGER, LONGER & UNCUT
1999, 80 mins, US Ⓥ ⊙
D: Trey Parker (Paramount/Warner)

South Park brings cable TV's most objectionable tykes to the silver screen with considerable aplomb. Pint-sized third-graders Stan, Kyle, Cartman, and Kenny are thrilled to discover their TV faves, Canadian *fartistes* Terrence and Philip, have a movie *Asses of Fire* at the local plex. The boys emerge with a whole new graphic vocabulary. Kyle's mom spearheads an anti-Canadian agitprop campaign and violent Canuck reprisal follows. Soon both nations are on the brink of full-scale combat. Kyle, Stan, and Cartman orchestrate La Résistance, a children's underground aimed at preventing war and possible biblical collapse. Screenplay ladles out high doses of xenophobia, knee-jerk patriotism, racism, homophobia, and whatever else comes to mind, in service of an earnest protoleature theme, however snarkily articulated.
1999: Nomination: Original Song (''Blame Canada'')

SOUTH RIDING
1938, 91 mins, UK Ⓥ
D: Victor Saville **A:** Edna Best, Ralph Richardson, Edmund Gwenn, Ann Todd, John Clements (London)

English melodrama is fairly familiar matter—the spoiled child whose father fears she will grow up to be like her stark-mad mother, the conniving contractor and real-estate operator, and the country gentleman whose intense love of his estate nearly enables the crooked plot to hatch. But all of this has been heightened by original twirls of acting and direction. Edna Best is tops as a schoolteacher. Ralph Richardson contributes one of his finer thespian jobs as the country gentleman.

SOUTH SEA FURY
See: Hell's Island

SOUTH SEAS ADVENTURE
1958, 120 mins, US ▭
D: Carl Dudley, Richard Goldstone, Francis D. Lyon, Walter Thompson, Basil Wrangell (Cinerama)

Cinerama still conveys its unique brand of pictorial experience, though distortion and seams persist. If *South Seas Adventure* were not No. 5 in a sequence of travelogues, its merits would no doubt seem more estimable. The voyage by liner, schooner, and aircraft adds up to a fairly diverting if not very exciting journey. Big physical thrill among the islands is the jump off the bamboo tower by the natives of the New Hebrides, the fall being broken by vine ropes attached to the men's ankles.

SOUVENIR
1989, 93 mins, UK
D: Geoffrey Reeve **A:** Christopher Plummer, Catherine Hicks, Michael Lonsdale, Christopher Casenove, Lisa Daniely (Fancy Free)

Earnest but bland film, about a former Nazi soldier's need to unburden himself of guilt 40 years after the war, sees German native Christopher Plummer leaving his adopted country of the US to see his daughter in Paris. His real mission, however, is to return to the French village where, as a young recruit, he had an unforgettable love affair with a local girl and played an unwitting part in the massacre of more than 100 townsfolk. Unfortunately, most of the first half of the picture has his immature, incredibly irritating daughter, played by Catherine Hicks, acting very intolerant and impatient with her old man.

SOYLENT GREEN
1973, 97 mins, US ♈ ⊙ ▱
D: Richard Fleischer **A:** Charlton Heston, Leigh Taylor-Young, Chuck Connors, Joseph Cotten, Brock Peters, Edward G. Robinson (M-G-M)

A good futuristic exploitation film. The year is 2022, the setting NY City, where millions of overpopulated residents exist in a smog-insulated police state and where real food is a luxury item. Charlton Heston is a detective assigned to the assassination of industrialist Joseph Cotten, who has discovered the shocking fact that the Soylent Corp is no longer making synthetic food from the dying sea. The substitute—the reconstituted bodies of the dead. The script bungles seriously by confining Heston's outrage to the secret of Soylent Green.

SPACEBALLS
1987, 96 mins, US ♈ ⊙ ▱
D: Mel Brooks **A:** Mel Brooks, John Candy, Rick Moranis, Bill Pullman, Daphne Zuniga, John Hurt (M-G-M/Brooksfilms)

Mel Brooks will do anything for a laugh. Unfortunately, what he does in a misguided parody of the *Star Wars* adventures isn't very funny. Pic features Bill Pullman as Lone Starr and Daphne Zuniga as Princess Vespa, former a composite of Harrison Ford and Mark Hamill, latter a Carrie Fisher clone. Pullman's partner is John Candy as Barf, a half-man, half-dog creature who is his own best friend. Barf is one of the better comic creations here.

SPACECAMP
1986, 107 mins, US ♈ ⊙
D: Harry Winer **A:** Kate Capshaw, Lea Thompson, Kelly Preston, Larry B. Scott, Tom Skerritt (ABC)

A youthful view of outer space set at the real-life United States Space Camp in Huntsville, AL for aspiring young astronauts. Pic never successfully integrates summer-camp high jinks with outer-space idealism in a dramatically compelling story. Hampered by cliché-ridden dialogue, performances suffer from a weightlessness of their own.

SPACEHUNTER: ADVENTURES IN THE FORBIDDEN ZONE
1983, 90 mins, US ♈ ⊙ ▱
D: Lamont Johnson **A:** Peter Strauss, Molly Ringwald, Ernie Hudson, Andrea Marcovicci, Michael Ironside (Columbia/Delphi)

Columbia's big-budget 3-D entry is a muddled science-fiction tale set in the mid-21st century on an earth colony reduced to rubble by wars and a plague. Weak story premise has salvage-ship pilot Wolff (Peter Strauss) and other "Earthers" including orphaned waif Niki (Molly Ringwald) searching the planet for three shipwrecked, later kidnapped girls. Episodic treatment pits them against many local dangers en route to a showdown at the lair of local tyrant Overdog (Michael Ironside).

SPANISH GARDENER, THE
1957, 97 mins, UK ♈
D: Philip Leacock **A:** Dirk Bogarde, Jon Whiteley, Michael Hordern, Cyril Cusack, Maureen Swanson, Bernard Lee (Rank)

A. J. Cronin's novel translates into absorbing screen entertainment with colorful Spanish backgrounds. Michael Hordern is the diplomat, continually passed up for promotion, who insists that his son is delicate, cannot join other children in games or at school, and is denied every form of companionship. Dirk Bogarde is hired as a gardener and his friendly attitude to the kid sparks a violent jealousy in the father.

SPANISH MAIN, THE
1945, 101 mins, US ♈ ⊙
D: Frank Borzage **A:** Paul Henreid, Maureen O'Hara, Walter Slezak, Binnie Barnes, John Emery (RKO)

Robust saga of swaggering pirates and beautiful girls. Story concentrates on action melodrama but occasionally takes a satirical slant. Paul Henreid does well by the dashing Dutchman who becomes the Spaniards' sea scourge. Maureen O'Hara hasn't much opportunity to show off her acting ability but fulfills the role's other requirements with lush beauty. Walter Slezak's cruel Spanish governor character is showy.

SPANISH PRISONER, THE
1997, 112 mins, US ♈ ⊙ ▱
D: David Mamet **A:** Campbell Scott, Rebecca Pidgeon, Steve Martin, Ricky Jay, Ben Gazzara, Felicity Huffman (Sweetlands)

David Mamet has a penchant for sleight-of-hand thrillers, and *The Spanish Prisoner* is his craftiest to date, a devilishly clever series of reversals that keeps you guessing to the very end. Joe Ross (Campbell Scott) arrives on a Caribbean isle for a secret meeting to unveil a new invention. While taking photos with Susan

(Rebecca Pidgeon), a company secretary, Joe is approached by Jimmy Dell (Steve Martin), who explains he's fearful Joe may have caught him on film in the midst of an illicit tryst. The friendship that develops between the reserved Joe and mercurial Jimmy is the perfect frame for Kafkaesque machinations. "The Spanish Prisoner," we're told by a seeming FBI agent, is the term for a classic confidence scam. Scott and Martin are a deliciously effective pairing. The support players, especially Pidgeon, provide the sort of mixed messages that bring both the on-screen characters and audience to the brink.

SPARROWS CAN'T SING
1963, 94 mins, UK Ⓥ
D: Joan Littlewood A: James Booth, Barbara Windsor, Roy Kinnear, George Sewell, Barbara Ferris (Carthage)

The story line is disarmingly slight. James Booth plays a tearaway merchant seaman who comes back to his East End home to find that it has been torn down and his wife (Barbara Windsor) has found herself another nest with a local bus driver. His arrival strikes uneasiness in the hearts of the locals, who know his uncertain temper. But Booth sets out to find his wife and collect his conjugal rights. Though there is a sober side to the film, this is mostly played for yocks. Booth is a striking personality, a punchy blend of toughness, potential evil, and irresistible charm. Barbara Windsor is a cute young blond who teeters delightfully through her role, on stiletto heels and with a devastating sense of logic.

SPARTACUS
1960, 197 mins, US Ⓥ ⊙ ▭
D: Stanley Kubrick [Anthony Mann] A: Kirk Douglas, Laurence Olivier, Jean Simmons, Charles Laughton, Peter Ustinov, Tony Curtis (Universal/Bryna)

A rousing testament to the spirit and dignity of man, dealing with a revolt by slaves against the pagan Roman Empire. In terms of spectacle, the clash between the slave army led by Kirk Douglas and the Romans commanded by Laurence Olivier is nothing short of flabbergasting. Douglas is the mainstay of the picture. He is not particularly expressive—not compared with the sophisticated Olivier, the conniving gladiator-ring operator portrayed by Peter Ustinov, or the slave maiden Jean Simmons. But Douglas succeeds admirably in giving an impression of a man who is all afire inside. Tony Curtis as the Italian slave who serves as houseboy to Olivier before running away to join Spartacus gives a nicely balanced performance. Charles Laughton is superbly wily and sophisticated as a Republican senator.

1960: Best Supp. Actor (Peter Ustinov), Color Cinematography, Color Art Direction, Color Costume Design
Nominations: Best Editing, Scoring of a Dramatic Picture

SPAWN
1997, 97 mins, US Ⓥ ⊙
D: Mark A. Z. Dippe A: John Leguizamo, Michael Jai White, Martin Sheen, Theresa Randle, Melinda Clarke, Nicol Williamson (New Line)

Spawn is a moodily malevolent, anything-goes revenge fantasy. On a mission to take out a North Korean biological weapons plant, US government operative Al Simmons (Michael Jai White) is blown to smithereens by his boss, Jason Wynn (Martin Sheen), who takes possession of the germ material to establish his bid for world domination. Five years later, Simmons is given the chance to return to Earth and see his beloved wife (Theresa Randle) and daughter if he accepts to lead the devil's army to conquer the world. He is influenced on behalf of the forces of darkness by the repellent Clown from Hell (John Leguizamo, unrecognizable in billowing fat and costumes). This is presented in a muddled way in Alan McElroy's screenplay, which has Simmons—transformed into the armor-plated, superhuman Spawn—get on the trail of the nefarious Wynn. Thesps have all been seen to better advantage elsewhere, to say the least.

SPAWN OF THE NORTH
1938, 105 mins, US
D: Henry Hathaway A: George Raft, Henry Fonda, Dorothy Lamour, Akim Tamiroff, John Barrymore (Paramount)

Plot recounts the battles of the Alaskan waters between licensed fishermen and pirates who steal the catch from the traps set for salmon at spawning time. George Raft and Henry Fonda, boyhood friends, are members of opposing factions, the former having fallen in with Russian thieves. Merit of the film is in the persuasive and authentic photographic record of Alaskan life and customs. Akim Tamiroff is a truly menacing pirate with a black heart and no regard for law and order.

1938: Special Award (special photographic and sound effects)

SPEAKING PARTS
1989, 92 mins, Canada ⓥ ⊙
D: Atom Egoyan **A:** Michael McManus, Arsinee Khanjian, Gabrielle Rose, David Hemblen (Ego)

A brooding, personal effort, adroitly blending film and video, but with mixed results overall. Hero cleans hotel rooms, sexually services female clients offscreen on orders from the housekeeper, and seeks a speaking part in films after playing extra roles.

SPECIALIST, THE
1994, 109 mins, US ⓥ ⊙
D: Luis Llosa **A:** Sylvester Stallone, Sharon Stone, James Woods, Rod Steiger, Eric Roberts (Warner)

Film delivers plenty of bright fireballs but fails to make good on the potential chemistry of Sylvester Stallone and Sharon Stone. Explosives specialists Ray Quick (Stallone) makes contact with a potential client (Stone) who is looking to eradicate three Cuban-American gangsters led by Tomas Leon (Eric Roberts). She begins by making herself available to Tomas, capably incarnated by Roberts, who again proves his aptitude at oozing sleaze from every pore. The killer's affair transpires under the increasingly watchful eyes of his crime boss father, Joe Leon (Rod Steiger), and Ray's former partner, Ned (Woods), who now appears to be simultaneously employed by the Leon family and the Miami police.

SPECIES
1995, 108 mins, US ⓥ ⊙ ⌨
D: Roger Donaldson **A:** Ben Kingsley, Michael Madsen, Alfred Molina, Forest Whitaker, Natasha Henstridge (M-G-M)

A gripping if not overly original account of an extraterrestrial species attempting to overwhelm our own. Sil, as the creature is known, morphs into a strikingly gorgeous blond (newcomer Natasha Henstridge, a Canadian model) whose mission is to reproduce as quickly as possible, fortunately in single-scene L.A. Sex, mayhem, and chases dominate tale's final hour. Thanks to high-velocity direction, lavishly realized effects, and sharp lensing, pic ends up an effective thrill machine.

SPECIES II
1998, 93 mins, US ⓥ ⊙
D: Peter Medak **A:** Michael Madsen, Na-
tasha Henstridge, Marg Helgenberger, Mykelti Williamson, George Dzundza, James Cromwell (FGM/M-G-M)

Species II, a half-baked rehash of the hit 1995 sci-fi shocker about a half-human, half-alien beauty with a murderous urge to mate, is an unsavory and unsatisfying blend of dumb plotting, leering lasciviousness and full-bore gore. Natasha Henstridge is half-breed Eve, cooked up in a top-secret government lab. Michael Madsen is Press Lennox, a freelance assassin hired to seek and destroy a killer alien. During a manned mission to Mars, astronaut Patrick Ross (Justin Lazard) is infected with the same DNA that figured in the birth of Eve. Back on Earth, he finds that each time he makes love to a woman, he instantly impregnates her, and each embryo rapidly develops to the size of a preschooler. Despite many messy deaths, some fairly impressive special effects and a surprising amount of softcore sex, *Species II* fails to generate much excitement. Madsen walks through his performance with all the enthusiasm of someone fulfilling a contractual obligation. Henstridge and Lazard are fine physical specimens, but their characters appear far more animated when the actors are replaced by tentacled, animatronic monsters.

SPECTER OF THE ROSE
1946, 90 mins, US ⓥ
D: Ben Hecht **A:** Judith Anderson, Michael Chekhov, Ivan Kirov, Lionel Stander (Republic)

Yarn concerns a ballet troupe. Okay mentally for periods, the top male dancer at times has hallucinations in which he hears music which forces him to dance the ballet *Spectre de la Rose* and, while terpin', he gets a desire to slit his wife's throat. One of the ballerinas is sure she can cure him. This is set against a seriocomic and satirical background of the ballet company's travails, financial and otherwise in staging a tour. Hecht's direction and dialogue give the acting a stylized artificiality that grows on the spectator as the picture progresses.

SPEECHLESS
1994, 99 mins, US ⓥ ⊙
D: Ron Underwood **A:** Michael Keaton, Geena Davis, Christopher Reeve, Bonnie Bedelia, Charles Martin Smith (M-G-M/Forge)

Likable but uneven romantic comedy. Davis and Keaton play warring speechwriters who have a chance encounter before realizing they're on opposite sides of the same New Mexico Senate race. Concern about fraternizing with the enemy creates tension between the pair even though they're perfect for each other. Another wrinkle gets thrown into the budding relationship when Davis's absentee boyfriend (Christopher Reeve) returns.

SPEED
1994, 115 mins, US Ⓥ ⊙ ▭
D: Jan De Bont **A:** Keanu Reeves, Dennis Hopper, Sandra Bullock, Joe Morton, Jeff Daniels (20th Century-Fox)

Although it hits any number of gaping credibility potholes on its careening journey around Los Angeles, pic still manages to deliver the goods as a no-stop actioner that scarcely pauses to take a breath. Main action is set on board a bus that's rigged to blow up if it slows to under 50 mph. Film's hallmark stunt has the huge bus building up a big head of steam so that it can bridge a 50-foot gap in a freeway overpass.
1994: Best Sound, Sound Effects Editing
Nomination: Best Film Editing

SPEED 2
CRUISE CONTROL
1997, 125 mins, US Ⓥ ▭
D: Jan De Bont **A:** Sandra Bullock, Jason Patric, Willem Dafoe, Temuera Morrison, Brian McCardie, Christine Firkins (Blue Tulip/20th Century-Fox)

Hampered by a derivative, cliché-ridden screenplay, waterbound sequel to the 1994 smash hit is a serviceable action thriller that takes too long to deliver the goods. Annie (Sandra Bullock) joins boyfriend Alex (Jason Patric) on a Caribbean cruise. Unbeknownst to her, he is a member of an elite SWAT unit. Yarn picks up some momentum once they get aboard the "world's most luxurious" cruise liner. John Geiger (Willem Dafoe), a mad computer mastermind, orchestrates a nasty takeover; most of the thrilling action scenes occur in the last 40 minutes, as a desperate effort is made to slow down the liner so it won't crash into another ship. Bullock and Patric don't generate much heat in their romantic scenes.

SPELLBOUND
1945, 116 mins, US Ⓥ ⊙
D: Alfred Hitchcock **A:** Ingrid Bergman, Gregory Peck, Rhonda Fleming, Leo G. Carroll, Norman Lloyd (United Artists)

Gregory Peck believes that he committed a murder but has no memory of the locale or circumstances surrounding the crime. Ingrid Bergman as a psychiatrist tries desperately to save him from punishment for the crime she is certain he could not have committed, and in doing so risks her career and almost her life. Salvador Dali designed the surrealistic dream sequence. Alfred Hitchcock handles his players and action in suspenseful manner.
1945: Best Score for a Dramatic Picture
Nominations: Best Picture, Director, Supp. Actor (Michael Chekhov), B&W Cinematography, Special Effects

SPENCER'S MOUNTAIN
1963, 121 mins, US Ⓥ ⊙ ▭
D: Delmer Daves **A:** Henry Fonda, Maureen O'Hara, James MacArthur, Donald Crisp, Mimsy Farmer (Warner)

Delmer Daves chooses the majestic Grand Tetons to background a quite ordinary, but generally enjoyable and often emotionally moving comedy-drama about a large, simple, hardworking family and its joys and disappointments from the cradle to the grave. With less ingratiating and expert performers than Henry Fonda and Maureen O'Hara, Daves might have found himself in trouble.

SPHERE
1998, 133 mins, US Ⓥ ⊙ ▭
D: Barry Levinson **A:** Dustin Hoffman, Sharon Stone, Samuel L. Jackson, Peter Coyote, Liev Schreiber, Queen Latifah (Baltimore/Constant/Warner)

Sphere is an empty shell. Derivative of numerous famous sci-fi movies and as full of false promises as the *Wizard of Oz*, this portentous underwater *Thing* swims along with reasonable good humor for its first hour, then descends into mechanical and routine "suspense" sequences. Psychologist Dr. Norman Goodman (Dustin Hoffman) is summoned to a remote Pacific site where group leader Barnes (Peter Coyote) throws him together with biochemist Beth Halperin (Sharon Stone)—with whom Goodman has a past—mathematician Harry Adams (Samuel L. Jackson) and astrophysicist Ted Fielding (Liev Schreiber). A thousand feet down they view an amazing sight: a submerged spacecraft nearly half a mile long that crashed there 288 years before. The main revelation is an enormous, shimmering, golden sphere seemingly made of liquid metal. Actors are all underused in shallow roles.

1154

SPHINX
1981, 117 mins, US ⊛ ▭
D: Franklin J. Schaffner **A:** Lesley-Anne Down, Frank Langella, Maurice Ronet, John Gielgud, Saeed Jaffrey (Orion)

An embarrassment. Contempo *Perils of Pauline* sees earnest, dedicated Egyptologist Lesley-Anne Down through countless situations of dire jeopardy as she travels from Cairo to Luxor's Valley of the Kings in pursuit of a mysterious tomb of riches, which also holds great interest for black marketers. Franklin J. Schaffner's steady and sober style is helpless in the face of the mounting implausibilities.

SPICE WORLD
1997, 92 mins, UK ⊛ ⊙
D: Bob Spiers **A:** The Spice Girls, Richard E. Grant, Alan Cumming, George Wendt, Claire Rushbrook, Roger Moore (Fragile/Spice Girls)

A bright and breezy movie as timely and evanescent as the Cool Britannia culture it celebrates, *Spice World* will delight the group's pre-pubescent fans and recall fond memories of the sixties to those who lived through them. Picture is not so much a story as a series of musical opportunities dotted with celeb cameos, following the Spices through five days leading up to their first live gig in London's Royal Albert Hall. En route, the movie takes potshots at the tabloid press, the capital's glitterati and the media in general, as well as stirring in beaucoup filmic refs to amuse oldsters while the young 'uns are transfixed by the girls and their music. The question of whether the Spices can act—they can't, but neither could the Beatles—is largely irrelevant. None is allowed to dominate, though the sultry Victoria (Posh), constantly griping about her wardrobe, gets the best of a so-so bunch of quips.

SPIES LIKE US
1985, 109 mins, US ⊛ ⊙
D: John Landis **A:** Chevy Chase, Dan Aykroyd, Steve Forrest, Donna Dixon, Bruce Davison (Paramount)

Spies is not very amusing. Chase and Aykroyd are a couple of bumbling bureaucrats with aspirations for spy work, but no talent for the job. They are chosen for a mission because they will make expendable decoys for a real spy team headed by pretty Donna Dixon. Much of the time Aykroyd is fooling with gadgets, Chase is fooling with Dixon, and director

John Landis is fooling with half-baked comedy ideas.

SPINSTER
See: Two Loves

SPIRAL ROAD, THE
1962, 145 mins, US
D: Robert Mulligan **A:** Rock Hudson, Burl Ives, Gena Rowlands, Geoffrey Keen, Neva Patterson (Universal)

Uninspiring tale of an atheist's conversion to God takes the devil's own time getting down to cases and the resolution. It concerns an opportunitist freshman medic (Rock Hudson) and his determination to ride to scientific fame on the research of a seasoned jungle physician (Burl Ives).

SPIRAL STAIRCASE, THE
1946, 83 mins, US ⊛
D: Robert Siodmak **A:** Dorothy McGuire, George Brent, Ethel Barrymore, Kent Smith, Rhonda Fleming, Elsa Lanchester (RKO)

Smooth production of a mass-murder story set in a small New England town of 1906. Director has retained a feeling for terror throughout the film by smart photography, camera angles, and sudden shifts of camera emphasis, abetted in this job by five performances of his cast. Dorothy McGuire's stature as actress is increased by her performance as a maidservant bereft of speech, and Ethel Barrymore's list of pic portraits will get another goldframer from her role of bedridden wealthy eccentric.
1946: Nomination: Best Supp. Actress (Ethel Barrymore)

SPIRIT OF ST. LOUIS, THE
1957, 135 mins, US ⊛ ▭
D: Billy Wilder **A:** James Stewart, Murray Hamilton, Patricia Smith (Warner)

Class-A picture-making doesn't manage to deliver entertainment wallop out of the story about one man in a single-engine plane over a 3,610-mile route. *Spirit* is a James Stewart one-man show. He portrays Charles Lindbergh with a toned-down performance intended as consistent with the diffident (i.e., noncommunicative) nature of the famed aviator. The flashback technique is used to convey some of Lindbergh's background.
1957: Nomination: Best Special Effects

SPIRIT OF THE BEEHIVE, THE
See: El Espiritu de la Colmena

SPITFIRE
See: The First of the Few

SPITFIRE
1934, 88 mins, US
D: John Cromwell **A:** Katharine Hepburn, Robert Young, Ralph Bellamy, Martha Sleeper, Sara Haden (RKO)

This is Hepburn with a picture built around her and the part she plays, that of a backwoods mountain girl of the south. Hepburn not only has to look the part of the hot-tempered woman but match a difficult accent with it throughout. In both respects, the performance is almost without flaw. The girl helps herself to a neighbor's baby. Her only thought is in giving it the care its parents are neglecting to bestow, but shortly after the child is returned to its native hearth, it dies. This arouses the mountaineers to lynching frenzy.

SPIVS, THE
See: I Vitelloni

SPLASH
1984, 111 mins, US Ⓥ ⊙
D: Ron Howard **A:** Tom Hanks, Daryl Hannah, John Candy, Eugene Levy, Dody Goodman (Touchstone)

Surprisingly charming mermaid yarn is notable for winning suspension of disbelief and fetching byplay between Daryl Hannah and Tom Hanks. Hannah couldn't be better cast if she were Neptune's daughter incarnate. Hanks, as a Gotham bachelor in search of love, makes a fine leap from sitcom land, and John Candy as an older playboy brother is a marvelous foil.
1984: Nomination: Best Original Screenplay

SPLENDOR
1935, 77 mins, US
D: Elliott Nugent **A:** Miriam Hopkins, Joel McCrea, Paul Cavanaugh, Helen Westley, Billie Burke, David Niven (Goldwyn/United Artists)

Well-written story, interpreted in skilled and sympathetic action under able direction. Miriam Hopkins marries Joel McCrea while he is on a business trip, and he proudly brings her home, not realizing that his ambitious mother (Helen Westley) is looking to a marriage with an heiress (Ruth Weston). Hopkins gets small welcome from her in-laws, and even McCrea is a bit impatient with her because of his own perplexities. His father and grandfather amassed money. He doesn't seem able to realize why he cannot. Helen Westley, as the mother, is the dominant figure.

SPLENDOR IN THE GRASS
1961, 124 mins, US Ⓥ ⊙
D: Elia Kazan **A:** Natalie Wood, Warren Beatty, Pat Hingle, Audrey Christie, Barbara Loden (Warner)

Elia Kazan's production of William Inge's original screenplay covers a forbidding chunk of ground with great care, compassion, and cinematic flair. Yet there is something awkward about the picture's mechanical rhythm. Inge's screenplay deals with a young couple deeply in love but unable to synchronize their opposing moral attitudes. Their tragedy is helped along by the influence of parental intervention. The children cannot consummate their relationship, either sexually or maritally. Natalie Wood and Warren Beatty (whom the picture "introduces") are the lovers. Both deliver convincing, appealing performances. The real histrionic honors, though, belong to Audrey Christie, who plays Wood's mother, and Pat Hingle, as Beatty's father.
1961: Best Original Story & Screenplay
Nomination: Best Actress (Natalie Wood)

SPLITTING HEIRS
1993, 86 mins, UK/US Ⓥ ⊙
D: Robert Young **A:** Rick Moranis, Eric Idle, Barbara Hershey, Catherine Zeta Jones, John Cleese, Sadie Frost (Prominent/Universal)

Breezy but lightweight comedy. Rick Moranis plays a motormouth Yank who becomes the 15th Duke of Bournemouth and head of the family bank when his father suddenly drowns. Unbeknownst to him, the real heir to the fortune is bank underling Eric Idle, who's become his best pal. When Idle stumbles across the truth, he tries every means to deep-six Moranis and claim his rightful fortune.

SPOILERS, THE
1942, 87 mins, US Ⓥ ⊙
D: Ray Enright **A:** Marlene Dietrich, Randolph Scott, John Wayne, Richard Barthelmess, Harry Carey (Universal)

Teeming, raw saga of Alaska in its 1898 Gold Rush days. It tells of Randolph Scott, as the crooked gold commissioner, an equally unscrupulous judge (Samuel S. Hinds), and their "legal" confiscation of the miners' claims. John Wayne plays a prospector who loses the mine he jointly owns with Harry Carey. Marlene Dietrich is the operator of a gin-and-gambling emporium. Dovetailed to this is the tempestuous romance between Wayne and Dietrich, with Scott as the bad third. The slugging match in the final reel between Wayne and Scott is something that apparently could be staged profitably at Madison Square Garden.

SPRING AND PORT WINE
1970, 101 mins, UK
D: Peter Hammond **A:** James Mason, Susan George, Diana Coupland, Rodney Bewes, Hannah Gordon (Memorial)

Set in the mill area of Lancashire and its moors, this is the story of a generational clash in a small family. James Mason plays a kindly but stubborn man who brings up his family with a startling strictness. Chief rebel is the high-spirited Susan George, whose refusal to eat a herring for tea sparks off a handful of situations that remind Mason that "you can spend a lifetime creating a family and break it up in a weekend."

SPRINGFIELD RIFLE
1952, 92 mins, US Ⓥ
D: Andre de Toth **A:** Gary Cooper, Phyllis Thaxter, David Brian, Paul Kelly, Lon Chaney (Warner)

The Springfield rifle and army counterespionage are the bases for the plot of this Gary Cooper starrer. Every time a cavalry outpost tries to supply the mounts needed to keep the government's army on the move, renegades ambush the soldiers and sell the horses to the Confederacy. Cooper, Union officer, is the key to the counterespionage plot. He's cashiered on charges bordering on cowardice and joins up with David Brian, leader of the herd raiders.

SPRING IN PARK LANE
1948, 91 mins, UK
D: Herbert Wilcox **A:** Anna Neagle, Michael Wilding, Tom Walls, Peter Graves, Nigel Patrick (British Lion)

Michael Wilding as a younger son of a noble family, needing money for a return trip to New York, becomes a temporary footman in a Park Lane mansion. Since Anna Neagle plays a secretary in the same house, everybody knows it will be love at first sight and that sooner or later the two will march altarward. It's a story in which the trimmings and incidentals are all-important. The gay harmless fun poked at the dinner-party bore, the housekeeper to whom bridge is a religion, the footman cutting in to dance or discussing art with his boss—incident upon incident carry merry laughter through the picture.

SPRINGTIME IN THE ROCKIES
1942, 90 mins, US Ⓥ ⊙
D: Irving Cummings **A:** Betty Grable, John Payne, Carmen Miranda, Cesar Romero, Charlotte Greenwood, Edward Everett Horton (20th Century-Fox)

Betty Grable and John Payne, costars in a Broadway musical, are romantically inclined—but he has a weakness for pretty girls, which keeps them continually battling. When the show closes, Grable joins her former dancing partner Romero for a western tour, but Payne follows to Lake Louise to woo her back to a new Broadway show. Script is studded with laugh lines that are well distributed among the cast.

SPY HARD
1996, 80 mins, US Ⓥ ⊙
D: Rick Friedberg **A:** Leslie Nielsen, Nicollette Sheridan, Charles Durning, Marcia Gay Harden, Barry Bostwick (Hollywood)

Spy Hard sticks closely to the *Naked Gun* formula. Title notwithstanding, the film is less a spoof of the ripe-for-parody *Die Hard*–style actioners than of the time-worn James Bonders (by way of *Get Smart*). Nielsen, ever reliable even when his material isn't, stars as Dick Steele, Agent WD-40. He's called out of retirement to hunt for his old nemesis, the evil General Rancor (Andy Griffith), an armless madman with plans for global takeover.

SPY IN BLACK, THE
(AKA: U-BOAT 29)
1939, 82 mins, UK Ⓥ ⊙
D: Michael Powell **A:** Conrad Veidt, Sebastian Shaw, Valerie Hobson, Marius Goring, June Duprez (Harefield/Korda)

Praiseworthy film about international espionage during World War I. Conrad Veidt, as captain of a German submarine, receives instructions to proceed to the Orkney Islands, where he's to meet a woman spy, from whom he's to take orders. Veidt has a strong role for which he's admirably suited.

SPYS
1974, 100 mins, UK/US Ⓥ
D: Irvin Kershner **A:** Donald Sutherland, Elliott Gould, Zou Zou, Joss Ackland, Shane Rimmer, Vladek Sheybal (Dymphana/Chartoff-Winkler/American Film Properties)

Spys is a mess. The production reteams Elliott Gould and Donald Sutherland, this time as a pair of bungling CIA agents. The script is tasteless, Irvin Kershner's direction is futile, and the whole effort comes across as vulgar, offensive, and tawdry. The "fun" of international espionage is depicted by a series of bomb explosions, lavatory homicide, police torture, kinky sex, a car chase, a search through canine feces, and a disrupted church wedding ceremony.

SPY WHO CAME IN FROM THE COLD, THE
1966, 112 mins, UK ⓥ ⊙
D: Martin Ritt **A:** Richard Burton, Claire Bloom, Oskar Werner, Sam Wanamaker, George Voskovec (Salem/Paramount)

Excellent espionage drama of the cold war achieves solid impact via emphasis on human values, total absence of mechanical spy gimmickry, and perfectly controlled underplaying. Film effectively socks over the point that East-West espionage agents are living in a world of their own, apart from the day-to-day existence of the millions whom they are serving. Richard Burton fits neatly into the role of the apparently burned-out British agent, ripe for cultivation by East German Communist secret police as a potential defector.
1965: Nominations: Best Actor (Richard Burton), B&W Art Direction

SPY WHO LOVED ME, THE
1977, 125 mins, UK ⓥ ⊙ ▭
D: Lewis Gilbert **A:** Roger Moore, Barbara Bach, Curt Jurgens, Richard Kiel, Caroline Munro (United Artists/Eon)

As always, story and plastic character are in the service of comic-strip parody, an excuse to star the prop department, set designer, stunt arrangers, the optical-illusion chaps, and such commercial suppliers as the maker of a sporty Lotus car that also converts to an underwater craft. When British and Russian nuclear subs start to mysteriously vanish, two agents are assigned by their collaborating governments to jointly crack the case. Curt Jurgens's arsenal includes the film's gimmick character, a monster human known as "Jaws," played with robotic finesse by Richard Kiel.
1977: Nominations: Art Direction, Original Score, Song ("Nobody Does It Better")

SPY WITH MY FACE, THE
1966, 86 mins, US
D: John Newland **A:** Robert Vaughn, Senta Berger, David McCallum, Leo G.

Carroll, Michael Evans, Sharon Farrell (M-G-M/Arena)

New footage was added to an old *Man from U.N.C.L.E.* episode to bring it up to 86 minutes for theatrical release. Thrush, that band of murderous renegades that would rule the world and is constantly combating U.N.C.L.E., fixes up one of its agents to be the exact double of Napoleon Solo, the good guy, and nearly succeeds in its purpose—whatever that is.

SQUEAKER, THE
1937, 79 mins, UK ⓥ
D: William K. Howard **A:** Edmund Lowe, Sebastian Shaw, Ann Todd, Tamara Desni, Robert Newton, Alastair Sim (London)

Fine Korda production from the Edgar Wallace play has been changed from a whodunit to a newer formula, that of revealing early the identity of the archcriminal who for years baffled Scotland Yard, and interest in the film is wholly dependent on how the Yard unravels the crime. Audience is asked to believe that a ruthless criminal, who doesn't even stop at murder, breaks down and confesses in a cowering, hysterical manner when confronted with the corpse of his victim.

SQUEEZE, THE
1977, 106 mins, UK ⓥ
D: Michael Apted **A:** Stacy Keach, Freddie Starr, Edward Fox, Stephen Boyd, David Hemmings, Carol White (Warner)

Stacy Keach plays a busted cop fighting the booze habit and some murderous thugs at the same time. Keach suffers some nasty lumps and sundry humiliations, all in the cause of Edward Fox as a security-firm exec whose wife and kid are hostages against a million-dollar-plus payoff. Pic has little in the way of style and no great surprises. It does, however, have a kind of gratuitous nasty tone.

SQUEEZE
1996, 100 mins, US ⓥ
D: Robert Patton-Spruill **A:** Tyrone Burton, Eddie Cutanda, Phuong Duong, Geoffrey Rhue, Russell G. Jones (Robbins/Cathartic Filmworks)

Pic represents the flowering of homegrown filmmaking in Boston. Tyson (Tyrone Burton), Hector (Eddie Cutanda), and Bao (Phuong Duong) are three poor 14-year-olds trying to figure out where they fit into life on the streets. What follows is a series of episodes as the three adolescents try to make sense of the conflicting messages they get from drug dealers, relatives, and officials. Patton-Spruill draws standout performances from his young cast. Pic boasts a surprisingly polished look.

SQUIRM
1976, 93 mins, US ⓥ
D: Jeff Lieberman A: John Scardino, Patricia Pearcy, R. A. Dow, Jean Sullivan, Peter MacLean (American International)

Average shock meller about some rampaging sand worms in the Georgia sticks. Some genuine creepy special effects are offset by clumsy and amateurish low-budget location production, yet there is an admirable earnestness to the effort.

STAGECOACH
1939, 95 mins, US ⓥ ⊙
D: John Ford A: Claire Trevor, John Wayne, Andy Devine, Thomas Mitchell, George Bancroft, John Carradine (United Artists)

John Ford in peak form. It's the adventures of a group aboard a stagecoach between two frontier settlements during the sudden uprising of the Apaches. Situation is a *Grand Hotel* on wheels. There's Claire Trevor, dancehall gal; driver, Andy Devine; gambler, John Carradine; inebriated medic, Thomas Mitchell; marshal, George Bancroft; wife of an army officer, Louise Platt; whiskey salesman, Donald Meek; and banker, Berton Churchill. John Wayne is picked up on the road shortly after the start. The running fight between the stagecoach passengers and the Apaches has been given thrilling and realistic presentation by Ford.
1939: Best Score, Supp. Actor (Thomas Mitchell)
Nominations: Best Picture, Director, B&W Cinematography, Art Direction, Editing

STAGECOACH
1966, 114 mins, US ▭
D: Gordon Douglas A: Ann-Margret, Red Buttons, Michael Connors, Alex Cord, Bing Crosby, Bob Cummings (Rackin/20th Century-Fox)

New version kicks off with a gory sequence establishing the brutality of Indians on the warpath, the menace that hangs over subsequent developments, after which the stagecoach starts loading its motley passenger crew. Ann-Margret is quite good as the saloon floozy bad-mouthed out of town. Bing Crosby, the boozy medic, is a similar victim. Bob Cummings, the gutless bank clerk absconding with a large payroll, is excellent. To Alex Cord goes the choice John Wayne role of Ringo. Cord underplays very well.

STAGE DOOR
1937, 83 mins, US/UK ⓥ
D: Gregory La Cava A: Katharine Hepburn, Ginger Rogers, Adolphe Menjou, Gail Patrick, Constance Collier, Andrea Leeds (RKO)

View of aspiring young actresses who live in a New York theatrical boardinghouse is funny in spots, emotionally effective occasionally, and generally brisk and entertaining. They're a high-strung, noisy bevy of showgirls, nightclub dancers, and embryo dramatic timber. Dialogue is caustic as they comment on each other and the passing world of show business. Ginger Rogers doea floor specialty in a nightclub which gives her an introduction to Adolphe Menjou, a hard-boiled theatrical producer and femme despoiler. Katharine Hepburn, stagestruck daughter of a wealthy westerner, becomes Ginger's roommate at the boardinghouse.
1937: Nominations: Best Picture, Director, Supp. Actress (Andrea Leeds), Screenplay

STAGE DOOR CANTEEN
1943, 132 mins, US ⓥ ⊙
D: Frank Borzage A: Cheryl Walker, William Terry, Marjorie Riordan, Lon McCallister, Margaret Early (United Artists)

Sock filmusical of great stature. Stars are introduced into the Stage Door Canteen on West 44th Street, just off Broadway, where Lunt and Fontanne and Sam Jaffe, George Raft and Allen Jenkins, Ned Sparks and Hugh Herbert, among others, are shown doing their menial back-in-the-kitchen chores. Then, up front, performing for the visiting men in uniform—no officers—is paraded six bands—Basie, Cugat, Goodman, Kyser, Lombardo, and Martin, in sock specialties all. And, to project the mechanics of the canteen, there are introduced Helen Hayes, Ina Claire, Tallulah Bankhead, Merle Oberon, Katharine Hepburn, and the others, intertwined into the lonely-soldier-boy-meets-romantic-stage-girl plot.
1943: Nominations: Best Scoring of a Musical Picture, Song ("We Mustn't Say Goodbye")

STAGE FRIGHT

1950, 110 mins, US/UK ⊙ ⊙

D: Alfred Hitchcock A: Jane Wyman, Marlene Dietrich, Michael Wilding, Richard Todd, Kay Walsh, Alistair Sim (Warner/Associated British)

Alfred Hitchcock doesn't stress melodrama throughout. He plays a surprising number of sequences strictly for lightness. Jane Wyman is a drama student sought out by a friend (Richard Todd) who is fleeing from the charge of murdering Marlene Dietrich's husband. Wyman and her father (Alistair Sim) hide Todd and attempt to prove Dietrich is guilty of the crime. Wyman is delightful as embryo actress but the choice femme spot goes to Dietrich. Michael Wilding clicks as a debonair detective.

STAGE STRUCK

1925, 70 mins, US ⊗

D: Allan Dwan A: Gloria Swanson, Lawrence Gray, Gertrude Astor, Ford Sterling (Paramount)

It's a fine piece of hoke. Watching the picture after the second of the six reels, you try to figure how this ever got past for over two reels. It's one of the old-time Keystone models padded out. One laugh is when Swanson tries to make up as an actress. And another after her prizefight, when she jumps overboard to be saved from drowning by her pants catching on a nail on the side of a riverboat. Barring her material, Swanson is not at all bad as a comedienne.

STAGESTRUCK

1936, 90 mins, US ⊙

D: Busby Berkeley A: Dick Powell, Joan Blondell, Warren William, Frank McHugh (Warner)

Picture takes a pretzellike course in recounting the conventional yarn about the unknown kid who makes good as the last-minute fill-in for the show's star. Musical interludes are kept to the minimum. With her material anything but surefire, Joan Blondell unlimbers a likable grade of comedy. Hers is the part of the dame whose only claim to fame is a penchant for drilling her troublesome boyfriends. She backs herself to the lead part in a musical show where Dick Powell functions as director.

STAGE STRUCK

1958, 95 mins, US ⊙ ⊙

D: Sidney Lumet A: Henry Fonda, Susan Strasberg, Joan Greenwood, Herbert Marshall, Christopher Plummer (RKO)

Remake of *Morning Glory*, a yester-year Katharine Hepburn starrer. Susan Strasberg plays the would-be actress who hounds producer Henry Fonda for a chance. He is intrigued by the girl but not as an actress and turns her down. Not so his playwright (Christopher Plummer), who sees her both as actress and romantic opposite. When the star of their show (Joan Greenwood) makes a temperamental exit, Plummer has Strasberg set to take over her role and she does with plot-predictable ease and success. Strasberg is not a conventional screen beauty but her face is expressive and lively.

STAGGERED

1994, 94 mins, UK ⊙

D: Martin Clunes A: Martin Clunes, Michael Praed, Anna Chancellor, Sylvia Syms, Griff Rhys Jones, Virginia McKenna (Big Deal)

Oddball comedy is a likable Brit item that produces a steady flow of mild gags but doesn't build a proper head of steam to go the distance as a feature. TV comic Martin Clunes (who also helms, after experience in legit directing) stars as toy demonstrator Neil, due to marry pretty, middle-class Hilary (Sarah Winman). At his stag party, supposed best friend Gary (Michael Praed) slips a mickey in his beer, and next day Neil wakes up on a remote Scottish beach wearing only his watch. Bulk of the pic consists of Neil's efforts to get back to London in the three days before his nuptials.

STAIRCASE

1969, 101 mins, US ⊙ ⊠

D: Stanley Donen A: Richard Burton, Rex Harrison, Cathleen Nesbitt, Beatrix Lehmann, Avril Angers (20th Century-Fox)

Staircase, investigating lonely, desperate lives of two aging male homosexuals in a drab London suburb, comes uncomfortably close to being depressing. Caustic wit, splendid photography, and fine direction serve only to point up weary plight of the middle-aged pair who cling to one another even while they clash. Homosexuality is not central theme of screenplay. Its basis is urgent need of neurotic individuals for consolation. Harrison and Burton have dared risky roles and triumphed.

STAIRWAY TO HEAVEN

See: *A Matter of Life and Death*

STAKEOUT
1987, 115 mins, US ⊗ ⊙

D: John Badham **A:** Richard Dreyfuss, Emilio Estevez, Madeleine Stowe, Aidan Quinn, Forest Whitaker (Touchstone)

Slick, surefooted entertainment, one part buddy comedy and one part police actioner stitched together with a dash of romance. Richard Dreyfuss is a reckless cop on familiar ground talking his way out of tight spots and jousting with partner Emilio Estevez. The wisecracking duo is assigned to a routine stakeout where they are supposed to wait for an escaped con (Aidan Quinn) to contact his ex-girlfriend (Madeleine Stowe). Dreyfuss is not a man to wait around for something to happen, and as he barrels into the case, he falls in love with Stowe.

STALAG 17
1953, 119 mins, US ⊗ ⊙

D: Billy Wilder **A:** William Holden, Don Taylor, Otto Preminger, Robert Strauss, Peter Graves (Paramount)

Lusty comedy-melodrama, loaded with bold, masculine humor. Producer-director Billy Wilder uses a suspense approach with plenty of humorous byplay springing from the confinement of healthy young males in a Nazi prison camp during the Second World War. Nub of the plot is the uncovering of an informer among the GIs in a particular barracks. Suspicion fastens on William Holden, a cynical character trying to make the best of his prison lot. Otto Preminger plays the camp commander, with obvious relish for its colorful cruelty.
1953: Best Actor (William Holden)
Nominations: Best Director, Supp. Actor (Robert Strauss)

STALKING MOON, THE
1969, 109 mins, US ⊗ ▭

D: Robert Mulligan **A:** Gregory Peck, Eva Marie Saint, Robert Forster (National General/Stalking Moon)

Seemingly was meant to be a chilling suspenser, pic does not achieve this goal, because of clumsy plot structuring and dialogue and tedious pacing. Gregory Peck is retiring as a vet Indian scout with the US Army. In an Indian roundup, Eva Marie Saint appears, with son Noland Clay. Years before, she was kidnapped and impressed into squaw service by Nathaniel Narcisco. Peck takes her and the boy to his retirement ranch, but the Indian brave stalks them.

STAND BY ME
1986, 87 mins, US ⊗ ⊙

D: Rob Reiner **A:** Wil Wheaton, River Phoenix, Corey Feldman, Jerry O'Connell, Richard Dreyfuss, Kiefer Sutherland (Act III)

Based on a novella by Stephen King, it is the experiences of four youths on a two-day trek through the woods to find the yet-undiscovered body of a dead teenager reported missing. Scripters have written inspired dialogue for this quartet of plucky boys at that hard-to-capture age when they're still young enough to get scared and yet old enough to want to sneak smokes and cuss. The introspective, sensitive "brain" of the bunch is Gordie Lachance (Wil Wheaton). His somber personality is matched by best friend Chris Chambers (River Phoenix), a toughie who is an abused child.
1986: Nomination: Best Adapted Screenplay

STAND-IN
1937, 90 mins, US ⊗

D: Tay Garnett **A:** Leslie Howard, Joan Blondell, Humphrey Bogart, Alan Mowbray, Marla Shelton (United Artists)

Hollywood studios and the people who make films receive some good-natured ribbing. Leslie Howard is a bespectacled representative of New York bankers who control a Hollywood film producing company. Howard comes west with a total ignorance of motion pictures. He volunteers to straighten out the production difficulties and save Colossal Films for the stockholders. Joan Blondell, a stand-in for the big star, takes him to one side and gives him the lowdown. Humphrey Bogart plays a producer who turns teetotaler.

STANDING ROOM ONLY
1944, 83 mins, US

D: Sidney Lanfield **A:** Fred MacMurray, Paulette Goddard, Edward Arnold, Roland Young, Anne Revere, Hillary Brooke (Paramount)

War-crowded Washington is the nucleus for a comedy based on the trouble people have in securing living accommodations and the red tape involved in getting in to see officials. MacMurray, as a butler, is especially funny in a scene where he drops a cherry from the fruit salad he is serving into the lap of one of the women and endeavors to snare the elusive fruit with a knife and spoon while she continues her conversation with one of the guests.

STANLEY AND IRIS

1990, 102 mins, US 🆅 ☒

D: Martin Ritt **A:** Jane Fonda, Robert De Niro, Swoosie Kurtz, Martha Plimpton (Lantana/M-G-M)

The elements are in place but they don't add up to great drama in this well-meant effort to personalize the plight of illiterate people. Project proves too small for a feature-film framework. Jane Fonda plays Iris, a recent widow still struggling with grief while trying to support a whole household. She catches the eye of Stanley Cox (Robert De Niro), a cafeteria cook who at middle age has never learned to read or write. Fired for being potentially dangerous, Stanley finally confronts his fears and asks Iris to teach him to read.

STANLEY AND LIVINGSTONE

1939, 100 mins, US 🆅

D: Henry King **A:** Spencer Tracy, Nancy Kelly, Cedric Hardwicke, Richard Greene, Walter Brennan, Charles Coburn (20th Century-Fox)

Lusty, pioneering adventure, detailing successful attempt of Tracy to find Hardwicke in the heart of Africa. Tracy gives persuasive portrayal as the reporter determined to get his story and inspired by love of Nancy Kelly. Kelly is a most adequate romantic interest; Walter Brennan is excellent as the Indian scout transposed to African plains.

STAR, THE

1952, 90 mins, US 🆅

D: Stuart Heisler **A:** Bette Davis, Sterling Hayden, Natalie Wood, Warner Anderson, Minor Watson, June Travis (Friedlob/20th Century-Fox)

A strong performance by Bette Davis, in a tailor-made role, gives a lift to a film that it might not have had otherwise. Davis gets drunk, is arrested, and bailed out by a boating man (Sterling Hayden). Hayden tries to get her to forget a film career and become a normal, natural woman. She tries, but fails at holding a department-store job, and wangles a screen test from a kindly producer.

1952: Nomination: Best Actress (Bette Davis)

STAR!
(AKA: THOSE WERE THE HAPPY TIMES)

1968, 169 mins, US 🆅 ⊙ ☒

D: Robert Wise **A:** Julie Andrews, Richard Crenna, Michael Craig, Daniel Massey, Robert Reed (Wise/20th Century-Fox)

Julie Andrews's portrayal of the late, great musicomedy idol Gertrude Lawrence occasionally sags between musical numbers, but the cast and team of redoubtable technical contributors have helped to turn out a pleasing tribute to one of the theater's most admired stars. Humor is more witty than boisterously funny, while the 16 musical numbers are staged in polished fashion.

1968: Nominations: Best Supp. Actor (Daniel Massey), Cinematography, Costume Design, Art Direction, Adapted Musical Score, Song ("Star!"), Sound

STAR CHAMBER, THE

1983, 109 mins, US 🆅 ⊙ ☒

D: Peter Hyams **A:** Michael Douglas, Hal Holbrook, Yaphet Kotto, Sharon Gless, James B. Sikking (20th Century-Fox)

Chamber starts out on an important note. The US criminal justice system is not only collapsing but what's left has been perverted until the victims of crime have no hope of satisfaction or protection. As a decent, conscientious judge, Michael Douglas deals with the problem daily, forced by straining legal precedent to free the obviously "guilty." Severely stricken by one event, Douglas turns to his friend and mentor, Hal Holbrook, who is secretly part of a group of judges who mete out their own fatal sentences on criminals who've been through their real courts and gone free.

STAR DUST

1940, 84 mins, US

D: Walter Lang **A:** Linda Darnell, John Payne, Roland Young, Charlotte Greenwood, William Gargan, Donald Meek (20th Century-Fox)

Yarn about Linda Darnell's experiences in getting a bid to Hollywood for a test, the resultant turndown because she is too young, and eventual connivance to stay and click in her first picture, closely parallels her experiences in real life. Darnell displays a wealth of youthful charm and personality. She handles her assignment in top-notch style. John Payne surprises with a crackerjack performance as the grid star scooted along for a test. Roland Young, Charlotte Greenwood and Donald Meek effectively carry comedy assignments.

STARDUST
1974, 113 mins, UK Ⓥ
D: Michael Apted **A:** David Essex, Adam Faith, Larry Hagman, Ines Des Longchamps, Marty Wilde (EMI/Goodtimes)

Singer-guitarist Jim Maclaine (David Essex), seen foretasting fame and fortune at the end of *That'll Be the Day,* is followed here on his rapid rise and fall as the eventual star of a heterogeneous pop group, the Stray Cats. En route, pic details the loves, joys and tribulations, hardships and achievements, jealousies and hypocrisies, as well as—and importantly—the damning effect of drugs, of the music scene.

STARDUST MEMORIES
1980, 89 mins, US Ⓥ ⊙
D: Woody Allen **A:** Woody Allen, Charlotte Rampling, Marie-Christine Barrault, Jessica Harper, Tony Roberts (United Artists)

No effort is made to pretend that Woody Allen's character of Sandy Bates is anybody but Allen himself—a filmmaker first adored for wacky comedies, then gradually appreciated as a cinematic genius. Though there are laughs along the way, this is a truly mean-spirited picture. Once a sympathetic nebbish, Allen here sees himself as a put-upon, embittered genius, disdainful of everything around him.

STAR 80
1983, 102 mins, US Ⓥ ⊙
D: Bob Fosse **A:** Mariel Hemingway, Eric Roberts, Cliff Robertson, Carroll Baker, David Clennon (Ladd Company)

Engrossing, unsentimental, and unavoidably depressing account of the short life and ghastly death of Playmate-actress Dorothy Stratten. As played here by Mariel Hemingway, Stratten is a virginal, extremely insecure teenager in Vancouver who is swooped down upon by small-time hustler Paul Snider. Although doubtlessly in love with his discovery, Snider uses Stratten as his ticket to the big time in L.A. Eric Roberts gives a startlingly fine performance as this pathetic loser.

STARGATE
1994, 120 mins, US Ⓥ ⊙ ▭
D: Roland Emmerich **A:** Kurt Russell, James Spader, Jaye Davidson, Viveca Lindfors, Alexis Cruz (Canal Plus/Centropolis)

What this $60-to-$70-million juvenile adventure has in spades is special effects and picturesque locations. What it lacks is an emotional link to make the Saturday-afternoon he-man posturing palatable, or at least bearable. Egyptologist Dr. Daniel Jackson (James Spader) is offered the job of translating an ancient stone lodged in a secret military complex. The ring is a portal to another dimension. Breaking the impenetrable code leads to a military probe commanded by Colonel Jack O'Neil (Kurt Russell). The inhabitants of this world are biblical-style slaves, the ruler a galactic hermaphrodite (Jaye Davidson).

STAR IS BORN, A
1937, 111 mins, US Ⓥ ⊙
D: William A. Wellman **A:** Janet Gaynor, Fredric March, Adolphe Menjou, May Robson, Lionel Stander (Selznick/United Artists)

Story relates the experiences of a young girl who rises to cinema fame while her husband, having touched the heights, is on a swift descent. Love is the heroine; alcohol, the villain. Janet Gaynor gives to her role, the small-town girl who makes good, a characterization of sustained loveliness. She is equally as good in the comedy passages. The same, without reservation, may be said for Fredric March and the manner in which he plays the passé star, Norman Maine. He creates a finely drawn portrait of weakness without viciousness.

1937: Best Original Story, Special Award (color cinematography)
Nominations: Best Picture, Director, Actor (Fredric March), Actress (Janet Gaynor), Screenplay, Assistant Director (Eric Stacey)

STAR IS BORN, A
1954, 154 mins, US Ⓥ ⊙ ▭
D: George Cukor **A:** Judy Garland, James Mason, Jack Carson, Charles Bickford, Tom Noonan (Warner/Transcona)

A great 1937 moneymaker is an even greater picture in its filmusical transmutation. Judy Garland glitters with that stardust which in the plot the wastrel star James Mason recognizes. And her loyalties are as Gibraltar amid the house of cards that periodically seems to collapse around her and upon him. From the opening drunken debacle at the Shrine benefit to the scandalous antics of a hopeless dipsomaniac when his wife (Garland) wins the Academy Award, there is an intense pattern of real-life mirrorings.

1954: Nominations: Best Actor (James Mason), Actress (Judy Garland), Color

Costume Design, Color Art Direction, Scoring of a Musical Picture, Song ("The Man That Got Away")

STAR IS BORN, A
1976, 140 mins, US ⓥ
D: Frank Pierson A: Barbra Streisand, Kris Kristofferson, Paul Mazursky, Gary Busey (Warner)

A superlative remake. Barbra Streisand's performance as the rising star is her finest screen work to date, while Kris Kristofferson's portrayal of her failing benefactor is magnificent. All the familiar plot turns are here, but updated to the spirit of the times. Plot picks up Kristofferson past his rock-superstar prime, unable or unwilling to make his tour commitments, raising hell, and alienating people. Barbra Streisand is discovered in a tacky nitery. There's a lot of music in the film, mostly by Paul Williams and Kenny Ascher.
1976: Best Song ("Evergreen")
Nominations: Best Cinematography, Adapted Score, Sound

STARLIGHT HOTEL
1987, 93 mins, New Zealand ⓥ ⊙
D: Sam Pillsbury A: Peter Phelps, Greer Robson, Marshall Napier, The Wizard, Alice Fraser (Challenge)

Road movie centers on the friendship between a man and a 13-year-old girl. Setting is the central South Island in 1930, with farmers forced to leave their land as the Depression bites. Kate (Greer Robson) runs away to try to find her father. She soon encounters Patrick (Peter Phelps), a man whose life was shattered by his experiences in the world war and later when his wife left him. He's wanted by the police, and is trying to get to a port and then passage to Australia. All the classic elements of this kind of film are here: jumping on trains, hiding out in barns, making friends and enemies along the way. The film benefits enormously from the charismatic performances in the leads.

STARMAN
1984, 115 mins, US ⓥ ⊙ ▭
D: John Carpenter A: Jeff Bridges, Karen Allen, Charles Martin Smith, Richard Jaeckel (Columbia-Delphi II)

There is little that is original in *Starman*, but at least it has chosen good models. The Starman (Jeff Bridges) arrives much like "E.T."—an alien in a hostile environment—but in an elaborate transformation scene he assumes human form. The body he chooses for his sojourn on

Earth happens to belong to the dead husband of Jenny Hayden (Karen Allen), who lives alone in a remote section of Wisconsin. Bridges and Allen set off on a trip across the country to Arizona, where the Starman must make his connection to return home.
1984: Nomination: Best Actor (Jeff Bridges)

STAR OF MIDNIGHT
1935, 90 mins, US ⓥ ⊙
D: Stephen Roberts A: William Powell, Ginger Rogers, Paul Kelly, Gene Lockhart, Leslie Fenton (RKO)

Noncamouflaged follow-up to *The Thin Man* (1934), although made by a different producer, hits a similar merry comedy-drama stride and attains practically the same effectiveness as screen entertainment. William Powell is once more the happy-go-lucky master sleuth. His romance this time is not so adult, but equally humorous, and, with Ginger Rogers opposite, always interesting. The mystery is double-barreled, concerning the disappearance of a show's leading lady and the killing of a Broadway columnist.

STARS AND STRIPES FOREVER
1952, 89 mins, US ⓥ
D: Henry Koster A: Clifton Webb, Debra Paget, Robert Wagner, Ruth Hussey, Finlay Currie (20th Century-Fox)

As spirited as any march John Philip Sousa ever led, film registers as top-notch entertainment, a kaleidoscopically presented career of the bandmaster. Enacting the late march king is Clifton Webb. It might not be an accurate Sousa, but it is good Webb. Generously sprinkled through the footage is a parade of Sousa tunes that start the feet marching.

STARSHIP TROOPERS
1997, 129 mins, US ⓥ ⊙
D: Paul Verhoeven A: Casper Van Dien, Dina Meyer, Denise Richards, Jake Busey, Neil Patrick Harris, Clancy Brown (Tri-Star/Touchstone)

Human culture and insect culture duel to the death in *Starship Troopers,* a gung-ho sci-fi epic that delivers two hours of good, nasty fun. It is, in the end, a picture about teenagers and giant bugs, but one with enough visual exhilaration and narrative wit to keep one thoroughly on board. Rich boy Johnny Rico (Casper Van Dien) enlists in the Mobile Infantry; his

girlfriend, Carmen Ibanez (Denise Richards), is heading for the Fleet Academy to become a pilot. Johnny finds himself in basic training with the sultry Dizzy Flores (Dina Meyer), who has the permanent hots for him. At the one-hour point, the invasion of the planet Klendathu begins, and pic shifts into fifth gear without ever looking back. The first encounter is a disaster, with some 100,000 dead. The bugs have sucked the brains out of the defeated humans, thereby acquiring all their knowledge. The soldiers are confronted with thousands of warrior bugs descending from the mountains with another brain-drain in mind. Young and virtually unknown cast is serviceable, with Van Dien a stalwart lead and Meyer standing out as Dizzy.
1997: Nomination: Best Visual Effects

STARS LOOK DOWN, THE
1939, 104 mins, UK Ⓥ
D: Carol Reed **A:** Michael Redgrave, Margaret Lockwood, Emlyn Williams, Nancy Price, Cecil Parker (Grafton/Grand National)

Splendid dramatic portrait of those who burrow for the black diamond in England's northland. Adapted from A. J. Cronin's novel of the mining town from where two sons seek different roads to success, one returning to foster misery, the other to fight on for its alleviation. Film unrolls at steady pace a wealth of dramatic incident.

STAR SPANGLED RHYTHM
1943, 99 mins, US
D: George Marshall **A:** Victor Moore, Betty Hutton, Eddie Bracken, Anne Revere (Paramount)

Tune pic on the grand scale, grand because of the personalities who wander in and out of the pic, because of the seven listenable tunes, because of the general lavishness of the production, and because of the downright gaiety of the whole affair. Among the names who deserve more than perfunctory billing are Bing Crosby, Bob Hope, Dorothy Lamour, Paulette Goddard, Veronica Lake, Betty Hutton, and Eddie Bracken.
1943: Nominations: Best Scoring of a Musical Picture, Song ("Black Magic")

STAR STRUCK
1982, 102 mins, Australia Ⓥ ⊙
D: Gillian Armstrong **A:** Jo Kennedy,

Ross O'Donovan, Pat Evison, Margo Lee, Max Cullen (Palm Beach)

Picture is a raucous, "let's put on a show" musical with a punk-rock beat. Story centers on an enterprising 14-year-old entrepreneur, Ross O'Donovan, who has big career plans for his cousin, singer Jo Kennedy. Grooming (?) her in the punk mode, O'Donovan has his sights on copping first prize on a New Year's television talent show. The film certainly doesn't lack energy. Camerawork is glossy and fluid and song-and-dance routines are loud and splashy. Regrettably, the choreography is uninspired.

STARTING OVER
1979, 106 mins, US Ⓥ ⊙
D: Alan J. Pakula **A:** Burt Reynolds, Jill Clayburgh, Candice Bergen, Charles Durning, Frances Sternhagen, Austin Pendleton (Paramount/Brook)

Pic takes on the subject of marital dissolution from a comic point of view, and succeeds admirably. Burt Reynolds plays a mild-mannered writer unwillingly foisted into a "liberated" condition by spouse Candice Bergen, feeling her feminine oats as a songwriter. Fleeing to protection of relatives Charles Durning and Frances Sternhagen, he meets spinster schoolteacher Jill Clayburgh. Reynolds is the core of the film, and underplays marvelously.
1979: Nominations: Best Actress (Jill Clayburgh), Supp. Actress (Candice Bergen)

STAR TREK—THE MOTION PICTURE
1979, 132 mins, US Ⓥ ⊙ ▭
D: Robert Wise **A:** William Shatner, Leonard Nimoy, DeForest Kelley, Stephen Collins, Persis Khambatta (Paramount)

The *Enterprise* has been completely reconditioned during a two-year dry dock, but must be prematurely dispatched to intercept an Earth-bound attacker destroying everything in its wake. William Shatner's Kirk is told to lead the mission along with other show regulars. Upshot is a search-and-destroy thriller that includes all of the ingredients the TV show's fans thrive on. But the expensive effects (under supervision of Douglas Trumbull) are the secret of this film, and the amazing wizardry throughout would appear to justify the whopping budget. Jerry Goldsmith's brassy score is the other necessary plus.

1979: Nominations: Best Art Direction, Original Score, Visual Effects

STAR TREK II: THE WRATH OF KHAN
1982, 113 mins, US Ⓥ ☉ ▭
D: Nicholas Meyer **A:** William Shatner, Leonard Nimoy, DeForest Kelley, Ricardo Montalban, James Doohan (Paramount)

Very satisfying space adventure, with starship *Reliant* landing on a planet on an exploration mission. This allows the evil Khan (Ricardo Montalban), who was marooned there with his family and crew 15 years before by Kirk (William Shatner), to take over the *Reliant* and vow revenge on Kirk. Latter, coaxed to take command once again of the starship *Enterprise* on a training mission, travels to the Regula space station on a rescue mission.

STAR TREK III: THE SEARCH FOR SPOCK
1984, 105 mins, US Ⓥ ☉ ▭
D: Leonard Nimoy **A:** William Shatner, DeForest Kelley, James Doohan, Walter Koenig, Leonard Nimoy (Paramount)

Emotionally satisfying science-fiction adventure centers upon a quest to bring Spock (Leonard Nimoy), the noble science officer and commander who, apparently, gave his life to save "the many," back to life.

1986: Nominations: Best Cinematography, Original Score, Sound, Sound Effects Editing

STAR TREK IV: THE VOYAGE HOME
1986, 119 mins, US Ⓥ ☉ ▭
D: Leonard Nimoy **A:** William Shatner, Leonard Nimoy, DeForest Kelley, James Doohan, Catherine Hicks, George Takei (Bennett)

Latest excursion is warmer, wittier, more socially relevant, and truer to its TV origins than prior odysseys. This voyage finds the crew Earthbound but they find the galaxy dark and messages from Earth distorted. Spock locates the source of the trouble in the bleating, eerie sounds of an unidentified probe and links them to a cry from Earth's past that has long been silenced. Scripters employ successful use of time travel.

STAR TREK V: THE FINAL FRONTIER
1989, 106 mins, US Ⓥ ☉ ▭
D: William Shatner **A:** William Shatner, Leonard Nimoy, DeForest Kelley, James Doohan, Nichelle Nichols, George Takei (Paramount)

Even die-hard Trekkies may be disappointed by *Star Trek V*, William Shatner's inauspicious feature directing debut. A major flaw in the story is that it centers on an obsessive quest by a character who isn't a member of the Enterprise crew. Recreations of Spock's rejection by his father after his birth and Kelley's euthanasia of his own father are moving highlights.

STAR TREK VI: THE UNDISCOVERED COUNTRY
1991, 109 mins, US Ⓥ ☉ ▭
D: Nicholas Meyer **A:** William Shatner, Leonard Nimoy, DeForest Kelley, Kim Cattrall, David Warner, Christopher Plummer (Paramount)

Weighed down by a midsection even flabbier than the long-in-the-tooth cast, director still delivers enough of what *Trek* auds hunger for. Following a Chernobyl-like disaster, a Klingon leader seeks peace with the Federation, the Klingon economy and environment having been depleted by constant warring—a not-at-all-veiled parable for the end of the cold war. Kirk & Co. are sent, reluctantly, to escort the leader to peace talks on earth, but conspirators seek to scuttle the détente by assassinating him and pinning the blame on the *Enterprise*.

1991: Nominations: Best Sound Effects Editing, Makeup

STAR TREK FIRST CONTACT
1996, 110 mins, US Ⓥ ☉ ▭
D: Jonathan Frakes **A:** Patrick Stewart, Jonathan Frakes, Brent Spiner, Gates McFadden, Marina Sirtis, Alice Krige (Paramount)

The Borgs are back, the future is in peril and the *Star Trek* mythos proceeds apace in a smashingly exciting sci-fi adventure that ranks among the very best in the long-running Paramount franchise. Captain Picard (Patrick Stewart) was captured and very nearly "assimilated" by the Borg, a marauding race of cyborgs, and as *First Contact* begins, he continues to be troubled by Borg bogeymen in his nightmares. After a battle, several of the Borg escape and head to Earth, where they hope to gain control of the present by sabotaging the past. Some others manage to board the USS *Enterprise* and set out to assimilate the entire crew for the greater good of their Borg Queen (Alice Krige). Stewart once again comports himself with all the gravity and panache you would expect from a Shakespearean-trained actor. Special-effects wizardry is by far the most elaborate seen in a *Star Trek* film.

1996: Nomination: Best Makeup (Michael Westmore, Scott Wheeler, Jake Garber)

STAR TREK: GENERATIONS

1994, 118 mins, US 🔞 ⊙ ⌨

D: David Carson **A:** Patrick Stewart, William Shatner, Malcolm McDowell, Jonathan Frakes, Whoopi Goldberg (Paramount)

Generations has enough verve, imagination, and familiarity to satisfy three decades' worth of Trekkers. The story begins at a PR-event maiden voyage of a ''New'' *Enterprise,* with Kirk (William Shatner), engineer Scotty (James Doohan), and Chekov (Walter Koenig) aboard as honored guests. When a distress signal summons the craft into action, the combination of an inexperienced captain and a not-yet-fully-equipped craft add up to catastrophe and the end, albeit heroic, of Kirk. Four generations after the disaster, the ''Next'' crew receives an emergency call. Rec center barkeep Guinan (Whoopi Goldberg) tells Captain Picard (Patrick Stewart) of the Nexus, a mysterious ribbon of energy. To regain its nirvana, fellow survivor Soran (Malcolm McDowell) is willing to do anything, including aligning with malevolent Klingons.

STAR TREK INSURRECTION

1998, 100 mins, US 🔞 ⊙ ⌨

D: Jonathan Frakes **A:** Patrick Stewart, Jonathan Frakes, Brent Spiner, Michael Dorn, F. Murray Abraham, Anthony Zerbe (Paramount)

The *Star Trek* feature franchise continues apace with a ninth installment aimed primarily at an audience of faithful fans. The Ba'ku, peaceful inhabitants of an idyllic planet, are in danger of forced relocation, thanks to an alliance between Federation leaders and the aging Son'a. Captain Picard (Patrick Stewart) leads the *Enterprise* crew to the Ba'ku planet and discovers that the 600 or so inhabitants remain eternally youthful. The age-reversal magic causes Commander Riker (Jonathan Frakes) and Lieutenant Commander Troi (Marina Sirtis) to get frisky in a candlelit bath, while Picard is briefly seized with an urge to mambo. Defying direct Federation orders, Picard leads the *Enterprise* officers in a defense of the Ba'ku. It's not always easy to make sense of what people are doing during the frenzied hurly-burly of the final half hour. However, the lead players manage to easily carry the audience along.

STAR WARS

1977, 121 mins, US 🔞 ⊙ ⌨

D: George Lucas **A:** Mark Hamill, Harrison Ford, Carrie Fisher, Peter Cushing, Alec Guinness, Anthony Daniels (20th Century-Fox)

A magnificent film. George Lucas set out to make the biggest possible adventure fantasy out of his memories of serials and older action epics, and he succeeded brilliantly. The story is an engaging space adventure which takes itself seriously while occasionally admitting an affectionate poke at the genre. The superb balance of technology and human drama is one of the many achievements: one identifies with the characters and accepts, as do they, the intriguing intergalactic world in which they live. Carrie Fisher is delightful as the regal but spunky princess on a rebel planet who has been kidnapped by Peter Cushing, would-be ruler of the universe. Mark Hamill is excellent as a farm boy who sets out to rescue Fisher in league with Alec Guinness, last survivor of a band of noble knights. Harrison Ford is outstanding as a likable mercenary pilot.

1977: Best Art Direction, Sound, Original Score, Editing, Costume Design, Visual Effects, Special Achievement Award (sound effects)

Nominations: Best Picture, Supp. Actor (Alec Guinness), Original Screenplay

STAR WARS: EPISODE I—THE PHANTOM MENACE

1999, 133 mins, US 🔞 ⊙ ⌨

D: George Lucas **A:** Liam Neeson, Ewan McGregor, Natalie Portman, Jake Lloyd, Pernilla August, Frank Oz (Lucasfilm/20th Century-Fox)

The first installment of George Lucas's three-part prequel to the original *Star Wars* trilogy is always visually diverting, but lacks any emotional pull and the sense of wonder and awe that marks the best works of sci-fi/fantasy. Action is set a generation prior to *Star Wars.* Conflict is triggered by the Trade Federation's decision to invade the peaceful planet of Naboo, ruled by teenage Queen Amidala (Natalie Portman). Jedi Master Qui-Gon Jinn (Liam Neeson) and his apprentice Obi-Wan Kenobi (Ewan McGregor) rescue the queen but become stranded on the desert planet of Tatooine, where they encounter the nine-year-old Anakin Skywalker. Qui-Gon Jinn suspects the boy is the Chosen One and will one day bring balance to the Force. As the story zigzags through its second hour, even more characters and creatures are introduced, notably lacking in charm or interest.

1999: Nominations: Sound, Sound Effects Editing, Visual Effects

STATE FAIR
1933, 80 mins, US
D: Henry King A: Will Rogers, Janet Gaynor, Lew Ayres, Sally Eilers, Norman Foster, Louise Dresser (Fox)

A production that has the charm of naturalness and the virtue of sincerity. No villain, little suspense, but a straightforward story of a rural family who find their great moments at the state fair, where paterfamilias captures the title for his prize hog, the mother makes a clean sweep in the pickle entries, the boy gets his first vicarious but satisfying taste of romance, and the girl finds a more lasting love. Of chief interest is the debut of a new romance team in Janet Gaynor and Lew Ayres. It is a charming romance between these two. There is just enough of Will Rogers's quaint humor and Louise Dresser's country dame to temper the more hectic moments.

1932/33: Nominations: Best Picture, Adaptation

STATE FAIR
1945, 100 mins, US ⊛
D: Walter Lang A: Jeanne Crain, Dana Andrews, Dick Haymes, Vivian Blaine, Charles Winninger, Fay Bainter (20th Century-Fox)

Latest screen version is still a boy-meets-girl yarn that has lost none of its flavor. And notably distinctive in the telling is the frequent punctuation of the story by Rodgers-Hammerstein tunes. Otherwise, the yarn is still the one of midwest rustication, concerning mainly the hoopla attendant to the annual state fair, at which products, from pickles to hogs, are displayed for judging and prizes.

1945: Best Song ("It Might As Well Be Spring")
Nomination: Best Scoring of a Musical Picture

STATE FAIR
1962, 118 mins, US ⊛ ⊐
D: Jose Ferrer A: Pat Boone, Bobby Darin, Pamela Tiffin, Ann-Margret, Tom Ewell, Alice Faye (20th Century-Fox)

Third time around on the screen for this vehicle. To the five original R&H refrains

retained in this version, five new numbers with both music and lyrics by Richard Rodgers have been added. The old songs are still charming, but they are not rendered with quite the zest and feeling of the 1945 cast. None of the four young stars comes off especially well. Ann-Margret makes perhaps the most vivid impression, particularly during her torrid song-dance rendition of "Isn't It Kind of Fun," the film's big production number.

STATE OF GRACE
1990, 134 mins, US ⊛ ⊙
D: Phil Joanou A: Sean Penn, Ed Harris, Gary Oldman, Robin Wright, John Turturro, Burgess Meredith (Cinehaus/Orion)

A handsomely produced, mostly riveting, but ultimately overlong and over-indulgent gangster picture. Sean Penn plays Terry, one of New York's Irish residents who grew up in Hell's Kitchen with his friends, brothers Frankie (Ed Harris) and Jackie (Gary Oldman) and their sister, Kathleen (Robin Wright). Terry's been away from New York for 12 years, but now he returns and signs up with the Irish Mob headed by the ruthless Frankie. In fact, Terry's an undercover cop assigned to get the goods on Frankie.

STATE OF THE UNION
(UK: THE WORLD AND HIS WIFE)
1948, 121 mins, US ⊛ ⊙
D: Frank Capra A: Spencer Tracy, Katharine Hepburn, Van Johnson, Angela Lansbury, Adolphe Menjou (M-G-M/Liberty)

Plot deals with a power-mad femme newspaper publisher who picks up a self-made plane magnate and shoves him toward the White House to satisfy her own interests. Cast is loaded with stalwarts who deliver in top form. Spencer Tracy fits his personality to the role of the presidential aspirant. Katharine Hepburn gives the role of Tracy's wife understanding and warmth. Van Johnson shines as the columnist turned political press agent. Capra's direction punches over the pictorial exposé of US politics and candidate manufacturers, the indifference of the average voter, and the need for more expression of true public opinion at the polls.

STATION SIX—SAHARA
1964, 97 mins, UK
D: Seth Holt A: Carroll Baker, Peter Van Eyck, Ian Bannen, Denholm Elliott, Mario Adorf (Allied Artists)

Story premise of a sexpot arriving at an

isolated desert oil pipeline station where five lonely men have only one thing in common—the nagging need for a woman—is generally well developed. Carroll Baker makes her work count. Peter Van Eyck, in charge of the station, is smooth and convincing. Ian Bannen, a Scotsman with a sour sense of humor, and Denholm Elliott, a paper-spined Englishman, persuasively portray their respective parts.

STAVISKY
1974, 115 mins, France/Italy ⓥ
D: Alain Resnais **A:** Jean-Paul Belmondo, Francois Perier, Anny Duperey, Michel Lonsdale, Claude Rich (Cerito/Ariane/Euro International)

This is an elegant, arresting film about the times and charm of a swindler who actually existed and almost brought down the French Third Republic in the 1930s. Political substance is there, for it was written by Jorge *(Z)* Semprun, but all is bathed in a study of the driving charm that turned an immigrant Jewish boy (Jean-Paul Belmondo) from a small-time embezzler with a prison record into the most dazzling of economic operators but whose frauds ultimately lead to his downfall.

STAY HUNGRY
1976, 102 mins, US ⓥ
D: Bob Rafelson **A:** Jeff Bridges, Sally Field, Arnold Schwarzenegger, R. G. Armstrong, Robert Englund (United Artists)

Pic features an excellent Jeff Bridges as a spoiled but affable rich young Alabama boy who gets involved in buying up small plots for a major development. But R. G. Armstrong's second-rate gym can't be had, so Bridges decides to infiltrate. There he falls for Sally Field and also is exposed to the barbell denizens who include real-life bodybuilding champ Arnold Schwarzenegger and good-natured staffer Robert Englund.

STAYING ALIVE
1983, 96 mins, US ⓥ ⊙
D: Sylvester Stallone **A:** John Travolta, Cynthia Rhodes, Finola Hughes, Steve Inwood, Frank Stallone (Stigwood/Paramount)

Nowhere as good as its 1977 predecessor, *Saturday Night Fever.* John Travolta's Tony Manero is now on the rounds of casting calls and auditions for Broadway dance shows. He's got a comfortable relationship going with fellow struggling dancer Cynthia Rhodes. Nevertheless, Travolta doesn't think twice about her feelings when he spots alluring British dancer Finola Hughes and hooks up with her while winning a background role in a show in which she will be starring.

STAYING TOGETHER
1989, 91 mins, US ⓥ
D: Lee Grant **A:** Sean Astin, Stockard Channing, Melinda Dillon, Jim Haynie (Feury)

Sincerely made coming-of-age tale serves up familiar homilies about family values in changing small-town America and the indomitable power of love. In a bucolic town somewhere in South Carolina, Mr. and Mrs. McDermott and their three strapping sons run a home-cooked-chicken restaurant. Mom is a tower of strength and a paragon of understanding, dad is gruff but caring, and the brothers confine their red-blooded oats-sowing, boozing, and pot-smoking to their off hours. Pop McDermott gets an offer he can't refuse for the restaurant and its choice land site.

STAY TUNED
1992, 87 mins, US ⓥ ⊙ ⊐
D: Peter Hyams **A:** John Ritter, Pam Dawber, Jeffrey Jones, David Tom, Bob Dishy (Morgan Creek)

Not diabolical enough for true black comedy, and witless in its send-up of obsessive TV viewing, *Stay Tuned* is a picture with nothing for everybody. As a Seattle couple trapped in a hellish cable system run by the devil himself, John Ritter and Pam Dawber look glum for more than plot reasons. One brief respite from the overall inanity is a six-minute cartoon interlude by the masterful Chuck Jones, with Ritter and Dawber portrayed as mice menaced by a robot cat. The animation has grace and depth.

STEAL BIG, STEAL LITTLE
1995, 135 mins, US ⓥ
D: Andrew Davis **A:** Andy Garcia, Alan Arkin, Rachel Ticotin, Joe Pantoliano, Ally Walker (Chicago Pacific/Savoy)

Bloated fairy tale of two brothers. The tug-of-war and tug-of-hearts in this comedy might best be described as Capra-grotesque. Ruben Martinez (Andy Garcia) is a dreamer with a big heart who, much to the chagrin of his slick, souless twin brother, Robby (also Garcia), inherits a vast spread in Santa Barbara from their wealthy stepmother. The bad bro has been skimming money from the estate and is in cahoots with local muck-a-mucks to create a sprawling real-estate development. Story is relayed in flashback, with Ruben telling a cable reporter how, through intimidation, bribery, and chicanery, Robby and his monied minions pushed him and his extended family off the land.

STEALING BEAUTY
(AKA: I DANCE ALONE)
1996, 118 mins, Italy/UK/France Ⓥ ⊙ ▭
D: Bernardo Bertolucci **A:** Liv Tyler, Sinead Cusack, Donal McCann, Jeremy Irons, Jean Marais, Rachel Weisz (Fiction/Recorded Picture/UGC)

Bertolucci returns to his native Italy after 15 years with a richly satisfying chamber piece. Liv Tyler plays Lucy Harmon, an American sent to Tuscany for the summer, ostensibly to have her portrait done by her host, Ian Grayson (Donal McCann). Lucy's real motive is to follow through on an incipient romance from an earlier visit with handsome neighbor Niccolo (Roberto Zibetti). The ripely sensual girl is waiting before giving up her virginity. Niccolo's return looks set to end that wait. The menagerie of expatriates camped out at the Graysons' hilltop farmhouse include Alex (Jeremy Irons), a playwright dying of a terminal illness.

STEALING HEAVEN
1989, 110 mins, UK/Yugoslavia Ⓥ ⊙
D: Clive Donner **A:** Derek de Lint, Kim Thomson, Denholm Elliott, Bernard Hepton, Rachel Kempson (Amy/Jadran)

This handsome historical pageant attempts to tell the ''true story'' behind one of history's most famous romances, that of 12th-century French philosopher Pierre Abelard and his beloved Heloise. Script pushes toward a sharp and witty, anticlerical, feminist tract. Abelard shuns emotional commitments as dangerous to his intellectual capacities. Heloise is the smart, intelligent, and unconventional girl with the courage to assume responsibility for her feelings.

STEALING HOME
1988, 98 mins, US Ⓥ ⊙
D: Steven Kampmann, Will Aldis **A:** Mark Harmon, Blair Brown, Jodie Foster, Jonathan Silverman, Harold Ramis (Mount)

Story of how a privileged boy's love for baseball dies with the sudden death of his father remains too remote emotionally to elicit more than a sigh of relief at its conclusion. For Billy (played at 10, teenage, and 38 by Thacher Goodwin, William McNamara, and Mark Harmon respectively), baseball takes priority. It's something he lives for and something he cherishes sharing with his equally fanatical baseball-loving dad (John Shea). Around for valuable lessons on how to grow up fast is the wayward and rebellious Katie (Jodie Foster), who becomes for Billy a mentor, lover, and tragic figure. The actress is perfect for the part.

STEAMBOAT BILL JR.
1928, 65 mins, US Ⓥ ⊙ d
D: Charles Riesner **A:** Buster Keaton, Ernest Torrence, Tom McGuire, Marion Byron (United Artists)

Pip of a comedy is one of Keaton's best. The story concerns the efforts of an old river captain (Ernest Torrence) to survive in the face of opposition from a brand-new modern boat. The old-timer hasn't seen his son (Keaton) since he was an infant. The son arrives and falls in love with the daughter of the rival owner. Matters reach a climax when the old tub of Steamboat Bill is condemned.

STEAMING
1985, 95 mins, UK Ⓥ
D: Joseph Losey **A:** Vanessa Redgrave, Sarah Miles, Diana Dors, Patti Love, Brenda Bruce (World Film Service)

On film, *Steaming* lacks the impact it had on stage. The ebullience and sheer fun of the original have mostly disappeared, and although this is by no means an earnest women's-lib tract, it's a lesser experience. All the action takes place in a run-down steam bath on ladies' day. Here we find the manager, Violet (Diana Dors), worried that the local council is going to close the place down.

STEEL
1980, 99 mins, US Ⓥ
D: Steve Carver **A:** Lee Majors, Jennifer O'Neill, Art Carney, George Kennedy, Harris Yulin (Davis-Panzer/New Line)

Lee Majors stars and exec-produced, and his well-crafted, restrained portrayal as the leader of constructioners provides a solid base for a series of involving relationships. There is an explosion and George Kennedy, the good-hearted company owner, plunges to a tragic death. Daughter Jennifer O'Neill is then left to take on the task of completing the project. Kennedy's friend Art Carney suggests O'Neill search out Majors to coordinate the job, and he rounds up the most famous workers in the business.

STEEL HELMET, THE
1951, 84 mins, US ⓥ
D: Samuel Fuller **A:** Gene Evans, Robert Hutton, Richard Loo, Steve Brodie, James Edwards (Deputy/Lippert)

Grim, hard-hitting tale is excellently told. A veteran top sergeant is the sole survivor of a small patrol. He and a young native boy start back for the lines. They are soon joined by a Negro medic, sole survivor of another group. Trio encounters a patrol of green GIs, help them out of an ambush, and go along to establish an observation post in a Korean temple. There they help direct artillery fire and capture a North Korean major. Film serves to introduce Gene Evans as the sergeant.

STEEL MAGNOLIAS
1989, 118 mins, US ⓥ ⊙ ▭
D: Herbert Ross **A:** Sally Field, Dolly Parton, Shirley MacLaine, Daryl Hannah, Olympia Dukakis, Julia Roberts (Rastar/Tri-Star)

As Sally Field's ever-hopeful seriously diabetic daughter, Julia Roberts has real freshness and charm of the sort that can't be faked. As the beauty-shop owner around whom all the action swirls, Dolly Parton is thoroughly in her element. Shirley MacLaine is a nicely bridled caricature as town curmudgeon. She looks a wreck, talks trash, and obviously loves every minute of it. As her partner in hamming-as-an-art-form, Olympia Dukakis just about walks away with the picture. Daryl Hannah has her hands full keeping up with this company as a gawky, nerdish beautician's assistant. Field does some spectacular underplaying, revealing layer after layer of the feelings of this kindly tempered, deeply worried mother.
1989: Nomination: Best Supp. Actress (Julia Roberts)

STEEL TRAP, THE
1952, 84 mins, US
D: Andrew L. Stone **A:** Joseph Cotten, Teresa Wright, Eddie Marr, Aline Towne (Thor/20th Century-Fox)

Suspense that is leavened with welcome chuckles of relief in telling improbable but entertaining events. Joseph Cotten is a minor bank exec who succumbs to an impulse to heist $1 million when the bank closes on Friday, then plans to fly off with his wife for Brazil. Suspense continues to mount as Cotten en-

counters passport trouble, delays that cause him to miss the Saturday plane, and, finally, customs curiosity that reveals to his wife he is a thief.

STEELYARD BLUES
1973, 92 mins, US ⓥ
D: Alan Myerson **A:** Jane Fonda, Donald Sutherland, Peter Boyle, Garry Goodrow, John Savage (Warner)

An erratically amusing slapstick comedy spotlights Donald Sutherland as ringleader of some dropouts who focus their energies on restoring an old US Navy amphibious plane; their search for spare parts leads to a climactic raid on a nearby naval air station. Jane Fonda is the town hooker whose customers include most of the city hall.

STELLA
1990, 114 mins, US ⓥ ⊙
D: John Erman **A:** Bette Midler, John Goodman, Trini Alvarado, Stephen Collins, Marsha Mason, Eileen Brennan (Touchstone/Goldwyn)

The semitragic *Stella Dallas* shows its years in this hopelessly dated and ill-advised remake. The idea of a lower-class mother who selflessly sends her daughter off to her upper-crust dad and his new wife—all so daughter can land the right beau—must sound like nails on a blackboard to Equal Rights Amendment proponents, and Bette Midler's ballsy wit completely misses the redeeming lower-class yearning Barbara Stanwyck gave the 1937 role.

STELLA DALLAS
1925, 108 mins, US ⓥ ⊗
D: Henry King **A:** Belle Bennett, Ronald Colman, Alice Joyce, Jean Hersholt, Douglas Fairbanks Jr. (Goldwyn/United Artists)

A mother picture. Not a great picture, but a great mother picture. Its sentiment is terrific, helped by two magnificent performances by Belle Bennett and Lois Moran. It tells of a mother who eliminates herself so that her child may enjoy the advantages of which the girl will not partake while knowing that her mother has no one to whom she can turn. Moran convinces as she plays the daughter at 10, 13, and as a young woman.

STELLA DALLAS
1937, 104 mins, US ⓥ ⊙
D: King Vidor **A:** Barbara Stanwyck, John Boles, Anne Shirley, Barbara O'Neil, Marjorie Main (Goldwyn/United Artists)

Goldwyn has pretty much followed his original. The sock scenes are still the same ones. These are, especially, a scene between Barbara Stanwyck and Anne Shirley in a train when the former has just heard playmates of the latter criticize the mother as a millstone around the child's head; a scene between the girl and her father, and the woman he wants to marry; and a scene between the mother and daughter at a birthday party to which no one has shown up because of one of the mother's indiscretions.

1937: Nominations: Best Actress (Barbara Stanwyck), Supp. Actress (Anne Shirley)

STELLA MARIS
1918, 77 mins, US ⊗
D: Marshall Neilan **A:** Mary Pickford, Conway Tearle, Camille Ankewich, Ida Waterman (Artcraft)

There are two characters of great importance. One is Stella Maris and the other Unity Blake. Pickford plays them both and proves a revelation. Stella Maris is a sweet child, an orphan, crippled in her nether limbs from birth. Her parents left her well provided for. As Unity Blake, she sees nothing but the harder side of the world's face, for Unity is also an orphan and the inmate of a home.

ST. ELMO'S FIRE
1985, 108 mins, US Ⓥ ⊙ ▭
D: Joel Schumacher **A:** Rob Lowe, Demi Moore, Andrew McCarthy, Judd Nelson, Ally Sheedy, Emilio Estevez (Columbia-Delphi IV/Channel)

All about a group of recent college graduates in Washington who were always the best of friends but now are drifting apart as real life approaches, discovering various reasons why they are so individually obnoxious. Rob Lowe is a saxophone player who refuses to assume any adult responsibility. The rest of the gang befriends him, especially virginal Mare Winningham. The other major problem is beautiful, coked-out Demi Moore, who lives in a pink apartment, sleeps with her boss, and calls her friends with wee-hour problems.

STEPFATHER, THE
1987, 98 mins, US Ⓥ ⊙
D: Joseph Ruben **A:** Terry O'Quinn, Jill Schoelen, Shelley Hack, Stephen Shellen (ITC)

Engrossing suspense thriller refreshingly doesn't cheat the audience in terms of valid clues and plot twists. Terry O'Quinn toplines as a mild-looking guy who immediately is revealed to be a psychotic who has murdered his entire family. A year later he has started a new life as Jerry Blake, married to young Susan (Shelley Hack), who has a teenage daughter Stephanie (Jill Schoelen). His past eventually catches up with him as his previous brother-in-law Jim (Stephen Shellen) is still researching the murder of his sister with the help of a reporter, the police, and (independently) Stephanie's psychiatrist (Charles Lanyer).

STEPFATHER II
1989, 86 mins, US Ⓥ ⊙
D: Jeff Burr **A:** Terry O'Quinn, Meg Foster, Caroline Williams, Jonathan Brandis, Henry Brown (ITC)

This dull sequel reduces the intriguing premise of the original to the level of an inconsequential, tongue-in-cheek slasher film. This time O'Quinn lifts the identity of a deceased family therapist from the newspaper obituary and moves into an L.A. suburb. He romances the pretty real-estate divorcée who's his neighbor (Meg Foster). Pic builds toward their impending marriage, but a neighbor (Caroline Williams), the postal delivery woman, is suspicious of O'Quinn.

STEPFORD WIVES, THE
1975, 114 mins, US Ⓥ
D: Bryan Forbes **A:** Katharine Ross, Paula Prentiss, Peter Masterson, Nanette Newman, Patrick O'Neal, Tina Louise (Palomar/Columbia)

Bryan Forbes's filmization of Ira Levin's potboiler is a quietly freaky suspense-horror story. Katharine Ross (in an excellent and assured performance), husband Peter Masterson, and kids depart NY's urban pressures to a seemingly bovine Connecticut existence. Trouble is, Ross and new friend Paula Prentiss (also excellent) find all the other wives exuding sticky hairspray homilies and male-chauvinist fantasy responses. The black humor and sophistication of the plot is handled extremely well.

STEPKIDS
See: *Big Girls Don't Cry . . . They Get Even*

STEP LIVELY
1944, 86 mins, US Ⓥ ▭
D: Tim Whelan **A:** Frank Sinatra, George Murphy, Adolphe Menjou, Gloria de Ha-

ven, Eugene Pallette, Walter Slezak (RKO)

Room Service has been resurrected for an RKO remake, with song trimming palpably designed to fit Frank Sinatra. The hectic machinations of theatrical shoestringers have been given a thorough going-over. But it is pleasant enough divertissement.

STEPPENWOLF
1974, 105 mins, US ⓥ ⊙
D: Fred Haines A: Max von Sydow, Dominique Sanda, Pierre Clementi, Carla Romanelli, Roy Bosier (Sprague)

Film remains as subjective and essentially plotless as the Hermann Hesse book. The weird effects produced from a sophisticated, electronic video mix translate Hesse's abstractions faithfully, if such a thing is at all possible. Max von Sydow as Harry Haller, the misanthrope who opts for one last try at life before reaching 50 and a preplanned suicide, makes the journey remarkable.

STEPPING OUT
1991, 106 mins, US ⓥ ⊙
D: Lewis Gilbert A: Liza Minnelli, Shelley Winters, Bill Irwin, Ellen Greene, Julie Walters (Paramount)

It's Liza-as-you-love-her in a modest heartwarmer about a bunch of suburban left-feeters getting it together for a charity dance spot. Fragile ensemble item often creaks under the Minnelli glitz, but results are likable enough. Minnelli is a former pro hoofer who's now teaching amateur dance classes on the side. She's lost none of her pizzazz. Looking as fresh-faced and gamine as ever, and in good voice and shape, she provides the pic's emotional highs in a solo dance spot and the finale's John Kander–Fred Ebb title song, but as an actress, she's one-note perky.

STEREO
1969, 63 mins, Canada
D: David Cronenberg A: Ronald Mlodzik, Jack Messinger, Iain Ewing, Clara Mayer, Paul Mulholland (Emergent)

Lensed for a paltry $3,500, initial feature-film effort by David Cronenberg tests the viewer's patience and endurance even with its hour's running time, due to its emphatically dry, scientific narration and deliberate emotional distancing. Film abstractly examines the situation at the Canadian Academy for Erotic Inquiry, where eight individuals have been subjected to telepathic surgery.

STERILE CUCKOO, THE
(UK: POOKIE)
1969, 108 mins, US ⓥ ⊙
D: Alan J. Pakula A: Liza Minnelli, Wendell Burton, Tim McIntire, Elizabeth Harrower (Paramount/Boardwalk)

The Sterile Cuckoo is a kook named Pookie, a wacky, wisecracking motherless, outrageously adorable, collegiate gamin. A first affair in a ramshackle upstate New York motel becomes high comedy with the hot-to-trot vamp Minnelli prodding the nervous-in-the-service Burton.

1969: Nominations: Best Actress (Liza Minelli), Song ("Come Saturday Morning")

STEVIE
1978, 102 mins, UK ⓥ
D: Robert Enders A: Glenda Jackson, Mona Washbourne, Alec McCowen, Trevor Howard (Bowden)

Well-acted and literate, but also talky and claustrophobic screen biography of British poet and novelist Stevie Smith. Glenda Jackson stars in the title role and her performance—in fact, the entire style of the film—seems better suited to the stage than the big screen. Most of the picture takes place inside a suburban residence Smith shared with her aunt, portrayed by Mona Washbourne in a charming and sympathetic performance.

STICKY FINGERS
1988, 97 mins, US ⓥ ⊙
D: Catlin Adams A: Helen Slater, Melanie Mayron, Danitra Vance, Eileen Brennan, Carol Kane (Hightop)

Snappy, offbeat urban comedy. Story casts Melanie Mayron and Helen Slater as struggling musicians on the verge of eviction from their NY walk-up until a bagful of drug money—nearly a million bucks—lands in their laps. They've been asked to "mind it." Initially panicked, they wind up using it to pay their rent; then to replace their instruments. As days pass, the urge to spend becomes insatiable, and they give in with gusto.

STIGMATA
1999, 103 mins, US ⓥ ⊙
D: Rupert Wainwright A: Patricia Arquette, Gabriel Byrne, Jonathan Pryce, Nia Long, Thomas Kopache, Rade Sherbedgia (FGM/M-G-M)

Aggressively silly, this possession thriller starts out promising a mix of unintentional laughs and visual hyperbole. But even those guilty pleasures soon pall.

In a Brazilian village, Vatican investigator Father Kiernan (Gabriel Byrne) discovers the "miracle" of a blood-weeping Virgin Mary statue. A thief steals a rosary from a cleric's corpse and an-American tourist mails it to her daughter, Frankie (Patricia Arquette), a larky 23-year-old Pittsburgh stylist, who soon experiences spooky visions and Christ-like mutilations. Father Kiernan is dispatched to examine her. In its early going, Stigmata whips up an entertaining hysteria of stylistic overkill, tittersome dialogue, and giddily outlandish situations. But the fun doesn't last.

STILL CRAZY
1998, 95 mins, UK Ⓥ
D: Brian Gibson A: Stephen Rea, Billy Connolly, Jimmy Nail, Timothy Spall, Bill Nighy, Juliet Aubrey (Marmot Tandy/Columbia)

Still Crazy is a chucklesome, warmly observed comedy about five middle-aged losers who reassemble their rock band that broke up in the seventies. Strange Fruit was a classic rock band, riven by drugs, booze, egos, and sex. The son of a fest promoter bumps into keyboard player Tony (Stephen Rea), now selling condoms in Spain, and suggests that the Fruits hold a reunion concert. Tony contacts their former PA, Karen (Juliet Aubrey), and the pair sets about rounding up the group. Guts of the picture is the band's odyssey through a series of low-rent continental clubs, marked by embarrassing disasters, the resurgence of old friction between guitarist composer Les (Jimmy Nail) and addled lead singer Ray (Bill Nighy), and a growing re-attraction between Tony and Karen. Pic's ambling style and humor takes a while to settle down but finds its focus with the second-reel appearance of Nighy, in an on-the-button portrait of a burned-out, middle-aged rocker whose brains are still fried by past excesses.

STILL OF THE NIGHT
1982, 91 mins, US Ⓥ
D: Robert Benton A: Roy Scheider, Meryl Streep, Jessica Tandy, Joe Grifasi, Sara Botsford, Josef Sommer (United Artists)

It comes as almost a shock to see a modern suspense picture so literate, well acted, and beautifully made. Roy Scheider effectively plays an introspective New York shrink whose life becomes endangered after one of his patients is found murdered. Meryl Streep—the neurotic mistress of the dead man—whose distressed, unpredictable behavior represents the source of most of the film's mystery, slowly insinuates herself into Scheider's relatively uneventful life.

STING, THE
1973, 127 mins, US Ⓥ ☉
D: George Roy Hill A: Paul Newman, Robert Redford, Robert Shaw, Charles Durning, Ray Walston, Eileen Brennan (Universal)

Paul Newman and Robert Redford are superbly reteamed as a pair of con artists in Chicago of the 1930s, out to fleece a big-time racketeer brilliantly played by Robert Shaw. The three stars make all the difference between simply a good film and a superior one. Newman's relationship with Eileen Brennan (in a sensational supporting role) rounds out his characterization of an old pro making his last big score. Redford works superbly. Shaw's taciturn menace commands attention. The film comes to a series of startling climaxes, piled atop one another with zest.
1973: Best Picture, Director, Original Story & Screenplay, Art Direction, Adapted Scoring, Editing, Costume Design (Edith Head)
Nominations: Best Actor (Robert Redford), Cinematography, Sound

STING II, THE
1983, 102 mins, US Ⓥ ☉
D: Jeremy Paul Kagan A: Jackie Gleason, Mac Davis, Teri Garr, Karl Malden, Oliver Reed, Bert Remsen (Universal)

Stars Jackie Gleason and Mac Davis come nowhere close to evoking the charming on-screen qualities of Paul Newman and Robert Redford. Combined with the slow pace and overdone exposition, sequel is mostly just a chore to watch. Gleason plays the master con man out to make a big score with the help of fellow huckster Davis. The chief patsy is nightclub owner Karl Malden. Teri Garr provides what little life there is as a slick, seasoned trickster who becomes involved in the scam.
1983: Nomination: Best Adapted Score

STIR CRAZY
1980, 111 mins, US Ⓥ ☉
D: Sidney Poitier A: Gene Wilder, Richard Pryor, JoBeth Williams, Georg Stanford Brown, Craig T. Nelson (Columbia)

Story setup has down-on-their-luck Richard Pryor and Gene Wilder dressing up as woodpeckers to make some cash.

Two baddies use the woodpecker suits to rob a bank, leaving Pryor and Wilder 120-year prison sentences and no alibi. Majority of the action focuses on the antics of prison life, with Pryor and Wilder at the center of a group of fairly stereotypical jail characters.

STIR OF ECHOES
1999, 110 mins, US Ⓥ ⊙
D: David Koepp **A:** Kevin Bacon, Kathryn Erbe, Illeana Douglas, Liza Weil, Kevin Dunn, Conor O'Farrell (Hofflund-Polone)

Stir of Echoes is a white-knuckle thriller propelled by Kevin Bacon's exceptional performance as a working-class Everyman who discovers dark secrets under his own roof after gaining precognitive powers. While Tom Witzky (Bacon) is bathing his young son, Jake (Zachary David Cope), moppet calmly converses with an unseen apparition. Shortly afterward, Tom is outspoken in his teasing of Lisa (Illeana Douglas), his metaphysical-minded sister-in-law. Lisa lulls him into a trance and encourages him to be more ''open'' in his thinking. But this makes Tom receptive to bad vibes. Koepp does a masterful job of grounding his intimations of the supernatural in persuasive, down-to-earth context. But the credibility quotient gets its biggest boost from Bacon's shrewdly detailed performance.

STITCH IN TIME, A
1963, 94 mins, UK
D: Robert Asher **A:** Norman Wisdom, Edward Chapman, Jeanette Sterke, Jerry Desmonde, Jill Melford (Rank)

String of farcical events puts the pint-sized Norman Wisdom through the full pratfalling routine. The thin thread linking the scenes has Wisdom as a hapless butcher's assistant causing constant commotion in a hospital. For sophisticated palates, Wisdom is mechanical, and he plays up the sentiment of the ''little man'' against authority to cloying effect.

ST. IVES
1976, 93 mins, US Ⓥ
D: J. Lee Thompson **A:** Charles Bronson, John Houseman, Jacqueline Bisset, Maximilian Schell, Harry Guardino, Harris Yulin (Warner)

Eliminate gratuitous, offensive, and overdone violence from a dull and plodding film story, and all you've got left is a dull and plodding film. Charles Bronson

stars as an ex–police reporter involved with wealthy crime dilettante John Houseman and partner Jacqueline Bisset. Plot progress is marred by lots of month-old red herrings.

ST. LOUIS BLUES
1939, 90 mins, US
D: Raoul Walsh **A:** Dorothy Lamour, Lloyd Nolan, Tito Guizar, Jerome Cowan (Paramount)

Behind-the-scenes Mississippi riverboat stuff in a modern setting lacks the charm of the background that keynotes Show Boat. There's quite a bit of stuff packed in, ranging from the 52nd street jitterbug motif (Maxine Sullivan) to Broadway injunction suits by Jerome Cowan against Dorothy Lamour. Latter eventually goes into her standard sarong routine as part of a South Seas sequence.

STOLEN HOURS
1963, 100 mins, US Ⓥ
D: Daniel Petrie **A:** Susan Hayward, Michael Craig, Diane Baker, Edward Judd, Paul Rogers (Mirisch/Barbican)

Smooth and slick production out of the story of a woman facing death as the result of brain disease. A remake of the 1939 Bette Davis starrer Dark Victory, the film moves easily from discovery to predetermined conclusion and gives Hayward a chance to do some effective emoting.

STOLEN KISSES
See: Baisers Voles

STOLEN LIFE, A
1946, 100 mins, US Ⓥ
D: Curtis Bernhardt **A:** Bette Davis, Glenn Ford, Dane Clark, Walter Brennan, Charles Ruggles (Warner/BD)

Bette Davis appears as a sweet, sincere, artistic girl, and as this girl's man-crazy sister. When the latter, by trickery, marries man with whom former has fallen in love and is later drowned in a boating accident, the sweet girl takes on her sister's identity in a try for happiness. Dialogue hands plenty of clichés to male players, particularly to Glenn Ford as the man in love with both sisters.
1946: Nomination: Best Special Effects

STONE BOY, THE
1984, 93 mins, US Ⓥ
D: Christopher Cain **A:** Robert Duvall, Jason Presson, Frederic Forrest, Glenn Close, Wilford Brimley (TLC)

Jason Presson plays a 12-year-old who accidentally slays his older, beloved brother with a shotgun in the opening moments of the film. Production never lapses into sentimentality or melodrama as family is rendered dazed and grief-stricken by the death of the older son, while young responsible brother retreats behind a wall of guilt. In its inarticulate characters whose feelings tear them apart, film is singular and highly accessible.

STONE KILLER, THE
1973, 95 mins, US Ⓥ ⊙
D: Michael Winner **A:** Charles Bronson, Martin Balsam, David Sheiner, Norman Fell, Ralph Waite (De Laurentiis)

Confused, meandering crime potboiler, starring Charles Bronson as a tough detective who starts out on a low-level gangster case only to find upper Mafia echelon also are involved. The story and direction reach for so many bases that the end result is a lot of cinema razzle-dazzle without substance.

STONEWALL
1995, 99 mins, US/UK Ⓥ
D: Nigel Finch **A:** Guillermo Diaz, Fred Weller, Brendan Corbalis, Bruce Mac-Vittie, Duane Boutte (Arena NY/BBC)

Film takes its name from the legendary Greenwich Village gay bar and its dramatic cue from the 1969 riot in which drag queens took on New York cops during a raid on the premises. Matty Dean (Fred Weller), a country boy, hooks up with LaMiranda (Guillermo Diaz), a sassy young drag queen, and Ethan (Brendan Corbalis), a member of an ineffectual gay activist group. A third track follows neighborhood drag-queen godmother Bustonia (Bruce MacVittie) and her relationship with Stonewall's owner, Vinnie (Duane Boutte). Characters are affectionately drawn, as is the sense of community and solidarity.

STOOGE, THE
1952, 100 mins, US
D: Norman Taurog **A:** Dean Martin, Jerry Lewis, Polly Bergen, Marion Marshall, Eddie Mayehoff, Richard Erdman (Paramount)

Dean Martin and Jerry Lewis venture into a straight story-line comedy. Martin plays a crooning, accordion-playing comic who only becomes a success when he acquires a dumb stooge to work with him from the audience. Lewis is the patsy, a wistful ugly duckling who adores the man who gave him a chance in show business.

STOP! OR MY MOM WILL SHOOT
1992, 87 mins, US Ⓥ ⊙
D: Roger Spottiswoode **A:** Sylvester Stallone, Estelle Getty, JoBeth Williams, Roger Rees, Martin Ferrero (Universal/Northern Lights)

This buddy cop picture casts budding comic actor Sylvester Stallone (Oscar) and proven laugh-getter Estelle Getty (TV's *Golden Girls*) as a beleaguered L.A. lawman and his aggravating mother. Visiting from the East Coast, the hyper-meddlesome Getty proves second to none in embarassing the pants off her Joey (Stallone). Before long she's pushed her way into Joey's business as his pistol-packing partner in some perilous escapades. Stallone is the model of the amiable, put-upon comic hero, while the tiny Getty is worth triple her weight in ticket stubs.

STORK CLUB, THE
1945, 98 mins, US Ⓥ
D: Hal Walker **A:** Betty Hutton, Barry Fitzgerald, Don DeFore, Andy Russell, Iris Adrian, Robert Benchley (Paramount)

Much occurs in the penthouse where Betty Hutton has been mysteriously ensconced. Interspersed is a blighted romance between Barry Fitzgerald and Mary Young, his wife of 40 years, who walked out on the eccentric Irish millionaire. A romantic crisis occurs between the checkroom gal (Hutton) and her bandleader-ex-marine (Don DeFore), who can't dope out her unaccustomed affluence. Hutton is capital throughout, vocally and histrionically, while Fitzgerald almost steals the picture.

STORM, THE
1930, 76 mins, US
D: William Wyler **A:** Lupe Velez, Paul Cavanaugh, William Boyd, Alphonz Ethier, Ernie S. Adams (Universal)

Lupe Velez is a French smuggler's daughter who is left with a friendly trapper by her father just before a bullet from a Mountie's gun lays him low. Story is that of a trapper-miner and his best friend who develop a serious rivalry over the girl ward left with the former. They both lean heavily toward the girl, finally hating each other.

STORM BOY
1976, 88 mins, Australia Ⓥ
D: Henri Safran **A:** Greg Rowe, Peter

Cummins, David Gulpilil, Judy Dick, Tony Allison (SAFC)

A gem of a film. Mike (Greg Rowe) is the 10-year-old son of Tom (Peter Cummins), a wifeless fisherman who inhabits a shanty on the beach and ekes out a living. A chance meeting with an Aborigine (David Gulpilil) affects Mike's life, and gives him the name Storm Boy. Fingerbone Bill lives a nomadic life pretty much along the lines of his ancestors. And he has retained the mystical insights of his forebears.

STORM OVER THE NILE
1955, 107 mins, UK ⍟ ▱
D: Terence Young, Zoltan Korda **A:** Anthony Steel, Laurence Harvey, Mary Ure, Ronald Lewis, Ian Carmichael, James Robertson Justice (London)

The Four Feathers ranked high among Alexander Korda's prewar successes and use of the widescreen process is probably the main justification for the remake, particularly as it enhances the vivid battle scenes in which Kitchener's troops rout the native armies at Khartoum, while imprisoned British officers capture the enemy arsenal. Generally, the acting hardly matches the lavish and spectacular qualities of the production. Laurence Harvey, as an officer who gets blinded by an overdose of sun, appears miscast. Only James Robertson Justice fits happily into the story.

STORM WARNING
1950, 93 mins, US
D: Stuart Heisler **A:** Ginger Rogers, Ronald Reagan, Doris Day, Steve Cochran, Lloyd Gough (Warner)

Pic weaves a hard-hitting plot around violence, murder, and the Ku Klux Klan. Ginger Rogers visits overnight with her married sister. She finds the streets strangely deserted, and while walking them inadvertently witnesses the brutal slaying of a newspaperman by Klansmen. Terrified and sick from the experience, she finds her sister and then discovers the husband is one of the killers.

STORMY MONDAY
1988, 93 mins, UK ⍟ ⊙
D: Mike Figgis **A:** Melanie Griffith, Tommy Lee Jones, Sting, Sean Bean, Prunella Gee (MovingPicture)

Attempt to come up with a stylish British film noir is all visual flash and no script, with comatose performances to boot. Melanie Griffith toplines as a sort of B-girl working for US gangster/real-estate magnate Tommy Lee Jones. Jones is trying to run Sting out of business, operating a local jazz club. Plot unfolds as a string of ridiculous coincidences. Jones walks through his idiotic role with barely hidden embarrassment. Griffith hasn't missed many meals, sporting an unbecoming figure.

STORMY WEATHER
1943, 77 mins, US ⍟ ⊙
D: Andrew L. Stone **A:** Lena Horne, Bill Robinson, Fats Waller, Dooley Wilson, Cab Calloway, Katherine Dunham (20th Century-Fox)

Chock-full of the cream-of-the-crop colored talent, with a deft story skein to hold it together. Story is told via the flashback formula. A 25th anniversary number of *Theatre World* is in tribute to the great trouper Bill Robinson. Via the number, Robinson crosses and recrosses paths with Lena Horne, in and out of shows, Hollywood filmusicals, etc., with Cab Calloway, Katherine Dunham and her expert troupe of ballet dancers, Fats Waller, the Nicholas Brothers, plus others.

STORY OF ADELE H., THE
See: L'Histoire D'Adele H.

STORY OF DR. WASSELL, THE
1944, 136 mins, US
D: Cecil B. DeMille **A:** Gary Cooper, Laraine Day, Signe Hasso, Dennis O'Keefe, Carol Thurston, Carl Esmond (Paramount)

Factual story of Dr. Wassell's heroic evacuation of 12 men, plus himself, from Java in earlier stages of the war has been brought to the screen on a lavish scale. Gary Cooper imparts to the role much vigor, color, and sympathetic interest. Instead of being court-martialed for having disobeyed orders to leave stretcher cases behind, Dr. Wassell was awarded the Navy Cross and his heroic deed made the subject of a broadcast by President Roosevelt.

1944: Nomination: Best Special Effects

STORY OF ESTHER COSTELLO, THE
1957, 104 mins, UK
D: David Miller **A:** Joan Crawford, Rossano Brazzi, Heather Sears, Lee Patterson, Denis O'Dea (Romulus/Valiant)

An all-out assault on the emotions. Joan Crawford is a rich American socialite who, revisiting her Irish birthplace, finds a young girl, deaf, dumb, and blind. Joan rescues the girl from her evil surroundings, takes her to the US, and devotes her life to the girl's recovery. This mercy campaign sparks the interest of the world, but Crawford's estranged husband (Rossano Brazzi) and a slick exploitation guy turn it into a giant racket. The acting is noteworthy for a remarkable debut by 21-year-old Heather Sears.

STORY OF G.I. JOE, THE
1945, 109 mins, US
D: William A. Wellman **A:** Burgess Meredith, Robert Mitchum, Freddie Steele, Wally Cassell (United Artists)

From the moment the infantrymen are picked out at "blanket drill" in the African desert until the last shot on the open highway to Rome, it's the foot-slogging soldier who counts most in this film. Real-life GI diarist Ernie Pyle is there, Burgess Meredith playing the simple little figure that's Pyle. Robert Mitchum is excellent as the lieutenant who grows to a captaincy. Freddie Steele is tops as the tough sergeant. Wally Cassell as the lothario of the company, and all the others are excellent.

STORY OF LOUIS PASTEUR, THE
1936, 85 mins, US Ⓥ
D: William Dieterle **A:** Paul Muni, Josephine Hutchinson, Anita Louise, Donald Woods, Fritz Leiber (Warner)

Paul Muni in the title role is at his very top form. Film skips his early life and struggles. He's propagandizing for sterilization of doctors' hands and instruments in childbirth. Doesn't get him very far because of general medical opposition and he turns to treatment of anthrax in sheep and cattle. Success here leads to admission to the French Academy, although still scoffed at by the majority of his confreres. Works on a cure for rabies for the rest of the picture. His reward finally is general acclaim.
1936: Best Actor (Paul Muni), Original Story & Screenplay
Nomination: Best Picture

STORY OF MANKIND, THE
1957, 99 mins, US
D: Irwin Allen **A:** Ronald Colman, Vincent Price, Agnes Moorehead, Peter Lorre, Dennis Hopper, Virginia Mayo (Cambridge/Warner)

Screenplay convokes the "High Tribunal of Outer Space" upon news that man has discovered the Super-H bomb 60

years too soon. The problem is whether to save mankind or let it go off and exterminate itself. To reach a decision, the tribunal permits both the Devil and the Spirit of Man to give evidence as to man's fitness to continue. In the dreary cataloging of man's crimes against humanity, the Devil makes a much better case. Best of the portrayals is Agnes Moorehead's Queen Elizabeth, and Cedric Hardwicke turns in a good performance as the High Judge. Ronald Colman a dignified personification of the Spirit of Man and Vincent Price is the sophisticated, sneering embodiment of Old Scratch.

STORY OF QIU JU, THE
See: Qiuju Da Guansi

STORY OF ROBIN HOOD, THE (AKA: THE STORY OF ROBIN HOOD AND HIS MERRIE MEN)
1952, 83 mins, UK Ⓥ ⊙
D: Ken Annakin **A:** Richard Todd, Joan Rice, Peter Finch, James Hayter, James Robertson Justice, Martita Hunt (Walt Disney/RKO)

A superb piece of entertainment, with all the action of a western and the romance and intrigue of a historical drama. Despite his modest stature, Richard Todd proves to be a first-rate Robin Hood, alert, dashing, and forceful, equally convincing when leading his outlaws against Prince John as he is in winning the admiration of Maid Marian.

STORY OF RUTH, THE
1960, 132 mins, US Ⓥ ▭
D: Henry Koster **A:** Stuart Whitman, Tom Tryon, Peggy Wood, Viveca Lindfors, Jeff Morrow, Elana Eden (20th Century-Fox)

Refreshingly sincere and restrained biblical drama elaborates on the romantic, political, and devotional difficulties encountered by the Old Testament heroine. Yet there is a sluggishness that is disturbing. The film introduces Elana Eden in the title role. She gives a performance of dignity, projecting an inner strength through a delicate veneer.

STORY OF THREE LOVES, THE
1953, 122 mins, US
D: Gottfried Reinhardt, Vincente Minnelli **A:** Pier Angeli, Ethel Barrymore, Leslie Caron, Kirk Douglas, James Mason, Moira Shearer (M-G-M)

Three yarns tied together by placing the key characters aboard an ocean liner. Opening episode is easily the most effective. Moira Shearer plays an aspiring ballerina prevented from dancing by a serious heart condition. When James Mason, a famous choreographer, sees her improvising on an empty stage, he asks her to perform for him.

STORY OF US, THE
1999, 94 mins, US Ⓥ ⊙
D: Rob Reiner **A:** Bruce Willis, Michelle Pfeiffer, Tim Matheson, Rob Reiner, Rita Wilson, Paul Reiser (Castle Rock/Universal)

The Story of Us is a seriocomic anatomy of the ups and downs of a 15-year marriage between two bright and attractive partners, credibly played by Michelle Pfeiffer and Bruce Willis. The tale is burdened by a complicated time scheme of flashbacks and flashforwards. About to celebrate their 15th anniversary, Ben and Katie Jordan have grown apart. They attempt a trial separation. Story unfolds as a series of reflections on their shared history, from their first, charming meeting in an office to the present, when each is in bed waiting for the other's call. The stylistic devices used, which recall early Woody Allen and Paul Mazursky, get increasingly tedious. Pfeiffer delivers a compelling performance. As a man who's more emotionally demonstrative than his wife, Willis is also good.

STORY OF VERNON AND IRENE CASTLE, THE
1939, 96 mins, US Ⓥ ⊙
D: H. C. Potter **A:** Fred Astaire, Ginger Rogers, Edna May Oliver, Walter Brennan, Lew Fields, Etienne Girardot (RKO)

Topflight cinematic entertainment deals with a much-in-love married pair of ballroomologists catapulted from dire straits in Paris to international acclaim and fortune. The medley of some 40 yesteryear pops is the common denominator for all types of audiences. Ginger Rogers and Fred Astaire are excellent.

STORYVILLE
1992, 110 mins, US Ⓥ
D: Mark Frost **A:** James Spader, Joanne Whalley-Kilmer, Jason Robards, Charlotte Lewis, Michael Warren (Davis Entertainment/Pressman)

A teeming cesspool of illicit sex, murder, suicide, family intrigue, and political chicanery in exotic Louisiana, this would-be *Chinatown* is so overloaded with outrageous implausibilities that the temptation

is very strong to consider it all a joke. James Spader plays Cray Fowler, a callow, good-looking kid trying to carry his rich, corrupt family's tradition of political service into a third generation. Cray does so many apparently stupid things, and the many jaw-dropping loopholes and implausibilities in the first half make the film systematically unconvincing.

STOWAWAY
1936, 87 mins, US Ⓥ
D: William A. Seiter **A:** Shirley Temple, Robert Young, Alice Faye, Eugene Pallette, Helen Westley, Arthur Treacher (20th Century-Fox)

In addition to her customary singing, dancing, and exceptional line reading for a child her age, Shirley Temple this time goes in for talking Chinese, quoting Oriental proverbs, and giving imitations of Jolson, Cantor, and Fred Astaire. She even handles a tearful dramatic exit expertly. Daughter of missionary parents who are slain by bandits, the kid meets up with a cruising American playboy in Shanghai and winds up marrying him off. The romantic leads are Robert Young, and Alice Faye, both very good.

STRADA, LA
1954, 115 mins, Italy Ⓥ ⊙
D: Federico Fellini **A:** Giulietta Masina, Anthony Quinn, Richard Basehart, Aldo Sivani, Marcella Rovena (Ponti, De Laurentiis)

Story of a blunt, brutal wandering carny performer (Anthony Quinn) who "buys" a girl (Giulietta Masina) to serve as his assistant. She's on the nutty side, but falls for him despite his many affairs with other women and his poor treatment of her. Her poetic conversations with a similarly dim-witted clown-trapezist (Richard Basehart) anger the brute, who finally accidentally kills his rival in a fistfight. Story is filled with pathetic and poetic moments, and often is both very touching and extremely amusing. Masina, one of Italy's best performers, easily steals show with her clownish mimicry.
1954: Best Foreign Language Film

STRAIGHT TIME
1978, 114 mins, US Ⓥ
D: Ulu Grosbard **A:** Dustin Hoffman, Theresa Russell, Gary Busey, Harry Dean Stanton, M. Emmet Walsh (First Artists/Sweetwall)

A most unlikable film because Dustin

Hoffman, starring as a paroled and long-time criminal, cannot overcome the essentially distasteful and increasingly unsympathetic elements in the character. Ulu Grosbard's sluggish direction doesn't help.

STRAIT-JACKET
1963, 93 mins, US ⓥ
D: William Castle A: Joan Crawford, Diane Baker, Leif Erickson, Howard St. John, George Kennedy (Columbia)

Heads really roll in this yarn, which commences with a dual hatchet job on a cheating husband and his lady friend who are discovered bedrooming by the wife (Joan Crawford), whose three-year-old daughter witnesses in horror the 40-some-odd whacks per victim administered by her mother. Mom goes to the insane asylum and daughter grows up into Diane Baker. They are reunited 20 years later when mom is released. Crawford does well by her role, delivering an animated performance. Most of the murders are suspensefully and chillingly constructed.

STRANGE AFFAIR, THE
1968, 102 mins, UK ▭
D: David Greene A: Michael York, Jeremy Kemp, Susan George, Jack Watson (Paramount)

Michael York is the "Strange" involved in an affair which finds Scotland Yard detective Pierce (Jeremy Kemp) trying to nail a trio of dangerous drug peddlers. Frustrated in various attempts at getting legal evidence, Kemp in desperation resorts to blackmailing Strange, who's been caught in a compromising situation with a girl, into planting a drug packet on one of the trio during a search. There are no lags in the action, with literate script ringing true all the way. It is, however, Susan George who captures most attention in a very appealing performance as an ebullient hippie.

STRANGE ALIBI
1941, 63 mins, US
D: D. Ross Lederman A: Arthur Kennedy, Joan Perry, Howard da Silva, Florence Bates (Warner/First National)

This rates high among the average run of B mellers. Everything in it has been seen before—particularly the sets—but the concoction has been tossed together again to become a speedy and delectable dish. Arthur Kennedy plays a detective who arranges with his chief for a publicized break between them so that he can go over to the Mob. Racket guys find out he's not playing them straight and kill the chief, planting the murder on Kennedy.

STRANGE BEDFELLOWS
1964, 99 mins, US
D: Melvin Frank A: Rock Hudson, Gina Lollobrigida, Gig Young, Edward Judd, Terry-Thomas (Panama-Frank/Universal)

Another of those romantic marital comedies based primarily on misunderstandings. Hudson is a trifle solemn as London-based US oil executive who can rise to extreme top echelon if his corporate image is whitewashed. This means he must patch up seven-year-marriage to Gina Lollobrigida, who more than compensates for Hudson's stuffiness by her enthusiastic rapport with zany causes.

STRANGE CARGO
1940, 111 mins, US ⓥ
D: Frank Borzage A: Joan Crawford, Clark Gable, Ian Hunter, Peter Lorre, Paul Lukas, Albert Dekker (M-G-M)

Strange melodramatic concoction endeavors to mix the adventures of an escaping group of convicts from a tropical-island prison with religious preaching through inclusion of a mysterious stranger with Christ-like attributes. The attempt is not successful. Crawford is provided with a particularly meaty role as a hardened dancehall gal. Gable is vigorous in his portrayal of the self-appointed head of the escaping convicts, a far-from-sympathetic assignment, and he is overshadowed by the reserved but strong-willed Hunter as the redeemer of the tough souls.

STRANGE DAYS
1995, 145 mins, US ⓥ ⊙ ▭
D: Kathryn Bigelow A: Ralph Fiennes, Angela Bassett, Juliette Lewis, Tom Sizemore, Vincent D'Onofrio (Lightstorm/20th Century-Fox)

Very dark vision of the very near future is a technical tour de force for director Kathryn Bigelow and her team. Pic is less accomplished in putting over its characters, emotions, and dubious sociopolitical themes. Black marketer Lenny Nero (Ralph Fiennes), a low-life hustler and former cop, offers customers "a piece of somebody's life" on a small disk and viewable via a compact headpiece. For his own personal pleasure, Nero prefers to replay scenes of happier times, when the saucy singer Faith (Juliette Lewis) was his eager-to-please girlfriend. Now, however, Faith has run off with the sadistic Philo Gant (Michael Wincott), a sinister gangster. Inevitably, all the major characters wind up at the mammoth party-to-end-all-parties in downtown L.A. to usher in the new millennium.

STRANGE HOLIDAY
1946, 62 mins, US

D: Arch Oboler A: Claude Rains, Bobbie Stebbins, Barbara Bate, Paul Hilton, Gloria Holden, Milton Kibbee (Elite)

A converted commercial film, turned out in wartime to boost morale of General Motors workers, poses thought that America's liberty must be carefully guarded. Message is hung on melodramatic plot that has John Stevenson (Rains) coming back to the city after a vacation. He finds the Nazis have taken over and he's kicked around, beaten, and subjected to other totalitarian stunts that show how great it is to live in a free United States. Heavy and lengthy dialogue that falls to Rains keeps general pace slow.

STRANGE INTERLUDE
(UK: STRANGE INTERVAL)
1932, 110 mins, US ⓥ

D: Robert Z. Leonard A: Norma Shearer, Clark Gable, Alexander Kirkland, Ralph Morgan, Robert Young, May Robson (M-G-M)

Norma Shearer, who shoulders the brunt of the histrionic burden, somehow misses in a vacillating characterization which was made, necessarily so, for censor purposes alone, if nothing else. The O'Neill asides, in screen treatment, might be said to be somewhat of an improvement over the stage original. The actual words are uttered, and then the subconscious thoughts are voiced by the same player on the soundtrack (with a different inflection, of course).

STRANGE INTERVAL
See: Strange Interlude

STRANGE LOVE OF MARTHA IVERS, THE
1946, 113 mins, US ⓥ

D: Lewis Milestone A: Barbara Stanwyck, Van Heflin, Lizabeth Scott, Kirk Douglas, Judith Anderson (Wallis/Paramount)

A forthright, uncompromising presentation of evil, greedy people, and human weaknesses with sharply drawn characters and direction that punches home suspense and excitement. Character portrayed by Stanwyck is evil and she gives it a high-caliber delineation. Douglas makes his weakling role interesting, showing up strongly among the more experienced players. Best performance honors, though, are divided between Heflin and Scott, latter as a Heflin pickup.

1946: Nomination: Best Original Story

STRANGER, THE
1946, 94 mins, US ⓥ

D: Orson Welles A: Orson Welles, Edward G. Robinson, Loretta Young, Philip Merivale (RKO/International)

Socko melodrama, spinning an intriguing web of thrills and chills. Plot moves forward at a relentless pace in depicting the hunt for a top Nazi who has removed all traces of his origin and is a professor in a New England school. Edward G. Robinson is the government man on his trail. Loretta Young is the New England girl who becomes the bride of the Nazi. The terror mounts as Robinson tries to trap Welles into revealing his true identity.

1946: Nomination: Best Original Story

STRANGER AMONG US, A
(UK: CLOSE TO EDEN)
1992, 111 mins, US ⓥ

D: Sidney Lumet A: Melanie Griffith, Eric Thal, John Pankow, Tracy Pollan, Mia Sara (Hollywood/Propaganda)

Fish-out-of-water mystery, about a case-hardened WASP female cop investigating a murder in New York's cloistered Hasidic community, tries to make up in local color what it lacks in dramatic plausibility. Plot is overloaded with hard-to-take factors, while the revelation of the killer is far from surprising. More importantly, the nature of the Hasidic community effectively prevents Melanie Griffith from conducting any kind of penetrating investigation. Griffith is at her best when she realizes that she may have a spiritual side that has never been acknowledged.

STRANGER IN THE HOUSE
1967, 104 mins, UK

D: Pierre Rouve A: James Mason, Geraldine Chaplin, Bobby Darin, Paul Bertoya, Ian Ogilvy (Rank)

This yarn is sparked by the antagonistic attitude of Geraldine Chaplin to her middle-aged father (James Mason), who was once a brilliant barrister. The idea is woven into a smooth, holding murder mystery, based on a story by Georges Simenon. Chaplin plays one of a small set that gets its kicks from whoop-it-up parties and drugs. A predatory, slightly nutty ship's steward (Bobby Darin) infiltrates the group and he's found murdered in the Mason home. Mason's performance is a fine study of disillusionment, self-disgust, and sly humor.

STRANGER ON THE THIRD FLOOR
1940, 67 mins, US ℗
D: Boris Ingster A: Peter Lorre, John McGuire, Margaret Tallichet, Elisha Cook Jr., (RKO)

Yarn concerns a stern newspaper reporter whose testimony provides the circumstantial evidence that convicts an innocent man. The familiar artifice of placing the scribe in parallel plight, arrested for two slayings and only clearing himself because of his sweetheart's persistent search for the real slayer, is used. It is only in the final footage that Peter Lorre, cast as the maniacal murderer, has much of anything to do. By that time the picture has lost its momentum. It's a film too arty for average audiences, and too humdrum for others.

STRANGERS
See: Viaggio in Italia

STRANGERS IN THE CITY
1962, 80 mins, US ℗
D: Rick Carrier A: Robert Gentile, Camilo Delgado, Rosita De Triana, Creta Margos, Robert Corso (Embassy/Carrier)

This shows a Puerto Rican family in a Manhattan slum. The father is a vain, proud man—and he has just lost his job. His teenage son and daughter go to look for work but he orders his wife to stay home. The boy runs into local racism as a delivery boy while the girl, a beauty, is used by factory workers and then becomes a sort of call girl for a dressmaker. It may sound overly melodramatic, but this has a neat insight into NY life, as this producer sees it.

STRANGER'S KISS
1983, 94 mins, US ℗
D: Matthew Chapman A: Peter Coyote, Victoria Tennant, Blaine Novak, Dan Shor, Richard Romanus (White)

A glowing homage to 1950s melodrama set in the film world. The love triangle is mirrored in both the real-life and

film-within-a-film structure of the production. Principals are Carole Redding (Victoria Tennant), a young woman kept by a gangster (Richard Romanus) who agrees to finance a film, and costar Stevie Blake (Blaine Novak, who also cowrote the script), a hustler who soon becomes consumed by Carole's mysterious background.

STRANGERS MAY KISS
1931, 82 mins, US
D: George Fitzmaurice A: Norma Shearer, Robert Montgomery, Neil Hamilton, Marjorie Rambeau, Irene Rich (M-G-M)

Sweet film deals with a girl's unwavering love for a roving newspaperman and their intimate relations in the hope (by the girl) of ultimate marriage. Here is a refined, thoroughly sophisticated picture. Shearer gives an extraordinarily fine performance. Only once does she overact, in a burst of hysteria. Neil Hamilton gives a very good account of himself as the newspaperman-hero and Robert Montgomery is very good as the swain, long courting the girl against great odds.

STRANGERS ON A TRAIN
1951, 100 mins, US ℗ ⊙
D: Alfred Hitchcock A: Farley Granger, Robert Walker, Ruth Roman, Leo G. Carroll, Patricia Hitchcock (Warner)

Given a good basis for a thriller in the Patricia Highsmith novel and a first-rate script, Hitchcock embroiders the plot into a gripping, palm-sweating piece of suspense. Two strangers meet on a train. One is Farley Granger, separated from his tramp wife (Laura Elliott) and in love with Ruth Roman. The other is Robert Walker, a neurotic playboy who hates his rich father. Walker proposes that he will kill Elliott if Granger will do away with the father. Granger treats the proposal as a bad joke but Walker is serious. Latter stalks down Elliott and strangles her. He then starts chasing Granger to make him fulfill the other end of the bargain.
1951: Nomination: Best B&W Cinematography

STRANGER'S RETURN
1933, 88 mins, US
D: King Vidor A: Lionel Barrymore, Miriam Hopkins, Franchot Tone, Stuart Erwin, Beulah Bondi (M-G-M)

It is the story of a New York girl who goes west after she leaves her husband, finds a new love, but loses out when the hero leaves to avoid temptation since he does not want to injure his wife and son. Overshadowing the love interest is a well-written story of a somewhat eccentric old farmer plagued by his fortune-seeking relatives. As the farmer Lionel Barrymore has a role he fits.

STRANGERS WHEN WE MEET
1960, 117 mins, US ⓥ ▭
D: Richard Quine A: Kirk Douglas, Kim Novak, Ernie Kovacs, Barbara Rush, Walter Matthau (Bryna-Quine/Columbia)

A pictorially attractive but dramatically vacuous study of infidelity is easy on the eyes but hard on the intellect. Brilliant architect Kirk Douglas is upset because his spouse (Barbara Rush) is overly concerned with balancing the family budget. Meanwhile, housewife Kim Novak is being taken for granted by her undersexed mate (John Bryant). A feverishly passionate affair blossoms between Douglas and Novak.

STRANGER THAN PARADISE
1984, 95 mins, US ⓥ ⊙
D: Jim Jarmusch A: John Lurie, Eszter Balint, Richard Edson, Cecilia Stark (Cinesthesia-Grokenberger)

A bracingly original, avant-garde black comedy starts with self-styled New York hipster Willie (John Lurie) being paid a surprise, and quite unwelcome, visit by Hungarian cousin Eva (Eszter Balint). But when she finally leaves after 10 days, there seems to be a strange sort of affection between them. Since plot doesn't count for much here, the style takes over, and Jarmusch has made such matters as camera placement, composition (in stunning black-and-white), and structure count for a lot.

STRANGE VENGEANCE OF ROSALIE, THE
1972, 107 mins, US
D: Jack Starrett A: Bonnie Bedelia, Ken Howard, Anthony Zerbe (20th Century-Fox/Cinecrest)

Offbeat film is centered around the fascinating, preposterous situation of a lonely adolescent girl (Bonnie Bedelia), naive and emotionally disturbed, who hitches a ride with a traveling salesman (Ken Howard) and leads him to her isolated ramshackle cabin, where she breaks his leg and holds him captive.

STRANGE WOMAN, THE
1946, 100 mins, US ⓥ
D: Edgar G. Ulmer A: Hedy Lamarr, George Sanders, Louis Hayward, Gene Lockhart, Hillary Brooke (United Artists)

Story deals with strong-willed Jenny Hager, who uses men for personal pleasure and as stepping-stones to wealth. It's told against a background of Bangor, ME, in the 1840s, a lusty, brawling town in the throes of growing pains. Hedy Lamarr scores as the scheming Hager. Louis Hayward gets across the weakling son of Hager's first husband, who is finally driven to suicide by the evil woman. George Sanders is out of his depth as Lamarr's second husband.

STRANGLER, THE
1964, 89 mins, US ⓥ
D: Burt Topper A: Victor Buono, David McLean, Diane Sayer, Ellen Corby (Allied Artists)

Scenario describes the latter phases of the homicidal career of a paranoid schizophrenic (Victor Buono) whose hatred of women has been motivated by a possessive mother. His fetish for dolls ultimately betrays him to the police just as he is in the act of applying the coup de grâce to distaff victim No. 11. Bueno for Buono, a convincing menace all the way.

STRAPLESS
1990, 97 mins, UK ⓥ ⊙
D: David Hare A: Blair Brown, Bruno Ganz, Bridget Fonda, Alan Howard, Michael Gough (Granada)

Central character is an American, Dr. Lillian Hempel (Blair Brown), who's lived in Britain for 12 years. Lillian's serious, well-ordered life is contrasted with her flighty younger sister Amy (Bridget Fonda), who has a series of Latin lovers. Lillian gradually is being drawn toward political activism as the British government's health-service cutbacks begin to hurt. Strapless (so named because both the sisters wind up with no visible means of support) is an intelligent, ironic, multilayered drama that's consistently intriguing. Performances are impeccable.

STRATEGIC AIR COMMAND
1955, 110 mins, US ⓥ ▭ ⊙
D: Anthony Mann A: James Stewart, June Allyson, Frank Lovejoy, Barry Sullivan, Alex Nicol, Jay C. Flippen (Paramount)

SAC is at its best when off the ground. Two giant ships engaging in a refueling operation and sweeping views of a B-36 with its jet engines skywriting long hyphens in blue smoke—this is visually stirring stuff. James Stewart as a hotshot third baseman for the St. Louis Cardinals is beckoned back to the air force. June Allyson scores as the wife, rebelling as the SAC takes hold on her mate, and then showing sympathy and understanding.

STRAWBERRY AND CHOCOLATE
See: Fresa y Chocolate

STRAWBERRY BLONDE
1941, 98 mins, US ⑦
D: Raoul Walsh A: James Cagney, Olivia de Havilland, Rita Hayworth, Jack Carson, George Tobias (Warner)

Gay-nineties period story is told in retrospect. James Cagney is a struggling dentist, when an emergency call comes to pull a molar of his worst enemy. While waiting for the patient's arrival, yarn goes back 10 years, when Cagney was enamored of the neighborhood's ''strawberry blonde.'' Jilted, he conveniently marries the understanding nurse (Olivia de Havilland) but carries a hate for the man who victimized him and stole his first girl. Rita Hayworth is an eyeful as the title character.
1941: Nomination: Best Scoring of a Musical Picture

STRAW DOGS
1971, 118 mins, UK ⑦ ⊙
D: Sam Peckinpah A: Dustin Hoffman, Susan George, Peter Vaughan, T. P. McKenna, David Warner (ABC/Talent Associates/Amerbroco)

Peckinpah indulges himself in an orgy of unparalleled violence and nastiness with undertones of sexual repression. Dustin Hoffman appears as a quiet American who has married a lively English girl (Susan George) and goes to live on her isolated West Country farm. When the village dolt accidentally kills a teenage miniskirted flirt, he takes refuge at the farm. Hoffman refuses to give him up to the inflamed villagers.
1971: Nomination: Best Original Score

STREAMERS
1983, 118 mins, US ⑦ ⊙
D: Robert Altman A: Matthew Modine, Michael Wright, Mitchell Lichtenstein, David Allen Grier, Albert Macklin (United Artists Classics)

Highly stylized set of theatricals describes an existentialist hell among a small group of men in a military barracks. Soldiers await orders to go to Vietnam and spending the time either lying around on their bunks or returning drunk from saloon or whorehouse outings. They taunt each other with tales of their own past history, but the taunts are socially, racially, and sexually loaded. Things explode in blood-gushing violence and general sadness in this overlong, overemphatic film.

STREET ANGEL
1928, 85 mins, US ⊗
D: Frank Borzage A: Janet Gaynor, Charles Farrell, Natalie Kingston, Henry Armetta, Guido Trento (Fox)

Janet Gaynor is in the title role. With the scene set in Italy and Naples for the opening, Gaynor is rescued from the police by a touring circus after receiving a year's sentence for soliciting to gain 20 lire to fill a prescription for her dying mother. Through that circumstance she meets a vagrant painter (Charles Farrell) who is showing in opposition to the little wagon oufit.

STREETCAR NAMED DESIRE, A
1951, 125 mins, US ⑦ ⊙
D: Elia Kazan A: Vivien Leigh, Marlon Brando, Kim Hunter, Karl Malden, Nick Dennis (Feldman)

Faithful adaptation from Tennessee Williams's play is the story of Blanche DuBois, a faded teacher, who seeks refuge with a sister in New Orleans. Because her presence intrudes on the husband-wife relationship, the husband, a crude brutal young Polish-American, becomes hostile. He also suspects she's lying about her past and embarks on a plan to force her from his home. Leigh gives a compelling performance. Brando at times captures strongly the brutality of the young Pole in a portrayal marked by frequent garbling of his dialogue. Kim Hunter and Karl Malden are excellent, as Blanche's sister and frantic suitor.
1951: Best Actress (Vivien Leigh), Supp. Actor (Karl Malden), Supp. Actress (Kim Hunter), B&W Art Direction
Nominations: Best Picture, Director, Actor (Marlon Brando), Screenplay, B&W Cinematography, B&W Costume Design, Scoring of a Dramatic Picture, Sound

STREETFIGHTER, THE
See: Hard Times

STREET FIGHTER
(AKA: STREET FIGHTER—THE ULTIMATE BATTLE)
1994, 97 mins, US ⑦ ▭
D: Steven E. de Souza A: Jean-Claude Van Damme, Raul Julia, Ming-Na Wen, Damian Chapa, Kylie Minogue (Capcom/Columbia)

Jean-Claude Van Damme takes a career step backward in a messy, basically plotless big-screen rendition of the popular multimedia game. Film is noisy, overblown and effects-laden, and lacks sustained action or engaging characters. Van Damme plays Colonel Guile, military commander of the Allied Nations forces, assigned to rescue 63 relief workers held hostage by a psychotic ruler. When the Allied Nations succumb to demands for a huge ransom, the fiesty fighter leads a commando force of tough street fighters on a covert mission.

STREET OF SORROW, THE
See: Die Freudlose Gasse

STREETS
1990, 83 mins, US ⊗
D: Katt Shea Ruben A: Christina Applegate, David Mendenhall, Eb Lottimer, Patrick Richwood (Concorde)

Despite its B-film framework involving a maniacal killer stalking street kids, *Streets* transcends its genre with a gritty and affecting portrait of a teenage throwaway struggling to exist in L.A.'s demimonde. Christina Applegate's solid performance as the jaded, but still sensitive, Dawn, who sells sex to survive and shoots up heroin to get through the day, speaks volumes about the scuzzy side of L.A. life.

STREET SCENE
1931, 80 mins, US ⊗
D: King Vidor A: Sylvia Sidney, William Collier Jr., Estelle Taylor, Max Montor, Russell Hopton (Goldwyn/United Artists)

Faithful reproduction of the Elmer Rice stage play. Opens on a sequence of city life with the introduction of a crashing symphonic musical setting, rather in the Gershwin manner, symbolizing the breadth and scope of the subject. Sylvia Sidney gives an even, persuasive performance, typifying the tragedy of budding girlhood cramped by sordid surroundings. In a purely acting sense the honors go to Beulah Bondi, as the malicious scandalmonger of the tenement.

STREETS OF FIRE
1984, 94 mins, US ⊗ ⊙
D: Walter Hill A: Michael Pare, Diane Lane, Rick Moranis, Amy Madigan, Willem Dafoe (Universal/RKO)

Pulsing, throbbing orchestration careens around the rescue of a kidnapped young singer. Movie has 10 original songs, and musically it is continually hot, with lyrics charting the concerns of the narrative line, simplistic as it is. Film also

has undeniable texture. Smoke, neon, rainy streets, platforms of elevated subway lines, alleys, and warehouses create an urban inferno in an unspecified time and place.

STREETS OF GOLD
1986, 95 mins, US ⊗
D: Joe Roth A: Klaus Maria Brandauer, Adrian Pasdar, Wesley Snipes (Ufland/Roth)

Likable, but hardly compelling story of not one, but two kids trying to box their way out of the slums. Klaus Maria Brandauer is a Russian Jew and former boxing champion who emigrated to the US and now works as a dishwasher and gets drunk a lot. A brash Irish tough named Timmy Doyle (Adrian Pasdar) asks him to be his coach.

STREETS OF SORROW
See: Die Freudlose Gasse

STREET WITH NO NAME, THE
1948, 94 mins, US ⊗
D: William Keighley A: Mark Stevens, Richard Widmark, Lloyd Nolan, Barbara Lawrence, Ed Begley (20th Century-Fox)

Double-barreled gangster film ranks at the top of the list of documentary-type productions that have been rolling out of the 20th-Fox lot. Richard Widmark commands complete interest with his interpretation of a psychotically ruthless character. His looks and personality have the latent menace of a loaded automatic. Mark Stevens plays the role of an all-American boy who, as an agent of the FBI, becomes a gang member. His efforts to collect the evidence for the police while exposing himself to the fate of a stool pigeon provide the basis for the plot structure and tension.

STRICTLY BALLROOM
1992, 92 mins, Australia ⊗ ⊙
D: Baz Luhrmann A: Paul Mercurio, Tara Morice, Bill Hunter, Barry Otto, Pat Thomson (M&A)

This bright, breezy, and immensely likable musical comedy is a behind-the-scenes look at a contest for ballroom dancers. A young dance star, Scott (Gus Mercurio), partnered with the lovely but waspish Liz (Gia Carides), blows the semifinals when he breaks federation rules by improvising on the floor. Enter Fran (Morice), a shy Spanish girl with bad skin and glasses. They work on a flamenco routine they know will be anathema to the federation honchos.

STRICTLY DISHONORABLE
1951, 94 mins, US
D: Melvin Frank, Norman Panama **A:** Ezio Pinza, Janet Leigh, Millard Mitchell, Gale Robbins (M-G-M)

Preston Sturges's venerable legit comedy comes to the screen as an amusing celluloid treatment of the loves and life of a romantic opera star back in the speakeasy days. Plot reprise finds Ezio Pinza famous for his opera notes and amours. Into his life comes Janet Leigh, a wide-eyed innocent from Mississippi, who has long worshiped him. Circumstance brings about a marriage of convenience between Pinza and Leigh, with both willing to make it more than that.

STRIKE ME PINK
1936, 99 mins, US
D: Norman Taurog **A:** Eddie Cantor, Ethel Merman, Sally Eilers, William Frawley, Brian Donlevy (Goldwyn)

Cantor is aces all the way, but he isn't singing so much, having only two numbers, one with Merman atop a Ferris wheel, the other (a production display) with Rita Rio, hotcha tapster, and the girls. Other two numbers are for Ethel Merman alone in the nitery setting, where she's spotted as the particular weakness of the hick Cantor. Merman is tops. Big-eyed comic plays a meek tailor whose efforts to overcome an inferiority complex land him in the job of general manager for an amusement park. Cantor's troubles with racketeers behind slot machines form the basis for most of the comedy.

STRIKE UP THE BAND
1940, 119 mins, US Ⓥ ⊙
D: Busby Berkeley **A:** Mickey Rooney, Judy Garland, Paul Whiteman, June Preisser, Ann Shoemaker (M-G-M)

Metro's successor to *Babes in Arms,* with Mickey Rooney, assisted by major trouping of Judy Garland, dominating every minute, details the enthusiastic musical talents of Rooney, who converts a high-school band into a swing orchestra, and then aims for a spot on the Paul Whiteman scholastic band broadcast. Young star is a socko personality, timing every movement for most effective reaction. In addition to a standout performance, he sings, dances, and plays both piano and drums in talented style. Garland's right there with him in much of the story as his mentoring girlfriend, teams with him in the production numbers for both songs and dances, and rings the bell

with several songs sold to the utmost.
1940: Best Sound Recording
Nominations: Best Score, Song ("Our Love Affair")

STRIPES
1981, 103 mins, US Ⓥ ⊙
D: Ivan Reitman **A:** Bill Murray, Harold Ramis, Warren Oates, Sean Young, John Candy, Judge Reinhold (Columbia)

Cheerful, mildly outrageous, and mostly amiable comedy. There's little in the way of art or comic subtlety here, but the film really seems to work. Bill Murray is an aimless layabout whose "Sad Sack" life prompts him to consider the army as a last-ditch passport to the career, romances, travels, and other delights painted in commercials. After he cons buddy Harold Ramis into enlisting, the sexy ads quickly prove to be Madison Avenue fiction, with basic training—under the grizzled glare of drill sergeant Warren Oates—taking the place of fraternity hell week as Murray heads deeper into trouble, cued by his amiably arrogant smart-assedness.

STRIPPER, THE
(UK: WOMAN OF SUMMER)
1963, 95 mins, US Ⓥ ▭
D: Franklin J. Schaffner **A:** Joanne Woodward, Richard Beymer, Claire Trevor, Carol Lynley, Robert Webber, Gypsy Rose Lee (20th Century-Fox)

The story is set in a small town in Kansas. Joanne Woodward, stranded by the abrupt deterioration of the little magician's unit of which she is part, is taken in by an old friend (Claire Trevor), now a widow. Her son (Richard Beymer), an ardent but inexperienced lad, fancies himself in love with the visitor and has a one-night affair with the fading, desperately accommodating and romantically vulnerable would-be actress. Woodward rivets attention and compassion to herself throughout with a forceful and vivacious portrayal. Beymer is adequate, little more.
1963: Nomination: Best B&W Costume Design

STRIPTEASE
1996, 115 mins, US Ⓥ ⊙
D: Andrew Bergman **A:** Demi Moore, Armand Assante, Ving Rhames, Robert Patrick, Burt Reynolds (Castle Rock/Columbia)

Dark comedy about sleaze, corruption, and naughty behavior below the Bible Belt doesn't quite come off. Erin Grant (Demi

Moore) takes up stripping at the Eager Beaver, a club where the girls have good backstage camaraderie and tough black bouncer Shad (Ving Rhames) protects them with vigilance. Sending everyone's lives into a different orbit is the arrival of sex-fiend congressman David Dilbeck (Burt Reynolds). After a teaser about 45 minutes in, Moore finally does her first full-fledged strip at the hour mark. Moore's dance routines have a rather overly calculated, too disciplined feel.

STRIPTEASE LADY
See: Lady of Burlesque

STROMBOLI
See: Stromboli, Terra Di Dio

STROMBOLI, TERRA DI DIO (US: STROMBOLI)
1950, 107 mins, Italy/US Ⓥ
D: Roberto Rossellini **A:** Ingrid Bergman, Mario Vitale, Renzo Cesana, Mario Sponzo (Be-Ro/RKO)

Rossellini purportedly denied responsibility for the film, claiming the American version was cut beyond recognition. Cut or not cut, the film reflects no credit on him. [Version reviewed was US one.] The only visible touch of the famed Italian director is in the hard photography, which adds to the realistic, documentary effect of life on the rocky, lava-blanketed island. Rossellini's penchant for realism, however, does not extend to Bergman. She's always fresh, clean, and well groomed. The story is of a girl (Bergman) in an Italian displaced-persons camp who marries a native fisherman (Mario Vitale) of Stromboli so that she may be released.

STRONGEST MAN IN THE WORLD, THE
1975, 92 mins, US
D: Vincent McEveety **A:** Kurt Russell, Joe Flynn, Eve Arden, Cesar Romero, Phil Silvers (Walt Disney)

The students of Medfield College concoct a scientific formula that gives people superhuman strength, a spoof on vitality and energy claims of cereal companies. The script rivets on situation of the school's reputation and financial stability tied in with sale of the formula to a cereal outfit and participating in an intercollegiate weight-lifting contest. The other team is sponsored by a rival cereal concern.

STRONG MAN, THE
1926, 75 mins, US Ⓥ ⊙ ⊗
D: Frank-Capra **A:** Harry Langdon, Pris-

cilla Bonner, Gertrude Astor, William V. Mong, Robert McKim (Langdon/First National)

A whale of a comedy production that has a wealth of slapstick, a rough-and-tumble finish, and in the earlier passages, bits of pantomimic comedy that are notable. Harry Langdon has a comic method distinct from other film fun makers. Pathos enters into it more fully than in the style of any other comedian with the possible exception of Chaplin. Langdon's gift for legitimate comedy here has a splendid vehicle.

STUART LITTLE
1999, 92 mins, US Ⓥ ⊙ ⊙
D: Rob Minkoff **A:** Geena Davis, Hugh Laurie, Jonathan Lipnicki, Brian Doyle-Murray, Estelle Getty, Julia Sweeney (Columbia)

Despite technically impressive animation, ample humor, and seamless special effects, the filmmakers have taken a slick, commercial approach to E. B. White's *Stuart Little* that turns the magical 1945 tale into a labored feel-good movie. Mr. and Mrs. Little (Hugh Laurie and Geena Davis) trot off to a Gotham adoption agency, promising to bring home a little brother for their son, George (Jonathan Lipnicki), who is less than thrilled when they return with a mouse named Stuart (voiced with boyish glee by Michael J. Fox). Even more irked is family feline Snowbell (Nathan Lane), who mistakes Stuart for dinner. Mr. Little reminds the cat that Stuart is family. Appalled, Snowbell's alley-cat pals insist the mouse must go, and consult feline crime boss Smokey (Chazz Palminteri), who brings in a pair of wayward mice (Bruno Kirby, Jennifer Tilly) to pose as Stuart's biological parents.
1999: Nomination: Visual Effects

STUART SAVES HIS FAMILY
1995, 95 mins, US Ⓥ
D: Harold Ramis **A:** Al Franken, Laura San Giacomo, Vincent D'Onofrio, Shirley Knight, Harris Yulin (Paramount)

Feeble comedy spun off from a *Saturday Night Live* sketch. Stuart Smalley, the lisping self-help specialist created and portrayed by Al Franken, simply isn't amusing or interesting enough to sustain a feature. And two thirds of the way through, pic suddenly becomes a maudlin drama about Stuart's intervention on behalf of his hard-drinking father (Harris Yulin).

STUD, THE
1978, 90 mins, UK Ⓥ
D: Quentin Masters **A:** Joan Collins, Oliver Tobias, Emma Jacobs, Sue Lloyd, Walter Gotell (Brent Walker)

The Stud goes a long way toward transcending the softcore sexpo genre, but ultimately doesn't quite make it. Based on the novel by Jackie Collins (sister of Joan, who toplines), production has Oliver Tobias in title role as a virile manager of a London nitery. Joan Collins is the lady who pulls the strings to manipulate him as her own sexual marionette.

STUDENT PRINCE, THE
1927, 105 mins, US Ⓥ ⊗ ▭
D: Ernst Lubitsch **A:** Ramon Novarro, Norma Shearer, Jean Hersholt, Gustav von Seyffertitz, Philippe De Lacy (M-G-M)

Ernst Lubitsch took his tongue out of his cheek when he directed this special. It's not farce and it's not drama. Just a pretty love story of peaches and cream. It concerns an heir to a throne who is forced to give up his love for a tavern maid because of duty to his country. Ramon Novarro's makeup is ghastly under certain lighting conditions. Shearer's efforts are a highlight.

STUDENT PRINCE, THE
1954, 107 mins, US Ⓥ ▭
D: Richard Thorpe **A:** Ann Blyth, Edmund Purdom, John Ericson, Louis Calhern, Edmund Gwenn (M-G-M)

The venerable operetta about a royal cutup in the beer gardens of Heidelberg has been given a brand-new look. This latest version is a fresh, beguiling musical, beautiful to hear and behold. The vocal personality of Mario Lanza doesn't jibe with the British starch of Edmund Purdom's physical appearance, but not many will mind because the latter's acting is good. Doing her own singing in a gracious, charming manner is Ann Blyth, who might not be everyone's idea of a barmaid who could charm a prince, but she's pert and pretty.

STUDS LONIGAN
1960, 103 mins, US Ⓥ
D: Irving Lerner **A:** Christopher Knight, Frank Gorshin, Helen Westcott, Dick Foran, Venetia Stevenson, Jack Nicholson (United Artists)

Compressing James T. Farrell's respected trilogy into a 103-minute film doesn't come off. Scenario is quite faithful to the book, which centers on an essentially decent hero who struggles against slum life of Chicago's South Side district in the 1920s. Christopher Knight, as the hero, has a disquieting tendency toward facial contortion and responsive exaggeration. Emphasis on startling composition is clever, but frequently distracting.

STUFF, THE
1985, 93 mins, US Ⓥ
D: Larry Cohen **A:** Michael Moriarty, Andrea Marcovicci, Paul Sorvino, Scott Bloom, Danny Aiello (Larco/New World)

Sci-fi with no hardware but lots of white goo seems to fly right out of the 1950s horror genre. It also has an underlying humor about it, plays around with satirizing fast foods, and cloaks a sly little subtext about people who ingest stuff they know is not good for them. The film enjoys a larky sense of innocence, some hideous gaping mouths full of a curdling, parasitic menace, and a fey performance by Michael Moriarty as an industrial saboteur.

STUNT MAN, THE
1980, 129 mins, US Ⓥ ⊙
D: Richard Rush **A:** Peter O'Toole, Steve Railsback, Barbara Hershey, Allen Garfield, Alex Rocco (Simon)

Offbeat tale has Vietnam vet Steve Railsback on the lam and accepting refuge from both benevolent and sinister film director Peter O'Toole, who puts the fugitive through some highly dangerous paces as a stuntman while shielding him from the cops. O'Toole smashingly delineates an omnipotent, godlike type whose total control over those around him makes him seem almost unreal.

1980: Nominations: Best Director, Actor (Peter O'Toole), Adapted Screenplay

STUNTS
1977, 90 mins, US Ⓥ
D: Mark L. Lester **A:** Robert Forster, Fiona Lewis, Joanna Cassidy, Darrell Fetty, Bruce Glover (New Line/Fleischman)

This is a tight-lipped actioner. Robert Forster is excellent as an ace stuntman who thwarts a maniac stalking a film crew making a police actioner on an ocean-side location in San Luis Obispo, CA. Fiona Lewis is a groupie journalist who initially causes friction in the group.

ST. VALENTINE'S DAY MASSACRE, THE
1967, 100 mins, US Ⓥ ▭
D: Roger Corman **A:** Jason Robards,

George Segal, Ralph Meeker, Jean Hale, Frank Silvera (20th Century-Fox)

A slam-bang, gutsy re-creation of a 1929 gangland sensation of Chicago. Well written, and presented in semidocumentary style, it features Jason Robards as Al Capone. Salty dialogue and violence are motivated properly, and solid production values evoke a bygone era. Robards is excellent, and Ralph Meeker, as Moran, is equally chilling.

SUBJECT WAS ROSES, THE
1968, 107 mins, US ⓥ
D: Ulu Grosbard **A:** Patricia Neal, Jack Albertson, Martin Sheen, Don Saxon (M-G-M)

Intimate, poignant, and telling drama of a young World War II vet, returning to an unhappy home, is superior in all departments. Neal and Albertson are outstanding as a Bronx Irish couple who, while not happy and loving, are not unloving either. Return from war of only son Sheen brings the festering crisis to a head, partly by a title-inspiring gift of flowers which releases pent-up emotions.

SUBSTITUTE, THE
1996, 114 mins, US ⓥ
D: Robert Mandel **A:** Tom Berenger, Ernie Hudson, Diane Venora, Marc Anthony, Cliff De Young (Dinamo/H2/Live)

The premise places an out-of-work soldier of fortune in a tough-as-nails high school to clean up the joint. Though the setup is largely preposterous, the filmmakers go whole hog for the idea and provide a kinetic entertainment. Berenger exacts revenge much in the style of the Man with No Name or the hero of *Death Wish*. It's a very satisfying fantasy scenario.

SUBTERRANEANS, THE
1960, 89 mins, US ▭
D: Ranald MacDougall **A:** Leslie Caron, George Peppard, Janice Rule, Roddy McDowall, Jim Hutton (M-G-M)

Those who have suspected all along that beatniks are dull, now have proof. Jack Kerouac's novel is the basis for the screenplay, which pokes around San Francisco's North Beach and dredges up some bargain-basement philosophy, B(eat)-girls, and bed ruminations. It's hero (George Peppard), a nervous novelist, finds his home-away-from-home with the local coffeehouse colony, and develops a crush on its most mixed-up member (Leslie Caron), whose Freudian slip shows every time she submits frigidly to the sexual advances of her pals. Music, all of the modern jazz variety, created by Andre Previn and interpreted by experts such as Gerry Mulligan and Shelly Manne, is the outstanding aspect of this film.

SUBURBAN COMMANDO
1991, 90 mins, US ⓥ ⊙
D: Burt Kennedy, Gary Davis **A:** Terry "Hulk" Hogan, Christopher Lloyd, Shelley Duvall, Larry Miller, Jack Elam (New Line)

Some funny gags enliven stupid sci-fi spoof. Lame vehicle for wrestler Hulk Hogan is a bad "high concept" effort marrying two elements. Hogan is an intergalactic warrior who travels to Earth for some R&R, instantly becoming a fish out of water boarding at suburbanites Christopher Lloyd and Shelley Duvall's house. Lloyd is a Caspar Milquetoast architect who briefly becomes the title character by donning Hogan's muscle-enhancing power suit.

SUBURBIA
1996, 118 mins, US ⓥ ⊙
D: Richard Linklater **A:** Jayce Bartok, Amie Carey, Nicky Katt, Ajay Naidu, Parker Posey, Giovanni Ribisi (Castle Rock)

subUrbia is a brooding, incisive comedy that blends the talents of helmer Richard Linklater and playwright Eric Bogosian, an acidly amusing account of 20-year-old losers acting out their miseries on the night one of their high school chums returns to town as a neophyte rock star. Jeff (Giovanni Ribisi) is the thinker in the bunch. Spinning his wheels in the rut between adolescence and adulthood, he's got apt company in Buff (Steve Zahn), a hedonistic goofball who works in a pizza joint, and Tim (Nicky Katt), a surly, tattooed hothead. The three rendezvous around nightfall in the parking lot of a 24-hour convenience store. Pony (Jayce Bartok) shows up as promised, ferried in a boat-sized limo and accompanied by a sleek L.A. publicist, Erica (Parker Posey). Bogosian's dialogue is rich and flavorful, capturing the pungent nuances of slang and the precise verbal textures of a world that seems like a giant invitation to "smoke a doob and hang out."

SUBWAY
1985, 104 mins, France ⓥ ⊙ ▭
D: Luc Besson **A:** Isabelle Adjani, Christopher Lambert, Richard Bohringer, Michel Galabru, Jean-Hugues Anglade (Gaumont/Films du Loup/TSF/TF1)

Feature may disappoint some for its singular lack of ambition or purpose and its ragged narrative, but proves a charmingly cartoonish escapade, strong on humor and rock rhythms. Pic's hero is Christopher Lambert, a dynamite-toting, punk-coiffed eccentric who has stolen some compromising documents belonging to Isabelle Adjani's influential husband. Lambert takes refuge in the subway at the moment of its early-morning closing. There he befriends some of the subterranean denizens and decides to realize his dream of managing a rock band, by recruiting the Métro's itinerant musicians. In the meantime he is sought by the thugs, the Paris transport police, and Adjani.

SUCCESS
See: The American Success Company

SUCCESS IS THE BEST REVENGE
1984, 90 mins, UK/France ⊘
D: Jerzy Skolimowski A: Michael York, Joanna Szczerbic, Michael Lyndon, Michel Piccoli, Anouk Aimee, John Hurt (De Vere/Gaumont)

Pic deals with how exile can become a trap, a temptation to coast along quite professionally on the artist-exile's most obvious obsession, and how the children of such exiles will sooner or later insist on exploring their roots. Story is told through parallels between teenager Adam (Michael Lyndon), who secretly prepares for combined punkdom and flight to Warsaw, and his father, Alex Rodak (Michael York), a Polish stage director about to put on another exile show at a London West End theater. The sad plight of the younger generation of refugees is a theme well worth exploring, but Skolimowski really has much more to say in a satirical way—about the older generation that has turned exile into business.

SUDBA CHELOVYEKA
(US: DESTINY OF A MAN)
1959, 98 mins, USSR
D: Sergei Bondarchuk A: Sergei Bondarchuk, Zinaida Kirienko, Pavlik Boriskin, Yuri Averin (Mosfilm)

Well-made, moving film details how a Russian prisoner of war (Sergei Bondarchuk) has only the thought of getting back alive to his family. After many adventures and privations he does find them, but all are dead. He adopts a homeless boy to give him the necessary love and reason to go on living.

SUDDEN DEATH
1995, 110 mins, US ⊘ ⊙ ▭
D: Peter Hyams A: Jean-Claude Van Damme, Powers Boothe, Raymond J. Barry, Whittni Wright, Ross Malinger (Signature/Universal)

Whipcord-taut actioner is bigger and better than its main star. Pacy opening sets the tone, with Jean-Claude Van Damme intro'd as Darren McCord, a fire marshal at Pittsburgh's Civic Arena, whither he and his two sprigs go for a game between the Pittsburgh Penguins and Chicago Blackhawks. Also due in the audience is the US vice-president (Raymond J. Barry). Smooth-talking psycho Joshua Foss (Powers Boothe) & Co. take over the VP's box and hold its human contents ransom for a cool $1.7 billion. Time limit for the transfer is the length of the hockey game. Basically, this is straight action stuff with a vague martial-arts riff in the fight scenes. Peter Hyams's restless camera has as good an eye for close-up drama as for big visual moments, like Van Damme's duel atop the arena's roof.

SUDDEN FEAR
1952, 110 mins, US
D: David Miller A: Joan Crawford, Jack Palance, Gloria Grahame, Bruce Bennett, Virginia Huston (RKO)

Suspense drama tailored for Joan Crawford is essentially a routine chiller, replete with more or less clever gimmicks, but mounted handsomely. Crawford as a playwright-heiress falls in love and marries an actor whom she had considered unsuited for the lead in her play. The union is idyllic until she discovers that her husband has only married her for her money and is planning her murder.

SUDDEN IMPACT
1983, 117 mins, US ⊘ ⊙ ▭
D: Clint Eastwood A: Clint Eastwood, Sondra Locke, Pat Hingle, Bradford Dillman, Paul Drake (Warner)

Fourth entry in the *Dirty Harry* series sends Harry out of his normal jurisdiction in San Francisco to research a case with connections to coastal San Paulo. While there, he bumps into Sondra Locke, who is extracting her own brand of vengeance on a group of individuals who, some years back, savagely raped both her and her younger sister. This is the first entry in the series to have been directed by Eastwood himself, and action is put over with great force, if also with some obviousness.

SUDDENLY
1954, 75 mins, US ✆

D: Lewis Allen **A:** Frank Sinatra, Sterling Hayden, James Gleason, Nancy Gates, Willis Bouchey (Libra)

This slick exploitation feature twirls about a fantastic plot to assassinate the president of the US. Frank Sinatra, as a professional gunman hired to kill the president as he debarks from his special train for a few days' fishing in neighboring mountains, is an offbeat piece of casting that pays off in lively interest. Thesp inserts plenty of menace into a psycho character, never too heavily done, and gets good backing from his costar, Sterling Hayden, as sheriff, in a less showy role but just as authoritatively handled.

SUDDENLY IT'S SPRING
1947, 87 mins, US

D: Mitchell Leisen **A:** Paulette Goddard, Fred MacMurray, Macdonald Carey, Arleen Whelan (Paramount)

Top-notch script, aptly cast and directed, concerns husband and wife who agreed to separate before the war. World strife delays the divorce and script picks them up again just as the WAC wife is returning from overseas. The husband has fallen for another gal and wants the divorce pronto. His wife would like to try again. Fun springs from Fred MacMurray's prodding of Paulette Goddard to get her to ink the necessary papers and her continual coy delay.

SUDDENLY, LAST SUMMER
1959, 112 mins, UK ✆ ◉

D: Joseph L. Mankiewicz **A:** Elizabeth Taylor, Katharine Hepburn, Montgomery Clift, Albert Dekker, Mercedes McCambridge (Horizon/Columbia)

Perversion and greed, Tennessee Williams's recurrent themes, are worked over again. The story is that of a doting mother (Katharine Hepburn) and her son. The son was a homosexual and his mother his procuress. When she passed the age when she could function effectively in this capacity, he enlisted the services of his beautiful cousin, Elizabeth Taylor. The question is whether Taylor is insane or sane. Hepburn wants a lobotomy performed on Taylor, to excise the memory of the son's death. It is the job of Montgomery Clift, as the neurosurgeon who would perform the operation, to decide if Taylor is deranged as Hepburn insists.

1959: Nominations: Best Actress (Ka-

tharine Hepburn, Elizabeth Taylor), B&W Art Direction

SUDDEN MANHATTAN
1996, 89 mins, US ✆

D: Adrienne Shelly **A:** Adrienne Shelly, Tim Guinee, Roger Rees, Louise Lasser, Hynden Walch (Kirkley)

Light, original, and at times amusing urban fantasy starts out searching for answers to life's Big Questions, ends up settling for much less. Donna (Adrienne Shelly) is a cute, single twentysomething woman living in the Village. She starts hearing earthquakelike rumblings emanating from a plate of scrambled eggs and witnesses a series of identical murders. Unsure whether it's her or the world that's gone crazy, she seeks the guidance of a lugubrious gypsy soothsayer (Louise Lasser). One by one, more characters are thrown into the self-consciously wacky mix.

SUDDEN TERROR
See: Eyewitness

SUEZ
1938, 100 mins, US

D: Allan Dwan **A:** Tyrone Power, Loretta Young, Annabella, J. Edward Bromberg, Joseph Schildkraut (20th Century-Fox)

Pic misses out on its epic aims. Its shortcomings are chiefly psychological, although a lethargic pace early on almost counts too heavily against it. The fictional liberties taken with history come under acceptable Hollywood license. There's considerable theatrical abracadabra with the manner in which the young Ferdinand de Lesseps (Tyrone Power), with his dream of a big ditch from the Mediterranean into the Red Sea, wins over the Egyptian viceroy's heir. The desert storm is an unquestionable boon.

SUGAR HILL
1993, 123 mins, US ✆ ◉

D: Leon Ichaso **A:** Wesley Snipes, Michael Wright, Theresa Randle, Clarence Williams III, Abe Vigoda (Beacon/South Street)

Self-indulgent drama, about a Harlem drug kingpin trying to go straight, exists in a netherworld between art and action films. Script tells of two brothers with giant chips on their shoulders. Having witnessed their mother overdose and white mobsters shoot their addict father, Roemello and Raynathan Skuggs (Wesley Snipes, Michael Wright) decided to get their own by becoming the biggest dealers in Harlem. Roemello persistently courts Melissa (Theresa Randle), who wants nothing more to do with him when she discovers his métier, but who can't ignore him either. It all ends in predictably bloody violence.

SUGARLAND EXPRESS, THE
1974, 109 mins, US Ⓥ ▭
D: Steven Spielberg A: Goldie Hawn, Ben Johnson, Michael Sacks, William Atherton, Gregory Walcott (Universal)
Film begins and plays for much of its length as a hilarious madcap caper chase comedy. Goldie Hawn stars as a young mother who helps husband William Atherton escape from prison so they may rescue their baby from involuntary adoption. Unfortunately, the film degenerates to heavy-handed social polemic and sound-and-fury shoot-out.

SUICIDE SQUAD
See: Dangerous Moonlight

SUITABLE CASE FOR TREATMENT, A
(AKA: MORGAN!; MORGAN (A SUITABLE CASE FOR TREATMENT))
1966, 97 mins, UK Ⓥ ⊙
D: Karel Reisz A: Vanessa Redgrave, David Warner, Robert Stephens, Irene Handl, Bernard Bresslaw (British Lion/Quintra)
Morgan follows the frequently funny, sometimes pathetic, but relentlessly lunatic exploits of an eccentric artist to his eventual, though not inevitable, incarceration in an insane asylum. Schizophrenia seems to have infected Reisz's direction. Instead of providing the subtle, gradually disintegrating character of Morgan, Reisz dwells on the comedic aspects of each prank, cunningly milked for maximum yaks, in the process ceding any hope of the observer taking character seriously.
1966: Nominations: Best Actress (Vanessa Redgrave), B&W Costume Design

SULLIVANS, THE
1944, 111 mins, US Ⓥ
D: Lloyd Bacon A: Anne Baxter, Thomas Mitchell, Ward Bond, Bobby Driscoll, Selena Royle (20th Century-Fox)
The story is that of the five Sullivan boys who enlisted in the US Navy immediately after Pearl Harbor and went down with their ship, later to be honored by the naming of a battlewagon after them. The true story has been done as a documentary account of heroism. Outstanding

on performance is that of Bobby Driscoll, playing youngest boy Al when he was perhaps five or six years old, although Thomas Mitchell, as the father, and others are fine in their work.

SULLIVAN'S TRAVELS
1941, 90 mins, US Ⓥ ⊙
D: Preston Sturges A: Joel McCrea, Veronica Lake, William Demarest, Franklin Pangborn, Porter Hall, Eric Blore (Paramount)
Curious but effective mixture of grim tragedy, slapstick of the Keystone brand, and smart, trigger-fast comedy. It is written and directed by Preston Sturges, who ties it all together neatly and keeps his audience on the go and on edge. Dialogue is trenchant, has drive, possesses crispness, and gets the laughs where that is desired. Hollywood director Joel McCrea, anxious to produce Oh, Brother, Where Art Thou?, an epic of hard times and troubles, disguises himself as a hobo and goes out to look for troubles, finding plenty for himself. He picks up Veronica Lake on the way and they travel the rails together, she in boy's clothes. Lake supplies the sex appeal and does a good acting job. McCrea turns in a swell performance.

SULT
(US: HUNGER)
1966, 111 mins, Denmark/Sweden/Norway Ⓥ
D: Henning Carlsen A: Per Oscarsson, Gunnel Lindblom, Birgitte Federspiel, Sigrid Horne-Rasmussen, Knud Rex (Carlsen/Sandrews/Svenska/Filminstitutet/Studio ABC)
Pic is a taut tour de force about a time of hunger and near breakdown of a talented writer in turn-of-the-century Norway. Its relentless dwelling on anguish, plus the brilliant playing of Per Oscarsson, keep this from ever being stilted or repetitive. Oscarsson is a scrawny, black-clad young man waiting for a reaction from an editor on an article he has written. He is reduced to eating paper, pawning his things, succumbing to hallucination, but still refusing to ask for help. A brief interlude with a girl who spurns him puts the last touch on his resistance.

SUMMER AND SMOKE
1961, 120 mins, US Ⓥ ⊙ ▭
D: Peter Glenville A: Laurence Harvey, Geraldine Page, John McIntire, Una Merkel, Rita Moreno, Thomas Gomez (Paramount)

Peter Glenville, who guided Tennessee Williams's play in Britain, gives this pic version a solid delineation. Performances are almost uniformly excellent, though Geraldine Page walks off with top honors in a repeat of her 1952 stage role as Alma Winemiller, the repressed spinster. Laurence Harvey, perhaps a bit young to play her opposite number, John, perhaps a bit too continental for a bayou boy, is nevertheless very good, and gives a solid and believeable rendering of the ne'er-do-well who reforms.

1961: Nominations: Best Actress (Geraldine Page), Supp. Actress (Una Merkel), Color Art Direction, Scoring of a Dramatic Picture

SUMMERFIELD
1977, 95 mins, Australia
D: Ken Hannam **A:** Nick Tate, John Walters, Elizabeth Alexander, Michelle Jarman, Charles Tingwell (Clare Beach)

Good-looking mystery starts slowly, introducing the characters while at the same time establishing an undefined menace in the locale—a remote island community off the coast of Victoria. Nick Tate is the replacement schoolteacher—his predecessor has disappeared in strange circumstances. Gradually he picks up clues to what everybody is not talking about. And, of course, once he starts, his curiosity gets the better of him.

SUMMER HOLIDAY
1948, 92 mins, US ⱴ ▭
D: Rouben Mamoulian **A:** Mickey Rooney, Gloria de Haven, Walter Huston, Frank Morgan, Agnes Moorehead, Marilyn Maxwell (M-G-M)

The Eugene O'Neill play *Ah! Wilderness*, with its account of a turn-of-the-century small-town New England family, provides admirable setting, story, color, and mood. The musical numbers, tastefully chosen and skillfully staged, stem naturally from the situations. The story emphasizes the puppy-love romance between the publisher's son (Mickey Rooney) and girl across the street (Gloria de Haven). Except for some laughable mugging by the former, they make an appealing pair.

SUMMER HOLIDAY
1963, 109 mins, UK ⱴ
D: Peter Yates **A:** Cliff Richard, Lauri Peters, Melvyn Hayes, Una Stubbs, the Shadows (Elstree)

Short-on-wit screenplay is simply an excuse for a lighthearted jaunt through sunny Europe. Cliff Richard and three mechanic buddies set out in a borrowed double-decker London bus. They pick up (in quite the nicest way) three stranded girls, a cabaret act en route to Athens. They also encounter a troupe of wandering entertainers and a stowaway in the shape of a young boy. "He" turns out to be an American girl tele singer. Richard has a warm presence and sings and dances more than adequately.

SUMMER MADNESS
(AKA: SUMMERTIME)
1955, 100 mins, UK/US ⱴ ⊙
D: David Lean **A:** Katharine Hepburn, Rossano Brazzi, Isa Miranda, Darren McGavin, Mari Aldon, Jeremy Spenser (Lopert/London)

Made in Venice, pic stacks up as promising entertainment—with some reservations. There is a lack of cohesion and some abruptness in plot transition without a too-clear buildup. Lesser characterizations, too, are on the sketchy side. Covering these flaws is a rich topsoil of drama as the proud American secretary who hits Venice as a tourist, falls for and is disillusioned by the middle-aged Italian charmer. Rossano Brazzi scores a triumph of charm and reserve. Hepburn turns in a feverish acting chore of proud loneliness.

1955: Nominations: Best Director, Actress (Katharine Hepburn)

SUMMER OF '42
1971, 102 mins, US ⱴ ⊙
D: Robert Mulligan **A:** Jennifer O'Neill, Gary Grimes, Jerry Houser, Oliver Conant, Katherine Allentuck (Warner)

The emotional and sexual awakening of teenagers is a dramatic staple. *Summer of '42* has a large amount of charm and tenderness; it also has little dramatic economy and much eye-exhausting photography which translates to forced and artificial emphasis on a strung-out story. Script tells of summer when Gary Grimes had his first sexual-romantic experience with war-widowed Jennifer O'Neill. O'Neill is wooden and stilted though her lines are few, so the handicap does not unduly mar the film.

1971: Best Original Score
Nominations: Best Story & Screenplay, Cinematography, Editing

SUMMER OF SAM
1999, 142 mins, US ⱴ ⊙
D: Spike Lee **A:** John Leguizamo, Adrien

Brody, Mira Sorvino, Jennifer Esposito, Anthony LaPaglia, Bebe Neuwirth (40 Acres & a Mule/Touchstone)

A hard-driving, combustible, collage-like drama about a notorious serial killer's traumatic effect on New York City in summer '77, *Summer of Sam* is never less than absorbing but feels like yesterday's news. Film is positioned as a period piece at the outset, set in the Bronx, and the many, largely Italian characters are brought on stage with relative dispatch. Vinny and Dionna (John Leguizamo, Mira Sorvino) are stylish young marrieds, but Vinny philanders compulsively. Ritchie (Adrien Brody) shocks his buddies by materializing as a London-style, spike-haired punk, and hooks up with lusty local Ruby (Jennifer Esposito). Son of Sam arrives as a force of terror. He soon kills again, and tempers soar with the temperature as a blackout occurs and riots ensue. Ensemble cast fits together snugly, with leads convincing as working-class types.

SUMMER PLACE, A
1959, 130 mins, US Ⓥ ⊙
D: Delmer Daves **A:** Richard Egan, Dorothy McGuire, Sandra Dee, Arthur Kennedy, Troy Donahue (Warner)

One of those big, emotional, slickly produced pictures that bites off a great deal more than it can chew. Characters, anguished most of the time, are unreal and totally devoid of depth. The film runs at least 20 minutes too long and has a tendency to use dialogue to preach what should be implied. With the single exception of Dorothy McGuire, who comes through with a radiant performance and is lovely to look at, the cast does an average job.

SUMMER RENTAL
1985, 88 mins, US Ⓥ ⊙
D: Carl Reiner **A:** John Candy, Rip Torn, Richard Crenna, Karen Austin, Kerri Green (Paramount)

Amusing in spots, *Summer Rental* is more a collection of bits about taking the family to the shore for the summer than a coherent story. John Candy manages to elevate some of those bits to the hilarious and therein lies the film's appeal. Best bits are supplied by Candy's wardrobe. As a modern-day pirate with a heart of gold, Rip Torn demonstrates once again that he can make any role believable regardless of how silly it is.

SUMMER'S TALE, A
See: Conte d'Ete

SUMMER STOCK
(UK: IF YOU FEEL LIKE SINGING)
1950, 108 mins, US ⊙
D: Charles Walters **A:** Judy Garland, Gene Kelly, Eddie Bracken, Gloria de Haven, Marjorie Main, Phil Silvers (M-G-M)

Background is a New England farm setting. Garland is the farmerette. Her younger sister (Gloria de Haven) brings a troupe of would-be thespians to the farm and they take over the barn to stage a new musical written by Kelly. Not only is Garland upset at such an invasion, so is the whole village of New Englanders.

SUMMER STORM
1944, 103 mins, US Ⓥ
D: Douglas Sirk **A:** George Sanders, Linda Darnell, Anna Lee, Edward Everett Horton, Hugo Haas (United Artists)

Carefully made drama of people and passion adapted from a Chekhov drama. Russian background displays intimate study in contrasts of local judge, George Sanders; young and impetuous siren, Linda Darnell; Edward Everett Horton, landowning aristocrat; estate superintendent, Hugo Haas; and Anna Lee, engaged to Sanders. All become engulfed in tragedy when Darnell marries Haas and immediately embarks on an affair with Sanders, while slyly playing Horton for the finery and jewels he can supply.
1944: Nomination: Best Scoring of a Dramatic Picture

SUMMER STORY, A
1988, 95 mins, UK/US Ⓥ
D: Piers Haggard **A:** Imogen Stubbs, James Wilby, Kenneth Colley, Sophie Ward, Susannah York (ITC)

Beautifully made pastoral romance, skillfully adapted from a John Galsworthy story, ''The Apple Tree.'' Screen version is set in Devon in 1902, portraying the ill-fated romance between young barrister Ashton (James Wilby) and a lovely country lass Megan (Imogen Stubbs). Stage actress Stubbs is a real find as the heartbroken heroine, while Wilby is a sympathetic version of the archetypal weak young aristocrat.

SUMMERTIME
See: Summer Madness

SUMMER WISHES, WINTER DREAMS
1973, 87 mins, US Ⓥ
D: Gilbert Cates **A:** Joanne Woodward,

Martin Balsam, Sylvia Sidney, Dori Brenner, Tresa Hughes (Columbia/ Rastar)

Pic begins with idle chatter between Joanne Woodward and her mother Sylvia Sidney. Eighty minutes later Woodward and husband Martin Balsam are reminiscing about the macaroons in Atlantic City. After the sudden death of mother, Woodward takes off for Europe with Balsam. Now the focus shifts from her woes to his as he searches for the only place his life had drama: 28 years earlier at Bastogne. Performances are first-rate. But only those approaching 50 or more are likely to feel the depth.

1973: Nominations: Best Actress (Joanne Woodward), Supp. Actress (Sylvia Sidney)

SUN ALSO RISES, THE
1957, 129 mins, US ⌐

D: Henry King **A:** Tyrone Power, Ava Gardner, Mel Ferrer, Errol Flynn, Eddie Albert, Juliette Greco (20th Century-Fox)

Transmutation of the Ernest Hemingway novel doesn't gloss over key plot twist that Tyrone Power plays an impotent newspaperman in frustrated love with Ava Gardner. But the script drags along their "love affair" instead of propelling it. Thus the yarn never comes off either as a love story or a definitive study of the "lost generation." Errol Flynn and Eddie Albert turn in topflight characterizations as drunken members of the gambling expatriates.

SUNA NO ONNA
(US: WOMAN IN THE DUNES;
WOMAN OF THE DUNES)
1964, 127 mins, Japan ⓥ

D: Hiroshi Teshigahara **A:** Eiji Okada, Kyoko Kishida, Koji Mitsui, Hiroko Ito (Teshigahara)

Offbeat adventure befalls an entomologist hunting insects in a barren part of the country. Some townspeople let him down to a house set in the side of a dune cliff. Here he finds a woman living alone. But next morning the ladder he came down on has been pulled up and he is told he must help this woman to fill lowered buckets with sand every night. Then the film shows the man's attempts to escape, his rage at the woman, and his finally giving in and even becoming her lover. Director displays a flawless feel for texture and observation. Underneath is a pulsating, if sometimes gritty, compassion for man's general fate and the state of his so-called liberty.

SUNBURN
1979, 99 mins, US ⓥ

D: Richard C. Sarafian **A:** Farrah Fawcett, Charles Grodin, Art Carney, Joan Collins, Eleanor Parker, Keenan Wynn (Paramount)

Film exists for no other reason than to provide a vehicle for Farrah Fawcett. Confection has Fawcett as a Gotham model posing as Charles Grodin's wife as he sleuths around chic Acapulco settings investigating the mysterious death of an industrialist on behalf of an insurance company.

SUNCHASER, THE
1996, 122 mins, US ⓥ ⌐

D: Michael Cimino **A:** Woody Harrelson, Jon Seda, Anne Bancroft, Alexandra Tydings, Matt Mulhern (Regency/Warner)

Conceptually bold tale is marked by visceral intensity and dramatic sloppiness. This is a film with a number of things on its mind, including Western medical practices vs. ancient treatments, and practical materialistic values contrasted with more mystical, spiritual ones. Dr. Michael Reynolds (Woody Harrelson) is a fastidious UCLA medic. Brandon "Blue" Monroe (Jon Seda) is a 16-year-old, shaven-headed half Navajo in the pen for killing his stepfather. When Blue learns he has inoperable cancer and only a month or two to live, he kidnaps the doc and forces him to drive toward the Navajo reservation in Arizona.

SUNDAY, BLOODY SUNDAY
1971, 110 mins, UK ⓥ ⊙

D: John Schlesinger **A:** Glenda Jackson, Peter Finch, Murray Head, Peggy Ashcroft, Maurice Denham (United Artists)

Low-key, delicately poised recital of triangular love. Glenda Jackson is a career femme on the rebound (separated from husband), Peter Finch is a Jewish doctor, and Murray Head, youngest of the trio, is a sculptor-designer oscillating between homo and hetero affairs and career. Sequence after vignette after sequence larded with deft little touches, all add to this story's cumulative message, namely that half a loaf is often better than none.

1971: Nominations: Best Director, Actor (Peter Finch), Actress (Glenda Jackson), Original Story & Screenplay

SUNDAY IN NEW YORK
1963, 105 mins, US

D: Peter Tewksbury **A:** Rod Taylor, Jane

Fonda, Cliff Robertson, Robert Culp, Jim Backus (M-G-M)

A maiden (Jane Fonda) is fretting over that age-old puzzler—should a girl before marriage? By now she has alienated herself from a well-heeled hometown beau (Robert Culp) upon whom she had matrimonial designs. Big brother (Cliff Robertson), an airline pilot, lauds the virtuous life, but when sis subsequently discovers flimsy negligee in her closet, she impulsively attempts to seduce the nearest male (Rod Taylor). The entire cast is equal to the challenge. Best of the lot is Taylor, who delivers a warm, flexible, and appealing performance.

SUNDAYS AND CYBELE
See: Les Dimanches de Ville d'Avray

SUNDAY TOO FAR AWAY
1975, 90 mins, Australia ⓥ
D: Ken Hannam A: Jack Thompson, Max Cullen, Reg Lye, John Ewart, Robert Bruning (SAFC)

Sheepshearers are journeymen who skim off the wool in backbreaking, dreary work. Foley (Jack Thompson) is a solid chap who would like to quit after his present job. But apparently that is not to be. The cutting of prices for shearers leads to a strike after the odyssey of their last contract. They finally win it. Pic gives an extraordinary insight into men at work.

SUNDOWN
1941, 90 mins, US ⓥ
D: Henry Hathaway A: Gene Tierney, Bruce Cabot, George Sanders, Harry Carey, Joseph Calleia (Wanger/United Artists)

Adventurous melodrama, unfolded in a colonial outpost of British East Africa, details the efforts of Nazi agents to foment native uprisings. Bruce Cabot is local commissioner of Manieka, joined by army officer George Sanders, detailed to uncover gunrunning plot to natives. Carl Esmond, secret Nazi agent, arrives posing as mining engineer; also Gene Tierney, operator of large caravans and network of native trading posts.
1941: Nominations: Best B&W Cinematography, B&W Art Direction, Scoring of a Dramatic Picture

SUNDOWNERS, THE
(UK: THUNDER IN THE DUST)
1950, 65 mins, US ⓥ
D: George Templeton A: Robert Preston, Robert Sterling, Chill Wills, Cathy

Downs, John Barrymore Jr. (Eagle Lion/LeMay-Templeton)

Story pits brother against brother to bring to a conclusion its account of a feud between rival cattlemen. Interesting is the film debut of John Barrymore Jr. He does well by his role of a kid who idolizes his bad, eldest brother but is held in line by the middle kin (Robert Sterling). Robert Preston gets his teeth into the colorful role of the daring, dashing eldest member of the family.

SUNDOWNERS, THE
1960, 133 mins, UK ⓥ
D: Fred Zinnemann A: Deborah Kerr, Robert Mitchum, Peter Ustinov, Glynis Johns, Dina Merrill, Chips Rafferty (Warner)

The story tells of a 1920s Irish-Australian sheep drover (Robert Mitchum) whose fondness for an itinerant existence clashes with the fervent hope of settling down shared by his wife (Deborah Kerr) and his son (Michael Anderson Jr.). The wife persuades her husband to accept stationary employment as a shearer. Mitchum's rugged masculinity is right for the part. Kerr gives a luminous and penetrating portrayal of the faithful wife.
1960: Nominations: Best Picture, Director, Actress (Deborah Kerr), Supp. Actress (Glynis Johns), Screenplay Adaptation

SUNFLOWER
1970, 105 mins, Italy/France ⓥ
D: Vittorio De Sica A: Sophia Loren, Marcello Mastroianni, Ludmila Savelyeva, Galina Andreeva (Champion/Concordia)

Tragedy of an ill-starred love destroyed by the horrors of war. Sophia Loren reaches a new high of mature, dramatic expression, particularly in contrast with Ludmila Savelyeva's briefer but beautifully contained portrait of a Russian woman who saves an Italian soldier (Marcello Mastroianni) on the Stalingrad front, to become his wife and mother of his child. The climactic confrontation between Loren, the wife Mastroianni left behind, and Savelyeva is a sterling credit to both femme performers.

SUNNY
1941, 97 mins, US
D: Herbert Wilcox A: Anna Neagle, Ray Bolger, John Carroll, Edward Everett Horton (RKO)

The Cinderella adventures of this musical comedy are set in New Orleans during Mardi Gras festivities. Anna Neagle is the star of a streamlined circus. She becomes engaged to John Carroll, heir to an auto fortune, and accompanies him to the family mansion to meet the relatives, especially gruff and eccentric auntie (Helen Westley). Wedding ceremony is blown up by arrival of the bride's circus friends. Ray Bolger scores in three solo routines and teams up with Neagle for a pair of numbers.

SUNNY SIDE UP
1929, 80 mins, US Ⓥ ⊙
D: David Butler **A:** Janet Gaynor, Charles Farrell, El Brendel, Marjorie White, Frank Richardson (Fox)

Buddy DeSylva, Lew Brown, and Ray Henderson have turned out an average Cinderella story for Janet Gaynor, and she plays it. And sings it. For delivery, Gaynor's ''I'm a Dreamer—Aren't We All?'' leads. Plenty of comedy. Some of it by Joe Brown as an undertaker.

SUNRISE
(US: A SONG OF TWO HUMANS)
1927, 95 mins, US Ⓥ ⊗
D: F. W. Murnau **A:** George O'Brien, Janet Gaynor, Margaret Livingston, Bodil Rosing, J. Farrell McDonald (Fox)

Murnau has tried to crystallize in dramatic symbolism those conflicts, adjustments, compromises, and complexities of man-and-woman mating experiences that ultimately grow into an endearing union. Story is as simple as it is human. The Woman from the City (Margaret Livingston) snares a young farmer (George O'Brien). Under her hypnotism he listens to a plan to drown his young wife (Janet Gaynor), sell the farm, and go off to the city.
1927/28: Best Actress (Janet Gaynor), Cinematography, Artistic Quality of Production
Nomination: Best Art Direction

SUNRISE AT CAMPOBELLO
1960, 144 mins, US Ⓥ ⊙
D: Vincent J. Donehue **A:** Ralph Bellamy, Greer Garson, Hume Cronyn, Jean Hagen, Ann Shoemaker (Warner)

In the journey from stage to screen, this chapter from the life of Franklin Delano Roosevelt loses none of its inspirational qualities, none of its humor and pathos. Dore Schary, as author-producer of play and film, can take just pride, shared by Ralph Bellamy, whose portrayal of Roosevelt clicked so resoundingly on Broadway. The period is 1921, when polio shatters a joyous family vacation on the island retreat of Campobello, to 1924, when Roosevelt reemerges in public. Greer Garson comes through as Eleanor Roosevelt with a deeply moving characterization. There is a third tower of strength in Hume Cronyn as the wizened, asthmatic friend and political Svengali.
1960: Nominations: Best Actress (Greer Garson), Color Costume Design, Color Art Direction, Sound

SUNSET
1988, 106 mins, US Ⓥ ⊙ ▭
D: Blake Edwards **A:** Bruce Willis, James Garner, Malcolm McDowell, Mariel Hemingway, Kathleen Quinlan (Hawk/Tri-Star)

Premise of teaming up righteous cowboy star Tom Mix and real-life lawman Wyatt Earp to solve an actual murder case may have looked good on paper, but it plays neither amusingly nor excitingly. Bruce Willis is one of the least likely choices imaginable to play Mix. That's just the beginning of the film's lack of plausibility, even on its own terms. Fortunately, there is James Garner as Earp as relief from all the nonsense around him. The actor's natural charm wins the day in virtually all his scenes.
1988: Nomination: Best Costume Design

SUNSET BOULEVARD
1950, 110 mins, US Ⓥ ⊙
D: Billy Wilder **A:** William Holden, Gloria Swanson, Erich von Stroheim, Nancy Olson (Paramount)

Pseudo-exposé of Hollywood. A young writer with a few minor credits and many creditors finds refuge in what he believes to be an abandoned mansion. It is occupied by a former great femme star. She takes a fancy to the young man, employs him to write a script that will return her to past glory. The association segues into an affair. Performances are exceptionally fine. Swanson socks hard with a silent-day technique to put over the decaying star. Erich von Stroheim, as her butler and original discoverer, delivers with excellent restraint.
1950: Best Story & Screenplay, B&W Art Direction, Score for a Dramatic Picture
Nominations: Best Picture, Director, Actor (William Holden), Actress (Gloria Swanson), Supp. Actor (Erich von Stroheim), Supp. Actress (Nancy Olson), B&W Cinematography, Editing

SUNSET PARK
1996, 99 mins, US ⊗

D: Steve Gomer A: Rhea Perlman, Fredro Starr, Carol Kane, Terrence Dashon Howard, Camille Saviola (Jersey/Tri-Star)

Sunset Park is by no means much of a new wrinkle. The venue is the basketball court, and the participants are an inexperienced female coach and a team of not terribly motivated, inner-city African-American kids. Phyllis Saroka (Rhea Perlman) knows little more than the shape of the ball. While her understanding of the game increases by leaps and bounds, she gains kids' trust by being there off the court. She advises them about girls, gets them tutors for class, visits them in the hospital, and gets them representation in court. The material makes its points with a sledgehammer, and they're obvious ones.

SUNSHINE BOYS, THE
1975, 111 mins, US ⊗

D: Herbert Ross A: Walter Matthau, George Burns, Richard Benjamin, Lee Meredith, Carol Arthur (M-G-M)

Extremely sensitive and lovable film version of Neil Simon's play, with Walter Matthau and George Burns outstanding as a pair of long-hostile vaudeville partners. Matthau, with some complex makeup artistry atop his own brilliant talent, gives his character its full dimension of rascality, stubbornness, heart, pride, and, eventually, humility. Burns provides the right complementing aspects to the pair's love-hate relationship.
1975: Best Supp. Actor (George Burns)
Nominations: Best Actor (Walter Matthau), Screenplay Adaptation, Art Direction

SUN SHINES BRIGHT, THE
1953, 90 mins, US ⊗

D: John Ford A: Charles Winninger, Arleen Wheelan, John Russell, Stepin Fetchit, Russell Simpson (Argosy/Republic)

Comedy-drama is poorly plotted and overlong. Characters are such stereotype figures as julep-drinking southerners, comic-opera darkies, and bigoted poor white trash. Script and John Ford's direction attempt to cloak these hackneyed types with a generous dose of schmaltz and a theme of "good triumphing over evil," but it fails to come off with any impact. Charles Winninger makes as much as possible of his Judge Priest character, the principal figure.

SUPER COPS, THE
1974, 95 mins, US ⊗

D: Gordon Parks A: Ron Leibman, David Selby, Sheila Frazier, Pat Hingle, Dan Frazer (M-G-M)

Essentially the real-life story of two NY police officers (Ron Liebman and David Selby) who brought their effective and original brand of justice to a crime-ridden section of Brooklyn, film is a gem of realism. Highlighted by smashing violence, story-line, though episodic, punches over its theme in first-rate fashion.

SUPERFLY
1972, 96 mins, US ⊗

D: Gordon Parks Jr. A: Ron O'Neal, Carl Lee, Sheila Frazier, Julius W. Harris, Charles McGregor (Warner)

This quickie is strictly action-adventure, alternating, like clockwork, drugs-sex-violence for its duration with hardly a plotline to hold it together. Ron O'Neal heads cast as Superfly, sluggin', lovin', needlin', and philosophizin' his way through the tale of the pusher with heart of gold, wanting to get out—but only after making his easy $1 million.

SUPERGIRL
1984, 105 mins, UK ⊗ ⊙ ▭

D: Jeannot Szwarc A: Faye Dunaway, Helen Slater, Peter O'Toole, Hart Bochner, Peter Cook, Brenda Vaccaro (Artistry/Cantharus)

Supergirl is Kara, Superman's cousin, who journeys to Earth to recover the Omegahedron Stone, life force of her world, which has fallen into the clutches of the evil Selena (Faye Dunaway). Landing near a boarding school for young ladies, Kara adopts the name of Linda Lee and rooms with Lois Lane's kid sister (Maureen Teefy). Dunaway has a ball as Selena. Helen Slater, blond as Supergirl, dark-haired as Linda Lee, is an appealing young heroine in either guise. Screenplay is filled with witty lines and enjoyable characters, but direction is rather flat.

SUPERMAN
1978, 143 mins, US ⊗ ⊙ ▭

D: Richard Donner A: Marlon Brando, Gene Hackman, Christopher Reeve, Margot Kidder, Ned Beatty, Glenn Ford (Warner/Salkind)

A wonderful, chuckling, preposterously exciting fantasy. As both the wholesome man of steel and his bumbling secret identity Clark Kent, Christopher Reeve is excellent. As newswoman Lois Lane,

Margot Kidder plays perfectly off both of his personalities. Superman's debut becomes a wild night, beginning with Lane's rescue from a skyscraper, the capture of assorted burglars, and the rescue of the president's airplane. Lurking in wacky palatial splendor in the sewers beneath Park Avenue, super-criminal Gene Hackman views this caped arrival as a super-threat. **1978:** Special Achievement Award (visual effects) **Nominations:** Best Editing, Original Score, Sound

SUPERMAN II
1981, 127 mins, UK Ⓥ ⊙ ⊑
D: Richard Lester **A:** Christopher Reeve, Gene Hackman, Margot Kidder, Ned Beatty, Terence Stamp (IFP/Salkind)

Solid, classy, cannily constructed piece of entertainment which gets down to action almost immediately. The film does an especially good job of picking up the strings of unexplored characters and plot left dangling from the first pic, taking its core plot from the three Kryptonian villains—Terence Stamp, Jack O'Halloran, and Sarah Douglas—briefly glimpsed in the first pic. The film builds to a battle between Christopher Reeve and the three super-villains in midtown Manhattan.

SUPERMAN III
1983, 123 mins, UK Ⓥ ⊙ ⊑
D: Richard Lester **A:** Christopher Reeve, Richard Pryor, Robert Vaughn, Annette O'Toole, Annie Ross, Margot Kidder (Salkind/Dovemead)

Surprisingly soft-cored disappointment, putting its emphasis on broad comedy at the expense of ingenious plotting and technical wizardry, has virtually none of the mythic or cosmic sensibility that marked its predecessors. The screenplay opts for the novelty of splitting the Clark Kent/Superman persona into two bodies, good and evil.

SUPERMAN IV: THE QUEST FOR PEACE
1987, 89 mins, US Ⓥ ⊙
D: Sidney J. Furie **A:** Christopher Reeve, Gene Hackman, Jackie Cooper, Mariel Hemingway, Margot Kidder (Cannon/Warner)

Superman addresses the United Nations to tell the world he personally is going to remove all nuclear weapons from the face of the earth. Meanwhile, Lex Luthor (Gene Hackman) has created an evil clone of Superman called Nuclear Man,

who wreaks havoc on famous landmarks around the world and does savage battle with the hero on the face of the moon until Superman discovers his nemesis's single flaw. The earlier films in the series had some flair and agreeable humor, qualities this one sorely lacks.

SUPER MARIO BROTHERS, THE
1993, 104 mins, US Ⓥ ⊙ ▭
D: Rocky Morton, Annabel Jankel **A:** Bob Hoskins, John Leguizamo, Dennis Hopper, Samantha Mathis, Fiona Shaw (Hollywood Pictures/Lightmotive/Allied Filmmakers)

Task of converting a nonnarrative video game into a $50-million motion picture was too much. Awkwardly constructed pic starts with the premise of a parallel world to New York created 65 million years ago by a meteorite. A miscast (he's not the only one) Dennis Hopper is intent upon retrieving a meteorite fragment and a young princess (Samantha Mathis) sent with it to our world. Mathis is kidnapped by Hopper's bumbling assistants and pursued into his world by the Mario Brothers, two Brooklyn plumbers. If you can believe that Bob Hoskins and John Leguizamo are brothers, let alone Italian, the rest of the film's leaps of faith are child's play.

SUPERNATURAL
1933, 65 mins, US
D: Victor Halpern **A:** Carole Lombard, Allan Dinehart, Vivienne Osborne, Randolph Scott, H. B. Warner (Paramount)

Ghost story dies after the first half hour. Carole Lombard's called on to change from a nice to a bad girl when the spirit of a dead murderess takes full possession of her. Her Jekyll-Hyde transposition depends on such flimsy devices as fainting spells, smirks, she-devil facial expressions, and double exposures. The villain, phony spiritualist (Allan Dinehart), is painted with a pretty broad brush all the way.

SUPERVIXENS
1975, 105 mins, US Ⓥ
D: Russ Meyer **A:** Shari Eubank, Charles Pitts, Charles Napier, Uschi Digard, Christy Hartburg (September 19)

Overlong and overly violent skin pic. Story involves Clint (Charles Pitts), whose foulmouthed girlfriend is electrocuted by a brutish cop (Charles Napier) with Clint getting the blame. Fleeing town, he has sexual encounters with a succession of busty amazons, then falls for Supervixen (Shari Eubank), whom he must eventually rescue from Napier.

SUPPORT YOUR LOCAL GUNFIGHTER
1971, 92 mins, US Ⓥ
D: Burt Kennedy **A:** James Garner, Suzanne Pleshette, Jack Elam, Joan Blondell, Harry Morgan, Marie Windsor (Cherokee/Brigade)

Follow-up to *Support Your Local Sheriff* has James Garner escaping from the clutches of Marie Windsor, only to become mistaken by competing mine owners Harry Morgan and John Dehner for a hired gun, played in a finale cameo by Chuck Connors. Jack Elam again is excellent in role of a befuddled but willing accomplice to Garner's maneuvers.

SUPPORT YOUR LOCAL SHERIFF
1969, 96 mins, US Ⓥ
D: Burt Kennedy **A:** James Garner, Joan Hackett, Walter Brennan, Harry Morgan, Jack Elam, Bruce Dern (United Artists/Cherokee)

Pic uses as the basis for its comedy the many clichés that have become part and parcel of the western genre. James Garner is delightful as the "stranger" riding into town on his way to Australia, so modest yet so perfect in his various abilities—never missing a shot, turning the town derelict into his deputy, outthinking the Danbys (a superb quartet of villains), outwitting the attempts of the mayor's daughter to land him until he's ready.

SUPPOSE THEY GAVE A WAR AND NOBODY CAME?
1970, 113 mins, US Ⓥ
D: Hy Averback **A:** Brian Keith, Tony Curtis, Ernest Borgnine, Ivan Dixon, Suzanne Pleshette, Tom Ewell (ABC)

A meandering comedy about three army tankmen in a missile base at war with the southern redneck town in which it is located. Ernest Borgnine is the heavy-handed southern sheriff. Tony Curtis keeps it lighthearted, but convincing. Suzanne Pleshette, a wisecracking "beer hustler," is very real, and her handling of tough snappy dialogue makes her appearances some of the best scenes in the film.

SURE THING, THE
1985, 94 mins, US Ⓥ ⊙
D: Rob Reiner **A:** John Cusack, Daphne Zuniga, Boyd Gaines, Tim Robbins, Viveca Lindfors (Embassy/Monument)

Sweetly old-fashioned look at the last lap of the coming-of-age ordeal in which the sure thing becomes less important than the real thing. Gib (John Cusack) is a beer-guzzling junk-food devotee with a flair for the outrageous. Alison (Daphne Zuniga) is a prim and proper coed who thinks that spontaneity is a social disease. They both arrange a ride, unbeknownst to each other, with a California-bound couple. Stranded together, the two travelers mix like oil and water, gradually realizing that their different personalities complement each other. Chemistry between Cusack and Zuniga is a plus.

SURF NAZIS MUST DIE
1987, 80 mins, US Ⓥ
D: Peter George **A:** Barry Brenner, Gail Neely, Michael Sonye, Dawn Wildsmith (Troma/Institute)

Pic hasn't one redeeming feature. Time is the near future and California's social fabric has been torn apart by a devastating earthquake. Striving for supremacy are the Surf Nazis, who live in a beach bunker, own beweaponed surfboards, bristle with knives and swastika tattoos, and are fueled by a surfing Führer—Adolf. Not much else is clear until a revenge-seeking mother (Bobby Bresee) takes on the Nazis after they kill her son.

SURF NINJAS
1993, 86 mins, US Ⓥ ⊙
D: Neal Israel **A:** Ernie Reyes Jr., Rob Schneider, Nicolas Cowan, Leslie Nielsen, Tone Loc (New Line)

Juvenile comedy-action pic. Action is relatively mild for the genre and, unfortunately, so are the jokes. Two California surfing dudes (Ernie Reyes Jr., Nicolas Cowan) are long-lost crown princes of the obscure nation of Patu San. To regain the throne, they must overthrow the dictator (Leslie Nielsen).

SURRENDER
1987, 95 mins, US Ⓥ ⊙
D: Jerry Belson **A:** Sally Field, Michael Caine, Steve Guttenberg, Peter Boyle, Jackie Cooper (Cannon)

Fifties sitcom dressed up in modern clothes. As the confused lovers, Michael Caine and Sally Field are good for a couple of laughs along the way, but production runs out of steam early. Caine is a casualty of too many marriages and too much success as a pop novelist. Field is a would-be artist who takes the easy way out in the form of a rich, unchallenging boyfriend (Steve Guttenberg). Opening skirmish is love at first fight. But once they've coupled, the series of complications can only lead to an inevitable happy ending.

SURVIVORS, THE
1983, 102 mins, US Ⓥ ⊙
D: Michael Ritchie A: Walter Matthau, Robin Williams, Jerry Reed, James Wainwright, Annie McEnroe (Delphi/Rastar)

Unfocused social comedy finds what laughs it has solely in the personal performing talents of Walter Matthau and Robin Williams. Exec Williams and gas station owner Matthau both become unemployed at the outset, and are thrown together as intended victims of professional hit man Jerry Reed. Confronted with the threat of another attack by Reed, Williams becomes a maniacal gun enthusiast.

SUSAN AND GOD
(UK: THE GAY MRS. TREXEL)
1940, 115 mins, US Ⓥ
D: George Cukor A: Joan Crawford, Fredric March, Ruth Hussey, John Carroll, Rita Hayworth (M-G-M)

Crawford returns from abroad a shallow and scatterbrained disciple of a "new thought" movement. She is faced with reconstructing her own marital happiness through personal practice of her tenets. Persistence of her husband to keep her in line and sincerity of the couple's youngster finally bring her to reason. Crawford provides a strong portrayal of Susan. March provides a capital presentation of the husband. Rita Quigley, as the daughter, is excellent.

SUSAN LENOX:
HER FALL AND RISE
1931, 75 mins, US Ⓥ
D: Robert Z. Leonard A: Greta Garbo, Clark Gable, Jean Hersholt, John Miljan (M-G-M)

Hot romance based on sexual antagonism. The Garbo Susan is a vital Swedish immigrant girl who flees her ignorant, self-righteous foster parents to take refuge with a prepossessing young engineer (Clark Gable). The young pair fall in love. Out of the curious antagonism that seems to be generated by their passion, she goes her errant way to become a famous courtesan, while he sinks from bad to worse. Gable plays with agreeable urbanity.

SUSAN SLADE
1961, 116 mins, US
D: Delmer Daves A: Troy Donahue, Connie Stevens, Dorothy McGuire, Lloyd Nolan, Bert Convy (Warner)

Plodding and predictable soap opera is a telling showcase for Connie Stevens. She enacts the virginal daughter of a devoted family man and engineer (Lloyd Nolan). The girl falls madly in love and finds herself with child but without husband. The family then tries a fake by moving to Guatemala, where Nolan dies and his wife (Dorothy McGuire) supposedly bears the child. The story returns to the US and boils down to who is worthy of Stevens's love—junior tycoon Bert Convy or poor stable operator Troy Donahue?

SUSAN SLEPT HERE
1954, 97 mins, US Ⓥ ⊙
D: Frank Tashlin A: Dick Powell, Debbie Reynolds, Anne Francis, Alvy Moore, Glenda Farrell (RKO)

Some 97 minutes of well-farced escapism involve Hollywood writer Dick Powell with juve delinquent Debbie Reynolds in sort of May-October romantic affair. Some chuckles are sly type since battle-of-sexes stuff is open to assorted interpretations. Debbie remains pure through all, managing to spoil Anne Francis's courtship of Powell and getting him for herself. 1954: Nominations: Best Song ("Hold My Hand"), Sound

SUSPECT, THE
1944, 85 mins, US
D: Robert Siodmak A: Charles Laughton, Ella Raines, Rosalind Ivan, Stanley C. Ridges (Universal)

Film is a murder mystery with all the suspense of a super-whodunit, a keen character study of a man whose married life has been a hell on earth and who sacrifices all to protect the one happiness in his middle age, a sensible young stenographer who later becomes his wife. Charles Laughton gives an impeccable performance as the kindly, law-abiding citizen. Matching his deft portrayal is Ella Raines as the youthful steno.

SUSPECT
1987, 121 mins, US Ⓥ ⊙
D: Peter Yates A: Cher, Dennis Quaid, Liam Neeson, John Mahoney, Joe Mantegna, Philip Bosco (Tri-Star)

Gimmicky suspense drama sabotaged by a flimsy script full of clichés. Cher stars as a hardworking public defender given a defendant charged with a brutal murder. Carl Wayne Anderson (Liam Neeson) has everything working against him: a Vietnam vet rendered deaf and speechless by the psychological toll of the war, and homeless—he has to be innocent.

SUSPICION
1941, 102 mins, US ⊗ ⊙
D: Alfred Hitchcock **A:** Cary Grant, Joan Fontaine, Cedric Hardwicke, Nigel Bruce, May Whitty (RKO)

Hitchcock's trademarked cinematic development of suspenseful drama is vividly displayed. Protected girl of an English country manor, Joan Fontaine falls in love and elopes with Cary Grant, an impecunious and happy-go-lucky individual, who figured her family would amply provide for both of them. Deeply in love, she overlooks his monetary irresponsibilities until her discovery that he has stolen a large sum from an estate.
1941: Best Actress (Joan Fontaine)
Nominations: Best Picture, Scoring of a Dramatic Picture

SUTURE
1993, 96 mins, US ⊗ ▭
D: Scott McGehee, David Siegel **A:** Dennis Haysbert, Mel Harris, Sab Shimono, Dina Merrill, Michael Harris (Kino-Korsakoff)

Exceedingly smart and elegant American indie in a very unusual vein. Part mystery thriller, part psychological investigation, and part avant-garde experiment, feature was shot in black-and-white 'scope. Vincent Towers (Michael Harris), a wealthy but cold white man living in an opulent home, has initiated a reunion with his half brother, Clay Arlington (Dennis Haysbert), who's black. Vincent plots to blow up his own car with Clay in it, and assumes a new identity after having planted his own papers with Clay.

SVENGALI
1931, 79 mins, US ⊗
D: Archie Mayo **A:** John Barrymore, Marian Marsh, Bramwell Fletcher, Donald Crisp, Carmel Myers (Warner)

Formerly well known as *Trilby*, story is well known, but Svengali (John Barrymore) here makes it clear that Trilby (Marian Marsh), the model, has been the houseguest of several artists, so that her desire to become legally attached to the pursuing young Englishman is not going to be without family difficulties. He hypnotizes her into running away with him and also into a career as a concert star. Barrymore's playing is interesting, sterling, and in broad strokes. Marsh flashes nothing unusual histrionically.
1930/31: Nominations: Best Cinematography, Art Direction

SWALLOWS AND AMAZONS
1974, 92 mins, UK ⊗
D: Claude , Whatham **A:** Virginia McKenna, Ronald Fraser, Brenda Bruce, Jack Woolgar, Simon West (EMI/Theatre Projects)

This charming, delightful film for both adults and children is faithfully based on the 1929 children's classic by Arthur Ransome. Essential plot involving four children (the Swallows) on holiday in the Lake District and their friendly rivalry with two tomboy girls (the Amazons) is simple but absorbing, and captures the spirit of the period.

SWAMP THING
1982, 90 mins, US ⊗ ⊙
D: Wes Craven **A:** Louis Jourdan, Adrienne Barbeau, Ray Wise, David Hess, Nicholas Worth (United Artists)

Adaptation of the DC Comics book to live-action feature filming is a childish programmer, short on thrills and laughs. Sci-fi premise has scientist Alec Holland (Ray Wise) developing a vegetable cell with an animal nucleus. The green mixture is accidentally poured on Holland who, catching fire (in pic's best special-effects scene), runs off into the swamp, later emerging as a big, green dude in a rubber suit, the Swamp Thing (Dick Durock). Pic disintegrates at this point into a series of contrived chases.

SWAMP WATER
(UK: THE MAN WHO CAME BACK)
1941, 90 mins, US
D: Jean Renoir **A:** Walter Brennan, Walter Huston, Anne Baxter, Dana Andrews, John Carradine (20th Century-Fox)

Jean Renoir's first job for an American company is less than an auspicious beginning. All the ingredients of an old-time meller have been thrown into the plot. Story has Walter Brennan hiding in a swamp after escaping hanging for a murder. Dana Andrews, Huston's son by a previous marriage, finds him while searching for his dog. Brennan convinces the kid of his innocence. They enter a fur-trapping partnership, the boy to give Brennan's share to the latter's daughter. But the lad's girl, in a fit of jealousy, gives the secret away.

SWAN, THE
1956, 107 mins, US ⓥ ▱
D: Charles Vidor A: Grace Kelly, Alec Guinness, Louis Jourdan, Agnes Moorehead, Jessie Royce Landis, Brian Aherne (M-G-M)

Genteel picture about genteel people in a never-never world of crowns, titles, and luxury living. There's subtle humor and broad humor, and several scenes that reach right into the heart. Costarring with Grace Kelly is Alec Guinness, who adds the correct, modified comedy touch to his role of the crown prince who must end up with the princess, and Louis Jourdan, who adds a romantic flavor to his character of the commoner-tutor who dares to love the princess. Kelly shines right along with her male stars as the princess.

SWANN IN LOVE
See: Un Amour de Swann

SWARM, THE
1978, 116 mins, US ⓥ ▱
D: Irwin Allen A: Michael Caine, Katharine Ross, Richard Widmark, Richard Chamberlain, Olivia de Havilland, Ben Johnson (Warner)

Killer bees periodically interrupt the arch writing, stilted direction, and ludicrous acting in a disappointing and tired nonthriller. Michael Caine heads the cast as a scientist who must contend with killer bees as well as with Richard Widmark, playing one of those cardboard military officers. Lots of other familiar names crop up. By the time the bees get to Houston, and the city is torched, few will care.
1978: Nomination: Best Costume Design

SWASHBUCKLER
(UK: THE SCARLET BUCCANEER)
1976, 101 mins, US ⓥ ◉ ▱
D: James Goldstone A: Robert Shaw, James Earl Jones, Peter Boyle, Genevieve Bujold, Beau Bridges, Anjelica Huston (Universal)

Coloring-book plot and formula characters as follows: genial lead pirates, Robert Shaw and James Earl Jones; wicked colonial governor, Peter Boyle; wronged noblelady, Genevieve Bujold; wronged noblelady's noble father, Bernard Behrens; and foppish soldier, Beau Bridges. This tacky pastepot job can't make up its mind whether it is serious, tongue-in-cheek, satirical, slapstick, burlesque, par-ody or travesty; but be assured it's all of the above.

SWEENEY!
1977, 97 mins, UK ⓥ
D: David Wickes A: John Thaw, Dennis Waterman, Barry Foster, Ian Bannen, Colin Welland (Euston)

Regular TV series topliners John Thaw and Dennis Waterman as two cops drift through an occasionally witty screenplay with no special flair following the unlikely story line. Oil and its sway on the world's political and economic situation is the plot. Ian Bannen plays a steely-eyed alcoholic government minister and easily gives the best performance.

SWEENEY 2
1978, 108 mins, UK ⓥ
D: Tom Clegg A: John Thaw, Dennis Waterman, Denholm Elliott, Georgina Hale, Nigel Hawthorne (Euston)

Excellent cops-and-robbers stuff in which a special squad of Scotland Yard detectives ultimately demolish a gang of bank robbers whose hallmarks include gold-plated shotguns. Good action well spaced and paced; good characterization played with finesse; a witty script and stylish direction all lend the production a degree of distinction. John Thaw is credible and appealing as the hard-bitten cop who leads the police team.

SWEET ADELINE
1935, 85 mins, US ⓥ
D: Mervyn LeRoy A: Irene Dunne, Donald Woods, Hugh Herbert, Ned Sparks, Winifred Shaw (Warner)

As a production, *Sweet Adeline* is in the big-time musical class, but strictly on merit it rates no better than fair. Adeline (Irene Dunne) and Sid (Donald Woods) have a love spat and spend more than an hour of footage scowling at each other. When they stop scowling the picture is over. That he's got to smirk most of the time makes it tough for Woods, who is no singer. Dunne, in fine voice, is comely as Adeline, and effective, also, despite that she's not suited to torch songs. "Here Am I" and "Why Was I Born?" are retained from the original score, but the music otherwise is mostly new.

SWEET AND LOWDOWN
1999, 95 mins, US ⓥ ◉
D: Woody Allen A: Sean Penn, Samantha Morton, Uma Thurman, Brian Markinson,

Anthony LaPaglia, Gretchen Mol (Magnolia/Sweetland)

Woody Allen is in mellow mood with *Sweet and Lowdown,* the fictional biopic of a legendary American jazz guitarist of the thirties and a wonderful showcase for some of the great jazz standards he loves so much. Film deals with Emmet Ray (Penn), a jazz guitarist considered to be second only to the great Django Reinhardt. A bombastic, self-centered extrovert with an ego a mile high, Ray finds himself touched by Hattie (Samantha Morton), a mute, orphaned laundress he meets in Atlantic City. But after a year he walks out on her and marries Blanche (Uma Thurman), a sultry, elegant writer. Penn gives a winning performance as the brash, unlikable Ray, redeemed only by the beautiful music he makes. British thesp Morton essays the touching character of Hattie with great distinction, and Thurman is amusing as the bitchy Blanche. The look and feel of the period are deftly caught.
1999: Nominations: Best Actor (Sean Penn), Supp. Actress (Samantha Morton)

SWEET BIRD OF YOUTH
1962, 120 mins, US ⓥ ⊙ ▭
D: Richard Brooks **A:** Paul Newman, Geraldine Page, Shirley Knight, Ed Begley, Rip Torn, Mildred Dunnock (M-G-M)

Tamer and tidied but arresting version of Tennessee Williams's play. Newman brings thrust and vitality to the role, but has some overly mannered moments that distract. This is Page's picture. Her portrayal of the fading actress seeking substitute reality in drink, sex, and what have you to offer is a histrionic classic. Shirley Knight is sympathetic and attractive as the distraught daughter of a corrupt political boss, and Ed Begley is outstanding as the latter.
1962: Best Supp. Actor (Ed Begley)
Nominations: Best Actress (Geraldine Page), Supp. Actress (Shirley Knight)

SWEET CHARITY
1969, 148 mins, US ⓥ ⊙ ▭
D: Bob Fosse **A:** Shirley MacLaine, John McMartin, Ricardo Montalban, Sammy Davis Jr,, Chita Rivera (Universal)

A terrific musical film, based on the 1966 legituner. Shirley MacLaine is a dancehall hostess who, at the outset, has just been sloughed off by a gigolo. An accidental encounter with an Italian screen idol, played superbly by Ricardo Montalban, precedes a blossoming romance with John McMartin. MacLaine's unique talents as a comic tragedienne are set off to maximum impact. The film strikes the correct balance between escapist fantasy and hard reality.
1969: Nominations: Best Costume Design, Art Direction, Adapted Musical Score

SWEET DREAMS
1985, 115 mins, US ⓥ ⊙
D: Karel Reisz **A:** Jessica Lange, Ed Harris, Ann Wedgeworth, David Clennon, James Staley (HBO/Silver Screen)

Jessica Lange's portrayal of country singer Patsy Cline is certainly equal to Sissy Spacek's Oscar-winning re-creation of Loretta Lynn. The film slants Cline's biography toward romance as likable redneck Harris meets Lange at a roadside inn and their initially blissful marriage tackles the rough, upward climb to stardom, with many a shabby way stop. Apart from the deftly interwoven singing sequences, most of Cline's career takes place off camera.
1985: Nomination: Best Actress (Jessica Lange)

SWEET HEREAFTER, THE
1997, 110 mins, Canada ⓥ ⊙ ▭
D: Atom Egoyan **A:** Ian Holm, Sarah Polley, Bruce Greenwood, Tom McCamus, Arsinee Khanjian, Alberta Watson (Ego/Alliance)

Canadian writer-director Atom Egoyan's most ambitious work to date, *The Sweet Hereafter* is a rich, complex meditation on the impact of a terrible tragedy on a small town. Egoyan shies away from the obvious tearjerker elements in this story of a bus crash that kills 14 children. Mitchell Stephens (Ian Holm) is a big-city lawyer who arrives to mount a class-action suit targeting the city authorities, the bus manufacturer and anyone else who can be made to pay for the accident. Stephens has also lost a child—in his case, to drugs. The one man staunchly opposed to Stephens's efforts is Billy Ansell (Bruce Greenwood), a widower who lost his two kids in the disaster. Pic is shot with no small amount of style.
1997: Nominations: Best Director, Screenplay Adaptation

SWEETIE
1989, 97 mins, Australia ⓥ ⊙
D: Jane Campion **A:** Genevieve Lemon, Karen Colston, Tom Lycos, Jon Darling, Dorothy Barry (Arenafilm)

Original, audacious tragicomedy about two sisters, one who's afraid of trees but believes in fortune-tellers, the other who's plump and plain and eager to make her mark in showbiz. At the beginning, focus is on Kay (Karen Colston), who becomes convinced that the man of her life is Louis (Tom Lycos). Kay sets about seducing him and before long they're living together. Enter Dawn (Genevieve Lemon), known as Sweetie, Kay's sister, who, with her drugged-out boyfriend Bob (Michael Lake), moves into the spare room.

SWEET LIBERTY
1986, 107 mins, US ⓥ ⊙
D: Alan Alda A: Alan Alda, Michael Caine, Michelle Pfeiffer, Bob Hoskins, Lillian Gish (Universal)

Comedic potential is too rarely realized in this story of a college professor who watches filming of his historical tome become bastardized by Hollywood into a lusty romp. Playing their true ages are Alan Alda as college professor who teaches history of the American Revolution, and Michael Caine as box-office draw Elliot James. When the film company arrives on location, Alda falls for leading lady Faith Healy (Michelle Pfeiffer).

SWEET MOVIE
1974, 99 mins, France/Canada ⓥ
D: Dusan Makavejev A: Carole Laure, Pierre Clementi, Anna Pruchnal, Sami Frey, John Vernon (VM/Mojack)

Sweet Movie is literally sweet, with lovemaking in a bed of sugar and a girl being bathed in chocolate for advertising purposes. But it also has an underpinning of scatology and a zany look at sensuality. Neither hard- nor softcore, Yugoslav filmmaker Dusan Makavejev's first pic in the West begins as broad, funny satire on the richest man in the world looking for a virgin to marry and then goes into the girl's hegira as she finds personal sensual liberation.

SWEET NOVEMBER
1968, 114 mins, US
D: Robert Ellis A: Sandy Dennis, Anthony Newley, Theodore Bikel, Burr DeBenning, Sandy Baron (Warner/Seven Arts)

A love story with a charming, almost fragile, and slightly nebulous premise. Screenplay focuses on the girl who takes to her heart—and her flat—for a month at a time some man with a problem. In doing so, she seeks to ease her own troubles. Sandy Dennis is delightful in role of the kindly femme and Anthony Newley shades his performance with subtle comedy.

SWEET REVENGE
1990, 93 mins, US/France ⓥ
D: Charlotte Brandstrom A: Rosanna Arquette, Carrie Fisher, John Sessions, Francois Eric Gendron, Myriam Moszko (Chrysalide/Canal Plus)

Stab at old-fashioned screwball romantic comedy comes off only halfheartedly because screenplay relies on squeaky contrivances. Carrie Fisher, playing Linda, a corporation lawyer, pays actress Kate Williams (Rosanna Arquette) to trap her ex-husband John (John Sessions), a struggling writer, into a mock marriage so that Linda can get out of paying him the alimony awarded him. The actress and the writer, of course, fall in real love right away.

SWEET RIDE, THE
1968, 111 mins, US ▭
D: Harvey Hart A: Anthony Franciosa, Michael Sarrazin, Jacqueline Bisset, Bob Denver, Michael Wilding (20th Century-Fox)

Flat programmer, with ragged scripting, papier-mâché characters, and routine direction. Tony Franciosa is a beachbum tennis hustler who is a sort of god to Malibu pad mates Sarrazin and draft-dodging musician Bob Denver. Enter Bisset, who has a running, masochistic affair with producer Warren Stevens. She takes to Sarrazin, though Charles Dierkop, a recurring motorcycle bum, gets an inordinate amount of attention from Bisset.

SWEET ROSIE O'GRADY
1943, 76 mins, US
D: Irving Cummings A: Betty Grable, Robert Young, Adolphe Menjou, Virginia Grey (20th Century-Fox)

Casting is tip-top, with Robert Young, as the Police Gazette reporter, the romantic vis-à-vis after forcing Betty Grable to jilt Reginald Gardner as an English duke. Adolphe Menjou is the volatile Gazette ed, but the rest of the cast is also-ran save for Virginia Grey as the star's pal and Phil Regan, marking his cinematic comeback effectively in a songsmithing role. Tunes by Mack Gordon and Harry Warren fit the action well.

SWEET SMELL OF SUCCESS
1957, 96 mins, US Ⓥ ⊙
D: Alexander Mackendrick **A:** Burt Lancaster, Tony Curtis, Susan Harrison, Marty Milner, Sam Levene, Barbara Nichols (Norma-Curtleigh/United Artists)

It's a no-holds-barred account of the sadistic fourth-estater played cunningly by Burt Lancaster. Failure to comply with his wishes means a broken career. Breaks in his column sustain the press agent, but for the mentions there are certain favors to be granted. To the p.a., the columnist's dictates are law; if the favors include framing a young musician on a narcotics rap, that's all right, too. Flaw concerns the newspaperman's devotion to his sister. It's not clear why he rebels at her courtship with a guitarist, who appears to be a nice kid.

SWEET SWEETBACK'S BAADASSSSS SONG
1971, 97 mins, US Ⓥ
D: Melvin Van Peebles **A:** Brer Soul [Melvin Van Peebles], Simon Chuckster, Hubert Scales, John Dullaghan, West Gale (Yeah)

Sweetback is first seen, aged 12, in the arms of an accommodating older woman, and soon thereafter as the adult lead performer in a sexual circus. He's selected by his employer to go along with a couple of white detectives who need an arrest for the evening, and on the way he's witness to a ghetto riot in which his friendly captors brutally beat a young black revolutionary. The moment of decision at hand, Sweetback smashes the detectives—and his own place in "the system." Thereafter, it's one long chase, and one long parable of the white man's brutality and duplicity.

SWEET WILLIAM
1980, 92 mins, UK Ⓥ
D: Claude Whatham **A:** Sam Waterston, Jenny Agutter, Anna Massey, Geraldine James, Arthur Lowe (Kendon)

Nice, ordinary English girl Jenny Agutter meets wild, romantic Scots divorcé Sam Waterston. Sadly for her—though the tone is never more than slightly bittersweet—he's a wolf with two not-so-ex-wives, and a compulsion to bed down anything he sees move. The screenplay is diligent without being distinguished. Direction tends to prefer lingering realism to dramatic pace.

SWELL GUY
1946, 96 mins, US
D: Frank Tuttle **A:** Sonny Tufts, Ann Blyth, Ruth Warrick, Thomas Gomez, Millard Mitchell (Universal)

Picture deals with a heel hero who doesn't reform. Sonny Tufts plays the title role, a departure from his usual casting. Story concerns stir caused in a small town when a war correspondent comes to visit his family and how his lack of scruples and inability to do the right thing affect all he meets. Ann Blyth comes through with a highly effective performance as the spoiled rich girl who is taken in by the phony hero. .

SWIMMER, THE
1968, 94 mins, US Ⓥ ⊙
D: Frank Perry **A:** Burt Lancaster, Janet Landgard, Janice Rule, Marge Champion, Kim Hunter, Joan Rivers (Columbia/Horizon)

Stylized, episodic, moody film, based on John Cheever's dramatic fantasy, is something of a minor triumph. Burt Lancaster pops up on a sunny Sunday morning at a suburban poolside, miles away from his house, and decides to "swim" home by visiting at each neighbor's house. Each self-contained sequence adds indirect light to Lancaster. Film is the story of a moral hangover, with the sobered-up, bewildered man retracing his steps to see what he has done.

SWIMMING TO CAMBODIA
1987, 87 mins, US Ⓥ ⊙
D: Jonathan Demme **A:** Spalding Gray (Demme)

Witnessed in its original incarnation as a staged monologue, Spalding Gray's free-associating recollection of his experiences in Thailand during the making of *The Killing Fields* had an exhilarating immediacy which is mostly absent in this compressed filmed performance. Gray elicits compassion and universal recognition for his seriocomic search for self.

SWIMMING WITH SHARKS
1995, 93 mins, US Ⓥ
D: George Huang **A:** Kevin Spacey, Frank Whaley, Michelle Forbes, Benicio Del Toro, Roy Dotrice (Cineville)

Revenge fantasy in which a much-put-upon flunky gets some of his own back when he holds his insufferable boss hostage and tortures him. Pic charts a recent Hollywood arrival's quick trip from idealism to murderous me-firstism. Kevin Spacey dominates, but Whaley makes a convincing transition from goody-goody to icy insider.

SWINDLE, THE
See: Il Bidone

SWINGER, THE
1966, 81 mins, US
D: George Sidney **A:** Ann-Margret, Anthony Franciosa, Robert Coote, Yvonne Romain, Horace McMahon (Paramount)

Very amusing original screen comedy. Direction spotlights Ann-Margret's singing-dancing talents. She is an aspiring mag writer who fakes her autobiog in the form of a mishmash of lurid paperback plots. Tony Franciosa, the editor, swallows the bait and tries to reform her, while nudie mag publisher Robert Coote seeks to exploit the gal. David Winters choreographed the terp sequences, one of which is a rather sexy bit in which Ann-Margret, in a fake orgy, rolls about on canvas with her body covered with paint.

SWING HIGH, SWING LOW
1937, 92 mins, US
D: Mitchell Leisen **A:** Carole Lombard, Fred MacMurray, Charles Butterworth, Jean Dixon, Dorothy Lamour (Paramount)

As an ex-soldier who can toot a mean horn, MacMurray, ably foiled by Carole Lombard, does much to sustain a story, which, in spots, looms as a bit dated. Sagas about kings of the nightclubs who, when they start to skid, go down fast, have become a bit familiar, as has the basic triangle situation when MacMurray goes the whoopee route and Lombard ultimately comes back to resurrect him from the sloughs. However, expert trouping by both more than sustains the story requirements.

SWING KIDS
1993, 112 mins, US
D: Thomas Carter **A:** Robert Sean Leonard, Christian Bale, Frank Whaley, Barbara Hershey, Kenneth Branagh (Hollywood Pictures)

A fascinating footnote to WWII Nazi Germany is trivialized and sanitized in this odd concoction of music and politics. Screenplay chronicles the development of a trio of young men whose passion for such American pop-music favorites as Benny Goodman, Artie Shaw, and Count Basie puts them in the unusual dilemma of embracing officially forbidden "decadent art."

SWING SHIFT
1984, 100 mins, US
D: Jonathan Demme **A:** Goldie Hawn, Kurt Russell, Christine Lahti, Fred Ward, Ed Harris, Holly Hunter (Lantana/Warner)

With all the heartwarming heroics to choose from on the homefront in World War II, *Swing Shift* tries instead to twist some consequence out of a tawdry adulterous tryst by a couple of self-centered sneaks, but the writing and acting are too flat for the challenge. Goldie Hawn and Ed Harris are your basic nice young couple living modestly until Pearl Harbor demands he immediately volunteer. Hawn sees him off to war and somewhat timidly goes to work at an aircraft factory, where she draws the immediate romantic interest of Kurt Russell.

1984: Nomination: Best Supp. Actress (Christine Lahti)

SWING TIME
1936, 103 mins, US
D: George Stevens **A:** Fred Astaire, Ginger Rogers, Victor Moore, Helen Broderick, Eric Blore (RKO)

Another winner for the Astaire-Rogers combo. It's smart, modern, and impressive in every respect, from its boy-loses-girl background to its tunefulness, dancipation, and production quality. There are six Jerome Kern tunes (Dorothy Fields's clever lyrics don't retard the motivation, either) and the tunes, as usual, have substance and quality.

1936: Best Song ("The Way You Look Tonight")
Nomination: Best Dance Direction ("Bo Jangles")

SWISS FAMILY ROBINSON
1960, 126 mins, US
D: Ken Annakin **A:** John Mills, Dorothy McGuire, James MacArthur, Janet Munro, Sessue Hayakawa, Cecil Parker (Walt Disney)

The rather modest 1813 Johann Wyss tale has been blown up to prodigious proportions. The essence and the spirit of the simple, intriguing story of a marvelously industrious family is all but snuffed out. The Robinson family seems to be enjoying a standard of living that would be the envy of an average modern family. Their famous tree house is almost outrageously comfortable (running water, no less), and seems to pop up overnight with virtually no effort. The climactic scrape with a band of Oriental buccaneers is the crushing blow to any semblance of credibility. Several sequences have a heap of genuine excitement, particularly the opening raft scene in which the family battles treacherous ocean currents to get from wrecked ship to island.

SWITCH
1991, 103 mins, US Ⓥ ⊙ ⊠
D: Blake Edwards **A:** Ellen Barkin, Jimmy Smits, JoBeth Williams, Lorraine Bracco, Tony Roberts (Beco/HBO)

Fainthearted sex comedy that doesn't have the courage of its initially provocative convictions. Undemanding audiences will get a few laughs from the notion of a man parading around in Ellen Barkin's body. Ladykiller Steve Brooks (Perry King) is murdered for his innumerable emotional crimes against women. Steve is given a chance to escape a fiery fate by returning to Earth and finding just one woman who genuinely likes him. Only catch is that he will henceforth inhabit the body of a woman, and that of an uncommonly sexy one. Barkin mugs and overdoes the grimacing and macho posturing.

SWITCHING CHANNELS
1988, 105 mins, US Ⓥ ⊙
D: Ted Kotcheff **A:** Kathleen Turner, Burt Reynolds, Christopher Reeve, Ned Beatty, Henry Gibson (Tri-Star)

Broad, sometimes silly, transfer of *The Front Page* or, more specifically, *His Girl Friday*, to the gleaming modern setting of a satellite TV-news station. Ace anchorwoman Kathleen Turner is swept off her feet by the dashing and obscenely rich Christopher Reeve. Turner announces to her crafty, manipulative boss (Burt Reynolds) that she is through with the news game and intends to settle down with her new love. Reynolds also is her ex-husband and, though he'd never admit it, still is in love with her, so he launches into a frantic campaign to keep her on the station.

SWOON
1992, 90 mins, US Ⓥ
D: Tom Kalin **A:** Daniel Schlachet, Craig Chester, Ron Vawter, Michael Kirby (Intolerance)

Studied, ultra-arty look at a notorious crime as seen through a thick filter of sexual politics. Story revolves around Nathan Leopold Jr. and Richard Loeb, two wealthy, brilliant, Jewish teenage lovers whose crime spree culminated in the murder of a kidnapped boy. Essentially equating gayness with outlaw status in a hostile society, Tom Kalin mixes in archival footage with his staged material.

SWORD AND THE SORCERER, THE
1982, 100 mins, US Ⓥ ⊙
D: Albert Pyun **A:** Lee Horsley, Kathleen Beller, Simon MacCorkindale, George Maharis, Nina Van Pallandt (Chase)

Combine beaucoup gore and an atrocity-a-minute action edited in fast-pace style. Then toss in a scantily clad cast of none-too-talented performers mouthing dim-witted dialogue and garnish with a touch of medieval gibberish. The result would be something resembling *The Sword and the Sorcerer*. The plot is needlessly complicated by a truly lackluster script. *Sword* is about the retaking by a group of ragtag medievalists of a once peaceable kingdom sadistically ruled by an evil knight named Cromwell.

SWORD IN THE STONE, THE
1963, 75 mins, US Ⓥ ⊙
D: Wolfgang Reitherman (Walt Disney)

Adaptation of the 1938 T. H. White book of the same title emerges as a tasty confection. Key figures are the boy who is to become King of England because he alone has the strength to remove the sword embedded in a stone in a London churchyard (he goes by the name of Wart), and Merlin, a magician and prophet, who's alternately wise and somewhat nutty. The songs by Richard M. and Robert B. Sherman are in the familiar Disney cartoon groove. They're agreeable tunes and go along nicely with the animated action.

SWORD OF LANCELOT
See: Lancelot and Guinevere

SYLVIA
1965, 115 mins, US
D: Gordon Douglas **A:** Carroll Baker, George Maharis, Joanne Dru, Peter Lawford, Viveca Lindfors, Edmond O'Brien (Paramount)

Story of a prostitute who turns to decency. The production is episodic until its closing reels, covering a period of 14 to 15 years as a private investigator digs into heroine's obscure past to learn who she really is. Carroll Baker is joined in stellar spot by George Maharis as the private eye who ultimately falls in love with the woman he is tracing.

SYLVIA SCARLETT

1936, 90 mins, US ⊗ ⊙

D: George Cukor **A:** Katharine Hepburn, Cary Grant, Brian Aherne, Edmund Gwenn, Dennie Moore (RKO)

Pic is puzzling in its tangents and sudden jumps, plus the almost poetic lines that are given to Katharine Hepburn. At moments it skirts the border of absurdity. Perhaps it is not valid to ask whether anybody would really fail to suspect the true sex of such a boy as Hepburn looks and acts. But while carrying this off well enough, she shines brightest and is most likable in the transition into womanhood inspired by her meeting with an artist (Brian Aherne). Cary Grant, doing a petty English crook, practically steals the picture.

SYMPHONY OF SIX MILLION
(UK: MELODY OF LIFE)

1932, 92 mins, US

D: Gregory La Cava **A:** Irene Dunne, Ricardo Cortez, Gregory Ratoff, Anna Appel, Lita Chevret (RKO)

A brilliant Jewish surgeon loses his nerve when his family virtually forces him to operate on his father for a brain tumor. The father dies on the table and the boy goes to pieces, vowing he will never touch an instrument again. His faith in himself is restored when he successfully performs a delicate spinal operation on the girl he loves. She has deliberately endangered her own life to force him to action. Ricardo Cortez is generally good as the young surgeon. Irene Dunne is meaningless, appearing but seldom and then always in forced and unreal situations.

SYNANON
(UK: GET OFF MY BACK)

1965, 105 mins, US

D: Richard Quine **A:** Edmond O'Brien, Chuck Connors, Stella Stevens, Alex Cord, Richard Conte, Eartha Kitt (Columbia)

Fictionized semidocumentary of a rehabilitation home for drug addicts. Producer-director Quine moved his cameras to the actual locale to ensure authenticity in this story of Synanon House, established by Charles E. Dederich, an ex-alcoholic, in 1958. Edmond O'Brien enacts the character of Dederich (who acted as technical adviser), plagued by debts and civil opposition as he goes about his seemingly thankless task.

SYSTEM, THE
(AKA: THE GIRL-GETTERS)

1964, 90 mins, UK

D: Michael Winner **A:** Oliver Reed, Jane Merrow, Barbara Ferris, Julia Foster, David Hemmings (BLC/Bryanston)

A bunch of local lads at a seaside resort every summer work a system by which they "take" the holidaying femmes for a lighthearted emotional ride. Tinker (Oliver Reed), a beach photographer, is leader of the "come up and see my pad" gang. The film tells how, one summer, he falls heavily in love with a fashion model, and that's against the "rules," even when the girl reciprocates. This thin yarn is an adroitly spun concoction of comedy, sentiment, and pathos.

SZEGENYLEGENYEK
(US: THE ROUND-UP)

1966, 94 mins, Hungary

D: Miklos Jancso **A:** Janos Gorbe, Tibor Molnar, Andras Kozak, Gabor Agardy, Zoltan Lastinovits (Mafilm)

Fable concerns Hungary of 1848. Gendarmes pen up several hundred suspects in a stockade. They have proof that one of the men is guilty of a double murder, and promise him a pardon if he will finger a bigger fry. Scared out of his wits, Janos Gajdor (Janos Gorbe) makes a try. This is a psycho pic, an anatomy of betrayal. Long-focusing and ingenious camerawork builds up tension. Emotional strength is given to the plot by the desolate horizon of the Hungarian lowlands.

SZERELEM
(US: Love)

1971, 92 mins, Hungary

D: Karoly Makk **A:** Lili Darvas, Mari Torocsik, Ivan Darvas, Tibor Bitskey, Eszter Szakacs (Mafilm 1)

Touching but never sentimental tale of three people, set in 1953, when there was some attempt to throw off the Stalinist yoke. Lili Darvas plays the dying octagenarian mother. It is a stroke of perfect casting. She is demanding without being shrewish or senile. She accepts the whopping letters of her son (Ivan Darvas) making a film in America and other outlandish things her daughter-in-law (Mari Torocsik) cooks up. Whether she ever suspects anything is left ambiguous.

T

TABLE FOR FIVE
1983, 122 mins, US 🆅 ⊙

D: Robert Lieberman **A:** Jon Voight, Richard Crenna, Marie-Christine Barrault, Millie Perkins, Roxana Zal, Robby Kiger (CBS Theatrical)

Well-written drama concerns an errant father who takes his three children on an ocean voyage in an effort to close the gap that's grown between them. Voight quickly realizes that he really doesn't know how to communicate with the kids who resent that he's more interested in chasing blondes in the bar than hanging out with them. Pic earns most of its emotional points honestly and will touch most anyone who's ever taken the responsibilities of parenting seriously.

TABU
1931, 81 mins, US 🆅 ⊙

D: F. W. Murnau **A:** Reri, Matahi, Hitu, Jean, Jules, Kong Ah (Paramount)

A strong love story set in the South Seas, with a native South Sea cast. The title, "Tabu," means "death." It's the fate that hangs over the romantic leads who flee from a distant isle and its barbaric customs after a girl has been handed over to Tabu, the ruler of one of the islands, as "the chosen one." Along with her goes the dictum "no man must touch her or cast eyes of desire upon her." *Tabu* is a silent film, with synchronization and sound effects.

1930/31: Best Cinematography

TAI-PAN
1986, 127 mins, US 🆅 ⊙ ▭

D: Daryl Duke **A:** Bryan Brown, Joan Chen, John Stanton, Tom Guinee, Bill Leadbitter (De Laurentiis)

Historical epic lost somewhere between 19th-century Hong Kong and 20th-century Hollywood. As the Tai-Pan, or trade leader of the European community, first in Canton and then later in Hong Kong, Aussie thesp Bryan Brown looks the part well enough, but lacks charisma. Within the exotic setting, the story is actually rather conventional. Brown is opposed by arch villains Brock (John Stanton) and his son Gorth (Bill Leadbitter) for the control of trading rights. At the same time, considerable politicking is going on with the Chinese over the opium trade and the British over trade regulations.

TAKE A GIRL LIKE YOU
1970, 101 mins, UK 🆅

D: Jonathan Miller **A:** Noel Harrison, Oliver Reed, Hayley Mills, Sheila Hancock, John Bird (Columbia)

Take a movie like this. It's about a virgin (Hayley Mills) and a guy (Oliver Reed) who is trying to make her, can't, and is obsessed about it. That's all there is to it. Basically, it's not a bad little English kitchen-sink drama with some strong but low-key performances, but the film lacks a sense of humor, contains generally wearisome development, and a downbeat ending.

TAKE A HARD RIDE
1975, 103 mins, US 🆅

D: Anthony M. Dawson [Antonio Margheriti] **A:** Jim Brown, Lee Van Cleef, Fred Williamson, Catherine Spaak, Jim Kelly, Barry Sullivan (20th Century-Fox)

Poly-formula period western dual-bill item. The script mixes several potboiler genres: Brown, gambler Fred Williamson, and mute Jim Kelly contribute black and karate elements; Lee Van Cleef provides menace as a callous bounty hunter; Catherine Spaak is briefly encountered and dropped on the trail, not before adding a Continental touch; crooked sheriff Barry Sullivan and Dana Andrews are in more conventional oater roles.

TAKE HER, SHE'S MINE
1963, 98 mins, US ▭

D: Henry Koster **A:** James Stewart, Sandra Dee, Audrey Meadows, Robert Morley, Philippe Forquet, John McGiver (20th Century-Fox)

The difficulty encountered by an older generation in comprehending the behavior of a younger generation is the business explored in this comedy. More specifically, the film explores one father's (James Stewart) trials and tribulations when he packs his precious daughter (Sandra Dee) off to college and observes, in long-distance dismay with an occasional globe-trot for closer inspection, her transition from adolescent to young woman.

TAKE ME OUT TO THE BALL GAME
(UK: EVERYBODY'S CHEERING)
1949, 83 mins, US 🆅 ⊙

D: Busby Berkeley **A:** Frank Sinatra, Esther Williams, Gene Kelly, Betty Garrett, Edward Arnold, Jules Munshin (M-G-M)

Backgrounded by an early-day baseball

yarn, pic is short on story but has some amusing moments—and Gene Kelly. Aided by Technicolor, Esther Williams is an eyeful, and Frank Sinatra cavorts pleasantly as shortstop Kelly's second baseman. Jules Munshin and Betty Garrett provide comedy relief, but the overall combination of talents is actually worthier of better material. There is no pretense that *Ball Game* is anything more than a romp for Kelly's virtuosity.

TAKE ME TO TOWN
1953, 80 mins, US
D: Douglas Sirk A: Ann Sheridan, Sterling Hayden, Philip Reed, Lee Patrick, Lee Aaker (Universal)

Ann Sheridan is a lady with a past, hiding out in a northwest lumber town. When the law gets close to her trail, she takes advantage of a proposition from three engaging young tykes who think she would make a good mother to look after them while their father (Sterling Hayden) is busy in the big timber. Papa gets wind of the situation from a jealous widow (Phyllis Stanley), who has set her own sights for him, and returns home. It doesn't take him long to see that his kids had the right idea. Since Sheridan is a saloon singer, there is ample reason for the sight values of the costumes she wears for display purposes.

TAKE THE HIGH GROUND
1953, 100 mins, US
D: Richard Brooks A: Richard Widmark, Karl Malden, Elaine Stewart, Russ Tamblyn, Steve Forrest (M-G-M)

Absorbing study of the training that makes tough, fighting GIs out of raw civilians has meticulous attention to detail and authenticity of incident. Richard Widmark comes over very strongly as the tough top sergeant. Karl Malden is the understanding sergeant, and he, too, gives the character life and feeling. Elaine Stewart is the mixed-up girl and, as the only credited femme in the cast, makes much of her part.
1953: Best Story & Screenplay

TAKE THE MONEY AND RUN
1969, 85 mins, US Ⓥ ⊙
D: Woody Allen A: Woody Allen, Janet Margolin, Marcel Hillaire, Jacquelyn Hyde (Palomar)

A few good laughs in an 85-minute film do not a comedy make. Woody Allen's *Take the Money and Run*, basically a running gag about hero Allen's ineptitude as a professional crook, scatters its

fire in so many directions that it has to hit at least several targets. But satire on documentary coverage of criminal flop is over-extended and eventually tiresome.

TAKING CARE OF BUSINESS (UK: FILOFAX)
1990, 103 mins, US Ⓥ ⊙
D: Arthur Hiller A: James Belushi, Charles Grodin, Anne DeSalvo, Loryn Locklin, Veronica Hamel, Hector Elizondo (Hollywood)

Brash Belushi and befuddled Grodin are perfect casting for yarn about a likable escaped con who assumes the identity of a stuffy, overworked ad agency exec. Though Belushi is set for release in days, he can't wait to see the World Series, so he escapes just as Grodin arrives in L.A. to pitch his agency to a Japanese tycoon. At the airport, Grodin loses his time-planning book—*Business* is one long commercial itself for a particular brand (Filofax, as pic is titled in the UK)—and Belushi finds it. Setting himself up in a Malibu mansion, Belushi proceeds to live Grodin's life just the opposite of how the businessman would do it.

TAKING OFF
1971, 92 mins, US Ⓥ
D: Milos Forman A: Lynn Carlin, Buck Henry, Linnea Heacock, Georgia Engel, Tony Harvey (Universal)

A very compassionate, very amusing contemporary comedy. The plot peg is the flight to Greenwich Village of Linnea Heacock, who's seeking something not provided in her home life. Lynn Carlin and Buck Henry (as the parents) enliven the many motivated and developing sequences: initial search for the girl; a large meeting of discarded parents where Vincent Schiavelli turns them all on to marijuana; and a funny strip poker game at home which ends abruptly when the runaway girl calmly appears from her bedroom.

TAKING OF PELHAM ONE TWO THREE, THE
1974, 10mins, US Ⓥ ⊙ ▭
D: Joseph Sargent A: Walter Matthau, Robert Shaw, Martin Balsam, Hector Elizondo, James Broderick (Palomar/Palladium)

Good action caper about a subway car heist under the streets of Manhattan. Walter Matthau heads the cast as a Transit Authority detective matching wits with the hijackers, headed by Robert Shaw. The major liability is a screenplay which develops little interest in either Matthau or Shaw's gang or in the innocent hostages.

TALENTED MR. RIPLEY, THE
1999, 139 mins, US Ⓥ ⊙
D: Anthony Minghella A: Matt Damon, Gwyneth Paltrow, Jude Law, Cate Blanchett, Philip Seymour Hoffman, Jack Davenport (Mirage/Timnick/Miramax/Paramount)

The Talented Mr. Ripley is an involving tale of intrigue and crime that loses its stride somewhat in the home stretch. This highly scenic adaptation of Patricia Highsmith's classic 1955 murder meller is splendidly served by a beautiful cast headed by Matt Damon, Gwyneth Paltrow, and Jude Law. Tom Ripley (Damon) is paid by shipbuilding tycoon Herbert Greenleaf (James Rebhorn) to fetch back his wastrel son, Dickie (Law). Ingratiating himself with Dickie and his beautiful writer girlfriend, Marge (Paltrow), Tom becomes a hanger-on in their idyllic seaside town south of Naples. On a boat ride, Tom finishes off the friend he has envied and obsessed over since he arrived in Italy. A new life opens up for him, one that includes trying to assume the identity (and bank account) of Dickie.
1999: Nominations: Best Supp. Actor (Jude Law), Adapted Screenplay, Art Direction, Costume Design, Original Score

TALE OF TWO CITIES, A
1936, 121 mins, US Ⓥ
D: Jack Conway A: Ronald Colman, Elizabeth Allan, Edna May Oliver, Reginald Owen, Basil Rathbone, Blanche Yurka (M-G-M)

A screen classic. The two yawning pitfalls of spectacle and dialogue have been adroitly evaded. The fall of the Bastille is breathtaking, but it is given no greater value than its influence on the plot warrants. The rabble at the guillotine is blood-chilling in its ferocity, but not for a moment does it overlie the principals, who are waiting in the shadow of the bloody platform for their turn to come. In the dialogue the lines are neither the often-stilted phrases of the book, nor yet the colloquial language of today. Ronald Colman makes his Carton one of the most pathetic figures in the screen catalog.
1936: Nominations: Best Picture, Editing

TALE OF TWO CITIES, A
1958, 117 mins, UK Ⓥ
D: Ralph Thomas A: Dirk Bogarde, Dorothy Tutin, Cecil Parker, Marie Versini, Stephen Murray (Rank)

Set against the Storming of the Bastille, Cities is primarily a character study of a frustrated young lawyer who fritters his life away in drink until the moment when he makes everything worthwhile by a supreme sacrifice for the girl he loves. Dirk Bogarde brings a lazy charm and nonchalance to the Sydney Carton role but tends to play in a surprisingly minor key throughout.

TALES AFTER THE RAIN
See: Ugetsu Monogatari

TALES FROM THE CRYPT PRESENTS DEMON KNIGHT
See: Demon Knight

TALES FROM THE DARKSIDE—THE MOVIE
1990, 93 mins, US Ⓥ ⊙
D: John Harrison A: Deborah Harry, Christian Slater, Rae Dawn Chong, James Remar, Steve Buscemi (Paramount)

Significantly gorier than its namesake television series, film has better production values. As Deborah Harry prepares to cook little boy Matthew Lawrence, he delays his fate by telling her a trio of horror stories. Most ambitious segment is last: artist James Remar witnessing a barman's extremely gory murder by a gargoyle come to life. To save his skin, he vows to the gargoyle not to tell anyone what happened, but 10 years later he spills the beans with tragic results.

TALES FROM THE HOOD
1995, 97 mins, US Ⓥ
D: Rusty Cundieff A: Clarence Williams III, Joe Torry, Wings Hauser, Anthony Griffith, Michael Massee, Tom Wright (40 Acres and a Mule/Savoy)

A smart and sassy horror anthology that mixes blunt shocks and sharp satire. As its title implies, pic is a clever commingling of elements from Boyz N the Hood and Tales from the Crypt. The filmmakers take dead-serious subjects—racism, child abuse, police brutality, gang violence—and lace them with dark comedy and supernatural horror. Result is a genre-bending pic that is fearsome and ferociously funny as well as socially conscious. The framing device for the four tales is a late-night visit by three street toughs (Joe Torry, De'Aundre Bonds, Samuel Monroe Jr.) to the inner-city funeral home of Mr. Simms (Clarence Williams III). While the hoods impatiently wait for the mortician to turn over a drug stash, Mr. Simms entertains them with spooky tales about his "clients." The second tale, the most discomforting, is about an abused youngster who claims a "monster" is responsible for his bruises. It turns out that the boy (well played by Brandon Hammond) and his helpless mother (Paula Jai Parker) are regularly victimized by the boy's brutal stepfather (David Alan Grier). Segment is quite simply one of the most terrifyingly realistic depictions of domestic violence ever seen in a feature film.

TALES OF BEATRIX POTTER (AKA: PETER RABBIT AND TALES OF BEATRIX POTTER)
1971, 90 mins, UK ⓥ

D: Reginald Mills A: Frederick Ashton, Alexander Grant, Ann Howard, Wayne Sleep, Michael Coleman (M-G-M/EMI)

The production partners conceived the happy notion of having Beatrix Potter's animals represented by members of the Royal Ballet, and the result is 90 minutes of style, fun, and enchantment. The episodes skip merrily along, the choreography by Frederick Ashton blends splendidly with Reginald Mills's direction, and John Lanchbery's bright—if tinkly—music has the right lilting note. But the whole might have fallen apart but for the lifelike masks designed by Rostislav Doboujinsky and Christine Edzard's gay costumes.

TALES OF HOFFMAN, THE
1951, 138 mins, UK ⓥ ⊙

D: Michael Powell, Emeric Pressburger A: Moira Shearer, Robert Rounseville, Robert Helpmann, Pamela Brown, Frederick Ashton, Leonide Massine (Archers/London)

The Jacques Offenbach fantasy opera has been transformed to the screen with great imagination and taste, with an unusual amount of inventiveness and effects, for a lush, resplendent production that's a treat to both eye and ear. Film is a brilliant integration of dance, story, and music. Fantastic nature of the story is highlighted by the excellent use of Technicolor. Prologue has Hoffman (Robert Rounseville) relating to a group of students "the three tales of my folly of love." One concerns the time, in Paris, when he fancied himself in love with Olympia (Moira Shearer). The second act, set in Venice, has Hoffman bewitched by a beautiful courtesan, Giulietta (Ludmilla Tcherina). The third act, set on a Grecian isle, has Hoffman in love with Antonia (Ann Ayars).

1951: **Nominations:** Color Costume Design, Color Art Direction

TALES OF MANHATTAN
1942, 117 mins, US

D: Julien Duvivier A: Charles Boyer, Rita Hayworth, Ginger Rogers, Henry Fonda, Charles Laughton, Edward G. Robinson (20th Century-Fox)

An expensive dress coat bears a curse, and the film recounts the fortunes and misfortunes of those who wear or come in possession of it. The coat was originally made for Charles Boyer, playing a Broadway matinee idol, and winds up on a scarecrow on a poor old Negro's farm.

TALES OF ORDINARY MADNESS
1981, 107 mins, ITALY ⓥ

D: Marco Ferreri A: Ben Gazzara, Ornella Muti, Susan Tyrrell, Tanya Lopert (23 Giugno/Ginis)

Marco Ferreri, the anarchically-inclined "Italo" filmmaker who has often delved into the human psyche in its mainly frustrated, exploited aspects in today's world, seems to have found a kindred spirit in the stories of the 1960s sub-culture writer-poet Charles Bukowski. Film is a distillation of Ferreri's themes. Ben Gazzara, in a knowing characterization of a poet (Charles), searches for the essence of love. He goes to L.A. to write, drink, and keep searching for women in an adventurous series of escapades reminiscent of Henry Miller but not as self-indulgent and with the notion of sex-for-its-own sake as the writings of Miller.

TALK OF THE TOWN
1942, 110 mins, US ⓥ ⊙

D: George Stevens A: Cary Grant, Jean Arthur, Ronald Colman, Edgar Buchanan, Rex Ingram (Columbia)

Cary Grant, the outspoken factory town soapbox "anti" worker, is being tried for arson and the death of factory foreman in the blaze. The case serves as a vehicle to introduce a pert schoolteacher (Jean Arthur) and a law school dean (Ronald Colman) in a procession of comedy dissertations on law, in both theory and practice. Plot has Grant escaping before his trial is completed and seeking refuge in the schoolmarm's home. Transition from serious or melodramatic to the slap-happy and humorous is sometimes a bit awkward, but in the main it is solid escapist comedy.

1942: **Nominations:** Best Picture, Original Story & Screenplay, B&W Cinematography, B&W Art Direction, Editing, Scoring of a Dramatic Picture

TALK RADIO
1988, 110 mins, US Ⓥ ⊙
D: Oliver Stone **A:** Eric Bogosian, Alec Baldwin, Ellen Greene, Leslie Hope, John C. McGinley (Cineplex Odeon/Ten Four)

Talk Radio casts a spotlight on the unpalatable underside of American public opinion and turns up an unlimited supply of anger, hatred, and resentment in the process. Most of the film unfolds in the studio of KGAB, a Dallas station from which the infamous Barry Champlain (Eric Bogosian) holds forth. Young, caustic, rude, insulting, grandstanding, flippant, and mercilessly cruel, the talk show host spews vitriol impartially on those of all races, colors, and creeds, and spares the feelings of no one. Bogosian commands attention in a patented tour de force.

TALL GUY, THE
1989, 92 mins, UK Ⓥ ⊙
D: Mel Smith **A:** Jeff Goldblum, Emma Thompson, Rowan Atkinson, Emil Wolk, Geraldine James (LWT/Virgin)

Cheery, ingratiating romantic comedy with Jeff Goldblum putting in a stellar performance as a bumbling American actor in London. The insecure goofball is earning a living but going nowhere fast when he comes under the care of hospital nurse Emma Thompson. Immediately smitten, Goldblum spends his time between weekly visits for injections and desperately concocting ways to ask her out. Throughout the entire film, the relationship evolves winningly, with so much believable give-and-take, mutual ribbing, and support that one roots for it heavily.

TALL IN THE SADDLE
1944, 84 mins, US Ⓥ ⊙
D: Edwin L. Marin **A:** John Wayne, Ella Raines, Audrey Long, George ''Gabby'' Hayes, Elisabeth Risdon (RKO)

Exciting and adventurous drama in the best western tradition. Story carries unusual twists. John Wayne shows up to take a job as a cow hand, only to find out his employer has been murdered. He refuses a position with Audrey Long, heiress at the ranch, and instead joins up with tempestuous Ella Raines, who operates an adjoining spread. Woman-hating Wayne is caught in the middle between the two girls while he gradually traces clues to the murder.

TALL MEN, THE
1955, 122 mins, US Ⓥ ⊠
D: Raoul Walsh **A:** Clark Gable, Jane Russell, Robert Ryan, Cameron Mitchell, Emile Meyer (20th Century-Fox)

Big, robust western that fills the wide screen with a succession of panoramic scenes of often incredible beauty. Story has brothers Clark Gable and Cameron Mitchell working for Robert Ryan, and they become partners driving a large herd of cattle from Texas to Montana. On the way north, the trio runs into Jane Russell. Gable seems to enjoy himself thoroughly. Russell goes through most of the film taunting both Gable and Ryan. It's probably only fair to assume that her pancake-flat acting is a secondary consideration.

TALL T, THE
1957, 78 mins, US Ⓥ
D: Budd Boetticher **A:** Randolph Scott, Richard Boone, Maureen O'Sullivan, Arthur Hunnicutt, Skip Homeier, Henry Silva (Columbia)

Unconventional western passes up most oater cliches. From a quiet start the yarn acquires a momentum that explodes in a stock climax. Modest and unassuming, Randolph Scott is a rancher who's been seized by a trio of killers led by Richard Boone. Also captured are newlyweds Maureen O'Sullivan and John Hubbard. Originally, the outlaws planned a stage robbery but are privately urged by the craven Hubbard to hold his heiress-wife for ransom in the hope that this move might save his skin. Scott impresses as the strong, silent type who ultimately vanquishes his captors.

TALL TALE
1995, 96 mins, US Ⓥ ⊠
D: Jeremiah Chechik **A:** Patrick Swayze, Oliver Platt, Roger Aaron Brown, Nick Stahl, Scott Glenn (Walt Disney/Caravan)

Lavishly produced, robustly entertaining Old West fantasy that is unlike anything else in recent memory. Pic is impressively larger than life, both in physical scale and heroic action. Nick Stahl is well cast as Daniel Hackett, a plucky young farm boy who takes off, hoping he can hide the deed to the family farm far from greedy land-grabbers. Magically, he meets Pecos Bill (Patrick Swayze), one of the many heroes in his father's tall tales. In the course of their travels, they rope logger Paul Bunyan (Oliver Platt) and steel driver John Henry (Roger Aaron

Brown) into their battle with the land-grabbers.

TAMARIND SEED, THE
1974, 123 mins, UK ⊗ ▱
D: Blake Edwards **A:** Julie Andrews, Omar Sharif, Anthony Quayle, Dan O'Herlihy, Sylvia Syms, Oscar Homolka (ITC/Jewel/Lorimar)

Some will see this as a love story against an espionage background, others as an excellent spy effort involving two people in love. Julie Andrews as a British civil servant on vacation in the Caribbean becomes fond of (but keeps at arm's length) a handsome Russian (Omar Sharif), also on leave. Sharif decides to defect. A major strong point of the film is the convincing performances of Andrews and Sharif as a pair of unlikely romantics.

TAMING OF THE SHREW, THE
1929, 63 mins, US ⊗
D: Sam Taylor **A:** Mary Pickford, Douglas Fairbanks, Edwin Maxwell, Joseph Cawthorn, Dorothy Jordan (United Artists)

Vastly extravagant burlesque of Shakespeare's best laugh, which the two leads often turn into a howl. Fairbanks and Pickford go to it knock-about. And Pickford takes the pratfalls. Fairbanks outlines a scheme when first meeting Katherine (Mary Pickford), the hell-raising daughter. He says, "Howdy, Kate." She says, "Katherine to you, mugg," or something near, and the warrior answers, "Kate, d'ya hear, plain Kate." Then to show her it stands, he and Katie roll down a flight of stairs.
1967: Nominations: Best Costume Design, Art Direction

TAMING OF THE SHREW, THE
1967, 122 mins, UK/Italy ⊗ ▱
D: Franco Zeffirelli **A:** Richard Burton, Elizabeth Taylor, Michael York, Michael Hordern, Cyril Cusack (Columbia/Royal Films International/F.A.I.)

Although version is a boisterous, often over-stagey frolic, it will strike many as a fair compromise between the original Shakespeare and, say, *Kiss Me Kate*. Screenwriters have done a neat job, infusing dialogue without rocking Bard's story overmuch. The two stars pack plenty of wallop, making their roles meaty and flamboyant.

TAMPOPO
1986, 114 mins, Japan ⊗ ⊙
D: Juzo Itami **A:** Ken Watanabe, Nobuko

Miyamoto, Tsutomu Yamazaki, Koji Yakusho, Rikiya Yasuoka (Itami)

Thoroughly offbeat but most enjoyable comedy on the subject of food. Main story line is pretty slight: a truck driver (Ken Watanabe) and his friend take pity on a pretty widow (Nobuko Miyamoto) who operates a rundown noodle shop, and undertake to teach her how to make her business a success. Along the way, Itami takes dozens of sidetracks, all of them on the theme of food. The viewer learns how to make noodle soup in three minutes flat and how to make the best turtle soup. This is a film that's as informative as it is funny.

TANGO & CASH
1989, 98 mins, US ⊗ ▱
D: Andrei Konchalovsky [Albert Magnoli] **A:** Sylvester Stallone, Kurt Russell, Teri Hatcher, Jack Palance, Michael J. Pollard (Guber-Peters/Warner)

Mindless buddy cop pic, loaded with nonstop action that's played mostly for laughs but delivers too few of them. Inane and formulaic, the film relies heavily on whatever chemistry it can generate between Sylvester Stallone and Kurt Russell, who repeatedly trade wisecracks while facing life-and-death situations. Jack Palance re-creates down to each gasp his role from *Batman* as a snarling crime boss.

TANG SHAN DAXIONG
(THE BIG BOSS; FISTS OF FURY)
1971, 100 mins, Hong Kong ⊗ ▱
D: Lo Wei **A:** Bruce Lee, Maria Yi, Nora Miao, James Tien, Han Ying-chieh (Golden Harvest)

Bruce Lee is compelled to avenge the deaths of friends and cousins who have been murdered for discovering that their employer traffics in drugs and prostitution. Despite the silly plot, dreadful supporting cast, and prim morality (or perhaps because of them), *Fists of Fury* is sometimes entertaining, with most of the credit due to Lee.

TANK
1984, 113 mins, US ⊗ ⊙
D: Marvin Chomsky **A:** James Garner, G. D. Spradlin, Shirley Jones, C. Thomas Howell (Lorimar)

The audience appeal of loners against corruption is here refashioned with the hero inside a marauding Sherman tank, taking on a maniacal southern sheriff in defense of integrity and family. James Garner's persona gives the events a soft, human, and at times bemused edge.

TANK GIRL

1995, 104 mins, US 🅥 ⊙

D: Rachel Talalay **A:** Lori Petty, Malcolm McDowell, Ice-T, Naomi Watts, Don Harvey (Trilogy/United Artists)

Coming to save the world in 2033 is that wild, wacky, and energetic Tank Girl. Film contains dazzling pyrotechnics, state-of-the-art makeup, a lavish song-and-dance production, nifty animation reflecting pic's comic book origins and a thumping rock soundtrack. What's missing from the mix is an engaging story to bind together its intriguing bits. And Lori Petty as Tank Girl, aka Rachel Buck, has the spunk but, sadly, not the heart of the post-apocalyptic heroine.

TAP

1989, 110 mins, US 🅥 ⊙

D: Nick Castle **A:** Gregory Hines, Suzzanne Douglas, Sammy Davis Jr., Savion Glover, Terrence McNally (Tri-Star)

Fim is a surprisingly rich and affecting blend of dance and story that transcends its respectful deference toward the great hoofers of a bygone era to deliver plenty of glowing contemporary entertainment. Gregory Hines plays Max, an ex-con torn between the high style and fast money of his former career as a jewel thief and the more deeply felt pleasures of tap dance. Trying to spark up an old romance with a dance teacher (Suzzanne Douglas), Max gets pulled into the world of the old-time hoofers who occupy the exalted third floor of a dance studio, a shabby shrine to the all-but-forgotten form.

TAPS

1981, 118 mins, US 🅥

D: Harold Becker **A:** George C. Scott, Timothy Hutton, Ronny Cox, Sean Penn, Tom Cruise (20th Century-Fox/Jaffe)

Portrait of military school education with a disturbing shoot-'em-up climax labors at an unbearably slow pace. Plot centers on a military academy whose students are angered that their school and its traditions are being sold out from under them in order to build condominiums. Timothy Hutton tries to lend some humanity to the headstrong cadet who leads his fellow students in forcibly taking over the school (weapons and all) in a last-ditch effort to save it, but he just appears too nice a guy.

TARANTULA

1955, 80 mins, US 🅥

D: William Alland **A:** John Agar, Mara

Corday, Leo G. Carroll, Nestor Paiva, Clint Eastwood (Universal)

A tarantula as big as a barn puts the horror into this well-made program science-fictioner, and it is quite credibly staged and played, bringing off the far-fetched premise with a maximum of believability. A tarantula injected with the yet unstabilized formula escapes and, while continuously increasing in size, starts living off cattle and humans.

TARAS BULBA

1962, 123 mins, US 🅥 ⊙ ▭

D: J. Lee Thompson **A:** Tony Curtis, Yul Brynner, Christine Kaufmann, Sam Wanamaker, Brad Dexter, Guy Rolfe (United Artists)

As powerful as they are, the spectacular features of *Taras Bulba* do not quite render palatable the wishy-washy subplot, seemingly devised to give Tony Curtis as much screen time as the far more colorful title role of Yul Brynner. Brynner's Taras Bulba is an arrogant, proud, physically powerful Cossack chief. The actor's allowed plenty of space in which to chew the scenery, and there's precious little of it in which he doesn't leave teethmarks. The battle sequences and, to a lesser extent, the Cossack camp scenes are the picture's greatest assets.

1962: Nomination: Best Original Music Score

TARGET

1985, 117 mins, US 🅥 ⊙

D: Arthur Penn **A:** Gene Hackman, Matt Dillon, Gayle Hunnicutt, Victoria Fyodorova, Josef Sommer (CBS)

Gene Hackman is a lumberyard owner in Dallas, and Matt Dillon is his sporty roughneck son. Mother Gayle Hunnicutt vacations in Paris alone because Hackman has an odd aversion to visiting Europe. While away, she hopes the two will make an effort to get to like each other. Then comes news that Mom has been kidnapped. Spy thriller is not only completely understandable and involving throughout, but also continually surprising along the way. It also strangely contains a few scenes of dreadful writing, acting, and direction.

TARGETS

1968, 90 mins, US 🅥

D: Peter Bogdanovich **A:** Boris Karloff, Tim O'Kelly, Nancy Hsueh, James Brown, Peter Bogdanovich (Saticoy)

A good programmer, within low-budget limitations, about a sniper and his innocent victims. A separate, concurrent subplot features Boris Karloff as a horror film star who feels he is washed up. Both plot lines converge in an exciting climax. Tim O'Kelly, a gun-loving, disturbed youth, hides in the screen tower of a drive-in theater, from which he terrorizes the audience. A press stunt has drawn Karloff to the theater for the climax.

TARNISHED ANGELS, THE
1957, 87 mins, US ▭
D: Douglas Sirk **A:** Rock Hudson, Robert Stack, Dorothy Malone, Jack Carson, Robert Middleton (Universal)

Based on William Faulkner's novel *Pylon*, screenplay carries an air circus setting. Rock Hudson is introduced as a seedy, but idealistic, New Orleans reporter covering a barnstorming show. He falls for Dorothy Malone, trick parachutist/wife of Robert Stack, speed flyer and World War I ace, still living in his past glory. Hudson appears in an unrealistic role to which he can add nothing, and Stack spends most of the time with eagles in his eyes.

TARNISHED LADY
1931, 80 mins, US
D: George Cukor **A:** Tallulah Bankhead, Clive Brook, Phoebe Foster, Alexander Kirkland, Osgood Perkins (Paramount)

This weepy and ragged meller about two society women, their lovers, and how all cross each other's paths has little outside its cast to recommend it. Tallulah Bankhead has personality, charm, and a voice loaded with s.a. Cast deports in a manner suggesting they were under orders to give way before Bankhead. Clive Brook slumps in trying to get over some of the silly dialogue. Phoebe Foster, in a totally unsympathetic role, gives an even performance.

TARZAN
1999, 88 mins, US Ⓥ ⊙
D: Kevin Lima, Chris Buck (Disney)

Disney's *Tarzan* swings, even if it doesn't always soar. Screenplay makes its obvious p.c. points right away, laying the groundwork for issues that will surface later, when Tarzan has to figure out whether he belongs among men or beasts. The tyke Tarzan neatly transforms into the ripply adult version (Tony Goldwyn) via one of Phil Collins's typically propulsive songs, in a show-off sequence in which Tarzan slips and slides through the jungle like a human roller coaster. Tone becomes more serious as a party of late-Victorian Brits begin teaching the deeply curious Tarzan about civilization, and the wild man senses that Jane (Minnie Driver), spirited daughter of nutty Professor Porter (Nigel Hawthorne), may be of interest to him in a way that no monkey ever has been. Voicings are first-class all round. Animation work is richly detailed and colorfully conceived.

1999: Original Song ("You'll Be in My Heart")

TARZAN AND HIS MATE
1934, 92 mins, US Ⓥ ⊙
D: Cedric Gibbons **A:** Johnny Weissmuller, Maureen O'Sullivan, Neil Hamilton, Paul Cavanagh (M-G-M)

Second of the Metro series with Johnny Weissmuller has a strange sort of power that overcomes its total lack of logic. The trouble starts as soon as the domain of Mr. and Mrs. Tarzan (Weissmuller and Maureen O'Sullivan) is trespassed upon by Neil Hamilton and Paul Cavanagh, a couple of heels from Mayfair. Boys are after a fortune in ivory which lies in a pachyderm graveyard.

TARZAN AND THE AMAZONS
1945, 76 mins, US
D: Kurt Neumann **A:** Johnny Weissmuller, Brenda Joyce, Johnny Sheffield, Henry Stephenson, Maria Ouspenskaya (Champion/RKO)

Story concerns Tarzan's efforts to keep faith with mysterious Palmyrians, whose valley hideout is populated only by women. Queen of the Amazons (Maria Ouspenskaya) trusts Tarzan (Johnny Weissmuller), knowing he will never reveal their secret. Unwittingly, the Tarzan household chimpanzee, Cheta, reveals to a group of Europeans that Palmyrians are somewhere in the neighborhood.

TARZAN AND THE GREAT RIVER
1967, 88 mins, US ▭
D: Robert Day **A:** Mike Henry, Jan Murray, Manuel Padilla Jr., Diana Millay, Rafer Johnson (Weintraub/Paramount)

Tarzan goes into upper reaches of the Amazon for his latest escapades, marking the first time that this location has been utilized for the Apeman series. Beautifully photographed, the production is strictly run-of-the-mill in story content and is often clumsily scripted. Mike Henry is the umpteenth thesp to portray the title character, doing well enough by the few demands of the role. In Rio de Janeiro, he's called upon to break an ancient killer cult which has been revived in the jungle by a vicious native leader (Rafer Johnson).

TARZAN AND THE GREEN GODDESS
1938, 72 mins, US
D: Edward Kull **A:** Herman Brix, Ula Holt, Frank Baker, Don Castello, Law Sargeant (Burroughs-Tarzan)

Herman Brix is at home in the Tarzan role, but even his robust endeavors fail to lift this production. The quest for a legendary "green goddess" that contains a valuable munitions formula rings in fights between natives, ambushes, captures, fist battles, and, as always, the colossal deeds of Tarzan. If he isn't able to defeat 12 men at a clip, it's an off day. Despite these episodes, told in old-time serial fashion, and a comparatively realistic storm at sea, this Tarzan story seldom impresses or even proves exciting.

TARZAN AND THE HUNTRESS
1947, 72 mins, US
D: Kurt Neumann **A:** Johnny Weissmuller, Brenda Joyce, Johnny Sheffield, Patricia Morison, Barton MacLane (Lesser/RKO)

Moderately entertaining adventure film. This time the Apeman flexes his muscles to repel the depredations of a zoological expedition that seeks to capture scores of animals for various zoos. Johnny Weissmuller's lines are confined to monosyllabic utterances, and his still-striking physique remains his top asset. Kurt Neumann could have directed at a faster pace.

TARZAN AND THE JUNGLE BOY
1968, 90 mins, US ▭
D: Robert Gordon **A:** Mike Henry, Rafer Johnson, Alizia Gur, Steve Bond, Ed Johnson (Banner/Paramount)

Tarzan is up to his customary brand of jungle antics in the latest entry in the Apeman series, which celebrates its 50th year on the screen. Lensed on location in South America, the production unspools along regulation lines for a fairly fast windup. Tarzan helps a female journalist (Alizia Gur) locate a supposed wild jungle boy (Ronald Gans), whose American father was drowned seven years before. The lad, then only about four, managed to survive. Search takes them into forbidden country.

TARZAN AND THE LEOPARD WOMAN
1946, 75 mins, US
D: Kurt Neumann **A:** Johnny Weissmuller, Brenda Joyce, Johnny Sheffield, Ac-

quanetta, Edgar Barrier (Lesser/RKO)

Tarzan is finally showing signs of age. This Tarzan film is bogged down by stock situations and unimaginative production and direction. The story has Tarzan out to break up a belligerent tribe of natives who dress up in leopard skins with iron claws—the situation found in quickie serials. Ape man dosen't give out with his famous call once during the picture. Brawny Johnny Weissmuller still makes a presentable Tarzan, but he, too, shows signs of age, with a growing waistline and a minimum of athletic antics.

TARZAN AND THE LOST SAFARI
1957, 80 mins, UK/US
D: H. Bruce Humberstone **A:** Gordon Scott, Robert Beatty, Yolande Donlan, Betta St. John, Wilfred Hyde White, George Coulouris (Croydon/Lesser)

Tarzan, perennial screen hero in black and white, takes to color and to authentic jungle backgrounds, and the antics come off entertainingly. Gordon Scott has the physique for the title role and does acceptably by it. The script finds the hero guiding a party of bored uppercrust socialites out of the jungle after their plane has crashed. To give the hero obstacles to overcome, plot introduces a hunter (Robert Beatty) who has a deal to turn over some white sacrifices to a native chief (Orlando Martins).

TARZAN AND THE MERMAIDS
1948, 68 mins, US
D: Robert Florey **A:** Johnny Weissmuller, Brenda Joyce, Linda Christian, John Laurenz, Fernando Wagner (Lesser/RKO)

Standard Johnny Weissmuller vehicle, produced in Mexico. This story is about a forbidden island where a white trader and his undercover cutthroat employ a fake tribal god to keep the natives subjugated in order to grab pearls. The crooks want Mara (Linda Christian) as a bride for this god, but she has other ideas. Tarzan fishes her out of the river accidentally and tells his wife (Brenda Joyce) he has bagged a mermaid. Tarzan ultimately unfrocks the phoney tribal priest and his helper.

TARZAN AND THE SHE-DEVIL
1953, 75 mins, US
D: Kurt Neumann **A:** Lex Barker, Joyce MacKenzie, Raymond Burr, Monique Van Vooren, Tom Conway (Lesser/RKO)

A much tamer Tarzan than heretofore results in this film being a tedious affair for a goodly portion of its 75 minutes.

Keeping the hero a tied-up captive for a long stretch wasn't hep scripting. Yarn pits Tarzan against a group of ivory thieves. Lex Barker looks like a Tarzan should, and consequently comes across okay in the lead, while Joyce MacKenzie is acceptable as his vis-à-vis. Raymond Burr is good as one of the heavies.

TARZAN AND THE SLAVE GIRL
1950, 74 mins, US
D: Lee Sholem A: Lex Barker, Vanessa Brown, Robert Alda, Denise Darcel, Hurd Hatfield, Arthur Shields (RKO/Lesser)

Lex Barker, as Tarzan, takes to the jungle on the trail of some female natives who are being held prisoner by a group of lost tribesmen. Vanessa Brown makes her bow in the Jane role and fills the bill on all counts.

TARZAN ESCAPES
1936, 90 mins, US Ⓥ
D: Richard Thorpe A: Johnny Weissmuller, Maureen O'Sullivan, John Buckler, Benita Hume, Herbert Mundin (M-G-M)

This plot permits Tarzan's idyllic romance with his mate (Maureen O'Sullivan) to be rudely interrupted by a couple of the missus' relatives from London. It so happens that their jungle guide is a dastardly rat who sees in Tarzan a cinch freak-show attraction for up north, and it takes not only Tarz himself but also a big zoo full of animal friends to clear up the mess, save the lives of the white folks, give the villain his just dues, and restore Tarzan's mate to Tarzan.

TARZAN FINDS A SON
1939, 81 mins, US Ⓥ
D: Richard Thorpe A: Johnny Weissmuller, Maureen O'Sullivan, Johnnie Sheffield, Ian Hunter, Laraine Day (M-G-M)

Tarzan Finds a Son carries more credulity and believable jungle adventure than the long list of preceding Tarzan features. Tarzan and the Missus save a baby in a plane that crashes in the jungle. Tarzan is proudly teaching his accepted son jungle lore, when a searching party arrives to establish the death of the baby, who has come into a heavy inheritance. Ian Hunter and Frieda Inescort are out to grab the inheritance for themselves and start plotting the death of Tarzan and the snatch of the youngster.

TARZAN GOES TO INDIA
1962, 88 mins, UK/US ▭
D: John Guillermin A: Jock Mahoney, Jai, Leo Gordon, Mark Dana, Simi (Weintraub/M-G-M)

Name's the same, but the character is counterfeit. Widespread appeal of the original primitive ape man will never be duplicated by his jet-age descendant, an articulate, subdued, businesslike troubleshooter in the jungles of the world. Still, the 36th in the venerable screen series that began in 1918, and the first to be endowed with CinemaScope, has a large-scale production sheen and exotic faraway flavor—it was filmed entirely in India. Loinclothed hero aids a young elephant boy in the rescue of a pack of pachyderms callously doomed to be submerged under the waters of a giant new jungle reservoir. Jock Mahoney is the best Tarzan in years.

TARZAN OF THE APES
1918, 130 mins, US Ⓥ
D: Scott Sidney A: Elmo Lincoln, Gordon Griffith, True Boardman, Colin Kenny, Enid Markey (National)

Occasional touches of the extraordinary are the film's greatest asset, and listed among these will have to be the work of Gordon Griffith as Tarzan as a 10-year-old boy. Lord and Lady Greystoke (True Boardman, Kathleen Kirkham) are in England in 1897. Greystoke is delegated to ferret out the inside of the slave trade. The final stage of his journey is on a sailing vessel. A mutiny is followed by the Greystokes' Robinson Crusoe existence; the birth of their child; the death of the parents, and the adoption of the baby by an ape. The film jumps 10 years. It is about equally divided between the development of the ape boy and the rearing of the son of the successor to the title in England. Then there is another leap, and Tarzan is 20. He has become King of the Apes, while in England the heir apparent is a dissipated youth. The ape family has been achieved by a flock of acrobats in skins and a number of closeups kill the illusion. Elmo Lincoln as Tarzan at 20 is all that could be asked for.

TARZAN'S DEADLY SILENCE
1970, 88 mins, US
D: Robert L. Friend A: Ron Ely, Jock Mahoney, Woody Strode, Manuel Padilla Jr., Gregorio Acosta

Old Tarzans don't disappear, they just end up in later Tarzan pix as villains. At least, that's the jump Jock Mahoney made from 1962's *Tarzan Goes to India* to this patchwork of three television shows, in which he plays a jungle dictator. Film painfully corroborates just how drab television techniques can be when subjected to the concentration level of a theater. Every action or piece of dialogue is redundantly reiterated (broadcast style) as the grenade-deafened Apeman (Ron Ely) attempts to escape from the evil "Colonel" (Mahoney).

TARZAN'S DESERT MYSTERY
1943, 70 mins, US
D: William Thiele **A:** Johnny Weissmuller, Nancy Kelly, Johnny Sheffield, Otto Kruger, Joe Sawyer (Lesser/RKO)

Tarzan's Desert Mystery doesn't miss a thing with its quota of Nazi agents and gruesome animals, plus the usual Tarzan jungle scenes. Tarzan (Johnny Weissmuller), Boy (Johnny Sheffield), and the chimp Cheta run into Connie Bryce (Nancy Kelly), an American vaudeville performer who is on her way to warn that Hendrix (Otto Kruger) and Karl (Joe Sawyer) are a couple of Nazi agents trying to stir up trouble. Things look tough for Tarzan and his crew when he is accused of stealing a stallion and Connie is framed on a murder charge.

TARZAN'S FIGHT FOR LIFE
1958, 86 mins, US
D: H. Bruce Humberstone **A:** Gordon Scott, Eve Brent, Rickie Sorensen, Jil Jarmyn, James Edwards, Woody Strode (Lesser/M-G-M)

This chapter has Tarzan involved with a medical outpost headed by Dr. Sturdy (Carl Benton Reid). The natives are wary of the scientific experiments, and their natural superstition is given an assist by witch doctor Futa (James Edwards). Gordon Scott again plays the title role and makes the athletic stunts believable and possible, and he also handles the few romantic scenes with Eve Brent with acceptable finesse.

TARZAN'S GREATEST ADVENTURE
1959, 90 mins, UK
D: John Guillermin **A:** Gordon Scott, Anthony Quayle, Sara Shane, Niall MacGinnis, Sean Connery (Solar)

Tarzan finally steps away from Hollywood's process screens to pound his chest amid authentic terrors in the heart of Africa. Tarzan (Gordon Scott) is a modern he-man, still adorned in loincloth but more conversational than Edgar Rice Burroughs pictured him. Scott puts little emotion into his greatest adventure, but, more than any-

thing else, he looks the part. Film's story line has Tarzan and another white man as mortal enemies. The antagonist (Anthony Quayle) is leading a five-member boat expedition to get rich in diamonds, and Tarzan, knowing of his bestial attitude, follows in hot pursuit.

TARZAN'S HIDDEN JUNGLE
1955, 72 mins, US
D: Harold Schuster **A:** Gordon Scott, Vera Miles, Peter Van Eyck, Jack Elam, Charles Fredericks (Lesser/RKO)

Stock entry in the Edgar Rice Burroughs Apeman marathon serves to introduce a new title hero. Gordon Scott is a well-muscled man but seldom convincing in the part. A pair of hunters (Jack Elam, Charles Fredericks), who have a contract to deliver fats, skins, heads, and ivory, are the heavies. Their purpose is to drive the vast number of animals out of this territory so they can slaughter them without fear of the natives. Tarzan defeats this intention.

TARZAN'S MAGIC FOUNTAIN
1949, 73 mins, US
D: Lee Sholem **A:** Lex Barker, Brenda Joyce, Albert Dekker, Evelyn Ankers, Charles Drake (Lesser/RKO)

The 10th screen Tarzan makes his appearance in the person of Lex Barker. A mythical fountain of youth is the springboard for adventure in this one. Plot has Tarzan rescuing an aviatrix (Evelyn Ankers) lost for 20 years in a mythical jungle valley where the residents never grow old. As important as the humans is the spotlighting of Cheta, the chimp, and her ape pal. For humor that jells, there's little that can match the human antics of the anthropoids.

TARZAN'S NEW YORK ADVENTURE
1942, 70 mins, US ⊘
D: Richard Thorpe **A:** Johnny Weissmuller, Maureen O'Sullivan, John Sheffield, Virginia Grey, Charles Bickford, Paul Kelly (M-G-M)

Like others in the series, this is in the groove for the juves and holds little for adults. Seventy minutes of jungle hoss opry is interspliced with Mr. and Mrs. Tarzan's adventures in New York regaining their adopted son, who was carried off by an unscrupulous hunter who figured he could clean up with the kid in a circus. All the situations are trite, even including Tarzan's 200-foot dive off the Brooklyn

Bridge to escape some cops who just don't understand the jungle man.

TARZAN'S PERIL
1951, 79 mins, US
D: Byron Haskin, Phil Brandon **A:** Lex Barker, Virginia Huston, George Macready, Douglas Fowley, Glenn Anders, Dorothy Dandridge (Lesser/RKO)

Lex Barker is a capable hero in the Tarzan character. He is called upon to mete out jungle justice to a gun runner who supplies forbidden weapons to a tribe of would-be warriors. Virginia Huston has only a few scenes as Tarzan's mate, Jane. There's more emphasis on Dorothy Dandridge, queen of a tribe that is saved by Tarzan from its warring rivals. George Macready is the able villain.

TARZAN'S REVENGE
1938, 70 mins, US ⓥ
D: D. Ross Lederman **A:** Glenn Morris, Eleanor Holm, George Barbier, C. Henry Gordon, George Meeker (Principal/20th Century-Fox)

Tarzan, Glenn Morris and the swimmer Eleanor Holm romp, swim, run, and swing through trees in another of Edgar Rice Burroughs's fables. Both human and animal dangers coat the action as it follows a safari across a part of Africa to the hidden mansion of a villainous king. Morris's feats on ropes between trees and elsewhere make him a highly acceptable Tarzan.

TARZAN'S SAVAGE FURY
1952, 81 mins, US
D: Cy Endfield **A:** Lex Barker, Dorothy Hart, Patric Knowles, Charles Korvin (Lesser/RKO)

Unexciting jungle heroics. Long-lived series introduces a sort of Tarzan Jr., in young Joey (Tommy Carlton), a jungle boy taken in by Tarzan and Jane (Lex Barker, Dorothy Hart). Moppet tags along when the jungle lord leads a party into dangerous country on a diamond hunt. Tarzan has been sold a bill of goods that the diamonds are for England's war industry.

TARZAN'S SECRET TREASURE
1941, 82 mins, US
D: Richard Thorpe **A:** Johnny Weissmuller, Maureen O'Sullivan, Johnny Sheffield, Reginald Owen, Barry Fitzgerald, Tom Conway (M-G-M)

Par entry in the series. The secret treasure turns out to be gold, which is plentiful among the rocks where the Tarzan group lives. After Tarzan saves a band of ex-

plorers and scientists from the nearby savage tribe, greedy members of the band figure to move in on the golden hill. Picture swings into straight meller for the second half, with several sequences devoted to Tarzan's miraculous escapes from death. Weissmuller adequately handles the Tarzan role in his usual style.

TARZAN'S THREE CHALLENGES
1963, 92 mins, UK/US ▭
D: Robert Day **A:** Jock Mahoney, Woody Strode, Tsuruko Kobayashi, Earl Cameron, Jimmy Jamal (Weintraub/M-G-M)

In an effort to prevent Tarzan from becoming a ludicrous anachronism, creative unit has gradually converted the character to a globe-trotting troubleshooter. Tarzan is a man without a country and with only a shred of his former personality. In *Tarzan's Three Challenges*, he has been transplanted to Thailand to escort a young spiritual heir (Ricki Der) from a monastery to his rightful throne at the head of an ancient land. To protect his charge, Tarzan must ward off the challenge of the brother of the dying ruler. Woody Strode is most impressive as the antagonist.

TARZAN THE APE MAN
1932, 70 mins, US ⓥ
D: W. S. Van Dyke **A:** Johnny Weissmuller, Maureen O'Sullivan, Neil Hamilton, C. Aubrey Smith, Doris Lloyd (M-G-M)

A jungle and stunt picture, done in deluxe style, with tricky handling of fantastic atmosphere and a fine, artless performance by the Olympic athlete that represents the absolute best that could be done with the character. Footage is loaded with a wealth of sensational wild animal stuff. Tarzan (Johnny Weissmuller) is pictured as achieving impossible feats of strength and daring. Story is slight. An English trader (C. Aubrey Smith) and his young partner (Neil Hamilton) are about to start in search of the traditional elephants' graveyard where ivory abounds, when the elder man's daughter from England (Maureen O'Sullivan) insists upon going along. The adventures grow out of their travels.

TARZAN, THE APE MAN
1959, 82 mins, US
D: Joseph Newman **A:** Denny Miller, Cesare Danova, Robert Douglas, Joanna Barnes (M-G-M)

Metro has remade its 1932 hit and the story is even more implausible than it was

27 years earlier. Tarzan meets Jane and ultimately takes her as his wife. It's quite a feat, considering that he's unable to mutter even "Me Tarzan!" There will be snickers when Jane, the rapacious but gentle Englishwoman, gives up the riches of ivory to spend her life in a paradise of crocodiles. But the adventure along the way is furious enough to result in an entertaining film. Denny Miller is able to get by without revealing whether or not he is as strong an actor as he is a tree-swinger. Joanna Barnes makes a fetching Jane.

TARZAN
THE APE MAN
1981, 112 mins, US Ⓥ ⊙
D: John Derek **A:** Bo Derek, Richard Harris, John Phillip Law, Miles O'Keeffe, Wilfrid Hyde White (M-G-M/Svengali)

This endless romp through the jungle, which lacks any focus, fun, or excitement (sexual or otherwise), seems to exist merely as a reason for husband John to find another 1,001 ways to photograph wife Bo in varying stages of undress. The Derek version has less to do with the jungle man (who doesn't show his face until halfway through the picture) than it does in dealing with Jane's (Bo's) rediscovery of her long-lost explorer father Richard Harris. The father-daughter relationship doesn't have a chance here with Bo's wooden recitation of her lines and Harris's ranting through any number of dreary, confusing speeches.

TARZAN THE FEARLESS
1933, 60 mins, US Ⓥ
D: Robert Hill, William Lord Wright **A:** Buster Crabbe, Jacqueline Wells, E. Alyn Warren, Edward Woods, Mischa Auer (Lesser/Principal)

Episode is loaded with shots clipped from hunt films and burdened with forced situations and yard after yard of Buster Crabbe doing his daily dozen in the jungle gym. Plot concerns Tarzan's interest in the daughter (Jacqueline Wells) of a scientist (E. Alyn Warren), who is looking for the people of Zar and is made prisoner. His safari is guided by a couple of scoundrels who are after the emeralds which tradition ascribes to Zar. Story is haltingly told in poor dialogue and no one in the cast gets a chance with the material at hand.

TARZAN THE MAGNIFICENT
1960, 82 mins, UK/US
D: Robert Day **A:** Gordon Scott, Jock Mahoney, Betta St. John, John Carradine, Lionel Jeffries, Alexander Stewart (Weintraub/Paramount)

A rather glum, unexciting version of the ape man in a slow-moving picture. Film concerns Tarzan's efforts to bring a criminal to justice through treacherous jungle terrain, pursued by the criminal's evil family and slowed up by the haggling of his own entourage, which includes a cowardly Britisher (Lionel Jeffries), whose unstable wife (Betta St. John) is sexually attracted to the captive. Only briefly, near the climax, does the reckless, tree-swinging Tarzan of old emerge. Gordon Scott, as Tarzan, seems uncomfortable in the role and brings it little more than an ample physique.

TARZAN TRIUMPHS
1943, 76 mins, US
D: William Thiele **A:** Johnny Weissmuller, Johnny Sheffield, Frances Gifford, Stanley Ridges, Sig Ruman (Principal/RKO)

Virtually all jungle stuff, *Tarzan Triumphs* has a good portion of stock animal shots and includes a hidden city for convenient takeover by a squad of Nazi paratroopers and a subsequent battle in which Tarzan, with the aid of the subjugated natives, knocks off the invaders and restores peace in the jungle territory. Weissmuller and Sheffield run around as usual without the necessity of displaying much acting ability.

TASK FORCE
1949, 116 mins, US Ⓥ
D: Delmer Daves **A:** Gary Cooper, Jane Wyatt, Wayne Morris, Walter Brennan, Julie London (Warner)

Task Force glorifies the birth and development of the American aircraft carrier, up to the part it played in World War II. This is a story about a handful of naval air heroes who, in the early 1920s, seek to assert naval air power but are stymied for years by Washington politics and navy protocol. Cooper is forthright as the naval hero, and Jane Wyatt is properly sacrificing as his wife.

TASTE OF HONEY, A
1961, 100 mins, UK Ⓥ
D: Tony Richardson **A:** Dora Bryan, Rita Tushingham, Robert Stephens, Murray Melvin (Woodfall)

Yarn primarily concerns five people and their dreams, hopes, and fears. They are Jo (Rita Tushingham); her flighty, sluttish, neglectful mother; the fancy man her mother marries; a young African-American ship's cook with whom Jo has a brief affair which leaves her pregnant; and a sensitive young homosexual who gives her the tenderness and affection lacking in her relationship with her mother. Film introduces 19-year-old Rita Tushingham as the 16-year-old schoolgirl. She plays with no makeup, her hair is untidy, and her profile is completely wrong by all accepted standards; but her expressive eyes and her warm, wry smile are haunting.

TASTE THE BLOOD OF DRACULA
1970, 95 mins, UK Ⓥ
D: Peter Sasdy **A:** Christopher Lee, Geoffrey Keen, Gwen Watford, Linda Hayden, Peter Sallis (Hammer)

Three old buffers, sated by their dingy little orgies in the East End, get entangled with one of Dracula's disciples and, with the aid of the blood of Dracula and some of his ''props,'' they start to dabble in Black Masses and Satanic rituals. They bump off Dracula's messenger in terror, and Dracula swears to dispose of the three men.

TATTOO
1981, 102 mins, US Ⓥ
D: Bob Brooks **A:** Bruce Dern, Maud Adams, Leonard Frey, Rikke Borge, John Getz (Levine)

Bruce Dern appears as a congenital cuckoo, who loves to put permanent pictures on people's bodies. Becoming enamored of fashion model Maud Adams, Dern decides she could be life's perfect companion, given a new paint job. So he kidnaps her.

TAXI!
1932, 70 mins, US
D: Roy Del Ruth **A:** James Cagney, Loretta Young, George E. Stone, Guy Kibbee, Dorothy Burgess (Warner)

An hour's entertainment for the boys in the established golden-hearted hoodlum manner of James Cagney. Foundation of the tale is the strife of the independent taxi owner whom the syndicates run off the most desirable corner stands. The dialogue is distinctly in the vernacular of the characters. Director Roy Del Ruth has given it pace, and Cagney jauntily carries the major burden.

TAXI DRIVER
1976, 113 mins, US Ⓥ ⊙
D: Martin Scorsese **A:** Robert De Niro, Cybill Shepherd, Peter Boyle, Albert Brooks, Harvey Keitel (Columbia)

Paul Schrader's original screenplay is a sociological horror story. Take a young veteran like Travis Bickle. A night cabbie, he prowls the New York streets until dawn, killing off-duty time in porno theaters. What prods Travis are a series of rejections, most notably by Cybill Shepherd and Jodie Foster, a teenage prostitute. In a climactic sequence, the madman exorcises himself. It's a brutal, horrendous, and cinematically brilliant sequence, capped by the irony that he becomes a media hero for a day. De Niro gives the role the precise blend of awkwardness, naivete, and latent violence. The pic has a quasi-documentary look, and Bernard Herrmann's final score is superb.
1976: Nominations: Best Picture, Actor (Robert De Niro), Supp. Actress (Jodie Foster), Original Score

TAXING WOMAN, A
See: Marusa No Onna

TAZA, SON OF COCHISE
1954, 79 mins, US
D: Douglas Sirk **A:** Rock Hudson, Barbara Rush, Gregg Palmer, Bart Roberts, Morris Ankrum (Universal)

Colorful 3-D Indian–US Cavalry entry alternating between hot action and passages of almost pastoral quality. This is the story of the great Apache chief's son, who promises at his father's deathbed that he will try to keep the peace. He is opposed here by his younger brother, who attempts to win the tribe over to Geronimo and take to the warpath again. Rock Hudson suffices in the action demands of his role of Taza, but his character is none too believable.

TEA AND SYMPATHY
1956, 122 mins, US Ⓥ ▭
D: Vincente Minnelli **A:** Deborah Kerr, John Kerr, Leif Erickson, Edward Andrews, Darryl Hickman (M-G-M)

This is the story of a youngster regarded by fellow students as ''not regular'' (i.e., not manly). The spotlight is on clearly implied homosexuality. The part is played with marked credibility by John Kerr. The housemaster's wife is a character study of equal sensitivity and depth. Deborah Kerr gives the role all it deserves.

TEACHERS
1984, 106 mins, US Ⓥ ⊙
D: Arthur Hiller **A:** Nick Nolte, JoBeth Williams, Judd Hirsch, Ralph Macchio,

Lee Grant, Richard Mulligan (United Artists)

Nick Nolte stars as a burned-out teacher who's drawn back to his ideals. Pic makes stinging, important points about the mess of secondary public education, but those points are diluted gradually by an overload of comic absurdity. Catalyst to this dark comedy is a lawsuit brought against the school district for awarding a diploma to a student who can't read or write. Nolte nicely captures the image of a rather shaggy 10-year veteran of the classroom.

TEACHER'S PET
1958, 120 mins, US ⊙
D: George Seaton A: Clark Gable, Doris Day, Gig Young, Mamie Van Doren, Nick Adams (Perlsea/Paramount)

There is rich new life and liveliness, and even a fresh approach with humor and heartiness, in Fay and Michael Kanin's original screenplay. Clark Gable is one of those crusty, old-line newspapermen who believes that nothing good comes out of schools of journalism. Invited to lecture by journalism professor Doris Day, he discovers that his ideas about female professors were wrong. For various reasons he must pretend he is not a city editor but a pupil. Gable frankly mugs through many of his comedy scenes, and it is effective low comedy. Day is as bright and fresh as a newly set stick of type.
1958: Nominations: Best Supp. Actor (Gig Young), Original Story & Screenplay

TEA FOR TWO
1950, 97 mins, US ⊙
D: David Butler A: Doris Day, Gordon MacRae, Gene Nelson, Eve Arden, Billy De Wolfe, S. Z. Sakall (Warner)

A generous sprinkling of songs, dances, and comedy makes *Tea for Two* beguiling musical nonsense. It wears its Technicolor dress well, the nostalgic numbers from the 1929 *No, No, Nanette* and other cleffing of the period listen well; the pacing is smooth and the cast able.

TEAHOUSE OF THE AUGUST MOON, THE
1956, 123 mins, US ⊙ ▭
D: Daniel Mann A: Marlon Brando, Glenn Ford, Machiko Kyo, Eddie Albert, Paul Ford, Harry Morgan (M-G-M)

Teahouse retains the basic appeal that made it a unique war novel and a legit hit. There is some added slapstick for those who prefer their comedy broader. The film unspools the tribulations of Ford, the young army officer assigned to bring the benefits of democracy and free enterprise to the little Okinawan town of Tobiki. The role represents a romp for Glenn Ford, who gives it an unrestrained portrayal that adds mightily to the laughs. Brando is excellent as the interpreter, limning the roguish character perfectly. Physically, however, he seems a bit too heavy for the role.

TED AND VENUS
1991, 100 mins, US ⊙
D: Bud Cort A: Bud Cort, Jim Brolin, Kim Adams, Carol Kane, Pamella D'Pella (Gondola/LA Dreams)

Bud Cort stars as Ted Whitley, a 35-year-old hippie on disability. A virginal, pathetically earnest nerd, Ted has a vision of a gorgeous young lady emerging from the sea, and when she turns out to be Linda (Kim Adams), the community service worker helping him find an apartment, he feels compelled to pursue her. Ted begins a romantic campaign that quickly degenerates into obscene phone calls and other antisocial acts. Aside from telling an actively off-putting story, Cort the director hasn't done a bad job of putting it up on the screen.

TEENAGE MUTANT NINJA TURTLES
1990, 93 mins, US ⊙ ⊙
D: Steve Barron A: Judith Hoag, Elias Koteas, Raymond Serra, Michael Turney, James Saito (Golden Harvest/Limelight)

Wacky live-action screen version of the cartoon characters scores with its generally engaging tongue-in-cheek humor. Supposedly mutated by radioactive goop, the turtles live in the sewers, eat pizza, dance to rock music, play Trivial Pursuit, and casually toss around such words as "awesome," "bodacious," and "gnarly." The screenplay makes all four of the green guys seem like clones, differentiated mostly by their variegated colored headbands. The martial-arts setpieces are amusingly outlandish, with the screen populated by hordes of attackers whom the nonchalant, graceful turtles have little trouble vanquishing as they toss off streams of surfer-lingo wisecracks.

TEENAGE MUTANT NINJA TURTLES II: THE SECRET OF THE OOZE
1991, 88 mins, US ⊙ ⊙
D: Michael Pressman A: Paige Turco, Da-

vid Warner, Michelan Sisti, Leif Tilden, Kenn Troum (Golden Harvest/Propper)

Although *Turtles II* suffers from a lack of novelty and an aimless screenplay, the bottom line is that the pic won't disappoint its core subteen audience. It gives more footage to Michelangelo, Donatello, Raphael, Leonardo, and their giant rat master Splinter than the original did, and adds two hilarious childlike monsters, Rahzar and Tokka, who virtually steal the show.

TEENAGE MUTANT NINJA TURTLES III: THE TURTLES ARE BACK . . . IN TIME
1993, 95 mins, US Ⓥ ⊙
D: Stuart Gillard **A:** Elias Koteas, Paige Turco, Stuart Wilson, Vivian Wu, Sab Shimono (Golden Harvest)

Bow-wow-abunga! Third installment is a decided case of diminishing returns. On a story and craft level, it borders on the unforgivably bad. The new installment is a time-travel yarn in which the four amphibian heroes and their pal, reporter April O'Neill (Paige Turco), switch places with five 17th-century samurai warriors. Writer-director Stuart Gillard inappropriately paces the action at tortoise speed.

TEEN AGENT
See: If Looks Could Kill

TEEN WOLF
1985, 91 mins, US Ⓥ ⊙
D: Rod Daniel **A:** Michael J. Fox, James Hampton, Scott Paulin, Susan Ursitti, Jerry Levine (Wolfkill/Atlantic)

Lightweight item is innocuous and well intentioned but terribly feeble. The Beacontown Beavers have the most pathetic basketball team in high school history, and pint-sized Michael J. Fox is on the verge of quitting when he notices certain biological changes taking place. Instead of turning into a horrific teen werewolf, however, Fox takes to trucking around school halls in full furry regalia, becoming more successful with the ladies and, most important, winning basketball games.

TELEFON
1977, 103 mins, US Ⓥ
D: Don Siegel **A:** Charles Bronson, Lee Remick, Tyne Daly, Donald Pleasence, Alan Badel, Sheree North (M-G-M)

Pleasant escapism stars Charles Bronson and Lee Remick as two spies trying to stop a diehard Stalinist (Donald Pleasence) from upsetting detente by triggering a war between the US and USSR. Tyne Daly is notable as a CIA staffer. Remick's

teaming with Bronson is a graceful one for both players.

TELL ME LIES A FILM ABOUT LONDON
1968, 118 mins, UK/US
D: Peter Brook **A:** Mark Jones, Pauline Munro, Robert Lloyd, Glenda Jackson, Paul Scofield, Kingsley Amis (Ronorus)

Tell Me Lies depicts a wide range of attitudes toward the war in Vietnam. While Peter Brook's emotional concern about the war seems unquestionable, his artistic sincerity is open to examination. Color and black-and-white footage is haphazardly alternated to no effect. Musical numbers are shouted-sung in a cacophonic manner that only underscores the lyrics' vacuity. Staged discussions are juxtaposed with cinema-verite encounters with British parliamentarians, Maoists, and blackpower advocate Stokeley Carmichael.

TELL ME THAT YOU LOVE ME, JUNIE MOON
1970, 112 mins, US
D: Otto Preminger **A:** Liza Minnelli, Ken Howard, Robert Moore, James Coco, Kay Thompson, Ben Piazza (Paramount)

This tale of a trio of handicapped, scarred, emotionally and psychologically marred humans is given a somewhat bland mounting and misses the poetics inherent in the tale. Liza Minnelli is Junie Moon, who has had acid poured over her face and arm by a perverted date. Robert Moore is a young man brought up by a queer (Leonard Frey) and wounded in an accident. Ken Howard had been sent to homes as retarded. They decide to live together. Moore is the brains; Minnelli, the heart and spunk; and Howard, the apparent breadwinner.

TELL THEM WILLIE BOY IS HERE
1969, 97 mins, US Ⓥ ▭
D: Abraham Polonsky **A:** Robert Redford, Katharine Ross, Robert Blake, Susan Clark, Barry Sullivan, John Vernon (Universal)

A powerful unfolding of an incident in US history, the film becomes, by extension, a deeply personal and radical vision of the past and future. Film tells the story of the tracking-down of a renegade Indian in California in 1909. Although Robert Blake is the title character, the film is really about Robert Redford, the deputy sheriff whose assignment is to track down Willie. Redford's presence is magnificent, always suggesting the classically structured, powerful-but-weak American.

TEMP, THE
1993, 95 mins, US Ⓥ ⊙
D: Tom Holland **A:** Timothy Hutton, Lara Flynn Boyle, Dwight Schultz, Oliver Platt, Faye Dunaway (Columbus Circle)

Moronic, derivative, artificial, and pointless are just the first adjectives that come to mind to describe this concoction. Lara Flynn Boyle temps for Timothy Hutton, a junior executive at a baked goods firm in Portland, run by the sleekly ruthless Faye Dunaway. Job uncertainty pits worker against worker, but provides room for Boyle to slither up the corporate ladder through stealth and, depending upon what you choose to believe, murder.

TEMPEST, THE
1979, 96 mins, UK Ⓥ
D: Derek Jarman **A:** Heathcote Williams, Karl Johnson, Toyah Wilcox, Elisabeth Welch (Boyd's)

Derek Jarman's film version of Shakespeare's most fanciful play is definitely one of a kind. Its greatest strength is its look, which offsets the director-adaptor's generally limp control of the narrative. Although heavily cut and reorganized, the Bard's lines are used virtually throughout. The plot remains intact. The most successful innovation is Toyah Wilcox's assault on the usually vacuous role of Miranda. Her reaction to the first eligible male she has ever seen is more lusty than wide-eyed, and thoroughly believable.

TEMPTATION
1946, 98 mins, US
D: Irving Pichel **A:** Merle Oberon, George Brent, Charles Korvin, Paul Lukas, Lenore Ulric, Ludwig Stossel (Universal)

Production is well stacked with solid values in every department except for the screenplay. Story is located in Egypt, where George Brent, newly married to Merle Oberon, is engaged in a British museum expedition. Overcome by boredom while her husband is out digging for a mummy, Oberon gets mixed up with an Egyptian dandy. Oberon in the role of the femme fatale scores a personal triumph. Her two male vis-à-vis register less successfully. Brent walks through his part with a wooden gait and frozen expression. Charles Korvin, as the Egyptian roué, lacks the polish and assurance for his role.

TEMPTRESS, THE
1926, 95 mins, US ⊗
D: Fred Niblo **A:** Greta Garbo, Antonio Moreno, Roy D'Arcy, Marc MacDermott, Lionel Barrymore, Virginia Brown Faire (Cosmopolitan/M-G-M)

A sumptuously produced picture, one unbroken succession of pictorial surprises in beauty. This flawlessness is unfortunately not matched by selection of story or star. Greta Garbo is scarcely the screen type of aggressive vitality the character demands. The story starts at a masquerade ball in Paris. Elena, unhappy wife of a Paris fop, and Robledo, Spanish engineer on leave from the Argentine, meet and fall in love, with Elena vowing she is free. When her married state is disclosed, Robledo breaks away, returning to South America. Thither Elena follows with her husband.

TEMPTRESS MOON
See: Feng Yue

10
1979, 122 mins, US Ⓥ ⊙ ▭
D: Blake Edwards **A:** Dudley Moore, Julie Andrews, Bo Derek, Robert Webber, Brian Dennehy, Dee Wallace (Orion/Geoffrey)

Blake Edwards's *10* is a shrewdly observed and beautifully executed comedy of manners and morals. Frustrated in his song writing and in his relationship with g.f. Julie Andrews, diminutive Dudley Moore decides to pursue the vision incarnated by Bo Derek despite that she's on her honeymoon with a jock type twice Moore's size.

1979: Nominations: Best Original Score, Song ("It's Easy to Say")

TENANT, THE
1976, 125 mins, France Ⓥ
D: Roman Polanski **A:** Roman Polanski, Isabelle Adjani, Melvyn Douglas, Jo Van Fleet, Bernard Fresson, Lila Kedrova (Marianne)

A tale of a paranoid breakdown of a little bureaucratic clerk that wastes no time in trying to be clinical. Director Roman Polanski plays the little man himself, who goes to look at an apartment. The girl who has it threw herself out the window. He is told he may have it if she does not come back. Polanski calls the hospital and learns that the girl is dead. He moves in, but mysterious things begin to happen.

TEN COMMANDMENTS, THE
See: Dekalog

TEN COMMANDMENTS, THE
1923, 160 mins, US ⓥ ⊗
D: Cecil B. DeMille **A:** Theodore Roberts, Charles De Roche, Estelle Taylor, Richard Dix, Rod La Rocque, Edythe Chapman (Paramount)

The biblical scenes of *The Ten Commandments* are irresistible in their assembly, breadth, color, and direction. This section is in color, and the big scenes are immense and stupendous, so big that the modern tale after that seems puny. The story is of two sons, one his mother's boy and the other an atheist. Cheating as a contractor, the atheist's defects in building material result in the collapse of church wall, with the mother killed by the falling debris. The best performance is given by Rod La Rocque as the atheist son. Theodore Roberts as Moses is but required to stride majestically, something he can do perhaps a little better than any one else.

TEN COMMANDMENTS, THE
1956, 219 mins, US ⓥ ⊙
D: Cecil B. DeMille **A:** Charlton Heston, Yul Brynner, Anne Baxter, Edward G. Robinson, Yvonne De Carlo, Debra Paget (Paramount)

Twenty-five thousand extras were employed on Cecil B. DeMille's superspectacular about the Children of Israel held in brutal bondage. Moses, prodded by the God of Abraham, delivers them from Egyptian bondage. The eyes of the audience are filled with amazing visuals, but emotional tug is sometimes lacking. More than two hours pass before the intermission, and the break is desperately welcome. Scenes of the greatness that was Egypt, and Hebrews by the thousands under the whip of taskmasters, are striking. But bigness wearies. There's simply too much. Performances meet requirements all the way, except for Anne Baxter, who leans close to old-school siren histrionics as the Egyptian princess Nefretiri.
1956: Best Special Effects
Nominations: Best Picture, Color Cinematography, Color Costume Design, Color Art Direction, Editing, Sound

TEN DAYS THAT SHOOK THE WORLD
See: Oktyabr

TENDER COMRADE
1943, 103 mins, US ⓥ
D: Edward Dmytryk **A:** Ginger Rogers, Robert Ryan, Ruth Hussey, Patricia Collinge, Mady Christians, Kim Hunter (RKO)

Centered around five women, all of whom have men in the armed services, Tender Comrade is a preachment for all that democracy stands for. The emotional impact is sometimes achieved with what may seem to be overdone dramatics. Ginger Rogers gives an unrestrained performance throughout. Ruth Hussey, Kim Hunter, and Patricia Collinge also give excellent portrayals. Dalton Trumbo contributes a screenplay replete with excellent dialogue.

TENDER IS THE NIGHT
1962, 146 mins, US ▱
D: Henry King **A:** Jennifer Jones, Jason Robards, Joan Fontaine, Tom Ewell, Cesare Danova, Jill St. John (20th Century-Fox)

This may not be a 100 proof distillation of F. Scott Fitzgerald, but *Tender Is the Night* is nonetheless on its own filmic terms a thoughtful, disturbing, and at times absorbing romantic drama. It depicts the deterioration of a brilliant and idealistic psychiatrist (Jason Robards), whose love for and marriage to a wealthy patient (Jennifer Jones) ultimately consumes and destroys him by engulfing him in the glamorous leisure of upper-class Americans adrift in Europe in the prosperous 1920s. Jones creates a striking character as the schizophrenic Nicole, and Robards plays with intelligence and conviction. Joan Fontaine is convincing as Nicole's shallow, older sister.
1962: Nomination: Best Song ("Tender Is the Night")

TENDER MERCIES
1983, 89 mins, US/UK ⓥ ⊙
D: Bruce Beresford **A:** Robert Duvall, Tess Harper, Allan Hubbard, Betty Buckley, Ellen Barkin, Wilford Brimley (Antron Media/EMI)

Tender Mercies is, in the best sense, an old-fashioned film. There's no sex, no violence. Robert Duvall is Mac Sledge, a down-and-out ex–country and western singer on the skids since his marriage broke up. Out on a drunken binge one night, he winds up in a small motel in Texas prairie country and accepts an offer of work from Rosa Lee (Tess Harper), the young widow who runs the place. Sledge stays on and the couple fall in love and marry. When tragedy unexpectedly touches his life, he finds he now has the strength to go on and achieves new peace of mind.

1983: Best Actor (Robert Duvall), Original Screenplay
Nominations: Best Picture, Director, Original Song ("Over You")

TENDER TRAP, THE
1955, 110 mins, US ⓥ ⊙ ▭
D: Charles Walters A: Frank Sinatra, Debbie Reynolds, David Wayne, Celeste Holm, Lola Albright, Carolyn Jones (M-G-M)

This is a fairly diverting, but considerably overlong, takeoff on the romantic didoes of bachelors and gals. Into the lives of Frank Sinatra—bachelor theatrical agent—and David Wayne—his married friend from Indiana—enters Debbie Reynolds, a determined girl who already has set the date for her wedding even without having found the right man. She decides Sinatra is it. Remainder of the footage details his capture. The title tune gets some consistent plugging in the film.
1955: Nomination: Best Song ("(Love Is) the Tender Trap")

TEN GENTLEMEN FROM WEST POINT
1942, 104 mins, US ⓥ
D: Henry Hathaway A: George Montgomery, Maureen O'Hara, John Sutton, Laird Cregar, Victor Francen, Ward Bond (20th Century-Fox)

This tells of the establishment of West Point as a military academy in the early 1800s, and the experiences of the original class of cadets. There's a fair amount of dramatic incident, and some comedy is injected to keep up audience interest, but overall the picture drops into the doldrums too many times. Only the patriotic angle helps it survive. Major difficulty encountered by scripter Richard Maibaum seems to be the requirement of jelling dramatic episodes with factual history.

TEN LITTLE INDIANS
1966, 92 mins, UK ⓥ
D: George Pollock A: Hugh O'Brian, Shirley Eaton, Fabian, Leo Genn, Stanley Holloway, Wilfrid Hyde White (Tenlit)

Second film version of Agatha Christie's endurable variation on the old idea of putting a group of disparate characters into a confined situation and letting them be killed one by one shapes up as a good suspenser. Director George Pollock works quite a bit of suspense into the restricted action, successfully hiding identity of the tenth Indian without resorting to too many red herrings. A "whodunit break" is inserted near the end, when the action is suspended while the audience is encouraged to guess the murderer's identity.

TEN LITTLE INDIANS
1975, 105 mins, Italy/W. Germany/France/Spain ⓥ
D: Peter Collinson A: Oliver Reed, Elke Sommer, Richard Attenborough, Gert Frobe, Stephane Audran, Herbert Lom (Talia/Coralta/Corona/Comeci)

Remake of Agatha Christie's whodunit classic, in which ten suspects find themselves incommunicado 300 kilometers from the nearest town in a luxurious hotel in the middle of a desert in Iran. The murders are all committed in the most discreet, unspectacular ways and cause only the mildest of trepidations among the remaining "Indians." Charles Aznavour manages to get in a song before drinking his poison, and the others dutifully plod through their parts.

TEN NORTH FREDERICK
1958, 102 mins, US ⓥ ▭
D: Philip Dunne A: Gary Cooper, Diane Varsi, Geraldine Fitzgerald, Tom Tully, Suzy Parker, Stuart Whitman (20th Century-Fox)

Ten North Frederick is a fairly interesting study of a man who is the victim of his own virtues. But the screen telling of the John O'Hara novel sacrifices detail and explanation at some loss to audience satisfaction. Joe Chapin (Gary Cooper) is a regional lawyer, rich but not apparently otherwise distinguished. Most of all he is a gentleman, and from this flows his troubles. After a series of disillusionments, including his beloved daughter's forced marriage, subsequent miscarriage, and annullment, the lawyer becomes involved in a bittersweet romance in New York with a younger woman. By the time the story is played out, the thesis makes sense—Joe Chapin has indeed been hopelessly handicapped in life by being a gentleman.

10 RILLINGTON PLACE
1971, 111 mins, UK ⓥ ⊙
D: Richard Fleischer A: Richard Attenborough, Judy Geeson, John Hurt, Pat Heywood, Isobel Black, Robert Hardy (Columbia)

In 1944, a woman was gassed, strangled, and ravished by John Christie, a seemingly quiet, respectable man living in a drab London district. Richard Fleischer has turned out a documentary feature which is an absorbing and disturbing picture. But the film has the serious flaw of not even attempting to probe the reasons that turned a man into a monstrous pervert. It could be that Fleischer found more interest in the other central figure in the case, Christie's lodger Timothy Evans. He was an illiterate who, duped by Christie, confessed and was executed. Though Richard Attenborough, playing the killer, is the central character, the acting honors are firmly wrapped up by John Hurt as Evans.

TEN SECONDS TO HELL
1959, 93 mins, UK
D: Robert Aldrich **A:** Jeff Chandler, Jack Palance, Martine Carol, Wesley Addy, Virginia Baker, Richard Wattis (Hammer)

Hazardous job of deactivating dud bombs after World War II appears sound material for a melodramatic and suspenseful film. But curiously, *Ten Seconds to Hell* emerges as a downbeat picture. Six former German soldiers form a bomb disposal unit in Berlin at the war's end. Jack Palance, leader of the unit, is a man of courage and conviction. But he's a moody individual who appears to be continually wrestling with inner problems. Ruthless and egotistical is Jeff Chandler, who has regard for no one except himself. With the film shot on location in Berlin, cameraman Ernest Laszlo has provided some realistic backgrounds.

TENSION
1950, 91 mins, US
D: John Berry **A:** Richard Basehart, Audrey Totter, Cyd Charisse, Barry Sullivan, Tom D'Andrea (M-G-M)

Tension lives up to its title. It's a tight, tersely stated melodrama that holds the attention. Plot has Richard Basehart, a drugstore manager married to wicked Audrey Totter, plotting a murder to do away with his wife's lover (Lloyd Gough). He creates himself a new identity and carefully shapes his crime so that no suspicion will be cast on him. Cyd Charisse is charming as the girl whom Basehart meets during the establishment of his new identity.

TENSION AT TABLE ROCK
1956, 93 mins, US
D: Charles Marquis Warren **A:** Richard Egan, Dorothy Malone, Cameron Mitchell, Billy Chapin, Royal Dano, Angie Dickinson (RKO)

There's more mood than pace in this western entry. Script abets the slow moodiness and takes quite a while to set the characters. Wes Tancred (Richard Egan) is on the run after having killed in self-defense the leader of a robber gang he is riding with. Main action takes place in Table Rock, where Egan brings a small boy (Billy Chapin) after the latter's dad had been killed by some holdup men. He finds the town prepping for the arrival of Texas trailherders, with the sheriff (Cameron Mitchell) frightened. The sheriff's wife (Dorothy Malone) could go for Egan.

TEN TALL MEN
1951, 97 mins, US
D: Willis Goldbeck **A:** Burt Lancaster, Jody Lawrance, Gilbert Roland, Kieron Moore, George Tobias, John Dehner (Norma/Columbia)

Yarn is tailor-made for the burly Burt Lancaster. Cast as a Foreign Legion sergeant, he picks up a tip while in jail that the Riffs plan an invasion of the city. With nine fellow prisoners he volunteers to harass the would-be invaders. Proceedings come off at a crisp pace under Willis Goldbeck's breezy direction. Cast handle their roles broadly, which at times achieves an almost satiric effect. Whether that was intentional or not is tough to determine.

10 THINGS I HATE ABOUT YOU
1999, 97 mins, US Ⓥ ◉
D: Gil Junger **A:** Heath Ledger, Julia Stiles, Joseph Gordon-Levitt, Larisa Oleynik, David Krumholtz, Andrew Keegan (Mad Chance/Janet/Touchstone)

Turning *The Taming of the Shrew* into a teen comedy sounds like a high-concept no-brainer. *10 Things I Hate About You* soon ditches its pitch idea in favor of a mishmash of newer formulas, never quite settling on a cogent game plan or directorial tone. Divorced Walter Stratford (Larry Miller) won't let his younger daughter, Bianca (Larisa Oleynik), date until his eldest, Kat (Julia Stiles), finds a beau. Everybody wants to date pretty Bianca. Kat, however, is into grrl rock, feminist theory, and other interests that somehow preclude the hormonal urge. Bianca's two would-be boyfriends—vain Joey (Andrew Keegan) and dweebish Cameron (Joseph Gordon-Levitt)—plot to fix up sis with whoever's willing, namely new kid in town Patrick (Heath Ledger), reputedly a very bad boy. Sitcom vet Gil

Junger's feature bow is high on energy, low on cohesion. Stiles and Aussie transplant Ledger make an assured lead duo.

10:30 P.M. SUMMER
1966, 85 mins, US
D: Jules Dassin **A:** Melina Mercouri, Romy Schneider, Peter Finch, Julian Mateos, Isabel Maria Perez, Beatriz Savon (Dassin-Litvak)

Jules Dassin's *10:30 P.M. Summer* is only 85 minutes long, but it seems longer. Dassin's direction is uncertain, frequently illogical and, for the most part, plodding; Melina Mercouri's thesping is in a similar vein. The thread of a plot concerns a married couple and a female friend traveling together in Spain under a mounting tension that is touched off by an incident with a fugitive in a village. There's some possibility of exploitation in the frankly erotic scenes of lovemaking between Romy Schneider (the reluctant guest) and Peter Finch (the husband).

10 TO MIDNIGHT
1983, 100 mins, US Ⓥ ⊙
D: J. Lee Thompson **A:** Charles Bronson, Lisa Eilbacher, Gene Davis, Andrew Stevens, Geoffrey Lewis, Wilford Brimley (Golan-Globus/City)

A sexually deranged killer slices up five young women like melons. The killer (well enough played by Gene Davis) is literally getting away with murder because of bureaucratic red tape and a pending insanity plea. So cop Charles Bronson takes matters into his own hands. William Roberts's screenplay, while it sags in the middle, is damnably clever at dropping in its vicious vigilante theme without being didactic, and J. Lee Thompson's direction, borrowing from Hitchcock's editing in *Psycho,* creates the horror of blades thrusting into naked bellies without the viewer actually seeing it happen.

TENUE DE SOIREE
(MENAGE; EVENING DRESS)
1986, 81 mins, France Ⓥ ▭
D: Bertrand Blier **A:** Gerard Depardieu, Michel Blanc, Miou-Miou, Bruno Cremer, Jean-Pierre Marielle, Jean-Francois Stevenin (Hachette Premiere/Dussart/Cine Valse/DD)

There's nothing like a good shot of insolence for getting one's flagging career out of a rut. *Tenue de soiree* is a tart black comedy of sexuality in which, among other things, writer-director Bertrand Blier energetically turns the French star system on its head. One did not quite expect to see Gerard Depardieu falling for another man, especially somebody so nebbishy as Michel Blanc. Depardieu, a burglar whose sexual tastes have undergone a change in prison, meets a down-and-out couple (Blanc and Miou-Miou), and drags them into a series of housebreakings. Blanc naturally is disturbed when their new friend begins making advances at him. He's even more unsettled when he finds himself giving in to Depardieu's husky wooing. They become lovers, with Depardieu secretly paying off a pimp to take the now intrusive wife off their hands. Blier's script is shot through with dark, ferocious humor. Depardieu has a field day as Blanc's exuberant dark angel, and as the odd-woman-out, Miou-Miou too has several outstanding scenes.

TEOREMA
(THEOREM)
1968, 100 mins, Italy Ⓥ
D: Pier Paolo Pasolini **A:** Silvana Mangano, Terence Stamp, Massimo Girotti, Anne Wiazemsky, Laura Betti, Ninetto Davoli (Aetos)

Teorema is an allegory in two acts that merges eros and religion in an up-to-date context. A visitor (Terence Stamp) to an upper bourgeois household has a heavenly divining rod enabling him to offer fulfilment and authenticity through physical love. For the provincial maid Emilia (Laura Betti), the sexual experience becomes a holy illumination. The deviate son, Pietro (Jose Cruz), is solaced. His mother (Silvana Mangano), disrobes on the country estate to partake of the visitor's magic. Teenage daughter Odette (Anne Wiazemsky) invites him to her room for her first fling. The father, Paolo (Massimo Girotti), a captain of industry, discovers his true and radically different personality in the arms of his supernatural guest. The narrative, almost silent in the first half, is unusually clear for a film by Pasolini. Performance by all members of the cast are praiseworthy.

TEQUILA SUNRISE
1988, 116 mins, US Ⓥ ⊙
D: Robert Towne **A:** Mel Gibson, Michelle Pfeiffer, Kurt Russell, Raul Julia, J. T. Walsh, Arliss Howard (Mount/Warner)

There's not much kick in this cocktail. Writer-director Robert Towne attempts a study of friendship and trust but gets lost in a clutter of drug dealings and police operations. Mel Gibson plays Dale "Mac" McKussic, a former big-time drug operator who's attempting to go straight just about the time his high school pal, cop Nick Frescia (Kurt Russell), is required to bust him. Frescia tries to dodge the duty by pressuring his friend to get out, but Mac owes one last favor to an old friend who's a Mexican cocaine dealer (Raul Julia). Gibson projects control skating atop paranoia, and Russell is fine as the slick cop who's confused by his own shifting values.

1988: Nomination: Best Cinematography

TERESA
1951, 101 mins, US

D: Fred Zinnemann **A:** Pier Angeli, John Ericson, Patricia Collinge, Bill Mauldin, Peggy Ann Garner, Ralph Meeker (M-G-M)

Bright news of *Teresa* is the American introduction of Pier Angeli, as the Italian war bride of the mixed-up John Ericson. There's enough of the waif in her appearance to generate tremendous audience sympathy. Fred Zinnemann handles the direction of the story too consciously like a documentary. Opening finds Ericson muddling his way through postwar life, resisting all aid. A flashback takes the plot to Italy, where he is a green replacement GI. During a stay in a small mountain village, he meets and falls in love with Angeli. When she arrives in the States, they make their home in cramped tenement quarters with his parents, and it is gradually revealed that his trouble is caused by a dominant mother and a false conception of his father.

1951: Nomination: Best Motion Picture Story

TERMINAL VELOCITY
1994, 100 mins, US Ⓥ ⊙

D: Deran Sarafian **A:** Charlie Sheen, Nastassja Kinski, James Gandolfini, Christopher McDonald, Gary Bullock, Melvin Van Peebles (Hollywood/Interscope/PFE)

Terminal Velocity is a snappy, thrill-packed political espionage/heist picture set in the spectacularly cinematic world of skydiving. Instructor Ditch Brodie (Charlie Sheen) takes winsome novice jumper Chris (Nastassja Kinski) on a danger-filled leap into post–cold war politics, murder, and a bounty of tongue-in-cheek homages to Hitchcock and Ian Fleming. Sheen finds himself a classically Hitchcockian wrong

man, employed as the ultimate fall guy (pun intended) for Kinski's earnest KGB agent, who's trying to save Russia from a massive hit on its already shaky treasury. Pic is filled with punchy gag-filled dialogue and sensational action bits, both in the air and on the ground.

TERMINATOR, THE
1984, 108 mins, US Ⓥ ⊙

D: James Cameron **A:** Arnold Schwarzenegger, Michael Biehn, Linda Hamilton, Paul Winfield, Lance Henriksen, Rick Rossovich (Hemdale)

The Terminator is a blazing, cinematic comic book, full of virtuoso moviemaking, terrific momentum, solid performances, and a compelling story. It opens in a post-holocaust nightmare, A.D. 2029, where brainy machines have crushed most of the human populace. Arnold Schwarzenegger as the cyborg Terminator is sent back to the present to assassinate a young woman named Sarah Connor (Linda Hamilton), who's soon-to-be-born son will become mankind's salvation. A human survivor in that black future (Michael Biehn), also drops into 1984 to stop the Terminator and save the woman and the future.

TERMINATOR 2: JUDGMENT DAY
1991, 136 mins, US Ⓥ ⊙ ⊡

D: James Cameron **A:** Arnold Schwarzenegger, Linda Hamilton, Edward Furlong, Robert Patrick, Earl Boen, Joe Morton (Carolco/Pacific Western)

As with *Aliens,* director James Cameron has again taken a first-rate science fiction film and crafted a sequel that's in some ways more impressive. The story finds the juvenile John Connor (Edward Furlong), future leader of the human resistance against machines that rule the war-devastated world of 2029, living with foster parents, his mother, Sarah (Linda Hamilton), having been committed to an asylum for insisting on the veracity of events depicted in the first film. The machines who rule the future dispatch a new cyborg to slay him while the human resistance sends its own reprogrammed Terminator back—this one bearing a remarkable resemblance to the evil one that appeared in 1984. The film's great innovation involves the second cyborg: an advanced model composed of a liquid metal alloy that can metamorphose into the shape of any person it contacts and sprout metal appendages to skewer its victims.

1991: Best Sound, Visual Effects, Sound Effects Editing, Makeup
Nominations: Best Cinematography, Editing

TERM OF TRIAL

1962, 130 mins, UK
D: Peter Glenville **A:** Laurence Olivier, Simone Signoret, Sarah Miles, Terence Stamp, Thora Hird, Hugh Griffith (Warner-Pathe/Romulus)

Olivier's an idealistic, but seedily unsuccessful, schoolmaster in a small mixed school in the north of England. He's afflicted with a sense of inferiority, a nagging scold of a wife, and a taste for hard liquor. He is delighted when he sees a desire to learn in a young 15-year-old girl (Sarah Miles) but, rather naively, fails to see that she is precociously sexually aroused by him. She feeds her mother with the tale that she has been indecently assaulted, and he lands in the courtroom. Overall, the characters are well drawn, the situations dramatic, and the thesping is tops.

TERMS OF ENDEARMENT

1983, 130 mins, US ⊗ ⊙
D: James L. Brooks **A:** Shirley MacLaine, Debra Winger, Jack Nicholson, Jeff Daniels, John Lithgow, Danny DeVito (Paramount)

Teaming of Shirley MacLaine and Jack Nicholson at their best makes *Terms of Endearment* an enormously enjoyable offering. At the core is mother MacLaine and daughter Debra Winger, fondly at odds from the beginning over the younger's marriage to likable, but limited, Jeff Daniels. Winger becomes a mother and moves away to Iowa, where she carries on an affair with John Lithgow while Daniels dallies at college with Kate Charleson. MacLaine and Nicholson are first introduced as she watches him come home drunk next door, but it's several years before she finally agrees to go out to lunch with him. *Terms of Endearment* is certainly special enough to overcome its own problems.
1983: Best Picture, Director, Actress (Shirley MacLaine), Supp. Actor (Jack Nicholson), Adapted Screenplay
Nominations: Best Actress (Debra Winger), Actor (John Lithgow), Art Direction, Editing, Original Score, Sound

TERRA TREMA, LA
EPISODIO DEL MARE

1948, 127 mins, Italy ⊗
D: Luchino Visconti (Universalia)

La Terra Trema, Luchino Visconti's second directorial effort, is a ponderous tale of Sicilian fishermen and their troubles. Artistically and technically the film is an important achievement, despite film's unnecessary caricaturization and confusing fragmentary quality. Visconti's direction of the Sicilian fisherfolk is magnificent; the entire cast is well chosen, and he's captured the grim and joyful sides of their daily lives with stark realism, aided by G. R. Aldo's superb lensing.

TERROR IN A TEXAS TOWN

1958, 80 mins, US
D: Joseph H. Lewis **A:** Sterling Hayden, Sebastian Cabot, Carol Kelly, Eugene Martin, Ned Young, Victor Millan (Seltzer)

Yarn revives the time-honored incident where the unscrupulous land-grabber attempts to toss the squatters off their property by hook or crook. In this case, Sebastian Cabot is the No. 1 heavy who carries on a campaign of intimidation with the aid of gunman Ned Young. But he fails to reckon with Sterling Hayden, a seafaring Swede whose farmer father has been shot down by Young. Producer Frank N. Seltzer evidently guided this one with an eye for economy since, while there are many scenes in a hotel and one on the town's street, seldom is anyone seen with exception of the immediate principals.

TERRORISTS, THE

See: Ransom!

TERROR TRAIN

1980, 97 mins, Canada/US ⊗ ⊙
D: Roger Spottiswoode **A:** Ben Johnson, Jamie Lee Curtis, Hart Bochner, David Copperfield (Astral-Bellevue-Pathe)

Roger Spottiswoode, vet editor, makes a competent directing debut here. Jamie Lee Curtis limns the feisty survivor character in a group of young people menaced by a psychotic while having a wild party on a train. Efficient screenplay sets up the premise by showing college med students perpetrating a sick joke on a sensitive youth who goes insane as a result. Three years later the kids take a train excursion to celebrate their graduation, and the chickens come home to roost.

TERRY FOX STORY, THE
1983, 96 mins, Canada ⑦
D: R. L. Thomas **A:** Robert Duvall, Eric Fryer, Michael Zelniker, Chris Makepeace, Rosalind Chao, Elva Mai Hoover (Astral)

The Terry Fox Story chronicles the heroic life of the young Canadian man whose 1980 Marathon of Hope resulted in raising more than $20 million for cancer research. Eric Fryer plays the title role with tremendous conviction. The story opens in Vancouver in 1977, before Fox lost his right leg to cancer. Despite initial parental and medical opposition, Fox's dream begins in April 1980. He enlists the aid of his friend, Doug Alward (Michael Zeiniker) to drive a camper and watch his progress but cannot convince his girlfriend, Rika (Rosalind Chao), to leave her job and join the marathon.

TESS
1979, 180 mins, France/UK ⑦ ⊙ ⊡
D: Roman Polanski **A:** Nastassja Kinski, Leigh Lawson, Peter Firth, John Collin, David Markham, Carolyn Pickles (Renn/Burrill)

Tess is a sensitive, intelligent screen treatment of a literary masterwork. Tess Durbeyfield is an uncommonly beautiful peasant girl whose derelict father learns of the family's descent from once-noble Norman ancestry. Her parents induce the girl to present herself to a rich family bearing the ancestral name in the hope of reaping profit from the family tree. The rakish young Alec d'Urberville gives her employment and seduces her. Tess bears a child who dies after a short time. She meets and falls in love with Angel Clare. But on the wedding night, Tess reveals her past. Angel reacts horribly and leaves her.
1980: Best Cinematography, Art Direction, Costume Design (Anthony Powell)
Nominations: Best Picture, Director, Original Score

TESS OF THE STORM COUNTRY
1914, 60 mins, US ⊗
D: Edwin S. Porter **A:** Mary Pickford, Harold Lockwood, Olive Golden (Famous Players)

In *Tess of the Storm Country*, Grace Miller White's human heart story, Mary Pickford comes into her own. As the little, expressive-eyed tatterdemalion of the Lake Cayuga shores, Pickford sticks another feather in her movie crown. There are some big scenes that give the picture

a k.o. wallop. The theft of the Bible from the mission, the fight with the real murderers of the gamekeeper, the struggle in the courtroom crowd, the hut fight with the shore bully, the break with her sweetheart, and the big situation in the church where Tess, realizing the baby is dying, makes a superhuman effort to have the kidlet baptized, are all well staged.

TESS OF THE STORM COUNTRY
1922, 110 mins, US ⊗
D: John S. Robertson **A:** Mary Pickford, Lloyd Hughes, Gloria Hope, David Torrence, Forrest Robinson, Jean Hersholt (Pickford/United Artists)

Mary Pickford fans will revel with her in *Tess of the Storm Country*. She acts with her head, hands, and feet; she pantomimes and plays the part all of the while, with the titles often lending a quiet though effective amusing touch. Nothing can be said against the least item in this film: everything has been done well, particularly the photography by Charles Rosher and the direction. After Pickford, the finest performance is that of Ben Letts by Jean Hersholt. Hersholt makes his villainous character real, shaggy and bearded, uncouth and rough.

TESTAMENT
1983, 89 mins, US ⑦ ⊚
D: Lynne Littman **A:** Jane Alexander, William Devane, Ross Harris, Roxana Zal, Lukas Haas, Kevin Costner (Entertainment Events/American Playhouse)

Testament is an exceptionally powerful film dealing with the survivors of a nuclear war. Pic depicts a normal, complacent community in the small California town of Hamlin. The town's calm is shattered when news comes that nuclear devices have exploded in New York and on the east and west coast. Isolated, Hamlin's residents attempt to survive, but within a month over 1,000 people have died from radiation sickness. A young couple (Rebecca DeMornay and Kevin Costner), whose baby has died, drive off in search of "a safe place."
1983: Nomination: Best Actress (Jane Alexander)

DAS TESTAMENT DES DR. MABUSE
(THE TESTAMENT OF DR. MABUSE; THE LAST WILL OF DR. MABUSE; THE CRIMES OF DR. MABUSE)
1933, 115 mins, Germany ⑦
D: Fritz Lang **A:** Rudolf Klein-Rogge,

Otto Wernicke, Oscar Beregi, Gustav Diessl, Vera Liessem, Karl Meixner (Nero)

This sequel to the silent picture, *Dr. Mabuse, the Gambler*, which had enormous success a decade earlier, certainly shows the influence of American mystery pictures. The story is very long winded, and even an ingenious director like Fritz Lang could not prevent its being rather slow-moving in places. Dr. Mabuse (Rudolf Klein-Rogge), great scientist and greater criminal, is confined in a lunatic asylum when the tale begins. Yet the mysterious crimes committed in his own style continue, even after the death of Mabuse. A doctor at the asylum finds the testament of Mabuse, with plans of crimes committed since his death, on the table of Dr. Baum (Oscar Beregi), the alienist who treated Mabuse and made a special study of his case.

LE TESTAMENT D'ORPHEE (THE TESTAMENT OF ORPHEUS)
1960, 80 mins, France
D: Jean Cocteau A: Jean Cocteau, Edouard Dermit, Henri Cremieux, Maria Casares, Francois Perier, Jean-Pierre Leaud (Editions Cinemato-graphiques)

Jean Cocteau, 70, poet/writer/ playwright/filmmaker, tries to explain the meaning of a poet's life and, incidentally, his own. Playing himself as an errant poet who roams through the ages, this is distinctly offbeat fare. He still has a flair for provoking strange moods in ordinary landscapes, as well as utilizing simple trick effects effectively and judiciously. He ribs himself at times but is quite clear in his summation that a poet is rarely recognized in his time.

TESTAMENT OF DR. MABUSE, THE
See: Das Testament Des Dr. Mabuse

TESTAMENT OF ORPHEUS, THE
See: Le Testament D'Orphee

TESTIMONY
1987, 157 mins, UK ▭
D: Tony Palmer A: Ben Kingsley, Sherry Baines, Magdalen Asquith, Mark Asquith, Terence Rigby, Ronald Pickup (Isolde/ Film Four)

Testimony is quite an undertaking: long, muddled, and abstract at times, it's ultimately a beautifully conceived and executed art film. In essence, the pic follows the life of the Russian composer Dmitri Shostakovich, played by Ben Kingsley sporting a dubious wig, but especially focuses on his relationship with Stalin. The young Shostakovich had success after success until Stalin took a dislike to the opera *Lady Macbeth*, after which his work is denounced. Stalin pours on further humiliation by sending him to an International Peace Congress in New York, where he is forced to denounce his fellow musicians, such as Stravinsky, who had fled Russia. Helmer Tony Palmer utilizes stunning technical skill to tell his story, though at times he seems to be a bit too clever for his own good.

TEST PILOT
1938, 120 mins, US ⊗
D: Victor Fleming A: Clark Gable, Myrna Loy, Spencer Tracy, Lionel Barrymore, Samuel S. Hinds, Marjorie Main (M-G-M)

Test Pilot is an actioner against a new approach to the aviation theme. Spencer Tracy is Clark Gable's ground aide—the Gunner. Gable as a crack but arrogant pilot is forced down on a Kansas farm, where Myrna Loy is introduced as a romantic interest. Ensuing action, backgrounded by ultra-modern aviation tests and experiments, vividly portrays the strong Loy-Gable romance.

1938: Nominations: Best Picture, Original Story, Editing

TEX
1982, 103 mins, US ⊗ ⊙
D: Tim Hunter A: Matt Dillon, Jim Metzler, Meg Tilly, Bill McKinney, Ben Johnson, Emilio Estevez (Walt Disney)

Tex will probably be best remembered for breaking new ground at Disney Studios in representing some of the real problems confronting today's young people. Family life is not necessarily rosy and well scrubbed. Where the picture goes awry is in trying to tackle all of these problems in the space of 103 minutes. Writers Charlie Haas and Tim Hunter seem intent on incorporating every conceivable adolescent and adult trauma into their script. Story centers on 15-year-old Oklahoma farm boy Tex, played admirably by Matt Dillon. Growing up with his older brother, while his father is traveling with the rodeo, he must deal with family skeletons, school, friends, class distinctions, drugs, love, sex, death, and responsibility.

TEXAN, THE
1930, 79 mins, US
D: John Cromwell **A:** Gary Cooper, Fay Wray, Emma Dunn, Oscar Apfel, James Marcus (Paramount)

Most of the action in this film centers in South America in a setting of rich Spanish ancestral life. The story concerns the Llano Kid, wanted bandit in the southwest. An agent of a rich widow in South America has been commissioned to find her long-lost son. Making a deal with the Llano Kid, who speaks Spanish and is possessed of Hispanic features sufficient to fool the widow, the two set out on their strange deception for dough. Fay Wray, as a cousin of the long-lost son, lends a pleasing touch to both eye and ear. Gary Cooper is great as the Llano Kid, registering by turn steely coldness, brutality, amazement, uneasiness, and tenderness.

TEXANS, THE
1938, 92 mins, US
D: James Hogan **A:** Joan Bennett, Randolph Scott, May Robson, Walter Brennan, Robert Cummings, Robert Barrat (Paramount)

The Texans is a story of Reconstruction and carpetbaggers following the Civil War, adopting a strong pro-Southern attitude. Plot deals with an old Texas family of ranchers who escapes from the homeland with 10,000 head of cattle to avoid onerous taxation. Most of the action covers the long and treacherous drive of the cattle through wild country up to the nearest railroad point in Kansas. Camera crew gets some beautiful outdoor shots on the cattle push from Texas to Kansas. Joan Bennett is too much the Fifth Avenue debbie in a cow hat to impart the desired touch. Randolph Scott, paired with Bennett for romantic interest, looks much more the pioneer type than the star opposite him.

TEXAS ACROSS THE RIVER
1966, 100 mins, US ⓥ ▭
D: Michael Gordon **A:** Dean Martin, Alain Delon, Rosemary Forsyth, Joey Bishop, Tina Marquand, Peter Graves (Universal)

Texas Across the River is a rootin', tootin' comedy western with no holds barred. Writers have developed a situation of a gallant Spanish nobleman (Alain Delon) with courtly ethics, set down in a world he can never quite understand. Taking in his stride wild Comanches and wilder longhorns, he finds Dean Martin, as a Texan, the most perplexing of all. Delon and Martin are faced with transporting guns across Comanche territory. Both Indians and the cavalry are satirized with countless slick touches.

TEXAS CARNIVAL
1951, 76 mins, US ⓥ
D: Charles Walters **A:** Esther Williams, Red Skelton, Howard Keel, Ann Miller, Paula Raymond, Keenan Wynn (M-G-M)

Plenty of laughs, dressed up to treat the eye and ear, are offered in Texas Carnival. For tunes film has Howard Keel as a virile cowpoke baritoning his way through the footage and Harry Warren–Dorothy Fields songs. Williams and Skelton are a carnival team struggling until proud Texan Keenan Wynn, in an alcoholic moment, takes a fancy to Skelton. Latter goes to a swank hotel to meet Wynn but, instead, is mistaken for the rich Texan.

TEXAS CHAINSAW MASSACRE, THE
1974, 83 mins, US ⓥ ⊙
D: Tobe Hooper **A:** Marilyn Burns, Allen Danziger, Paul A. Partain, William Vail, Teri McMinn, Gunnar Hansen (Vortex)

Despite heavy doses of gore in The Texas Chainsaw Massacre, Tobe Hooper's pic is well made for an exploiter of its type. Disaster strikes when Marilyn Burns makes a side trip to her deserted Texas family home. A family of graverobbers, led by chainsaw-wielding Gunnar Hansen, butchers everyone but Burns, who makes a narrow escape. Sharp sense of composition and careful accumulation of detail help enliven the crude plot, and the acting is above par for this type of film.

TEXAS CHAINSAW MASSACRE PART 2, THE
1986, 95 mins, US ⓥ ⊙
D: Tobe Hooper **A:** Dennis Hopper, Caroline Williams, Bill Johnson, Jim Siedow, Bill Moseley, Lou Perry (Cannon)

With Chainsaw 2, director Tobe Hooper is back on the Texas splatterfest turf he knows. Also a big help is L. M. Kit Carson's tongue-in-cheek script. The family is just an ordinary American hard luck story—butchers who have fallen on hard times and take their resentment out on the human race. Although Dennis Hopper gets top billing, his role is surprisingly limited. Performances of the family are fine, but the real star here is carnage.

TEXASVILLE
1990, 123 mins, US Ⓥ ⊙
D: Peter Bogdanovich **A:** Jeff Bridges, Cybill Shepherd, Annie Potts, Timothy Bottoms, Cloris Leachman, Randy Quaid (Nelson)

Peter Bogdanovich's sequel to 1971's *The Last Picture Show* is long on folksy humor and short on plot. Set in 1984, film revolves around the non-adventures of oil tycoon Jeff Bridges. He's $12 million in debt, and his loyal assistant (Cloris Leachman) is ready to quit. Bogdanovich has rounded up many of the first film's players, but the plum role goes to Annie Potts as Bridges's domineering wife. Less successful is Cybill Shepherd, whose career was launched with the 1971 pic, as Bridges's old flame. Apart from a few set pieces involving the Archer County pageant parade, pic is static and poorly lensed.

THANKS A MILLION
1935, 85 mins, US Ⓥ
D: Roy Del Ruth **A:** Dick Powell, Ann Dvorak, Fred Allen, Patsy Kelly, Raymond Walburn, Paul Whiteman (20th Century-Fox)

Thanks a Million is corking entertainment. Fred Allen's radio rep as a pungent comedy deliverer is well capitalized here as the manager of a near-stranded unit which includes Ann Dvorak and Patsy Kelly as a sister team. Nunnally Johnson's script deserves some sort of award as a sample of celluloid writing. Punchy, pithy, and punctuated with a flock of telling nifties, the comedy wordage doesn't sacrifice the story. The title song is the best of Gus Kahn-Arthur Johnston's five numbers.
1935: Nomination: Best Sound

THANK YOU, MR. MOTO
1938, 68 mins, US
D: Norman Foster **A:** Peter Lorre, Thomas Beck, Pauline Frederick, Jayne Ryan, Sidney Blackmer, John Carradine (20th Century-Fox)

Moto wriggles through another mass of Oriental-Occidental intrigue in the Far East for the second of 20th Century-Fox's rival series to the well-established Charlie Chans. Peter Lorre is ideal in the role of the sly Oriental who pursues smuggling outfits trying to steal his country's treasures. Moto can use his fists, his feet, his gun, or his knife, which makes colorful film material.

THANK YOUR LUCKY STARS
1943, 127 mins, US Ⓥ ⊙
D: David Butler **A:** Eddie Cantor, Dinah Shore, Joan Leslie, Dennis Morgan, Edward Everett Horton, S. Z. Sakall (Warner)

As an Eddie Cantor vehicle, this has long stretches that are under par; the musical and star participation interludes are dovetailed together by a story that often gets lost in the shuffle. But even the most captious will admit to its many moments of diversion. Cantor plays a dual role, on the one hand a film star portrayed strictly as a heel, and on the other a film colony bus guide who can't land a picture job because he looks "too much like that Cantor guy." But that idea goes astray, too.

THAT CERTAIN AGE
1938, 100 mins, US
D: Edward Ludwig **A:** Deanna Durbin, Melvyn Douglas, Jackie Cooper, Irene Rich, Nancy Carroll, John Halliday (Universal)

That Certain Age brims with substantial entertainment, carrying all of the charm and wholesomeness which characterizes Deanna Durbin's previous pictures. Durbin develops a romantic crush for Melvyn Douglas's globetrotting reporter and tosses aside Jackie Cooper, her loyal puppy-love admirer. By her attentions she keeps Douglas amused and away from social affairs, for which he is grateful. Douglas turns in a sterling performance. Cooper clicks resoundingly.

THAT CERTAIN FEELING
1956, 102 mins, US Ⓥ
D: Norman Panama, Melvin Frank **A:** Bob Hope, Eva Marie Saint, George Sanders, Pearl Bailey, David Lewis, Al Capp (Paramount)

What's fashioned here overall is amusingly frothy, with an occasional touch of heart to add depth. A big asset is Pearl Bailey, maid in the household of renowned cartoonist George Sanders, for whom Eva Marie Saint is secretary-fiancée. Sanders has himself a freewheeling ball as the sophisticated cartoonist who has lost the common touch and calls in ghoster Bob Hope, a neurotic who wants to upchuck every time he tries to stand up to the boss. Complicating his employment is the fact that Saint's his ex-wife.

THAT CERTAIN WOMAN
1937, 91 mins, US
D: Edmund Goulding **A:** Bette Davis, Henry Fonda, Ian Hunter, Anita Louise, Donald Crisp, Hugh O'Donnell (Warner)

Appeal is aimed strictly at the emotions, as the plot is another variation of self-sacrificing mother love. Film relates the adventures of a self-reliant young woman (Bette Davis), who as a girl of 16 married a gangster, since deceased. She falls in love with a wealthy young wastrel and marries him, but his father compels the young woman to reveal her past. It's a synthetic tale that does not stand up under close analysis. The story's deficiencies are not so important, however, because the characters are made credible by the cast, and by Goulding's smooth direction.

THAT COLD DAY IN THE PARK
1969, 115 mins, Canada ⱱ
D: Robert Altman **A:** Sandy Dennis, Michael Burns, Susanne Benton, Luana Anders, John Garfield Jr. (Factor-Altman-Mirell)

A pretty, reserved, rich spinster in Vancouver, BC, spots a teenager sitting in the park in the rain. She invites the boy to her apartment and a strange relationship starts that ends in breakdown and tragedy. This mixing of themes and social strata is too literary to gain a true insight into the story's many layers. It tries to bring in too much and waters down the interesting personal relations, turning the denouement into grand guignol.

THAT FORSYTE WOMAN
1950, 112 mins, US ⱱ
D: Compton Bennett **A:** Errol Flynn, Greer Garson, Walter Pidgeon, Robert Young, Janet Leigh, Harry Davenport (M-G-M)

Metro has fashioned a long, elaborate, and costly class feature out of John Galsworthy's writings about his Victorian family, the Forsytes. Compton Bennett's direction unfolds, at a measured pace, the story of an outsider femme who marries into the family, then falls in love with a man engaged to one of the Forsyte women, bringing discord into an ordered way of life. Greer Garson, Errol Flynn, and their co-stars approach the characters with all the dignified stuffiness that distinguishes Galsworthy's people.
1950: Nomination: Best Color Costume Design

THAT HAMILTON WOMAN
(UK: LADY HAMILTON)
1941, 124 mins, US ⱱ ⊙
D: Alexander Korda **A:** Vivien Leigh, Laurence Olivier, Alan Mowbray, Sara Allgood, Gladys Cooper, Henry Wilcoxon (Korda Inc./United Artists)

Alexander Korda dips into British history for this biographical drama of Lady Hamilton and her amorous affair with naval hero Lord Nelson. He makes out a sympathetic case for the scandalous romance between the wife of a British ambassador and the great Lord Nelson. Vivien Leigh hits the peaks with her delineation of the vivacious Lady Hamilton, while Laurence Olivier's characterization of Nelson carries the full dignity and reserve of the historical figure. Picture shows plenty of production outlay with its series of elaborate settings.
1941: Best Sound Recording
Nominations: Best B&W Cinematography, B&W Art Direction, Special Effects

THAT'LL BE THE DAY
1973, 90 mins, UK ⱱ ⊙
D: Claude Whatham **A:** David Essex, Ringo Starr, Rosemary Leach, James Booth, Billy Fury, Keith Moon (Anglo-EMI/Goodtimes)

Here's a nice bit of nostalgia (late 1950s) with a superior period feel: a serious, loving, but not sticky-sweet probe of a youngster's torment in finding himself, complete with parental problems, friendships gained and lost, puppy love hangups, and first sex. A major asset is having David Essex as star and key ingredient. Ringo Starr is excellent as his sometime sidekick.

THAT LUCKY TOUCH
1975, 93 mins, UK ⱱ
D: Christopher Miles **A:** Roger Moore, Susannah York, Shelley Winters, Lee J. Cobb, Jean-Pierre Cassel, Raf Vallone (Rank)

This light comedy of love-against-the-odds, which evokes the Hollywood genre of the 1930s, falls short of its target. It concerns the entanglements of an arms dealer (Roger Moore) and a leftist women's libber (Susannah York) covering NATO war games for the *Washington Post*. Moore just about copes as the high-living gun merchant, but where finesse is called for he is merely workmanlike. York makes the best of her chances as the sex-shunning pacifist.

THAT MIDNIGHT KISS
1949, 96 mins, US
D: Norman Taurog **A:** Kathryn Grayson, Mario Lanza, Jose Iturbi, Ethel Barrymore, Keenan Wynn, J. Carrol Naish (M-G-M)

The film introduces tenor Mario Lanza, recruited from grand opera. His singing voice is excellent, though he's no great actor. Ethel Barrymore is a wealthy Philly blueblood who finances an opera company to star her granddaughter, Kathryn Grayson. When the tenor originally booked to costar with Grayson quits, she convinces maestro Jose Iturbi to give Lanza her big chance.

THAT NIGHT IN RIO
1941, 90 mins, US
D: Irving Cummings **A:** Alice Faye, Don Ameche, Carmen Miranda, J. Carrol Naish, S. Z. Sakall, Curt Bois (20th Century-Fox)

This successor to *Down Argentine Way* is a remake of *Folies Bergere* (1935). Don Ameche takes the dual role of an American night club m.c. performing in Rio, and a native financier. When a business crisis arrives, the tycoon's associates secure the entertainer to impersonate the absent Baron, with the stand-in innocently completing a deal that prevents financial ruin. Ameche is very capable in his dual role, but it's the tempestuous Carmen Miranda who gets away to a flying start.

THAT OBSCURE OBJECT OF DESIRE
See: Cet Obscur Objet du Desir

THAT'S DANCING!
1985, 105 mins, US Ⓥ ⊙ ▭
D: Jack Haley Jr. **A:** Gene Kelly, Sammy Davis Jr., Mikhail Baryshnikov, Liza Minnelli, Ray Bolger (M-G-M)

Big-screen terpsichorean art at its best. M-G-M has not only dipped into its own collection but has also borrowed from most of the other studios of the golden years of movie musicals. There is a lot of Busby Berkeley, plus Ruby Keeler and Dick Powell, followed by the wonderful work of Fred Astaire and Ginger Rogers, and on through an absolutely complete list of the greats.

THAT'S ENTERTAINMENT!
1974, 132 mins, US Ⓥ ⊙ ▭
D: Jack Haley Jr. **A:** Fred Astaire, Bing Crosby, Gene Kelly, Frank Sinatra, Liza Minnelli, Donald O'Connor (M-G-M)

Metro-Goldwyn-Mayer celebrated its 50th anniversary with *That's Entertainment!*, an outstanding, colorful, spirit-lifting, tuneful and richly satisfying feature documentary commemorating its filmusicals. From the musical library, about 100 films were selected from the 1929–58 era, enough to satisfy nearly every memory. Each segment has a particular theme (usually film highlights of a particular star), and each has its narrator.

THAT'S ENTERTAINMENT, PART II
1976, 133 mins, US Ⓥ ⊙ ▭
D: Gene Kelly **A:** Fred Astaire, Gene Kelly (M-G-M)

That's Entertainment, Part II, the handsome and polished sequel to *That's Entertainment!*, features excerpts from perhaps $100 million worth of classic Metro library footage. In addition, Fred Astaire and Gene Kelly shine in sharp bridging footage, which was well directed by Kelly. Bulk of the footage is Metro musicals. However, there are periodic brief collages including The Marx Brothers, Spencer Tracy–Katharine Hepburn, Clark Gable, Laurel & Hardy, and Buster Keaton.

THAT'S ENTERTAINMENT! III
1994, 110 mins, US Ⓥ ⊙
D: Bud Friedgen, Michael J. Sheridan **A:** Cyd Charisse, Lena Horne, Gene Kelly, Ann Miller, Debbie Reynolds, Esther Williams (M-G-M)

A bang-up third anthology of golden-era musical highlights that capably holds its own with its predecessors. Format is the same as before, as stars from M-G-M's musical heyday introduce different chapters in the story, which encompasses 62 musical numbers culled from more than 100 films. Metro was reportedly the only major studio to systematically save its outtakes, and examples of these—by Debbie Reynolds, Lena Horne, Judy Garland, and Cyd Charisse among others—will draw the buffs.

THAT SINKING FEELING
1979, 80 mins, UK Ⓥ
D: Bill Forsyth **A:** Robert Buchanan, John Hughes, Billy Greenlees, Douglas Sannachan, Alan Love, John Gordon Sinclair (Minor Miracle)

The first wholly Scottish feature for many a year proves that debuting filmmaker Bill Forsyth has an entertaining touch. A motley bunch of unemployed lads, amiably led by Robert Buchanan, heist a hundred stainless steel sinks in a boisterous bid to embark on an essentially light-hearted life of crime. Forsyth's incidental observations and the generally high standard of playing by non-professionals help to offset that most scenes could have been pruned to advantage.

THAT'S LIFE!
1986, 102 mins, US ⓥ ⊙ ☐
D: Blake Edwards **A:** Jack Lemmon, Julie Andrews, Sally Kellerman, Robert Loggia, Jennifer Edwards, Rob Knepper (Paradise Cove/Ubilam)

Personal virtually to the point of being a home movie, film proves absorbing and entertaining and benefits from a terrific lead performance by Jack Lemmon. Story opens with Lemmon's wife (Julie Andrews) awaiting the results of a biopsy, while Lemmon dreads the arrival of his 60th birthday, can't face the big party planned for him over the weekend, and is fretting because he can't perform sexually these days.
1986: Nomination: Best Song ("Life in a Looking Glass")

THAT THING YOU DO!
1996, 110 mins, US ⓥ ⊙
D: Tom Hanks **A:** Tom Everett Scott, Liv Tyler, Johnathon Schaech, Steve Zahn, Ethan Embry, Tom Hanks (Clinica Estetico/20th Century-Fox)

That Thing You Do! is an immensely likable, sweet-natured tale of the quick rise to fame—and just as quick demise—of a small-town rock band, set in 1964. Tom Hanks's directing debut bears all the elements that have made him a movie star: boyish charm, natural ease, comic precision and generosity of spirit. In Erie, PA, Guy's (Tom Everett Scott) heart has been set on music ever since he listened to a jazz album by Del Paxton (Bill Cobbs). Opportunity knocks when a local drummer breaks his arm and Guy is approached to replace him. What follows is an episodic chronicle that is as shallow as it is engaging, a collective portrait of the white boys in the band from the early days to their ultimate collapse—all in a matter of months. Score consists entirely of original songs, some written by Hanks.

THAT TOUCH OF MINK
1962, 99 mins, US ⓥ ☐
D: Delbert Mann **A:** Cary Grant, Doris Day, Gig Young, Audrey Meadows, John Astin, Dick Sargent (Universal)

The recipe is potent: Cary Grant and Doris Day in an old cat-and-mouse game. The gloss of *That Touch of Mink*, however, doesn't obscure an essentially threadbare lining. He's a company-gobbling financier; she's a trim chick legging it through Manhattan's canyons in search of a job. It starts when his limousine splatters her with puddle water. Fortuitous meeting and mating maneuvres follow, with the action shuttling between Gotham and Bermuda or Gotham and New Jersey suburbia. As written, Day's clowning has the better of it.
1962: Nominations: Best Original Story & Screenplay, Color Art Direction, Sound

THAT UNCERTAIN FEELING
1941, 89 mins, US ⓥ
D: Ernst Lubitsch **A:** Merle Oberon, Melvyn Douglas, Burgess Meredith, Alan Mowbray, Olive Blakeney, Harry Davenport (United Artists)

That Uncertain Feeling tackles the problem of a husband who doesn't pay his wife enough attention in a light and singularly satirical vein. The famed Lubitsch touch is present, but the entertainment value isn't. Merle Oberon and Melvyn Douglas are apparently happily married. He is a prosperous, settled insurance man who fails to fulfill the more romantic duties of a spouse. Into Oberon's life comes a wacky pianist (Burgess Meredith) with a strange, impudent dislike for a lot of things. The picture is tiring, slow, and embraces numerous situations that are basically weak.
1941: Nomination: Best Scoring of a Dramatic Picture

THAT WAS THEN . . . THIS IS NOW
1985, 102 mins, US ⓥ ⊙
D: Christopher Cain **A:** Emilio Estevez, Craig Sheffer, Kim Delaney, Jill Schoelen, Barbara Babcock, Frank Howard (Media Ventures/Belkin)

God save the kids who live in an S. E. Hinton novel. They're firecrackers waiting to go off. Most troubled of the kids here is Emilio Estevez as Mark Jennings, a lonely, brooding child anxious to be through with his adolescence. His friendship with Bryon Douglas (Craig Sheffer) is falling apart as Bryon takes on a girlfriend and starts to accept adult responsibility. Dark tone is reinforced by cinematographer Juan Ruiz-Anchia, who captures well the look of the street, but that's all one sees. It's an oppressive world without being particularly insightful.

THAT WONDERFUL URGE
1948, 82 mins, US
D: Robert B. Sinclair **A:** Tyrone Power, Gene Tierney, Reginald Gardiner, Gene Lockhart (20th Century-Fox)

Mounted in a slick production, the screenplay is a variation of the poor-little-rich-girl theme against a newspaper background. Tyrone Power makes the most of his comedy chances as a cynical reporter assigned to assassinate the character of a grocery chain heiress. But he becomes tangled in his own web when the gal (Gene Tierney) snaps back and turns him into a national laughing stock. This is one of Tierney's most successful performances, and she polishes off her role with considerable grace.

THEATER OF BLOOD
1973, 104 mins, US/UK ⊗ ⊙
D: Douglas Hickox **A:** Vincent Price, Diana Rigg, Ian Hendry, Harry Andrews, Coral Browne, Robert Coote (Harbor/Cineman)

Theater of Blood is black comedy played for chills and mood and emerges a macabre piece of wild melodramatics. A demented Shakespearean actor (Vincent Price) takes revenge on eight London critics whom he believes denied him a Best Actor of the Year award. He uses gory Shakespeare-inspired deaths to systematically murder each of them. Price delivers with his usual enthusiasm, and Diana Rigg is good as his daughter.

THELMA & LOUISE
1991, 128 mins, US ⊗ ▭
D: Ridley Scott **A:** Susan Sarandon, Geena Davis, Harvey Keitel, Michael Madsen, Christopher McDonald, Brad Pitt (Pathe/Main)

Thelma & Louise is a thumpingly adventurous road pic about two regular gals who shoot down a would-be rapist and wind up on the lam in their 1966 T-bird. Arkansas housewife Thelma (Geena Davis) and waitress Louise (Susan Sarandon) set out for a weekend trip away from the drudgery of their lives. At a roadside honkytonk things turn ugly. They hit the highway, dazed and in trouble. Despite some delectably funny scenes between the sexes, Ridley Scott's pic isn't about women vs. men. It's about freedom, like any good road picture, and it maintains the sense of reckless exhilaration to the end.
1991: Best Original Screenplay
Nominations: Best Director, Actress (Geena Davis, Susan Sarandon), Cinematography, Editing

THEM!
1954, 93 mins, US ⊗ ⊙
D: Gordon Douglas **A:** James Whitmore, Edmund Gwenn, Joan Weldon, James Arness, Onslow Stevens, Sean McClory (Warner)

This science-fiction shocker has a well-plotted story, expertly directed and acted in a matter-of-fact style. The title monsters are giant ants, mutations caused by radiation from the detonation of an atomic bomb in the desert. James Whitmore, sergeant in the New Mexico State Police, first gets on their track. Into the picture then arrives Edmund Gwenn and Joan Weldon, entomologists; and James Arness, FBI man. Whitmore, Gwenn, Weldon, and Arness wrap up the acting chores in first-rate fashion, and Sid Hickox's photography gives the fantastic monsters plenty of menace.
1954: Nomination: Best Special Effects

THEODORA GOES WILD
1936, 94 mins, US
D: Richard Boleslawski **A:** Irene Dunne, Melvyn Douglas, Thomas Mitchell, Spring Byington, Elisabeth Risdon, Margaret McWade (Columbia)

A comedy of steady tempo and deepening laughter. Theodora (Irene Dunne) may superficially be compared to the *Mr. Deeds Goes to Town* (1936) character in that both come from small New England villages. Eccentric figures and customs are exploited for laughs and background in both cases, and the experiences of the small-town character when hitting Manhattan form the main content of the story. Richard Boleslawski's direction brings out the nuances, and Dunne's playing of Theodora's New York escapades makes for diverting light-and-shade farce.
1936: Nominations: Best Actress (Irene Dunne), Editing

THEOREM
See: Teorema

THERE'S A GIRL IN MY SOUP
1971, 94 mins, UK ⊗
D: Roy Boulting **A:** Peter Sellers, Goldie Hawn, Tony Britton, Nicky Henson, John Comer, Diana Dors (Columbia)

There's a Girl in My Soup is a delightful surprise: a rather simple legit sex comedy (by Terence Frisby) transformed into breezy and extremely tasteful screen fun. Peter Sellers is a television personality whose roving eye misses few femme specimens. Accidental encounter with Goldie Hawn, who is having some free-love domestic problems with mate Nicky Henson, blossoms into unexpected love and compassion between the unlikely pair.

THERE'S ALWAYS A WOMAN
1938, 81 mins, US

D: Alexander Hall A: Joan Blondell, Melvyn Douglas, Mary Astor, Frances Drake, Jerome Cowan (Columbia)

A briskly paced battle-of-the-sexes comedy against a background of a murder mystery. Smart production and the direction of Alexander Hall have imbued a basically incredible plot with the tempo and animation necessary to make people either believe or forget to disbelieve. Melvyn Douglas and Joan Blondell are man and wife. He's professionally a detective; she's an amateur detective who gums up the works repeatedly. Plenty of slapstick in the tradition of *The Thin Man*.

THERESE DESQUEYROUX
1962, 109 mins, France

D: Georges Franju A: Emmanuelle Riva, Philippe Noiret, Edith Scob, Sami Frey, Renee Devillers, Lucien Nat (Filmel)

This is a social and psychological drama that remains taut and absorbing throughout, due to observant direction, expert thesping, and an insight into the characters. A woman has tried to poison her husband in a provincial section of France. She is freed when he does not press charges. But on her way back to him she thinks over what led to it. Emmanuelle Riva overcomes her ordinary looks by an intense projection of internal sincerity and etches a brilliant picture of this fragile, tragic woman almost destroyed by human pettiness, pride, and indifference.

THERESE RAQUIN
1953, 110 mins, France

D: Marcel Carne A: Simone Signoret, Raf Vallone, Jacques Duby, Roland Lesaffre, Sylvie (Paris/Lux)

Marcel Carne has conceived a brilliant but curiously cold film. A modernization of the Emile Zola novel, this evokes the infatuation and love between a manly truck driver and the wife of his officious,

petty, and sickly superior. The affair leads to the murder of the husband and the final destruction of the lovers. Carne's direction builds a heavy, brooding atmosphere of the self-indulgent, dreary life of the woman whose attempt at escape and gratification leads to her eventual destruction. Lensing is brilliant, and the studio reconstructions matches the heavy atmosphere of the bleak Lyon streets.

THERE'S NO BUSINESS LIKE SHOW BUSINESS
1954, 117 mins, US ⊘ ⊙ ▭

D: Walter Lang A: Ethel Merman, Donald O'Connor, Marilyn Monroe, Dan Dailey, Johnnie Ray, Mitzi Gaynor (20th Century-Fox)

This is a film palpably primed to point up the "heart" of showfolk. Ethel Merman and Dan Dailey are capital as the vaudeville Donahues, who bring our first one, then two, then three of their offspring for that extra bow. *Show Business* gets the works in every respect. The orchestral-vocal treatments of the Irving Berlin standards are so richly endowed as to give them constantly fresh values.

1954: Nominations: Best Motion Picture Story, Color Costume Design, Scoring of a Musical Picture

THERE'S SOMETHING ABOUT MARY
1998, 118 mins, US ⊘ ⊙

D: Peter Farrelly, Bobby Farrelly A: Cameron Diaz, Matt Dillon, Ben Stiller, Lee Evans, Chris Elliott, Lin Shaye (20th Century-Fox)

Crudely made, overlong and larded with plenty of things that don't work, pic still hits the bull's-eye in delivering in its big scenes. In 1985, Ted (Ben Stiller), a geeky teen in small-town Rhode Island, is asked by class knockout Mary (Cameron Diaz) to the senior prom. But they never make it to the dance. Instead, Ted has the misfortune to catch his private parts in his pants' zipper. Thirteen years later, a depressed Ted hires a sleazy private dick, Pat Healy (Matt Dillon), to find her. But when Pat locates Mary in Miami and sees that she's not only a sexy babe but is unattached, he reports back to Ted that his inamorata now weighs 200 pounds and is confined to a wheelchair. Mary begins falling for the conmeister, but when Ted hears that Mary is still a fox after all, he heads for Miami himself. Much of the silliness involves crossing many lines of taste. But the sense of violation becomes explosively liberating to audiences. Diaz is dazzling throughout, sexy, insouciant, and always a good sport.

THERE WAS A CROOKED MAN
1960, 90 mins, UK ✉
D: Stuart Burge A: Norman Wisdom, Alfred Marks, Andrew Cruickshank, Reginald Beckwith, Susannah York, Jean Clarke (Knightsbridge)

There are so many holes in this yarn that it's like a fishing net, but the result is amiable comedy. Norman Wisdom is a down-and-out who runs into a gang of crooks who want his help because he is a demolitions expert and who con him into assisting them in cracking a bank vault. He alone is caught holding the loot, and he goes to jail. Let out after five years, he goes to take a job in a Northern seaside factory and discovers that the town is under the control of a swindler (Andrew Cruickshank). Wisdom enlists the help of his crook friends on a wild enterprise to outwit Cruickshank.

THERE WAS A CROOKED MAN . . .
1970, 128 mins, US Ⓥ ✉
D: Joseph L. Mankiewicz A: Kirk Douglas, Henry Fonda, Hume Cronyn, Warren Oates, Burgess Meredith, Arthur O'Connell (Warner)

There Was a Crooked Man . . . has a crooked plot that is neither comedy nor convincing drama. It is the type of action drama in which neither the actors nor director appear to believe the script or characters. Douglas is the crooked man of the title who steals $500,000 and is caught in a bordello literally with his pants down. Fonda plays it straight as the saintly sheriff who becomes an idealistic prison reformer only to have his principles blow up in his face when Douglas organizes a riot and break-out.

THESE ARE THE DAMNED
See: The Damned

THESE THREE
1936, 90 mins, US Ⓥ ⊙
D: William Wyler A: Miriam Hopkins, Merle Oberon, Joel McCrea, Catherine Doucet, Alma Kruger, Bonita Granville (Goldwyn/United Artists)

A thoroughly fine cinematic transmutation of Lillian Hellman's dramatic Broadway smash *The Children's Hour*, reedited and retitled for Haysian purposes as *These Three*. Stripped of its original theme of lesbianism, the film is fortified by a socko trio in Miriam Hopkins, Merle Oberon, and Joel McCrea. As two adolescents, respectively odious and inhibited, Bonita Granville and Marcia Mae Jones give inspired performances. Hellman, if anything, has improved upon the original in rescripting it as a triangle of romantic frustration.

1936: Nomination: Best Supp. Actress (Bonita Granville)

THEY ALL KISSED THE BRIDE
1942, 84 mins, US
D: Alexander Hall A: Joan Crawford, Melvyn Douglas, Roland Young, Billie Burke, Helen Parrish, Allen Jenkins (Columbia)

Picture is adult entertainment that veers from the general run of pictures of its type to sufficiently get the audience's attention. Joan Crawford is in command of the vast business interests left by her father and is shaken by the writings of Melvyn Douglas, a happy-go-lucky scribbler who rattles the family's personal and business skeletons. Script is studded with amusing dialogue, containing intimate content and double entendres. Alexander Hall's direction is snappy and speedy all along the line.

THEY ALL LAUGHED
1981, 115 mins, US Ⓥ ⊙
D: Peter Bogdanovich A: Audrey Hepburn, Ben Gazzara, John Ritter, Colleen Camp, Dorothy Stratten, Patti Hansen (20th Century-Fox/Time-Life)

This *La Ronde*–like tale is intensely devoted to the sexual and amorous sparks struck among some unusually magnetic people. It takes a while to figure out where the story is headed, but basic framework has Ben Gazzara, John Ritter, and Blaine Novak working for the Odyssey Detective Agency. Gazzara's assigned to track Gotham visitor Audrey Hepburn by her husband, while Ritter and Novak trail Dorothy Stratten as she slips away from her husband to rendezvous with young Sean Ferrer. Certain plot contrivances bear eerie resemblances to the circumstances leading up to Stratten's real-life 1980 murder.

THEY CALL ME MISTER TIBBS!
1970, 108 mins, US
D: Gordon Douglas A: Sidney Poitier, Martin Landau, Barbara McNair, Anthony

Zerbe, Edward Asner, Jeff Corey (Mirisch)

A Nob Hill prostitute is murdered in her apartment. Under suspicion is Martin Landau, a minister in the midst of an activist campaign to reform local government. Landau is a close personal friend of Sidney Poitier, who is assigned to investigate the case. The detective is a tough, efficient cop, and the portrayal might be dramatically deadly. However, script switches back and forth between the case and the cop's everyday domestic problems.

THEY CAME FROM WITHIN
See: Shivers

THEY CAME TO CORDURA
1959, 123 mins, US ⓥ ⊙ ▭
D: Robert Rossen **A:** Gary Cooper, Rita Hayworth, Van Heflin, Tab Hunter, Richard Conte, Michael Callan (Columbia)

Film is a bitter and realistic drama set during the 1916 border action between US troops and Pancho Villa's Mexican rebels. Gary Cooper is the U.S. Army officer detailed to lead five Medal of Honor candidates back from the front lines of the war. Cooper has been made awards officer after showing cowardice in battle. Also on the party is Rita Hayworth, the disillusioned daughter of a disgraced politician. Gary Cooper is very good as the central figure, and Hayworth, looking haggard and defeated, gives the best performance of her career. Van Heflin does a brilliantly evil job as one of the "heroes," and Richard Conte, as his malevolent sidekick, is almost equally impressive.

THEY DIED WITH THEIR BOOTS ON
1941, 140 mins, US ⓥ ⊙
D: Raoul Walsh **A:** Errol Flynn, Olivia de Havilland, Arthur Kennedy, Charley Grapewin, Gene Lockhart, Anthony Quinn (Warner)

They Died with Their Boots On is the Custer story, full of action, Indians, and anachronisms. It's a long time getting to the tragic engagement in the Black Hills when Custer (Errol Flynn) with a third of his command, numbering 264 members of the 7th Cavalry, fell into ambush and were slaughtered by the Sioux. The liberties the screen writers have taken with well-established and authenticated facts are likely to be a bit trying in spots. But the test of the yarn is not its accuracy, but its

speed and excitement. Of these it has plenty.

THEY DRIVE BY NIGHT
1940, 93 mins, US ⓥ ⊙
D: Raoul Walsh **A:** George Raft, Ann Sheridan, Humphrey Bogart, Ida Lupino, Gale Page, Alan Hale (Warner)

Fast moving and action-packed melodrama of the long-haul trucking biz, *They Drive* divides into two sections. First half is adventure of George Raft and Humphrey Bogart as brothers operating a freelance highway truck, culminating with a wreck in which Bogart loses an arm. Second half is a triangle melodrama, with Raft on the receiving end of the persistent amorous advances of the married Ida Lupino. Raoul Walsh provides deft direction that accentuates dramatic moments. Raft turns in a top-notch performance as the vigorous and determined trucking indie. Equal in importance is Lupino, who gives an exceptionally outstanding portrayal, unsympathetic though it is.

THEY GOT ME COVERED
1943, 96 mins, US ⊙
D: David Butler **A:** Bob Hope, Dorothy Lamour, Lenore Aubert, Otto Preminger, Eduardo Ciannelli, Marion Martin (RKO/Goldwyn)

A farce of the broadest stripe. Sometimes it takes and sometimes it doesn't. It's just too clear how hard the writers were trying. Bob Hope is a newspaperman who's fired as a Moscow correspondent for completely missing the German invasion of Russia. He returns and goes to Washington in the hope of re-establishing his rep. No asset to the film is the quality of much of the acting, particularly that of Dorothy Lamour. Director David Butler succeeds in keeping the film moving, despite the episodic construction of the situation gags.

THEY LIVE
1988, 93 mins, US ⓥ ⊙ ▭
D: John Carpenter **A:** Roddy Piper, Keith David, Meg Foster, George "Buck" Flower, Peter Jason (Carolco/Alive)

Conceived on 1950s B-movie sci-fi terms, *They Live* is a fantastically subversive film. It takes the clever premise that those in control of the global economic power structure are secretly aliens. The pretentiously named Nada (Roddy Piper) is a heavily muscled working Joe who happens upon some sunglasses which reveal an alternate existence in which certain individuals—the ruling class—are instantly recognizable due to their hideously decomposed, skeletal faces. Nada becomes an outlaw, picking off aliens wherever he can. He seeks an accomplice, first in Meg Foster, who unwillingly rescues him from the police, and then in co-worker Keith David, another bodybuilder.

THEY LIVE BY NIGHT (AKA: THE TWISTED ROAD)
1948, 95 mins, US ⊛ ⊙
D: Nicholas Ray A: Cathy O'Donnell, Farley Granger, Howard da Silva, Jay C. Flippen, Helen Craig, Will Wright (RKO)
  They Live by Night is a moving, somber story of hopeless young love. There's no attempt at sugarcoating a happy ending, and yarn moves toward its inevitable, tragic climax without compromise. Farley Granger plays a young escaped convict who falls in love and marries a girl (Cathy O'Donnell) whose circumstances are little better than his own. Nicholas Ray directed, demonstrating a complete understanding of the characters. It's a first-rate job of moody storytelling.

THEY LOVED LIFE
See: Kanal

THEY MET IN BOMBAY
1941, 92 mins, US
D: Clarence Brown A: Clark Gable, Rosalind Russell, Peter Lorre, Reginald Owen, Matthew Boulton, Jessie Ralph (M-G-M)
  Action-packed adventure yarn picks up Clark Gable and Rosalind Russell in Bombay, both bent on lifting a famous jewel during the Empire Day celebration. Pair meet, and Gable proceeds to let her grab the gem so he can conveniently take it from her. But his scheming is discovered by Russell, and the pair take it on the lam, grabbing a tramp steamer bound for Hong Kong. Early episodes present much rapidfire and sparkling by-play between Gable and Russell. But when the pair reach Hong Kong, story strays through fields of corn in an attempt to reform the pair.

THEY MIGHT BE GIANTS
1971, 91 mins, US ⊛
D: Anthony Harvey A: George C. Scott, Joanne Woodward, Jack Gilford, Lester Rawlins, Rue McClanahan, Ron Weyand (Universal)
  They Might Be Giants starts off splendidly, with George C. Scott at his impos-

ing best as a former jurist who thinks he's Sherlock Holmes, and Joanne Woodward charming as the psychiatrist who just happens to be named Dr. (Mildred) Watson. After that, it's all downhill, becoming increasingly preachy and sentimental—hammering at the cliched tale of the good-hearted nut who's saner, and nicer, than the meanies who attempt to defeat him. Scott and Woodward battle the script valiantly, but they're not helped much by Anthony Harvey's visually unimaginative direction.

THEY'RE A WEIRD MOB
1966, 109 mins, Australia/UK ⊛
D: Michael Powell A: Walter Chiari, Clare Dunne, Chips Rafferty, Alida Chelli, Ed Devereaux, Slim de Grey (Williamson/Powell International)
  Italian import Walter Chiari plays an Italian journalist who immigrates to Australia to write for a Sydney journal edited by his cousin. Much amusement is caused by his taking some of the Aussie slang literally. Chiari finds that his cousin has fled, leaving an irate young lady, Clare Dunne, who had invested in the journal. Determined to repay his cousin's debts, Chiari gets a job as a bricklayer, while seeking Dunne on Sydney's beaches and elsewhere. For the first half, the film strives too hard to be funny. Once it settles down to telling a story, it is stronger entertainment.

THEY SHOOT HORSES, DON'T THEY?
1969, 129 mins, US ⊛ ⊡
D: Sydney Pollack A: Jane Fonda, Michael Sarrazin, Susannah York, Gig Young, Red Buttons, Bonnie Bedelia (Palomar/ABC)
  Horace McCoy's 1935 novel of a depression-era dance marathon becomes, in a recreated old ballroom, a kind of existentialist allegory of life. Gig Young is the promoter-emcee with an endless patter of cliches. Puffy-eyed, unshaven, reeking of stale liquor and sweat, he has never acted better. Jane Fonda, as the unremittingly cynical loser, gives a dramatic performance that gives the film a personal focus and an emotionally gripping power. Pollack turns the marathon into a vulgar, sleazy, black microcosm of life in 1932.
1969: Best Supp. Actor (Gig Young)
Nominations: Best Actress (Jane Fonda), Supp. Actress (Susannah York), Screenplay Adaptation, Costume Design, Art Direction, Editing, Adapted Music Score

THEY WERE EXPENDABLE
1945, 135 mins, US ⓥ ⊙
D: John Ford **A:** Robert Montgomery, John Wayne, Donna Reed, Cameron Mitchell, Ward Bond, Leon Ames (M-G-M)

They Were Expendable, dealing with the Japanese overrunning of the Philippines, primarily concerns the part played by US torpedo boats. Robert Montgomery and his buddy (John Wayne) are naval lieutenants in command of P-T boats. While the squadron of P-T tubs stationed at Manila Bay prior to Pearl Harbor were looked upon doubtfully by naval officers, invasion by the Japanese gave them their chance to show what they could do. Most of the rest of the picture vividly portrays the big job the little boats did. The battle scenes in which the P-Ts go after Japanese cruisers and supply ships are exceptionally well directed.
1945: Nominations: Best Sound, Special Effects

THEY WON'T FORGET
1937, 95 mins, US ⓥ
D: Mervyn LeRoy **A:** Claude Rains, Edward Norris, Allyn Joslyn, Linda Perry, Cy Kendall, Clinton Rosemond (Warner Bros.)

This film pulls no punches, indicting lynch law and mob fury with scalpel-like precision. The locale is the Deep South. A young business-school student is assaulted and murdered after classes are out. The two most likely suspects are a black janitor (Clinton Rosemond) and a young Yankee professor (Edward Norris) at the school. The d.a. (Claude Rains), driven by political ambition, decides by a hair's breadth that the young teacher is the better bait. In the punch-packed courtroom scenes, the film really implants its wallop. The cast is uniformly fine. Rains especially stands out.

THIEF, THE
1952, 85 mins, US ⓥ
D: Russell Rouse **A:** Ray Milland, Rita Gam, Martin Gabel, Harry Bronson, Rex O'Malley, Rita Vale (Fran/United Artists)

This has an offbeat approach to film storytelling (a complete absence of dialogue), a good spy plot, and a strong performance by Ray Milland. The film is not soundless. A strident telephone bell plays an important part, and there's a top-notch musical score by Herschel Gilbert. Missed in the story is the reason why Milland, a respected scientist in the field of nuclear physics, should turn traitor and deliver nuclear secrets to foreign agents.
1952: Scoring of a Dramatic Picture

THIEF
1981, 122 mins, US ⓥ ⊙
D: Michael Mann **A:** James Caan, Tuesday Weld, Willie Nelson, James Belushi, Robert Prosky, Tom Signorelli (United Artists)

A slick Chicago crime-drama with a well-developed sense of pathos running throughout. James Caan gives a particularly convincing portrait of the central figure. As exec producer-director-writer, Mann has woven a fine story around an honorable man who just happens to be an expert thief with an extensive prison record. In terms of story, Caan is a highly successful crook who takes pains to maintain his professional independence. Against his better judgment he gives in to "godfather" Robert Prosky's request to join forces. Mann's major flaw is being a bit too meticulous in delineating the process Caan must go through in order to make a big score.

THIEF OF BAGDAD, THE
1924, 155 mins, US ⓥ ⊗
D: Raoul Walsh **A:** Douglas Fairbanks, Snitz Edwards, Julanne Johnston, Anna May Wong, Charles Belcher, Sojin (Fairbanks/United Artists)

An absorbing picture, totally different from any of its predecessors. Nearly all of it is fairytale-like or fantasy, derived from the classic stories of the Arabian Nights. There is a magic rope with which the thief (Douglas Fairbanks) climbs up high walls. There is a magic carpet upon which he sails away with his princess. And there is a magic chest which he retrieves after heroic struggles. Now a prince, he returns at the seventh moon to win his princess against the wiles of Oriental potentates. Sojin in the role of the Mongol prince gives a really fine characterization, and Anna May Wong as the little slave girl proves herself a fine actress.

**THIEF OF BAGDAD, THE
AN ARABIAN FANTASY**
1940, 106 mins, UK/US ⓥ ⊙
D: Ludwig Berger, Michael Powell, Tim Whelan, Geoffrey Boothby, Charles David, [Zoltan Korda, William Cameron Menzies, Alexander Korda] **A:** Conrad Veidt, Sabu, June Duprez, John Justin, Rex Ingram, Miles Malleson (Korda)

The Thief of Bagdad is a colorful, lav-

ish and eye-appealing spectacle. Huge sets, amazing special effects and process photography, and vivid Technicolor completely submerge the stolid, slow, and rather disjointed fairy tale. As a result, in Alexander Korda's version of the picture originally turned out by Douglas Fairbanks in 1924, the unimpressive story and stagey acting fail to measure up to the general production qualities. The story combines many imaginative incidents culled from Arabian Nights fables. There's the mechanical flying horse; the giant genie of the bottle; the huge spider that guards the all-seeing eye; the six-armed dancing doll; and the famous magic carpet. Conrad Veidt is most impressive as the sinister grand vizier, sharing honors with Sabu, who capably carries off the title role.
1940: Best Color Cinematography, Color Interior Decoration (Vincent Korda), Special Effects (Lawrence Butler, Jack Whitney)
Nomination: Best Original Score

THIEF WHO CAME TO DINNER, THE
1973, 105 mins, US Ⓥ
D: Bud Yorkin **A:** Ryan O'Neal, Jacqueline Bisset, Warren Oates, Jill Clayburgh, Charles Cioffi, Ned Beatty (Tandem/Warner)

The Thief Who Came to Dinner has a good title and a helpful supporting cast. Otherwise, it's a tepid caper comedy, starring Ryan O'Neal as a computer-age society gem burglar, Jacqueline Bisset as his girl, and Warren Oates as a befuddled insurance detective. The episodic script focusses on O'Neal, who blackmails magnate Charles Cioffi for entree into rich circles where he can plot his heists. The film exudes the lethargy of a project where some actors' commitments are being exercised.

THIEVES
See: Les Voleurs

THIEVES' HIGHWAY
1949, 93 mins, US
D: Jules Dassin **A:** Richard Conte, Valentina Cortese, Lee J. Cobb, Jack Oakie, Millard Mitchell (20th Century-Fox)

Script stresses realism, as does Jules Dassin's direction in the no-holds-barred love sequences between Richard Conte and Hollywood newcomer Valentina Cortese, the high action trucking scenes, and the barroom fight finale. The screenplay is guttily dialogued and plays fast. Conte

plays a trucker whose father has lost his legs in an accident staged by heavy Lee J. Cobb, produce commission man. Cortese is a prostitute hired by Cobb to lure Conte from his game of revenge.

THIEVES LIKE US
1974, 123 mins, US
D: Robert Altman **A:** Keith Carradine, Shelley Duvall, John Schuck, Bert Remsen, Louise Fletcher, Tom Skerritt (United Artists)

Thieves Like Us proves that when Robert Altman has a solid story and script, he can make an exceptional film, and one mostly devoid of auteurist mannerisms. It's a better film than Nicholas Ray's first jab at the story in 1948 [*They Live By Night*], the mid-1930s tale of lower-class young love and Dixie bank-robbing. Keith Carradine plays a young prison trustee who escapes with John Schuck to join Bert Remsen in a spree of small-town bank heists. Shelley Duvall and Carradine fall in love, their romance clearly destined for tragedy.

THIEVES QUARTET
1994, 90 mins, US Ⓥ
D: Joe Chappelle **A:** Phillip Van Lear, Joe Guastaferro, Michele Cole, James ''Ike'' Eichling, Richard Henzel, Jamie Denton (Mooncoin)

Thieves Quartet drives a familiar neo-noir road, where down-and-dirty crooks conspire, connive, and ultimately square-off over their ill-gotten gains. When aging hippie bartender Art Bledsoe (Joe Guastaferro) dreams up a kidnapping plot to score a quick $2 million, he turns to three partners (Phillip Van Lear, James ''Ike'' Eichling, and Michele Cole) in his hometown of Chicago to help him pull off the heist. Ostensibly a character study that gets inside the heads of the ''Thieves Quartet,'' film suffers from there not being much of interest once the audience is inside the characters' heads.

THIN BLUE LINE, THE
1988, 106 mins, US Ⓥ ⊙
D: Errol Morris (American Playhouse/Third Floor)

The Thin Blue Line constitutes a mesmerizing reconstruction and investigation of a senseless murder. It employs strikingly original formal devices to pull together interviews, film clips, photo collages, and re-creations of the crime. Case in question centers upon the 1976 murder of a Dallas policeman. David Harris, 16, was arrested after bragging to friends that he'd killed a Dallas cop. Harris insisted his boasting was only meant to impress his buddies and that the real murderer was a hitchhiker he'd picked up, one Randall Adams. Despite Harris's criminal history, he got off scot-free, while Adams was convicted and sentenced to death.

THING, THE
1982, 108 mins, US Ⓥ ⊙
D: John Carpenter A: Kurt Russell, A. Wilford Brimley, T. K. Carter, David Clennon, Keith David, Richard Dysart (Universal/Turman-Foster)

If it's the most vividly gruesome monster ever to stalk the screen that audiences crave, then *The Thing* is the thing. On all other levels, however, John Carpenter's remake of Howard Hawks's 1951 sci-fi classic comes as a letdown. A group of American scientists and researchers at an isolated station in Antarctica are infested by a creature from a space ship that had remained buried in ice for 100,000 years. It soon becomes clear that The Thing is capable of ingesting, then assuming the bodily form of, any living being. What the old picture delivered—and what Carpenter missed—was a sense of intense dread, a fear that the loathed creature might be lurking behind any door.

THING CALLED LOVE, THE
1993, 116 mins, US Ⓥ ⊙
D: Peter Bogdanovich A: River Phoenix, Samantha Mathis, Dermot Mulroney, Sandra Bullock, K. T. Oslin, Anthony Clark (Paramount)

A fairly typical tale of young talent on the rise in Nashville is given nicely nuanced treatment in *The Thing Called Love*. Aspiring singer-songwriter Miranda Presley (Samantha Mathis) Greyhounds from New York City to Nashville. Moving in with the buoyantly untalented Linda Lue Linden (Sandra Bullock), Miranda attracts the attention of two good-looking dudes, the moody, gifted James Wright (River Phoenix) and soulful Kyle Davidson (Dermot Mulroney), who writes better than he sings. Kyle brings Miranda to a big country dance, but loses her after James, who is performing that night, invites her onstage to join him in one of his numbers.

THING (FROM ANOTHER WORLD), THE
1951, 89 mins, US Ⓥ ⊙
D: Christian Nyby A: Margaret Sheridan, Kenneth Tobey, Robert Cornthwaite,

Douglas Spencer, Dewey Martin, James Arness (Winchester/RKO)

Offbeat subject matter concerns an outlandish interplanetary space-hopper that descends upon earth in a flying saucer. Christian Nyby's direction sustains a mood of tingling expectancy as a group of US airmen and scientists stationed near the North Pole learn that a new, mysterious element is playing tricks with their compass readings. But the resourcefulness shown in building the plot groundwork is lacking as the yarn gets into full swing. Cast members fail to communicate any real terror as the "Thing" makes its appearance and its potential to destroy the world is revealed.

THINGS CHANGE
1988, 100 mins, US Ⓥ ⊙
D: David Mamet A: Don Ameche, Joe Mantegna, Robert Prosky, J. J Johnston, Ricky Jay, Mike Nussbaum (Filmhaus/Columbia)

David Mamet's *Things Change* is a dry, funny, and extremely intelligent comedy of mistaken identity. The elderly Gino (Don Ameche), a shoeshine boy, is invited to meet a Mafia boss whom he resembles. He wants Gino to take the rap for a murder, and as a reward he can have his heart's desire. Gino is handed over to Jerry (Joe Mantegna), a very junior Mafioso. Jerry decides to give the oldster a final fling at Lake Tahoe where, unknown to him, a Mafia convention is about to take place. Gino is mistaken for a senior Don and invited to meet the local Mafia kingpin (Robert Prosky), with whom he strikes up a close rapport. The comedy centers around a beautifully modulated performance from Ameche. As the dimwitted Jerry, Mantegna is consistently funny and touching.

THINGS OF LIFE, THE
See: Les Choses de la Vie

THINGS TO COME
1936, 97 mins, UK Ⓥ
D: William Cameron Menzies A: Raymond Massey, Cedric Hardwicke, Edward Chapman, Ralph Richardson, Margaretta Scott, Maurice Braddell (London)

This is England's first $1 million picture, an impressive but dull exposition of a bad dream. H. G. Wells's script predicts that in 1946 there will be a disastrous world war. At the end of it, civilization will be reduced to nothingness, disease having scourged the world. A group of engineers and aviators, however, think things over and decide to work for the world's salvation. They take over, do away with the petty little fascistic states that have sprung up, and create a brave new world of science. It is all very pictorial, very imaginative, very artificial, and it runs on and on.

THINGS TO DO IN DENVER WHEN YOU'RE DEAD
1995, 114 mins, US Ⓥ ⊙
D: Gary Felder **A:** Andy Garcia, Christopher Walken, William Forsythe, Bill Nunn, Treat Williams, Jack Warden (Miramax/Woods Entertainment)

Tartly written and vividly performed by a fine ensemble cast, Gary Felder's bracingly entertaining first feature covers familiar ground in a fresh, breezy way. Jimmy the Saint (Andy Garcia) is a smooth-talking, sharp-dressing hipster who has retired from crime. He is paged by his former boss (Christopher Walken), an ailing criminal kingpin who asks him to do a small favor in return for a big payday: to put a scare into the new boyfriend of the boss's son's ex-girlfriend. To this end, Jimmy rounds up his old gang. But the action goes awry, pushing the big boss into issuing death warrants for all the boys, to be executed by hit man Mr. Shhh (Steve Buscemi). Given 48 hours, Jimmy urgently sets about trying to do right by his friends.

THIN ICE
1937, 78 mins, US
D: Sidney Lanfield **A:** Sonja Henie, Tyrone Power, Arthur Treacher, Raymond Walburn, Joan Davis, Sig Ruman (20th Century-Fox)

Sonja Henie is the skating and skiing instructor at an Alpine hotel, the meeting place of a group of European diplomats. Tyrone Power is a young prince sent by his prime minister. While politics are being discussed, he slips out with his skis. Sliding down a glacier he meets Sonja traveling in the same direction. Mistaken identities, threatened international complications, and old-fashioned romance ensue. Production features three elaborate ice ballets, engaging a skating corps of 100 men and women.

THINK FAST, MR. MOTO
1937, 66 mins, US
D: Norman Foster **A:** Peter Lorre, Virginia Field, Thomas Beck, Sig Ruman, Murray Kinnell, John Rogers (20th Century-Fox)

Peter Lorre's new characterization, that of an educated Japanese merchant and amateur sleuth, gets away from the grim villainy of his previous film efforts. In *Mr. Moto* he carries the title role, as a San Francisco importer who decides to run down a vast ring of gem smugglers. Lorre is surrounded by a capable cast. Virginia Field is the gang's unwilling undercover operative. Sig Ruman plays the cabaret owner and king of the smugglers.

THIN MAN, THE
1934, 80 mins, US Ⓥ ⊙
D: W. S. Van Dyke **A:** William Powell, Myrna Loy, Maureen O'Sullivan, Nat Pendleton, Minna Gombell, Porter Hall (M-G-M/Cosmopolitan)

The Thin Man was an entertaining novel, and it's also an entertaining picture. The adapters capture the spirit of the jovial, companionable relationship of the characters Nick, retired detective, and Nora, his wife. Their very pleasant manner of loving each other is used as a light comedy structure upon which the screen doctors perform their operation on the Hammett novel. The comedy as directed by W. S. Van Dyke and played by William Powell and Myrna Loy gives it an impetus which sweeps the meat of the mystery story through to a fast finish. No changes were made in the basic plot nor in the murder mystery developments.

1934: Nominations: Best Picture, Director, Actor (William Powell), Writing Adaptation

THIN MAN GOES HOME, THE
1944, 100 mins, US Ⓥ ⊙
D: Richard Thorpe **A:** William Powell, Myrna Loy, Gloria de Haven, Anne Revere, Harry Davenport, Edward Brophy (M-G-M)

Based on the characters originally created by Dashiell Hammett, the story emerges as a neatly fashioned whodunit. Richard Thorpe paces the plot nicely, overcoming a rather slow opening. Production as a whole lacks much of the sophistication and smartness which characterized the early Thin Man films. Yarn deals with an espionage ring working for a foreign power. Battle of wits to secure a group of paintings leads to a couple of killings.

THIN RED LINE, THE
1964, 90 mins, US ▭
D: Andrew Marton **A:** Keir Dullea, Jack Warden, James Philbrook, Ray Daley,

Robert Kanter, Merlyn Yordan (Allied Artists)

Action-packed war film is an explosive melodramatization of the American assault on Guadalcanal in World War II. Bernard Gordon's scenario focuses on two figures implicated in the taking of the Pacific island. One is a resourceful private (Keir Dullea), the other a war-wise, sadistic sergeant (Jack Warden). The two quickly become enemies but ultimately one dies in the other's arms after saving the other's life. Dullea and Warden are colorful antagonists, the former's intensity contrasting sharply with the latter's easygoing air.

THIN RED LINE, THE
1998, 170 mins, US Ⓥ ⊙ ▱
D: Terrence Malick **A:** Sean Penn, Adrien Brody, Jim Caviezel, Ben Chaplin, George Clooney, John Cusack (Geisler-Roberdeau/Phoenix/Fox 2000)

Terrence Malick's much anticipated return to films after a 20-year hiatus is a complex, highly skilled piece of work that will captivate some critics and serious viewers. Its abstract nature, emotional remoteness and lack of dramatic focus will frustrate mainstream audiences. In WWII, surprised to encounter no initial resistance on the Pacific island of Guadalcanal, the Americans are forced to pursue the Japanese up toward their dug-in positions in the hills. Structurally, the film is lumpy, with confrontations and climaxes coming and going, and a final 45 minutes in which the dramatic momentum slides noticeably downhill. Characters get special attention then disappear for lengths of time—Sean Penn's stand-apart sergeant is a particular victim of this choppiness. Visually, the film is ravishing, and Malick's ability to build dense, multilayered sequences proves as supple as ever.
1998: Nominations: Best Picture, Director, Adapted Screenplay, Cinematography, Editing, Original Dramatic Score, Sound

THIRD DAY, THE
1965, 119 mins, US ▱
D: Jack Smight **A:** George Peppard, Elizabeth Ashley, Roddy McDowall, Arthur O'Connell, Mona Washbourne, Herbert Marshall (Warner)

Interesting and sometimes suspenseful drama about a man fighting amnesia and faced with a manslaughter rap. Film opens on George Peppard climbing out of a river, but he cannot remember what happened to him or who he is. He learns he's married to a beautiful aristocrat whom he's about to

lose because he's a drunk and is about to be talked into selling the family business. Peppard delivers an expert enactment, and Elizabeth Ashley, as his wife, lends a colorful note. Roddy McDowall is convincing as a conniving character, and Mona Washbourne offers a standout performance in a warm and understanding characterization.

THIRD FINGER, LEFT HAND
1940, 96 mins, US
D: Robert Z. Leonard **A:** Myrna Loy, Melvyn Douglas, Raymond Walburn, Lee Bowman, Bonita Granville, Felix Bressart (M-G-M)

Third Finger, Left Hand is sufficiently light and fluffy in its farcical setup to provide diverting entertainment. Story is obvious from the opening reel, but still displays several corking comedy episodes. Myrna Loy is a magazine editor who invents a fictitious husband to ensure her job against the jealousy of the boss's wife. She meets Melvyn Douglas, a roaming artist, and the pair fall in love. He moves into her home as the missing husband, and from there on it's a melange of provoking situations. Robert Z. Leonard directs with a capable hand, and does much to overcome the lightweight script.

THIRD MAN, THE
1949, 93 mins, UK Ⓥ ⊙
D: Carol Reed **A:** Joseph Cotten, Alida Valli, Orson Welles, Trevor Howard, Bernard Lee, Wilfrid Hyde White (London)

A full-blooded, absorbing story set in occupied postwar Vienna and revolving around the black market and its unsavory ramifications. Holly Martins, an American writer, comes to join his friend Harry Lime but arrives in time to attend his funeral. Suspecting that Harry was murdered, Holly decides to unravel the mystery. Orson Welles manifests as the supposed corpse. Joseph Cotten makes a pleasing personality of the loyal friend, and Trevor Howard, as the detached British officer, displays just the right amount of human sympathy and understanding.
1950: Best B&W Cinematography
Nominations: Best Director, Editing

THIRD SECRET, THE
1964, 103 mins, UK
D: Charles Crichton **A:** Stephen Boyd, Jack Hawkins, Richard Attenborough, Diane Cilento, Pamela Franklin, Paul Rogers (20th Century-Fox)

When a renowned psychoanalyst is deemed a suicide, the puzzle surrounding his death, pieced together by one of his patients, is the plot pursued by *The Third Secret*, an engrossing—if not wholly convincing—psychological mystery melodrama. Stephen Boyd, as the inquisitive patient, conducts a private investigation to determine whether the death was a suicide or a murder committed by one of his patients. The investigation leads Boyd from patient to patient until he unearths "the third secret." A lack of animation is evident in Boyd's performance, but at moments he catches the spark of the character. Pamela Franklin does a highly professional job as the analyst's daughter.

THIRTEEN CHAIRS, THE
See: 12 Plus 1

13 RUE MADELEINE
1946, 95 mins, US Ⓥ
D: Henry Hathaway **A:** James Cagney, Annabella, Richard Conte, Frank Latimore, Walter Abel, Sam Jaffe (20th Century-Fox)

Producer Louis de Rochemont, an alumnus of the Time-Life technique, here utilizes the same off-screen documentary exposition as he did in *The House on 92nd Street* to set his theme: a Nazi-Allies cops-and-robbers tale of bravery and bravado. James Cagney plays one of the strategic services' masterminds, up against Richard Conte, the crack Gestapo agent who has insinuated himself into the American espionage school as a means to learn Allied invasion plans. The training methods, as indoctrinated into the plot's development, are arresting stuff.

THIRTEENTH FLOOR, THE
1999, 120 mins, US Ⓥ ⊙ ▭
D: Josef Rusnak **A:** Craig Bierko, Armin Mueller-Stahl, Gretchen Mol, Vincent D'Onofrio, Dennis Haysbert, Steven Schub (Centropolis)

The makers of this pic are clearly entranced with the notion of a supercomputer designed to provide the user with simulated time travel, but never figured out how to build a dramatically intriguing story around the concept. The prologue is set in a sepia-toned 1937 Los Angeles, where dapper Fuller (Armin Mueller-Stahl) gives a letter about "the awful truth" to barkeep Ashton (Vincent D'Onofrio) with instructions that it is only for the eyes of Douglas Hall (Craig Bierko). Fuller zaps back into the present, but is murdered soon after phoning Hall. Hall is intrigued by Jane Fuller (Gretchen Mol), who arrives claiming to be Fuller's

daughter, and zaps back into Fuller's simulated 1937 reality to uncover the truth behind the murder. The pic's highlight is an astonishing re-creation of a bygone City of the Angels, stuffed with period detail.

13TH LETTER, THE
1951, 85 mins, US
D: Otto Preminger **A:** Linda Darnell, Charles Boyer, Michael Rennie, Constance Smith, Francoise Rosay (20th Century-Fox)

Interesting account of the effects of poison pen letters on a small Quebec village. Plot deals principally with Michael Rennie, a doctor; Charles Boyer, an older doctor; and his young wife (Constance Smith). Their village becomes a gossip mill when poison pen letters, indicating that Rennie and Smith are having an affair, are widely distributed. Further letters eventually cause a wounded war hero to commit suicide. Boyer slips into the character of the elderly French-Canadian doctor with wonderful ease.

13TH WARRIOR, THE
1999, 103 mins, US Ⓥ ⊙ ▭
D: John McTiernan **A:** Antonio Banderas, Diane Venora, Dennis Storhoi, Vladimir Kulich, Omar Sharif, Anders T. Andersen (Touchstone)

The 13th Warrior emerges as a bloody but anemic story of he-men with broadswords and long ships fighting off marauding cannibals dressed in bearskins. Yarn moves along in orderly three-act fashion and delivers the expected quotient of blood and guts, plus an odd combo of civilized rather than primitive-minded talk, some mumbo jumbo about unmentionable flesh-eating beasts, and a promising but finally unrealized contrasting of 10th-century Western and Eastern cultures. The hero is a cultured poet from Baghdad (Antonio Banderas) exiled to a distant land and coerced into joining a band of blond fellows who require a non-Nordic 13th warrior to help them fight fiends terrorizing their land. Banderas cuts a fine figure with his black robes and white horse.

30 IS A DANGEROUS AGE, CYNTHIA
1968, 85 mins, UK Ⓥ
D: Joseph McGrath **A:** Dudley Moore, Eddie Foy Jr., Suzy Kendall, John Bird, Duncan MacRae (Columbia)

Generously endowed with the better comedic elements of satire, knockabouts, subtleties, and slapstick, film is almost a virtuoso performance by Dudley Moore. Close to his 30th birthday, Moore launches a desperation drive to achieve two ambitions: writing a successful musical comedy and getting married. From this plot establishment, Moore and friends take off on a romp with such a sense of camp that audiences are bound to be laughing long after the last frame. Moore's versatility is the central focus, with a remarkably underplayed performance that sets pace and keeps it on track.

39 STEPS, THE
1935, 86 mins, UK Ⓥ ⊙
D: Alfred Hitchcock **A:** Robert Donat, Madeleine Carroll, Godfrey Tearle, Peggy Ashcroft, Lucie Mannheim, Wylie Watson (Gaumont-British)

A zippy, punchy, romantic melodrama, at times far-fetched and improbable, *The 39 Steps* twists and spins artfully from one high-powered sequence to another and holds like a steel cable from start to finish. A Canadian rancher (Robert Donat), embroiled in an English military secrets plot, is simultaneously fleeing an accusation of murder and hunting down the leader of the spies. In his wanderings through Scotland's hills and moors, he has a series of spectacular escapes and encounters. Donat's performance, ranging from humor to horror, reveals acting ability behind that good-looking facade.

39 STEPS, THE
1959, 93 mins, UK Ⓥ
D: Ralph Thomas **A:** Kenneth More, Taina Elg, Brenda de Banzie, Barry Jones, Reginald Beckwith, James Hayter (Rank)

This version of John Buchan's novel stands up very well. Kenneth More finds himself involved in a mysterious adventure involving espionage and murder. All he knows is that the top spy is somewhere in Scotland and that the tangle is tied up with the strange words "the 39 steps." Suspected of murder, More has just 48 hours to find out the secret of the 39 steps, expose the gang, and clear himself of the murder rap. More's performance is a likeable mixture of humor and toughness, while Taina Elg is appealing as a pretty schoolmistress dragged into the adventure against her will. The rest of the cast all pitch in splendidly in a well-acted picture.

THIRTY NINE STEPS, THE
1978, 102 mins, UK Ⓥ ⊙
D: Don Sharp **A:** Robert Powell, David Warner, Eric Porter, Karen Dotrice, John Mills, George Baker (Rank/Norfolk)

Okay period suspense, directed with a smooth but unremarkable touch by Don Sharp. For the short of memory, *Steps* is the melodramatic tale of a man on the run from Prussian assassins plotting World War I. It was first a classic novel by John Buchan, then a classic film by Alfred Hitchcock, with Robert Donat as the elusive hero and Madeleine Carroll as the romantic interest. This third version has attractive young Robert Powell and Karen Dotrice, but nothing like the Donat-Carroll chemistry or flourish.

THIRTY SECONDS OVER TOKYO
1944, 138 mins, US Ⓥ
D: Mervyn LeRoy **A:** Van Johnson, Robert Walker, Phyllis Thaxter, Tim Murdock, Robert Mitchum, Spencer Tracy (M-G-M)

Lieutenant Colonel James Doolittle mapped his blitz on Japan 131 days after Pearl Harbor. There is suspense as the flyers prepare themselves for their long-range training in anticipation of the secret mission. Spencer Tracy's appearance as Doolittle is basically a cameo. Van Johnson is Ted Lawson, and Phyllis Thaxter is his wife. His plane, the *Ruptured Duck*, and its pleasant little family of crew become the focal attention henceforth. After Doolittle finally tells them of their mission to bomb Japan, the war becomes highly personalized through the actions of these crew members.
1944: Best Special Effects
Nomination: Best B&W Cinematography

3702 LE MATIN
(BETTY BLUE)
1986, 120 mins, France Ⓥ ⊙
D: Jean-Jacques Beineix **A:** Jean-Hugues Anglade, Beatrice Dalle, Gerard Darmon, Consuelo de Haviland, Clementine Celarie, Vincent Lindon (Gaumont/Constellation/Cargo)

This feverish tale of amour fou begins with the animal attraction between Zorg (Jean-Hugues Anglade), a young would-be writer living off odd jobs in a coastal bungalow colony, and Betty (Beatrice Dalle), a waitress. They move into a Paris suburban house shared by a girlfriend of Betty's (Consuelo de Haviland) and her mate (Gerard Darmon). Betty sends off Zorg's manuscript to numerous publishers, but the response is negative. They try to settle down, but Betty's failed pregnancy and her dreams of stability push her into madness. Dalle makes a moving debut as the desperate baby doll who fails to mold reality to her own conceptions of happiness. Anglade is more introvertedly affecting as the casual, but devoted, Zorg.

36 CHOWRINGHEE LANE
1982, 122 mins, India
D: Aparna Sen **A:** Jennifer Kendall, Dhritiamn Chatterjee, Debashree Roy, Geoffrey Kendall (Kapoor/Vilas)

In Aparna Sen's first directorial stint, Jennifer Kendall is effective as a lonely Anglo-Indian old lady. She teaches Shakespeare in a private girls' school and has befriended a couple. She does not realize they have been using her for her apartment rather than for the friendship that has warmed her lonely life. They marry and then gently put her off until she realizes they do not need her any more. Full of visual ideas, film does not quite transcend them to achieve a more piercing insight into aging and loneliness.

36 HOURS
1964, 115 mins, US/W. Germany ⌑
D: George Seaton **A:** James Garner, Eva Marie Saint, Rod Taylor, Werner Peters, John Banner, Alan Napier (M-G-M/Perlberg-Seaton/Cherokee)

A fanciful war melodrama set during the hours immediately preceding D day. The title indicates the time allotted a German psychiatrist to learn from a captured US intelligence officer the exact point of the Allied landings. James Garner plays the American sent to Lisbon who is captured and drugged by the Germans. Upon regaining consciousness, he's led to believe he has been an amnesia victim for six years. Rod Taylor registers most effectively in the offbeat role of the German, playing it realistically for sympathy.

THIRTY-TWO SHORT FILMS ABOUT GLENN GOULD
1993, 93 mins, Canada
D: Francois Girard **A:** Colin Feore, Gale Garnett, Katya Ladan, David Hughes, Gerry Quigley, Carlo Rota (Max)

Thirty-Two Short Films About Glenn Gould is an impressionistic approach to the life and times of the iconoclastic classical pianist. An assured melange of dramatic recreation, archival material, and interviews, it is a uniquely entertaining venture. There are a couple of Gould's non-musical ventures for radio and a segment of his film collaboration with animator Norman MacLaren. There's also the dramatic reconstruction of key events in his life, including his last live perfor-

mance. Woven into an already rich tapestry are a handful of recollections from real-life colleagues and friends.

THIS ABOVE ALL
1942, 110 mins, US
D: Anatole Litvak **A:** Tyrone Power, Joan Fontaine, Thomas Mitchell, Henry Stephenson, Nigel Bruce, Gladys Cooper (20th Century-Fox)

This Above All is set in England in that tense interval between Dunkirk and the London blitz of September 1940. It tells of the romance between a beautiful daughter of the aristocracy and a lowly-born soldier who has deserted after fighting honorably through the shattering battle of Flanders and the tragic evacuation of Dunkirk. The subject of the democratic aims in the war, the problem of the conflict of social classes, and the question of pacifism against duty to one's country are expertly focused in personal terms.

1942: Best B&W Art Direction (Richard Day, Joseph Wright)
Nominations: Best B&W Cinematography, Editing, Sound

THIS BOY'S LIFE
(A TRUE STORY)
1993, 115 mins, US Ⓥ ⊙
D: Michael Caton-Jones **A:** Robert De Niro, Ellen Barkin, Leonardo DiCaprio, Jonah Blechman, Eliza Dushku, Chris Cooper (Warner)

This Boy's Life is a nicely acted but bland coming-of-age memoir about a young man's escape from domestic turmoil and abuse, narrated in writerly style by young Toby (Leonardo DiCaprio). Hitting the road in 1957 with his working-class mother, Caroline (Ellen Barkin), Toby begins hanging out with a bad crowd once they settle in Seattle. Then mom meets Dwight (Robert De Niro), a man's man with a crewcut. Dwight devotes himself to cutting the sullen ''hot shot'' down to size. After a relatively promising warm-up, pic actually proceeds to flatten out the characters in the latter sections. Film's strength lies in its portrait of the father-stepson struggle, how each pushes the other toward even worse behavior.

THIS DAY AND AGE
1933, 82 mins, US
D: Cecil B. DeMille **A:** Charles Bickford, Judith Allen, Richard Cromwell, Eddie Nugent, Ben Alexander (Paramount)

A highly improbable and fantastic story about the crusading student body of a high school which, aroused by racketeering activities, sets out to deal justice in its own way. Charles Bickford supplies the major menace as a gunman who starts the first reel off with a couple of ruthless murders. Trying to exact tribute from tailors, Bickford makes the mistake of murdering a high-school pants presser who's beloved by the students. Principal student assignment goes to Richard Cromwell, lessers being Eddie Nugent, Ben Alexander, and Lester Arnold, all well cast. Bickford turns in one of his best performances as the heavy.

THIS EARTH IS MINE
1959, 123 mins, US ◻
D: Henry King **A:** Rock Hudson, Jean Simmons, Dorothy McGuire, Claude Rains, Kent Smith, Anna Lee (Universal/Vintage)

This film is almost completely lacking in dramatic cohesion. Its complex plot relationships begin with confusion and end in tedium. The setting is the Napa Valley wine country in the waning years of Prohibition. The basic plot is a conflict between generations—the older, European-born vintners, headed by Claude Rains, with traditions of dedication to the craft, and the younger men, represented by Rock Hudson, who are interested in selling their crop to the highest bidders, even if it means their grapes will be made into bootleg liquor. What's lacking mostly in the script, and not supplemented in the direction, is an overall intelligence that would have appraised these complexities.

THIS GUN FOR HIRE
1942, 86 mins, US ⓥ ◉
D: Frank Tuttle **A:** Veronica Lake, Robert Preston, Laird Cregar, Alan Ladd, Tully Marshall, Mikhail Rasumny (Paramount)

A very complicated yarn by Graham Greene about international intrigue and treason concerning the sale of a secret chemical formula to the Japanese. The screenplay is a succession of gunplay scenes in which Veronica Lake becomes the unwilling accomplice of a young killer (Alan Ladd). Robert Preston plays a policeman who is too easily outwitted to deserve Lake in the end. Laird Cregar is an interesting heavy, and Tully Marshall a reprobate of the worst kind.

THIS HAPPY BREED
1944, 116 mins, UK ⓥ
D: David Lean **A:** Robert Newton, Celia Johnson, John Mills, Kay Walsh, Stanley Holloway, Amy Veness (Two Cities/Cineguild)

Based on Noel Coward's legit London hit, film is the history of an average British family, with its pleasures and pains, during the 1920s and 1930s. A bit episodic and choppy at the start, it soon settles down to an absorbing chronicle. Film's excellence comes mainly in the performances. Celia Johnson, as the mother of three and the center around which the family revolves, presents a masterful, poignant portrayal. Robert Newton, as the head of the house, is also superb as the steady, grounded but intelligent Britisher. Kay Walsh as the flighty daughter, John Mills as the loyal sailor in love with her, and Stanley Holloway as the nextdoor neighbor all give fine support.

THIS IS ELVIS
1981, 88 mins, US ⓥ
D: Malcolm Leo, Andrew Solt **A:** Johnny Harra, David Scott, Paul Boensch III, Lawrence Koller, Rhonda Lyn (Warner)

This Is Elvis is a fast-paced gloss on Presley's life and career, packed with fine music and unusual footage. Pic opens with Presley's death at the age of 42 and the subsequent funeral mob scene and is thereafter narrated by uncanny Elvis sound-alike Ral Donner, even though the character is dead. Included are glimpses of the 1950s sensation in his earliest television appearance, some previously unseen press conference footage, the celebrated Ed Sullivan performance, extensive coverage of his army indoctrination and stint in Germany, his comeback appearance with Frank Sinatra, and clips of a few feature films and a look at his smash 1968 television special.

THIS ISLAND EARTH
1955, 87 mins, US ⓥ ◉ ◻
D: Joseph M. Newman **A:** Jeff Morrow, Faith Domergue, Rex Reason, Lance Fuller, Russell Johnson, Douglas Spencer (Universal)

Plot motivation is derived from the frantic efforts of the men of the interstellar planet Metaluna to find on Earth a new source of atomic energy by recruiting the outstanding scientists in the field. A thrilling sequence occurs as huge meteors bombard the space ship as it makes its way to Metaluna. Ingeniously constructed props and equipment and strange sound effects are also responsible for furthering edge-of-the-seat interest during the latter half of the film.

THIS IS MY AFFAIR
See: I Can Get It for You Wholesale

THIS IS MY LIFE
1992, 105 mins, US Ⓥ
D: Nora Ephron **A:** Julie Kavner, Samantha Mathis, Gaby Hoffmann, Carrie Fisher, Dan Aykroyd, Danny Zorn (20th Century-Fox)

A deftly accomplished directorial debut from scripter Nora Ephron. The glib urban sensibility that informed Ephron's screenplay for *When Harry Met Sally* is toned down in favor of humbler, texture-of-life comedy. Julie Kavner stars as a New Jersey divorcée who shares her excess comic energy with her 16- and 10-year-old daughters (Samantha Mathis, Gaby Hoffmann) as they dream of her comedy breakthrough. When an aunt leaves Kavner some money, she packs the kids up for Manhattan, and before long her dreams start to come true. But it's more than the introverted and dependent teenage daughter can handle.

THIS IS SPINAL TAP
1984, 82 mins, US Ⓥ ⊙
D: Rob Reiner **A:** Rob Reiner, Michael McKean, Christopher Guest, Harry Shearer, R. J. Parnell, David Kaff (Spinal Tap)

This Is Spinal Tap is a vastly amusing satire of heavy metal bands. Director Rob Reiner casts himself as Marty DiBergi, a filmmaker intent upon covering the long-awaited American return of the eponymous 17-year-old British rock band. Pic takes the form of a cinema-verité documentary, recording the fictional musicians' increasingly disastrous tour and the group's internal strife. The film has loads of fun creating mock 1960s television videotapes of early gigs and filling the fringes with hilariously authentic music-biz types.

THIS IS THE ARMY
1943, 120 mins, US Ⓥ
D: Michael Curtiz **A:** George Murphy, Joan Leslie, Ronald Reagan, George Tobias, Julie Oshins, Una Merkel (Warner)

A dynamic linking of World Wars I and II with their respective soldier shows—*Yip Yip Yaphank* and *This Is the Army*, both by Irving Berlin. Skillfully linked are both generations, with George Murphy as the yesteryear musicomedy star who suffers a leg injury, which doesn't curb his skill as a theatrical impresario after 1918, and Ronald Reagan, as Johnny Jones, his

son, who carries the romantic interest in World War II. The socko Berlin songs—17 of them—tie the whole package together.
1943: Best Scoring of a Musical Picture
Nominations: Best Color Art Direction, Sound

THIS LAND IS MINE
1943, 103 mins, US Ⓥ ⊙
D: Jean Renoir **A:** Charles Laughton, Maureen O'Hara, George Sanders, Walter Slezak, Kent Smith, Una O'Connor (RKO)

This Land is a steadily engrossing film based on the inner drama of character rather than the exciting physical action of some war films. Its theme is the invincibility of ideas over brute force, and it is given sincere, dignified, and eloquent treatment. Not that the picture is by any means perfect. Some of its incidents tax belief, and the presentation at times is ultra-obvious. Such scenes as Charles Laughton's courtroom espousal of the cause of patriotism and civil disobedience, or his defiant schoolroom reading of "The Rights of Man," are suspiciously theatrical. As the blubbering coward who rises to heroism in a crisis, Laughton gives a shrewdly conceived and developed portrayal, although he occasionally mugs a bit.
1943: Best Sound Recording (Stephen Dunn)

THIS LOVE OF OURS
1945, 90 mins, US
D: William Dieterle **A:** Merle Oberon, Charles Korvin, Claude Rains, Carl Esmond, Sue England, Ralph Morgan (Universal)

Most commendable feature of this film is the plot's originality. Charles Korvin plays a famous doctor whose young daughter (Sue England) has sanctified the memory of her presumably dead mother. Visiting a Chicago nitery while attending a doctors' convention, Korvin meets Merle Oberon, his "dead" wife, working as accompanist for Claude Rains, an artist who does flash sketches of the bistro's patrons. She tries suicide after the meeting, and Korvin saves her through an intricate operation. Film could have been a trite tearjerker, but that's prevented by Dieterle's expert handling.

THIS PROPERTY IS CONDEMNED
1966, 110 mins, US ✆ ☉
D: Sydney Pollack A: Natalie Wood, Robert Redford, Charles Bronson, Kate Reid, Mary Badham, Alan Baxter (Seven Arts/ Stark)

A handsomely mounted Depression-era drama about the effect of railroad retrenchment on people in a boarding house. Derived from a Tennessee Williams one-acter, the production is adult without being sensational, touching without being maudlin. Natalie Wood stars as the young Dixie belle, older daughter of Kate Reid, sleazy landlady to some railroad men. Wood dreams of another life while she acts as the shill for her mother. Robert Redford gives an outstanding performance as the railroad efficiency expert sent to town to lay off most of the crew. Charles Bronson is excellent as the earthy boarder.

THIS RECKLESS AGE
1932, 63 mins, US
D: Frank Tuttle A: Charles "Buddy" Rogers, Richard Bennett, Peggy Shannon, Charles Ruggles, Frances Dee, Frances Starr (Paramount)

Film is completely lacking in anything resembling dramatic force, and what plot is present is largely synthetic, but in the place of drama there is an abundance of sentimentality. It is in the sympathetically drawn family picture that the punch of the story lies. The mother's role is engagingly played by Frances Starr, who is borne along through life by an abiding affection for her husband and a splendid faith and happiness in the integrity of her two children. Story is expertly told within its modest comedy limits, and the playing by the cast is flawless.

THIS SPORTING LIFE
1963, 134 mins, UK ✆
D: Lindsay Anderson A: Richard Harris, Rachel Roberts, Alan Badel, William Hartnell, Colin Blakely, Arthur Lowe (Independent Artists)

Set in the raw, earthy mood of *Saturday Night and Sunday Morning*, *Taste of Honey*, and *Room at the Top*, this film has a gutsy vitality. Lindsay Anderson, making his debut as a feature director, brings the keen, observant eye of a documentarian without sacrificing the story line. The yarn concerns professional rugby football. Richard Harris plays miner Frank Machin, who becomes the ruthless star of his team. He revels in his new prosperity, but

doesn't realize he is being used by local businessmen opportunists. Anderson directs with fluid skill, and sharp editing keeps the film moving, even at its more leisurely moments, Denys Coop's lensing is graphic, and the atmosphere of a northern town is captured soundly. Harris gives a dominating, intelligent performance as the blustering, fundamentally simple and insecure footballer. Roberts, as a repressed widow, brings light and shade and poignance to a role that might have been shadowy and overly downbeat.
1963: Nominations: Best Actor (Richard Harris), Actress (Rachel Roberts)

THIS STRANGE PASSION
See: El

THIS THING CALLED LOVE
1940, 98 mins, US
D: Alexander Hall A: Rosalind Russell, Melvyn Douglas, Binnie Barnes, Allyn Joslyn, Gloria Dickson, Lee J. Cobb (Columbia)

Here is fun with a capital F. It's adult, it's amusing, it has sparkle, and it has vim. Rosalind Russell and Melvyn Douglas are a couple who, though legally wedded, don't know what to do about sex. Or, to be specific, only one of them (at a time) knows what to do, while the other is coy. Roz starts off by having a theory: they will test their love by a three-month abstainment period. Douglas can't see that at all and decides to break her down. Alexander Hall pilots the picture with considerable spirit and a furious pace; so much so that it seems a bit overlong, and some of the biz is repetitious. Both are about evenly divided on the acting honors, managing to point up their laughs beautifully, although a top scene in which Douglas does a rumba as a cover-up for scratching (having contracted oak poisoning) is outstanding.

THIS WOMAN IS DANGEROUS
1952, 97 mins, US
D: Felix Feist A: Joan Crawford, Dennis Morgan, David Brian, Richard Webb, Mari Aldon, Philip Carey (Warner)

This is the story of a woman (Joan Crawford), the mastermind of a criminal gang, who, after the holdup of a New Orleans gambling house, goes to hospital for a dangerous operation to restore her failing sight. She leaves behind a violent, jealous lover (David Brian), plus a clue that tips the FBI that she might have been in on the robbery. Her medico is Dennis Morgan, and the forced association with him leads to an unwilling romance.

THOMAS CROWN AFFAIR, THE
1968, 102 mins, US Ⓥ ⊙

D: Norman Jewison A: Steve McQueen, Faye Dunaway, Paul Burke, Jack Weston, Yaphet Kotto, Biff McGuire (United Artists/Mirisch)

Free of social-conscious pretensions, this Norman Jewison film tells a cracker-jack story, well tooled, professionally crafted, and fashioned with obvious meticulous care. Steve McQueen is a rich, young Boston industrialist who masterminds a bank heist. Paul Burke delivers an excellent performance as a detective who works with Faye Dunaway, an insurance company bounty hunter whose job is to trap McQueen. McQueen is neatly cast as the likable, but lonely, heavy. Dunaway makes an excellent detective who gradually develops a conflict of interests regarding her prey. The only message in this film: enjoy it.
1968: Best Song ("The Windmills of Your Mind")
Nomination: Best Original Score

THOMAS CROWN AFFAIR, THE
1999, 111 mins, US Ⓥ ⊙ ⊡

D: John McTiernan A: Pierce Brosnan, Rene Russo, Denis Leary, Ben Gazzara, Frankie Faison, Fritz Weaver (Irish DreamTime/M-G-M)

This redo of Norman Jewison's 1968 Steve McQueen–Faye Dunaway hit is an ultraslick thriller that shifts the focus from the caper elements to the psychological and emotional factors that compel two hard-shelled professional adversaries to risk a romantic entanglement. Playboy tycoon Thomas Crown (Pierce Brosnan) is a self-made man who can never settle down with a woman because he can't trust anyone. He pulls the theft of a $100 million Monet from New York's Metropolitan Museum of Art. Insurance company investigator Catherine Banning (Rene Russo) is positive that Crown is the culprit. The twists and turns of their relationship are not without interest. Russo takes seriously her rare opportunity at a part more substantial than her usual superstar pairings. Brosnan's Thomas Crown is carved out of ice and thesp's charisma is insufficient to melt it much.

THOMAS L'IMPOSTEUR
(THOMAS THE IMPOSTER)
1965, 93 mins, France

D: Georges Franju A: Emmanuelle Riva, Fabrice Rouleau, Jean Servais, Sophie Dares, Rosy Varte, Michel Vitold (Filmel)

This is a poetic film, drawn from a novel by Jean Cocteau about a teenage boy impersonating an officer during World War I. It also embodies a gentle love story and a biting feel for war's horrors, as well as its strangeness. A headstrong widow princess (Emmanuelle Riva) organizes a caravan to go to the front to pick up wounded men and bring them back to her chateau near Paris for treatment. Stymied by red tape, she is helped by a 16-year-old boy (Fabrice Rouleau) in an officer's uniform who says he is the nephew of a noted general. The boy becomes indispensable to the princess who feels a strange attachment for him. Franju is true to the poetic, artful world of Cocteau but adds his own talent for imbuing the narrative with an underlying strangeness that makes it constantly eye-filling and sometimes disturbing.

THOMAS THE IMPOSTER
See: Thomas L'Imposteur

THOROUGHLY MODERN MILLIE
1967, 138 mins, US Ⓥ ⊙

D: George Roy Hill A: Julie Andrews, James Fox, Mary Tyler Moore, Carol Channing, John Gavin, Beatrice Lillie (Universal)

The first half of *Thoroughly Modern Millie* is quite successful in maintaining a gay spirit and pace. There are many beguiling satirical references to the flapper age and some quite funny bits. But the sudden thrusting of the hero, played by James Fox in hornrimmed glasses, into a skyscraper-climbing, flagpole-hanging acrobat, à la Harold Lloyd, has little of Lloyd but the myth. Musically, *Millie* is a melange. Standards such as "Baby Face" mingle with specials by Jimmy Van Heusen and Sammy Cahn. Julie Andrews is the leading lady of the story but hardly more than a bystander when Carol Channing commands the scene.
1967: Best Original Score
Nominations: Best Supp. Actress (Carol Channing), Costume Design, Scoring of Music, Song ("Thoroughly Modern Millie"), Sound

THOSE MAGNIFICENT MEN IN THEIR FLYING MACHINES OR HOW I FLEW FROM LONDON TO PARIS IN 25 HOURS 11 MINUTES
1965, 131 mins, UK ⓥ ⊙ ⌑
D: Ken Annakin **A:** Stuart Whitman, Sarah Miles, James Fox, Alberto Sordi, Robert Morley, Gert Frobe (20th Century-Fox)

This backward look into the pioneer days of aviation, when most planes were built with spit and bailing wire, is a warming entertainment experience. A London newspaper publisher offers a 10,000 prize to winner of an event which will focus worldwide attention on the fledgling sport of flying (circa 1910), subsequently attracting a flock of international contestants. While there is naturally a story line and a nice romance, the planes themselves, a startling collection of uniquely designed oddities which actually fly, probably merit the most attention.
1965: Nomination: Best Story & Screenplay

THOSE WERE THE HAPPY TIMES
See: Star!

THOUSAND CLOWNS, A
1965, 117 mins, US ⓥ
D: Fred Coe **A:** Jason Robards, Barbara Harris, Martin Balsam, Gene Saks, William Daniels, Barry Gordon (Harrell/United Artists)

A Thousand Clowns depicts a happy-go-lucky nonconformist who attains maturity when a child welfare board threatens to take away his young resident nephew. Jason Robards plays the ex-vidscripter trying to prevent nephew Barry Gordon from becoming one of the "dead people," i.e., conformists. Terrific dialogue to match Robards's scenery-chewing create a strong impact as he lectures the 12-year-old, ignores the pleas of brother-agent Martin Balsam to return to work, and pierces the outstanding social worker bureaucratic shell of Barbara Harris and William Daniels, who've arrived to check on the kid's home life.
1965: Best Supp. Actor (Martin Balsam)
Nominations: Best Picture, Screenplay Adaptation, Adapted Music Score

THOUSANDS CHEER
1943, 124 mins, US ⓥ ⊙
D: George Sidney **A:** Kathryn Grayson, Gene Kelly, Mary Astor, John Boles, Jose Iturbi, Frances Rafferty (M-G-M)

Kathryn Grayson is the colonel's (John Boles) daughter who puts on a super-duper camp show which not only introduces Jose Iturbi as part of the entertainment but brings forth Mickey Rooney, Judy Garland, Red Skelton, Eleanor Powell, and others. Paramount keynote of this expert musical is the tip-top manner in which young George Sidney has marshalled his multiple talents so that none trips over the other. It's a triumph for Sidney on his first major-league effort. Grayson, making her long-hair farewell at an Iturbi concert, decides to move with papa Boles to his camp, in an endeavor to reconcile him and Mary Astor (the mother).
1943: Nominations: Best Color Cinematography, Color Art Direction, Scoring of a Musical Picture

THREE
1969, 105 mins, UK
D: James Salter **A:** Charlotte Rampling, Robie Porter, Sam Waterston, Pascale Roberts (United Artists/Obelisk)

Three is a rare pic about youth that deals with a romantic summer idyll sans sentimentality and with a freshness and easy charm that pinpoints character without affectation. Two young men, Robie Porter and Sam Waterston, set off in an old car one summer to tour Italy and France. They meet a pretty English girl (Charlotte Rampling) and make a pact to keep her a friend rather than a sexual or love target. But Waterston begins to fall for her, and their triple idyll deteriorates as she succumbs to Porter.

THREE AGES, THE
1923, 67 mins, US ⊗
D: Buster Keaton, Edward Cline **A:** Buster Keaton, Margaret Leahy, Wallace Beery, Lillian Lawrence, Joe Roberts, Horace "Cupid" Morgan, Oliver Hardy (Schenck/Metro)

The three periods are the Stone Age, the pompous days of Rome, and the modern age. A brief foreword explains that, although customs and times change, love-making and loving are always the same. First we have the young lover of the Stone Age up to a certain point in his courtship; then the Roman dandy up to the same point; and finally the modern swain in a similar cross section of his love affair. In all three cases the situation is the same—a humble but faithful lover (Buster Keaton) struggles for his lady fair against the unscrupulous unworthy adventurer (Wallace Beery) and in his efforts stumbles into all sorts of scrapes. The stories are worked out with the most ingenious incidents.

¡THREE AMIGOS!
1986, 105 mins, US Ⓥ ⊙
D: John Landis **A:** Chevy Chase, Steve Martin, Martin Short, Patrice Martinez, Alfonso Arau, Joe Mantegna (LA Films/Orion)

A few choice morsels of brilliant humor can't save *¡Three Amigos!* from missing the whole enchilada. It has three funny guys, Steve Martin, Chevy Chase, and Martin Short playing the three wimpy matinee idols known as the "Three Amigos," each doing his particular brand of shtick that is priceless in some scenes but not at all amusing in others. These singing cowboy stars of the silent screen have just been fired by the flamboyant Goldsmith Studios mogul Harry Flugelman (Joe Mantegna) when they get a cryptic telegram from a Mexican woman (Patrice Martinez) offering them 100,000 pesos to come to her dusty desert town of Santa Poco. It turns out she's hired them under the mistaken belief that they are as macho in real life as they are on screen.

THREE BITES OF THE APPLE
1967, 98 mins, US ▭
D: Alvin Ganzer **A:** David McCallum, Sylva Koscina, Tammy Grimes, Harvey Korman, Domenico Modugno (M-G-M)

As a travelogue, *Three Bites of the Apple* has certain merit; as a madcap comedy, its intended goal, it hasn't. The screenplay is based on the flimsiest of premises. David McCallum, a mild-mannered tour guide, wins 1,200 in an Italian casino and is then faced with the question of how to save it from taxes so he'll be able to return to his native Britain with more than a pittance. A pretty young adventuress, Sylva Koscina, out to get the coin for herself, sells him on allowing a "friend" to help him in this matter.

THREE CABALLEROS, THE
1945, 71 mins, US Ⓥ ⊙
D: Norman Ferguson **A:** Aurora Miranda, Carmen Molina, Dora Luz (RKO/Walt Disney)

Walt Disney in *The Three Caballeros* reveals a new form of cinematic entertainment in which he blends live action with animation into a socko feature production. Neatly conceived, it ties in many pan-American highlights through the medium of irascible Donald Duck, the wiseguy Joe Carioca (first introduced in *Saludos Amigos*), and a lovable character in Panchito, the little South American boy. It's DD's birthday, and he gets three huge packages of gifts from his friends in Latin America. What he unwraps as his "gifts" are transplanted to this live action-animation feature. The off-screen narration is skillfully blended with the dialogue between Donald, Joe Carioca, and others.
1945: Nominations: Best Scoring of a Musical Picture, Sound

THREE CAME HOME
1950, 106 mins, US Ⓥ
D: Jean Negulesco **A:** Claudette Colbert, Patric Knowles, Sessue Hayakawa, Florence Desmond (20th Century-Fox)

Agnes Newton Keith's deeply affecting autobiography of hardships in a Japanese prison camp has been filmed without any easing of the book's harrowing impact. Particularly effective is the sequence which portrays the principal character, an American woman (Claudette Colbert), married to a British administrator, crawling under barbed wire and through the jungle to keep a tryst with her husband. The implacable conduct of the jailers is related convincingly.

THREE COINS IN THE FOUNTAIN
1954, 101 mins, US Ⓥ ⊙ ▭
D: Jean Negulesco **A:** Clifton Webb, Dorothy McGuire, Jean Peters, Louis Jourdan, Maggie McNamara, Rossano Brazzi (20th Century-Fox)

Three Coins in the Fountain has warmth, humor, a rich dose of romance, and almost incredible pictorial appeal. There is a trio of female stars—Dorothy McGuire, Jean Peters, and Maggie McNamara—in expensive-looking clothes. As their male counterparts they have Clifton Webb, debonair and fun as always; Rossano Brazzi, an appealing young Italian; and suave Louis Jourdan, appealing as the romantic lead. Story introduces McNamara, an American coming to take a secretarial job to Rome. She's met by Peters and is later introduced to her third roommate, McGuire, in their sumptuous apartment. They all toss a coin in the fountain, and it grants them their wish.
1954: Best Color Cinematography, Song ("Three Coins in the Fountain")
Nomination: Best Picture

THREE COLORS
BLUE
See: Trois Couleurs Bleu

THREE COLORS
RED
See: Trois Couleurs Rouge

THREE COLORS
WHITE
See: Trois Couleurs Blanc

THREE COMRADES
1938, 100 mins, US
D: Frank Borzage **A:** Robert Taylor, Margaret Sullavan, Franchot Tone, Robert Young, Guy Kibbee, Lionel Atwill (M-G-M)

There must have been some reason for making this picture, but it certainly isn't in the cause of entertainment. Film deals with the psychological subtleties of German youth lately released from the armies of World War I; of the political struggle in establishing the republic; of the futility of the army-bred boys to cope with civilian connivance; and finally, the tragedy of a love affair between one of the youths and a young woman dying of tuberculosis (Margaret Sullavan). It is a film of characterization, rather than plot. The titular comrades are Robert Taylor, Franchot Tone, and Robert Young. After Young is killed in a street riot, the other two look forward to a dark, unhappy, and lonely future.
1938: Nomination: Best Actress (Margaret Sullavan)

THREE DAYS OF THE CONDOR
1975, 117 mins, US Ⓥ ⊙ ▭
D: Sydney Pollack **A:** Robert Redford, Faye Dunaway, Cliff Robertson, Max von Sydow, John Houseman, Addison Powell (Paramount)

Robert Redford, working in a CIA front, discovers all his associates massacred. He runs, pants, thinks, schemes, evades, and ultimately exposes an agency insider who has been plotting on the side. Disenchanted, Redford walks into a newspaper to expose the whole thing. The film is a perfect contemporary example of an old studio formula approach to filmmaking. Basically a B movie, it has been elevated in form—but not in substance—via bigger names, location shooting, and higher production values. Sometimes the trick works, but not here.
1975: Nomination: Best Editing

THREE FACES OF EVE, THE
1957, 91 mins, US Ⓥ ▭
D: Nunnally Johnson **A:** Joanne Woodward, David Wayne, Lee J. Cobb, Edwin Jerome, Alena Murray, Nancy Kulp (20th Century-Fox)

The Three Faces of Eve is based on a true-life case history. It is frequently an intriguing, provocative motion picture, but director Nunnally Johnson's treatment shifts back and forth—striving for comedy at one point and presenting a documentary case history at another. However, it is notable for the performance of Joanne Woodward as the woman with the triple personality. The psychiatric sessions, while possibly authentic, could readily confuse the layman. The manner in which the doctor (Lee J. Cobb) can hypnotize and alter his patient's personality seems so easy and pat as to appear hard to believe.
1957: Best Actress (Joanne Woodward)

THREE FUGITIVES
1989, 96 mins, US ⊙
D: Francis Veber **A:** Nick Nolte, Martin Short, Sarah Rowland Doroff, James Earl Jones, Alan Ruck, Kenneth McMillan (Touchstone)

French director Francis Veber remakes his own 1986 comedy *Les Fugitifs* American-style. Clever premise starts pic off on a roll, as master bankrobber Lucas (Nick Nolte) gets out of the slammer determined to go straight, only to get involved in another heist in the very first bank he enters as an innocent bystander taken hostage by a hysterically inept gunman (Martin Short). Short, once he figures out Nolte's predicament, blackmails him into aiding and abetting his escape from the country. Nolte, not really a comic natural, gruffs and grumbles his way as hunky straight man to Short's calamitous comedian. Short runs with the slapstick style.

300 SPARTANS, THE
1962, 108 mins, US ▭
D: Rudolph Mate **A:** Richard Egan, Ralph Richardson, Diane Baker, Barry Coe, David Farrar, Donald Houston (20th-Century Fox)

The hopeless but inspiring defense of their country by a 300 Spartan soldiers against an immense army of Persian invaders in 480 B.C.—known to history as the Battle of Thermopylae—is the nucleus around which this film is constructed. The inherent appeal and magnitude of the battle itself dwarfs and sweeps aside all attempts at romantic byplay. Richard Egan, as King Leonidas of Sparta, is physically suitable for the character, but the heroic mold of his performance is only skin deep. Ralph Richardson, as might be expected, does the best acting in the picture, but no one is going to list this portrayal as one of the great achievements in his career.

THREE IN THE ATTIC
1968, 90 mins, US ⓥ
D: Richard Wilson **A:** Yvette Mimieux, Christopher Jones, Judy Pace, Maggie Thrett, Nan Martin, John Beck (American International)

Three in the Attic apparently starts out as a tragicomedy about physical sex versus love. It is littered with padding optical effects, hampered by an uneven dramatic concept, and redundant in its too-delicious sex teasing. Christopher Jones, a college campus lover type, gets hung up on Yvette Mimieux. He won't admit he loves her, and adds Judy Pace, an African-American charmer, and Maggie Thrett, a Jewish hippie, to his harem. The gals learn of the bed rotation plan and lock Jones in an attic, where they attempt to exhaust him with regular, clock-timed sex visits.

3 INTO 2 WON'T GO
1969, 93 mins, UK
D: Peter Hall **A:** Rod Steiger, Claire Bloom, Judy Geeson, Peggy Ashcroft, Paul Rogers (Universal)

Superb British film, *3 into 2 Won't Go* is an examination of a shattered marriage between career-oriented Rod Steiger, an appliance salesman, and his childless, schoolteacher-wife, Claire Bloom. Judy Geeson, 19-year-old hitchhiker with no social or moral ties, seduces Steiger on an overnight sales trip. With dialogue that has the banal sound of realistic human exchanges, Edna O'Brien's script investigates all sorts of suggestions and shifts in audience reaction. Film is brisk and emotionally stirring.

THREE KINGS
1999, 115 mins, US ⓥ ⊙ ▭
D: David O. Russell **A:** George Clooney, Mark Wahlberg, Ice Cube, Spike Jonze, Nora Dunn, Jamie Kennedy (Coast Ridge/Atlas/Warner)

Three Kings takes on the 1991 Gulf War in an impudently comic, stylistically aggressive, and, finally, very thoughtful manner. David O. Russell's individualistic first studio picture discharges black humor, startling action, genre subversion, anarchic attitude, and barbed political commentary while making cogent points about the cynical nature of war and America's role as the world's policeman. Special Forces Captain Archie Gates (George Clooney) discovers that three GIs (Mark Wahlberg, Ice Cube, Spike Jonze) have a map identifying a stash of gold bullion snatched from Kuwait by Saddam's army. The four men encounter a confusing situation, welcomed with open arms by Iraqi civilians whom the soldiers treat brusquely in their quest for the gold bricks. Underlying it all are sentiments concerning the amorality and lack of consistent principles in American foreign policy.

THREE LITTLE WORDS
1950, 100 mins, US ⓥ ⊙
D: Richard Thorpe **A:** Fred Astaire, Red Skelton, Vera-Ellen, Arlene Dahl, Keenan Wynn, Debbie Reynolds (M-G-M)

A biopic of the songwriting team of Harry Ruby and Bert Kalmar, the picture is a charmful, entertaining cavalcade of show business. Fred Astaire is Kalmar and Red Skelton is Ruby, and the entire cast does fine work under the skillful direction of Richard Thorpe. Vera-Ellen matches Astaire tap for tap in their terping duets, which is no mean achievement, and looks to be possibly the best partner he's ever had. Arlene Dahl plays Eileen Percy and also turns in a standout performance.

1950: Nomination: Best Scoring of a Musical Picture

THREE LOVES HAS NANCY
1938, 70 mins, US
D: Richard Thorpe **A:** Janet Gaynor, Robert Montgomery, Franchot Tone, Guy Kibbee, Claire Dodd, Reginald Owen (M-G-M)

Three Loves Has Nancy is a completely daffy, reasonably entertaining romp by Janet Gaynor, Robert Montgomery, Franchot Tone, and a group of familiar supporting players. It's about a small-town gal who gets stranded in New York and becomes the object of a furious contest between a flighty author and his hell-raising publisher. On that slender framework have been scribbled all the balmy situations, crackpot gags, and slapstick whimsy that six frenzied scripters could concoct. Director Richard Thorpe and the cast play it with broad relish.

3 MEN AND A BABY
1987, 102 mins, US ⓥ ⊙
D: Leonard Nimoy **A:** Tom Selleck, Steve Guttenberg, Ted Danson, Nancy Travis,

Margaret Colin, Celeste Holm (Touchstone/Interscope)

3 Men and a Baby is about as slight a feature comedy as is made, an Americanized version of the 1985 French sleeper hit *3 Hommes et un Couffin* that parallels the original's story line almost exactly. Three confirmed bachelors are thrown into confusion when a baby is left at their front door. As it happens, actor and suspected father of the infant (Ted Danson) is conveniently out of town on a shoot, leaving architect Peter (Tom Selleck) and cartoonist Michael (Steve Guttenberg) all in a quandary about what to do with the precious little thing. Big macho men tripping all over themselves trying to successfully feed, diaper, and bathe a bundle of innocence and helplessness are ripe for comic development.

3 MEN AND A CRADLE
See: 3 Hommes et un Couffin

3 MEN AND A LITTLE LADY
1990, 100 mins, US ⊗ ⊙
D: Emile Ardolino **A:** Tom Selleck, Steve Guttenberg, Ted Danson, Nancy Travis, Robin Weisman, Christopher Cazenove (Touchstone/Interscope)

Back in their places for this two-dimensional sequel are the three bachelor dads of the waif who landed on their doorstep in part one: vain actor and biological dad Ted Danson, architect Tom Selleck, and illustrator Steve Guttenberg. What's new is that Selleck has fallen in love with the baby's mom, Sylvia (Nancy Travis), the actress who shares their new apartment. Mom decides that she must marry. She accepts a proposal from her director friend, Edward (Christopher Cazenove), and plans to move to England with little Mary (Robin Weisman), since Selleck is too confused to pop the question. Rest of the pic is standard romantic comedy.

THREE MEN ON A HORSE
1936, 85 mins, US
D: Mervyn LeRoy **A:** Frank McHugh, Joan Blondell, Guy Kibbee, Carol Hughes, Allen Jenkins, Sam Levene (Warner)

Mervyn LeRoy, in producing this screen version of the legit hit, adhered pretty closely to the original. Instead of the radio broadcast finish, the screen permits carrying the action directly to the racetrack, which opens the way for some extra comedy. Another improvement is the handling of the lead, "Oiwin," by Frank McHugh. He does splendidly in the sap

assignment without changing the character of the timid man who always picks winners. Other cast standouts include Sam Levene's wise guy and Teddy Hart's softhearted chiseler, both highly enjoyable.

THREE MUSKETEERS, THE
1921, 140 mins, US ⊗
D: Fred Niblo **A:** Douglas Fairbanks, Leon Bary, George Siegmann, Eugene Pallette, Marguerite De La Motte, Adolphe Menjou (Fairbanks/United Artists)

This story of Dumas has been ideally approximated in this screen version. There is a flare and sweep about the film. Douglas Fairbanks and D'Artagnan are a happy combination. Nigel de Brulier as Richelieu develops a real creation. Excepting only the star, he dominates the picture. Adolphe Menjou does excellently as Louis XIII, gaining a sympathetic response.

THREE MUSKETEERS, THE
1931, 97 mins, US ⊙
D: Rowland V. Lee **A:** Walter Abel, Paul Lukas, Margot Grahame, Heather Angel, Ian Keith, Moroni Olsen (RKO)

The impotency of the sound medium in the field of romantic adventure comedy, when inexpertly handled, is revealed with melancholy effect in this famous Dumas story, remade with dialogue. *The Three Musketeers* is dull entertainment. Walter Abel, a well-regarded young player from Broadway, is unsuited in nearly every respect for the role of D'Artagnan. Nigel de Brulier is convincing as Richelieu, the same role he played in the 1921 Fairbanks picture. Ian Keith as the villainous de Rochefort is excellent as always.

THREE MUSKETEERS, THE
1939, 71 mins, US
D: Allan Dwan **A:** Don Ameche, Ritz Bros, Binnie Barnes, Lionel Atwill, Pauline Moore (20th Century-Fox)

Utilizing the broadest strokes of comedy technique, this version of Dumas' romantic adventure presents Don Ameche as a rather personable D'Artagnan, and the Ritz Bros as a helter-skelter trio performing their standard screwball antics. There is little seriousness or suspense generated in the slender story and not much interest in the adventures of D'Artagnan and his pals to regain the queen's brooch in the possession of the Duke of Buckingham. Main excuse for the yarn is apparently to provide Ameche with an opportunity to be a dashing hero, while the Ritz clown through the footage as phoney musketeers.

THREE MUSKETEERS, THE
1948, 126 mins, US Ⓥ ⊙
D: George Sidney **A:** Gene Kelly, Lana Turner, June Allyson, Van Heflin, Angela Lansbury, Vincent Price (M-G-M)

A swaggering, tongue-in-cheek treatment of picturesque fiction, extravagantly presented. The fanciful tale is launched with a laugh and swings into some exciting sword duels as the pace is set for the adventures of D'Artagnan and his three cronies. There are acrobatics by Gene Kelly that would give Douglas Fairbanks pause. His first duel with Richelieu's cohorts is almost ballet, yet never loses the feeling of swaggering swordplay. Lana Turner is a perfect visualization of the sexy, wicked Lady de Winter, sharply contrasting with the sweet charm of June Allyson as the maid Constance. The musketeers of the title are dashingly portrayed by Van Heflin, Gig Young, and Robert Coote as Athos, Porthos, and Aramis, respectively.
1948: Nomination: Best Color Cinematography

THREE MUSKETEERS, THE
1993, 105 mins, US Ⓥ ⊙ ▭
D: Stephen Herek **A:** Charlie Sheen, Kiefer Sutherland, Chris O'Donnell, Oliver Platt, Tim Curry, Rebecca DeMornay (Walt Disney)

Fifth major screen version of Alexandre Dumas' classic swashbuckling saga is a handsome but pallid affair. Although filmed on beautiful locations in Austria and elsewhere, pic has an Americanized slant. Possibly the most faithful rendition of the perennial favorite, it is tame compared with Richard Lester's wild and woolly 1974 version. Set in 16th-century France, yarn begins as the noble Musketeers, guardians of the king, are disbanded by Cardinal Richelieu (Tim Curry), who is conniving to wrest the throne from the weak teenaged monarch. Dashing D'Artagnan (Chris O'Donnell) is hoping to join their ranks, but the only ones left are renegades Aramis (Charlie Sheen), Athos (Kiefer Sutherland), and Porthos (Oliver Platt). Chased to Calais, they intercept his eminence's messenger and return to Paris to disrupt Richelieu's plans.

THREE MUSKETEERS, THE
THE QUEEN'S DIAMONDS
1973, 105 mins, Panama/Spain Ⓥ
D: Richard Lester **A:** Oliver Reed, Charlton Heston, Raquel Welch, Faye Dunaway, Richard Chamberlain, Michael York (Fox Film Trust)

The Three Musketeers take very well to Richard Lester's provocative version that does not send it up but does add comedy to Dumas' adventure tale. D'Artagnan, played with brio by Michael York, is a country bumpkin; the musketeers themselves are more interested in money, dames, and friendship than fidelity to the king—a simple-minded type—and their fight scenes are full of flailing, kicks, and knockabout. Behind it, however, is a look at an era of poverty and virtual worker slavery to fulfill the king's whims. Musketeers are played with panache by Richard Chamberlain as the haughty ladies' man, Oliver Reed as the gusty one, and Frank Finlay as the dandyish type. Raquel Welch has comedic timing as D'Artagnan's maladroit girl while Faye Dunaway has less to do as the perfidious Milady.

3 NINJAS
1992, 84 mins, US Ⓥ ⊙
D: Jon Turteltaub **A:** Victor Wong, Michael Treanor, Max Elliott Slade, Chad Power, Rand Kingsley, Alan McRae (Global Venture Hollywood)

Though the plot is thin and formulaic, the gracefully choreographed spectacle of three little boys outfighting hordes of evil adult ninjas is a sure-fire juvenile crowd-pleaser. Borrowing liberally from *The Karate Kid* and *Home Alone*, the filmmakers show little guys Michael Treanor, Max Elliott Slade, and Chad Power hurling baddies through the air and flattening the massive, seemingly invincible Toru Tanaka. Director Jon Turteltaub keeps things zipping along, wisely not wasting much time with the ninjas' arms dealer boss (Rand Kingsley) or with his antagonist, the boys' blandly inattentive FBI agent father (Alan McRae).

3 NINJAS KICK BACK
1994, 99 mins, US Ⓥ ⊙
D: Charles T. Kanganis **A:** Victor Wong, Max Elliott Slade, Sean Fox, Evan Bonifant, Caroline Junko King, Sab Shimono (Sheen)

Set mostly in Japan and adding a female ninja to the three boys, this is a high-spirited sequel to Disney's 1992 sleeper. Its three cute ninjas, Rocky (Sean Fox), Colt (Max Elliott Slade), and Tum Tum (Evan Bonifant), have to help Grandpa Mori (Victor Wong) return to Japan to present a ceremonial dagger to the new winner of a ninja tournament. And they have to return to L.A. on time to aid their baseball team, the Dragons, against the rival Mustangs. In pursuit of the dagger, Grandpa's old enemy Koga (Sab Shimono) recruits a trio of spaced-out heavy-metal rockers. A young girl, Miyo (Caroline Junko King), teaches the boys a lesson or two in the ninja arts.

3 NINJAS KNUCKLE UP
1995, 85 mins, US Ⓥ
D: Simon S. Sheen **A:** Victor Wong, Charles Napier, Michael Treanor, Max Elliott Slade, Chad Power, Crystle Lightning (Sheen)

The third time isn't the charm for this latest adventure of the pint-size chopsocky heroes. *Knuckle Up* is thoroughly second-rate in all regards, with slapdash production values, cartoonish performances, by-the-numbers scripting, and ridiculous martial-arts fight scenes. The silliness is strained and witless. Once again, brothers Rocky (Treanor), Tum Tum (Power), and Colt (Max Elliot Slade) spend an eventful summer vacation with their Grandpa Mori (Victor Wong), a sage martial-arts instructor. Formulaic script has the young heroes defending a Native American tribe against a ruthless businessman (Charles Napier) who's dumping toxic waste on their land.

THREE OF HEARTS
1993, 102 mins, US Ⓥ
D: Yurek Bogayevicz **A:** William Baldwin, Kelly Lynch, Sherilyn Fenn, Joe Pantoliano, Gail Strickland, Cec Verrell (New Line)

The comic triangle of *Three of Hearts* offers a male prostitute and a lesbian nurse enamored of a seemingly bisexual woman. The film gets off to a good start, when Sherilyn Fenn dumps g.f. Kelly Lynch in Washington Square Park. Lynch, who intended to officially come out at her sister's wedding by bringing Fenn, hires William Baldwin, a good-looking hustler, to accompany her. Before long, Baldwin moves into Lynch's apartment and a new friendship is formed to win Fenn back. For viewers willing to suspend disbelief, this aspiring screwball comedy is immensely likable. Baldwin delivers a knockout performance in film's richest role. Lynch also shines as a droll, slightly obsessive lesbian.

THREE ON A WEEKEND
See: Bank Holiday

THREEPENNY OPERA, THE
See: Die Dreigroschenoper

3 RING CIRCUS
1954, 103 mins, US ▭
D: Joseph Pevney **A:** Dean Martin, Jerry Lewis, Joanne Dru, Zsa Zsa Gabor, Elsa Lanchester, Wallace Ford (Paramount)

Circus background gives Dean Martin and Jerry Lewis slick opportunity to disport themselves along familiar lines. Lewis reports as a lion tamer's assistant in the hope he'll get to be a clown. Martin tags along, catching the eye of the beautiful but temperamental trapeze artist (Zsa Zsa Gabor), who makes him her "assistant." Comics as a team are somewhat less zany than in previous productions.

THREE SAILORS AND A GIRL
1953, 94 mins, US
D: Roy Del Ruth **A:** Jane Powell, Gordon MacRae, Gene Nelson, Sam Levene, George Givot, Veda Ann Borg (Warner)

This musical deals with a group of submarine sailors (including Gordon MacRae and Gene Nelson) who put their savings into a musical being promoted by Sam Levene. The three sailors are babes in the woods on Broadway but soon learn the ropes, and a flop show is turned into a hit starring the boys and with Jane Powell, after its hambone leading man (George Givot) has joined the setup. The big production finale is a dressed-up, tuneful affair with Powell and MacRae doing "Home Is Where the Heart Is" before Nelson takes over the terping with line dancers. LeRoy Prinz staged and directed the musical numbers for sight appeal.

THREE SMART GIRLS
1937, 86 mins, US
D: Henry Koster **A:** Deanna Durbin, Binnie Barnes, Alice Brady, Ray Milland, Charles Winninger, Mischa Auer (Universal)

Film is a sentimental comedy and has that rare quality of making an audience feel better for having seen it. Story merely tells of three girls' attempts to reconcile their estranged parents. Deanna Durbin is the prime schemer, and the other two daughters find future husbands as the action progresses. Film ends on a happy tear as the youngest reintroduces her mother to her dad. Durbin stands out not only as a "darling child" personality, but as a winsome little dramatic actress whose talents do not end with an ability to hit the high registers.

1936: Nominations: Best Picture, Original Story, Sound

THREESOME
1994, 93 mins, US 🆅 ⊙
D: Andrew Fleming A: Lara Flynn Boyle, Stephen Baldwin, Josh Charles, Alexis Arquette, Martha Gehman, Mark Arnold (Motion Picture Corp. of America)

Cute, sexy, and funny, *Threesome* also manages to deftly capture the working out of personality and sexual identity that is part and parcel of the college years. Because of her male-sounding name, sharp-looking Alex (Lara Flynn Boyle) is assigned a room in the same UCLA dorm suite shared by hot-looking party boy Stuart (Stephen Baldwin) and handsome intellectual Eddy (Josh Charles). Alex becomes infatuated with Eddy, who backs off, admitting he's actually attracted to Stuart, not Alex. Stuart tries to seduce Alex, but she spurns him, still intent upon molding Eddy into a heterosexual. Before long, the trio is locked in three-way embraces and gropings, supplemented by separate sessions between Alex and the two young men.

THREE STRANGERS
1946, 91 mins, US
D: Jean Negulesco A: Sydney Greenstreet, Peter Lorre, Geraldine Fitzgerald, Joan Lorring, Robert Shayne, Marjorie Riordan (Warner)

Three Strangers employs a rather complicated episodic plot, depending mostly on the fine cast performances to carry it. Sydney Greenstreet overplays as the attorney who has raided a trust fund, but he still does a good job. Peter Lorre is tops as a drunk who gets involved in a murder of which he's innocent, while Geraldine Fitzgerald plays the victim. The three have equal shares in a sweepstakes ticket, but are strangers. They win on the ticket, but Greenstreet murders the girl in a fit of rage, in Lorre's presence, thus leaving Lorre also a loser, since he cannot risk trying to cash the ticket because it would involve him in the killing.

3:10 TO YUMA
1957, 92 mins, US 🆅 ⊙
D: Delmer Daves A: Glenn Ford, Van Heflin, Felicia Farr, Leora Dana, Henry Jones, Richard Jaeckel (Columbia)

3:10 to Yuma will strike many for its resemblance to *High Noon*. Glenn Ford portrays the leader of an outlaw gang that holds up a stagecoach. Van Heflin, impoverished rancher, helps capture him. But Ford's gang is too strong for local lawmen to handle. Stagecoach owner Robert Emhardt promises a large reward to Heflin to hold Ford in another town, unknown to his gang, until the 3:10 train can take him to Yuma for a trial. Ford's switch-casting, as the quietly sinister gang leader, is authoritative, impressive, and successful. Heflin measures up fully and convincingly to the rewarding role of the proud and troubled rancher.

THREE VIOLENT PEOPLE
1956, 100 mins, US
D: Rudolph Mate A: Charlton Heston, Anne Baxter, Gilbert Roland, Tom Tryon, Forrest Tucker, Bruce Bennett (Paramount)

Demobilized Confederate soldiers are being taunted and abused by Yankee soldiers and carpetbaggers in Texas. The proud captain, mellowed from four years of war and retreating, holds his temper and his gunfire. The plot twist concerns the precipitate marriage of the proud Texan to a former fille de nuit. One of the occupation army camp-followers spills the beans. Anne Baxter has the requisite sauciness combined with sincerity to make the woman's part stand up. Her relationship with Charlton Heston, who offers a rugged and believable characterization, gives the production its underpinning.

THREE WISE GIRLS
1932, 67 mins, US
D: William Beaudine A: Jean Harlow, Mae Clarke, Walter Byron, Marie Prevost, Andy Devine, Natalie Moorhead (Columbia)

Three small-town girls come to New York. One gets an apartment on Park Avenue, with a banker paying the bills. The second girl addresses envelopes for a living and marries a chauffeur. The third goes back home disgusted because her boyfriend can't get a divorce from his wife, but he gets his freedom and comes after her. Jean Harlow plays the girl who keeps straight. She does her best to suggest the innocent young thing but fails to be convincing, while Mae Clarke takes the acting honors as the banker's wife.

THREE WOMEN
1924, 82 mins, US ⊗
D: Ernst Lubitsch A: May McAvoy, Pauline Frederick, Lew Cody, Marie Prevost, Willard Louis (Warner Bros)

Three Women is a pretty piece of direction. Lew Cody plays a penniless Don Juan who lays siege to the heart of a millionaire widow (Pauline Frederick). He is not aware that she has a daughter (May McAvoy) until she returns from school unawares and steps right into her mother's romance. When Cody hears that the daughter is to receive half of the family fortune on her marriage, he lays plans to win her. As soon as the ceremony is set, he begins another affair, which is where the third woman comes in.

THREE WOMEN
1977, 122 mins, US ▢
D: Robert Altman **A:** Shelley Duvall, Sissy Spacek, Janice Rule, Robert Fortier, Ruth Nelson, John Cromwell (20th Century-Fox)

Absorbing, moody, and often compelling story about psychological dependence and transference, film is set in the desert where Shelley Duvall works as an attendant in an old-folks' health center and new staffer Sissy Spacek becomes her roommate. Janice Rule is the mural-painting wife of retired stuntman Robert Fortier, the two of them being catalysts to the changing relationship between Spacek and Duvall.

THREE WORLDS OF GULLIVER, THE
1960, 98 mins, UK ⊘ ⊙
D: Jack Sher **A:** Kerwin Mathews, Jo Morrow, June Thorburn, Basil Sydney, Gregoire Aslan, Lee Patterson (Columbia)

Jonathan Swift's 18th-century satire has been softened and drastically romanticized, but enough of its caustic comment remains. The work has been trimmed to the familiar twosome of Lilliput, land of little people, and Brobdingnag, where the natives are gigantic. The picture is notable for its visuo-cinematic achievements and its bold, bright, and sweeping score by Bernard Herrmann. Special visual effects expert Ray Harryhausen's Superdynamation process makes the motion-pictured Gulliver plausible and workable.

THRESHOLD
1981, 106 mins, Canada ⊘
D: Richard Pearce **A:** Donald Sutherland, John Marley, Sharon Ackerman, Jeff Goldblum, Mare Winningham, Michael Lerner (Paragon)

Donald Sutherland plays a heart specialist involved in the development of a mechanical heart for transplants. The device is the brainchild of fanatical medical biologist Jeff Goldblum. When current practices fail on patient Mare Winningham, Sutherland decides to defy the board and bring out the miracle device. Writer James Salter and director Richard Pearce have strenuously avoided a melodramatic approach. At times one wishes the film had opted for a more dramatic tone.

THRILL OF IT ALL
1963, 108 mins, US ⊘
D: Norman Jewison **A:** Doris Day, James Garner, Arlene Francis, Edward Andrews, ZaSu Pitts, Reginald Owen (Universal/Arwin)

Writer Carl Reiner's scenario is peppered with digs at various institutions of American life. But these pinpricks of satiric substance are primarily bonuses. Ultimately it is in the engineering of cumulative sight gag situations that *Thrill of It All* excels. Doris Day scores as the housewife with two children who is suddenly thrust into the position of $80,000-a-year pitch woman for an eccentric soap tycoon who is impressed by her unaffected quality. James Garner plays her husband, a gynecologist whose domestic tranquility is shattered by his wife's sudden transition to career girl.

THRONE OF BLOOD
See: Kumonosu-jo

THROUGH A GLASS DARKLY
See: Sasom I En Spegel

THROW MOMMA FROM THE TRAIN
1987, 88 mins, US ⊘ ⊙
D: Danny DeVito **A:** Danny DeVito, Billy Crystal, Anne Ramsey, Kim Greist, Kate Mulgrew, Annie Ross (Orion)

Throw Momma from the Train is a fun and delightfully venial comedy. The idle death threats of a junior college professor (Billy Crystal) against his ex-wife are overheard by one of his dimwitted and impressionable students (Danny DeVito), whose limited creative abilities are stifled by his crazy, overbearing momma (Anne Ramsey). He seeks out Crystal for help on his writing, is told to go see Alfred Hitchcock's *Strangers on a Train*, and comes away with a ridiculous scheme to kill Crystal's wife and then ask for a like favor in return.
1987: Nomination: Best Supp. Actress (Anne Ramsey)

THUNDER AND LIGHTNING
1977, 93 mins, US ⊘
D: Corey Allen **A:** David Carradine, Kate Jackson, Roger C. Carmel, Sterling Holloway, Ed Barth, Ron Feinberg (20th Century-Fox)

Thunder and Lightning has just about everything in the action department, packing thrills and fast movement as stunt drivers have their day in some wild pic mileage. David Carradine, an irrepressible booze runner, competes with girlfriend Kate Jackson's pop in his chosen field. Director Corey Allen expertly maneuvers the chase sequences.

THUNDERBALL
1965, 130 mins, UK ⊘ ⊚ ⊟
D: Terence Young **A:** Sean Connery, Claudine Auger, Adolfo Celi, Luciana Paluzzi, Rik Van Nutter, Bernard Lee (McClory)

Sean Connery plays his indestructible James Bond for the fourth time in the manner born, faced here with a $280 million atomic bomb ransom plot. Action gets rougher before the credits even begin. Underwater weapon-carrying sea sleds provide an imaginative note. Connery is up to his usual stylish self as he lives up to his past rep, in which mayhem is a casual affair. Terence Young's direction maintains action at a fever pitch.
1965: Best Visual Effects (John Stears)

THUNDER BAY
1953, 103 mins, US ⊘
D: Anthony Mann **A:** James Stewart, Joanne Dru, Gilbert Roland, Dan Duryea, Jay C. Flippen, Marcia Henderson (Universal)

A regulation outdoor actioner with an interesting switch. James Stewart and Dan Duryea are a couple of ex-GIs with a dream of extracting oil from the bottom of the Gulf of Mexico off the coast of Louisiana. Having talked Jay C. Flippen, head of an oil company, into backing the offshore exploration, the two adventurers plunge into their work against the wishes of shrimp fishermen, who see their livelihood threatened. Anthony Mann's direction manages considerable action to balance a script tending toward verbosity.

THUNDERBOLT AND LIGHTFOOT
1974, 114 mins, US ⊘ ⊚ ⊟
D: Michael Cimino **A:** Clint Eastwood, Jeff Bridges, George Kennedy, Geoffrey Lewis, Catherine Bach, Gary Busey (United Artists)

Thunderbolt and Lightfoot is an over-long, sometimes hilariously vulgar comedy-drama about a safecracking heist. Clint Eastwood plays a cowtown preacher, a survivor of an earlier caper in which the loot was hidden and never found. He meets Bridges, on the lam from a car theft, then his former accomplices. Together the team plans one more heist.
1974: Nomination: Best Supp. Actor (Jeff Bridges)

THUNDERHEAD—SON OF FLICKA
1945, 78 mins, US
D: Louis King **A:** Roddy McDowall, Preston Foster, Rita Johnson, Diana Hale (20th Century-Fox)

Thunderhead—Son of Flicka, 20th Century-Fox's sequel to *Flicka*, is a worthy successor. Though story is a simple one of a boy rearing a colt in hopes of making him a racer, pic contains drama throughout, as in various stages of breaking in the horse or the hunt for an equine killer. Roddy McDowall again plays the rancher's son, with shy appeal.

THUNDERHEART
1992, 118 mins, US ⊘ ⊚
D: Michael Apted **A:** Val Kilmer, Graham Greene, Sam Shepard, Sheila Tousey, Fred Ward, Fred Dalton Thompson (Tribeca/Waterhorse)

Dances with the Evidence could be the title of this pic. Reasonably engrossing as a mystery-thriller, *Thunderheart* succeeds most in its portrayal of mystical Native American ways. Val Kilmer stars as a sharp but surly young fed who bristles when he's expected to use his long-suppressed Indian heritage to help quell violence on a South Dakota reservation. Partnered with a crack FBI vet (Sam Shepard), he travels to the reservation, where the two city sharpies excel at shockingly insensitive behavior. Befriended by a wary but compassionate Sioux sheriff (Graham Greene, in a standout portrayal), Kilmer is introduced to a tribal spiritual elder (Chief Ted Thin Elk), who points him toward his true self.

THUNDERING HERD, THE
1925, 70 mins, US ⊗
D: William K. Howard **A:** Jack Holt, Lois Wilson, Noah Beery, Raymond Hatton, Col. Tim McCoy, Eulalie Jensen (Paramount)

Here is the greatest western picture since *The Covered Wagon*. Director William K. Howard has achieved groupings and scenes that rival the best of Frederic Remington. But it isn't the cast, the director, the story, or the photography that makes *The Thundering Herd* a truly great picture. It's the thrills.

THUNDER IN THE CITY
1937, 86 mins, UK ⓥ
D: Marion Gering **A:** Edward G. Robinson, Luli Deste, Nigel Bruce, Constance Collier, Ralph Richardson, Arthur Wontner (Atlantic/Columbia)

Edward G. Robinson plays an American ballyhoo artist who invades the staid calm of business methods in England and promotes a metal mine in Africa into a big proposition. Robinson's rival ties him up under patents, and it looks as though the Horatio Algerian hero is stymied. The writers have provided numerous comedy situations that are ably maneuvered by director Marion Gering. Ralph Richardson renders a good job as a British banker.

THUNDER IN THE DUST
See: The Sundowners

THUNDER ROCK
1942, 110 mins, UK
D: Roy Boulting **A:** Michael Redgrave, Barbara Mullen, James Mason, Lilli Palmer, Finlay Currie, Frederick Valk (M-G-M/Charter)

Thunder Rock is a remarkable piece of technical work. Its treatment of the subject (a newspaperman gaining new hope through visions of drowned people) is realistic. Acting credits are headed by Michael Redgrave, who enacted the same role in the stage play.

THX 1138
1971, 88 mins, US ⓥ ⊙ ▭
D: George Lucas **A:** Robert Duvall, Donald Pleasence, Don Pedro Colley, Maggie McOmie, Ian Wolfe, Sid Haig (American Zoetrope)

THX 1138 is a psychedelic science fiction horror story about a future civilization regimented into computer-programmed slavery and the story of one man's determination to crash out of his worldly prison. Robert Duvall heads the cast as the defector forced into action after his mate Maggie McOmie is programmed into the cell of Donald Pleasence, a corrupt computer technician.

TIARA TAHITI
1962, 100 mins, UK ⓥ
D: Ted Kotcheff **A:** James Mason, John Mills, Claude Dauphin, Herbert Lom, Rosenda Monteros, Jacques Marin (Rank)

In Germany, just after the war, a pompous lieutenant colonel (Mills) clashes with a sophisticated, care-free junior officer (Mason). Mills catches Mason trying to smuggle loot back to London, and Mason is cashiered. He finds a life of dissolute ease and enchantment in Tahiti. Mills arrives to negotiate a deal to build a hotel and finds to his intense irritation that Mason still has the effect of reducing him to fumbling ineptitude. The two male stars have a field day.

TIE ME UP! TIE ME DOWN!
See: Atame!

TIE THAT BINDS, THE
1995, 98 mins, US ⓥ
D: Wesley Strick **A:** Daryl Hannah, Keith Carradine, Moira Kelly, Vincent Spano, Julia Devin, Cynda Williams (Interscope/PolyGram/Hollywood)

A nasty and violent take on the real versus adoptive parents issue, *The Tie That Binds* is simply dull for most of its running time before turning downright nauseating. Tale has outlaw team of John and Leann Netherwood (Keith Carradine, Daryl Hannah) forced to flee a crime scene, leaving their young daughter, Janie (Julia Devin), behind. Taken in by professional couple Russell and Dana Clifton (Vincent Spano, Moira Kelly) with an eye to adoption, Janie begins to adapt to her new surroundings. Her white trash parents set out, not just to recapture their daughter, but to murder everyone who had anything to do with their separation.

TIGER AND THE PUSSYCAT, THE
1967, 105 mins, Italy/US ⓥ
D: Dino Risi **A:** Vittorio Gassman, Ann-Margret, Eleanor Parker (Fair/Embassy)

A timeworn three-point relationship, bulwarked with many physical gag situations and flash comic inserts. Plot concerns the extra-marital fling between a middle-aged captain of industry (Vittorio Gassman) and a 20-year-old Bohemian ball of fire (Ann-Margret). For about two-thirds of the film, *The Tiger* is a swiftly paced romp of deceit. But the charm and tempo slacken with Gassman's dilemma, when he's prodded by his young mistress to give up his wife and family.

TIGER BAY
1959, 105 mins, UK ⓥ
D: J. Lee Thompson **A:** John Mills, Horst Buchholz, Hayley Mills, Yvonne Mitchell, Megs Jenkins, Anthony Dawson (Rank)

Story concerns a Polish seaman who,

returning from a voyage, finds that his mistress has moved in with another man. In a burst of anger he kills her. The slaying is witnessed by a child (Hayley Mills, in her screen debut), a lonely youngster whose attachment for the killer seriously complicates the police investigation. Young Mills gives a lift to a pic which, anyway, stacks up as a lively piece of drama.

TIGER MAKES OUT, THE
1967, 94 mins, US
D: Arthur Hiller **A:** Eli Wallach, Anne Jackson, Bob Dishy, John Harkins, Ruth White, Roland Wood (Columbia)

A distended, uneven pic. *The Tiger*, a two-character comedy-drama, concerns the kidnapping of Anne Jackson, a suburban housefrau, by frustrated mailman Eli Wallach, after which some genuinely tender dialogue brings together the two spirits.

TIGER SHARK
1932, 78 mins, US
D: Howard Hawks **A:** Edward G. Robinson, Richard Arlen, Zita Johann, Leila Bennett, J. Carrol Naish, Vince Barnett (First National)

A strong and exceedingly well played and directed sea drama. A sea captain, Edward G. Robinson, loses his hand to a tiger shark. The shady lady who marries him bears no love but only appreciation for his kindness, and soon falls for Robinson's personable best friend (Richard Arlen). The captain's feelings toward his first mate turn to hatred when the boy and the missus are caught in a clinch.

TIGHT LITTLE ISLAND
See: Whisky Galore!

TIGHTROPE
1984, 117 mins, US ⓥ ⊙
D: Richard Tuggle **A:** Clint Eastwood, Genevieve Bujold, Dan Hedaya, Alison Eastwood, Jennifer Beck, Marco St. John (Malpaso/Warner)

Clint Eastwood plays a big-city homicide cop, a man whose taste for seamy sex nearly brings him down. An anonymous killer stalks prostitutes and massage parlor girls in New Orleans' French Quarter. Eastwood has been accustomed to taking his pleasure with the very sort of women upon whom the murderer is preying. It all leads up to a rather predictable assault on the cop's home and daughters, and some sweating and soul-searching on his part. Overall, however, action is well handled.

TILLIE AND GUS
1933, 58 mins, US
D: Francis Martin **A:** W. C. Fields, Alison Skipworth, Baby LeRoy, Jacqueline Wells, George Barbier, Clarence Wilson (Paramount)

This is an effort to stretch a brief idea to feature length with horseplay and mechanical punch which doesn't quite register. W. C. Fields and Alison Skipworth are a married couple who reunite when called to the old home for a presumed legacy. Local bad boy is trying to hog the fortune and oust a young couple from their home. In between it's some of Fields's old vaudeville gags, comedy not helped by efforts to inject a dramatic story.

TILLIE'S PUNCTURED ROMANCE
1914, 70 mins, US ⓥ ⊙ ⊗
D: Mack Sennett **A:** Marie Dressler, Charles Chaplin, Mabel Normand, Mack Sennett, Mack Swain, Keystone Kops (Keystone)

Tillie's Punctured Romance came from the title role Marie Dressler played in *Tillie's Nightmare*. She is splendidly supported by the Keystone Company, including Charles Chaplin, Mabel Normand, Mack Sennett, Mack Swain, and others. Dressler is the central figure, but Chaplin's camera antics are an essential feature in putting the picture over. The picture runs a trifle too long, but the hilarious comedy finale is worth waiting for.

TILL THE CLOUDS ROLL BY
1946, 120 mins, US ⓥ ⊙
D: Richard Whorf, [George Sidney, Vincente Minnelli] **A:** Robert Walker, Judy Garland, Lucille Bremer, Joan Wells, Van Heflin, Dorothy Patrick (M-G-M)

The Jerome Kern saga reminds one of Cole Porter's *Night and Day*—both apparently enjoyed a monotonously successful life: no early-life struggles, no frustrations, nothing but an uninterrupted string of Broadway and West End show successes. Robert Walker is completely sympathetic as Kern. Picture actually opens with *Show Boat*, a 1927 whammo. A virtually tabloid version of that operetta is utilized for the opener, and the rest of the story is a success-story flashback.

TILL THERE WAS YOU
1991, 93 mins, Australia ⓥ
D: John Seale **A:** Mark Harmon, Deborah Unger, Jeroen Krabbe, Shane Briant (Ayer/Five Arrow/AFFC)

An expensive, high-concept affair that

falls between several categories. The familiar plot has Mark Harmon playing a New York sax player who wings off to a Pacific island on his brother's invitation. When he arrives he discovers that his brother has been killed, and that he's not very welcome on the island. Camerawork on little-seen island locations is often spectacular, and the local Vanuatans prove to be natural actors.

TILL WE MEET AGAIN
1944, 85 mins, US
D: Frank Borzage **A:** Ray Milland, Barbara Britton, Walter Slezak, Mona Freeman, Lucile Watson, Vladimir Sokoloff (Paramount)

A different sort of war romance. Its heroine is a novice nun, and Ray Milland is a happily married—albeit dashing—American aviator, forced down in occupied France. Milland's love for his wife and child sends a wholesome message of the American standard of love and marriage to the young French convent girl as she accompanies Milland as his pseudo-wife to aid his escape with valuable secret papers from the French Underground for London.

'TIL WE MEET AGAIN
1940, 99 mins, US
D: Edmund Goulding **A:** Merle Oberon, George Brent, Pat O'Brien, Geraldine Fitzgerald, Binnie Barnes, Frank McHugh (Warner)

This remake of *One Way Passage* still has plenty of punch. Story opens in Hong Kong with Merle Oberon falling for George Brent, a total stranger, in a bar. She meets him again on the ship bound for the United States and chases after him in a manner that is just as implausible as their original meeting. Brent is being returned to San Quentin to hang for murder, while Oberon is in final stages of a cardiac ailment.

TIM BURTON'S THE NIGHTMARE BEFORE CHRISTMAS
See: The Nightmare Before Christmas

TIME AFTER TIME
1980, 112 mins, UK Ⓥ ⊙ ▭
D: Nicholas Meyer **A:** Malcolm McDowell, David Warner, Mary Steenburgen, Charles Cioffi, Patti D'Arbanville, Corey Feldman (Warner/Orion)

Time After Time is a delightful, entertaining trifle of a film that shows the possibilities and limitations of taking liberties with literature and history. H. G. Wells and Jack The Ripper abandon London circa 1893 in Wells's famous time machine. Their arrival in 1979 San Francisco is played for all the inevitable anachronisms, with results that are both witty and pointed.

TIME BANDITS
1981, 110 mins, UK Ⓥ ⊙
D: Terry Gilliam **A:** John Cleese, Sean Connery, Shelley Duvall, Ralph Richardson, David Warner, Michael Palin (Handmade)

Time Bandits is a kind of potted history of man, myth, and the eternal clash between good and evil as told in the inimitable idiom of Monty Python. The premise has an English youngster and a group of dwarfs passing through time holes on assignment by the Maker to patch up the shoddier parts of His creation. What results, unfortunately, is a hybrid neither sufficiently hair-raising or comical. A costume-heavy David Warner, as Ultimate Evil is one of nine cameo parts, the funniest of which is the Maker Himself played by none other than Ralph Richardson in a business suit.

TIMECOP
1994, 98 mins, US Ⓥ ⊙
D: Peter Hyams **A:** Jean-Claude Van Damme, Mia Sara, Ron Silver, Bruce McGill, Gloria Reuben, Scott Bellis (Largo/Signature/Renaissance/Dark Horse)

Director Peter Hyams delivers a curiously flat sci-fi comic-book actioner. The ever limber Jean-Claude Van Damme plays Max Walker, a D.C. cop whose wife (Mia Sara) is apparently murdered in an explosion. Ten years later, in 2004, we find Walker functioning as a "timecop," policing those who have gone back in time to strike it rich or influence the course of history. He discovers that the mastermind behind the time-crime wave is the US senator (Ron Silver) responsible for overseeing the enforcement program and seeking to use his ill-gotten gains to finance a run for the presidency.

TIME FOR ACTION
See: Tip on a Dead Jockey

TIME LOST AND TIME REMEMBERED
See: I Was Happy Here

TIME MACHINE, THE
1960, 103 mins, US Ⓥ ⊙
D: George Pal A: Rod Taylor, Alan Young, Yvette Mimieux, Sebastian Cabot, Tom Helmore, Whit Bissell (M-G-M/Galaxy)

In utilizing contemporary knowledge to update H. G. Wells's durable novel, scenarist David Duncan has brought the work into modern focus. But the basic spirit of Wells's work has not been lost. The film's chief flaw is its somewhat palsied pace. It perks to a fascinating peak when the Time Traveller (Rod Taylor) plants himself in his machine and begins his enviable tour of time, visiting World Wars I, II, and III. But things slow down to a walk when Taylor arrives at the year 802,701 and becomes involved generally with a group of tame, antisocial towheads, the Eloi.
1960: Best Special Effects

TIME OF THEIR LIVES, THE
1946, 82 mins, US Ⓥ
D: Charles T. Barton A: Lou Costello, Bud Abbott, Marjorie Reynolds, Binnie Barnes, Gale Sondergaard (Universal)

A picnic for Abbott & Costello fans, replete with trowelled-on slapstick, corned-up gags, and a farcical plot. Shot as a traitor in the American Revolutionary War and doomed to remain an earthbound ghost until proved innocent, Costello turns up in 1946 still looking for the evidence. In a similar fix, Marjorie Reynolds floats through the film like a Sears-Roebuck model ghost. Abbott plays a 1780s heel and turns up in modern times as a psychiatrist, house-guesting in the mansion Costello and his girlfriend are haunting.

TIME OF YOUR LIFE, THE
1948, 108 mins, US Ⓥ
D: H. C. Potter A: James Cagney, William Bendix, Wayne Morris, Jeanne Cagney, Broderick Crawford, Ward Bond (United Artists/William Cagney)

The Time of Your Life is as full of humor and entertainment as the frothiest of comedies. The catch is that it is presented in the unconventional and formless pattern of William Saroyan's stage writing. The difference between Life and a standard film is that this one has no story in the accepted sense of the term. It merely introduces, one by one, a series of "characters." It doesn't even delve into what makes them tick but presents their amusing exterior sides as they spout the Saroyan views on life and living.

TIME, THE PLACE AND THE GIRL, THE
1946, 105 mins, US
D: David Butler A: Dennis Morgan, Jack Carson, Janis Paige, Martha Vickers (Warner)

The·Time, the Place and the Girl is snappy tomfoolery, tunefully embroidered with six numbers by Leo Robin and Arthur Schwartz. David Butler's direction punches over the comedy, getting the most from bright lines and situations in the script. Plot is thin but neatly put together to support the musical sequences. Story line has Dennis Morgan and Jack Carson trying to put on a musical show against the opposition of Florence Bates, old-time opera star, and her priggish manager, Donald Woods.

TIME TO KILL, A
1996, 150 mins, US
D: Joel Schumacher A: Sandra Bullock, Samuel L. Jackson, Matthew McConaughey, Kevin Spacey, Brenda Fricker, Oliver Platt (Warner Bros.)

A Time to Kill is generally the most satisfying of the John Grisham screen adaptations to date. Although it's as much of a synthetic fabrication as other Grisham yarns, this one emerges as more substantial due to the social fabric. Two bad ol' boys beat and rape a 10-year-old black girl. The girl's father (Samuel L. Jackson) guns down the goons in the county courthouse. Young, good-looking Jake Brigance (Matthew McConaughey) takes on the murder case, which inspires a revival of the local Ku Klux Klan. Perky rich-girl law student Ellen Roark (Sandra Bullock) keeps pestering Brigance to let her pitch in. The trial is intense and provides numerous surprises and twists. In the film's most riveting performance, Jackson capitalizes on his role's potent dramatic opportunities.

TIME TO LOVE AND A TIME TO DIE, A
1958, 133 mins, US Ⓥ ▭
D: Douglas Sirk A: John Gavin, Lilo Pulver, Keenan Wynn, Erich Maria Remarque, Thayer David, Jock Mahoney (Universal)

A Time to Love and a Time to Die is less a panorama of the battle horrors of World War II than a poignant telling of the anguish of being in love while civilian bombings rage and decency is being held hostage by vicious character traits. The story is somewhat slow in development. It opens with the hero German soldier (John Gavin) on the Russian front under the cloud of defeat in 1944. He gets his furlough and goes to his native town to find his home is rubble and his parents disappeared. Nearly all the action comprises the experiences of the furloughed soldier.

1958: Nomination: Best Sound

TINA
WHAT'S LOVE GOT TO DO WITH IT
See: What's Love Got to Do with It

TIN CUP
1996, 93 mins, US Ⓥ ⊙ ▭
D: Ron Shelton A: Kevin Costner, Rene Russo, Cheech Marin, Linda Hart, Don Johnson, Dennis Burkley (Regency/Warner)

Amiable and constantly amusing, this mangy tale of a ne'er-do-well's fitful assault on personal and professional respectability benefits greatly from Kevin Costner's ingratiatingly comic star turn. With more armadillos than customers at his dilapidated desert golf range outside of Salome, Texas, life is passing Rod McAvoy (Costner) by, when Dr. Molly Griswold (Rene Russo) turns up for a lesson. Roy's old college partner, David Simms (a credible Don Johnson), now a top pro, comes around to ask him to caddy for him in a celebrity tourney, Roy accepts the humiliating job. When he learns that Molly is David's girlfriend, Roy uses this as added inspiration to make it to the US Open. Pic runs a bit long for what it is and appears rather untidy directorally, with mismatched shots and less than totally coherent coverage at times.

TIN DRUM, THE
See: Die Blechtrommel

TIN MEN
1987, 112 mins, US Ⓥ ⊙
D: Barry Levinson A: Richard Dreyfuss, Danny DeVito, Barbara Hershey, John Mahoney, Jackie Gayle, Stanley Brock (Touchstone)

The improbable tale of a pair of feuding aluminum siding salesmen, *Tin Men* is packed with laughs, thanks to taut scripting and superb character depictions by Richard Dreyfuss, Danny DeVito, and a fascinating troupe of sidekicks. These fast-buck hustlers collectively fashion a portrait of superficial greed so pathetic it soars to a level of black humor. Story line finds Dreyfuss and DeVito tangling from the start after an accident damages both of their Cadillacs. Conflict escalates to the point where Dreyfuss seeks to get even by wooing DeVito's unhappy wife (Barbara Hershey) into bed.

TIN PAN ALLEY
1940, 94 mins, US
D: Walter Lang A: Alice Faye, Betty Grable, Jack Oakie, John Payne, Allen Jenkins, Esther Ralston (20th Century-Fox)

Story set in the noisy but colorful stretch of 46th Street and 8th Avenue, headquartering song publishers in 1915. Jack Oakie is a breezy ex-vaudevillian teamed with tunesmith John Payne in a publishing venture. The pair hit the jackpot with a pop tune, with the song-plugging end handled by Alice Faye, who warms up to Payne. But there's the inevitable romantic split. Faye hops to London to become a music hall sensation with Betty Grable.

1940: Best Score

TIN STAR, THE
1957, 92 mins, US Ⓥ
D: Anthony Mann A: Henry Fonda, Anthony Perkins, Betsy Palmer, Michael Ray, Neville Brand, John McIntire (Perlsea/Paramount)

The Tin Star is a quality western that unfolds interestingly under the smooth direction of Anthony Mann. Screenplay centers around Anthony Perkins's insistence on keeping his sheriff's badge despite the pleading of his sweetheart, and Henry Fonda, a former lawman turned bounty hunter, reluctantly teaching him the tricks of the trade.

1957: Nomination: Best Original Story & Screenplay

TIP ON A DEAD JOCKEY
(UK: TIME FOR ACTION)
1957, 98 mins, US ▭
D: Richard Thorpe A: Robert Taylor, Dorothy Malone, Gia Scala, Martin Gabel, Marcel Dalio, Jack Lord (M-G-M)

Once this *Jockey* spurs up momentum, film shapes as a solid, satisfactory action picture. In expatriate society of Madrid, Robert Taylor is an ex-pilot, afraid of emotional entanglements because his war job was sending pilots to their deaths. He's eking out a precarious existence on the fringes of Spain's precarious economy. Dorothy Malone is his wife, fighting to regain his love after he requests a divorce. Taylor undertakes a currency-smuggling caper proposed by sinister Martin Gabel.

TIREZ SUR LE PIANISTE (SHOOT THE PIANO PLAYER; SHOOT THE PIANIST)
1960, 80 mins, France Ⓥ ⊙ ▭
D: François Truffaut **A:** Charles Aznavour, Nicole Berger, Marie Dubois, Michele Mercier, Albert Remy, Claude Mansard (Pleiade)

François Truffaut's second film is done with the same freewheeling, inventive quality as his *400 Blows*. Charlie (Charles Aznavour) is a pianist in a little bar. The waitress, who loves him, knows he was once a noted concert pianist before his inability to forgive his wife for her affair with his sleazy impresario. He is content to play in the bar until his brother brings in two gangsters whom he has doublecrossed. The gangsters go after Charlie and eventually slay the waitress. Charlie inadvertently kills his boss in self-defense. He goes back to his piano and a new serving girl after it is all over. The meandering script only intermittently makes its point. Aznavour is excellent as the pianist.

TITANIC
1953, 97 mins, US
D: Jean Negulesco **A:** Clifton Webb, Barbara Stanwyck, Robert Wagner, Audrey Dalton, Thelma Ritter, Richard Basehart (20th Century-Fox)

The sinking of HMS *Titanic* provides a factual basis for this screen drama reenacting the tragic voyage. Story line is built around fictional characters aboard the supposedly unsinkable British luxury liner on its maiden voyage from Southampton to New York in 1912. During the first half the film is inclined to dawdle, but the impending disaster begins to take a firm grip on the imagination and builds a compelling expectancy. Jean Negulesco's direction and the script really shine after the ship's bottom is opened by an iceberg, bringing out the drama in the confusion of shipwreck and passengers' reaction to certain doom.
1953: Best Story & Screenplay
Nomination: Best B&W Art Direction

TITANIC
1997, 194 mins, US Ⓥ ⊙ ▭
D: James Cameron **A:** Leonardo DiCaprio, Kate Winslet, Billy Zane, Kathy Bates, Frances Fisher, Gloria Stuart (Lightstorm/Paramount/20th Century-Fox)

A spectacular demonstration of what modern technology can contribute to dramatic storytelling, James Cameron's $200 million-plus romantic epic is the biggest roll of the dice in film history. Cameron's swooping camera takes an interest in two people boarding the giant ship: Rose DeWitt Bukater (Kate Winslet), a haughty society girl returning to Philadelphia to marry her rich snob fiancé, Cal Hockley (Billy Zane), and penniless, devil-may-care American Jack Dawson (Leonardo DiCaprio). Rose rebels against her fiancé and class-obsessed mother (Frances Fisher). She is rescued from jumping overboard by none other than Jack. And so it goes with their schematic romance. The *Titanic* hits the iceberg 100 minutes into the film, and the next 80 minutes represent uninterrupted excitement and spectacle. The film misses a suspenseful beat by largely ignoring the presence of other boats in the vicinity and why they never made it to the *Titanic*. The ship's final plunge is utterly stunning and effectively places the viewer in the jaws of death. The integration of digital special effects into the live filming is seamless.
1997: Best Picture, Director, Cinematography, Editing, Original Dramatic Score, Original Song ("My Heart Will Go On"), Art Direction, Costume Design (Deborah L. Scott), Sound, Sound Effects Editing, Visual Effects
Nominations: Best Actress (Kate Winslet), Supp. Actress (Gloria Stuart), Makeup

TITFIELD THUNDERBOLT, THE
1953, 84 mins, UK Ⓥ
D: Charles Crichton **A:** Stanley Holloway, George Relph, Naunton Wayne, John Gregson, Godfrey Tearle, Hugh Griffith (Ealing)

Titfield is a small English village which gets worked up when the government decides to close an unprofitable branch railway line. The vicar and the squire, both railway enthusiasts, are heartbroken at the news. The only ones cheered by the decision are the partners of a transport company who hope to profit from their bus service. The *Thunderbolt* is the railway engine involved in the story. Once the basic situation is accepted, the entire yarn concentrates on the feuding between the rival factions.

T-MEN
1947, 91 mins, US Ⓥ
D: Anthony Mann **A:** Dennis O'Keefe,

Mary Meade, Charles McGraw, Alfred Ryder, Wally Ford, June Lockhart (Reliance/Small)

Producer Edward Small has taken a case out of the Treasury Dept. files, reenacted it in documentary fashion, and the result is an entertaining action film. Dennis O'Keefe's characterization of a Treasury agent is finely drawn. Cast as his partner is Alfred Ryder. They're undercover agents assigned to break the "Shanghai Paper Case." Masquerading as mobsters, they join a ring of liquor cutters in Detroit who are using phony revenue stamps. The final reel is a corker.

1947: Nomination: Best Sound

TOAST OF NEW YORK, THE
1937, 93 mins, US Ⓥ ⊙

D: Rowland V. Lee **A:** Edward Arnold, Cary Grant, Frances Farmer, Jack Oakie, Donald Meek, Clarence Colb (RKO)

Here is the life of Jim Fisk, Wall Street operator of the 1880s. It's absurd biography but good entertainment despite its inanities, extravagances, and exaggerations. Fisk (Edward Arnold) and his stooges are introduced as medicine show fakers in the South just before the Civil War. When hostilities commence, the trio smuggle raw cotton across the frontier for New England mills. They make a fortune, which is soon lost and won again in the purchase and sale of steamships. Thereafter, on the floor of the New York stock exchange, Fisk devises various schemes which culminate in a struggle with Cornelius Vanderbilt for control of the Erie railroad.

TOBACCO ROAD
1941, 91 mins, US

D: John Ford **A:** Charley Grapewin, Marjorie Rambeau, Gene Tierney, William Tracy, Elizabeth Patterson, Dana Andrews (20th Century-Fox)

Tobacco Road as a motion picture falls far short of its promises. The sensational pulling elements of the play by Jack Kirkland from Erskine Caldwell's saga—the dialogue and the low-life manners of its people—have been deleted, altered, or attenuated to the point of dullness. What remains of the story is a back-in-the-hills comedy of shiftless folk, with a trite comedy theme about the dubious efforts by which old Jeeter (Charley Grapewin) hopes to raise $100 for the annual rent of the old farm.

TO BEGIN AGAIN
See: Volver a Empezar

TO BE OR NOT TO BE
1942, 99 mins, US Ⓥ

D: Ernst Lubitsch **A:** Carole Lombard, Jack Benny, Robert Stack, Lionel Atwill, Sig Ruman, Felix Bressart (Korda)

To Be or Not to Be is absorbing drama with farcical trimmings, a triumph for Carole Lombard, who delivers an effortless and highly effective performance that provides a memorable finale to her brilliant screen career. Story recounts the adventures of a legit stock company in Warsaw, before and during the Nazi invasion. Carole Lombard is the female lead, with husband Jack Benny a hammy matinee idol with a penchant for playing Hamlet. Lubitsch provides a tense dramatic pace with events developed deftly and logically throughout. The farcical episodes display him in best form.

1942: Nomination: Best Scoring of a Dramatic Picture

TO BE OR NOT TO BE
1983, 108 mins, US Ⓥ ⊙

D: Alan Johnson **A:** Mel Brooks, Anne Bancroft, Tim Matheson, Charles Durning, Jose Ferrer, George Gaynes (Brooksfilms)

To Be or Not to Be, Mel Brooks's glossy remake of Lubitsch's 1942 Carole Lombard–Jack Benny starrer, is very funny stuff indeed. Played mostly for Brooks-style laughs, the tale of a Warsaw theatrical troupe that winds up saving the Polish underground during the Nazi occupation does have some potential hurdles to clear. Cute Nazis and roly-poly Gestapo officers hardly have universal lure. Brooks sustains, with varying success, his role as Frederick Bronski, vainglorious head of a tawdry theatrical company. Mainstay of the film is a superbly sustained comic performance by Anne Bancroft, as Bronski's wife.

1983: Nomination: Best Supp. Actor (Charles Durning)

TOBRUK
1967, 107 mins, US Ⓥ ▭

D: Arthur Hiller **A:** Rock Hudson, George Peppard, Nigel Green, Guy Stockwell, Jack Watson, Norman Rossington (Gibraltar/Universal)

Tobruk is a colorful, hard-hitting World War II melodrama with plenty of guts and suspense to hold action buffs. Screenplay projects the protagonists on a suicidal mission in the North African war of 1942. Daring plan calls for a British column composed of commandos and German-

born Jews to form a special unit to cross the desert to Tobruk, held by German and Italian troops. Once there, they are to hold its key fortified positions pending arrival of a British naval force, and blow up the gigantic German fuel bunkers upon which Rommel depends for his push to the Suez canal.
1967: Nomination: Best Sound Effects

TO CATCH A THIEF
1955, 103 mins, US Ⓥ ⊚
D: Alfred Hitchcock **A:** Cary Grant, Grace Kelly, Jessie Royce Landis, John Williams, Charles Vanel, Brigitte Auber (Paramount)
Cary Grant is a reformed jewel thief, now living quietly in Cannes. When burglaries occur that seem to bear his old trademark, he has to catch the thief to prove his innocence, assisted by Grace Kelly, a rich American girl; her mother, Jessie Royce Landis; and insurance agent John Williams. While a suspense thread is present, director Alfred Hitchcock doesn't emphasize it, letting the yarn play lightly for comedy more than thrills.
1955: Best Color Cinematography
Nominations: Best Color Costume Design, Color Art Direction

TO DIE FOR
1995, 103 mins, US Ⓥ ⊚
D: Gus Van Sant **A:** Nicole Kidman, Matt Dillon, Joaquin Phoenix, Casey Affleck, Illeana Douglas, Alison Folland (Rank/Columbia)
Gus Van Sant's *To Die For* delivers continuous pinpricks of irreverent humor and subversive cultural commentary. Although this is his first film for a major studio, the picture retains the idiosyncratic, charmingly ragged feel of his previous, lower-budget productions. Presented in faux-documentary style, pic is narrated straight-to-camera by parties acquainted with the sordid murder of Larry Maretto (Matt Dillon), working-class husband of glamorous Suzanne Stone (Nicole Kidman), who has been charged with the crime. Suzanne is a modern monster, a big-timer dabbling with small-timers, a woman who believes that something is important only if it's seen on televison. Kidman rises to the occasion, displaying great facility at conveying a winning personality, seductiveness, sincerity, and utter heartlessness.

TO DIE IN MADRID
See: Mourir a Madrid

**TODO SOBRE MI MADRE
(ALL ABOUT MY MOTHER)**
1999, 99 mins, Spain/France Ⓥ ⊚
D: Pedro Almodovar **A:** Cecilia Roth, Eloy Azorin, Marisa Paredes, Penelope Cruz, Candela Pena, Antonia San Juan (El Deseo/Renn/France 2)
Pedro Almodovar's 13th outing is an emotionally satisfying and brilliantly played take on the ups and downs of a group of less-than-typical female friends, full of profound empathy for offbeat characters whom he once treated merely as vehicles for comedy. Cecilia Roth plays Manuela, a single mother in her late thirties whose son Esteban (Eloy Azorin) is killed by a passing car. Trying to get in touch with Esteban's father (Toni Canto), who has become a transvestite called Lola, Manuela returns to Barcelona, where she meets Huma (Marisa Paredes), who's playing Blanche in *A Streetcar Named Desire;* Huma's junkie g.f., Nina (Candela Pena); do-gooder nun Sister Rosa (Penelope Cruz); and her hysterical mother (Rosa Maria Sarda). All the women have some emotional burden to bear. The tone is predominantly dark, with death, pain, and disease just around the corner. But thanks to a witty script, pic doesn't become depressing.
1999: Best Foreign Language Film

TO EACH HIS OWN
1946, 122 mins, US
D: Mitchell Leisen **A:** Olivia de Havilland, Mary Anderson, Roland Culver, John Lund, Philip Terry, Griff Barnett (Paramount)
Start and finish of story are laid against a war-time London background but flashes back to a World War I small-town locale. It depicts the love and sacrifices of an unwed mother for her son, born out of a one-night romance with a war hero in 1918. It carries her through the years to London where, the relationship still unacknowledged, she waits to catch a brief glimpse of the young man as he comes to town on leave. Artistry of Olivia de Havilland as the mother is superb.

TOGETHER AGAIN
1944, 93 mins, US
D: Charles Vidor **A:** Irene Dunne, Charles Boyer, Charles Coburn, Mona Freeman, Elizabeth Patterson (Columbia)
Plot is a light affair, displaying Irene Dunne as the widow of the former mayor of a small town in Vermont who goes to

New York to hire a sculptor to make a statue of her late husband for the town square. She hires Charles Boyer, is mistaken for a striptease artist, and fires the sculptor. He shows up in town later to do the job and carries his romantic pitches to the mayoress. Story, developed in broad farcical vein, romps along at a good clip and is so generally crazy-quilt that the overall effect is very entertaining.

TO HAVE AND HAVE NOT
1944, 100 mins, US ⊗ ⊙
D: Howard Hawks **A:** Humphrey Bogart, Walter Brennan, Lauren Bacall, Dolores Moran, Hoagy Carmichael, Marcel Dalio (Warner)

To Have and Have Not introduces Lauren Bacall in her first picture. She's an arresting personality. She can slink, brother, and no fooling! Yarn deals with the intrigue centering around the Caribbean island of Martinique, owned by France, and the plotting that ensued there prior to its ultimate capitulation to Allied pressure. Bogart is an American skipper who hires out his boat to anyone who meets his price. When he becomes involved in the local Free French movement, the story's pattern becomes woven around him. Warners give the pic its usually nifty production accoutrements, but the basic story is too unsteady.

TO HELL AND BACK
1955, 106 mins, US ⊗ ▭
D: Jesse Hibbs **A:** Audie Murphy, Marshall Thompson, Charles Drake, Jack Kelly, Gregg Palmer, David Janssen (Universal)

This biopic on the World War II exploits that made Audie Murphy the most decorated soldier in American history is gripping drama with the original playing himself. There are no blustering heroics, and the action shown is that of a modest, unassuming young man. He enters the army in 1942 at age 18. In 1943, Murphy joined Company B, 15th Infantry Regiment, in North Africa, and served with the unit throughout the war in Tunisia, Italy, France, Germany, and Austria. His decorations total 24, from the Congressional Medal of Honor on down. Aside from the fighting, footage works in some touching moments during too-short leaves from combat.

TO KILL A MOCKINGBIRD
1962, 129 mins, US ⊗ ⊙
D: Robert Mulligan **A:** Gregory Peck, Mary Badham, Phillip Alford, John Megna, Robert Duvall, Brock Peters (Universal)

Harper Lee's highly regarded first novel has been artfully and delicately translated to the screen. A telling indictment of racial prejudice in the Deep South, it is also a charming tale of the emergence of two youngsters from the realm of wild childhood fantasy into maturity, compassion, and social insight. It is also the story of a wise, gentle, soft-spoken Alabama lawyer (Gregory Peck) entrusted with the defence of an African American falsely accused of rape while raising his own impressionable, motherless children in an environment of bigotry and economic depression. For Peck, it is an especially challenging role, requiring him to project through a veneer of civilized restraint the fires of social indignation and humanitarian concern. He not only succeeds, but makes it appear effortless. But by no means is this entirely Peck's film. The two youngsters (Mary Badham and Phillip Alford) just about steal it away.

1962: Best Actor (Gregory Peck), Adapted Screenplay, B&W Art Direction **Nominations:** Best Picture, Director, Supp. Actress (Mary Badham), B&W Cinematography, Original Music Score

TO KILL A PRIEST
1988, 116 mins, France/US ⊗ ⊙ ▭
D: Agnieszka Holland **A:** Christopher Lambert, Ed Harris, Joanne Whalley-Kilmer, Joss Ackland, David Suchet, Tim Roth (JP/FR3/Columbia)

To Kill a Priest is an ambitious political thriller emptied of substance by its heterogeneous components and hybrid dramaturgy. This is a fictional re-creation of the murder of Polish priest Jerzy Popieluszko by security police in 1984. But Polish helmer Agnieszka Holland's recreation on French soil of her homeland lacks a sense of time and place. Central weakness is the casting of France's Christopher Lambert, playing a rather bland priest and Solidarity apostle, and America's Ed Harris, not quite the right stuff as the Polish militia officer who engineers the plot to assassinate him. Film picks up some steam in the second half, though by this time one's empathy for the principals of the story has been severely tried.

TOKYO JOE
1949, 87 mins, US ⊗ ⊙
D: Stuart Heisler **A:** Humphrey Bogart, Alexander Knox, Florence Marley, Sessue Hayakawa (Columbia/Santana)

Tokyo Joe has been given a documentary flavor by footage shot in Tokyo. Stuart Heisler's direction develops a neat air of anticipation that climaxes in a gripping fight finale. Story opens with Bogart returning to Tokyo, where he owns a night club, after service in the war. He finds the wife he had left has married another man. Out to win her back, Bogart starts a small freight airline and soon becomes involved in smuggling war criminals back into Japan.

TOKYO OLYMPIAD
See: *Tokyo Orimpikku*

TOKYO ORIMPIKKU (TOKYO OLYMPIAD)
1965, 165 mins, Japan
D: Kon Ichikawa (Toho/Organising Committee)

It was a good idea to give the filming of the 1964 Olympics in Tokyo to proven filmmaker Kon Ichikawa. He gives it a balance, drama and realism, laying bare the competitive dash, the human endeavor and beauty, as well as the underside of sweat, suffering and pain. A rapid-fire volleyball game between women's Japanese and Russian teams is a highly suspenseful affair. Intercut audience reactions are knowingly used and seldom overdone. A marathon brings this admirable pic to a glowing climax.

TOL'ABLE DAVID
1930, 78 mins, US
D: John G. Blystone A: Richard Cromwell, Noah Beery, Joan Peers, Henry B. Walthall, Tom Keene (Columbia)

Columbia execs and director John Blystone must have sat through the 1921 silent print of the original *Tol'able David* time after time. The studio evidently decided it couldn't improve on Henry King's superb silent job. The story borders on the feud theme and is set in the Virginia hills. Young David, chafing at being the youngest of the family, finally comes into his own when his elder brother is crippled and his father dies as he is about to launch a vengeance campaign.

TO LIVE
See: *Ikiru*

TO LIVE
See: *Huozhe*

TO LIVE AND DIE IN L.A.
1985, 116 mins, US Ⓥ ⊙
D: William Friedkin A: William L. Petersen, Willem Dafoe, John Pankow, Debra Feuer, John Turturro, Darlanne Fluegel (United Artists/New Century/SLM)

To Live and Die in L.A. looks like a rich man's *Miami Vice*, engrossing and diverting enough on a moment-to-moment basis but overtooled. William L. Petersen plays a Secret Service agent who decides to nail a notorious counterfeiter responsible for the murder of his partner. His search leads him into the kinky, high-tech world of Willem Dafoe, a supremely talented artist whose tentacles reach into surprising areas of the criminal underworld, both high and low-class.

TOM & VIV
1994, 125 mins, UK/US Ⓥ ⊙ ▭
D: Brian Gilbert A: Willem Dafoe, Miranda Richardson, Rosemary Harris, Tim Dutton, Nickolas Grace, Philip Locke (Samuelson/Kass/IRS Media)

Passion of only the driest and most cerebral kind peeks through the lace curtains of *Tom & Viv*, a handsomely appointed but overly starchy love story that attains real clout only in the final reel. Tale opens in 1914, with spoiled socialite Vivienne Haigh-Wood (Miranda Richardson) visiting Merton College, Oxford, with her soppy brother, Maurice (Tom Dutton), to see American student Tom Eliot (Willem Dafoe). Following a whirlwind affair, the couple marry, but Viv's wild mood swings continue, even in public. Tom finally has her committed to an asylum.
1994: Nominations: Best Actress (Miranda Richardson), Supp. Actress (Rosemary Harris)

TOMB OF LIGEIA, THE
1965, 80 mins, UK/US Ⓥ ▭
D: Roger Corman A: Vincent Price, Elizabeth Shepherd, John Westbrook, Oliver Johnston, Derek Francis, Richard Vernon (American International/Alta Vista)

''More Poe but no go'' about sums up *The Tomb of Ligeia*, a tedious and talky addition to American International's series of chillpix based on tales by the 19th-century US author. Amid ruins of English abbey lives widower Vincent Price, near the grave of first wife Ligeia, who was buried under strange circumstances some years before. Price disappoints in an attempt to project his character's inner struggle, since no one knows why he's acting kooky. Elizabeth Shepherd as his second wife vacillates between too-stiff patrician elegance and unconvincing terror.

TOM BROWN'S SCHOOL DAYS
(AKA: ADVENTURES AT RUGBY)
1940, 88 mins, US ⓥ

D: Robert Stevenson **A:** Cedric Hardwicke, Freddie Bartholomew, Jimmy Lydon, Josephine Hutchinson, Billy Halop, Polly Moran (The Play's The Thing/RKO)

Much can be said for this treatment of the Thomas Hughes yarn. While remaining faithful to the spirit of the original, it contrives to vitalize the action and humanize the characters. Although *Tom Brown* is not a lavish production, it is sympathetically and skillfully made, with many touching moments and an excellent cast. It alters the emphasis somewhat from the development of the boy to the character of the headmaster, Arnold. But that probably results in a better picture, since Cedric Hardwicke, who plays the wise and kindly teacher, is much better qualified to carry a story than is any Hollywood prodigy, and his performance is one of the best he has ever given on the screen.

TOM BROWN'S SCHOOLDAYS
1951, 96 mins, UK ⓥ

D: Gordon Parry **A:** John Howard Davies, Robert Newton, Diana Wynyard, Francis De Wolff, Kathleen Byron, Hermione Baddeley (Renown)

England's classic story of public school life is acted with great sincerity by a well-known cast, but script and direction go all out to emphasize the obvious tear-jerker angles. Almost the entire script hinges on the popular angle of the new boy versus the bully. John Howard Davies makes Tom Brown a lovable and sympathetic youngster without a shade of priggishness. Robert Newton as the reforming headmaster Dr. Arnold fills his role with commendable restraint.

TOMBSTONE
1994, 127 mins, US ⓥ ⊙ ▭

D: George Pan Cosmatos **A:** Kurt Russell, Val Kilmer, Michael Biehn, Powers Boothe, Dana Delaney, Sam Elliott (Hollywood/Cinergi)

A decent addition to the current cycle of screen and television Westerns, *Tombstone* is a tough-talking but soft-hearted tale that is entertaining in a sprawling, old-fashioned manner, and is not so much a revisionist view of the Old West as a retelling of the famous story that blends drama, comedy, action, and romance the way that 1950s movies did. Story begins in 1879, when Wyatt Earp (Kurt Russell) arrives in the lawless boom town of Tombstone, AZ, determined to settle down into domesticity and open a business with his brothers Virgil (Sam Elliott) and Morgan (Bill Paxton). But the town is terrorized by a bunch of villains, headed by the McLaurys and Clantons. Earp is assisted by the unpredictable Doc Holliday (Val Kilmer).

TOM, DICK AND HARRY
1941, 85 mins, US ⓥ ⊙

D: Garson Kanin **A:** Ginger Rogers, George Murphy, Alan Marshal, Burgess Meredith, Phil Silvers, Jane Seymour (RKO)

Director Garson Kanin steers his tale through a series of spontaneous episodes to deliver a surprise finish in this cleverly contrived version of a modern Cinderella. Ginger Rogers, telephone operator, aims for romance with a millionaire but accepts the proposal of breezy and ambitious auto salesman George Murphy. Mistaking Burgess Meredith for her rich Romeo, she nonchalantly becomes engaged to him, also. Then she meets the young millionaire (Alan Marshal) and neatly wangles a proposal from him—but eventually she has to decide among the three.

TOM HORN
1980, 98 mins, US ⓥ ▭

D: William Wiard, [James William Guercio] **A:** Steve McQueen, Richard Farnsworth, Linda Evans, Billy Green Bush, Slim Pickens, Elisha Cook (Warner/First Artists)

Steve McQueen's *Tom Horn* is a sorry ending to the once high hopes of the star-studded founding of First Artists Productions. Imagine a film that opens up with dialogue that can't be heard at all, then proceeds to build up to a fist fight that's never seen, and that cuts away to sunsets to fill in other scenes that have no dramatic point, and you have just the beginning of what's wrong with *Tom Horn*. Pic takes up in the final days of the life of the legendary Western hero. And the only plus at all is a couple of good, bloody shoot-out sequences.

TOM JONES
1963, 128 mins, UK ⓥ ⊙

D: Tony Richardson **A:** Albert Finney, Susannah York, Hugh Griffith, Edith Evans, Joan Greenwood, Diane Cilento (Woodfall)

Based on Henry Fielding's enduring novel, story is set in Somerset and London during the 18th century. Hero is Tom

Jones (Albert Finney), born under suspicious circumstances. He is brought up by Squire Allworthy (George Devine) and leads a rollicking life in which women play a prominent part before he finally escapes the gallows after being framed. The somewhat sprawling, bawdy, and vivid screenplay provides meaty acting opportunities, and the thesps grasp their chances with zest. Director Tony Richardson has occasionally pressed his luck with some over-deliberate arty camera bits.
1963: Best Picture, Director, Adapted Screenplay, Original Music Score
Nominations: Best Actor (Albert Finney), Supp. Actor (Hugh Griffith), Supp. Actress (Diane Cilento, Dame Edith Evans, Joyce Redman), Color Art Direction

TOMMY
1975, 111 mins, UK 🎬 ⊙
D: Ken Russell **A:** Ann-Margret, Oliver Reed, Roger Daltrey, Elton John, Eric Clapton, Jack Nicholson (Columbia)

Ken Russell's *Tommy* is spectacular in nearly every way. The appeal of the original 1969 record album by The Who has been complemented in a superbly added visual dimension. Young Tommy, traumatized when he sees his real father Robert Powell accidentally killed in an argument with stepfather Oliver Reed as mother Ann-Margret watches in horror, grows up amid an atmosphere of cruel exploitation and abuse. Elton John plays the pinball wizard and Tina Turner virtually rips the screen apart with her animalistic Acid Queen.
1975: Nominations: Best Actress (Ann-Margret), Adapted Score

TOMMY THE TOREADOR
1959, 90 mins, UK
D: John Paddy Carstairs **A:** Tommy Steele, Janet Munro, Sidney James, Bernard Cribbins, Kenneth Williams, Eric Sykes (Associated-British/Fanfare)

Tailored for the talents of Tommy Steele, *Tommy the Toreador* emerges as a brisk, disarming little comedy. Steele plays a young seaman who gets stranded in Spain and through a string of highly fortuitous circumstances gets conned into making a one-performance-only appearance as a toreador.

TOMORROW IS FOREVER
1946, 102 mins, US 🎬
D: Irving Pichel **A:** Claudette Colbert, Orson Welles, George Brent, Lucile Watson,

Richard Long, Natalie Wood (RKO/International)

International Pictures takes its audience through a deep emotional bath in this moving film. In World War I, Orson Welles and Claudette Colbert are newlyweds when the bugle's note separates them. Disfigured and crippled, Welles allows himself to be declared dead and makes a new life for himself in Austria. Colbert, meanwhile, marries George Brent and is happily married until shortly before World War II, when Welles returns to the States and he and Colbert come face-to-face.

TOMORROW NEVER DIES
1997, 119 mins, UK/US 🎬 ⊙ ▭
D: Roger Spottiswoode **A:** Pierce Brosnan, Jonathan Pryce, Michelle Yeoh, Teri Hatcher, Joe Don Baker, Judi Dench (Eon/United Artists)

There is plenty of bang-bang but very little kiss-kiss in this solid but somewhat by-the-numbers 18th entry in the James Bond cycle. Villain is a megalomaniacal communications tycoon, Elliot Carver (Jonathan Pryce). Carver sinks a British naval vessel in a way that pins the blame on the Chinese. The Brits send Bond to Hamburg to infiltrate a party Carver is throwing, where he makes the acquaintance of a striking Chinese woman, Wai Lin (Malaysian–Hong Kong favorite Michelle Yeoh). Action shifts to Southeast Asia, where Bond runs into Wai Lin scuba diving in the sunken remains of the British ship. The two secret agents reunite to prevent World War III by locating Carver's stealth ship, from which a cruise missile is about to be launched toward Beijing. Filmmakers have steered almost exclusively toward action at the expense of sex, humor or jet-set glamor. Yeoh proves a worthy equal partner to Bond, displaying snappy martial arts moves and not falling into the compliant-bimbo mode.

TOMORROW THE WORLD
1944, 96 mins, US
D: Leslie Fenton **A:** Fredric March, Betty Field, Agnes Moorehead, Skip Homeier, Joan Carroll, Boots Brown (United Artists)

Reformation of Nazi youth is assiduously dealt with in this vivid story of a youngster brought to America from Germany by a college professor whose philosophies have been governed by those of the boy's father, a well-known liberal killed by the Nazis. The boy has been taught that his father had been a traitor to the Third Reich. An attempt to inculcate Nazi fears into the minds of his American schoolfellows almost succeeds, as does his bid to break up the impending marriage between the professor and his Jewish fiancée. Fredric March and Betty Field give dignity to the parts of the professor and his bride-to-be. But the main accolade must go to Skippy Homeier, as the young Nazi.

TOM SAWYER
1930, 82 mins, US ⓥ
D: John Cromwell **A:** Jackie Coogan, Junior Durkin, Mitzi Green, Lucien Littlefield, Tully Marshall, Clara Blandick (Paramount)

This Mark Twain classic has been shrewdly molded to the screen. It crystallizes the essence of a work that is timeless in its human appeal and has all the marks of a labor of love. Story is splendidly acted by a great group of youngsters. Young Jackie Coogan plays Tom to the hilt.

TOM SAWYER
1973, 100 mins, US ⓥ
D: Don Taylor **A:** Johnny Whitaker, Celeste Holm, Warren Oates, Jeff East, Jodie Foster, Lucille Benson (Reader's Digest/ United Artists)

The strikingly handsome $2.5 million production, directed with discreet and appealing folksiness by Don Taylor, boasts an excellent cast. Jeff East is most effective as Huck Finn, and Jodie Foster is great as Becky Thatcher. Celeste Holm, as Aunt Polly, returns to the screen in a personal triumph. Few actresses project so well warmth-with-backbone and a ladylike gentility not immune to kicking up the heels occasionally. Also superbly cast is Warren Oates as Muff Potter, the likable boozy philosopher.
1973: Nominations: Best Costume Design, Art Direction, Adapted Score

TOM THUMB
1958, 92 mins, US ⓥ
D: George Pal **A:** Russ Tamblyn, Alan Young, Terry-Thomas, Peter Sellers, Jessie Matthews, June Thorburn (M-G-M)

The only thing lower case about this production is the Metro spelling of "tom thumb." Otherwise, film is top-drawer, a comic fairy tale with music that stacks up alongside some of the Disney classics. A childless couple (Bernard Miles and Jessie Matthews) get a miniature son (Russ Tam-

blyn) when wood-cutter Miles spares a special tree in the forest surrounding their home and is rewarded by the Forest Queen (June Thorburn). Complications in the story come from Tom's size—only five and one-half inches tall. Villain (Terry-Thomas and Peter Sellers) attempt to use tom for their own evil purposes. The miniature work was done in Hollywood, based on George Pal's Puppetoon figures, with the life-size work done in London.
1958: Best Special Effects

TONGNIAN WANGSHI
(THE TIME TO LIVE AND THE TIME TO DIE)
1985, 137 mins, Taiwan
D: Hou Hsiao-hsien **A:** Tien Feng, Mei Fang, Tang Ju-yun, Yu An-shun, Hsiao Ai, Hsin Shu-fen (CMPC)

After the success of his *Summer At Grandpa's,* Hou Hsiao-hsien is back with another beautifully controlled and highly nostalgic picture of childhood, based on his own boyhood during the last years of the Chinese revolution and the establishment of an independent Taiwan. The script is mostly concerned with growing up in a lower-middle-class family, culturally bridging ancient superstitions and modern methods of education. It is also about the economic struggle to keep afloat in those difficult years. The film impresses by its exquisite camerawork, which suggests perfectly framed paintings.

TONI
1935, 80 mins, France ⓥ
D: Jean Renoir **A:** Charles Blavette, Celia Montalvan, Jenny Helia, Edouard Delmont, Max Dalban (Films d'Aujourd'hui)

Full of atmosphere, intensely tragic, studded with artistic touches of direction, acting, and photography, this story takes place in the south of France and was filmed on location. Not a single scene was made in a studio. Locale is a region not far from Marseilles. The leading character, Toni (Charles Blavette), is Italian. He gets entangled with a girl (Jenny Helia) who keeps his boarding house, but falls in love with a young Spanish girl, Josepha (Celia Montalvan). She loves him but is taken away by the Belgian quarry foreman, Albert (Max Dalban). Toni goes to live in the woods from where he can see Josepha's house. There things come to a climax.

TONIGHT AND EVERY NIGHT
1945, 89 mins, US ⊗
D: Victor Saville **A:** Rita Hayworth, Lee Bowman, Janet Blair, Marc Platt, Florence Bates, Shelley Winters (Columbia)

Setting is a five-a-day music hall in London, which carries on with daily performances during the blitz through the courage of the performers, headed by American-born Rita Hayworth and impresario Florence Bates. Romance is quickly developed between Hayworth and RAF pilot Lee Bowman. *Tonight and Every Night* has plenty of pace in its back-stage tale.

TONIGHT FOR SURE
1962, 69 mins, US ⊗
D: Francis Ford Coppola **A:** Don Kenney, Karl Schanzer, Virginia Gordon, Marti Renfro, Sandy Silver, Linda Gibson (Searchlight)

Francis Coppola's first feature film effort, the nudie pic *Tonight for Sure*, preceded the director's "official" first film, *Dementia 13,* by at least a year. Surprisingly, unlike most of the "adults only" features of the period, *Tonight for Sure* is chock full of nudity. Story line is ridiculous, to be sure. Two dirty old men posing as moral crusaders slip into a Hollywood burlesque house to plot the cessation of the indecent behavior transpiring therein. In the meantime, they relate how they've each arrived at their righteous beliefs.

TONIGHT WE SING
1953, 109 mins, US
D: Mitchell Leisen **A:** David Wayne, Ezio Pinza, Roberta Peters, Tamara Toumanova, Anne Bancroft, Isaac Stern (20th Century-Fox)

This is a top-flight musical drama, based on the career of Sol Hurok, a renowned impresario in the concert field. It establishes Hurok's early love for music, though he has no talent to express it through instrument or voice, hence his determination to bring the world's top artists to the common working man as well as to the top-hatted music lover. From his native Russia he comes to America and, with the backing and encouragement of his wife and a few friends, he achieves his goal.

TONY ROME
1967, 110 mins, US ⊗ ▱
D: Gordon Douglas **A:** Frank Sinatra, Jill St. John, Richard Conte, Gena Rowlands, Simon Oakland, Jeffrey Lynn (20th Century-Fox/Arcola-Millfield)

Tony Rome is a flip gumshoe on the Miami scene. Film has a busy, heavily populated script; zesty Gordon Douglas direction; and solid production values. This fast-moving whodunit is far less intriguing than the individual scenes en route to the climax. There is an abundance of double-entendre dialogue which in reality can be taken only one way.

TOO BEAUTIFUL FOR YOU
See: Trop Belle Pour Toi

TOO FAR TO GO
1982, 100 mins, US ⊗
D: Fielder Cook **A:** Michael Moriarty, Blythe Danner, Glenn Close, Ken Kercheval, Josef Sommer, Kathryn Walker (Sea Cliff/Polytel)

Too Far to Go is an affecting feature film dealing with marital breakup. Scripted from stories by John Updike, pic utilizes witty, arch dialogue in limning the separation and divorce of New England couple Richard and Joan Maple (Michael Moriarty and Blythe Danner). Flashbacks detail happier times for the duo, with sexual matters ranging from infidelity to cessation of marital relations for several years.

TOO HOT TO HANDLE
See: The Marrying Man

TOO HOT TO HANDLE
1938, 106 mins, US ⊗
D: Jack Conway **A:** Clark Gable, Myrna Loy, Walter Pidgeon, Walter Connolly, Leo Carrillo, Marjorie Main (M-G-M)

Adventures of a newsreel cameraman are the basis for this Clark Gable–Myrna Loy costarrer. It has driving excitement, crackling dialogue, glittering performances, and inescapable romantic pull. The story has Gable and Walter Pidgeon as rival newsreelers and Loy as the woman who entangles their already frenzied competition. When Gable hijacks Pidgeon's girl and they both land in the doghouse through Pidgeon's efforts to get even, the girl goes to South America to search for her long-lost aviator brother. Best parts are the early sequences, up to the sequence of a shipload of dynamite exploding directly underneath a tiny plane.

TOO LATE BLUES
1962, 100 mins, US
D: John Cassavetes **A:** Bobby Darin, Stella Stevens, Everett Chambers, Cliff Carnell, Seymour Cassel, Marilyn Clark (Paramount)

John Cassavetes's first Hollywood-made project shows a tendency to force casebook psychology on the characters at the cost of spontaneity. An idealistic small-time jazz pianist and composer (Bobby Darin) loses his way when he is left by his girl due to a cowardly act. A chance for a record deal is blown sky high when Darin's insistence on doing what he wants is compromised by his girl's quitting him. He becomes the gigolo of an aging woman but finds his spark dampened. He finally seeks out his old girl, now a tramp. Film never makes it clear whether the Darin character truly has talent or whether he should accept what he has and do his best at it.

TOO LATE THE HERO
1970, 133 mins, US Ⓥ ▯
D: Robert Aldrich A: Michael Caine, Cliff Robertson, Henry Fonda, Ian Bannen, Harry Andrews, Denholm Elliott (ABC/ Palomar)

An okay World War II melodrama featuring Michael Caine and Cliff Robertson as antagonists who come to respect each other in the course of destroying a Japanese radio transmitter. Their patrol must cross a no-man's-land where both Japanese and Allied soldiers occasionally exchange fire.

TOO MANY CHEFS
See: Who Is Killing the Great Chefs of Europe?

TOO MANY HUSBANDS
1940, 80 mins, US
D: Wesley Ruggles A: Jean Arthur, Fred MacMurray, Melvyn Douglas, Harry Davenport, Dorothy Peterson, Edgar Buchanan (Columbia)

Too Many Husbands is a light, fluffy, and amusing triangle with complications. A woman finds herself with two husbands, as the first turns up after reportedly drowning a year earlier. Picture is studded with explosive dialogue and situations. Husbands is very light in texture but keeps going at a merry pace, mainly through deft direction by Wesley Ruggles. Finish is rather inconclusive.

TOOTSIE
1982, 116 mins, US Ⓥ ⊙ ▯
D: Sydney Pollack A: Dustin Hoffman, Jessica Lange, Teri Garr, Dabney Coleman, Charles Durning, Bill Murray (Mirage/Punch/Columbia)

Tootsie is a lulu. Remarkably funny and entirely convincing, film pulls off the rare accomplishment of being an in-drag comedy which emerges with three-dimensional characters. Dustin Hoffman

portrays a struggling New York stage actor who auditions for a popular soap opera as a woman. Becoming a hit on the show, "Dorothy Michaels" develops into a media celebrity. Hoffman finds it hard to devote much time to girlfriend Teri Garr, and all the while is growing attracted to soap co-star Jessica Lange. Hoffman triumphs in what must stand as one of his most brilliant performances.
1982: Best Supp. Actress (Jessica Lange)
Nominations: Best Picture, Director, Actor (Dustin Hoffman), Supp. Actress (Teri Garr), Original Screenplay, Cinematography, Editing, Original Song ("It Might Be You"), Sound

TOPAZ
1969, 126 mins, US Ⓥ ⊙
D: Alfred Hitchcock A: Frederick Stafford, Dany Robin, John Vernon, Karin Dor, Michel Piccoli, Philippe Noiret (Universal)

Topaz tends to move less infectiously than many of Alfred Hitchcock's best remembered pix. Yet Hitchcock brings in a full quota of twists and tingling moments. Story, from Leon Uris's heavily plotted novel, centers around high politics, with intrigue and trickery involving French, American, Russian, and Cuban security. Action is triggered by defection of a Russian scientist in Copenhagen to the Americans.

TOP GUN
1986, 110 mins, US Ⓥ ⊙ ▯
D: Tony Scott A: Tom Cruise, Kelly McGillis, Val Kilmer, Anthony Edwards, Tom Skerritt, Meg Ryan (Paramount)

Set in the world of naval fighter pilots, pic has strong visuals and pretty young people in stylish clothes and a non-stop sound track. Tom Cruise is a hot-shot fighter pilot with something to prove, assigned to the prestigious Top Gun training school. Romantic interest is Kelly McGillis, a civilian astrophysicist brought in to teach the boys about negative Gs and inverted flight tanks. McGillis is blessed with an intelligent and mature face that doesn't blend well with Cruise's one-note grinning. There is nothing menacing or complex about his character.
1986: Best Song ("Take My Breath Away")
Nominations: Best Editing, Sound, Sound Effects Editing

TOP HAT
1935, 101 mins, US Ⓥ ☉
D: Mark Sandrich **A:** Fred Astaire, Ginger Rogers, Edward Everett Horton, Erik Rhodes, Helen Broderick, Eric Blore (RKO)

This one can't miss and the reasons are three—Fred Astaire, Irving Berlin's songs, and sufficient comedy between numbers to hold the film together. The danger sign is in the story and cast. Substitute Alice Brady for Helen Broderick and it's the same lineup of players as was in *The Gay Divorcee* (1934). Besides which, the situations in the two scripts parallel each other closely. Rogers never opens her mouth vocally until the concluding "Piccolino." She is again badly dressed while her facial makeup and various coiffeurs give her a hard appearance.
1935: Nominations: Best Picture, Art Direction, Song ("Cheek to Cheek"), Dance Direction ("Top Hat," "Piccolino")

TOPKAPI
1964, 120 mins, US Ⓥ
D: Jules Dassin **A:** Melina Mercouri, Peter Ustinov, Maximilian Schell, Robert Morley, Akim Tamiroff, Gilles Segal (United Artists/Filmways)

Jules Dassin has taken a minor novel by Eric Ambler and turned it into a delightful and suspenseful comedy spoof of his own *Rififi*. The band of thieves includes Melina Mercouri, Maximilian Schell, Robert Morley, Gilles Segal, and Jess Hahn. Peter Ustinov is an unwitting accomplice. The basically simple plot has the gang attempting to steal a fabulous jeweled dagger from the Topkapi Palace museum in Istanbul. The actual theft is depicted in a long sequence reminiscent of the one in *Rififi* but with a bit more levity. Ustinov has probably the meatiest part in the film and one that allows him to use many of the unsubtleties in dominating the scenes he has at his command.
1964: Best Supp. Actor (Peter Ustinov)

TOPPER
1937, 98 mins, US Ⓥ ☉
D: Norman Z. McLeod **A:** Cary Grant, Constance Bennett, Roland Young, Billie Burke, Alan Mowbray, Eugene Pallette (Roach/M-G-M)

Topper is carefully made, excellently photographed, and adroitly employs mechanical illusions and trick sound effects. Story is about the adventures of a young married couple, George and Marion Kerby, who are killed in an automobile ac-

cident as the climax of a wild night of carousing. Their astral bodies rise from the ruins, and they agree that until they have done someone a good deed they are likely to remain indefinitely in a state of double exposure (both dead and alive). They decide that their friend, Cosmo Topper, a hen-pecked bank president who has lived a dull, routine life, shall have the benefit of their assistance.
1937: Nomination: Best Sound

TOPPER RETURNS
1941, 95 mins, US Ⓥ
D: Roy Del Ruth **A:** Joan Blondell, Roland Young, Carole Landis, Billie Burke, Dennis O'Keefe, Patsy Kelly (Roach/United Artists)

This is the third film produced from the ideas and characters conceived by Thorne Smith. Roland Young again appears as Topper, the mild-mannered suburbanite whose quiet life is rudely upset by his affinity for spirits that lead him into weird complications. Joan Blondell is murdered, having been mistaken for her friend Carole Landis, and in shadowy form appeals to Young for aid in capturing the villain and saving the intended victim. Film begins to miss out when the story veers to the level of a conventional mystery farce. Direction by Roy Del Ruth is uneven and lacking in improvisations.

TOPPER TAKES A TRIP
1938, 80 mins, US Ⓥ
D: Norman Z. McLeod **A:** Constance Bennett, Roland Young, Billie Burke, Alan Mowbray, Veree Teasdale, Franklin Pangborn (Roach/United Artists)

A delightful, very entertaining comedy built around several of the characters who appear in *Topper*, to which this is a sequel. Roland Young, as Topper, is trying to offer a defense in a divorce case Billie Burke has brought against him because he had a woman in his room. Thereafter, with the action shifting to Europe, where Burke has gone to get her divorce, the spirit of Constance Bennett and her dog Skippy remain to keep him company. Norman McLeod's adroit direction throughout keeps the film at a nice pace.
1939: Nomination: Best Special Effects

TOP SECRET!
1984, 90 mins, US Ⓥ ☉
D: Jim Abrahams, David Zucker, Jerry Zucker **A:** Val Kilmer, Lucy Gutteridge, Christopher Villiers, Omar Sharif, Peter Cushing, Jeremy Kemp (Paramount)

Top Secret! is a tribute to all that was odd in old movies. Followers of the *Airplane!* writer-director trio will probably be happy with this effort, yet short of overjoyed. The target this time is a combination of the traditional spy film and Elvis Presley musical romps. *Top Secret!* shares the same wonderful, wacky attitude that allows just about any kind of gag to come flowing in and out of the picture. Val Kilmer plays an American pop idol drawn into a plot to reunite Germany under one rule. How all of this gets started on the beach when "skeet surfing" is beyond easy description, along with the parachuting fireplace and the unexpected sexual delights in dressing up like a cow.

TORA! TORA! TORA!
1970, 144 mins, US ⑰ ◉ ▱
D: Richard Fleischer, Toshio Masuda, Kinji Fukasaku **A:** Martin Balsam, Soh Yamamura, Joseph Cotten, Tatsuya Mihashi, E. G. Marshall, Takahiro Tamura (20th Century-Fox)

Lavish and meticulous restaging of the Japanese airborne attack on Pearl Harbor on December 7, 1941, constitutes a brilliant logistics achievement which is not generally matched by the handling of the dramatic narrative. Overall director Richard Fleischer and his Japanese counterparts do a dull job, and the monotonously low-key tone of scene after scene almost suggests that each was filmed without a sense of ultimate placement in the finished form.
1970: Best Special Visual Effects (A. D. Flowers, L. B. Abbot)
Nominations: Best Cinematography, Art Direction, Editing, Sound

TORCHLIGHT
1984, 91 mins, US ⑰ ◉
D: Tom Wright **A:** Pamela Sue Martin, Steve Railsback, Ian McShane, Al Corley, Rita Taggart, Arnie Moore (UCO)

Torchlight opens on a deceptively light-hearted note but develops in downbeat style. The plot depicts the love-at-first-sight romance and marriage of Pamela Sue Martin and Steve Railsback. Enter McShane, a sinister and larger than life pusher, and Railsback's downfall progresses until he becomes a physical and mental wreck, without wife or home. McShane as the sinister pusher is a grossly overdrawn character.

TORCH SONG
1953, 89 mins, US ⑰ ◉
D: Charles Walters **A:** Joan Crawford, Michael Wilding, Gig Young, Marjorie Rambeau, Henry Morgan, Dorothy Patrick (M-G-M)

Torch Song tells a backstage story of Jenny Stewart (Joan Crawford), a successful musical comedy star on Broadway. The career drive has left her lonely, but too self-sufficient to acknowledge needs outside of herself. This tough veneer begins to crack when Tye Graham (Michael Wilding), a war-blinded pianist, substitutes for her regular vocal arranger and accompanist. Her reluctant interest in this man builds to a tremendous scene in which she, alone in her bedroom, simulates blindness to discover what it must be like to live in a world of darkness.

TORCH SONG TRILOGY
1988, 117 mins, US ⑰ ◉
D: Paul Bogart **A:** Anne Bancroft, Matthew Broderick, Harvey Fierstein, Brian Kerwin, Karen Young, Charles Pierce (New Line)

Torch Song Trilogy is bracing in its frank depiction of the gay sex life. Harvey Fierstein repeats his Tony Award–winning performance as Arnold Beckoff, a flamboyant drag queen looking for love and respect. Nervous, mannered, gravelly voiced, campy, and with a taste for eye rolling rivaled only by Groucho Marx, Arnold appears a bit gun-shy of romance, but allows himself to be picked up in a gay bar by Ed (Brian Kerwin), a good-looking, straight-seeming fellow who openly announces his bisexuality. He later meets Alan (Matthew Broderick), who actively seeks out Arnold for his human, as opposed to superficial, qualities. Act Three is given over to Arnold's efforts to handle an adopted teenage son and sort out his strained relations with his mother (Anne Bancroft).

TORN CURTAIN
1966, 126 mins, US ⑰ ◉
D: Alfred Hitchcock **A:** Paul Newman, Julie Andrews, Lila Kedrova, Hansjoerg Felmy, Tamara Toumanova, Wolfgang Kieling (Universal)

Torn Curtain is an okay cold war suspenser with Paul Newman, who fakes defection to East Germany in order to obtain Communist defense secrets. Alfred Hitchcock's direction emphasizes suspense and ironic comedy flair, but some good plot ideas are marred by routine dialogue, and a too-relaxed pace contributes to dull over-length. Hitchcock freshens up his bag of tricks in a good potpourri, which becomes a bit stale through a noticeable lack of zip and pacing.

TORRENT, THE
1926, 68 mins, US ⊗
D: Monta Bell **A:** Ricardo Cortez, Greta Garbo, Gertrude Olmstead, Edward Connelly, Martha Mattox (Cosmopolitan/MGM)

Greta Garbo, making her American debut as a screen star, has everything with looks, acting ability, and personality. When one is a Scandinavian and can put over a Latin characterization with sufficient power to make it most convincing, need there be any more said regarding her ability? It is evident that the great scene of the rush of waters was counted on to carry the picture, but a bursting dam doesn't mean anything in a picture except as an incident. The tale of the unrequited love of the little Spanish peasant girl who develops into a great operatic star will hold because of its love twist.

TORTILLA FLAT
1942, 105 mins, US ⓥ
D: Victor Fleming **A:** Spencer Tracy, Hedy Lamarr, John Garfield, Frank Morgan, Akim Tamiroff, Donald Meek (M-G-M)

From John Steinbeck's book of related stories, Metro has made a sincere, tender, beguiling, and at times exalting picture. Steinbeck's stories have been compressed into a single narrative, with dramatic form, steadily heightening interest and a fairly moving, if obvious, climax. Title refers to a locale near Monterey, in northern California, and the story deals with the paisanos, lowly descendants of early Spanish settlers. Spencer Tracy is superb as the leader of the group, retaining sympathy for the character even when he's behaving with shameless selfishness. Hedy Lamarr not only looks stunning as the Portuguese girl, but gives easily her best dramatic performance to date.

TORTURE GARDEN
1968, 92 mins, UK ⓥ
D: Freddie Francis **A:** Jack Palance, Burgess Meredith, Beverly Adams, Peter Cushing, Michael Bryant, Barbara Ewing (Amicus)

Burgess Meredith is a sideshow mystic who gives a special after-hours show to five patrons. Jack Palance is an Edgar Al-

lan Poe buff who will do almost anything to achieve eminence in his hobby. Michael Bryant's sequence involves a man-eating house cat with whom he tangles after greed induces him to permit the death of a supposedly wealthy relative. The situations are developed economically and inventively, both from script and Freddie Francis's very good direction. Sets range from well thought-out to skimpy.

TO SIR, WITH LOVE
1967, 104 mins, UK ⓥ ⊙
D: James Clavell **A:** Sidney Poitier, Christian Roberts, Judy Geeson, Suzy Kendall, Lulu, Faith Brook (Columbia)

To Sir, with Love is a well-made, sometimes poignant drama about an African-American teacher (Sidney Poitier) working in a London slum who transforms an unruly class into a group of youngsters better prepared for adult life. Scrapping the formal agenda, Poitier institutes what he rightly calls "survival training."

TOTAL ECLIPSE
1996, 110 mins, France/UK/Belgium ⓥ
D: Agnieszka Holland **A:** Leonardo DiCaprio, David Thewlis, Romane Bohringer, Dominique Blanc (Fit/Portman/SFP/K2)

Total Eclipse has the effect of making one never want to hear about its protagonists again. This misbegotten look at the mutually destructive relationship between the 19th-century French poets Arthur Rimbaud and Paul Verlaine is a complete botch in all respects. The two become lovers, and the poets' ugly sado-masochistic seesawing is intercut with interludes in which a drunken, guilt-ridden Verlaine returns to ingratiate himself with his wife (Romane Bohringer). Kissing and sodomy scenes between the two men are photographed in frankly embarrassing close-up. Given their desultory personal relationship, it comes as a relief when Verlaine's two-year imprisonment, for shooting his friend, forces a break.

TOTAL RECALL
1990, 113 mins, US ⓥ ⊙
D: Paul Verhoeven **A:** Arnold Schwarzenegger, Rachel Ticotin, Sharon Stone, Ronny Cox, Michael Ironside, Marshall Bell (Carolco)

This futuristic extravaganza features gargantuan movie sets depicting Mars and a futuristic Earth society, grotesque creatures galore, genuinely weird and mostly seamless visual effects, and enough gunshots, grunts, and explosions to keep anyone in a high state of nervous exhilaration. Arnold Schwarzenegger's character, a working stiff in the year 2084, has strange nightmares about living on Mars. It happens that he once worked in the colony as an intelligence agent before rebelling against dictator Ronny Cox. Schwarzenegger had most, but not quite all, of his bad memories erased and was sent to Earth to work on a construction crew, with a sexy but treacherous wife (Sharon Stone). The fierce and unrelenting pace, accompanied by a tongue-in-cheek strain of humor in the roughhouse screenplay, keeps the film moving like a juggernaut.

1990: Special Achievement Award (visual effects)
Nomination: Best Sound

TO THE DEVIL A DAUGHTER
1976, 92 mins, UK/W. Germany Ⓥ
D: Peter Sykes **A:** Richard Widmark, Christopher Lee, Honor Blackman, Denholm Elliott, Michael Goodliffe, Nastassja Kinski (Hammer/Terra)

To the Devil a Daughter is a lackluster occult melodrama in which Christopher Lee is up to his old tricks as an excommunicated priest who takes up Satan's cause in order to save the world from its own decadent folly. Lee is ever-dependable in this sort of menace routine. Nastassja Kinski is moderately appealing as the child-woman novice, and Denholm Elliott turns on the requisite anguish as the father who signed the girl over to Lee to spare his own hide.

TOTO LE HEROS
(TOTO THE HERO)
1991, 89 mins, Belgium/France/Germany
Ⓥ ⊙
D: Jaco van Dormael **A:** Michel Bouquet, Jo De Backer, Mireille Perier, Sandrine Blancke, Peter Boehlke, Fabienne Loriaux (Iblis/Dussart/Metropolis)

Toto the Hero is a winning blend of kid's fantasy and adult comedy that's as fresh as a hot croissant. Multilayered plot kicks off with Thomas van Hasebroeck (Michel Bouquet) soliloquizing about childhood buddy Alfred Kant "stealing" his life. Thomas reckons he was given to the wrong family because of chaos during a hospital fire. The Kant family went on to become rich and famous, while Thomas was stuck with a workaday middle-class upbringing in a dull Belgian nabe. Pic often plays like a European version of *The World According to Garp*. The tempo

slows in the long central section dominated by the adult Thomas's affair with Evelyne (Mireille Perier), who may be his sister; but the pacey final reels rediscover the opening's elan and spring some neat twists in the bargain.

TOTO THE HERO
See: Toto le Heros

TO TRAP A SPY
1966, 92 mins, US
D: Don Medford **A:** Robert Vaughn, Luciana Paluzzi, Patricia Crowley, Fritz Weaver, William Marshall, David McCallum (M-G-M)

To Trap a Spy is an elaborated version of MGM-TV's *The Man From U.N.C.L.E.* pilot. Much of the new footage is devoted to build Robert Vaughn, the agent from U.N.C.L.E., into a glamor boy with a roving eye for beautiful femmes. Whatever plot there is revolves around efforts to prevent the assassination of a visiting African dignitary, but the refurbished entry isn't much better than the original.

TOUCH, THE
1971, 113 mins, Sweden/US Ⓥ
D: Ingmar Bergman **A:** Bibi Andersson, Elliott Gould, Max von Sydow, Sheila Reid, Steffan Hallerstram, Maria Nolgard (ABC/Persona)

Shot in English with occasional Swedish dialogue and splendidly acted and lensed, *The Touch* is both a romantic film of great poignancy and strength and as example of masterful cinema honed down to deceptively simple near-perfection. In telling what is basically a straight triangle tale, Bergman seems to be appealing to the emotions rather than the intellect. Bibi Andersson walks away with pic thanks to one of those immense, bigger-than-life performances. Elliott Gould is a perfect choice as the somewhat neurotic foreign archeologist. Max von Sydow does wonders with the normally unplayable role of the silently strong husband.

TOUCH AND GO
1986, 101 mins, US Ⓥ ⊙
D: Robert Mandel **A:** Michael Keaton, Maria Conchita Alonso, Ajay Naidu, Maria Tucci, Max Wright, Jere Burns (Tri-Star)

Touch and Go mixes humor, heart, and considerable hokum in an engaging story. Michael Keaton is a hot-shot hockey jock with the Chicago Eagles. One night, a punk kid (Ajay Naidu) acts as the innocent front for his thug friends as they try to mug the sports star. Keaton fends the rascals off and returns the 11-year-old home to his slummy neighborhood and to Mom (Maria Conchita Alonso) for discipline, opening the way for romance.

TOUCHEZ PAS AU GRISBI
1954, 95 mins, France/Italy
D: Jacques Becker A: Jean Gabin, Rene Dary, Paul Frankeur, Lino Ventura, Jeanne Moreau, Dora Doll (Del Duca/Silver/Antares)

Max the Liar (Jean Gabin) is an aging racketeer who has made a big haul in gold bullion and wants to retire. Friendship, gang codes, and women mess up this dream when Max's best friend (Rene Dary) gets kidnapped by a rival gang, who will only release him in return for the gold. The element of keen insight into gang behavior puts this into a measured pacing which crescendos in a final well-staged gunfight. Gabin brings all his authority to bear in making Max a sturdy, noble crook whose code carries him through. Jeanne Moreau turns in a neat bit as a moll, and Dary as the inarticulate aging Romeo friend is memorable.

TOUCH OF CLASS, A
1973, 106 mins, UK Ⓥ ⌷
D: Melvin Frank A: George Segal, Glenda Jackson, Paul Sorvino, Hildegard Neil, Cec Linder, K. Callan (Brut)

A Touch of Class is sensational and revitalizing, updating and invigorating an earlier film genre to smash results. George Segal superbly justifies a reputation for comedy while Glenda Jackson's full-spectrum talent is again confirmed. An accidental London meeting between Segal and Jackson leads to a casual pass by Segal, thence to a frustrated rendezvous in a Spanish resort. Pair's romance flourishes into a full-blown affair at home, with Segal wearing himself out dashing between two beds.
1973: Best Actress (Glenda Jackson)
Nominations: Best Picture, Story & Screenplay, Original Dramatic Score, Song ("All That Love Went to Waste")

TOUCH OF EVIL
1958, 95 mins, US Ⓥ ⊙
D: Orson Welles, Harry Keller A: Charlton Heston, Janet Leigh, Orson Welles, Joseph Calleia, Akim Tamiroff, Joanna Moore (Universal)

Touch of Evil smacks of brilliance but ultimately flounders in it, proving it takes more than good scenes to make a good picture. Welles portrays an American cop who has the reputation of always getting his man, hot on the trail of scoundrels who blew to smithereens the "owner" of a Mexican border town. Charlton Heston, a bigwig in the Mexican government, happens to be around with his new American bride (Janet Leigh) and gets himself involved in the proceedings, suspecting that the dynamiting has something to do with a narcotics racket he's investigating. Welles turns in a unique and absorbing performance. Heston combines a dynamic quality with a touch of Latin personality. Leigh, sexy as all get-out, switches from charm to fright with facility. Dennis Weaver, as the night man, is fine though exaggerated.

TOUCH OF LOVE, A
1969, 102 mins, UK Ⓥ
D: Waris Hussein A: Sandy Dennis, Ian McKellen, Michael Coles, John Standing, Eleanor Bron (Palomar)

Story deals with a philosophy student whose seduction by a chance acquaintance leaves her pregnant, while each of her steady but platonic suitors thinks her rival is the father. Pic details girl's solo battle against society and herself to decide whether to keep the child and bring it up sans a father. Sandy Dennis' performance is pinpoint accurate in conveying the tremendous inner strength which helps her character win through against hostile society and family.

TOUCH OF ZEN, A
See: Xia Nu

TOUGH GUYS
1986, 104 mins, US Ⓥ ⊙ ⌷
D: Jeff Kanew A: Burt Lancaster, Kirk Douglas, Charles Durning, Alexis Smith, Dana Carvey, Darlanne Fluegel (Touchstone/Silver Screen/Bryna)

Tough Guys is unalloyed hokum that proves a sad waste of talent on the parts of costars Burt Lancaster and Kirk Douglas. The two venerable thesps turn up as gentleman crooks celebrated for having been the last outlaws to rob a train. Pic pokes along with Lancaster provoking havoc at his old folks' home and Douglas quitting a series of jobs in disgust until scripters decide that perhaps a plot would be nice, so the guys get together and—surprise—decide to rob the train again. It's all silly, meaningless, and vaguely depressing.

TOUGH GUYS DON'T DANCE
1987, 108 mins, US Ⓥ ⊙
D: Norman Mailer **A:** Ryan O'Neal, Isabella Rossellini, Debra Sandlund, Wings Hauser, John Bedford Lloyd, Frances Fisher (Cannon/Zoetrope)

Tough Guys is part parody and part serious, with a nasty streak running right down the middle. Set in a small coastal town in Massachusetts where business is bad for Tim Madden (Ryan O'Neal), story has something to do with a botched drug deal, men who love the wrong women, and women who love the wrong men. In the course of it, Madden's wealthy wife (Debra Sandlund), a washed up porno star (Frances Fisher), a suicidal southerner (John Bedford Lloyd), a gay sugar daddy (R. Patrick Sulliva) and a corrupt police chief (Wings Hauser) all get blown away.

TOVARICH
1937, 94 mins, US
D: Anatole Litvak **A:** Claudette Colbert, Charles Boyer, Basil Rathbone, Anita Louise, Melville Cooper, Isabel Jeans (Warner)

Tovarich emerges as a piece of popular entertainment. It also has the very considerable drawing value of Claudette Colbert and Charles Boyer. Boyer's diction is difficult to comprehend in several places. Only in brief moments does Colbert convey the dignity, bearing, and fine humor of a Russian imperial princess. Litvak seems imbued with the idea that he had to make Tovarich look like a big picture, whereas the story of the royal refugee couple who enter domestic service in the household of a Paris banker is a yarn of charming and finely shaded characterizations.

TOWERING INFERNO, THE
1974, 165 mins, US Ⓥ ⊙ ▭
D: John Guillermin, Irwin Allen **A:** Steve McQueen, Paul Newman, William Holden, Faye Dunaway, Fred Astaire, Richard Chamberlain (20th Century-Fox/Warner)

The Towering Inferno is one of the greatest disaster pictures made, a personal and professional triumph for producer Irwin Allen. Steve McQueen, as the fireman in charge of extinguishing the runaway fire in a 130-story San Francisco building; Paul Newman, as the heroic and chagrined architect of the glass and concrete pyre; William Holden, as its builder; and Faye Dunaway, as Newman's fiancée, get and deserve their star billing.

1974: Best Cinematography, Song ("We

May Never Love Like This Again"), Editing
Nominations: Best Picture, Supp. Actor (Fred Astaire), Art Direction, Original Dramatic Score, Sound

TOWER OF LIES, THE
1925, 80 mins, US ⊗
D: Victor Seastrom **A:** Norma Shearer, Lon Chaney, Ian Keith, Claire McDowell, William Haines, David Torrence (M-G-M)

The fault with this film is that it isn't a movie story by any stretch of the imagination. The locale is some Scandinavian country. Jan, a rough farmer, finds love playing an important part in his life when a baby daughter is born. She grows to be his pride, but when the nephew of their former landlord gets bad over back rents, the girl goes to the city to make money. That a woman, well bred, with parental love always about her, would turn prostitute for purely pecuniary reasons is silly. The acting is aces, and the direction masterful. But *Tower of Lies* can never be anything more than a soggy picture made bearable by the leavening forces of director Victor Seastrom and actors Lon Chaney and Norma Shearer.

TOWER OF LONDON
1939, 92 mins, US Ⓥ
D: Rowland V. Lee **A:** Basil Rathbone, Boris Karloff, Vincent Price, Barbara O'Neill, Ian Hunter, Nan Grey (Universal)

Tower of London emerges as a spinechiller with an accent on gruesomeness. Boris Karloff plays a clubfooted and misshapen giant, chief executioner and torturer for the conniving Basil Rathbone. Story delves into the court intrigues during the reign of King Edward IV. Everyone seems to be indulging in undercover manipulations except the king, with latter's brother Richard, Duke of Gloucester (Rathbone), hatching a plot to become ruler.

TOWN LIKE ALICE, A
(THE RAPE OF MALAYA)
1956, 117 mins, UK Ⓥ ⊙
D: Jack Lee **A:** Virginia McKenna, Peter Finch, Marie Lohr, Renee Houston, Jean Anderson, Maureen Swanson (Rank/Vic)

Film describes how a handful of women and children were marched through Malaya at the hands of the Japanese. During the period of their cross-country march, the women and kids are befriended by a couple of Australian POWs who have been assigned to truck driving duties, and a bond develops between Virginia McKenna and Peter Finch. The subject matter is necessarily grim, but, wherever possible, the script and direction endeavor to infuse a touch of lighter relief.

TOWN WITHOUT PITY
1961, 112 mins, US
D: Gottfried Reinhardt A: Kirk Douglas, E. G. Marshall, Robert Blake, Richard Jaeckel, Christine Kaufmann, Frank Sutton (United Artists/Mirisch/Gloria)

Town Without Pity appears to be a straight courtroom drama of a gang rape case and its repercussions on a German community incensed that the rapists are American GIs and the victim is a local girl. But the production attempts to go much deeper than that. The screenplay dramatizes the story of a military defense attorney who must against his will bring about the destruction of the innocent raped girl who becomes a victim of her own human fallibility and the fallibility of German witnesses who lie, exaggerate, or conceal on the stand. A picture that raises important moral and judicial questions must do so in terms of rounded, dimensional characters if it is to register with impact. *Town without Pity* fails in this regard.
1961: Nomination: Best Song ("Town Without Pity")

TO WONG FOO, THANKS FOR EVERYTHING! JULIE NEWMAR
1995, 108 mins, US
D: Beeban Kidron A: Wesley Snipes, Patrick Swayze, John Leguizamo, Stockard Channing, Blythe Danner, Arliss Howard (Amblin/Universal)

To Wong Foo, Thanks for Everything! Julie Newmar, the American response to *The Adventures of Priscilla, Queen of the Desert,* is not as outrageous or funny as the Aussie pic, but it still offers some rewards as mainstream entertainment, toplined by macho actors Wesley Snipes, Patrick Swayze and John Leguizamo as drag queens in fabulous costumes. In a New York drag queen beauty pageant, a tie is declared between Vida Boheme (Swayze) and Noxeema Jackson (Snipes). The pair meet Chi Chi Rodriguez (Leguizamo), a poor Hispanic queen, and the trio buy a '67 Cadillac convertible and hit the open road. The car breaks down in the middle of nowhere and they find themselves stuck in Snydersville, a reactionary Midwestern town. Over the course of one long weekend, the three end up performing miracles. The movie unfolds at a deliberate and unvarying pace, but the material is too thin to merit such extended treatment.

TOXIC AVENGER, THE
1985, 100 mins, US
D: Michael Herz, Samuel Weil A: Andree Maranda, Mitchell Cohen, Jennifer Baptist, Cindy Manion, Robert Prichard, Mark Torgl (Troma)

This madcap spoof on The Incredible Hulk is an outlandish mix of gory violence and realistic special effects. Melvin, a 90-pound weakling, works in a body-building club and is hated by the muscular and healthy types that flaunt their bodies before him. Humiliated by the bodybuilders, Melvin jumps out of a window and lands in a truck carrying toxic waste. This transforms him into a hulking monster seeking only to right wrongs in his town and persecute the meanies.

TOXIC AVENGER, PART II, THE
1989, 95 mins, US
D: Lloyd Kaufman, Michael Herz A: Ron Fazio, John Altamura, Phoebe Legere, Rick Collins, Rikiya Yasuoka, Lisa Gaye (Troma)

Even die-hard Troma fans will have a hard time stomaching *The Toxic Avenger, Part II.* A weak script and sluggish direction turn this sequel to the 1985 spoof into an endless, stultifying mess. *Toxic II* finds 90-pound weakling Melvin suffering from emotional problems, unable to save a home for the blind from an evil drug magnate who razed the center and killed its inhabitants in his march to conquer Tromaville. Because each limited spoof is telegraphed and laboriously executed, this toxic sequel can be hazardous to your health.

TOYS
1992, 121 mins, US
D: Barry Levinson A: Robin Williams, Michael Gambon, Joan Cusack, Robin Wright, LL Cool J, Donald O'Connor (20th Century-Fox/Baltimore)

Barry Levinson, a director most at home with slice-of-life portraits relating to his Baltimore roots, tries his hand here at a darkly satiric fable and ends up doing an extremely poor impression of Terry Gilliam. The story has aging toymaker Kenneth Zevo (a cameo by Donald O'Connor) leave his factory to his army-general brother (Michael Gambon), fearing that his two children (Robin Williams and Joan

1288

Cusack) are too immature for the job. The General goes about converting the plant into a factory producing war toys and machines of war. Williams and Cusack, the supposed spirits of innocence, are for the most part annoying—particularly Cusack's adult-as-child antics. The movie's real star, production designer Ferdinando Scarfiotti, nevertheless deserves enormous credit.

1992: Nominations: Best Art Direction, Costume Design

TOYS IN THE ATTIC
1963, 88 mins, US Ⓥ ▭
D: George Roy Hill **A:** Dean Martin, Geraldine Page, Yvette Mimieux, Wendy Hiller, Gene Tierney, Frank Silvera (United Artists)

Toys in the Attic is a watered-down version of Lillian Hellman's play, but enough of the original emotional savagery has been retained to satisfy those who prefer their melodramatic meat raw and chewy. *Toys* is laid in the Deep South and is liberally crammed with incest, adultery, imbecility, lust, and a few other folk pleasantries. Hellman's heavyweight drama examines the tragedy that transpires as a result of a spinster sister's secret lust for her younger brother, whose monetarily motivated marriage to a simple-minded girl sets in operation the mechanism for his ultimate disaster. The new ending is thoroughly artificial.

1963: Nomination: Best B&W Costume Design

TOY SOLDIERS
1991, 112 mins, US Ⓥ ⊙
D: Daniel Petrie Jr. **A:** Sean Astin, Wil Wheaton, Keith Coogan, Andrew Divoff, Louis Gossett Jr., Denholm Elliott (Tri-Star)

Toy Soldiers is a very entertaining action film, presenting rich kids at a Virginia prep school who have to develop some backbone and defend themselves when Andrew Divoff's group of Colombian terrorists take over their school and hold them hostage. Seeing Sean Astin and his pranksters turn into commandos who wipe out the nasty invaders makes for purely escapist, crowd-pleasing pleasure. Young villain Divoff is terrific at creating a brutal figure of hate.

TOY STORY
1995, 80 mins, US Ⓥ ⊙
D: John Lasseter (Pixar/Walt Disney)

Walt Disney continues its long tradition of cutting-edge animation with the computer-generated *Toy Story*. The film is a modern parable that masks its serious side with a fun house full of colorful characters and thrilling adventures. The story involves a group of toys owned by a boy named Andy. Woody, a cowboy marionette, has been the boy's long-time, sentimental favorite. He's put to the test with the arrival of Buzz Lightyear, a galactic superhero with an arsenal of flashy gadgets, a gung-ho type with an annoyingly helpful attitude. The camera loops and zooms in a dizzying fashion that fairly takes one's breath away. But the filmmakers dispense with the most dazzling elements of computer-generated graphics and concentrate on telling an effective story, helped by a first-rate voice cast.

Nominations: Best Original Screenplay, Original Musical or Comedy Score, Original Song ("You've Got a Friend")

TOY STORY 2
1999, 92 mins, US Ⓥ ⊙
D: John Lasseter, Lee Unkrich, Ash Brannon (Pixar/Walt Disney)

As a sequel to *Toy Story*, *Toy Story 2* is a richer, more satisfying film in every respect. The affable Woody (voiced by Tom Hanks) anticipates being taken to Cowboy Camp by his owner, Andy (John Morris). But a "broken" arm causes Woody to be left behind, and he inadvertently lands in a yard-sale bin, where he's kidnapped by the greedy Al McWhiggin (Wayne Knight), who knows Woody was a big TV star back in the fifties. In a downtown building, Woody meets cowgirl Jessie (Joan Cusack), Stinky Pete the Prospector (Kelsey Grammer), and a horse named Bullseye and learns of his long-ago celebrity. Al plans to cash in by selling the whole set to a museum in Japan. It's up to spaceman Buzz Lightyear (Tim Allen), Rex the Dinosaur (Wallace Shawn), Hamm the Pig (John Ratzenberger), Mr. Potato Head (Don Rickles), and Slinky Dog (Jim Varney) to mount a rescue expedition. A sense of spirited invention permeates the proceedings from top to bottom.

1999: Nomination: Original Song ("When She Loved Me")

TRACK OF THE CAT
1954, 102 mins, US ▭
D: William A. Wellman **A:** Robert Mitchum, Teresa Wright, Diana Lynn, Tab Hunter, Beulah Bondi, Philip Tonge (Warner)

The novelty of lensing, in color, a picture designed to reproduce black-and-white is rather dissipated in this production. If there had been some entertainment to accompany the photographic treatment, the combination might have paid off strongly. Story deals with a farm family of three brothers, an old-maid sister, a drunken father, and a Bible-reading mother, plus a girl from a neighboring farm. First the older brother, William Hopper, is killed by a mountain lion. Then the middle brother, Robert Mitchum, dies while looking for the "cat."

TRACKS
1976, 90 mins, US Ⓥ ⊙
D: Henry Jaglom A: Dennis Hopper, Taryn Power, Dean Stockwell, Topo Swope, Alfred Ryder, Michael Emil (Rainbow)

Henry Jaglom abandons the poseur excesses that marred his first film, *A Safe Place*, for an incisive, revelatory film about a returning Vietnam veteran transporting the body of a friend across the US for burial. Dennis Hopper gives an excellent rendering of a soldier needing tenderness but hiding it until he finds it with a headstrong but knowing girl, played by Tyrone Power's daughter, Taryn, who shows an offbeat beauty and presence.

TRACK 29
1988, 86 mins, UK Ⓥ
D: Nicolas Roeg A: Theresa Russell, Gary Oldman, Sandra Bernhard, Christopher Lloyd, Colleen Camp, Seymour Cassel (HandMade)

Track 29 is set in a Southern town where strange things happen every day. Linda (Russell) and husband Henry (Christopher Lloyd) are at odds over Linda's desire for a child and Henry's preference for his model trains. He also enjoys being spanked by Nurse Stein (Sandra Bernhard). Into this world of normal absurdity arrives a stranger (Gary Oldman), who convinces Linda he's her baby boy born out of wedlock and taken from her at birth, but viewers begin to have doubts that the weirdo isn't a figment of her imagination. Perverse humor is the keynote of the Oedipal complexed duo.

TRADER HORN
1931, 123 mins, US
D: W. S. Van Dyke A: Harry Carey, Edwina Booth, Duncan Renaldo, Mutia Omoolu, Olive Golden, C. Aubrey Smith (M-G-M)

A good-looking animal picture. The story doesn't mean anything other than a connecting link for a series of sequences which, at one point, become nothing more than an out-and-out lecture. Light love vein is introduced between Harry Carey's young companion, Duncan Renaldo, and Edwina Booth as the queen of a tribe from whom she and the men escape when her followers turn on her after she countermands an order of death by torture for Carey, Renaldo, and Rencharo, the former's native gun boy. Sound effects are outstanding. Andy Anderson, the sound man, accompanied director W. S. Van Dyke's unit to Africa. The camera work is also swell marksmanship.
1930/31: Nomination: Best Picture

TRADING PLACES
1983, 106 mins, US Ⓥ ⊙
D: John Landis A: Dan Aykroyd, Eddie Murphy, Ralph Bellamy, Don Ameche, Denholm Elliott, Jamie Lee Curtis (Paramount)

Trading Places is a light romp geared up by the schtick shifted by Dan Aykroyd and Eddie Murphy. But even those two popular young comics couldn't have brought this one off without the contributions of three veterans—Ralph Bellamy, Don Ameche, and the droll Englishman Denholm Elliott. Aykroyd plays a stuffy young financial wizard who runs a Philadelphia commodities house for two scheming brothers, Bellamy and Ameche. Murphy has grown up in the streets and lives on the con. On a whim motivated by disagreement over the importance of environment versus breeding, Bellamy bets Ameche that Murphy could run the complex commodities business just as well as Aykroyd, given the chance, while Aykroyd would resort to crime and violence if suddenly all friends and finances were stripped away from him.
1983: Nomination: Best Adapted Score

TRAIL OF THE LONESOME PINE, THE
1916, 70 mins, US ⊗
D: Cecil B. DeMille A: Charlotte Walker, Theodore Roberts, Earle Foxe, Thomas Meighan (Lasky)

The Trail of the Lonesome Pine is a remarkable motion picture. Theodore Roberts, who plays the aged head of the clan of Tollivers who make their headquarters in the lonesome by-ways of the Tennessee mountains, must be given the credit for the star performance. Charlotte Walker plays

June, and Thomas Meighan is the young revenue officer with whom she falls in love. Scenically the picture is wonderful. The sheriff of the county in which the Tollivers hold sway is certain that they are running a still for illicit whiskey, but he cannot obtain the evidence. So he applies to the federal authorities, and John Hale (Meighan) is sent into the mountains to assist the sheriff and run down the case.

TRAIL OF THE LONESOME PINE, THE
1936, 100 mins, US
D: Henry Hathaway **A:** Sylvia Sidney, Henry Fonda, Fred MacMurray, Fred Stone, Nigel Bruce, Beulah Bondi (Paramount)

The Trail of the Lonesome Pine is the first all-Technicolor feature produced 100 percent outdoors, faithfully preserving the curt mien of the feuding Tolliver and Falin clans. Sylvia Sidney's performance as the hillbilly looker is uncompromising in every detail. After a brief spell of schooling in Louisville, she reverts to type. Upon hearing how Buddy (Spanky McFarland) has been murdered, she too cries for a Falin's blood. Henry Fonda, as her mountaineer vis-à-vis, is equally consistent in his scowling hate for the Falin clan, as well as for the advent of the city engineer (Fred MacMurray).
1936: Nomination: Best Song ("A Melody from the Sky")

TRAIL OF THE PINK PANTHER
1983, 97 mins, UK Ⓥ ⊙ ▭
D: Blake Edwards **A:** Peter Sellers, David Niven, Herbert Lom, Richard Mulligan, Joanna Lumley, Capucine (Titan)

A patchwork of out-takes, reprised clips, and new connective footage, *Trail of the Pink Panther* is a thin, peculiar picture unsupported by the number of laughs one is accustomed to in this series. Stitched together after Peter Sellers's death, this is by far the slightest of the six Inspector Clouseau efforts. Story's structure is strange, to say the least. The fabulous Pink Panther gem is stolen yet again from an Arab museum, which sparks immediate interest from the haplessly effective French detective. Clouseau's plane is reported missing. French television reporter Joanna Lumley sets out to interview many of those who had known the inspector in earlier pics.

TRAIN, THE
1965, 140 mins, US/France/Italy Ⓥ
D: John Frankenheimer **A:** Burt Lancaster, Paul Scofield, Jeanne Moreau, Michel Simon, Suzanne Flon, Wolfgang Preiss (Artistes Associes/Ariane/Dear)

After a slow start, *The Train* picks up to become a colorful, action-packed big-scale adventure opus. Pic concerns an elaborate railroad resistance plot to keep a train full of French art treasures from being shipped to Germany near the end of World War II. An earthy stationmaster (Burt Lancaster) in the resistance is reluctant to sacrifice men for paintings. But he finally gives in when an old engineer is killed by the Germans for trying to hold up the art train. Lancaster himself is made to drive the train by the fanatic German colonel (Paul Scofield), for whom the art has become bigger than the war itself.
1965: Best Original Story & Screenplay

TRAIN OF EVENTS
1949, 89 mins, UK
D: Sidney Cole, Charles Crichton, Basil Dearden **A:** Jack Warner, Valerie Hobson, John Clements, Peter Finch, John Gregson, Susan Shaw (Ealing)

This is an absorbing human drama featuring multiple plots. Story concerns a train wreck and the lives of four sets of people immediately prior to their presence on the doomed train. There is sufficient light and shade to preclude top-heaviness, but accent is more on the grave than gay. Acting plum falls to Peter Finch. His tense overwrought emotions, depicting how war can turn a harmless nonentity into a murderer, are convincingly and forcefully portrayed.

TRAIN ROBBERS, THE
1973, 92 mins, US Ⓥ ⊙ ▭
D: Burt Kennedy **A:** John Wayne, Ann-Margret, Rod Taylor, Ben Johnson, Christopher George, Bobby Vinton (Batjac)

The Train Robbers is an above-average John Wayne actioner, written and directed by Burt Kennedy with suspense, comedy, and humanism not usually found in the formula. Wayne recruits a group to recover gold stolen from a train by Ann-Margret's deceased outlaw husband so that her name and that of her child can be clear. Kennedy has provided a series of rich, deep characterizations, plus some intriguing red-herring plot twists.

TRAINSPOTTING
1996, 94 mins, UK Ⓥ ⊙
D: Danny Boyle **A:** Ewan McGregor, Ewen Bremner, Johnny Lee Miller, Kevin McKidd, Robert Carlyle, Kelly Macdonald (Figment/Channel 4)

Scabrous, brutal, and hip, *Trainspotting* is a *Clockwork Orange* for the nineties. Set among a group of self-destructive no-hopers and junkies in Edinburgh's under-belly, action centers on Mark Renton (Ewan McGregor), an on-off junkie who acts as a funnel to the surreal world of his friends and regales the audience with his anti-middle-class values and idiosyncratic philosophy of life. The tone is set by the rough, self-deprecating Scottish humor de-livered in heavy accents. Film's most striking accomplishment is the way it takes a bunch of goal-less losers and turns the material into a sustained piece of cin-ema that's often wildly funny and, at a character level, extremely involving. Dominating the film is Robert Carlyle, genuinely terrifying as the psychopathic Begbie, a walking time bomb who's half-way to hell.

TRANCERS
(AKA: FUTURE COP)
1985, 85 mins, US Ⓥ ⊙
D: Charles Band **A:** Tim Thomerson, He-len Hunt, Michael Stefani, Art La Fleur, Biff Manard, Anne Seymour (Empire)

Trancers works out of a central idea closely akin to *The Terminator,* but this film in no way can match the Arnold Schwarzenegger vehicle in gritty action, wit, and technical know-how. Plot centers on Angel City in A.D. 2247. A sinister mystic (Michael Stefani), who threatens the peace with his legion of controlled trancers, retreats in time to 1985 with a plan to murder the ancestors of the rulers of Angel City. Trooper Jack Deth (Tim Thomerson) is sent back to stop him.

TRANSYLVANIA TWIST
1989, 82 mins, US
D: Jim Wynorski **A:** Robert Vaughn, Teri Copley, Steve Altman, Monique Gabrielle, Angus Scrimm, Ace Mask (Concorde)

Transylvania Twist is an occasionally hilarious horror spoof notable for the range of its comical targets. Robert Vaughn is delightful as a Dracula-styled vampire. His beautiful niece Teri Copley is an American singing star who travels to his castle in Transylvania upon the death of her father. Mixed into the comic stew

are many delightful reflexive bits: a track-ing camera that gets sidetracked on boda-cious women passing by, a black & white sequence when the star visits a set that looks left over from *The Honeymooners,* and a terrifically edited appearance by Boris Karloff.

TRAP, THE
1966, 106 mins, UK Ⓥ ⋈
D: Sidney Hayers **A:** Rita Tushingham, Oliver Reed, Rex Sevenoaks, Barbara Chilcott, Linda Goranson, Blain Fairman (Rank)

This Anglo-Canadian earthy adventure yarn is set in the mid-1890s when British Columbia was wild and untamed. Jean La Bete (Oliver Reed), a lusty French-Canadian trapper, returns to the trading post too late for the once-a-year "auc-tion" of harlots. So he settles for a young mute orphan, a servant in the trader's house, and sets off for the wastes. There follows an edgy *Taming of the Shrew* sit-uation, as the hunter tries to win her af-fection by cajoling, bullying, and occasionally sweet-talking her.

TRAPEZE
1956, 106 mins, US Ⓥ ⋈
D: Carol Reed **A:** Burt Lancaster, Tony Curtis, Gina Lollobrigida, Katy Jurado, Thomas Gomez, Minor Watson (Susan/United Artists)

Trapeze is a high-flying screen enter-tainment equipped with circus thrills and excitement, a well-handled romantic tri-angle, and a cast of potent marquee names. Reed's direction loads the aerial scenes with suspense, and stars Burt Lancaster and Tony Curtis simulate big-top aristo-crats realistically. The script tells how Curtis, son of an aerialist, comes to Paris to learn from Lancaster, one of the few fliers able to achieve the triple somersault, a feat which had left him crippled. To-gether, they start to work up an act when the tumbler (Gina Lollobrigida) moves in, using her wiles on the young man but lov-ing the older.

TRASH
1970, 103 mins, US Ⓥ
D: Paul Morrissey **A:** Joe Dallesandro, Holly Woodlawn, Jane Forth, Michael Sklar, Geri Miller, Andrea Feldman (War-hol)

Andy Warhol surfaces from the camp underground with *Trash,* the most com-prehensible, and least annoying, of a long line of quasi-porno features from *Chelsea Girls* to *Lonesome Cowboys*. Once again, stud-in-residence is Joe Dallesandro, this time as a strung-out heroin addict unable to function sexually despite numerous provocations.

TRAVELING EXECUTIONER, THE
1970, 94 mins, US ⓥ ☐
D: Jack Smight **A:** Stacy Keach, Marianna Hill, Bud Cort, Graham Jarvis, James J. Sloyan, M. Emmet Walsh (M-G-M)

The Traveling Executioner is a macabre, tastefully seamy comedy-drama about bayou prison life, circa 1918. Film is dominated by Stacy Keach, the professional executioner who makes $100 per client. He's a promoter from the word go, but an underlying, disarming sincerity about the job makes the character believable and sympathetic. A literal description of the story does injustice to the whole; film contains some gritty elements and some broad comedy elements.

TRAVELLING NORTH
1987, 96 mins, Australia ⓥ
D: Carl Schultz **A:** Leo McKern, Julia Blake, Graham Kennedy, Henri Szeps, Michelle Fawdon, Diane Craig (View)

This is a mature, frequently funny, and ultimately most moving story of old age and retirement. Leo McKern plays Frank, a cantankerous ex-Communist and retired civil engineer. A widower, he persuades his close friend Frances (Julia Blake), a younger widow, to accompany him to subtropical northern Queensland. McKern gives a remarkable performance as the crotchety yet endearing Frank. As Frances, Blake positively glows; she plays a patient, loving woman with a determination of her own.

TRAVELS WITH MY AUNT
1972, 109 mins, UK ☐
D: George Cukor **A:** Maggie Smith, Alec McCowen, Lou Gossett, Robert Stephens, Cindy Williams, Robert Flemyng (M-G-M)

Travels with My Aunt is the story of an outrageous woman of indeterminate years cavorting in a set of outrageous situations which spell high comedy. It may also be regarded as utter nonsense in a hammed-up set of overly contrived circumstances. Maggie Smith plays the title role in an overdrawn but delightful manner. Film opens at the funeral services of her nephew's mother, but the disrupting arrival of the over-dressed, over-cosmeticked Aunt Augusta sets the stage for a comedy spree.

1972: Best Costume Design (Anthony Powell)
Nominations: Best Actress (Maggie Smith), Cinematography, Art Direction

T. R. BASKIN
(UK: A DATE WITH A LONELY GIRL)
1971, 89 mins, US ⓥ
D: Herbert Ross **A:** Candice Bergen, Peter Boyle, James Caan, Marcia Rodd, Erin O'Reilly, Howard Platt (Paramount)

T. R. Baskin makes a few good comedic comments on modern urban existence, but these are bits of rare jewelry lost on a vast beach of strung-out, erratic storytelling. Candice Bergen is a rural girl in the big city. Peter Hyams's debut production is handsomely mounted, but his screenplay is sterile, superficial, and inconsistent. Bergen's screen presence is too sophisticated for the role, and her acting, direction, and dialogue result in confusion. Peter Boyle, whose contribution is little more than a foil, tries to get some depth into the role of a square salesman.

TREASURE ISLAND
1934, 105 mins, US ⓥ
D: Victor Fleming **A:** Wallace Beery, Jackie Cooper, Lionel Barrymore, Otto Kruger, Lewis Stone, Nigel Bruce (M-G-M)

It's pretty dangerous to put an old classic as popular as this Robert Louis Stevenson yarn on the screen. It is hard to imagine anyone else in the Long John Silver role than Wallace Beery. It is hard to think of anyone who might have replaced Jackie Cooper as Jim Hawkins. Yet neither of the two completely convinces. *Treasure Island* is a grand, blood-curdling adventure yarn. In portions where it is so played, it's genuinely thrilling and good entertainment.

TREASURE ISLAND
1950, 96 mins, UK ⓥ ⊙
D: Byron Haskin **A:** Bobby Driscoll, Robert Newton, Basil Sydney, Walter Fitzgerald, Denis O'Dea, Finlay Currie (RKO/Walt Disney)

Treasure Island, Robert Louis Stevenson's classic, has been handsomely mounted. A British cast headed by American moppet Bobby Driscoll faithfully recaptures the bloodthirsty 18th-century era when pirates vied for the supremacy of the seas. Yarn revolves around a squire and a doctor who fit out a ship to search for South Seas treasure on the strength of a chart obtained from a dying pirate. Robert Newton racks up a virtual tour de force as Long John Silver. There's no dearth of action in the footage.

TREASURE OF THE GOLDEN CONDOR

1953, 93 mins, US ⓥ
D: Delmer Daves **A:** Cornel Wilde, Constance Smith, Finlay Currie, Walter Hampden, Anne Bancroft, Fay Wray (20th Century-Fox)

A moderate round of entertainment is offered in this adventure-swashbuckler set in early France and Guatemala. Plot deals with Wilde's efforts to oust a cruel uncle (George Macready) who has usurped his French estates and title. Needing money to prove his rights, Wilde joins forces with Finlay Currie, possessor of a map to a fabulous Mayan treasure, and his daughter (Constance Smith). Back in France, his plans are exposed by Anne Bancroft, a selfish girl he hopes to wed.

TREASURE OF THE SIERRA MADRE, THE

1948, 124 mins, US ⓥ ⊙
D: John Huston **A:** Humphrey Bogart, Walter Huston, Tim Holt, Bruce Bennett, Barton MacLane (Warner)

Sierra Madre, adapted from the popular novel by B. Traven, is a story of psychological disintegration under the crushers of greed and gold. John Huston, with an extraordinary assist in the thesping department from his father, Walter Huston, has fashioned this standout film with unfailing sensitivity for suggestive detail and uncompromising commitment to reality. Cast is headed by Humphrey Bogart, Walter Huston, and Tim Holt as three gold prospectors who start out in the Mexican mountains as buddies but wind up in a murderous tangle at the finish. In a remarkable, controlled portrait, Bogart progresses to the edge of madness without losing sight of the subtle shadings needed to establish persuasiveness.
1948: Best Director, Best Supp. Actor (Walter Huston), Screenplay
Nomination: Best Picture

TREE GROWS IN BROOKLYN, A

1945, 132 mins, US ⓥ ⊙
D: Elia Kazan **A:** Dorothy McGuire, Joan Blondell, James Dunn, Lloyd Nolan, Peggy Ann Garner (20th Century-Fox)

This is the story of the poverty-ridden Nolan family. *Tree* recalls an absorbing period of a colorful tribe of a Brooklyn neighborhood that was tough in its growing-up, where kids fought and on Saturday nights fathers and husbands loped uncertainly from the corner quenchery. Some of this might have acquired the tinge of travesty in hands less skilled than those of director Elia Kazan, but never does the serio-comic make a false note; and never does this story become maudlin. To Dorothy McGuire went the prize part of Katie Nolan. It is a role that she makes distinctive by underplaying.
1945: Best Supp. Actor (James Dunn)
Nomination: Best Screenplay

TREES LOUNGE

1996, 94 mins, US ⓥ
D: Steve Buscemi **A:** Steve Buscemi, Mark Boone Jr., Chloe Sevigny, Michael Buscemi, Anthony LaPaglia, Elizabeth Bracco (Live)

A serio-comedy about a ne'er-do-well barfly, *Trees Lounge* represents a modest, agreeable directorial debut by indie acting stalwart Steve Buscemi. Pic takes a rueful, kaleidoscopic look at the petty feuds and minimal ambitions that dominate people's lives in a working-class New York suburb. Tommy (Buscemi) is a joker, an alcoholic, and, at 31, a loser. He spends most of his time downing drinks at the neighborhood watering hole, the Trees Lounge. Neither the comedy nor the melodrama of the situations is punched up in a manipulative way as Buscemi, seemingly taking his cue from indie pioneer John Cassavetes, roots everything in his characters and actors.

TREMORS

1990, 96 mins, US ⓥ ⊙
D: Ron Underwood **A:** Kevin Bacon, Fred Ward, Finn Carter, Michael Gross, Reba McEntire, Bobby Jacoby (No Frills)

An affectionate send-up of schlocky 1950s monster pics, *Tremors* has a few clever twists but ultimately can't decide what it wants to be—flat-out funny or scarey. The threat comes in the form of four house-trailer-sized worm creatures with multiple serpent-like tongues that tunnel underground before bursting up to devour human prey. All the conventions of the genre are here: a small town in the middle of nowhere isolated from outside help with a scientist on hand to study strange seismic phenomena. After that, however, the scripters begin to play with those cliches. The pacing and action improve considerably as the film goes on, maintaining a tongue-in-cheek approach while the situation becomes more dire.

TRESPASS
1992, 101 mins, US Ⓥ ⊙
D: Walter Hill **A:** Bill Paxton, Ice T, William Sadler, Ice Cube, Art Evans, De'voreaux White (Universal)

After a brief prologue, the film is entirely set in a huge abandoned factory in East St. Louis, IL. Learning that a huge stash of gold is supposedly buried somewhere in the bombed-out building, good ol' boy firemen Bill Paxton and William Sadler set out to recover the loot. But the two Arkansas crackers stumble on a gangland murder and become marked men. Pursued by some well-armed blacks led by a resplendent Ice T, Paxton and Sadler manage to nab T's brother (De'voreaux White). Holed up in one room, the white guys squabble about what to do with the gold. Director Walter Hill's handling of the action is fluid and kinetic, making the film a pleasure to watch for the expertness of its craft.

TRESPASSER, THE
1929, 120 mins, US
D: Edmund Goulding **A:** Gloria Swanson, Robert Ames, Purnell Pratt, William Holden, Henry B. Walthall (United Artists)

There is likely no picture with as many anti-climaxes as *The Trespasser*. At least four times the film goes to a finish, as one might suspect, to take another interesting tack. That is one of the novelties of the story. Three others are Gloria Swanson, her voice, and her clothes. Marion Donnell (Swanson), stenographer to Hector Ferguson (Purnell Pratt), elopes with Jack Merrick (Robert Ames), a rich man's son, and a few days afterwards father Merrick (William Holden) returns and persuades Jack that annulment followed by building up of Marion through publicity and remarriage later is socially essential. The pic is framed to carry a sob at the close of every sequence.

TRIAL, THE
1962, 115 mins, France/W. Germany/Italy Ⓥ ⊙
D: Orson Welles **A:** Anthony Perkins, Jeanne Moreau, Romy Schneider, Elsa Martinelli, Akim Tamiroff, Orson Welles (Paris-Europa/Hisa/FICIT)

Orson Welles's film may well delight film buffs and startle or irritate others. A young white-collar worker, Joseph K, wakes up to find a sinister police inspector and two seedy detectives in his room. He is technically under arrest, but he is not told why. The film gets progressively more expressionistic and surreal as he is caught up in his impending trial and gets deeper into the complex setup of the law. Anthony Perkins as K is on screen practically all the time, a timid but priggish type who faces up to an impersonal court. Welles has given intimations that this could be a totalitarian nation or one of over-automation. It also may be a man's awakening to consciousness and finding himself alienated in the world. Pic is uneven and sometimes filled with arid dialogue but has enough visual vitality to keep it engrossing in its first part.

TRIAL, THE
1993, 118 mins, UK Ⓥ
D: David Jones **A:** Kyle MacLachlan, Anthony Hopkins, Jason Robards, Jean Stapleton, Polly Walker, Juliet Stevenson (BBC/Europanda)

The Trial is just that. Despite a fine cast, superior Prague locations, and a faithful Harold Pinter screenplay, this second film adaptation of Kafka's landmark 1913 novel is dull, lifeless, and strictly television-bound in its aesthetics. Up against the brick wall of an authoritarian regime and an unknowable Law, K (Kyle MacLachlan) has experiences that are positively illogicial and evocative of modern man's absurd status in the universe. But, as structured, the script evolves as a tedious series of mostly two-character scenes. Performances are acceptable without being at all electrifying.

TRIAL AND ERROR
See: The Dock Brief

TRIAL BY JURY
1994, 92 mins, US Ⓥ ⊙
D: Heywood Gould **A:** Joanne Whalley-Kilmer, Armand Assante, Gabriel Byrne, William Hurt, Kathleen Quinlan, Ed Lauter (Morgan Creek/Warner)

Even charismatic top-rank stars can't resuscitate this leaden-paced legal thriller. The script's troubles begin when the key government witness in the trial of crime boss Rusty Pirone (Armand Assante) is murdered in an unbelievable fashion. Trying hard to put Pirone away is Gabriel Byrne's US Attorney Daniel Graham, a crusading good boy from the same bad neighborhood as Pirone. Valerie Alston (Joanne Whalley-Kilmer) strolls into the trial as an idealistic single mom. Disgraced ex-cop Tommy Vesey (William Hurt) kidnaps her to scare her into rigging the jury. With cinematographer Frederick Elmes's atmospheric lensing and enough laughable dialogue to fill a camp film festival, all *Jury* needed was a director willing to take the film all the way into the realm of courtroom-thriller parody. Director Heywood Gould apparently didn't see the possibilities.

TRIAL OF BILLY JACK, THE
1974, 170 mins, US ⓥ ▭
D: Frank Laughlin [Tom Laughlin] A: Tom Laughlin, Delores Taylor, Victor Izay, Teresa Laughlin, William Wellman Jr., Russell Lane (Taylor-Laughlin)

   The Trial of Billy Jack is a violent, antiestablishment sequel to *Billy Jack* (1971). Like its predecessor, starring the same two principals, it pinpoints community prejudices against the American Indian. *Trial* takes up where *Billy* ended, when Tom Laughlin as the half-breed Billy Jack was arrested for murder. Much of the footage unfolds at the Freedom School, a reservation institution headed by white women. The production enjoys extraordinary pictorial interest, having been photographed in Arizona's Monument Valley. But it is only when Laughlin is on-camera that the picture picks up.

TRIAL OF JOAN OF ARC, THE
See: *Proces De Jeanne D'Arc*

TRIAL OF SERGEANT RUTLEDGE
See: *Sergeant Rutledge*

TRIAL OF THE CATONSVILLE NINE, THE
1972, 85 mins, US ⓥ
D: Gordon Davidson A: Gwen Arner, Ed Flanders, Barton Heyman, Richard Jordan, Nancy Malone, Donald Moffat (Melville)

   The Trial of the Catonsville Nine is potent in its look at the reasons behind the burning of draft records and the trial that followed. Though based on a play by Father Daniel Berrigan, it reportedly draws heavily on actual court proceedings. Berrigan delves into the backgrounds of those involved and why they thought participation in the Vietnam War was wrong. Direction by Gordon Davidson gives this a dramatic impetus despite static qualities and literary dialogue.

TRIALS OF OSCAR WILDE, THE (THE MAN WITH THE GREEN CARNATION)
1960, 123 mins, UK ▭
D: Ken Hughes A: Peter Finch, Yvonne Mitchell, James Mason, Nigel Patrick, Lionel Jeffries, John Fraser (Warwick)

   Film starts where the scandalous friendship between Wilde and Lord Douglas is well established, introduces Wilde's retrial and, in one brilliant scene at Brighton, shows his anguish when he realizes he is merely being used by his young friend as a weapon in his vindictive struggle with his brutal father. Peter Finch gives a moving and subtle performance as the ill-starred playwright. Before his downfall, he gives the man the charm that he undoubtedly had. John Fraser as handsome young Lord Alfred Douglas is suitably vain, selfish, and petulant. James Mason never provides the strength and bitter logic necessary for the dramatic cut-and-thrust when Wilde is in the witness box.

TRIBUTE
1980, 123 mins, Canada ⓥ ⊙
D: Bob Clark A: Jack Lemmon, Robby Benson, Lee Remick, Kim Cattrall, Colleen Dewhurst, John Marley (20th Century-Fox)

   Film begins with Scottie Templeton (Jack Lemmon) learning of his fatal illness just as the young son he hasn't seen for several years arrives for a visit. Robby Benson is excellent in the complex part of the intellectual, introspective boy, both repelled by his father's superficial, even pimpish, existence as a Broadway press agent and attracted, as everyone is, to his charm. Most of all he's resentful of the years lost since his father divorced his mother (Lee Remick).

TRIBUTE TO A BAD MAN
1956, 95 mins, US ▭
D: Robert Wise A: James Cagney, Don Dubbins, Stephen McNally, Irene Papas, Vic Morrow, Lee Van Cleef (M-G-M)

   A rugged frontier drama of the early west, *Tribute to a Bad Man* is a sight to behold, using the location sites for full visual value. Critically, *Bad Man* is both fast and slow paced, due to a feeling of repetition in some of the story points and in some scene-prolonging by Robert Wise's direction. The title is somewhat of a misnomer. The man portrayed so well by Cagney is a hard-bitten pioneer who must enforce his own law on the limitless range he controls. He is seen through the eyes of young Don Dubbins, eastern lad come west to make his fortune.

TRICK OR TREAT
1986, 97 mins, US ⊚
D: Charles Martin Smith A: Marc Price, Tony Fields, Lisa Orgolini, Ozzy Osbourne (De Laurentiis)

Like a dark street on Halloween night, *Trick or Treat* is ripe for howls and hoots but only manages to deliver them when the festivities are just about over. A recently killed rock star (Tony Fields), comes back to life when his last, awful unreleased record is played backwards, determined to seek revenge on his most ardent critics. The satanic rocker takes himself seriously in reincarnation and ends up acting out all those evil acts he's been singing about for years, drawing his power from the megawatts that surge through his guitar.

TRIO
1950, 91 mins, UK ⊚
D: Ken Annakin, Harold French A: James Hayter, Anne Crawford, Nigel Patrick, Jean Simmons, Michael Rennie, Kathleen Harrison (Gainsborough)

The success of *Quartet*, in which four Somerset Maugham short stories were strung together in a single picture, encouraged the producers to repeat the formula with three more. The first two vignettes, "The Verger" and "Mr. Know-All," occupy roughly half the screen time. The third, Sanatorium, deals with the treatment of tuberculosis.
1950: Nomination: Best Sound

TRIP, THE
1967, 85 mins, US ⊚
D: Roger Corman A: Peter Fonda, Susan Strasberg, Bruce Dern, Dennis Hopper, Salli Sachse, Katherine Walsh (American International)

Peter Fonda, a director of television commercials, whose wife is about to divorce him, goes with friend Bruce Dern to the hippie house of a pusher, played by Dennis Hopper, to buy LSD. Guarded by Dern, Fonda's trip begins. Scenes rapidly cut from Fonda climbing lofty sand dunes, being chased by black-hooded horsemen

through forests, and being the sacrificial victim at a medieval rite in a torch-lit cave. Unconnected scenes spin off the screen with increasing speed and with no attempt at explanation.

TRIPLE CROSS
1966, 140 mins, France/UK ⊚
D: Terence Young A: Christopher Plummer, Yul Brynner, Romy Schneider, Claudine Auger, Trevor Howard, Gert Frobe (Cineurop)

Though based on a true story of a British safecracker who worked as a double spy during World War II, *Triple Cross* is made in the standard spy pattern of having the lead be a ladies' man, fast with his mitts, glib and shrewd, with overloaded and obvious suspense bits thrown in. Cracksman Christopher Plummer is arrested on Jersey. Along comes the war, and the Germans take over the island. He gulls them into letting him work for them and is entrusted with a mission. Once in Britain he goes to work for the British security people in return for a big sum and a promise to wipe out his criminal record. Plummer does not quite have the impassive mask for the pro criminal or the lightness to give the romantic dash the role calls for.

TRIPLE ECHO, THE
1972, 102 mins, UK ⊚
D: Michael Apted A: Glenda Jackson, Oliver Reed, Brian Deacon, Anthony May, Gavin Richards, Jenny Lee Wright (Hemdale/Senta)

Story is set on an English farm in 1943. Alice (Glenda Jackson) lives alone, her husband taken prisoner by the Japanese. One day a young soldier, Barton (Brian Deacon), comes along, and she invites him in for tea. He decides to go AWOL and stay with Alice. So as not to be discovered, he dons female clothes. A stray tank shows up with a sergeant (Oliver Reed) in it. He believes Barton to be Alice's sister and announces he's going to take her out dancing. One never really gets into the motivations of the two main characters.

TRIP TO BOUNTIFUL, THE
1985, 106 mins, US ⊚ ⊙
D: Peter Masterson A: Geraldine Page, John Heard, Carlin Glynn, Richard Bradford, Rebecca DeMornay, Kevin Cooney (FilmDallas/Bountiful Film Partners)

The Trip to Bountiful is a superbly crafted drama featuring the performance

of a lifetime by Geraldine Page. She plays a woman determined to escape the confines of life in a small Houston apartment with her selfless son (John Heard) and his domineering wife (Carlin Glynn). She sets out on a moving and memorable journey across the Gulf Coast to Bountiful, the town where she was born and raised. The 1947-set film recalls the days of scripts with rich plots and dialogue.
1985: Best Actress (Geraldine Page)
Nomination: Best Screenplay Adaptation

TRISTANA

1970, 105 mins, Spain/Italy/France Ⓥ
D: Luis Buñuel **A:** Catherine Deneuve, Fernando Rey, Franco Nero, Lola Gaos, Antonio Casas, Jesus Fernandez (Epoca/Talia/Selenia/Corona)

Those seeking the Buñuel touches of black humor, digs at church and establishment, irreverence and criticism, and an overall condemnation of Spanish mores and hypocrisy, will find a modicum of scenes here to titillate their palates. Yet Buñuel, despite occasional digs, has remained more or less respectful. Much of the pic, which deals with the love-hate relationship between an orphaned girl and her guardian, is rather somber, weighed down by a vision of life in Spain in the 1920s. As the guardian, Don Lope, Fernando Rey is superb. He seems completely at ease in the part.

TRIUMPH OF THE SPIRIT

1989, 120 mins, US Ⓥ
D: Robert M. Young **A:** Willem Dafoe, Edward James Olmos, Robert Loggia, Wendy Gazelle, Kelly Wolf, Costas Mandylor (Nova/Arama/Kopelson)

Film's true story of Greek boxing champ Arouch (Willem Dafoe), who survived life-and-death bouts in the ring at Auschwitz, is murkily underplayed within the harrowing chronicle of death-camp suffering. Writers were hamstrung by history, as Arouch did not take part in the film's climactic event—an uprising that leads to the blowing up of the crematorium. Focus is therefore spread among Arouch's family and friends, including his love interest, Allegra (Wendy Gazelle). Arouch's fights don't commence until 45 minutes into a very slow film. Dafoe finds little to do; like the other actors, he just tries to exude sorrowful stamina.

TROIS COULEURS BLANC (THREE COLORS WHITE)

1994, 89 mins, France/Switzerland/Poland Ⓥ ⊙
D: Krzysztof Kieslowski **A:** Zbigniew Zamachowski, Julie Delpy, Janusz Gajos, Jerzy Stuhr, Florence Pernel, Juliette Binoche (MK2/Cab/Tor)

The entertaining second segment of Krzysztof Kieslowski's *Three Colors* trilogy, *White* is involving, bittersweet, and droll. Pic begins in a Paris law court where cruel French beauty Dominique (Julie Delpy) is divorcing her bumbling Polish hubby Karol (Zbigniew Zamachowski). Karol is offered a lucrative job by fellow countryman Mikolaj (Janusz Gajos) of killing an unnamed Pole. He declines, but Mikolaj agrees to smuggle Karol back home as "checked baggage." Karol gets a rude introduction to the new Poland in which anything and everything can be bought and sold. At the pinnacle of his career, Karol hatches a plot to fake his own death and leave his financial empire to his ex-wife. Although Delpy is fine as the wife, the pic is Zamachowski's through and through.

TROIS COULEURS BLEU (THREE COLORS BLUE)

1993, 97 mins, France/Switzerland/Poland Ⓥ ⊙
D: Krzysztof Kieslowski **A:** Juliette Binoche, Benoit Regent, Florence Pernel, Charlotte Very, Emmanuelle Riva, Hugues Quester (MK2/CED/France 3/CAB/Tor)

The first installment in Kryzsztof Kieslowski's trilogy boasts a riveting central performance by a carefully controlled, lovingly lit Juliette Binoche, as a woman who streamlines her life after surviving the accident that kills her young daughter and composer husband. Julie (Binoche) instructs her lawyer to sell every last shred of property. But is she at liberty to discard the *Concerto for Europe* that her late husband left unfinished? Julie wants only to blend into Paris, but a sex-attuned neighbor (Charlotte Very) and her late husband's assistant (Benoit Regent) exert a pull on her.

TROIS COULEURS ROUGE (THREE COLORS RED)

1994, 99 mins, France/Switzerland/Poland Ⓥ ⊙

D: Krzysztof Kieslowski **A:** Irene Jacob, Jean-Louis Trintignant, Frederique Feder, Jean-Pierre Lorit, Juliette Binoche, Julie Delpy (MK2/France 3/Cab/Tor)

Red, a beautifully spun and splendidly acted tale, is another deft, deeply affecting variation on Krzysztof Kieslowski's recurring theme that people are interconnected in ways they can barely fathom. Swiss law student Auguste (Jean-Pierre Lorit) lives across the street from fashion model Valentine (Irene Jacob), who communicates via telephone with her boyfriend in England. Auguste loves Karin (Frederique Feder), who runs a "personalized weather service." Auguste and Valentine pass each other on countless occasions but have never noticed each other. Valentine meets a former judge (Jean-Louis Trintignant), who listens in on his neighbors' telephone conversations. The innocent, troubled young woman and the resigned older man explore the implications of extending a fraternal hand.

1994: Nominations: Best Director, Original Screenplay, Cinematography

3 HOMMES ET UN COUFFIN (3 MEN AND A CRADLE)
1985, 104 mins, France ⓥ ⊙
D: Coline Serreau **A:** Roland Giraud, Michel Boujenah, Andre Dussollier, Philippine Leroy Beaulieu, Dominique Lavanant, Marthe Villalonga (Flach/Soprofilms/TF1)

Coline Serreau's comedy about three hardened bachelors saddled with a newborn baby is warm, hilarious, and well-made. Serreau's direction is bright and confident, avoiding the saccharine pitfalls of the material. Story is set in the sprawling Paris apartment of the three liberty-loving bucks. The baby is the unannounced deposit of a girl whom airline pilot Jacques (Andre Dussollier, the alleged father) bedded and forgot. With Jacques away, Pierre (Roland Giraud) and Michel (Michel Boujenah) react with expected panic, and their calamitous first attempts to take care of their new ward are chronicled with a sure sense of farce pacing. Added complications arise in the form of a small package of heroin, which the trio has been unwittingly harboring.

TROJAN WOMEN, THE
1971, 111 mins, Greece/US ⓥ
D: Michael Cacoyannis **A:** Katharine Hepburn, Genevieve Bujold, Vanessa Redgrave, Irene Papas, Brian Blessed, Patrick Magee (Shaftel)

Pic has a surface resonance but not enough of the tragic sweep and force its outcry against war and oppression call for. Katharine Hepburn is the proud Queen of Troy, Hecuba, whose husband and sons have been killed. Only a daughter, Cassandra, and Andromache, the wife of her son Hector, are alive. She valiantly tries to lament and stand up to the fates in dignity, but the force and the needed tragic depth elude her. Vanessa Redgrave is lacking in passion as Andromache. Nor is Genevieve Bujold, as Cassandra, up to the frenzy and needed steely quality of her preachments and prophecies. Irene Papas, probably the true tragedienne among them, plays Helen of Troy.

TROLL
1986, 86 mins, US ⓥ ⊙
D: John Carl Buechler **A:** Noah Hathaway, Michael Moriarty, Shelley Hack, Jenny Beck, Sonny Bono, June Lockhart (Empire)

Troll is a predictable, dim-witted premise executed for the most part with surprising style. Fantasy of a universe of trolls taking over a San Francisco apartment house is far-fetched even for this genre. No sooner does the Potter family move into an ordinary-looking building than the young daughter (Jenny Beck) is possessed by a troll. Where the film rises above the ordinary is in the domestic scenes when, thanks to her acquired personality, young Beck can flout all the conventions of how a good girl should act.

TROLLENBERG TERROR, THE (US: THE CRAWLING EYE)
1958, 85 mins, UK ⓥ ⊙
D: Quentin Lawrence **A:** Forrest Tucker, Laurence Payne, Janet Munro, Jennifer Jayne, Warren Mitchell, Andrew Faulds (Eros)

Yarn concerns a creature from outer space secreted in a radioactive cloud on the mountain of Trollenberg in Switzerland. The mysterious disappearance of various climbers brings Forrest Tucker to the scene as a science investigator for UNO. During investigations, two headless corpses are discovered, and a couple of ordinary citizens go berserk and turn into killers. Main object of the two is Janet Munro, who is half of a sister mind-reading act and presents a threat to the sinister visitor. The taut screenplay extracts the most from the situations and is helped by strong, resourceful acting from a solid cast.

TRON
1982, 96 mins, US Ⓥ ⊙ ▭
D: Steven Lisberger **A:** Jeff Bridges, Bruce Boxleitner, David Warner, Cindy Morgan, Barnard Hughes, Dan Shor (Walt Disney)

Tron is loaded with visual delights but falls way short of the mark in story and viewer engagement. Computer games designer Kevin Flynn (Jeff Bridges) has had his series of fabulously successful programs stolen by Ed Dillinger (David Warner). Dillinger has seized corporate power and with his Master Control Program has increasingly dominated other programmers and users. To obtain the evidence that Dillinger has appropriated his work, Flynn has himself transformed into a computer-stored program, bringing the viewer into a parallel world inside a computer. Computer-generated visuals are impressive, but pic's design work and execution lack the warmth and humanity of classical animation.

1982: Nominations: Best Costume Design, Sound

TROP BELLE POUR TOI
(TOO BEAUTIFUL FOR YOU)
1989, 93 mins, France Ⓥ ⊙ ▭
D: Bertrand Blier **A:** Gerard Depardieu, Josiane Balasko, Carole Bouquet, Roland Blanche, Francios Cluzet, Myriam Boyer (Cine Valse/DD)

Bertrand Blier has come up with a new charmer in *Too Beautiful for You*, bringing fresh insight to the old story of marital infidelity. Gerard Depardieu is married to a sublimely beautiful woman (Carole Bouquet), to the envy of all his friends. But he falls passionately in love with his temporary secretary—a plump, somewhat plain, middle-aged woman. Josiane Balasko plays the sweet, sensual mistress with a warmth which makes Depardieu's passion acceptable. Blier keeps his audience in a constant state of surprise and delight, with the complex but funny way he tells his essentially banal story. Depardieu, in his fifth Blier film, brings the right comic touch to his impassioned, confused character.

LE TROU
(THE HOLE)
1960, 145 mins, France/Italy
D: Jacques Becker **A:** Michel Constantin, Jean Keraudy, Philippe Leroy, Raymond Meunier, Marc Michel (PlayArt/Filmsonor/Titanus)

The late Jacques Becker left behind a solidly built film, based on a true story of a jailbreak. Using non-actors, picture is a tale of human endeavor and cooperation that transcends its actual locale. Five men awaiting sentencing break through their cell floor and reach the sewer system from which they escape to freedom. But the plans are foiled by a newcomer who turns them in. The intricate breakout and digging aspects are dynamically detailed. The acting is uncannily clear for non-actors, and the prisoners are all well depicted and acceptable. Becker, sans music, holds the tension firmly in hand.

TROUBLE ALONG THE WAY
1953, 109 mins, US Ⓥ
D: Michael Curtiz **A:** John Wayne, Donna Reed, Charles Coburn, Tom Tully, Sherry Jackson, Marie Windsor (Warner)

A delightful comedy-drama about a Catholic college that saves itself from bankruptcy with a football team. Charles Coburn heads St. Anthony's College in New York, ordered closed because he's $170,000 in debt. The rector decides a football team is needed, and uncovers John Wayne, a cynical ex-coach kicked out of several big colleges for being unable to conform. Wayne spurns Coburn's offer until he sees the job as a way to defeat the threats of his ex-wife Marie Windsor of taking custody of their daughter.

TROUBLE IN MIND
1985, 111 mins, US Ⓥ ⊙
D: Alan Rudolph **A:** Kris Kristofferson, Keith Carradine, Lori Singer, Genevieve Bujold, Joe Morton, Divine (Island Alive)

Trouble in Mind is a stylish urban melodrama instantly recognizable as an Alan Rudolph picture, peopled by a strange collection of off-center characters living in a stylish, almost-real location. Set in RainCity, action could be taking place in the 1950s, 1980s or 1990s, so stylized is the production design. At the core of the film is a not-so-classic romantic triangle involving Hawk (Kris Kristofferson), Georgia (Lori Singer) and her boyfriend, Coop (Keith Carradine). Rudolph stirs all the ingredients—love, crime, friendship, responsibility—and ties them together with a charged score by Mark Isham.

TROUBLE IN PARADISE
1932, 81 mins, US
D: Ernst Lubitsch **A:** Miriam Hopkins, Kay Francis, Herbert Marshall, Charles Ruggles, Edward Everett Horton, C. Aubrey Smith (Paramount)

Despite the Lubitsch artistry, much of which is technically apparent, it's not good cinema in toto. For one thing, it's predicated on a totally meretricious premise. Herbert Marshall is the gentleman crook. Miriam Hopkins is a light-fingered lady. Kay Francis is a rich young widow who owns the largest parfumerie in Paris. Marshall's appointment as her "secretary" inspires beaucoup gossip. The dialogue is bright, and the Lubitsch montage is per usually *tres artistique*, but somehow the whole thing misses.

TROUBLE IN STORE
1953, 85 mins, UK Ⓥ
D: John Paddy Carstairs **A:** Norman Wisdom, Margaret Rutherford, Moira Lister, Derek Bond, Lana Morris, Jerry Desmonde (Two Cities)

This British piece of slapstick marks the debut of Norman Wisdom. He clowns his way through, playing the most humble member of a big department store who falls foul of his new boss. But he gets his girl and rounds up some gangsters. Margaret Rutherford has some nice comedy scenes as an inveterate shoplifter. Jerry Desmonde is little more than a comedy stooge as the boss, but he plays the role for all it is worth.

TROUBLE WITH ANGELS, THE
1966, 111 mins, US Ⓥ ⊙
D: Ida Lupino **A:** Rosalind Russell, Hayley Mills, Binnie Barnes, Gypsy Rose Lee, Camilla Sparv, June Harding (Columbia)

The trouble with *The Trouble with Angels* is hard to pinpoint. An appealing story idea—hip Mother Superior nun who outfoxes and matures two rebellious students in a Catholic girls' school—has lost impact via repetitious plotting and pacing, plus routine direction. Story takes the extrovert Hayley Mills and pal—sensitive, introverted June Harding—through three full years of school under the watchful eye of Rosalind Russell.

TROUBLE WITH HARRY, THE
1955, 96 mins, US Ⓥ ⊙
D: Alfred Hitchcock **A:** Edmund Gwenn,

John Forsythe, Shirley MacLaine, Mildred Natwick, Mildred Dunnock, Royal Dano (Paramount)

This is a blithe little comedy, produced and directed with affection by Alfred Hitchcock, about a bothersome corpse that just can't stay buried. Edmund Gwenn is a delight as a retired sea captain who stumbles on Harry's corpse while rabbit hunting. Believing he did the killing, he decides to bury the cadaver on the spot. Harry goes in and out of the ground three or four times and is responsible for two romances and not a little consternation and physical exercise.

TRUCK STOP WOMEN
1974, 82 mins, US Ⓥ ▭
D: Mark L. Lester **A:** Claudia Jennings, Lieux Dressler, John Martino, Dennis Fimple, Dolores Dorn, Gene Drew (Lester)

Truck Stop Women spoofs the mindless sensationalism involved in films of its type while it also exploits sex and violence. Pic deals with bloody territorial warfare in New Mexico between Mafia hit man John Martino and indie gang leader Lieux Dressler over Dressler's lucrative theft and prostitution operation, conducted out of a highway truck stop with henchpersons including her daughter Claudia Jennings. Direction is highly uneven, with many scenes handled in perfunctory fashion and others with care and skill.

TRUE COLORS
1991, 111 mins, US Ⓥ ⊙
D: Herbert Ross **A:** John Cusack, James Spader, Imogen Stubbs, Mandy Patinkin, Richard Widmark, Dina Merrill (Paramount)

True Colors represents a cloyingly schematic attempt to portray the political and moral bankruptcy of the 1980s in a neat little package. Paired off at law school at the University of Virginia in 1983, James Spader is a rich boy with the daughter of US senator Richard Widmark as a girlfriend, while John Cusack is pretender, a social climber whose lower-class roots are quickly exposed. Cusack launches a political career based upon trickery, blackmail, and betrayal, with backing from oily developer Mandy Patinkin. Having scooped Spader's g.f. (Imogen Stubbs) out from under him, Cusack loses her when he threatens her powerful father. Cusack does what he can, but the character is simply weighed down with too much symbolic baggage.

TRUE CONFESSIONS
1981, 108 mins, US ⊗ ⊙
D: Ulu Grosbard **A:** Robert De Niro, Robert Duvall, Charles Durning, Burgess Meredith, Cyril Cusack, Rose Gregorio (United Artists)

Given the powerhouse casting combo and provocative theme, *True Confessions* has to be chalked up as a disappointment. Pic features corrupt cops, whores, pimps, sibling rivalry, pornography, and political intrigue within the Roman Catholic Church, but still comes off as mild fare which fails to pack a dramatic or emotional wallop. Main body of pic flip-flops between police detective Duvall handling two bizarre deaths and ambitious Monsignor De Niro negotiating the delicate waters of church diplomacy. Nowhere near the full weight of these considerations is ever felt in Ulu Grosbard's muted, unmuscular telling of the sordid, fateful events. Script is deliberately structured to build to a big dramatic payoff, but this never comes. Failings cannot be attributed to the actors, all of whom have clearly immersed themselves in their roles.

TRUE CRIME
1999, 127 mins, US ⊗ ⊙
D: Clint Eastwood **A:** Clint Eastwood, Isaiah Washington, Denis Leary, Lisa Gay Hamilton, James Woods, Bernard Hill

Clint Eastwood's *True Crime,* a capital-punishment yarn much more concerned with character issues than with moral or legal matters, boasts tight storytelling, sharp acting, and an eye for unexpected detail. Yarn covers a 24-hour period and follows the fortunes of two men, black inmate Frank Beachum (Isaiah Washington), scheduled for execution at midnight, and white newspaper reporter Steve Everett (Eastwood), who becomes convinced that the prisoner is innocent. Pic contrasts the respective family relationships of Steve and Frank. Steve, who's free, throws it all away through his irresponsibility and selfishness; Frank is doomed, but exhibits unlimited love and care for his family even while staring death in the face. Eastwood takes evident delight in portraying a sympathetic but amoral scoundrel.

TRUE GRIT
1969, 128 mins, US ⊗ ⊙
D: Henry Hathaway **A:** John Wayne, Glen Campbell, Kim Darby, Jeremy Slate, Robert Duvall, Dennis Hopper (Paramount)

Story centers on young girl (Kim Darby) of the 1830s starting out from Arkansas to avenge the murder of her father with the aid of John Wayne, whom she pays, and Texas Ranger Glen Campbell, who wants to claim the murderer (Jeff Corey) for a reward. Darby is refreshingly original, sticking relentlessly to the strong character of Mattie. Campbell holds his own as a foil for Wayne. But it's Wayne all the way in the role of the "fat old man."

1969: Best Actor (John Wayne)
Nomination: Best Song ("True Grit")

TRUE HEART SUSIE
1919, 72 mins, US ⊗
D: D. W. Griffith **A:** Lillian Gish, Loyola O'Connor, Robert Harron, Wilber Higby, Clarine Seymour, Kate Bruce (Artcraft)

D. W. Griffith chose Lillian Gish for the role of plain little country girl and Robert Harron as the "boy across the road." There is an early love affair, and the girl sacrifices part of her farm to send the boy to college. On his return he falls in love with a milliner from Chicago and marries her. She leads him a decidedly merry life and slips out of an evening to play with the boys. The story carries a role of tremendous sympathy in *True Heart Susie,* which Gish portrays most successfully. Griffith has handled the picture in the same masterly way as usual. The comedy elements are splendidly handled, with a number of real laughs mixed with the action.

TRUE LIES
1994, 141 mins, US ⊗ ⊙
D: James Cameron **A:** Arnold Schwarzenegger, Jamie Lee Curtis, Tom Arnold, Bill Paxton, Tia Carrere, Art Malik (Lightstorm/20th Century-Fox)

A reunion of *Terminator 2* star Arnold Schwarzenegger and writer/director James Cameron creates obvious expectations, and this 2 1/2-hour $100 million-plus action comedy tries way too hard to live up to them. Providing its share of fun in stretches, pic ultimately overstays its welcome. *Lies* is really two movies in one. An impressive Bondian opening sequence introduces us to secret agent Harry Tasker (Schwarzenegger), who leads a double life, having convinced his wife (Jamie Lee

Curtis) and teenage daughter (Eliza Dushku) that he's a staid computer salesman. Harry and sidekick Gib (Tom Arnold) get on the trail of an Arab terrorist (Art Malik) who's acquired four nuclear weapons. The script veers into a periodically amusing but staggeringly drawn-out tangent that has Harry suspecting his wife of infidelity and using all his agenting wiles to investigate. An hour long on its own, this foray into romantic comedy doesn't jibe with what precedes or follows it.

1994: Nomination: Best Visual Effects

TRUE LOVE
1989, 104 mins, US Ⓥ ⊙
D: Nancy Savoca **A:** Annabella Sciorra, Ron Eldard, Star Jasper, Aida Turturro, Roger Rignack, Michael J. Wolfe (Forward)

True Love is anything but traditional, even though it's solidly rooted in a Bronx working-class Italian community. Annabella Sciorra and her friends aren't as starry-eyed about the men available for matrimony. Certainly her fiancé (Ron Eldard) is no bargain, except perhaps in bed. For most of the picture, Sciorra frets about why she's marrying the immature, self-centered lout and never comes up with a good reason, except that he's good-looking and says he loves her even though he doesn't act like it. This is Savoca's first feature, with first-rate performances out of his cast of neophytes.

TRUE ROMANCE
1993, 116 mins, US Ⓥ ⊙ ▭
D: Tony Scott **A:** Christian Slater, Patricia Arquette, Dennis Hopper, Gary Oldman, Brad Pitt, Christopher Walken (Morgan Creek/Warner)

The footprints of dozens of classic thrillers are imprinted on the slick, violent, and energetic *True Romance*, a variation on the couple-on-the-run subgenre. The couple here are Clarence (Christian Slater) and Alabama (Patricia Arquette), a young man working in a comic-book store and a prostitute on the streets of Detroit. Clarence kills Alabama's former pimp Drexl (Gary Oldman) and grabs her suitcase—except it's the wrong one, containing a fortune in uncut cocaine. The young man foolishly believes he can sell the stash and escape to some remote paradise—in this case, Hollywood. *True Romance* rides along largely on the power of its colorful rogues' gallery. Movie mavens have a veritable field to plow in the Quentin Taran-

tino screenplay. Tony Scott's slick style is visually arresting, if too obvious.

TRUE STORIES
A FILM ABOUT A BUNCH OF PEOPLE IN VIRGIL TEXAS
1986, 90 mins, US ⊙ ⊙
D: David Byrne **A:** David Byrne, John Goodman, Swoosie Kurtz, Spalding Gray, Alix Elias, Annie McEnroe (True Stories)

In his feature directorial debut, ex–Talking Head David Byrne takes a bemused and benevolent view of provincial America's essential goodness in a loosely connected string of vignettes that amount to sophisticated music video concepts dressed up as filmmaking. Byrne uses the cartoonish conceit of examining life in the hypothetical town of Virgil, Texas, with the human-interest perspective of a supermarket tabloid feature, driving into Virgil during its sesquicentennial "celebration of specialness" for a series of close encounters with the town's peculiar denizens.

TRUE STORY OF JESSE JAMES, THE
(UK: THE JAMES BROTHERS)
1957, 92 mins, US ▭
D: Nicholas Ray **A:** Robert Wagner, Jeffrey Hunter, Hope Lange, Agnes Moorehead, Alan Hale, John Carradine (20th Century-Fox)

On celluloid, Jesse James has had more lives than a cat, and *The True Story of Jesse James* suggests it's time screenwriters let him roll over and play dead for real. This attempt to view the James character through the eyes of pro and con contemporaries only makes for confusion, depriving an audience of clear-cut plot line that might keep them interested. Nicholas Ray directs in stock fashion, adding little of substance. As Jesse and Frank James, Robert Wagner and Jeffrey Hunter go through the motions of telling why the former took up the gun when Northern sympathizers made it difficult for them to live in Missouri after the Civil War.

TRUE TO LIFE
1943, 94 mins, US
D: George Marshall **A:** Mary Martin, Franchot Tone, Dick Powell, Victor Moore, William Demarest, Ernest Truex (Paramount)

Taking the premise that life should mirror the movies, instead of the movies reflecting life, the escapist theme of *True to Life* is quickly set. The plot has the radio soap opera appeal of a frothy film. Franchot Tone and Dick Powell are the all-written-out radio scripters on the verge of losing their jobs because their Kitty Farmer serial has become too phoney. Powell, in search of down-to-the-peasants material, runs into hash-house waitress Mary Martin, whose real-life family in Sunnyside—a suburb of New York—and their zany behavior provide the authors with almost literal libretto. Well-paced direction by George Marshall and some excellent scripting do much to hold the madcap proceedings together.

TRULY MADLY DEEPLY (AKA: CELLO)
1991, 105 mins, UK ⓥ
D: Anthony Minghella A: Juliet Stevenson, Alan Rickman, Bill Paterson, Michael Maloney, Jenny Howe, Stella Maris (BBC)

This sharply scripted study of a bereaved woman who literally wishes her partner back from the grave is an impressive directorial bow by British playwright Anthony Minghella. Nina (Juliet Stevenson) is cut up about losing her longtime partner, virtuoso cellist Jamie (Alan Rickman). She still feels his presence in her tiny London flat. One day Jamie literally reappears and they relive their idyllic relationship until it's time for both to move on—he to a higher plane, she to a new relationship. Sans special effects, pic manages to suspend belief through fine ensemble playing and sheer strength of the main performances. Rickman gives subtle support, but it's Stevenson's movie through and through, a tour de force of sustained playing.

TRUMAN SHOW, THE
1998, 102 mins, US ⓥ ⊙
D: Peter Weir A: Jim Carrey, Laura Linney, Noah Emmerich, Natascha McElhone, Holland Taylor, Ed Harris (Rudin/Paramount)

A gemlike picture crafted with rare and immaculate precision, *The Truman Show* is a fable about a man whose entire life, unbeknownst to him, has been the subject of a staggeringly popular, 24-hour-per-day television show. Pic trades in issues of personal liberty vs. authoritarian control, safe happiness vs. the excitement of chaos, manufactured emotions, the penetration of media to the point where privacy vanishes and the fascination of fabricated images over real things. Truman Burbank (Jim Carrey), a clean-cut, "normal" guy married to the perenially perky Meryl (Laura Linney), lives in the immaculate community of Seahaven, an antiseptic island "paradise" where people are forever cheery and nothing untoward ever happens. When slight cracks appear in this perfect veneer that arouse his suspicion, those around him go into panicky damage-control mode, and the hand of Truman's "inventor" and manipulator, Christof (Ed Harris), becomes increasingly evident. Carrey delivers an impressively disciplined performance that is always engaging.

TRUST
1990, 103 mins, US/UK ⓥ
D: Hal Hartley A: Adrienne Shelly, Martin Donovan, Merritt Nelson, John MacKay, Edie Falco, Marko Hunt (True Fiction/Zenith)

A bleak, off-center comedy about dysfunctional families in working-class suburbia. When Maria (Adrienne Shelly) gets pregnant by the high school quarterback, she drops out of school, her father drops dead of a heart attack, and her mother treats her like a pariah. Matthew (Martin Donovan), an intellectually inclined reform school graduate with a talent for fixing things, quits his mind-numbing job assembling computers, encounters Maria, and takes the shattered girl to his home. Donovan is excellent as the brooding misfit, and Shelly is tangibly right as the suburban brat. Also very good are Merritt Nelson as Maria's emotionally alienated mother and John MacKay as Matthew's bullying father.

TRUTH, THE
See: La Verite

TRUTH ABOUT CATS AND DOGS, THE
1996, 97 mins, US ⓥ
D: Michael Lehmann A: Uma Thurman, Janeane Garofalo, Ben Chaplin, Jamie Fox, James McCaffrey, Richard Coca (Noon Attack/20th Century-Fox)

Yet another modern riff on the Cyrano de Bergerac theme, this thinly conceived comedy climbs above its material thanks to charming performances and a genial tone. Janeane Garofalo plays Abby, host of a radio talk show about pets who talks a caller, photographer Brian (Ben Chaplin), through a threatening experience with a dog he's acquired for a photo shoot. Brian suggests the two meet, yet when asked what she looks like, Abby describes her model neighbor, Noelle (Uma Thurman)—a blonde who can literally stop traffic. A confusing situation is made worse when both women become interested in Brian. What makes the pic special in places is Garofalo's dry, self-effacing wit and Thurman's ditzy, old-style Hollywood glamour.

TRUTH OR DARE
IN BED WITH MADONNA
See: In Bed with Madonna

TRYGON FACTOR, THE
1967, 87 mins, UK
D: Cyril Frankel A: Stewart Granger, Susan Hampshire, Robert Morley, Cathleen Nesbitt, Brigitte Horney, James Robertson Justice (Warner/Seven Arts/Rialto)

The Trygon Factor, its title totally meaningless, is a complicated Scotland Yard whodunit which the spectator will find taxing to follow. Stewart Granger, the Yard superintendent investigating a rash of unsolved robberies, is assigned to a large country house where a gang is operating under the cloak of respectability. Script is pocketed with story loopholes and attempts to confuse, plus motivations and bits of business impossible to fathom.

TSUBAKI SANJURO
(SANJURO)
1962, 96 mins, Japan ⓥ ⊙ ▭
D: Akira Kurosawa A: Toshiro Mifune, Yuzo Kayama, Tatsuya Nakadai, Keiju Kobayashi, Reiko Dan, Takashi Shimura (Kurosawa/Toho)

Roughly the Japanese equivalent of an American western. The charm of this fascinating Toho production, stylishly directed by Akira Kurosawa, is the personality of the hero, powerfully played by Toshiro Mifune. Story is set in the turbulent mid-1800s and describes the remarkable manner in which one man, the warrior Sanjuro, destroys a corrupt ruling faction. As usual, Kurosawa doesn't compromise in the battle and brutality area. This one features a rousing climactic duel between Mifune and his chief adversary that outdoes the average Western showdown by a dramatic mile.

TSUI KUN
(DRUNK MONKEY IN THE
TIGER'S EYES; DRUNKEN
MASTER)
1978, 110 mins, Hong Kong ⓥ
D: Yuen Woo-ping A: Jackie Chan, Simon Yuen, Hwang Jeong-ri, Sek Tin, Tsui Ha, Lam Ying (Seasonal)

Pic is kung fu with a big difference, in the sense that unusual drunken martial arts techniques are mixed with high Cantonese comedy. Lead star Jackie Chan, an excellent acrobat, has the stamina and movements of an experienced kung-fu specialist. His charming boyish appeal and talent for comedy routines help in captivating audiences. He makes a very human hero since he doesn't win all the fights, with the exception of the required finale. Highlights include practice sessions with an eccentric teacher (Simon Yuen). The story line is practically nil, but the humor is universal.

TUCKER
THE MAN AND HIS DREAM
1988, 111 mins, US ⓥ ⊙ ▭
D: Francis Ford Coppola A: Jeff Bridges, Joan Allen, Martin Landau, Frederic Forrest, Dean Stockwell, Lloyd Bridges (Lucasfilm/Zeotrope)

The true story of a great American visionary who was thwarted, if not destroyed, by the established order, *Tucker* represents the sunniest imaginable telling of an at least partly tragic episode in recent history. After World War II, seemingly on the strength of his enthusiasm alone, Tucker got a small core of collaborators to work on his dream project, "the first completely new car in 50 years." With a factory in Chicago, Tucker managed to turn out 50 of his beauties, but vested interests in Detroit and Washington dragged him into court on fraud charges, shutting him down and ending his automobile career. Jeff Bridges's Tucker is inspiring because he won't be depressed or defeated by anything.
1988: Nominations: Best Supp. Actor (Martin Landau), Art Direction, Costume Design

TUFF TURF
1985, 112 mins, US ⓥ ⊙
D: Fritz Kiersch A: James Spader, Kim Richards, Paul Mones, Robert Downey Jr., Matt Clark, Claudette Nevins (New World)

This modestly budgeted youth pic is a poor man's *Rebel Without a Cause*. Rebellious newcomer James Spader is the James Dean character, and saucy gang moll Kim Richards is the Natalie Wood character. They go through social and romantic hell for each other, and a large slice of suburban L.A. and uncomprehending parenthood embellish a story that is deceptively compelling despite, in this case, a distracting mix of comedy and music. The on-screen music, however, lurches the film off balance.

TUGBOAT ANNIE
1933, 85 mins, US
D: Mervyn LeRoy A: Marie Dressler, Wallace Beery, Robert Young, Maureen O'Sullivan, Willard Robertson, Tammany Young (M-G-M)

Tugboat Annie, while weak in many respects, is on the whole perfectly suited to the Dressler-Beery requirements. In the hands of the co-starring couple, its deficiencies are barely noticeable. Making Marie Dressler the femme skipper of a harbor tugboat; Wallace Beery her shiftless, soused but likable husband; and giving them a son of which to be proud, was not asking much of the two actors.

TUMBLEWEEDS
1925, 76 mins, US ⓥ ⊛
D: King Baggot A: William S. Hart, Barbara Bedford, Lucien Littlefield, J. Gordon Russell, Richard R. Neill (Hart/United Artists)

This is a typical Hart western, although the story carries something of a different angle. Its punch is a stampede of homesteaders claim-staking the Cherokee Strip, an area famed in the annals of the Old West. The heroine, not getting into any serious difficulties, has eliminated the need of any ultra-heroic measures to save her. The love theme of the tale may be said to be secondary to its historical interest.

TUNE IN TOMORROW
(AUNT JULIA AND THE SCRIPTWRITER)
1990, 102 mins, US ⓥ ⊙
D: Jon Amiel A: Barbara Hershey, Keanu Reeves, Peter Falk, Hope Lange, Peter Gallagher, Elizabeth McGovern (Polar)

Tune in Tomorrow is lusty and full of zany characters, but cluttered and overdone. Aunt Julia (Barbara Hershey) a divorcée, returns to New Orleans in 1951 at age 36 to find a rich third husband. Instead, she finds her 21-year-old nephew by marriage (Keanu Reeves), a local radio newswriter, who falls in love with her. The aunt succumbs, incurring her family's anger. On top of that is the more complicated story of a disheveled writer (Peter Falk), who creates a successful radio soap opera laced with incest and anti-Albanian sentiment. Falk manipulates the nephew-aunt relationship and, to Reeves's anger, reproduces the couple's arguments in his soap. While the action is fun for much of the first half, the story lines ultimately smother each other.

TUNES OF GLORY
1960, 105 mins, UK ⓥ ⊙
D: Ronald Neame A: Alec Guinness, John Mills, Dennis Price, John Fraser, Susannah York, Kay Walsh (United Artists)

Alec Guinness and John Mills are colonels, the former a man of humble origin who has risen from the ranks, the latter a product of Eton, Oxford, and a classy military academy. A peacetime Scottish regiment is commanded by Guinness. When he is superseded by Mills, the clash is inevitable. Guinness finds his daughter in a public house with a young corporal and strikes the soldier. Though Mills has the power to deal with the case, he chooses to submit a report to higher authority, which would inevitably lead to a court-martial. Guinness, as always, is outstanding. He assumes an authentic Scottish accent and never misses a trick to win sympathy, even when he behaves foolishly. It's a tough assignment for Mills, particularly in a fundamentally unsympathetic role, but he is always a match for his co-star.
1960: Nomination: Best Adapted Screenplay

TUNNEL OF LOVE, THE
1958, 98 mins, US ▭
D: Gene Kelly A: Doris Day, Richard Widmark, Gig Young, Gia Scala, Elisabeth Fraser, Elizabeth Wilson (M-G-M)

Richard Widmark is a would-be cartoonist for a *New Yorker*–type magazine. He and his wife (Doris Day) want a child but cannot conceive. They have friends (Gig Young and Elisabeth Fraser) whom they envy. Young is an editor of the magazine Widmark aspires to crack, and he and Fraser regularly add to their brood. Young, whose home life has been stimulated by extramarital affairs, urges his system on Widmark. Widmark is visited by an adoption home investigator (Gia Scala) and spends a night on the town with her. Just a little over nine months later, the adoption agency presents a baby to Day and Widmark. Gene Kelly emerges as an inventive and capable comedy director.

TUNTEMATON SOTILAS
(THE UNKNOWN SOLDIER)
1955, 181 mins, Finland
D: Edvin Laine A: Kosti Klemela, Jussi Jurkka, Heikki Savolainen, Matti Ranin,

Reino Tolvanen, Veikko Sinisalo (SF)

Film has actually no plot and may be better classified as a documentary. It is a recklessly open and hard-hitting production about victory and defeat and life and death of Finnish soldiers during World War II. The camera follows a group of soldiers and shows through very impressive scenes how they go through the murderous phase of modern warfare. But the constant battling becomes monotonous and even dull toward the end.

TURK 182!
1985, 98 mins, US Ⓥ ✉

D: Bob Clark **A:** Timothy Hutton, Robert Urich, Kim Cattrall, Robert Culp, Darren McGavin, Steven Keats (20th Century-Fox)

Taking aim at the theme of the working man's struggle against the inequities of the system, *Turk 182!*, a cleverly conceived story of a mystery rebel in New York City whose popularity reaches almost mythic proportions, convincingly hits its mark. Timothy Hutton plays a 20-year-old whose fireman older brother (Robert Urich), when off-duty in a bar, goes into a burning building to save a young girl. Urich is severely injured but the city maintains he should not have entered the premises in his intoxicated state. Hutton begins a one-man quest to embarrass and discredit the mayor (Robert Culp).

TURNER & HOOCH
1989, 100 mins, US Ⓥ ⊙

D: Roger Spottiswoode **A:** Tom Hanks, Mare Winningham, Craig T. Nelson, Reginald Veljohnson, Scott Paulin, J. C. Quinn (Touchstone)

Until its grossly miscalculated bummer of an ending, *Turner & Hooch* is a routine but amiable comedy enlivened by the charm of Tom Hanks and his homely-assin canine partner. Hanks plays a fussy small-town California police investigator whose life is disrupted by a messy junkyard dog with a face only a furry mother could love. The dog witnesses a double murder and is Hanks's only means of catching the drug smugglers responsible for the slayings.

TURNING POINT, THE
1952, 85 mins, US

D: William Dieterle **A:** William Holden, Edmond O'Brien, Alexis Smith, Tom Tully, Ed Begley, Ray Teal (Paramount)

Paramount trains its cameras on a fictional crime syndicate in *The Turning Point*. Armed with a college education and a law degree, Edmond O'Brien tackles his new job as crime committee chairman with a youthful enthusiasm. William Holden, a cynical reporter, warns O'Brien of the pitfalls that lie ahead. The closing reels are highlighted by a suspenseful hunt for an "all-important" witness, plus Holden's frantic efforts to escape from an assassin in a stadium.

TURNING POINT, THE
1977, 119 mins, US Ⓥ

D: Herbert Ross **A:** Anne Bancroft, Shirley MacLaine, Mikhail Baryshnikov, Leslie Browne, Tom Skerritt, Martha Scott (20th Century-Fox)

The Turning Point is one of the best films of its era, a rare example of synergy in which every key element is excellent and the ensemble is an absolute triumph. Anne Bancroft and Shirley MacLaine star as longtime friends with unresolved problems. Bancroft is a ballet star just reaching an uneasy age. MacLaine long ago abandoned a similar career to marry Tom Skerritt, and now their teenage daughter (Leslie Browne) shows promise as a dancer. This triggers an explosion of new and old conflicts.

1977: Nominations: Best Picture, Director, Actress (Anne Bancroft, Shirley MacLaine), Supp. Actor (Mikhail Baryshnikov), Supp. Actress (Leslie Browne), Original Screenplay, Cinematography, Art Direction, Editing, Sound

12 ANGRY MEN
1957, 95 mins, US Ⓥ ⊙

D: Sidney Lumet **A:** Henry Fonda, Lee J. Cobb, Ed Begley, E. G. Marshall, Jack Warden, Martin Balsam (Orion-Nova)

The 12 angry men are a jury chosen to decide the guilt or innocence of a teenager accused of murdering his father. They have heard the arguments and have received instructions from the presiding judge. Now they are on their own. What will they do? To most of them, it is an open-and-shut case. The boy is guilty, and they demand a quick vote. On the first ballot it is 11 to 1 for a conviction. Henry Fonda is the lone holdout. Most of the action takes place in the one room on a hot summer day. The effect, rather than being confining, serves to heighten the drama. Sidney Lumet, making his bow as a film director, cleverly maneuveres his players in the small area. The film leaves a tremendous impact.

1957: Nominations: Best Picture, Director, Screenplay Adaptation

TWELVE CHAIRS, THE
1970, 94 mins, US ⓥ ⊙
D: Mel Brooks **A:** Ron Moody, Frank Langella, Dom DeLouise, Mel Brooks, Andreas Voutsinas, David Lander (UMC/Crossbow)

The Twelve Chairs is a nutty farce, frequently slapstick and often tongue-in-cheek. Mel Brooks directed, scripted, plays a leading role, and authored a song. Simple story is of three men trying to locate 12 dining-room chairs, once owned by a wealthy woman who confesses on her deathbed that years before she had secreted all her jewels in the upholstery of one of them. Voila, the plot.

TWELVE MONKEYS
1995, 131 mins, US ⓥ ⊙
D: Terry Gilliam **A:** Bruce Willis, Madeleine Stowe, Brad Pitt, Christopher Plummer, Jon Seda, Joseph Melito (Atlas/Classico/Universal)

A dark and somber sci-fier in the mold of *Blade Runner*, Terry Gilliam's *Twelve Monkeys* is a spectacular mess, an excessively complicated film that attempts to be timely by blending a "virus" thriller with a post-apocalyptic anti-science drama. Story is set in a subterranean nether world in 2035, following the eradication of 99% of the Earth's population. A group of scientists living beneath Philadelphia send prisoner James Cole (Bruce Willis) on a dangerous trip back to 1996. Cole lands in a mental institution under the supervision of Dr. Kathryn Railly (Madeleine Stowe). Cole himself questions his sanity, but bizarre clues continue to torment him. In the course of an overly long and convoluted plot, Dr. Railly falls for the tortured man. But the stellar cast can't overcome the cartoonish nature of their characters. The joys to be had are in observing the majestic peculiarities of Gilliam's ever-fanciful universe.
1995: Nominations: Best Supporting Actor (Brad Pitt), Costume Design

TWELVE O'CLOCK HIGH
1949, 132 mins, US ⓥ ⊙
D: Henry King **A:** Gregory Peck, Hugh Marlowe, Gary Merrill, Millard Mitchell, Dean Jagger, Robert Arthur (20th Century-Fox)

Picture addresses a general's concern for his men's morale during the man-killing daylight bombing raids of 1942. Gregory Peck heads up the operations of a bombing squadron from a base in England. Peck gives the character much credence as he suffers and sweats with his men. Standout performance comes from Dean Jagger as a retread still determined to do his bit. Story comes to life through his eyes as he revisits the base in 1948.
1949: Best Supp. Actor (Dean Jagger), Sound Recording (20th Century-Fox Sound Dept)
Nominations: Best Picture, Actor (Gregory Peck)

12 PLUS 1
(THE THIRTEEN CHAIRS)
1970, 95 mins, Italy/France ⓥ
D: Nicholas Gessner **A:** Vittorio Gassman, Sharon Tate, Orson Welles, Vittorio De Sica, Terry-Thomas, Mylene Demongeot (CEF/COFCI)

Film is mainly of interest as being the last of the tragically fated Sharon Tate. It is a sort of madcap romantic comedy in the form of a chase for treasure hidden in a chair. Gassman is a Yank barber left an estate in Britain by an eccentric aunt. But he finds only a rundown house and some antique chairs that he immediately sells. He finds a note saying a fortune is hidden in one of the chairs. Tate, who works in the gallery he sold the chairs to, teams up with him for a share of the loot. Pic has some good moments, but overall misses the light touch and forward-propelling zest to keep this comedy from lagging.

TWENTIETH CENTURY
1934, 91 mins, US ⓥ
D: Howard Hawks **A:** John Barrymore, Carole Lombard, Walter Connolly, Roscoe Karns, Etienne Girardot, Ralph Forbes (Columbia)

It's John Barrymore's picture, no doubt, with something left over for Carole Lombard, who manages to shine despite practically stooging. Lily Garland (Lombard) walks out on producer Oscar Jaffe (Barrymore) to go Hollywood shortly after he helps make her career. From then on it's a chase. Jaffe goes broke trying to land another Lily Garland, and Lily goes big in Hollywood. The way Jaffe and his boys try to frame Lily into coming back into the legitimate fold paves the road for some crazy trouping.

TWENTY-ONE
1991, 101 mins, US ⓥ ⊙
D: Don Boyd **A:** Patsy Kensit, Jack Shepherd, Patrick Ryecart, Rufus Sewell, So-

phie Thompson, Maynard Eziashi (Anglo International)

Twenty-One mirrors the character of its cheeky protagonist: bored, cynical, and operating chiefly for self-amusement. A worldly young Brit (Patsy Kensit) leaves her life in London for a fresh start in New York. Boyd employs a technique in which the salty-tongued heroine talks to the camera while having her facial, tending to nature's call, and so on. If only she were more compelling. This rather vapid lass hasn't much on her mind, and her intimate revelations are forgettable. Camera also operates in pic's spirit—with flash and style but no real purpose.

20,000 LEAGUES UNDER THE SEA
1954, 120 mins, US Ⓥ ⊙ ▭
D: Richard Fleischer **A:** Kirk Douglas, James Mason, Paul Lukas, Peter Lorre, Robert J. Wilke, Carleton Young (Walt Disney)

Walt Disney's production of *20,000 Leagues Under the Sea* is a very special kind of picture, combining photographic ingenuity, imaginative story-telling, and fiscal daring. James Mason is the captain of the *Nautilus* and a genius who fashioned and guides the out-of-this-world craft. Kirk Douglas is a freewheeling, roguish harpoonist. Paul Lukas is a gentle man of science, and Peter Lorre is his fretting apprentice. But the production itself is the star. Technical skill was lavished in fashioning the fabulous *Nautilus*. The underwater lensing is remarkable on a number of counts. Story opens in San Francisco, where maritime men are terrorized by reports of a monstrous denizen of the seas which has been sinking their ships. An armed frigate sets out in pursuit and is itself destroyed, with Lukas, Douglas, and Lorre the survivors.

1954: Best Color Art Direction, Special Effects

Nomination: Best Editing

20,000 YEARS IN SING SING
1932, 78 mins, US
D: Michael Curtiz **A:** Spencer Tracy, Bette Davis, Arthur Byron, Lyle Talbot, Warren Hymer, Louis Calhern (First National)

Of pictures having inside of penal institutions as their locale, this is one of the best. It covers a lot of routine that's unknown to most outsiders. It appears that Sing Sing wouldn't be a bad place at all to spend a vacation during the Depression. Arthur Byron's paternal smile as the war-

den, his anxiety to create reform and allow plenty of leeway even to tough ones among his charges, would make it quite a resort. Though let out to visit his dying gal friend and committing murder in the meantime, convict Tom Connors (Spencer Tracy) returns, putting the warden's honor system to the strongest test imaginable. In the end it's the chair for the reformed bad boy whose only regret seems to be his parting from the warden's shelter and benevolence. Far-fetched, but it sells.

TWICE IN A LIFETIME
1985, 117 mins, US Ⓥ ⊙
D: Bud Yorkin **A:** Gene Hackman, Ann-Margret, Ellen Burstyn, Amy Madigan, Ally Sheedy, Stephen Lang (Yorkin)

An edgy, shifty-eyed 50th birthday tribute for the hero gets this midlife-crisis film off to a sentimental start, and from there on it's Ellen Burstyn, the abandoned wife, versus Gene Hackman, the not-unsympathetic-but-risk-taking husband, vying for audience affections. Burstyn claims the film as Kate, who has to cope with her own life and family and some rather mediocre lines. Hackman is stalwart in his resolve to make a new life with Ann-Margret, but she is far too sexy and he far too underdeveloped for anybody to understand what she sees in him.

1985: Nomination: Best Supp. Actress (Amy Madigan)

TWILIGHT
1998, 94 mins, US Ⓥ ⊙
D: Robert Benton **A:** Paul Newman, Susan Sarandon, Gene Hackman, Reese Witherspoon, Stockard Channing, James Garner (Cinehaus/Paramount)

Twilight is an autumnal murder mystery awash in rueful intimations of mortality. Paul Newman plays longtime cop and private dick Harry Ross, divorced, broke and formerly alcoholic, reduced to living above the garage on the estate of his movie star friends Jack and Catherine Ames (Gene Hackman, Susan Sarandon). Harry encounters a gunshot old man (M. Emmet Walsh), who empties his pistol at him before expiring. The dead man was investigating the disappearance 20 years before of Catherine's first husband. Writers consciously connect the dots by directly explaining almost everyone's motivations at one point or another, and *Twilight* is similarly explicit about its meanings. Newman's work is sly, stealthy and subtle, and his rapport with his costars is a pleasure to watch.

TWILIGHT FOR THE GODS

1958, 120 mins, US
D: Joseph Pevney **A:** Rock Hudson, Cyd Charisse, Arthur Kennedy, Leif Erickson, Charles McGraw, Richard Haydn (Universal)

Twilight for the Gods emerges as a routine sea adventure drama. It assembles a group of passengers of different personalities and backgrounds, including several with shady pasts, headed by Rock Hudson, a court-martialed ship's captain fighting alcoholism, as the skipper of the battered sailing ship, and Cyd Charisse as a Honolulu call girl running away from the authorities. Film studies cast's reactions to the dangers encountered during a long sea voyage. Filmed on location in the Hawaiian islands, the photography is a delight to the eyes.

TWILIGHT OF HONOR

1963, 105 mins, US ▭
D: Boris Sagal **A:** Richard Chamberlain, Joey Heatherton, Nick Adams, Claude Rains, Joan Blackman, James Gregory (M-G-M)

Twilight of Honor casts Richard Chamberlain in his first starring role, as a court-appointed defense attorney who takes on an entire New Mexico town to save his client from the gas chamber. Defense under New Mexico's criminal code is that Chamberlain's client killed the town's most respected citizen after he found him in bed with his trampish teenage spouse. One of pic's highlights is the introduction of Joey Heatherton. In the part of the two-timing wife of the accused, she registers impressively.

1963: Nominations: Best Supp. Actor (Nick Adams), B&W Art Direction

TWILIGHT'S LAST GLEAMING

1977, 146 mins, US/W. Germany ⓥ ⊙
D: Robert Aldrich **A:** Burt Lancaster, Richard Widmark, Charles Durning, Melvyn Douglas, Paul Winfield, Burt Young (Lorimar-Bavaria/Geria)

Robert Aldrich's *Twilight's Last Gleaming* is an intricate, intriguing, and intelligent drama. Burt Lancaster stars as a cashiered US Air Force officer who seizes a nuclear missile site to force public disclosure of secret Vietnam War policy goals. Charles Durning is outstanding as the US president who must respond to the challenge. A suspenseful and taut confrontation.

TWILIGHT ZONE
THE MOVIE

1983, 102 mins, US ⓥ ⊙
D: John Landis, Steven Spielberg, Joe Dante, George Miller **A:** Dan Aykroyd, Albert Brooks, Vic Morrow, Scatman Crothers, Kathleen Quinlan, John Lithgow (Warner)

Twilight Zone, the feature film spin-off from Rod Serling's popular 1960s television series, plays like a traditional vaudeville card, with its tantalizing teaser opening followed by three sketches of increasing quality, building up to a socko headline act. John Landis gets things off to a wonderful start with a comic prologue starring Dan Aykroyd and Albert Brooks. His principal episode, however, is a downbeat, one-dimensional fable about racial and religious intolerance. Vic Morrow spouts a torrent of racial epithets aimed at Jews, blacks, and Orientals while drinking at a bar. Upon exiting, he finds himself in Nazi-occupied Paris as a suspected Jew on the run. Steven Spielberg's entry is the most down-to-earth. In a retirement home filled with oldsters, spry Scatman Crothers encourages various residents to think young and actually transforms them into their childhood selves. The most bizarre contribution comes from Joe Dante. Kathleen Quinlan enters the Twilight Zone courtesy of little Jeremy Licht, who lords it over a Looney-Tune household through his power to will anything into existence except happiness. George Miller's episode, about a man who sees a gremlin tearing up an engine wing of an airplane, is electrifying from beginning to end.

TWIN PEAKS
FIRE WALK WITH ME

1992, 135 mins, US ⓥ ⊙
D: David Lynch **A:** Sheryl Lee, Chris Isaak, Ray Wise, Moira Kelly, Kyle MacLachlan, Kiefer Sutherland (Lynch-Frost/CiBy)

A feature prequel to the celebrated televsion series, pic is like an R-rated episode embodying the pros and cons of the intriguingly offbeat television program. It recounts the final week in the life of the quasi-legendary Laura Palmer, with plenty of digressions and artistic doodlings, as well as the occasional striking sequence. Events largely center on Laura's downward spiral of drug use, promiscuity, and crime, up to the moment of her killing, which leaves things off where they all started on television. Suspense is clearly lacking in this story with a preordained outcome. Another significant drawback is that long before the climax, Laura has become a tiresome teen.

TWINS
1988, 112 mins, US Ⓥ ⊙
D: Ivan Reitman **A:** Arnold Schwarzenegger, Danny DeVito, Kelly Preston, Chloe Webb, Bonnie Bartlett, Trey Wilson (Universal)

Arnold Schwarzenegger plays Julius Benedict, a perfect specimen of a man in both body and soul, raised as an orphan in pristine innocence on a tropical isle. Created in a genetic experiment, he has a twin brother on the mainland. Danny DeVito's Vincent Benedict is a major creep, a guy you wouldn't mind seeing get hit by a car. To him, Julius is a dopey nut who makes a good bodyguard. They set out to locate their mother. Schwarzenegger is a delightful surprise in this transitional role to comedy, so strongly does he project the tenderness, nobility, and puppy-dog devotion that make Julius tick. DeVito is a blaze of energy and body language as Vince, articulating the part as though he'd written it himself.

TWINS OF EVIL
1971, 87 mins, UK Ⓥ
D: John Hough **A:** Peter Cushing, Madelaine Collinson, Mary Collinson, Kathleen Byron, Dennis Price, Damien Thomas (Hammer)

Blood flows and thunder roars as Mary and Madelaine Collinson, attractive identical twins, come to live with their witch-hunting, God-fearing uncle (Peter Cushing), in the shadow of dreaded Karnstein Castle. One sister is good and timid while the other is bold and brazen. The latter cannot wait to find out more about the castle and the handsome young count (Damien Thomas). He is one of the undead, and soon she is his victim. The question becomes, which twin is the vampire?

TWISTED NERVE
1968, 118 mins, UK Ⓥ
D: Roy Boulting **A:** Hayley Mills, Hywel Bennett, Billie Whitelaw, Phyllis Calvert, Frank Finlay, Barry Foster (British Lion)

Twisted Nerve has Hayley Mills involved in some fairly gruesome *Psycho*-like proceedings. She's a bit shocked when the young anti-hero (Hywel Bennett) catches her off guard and kisses her fiercely; she's sweetly reasonable when he suddenly turns to her stark naked; and she

eventually faces near-rape and imminent murder not with displeasure, but aplomb. Film stands as a reasonably tough chilling suspenser, a compelling study of a warped young psychopath. Roy Boulting lacks the subtleties of a Hitchcock but manages to bring some brooding menace into his direction.

TWISTED ROAD, THE
See: They Live By Night

TWISTER
1989, 94 mins, US Ⓥ ⊙
D: Michael Almereyda **A:** Harry Dean Stanton, Suzy Amis, Crispin Glover, Dylan McDermott, Jenny Wright, Lois Chiles (Vestron)

Twister is an oddball family drama about some Kansas nuts who bounce off the walls of their mansion while a storm brews outside. Appealing for its ambition to achieve a unique tone and for its wildly disparate cast, pic never entirely comes together. Harry Dean Stanton is a retired soda pop tycoon who presides over a brood consisting of his layabout daughter Suzy Amis, the latter's eight-year-old daughter, his pretentious would-be artiste son Crispin Glover, the latter's fiancée Jenny Wright, unconventional black maid Charlaine Woodard, and his own fiancée, children's television evangelist Lois Chiles. Also present is Dylan McDermott, father of Amis's child, a ne'er-do-well who seems too nice a guy for the fruitcakes of Stanton's family.

TWISTER
1996, 114 mins, US Ⓥ ⊙ ▭
D: Jan De Bont **A:** Helen Hunt, Bill Paxton, Cary Elwes, Jami Gertz, Lois Smith, Alan Ruck (Amblin/Warner/Universal)

Another theme park ride of a movie without an ounce of emotional credibility to it, *Twister* succeeds on its own terms by taking the audience somewhere it has never been before: into a tornado's funnel. The time between tornadoes is just dead air. A group headed by scientist Helen Hunt is attempting to place sensors directly inside a funnel. Jo's almost-ex, Bill Paxton, who was the group leader before opting for the soft life as a broadcast weather man, turns up in the middle of the Oklahoma farmlands as bad weather is brewing. The competition, in the guise of hot-shot Cary Elwes and his corporate-sponsored caravan of black vans, roars onto the scene with their own sensors to launch. Remainder of film is taken up with the two crews racing around the country-side trying to intercept tornadoes. Pic never lets up, even in the so-called quiet scenes, which are generally filled with bickering and characters shouting to be heard over either the weather or one another. The effects set a new standard in their field.

TWO BITS
1995, 85 mins, US ⑰
D: James Foley A: Jerry Barone, Mary Elizabeth Mastrantonio, Al Pacino, Joe Grifasi, Joanna Merlin, Andy Romano (Connexion)

A mild, nostalgic Depression-era memoir, *Two Bits* has the impact of a sweet little short story rather than a thoroughly fleshed-out drama. Grizzled and rumpled, sitting in an overgrown garden, an elderly Italian gent (Al Pacino) announces that this summer day will be his last. Of more pressing concern to his 12-year-old grandson (Jerry Barone) is how he's going to raise the 25 cents he needs to attend the opening day of the new local movie palace. His escapades comprise the bulk of the picture, as the kid tries gambits of varying legitimacy and precariousness. A great deal of loving care clearly has gone into this re-creation of a long-vanished South Philly, but it's so prettified and idealized as to go over the top.

TWO ENGLISH GIRLS
See: Deux Anglaises et le Continent

TWO-FACED WOMAN
1941, 94 mins, US ⑰
D: George Cukor A: Greta Garbo, Melvyn Douglas, Constance Bennett, Ruth Gordon, Roland Young, Frances Carson (M-G-M)

Metro presents the one-time queen of mystery in a wild, and occasionally very risque, slap farce entitled *Two-Faced Woman*. That the experiment of converting Greta Garbo into a comedienne is not entirely successful is no fault of hers. Had the script writers and the director, George Cukor, entered into the spirit of the thing with as much enthusiasm, lack of self-consciousness, and abandon as the star, the result would have been a smash hit. The story is one of those imports from the Continent wherein the wife masquerades as her own twin sister just to test the fiber of her husband's adoration. There's a double entendre to nearly everything that is said between the two, and nearly everything is said.

TWO FLAGS WEST
1950, 92 mins, US
D: Robert Wise A: Joseph Cotten, Linda Darnell, Jeff Chandler, Cornel Wilde, Dale Robertson, Jay C. Flippen (20th Century-Fox)

The Civil War is carried into the west for Indian-fighting, giving *Two Flags West* an interesting premise for solid action and a fast pace. Basis for the plot is the recruiting of Confederate prisoners to man western army outposts under the Union flag. Joseph Cotten, a Confederate colonel, and a group of his soldiers accept the deal to escape prison and as an opportunity to eventually get back to fighting for the South. They are taken west under the guidance of Cornel Wilde, a Union officer, to the fort commanded by Jeff Chandler, a bitter, brooding man crippled in his first clash of arms.

TWO FOR THE ROAD
1967, 112 mins, UK ⑰ ⊙ ▭
D: Stanley Donen A: Audrey Hepburn, Albert Finney, Eleanor Bron, William Daniels, Claude Dauphin, Georges Descrieres (20th Century-Fox)

As far as producer, director, female lead, and screenwriter are concerned, this attempt to visually analyze what goes into making a marriage, and making it work, is successful. If it drags a bit here and there, blame it on the stodgy performance of Albert Finney, who is unable to convey the lightness, gaiety, and romanticism needed. The same married couple make basically the same trip, from London to the Riviera, at three different stages in their lives, with continual cross-cutting and flashing backward and forward from one period to another. Finney remains the same throughout, but Audrey Hepburn is amazing in her ability to portray a very young girl, a just pregnant wife of two years, and a beginning-to-be-bored wife of five years. **1967: Nomination:** Best Original Story & Screenplay

TWO FOR THE SEESAW
1962, 119 mins, US ▭
D: Robert Wise A: Robert Mitchum, Shirley MacLaine, Edmon Ryan, Elisabeth Fraser, Eddie Firestone, Billy Gray (United Artists)

There is a fundamental torpor about *Seesaw* that is less troublesome on stage than it is on screen. On film, it drags in spite of the charm, insight, wit, and compassion of William Gibson's play, the infectious friskiness of Shirley MacLaine's

1312

performance, and the consummate care taken by those who shaped and mounted the film. The basic flaws appear to be the play's innate talkiness and the selection of Robert Mitchum for the role of Jerry Ryan. The strong attraction Gittel is supposed to feel for Jerry becomes less plausible because of Mitchum's lethargic, droopy-eyed enactment. MacLaine's performance in the meaty role of the disarmingly candid, stupendously kindhearted Gittel Mosca is a winning one.

1962: Nominations: Best B&W Cinematography, Song ("Second Chance")

TWO GENTLEMEN SHARING
1969, 106 mins, UK

D: Ted Kotcheff **A:** Robin Phillips, Judy Geeson, Esther Anderson, Hal Frederick, Norman Rossington, Rachel Kempson (American International)

Film boasts a solid and well-chosen cast, strong physical values for such a medium-scaled item, and a racial story delivered with unhysterical acumen and considerable barbed humor. The two "gentlemen" who share the London pad in question are a young white ad exec with a liberal outlook and a certain mistrust for his middle-class background and a black lawyer with a youthfully unblunted hope of making a go of things in his profession on his own merits.

TWO GIRLS AND A SAILOR
1944, 124 mins, US ⓥ ⊙

D: Richard Thorpe **A:** Van Johnson, June Allyson, Gloria DeHaven, Jimmy Durante, Lena Horne, Jose Iturbi (M-G-M)

Weakness of story, a very thin one in this instance, reduces *Two Girls and a Sailor* to little more than a salmagundi of band numbers by Harry James and Xavier Cugat, plus Jimmy Durante, of whom there isn't enough. Film is too long and generally slow. June Allyson and Gloria DeHaven play a sister act. Headliners at a nightclub with the James and Cugat orchestras, they turn their home into a place where servicemen may be entertained.

1944: Nomination: Best Original Screenplay

TWO-HEADED SPY, THE
1958, 93 mins, UK

D: Andre de Toth **A:** Jack Hawkins, Gia Scala, Erik Schumann, Alexander Knox, Felix Aylmer, Donald Pleasence (Sabre)

Based on a real-life story, this film pursues a fairly pedestrian beat, but it builds its tension excellently and without too bla-

tant use of the usual cloak-and-dagger methods. Hawkins, a British spy in both wars, has built up confidence as an astute, loyal, and resourceful member of the Nazi machine. At the same time he is feeding the Allies invaluable information through a British agent, neatly played by Felix Aylmer. When Aylmer is arrested and murdered, suspicion falls on Hawkins.

200 MOTELS
1971, 98 mins, UK ⓥ

D: Frank Zappa, Tony Palmer **A:** The Mothers of Invention, Theodore Bikel, Ringo Starr, Janet Ferguson, Lucy Offerall, Pamela Miller (United Artists)

Frank Zappa's *200 Motels*, featuring his group, The Mothers of Invention, plus Theodore Bikel and Ringo Starr, is the zaniest. The film is a series of surrealistic sequences allegedly inspired by the experiences of a rock group on the road. The incidents are often outrageously irreverent. The comedy is fast and furious, both sophisticated and sophomoric. Bikel appears to superior advantage in several characterizations: a television m.c., an officious military bureaucrat, and something resembling a British secret agent or banker. Starr's okay cameo has him dressed up like Zappa.

TWO IF BY SEA
1996, 96 mins, US ⓥ

D: Bill Bennett **A:** Denis Leary, Sandra Bullock, Stephen Dillane, Yaphet Kotto, Wayne Robson, Jonathan Tucker (Morgan Creek/Warner)

An inert tale of a criminal couple, *Two If by Sea* is suitable for incarceration, provided the jailer loses the key. Denis Leary plays a petty thief, Frank, who steals a Matisse painting three days earlier than planned and spends the extra time vacationing in a remote New England enclave with his long-suffering girlfriend (Sandra Bullock). The FBI, led by the obsessive O'Malley (Yaphet Kotto), is convinced this is the work of a seasoned professional. Leary's work feels like catching a seasoned comic on a bad night. Bullock, playing dumb but good-hearted, displays none of the qualities that propelled her to recent stardom.

TWO JAKES, THE
1990, 138 mins, US ⓥ ⊙ ▭

D: Jack Nicholson **A:** Jack Nicholson, Harvey Keitel, Meg Tilly, Madeleine Stowe, Eli Wallach, Frederic Forrest (Paramount)

This oft-delayed sequel proves a jumbled, obtuse yet not entirely unsatisfying follow-up to *Chinatown*. Like much of the film noir of the 1940s, *Jakes* simply spins a web of intrigue so thick its origins become imperceptible. Picking up in 1948, 11 years after the events in *Chinatown*, Jake Gittes (Jack Nicholson) has become a prosperous and respected private investigator. When the name of Katherine Mulwray turns up on an audiotape, it revives Gittes's ghosts of events that occurred in Chinatown, linking sex, murder, and deceit to the role of precious resources in a developing Southern California. The film then takes on a dual structure, with Gittes in the eye of the hurricane as holder of the incriminating tape while seeking to unravel its connection to Mulwray, product of the coupling of father and daughter in Roman Polanski's earlier film.

TWO-LANE BLACKTOP
1971, 102 mins, US ⊑
D: Monte Hellman **A:** James Taylor, Warren Oates, Laurie Bird, Dennis Wilson, Harry Dean Stanton, Alan Vint (Universal/Laughlin)

The strange and sometimes pathetic world of hustling street-racing is explored with feeling by director-editor Monte Hellman in *Two-Lane Blacktop*. James Taylor is a modern dropout, living on winnings from impromptu pavement racing challenges. Dennis Wilson is his expert mechanic. En route to nowhere in particular, they are latched onto by Laurie Bird. The compelling plot is supplied by the good writing and direction, along with a wonderful performance of Warren Oates as an older man roaming the country in a souped-up Detroit vehicle. When Oates challenges Taylor to a cross-country run, with vehicle ownership the payoff, the story becomes a superior interplay of basic human nature. Much of the story's import is on Oates's back, and he carries it like a champion.

TWO LEFT FEET
1965, 93 mins, UK ⊛
D: Roy Ward Baker **A:** Michael Crawford, Nyree Dawn Porter, Julia Foster, Michael Craze, David Hemmings, Dilys Watling (British Lion)

This is a very fly-weight, trite pic. A callow youth is infatuated with a teasing waitress, but his attempt to seduce her ends in disaster. She turns to brighter young men at a jazz club, and he finds consolation in a naive young shop assistant. An attempt to satirize an appalling suburban wedding party becomes more of a caricature. Director Baker seems to have been unable to pull together a limp script.

TWO LOVES
(SPINSTER)
1961, 100 mins, US ⊑
D: Charles Walters **A:** Shirley MacLaine, Laurence Harvey, Jack Hawkins, Juano Hernandez, Norah Howard, Nobu McCarthy (M-G-M)

Frigidity is the subject broached by *Two Loves*. Shirley MacLaine plays a dedicated American school teacher in an isolated settlement in northern New Zealand. Her dogged innocence is threatened by the amorous advances of Laurence Harvey, an immature fellow teacher unhappy with his lot. She seems on the verge of giving herself to Harvey when he rather conveniently comes to a violent end in a motorcycle mishap. On the rebound, she is coaxed out of self-guilt pangs by senior school inspector Jack Hawkins. MacLaine, although not ideally suited to the role, manages for the most part to rise above the miscasting.

TWO-MINUTE WARNING
1976, 115 mins, US ⊛ ⊙ ⊑
D: Larry Peerce **A:** Charlton Heston, John Cassavetes, Martin Balsam, Beau Bridges, Marilyn Hassett, David Janssen (Universal)

An off-the-beaten-track story of a football stadium crowd menaced by a sniper, combined with above-average plotting, acting, and direction. Among the prominent players are stadium manager Martin Balsam and assistant Brock Peters; unmarried but long-time lovers David Janssen and Gena Rowlands; and unemployed young father Beau Bridges.
1976 Nomination: Best Editing

TWO MOON JUNCTION
1988, 104 mins, US ⊛ ⊙
D: Zalman King **A:** Sherilyn Fenn, Richard Tyson, Louise Fletcher, Kristy McNichol, Martin Hewitt, Burl Ives (DDM/Lorimar)

Two Moon Junction is a bad hick version of *Last Tango in Paris*, down to the poor imitative scoring. Sexual obsession might be the aim, but the result is anything but hot. Sherilyn Fenn decides to give her virginity to a guy who works at the traveling midway (Richard Tyson) instead of her fiancé (Martin Hewitt). Plot has all the ingredients of a 1940s meller with the obvious exception that Fenn defrocks at the drop of a hat while Tyson never bares much more than his chest. Shot in and around Los Angeles, pic seldom looks like Alabama.

TWO MRS. CARROLLS, THE
1947, 100 mins, US ⓥ
D: Peter Godfrey A: Humphrey Bogart, Barbara Stanwyck, Alexis Smith, Nigel Bruce, Isobel Elsom (Warner)

The Two Mrs. Carrolls is more stage play than motion picture. Overladen with dialogue as a substitute for action, it talks itself out of much of the suspense that should have developed. Humphrey Bogart, Barbara Stanwyck, and Alexis Smith feel the burden of dialogue and unnatural characters but manage to give the material an occasional lift. Plot deals with married artist who meets a new love while vacationing in Scotland. He returns to London, murders his wife, and marries the new flame. Second marriage works okay until another attractive girl appears.

TWO MUCH
1995, 115 mins, Spain ⓥ ▢
D: Fernando Trueba A: Melanie Griffith, Antonio Banderas, Daryl Hannah, Danny Aiello, Joan Cusack, Eli Wallach (Andres Vicente Gomez/Interscope/PFE)

Antonio Banderas plays Art Dodge, a failed painter and brash owner of a modern-art gallery in Miami. A scam fails to fool shady businessman Gene Paletto (Danny Aiello). Threatened by the man's thugs, Art escapes in the convertible of Paletto's impulsive ex-wife, Betty (Melanie Griffith). Closer acquaintance between the sheets follows, and Betty hears wedding bells, but he meets and is attracted to Betty's more level-headed sis, Liz (Daryl Hannah). To assist in his courtship of Liz, Art invents a brother, Bart, who also proves handy in escaping Paletto and his henchmen. Banderas reveals himself to be remarkably adept at physical comedy, giving the slapstick antics considerably more vigor than they might otherwise have mustered.

TWO MULES FOR SISTER SARA
1970, 116 mins, US ⓥ ▢
D: Don Siegel A: Shirley MacLaine, Clint Eastwood, Manolo Fabregas, Alberto Morin, Armando Silvestre, John Kelly (Universal/Malpaso)

Two Mules for Sister Sara might have worked. But with Clint Eastwood as an American mercenary looking for a fast peso in old French-occupied Mexico, Shirley MacLaine as a scarlet sister disguised in a nun's habit, and Don Siegel's by-the-old-book direction, it doesn't. It needed a Lee Marvin, or a portrayal like Humphrey Bogart's in The African Queen to work. MacLaine is unbelievable as a nun, and the story's main thread of tension, the relationship between her and Eastwood, simply dissipates.

TWO OF A KIND
1983, 87 mins, US ⊙
D: John Herzfeld A: John Travolta, Olivia Newton-John, Charles Durning, Beatrice Straight, Scatman Crothers, Oliver Reed (20th Century-Fox)

Aside from the presence of the two stars, Two of a Kind has all the earmarks of a bargain-basement job. Script's only vaguely amusing conceit presents itself at the beginning, when God returns from a vacation and, finding the world gone to seed in the interim, announces he's going to wipe out the human race and start over again. The angels urge Him to reconsider His decision based on whether or not a random man can prove capable of genuine goodness. John Travolta, a self-styled inventor, is selected as the guinea pig, just in time to find him robbing a bank in order to pay off a debt to the mob. Bank teller Olivia Newton-John, fired for flirting with the stick-up man, actually makes off with the dough.

TWO PEOPLE
1973, 100 mins, US
D: Robert Wise A: Peter Fonda, Lindsay Wagner, Estelle Parsons, Alan Fudge, Philippe March, Frances Sternhagen (Filmakers/Universal)

Two People is a major disappointment. Film clearly aimed to develop a love-at-first-sight romance between two characters whose different life styles run parallel in a brief encounter. However, sluggish pacing and ludicrous dialogue turn the film into a travesty. Peter Fonda, a repentant Vietnam War field deserter, is tired of running and ready to return to face his punishment. In Marrakech, he meets fashion model Lindsay Wagner. The film's pacing turns the desired audience wish—that the couple make physical love—into barely concealed impatience.

TWO RODE TOGETHER
1961, 108 mins, US ⓥ ⊙
D: John Ford A: James Stewart, Richard Widmark, Shirley Jones, Linda Cristal,

Andy Devine, John McIntire (Columbia)

John Ford's western is a story of the ill-advised attempt to haul white prisoners back to civilized society in the 1880s after they have spent a decade or more in Comanche Indian captivity. This is fairly fresh sagebrush fiction, but somehow the production misfires in the process. Parts of the film zoom into the heavy, psychological sphere of the modern western, others revert to the outmoded innocence and directness of a 1930s sagebrush style. Compensation is the unusually practical, non-heroic nature of the central character, most disarmingly and authoritatively enacted by James Stewart.

TWO SISTERS FROM BOSTON
1946, 112 mins, US
D: Henry Koster A: Kathryn Grayson, June Allyson, Lauritz Melchior, Jimmy Durante, Peter Lawford (M-G-M)

Two Sisters from Boston is both an operatic and a low comedy treat. Kathryn Grayson tees off as "High C Susie," a hotsy singer who's quite a click in a Bowery joint until her staid Back Bay family descends on New York. With the somewhat outlandish assistance of Spike (Jimmy Durante), the pianist-impresario of the Bowery bistro, she makes the Met. In between, Lautritz Melchior indulges in temperamental outbursts. There's a close-up on the prehistoric method of His Master's Voice recording, a great sequence, and some good turn-of-the-century song hokum to carry the action along.

TWO STAGE SISTERS
See: Wutai Jiemei

2001: A SPACE ODYSSEY
1968, 139 mins, UK/US
D: Stanley Kubrick A: Keir Dullea, Gary Lockwood, William Sylvester, Daniel Richter, Douglas Rain, Leonard Rossiter (M-G-M)

A major achievement in cinematography and special effects, *2001* lacks dramatic appeal and only conveys suspense after the halfway mark; Kubrick must receive all the praise—and take all the blame. The plot uses up almost two hours in exposition of scientific advances in space travel and communications before anything happens. The dull prologue deals with the "advancement of man," centering around a group of apes. A huge black monolith is shown briefly (to reappear later as the key to possible life on other planets). A computer named HAL that can talk is one of the film's best effects and is surprisingly acceptable. Dullea and Gary Lockwood are the two principal astronauts. Their complete lack of emotion becomes rather implausible during scenes in which they discover the villainy of the computer. Film ends on a confused note, never really tackling the "other life" situation and evidently leaving interpretation up to the viewer. The over-long running time could have been shortened by some slicing in the lengthy introduction. *2001* compares with, but does not best, previous efforts at science fiction, lacking the humanity of *Forbidden Planet*, the imagination of *Things to Come*, and the simplicity of *Of Stars and Men*. It actually belongs to the technically slick group previously dominated by George Pal and the Japanese.
1968: Special Visual Effects
Nominations: Best Director, Original Story & Screenplay, Art Direction

2010
1984, 114 mins, US
D: Peter Hyams A: Roy Scheider, John Lithgow, Helen Mirren, Bob Balaban, Keir Dullea, Douglas Rain (M-G-M)

2010 begins nine years after something went wrong with the Jupiter voyage of Discovery. US and Russian scientists have united in a venture to return to Jupiter to seek an answer to Discovery's fate and the significance of the huge black monolith that orbits near it. American crew is headed by Roy Scheider, John Lithgow, and Bob Balaban. The Soviets want them along mainly for their understanding of HAL 9000, whose mutiny remains unexplained. In Peter Hyams's hands, the HAL mystery is the most satisfying substance of the film. Unfortunately, it lies amid a hodge-podge of bits and pieces.
1984: Nominations: Best Costume Design, Art Direction, Sound, Visual Effects, Makeup

TWO WAY STRETCH
1960, 87 mins, UK
D: Robert Day A: Peter Sellers, Wilfrid Hyde White, David Lodge, Bernard Cribbins, Maurice Denham, Lionel Jeffries (British Lion/Shepperton)

Peter Sellers gives another deft, very funny performance in *Two Way Stretch*. The thin story line concerns a free-and-easy prison run by a governor more interested in gardening than discipline. Occupying a luxury cell are three partners in crime—Sellers, David Lodge, and Bernard Cribbins. They have the prison completely sewn up. An outside partner arrives with a scheme for stealing $5 million in diamonds. It needs the trio to break jail the night before their release, pull off the job, return to prison with their loot, and next morning walk out free men with a perfect alibi. The arrival of a tough new chief warden frustrates their plans. Success of this film depends largely on the actors and Robert Day's brisk direction. Sellers has himself a ball as the leader of the crafty trio of crooks, while Lodge and Cribbins make perfectly contrasted partners.

TWO WEEKS IN ANOTHER TOWN
1962, 106 mins, US ⓋⓄ▭
D: Vincente Minnelli **A:** Kirk Douglas, Edward G. Robinson, Cyd Charisse, George Hamilton, Daliah Lavi, Claire Trevor (M-G-M)

Two Weeks in Another Town is not an achievement about which any of its creative people are apt to boast. Kirk Douglas stars as an unstable actor, fresh off a three-year hitch in sanitariums, who goes to Rome to rejoin the director (Edward G. Robinson) with whom, years earlier, he's scored his greatest triumphs. Douglas emotes with his customary zeal and passion, largely in vain to illuminate an unbelievable character. Even less believable is his ex-wife, a hard-as-nails seductress exotically overplayed by Cyd Charisse. Only remotely lifelike characters in the story are Robinson and Claire Trevor as an ambivalent married couple whose personalities transform under the cover of night. Footage from *The Bad and the Beautiful* is cleverly incorporated into the drama and is livelier than just about anything else in the film.

TWO YEARS BEFORE THE MAST
1946, 96 mins, US
D: John Farrow **A:** Alan Ladd, Brian Donlevy, William Bendix, Barry Fitzgerald, Howard da Silva, Esther Fernandez (Paramount)

Chief credit for this one belongs to director John Farrow, with the emphasis on action throughout. Although Alan Ladd and the other stars top the cast, it's Howard da Silva, as the pitiless ship's captain, who walks off with the blue ribbon. Ladd does a nice job as the fop who finds regeneration fighting to get human treatment for the merchant seamen of the day. Bendix gives a restrained reading to his role as the tough but sympathetic first mate, and Barry Fitzgerald adds the comedy touches as the ship's cook.

TYSTNADEN
(THE SILENCE)
1963, 95 mins, Sweden ⓋⓄ
D: Ingmar Bergman **A:** Ingrid Thulin, Gunnel Lindblom, Jorgen Lindstrom, Hakan Jahnberg, Birger Malmsten, Eduardo Gutierrez (Svensk Filmindustri)

In *The Silence*, Ingmar Bergman turns his attention exclusively to the body and its passions. Two lonely sisters, Ann and Ester, traveling home to Sweden, stop in the town of Timuku in a fictitious country. The town is full of soldiers, tanks, and crowded cafe halls. The sisters, and Ann's seven-year-old son Johan, are installed in an old hotel with stuffy majestic rooms, deep beds, and mile-long corridors. The older sister, Ester (Ingrid Thulin), is an intellectual with a lesbian fixation on Ann (Gunnel Lindblom), a seductive, sex-hungry animal more interested in adventures in the town. Distressed by the antics of her amorous sister, Ester tries to forget her love in alcohol and degradation. There is not much dialogue, almost no music, but the sex scenes have vigor and primitive power. Lindblom has the fury of an Anna Magnani and the beauty of a Sophia Loren; for the first time she has a big role in a Bergman picture.

U-BOAT 29
See: The Spy in Black

UGETSU
See: Ugetsu Monogatari

UGETSU MONOGATARI (UGETSU; TALES AFTER THE RAIN)
1953, 96 mins, Japan ⓥ
D: Kenji Mizoguchi **A:** Machiko Kyo, Masayuki Mori, Kinuyo Tanaka, Sakae Ozawa, Mitsuko Mito (Daiei)

Tale of two men in seething 16th-century Japan has a color and panorama which makes this absorbing film fare. The trials of the two men, one a potter (Masayuki Mori) who gets involved with a phantom princess (Machiko Kyo), and the other a merchant (Sakae Ozawa) who yearns to be a Samurai warrior, are unfolded on the teeming tile of the clan wars. Direction of Kenji Mizoguchi keeps the complicated proceedings coherent. Acting is good right down the line.

UGLY AMERICAN, THE
1963, 120 mins, US ⓥ
D: George Englund **A:** Marlon Brando, Eiji Okada, Sandra Church, Arthur Hill, Pat Hingle, Jocelyn Brando (Universal)

Some of the ambiguities, hypocrisies, and perplexities of cold war politics are observed, dramatized, and, to a degree, analyzed in *The Ugly American*. Focal figure is an American ambassador (Marlon Brando) to a southeast Asian nation who comes to understand that there is more to modern political revolution than meets the casual or jaundiced bystander's eye. Although skillfully and often explosively directed by George Englund and well played by Brando and others, the film tends to be overly talkative and lethargic in certain areas, vague and confusing in others.

UGLY DACHSHUND, THE
1965, 93 mins, US ⓥ
D: Norman Tokar **A:** Dean Jones, Suzanne Pleshette, Charles Ruggles, Kelly Thordsen, Farley Baer, Robert Kino (Walt Disney)

Walt Disney, who knows his way with a dog as well as a family, has turned out a rollicking piece of business in this comedy about a Great Dane who thinks he's a dachshund. Dean Jones and Suzanne Pleshette are the two principals, a young married couple faced with the Dane (his) being raised with four dachs (hers). Action is light and airy as the couple go their own way with their respective pets.

ULEE'S GOLD
1997, 111 mins, US ⓥ ⊙
D: Victor Nunez **A:** Peter Fonda, Patricia Richardson, Jessica Biel, J. Kenneth Campbell, Christine Dunford, Steven Flynn (Clinica Estetico)

A gem of rare emotional depth and integrity, *Ulee's Gold* is graced by a performance from Peter Fonda that is the best of his career. Ulysses (Ulee) Jackson (Fonda) is a middle-aged Vietnam vet living in a rural area of the Florida panhandle. Devastated by the death of his wife and the long-term imprisonment of his son Jimmy (Tom Wood), Ulee puts most of his attention into his work as a beekeeper. His daughter-in-law, Helen (Christine Dunford), has disappeared, and Ulee is obliged to look after his two granddaughters. Their mundane lives change when Jimmy asks his father to fetch Helen and he is confronted with two low-rent criminals (Steven Flynn, Dewey Weber) who demand, at gunpoint, that Ulee produce the $100,000 Jimmy has hidden from them. Writer-director Victor Nunez (*Ruby in Paradise*) achieves a rare emotional depth. Fonda responds splendidly, with work that is reserved yet revealing. It's impossible not to compare the actor here to his father.
1997: Nomination: Best Actor (Peter Fonda)

ULTIMATE SOLUTION OF GRACE QUIGLEY, THE (AKA: GRACE QUIGLEY)
1984, 102 mins, US ⓥ
D: Anthony Harvey **A:** Katharine Hepburn, Nick Nolte, Elizabeth Wilson, Chip Zien, Kit Le Fever, William Duell (Cannon/Northbrook)

Black comedy dealing with voluntary euthanasia by the Geritol set. Katharine Hepburn is the spry, entrepreneurial mother figure who arranges for her peers' demise, and Nick Nolte plays the gruff, hard-bitten, and sarcastic hit man she hires. Sitting across from her apartment one day, Hepburn inadvertently witnesses Nolte put a bullet into her money-grubbing landlord and subsequently enlists him in her scheme to provide a "service" for her aging compatriots who wish to meet the hereafter ahead of schedule.

ULYSSES
1954, 104 mins, Italy ⓥ
D: Mario Camerini **A:** Kirk Douglas, Silvana Mangano, Anthony Quinn, Rossana Podesta, Jacques Dumesnil (Lux/Ponti-De Laurentiis)

Perhaps too much money went into the making of *Ulysses*, but expense aside. Only a few of the w.k. Homeric episodes have been included in the already lengthy pic, but material covered makes for plenty of action, dominated by a virile performance by Kirk Douglas. Others include costar Silvana Mangano as both Circe and Penelope, limited by both parts to expressing monotonous unhappiness until the finale. For a spectacle, the pic runs too many close-ups, with longish stretches of dialogue between the two principals.

ULYSSES
1967, 140 mins, Ireland ⓥ ⊙ ▭
D: Joseph Strick **A:** Barbara Jefford, Milo O'Shea, Maurice Roeves, T. P. McKenna, Martin Dempsey, Sheila O'Sullivan (Continental/Walter Reade)

Ulysses is a healthy, promising cinematic piece of flora, nightblooming and carnivorous. Filmed entirely in Ireland, the picture concentrates on the trio of primary characters—Leopold and Molly Bloom and student Stephen Dedalus. Although their tales overlap, the primary emphasis is on the two males, leaving the last 20 or 30 minutes to Molly's famous libidinous soliloquy. Barbara Jefford's Molly is handsomely overblown, a wasted garden of a woman who yearns for a man with a passion that almost causes the screen to pulsate. Milo O'Shea's Leopold Bloom is a realized example of the degraded, dejected husband.
1967: Nomination: Best Adapted Screenplay

ULZANA'S RAID
1972, 103 mins, US ⓥ ⊙
D: Robert Aldrich **A:** Burt Lancaster, Bruce Davison, Jorge Luke, Richard Jaeckel, Joaquin Martinez, Lloyd Bochner (Universal)

Ulzana's Raid is the sort of pretentious US Army-versus-Indians potboiler that invites derision from its own dialogue and situations. The production is ponderous in its formula action-sociology-violence, routine in its acting and direction, and often confusing in its hokey storytelling. A weathered old frontier scout (Burt Lancaster) is saddled with a greenhorn young army officer (Bruce Davison) as the patrol attempts to round up some marauding Apaches. The effect is simply another exploitation western in which plot suspense is not predicated on what is going to happen, but on how bestial it can be.

UMBERTO D.
1952, 82 mins, Italy ⓥ ⊙
D: Vittorio De Sica **A:** Carlo Battisti, Maria Pia Casilio, Lina Gennari (Dear)

A simple tale of a poor pensioner's search for friendship and a means of sustenance. Umberto D., played by Carlo Battisti, has only two friends in the world: the maid in the apartment in which he boards, and his dog. It is the dog, and the problem of its disposal, variously attempted, which finally persuades him to give up his tragic idea of committing suicide. The ending is happy, but the general effect of the film is disturbing, so compelling is De Sica's description of a man's solitude.

UMBRELLAS OF CHERBOURG, THE
See: Les Parapluies De Cherbourg

UNBEARABLE LIGHTNESS OF BEING, THE
1988, 171 mins, US ⓥ ⊙
D: Philip Kaufman **A:** Daniel Day-Lewis, Juliette Binoche, Lena Olin, Derek de Lint, Erland Josephson, Donald Moffat (Zaentz)

A richly satisfying adaptation of Milan Kundera's international bestseller of love and erotica set against the Russian invasion of Czechoslovakia. Tomas (Daniel Day-Lewis), a top surgeon and compulsive ladies' man, marries a lovely country girl, Tereza. He continues his womanizing, however, particularly with his voluptuous mistress Sabina, an artist who takes off for Geneva when Russian tanks put a halt to the Prague Spring of 1968. The sexuality which drenches the entire film possesses a great buoyancy and spirit. As played by Juliette Binoche and Lena Olin, the two women are absolutely enchanting. Attractive in some ways, Tomas is irritatingly uncommunicative and opaque in others. Day-Lewis at times overdoes the self-consciously smug projection of his own appeal.
1988: Nominations: Best Adapted Screenplay, Cinematography

UNBELIEVABLE TRUTH, THE
1989, 98 mins, US ⊗

D: Hal Hartley **A:** Adrienne Shelly, Robert Burke, Christopher Cooke, Julia McNeal, Gary Sauer, Mark Bailey (Action)

The Unbelievable Truth has a minor-key feel to it. Josh, a good-looking, taciturn guy, shows up in his small New York hometown after a spell in the slammer. He lands a job in a garage owned by Vic, whose daughter Audry is a 17-year-old sexpot due to enter Harvard. Audry drops her long-time boyfriend, moans about the impending end of the world, then shocks everyone by going materialistic and hitting it big as a model in Manhattan, where she shacks up with a photographer she detests. She also makes passes at Josh. Framing the middle-class melodrama is director Hal Hartley's manipulative artistry, which uses such devices as orchestrated color schemes, unrealistic sound, Godardian intertitles, repeated motifs, and careful scoring.

UNCENSORED
1944, 82 mins, UK ⊗

D: Anthony Asquith **A:** Eric Portman, Phyllis Calvert, Griffith Jones, Irene Handl, Peter Glenville, Walter Hudd (Gainsborough)

Efforts of the Belgian underground to thwart the Nazi grip form the basis for this thrilling melodrama. Belgium's patriots maintain regular publication of an underground paper as a constant thorn to the Nazi occupational troops, thanks to the apparently unpatriotic Eric Portman, who quietly continues his underground operations while entertaining nightly at a cabaret for Nazi toppers. Portman contributes a standout performance. Phyllis Calvert, as the faithful Belgian worker, provides several romantic interludes.

UNCERTAIN GLORY
1944, 102 mins, US ⊗

D: Raoul Walsh **A:** Errol Flynn, Paul Lukas, Jean Sullivan, Lucile Watson, Faye Emerson, Douglass Dumbrille (Warner)

France under the Nazis is portrayed in *Uncertain Glory*, a psychological, melodramatic study that is lengthy and frequently tedious. Story is complicated, dealing with a Surete inspector (Lukas) and the object of his long-time chase (Errol Flynn). The film's opening finds Flynn being led to the guillotine for murder. A British flying squadron bombs the prison, leading to Flynn's escape. Then follows

the chase by Paul Lukas, the capture and the subsequent plan by Flynn to give himself up as a saboteur so that 100 French hostages could go free.

UNCLE, THE
1966, 87 mins, UK

D: Desmond Davis **A:** Rupert Davies, Brenda Bruce, Robert Duncan, William Marlowe, Ann Lynn, Maurice Denham (British Lion/Lenart)

Most of *The Uncle* deals with the loss of innocence of a small boy over one summer. Gus (Robert Duncan), a seven-year-old, finds himself in a catastrophic situation—Gus is totally unprepared to be an uncle to a nephew the same age. The position presents many difficulties. The entire film is done from the perspective of the pint-sized hero. Director Davis has been fortunate in having a cast that is entirely excellent, particularly young Robert Duncan (only a British child could look so profound at seven).

UNCLE BUCK
1989, 100 mins, US ⊗ ⊙

D: John Hughes **A:** John Candy, Amy Madigan, Jean Louisa Kelly, Gaby Hoffman, Macaulay Culkin, Elaine Bromka (Universal)

John Hughes unsuccessfully tries to mix a serious generation gap message between the belly laughs in *Uncle Buck*, a warm-weather John Candy vehicle. Candy is a ne'er-do-well black sheep of the family pressed into service when his relatives (Elaine Bromka, Garrett M. Brown) have to rush off to visit Bromka's dad, who's stricken with a heart attack. Enter Uncle Buck, in charge of the three youngsters for an indefinite period of time. The kids wear down Buck's rough edges, and he teaches them some seat-of-the-pants lessons about life. Candy is too likable to give the role any edge. When called upon to be tough or mean, he's unconvincing.

UNCOMMON VALOR
1983, 105 mins, US ⊗ ⊙

D: Ted Kotcheff **A:** Gene Hackman, Robert Stack, Fred Ward, Reb Brown, Randall ''Tex'' Cobb, Patrick Swayze (Paramount)

The top talent involved—especially Gene Hackman—is hardly needed to make *Uncommon Valor* what it is, a very common action picture. Hackman is a grieving father obsessed with the idea that his son remains a prisoner 10 years after he was reported missing in action in Vietnam. Financed by oil tycoon Robert Stack, whose son is also missing, Hackman puts together his small invasion force. By the time the tough really get going it's only a question of who won't come back from the dangerous mission.

UNCONQUERED
1947, 135 mins, US ·
D: Cecil B. DeMille **A:** Gary Cooper, Paulette Goddard, Howard da Silva, Boris Karloff, Ward Bond, Cecil Kellaway (Paramount)

Cecil B. DeMille's *Unconquered* is a pre-Revolutionary western with plenty of Indians which, for all the vacuousness and shortcomings, has its gripping moments. Howard da Silva is the arch-knave whose marriage to Indian chief Boris Karloff's daughter (Katherine DeMille) puts him in the black with the redskins on fur-trading. Paulette Goddard is the proud slave girl whose freedom Gary Cooper purchases on the British slave ship, only to cross paths with da Silva and his number-two menace (Mike Mazurki). Although a bond slave, Goddard spurns da Silva and sufficiently attracts Cooper to make for a romantic angle.
1947: Nomination: Best Special Effects

UNDEFEATED, THE
1969, 118 mins, US ⊙ ▭
D: Andrew V. McLaglen **A:** John Wayne, Rock Hudson, Tony Aguilar, Roman Gabriel, Marian McCargo, Lee Meriwether (20th Century-Fox)

Film has a basic story line, characters, and dialogue for what might have been a superior drama and possibly a great western. But Andrew McLaglen's direction seems to consist of splicing together cliches, static camera work, and Central Casting of the bit parts. John Wayne is the leader of the ragtag remnants of a troop of Union cavalry who make a bloody charge against a thin line of Confederate soldiers, only to find after the massacre that the war has been over for three days.

UNDER CAPRICORN
1949, 116 mins, UK Ⓥ ⊙
D: Alfred Hitchcock **A:** Ingrid Bergman, Joseph Cotten, Michael Wilding, Margaret Leighton, Cecil Parker (Transatlantic)

Under Capricorn is overlong and talky, with scant measure of the Alfred Hitchcock thriller tricks. Time of the plot is 1831, in Sydney, Australia. Joseph Cotten is an ex-convict, former groom, and now Ingrid Bergman's husband. Cotten has become a man of wealth but is not accepted socially. That, and his crime—the killing of his wife's brother, a deed committed by Bergman but for which he took the blame—have caused his wife's addiction to the bottle.

UNDERCOVER BLUES
1993, 89 mins, US Ⓥ ⊙
D: Herbert Ross **A:** Kathleen Turner, Dennis Quaid, Fiona Shaw, Stanley Tucci, Larry Miller, Tom Arnold (M-G-M)

The moderately enjoyable *Undercover Blues* plays like a big-screen pilot for a television series. Former spies Jane and Jeff Blue (Kathleen Turner, Dennis Quaid) are lured back into the espionage business to help foil an international terrorist ring led by Novacek (Fiona Shaw). The film spends about four minutes on the plot, with the rest devoted to comic scenes of Quaid and Turner playing kissy-face and cooing over their baby, sidestepping the New Orleans police, and fending off the assaults of street mugger Muerte (Stanley Tucci, who garners the lion's share of laughs).

UNDERCOVER GIRL
1950, 83 mins, US
D: Joseph Pevney **A:** Alexis Smith, Scott Brady, Richard Egan, Gladys George, Royal Dano, Regis Toomey (Universal)

Undercover Girl, by its very title, suggests a conventional melodrama with a twist in that a girl is the gangsters' foil. Alexis Smith plays Christine Miller, who interrupts her police training in New York to go to California to avenge the death of her policeman father, killed by a narcotics ring. Working with the Los Angeles police, she gets into the confidence of the gang, posing as a dope buyer.

UNDERCOVER MAN, THE
1949, 80 mins, US
D: Joseph H. Lewis **A:** Glenn Ford, Nina Foch, James Whitmore, Barry Kelley, David Wolfe, Frank Tweddell (Columbia)

The Undercover Man is a good crime-busting saga. Fresh, natural dialogue helps to cover up the formulaic yarn. Joseph H. Lewis's direction also mutes the melodramatic elements but manages to keep the tension mounting through a series of violent episodes. Glenn Ford plays a government Treasury agent on the trail of an underworld czar. Aiming to nail the racketeer on a tax-evasion rap, Ford attempts to contact some stool pigeons, but the syndicate knocks them off before they can squeal.

UNDERCURRENT
1946, 111 mins, US Ⓥ
D: Vincente Minnelli **A:** Katharine Hepburn, Robert Taylor, Robert Mitchum, Edmund Gwenn, Marjorie Main, Jayne Meadows (M-G-M)

Undercurrent is heavy drama with femme appeal. Picture deals with psychological angle in which a weak man uses lies, theft, and even murder to obtain power and acclaim. Robert Taylor, warmade industrialist, marries Katharine Hepburn, daughter of a scientist, after a whirlwind courtship. After marriage, the bride begins to discover odd incidents in her husband's past, including his brother's mysterious disappearance and the fear that dogs and other animals have for the man.

UNDER FIRE
1983, 100 mins, US Ⓥ ◎
D: Roger Spottiswoode **A:** Nick Nolte, Gene Hackman, Joanna Cassidy, Jean-Louis Trintignant, Ed Harris, Richard Masur (Lion's Gate)

Three individuals cover the Chad conflict in the late 1970s: photographer Russell Price (Nick Nolte), senior correspondent for *Time* magazine Alex Grazier (Gene Hackman), and radio newslady Claire Stryder (Joanna Cassidy). All are tough professionals. There's a hired mercenary who surfaces now and then, first in Chad and later in Nicaragua. In the course of covering the Nicaraguan events, Nolte and Cassidy opt to search for a rebel leader named Rafael among the Sandinistas. Nolte's photos of the rebels play into the hands of a double-agent (Jean-Louis Trintignant), who uses them to hunt down and kill key Sandinista leaders.
1983: Nomination: Best Original Score

UNDERGROUND
1941, 95 mins, US
D: Vincent Sherman **A:** Jeffrey Lynn, Philip Dorn, Karen Verne, Mona Maris, Frank Reicher, Martin Kosleck (Warner)

Underground deals with the underground anti-Nazi movement in the Reich, specifically, with the outlaw shortwave radio stations that helped to spread the voice of truth and freedom and thus keep Nazi officialdom in a state of frenzy. It's a story of brother against brother; of forbidden love between a young, idealistic Nazi zealot and a girl of the underground movement; and of a tragic death of several leaders of the group serving to open the eyes of the hero to the real evil of Nazism. It has the integrity that indicates its makers believed in what they were doing.

UNDERGROUND
1995, 178 mins, France/Germany/Hungary Ⓥ
D: Emir Kusturica **A:** Miki Manojlovic, Lazar Ristovski, Mirjana Jokevic, Slavko Stimac, Ernst Stotzner, Srdan Todorovic (Ciby 2000/Pandora/Novo)

Emir Kusturica's epic black comedy about Yugoslavia from 1941 to 1992 is a three-hour steamroller that leaves the viewer dazed and exhausted, but mightily impressed. Pic kicks off to a wild and joyous start. Leading the band is Marko (Miki Manojlovic), dancing and whoring his way through 1941 Belgrade. He and his best pal, Blacky (Lazar Ristovski), are patriots and gangsters, directing a black market operation from a warren of underground tunnels. They hide their families in a cellar, where refugees have put together an underground munitions factory. When Blacky is captured and tortured by the Gestapo, Marko rescues him. While Blacky recuperates in the cellar, Marko seduces Blacky's beloved, headstrong actress Natalija (Mirjana Jokovic). As Allied bombers destroy what's left of Belgrade, Marko completes his betrayal: he makes the refugees in the cellar believe the war is still going on. Twenty years later, Marko has become an important party boss. In the cellar, Blacky and the others keep manufacturing arms while they wait for Tito's call to "the final battle."

UNDER MILK WOOD
1971, 90 mins, UK Ⓥ
D: Andrew Sinclair **A:** Richard Burton, Elizabeth Taylor, Peter O'Toole, Glynis Johns, Vivien Merchant, Sian Philips (Timon)

Screen adaptations of hard-to-slot items such as Dylan Thomas's *Under Milk Wood* have long been tricky affairs, so it's a tribute to the makers of this pic that it comes off this well. Normal screen conventions are broken as writer-director Andrew Sinclair chooses to follow Thomas instead in his dissection of a Welsh seaside village and its inhabitants in boisterously, earthily humorous vein. Richard Burton speaks the bulk of Thomas's voice-over lines with feeling and obvious love. Through him principally, the purr and the occasional soar of the poet's phrase flows and satisfies.

UNDERNEATH, THE
1995, 99 mins, US Ⓥ ▭
D: Steven Soderbergh **A:** Peter Gallagher, Alison Elliott, William Fichtner, Adam Trese, Joe Don Baker, Elisabeth Shue (Populist/Gramercy)

A remake of the superb 1949 film noir *Criss Cross, The Underneath* downplays the boilerplate genre elements in favor of something akin to a meditation on personal responsibility and culpability. Michael Chambers (Peter Gallagher) arrives back home in Austin, Texas, to attend the wedding of his mother (Anjanette Gomer) to a nice older fellow, Ed Dutton (Paul Dooley). But his ulterior motive is to see what's cooking with his former flame, the slinky Rachel (Alison Elliott), whom he tracks down at a nightclub owned by Rachel's snaky new beau, Tommy Dundee (William Fichtner). All these plot strands are deftly orchestrated. At the same time, however, Soderbergh has curiously crimped the story's most exploitable genre ingredients, i.e., the sex and violence, from what they were in the 1949 telling. The original ending has been entirely reworked.

UNDER SIEGE
1992, 102 mins, US Ⓥ ⊙
D: Andrew Davis **A:** Steven Seagal, Tommy Lee Jones, Gary Busey, Erika Eleniak, Patrick O'Neal, Nick Mancuso (Warner)

Under Siege is an immensely slick, if also old-fashioned and formulaic, entertainment. Steven Seagal plays a cook on the USS *Missouri*, the Navy's largest and most powerful battleship. En route to decommission, the journey turns out to be volatile and dangerous when two corrupt psychopaths, both top military experts, hijack the ship and steal its nuclear arsenal. Seagal's rebellious cook is actually a decorated Navy Seal. In between battles and explosions, scripter J. F. Lawton has shrewdly placed the funny one-liners, delivered by Seagal in his customary tongue-in-cheek style.
1992: Nominations: Best Sound, Sound Effects Editing

UNDER SIEGE 2
DARK TERRITORY
1995, 100 mins, US Ⓥ ⊙
D: Geoff Murphy **A:** Steven Seagal, Eric Bogosian, Katherine Heigl, Everett McGill, Nick Mancuso, Brenda Bakke (Warner/Regency/Nasso)

The second Steven Seagal *Under Siege* foray is muscle-bending, mind-numbing action at high-decibel levels for the lowest and least discerning common denominator, casting reason, plot, character, and sanity aside. This time, Seagal's former CIA Black Op, Casey Ryback, is on a train that gets hijacked by wacko terrorists with diabolical plans for world devastation. The script cribs mercilessly from the structure devised by Jon Lawton in the original. Once again there are a civilian sidekick, eccentric bad guys, and spectacular stunts. Director Geoff Murphy handles the action with the precision of a good traffic cop.

UNDER SUSPICION
1991, 99 mins, UK Ⓥ ⊙ ▭
D: Simon Moore **A:** Liam Neeson, Laura San Giacomo, Kenneth Cranham, Alphonsia Emmanuel, Stephen Moore, Maggie O'Neill (Carnival)

Under Suspicion is an old-fashioned murder mystery flawed by wobbly playing from Irish actor Liam Neeson. Neeson is a down-at-the-heels private investigator arranging phoney divorce evidence. His wife (Maggie O'Neill), who poses as the other woman in hotel setups to get photographic court evidence, ends up with her brain splattered on the sheets next to an equally dead client. Enter the client's mysterious American mistress (Laura San Giacomo), who hires Neeson to investigate her lover's murder. Pic plays like a loving tribute to every film noir in the book. But it's more like a rainy-day Brit cross between *Jagged Edge* and *Body Heat*.

UNDER THE CHERRY MOON
1986, 98 mins, US Ⓥ ⊙
D: Prince **A:** Prince, Steven Berkoff, Francesca Annis, Kristin Scott Thomas, Jerome Benton, Alexandra Stewart (Warner)

In *Under the Cherry Moon*, Prince tries to direct, too, giving himself a lot of closeups kissing and hardly any of him singing. What is left is a trite story about a rich girl and a poor musician (Prince) set on the Riviera and shot in black and white. Story has less plot than the average music video, with Prince as a pianist at a Nice hotel who sets his sights on meeting a young, wealthy woman. Film comes out looking about as flat and uninteresting as a newsreel from the 1930s about vacationing in the south of France.

UNDER THE CLOCK
See: The Clock

UNDER THE RED ROBE
1937, 80 mins, UK ⊙
D: Victor Seastrom **A:** Conrad Veidt, Annabella, Raymond Massey, Romney Brent, Sophie Stewart, F. Wyndham Goldie (20th Century-Fox)

Considering that it may be erroneously tabbed as a costume production, *Under the Red Robe* turns out to be surprisingly fine entertainment. Direction never wastes a move, holding proper suspense and mixing droll comedy with exciting and dramatic moments. Conrad Veidt, the "black death" and chief undercover killer for Cardinal Richelieu (Raymond Massey), is sent to corral an elusive duke and rebel. He weaves a romantic thread which eventually leads to the duke's capture. Veidt turns in one of his most polished portrayals.

UNDER THE VOLCANO
1984, 109 mins, US ⊙ ⊙
D: John Huston **A:** Albert Finney, Jacqueline Bisset, Anthony Andrews, Ignacio Lopez Tarzo, Katy Jurado, James Villiers (Ithaca-Conacine)

Story unfolds over a 24-hour period in November 1938 in the Mexican village of Cuernavaca, where the former British Consul, Geoffrey Firmin (Albert Finney), guilt-ridden over the past and abandoned by his wife, is drinking himself to death. It's a time of celebration, the Day of the Dead. Firmin returns home to discover that his wife, Yvonne (Jacqueline Bisset), has unexpectedly returned. The occasion provides only a momentary interval from hard liquor. Although this voyage into self-destruction won't be to the taste of many; there will be few unmoved by Finney's towering performance as the tragic Britisher.
1984: Nominations: Best Actor (Albert Finney), Original Score

UNDER THE YUM YUM TREE
1963, 110 mins, US
D: David Swift **A:** Jack Lemmon, Carol Lynley, Dean Jones, Edie Adams, Imogene Coca, Paul Lynde (Columbia)

Two young people in love (Carol Lynley and Dean Jones) agree to determine their "character compatibility" prior to marriage by living together platonically. The project is complicated by the intrusion of the lecherous landlord (Jack Lemmon) of their apartment building. The film's cardinal error is its lack of restraint. There is a tendency to embellish, out of all proportion, situations that, kept simple, would have served the comic purposes far more effectively. For Lemmon, the role of amorous landlord is a tour-de-farce, and he plays it to the hilt.

UNDER TWO FLAGS
1936, 111 mins, US
D: Frank Lloyd **A:** Ronald Colman, Claudette Colbert, Victor McLaglen, Rosalind Russell, Gregory Ratoff, Nigel Bruce (20th Century-Fox)

A pioneer saga of the Foreign Legion. Not the tempestuous Cigarette of the Theda Bara vintage when *Under Two Flags* was a highlight in that silent film vamp's career, Claudette Colbert nonetheless makes the somewhat bawdy cafe hostess stand up. Twixt her and Rosalind Russell as the English lady, Ronald Colman does all right as the romantic interest. Victor McLaglen turns in an expert chore as the scowling Major Doyle, jealous of Cigarette's two-timing. Highlight is the pitched battle between the marauding Arabs and the legionnaires defending the fort.

UNDERWATER!
1955, 98 mins, US ⊙ ⊙ ▭
D: John Sturges **A:** Jane Russell, Gilbert Roland, Richard Egan, Lori Nelson, Robert Keigh, Joseph Calleia (RKO)

Richard Egan and Gilbert Roland are diving for treasure aboard a sunken galleon. As Egan's wife, Jane Russell is a fetching sight, whether plumbing the depths or lounging comfortably aboard ship. The treasure-hunters are threatened by a Cuban shark fisherman (Joseph Calleia) and his crew. Once some unnecessary talk and extraneous sequences are out of the way, the pace tightens, and thrills are consistent. Film is RKO's first SuperScope release.

UNDERWORLD
1927, 75 mins, US ⊗
D: Josef von Sternberg **A:** George Bancroft, Clive Brook, Evelyn Brent, Larry Semon, Fred Kohler (Paramount)

Underworld evidently is a page out of Ben Hecht's underworld acquaintance with the Chicago Cicero and South Side gun mob. Hecht could have made *Underworld* a true biography of Cicero with the "alky" gun mob, but instead our hero is a jewelry store sampler. George Bancroft plays Bull Weed, a sympathetic crook.

Clive Brook as the regenerated drunkard and Evelyn Brent as Bancroft's girl complete the outstanding trio.

UNDERWORLD INFORMERS
See: The Informers

UNDERWORLD, U.S.A.
1961, 98 mins, US Ⓥ
D: Samuel Fuller **A:** Cliff Robertson, Dolores Dorn, Beatrice Kay, Paul Dubov, Richard Rust, Larry Gates (Globe/Columbia)

Underworld, U.S.A. is a slick gangster melodrama made to order for filmgoers who prefer their screen fare explosive and uncomplicated. The yarn concerns a supposedly decent but hate-motivated fellow (Cliff Robertson) who, as a youngster, witnessed the gangland slaying of his father by four budding racketeers. Director Samuel Fuller's screenplay has its lags, character superficialities, and unlikelihoods, but it is crisp with right-sounding gangster jargon and remains absorbing.

UNFAITHFULLY YOURS
1948, 105 mins, US Ⓥ ⊙
D: Preston Sturges **A:** Rex Harrison, Linda Darnell, Barbara Lawrence, Rudy Vallee, Lionel Stander, Edgar Kennedy (20th Century-Fox)

Unfaithfully Yours misses that stamp of originality which marked the scripting and direction of Preston Sturges's previous films. The yarn is too slight to carry its long running time. Sturges executes some amusing highjinks with serious music, but the humor is mild and unsustained. Rex Harrison plays a symphony orchestra leader, jealous of his beautiful wife (Linda Darnell). Three long revenge fantasies race through his brain while he batons his way through a concert, to music by Rossini, Wagner, and Tchaikovsky. Stylization of the fantasies would have given these sequences the comic energy that is lacking.

UNFAITHFULLY YOURS
1984, 96 mins, US Ⓥ ⊙
D: Howard Zieff **A:** Dudley Moore, Nastassja Kinski, Armand Assante, Albert Brooks, Cassie Yates, Richard Libertini (20th Century-Fox)

Unfaithfully Yours is a moderately amusing remake of Preston Sturges's wonderful comedy which was a commercial bust upon its release in 1948. Dudley Moore plays a big-time orchestra conductor with a much younger Italian screen star, Nastassja Kinski, as his bride. Moore

suspects her of fooling around with dashing violinist Armand Assante, and core of the film consists of a fantasy in which Moore murders his wife but makes it look as though Assante did it.

UNFAITHFUL WIFE
See: La Femme Infidele

UNFINISHED BUSINESS
1984, 99 mins, Canada
D: Don Owen **A:** Isabelle Mejias, Peter Spence, Leslie Toth, Peter Kastner, Julie Biggs, Chuck Shamata (Zebra Films/NFBC)

A high school senior (Isabelle Mejias), days away from her finals, finds diversions in dope, friends, a rock club, and anti-nuke activists. The clash between parental pressure and the seemingly more meaningful pursuits of the radicals sends her into the streets for a different kind of education. Although a common enough story, *Unfinished Business* has a raw energy which is touching and deeply felt.

UNFINISHED SYMPHONY, THE
1934, 90 mins, UK/Germany
D: Willy Forst, Anthony Asquith **A:** Helen Chandler, Marta Eggerth, Hans Jaray, Ronald Squire, Beryl Laverick, Brember Wills (Gaumont-British/UFA)

A thing of arresting beauty in pictorial and musical conception, *The Unfinished Symphony* should attract the musically appreciative, particularly those who love the melodies of Franz Schubert, which are brilliantly woven into the fine costume mosaic turned out by director Willy Forst. Story has been aptly cast, even if the players constitute a babel of dialects.

UNFORGETTABLE
1996, 116 mins, US Ⓥ ⊙
D: John Dahl **A:** Ray Liotta, Linda Fiorentino, Peter Coyote, Christopher McDonald, Kim Cattrall, Kim Coates (De Laurentiis/Spelling)

Unforgettable doesn't linger in the memory. Cult modern noir-meister John Dahl's yarn of a forensic scientist (Ray Liotta) obsessed with discovering his wife's murderer packs an explosive punch in its opening reels but becomes progressively less impressive as the twists and body count mount. The first few reels are stunners, but problems start to mount in the second and third acts as the movie simply settles into an off-beat whodunit. The movie is so plot-intensive that there's little room for real character development.

UNFORGIVEN, THE
1960, 125 mins, US ℗ ▱
D: John Huston **A:** Burt Lancaster, Audrey Hepburn, Audie Murphy, John Saxon, Charles Bickford, Lillian Gish (James/United Artists)

There are many aspects of *The Unforgiven* that elicit comparison with *Shane*. Audrey Hepburn gives a shining performance as the foundling daughter of a frontier family. The scene is the Texas panhandle immediately after the Civil War during a time of unbending hatred between the white settlers and the local Kiowa Indians. In the midst of this tension, it's discovered that Hepburn is actually a full-blooded Indian. The desire of the Indians to recover their own "blood," the resentment of the settlers in having an "enemy" in their midst, and the determination of the family to hold on to the girl provides the crux of the conflict.

UNFORGIVEN
1992, 130 mins, US ℗ ⊙ ▱
D: Clint Eastwood **A:** Clint Eastwood, Gene Hackman, Morgan Freeman, Richard Harris, Jaimz Woolvett, Saul Rubinek (Warner/Malpaso)

Unforgiven is a classic western for the ages. Clint Eastwood has crafted a tense, hard-edged, superbly dramatic yarn that is also an exceedingly intelligent meditation on the West, its myths, and its heroes. When a $1,000 reward is offered for the hides of two men who sliced up a prostitute in the town of Big Whiskey, ageing gunman Bill Munny (Eastwood) reluctantly straps on his holster for the first time in years. The town is ruled by Sheriff Little Bill Daggett (Gene Hackman), a brutal ex-badman who allows no one to carry guns. Resolution comes not in an expected, standard showdown, but much more complexly, in a series of alternately tragic and touching confrontations. Eastwood is outstanding in his best clipped, understated manner. Hackman deliciously realizes the two sides of the sheriff's quicksilver personality, the folksy raconteur and the vicious sadist.
1992: Best Picture, Director, Supp. Actor (Gene Hackman), Editing
Nominations: Best Actor (Clint Eastwood), Original Screenplay, Cinematography, Art Direction, Sound

UNHOLY ROLLERS, THE
1972, 88 mins, US ℗
D: Vernon Zimmerman **A:** Claudia Jennings, Louis Quinn, Betty Anne Rees, Roberta Collins, Alan Vint, Candice Roman (American International)

Unholy Rollers is a gander into the rough, tough world of women's roller derby. Yarn focuses on Claudia Jennings, who leaves her factory job to win a place on a roller derby team and almost immediately becomes its star by scorning the routinely planned phony action of opponents on the track and playing for real.

UNION CITY
1980, 87 mins, US ℗ ⊙
D: Mark Reichert **A:** Dennis Lipscomb, Deborah Harry, Irina Maleeva, Everett McGill, Sam McMurray, Pat Benatar (Kinesis)

While indie helmer Mark Reichert exploits the strangeness of his story very well, he fails to flesh out the short, one-actor sketch into a full-length feature. Pic concerns a paranoid businessman (Dennis Lipscomb), obsessed with catching the culprit who steals a drink out of his milk bottle every morning. He captures a young war vet vagrant (Sam McMurray) in the act and kills him. The Hitchcockian body removal footage provides fine black humor.

UNION DEPOT
1932, 66 mins, US
D: Alfred E. Green **A:** Douglas Fairbanks Jr., Joan Blondell, Guy Kibbee, Alan Hale, George Rosener, David Landau (First National)

An action melodrama set in a big bustling railway terminal. Chic (Douglas Fairbanks Jr.), a carefree knight of the road, finds the windfall of a forgotten handbag in a washroom, then falls for Ruth (Joan Blondell), a stranded chorus girl. Meanwhile, the police have been closing in on a counterfeiter gang. A few turns of fate and the spurious fortune is in Chic's hands, just as the police begin to close in.

UNION PACIFIC
1939, 133 mins, US ℗
D: Cecil B. DeMille **A:** Barbara Stanwyck, Joel McCrea, Akim Tamiroff, Robert Preston, Brian Donlevy, Anthony Quinn (Paramount)

A super western, with cowboys and Indians backgrounded by the epochal building of the Union Pacific. Henry Kolker is the banker menace who foments sabotage to favor the competitive Central Pacific. Joel McCrea comes on the scene as a trouble-shooter. Barbara Stanwyck sustains the femme interest as the railroad engineer's daughter.

1939: Nomination: Best Special Effects

UNION STATION
1950, 81 mins, US ⓥ
D: Rudolph Mate **A:** William Holden, Nancy Olson, Barry Fitzgerald, Lyle Bettger, Jan Sterling, Allene Roberts (Paramount)

Union Station is a melodrama set in a big city railway terminal. William Holden heads up the railway policing department. A passenger (Nancy Olson), secretary to a rich man and his blind daughter (Allene Roberts), reports two suspicious characters. Events prove that Roberts has been kidnapped and the terminal is to be used as the payoff location.

UNIVERSAL SOLDIER
1992, 104 mins, US ⓥ ⊠
D: Roland Emmerich **A:** Jean-Claude Van Damme, Dolph Lundgren, Ally Walker, Ed O'Ross, Jerry Orbach, Leon Rippy (Carolco/IndieProd)

The story feels like a late-night sci-fi movie patched together with a mix of elements from *RoboCop* and *The Terminator*, with a dash of Captain America comic books. A crazed Vietnam platoon leader (Dolph Lundgren) and his subordinate (Jean-Claude Van Damme), killed in Vietnam in 1969, pop up 23 years later as re-animated corpses, brought back by the Defense Department to act as an elite terrorism-fighting unit. But Van Damme begins to recover his memory, taking off accompanied by a pretty reporter (Ally Walker), with Lundgren—his mind still addled with 'Nam hysteria—and other brigade members in hot pursuit.

UNIVERSAL SOLDIER
THE RETURN
1999, 82 mins, US ⓥ ⊙
D: Mic Rodgers **A:** Jean-Claude Van Damme, Michael Jai White, Heidi Schanz, Xander Berkeley, Justin Lazard, Kiana Tom (Baumgarten Prophet/Tri-Star)

An underwhelming follow-up to one of Jean-Claude Van Damme's better efforts, *Return* picks up a few years later, reintroducing Luc Deveraux as a kinder, gentler, and more human hero. Deveraux and his employers at a Dallas research facility try to perfect a new breed of UniSol. The brain of the outfit is a super-duper computer: the Self-Evolving Thought Helix, aka SETH. Van Damme struggles mightily to inject a touch of soulfulness into his

macho-man heroics, but he ends up looking faintly ridiculous each time he gets all teary-eyed over a casualty. Vet stunt director Mic Rodgers places great emphasis on frenetic action and deafening explosions, but fails to instill a sense of urgency in the routine and occasionally incoherent goings-on.

UNKNOWN, THE
1927, 55 mins, US ⊗
D: Tod Browning **A:** Lon Chaney, Norman Kerry, Joan Crawford, Nick De Ruiz, John George, Frank Lanning (M-G-M)

A good Lon Chaney film that might have been great, concerning an armless fakir in a gypsy circus who loves the proprietor's daughter. The girl has come to detest all men for their constant pawing, hence the welcome companionship of Alonzo (Chaney). None of the circus troupe knows that Alonzo is physically normal, faking by strapping his arms to his sides.

UNKNOWN SOLDIER, THE
See: Tuntematon Sotilas

UNLAWFUL ENTRY
1992, 111 mins, US ⓥ ⊙
D: Jonathan Kaplan **A:** Kurt Russell, Ray Liotta, Madeleine Stowe, Roger E. Mosley, Ken Lerner, Deborah Offner (Largo)

After an intruder breaks into the L.A. home of attractive married couple Kurt Russell and Madeleine Stowe, the policemen (Ray Liotta and Roger E. Mosley) are the picture of helpfulness. But Liotta becomes excessively solicitous, coming on to Stowe in a quiet but insidious way, and will stop at nothing to get Russell out of the way and have Stowe for himself. Story might have achieved genuinely chilling dimensions, but Liotta being clearly off-base and demented from the beginning gets everyone off the hook.

UNMAN, WITTERING AND ZIGO
1971, 100 mins, US
D: John Mackenzie **A:** David Hemmings, Carolyn Seymour, Douglas Wilmer, Hamilton Dyce, Anthony Haygarth, Donald Gee (Mediarts)

Unman, Wittering, and Zigo are pupils at a British school for teenage boys, but Zigo is constantly marked absent, for reasons unexplained. The rest of the class make for a sinister lot, blatantly threatening their new teacher, David Hemmings, with the same kind of death that has befallen his predecessor. The viewer may be both intrigued and puzzled, for while the film is a compelling piece of drama about innocent-looking terrorists, it asks a great deal of credence.

UNMARRIED WOMAN, AN
1978, 124 mins, US ⊙
D: Paul Mazursky **A:** Jill Clayburgh, Alan Bates, Michael Murphy, Cliff Gorman, Pat Quinn, Kelly Bishop (20th Century-Fox)

Jill Clayburgh is torn between conflicting forces following the surprise confession of husband Michael Murphy that he has fallen in love with another woman. Daughter Lisa Lucas needs her mother's support as she herself is coming on to adolescent love; Clayburgh's girlfriends offer well-meaning advice; a blind date's pass falls flat; therapist Penelope Russianoff's probing strikes raw nerves. Finally, artist Alan Bates arrives in Clayburgh's life, and a thoughtful and deep attachment evolves.
1978: Nominations: Best Picture, Actress (Jill Clayburgh), Original Screenplay

LES UNS ET LES AUTRES (BOLERO)
1981, 184 mins, France ⊙
D: Claude Lelouch **A:** Robert Hossein, Nicole Garcia, Geraldine Chaplin, Jacques Villeret, James Caan, Evelyne Bouix (Films 13/TF1)

This surface album of criss-crossed destinies is heavy-footed, innocent, syrupy thumbnail history. There is a couple in Russia, one in Germany, one in France, and one in the US. It begins in 1936, and soon comes the war and all are, of course, embroiled. The Russian couple has the man die but she has a son; the German (Daniel Olbrychski), a conductor, loses his son; the French couple (Robert Hossein, Nicole Garcia) are deported to a concentration camp; and the Yank couple (James Caan, Geraldine Chaplin) are patterned on Glenn Miller and his wife. Caan brings swing to liberated Paris, but his wife dies in an accident. The German finds himself giving a concert in New York, where the house is empty. The Russian boy turns out to be Nureyev. Film is reportedly part of a French television miniseries. That may explain the many holes in the lives and growth of the many characters.

UNSINKABLE MOLLY BROWN, THE
1964, 128 mins, US ⊙ ⊙ ⊡
D: Charles Walters **A:** Debbie Reynolds, Harve Presnell, Ed Begley, Jack Kruschen, Hermione Baddeley, Martita Hunt (M-G-M)

The *Unsinkable Molly Brown* is a rowdy and sometimes rousing blend of song and sentiment. It relates the adventures of Molly Brown (Debbie Reynolds), a hillbilly heroine who rises from poverty to become one of the most celebrated women of her time. Shortly after her marriage to Leadville Johnny Brown (Harve Presnell), he strikes it rich, and the rest of the picture depicts her feverish efforts to cut the mustard with snooty Denver society. In essence, it's a pretty shallow story.
1964: Nominations: Best Actress (Debbie Reynolds), Color Cinematography, Color Costume Design, Color Art Direction, Adapted Music Score

UNSTRUNG HEROES
1995, 94 mins, US ⊙ ⊙
D: Diane Keaton **A:** Andie MacDowell, John Turturro, Michael Richards, Maury Chaykin, Nathan Watt, Kendra Krull (Hollywood)

A coming-of-age piece that is slight to the point of anemia, *Unstrung Heroes* sports a willful eccentricity that almost immediately becomes annoying. Set in middle-class Los Angeles in 1962, yarn focuses on 12-year-old Steven Lidz (Nathan Watt), a bright kid whose life at home becomes too much to take. After mom Selma (Andie MacDowell) becomes ill, Steven feels compelled to run away to the home of his seriously goofy uncles Danny (Michael Richards) and Arthur (Maury Chaykin). MacDowell floats through it all in a nearly blissful daze.
1995: Nomination: Original Musical or Comedy Score

UNSUITABLE JOB FOR A WOMAN, AN
1982, 94 mins, UK ⊙
D: Christopher Petit **A:** Pippa Guard, Billie Whitelaw, Paul Freeman, Dominic Guard, Dawn Archibald, David Horovitch (Boyd's/NFE)

Cordelia Gray (Pippa Guard), assistant to a shabby gumshoe, finds her boss dead, an apparent suicide. A posthumous tape asks her to take over. An intense woman (Billie Whitelaw) asks her to take on a case, the suicide of her boss's son. Gray is slowly fascinated by the dead boy. She gets thrown into a well but muddles through. Tale is handled from a distance by director Christopher Petit, robbing it of a more forceful narration, timing, and revelation.

UNSUSPECTED, THE
1947, 103 mins, US
D: Michael Curtiz **A:** Joan Caulfield, Claude Rains, Audrey Totter, Constance Bennett, Hurd Hatfield, Michael North (Warner)

Story deals with suave mayhem, with murderer Claude Rains known from the opening crime. Rains is radio narrator of murder mysteries who's not above making his stories actually true. An apparently suave, kindly soul, he's unsuspected in the death of his secretary, niece, and latter's husband. Rains pulls out all his thesping tricks to sustain the character, and makes it believable.

UNTAMED HEART
1993, 102 mins, US ⓥ ⊙
D: Tony Bill **A:** Christian Slater, Marisa Tomei, Rosie Perez, Kyle Secor, Willie Garson (M-G-M)

Appealing lead performances elevate this modestly scaled romantic tear-jerker. Marisa Tomei plays a Minneapolis waitress who is assaulted one night by two creeps, only to be rescued by Christian Slater, an introverted busboy enamored of her. An awkward and unlikely romance develops, Tomei slowly penetrating Slater's protective shell. The story sometimes seems like an excuse to get out the can opener and serve up the corn. But the performances prove so earnest that the movie largely works on its own terms.

UNTIL SEPTEMBER
1984, 95 mins, US ⓥ
D: Richard Marquand **A:** Karen Allen, Thierry Lhermitte, Christopher Cazenove, Marie Catherine-Conti, Hutton Cobb, Michael Mellinger (M-G-M/United Artists)

A young American woman (Karen Allen) is stranded in Paris when she becomes separated from a tour group and takes refuge in a modest hotel. Temporary setback is put aright when a suave banker (Thierry Lhermitte) checks on the woman's story for verification. It doesn't take much to guess that the two tenants are destined to hit it off romantically, and a fanciful, unconvincing "love-conquers-all" scenario emerges.

UNTIL THE END OF THE WORLD
1991, 158 mins, Germany/France/Australia ⓥ ⊙
D: Wim Wenders **A:** William Hurt, Solveig Dommartin, Sam Neill, Max von Sydow, Rudiger Vogler, Jeanne Moreau (Road Movies/Agos/Village Roadshow)

Until the End of the World is described by director Wim Wenders as "the ultimate road movie." The production was intended to shoot in 17 countries, but budget limitations forced a cutback to nine nations. Narration by Sam Neill wallpapers the gaps in the globetrotting of William Hurt, Solveig Dommartin, and other actors. Set in 1999, script presents a world threatened by a nuclear satellite careening toward Earth. Party girl Claire Tourneur (Dommartin) is given stolen money by bank robbers and picks up a stranger, Trevor McPhee (Hurt), while transporting the loot to Paris. Pursuing Trevor to Lisbon, Claire gets him into bed, but he takes off again. One step behind him to Berlin, Moscow, China, and Japan, Claire finally wins Trevor's trust. Detouring to San Francisco, pic comes to a rest in Australia's outback. The grand emotion needed to carry the two lovers around the world isn't apparent. Pair strike no sparks, and Hurt seems blank most of the time.

UNTOUCHABLES, THE
1987, 119 mins, US ⓥ ⊙ ▭
D: Brian De Palma **A:** Kevin Costner, Sean Connery, Charles Martin Smith, Andy Garcia, Robert De Niro, Richard Bradford (Linson/Paramount)

The Untouchables is a beautifully crafted portrait of Prohibition-era Chicago. Robert De Niro's Al Capone professes to be just "a businessman" giving people the product they want. This is prelude to arrival of idealistic law enforcer Eliot Ness (Kevin Costner). A dichotomy of values is thus established between these two adversaries, but it is the introduction of street cop Jim Malone (Sean Connery) that truly gives the film its momentum. Connery delivers one of his finest performances, filled with nuance, humor, and abundant self-confidence. De Palma has brought his sure and skilled hand to a worthy enterprise.
1987: Best Supp. Actor (Sean Connery)
Nominations: Best Costume Design, Art Direction, Original Music Score

UNVANQUISHED, THE
See: Aparajito

UP!
1976, 80 mins, US
D: Russ Meyer **A:** Robert McLane, Edward Schaaf, Mary Gavin, Elaine Collins, Su Ling, Janet Wood (RHM)

Director Russ Meyer habitually casts the most incredibly endowed actresses who bounce and jiggle through a primitive world, driving men to violence and murder. The men are rarely a match for the women. The violence, like much of the sex, is too outrageous to be believable. At one point, an axe is buried in a man's back, but he pulls it out and buries it in his attacker's chest who then pulls it out and finishes the job with a buzzsaw to the groin. Fun stuff.

UP CLOSE AND PERSONAL
1996, 124 mins, US Ⓥ ⊚
D: Jon Avnet **A:** Robert Redford, Michelle Pfeiffer, Stockard Channing, Joe Mantegna, Kate Nelligan, Glenn Plummer (Touchstone)

Up Close and Personal is *A Star is Born* meets *The Way We Were,* loosely based on writer Alanna Nash's Jessica Savitch bio, *Golden Girl.* Sally Atwater (Michelle Pfeiffer) is fresh out of Reno and has landed a television job in Miami. Her debut's a catastrophe, but her boss Warren Justice (Robert Redford) takes her under his wing, and she begins to improve. Director Jon Avnet does a fair job of substituting pace and scenery for logic. This piece of recycled goods isn't nearly as accomplished as its inspiration.

UP IN ARMS
1944, 100 mins, US Ⓥ
D: Elliott Nugent **A:** Danny Kaye, Dinah Shore, Dana Andrews, Constance Dowling, Louis Calhern, Elisha Cook Jr. (RKO/Goldwyn)

Up in Arms is a filmusical expertly showcasing the comedic talents of Danny Kaye in his first film. Kaye is a wacky hypochondriac who's inducted by the army for a series of wild misadventures. He's a reticent suitor for Constance Dowling, while Dinah Shore has designs on snagging Kaye, and Dana Andrews is in love with Dowling. The girls enlist as army nurses. On transport to the South Pacific, quartet are thrown together, with main ship-board routine being a wild chase. Kaye has a great sense of timing and smartly delivers three song specialities.

UP IN SMOKE
1978, 86 mins, US Ⓥ ⊚
D: Lou Adler **A:** Cheech Marin, Tommy Chong, Stacy Keach, Edie Adams, Tom Skerritt, Strother Martin (Paramount)

Up in Smoke is essentially a drawn-out version of the drug-oriented comedy routines of Tommy Chong and Cheech Marin. Hippie rich kid Chong teams up with barrio boy Cheech in search for some pot to puff on to aid them in putting together a rock band. Pursuit takes them to Tijuana, where they end up driving back a van constructed out of treated marijuana. In diligent pursuit is narcotics detective Stacy Keach, saddled with the usual crew of incompetent assistants. Once the more obvious drug jokes are exhausted, director Lou Adler lets the film degenerate into a mixture of fitful slapstick and toilet humor.

UP THE DOWN STAIRCASE
1967, 120 mins, US Ⓥ
D: Robert Mulligan **A:** Sandy Dennis, Patrick Bedford, Eileen Heckart, Ruth White, Jean Stapleton (Warner)

Up the Down Staircase concerns troubles of a beginning teacher in a tough city high school. And it is very good, almost in spite of itself. Director Robert Mulligan has for the most part avoided sentimentalism and presents his story honestly and directly. As pretty young Miss Barrett, fresh from college training as an English teacher, Sandy Dennis is plopped into a multi-racial institution where most of the teachers feel they are successful if they manage to keep their classrooms fairly civilized. Though many of the characters are familiar stock ones, their treatment is generally successful.

UP THE JUNCTION
1968, 119 mins, UK
D: Peter Collinson **A:** Suzy Kendall, Dennis Waterman, Adrienne Posta, Maureen Lipman, Michael Gothard, Alfie Bass (British Home Entertainment)

Up the Junction concerns an affluent girl (Suzy Kendall) who goes to live in a seedy area of London. There she works in a factory and falls for a good-looking van driver. The irony is that the boy wants the lush life she's left behind, and she is quite unsympathetic, feeling that underprivileged life is more real. The treatment introduces an air of patronage, a condescending class-conscious view of the British working classes.

UP THE RIVER
1930, 90 mins, US
D: John Ford **A:** Spencer Tracy, Claire Luce, Warren Hymer, Humphrey Bogart, William Collier Sr., Joan Lawes (Fox)

A comedy prison picture. Funny idea has two escaped prisoners returning of their own volition just in time to save the big ball game against an opposition jail. This is Tracy's first talker, and he easily makes the grade. Humphrey Bogart and Claire Luce are also in the prison, but really don't belong.

UP THE SANDBOX
1972, 97 mins, US ♥
D: Irvin Kershner **A:** Barbra Streisand, David Selby, Jane Hoffman, John C. Becher, Jacobo Morales, Iris Brooks (First Artists)

Forget the euphemisms, *Up the Sandbox* is an overproduced, heavy-handed fantasy concerning a married woman's identity crisis. Barbra Streisand, married to professor David Selby, is harried by two children and fears the effect of accommodating the birth of a third child. Had Streisand been working off some old contractual commitment, there would be much sympathy. But the star is the producer.

UPTOWN SATURDAY NIGHT
1974, 104 mins, US ♥
D: Sidney Poitier **A:** Sidney Poitier, Bill Cosby, Harry Belafonte, Flip Wilson, Richard Pryor, Rosalind Cash (First Artists)

Uptown Saturday Night is an uneven black melodramatic comedy. Its assets include an unwavering ragamuffin charm and some amusing bits. Its debits stem from a helter-skelter screenplay and Sidney Poitier's lifeless performance and unimaginative comic direction. Factory worker Poitier and cab driver Cosby visit an after-hours gambling club, where the customers are held up by thieves. When Poitier realizes that a $50,000 winning lottery ticket was in his stolen wallet, he and Cosby decide to track down the hold-up men.

UPTURNED GLASS, THE
1947, 86 mins, UK
D: Lawrence Huntington **A:** James Mason, Rosamund John, Pamela Kellino, Jane Hylton, Ann Stephens, Henry Oscar (Sydney Box)

Michael, a brilliant young surgeon (James Mason), falls in love with Emma (Rosamund John), whose child he has saved from blindness. But Emma decides she cannot shirk her responsibilities to her husband, and she and Michael agree to say good-bye. Then Michael learns that Emma is dead, having fallen from a high window in her country house, and he realizes that Emma was killed by her jealous, widowed sister-in-law, Kate (Pamela Kellino). He decides to murder Kate, begins an affair with her instead, and eventually murders

her in a similar manner, throwing her from a window.

URBAN COWBOY
1980, 135 mins, US ♥ ⊙ ▭
D: James Bridges **A:** John Travolta, Debra Winger, Scott Glenn, Madolyn Smith, Barry Corbin, Bonnie Raitt (Paramount)

Director James Bridges has ably captured the atmosphere of Gilley's Club on the outskirts of Houston. John Travolta, fresh from a west Texas farm and working his first job in an oil refinery, quickly learns that Gilley's is where everybody heads after work. Debra Winger is outstanding as a fetching little slut who marries Travolta. In one way or another, the story revolves around Gilley's mechanical bucking bull, a menacing device that tests the courage of all the would-be cowboys.

USED CARS
1980, 113 mins, US ♥ ⊙
D: Robert Zemeckis **A:** Kurt Russell, Jack Warden, Frank McRae, Gerrit Graham, Deborah Harmon, Joseph P. Flaherty (Columbia)

A great idea on paper has been tackled by filmmakers who haven't expanded it much beyond the one joke inherent in the premise. Fat cat car dealer Jack Warden is desperate to knock out competition provided by a brother (also Warden). Latter dies but operator Kurt Russell and his partners disguise that to prevent their slimy neighbor from inheriting the property. Robert Zemeckis directs with vigor, if insufficient control and discipline.

USED PEOPLE
1992, 115 mins, US ♥ ⊙
D: Beeban Kidron **A:** Shirley MacLaine, Kathy Bates, Jessica Tandy, Marcello Mastroianni, Marcia Gay Harden, Sylvia Sidney (Largo/20th Century-Fox)

Set in 1969 in the New York borough of Queens, film limns the colorful family life of a Jewish matriarchy: newly widowed Shirley MacLaine, her protective mom (Jessica Tandy), dysfunctional, divorced children (Kathy Bates and Marcia Gay Harden) and Tandy's best friend (Sylvia Sidney). Enter Marcello Mastroianni, MacLaine's secret admirer, who now makes his platonic affections for her manifest. There is some effective comedy in the middle reels but film is built around highly dramatic confrontation scenes. Mastroianni has his best English-language role by far.

U.S. MARSHALS

1998, 133 mins, US ⓥ ⊙ ▭
D: Stuart Baird **A:** Tommy Lee Jones, Wesley Snipes, Robert Downey Jr., Kate Nelligan, Joe Pantoliano, Irene Jacob (Kopelson-Barish/Warner)

U.S. Marshals is a disappointing sequel to the 1993 *The Fugitive*. Stuart Baird's new thriller is inferior to the Andrew Davis movie in every respect: script, acting, rhythm and even tech credits. Tommy Lee Jones reprises his Oscar-winning role as Chief Deputy Marshal Sam Gerard, a dogged pursuer who this time around is chasing the ruthless Sheridan (Wesley Snipes), accused of murdering two top agents. Gerard's elite law enforcement crew is newly joined by Cooper (Latanya Richardson), a black female, and John Royce (Robert Downey Jr.), a cocky special agent who's not completely trustworthy. Not much info is provided about Sheridan, who remains enigmatic throughout the film. An hour into the movie almost everything is disclosed, which means the story has nowhere to go.

U.S.S. TEAKETTLE

1951, 92 mins, US
D: Henry Hathaway **A:** Gary Cooper, Jane Greer, Millard Mitchell, Eddie Albert, John McIntire, Ray Collins (20th Century-Fox)

Gary Cooper is assigned to a craft to conduct trials with an experimental steam engine simply because he studied engineering in college, not because of any nautical knowledge. Crew of the craft, with the exception of Navy vet Millard Mitchell, is in the landlubber class. String of incidents developed around the situation are run off smartly and help to disguise that there's practically no plot.

USUAL SUSPECTS, THE

1995, 105 mins, US ⓥ ⊙ ▭
D: Bryan Singer **A:** Stephen Baldwin, Gabriel Byrne, Chazz Palminteri, Kevin Pollak, Pete Postlethwaite, Kevin Spacey (Blue Parrot/Bad Hat Harry/PFE/Spelling)

The Usual Suspects is an ironic, bang-up thriller about the wages of crime, an absorbingly complicated yarn spun in seductively slick fashion by director Bryan Singer. The pleasures begin from the opening moments, with a huge fire dockside in San Pedro. Pic then jumps back six weeks. A highjacking in New York results in a police round-up of suspects, who include corrupt cop-turned-thief Keaton (Byrne), the hot-headed McManus (Stephen Baldwin), the impudent Hockney (Kevin Pollak), the unpredictable Latin Fenster (Benicio Del Toro) and a crippled squealer appropriately named Verbal (Kevin Spacey). Christopher McQuarrie's ingeniously structured script then begins cutting back and forth between Gotham and the events leading up to the ship-board inferno.

1995: Best Supp. Actor (Kevin Spacey), Original Score
Nomination: Best Original Screenplay

UTU

1983, 120 mins, New Zealand ⓥ
D: Geoff Murphy **A:** Anzac Wallace, Bruno Lawrence, Kelly Johnson, Wi Kuki Kaa, Tim Elliott, Ilona Rodgers (Glitteron)

A New Zealand western. Geoff Murphy has fashioned a fast-moving visual tale of archetypal passion and action. "Utu" is the Maori word for "revenge." Central figure is rebel leader Te Wheke (Anzac Wallace) during the wars between European settlers and the native Maoris in the late 19th century. At first sympathetic to the European cause, Te Wheke turns guerrilla when his village is wiped out by British soldiers protecting the settlers. As his actions become more despotic and cruel, he is hunted, captured, and finally shot.

U-TURN

1997, 125 mins, US ⓥ ⊙
D: Oliver Stone **A:** Sean Penn, Nick Nolte, Jennifer Lopez, Powers Boothe, Claire Danes, Jon Voight (Illusion/Phoenix/TriStar)

A sun-baked film noir in the style of a demented fever dream, *U-Turn* lives almost as dangerously as its wild characters—and gets away with it. Exceedingly raw, imaginative, daring and energized, this rare straight genre exercise by Oliver Stone is loaded with twisted motives, brazen amorality, double dealing, incestuous relationships, subversive intent and hilarious surreal asides. Two-bit criminal Bobby Cooper (Sean Penn) lands in godforsaken Superior, AZ, with an overheated engine. Downtown, Bobby picks up Grace (Jennifer Lopez), a looker who invites the drifter home. Enter Grace's gruff husband, Jake (Nick Nolte), who kicks him out. Moments later, however, Jake picks Bobby up on the road and asks him if he'd care to murder his wife for a price. Pic could easily be mistaken for the work of an adventurous artist making his first or second film. Few directors with as many films under their belt are displaying this kind of stylistic urgency. In addition, there are enormous pleasures to be taken from the performances.

U2 RATTLE AND HUM
1988, 99 mins, US Ⓥ
D: Phil Joanou (Midnight)

Visionary Irish rock band U2 has not sold itself short with this cinematic treatment of the band's music and concerns, infused with a striking visual style and electric momentum. Film follows the band through the landscape of American roots music, encountering street musicians in Harlem, collaborating with a gospel choir, performing with bluesmaster B. B. King, and recording "Angel of Harlem," a poignant remembrance of Billie Holiday at Sun Studios in Memphis. Director Phil Joanou films mostly in black and white, save one color concert sequence where he uses a startling mixture of silhouette and shadow.

V

ther's mysterious death at Auschwitz, and the sinister presence of their mother's second husband, Gilardini (Renzo Ricci). Ambiguity prevails in many of Visconti's situations, and while this may irk some, it does confer an air of mystery and suspense on a feature that might otherwise be merely morbid.

LES VACANCES DE MONSIEUR HULOT
(MR. HULOT'S HOLIDAY)
1953, 90 mins, France ⓥ ⊙
D: Jacques Tati **A:** Jacques Tati, Nathalie Pascaud, Louis Perrault, Michele Rolla, Andre Dubois, Valentine Camax (Cady/Discina/Eclair Journal)

Jacques Tati, whose comic talents were revealed in *Jour de Fete*, confirms them in his second pic, with fine observation of types at a vacation resort. Tati builds his gags with sureness, and clever timing and pantomime bring most of them off. Tati is the semi-articulate, blundering, but well-meaning clown. Whether he is being chased by dogs, setting off a cabin full of fireworks, or blundering into a staid funeral, he is a very funny man.

VAGABOND KING, THE
1930, 100 mins, US
D: Ludwig Berger **A:** Dennis King, Jeanette MacDonald, O. P. Heggie, Lillian Roth, Warner Oland (Paramount)

This ornate operetta is founded upon "If I Were King," a story which has been done three or four times earlier in pictures. This time the protagonist is Englishman Dennis King. *The Vagabond King,* as an operetta, regards itself as a melodrama. Touches of grim realism are sapped of their power by girls in tights as pages in the royal court and dwarfs turning cartwheels. Lillian Roth has neither the necessary age nor emotional maturity to play the passionate Huguette.

1929/30: Nomination: Best Art Direction

VAGHE STELLE DELL'ORSA
(SANDRA; OF A THOUSAND DELIGHTS)
1965, 95 mins, Italy
D: Luchino Visconti **A:** Claudia Cardinale, Michael Craig, Jean Sorel, Marie Bell, Renzo Ricci, Fred Williams (Vides)

An admitted steal from Electra, Luchino Visconti's modernized story is set in a small Italian town where Sandra (Claudia Cardinale) brings her new husband, Andrew (Michael Craig), for a visit to the family. Family's disintegration emerges in rapid strokes, via a love affair between Sandra and her brother, Gianni (Jean Sorel), their mother's near-insanity, their fa-

VALACHI PAPERS, THE
1972, 123 mins, Italy ⓥ
D: Terence Young **A:** Charles Bronson, Lino Ventura, Jill Ireland, Walter Chiari, Joseph Wiseman, Gerald S. O'Loughlin (Columbia/De Laurentiis)

The Valachi Papers, based upon the revelations of the mobster who disclosed details of Cosa Nostra organized crime in the US, is a hard-hitting, violence-ridden documented melodrama of the underworld covering more than three decades. Flashback technique is utilized as Charles Bronson, as Valachi, recounts to a Federal agent the innermost secrets of the mob, of which he was a constant but unimportant soldier.

VALAHOL EUROPABAN
(SOMEWHERE IN EUROPE)
1948, 85 mins, Hungary
D: Geza Radvanyi **A:** Arthur Somlay, Miklos Gabor, Zsuzsa Banki, Gyorgy Bardi, Laszlo Horvath, Laszlo Kemeny (Mafirt)

Geza Radvanyi, the director who made many films in Italy during the war, has touched with great skill and ability on one of the most important problems of Europe—children who were lost in the welter of World War II. Story shows children of various origins forced to roam the highways. They form a gang and are forced to rob for food. Kids find a ruined castle and decide to live there. However, it's not deserted as they thought; an elderly pianist living there too wants to escape from the world into this asylum. The artist begins to lead them back to the right way.

VALDEZ IS COMING
1971, 90 mins, US ⓥ
D: Edwin Sherin **A:** Burt Lancaster, Susan Clark, Jon Cypher, Barton Heyman, Richard Jordan, Hector Elizondo (United Artists)

Valdez Is Coming is a sluggish meller starring Burt Lancaster. Story collapses due to the uninspired premise of a man attempting to right a wrong and reels of boring mayhem. An ethnic southwestern constable (Lancaster) accidentally kills suspected murderer Lex Monson, who has been cornered by Jon Cypher, who also happens to have stolen away Susan Clark, wife of the man Monson is accused of having killed. Cypher has Lancaster brutally beaten. Latter's vengeance comprises the main thrust of the story.

VALENTINO
1951, 103 mins, US
D: Lewis Allen **A:** Anthony Dexter, Eleanor Parker, Richard Carlson, Patricia Medina, Joseph Calleia, Lloyd Gough (Small/Columbia)

Valentino is a full-blown romantic drama that makes little pretense of accurately biographing the screen star's life. Anthony Dexter bears a remarkable resemblance to the man he impersonates. The story gets underway with a meeting between Dexter and Eleanor Parker on board a ship to New York from Naples. Parker is a film star traveling incognito, and Dexter is a member of a dance troupe. In the big city, Dexter has a period of dishwashing and gigoloing before he again finds Parker and gets his first taste of film work. He goes to Hollywood and works as an extra until winning the gaucho role in *Four Horsemen of the Apocalypse*, the part that skyrocketed Valentino to fame. Parker brings to her role a quiet warmth and quality that helps make Dexter look better than he actually is.

VALENTINO
1977, 132 mins, UK Ⓥ
D: Ken Russell **A:** Rudolf Nureyev, Leslie Caron, Michelle Phillips, Carol Kane, Felicity Kendal, Seymour Cassel (United Artists)

Director Ken Russell seems less interested in nostalgia and early Hollywood than in trying to find the essence of a certain charisma of a world sex symbol. Casting of ballet dancer Rudolf Nureyev as Valentino works despite the elimination of the Latino darkness and smoldering looks. Using him also excuses the film a slavish need to hue to Valentino's factual life. Yet Russell has now and then opted for the lyric, even the outrageous.

VALERIE
1957, 81 mins, US
D: Gerd Oswald **A:** Sterling Hayden, Anita Ekberg, Anthony Steel, Peter Walker (United Artists)

Tale, briskly and imaginatively directed by Gerd Oswald, is set in the west but is by no means a western. Rather, it is a gothic and somber psychological tale that repeats the same theme three times, each time from the viewpoint of a different character. Sterling Hayden and his henchmen wipe out the family of his estranged wife (Anita Ekberg) and seriously wound her. At the trial, sympathy is on his side, since Ekberg was supposedly running away with handsome preacher Anthony Steel. But Steel's testimony relates that he was helping an ill and neglected parishioner by taking her to her parents. Ekberg, supposedly near death, regains consciousness and gives her testimony.

VALLEY GIRL
1983, 95 mins, US Ⓥ ⊙
D: Martha Coolidge **A:** Nicolas Cage, Deborah Foreman, Elizabeth Daily, Michelle Meyrink, Colleen Camp, Frederic Forrest (Valley 9000/Atlantic)

Valley Girl is very good simply because director Martha Coolidge obviously cares about her two lead characters and is privileged to have a couple of fine young performers—Nicolas Cage and Deborah Foreman—to make the audience care. She's a definitive valley girl. He's a Hollywood punker who normally wouldn't venture over the hills into the square valley, except to crash a party where they meet. Their blazing romance ultimately becomes too socially threatening for Foreman, and she cuts it off.

VALLEY OF DECISION, THE
1945, 118 mins, US
D: Tay Garnett **A:** Greer Garson, Gregory Peck, Donald Crisp, Lionel Barrymore, Preston Foster, Dan Duryea (M-G-M)

Plot picks up the Scott clan, a Pittsburgh pioneer steel family, at the time Irish Mary Rafferty (Greer Garson) comes to join it as a maid. The tale of unfulfilled love between the servant girl and young Paul Scott (Gregory Peck), one of the family's sons, is movingly dealt with.

VALLEY OF THE DOLLS
1967, 123 mins, US Ⓥ ⊙ ▭
D: Mark Robson **A:** Barbara Parkins, Patty Duke, Paul Burke, Sharon Tate, Tony Scotti, Susan Hayward (20th Century-Fox/Red Lion)

Plot meanders between New England country girl Barbara Parkins, who comes to the big city and is eventually seduced by urban social patterns; Patty Duke, rising young singing star who gets hung up on pills; and Sharon Tate, playing a big-breasted, untalented, but basically sensitive girl who never finds happiness. Main body of the story concerns the rise, plateau, and erratic performance of Duke's character.

1967: Nomination: Best Adapted Music Score

VALLEY OF THE KINGS
1954, 85 mins, US

D: Robert Pirosh **A:** Robert Taylor, Eleanor Parker, Carlos Thompson, Samia Gamal, Kurt Kasznar, Victor Jory (M-G-M)

Spectators are given a tour of the land of the Nile in this suspense drama, and the backgrounds offer more freshness to the film than does the routine story, which deals with robbers of the tombs of the pharaohs. Robert Taylor plays a rugged American archaeologist who agrees to help Eleanor Parker search for the tomb of Pharaoh Ra-hotep. A mysterious gang headed by sinister Kurt Kasznar puts obstacles in the way of the search. Plot period is 1900, and ageless wonders of the land of the Nile fit perfectly.

VALMONT
1989, 137 mins, France/UK ⓥ ⊙ ▭

D: Milos Forman **A:** Colin Firth, Annette Bening, Meg Tilly, Fairuza Balk, Sian Phillips, Fabia Drake (Renn/Burrill)

Milos Forman's meticulously produced *Valmont* is an extremely well-acted period piece that suffers from stately pacing and lack of dramatic high points. Basic story revolves around a bet by two 18th-century French aristocrats, Valmont (Colin Firth) and his old flame Marquise de Merteuil (Annette Bening). She wants Valmont to seduce 15-year-old Cecile (Fairuza Balk) to cuckold Cecile's fiancé, Gercourt (Jeffrey Jones), who is Merteuil's unfaithful lover. What keeps the film interesting, if not riveting, is the generally on-target casting.

LES VALSEUSES
(GOING PLACES; MAKING IT)
1974, 118 mins, France ⓥ ⊙

D: Bertrand Blier **A:** Gerard Depardieu, Miou-Miou, Patrick Dewaere, Jeanne Moreau, Jacques Chailleux, Isabelle Huppert (CAPAC/UPF/Prodis)

A rather raunchy tale of two drifters in their twenties who live off the land, women, and small-time extortion and theft. The jovial and sometimes menacing duo are first seen terrorizing a middle-aged woman and running off with her bag. They take a joy ride in a car. The owner

has a gun, but they manage to escape with his girl, who becomes part of their group. An older woman, played with a mixture of weariness and gusto by Jeanne Moreau, has an interlude with the two. Director Bertrand Blier shows a sure hand, brio, and an anarchic bounce.

VAMP
1986, 94 mins, US ⓥ ⊙

D: Richard Wenk **A:** Chris Makepeace, Sandy Baron, Robert Rusler, Dedee Pfeiffer, Gedde Watanabe, Grace Jones (New World)

Vamp is an extremely imaginative horror film styled as jet-black comedy. Film opens deceptively with the format of a teenage sex comedy. Two fraternity pledges (Chris Makepeace and Robert Rusler) agree to find a stripper for a frat party. They team up with a friend (Gedde Watanabe) who has a car. Upon arrival in the big city, their car skids and bright daylight suddenly turns to spooky night-time. Trio heads for the After Dark Club, which turns out to be a den of vampires.

VAMPIRA
(OLD DRACULA)
1975, 89 mins, UK ⓥ

D: Clive Donner **A:** David Niven, Teresa Groves, Peter Bayliss, Jennie Linden, Nicky Henson, Linda Hayden (World)

David Niven goes the way of Vincent Price in *Vampira*. His present day Dracula reads *Playboy,* sleeps in an automated coffin, and gives tours of his castle as a means of luring fresh victims. All of this might have made a good high-comedy satire if the dialogue were sharper and if the plot didn't revolve around Niven's attempts to revive his long-dead mate Vampira, played witlessly by Teresa Graves.

VAMPIRE IN BROOKLYN
1995, 101 mins, US ⓥ ⊙

D: Wes Craven **A:** Eddie Murphy, Angela Bassett, Allen Payne, Kadeem Hardison, John Witherspoon, Zakes Mokae (Paramount)

Striking a good balance between horror and comedy, this contemporized vampire tale flits along in entertaining fashion before making like a ghoul and falling apart at the end. Maximillian (Eddie Murphy) is the last of a breed of Caribbean vampires, descending on Brooklyn in search of a half-human, half-vampire woman who's unaware of her lineage to be his bride. Rita (Angela Bassett) and her partner Justice (Allen Payne) are cops investigating the murder spree Maximillian has caused, with furtive romantic interest between the two partners complicated by Rita's attraction to Maximillian.

VAMPIRE LOVERS, THE
1970, 91 mins, UK/US ✇
D: Roy Ward Baker **A:** Ingrid Pitt, George Cole, Kate O'Mara, Peter Cushing, Ferdy Mayne, Dawn Addams (Hammer/American International)

The vampire anti-heroine, played by Ingrid Pitt, has distinct lesbian tendencies. She prefers sinking her fangs into the bosoms of comely young women, though when required she's not averse to giving the works to an interfering local doctor and a manservant. Not much of a story, but the screenplay has all the needed ingredients. Fairly flat dialogue doesn't provide much of the unconscious humor that usually gives a lift to this type of entertainment.

VAMPIRES
(AKA: JOHN CARPENTER'S VAMPIRES)
1998, 104 mins, US ✇ ⊙ ⌑
D: John Carpenter **A:** James Woods, Daniel Baldwin, Sheryl Lee, Thomas Ian Griffith, Tim Guinee, Maximilian Schell (Storm King/Largo/Film Office)

The pleasures are modest but consistent in *Vampires,* a part-western, part-horror flick that doesn't aim too high but nails the range it occupies. In New Mexico, Jack Crow (James Woods) and his team of specially equipped mercenaries attack a vampire "nest." Master vampire Valek (Thomas Ian Griffith, who is very tall and very Gothic) breaks up the party along with the chests and spines of most of the revelers. The only ones to get out alive are Jack, his buddy Montoya (Daniel Baldwin) and Katrina (Sheryl Lee), a hooker Valek has already bitten. *Vampires* taps into an appealing mix of anti-clerical sentiment, unsentimental rebel codes and gung-ho gouging and splattering. Unlike garlic, Carpenter's humor-leavened handling of evil doesn't leave a bad taste in the mouth. Woods is a laconic delight.

VAMPIRE'S KISS
1988, 103 mins, US ✇ ⊙
D: Robert Bierman **A:** Nicolas Cage, Maria Conchita Alonso, Jennifer Beals, Elizabeth Ashley, Kasi Lemmons, Bob Lujan (Magellan)

Nicolas Cage is a New York literary agent who works hard and plays hard. One night his latest pickup (Jennifer Beals) exposes her fangs. She keeps him alive so that she may continue to feed. As a result, he starts getting the urge for blood himself. The film then takes a major U-turn, suddenly getting deadly serious as it appears that Loew is not turning into a vampire at all but is becoming a full-blown psychotic. Latter portion of the film shows him raping, murdering, and pleading with people to kill him.

VAN, THE
1996, 105 mins, UK ✇
D: Stephen Frears **A:** Colm Meaney, Donal O'Kelly, Ger Ryan, Caroline Rothwell, Neili Conroy, Ruaidhri Conroy (Deadly/BBC)

The Van is set in the now-familiar suburbs of North Dublin, as seen from the perspective of author Roddy Doyle. Unfortunately, the new film turns out to be a minor affair that tries hard but fails to recapture the wild humor of earlier outings. Larry (Colm Meaney) has become used to being on welfare; best friend Bimbo (Donal O'Kelly) has, until now, held down a job in a bakery. The discovery of an abandoned fast-food van spurs Bimbo to a bold idea: if he and Larry can refurbish the van, they can cook fish and chips, hamburgers, and other delights for sporting crowds. There are plenty of amusing moments in *The Van,* but ultimately the jokes remain anecdotal and don't build into a satisfying narrative. Meaney and O'Kelly give robust, larger-than-life performances, but they have an unfortunate tendency to shout at one another.

IL VANGELO SECONDO MATTEO
(THE GOSPEL ACCORDING TO ST. MATTHEW)
1964, 142 mins, Italy/France ✇ ⊙
D: Pier Paolo Pasolini **A:** Enrique Irazoqui, Margherita Caruso, Susanna Pasolini, Marcello Morante, Mario Socrate, Otello Sestili (Arco/Lux)

Offbeat, almost neo-realistic film version of the St. Matthew Gospel. Pier Paolo Pasolini has made a pic poles apart from the many which have told the story of Christ—though remaining faithful in its development and spoken text. Pic was filmed in southern Italy, and the faces are deliberately those of Italians. Thesps are all non-actors, and Enrique Irazoqui is a find as the man who plays Christ. Faces have the craggy, unglamorous, rugged look of the working man or peasant. Lensing by Tonino Delli Colli is fine, its grey tone giving it a timelessness in keeping with Pasolini's choice of bleakly beautiful settings.

VANISHING, THE
1993, 110 mins, US ⓥ ⊙
D: George Sluizer **A:** Jeff Bridges, Kiefer Sutherland, Nancy Travis, Sandra Bullock, Maggie Linderman, Lisa Eichhorn (20th Century-Fox)

Dutch director George Sluizer had the rare chance to remake his own 1988 *Spoorloos* in America. Unfortunately, this version is schematic and unconvincing. Film introduces Jeff Bridges as the villain at the outset, a happily married school teacher with a Nietzschean complex. Parallel story has Kiefer Sutherland and g.f. Sandra Bullock on vacation from Seattle. She suddenly disappears from a rest stop. Sutherland goes crazy looking for her. Fade out to three years later and Sutherland's obsession with finding her has continued. The chilling climax of the original is repeated in the remake, but with very little impact. Unlike the subtle acting of Bernard-Pierre Donnadieu in the original, Bridges adopts an odd gait, curious manner, and an on-and-off accent that spoil his performance.

VANISHING POINT
1971, 107 mins, US ⓥ ⊙
D: Richard C. Sarafian **A:** Barry Newman, Cleavon Little, Charlotte Rampling, Dean Jagger, Victoria Medlin, Paul Koslo (Cupid)

According to this lackluster action effort, the "wasteland" between Denver and the California border is peopled only with uniformed monsters, aided and abetted by an antagonistic citizenry with the only "good" people being a few hippies, motorcycle gangs, and dope pushers. The action is almost entirely made up of one man driving a car at maximum speed from Denver to San Francisco against various odds, from the police who try to intercept him to the oddball individuals he meets along the way.

VANYA ON 42ND STREET
1994, 119 mins, US ⓥ ⊙
D: Louis Malle **A:** Wallace Shawn, Julianne Moore, Brooke Smith, Larry Pine, George Gaynes, Lynn Cohen (Berner)

The performances are precise, the language is alive and well spoken, and the setting is striking, but *Vanya on 42nd Street* still suffers from the limitations of

filmed theater. Louis Malle has unobtrusively recorded a theater piece that Andre Gregory and this cast rehearsed and performed for more than four years, an adaptation of Chekov's classic drama by David Mamet. Wallace Shawn is the 47-year-old Vanya, who vainly pursues the affections of the beautiful Yelena (Julianne Moore), faithfully married to aging scientist and writer Serybryakov (George Gaynes). Latter's daughter by his first marriage, Sonya (Brooke Smith), pines for a frequent visitor to the estate, Dr. Astrov (Larry Pine), while other members of the family and staff have their say about the unhappy goings-on.

VELVET GOLDMINE
1998, 123 mins, UK/US ⓥ ⊙
D: Todd Haynes **A:** Ewan McGregor, Jonathan Rhys Meyers, Toni Collette, Christian Bale, Eddie Izzard, Emily Woof (Zenith/Killer)

Iconoclastic American indie filmmaker Todd Haynes takes a highly personal look at the British glam rock scene of the early 1970s in *Velvet Goldmine*, an imaginative, stylistically lively but dramatically inert chronicle of cultural and sexual rebellion. Boldly conceived film boasts an arresting first half but bogs down thereafter. Megastar glam rocker Brian Slade (Jonathan Rhys Meyers) is seemingly shot dead during a concert. Ten years later, Brit newspaper reporter Arthur Stuart (Christian Bale) is assigned to write a "Whatever Happened to Brian Slade?" feature. Arthur visits the man who discovered Slade, Cecil (Michael Feast). Cecil covers the star's encounter with the outlandish American singer Curt Wild (Ewan McGregor), whose audacious act makes Slade realize he's seen the future. No one will have any trouble identifying David Bowie as the inspiration for Slade. Pic is loaded with music, much of it excitingly staged and performed. McGregor seems vaguely off the mark as the unhinged but inspired American performer. —

VENETIAN AFFAIR, THE
1967, 92 mins, US ▢
D: Jerry Thorpe **A:** Robert Vaughn, Elke Sommer, Felicia Farr, Karl Boehm, Ed Asner, Boris Karloff (M-G-M)

The Venetian Affair is a tepid programmer about international espionage in Venice. Pacing is tedious and the plotting routine, but the production is enlivened by some footage of Venice. Vaughn, ex-CIA agent now a reporter, is sent to Venice after a diplomatic meeting has been bombed. Ed Asner, CIA boss there, once canned Vaughn because the latter's then-wife, Elke Sommer, was a Communist agent. Now she has disappeared.

VENGEANCE IS MINE
See: Fukushu Sure Wa Ware Ni Ari

VENICE/VENICE
1992, 92 mins, US Ⓥ
D: Henry Jaglom **A:** Nelly Alard, Henry Jaglom, Melissa Leo, Suzanne Bertish, Daphna Kastner, David Duchovny (International Rainbow)

Venice/Venice represents the definition of a vanity production. Henry Jaglom's ninth feature lacks the colorful characters and innately interesting subject matter of his better films. As the director of the only American film in competition at the Venice Film Festival, Jaglom announces: "I am the representative of the anti-establishment," and builds a fragile little story about his relationship with attractive French journalist Nelly Alard, who is obsessed with his work. Jaglom gives her an interview that allows him to expound upon his own talents, pursue her at lunch and around the pool, and finally make out with her during a scenic gondola ride. After an hour, setting shifts to Venice, CA, as Alard wanders in on a party Jaglom is throwing.

VENOM
1982, 93 mins, UK Ⓥ
D: Piers Haggard **A:** Klaus Kinski, Oliver Reed, Nicol Williamson, Sarah Miles, Sterling Hayden, Susan George (Venom/Paramount)

Venom is an engrossing traditional suspense thriller. Klaus Kinski toplines as a German criminal who kidnaps a young American boy (Lance Holcomb) living in London, aided in the inside job by the boy's servants (Oliver Reed and Susan George). Unbeknownst, the boy has accidentally acquired a poisonous snake intended for toxicologist Dr. Marion Stowe (Sarah Miles), and the lethal reptile gets loose in the house.

VENUS PETER
1989, 92 mins, UK Ⓥ
D: Ian Sellar **A:** Gordon R. Strachan, Ray McAnally, David Hayman, Sinead Cusack, Caroline Paterson, Peter Caffrey (BFI)

Ian Sellar's first feature, shot in the wind-swept Orkney Islands, is a film about childhood that moves very slowly to a quite moving climax. Central character is young Peter, who lives with his mother and fisherman grandfather; he's not certain where his father is, but imagines him to be a ship's captain. When the father returns, it seems that he'd simply tired of island life and had gone to the mainland. The evocative background of the Orkneys is a major asset to the film.

VERA CRUZ
1954, 94 mins, US Ⓥ ▭
D: Robert Aldrich **A:** Gary Cooper, Burt Lancaster, Denise Darcel, Cesar Romero, Sarita Montiel, George Macready (United Artists)

Vera Cruz, the first release in Super-Scope, stresses the violence and suspenseful action of Mexico's revolutionary period when the Juaristas were trying to free the country of the French-supported Emperor Maximilian. Gary Cooper, ex-Confederate major, joins forces with Burt Lancaster, western outlaw, to escort a countess from Mexico City to the port of Vera Cruz. Secretly, the countess has a load of gold to be used in Europe to bring more troops to Maximilian's aid.

VERBOTEN!
1959, 86 mins, US
D: Samuel Fuller **A:** James Best, Susan Cummings, Tom Pittman, Paul Dubov, Harold Daye, Dick Kallman (Globe/RKO)

A photographic record of Nazi atrocities is incorporated in *Verboten!*, set in a German city in the first days of US occupation following World War II. The initial scenes build a troubled romance between a GI (James Best) and a sympathetic German girl (Susan Cummings), with the latter part of the film devoted to the resurgence of the Hitler Youth into a "Werewolf" band that loots, kills, and aids escaped war criminals. The girl's 15-year-old brother, a member of the gang, becomes disillusioned upon attending the Nuremberg War Criminal Trials and seeing the captured German film of Nazi horrors.

VERDICT, THE
1946, 86 mins, US
D: Don Siegel **A:** Sydney Greenstreet, Peter Lorre, Joan Lorring, George Coulouris, Arthur Shields, Rosalind Ivan (Warner)

Stock mystery tale with period background, *The Verdict* aims at generating suspense and thrills, succeeding modestly. Sydney Greenstreet plays a Scotland Yard superintendent who is fired when he convicts and hangs a man on circumstantial evidence. To show up the Yard and the man who replaced him, Greenstreet commits the perfect crime. Only the conviction of an innocent man for the murder makes Greenstreet reveal how the killing was done and the reason for it.

VERDICT, THE
1982, 122 mins, US Ⓥ ⊙
D: Sidney Lumet A: Paul Newman, Charlotte Rampling, Jack Warden, James Mason, Milo O'Shea, Edward Binns (20th Century-Fox/Zanuck-Brown)

There are many fine performances and sensitive moral issues contained in The Verdict, but that isn't enough to make it the compelling film it should be. Paul Newman is a cloudy-headed boozer who was once a top lawyer. Colleague Jack Warden hands him a case that could put him back on the straight and narrow. A young woman lies in a respected Boston hospital—a vegetable thanks to anesthesia she received from doctors while delivering a baby. Her sister wants to sue the hospital and the Catholic Church (which owns the facility) for the money to enable her to start a new life. Newman becomes convinced that the church and hospital have conspired to cover up medical malpractice.
1982: Nominations: Best Picture, Director, Actor (Paul Newman), Supp. Actor (James Mason), Screenplay Adaptation

LA VERITE
(THE TRUTH)
1960, 130 mins, France/Italy
D: Henri-Georges Clouzot A: Brigitte Bardot, Charles Vanel, Paul Meurisse, Louis Segnier, Marie-Jose Nat, Sami Frey (Iena/CEIAP)

Using the background of a murder trial, director Henri-Georges Clouzot details a young provincial girl's adventures in Paris and the eventual murder of her lover and her own suicide. It stars Brigitte Bardot, forced into one of her most dramatic roles as a dissatisfied small-town girl who goes to Paris. She sinks into a Bohemian life and affairs with intellectuals. Her sister's boyfriend falls for her. They finally fight and part, but she tries to come back to him.

VERTIGO
1958, 126 mins, US Ⓥ ⊙
D: Alfred Hitchcock A: James Stewart, Kim Novak, Barbara Bel Geddes, Tom Helmore, Henry Jones, Ellen Corby (Paramount)

Vertigo is prime though uneven Hitchcock. James Stewart gives a startlingly fine performance as the ex-cop who suffers from acrophobia. Kim Novak is a shop girl who involves Stewart in what turns out to be a case of murder. Unbilled is the city of San Francisco, photographed extensively and in exquisite color. The film's first half is too slow and too long. Film opens with a striking scene in which Stewart's acrophobia is explained. But for the next hour the action is mainly psychic, with Stewart hired by a rich ship builder to watch the ship owner's wife (Novak) as she loses her mental moorings, attempts suicide, and immerses herself in the gloomy maunderings of her mad great-grandmother.
1958: Nominations: Best Art Direction, Sound

VERY BRADY SEQUEL, A
1996, 89 mins, US Ⓥ ⊙ ▭
D: Arlene Sanford A: Shelley Long, Gary Cole, Tim Matheson, Christopher Daniel Barnes, Christine Taylor, Paul Sutera (Ladd-Schwartz/Paramount)

In this new installment, Carol's (Shelley Long) first husband, an archaeologist presumed lost at sea, returns unexpectedly. Roy Martin (Tim Matheson) says the fateful expedition left him an amnesiac. New hubby Mike (Gary Cole) insists that Roy bunk with the bunch. But Roy's an imposter searching for an ancient carved horse the real Roy sent home prior to his untimely demise. The Bradys have no idea it's worth millions. Director Arlene Sanford and her first-rate cast make A Very Brady Sequel work by keeping a stony face. Pic is surprisingly hip. Double entendres abound, and references to pop culture and television lore are rife. The story slows and goes slightly off course as the family pursues the kidnapped Carol to Hawaii. But this is a mere cavil about an otherwise entertaining diversion.

VERY SPECIAL FAVOR, A
1965, 105 mins, US
D: Michael Gordon A: Rock Hudson, Leslie Caron, Charles Boyer, Walter Slezak, Dick Shawn, Larry Storch (Universal)

This beautifully mounted feature stars Rock Hudson as an American oil man who bests French lawyer Charles Boyer in a Paris court case simply by romancing the female judge and who later admits to Boyer on a plane en route back to the US that he feels he owes him a favor. Boyer, in New York to visit his daughter, sees in her a spinster with the spirit of an old maid who has never tasted the life her French father thinks every woman should know. He calls on Hudson to make good his offer.

VIAGGIO IN ITALIA
(VOYAGE TO ITALY; STRANGERS; THE LONELY WOMAN)
1954, 100 mins, Italy Ⓥ
D: Roberto Rossellini **A:** Ingrid Bergman, George Sanders, Leslie Daniels, Natalia Ray, Anna Proclemer, Maria Mauban (Sveva/Junior)

Story tells of an English couple who are coldly moving close to divorce because of mutual incomprehension, who inherit a house near Naples. They begin to warm to the southern climate and the boisterous humanity about them. Film alternates brilliant bits with long stretches of so-so scenes. Rapid change from grit to grin, especially in George Sanders, as Ingrid Bergman's husband, mars the effect of the warm-up process by overspeeding. Tale is unevenly told, has some unhappy bits of dialogue, and is sometimes roughly shot, which for its director is the final version.

VICE SQUAD
1953, 88 mins, US
D: Arnold Laven **A:** Edward G. Robinson, Paulette Goddard, K. T. Stevens, Porter Hall, Adam Williams, Mary Ellen Kay (United Artists/Sequoia)

The workaday world of a police captain, complete with murder, bank robbery, and sundry other crimes, is the basis for this adequate melodrama. Edward G. Robinson does the expected competent job as the police captain who arrives at work to find his men looking for the gunmen who killed a cop during the early hours. The killing is tied in with a planned bank robbery, a scheme thwarted by police vigilance, but which doesn't prevent the kidnapping of a female bank clerk as a shield.

VICE VERSA
1988, 98 mins, US Ⓥ ⊙
D: Brian Gilbert **A:** Judge Reinhold, Fred Savage, Corinne Bohrer, Swoosie Kurtz, David Proval, Jane Kaczmarek (Columbia)

Vice Versa finds Judge Reinhold, a tony Chicago department store executive, and his junior high school–aged son (Fred Savage), ending up with each other's personalities after they both touch a mystical oriental skull. Reinhold is in his element acting like an 11-year-old more interested in heavy metal rock and his pet frog than girls. The store's chief honcho is ready to fire him, but his fellow execs, all coveting his job, are relishing his antics.

VICTIM
1961, 100 mins, UK Ⓥ
D: Basil Dearden **A:** Dirk Bogarde, Sylvia Syms, Dennis Price, Anthony Nicholls, Peter McEnery, Nigel Stock (Allied Film Makers)

Victim is a taut, holding thriller about blackmailers latching on to homosexuals that takes several critical swipes at the British law that encourages blackmail by making homosexuals criminal outcasts. Dirk Bogarde plays a barrister on the verge of becoming a Queen's Counsel, happily married to a wife (Sylvia Syms) who knew of his homosexual leanings when she married him but has helped him lead a normal life. He refuses to see a youth (Peter McEnery) with whom he previously associated because he fears blackmail. Instead, the boy is trying to protect the barrister from blackmail. The youth commits suicide, and Bogarde sets out to break the blackmailers even though he knows that if the facts come out, they will ruin his marriage and his career. Bogarde is subtle, sensitive, and strong. Syms handles a difficult role with delicacy. This is telling, moving stuff.

LA VICTOIRE EN CHANTANT
(BLACK AND WHITE IN COLOR)
1976, 100 mins, France/W. Germany/ Ivory Coast Ⓥ ⊙
D: Jean-Jacques Annaud **A:** Jean Carmet, Jacques Dufilho, Catherine Rouvel, Jacques Spiesser, Dora Doll, Maurice Barrier (Raggane/SFP/FR3/Smart/Societe Ivorienne de Cinema)

A cutting pic dealing in racism, colonialism, imperialism, and war. Film takes place in a remote corner of Africa during World War I when a handful of bored Frenchmen belatedly find they are at war with Germany and decide to attack the neighboring Germans in a nearby colony. They press natives into their armies who do the fighting and dying for no reason. Finally, an English group moves in and tells them the war is over. The film avoids overdoing its satirical thrust and is a moral fable about man's inhumanity to man.
1976: Best Foreign Language Film

VICTORIA THE GREAT
1937, 112 mins, UK

D: Herbert Wilcox **A:** Anna Neagle, Anton Walbrook, Walter Rilla, Mary Morris, H. B. Warner, Felix Aylmer (Imperator)

Victoria the Great travels a long way toward a full explanation of the most popular ruler England ever had. Her career is traced from 20 June 1837, when she ascended the throne, until her 60th anniversary as queen, shortly before her demise. Anna Neagle, in the title role, gives an unwavering performance. Anton Walbrook as Albert, the Prince Consort, is superb. The film wisely puts its prime focus on the private life of Victoria, her romance, marriage, and personal characteristics. Backgrounded is her public life, and her gradual rise to such high estimation by her people.

VICTORS, THE
1963, 175 mins, US

D: Carl Foreman **A:** George Hamilton, George Peppard, Eli Wallach, James Mitchum, Romy Schneider, Jeanne Moreau (Highroad/Columbia)

Carl Foreman's tale of war concentrates on homesickness; woman-hunger; civilian starvation; and the "nice" girls who shack up with the GI smoothies for food, cigarettes, and kicks. One of these is played by Romy Schneider, indifferent to the decent soldier (George Hamilton) and bumming around with a slicker, causing the decent GI's own ultimate hardening. Foreman has designed his narrative with great filmmaking skill and considerable daring, recalling the early 1940s both for nostalgia and irony.

VICTOR/VICTORIA
1982, 133 mins, UK ⊗ ⊙ ▭

D: Blake Edwards **A:** Julie Andrews, James Garner, Robert Preston, Lesley Ann Warren, Alex Karras, John Rhys-Davies (M-G-M/Peerford/Artista)

Victor/Victoria is sparkling, ultrasophisticated entertainment from Blake Edwards. Set in Paris of 1934, tale introduces Julie Andrews as a down-on-her-luck chanteuse. Tres gai nightclub entertainer Robert Preston remakes her as a man who in short order becomes celebrated as Paris's foremost female impersonator. Enter Windy City gangster James Garner. Not knowing he's in one of "those" clubs, the tough guy falls hard for Andrews, only to experience a severe blow to his macho ego when it becomes apparent that she's a he.

1982: Best Original Song Score
Nominations: Best Actress (Julie Andrews), Supp. Actor (Robert Preston), Supp. Actress (Lesley Ann Warren), Screenplay Adaptation, Costume Design, Art Direction

VICTORY
1940, 77 mins, US ▭

D: John Cromwell **A:** Fredric March, Betty Field, Cedric Hardwicke, Jerome Cowan, Sig Rumann, Rafaela Ottiano (Paramount)

This film version of Joseph Conrad's novel impresses with several strongly individual performances rather than with the story itself. Fredric March is the recluse living on a small East Indian island. Under his protection comes Betty Field, a stranded musician, and when March finds himself falling in love with the girl, he prepares to ship her away on a trading schooner. Cedric Hardwicke and his outlaw companions arrive to rob and kill March for his buried fortune. Direction by John Cromwell employs a stagey technique with burdensome dialogue and a slow pace until the final episodes, which pick up dramatic interest.

VICTORY
(ESCAPE TO VICTORY)
1981, 117 mins, US ⊗

D: John Huston **A:** Sylvester Stallone, Michael Caine, Max von Sydow, Pele, Daniel Massey, Carole Laure (Lorimar/Victory)

Victory amounts to a frankly old-fashioned World War II morality play, hinging on soccer as a metaphor for the game of war. Set in a German p.o.w. camp in 1943, plot hinges on a morality-building ploy by a genteel propaganda officer (Max von Sydow) to pit a team of Allied prisoners against the local German troops. When his superiors get wind of the plan, they quickly see the worldwide propaganda potential and insist on expanding the plan to square off a p.o.w. "all-star" team drawn from imprisoned footballers throughout Europe against the German national team.

VICTORY AT SEA
1954, 97 mins, US ⊗
(NBC Film Division)

Originally presented on NBC as a 26-part filmed documentary of World War II naval history, the television series *Victory at Sea* was compressed to 97 minutes for theatrical release. But despite the loss of many fine scenes of the original, the edited print is still a forceful pictorial chronicle of the Axis Powers' global sea campaigns against the Axis Powers, covering the period from the Axis's 1939 ascendancy to its defeat in 1945. Quality of the print is good considering the varied origin and age of the footage.

VICTORY THROUGH AIR POWER
1943, 65 mins, US
D: H. C. Potter, Clyde Geronimi, Jack Kinney, James Algar **A:** Alexander P. de Seversky (Walt Disney)

Disney and Major Alexander P. de Seversky trace the progress of aviation in 65 snappy minutes, a combination of super-animation in color and Technicolored photography with the major himself participating. Film flashes back to 1903, when the Wright brothers first succeeded in lifting a heavier-than-air craft off the ground. In cartoon and narration is traced the Luftwaffe's exploits, plus the concluding arguments by de Seversky of how to beat Hitler in his Fortress Europa and how to overcome Japan's air-based advantages. There are the usual imaginative complement of Disneyisms in the cartoons, and an excellent musical score to spice it up.
1943: Nomination: Best Scoring of a Dramatic Picture

VIDEODROME
1983, 88 mins, Canada ⊗
D: David Cronenberg **A:** James Woods, Sonja Smits, Deborah Harry, Peter Dvorsky, Les Carlson, Jack Creley (Filmplan)

Story concerns a small-time cable television outlet in Toronto run by Max Renn (James Woods), ever on the lookout for offbeat and erotic material. He becomes fascinated with a program called *Videodrome*, which appears to be a series of torture sequences, primarily involving women. One of Renn's suppliers assures him that the activities on the show are not staged. However, he perseveres, making contact with a McLuhanesque media guru named Brian O'Blivion (Jack Creley). Cronenberg amplifies the freaky situation with a series of stunning visual effects.

LA VIE DEVANT SOI
(MADAME ROSA)
1977, 105 mins, France ⊗
D: Moshe Mizrahi **A:** Simone Signoret, Claude Dauphin, Samy Ben Youb, Gabriel Jabbour, Michal Bat-Adam, Constantin Costa-Gavras (Lira)

Film traces the relationship between an ailing old Jewish woman who cares for the children of prostitutes and one of her charges, an Arab boy. Direction is unobtrusive and leaves the film to its actors, which works, due to the canny, insightful playing of Simone Signoret. Rose (Signoret), once in a concentration camp and a prostitute for 35 years, is very ill. One of her charges is a handsome, brooding boy who loves her, but whose stifled tenderness makes him unruly. When she dies, he stays with her for weeks. He spreads toilet water to kill the smell, but firemen finally break in and take her away.
1977: Best Foreign Language Film

VIETNAM, TEXAS
1990, 85 mins, US ⊗
D: Robert Ginty **A:** Robert Ginty, Haing S. Ngor, Tim Thomerson, Kiev Chinh, Tamlyn Tomita (Epic)

Good intentions are roughly served in this uneven actioner that displays compassion for the stateside Vietnamese community while exploiting its violent elements. Robert Ginty stars as Father Thomas McCain, a Vietnam vet turned priest who suffers guilt about the Vietnamese woman he abandoned—pregnant with his child—when he returned to the States. Fifteen years later, he tracks them down in Houston's Little Saigon and forces himself into their lives, despite his former flame Mailan (Kieu Chinh) being comfortably established as the wife of a vicious drug runner (Haing S. Ngor).

VIEW TO A KILL, A
1985, 131 mins, UK ⊗ ⊙ ▭
D: John Glen **A:** Roger Moore, Christopher Walken, Tanya Roberts, Grace Jones, Patrick Macnee, Fiona Fullerton (Eon/United Arists)

Bond's adversary this time is international industrialist Max Zorin (Christopher Walken) and his love-hate interest, May Day (Grace Jones). Bond uncovers their profitable scheme in which microchips are surgically implanted in racehorses to assure easy victory. Action jumps abruptly to San Francisco to reveal Zorin's true master plan to pump seawater into the San Andreas fault, causing a major earthquake, destroying Silicon Valley, and leaving him with the world's microchip monopoly. Roger Moore, making his seventh appearance as Bond, is right about half the time. He is still suave and cool enough for the part, but he looks a bit old, and his womanizing seems dated.

VIGIL
1984, 90 mins, New Zealand ⱱ

D: Vincent Ward **A:** Penelope Stewart, Frank Whitten, Bill Kerr, Fiona Kay (Film Investment/NZFC)

Central figure is 11-year-old Toss (Fiona Kay), caught in the tragedy of the death of her father and the coincidental arrival of a stranger, Ethan (Frank Whitten). While Toss is fascinated by Ethan's mysterious aura, her mother, Elizabeth (Penelope Stewart), is reawakened from a joyless marriage, and her grandfather Birdie (Bill Kerr) finds a comrade for his grandiose mechanical inventions. The film gives fresh resonance to universal themes.

VIKINGS, THE
1958, 114 mins, US ⱱ ▱ ▭

D: Richard Fleischer **A:** Kirk Douglas, Tony Curtis, Ernest Borgnine, Janet Leigh, Alexander Knox, Frank Thring (United Artists/Bryna)

The Vikings is spectacular, rousing, and colorful. Blood flows freely, and there's no hesitation about throwing a victim into a wolf pit or a pool of crabs. It starts with a Viking army of 200 raiding the Kingdom of Northumbria and the death of the English king. The widowed queen is with child, the father being Ernest Borgnine, head of the marauding Vikings. To escape the new king's wrath, she flees to another land and with the proper passage of time the child, now a young man (Tony Curtis), turns up in the Viking village as a slave. He encounters Kirk Douglas, heir to the Viking throne. Neither is aware that they are brothers. Douglas, doing a bang-up, freewheeling job as the ferocious and disfigured Viking fighter, fits the part splendidly.

VIKTOR UND VIKTORIA
1933, 90 mins, Germany

D: Reinhold Schunzel **A:** Renate Muller, Hermann Thimig, Hilde Hildebrand, Friedel Pisetta, Fritz Odemar, Aribert Wascher (UFA)

Real fast comedy put over with pace and pleasant lightness. A splendid vehicle for Renate Muller in trousers, who develops extraordinary talents in the nonchalant representation of a would-be unconcerned aristocrat. Hermann Thiming plays the fool wherever the plot gives him a chance in the part of the original "Viktoria," overdoing it at times. Adolf Wohlbruck, the suspecting lover, plays with agreeable unobtrusiveness.

VILLAGE OF THE DAMNED
1960, 77 mins, US ⱱ

D: Wolf Rilla **A:** George Sanders, Barbara Shelley, Michael Gwynn, Laurence Naismith, John Phillips, Richard Vernon (M-G-M)

Plot kicks around what is not an uninteresting idea. A little British village comes under the spell of some supernatural force that makes all the women pregnant. The children are little monsters. They all look alike—fair haired, unblinking stare, and with intellects the equivalent of adults, plus telepathy. George Sanders, a physicist, is intimately involved, since his wife is the mother of the leader of the little gang of abnormal moppets. This just tapers off from a taut beginning into soggy melodrama. Wolf Rilla's direction is adequate, but no more.

VILLAGE OF THE DAMNED
1995, 98 mins, US ⱱ ▭

D: John Carpenter **A:** Christopher Reeve, Kirstie Alley, Linda Kozlowski, Michael Pare, Meredith Salenger, Mark Hamill (Alphaville/Universal)

Village of the Damned is a risible remake of the British 1960 sci-fi classic about malevolent children mysteriously born at the same time who employ superior cerebral skills and mental telepathy to gain the upper hand over adults. Unlike the subversively anti-Reaganite undercurrents in Carpenter's 1988 *They Live*, there are no unsettling frissons here to lend any dimension to the minimal surface thrills. The town of Midwich, a small Northern California community, is hit by a mysterious force that knocks out the entire population for six hours. Soon thereafter, 10 women in town turn up pregnant. Pic's one notable adjustment lies in shifting more importance to the women in the story, which would have been fine were it not for the silly roles and atrocious dialogue.

VILLAIN
1971, 98 mins, UK ⱱ

D: Michael Tuchner **A:** Richard Burton, Ian McShane, Nigel Davenport, Donald Sinden, Fiona Lewis, T. P. McKenna (Anglo-EMI)

Villain uses a frayed shoestring plot of a payroll stick-up to flesh out the sadistic actions of Richard Burton as a one-time nightclub bouncer who has become one of the major figures of the London underworld. Tied to a dying mother (Cathleen Nesbitt) by a silver cord stronger than steel cable, he is also a homosexual with a thing about a petty criminal (Ian McShane) that makes him beat him up, then bed down with him. His bete noir, however, is a dedicated police inspector (Nigel Davenport) whose sole duty is to pin something on him.

VILLAIN, THE
1979, 93 mins, US ⊗
D: Hal Needham **A:** Kirk Douglas, Ann-Margret, Arnold Schwarzenegger, Paul Lynde, Ruth Buzzi, Jack Elam (Columbia/Rastar)

Idea for this satire must have looked great on paper. Why not take all the standard sagebrush types—the handsome stranger, the décolleté femme, the evil outlaw—and put them through a parody of their usual paces? But without any depth of characterization, and only the flimsiest plot structure, a take-off has nowhere to go. With Kirk Douglas in the title role, Arnold Schwarzenegger as the good guy, and Ann-Margret as the lascivious girl who loves being fought over, *The Villain* becomes even more of a disappointment. Rarely has so much talent been used to so little purpose.

VILLA RIDES
1968, 125 mins, US ⊗ ⊡
D: Buzz Kulik **A:** Yul Brynner, Robert Mitchum, Grazia Buccella, Charles Bronson, Robert Viharo, Herbert Lom (Paramount)

Villa Rides is a pseudo-biopic of a portion of the bandit career of Mexico's folk hero Pancho Villa, with Yul Brynner in the title role. Ted Richmond's handsome exterior production, filmed in 1967 in Spain, is competently, if routinely, directed. With the aid of Charles Bronson and Robert Viharo, Brynner is responsible for the on-screen deaths of literally dozens of men. Brynner makes Villa sympathetic at times, as a man fighting for human rights, though that's a bit hard to swallow since those he killed were "traitors" by his convenient self-excusing definition.

VINCENT & THEO
1990, 138 mins, UK/France/Netherlands/Italy ⊗
D: Robert Altman **A:** Tim Roth, Paul Rhys, Jip Wijngaarden, Johanna Ter Steege, Jean-Pierre Cassel, Anne Canovas (Belbo/Central/La Sept/Telepool/RAI Uno/Vara/Sofica Valor)

A study of Vincent Van Gogh's last years as seen through his tortured relationship with his brother, *Vincent and Theo* is one of Robert Altman's most cinematically conventional films as well as one of his most deeply personal. Altman and his scripter Julian Mitchell focus on Vincent's obsessive devotion to his craft and the failure of his timid art dealer/brother to win him acceptance in an art world that scorned his idiosyncratic genius. As Theo, Paul Rhys skillfully inhabits a character even more wretchedly unhappy than his brother, who at least has the consolation of his art, and Tim Roth powerfully conveys Vincent's heroic, obsessive concentration on his work.

VINCENT, FRANCOIS, PAUL . . . ET LES AUTRES
(VINCENT, FRANCOIS, PAUL AND THE OTHERS)
1974, 118 mins, France/Italy ⊗
D: Claude Sautet **A:** Yves Montand, Michel Piccoli, Serge Reggiani, Gerard Depardieu, Stephane Audran, Marie Dubois (Lira/President)

Claude Sautet seems to be turning into the chronicler of middle-class, middle-aged manners and mores. Character is etched fleetingly, with Vincent (Yves Montand) being the most developed since he is losing his business, is separated from his wife, and is drifting away from a young mistress. Francois (Michel Piccoli), a doctor, is also losing his wife, while Paul (Serge Reggiani), a failed writer, has a woman who loves him. A young friend, Jean (Gerard Depardieu), a boxer, gives the film its final burst of action as all assist at his victory. Pic has an insistent feel for the ordinary, is well played, but misses a transcending dramatic insight to make the fates of these old-time friends more revealing.

VINCENT, FRANCOIS, PAUL AND THE OTHERS
See: Vincent, Francois, Paul . . . et les Autres

VINCENT
THE LIFE AND DEATH OF VINCENT VAN GOGH
1987, 103 mins, Australia/Netherlands ⊗
D: Paul Cox (Illumination/Look/Ozfilms/Dasha)

This very special art film is neither documentary nor fiction. Paul Cox, one of Australia's foremost directors, has made an exquisite tribute to Vincent Van Gogh using as text his letters to his brother Theo, beautifully read by John Hurt. Van Gogh worked as a painter for only 10 years, producing about 1,800 works, but when he killed himself at age 37, he had only sold one of them and was unknown and impoverished. Cox's film covers those last 10 years. Van Gogh's thoughts and philosophies are enunciated superbly on the soundtrack. The images accompanying the text are of trees and fields and birds in flight, and the inevitable sunflowers.

VIOLENT PLAYGROUND
1958, 108 mins, UK
D: Basil Dearden **A:** Stanley Baker, Anne Heywood, David McCallum, Peter Cushing, John Slater, Clifford Evans (Rank)

Violent Playground brings a sincere semi-documentary touch to the matter of juvenile delinquency and is convincingly acted against authentic Liverpool backgrounds. Result is an absorbing film that works up to an overlong but tense climax. Film concerns an experiment made in Liverpool in 1949. Policemen have become Juvenile Liaison Officers whose job is to keep an eye on mischievous youngsters. Stanley Baker gives a vigorous and sympathetic performance as a cop who is taken off the investigation of a series of unexplained fires for this work. He becomes particularly involved with one family and discovers who is responsible for the arson.

VIOLENT SATURDAY
1955, 90 mins, US ▭
D: Richard Fleischer **A:** Victor Mature, Richard Egan, Stephen McNally, Virginia Leith, Lee Marvin, Sylvia Sidney (20th Century-Fox)

Film concerns a bank robbery planned by a cool trio played by Stephen McNally, Lee Marvin, and J. Carrol Naish. As preparations for the hold-up unfold, several subplots are set up to set the stage for the hold-up. They're highly contrived and unconvincing, but they do give the film a greater sense of scope and power. Climax comes with the robbery itself and the getaway. It's here that the film strips the action of the non-essentials and turns on the heat in a powerful wind-up that's worth the wait.

VIOLENT STRANGER
See: Wetherby

V.I.P.S, THE
1963, 119 mins, UK ▭
D: Anthony Asquith **A:** Elizabeth Taylor, Richard Burton, Louis Jourdan, Margaret

Rutherford, Maggie Smith, Rod Taylor (M-G-M)

Setting is London Airport, and the basic problem is the necessity for at least four Very Important Passengers bound for the States to get out of the country pronto. Their plans go haywire when a thick fog grounds all planes overnight. Terence Rattigan's screenplay juggles these situations and does not neglect many of the star performers. The script has literate, witty, and sometimes touching dialogue, and Anthony Asquith has directed skillfully. Principal story, that of a business tycoon who has taken his wife for granted and now looks set to lose her, is played out by Richard Burton, Elizabeth Taylor, and Louis Jourdan as the lover. Maybe Taylor needs a sabbatical—there is a feeling of ordinariness about her thesping.

1963: Best Supp. Actress (Margaret Rutherford)

VIRGIN AND THE GYPSY, THE
1970, 95 mins, UK ⊗
D: Christopher Miles **A:** Joanna Shimkus, Franco Nero, Honor Blackman, Mark Burns, Maurice Denham, Fay Compton (De Grunwald)

D. H. Lawrence's novella *The Virgin and the Gypsy* is about a young English girl's awakening to adult life in northern England, circa 1921. While faithful perhaps to the author, film is a stilted period piece. Joanna Shimkus and Harriett Harper are two rural sisters returning from a French school to a provincial environment, ruled by grandmother Fay Compton. Shimkus grows restive and finds a sexual stirring under Franco Nero's gaze.

VIRGINIA CITY
1940, 123 mins, US ⊗
D: Michael Curtiz **A:** Errol Flynn, Miriam Hopkins, Randolph Scott, Humphrey Bogart, Frank McHugh, Alan Hale (Warner)

As a shoot-'em-up, this picture is first class; as a bit of cinematic history telling, it is far short of the possibilities indicated by the title and cast. It's about a cache of $5 million in gold bullion which Confederate sympathizers have offered to the Southern cause during the Civil War. The catch is how to get the gold out of Nevada and through Union lines. Errol Flynn is assigned to intercept the gold. Miriam Hopkins is a singer traveling on the stage with Flynn. She is a rebel spy. The stage is held up by outlaw Humphrey Bogart (behind a slick-waxed mustache). And in Virginia City is Randolph Scott, planning the removal of the gold. Scott is much in love with Hopkins, who leans toward Flynn but betrays him, placing patriotism ahead of love. Michael Curtiz, the director, has steamed all this up with some noisy trigger work, charging cavalry, dance-hall intimacies, and the sands of the desert into a bustling western replete with action, though short on credulity.

VIRGINIAN, THE
1929, 92 mins, US ⓥ
D: Victor Fleming A: Gary Cooper, Walter Huston, Mary Brian, Chester Conklin, Eugene Pallette, E. H. Calvert (Paramount)
This Paramount production makes of the Owen Wister and Kirk La Shelle story 92 minutes of drama and comedy. Toward the middle there's one of the most harrowing and vivid sequences ever before the lense when the silent and lanky Virginian (Gary Cooper) is forced to give the signal which sends his pal, Steve (Richard Arlen) to his death in a noose. Trampas (Walter Huston), the menace, is saved from the hanging to bait along the story for the vengeance-filled climax.

VIRGINIAN, THE
1946, 83 mins, US
D: Stuart Gilmore A: Joel McCrea, Brian Donlevy, Sonny Tufts, Barbara Britton, Fay Bainter, Henry O'Neill (Paramount)
The Virginian stands up pretty well over the years. This version of the Owen Wister novel is still a pleasant, flavorsome western, with much of the old charm of a daguerreotype and enough shooting and suspense to offset the plodding pace. Yarn is still the story of the schoolmarm from Vermont and the cowboy from Virginia, who meet in Montana and wed, after the hero has disposed of a few troublesome cow rustlers. Joel McCrea follows soundly in the footsteps of Dustin Farnum and Gary Cooper as The ("When You Call Me That, Smile") Virginian.

VIRGIN SOLDIERS, THE
1969, 96 mins, UK ⓥ
D: John Dexter A: Lynn Redgrave, Hywel Bennett, Nigel Davenport, Nigel Patrick, Rachel Kempson, Jack Shepherd (Columbia/Foreman)
The Virgin Soldiers comes out as a bright and affectionate peek at the trials and tribulations of young National Service rookies. Though the writers have concentrated mainly on making the film ruefully funny, the serious side has not been ne-

glected. The smell of death is often just around the corner, and violence in the jungle and streets of terrorist-infested Malaya is in striking, effective contrast to the boisterous, bawdy, barrack-room atmosphere.

VIRGIN SPRING, THE
See: Jungfrukallan

VIRIDIANA
1961, 90 mins, Spain/Mexico ⓥ
D: Luis Buñuel A: Silvia Pinal, Fernando Rey, Francisco Rabal, Margarita Lozano, Victoria Zinny, Teresa Rabal (Uninci/Films 59/Alatriste)
Brilliantly carpentered offbeat pic is sure to be controversial. Theme is about charity and its uses and misuses, with an insight into human reasons. A girl about to take her vows as a nun visits a rich uncle. He begs her to be his wife, drugs her, and almost makes advances to her, then hangs himself, leaving her his large estate. The would-be nun tries to become a saintly creature by bringing in a flock of derelicts. But they almost rape her, and she decides to become a human being first before trying to be a selfless saint. Director Luis Buñuel returned to Spain for the first time since 1938 to make this film.

VIRTUOSITY
1995, 105 mins, US ⓥ ⊙
D: Brett Leonard A: Denzel Washington, Kelly Lynch, Russell Crowe, Stephen Spinella, William Forsythe, Louise Fletcher (Paramount)
A futuristic actioner, Virtuosity exhibits the perils of putting technology ahead of virtues like emotion and character. Parker Barnes (Denzel Washington), an ex-cop, is taking part in a virtual reality simulation designed to train police officers for violent situations. His nemesis is a VR fabrication Sid 6.7 (Russell Crowe), designed to combine the least savory character traits of Hitler, Manson, and 181 other psychopaths. Predictably, Sid 6.7 escapes into the real world in a cyber-body that makes him virtually invulnerable, and Barnes is chosen to hunt him down. Like too many other such movies, pic climaxes with a battle atop a tall building. Helmer Brett Leonard's handling is competent but undistinctive.

VISIONS OF EIGHT
1973, 110 mins, US ⓥ
D: Milos Forman, Kon Ichikawa, Claude Lelouch, Yuri Ozerov, Arthur Penn, Michael Pfleghar, John Schlesinger, Mai Zetterling (Wolper)
Producer David Wolper recruited eight

name directors to choose a segment of the 1972 Munich Olympics and give his/her view of the event. The problem is that many of the sketches sometimes forget the idea of sport and competition itself to indulge in ideas. But the flurry, crowds, and human endeavor are there, and in the background are the tragic terrorist events that led to the massacre of Israeli athletes by Arab terrorists.

LES VISITEURS DU SOIR
(THE DEVIL'S ENVOYS)
1942, 118 mins, France
D: Marcel Carne **A:** Arletty, Jules Berry, Marie Dea, Fernand Ledoux, Alain Cuny, Gabriel Gabrio (Superfilm)

This story is a romantic legend about two damned souls who return to earth to corrupt the human race but remain long enough for one to be saved by a girl's love. The early scenes, in which the two Devil's disciples arrive at the castle in time to entertain the banquet guests and presently disrupt the household, are promising. Some of the Devil's later scenes are amusing, too. But the yarn itself is slow, and the direction further retards it. Arletty plays an enigmatic femme fatale, handling the assignment with skill and poise. Jules Berry, as Satan, gives a standout performance, revealing excellent range, flexibility, and personal impact.

VISKNINGAR OCH ROP
(CRIES AND WHISPERS)
1973, 91 mins, Sweden ⓥ
D: Ingmar Bergman **A:** Harriet Andersson, Kari Sylwan, Ingrid Thulin, Liv Ullmann, Erland Josephson, Henning Moritzen (Cinematograph)

Ingmar Bergman's dark vision of the human condition focuses on individuals crying for help in a world they can neither cope with nor comprehend. In *Cries and Whispers* he provides a bravado portrait of four women in this barren emotional landscape. Two sisters (Ingrid Thulin and Liv Ullmann) return to their family home to await the death of a third (Harriet Andersson), a spinster long cared for by a peasant housekeeper (Kari Sylwan). The women represent varying degrees of alienation, ranging from Thulin's suicidal despair to Sylwan's benign acceptance of God's will. The atmosphere of imminent death cues memories of past events which occurred in the house. Bergman's lean style, his use of lingering close-ups, fades to red, and a soundtrack echoing with the ticking of clocks, the rustle of dresses, and the hushed cries of the lost gives pic a hypnotic impact.

VITAL SIGNS
1990, 103 mins, US ⓥ ⊙
D: Marisa Silver **A:** Adrian Pascar, Diane Lane, Jimmy Smits, Norma Aleandro, Jack Gwaltney, Laura San Giacomo (20th Century-Fox)

Vital Signs is a strikingly well-done ensemble piece about a pivotal year in the lives of a group of medical students. As a gifted doctor-to-be who oozes charm and good looks, Adrian Pasdar is the focus of a group navigating their tough third year at L.A. Central's med school. Diane Lane is the crisp but compassionate fellow student he falls in love with. Jack Gwaltney plays the fellow from a less-advantaged background who's determined not to let Pasdar surpass him. Director Marisa Silver does a good job of getting across characters' emotional lives and fashions a crisply moving story.

I VITELLONI
(THE SPIVS; THE YOUNG AND THE PASSIONATE)
1953, 105 mins, Italy/France ⊙
D: Federico Fellini **A:** Alberto Sordi, Franco Interlenghi, Franco Fabrizi, Leopoldo Trieste, Eleonora Ruffo, Riccardo Fellini (PEG/Cite)

Federico Fellini's second feature film satirizes the "wastrels," the do-nothing sons of middle-class Italian provincials whose life ranges from schoolroom to poolroom. Fellini has mirrored this atmosphere and its characters sharply. Such sequences as the carnival ball, the visit to the village of the broken-down vaudeville troupe, and many others are good entertainment. Scene of Alberto's drunken wanderings is a classic of the genre. Thesping throughout points up the strong direction.

VIVACIOUS LADY
1938, 90 mins, US ⓥ
D: George Stevens **A:** Ginger Rogers, James Stewart, James Ellison, Beulah Bondi, Charles Coburn, Frances Mercer (RKO)

Vivacious Lady is entertainment of the highest order and broadest appeal. Story tells the romantic adventures and tribulations of a New York cabaret singer and a youthful college professor. After love at first sight, a speedy wooing, and a hasty marriage, the young man takes his bride to the small town and introduces her to his family and associates. Prejudice and stern respectability resist the invasion. Manner in which approval of the marriage is won from the boy's parents is amusingly accomplished.

1938: Nominations: Best Cinematography, Sound

VIVA KNIEVEL!
1977, 104 mins, US Ⓥ ⊑

D: Gordon Douglas **A:** Evel Knievel, Gene Kelly, Marjoe Gortner, Lauren Hutton, Leslie Nielsen, Red Buttons (Warner/Corwin)

In the most daring feat of his career, Evel Knievel leaps over a mountain of blazing cliches and a cavernous plot, somehow landing upright to the cheers of his legions of fans. Evel the actor emerges from the wreck in better shape than the bent careers of his costars Gene Kelly, Marjoe Gortner, Red Buttons, Lauren Hutton, and Leslie Nielsen, for whom it's a credit best forgotten. Plot: evil Leslie Nielsen will lure the leaper to Mexico where he'll kill Knievel and steal his truck, substituting an identical truck whose sides are packed with illegal white powder.

VIVA LAS VEGAS
1964, 85 mins, US ⊙ ⊑

D: George Sidney **A:** Elvis Presley, Ann-Margret, Cesare Danova, William Demarest, Nicky Blair, Jack Carter (M-G-M)

The sizzling combination of Elvis Presley and Ann-Margaret is enough to carry *Viva Las Vegas* over the top. The picture is fortunate in having two such commodities for bait, because the production is a pretty trite and heavy-handed affair, puny in story development and distortedly preoccupied with anatomy. Vegas is the setting of this superficial contrivance about an auto racing buff (Presley) trying to raise funds to purchase an engine for the racer with which he hopes to win the Grand Prix. His main obstacle is a swimming instructress (Ann-Margret) who doesn't approve of his goal, but ultimately softens.

VIVA MARIA!
1965, 120 mins, France/Italy ⊑

D: Louis Malle **A:** Jeanne Moreau, Brigitte Bardot, George Hamilton, Claudio Brooks, Gregor Von Rezzoni, Carlos Lopez Moctezuma (NEF/Artistes Associes/Vides)

Pic has Brigitte Bardot in her best form since *And God Created Woman*, brilliantly matched by Jeanne Moreau. They are backed by a rollicking, comic adventure opus impeccably brought off by director Louis Malle. Bardot is the daughter of a life-long anarchist who has spent his life blowing up bridges and police stations. She finds herself hunted in some Latin American country in 1910 and is taken up by Moreau, a dancer in a traveling music hall cum circus. The two, both named Maria, team up. There follows some knowing take-offs on the songs of the era, with Bardot unwittingly seeming to invent the striptease in one show, and the circus gets involved in a local revolution.

VIVA MAX
1969, 92 mins, US/UK Ⓥ

D: Jerry Paris **A:** Peter Ustinov, Pamela Tiffin, Jonathan Winters, John Astin, Keenan Wynn, Harry Morgan (Commonwealth United)

This satirical saga of a ragtag platoon of Mexican soldiers who recapture the Alamo in 1969 is a captivatingly original idea, well produced but questionably cast with Peter Ustinov in the lead. Ustinov is the Mexican general who leads his small band of grousing troops across the border on the pretext of marching in a Washington's Birthday parade in Laredo. Both he and John Astin, as his tough sergeant, have that vague aura of embarrassment of good actors who wonder what the director has wrought. The film has something to offend a wide variety of groups—Texans, the National Guard, right-wing paramilitary groups, and even John Wayne.

VIVA VILLA!
1934, 112 mins, US

D: Jack Conway **A:** Wallace Beery, Leo Carrillo, Fay Wray, Donald Cook, Joseph Schildkraut, Stuart Erwin (M-G-M)

Viva Villa! is a big, impressive production which sets out to make Wallace Beery's Pancho Villa appear as a sympathetic and quasi-patriotic bandit. But Beery's characterization lets Pancho down too much. His Villa is a hybrid dialectician with a vacillating accent that suffers alongside of Leo Carrillo's charming dialect or the contra-renegade version as done by Joseph Schildkraut as Pascal. Both impart an unction and a style to their cruelties that show up Beery's boorish Villa. There is no denying the mass-movement impressiveness of the production. The handling of the mob scenes on field of battle was no mean task.

1934: Best Assistant Director

Nominations: Best Picture, Writing Adaptation, Sound

VIVA ZAPATA!

1952, 112 mins, US Ⓥ ⊙

D: Elia Kazan **A:** Marlon Brando, Jean Peters, Anthony Quinn, Joseph Wiseman, Arnold Moss, Margo (20th Century-Fox)

The story of Emiliano Zapata, Mexican revolutionary, is a hard, cruel, curiously unemotional account of Mexican banditry and revolt against an oppressive government. Elia Kazan's direction strives for a personal intimacy, but neither he nor the John Steinbeck scripting achieves in enough measure. Marlon Brando brings to the Zapata character the same type of cold objectivity. There's a stark quality to the photography that suggests the raw, hot atmosphere of Mexico.

1952: Best Supp. Actor (Anthony Quinn)

Nominations: Best Actor (Marlon Brando), Story & Screenplay, Art Direction, Scoring of a Dramatic Picture

VIVRE POUR VIVRE
(LIVE FOR LIFE)

1967, 120 mins, France

D: Claude Lelouch **A:** Yves Montand, Annie Girardot, Candice Bergen, Irene Tunc, Uta Taeger, Anouk Ferjac (Ariane/Artistes Associes/Vides)

Live for Life is very similar in subject matter and style to Claude Lelouch's previous hit, *A Man and a Woman*, but lacks the lyric sweep and charm and falters technically despite a sizable budget. The hero (Yves Montand), self-absorbed and emotionally sterile, is a married man whose adulteries unexpectedly culminate in a serious love affair. The American girl (Candice Bergen) whom he loves is equally immature, given to pouting and aimless tear-ridden sessions in which she berates him for not leaving his spouse. Montand's acting consists of who-cares shrugs, a downturned mouth, eyebrows raised in boredom, and tired line readings. Bergen has seemingly been asked to improvise many of her scenes, but she lacks spontaneity and self-confidence. Much better is Annie Girardot in the hazily defined role of Montand's long-suffering wife.

VIVRE SA VIE
FILM EN DOUZE TABLEAUX
(MY LIFE TO LIVE; IT'S MY LIFE)

1962, 80 mins, France Ⓥ

D: Jean-Luc Godard **A:** Anna Karina, Saddy Rebbot, Andre Labarthe, G.

Schlumberger, Gerard Hoffman, Monique Messine (Braunberger)

As he looked at a young, cynical hoodlum in *Breathless*, director Jean-Luc Godard brings his dispassionate outlook to a pretty girl who slips into prostitution. Nothing sentimental here but a knowing series of episodes that skillfully probes the girl's character and life. First she breaks with a weak, self-indulgent boyfriend (Andre Labarthe). She then gets locked out of her apartment, leaves her job, and goes into prostitution. She ends up with a procurer (Saddy Rebot). When she tries to break with him for a young man, she is sold to another group, only to be shot down when they fight over money. Godard mixes titles, unusual use of sound, and long scenes of dialogue. Anna Karina gives the girl a ring of truth and depth.

V.I. WARSHAWSKI

1991, 89 mins, US Ⓥ ⊙

D: Jeff Kanew **A:** Kathleen Turner, Jay O. Saunders, Charles Durning, Angela Goethals, Nancy Paul, Frederick Coffin (Hollywood/Chestnut Hill)

You can't be much worse-offski than to sit through *V.I. Warshawski*. Klutzy murder mystery was obviously intended to be the first in a series about the eponymous femme detective impersonated by Kathleen Turner. The story has Warshawski getting involved in dirty business among three warring brothers. One brother, a former hockey player for whom V.I. has eyes, is killed in a suspicious dockside explosion. Warshawski is responsible for his 13-year-old daughter Kat (Angela Goethals), whom she was babysitting when the girl's father was sent into permanent slumber. From a filmmaking point of view, it is all uninspired and perfunctory, utterly lacking in a sense of style that might have made this punchy fun. Turner would seem to have been perfectly cast in such a sassy, confident part, but even she can't drive a totally rusty vehicle.

VIXEN!

1968, 71 mins, US

D: Russ Meyer **A:** Erica Gavin, Harrison Page, Garth Pillsbury, Michael O'Donnell, Vincene Wallace, Robert Aiken (Eve/Coldstream)

Russ Meyer's film is another of his technically polished sexploit dramas, this time free of physical violence and brutality. Vixen is a girl who can't say no, and she proves it every seven minutes. She finds time for her husband, too. There is a frankness to Meyer's sex scenes, in that they are unabashed in their frequent amorality, motivated without hypocrisy, and executed with dispatch. No tortured rationalizing here (Meyer's budget—$70,000— couldn't afford it anyway), nor any so phisticated gloss-over. His people simply meet, rut a bit, then move along. The se quences are often hilarious in their unbe lievability.

VOGUES OF 1938
1937, 108 mins, US Ⓥ
D: Irving Cummings **A:** Warner Baxter, Joan Bennett, Helen Vinson, Mischa Auer, Alan Mowbray, Jerome Cowan (Wanger/ United Artists)

A distinct departure from routine pic ture producing, *Vogues of 1938* has an in genious script of surprising elasticity. The screenplay is more of a libretto than a tightly knit story, exposing the inner work ings of the fashion racket, the rivalry for the latest Paris designs and models, the methods of exploiting styles, and the salesmanship necessary to convince fickle women that they must buy only what the establishments have for sale. Production numbers are incorporated in the public showings of new styles in costumes, furs, and lingerie. Warner Baxter plays the pro prietor of the House of Curson. When Joan Bennett's society girl pleads with him to delay delivery of her wedding cos tume, he refuses to fall down on an order, but hires her as a model after she walks out.

VOLCANO
1997, 102 mins, US Ⓥ ⊙
D: Mick Jackson **A:** Tommy Lee Jones, Anne Heche, Gaby Hoffmann, Don Chea dle, Jacqueline Kim, Keith David (Shuler Donner-Donner/Moritz Original/20th Century- Fox)

A furiously paced popcorn picture whose outrageous implausibility is some what amusing, *Volcano* never generates a head of true excitement, partly because the characters remain constructs to perform designed functions. A nerve-jangling morning earthquake puts city workers on alert. Mike Roark (Tommy Lee Jones), di rector of L.A.'s Office of Emergency Management, takes remarkably efficient control of the situation. Turning up to help out is crack seismologist Dr. Amy Barnes (Anne Heche). Less than a half-hour in, the Big One hits. A fiery geyser erupts from the La Brea Tar Pits, producing a lava flow that heads right onto Wilshire Boulevard (fortunately, in the opposite di rection from the offices of *Variety,* just a block to the east). Remaining hour is oc cupied by the frantic battle to stem the molten tide. Production delivers the goods on the physical side, although lava is not the most exciting of the destructive natural forces to watch on screen.

LES VOLEURS (THIEVES)
1996, 118 mins, France Ⓥ
D: Andre Techine **A:** Daniel Auteuil, Catherine Deneuve, Laurence Cote, Be noit Magimel, Julien Riviere, Didier Be zace (Sarde/TF1/Rhone-Alpes/DA)

Director Andre Techine's *Thieves* ele vates a seemingly routine police drama into a *Rashomon*-style exploration of fam ily and amorous ties. The drama is initially viewed from the perspective of Justin (Ju lien Riviere), a 10-year-old boy, but Alex (Daniel Auteuil), a Lyon detective, contin ues the story with his encounter with Ju liette (Laurence Cote), a young woman whose brother works for Alex's brother Ivan (Didier Bezace), a crime boss. Alex and Juliette carry on a tortured relation ship, complicated by the young woman's affair with Marie (Catherine Deneuve), a professor. The film demands a chess mas ter's concentration. Techine never favors any of the four primary characters, letting the viewer decide where to place empha sis. While a knockout of fluid direction, the technical virtuosity never stands in the way of the highly emotional plot.

VOLUNTEERS
1985, 106 mins, US Ⓥ ⊙
D: Nicholas Meyer **A:** Tom Hanks, John Candy, Rita Wilson, Tim Thomerson, Gedde Watanabe, George Plimpton (HBO)

Volunteers is a very broad and mostly flat comedy about hijinx in the Peace Corps, circa 1962. Tom Hanks plays an arrogant, snide rich boy from Yale who trades places with an earnest Peace Corps designate when his gambling debts land him in danger of his life at home. Once ensconced in a remote village, contentious couple Hanks and cohort Rita Wilson and ultra do-gooder John Candy set out to build a bridge across a river. Kidnapped and brainwashed by the commies, the gung-ho Candy disappears for a long stretch. Lensed in Mexico, pic features a muddy, ugly look, and the most offensively blatant plug for Coca-Cola yet seen in the new era of Coke-owned entertainment companies.

VOLVER A EMPEZAR
(TO BEGIN AGAIN; BEGIN THE
BEGUINE)
1982, 90 mins, Spain
D: Jose Luis Garci A: Antonio Ferrandis, Encarna Paso, Jose Bodalo, Agustin Gonzalez, Pablo Hoyo, Marta Fernandez Muro (Nickel Odeon)

Pic seems simple in its plot and characterizations but is buoyed by outstanding performances; a script that is sensitive, eloquent, and pointed; and flawless direction, cinematography, and editing. Story concerns an exiled Spanish novelist and Nobel prize-winner who returns to his northern native town after 40 years for a two-day trip into the past. The reason is that he's terminally ill. The writer walks about the town, looks up an old girlfriend from pre-war days, watches a soccer game, and is showered with honors. Though subject is maudlin and once or twice director Jose Luis Garci veers close to the lachrymose, he succeeds in keeping the story upbeat.
1982: Best Foreign Language Film

VON RYAN'S EXPRESS
1965, 114 mins, US ⊗ ▭
D: Mark Robson A: Frank Sinatra, Trevor Howard, Raffaella Carra, Brad Dexter, Sergio Fantoni, John Leyton (20th Century-Fox)

Mass escape of 600 American and British prisoners-of-war across 1943 Nazi-controlled Italy lends colorful backing to this fast, suspenseful, and exciting World War II tale. Frank Sinatra and Trevor Howard co-star as leaders of the escape who seize a freight train bearing prisoners for delivery to the Germans in Austria and divert it across northern Italy in an attempt to find haven in Switzerland. Sinatra plays a hard-boiled American Air Force colonel named Ryan, imprisoned in the Italian camp where Howard, an equally tough British major, is senior officer.
1965: Nomination: Best Sound Effects

VOYAGE OF THE DAMNED
1976, 155 mins, UK ⊗
D: Stuart Rosenberg A: Faye Dunaway, Max von Sydow, Oskar Werner, Malcolm McDowell, Orson Welles, James Mason (ITC/Associated Pictures)

Voyage of the Damned is a sluggish melodrama, loaded with familiar film names who flesh out the diverse formula characters involved in this story about a ship carrying Jews away from Nazi Germany, to which Cuba will deny entry per-

mit, thereby fulfilling a Nazi propaganda plan. Max von Sydow, a non-Nazi German, is skipper of the ship. That the story is based on an actual incident makes its transfer to the screen all the more disappointing.
1976: Nominations: Best Supp. Actress (Lee Grant), Adapted Screenplay, Original Score

VOYAGER
1991, 117 mins, Germany/France ⊗
D: Volker Schlondorff A: Sam Shepard, Julie Delpy, Barbara Sukowa, Dieter Kirchlechner, Traci Lind, Deborra-Lee Furness (Bioskop/Action)

Equal parts road movie and Greek tragedy, Volker Schlondorff's latest literary adaptation makes good use of fine material. Walter Faber (Sam Shepard) is an inveterate traveler in 1950s Europe, the quintessentially cool cowboy-loner-businessman. He recalls his student days in Zurich before the war: he was in love with Hanna, a German Jew pregnant with his child. Waiting for a flight to Venezuela, Faber learns that his friend Joachim married Hanna, and they had a daughter but divorced shortly afterward. Back in New York, he decides to travel to Paris by ship. On board he meets Sabeth (Julie Delpy), in her twenties and returning home after studying in the States. Her charm and fragile beauty begin to take effect.

VOYAGE TO ITALY
See: Viaggio in Italia

VOYAGE TO THE BOTTOM OF THE SEA
1961, 105 mins, US ⊗ ▭
D: Irwin Allen A: Walter Pidgeon, Joan Fontaine, Barbara Eden, Peter Lorre, Michael Ansara, Frankie Avalon (20th Century-Fox)

Voyage is a crescendo of mounting jeopardy. A brilliant admiral (Walter Pidgeon), commander of an atomic submarine, devises a scheme to save mankind when life on earth is threatened when the Van Allen Belt of Radiation encircling the globe goes berserk and erupts. Pidgeon heads for a spot near the Marianas, where he plans to orbit a Polaris and explode the heavenly blaze out into space. Viewers who expect an advanced course in oceanography will discover only an occasional giant squid and a lot of rubbery vegetation. The bottom of director Irwin Allen's sea is merely the setting for the kind of emotional calisthenics that might just as easily break out on the top of Mount Everest. The acting is about the best it can be under the trying dramatic circumstances.

VOYNA I MIR I
ANDREI BOLKONSKY
(WAR AND PEACE, PART I)
1966, 140 mins, USSR Ⓥ ▭

D: Sergei Bondarchuk A: Lyudmila Savelyeva, Sergei Bondarchuk, Vyacheslav Tikhonov, Anatoli Ktorov, Boris Smirnov, Kira Ivanova-Golovko (Mosfilm)

More than three years in the making, *War and Peace* is a sumptuous and lavish spectacular, making brilliant use of the 70mm screen. Sergei Bondarchuk has kept to his intention of making a faithful film of Leo Tolstoy's famous novel, and the film suffers occasionally from being too literary. The production is superb. The two great battle scenes in the first part are nothing short of breathtaking. But in his determination to translate the novel literally, Bondarchuk tries to be too poetic and overdoes it with endless shots of clouds, trees, and the countryside. Bondarchuk's own performance in the demanding role of the shy, tongue-tied Pierre is quite remarkable, from a drunk scene with fellow officers in the opening stages to his embarrassed proposal to the beautiful Helene (Irina Skobtseva).

VOYNA I MIR II
NATASHA ROSTOVA
(WAR AND PEACE, PART II)
1966, 90 mins, USSR Ⓥ ▭

D: Sergei Bondarchuk A: Lyudmila Savelyeva, Sergei Bondarchuk, Vyacheslav Tikhonov, Anastasia Vertinskaya, Vladislav Strzhelchik, Irina Skobtseva (Mosfilm)

The spectacle in *War and Peace* is not confined to battle sequences. In *Natasha Rostova*, there is a superbly staged and photographed ballroom scene and a magnificent hunt. Lyudmila Savelyeva, the Leningrad ballerina who plays the part of Natasha, is a joy to behold. All the fresh, impetuous eagerness of youth comes out in her performance, and it comes out naturally. There's an incandescent glow whenever she's on screen. Another imposing performance comes from Vyacheslav Tikhonov as Prince Andrei Bolkonsky.

VOYNA I MIR III
1812 GOD
(WAR AND PEACE, PART III)
1967, 85 mins, USSR Ⓥ ▭

D: Sergei Bondarchuk A: Lyudmila Savelyeva, Sergei Bondarchuk, Vyacheslav Tikhonov, Boris Zakhava, V. Stanitsyn, Vladislav Strzhelchik (Mosfilm)

Part III deals with the death of Prince Andrei's father; Pierre's visit to the young Natasha; and the battlefield of Borodino, where Pierre wanders amidst the carnage. The film remains posey and conventional, often opting for tableaus rather than a more personal look at the war and its effect on the Russian people and country. But its sheer size soon casts a spell. The camera will suddenly zoom up from the field, disclosing thousands of scurrying men, horses and battle gear, or watch one character face death. All this takes on a hypnotic quality, and somehow the logistics of battle are clear. Napoleon, brooding in the midst of hundreds of bodies, is the final shot while a stentorian voice extols the victory of the Russian moral drive over the French will of conquest.

VOYNA I MIR IV
PYER BEZUKHOV
(WAR AND PEACE, PART IV)
1967, 95 mins, USSR Ⓥ ▭

D: Sergei Bondarchuk A: Lyudmila Savelyeva, Sergei Bondarchuk, Vyacheslav Tikhonov, Boris Zakhava, Vladislav Strzhelchik (Mosfilm)

Fourth and final part of the massive Russian costumer is an impressive windup to this super spectacle, with a cumulative force that overcomes some of its academic and posey qualities. It deals with Pierre's capture and near-execution when Napoleonic troops invade and burn Moscow, the death of Prince Andrei, and Pierre's final uniting with Natasha after the retreat of Napoleon's troops in the terrible Russian winter. It reaches grandiose proportions and an operatic, almost ecstatic, quality that is in keeping with the book via Tolstoy's cosmic vision. The camera zooming through a burning building, Pierre's rage at soldierly inhumanity, the prince's death, a mother's mourning, the young girl's anguish—all work as comments on man's prevailing end and overcome the sentimentality and overdone aspects in some of the earlier segments.

1968: Best Foreign Language Film

WABASH AVENUE
1950, 90 mins, US

D: Henry Koster **A:** Betty Grable, Victor Mature, Phil Harris, James Barton, Reginald Gardiner, Margaret Hamilton (20th Century-Fox)

Plot is a satisfactory backdrop for a deluge of tunes. There's nothing in the writing to tax the dramatic skill of the players, and they romp along neatly. Phil Harris and Victor Mature portray friendly enemies, out to beat each other with a smile. It's all good fun as long as they cheat each other at cards and win and lose their various business enterprises. It's more serious, though, when they compete for Grable and skulduggery runs high.

WAGES OF FEAR
See: Sorcerer

WAGES OF FEAR, THE
See: Le Salaire de la Peur

WAGNER
1983, 300 mins, UK/Austria/Hungary ⊙

D: Tony Palmer **A:** Richard Burton, Vanessa Redgrave, Gemma Craven, Marthe Keller, John Gielgud, Ralph Richardson (London Trust Cultural)

There's nothing particularly intimate or revelatory about this five-hour biopic of the German 19th-century composer. It begins in Dresden in 1848 when Richard Wagner (Richard Burton) was beginning to gain notoriety for his compositions and grand, heroic operas. He was also actively involved in the movement for a unified Germany. So begins Wagner's 40-year trek across Europe for the most part as a stateless artist. Ludwig II becomes his patron. Along the way there are mounting bills, political scandals, and Faustian pursuits. Burton's performance as Wagner presents an almost entirely unsympathetic picture.

WAGON MASTER
1950, 85 mins, US ⊙

D: John Ford **A:** Ben Johnson, Harry Carey Jr., Ward Bond, Joanne Dru, Alan Mowbray, Jane Darwell (RKO/Argosy)

Wagon Master is a good outdoor action film, done in the best John Ford manner. That means careful character development and movement, spiced with high spots of action, good drama and leavening comedic moments. The story deals with a wagon train of Mormons seeking a rich valley in which to locate. They are led by Ward Bond, who hires horsetraders Ben Johnson and Harry Carey Jr. to guide the pioneers to their new land.

WAGONS EAST!
1994, 106 mins, US ⊙

D: Peter Markle **A:** John Candy, Richard Lewis, John C. McGinley, Ellen Greene, Robert Picardo, Ed Lauter (Carolco/Outlaw)

Wagons East! records John Candy's final hours spent before the cameras. Unfortunately, they were far from his finest. Everyone's creative burners were on low heat for this woeful outing. Gag is completely related by the title: a bunch of Old West pioneers who have had enough of bank robbers, cattle rustlers, drunken boors, and intolerant know-nothings decide to head back from whence they came. To guide them east, they hire wagonmaster James Harlow (Candy), who has a pretty shaky sense of direction. Trek is opposed by the big-money rail interests, who fear bad publicity if word of the malcontents gets around.

WAGONS ROLL AT NIGHT, THE
1941, 83 mins, US

D: Ray Enright **A:** Humphrey Bogart, Sylvia Sidney, Eddie Albert, Joan Leslie, Sig Ruman, Cliff Clark (Warner)

The Wagons Roll at Night is a fast-moving meller. Background is supplied by a traveling carnival operated by the tough and calloused Humphrey Bogart, who succeeds in evading successive sheriffs to keep the show moving. Bogart delivers his usually capable characterization, putting plenty of zest into his role of the carny operator. Eddie Albert is excellent as the bumpkin, providing plenty of lightness and humor to the part.

WAG THE DOG
1997, 97 mins, US ⊙ ⊙

D: Barry Levinson **A:** Dustin Hoffman, Robert De Niro, Anne Heche, Woody Harrelson, Denis Leary, Willie Nelson (Tribeca/Baltimore/Punch)

Glib cynicism isn't a tremendously appealing quality, but in *Wag the Dog* it at least has the benefit of comic precision and polished handling. Two weeks before he's up for re-election, the president (Michael Belson) is accused of accosting a

Girl Scout in the Oval Office. Before the news reaches the media, his advisors, led by Winifred Ames (Anne Heche), call in a mysterious political consultant, Conrad Brean (Robert De Niro), who specializes in near-impossible image rescues. His ruse is to buy time by whipping up an aura of impending national crisis. Brean jets off to Hollywood producer Stanley Motss (Dustin Hoffman), a caricature come to life with his carefully cultivated tan, tennis togs and upswept hairdo. Motss jumps at orchestrating a patriotic campaign against the enemy du jour picked by Brean: Albania. De Niro seems to hang back to let his costar have a clear field.

1997: Nominations: Best Actor (Dustin Hoffman), Screenplay Adaptation

WAITING TO EXHALE
1995, 121 mins, US Ⓥ ⊙
D: Forest Whitaker **A:** Whitney Houston, Angela Bassett, Loretta Devine, Lela Rochon, Gregory Hines, Dennis Haysbert (20th Century-Fox)

Waiting to Exhale smoothly combines the elan and emotional luxuriance of old-fashioned women's mellers with a modern black-pop sensibility in a tale of four women beset by romantic perplexities. The four friends here are well-off Southwestern suburbanites whose only want is romance: all complain of the dearth of black men able to forge long-term commitments. Briskly paced, pic deftly interweaves stories of the four women over a year. Assigned the pic's meatiest role, Angela Bassett gives a performance at once fiery and delicate. Whitney Houston follows her *Bodyguard* debut with another glamorous turn, while Lela Rochon's spunky charm and Loretta Devine's earthy aplomb round out the quartet of well-matched performances.

WAIT UNTIL DARK
1967, 107 mins, US Ⓥ
D: Terence Young **A:** Audrey Hepburn, Alan Arkin, Richard Crenna, Efrem Zimbalist Jr., Jack Weston, Samantha Jones (Warner)

Wait Until Dark emerges as an excellent suspense drama, effective in casting, scripting, direction and genuine emotional impact. Audrey Hepburn stars as the not-so-helpless blind heroine. Hubby Efrem Zimbalist Jr. has made his wife self-sufficient and able to fend for herself in their apartment. Heroin-smuggling Samantha Jones plants a dope-loaded doll in his possession. Alan Arkin sets out to intimidate Hepburn into surrendering the doll.

1967: Nomination: Best Actress (Audrey Hepburn)

WAKE ISLAND
1942, 87 mins, US Ⓥ
D: John Farrow **A:** Brian Donlevy, Robert Preston, Macdonald Carey, Albert Dekker, Barbara Britton, William Bendix (Paramount)

The heroic defense of Wake Island in December 1941 by some 385 US marines has been reproduced as a screen feature almost minutely faithful to the facts and without stooping to cheapness in any way. Brian Donlevy is excellent as the unexcitable major who commanded the post. Albert Dekker overdoes things just a bit as a tough construction superintendent, while Macdonald Carey shows fine restraint as a flier who is trying to even the score for the death of his wife at Pearl Harbor.

1942: Nominations: Best Picture, Director, Supp. Actor (William Bendix), Original Screenplay

WAKE OF THE RED WITCH
1949, 106 mins, US Ⓥ
D: Edward Ludwig **A:** John Wayne, Gail Russell, Gig Young, Luther Adler, Adele Mara, Eduard Franz (Republic)

Wake of the Red Witch, with its Polynesian locale, is replete with action, drama, and adventure. Story is a gripping account of deadly rivalry between two men. Struggle between John Wayne, an impetuous sea captain, and his employer, shipping tycoon Luther Adler, should have been stressed more fully.

WAKE UP AND LIVE
1937, 91 mins, US
D: Sidney Lanfield **A:** Walter Winchell, Ben Bernie and His Band, Alice Faye, Patsy Kelly, Ned Sparks, Jack Haley (20th Century-Fox)

Both Alice Faye and Jack Haley are capital as the love interest, the former never looking better and handling light emotional scenes with conviction. Walter Winchell and bandleader Ben Bernie play themselves, and are swell. This duel holds up in the picture, especially since it's deftly tied with the story. Patsy Kelly, as Winchell's girl Friday, and Ned Sparks, as his chief spy, are corking comedy support.

WALKABOUT
1971, 95 mins, UK Ⓥ
D: Nicolas Roeg **A:** Jenny Agutter, Lucien John, David Gulpilil, John Meillon, John Illingsworth (Raab-Litvinoff)

Walkabout is a tepid artistic effort

about two children, lost in the Australian wilds, who are befriended by an aborigine. Nicolas Roeg directed and photographed on authentic locations. But pretty pictures alone cannot sustain this fragile and forced screen adaptation of a James Vance Marshall novel. Jenny Agutter and Lucien John find themselves alone in the desert after father John Meillon tries to kill the boy and then shoots himself. On the kids' long trek in search of civilization, they encounter David Gulpilil, an aborigine who guides them toward rescue. In an effort to pump up the plot, Roeg resorts to ad nauseam inserts of insects, reptiles, and assorted wild beasts, in varying stages of life and decay.

WALK A CROOKED MILE
1948, 90 mins, US
D: Gordon Douglas **A:** Louis Hayward, Dennis O'Keefe, Louise Allbritton, Raymond Burr, Onslow Stephens (Columbia)

The documentary technique gives a factual gloss to the high melodramatics of *Walk a Crooked Mile*. A Southern California atom plant is losing its top secrets, and the FBI and Scotland Yard, in the respective persons of Dennis O'Keefe and Louis Hayward, join forces to run down the criminals. Dialogue is good and situations believably developed, even the highly contrived melodramatic finale.

WALK DON'T RUN
1966, 114 mins, US ⊗ ⊙ ▭
D: Charles Walters **A:** Cary Grant, Samantha Eggar, Jim Hutton, John Standing, Miiko Taka, Ted Hartley (Columbia/Granley)

Walk Don't Run is a completely entertaining, often hilarious romantic comedy. This fast-moving and colorful production pegs its laughs on a Tokyo housing shortage during the 1964 Olympics. Cary Grant is an English industrialist who arrives two days before his Tokyo hotel suite will be available. Noting an apartment-to-share sign, he finds it to be the diggings of prim, schedule-conscious Samantha Eggar. She is engaged to a stuffy embassy functionary, played by John Standing, with whom Grant has already had a run-in.

WALKER
1987, 95 mins, US ⊗
D: Alex Cox **A:** Ed Harris, Marlee Matlin, Peter Boyle, Bianca Guerra, Richard Masur, Rene Auberjonois (Incine/Universal)

The potentially fascinating story of an American adventurer who installed himself as president of Nicaragua, *Walker* unfortunately exists for one reason only—for director Alex Cox to vent his spleen about continued American interference with the Central American country. The comic, idiosyncratic approach has merit in theory, but the result onscreen is a fiasco. With the financial backing of tycoon Cornelius Vanderbilt, Walker led a mercenary band of 58 men to Nicaragua in 1855 and ruled the tiny nation with an increasingly heavy hand for two years until being kicked out. Cox makes a muddled attempt to paint Walker as an idealist who becomes fatally twisted after the premature death of his fiancée.

WALKING AND TALKING
1996, 83 mins, US/UK ⊗
D: Nicole Holofcener **A:** Catherine Keener, Anne Heche, Todd Field, Liev Schreiber, Kevin Corrigan, Randall Batnikoff (Good Machine/Zenith)

Walking and Talking is a glibly observant comedy about the anxieties of romance and the evolution of a female friendship. Written and cut with an eye more toward jokes than on developing much emotional depth, writer-director Nicole Holofcener's first feature is boosted by uniformly droll lead performances as well as by impressively confident filmmaking savvy. Zippy script charts the relationship of best friends Amelia (Catherine Keener) and Laura (Anne Heche), young Manhattan professionals. Laura's upcoming marriage to Frank (Todd Field) gives her much less time to counsel Amelia about her romantic woes. The two young actresses have been seen to favorable advantage before but haven't had such an opportunity to fly until now.

WALKING DEAD, THE
1936, 62 mins, US ⊗
D: Michael Curtiz **A:** Boris Karloff, Ricardo Cortez, Edmund Gwenn, Marguerite Churchill, Warren Hull, Barton MacLane (Warner)

Boris Karloff plays a sensitive musician who twice gets himself into prison. After his discharge, he artlessly becomes embroiled with a racketeering gang and in the murder of the judge who had sent him away. Karloff protests his innocence, but the governor's pardon doesn't get to the prison until after the first electric shock has been applied. An operation brings the executed man back to life. The living dead man has acquired a supernatural power to recognize his enemies and to track them down one by one.

WALKING DEAD, THE
1995, 89 mins, US ⌑
D: Preston A. Whitmore II **A:** Allen Payne, Eddie Griffin, Joe Morton, Vonte Sweet, Roger Floyd (Price)

Playing tribute to the black combat soldier, *The Walking Dead* is an earnest, socially conscious pic that is not terribly effective as an actioner or personal drama. Set in 1972, tale centers on Sergeant Barkley (Joe Morton) and his fellow Marines as they are assigned their last mission, which involves evacuating all remaining survivors from a p.o.w. camp abandoned by the Viet Cong.

WALKING HILLS, THE
1949, 78 mins, US
D: John Sturges **A:** Randolph Scott, Ella Raines, Arthur Kennedy, John Ireland, William Bishop, Edgar Buchanan (Columbia)

An out-of-the-way westerner opening in a Mexican border town, *The Walking Hills* introduces eight men who accidentally stumble on some information pointing to the location in the desert of a 100-year-old wagon train loaded with bullion. Attempt to handle the cross-currents of greed for gold and a three-way romantic tangle is not fully successful due to a slightly hazy plot.

WALKING STICK, THE
1970, 100 mins, US ⌑
D: Eric Till **A:** David Hemmings, Samantha Eggar, Emlyn Williams, Phyllis Calvert, Ferdy Mayne, Dudley Sutton (Winkast/M-G-M)

The Walking Stick concerns a physically handicapped girl who finds love, then betrayal, in a jewel robbery. Hemmings plays a tool of Emlyn Williams, an art dealer whose night acquisitions come via robbery. Eggar, who works in a gallery, is pressured into the heist. Her dilemma—should she give up her happiness by reporting to the police?—is resolved in a somewhat melodramatic way.

WALK IN THE CLOUDS, A
1995, 103 mins, US ⓥ ⊙
D: Alfonso Arau **A:** Keanu Reeves, Aitana Sanchez-Gijon, Anthony Quinn, Giancarlo Giannini, Angelica Aragon, Evangelina Elizondo (Zucker/20th Century-Fox)

At the end of World War II, returning vet Paul Sutton (Keanu Reeves) is left stranded roadside with a beautiful fellow traveler, Victoria (Aitana Sanchez-Gijon). She's pregnant by a departed lover, and Paul gallantly agrees to appear as her husband. Alberto Aragon (Giancarlo Giannini) at first spurns his supposed son-in-law. Paul is welcomed by the rest of the clan, especially gregarious patriarch Don Pedro (Anthony Quinn). Arau stages all this with a determined gusto that at least has the virtue of consistency, with winning performances from Giannini, Quinn, and Sanchez-Gijon. It's hardly her fault that the drama founders on a lack of electricity between the lovers, because Reeves offers more in the way of looks and presence than thesping savvy.

WALK IN THE SHADOW
See: Life for Ruth

WALK IN THE SPRING RAIN, A
1970, 98 mins, US ⓥ ⌑
D: Guy Green **A:** Anthony Quinn, Ingrid Bergman, Fritz Weaver, Katherine Crawford, Tom Fielding, Virginia Gregg (Columbia)

Ingrid Bergman and hubby Fritz Weaver go on sabbatical to the Tennessee mountain country so he can write a law text. Bergman finds love beating again in her bosom. The reason is Anthony Quinn, a Zorba-like hillbilly. Quinn has a cackling wife, played terribly by Virginia Gregg. He also has a son, played by Tom Fielding in the style of a method actor satire. At least he doesn't even bother faking a Dixie accent.

WALK IN THE SUN, A
1945, 117 mins, US ⓥ ⊙
D: Lewis Milestone **A:** Dana Andrews, Richard Conte, John Ireland, Norman Lloyd, Lloyd Bridges, Huntz Hall (20th Century-Fox)

As a film, *Walk* is not so sunny. Too frequently the author is given to spieling the colorful talk of the enlisted man, and thus allows his yarn to flounder. Film concerns an operation by a platoon of American soldiers after they hit the beach at Salerno. They're detailed to wipe out a farmhouse and its Nazi occupants. The rest of the pic is concerned with reactions of the GIs to the conditions under which they're fighting, their thoughts, and so forth. Dana Andrews gives a forthright performance as a sergeant, and the rest of the impressive cast know their way around a script—particularly Richard Conte, who has the best lines.

WALK LIKE A DRAGON
1960, 95 mins, US
D: James Clavell **A:** Jack Lord, Nobu Mc-
Carthy, James Shigeta, Mel Torme, Benson Fong (Paramount)

Producer-director-writer James Clavell
sets his story in the Old West, and utilizes
some interesting, offbeat historical data.
Film is based on an interracial romantic
triangle consisting of one tall, strapping
American (Jack Lord); one proud, rebellious Chinaman (James Shigeta); and one
frail, would-be Chinese slave girl (Nobu
McCarthy). Rescuing the latter from enforced prostitution, Lord bumps into mass
discrimination and an emotional duel with
Shigeta when he brings the girl to live in
his home. Mel Torme, as a gun-totin',
scripture-spoutin' deacon, plays the offbeat role with a flourish, but appears
bewildered by the nebulous nature of the
character. As director, Clavell's approach
tends to form predictably repetitive patterns such as following each soft, tender
sequence with an explosion of gunfire to
open the next one.

WALK ON THE WILD SIDE
1962, 114 mins, US Ⓥ
D: Edward Dmytryk **A:** Laurence Harvey,
Capucine, Jane Fonda, Anne Baxter, Barbara Stanwyck, Joanna Moore (Columbia)

Laurence Harvey plays a drifter in
search of his lady, Capucine, who it turns
out is a member of the Doll House in New
Orleans. She shows a classic, Garbo-type
beauty but is limited in emotional range.
Jane Fonda cops the show with her hoydenish behavior as another member of the
house. Barbara Stanwyck is steely as the
madame who looks to Capucine for the
"affection" she cannot find in her maimed
husband. Dmytryk maintains a steady
pace, but more forcefulness in both direction and writing might have provided more
dramatic impact.
1962: Nomination: Best Song ("Walk on
the Wild Side")

**WALK WITH LOVE AND DEATH,
A**
1969, 90 mins, US
D: John Huston **A:** Anjelica Huston, Assaf
Dayan, Anthony Corlan, John Hallam,
Robert Lang, Michael Gough (20th
Century-Fox)

A Walk with Love and Death is set in
the French Middle Ages when human life
was valueless, social order unbending, and
individual outlook bleak. Director John
Huston tells his story unhurriedly, lingering over details of style and torture. His
young hero, Assaf Dayan, obeying a mystic call from the sea, leaves Paris and studies behind to journey on foot through the
war-scarred French countryside. His meeting with Anjelica Huston, daughter of a
nobleman, is the beginning of the end for
the scholar and the lady. The slow pace
and gloomy atmosphere tend to dull
viewer interest.

WALL STREET
1987, 124 mins, US Ⓥ
D: Oliver Stone **A:** Michael Douglas,
Charlie Sheen, Daryl Hannah, Martin
Sheen, Terence Stamp, Sean Young
(Pressman/American Entertainment/20th
Century-Fox)

Watching Oliver Stone's Wall Street is
about as wordy and dreary as reading the
financial papers. Young broker (Charlie
Sheen) is seduced by the power and financial stature of megalomaniacal arbitrageur
Gordon Gekko (Michael Douglas), a nasty
manipulator barking orders to buy and sell
and delivering declamatory speeches on
how greed is what makes America great.
As the easily duped sort, Sheen doesn't
elicit much sympathy. Martin Sheen as his
father, an airplane mechanic, is the only
person worth caring about.
1987: Best Actor (Michael Douglas)

WALTZ OF THE TOREADORS
1962, 104 mins, UK Ⓥ
D: John Guillermin **A:** Peter Sellers, Dany
Robin, Margaret Leighton, John Fraser,
Cyril Cusack, Prunella Scales (Rank/In-
dependent Artists)

Too many moods jostle in this pic for
it to be a complete success. Slapstick,
farce, high comedy, drama, and tragedy
are all present, but they don't make easy
companions. Film concerns an elderly
general about to retire before World War
I. He is a man with a roving eye for the
girls, trapped by a neurotic, shrewish,
sham-invalid of a wife and two unprepossessing daughters. For 17 years, he has
had a platonic romance with a Frenchwoman, never having an opportunity to
consummate their love. She turns up determined that this sad state of affairs
should end. Sellers extracts laughs and
compassionate pity with equal ease.

WANDA
1970, 105 mins, US
D: Barbara Loden **A:** Barbara Loden, Michael Higgins (Foundation for Filmakers)

Wanda is a wanderer, a loser in a heavily industrialized part of the US. Barbara Loden shows a calm, dispassionate feel for direction and an insight into the psyche of an inarticulate woman. She does not force blame on anyone but denotes the growing conflicts between puritanism and promiscuity, poverty within plenty, and ignorance alongside the more educated. She has the vulnerability and yet inner resiliency that keeps her character from being a drudge.

WANDERER, THE
See: Le Grand Meaulnes

WANDERERS, THE
1979, 113 mins, US Ⓥ
D: Philip Kaufman **A:** Ken Wahl, John Friedrich, Karen Allen, Linda Manz, Toni Kalem, Tony Ganios (Orion)

Despite an uneasy blend of nostalgia and violence, *The Wanderers* is a well-made and impressive film, capturing the urban angst of growing up in the 1960s. Thesping is first-rate from the largely unknown cast. Disturbing elements crop up in the explicitly violent episodes, including those involving the symbolic Ducky Boys, a murderous pint-sized gang, and the Fordham Baldies, bald behemoths.

WANDERING JEW, THE
1923, 111 mins, UK ⊗
D: Maurice Elvey **A:** Matheson Lang, Hutin Britton, Malvina Longfellow, Isobel Elsom, Florence Sanders, Shayle Gardner (Stoll)

Matheson Lang's impersonation of the Jew, condemned to wander through the ages, arrogant, proud, though broken-hearted, is masterly. In the opening scenes we see his reviling of the Saviour on His way to Calvary and the dreadful outlawry which sent him into the world a wanderer. So the story goes down the years until at last the Inquisition gives him the peace and eternal rest which have always been denied him. Spectacularly, the production is very fine and the subject is treated with great reverence by Maurice Elvey.

WANDERING JEW, THE
1933, 110 mins, UK
D: Maurice Elvey **A:** Conrad Veidt, Marie Ney, Anne Grey, Joan Maude, Peggy Ashcroft (Twickenham/Gaumont-British)

The film is divided into four episodes: Jerusalem on the day of the Crucifixion; Antioch during the first crusade; Palermo, Sicily, in 1290; and Seville in 1560, during the Inquisition. It is a massive, artistic, and well-acted film, flavored perhaps by a surplus of scenes and detail. Conrad Veidt in the first half of the picture is guilty of scene-chewing, counteracted before the finish by a restrained, moving dignity. Peggy Ashcroft as the Magdalene in the fourth phase, who is converted by the Christ-like nobility of Battadios (Veidt), offers a fine characterization rich in feeling.

WANTON CONTESSA, THE
See: Senso

WAR, THE
1994, 125 mins, US Ⓥ ⊙
D: Jon Avnet **A:** Elijah Wood, Kevin Costner, Mare Winningham, Lexi Randall, Christine Baranski, Raynor Scheine (Island World/Universal)

Despite Kevin Costner's presence, *The War* really belongs to its child cast. The parallel between the Vietnam War and the children's feud with a local clan of kids feels heavy-handed and its attempts to infuse the narrative with a sense of spirituality is blatantly manipulative. Set in Mississippi in 1970, the story focuses on a poor family whose patriarch (Costner) has returned from Vietnam bearing emotional scars that make it difficult for him to hold a job. His wife (Mare Winningham) struggles to keep the family afloat, while the kids feud with the despised Lipnickis—an almost feral family of dirt-poor bullies. Elijah Wood, a gifted child actor, proves to be about the only cast member who doesn't stumble over his Southern drawl.

WAR AND PEACE
1956, 208 mins, US/Italy Ⓥ ⊙
D: King Vidor **A:** Audrey Hepburn, Henry Fonda, Mel Ferrer, Vittorio Gassman, John Mills, Anita Ekberg (Ponti-De Laurentiis/Paramount)

Hollywood and Italian know-how have produced a visual epic. The classic Tolstoy novel is digested into three-and-a-half hours of vivid cinematic magic, maintaining cohesiveness and fluidity of story and conveying the size and sweep of Bonaparte's armies at Austerlitz and Borodino. Audrey Hepburn is the epitome of wholesome young love under benevolent aristocratic rearing. Henry Fonda, the confused young liberal, is perhaps sometimes too literally the confused character.
1956: Nominations: Best Director, Color Cinematography, Color Costume Design

WAR AND PEACE, PART I
See: Voyna I Mir I
Andrei Bolkonsky

WAR AND PEACE, PART II
See: Voyna I Mir II
Natasha Rostova

WAR AND PEACE, PART III
See: Voyna I Mir III
1812 God

WAR AND PEACE, PART IV
See: Voyna I Mir IV
Pyer Bezukhov

WAR BETWEEN MEN AND WOMEN, THE
1972, 105 mins, US
D: Melville Shavelson **A:** Jack Lemmon, Barbara Harris, Jason Robards, Herb Edelman, Severn Darden, Lisa Eilbacher
(Cinema Center)

An amusing clambake of a James Thurber–like character portrayed by Jack Lemmon, *The War Between Men and Women* comes off as a first-rate comedy peopled by some delicious humans, as well as a pregnant pooch. Lemmon is an acerbic and grumpy New York writer and cartoonist whose failing eyesight and unflattering treatment of women in his works arouse the interest of Barbara Harris. Her children and the dog are unfriendly, and further problems arise when her former spouse arrives during the marriage ceremony.

WAR GAME, THE
1966, 50 mins, UK Ⓥ
D: Peter Watkins (BBC-TV)

A wholly imaginary picture of what could happen immediately before, during, and after a nuclear attack on Britain, *The War Game* is grim, gruesome, horrific, and realistic. It is not a pleasant picture to watch, but yet it is one that needs to be shown as widely as possible. The attack itself is predictably grim, but the most telling part is the aftermath of the bomb—the severely burned are killed off and their bodies burned, and looters face the firing squad. Watkins does an excellent and imaginative job, based on considerable research.
1966: Best Feature Documentary

WARGAMES
1983, 110 mins, US Ⓥ ⊚
D: John Badham **A:** Matthew Broderick, Dabney Coleman, John Wood, Ally Sheedy, Barry Corbin, Dennis Lipscomb
(United Artists)

Although the script has more than its share of short circuits, director John Badham solders the pieces into a terrifically exciting story. Matthew Broderick is a bright teenager, brilliant with computers. Aiming to sneak an advance look at a new line of video games, he taps into the country's Norad missile-defense system to challenge its computer to a game of global thermonuclear warfare. Ally Sheedy is perfectly perky as Broderick's girlfriend; Dabney Coleman brings his usual dissonance to the role of the computer-reliant defense specialist; but John Wood's large talents aren't fully used as the misanthropic eccentric who designed the computer.
1983: Nominations: Best Original Screenplay, Cinematography, Sound

WAR IS OVER, THE
See: La Guerre Est Finie

WARLOCK
1989, 102 mins, US Ⓥ ⊚
D: Steve Miner **A:** Richard E. Grant, Julian Sands, Lori Singer, Kevin O'Brien, Richard Kuse, Mary Woronov (New World)

Warlock is an attempt to concoct a pic from a pinch of occult chiller, a dash of fantasy thriller, and a splash of "stalk and slash." But what could have been a heady brew falls short, despite some gusto thesping from Richard E. Grant and Lori Singer. Pic opens in Massachusetts in 1691 where a contemptuous warlock (Julian Sands) is being readied for execution. But with a bit of nifty hocus-pocus, both he and witch-hunter Grant are sent to 1988 L.A. Sands gets back to his nasty habits as he pursues the magical book the Grand Grimoire. Director Steve Miner directs ably but doesn't avoid some of the horror cliches.

WARLOCK: THE ARMAGEDDON
1993, 93 mins, US Ⓥ ⊚
D: Anthony Hickox **A:** Julian Sands, Chris Young, Paula Marshall, Steve Kahan, Charles Hallahan, R. G. Armstrong
(Trimark/Tapestry)

Julian Sands remains unrepentantly evil in *Warlock: The Armageddon*. Though not specifically linked to the earlier horror thriller, this outing should satisfy fans of hokum-filled good-and-evil conflicts. The current mumbo jumbo involves the struggle for control of six Druidic runestones. The baubles not only have the ability to summon Satan's emissary but also to quell his nefarious activities. The Warlock's path leads to a Northern California hamlet that is one of the last enclaves of the virtually extinct sect. Its young designated defenders, Chris Young and Paula Marshall, are neither aware of nor trained in their roles. These scrubbed, wholesome teens are bland beside Sands's sinister histrionics. Director Tony Hickox, too, seems more at home with the bad guy.

WAR LORD, THE
1965, 120 mins, US Ⓥ ⊙ ▭
D: Franklin J. Schaffner **A:** Charlton Heston, Richard Boone, Rosemary Forsyth, Maurice Evans, Guy Stockwell, Niall MacGinnis (Universal/Court)

Franklin Schaffner's direction, while not always overcoming deficiencies of dialogue and Charlton Heston's sometimes vacillating characterization, in the main projects the proper spirit of a days-of-yore melodrama. His battle scenes, utilizing the weapons and tactics of the period, are particularly well handled. Script, set in the 11th century, presents Heston as war lord of the Duke of Normandy, detailed to oversee a primitive Druid village on the North Sea, whose inhabitants are constantly harassed by invaders from the north. Plot dwells on his mad passion for a village girl, claiming her on her wedding night according to custom of "droit de seigneur"—a lord's right of the first night. Heston is more convincing in his battle scenes than in romancing Rosemary Forsyth.

WARLORDS OF ATLANTIS
1978, 96 mins, UK Ⓥ
D: Kevin Connor **A:** Doug McClure, Peter Gilmore, Shane Rimmer, Lea Brodie, Michael Gothard, Cyd Charisse (EMI)

In *Warlords of Atlantis*, Doug McClure and other earthlings suffer a close encounter with Cyd Charisse and Daniel Massey, who rule over the legendary lost city. More terrifying were their brushes with various marine monsters on periodic rampages. And a good thing, too, in an otherwise skimpy reworking of the hoary Atlantis legend. The one virtue of the script is that it keeps the pot boiling. The cliched characters are played in workmanlike fashion by all hands.

WARLORDS OF THE 21ST CENTURY
See: Battletruck

WAR LOVER, THE
1962, 105 mins, US Ⓥ ⊙
D: Philip Leacock **A:** Steve McQueen, Robert Wagner, Shirley Anne Field, Gary Cockrell, Michael Crawford, Jerry Stovin (Columbia)

The scenario seems reluctant to come to grips with the chief character's unique personality—a "war lover" whose shell of heroic masculinity covers up a psychopathic inability to love or enjoy normal relationships with women. The story, set in 1943 England, focuses on B-17 bombing raids over Germany, with the title character (Steve McQueen) a pilot of one of the planes. That he emerges more of an unappealing symbol than a sympathetic flesh-and-blood portrait is no fault of McQueen, who plays with vigor and authority, although occasionally with too much eyeball emotion. Scenes of the bombing raids and accompanying aerial incidents are adroitly and authentically executed.

WARNING SHOT
1967, 100 mins, US
D: Buzz Kulik **A:** David Janssen, Ed Begley, Keenan Wynn, Sam Wanamaker, Lillian Gish, Stefanie Powers (Paramount)

Warning Shot is a police drama in which fine production, direction, and performances overcome a flawed script. David Janssen plays a cop accused of killing an apparently innocent medic. His only hope of vindication is proving the existence of a missing gun and the discovery of evidence to prove that the medic was breaking the law. Pic has the immediacy of headlines about police brutality and irresponsibility.

WAR OF THE BUTTONS
See: La Guerre des Boutons

WAR OF THE BUTTONS
1994, 90 mins, UK/France Ⓥ
D: John Roberts **A:** Liam Cunningham, Gregg Fitzgerald, Colm Meaney, John Coffey, Eveanna Ryan, Paul Batt (Enigma/Hugo)

This remake of the 1962 Gallic kidpic about warring tykes is old-fashioned in the best sense and manages to avoid almost every obstacle that time and changing values can throw in its path. Producer David Puttnam and writer Colin Welland have set it deep in rural Ireland, excluding all signs of modern adult life, giving the movie a sense of timelessness. Two villages, Carrickdowse and Ballydowse, straddle a stretch of tidal water. The scruffy Ballys are engaged in a permanent kids' war with the neighboring Carricks. To the movie's credit, any allegory to the present Irish troubles is simply there for the taking rather than being forced onto center stage. By keeping the focus tight on his young players, all non-professionals, debuting director John Roberts constructs a self-sufficient world.

WAR OF THE ROSES, THE
1989, 116 mins, US Ⓥ ⊙
D: Danny DeVito **A:** Michael Douglas, Kathleen Turner, Danny DeVito, Marianne Sagebrecht, Sean Astin, Heather Fairfield (Gracie/20th Century-Fox)

What Michael Douglas does to the fish at Kathleen Turner's dinner party in *War of the Roses,* director Danny DeVito does to the audience. Everything beautiful on screen in this glossily photographed film, from Douglas's antique sports car to the ravishingly leonine Turner herself, is thoroughly trashed by DeVito, whose sicko humor will wind up alienating everyone in the audience. Douglas is a workaholic D.C. lawyer married to Turner, a saucy former college gymnast. She realizes the marriage is a shell, but Douglas refuses to change his ways and causes her to seek a divorce. What keeps the film fresh are the sexually charged performances of the two attractive leads and the sarcastic twists DeVito and scripter Michael Leeson pull from the material.

WAR OF THE WORLDS, THE
1953, 85 mins, US Ⓥ
D: Byron Haskin **A:** Gene Barry, Ann Robinson, Les Tremayne, Lewis Martin, Robert Cornthwaite, Jack Kruschen (Paramount)

The War of the Worlds is a socko science-fiction feature, a story of the invasion of the earth by spider-like characters from Mars, against whom even the atom bomb is of no avail. The special effects group headed by Gordon Jennings loosens a reign of screen terror, of futile defense, demolished cities, charred landscapes, and people burned to ashes by the invaders' weapons. What is believed to be a huge meteor lands near a small town in Southern California, but turns out to be a Martian machine that turns deadly heat waves on humans, buildings, and anything else within range. An ominous commentary is spoken by Cedric Hardwicke.
1953: Best Special Effects
Nominations: Best Editing, Sound

WAR PARTY
1988, 99 mins, US Ⓥ ⊙
D: Franc Roddam **A:** Kevin Major Howard, M. Emmet Walsh (Hemdale)

A lethal contemporary game of Cowboys and Indians is played out in this revisionist western. Opening scene is the aftermath of a massacre 100 years ago. We move to present-day Montana and a small town with a large Indian population. The (white) Mayor has planned, as a tourist attraction, a re-enactment of that old battle; but racial hatreds run deep, and a drunken white boy kills an Indian youth whose pals quickly avenge him. Pic then develops into a manhunt as five Indian youths take off on horseback. Despite its interesting depiction of modern Indian life, *War Party* is basically just another pursuit movie, no better or worse than the average.

WARRENDALE
1967, 105 mins, Canada
D: Allan King (King)

A shattering documentary of a home for disturbed children and adolescents in Canada. Film deals with a group of young, dedicated workers who stay with these emotionally mixed-up youngsters and emerges as an engrossing, stark film. It is the treatment in this institution that is noteworthy in this psychologically absorbing, well-made, and incisive documentary.

WAR REQUIEM
1988, 85 mins, UK Ⓥ
D: Derek Jarman **A:** Nathaniel Parker, Tilda Swinton, Laurence Olivier, Patricia Hayes, Rohan McCullough, Nigel Terry (Anglo International/BBC)

A stunning visual and serious music treat, *War Requiem* is a visualization of Benjamin Britten's oratorio. It has no dialogue, though it opens with Laurence Olivier reciting Wilfred Owen's poem "Strange Meeting." Live-action footage is intercut with documentary footage from the Imperial War Museum. Pic uses the story of Owen's experiences in World War I, up to his death by a sniper bullet one week before the war ended, as its structure, while a nurse and unknown soldier are introduced to supplement Britten's musical scenarios.

WARRIORS, THE
1979, 90 mins, US Ⓥ ⊙
D: Walter Hill **A:** Michael Beck, James Remar, David Patrick Kelly, Deborah Van Valkenburgh, Mercedes Ruehl, Brian Tyler (Paramount)

Theme of this pic is a variation on

countless westerns and war films. The slaying of a hood is pinned on a Coney Island gang, the Warriors, and word goes out that the group's members are to be eliminated. It's a long subway ride to Coney Island, so for at least 70 of the film's 90 minutes, the boys in this band experience a variety of macho passage rites. As with his previous pix, director Walter Hill demonstrates outstanding visual sense.

WAR ROOM, THE
1993, 94 mins, US ⓥ ⊙
D: D. A. Pennebaker, Chris Hegedus **A:** James Carville, George Stephanopolous (Pennebaker)

If *The War Room* were a fictional feature, it would be a sure-fire star-making vehicle for James Carville. President Clinton's crafty, straight-talking campaign manager dominates this absorbing but basically unrevelatory behind-the-scenes look at the former Arkansas governor's long push for the presidency. With Clinton as a secondary character who pops in periodically, pic charts his nine-month campaign for the White House from the perspective of his key strategists, Carville, and communications director George Stephanopoulos. Cinema verite pioneer Pennebaker has valuably added to the official record with this fresh angle on the US political process.
1993: Nomination: Best Documentary Feature

WAR WAGON, THE
1967, 100 mins, US ⓥ ⊙ ▭
D: Burt Kennedy **A:** John Wayne, Kirk Douglas, Howard Keel, Robert Walker, Keenan Wynn, Bruce Cabot (Universal)

The War Wagon is an entertaining, exciting western drama of revenge, laced with action and humor. Burt Kennedy directs with an eye for panorama, as well as intimate, personal interaction. John Wayne, framed into prison by Bruce Cabot who then seizes his land to make a fortune in gold, returns for revenge. Together with Kirk Douglas, a hired gun, he plans a heist of Cabot's armored gold wagon.

WATCHER IN THE WOODS, THE
1980, 100 mins, UK
D: John Hough **A:** Bette Davis, Carroll Baker, David McCallum, Ian Bannen, Lynn-Holly Johnson, Kyle Richards (Walt Disney)

Teenager Lynn-Holly Johnson happens to resemble Bette Davis's long-lost daughter. Johnson's family rents the huge country house belonging to Davis, who lives in a nearby cottage. The pre-title sequences establish the house and woods as being something less than fun city. Whatever is out there, however, remains undiscovered, even after the film has ended. The acting and writing are barely professional, but the art direction gives the pic a gloss.

WATCH ON THE RHINE
1943, 109 mins, US ⓥ
D: Herman Shumlin **A:** Bette Davis, Paul Lukas, Geraldine Fitzgerald, George Coulouris, Lucile Watson, Beulah Bondi (Warner)

Watch on the Rhine is a distinguished picture, made with passionate conviction and enormous skill. There is no compromise on controversial matters. Fascists are identified as such, and the industrial-financial support that makes fascism possible is also mentioned. Paul Lukas is the outstanding star of the film. His portrayal of the heroic German has quiet strength and slowly gathering force. In the lesser part of the wife, Bette Davis gives a performance of genuine distinction.
1943: Best Actor (Paul Lukas)
Nominations: Best Picture, Supp. Actress (Lucile Watson), Screenplay

WATCH YOUR STERN
1960, 88 mins, UK
D: Gerald Thomas **A:** Kenneth Connor, Eric Barker, Leslie Phillips, Joan Sims, Hattie Jacques, Spike Milligan (Anglo Amalgamated)

The team responsible for the successful *Carry On* series are up to their profitable yuk-raising larks with *Watch Your Stern*. The yarn concerns a top-secret test on an acoustic torpedo which, when fired, doubles in its tracks and blows up the firing ship. An Admiralty buffoon is detailed to modify the torpedo, the plan gets destroyed, and the destroyer's officers manage to bluff the admiral with the plans of the ship's refrigeration plant. Sidney James, guest-starring as a chief petty officer, enlivens his scenes as always, and there are standout cameos by Spike Milligan and Eric Sykes as a couple of gabby electricians.

WATER
1985, 95 mins, UK ⓥ
D: Dick Clement **A:** Michael Caine, Valerie Perrine, Brenda Vaccaro, Billy Con-

nolly, Leonard Rossiter, Maureen Lipman (HandMade)

A British satire of political muddle on a Caribbean island, *Water* is a frenetic mishmash. Michael Caine is fine as a laid-back British governor, but he can't salvage a production that's top-heavy with multi-national plots threatening the island's harmony. The filmmakers, who shot on the island of St. Lucia, obviously were targeting the invasions of Grenada and the Falkland Islands as subjects of satire. As Caine's hysterical South American wife, Brenda Vaccaro hits the nadir of her career in a performance that is one unrelieved shriek.

WATER BABIES, THE
1979, 93 mins, UK ✆
D: Lionel Jeffries A: James Mason, Billie Whitelaw, Bernard Cribbins, Joan Greenwood, David Tomlinson, Samantha Gates (Pethurst/Production Associates/Ariadne)

The musical screen version of *The Water Babies,* Charles Kingsley's children's novel, combines live action footage and—for the underwater sequences—animation. A 12-year-old apprentice chimney sweep, wrongly accused of theft, dives into a pool to escape his pursuers. Below the surface he meets a succession of human stereotypes, jokily animated as underwater creatures, and battles to free the water babies, who have been captured by a shark and an electric eel. Animated sequences are garish but effective.

WATERBOY, THE
1998, 88 mins, US ✆ ⊙
D: Frank Coraci A: Adam Sandler, Kathy Bates, Henry Winkler, Fairuza Balk, Jerry Reed, Larry Gilliard Jr. (Touchstone)

The *Waterboy* is a formulaic mix of mirth and mayhem aimed way down the MTV food chain. The big laughs come from a ragtag football team that's so poor its players share a single protective cup. As for Adam Sandler, he remains an acquired (lack of) taste. His recycled Jerry Lewis shtick would test the patience of even the French. He plays Bobby Boucher, who's a tackling dummy used by Louisiana University's football team. Fired for fighting back, Bobby signs on with the underdog Mud Dogs, led by a hallucinating coach (Henry Winkler), and overcomes 11th-hour adversity to lead his team to victory in the big game. Fairuza Balk is sexy and funny as Bobby's bad-girl girlfriend, and Winkler underplays nicely as the coach who sports a tattoo of

Roy Orbison on his tush. Tech credits are what you'd expect of a low-grade genre entry.

WATERDANCE, THE
1992, 106 mins, US ✆ ⊙
D: Neal Jimenez, Michael Steinberg A: Eric Stoltz, Helen Hunt, William Forsythe, Wesley Snipes, Elizabeth Pena (JBW)

Set in a hospital for paralyzed men where a young novelist (Eric Stoltz) lands after a hiking accident, pic is about his coming to terms with the fate he shares with others in the ward, among them, a hostile white redneck biker (William Forsythe) and a restless, fast-talking black man (Wesley Snipes). Script unfolds with a spirit and sparkle devoid of self-indulgence, and Stoltz plays the lead with lightness, wit, and balance.

WATERHOLE #3
1967, 95 mins, US ✆ ⊏
D: William Graham A: James Coburn, Carroll O'Connor, Maggie Blye, Claude Akins, Timothy Carey, Bruce Dern (Paramount)

Waterhole #3 is a slow-building, deliberate oater comedy blending satire, slapstick, and double entendres for laughs. Distended story line turns on two gags: gold heist by crooked army sergeant Claude Akins, dirty outlaw Timothy Carey, and unwilling hostage Harry Davis; and the casual seduction by gambler James Coburn of Carroll O'Connor's daughter, Margaret Blye.

WATERLAND
1992, 95 mins, UK/US ✆ ⊙ ⊏
D: Stephen Gyllenhaal A: Jeremy Irons, Ethan Hawke, Sinead Cusack, John Heard, Cara Buono, Grant Warnock (Palace/Fine Line)

High school teacher Jeremy Irons walks his students through the physical and emotional landscapes of his troubled life in *Waterland*, a talented but terminally parched piece of literary cinema. This twisted, inbred yarn is not the sort of thing normally associated with British accents, scarfed pipe-smokers, and memory flashbacks. At its heart, the tale is a Southern gothic of sordid family secrets. Finding his Pittsburgh students bored with his lectures about the French Revolution, teacher Irons begins telling them about his own upbringing in the odd area called the Fens, bleak, flat marshlands in East Anglia. Irons does his best, but he can't entirely break through the project's fundamental weakness.

WATERLOO
1970, 132 mins, Italy/USSR ⊗ ▭
D: Sergei Bondarchuk **A:** Rod Steiger, Christopher Plummer, Orson Welles, Jack Hawkins, Virginia McKenna, Dan O'Herlihy (De Laurentiis/Mosfilm)

Directed by Russia's Sergei Bondarchuk, the long-nursed Dino De Laurentiis project has an international flavor. The battle is the focal point, and a striking din-laden affair it is, but the film is raised from being just another historical war epic by the performances of Rod Steiger as Napoleon and Christopher Plummer as Wellington. Steiger gives a remarkably powerful portrayal, with sudden blazes of rage highlighting his moody introspection. Dan O'Herlihy stands out as Marshal Ney, devoted loyalist to Napoleon, and Orson Welles makes much of two minor moments as Louis XVIII.

WATERLOO BRIDGE
1940, 103 mins, US ⊗ ⊙
D: Mervyn LeRoy **A:** Vivien Leigh, Robert Taylor, Lucile Watson, Virginia Field, Maria Ouspenskaya, C. Aubrey Smith (M-G-M)

This is a persuasive and compelling romantic tragedy about a love affair launched on Waterloo Bridge during World War I. Vivien Leigh, a ballet dancer, meets and falls in love with British officer Robert Taylor on the eve of his departure for the front. There's a whirlwind romance with immediate marriage delayed until his first furlough. Fate intervenes, and erroneous report of his death eventually sends her onto the streets, but Taylor returns, meets her at the station where she is soliciting, and the romance flares again for an instant.
1940: Nominations: Best B&W Cinematography, Original Score

WATERLOO ROAD
1945, 76 mins, UK
D: Sidney Gilliat **A:** John Mills, Stewart Granger, Alastair Sim, Joy Shelton, Beatrice Varley, George Carney (Gainsborough)

Played against the drab, bomb-shattered background of a London slum, story is the familiar triangle theme. But it's acted with such sincerity and is so true-to-life in its characterization that the picture grips throughout. There is a terrific climax in which two men (John Mills and Stewart Granger) fight for one woman as the bombs thunder down. A soldier deserts when he learns his wife is receiving attentions from another man. Story depicts his day spent in pursuit of the pair, finally confronting them in a sports arcade.

WATERWORLD
1995, 135 mins, US ⊗ ⊙
D: Kevin Reynolds **A:** Kevin Costner, Dennis Hopper, Jeanne Tripplehorn, Tina Majorino, Michael Jeter, Gerard Murphy (Universal/Gordon/Davis/Licht-Mueller)

Waterworld is a not-bad futuristic actioner with three or four astounding sequences, an unusual hero, a nifty villain, and less mythic and romantic resonances than might be delivered. Premise is a world whose land masses have been entirely covered by water. The Mariner (Kevin Costner) sails the endless seas. From an attack by the savage Smokers, who take orders from the maniacal Deacon (a bald-headed, eye-patched Dennis Hopper), he rescues Helen (Jeanne Tripplehorn), and her adopted daughter, Enola (Tina Majorino), on whose back is tatooed a symbol that may indicate the whereabouts of the mythical Dryland. The story has a sort of grim obsessiveness about it. Humor could have derived from the central male-female relationship. But Tripplehorn provides a serious, overwrought woman quite unable to leaven Kevin. The sets, costumes, and many of the effects are stupendous.
Nomination: Best Sound

WAY AHEAD, THE
(IMMORTAL BATTALION)
1944, 115 mins, UK ⊗
D: Carol Reed **A:** David Niven, Raymond Huntley, Billy Hartnell, Stanley Holloway, James Donald, Leo Genn (Two Cities)

There is no story in the accepted sense, which heightens the documentary value of this wartime slice of English life. David Niven, far less obtrusive than his star's status might seem to justify, is a subaltern in command of a platoon. Covering the period from early 1939 to the Tunisian campaign of 1943, *The Way Ahead* shows how a totally unprepared, peace-loving people were suddenly catapulted into war and how a score of widely different individuals reacted to it.

WAY DOWN EAST
1920, 150 mins, US ⊗ ⊗
D: D. W. Griffith **A:** Lillian Gish, Richard Barthelmess, Lowell Sherman, Burr Mc-

Intosh, Creighton Hale, Kate Bruce (Griffith/United Artists)

Way Down East by D. W. Griffith is a film poem. Without the aid of any spectacular mechanical effects, with a relatively small cast and less than half a dozen stellar film artists, Griffith has taken a simple, old-fashioned, bucolic melodrama and milked it for 12 reels of absorbing entertainment. First honors for acting belong to Lillian Gish, who reveals hitherto unsuspected emotional powers. Richard Barthelmess, as David, has little to do until almost the finish, when he rescues Gish from an ice floe about to be precipitated over a seething waterfall.

WAYNE'S WORLD
1992, 95 mins, US ⓥ ⊙ ▱
D: Penelope Spheeris **A:** Mike Myers, Dana Carvey, Rob Lowe, Tia Carrere, Lara Flynn Boyle, Colleen Camp (Paramount)

Saturday Night Live regular Mike Myers created the characters of two overage heavy metal teens fronting a cable-access television show in Aurora, IL. Plot has Rob Lowe as a slimy opportunist who buys the heroes' *Wayne's World* show and restructures it to plug Brian Doyle-Murray's video arcade business. Wayne (Myers) falls in love with beautiful Hong Kong rock singer Tia Carrere and has to worry about womanizer Lowe stealing her away. Director Penelope Spheeris delivers a colorful but uneventful picture. Guest stars add almost nothing to the proceedings.

WAYNE'S WORLD 2
1993, 94 mins, US ⓥ ⊙
D: Stephen Surjik **A:** Mike Myers, Dana Carvey, Christopher Walken, Tia Carrere, Ralph Brown, Kim Basinger (Paramount)

The latest chapter in the saga of Aurora, IL, twosome Wayne and Garth is a puerile, misguided, and loathsome effort . . . NOT! Wayne Campbell (Mike Myers) and Garth Algar (Dana Carvey) have been turfed out of high school and entered the big world. Wayne is visited in his dreams by a Native American guide who leads him into the desert where he encounters late rock star Jim Morrison (Michael Nickles). The singer tells him to put on a concert. He sagely advises, "If you book them, they will come." Thus is born Waynestock. The mad pursuit to put on the show fuels subplots, asides, digressions, and 100 percent unadulterated non sequiturs.

WAY OF ALL FLESH, THE
1927, 90 mins, US ⊗
D: Victor Fleming **A:** Emil Jannings, Belle Bennett, Phyllis Haver, Donald Keith, Fred Kohler (Paramount)

Emil Jannings plays a middle class character who succumbs, just once, to the feminine wiles and must forever after live in hiding while his family believes him dead. Starting in 1910, the story weaves its way up to 1927, giving star opportunity to display three characterizations in as many makeups: as the bewhiskered and trusted cashier of a Milwaukee bank, as under the influence of a demi-mondaine and shorn of his facial growth, and finally as a broken example of indiscretion cleaning up park playgrounds and peddling chestnuts. As regards Jannings, this, his first domestic-made picture, is assuredly creditable.
1927/28: Best Actor (Emil Jannings)
Nomination: Best Picture

WAY OF THE DRAGON, THE
See: Meng Long Guo Jiang

WAY OUT WEST
1937, 64 mins, US ⓥ ⊙
D: James W. Horne **A:** Stan Laurel, Oliver Hardy, Sharon Lynn, James Finlayson, Stanley Fields, Vivian Oakland (M-G-M)

Manner in which this comedy stumbles along is probably due both to formula direction and scripting. This Laurel and Hardy entry follows closely the old methods used on their feature shorts. There's too much driving home of gags. They sing and dance in this one, both to neat returns. The two are commissioned to deliver a deed to a gold mine. They find out, after handing it over, that the valuable paper has been given to the wrong girl. Hence, the mad race to readjust matters. On this thin framework hang all of the quips.
1937: Nomination: Best Score

WAY TO THE STARS, THE (JOHNNY IN THE CLOUDS)
1945, 107 mins, UK
D: Anthony Asquith **A:** John Mills, Michael Redgrave, Douglass Montgomery, Trevor Howard, Rosamund John, Stanley Holloway (Two Cities)

This straight tale of what happened to an RAF airdrome when it was taken over by the 8th USAAF is outstanding. Not the least interesting thing is the camera technique. Instead of many aerial shots, the camera is entirely grounded, concentrating on how the forces lived on terra firma. Despite technically perfect performances by the three male principals—Michael Redgrave, John Mills, and Douglass Montgomery—Rosamund John actually walks away with the acting honors in a part as devoid of glamor as it is rich in feminine charm.

WAY WEST, THE
1967, 122 mins, US ⓥ ▭
D: Andrew V. McLaglen **A:** Kirk Douglas, Robert Mitchum, Richard Widmark, Lola Albright, Jack Elam, Sally Field (United Artists)

Story takes a group of Missouri farmers, under martinet Kirk Douglas, to the promised land of Oregon. Robert Mitchum is the trail scout who leads them despite fading eyesight, and Richard Widmark plays an irascible member of the party. Project probably looked good on paper but washed out in scripting, direction, and pacing. Incidents do not build to a climax; excepting the first and last reels, others could be shown out of order with no apparent discontinuity. The three male stars could all have phoned in their acting.

WAY WE WERE, THE
1973, 118 mins, US ⓥ ⊙ ▭
D: Sydney Pollack **A:** Barbra Streisand, Robert Redford, Bradford Dillman, Patrick O'Neal, Viveca Lindfors, Lois Chiles (Columbia/Rastar)

This is a distended, talky, redundant, and moody melodrama, combining young love, relentless 1930s and 1940s nostalgia, and spiced with Hollywood Red-hunt pellets. The story follows the stars from the late 1930s—on a college campus where Barbra Streisand is a young Communist activist, and Robert Redford a casual, shallow type—through World War II and finally to Hollywood where liberal activities lead to blacklisting and marriage breakups. The overemphasis on Streisand makes the film just another of those Streisand vehicles where no other elements ever get a chance.
1973: Best Original Score, Song ("The Way We Were")
Nominations: Best Actress (Barbra Streisand), Cinematography, Costume Design, Art Direction

WEB, THE
1947, 87 mins, US
D: Michael Gordon **A:** Ella Raines, Edmond O'Brien, William Bendix, Vincent Price, Maria Palmer (Universal-International)

Picture presents a crook who kills because he wants money and power and not because of some psycho-quirk springing from a past incident. The pace is tight and fast, accentuating intrigue and excitement. Edmond O'Brien is outstanding as the hero who becomes enmeshed in Vincent Price's schemes. Plot deals with efforts of a young attorney and the police to trap Price into confession of two murders and the theft of a million bucks. Former stage director Michael Gordon makes an effective first try at screen directing that gets the best from the suspense ingredients.

WEDDING, A
1978, 125 mins, US ⓥ ▭
D: Robert Altman **A:** Carol Burnett, Mia Farrow, Lillian Gish, Howard Duff, Geraldine Chaplin, Lauren Hutton (Lion's Gate)

If *Nashville* is ensemble Altman at its best, then *A Wedding* is the other extreme. Altman's loose, unstructured style backfires in this comedy-drama of a wedding between the daughter of a nouveau rich southern family and the son of old midwestern money. Unlike *Nashville*, this film lacks a core. Nothing builds; the characters, except for Lillian Gish as the old money matriarch and Mia Farrow as the silent sister of the bride, are uninteresting and unsympathetic.

WEDDING BANQUET, THE
See: Xi Yan

WEDDING BELLS
See: Royal Wedding

WEDDING MARCH, THE
1928, 115 mins, US ⓥ
D: Erich von Stroheim **A:** Erich von Stroheim, Fay Wray, George Fawcett, George Nichols, ZaSu Pitts, Maude George (Paramount)

A ponderous, slow-moving production and some beautiful photography tell a very familiar story, the tip-off for which is the lead title, "Vienna 1914." It's the well-known blue-blooded Austrian army officer having his fling with the country maiden and then wedding a limping heiress as the seduced rural miss promises marriage to pacify the brow-beating butcher who has threatened the life of the hit-and-run army lieutenant. Fay Wray is appealing and convincing as the shy, pretty, and innocent victim, while Stroheim's scoundrel is interesting.

WEDDING NIGHT, THE
1935, 81 mins, US

D: King Vidor A: Gary Cooper, Anna Sten, Helen Vinson, Ralph Bellamy, Sig Ruman, Esther Dale (Goldwyn/United Artists)

Gary Cooper is a young author who sells a piece of his land to a Polish tobacco grower, who wants it as a dowry for his daughter. He goes to the farmhouse to make the sale and the theme for his new book in the family. The Polish girl becomes interested in the man and is flattered by the novel in which she, the heroine, works the spiritual regeneration of the author. King Vidor handles the incidents with a fine touch, keeping each character whole and consistent and developing a fluid action which moves easily from America to Poland and back again.

WEDDING PARTY, THE
1969, 90 mins, US Ⓥ

D: Cynthia Munroe, Brian De Palma, Wilford Leach A: Jill Clayburgh, Charles Pflugar, Valda Setterfield, Ray McNally, Robert De Niro, Judy Thomas (Ondine)

Story dwells on a young man who, accompanied by two friends, arrives at the island estate of his soon-to-be bride. Apparently a script was employed, but the dialogue itself was produced by taping ad-libbed scenes. The film suffers from this technique. Tightness and direction of the dialogue is sacrificed for a certain spontaneity that is seldom forthcoming. Film was actually completed in 1963.

WEDDING SINGER, THE
1998, 96 mins, US Ⓥ ⊙

D: Frank Coraci A: Adam Sandler, Drew Barrymore, Christine Taylor, Allen Covert, Matthew Glave, Ellen Albertini Dow (New Line)

The aptly named Robbie Hart (Adam Sandler) sings the hits of the eighties and elevates the fun level at weddings, bar mitzvahs, and other celebrations. *The Wedding Singer* captures that joie de vivre in an unabashedly romantic comedy. Julia Sullivan (Drew Barrymore), a waitress at events where Robbie performs, believes in love and family and has convinced herself that marriage to boorish Glen (Matthew Glave) will fulfill her life. After Robbie is stood up at his own wedding, it's clear that these two are the right people with the wrong mates. Structurally, pic's like a series of syncopated opening and closing doors. The skill is in the filmmakers' ability to camouflage the mechanical parts by

means of digression, red herrings, and simple sleight of hand. Sandler is a revelation, playing a character with innate decency. Barrymore also covers new ground as a light comic actress.

WE DIVE AT DAWN
1943, 92 mins, UK Ⓥ

D: Anthony Asquith A: Eric Portman, John Mills, Reginald Purdell, Niall MacGinnis, Jack Watling, Leslie Watson (Gainsborough)

A submarine is sent out to sink a Nazi battleship off the German coast. The attack results in a leakage in the sub's oil tanks and the Britisher decides to blow her up and escape to Denmark. One of the seamen dons the uniform of a dead German airman, finds a tanker, and signals to his ship to come in shore. They refuel and return home, where they discover they have sunk the German vessel they were after. John Mills enacts the lieutenant with not only requisite dignity, but with a human touch. But it is Eric Portman, as the seaman, who has the outstanding role and scores best.

WEEK-END
(WEEKEND)
1968, 95 mins, France/Italy Ⓥ

D: Jean-Luc Godard A: Mireille Darc, Jean Yanne, Jean-Pierre Kalfon, Valerie Lagrange, Paul Gegauff, Jean Eustache (Copernic/Ascot Cineraid)

Jean-Luc Godard looks at the collective hysteria of weekend drivers. He also laces it with his personalized symbols of the consumer world, the class battle, guerilla warfare, growing human violence, and pettiness and meanness in a grating, disturbing, funny, witty, and controversial package that tackles too much but has enough sheer talent to justify the usual pros and cons. Star Mireille Darc is seen confessing to a psychoanalyst, who might also be her lover. Her husband phones a mistress, before the couple set out to see his dying father. On the road, there is a tremendous traffic jam that turns into what looks like the end of the world. After this, pic turns into a series of adventures. The group meets figures from the French Revolution and are captured by a gang of revolutionary hippie beatniks.

WEEKEND AT BERNIE'S
1989, 97 mins, US Ⓥ ⊙

D: Ted Kotcheff A: Andrew McCarthy, Jonathan Silverman, Catherine Mary

Stewart, Terry Kiser, Don Calfa, Catherine Parks (Gladden)

As shlepping-the-stiff pics go, *Weekend at Bernie's* ranks below the classic black comedy of *The Trouble with Harry* and *S.O.B.*, but there's enough farcical fun. When Gotham insurance company go-getters Andrew McCarthy and Jonathan Silverman show up for a weekend in the Hamptons with slimy boss Terry Kiser, only to find him bumped off by the mob, it's a scream for a few minutes before the gags become repetitive. Gross caricatures abound as Kiser's decadent party guests fail to notice their host is much more laid-back than usual.

WEEKEND AT BERNIE'S II
1993, 90 mins, Italy/US Ⓥ ⊙
D: Robert Klane A: Andrew McCarthy, Jonathan Silverman, Terry Kiser, Tom Wright, Steve James, Troy Beyer (Artimm/Drai)

Hitching a routine rehash of the first installment's cavorting cadaver antics to a frantic hunt for the defunct's cash stash, writer-director Robert Klane delivers a mildly diverting farcical caper in *Weekend at Bernie's II*. Ambitious insurance company stooges Andrew McCarthy and Jonathan Silverman are back in Gotham to check boss Bernie (Terry Kiser) into the morgue and return to work as heroes after uncovering his $2 million plunder. But instead of a promotion, they get fired, with company snoop Barry Bostwick tailing them to track down the missing loot. Also after the cash are Kiser's mob cohorts.

WEEK-END AT THE WALDORF
1945, 130 mins, US Ⓥ
D: Robert Z. Leonard A: Ginger Rogers, Lana Turner, Walter Pidgeon, Van Johnson, Edward Arnold, Keenan Wynn (M-G-M)

Everything happens during this particular weekend at the famed Park Avenue hostelry. Bob Benchley's scottie has pups; a benevolent tycoon lets a honeymooning couple utilize his apartment while he weekends in the country; Edward Arnold tries to gyp a visiting Egyptian bey; stenographer Lana Turner falls in love with the war-wounded Van Johnson; Phyllis Thaxter solves her own romance; Keenan Wynn, reporter, gets his scoop; and movie star Ginger Rogers and cynical war correspondent Walter Pidgeon find a throbbing romance. Never a dull moment in this weekend.

WEEKEND WITH KATE
1990, 95 mins, Australia Ⓥ
D: Arch Nicholson A: Colin Friels, Catherine McClements, Jerome Ehlers, Helen Mutkins (Emanuel)

Film's well-constructed script indicates a knowledge of romantic comedies of another era. Journalist turned rock music promoter Colin Friels is torn between beautiful wife Catherine McClements, who wants a baby, and ambitious mistress Helen Mutkins, who wants Friels. He decides to tell his wife he's leaving her during a weekend alone at a beach house. She has decided to use the intimacy of the weekend to get pregnant. Both plans go astray when British rock idol Jerome Ehlers arrives and moves in for a peaceful weekend of fishing. The sexual adventures are exuberantly captured on screen. Dialogue is sharp and witty, direction is brisk and well timed, and performances are top-notch.

WEE WILLIE WINKIE
1937, 105 mins, US Ⓥ
D: John Ford A: Shirley Temple, Victor McLaglen, C. Aubrey Smith, June Lang, Michael Whalen, Cesar Romero (20th Century-Fox)

This Rudyard Kipling story is an adventure yarn about a young American widow and her daughter who journey to India and the protection of the child's grandfather, a colonel of a Highland regiment stationed on the frontier. The menace of native insurrection and massacre provides melodramatic suspense. When open warfare is threatened, Shirley Temple on a peace-pleading mission is delivered into enemy hands. She is the means of reconciling the two factions.

WEIRD SCIENCE
1985, 94 mins, US Ⓥ ⊙
D: John Hughes A: Anthony Michael Hall, Kelly Le Brock, Ilan Mitchell-Smith, Bill Paxton, Suzanne Snyder, Robert Downey Jr. (Universal)

Helplessly horny high school nerds Gary (Anthony Michael Hall) and Wyatt (Ilan Mitchell-Smith) put their brains together and through some inexplicable computer hocus-pocus create the answer to their fantasies—the beautiful and very available Lisa (Kelly Le Brock). The trouble is that the boys hardly use her, and the film goes nowhere with its central conceit. Director John Hughes never capitalizes on the idea that Lisa is a creation of 15-year-old psyches or examines the intriguing question of who controls whom in this relationship.

WELCOME HOME
1989, 87 mins, US Ⓥ
D: Franklin J. Schaffner A: Kris Kristofferson, JoBeth Williams, Brian Keith, Sam Waterston, Trey Wilson, Thomas Wilson Brown (Columbia/Rank)

A fine opportunity to explore the emotional conflict of US soldiers recorded as dead in Vietnam and Cambodia is missed almost totally in Franklin J. Schaffner's *Welcome Home*. Kris Kristofferson looks suitably haggard as Lieutenant Jake Robbins, who returns home after 17 years in Cambodia, where he settled down to married life with Cambodian Leang (Kieu Chinh Nguyen) who bore him two children. He had just married his American sweetheart Sarah (mournfully played by JoBeth Williams) before he set out on his tour of duty. Now remarried, she lives happily in Vermont with her second husband (Sam Waterston) and a 17-year-old son (Thomas Wilson Brown), who is actually Jake's. An uninspired screenplay does not help Schaffner in making the film move forward more than sluggishly.

WELCOME HOME, ROXY CARMICHAEL
1990, 98 mins, US Ⓥ ◉
D: Jim Abrahams A: Winona Ryder, Jeff Daniels, Laila Robins, Thomas Wilson Brown, Joan McMurtrey, Frances Fisher (ITC)

Winona Ryder plays 15-year-old Dinky Bossetti, a moody, glowering misfit. Her nowheresville hometown of Clyde, OH, is all in a dither about the impending return of local legend Roxy Carmichael, and Dinky decides that Roxy must have been her real mother. Also certain that Roxy is coming back for him is Jeff Daniels, formerly the teenaged boyfriend with whom she had a baby, and who is now married with a family. As gossip turns to Roxy and her precocious deeds, Daniels's wife (Joan McMurtrey) gets fed up and leaves him. Ryder's performance has a subtle glow and maturity that mesmerizes. As the spooky, androgynous Dinky, with her low voice and deadpan delivery, she injects her scenes with a natural comedy far more satisfying than the hysterical efforts being made around her.

WELCOME TO BLOOD CITY
1977, 96 mins, UK/Canada Ⓥ
D: Peter Sasdy A: Jack Palance, Keir Dullea, Samantha Eggar, Barry Morse, Hollis McLaren, Chris Wiggins (EMI/Herberman)

An anonymous totalitarian organization kidnaps Keir Dullea and transports him to a fantasized oater settlement (Blood City) where a person's status accrues according to the number of people he/she can murder. Sheriff Jack Palance is classified as Immortal, having 20 killings to his score. Although the initial conception may have held traces of intelligence, swiss-cheese script strains coherence and interest with each development.

WELCOME TO HARD TIMES
1967, 103 mins, US
D: Burt Kennedy A: Henry Fonda, Janice Rule, Keenan Wynn, Janis Paige, Warren Oates, Fay Spain (M-G-M)

Welcome to Hard Times is more than a western title; it is a pretty fair evaluation of this production. Burt Kennedy's direction is as inept as his script, an adaptation of E. L. Doctorow's novel about sadistic tough Aldo Ray who burns down a western town. Mayor Henry Fonda inspires the town to rebuild. Presence of many pro names—Lon Chaney, Elisha Cook, Paul Fix—only serves to emphasize the lack of depth and perception in script and direction.

WELCOME TO L.A.
1976, 103 mins, US Ⓥ
D: Alan Rudolph A: Keith Carradine, Sally Kellerman, Geraldine Chaplin, Harvey Keitel, Lauren Hutton, Viveca Lindfors (United Artists)

Welcome to L.A. has a studied, calculated, over-designed look that drains the vitality from the cast as director Alan Rudolph puts them through their predictable paces in an amorphous story which has something to do with the music industry. There's lots of aimless driving around town, gloomy sex encounters, mumbled dialogue, and showy camera movements. Carradine exerts a mysterious attraction on every woman in sight.

WELCOME TO THE DOLLHOUSE
1995, 87 mins, US Ⓥ
D: Todd Solondz A: Heather Matarazzo, Darina Kalinina, Matthew Faber, Angela Pietropinto, Bill Buell, Brendan Sexton Jr. (Suburban)

Welcome to the Dollhouse is a stark, often funny, and poignant comedy about how to survive junior high school and life in the 'burbs. Eleven-year-old Dawn Wiener (Heather Matarazzo) is the middle child of a Jewish family in suburban New Jersey. As a seventh-grader in Benjamin Franklin Junior High, the unattractive slump-shouldered girl is tortured and humiliated by the rest of her class. Her little sister, Missy (Daria Kalinina), always dressed in a pink tutu, is her mother's favorite, while her older brother, Mark (Matthew Faber), is a computer whiz who has his own garage band. Solondz explores an idea that is seldom depicted in American films—that parents might not really love their children equally. Every creepy detail encountered by children in this difficult transitional phase is conveyed with stark accuracy.

WELCOME TO SARAJEVO
1997, 101 mins, UK/US ⓥ ⊙ ▭
D: Michael Winterbottom **A:** Stephen Dillane, Woody Harrelson, Marisa Tomei, Emira Nusevic, Kerry Fox, Emily Lloyd (Dragon Pictures/Channel 4/Miramax)

Seen through the eyes of a cool British war journalist who becomes emotionally attached to his subject, *Welcome to Sarajevo* hits a whole range of emotional buttons. The city itself is an active participant in the drama, and it's the revival of its communal soul that the pic celebrates. At the center is hot-spot hotshot Michael Henderson (Stephen Dillane) and his team, who happen upon an orphanage near the front lines. Henderson makes plans to take one of the children, Emira (Emira Nusevic), illegally back to England. The film's persistent skimming from one vantage point to another will unsettle audiences expecting something on which to hook their emotions over the long term. But the movie unquestionably delivers in its final half-hour, and especially during Henderson's return to Sarajevo.

WE LIVE AGAIN
1934, 85 mins, US
D: Rouben Mamoulian **A:** Anna Sten, Fredric March, Jane Baxter, C. Aubrey Fish, Sam Jaffe, Jessie Ralph (Goldwyn)

We Live Again is Tolstoy's *Resurrection* beautifully re-created in dialogue and endowed with lavish Goldwynesque artistry. The nobleman that Fredric March portrays is well depicted to illustrate how the youth's natural instincts are sated by power and pleasure to the degree that he betrays the peasant girl (Anna Sten) with whom he had been reared in equal companionship. March's resurrection and regeneration is handled with unusual

restraint. Director Rouben Mamoulian has held him in fine check, at the same time not sacrificing Sten.

WELL, THE
1951, 84 mins, US ⓥ
D: Russell Rouse, Clarence Greene **A:** Richard Rober, Gwendolyn Laster, Maidie Normon, George Hamilton, Ernest Anderson, Dick Simmons (Popkin/United Artists)

High drama and suspense are embodied strongly in this production. Writers took a true-life episode, in which a California child was trapped in an old well, to create a tense and gripping screenplay. For purposes of drama, they have made this key character a Negro child. Plot has for its motivation the measures taken by Negro populace of a small town, after a white man comes under suspicion of having kidnapped the girl.

WE'LL SMILE AGAIN
1942, 93 mins, UK
D: John Baxter **A:** Bud Flanagan, Chesney Allen, Phyllis Stanley, Peggy Dexter (British National)

Anglo-American Film Corporation "announces proudly that no expense has been spared to save money on this production." So begins this Flanagan and Allen starring vehicle, in which the pair do their stuff against a background of Nazi spies at work in a British film studio. The chief fault is in the miscasting of the two principal females. Phyllis Stanley, as a film star and a leader of the spy gang, is not only almost a head taller than Chesney Allen, but she has a poor singing voice, cannot dance, and is sadly lacking in the required glamor. As Googie, an extra girl supposed to have what it takes, Peggy Dexter acts much too much like an extra suddenly shoved into a part worthy of a Barbara Stanwyck.

WENT THE DAY WELL?
(48 HOURS)
1942, 93 mins, UK
D: Alberto Cavalcanti **A:** Leslie Banks, Basil Sydney, Frank Lawton, Elizabeth Allan, Valerie Taylor, John Slater (Ealing)

This Ealing Studios tale deals with the airborne invasion of a small village in a sparsely peopled part of England. Settings, exterior and interior, smack of the real thing, from the 13th-century church to the village grocery store. Direction by Alberto Cavalcanti is workmanlike, but to the men of the Gloucestershire Regiment (cast as both German invaders and members of the local Home Guard) must go chief credit for the realistic note underlying the film, which is almost as factual as a propaganda short.

WE OF THE NEVER NEVER
1982, 136 mins, Australia Ⓥ ▭
D: Igor Auzins A: Angela Punch McGregor, Arthur Dignam, Tony Barry, Tommy Lewis, Lewis Fitz-Gerald, Martin Vaughan (Adams Packer/FCWA)

We of the Never Never is a stirring historical drama that explores racism, women's emancipation, and man's struggle to come to terms with an alien environment. In the lead role, Arthur Dignam lacks the authority and ruggedness to be credible as a turn-of-the-century explorer and adventurer. Compensating for that weakness is the top-line performance of Angela Punch McGregor, an actress with a commanding presence. Film concerns a 30-year-old city-bred woman, Jeannie, forced to make the transition from civilized Melbourne to the barren outback of the Northern Territory when she marries station owner Aeneas Gunn. Director Igor Auzins has created a big, bold, and magnificently scenic picture.

WE'RE BACK!
A DINOSAUR'S STORY
1993, 72 mins, US Ⓥ ⊙
D: Dick Zondag, Ralph Zondag, Phil Nibbelink, Simon Wells (Amblin/Universal)

This film's chief appeal is its central conceit—that giant prehistoric monsters can be transformed into intelligent, talking tourists who like to play with children. The source of this miracle is a special cereal invented by Captain NewEyes (voice of Walter Cronkite), who brings Rex (John Goodman) and his friends to New York so that children who want to see a real dinosaur can have their wish come true. Problems ensue when they are trapped by the Captain's evil brother, Professor ScrewEyes (Kenneth Mars). The animation is a bravura mix of traditional cel animation and computer-generated material.

WE'RE NO ANGELS
1955, 103 mins, US Ⓥ ⊙ ▭
D: Michael Curtiz A: Humphrey Bogart, Aldo Ray, Peter Ustinov, Joan Bennett, Basil Rathbone, Leo G. Carroll (Paramount)

Three convicts of Devil's Island find themselves playing Santa Claus to a family they came to rob. At times proceedings

are too consciously cute, and the stage origin of the material still clings. However, Michael Curtiz's directorial pacing and top-flight performances from Humphrey Bogart, Aldo Ray, and Peter Ustinov help minimize the flaws.

WE'RE NO ANGELS
1989, 108 mins, US Ⓥ ⊙
D: Neil Jordan A: Robert De Niro, Sean Penn, Demi Moore, Wallace Shawn, Ray McAnally, James Russo (Paramount)

We're No Angels is about a pair of jailbirds on the run. The year is 1935, and Robert De Niro and Sean Penn are hardtimers in a hellish north country penitentiary that may be a metaphor for Depression-era America. They pull an improbable breakout and reach a remote border town renowned for a shrine of "the weeping Madonna" and a monastery. The cons are happily mistaken for visiting ecclesiastical scholars. Director Neil Jordan and screenwriter David Mamet thus set the stage for a parable about virtue, wisdom, faith, and redemption. De Niro and Penn mug their semiarticulate roles with relish, but as religious fish out of water, their con game becomes a tiresome joke.

WE'RE NOT DRESSING
1934, 80 mins, US
D: Norman Taurog A: Bing Crosby, Carole Lombard, George Burns, Gracie Allen, Ethel Merman, Leon Errol (Paramount)

Plot is one of those familiar patterns of the fabulously rich heiress on whose yacht Bing is a gob. His particular chore is to exercise a bear, pet of the female owner. Comes the wreck and strangely enough none of the crew survives but Crosby, although somehow all the less-expert passengers manage to reach shore safely. Crosby asserts himself, with the gob alone knowing how to wrest food and comfort from the natural sources, thus making the proud heiress capitulate.

WES CRAVEN'S NEW NIGHTMARE
1994, 112 mins, US Ⓥ ⊙
D: Wes Craven A: Robert Englund, Heather Langenkamp, Miko Hughes, David Newsom, Tracy Middendorf, John Saxon (New Line)

Wes Craven's New Nightmare is an ingeniously conceived and devilishly clever opus. Craven's audacious conceit is that his first *Nightmare* (1984) and the five sequels were works of fiction that inadvertently summoned, and briefly contained, a real supernaturally evil force. After Krueger was decisively killed in the series finale, the evil force was freed to wreak havoc on an unsuspecting world. For that reason, Craven explains, while playing himself in the pic's most darkly comical sequence, that he simply must make another *Nightmare* pic. Heather Langenkamp, star of the first *Nightmare*, returns to star as Heather Langenkamp. Even though she wants no part of another Freddy pic, Freddy just won't stay out of her dreams. When she seeks help from Craven, he admits he is transforming those nightmares into a new script.

WEST 11
1963, 93 mins, UK
D: Michael Winner **A:** Alfred Lynch, Kathleen Breck, Eric Portman, Diana Dors, Harold Lang (Associated-British)

This is a hackneyed drama about a young man (Alfred Lynch) who is a layabout, a misfit, a self-pitier. He gets involved with chicks, can't keep a job, and gets mixed up with jazz clubs and seedy parties. Turning point in his life is when he meets up with an ex-army con-man (Eric Portman) who wants his aunt bumped off. The sleazy London locations are very authentically shown. Perhaps too authentically.

WESTERNER, THE
1940, 97 mins, US Ⓥ ⊙
D: William Wyler **A:** Gary Cooper, Walter Brennan, Doris Davenport, Fred Stone, Forrest Tucker, Lilian Bond (Goldwyn/United Artists)

Although Gary Cooper stars, Walter Brennan commands major attention as Judge Roy Bean, the dispenser of law west of the Pecos. Brennan turns in a socko job that does much to hold together a not-too-impressive script. The story, of cattlemen's resentment against the migration of settlers to Texas in the post–Civil War days, is a rather familiar one cinematically. Cooper is a wandering cowhand who comes before the two-gun judge charged with horse-stealing. But the latter is a worshipper of actress Lily Langtry, and when Cooper professes intimate acquaintance with the lady, the sentence is suspended. A strange friendship develops between the cantankerous old judge and the cowboy.
1940: Best Supp. Actor (Walter Brennan)
Nominations: Best Original Story, B&W Art Direction

WESTERN UNION
1941, 93 mins, US Ⓥ
D: Fritz Lang **A:** Robert Young, Randolph Scott, Dean Jagger, Virginia Gilmore, Barton MacLane, John Carradine (20th Century-Fox)

Western Union is another epic of the early American frontier. This time the stringing of telephone lines in the 1860s, between Omaha and Salt Lake City, provides the background for adventures and excitement in empire building. Randolph Scott, an ex-outlaw who joins the expedition as a scout, turns in a strong characterization. Dean Jagger is the company engineer in charge of construction, Robert Young a dudish easterner who toughens up under western ways, and Barton MacLane is the renegade outlaw whose band continually harasses the camp.

WEST OF ZANZIBAR
1928, 70 mins, US
D: Tod Browning **A:** Lon Chaney, Lionel Barrymore, Warner Baxter, Mary Nolan, Jane Daly, Roscoe Ward (M-G-M)

West of Zanzibar will satisfy Lon Chaney fans who like their color regardless of the way it is daubed. Lionel Barrymore captures the magician's bride, just after Chaney has subtitled his affection for her. Then, for no particular reason, the action is transferred to another world. Chaney is shown as an ivory robber, and just as mysteriously Barrymore suddenly appears as a white trader in Africa. Jungle scenes with crocodiles oozing through slime and a score or so of vaselined black extras doing their dances and attending to their funeral pyres are what get this by.

WEST POINT STORY, THE (FINE AND DANDY)
1950, 106 mins, US
D: Roy Del Ruth **A:** James Cagney, Virginia Mayo, Doris Day, Gordon MacRae, Gene Nelson, Alan Hale Jr. (Warner)

Fresh treatment and new twists to the musical formula make *The West Point Story* worthwhile entertainment. There are several production numbers in keeping with the cadet background of the story, which has James Cagney as a brash Broadway director down on his luck who accepts the assignment to stage the annual West Point show. Gordon MacRae, a cadet, wrote the show's book and tunes, and his producer uncle wants it and the young man for a Broadway staging.
1950: Nomination: Best Score of a Musical Picture

WEST SIDE STORY
1961, 153 mins, US Ⓥ ⊙ ▱

D: Robert Wise, Jerome Robbins **A:** Natalie Wood, Richard Beymer, Russ Tamblyn, Rita Moreno, George Chakiris, Simon Oakland (Mirisch/Beta)

West Side Story is a beautifully mounted, impressive, emotion-ridden, and violent musical. The *Romeo and Juliet* theme, set against the seething background of rival Puerto Rican and American gangs on the upper West Side of Manhattan, makes for both a savage and tender mixture of romance and war-to-the-death. Even more notable, however, is the music of Leonard Bernstein and most of all the breathtaking choreography of Jerome Robbins. Bernstein's score, with Stephen Sondheim's expressive lyrics, accentuates the tenseness that constantly builds. Plottage focuses on the romance of a young Puerto Rican girl with a mainland boy, which fans the enmity between the two gangs and ultimately leads to the rumble that leaves both gang leaders dead of knife wounds. Natalie Wood offers an entrancing performance as the Puerto Rican who falls in love with Richard Beymer, forbidden by a strict neighborhood ban against group intermingling, and later impresses with his singing. Most colorful performance, perhaps, is by George Chakiris, leader of the Puerto Rican gang the Sharks.

1961: Best Picture, Directors, Supp. Actor (George Chakiris), Supp. Actress (Rita Moreno), Color Cinematography, Color Art Direction, Sound (Todd-AO Sound Dept, Samuel Goldwyn Sound Dept), Scoring of a Musical Picture, Editing, Color Costume Design

Nomination: Best Adapted Screenplay

WESTWARD THE WOMEN
1951, 116 mins, US Ⓥ

D: William A. Wellman **A:** Robert Taylor, Denise Darcel, Hope Emerson, John McIntire, Julie Bishop, Lenore Lonergan (M-G-M)

This picture graphically depicts the women who helped settle the west, over a somewhat lengthy 116-minute course. John McIntire's California settler conceives the idea of going east to Chicago and picking up a group of women who will be brought west as wives for the mateless men peopling his rich valley. He hires Robert Taylor, a rough, tough trail guide, to lead the women into the sun. They battle Indians, the elements, and haz-ardous crossing of mountains, rivers, and deserts.

WESTWORLD
1973, 88 mins, US Ⓥ ⊙ ▱

D: Michael Crichton **A:** Yul Brynner, Richard Benjamin, James Brolin, Alan Oppenheimer, Victoria Shaw, Dick Van Patten (M-G-M)

Westworld combines solid entertainment, chilling topicality, and superbly intelligent serio-comic story values. Michael Crichton's original script is as superior as his direction. *Westworld* is a gigantic theme park where, for $1,000 a day, tourists may indulge their highest and lowest appetites. Automated robots move about as real people. These automatons may be raped, shot to death, befriended, or betrayed. They never strike back. Richard Benjamin and James Brolin arrive to live out the screen life depicted by John Wayne and Clint Eastwood. Yul Brynner plays a black-clothed bad guy whom Benjamin kills in a saloon confrontation. But things begin to go wrong. An unidentified computer casualty spreads like a plague. The automatons strike back.

WETHERBY
(AKA: VIOLENT STRANGER)
1985, 97 mins, UK Ⓥ

D: David Hare **A:** Vanessa Redgrave, Ian Holm, Judi Dench, Stuart Wilson, Tim McInnerny, Suzanna Hamilton (Greenpoint/Film Four)

Wetherby is a small town in Yorkshire where Jean Travers (Vanessa Redgrave), a lonely schoolteacher, lives. The film opens with a dinner party hosted by Jean in her little cottage. Present are two couples and a young stranger, John Morgan, whom Jean assumes came with one of the couples, while they in turn assume he is her guest. The next day, Morgan returns to the cottage, pulls out a gun, and kills himself. Hare initially allows us to assume that what we saw of the dinner party was the whole story. Gradually, however, we realize we only saw a highly selected part of that evening, and as we return to it again and again, the whole story takes on a different complexion.

WE WERE STRANGERS
1949, 106 mins, US

D: John Huston **A:** Jennifer Jones, John Garfield, Pedro Armendariz, Gilbert Roland, Ramon Novarro (Columbia/Horizon)

While relating the overthrow of the Machado dictatorship in Cuba, *Strangers'* distillation of political and social overtones serve as a foil to the revolutionary stalwarts versus state gestapo duelling that makes up the body of the film. Film could have packed considerably more documentary wallop if the revolt which did in fact occur had been woven into the main story.

WHALE MUSIC
1994, 100 mins, US Ⓥ
D: Richard J. Lewis **A:** Maury Chaykin, Cyndy Preston, Jennifer Dale, Kenneth Walsh, Paul Gross, Blu Mankuma (Alliance/Cape Scott)

The oddball saga of a burned-out rock star and the tough runaway who invades his tumbledown estate, *Whale Music* is an offbeat, tuneful romance just a shade too quirky to swim in the mainstream. In the Pacific Northwest, Desmond Howl (Maury Chaykin) has retreated from the grind of recording studios and concert tours to create a symphonic piece for whales. The ramshackle harmony is threatened by the arrival of Claire (Cyndy Preston), a frank young woman on the run from the law. Their potential union is muddied by the myriad demons that haunt Desmond. The film's song score just isn't of a quality to convince viewers that Howl is a major talent. The filmmaker also feels compelled to give inordinate weight to secondary concerns.

WHALES OF AUGUST, THE
1987, 90 mins, US Ⓥ Ⓞ
D: Lindsay Anderson **A:** Bette Davis, Lillian Gish, Vincent Price, Ann Sothern, Harry Carey Jr., Frank Grimes (Alive)

Muted but engrossing tale about the balance of power between two elderly sisters boasts superior lead performances from two of the screen's most legendary actresses, Bette Davis and Lillian Gish. The sisters live alone in the home they have occupied for decades on the coast of Maine. Sarah (Gish) is a doting busybody who is obliged to care for her sister Libby (Davis), because the latter is blind. Trouble rears its head in the form of Vincent Price, a White Russian of considerable charm and gentlemanliness.
1987: Nomination: Best Supp. Actress (Ann Sothern)

WHAT ABOUT BOB?
1991, 99 mins, US Ⓥ Ⓞ
D: Frank Oz **A:** Bill Murray, Richard Dreyfuss, Julie Hagerty, Charlie Korsmo, Kathryn Erbe, Tom Aldredge (Touchstone Pacific Partners I)

Richard Dreyfuss's Dr. Leo Marvin, a tightly wound, egotistical psychiatrist, gets irked when a persistent ''multiphobic'' patient (Bill Murray) follows him to a rustic New Hampshire retreat, then grows increasingly outraged as Murray proceeds to win over his family. He helps the doc's death-obsessed son (Charlie Korsmo) to learn to enjoy life and shows compassion to his daughter (Kathryn Erbe) and unappreciated wife (Julie Hagerty). Murray has a field day with the character.

WHAT A MAN
See: Never Give a Sucker an Even Break

WHAT A WAY TO GO!
1964, 111 mins, US ▭
D: J. Lee Thompson **A:** Shirley MacLaine, Paul Newman, Robert Mitchum, Dean Martin, Gene Kelly, Dick Van Dyke (Apjac/Orchard/20th Century-Fox)

What a Way to Go! is a big, gaudy, gimmicky comedy which promises more than it delivers by way of wit and belly laughs. It's the story of a little poor girl from Ohio who, although she wants only true love, is married and widowed in succession by four diverse types who eventually make her the richest woman in the world. Essentially, the film is a series of blackout sketches, enlivened from time to time as Shirley MacLaine tells of her marriages in styles of various types of films. Some of these parodies are very funny, but there often isn't much difference between the style of the parody and that of the encasing flashback.
1964: Nominations: Best Color Costume Design, Best Color Art Direction

WHAT A WIDOW!
1930, 90 mins, US
D: Allan Dwan **A:** Gloria Swanson, Owen Moore, Lew Cody, Margaret Livingston, William Holden (Kennedy/United Artists)

Gloria Swanson is a youthful widow left $5 million when her 60-year-old husband passes away. Seemingly, New York isn't big enough for the corking-looking widow. So she switches to Paris. Into all of this come three men: an American lawyer, a Russian violinist, and a Spanish piano-playing warbler. Director Allan Dwan has given an unusually fast tempo to the entire direction.

WHAT DID YOU DO IN THE WAR, DADDY?
1966, 115 mins, US ▭
D: Blake Edwards **A:** James Coburn, Dick Shawn, Sergio Fantoni, Aldo Ray, Giov-

anna Ralli, Carroll O'Connor (United Artists/Mirisch)

What Did You Do in the War, Daddy? is a thinly devised comedy without much substance. Set in Sicily, 1943, the screenplay dwells on a situation which holds promise but is never sufficiently realized. A war-weary American company, commanded by a by-the-book officer, is detailed to take a town held by a large Italian force, and are welcomed by the Italians who are agreeable to surrendering willingly. But first, they must hold their wine festival. No festival, no surrender.

WHATEVER HAPPENED TO AUNT ALICE?
1969, 101 mins, US Ⓥ
D: Lee H. Katzin **A:** Geraldine Page, Ruth Gordon, Rosemary Forsyth, Robert Fuller, Mildred Dunnock (Palomar/Associates & Aldrich)

Widow Geraldine Page invites in unencumbered women as companions, to take their life savings and murder them. Trouble starts when she eliminates wistful Mildred Dunnock. Suspicious Ruth Gordon, former employer of Dunnock, takes on the guise of yet another housekeeper. The two ladies play off each other relentlessly and the audience reaps the rewards. A fine tale of suspense, rounded off with a twist ending.

WHAT EVER HAPPENED TO BABY JANE?
1962, 132 mins, US Ⓥ ⊙
D: Robert Aldrich **A:** Bette Davis, Joan Crawford, Victor Buono, Marjorie Bennett, Anna Lee (Seven Arts-Associates)

The plot of *Baby Jane* allows Bette Davis to run unfettered through all the stages of oncoming insanity. Joan Crawford gives a quiet, remarkably fine interpretation of the crippled Blanche. The tale is of two sisters, complete opposites. As children, Jane is Baby Jane, a vaudeville star and the idol of the public. Eventually both girls go into film, where Blanche blossoms into a beauty and fine actress and becomes Hollywood's top star. As a result of an accident, Blanche is permanently crippled. Jane is forced to care for her, her hate growing with the years. The chain of circumstances grows, violence creating violence. Once the inept, draggy start is passed, the film's pace builds with ever-growing force.
1962: Best B&W Costume Design
Nominations: Best Actress (Bette Davis),

Supp. Actor (Victor Buono), B&W Cinematography, Sound

WHAT EVERY WOMAN KNOWS
1934, 90 mins, US
D: Gregory La Cava **A:** Helen Hayes, Brian Aherne, Madge Evans, Lucile Watson, Dudley Digges, Donald Crisp (M-G-M)

It's the "lil woman" all over again, the helpmeet who humbly does her quiet bit in balancing an impulsive man's judgments or, rather, misjudgments. Egotistical but knowledge-hungry young barrister (Brian Aherne) comes out of Scotland into Parliament, where he thinks he finds new romance with power but is actually catapulted into even greater glory by the brainy Maggie (Helen Hayes), who types and edits his speeches. Aherne is a vigorous zealot who makes his upstartishness respected.

WHAT LOLA WANTS
See: Damn Yankees

WHAT PRICE GLORY?
1926, 116 mins, US ⊗
D: Raoul Walsh **A:** Victor McLaglen, Edmund Lowe, Dolores Del Rio, William V. Mong, Phyllis Haver, Leslie Fenton (Fox)

There is a wallop right at the beginning in the two short sequences showing Flagg and Quirt as sergeants of the marines in China and the Philippines. The conflict between the two soldiers over women is set down with a light touch of comedy. Victor McLaglen stands out as the hard-boiled Captain Flagg, and his role gets far greater sympathy than that of Sergeant Quirt, which Edmund Lowe plays. As for the Charmaine of Dolores Del Rio, she registers like a house afire.

WHAT PRICE GLORY?
1952, 110 mins, US ⊗
D: John Ford **A:** James Cagney, Dan Dailey, Corinne Calvet, Robert Wagner, Marisa Pavan (20th Century-Fox)

James Cagney, a corpulent Captain Flagg who looks like he'll burst out of his britches any minute, and Dan Dailey, the braggard Sergeant Quirt, play rivals for gals and glory. Both are inclined to mumble or shout their dialogue. Corinne Calvet's charms are freely displayed as the ever-loving Charmaine. Episodic story deals with the marines in World War I and the professional and amatory rivalry of Cagney and Dailey. Over the entire production is a feeling that any second the picture will break into a musical number. This doesn't happen, but it still serves as a subconscious distraction.

WHAT PRICE HOLLYWOOD?
1932, 87 mins, US Ⓥ ⊙
D: George Cukor **A:** Constance Bennett, Lowell Sherman, Neil Hamilton, Gregory Ratoff, Brooks Benedict (RKO)

A fan magazine-ish interpretation of Hollywood plus a couple of twists. A waitress becomes a picture star, marries a wealthy playboy, loses him and gets him back when her screen career founders on the suicide of the director who gave her a start. Story has its exaggerations, but they can sneak under the line as theatrical license. Gregory Ratoff is closer to some film producers than the average audience will realize, and Lowell Sherman gives a fine interpretation of a derelict director.
1931/32: Nomination: Best Original Story

WHAT'S EATING GILBERT GRAPE?
1993, 118 mins, US Ⓥ ⊙
D: Lasse Hallstrom **A:** Johnny Depp, Juliette Lewis, Mary Steenburgen, Leonardo DiCaprio, Darlene Cates, Laura Harrington (Matalon-Teper-Ohlsson)

What's Eating Gilbert Grape?, an offbeat middleweight charmer, depicts a dysfunctional rural family. They cope reasonably well due to the self-sacrificial ministrations of eldest son Gilbert (Johnny Depp), who carries on a discreet affair with an older woman and can't even think of leaving due to how much Momma (Darlene Cates) and Arnie (Leonardo DiCaprio) depend upon him. Becky (Juliette Lewis) pitches tent outside town in a shiny trailer and gently entices the reticent Gilbert into a tentative romantic relationship just as his lover (Mary Steenburgen) is moving away. Swedish director Lasse Hallstrom and his fine cast have endowed the story with a good deal of behavioral truth and unstressed comedy.
1993: Nomination: Best Supp. Actor (Leonardo DiCaprio)

WHAT'S LOVE GOT TO DO WITH IT
(TINA: WHAT'S LOVE GOT TO DO WITH IT)
1993, 118 mins, US Ⓥ ⊙
D: Brian Gibson **A:** Angela Bassett, Laurence Fishburne, Vanessa Bell Calloway, Jenifer Lewis, Phyllis Yvonne Stickney, Khandi Alexander (Touchstone)

This immensely enjoyable biography of songstress Tina Turner hits both the high and low notes of an extraordinary career. Young Tina (Angela Bassett), is first seen as a precocious youngster. In St. Louis, circa 1958, she encounters charismatic R&B singer-songwriter Ike Turner (Laurence Fishburne), who coaxes her to the mike. When she lets loose, Ike sees a potent meal ticket. Nothing in Bassett's earlier repertoire suggested the consummate skill she brings to the part.
1993: Nominations: Best Actor (Laurence Fishburne), Actress (Angela Bassett)

WHAT'S NEW, PUSSYCAT?
1965, 108 mins, US Ⓥ
D: Clive Donner **A:** Peter Sellers, Peter O'Toole, Romy Schneider, Capucine, Paula Prentiss, Woody Allen (United Artists)

What's New, Pussycat? is a zany farce that goes overboard in pressing for its goal and suffers from over-contrived treatment. Peter Sellers is a Viennese professor to whom Peter O'Toole, editor of a Parisian fashion magazine, goes for help in solving his women problems, which keep piling up as he finds more pretty girls. Sellers has a jealous wife and a roving eye which gets him into trouble. Woody Allen plays an undresser for strippers at the Crazy Horse Saloon similarly afflicted with girl troubles. Sellers's nuttiness knows no bounds as he speaks with a thick German accent, and O'Toole proves his forte in drama rather than comedy.
1965: Nomination: Best Song ("What's New, Pussycat?")

WHAT'S THE MATTER WITH HELEN?
1971, 101 mins, US
D: Curtis Harrington **A:** Debbie Reynolds, Shelley Winters, Dennis Weaver, Agnes Moorehead, Micheal MacLiammoir, Sammee Lee Jones (Filmways/Raymax)

What's the Matter with Helen? is an adequate exploitation shocker starring Debbie Reynolds and Shelley Winters as two Hollywood types of the early sound era caught up in mayhem and mutual suspicion. Pair run a Hollywood terp studio for would-be Shirley Temples. Reynolds finds romance with Dennis Weaver, the father of one of her pupils. His Texas millionaire accent is a few feet too thick. Winters turns more to the radio preachings of Agnes Moorehead, excellent in the hard-sell evangelist role.

WHAT'S UP, DOC?
1972, 94 mins, US ⓥ ⊙
D: Peter Bogdanovich A: Barbra Streisand, Ryan O'Neal, Kenneth Mars, Austin Pendleton, Sorrell Booke, Stefan Gierasch (Saticoy/Warner)

What's Up, Doc? is a contemporary comedy in the screwball 1930s style, with absolutely no socially relevant values. This picture is a total smash. Gimmick is a quartet of identical suitcases which of course get into the wrong hands. Barbra Streisand is conning some food out of a hotel, where Ryan O'Neal and fiancée (Madeline Kahn) are attending a musicologists' convention. There is an unending stream of opening and closing doors, perilous balcony walks, and two terrific chases through San Francisco streets. One of them is virtually a Road Runner storyboard, and there's absolutely nothing wrong with that.

WHAT'S UP, TIGER LILY?
1966, 79 mins, US ⓥ ⊙ ⊠
D: Woody Allen A: Woody Allen, Tatsuya Mihashi, Mie Hama, Akiko Wakabayashi, Tadao Nakamura, Susumu Korobe (American International/Benedict)

Take a Toho Films (Japan) crime meller in the James Bond tradition for the domestic market there, turn loose Woody Allen and associates to dub and re-edit in camp-comedy vein, and the result is *What's Up, Tiger Lily?* The production has one premise—deliberately mismatched dialogue—which is sustained reasonably well through its brief running time.

WHEN A MAN LOVES A WOMAN
1994, 124 mins, US ⓥ ⊙
D: Luis Mandoki A: Andy Garcia, Meg Ryan, Lauren Tom, Philip Seymour Hoffman, Tina Majorino, Ellen Burstyn (Touchstone)

This tale of alcoholism and substance abuse does have an underlying tenderness, but its core is sober, vivid, and gutwrenching. Michael (Andy Garcia) and Alice (Meg Ryan) are the seeming paradigm of the yuppie lifestyle. But the cracks in the veneer become obvious. Alice cannot face a social situation without at least one drink too many. After a near-fatal boating incident, she promises to reform—meaning only that she will hide her drinking problem more ferociously. The ambition of the screenplay is often staggering. It's more a case study than a traditional three-act movie fable. Ryan has

one of those rollercoaster roles that demands attention.

WHEN A STRANGER CALLS
1979, 97 mins, US ⓥ ⊙
D: Fred Walton A: Carol Kane, Charles Durning, Colleen Dewhurst, Tony Beckley, Rachel Roberts, Ron O'Neal (Columbia/Simon-Krost)

Stranger is unquestionably a scary film. But something seems lacking overall. By the film's end, the deficiency seems clear—key actions and motivations just don't make sense. Carol Kane is quite good as the terrified baby sitter who grows up to have the same chilling chain of events begin all over again. More than anything else, *Stranger* resembles a good, old-fashioned grade-B thriller.

WHEN DINOSAURS RULED THE EARTH
1970, 100 mins, UK ⓥ ⊙
D: Val Guest A: Victoria Vetri, Robin Hawdon, Patrick Allen, Sean Caffrey, Magda Konopka, Imogen Hassall (Hammer)

This is one of those simple sci-fi prehistoric films which do no harm. What the story is all about is subject to debate since Val Guest, who directed and wrote the original screenplay, has elected to invent a "prehistoric" lingo for the dialogue. A blonde (Victoria Vetri) is blamed for a huge upheaval in the Sun and is condemned to death, but is rescued by a neighboring Sand Tribe. Fisherman Tara (Robin Hawdon) falls for the cutie, which irritates his girlfriend (Imogen Hassall). Amid the animals, special effects, and tribal rituals, the human thesps don't stand much chance of scoring. There are a lot of very nubile, scantily clad dames.

WHEN EIGHT BELLS TOLL
1971, 94 mins, UK ⓥ ⊠
D: Etienne Perier A: Anthony Hopkins, Robert Morley, Nathalie Delon, Jack Hawkins, Corin Redgrave, Derek Bond (Winkast)

Alistair MacLean's two-fisted, no-holds-barred adventure yarns are a natural for the screen. Anthony Hopkins plays a naval secret service agent assigned to find out how millions of pounds in gold bullion are being pirated. The obvious suspect is a suave Greek tycoon (Jack Hawkins), whose luxury yacht guests some odd characters. Nathalie Delon is allegedly Hawkins's wife but apparently goes over to the Hopkins camp. Hawkins himself, as the

Greek tycoon, retains his usual stature. Comedy relief comes from Robert Morley, as Hopkins's snobbish, stuffy chief.

WHEN FATHER WAS AWAY ON BUSINESS
See: Otac Na Sluzbenom Putu

WHEN HARRY MET SALLY . . .
1989, 95 mins, US ⑫ ◉
D: Rob Reiner **A:** Billy Crystal, Meg Ryan, Carrie Fisher, Bruno Kirby, Steven Ford, Lisa Jane Persky (Castle Rock/Nelson)

Can a man be friends with a woman he finds attractive? Can usually acerbic scripter Nora Ephron sustain 95 minutes of unrelenting cuteness? Can the audience sit through 11 years of emotional foreplay between adorable Billy Crystal and Meg Ryan? Two characters who seem to have nothing on their minds but each other (even though they won't admit it), Harry and Sally are supposed to be a political consultant and a journalist, but it's hard to tell from the evidence presented. Rob Reiner directs with deftness and sincerity, making the material seem more engaging than it is.
1989: Nomination: Best Original Screenplay

WHEN I FALL IN LOVE
See: Everybody's All-American

WHEN LADIES MEET
1933, 73 mins, US
D: Harry Beaumont **A:** Ann Harding, Robert Montgomery, Myrna Loy, Alice Brady, Frank Morgan, Luis Alberni (M-G-M)

Story gets off to a typical start, but soon steadies down into nicely paced action punctuated by plenty of laughs that arise from the lines instead of horseplay. The chat might be overlong, but it's interesting and holds quiet attention. Myrna Loy does an excellent job as the ambitious young writer who has fallen in love with her publisher. Robert Montgomery does not quite get into his character. Alice Brady, in a fat part as a socialite, is dangerously close to running away with the film now and then.
1932/33: Nomination: Best Art Direction

WHEN LADIES MEET
1941, 103 mins, US ⑫
D: Robert Z. Leonard **A:** Joan Crawford, Robert Taylor, Greer Garson, Herbert Marshall, Spring Byington, Rafael Storm (M-G-M)

Pic is long on talk and slim on action,

with plot unfolding entirely via dialogue. Joan Crawford is Mary Howard, a young authoress, admired and loved by Jimmy Lee (Robert Taylor), having a romance with publisher Woodruff (Herbert Marshall). Deciding that the affair has gone far enough, Lee introduces Woodruff's wife to Howard, with both women unaware of their triangle corners. Greer Garson is outstanding as the wife, catching major honors. Spring Byington adds comedy as the flustery matron who becomes bewildered by the mix-up.

WHEN SATURDAY COMES
1996, 97 mins, UK ⑫
D: Maria Giese **A:** Sean Bean, Emily Lloyd, Pete Postlethwaite, John McEnery, Ann Bell, Melanie Hill (Capitol)

When Saturday Comes is a northern working-class drama about a young guy trying to better himself. Jimmy Muir (Sean Bean) still lives at home, with his younger brother Russell (Craig Kelly), embittered father (John McEnery) and downtrodden mom (Ann Bell). His dream is to make it as a professional soccer player with Sheffield United. Jimmy starts making headway with the perky Annie (Emily Lloyd). The big time beckons Jimmy with an invitation to try out for Sheffield United, but he blows his chances on all fronts. Bean plays his part to the hilt, and Lloyd makes quite a mark as the sassy, self-possessed Annie.

WHEN STRANGERS MARRY (AKA: BETRAYED)
1944, 67 mins, US
D: William Castle **A:** Dean Jagger, Kim Hunter, Robert Mitchum, Neil Hamilton, Lou Lubin, Milt Kibbee (Monogram)

When Strangers Marry is a taut psychological thriller full of suspense and excitement. Two strangers are married after three meetings and are immediately separated. The girl goes off to find her man. Then begins another type of manhunt, the police on the trail of a killer who for all intents and purposes is the disappearing husband. Dean Jagger has the soft menacing air that befits the suspect. Kim Hunter, a comparative newcomer, is attractive as well as immensely appealing as the disraught but loyal wife.

WHEN THE BOYS MEET THE GIRLS
1965, 97 mins, US ▭
D: Alvin Ganzer **A:** Connie Francis, Harve Presnell, Herman's Hermits, Louis

Armstrong, Sam the Sham and the Pharoahs, Sue Ane Langdon (Four Leaf/M-G-M)

When the Boys Meet the Girls is a spotty comedy film, loaded with often extraneous tunes and some okay performances and gags. Top-featured Connie Francis and Harve Presnell (seemingly cast more from contractual commitments than suitability) are adequate; she as the backwoods Nevada US mail woman while Presnell is the big city playboy exiled to the boondocks to avoid a breach-of-promise suit. Among the 11 tunes are five vintage Gershwin numbers, including "I Got Rhythm," subject of what is the big production number.

WHEN THE WHALES CAME
1989, 99 mins, UK ⓥ ⊙
D: Clive Rees **A:** Paul Scofield, David Thelfall, Helen Mirren, David Suchet, Helen Pearce, Jeremy Kemp (Golden Swan/Central)

When the Whales Came is a slight story beautifully dressed to give the appearance of more substance. Film opens on the island of Samson in the Scilly Isles in 1844, which the locals leave believing the island is cursed. Then in 1914 on the neighboring island of Bryher, youngsters Daniel (Max Rennie) and Gracie (Helen Pearce) play on the beach, watched by the mysterious Birdman (Paul Scofield). He warns them about never going to Samson. When a whale is beached on the shore it seems the curse of Samson will strike Bryher. Paul Scofield's portrayal of the deaf Birdman has the quality of sadness and pride that only he can give a role. The most endearing performance is by radiant young Pearce, a non-actor.

WHEN WILLIE COMES MARCHING HOME
1949, 82 mins, US
D: John Ford **A:** Dan Dailey, Corinne Calvet, Colleen Townsend, William Demarest, Mae Marsh (20th Century-Fox)

Dan Dailey plays a small-town lad who becomes a hero when he is first to enlist after Pearl Harbor. But he is shipped back to an air base in the same home town, and the population turns against him when he is held there for over two years as a gunnery instructor. Credit for the laugh-fest can be spread among Dailey and the rest of the cast. But the major share goes to John Ford, demonstrating that comedy can also be his forte.

WHEN WORLDS COLLIDE
1951, 81 mins, US ⓥ ⊙
D: Rudolph Mate **A:** Richard Derr, Barbara Rush, Peter Hanson, John Hoyt, Larry Keating, Judith Ames (Paramount)

Top honors for this interplanetary fantasy rest with the cameramen and special effects technicians rather than with performances of the no-name cast. A scientist (Hayden Rorke) discovers that a planet, Zyra, will pass so close to the earth that oceans will be pulled from their beds. Soon after this catastrophe, the star Bellus will collide with whatever remains of the world. Unfortunately, scripter Sydney Boehm chose to work in a romance between Barbara Rush, daughter of astronomer Larry Keating, and Richard Derr, a plane pilot. Flight and landing upon Zyra represent the high point of the picture.
1951: Best Special Effects
Nomination: Best Color Cinematography

WHERE ANGELS FEAR TO TREAD
1991, 112 mins, UK ⓥ
D: Charles Sturridge **A:** Helena Bonham Carter, Judy Davis, Rupert Graves, Giovanni Guidelli, Barbara Jefford, Helen Mirren (Sovereign)

A turn-of-the-century costumer about cold-blooded Brits thawing out in sunny Italy, *Where Angels Fear to Tread* is a far more rewarding dip into the E. M. Forster tub than some of its predecessors. Feisty widow Lilia (Helen Mirren) goes to Italy for some rest and relaxation with younger companion Caroline (Helena Bonham Carter) and tangles with Tuscan boy toy Gino (Giovanni Guidelli). When news reaches home, Lilia's bossy mother-in-law, Mrs. Herriton (Barbara Jefford), dispatches milquetoast son Philip (Rupert Graves) to buy off the hot-blooded Italian. That idea goes down the tubes when the pair reveal they're already hitched. Helmer Charles Sturridge tweaks what could have been a talky telepic into a proper theatrical product. Bonham Carter gives her strongest performance to date, ably supported by Graves.

WHERE EAGLES DARE
1969, 158 mins, UK/US ⓥ ⊙ ▭
D: Brian G. Hutton **A:** Richard Burton, Clint Eastwood, Mary Ure, Michael Hordern, Patrick Wymark, Anton Diffring (M-G-M/Winkast)

Pic is highly entertaining, thrilling, and rarely lets down for a moment. It's a tale of rescuing a captured American general from a stronghold in Bavaria during World

War II by a team of experts. Richard Burton, a British agent, and Clint Eastwood, an OSS "assassin," head the crew which includes female agent Mary Ure. The killings and explosions are so integrated into the story that they never appear overdone. It's more of a saga of cool courage than a glorification of war. Burton never treats his role, though full of cliches, as anything less than Hamlet. Eastwood seems rather wooden in the early scenes, but snaps out of it when action starts piling up.

WHERE LOVE HAS GONE
1964, 111 mins, US Ⓥ ▭
D: Edward Dmytryk **A:** Susan Hayward, Bette Davis, Michael Connors, Joey Heatherton, Jane Greer, DeForest Kelley (Paramount)

Yarn revolves around a bitter divorced couple that come together again briefly to save their daughter after the 15-year-old girl kills her mother's lover. Susan Hayward and Bette Davis share top honors in impressive performances, the former as the daughter whose life is a story of indiscretions. Davis plays the autocratic mother, a scheming woman of unscrupulous methods and seemingless inexhaustible means. As the mixed-up teenager who never knew domestic happiness, Joey Heatherton is ideally cast and delivers a compelling portrayal.
1964: Nomination: Best Song ("Where Love Has Gone")

WHERE NO VULTURES FLY (IVORY HUNTER)
1951, 106 mins, UK
D: Harry Watt **A:** Anthony Steel, Dinah Sheridan, Harold Warrender, Meredith Edwards, William Simons, Orlando Martins (Ealing)

Excellent Technicolor photography and thrilling wild animal sequences are the highlights of *Where No Vultures Fly*. It's a soundly made film, lensed in the attractive East African setting of the Kenya National Park. An insignificant though basically true story is tagged on of a game warden who starts the national park after fighting local prejudice, hunters, and ivory poachers. Harry Watt's direction of the game sequences is top grade, but he tends to flounder when handling human characters.

WHERE'S JACK?
1969, 113 mins, UK
D: James Clavell **A:** Tommy Steele, Stanley Baker, Fiona Lewis, Alan Badel, Dudley Foster, Noel Purcell (Paramount/Oakhurst)

Where's Jack?, the story of Jack Sheppard, notorious 18th-century London highwayman, does not move speedily or with tremendous dramatic climaxes, but it has an authentic sense of atmosphere. Tommy turns in a good acting performance. Unfortunately, the script does not give him much chance to give the role any depth. *Where's Jack?* could well have been a more impressive picture about a colorful era in bawdy, criminal, corrupt London. But film has settled for a single adventure.

WHERE SLEEPING DOGS LIE
1992, 89 mins, US Ⓥ
D: Charles Finch **A:** Dylan McDermott, Tom Sizemore, Sharon Stone, Mary Woronov, David Combs, Shawne Rowe (Sotela)

Dylan McDermott portrays an unsuccessful writer in Hollywood who decides to write a detailed novel about a mass killer. He moves into a creepy old mansion and uses the house for inspiration, basing his novel on a notorious murder case that took place there. Before the film can turn into a haunted house suspenser, Tom Sizemore shows up as a twitchy boarder. Insidious relationship that develops between the two protagonists is reminiscent of the classic *The Servant*. Film reportedly was heavily trimmed to reach its release version.

WHERE'S POPPA?
1970, 83 mins, US Ⓥ ◉
D: Carl Reiner **A:** George Segal, Ruth Gordon, Ron Liebman, Trish Van Devere, Barnard Hughes, Vincent Gardenia (United Artists)

Where's Poppa? is a black comedy with George Segal as a young lawyer with an active death wish for his old Jewish mother, played by Ruth Gordon, whose senile eccentricities are ruining his career, sex life, and health. Screenplay is very close to tragedy, except that it works from the conviction that everyone, at least everyone living in New York City, is insane. Gordon is constantly asking "Where's Poppa?" and scaring off nurses and Segal's girlfriends with her bawdy eccentricities. She can't remember that her son is a grown man, and when he brings home Trish Van Devere, the mother suddenly describes the size of her son's sex organs as if he were a child.

WHERE THE BOYS ARE
1960, 99 mins, US ♥ ☉ ✉
D: Henry Levin A: Dolores Hart, George Hamilton, Yvette Mimieux, Jim Hutton, Barbara Nichols, Paula Prentiss (M-G-M)

The boys of today, according to the screenplay, are generally in irresponsible sexual orbit, and it is up to the girls of today to bring them down to earth. Fort Lauderdale, FL, is site of an annual spring invasion by Easter-vacationing collegians from all over the East and Midwest. Most of the girls manage to avoid the primitive passion, but there is an occasional casualty, in this case Yvette Mimieux, who gets in too deep with a pair of those unscrupulous "Yalies."

WHERE THE BUFFALO ROAM
1980, 96 mins, US ♥
D: Art Linson A: Peter Boyle, Bill Murray, Bruno Kirby, Rene Auberjonois, R. G. Armstrong, Leonard Frey (Universal)

Where the Buffalo Roam is based on the self-described antics of flip journalist Hunter S. Thompson. Pic features a number of amusing set-pieces of irreverent lunacy, but lack of serious substance renders film too frivolous and detached from reality. Sole exceptional element is Bill Murray's clearly studied but provocatively off-beat performance as Thompson, which rings absolutely true.

WHERE THE DAY TAKES YOU
1992, 92 mins, US ♥ ☉
D: Marc Rocco A: Dermont Mulroney, Lara Flynn Boyle, Balthazar Getty, Sean Astin, James LeGros, Kyle MacLachlan (Cintel)

Attempting a hard-hitting pic on the grimy realities of Hollywood street life, *Where the Day Takes You* winds up giving the runaway's life the kind of romantic-tragic scope that appeals to troubled teens. Dermot Mulroney plays King, a 21-year-old parolee who returns to his position as a natural leader of street dwellers. He has his hands full watching a gun-happy youth (Balthazar Getty) and a middle-class runaway (Sean Astin) totally "tweaked" on speed. King takes up with the newest and prettiest chick off the bus from Chicago (a bra-less Lara Flynn Boyle). Steven Tobolowsky turns in a memorably chilly performance as a wealthy gay man who pays Getty for titillation.

WHERE THE HEART IS
1990, 94 mins, US ♥ ☉
D: John Boorman A: Dabney Coleman, Uma Thurman, Joanna Cassidy, David Hewlett, Suzy Amis, Christopher Plummer (Touchstone/Silver Screen Partners IV)

Tyrannical buildings demolitions expert Dabney Coleman gets fed up with his spoiled, grown-up kids. He throws them out of the mansion and (unconvincingly) orders them to live in a Brooklyn tenement. Kids, led by Uma Thurman, are determined to make it on their own. Her sister (Suzy Amis) gets a gig doing a calendar for an insurance company, with Thurman the chief nude model for her body-painting and photography artwork. Pic succeeds in capturing a 1960s ambience. Besides Thurman, perfectly cast as a sexy kook, Amis makes a very good impression as her artistic, romantic sister.

WHERE THE RIVER BENDS
See: Bend of the River

WHERE THE RIVER RUNS BLACK
1986, 100 mins, US ♥
D: Christopher Cain A: Charles Durning, Alessandro Rabelo, Ajay Naidu, Peter Horton, Conchata Ferrell, Dana Delaney (M-G-M)

Where the River Runs Black is a beautifully simple film that celebrates an innocent boy's peaceful co-existence with nature while subtly despairing about man's abuse of it. Film revolves around a boy with roots in modern civilization raised by Amazon tribespeople without knowing he is the child of two very distinct worlds. Ten-year-old Rabelo, a waif-like Brazilian swimmer, is perfectly cast to portray the physically and emotionally confused dolphin boy traumatized by competing forces.

WHERE THE SIDEWALK ENDS
1950, 95 mins, US ☒
D: Otto Preminger A: Dana Andrews, Gene Tierney, Gary Merrill, Karl Malden, Tom Tully, Ruth Donnelly (20th Century-Fox)

Story, by Ben Hecht, unwinds with a maximum of suspense and swiftly paced action and an excellent performance by Dana Andrews. On the carpet for slugging too many hoodlums, Andrews accidentally kills a man in self-defense. Victim is Craig Stevens, former war hero and ne'er-do-well estranged husband of Gene Tierney, a lush model. Otto Preminger, director, does an excellent job of pacing the story and of building sympathy for Andrews.

WHERE THE SPIES ARE
1966, 113 mins, UK ▭
D: Val Guest **A:** David Niven, Francoise Dorleac, Cyril Cusack, John Le Mesurier, Nigel Davenport, Eric Pohlmann (M-G-M)

David Niven stars as a mild-mannered English doctor pressed into Middle East espionage. The production carries suspense, after a slow and talky start, and action is fast-paced once story gets underway. Niven is sent to Lebanon to try to learn what urgent information the agent there had uncovered before he was bumped off by the Russians. Niven delivers one of his customary competent performances and is able to cope with the melodramatic demands of the character.

WHERE WERE YOU WHEN THE LIGHTS WENT OUT?
1968, 90 mins, US ▭
D: Hy Averback **A:** Doris Day, Robert Morse, Terry-Thomas, Patrick O'Neal, Lola Albright, Jim Backus (M-G-M)

On November 9, 1965, large parts of the eastern US were blacked out. In this script, the blackout is less than a prop for a routine marital mix-up. Doris Day, an actress, is married to architect Patrick O'Neal. Latter lingers a bit too long with sexy magazine interviewer Lola Albright, cueing Day's stormy exit to a Connecticut hideaway. Simultaneously, Robert Morse, aced out of being made president of his company by nepotism, steals a pile of money. An amusing, though never hilarious, film.

WHILE THE CITY SLEEPS
1956, 99 mins, US Ⓥ ▭
D: Fritz Lang **A:** Dana Andrews, Ida Lupino, Rhonda Fleming, George Sanders, Vincent Price, Howard Duff (RKO)

Newspaper yarn weaves several story lines together: the activities of a homicidal maniac, played by John Barrymore Jr.; a scramble for power among the top brass of a newspaper empire; and a good-natured love story between the paper's top reporter, played by Dana Andrews, and Sally Forrest, the secretary of one of the contestants. The empire's new chieftain, Vincent Price, decides to set up a new top executive post for grabs, and lets it be known that the one to crack the wave of murders being committed by Barrymore gets the job. Plot intricacies are deftly interwoven, with director Fritz Lang doing a top-flight job of balancing the ingredients without dragging the pace.

WHILE YOU WERE SLEEPING
1995, 103 mins, US Ⓥ ☉
D: Jon Turteltaub **A:** Sandra Bullock, Bill Pullman, Peter Gallagher, Peter Boyle, Jack Warden, Glynis Johns (Hollywood)

While You Were Sleeping has all the trappings of a lighthearted romantic comedy. The film's complete embrace of love's ability to break through all barriers is undeniably infectious. Lucy (Sandra Bullock) is lonely in Chicago, working as a toll-taker for the Chicago Transit Authority. Her dreamboat is a handsome guy (Peter Gallagher) who's never so much as said hello. After she saves his life, a series of misunderstandings result in her being presented as the comatose man's fiancée, as well as his savior. The twist that keeps the audience off balance is the budding romance between Lucy and Mr. Coma's brother Jack (Bill Pullman). Bullock's first romantic starring vehicle reveals a high likability quotient. Pullman, rarely used effectively onscreen, takes great relish in his plum role.

WHIRLPOOL
1949, 97 mins, US
D: Otto Preminger **A:** Gene Tierney, Richard Conte, Jose Ferrer, Charles Bickford, Barbara O'Neil, Fortunio Bonanova (20th Century-Fox)

Whirlpool is a highly entertaining, exciting melodrama. Subject is the wife of a prominent psychiatrist who, since adolescence, has been plagued by kleptomania. As the young wife, Gene Tierney gives a plausible performance, though at times she fails to achieve the intensity that the entranced woman should have. Richard Conte, as her husband, is a little out of his metier here. The acting honors go to Jose Ferrer as the blackguard hypnotist.

WHISKY GALORE!
(TIGHT LITTLE ISLAND)
1949, 82 mins, UK Ⓥ
D: Alexander Mackendrick **A:** Basil Radford, Joan Greenwood, Gordon Jackson, James Robertson Justice, Bruce Seaton, Gabrielle Blunt (Ealing)

Pic unfolds on a Hebridean island in 1943. A major disaster occurs when the island runs out of whisky. When a freighter laden with Scotch runs aground off the island, the natives organize a midnight expedition and lay in a tremendous store for future consumption. Sustained comedy treatment successfully carries the film forward to the point where the islanders outwit the Home Guard captain who regards the adventure as the worst type of looting. Basil Radford gives a flawless performance as the misunderstood Home Guard chief.

WHISPERERS, THE
1966, 103 mins, UK
D: Bryan Forbes **A:** Edith Evans, Eric Portman, Nanette Newman, Gerald Sim, Avis Bunnage, Ronald Fraser (United Artists)

Low-budgeter centers around an old woman who lives alone in a broken-down, tiny flat in a slummy outskirt of a British town, Her dream of sudden riches comes true one day when her son hides the haul of a robbery in her spare room, and she finds it. Few other films have attacked the unglamorous but poignant theme of old-age loneliness with such unsentimental taste and discretion. It has in Edith Evans's great performance an invaluable asset.
1967: Nomination: Best Actress (Edith Evans)

WHISPERS IN THE DARK
1992, 102 mins, US ⊘ ⊙
D: Christopher Crowe **A:** Annabella Sciorra, Jamey Sheridan, Anthony LaPaglia, Jill Clayburgh, John Leguizamo, Deborah Unger (Paramount)

A turn-off psycho-sexual thriller, *Whispers in the Dark* grows steadily more absurd by the reel until literally stumbling into the ocean at its climax. Annabella Sciorra essays a meek Gotham shrink who gets turned on by tales of bondage and great sex confided by her patient Deborah Unger. Sciorra falls for straight-arrow pilot Jamey Sheridan, but discovers he is the sex partner Unger so deliciously describes. Before she can say "ropes and handcuffs," Sciorra finds Unger murdered in her gallery. Some initial interest is generated by the intensely erotic performance of Unger, and by the voyeuristic appeal of the numerous private sexual revelations. But writer-director Christopher Crowe nudges the picture along a very narrow track without coupling the viewer to the train.

WHISTLE BLOWER, THE
1987, 104 mins, UK ⊘ ⊙
D: Simon Langton **A:** Michael Caine, James Fox, Nigel Havers, Felicity Dean, John Gielgud, Gordon Jackson (Portreeve)

The Whistle Blower is a highly charged conspiracy theory drama. A murdered man, played by Nigel Havers, worked as a Russian translator at the top-secret listening center, GCHQ, in Cheltenham. Michael Caine is excellent as his father, a non-political, middle-aged man driven to radical action as a result of what the government he once trusted has done to his son. Unfortunately, the film ends rather lamely, almost as if the writer wasn't sure how to finish it.

WHISTLE DOWN THE WIND
1961, 99 mins, UK ⊘
D: Bryan Forbes **A:** Hayley Mills, Alan Bates, Bernard Lee, Norman Bird, Elsie Wagstaff, John Arnatt (Rank/Allied Film Makers)

Whistle Down the Wind takes a modern, sentimental-religious subject and treats it with care, taste, sincerity, imagination, and good humor. Three small children, leading a lonely life on their father's farm, stumble on a ragged, unshaven man taking refuge in their barn. Startled when a terrified Hayley Mills asks who he is, the stranger involuntarily swears "Jesus Christ." The children take the remark literally. In fact, the man is a murderer on the run. Bryan Forbes in his debut as a director coaxes some outstanding performances from a bunch of local kids. Only their leader, young Mills, ever saw a script before. The result is complete authenticity.

WHISTLE STOP
1946, 84 mins, US ⊘
D: Leonide Moguy **A:** George Raft, Ava Gardner, Victor McLaglen, Tom Conway (United Artists)

Somber melodrama, vignetting a seamy side of life in a small town. Characters are all little people and not very nice. Story opens with Ava Gardner returning to the whistle-stop town of Ashbury to renew her romance with the shiftless George Raft. Pair had broken off the romance because he refused to change his habits. A prosperous rival, Tom Conway, owner of the town's hotel and saloon, starts to move in. Score aids in projecting the somber mood.

WHITE BUFFALO, THE
1977, 97 mins, US ⊘
D: J. Lee Thompson **A:** Charles Bronson, Jack Warden, Will Sampson, Kim Novak, Clint Walker, Stuart Whitman (De Laurentiis)

Charles Bronson stars as Wild Bill Hickok, returned to the West to hunt down an albino buffalo that haunts his dreams. Production features arch scripting by Richard Sale, stilted acting, and forced direction by J. Lee Thompson. The title beast looks like a hung-over carnival prize despite attempts at camouflage via hokey sound track noise, busy John Barry scoring, murky photography, and fast editing.

WHITE CARGO
1942, 89 mins, US

D: Richard Thorpe **A:** Hedy Lamarr, Walter Pidgeon, Frank Morgan, Richard Carlson, Reginald Owen (M-G-M)

Action revolves around the passion of a white man, disintegrating in a tropical English colony, for a half-breed. Walter Pidgeon plays well the part of the tough English magistrate of the colony who has to wet-nurse a succession of novices from the home country. Hedy Lamarr as the only woman in the film does her best acting to date.

WHITE CHRISTMAS
1954, 120 mins, US Ⓥ ◉

D: Michael Curtiz **A:** Bing Crosby, Danny Kaye, Rosemary Clooney, Vera-Ellen, Dean Jagger, Mary Wickes (Paramount)

Bing Crosby and Danny Kaye, along with VistaVision, keep the entertainment going in this fancifully staged production, a smooth blend of music and drama. The plot has Crosby and Kaye, Army buddies, joining forces after the war and becoming a big musical team. They get together with the girls and trek to Vermont for a white Christmas. The inn at which they stay is run by Dean Jagger, their old general, and the boys put on a show to pull him out of a financial hole.

1954: Nomination: Best Song ("Count Your Blessings Instead of Sheep")

WHITE CLIFFS OF DOVER, THE
1944, 126 mins, US

D: Clarence Brown **A:** Irene Dunne, Alan Marshall, Frank Morgan, Roddy McDowall, Van Johnson, Peter Lawford (M-G-M)

The White Cliffs of Dover is the saga of an American girl who went to England for a vacation in 1914, fell in love, learned to love Britain, and remained there through World War I and the coming of World War II. As the story opens, Irene Dunne, a Red Cross supervisor in an English Army hospital, is awaiting the arrival of casualties. She begins to muse about the white cliffs and the first time she saw them as a young girl. Dunne gives an excellent performance, as does Alan Marshal as her husband, while Roddy McDowall stands out sharply as their son.

WHITE DAWN, THE
1974, 109 mins, US Ⓥ ◉

D: Philip Kaufman **A:** Warren Oates, Timothy Bottoms, Lou Gossett, Simonie Kopapik, Joanasie Salomone, Pilitak (Paramount)

Film limns the tale of trio of whale boaters, stranded in the late 1890s near the North Pole, who interact with and nearly destroy the Eskimos who saved their lives. Film emerges with a static narrative. The three whalers bring familiar baggage to the Eskimo village—they find ways of making booze, they gamble, they take advantage of village women, and they steal. Warren Oates is properly blustery as the roistering oldest sea hand.

WHITE DOG
1982, 90 mins, US Ⓥ

D: Samuel Fuller **A:** Kristy McNichol, Paul Winfield, Burl Ives, Jameson Parker, Lynne Moody, Marshall Thompson (Paramount)

White Dog is an unusual, often powerful study of racism, an intense yarn about an up-and-coming L.A. actress (Kristy McNichol) who takes in a German shepherd, only to discover that her new pet is a deadly White Dog, trained from birth to hate anyone with black skin. Scientist-trainer Paul Winfield becomes obsessed with the idea of curing the beast of its racism. His very physical attempts to wear the dog down are effectively elemental.

WHITE FANG
1936, 70 mins, US

D: David Butler **A:** Michael Whalen, Jean Muir, Slim Summerville, Charles Winninger, John Carradine, Jane Darwell (20th Century-Fox)

This is a sequel to *The Call of the Wild*, a yarn of the north country. Michael Whalen isn't altogether a sympathetic character, trying to cheat a girl out of the mine her uncle left her up in Yukon. She not only forgives him for this but refuses to believe that he murdered her own brother. Girl is Jean Muir, a rather brittle type for the tough north country. Excellent heavy is John Carradine. Much more in her place up in the arctic country than Muir is hotel keeper Jane Darwell, a rugged lady.

WHITE FANG
1990, 107 mins, US ♥ ⊙

D: Randal Kleiser **A:** Klaus Maria Brandauer, Ethan Hawke, Seymour Cassel, Susan Hogan, James Remar, Bill Moseley (Hybrid/Walt Disney)

Disney's workmanlike remake of Jack London's adventure *White Fang* boasts enough nature footage and a strong central performance by Ethan Hawke. He plays a would-be prospector who heads to the Alaska gold rush just before the turn of the century to find and work his late father's claim. He teams up with veteran miner Klaus Maria Brandauer and his Gabby Hayes-esque sidekick Seymour Cassel to trek across the snow. Pic never adds up to more than a series of individual moments.

WHITE FANG 2
MYTH OF THE WHITE WOLF
1994, 106 mins, US ♥ ⊙

D: Ken Olin **A:** Scott Bairstow, Charmaine Craig, Al Harrington, Anthony Michael Ruivivar, Victoria Racimo, Alfred Molina (Walt Disney)

Henry Casey (Scott Bairstow) is the new human companion of the titular half-dog, half-wolf. When Casey and White Fang nearly drown while paddling up-river for supplies, Casey is saved by a Haida Indian princess, Lily Joseph (Charmaine Craig). Tribal leader Moses Joseph (Al Harrington) contends that Casey is the one who will help his hunger-ravaged community by finding out why the caribou no longer graze nearby. Script develops a chaste romance between Casey and Lily, and even allows White Fang to find a mate.

WHITE FEATHER
1955, 102 mins, US ⌑

D: Robert D. Webb **A:** Robert Wagner, John Lund, Debra Paget, Jeffrey Hunter, Eduard Franz, Noah Beery (Panoramic/20th Century-Fox)

Plot depicts Robert Wagner as Josh Tanner, a surveyor who is with a government party about to sweep west from Fort Cheyenne. They are stalled until the Cheyennes agree to move from their hunting grounds to a southern area. The big chief's son and his young fighter pal challenge the whole cavalry contingent to pitched battle. It is only through the successful intervention of Tanner and Indian girl Appearing Day (Debra Paget) that needless slaughter is averted.

WHITE HEAT
1949, 114 mins, US ♥ ⊙

D: Raoul Walsh **A:** James Cagney, Virginia Mayo, Edmond O'Brien, Steve Cochran, Margaret Wycherly, John Archer (Warner)

White Heat is about a killer (James Cagney) over whom only his mother can wield any influence. He heads a western gang, with his mother and his double-dealing wife along for company. Steve Cochran makes a good-looking, double-crossing mobster's aide whose ambition for the gang leadership, and the leader's wife, ends in a rain of bullets. Virginia Mayo has little to do except look sexy as the wife.

1949: Nomination: Best Motion Picture Story

WHITE HUNTER, BLACK HEART
1990, 110 mins, US ♥ ⊙

D: Clint Eastwood **A:** Clint Eastwood, Jeff Fahey, George Dzundza, Alun Armstrong, Marisa Berenson, Timothy Spall (Malpaso/Rastar/Warner)

Clint Eastwood's film is an intelligent, affectionate study of an obsessive American film director who, while working on a film in colonial Africa, becomes sidetracked by his compulsion to hunt elephants. This is clearly a story about John Huston and the preproduction period for *The African Queen*. Eastwood plays the Huston character with obvious appreciation of the man: he wears Huston's clothes and hats, assumes Huston's mannerisms, and speaks with the characteristic Huston timbre. The first 20 minutes of the pic unfold in England, where Wilson (Eastwood) welcomes Pete Verrell (Jeff Fahey), his biographer, and it's from Verrell's perspective that the events unfold.

WHITE LIGHTNING
1973, 100 mins, US ♥

D: Joseph Sargent **A:** Burt Reynolds, Jennifer Billingsley, Ned Beatty, Bo Hopkins, Matt Clark, Diane Ladd (United Artists)

An expert auto driver doing time in a Southern state prison for running bootleg whiskey, Burt Reynolds makes a deal with US Treasury agents to help them trap a gang of bootleggers on income tax evasion. Joseph Sargent's direction is particularly effective in the auto-chasing sequences, latter a field day for stunt drivers and occasionally incorporating humorous bits of biz. Reynolds is quite up to all the demands of his smashing role.

WHITE LINE FEVER

1975, 89 mins, US/Canada ⓥ ⊙

D: Jonathan Kaplan **A:** Jan-Michael Vincent, Kay Lenz, Slim Pickens, L. Q. Jones, Don Porter, Sam Laws (Columbia/International Cinemedia)

Air Force vet Jan-Michael Vincent returns home to marriage with Kay Lenz and work as an independent trucker. He soon finds smuggling to be endemic to the career and is violently hassled when he refuses to participate. What seems missing from the film is more depth and logical transition: Vincent passes too rapidly from a stubborn honest lone wolf to practically a union leader. Stunt experts create some powerful action footage.

WHITE MAN'S BURDEN

1995, 89 mins, US/France ⓥ ⊙

D: Desmond Nakano **A:** John Travolta, Harry Belafonte, Kelly Lynch, Margaret Avery, Tom Bower, Carrie Snodgress (A Band Apart/UGC)

White Man's Burden imagines an American society in which the wealthy, privileged classes are predominantly black, and whites occupy the lower strata. But once this challenging food for thought is on the table, debuting writer-director Desmond Nakano fails to make a substantial meal of it. John Travolta plays a factory hand employed at a chocolate manufacturing plant owned by Harry Belafonte. When Travolta makes a bid for a soon-to-be vacant foreman's job, he finds himself fired instead. Robbed of his livelihood, home, and family, he is driven to hijack Belafonte at gunpoint, demanding the money he feels is due him for his years of undeclared overtime. Both talented actors have been denied the chance to take their roles in more interesting directions.

WHITE MISCHIEF

1987, 107 mins, UK ⓥ ⊙

D: Michael Radford **A:** Greta Scacchi, Charles Dance, Sarah Miles, Joss Ackland, John Hurt, Trevor Howard (Nelson/Goldcrest/Umbrella)

White Mischief glossily portrays the flip side of colonial life, exposing the opulent and lush—but downright debauched—lifestyle of the British "Happy Valley" crowd in Kenya during the war years. Pic opens in 1940 with newlyweds "Jock" Broughton (Joss Ackland) and Diana (Greta Scacchi) about to leave England for the British colony in Nairobi. When Diana meets handsome Erroll (Charles Dance), the scene is set for philandering. Brough-

ton seemingly accepts the affair, even when the couple announce their plans to go away together. Later that night Erroll is shot through the head while in his car. The scandal means the end of the Happy Valley set and their dalliances.

WHITE NIGHTS

1985, 135 mins, US ⓥ ⊙

D: Taylor Hackford **A:** Mikhail Baryshnikov, Gregory Hines, Jerzy Skolimowski, Helen Mirren, Geraldine Page, Isabella Rossellini (Columbia-Delphi V/New Visions)

At its core, *White Nights* is a political thriller about the dilemma of a famous Russian defector (Mikhail Baryshnikov) who finds himself trapped back in his mother country. However, pic shies away from the world of classical dance in favor of assorted modern stuff in blatant music video contexts. Mix all this in with KGB intrigue, racial tensions, numerous emotional breakdowns, and several suspense sequences, all played at the broadest levels of melodrama, and one has quite a mishmash indeed. Baryshnikov is moved to the dingy Siberian residence of Hines, a black American tap dancer who jumped to the other side during Vietnam, and his Russian wife Isabella Rossellini. Inevitably, an escape attempt is the climax.

1985: Best Song ("Say You, Say Me")
Nomination: Best Song ("Separate Lives")

WHITE OF THE EYE

1987, 110 mins, UK ⓥ

D: Donald Cammell **A:** David Keith, Cathy Moriarty, Art Evans, Alan Rosenberg, Alberta Watson, Michael Greene (Kastner/Cannon)

White of the Eye is an intriguing thriller. Beneath the layers of flashbacks and, at times, almost subliminal imagery is a conventional story line. Sound expert Paul White (David Keith), living in a small Arizona town, is having marital problems with frau Joan (Cathy Moriarty). Circumstantial evidence implicates him in the case of a serial murderer who mutilates the corpses of his wealthy house wife victims. With lots of clues and red herrings introduced in the early reels, picture maintains considerable suspense.

WHITE PALACE

1990, 104 mins, US ⓥ ⊙

D: Luis Mandoki **A:** Susan Sarandon, James Spader, Jason Alexander, Kathy

Bates, Eileen Brennan, Steven Hill (Universal/Mirage)

Outstanding performances by Susan Sarandon and James Spader, working from a relentlessly witty script, make *White Palace* one of the best films of its kind. Sarandon is Nora, a 43-year-old fast-food worker who gets involved with a 27-year-old advertising executive. They share a magnetic sexual attraction. Their differences include class, religion, and hygiene in addition to the age discrepancy. The ferocity that director Luis Mandoki brings to the pair's early love scenes helps establish how two people can fall into lust and worry about love later.

WHITE PARADE, THE
1934, 80 mins, US
D: Irving Cummings A: Loretta Young, John Boles, Dorothy Wilson, Muriel Kirkland, Astrid Allwyn, Frank Conroy (Fox)

The stern curriculum that goes toward the molding of present-day Florence Nightingales and all the other details that go toward the schooling of the modern nurse are graphically and sometimes heartthrobbingly depicted. Loretta Young is altogether convincing as the sympathetic novice who has consecrated herself to her profession. John Boles, the featured vis-à-vis, is handicapped by his role. Polo-playing Boston playboys who fall for nurses are tough to make real, but he manages quite well.
1934: Nomination: Best Picture

WHITE SANDS
1992, 101 mins, US ⓥ ⊙ ▭
D: Roger Donaldson A: Willem Dafoe, Mary Elizabeth Mastrantonio, Mickey Rourke, Samuel L. Jackson, M. Emmet Walsh, Mimi Rogers (Morgan Creek)

The plot shifts as often as the desert in *White Sands*, an absorbing, tightly coiled thriller not always easy to follow. Willem Dafoe finds a dead Indian with $500,000 in cash in the middle of nowhere and assumes the victim's identity in an effort to solve the case. He is robbed of the loot by two babes and is then abducted by the FBI, who demand that the stash be recovered. Pic builds tautly to a powerful first-act peak. Some thrillers have gone down as classics despite their lack of total narrative coherence, and while *White Sands* doesn't rate that high, it can hold its own with Donaldson's *No Way Out* as an audience-pleasing cliffhanger.

WHITE SISTER, THE
1933, 105 mins, US
D: Victor Fleming A: Helen Hayes, Clark Gable, Lewis Stone, Louise Closser Hale, May Robson, Edward Arnold (M-G-M)

Helen Hayes is the sorrowing Angela. Clark Gable is a gallant soldier hero. The studio has given the story a superlative production, making the most of its Rome setting with a background of the church's pomp and pageantry. Central theme is the separation of the lovers. The girl, believing her lover is dead, enters a nunnery from which, upon his return, she cannot bring herself to depart.

WHITE SQUALL
1996, 127 mins, US ⓥ ⊙
D: Ridley Scott A: Jeff Bridges, Caroline Goodall, John Savage, Scott Wolf, Jeremy Sisto, Ryan Phillippe (Scott Free/Hollywood)

Call it *Floating Poets Society*, or perhaps *Dead Sailors Society*. This coming-of-age story, circa 1960, has a group of teenage boys undergoing a rite of passage—under the tutelage of a stern mentor—by sailing around the Caribbean for a year. Scott Wolf is Chuck Gieg, a high-school senior through whose eyes the audience sees the Skipper (Jeff Bridges) and his other classmates aboard the Albatross. In a storm the boat is sunk, and various members of the crew are lost. That is followed by a brief, anticlimactic courtroom tribunal—a sort of poor man's *Caine Mutiny*.

WHITE TOWER, THE
1950, 98 mins, US ⓥ
D: Ted Tetzlaff A: Glenn Ford, Alida Valli, Claude Rains, Oscar Homolka, Cedric Hardwicke, Lloyd Bridges (RKO)

Magnificent scenic Swiss backgrounds and a gripping yarn are welded together in *The White Tower* for a powerful emotional impact. Plot opens in a peasant village, where a small group of Europeans and one American (Glenn Ford) have gathered to scale a nearby summit. In the case of the German member of the party (Lloyd Bridges), the pic frankly exploits the opportunity to blast the cold brutality and superman pretensions of the Herrenvolk.

WHO?
1974, 93 mins, UK/W. Germany ⓥ
D: Jack Gold A: Elliott Gould, Trevor Howard, Joseph Bova, Ed Grover, James Noble, Lyndon Brook (Lion International/Hemisphere)

Who? is an action-espionage thriller

examining, from a science-fiction perspective, the nature of identity. Joe Bova plays US scientist Martino, whose face and arm are remade in metal after an accident in Berlin. Iterated flashbacks show Martino grilled or indoctrinated by East German intelligence officer Azarin (Trevor Howard). Back in the US, Martino is subjected to gruelling questioning and investigation by FBI operative Rogers (Elliott Gould).

WHO DARES WINS
1982, 125 mins, UK Ⓥ
D: Ian Sharp A: Lewis Collins, Judy Davis, Richard Widmark, Edward Woodward, Robert Webber, Tony Doyle (Rank)

Who Dares Wins is pulp fare about the politics of terrorism in which the anti-war movement is discredited as prone to reckless murder in the ironic name of peace. The simple-minded plot has a militant anti-nuke organization take over a US diplomatic facility in London and demand the wipeout of a US sub base in Scotland. Wiped out instead, by a crack British commando team, are the peaceniks.

WHO FRAMED ROGER RABBIT?
1988, 103 mins, US Ⓥ ⊙
D: Robert Zemeckis A: Bob Hoskins, Christopher Lloyd, Joanna Cassidy, Stubby Kaye, Alan Tilvern (Touchstone/Amblin/Silver Screen Partners III)

Who Framed Roger Rabbit? is an unparalleled technical achievement in which animation is brilliantly integrated into live action. The story amounts to little more than inspired silliness. Things aren't going well for poor Roger Rabbit, a famous contract Toon player (as in cartoon) for Maroon Studios. Ever since he became estranged from his voluptuous human character Toon wife Jessica (sultry, uncredited voice courtesy of Kathleen Turner), he just can't act. He becomes an innocent murder suspect, with a disheveled, alcoholic private eye (Bob Hoskins) his only hope to help him beat the rap. The real stars are the animators, under British animation director Richard Williams, who pull off a technically amazing feat.
1988: Best Editing, Sound Effects Editing, Visual Effects
Nominations: Best Cinematography, Art Direction, Sound

WHO IS KILLING THE GREAT CHEFS OF EUROPE?
(TOO MANY CHEFS)
1978, 112 mins, US/W. Germany Ⓥ
D: Ted Kotcheff A: George Segal, Jacqueline Bisset, Robert Morley, Jean-Pierre Cassel, Philippe Noiret, Jean Rochefort (Aldrich/Lorimar)

Who Is Killing the Great Chefs of Europe? is a happy combination of the macabre and the merry, a fast-moving, witty film. While George Segal and Jacqueline Bisset carry star billing, it is Robert Morley as a massive, dedicated gourmet who provides the finest moments. The murders are the responsibility of some of France and Italy's most outstanding character actors. Philippe Noiret underplays in a manner that gives him a slight edge over the more voluble Italians. The other endangered chef is Jean-Pierre Cassel, while Jean Rochefort is a red herring who'll fool no one.

WHOLE TOWN'S TALKING, THE
(PASSPORT TO FAME)
1935, 95 mins, US
D: John Ford A: Edward G. Robinson, Jean Arthur, Wallace Ford, Arthur Hohl, Donald Meek, Etienne Girardot (Columbia)

Edward G. Robinson plays a dual role, soft in one part and tough in the other. The softie bookkeeper is a dead ringer for a gangster wanted by the police. So the bookkeeper gets a pass identifying him as legitimate. The real criminal, of course, shows up and quietly takes over the passport as a shield to continue his activities. Robinson's characterization of the submerged, over-polite, and indecisive office worker is human and believable. Jean Arthur is typically the young and rather sassy American stenographer.

WHOLE WIDE WORLD, THE
1996, 111 mins, US Ⓥ ▭
D: Dan Ireland A: Vincent D'Onofrio, Renee Zellweger, Ann Wedgeworth, Harve Presnell, Benjamin Mouton, Helen Cates (Kushner-Locke)

Superbly acted by Vincent D'Onofrio and Renee Zellweger, this well-appointed indie production recounts the true-life relationship between a small-town Texas schoolteacher and Robert E. Howard, creator of *Conan the Barbarian* and other 1930s pulp-fiction classics. Tale is told from the p.o.v. of Novalyne Price (Zellweger), a proper young Texas woman who teaches school but aspires to be a writer, and so arranges to be introduced to Howard (D'Onofrio), a rather mysterious and wild figure. Pic has no dramatic aspirations other than to chart the course of the pair's three-year relationship. There is no suggestion that they ever slept together. Film's main drawback is that it can never truly get under the skin of Howard's weirdness.

WHO'LL STOP THE RAIN (DOG SOLDIERS)
1978, 125 mins, US ⓥ ⊙
D: Karel Reisz **A:** Nick Nolte, Tuesday Weld, Michael Moriarty, Anthony Zerbe, Richard Masur, Ray Sharkey (United Artists)

This is a corking couple-on-the-run adventure pic, given depth in its focus on personal disarray, growing governmental corruption, and the effects of the Vietnam war on America. Michael Moriarty, a journalist and photographer during the Vietnam War, suffers trauma under a deadly enemy barrage. He decides to try to smuggle heroin to the US. An old Marine buddy (Nick Nolte) is to get in touch with Moriarty's wife (Tuesday Weld) and wait for Moriarty to get back. But back in the US, Nolte is followed. He and Weld go on the lam. Film has a hardnose progression and solidity in its characterizations. Nolte earns his star stripes here.

WHORE
1991, 84 mins, US ⓥ ⊙
D: Ken Russell **A:** Theresa Russell, Benjamin Mouton, Antonio Fargas, Sanjay, Elizabeth Moorehead, Michael Crabtree (Trimark)

Given the possibilities afforded by the subject matter, *Whore* features little of the kinkiness and bravura stylistics one expects from director Ken Russell, and no compensating psychological or documentary insight into the lead character or her lifestyle. The setting is Los Angeles, where the consummately vulgar Liz (Theresa Russell) plies her trade on downtown streets. In flashbacks, Liz covers her initial tricks, hooks up with her pimp and sometime boyfriend, Blake (Benjamin Mouton), and has failed marriage. Overriding problem is a pervasive feeling of utter inauthenticity. Russell's strident, stops-out performance sets the tone for the entire picture.

WHO'S AFRAID OF VIRGINIA WOOLF?
1966, 131 mins, US ⓥ ⊙
D: Mike Nichols **A:** Elizabeth Taylor, Richard Burton, George Segal, Sandy Dennis (Warner)

Keen adaptation of Edward Albee's incisive, inhuman drama by Ernest Lehman; outstanding direction by Mike Nichols in his feature debut; and four top-flight performances score an artistic bull's-eye. Elizabeth Taylor is at once sensual, spiteful, cynical, pitiable, loathsome, lustful, and tender. Richard Burton evokes sympathy during the public degradations to which his wife subjects him, and his outrage and deliberate vengeance are totally believable. Provoking the exercise in exorcism is the visit of Sandy Dennis and George Segal. The latter, in the course of one night, is seduced by his hostess, exposed by his host, but enlightened as to the more mature aspects of love and marriage. Segal is able to evoke sympathy, then hatred, then pity. Dennis makes an impressive screen debut as the young bride, with the intended subtlety of a not-so-Dumb Dora.

1966: Best Actress (Elizabeth Taylor), Supp. Actress (Sandy Dennis), B&W Cinematography, B&W Art Direction, B&W Costume Design (Irene Sharaff)
Nominations: Best Picture, Director, Actor (Richard Burton), Supp. Actor (George Segal), Screenplay Adaptation, Editing, Original Music Score, Sound

WHO'S BEEN SLEEPING IN MY BED?
1963, 103 mins, US ▭
D: Daniel Mann **A:** Dean Martin, Elizabeth Montgomery, Martin Balsam, Jill St. John, Carol Burnett, Macha Meril (Paramount)

Dean Martin is right for the part of an actor who appears on television as a doctor, then moonlights into the field of psychiatric advice (and perhaps romantic stimulation) for the glamorous dames married to his television-business associates. But what might have been mischievous, zesty comedy in a couple of instances is permitted to sink in its quest for sophisticated hilarity. Martin is an amiable performer in light comedy and does fine with the material at hand.

WHOSE LIFE IS IT ANYWAY?
1981, 118 mins, US ⓥ ▭
D: John Badham **A:** Richard Dreyfuss, John Cassavetes, Christine Lahti, Bob Balaban, Kenneth McMillan, Kaki Hunter (M-G-M)

Richard Dreyfuss delivers a sensitive portrait of a young sculptor cut down in an automobile accident at the height of his life and paralyzed from the neck down. An opening sequence establishes his idyllic relationship with dancer Janet Eilber, and there are glimpses at Dreyfuss's former life, particularly through his artist's studio. All the action leads to the unresolvable issue of who has the power to decide the fate of the patient—the hospital or the patient. Dreyfuss demands a legal hearing in his fight to be rid of all life-sustaining methods.

WHO'S HARRY CRUMB?
1989, 98 mins, US Ⓥ ⊙
D: Paul Flaherty **A:** John Candy, Jeffrey Jones, Annie Potts, Tim Thomerson, Barry Corbin, Shawnee Smith (Tri-Star/NBC/Frostbacks)

Foolishness in the right hands can be sublimely funny. John Candy plays Crumb, a complete idiot related to a line of crack detectives who finally gets assigned to a lucrative kidnapping case—but only because his beady-eyed boss (Jeffrey Jones), who's the kidnapper, doesn't want it solved. He lusts after the golddigging newlywed wife (deliciously played by Annie Potts) of a benign, trusting multimillionaire (Barry Corbin). The plot is to get $10 million ransom for the return of Corbin's slinky daughter (Renee Coleman) and use the riches to pry Potts away from her main meal-ticket.

WHO'S MINDING THE STORE?
1963, 90 mins, US
D: Frank Tashlin **A:** Jerry Lewis, Jill St. John, Agnes Moorehead, John McGiver, Ray Walston, Francesca Bellini (Paramount/York/Lewis)

Jerry Lewis goes to work in a department store and wrecks it department by department. He has an especially attractive romantic vis-à-vis in Jill St. John, who takes a job as elevator operator to hide that she's really the daughter of the store's owner. Agnes Moorehead plays the owner's domineering wife, who regards Lewis as an idiot. Accent is on broad comedy, with the spotlight mainly on havoc-wreaking Lewis.

WHO'S THAT GIRL?
1987, 94 mins, US Ⓥ ⊙
D: James Foley **A:** Madonna, Griffin Dunne, Haviland Morris, John McMartin, Bibi Besch, John Mills (Warner)

Madonna plays a just-out-of-jail petty thief bent on avenging the thugs who made her take the rap for a murder she didn't commit. Weak-kneed lawyer-type Griffin Dunne is sent by his megabucks soon-to-be-father-in-law (John McMartin) to pick her up and make sure she's on the next bus home. Madonna turns Dunne into a near nut case, bashing up his future mother-in-law's Corniche, buying stolen goods in Harlem, and stealing right and left. Fortunately, Dunne's playful personality eventually counter-balances Madonna's shrillness. What's lacking is pure and simple good humor.

WHO'S THAT KNOCKING AT MY DOOR?
1968, 90 mins, US Ⓥ
D: Martin Scorsese **A:** Zina Bethune, Harvey Keitel, Lennard Kuras, Ann Collette, Michael Scala, Harry Northup (Trimod)

The tale is the inner struggle of a young Italian-American, J. R., torn between a Roman Catholic upbringing and the temptations of modern life. He's portrayed as a crude, carousing lout who never works but devotes himself to drinking and drifting or spending time with a "good" girl, until he finds that she's not the virgin he imagined. Harvey Keitel, as the anti-hero, is alternately boorish and bewildered. Scorsese occasionally brings the film to life. Generally, however, his script and direction lack dramatic value and give far too much exposure to sexual fantasies on the part of the boy.

WHO WAS THAT LADY?
1960, 116 mins, US
D: George Sidney **A:** Tony Curtis, Dean Martin, Janet Leigh, James Whitmore, John McIntire, Barbara Nichols (Ansark/Columbia)

Who Was That Lady? is an often hilarious romp made somewhat sedate only in a compromise between farce and romantic comedy. Tony Curtis is an assistant professor of chemistry. When his wife, Janet Leigh, catches him kissing a pretty student, she threatens divorce. In his desperation for an acceptable alibi, Curtis turns to a friend (Dean Martin), a television writer. James Whitmore, not ordinarily thought of as a comedian, gets the film's biggest laughs, mostly on reaction shots of no lines, just looks.

WICKED LADY, THE
1945, 102 mins, UK Ⓥ
D: Leslie Arliss **A:** Margaret Lockwood, James Mason, Patricia Roc, Griffith Jones,

Michael Rennie, Felix Aylmer (Gainsborough)

Producers claim that this story is "set in the days of Charles II," but the period atmosphere is not convincing. James Mason as a Robin Hood–type highwayman scores in spite of the weak script. The other performance lending credibility to the period comes from Felix Aylmer as an old retainer who tumbles to the villainy of Margaret Lockwood in the title role. Lockwood shoots, poisons, and betrays all who get in her way. Between murders, she steals the fiancé of her best girl friend.

WICKED LADY, THE
1983, 98 mins, US Ⓥ

D: Michael Winner **A:** Faye Dunaway, Alan Bates, John Gielgud, Denholm Elliott, Prunella Scales, Oliver Tobias (Cannon)

Sex, humor, and even a facsimile of style distinguish Michael Winner's entertaining remake of *The Wicked Lady* as a comedy-drama of rogue-ridden 17th-century England with Faye Dunaway an effective title star. After marrying Denholm Elliott for his money, Dunaway turns to a life of nocturnal crime, solo at first, later in cahoots with legendary stagecoach robber Alan Bates. Dunaway performs with satisfying conviction, straight face and all. So does Elliott as her scorned and cuckolded husband. Bates makes for a charming but all-too-brief rogue, while John Gielgud as a God-fearing retainer has a marvelous deadpan time of it kidding himself.

WICKER MAN, THE
1973, 87 mins, UK Ⓥ

D: Robin Hardy **A:** Edward Woodward, Britt Ekland, Diane Cilento, Ingrid Pitt, Christopher Lee, Roy Boyd (British Lion/Brut)

The Wicker Man, lensed entirely on location in Scotland, is possessed of a weird and paganistic story which, for sheer imagination and near-terror, has seldom been equalled. A Scottish police sergeant arrives on a little off-shore island to investigate the disappearance of a young girl. He finds a sinister situation dating back to the days of pagan practices and fertility rites. Edward Woodward plays the sergeant who is forced into a fatal part in the paganistic rituals. Christopher Lee is the cultured lord of the island. Both score in their roles.

WIDE SARGASSO SEA
1993, 96 mins, Australia Ⓥ ⊙

D: John Duigan **A:** Karina Lombard, Nathaniel Parker, Rachel Ward, Michael York, Martine Beswick, Claudia Robinson (Laughing Kookaburra)

An exotic and erotic melodrama, *Wide Sargasso Sea* is an uneven but ultimately engrossing feature. Production boasts stunning location photography in Jamaica and the north of England, but the editing looks like the film was put through a shredder. A mad French woman (Rachel Ward) in Jamaica marries an Englishman (Michael York). Her daughter (lovely model Karina Lombard) is stuck in a marriage arranged by her uncle to Englishman Edward Rochester (Nathaniel Parker), the brooding hero of Charlotte Bronte's *Jane Eyre*. The local form of voodoo seems to hold each of them in thrall. Thesping honors go to Claudia Robinson as Lombard's sharp-tonged black nanny.

WIDOWS' PEAK
1994, 102 mins, UK/US Ⓥ ⊙

D: John Irvin **A:** Mia Farrow, Joan Plowright, Natasha Richardson, Adrian Dunbar, Jim Broadbent, Anne Kent (Rank/Fine Line)

There's more old-fashioned blarney on show in *Widows' Peak* than at a shamrock-growers' convention. Teaming of Mia Farrow, Joan Plowright, and Natasha Richardson manages to keep the dramatically rickety craft afloat through star power alone. Yarn is set during the mid-1920s in the spa resort of Kilshannon, a stuffy, middle-class enclave socially ruled by a Mrs. Doyle Counihan (Joan Plowright), high priestess of a section dubbed Widows' Peak, whose members also include penurious spinster Miss O'Hare (Mia Farrow). Enter American Edwina Broome (Natasha Richardson), a glamorous World War I widow who soon has D.C.'s son, Godfrey (Adrian Dunbar), dancing on a string but is seemingly loathed by the dowdy O'Hare. Pic needs a sharper script and pacier direction to counter the earth-bound realism of locations on display here.

WIFE VS. SECRETARY
1936, 88 mins, US

D: Clarence Brown **A:** Clark Gable, Jean Harlow, Myrna Loy, May Robson, Hobart Cavanaugh, James Stewart (M-G-M)

Here Jean Harlow is no siren, but a perfectly competent secretary, very much in love with her job and her boss (Gable), but not on the make for him. Myrna Loy, as the wife, is much in love with Clark Gable, and he with her. They are an ideal couple until his mother plants seeds of suspicion. Gable's part might have been tailored to his order. Loy gets a part which suits her, but it is Harlow who profits most. She clicks in every scene.

WILBY CONSPIRACY, THE
1975, 101 mins, UK ⊗
D: Ralph Nelson A: Sidney Poitier, Michael Caine, Nicol Williamson, Prunella Gee, Persis Khambatta, Saeed Jaffrey (United Artists)

The Wilby Conspiracy is a good action melodrama about apartheid in South Africa. The stars Sidney Poitier and Michael Caine are relentlessly stalked by Nicol Williamson, superb as a coldly dedicated and brutal policeman out after racial agitators. Caine is an Englishman whose girlfriend (Prunella Gee)—Poitier's lawyer—has Poitier freed from a decade in prison. Williamson expects Poitier to lead him to his political guerrilla partner. Somehow the story comes out too much of a potboiler undeserving of the fine work that Williamson, Caine, and Poitier put into it.

WILD AND THE WILLING, THE (YOUNG AND WILLING)
1962, 123 mins, UK
D: Ralph Thomas A: Virginia Maskell, Paul Rogers, Ian McShane, Samantha Eggar, John Hurt, Richard Warner (Rank)

The Wild and the Willing has nothing much new to say on its chosen theme—youth trying to find their place in society. Film concerns a brilliant young student from a poor working class family who rebels against the university, its professors, and the opportunities they offer. He is arrogantly content to drift along raising Cain. He has a particular influence on his roommate, a shyer, more introspective lad. The students, the professors, and the townsfolk are real people about whose problems audiences will care. Ian McShane plays the leading role. He is a virile, good-looking young man with authority who is a real discovery, as is John Hurt, also a first-timer, who plays his sensitive roommate.

WILD ANGELS, THE
1966, 83 mins, US ⊗ ⊙
D: Roger Corman A: Peter Fonda, Nancy Sinatra, Bruce Dern, Diane Ladd, Michael J. Pollard, Gayle Hunnicutt (American International)

Pinpointed here, the Hell's Angels, in vicious stride and without regard for law and order, operate in a southern California beach community, and it is upon this particular segment that Corman directs his clinical eye in dissecting their rebellion. Corman tackles his assignment with realism, taking apart the cult and giving its members an in-depth study as he follows a gang headed by Peter Fonda in their defiance of common decencies.

WILD AT HEART
1990, 127 mins, US ⊗ ⊙ ▭
D: David Lynch A: Nicolas Cage, Laura Dern, Diane Ladd, Willem Dafoe, Isabella Rossellini, Harry Dean Stanton (Polygram/Propaganda)

Joltingly violent, wickedly funny, and rivetingly erotic, David Lynch's *Wild at Heart* is a rollercoaster ride to redemption through an American gothic heart of darkness. Sailor (Nicolas Cage), an Elvis acolyte, and his seethingly sexy 18-year-old girlfriend Lula (Laura Dern) are waylaid leaving a dance hall somewhere in the Carolinas. Sailor literally cracks open the assassin with his bare hands and does two years for manslaughter. Sailor breaks parole and absconds with Lula to New Orleans, pursued by private eye Johnnie Farragut (Harry Dean Stanton), who's hired by Lula's insanely obsessive mother Marietta (Diane Ladd), his sometime lover.

1990: Nomination: Best Supp. Actress (Diane Ladd)

WILD BILL
1995, 97 mins, US ⊗ ⊙
D: Walter Hill A: Jeff Bridges, Ellen Barkin, John Hurt, Diane Lane, David Arquette, Christina Applegate (Zanuck/United Artists)

Wild Bill is an art-western that manages to shoot itself in both feet. This awkwardly structured look at one of the west's most famous gunmen presents Buffalo Bill, as impersonated with great physical conviction by Jeff Bridges, as one ornery, soreheaded s.o.b. In Deadwood Gulch, Bill resumes his old quasi-romance with Calamity Jane (Ellen Barkin), suffers an opium-induced crisis of conscience, and faces a recurring challenge from green would-be assassin Jack McCall (David Arquette), who, it appears, may be Wild Bill's son. Pic comes to a near dead-stop as Wild Bill, Calamity Jane, and Jack's band of killers sit around all night in a saloon while Jack decides whether or not to kill his nemesis.

WILD BUNCH, THE
1969, 145 mins, US ♥ ⊚ ▭
D: Sam Peckinpah A: William Holden, Ernest Borgnine, Robert Ryan, Edmond O'Brien, Warren Oates, Jaime Sanchez (Warner/Seven Arts)

Plot concerns a small band of outlaws headed by William Holden who hijack a US ammunition train crossing the border into Mexico in 1913 to supply the revolutionary army of Pancho Villa, while Robert Ryan, former member of Holden's gang and a temporarily released convict, tracks down his former chief to "buy" his freedom from jail. Sam Peckinpah's forceful direction is a definite asset, particularly in later sequences in which Holden deals with a vicious Mexican general over the hijacked guns and ammo.
1969: Nominations: Best Original Story & Screenplay, Original Music Score

WILDCATS
1986, 107 mins, US ♥
D: Michael Ritchie A: Goldie Hawn, James Keach, Swoosie Kurtz, Nipsey Russell, Bruce McGill, M. Emmet Walsh (Warner)

When Goldie Hawn tangles with high school varsity coach Bruce McGill, who has her appointed football coach at an unspeakable ghetto school, Central High, it's an inevitable collision course. Along the way crises pop up at carefully placed intervals, the first being winning the confidence of the ragtag collection of players. Michael Ritchie's direction lacks his usual bite and eye for detail. Hawn is fun to watch as she runs her team through aerobics and mugs for the camera, but even better is Nipsey Russell as the rough-hewn high school principal.

WILD CHILD
See: L'Enfant Sauvage

WILDE
1997, 115 mins, UK ♥ ⊚ ▭
D: Brian Gilbert A: Stephen Fry, Jude Law, Vanessa Redgrave, Jennifer Ehle, Gemma Jones, Judy Parfitt (Samuelson)

Wilde is the full monty on Oscar-toplining British comedian/wit Stephen Fry in a once-in-a-lifetime role as the brilliant,

acerbic playwright. Mounted with care and affection in all departments, movie manages to combine an upfront portrayal of the scribe's gayness with an often moving examination of his broader emotions and artistic ideals. Pic is the first to go the whole enchilada on Wilde's homosexuality, with reasonably forthright, though far from full-frontal, sex scenes. Script equally addresses Wilde's love for his wife and children. It's when he's introduced to the upper-crust Alfred (Bosie) Douglas (Jude Law) that Fry's performance really kicks in. Behind the man's overweening arrogance lies a real sadness that his affection for Bosie—prone to childish tantrums and sexual philandering—is to be the vehicle for his downfall. Brian Gilbert brings to the picture visual fluency, deep-seated emotion, and first-rate playing from his cast.

WILDER NAPALM
1993, 109 mins, US ♥
D: Glenn Gordon Caron A: Debra Winger, Dennis Quaid, Arliss Howard, M. Emmet Walsh, Jim Varney, Mimi Lieber (Tri-Star)

If nothing else, *Wilder Napalm* deserves a special mention in the history books as the first and only pyrokinetic romantic comedy-drama. Beyond that, there's little to recommend in this slow-moving, fuzzy-minded yarn. The Foudroyant brothers—Wallace (Dennis Quaid) and Wilder (Arliss Howard)—have the gift of thinking real hard and making things explode in flames. Wallace has managed to incorporate such shenanigans into a clown act he performs in a low-grade traveling carnival. There's mysterious bad blood involving a prank Wallace inflicted on his brother. The carnival arrives in town and parks itself in the mall where Wilder works. It's painful to watch such gifted actors struggling to maintain their dignity.

WILD GEESE, THE
1978, 132 mins, UK ♥ ⊚
D: Andrew V. McLaglen A: Richard Burton, Roger Moore, Richard Harris, Hardy Kruger, Stewart Granger, Jack Watson (Rank)

Euan Lloyd's actioner attempts to be a cornucopia of tried box-office hooks but ultimately fails to meld its comedy, adventure, pathos, violence, heroics, or even its political message, into a credible whole. The story—about mercenaries who parachute into the African bush to snatch a deposed African president for reinstatement to suit British business interests—is routinely predictable and, in the end, cornily incredible.

WILD GEESE II
1985, 125 mins, UK Ⓥ ⊙
D: Peter Hunt A: Scott Glenn, Barbara Carrera, Edward Fox, Laurence Olivier, Robert Webber, Robert Freitag (Thorn-EMI/Frontier)

Script has a promising basic premise. An American television station commissions mercenary John Haddad (Scott Glenn) to kidnap the nonagenarian Nazi leader Rudolf Hess from the impregnable Spandau prison in Berlin, but the followthrough never arrives. Despite these structural problems, film contains a wealth of incidents. Haddad is the object of assassination attempts organized by the German Heinrich Stroebling (Robert Freitag), who is in league with Russians and Palestinian terrorists. The British are after Hess, too. There's also a supporting role for members of the Irish Republican Army. Unintentionally, perhaps, Laurence Olivier extracts laughs from his cameo as Hess.

WILD HEART, THE
See: Gone to Earth

WILD IN THE COUNTRY
1961, 112 mins, US Ⓥ ▱
D: Philip Dunne A: Elvis Presley, Hope Lange, Tuesday Weld, Millie Perkins, John Ireland, Gary Lockwood (20th Century-Fox)

Dramatically, there simply isn't substance, novelty, or spring to this wobbly and artificial tale of a maltreated country boy (Elvis Presley) who, supposedly, has the talent to become a great writer but lacks the emotional stability and the encouragement until he meets a beautiful psychiatric consultant (Hope Lange) who develops traumas of her own in the process. Clifford Odets penned the screenplay. The writing has its occasional rewards. Presley uses what dramatic resources he has to his best advantage. Tuesday Weld contributes a flashy and arresting portrait of a sexy siren enamored of Mr. P.

WILD IN THE STREETS
1968, 96 mins, US Ⓥ
D: Barry Shear A: Shelley Winters, Christopher Jones, Diane Varsi, Ed Begley, Hal Holbrook, Millie Perkins (American International)

An often-chilling political science-fiction drama, with comedy, this film considers the takeover of the American government by a preponderant younger population. Christopher Jones plays a rock 'n' roll hero who exceeds the bounds of electioneering help by mobilizing teenagers into legalized voters. Shelley Winters plays his sleazy, selfish mother. Actual footage from real-life demonstrations was shot for pic, some of it matched quite well with internal drama.
1968: Nomination: Best Editing

WILD IS THE WIND
1957, 110 mins, US
D: George Cukor A: Anna Magnani, Anthony Quinn, Anthony Franciosa, Dolores Hart, Joseph Calleia, Lili Valenty (Paramount)

Wild Is the Wind, a story of earthy passion, starts off on a comedy level before abruptly switching to drama. Long early portions are almost entirely in Italian. Anthony Quinn, a wealthy sheep rancher in Nevada, goes back to the old country to wed the sister of his long-dead wife, but the shadow of the first wife is constantly between them. The sister's urgent need to be loved leads to a growing attraction between herself and Anthony Franciosa, young Basque sheepherder who had been raised by Quinn.
1957: Nominations: Best Actor (Anthony Quinn), Actress (Anna Magnani), Song ("Wild Is the Wind")

WILD ONE, THE
1953, 79 mins, US Ⓥ ⊙
D: Laslo Benedek A: Marlon Brando, Mary Murphy, Robert Keith, Lee Marvin, Jay C. Flippen, Hugh Sanders (Columbia)

This feature is long on suspense, brutality, and sadism. Marlon Brando plays a hard-faced "hero" who never knew love as a boy and is now plainly in need of psychoanalysis. The young cyclists are a motley mob of jivesters, some carrying their own female cargo. Reckless, impudent, cruel, and knife-carrying, they break and borrow things and drive motorcycles into and through saloons. However intolerable and barbarian the cyclists are, nothing they do is as vicious and vindictive as the vigilante spirit that develops among the merchants of the village. These adults joyously beat Brando to a pulp and then try to frame him for a manslaughter rap. A second band of ruffians comes along later, led by colorful young actor named Lee Marvin.

WILD ORCHID
1990, 100 mins, US Ⓥ ⊙
D: Zalman King **A:** Mickey Rourke, Jacqueline Bisset, Carre Otis (Vision)

If *Wild Orchid* aims to grab audiences with a hot-house atmosphere of erotica, it mainly teases until a pay-off in the last sequence. Claudia (Jacqueline Bisset) is a jet-set businesswoman who hires tyro lawyer Emily (Carre Otis) to help her close a deal. Emily finds herself on a plane to Rio, where she meets Claudia's old flame Wheeler (Mickey Rourke), a self-made millionaire with perverse sexual tastes. What doesn't work is the hold Rourke is supposed to have on Otis. Pudgy and puffy-faced, with a little gold earring, he is anything but an appetizing sex object. Only when Emily breaks through his reserve in the last sequence does pic deliver in a torrid, highly choreographed but explicit bedroom session between the two.

WILD PARTY, THE
1975, 100 mins, US Ⓥ
D: James Ivory **A:** James Coco, Raquel Welch, Perry King, Tiffany Bolling, Royal Dano, David Dukes (American International)

The Wild Party is an extremely handsome, overly talky musical drama starring James Coco as a faded 1920s film comic whose disastrous premiere house party for a comeback film leads to murder. Coco covers a spectrum from silly comedy, warm humor, sober anger, and maddening frustration to drunken psychosis. Holding her own as his mistress is Raquel Welch, who registers very strongly.

WILD RIVER
1960, 115 mins, US ▭
D: Elia Kazan **A:** Montgomery Clift, Lee Remick, Jo Van Fleet, Albert Salmi, Jay C. Flippen, Barbara Loden (20th Century-Fox)

Wild River is the tragic tale, set in the 1930s, of an 80-year-old rugged individualist (Jo Van Fleet) who refuses to give ground (a small island on the Tennessee River smack dab in the Tennessee Valley Authority's dam-building path) to an understanding, but equally firm, TVA agent (Montgomery Clift). Clift gets into scrapes with local Tennessee bigots over his decent treatment of blacks and squeezes sufficient romance into his tight schedule to wind up the spouse of the old woman's pretty granddaughter (Lee Remick). Where the film soars is in its clean, objective approach to the basic conflict between

progress and tradition. The result is that rare element of tragedy, where an indomitable individual must cede to an irresistible but impersonal edict designed for universal good.

WILD ROVERS
1971, 110 mins, US Ⓥ ▭
D: Blake Edwards **A:** William Holden, Ryan O'Neal, Karl Malden, Lynn Carlin, Tom Skerritt, Joe Don Baker (M-G-M)

Film tells a sentimental story about an aging cowpoke (William Holden) and a younger buddy (Ryan O'Neal) whose dreams of crashing out of their rut lead to violence and death. The mood is broken regularly with pratfall humor and some dehumanizing slow-motion ballets of death. O'Neal's character is not always well defined, since the boyish naïveté also exhibits some jarring evidence of cruelty.

WILD STRAWBERRIES
See: Smultronstallet

WILD THINGS
1998, 108 mins, US Ⓥ ⊙ ▭
D: John McNaughton **A:** Kevin Bacon, Matt Dillon, Neve Campbell, Theresa Russell, Denise Richards, Bill Murray (Columbia/Mandalay)

In the blue-chip Florida enclave of Blue Bay, the sex is as steamy as the climate. *Wild Things* captures the passions of the area's haves and have-nots and gives them a wicked comic spin. High-nosed teen socialite Kelly Van Ryan's (Denise Richards) moves on guidance counselor Sam Lombardo (Matt Dillon) have been met with indifference. But that doesn't stop her from crying rape. Lombardo enlists personal-injuries lawyer Ken Bowden (Bill Murray), who proves more shrewd than the army of legal eagles Kelly's mother—Sam's former lover (Theresa Russell)—employs to destroy the teacher. Another teen, trailer-trash Suzie Toller (Neve Campbell), comes forward with a carbon-copy tale of Sam's advances. The story demands investigation by cop Ray Duquette (Kevin Bacon). Director John McNaughton casts his four principals against type. There's not a wrong note struck by the game group of players.

WILD WILD WEST
1999, 107 mins, US Ⓥ ⊙
D: Barry Sonnenfeld **A:** Will Smith, Kevin Kline, Kenneth Branagh, Salma Hayek, Ted Levine, M. Emmet Walsh (Peters/Sonnenfeld-Josephson/Warner)

Some very talented people stub their

collective toes quite elaborately and expensively in *Wild Wild West*, in turning the 1964–68 TV series into a Jules Verne–like 19th-century quasi-sci-fier equipped with hip refs and contempo attitude. In 1869, special government agents James West (Will Smith) and Artemus Gordon (Kevin Kline) are thrown together by President Grant (Kline again) to prevent Confederate General "Bloodbath" McGrath (Ted Levine) from developing a highly advanced weapons system that threatens the Union. But their real foe is Dr. Arliss Loveless (Kenneth Branagh), a paraplegic who has kidnapped all the top scientists. Kline has fun with his disguises but fights an uphill battle with undernourished dialogue. Branagh supplies all the vinegar he can to his Prussian-style villain.

WILLARD
1971, 95 mins, US ✆ ⊙
D: Daniel Mann **A:** Bruce Davison, Ernest Borgnine, Elsa Lanchester, Sondra Locke, Michael Dante, Jody Gilbert (BCO)

Neat little horror tale. Bruce Davison, working for wheeler-dealer Ernest Borgnine, who took foundry over from Davison's dead father, lives with invalid, unrelenting mother Elsa Lanchester. Davison makes friends with resident rats, who learn to obey his commands. Davison, after death of his mother and killing of one of the chief rats at Borgnine's hands, begins to fight back. Davison supplies nicely controlled characterization.

WILLIAM SHAKESPEARE'S A MIDSUMMER NIGHT'S DREAM
See: A Midsummer Night's Dream

WILLIAM SHAKESPEARE'S ROMEO + JULIET
See: Romeo + Juliet

WILLIE & PHIL
1980, 116 mins, US ✆
D: Paul Mazursky **A:** Michael Ontkean, Margot Kidder, Ray Sharkey, Jerry Hall, Natalie Wood, Tom Brennan (20th Century-Fox)

Willie & Phil is an amiable and humane film about a ménage à trois spanning the 1970s. Michael Ontkean and Ray Sharkey play the title characters, and Margot Kidder completes the romantic triangle, which forms in Greenwich Village at the beginning of the 1970s and winds up in Malibu nine years later. Along the way, Mazursky deftly traces changing sexual mores and other social values while portraying the trio as typical representative of

their generation's hopes and confusions. It's all handled in very civilized and low-key fashion by Mazursky and his characters.

WILLOW
1988, 125 mins, US ✆ ⊙ ▭
D: Ron Howard **A:** Val Kilmer, Joanne Whalley-Kilmer, Warwick Davis, Patricia Hayes, Jean Marsh, Billy Barty (Lucasfilm)

Willow is medieval mishmash from George Lucas, a sort of 10th-century *Star Wars* tossed together with a plethora of elements taken from numerous classic fables. Willow is a Nelwyn, one of a community of midgets saving their kingdom from an evil queen (Jean Marsh) who makes her crusade to kill every newborn in the land to ensure that baby Elora Danan, a princess, never ascends to the throne. Dialogue wavers from the truly banal to some clever interplay between the secondary characters. Ron Howard directed, but only Lucas's touch shows up on the screen, particularly toward the end when the special effects start to come on at full bore.
1988: Nominations: Best Sound Effects Editing, Visual Effects

WILL PENNY
1968, 108 mins, US ✆ ⊙
D: Tom Gries **A:** Charlton Heston, Joan Hackett, Donald Pleasence, Lee Majors, Bruce Dern, Ben Johnson (Paramount)

Will Penny is not a straight out-and-out western but more a character study of an aging cowpoke who for the first time feels the stirrings of romance. Charlton Heston in the title role is persuasively effective as the cowpoke who finally rides away from romance. Joan Hackett as the woman traveling across the plains to join her farmer-husband in Oregon, willing to renounce that marriage to wed the penniless range rider, is quietly commanding. Donald Pleasence is a scavenging rawhider who, with his three sons, would rather murder than not. This is not a story of the wild west but the west as lived in by real-life characters.

WILL SUCCESS SPOIL ROCK HUNTER? (OH! FOR A MAN)
1957, 94 mins, US ▭
D: Frank Tashlin **A:** Jayne Mansfield, Tony Randall, Betsy Drake, Joan Blondell, Mickey Hargitay, Groucho Marx (20th Century-Fox)

In converting the stage play *Will Success Spoil Rock Hunter?* to his purposes, Frank Tashlin turns out a vastly amusing comedy. Story has Tony Randall as a television commercial writer about to be fired because his agency is threatened with the loss of its big lipstick account. He saves the situation by getting an endorsement from a famous movie star. Betsy Drake is cute and displays a strong sense of comedy as Randall's fiancée; Joan Blondell is a standout in a small part, and Mickey Hargitay is properly pompous as the Tarzan he-man who triggers Randall's troubles.

WILLY/MILLY
1986, 90 mins, US ⓥ
D: Paul Schneider **A:** Pamela Segall, Eric Gurry, Mary Tanner, Patty Duke, John Glover, Seth Green (Cinema)

A charming and substantial kidpic about sex roles. Rather than face the trauma of crossing the threshold of womanhood, 14-year-old Milly (Pamela Segall) turns into a boy under the effect of a magic spell she tries out during an eclipse. The effects of the kid's crossover are explored on all fronts, going beyond locker room humor and capturing the kinds of expectations that spark the war between the sexes at all ages.

WILLY WONKA & THE CHOCOLATE FACTORY
1971, 98 mins, US ⓥ ⊙
D: Mel Stuart **A:** Gene Wilder, Jack Albertson, Peter Ostrum, Roy Kinnear, Julie Dawn Cole, Leonard Stone (Wolper/Quaker)

Willy Wonka & the Chocolate Factory is an adequate family musical fantasy featuring Gene Wilder as an eccentric candy maker who makes a boy's dreams come true. The film has a fair score by Leslie Bricusse and Anthony Newley. Plot hook is a merchandising gimmick by Wilder who puts five golden tickets into a candy bar run, and tests the honesty of the winners. Ultimately, Peter Ostrum, the kids' hero, and grandpa Jack Albertson pass the honesty test. Sidebar incidents and dialogue are the sharpest elements, particularly the running satire on television news programming.
1971: Nomination: Best Adapted Score

WILSON
1944, 136 mins, US
D: Henry King **A:** Alexander Knox, Charles Coburn, Geraldine Fitzgerald, Thomas Mitchell, Cedric Hardwicke, Vincent Price (20th Century-Fox)

When the period of 1912–20 is re-created in Technicolor, it is as authentic as it is splendid. All the details of the White House decor of the Wilson administration and all the local color of the era are faithfully brought to the canvas in a nostalgic, authentic fashion. In fact, that is the keynote of *Wilson*—authority, warmth, idealism, a search for a better world. Through it all stalks a potent personality in Alexander Knox, a newborn star, supported by a flawless cast.
1944: Best Original Screenplay, Color Cinematography, Color Art Direction, Editing, Sound
Nominations: Best Picture, Director, Actor (Alexander Knox), Scoring of a Dramatic Picture, Special Effects

WILT
1989, 91 mins, UK ⓥ
D: Michael Tuchner **A:** Griff Rhys Jones, Mel Smith, Alison Steadman, Diana Quick, Jeremy Clyde (Carnival/LWT)

There is a good deal of enjoyment to be derived from *Wilt*. Griff Rhys Jones plays the title character, a disillusioned college lecturer who spends his spare time walking his dog and dreaming about murdering his domineering wife (Alison Steadman). When the couple attend a party at a posh country home, Rhys Jones gets dead-drunk and finds himself locked in naked passionate embrace with a life-size inflatable doll named Angelique. The next day, Steadman is missing and Rhys Jones's nocturnal activities are noted, especially by ambitious inspector Mel Smith.

WINCHESTER '73
1950, 92 mins, US ⓥ ⊙
D: Anthony Mann **A:** James Stewart, Shelley Winters, Dan Duryea, Stephen McNally, Rock Hudson, Tony Curtis (Universal)

Story is centered on a manhunt, the search of Lin McAdam (James Stewart) for the cowardly murderer of his father. Film opens with Lin riding into Dodge City in time for a July 4th celebration. The big event is a rifle match, with first prize a priceless 1873 model Winchester rifle. Lin's brother Dutch (Stephen McNally), however, makes off with the precious rifle.

WIND, THE
1928, 70 mins, US ⓥ ⊙ ⊗
D: Victor Seastrom **A:** Lillian Gish, Lars

Hanson, Montagu Love, Dorothy Cumming, Edward Earle, William Orlamond (M-G-M)

Everything a high-pressure, lavishly equipped studio, expert director, and reputable star could contribute was showered on this production. Everything about the picture breathes quality. Yet it flops dismally. It may be a true picture of life on the prairie, but it still remains lifeless and unentertaining. The story opens with Letty (Lillian Gish), a girl from Virginia trainbound for her cousin's ranch. There she becomes too popular with Cora's (Dorothy Cummings) children and is forced to leave. The girl then accepts a proposal from Lige (Lars Hanson), whom she had laughed at the night before.

WIND
1992, 125 mins, US/Japan Ⓥ ⊙
D: Carroll Ballard **A:** Matthew Modine, Jennifer Grey, Stellan Skarsgard, Rebecca Miller, Cliff Robertson, Jack Thompson (American Zoetrope/Filmlink)

The elements prove far more stimulating than the people in *Wind*, a sail-racing saga that could have used a great deal more dramatic rigging. Uncompelling protagonists are Matthew Modine, a young sailor with a knack for choking when things get tough, and Jennifer Grey, his spunky g.f., who is seemingly a sailing genius but is kept off the crew due to sexism. Having lost the race and his lady, Modine turns up six months later at Deadman's Flat, NV, where Grey and new b.f./engineering whiz Stellan Skarsgard are designing aircraft. Modine convinces them to develop a new yacht to compete in the next America's Cup race, more than three months hence.

WIND ACROSS THE EVERGLADES
1958, 91 mins, US
D: Nicholas Ray **A:** Burl Ives, Christopher Plummer, Gypsy Rose Lee, George Voskovec, Emmett Kelly, Peter Falk (Warner)

Wind Across the Everglades is a worthy attempt to make a picture about the early efforts of the Audubon Society to preserve the bird wildlife of Florida. It should have been far better. The action revolves around the almost single-handed efforts of an agent (Christopher Plummer) to stop the mass killings of plume birds for women's hats, and in particular his battle with the leader of one band of bird-hunters, one of which is played by Burl Ives. Plummer does a good job as the idealistic bird warden, although not much

motivation is ever given for his dedication. Ives, looking like Henry VIII with a red beard, eyebrows, and hair, does a characteristically intense job, and his character, as a free-booting, civilization-hating rugged individualist, makes sense if it doesn't evoke sympathy.

WIND AND THE LION, THE
1975, 119 mins, US Ⓥ ⊙ ▭
D: John Milius **A:** Sean Connery, Candice Bergen, Brian Keith, John Huston, Geoffrey Lewis, Steve Kanaly (M-G-M)

The Wind and the Lion is a generally literate and very commercial period action drama. Film stars Sean Connery as a Berber chieftain who in 1904 kidnaps Candice Bergen and her children, provoking Brian Keith (as Theodore Roosevelt) into dramatic power politics, which confound European moves into North Africa. The film sustains itself throughout, carefully laying out the diverse attitudes and motivations of the principals and depicting the ultimate and daring rescue ploy that frees both Bergen and Connery while sparking Keith's own political career. Connery scores one of his major screen impressions, while Bergen handles with assured excellence the subtleties of a woman who is first outraged at her captor but later becomes his benefactor. Keith's performance is marvelous.

1975: Nominations: Best Original Score, Sound

WIND CANNOT READ, THE
1958, 115 mins, UK
D: Ralph Thomas **A:** Dirk Bogarde, Yoko Tani, Ronald Lewis, John Fraser, Anthony Bushell, Michael Medwin (Rank)

Richard Mason's novel shapes up as a useful romantic drama. The pic is a love story told against a Burma war background. Dirk Bogarde is a grounded flyer sent to learn Japanese in order to be able to interrogate Japanese POWs. He falls for Yoko Tani, one of the instructors, marries her in secret, and is then sent off to the front where he is captured, tortured, and humiliated before escaping.

WINDOM'S WAY
1957, 108 mins, UK Ⓥ
D: Ronald Neame **A:** Peter Finch, Mary Ure, Natasha Parry, Robert Flemyng, Michael Hordern, Gregoire Aslan (Rank)

Peter Finch is a dedicated doctor working in the village of Selim on a Far East island. He is loved and trusted by the villagers and finds himself involved in their political problems. He tries to prevent the villagers from taking up arms against the local police and plantation manager. The acting throughout this drama is first class, with Finch particularly convincing. Natasha Parry as a native nursing sister in love with Finch is warm, sensitive, and technically very sound.

WINDOW IN THE SKY
See: The Other Side of the Mountain

WINDY CITY
1984, 102 mins, US ⓥ ⊙
D: Armyan Bernstein **A:** John Shea, Kate Capshaw, Josh Mostel, Jim Borrelli, Jeffrey DeMunn, Eric Pierpoint (CBS)

Windy City marks writer Armyan Bernstein's maiden voyage as director of his own tales. The heartfelt nature of his subject is generally strong enough to weather the awkwardness of this story of romance, friendship, and shattered dreams. Focus is on Danny Morgan (John Shea), a writer forced to take odd jobs including delivering mail. In the latter capacity he meets Emily (Kate Capshaw), the woman who finally accelerates his maturation which ironically forces their estrangement.

WINGED SERPENT, THE
See: Q

WINGED VICTORY
1944, 130 mins, US
D: George Cukor **A:** Mark Daniels, Lon McCallister, Don Taylor, Red Buttons, Edmond O'Brien, Jeanne Crain (20th Century-Fox)

This is the tale of American youth fighting for the preservation of American ideals, learning to fly for victory. The story of six boys from diverse parts of America and how they left behind wives and sweethearts and mothers to join the AAF, *Victory* is an honest portrait of American youth with the insatiable urge to ride the clouds. The narrative follows them through basic training, the rigorous aptitude tests, the solo flights, and, ultimately, graduation day, followed by their assignments as either pilots, navigators, or bombardiers, all significantly told.

WINGS
1927, 139 mins, US ⓥ ⊗
D: William A. Wellman **A:** Clara Bow, Charles "Buddy" Rogers, Richard Arlen, Jobyna Ralston, Gary Cooper, El Brendel (Paramount)

When the action settles on terra firma, there is nothing present that other great war movies haven't had. But nothing has possessed the graphic descriptive powers of aerial flying and combat that have been poured into this effort. Richard Arlen goes through the picture minus makeup. Consequently, he looks like the high-bred, high-strung youngster who would dote on aviation and backs it up with a splendid performance that never hints of the actor. Charles Rogers's effort is also first rate. There not being so much of Clara Bow in the picture, she gives an all-around corking performance. Gary Cooper is on and off within half a reel.

1927/28: Best Picture, Engineering Effects

WINGS OF DESIRE
See: Der Himmel Uber Berlin

WINGS OF THE APACHE
See: Fire Birds

WINGS OF THE DOVE, THE
1997, 101 mins, UK/US ⓥ ⊙ ▭
D: Iain Softley **A:** Helena Bonham Carter, Linus Roache, Alison Elliott, Elizabeth McGovern, Charlotte Rampling, Michael Gambon (Renaissance Dove/Miramax)

This handsomely produced release renders one of Henry James's lesser romantic novels into a mostly satisfying romantic melodrama. The character of the willful Kate gives Helena Bonham Carter one of her best opportunities in a while. It's 1910, and Kate is taken in hand by her conservative Aunt Maud (Charlotte Rampling), determined to find her a place in high society. Kate, however, is in love with Merton Densher (Linus Roache), an impoverished journalist. The arrival of Millie (Alison Elliott), a fabulously wealthy and beautiful young orphaned American touring Europe, offers the lovers new opportunities. Discovering that Millie is terminally ill, Kate decides to push Merton into the sick woman's arms in order to make him, eventually, a widower of social standing. The characters are driven by very contemporary needs and passions, and the bitter climax is carefully prepared. Roache makes Merton rather too vacillating and feeble a character.

1997: Nominations: Best Actress (Helena Bonham Carter), Screenplay Adaptation, Cinematography, Costume Design

WINNING
1969, 123 mins, US ⓥ ▭
D: James Goldstone **A:** Paul Newman, Joanne Woodward, Robert Wagner, Richard Thomas, David Sheiner, Clu Gulager (Universal)

Winning, a love story set against an

auto racing background, is overlong, but suspenseful racing sequences and a realistically developed marital romance score strongly. Paul Newman is ideally cast as the racer, and those sequences in which he is racing are convincingly portrayed. Joanne Woodward, who makes no attempt at glamor or any other goal except as Newman's earthy wife, turns in a ringingly effective characterization.

WINNING OF BARBARA WORTH, THE
1926, 90 mins, US ⊗
D: Henry King A: Ronald Colman, Vilma Banky, Charles Lane, Gary Cooper (Goldwyn/United Artist)

Henry King told Samuel Goldwyn he thought this epic of the reclamation of the desert lands was a highly dramatic incident for interpretation on the screen by him. Instead of going to Arizona and making his picture, he went into the arid lands of Nevada and put every dollar necessary into the production. King has performed a miraculous task. Putting over the fine points of the yarn by showing a desert sandstorm and then showing the progress of reclamation work and the destruction done by faulty construction was a well-executed mountainous job. This film is incomparable in telling a new angle of the development of the west.

WINSLOW BOY, THE
1948, 117 mins, UK ⓥ
D: Anthony Asquith A: Robert Donat, Margaret Leighton, Cedric Hardwicke, Basil Radford, Kathleen Harrison, Francis L. Sullivan (British Lion/London)

Story tells of a 13-year-old naval cadet, expelled from school for the alleged theft of a postal order. The boy's father, certain of his innocence, invokes the whole machinery of British democracy by arranging a full-scale parliamentary debate and subsequently bringing a successful action against the king. It's more the father's conviction of his son's innocence, rather than the incident itself, which forms the background of this well-knit story. A flawless cast portrays the principal characters to perfection, and minor roles have been painstakingly filled.

WINSTANLEY
1975, 95 mins, UK
D: Kevin Brownlow, Andrew Mollo A: Miles Halliwell, Jerome Wills (BFI)

The very opposite of the typical, commercial costume drama, Winstanley depicts the hardships and political turmoil in 17th-century England following the Civil War and the victory of the Puritans. Winstanley was a leader of a dissident religious sect known as the Diggers, a commune set up in Surrey to proclaim equality and the right to work ''free'' land. The parson, upon whose land the Diggers squatted, takes a different view and sends ruffians to destroy their crops, beat them, and burn down their makeshift hovels.

WINTER KILLS
1979, 97 mins, US ⓥ ⊙ ▭
D: William Richert A: Jeff Bridges, John Huston, Anthony Perkins, Sterling Hayden, Eli Wallach, Elizabeth Taylor (Avco Embassy)

If there's a decent film lurking somewhere in Winter Kills, writer-director William Richert doesn't want anyone to see it. Tale of wealthy family patriarch John Huston, whose elder son was a president slain 19 years before the pic's beginning, and younger sibling Jeff Bridges, now after his brother's killer(s), is an exercise in methodical obfuscation. Huston gives a powerhouse performance, and Bridges, always likable, runs through his repertoire of facial expressions and grimaces, but it's a lost cause.

WINTER PEOPLE
1989, 110 mins, US ⓥ ⊙ ▭
D: Ted Kotcheff A: Kurt Russell, Kelly McGillis, Lloyd Bridges, Mitchell Ryan, Amelia Burnette (Nelson/Columbia)

Winter People is a grimly unappetizing melodrama that forwards themes and concerns as remote as its time and place, North Carolina in 1934. Widower Kurt Russell decamps from his native town with little daughter in tow and alights at the remote cabin of Kelly McGillis, who has an illegitimate baby son. Russell has to prove himself to McGillis's three brothers by joining them on a bear hunt, and wins the approval of her pa (Lloyd Bridges) by designing and building a clock tower for the little community. But the demented Campbell clan lives across the river, and McGillis's dark secret is then revealed.

WINTERTIME
1943, 82 mins, US
D: John Brahm A: Sonja Henie, Jack Oakie, Cornel Wilde, Cesar Romero, Carole Landis, S. Z. Sakall (20th-Century-Fox)

Story revolves about a Norwegian refugee and his daughter (Sonja Henie), whose destination is the Chateau Frontenac, Quebec. Jack Oakie, who, in partnership with Cornel Wilde, operates a small, shabby hostelry called the Chateau Promenade, detours the party to his own place in order to build trade through the presence of the distinguished refugees. Henie's blade sequences, solo and with a partner, enhanced by gorgeous settings, are socko as always.

WIRED
1989, 108 mins, US Ⓥ ⊙
D: Larry Peerce **A:** Michael Chiklis, Ray Sharkey, J. T. Walsh, Patti D'Arbanville, Lucinda Jenney, Alex Rocco (F/M/Lion)

In a brief but estimable career, John Belushi was an engaging personality. His drug overdose death further enthralled the public. *Wired*, however, told in episodes, flashbacks, and dream sequences, is relentlessly off-putting. It begins after Belushi (Michael Chiklis) has died. He rises, dressed in an autopsy gown to join another "spirit," Angel Valesquez (Ray Sharkey), in a cab ride down memory lane. Chiklis ekes out an estimable performance as the doomed comic actor, sweating flashes of Belushi's intensity and vulnerability.

WISE BLOOD
1979, 108 mins, US/W. Germany Ⓥ
D: John Huston **A:** Brad Dourif, Ned Beatty, Harry Dean Stanton, Dan Shor, Amy Wright, John Huston (Ithaca/Anthea)

John Huston, with uncluttered direction and expert handling of actors, has fashioned a disturbing tale of the fringe side of overzealous religious preachers in the deep South. Film is grim and Gothic in feeling, but balanced by an underlying tenderness for these fringe people. Brad Dourif is effective as a young man home from the wars, who doffs his uniform to buy clothes making him look like a preacher. He goes to a city where he is attracted by a blind preacher with a teenage daughter who gives him lubricious looks.

WISH YOU WERE HERE
1987, 91 mins, UK Ⓥ ⊙
D: David Leland **A:** Emily Lloyd, Tom Bell, Clare Clifford, Barbara Durkin, Geoffrey Hutchings, Jesse Birdsall (Zenith/Working Title)

Set in an up-tight, provincial British seaside resort in the 1950s, this is a touching account of a girl's growing pains. What makes it interesting is the character of the heroine, a spunky but troubled 16-year-old girl named Lynda (played with exasperating charm by newcomer Emily Lloyd). Her mother died when she was 11, and no one has replaced that essential loss. Lynda's reaction to her plight is to shock people with her rudeness and to taunt the opposite sex. Lynda's rebelliousness eventually leads to a sinister liaison with a seedy older man (played with taciturn intensity by Tom Bell), as much a misfit as she is.

WITCHCRAFT
See: Haxan

WITCHCRAFT THROUGH THE AGES
See: Haxan

WITCH DOCTOR
See: Men of Two Worlds

WITCHES, THE
1966, 91 mins, UK
D: Cyril Frankel **A:** Joan Fontaine, Kay Walsh, Alec McCowen, Ann Bell, Gwen Ffrangcon-Davies, Ingrid Brett (Hammer)

Despite a very professional cast, this Nigel Kneale script doesn't spark off enough horror and tension to make the picture more than routine entertainment. Joan Fontaine is a schoolmistress who endures a horrible traumatic witch-doctor experience in an African mission. She seeks a new, peaceful life in a British village as headmistress of the local school, but she realizes that the village is under some strange spell.

WITCHES, THE
1990, 92 mins, US Ⓥ ⊙
D: Nicolas Roeg **A:** Anjelica Huston, Mai Zetterling, Jasen Fisher, Rowan Atkinson, Bill Paterson, Jane Horrocks (Lorimar/Henson)

The wizardry of Jim Henson's Creature Shop and a superbly over-the-top performance by Anjelica Huston gives *The Witches* a good deal of charm and enjoyment. Nine-year-old Luke's (Jasen Fisher) parents die in a car crash, and he and grandmother Helga (Mai Zetterling) travel to a stark Cornish hotel for a holiday. Also checking in is the annual ladies' meeting of the Royal Society for the Prevention of Cruelty to Children; in fact a meeting of British witches, due to be addressed by the Grand High Witch, Huston. In a tight black dress and vampish haircut, Huston enjoys herself, and the pic plods along until she arrives on the scene.

WITCHES OF EASTWICK, THE
1987, 118 mins, US Ⓥ ⊙ ✉
D: George Miller **A:** Jack Nicholson, Cher, Susan Sarandon, Michelle Pfeiffer, Veronica Cartwright, Richard Jenkins (Warner/Guber-Peters/Kennedy Miller)

The Witches of Eastwick is a brilliantly conceived metaphor for the battle of the sexes that poses the question, must a woman sell her soul to the devil to have a good relationship? With a no-holds-barred performance by Jack Nicholson as the horny Satan, it's a very funny and irresistible set-up. Michelle Pfeiffer is the intellectual; Susan Sarandon is the woman of feeling; and Cher represents the sensual side. They're all divorced and looking for Mr. Right. Enter Daryl Van Horn (Nicholson), the answer to their longing for a man of wit, charm, and intelligence. Dressed in eccentric flowing robes and odd hats and installed in a lush mansion, Nicholson is larger than life, as indeed the devil should be.

1987: Nominations: Best Original Score, Sound

WITCHFINDER GENERAL (THE CONQUEROR WORM)
1968, 88 mins, UK Ⓥ
D: Michael Reeves **A:** Vincent Price, Ian Ogilvy, Rupert Davies, Hilary Dwyer, Robert Russell, Nicky Henson (Tigon)

Story is about witchcraft, inquisitions, and executions as performed by Vincent Price and his thuggish henchman (Robert Russell) during the days when Cromwell was deposing the king of England. Ian Ogilvy is the soldier-hero who stops them after lots of bloody executions and the rape of his sweetheart (Hilary Dwyer). Price is an excellent heavy, but while sometimes he seems to piously believe he is rooting out witches, most of the time he's simply killing for the fun of it. Dwyer gives evidence of acting talent, but she and all the principals are hampered by Michael Reeves's mediocre script and ordinary direction.

WITH A SONG IN MY HEART
1952, 116 mins, US
D: Walter Lang **A:** Susan Hayward, Rory Calhoun, David Wayne, Thelma Ritter, Robert Wagner, Helen Westcott (20th Century-Fox)

The story of Jane Froman, a songbird who started her rise to fame in 1936 as a penny-ante singer of radio commercials, comes to the screen in this film version of her career. In the first half, the pattern is the rather pat one of an unknown woman coming into prominence. The rest, however, has the ring of sincere dramatics from the time Froman was nearly fatally injured in a plane crash in 1943. Her fight back to life and the only partial recovery of the use of her limbs, the birth of a new love, and the resumption of a career to pay the enormous medical bills come over on the screen as heartening drama.

1952: Best Scoring of a Musical Picture
Nominations: Best Actress (Susan Hayward), Supp. Actress (Thelma Ritter), Color Costume Design, Sound

WITHNAIL & I
1986, 108 mins, UK Ⓥ ⊙
D: Bruce Robinson **A:** Richard E. Grant, Paul McGann, Richard Griffiths, Ralph Brown, Michael Elphick (HandMade)

Withnail & I is about the end of an era. Set in England in 1969, it mirrors the seedy demise of the hippie period, delivering some comic gems along the way. Pic opens in the disgusting London flat of out-of-work actors Withnail and Marwood. Marwood (Paul McGann) is the nervous type trying to look like John Lennon, while Withnail (Richard E. Grant) is gaunt, acerbic, and never without a drink in his hand. A visit to Withnail's Uncle Monty secures them the loan of his country cottage. They eventually arrive there only to discover there is no light, no heat, and no water. Uncle Monty (a standout performance by the portly Richard Griffiths) arrives with a twinkle in his eye when he is sidling up closer to Marwood. The humor is both clever and brutal, and the acting uniformly excellent.

WITHOUT LOVE
1945, 111 mins, US
D: Harold S. Bucquet **A:** Spencer Tracy, Katharine Hepburn, Keenan Wynn, Gloria Grahame, Patricia Morison, Lucille Ball (M-G-M)

There's no gainsaying the general obviousness of it all, along with a somewhat static plot, despite the adult trouping of the lady scientist who aids the gentleman scientist. It's a foregone conclusion that behind their mutual shells of yesteryear amours they'll clinch eventually. Interspersed is an intelligent pooch who has been trained to curb Tracy's somnambulism, which is planted early for boudoir usage later.

WITHOUT RESERVATIONS
1946, 107 mins, US Ⓥ ⊙
D: Mervyn LeRoy **A:** Claudette Colbert, John Wayne, Don DeFore, Dona Drake, Louella Parsons, Thurston Hall (RKO)

Plot concerns a female author who meets the real-life counterpart of her tome's hero. Claudette Colbert, the writer, is tripping west to adapt her book to the screen. On a crowded train she is picked up by two Marine fliers, John Wayne and Don DeFore. Without realizing her identity, the boys proceed throughout the footage to impress her with how wrong the book's slant on life, love, and returned heroes actually is. Mervyn LeRoy's direction doesn't miss a beat in underlying the laughs with a solid feeling of reality, and the players troupe the roles to the hilt. Colbert and Wayne prove particularly facile in building to a solid laugh.

WITHOUT YOU I'M NOTHING
1990, 90 mins, US Ⓥ
D: John Boskovich **A:** Sandra Bernhard, Steven Antin, Lu Leonard (MCEG)

Sandra Bernhard's screen adaptation of her one-woman show is a rigorous, experimental examination of performance art, a remote, self-absorbed, and often cryptic picture. Film unfolds in performance on stage at a large, ersatz night club before a predominantly black audience. Crowd reacts only with silent, quizzical expressions or files out apparently not enjoying the show. Pic's highlight is a 1978-set "I Feel Real" monologue/song with Bernhard pretending to be two guys in a disco, one of whom gets turned on by a black man and comes out of the closet.

WITNESS
1985, 112 mins, US Ⓥ ⊙
D: Peter Weir **A:** Harrison Ford, Kelly McGillis, Josef Sommer, Lukas Haas, Danny Glover, Alexander Godunov (Paramount)

Witness is at times a gentle, affecting story of star-crossed lovers within the fascinating Amish community. Too often, however, this fragile romance is crushed by a thoroughly absurd shoot-'em-up, like ketchup poured over a Pennsylvania Dutch dinner. Venturing outside the community on a trip to see her sister, recently widowed Kelly McGillis is drawn into the 20th century when her young son (Lukas Haas), witnesses a murder in the men's room in a Philadelphia train station. Enter gruff, foul-mouthed, streetwise detective Harrison Ford. *Witness* warms up as the attraction builds between Ford, McGillis, and Haas. Admirable, too, is Ford's growing admiration for the people he's been thrown among.

1985: Best Original Screenplay, Editing **Nominations:** Best Picture, Director, Actor (Harrison Ford), Cinematography, Art Direction, Original Score

WITNESS FOR THE PROSECUTION
1957, 114 mins, US Ⓥ ⊙
D: Billy Wilder **A:** Tyrone Power, Marlene Dietrich, Charles Laughton, Elsa Lanchester, Una O'Connor, Ian Wolfe (United Artists)

A courtroom meller played engagingly and building evenly to a surprising and arousing, albeit tricked-up, climax, *Witness for the Prosecution* unfolds realistically, generating a quiet and steady excitement. Story line has defense attorney Charles Laughton wholly convinced that the likable chap played by Tyrone Power is innocent, that he couldn't have murdered the rich widow who had taken a fancy to him. A disturbing note, however, is the unexpected attitude taken by Power's wife (Marlene Dietrich). Laughton's reputation for scenery chewing is unmarred via this outing.

1957: Nominations: Best Picture, Director, Actor (Charles Laughton), Supp. Actress (Elsa Lanchester), Editing, Sound

WITTGENSTEIN
1993, 71 mins, UK Ⓥ
D: Derek Jarman **A:** Karl Johnson, Michael Gough, Tilda Swinton, John Quentin, Kevin Collins, Clancy Chassay (Channel 4/BFI/Bandung)

Shot on minimalist sets, this gabby but sophisticated riff on the tortured life of philosopher Ludwig Wittgenstein is an immaculately lensed, intellectual jape that's diverting, but not a substantial addition to Derek Jarman's quirky oeuvre. Pic's opening, with young Ludwig (confidently played by 12-year-old Clancy Chassay) introducing the members of his ill-fated family, promises a Ken Russell–like irreverence that never really develops. With the appearance of the adult Wittgenstein (Karl Johnson), things settle down into a series of talky tableaux against black backdrops. Running parallel with the intellectual stuff is an exploration of Wittgenstein's repressed homosexuality, per his friendship with a handsome, working-class student (Kevin Collins) and Maynard Keynes (John Quentin), portrayed as a flouncing gay.

WIVES AND LOVERS
1963, 102 mins, US
D: John Rich **A:** Janet Leigh, Van Johnson, Shelley Winters, Martha Hyer, Ray Walston, Claire Wilcox (Paramount)

Failure to be consistent with itself mars *Wives and Lovers,* an otherwise highly polished and pleasurable sophisticated comedy that contains some of the sharpest, wittiest, most perceptive comedy dialogue to pop out of a soundtrack in some time. An unsuccessful writer (Van Johnson), who for three years has been lovingly and uncomplainingly supported by his wife (Janet Leigh) while he pens a novel, suddenly hits the book-of-the-month jackpot. In a flash, the couple and their precocious tot have moved from a cramped Gotham cold-water flat to the luxury living of the fashionable Connecticut suburbs. Johnson becomes entangled in an affair with his glamorous agent (Martha Hyer); in retaliation, Leigh apparently gets herself voluntarily seduced by the star (Jeremy Slate) of her husband's play.
1963: Nomination: Best B&W Costume Design

WIZ, THE
1978, 133 mins, US Ⓥ ⊙
D: Sidney Lumet **A:** Diana Ross, Michael Jackson, Nipsey Russell, Lena Horne, Richard Pryor, Ted Ross (Motown)

Frank Baum would never recognize his simple little story in this fantastically blown-up version of *The Wizard of Oz,* but the heart of his tale—that a person must find what he's searching for within himself—is still there. Director Sidney Lumet has created what amounts to a love letter to the city of New York, which he equates with Oz. Diana Ross is believable as a 24-year-old Harlem school teacher. Vocally, she's superb but, surprise, she also dances with all the abandon of an Alvin Ailey protégé. Of the supporting players and, despite their billing, that's what they amount to—Richard Pryor's Wiz, Ted Ross's Lion, and Mabel King's Evillene make the heaviest impressions.
1978: Nominations: Best Cinematography, Costume Design, Art Direction, Adapted Score

WIZARD OF OZ, THE
1939, 100 mins, US Ⓥ ⊙
D: Victor Fleming [King Vidor] **A:** Judy Garland, Frank Morgan, Ray Bolger, Bert Lahr, Jack Haley, Billie Burke (M-G-M)

Except for the prologue and epilogue, which are visioned in a rich sepia, the greater portion of *The Wizard of Oz* is in Technicolor. Such liberties that have been taken with the original story vest the yarn with constructive dramatic values. What is on the screen is an adventure story about a small girl who lives on a Kansas farm. She and her dog, Toto, are caught in a twister and whisked into an eerie land in which she encounters strange beings, good and evil fairies, and prototypes of some of the adults who comprised her farm world, and makes the long trek to the mighty wizard's castle, where she and her companions seek fulfillment of desire. Judy Garland is an appealing figure as the wandering waif.
1939: Best Original Score, Song ("Over the Rainbow")
Nominations: Best Picture, Art Direction, Special Effects

WOLF
1994, 125 mins, US Ⓥ ⊙
D: Mike Nichols **A:** Jack Nicholson, Michelle Pfeiffer, James Spader, Kate Nelligan, Richard Jenkins, Christopher Plummer (Columbia)

Wolf is a decidedly upscale horror film, a tony werewolf movie in which a full roster of fancy talents tries to mate with unavoidably hoary, not to say hairy, material. Offspring of this union is an intriguing thriller more enjoyable for its humor and sophistication than for its scare quotient. Editor Will Randall (Jack Nicholson) hits a wolf with his car on a lonely Vermont road. The animal bites him on the hand before lighting out into the woods. Back in New York, Will is facing the dreaded prospect of being ousted from his position following a takeover by billionaire tycoon Raymond Alden (Christopher Plummer). At a swank dinner party at Alden's estate, Randall has a chance meeting with Raymond's edgy, beautiful daughter, Laura (Michelle Pfeiffer). Nicholson begins his performance in a low key and cranks it up only by degrees. By contrast, Pfeiffer's Laura comes across as hard and brittle.

WOLFEN
1981, 114 mins, US Ⓥ ⊙ ▭
D: Michael Wadleigh **A:** Albert Finney, Diane Venora, Edward James Olmos, Gregory Hines, Tom Noonan, Dick O'Neill (Orion)

Wolfen is consistently more interesting than it is thrilling. Policeman Albert Finney is confronted with a series of baffling, grisly murders, gradually realizing they are not the work of mere mortals. As always in the best of pictures like this, the build-up is the most fun. Michael Wadleigh creates a surreal point-of-view for the killers that works effectively, accented by handy digital sound. Overall, Paul Sylbert's production design is also a major plus.

WOLF MAN, THE
1941, 69 mins, US ⓥ ⊙
D: George Waggner A: Lon Chaney, Claude Rains, Ralph Bellamy, Bela Lugosi, Maria Ouspenskaya (Universal)

The legendary English werewolf provides the basis for another cinematic adventure into the horrific chiller-diller realm. *The Wolf Man* is a compactly knit tale of its kind, but dubious entertainment. Young Lon Chaney returns to the family's English castle after a long absence in America, to stand in line as heir to the estate. According to legend, a person bitten by a werewolf assumes the dual personality of the latter—and Chaney is the victim of a bite.

WOLVES OF WILLOUGHBY CHASE, THE
1989, 93 mins, UK ⓥ ⊙
D: Stuart Orme A: Stephanie Beacham, Mel Smith, Emily Hudson, Aleks Darowska, Geraldine James, Richard O'Brien (Zenith)

The Wolves of Willoughby Chase is a thoroughly enjoyable children's fantasy-adventure. Pic has a suitable Dickensian feel, set some time in the last century in a snow-bound part of North Yorkshire where wolves rule the countryside. It has an attractively sinister quality and centers on the fight by two young girls to foil a dastardly plot hatched by their evil governess, Slighcarp. Emily Hudson and Aleks Darowska are excellent as the plucky youngsters, but best of all is Stephanie Beacham who outdoes herself as the wicked Slighcarp.

WOMAN CHASES MAN
1937, 71 mins, US
D: John G. Blystone A: Miriam Hopkins, Joel McCrea, Charles Winninger, Erik Rhodes, Ella Logan, Broderick Crawford (Goldwyn/United Artists)

Three top-flight players, Miriam Hopkins, Joel McCrea, and Charles Winninger, simply run out of material. As a comedienne, Hopkins displays exceptional skill, charm, and resource. She is effective and amusing as long as she has something to do. She brings to Winninger, as the fa-

ther, a set of architectural plans of her own designing, which will turn his suburban development into a success if he can obtain a $100,000 loan to hold off creditors. McCrea, as the son, has the money but not the inclination to invest. Hopkins volunteers to persuade him. She plays on the boy's weakness for drink and obtains his signature to a contract. It isn't much funnier than it reads, but that's *Woman Chases Man*.

WOMAN IN A DRESSING GOWN
1957, 98 mins, UK
D: J. Lee Thompson A: Yvonne Mitchell, Sylvia Syms, Anthony Quayle, Andrew Ray, Carole Lesley, Olga Lindo (Godwin-Willis)

The principal character in Ted Willis's screenplay is reminiscent of the Shirley Booth role in *Come Back, Little Sheba*. Yvonne Mitchell plays an endearing slut on the verge of losing her husband to a younger, more attractive, and more wholesome girl. The uncanny depth of her portrayal lifts the story from a conventional rut and gives it a classy stature. Every day she tries to make her home attractive for her husband and son, but the odds are always overwhelming. Inevitably, her husband (Anthony Quayle) is attracted to a girl in the office (Sylvia Syms) but at the moment of crisis cannot make the break.

WOMAN IN RED, THE
1984, 87 mins, US ⓥ ⊙
D: Gene Wilder A: Gene Wilder, Charles Grodin, Joseph Bologna, Judith Ivey, Michael Huddleston, Kelly Le Brock (Orion)

The woman in red is the very sexy Kelly Le Brock, hired as a model by a San Francisco city agency, bringing her into contact with a mundane bureaucrat, Gene Wilder, heretofore a contented family man. But one look at Le Brock, and Wilder is ready to risk all for illicit romance: he is not very adept at adultery. The laughs roll along readily.
1984: Best Song ("I Just Called to Say I Love You")

WOMAN IN THE DUNES
See: Suna No Onna

WOMAN IN THE WINDOW, THE
1945, 90 mins, US ⓥ
D: Fritz Lang A: Edward G. Robinson, Joan Bennett, Raymond Massey, Dan Duryea, Edmond Breon, Robert Blake, Thomas E. Jackson (RKO/International)

A strong and decidedly suspenseful murder melodrama, with especially fine timing in the direction by Fritz Lang and outstanding performances by Edward G. Robinson, Joan Bennett, Raymond Massey, and Dan Duryea. Robinson, a staid and middle-aged college professor, pauses to admire a painting in a store window adjoining his club, only to find the model standing beside him. He visits her apartment to look over other sketches; a stranger breaks in to accuse the girl of infidelity and attacks Robinson, who stabs the visitor in self-defense, then connives with the girl to dispose of the body.

1945: Nomination: Best Scoring of a Dramatic Picture

WOMAN IS A WOMAN, A
See: Une Femme Est Une Femme

WOMAN OF AFFAIRS, A
1929, 90 mins, US Ⓥ
D: Clarence Brown **A:** Greta Garbo, John Gilbert, Lewis Stone, John Mack Brown, Douglas Fairbanks Jr., Dorothy Sebastian (M-G-M)

A sensational array of screen names and the intriguing nature of the story, together with magnificent acting by Greta Garbo, carries through this vague and sterilized version of Michael Arlen's erotic play. Here is a woman who, disappointed in her first love, plunges into an orgy of amorous adventures from Calais to Cairo. Garbo saves an unfortunate situation throughout by subtle playing that suggests just the erotic note that is essential to the whole theme and story. John Gilbert has an utterly boring role. In most of the footage he merely stands around rather sheepishly. Production is noteworthy for its beauty of setting and atmosphere.

WOMAN OF DISTINCTION, A
1950, 89 mins, US Ⓥ ⊙
D: Edward Buzzell **A:** Ray Milland, Rosalind Russell, Edmund Gwenn, Janis Carter, Mary Jane Saunders, Francis Lederer (Columbia)

A *Woman of Distinction* is a loosely tied grab bag of screwball and nonsensical events about two warring-but-loving pedagogues. Featured is a running duel between Rosalind Russell, the woman of distinction too busy for romance, and professor Ray Milland, who is dragged into a faked news-headlined affair with the dean of a woman's college through the connivings of an overly diligent press agent.

WOMAN OF PARIS, A
1923, 84 mins, US Ⓥ ⊗
D: Charles Chaplin **A:** Edna Purviance, Adolphe Menjou, Carl Miller, Lydia Knott, Charles K. French, Clarence Geldert (United Artists)

A *Woman of Paris* is a serious, sincere effort, with subtlety of expression. Edna Purviance looks and acts well enough, but she falls short of the fine pace set by the rest of the endeavor. However, this is not a conspicuous drag on *A Woman of Paris*. Charlie Chaplin comes forth as a genius both as a producer and a director. The finish is as brilliant and as memorable as the Mexico-line finale of *The Pilgrim*.

WOMAN OF STRAW
1964, 117 mins, UK
D: Basil Dearden **A:** Gina Lollobrigida, Sean Connery, Ralph Richardson, Johnny Sekka, Laurence Hardy, Danny Daniels (United Artists)

Best that can be said of *Straw* is that it looks handsome. But the film gets bogged down by stilted dialogue and situations. Ralph Richardson is a multimillionaire, an ill-mannered, sour tycoon condemned to spend his life in a wheelchair. He takes it out on anybody handy, including his nephew-secretary (Sean Connery). Gina Lollobrigida is hired by the nephew as the old man's nurse. There are several people who are not unhappy when he is found dead in the bunk of his yacht. Richardson manages to extract what fun there is out of the desultory proceedings. Lollobrigida is out of her depth, while Connery has the air of a man who can't wait to get back to being James Bond again.

WOMAN OF SUMMER
See: The Stripper

WOMAN OF THE DUNES
See: Suna No Onna

WOMAN OF THE YEAR
1942, 112 mins, US Ⓥ ⊙
D: George Stevens **A:** Spencer Tracy, Katharine Hepburn, Fay Bainter, Reginald Owen, William Bendix, Dan Tobin (M-G-M)

Woman of the Year is an entertaining film with superb work by Katharine Hepburn and Spencer Tracy. Director George Stevens merits small praise. Screenwriters had an amusing starting point—a sports writer and a young and beautiful female politico spatting, falling in love, and marrying—but wend it tortuously through every hackneyed plot device. Picture runs 112 minutes and frequently seems every moment of that. Tracy and Hepburn go a

long way toward pulling the chestnut out of the fire.
1942: Best Original Screenplay
Nomination: Best Actress (Katharine Hepburn)

WOMAN ON PIER 13, THE
See: I Married a Communist

WOMAN ON THE BEACH, THE
1947, 71 mins, US
D: Jean Renoir **A:** Joan Bennett, Robert Ryan, Charles Bickford (RKO)

Film is more mood than meaning, a narrative drawn with invisible lines around characters without motivation in a plot only hazily defined. But beneath the surface, cinematic elements are brilliantly fused by Jean Renoir into an intense and compelling emotional experience. The yarn is a variation of the eternal triangle theme, but it unfolds elusively through implication and suggestion, only occasionally emerging to the level of full clarity. Charles Bickford plays a blind artist, brutally strong and madly jealous of his wife. Joan Bennett is a callous tart tied to her husband only through guilt. Robert Ryan is a coast guard officer stationed near the blind man's home, recovering from a mental shock obtained in naval combat during the war.

WOMAN'S FACE, A
1941, 105 mins, US Ⓥ
D: George Cukor **A:** Joan Crawford, Melvyn Douglas, Conrad Veidt, Osa Massen, Reginald Owen, Albert Bassermann (M-G-M)

Opening with the court trial of Joan Crawford for murder, this story is developed through testimony of the several witnesses and finally of the defendant herself. Crawford is the victim of a childhood accident which left her face distorted and disfigured. She drops into a criminal career. Romantic approach of Conrad Veidt is the first she has had, and she accepts his flattery with love-hungry adoration. Plastic surgeon Melvyn Douglas's offer of an operation is gladly accepted. Veidt then persuades her to take a job as governess on his uncle's estate—and to murder the child-heir that stands in his path to inheritance.

WOMAN'S SECRET, A
1949, 84 mins, US Ⓥ
D: Nicholas Ray **A:** Maureen O'Hara, Melvyn Douglas, Gloria Grahame, Bill Williams, Victor Jory, Jay C. Flippen (RKO)

There's too much unintended mystery about *A Woman's Secret* for it to be anything but spotty entertainment. Story opens with Maureen O'Hara confessing to the shooting of Gloria Grahame, a trollop-minded singer she has coached into the big time. O'Hara's friend (Melvyn Douglas) doesn't believe she did the shooting, and picture then goes into a confusing flashback account of her life.

WOMAN'S TALE, A
1991, 93 mins, Australia Ⓥ
D: Paul Cox **A:** Sheila Florance, Gosia Dobrowolska, Norman Kaye, Chris Haywood, Myrtle Woods, Ernest Gray (Illumination)

Paul Cox's *A Woman's Tale* bears all the director's hallmarks. Martha (Sheila Florance) is terminally ill yet fiercely determined to hold on to her independence. She lives alone in a small city apartment with her cat, canary, and memories. A nurse, Anna, visits her every day, and Martha even lets her use her apartment for afternoon trysts with her married lover. Next door lives the equally old and even frailer Billy (Norman Kaye, in a tremendously touching performance). Anna also visits Billy, but is unamused when he makes pathetic sexual advances toward her.

WOMAN'S WORLD
1954, 94 mins, US ▭
D: Jean Negulesco **A:** Clifton Webb, June Allyson, Van Heflin, Lauren Bacall, Fred MacMurray, Arlene Dahl (20th Century-Fox)

Woman's World is Hollywood at its commercial best, a highly polished product, technically and story-wise. Clifton Webb, as president of Gifford Motors, brings three of his district managers to New York to select a successor to a recently deceased sales manager. He invites their wives along since he believes that the right wife is just as important as the right man for the job. There's June Allyson and Cornel Wilde from Kansas City, Lauren Bacall and Fred MacMurray from Philadelphia, and Arlene Dahl and Van Heflin from Dallas. All the men in Webb's estimation are equally capable of handling the number-one post. The final decision rests on their wives. The choice is left to the very end and will come as a surprise to many.

WOMAN TIMES SEVEN
1967, 99 mins, US Ⓥ
D: Vittorio De Sica **A:** Shirley MacLaine, Peter Sellers, Alan Arkin, Rossano Brazzi, Michael Caine, Vittorio Gassman (Embassy)

Woman Times Seven is a seven-segment showcase for the talents of Shirley MacLaine, who plays a variety of female types. MacLaine is spotted in many different adult situations—such as the bereaved widow and the enraged female set on revenge—and largely convinces with each switcheroo. Major tour-de-force segment finds MacLaine and Alan Arkin alone in a flophouse room, plotting suicide together.

WOMAN UNDER THE INFLUENCE, A
1974, 155 mins, US
D: John Cassavetes **A:** Peter Falk, Gena Rowlands, Matthew Cassel, Matthew Laborteaux, Christina Grisanti, Katherine Cassavetes (Faces International)

This is a disturbing portrait of a slightly mad housewife. Gena Rowlands plays a lower-middle-class L.A. housewife whose sense of identity is so impoverished that she defines herself only in terms of her husband's love and the devotion of her children. Her performance is one of those tour-de-force numbers available only to screen players of alcoholics and lunatics. Peter Falk is outstanding in a role that calls for him to be loving and callous at the same time.

1974: Nominations: Best Director, Actress (Gena Rowlands)

WOMEN, THE
1939, 132 mins, US Ⓥ ⊙
D: George Cukor **A:** Norma Shearer, Joan Crawford, Rosalind Russell, Paulette Goddard, Joan Fontaine, Hedda Hopper (M-G-M)

No man appears—it's a field day for the gals to romp intimately in panties, scanties, and gorgeous gowns. Most of them deport themselves in a manner best described by Joan Crawford at the end: "There's a name for you ladies, but it's not used in high society outside of kennels." Story is essentially light-weight and trivial and covers a wide range of female conversations—barbed shafts at friends, whisperings of husbands' indiscretions, maligning gossip, and catty asides.

WOMEN IN LOVE
1969, 130 mins, UK Ⓥ ⊙
D: Ken Russell **A:** Alan Bates, Oliver Reed, Glenda Jackson, Jennie Linden, Eleanor Bron, Vladek Sheybal (United Artists)

D. H. Lawrence's pungent thoughts about love and marriage, and the attitudes of the two sexes toward them, are not highly original but are shrewdly delivered. The rough, tough coal-mining area of the Midlands is effectively evoked. Two sisters are wooed and won by two men, and the film addresses their relationships. One settles down to a marriage on happy but uneasy terms. The other, more questing, has an equally uneasy yet gleeful romance which ends in tragedy.

1970: Best Actress (Glenda Jackson)
Nominations: Best Director, Screenplay Adaptation, Cinematography

WOMEN ON THE VERGE OF A NERVOUS BREAKDOWN
See: Mujeres al Borde de un Ataque de Nervios

WOMEN'S PRISON
1955, 80 mins, US
D: Lewis Seiler **A:** Ida Lupino, Jan Sterling, Cleo Moore, Audrey Totter, Phyllis Thaxter, Howard Duff (Columbia)

Villain of this film is Amelia (Ida Lupino), supervisor of a women's prison. A "borderline psychopath" who's never been able to hit it off socially with men, she takes it out on her female inmates who apparently have done better with the opposite sex. Among the objects of her ire are Helene (Phyllis Thaxter), in for manslaughter with an automobile; Joan (Audrey Totter), doing time for a gun possession charge and wife of convict Glen (Warren Stevens); and forger Brenda (Jan Sterling).

WONDERFUL LIFE
1964, 113 mins, UK ⊡
D: Sidney J. Furie **A:** Cliff Richard, Walter Slezak, Susan Hampshire, The Shadows, Una Stubbs, Melvyn Hayes (Elstree/Ivy)

Film musicals often get by on shaky story lines but are usually decked out with lively jokes and badinage. *Wonderful Life* proves somewhat sparing in this department. Cliff Richard and friends are merchant sailors stranded in the Canaries, where they come across Walter Slezak directing a diabolical *Beau Geste* epic. Leading lady Susan Hampshire is having a rough time. For love of the young lady the lads decide to boost her confidence by making an off-the-cuff musical version of the director's film. The happiest flight of fancy is a sequence that sends up films down the ages.

WONDERFUL WORLD OF THE BROTHERS GRIMM, THE
1962, 135 mins, US ⊗ ▭
D: Henry Levin, George Pal **A:** Laurence Harvey, Karl Boehm, Claire Bloom, Walter Slezak, Yvette Mimieux, Russ Tamblyn (M-G-M/Cinerama)

Grimm is delightful, refreshing entertainment. The traditional tale of the princess who finds her true love in the humble woodsman is charmingly interpreted by Yvette Mimieux and Russ Tamblyn. Laurence Harvey, in addition to playing Wilhelm Grimm, also enacts the title role in "The Cobbler and the Elves." This sequence is entirely enchanting. "The Singing Bone," dealing with an encounter between a supercilious knight, his servant, and a fire-spouting dragon, is full of exaggerated chills and wry humor.
1962: Best Color Costume Design (Mary Wills)
Nominations: Best Color Cinematography, Color Art Direction, Scoring of Music

WONDERLAND
1999, 108 mins, UK ⊗ ⊙ ▭
D: Michael Winterbottom **A:** Shirley Henderson, Gina McKee, Molly Parker, Ian Hart, John Simm, Stuart Townsend (Kismet/Revolution/PolyGram/BBC)

Michael Winterbottom's ironically titled *Wonderland* is a wonderfully acted and emotionally rewarding slice of London life in which the versatile director enters Mike Leigh territory with considerable success. The story of a family in crisis unfolds over four days in November. Nadia (Gina McKee) meets men via a dating agency, usually with disappointing results. Her older sister, Debbie (Shirley Henderson), is separated from her oafish husband, Dan (Ian Hart). Molly (Molly Parker), the youngest sister, is nine months pregnant and her partner, Eddie (John Simm), leaves after an argument. The sisters' parents (Kika Markham, Jack Shepherd) are unhappy as well. The film is suffused with stoic humor and ends on a note of guarded optimism; there's no sense of defeat or despair. Performances by the ensemble cast are just about flawless.

WONDER MAN
1945, 95 mins, US ⊗
D: H. Bruce Humberstone **A:** Danny Kaye, Virginia Mayo, Vera-Ellen, Steve Cochran, Huntz Hall, Donald Woods (Goldwyn)

Wonder Man finds Danny Kaye in a dual role, as twins, one being a nitery performer bumped off by yeggs because of information he was going to give the district attorney; the other a mild-mannered, studious type who, after his brother's slaying, is belabored by the latter's spirit into taking his place and thus help run down the thugs. Several of the comedy situations are rewrites of oldies, but Kaye makes them capital. There's no mistaking that without him this film would be decidedly commonplace.
1945: Best Special Effects
Nominations: Best Scoring of a Musical Picture, Song ("So in Love"), Sound

WOODEN HORSE, THE
1950, 101 mins, UK ⊗
D: Jack Lee **A:** Leo Genn, David Tomlinson, Anthony Steel, Bryan Forbes, David Greene, Peter Finch (London/Wessex)

A commendable degree of documentary fidelity is established in this film of the escape of three prisoners-of-war from a German camp. Yarn traces the exploits of three officers who, after receiving approval from the camp's "escape committee," cover up their tunnel-digging by means of a vaulting horse. Some of the best drama comes after the prison break, when the two ex-airmen make for a port and board a boat for Copenhagen en route to freedom.

WOODSTOCK
1970, 183 mins, US ⊗ ⊙ ▭
D: Michael Wadleigh (Warner)

Woodstock is a virtually perfect record of the music festival held in Bethel, NY, in the summer of 1969. As a documentary, the film is a milestone in artistic collation of raw footage into a multipanel, variable-frame, dazzling montage that engages the senses with barely a let-up. Of no mean help, of course, are the outstanding musical talents. The individual and collective effect is spine-tingling.
1970: Best Feature Documentary
Nominations: Best Editing, Sound

WORDS AND MUSIC
1948, 119 mins, US ⊗ ⊙
D: Norman Taurog **A:** Tom Drake,

Mickey Rooney, Betty Garrett, Ann Sothern, Janet Leigh, Marshall Thompson (M-G-M)

The saga of Rodgers and Hart is itself neither very interesting nor exceptional. Screenwriter Fred Finklehoffe therefore acted wisely in reducing the biographical aspects to a minimum, using them as a rack around which to weave production numbers, dancing routines, and lyric assignments. Tom Drake plays the serious, businesslike, and home-loving Rodgers, the melodist of the pair. Mickey Rooney plays Hart, giving the role at least some partial physical verisimilitude in that his tiny stature was a near-tragedy in the lyricist's life. Biography sticks to truth about as closely as can be presented on the screen. Hart, who never married, was the more colorful of the pair, and the camera faithfully catches that. Rooney plays Rooney, however, rather than Hart, almost turning the role into a burlesque.

WORKING GIRL
1988, 113 mins, US ⓥ ⊙
D: Mike Nichols **A:** Sigourney Weaver, Harrison Ford, Melanie Griffith, Joan Cusack, Alec Baldwin, Philip Bosco (20th Century-Fox)

Working Girl is enjoyable largely due to the fun of watching scrappy, sexy, unpredictable Melanie Griffith rise from Staten Island secretary to Wall Street whiz. She stands apart, both for her eagerness to break out of her clerical rut and her tenacity in dealing with whomever seems to be thwarting her. This is not a laugh-out-loud film, though a lighthearted tone runs consistently throughout.
1988: Best Song ("Let the River Run")
Nominations: Best Picture, Director, Actress (Melanie Griffith), Supp. Actress (Joan Cusack), Sigourney Weaver

WORKING GIRLS
1986, 90 mins, US ⓥ
D: Lizzie Borden **A:** Louise Smith, Ellen McElduff, Amanda Goodwin, Marusia Zach, Janne Peters, Helen Nicholas (Alternative Current)

Working Girls is a simulated documentary-style feature covering one day and part of the evening in a Manhattan brothel staffed by about 10 whores charging $50 per half hour when special services are not required. When their shifts are over, the girls go home to private life with or without husbands or boyfriends. Director Lizzie Borden neither glamorizes, romanticizes, nor condemns anything or anybody connected to the brothel.

WORK IS A FOUR LETTER WORD
1968, 93 mins, UK
D: Peter Hall **A:** David Warner, Cilla Black, Elizabeth Spriggs, Zia Mohyeddin, David Waller, Alan Howard (Cavalade/Universal)

Work Is a Four Letter Word is a way-out comedy fantasy. There is an irritating air of improvisation about much of the picture. The thin story line visualizes man's struggle against automation. Overwhelmed by the DICE organization, which makes such horrors as plastic daffodils and whose skyscraper offices and factories are automated to the point of frenzy, one young man holds out against the system. The plot and message are merely hooks for a series of offbeat situations. Director Peter Hall often hangs on to a point just long enough to blunt it.

WORLD ACCORDING TO GARP, THE
1982, 136 mins, US ⓥ
D: George Roy Hill **A:** Robin Williams, Mary Beth Hurt, Glenn Close, John Lithgow, Hume Cronyn, Jessica Tandy (Pan Arts)

The World According to Garp has taste, intelligence, craft, and numerous other virtues going for it. Tale is that of young Garp, bastard son of independent-minded nurse Jenny Fields, who becomes a media celebrity on publication of her autobiography. Garp (Robin Williams) meets and marries Mary Beth Hurt, raises his family, fitfully pursues his writing, and all the while tries to avoid the "undertoad," the unseen threat that lurks everywhere and strikes without warning. Physically, Williams is fine, but much of the performance is hit-and-miss. Glenn Close proves a perfect choice as Jenny Fields, a woman of almost ethereal simplicity. Best of all, perhaps, is John Lithgow as Roberta Muldoon, a former football player, now a transsexual.
1982: Nominations: Best Supp. Actor (John Lithgow), Supp. Actress (Glenn Close)

WORLD AND HIS WIFE, THE
See: State of the Union

WORLD APART, A
1988, 113 mins, UK ⓥ ⊙
D: Chris Menges **A:** Barbara Hershey, Jodhi May, David Suchet, Jeroen Krabbe,

Paul Freeman, Tim Roth (British Screen/ Working Title)

A World Apart provides a sharp glimpse of what it was like to be politically contrary in the early 1960s in South Africa. It is mostly told from the p.o.v. of a 13-year-old girl, Molly (Jodhi May), whose life becomes dramatically disrupted as a result of her parents' subversive activities. Pic traces the growing emotional and political awareness of the youngster but also represents her critique of what she perceives as her mother's selfish absorption in concerns she condescendingly considers above her offspring's head. Barbara Hershey (as the mother) represents a solid central figure for the film. Nevertheless, the limited, daughter's-eye viewpoint restricts one's access to the woman's inner self. Happily, May is at all times engaging as Molly, sustaining the film with no problem.

WORLD IN HIS ARMS, THE
1952, 104 mins, US

D: Raoul Walsh **A:** Gregory Peck, Ann Blyth, Anthony Quinn, John McIntire, Andrea King, Carl Esmond (Universal)

Rex Beach's novel of romance and adventure in early-day Alaska comes to the screen as a hearty, salty, action film. Gregory Peck, as a daring sea captain, sails into San Francisco Harbor with a load of seal pelts taken in the waters off Russian-owned Alaska. He meets Ann Blyth, a Russian countess fleeing from a Czar-arranged marriage. Love blooms between the two, but on the day they are to be married, the pursuing Russian prince arrives, carts her off, and leaves Peck believing he has been jilted.

WORLD IS FULL OF MARRIED MEN, THE
1979, 107 mins, UK ⊗

D: Robert Young **A:** Anthony Franciosa, Carroll Baker, Sherrie Cronn, Paul Nicholas, Gareth Hunt, Georgina Hale (New Realm/Married Men)

Set in a glossy world of penthouses and charge accounts, this sexploitation melodrama will titillate both sexes. Anthony Franciosa brings a mercifully light touch to the central antihero, an errant advertising executive who trips over one floozie too many and falls in love. Carroll Baker works hard as Franciosa's oft-betrayed spouse who conveniently finds affection with a teen-idol some 15 years her junior. Paul Nicholas in that role is uncharismatic.

WORLD IS NOT ENOUGH, THE
1999, 125 mins, UK/US ⊗ ⊙ ▭

D: Michael Apted **A:** Pierce Brosnan, Sophie Marceau, Robert Carlyle, Denise Richards, Robbie Coltrane, Judi Dench (Eon/M-G-M)

The World Is Not Enough, and neither is this new entry in the James Bond cycle. Although not without its moments, particularly an exciting precredits high-speed boat chase and some solid work by Pierce Brosnan and Sophie Marceau, 19th assignment of Bond's screen career sees 007 undone by villainous scripting and misguided casting. Story launch has Bond (Brosnan) in Bilbao, Spain, to collect a stash of money recovered from a killed MI6 agent. He returns to London with the loot, only to see the rightful owner blown up. The dead man was a wealthy industrialist whose daughter, Elektra (Marceau), Bond seeks out. But her old tormentor, the terrorist Renard (Robert Carlyle), also turns up. The gifted Carlyle is saddled with a role that is more annoying than imposing. Further beyond the pale is bimbette Denise Richards, as high-level nuclear-weapons expert in regulation nuke-scientist shorts and midriff-revealing shirt.

WORLD MOVES ON, THE
1934, 90 mins, US

D: John Ford **A:** Madeleine Carroll, Franchot Tone, Lumsden Hare, Raul Roulien, Reginald Denny, Sig Rumann (Fox)

A pacifist tale concluding with a religious aspect, its story is more frail than its message. The first half hour is undeniably slow, and to follow such war action is not easy. Madeleine Carroll's role is not overboard on color in the first place, and the result is a pleasant if tepid performance. Franchot Tone takes his war stuff with a pipe and three fingers of reserve. Story starts in New Orleans in 1825 with the reading of a will that combines the Girard and Warburton families through business. Establishment of branches of the Girards in France and Germany paves the way to the complex situation brought on by the war.

WORLD OF APU, THE
See: *Apar Sansar*

WORLD OF HENRY ORIENT, THE
1964, 115 mins, US ⊗ ⊙

D: George Roy Hill **A:** Peter Sellers, Paula Prentiss, Angela Lansbury, Tippy

Walker, Merrie Spaeth, Tom Bosley (Pan Arts/United Artists)

Orient comes off as an often-funny and always fetching production. It deals with two young schoolgirls in Manhattan and their infatuation with a nutty avant-garde pianist named Henry Orient (Peter Sellers). One of the girls (Tippy Walker) is given to wild flights of fancy. She befriends a more stable youngster (Merrie Spaeth), and the two become best friends. Pic traces the duo in their pursuit of Orient, whose talent at the piano is less than distinctive but whose ardor for ladies is unbounded. The young women develop the knack of showing up at just the wrong time. It is primarily the girls' picture, probably the first time anyone has stolen a pic from Sellers.

WORLD OF SUZIE WONG, THE
1960, 130 mins, US ⑆ ⊚

D: Richard Quine **A:** William Holden, Nancy Kwan, Sylvia Syms, Michael Wilding, Jacqui Chan, Laurence Naismith (Paramount)

The advantage of on-the-spot geography does a great deal for *The World of Suzie Wong*, the story of an artist (William Holden) who comes to Hong Kong to devote one year to "learning something about painting and something about myself." Before long, he is also learning a great deal about Suzie (Nancy Kwan), leader of a band of lovable, warm-hearted prostitutes (are there any other kind?). After resisting temptations of the flesh for an admirable period, Holden eventually succumbs to the yen. Holden gives a restrained and sincere first-class performance. Kwan is not always perfect in her timing of lines, but on the whole she manages a fairly believable portrayal.

WORLD'S GREATEST ATHLETE, THE
1973, 92 mins, US ⑆

D: Robert Scheerer **A:** Tim Conway, Jan-Michael Vincent, John Amos, Roscoe Lee Browne, Dayle Haddon, Billy De Wolfe (Walt Disney)

The World's Greatest Athlete features Jan-Michael Vincent in the title role of a jungle boy transplanted to an American campus where he becomes a one-man track squad. Emphasis is on visual comedy, from sublime to campy. Coach John Amos and assistant Tim Conway, with a terrible record behind them in all sports, discover Vincent during a trip to Africa.

Vincent's godfather, witchdoctor Roscoe Lee Browne, is tricked into letting him go back to the USA.

WORLD'S GREATEST LOVER, THE
1977, 89 mins, US ⑆

D: Gene Wilder **A:** Gene Wilder, Carol Kane, Dom DeLuise, Fritz Feld, Carl Ballantine, Michael Huddleston (20th Century-Fox)

The World's Greatest Lover is a good period comedy starring Gene Wilder, who competes in a Hollywood studio talent search of 50 years ago to be a rival of Rudolph Valentino. The individual sketches emerge as varyingly humorous episodes strung out on a skimpy story line. Dom DeLuise and Michael Huddleston repeatedly bring up the laughs.

WORLD TEN TIMES OVER, THE (PUSSYCAT ALLEY)
1963, 93 mins, UK

D: Wolf Rilla **A:** Sylvia Syms, Edward Judd, June Ritchie, William Hartnell (Cyclops/Associated-British)

Story concerns two girls, euphemistically called nightclub hostesses, who share an apartment. One (June Ritchie) is a flighty young extrovert having an affair with the married son of a property tycoon. The other (Sylvia Syms) is an older girl, daughter of a country schoolmaster, who is disgusted with her job but cannot break away from it. Syms gives an intelligent and often moving performance. Her scenes with her father (William Hartnell) are excellent.

WORLD, THE FLESH AND THE DEVIL, THE
1959, 95 mins, US ⑆ ▭

D: Ranald MacDougall **A:** Harry Belafonte, Inger Stevens, Mel Ferrer (M-G-M/HarBel)

This is a provocative story dealing with some pertinent issues (racism, atomic destruction) in the frame of a suspense melodrama. Harry Belafonte is a coal miner who fights his way out of a wrecked Pennsylvania mine shaft to find himself apparently alone in a devastated world. Inger Stevens turns up, spared because she was in a decompression chamber when the bombs burst. Later, Mel Ferrer arrives in a small power boat from a fishing expedition. Although overall the film is engrossing, it gets curiously less effective as additional survivors turn up.

WRATH OF GOD, THE
1972, 111 mins, US

D: Ralph Nelson **A:** Robert Mitchum, Frank Langella, Rita Hayworth, John Colicos, Victor Buono, Ken Hutchison (M-G-M)

The Wrath of God is a good solid action-adventure film, starring Robert Mitchum as a renegade priest who frees a Latin-American town of fear and terror during a rebellion in the 1920s. With Victor Buono and Ken Hutchison, likable soldiers of fortune, Mitchum is forced by army colonel John Colicos to attempt the assassination of Frank Langella, who rules his mountain retreat with vicious authority.

WRECKING CREW, THE
1969, 105 mins, US

D: Phil Karlson **A:** Dean Martin, Elke Sommer, Sharon Tate, Nancy Kwan, Nigel Green, Tina Louise (Columbia/Meadway-Claude)

Fourth in the Matt Helm series, *The Wrecking Crew* emerges as a very entertaining, relaxed spy comedy. It features Dean Martin, Elke Sommer, Nancy Kwan, and Sharon Tate, the latter in a delightful comedy performance. Nigel Green is the heavy, the mastermind of a gold theft. Sommer and Kwan are his principal aides, while Tate is a British agent in support of Martin.

WRECK OF THE MARY DEARE, THE
1959, 105 mins, US

D: Michael Anderson **A:** Gary Cooper, Charlton Heston, Michael Redgrave, Emlyn Williams, Richard Harris, Ben Wright (M-G-M)

The mystery of a "ghost" ship looming out of the night, with only a crazed and battered captain aboard, is solved skillfully and with a good deal of suspense in *The Wreck of the Mary Deare*. Gary Cooper is Gideon Patch, the captain who's been the victim of foul play but stands accused of negligence. Charlton Heston plays the skipper of a salvage boat who becomes involved in the mystery and helps solve it. There's a letdown in pace at the middle of the film when the Court of Inquiry appears stacked against Cooper. But the climax comes off with bang-up effects.

WRESTLING ERNEST HEMINGWAY
1993, 122 mins, US

D: Randa Haines **A:** Robert Duvall, Richard Harris, Shirley MacLaine, Sandra Bullock, Nicole Mercurio, Piper Laurie (Warner)

A poignant tale of intimate friendship between two elderly, eccentric men, *Wrestling Ernest Hemingway* serves mostly as a showcase for its two stars, Robert Duvall and Richard Harris. Duvall, a retired Cuban barber, and Harris, a flamboyant ex-sea captain, meet in a public park. Shy, dignified, and gentlemanly, Duvall leads a quiet, orderly life. He's secretly enamored of a much younger waitress (Sandra Bullock). Harris is still an amorous daredevil, who exhaustingly relishes telling the story of how as a youngster he wrestled Ernest Hemingway. Script has inspired scenes and some poignant dialogue, but not enough to conceal the clanky machinery of the plot.

WRITTEN ON THE WIND
1956, 99 mins, US

D: Douglas Sirk **A:** Rock Hudson, Lauren Bacall, Robert Stack, Dorothy Malone, Robert Keith, Grant Williams (Universal)

This outspoken drama probes into the morals and passions of an uppercrust Texas oil family. Rock Hudson, Lauren Bacall, Robert Stack, and Dorothy Malone add a zing to the characters that pays off in audience interest. Hudson plays the normal, lifelong friend of profligate Stack. The latter draws a compelling portrait of a psychotic man ruined by wealth and character weaknesses. Bacall registers strongly as a sensible girl swept into the madness of the oil family when she marries Stack, while Malone hits a career high as the completely immoral sister.

1956: Best Supp. Actress (Dorothy Malone)

Nominations: Best Supp. Actor (Robert Stack), Song ("Written on the Wind")

WR: MISTERIJE ORGANIZMA (WR: MYSTERIES OF THE ORGANISM)
1971, 80 mins, Yugoslavia

D: Dusan Makavejev **A:** Milena Dravic, Jagoda Kaloper, Ivica Vidovic, Zoran Radmilovic, Miodrag Andric, Tuli Kupferberg (Neoplanta)

Yugoslav filmmaker Dusan Makavejev has brought off a most unusual film built around the late Wilhelm Reich, proponent of cosmic life, the energy of love, and the power of the orgasm. It is handled with shrewd association, charm, and sheer fun. Tale centers on a Yugoslav beautician who harangues her household about the need for sex that would cure all the ills of repression. She develops a crush on a Russian champion skater and literally loses her head over him. Makavejev fills the 80 minutes with much brash and sly wit, dynamic dialectics, and excerpts from a Russian cult film, intercut with Nazi films showing backward or deranged people.

WR: MYSTERIES OF THE ORGANISM
See: WR: Misterije Organizma

WRONG ARM OF THE LAW, THE
1963, 94 mins, UK ⊗
D: Cliff Owen **A:** Peter Sellers, Lionel Jeffries, Bernard Cribbins, Bill Kerr, Davy Kaye, Nanette Newman (Romulus)

A slightweight cops and robbers idea is pepped up into a briskly amusing farce thanks to a combo of deft direction, thesping, and writing. Peter Sellers runs a top West End dress salon as Monsieur Jules. But as Pearly Gates, he is the Cockney King of the Underworld, with a gang run on Welfare State lines, with free luncheon vouchers and holidays with pay on the Costa Brava. Everything's fine until the police swoop on the gang job after job. Sellers realizes that an IPO (Impersonating Police Officers) mob is in town. He calls an extraordinary general meeting of London's crime syndicates, negotiates with Scotland Yard, and arranges for a 24-hour crime truce so that the police can concentrate on running in the IPO gang.

WRONG BOX, THE
1966, 110 mins, UK ⊗
D: Bryan Forbes **A:** John Mills, Ralph Richardson, Michael Caine, Peter Cook, Dudley Moore, Peter Sellers (Columbia/Salamander)

Robert Louis Stevenson's macabre Victorian yarn has been impressively mounted by producer-director Bryan Forbes. Story line concerns a macabre lottery in which 20 parents each toss some money into a kitty for their children, the last survivor to draw the loot. Eventual survivors are two estranged brothers. One of them (John Mills) makes ineffective attempts to bump off his brother (Ralph Richardson), and their offspring take a more than casual interest in the proceedings. Mills amusingly hams his way through two or three sequences. Richardson, bland, imperturable old bore, is superb. He and Wilfrid Lawson, portraying a decrepit butler, virtually carry away the acting honors.

WRONG IS RIGHT
(THE MAN WITH THE DEADLY LENS)
1982, 117 mins, US ⊗ ⊙
D: Richard Brooks **A:** Sean Connery, George Grizzard, Robert Conrad, Katharine Ross, G. D. Spradlin, John Saxon (Columbia)

Wrong Is Right represents Richard Brooks's shriek of protest at what he sees as the insane, downward spiral of world history over the past decade. Part political satire, part doomsday melodrama, and part intellectual graffiti scribbled on the screen, film is impossible to pigeon-hole. Sean Connery plays a globe-trotting television commentator who enjoys total access to world leaders of all persuasions. An Arab king is ready to turn over two mini-atom bombs to a Khaddafi-like revolutionary leader, to be detonated in Israel and New York, unless the US president, who has admitted ordering the killing of the king, resigns from office. Wild proceedings are packed with convoluted intrigue.

WRONG MAN, THE
1958, 110 mins, US ⊗ ⊙
D: Alfred Hitchcock **A:** Henry Fonda, Vera Miles, Anthony Quayle, Harold J. Stone, Charles Cooper, Richard Robbins (Warner)

Alfred Hitchcock draws upon real-life drama for this gripping piece of realism. Subject is Manny Balestrero, the bass fiddle player whose story hit Gotham headlines in 1953 when he was arrested for crimes he did not commit and was not freed until the actual culprit was found during his trial, Hitchcock drains the dramatic possibilities with often frightening overtones, as the spectator comes to realize that the very same could happen to him. The musician is played with a stark kind of impersonation by Henry Fonda.

WRONG MAN, THE
1993, 110 mins, US ⊗ ⊙
D: Jim McBride **A:** Rosanna Arquette, Kevin Anderson, John Lithgow, Jorge Cervera Jr., Ernesto Laguardia, Robert Harper (Viacom)

A sultry sex-suspenser about gringos

on the run south of the border, *The Wrong Man* teeters back and forth over the line between good, dirty, genre fun, and outright silliness. Kevin Anderson is in the wrong place at the wrong time, standing with a gun in his hand over a dead man who robbed him of his wallet. Rosanna Arquette and hubby John Lithgow agree to let him hitch a ride, and Arquette gets him heated up by frolicking topless in the surf. Script is low on believability and high on goofy contrivance; there's so little realistically at stake that no tension is generated.

W USA
1970, 114 mins, US ▭
D: Stuart Rosenberg **A:** Paul Newman, Joanne Woodward, Anthony Perkins, Laurence Harvey, Pat Hingle, Don Gordon (Paramount)

W USA has some serious liabilities, but it's a breath of fresh air. Title derives from call letters of a New Orleans radio station that spews forth propaganda. The cynical profession of crowd manipulation and psychology is the primary plot. Paul Newman is a drifter with radio experience. His buddy, Laurence Harvey, a con-man mission preacher, sends him to the radio station dedicated to exposing "welfare chiselers" and other social evils. As Newman's star rises, his affair with Joanne Woodward becomes strained.

WUTAI JIEMEI
(TWO STAGE SISTERS)
1965, 114 mins, China
D: Xie Jin **A:** Xie Fang, Cao Yindi, Feng Ji, Gao Yuansheng, Shen Fengjuan, Shangguan Yunzhu (Tianma)

Story spans 15 years in the relationship of two young actresses. A girl joins a group of traveling players and develops a close friendship with the daughter of the troupe's manager. The young women go to Japanese-occupied Shanghai in 1941 and become well-regarded thesps. But by 1944, a rift occurs, with one coming under the influence of corrupt, Western-style gangster types and the other beginning to display revolutionary awareness. Tale jumps to the revolutionary China of 1950. One actress tracks down the other in the provinces and, after their emotional reunion, pair makes a joint resolve in a classic final line—"Let us remold ourselves and always perform revolutionary operas." Last section is fortunately the only one with overt political content.

WUTHERING HEIGHTS
1939, 103 mins, US ▨ ⊙
D: William Wyler **A:** Merle Oberon, Laurence Olivier, David Niven, Flora Robson, Geraldine Fitzgerald, Donald Crisp (United Artists/Goldwyn)

Emily Brontë's novel tells a haunting tale of love and tragedy. Samuel Goldwyn's film version retains all of the grim drama of the book. It's heavy fare throughout. Merle Oberon has two loves—stableboy Laurence Olivier and affluent David Niven. After unsuccessfully goading Olivier to make something of himself, girl turns to Niven. Olivier disappears, to return several years later with a moderate fortune. Oberon keeps her smouldering passions under control, and Olivier marries Niven's sister (Geraldine Fitzgerald) for spite. Direction by William Wyler is slow and deliberate, accenting the tragic features of the piece.
1939: Best B&W Cinematography
Nominations: Best Picture, Director, Actor (Laurence Olivier), Supp. Actress (Geraldine Fitzgerald), Screenplay, Art Direction, Original Score

WUTHERING HEIGHTS
1971, 105 mins, UK/US ▨
D: Robert Fuest **A:** Anna Calder-Marshall, Timothy Dalton, Julian Glover, Ian Ogilvy, Hilary Dwyer, Judy Cornwell (American International)

Wuthering Heights is a competent, tasteful, frequently even lovely re-adaption of Emily Brontë's Gothic, mystical love story. But the brooding tension, the electric passion of two lovers compelled to an inevitable tragedy is not generated. Anna Calder-Marshall as Catherine gives the role a wild young animal look and spirit. Timothy Dalton has a dark gypsy brooding look appropriate for Heathcliff. But his sullen portrayal is often that of a hurt boy rather than a man seething with resentment and frustrated passion.

WUTHERING HEIGHTS
1992, 105 mins, UK/US ▨ ⊙
D: Peter Kosminsky **A:** Juliette Binoche, Ralph Fiennes, Janet McTeer, Sophie Ward, Simon Shepherd, Simon Ward (Paramount)

UK-lensed *Wuthering Heights* is a by-the-numbers telling of the Emily Brontë classic that's as cool as a Yorkshire moor, weakened by a wobbly central performance by Gallic thesp Juliette Binoche. Film misses out on atmosphere and passion. With an uncontrolled accent, Binoche misses spontaneity and feeling. Screen newcomer Ralph Fiennes makes a good stab at the Heathcliff part. Sprawling story moves at quite a clip to get everything in. A late-on fantasy sequence of Heathcliff reunited with the dead Cathy has some of the romantic panache badly missing elsewhere.

W.W. AND THE DIXIE DANCEKINGS

1975, 91 mins, US
D: John G. Avildsen **A:** Burt Reynolds, Conny Van Dyke, Jerry Reed, Ned Beatty, James Hampton, Don Williams (20th Century-Fox)

Burt Reynolds stars as a 1950s con artist. A footloose character, he robs gas stations and divides the loot with the underpaid attendants in return for their giving phony descriptions. Sherman G. Lloyd, redneck oil magnate, recruits Art Carney, lawman turned fundamentalist preacher, to catch him. This plot angle alternates with Reynolds's growing attachment to the Dixie Dancekings, a c&w band headed by Jerry Reed.

WYATT EARP

1994, 189 mins, US ⊗ ⊙ ▭
D: Lawrence Kasdan **A:** Kevin Costner, Dennis Quaid, Gene Hackman, Jeff Fahey, Mark Harmon, Michael Madsen (Tig/Kasdan/Warner)

Wyatt Earp is a stately, handsome, grandiose gentleman's western that evenhandedly but too doggedly tries to tell more about the famous Tombstone lawman than has ever before been put on screen. After losing his pregnant young wife to typhoid, Wyatt (Kevin Costner) goes into a drunken, criminal downward spin. With his father's help, he pulls himself out of his stupor and lands in Wichita, where he almost inadvertently becomes a lawman. Pic begins treading on more familiar territory as Bat and Ed Masterson enter the story, followed by Doc Holliday (Dennis Quaid), the gunslinging dentist who forms an unlikely partnership with the brothers Earp in trying to tame lawlessness in the boom towns of Dodge City and Tombstone. Standout performance comes from Quaid as Doc Holliday. Pic jumps to life whenever he's around.
1994: Nomination: Cinematography

X
(THE MAN WITH THE X-RAY EYES)
1963, 80 mins, US ⓥ
D: Roger Corman A: Ray Milland, Diana van der Vlis, Harold J. Stone, Don Rickles, John Hoyt (American International/ Alta Vista)

Ray Milland is a doctor who devises a drug he thinks will allow men's eyes to see infinitely more. He tries it on himself and finds he can see inside human tissue and through clothes. Things get worse when he inadvertently kills a friend and has to hide out in a carnival as a mind-reader. Interesting comic, dramatic, and philosophical ideas are touched on but only on the surface. However, director Roger Corman keeps things moving, and Milland is competent as the doomed man.

XANADU
1980, 92 mins, US ⓥ ⊙
D: Robert Greenwald A: Olivia Newton-John, Gene Kelly, Michael Beck (Universal)

Xanadu is truly a stupendously bad film whose only salvage is the music. Olivia Newton-John plays a muse whose task is to inspire Michael Beck's work as an artist. He thinks she's a real girl, and love is threatening, so she decides it's best if she bids him farewell. But he pursues her into the wall on which her image is painted and winds up somewhere near Mount Olympus.

X-FILES, THE
1998, 120 mins, US ⓥ ⊙ ▱
D: Rob Bowman A: David Duchovny, Gillian Anderson, Martin Landau, Armin Mueller-Stahl, Blythe Danner, William B. Davis (Ten Thirteen/20th Century-Fox)

The X-Files falls somewhere in between standing on its own feet as a real movie and merely being a glorified television episode refitted for theaters. Film lacks the excitement, scope, and style expected from event movies. Initial sequence reveals a ferocious creature killing a caveman; second hook shows a young boy falling into a pit and being infected by a black goo. Third deals with the discovery of a bomb at the Federal Building in Dallas. FBI agent Fox Mulder (David Duchovny) is approached by a conspiracy theorist (Martin Landau), who hints at the existence of a "secret government" poised to take over after it unleashes a plague upon the world. Thus resumes Mulder and Scully's (Gillian Anderson) ongoing probe into the presence of aliens on Earth. Director Rob Bowman relies far too much on dark alleys and rain-slicked streets for atmospherics, and on shocks achieved by quick cutting, out-of-the-blue attacks, and blasts of sound. Climax, set in a vast chamber under the Antarctic ice, unfolds as a routine action finale with unfulfilled James Bondian aspirations. Duchovny and Anderson's appeal carries over intact to the big screen.

XIA NU
(A TOUCH OF ZEN)
1969, 177 mins, Taiwan
D: King Hu A: Hsu Feng, Shih Chun, Pai Ying, Tien Peng, Hsueh Han, Roy Chiao (Union)

Kung fu proves itself here as material for a serious, thoughtful film yet with its exciting, dynamic effects and drive undiminished. Set in the 14th-century Ming Dynasty, leisurely tale is of people fighting the tyranny of a vicious secret police. A local artist gets mixed up in the intrigues of the higher echelons when he befriends a girl living near him, the daughter of a nobleman killed by the secret police. The battles, with their swirling airborne bodies, swishing sounds, and balletic grace, serve as codas to this tale of love and tyranny. [Pic was originally released in Taiwan in two parts, in 1970 and 1973. Above review is of combined version first shown in competition at Cannes in 1975.]

XI YAN
(THE WEDDING BANQUET)
1993, 107 mins, Taiwan ⓥ ⊙
D: Ang Lee A: Winston Chao, May Chin, Mitchell Lichtenstein, Sihung Lung, Ah-leh Gua (CMPC)

A slickly mounted Gotham comedy about two gays who try to hoodwink the Chinese partner's parents with a phony marriage. To fend off his overseas mom's nagging to get married, Wai-tung (Winston Chao), a Taiwanese with a comfy lifestyle in Manhattan and a white US lover, Simon (Mitchell Lichtenstein), agrees to a green-card deal with one of his tenants, ambitious but broke Wei-wei (May Chin). Complications arise when Wai-tung's parents suddenly fly over from Taiwan to attend the marriage.

X, Y AND ZEE
See: Zee & Co.

YAKUZA, THE
1975, 112 mins, US Ⓥ ⊙ ▭
D: Sydney Pollack **A:** Robert Mitchum, Ken Takakura, Brian Keith, Herb Edelman, Richard Jordan, Kishi Keiko (Warner)

The Yakuza is a confused film that bites off more than it can artfully chew. Robert Mitchum plays a private eye returning to Japan to unravel some international crimes, as well as a long-ago love affair. The result is an uneasy combination of an oriental Mafia story overlaid on a formula international business swindle, mixed up with a 20-years-later update of *Sayonara*.

YANGTSE INCIDENT
(BATTLE HELL)
1957, 113 mins, UK Ⓥ
D: Michael Anderson **A:** Richard Todd, William Hartnell, Akim Tamiroff, Donald Houston, Keye Luke, Sophie Stewart (British Lion)

Story is of the *Amethyst*, which, battered though not beaten, broke the Chinese Communist blockade and rejoined the British fleet. The *Amethyst* is sailing up the Yangtse, headed for Nanking on a lawful mission delivering supplies to the British Embassy. Suddenly the Red shore batteries open fire and the frigate is grounded in the mud. All attempts to persuade the British to issue an apology for "unprovoked aggression" are resolutely turned down, and both sides play a waiting game until the British commander decides to run for it.

YANK AT OXFORD, A
1938, 100 mins, UK
D: Jack Conway **A:** Robert Taylor, Maureen O'Sullivan, Lionel Barrymore, Vivien Leigh, Edmund Gwenn, Griffith Jones (M-G-M)

Robert Taylor brings back from Oxford an entertaining rah-rah film that is full of quarter-mile dashes, boat race finishes, and surefire sentiment—Metro's first British-made film under Hollywood supervision and with Hollywood principals and director. What Jack Conway has caught is the humor of student life at the university. This is the background for Taylor's adventures, the wall against which a cocky Yank bounces his somewhat enlarged head, eventually regaining his poise as a better and tamed human being.

YANKEE DOODLE DANDY
1942, 126 mins, US Ⓥ ⊙
D: Michael Curtiz **A:** James Cagney, Joan Leslie, Walter Huston, Richard Whorf, Irene Manning, Jeanne Cagney (Warner)

Yankee Doodle Dandy is shamelessly nationalistic, no matter how you slice it. It's a tribute to a grand American gentleman of the theater, George M. Cohan, and it's a tribute to all show business. James Cagney does a Cohan of which the original George M. might well be proud. That Robert Buckner and his coscripter Edmund Joseph jazzed up a little of the latter-day chronology is beside the point.

1942: Best Actor (James Cagney), Scoring of a Musical Picture, Sound Recording

Nominations: Best Picture, Director, Supp. Actor (Walter Huston), Original Story, Editing

YANKEE IN KING ARTHUR'S COURT, A
See: A Connecticut Yankee in King Arthur's Court

YANK IN LONDON, A
See: I Live in Grosvenor Square

YANK IN THE R.A.F., A
1941, 97 mins, US Ⓥ
D: Henry King **A:** Tyrone Power, Betty Grable, John Sutton, Reginald Gardiner, Donald Stuart, Morton Lowry (20th Century-Fox)

Picture neatly mixes the adventures of cocky and carefree Tyrone Power, former airline pilot, with the inner workings of the RAF squadrons during the hectic times of the German blitz against the low countries and France. Producer Darryl F. Zanuck sidesteps overloading the picture with flying sequences. Power enlists as a pilot to ferry bombers to England. On his first trip, he meets a former sweetheart (Betty Grable), a Texas girl performing in a night club and a member of the ambulance reserve. Power pursues his former attention, and enlists in the RAF for fighter duty.

1941: Nomination: Best Special Effects

YANKS
1979, 141 mins, UK Ⓥ ⊙
D: John Schlesinger **A:** Richard Gere, Lisa Eichhorn, Vanessa Redgrave, William Devane, Rachel Roberts, Annie Ross (CIP/Universal)

Director John Schlesinger has done a beautiful job with both cast and craft in *Yanks*, a multiple love story set in England in World War II. Yet little that's exciting ever happens in the picture. The British director vividly re-creates the atmosphere in a small English village inundated by thousands of American troops prepping for the invasion of Europe. The six lovers are played excellently, and Schlesinger and crew have created an extravagantly authentic period setting.

YAO A YAO YAO DAO WAIPO QIAO (SHANGHAI TRIAD)

1995, 108 mins, China/France Ⓥ

D: Zhang Yimou **A:** Gong Li, Li Baotian, Li Xuejian, Shun Chun, Wang Xiaoxiao, Jiang Baoying (Shanghai/Alpha/UGC Images/La Sept)

Poised somewhere between the visual flamboyance of *Red Sorghum* and the interior tension of the later *Raise the Red Lantern*, *Triad*—a stylized but gripping portrait of mob power play and lifestyles in 1930 Shanghai—oozes a confidence that carries the viewer almost without pause to its shocking climax and ironic finish. Covering eight days in the fortunes of Shanghai's most powerful triad, yarn starts with the arrival from the countryside of young Tang Shuisheng (Wang Xiaoxiao), a naive member of the Tang clan placed under the care of Uncle Liu (Li Xuejian). Shuisheng sees almost every aspect of the closed, violent world. Over the next couple of days, this rigorously controlled world is shown to be as shaky as some of songstress Xiao's (Gong Li) onstage crooning. As in Greek tragedies, all the important events are actually taking place offstage, as we finally learn with a wallop at the end.

YEARLING, THE

1946, 134 mins, US Ⓥ ☉

D: Clarence Brown **A:** Gregory Peck, Jane Wyman, Claude Jarman Jr., Chill Wills, Forrest Tucker, Margaret Wycherly (M-G-M)

This is a heart-warming story of good earth, family ties, and the love of the 11-year-old Jody Baxter for the fawn which he is compelled to put out of his life as it becomes a yearling. In the Florida scrub country, Gregory Peck and Jane Wyman fight for existence, while raising meager patches of crops and their offspring Jody (Claude Jarman Jr.). The lad becomes a man, who with great love and effort wards off the destruction of his pet.

1946: Best Color Cinematography, Art Direction, Honorary (Claude Jarman Jr., outstanding child actor)
Nominations: Best Picture, Director, Actor (Gregory Peck), Actress (Jane Wyman), Editing

YEAR MY VOICE BROKE, THE

1987, 103 mins, Australia Ⓥ ☉

D: John Duigan **A:** Noah Taylor, Loene Carmen, Ben Mendelsohn, Graeme Blundell, Lynette Curran, Bruce Spence (Kennedy Miller)

Setting is a small New South Wales country town in 1962. Danny (Noah Taylor) and Freya (Loene Carmen) have been friends from childhood. Danny is troubled because Freya, though the same age he is, is maturing far more rapidly. She falls heavily for Trev (Ben Mendelsohn), an older football coach. Freya gets pregnant, and Trev gets into trouble with the law. Danny tries to help, but an old scandal involving Freya's mother surfaces, which causes more distress. All of this is handled by John Duigan with insight and understatement. The characters are beautifully played by the three young newcomers.

YEAR OF LIVING DANGEROUSLY, THE

1982, 114 mins, Australia/US Ⓥ ☉ ⌑

D: Peter Weir **A:** Mel Gibson, Sigourney Weaver, Linda Hunt, Michael Murphy, Bill Kerr, Noel Ferrier (McElroy & McElroy/M-G-M)

Peter Weir's *The Year of Living Dangerously* is set in Indonesia in 1965 in the turbulent months leading to the fall of the Sukarno government. Mel Gibson, a young Australian journalist on his first posting as a foreign correspondent, is befriended by an astute Chinese-Australian cameraman, a dwarf who seeks to manipulate people as deftly as he handles shadow puppets—an astonishing feat of acting by Linda Hunt, cast by Weir because he could not locate a short male actor to fit the bill. A bizarre romantic triangle develops between Gibson, Hunt, and Sigourney Weaver as a British Embassy official. Gibson learns that the Communists are bringing in arms for a coup against Sukarno and in broadcasting the story blows a confidence from Weaver, who rejects him.

1983: Best Supp. Actress (Linda Hunt)

YEAR OF THE COMET

1992, 89 mins, US Ⓥ ☉ ⌑

D: Peter Yates **A:** Penelope Ann Miller, Timothy Daly, Louis Jourdan, Art Malik,

Ian Richardson, Ian McNeice (Castle Rock)

Harvested from the same field as *Romancing the Stone*, this wine-soaked comedy-adventure never really ferments. The film's problems begin with its title, a reference to the vintage of a 150-year-old bottle of wine that sounds more like a sci-fi thriller. That bottle brings together a wine auctioneer's daughter (Penelope Ann Miller), who discovers it, and a Texas millionaire's troubleshooter (Tim Daly), assigned to bring it back to his boss.

YEAR OF THE DRAGON
1985, 136 mins, US Ⓥ ⊙ ▭
D: Michael Cimino **A:** Mickey Rourke, John Lone, Ariane, Leonard Termo, Ray Barry, Caroline Kava (De Laurentiis)

Year of the Dragon is never as important as director Michael Cimino thinks it is, but there's a fair amount of solid action and gunplay, all set securely in the intricate, mysterious enigma of New York's Chinatown and its ties to worldwide drug dealing. Assigned to Chinatown to clear up a problem of murderous youth gangs, Mickey Rourke proves to be one of those lone renegade cops that fiction favors more than real life. He wants to undo a criminal system rooted in a culture for thousands of years. Beyond the color and the corpses, though, Cimino fails to focus on an idea and stick with it.

YEAR OF THE GUN
1991, 111 mins, US Ⓥ ⊙
D: John Frankenheimer **A:** Andrew McCarthy, Valeria Golino, Sharon Stone, John Pankow, Mattia Sbragia, George Murcell (Pressman)

Year of the Gun is a competent but routine thriller about a young American novelist in Rome in 1978 who hits upon a terrorist kidnapping plot. Andrew McCarthy plays an expatriate US journalist with a rich Italian g.f. (Valeria Golino) and the insistent attentions of a beautiful American photojournalist (Sharon Stone). Stone wants in on a book she believes he's writing about the Red Brigade terrorists. She leaks it to a mutual friend (John Pankow), a university professor who leaks it to the Red Brigade, and the two Yanks are imperiled. Director John Frankenheimer and cinematographer Blasco Giuarto do a standout job with the taut, hysterical action scenes.

YEARS WITHOUT DAYS
See: Castle on the Hudson

YELLOW BALLOON, THE
1953, 80 mins, UK
D: J. Lee Thompson **A:** Andrew Ray, Kathleen Ryan, Kenneth More, Bernard Lee, William Sylvester, Sydney James (Associated British/Marble Arch)

This British pic is a depressing study of a child who falls into the clutches of a modern Fagin and is forced to steal from his own parents before being used as a decoy in a hold-up that leads to murder. Andrew Ray plays the part of the boy almost on a single key, but his static expression captures the story's spirit. Sydney James gives a rich performance as a cockney trader.

YELLOW CANARY, THE
1943, 95 mins, UK
D: Herbert Wilcox **A:** Anna Neagle, Richard Greene, Nova Pilbeam, Albert Lieven, Margaret Rutherford (Imperator)

Direction, cast, production, and camerawork are so good it is a pity the suspenseful story is not on the same plane of excellence. Anna Neagle plays Sally Maitland, daughter of an aristocratic British family, notorious for her pre-war association with the Nazis. Public antagonism against her is so violent that she is forced to leave Britain. It is a role altogether different from her previous film appearances.

YELLOW CANARY, THE
1963, 93 mins, US ▭
D: Buzz Kulik **A:** Pat Boone, Barbara Eden, Steve Forrest, Jack Klugman, Jesse White, Steve Harris (20th Century-Fox)

Hero of the piece is Pat Boone, a surly singing idol whose loose ways have him on the brink of divorce with his wife (Barbara Eden). Their baby is kidnapped by Boone's psychotic bodyguard (Steve Forrest). Rod Serling's screenplay is reasonably strong in dramatic anatomy, but limp and fuzzy in character definition. Boone warbles several old standards pleasantly.

YELLOW EARTH
See: Huang Tudi

YELLOW ROLLS-ROYCE, THE
1964, 122 mins, US ▭
D: Anthony Asquith **A:** Rex Harrison, Jeanne Moreau, Shirley MacLaine, George C. Scott, Ingrid Bergman, Omar Sharif (M-G-M)

A sleek piece of entertainment, handsomely tinted, lushly lensed, and, though leisurely in its approach, has style, humor, and some effective thesping. Film consists of three separate anecdotes, linked only by ownership of the elegant auto. Rex Harrison, a Foreign Office big shot, buys the car as an anniversary gift for his wife (Jeanne Moreau) and discovers her and a minion (Edmund Purdom) in passionate embrace in its back seat. The car is bought in Italy by gangster George C. Scott as a present for his current moll, Shirley MacLaine, who falls for a street photographer (Alain Delon), and again the back seat of the Rolls is pressed into service. In 1942 the car is acquired by Ingrid Bergman playing a hectoring American woman. Hitler is attacking Yugoslavia, and she finds she has smuggled an arch-patriot (Omar Sharif) across the border.

YELLOW ROSE OF TEXAS, THE
1944, 69 mins, US ⓥ ⊙
D: Joseph Kane **A:** Roy Rogers, Dale Evans, Grant Withers, Harry Shannon (Republic)

Roy Rogers is an investigator for an insurance company trying to locate a payroll stolen five years ago. He obtains a job singing on the showboat *Yellow Rose of Texas* from Betty Weston (Dale Evans), whose father was imprisoned for the robbery. When Sam Weston (Harry Shannon) breaks jail to clear himself, Rogers helps get the evidence that traps the real culprit. The musical sequences are pleasant and well staged, and there is enough action to satisfy those who like excitement in their westerns.

YELLOW SKY
1948, 99 mins, US
D: William A. Wellman **A:** Gregory Peck, Anne Baxter, Richard Widmark, Robert Arthur, John Russell, Harry Morgan (20th Century-Fox)

Setting for the story is the west of 1867, and the outdoor locations have been magnificently lensed. The direction by William A. Wellman is vigorous, potently emphasizing every element of suspense and action. Plot traces a group of outlaws who rob a bank, flee across a desert, and seek refuge in a ghost mining town. There they find a girl and her grandfather, learn they have gold, and seek to steal it. Peck shines as the outlaw leader and matching dramatic stride for stride with him is Baxter as the ghost town girl.

YELLOWSTONE KELLY
1959, 91 mins, US
D: Gordon Douglas **A:** Clint Walker, Edward Byrnes, John Russell, Ray Danton, Andra Martin, Claude Akins (Warner)

Yellowstone Kelly is a well-made western about a fur trapper, Kelly, who is on good terms with the Sioux Indians. He refuses to help the US Cavalry's punitive expedition of 1876 but ultimately has to help the arrogant white men after they have been trounced by the righteous red men. Director Gordon Douglas moves the story along with a speed sufficient to cover up weak plot points.

YELLOW SUBMARINE
1968, 89 mins, UK ⓥ ⊙
D: George Dunning (Apple/King/Suba-films)

This is a full-length cartoon in which the Beatles appear in caricature form. Story consists of a fantastic voyage in a yellow submarine through sky and sea, manned by the skipper and The Beatles, to Pepperland, where the inhabitants are up against thugs known as the Blue Meanies. Time travel, science fiction, outer space, monsters, war, and their own idiom of pop music are all taken for a ride. The film makes no concession to sentiment. Characters are mostly matter-of-fact, grotesque, and anti-heroic.

YENTL
1983, 134 mins, US ⓥ ⊙
D: Barbra Streisand **A:** Barbra Streisand, Mandy Patinkin, Amy Irving, Nehemiah Persoff, Steven Hill, Allan Corduner (Barwood/United Artists)

Yentl tells the tale of a young Eastern European woman, circa 1904, who disguises herself as a boy to pursue her passion for studying holy scripture, an endeavor restricted exclusively to men in orthodox Jewish culture. Befriended by her brash, attractive fellow student Avigdor, wonderfully played by Mandy Patinkin, Yentl falls in love with him. When Avigdor is prevented from marrying his fiancée Hadass (Amy Irving), he asks Yentl to marry her in his stead. Streisand has created a fine-looking period piece, working on Czech locations and in English studios.
1983: Best Original Song Score
Nominations: Best Supp. Actress (Amy Irving), Art Direction, Song ("Papa, Can You Hear Me?" "The Way He Makes Me Feel")

YESTERDAY, TODAY AND TOMORROW
See: Ieri, Oggi, Domani

LES YEUX SANS VISAGE
(EYES WITHOUT A FACE; THE HORROR CHAMBER OF DR. FAUSTUS)
1959, 90 mins, France 🆅 ⊙
D: Georges Franju **A:** Pierre Brasseur, Alida Valli, Edith Scob, Francois Guerin, Juliette Mayniel, Beatrice Altariba (Champs-Elysees/Lux)

Ambitious horror pic has some queasy scenes, but unclear progression and plodding direction give this film an old-fashioned air. The face of a plastic surgeon's daughter is destroyed in an accident. He gets young girls, lured in by a woman whose face he has saved, and tries to transpose their faces to that of his daughter. The operations fail. Director Georges Franju has given this some suspense and not spared any shock details. But the stilted acting and a repetition of effects lose the initial impact.

YIELD TO THE NIGHT
(US: BLONDE SINNER)
1956, 100 mins, UK 🆅
D: J. Lee Thompson **A:** Diana Dors, Yvonne Mitchell, Michael Craig, Marie Ney, Geoffrey Keen, Liam Redmond (Associated British)

Diana Dors plays a heavy dramatic role in *Yield to the Night*, which calls for a drastic de-glamorizing treatment. The killing which leads her to the death cell is depicted before the credit titles, but the events which led her to it are shown in flashbacks. Main footage, inside the condemned cell, illustrates her anguish, the wardresses who guard her night and day, the members of her family and the husband whom she deserted. On the whole, Dors rises to the occasion and shows up as a dramatic actress better than anticipated.

YINGHUNG BUNSIK
(A BETTER TOMORROW)
1986, 98 mins, Hong Kong 🆅 ⊙
D: John Woo **A:** Ti Lung, Leslie Cheung, Chow Yun-fat, Emily Chu, Waise Lee, Kent Tseng (Cinema City)

A contemporary cop and gangster action drama burdened with an excess of practically everything except sex, *A Better Tomorrow* is a contrived bang-bang thriller with overdone violence and bloodshed. Chow Yun-fat and perennial teenager Leslie Cheung both overact. But Ti Lung shines in his comeback role as a reformed ex-gangster, lacing his portrayal with inner strength and vulnerability. It's

a fine vehicle for director John Woo, who has changed his style from light comedy to the "macho" genre. Film is about two brothers in conflicting roles. Kit (Cheung) is a dedicated policeman who blames his elder brother (Ti Lung) for their father's death and for obstructing his career in the police force. After serving a jail term, repentant Ti Lung returns to Hong Kong to lead a new life.

YINGHUNG BUNSIK II
(A BETTER TOMORROW II)
1987, 103 mins, Hong Kong 🆅 ⊙
D: John Woo **A:** Dean Shek, Ti Lung, Leslie Cheung, Chow Yun-fat, Kwan San, Emily Chu (Film Workshop/Cinema City/Golden Princess)

This is a highly commercial, overblown but entertaining follow-up to the 1986 gangster attraction. Chow Yun-fat (his character died in Part I), returns as a twin brother called Ken, who lives in New York. Kid brother of Ti Lung, young cop Leslie Cheung is still stubborn as ever and dies a hero's death. Ti Lung is forced to join an international counterfeit syndicate, his way out of prison. His brother (Cheung) is assigned to collect evidence by the police department against the illegal activities of the shipbuilding company headed by Dean Shek. Villain Ko plans to have Shek murdered to take over his shipyard and full control of the profitable trading.

YINGHUNG BUNSIK III TSIKYEUNG TSI GO
(A BETTER TOMORROW III; LOVE AND DEATH IN SAIGON)
1989, 108 mins, Hong Kong 🆅 ⊙
D: Tsui Hark **A:** Chow Yun-fat, Anita Mui, Tony Leung Kar-fai, Saburo Tokito, Shek Kin, Maggie Cheung (Film Workshop/Golden Princess)

Tsui Hark has taken the series in a somewhat surprising direction with this entry, scaling down the action and tossing in a romantic subplot. Pic takes place in Vietnam during the chaotic withdrawal of US troops in 1974. Plot follows the efforts of Hong Hong hustler Mark (Chow Yun-fat) to secure exit visas for his uncle and cousin. Requiring large sums of cash for bribery, he becomes involved in smuggling US currency with his cousin Mun (Tony Leung) and black market temptress Kitty Chow (Anita Mui). In many ways, Mui emerges as the most memorable performer in the film. Even in her love scenes, she seems almost invulnerable.

The action scenes that serve as denouement are almost overwhelming by Western standards, but they are subtle in comparison to the kill-fest that capped *A Better Tomorrow II*.

YINSHI NANNU
(EAT DRINK MAN WOMAN)
1994, 123 mins, Taiwan Ⓥ
D: Ang Lee **A:** Sihung Lung, Yang Kuei-mei, Wu Chien-lien, Gua Ah-leh, Sylvia Chang, Winston Chao (CMPC)

After the international success of *The Wedding Banquet*, Ang Lee directed the ambitious and entertaining *Eat Drink Man Woman*. Again his focus is the family. Chu (Sihung Lung), a master chef who's literally lost his sense of taste, lives in Taipei with his three adult daughters, each of whom is itching to leave the nest. As one of the daughters notes, "We communicate by eating." In fact, the ritual of preparing food is a means to avoid interaction. The technical sheen and visual assurance of Lee's third film is a quantum leap from earlier credits. He also elicits deeper, more textured performances from his actors.
1994: Nomination: Best Foreign Language Film

YOJIMBO
(THE BODYGUARD)
1961, 110 mins, Japan Ⓥ ⊙ ▭
D: Akira Kurosawa **A:** Toshiro Mifune, Eijiro Tono, Tatsuya Nakadai, Isuzu Yamada, Daisuke Kato, Kamatari Fujiwara (Kurosawa/Toho)

Story, set in 1800s, is told with vigor and visual excitement by Akira Kurosawa and is splendidly acted by Toshiro Mifune. A wandering samurai arrives in a village split into two warring factions. He offers his services to one, then to the other gang leader, and starts a series of fights, duels, and kidnappings until he unselfishly frees some prisoners. Kurosawa again shows his mastery of the medium. His choice of secondary characters is also adroit and colorful, as is his ever-exciting use of the camera. Music by Masaru Sato rates a special nod for the way it keys the serio-comic tone.

YOLANDA AND THE THIEF
1945, 108 mins, US Ⓥ ⊙
D: Vincente Minnelli **A:** Fred Astaire, Lucille Bremer, Frank Morgan, Mildred Natwick, Mary Nash, Leon Ames (M-G-M)

Arthur Freed produced with lavishness, and the casting has an eye toward marquee values, but the basic yarn doesn't lend itself toward the screen. A Latin-American heiress, after being brought up in a convent, assumes charge of her fortune upon coming of age. Her sheltered childhood makes her easy prey for a fraud. There's an idea in this yarn, but it only suggests itself. The story strains credibility.

YOU AND ME
1938, 90 mins, US
D: Fritz Lang **A:** Sylvia Sidney, George Raft, Robert Cummings, Barton MacLane, Roscoe Karns, Harry Carey (Paramount)

Fritz Lang's *You and Me* is a curious cinematic adventure, a sort of cinematic Mercury Theater with European flavoring. It's set in a department store where Harry Carey, as the boss, runs on a rehabilitation basis. Some 50 of his 2,500 employees are ex-convicts out on parole. George Raft is one, and finally his parole is clear; he may even marry. Sylvia Sidney is the girl. She, too, is a paroled penitentiary inmate, but Raft never knew that.

YOU BELONG TO ME
1941, 93 mins, US
D: Wesley Ruggles **A:** Barbara Stanwyck, Henry Fonda, Edgar Buchanan, Roger Clark, Ruth Donnelly, Melville Cooper (Columbia)

They've been laughing at gags about the doctor and his jealous wife since way back, and in this case the wife is the doctor to give it a reverse twist. So long as the story sticks to its comedy angle it beats a pleasant tattoo. But it veers off on a socio-economic tangent, the result being a sharp shift in mood and a letdown in entertainment. The performances of Barbara Stanwyck and Henry Fonda merit fulsome praise. Fonda, cast as a rich playboy who suffers a skiing fall and recovers with a medical wife, proves again that he is endowed with a high flair for comedy.

YOU CAN'T HAVE EVERYTHING
1937, 100 mins, US Ⓥ
D: Norman Taurog **A:** Alice Faye, Ritz Bros., Don Ameche, Charles Winninger, Gypsy Rose Lee, Rubinoff (20th Century-Fox)

Another backstage story with all the principals being familiar types of the theater. This time the heroine (Alice Faye) is a young dramatist of serious plays, who sells a script because of her good looks. Don Ameche is the successful Broadway librettist who persuades Charles Winninger to make the investment. When her serious play is made the basis of a satiric musical, Faye returns to town to protest and discovers herself the author of a hit. Five numbers are contributed by Mack Gordon and Harry Revel.

YOU CAN'T SLEEP HERE
See: I Was a Male War Bride

YOU CAN'T TAKE IT WITH YOU
1938, 126 mins, US ⓥ ⊙
D: Frank Capra **A:** Jean Arthur, Lionel Barrymore, James Stewart, Edward Arnold, Mischa Auer, Ann Miller (Columbia)

This comedy is wholly American, wholesome, homespun, human, appealing, and touching. The wackier comedy side contrasts with a somewhat serious, philosophical note that may seem a little overstressed on occasion. The Vanderhoff tribe is played appealingly but screwily, the antics of the polyglot combination of grandpa, daughter, son-in-law, grandchildren, and hangers-on being basically for the creation of fun. The romance between James Stewart and Jean Arthur is the keystone of the comedy. Other comedy elements are registered at the expense of Edward Arnold, the stuff-shirt banker, and his wife. Arthur acquits herself creditably. Stewart is not a strong romantic lead opposite her but does satisfactorily in the love scenes.
1938: Best Picture, Director
Nominations: Best Supp. Actress (Spring Byington), Screenplay, Cinematography, Editing, Sound

YOU LIGHT UP MY LIFE
1977, 90 mins, US ⓥ
D: Joseph Brooks **A:** Didi Conn, Joe Silver, Michael Zaslow, Stephan Nathan, Melanie Mayron, Amy Letterman (Brooks)

You Light Up My Life has all the virtues and the liabilities of a low-budget effort. There's an earnest sincerity in the story of washed-up juvenile comedienne Didi Conn working out an adult identity. There's also a lot of cutesy, cornball, convenient, and compacted plotting. As the burnt-out child of stage-father Joe Silver, she is headed for a dull marriage to Stephan Nathan when film producer Michael Zaslow sponsors her breakthrough into pop music. She falls for Zaslow, but his mind is on his own career.

YOU'LL LIKE MY MOTHER
1972, 93 mins, US
D: Lamont Johnson **A:** Patty Duke, Rosemary Murphy, Richard Thomas, Sian Barbara Allen, Dennis Rucker, Harold Congdon (Crosby/Universal)

You'll Like My Mother is a quietly intense thriller. The film avoids explicit physical gore, instead stimulating intellectual and unseen menace. The plot logically piles confusion on Duke, a pregnant widow who comes for a first-time visit to her mother-in-law (Murphy). The latter's cold, gushing, and blasé attitude, compounded by the presence of Richard Thomas as a deranged rape-murderer relative, add up to a situation which finds an audience rooting for Duke and her nursing infant.

YOU'LL NEVER GET RICH
1941, 87 mins, US ⓥ ⊙
D: Sidney Lanfield **A:** Fred Astaire, Rita Hayworth, Robert Benchley, John Hubbard, Osa Massen, Frieda Inescort (Columbia)

Fred Astaire is staging a musical for producer Robert Benchley. The latter, struck by Rita Hayworth, gets in a jam with his wife, and has Astaire get him out of the predicament. Girl, with a crush on Astaire, is disillusioned by the proceedings, and gives him the heave-ho. When Astaire is inducted into the selective service camp, Benchley makes a deal to stage a show for the boys. Script is studded with humorous lines and situations, and despite a familiar ring, it's all sufficiently refurbished by Sidney Lanfield's direction to go over in good style.
1941: **Nominations:** Best Scoring of a Musical Picture, Song ("Since I Kissed My Baby Goodbye")

YOUNG AMERICANS, THE
1993, 103 mins, UK ⓥ ⊙ ▭
D: Danny Cannon **A:** Harvey Keitel, Iain Glen, John Wood, Terence Rigby, Keith Allen, Viggo Mortensen (PFE/Live/Working Title/Trijbits-Worrell)

Harvey Keitel hits the mean, mixed-race streets of London in *The Young Americans*, a high-octane, in-your-face cop thriller that's got everything going for it except a well-rounded script. Keitel is New York–out-of-L.A. cop John Harris, seconded from the DEA as an adviser to London's boys in blue on the current spate of London clubland killings. The real villain is psychotic Yank drugster Frazer (Viggo Mortensen), whom Harris has been trailing from the US and who is trying to move in on the London drug scene. Pic's strength is its vivid sense of place and identity.

YOUNG AND THE DAMNED, THE
See: Los Olvidados

YOUNG AND THE PASSIONATE, THE
See: I Vitelloni

YOUNG AND WILLING
See: The Wild and the Willing

YOUNG BESS
1953, 111 mins, US
D: George Sidney A: Jean Simmons, Stewart Granger, Deborah Kerr, Charles Laughton, Kay Walsh, Guy Rolfe (M-G-M)

Young Bess is a romantic drama told against a Tudor setting. Romance phases are rich in emotion, court intrigue conjures suspense, and there is a suggestion of action throughout. It is not until gracious Catherine Parr (Deborah Kerr) becomes queen that Bess (Jean Simmons) takes up residence in the palace, finding love and happiness with the queen and her little stepbrother, the sickly Edward. When Henry VIII (Charles Laughton) dies, the queen marries the heroic Lord Admiral (Stewart Granger). Bess conceals her own infatuation for the dashing hero, but her feelings are found out and used by his evil brother.
1953: Nominations: Best Color Costume Design, Color Art Direction

YOUNG BILLY YOUNG
1969, 89 mins, US
D: Burt Kennedy A: Robert Mitchum, Angie Dickinson, Robert Walker, David Carradine, Jack Kelly, John Anderson (Talbot-Youngstein/United Artists)

Standard western plot undergoes generally good polishing. Burt Kennedy, who directed and scripted, could have tightened film for better effect. His climax lacks the suspense it should have carried. Robert Mitchum takes on a marshal's job in Lordsburg after he learns that his quarry may be found there. Robert Walker, an ornery youngster who wants his way, leaves Mitchum to his own devices until he discovers that a dozen gunmen have arrived to mow down the marshal.

YOUNGBLOOD
1986, 109 mins, US ⓥ ⊙
D: Peter Markle A: Rob Lowe, Cynthia Gibb, Patrick Swayze, Ed Lauter, Jim Youngs, Fionnula Flannagan (United Artists/Guber-Peters)

Picture has a simple premise: Rob Lowe yearns to leave the hard life on his father's farm to join a minor league Ca-

nadian hockey team. He is an innocent who, after less than a week, is seduced by his landlady (Fionnula Flanagan), ridiculed by his teammates, and enamored of the first girl he meets (Cynthia Gibb). Scenes on the ice look great, and Lowe truly looks like the son-of-a-gun hockey player he's supposed to be.

YOUNG CASSIDY
1965, 107 mins, US
D: Jack Cardiff, John Ford A: Rod Taylor, Julie Christie, Edith Evans, Michael Redgrave, Flora Robson, Maggie Smith (M-G-M)

Young Cassidy, biopic of Irish playwright Sean O'Casey in his sprouting years, like the majority of screen bio narratives, is episodic; in attempting to cover the many facets of his career, the film lacks the cohesion necessary for a full dramatic enactment of a historic personality. Started under John Ford's direction but taken over by Jack Cardiff when illness forced Ford to withdraw, pic opens in 1911 Dublin when O'Casey was feeling the stirrings of a talent which was to make him one of Ireland's great playwrights. Rod Taylor delivers a fine, strongly-etched characterization, believable both in his romantic scenes and as the writer who comes up the hard way. Splendid support is afforded by Maggie Smith.

YOUNG DOCTORS, THE
1961, 103 mins, US
D: Phil Karlson A: Fredric March, Ben Gazzara, Dick Clark, Ina Balin, Eddie Albert, Phyllis Love (Drexel/Millar-Turman)

The Young Doctors is an enlightening motion picture executed with restraint and clinical authenticity. The story represents an idealistic clash between two pathologists, one (Fredric March) the vet department head whose ideals have been blunted by years of red tape and frustration; the other (Ben Gazzara), his new assistant, young, aggressive, up-to-date and meticulous in his approach to the job. Veteran March creates a character of dimension and compassion. Gazzara, in another fine portrayal, plays with great reserve and intensity.

YOUNG EINSTEIN
1988, 89 mins, Australia ⓥ ⊙
D: Yahoo Serious A: Yahoo Serious, Odile Le Clezio, John Howard, Pee Wee Wilson, Su Cruickshank (Serious)

This wild, cheerful, off-the-wall comedy showcases the many talents of Australian satirist Yahoo Serious, who not only directed and plays the leading role, but also co-wrote, co-produced, edited, and handled the stunts. Pic posits young Einstein as the only son of eccentric apple farmers from Tasmania. He has a fertile mind and is forever discovering things. He sets off for mainland Australia to patent an invention and meets French genius Marie Curie (Odile Le Clezio) on a train; he also meets patents stealer Preston Preston (John Howard). Serious (born Greg Pead), a long-haired gangly clown, exhibits a brash and confident sense of humor, endearing personality, and a fondness for sight gags.

YOUNGER AND YOUNGER
1993, 99 mins, US ⓥ ⊙
D: Percy Adlon **A:** Donald Sutherland, Lolita Davidovich, Brendan Fraser, Julie Delpy, Sally Kellerman, Linda Hunt (Pelemele/BR/Duckster/Leora)

Superficially a family drama of a philandering father, *Younger and Younger* spins out from its simple premise into fantasy, music, black comedy and innumerable offbeat digressions. Although the film misses the bull's-eye, it's filled with intriguing elements and echoes of Adlon's earlier *Bagdad Cafe*. Film is set in a storage facility where the forgotten and marginal mingle with the hoi polloi. Jonathan Younger (Donald Sutherland) is the titular overseer, comporting himself in the manner of some exiled European royal. The real work falls upon his neglected wife, Penelope (Lolita Davidovich). Jonathan cares only about their son, Winston (Brendan Fraser), who is studying economics in England. He dreams of Winston's graduation and return to carry on the family business.

YOUNG FRANKENSTEIN
1974, 108 mins, US ⓥ ⊙
D: Mel Brooks **A:** Gene Wilder, Peter Boyle, Marty Feldman, Madeline Kahn, Cloris Leachman, Gene Hackman (20th Century-Fox)

Young Frankenstein emerges as a reverently satirical salute to the 1930s horror film genre. Gene Wilder plays the grandson of Baron Victor Frankenstein, creator of the monster. Wilder, an American medical college teacher, is lured back to Transylvania by old family retainer Richard Haydn. Wilder's assistant, the namesake descendant of Igor, is played by Marty Feldman. Peter Boyle is the mon-

ster, an artistically excellent blend of malice, pity, and comedy.
1974: Nominations: Best Adapted Screenplay, Sound

YOUNG GIRLS OF ROCHEFORT, THE
See: Les Demoiselles de Rochfort

YOUNG GUNS
1988, 107 mins, US ⓥ ⊙
D: Christopher Cain **A:** Emilio Estevez, Kiefer Sutherland, Lou Diamond Phillips, Charlie Sheen, Jack Palance, Terence Stamp (Morgan Creek)

Young Guns is a lame attempt at a brat pack *Wild Bunch*, executed without style or feel for the genre. British gang ringleader Terence Stamp seeks to better the lot of his renegade boys. His murder by town big shots prompts quick retaliation by the trigger-happy kids. Irresponsibility and inclination toward gunplay brand them as outlaws and sets in motion a chain of violence that leads to a fateful confrontation. As Billy the Kid, Emilio Estevez is the nominal star here, but no one really shines.

YOUNG GUNS II (YOUNG GUNS II—BLAZE OF GLORY)
1990, 103 mins, US ⓥ ⊙ ▭
D: Geoff Murphy **A:** Emilio Estevez, Kiefer Sutherland, Lou Diamond Phillips, Christian Slater, William Petersen, James Coburn (Morgan Creek)

Young Guns II exhausts its most inspired moment during the opening credits and fades into a copy of its predecessor—a slick, glossy MTV-style western. Oater picks up the adventures of Billy Bonney's Lincoln County gang a few years after the events in *Young Guns*. The story essentially involves the gang's hell-bent rush toward Mexico with a band of government men in hot pursuit. Christian Slater has a nice recurring bit as a gun with an inferiority complex over his lack of notoriety.
1990: Nomination: Best Song ("Blaze of Glory")

YOUNG HEARTS
See: Promised Land

YOUNG IN HEART, THE
1938, 91 mins, US ⓥ
D: Richard Wallace **A:** Janet Gaynor, Douglas Fairbanks Jr., Paulette Goddard, Roland Young, Billie Burke, Richard Carlson (Selznick/United Artists)

The Young in Heart takes its title from the little old woman whose pathetic eagerness for companionship touches the affections of a conniving and indolent family. When she meets them on a Paris train after they have been expelled from a Riviera resort, she is captivated by their tall tales of troubles and delighted with their courage in their predicament. Acting of the entire cast is superb. Janet Gaynor and Douglas Fairbanks Jr. sparkle as the pseudo-thick-skinned children of the worthless family, while Roland Young and Billie Burke are brilliant as the parents who are soft-hearted in spite of their worst intentions.

YOUNG LIONS, THE
1958, 167 mins, US ♥ ⊙ ▭
D: Edward Dmytryk A: Marlon Brando, Montgomery Clift, Dean Martin, Hope Lange, May Britt, Barbara Rush (20th Century-Fox)

The Young Lions is a canvas of World War II of scope and stature. Marlon Brando's interpretation of the young Nazi officer; Montgomery Clift, the drafted GI of Jewish heritage; and Dean Martin as a frankly would-be draft-dodger until the realities of war catch up with him are standout all the way. Dmytryk effectively highlights the human values on both the German and American homefronts. Film gravitates from the boot camp in the States to the fall of France, the North African campaign, the deterioration of the Third Reich, and the gradual disillusionment of the once ardent Nazi as symbolized by Brando. Edward Anhalt's screenplay captures shade and nuance of role in pithy, pungent dialogue.
1958: Nominations: Best B&W Cinematography, Scoring of a Dramatic Picture, Sound

YOUNG LOVERS, THE
1954, 95 mins, UK
D: Anthony Asquith A: Odile Versois, David Knight, David Kossoff, Joseph Tomelty, Theodore Bikel, Paul Carpenter (Group)

The political conflict between east and west is brought home in this moving romantic drama. The boy (David Knight) works in the code room of the American Embassy in London; the girl (Odile Versois) is the daughter of the minister of an Iron Curtain legation. She finds she's being followed; his telephone messages are being intercepted. Both the embassy and the legation fear that confidential information is getting into the hands of the wrong people, so the girl is ordered home

and the boy is placed under arrest. The plot pinpoints the emotions of the young lovers without indulging in unnecessary politics, using rare touches of humor to relieve a tense situation with great skill.

YOUNG LOVERS, THE
1964, 110 mins, US
D: Samuel Goldwyn Jr. A: Peter Fonda, Sharon Hugueny, Nick Adams, Deborah Walley, Beatrice Straight, Malachi Throne (M-G-M)

Samuel Goldwyn Jr.'s The Young Lovers has a lot of things going for it. While the story about young, unwed parents-to-be is no shocker, the talk is frank, and the film's focus on the problems of the unwed father rather than the mother is the twist. Fonda has uncomfortable moments as an art student who intends to live a free, bachelor life, and his voice doesn't carry conviction in several scenes. Sharon Hugueny also suffers acting lapses, but scores by making apparent her transition from shy teenager to mature young adult.

YOUNG MAN OF MUSIC
See: Young Man with a Horn

YOUNG MAN WITH A HORN (YOUNG MAN OF MUSIC)
1950, 111 mins, US ♥
D: Michael Curtiz A: Kirk Douglas, Lauren Bacall, Doris Day, Hoagy Carmichael, Juano Hernandez (Warner)

For the jazz devotee this is nearly two hours of top trumpet notes. For the regular filmgoer, it is good drama. Kirk Douglas's single-minded concentration on a horn and the notes that come from it sets the character up for an eventual downfall. When his marriage to Lauren Bacall falls apart, he hits the bottle, only to be saved by the wholesome affection that band canary Doris Day has had for him over the years.

YOUNG MR. LINCOLN
1939, 101 mins, US ♥ ⊙
D: John Ford A: Henry Fonda, Alice Brady, Marjorie Weaver, Arleen Whelan, Richard Cromwell, Donald Meek (20th Century-Fox/Cosmopolitan)

As the title implies, this deals with the Great Emancipator's early days, emphasizing his inherent honesty, fearlessness, shrewdness, plus such homely qualities as being a champ rail-splitter mixed with an avid hunger for book learning. As motion picture entertainment, however, Young Mr. Lincoln resolves itself down to a courtroom drama. He's called upon to extricate Richard Cromwell and Eddie Quillan from a murder rap. Henry Fonda is capital in the highlight scenes in which he languorously addresses the small group in front of the general store. The major shortcoming of this film is the rather lethargic production and direction.

1939: Nomination: Best Original Story

YOUNG MR. PITT, THE
1942, 110 mins, UK
D: Carol Reed A: Robert Donat, Robert Morley, Phyllis Calvert, John Mills, Max Adrian, Felix Aylmer (20th Century-Fox)

There is so much to acclaim and so little with which to find fault in this production. The 18th-century period details have seldom been better reproduced. Story is based on the political career of William Pitt Jr. (Robert Donat), who was Prime Minister of England at age 24. Robert Morley towers above the rest of the excellent cast. Donat acts with meticulous earnestness and sincerity, but seemingly lacks inspiration. In sharp contrast, John Mills, in a relatively minor role, is impressive without resorting to heroics.

YOUNG ONE, THE
1961, 94 mins, US/Mexico
D: Luis Buñuel A: Zachary Scott, Key Meersman, Bernie Hamilton, Crahan Denton, Claudio Brook (Werker/Olmeca)

The Young One is an odd, inconclusive attempt to interweave two sizzling themes—race prejudice in the deep South and an almost *Lolita*-like sex situation. The story takes place on an island wild game preserve off South Carolina, occupied by an unsavory gamekeeper (Zachary Scott) and a 14-year-old orphan girl whose grandfather has just expired. Into this potentially explosive scene drifts a hip-talking black (Bernie Hamilton), falsely accused of rape and on the run. Luis Buñuel does an alert, perceptive job of directing, succeeding in getting the Carolina geographical flavor out of the Mexican location. But his efforts are lamentably diluted by the unsatisfactory nature of the story.

YOUNG ONES, THE
1962, 108 mins, UK ⓥ ▭
D: Sidney J. Furie A: Cliff Richard, Robert Morley, Carole Gray, Richard O'Sullivan, Melvyn Hayes, The Shadows (Associated British)

Cliff Richard is the leader of a youth club whose humble little clubhouse is endangered when a millionaire property tycoon, Richard's father, buys the land on which it is situated. The club decides to fight him, and this involves raising $4,000 to challenge the lease. To do this, they take over a derelict theater to stage a show. The choreography is agile and sharp. Main fault of the film is that the screenplay and dialogue are uneven. However, Robert Morley, as the tycoon, brings some adult wit and irony to the screen. Richard is inexperienced as an actor but has a pleasant charm and sings well within his range.

YOUNG POISONER'S HANDBOOK, THE
1995, 106 mins, UK/Germany ⓥ
D: Benjamin Ross A: Hugh O'Conor, Antony Sher, Ruth Sheen, Roger Lloyd Pack, Charlotte Coleman, Paul Stacey (Mass/Kinowelt/Haut & Court)

An expressive piece of grotesquerie, *The Young Poisoner's Handbook* takes a darkly comic look at a sinister British lad who, in the 1960s, pursued "a career as a poisoner." Based on a true story, the film has a lively sense of style and is cuttingly satiric about established norms of British life and medical practise. Fourteen-year-old chemistry genius Graham Young (Hugh O'Conor) lives with his father, step-mother, and sister, all caricatured to the nth degree of hideousness. The dispassionate youngster murders his step-mother with poisoned chocolates. Convicted, Graham lands in a hospital for the criminally insane, where Dr. Zeigler (Antony Sher) believes that Graham's outstanding intellect makes him a prime candidate for salvation. He's reintroduced to society and resumes his "career" on a wider scale than before.

YOUNG SAVAGES, THE
1961, 103 mins, US
D: John Frankenheimer A: Burt Lancaster, Dina Merrill, Shelley Winters, Edward Andrews, Larry Gates, Telly Savalas (United Artists)

The Young Savages is a kind of nonmusical east side variation on *West Side Story*, set against the backdrop of New York's teeming East Harlem district. Director John Frankenheimer and cameraman Lionel Lindon catch the wild fury of gang warfare, twisting, tilting, pulling way back and zeroing in to follow and frame the excitement. But there is nothing Frankenheimer can do to make the yarn itself stand tall as screen fiction. The story is that of three teenage Italian lads who murder a blind Puerto Rican boy of 15, the top warlord of a rival gang. Scrupulous d.a.'s assistant Burt Lancaster's search for truth and justice and familiarity with the asphalt jungle lead him to make a valiant courtroom stand on behalf of the boys he is supposed to be trying to convict.

YOUNG SCARFACE
See: Brighton Rock

YOUNG SHERLOCK HOLMES (YOUNG SHERLOCK HOLMES AND THE PYRAMID OF FEAR)
1985, 109 mins, US Ⓥ ⊙
D: Barry Levinson **A:** Nicholas Rowe, Alan Cox, Sophie Ward, Anthony Higgins, Susan Fleetwood, Freddie Jones (Paramount)

Young Sherlock Holmes is another Steven Spielberg film that functions as those lamps made from driftwood and coffee tables made from redwood burl and hatchcovers: it's not art but they serve their purpose and sell by the millions. The formula this time is, what might have happened had Sherlock Holmes and John Watson first met as teenagers? As usual, Spielberg's team isn't really as interested in the answer as it is in fooling around with the visual possibilities conjured by George Lucas's Industrial Light & Magic shop.
1985: Nomination: Best Visual Effects

YOUNG STRANGER, THE
1956, 83 mins, US Ⓥ ⊙
D: John Frankenheimer **A:** James MacArthur, Kim Hunter, James Daly, James Gregory, Whit Bissell, Jeff Silver (RKO)

A story of conflict between youth and parents, the plot indulges in one-note dramatics that provide very little shading between the black and white of the problem, yet which are effective within the aim of entertainment. James MacArthur plays the rebellious son of picture producer James Daly and Kim Hunter. Filmmaking keeps the father too busy to give much time to his son, but he realizes the error after the son is arrested for socking a theater manager and a cop.

YOUNG TOM EDISON
1940, 85 mins, US
D: Norman Taurog **A:** Mickey Rooney, Fay Bainter, George Bancroft, Virginia Weidler, Eugene Pallette (M-G-M)

Young Tom Edison covers the inventor's life as a boy in Port Huron, Michigan, around 1863. It details his inquisitiveness on chemicals and labor-saving gadgets and his disregard for school curriculum and rules. No attempt is made to paint him as a youthful genius. He's an all-American boy; an inventive opportunist. Mickey Rooney plays the young inventor with sympathetic restraint, with no obvious stunts or gags. Story revolves around the home life of the Edison family. There's the lovable and protecting mother (Fay Bainter), the stern father (George Bancroft) who fails to understand his son, and a younger sister (Virginia Weidler) sympathetic to her brother and his problems.

YOUNG WINSTON
1972, 157 mins, UK Ⓥ ▭
D: Richard Attenborough **A:** Simon Ward, Robert Shaw, Anne Bancroft, Jack Hawkins, Ian Holm, Anthony Hopkins (Columbia/Open Road)

Rate this biopic of Winston Churchill's early years as both a brilliant artistic achievement and a fascinating, highly enjoyable film. It touches on his lonely childhood and only occasional contact with his politician father and socialite American mother, school experience, war correspondent stints in India and the Sudan, and on to his first political defeat and ultimate vindication. Far from a sycophantic paean to a great man in the bud, pic manages a believable portrait of an ambitious and sometimes arrogant young man.
1972: Nominations: Best Original Story & Screenplay, Costume Design, Art Direction

YOU ONLY LIVE ONCE
1937, 85 mins, US Ⓥ
D: Fritz Lang **A:** Sylvia Sidney, Henry Fonda, Barton MacLane, Jean Dixon, William Gargan, Warren Hymer (Wanger/United Artists)

You Only Live Once is full of stark and bitter moments, but these bite no more deeply than deftly wrought scenes of tenderness. The self-sacrificing love of the girl for the ex-convict reaches a high level of heart-tugging during their flight as fugitives from the law. Fritz Lang's penchant for mob scenes is indulged in only one sequence after Henry Fonda has been found guilty of causing the death of six men in a holdup. On the spectacular side are the gas bombing of money-truck guards in a one-man robbery, the guile used by Fonda in getting out of the deathhouse, and the bartering which goes on between the escaped convict and the warden just inside the prison gates.

YOU ONLY LIVE TWICE

1967, 117 mins, UK ⓥ ⊙ ▭

D: Lewis Gilbert **A:** Sean Connery, Akiko Wakabayashi, Tetsuro Tamba, Mie Hama, Karin Dor, Donald Pleasence (United Artists/Eon)

Film begins with a prologue in which a US astronaut's space walk is interrupted by another spacecraft that, crocodile-style, opens its jaws and swallows the capsule. US government is peeved at what it assumes to be Russian aggression, and 007 is assigned to locate the missing rocket before war breaks out between the two nuclear powers. Sean Connery plays 007 with his usual finesse. Donald Pleasence makes a suitably menacing heavy.

YOU'RE A BIG BOY NOW

1966, 98 mins, US ⓥ

D: Francis Coppola **A:** Elizabeth Hartman, Geraldine Page, Julie Harris, Peter Kastner, Rip Torn, Michael Dunn (Seven Arts)

You're a Big Boy Now has a simple premise—a virginal young man growing into manhood, not so much through his own efforts as through those about him. Peter Kastner plays a roller-skating stack boy in a New York public library and is somewhat of a dreamer. Father Rip Torn decides the best way for his son to grow up would be to move out of the family home. Lad becomes ensconced in a rooming house run by Julie Harris. With the help of his dope-inclined pal (Tony Bill) and a pretty library assistant (Karen Black), the boy is launched on his road to manhood, which takes him into the arms of a way-out, Greenwich Village discotheque dish (Elizabeth Hartman).

1966: Nomination: Best Supp. Actress (Geraldine Page)

YOU'RE IN THE ARMY NOW [1937]

See: O.H.M.S.

YOU'RE IN THE ARMY NOW

1941, 79 mins, US

D: Lewis Seiler **A:** Jimmy Durante, Jane Wyman, Phil Silvers, Regis Toomey, George Meeker, Donald MacBride (Warner)

Though it is a bit corny in spots and lays the slapstick on heavily, here is a comedy of soldier life that completely entertains. Jimmy Durante and Phil Silvers, trying to interest a recruiting officer in a vacuum cleaner, accidentally get themselves enlisted. As buck privates, they become guardhouse regulars by getting themselves into one jam after another.

YOU'RE MY EVERYTHING

1949, 94 mins, US

D: Walter Lang **A:** Dan Dailey, Anne Baxter, Anne Revere, Buster Keaton, Stanley Ridges, Alan Mowbray (20th Century-Fox)

You're My Everything is practically a synthesis of all the backstage musicals ever filmed, including the songs. The direction doesn't perceptibly freshen the material. Dan Dailey plays a hoofer who meets and marries Anne Baxter when his show is playing the Hub. As an inductee into the chorus she's an enthusiastic wife, but when he's screen tested, she's drafted for a love scene opposite him, thereby getting the picture contract and becoming the hot sensation of the 1920s.

YOU'RE NEVER TOO YOUNG

1955, 102 mins, US

D: Norman Taurog **A:** Dean Martin, Jerry Lewis, Diana Lynn, Nina Foch, Raymond Burr (Paramount)

In *You're Never Too Young*, Dean Martin and Jerry Lewis star in one of their funniest pictures. Screenplay is inconsequential, but who cares as long as it provides Lewis with the skeleton for his madcap antics. He has a field day as a barber's apprentice who unknowingly obtains possession of a stolen diamond. He romps around a girls' school, falls in a pool, vies with Martin for Diana Lynn's affections, disrupts a faculty meeting, does a take-off on Humphrey Bogart, and upsets Martin in an unmanageable barber's chair.

YOU'RE ONLY YOUNG ONCE

1938, 77 mins, US

D: George B. Seitz **A:** Lewis Stone, Cecilia Parker, Mickey Rooney, Fay Holden, Frank Craven, Ann Rutherford (M-G-M)

First of the series involving the Hardy family is *You're Only Young Once*. There's the kindly judge, the daughter suffering all the exquisite torture of young love, the son in his first long pants, the mother who rules, and the old maiden aunt with a few ideas. The judge (Lewis Stone) maneuvers his family into a trip to Catalina, where he wants to catch a swordfish. There Mickey Rooney encounters womanly Eleanor Lynn and almost becomes a man. Cecilia Parker romances with Ted Pearson, a life guard, who is already married, and the judge has a patience-disturbing time with the fish not biting.

YOU'RE TELLING ME
1934, 66 mins, US
D: Erle C. Kenton **A:** W. C. Fields, Joan Marsh, Buster Crabbe, Adrienne Ames, Louise Carter, Kathleen Howard (Paramount)

The kind of comedy that Chaplin used to do in two reels, but stretched out to run an even six. Thanks to J. P. McEvoy's dialogue and the sustained pantomiming of W. C. Fields, it's passable comedy. Fields is a dumb but likeable guy who invents things and ruins his daughter's social chances by getting stewed and taking off his shoes in the parlor. Papa's big invention is a puncture-proof tire that finally nets him a million.

YOURS, MINE AND OURS
1968, 111 mins, US Ⓥ ⊙
D: Melville Shavelson **A:** Lucille Ball, Henry Fonda, Van Johnson, Tom Bosley, Jennifer Leak, Timothy Matthieson (United Artists/Desilu-Walden)

Yours, Mine and Ours is socko family entertainment. Literate scripting, excellent performances, and superior direction are underscored by a top-notch production. Director Shavelson and Mort Lachman adroitly intermingle the amusing, as well as dramatic, angles of mature second love, raising a family, and adolescence. Lucille Ball plays a widow, old enough to know her responsibilities but young enough to want male companionship. Henry Fonda is cast perfectly as the widower. Thereafter, the sometimes-awkward, always-loving melding of the two families proceeds.

YOU'VE GOT MAIL
1998, 119 mins, US Ⓥ ⊙
D: Nora Ephron **A:** Tom Hanks, Meg Ryan, Parker Posey, Greg Kinnear, Jean Stapleton, Steve Zahn (Warner)

The long-awaited reteaming of the *Sleepless in Seattle* combo of Tom Hanks and Meg Ryan and director Nora Ephron puts a fine contempo spin on the time-tested premise of anonymous, affectionate pen pals who dislike each other in person. In many ways, new pic is the most successful version yet of this familiar premise. Corporate heir Joe Fox (Hanks) and shop owner Kathleen Kelly (Ryan) both work on the Upper West Side. Joe is planning to open a mammoth book store, while Kathleen runs a tiny children's bookshop.

When she learns that he's about to steamroll her shop, her appreciation of his quick-witted charm gives way to disapproval of his soulless guile. Unwittingly, however, Joe and Kathleen are each other's cyber soul mates, exchanging daily E-mail under pseudonymous screen names. Pic makes a good point about the difference between public personae and private selves, indicating correctly how we can be more open with people we barely know.

YOU WERE NEVER LOVELIER
1942, 98 mins, US Ⓥ
D: William A. Seiter **A:** Fred Astaire, Rita Hayworth, Adolphe Menjou, Larry Parks, Xavier Cugat, Leslie Brooks (Columbia)

A Jerome Kern–Johnny Mercer score, Fred Astaire and Rita Hayworth dancing and singing, and Xavier Cugat's crack rhumba band are an excellent combination of entertainment vitamins. This yarn concerns the efforts of hotel magnate Adolphe Menjou to get his daughter (Rita Hayworth) interested in romance. Until she takes the plunge, his two lovesick youngest girls must wait. This is purely escapist screen fare, with Buenos Aires for a background. There isn't even a hint of the war, and that is some compensation for the few slow spots in the story's unfolding.

YUKINOJO HENGE
(AN ACTOR'S REVENGE;
YUKINOJO'S REVENGE)
1963, 113 mins, Japan Ⓥ ▢
D: Kon Ichikawa **A:** Kazuo Hasegawa, Fujiko Yamamoto, Ayako Wakao, Raizo Ichikawa, Shintaro Katsu, Ganjiri Nakamura (Daiei)

A stylized film, *An Actor's Revenge* mixes Kabuki theater with ritual, action, and humor into an entertaining opus. The hero is an actor who impersonates women, for there are no women in Kabuki. But he carries his impersonations into real life, too. He has sworn vengeance on those who ruined his father's business and drove him to suicide. Director Kon Ichikawa has done a sort of play-within-a-play pic. Outdoor shots are staged on sets which add to the ambiguity but are a visual delight. Kazuo Hasegawa is extraordinary as the actor.

YUKINOJO'S REVENGE
See: Yukinojo Henge

Z

1969, 126 mins, France/Algeria Ⓥ ⊙

D: Constantin Costa-Gavras **A:** Yves Montand, Irene Papas, Jean-Louis Trintignant, Jacques Perrin, Francois Perrier, Charles Denner (Reganne/ONCIC)

Z is a punchy political pic that mixes action, violence, and conspiracy on a robust, lavish scale. Originally subtitled "the anatomy of a political assassination," it is based on the murder of a noted progressive Greek political figure some years earlier. There is an idealistic professor fighting against A-bombs (Yves Montand), his wife who fears for his safety (Irene Papas), and a young judge (Jean-Louis Trintignant) put on the case on the theory he will not upset things after the professor is killed, but who turns out to be surprisingly strong and obdurate. Director Costa-Gavras manages not to exploit violence and political innuendo for its own sake.
1969: Best Foreign Language Film

ZABRISKIE POINT

1970, 112 mins, US Ⓥ ⊙ ▭

D: Michelangelo Antonioni **A:** Mark Frechette, Daria Halprin, Paul Fix, G. D. Spradlin, Bill Garaway, Kathleen Cleaver (M-G-M)

Michelangelo Antonioni makes the US social scene, and distills from his notes some arresting photographic moments. Antonioni has sought to bring into focus the student versus establishment conflict. Probably the most compelling footage of *Zabriskie Point* is the ending, in which things representative of the ultra "haves" go up in explosions as the remnants of modern big business hit the sky, piece by piece, and hang in a dangling collage of symbolism.

ZANDY'S BRIDE

1974, 116 mins, US ▭

D: Jan Troell **A:** Gene Hackman, Liv Ullmann, Eileen Heckart, Susan Tyrrell, Sam Bottoms, Joe Santos (Warner)

Zandy's Bride is a good period frontier romantic melodrama starring Gene Hackman as a gruff cattle rancher and Liv Ullmann as the mail-order bride who softens him up. Star performances sustain Jan Troell's delicate but placid direction. Set in 1870 in upstate California's rugged Big Sur, story takes Hackman from a crude, thoughtless hermit to a loving husband and father. The plot line is thin but sufficient.

ZARDOZ

1974, 104 mins, UK/US Ⓥ ⊙ ▭

D: John Boorman **A:** Sean Connery, Charlotte Rampling, Sara Kestelman, John Alderton, Sally Anne Newton, Niall Buggy (20th Century-Fox)

Zardoz is a futuristic, metaphysical, and anthropological drama. The direction is good; the script, a brilliant premise which unfortunately washes out in climactic sound and fury; the production, outstanding, particularly special visual effects which belie the film's modest cost. The story, set in 2293, postulates a world in which the highest order beings are an elite group of effete aesthetes, eternally youthful on a spiritual plane. Sean Connery rises from the lower ranks to overthrow the new order and recycle mankind into its older pattern.

ZAZA

1939, 83 mins, US

D: George Cukor **A:** Claudette Colbert, Herbert Marshall, Bert Lahr, Helen Westley, Constance Collier, Genevieve Tobin (Paramount)

Zaza is a mischievous and flirtatious vaudville soubrette in France. Forcing introduction with Herbert Marshall, pair fall in love and launch an affair. Claudette Colbert hits a sincere and scintillating portrayal of the tempestuous Zaza. Her coy flirtation with Marshall and her later dramatic passages are a finely tempered characterization. Play does not lend itself to fast-paced picture technique, and director George Cukor wisely steers away from such a radical change.

ZAZIE DANS LE METRO

1959, 92 mins, France Ⓥ ⊙

D: Louis Malle **A:** Catherine Demongeot, Philippe Noiret, Carla Marlier, Vittorio Caprioli, Hubert Deschamps, Jacques Dufilho (Nouvelles Editions)

Director Louis Malle's first comedy is a sort of intellectual slapstick entry. It has some risible bits but is, in all, somewhat diffuse. Zazie (Catherine Demongeot) is a 12-year-old girl whose mother leaves her with an uncle (Philippe Noiret) when she comes into Paris for a day with her latest lover. Zazie is off on a round of adventures in a weird, colorful Paris. Pic has obviously been influenced in style by the better Yank animated pictures and Mack

Sennett comedies. Malle shows a wealth of invention and uses color artfully. Vehicle moves at whirlwind pace.

ZED AND TWO NOUGHTS, A
1985, 115 mins, UK/Netherlands ⊗
D: Peter Greenaway A: Andrea Ferreol, Brian Deacon, Eric Deacon, Frances Barber, Joss Ackland, Gerard Thoolen (Artificial Eye/BFI/Channel Four/Allarts/VPRO)

Despite its visual pyrotechnics and an impressively woven texture of intellectual allusions, Peter Greenaway's feature remains the work of a highly talented British eccentric who hasn't managed to thresh out his obscurantist preoccupations to connect with major concerns or touch the emotions. The action centers on a zoo where Greenaway is intent on upturning the seamier side of animal existence in captivity (including that of homo sapiens). Meanwhile, pseudo-philosophical conundrums are tossed at the audience like peanuts to caged animals. Needless to say, the resulting stilted dialogue does not make the acting much of a treat.

ZEE & CO.
(X, Y & ZEE)
1972, 110 mins, UK ⊗
D: Brian G. Hutton A: Elizabeth Taylor, Michael Caine, Susannah York, Margaret Leighton, John Standing, Mary Larkin (Columbia)

Not in years have three people more deserved the star billing they get in this Love Story for adults. Elizabeth Taylor and Susannah York both turn in performances that fully capture the characters of Edna O'Brien's screenplay. Michael Caine keeps up beautifully with the pace set by his co-stars. Taylor, the "Zee" of the title, and Caine are a long-married couple whose relationship has turned into a love-hate affair that leads into Caine's affair with York.

ZELIG
1983, 84 mins, US ⊗ ⊙
D: Woody Allen A: Woody Allen, Mia Farrow, Garrett Brown, Stephanie Farrow, Will Holt, Sol Lomita (Rollins-Joffe/Orion)

Lampooning documentary tradition by structuring the entire film as a meticulously crafted bogus documentary, Woody Allen tackles some serious stuff en route. More positively, Zelig is consistently funny, though more academic than boulevardier. Allen plays the eponymous Leonard Zelig, a one-time legend of the 1920s-30s whose weak personality and need to be liked caused him to become the ultimate conformist. Through the use of doctored photos and staged black and white footage cannily—and usually undetectably—matched with authentic newsreels and stock footage of the period, Allen is seen intermingling with everyone from the Hearst crowd at San Simeon to the likes of Pope Pius XI and even Adolf Hitler.

1983: Nomination: Best Cinematography, Costume Design

ZENOBIA
1939, 71 mins, US
D: Gordon M. Douglas A: Oliver Hardy, Harry Langdon, Billie Burke, Alice Brady (United Artists)

Hal Roach introduces Oliver Hardy in straight comedy. Teamed with Harry Langdon, Hardy gives out with a minimum of slapstick antics and knockabout stunts. Slender story does not warrant the amount of footage. Script is a series of incidents tied together in not-too-compact form. As the doctor in an 1870s Mississippi town, Hardy is called on to treat Zenobia, an elephant belonging to a carnival pitchman (Langdon). Pachyderm gratefully follows Hardy around, through buildings and into a reception for his daughter. Matter winds up in court, with Langdon suing Hardy for alienation of the beast's affections.

ZENTROPA
See: Europa

ZEPPELIN
1971, 97 mins, UK ⊗ ⊠
D: Etienne Perier A: Michael York, Elke Sommer, Peter Carsten, Marius Goring, Anton Diffring, Andrew Keir (Getty & Fromkess/Warner)

Zeppelin settles for being just another wartime melodrama. Story deals with Britain's concern about German's new World War I weapon, the Zeppelin, the monstrous, looming airship that made Britain vulnerable. Indication that the Germans have perfected a new and even more effective Zeppelin jerks the British high-ups into swift action. A young Scottish lieutenant of Anglo-German parentage (Michael York) looks the perfect spy. When called on to volunteer to "defect" to the Germans and dig out the secrets of the new Zeppelin, he reluctantly agrees.

ZIEGFELD FOLLIES
1945, 116 mins, US Ⓥ ⊙
D: Vincente Minnelli [George Sidney, Norman Taurog, Roy Del Ruth, Lemuel Ayers] **A:** Fred Astaire, Lucille Ball, Fanny Brice, Judy Garland, Gene Kelly, William Powell (M-G-M)

Even Florenz Ziegfeld (William Powell) would be dazzled by this film's color, sets, and routines, which are far above the capacities of his day. But Zieggy would have missed his nudes, his pleasantly risque interludes, and a certain heartwarming which came with the old productions. Pic opens with a dreamland set out of which Powell emerges, apparently comfortably fixed in celestial heights à la Ziegfeld. As the great producer, he reflects on his greatest successes. It's all stupendous, terrific, colossal—practically everyone would agree. Even Zieggy.

ZIEGFELD GIRL
1941, 135 mins, US Ⓥ ⊙
D: Robert Z. Leonard, Busby Berkeley **A:** James Stewart, Judy Garland, Hedy Lamarr, Lana Turner, Tony Martin, Jackie Cooper (M-G-M)

The attempt to balance three parallel dramas of the lives of three Ziegfeld showgirls, plus interpolation of two extended displays of Ziegfeldian production sequences, prevents smooth unfolding of the piece and results in several dull passages. Smart casting provides vivid contrast. There's Judy Garland, youthful but veteran trouper, with showmanship, personality, and talent; Hedy Lamarr, with her striking and reserved beauty; and the sexy Lana Turner, who succumbs to the easiest way for a brief fling at luxury. Director Robert Z. Leonard provides a most capable directorial job.

ZIMLYA
(EARTH)
1930, 63 mins, USSR ⊗
D: Aleksandr Dovzhenko **A:** Semyon Svashenko, Stepan Shkurat, Mikola Nademsky, Yelena Maksimova, Pyotr Masokha (VUFKU)

Earth embodies the quintessence of Aleksandr Dovzhenko's philosophy of life: that Marxist tenets are related to the attachment of simple men to the land of their forefathers. Showing how the machines help the collectivization of farms in the Ukraine, *Earth* remains one of the finest examples of the poetic cinema of the silent period.

ZOMBIES
See: Dawn of the Dead

ZOO IN BUDAPEST
1933, 82 mins, US
D: Rowland V. Lee **A:** Loretta Young, Gene Raymond, O. P. Heggie, Wally Albright, Paul Fix (Fox)

Seemingly what producer Jesse Lasky has tried to do is to make a picture which has in it something of the strange romance and atmosphere of *Liliom* and an element of Hollywood punch. He has gotten both things, and they don't blend. The story has still another facet, a submotif of bitter social satire in suggestions of similarities between the animals in the zoo and some of the people that cross the screen. However, there can be no two views of the picture's pictorial beauty. There are several sequences of night falling over a lake in a zoo peopled with strange creatures that are a knockout.

ZORBA THE GREEK
1964, 142 mins, US Ⓥ
D: Michael Cacoyannis **A:** Anthony Quinn, Alan Bates, Irene Papas, Lila Kedrova, George Foundas, Eleni Anousaki (20th Century-Fox)

Zorba the Greek is a paean to life in all its diverse aspects, ranging from the farcical to the tragic, as epitomized by the title character. This Zorba, beautifully played by Anthony Quinn, is a free soul who is totally committed to life no matter what it holds. Michael Cacoyannis' screenplay is so packed with incidents of varying moods that some of the more important ones cannot be developed fully. The story takes place in a remote part of Crete where Zorba has come as the self-appointed aide-de-camp to a young, inhibited Englishman of Greek parentage (Alan Bates), who intends to reopen an old lignite mine he has inherited. Their subsequent adventures, wherein Bates finally learns to live à la Zorba, comprise the body of the film.

1964: Best Supp. Actress (Lila Kedrova), B&W Cinematography, B&W Art Direction

Nominations: Best Picture, Director, Actor (Anthony Quinn), Adapted Screenplay

ZORRO, THE GAY BLADE
1981, 93 mins, US Ⓥ
D: Peter Medak **A:** George Hamilton, Lauren Hutton, Brenda Vaccaro, Ron Leibman, Donovan Scott, James Booth (20th Century-Fox/Simon)

Despite an inspired, offbeat performance by George Hamilton, *Zorro, the Gay Blade* doesn't have nearly enough gags to sustain its 93 minutes. This is a *Zorro* with a very dull edge. Film is set years ago in California where Don Diego Vega, offspring of the legendary Zorro, is called upon to pick up his father's sword. But Hamilton's Vega, righting the wrongs of the poor villagers against leader Ron Leibman, injures his foot and can no longer carry on his heroic deeds. Luckily, his long-lost English brother appears out of nowhere and takes on the Zorro persona. The contrast between the two Zorros is initially quite funny, but there is nothing intriguing or original through the rest of the action.

ZULU

1964, 135 mins, UK ⓥ ⊙ ▭
D: Cy Endfield **A:** Stanley Baker, Jack Hawkins, Ulla Jacobsson, James Booth, Michael Caine, Nigel Green (Paramount/ Diamond)

Based on a famous heroic exploit of 1879, when a handful of British soldiers withstood an onslaught by 4,000 Zulu warriors at Rorke's Drift, *Zulu* is distinguished by its notable onscreen values, enhanced by top-quality lensing by Stephen Dade. It also has an intelligent screenplay that avoids most of the obvious cliches. It keeps the traditional British stiff upper-lip attitudes down to the barest minimum. The high all-around standard of acting is one of the notable features. Stanley Baker turns in a thoroughly convincing portrayal as the resolute Royal Engineers officer, with an effective contrasting study by Michael Caine as a supercilious lieutenant.

ZULU DAWN

1979, 117 mins, UK ⓥ ⊙ ▭
D: Douglas Hickox **A:** Burt Lancaster, Peter O'Toole, Simon Ward, John Mills, Nigel Davenport, Denholm Elliott (Lamitas/ Samarkand)

The subject of *Zulu Dawn* is the Battle of Islandlhwana, wherein some 1,500 redcoats were slaughtered by 16 times their number of Zulu warriors led by legendary chief Cetshwayo. The film is a sort of "prequel" to the 1964 picture *Zulu*. The action sequences are superbly handled, as are the scenes in which the men and material are assembled and manoeuvered. Such banality as there is is confined to the expositional sequences, which are quickly gotten out of the way.

Directors Index

ing Man, The; It Came from Outer Space; Mouse that Roared, The; Revenge of the Creature

Arnold, Newt *Allan Quatermain and the Lost City of Gold*

Arzner, Dorothy *Anybody's Woman; Honor Among Lovers; Nana*

Ashby, Hal *Being There; Bound for Glory; Coming Home; 8 Million Ways to Die; Harold and Maude; Landlord, The; Last Detail, The; Lookin' to Get Out; Shampoo*

Asher, Robert *Bulldog Breed, The; Make Mine Mink; Stitch in Time, A*

Asher, William *Beach Party; How to Stuff a Wild Bikini; Johnny Cool; Muscle Beach Party; Night Warning*

Ashley, Christopher *Jeffrey*

Asquith, Anthony *Browning Version, The; Carrington V. C.; Demi-Paradise, The; Doctor's Dilemma, The; Fanny by Gaslight; Guns of Darkness; Importance of Being Earnest, The; Libel; Millionairess, The; Moscow Nights; Pygmalion; Uncensored; Unfinished Symphony, The; V.I.P.s, The; Way to the Stars, The; We Dive at Dawn; Winslow Boy, The; Yellow Rolls-Royce, The; Young Lovers, The*

Attenborough, Richard *Bridge Too Far, A; Chaplin; Chorus Line, A; Cry Freedom; Gandhi; In Love and War; Magic; Oh! What a Lovely War; Shadowlands; Young Winston*

Auer, John H. *City that Never Sleeps*

August, Bille *House of the Spirits, The; Pelle Erobreren*

Auster, Paul *Blue in the Face*

Austin, Michael *Killing Dad; Princess Caraboo*

Auzins, Igor *We of the Never Never*

Avakian, Aram *11 Harrowhouse*

Avary, Roger *Killing Zoe*

Averback, Hy *I Love You, Alice B. Toklas!; Suppose They Gave a War and Nobody Came?; Where Were You When the Lights Went Out?*

Avildsen, John G. *Formula, The; Happy New Year; Joe; Karate Kid, The; Karate Kid Part II, The; Karate Kid Part III, The; Neighbors; Power of One, The; Rocky; Rocky V; Save the Tiger; Slow Dancing in the Big City; W. W. and the Dixie Dancekings*

Avis, Meiert *Far from Home*

Avnet, Jon *Fried Green Tomatoes; Up Close and Personal; War, The*

Axel, Gabriel *Babettes Gaestebud*

Axelrod, George *Lord Love a Duck; Secret Life of an American Wife, The*

Ayers, Roy Del Ruth, Lemuel *Ziegfeld Follies*

Aykroyd, Dan *Nothing But Trouble*

Babenco, Hector *At Play in the Fields of the Lord; Ironweed; Kiss of the Spider Woman; Pixote*

Bachmann, Gideon *Ciao, Federico!*

Bacon, Lloyd *Boy Meets Girl; Call Me Mister; Footlight Parade; Footsteps in the Dark; 42nd Street; French Line, The; Frisco Kid; Frogmen, The; Give My Regards to Broadway; Gold Diggers of 1937; Here Comes the Navy; He Was Her Man; Knute Rockne All American; Marked Woman; Moby Dick; Picture Snatcher; San Quentin; Say it with Songs; Singing Fool, The; Sullivans, The*

Badger, Clarence *It*

Badham, John *American Flyers; Another Stakeout; Bingo Long Traveling All-Stars and Motor Kings, The; Bird on a Wire; Blue Thunder; Dracula; Drop Zone; Hard Way, The; Nick of Time; Point of No Return; Saturday Night Fever; Short Circuit; Stakeout; WarGames; Whose Life Is it Anyway?*

Baer, Max *Ode to Billy Joe*

Baggot, King *Tumbleweeds*

Bail, Chuck *Gumball Rally, The*

Bailey, John *China Moon*

Baird, Stuart *Executive Decision; U.S. Marshals*

Baker, Graham *Alien Nation; Final Conflict, The; Impulse*

Baker, Robert S. *Siege of Sidney Street, The*

Baker, Roy Ward *Anniversary, The; Asylum; Don't Bother to Knock; Dr. Jekyll and Sister Hyde; Flame in the Streets; Inferno; Moon Zero Two; Night to Remember, A; October Man, The (1947); Quatermass and the Pit; Singer Not the Song, The; Two Left Feet; Vampire Lovers, The*

Moon; Girl Crazy; Gold Diggers of 1933; Gold Diggers of 1935; Gold Diggers of 1937; Hollywood Hotel; Me and My Gal; Roman Scandals; Stage-struck; Strike up the Band; Take Me Out to the Ball Game; Ziegfeld Girl

Berman, Monty Siege of Sidney Street, The

Berman, Ted Black Cauldron, The

Bernard, Chris Letter to Brezhnev

Bernard, Raymond Les Miserables

Brends, Edward Queen of Outer Space

Bernds, Edward L. Return of the Fly

Bernhardt, Curtis, Blue Veil, The; Conflict; Devotion; Happy Go Lucky; High Wall; Miss Sadie Thompson; My Reputation; Payment on Demand; Possessed; Sirocco; Stolen Life, A

Bernstein, Armyan Cross My Heart; Windy City

Bernstein, Walter Little Miss Marker

Berri, Claude Germinal; Jean de Florette; Manon des Sources

Berry, John Bad News Bears go to Japan, The; Casbah; Claudine; From This Day Forward; Tension

Bertolucci, Bernardo Il Conformista; La Luna; Last Emperor, The; Last Tango in Paris; Little Buddha; Novecento; Sheltering Sky, The; Stealing Beauty

Besson, Luc Fifth Element, The; Le Grand Bleu; Jeanne D'Arc; Leon; Nikita; Subway

Bharadwaj, Radha Closet Land

Bianchi, Edward Fan, The

Biberman, Herbert J. Master Race, The; Salt of the Earth

Bierman, Robert Vampire's Kiss

Bigelow, Kathryn Blue Steel; Near Dark; Point Break; Strange Days

Bill, Tony Crazy People; Five Corners; My Bodyguard; Six Weeks; Untamed Heart

Billington, Kevin Interlude; Light at the Edge of the World, The

Binder, Mike Indian Summer

Binyon, Claude Here Come the Girls

Birch, Patricia Grease 2

Bird, Antonia Mad Love; Priest

Birkin, Andrew Burning Secret; Cement Garden, The; Salt on Our Skin

Black, Noel Change of Seasons, A; Jennifer on My Mind; Pretty Poison

Blair, Les Bad Behaviour

Blashfield, Jim Moonwalker

Blatt, Edward A. Between Two Worlds

Blatty, William Peter Exorcist III, The; Ninth Configuration, The

Blier, Bertrand Preparez Vos Mouchoirs;

Tenue de Soiree; Trop Belle Pour Toi; Les Valseuses

Bloom, Jeffrey Flowers in the Attic

Bluth, Don American Tail, An; Anastasia; Land Before Time, The; Secret of NIMH, The

Blystone, John G. Charlie Chan's Chance; Our Hospitality; Tol'able David; Woman Chases Man

Bochner, Hart PCU

Boetticher, Budd Bronco Buster; Buchanan Rides Alone; Bullfighter and the Lady; City Beneath the Sea; Comanche Station; Decision at Sundown; Horizons West; Man from the Alamo, The; Ride Lonesome; Tall T, The

Bogart, Paul Class of '44; Marlowe; Oh, God! You Devil; Torch Song Trilogy

Bogayevicz, Yurek Three of Hearts

Bogdanovich, Peter At Long Last Love; Daisy Miller; Illegally Yours; Last Picture Show, The; Mask; Nickelodeon; Noises Off; Paper Moon; Saint Jack; Targets; Texasville; They All Laughed; Thing Called Love, The; What's Up, Doc?

Boleslawski, Richard Clive of India; Garden of Allah; Last of Mrs. Cheyney, The; Men in White; Les Miserables; Painted Veil, The; Theodora Goes Wild

Bolognini, Mauro Arabella

Bolt, Robert Lady Caroline Lamb

Bondarchuk, Sergei Sudba Chelovyeka; Voyna I Mir I Andrei Bolkonsky; Voyna I Mir II Natasha Rostova; Voyna I Mir III 1812 God.; Voyna I Mir IV Pyer Bezukhov; Waterloo

Bonerz, Peter Police Academy 6 City Under Siege

Boorman, John Beyond Rangoon; Catch Us If You Can; Deliverance; Emerald Forest, The; Excalibur; Exorcist II The Heretic; General, The; Hell in the Pacific; Hope and Glory; Leo the Last; Point Blank; Where the Heart Is; Zardoz

Borden, Lizzie Born in Flames; Love Crimes; Working Girls

Boris, Robert Oxford Blues

Borsos, Phillip Bethune The Making of a Hero; Far from Home The Adventures of Yellow Dog; Grey Fox, The; Mean Season, The

Borzage, Frank Bad Girl; Big Fisherman, The; China Doll; Desire; Farewell to Arms, A; Flirtation Walk; His Butler's Sister; Magnificent Doll; Mannequin; Man's Castle; Mortal Storm, The; 7th Heaven; Shining Hour, The; Song O' My Heart; Spanish Main, The; Stage

Borzage, Frank (cont.)
Door Canteen; Strange Cargo; Street Angel; Three Comrades; Till We Meet Again

Boskovich, John *Without You I'm Nothing*

Boulting, John *Brighton Rock; Heavens Above!; I'm All Right Jack; Journey Together; Lucky Jim; Magic Box, The; Private's Progress; Rotten to the Core; Seven Days to Noon*

Boulting, Roy *Brothers in Law; Carlton-Browne of the F.O.; Fame Is the Spur; Family Way, The; Run for the Sun; Seven Days to Noon; There's a Girl in My Soup; Thunder Rock; Twisted Nerve*

Bourguignon, Serge *Les Dimanches de Ville d'Avray; Reward, The*

Bowman, Rob *X-Files, The*

Box, Muriel *Rattle of a Simple Man*

Boyd, Don *Twenty-One*

Boyle, Danny *Life Less Ordinary, A; Shallow Grave; Trainspotting*

Brabin, Charles *Mask of Fu Manchu, The*

Brahm, John *Face to Face; Guest in the House; Hangover Square; Locket, The; Lodger, The; Wintertime*

Brambilla, Marco *Demolition Man*

Branagh, Kenneth *Dead Again; Frankenstein; Hamlet; Henry V; In the Bleak Midwinter; Much Ado about Nothing; Peter's Friends*

Brand, Joshua *Pyromaniac's Love Story, A*

Brando, Marlon *Mutiny on the Bounty; One-Eyed Jacks*

Brandon, Phil *Tarzan's Peril*

Brannon, Ash *Toy Story 2*

Brass, Tinto *Caligula*

Brecher, Irving *Somebody Loves Me*

Brenon, Herbert *Beau Geste*

Bresson, Robert *Le Journal d'Un Cure de Campagne; Mouchette; Proces De Jeanne D'Arc*

Brest, Martin *Beverly Hills Cop; Meet Joe Black; Midnight Run; Scent of a Woman*

Bretherton, Howard *Hills of Kentucky*

Brickman, Marshall *Lovesick; Manhattan Project, The*

Brickman, Paul *Men Don't Leave; Risky Business*

Bridges, Alan *Hireling, The; Out of Season; Return of the Soldier, The; Shooting Party, The*

Bridges, James *Baby Maker, The; Bright Lights, Big City; China Syndrome, The; Mike's Murder; 9/30/55; Paper Chase, The; Perfect; Urban Cowboy*

Brook, Peter *Beggar's Opera, The; Lord of the Flies; Persecution and Assassi-*

nation of Jean-Paul Marat as Performed by the Inmates of the Asylum of Charenton under the Direction of the Marquis de Sade, The; Tell Me Lies A Film About London*

Brookner, Howard *Bloodhounds of Broadway*

Brooks, Albert *Defending Your Life; Lost in America; Modern Romance*

Brooks, Bob *Tattoo*

Brooks, James L. *As Good As It Gets; Broadcast News; I'll Do Anything; Terms of Endearment*

Brooks, Joseph *You Light Up My Life*

Brooks, Mel *Blazing Saddles; High Anxiety; History of the World—Part I; Life Stinks; Producers, The; Robin Hood Men in Tights; Silent Movie; Spaceballs; Twelve Chairs, The; Young Frankenstein*

Brooks, Richard *Bite the Bullet; Blackboard Jungle; Brothers Karamazov, The; Catered Affair, The; Cat on a Hot Tin Roof; Crisis; Deadline U.S.A.;$; Elmer Gantry; Fever Pitch; Happy Ending, The; In Cold Blood; Last Time I Saw Paris, The; Looking for Mr. Goodbar; Lord Jim; Professionals, The; Sweet Bird of Youth; Take the High Ground; Wrong Is Right*

Broomfield, Nick *Diamond Skulls; Monster in a Box*

Brower, A. *Edward Sutherland, Otto Paramount on Parade*

Brower, Otto *Gay Caballero, The*

Brown, Clarence *Angels in the Outfield; Anna Christie; Anna Karenina; Come Live with Me; Conquest; Eagle, The; Edison, The Man; Emma; Flesh and the Devil; Gorgeous Hussy, The; Human Comedy, The; Idiot's Delight; Inspiration; Intruder in the Dust; National Velvet; Night Flight; Of Human Hearts; Plymouth Adventure; Rains Came, The; Romance; Sadie McKee; Song of Love; They Met in Bombay; White Cliffs of Dover, The; Wife vs. Secretary; Woman of Affairs, A; Yearling, The*

Brown, Harry Joe *Knickerbocker Holiday; Sitting Pretty*

Brown, Rowland *Hell's Highway; Quick Millions*

Browning, Tod *Black Bird, The; Devil-Doll, The; Dracula; Freaks; Unkown, The; West of Zanzibar*

Brownlow, Kevin *It Happened Here; Winstanley*

Bruckman, Clyde *Feet First; General, The*

Brunel, Adrian *Constant Nymph, The*

1442

Bryant, Charles *Salome*

Bryden, Derek *Jarman, Bill Aria*

Buchanan, Larry *Goodbye, Norma Jean*

Buck, Chris *Tarzan*

Bucksey, Colin *Dealers*

Bucquet, Harold S. *Dragon Seed; Without Love*

Buechler, John Carl *Friday the 13th Part VII—The New Blood; Troll*

Buntzman, Mark *Exterminator 2*

Bunuel, Luis *L'Age D'Or; El Angel Exterminador; Belle De Jour; Cet Obscur Object du Desir; Le Charme Discret De La Bourgeoisie; El; Le Journal D'Une Femme De Chambre; Nazarin; Los Olvidados; Tristana; Viridiana; Young One, The*

Burge, Stuart *Julius Caesar; There Was a Crooked Man*

Burnett, Charles *Glass Shield, The*

Burns, Edward *She's the One*

Burr, Jeff *Stepfather II*

Burrows, James *Partners*

Burton, Tim *Batman; Batman Returns; Beetlejuice; Edward Scissorhands; Ed Wood; Mars Attacks!; Pee-Wee's Big Adventure; Sleepy Hollow*

Bushell, Anthony *Richard III*

Butler, David *Bottoms Up; Calamity Jane; Command, The; Connecticut Yankee, A; Fox Movietone Follies of 1929; King Richard and the Crusaders; Little Colonel, The; Littlest Rebel, The; Lullaby of Broadway; Princess and the Pirate, The; Road to Morocco; San Antonio; Sunny Side Up; Tea for Two; Thank Your Lucky Stars; They Got Me Covered; Time, the Place and the Girl, The; White Fang*

Butler, George *Pumping Iron; Pumping Iron II The Women*

Butler, Robert, *Computer Wore Tennis Shoes, The; Night of the Juggler; Now You See Him, Now You Don't*

Butoy, Hendel *Rescuers Down Under, The*

Buzzell, Edward *At the Circus; Best Foot Forward; Easy to Wed; Go West; Neptune's Daughter; Paradise for Three; Woman of Distinction, A*

Byrne, David *True Stories A Film About a Bunch of People in Virgil, Texas*

Byrum, John *Heart Beat; Inserts; Razor's Edge, The*

Caan, James *Hide in Plain Sight*

Cacoyannis, Michael *Trojan Women, The; Zorba the Greek*

Cagney, James *Short Cut to Hell*

Cahn, Edward L. *It! The Terror from Beyond Space*

Cain, Christopher *Amazing Panda Adventure, The; Next Karate Kid, The; Pure Country; Sixth and Main; Stone Boy, The; That Was Then . . . This Is Now; Where the River Runs Black; Young Guns*

Callow, Simon *Ballad of the Sad Cafe, The*

Camerini, Mario *Ulysses*

Cameron, James *Abyss, The; Aliens; Piranha II The Spawning; Terminator, The; Terminator 2 Judgement Day; Titanic; True Lies*

Cameron, Julia *God's Will*

Cameron, Ken *Good Wife, The*

Cammell, Donald *Demon Seed; Performance; White of the Eye*

Camp, Joe *Benji; For the Love of Benji*

Campanile, Pasquale Festa *On My Way to the Crusades, I Met a Girl Who . . .*

Campbell, Martin *Criminal Law; Defenseless; GoldenEye; Mask of Zorro, The*

Campion, Jane *Angel at My Table, An; Piano, The; Portrait of a Lady, The; Sweetie*

Campus, Michael *Passover Plot, The*

Camus, Marcel *Orfeu Negro*

Cannon, Danny *Judge Dredd; I Still Know What You Did Last Summer; Young Americans, The*

Cannon, Dyan *End of Innocence, The*

Capra, Frank *Arsenic and Old Lace; Battle for Russia, The; Bitter Tea of General Yen, The; Broadway Bill; Dirigible; Here Comes the Groom; It Happened One Night; It's a Wonderful Life; Lady for a Day; Long Pants; Lost Horizon; Meet John Doe; Miracle Woman, The; Mr. Deeds Goes to Town; Mr. Smith Goes to Washington; Negro Soldier, The; Platinum Blonde; Pocketful of Miracles; Power of the Press; Prelude to War; Riding High; State of the Union; Strong Man, The; You Can't Take It with You*

Cardiff, Jack *Girl on a Motorcycle, The; Liquidator, The; Long Ships, The; Mercenaries, The; My Geisha; Scent of Mystery; Sons and Lovers; Young Cassidy*

Cardos, John *Kingdom of the Spiders*

Carlei, Carlo *Fluke*

Carlino, Lewis John *Class; Great Santini, The; Sailor Who Fell from Grace with the Sea, The*

Carlsen, Henning *Sult*

Carne, Marcel *Les Enfants du Paradis; Le Jour Se Leve; Therese Raquin; Les Visiteurs du Soir*

Caro, Marc *La Cite des Enfants Perdus; Delicatessen*

Caron, Glenn Gordon *Clean and Sober; Love Affair; Wilder Napalm*

Carpenter, John *Assault on Precinct 13; Big Trouble in Little China; Christine; Dark Star; Escape from L.A.; Escape from New York; Fog, The; Halloween; In the Mouth of Madness; Memoirs of an Invisible Man; Prince of Darkness; Starman; They Live; Thing, The; Vampires; Village of the Damned*

Carreras, Michael *Blood from the Mummy's Tomb; Curse of the Mummy's Tomb, The*

Carrier, Rick *Strangers in the City*

Carson, David *Star Trek Generations*

Carstairs, John *Paddy Saint in London, The; Tommy the Toreador; Trouble in Store*

Carter, Thomas *Swing Kids*

Carver, Steve *Big Bad Mama; Capone; Drum; Eye for an Eye, An; Lone Wolf McQuade; Steel*

Cass, Henry *Glass Mountain, The*

Cassavetes, John *Child Is Waiting, A; Faces; Gloria; Husbands A Comedy About Life, Death & Freedom; Killing of a Chinese Bookie, The; Love Streams; Minnie and Moscowitz; Opening Night; Shadows; Too Late Blues; Woman Under the Influence, A*

Castle, Nick *Boy Who Could Fly, The; Dennis the Menace; Last Starfighter, The; Major Payne; Mr. Wrong; Tap*

Castle, William *House on Haunted Hill; Serpent of the Nile; Strait-Jacket; When Strangers Marry*

Cates, Gilbert *I Never Sang For My Father; Last Married Couple in America, The; Oh, God! Book II; Promise, The; Summer Wishes, Winter Dreams*

Caton-Jones, Michael *Doc Hollywood; Jackal, The; Memphis Belle; Rob Roy; Scandal; This Boy's Life*

Cattaneo, Peter *Full Monty, The*

Cavalcanti, Alberto *Dead of Night; Nicholas Nickleby; Went the Day Well?*

Cavani, Liliana *Night Porter, The*

Cavara, Paolo *Mondo Cane*

Chabrol, Claude *Le Beau Serge; Les Biches; Blood Relatives; Le Boucher; La Ceremonie; Les Cousins; La Femme Infidele; Juste Avant la Nuit*

Chaffey, Don *Greyfriars Bobby; Jason and the Argonauts; One Million Years B.C.; Persecution; Pete's Dragon*

Chaplin, Charles *Circus; City Lights; Countess from Hong Kong, A; Easy Street; Gold Rush, The (1942); Great Dictator, The; Immigrant, The; Kid, The; King in New York, A; Limelight; Modern Times; Monsieur Verdoux; Shoulder Arms; Woman of Paris; A*

Chapman, Brenda *Prince of Egypt, The*

Chapman, Matthew *Heart of Midnight; Hussy; Stranger's Kiss*

Chapman, Michael *All the Right Moves; Clan of the Cave Bear, The*

Chappelle, Joe *Halloween The Curse of Michael Myers; Thieves Quartet*

Charell, Erik *Kongress Tanzt, Der*

Chauvel, Charles *Forty Thousand Horsemen*

Che-Kirk Wong *Big Hit, The*

Chechik, Jeremiah *Avengers, The; Benny & Joon; Diabolique; National Lampoon's Christmas Vacation; Tall Tale*

Chelsom, Peter *Funny Bones; Hear My Song*

Chen Kaige *Bawang Bie Ji; Feng Yue; Huang Tudi*

Chereau, Patrice *La Reine Margot*

Chetwynd, Lionel *Hanoi Hilton*

Chivers, Colin *Moonwalker*

Chomsky, Marvin *Tank*

Christensen, Benjamin *Haxan*

Christian, Roger *Nostradamus; Sender, The*

Christian-Jaque, *Fanfan La Tulipe*

Chukhrai, Grigori *Ballada O Soldatye; Sorok Pyervi*

Chytilova, Vera *Sedmikrasky*

Cimber, Matt *Butterfly*

Cimino, Michael *Deer Hunter, The; Desperate Hours; Heaven's Gate; Sicilian, The; Sunchaser, The; Thunderbolt and Lightfoot; Year of the Dragon*

Clair, Rene *And Then There Were None; Nous La Liberte, A; Flame of New Orleans; The; Ghost Goes West, The; I Married a Witch; It Happened Tomorrow; Le Million; Porte des Lilas; Sous les Toits de Paris*

Clark, Bob *Black Christmas; Loose Cannons; Murder by Decree; Porky's; Porky's II The Next Day; Rhinestone; Tribute; Turk 182!*

Clark, James B. *Flipper*

Clark, Larry *Kids*

Clark, Matt *Da*

Clarke, Alan *Rita, Sue and Bob Too; Scum*

Clarke, Frank *Blonde Fist*

Clarke, Shirley *Cool World, The*

Clavell, James *Last Valley, The; To Sir, with Love; Walk Like a Dragon; Where's Jack?*

1445

Cosmatos, George (cont.)
Crossing, The; Cobra; Escape to Athena; Leviathan; Massacre in Rome; Rambo First Blood Part II; Tombstone

Costa-Gavras, Constantin *Betrayed; Missing; Music Box; Z*

Costner, Kevin *Dances with Wolves; Postman, The*

Couffer, Jack *Living Free; Ring of Bright Water*

Couturie, Bill *Ed*

Coward, Noel *In Which We Serve*

Cox, Alex *Repo Man; Sid and Nancy; Walker*

Cox, Paul *Golden Braid; Lonely Hearts; Man of Flowers; My First Wife; Nun and the Bandit, The; Vincent The Life and Death of Vincent Van Gogh; Woman's Tale, A*

Cozzi, Luigi *Hercules*

Crabtree, Arthur *Quartet*

Crain, William *Blacula*

Crane, Peter *Moments*

Craven, Wes *Deadly Friend; Hills Have Eyes, The; Hills Have Eyes Part II, The; Music of the Heart; Nightmare on Elm Street, A; People under the Stairs, The; Scream; Scream 2; Serpent and the Rainbow, The; Shocker; Swamp Thing; Vampire in Brooklyn; Wes Craven's New Nightmare*

Crame, Lol *Lunatic, The*

Crichton, Charles *Boy Who Stole a Million, The; Dead of Night; Divided Heart, The; Fish Called Wanda, A; He Who Rides a Tiger; Hue and Cry; Lavender Hill Mob, The; Law and Disorder; Third Secret, The; Titfield Thunderbolt, The; Train of Events*

Crichton, Michael *Coma; First Great Train Robbery, The; Looker; Physical Evidence; Runaway; Westworld*

Crisp, Donald *Don Q. Son of Zorro; Navigator, The*

Croghan, Emma-Kate *Love and Other Catastrophes*

Crombie, Donald *Caddie; Cathy's Child; Irishman, The; Killing of Angel Street, The; Kitty and the Bagman*

Cromwell, John *Algiers; Anna and the King of Siam; Caged; Dead Reckoning; Enchanted Cottage, The; In Name Only; Little Lord Fauntleroy; Made for Each Other; Of Human Bondage; Prisoner of Zenda, The; Racket, The; Since You Went Away; Son of Fury The Story of Benjamin Blake; Spitfire; Texan, The; Tom Sawyer; Victory*

Cronenberg, David *Brood, The; Crash; Crimes of the Future; Dead Ringers;*

Dead Zone, The; eXistenZ; Fly, The; M. Butterfly; Naked Lunch; Rabid; Scanners; Shivers; Stereo; Videodrome

Crosland, Alan *Don Juan; Jazz Singer, The*

Crowe, Cameron *Jerry Maguire; Say Anything . . . ; Singles*

Crowe, Christopher *Off Limits; Whispers in the Dark*

Cruze, James *Covered Wagon, The; Great Gabbo, The; Hollywood; I Cover the Waterfront; Pony Express, The; Ruggles of Red Gap*

Crystal, Billy *Forget Paris; Mr. Saturday Night*

Cuaron, Alfonso *Great Expectations; Little Princess, A*

Cui, Yan *Chinese Chocolate*

Cukor, George *Actress, The; Adam's Rib; Bhowani Junction; Bill of Divorcement, A; Blue Bird, The; Born Yesterday; Camille; Chapman Report, The; David Copperfield; Desire Me; Dinner at Eight; Double Life, A; Edward, My Son; Edward, My Son (1949); Gaslight; Girls About Town; Gone With the Wind; Heller in Pink Tights; Holiday; It Should Happen to You; Justine; Les Girls; Let's Make Love; Life of Her Own, A; Little Women; Marrying Kind, The; My Fair Lady; Pat and Mike; Philadelphia Story, The; Rich and Famous; Romeo and Juliet; Song Without End; Star Is Born, A; Susan and God; Sylvia Scarlett; Tarnished Lady; Travels with My Aunt; Two-faced Woman; What Price Hollywood?; Wild Is the Wind; Winged Victory; Woman's Face, A; Women, The; Zaza*

Culp, Robert *Hickey & Boggs*

Cummings, Irving *Dolly Sisters, The; Hollywood Cavalcade; Hollywood Cavalcade (1939); In Old Arizona; Little Miss Broadway; Louisiana Purchase; Mad Game, The; My Gal Sal; Springtime in the Rockies; Sweet Rosie O' Grady; That Night in Rio; Vogues of 1938; White Parade, The*

Cundieff, Rusty *Tales from the Hood*

Cunningham, Sean S. *Deepstar Six; Friday the 13th*

Curteis, Ian *Projected Man, The*

Curtis, Dan *Burnt Offerings*

Curtiz, Michael *Adventures of Robin Hood, The; Angels with Dirty Faces, The; Best Things in Life Are Free, The; Black Fury; British Agent; Cabin in the Cotton; Captain Blood; Captains of the Clouds; Casablanca; Charge of the Light Brigade, The; Comancheros,*

The; Doctor X; Dodge City; Egyptian, The; Flamingo Road; Force of Arms; Four Daughters; Four's a Crowd; Front Page Woman; Helen Morgan Story, The; Jazz Singer, The; Jimmy the Gent; Jim Thorpe—All-American; Kennel Murder Case, The; Key, The; Kid Galahad; King Creole; Life with Father; Mammy; Mandalay; Mildred Pierce; Mission to Moscow; Mystery of the Wax Museum, The; Night and Day; Noah's Ark The Story of the Deluge; Passage to Marseille; Private Lives of Elizabeth and Essex, The; Proud Rebel, The; Santa Fe Trail; Sea Hawk, The; Sea Wolf, The; This Is the Army; Trouble along the Way; 20,000 Years in Sing Sing; Unsuspected, The; Virginia City; Walking Dead, The; We're No Angels; White Christmas; Yankee Doodle Dandy; Young Man with a Horn

Czinner, Paul Escape Me Never; Rise of Catherine the Great, The

DaCosta, Morton Auntie Mame; Music Man, The

Dahl, John Kill Me Again; Last Seduction, The; Red Rock West; Rounders; Unforgettable

Dalen, Zale Skip Tracer

Dalva, Robert Black Stallion Returns, The

Damiani, Damiano Amityville II The Possession

Damiano, Gerard Deep Throat; Devil in Miss Jones, The

Daniel, Rod Beethoven's 2nd; K-9; Teen Wolf

Dante, Joe Amazon Women on the Moon; 'Burbs, The; Explorers; Gremlins; Gremlins 2 The New Batch; Hollywood Boulevard; Howling, The; Innerspace; Matinee; Piranha; Twilight Zone The Movie

Darabont, Frank Green Mile, The; Shawshank Redemption, The

Darling, Joan First Love

Darnborough, Antony So Long at the Fair

Darnell, Eric Antz

Dassin, Jules Brute Force; Canterville Ghost, The; Dream of Passion, A; Du Rififi Chez les Hommes; Naked City, The; Night and the City; Pote Tin Kyriaki; Reunion; 10:30 P.M. Summer; Thieves' Highway; Topkapi

Daves, Delmer Badlanders, The; Battle of the Villa Fiorita, The; Bird of Paradise; Broken Arrow; Dark Passage; Demetrius and the Gladiators; Destination Tokyo; Drum Beat; Hanging Tree, The; Hollywood Canteen; Jubal;

Kings Go Forth; Last Wagon, The; Never Let Me Go; Parrish; Pride of the Marines; Red House, The; Spencer's Mountain; Summer Place, A; Susan Slade; Task Force; 3:10 to Yuma; Treasure of the Golden Condor

David, Charles Lady on a Train

David, Geoffrey The Thief of Bagdad An Arabian Fantasy

Davidson, Boaz Lemon Popsicle

Davidson, Gordon Trial of the Catonsville Nine, The

Davidson, Martin Eddie And the Cruisers; Lord's of Flatbush, The

Davies, Howard Secret Rapture, The

Davies, Terence Distant Voices, Still Lives; Long Day Closes, The; Neon Bible, The

Davies, Valentine Benny Goodman Story, The

Davis, Andrew Above the Law; Code of Silence; Fugitive, The; Package, The; Perfect Murder, A; Steal Big, Steal Little; Under Siege

Davis, Desmond Clash of the Titans; Girl with Green Eyes; I Was Happy Here; Nice Girl Like Me, A; Smashing Time; Uncle, The

Davis, Eddie Panic in the City

Davis, Gary Suburban Commando

Davis, Ossie Cotton Comes to Harlem

Davis, Philip i.d.

Davis, Tamra Billy Madison; CB4; Guncrazy

Day, Robert Man with Bogart's Face, The; Rebel, The; She; Tarzan and the Great River; Tarzan's Three Challenges; Tarzan the Magnificent; Two Way Stretch

De Antonio, Emile Rush to Judgement

De Bello, John Attack of the Killer Tomatoes

De Bont, Jan Haunting, The; Speed; Speed 2 Cruise Control; Twister

De Bosio, Gianfranco Moses

De Concini, Ennio Hitler The Last Ten Days

De Cordova, Frederick Frankie and Johnny

De Heer, Rolf Bad Boy Bubby; Quiet Room, The

De Jarnatt, Steve Cherry 2000

De Jong, Ate Drop Dead Fred

De Leon, Marcus Big Squeeze, The

De Martino, Alberto Holocaust 2000

De Niro, Robert Bronx Tale, A

De Palma, Brian Blow Out; Body Double; Bonfire of the Vanities, The; Carlito's Way; Carrie; Casualties of War; Dressed to Kill; Fury, The; Home Mov-

De Palma, Brian (cont.)
ies; Mission Impossible; Obsession; Phantom of the Paradise; Raising Cain; Scarface; Sisters; Snake Eyes; Untouchables, The; Wedding Party, The

De Seta, Vittorio *Banditi a Orgosolo*

De Sica, Vittorio *After the Fox; Boccaccio 70; La Ciociara; Condemned of Altona, The; Il Giardino Dei Finzi-Contini; Ieri, Oggi, Domani; Indiscretion of an American Wife; Ladri di Biciclette; Miracolo A Milano; Place for Lovers, A; Sciuscia; Sunflower; Umberto D.; Woman Times Seven*

De Toth, Andre *Dark Waters; House of Wax; Indian Fighter, The; Play Dirty; Ramrod; Springfield Rifle; Two-Headed Spy, The*

Dean, Basil *Constant Nymph, The; Escape; Lorna Doone*

Dear, William *Angels in the Outfield; Harry and the Hendersons; If Looks Could Kill*

Dearden, Basil *Assassination Bureau Limited, The; Bells Go Down, The; Blue Lamp, The; Captive Heart, The; Dead of Night; Frieda; Khartoum; League of Gentlemen, The; Life for Ruth; Man Who Haunted Himself, The; Masquerade; Mind Benders, The; My Learned Friend; Only When I Larf; Pool of London; Sapphire; Saraband for Dead Lovers; Smallest Show on Earth, The; Train of Events; Victim; Violent Playground; Woman of Straw*

Dearden, James *Cold Room, The; Kiss before Dying, A; Pascali's Island*

Dehlavi, Jamil *Immaculate Conception*

Deitch, Donna *Desert Hearts*

Dekker, Fred *Robocop 3*

Del Toro, Guillermo *Mimic*

DeLacey, Philippe *Cinerama Holiday*

Delannoy, Jean *Hunchback of Notre Dame, The*

Dell, Jeffrey *Carlton-Browne of the F.O.*

Dembo, Richard *La Diagonale du Fou*

DeMille, Cecil B. *Cleopatra; Crusades, The; Dynamite; Four Frightened People; Greatest Show on Earth, The; King of Kings, The; Male and Female; North West Mounted Police; Plainsman, The; Reap the Wild Wind; Road to Yesterday, The; Samson and Delilah; Sign of the Cross, The; Story of Dr. Wassell, The; Ten Commandments, The; Ten Commandments, The (1956); This Day and Age; Trail of the Lonesome Pine, The; Unconquered; Union Pacific*

Demme, Jonathan *Citizens Band; Crazy Mama; Last Embrace; Married to the Mob; Melvin and Howard; Philadelphia; Silence of the Lambs, The; Something Wild; Swimming to Cambodia; Swing Shift*

Demme, Ted *Beautiful Girls; Life; Ref, The*

Demy, Jacques *Les Demoiselles de Rochefort; Lady Oscar; Lola; Model Shop; Les Parapluies De Cherbourg; Pied Piper, The*

Densham, Pen *Kiss, The; Moll Flanders*

Deray, Jacques *Borsalino*

Derek, John *Bolero; Tarzan the Ape Man*

Deschanel, Caleb *Escape Artist, The*

DeSimone, Tom *Reform School Girls*

Deutch, Howard *Article 99; Getting Even with Dad; Great Outdoors, The; Grumpier Old Men; Pretty in Pink; Some Kind of Wonderful*

Deville, Michel *La Lectrice; Peril en la Demeure*

DeVito, Danny *Hoffa; Throw Momma from the Train; War of the Roses, The*

Dewolf, Patrick *Innocent Lies*

Dexter, John *Virgin Soldiers, The*

DiCillo, Tom *Johnny Suede*

Dickerson, Ernest *Demon Knight; Juice*

Dickinson, Thorold *Gaslight; Men of Two Worlds; Queen of Spades, The; Secret People*

Dieterle, William *Accused, The; Blockade; Boots Malone; Dark City; Devil and Daniel Webster, The; Dr. Ehrlich's Magic Bullet; Dr. Socrates; Elephant Walk; Fashions of 1934; Great O'Malley, The; Her Majesty Love; Hunchback of Notre Dame, The; Juarez; Kismet; Last Flight, The; Lawyer Man; Life of Emile Zola, The; Louis Pasteur; Love Letters; Madame Dubarry; Midsummer Night's Dream, A; Omar Khayyam; Peking Express; Portrait of Jennie; Salome; Satan Met a Lady; Searching Wind, The; September Affair; Story of Louis Pasteur, The; This Love of Ours; Turning Point, The*

Dinner, Michael *Heaven Help Us; Off Beat*

Dippe, Mark A. Z. *Spawn*

DiSalle, Mark *Kickboxer*

Dmytryk, Edward *Alvarez Kelly; Anzio; Back to Bataan; Behind the Rising Sun; Blue Angel, The; Bluebeard; Broken Lance; Caine Mutiny, The; Carpetbaggers, The; Cornered; Crossfire; Give Us This Day; Hitler's Children; Juggler, The; Left Hand of God, The; Mirage; Murder, My Sweet; Ob-*

session; Raintree County; Shalako; Soldier of Fortune; Tender Comrade; Walk on the Wild Side; Where Love Has Gone; Young Lions, The

Donaldson, Roger Bounty, The; Cadillac Man; Cocktail; Dante's Peak; Getaway, The; Marie; No Way Out; Sleeping Dogs; Smash Palace; Species; White Sands

Donehue, Vincent J. Sunrise at Campobello

Donen, Stanley Arabesque; Bedazzled; Blame it on Rio; Charade; Damn Yankees; Funny Face; Give a Girl a Break; Grass Is Greener, The; Indiscreet; It's Always Fair Weather; Kismet; Little Prince, The; Lucky Lady; Movie Movie; Once More, with Feeling; On the Town; Pajama Game, The; Royal Wedding; Saturn 3; Seven Brides for Seven Brothers; Singin' in the Rain; Staircase; Two for the Road

Donner, Clive Alfred the Great; Caretaker, The; Here We Go Round the Mulberry Bush; Luv; Nothing But the Best; Some People; Stealing Heaven; Vampira; What's New Pussycat

Donner, Richard Assassins; Conspiracy Theory; Goonies, The; Inside Moves The Guys From Max's Bar; LadyHawke; Lethal Weapon; Lethal Weapon 2; Lethal Weapon 3; Lethal Weapon 4; Maverick; Omen, The; Radio Flyer; Scrooged; Superman

Donoghue, Mary Agnes Paradise

Donohue, Jack Assault on a Queen; Babes in Toyland; Lucky Me

Donovan, Martin Apartment Zero; Mad at the Moon

Dorfmann, Jacques Shadow of the Wolf

Dornhelm, Robert Echo Park

Douglas, Bill Comrades A Lanternist's Account of the Tolpuddle Martyrs and What Became of Them

Douglas, Gordon Barquero; Black Arrow, The; Call Me Bwana; Come Fill the Cup; Detective, The; Dick Tracy vs. Cueball; Follow That Dream; Gold of the Seven Saints; Harlow; In Like Flint; I Was a Communist for the F.B.I.; Kiss Tomorrow Goodbye; Lady in Cement; Only the Valiant; Rio Conchos; Robin and the 7 Hoods; San Quentin; Sins of Rachel Cade, The; Stagecoach; Them!; They Call Me Mister Tibbs!; Tony Rome; Viva Knievel!; Walk a Crooked Mile; Yellowstone Kelly

Douglass, Gordon M. Zenobia

Douglas, Kirk Posse

Dovzhenko, Aleksandr Zimlya

Downey, Robert Putney Swope

Dragoti, Stan Love at First Bite; Mr. Mom; Necessary Roughness; She's Out of Control

Drake, Jim Police Academy 4 Citizens on Patrol

Drazen, Anthony Imaginary Crimes

Dreifuss, Arthur Quare Fellow, The

Dreville, Jean La Reine Margot

Dreyer, Carl Gertrud; Le Passion de Jeanne D'Arc

Drury, David Defence of the Realm

Dudley, Carl South Seas Adventure

Duffell, Peter England Made Me

Dugan, Dennis Brain Donors; Problem Child

Dugan, Michael Mausoleum

Duigan, John Flirting; One Night Stand; Sirens; Wide Sargasso Sea; Year My Voice Broke, The

Duke, Bill Deep Cover; Rage in Harlem, A; Sister Act 2 Back in the Habit

Duke, Daryl Silent Partner, The; Tai-Pan

Dunham, Duwayne Homeward Bound; Little Giants

Dunne, Philip Blindfold; Blue Denim; In Love and War; Prince of Players; Ten North Frederick; Wild in the Country

Dunning, George Yellow Submarine

Dupont E. A. Moulin Rouge; Piccadilly

Duvall, Robert Apostle, The

Duvivier, Julien Anna Karenina; Flesh and Fantasy; Great Waltz, The; Impostor, The; Lydia; Pepe le Moko; Tales of Manhattan

Dwan, Allan Big Noise, The; Brewster's Millions; Cattle Queen of Montana; Getting Gertie's Garter; Human Cargo; I Dream of Jeanie; Iron Mask, The; Josette; Manhandled; Rebecca of Sunnybrook Farm; Robin Hood; Sands of Iwo Jima; Stage Struck; Suez; Three Musketeers, The; What a Widow!

D'Antoni, Philip Seven Ups, The

D'Arrast, Harry Laughter; Raffles

Eastwood, Clint Absolute Power; Bird; Breezy; Bridges of Madison County, The; Bronco Billy; Eiger Sanction, The; Firefox; Gauntlet, The; Heartbreak Ridge; High Plains Drifter; Honkytonk Man; Midnight in the Garden of Good and Evil; Outlaw Josey Wales, The; Pale Rider; Perfect World, A; Play Misty for Me; Rookie, The; Sudden Impact; True Crime; Unforgiven; White Hunter Black Heart

Eberhardt, Thom Gross Anatomy; Night of the Comet

Edel, Uli *Body of Evidence; Last Exit to Brooklyn*

Edwards, Blake *Blind Date; Breakfast at Tiffany's; Carey Treatment, The; Curse of the Pink Panther; Darling Lili; Days of Wine and Roses; Experiment in Terror; Fine Mess, A; Great Race, The; Gunn; High Time; Man Who Loved Women, The; Micki + Maude; Operation Petticoat; Party, The; Pink Panther, The; Pink Panther Strikes Again, The; Return of the Pink Panther, The; Revenge of the Pink Panther; Shot in the Dark, A; Skin Deep; S.O.B.; Son of the Pink Panther; Sunset; Switch; Tamarind Seed, The; 10; That's Life!; Trail of the Pink Panther; Victor/Victoria; What Did You Do in the War, Daddy?; Wild Rovers*

Edzard, Christine *Fool, The; Little Dorrit*

Egleson, Jan *Shock to the System, A*

Egoyan, Atom *Adjuster, The; Family Viewing; Speaking Parts; Sweet Hereafter, The*

Eisenstein, Sergei *Aleksandr Nyevski; Bronenosets 'Potyomkin'; Ivan Grozni; Ivan Grozni, II; Oktyabr*

Elliott, Stephan *Adventures of Priscilla, Queen of the Desert, The; Frauds*

Ellis, David R. *Homeward Bound II Lost in San Francisco*

Ellis, Robert *Sweet November*

Ellison, Joseph *Joey*

Elorrieta, Javier *Blood and Sand*

Elvey, Maurice *Lodger, The; Sally in Our Alley; Wandering Jew, The; Wandering Jew, The (1933)*

Emmerich, Roland *Godzilla; Independence Day; Stargate; Universal Soldier*

Enders, Robert *Stevie*

Endfield, Cy *De Sade; Hell Drivers; Mysterious Island; Sands of the Kalahari; Tarzan's Savage Fury; Zulu*

Engel, Andi *Melancholia*

Englund, George *Ugly American, The*

Enright, Ray *China Sky; Dames; Gung Ho!; Havana Widows; Naughty But Nice; Spoilers, The; Wagons Roll at Night, The*

Ephron, Nora *Mixed Nuts; Sleepless in Seattle; This Is My Life; You've Got Mail*

Epstein, Rob *Celluloid Closet, The*

Erice, Victor *El Espiritu De La Colmena*

Erman, John *Stella*

Erskine, Chester *Androcles and the Lion; Egg and I, The; Girl in Every Port, A*

Essex, Harry I, *The Jury*

Evans, Bruce A. *Kuffs*

Evans, David Mickey *Sandlot, The*

Eyre, Richard *Loose Connections; Ploughman's Lunch, The*

Fabri, Zoltan *Korhinta*

Faiman, Peter *Crocodile Dundee; Dutch*

Fairchild, William *Silent Enemy, The*

Fanaka, Jamaa *Penitentiary*

Fargo, James *Caravans; Enforcer, The; Every Which Way But Loose; Private Lessons*

Farrelly, Bobby *There's Something about Mary*

Farrelly, Peter *Dumb and Dumber; There's Something about Mary*

Farrow, John *Big Clock, The; Bill of Divorcement, A; China; Commandos Strike at Dawn, The; His Kind of Woman; Hondo; John Paul Jones; Night Has a Thousand Eyes; Ride; Vaquero; Sea Chase, The; Two Years Before the Mast; Wake Island*

Fassbinder, Rainer Werner *Angst Essen Seele Auf; Despair; Querelle*

Feist, Felix *George White's Scandals; This Woman Is Dangerous*

Fejos, Paul *Broadway*

Felder, Gary *Things to Do in Denver When You're Dead*

Feldman, John *Dead Funny*

Feldman, Marty *In God We Trust or Gimme That Prime Time Religion; Last Remake of Beau Geste, The*

Fellini, Federico *Amarcord; Il Bidone; Boccaccio 70; Casanova; La Dolce Vita; 8 ½; Giulietta degli Spiriti; Satyricon; La Strada; I Vitelloni*

Fenton, Leslie *On Our Merry Way; Pardon My Past; Saigon; Tomorrow the World*

Ferguson, Norman *Three Caballeros, The*

Ferrara, Abel *Addiction, The; Bad Lieutenant; Body Snatchers; Cat Chaser; China Girl; Dangerous Game; Driller Killer, The; Fear City; King of New York; Ms. 45*

Ferrer, Jose *Cockleshell Heroes; Great Man, The; I Accuse; Return to Peyton Place; State Fair*

Ferrer, Mel *Green Mansions*

Ferreri, Marco *Tales of Ordinary Madness*

Fessenden, Larry *Habit*

Feyder, Jacques *Daybreak; La Kermesse Heroique; Kiss, The; Knight without Armour*

Fields, Michael *Bright Angel*

Figgis, Mike *Browning Version, The; Internal Affairs; Leaving Las Vegas; Liebestraum; Mr. Jones; Stormy Monday*

Finch, Charles *Where Sleeping Dogs Lie*

Finch, Nigel *Stonewall*

Fincher, David *Alien 3; Fight Club; Game, The; Seven*

Finkleman, Ken *Airplane II The Sequel*

Finney, Albert *Charlie Bubbles*

Fiore, Robert *Pumping Iron*

Firstenberg, Sam *American Ninja; American Ninja 2 The Confrontation; Breakin' 2 Electric Boogaloo; Ninja III The Domination; Revenge of the Ninja*

Fisher, Terrence *Curse of Frankenstein, The; Curse of the Werewolf, The; Devil Rides Out, The; Dracula; Dracula—Prince of Darkness; Frankenstein Must Be Destroyed; Hound of the Baskervilles, The; Phantom of the Opera, The; Revenge of Frankenstein, The; So Long at the Fair*

Fisk, Jack *Daddy's Dyin' . . . Who's Got the Will? Raggedy Man*

Fitzmaurice, George *Arsene Lupin Returns; As You Desire Me; Lilac Time; Mata Hari; Raffles; Son of the Sheik, The; Strangers May Kiss*

Flaherty, Paul *Who's Harry Crumb?*

Flaherty, Robert *Elephant Boy; Louisiana Story; Man of Aran; Moana; Nanook of the North*

Fleder, Gary *Kiss the Girls*

Fleischer, Dave *Gulliver's Travels*

Fleischer, Richard *Amityville 3–D; Armored Car Robbery; Ashanti; Bandido; Barabbas; Between Heaven and Hell; Big Gamble, The; Boston Strangler, The; Che!; Compulsion; Conan the Destroyer; Crack in the Mirror; Doctor Dolittle; Don Is Dead, The; Fantastic Voyage; Incredible Sarah, The; Jazz Singer, The; Last Run, The; Mandingo; Mr. Majestyk; Narrow Margin, The; New Centurions, The; Prince and the Pauper, The; Red Sonja; See No Evil; Soylent Green; 10 Rillington Place; Tora! Tora! Tora!; 20,000 Leagues under the Sea; Vikings, The; Violent Saturday*

Fleming, Andrew *Craft, The; Dick; Threesome*

Fleming, Victor *Abie's Irish Rose; Abie's Irish Rose (1928); Adventure; Captains Courageous; Dr. Jekyll and Mr. Hyde; Farmer Takes a Wife, The; Gone With the Wind; Guy Named Joe, A; Joan of Arc; Mantrap; Reckless; Red Dust; Test Pilot; Tortilla Flat; Treasure Island; Virginian, The; Way of All Flesh, The; White Sister, The; Wizard of Oz, The*

Flemyng, Gordon *Daleks' Invasion Earth 2150 A.D.; Dr. Who & the Daleks; Great Catherine*

Flicker, Theodore J. *President's Analyst, The*

Flood, James *Life Begins*

Florey, Robert *Beast with Five Fingers, The; Cocoanuts, The; Dangerously They Live; Desert Song, The; Face Behind the Mask; God Is My Co-Pilot; Murders in the Rue Morgue; Tarzan and the Mermaids*

Flynn, John *Best Seller; Brainscan; Lock Up; Outfit, The; Out for Justice; Rolling Thunder; Sergeant, The*

Foley, James *After Dark, My Sweet; At Close Range; Chamber, The; Fear; Glengarry Glen Ross; Two Bits; Who's That Girl?*

Fonda, Peter *Hired Hand, The*

Forbes, Bryan *Deadfall; International Velvet; King Rat; L-Shaped Room, The; Madwoman of Chaillot, The; Raging Moon, The; Sance on a Wet Afternoon; The Slipper and the Rose The Story of Cinderella; Stepford Wives, The; Whisperers, The; Whistle Down the Wind; Wrong Box, The*

Ford, John *Air Mail; Alamo, The; Arrowsmith; Black Watch, The; Cheyenne Autumn; Donovan's Reef; Drums Along the Mowhawk; Flesh; Fort Apache; Four Sons; Fugitive, The; Gideon's Day; Grapes of Wrath, The; Hell Bent; Horse Soldiers, The; How Green Was My Valley; How the West Was Won; Hurricane, The; Informer, The; Iron Horse, The; Judge Priest; Last Hurrah, The; Long Gray Line, The; Long Voyage Home, The; Lost Patrol, The; Man Who Shot Liberty Valance, The; Mary of Scotland; Men without Women; Mister Roberts; Mogambo; My Darling Clementine; Pilgrimage; Plough and the Stars, The; Prisoner of Shark Island, The; Quiet Man, The; Rio Grande; Searchers, The; Sergeant Rutledge; 7 Women; She Wore a Yellow Ribbon; Stagecoach; Sun Shines Bright, The; They Were Expendable; Tobacco Road; Two Rode Together; Up the River; Wagon Master; Wee Willie Winkie; What Price Glory; When Willie Comes Marching Home; Whole Town's Talking, The; World Moves On, The; Young Cassidy; Young Mr. Lincoln*

Forde, Eugene *Charlie Chan in London; Charlie Chan on Broadway*

Forde, Walter *Chu Chin Chow; Four Just Men, The; Rome Express*

Foreman, Carl *Victors, The*

Forman, Milos *Amadeus; Hair; Hori, Ma*

Forman, Milos (cont.)
Panenko; Lasky Jedne Plavovlasky; Man on the Moon; One Flew over the Cuckoo's Nest; People vs. Larry Flynt, The; Ragtime; Taking Off; Valmont

Forst, Willy *Unfinished Symphony, The*

Forsyth, Bill *Being Human; Breaking In; Comfort and Joy; Gregory's Girl; Housekeeping; Local Hero; That Sinking Feeling*

Fortenberry, John *Jury Duty*

Fosse, Bob *All That Jazz; Cabaret; Lenny; Star 80; Sweet Charity*

Foster, Jodie *Home for the Holidays; Little Man Tate*

Foster, Norman *Charlie Chan at Treasure Island; Journey into Fear; Kiss the Blood off My Hands; Mr. Moto's Last Warning; Mr. Moto Takes a Chance; Mr. Moto Takes a Vacation; Mysterious Mr. Moto; Rachel and the Stranger; Thank You, Mr. Moto; Think Fast, Mr. Moto*

Fowler, Gene Jr. *I Married a Monster from Outer Space; I Was a Teenage Werewolf*

Foy, Bryan *Lights of New York*

Fraker, William A. *Monte Walsh*

Frakes, Jonathan *Star Trek First Contact; Star Trek: Insurrection*

Francis, Freddie *Deadly Bees, The; Dr. Terror's House of Horrors; Evil of Frankenstein, The; Mumsy, Nanny, Sonny & Girly; Nightmare; Paranoiac; Torture Garden*

Francis, Karl *Giro City; Rebecca's Daughters*

Franju, Georges *Judex; Therese Desqueyroux; Thomas L'imposteur; Les Yeux Sans Visage*

Frank, Melvin *Buona Sera, Mrs. Campbell; Court Jester, The; Duchess and the Dirtwater Fox, The; Li'l Abner; Prisoner of Second Avenue, The; Strange Bedfellows; Strictly Dishonorable; That Certain Feeling; Touch of Class, A*

Frankel, Cyril *Don't Bother to Knock; Man of Africa; Never Take Sweets from a Stranger; Trygon Factor, The; Witches, The*

Frankel, David *Miami Rhapsody*

Frankenheimer, John *All Fall Down; Birdman of Alcatraz; Black Sunday; Challenge, The; Extraordinary Seaman, The; 52 Pick-Up; Fixer, The; Fourth War, The; French Connection II; Grand Prix; Gypsy Moths, The; Holcroft Covenant, The; Horsemen, The; Impossible Object; I Walk the Line; Is-*
land of Dr. Moreau, The; Manchurian Candidate, The; 99 and 44/100% Dead; Prophecy; Ronin; Seconds; Seven Days in May; Train, The; Year of the Gun; Young Savages, The; Young Stranger, The*

Franklin, Carl *Devil in a Blue Dress; One False Move*

Franklin, Howard *Public Eye, The; Quick Change*

Franklin, Richard *F/X2; Link; Patrick; Psycho II; Road Games*

Franklin, Sidney *Barretts of Wimpole Street, The; Barretts of Wimpole Street, The (1957); Dark Angel, The; Good Earth, The; Lady's Morals, A; Last of Mrs. Cheyney, The; Private Lives; Smilin' Through*

Frawley, James *Big Bus, The; Muppet Movie, The*

Frears, Stephen *Dangerous Liasons; Grifters, The; Gunshoe; Hero; Hit, The; Mary Reilly; My Beautiful Laundrette; Prick up Your Ears; Sammy and Rosie Get Laid; Van, The*

Freedman, Jerrold *Borderline; Kansas City Bomber*

Freeland, Thornton *Flying down to Rio; Gang's All Here, The; George White's Scandals*

Freeman, Morgan *Bopha!*

Fregonese, Hugo *Decameron Nights; My Six Convicts*

French, Harold *Encore; Major Barbara; Man Who Watched Trains Go By, The; Quartet; Rob Roy; Trio*

Frend, Charles *Cruel Sea, The; Loves of Joanna Godden, The; San Demetrio-London; Scott of the Antarctic*

Freund, Karl *Mad Love; Mummy, The*

Friedberg, Rick *Spy Hard*

Friedgen, Bud *That's Entertainment! III*

Friedkin, William *Birthday Party, The; Blue Chips; Boys in the Band, The; Cruising; Exorcist, The; French Connection, The; Guardian, The; Jade; Night They Raided Minsky's, The; Rampage; Sorcerer; To Live and Die in L.A.*

Friedman, Jeffrey *Celluloid Closet, The*

Friedmann, Anthony *Bartleby*

Friend, Robert L. *Tarzan's Deadly Silence*

Friggis, Mike *One Night Stand*

Fritsch, Gunther von *Curse of the Cat People, The*

Frost, Mark *Storyville*

Fuest, Robert *Abominable Doctor Phibes, The; And Soon the Darkness; Dr. Phibes Rises Again; Final Programme, The; Wuthering Heights*

Fukasaku, Kinji *Tora! Tora! Tora!*

Fuller, Samuel *Big Red One, The; China Gate; Crimson Kimono, The; Fixed Bayonets!; Forty Guns; Hell and High Water; House of Bamboo; I Shot Jesse James; Merrill's Marauders; Naked Kiss, The; Pickup on South Street; Run of the Arrow; Shock Corridor; Steel Helmet, The; Underworld, U.S.A.; Verboten!; White Dog*

Fuqua, Antoine *Replacement Killers, The*

Furie, Sidney J. *Boys in Company C, The; Gable and Lombard; Hit!; Ipcress File, The; Iron Eagle; Iron Eagle II; Iron Eagle IV; Jazz Singer, The; Ladybugs; Lady Sings the Blues; Leather Boys, The; Little Fauss and Big Halsy; Naked Runner, The; Purple Hearts; Superman IV The Quest for Peace; Wonderful Life; Young Ones, The*

Gabor, Pal *Angi Vera*

Gabriel, Mike *Pocahontas; Rescuers Down Under, The*

Gance, Abel *Napoleon*

Gans, Christophe *Necronomicon*

Ganzer, Alvin *Three Bites of the Apple; When Boys Meet the Girls*

Garci, Jose Luis *Volver A Empezar*

Gardner, Herb *Goodbye People, The*

Garland, Patrick *Doll's House, A*

Garmes, Lee *Angels over Broadway*

Garnett, Tay *Bataan; China Seas; Connecticut Yankee in King Arthur's Court, A; Mrs Parkington; Postman Always Rings Twice, The; 7 Wonders of the World; Slave Ship; Soldiers Three; S.O.S. Iceberg; Stand-In; Valley of Decision, The*

Garnett, Tony *Handgun*

Garris, Mick *Critters 2 The Main Course; Sleepwalkers*

Gary, Romain *Kill*

Gazcon, Gilberto *Rage*

Geller, Bruce *Harry in Your Pocket*

George, Peter *Surf Nazis Must Die*

George, Terry *Some Mother's Son*

Gering, Marion *Thunder in the City*

Geronimi, Clyde *Alice in Wonderland; Cinderella; Lady and the Tramp; Make Mine Music; One Hundred and One Dalmations; Peter Pan; Sleeping Beauty; Victory through Air Power*

Gessner, Nicholas *Little Girl Who Lives down the Lane, The; 12 Plus 1*

Gibbons, Cedric *Tarzan and His Mate*

Gibson, Brian *Breaking Glass; Juror, The; Poltergeist II The Other Side; Still Crazy; What's Love Got to Do with It*

Gibson, Mel *Braveheart; Man without a Face, The*

Giese, Maria *When Saturday Comes*

Gilbert, Brian *Not without My Daughter, Tom & Viv; Vice Versa; Wilde*

Gilbert, Lewis *Admirable Crichton, The; Adventurers, The; Albert, R.N.; Alfie; Carve Her Name with Pride; Educating Rita; Good Die Young, The; Greengage Summer, The; Haunted; H.M.S. Defiant; Moonraker; Reach for the Sky; Seven Nights in Japan; 7th Dawn, The; Shirley Valentine; Sink the Bismarck!; Spy Who Loved Me, The; Stepping Out; You Only Live Twice*

Giler, David *Black Bird, The*

Gillard, Stuart *Teenage Mutant Ninja Turtles III The Turtles Are Back . . . In Time*

Gillespie, Jim *I Know What You Did Last Summer*

Gilliam, Terry *Adventures of Baron Munchausen, The; Brazil; Fear and Loathing in Las Vegas; Fisher King, The; Jabberwocky; Monty Python and the Holy Grail; Time Bandits; Twelve Monkeys*

Gilliat, Sidney *Blue Lagoon, The; Constant Husband, The; Great St. Trinian's Train Robbery, The; Green for Danger; London Belongs to Me; Millions Like Us; Only Two Can Play; Rake's Progress, The; Waterloo Road*

Gilling, John *Plague of the Zombies, The*

Gilmore, Stuart *Virginian, The*

Gilroy, Frank D. *From Noon Til Three; Gig, The; Once in Paris*

Ginty, Robert *Vietnam, Texas*

Girard, Bernard *Dead Heat on a Merry-Go-Round; Mad Room, The*

Girard, Francois *Thirty-two Short Films about Glenn Gould*

Girdler, William *Manitou, The*

Gish, Lillian *Remodeling Her Husband*

Gladwell, David *Memoirs of a Survivor*

Glaser, Paul Michael *Cutting Edge, The; Running Man, The*

Glatter, Lesli *Linka Now and Then*

Glatzer, Richard *Grief*

Glen, John *Aces Iron Eagle III; Christopher Columbus The Discovery; For Your Eyes Only; Licence to Kill; Living Daylights, The; Octopussy; View to a Kill, A*

Glenville, Peter *Becket; Comedians, The; Hotel Paradiso; Prisoner, The; Summer and Smoke; Term of Trial*

Glickenhaus, James *Exterminator, The; McBain; Protector, The*

Glimcher, Arne *Just Cause; Mambo Kings, The*

Godard, Jean-Luc *Bout De Souffle, A; Alphaville Une Etrange Aventure de Lemmy Caution; Detective; Une Femme Est Une Femme; Le Mepris; Passion; Pierrot le Fou; Prenom Carmen; Vivre sa Vie Film en Douze Tableaux; Week-End*

Godard, Nicholas Roeg, Charles Sturridge, Jean-Luc *Aria*

Goddard, Gary *Masters of the Universe*

Goddard, Jim *Shanghai Surprise*

Godfrey, Peter *Escape Me Never; Hotel Berlin; Two Mrs. Carrolls, The*

Golan, Menahem *Delta Force, The; Diamonds; Enter the Ninja; Hanna's War; Hit the Dutchman; Over the Brooklyn Bridge; Over the Top*

Gold, Jack *Aces High; Bofors Gun, The; Man Friday; Medusa Touch, The; Reckoning, The; Sailor's Return, The; Who?*

Goldbeck, Willis *Love Laughs at Andy Hardy; Ten Tall Men*

Goldberg, Dan *Feds*

Goldberg, Eric *Pocahontas*

Goldberg, Gary David *Dad*

Goldblatt, Mark *Punisher, The*

Goldenberg, Michael *Bed of Roses*

Goldschmidt, John *She'll Be Wearing Pink Pajamas*

Goldstein, Allan A. *Death Wish V The Face of Death*

Goldstone, James *Rollercoaster; Swashbuckler; Winning*

Goldstone, Richard *South Seas Adventure*

Goldwyn, Samuel, Jr. *Young Lovers, The*

Gomez, Nick *New Jersey Drive*

Gordon, Bert I. *Empire of the Ants*

Gordon, Bryan *Career Opportunities*

Gordon, Michael *Another Part of the Forest; Boys' Night Out; Cyrano de Bergerac; For Love or Money; I Can Get It for You Wholesale; Lady Gambles, The; Move Over, Darling; Pillow Talk; Texas across the River; Very Special Favor, A; Web, The*

Gordon, Robert *Joe Louis Story, The; Tarzan and the Jungle Boy*

Gordon, Steve *Arthur*

Gordon, Stuart *Fortress; Re-Animator*

Goretta, Claude *La Dentelliere*

Gornick, Michael *Creepshow 2*

Gorris, Marleen *Antonia's Line*

Gosnell, Raja *Home Alone 3*

Gottlieb, Carl *Amazon Women on the Moon*

Gottlieb, Lisa *Just One of the Guys*

Gottlieb, Michael *Mannequin; Mr. Nanny*

Gould, Heywood *One Good Cop; Trial by Jury*

Goulder, Stanley *Silent Playground, The*

Goulding, Alfred *Chump at Oxford, A*

Goulding, Edmund *Blondie of the Follies; Constant Nymph, The; Dark Victory; Dawn Patrol, The; Grand Hotel; Great Lie, The; Love; Nightmare Alley; Of Human Bondage; Old Maid, The; Razor's Edge, The; Sally, Irene and Mary; That Certain Woman; 'Til We Meet Again; Trespasser, The*

Goulding, Edwin H. Knopf, Lothar Mendes, Edmund *Paramount on Parade*

Goulding, Rene Clair, Edmund *Forever and a Day*

Graef, Roger *Secret Policeman's Ball, The*

Graham, William *Waterhole #3*

Graham, William A. *Return to the Blue Lagoon*

Grant, James Edward *Angel and the Badman*

Grant, Lee *Staying Together*

Grauman, Walter *Lady in a Cage; Rage to Live, A; 633 Squadron*

Gray, F. Gary *Friday; Negotiator, The*

Gray, James *Little Odessa*

Green, Alfred E. *Colleen; Dangerous; Disraeli; Girl from Tenth Avenue, The; Invasion U.S.A.; Jolson Story, The; King of the Turf; Little Lord Fauntleroy; Union Depot*

Green, David *Buster; Fire Birds*

Green, Guy *Angry Silence, The; Diamond Head; Light in the Piazza; Magus, The; Once Is Not Enough; Patch of Blue, A; Pretty Polly; Sea of Sand; Walk in the Spring Rain, A*

Greenaway, Peter *Baby of Macon, The; Belly of an Architect, The; Cook The Thief His Wife & Her Lover, The; Draughtsman's Contract, The; Drowning by Numbers; Pillow Book, The; Prospero's Books; Zed and Two Noughts, A*

Greene, Clarence *Well, The*

Greene, David *Count of Mount Cristo, The; Godspell; Gray Lady Down; I Start Counting; Sebastian; Shuttered Room, The; Strange Affair, The*

Greenwald, Maggie *Ballad of Little Jo, The; Kill-Off, The*

Greenwald, Robert *Hear No Evil; Xanadu*

Green, Guy *55 Days at Peking*

Gries, Tom *Breakheart Pass; Breakout; Greatest, The; Hawaiians, The; Lady Ice; Will Penny*

Grieve, Andrew *On the Black Hill*

Griffith, D. W. *Abraham Lincoln; Battle of the Sexes, The; Birth of a Nation,*

The; Birth of a Nation, The (1930); Broken Blossoms or The Yellow Man and the Girl; Dream Street; Escape, The; Fall of Babylon, The; Hearts of the World; Intolerance; Isn't Life Wonderful; Judith of Bethulia; Orphans of the Storm; Sally of the Sawdust; Sorrows of Satan, The; True Heart Susie; Way Down East

Grosbard, Ulu Deep End of the Ocean, The; Falling in Love; Georgia; Straight Time; Subject Was Roses, The; True Confessions

Guercio, James William Electra Guide in Blue; Tom Horn

Guest, Christopher Big Picture, The

Guest, Val Beauty Jungle, The; Camp on Blood Island, The; Casino Royale; Day the Earth Caught Fire, The; 80,000 Suspects; Expresso Bongo; Hell Is a City; Quatermass Experiment, The; Quatermass 2; When Dinosaurs Ruled the Earth; Where the Spies Are

Guillermin, John Blue Max, The; Bridge at Remagen, The; Death on the Nile; El Condor; Guns at Batasi; House of Cards; I Was Monty's Double; King Kong; King Kong Lives; Shaft in Africa; Sheena; Skyjacked; Tarzan Goes to India; Tarzan's Greatest Adventure; Towering Inferno, The; Waltz of the Toreadors

Gyllenhaal, Stephen Dangerous Woman, A; Losing Isaiah; Paris Trout; Waterland

Haas, Philip Angels and Insects; Music of Chance, The

Hackford, Taylor Against All Odds; Blood In Blood Out; Devil's Advocate, The; Dolores Claiborne; Everybody's All-American; Hail! Hail! Rock 'n' Roll; Idolmaker, The; Officer and a Gentleman, An; White Nights

Haggard, Piers Summer Story, A; Venom

Haines, Fred Steppenwolf

Haines, Randa Children of a Lesser God; Doctor, The; Wrestling Ernest Hemingway

Haines, Richard W. Class of Nuke 'em High

Halas, John Animal Farm

Hale, Sonnie Head over Heels

Haley, Jack Jr That's Entertainment!; That's Dancing!

Hall, Alexander Bedtime Story; Down to Earth; Great Lover, The; Heavenly Body, The; Here Comes Mr. Jordan; Love That Brute; My Sister Eileen; There's Always a Woman; They All Kissed the Bride; This Thing Called Love

Hall, Peter Akenfield; Never Talk to Strangers; Perfect Friday; 3 into 2 Won't Go; Work Is a Four-Letter Word

Halliday, Mark Just Like in the Movies

Hallstrom, Lasse ABBA The Movie; Mitt Liv Som Hund; Once Around; Something to Talk About; What's Eating Gilbert Grape

Halperin, Victor Party Girl

Halpern, Victor Supernatural

Hamer, Robert Dead of Night; Father Brown; Kind Hearts and Coronets; Pink String and Sealing Wax; School for Scoundrels or How to Win without Actually Cheating

Hamilton, Guy Battle of Britain; Best of Enemies, The; Colditz Story, The; Devil's Disciple, The; Diamonds Are Forever; Evil under the Sun; Force 10 from Navarone; Funeral in Berlin; Goldfinger; Intruder, The; Live and Let Die; Man with the Golden Gun, The; Mirror Crack'd, The; Party's Over, The; Remo Williams The Adventure Begins . . .

Hamilton, Strathford Blueberry Hill

Hammond, Peter Spring and Port Wine

Hampton, Christopher Carrington

Hand, David Bambi; Snow White and the Seven Dwarfs

Hanks, Tom That Thing You Do!

Hannam, Ken Summerfield; Sunday Too Far Away

Hanson, Curtis Bad Influence; Bedroom Window, The; Hand That Rocks the Cradle, The; L.A. Confidential; Losin' It; River Wild, The

Hardy, Robin Wicker Man, The

Hare, David Paris by Night; Strapless; Wetherby

Hark, Tsui Yinghung Bunsik III Tsikyeung Tsi Go

Harlin, Renny Adventures of Ford Fairlane, The; Cliffhanger; CutThroat Island; Deep Blue Sea; Die Hard 2; Long Kiss Goodnight, The; Nightmare on Elm Street 4, A: The Dream Master; Prison

Harmon, Robert Hitcher, The; Nowhere to Run

Harrington, Curtis Games; Night Tide; Ruby; What's the Matter with Helen?

Harris, Damian Bad Company; Deceived; Rachel Papers, The

Harris, James B. Bedford Incident, The; Boiling Point; Cop; Fast-Walking

Harris, Leslie Just Another Girl on the I.R.T.

Harrison, John *Tales from the Darkside The Movie*

Harron, Mary *I Shot Andy Warhol*

Hart, Harvey *Bus Riley's Back in Town; Shoot; Sweet Ride, The*

Hartford-Davis, Robert *Sandwich Man, The; Saturday Night Out*

Hartley, Hal *Amateur; Flirt; Henry Fool; Simple Men; Trust; Unbelievable Truth, The*

Hartman, Don *Every Girl Should Be Married*

Harvey, Anthony *Abdication, The; Dutchman; Eagle's Wing; Lion in Winter, The; Players; They Might Be Giants; Ultimate Solution of Grace Quigley, The*

Harvey, Hark *Carnival of Souls*

Harvey, Laurence *Ceremony, The; Dandy in Aspic, A*

Has, Wojciech J. *Rekopis Znaleziony W Saragossie*

Haskin, Byron *Conquest of Space; His Majesty O'Keefe; I Walk Alone; Naked Jungle, The; Power, The; Tarzan's Peril; Treasure Island; War of the Worlds, The*

Hathaway, Henry *Black Rose, The; Bottom of the Bottle, The; Brigham Young; Call Northside 777; China Girl; Circus World; Desert Fox, The; Diplomatic Courier; Down to the Sea in Ships; 5 Card Stud; Fourteen Hours; Garden of Evil; Go West, Young Man; House on 92nd Street, The; How the West Was Won; Kiss of Death; Lives of a Bengal Lancer, The; Nevada Smith; Niagara North to Alaska; Now and Forever; Of Human Bondage; O. Henry's Full House; Peter Ibbetson; Prince Valiant; Rawhide; Real Glory, The; Sons of Katie Elder, The; Souls at Sea; Spawn of the North; Sundown; Ten Gentlemen from West Point; 13 Rue Madeleine; Trail of the Lonesome Pine, The; True Grit; U.S.S. Teakettle*

Hawks, Howard *Air Force; Ball of Fire; Barbary Coast; Big Sky, The; Big Sleep, The; Bringing Up Baby; Ceiling Zero; Criminal Code, The; Crowd Roars, The; Dawn Patrol, The; El Dorado; Gentlemen Prefer Blondes; Girl in Every Port, A; Hatari!; His-Girl Friday; I Was a Male War Bride; Land of the Pharaohs; Man's Favorite Sport?; Monkey Business; O. Henry's Full House; Only Angels Have Wings; Red Line 7000; Red River; Rio Bravo; Rio Lobo; Road to Glory, The; Scarface; Sergeant York; Song Is Born, A; Tiger*

Shark; To Have and Have Not; Twentieth Century

Haydn, Richard *Miss Tatlock's Millions; Mr. Music*

Hayers, Sidney *Finders Keepers; Trap, The*

Haynes, Todd *Poison; Velvet Goldmine*

Hazan, Jack *Bigger Splash, A*

Heap, Jonathan *Benefit of the Doubt*

Hecht, Ben *Actors and Sin; Angels over Broadway; Crime without Passion; Scoundrel, The; Specter of the Rose*

Heckerling, Amy *Clueless; Fast Times at Ridgemont High; Johnny Dangerously; Look Who's Talking Too; National Lampoon's European Vacation*

Hedden, Rob *Friday the 13th, Part VIII Jason Takes Manhattan*

Heerman, Victor *Animal Crackers*

Heffron, Richard T. *Futureworld; I, The Jury; Outlaw Blues*

Hegedus, Chris *War Room, The*

Heisler, Stuart *Along Came Jones; Blue Skies; Burning Hills, The; Dallas; Glass Key, The; Star, The; Storm Warning; Tokyo Joe*

Helgeland, Brian *Payback*

Hellman, Jerome *Promises in the Dark*

Hellman, Monte *China 9 Liberty 37; Ride in the Whirlwind; Two-Lane Blacktop*

Hemmings, David *Just a Gigolo*

Henderson, John *Loch Ness*

Henenlotter, Frank *Basket Case; Basket Case 2; Basket Case 3 The Progeny; Frankenhooker*

Henkel, Kim *Return of the Texas Chainsaw Massacre, The*

Henry, Buck *Heaven Can Wait*

Henson, Brian *Muppet Christmas Carol, The; Muppet Treasure Island*

Henson, Jim *Dark Crystal, The; Great Muppet Caper, The; Labyrinth*

Herek, Stephen *Bill & Ted's Excellent Adventure; Critters; Don't Tell Mom the Babysitter's Dead; Mighty Ducks, The; 101 Dalmations; Three Musketeers, The*

Herman, Mark *Blame It on the Bellboy; Brassed Off*

Herrington, Rowdy *Gladiator; Road House*

Herskovitz, Marshall *Jack the Bear*

Hertz, Nathan *Attack of the 50 Foot Woman*

Herz, Michael *Toxic Avenger, The; Toxic Avenger, Part II, The*

Herzfeld, John *Two of a Kind*

Herzog, Werner *Aguirre, Der Zorn Gottes; Scream of Stone*

Hessler, Gordon *Girl in a Swing, The;*

Golden Voyage of Sinbad, The; Oblong Box, The

Heston, Charlton *Anthony and Cleopatra; Mother Lode*

Heston, Fraser C. *Needful Things*

Hewitt, Peter *Bill & Ted's Bogus Journey*

Heyes, Douglas *Beau Geste; Kitten with a Whip*

Hibbs, Jesse *To Hell and Back*

Hickenlooper, George *Big Brass Ring, The*

Hickox, Anthony *Hellraiser III Hell on Earth; Invasion of Privacy; Warlock: The Armageddon*

Hickox, Douglas *Brannigan; Entertaining Mr. Sloane; Sitting Target; Sky Riders; Theater of Blood; Zulu Dawn*

Hicks, Scott *Shine*

Higgins, Colin *Best Little Whorehouse in Texas, The; Foul Play; Nine to Five*

Hill, George *Big House, The*

Hill, George Roy *Butch Cassidy and the Sundance Kid; Funny Farm; Great Waldo Pepper, The; Hawaii; Little Drummer Girl, The; Little Romance, A; Period of Adjustment; Slap Shot; Slaughterhouse-Five; Sting, The; Thoroughly Modern Millie; Toys in the Attic; World According to Garp, The; World of Henry Orient, The*

Hill, Jack *Coffy; Foxy Brown*

Hill, James *Black Beauty; Born Free; Dock Brief, The*

Hill, Jerome *Sand Castle, The*

Hill, Robert *Tarzan the Fearless*

Hill, Tim *Muppets from Space*

Hill, Walter *Another 48HRS.; Brewster's Millions; Crossroads; Driver, The; Extreme Prejudice; 48HRS.; Geronimo An American Legend; Hard Times; Johnny Handsome; Last Man Standing; Long Riders, The; Red Heat; Southern Comfort; Streets of Fire; Trespass; Warriors, The; Wild Bill*

Hillcoat, John *Ghosts . . . of the Civil Dead*

Hiller, Arthur *Alan Smithee Film—Burn, Hollywood, Burn, An; Americanization of Emily, The; Author! Author!; Babe, The; Hospital, The; In-Laws, The; Lonely Guy, The; Love Story; Making Love; Man of La Mancha; Married to It; Out of Towners, The; Outrageous Fortune; Penelope; Plaza Suite; Popi; Promise Her Anything; See No Evil, Hear No Evil; Silver Streak; Taking Care of Business; Teachers; Tiger Makes Out, The; Tobruk*

Hilliard, Richard L. *Psychomania*

Hilton, Arthur *Cat-Women of the Moon*

Hitchcock, Alfred *Birds, The; Blackmail; Dial M for Murder; Family Plot; Foreign Correspondent; Frenzy; I Confess; Jamaica Inn; Juno and the Paycock; Lady Vanishes, The; Lifeboat; Man Who Knew Too Much, The; Man Who Knew Too Much, The (1956); Manxman, The; Marnie; Mr. & Mrs. Smith; Murder; North by Northwest; Notorious; Paradine Case, The; Psycho; Rear Window; Ring, The; Rope; Sabotage; Saboteur; Secret Agent; Shadow of a Doubt; Skin Game, The; Spellbound; Stage Fright; Strangers on a Train; Suspicion; 39 Steps, The; To Catch a Thief; Topaz; Torn Curtain; Trouble with Harry, The; Under Capricorn; Vertigo; Wrong Man, The*

Hoblit, Gregory *Primal Fear*

Hodges, Mike *Black Rainbow; Flash Gordon; Get Carter; Prayer for the Dying, A; Pulp*

Hoellering, George *Murder in the Cathedral*

Hoffman, Michael *One Fine Day; Midsummer Night's Dream, A; Promised Land; Restoration; Soapdish; Some Girls*

Hofsiss, Jack *I'm Dancing as Fast as I Can*

Hogan, David *Barb Wire*

Hogan, James *Texans, The*

Hogan, P. J. *Muriel's Wedding; My Best Friend's Wedding*

Holden, Lansing C. *She*

Holland, Agnieszka *Secret Garden, The; To Kill A Priest; Total Eclipse*

Holland, Tom *Child's Play; Fright Night; Temp, The*

Holmes, Ben *Saint in New York, The*

Holofcener, Nicole *Walking and Talking*

Holt, Seth *Blood from the Mummy's Tomb; Danger Route; Nanny, The; Station Six-Sahara*

Hook, Harry *Kitchen Toto, The; Lord of the Flies*

Hooks, Kevin *Passenger 57*

Hooper, Tobe *Funhouse, The; Invaders from Mars; Lifeforce; Poltergeist; Texas Chain Saw Massacre, The; Texas Chain Saw Massacre Part 2, The*

Hopkins, Anthony *August*

Hopkins, Stephen *Blown Away; Ghost and the Darkness, The; Judgement Night; Lost in Space; Nightmare on Elm Street, A; Dream Child, The; Predator 2*

Hopper, Dennis *Catchfire; Chasers; Colors; Easy Rider; Hot Spot, The; Last Movie, The; Out of the Blue*

Hopper, Jerry *Atomic City, The*

Horn, Buddy Van *Any Which Way You Can; Dead Pool, The*

Hornaday, Jeffrey *Shout*

Horne, James W. *Way Out West*

Horner, Harry *Red Planet Mars*

Horton, Peter *Amazon Women on the Moon*

Hoskins, Bob *Raggedy Rawney, The*

Hoskins, Dan *Chopper Chicks in Zombietown*

Hossein, Robert *Les Miserables*

Hou Hsiao-hsien *Tongnian Wangshi*

Hough, John *Biggles; Brass Target; Dirty Mary Crazy Larry; Escape to Witch Mountain; Eyewitness; Legend of Hell House, The; Return from Witch Mountain; Twins of Evil; Watcher in the Woods, The*

Hovde, Ellen *Enormous Changes at the Last Minute*

Howard, Cy *Lovers and Other Strangers*

Howard, Leslie *First of the Few, The; Gentle Sex, The; Pygmalion*

Howard, Ron *Apollo 13; Backdraft; Cocoon; EdTV; Far and Away; Grand Theft Auto; Gung Ho; Night Shift; Paper, The; Parenthood; Ransom; Splash; Willow*

Howard, William K. *Fire over England; First Year, The; Johnny Come Lately; Power and the Glory, The; Rendezvous; Squeaker, The; Thundering Herd, The*

Howitt, Peter *Sliding Doors*

Howley, John *Happily Ever After*

Hu, King *Xia Nu*

Huang, George *Swimming with Sharks*

Hubert, Jean-Loup *Le Grand Chemin*

Hudlin, Reginald *Boomerang; Great White Hype, The; House Party*

Hudson, Hugh *Chariots of Fire; Greystoke The Legend of Tarzan Lord of the Apes; Lost Angels; Revolution*

Hughes, Albert *Dead Presidents*

Hughes, Allen *Dead Presidents*

Hughes, Howard *Hell's Angels; Outlaw, The*

Hughes, John *Breakfast Club, The; Curly Sue; Ferris Bueller's Day Off; Planes, Trains & Automobiles; She's Having a Baby; Sixteen Candles; Uncle Buck; Weird Science*

Hughes, Ken *Casino Royale; Chitty Chitty Bang Bang; Cromwell; Drop Dead Darling; Joe Macbeth; Of Human Bondage; Sextette; Small World of Sammy Lee, The; Trials of Oscar Wilde, The*

Hughes, Terry *Butcher's Wife, The*

Humberstone, H. Bruce *Charlie Chan at the Opera; Desert Song, The; Hello Frisco, Hello; Hot Spot; If I Had a Million; I Wake Up Screaming; Pin Up Girl; Tarzan and the Last Safari; Tarzan's Fight for Life; Wonder Man*

Hung, Tran Anh *Mui Du Du Xanh*

Hunt, Maurice *Pagemaster, The*

Hunt, Peter *Gold; On Her Majesty's Secret Service; Shout at the Devil; Wild Geese II*

Hunter, Tim *River's Edge; Tex*

Huntington, Lawrence *Upturned Glass, The*

Hurst, Brian Desmond *Black Tent, The; Dangerous Moonlight; Malta Story*

Hussein, Waris *Henry VIII and his Six Wives; Melody; Possession of Joel Delaney, The; Touch of Love, A*

Huston, Anjelica *Bastard out of Carolina*

Huston, Danny *Mr. North*

Huston, John *Across the Pacific; African Queen, The; Annie; Asphalt Jungle, The; Barbarian and the Geisha, The; Beat the Devil; The Bible in the Beginning . . . ; Casino Royale; Dead, The; Fat City; Freud; Heaven Knows, Mr. Allison; In This Our Life; Key Largo; Kremlin Letter, The; Life and Times of Judge Roy Bean, The; List of Adrian Messenger, The; Mackintosh Man, The; Maltese Falcon, The; Man Who Would Be King, The; Misfits, The; Moby Dick; Moulin Rouge; Night of the Iguana, The; Prizzi's Honor; Red Badge of Courage, The; Reflections in a Golden Eye; Roots of Heaven, The; Sinful Davey; Treasure of the Sierra Madre, The; Under the Volcano; Unforgiven, The; Victory; Walk with Love and Death, A; We Were Strangers; Wise Blood*

Hutton, Brian G. *First Deadly Sin, The; High Road to China; Kelly's Heroes; Night Watch; Pad (And How to Use It), The; Sol Madrid; Where Eagles Dare; Zee & Co.*

Huyck, Willard *Howard the Duck*

Hyams, Peter *Busting; Capricorn One; End of Days; Hanover Street; Narrow Margin; Outland; Peeper; Presidio, The; Running Scared; Star Chamber, The; Stay Tuned; Sudden Death; Timecop; 2010*

Hytner, Nicholas *Crucible, The; Madness of King George, The*

Ichaso, Leon *Sugar Hill*

Ichikawa, Kon *Biruma No Tategoto; Nobi; Sasame Yuki; Yukinojo Henge*

Ichikawa, Kon Milos Forman *Visions of Eight*

Imamura, Shohei *Fukushu Sure Wa Ware Ni Ari; Narayama Bushi-ko*

Ingram, Rex *Arab, The; Four Horsemen of the Apocalypse, The; Garden of Allah, The; Mare Nostrum; Prisoner of Zenda, The; Scaramouche*

Ingster, Boris *Stranger on the Third Floor*

Ireland, Dan *Whole Wide World, The*

Irvin, John *Dogs of War, The; Ghost Story; Hamburger Hill; Next of Kin; Raw Deal; Robin Hood; Widows' Peak*

Israel, Neal *Bachelor Party; Surf Ninjas*

Itami, Juzo *Marusa No Onna; Tampopo*

Ivory, James *Bostonians, The; Europeans, The; Guru, The; Heat and Dust; Howards End; Jefferson in Paris; Maurice; Mr. & Mrs. Bridge; Quartet; Remains of the Day, The; Room with a View, A; Roseland; Savages; Shakespeare Wallah; Wild Party, The*

Jackson, George *House Party 2*

Jackson, Mick *Bodyguard, The; Chattahoochee; Clean Slate; L.A. Story; Volcano*

Jackson, Pat *Encore*

Jackson, Peter *Braindead; Heavenly Creatures*

Jackson, Wilfred *Alice in Wonderland; Cinderella; Lady and the Tramp; Peter Pan*

Jacopetti, Gualtiero *Mondo Cane*

Jaeckin, Just *Emmanuelle; Lady Chatterley's Lover*

Jaglom, Henry *Always; Babyfever; Can She Bake a Cherry Pie?; Eating; Last Summer in the Hamptons; New Year's Day; Safe Place, A; Sitting Ducks; Someone to Love; Tracks; Venice/Venice*

Jameson, Jerry *Airport '77; Raise the Titanic*

Jancso, Miklos *Csillagosok, Katonak; Szegenylegenyek*

Jankel, Annabel *D.O.A.; Super Mario Bros.*

Jann, Michael Patrick *Drop Dead Gorgeous*

Jarman, Derek *Blue; Caravaggio; Edward II; Garden, The; Jubilee; Last of England, The; Tempest, The; War Requiem; Wittgenstein*

Jarmusch, Jim *Dead Man; Down by Law; Mystery Train; Night on Earth; Stranger Than Paradise*

Jarrott, Charles *Anne of the Thousand Days; Dove, The; Lost Horizon; Mary, Queen of Scots; Other Side of Midnight, The*

Jean, Vadim *Beyond Bedlam; Clockwork Mice; Leon the Pig Farmer*

Jeffrey, Tom *Odd Angry Shot, The*

Jeffries, Lionel *Baxter!; Railway Children, The; Water Babies, The*

Jenkins, Michael *Heartbreak Kid, The*

Jeunet, Jean-Pierre *Alien Resurrection; La Cite des Enfants Perdus; Delicatessen*

Jewison, Norman *Agnes of God; . . . And Justice for All; Art of Love, The; Best Friends; Cincinnati Kid, The; Fiddler on the Roof; F.I.S.T.; Forty Pounds of Trouble; Gaily, Gaily; Hurricane, The; In Country; In the Heat of the Night; Jesus Christ Superstar; Moonstruck; Only You; Other People's Money; Rollerball; Russians Are Coming! The Russians Are Coming!, The; Send Me No Flowers; Soldier's Story, A; Thomas Crown Affair, The; Thrill of It All*

Jimenez, Neal *Waterdance, The*

Jin, Xie *Wutai Jiemei*

Joanou, Phil *Final Analysis; Heaven's Prisoners; State of Grace; U2 Rattle and Hum*

Joffe, Arthur *Harem*

Joffe, Roland *City of Joy; Fat Man and Little Boy; Killing Fields, The; Mission, The; Scarlet Letter, The*

Johnson, Alan *To Be or Not to Be*

Johnson, Jed *Bad*

Johnson, Kenneth *Short Circuit 2*

Johnson, Lamont *Cattle Annie and Little Britches; Groundstar Conspiracy, The; Gunfight, A; Last American Hero, The; Lipstick; McKenzie Break, The; One on One; Spacehunter Adventures in the Forbidden Zone; You'll Like My Mother*

Johnson, Nunnally *Black Widow; How to Be Very, Very Popular; Man in the Gray Flannel Suit, The; Night People; Three Faces of Eve, The*

Johnson, Patrick *Read Baby's Day Out*

Johnson, Tim *Antz*

Johnston, Aaron Kim *Last Winter, The*

Johnston, Joe *Honey, I Shrunk the Kids; Jumanji; Pagemaster, The; Rocketeer, The*

Jones, Amy *Love Letters; Slumber Party Massacre*

Jones, David *Betrayal; 84 Charing Cross Road; Jacknife; Trial, The*

Jones, F. Richard *Bulldog Drummond; Gaucho, The; Mickey*

Jones, James Cellan *Bequest to the Nation*

Jones, Terry *Erik the Viking; Life of Brian; Monty Python and the Holy*

Greenwich Village; Jackpot, The; King and I, The; Little Princess, The; Love Before Breakfast; Marriage-Go-Round, The; Mighty Barnum, The; Mother Wore Tights; On the Riviera; Sitting Pretty; Song of the Islands; Star Dust; State Fair; There's No Business Like Show Business; Tin Pan Alley; With a Song in My Heart; You're My Everything

Langley, Noel *Our Girl Friday; Pickwick Papers, The*

Langton, Simon *Whistle Blower, The*

Lapine, James *Impromptu; Life with Mikey*

Lasseter, John *Bug's Life, A; Toy Story; Toy Story 2*

Laughlin, Tom *Billy Jack; Billy Jack Goes to Washington; Born Losers; Master Gunfighter, The; Trial of Billy Jack, The*

Laughton, Charles *Night of the Hunter, The*

Launder, Frank *Belles of St. Trinian's, The; Blue Lagoon, The; Blue Murder at St. Trinians; Great St. Trinian's Train Robbery, The; Happiest Days of Your Life, The; Millions Like Us; Pure Hell of St. Trinian's, The*

Lautner, Georges *La Cage aux Folles 3*

Laven, Arnold *Geronimo; Glory Guys, The; Rough Night in Jericho; Slaughter on Tenth Avenue; Vice Squad*

Lawrence, Quentin *Secret of Blood Island, The; Trollenberg Terror, The*

Lawrence, Ray *Bliss*

Lawton, J. F. *Hunted, The*

Layton, Joe *Richard Pryor Live on the Sunset Strip*

Lazarus, Ashley *Golden Rendezvous*

Leach, Wilford *Pirates of Penzance, The; Wedding Party, The*

Leacock, Philip *Reach for Glory; Spanish Gardener, The; War Lover, The*

Leader, Anton M. *Children of the Damned*

Lean, David *Blithe Spirit; Bridge on the River Kwai, The; Brief Encounter; Doctor Zhivago; Great Expectations; Greatest Story Ever Told, The; Hobson's Choice; In Which We Serve; Lawrence of Arabia; Major Barbara; Oliver Twist; Passage to India, A; Passionate Friends, The; Ryan's Daughter; Sound Barrier, The; Summer Madness; This Happy Breed*

LeChanois, Jean Paul *Les Miserables*

Leconte, Patrice *Le Mari de la Coiffeuse; Mosieur Hire; Ridicule*

Leder, Herbert J. *Pretty Boy Floyd*

Leder, Mimi *Deep Impact; Peacemaker, The*

Lederman, D. Ross *Strange Alibi; Tarzan's Revenge*

Lee, Ang *Ice Storm, The; Ride with the Devil; Sense and Sensibility; Xi Yan; Yinshi Nannu*

Lee, Bruce *Meng Long Guo Jiang*

Lee, Jack *Robbery under Arms; Town Like Alice, A; Wooden Horse, The*

Lee, Rowland V. *Captain Kidd; Count of Monte Cristo, The; Dr. Fu Manchu; Return of Dr. Fu Manchu, The; Son of Frankenstein; Three Musketeers, The; Toast of New York, The; Tower of London; Zoo in Budapest*

Lee, Spike *Clockers; Crooklyn; Do the Right Thing; Get on the Bus; Girl 6; He Got Game; Jungle Fever; Malcolm X; Mo' Better Blues; School Daze; She's Gotta Have It; Summer of Sam*

Leeds, Herbert I. *Danger Island; It Shouldn't Happen to a Dog*

Lehman, Ernest *Portnoy's Complaint*

Lehmann, Michael *Airheads; Heathers; Hudson Hawk; Meet the Applegates; Truth about Cats and Dogs, The*

Leigh, Mike *Bleak Moments; High Hopes; Life Is Sweet; Naked; Secrets & Lies*

Leight, Warren *Night We Never Met, The*

Leisen, Mitchell *Big Broadcast of 1937, The; Big Broadcast of 1938, The; Bride of Vengeance; Captain Carey, U.S.A.; Death Takes a Holiday; Dream Girl; Eagle and the Hawk, The; Easy Living; Frenchman's Creek; Hold Back the Dawn; Kitty; Lady in the Dark; Lady Is Willing, The; Mating Season, The; Midnight; Murder at the Vanities; No Man of Her Own; No Time for Love; Remember the Night; Suddenly It's Spring; Swing High, Swing Low; To Each His Own; Tonight We Sing*

Leland, David *Big Man, The; Checking Out; Wish You Were Here*

Lelouch, Claude *Un Autre Homme Une Autre Chance; Un Homme et une Femme; Les Miserables; Les Uns Et Les Autres; Vivre pour Vivre*

Lemmon, Jack *Kotch*

Lemont, John *Frightened City, The*

Leo, Malcolm *This Is Elvis*

Leonard, Brett *Lawnmower Man, The; Virtuosity*

Leonard, Herbert B. *Going Home*

Leonard, Robert Z. *Bachelor Father; B.F.'s Daughter; Cynthia; Dancing Lady; Divorcee, The; Escapade; Everything I Have Is Yours; Girl of the Golden West, The; Great Ziegfeld, The; Maytime; Nancy Goes Rio; Pride and*

Leonard, Robert (cont.)
Prejudice; Secret Heart, The; Strange Interlude; Susan Lenox Her Fall and Rise; Third Finger, Left Hand; Weekend at the Waldorf; When Ladies Meet; Ziegfeld Girl

Leone, John Last of the Cowboys, The

Leone, Sergio Fistful of Dollars; Fistful of Dynamite, A; For a Few Dollars More; Good, the Bad and the Ugly, The; Once Upon a Time in America; Once Upon a Time in the West

Lepage, Robert Le Confessional

Lerner, Irving Murder by Contract; Royal Hunt of the Sun, The; Studs Lonigan

LeRoy, Mervyn Anthony Adverse; Any Number Can Play; Bad Seed, The; Blossoms in the Dust; Desire Me; Devil at 4 O'Clock, The; East Side, West Side; Escape; FBI Story, The; Five Star Final; Gold Diggers of 1993; Gypsy; Hard to Handle; High Pressure; Home before Dark; Homecoming; I Am a Fugitive from a Chain Gang; I Found Stella Parish; Johnny Eager; King and the Chorus Girl, The; Latin Lovers; Little Caesar; Little Women; Lovely to Look At; Madame Curie; Majority of One, A; Million Dollar Mermaid; Mister Roberts; Moment to Moment; Oil for the Lamps of China; Page Miss Glory; Quo Vadis; Random Harvest; Rose Marie; Sweet Adeline; They Won't Forget; Thirty Seconds over Tokyo; Three Men on a Horse; Tugboat Annie; Waterloo Bridge; Without Reservations

Lessac, Michael House of Cards

Lester, Mark L. Armed and Dangerous; Class of 1984; Class of 1999; Commando; Firestarter; Showdown in Little Tokyo; Stunts; Truck Stop Women

Lester, Richard Bed Sitting Room, The; Butch and Sundance The Early Days; Cuba; Finders Keepers; The Four Musketeers The Revenge of Milady; Funny Thing Happened on the Way to the Forum, A; Get Back; Hard Day's Night, A; Help!; How I Won the War; Juggernaut; The Knack . . . And How to Get It; Petulia; Return of the Musketeers, The; Ritz, The; Robin and Marian; Royal Flash; Superman II; Superman III; Three Musketeers, The; Queen's Diamonds, The

Lettich, Sheldon Double Impact

Levant, Brian Beethoven; Flinstones, The; Jingle All The Way; Problem Child 2

Leven, Jeremy Don Juan DeMarco

Levin, Henry Ambushers, The; And Baby Makes Three; Bandit of Sherwood Forest, The; Come Fly with Me; Convicted; Farmer Takes a Wife, The; Genghis Khan; Holiday for Lovers; Jolson Sings Again; Journey to the Center of the Earth; Murderers' Row; President's Lady, The; Where the Boys Are; Wonderful World of the Brothers Grimm, The

Levin, Sid Let the Good Times Roll

Levinson, Barry Avalon; Bugsy; Diner; Disclosure; Good Morning, Vietnam; Jimmy Hollywood; Liberty Heights; Natural, The; Rain Man; Sleepers; Sphere; Tin Men; Toys; Wag the Dog; Young Sherlock Holmes

Levy, Eugene Once Upon a Crime

Levy, Jefery Inside Monkey Zetterland; S.F.W.

Levy Ralph Bedtime Story; Do Not Disturb

Levy, Raoul Defector, The

Lewin, Albert Moon and Sixpence, The; Pandora and the Flying Dutchman; Picture of Dorian Gray, The; Private Affairs of Bel Ami, The

Lewis, Jay Invasion Quartet; Live Now Pay Later

Lewis, Jerry Bellboy, The; Errand Boy, The; Family Jewels, The; Ladies' Man, The; Nutty Professor, The; Patsy, The

Lewis, Joseph H. Big Combo, The; Gun Crazy; Lady without Passport, A; My Name Is Julia Ross; Retreat, Hell!; So Dark the Night; Terror in a Texas Town; Undercover Man, The

Lewis, Richard J. Whale Music

Lewis, Robert Anything Goes

Lieberman, Jeff Squirm

Lieberman, Robert D3: The Mighty Ducks; Table for Five

Lima, Kevin Tarzan

Lilley, Edward Never a Dull Moment

Liman, Doug Go

Lindsay-Hogg, Michael Frankie Starlight; Let It Be; Nasty Habits; Object of Beauty, The

Linklater, Richard Before Sunrise; Dazed and Confused; Slacker; Suburbia

Linson, Art Where the Buffalo Roam

Lipstaft, Aaron Android; City Limits

Lisberger, Steven Slipstream; Tron

Little, Dwight Free Willy 2 The Adventure Home

Little, Dwight H. Halloween 4 The Return of Michael Myers; Marked for Death; Murder at 1600; Phantom of the Opera, The; Rapid Fire

Littlewood, Joan Sparrows Can't Sing

Littman, Lynne Testament

Maas, Dick *De Lift*

MacArthur, Charles *Crime without Passion; Scoundrel, The*

Macdonald, David *Cairo Road; Christopher Columbus; Petticoat Pirates*

Macdonald, Hettie *Beautiful Thing*

Macdonald, Mace *Neufeld Saint, The*

Macdonald, Peter *Mo' Money; Neverending Story III, The; Rambo III*

MacDougall, Ranald *Go Naked in the World; Man on Fire; Subterraneans, The; World, the Flesh and the Devil, The*

MacFadden, Hamilton *Charlie Chan Carries On*

MacGrath, Jospeh *Bliss of Mrs. Blossom, The*

Machaty, Gustav *Extase*

Mack, Willard *Broadway to Hollywood*

Mackendrick, Alexander *Don't Make Waves; High Wind in Jamaica, A; Ladykillers, The; 'Maggie', The; Mandy; Man in the White Suit, The; Sammy Going South; Sweet Smell of Success; Whisky Galore!*

Mackenzie, John *Fourth Protocol, The; Honorary Consul, The; Last of the Finest, The; Long Good Friday, The; Ruby; Unman, Wittering and Zigo*

MacKinnon, Gillies *Playboys, The; Simple Twist of Fate, A; Small Faces*

Madden, David *Separate Lives*

Madden, John *Mrs. Brown; Shakespeare in Love*

Maddow, Ben *Savage Eye, The*

Magnoli, Albert *Purple Rain; Tango & Cash*

Mailer, Norman *Tough Guys Don't Dance*

Main, Stewart *Desperate Remedies*

Makavejev, Dusan *Coca-Cola Kid, The; Nevinost Bez Zastite; Sweet Movie; WR: Misterije Organizma*

Makin, Kelly *Brain Candy; Mickey Blue Eyes; National Lampoon's Senior Trip*

Makk, Karoly *Szerelem*

Malick, Terrence *Badlands; Days of Heaven; Thin Red Line, The*

Malle, Louis *Alamo Bay; Les Amants; Atlantic City; Au Revoir, Les Enfants; Crackers; Damage; Lacombe Lucien; My Dinner with Andre; Pretty Baby; Le Souffle au Coeur; Vanya on 42nd Street; Viva Maria!; Zazie Dans Le Metro*

Mallon, Jim *Mystery Science Theater 3000: The Movie*

Malmuth, Bruce *Hard to Kill; Nighthawks*

Malone, Mark *Killer*

Malone, William *House on Haunted Hill*

Mamet, David *Homicide; House of Games; Oleanna; Spanish Prisoner The; Things Change*

Mamoulian, Rouben *Applause; Beck Sharp; Blood and Sand; City Streets Dr. Jekyll and Mr. Hyde; Gay Desper ado, The; High, Wide and Handsome Love Me Tonight; Mark of Zorro, The Queen Christina; Rings on Her Fin gers; Silk Stockings; Song of Songs Summer Holiday; We Live Again*

Manchevski, Milcho *Before the Rain*

Mandel, Robert *F/X; Independence Day Substitute, The; Touch and Go*

Mandoki, Luis *Born Yesterday; When Man Loves a Woman; White Palace*

Manduke, Joseph *Gumshoe Kid, The*

Mangold, James *Cop Land; Girl, Inter rupted*

Mankiewicz, Joseph L. *All about Eve Barefoot Contessa, The; Cleopatra Dragonwyck; 5 Fingers; Ghost an Mrs. Muir, The; Guys and Dolls Honey Pot, The; House of Strangers Julius Caesar; Letter to Three Wives A; No Way Out; People Will Talk Quiet American, The; Sleuth; Sud denly, Last Summer; There Was Crooked Man . . .*

Mankiewicz, Tom *Delirious; Dragnet*

Mann, Anthony *Bend of the River; Borde Incident; Cimarron; Dandy in Aspic A; Desperate; Devil's Doorway; E Cid; Fall of the Roman Empire, The Far Country, The; Furies, The; Glen Miller Story, The; God's Little Acre Heroes of Telemark, The; Man from Laramie, The; Man of the West; Mer in War; Naked Spur, The; Spartacus Strategic Air Command; Thunder Bay Tin Star, The; T-Men; Winchester '73*

Mann, Daniel *Butterfield 8; Come Back Little Sheba; Dream of Kings, A; Fiv Finger Exercise; For Love of Ivy; I'l Cry Tomorrow; Judith; Last Angry Man, The; Our Man Flint; Rose Tat too, The; Teahouse of the Augus Moon, The; Who's Been Sleeping ir My Bed?; Willard*

Mann, Delbert *Bachelor Party, The; Dark at the Top of the Stairs, The; Davic Copperfield; Desire under the Elms, Fitzwilly; Gathering of Eagles, A; Jane Eyre; Kidnapped; Lover Come Back, Marty; Night Crossing; Separate Ta bles; That Touch of Mink*

Mann, Farhad *Lawnmower Man 2 Beyonc Cyberspace*

Mann, Michael *Heat; Insider, The; Keep The; Last of the Mohicans, The; Man hunter; Thief*

Marcus, Adam *Jason Goes to Hell The Final Friday*

Margheriti, Antonio *Take a Hard Ride*

Marin, Edwin L. *Abilene Town; Everybody Sing; Johnny Angel; Listen, Darling; Nocturne; Paris Calling; Tall in the Saddle*

Maris, Peter *Hangfire*

Marker, Chris *Le Joli Mai*

Markle, Fletcher *Incredible Journey, The*

Markle, Peter *BAT 21; Personals, The; Wagons East!; Youngblood*

Marks, Arthur *Friday Foster*

Marks, Ross Kagan *Homage*

Marquand, Richard *Eye of the Needle; Hearts of Fire; Jagged Edge; Legacy, The; Return of the Jedi; Until September*

Marshall, Frank *Alive; Arachnophobia; Congo*

Marshall, Garry *Beaches; Exit to Eden; Flamingo Kid, The; Frankie and Johnny; Overboard; Pretty Woman; Runaway Bride*

Marshall, George *Blue Dahlia, The; Boy, Did I Get a Wrong Number!; Destry; Destry Rides Again; Fancy Pants; Gazebo, The; Goldwyn Follies, The; Houdini; How The West Was Won; Incendiary Blonde; In Old Kentucky; It Started with a Kiss; Mating Game, The; Millionare for Christy, A; Monsieur Beaucaire; Murder, He Says; Never a Dull Moment; Off Limits; Pack up Your Troubles; Perils of Pauline, The; Riding High; Savage, The; Scared Stiff; Star Spangled Rhythm; True to Life; Variety Girl*

Marshall, Noel *Roar*

Marshall, Penny *Awakenings; Big; Jumpin' Jack Flash; League of Their Own, A; Preacher's Wife; Renaissance Man*

Martin, Darnell *I Like It Like That*

Martin, Francis *Tillie and Gus*

Martinson, Leslie *Batman; Fathom*

Marton, Andrew *Africa—Texas Style; Ben-Hur; Crack in the World; Devil Makes Three, The; 55 Days at Peking; Green Fire; King Solomon's Mines; Longest Day, The; 7 Wonders of the World; Thin Red Line, The*

Maselli, Francesco *Fine Pair, A*

Masters, Quentin *Stud, The*

Masterson, Peter *Blood Red; Trip to Bountiful, The*

Masuda, Toshio *Tora! Tora! Tora!*

Mate, Rudolph *Branded; Dark Past, The; D.O.A.; Mississippi Gambler, The; 300 Spartans, The; Three Violent People; Union Station; When Worlds Collide*

Matthau, Charles *Grass Harp, The*

Mattinson, Burny *Great Mouse Detective, The*

Maxwell, Ronald F. *Gettysburg; Little Darlings*

May, Elaine *Heartbreak Kid, The; Ishtar; Mikey and Nicky; New Leaf, A*

May, Joe *Invisible Man Returns, The*

Mayersberg, Paul *Captive*

Mayfield, Les *Encino Man; Flubber; Miracle on 34th Street*

Mayo, Archie *Adventures of Marco Polo, The; Angel on My Shoulder; Black Legion, The; Bordertown; Charley's Aunt; Crash Dive; Go into Your Dance; Great American Broadcast, The; It's Love I'm After; Moontide; Night in Casablanca, A; Svengali*

Mayo, Archie L. *Petrified Forest, The*

Mayron, Melanie *Baby-sitters Club, The*

Maysles, Albert *Gimme Shelter*

Maysles, David *Gimme Shelter*

Mazursky, Paul *Alex in Wonderland; Blume in Love; Bob & Carol & Ted & Alice; Down and Out in Beverly Hills; Enemies A Love Story; Harry and Tonto; Moon over Parador; Moscow on the Hudson; Next Stop, Greenwich Village; Pickle, The; Scenes from a Mall; Unmarried Woman, An; Willie & Phil*

McBride, Jim *Big Easy, The; Breathless; Great Balls of Fire!; Wrong Man, The*

McCall, Rod *Paper Hearts*

McCarey, Leo *Affair to Remember, An; Awful Truth, The; Belle of the Nineties; Bells of St. Mary's, The; Duck Soup; Going My Way; Good Sam; Indiscreet; Love Affair; Make Way for Tomorrow; Milky Way, The; Once upon a Honeymoon; Rally 'Round the Flag, Boys!; Ruggles of Red Gap; Satan Never Sleeps*

McCarey, Raymond *Pack up Your Troubles*

McCowan, George *Frogs*

McEveety, Vincent *Herbie Goes to Monte Carlo; Strongest Man in the World, The*

McGaugh, W. F. *New Adventures of Tarzan, The*

McGehee, Scott *Suture*

McGrath, Douglas *Emma*

McGrath, Joseph *Cynthia; Magic Christian, The; 30 Is a Dangerous Age*

McGrath, Robert Parrish, Joseph *Casino Royale*

McHenry, Doug *House Party 2*

McKay, Jim *Girls Town*

McLaglen, Andrew V. *Bandolero!; Cahill,*

McLaglan, Andrew V. (cont.)
United States Marshal; Chisum; Devil's Brigade, The; Last Hard Men, The; McLintock!; Monkeys, Go Home!; North Sea Hijack; Rare Breed, The; Sahara; Sea Wolves, The; Last Charge of the Calcutta Light Horse, The; Shenandoah; Undefeated, The; Way West, The; Wild Geese, The

McLeod, Norman Z, Horse Feathers; It's a Gift; Kid from Brooklyn, The; Lady Be Good; Let's Dance; Merrily We Live; Monkey Business; My Favorite Spy; Paleface, The; Road to Rio; Secret Life of Walter Mitty, The; Topper; Topper Takes a Trip

McLeod, Stephen Roberts, Norman Z. If I Had a Million

McLoughlin, Tom Jason Lives Friday the 13th Part VI

McNaughton, John Henry Portrait of a Serial Killer; Mad Dog and Glory; Wild Things

McTiernan, John Die Hard; Die Hard with a Vengeance; Hunt for Red October, The; Last Action Hero; Medicine Man; Nomads; Predator; 13th Warrior, The; Thomas Crown Affair, The

Meador, Bob Cormack, Josh Make Mine Music

Medak, Peter Changeling, The; Day in the Death of Joe Egg, A; Krays, The; Let Him Have It; Men's Club, The; Pontiac Moon; Romeo Is Bleeding; Ruling Class, The; Species II; Zorro, the Gay Blade

Medford, Don Hunting Party, The; Organization, The; To Trap a Spy

Megahey, Leslie Hour of the Pig, The

Mehta, Deepa Camilla

Meins, Gus Babes in Toyland

Meisel, Myron It's All True

Mekas, Adolfas Hallelujah The Hills

Melendez, Bill Snoopy, Come Home

Melford, George Sheik, The

Melkonian, James Jerky Boys, The

Melville, Jean-Pierre Bob Le Flambeur; Le Deuxieme Souffle; Les Enfants Terribles; Leon Morin, Pretre; Le Samourai

Menaul, Christopher Feast of July

Mendes, Lothar Jew Suss; Moonlight Sonata

Mendes, Sam American Beauty

Menendez, Ramon Money for Nothing

Menges, Chris Criss Cross; Second Best; World Apart, A

Menotti, Gian-Carlo Medium, The

Menshov, Vladimir Moskva Slezam Ne Verit

Menzel, Jiri Ostre Sledovane Vlaky

Menzies, William Cameron Invaders from Mars; Thief of Bagdad An Arabian Fantasy, The; Things to Come

Merek, Stephen Mr. Holland's Opus

Metcalfe, Tim Killer Journal of Murder, A

Metter, Alan Police Academy Mission to Moscow

Meyer, Muffie Enormous Changes at the Last Minute

Meyer, Nicholas Company Business; Deceivers, The; Star Trek II The Wrath of Khan; Star Trek VI The Undiscovered Country; Time after Time; Volunteers

Meyer, Russ Beneath the Valley of the Ultra Vixens; Beyond the Valley of the Dolls; Cherry, Harry & Raquel!; Faster, Pussycat! Kill! Kill!; Lorna; Motor Psycho; Seven Minutes, The; Supervixens; Up!; Vixen!

Meyers, Sidney Savage Eye, The

Meza, Eric House Party 3

Michell, Roger Notting Hill

Michell, Scott Innocent Sleep, The

Michener, Dave Great Mouse Detective, The

Mikels, Ted V. Corpse Grinders, The

Miles, Christopher Priest of Love; That Lucky Touch; Virgin and the Gypsy, The

Milestone, Lewis All Quiet on the Western Front; Anything Goes; Arch of Triumph; Edge of Darkness; Front Page, The; General Died at Dawn, The; Hallelujah, I'm a Bum!; Halls of Montezuma; Les Miserables; Mutiny on the Bounty; North Star, The; Ocean's Eleven; Of Mice and Men; Pork Chop Hill; Purple Heart, The; Racket, The; Rain; Red Pony, The; Strange Love of Martha Ives, The; Walk in the Sun, A

Milius, John Big Wednesday; Conan the Barbarian; Dillinger; Farewell to the King; Flight of the Intruder; Red Dawn; Wind and the Lion, The

Milland, Ray Lisbon; Man Alone, A; Panic in Year Zero

Millar, Stuart Rooster Cogburn

Miller, David Captain Newman, M.D.; Diane; Executive Action; Flying Tigers; Lonely Are the Brave; Love Happy; Midnight Lace; Story of Esther Costello, The; Sudden Fear

Miller, George Aviator, The; Babe: Pig in the City; Lorenzo's Oil; Mad Max; Mad Max 2; Mad Max Beyond Thunderdome; Man From Snowy River, The; Neverending Story II The Next

Chapter, The; Twilight Zone The Movie; Witches of Eastwick, The

Miller, Harvey *Getting Away with Murder*

Miller, Jonathan *Take a Girl Like You*

Miller, Michael *Jackson County Jail; National Lampoon's Class Reunion; Silent Rage*

Miller, Randall *Class Act; Houseguest*

Miller, Robert Ellis *Any Wednesday; Baltimore Bullet, The; Buttercup Chain, The; Hawks; Heart Is a Lonely Hunter, The; Reuben, Reuben*

Mills, John *Sky West and Crooked*

Mills, Reginald *Tales of Beatrix Potter*

Milton, Robert *Outward Bound*

Miner, Steve *Forever Young; Friday the 13th Part 2; Friday the 13th Part III; Halloween: H20 Twenty Years Later; House; Lake Placid; My Father, the Hero; Soul Man; Warlock*

Minghella, Anthony *English Patient, The; Mr. Wonderful; Talented Mr. Ripley, The; Truly Madly Deeply*

Minkoff, Rob *Lion King, The; Stuart Little*

Minnelli, Vincente *American In Paris, An; Bad and the Beautiful, The; Band Wagon, The; Bells Are Ringing; Brigadoon; Cabin in the Sky; Clock, The; Cobweb, The; Courtship of Eddie's Father, The; Designing Woman; Father of the Bride; Four Horsemen of the Apocalypse, The; Gigi; Goodbye Charlie; Home from the Hill; I Dood It; Kismet; Lust for Life; Madame Bovary; Meet Me in St. Louis; On a Clear Day You Can See Forever; Pirate, The; Reluctant Debutante, The; Sandpiper, The; Some Came Running; Story of Three Loves, The; Tea and Sympathy; Till the Clouds Roll By; Two Weeks in Another Town; Undercurrent; Yolanda and the Thief; Ziegfeld Follies*

Mirkin, David *Romy and Michele's High School Reunion*

Mitchell, Art *Behind the Green Door*

Mitchell, Jim *Behind the Green Door*

Mizoguchi, Kenji *Sansho Dayu; Ugetsu Monogatari*

Mizrahi, Moshe *Every Time We Say Goodbye; La Vie Devant Soi*

Moguy, Leonide *Whistle Stop*

Molander, Gustaf *Intermezzo*

Molinaro, Edouard *La Cage aux Folles; La Cage aux Folles II*

Mollo, Andrew *It Happened Here; Winstanley*

Monger, Christopher *Englishman Who Went up a Hill But Came Down a Mountain; Just Like a Woman*

Montagne, Edward J. *McHale's Navy*

Montgomery, Robert *Lady in the Lake; Once More, My Darling*

Moore, Michael *Canadian Bacon; Paradise, Hawaiian Style; Roger and Me*

Moore, Robert *Chapter Two; Cheap Detective, The; Murder by Death*

Moore, Simon *Under Suspicion*

Moorhouse, Jocelyn *How to Make an American Quilt; Proof*

Mora, Philippe *Beast Within, The; Breed Apart, A; Howling II Your Sister Is a Werewolf*

Morahan, Andy *Highlander III The Sorcerer*

Morahan, Christopher *All Neat in Black Stockings; Clockwise; Diamonds for Breakfast; Paper Mask*

Morris, David Burton *Jersey Girl; Loose Ends; Patti Rocks*

Morris, Errol *Dark Wind, The; Thin Blue Line, The*

Morrison, Bruce *Constance*

Morrissey, Paul *Blood for Dracula; Flesh; Flesh for Frankenstein; Heat; Mixed Blood; Trash*

Morton, Rocky *D.O.A.; Super Mario Bros.*

Mostow, Jonathan *Breakdown*

Mowbray, Malcolm *Private Function, A*

Moyle, Allan *Gun in Betty Lou's Handbag, The; Pump Up the Volume*

Mulcahy, Russell *Blue Ice; Highlander; Highlander II The Quickening; Razorback; Real McCoy, The; Ricochet; Shadow, The*

Mulligan, Robert *Baby the Rain Must Fall; Bloodbrothers; Clara's Heart; Come September; Fear Strikes Out; Inside Daisy Clover; Kiss Me Goodbye; Love with the Proper Stranger; Man in the Moon, The; Other, The; Same Time, Next Year; Spiral Road, The; Stalking Moon, The; Summer of '42; To Kill a Mockingbird; Up the Down Staircase*

Munk, Andrzej *Eroica*

Munroe, Cynthia *Wedding Party, The*

Murakami, Jimmy T. *Battle Beyond the Stars*

Murch, Walter *Return to Oz*

Murnau, F. W. *Nosferatu Eine Symphonie des Grauens; Sunrise; Tabu*

Murphy, Eddie *Harlem Nights*

Murphy, Geoff *Freejack; Goodbye Pork Pie; Quiet Earth, The; Under Siege 2 Dark Territory; utu; Young Guns II*

Murray, Bill *Quick Change*

Musker, John *Aladdin; Great Mouse De-

Musker, John (cont.)
tective, The; Hercules; Little Mermaid, The

Myerson, Alan Police Academy 5 Assignment: Miami Beach; Private Lessons; Steelyard Blues

Myrick, Daniel Blair Witch Project, The

Nagy, Ivan Deadly Hero

Nair, Mira Mississipi Masala; Perez Family, The; Salaam Bombay

Nakano, Desmond White Man's Burden

Nakasako, Spencer Life Is Cheap . . . But Toilet Paper Is Expensive

Narizzano, Silvio Blue; Choices; Class of Miss MacMichael, The; Fanatic; Georgy Girl; Loot

Nava, Gregory El Norte

Neame, Ronald Card, The; Chalk Garden, The; First Monday in October; Foreign Body; Gambit; Hopscotch; I Could Go on Singing; Man Who Never Was, The; Meteor; Million Pound Note, The; Mister Moses; Odessa File, The; Poseidon Adventure, The; Prime of Miss Jean Brodie, The; Scrooge; Tunes of Glory; Windom's Way

Needham, Hal Cannonball Run, The; Cannonball Run II; Hooper; Smokey and the Bandit; Smokey and the Bandit II; Villain, The

Negulesco, Jean Best of Everything, The; Boy on a Dolphin; Britannia Mews; Certain Smile, A; Daddy Long Legs; Greatest Story Ever Told, The; How to Marry a Millionaire; Humoresque; Jessica; Johnny Belinda; Lydia Bailey; Mask of Dimitrios, The; Mudlark, The; Nobody Lives Forever; O. Henry's Full House; Phone Call from a Stranger; Pleasure Seekers, The; Rains of Ranchipur, The; Road House; Scandal at Scourie; Three Came Home; Three Coins in the Fountain; Three Strangers; Titanic; Woman's World

Neilan, Marshall Rebecca of Sunnybrook Farm; Stella Maris

Neill, Roy William Frankenstein Meets the Wolf Man

Neilson, James Moon-Spinners, The; Night Passage

Nelson, Gary Allan Quatermain and the Lost City of Gold; Black Hole, The; Freaky Friday

Nelson, Gene Kissin' Cousins

Nelson, Jessie Corrina, Corrina

Nelson, Ralph Charly; Counterpoint; Duel at Diablo; Embryo; Fate Is the Hunter; Father Goose; Flight of the Doves; Lilies of the Field; Once a Thief; Requiem for a Heavyweight; Soldier Blue; Soldier in the Rain; Wilby Conspiracy, The; Wrath of God, The

Neumann, Kurt Fly, The; Kronos; Ring, The; Tarzan and the Amazons; Tarzan and the Huntress; Tarzan and the Leopard Woman; Tarzan and the She-Devil

Nevin, Robyn More Things Change, The

Newell, Mike Amazing Grace and Chuck; Awakening, The; Awfully Big Adventure, An; Bad Blood; Dance with a Stranger; Donnie Brasco; Enchanted April; Four Weddings and a Funeral; Into the West; Pushing Tin; Soursweet

Newland, John Spy with My Face, The

Newley, Anthony Can Heironymus Merkin Ever Forget Mercy Humppe and Find True Happiness?

Newman, Joseph M. Human Jungle, The; 711 Ocean Drive; This Island Earth

Newman, Paul Effect of Gamma Rays on Man-in-the-Moon Marigolds, The; Glass Menagerie, The; Harry & Son; Rachel, Rachel; Sometimes a Great Notion

Newmeyer, Fred Fast and Loose; Safety Last

Nibbelink, Phil American Tail: Fievel Goes West, An; We're Back! A Dinosaur's Story

Niblo, Fred Ben-Hur A Tale of the Christ; Blood and Sand; Camille; Mysterious Lady, The; Temptress, The; Three Musketeers, The

Niccol, Andrew Gattaca

Nichols, Charles A. Charlotte's Web

Nichols, Dudley Mourning Becomes Electra

Nichols, Mike Biloxi Blues; Birdcage, The; Carnal Knowledge; Catch-22; Day of the Dolphin, The; Fortune, The; Graduate, The; Heartburn; Postcards from the Edge; Primary Colors; RegardingHenry; Silkwood; Who's Afraid of Virginia Woolf?; Wolf; Working Girl

Nicholls, George, Jr. Anne of Green Gables; Flying Down to Rio

Nicholson, Arch Weekend with Kate

Nicholson, Jack Drive, He Said; Goin' South; Two Jakes, The

Nicholas, Paul Chained Heat

Nimoy, Leonard Funny About Love; Good Mother, The; Holy Matrimony; Star Trek III: The Search for Spock; Star Trek IV: The Voyage Home; 3 Men and a Baby

Noonan, Chris Babe

Norman, Leslie Dunkirk; Long and the Short and the Tall, The

Robson, Mark (cont.)
Birthday, Wanda June; Harder They Fall, The; Inn of the Sixth Happiness, The; Isle of the Dead; Limbo; Little Hut, The; Lost Command; My Foolish Heart; Nine Hours to Rama; Peyton Place; Phffft; Prize, The; Prize of Gold, A; Return to Paradise; Seventh Victim, The; Valley of the Dolls; Von Ryan's Express

Rocco, Marc Murder in the First; Where the Day Takes You

Rockwell, Alexandre Four Rooms; Somebody to Love

Roddam, Franc Bride, The; K2; Lords of Discipline, The; Quadrophenia; War Party

Rodgers, Mic Universal Soldier: The Return

Rodriguez, Robert Desperado; El Mariachi; Faculty, The; Four Rooms; From Dusk Till Dawn

Roeg, Nicholas Bad Timing; Castaway; Cold Heaven; Don't Look Now; Eureka; Insignificance; Man Who Fell to Earth, The; Performance; Track 29; Walkabout; Witches, The

Roemer, Michael Plot against Harry, The

Rogell, Albert S. Heaven Only Knows; Hit Parade of 1943

Rogers, Charles Babes in Toyland; Bohemian Girl, The

Rohmer, Eric L'Amour, L'Apres-Midi; Conte D'ete; Le Genou de Claire; Ma Nuit Chez Maud

Romero, George A. Creepshow; Dark Half, The; Dawn of the Dead; Day of the Dead; Knightriders; Martin; Monkey Shines; Night of the Living Dead

Romm, Mikhail Lyenin V Oktyabrye

Roodt, Darrell James Cry, the Beloved Country; Sarafina!

Rooks, Conrad Siddhartha

Ropelewski, Tom Look Who's Talking Now

Rose, Bernard Candyman; Chicago Joe and the Showgirl; Immortal Beloved; Paperhouse

Rosen, Phil Black Beauty

Rosenberg, Stuart Amityville Horror, The; April Fools, The; Brubaker; Cool Hand Luke; Drowning Pool, The; Laughing Policeman, The; Let's Get Harry; Love and Bullets; Murder, Inc.; My Heroes Have Always Been Cowboys; Pope of Greenwich Village, The; Voyage of the Damned; W USA

Rosenthal, Rick Bad Boys; Halloween II

Rosi, Francesco Cadaveri Eccellenti; Carmen; Lucky Luciano; La Mani Sulla

Citta; More Than a Miracle; Salvatore Giuliano

Rosmer, Milton Dreyfus

Ross, Benjamin Young Poisoner's Handbook, The

Ross, Herbert Boys on the Side; California Suite; Footloose; Funny Lady; Goodbye Girl, The; Goodbye, Mr. Chips; I Ought to Be in Pictures; Last of Sheila, The; Max Dugan Returns; My Blue Heaven; Nijinsky; Owl and the Pussycat, The; Pennies from Heaven; Play It Again, Sam; Protocol; Secret of My Succe$s, The; Seven-Per-Cent Solution, The; Steel Magnolias; Sunshine Boys, The; T. R. Baskin; True Colors; Turning Point, The; Undercover Blues

Rossellini, Roberto Germania Anno Zero; Paisa; Roma, Citta Aperta; Stromboli, Terra Di Dio; Viaggio in Italia

Rossen, Robert Alexander the Great; All the King's Men; Body and Soul; Brave Bulls, The; Hustler, The; Island in the Sun; Johnny O'Clock; Lilith; Mambo; They Came to Cordura

Rossif, Frederic Mourir a Madrid

Rosso, Franco Babylon

Rosson, Arthur North West Mounted Police; Red River

Roth, Joe Streets of Gold

Rouse, Russell New York Confidential; Oscar, The; Thief, The; Well, The

Rouve, Pierre Stranger in the House

Rowland, Roy 5,000 Fingers of Dr. T., The; Girl Hunters, The; Hit the Deck; Killer McCoy; Lost Angel; Outriders, The; Scene of the Crime

Rozema, Patricia I've Heard the Mermaids Singing; Mansfield Park

Ruben, J. Walter Public Hero No. 1

Ruben, Joseph Dreamscape; Good Son, The; Money Train; Sleeping with the Enemy; Stepfather, The

Ruben, Katt Shea Poison Ivy; Streets

Rubin, Bruce Joel My Life

Rudolph, Alan Afterglow; Breakfast of Champions; Equinox; Love at Large; Made in Heaven; Moderns, The; Mortal Thoughts; Mrs. Parker and the Vicious Circle; Remember My Name; Songwriter; Trouble in Mind; Welcome to L.A.

Ruggles, Wesley Bride Comes Home, The; Cimarron; Gilded Lily, The; I Met Him in Paris; I'm No Angel; No Man of Her Own; Somewhere I'll Find You; Too Many Husbands; You Belong to Me

Rush, Richard Color of Night; Freebie

and the Bean; Getting Straight; Psych-Out; Stunt Man, The

Rusnak, Josef *Thirteenth Floor, The*

Russell, Charles *Eraser; Mask, The*

Russell, Chuck *Blob, The; Nightmare on Elm Street 3, A; Dream Warriors*

Russell, David O. *Flirting with Disaster; Three Kings*

Russell, Franc Roddam, Ken *Aria*

Russell, Ken *Altered States; Billion Dollar Brain; Boy Friend, The; Crimes of Passion; Devils, The; French Dressing; Gothic; Lair of the White Worm, The; Rainbow, The; Savage Messiah; Tommy; Valentino; Whore; Women in Love*

Russell, William D. *Bride For Sale*

Ruth, Roy Del *Blonde Crazy; Born to Dance; Broadway Melody of 1936; Broadway Melody of 1938; Broadway Rhythm; Bureau of Missing Persons; Desert Song, The; Du Barry Was a Lady; Folies Bergere; Gold Diggers of Broadway; Kid Millions; Lady Killer; Maltese Falcon, The; On Moonlight Bay; On the Avenue; Phantom of the Rue Morgue; Taxi!; Thanks a Million; Three Sailors and a Girl; Topper Returns; West Point Story, The*

Ryan, Frank *Can't Help Singing; Hers to Hold; Patrick the Great*

Rydell, Mark *Cinderella Liberty; Cowboys, The; For the Boys; Fox, The; Harry and Walter Go to New York; Intersection; On Golden Pond; Reivers, The; River, The; Rose, The*

Sachs, William *Exterminator 2*

Safran, Henri *Storm Boy*

Sagal, Boris *Made in Paris; Omega Man, The; Twilight of Honor*

Sagan, Leontine *Maedchen in Uniform*

Saks, Gene *Barefoot in the Park; Brighton Beach Memoirs; Cactus Flower; Last of the Red Hot Lovers; Mame; Odd Couple, The*

Sale, Richard *Let's Make It Legal; Meet Me after the Show*

Salle, David *Search and Destroy*

Salles, Walter *Central do Brasil*

Salter, James *Three*

Salva, Victor *Powder*

Salvatores, Gabriele *Mediterraneo*

Sandrich, Mark *Carefree; Follow the Fleet; Gay Divorce, The; Holiday Inn; I Love a Soldier; Shall We Dance; Skylark; So Proudly We Hail!; Top Hat*

Sanford, Arlene *Very Brady Sequel, A*

Santell, Alfred *Breakfast for Two; Daddy Long Legs; Dictator, The; Hairy Ape, The; Jack London*

Santley, Joseph *Brazil; Cocoanuts, The; Down Mexico Way*

Sarafian, Deran *Back in the USSR; Gunmen; Terminal Velocity*

Sarafian, Richard C. *Eye of the Tiger; Lolly-Madonna XXX; Man Who Loved Cat Dancing, The; Next Man, The; Run Wild, Run Free; Sunburn; Vanishing Point*

Sargent, Joseph *Jaws The Revenge; MacArthur; Man, The; One Spy Too Many; Taking of Pelham One Two Three, The; White Lightning*

Sarne, Michael *Joanna; Myra Breckinridge*

Sasdy, Peter *Hands of the Ripper; I Don't Want to Be Born; Taste the Blood of Dracula; Welcome to Blood City*

Sassone, Oley *Bloodfist III Forced to Fight*

Sautet, Claude *Les Choses de la Vie; Un Coeur en Hiver; Une Histoire Simple; Nelly & Monsieur Arnaud; Vincent, Francois, Paul . . . et les Autres*

Savani, Tom *Night of the Living Dead*

Saville, Philip *Fellow Traveller; Oedipus the King*

Saville, Victor *Conspirator; Dictator, The; Evensong; Evergreen; First a Girl; Friday the Thirteenth; Good Companions, The; Green Dolphin Street; Green Years, The; It's Love Again; I Was a Spy; Kim; Silver Chalice, The; South Riding; Tonight and Every Night*

Savoca, Nancy *Dogfight; True Love*

Sayles, John *Baby, It's You; Brother from Another Planet, The; City of Hope; Eight Men Out; Lianna; Lone Star; Matewan; Passion Fish; Return of the Secaucus Seven; Secret of Roan Inish, The*

Schaefer, George *Enemy of the People, An; Pendulum*

Schaffner, Franklin J. *Best Man, The; Boys from Brazil, The; Double Man, The; Islands in the Stream; Lionheart; Nicholas and Alexandra; Papillon; Patton; Planet of the Apes; Sphinx; Stripper, The; War Lord, The; Welcome Home*

Schatzberg, Jerry *Blood Money; Honeysuckle Rose; Misunderstood; No Small Affair; Panic in Needle Park, The; Puzzle of a Downfall Child; Reunion; Scarecrow; Seduction of Joe Tynan, The*

Scheerer, Robert *World's Greatest Athlete, The*

Schepisi, Fred *Barbarosa; Chant of Jimmie Blacksmith, The; Cry in the Dark, A; Devil's Playground, The; I.Q.; Mr. Baseball; Plenty; Roxanne; Russia House, The; Six Degrees of Separation*

Schertzinger, Victor *Birth of the Blues; Fleet's In, The; Kiss the Boys Goodbye; One Night of Love; Road to Singapore; Road to Zanzibar; Something to Sing About*

Schiller, Tom *Nothing Lasts Forever*

Schlamme, Thomas *Miss Firecracker; So I Married an Axe Murderer*

Schlesinger, John *Billy Liar; Darling; Day of the Locust, The; Eye for an Eye; Falcon and the Snowman, The; Far from the Madding Crowd; Honky Tonk Freeway; Innocent, The; Kind of Loving, A; Madame Sousatzka; Marathon Man; Midnight Cowboy; Pacific Heights; Sunday Bloody Sunday; Yanks*

Schlondorff, Volker *Un Amour de Swann; Die Blechtrommel; Handmaid's Tale, The; Voyager*

Schmitt, Bernard *Pacific Palisades*

Schneider, Paul *Willy/Milly*

Schoedsack, Ernest B. *Chang; Dr. Cyclops; Four Feathers; King Kong; Last Days of Pompeii, The; Mighty Joe Young; Most Dangerous Game, The; Son of Kong, The*

Schrader, Leonard *Naked Tango*

Schrader, Paul *American Gigolo; Blue Collar; Cat People; Comfort of Strangers, The; Forever Mine; Hardcore; Light of Day; Light Sleeper; Mishima A Life in Four Chapters; Patty Hearst*

Schroeder, Barbet *Barfly; Before and After; Kiss of Death; More; Reversal of Fortune; Single White Female*

Schultz, Carl *Careful He Might Hear You; Travelling North*

Schultz, Michael *Car Wash; Cooley High; Greased Lightning; Sgt. Pepper's Lonely Hearts Club Band*

Schumacher, Joel *Batman & Robin; Batman Forever; Client, The; Cousins; Dying Young; 8MM; Falling Down; Flatliners; Flawless; Incredible Shrinking Woman, The; Lost Boys, The; St. Elmo's Fire; Time to Kill, A*

Schunzel, Reinhold *Ice Follies of 1939; Viktor und Viktoria*

Schuster, Harold *My Friends Flicka; Tarzan's Hidden Jungle*

Schwartz, Stefan *Soft Top Hard Shoulder*

Scola, Ettore *Macaroni*

Scorsese, Martin *After Hours; Age of Innocence, The; Alice Doesn't Live Here Anymore; Boxcar Bertha; Bringing Out the Dead; Cape Fear; Casino; Color of Money, The; Goodfellas; King of Comedy, The; Kundun; Last Temptation of Christ, The; Last Waltz, The; Mean Streets; New York New York; New York Stories; Raging Bull; Taxi Driver; Who's That Knocking At My Door*

Scott, Cynthia *Company of Strangers, The*

Scott, George C. *Rage*

Scott, Oz *Bustin' Love*

Scott, Peter Graham *Bitter Harvest; Cracksman, The; Pot Carriers, The*

Scott, Ridley *Alien; Black Rain; Blade Runner; Duelists, The; 1492 Conquest of Paradise; G.I. Jane; Legend; Someone to Watch over Me; Thelma & Louise; White Squall*

Scott, Tony *Beverly Hills Cop II; Crimson Tide; Days of Thunder; Enemy of the State; Fan, The; Hunger, The; Last Boy Scout, The; Revenge; Top Gun; True Romance*

Seacot, Sandra *In the Spirit*

Seagal, Steven *On Deadly Ground*

Seale, John *Till There Was You*

Sears, Fred F. *Earth vs. the Flying Saucers; Rock around the Clock*

Seastrom, Victor *Divine Woman, The; Scarlet Letter, The; Tower of Lies, The; Under the Red Robe; Wind, The*

Seaton, George *Airport; Anything Can Happen; Apartment for Peggy; Country Girl, The; Diamond Horseshoe; Junior Miss; Miracle on 34th Street; Pleasure of His Company, The; Teacher's Pet; 36 Hours*

Sedgwick, Edgar *Speak Easily*

Sedgwick, Edward *Cameraman, The; Passionate Plumber, The; Phantom of the Opera, The*

Segal, Alex *Harlow; Joy in the Morning; Ransom*

Segal, Peter *Naked Gun 33 1/3 The Final Insult*

Seidelman, Susan *Cookie; Desperately Seeking Susan; Making Mr. Right; She-Devil*

Seiler, Lewis *Guadalcanal Diary; Last Trail, The; Molly and Me; Something for the Boys; Women's Prison; You're in the Army Now*

Seiter, William A. *Affairs of Susan, The; Appointment for Love; Belle of the Yukon; Broadway; If I Had a Million; Life Begins in College; One Touch of Venus; Roberta; Room Service; Sally,*

1479

Silver, Joan Micklin (cont.)
Big Girls Don't Cry...They Get Even; Crossing Delancey; Head over Heels; Hester Street

Silver, Marcel *Fox Movietone Follies of 1929*

Silver, Marisa *He Said She Said; Old Enough; Permanent Record; Vital Signs*

Silverstein, Elliot *Cat Ballou; Happening, The; Man Called Horse, A*

Simmons, Anthony *Four in the Morning; Optimists of Nine Elms, The*

Simon, Adam *Carnosaur*

Simon, S. Sylvan *Abbott and Costello in Hollywood; Dancing Co-Ed; Her Husband's Affairs; Rio Rita; Son of Lassie*

Simoneau, Yves *Mother's Boys*

Sinatra, Frank *None But the Brave*

Sinclair, Andrew *Under Milk Wood*

Sinclair, Robert B. *That Wonderful Urge*

Singer, Alexander *Cold Wind in August, A; Love Has Many Faces*

Singer, Bryan *Apt Pupil; Public Access; Usual Suspects, The*

Singleton, John *Boyz N the Hood; Higher Learning; Poetic Justice*

Sinise, Gary *Of Mice and Men*

Sinyor, Gary *Bachelor, The; Leon the Pig Farmer*

Siodmak, Robert *Christmas Holiday; Cobra Woman; Crimson Pirate, The; Criss Cross; Cry of the City; Cluster of the West; Dark Mirror, The; File on Thelma Jordon, The; Fly by Night; Killers, The; Phantom Lady; Son of Dracula; Spiral Staircase, The; Suspect, The*

Sipes, Andrew *Fair Game*

Sirk, Douglas *All I Desire; All That Heaven Allows; Battle Hymn; Has Anybody Seen My Gal; Imitation of Life; Magnificent Obsession; Meet Me at the Fair; Shockproof; Sign of the Pagan; Sleep, My Love; Summer Storm; Take Me to Town; Tarnished Angels, The; Taza, Son of Cochise; Time to Love and a Time to Die, A; Written on the Wind*

Sjoberg, Alf *Froken Julie*

Skolimowski, Jerzy *Deep End; King, Queen, Knave; Lightship, The; Moonlighting; Shout, The; Success Is the Best Revenge*

Sluizer, George *Crimetime; Vanishing, The*

Smallwood, Ray C. *Camille*

Smart, Ralph *Quartet*

Smight, Jack *Airport 1975; Damnation Alley; Harper; Illustrated Man, The; Kaleidoscope; Loving Couples;*

Midway; No Way to Treat a Lady; Secret War of Harry Frigg, The; Third Day, The; Traveling Executioner, The

Smith, Charles *Martin Trick or Treat*

Smith, John N. *Dangerous Minds*

Smith, Kevin *Mallrats*

Smith, Mel *Bean; Radioland Murders; Tall Guy, The*

Soderbergh, Steven *Kafka; King of the Hill; Limey, The; Out of Sight; Schizopolis; sex, lies, and videotape; Underneath, The*

Softley, Iain *Backbeat; Hackers; Wings of the Dove, The*

Solondz, Todd *Happiness; Welcome to the Dollhouse*

Solt, Andrew *This Is Elvis*

Sommers, Stephen *Adventures of Huck Finn, The; Jungle Book, The; Mummy, The*

Sonnenfeld, Barry *Addams Family, The; Addams Family Values; For Love or Money; Get Shorty; Men in Black; Wild Wild West*

South, Colin *In Too Deep*

Souza, Steven E. de *Street Fighter*

Spencer, Alan *Hexed*

Spheeris, Penelope *Beverly Hillbillies, The; Boys Next Door, The; Decline of Western Civilization, The; Dudes; Little Rascals, The; Wayne's World*

Spicer, Bryan *Mighty Morphin Power Rangers The Movie*

Spielberg, Steven *Always; Amistad; Close Encounters of the Third Kind; Color Purple, The; Duel; Empire of the Sun; E.T. The Extra-Terrestrial; Hook; Indiana Jones and the Last Crusade; Indiana Jones and the Temple of Doom; Jaws; Jurassic Park; Lost World, The Jurassic Park; 1941; Raiders of the Lost Ark; Saving Private Ryan; Schindler's List; Sugarland Express, The; Twilight Zone The Movie*

Spiers, Bob *Spice World*

Spottiswoode, Roger *Air America; Mesmer; Pursuit of D. B. Cooper, The; Shoot to Kill; Stop! Or My Mom Will Shoot; Terror Train; Tomorrow Never Dies; Turner & Hooch; Under Fire*

Stacey, Eric *North West Mounted Police*

Stahl, John M. *Back Street; Eve of St. Mark, The; Foxes of Harrow, The; Holy Matrimony; Imitation of Life; Immortal Sergeant, The; Keys of the Kingdom, The; Leave Her to Heaven; Magnificent Obsession; Only Yesterday; Our Wife*

Stallone, Sylvester *Paradise Alley; Rocky II; Rocky III; Rocky IV; Staying Alive*

Stanley, Richard *Dust Devil The Final Cut; Hardware*

Starett, Jack *Cleopatra Jones; Losers, The; Race with the Devil; Small Town in Texas, A; Strange Vengeance of Rosalie, The*

Staudte, Wolfgang *Die Moerder Sind unter Uns*

St. Clair, Malcom *Canary Murder Case*

Steinberg, David *Paternity*

Steinberg, Michael *Bodies, Rest & Motion; Waterdance, The*

Steinmann, Danny *Friday the 13th, Part V: A New Beginning; Savage Streets*

Sterling, William *Alice's Adventures in Wonderland*

Stern, Bert *Jazz on a Summer's Day*

Stern, Daniel *Rookie of the Year*

Stern, Steven *Morning Glory*

Stern, Tom *Freaked*

Sternberg, Josef von *American Tragedy, An; Der Blaue Engel; Blonde Venus; Blue Angel, The; Crime and Punishment; Devil Is a Woman, The; Dishonored; Docks of New York, The; Drag Net, The; Jet Pilot; Last Command, The; Macao; Morocco; Scarlet Empress, The; Shanghai Express; Shanghai Gesture, The; Underworld*

Steven, Geoff *Skin Deep*

Stevens, Art *Rescuers, The*

Stevens, George *Alice Adams; Annie Oakley; Annie Oakley (1935); Damsel in Distress, A; Diary of Anne Frank, The; Giant; Greatest Story Ever Told, The; Gunga Din; I Remember Mama; More the Merrier, The; Only Game in Town, The; Penny Serenade; Place in the Sun, A; Quality Street; Shane; Swing Time; Talk of the Town; Vivacious Lady; Woman of the Year*

Stevens, Robert *In the Cool of the Day; Never Love a Stranger*

Stevenson, Robert *Absent Minded Professor, The; Back Street; Bedknobs and Broomsticks; Blackbeard's Ghost; Dishonored Lady; Herbie Rides Again; I Married a Communist; In Search of the Castaways; Island at the Top of the World, The; Jane Eyre; Joan of Paris; Kidnapped; King Solomon's Mines; Love Bug, The; Mary Poppins; My Forbidden Past; Old Yeller; Shaggy D.A., The; Tom Brown's School Days*

Stevenson, Victor *Saville, Robert Forever and a Day*

Stiller, Ben *Cable Guy, The; Reality Bites*

Stiller, Mauritz *Hotel Imperial*

Stillman, Whit *Barcelona; Last Days of Disco, The; Metropolitan*

Stone, Andrew L. *Bedside Manner; Decks Ran Red, The; Password Is Courage, The; Secret of My Success, The; Sensations of 1945; Song of Norway; Steel Trap, The; Stormy Weather*

Stone, Oliver *Any Given Sunday; Born on the Fourth of July; Doors, The; Hand, The; Heaven & Earth; JFK; Natural Born Killers; Nixon; Platoon; Salvador; Talk Radio; U-Turn; Wall Street*

Stoppard, Tom *Rosencrantz and Guildenstern Are Dead*

Stoumen, Louis Clyde *Naked Eye, The*

Streisand, Barbra *Mirror Has Two Faces, The; Prince of Tides, The; Yentl*

Streitfeld, Susan *Female Perversions*

Strick, Joseph *Balcony, The; Savage Eye, The; Ulysses*

Strick, Wesley *Tie That Binds, The*

Stroheim, Erich von *Foolish Wives; Greed; Merry Widow, The; Queen Kelly; Wedding March, The*

Stuart, Mel *If It's Tuesday, This Must Be Belgium; One Is a Lonely Number; Willy Wonka & the Chocolate Factory*

Sturges, John *Backlash; Bad Day at Black Rock; By Love Possessed; Capture, The; Eagle Has Landed, The; Girl Named Tamiko, A; Great Escape, The; Gunfight at the O.K. Corral; Hallelujah Trail, The; Hour of the Gun; Ice Station Zebra; Jeopardy; Joe Kidd; Last Train from Gun Hill; Le Mans; Magnificent Seven; Magnificent Yankee, The; Marooned; McQ; Never So Few; Old Man and the Sea, The; People against O'Hara, The; Right Cross; Satan Bug, The; Sergeants 3; Underwater!; Walking Hills, The*

Sturges, Preston *Beautiful Blonde from Bashful Bend, The; Christmas in July; Great McGinty, The; Great Moment, The; Hail the Conquering Hero; Lady Eve, The; Miracle of Morgan's Creek, The; Palm Beach Story, The; Sin of Harold Diddlebock, The; Sullivan's Travels; Unfaithfully Yours*

Sturridge, Charles *Handful of Dust, A; Runners; Where Angels Fear to Tread*

Sullivan, Kevin Rodney *How Stella Got Her Groove Back*

Sullivan, Tim *Jack & Sarah*

Summers, Jeremy *Punch and Judy Man, The*

Sundstrom, Cedric *American Ninja 3 Blood Hunt*

Surjik, Stephen *Wayne's World 2*

Suso, Henry *Deathsport*

Sutherland, A. Edward *Abie's Irish Rose; Boys from Syracuse, The; Dixie; Every*

Sutherland, A. Edward (cont.)
Day's a Holiday; Flying Deuces, The; Follow the Boys; Mississippi; Poppy; Secret Command

Sverak, Jan *Kolya*

Swaim, Bob *La Balance; Half Moon Street; Masquerade*

Swift, David *Good Neighbor Sam; How to Succeed in Business Without Really Trying; Interns, The; Love Is a Ball; Parent Trap, The; Pollyanna; Under the Yum Yum Tree*

Sykes, Peter *To the Devil a Daughter*

Szabo, Istvan *Apa; Meeting Venus; Mephisto*

Szwarc, Jeannot *Bug; Enigma; Jaws 2; Santa Claus; Somewhere in Time; Supergirl*

Tabeo, Juan Carlos *Fresa y Chocolate*

Tabet, Sylvio *Beastmaster 2: Through the Portal of Time*

Tacchella, Jean-Charles *Cousin Cousine*

Takamoto, Iwao *Charlotte's Web*

Talalay, Rachel *Freddy's Dead The Final Nightmare; Ghost in the Machine; Tank Girl*

Tamahori, Lee *Edge, The; Mulholland Falls; Once Were Warriors*

Tarantino, Quentin *Four Rooms; Jackie Brown; Pulp Fiction; Reservoir Dogs*

Tarkovsky, Andrei *Andrei Rublyov; Ivanovo Dyetstvo; Offret; Solyaris*

Tashlin, Frank *Alphabet Murders, The; Artists and Models; Bachelor Flat; Caprice; Cinderfella; Disorderly Orderly, The; Geisha Boy, The; Girl Can't Help It, The; Glass Bottom Boat, The; Hollywood or Bust; It'\$ Only Money; Lieutenant Wore Skirts, The; Private Navy of Sgt. O'Farrell, The; Son of Paleface; Susan Slept Here; Who's Minding the Store?; Will Success Spoil Rock Hunter?*

Tass, Nadia *Big Steal, The; Rikky and Pete*

Tati, Jacques *Jour de Fete; Mon Oncle; Play Time; Les Vacances de Monsieur Hulot*

Tatoulis, John *In Too Deep*

Taurog, Ernst Lubitsch, Norman *If I Had a Million*

Taurog, Norman *Adventures of Tom Sawyer, The; Beginning or the End, The; Big Broadcast of 1936, The; Blue Hawaii; Boys Town; Broadway Melody of 1940; Caddy, The; Design for Scandal; Double Trouble; G.I. Blues; Girl Crazy; Girls! Girls! Girls!; Hoodlum Saint, The; Huckleberry Finn; It Happened at the World's Fair; Jumping Jacks; Mad about Music; Men of Boys Town; Phantom President, The; Presenting Lily Mars; Room for One More; Skippy; Stooge, The; Strike Me Pink; That Midnight Kiss; We're Not Dressing; Words and Music; You Can't Have Everything; Young Tom Edison; You're Never Too Young; Ziegfeld Follies*

Tavernier, Bertrand *L'Appat; Death Watch; La Fille de D'Artagnan; L.627; 'Round Midnight*

Taviani, Paolo *Padre Padrone*

Taviani, Vittorio *Padre Padrone*

Taylor, Don *Damien Omen II; Escape from the Planet of the Apes; Final Countdown, The; Great Scout & Cathouse Thursday, The; Island of Dr. Moreau, The; Tom Sawyer*

Taylor, Robert *Nine Lives of Fritz the Cat, The*

Taylor, Sam *Cat's Paw, The; For Heaven's Sake; My Best Girl; Nothing But Trouble; Safety Last; Taming of the Shrew*

Teague, Lewis *Alligator; Cat's Eye; Cujo; Jewel of the Nile, The; Lady in Red, The; Navy Seals*

Temple, Julien *Absolute Beginners; Earth Girls Are Easy; Great Rock 'n' Roll Swindle, The; Secret Policeman's Other Ball, The*

Templeton, George *Sundowners, The*

Tennant, Andy *Anna and the King; It Takes Two*

Tenney, Kevin S. *Peacemaker*

Teshigahara, Hiroshi *Suna No Onna*

Tetzlaff, Ted *Johnny Allegro; 7 Wonders of the World; White Tower, The*

Tewkesbury, Joan *Old Boyfriends*

Tewksbury, Peter *Sunday in New York*

Thiele, Wilhelm *Love Waltz, The*

Thiele, William *London by Night; Tarzan's Desert Mystery; Tarzan Triumphs*

Thomas, Betty *Brady Bunch Movie, The*

Thomas, Gerald *Carry On Again Doctor; Carry On Cabby; Carry On Camping; Carry On Cleo; Carry On Columbus; Carry On, Constable; Carry On Cowboy; Carry On Cruising; Carry On Doctor; Carry On Emmannuelle; Carry On England; Carry On Jack; Carry On Loving; Carry On Nurse; Carry On Regardless; Carry On Screaming; Carry On, Sergeant; Carry On Spying; Carry On, Teacher; Carry On Up The Jungle; Carry On Up ... The Khyber; Don't Lose Your Head; Duke Wore Jeans, The; Follow That Camel; Watch Your Stern*

Thomas, R.L. *Terry Fox Story, The*

Thomas, Ralph *Campbell's Kingdom; Clouded Yellow, The; Deadlier Than the Male; Doctor at Large; Doctor at Sea; Doctor in the House; High Bright Sun, The; Hot Enough for June; Nobody Runs Forever; Tale of Two Cities, A; 39 Steps, The; Wild and the Willing, The; Wind Cannot Read, The*

Thompson, Caroline *Black Beauty*

Thompson, Ernest *1969*

Thompson, J. Lee *As Long As They're Happy; Battle for the Planet of the Apes; Before Winter Comes; Cape Fear; Chairman, The; Conquest of the Planet of the Apes; Country Dance; Death Wish 4 The Crackdown; Eye of the Devil; Good Companions, The; Greek Tycoon, The; Guns of Navarone, The; Ice Cold in Alex; Kings of the Sun; King Solomon's Mines; Mackenna's Gold; Murphy's Law; North West Frontier; No Trees in the Street; Reincarnation of Peter Proud, The; Return from the Ashes; St. Ives; Taras Bulba; 10 to Midnight; Tiger Bay; What a Way to Go!; White Buffalo, The; Woman in a Dressing Gown; Yellow Balloon, The; Yield to the Night*

Thompson, Paul Mantz, Walter *7 Wonders of the World*

Thomson, Chris *Delinquents, The*

Thorpe, Jerry *Venetian Affair, The*

Thorpe, Richard *Above Suspicion; All the Brothers Were Valiant; Ben-Hur; Crowd Roars, The; Cry Havoc; Date with Judy, A; Double Wedding; Fiesta; Follow the Boys; Fun in Acapulco; Great Caruso, The; Huckleberry Finn; Ivanhoe; Jailhouse Rock; Knights of the Round Table; Malaya; Man-Proof; Prisoner of Zenda, The; Prodigal, The; Quentin Durward; Student Prince, The; Tarzan Escapes; Tarzan Finds a Son; Tarzan's New York Adventure; Tarzan's Secret Treasure; Thin Man Goes Home, The; Three Little Words; Three Loves Has Nancy; Tip on a Dead Jockey; Two Girls and a Sailor; White Cargo*

Thorsen, Jens-Jorgen *Quiet Days in Clichy*

Thorton, Billy Bob *Sling Blade*

Till, Eric *Hot Millions; Improper Channels; Walking Stick, The*

Tinling, James *Charlie Chan in Shanghai; Mr. Moto's Gamble*

Title, Stacy *Last Supper, The*

Toback, James *Exposed; Love and Money; Pick-up Artist, The*

Tobin, Thomas J. *Fraternity Row*

Tokar, Norman *Cat from Outer Space, The; Happiest Millionaire, The; Ugly Dachshund, The*

Tolkin, Michael *New Age, The; Rapture, The*

Tong, Stanley *Hung Fan Kui; Police Story 4 First Strike*

Topper, Burt *Strangler, The*

Tornatore, Guiseppe *Nuovo Cinema Paradiso*

Totten, Robert *Death of a Gunfighter*

Tourneur, Jacques *Anne of the Indies; Berlin Express; Cat People; Circle of Danger; Experiment Perilous; Flame and the Arrow, The; I Walked with a Zombie; Leopard Man, The; Out of the Past*

Tourneur, Maurice *Christian, The*

Towbin, Bram *Just Like in the Movies*

Towne, Robert *Personal Best; Tequila Sunrise*

Townsend, Robert *Five Heartbeats, The; Hollywood Shuffle; Meteor Man, The*

Tramont, Jean-Claude *All Night Long*

Trauberg, Leonid *Novi Vavilon*

Trenchard-Smith, Brian *Man from Hong-Kong, The*

Trent, John *Middle Age Crazy*

Trier, Lars Von *Breaking the Waves; Europa*

Trikonis, Gus *Evil, The*

Troche, Rose *Go Fish*

Troell, Jan *Hurricane; Zandy's Bride*

Tronson, Robert *Ring of Spies*

Trousdale, Gary *Beauty and the Beast; Hunchback of Notre Dame, The*

Trueba, Fernando *Two Much*

Truffaut, Francois *Baisers Voles; Le Dernier Metro; Deux Anglaises et le Continent; Domicile Conjugal; L'Enfant Sauvage; Fahrenheit 451; L'Histoire D'Adele H.; Jules et Jim; La Nuit Americaine; La Peau Douce; Les Quatre Cents Coups; Tirez Sur Le Pianiste*

Trumbull, Douglas *Brainstorm; Silent Running*

Tsukerman, Slava *Liquid Sky*

Tuchner, Michael *Fear Is the Key; Mister Quilp; Villain; Wilt*

Tucker, Phil *Robot Monster*

Tuggle, Richard *Tightrope*

Tully, Montgomery *Battle beneath the Earth*

Turkiewicz, Sophia *Silver City*

Turman, Lawrence *Marriage of a Young Stockbroker, The*

Turner, Ann *Celia*

Turteltaub, Jon *Cool Runnings; Phenomenon; 3 Ninjas; While You Were Sleeping*

Turturro, John *Mac*

Tuttle, Frank *Big Broadcast, The; Glass Key, The; Great John L., The; Her Wedding Night; Roman Scandals; Swell Guy; This Gun for Hire; This Reckless Age*

Tuttle, Rowland V.; Lee, Victor; Schertzinger, Frank *Paramount on Parade*

Ulmer, Edgar G. *Black Cat, The; Carnegie Hall; Detour; Hannibal; Man from Planet X, The; Ruthless; Strange Woman, The*

Underwood, Ron *City Slickers; Speechless; Tremors; Mighty Joe Young*

Unkrish, Lee *Toy Story 2*

Ustinov, Peter *Billy Budd; Hammersmith Is Out; Lady L; Romanoff and Juliet*

Uys, Jamie *Gods Must Be Crazy, The; Gods Must Be Crazy II, The*

Vadim, Roger *And God Created Woman; Barbarella; Et Dieu . . . Crea la Femme; Game Is Over, The; Les Liaisons Dangereuses; Pretty Maids All in a Row; La Ronde*

Valdez, Luis *La Bamba*

Van Damme, Jean-Claude *Quest, The*

Van Diem *Karakter*

Van Dormael, Jaco *Le Huitieme Jour; Toto le Heros*

Van Dyke, W. S. *After the Thin Man; Bitter Sweet; Devil Is a Sissy, The; Feminine Touch, The; Forsaking All Others; His Brother's Wife; I Live My Life; It's a Wonderful World; Love on the Run; Manhattan Melodrama; Marie Antoinette; Naked Eye, The; Naughty Marietta; Penthouse; Personal Property; Rosalie; Rose-Marie; San Francisco; Shadow of the Thin Man; Tarzan the Ape Man; Thin Man, The; Trader Horn*

Van Sant, Gus *Drugstore Cowboy; Even Cowgirls Get the Blues; Good Will Hunting; My Own Private Idaho; Psycho; To Die For*

Varda, Agnes *Cleo de 5 a 7; Lions Love*

Varnel, Marcel *Ask a Policeman; Oh, Mr. Porter!*

Vasiliev, Dmitri *Aleksandr Nyevski; Lyenin V Oktyabrye*

Vasquez, Joseph P. *Hangin' with the Homeboys*

Veber, Francis *Three Fugitives*

Verhoeven, Michael *Mutters Courage*

Verhoeven, Paul *Basic Instinct; Flesh + Blood; RoboCop; Showgirls; Starship Troopers; Total Recall*

Verneuil, Henri *Guns for San Sebastian*

Verona, Stephen *Boardwalk; Lord's of Flatbush, The*

Verow, Todd *Frisk*

Vidor, Charles *Blind Alley; Cober Girl; Desperadoes, The; Farewell to Arms, A; Gilda; Hans Christian Andersen; Joker Is Wild, The; Love Me or Leave Me; Song to Remember, A; Song Without End; Swan, The; Together Again*

Vidor, King *American Romance, An; Beyond the Forest; Big Parade, The; Billy the Kid; Bird of Paradise; Champ, The; Citadel, The; Comrade X; Crowd, The; Cynara; Duel in the Sun; Fountainhead, The; Hallelujah; H. M. Pulham, Esq.; Japanese War Bride; La Boheme; Man without a Star; Northwest Passage; On Our Merry Way; Our Daily Bread; Patsy, The; Peg O' My Heart; Ruby Gentry; Show People; Solomon and Sheba; Stella Dallas; Stranger's Return; Street Scene; War and Peace; Wedding Night, The; Wizard of Oz, The*

Vincent, Chuck *Hollywood Hot Tubs*

Vinton, Will *Moonwalker*

Visconti, Luchino *Bellissima; Boccaccio 70; Conversation Piece; Damned, The; Death in Venice; Il Gattopardo; Ludwig; Ossessione; Rocco E I Suoi Fratelli; Senso; La Terra Trema Episodio del Mare; Vaghe Stelle Dell'Orsa*

Vogel, Virgil *Land Unknown, The*

Wachowski, Andy *Bound; Matrix, The*

Wachowski, Larry *Bound; Matrix, The*

Wadleigh, Michael *Wolfen; Woodstock*

Waggner, George *Fighting Kentuckian, The; Man Made Monster; Wolf Man, The*

Wagner, Jane *Moment by Moment*

Wainwright, Rupert *Stigmata*

Wajda, Andrzej *Czlowiek z Marmuru; Czlowiek Z Zelaza; Danton; Kanal; Pokolenie; Popiol I Diament*

Walas, Chris *Fly II, The*

Walker, Hal *Road to Bali; Road to Utopia; Sailor Beware; Stork Club, The*

Walker, Nancy *Can't Stop the Music*

Walker, Stuart *Eagle and the Hawk, The*

Wallace, Randall *Man in the Iron Mask, The*

Wallace, Richard *Because of Him; Framed; Shopworn Angel, The; Sinbad the Sailor; Young in Heart, The*

Wallace, Stephen *Blood Oath*

Wallace, Tommy Lee *Fright Night, Part 2; Halloween III: Season of the Witch*

Walsh, Raoul *Along the Great Divide; Artists and Models; Band of Angels; Battle Cry; Big Trail, The; Blackbeard,* the Pirate; Bowery, The; Captain Horatio Hornblower R.N.; Distant Drums; Distant Trumpet, A; Enforcer, The; Fighter Squadron; Gentleman Jim; High Sierra; Horn Blows at Midnight, The; In Old Arizona; Klondike Annie; Lawless Breed, The; Lion Is in the Streets, A; Manpower; Me and My Gal; Naked and the Dead, The; Northern Pursuit; Objective, Burma!; O.H.M.S.; Pursued; Roaring Twenties, The; Sadie Thompson; Sheriff of Fractured Jaw, The; St. Louis Blues; Strawberry Blonde; Tall Men, The; They Died with Their Boots On; They Drive by Night; Thief of Bagdad, The; Uncertain Glory; What Price Glory?; White Heat; World in His Arms, The

Walters, Charles Barkleys of Broadway, The; Belle of New York, The; Dangerous When Wet; Easter Parade; Easy to Love; Gigi; Glass Slipper, The; High Society; Jumbo; King of Kings; Lili; Please Don't Eat the Daisies; Summer Stock; Tender Trap, The; Texas Carnival; Torch Song; Two Loves; Unsinkable Molly Brown, The; Walk Don't Run

Walton, Fred Rosary Murders, The; When a Stranger Calls

Wanamaker, Sam Executioner, The; Sinbad and the Eye of the Tiger

Wang, Peter Great Wall, A; Laser Man, The

Wang, Wayne Anywhere But Here; Blue in the Face; Chan Is Missing; Dim Sum A Little Bit of Heart; Eat a Bowl of Tea; Joy Luck Club, The; Life Is Cheap . . . But Toilet Paper Is Expensive; Slam Dance; Smoke

Ward, David S. Cannery Row; King Ralph; Major League; Major League II

Ward, Vincent Map of the Human Heart; Navigator, The A Medieval Odyssey; Vigil

Wargnier, Regis Indochine

Warhol, Andy Chelsea Girls, The; My Hustler

Warren, Charles Marquis Arrowhead; Hellgate; Tension at Table Rock

Warren, Mark Come Back Charleston Blue

Waters, John Cry-Baby; Female Trouble; Hairspray; Pink Flamingos; Polyester; Serial Mom

Watkins, Peter Privilege; Punishment Park; War Game, The

Watt, Harry Eureka Stockade; Overlanders, The; Where No Vultures Fly

Wayne, John Alamo, The; Green Berets, The

Webb, Jack Dragnet; Pete Kelly's Blues

Webb, Robert D. Beneath the 12 Mile Reef; Love Me Tender; Proud Ones, The; White Feather

Wei, Lo Jingwu Men; Tang Shan Daxiong

Weiderhorn, Ken Return of the Living Dead, Part II

Weil, Samuel Toxic Avenger, The

Weiland, Paul City Slickers II: The Legend of Curly's Gold

Weill, Claudia Girlfriends; It's My Turn

Wein, Chuck My Hustler

Weir, Peter Cars That Ate Paris, The; Dead Poets Society; Fearless; Gallipoli; Green Card; Last Wave, The; Mosquito Coast, The; Picnic at Hanging Rock; Truman Show, The; Witness; Year of Living Dangerously, The

Weis, Don Billie; I Love Melvin; King's Pirate, The; Pajama Party

Weisman, David Ciao Manhattan

Weisman, Sam D2 The Mighty Ducks; Out-of-Towners, The

Weitz, Paul American Pie

Welles, Orson Chimes at Midnight; Citizen Kane; Confidential Report; F for Fake; Journey into Fear; Lady from Shanghai, The; Macbeth; Magnificent Ambersons, The; Othello; Stranger, The; Touch of Evil; Trial, The

Wellman, William A. Across the Wide Missouri; Battleground; Beau Geste; Buffalo Bill; Call of the Wild, The; Great Man's Lady, The; High and the Mighty, The; Iron Curtain, The; Island in the Sky; Lady of Burlesque; Love Is a Racket; Magic Town; Men with Wings; Next Voice You Hear . . . , The; Night Nurse; Nothing Sacred; Ox-Bow Incident, The; Public Enemy, The; Roxie Hart; Small Town Girl; Star Is Born, A; Story of G.I. Joe, The; Track of the Cat; Westward the Women; Wings; Yellow Sky

Wells, Audrey Guinevere

Wells, Peter Desperate Remedies

Wells, Simon American Tail: Fievel Goes West, An; Balto; We're Back! A Dinosaur's Story

Wenders, Wim Hammett; Himmel Ueber Berlin; Im Lauf der Zeit; Par-Dela Les Nuages; Paris, Texas; Until the End of the World

Wendkos, Paul Burglar, The; Cannon for Cordoba; Gidget; Gidget Goes Hawaiian; Guns of the Magnificent Seven; Mephisto Waltz, The

Wenk, Richard Vamp

Werker, Alfred *Adventures of Sherlock Holmes, The; He Walked by Night; House of Rothschild, The; Reluctant Dragon, The*

Werner, Peter *No Man's Land*

West, Raymond B. *Civilization*

West, Roland *Alibi; Bat, The; Bat Whispers, The*

West, Simon *Con Air; General's Daughter, The*

Wexler, Haskell *Medium Cool*

Whale, James *Bride of Frankenstein; Frankenstein; Great Garrick, The; Great Garrick, The (1937); Invisible Man, The; Man in the Iron Mask, The; Old Dark House, The; Show Boat*

Whatham, Claude *Swallows and Amazons; Sweet William; That'll Be the Day*

Whelan, Ludwig Berger, Michael Powell, Tim *The Thief of Bagdad An Arabian Fantasy*

Whelan, Tim *Divorce of Lady X, The; Higher and Higher ; Q Planes; Step Lively*

Whitaker, Forest *Waiting to Exhale*

White, George *George White's 1935 Scandals; George White's Scandals*

Whitesell, John *Calendar Girl*

Whitmore, Preston A., III *Walking Dead, The*

Whorf, Richard *Champagne for Caesar; It Happened in Brooklyn; Sailor Takes a Wife, The; Till the Clouds Roll By*

Wiard, William *Tom Horn*

Wickes, David *Silver Dream Racer; Sweeney!*

Wicki, Bernhard *Longest Day, The; Morituri*

Widerberg, Bo *Elvira Madigan; Kvarteret Korpen*

Wiene, Robert *Das Cabinett des Dr. Caligari; Orlacs Haende*

Wilcox, Fred M. *Forbidden Planet; Lassie Come Home; Secret Garden, The*

Wilcox, Herbert *Bitter Sweet; Courtneys of Curzon Street, The; Forever and a Day; I Live in Grosvenor Square; Irene; Lady with the Lamp, The; Limelight; Nell Gwyn; No, No, Nanette; Odette; Spring in Park Lane; Sunny; Victoria the Great; Yellow Canary, The*

Wilde, Cornel *Beach Red; Lancelot and Guinevere; Naked Prey, The*

Wilde, Ted *Kid Brother, The*

Wilder, Billy *Ace in the Hole; Apartment, The; Avanti!; Buddy Buddy; Double Indemnity; Emperor Waltz, The; Fedora; Five Graves to Cairo; Foreign Affair, A; Fortune Cookie, The; Front Page, The; Irma La Douce; Kiss Me, Stupid; Lost Weekend, The; Love in the Afternoon; Major and the Minor, The; One, Two, Three; Private Life of Sherlock Holmes, The; Sabrina; Seven Year Itch, The; Some Like It Hot; Spirit of St. Louis, The; Stalag 17; Sunset Blvd.; Witness for the Prosecution*

Wilder, Gene *Adventure of Sherlock Holmes' Smarter Brother, The; Haunted Honeymoon; Woman in Red, The; World's Greatest Lover, The*

Wiley, Ethan *House II The Second Story*

Williams, Paul *November Men, The*

Williams, Richard *Arabian Night*

Williams, Wade *Detour*

Wilson, Hugh *Dudley Do-Right; First Wives Club, The; Guarding Tess; Police Academy*

Wilson, Richard *Al Capone; It's All True; Three in the Attic*

Wincer, Simon *D.A.R.Y.L.; Free Willy; Harley Davidson and The Marlboro Man; Lighthorsemen, The; Phantom, The; Phar Lap; Quigley Down Under*

Windust, Bretaigne *Enforcer, The; Face to Face; June Bride; Perfect Strangers*

Winer, Harry *Spacecamp*

Winkler, Irwin *At First Sight; Guilty by Suspicion; Net, The; Night and the City*

Winner, Michael *Appointment with Death; Big Sleep, The; Chato's Land; Chorus of Disapproval, A; Death Wish; Death Wish II; Death Wish 3; Dirty Weekend; Firepower; Games, The; Hannibal Brooks; I'll Never Forget What's 'is name; Jokers, The; Lawman; Mechanic, The; Nightcomers, The; Scorpio; Sentinel, The; Stone Killer, The; System, The; West 11; Wicked Lady, The*

Winter, Alex *Freaked*

Winterbottom, Michael *Butterfly Kiss; Jude; Welcome to Sarajevo; Wonderland*

Wise, Kirk *Beauty and the Beast; Hunchback of Notre Dame, The*

Wise, Robert *Andromeda Strain, The; Audrey Rose; Blood on the Moon; Body Snatcher, The; Captive City, The; Curse of the Cat People, The; Day the Earth Stood Still, The; Desert Rats, The; Destination Gobi; Executive Suite; Game of Death, A; Haunting, The; Helen of Troy; Hindenburg, The; House on Telegraph Hill, The; I Want to Live!; Odds Against Tomorrow; Run Silent, Run Deep; Sand Pebbles, The; Set-Up, The; So Big; Somebody Up There Likes Me; Sound of Music, The; Star!; Star Trek The Motion Picture;*

Ziehm, Howard *Flesh Gordon*
Zielinski, Rafal *Fun; Screwballs*
Zimmerman, Vernon *Unholy Rollers, The*
Zinnemann, Fred *Act of Violence; Behold a Pale Horse; Day of the Jackal, The; Five Days One Summer; From Here to Eternity; Hatful of Rain, A; High Noon; Julia; Kid Glove Killer; Man for All Seasons, A; Men, The; Nun's Story, The; Oklahoma!; Search, The; Seventh Cross, The; Sundowners, The; Teresa*

Zito, Jospeh *Friday the 13th The Final Chapter; Invasion U.S.A.; Missing in Action; Red Scorpion*

Zondag, Dick *We're Back! A Dinosaur's Story*
Zsigmond, Vilmos *Long Shadow, The*
Zucker, David *Airplane!; The Naked Gun From the Files of Police Squad!; The Naked Gun 2½ The Smell of Fear; Ruthless People; Top Secret!*
Zucker, Jerry *Airplane!; First Knight; Ghost; Ruthless People; Top Secret!*
Zulawski, Andrzej *La Femme Publique; Possession*
Zwerin, Charlotte *Gimme Shelter*
Zwick, Edward *About Last Night . . . ; Courage Under Fire; Glory; Leaving Normal; Legends of the Fall; Siege, The*